Business French Dictionary

French ⟶ English
English ⟶ French

Edited by
Marianne Chalmers
Martine Pierquin

OXFORD
UNIVERSITY PRESS

OXFORD
UNIVERSITY PRESS

Great Clarendon Street, Oxford OX2 6DP

Oxford University Press is a department of the University of Oxford.
It furthers the University's objective of excellence in research, scholarship,
and education by publishing worldwide in

Oxford New York

Auckland Bangkok Buenos Aires Cape Town Chennai
Dar es Salaam Delhi Hong Kong Istanbul Karachi Kolkata
Kuala Lumpur Madrid Melbourne Mexico City Mumbai Nairobi
São Paulo Singapore Taipei Tokyo Toronto

with an associated company in Berlin

Oxford is a registered trade mark of Oxford University Press
in the UK and in certain other countries

Published in the United States
by Oxford University Press Inc., New York

© *The Oxford Business French Dictionary* Oxford University Press 2002
Updated, adapted, and abridged from the *Routledge French Dictionary of
Business, Commerce and Finance* © Routlege 1996.

The moral rights of the author have been asserted

Database right Oxford University Press (maker)

First published 2002

British Library Cataloguing in Publication Data
Data available

Library of Congress Cataloging in Publication Data
Data available

ISBN 0-19-860483-1

10 9 8 7 6 5 4 3 2 1

Typeset in Nimrod, Arial and Meta
by Morton Word Processing Ltd
Printed in Great Britain by Clays Ltd, Bungay, Suffolk

Preface

This dictionary has been written to meet the challenges of the new economy and to embrace the changes taking place in business practices with the rise of new information and communications technologies. Designed to meet the needs of the business studies student, the business professional, and all who need to understand the language of business, it combines an extensive word list with clearly presented examples of business language in use.

The dictionary offers the user comprehensive coverage of core business vocabulary from a wide range of fields, including accountancy, banking, economics, human resource management, law, sales and marketing, the stock market, management, taxation, insurance, and information technology. The word list is further enhanced by the addition of vocabulary generated by the Internet revolution and the growth of the digital economy. Where appropriate American variations in spelling and usage are highlighted.

Presentation of the entries is streamlined to provide ease of reference. Essential information is provided in brackets to guide the user to the most appropriate translation. Field labels, e.g. **FIN, INS, COMP**, help the user navigate through the entry to the relevant category of information. Examples of typical structures and phrases in which a word is frequently found allow the user to deploy the term accurately and effectively in a sentence. Compounds are grouped alphabetically in a block for ease of consultation. Where a compound contains a preposition, the preposition is ignored for the purposes of alphabetical ordering.

English compounds and adjective-noun combinations are listed under their first elements.

In recognition of the greater degree of mobility within the labour market, a section of the dictionary is devoted to the presentation of curricula vitae with covering letters in English and French. This section equips the user with a wide variety of expressions and vocabulary for describing their career path, achievements, and skills which can be tailored to suit individual requirements.

An additional feature of the dictionary is the sample business correspondence. The letters are presented in pairs on similar themes for ease of comparison and exemplify the different conventions prevalent in each language. The material covers standard business correspondence as well as email, memoranda, fax, invoices, and statements.

'Using the telephone' provides a wealth of information on the vocabulary of telecommunications, including mobile communications, and on how to use the French telephone system. A list of the world's major countries, nationalities, languages, and currencies is also supplied in the central section of the dictionary, as is an overview of the euro currency and details on conversion.

The dictionary is designed to be a practical, effective and user-friendly tool both for study purposes and for tackling business assignments.

Préface

Ce dictionnaire a pour ambition de répondre aux demandes de la nouvelle économie et de prendre en compte les changements survenus dans le monde des affaires avec l'arrivée des nouvelles technologies de l'information et de la communication. Le dictionnaire a été conçu pour répondre aux besoins des étudiants comme des professionnels ainsi que de tous ceux qui s'intéressent à la langue des affaires. Il offre une importante nomenclature, illustrée d'exemples clairs.

Le dictionnaire met à la disposition de l'utilisateur un ensemble de termes-clé dans des domaines tels que la comptabilité, le domaine bancaire, l'économie, la gestion du personnel, le droit, la vente, le marketing, la Bourse, la gestion, la fiscalité, les assurances, et les technologies de l'information. À ce vaste lexique, s'ajoute le vocabulaire généré par la révolution Internet et l'expansion rapide de la e-économie. De nombreuses variantes de l'anglais américain sont également signalées.

La présentation sobre des entrées permet de se référer rapidement au terme recherché. Des informations indispensables au choix de la bonne traduction sont données entre parenthèses. Des indicateurs de champs sémantiques tels que **FIN**, **ASSUR**, **INFO** orientent également l'utilisateur à l'intérieur de chaque entrée jusqu'à la catégorie recherchée. Des exemples de constructions et d'expressions typiques utilisant un mot particulier permettent d'utiliser ce mot correctement et à bon escient. Quand un nom composé contient une préposition, celle-ci n'est pas prise en compte dans le classement par ordre alphabétique. Pour faciliter encore la recherche, les mots composés sont regroupés au bas de chaque entrée.

En accord avec le degré croissant de mobilité dans le monde du travail, une section du dictionnaire est consacrée à la présentation de curriculum vitae et de lettres de motivation en français et en anglais. Cette section fournit à l'utilisateur un grand nombre de termes et expressions indispensables à la description de leur parcours professionnel, de leurs compétences et de leurs réussites. Tout ce vocabulaire peut s'adapter aisément aux besoins individuels.

Le supplément sur la correspondance commerciale a pour objectif d'aider à communiquer avec plus d'efficacité quel que soit le moyen de communication choisi. Pour chaque thème abordé, deux exemplaires de lettres sont proposés, l'un en français l'autre en anglais, afin de faciliter la comparaison et de mettre en évidence les conventions propres à chaque langue. Dans cette section, on trouvera des lettres commerciales standard ainsi que des exemples d'e-mails, de memos, facsimilés, factures et relevés de compte.

Dans un souci d'aide pratique, une partie traitant des télécommunications, y compris la téléphonie mobile, a été ajoutée. On y trouvera de nombreuses informations aussi bien sur le vocabulaire de la téléphonie que sur l'utilisation du téléphone en Grande-Bretagne et aux États-Unis. Une liste des pays, nationalités, langues et monnaies du monde actuel est également fournie dans les pages centrales.

Ce dictionnaire est un outil pratique et efficace, d'utilisation facile pour les travaux d'étudiant comme pour les tâches quotidiennes du monde des affaires.

Editors and Contributors/Rédactrices et collaboratrices

Chief Editors/Direction éditoriale
Marianne Chalmers
Martine Pierquin

Editor/Rédactrice
Isabelle Stables

Proofreader/Correctrice
Genevieve Hawkins

Data Capture/Saisie des données
Anne McConnell
Catherine Hindson
Susan Wilkin
Sandy Vaughan

Note on proprietary status/Les marques déposées

This dictionary includes some words which have, or are asserted to have, proprietary status as trademarks or otherwise. Their inclusion does not imply that they have acquired for legal purposes a non-proprietary or general significance, nor any other judgement concerning their legal status. In cases where the editorial staff have some evidence that a word has proprietary status, this is indicated in the entry for that word by the symbol ®, but no judgement concerning the legal status of such words is made or implied thereby.

Les mots qui, à notre connaissance, sont considérés comme des marques ou des noms déposés sont signalés dans cet ouvrage par ®. La présence ou l'absence de cette mention ne peut pas être considérée comme ayant valeur juridique.

Contents/Table des matières

Abbreviations/Abréviations

English/anglais	Abbreviation/Abréviation	French/français
abbreviation	abbr	abréviation
abbreviation	abrév	abréviation
Accountancy	Acc	Comptabilité
adjective	adj	adjectif
Business Administration	Admin	Administration
adverb	adv	adverbe
American English	AmE	anglais américain
Insurance	Assur	Assurance
Australian English	Aus	anglais australien
In Australia	Australia	En Australie
Banking	Bank	Banque
Banking	Banque	Banque
Belgian	Bel	Belge
In Belgium	Belgique	En Belgique
Stock Market	Bourse	Bourse
British English	BrE	anglais britannique
Patents	Brevets	Brevets
Canadian English	Can	anglais canadien
In Canada	Canada	Au Canada
General Commerce	Com	Commerce
Communications	Comms	Communications
Computing	Comp	Informatique
Accountancy	Compta	Comptabilité
conjunction	conj	conjonction
dated	dat	vieilli
Law	Droit	Droit
Economics	Econ	Économie
Environment	Envir	Environnement
feminine	f	féminin
feminine plural	f pl	féminin pluriel
Finance	Fin	Finance
Taxation	Fisc	Fiscalité
French	Fra	français
In France	France	En France
formal	frml	formel
General Commerce	Gen Comm	Commerce
Management	Gestion	Gestion
Human Resource Management	HRM	Gestion des Ressources Humaines
Property	Immob	Immobilier
Import & Export	Imp/Exp	Import & Export
Industry	Ind	Industrie
Computing	Info	Informatique
informal	infrml	informel

English/anglais	Abbreviation/Abréviation	French/français
Insurance	Ins	Assurance
invariable	inv	invariable
jargon	jarg	jargon
Law	Law	Droit
Leisure and Tourism	Leis	Loisirs
phrase	loc	locution
Leisure and Tourism	Loisirs	Loisirs
masculine	m	masculin
masculine, feminine	mf	masculin, féminin
masculine and feminine	m,f	masculin et féminin
masculine plural	m pl	masculin pluriel
Mathematics	Math	Mathématiques
Media	Media	Médias
Management	Mgmnt	Gestion
noun	n	nom
noun plural	n pl	nom pluriel
proper noun	n pr	nom propre
Patents	Patents	Brevets
pejorative	pej	péjoratif
péjoratif	péj	pejorative
phrase	phr	locution
plural	pl	pluriel
Politics	Pol	Politique
proper noun	pr n	nom propre
prefix	pref	préfixe
prefix	préf	préfixe
preposition	prep	préposition
preposition	prép	préposition
Property	Prop	Immobilier
Human Resource Management	Res Hum	Gestion des Ressources Humaines
Sales and Marketing	S&M	Vente & Marketing
singular	sing	singulier
Stock Market	Stock	Bourse
Taxation	Tax	Fiscalité
Transport	Transp	Transport
In the UK	UK	Au Royaume-Uni
In the US	US	Aux États-Unis
verb	v	verbe
Sales and Marketing	V&M	Vente & Marketing
intransitive verb	vi	verbe intransitif
dated	vieilli	vieilli
reflexive verb	v pron	verbe pronominal
reflexive verb	v refl	verbe pronominal
transitive verb	vt	verbe transitif
transitive and intransitive verb	vti	verbe transitif et intransitif

Aa

a: ~ **commercial** *m* at sign

A3 *m* (format) A3

A4 *m* (format) A4

abaisser *vt* (prix, taux) reduce; (niveau) lower; ~ **l'âge de la retraite à 60 ans** lower the retirement age to 60

abandon *m* (de navire, fret, projet, méthode, d'idée, d'option) abandonment; (de dette) deletion; (Info) abort; **à l'**~ (usine) in a state of neglect; ~ **de créance** composition between debtor and creditor; ~ **progressif** phasing out

abandonnataire *mf* (Assur) abandonee

abandonner *vt* (navire, fret, projet, méthode, idée, option) abandon; (dette) delete; (Info) abort; ~ **progressivement** phase out

abattement *m* (réduction) deduction; (d'impôts) allowance; ~ **fiscal** tax allowance BrE, tax deduction AmE; ~ **fiscal sur les intérêts versés** interest relief; ~ **sur les plus-values** capital gains allowance; ~ **sur le prélèvement** abatement of the levy

ab intestat *adj* (Droit) (succession) intestate

abolir *vt* (loi, impôt, droit) abolish

abolition *f* abolition

abonné, e *m,f* (à un magazine) subscriber; (à une association) season ticket holder BrE; (à l'électricité, au gaz) consumer; ~ **au téléphone/à l'Internet** telephone/Internet subscriber

abonnement *m* (à un magazine) subscription; (pour téléphone) rental charge; (pour gaz, électricité) standing charge; **prendre/souscrire un** ~ take out a subscription; ~ **annuel à l'essai** annual trial subscription

abonner: s'~ **à** *v pron* subscribe to

abordable *adj* (prix) affordable

abordage *m* (navigation) collision

aborder *vt* (problème) address, tackle

aboutir *vi* be successful; ~ **à** result in; ~ **à un compromis/accord** reach a compromise/an agreement

aboutissement *m* (de carrière, d'évolution) culmination; (de conférence, parcours) outcome; (résultat satisfaisant) success

abrégé *m* abstract, summary

abréviation *f* abbreviation

abri *m* shelter; **être à l'**~ **de** (concurrence) to be safe *ou* sheltered from; ~ **fiscal** tax shelter

abrogation *f* (de loi) abrogation, repeal; (de décret) annulment

abroger *vt* (loi) abrogate, repeal; (décret) annul; ~ **un impôt** repeal a tax

ABSAR *abrév* (**Actions à bons de souscription d'actions avec facilité de rachat**) *shares with redeemable share warrants*

absence *f* (disparition, inexistence) absence; (défaut) lack; **en l'**~ **de** in the absence of; ~ **d'accord** failure to agree; ~ **de communication** lack of communication, communication gap; ~ **de contrepartie** absence of consideration; ~ **non justifiée** absence without leave; ~ **de responsabilité** nonliability

absent¹, e *adj* absent; **être** ~ **pour cause de maladie** be absent due to illness, be off sick (infrml)

absent², e *m,f* absentee

absentéisme *m* absenteeism; **taux d'**~ absenteeism rate

absenter: s'~ *v pron* (longtemps) go away; (brièvement) go out; **s'**~ **pour affaires** go away on business

ABSOC *abrév* (**Actions à bons de souscription d'obligations convertibles**) *shares with convertible bond warrants carrying preferential subscription rights*

absorber *vt* (émission) take over; (une autre société) absorb, take over, acquire; (perte) cover

absorption *f* (d'une société) absorption, takeover, acquisition; (Compta) merger accounting BrE, pooling of interests AmE

abstenir: s'~ *v pron* (dans une élection) abstain; **s'**~ **de** refrain from

abstention *f* abstention

abus *m* (de brevets) abuse; (Envir) overuse; ~ **de confiance** breach of trust; ~ **de droits** abuse of rights; ~ **d'influence** undue influence; ~ **de pouvoir** abuse of power

abuser *vt* (client) mislead; ~ **de** (privilège) abuse

abusif, -ive *adj* (prix) excessive, prohibitive; (usage, pratique) improper

a.c. *abrév* (▸**avarie commune**) GA (general average)

à/c *abrév* (▸**à compter de**) A/D (after date)

acc. *abrév* (▸**acceptation**) acpt., acce. (acceptance)

accabler *vt* overwhelm; ~ **qn d'accusations** throw the book at sb

accalmie *f* lull

accaparement *m* ~ **du marché** cornering of the market

accaparer *vt* (marché) corner; (pouvoir) seize; (marchandises) hoard; **être accaparé par son travail** be taken up by one's work

accéder *vi* ~ **à** (grade) rise to; (requête) comply with, grant; (responsabilité) accede to; (Info) (base de données, fichier, dossier) access; ~ **à la propriété** become a home-owner

accélérateur *m* (Info) accelerator

accélération *f* acceleration; (de processus, projet, production) acceleration, speeding-up; ~ **de** (croissance, consommation, prix) sharp increase in

accéléré, e *adj* (formation professionnelle) fast-track

accélérer **1** *vt* accelerate; (processus, projet, production) accelerate, speed up
2 **s'accélérer** *v pron* (travail, production) accelerate, speed up

accent *m* emphasis; **mettre l'**~ **sur** stress, put the emphasis on

acceptable *adj* acceptable; (Droit) permissible

acceptant, e *adj* (banquier) accepting

acceptation *f* acceptance; **sous réserve d'**~ subject to acceptance; **refus d'**~ non-acceptance; ~ **de cautionnement** collateral acceptance; ~ **commerciale** trade acceptance; ~ **conditionnelle** qualified acceptance; ~ **définitive** final acceptance; ~ **d'une hypothèque** mortgage assumption; ~ **inconditionnelle** unconditional acceptance; ~ **par intervention** acceptance for honour; ~ **provisoire** provisional acceptance

accepter *vt* agree; (conditions, contrat, devis) agree to; (défi, pari) take up; (offre, traite, appel) accept; **ne pas** ~ (traite) disallow; ~ **du travail supplémentaire** take on extra work; **est-ce que vous acceptez les chèques?** do you take cheques?

accepteur *m* (d'une traite) acceptor, drawee

accès *m* admittance; (Info) access; **avoir** ~ **à** (une base de données, un fichier) be able to access; **avoir** ~ **à l'information** have access to information; **avoir** ~ **à l'Internet** (chez soi) be on the Internet; (au travail) have access to the Internet; ~ **aléatoire** random access; ~ **direct** direct access; ~ **à distance** remote access; ~ **immédiat** immediate access; ~ **onlÌne** online access; ~ **libre** unrestricted access; ~ **multiple** multiaccess; ~ **du public** public access; ~ **séquentiel** (Info) serial access

accessibilité *f* (de l'information) accessibility; (d'un prix) affordability; (droit) right; **l'**~ **de tous à l'emploi** everybody's right to a job

accessible *adj* accessible, available; (prix, tarif) affordable

accession *f* (au pouvoir) accession; ~ **à la propriété** home ownership

accessoire¹ *adj* (problème, détail, avantage) incidental; (Droit) (cause) appurtenant, contributory

accessoire² *m* (d'équipement auto, de tenue vestimentaire) accessory; (de machine) attachment, accessory; ~ **de bureau** desk accessory

accident *m* accident; **avoir un** ~ have an accident; **faire une déclaration d'**~ make an accident claim; ~ **corporel** accident involving injury; ~ **de mer** accident at sea; ~ **du travail** industrial accident, occupational injury, industrial injury

accommodement *m* (accord) compromise; (avec créanciers) composition

accompagnateur, -trice *m,f* (d'enfants) accompanying adult; (de touristes) guide

accompagné, e *adj* (bagage) accompanied; **non** ~ unaccompanied; ~ **de/par** accompanied by

accompagner *vt* accompany; (escorter) escort

accomplir *vt* (tâche, mission) accomplish; (contrat) discharge; ~ **des démarches/formalités** go through procedures/formalities

accomplissement *m* (d'une tâche, mission) accomplishment; (d'un contrat) discharge

accord *m* arrangement; (contrat) deal; (Droit) accord; (consentement, pacte) agreement; (Bourse) indenture; **avec l'**~ **des parties** by mutual agreement; **donner son** ~ agree; **en** ~ **avec** in keeping with, in accordance with; **être d'**~ agree, concur; **se mettre d'**~ come to an agreement; **l'**~ **n'est pas fait** the deal is off; **ne pas être d'**~ disagree; **par** ~ **tacite** by tacit agreement; ~ **à l'amiable** friendly agreement, gentleman's agreement; ~s **entre banques régionales** regional banking pacts; ~ **de base** substantive agreement; ~ **bilatéral** reciprocal agreement; ~ **commercial** trade agreement; ~ **de commercialisation** marketing agreement; ~s **commerciaux de réciprocité** reciprocal trading agreements; ~s **communs de l'assurance corps** Joint Hull Understandings; ~ **de compensation** (commerce international) barter agreement, buy-back agreement; ~ **de compte en commun** joint account agreement; ~ **de confidentialité** confidentiality agreement; ~ **à durée déterminée** fixed-term agreement; ~ **écrit** written agreement; ~ **financier à terme** financial futures contract; ~ **de fond** substantive agreement; ~ **général** consensus; **Accord général d'emprunt** General Agreement to Borrow; **Accord général sur les tarifs et le commerce** General Agreement on Tariffs and Trade; ~s **généraux d'emprunt** general arrangements to borrow; ~ **global** blanket agreement; ~ **implicite** unspoken agreement, tacit agreement; ~ **d'indemnisation** compensation settlement; ~s **interbancaires** inter-bank arrangements; **Accord international sur le blé** International Wheat Agreement; **Accord international sur le sucre** ≈ International Sugar Agreement; ~s **internationaux sur les matières premières** International Commodity Agreements; ~s **internationaux sur les produits de base** International

Commodity Agreements; **~ interne** domestic agreement; **~s intersyndicaux et d'industrie en matière de politique sociale** custom and trade practices; **Accord de la Jamaïque** Jamaica Agreement; **~ de libre-échange** free-trade agreement; **Accord de libre-échange nord-américain** North American Free Trade Area; **les Accords de Lomé** Lomé Convention; **Accord du Louvre** Louvre Accord; **~ de marketing** marketing agreement; **~ sur les matières premières** commodity agreement; **Accord monétaire européen** European Monetary Agreement; **~ moratoire** standstill agreement; **~ multilatéral** multilateral agreement; **~ de non-recours à la grève** no-strike agreement; **~ de normalisation** standardization agreement; **~ officiel** formal agreement, formal arrangement; **~ officieux** informal agreement, informal arrangement; **~ patronat-syndicats** collective agreement; **~ de perception** (Fisc) collection agreement; **~s privés** private terms; **~ sur les prix** price-fixing; **~ sur les prix et les revenus** prices and incomes agreement; **~ de procédure** procedural agreement; **~ provisoire** interim agreement; **~ de rachat** buy-back agreement; **~ de rachat et de vente** (entre les actionnaires d'une société) buy-and-sell agreement; **~ de réciprocité fiscale** reciprocal taxation agreement; **~ réglementé** regulated agreement; **~ de régulation du marché** orderly market agreement; **~ de rendement** productivity agreement; **~ de représentation** agency agreement; **~ sur le salaire initial** threshold agreement; **~ salarial** wage agreement; **~ de savoir-faire** (propriété intellectuelle) know-how agreement; **~ supplémentaire** supplemental agreement; **~ syndical** union agreement; **~ de taux à terme** forward rate agreement, future rate agreement; **~ sur les taux de change** exchange rate agreement; **~ à terme fixe** fixed-term agreement; **~ de troc** (commerce international) barter agreement; **~ de tutelle** buy-and-sell agreement; **~ type** pattern settlement; **~ verbal** unwritten agreement, verbal agreement

accord-cadre *m* outline agreement, framework agreement

accorder *vt* (prêt) advance, grant; (argent) allow; (droits) confer; (Banque) extend, grant; (subvention) allot, grant; (location) grant; **~ une charte à** (compagnie) grant a charter to; **~ un crédit** grant credit; **~ un crédit de longue durée** grant extended credit; **~ des dommages-intérêts** (Assur) award damages; **~ à qn le droit de faire** give sb the right to do; **~ le droit de vote** enfranchise; **~ les écritures** (Compta) agree the books; **~ une journée de congé aux employés** give the employees a day off; **~ une licence** grant a

licence; **~ à qn 8 000 euros de dommages et intérêts** allow sb 8,000 euros in damages; **~ un prêt à qn** grant a loan to sb, make a loan to sb, provide sb with a loan; **~ la priorité à** give priority to; **~ une promotion à** promote; **~ une remise sur** give a discount on

accostage *m* (navigation) docking, berthing

accoster *vt* (quai) come alongside; **~ des clients** tout for trade

accréditer *vt* (représentant) accredit

accréditif *m* cheque credit

accrochage *m* (affrontement) clash; **~ initial** (publicité) attention getter

accroche *f* slogan

accrocheur, -euse *adj* eye-catching

accroissement *m* growth, increase; (du capital) accumulation; **~ de la demande** expansion of demand; **~ interne** internal expansion; **~ naturel** natural increase; **~ de la valeur** appreciation

accroître [1] *vt* increase; (Econ) boost; (productivité) increase, raise; **~ l'offre** increase the supply
[2] **s'accroître** *v pron* increase, grow; (Banque, Compta) accrue; (Econ) climb; (population, pouvoir) increase

accru, e *adj* (besoin, présence, stabilité) increased, greater

accueil *m* reception; (Res Hum) induction; **faire bon ~ à qn** make sb welcome; **faire bon ~ à qch** welcome sth; **faire bon ~ à une traite** (Fin) honour *ou* meet a bill; **passer à l'~** go to the reception desk; **~ favorable** favourable reception; (d'un produit) acceptance; **~ des passagers** passenger care; **~ réservé à la marque** brand acceptance

accueillir *vt* (recevoir) welcome, greet; (héberger, contenir) accommodate; (aller chercher) meet, collect; **bien/mal ~ qn/qch** give sb/ sth a good/bad reception; **(bien) ~ une traite** meet *ou* honour a bill; **l'idée a été accueillie avec méfiance/intérêt** the idea was received with suspicion/interest

acculer *vt* **~ qn à la faillite** push sb into bankruptcy

accumulateur *m* (Info) accumulator

accumulation *f* accumulation; (de commandes, de travail) backlog; (de stocks) build-up; (Fin) accruals; **~ de capital** capital accumulation; **~ d'épargne non productive** monetary overhang; **~ d'intérêts** accrual of interest

accumuler [1] *vt* accumulate; (marchandises) stockpile; (stocks) build up; **~ un déficit** run up a deficit
[2] **s'accumuler** *v pron* accumulate; (commandes en souffrance, travail) pile up, back up; (Fin) accrue

accusation *f* accusation

accusé, e *m,f* accused; (procédure pénale) ⋯⋗

defendant; ∼ **de réception**
acknowledgement of receipt; ∼ **de**
réception d'une commande
acknowledgement of receipt of an order,
confirmation of receipt of an order

accuser *vt* accuse (**de** of); ∼ **une plus-**
value (actif) appreciate; ∼ **réception de**
(courrier, marchandises) acknowledge receipt of,
confirm receipt of

achalandage *m* (clientèle) clientele, custom;
(fonds de commerce) goodwill

acharné, e *adj* (concurrence) fierce

achat *m* (action) buying, purchasing; (objet)
purchase; (d'une immobilisation) addition;
(Bourse) buy transaction; **faire un** ∼ make a
purchase; **faire un** ∼ **à crédit** buy sth on
credit; ∼ **à la clôture** (Bourse) closing
purchase; ∼ **de compensation** counter
purchase; ∼ **au comptant** cash purchase; ∼
à crédit credit purchase, term purchase;
(Bourse) buying on margin; ∼ **à découvert**
margin buying, margin purchase; ∼ **en**
dessous du cours buy minus; ∼ **avec**
effet de levier leveraged buyout; ∼
d'endettement leveraged buyout; ∼
d'espace (publicité) space buying; ∼ **et vente**
par correspondance mail-order; ∼ **en**
gros bulk buying; ∼ **groupé** block
purchase; ∼ **à la hausse** bull buying, bull
purchase; ∼ **impulsif** impulse buying; ∼
d'impulsion impulse buying; ∼ **en ligne**
online shopping; (d'un article) online purchase;
∼ **de liquidation** closing purchase
transaction; ∼ **pour liquidation** purchase
for settlement; ∼ **à montant global** lump-
sum purchase; ∼ **mutuel entre institutions**
back-to-back placement; ∼ **d'une option**
d'achat call purchase, synthetic long call; ∼
d'option couverte covered long; ∼ **d'une**
option de vente synthetic long put; ∼
d'options de vente put writing; ∼ **à un**
prix forfaitaire/global basket purchase; ∼
public d'objets précieux nonmonetary
investment; ∼ **réfléchi comparatif**
comparison shopping; ∼ **spontané** impulse
buy, impulse purchase; ∼ **à tempérament**
instalment purchase BrE, installment
purchase AmE; ∼ **à terme** forward buying,
purchase for settlement; ∼ **de valeurs**
purchase of assets; ∼**-vente d'une valeur**
wash sale

achats *m pl* (service) procurement
department, purchasing department; **faire**
des ∼ go shopping; **faire ses** ∼ **à l'extérieur**
do one's shopping out of town; ∼ **de**
précaution panic buying; ∼ **publics** public
procurement; ∼ **répétés** (marketing) repeat
buying; ∼ **de soutien** supporting purchases

acheminement *m* dispatching,
forwarding, sending; ∼ **de l'envoi** route
order; ∼ **intérieur** inland haulage; ∼ **par le**
négociant merchant haulage; ∼ **par le**
transporteur maritime carrier haulage

acheminer *vt* (courrier, marchandises)

dispatch, forward, send

acheter *vt* (marchandises) buy; (corrompre)
bribe; ∼ **des actions en bourse** buy shares
on the open market; ∼ **à la baisse** buy on a
fall, buy on a falling market; ∼ **à la baisse**
et vendre à la hausse buy low and sell high;
∼ **à la clôture** buy on close; ∼ **au cours du**
marché buy at market; ∼ **à crédit** buy on
credit; ∼ **par échelons de baisse** average
down; ∼ **par échelons de hausse** average
up; ∼ **aux enchères** buy at auction, (stock)
buy on bid; ∼ **de l'espace** buy space; (radio,
télévision) buy airtime; ∼ **à l'essai** buy on
approval; ∼ **en grandes quantités** buy in
large quantities; ∼ **à la hausse** buy for a
rise, buy on a rise; ∼ **l'inventaire** buy the
book; ∼ **en ligne** buy online; ∼ **en**
liquidation buy for the account; ∼ **au**
marché noir buy on the black market; ∼ **sur**
marge buy on margin; ∼ **au prix fort** buy at
the top of the market; ∼ **qch comptant** buy
and pay immediately; ∼ **au rabais** buy at a
reduced price; ∼ **au son du canon** buy on
the bad news; ∼ **à tempérament** buy on hire
purchase BrE, buy on the installment plan
AmE; ∼ **à terme** buy forward

acheteur, -euse *m,f* buyer, purchaser;
(d'options) buyer; (Jur) vendee; ∼ **d'art** art
buyer; ∼ **à la baisse** bear operator; ∼ **de**
bonne foi bona fide purchaser; ∼ **d'un call**
call buyer; ∼ **au comptant** cash buyer; ∼ **à**
crédit charge buyer BrE, credit buyer AmE; ∼
de double option straddle buyer; ∼
d'espace space buyer; (radio, télévision)
airtime buyer; ∼ **d'espace publicitaire**
advertising space buyer; ∼ **ferme** (Bourse)
firm buyer; ∼ **en gros** bulk buyer, bulk
purchaser; ∼ **à la hausse** (Bourse) bull, bull
operator; ∼ **impulsif** impulse buyer; ∼
industriel industrial buyer, producer buyer;
∼ **en ligne** online shopper, e-shopper; ∼
multiple multiple buyer; ∼ **occasionnel**
one-time buyer; ∼ **d'option** option buyer,
option holder; ∼ **d'une option d'achat**
giver for a call; ∼ **d'option d'achat** call
writer, put seller; ∼ **d'option de vente** put
buyer, put writer; ∼ **potentiel** potential
buyer, prospective buyer

acheteur-cible *m* target buyer

achevé, e *adj* complete, completed

achèvement *m* (d'un travail, d'un projet)
completion; ∼ **de tâche** task closure

achever *vt* (travail, projet) complete, finish

acier *m* steel; ∼ **inoxydable** stainless steel

aciérie *f* steelworks

acompte *m* (paiement échelonné) instalment
BrE, installment AmE; (premier paiement) down
payment; ∼ **trimestriel** (Fisc) quarterly
instalment BrE, quarterly installment AmE; ∼
sur salaire advance on salary; **verser un** ∼
de make a down payment of; **3 000 euros**
d'∼ *or* **en** ∼ a 3,000 euro down payment; ∼
sur dividende interim dividend; ∼ **non**

remboursable nonrefundable deposit; ~ **permanent** (Imp/exp) standing deposit UK; ~ **provisionnel** (d'impôt) tax instalment BrE, tax installment AmE; ~ **provisionnel insuffisant** deficient tax instalment BrE, deficient tax installment AmE; ~ **remboursable** refundable deposit

acquéreur, -euse *m,f* buyer, purchaser; (entreprise) acquiring company; (Droit) preemptor; **se porter ~ de** state one's intention to buy *ou* purchase

acquérir *vt* acquire; (en achetant) acquire, buy; (réputation) acquire, earn; ~ **de l'expérience** gain experience

acquêt *m* acquest, property acquired after marriage

acquis¹, e *adj* acquired

acquis² *m* knowledge, experience; ~ **à caution** excise bond

acquisition *f* acquisition; (nouvel avoir) acquisition, addition; ~ **d'actions** acquisition of shareholdings, acquisition of stock; ~ **de données** data acquisition; ~ **d'immobilisations** acquisition of assets; ~ **nette d'actifs financiers** net acquisition of financial assets; ~**s nettes** net acquisitions; ~ **partielle** partial taking

acquit *m* receipt; **pour ~** received; (sur une facture) paid in full, received with thanks; ~ **libératoire** (Assur) no risk after discharge; ~ **de paiement** receipt; ~ **de transit** transhipment bond, transit bond note

acquit-à-caution *m* (douanes) bond

acquitté, e *adj* (Fin) paid

acquittement *m* (d'une dette) discharge; (d'un accusé) acquittal

acquitter [1] *vt* (taxe) pay; (dette) discharge, pay off; (facture) settle, pay; (accusé) acquit; ~ **une dette intégralement** pay a debt in full; ~ **qn d'une dette** release sb from a debt [2] **s'acquitter de** *v pron* (devoir) discharge; (engagement, obligation) fulfil BrE, fulfill AmE; (Droit) (dette) clear, pay off, discharge

acronyme *m* acronym

act. *abrév* (▸**action**) shr. (share)

acte *m* (Admin) certificate; (Droit) act, deed; (Pol) act; **faire ~ d'autorité** exercise one's authority; **faire ~ de candidature** put oneself forward as a candidate; **passer des** ~**s** execute deeds; **prendre ~ de** take note of; (Droit) take cognizance of; ~ **ab intestat** administrator's deed; ~ **d'association** deed of partnership; ~ **authentique** deed, legal document; (Immob) deed; ~ **de cautionnement** guarantee deed; ~ **de cession** act of cession, deed of assignation; ~**s de conférence** conference proceedings; ~ **constitutif d'une personne morale** certificate of incorporation; ~ **constitutif de société** memorandum of association; ~ **de décès** death certificate; ~ **délictueux** actus reus; ~ **dommageable** nuisance; ~ **de donation** gift deed, deed of covenant UK;

~ **de faillite** act of bankruptcy; ~ **fiduciaire** deed of trust; ~ **de garantie de tranquillité** quitclaim deed; ~ **illégal** unlawful act; ~**s illicites** illegal practices; ~ **juridique** instrument; ~ **manifeste** positive action; ~ **de mise en faillite** act of bankruptcy; ~ **de naissance** birth certificate; ~ **d'opposition** notice of opposition; ~ **de procédure** proceedings; ~ **de propriété** deed; ~ **de reconnaissance** act of acknowledgement; ~ **de recours** notice of appeal; ~ **sous seing privé** private treaty; ~ **tenant lieu de saisie d'hypothèque** deed in lieu of foreclosure; ~ **de tutelle** guardian deed; ~ **unilatéral** deed poll; **Acte unique européen** *m* Single European Act

acteur, -trice *m,f* (participant) player

actif¹, -ive *adj* (personne) active; (population) working; (marché) brisk; (Econ) (secteur) buoyant; (Info) (fichier) active; **jouer un rôle ~ dans qch** play an active role in sth; **peu ~** (Bourse) inactive

actif² *m* assets; **à l'~ du bilan** on the assets side; ~ **amortissable** depreciable assets; ~ **brut** gross assets; ~ **circulant** current assets; ~ **commercial** business assets; ~ **consommable** wasting assets; ~ **corporel** tangible assets, physical assets; ~ **détenu à l'étranger** overseas assets; ~ **disponible** liquid assets, quick assets; ~ **dormant** inactive assets; ~ **fictif** nominal assets; ~ **financier** financial assets; ~ **gelé** frozen assets; ~ **immatériel** intangible asset; ~ **immobilisé** (Compta) fixed assets; (Fin) capital assets; ~ **incorporel** intangible asset, intangible property; ~ **liquide** cash assets; ~ **à long terme** noncurrent assets; ~ **monétaire** monetary item; ~ **national** domestic assets; ~ **négociable** (Compta) quick assets; (Fin) liquid assets, quick assets; ~ **net** (Bourse) equity; (Compta) net assets; (Fin) net assets, residue; ~ **non disponible** illiquid assets; ~ **potentiel** contingent asset; ~ **principal** chief assets, principal assets; ~ **réalisable** liquid assets, quick assets; ~ **réel net par action** net tangible assets per share; ~**s des réserves monétaires mondiales** world monetary reserve assets

actif³, -ive *m,f* (personne qui travaille) working person; **les ~s** the working population

action *f* action; (Droit) lawsuit; (Bourse) share; **par ~** per share; **avoir des ~s dans une société** have shares in a company; ~**s qui augmentent/baissent** rising/falling shares; **émettre des ~s** issue shares; ~ **annulée** cancelled share AmE, cancelled share BrE; ~ **antitrust** trustbusting US (infrml); ~ **approuvée** approved share; ~ **attribuée** allotted share; ~ **d'avarie** (Assur) average claim; ~ **bêta** beta share, beta stock UK; ~ **de capital non-émise** unissued treasury share; ~ **civile** (Droit) civil action; ~ **collective** community action; (Droit) joint ⋯▸

action; ~ **communautaire** community action; ~ **concertée** joint venture; ~ **contre X** action against X; ~ **convertible** convertible share, convertible stock; ~ **cotée** listed share, quoted share; ~ **à deux sous** (infml) penny share, penny stock AmE; ~ **de dividende** junior share; ~ **à dividende différé** deferred share, deferred stock; ~ **à dividende prioritaire** preference share BrE, preferred stock AmE; ~ **à dividende prioritaire non-cumulative** noncumulative preferred stock; ~ **en dommages et intérêts** action for damages; ~ **dormante** inactive stock; ~ **sans droit de vote** nonvoting share, nonvoting stock; ~ **étrangère** foreign share, foreign stock; ~ **fictive** phantom share; ~ **fluctuante** yo-yo stock; ~ **garantie** guaranteed share; ~ **gratuite** bonus share, bonus stock; ~ **inactive** inactive stock; ~ **en justice** action, legal action, legal proceedings; ~ **nécessaire** required action; ~ **nominative** personal share; (Compta) registered share; ~ **non-cotée** unlisted share, unquoted share; ~ **non-échangeable en bourse** letter stock; ~ **non-entièrement libérée** partly-paid share; ~ **non-pair** no-par stock; ~ **non-participant** nonparticipating share; ~ **non-participative** nonparticipating share; ~ **de numéraire** share issued for cash; ~ **ordinaire** ordinary share BrE, common stock AmE; ~ **ordinaire classée** classified stock; ~ **ordinaire entièrement libérée** paid-up common share; ~ **ordinaire sans droit de vote** A-share UK; ~ **de participation** equity share; ~ **sans participation** nonparticipating preferred stock; ~ **peu active** gamma stock UK, inactive stock; ~ **au porteur** bearer share, bearer stock; ~ **prioritaire** priority share; ~ **de priorité** preference share BrE, preferred stock AmE; ~ **privilégiée avec garantie** collateralized preferred share; ~ **privilégiée imposable** taxable preferred share; ~ **privilégiée de premier rang** first preference share, first preferred stock; ~ **à prix élevé** heavy share; ~ **publique** (Droit) prosecution; ~ **rachetable au gré du porteur** retractable share; ~ **revendicative** industrial action; ~ **à revenu variable** equity share; ~ **sans risque** widow-and-orphan stock; ~ **de seconde catégorie** junior share; ~ **de société étrangère** foreign share, foreign stock; ~ **de soutien** sympathetic action; ~ **spécifique** golden share; ~ **superprivilégiée** prior-preferred stock; ~ **totalement libérée** fully-paid share; ~ **à valeur nominale** par stock, par value share, par value stock; ~ **sans valeur nominale** no-par-value share

actionnaire *mf* shareholder, stockholder; ~ **désigné** specified shareholder; ~ **déterminé** designated shareholder; ~ **intermédiaire** nominee shareholder; ~ **majoritaire** controlling shareholder, majority shareholder, majority stockholder; ~ **minoritaire** minority shareholder, minority stockholder; ~**-paravent** nominee shareholder; ~ **principal** principal stockholder

actionnariat *m* shareholding; ~ **majoritaire** majority shareholding; ~ **des salariés** employee shareholding scheme

actionner *vt* (mécanisme) activate; (système) operate

activé, e *adj* (Info) activated

activement *adv* actively; **participer** ~ **à** take an active part in; ~ **négocié** heavily traded

activer *vt* (production, travail, processus) speed up; (Info) (programme) activate

activiser *vt* capitalize

activiste *mf* activist

activité *f* activity; **entrer en** ~ (entreprise) start trading; **cesser ses** ~**s** (entreprise) cease trading, stop trading; (avocat) stop working; **reprendre ses** ~**s** (entreprise, commerçant) resume trading; **l'entrée en** ~ **de l'entreprise** the company's entry into the market; **en** ~ (employé) in active employment; ~ **d'audit** audit activity; ~ **bancaire** banking business; ~ **bénévole** voluntary work; ~ **de bienfaisance** charitable activity; ~ **boursière fictive** daisy chain; ~ **commerciale** trading, commercial activity; ~ **économique** economic activity; ~ **écran** (pour en cacher une autre) dummy activity; ~ **industrielle** industrial activity; ~ **de location d'ordinateurs** computer-leasing business; ~ **lucrative** lucrative activity, money-spinner; ~ **manufacturière** manufacturing activity; ~ **du marché** trading activity; ~ **principale** core business, principal business

activités *f pl* (Com) business, operations; ~ **accessoires** ancillary activities; ~ **boursières** securities business; ~ **habituelles** routine business, ordinary business; ~ **sur un marché** market dealing; ~ **quotidiennes de l'entreprise** daily business activities, routine company business; ~ **du secteur primaire/secondaire/tertiaire** primary/secondary/tertiary activities

actuaire *m* actuary

actualisation *f* update, updating; (des produits et charges à venir) discounting; (Info) update

actualiser *vt* bring up to date, update

actualité *f*: **l'**~ current events; (Media, Pol) current affairs

actualités *f pl* news

actuariat *m* actuarial science

actuariel, -elle *adj* actuarial

actuel, -elle *adj* current, present

actuellement *adv* at the present time, currently; ~ **en stock** currently available, currently in stock

adaptabilité *f* adaptability; ∼ **fonctionnelle** task flexibility

adaptable *adj* adaptable

adaptateur *m* adaptor; ∼ **secteur** mains adaptor BrE, current adaptor AmE; ∼ **série** serial adaptor

adaptation *f* adaptation, adjustment; (Info) localization; ∼ **du produit** product adaptation; ∼ **du travail à l'homme** human engineering

adapté, e *adj* (moyens) adequate; (contrat) custom-made; (aux exigences du client, à la demande du marché) tailored, personalized

adapter: s'∼ *v pron* adapt; **s'∼ à** (situation) adapt to, adjust to; **doit s'∼** (Brevets) must fit, must match

additif *m* (Ind) additive; (Droit) addendum; ∼ **budgétaire** supplemental budget

addition *f* (restaurant) bill BrE, check AmE; (Compta) adding, addition; (Info) addition; ∼ **binaire** binary addition

additionnel, -elle *adj* (taxe, clause) additional

additionner *vt* add, add up, tot up

adéquat, e *adj* adequate

adéquation *f* adequacy; (entre l'offre et la demande) balance; ∼ **du capital** capital adequacy; ∼ **de couverture** adequacy of coverage

adhérent, e *m,f* member; ∼ **compensateur** clearing member BrE; ∼ **mainteneur de marché** *m* market maker UK

adhérer *vi*: ∼ **à** (politique) support, adhere to; (s'inscrire à) join; (être membre de) be a member of

adhésion *f* membership; ∼ **à un syndicat** trade union membership, union affiliation; **donner son ∼ à** (projet) support

ad hoc *adj* ad hoc

adjoint, e *m,f* assistant; (au directeur) assistant manager; ∼ **administratif** *m*, **∼e administrative** *f* administrative assistant

adjudicataire *mf* (dans une vente) successful buyer; (de contrat) successful bidder

adjudicateur, -trice *m,f* awarder

adjudication *f* (attribution d'un contrat) allocation, award; (vente aux enchères) sale by auction, auction; ∼ **de bons du Trésor** Treasury bill tender UK, tap stock tender; ∼ **de gré à gré** tender by private contract; ∼ **au soumissionnaire le moins-disant** allocation to the lowest tenderer

adjuger *vt* (contrat) award; (objet à une vente aux enchères) knock down

admettre *vt* (retard) acknowledge; (tort) admit; (personne) admit; ∼ **le bien-fondé d'une réclamation** uphold a claim, allow a claim; ∼ **une entreprise à la cote** list a company, admit a company to listing

administrateur, -trice *m,f* administrator; (d'une fondation) trustee; (d'une société) member of the board; ∼ **de biens** property manager, estate manager; ∼ **chargé du développement** development director; ∼ **commercial** sales director; ∼ **des exportations** export director, export manager; ∼ **externe** nonexecutive director; ∼ **de faillite**, ∼ **judiciaire** official receiver, receiver and manager; ∼ **non-dirigeant** nonexecutive director; ∼ **système** (Info) system administrator; ∼ **des valeurs mobilières** securities administrator

administratif, -ive *adj* (bâtiment, personnel, réforme) administrative; (courrier, document, rapport) official

administration *f* (fonction publique) civil service; (Gestion) administration, management; (gouvernement) administration, government; **l'∼** the authorities; ∼ **centrale** central government; ∼ **commerciale** business administration; ∼ **des domaines** land office; ∼ **des douanes** Customs and Excise UK; ∼ **d'entreprise** business management; ∼ **fiscale** taxation authorities; ∼ **judiciaire** receivership; ∼ **locale** local government; ∼ **du personnel** personnel management, staff management; ∼ **publique** public administration; ∼ **des ventes** sales management

administrer *vt* (Gestion) manage; (patrimoine) administer

admis, e *adj* (déduction) allowed; ∼ **à faire valoir ses droits à la retraite** eligible for retirement

admissibilité *f* (à un concours) eligibility

admissible *adj* (candidat) eligible; (idée, plan) acceptable; (Droit) (preuve, témoignage, recours) admissible; ∼ **pour** eligible for

admission *f* admission, entry; ∼ **à la cote** admission to listing UK, admission to quotation; ∼ **en franchise** (douane) duty-free entry; **l'∼ d'un pays dans l'Union Européenne** the entry of a country into the European Union

adopter *vt* (enfant) adopt; (loi) pass; (produit) adopter; **faire ∼** pass; ∼ **une position** take up a position; ∼ **une position commune** adopt a joint stance; ∼ **un profil bas** keep a low profile; ∼ **progressivement** phase in; ∼ **le système métrique** go metric

adoption *f* (d'enfant) adoption; (de loi) passing; (d'un produit) adoption; ∼ **progressive** (Econ, Info) phasing in

ADP *abrév* (▸**action à dividende prioritaire**) preference share BrE, preferred stock AmE

adressable *adj* (Info) addressable

adressage *m* (Info) addressing; ∼ **absolu** absolute addressing; **mode d'∼** address mode

adresse *f* (d'une personne, d'une entreprise) address; (Info) (de données en mémoire) address; ∼ **ci-dessous** address as below; ∼ **ci-dessus** ···⟩

address as above; **l'~ précitée** the above address; **~ absolue** (Info) absolute address; **~ de base** (Info) base address; **~ commerciale** business address; **~ du destinataire** shipping address; **~ électronique, ~ e-mail** e-mail address; **~ émettrice** source address; **~ d'envoi** mailing address; **~ de l'expéditeur** return address; **~ personnelle** home address; **~ professionnelle** business address; **~ de publipostage** mailing address; **~ de réexpédition** forwarding address; **~ du siège social** registered address

adresser ① *vt* (discours, paquet) address; **~ ses réclamations à** address one's complaints to
② **s'adresser à** *v pron* (journal, programme) cater for; (V&M) appeal to; **s'~ à qn** to speak to sb; **s'~ au bureau** apply at the office, inquire at the office; **s'~ à qn pour obtenir qch** apply to sb for sth

adulte *mf* adult

ad valorem *adj* ad valorem

adversaire *mf* adversary

AELE *abrév* (▸**Association européenne de libre-échange**) EFTA (European Free Trade Association)

aérogare *f* (air) terminal

aéroglisseur *m* hovercraft

aérogramme *m* aerogram

aérographie *f* (publicité) airbrush technique

aéroport *m* airport; **~ d'arrivée** destination airport

aérosol *m* aerosol

aérospatial, e *adj* aerospace

AFC *abrév* (▸**Agence française de codification**) ≈ CUSIP US (Committee on Uniform Securities Identification Procedures)

affacturage *m* factoring

affaiblir ① *vt* (Econ) impair, weaken
② **s'affaiblir** *v pron* **l'euro s'est affaibli face au dollar** the euro has fallen against the dollar

affaiblissement *m* (de la demande) slackening

affaire *f* (ensemble de faits) matter; (transaction) deal; (commerce) business concern; (Droit) case; (scandale) affair; **faire l'~** serve the purpose; **faire une ~ avec qn** make a deal (with sb); **l'~ est annulée** the deal is off; **~ à saisir** business opportunity; **l'~ de la semaine** this week's super saver; **~ sérieuse** serious matter

affaires *f pl* business; **~ à régler** business to be transacted; **être dans les ~** be in business; **être en relations d'~ avec** do business with, deal with; **se lancer dans les ~** go into business, set up in business; **parler ~** talk business, talk shop; **le français des ~** business French; **lettre/rendez-vous d'~** business letter/appointment; **axé sur les ~** business-orientated; **~ de l'entreprise**

company's affairs; **faire des ~** do business; **les ~ ne marchent pas** business is slack; **pour ~** on business; **~ d'argent** money matters; **~ commerciales** mercantile affairs; **~ courantes** daily business, routine business; **~ en cours** pending business; **~ électroniques** e-business; **~ étrangères** foreign affairs; **~ européennes** European affairs; **~ intérieures** domestic business; (Pol) home affairs

affairisme *m* wheeling and dealing

affairiste *mf* wheeler-dealer

affaissement *m* (de marché) slump

affectation *f* (de fonds, ressources) allocation, appropriation; (de frais) apportionment; (publique) allotment; (Info) allocation, assignment; (d'un employé) appointment; (d'une équipe) deployment, posting; (à un poste ailleurs) posting; **~ des bénéfices/frais** appropriation of income/costs; **~ budgétaire** budget appropriation; **~ courante** standard allotment; **~ d'un coût** cost application; **~ pour dépenses en capital** capital allotment; **~ réglementaire** statutory allocation; **~ de ressources** resource allocation; **~ des salaires** wage assignment; **~ des tâches** job assignment

affecté, e *adj* affected; (Compta) absorbed; **~ négativement** adversely affected

affecter *vt* (fonds, ressources) allocate, appropriate; (frais) apportion; (employé) appoint; (équipe) deploy; (à un poste ailleurs) post

afférent, e *adj* (revenu, dépenses) accruing

affermage *m* leasing

affichage *m* billposting; (Droit) (procédure civile) posting; (Info) display; (publicité) poster display; **~ sur écran** soft copy

affiche *f* bill, poster; **par voie d'~** by public notice

afficher ① *vt* display, post; (Info) display; **~ une marge** post a margin; **~ ses idées** air one's opinions, air one's views
② **s'afficher** *v pron* (Info) to be displayed

affiliation *f* affiliation

affilié¹, e *adj* affiliated; **non ~** (syndicat) unaffiliated; **membre ~** affiliated member

affilié², e *adj m,f* (personne) affiliated member; (company) affiliated company

affilier ① *vt* affiliate; **~ à** affiliate to
② **s'affilier à** *v pron* affiliate oneself to

affiné, e *adj* refined

affirmation *f* assertion; **~ a priori** a priori statement

affirmer *vt* assert

affluer *vi* (argent, capitaux) flow

afflux *m* flow; **~ de capitaux/fonds** capital inflow; **~ de commandes** flow of orders

affranchir *vt* stamp; (à la machine) frank; **une lettre insuffisamment affranchie** a letter with insufficient postage

affranchissement *m* postage; **~**

supplémentaire extra postage
affrètement *m* charter, chartering; (navigation) affreightment; ~ **partagé** (fret aérien) split charter; ~ **total** whole cargo charter
affréter *vt* (avion, bateau, camion) charter
affréteur *m* charterer
affrontement *m* (conflit) confrontation
affronter *vt* confront, face up to
affût: être à l'~ de be on the lookout for, be watching out for
AFNOR *abrév* (▸**Association française de normalisation**) *French standards authority*, ≈ ANSI (American National Standards Institute), ≈ ASA (American Standards Association), ≈ BSI (British Standards Institution), ≈ National Bureau of Standards US
AFP *abrév* (▸**Agence France-Presse**) *official French news agency*
ag. *abrév* (▸**agence**) agcy (agency); (Banque) branch
AG *abrév* (▸**assemblée générale**) GA (General Assembly), GM (general meeting)
âge *m* age; ~ **atteint** attained age; ~ **d'effet de la retraite** pensionable age; ~ **à l'entrée** age at entry; ~ **limite** age limit; ~ **d'or** golden age; ~ **de la retraite** retirement age
AGE *abrév* (▸**accords généraux d'emprunt**) GAB (general arrangements to borrow); (▸**assemblée générale extraordinaire**) EGM (extraordinary general meeting)
âgé, e *adj* (homme, femme) old, elderly; **personne ~e** (Admin) senior citizen
agence *f* agency; (d'une banque) branch; ~ **bénévole** voluntary agency; ~ **centrale** head office; ~ **commerciale** sales agency, sales office; ~ **de commercialisation** marketing board; ~ **de design** design agency; ~ **donatrice** (aidant une région, un pays) donor agency; **Agence pour l'Emploi des Cadres** executive employment agency; **Agence européenne de productivité** European Productivity Agency; **Agence France-Presse** *f official French news agency*; ~ **gouvernementale** government agency; ~ **immobilière** estate agency BrE, real estate agency AmE; ~ **internationale** international agency; ~ **locale** branch office; ~ **de logement** accommodation agency, accommodations agency AmE; ~ **maritime** shipping agency, shipping office; ~ **de marketing** marketing agency; ~ **de messageries** express delivery agency, courier company; ~ **nationale** national agency; **Agence nationale pour l'emploi** ≈ Employment Service UK, ≈ Jobcentre UK; **Agence nationale pour la valorisation de la recherche** *national development research centre*; ~ **de notation** credit bureau, credit reference agency, rating agency; ~ **de**

placement employment agency, employment bureau; ~ **de presse** news agency BrE, wire service AmE; ~ **pour la protection de l'environnement** environmental protection agency; ~ **de publicité** advertising agency; ~ **de relations publiques** public relations agency, PR agency; **Agence spatiale européenne** European Space Agency; ~ **de transit en douane** customs agency; ~ **de tutelle** regulatory agency; ~ **de voyages** travel agency, travel agent
agenda *m* diary; ~ **électronique** (electronic) personal organizer
agent *m* agent; (Fin) broker, dealer; ~ **acquisiteur** acquisition agent; ~ **administratif** administration officer; ~ **d'affaires** business agent; ~ **agréé** authorized representative; ~ **d'assurance** insurance broker, insurance agent; ~ **d'assurance-vie agréé** chartered life underwriter US; ~ **en brevet d'invention** patent agent; ~ **certificateur** Certification Officer UK, certifying officer; ~ **de change** stockbroker; ~ **commercial** sales rep (infrml), sales representative; ~ **commercial exclusif** sole agent; ~ **comptable** accountant; ~ **comptable du Trésor** *government official responsible for revenue collection and administration*; ~ **en douane** customs officer; ~ **économique** economic agent; ~ **à l'étranger** foreign agent, overseas agent; ~ **exclusif** sole agent; ~ **financier** financial officer; ~ **fondé de pouvoir** authorized agent; ~ **immobilier** estate agent BrE, realtor AmE; ~ **de l'impôt** taxation officer; ~ **de listage** listing agent US; ~ **de maîtrise** first-line supervisor; ~ **maritime** shipping agent; ~ **maritime-transitaire** shipping and forwarding agent; ~ **de marques** (propriété intellectuelle) trademark agent; ~ **négociateur** bargaining agent; ~ **payeur** paymaster; ~ **de placement** selling agent; ~ **de la Police de l'air et des frontières** immigration officer; ~ **portuaire** port agent; ~ **de prêts** lending officer, loan officer; ~ **de recouvrement** debt collector; ~ **tireur** drawing officer; ~ **de voyage** travel agent
agétac *abrév* (**Accord général sur les tarifs douaniers et le commerce**) General Agreement on Tariffs and Trade, GATT
agglomération *f* (Admin) town; **l'~ lyonnaise** Lyons and its suburbs; ~ **urbaine** built-up area, urban area
aggloméré *m* chipboard
aggravation *f* (d'une situation) worsening; (du chômage) increase; ~ **unique** (Assur) unique impairment
aggraver: s'~ *v pron* worsen, deteriorate
aggrégat *m*: ~ **de la production** aggregate output
agio *m* (échange de devises) agio
agios *m pl* (intérêts débiteurs) bank charges, ···❯

bank commission

agiotage m (Bourse) speculation, gambling

agiotager vi speculate, gamble

agioteur m speculator, gambler

agir vi act; ~ **de bonne foi** act in good faith; ~ **pour le compte de qn**, ~ **au nom de qn** act on sb's behalf; ~ **dans l'exercice de ses fonctions** act in one's official capacity; **faire** ~ actuate; ~ **illégalement** act illegally, engage in illegal activity; ~ **sur le marché** manipulate the market; ~ **en médiateur** mediate

âgisme m ageism BrE, agism AmE

agitation f unrest; (Bourse) flurry of activity

AGO abrév (▶**assemblée générale ordinaire**) OGM (ordinary general meeting)

agrafe f (pour papiers) staple

agrafer vt staple

agrafeuse f stapler

agrandir [1] vt (entreprise) expand, grow; (Info) (fenêtre) maximize [2] **s'agrandir** v pron (entreprise) expand, grow; (marge) widen

agrandissement m (d'une entreprise) expansion; (d'une photo) enlargement

agréé, e adj (Admin) authorized, registered; (contrat, requête) approved; (institution, qualification) accredited

agréer vt (Admin) authorize, register; (réclamation, contrat, requête) approve; (institution, qualification) accredit; **je vous prie d'**~, **Madame/Monsieur, l'expression de mes sentiments les meilleurs** (personne nommée) Yours sincerely BrE, Sincerely yours AmE; (personne non nommée) yours faithfully BrE, faithfully yours AmE

agrégat m aggregate; ~**s monétaires** monetary aggregates

agrément m (d'un contrat, d'une requête) approval; (d'une qualification) accreditation; **lettre d'**~ letter of acceptance; **donner son** ~ to give one's consent; ~ **fiscal** tax relief

agréments m pl amenities

agressif, -ive adj aggressive

agricole adj agricultural

agriculteur, -trice m,f farmer; ~ **admissible/qualifiable** qualifying farmer

agriculture f agriculture, farming; ~ **biologique** organic farming; ~ **industrielle** factory farming; ~ **intensive** intensive farming; ~ **de subsistance** subsistence farming

agroalimentaire m food-processing industry

agro-industries f pl agribusiness

agronome mf agronomist

agronomie f agronomy

aguiche f (V&M) teaser

AIB abrév (▶**Accord international sur le blé**) IWA (International Wheat Agreement)

AIDA abrév (▶**attention, intérêt, désir, action**) AIDA (attention, interest, desire, action)

aide f help; (en argent) aid, assistance; (subvention) grant, subsidy; (Info) help, support; **bénéficiant d'une** ~ **publique** government-backed; ~ **alimentaire** food aid; ~ **bilatérale** bilateral aid; ~ **communautaire** Community aid; ~ **complémentaire** supplementary assistance; ~ **contextuelle** context-sensitive help; ~ **à la création d'entreprise** business start-up grant, enterprise allowance UK; ~ **à la décision** decision support; ~ **au développement** development aid, donor aid; ~ **de l'État** state help; ~ **à l'étranger** foreign aid; ~ **étrangère** foreign aid; ~ **extérieure** overseas aid; ~ **financière** financial aid, financial assistance; ~ **financière en capital** capital aid; ~ **fiscale** tax assistance; ~ **gouvernementale** government assistance; ~ **d'interfinancement** cross subsidy; ~ **judiciaire**, ~ **juridique** legal aid; ~ **liée** tied aid; ~ **en ligne** online help; ~ **au logement** housing benefit UK, housing subsidy; ~ **en nature** aid in kind; ~ **publique au développement** official development assistance; ~ **à la réinsertion** workfare; ~ **sociale** social security; ~ **structurelle** structural aid; ~ **d'urgence** emergency aid

aide-caissier, -ière m,f assistant cashier BrE, assistant teller AmE

aide-comptable mf accounting clerk, book-keeper

aide-programme f programme aid BrE, program aid AmE

aider vt help; (industrie) aid; (pays pauvre) give aid to; ~ **à** help towards; ~ **à faire** help in doing; ~ **qn financièrement** help sb financially; ~ **qn de ses conseils** give sb helpful advice; **l'état aide les agriculteurs** farmers are subsidized by the government; **le temps aidant** with time

aiguillage m (Transp) points BrE, switch AmE; (Info) switch; **une erreur d'**~ (Transp) a signalling error; (confusion) a mix-up

aiguilleur m pointsman BrE, switchman AmE; ~ **du ciel** air-traffic controller

aimable adj polite

aîné, e adj Snr, senior

air m air; ~ **conditionné** air conditioning

aire f area; ~ **de chargement** loading bay; ~ **de détente** recreational facility; ~ **d'embarquement** departure lounge; ~ **ouverte** (dans une zone bâtie) open space; ~ **de stationnement** car park; ~ **de stockage** storage area

AIS abrév (▶**Accord international sur le sucre**) ≈ ISA (International Sugar Agreement)

aisé, e adj (facile) easy; (riche) affluent

ajournement m (de voyage, décision)

postponement; (**Droit**) (de débat, procès) adjournment; **∼ de peine** *or* **du prononcé de la peine** non-imposition of a sentence

ajourner *vt* (voyage, projet, décision) postpone, put off; (**Droit**) (débat, procès) adjourn; **∼ une sentence** adjourn sentence; **les débats sont ajournés d'une semaine** discussions are adjourned for a week; **un procès ajourné** an adjourned trial

ajout *m* addition; **faire des ∼s à** make additions to

ajouter ① *vt* add; **∼ qch à** add sth to; **je n'ai rien à ∼** I've nothing to add; **j'ajouterais que** I would add that; **si l'on ajoute à cela que** if you add the fact that; **permettez-moi d'∼ une remarque** allow me to make an additional comment; **∼ foi à qch** put faith in sth; **∼ à la confusion** add to the confusion ② **s'ajouter** *v pron* **s'∼ à** be added to; **les désordres sociaux viennent s'∼ aux difficultés économiques** on top of the economic difficulties there is social unrest

ajustage *m* adjustment

ajustement *m* (de prix, salaires) adjustment; **∼ budgétaire** budgetary adjustment; **∼ d'impôt** tax adjustment; **∼ du marché** market adjustment; **∼ monétaire** monetary accommodation

ajuster *vt* adjust; **∼ l'économie en fonction de la demande globale** fine-tune the economy in line with demand

alarme *f* alarm; **donner l'∼** raise the alarm

aléatoire *adj* (Assur) aleatory; (hasardeux) risky, uncertain; (résultat) unpredictable; (sondage, échantillon, nombre) random

ALENA *abrév* (▶**Accord de libre-échange nord-américain**) NAFTA (North American Free Trade Area)

alerte *f* alarm, alert; **donner l'∼** raise the alarm; **∼ à la bombe** bomb scare

algèbre *f* algebra; **∼ de Boole** Boolean algebra

algorithme *m* algorithm

algorithmique *adj* algorithmic

alias *adv* also known as, a.k.a., alias

aliénable *adj* (Droit) alienable

aliénataire *mf* (Droit) alienee

aliénation *f* alienation; **∼ de titres** security disposal

aligné, e *adj* in a line; **∼ à droite** (Info) right-justified; **∼ à gauche** (Info) left-justified

alignement *m* alignment; (Info) array; (des salaires) comparability; **∼ sur la concurrence** competitive parity UK, defensive budgeting; **∼ sur les prix du marché** market comparison approach; **∼ des salaires sur le coût de la vie** cost of living adjustment

aligner ① *vt* (Info) align, aline AmE; **∼ qch sur qch** bring sth into line with sth; **∼ à droite** right-justify; **∼ à gauche** left-justify

② **s'aligner** *v pron* **s'∼ sur** (concurrents) fall into line with; (Bourse) shadow

aliment *m* food, foodstuff; **∼ tout préparé** convenience food; **∼s pour bétail** (agriculture) feedstuffs; **∼s biologiques** organic food; **∼s macrobiotiques** health food; **∼s naturels** health food

alimentation *f* diet; (en eau, énergie) supply; **l'∼** (commerce) food trade; **magasin d'∼** grocery (store); **∼ de base** basic foodstuffs; **∼ continue** (Info) chain feeding; **∼ feuille à feuille** sheet feeding; **∼ non-interruptible** uninterruptible power supply; **∼ du papier** paper feed; **∼ de secours** battery backup; **∼ secteur** mains BrE, supply network AmE

alimenter *vt* (personne) feed; (inflation) fuel; **∼ en papier** (imprimante) feed with paper

alinéa *m* paragraph; (espace) indent

allée *f* aisle

allégation *f* allegation

allègement *m* (de structure, procédure) simplification; (de l'impôt) reduction; (de contrôle) relaxing; **∼ de la dette** debt relief; **∼ fiscal** tax relief

alléger *vt* (structure, procédure) simplify; (impôt) cut, reduce; (contrôle) relax; **qui allège le travail** labour-saving BrE, labor-saving AmE

allégué, e *adj* alleged

aller¹ *vi* go; **∼ contre** go against; **∼ à contre-courant** go against the stream; **∼ à l'encontre de la tendance générale** buck the trend; **∼ jusqu'au bout de qch** follow sth through; **∼ mal** (économie) go downhill; **∼ mieux** take a turn for the better; **∼ de pair avec** go hand in hand with; **∼ à vau-l'eau** (économie) go to rack and ruin

aller² *m* one-way ticket; **∼ plein-tarif** standard single; **∼-retour** return ticket BrE, round-trip ticket AmE; **∼-retour de fin de semaine** (tarif) weekend return; **∼ simple** single BrE, single ticket BrE, one-way ticket AmE; **∼ simple plein-tarif** standard single

alliance *f* alliance; **∼ de coalition** coalition alliance; **∼ stratégique** strategic alliance

allier *vt* ally, unite

allocataire *mf* benefit recipient, welfare recipient AmE

allocation *f* (aide sociale) allowance, benefit; (des ressources) allocation, appropriation; **∼s allouées** allocated benefits UK; **∼ chômage** unemployment benefit BrE, unemployment compensation AmE; **∼ de devises** foreign currency allowance; **∼ efficiente** efficient allocation; **∼s familiales** child benefit UK, family allowance payments; **∼ des fonds** budget appropriation; **∼ pour frais** expense allowance; **∼ de garantie** collateral assignment; **∼ imposable** taxable allowance; **∼ journalière** daily allowance; **∼ logement** housing benefit UK, housing subsidy; **∼ maladie** sickness benefit; **∼ de** ⸭⸭⸭⸭

maternité maternity benefit; ~**s et prestations imposables** taxable allowances and benefits; ~ **des ressources** resource allocation; ~**s de la Sécurité Sociale** Social Security benefits, welfare benefits; ~ **de subsistance** subsistence allowance

allocution *f* address; **une** ~ **de bienvenue/clôture** a welcoming/closing address

allonger *vt* lengthen

allouer *vt* allocate; (prêt) grant; (temps) allocate, allow; (Info) assign; ~ **des dommages et intérêts** adjudge damages

allumé, e *adj* (voyant) on; (infrml), lit

almanach *m* yearbook

alphabétique *adj* alphabetical

altération *f* (de faits, texte, chiffres) distortion; (de monnaie) falsification; (Info) (de fichier) corruption

altérer *vt* (fait, texte, chiffres) distort; (monnaie) falsify

alternance *f* alternation; **en** ~ **avec** alternately with

alternatif, -ive *adj* alternate

alternative *f* alternative; **il n'y a pas d'**~ there is no alternative

alterné, e *adj* alternate

alterner *vt* alternate

altruisme *m* altruism

aluminium *m* aluminium BrE, aluminum AmE

AM *abrév* (▶**Assurance maladie**) health insurance

amalgamation *f* (d'entreprises) merger

amalgamer *vt* (entreprises) merge

amarrage *m* (d'un navire) mooring; (dans un dock) docking

amassé, e *adj* accrued

amasser *vt* (fortune, papiers) accumulate, amass

amateur¹, -trice *adj* (sport) amateur

amateur², -trice *m,f* (sport) amateur; ~ **de risques** risk-taker

ambassade *f* embassy

ambassadeur, -drice *m,f* ambassador

ambiance *f* atmosphere; (Bourse) tone; ~ **de travail** work atmosphere; ~ **à la baisse** bearish tone, bearishness; ~ **à la hausse** bullish tone, bullishness; ~ **du marché** market tone

AME *abrév* (▶**Accord monétaire européen**) EMA (European Monetary Agreement)

amélioration *f* improvement; (apportée à un bien immobilier) improvement; (Info) upgrade; ~ **de l'habitat** home improvement; ~ **locative** leasehold improvement; ~ **matérielle** hardware upgrade; ~ **sensible** (Econ) marked upswing, marked upturn

améliorer 1 *vt* (situation, résultat, performance) improve; (Info) upgrade

2 **s'améliorer** *v pron* improve

aménagement *m* (de région, ville) development; (de magasin, bureau) fitting out; (d'horaire) arrangement; (par rapport à la loi, au règlement) adjustment; ~ **urbain/régional** urban/regional development; **l'**~ **du temps de travail** flexible working hours; ~ **du commerce** trade fixture; ~ **de l'environnement** environmental planning; ~**s fiscaux** tax adjustments; ~ **du territoire** land-use planning, town and country planning UK

aménager *vt* (région, ville) develop; (magasin, bureau) fit out; (horaire) arrange; (règlement) adjust

amende *f* fine; (pour retard) penalty; **infliger une** ~ **à qn** fine sb; (pour retard) penalize sb

amendement *m* (Droit) amendment; ~ **provisoire** draft amendment

amender *vt* (loi, contrat) amend

amener *vt* bring; ~ **à la grève** bring out on strike

amenuisement *m* dwindling; ~ **de la demande** contraction of demand

américain, e *adj* American

Américain, e *m,f* American

Amérique *f* America; ~ **centrale** Central America; ~ **du Nord** North America; ~ **du Sud** South America

amiable *adj* amicable; **à l'**~ amicably, by mutual consent; ~ **compositeur** *m* (Droit) arbitrator

amical, e *adj* amicable

AMM *abrév* (▶**adhérent mainteneur de marché**) market maker UK; (▶**autorisation de mise sur le marché**) (industrie pharmaceutique) marketing authorization

amont *m* (de cours d'eau) upper reaches; **en** ~ upstream; **dès l'**~ (dans un processus) from the initial stages

amorçage *m* (Info) booting, bootup; ~ **automatique** autoboot

amorce *f* beginning; (Média) standfirst (jarg)

amorcer *vt* begin; (processus, discussion, changement) begin, initiate; (Info) boot, boot up

amortir *vt* (action, emprunt) redeem; (son, choc) absorb; (actif) amortize; (dette) amortize, liquidate

amortissable *adj* (Bourse) redeemable; (Compta) amortizable

amortissement *m* (d'action, d'emprunt) redemption; (de son, choc) absorption; (d'actif) amortization; (Compta) (perte de valeur) depreciation; (de dette) amortization; ~ **accéléré** accelerated depreciation; ~ **comptable** book depreciation; ~ **dégressif** accelerated cost recovery system, reducing balance; ~ **dérogatoire** exceptional depreciation, tax-based depreciation; ~ **économique franc** free depreciation; ~ **d'un emprunt** amortization of a loan; ~ **du fonds de commerce** goodwill amortization;

~ linéaire straight-line amortization, straight-line depreciation; **~ récupérable** recapturable depreciation

ampleur f (du marché) breadth

amplification f intensification

amplitude f amplitude; **~ de fluctuation** degree of fluctuation

an m year; **par ~** per annum; **sur un ~** over one year

analogique adj (Info) analog; **~-numérique** analog-digital

analogue adj similar; **~ à** similar to

analyse f analysis; (Info) scanning; **~ approfondie** in-depth analysis; **~ commerciale économique** commercial economic analysis; **faire l'~ de** analyse BrE, analyze AmE in the final analysis; **~ d'activité** activity analysis; **~ de l'année de base** base year analysis; **~ des besoins** needs analysis; **~ budgétaire** budget analysis; **~ comptable** accounting analysis; **~ d'un compte** account analysis; **~ des concurrents** competitor analysis; **~ de conjoncture** analysis of time series; **~ des coûts** cost analysis; **~ coûts-avantages** cost-benefit analysis; **~ des coûts de distribution** distribution cost analysis; **~ coûts-rendements** cost-benefit analysis; **~ de crédit** credit analysis; **~ différentielle** differential analysis; **~ dynamique** dynamic evaluation; **~ des écarts** variance analysis; **~ des écarts de coûts** analysis of cost variances; **~ électronique des données** electronic data processing; **~ d'entrée/de sortie** input/output analysis; **~ d'équilibre général** general equilibrium analysis; **~ des facteurs de profit** profit-factor analysis; **~ factorielle** factor analysis; **~ financière** financial analysis; **~ fonctionnelle** functional analysis, systems analysis; **~ des forces, des faiblesses, des opportunités et des menaces** strengths, weaknesses, opportunities and threats analysis, SWOT analysis; **~ intrants-extrants** input/output analysis; **~ des marchandises** commodity analysis UK; **~ de marché** market analysis; **~ des marchés** market research; **~ marginale** incremental analysis; (de la valeur marchande) marginal analysis; **~ des matières premières** commodity analysis UK; **~ matricielle** matrix analysis; **~ des méthodes** process analysis; **~ modulée** differential analysis; **~ des motivations** motivational analysis; **~ par secteur d'activité** business segment reporting; **~ par segments** (étude de marché) cluster analysis; **~ du point mort** break-even analysis; **~ préalable** feasibility report; **~ de produit** product analysis; **~ qualitative** qualitative analysis; **~ quantitative** quantitative analysis; **~ de rapport** ratio analysis; **~ du rapport coût-efficacité** cost-effectiveness analysis; **~ de rentabilité**

break-even analysis; **~ de réseau** network analysis; **~ sectorielle** sector analysis; **~ séquentielle** sequential analysis; **~ d'une situation comptable** statement analysis; **~ des tâches** job analysis, operations analysis; **~ technique** technical analysis; **~ de tendance** trend analysis; **~ de valeur** value analysis; **~ de variance** variance analysis; **~ des ventes** sales analysis; **~ des ventes au détail** retail sales analysis; **~ verticale** vertical analysis

analyser vt (ventes, coûts, résultats) analyse BrE, analyze AmE

analyseur m analyser BrE, analyzer AmE

analyste mf analyst; **~ commercial** m sales analyst; **~ pétrolier** m oil analyst; **~ de placements** m investment analyst; **~ de systèmes** m systems analyst; **~ des ventes** m sales analyst

analyste-programmeur m analyst programmer

analytique adj analytical

anarcho-syndicalisme m anarcho-syndicalism

ancêtre mf ancestor

ancien, -enne adj old; **~ affrètement** m (maritime) old charter; **~ client** m former customer; **~ employé** m ex-employee; **~ne loi** f old law; **~ numéro** m (édition) back issue, back number

ancienneté f seniority; **avoir de l'~** be senior; **promotion à la ~** promotion based on seniority; **trois ans d'~** three years' service

ancrage m anchorage

angle m angle; **~ d'attaque** line of attack

animateur, -trice m,f (radio, télévision) announcer; (de cours, stage) instructor, facilitator; **~ de groupe** group leader

animation f: **~ des ventes** sales drive

animé, e adj (marché) active, brisk; (currency) buoyant

animer vt (débat, cérémonie) lead; (stage) run, teach; (quartier, réunion) liven up; **animé par** (association, stage) run by

année f year; **chaque ~** annually, every year; **d'une ~ sur l'autre** year-to-year; **dans les dix ~s qui ont précédé 2001** in the decade to 2001; **depuis les dix dernières ~s** over the last decade; **une ~ accomplie** one completed year; **~ d'acquisition** year of acquisition; **~ de base** base year; **~ bissextile** leap year; **~ budgétaire** financial year, fiscal year; **~ civile** calendar year; **~ complète d'imposition** full taxation year; **l'~ considérée** the year under review; **~ en cours** current year; **~ difficile** lean year; **~ d'émission** year of issue; **~ exceptionnelle** banner year, bumper year; **~ fiscale** natural business year, tax year; **~ précédente** preceding

⋯⋗

year, previous year; ~ **de référence** base year

annexe¹ *adj* (document) attached; (budget, activités, revenus) additional; (industries) subsidiary

annexe² *f* appendix; (bâtiment, document) annexe BrE, annex AmE; **en ~** in an appendix; **~ à porter sur les comptes** notes to the accounts

annexer *vt* (joindre) append (**à** to); (Pol) annex

annonce *f* (information) announcement; (publicité) advertisement, advert (infrml), ad (infrml); **mettre/passer une ~ dans un journal** put/place an advertisement in a newspaper; **~ classée** classified advertisement, classified ad (infrml); **~ mensongère** false advertising claim; **~ publicitaire** advertisement, advert (infrml); **~ radiophonique/par voie de presse** (information) radio/press announcement

annoncer *vt* (information) announce; **~ la nouvelle** break the news; **comme annoncé** as reported

annonceur, -euse *m,f* (radio, télévision) announcer; (V&M) advertiser

annoter *vt* annotate, write sth in the margin of

annuaire *m* directory; (Média) yearbook; **~ du commerce** trade directory; **~ de données commerciales de base** Trade Data Elements Directory; **~ électronique** online directory; **~ professionnel** trade directory, Red Book US (infrml); **~ de statistiques** annual abstract of statistics; **~ téléphonique** phone book, telephone directory

annualiser *vt* annualize

annuel, -elle *adj* annual, yearly

annuellement *adv* annually, yearly

annuité *f* annual instalment BrE, annual installment AmE; (année de service) year of pensionable service; **~ d'amortissement** annual amortization; **~ d'assurance** insurance annuity; **~ complémentaire** wraparound annuity; **~ conditionnelle** qualifying annuity; **~ de remboursement** annual repayment

annulation *f* (d'une commande, d'un ordre, d'un projet) cancellation; (d'un accord, d'un contrat) invalidation, voidance; (d'une dette) writing off; (Droit) (d'une loi) repeal, rescission; (d'un verdict) revocation; (d'une amende) waive; (d'une décision) annulment; (Pol) overruling

annuler *vt* (commande, ordre, projet) cancel; (accord, contrat) invalidate, void; (dette) write off; (Droit) (loi) repeal, rescind; (ordonnance, verdict) revoke; (amende) waive; (décision) annul; (Pol) (décision) overrule

anomalie *f* anomaly, irregularity; (Info) fault

anomie *f* anomie

anonymat *m* anonymity; **garder l'~** remain anonymous

anonyme *adj* (don) anonymous

anormal, e *adj* abnormal

ANPE *abrév* (▸**Agence nationale pour l'emploi**) ≈ Employment Service UK, ≈ Jobcentre UK

antécédent¹, e *adj* previous

antécédent² *m* previous occurrence, past history; **elle a un ~ judiciaire** she has a criminal record

antécédents *m pl* previous history, track record; **~ financiers** financial history; **~ en matière de crédit** credit history

antémémoire *f* cache memory

antenne *f* (de radio, TV) aerial; (de radar, satellite) antenna; (poste détaché) branch; **~s locales/régionales** local/regional branches; **être à l'~** be on the air; **passer à l'~** go on the air; **~s commerciales** commercial outlets; **~ financière** money desk; **~ sur le terrain** field organization

anticipation *f* anticipation, expectation; **~ des prix** anticipatory pricing; **~ stratégique** anticipatory response

anticipé, e *adj* early; (Fin) before due date; **avec mes remerciements ~s** thanking you in advance; **faire qch de façon ~e** do sth in advance

anticiper *vt* (paiement) anticipate; **~ l'action de** second-guess (infrml)

anticoncurrentiel, -elle *adj* anticompetitive

anticrénelage *m* (Info) antialiasing

anticyclique *adj* anticyclical

antidatation *f* backdating, predating

antidater *vt* backdate, predate

anti-inflationniste *adj* anti-inflationary

antiréfléchissant, e *adj* glare-free

antireflet *adj inv* (Info) anti-glare

antirequins *m pl* shark repellents, porcupine provisions

antisélection *f* adverse selection

antisyndicalisme *m* union-bashing (infrml)

antitrust *adj inv* (loi) anti-monopoly UK, antitrust US

antivirus *m* antivirus software

antivol *m* antitheft device

AOC *abrév* (▸**appellation d'origine contrôlée**) *guaranteed quality label for wine*

AP *abrév* (▸**Assistance publique**) *authority which manages state-owned hospitals and Social Services*

apaiser *vt* conciliate, pacify

apathie *f* sluggishness

apatride *adj* nationless, stateless

APE *abrév* (▸**Assemblée Parlementaire Européenne**) EP (European Parliament)

APEC *abrév* (▸**Agence Pour l'Emploi des Cadres**) executive employment agency

aperçu *m* (de situation) outline, overview; ∼ **avant impression** print preview; ∼ **du marché** market view; ∼ **stratégique** strategic overview

apériteur *m* leading underwriter

aplanir *vt* (difficultés) iron out, smooth out

aplatir ⟦1⟧ *vt* (carton, tôle) flatten
⟦2⟧ **s'aplatir** *v pron* **s'**∼ **devant qn** grovel in front of sb

appareil *m* device; (pour la maison) appliance; (téléphone) phone, telephone; **qui est à l'**∼**?** who is speaking?; ∼ **en service** (Info) busy; ∼ **de chauffage** heater; ∼ **électrique** electrical appliance; ∼**s ménagers** household appliances, white goods; ∼ **de surveillance** monitor

appareiller *vi* (navire) leave port

apparenté, e *adj* (société) affiliated

appartement *m* flat BrE, apartment AmE; ∼ **en rez-de-jardin** garden flat BrE, garden apartment AmE

appartement-témoin *m* show flat

appartenir *vi:* ∼ **à** belong to

appauvri, e *adj* impoverished

appauvrissement *m* impoverishment

appel *m* call; (téléphonique) call; (Droit) appeal; **à l'**∼ **du marché** at the market call; **faire** ∼ (Droit) appeal, enter an appeal; **faire** ∼ **d'une décision** appeal against a judgement; **faire** ∼ **au marché pour** tap the market for; **faire un** ∼ **d'offres** appeal for tenders; **faire un** ∼ **de fonds** appeal for funds; **sur** ∼ on a per call basis; ∼ **en attente** call waiting; ∼ **de capitaux** capital-raising (operation); ∼ **de départ** outgoing call; ∼ **de l'extérieur** incoming call; ∼ **de fonds** call for capital, appeal for funds; ∼ **gratuit** Freefone call BrE, toll-free call AmE; ∼ **d'impôts** tax appeal; ∼ **international** international call; ∼ **local** local call; ∼ **longue distance** long-distance call, toll call US; ∼ **de marge du jour** mark to market, value to the market; ∼ **d'offres** (pour un marché) appeal for tenders, call for bids; ∼ **en PCV** reverse charge call BrE, collect call AmE; ∼ **sélectif numérique** digital selective calling; ∼ **téléphonique** phone call, telephone call; ∼ **à trois** three-way call; ∼ **d'urgence** emergency call

appeler *vt* call, phone; ∼ **en PCV** make a reverse charge call BrE, make a collect call AmE; ∼ **à la grève** call a strike; **en** ∼ **d'un jugement** appeal against a judgement; ∼ **qn par l'interphone** call sb over the intercom

appellation *f* name; ∼ **d'origine** (de produit) indication of country of origin; ∼ **d'origine contrôlée** *label guaranteeing quality of wine*; ∼ **d'origine protégée** Protected Designation of Origin

appendice *m* appendix

applicable *adj* applicable; (Droit) enforceable; ∼ **à** applicable to; **être** ∼ come into force; **facilement/difficilement** ∼ easy/

difficult to implement

application *f* (de décision, mesure) application; (d'un règlement) implementation, application; (Info) application; (programme) applications program; ∼ **logicielle** software application; ∼ **des stratégies** strategy implementation

appliquer ⟦1⟧ *vt* apply; (loi) apply, enforce
⟦2⟧ **s'appliquer** *v pron* **s'**∼ **à** concentrate on; (Info) apply to; **ne s'applique pas à** is not applicable to

appliquette *f* (Info) applet

appoint *m* (monnaie) exact change; **faire l'**∼ give the exact change; **faire l'**∼ **à** (économies, finances) top up UK

appointements *m pl* salary

apport *m* (financier, personnel) contribution; **faire un** ∼ (en capital) make a contribution; ∼ **de capital** capital contribution, contribution of capital; ∼ **chimique** chemical input; ∼ **en espèces** (investissement) cash contribution; ∼ **de gestion** management buy-in; ∼ **de main-d'œuvre** additional labour BrE, additional labor AmE

apporter *vt* (fonds) contribute; (preuve) adduce; ∼ **une aide à** (pays) aid; ∼ **une contribution à** (œuvre, programme) make a contribution to; ∼ **des éléments sur** carry information on

apporteur, -euse *m,f* acquisition agent; ∼ **de capitaux** contributor of capital

apposer *vt* affix, append; ∼ **la date au tampon** stamp the date; ∼ **sa signature** affix *ou* append one's signature, sign; ∼ **son sceau sur qch** put one's seal to sth

appréciable *adj* appreciable

appréciation *f* (évaluation, jugement) assessment; (d'une monnaie) appreciation; ∼ **d'une devise** currency appreciation; ∼ **des investissements** investment appraisal; ∼ **limitée** limited discretion; ∼ **du mérite** merit rating; ∼ **monétaire** currency appreciation; ∼ **du personnel** staff appraisal; ∼ **restreinte** (ordre) limited discretion; ∼ **des risques** risk assessment

apprécier ⟦1⟧ *vt* (aimer) appreciate; (évaluer) estimate; ∼ **qch au-dessus de sa valeur** overvalue sth; ∼ **qch au-dessous de sa valeur** undervalue sth
⟦2⟧ **s'apprécier** *v pron* (augmenter de valeur) appreciate

apprendre *vt* learn; (être informé de) hear, learn; ∼ **qch de manière indirecte** hear sth through the grapevine; ∼ **que** hear *ou* learn that

apprenti, e *m,f* apprentice; ∼ **programmeur** *m* trainee programmer

apprentissage *m* apprenticeship; **faire son** ∼ **chez** serve an apprenticeship with; ∼ **sur le tas** learning-by-doing, on the job training; **être en** ∼ **chez qn** be apprenticed to sb; ∼ **à distance** distance learning; ∼ ···⟩

des langues assisté par ordinateur computer-aided language learning, computer-assisted language learning; **~ pratique** hands-on training; **~ de produit** product initiation

approbation f (d'un document, des comptes) approval; **pour ~** for approval; **donner son ~ à qch** give sth one's approval; **~ de comptes** accounts certification; **~ modérée** qualified approval; **~ de projet** project approval

approche f (d'un client, problème) approach; **~ des excédents** surplus approach, surplus value; **~ par les coûts** cost approach; **~ par l'enquête** investigative approach; **~ personnalisée** person-to-person approach, one-to-one approach; **~ du produit** (marketing) commodity approach; **~ pyramidale d'investissement** bottom-up approach to investing; **~ qualitative** qualitative approach; **~ de rendement** income approach

approcher vt **~ qn au sujet de** approach sb about sth; **nous approchons du but** we're nearly there; **nous approchons du marché unique** the single market will soon be with us; **~ de** (Compta) approximate

approfondi, e adj in-depth

approfondir vt (recherches, étude) extend

appropriation f (de fonds) appropriation

approprié, e adj appropriate

approprier: s'approprier v pron appropriate

approuvé, e adj approved; **lu et ~** read and approved

approuver vt (être favorable à) be in favour of BrE, be in favor of AmE; (donner son approbation) approve; **~ les comptes** agree the books

approvisionnement m (réserve) supply; (activité) supplying; (V&M) purchasing, procurement; (d'un commerce) stocking; (fournisseur) supplier; **assurer l'~ en pétrole/eau potable** ensure the supply of oil/drinking water; **les industriels diversifient leurs ~s** industrialists vary their suppliers; **directeur de l'~** purchasing manager, procurement manager; **service des ~s** purchasing department, supplies department; **~ à l'extérieur** (Gestion) outsourcing; **~ invisible** invisible supply

approvisionner ① vt supply; (commerce) stock, supply; (compte) pay money into; **une boutique mal approvisionnée** a badly stocked shop; **votre compte n'est plus approvisionné depuis trois mois** your account has not been in credit for three months ② **s'approvisionner** v pron **s'~ en** buy in, stock up on

approximation f approximation, rough guide

approximativement adv approximately

appui m support, backup; **~ financier** financial backing; **~ populaire** grass-roots support

appuyer ① vt (sur un bouton) press; (raisonnement) support, back up; (candidat) back, support; **~ financièrement** back ② **s'appuyer** v pron lean; **s'~ sur** (personne, argument, témoignage) rely on

âpre adj harsh; **~ au gain** greedy

après¹ adv afterwards; **par ~** ex post facto (frml)

après² prép after; **d'~** according to; **d'~ les règles** according to the rules, under the rules US; **~ bourse** after-hours, after-market; **~ examen** on examination; **~ faillite** post-bankruptcy; **~ impôts** after-tax

après-guerre m or f postwar period; **d'après-guerre** postwar

après-vente adj inv after-sales

apte adj (capable) capable; (ayant les qualifications requises) qualified; **être ~ à qch** (Droit) have legal capacity to do sth; **~ au travail** able to work

aptitude f ability, aptitude; (dans le travail) competence; (savoir-faire) skill; (Droit) legal capacity; **~s à la communication** communication skills; **~ manuelle** manual skill; **~ professionnelle** aptitude, capacity

apurer vt (comptes) audit; (dette, passif) discharge

aquaculture f aquaculture

AR abrév (▶**accusé de réception**) acknowledgement of receipt

arbitrage m (Fin, Bourse) arbitrage; (Droit) arbitration, mediation; **~ sur actions** stock arbitrage; **~ de change** arbitration of exchange, currency arbitrage; **~ par compensation** pendulum arbitration; **~ comptant-terme** cash and carry arbitrage; **~ de fusion** merger arbitrage; **~ d'indice** stock index arbitrage; **~ en matière de conflits du travail** industrial arbitration; **~ d'office** compulsory arbitration UK; **~ de portefeuille** portfolio switching; **~ des risques** risk arbitrage; **~ sur titres** arbitrage in securities UK

arbitragiste mf arbitrager; **~ d'investissement** investment hedger; **~ de place en place** shunter

arbitral, e adj arbitral; **commission ~e** arbitration board; **sentence ~e** ruling of the arbitration board; **tribunal ~** arbitration tribunal

arbitre m (Droit) arbitrator, mediator; **être ~ de** (concours) adjudicate; **~ unique** sole arbitrator

arboriculture f: **~ fruitière** fruit farming

arbre m (Info) tree

architecte mf architect; **~ naval** naval architect

architecture f architecture; **~ de réseau** (Info) network architecture

archivage *m* archiving

archive *f* record; (Info) archive

archiver *vt* file; (Info) archive

archives *f pl* archives, records; ～ **de l'État** public records

archiviste *mf* archivist, record keeper

argent *m* money; (métal) silver; **avoir de l'～ à ne plus savoir qu'en faire** have money to burn; **en avoir pour son ～** get good value for money; **faire de l'～** make money; **le temps c'est de l'～** time is money; **～ en caisse** cash in hand; **～ comptant** cash; **～ devant soi** money up front; **～ qui dort** idle money; **～ électronique** e-money, e-cash; **～ facile** easy money; **～ improductif** idle money; **～ au jour le jour** day-to-day money; **～ liquide** cash, ready money; **～ de poche** pocket money, spending money; **～ en trop** spare cash; **～ virtuel** e-money, e-cash

argument *m* argument; **trouver de bons ～s en faveur de/contre** make a good case for/against; **～ de vente** selling point

argumentaire *m* (dossier) promotional material, sales portfolio; **～ de vente** sales presentation, sales talk

argus *m* (Transp) used car price guide

armateur, -trice *m,f* shipowner; **～-gérant** (d'un navire) managing owner, ship's husband

arme *f* (objet, moyen) weapon; **l'～ absolue** the ultimate weapon; **une ～ à double tranchant** a double-edged sword, a whipsaw AmE; **à ～s égales** on equal terms; **～ publicitaire** advertising weapon

armement *m* (commerce maritime) shipping trade; (d'un navire) fitting out

armer *vt* (navire) fit out

armoire *f* (Info) rack

arobas(e) *m* at sign

arr. *abrév* (▸**arrondissement**) (de Paris, Lyon, Marseille) *administrative subdivision of the commune*

arrachement *m* (Immob) avulsion

arrangement *m* agreement; (Droit) settlement; (pour dettes) composition; **arriver/ parvenir à un ～** come to/reach an agreement; **～ à l'amiable** amicable settlement

arranger ⓵ *vt* (voyage, réunion) arrange; **～ des rencontres entre hommes d'affaires** arrange meetings between businessmen
⓶ **s'arranger** *v pron* (situation) get better; **s'～ à l'amiable** come to an amicable settlement

arrérages *m pl* arrears, back payment

arrestation *f* arrest

arrêt *m* (d'une machine, usine) shutdown; (d'une décision) adjudication, judgment; (d'une cour) order; (des poursuites) abatement; (Info) shutdown; **～ des comptes** closing of the accounts; **～ d'expulsion** eviction order; **～ des opérations** halt of trading; **～ prématuré** (Info) abort; **～ de travail** stoppage, work stoppage; **～ de travail symbolique** token stoppage

arrêté¹, e *adj* (Fin) balanced; (Ind) idle; (Info) down

arrêté² *m* (Droit) decree, order; **～ de compte** settlement of account; **～ ministériel** ministerial order; **～ municipal** bye-law, bylaw, ordinance US

arrêter ⓵ *vt* stop; (production) discontinue, stop; (Info) stop; (Droit) arrest; **～ prématurément** (Info) abort; **～ de travailler** stop work; **～ les comptes** balance the books; **～ des dispositions** lay down the rules
⓶ **s'arrêter** *v pron* stop; (Info) abort

arrhes *f pl* deposit; **verser des ～** pay a deposit

arriéré¹, e *adj* outstanding, overdue

arriéré² *m* (dettes) arrears, overdue payment; (travail) backlog; **～ de dividendes** arrearage; **～ d'impôt** tax arrears; **～ d'intérêts** arrears of interest, back interest; **～ de loyer** back rent; **～ de paiements** backlog of payments

arrière-plan *m* background; **en ～** in the background

arriérer *vt* (paiement) defer

arrimage *m* stowage

arrimer *vt* (cargaison) stow

arrivage *m* (de marchandises) delivery, consignment; (de personnes) influx; **le dernier ～ de fruits** the last delivery of fruit; **attendre un ～** expect a delivery

arrivée *f* (de nouvelles commandes) intake; (de marchandises, voyageurs) arrival; **～ tardive** lateness

arriver *vi* arrive, come; **～ à un accord** come to an understanding; **～ à un compromis avec qn** reach an accommodation with sb; **～ au compte-gouttes** trickle in; **～ à destination** reach one's destination; **～ à échéance** come to maturity, expire; (engagement) become due; (contrat) cease to have effect; **～ sur le marché** hit the market; (maison) come onto the market; **～ sur le marché du travail** enter the labour market BrE, enter the labor market AmE; **～ en même temps** concur; **～ au port** (navigation) make port; **～ à saturation** reach saturation point

arriviste *mf* careerist

arrondir *vt* (chiffre, résultat) round off; (vers le bas) round down; (vers le haut) round up; (patrimoine) increase; **～ son revenu en faisant** supplement one's income by doing

arrondissement *m* (de ville) administrative subdivision

art *m* (savoir-faire) art; (habileté) skill; **～ du compromis** art of the compromise; **～ de la vente** salesmanship

article *m* article, item; (d'une loi) article, section; (d'un contrat) clause; (dans un journal) article; (découpé) cutting BrE; **～ de** ⋯⋯⟫

consommation consumer item; ~ **de consommation courante** staple product; ~ **courant** standard item; ~ **défectueux** faulty item; ~ **dépareillé** oddment; ~ **de dessous de ligne** below-the-line item; ~ **de dessus de ligne** above-the-line item; ~ **de fond** (presse) feature, feature article; ~ **à forte rotation** fast mover; ~ **de forum** (Info) news posting, news article; ~ **générateur de pertes** loss-maker; ~ **à grand débit** fast-moving article; ~ **imposable** taxable article; ~**s de marque** branded goods; ~ **de ménage** household commodity; ~ **en réclame** special offer, bargain; ~ **en solde** bargain, sale item

articles *m pl* goods; ~ **en cuir** leather goods; ~ **démarqués** knockoffs (infrml); ~ **dépareillés** broken lots; ~ **de luxe** luxury goods; ~ **de marque** branded goods

artificiel, -elle *adj* artificial; (Ind) man-made

artisan *m* craftsman

artisanat *m* craft industry; ~ **local** local crafts

ascenseur *m* lift BrE, elevator AmE; (Info) slider, scroll box; **renvoyer l'**~ return a favour

ascots *m pl* (Fisc) ascots UK

ASE *abrév* (▸**Agence spatiale européenne**) ESA (European Space Agency)

asiatique *adj* Asian

Asiatique *mf* Asian

Asie *f* Asia; ~ **du Sud-Est** Southeast Asia

assainir *vt* (économie, marché) stabilize; (entreprise, gestion) streamline; (situation) improve; (région, rivière, quartier) clean up; ~ **les finances** make the finances healthier

assainissement *m* (d'économie, de marché) stabilization; (d'entreprise, de gestion) streamlining; (de région, rivière, quartier) cleaning up; (de situation) improvement; ~ **écologique** ecological recovery

asse. *abrév* (▸**assurance**) ins. (insurance)

ASSEDIC *abrév* France (▸**Association pour l'emploi dans l'industrie et le commerce**) *organization managing unemployment contributions and payments*; **toucher les** ~ get unemployment benefit BrE, get unemployment compensation AmE

assemblage *m* (Ind) assembly

assemblée *f* meeting; ~ **extraordinaire** extraordinary meeting, special meeting; ~ **générale** General Assembly, general meeting; ~ **générale ordinaire** ordinary general meeting; ~ **générale des actionnaires** shareholders' meeting; ~ **générale annuelle** annual general meeting, AGM BrE; **Assemblée Parlementaire Européenne** European Parliament; ~ **générale extraordinaire** extraordinary general meeting; ~ **plénière** full session; ~ **statutaire** statutory meeting

assembleur *m* (Info) assembler

assentiment *m* approval, consent; (de la Chambre) assent

asseoir *vt* (impôt) base (**sur** on)

assiette *f* (Fisc) basis, base; (hypothèque) property on which a mortgage is secured; ~ **fiscale** tax base; ~ **de l'impôt** tax base

assignation *f* assignment; (Droit) writ of subpoena; ~ **à comparaître** subpoena, summons

assigner *vt* (besogne) assign; (crédits) allocate; ~ **qch à qn** vest sth in sb; ~ **à comparaître** (défenseur) summons; (témoin) subpoena; **faire** ~ take out a summons against; ~ **qn en justice** issue a writ against sb; ~ **en justice pour contrefaçon** sue for infringement of patent; ~ **à résidence** put under house arrest

assimilation *f* (UE) assimilation

assimilé, e *adj* assimilated, integrated; (Compta) absorbed; **être** ~ **cadre** have executive status

assistance *f* assistance; (à l'étranger) aid; ~ **à la clientèle** customer support, field support; ~ **au développement** development assistance; ~ **financière** financial assistance; ~ **judiciaire** legal aid; ~ **en ligne** online help; ~ **médicale** medical assistance; ~ **publique** public welfare; **Assistance Publique** *authority which manages state-owned hospitals and Social Services*; ~ **sociale** social work; ~ **technique** technical support; ~ **téléphonique** hot line, helpline

assistant, e *m,f* assistant; ~ **au chef de projet** project agent; ~ **machiniste** assistant engineer; ~ **personnel** personal assistant, PA; ~ **social** social worker

assisté, e *adj* (recevant prestations sociales) receiving benefit BrE, on welfare AmE; ~ **par ordinateur** computer-aided, computer-assisted

assister *vt* assist; (refugié, pays) aid; ~ **à** (une réunion) attend

assisté social *m* benefit recipient BrE, welfare recipient AmE

association *f* (organisation) association; (partenariat) partnership; **en** ~ **avec** in association with; ~ **communautaire** community association; ~ **coopérative de crédit** cooperative credit association; **Association de défense du consommateur** ≈ Consumers' Association; **Association pour l'emploi dans l'industrie et le commerce** ≈ Employment Service UK; ~ **d'employés** staff association; **Association européenne de libre-échange** European Free Trade Association; **Association pour la formation professionnelle des adultes** ≈ Training Agency UK; **Association française de codification** Committee on Uniform Securities Identification Procedures;

Association française de normalisation *French standards authority,* ≈ American National Standards Institute US, ≈ American Standards Association, ≈ British Standards Institution UK, ≈ National Bureau of Standards US; **Association française des sociétés de Bourse** *French association of stock exchange member firms;* **Association internationale pour le développement** International Development Association; **Association internationale des ports** International Association of Ports and Harbours; **Association internationale des transports aériens** International Air Transport Association; **Association des Nations Unies** United Nations Association; **Association de normalisation des télécommunications** European Telecommunications Standards Institute; ∼ **professionnelle** trade association; ∼ **de secours mutuel** friendly society BrE, benefit society AmE

associé¹, e *adj* associated; **être** ∼ **à** be associated with

associé², e *m,f* associate, partner; (d'une association) member, shareholder; ∼ **commanditaire** sleeping partner BrE, silent partner AmE; ∼ **commandité** acting partner; ∼ **gérant** managing partner; ∼ **majoritaire** senior partner; ∼ **minoritaire** junior partner

associer ① *vt* combine; ∼ **à** associate with

② **s'associer** *v pron* (personnes) form a partnership; (sociétés) join together; **s'**∼ **à/ avec** associate with

assolement *m* crop rotation; ∼ **triennal** (agriculture) three-course rotation

assortiment *m* (Com) stock; (sélection de marchandises) selection, assortment; (série) range; ∼ **de denrées** basket of goods; ∼ **de produits** selection of goods, assortment of goods

assouplir *vt* (politique, loi) relax

assouplissement *m* (d'une loi, politique) relaxation; (des procédures commerciales) facilitation

assujetti, e *adj*: ∼ **à** liable for, subject to; ∼ **à l'impôt** liable for tax, taxed; **ne pas être** ∼ **à la TVA** be zero-rated for VAT

assujettissement *m*: ∼ **à l'impôt** liability for tax

assumer *vt* (conséquences) abide by; (engagement, risques) assume; (responsabilité) take on

assurable *adj* insurable; **non** ∼ uninsurable

assurance *f* insurance;

(**assurance a...**) ∼ **accidents** accident insurance; ∼ **accidents et maladies** accident and health insurance US; ∼ **accidents et risques divers** casualty insurance; ∼ **accidents du travail**
industrial injury insurance; ∼ **automobile** automobile insurance AmE, motor vehicle insurance;

(**b...**) ∼ **des biens commerciaux** commercial property policy;

(**c...**) ∼ **à capital différé** endowment policy; ∼ **chômage** unemployment insurance; ∼ **contre le chantage** extortion insurance; ∼ **combinée** comprehensive insurance; ∼ **commerciale** commercial insurance policy; ∼ **commerciale contre le vol** mercantile robbery insurance; ∼ **complémentaire** excess insurance; ∼ **de consignation** consignment insurance; ∼ **en cours** current insurance, insurance in force; ∼ **du crédit à l'exportation** export credit insurance; ∼ **cumulative** double insurance;

(**d...**) ∼ **défense et recours** legal expense insurance; ∼ **dentaire** dental insurance; ∼ **détournement et vol** fidelity insurance; ∼ **contre les détournements** fidelity guarantee;

(**e...**) ∼ **des expositions** exhibition risks insurance;

(**f...**) ∼ **facultative** voluntary insurance; ∼ **des frais d'hospitalisation** (assurance maladie) hospital care insurance plan; ∼ **contre la fraude informatique** computer crime insurance; ∼ **du fret** freight insurance;

(**g...**) ∼ **de garantie** (assurance caution, assurance vol) fidelity bond; ∼ **globale** blanket insurance; ∼ **globale des frais médicaux** blanket medical expense insurance; ∼ **contre la grêle** crop hail insurance;

(**h...**) ∼ **habitation** homeowner's policy; ∼ **hospitalisation** (assurance maladie) hospital care insurance plan; ∼ **d'hypothèque** mortgage insurance;

(**i...**) ∼ **incapacité** disability insurance; ∼ **informatique** data processing insurance; ∼ **contre les inondations** flood insurance; ∼ **contre les intempéries** qualified insurance corporation, rain insurance; ∼ **invalidité** disability insurance, disability cover;

(**l...**) ∼ **livraison** consignment insurance; ∼ **locative** leasehold insurance; ∼ **loisirs** holiday and leisure insurance;

(**m...**) ∼ **maladie** health insurance; ∼ **maladie de l'entreprise** company sickness insurance scheme; ∼ **maritime** sea insurance, marine insurance; ∼ **maternité** maternity protection; ∼ **médicale** medical insurance; ∼ **mixte** endowment assurance; ∼ **mixte avec participation aux bénéfices** with-profits endowment assurance; ∼ **multirisque** comprehensive policy, multirisk insurance;

(**o...**) ∼ **obligatoire** compulsory insurance;

(**p...**) ∼ **avec participation aux bénéfices** composite insurance, participating insurance; ∼ **perte d'exploitation** business interruption insurance, business interruption ⸱⸱⸱⸸

policy; ~ **perte de revenu** loss-of-income insurance; ~ **de portefeuille** portfolio insurance; ~ **à la prime de risque** risk-based premium; ~ **de la protection juridique** legal expense insurance;

(**q...**) ~ **de la qualité** quality assurance;

(**r...**) ~ **RC de l'employeur** (▸**assurance responsabilité civile de l'employeur**) employer's liability insurance; ~ **RC obligatoire** (▸**assurance responsabilité civile obligatoire**) compulsory third-party insurance; ~ **de responsabilité** carrier's liability, liability insurance; ~ **responsabilité civile** liability insurance; ~ **responsabilité civile complémentaire et excédentaire** umbrella liability insurance; ~ **responsabilité civile de l'employeur** employer's liability insurance; ~ **responsabilité civile générale** comprehensive general liability insurance; ~ **responsabilité civile obligatoire** compulsory third party insurance; ~ **responsabilité civile des particuliers** comprehensive personal liability insurance; ~ **de responsabilité professionnelle** professional liability insurance;

(**s...**) ~ **sociale** National Insurance UK, social insurance; ~ **soins dentaires** dental insurance;

(**t...**) ~ **au tiers** third-party insurance; ~ **tous risques** all risks insurance, comprehensive insurance; ~ **sur le traitement des données** data processing insurance; ~ **transport aérien** air transport insurance;

(**v...**) ~ **vacances** holiday and leisure insurance; ~ **valeur agréée** agreed value insurance; ~ **des valeurs différentes** difference-in-value insurance; ~ **vieillesse** old age pension; ~ **en vigueur** current insurance, insurance in force; ~ **voyage** travel insurance

assurance-vie *f* life insurance, life assurance BrE; ~**-vie sur deux têtes** survivor policy; ~**-vie de groupe** group life insurance; ~**-vie individuelle** individual life insurance; ~**-vie avec option rente viagère** annuity insurance; ~**-vie à prestations variables** variable life insurance; ~**-vie à prime unique** single-premium life insurance; ~**-vie voyage aérien** aviation trip life insurance

assuré, e *m,f* policyholder; l'~ the insured, the claimant

assurer ⌐1⌐ *vt* (affirmer) assure, claim; (Assur) (personne, bien) insure; (effectuer) (entretien) carry out; (réparations) carry out; (service) provide; (monopole, revenu) give; (garantir) ensure; **non assuré** (Assur) uninsured; ~ **sa voiture contre le vol** insure one's car against theft; ~ **qn sur la vie** insure sb's life; ~ **la correspondance avec** connect with; ~ **l'entretien de** maintain; ~ **la manœuvre de**

man; ~ **la permanence de** (stand) man; ~ **la subsistance de** support; ~ **le suivi** follow up; **ils n'assurent que les réparations urgentes** they only carry out urgent repairs; **le service après-vente est assuré par nos soins** we provide the after-sales service; ~ **la gestion/sauvegarde de qch** manage/safeguard sth; ~ **les fonctions de directeur/président** be director/chairman; **pour ~ le succès commercial** in order to ensure commercial success; **il est là pour ~ la bonne marche du projet** his role is to make sure *ou* to ensure that the project runs smoothly; **ce rachat assure à l'entreprise le monopole** the takeover gives the company a guaranteed monopoly

⌐2⌐ **s'assurer** *v pron* (avantage, bien, aide, monopole) secure; (Assur) take out insurance (contre against); **s'~ contre l'incendie** insure oneself against fire; **s'~ contre un risque** insure oneself against risk, provide against a risk; **s'~ les services de** enlist the services of

assureur *m* insurer, (insurance) underwriter; (intermédiaire) insurance agent; (compagnie) insurance company, insurer; ~ **de biens** property insurer; ~ **direct** direct insurer; ~ **immobilier** property insurer; ~ **mutuel** mutual insurer; ~ **principal** leader

assureur-vie *m* life insurer

astreinte *f* standby; **être d'~** be on standby

astuce *f* trick; ~ **publicitaire** advertising gimmick, publicity stunt

asynchrone *adj* asynchronous

atelier *m* workshop; (dans une usine) factory floor, shop floor; ~ **de carrosserie** body shop; ~ **d'outillage** toolroom; ~ **de réparation** repair shop; ~ **de tissage** weaving mill

atmosphère *f* atmosphere

atomicité *f* atomicity

atout *m* asset, trump card

attaché¹, e *m,f* attaché; ~ **fonctionnel** staff assistant; ~ **militaire** defence attaché BrE, defense attaché AmE; ~ **de presse** press agent

attaché², e *adj* **être ~ à** (principe) adhere to

attacher ⌐1⌐ *vt* (étiquette) affix; ~ **de l'importance à** attach importance to ⌐2⌐ **s'attacher** *v pron* **s'~ les services de qn** retain sb's services

attaquant *m* (Bourse) raider

attaque *f* (Bourse) raid; ~ **à l'ouverture** dawn raid

attaquer ⌐1⌐ *vt* contest; (testament) contest, dispute; ~ **le marché** raid the market, tap the market; ~ **qn en justice** bring a lawsuit against sb ⌐2⌐ **s'attaquer à** *v pron* (problème) address, tackle

atteindre *vt* (but) achieve; (le cours le plus haut) achieve, record; (toucher) affect; ~ **une jolie somme** (rapporter) fetch a good price; ~ **son maximum** peak; ~ **son niveau le plus bas** bottom, bottom out; ~ **son niveau record** peak; ~ **un total de** reach a total of

atteint, e *adj* (affecté) affected; **une région très ~e par la pollution** a region badly affected by pollution; ~ **d'incapacité** disabled, incapacitated

atteinte *f* attack; ~ **à** attack on; **porter ~ à** (réputation) damage; (droit) infringe; (sécurité) endanger, breach; **qui ne porte pas ~ à l'environnement** environmentally-friendly; ~ **aux droits d'un individu** civil wrong; ~ **à l'environnement** environmental damage; ~ **flagrante aux droits d'une partie** gross miscarriage of justice; ~ **à la libre concurrence** restrictive practice

attenant, e *adj* adjoining

attendre ① *vt* wait for ② *vi* wait ③ **s'attendre à** *v pron* anticipate, expect

attendu¹ *prép* given, considering; ~ **que** given *ou* considering that; (Droit) whereas

attendu², e *adj* (résultat) anticipated, expected

attendu³ *m*: ~**s d'un jugement** grounds for a decision; **les ~s** the whereas clauses

attente *f* (période) wait; (espoir) expectations; (impatience) anticipation; **l'~ du verdict** waiting for the verdict; **dans l'~ de notre rencontre/de vous lire** looking forward to our meeting/to hearing from you; **en ~** (passenger) waiting; (dossier, affaire) pending; **répondre à/dépasser l'~** live up to/exceed sb's expectations; **contrairement à toute ~** contrary to expectations; **commandes en ~** back orders; ~**s du consommateur** consumer expectations; ~**s professionnelles** career expectations

attention *f* attention, care; ~, **intérêt, désir, action** attention, interest, desire, action; ~ **portée aux besoins de la clientèle** customer care

attentisme *m* wait-and-see policy

atténuation *f* mitigation; ~ **d'impôts** mitigation of taxes

atterrissage *m* (aviation) landing; ~ **brutal** hard landing; ~ **en douceur** soft landing; ~ **forcé** (aviation) emergency landing, forced landing

attestation *f* attestation; (sous serment) affidavit; (dans les déclarations) certification; ~ **d'assurance** certificate of insurance, insurance certificate; **l'~ ci-jointe** the affixed testimonial; ~ **de conformité** certificate of conformity; ~ **médicale** medical certificate; ~ **de prise en charge** acceptance certificate; ~ **de titre** warranty of title; ~ **de valeur** certificate of value; ~ **de valeur et d'origine** certificate of value and origin

attester *vt* testify; (prouver) prove, attest to; ~ **que** testify that; **fait attesté** attested fact; **les chiffres attestent notre succès** the figures are proof of our success; ~ **par la présente que** I, the undersigned, hereby testify that

attirer ① *vt* attract; (attention) attract, grab; (personne) appeal to; ~ **l'attention de qn** attract sb's attention; ~ **de nouveaux contrats** attract new business ② **s'attirer** *v pron* **s'~ le mécontentement de qn** incur sb's displeasure, fall foul of sb; **s'~ les bonnes grâces de qn** win sb's favour BrE, win sb's favor AmE

attitré, e *adj* (agent, président) appointed

attitude *f* (vis-à-vis de produits, d'idées) attitude; ~ **anti-inflationniste** anti-inflation stance; ~ **des utilisateurs** user attitude

attractif, -ive *adj* attractive

attraction *f* (pour un produit) attraction; **centre d'~** centre of attraction; ~ **commerciale** sales appeal; ~ **touristique** tourist attraction

attrait *m* (d'un produit) appeal; ~ **commercial** sales appeal; ~ **visuel** visual appeal

attrayant, e *adj* attractive

attribuer *vt* (action) allot; (récompense) award; (prêt) grant; (salaire, prime) allocate, assign; ~ **qch à qn** (œuvre) attribute sth to sb; **attribué à** attributed to; ~ **la responsabilité de qch à qn** hold sb responsible for sth, blame sb for sth; **non attribué** (Bourse) unallotted

attribut *m* attribute

attributaire *mf* (Bourse) allottee

attribution *f* (de récompense) award; (de prêt) granting; (de salaire, prime) allocation, assignment; ~ **d'actions** allotment of shares; ~ **des recettes** revenue allocation; ~ **de titres** allotment of securities; ~ **de valeurs** allotment of securities

attributions *f pl* (de personne) remit; (de tribunal) competence; **ce n'est pas dans mes ~** it is outside my remit

aubaine *f* windfall

aube *f* (d'un navire) paddle

AUD *abrév* (**administration de l'union des douanes**) (UE) ACU (administration of the customs union)

au-dessous: ~ **de** *prép* below; ~ **de la barre de 5%** below the 5% mark; ~ **de la ligne** below the line; ~ **de la moyenne** below average; ~ **de la norme** below the norm; ~ **de la valeur** underpriced; ~ **du cours** below-market price; ~ **du pair** (prix d'actions) below par; ~ **du quota** below quota

au-dessus: ~ **de** *prép* above; ~ **de la ligne** above the line; ~ **de la moyenne** above average; ~ **de la norme** above the norm; ~ **du cours** above-market price; ~ **du pair** (obligation, action) at a premium; (prix d'actions) above par; ~ **du quota** above quota; **être ~** ⋯⦂

de sa valeur nominale stand at a premium

audience f audience; (Droit) hearing; (Média) audience; (chiffres) audience ratings; **indicateurs d'~** audience ratings; **35% d'~** 35% in the audience ratings; **~ cible** target audience; **~ cumulée** (marketing) cumulative audience, reach; **~ à huis clos** in camera hearing; **~ radiophonique** radio audience

audimétrie f audience measurement

audioconférence f audio conference, audio-conferencing

audiotypie f audiotyping

audiovisuel, -elle adj audiovisual

audit m audit; (contrôleur) auditor; **faire un ~ de** (comptes) audit; **~ analytique** analytical audit, systems-based auditing; **~ de conformité** compliance audit; **~ en continu** continuous audit; **~ de fin d'exercice** year-end audit; **~ à l'insu** undercover audit; **~ interne** internal audit, administrative audit; **~ légal** statutory audit; **~ des opérations** operations audit; **~ sur place** field audit; **~ restreint** limited audit; **~ sur site** site audit

auditabilité f auditability

auditer vt audit; **non audité** unaudited

auditeur, -trice m,f auditor; **~ indépendant** independent auditor

auditeurs m pl (radio) radio audience

audition f (Droit) hearing

AUE abrév (▸**Acte unique européen**) SEA (Single European Act)

augmentation f increase; (de prix) increase, rise; (de salaires) increase, rise BrE, raise AmE; (en marketing) mark-up; **par ~** incremental; **~ de capital** capital gain; **~ des dépenses** incremental spending; **~ générale/globale** across-the-board increase; **~ au mérite** merit increase, merit rise BrE, merit raise AmE; **~ des prix** price rise, increase in prices, rise in prices; **~ du prix du pétrole** oil price increase, oil price rise; **~ d'un prix de vente** mark-up; **~ de salaire** salary increase, wage increase; **~ toutes catégories** across-the-board increase

augmenté, e adj (offre) increased, stepped-up; (revenu) supplemented

augmenter ⊡ vt increase; **~ de** increase by; (offre) increase, up; (prix) increase, raise; (production) increase, build up; (revenus) supplement; (Info) (capacité mémoire) upgrade ⊡ vi increase; **~ de** increase by

aujourd'hui adv today; **~ en huit** a week today

aussitôt adv immediately; **~ que possible** as soon as possible, a.s.a.p.

austérité f austerity; **~ budgétaire/ économique** fiscal/economic austerity

autarcie f autarky; **vivre en ~** be self-sufficient

auteur m (de réforme, loi) author; (de découverte) inventor; (de crime, délit)

perpetrator; **~ d'un tort** tort feasor

authentification f authentication, certification; **~ d'une obligation** (Bourse) authentication

authentifier vt (signature, document) authenticate

auto-amortissable adj self-liquidating

auto-assistance f self-help

auto-assurance f self-insurance

autobus m bus; **~ à impériale** double-decker

autocommutateur m: **~ privé** automatic private branch exchange

autoconsommation f subsistence farming; **~ par l'entreprise productrice** in-house consumption

autocotisation f self-assessment

autocritique f self-appraisal

autodidacte adj self-taught

auto-évaluation f self-assessment

autofinancé, e adj self-financing

autofinancement m ploughback BrE, plowback AmE, self-financing; **~ net annuel** annual net cash inflow

autogénéré, e adj self-generated

autogestion f self-management; (Res Hum) worker control

automatique adj automatic

automatiquement adv automatically

automatisation f automation

automatisé, e adj automated

automatiser vt automate

automne m autumn BrE, fall AmE

automobile adj (industrie) automotive, car, automobile AmE; (assurance, constructeur) car, motor, automobile AmE

automotivation f self-motivation

automotrice f (chemin de fer) railcar

autonome adj autonomous; (filiale, gestion) independent, autonomous; (syndicat) independent, non-affiliated; (système, équipement) off-line; (unité) stand-alone

autonomie f autonomy, self-government

autoréglementation f self-regulation

autorépondeur m autoresponder

autorisation f authorization; (d'un prêt) approval; (d'un permis) licensing; (d'exercer une activité) licence BrE, license AmE; (Info) permission; **qui n'est pas soumis à ~** permit-free; **~ d'absence** leave of absence; **~ d'accès** entry permit; **~ d'achat** authority to buy; **~ de congé** leave authorization, furlough AmE; **~ de crédit** bank line, credit line, line of credit AmE; **~ de déchargement** (au port) landing order; **~ de découvert** overdraft facility; **~ de dépense** authorization for expenditure; **~ d'exercer un commerce/métier** trading authorization; **~ d'exporter** export permit; **~ expresse** express authority; **~**

d'importation import licensing; ~ **de mise sur le marché** (médicaments) marketing authorization; ~ **permanente** standing authorization; ~ **de prêt** loan authorization; ~ **de prospection pétrolière** oil exploration licence BrE, oil exploration license AmE; ~ **de sortie** release for shipment; ~ **de sortie de marchandises** gate pass; ~ **de virement** transfer advice, payment notice

autorisé, e *adj* authorized, (prêt) approved; (revendication) permitted; (qui a un permis) licensed; **personne** ~**e** authorized person

autoriser *vt* authorize; (prêt) approve; (par permis) license; ~ **qn à faire** allow sb to do, give sb the right to do; (par permis) license sb to do

autorité *f* authority (sur over); **être sous l'**~ **de qn** be under sb's authority; **de sa propre** ~ on one's own authority; **qui s'exerce en douceur** free-rein leadership; **les** ~**s** the authorities; ~ **compétente** relevant authority; ~ **européenne de l'énergie nucléaire** European Nuclear Energy Authority; ~ **fragmentée** splintered authority; ~ **hiérarchique** line authority; ~ **de parquet** floor official; ~ **portuaire** harbour authority BrE, harbor authority AmE; ~ **réglementaire** (Droit) regulatory body; (Pol) statutory authority; ~**s locales** local authority, local government; ~**s monétaires** monetary authorities

autoroute *f* motorway BrE, freeway AmE; ~ **d'information** (Info) information highway; ~ **à péage** toll motorway BrE, turnpike AmE

autosuffisance *f* self-sufficiency

autosuffisant, e *adj* self-sufficient

autour *adv* around; ~ **de** around

autre *adj* alternative, other; **à d'**~**s égards** in other respects; **et** ~**s** et al, et alii; ~ **bénéficiaire** other beneficiary; ~ **revenu** other income; ~**s comptes financiers** (actif) other receivables; ~**s dépôts vérifiables** other checkable deposits; ~**s dettes** other liabilities; ~**s éléments d'actif** other assets; ~**s produits** other income; ~**s produits de gestion courante** nonoperating revenue; ~**s questions à l'ordre du jour** any other competent business

auxiliaire¹ *adj* subsidiary; (service, opération) ancillary; (Info) auxiliary

auxiliaire² *mf* assistant; (navigation) auxiliary; ~ **clients** *m* accounts receivable ledger; ~ **fournisseurs** *m* accounts payable ledger; ~ **des postes** postal assistant

a.v.a. *abrév* (▶**agent d'assurance-vie agréé**) chartered life underwriter

aval: **en** ~ downstream; **industrie en** ~ downstream industry

avaliser *vt* back; (Banque) guarantee

avaliseur *m* backer; (Banque) guarantor

avance *f* (argent) advance, subvention BrE (frml); (avantage) lead; **conserver son** ~ keep one's lead, maintain one's lead; **avoir de l'**~ **sur** be ahead of; **prendre de l'**~ **sur** pull ahead of; **d'**~ in advance; **en** ~ in advance; **en** ~ **sur le calendrier établi** ahead of schedule; **en** ~ **sur les prévisions** ahead of schedule; **faire une** ~ (d'argent) make an advance; **par** ~ in advance; ~ **automatique** autofeed; ~ **bancaire** bank advance; ~ **sur les concurrents** competitive edge; ~ **sur contrat** policy loan; ~ **en cours** outstanding advance; ~ **à découvert** unsecured advance; uncovered advance; ~ **de fonds de roulement** working capital advance; ~ **sur garantie** secured advance; ~ **sur marchandises** advance against goods, advance on goods; ~ **sur nantissement** advance against security; ~ **permanente** standing advance; ~ **sur police** policy loan; ~ **sur salaire** advance on salary; ~ **technologique** technological advance; ~ **sur titres** advance on securities; ~ **de trésorerie** cash advance

avancé, e *adj* advanced

avancée *f* (technologique) advance

avancement *m* (dans une carrière) promotion; (dans des travaux, des connaissances) progress; **obtenir de l'**~ get promoted; **il a reçu de l'avancement** he was promoted; **un rapport sur l'état d'**~ **du projet** a progress report on the project; ~ **de l'âge de la retraite** lowering of the retirement age

avancer *vt* (dans le temps) bring forward; (travail) get ahead with, make progress with; (proposition) put forward; (ses opinions) air; ~ **une proposition** put forward a proposal; **faire** ~ advance; ~ **à pas de géant** make quick progress; ~ **de l'argent à qn** advance money to sb

avant *prép* before, prior to; ~ **bourse** before-hours; ~ **l'échéance** before due date, before maturity; ~ **impôt** before-tax; ~ **midi** am, ante meridiem

avantage *m* advantage; (Fisc, Gestion) benefit; **avoir l'**~ have the upper hand; **avoir l'**~ **sur qn** have the edge on/over sb; **faire partie des** ~**s du métier** be a perk of the job; ~ **absolu** (économie internationale) absolute advantage; ~ **commercial** commercial advantage; ~ **concurrentiel** competitive edge; ~**s divers** fringe benefits; ~ **économique** economic benefit; ~ **en espèces** allowance in kind; ~**s et inconvénients** advantages and drawbacks; ~ **fiscal** tax incentive; ~ **imposable** taxable benefit; ~ **matériel/en nature** allowance in kind; ~ **personnel** personal benefit; ~ **réciproque** mutual benefit; ~**s sociaux** social benefits; (pour employés) company benefits

avantageux, -euse *adj* advantageous, beneficial

avant-faillite f pre-bankruptcy

avant-garde f leading edge; **à l'~** at the forefront, at the leading edge

avant-plan m foreground

avant-première f preview; **~ surprise** sneak preview

avant-projet m draft project

avarie f damage; **~ commune** common average, general average; **~ commune étrangère** foreign general average; **~ avant embarcation** country damage; **~ grosse** general average in full

avarié, e adj damaged; **~ en cours de route** damaged in transit

avatar m (Info) avatar

avec prép with; (Droit) cum

avenant m clause, extended coverage endorsement US; (Droit) additional clause; **~ d'exclusion de la masse salariale** ordinary payroll exclusion endorsement

avenir m future; **à l'~** in the future; **dans l'~** at some time in the future; **dans un ~ prévisible** in the foreseeable future; **dans un proche ~** in the near future; **qui regarde vers l'~** forward-thinking

avérer: s'~ v pron **s'~ faux** prove wrong; **s'~ vrai** prove right

avertir vt inform, notify; (d'un problème grave) warn; **~ qn de qch** notify sb of sth, inform sb of sth

avertissement m (avis) warning; (mise en garde) caveat; (Droit) caution; **~ écrit** written warning; **~ préalable** notice of intention; **~ public** public warning

aviation f aviation; **~ civile** civil aviation

avion m aircraft, aeroplane BrE, airplane AmE, plane; **par ~** by air; (courrier) by airmail; **~ affrété** chartered aircraft, chartered airplane AmE; **~ charter** chartered aircraft, chartered airplane AmE; **~ de fret** cargo plane; **~ de ligne** airliner; **~ passagers** passenger aircraft

avion-cargo m cargo plane

avion-taxi m air taxi

avis m (avis) opinion (**sur** about); (conseil) advice (**sur** about); (annonce) notice; (d'arrivée, de livraison, de réception) advice; (Droit) notice; (émanant d'un juriste) opinion; **à mon ~** in my opinion; **~ d'annulation** cancellation notice; **~ d'appel** notice of appeal; **~ d'assignation/de levée** assignment notice; **~ bancaire** bank advice; **~ de cession** letter of assignment; **~ de compte** account statement; **~ de confirmation** confirmation notice; **~ de congé** notice to quit; **~ de cotisation** notice of assessment; **~ défavorable** adverse opinion; **~ de délaissement** notice of abandonment; **~**

divergent divergent thinking; **~ d'expédition** notice of shipment, advice of dispatch; **~ d'expiration** expiration notice; **~ de faillite** bankruptcy notice; **~ d'interdiction** prohibition notice; **~ juridique** legal opinion; **~ de levée** exercise notice; **~ de licenciement** termination papers; **~ de livraison** delivery notice; **~ de prélèvement** direct debit advice; **~ de requête** notice of application; **~ de résiliation** notice of cancellation; **~ de révocation** notice of revocation; **~ de vente** announcement of sale

aviser vt advise, notify; **~ qn de qch** advise sb of sth, notify sb of sth

avitaillement m (d'un navire) victualling

avocat, e m,f lawyer, solicitor UK, attorney at law US; (à la cour) trial attorney US, barrister UK; **~ commis d'office** court-appointed lawyer, kite (infrml); **~-conseil** legal adviser, legal advisor; **~ de la défense** defence lawyer UK, defense attorney US; **~ d'entreprise** corporate lawyer; **~ général** counsel for the prosecution UK, prosecuting attorney US; **~ stagiaire** trainee solicitor UK

avoir m asset, equity; **~ des actionnaires** shareholders' equity; **~ à échéance plus longue** longer-term asset; **~ extérieur net** net foreign assets; **~ fiscal** tax credit; **~ horizontal** horizontal equity; **~ inactif** inactive asset; **~ non-productif** nonperforming credit; **~ des propriétaires** equity capital; **~ de qualité** quality asset; **~ en valeurs d'anticipation à long terme** long-term equity anticipation securities; **~ vertical** vertical equity; **~s en actions** equity holdings; **~s en devises** foreign exchange holdings, currency holdings; **~s dormants** sleeping economy; **~s à l'étranger** assets held abroad; **~s extérieurs** foreign assets, overseas assets; **~s financiers libellés en dollars américains** US dollar financial assets; **~s liquides admissibles** allowable liquid assets; **~s du ministère** departmental assets; **~s non-productifs** nonperforming assets; **~s en obligations** bond holdings

avoisinant, e adj adjoining

avouer vt admit; **~ qu'on est dans son tort** admit one is wrong

axe m axis; **~ de la campagne** copy platform; **~ publicitaire** advertising message, advertising concept

ayant: ~ cause m assignee, successor in title; **~ droit** m (à une prestation, une allocation) legal claimant; **~ droit économique** beneficial owner

Bb

B/. *abrév* (▸**billet à ordre**) PN (promissory note)

B: ∼ **to B** *m* B2B, B to B, business to business; ∼ **to C** *m* B2C, B to C, business to consumer

BAB *abrév* (**bord à bord**) FIO (free in and out)

baby-boom *m* baby boom

bac *m* baccalaureate; ∼ **+ 2/4** baccalaureate plus 2/4 years' higher education; ∼ **professionnel** *secondary school vocational diploma*

baccalauréat *m* baccalaureate, ≈ A level UK

bachelier, -ière *m,f holder of the (French) baccalaureate*

BAD *abrév* (▸**bon à délivrer**) F/R (freight release)

badge *m* badge; ∼ **d'identification** name badge; (carte magnétique) swipe card

bagage *m* luggage, baggage; (diplômes) qualifications; (expérience) credentials; **avoir un bon** ∼ have good qualifications, be well qualified; ∼**s accompagnés** accompanied baggage; ∼**s enregistrés** registered baggage; ∼**s à main** hand luggage, carry-on baggage AmE; ∼**s non-accompagnés** unaccompanied baggage; ∼**s non-enregistrés** unchecked baggage

bagarrer: se ∼ **pour** *v pron* (infrml) battle for, fight for

bagne *m* (infrml) sweatshop

baie *f* (Info) bay

bail *m* lease; (à loyer) rental agreement; **donner à** ∼ lease out; **prendre à** ∼ lease; **renouveler un** ∼ renew a lease; ∼ **assuré** security of tenure; ∼ **à céder** lease for sale; ∼ **commercial** business lease, commercial lease; ∼ **à court terme** short lease; ∼ **à effet de levier** leverage lease; ∼ **d'exploitation** operation lease; ∼ **financier** financial lease; ∼ **implicite** (immobilier) tenancy at will; ∼ **à long terme** long lease; ∼ **avec option d'achat** lease with option to purchase; ∼ **perpétuel** perpetual lease; ∼ **à vie** life tenancy

bailleur, -eresse *m,f lessor;* ∼ **de fonds** (officiel) financial backer; (passif) sleeping partner BrE, silent partner AmE

baisse *f* (de qualité) decline; (de ventes) drop, decline; (de productivité, taux) drop; (des prix, cours) fall; **en** ∼ (ventes) falling, declining; (demande) flagging; **une** ∼ **de 50%** a drop/fall of 50%; **une** ∼ **des salaires** a fall in wages; **être en** ∼ (taux, actions, valeurs) be going down;

(résultats) be falling, be dropping; **le marché est à la** ∼ the market is bearish; **tendance à la** ∼ downward *ou* bearish trend; **réviser des prévisions à la** ∼ revise estimates downwards; **opérations/spéculations à la** ∼ bear transactions/speculation; **spéculer à la** ∼ go a bear, go for a fall; ∼ **de clientèle** loss of custom; ∼ **de cours** price drop, price loss; ∼ **de la monnaie** fall of currency; ∼ **de la population** fall in population; ∼ **de tension** (Info) brownout US; ∼ **de valeur** (Banque, Bourse) impairment of value; ∼ **de volume** drop

baisser ① *vt* (prix) reduce, mark down ② *vi* drop, fall; **le dollar a baissé de 1%** the (value of the) dollar has fallen by 1%; **faire** ∼ bring down; (prix) drive down; ∼ **de valeur** fall in value

baissier¹, -ière *adj* **être** ∼ be bearish

baissier² *m* bear, bear operator; ∼ **à découvert** uncovered bear

balance *f* (pour peser) scales; (équilibre) balance; (Banque, Compta) balance; **faire pencher la** ∼ tip the scales; ∼ **après clôture** post-closing trial balance; ∼ **chronologique** aged trial balance; ∼ **de clôture** final balance; ∼ **du commerce extérieur** balance of trade; ∼ **commerciale** balance of trade; ∼ **commerciale déficitaire** unfavourable balance of trade BrE, unfavorable balance of trade AmE; ∼ **commerciale excédentaire** favourable balance of trade BrE, favorable balance of trade AmE; ∼ **de compte courant** current account balance, balance on current account; ∼ **des financements officiels** Balance for Official Financing; ∼ **des marchandises** merchandise balance of trade; ∼ **matières** material balance; ∼ **des opérations courantes** balance on current account; ∼ **des paiements** balance of payments; ∼ **des pouvoirs** balance of power

balancer *vt* (comptes) balance

balayage *m* (Info) scanning; **faire un** ∼ (Info) scan; ∼ **de l'environnement** environment scan

balcon *m* (théâtre) circle

bale *m* bale cubic metres BrE, bale cubic meters AmE

balise *f* beacon; (Info) tag

baliser *vt* (Info) tag

ballast *m* (d'un navire) ballast tank

balle *f* bale

ballot *m* (de marchandises) bundle; (navigation) ballot

b

BALO *abrév* (▸Bulletin des annonces légales obligatoires) *official stock exchange bulletin where French quoted companies must disclose financial information*

banc: ∼ **des accusés** *m* dock UK; ∼ **d'essai** *m* test bench

bancable *adj* (Fin) bankable

bancaire *adj* (activité, secteur, service) banking; (carte, compte, chèque, prêt) bank

bancarisation *f* spread of banking services

bancarisé, e *adj* (personne, entreprise) using bank services

bancassurance *f* bankassurance

bancassureur *m* bankassurer

bancatique *f* computerized banking, electronic banking

bande *f* (Info, Média) tape; (TVA) band; ∼**-annonce** (TV, cinéma) trailer, preview; ∼ **audionumérique** digital audio tape; ∼ **de base** (Info) baseband; ∼ **de défilement** (Info) scroll bar; ∼ **passante** bandwidth; ∼ **témoin** (Info) audit trail; **très large** ∼ (Info) broadband

bandeau *m* (sur Internet) banner; ∼ **publicitaire** (advertising) banner

banderole *f* banner

banlieue *f* (périphérie) suburbs; (quartier) suburb; **en grande** ∼ in the outer suburbs

banlieusard, e *m,f* person from the suburbs

bannière *f* (sur Internet) banner; ∼ **publicitaire** (advertising) banner

banquable *adj* ▸bancable

banque *f* bank; ∼ **d'acceptation** acceptance bank, accepting bank; ∼ **d'affaires** investment bank US, merchant bank UK; ∼ **d'affaires en participation** joint-venture investment bank; ∼ **affiliée** affiliated bank, member bank; ∼ **agréée** authorized bank; ∼ **agricole** agricultural bank; **Banque asiatique de développement** Asian Development Bank; **Banque centrale européenne** European Central Bank; **Banque européenne pour la reconstruction et le développement** European Bank for Reconstruction and Development; ∼ **à charte** chartered bank US; ∼ **de commerce** mercantile bank; ∼ **commerciale** commercial bank, merchant bank UK; ∼ **de crédit** borrowing bank; ∼ **de dépôt** deposit institution; ∼ **de détail** retail banking; ∼ **à domicile** home banking; ∼ **de données** data bank; ∼ **électronique** computerized banking, electronic banking; ∼ **émettrice** issuing bank; ∼ **d'émission** bank of issue; ∼ **d'entreprise** corporate banking; ∼ **d'épargne** savings bank, thrift institution US; ∼ **d'escompte** acceptance house; **Banque européenne d'investissement** European Investment Bank; **Banque de France** Bank of France (*French central bank*); ∼ **habilitée** authorized bank; **Banque internationale pour la reconstruction et le développement** International Bank for Reconstruction and Development; ∼ **d'investissement** investment bank US, trust bank; ∼ **mandataire** agency bank UK, agent bank; ∼ **mère** parent bank; **Banque Mondiale** World Bank; ∼ **nationale** domestic bank, national bank US; ∼ **non-affiliée** nonmember bank; ∼ **notificatrice** advising bank; ∼ **en participation** joint-venture bank; ∼ **payeuse** paying bank; ∼ **de placement** issuing bank; ∼ **de recouvrement** collecting bank; **Banque des Règlements Internationaux** Bank for International Settlements; ∼ **de réseau** retail bank, wholesale bank; ∼ **de réserve** reserve bank; ∼ **résidente** resident bank; ∼ **secondaire** fringe bank; ∼ **à succursales** branch bank

banqueroute *f* bankruptcy; **faire** ∼ go bankrupt; ∼ **frauduleuse** fraudulent bankruptcy

banqueroutier, -ière *m,f* bankrupt

banquier, -ière *m,f* banker; ∼ **acceptant** accepting banker; ∼ **d'affaires** investment banker US, merchant banker UK; ∼ **émetteur** issuing banker; ∼ **hypothécaire** mortgage banker US

b. à p. *abrév* (▸billet à payer) bp (bill payable)

b. à r. *abrév* (▸billet à recevoir) br (bill receivable)

baratin *m* (infrml) (pour vendre) sales pitch, spiel (infrml); ∼ **commercial** sales pitch; ∼ **publicitaire** (publicité) blurb

barème *m* (tableau) set of tables; (méthode de calcul) scale; ∼ **de calculs** ready reckoner; ∼ **de commission** scale of commission; ∼ **d'imposition** tax rate schedule; ∼ **d'invalidité** disability percentage table; ∼ **par points** points rating; ∼ **des prix** price schedule; ∼ **progressif** progressive scale

baril *m* (unité de capacité, récipient) barrel; (pour poudre) keg; (de vin) cask; ∼**s par jour** barrels per day

baromètre *m* barometer; ∼ **économique** economic barometer

barre *f* (des avocats) bar; (des témoins) ≈ witness box UK, ≈ witness stand US; (seuil) mark; (de gouvernail) helm; **être appelé à la** ∼ be called to the witness box; **passer la** ∼ **des 13%** go over the 13% mark; **c'est de l'or en** ∼ it's a golden opportunity; ∼ **de défilement** scroll bar; ∼ **d'espacement** space bar; ∼ **d'état** status bar; ∼ **des menus** menu bar; ∼ **oblique** slash; ∼ **oblique inverse**, ∼ **oblique inversée** backslash; ∼ **d'outils** tool bar; ∼ **des tâches** task bar

barreau *m*: **le** ∼ (avocats) ≈ the Bar UK; **le** ∼ **de Toulouse** barristers practising in Toulouse

barrer *vt* (chèque) cross; ∼ **spécialement** cross specially; **chèque barré** crossed cheque BrE, crossed check AmE; **chèque non barré** uncrossed cheque BrE, uncrossed check AmE

barrière *f* (obstacle) barrier; ∼ **commerciale** trade barrier; ∼ **douanière** tariff barrier; ∼ **fiscale** (commerce) tax barrier; ∼ **non-douanière** nontariff barrier; ∼ **de sécurité** (Info) firewall; ∼ **tarifaire** tariff barrier

barrique *f* hogshead

bas¹, -se *adj* low; **à** ∼ **prix** low-priced; **les** ∼ **salaires** the low-paid; **de** ∼ **en haut** (hiérarchie) across-the-board; ∼ **de gamme** bottom-of-the-range; ∼ **échelon** basic grade; ∼ **salaire** low pay

bas² *m* bottom; ∼ **de casse** lower case; ∼ **de gamme** (options d'achat) bottom end of the range; ∼ **de laine** nest egg; ∼ **niveau sans précédent** (marché) all-time low; ∼ **de page** footer

bascule *f* weighing machine; ∼ **électronique** flip-flop; (Info) toggle

basculer 1 *vt* (appel) transfer; (d'une chose à l'autre) switch
2 *vi* (Info) (touche, fonction) toggle

basculeur *m* (Info) toggle key

base *f* basis; (d'un étalement) leg; **la** ∼ (Pol) the grass-roots; **en partant de la** ∼ bottom-up; **sur la** ∼ **de** on the basis of; **sur la** ∼ **du bénévolat** voluntary; (fonction) honorary; **sur une** ∼ **d'escompte** on a discount basis; **sur une** ∼ **saine** on a sound footing; ∼ **d'amortissement** depreciable basis; ∼ **augmentée** stepped-up basis; ∼ **de bénéfices** earnings base; ∼ **de calcul** base of calculation; ∼ **de calcul de prime** basis of premium calculation; ∼ **du capital** source of capital; ∼ **de clientèle** client base; ∼ **commune de données** shared database; ∼ **de connaissance** knowledge base; ∼ **de crédit** instalment base BrE, installment base AmE; ∼ **de dépenses** expenditure base; ∼ **de discussion** basis for discussion; ∼ **de données** database; ∼ **de données d'entreprise** corporate database; ∼ **de données graphiques** graphic database; ∼ **de données juridiques** legal database; ∼ **de données en ligne** online database; ∼ **de données relationnelles** relational database; ∼ **d'équilibre** equilibrium basis; ∼ **d'imposition** tax base, tax basis; ∼ **monétaire** monetary base; ∼ **de participation** equity base; ∼ **de réserve** reserve base; ∼ **salariale** salary base

baser *vt* base; **être basé à** be based in; **l'entreprise est basée à Bourges** the company is based in Bourges; **basé sur des faits** factual

basic, BASIC *m* BASIC

bassin *m* (port) basin, dock; ∼ **d'amarrage** (port) mooring basin; ∼ **de commerce** commercial dock

bastingage *m* ship's rail

BAT *abrév* (▸**bon à tirer**) (épreuve) final proof; (formule) pass for press

bateau *m* boat; ∼ **à aubes** paddle steamer; ∼**-citerne** tanker; ∼ **fluvial** inland waterway vessel; ∼ **à vapeur** steamboat, steamer

bâtiment *m* building; (navigation) vessel; **le** ∼ (industrie) construction industry; ∼ **agricole** farm building, agricultural building; ∼ **et travaux publics** building and public works

bâtir *vt* (Ind) build; (réputation) build up

battage *m* publicity, hype (infrml); ∼ **médiatique** media hype; ∼ **publicitaire** hype

battant, e *m,f* achiever

batterie *f* battery; ∼ **sèche** dry battery

battre 1 *vt* (concurrent) beat; (record) break; (monnaie) mint; ∼ **son plein** be in full swing
2 **se battre** *v pron* fight; **se** ∼ **pour/contre** fight for/against; **se** ∼ **en pure perte** fight a losing battle

baud *m* (Info) baud

bavardage *m* (sur Internet) chat

BBS *m* (Info) BBS (bulletin board system)

bcbg *abrév* (**bon chic bon genre**) (personne, restaurant) chic and conservative

bce. *abrév* (▸**balance**) bal. (balance)

BCE *abrév* (▸**Banque Centrale Européenne**) European Central Bank

BD *abrév* (Info) (▸**base de données**) database

BDR *abrév* (▸**base de données relationnelles**) RDB (relational database)

BEI *abrév* (▸**Banque européenne d'investissement**) EIB (European Investment Bank)

bénéfice *m* (gain financier) profit; (avantage) advantage; (action bénéfique) benefit; **le** ∼ **de l'ancienneté** the advantage of seniority; **pour un** ∼ **de** at a profit of; **faire 5 000 euros de** ∼ make a profit of 5,000 euros (**sur** on); **faire un** ∼ **énorme** make a huge profit, make a killing (infrml); ∼ **accumulé** accumulated surplus; ∼ **brut** gross profit; (revenue) net income; ∼ **budgété** budgeted profit; ∼ **commercial** profit; ∼ **comptable** accounting income, book profit; ∼ **consolidé** group profit; ∼ **de conversion** (commerce international) translation profit; ∼ **courant** profit for the year; ∼ **disponible** available cash flow; ∼ **économique** economic profit; ∼ **de l'exercice** annual net profit, profit for the financial year; ∼ **d'exploitation** operating profit; ∼ **fiscal** tax advantage, tax benefit; ∼ **imposable** taxable profit; ∼ **inattendu** windfall profit; ∼ **marginal** marginal profit; ∼ **net** net profit; (revenu) net income; ∼ **net annuel** annual net profit; ∼ **net consolidé** consolidated net profit; ∼ **non-dilué par action** basic

···﹥

earnings per share; ~ **non-réalisé** unrealized profit, paper profit; ~ **nul** zero profit; ~ **réinvesti** reinvested profit, ploughback BrE, plowback AmE; ~ **sectoriel** segment margin; ~ **sur transactions** (commerce international) transaction profit; ~ **théorique** paper profit

bénéfices *m pl* profit; **les ~ du premier trimestre ont dépassé les prévisions** first quarter profits exceeded forecasts; **faire des ~** make a profit; **vendre à ~** sell at a profit; **~ par action** earnings per share; ~ **attribués aux actionnaires** distributed profit; ~ **distribués** distributed profit; ~ **de l'entreprise** corporate earnings; ~ **en espèces** cash earnings; ~ **de fabrication et de transformation** manufacturing and processing profits; ~ **après impôts** after-tax profit; ~ **avant impôts** pre-tax profit, profit before tax; ~ **industriels et commerciaux** business profits; ~ **en monnaie constante** inflation-adjusted income; ~ **non-commerciaux** non-business income; ~ **non-distribués,** ~ **non-répartis** undistributed profit; ~ **prévus** anticipated profit; ~ **de revenus** income gain

bénéficiaire *mf* beneficiary; (de chèque) payee; ~ **assimilé** designated beneficiary; ~ **d'une fiducie** beneficiary under a trust; ~ **net** net beneficiary; ~ **d'un prêt** loan recipient; ~ **privilégié** preferred beneficiary; ~ **de redevances** royalty holder; ~ **à titre onéreux** (assurance-vie) creditor rights life insurance; ~ **du trust** beneficiary of a trust, cestui que trust (frml)

bénéficier *vt* ~ **de** (aide financière, appui) receive; (immunité diplomatique) enjoy; (conjoncture favorable) benefit from; **faire ~ qn d'une remise** allow sb a discount

bénévolat *m* voluntary work, volunteer work

bénévole *adj* (travail, service) voluntary; **travailleur ~** voluntary worker, volunteer worker

benne *f* (de chantier) skip BrE, dumpster AmE; ~ **à ordures** dustbin lorry BrE, garbage truck AmE

BEP *m* (▸**brevet d'études professionnelles**) *vocational qualification*

BERD *abrév* (▸**Banque européenne pour la reconstruction et le développement**) EBRD (European Bank for Reconstruction and Development)

besoin *m* need; **avoir un ~ urgent de** be in urgent need of; **~s en biens tutélaires** merit wants; **~s en capitaux** capital requirements; **~s de la clientèle/des consommateurs** customer/consumer needs; **~s concurrents** competing requirements; **~s de crédit** borrowing requirement; **~s en financement** capital requirements; **~s financiers** financial requirements; **~s fondamentaux** basic needs; **~s en**

formation training needs; **~s de liquidités** cash needs, cash requirements; **~s en main-d'œuvre** manpower requirements; **~s en personnel** staffing requirements; **~s sociaux** social wants

bêta *adj* (actions, valeurs) beta; ~ **test** *m* beta test

bétail *m* livestock; (bovins) cattle

bétaillère *f* cattle truck, stock car AmE

BF *abrév* (▸**Banque de France**) Bank of France (*French central bank*)

bibliothèque *f* library; ~ **de données** data library

BIC *abrév* (▸**bénéfices industriels et commerciaux**) business profits

biclic *m* (Info) double click

bicliquer *vi* (Info) double-click

bide *m* flop; **faire un ~** be a flop

bien[1] *adv* well; ~ **connaître qch** be familiar with sth; ~ **connaître son client** know your customer; ~ **fonctionner** run smoothly; ~ **insister sur** (point) hammer home; ~ **réfléchir à** give serious thought to; ~ **approvisionné** well-stocked; ~ **établi** well-established; ~ **fondé** well-grounded; ~ **intentionné** well-meaning; ~ **rémunéré** well-paid; ~ **renseigné** well-informed

bien[2] *m* (avantage) good; (possession) possession; (maison, terres) property; ~ **acquis** purchased good; ~ **d'assurance** insurance property; ~ **en communauté** joint estate, communal estate, community property US; ~ **de la concurrence** rival good; ~ **économique** economic good; ~ **étalon** standard commodity; ~ **immobilier** immovable estate, real estate; ~ **en immobilisation** capital property; ~ **en immobilisation corporel** tangible capital property; ~ **incorporel** incorporeal property; ~ **meuble** personal property; ~ **privé** private good; ~ **public** collective good, public good, social good; ~ **reçu en héritage** inherited property; ~ **social** public good, social good; ~ **transporté en gage/nantissement** pledge; ~ **tutélaire** merit good

bien-être *m* welfare; ~ **économique/mondial** economic/world welfare

bienfaisance *f* charity; **société de ~** charity, charitable organization; **soirée de ~** charity gala

bien-fonds landed property; ~ **loué à bail** leasehold interest

biennal, e *adj* biennial

biens *m pl* (avoirs) assets; (ensemble des possessions) property; (domaine) estate; (patrimoine) fortune; ~ **amortissables** depreciable property; ~ **d'assistance** relief goods; ~ **communs** joint estate; ~ **de consommation** consumer goods; ~ **de consommation courante** fast-moving consumer goods; ~ **corporels** physical

assets; **~ durables** durables; **~
d'environnement** environmental goods; **~
d'équipement** capital goods, hard goods; **~
d'équipement ménager** durable household
goods, consumer durables; **~ immeubles**
real property; **~ immobiliers** real estate; **~
indivisibles** undivided property; **~
industriels** industrial goods; **~
matrimoniaux** after-marriage acquired
property; **~ meubles** (Fisc) goods and
chattels; (Immob) movable property; **~
mobiliers** movable property; **~ non-
durables** expendable goods; **~ non-
marchands** nontradeables; **~ personnels**
personal property; **~ physiques** actuals; **~
de production** production goods; **~ et
services** goods and services

bihebdomadaire *adj* biweekly

bilan *m* (Compta) balance sheet; (évaluation)
assessment; (aboutissement) outcome; (compte
rendu) report; **établir un ~** draw up a balance
sheet; **déposer le ~** file a petition in
bankruptcy; **ne pas apparaître dans le ~** be
unaccounted for in the balance sheet; **~ bien
équilibré** ungeared balance sheet; **~
certifié** certified financial statement; **~ en
forme de compte** horizontal balance sheet;
~ d'inventaire balance sheet; **~ de
liquidation** statement of affairs; **~ en liste**
vertical balance sheet; **~ de mi-année**
interim balance sheet; **~ provisoire** interim
balance sheet

bilatéral, e *adj* bilateral

billet *m* (Loisirs, Transp) ticket; **~ aller-
retour** return ticket BrE, round-trip ticket
AmE; **~ de banque** banknote BrE, bank bill
AmE; **~ en classe économique** economy-
class ticket; **~ collectif** group ticket, party
ticket; **~ de complaisance** accommodation
note; **~ d'entrée** entrance ticket; **~ à
escompte** discount bill; **~ à note**
promissory note; **~ à ordre** promissory
note, bill to order; **~ à ordre payable à
vue** demand note; **~ ouvert** (Transp) open
ticket; **~ à payer** bill payable; **~ plein-tarif**
ordinary ticket; **~ à recevoir** bill
receivable; **~ de trésorerie** (retail)
commercial paper; (Bourse) Treasury note; **~
de trésorerie euro** Eurocommercial paper;
~ vert (infrml) greenback US (infrml)

billétique *f* cash dispenser technology

billetterie *f* (chemin de fer) booking office,
ticket office; **~ automatique** (de billets de
banque) automated cash dispenser, cashpoint

BIM *abrév* (▸**bon à intérêts mensuels**)
bond with monthly-paid interest

bimensuel, -elle *adj* fortnightly BrE,
semimonthly AmE

bimestriel, -elle *adj* bimonthly

binaire *adj* binary

biodégradable *adj* biodegradable

bioéconomie *f* bioeconomics

bioingénierie *f* bioengineering

biopuce *f* (Info) biochip

biotechnologie *f* biotechnology

biotope *m* biotope

bip *m* (son) beep; (appareil) pager; **faire un ~**
beep; **appeler qn au ~** page sb; **~ sonore**
tone

BIPA *abrév* (▸**bon à intérêts payés
d'avance**) bond with interest paid in
advance

biper *vt* page

bipolaire *adj* bipolar

BIRD *abrév* (▸**Banque internationale
pour la reconstruction et le
développement**) IBRD (International Bank
of Reconstruction and Development)

bisannuel, -elle *adj* biennial

bit *m* (Info) bit; **~ d'arrêt** stop bit; **~ de
contrôle** check bit; **~ de début** start bit; **~
de départ** start bit; **~ d'information** data
bit, information bit; **~ de parité** parity bit

BIT *abrév* (▸**Bureau International du
Travail**) ILO

BITD *abrév* (▸**Bureau international des
tarifs douaniers**) ICTB (International
Customs Tariffs Bureau)

blanc, blanche *adj* blank

blanchiment *m* (de l'argent) laundering; **~
de capitaux** money laundering

blanchir *vt* (argent) launder; **argent blanchi**
laundered money

blessure *f* injury; **~ liée à l'exercice d'une
profession** occupational injury, work-related
injury; **~ corporelle** bodily injury

blister *m* blisterpack

bloc *m* (Fin, Pol, Info) block; **~ d'actions**
block of shares; **~ commercial monétaire**
trading monetary bloc; **~ side together;
faire ~ avec qn** side with sb; **faire ~ contre
qn** (s'unir) unite against sb; (être unis) be united
against sb; **acheter en ~** buy the whole
stock; **~ de contrôle** control block,
controlling interest; **~ de mémoire** memory
bank; **~ monétaire** monetary bloc; **~ de
touches numériques** numeric keypad

blocage *m* (des prix, salaires) freeze; (Info)
deadlock (jarg); **faire ~** (projet de loi) block; **~
de titres** escrow

bloc-notes *m* writing pad; (Info) notepad

blocus *m* blockade

bloquer *vt* block; **~ un chèque** stop a check
AmE, stop a cheque BrE; **~ un compte** freeze
an account; **~ un cours** lock in a rate; **~ les
prix** peg prices; **~ les salaires** freeze wages

BMT *abrév* (▸**bon des maisons de titres**)
securities houses bond

BNC *abrév* (▸**bénéfices non-
commerciaux**) non-business income

BOCB *abrév* France (▸**Bulletin officiel des
cours de la Bourse**) ≈ SEDOL UK (Stock
Exchange Daily Official List)

bogue *mf* (Info) bug

b

bogué, e *adj* (Info) bug-ridden, buggy

boire *vt* drink; **je bois à la santé de notre projet** I drink to the success of our project; ~ **la tasse** (infrml) (Bourse) take a bath (infrml)

boîte *f* (pour ranger) box; ~ **de dialogue** (Info) dialog box AmE, dialogue box BrE; ~ **d'envoi** out-box; ~ **à idées** suggestion box; ~ **aux lettres** post box BrE, mailbox AmE; ~ **à lettres électronique** mailbox; ~ **noire** black box; ~ **postale** post office box; ~ **de réception** in-box; ~ **de requête** query box, query window

boîtier *m* (Info) case, casing; ~ **vertical** tower

bombardement *m* (Info) (de messages) bombing

bombe *f* (pour insecticide, peinture) spray; **peindre à la** ~ spray-paint; ~ **aérosol** aerosol, spray; ~ **électronique** (Info) mail bomb

bon[1], **-ne** *adj* (compétent, efficace) good; (moment, numéro, outil) right; (billet) valid; **bonne affaire** bargain; **ce serait une bonne chose** it would be a good thing; **bonne couverture** (informations) full coverage; **bonne délivrance** (d'un certificat) good delivery; **en** ~ **état de marche** in good working order; **bonne expérience des affaires** good business background; **bonne foi** good faith, bona fides (frml); **bonne foi absolue** utmost good faith; **de bonne foi** in good faith; ~ **fonctionnement** smooth running; **bonne gestion** good management; (de données, fichiers) good housekeeping; ~ **à jeter à la poubelle** fit for the bin BrE, fit for the garbage AmE; ~ **marché** cheap; **bonne monnaie** good money; ~ **pour acceptation** accepted; **être** ~ **pour la casse** (infrml) be a write-off (infrml); ~ **rendement** good return; ~ **risque** good risk; **en bonne santé** healthy; ~ **sens** common sense; **aux** ~**s soins de** care of, c/o; ~ **à tirer** pass for press; **être en bonne voie** be under way; **au** ~ **vouloir de** at the discretion of; **si vous le jugez** ~ if you think it advisable

bon[2] *m* bond; ~ **de caisse** (formule) (dans un magasin) certificate of deposit; (Fin) cash certificate; ~ **de cautionnement** guaranty bond; ~ **de chargement** (maritime) mate's receipt; ~ **de commande** purchase order, order form; ~ **à délivrer** (marchandises) freight release; ~ **d'échange** voucher; ~ **d'épargne** savings bond, savings certificate; ~ **à intérêts mensuels** bond with monthly-paid interest; ~ **à intérêts payés d'avance** bond with interest paid in advance; ~ **de livraison** delivery note, delivery order; ~ **des maisons de titres** *securities houses bond*; ~ **à moyen terme négociable** medium-term note; ~ **normalisé** (Lloyd's) standard slip; ~ **à ordre négociable** tradable promissory note; ~ **de réception** goods received note; ~ **de réduction** (publicité) money-off voucher, coupon; ~ **de sortie de stock** issue

voucher; ~ **de souscription** stock purchase warrant; ~ **de souscription au porteur** bearer warrant; ~ **à taux annuel** annual rate note; ~ **à taux annuel normalisé** France *French government bond*; ~ **à taux fixe** fixed-rate bond; ~ **à taux mensuel** monthly rate note; ~ **à taux trimestriel** quarterly rate bond; ~ **à taux variable** floating-rate bond; ~ **à tirer** (épreuve) final proof; ~ **du Trésor** government bond, Treasury bill US; ~ **du Trésor négociable** tradable treasury bond

BON *abrév* (▸**bon à ordre négociable**) tradable promissory note

bonbonne *f* carboy; ~ **de gaz/d'oxygène** gas/oxygen cylinder

bonification *f* bonus; (d'intérêt) rebate; ~ **d'ancienneté** seniority premium; ~ **d'assurance libérée** paid-up addition; ~ **d'intérêt** interest rebate; ~ **de police** policy dividend; ~ **du taux d'intérêt** interest rate rebate

bonus *m* (Assur) no-claim bonus UK

bonus-malus *m* (Assur) no-claim bonus system

boom *m* boom; ~ **économique** economic boom

bordereau *m* (Admin) slip; (de marchandises) invoice; (Fin) note; ~ **d'acceptation** acceptance slip; ~ **d'achat** (Bourse) bought note; (Commerce) purchase note; ~ **d'acheminement** (marchandises) routing order; ~ **de caisse** cash statement; ~ **de cargaison (soumise aux droits de douane)** dutiable cargo list; ~ **de charge** load sheet; ~ **de chèque de guichet** counter cheque form BrE, counter check form AmE; ~ **de dépôt** paying-in slip BrE, pay-in slip AmE; ~ **d'enlèvement** removal note; ~ **d'expédition** consignment note, despatch note, dispatch note; ~ **de livraison** release note, delivery note; ~ **de paiement** remittance slip; ~ **de retrait** withdrawal slip; ~ **de signature** signature slip; ~ **de sortie de frais** out-of-charge note; ~ **de vente** (Bourse) contract note; ~ **de versement** paying-in slip BrE, deposit slip, pay-in slip AmE

borne *f* landmark; ~ **d'appel d'urgence** emergency telephone; ~ **interactive** interactive terminal

Bottin® *m* France phone book, telephone directory

bouche-à-oreille *m inv* word of mouth

boucher *vt* (marché) clog; ~ **le trou** (dans un budget) plug the gap; **le marché est bouché** the market is clogged

bouchon *m* (Transp) traffic jam; ~ **de sécurité** safety cap, child-proof cap

bouclage *m* (Info) wraparound; ~ **rapide** quick fix

boucle *f* (Info) loop; ~ **de courant** current loop; ~ **locale** local loop; **la** ~ **est bouclée**

the wheel has come full circle

boucler *vt* (Bourse) (position) close (out)

bouder *vt* (produit) refuse to buy

bouger *vi* move; (secteur, entreprise) stir; **faire ~ une entreprise** shake up a company; **ça bouge dans l'audiovisuel/en Espagne** things are stirring in the audiovisual sector/in Spain; **ne pas ~** sit tight, stand firm

boule *f* (de machine à écrire) head; **faire ~ de neige** snowball; **effet ~ de neige** snowball effect; **~ de commande** (Info) trackball, trackerball

bouleversement *m* (dans organisation) upheaval

bourrage *m* (dans imprimante) jam; **~ papier** paper jam

bourreau *m*: **~ de travail** workaholic

bourse *f* (porte-monnaie) purse; (Bourse) exchange; (soutien financier) grant; **dénouer les cordons de sa ~** loosen one's purse strings; **être à la portée de toutes les ~s** be within everybody's means; **en ~** (Bourse) on the stock exchange; **~ de commerce** commodity exchange; **~ à découvert** short; **~ d'études** scholarship; **~ aux grains** grain exchange; **~ professionnelle** workshop; **~ du travail** *local trade union information centre*; **~ de valeurs mobilières** stock exchange

Bourse *f* stock exchange, securities exchange, stock market; **la ~ de Paris** the Paris Stock Exchange; **~ d'options européenne** European Options Exchange

boursicotage *m* dabbling in stocks and shares

boursicoter *vi* dabble in stocks and shares

boursicoteur, -euse *m,f* punter, small-scale speculator

bout *m* (dernière partie) end; (pointe) tip; (morceau) piece; **~ d'essai** (télévision, cinéma) screen test

boutique *f* shop BrE; **~ hors taxes** duty-free shop; **~ de proximité** convenience store, convenience shop BrE

boutiquier, -ière *m,f* shopkeeper BrE, storekeeper AmE

bouton *m* (sur un appareil) button, knob; (Info) button; **~ publicitaire** ad button; **~ de remise à zéro** reset button

boycott *m* boycott; **~ complémentaire** secondary boycott; **~ primaire** primary boycott

boycottage *m* boycott

boycotter *vt* boycott

BP *abrév* (▶**boîte postale**) POB (post office box), PO box

BPA *abrév* (▶**bénéfices par action**) EPS (earnings per share)

bps *abrév* (**bits par seconde**) bps (bits per second)

brader *vt* (liquider) sell off; (vendre à bas prix)

sell cheaply; (prix) cut; **prix bradés** knockdown prices

braderie *f* (marché) street market; (magasin) discount store; (vente) clearance sale; (liquidation) selling off; **~ d'objets usagés** jumble sale BrE, rummage sale AmE

brainstorming *m* brainstorming

branche *f* (d'organigramme) path; **~ d'activité** field of activity; **~ d'assurance** class of insurance

branché, e *adj* trendy (infrml)

branchement *m* (Info) branch; **~ conditionnel** conditional branch

brancher *vt* plug in

branlant, e *adj* (situation, projet) shaky

braquer: se ~ *v pron* dig in one's heels (infrml)

brassage *m* (de bière) brewing; (de personnes) intermingling; (d'idées) cross-fertilization; **~ d'affaires louches** wheeling and dealing (infrml)

brasseur *m* (de bière) brewer; **~ d'affaires** business tycoon

brevet *m* (d'invention) patent; (diplôme) certificate; **déposer un ~ pour** take out a patent on; **après le dépôt du ~** after patenting; **~ déposé** patent pending; **~ d'études professionnelles** *vocational qualification*; **~ européen** European patent; **~ d'invention** patent of invention; **~ de perfectionnement** improvement patent; **~ professionnel** *specialized technical qualification*; **~ de technicien supérieur** *advanced vocational qualification diploma*

brevetabilité *f* patentability

brevetable *adj* patentable

breveter *vt* faire **~** (invention) patent; **non breveté** (invention) unpatented; **qui peut être breveté** patentable

BRI *abrév* (▶**Banque des Règlements Internationaux**) BIS (Bank for International Settlements)

bricolage *m* do-it-yourself, DIY

briefer *vt* brief

briefing *m* briefing; **~ d'équipe** team briefing

briseur *m* **~ de grève** strikebreaker

brocante *f* second-hand market

brochure *f* booklet, brochure; **~ publicitaire** publicity brochure

brouillage *m* (radio, télévision) signal jamming; (involontaire) interference

brouillon *m* (de texte, discours) (*rough*) draft; (d'une déclaration d'impôt) working copy

broyeur *m* (de papier) shredder

brut, e *adj* (bénéfice, valeur) gross; (Info) (données) raw; **salaire ~** gross income; **poids ~** gross weight

BSF *abrév* France (**bon des sociétés financières**) *note issued by certain financial institutions*

b

BT *abrév* (▶**billet de trésorerie**) CP
(commercial paper); (Bourse) Treasury note
BTA *abrév* (▶**bon à taux annuel**) annual
rate bond
BTAN *abrév* France (▶**bon à taux annuel
normalisé**) *French government bond*
BTF *abrév* (▶**bon à taux fixe**) fixed-rate
bond
BTM *abrév* (▶**bon à taux mensuel**)
monthly rate note
BTN *abrév* (▶**bon du Trésor négociable**)
tradable Treasury bond
BTP *abrév* (▶**bâtiment et travaux publics**)
building and public works
BTS *abrév* (▶**brevet de technicien
supérieur**) *advanced vocational diploma*
BTT *abrév* (▶**bon à taux trimestriel**)
quarterly rate bond
BTV *abrév* (▶**bon à taux variable**) floating
rate bond
budget *m* budget; (de publicité) account; **gérer
un** ~ administer a budget; **un petit** ~ a tight
budget; ~ **de base** base budget; ~
commercial sales budget; ~ **conjoncturel**
contingent budget; ~ **des dépenses**
expense budget; ~ **directeur** comprehensive
budget; ~ **équilibré** balanced budget; ~
d'équipement capital budget; **le** ~ **de
l'État** the Budget; ~ **d'exploitation**
operating budget, operational budget; ~
familial household budget; ~ **flexible**
variable budget; ~ **fonctionnel** performance
budget; ~ **de fonctionnement** operating
budget; ~ **général** comprehensive budget; ~
des immobilisations capital budget; ~
d'investissement capital budget; ~
perpétuel continuous budget; ~ **principal**
master budget; ~ **de recettes** revenue
budget; ~ **réel** (calculs économiques) actual
budget; ~ **serré** tight budget; ~ **de
trésorerie** cash budget; ~ **variable** flexible
budget, variable budget; ~ **de ventes**
revenue budget; ~ **des ventes** sales budget
budgétaire *adj* (prévisions, déficit, excédent)
budget; (contrôle, contraintes, restrictions)
budgetary; (année) fiscal
budgétisation *f* (entreprises) budgeting; ~
base zéro zero-base budgeting; ~ **en
fonction de la gestion** responsibility
budgeting; ~ **des immobilisations/
investissements** capital budgeting
budgétiser *vt* (dépense, recette) include in
the budget
bug *m* (Info) bug
bulle *f* bubble; ~ **financière/spéculative**
bubble
bulletin *m* (communiqué) bulletin;
(d'informations) newsletter; **Bulletin des
annonces légales obligatoires** *official
stock exchange bulletin where French quoted
companies must disclose financial information*;
~ **de bagages** baggage check; ~ **de**

consigne (commercial) warehouse warrant; ~
de dépôt (port) dock warrant; ~
d'expédition despatch note, dispatch note;
~ **financier** market review; ~
d'informations bulletin, news bulletin; ~
de livraison delivery note; ~
météorologique weather report; **Bulletin
officiel des cours de la Bourse** ≈ Stock
Exchange Daily Official List UK; ~ **de paie**
payslip BrE, pay bill AmE; ~ **de salaire**
payslip BrE, pay bill AmE; ~ **de salaire
analytique** itemized pay statement; ~
scolaire school report; ~ **de souscription**
application form; ~ **de versement** credit
slip; ~ **de vote** ballot paper
bulletin-réponse *m* reply form
bureau *m* (de travail, agence) office; (meuble)
desk; (Info) desktop; **ouvrir un** ~ **à Londres**
open an office in London; ~**x transférés à**
business transferred to; ~**x à vendre** offices
for sale; ~ **d'aide sociale** social security
office BrE, welfare office AmE; ~ **d'avocats**
law firm, law practice; ~ **du cadastre** land
registry; ~ **du caissier** cash office; ~
central (agence) main office; (guichet) front
office; ~ **central des réservations** central
reservation office; ~ **central de transport**
central freight bureau; ~ **de change** bureau
de change, foreign exchange office; ~
commercial business office; ~ **des
contributions** revenue office; ~ **de
cotation** credit bureau, credit reference
agency; ~ **des dépêches** (Média) desk; ~
du directeur manager's office; ~
électronique electronic office; ~ **de
l'état civil** register office, registrar's office,
registry office UK; ~ **d'études** (recherche)
research department; (conception) design office;
~ **d'étude technique** engineering and
design department; ~ **exécutif** executive
board; ~ **d'exportation** export office; ~
d'imposition taxation office; **Bureau
International du Travail** International
Labour Office; **Bureau international des
tarifs douaniers** International Customs
Tariffs Bureau; ~ **de messageries**
receiving office; ~ **paysager** open-plan
office; ~ **de placement** employment agency;
~ **de poste** post office; ~ **de prêteur sur
gages** pawnshop; ~ **de réception** (des
marchandises) goods-in office; ~ **du receveur**
collector's office; ~ **de recrutement**
recruiting office; ~ **régional** branch office,
regional office; ~ **de renseignements**
information desk, inquiry desk; ~ **des
réservations** booking office; ~ **de vote**
polling station
bureaucrate *mf* bureaucrat
bureaucratie *f* bureaucracy
bureaucratique *adj* bureaucratic
bureaucratisation *f* bureaucratization
bureautique *f* office automation

bus *m* (Info) bus, busbar; ~ **d'adresses** address bus; ~ **de données** data bus
business *m* (affaires commerciales) business; ~ **angel** business angel; ~ **en ligne** online business; ~ **plan** business plan
but *m* aim, purpose; ~ **de l'entreprise** company goal; **à** ~ **non-lucratif** non-profit-making BrE, not-for-profit AmE

Cc

c *abrév* (▸**carré**) sq (square)
c. *abrév* (▸**centime**) c. (centime); (▸**coupon**) c., CP (coupon)
ca *abrév* (▸**courant alternatif**) AC (alternating current)
CA *abrév* (▸**conseil d'administration**) (d'une société) board of directors, administrative board; (▸**chiffre d'affaires**) turnover; ~ **tournant** staggered board of directors
cabine *f* (avion, navire) cabin; ~ **de conduite** driver's cab; ~ **téléphonique** phone box BrE, call box, phone booth
cabinet *m* office; (collectif) firm; (de profession libérale) practice; (Droit) (d'avocat, de notaire) office; (de juge) chambers; (Pol) cabinet; ~ **d'affaires** business consultancy; ~ **d'assurances** insurance agency, insurance firm; ~ **d'avocats** law firm, law practice; ~ **d'experts** consulting firm; ~ **d'experts-comptables** accounting firm, accounting practice; ~ **juridique** law firm, law practice; ~ **ministériel** minister's advisers; ~ **de placement** outplacement agency; ~ **de recrutement** recruitment agency
cabinet-conseil *m* consultancy, consultancy practice; ~ **en gestion** management consultancy
câble *m* (fil) cable; (câblogramme) cable, cablegram (frml); **votre** ~ y/c, your cable; ~ **coaxial** (Info) coaxial cable
câblé, e *adj* (Info) hardwired; (immeuble) with cable television
câbler *vt* (connecter) wire; (TV) install cable television in; (Info) hardwire; (Comms) cable
câblogramme *m* cable, cablegram (frml)
câblo-opérateur *m* cable television company
cabotage *m* (Transp) (maritime) coasting, short sea shipping; (navigation) cabotage; **de** ~ (navigation) intercoastal
caboteur *m* coaster, coasting broker
CAC *abrév* (▸**cotation assistée en continu**) automated quotation; (▸**Compagnie des agents de change**) Institute of Stockbrokers
cache *m* (Info) cache
cacher *vt* conceal, cover up; (cinéma,

télévision) mask
cachet *m* (d'une société) seal; (d'un acteur, musicien) fee; ~ **pour colis de titres** remittance seal; ~ **de numéraire** remittance seal; ~ **de la poste** postmark
cacheter *vt* seal; **sous pli cacheté** in a sealed envelope
c-à-d *abrév* (▸**c'est-à-dire**) i.e. (id est)
CAD *abrév* (▸**comité d'aide au développement**) development aid committee
cadastrage *m* land registration
cadastral, e *adj* cadastral
cadastre *m* (bureau) land registry BrE, real estate registry AmE; (registre) land register BrE, real estate register AmE
cadastrer *vt* enter in the land register BrE, enter in the real estate register AmE
cadeau *m* gift, present; (publicité) free gift, freebie (infrml)
cadence *f* rate; ~ **de production** rate of production; ~ **de travail** work rate; ~ **de frappe** keystroke rate
cadre *m* context; (institutionnel) framework; (Info) frame; (Admin) executive; **dans le** ~ **de** (enquête, plan, campagne) as part of; (lutte, politique, négociations, organisation) within the framework of; (rencontre) on the occasion of; ~ **adjoint** (Admin) executive assistant; ~ **de banque** bank officer; ~ **chargé de la formation** training officer; ~ **commercial** sales executive; ~ **conceptuel** conceptual framework; ~ **d'échantillonnage** sampling frame; ~ **d'entreprise** company executive; ~ **d'exploitation** operational environment; ~ **juridique** legal framework; ~ **moyen** middle manager; ~ **stagiaire** management trainee; ~ **supérieur** senior executive, senior manager
cadrer *vi* correspond, tally
cadres *m pl* (Admin) management, managerial staff; ~ **moyens** middle management; ~ **supérieurs** senior management, top management
caduc, caduque *adj* (Droit) (accord, contrat) lapsed
CAF *abrév* (▸**coût, assurance, fret**) CIF (cost, insurance and freight); (▸**caisse** ⋯⟩

d'allocations familiales) ≈ social security office; ~ **à quai** CIF landed

cage f (Info) scroll box

cahier m notebook; ~ **des charges** brief; (pour construction, fabrication) specifications, requirements; (contrat) terms of reference

caisse f (de banque) cashier's desk; (d'un magasin) cash desk; (d'un supermarché) cash register, checkout, till; (boîte) cash box; (machine) cash register, till; (capital) fund; (argent) cash; (pour le transport de marchandises) case, crate; **faire la** ~ balance the cash; **passer à la** ~ (pour payer) go to the cash desk, go to the till; (pour être payé) collect one's money; **avoir de l'argent en** ~ have money in hand, have money in the till; ~ **d'allocations familiales** child benefit office; ~ **d'assurance maladie contributive** contributory health insurance fund; ~ **de crédit** credit union; ~ **de crédit mutuelle** mutual savings bank US; ~ **enregistreuse** cash register; ~ **d'épargne** thrift institution US, savings bank; ~ **d'épargne de la poste** post office savings bank; **les ~s de l'État** the Treasury coffers, the Thrifts US (infrml); ~ **de garantie** compensation fund; ~ **maladie propre à l'entreprise** company health insurance scheme; **Caisse nationale d'épargne** ≈ National Savings Bank UK; ~ **noire** slush fund; ~ **privée d'assurance maladie** private health insurance fund; ~ **de règlement des sinistres** claims settlement fund; ~ **de retraite** pension fund, superannuation fund; ~ **de secours** relief fund

caissier, -ière m,f (dans une banque) cashier, teller; (dans un supermarché) checkout assistant BrE, checkout clerk AmE; ~ **adjoint** assistant cashier, assistant teller

calcul m calculation; **faire un** ~ to make a calculation; **faire une erreur de** ~ miscalculate; ~ **comptable** number crunching; ~ **de l'impôt** tax calculation; ~**s d'intérêts** (profits et pertes) interest operations; ~ **de probabilités** calculus of probabilities; ~ **de la valeur des stocks** inventory computation

calculable adj calculable

calculateur m calculator; ~ **électronique** electronic computer; ~ **numérique** digital computer

calculatrice f calculator; ~ **de poche** pocket calculator

calculer vt calculate, work out; ~ **les intérêts** work out the interest; **calculé annuellement** annualized

calculette f pocket calculator

cale f (d'un navire) hold, lower hold; (port) slipway; ~ **sèche** (navigation) dry dock

calendrier m calendar; (programme) schedule, timetable; **un** ~ **chargé** a busy timetable; **prendre du retard sur le** ~ fall behind schedule; **être en avance par rapport**

au ~ be ahead of schedule; ~ **d'amortissement** repayment schedule; ~ **de contrôle** audit schedule; ~ **d'encaissement** encashment schedule; ~ **de remboursement** repayment schedule; ~ **des travaux** work schedule

calibrer vt (boulons, fruits) grade

calme adj (marché) inactive; quiet; (demande) slack

calomnier vt defame

calomnieux, -euse adj (écrit) libellous BrE, libelous AmE; (propos) slanderous

camarade mf (ami) friend; (Pol) comrade; ~ **de travail** workmate

cambiste mf foreign exchange broker ou dealer

cambriolage m burglary

camelote f (infrml) trashy goods, junk (infrml)

camembert m (infrml) (graphique) pie chart

caméra f camera, movie camera AmE; ~ **de télévision** TV camera; ~ **vidéo** video camera

camion m lorry BrE, truck; ~ **de déménagement** moving van, removal van; ~ **frigorifique** refrigerated lorry BrE, refrigerated truck; ~ **isotherme** refrigerated lorry BrE, refrigerated truck; ~ **de messageries** parcels van; ~ **pour transport d'automobiles** car transporter

camion-citerne m tanker (lorry) BrE, tank truck AmE

camionnage m haulage, truckage AmE

camionner vt haul, truck AmE

camionneur m (chauffeur) lorry driver BrE, truck driver, trucker; (entrepreneur) carrier, haulier BrE, trucking company AmE

camp m camp; ~ **écologique** conservation camp

campagne f (de ventes, publicitaire) campaign; ~ **arrêt buffet** whistlestop campaign; ~ **d'assainissement** cleanup campaign; ~ **centrée sur un secteur** zoned campaign; ~ **diffamatoire** dirty tricks campaign; ~ **d'efficacité** efficiency drive; ~ **électorale** election campaign; ~ **de matraquage** (publicité) burst campaign; ~ **de presse** press campaign; ~ **promotionnelle** (marketing) promotional exercise; ~ **de publicité** advertising campaign; ~ **de saturation** (publicité) saturation campaign

canal m (télévision) channel; (cours d'eau) canal; ~ **de distribution** distribution channel; ~ **publicitaire** advertising channel, advertising medium; ~ **de retour** (Info) reverse channel

canaliser vt (fonds, informations) channel, funnel

canard m (infrml) (journal) rag (infrml), down-market newspaper; ~ **boiteux** (infrml) (spéculateur, société) lame duck

C&A abrév (▶**coût et assurance**) C&I (cost and insurance)

C&F *abrév* (▸**coût et fret**) C&F (cost and freight)

candidat, e *m,f* (à un poste) applicant; (Bourse) (à l'inscription) applicant; (Pol) candidate; (à un examen) candidate; **∼ retenu** appointee, successful applicant

candidature *f* application; **faire acte de ∼** apply, submit an application; **formulaire de ∼** application form; **lettre de ∼** letter of application; **∼ spontanée** unsolicited application

cannibalisation *f* (d'une entreprise) asset stripping

canot: **∼ à moteur** *m* (navigation) motor launch; **∼ de sauvetage** *m* lifeboat

cantine *f* canteen

canton *m* canton

CAO *abrév* (▸**conception assistée par ordinateur**, ▸**création assistée par ordinateur**) CAD (computer-aided design, computer-assisted design), D/A (design automation)

cap¹ *abrév* (▸**capital**) cap (capital)

cap² *m* cap, restriction

CAP *abrév* (▸**Certificat d'aptitude professionnelle**) *vocational qualification*

capable *adj* capable; **∼ de faire qch** capable of doing sth; **bon salaire si ∼** good salary for the right person

capacité *f* (compétence) ability; (potentiel) capacity; (qualification) qualification; (Info) (de la mémoire) capacity; (contenance) capacity; (Droit) capacity; **∼ de qn/qch à faire** capacity of sb/sth to do; **la ∼ d'évolution des employés** the employees' capacity to progress; **avoir ∼ à faire** (Droit) be qualified to do, have the capacity to do; **∼ d'absorption** (du marché) absorption capacity; **∼ de chargement** (d'un navire) cargo capacity; **∼ de crédit** borrowing power; **∼ de distribution** distributive ability; **∼ d'emprunt** borrowing power; **∼ d'endettement** borrowing capacity; **∼ exportatrice** export capacity; **∼ financière** financial capacity; **∼ fiscale** tax capacity; **∼ de fonctionnement** operating capacity; **∼ inutilisée** excess capacity, spare capacity; **∼ de mémoire** (Info) storage capacity, memory capacity; **∼ de paiement** (des salaires) ability to pay; **∼ de production** manufacturing capacity, production capacity; **∼ de stockage des données** information storage capacity; **∼ de traitement** throughput; **∼ de l'usine** plant capacity

capacités *f pl* (talent) abilities; (savoir-faire) skills; **je ne doute pas de vos ∼ I** have no doubts as to your ability *ou* abilities; **∼ locales** local skills

CAPAFE *abrév* (▸**comptes à payer à la fin de l'exercice**) PAYE AmE (Payables at Year-End)

capitaine *m* (d'un navire de commerce) captain, master; **∼ d'industrie** captain of industry

capital *m* capital; **société au ∼ de 500 000 francs** company with (a) capital of 500,000 francs; **procéder à une augmentation de ∼** increase capital; **impôt sur le ∼** capital levy; **∼ actif** active capital; **∼ actions** capital stock, equity capital, share capital; **∼ actions remboursable** redeemable stock; **∼ d'amorçage** seed capital; **∼ appelé** called-up capital; **∼ d'apport** start-up capital; **∼ bancaire** primary capital; **∼ de base** base capital; **∼ constitutif** consideration; **∼ de courtage** broker fund; **∼ décès** death benefit; **∼ de démarrage** start-up capital; **∼ de départ** initial capital, seed money; **∼ échu** matured endowment; due capital; **∼ d'emprunt** loan capital; **∼ fictif** phantom capital; **∼ humain** human capital, human resources; **∼ imposable** taxable capital; **∼ industriel** industrial resources; **∼ libéré** paid-up capital; **∼ nominal** (assurance-vie) face amount, face of policy; **∼ permanent** invested capital; **∼ risque** risk capital, venture capital; **∼ risqueur** venture capitalist; **∼ social** authorized capital, share capital, social overhead capital; **∼ social autorisé** authorized capital stock, authorized capital share; **∼ social souscrit** issued share capital; **∼ souscrit** issued share capital; **∼ utilisé** (Compta) capital employed; (Fin) capital employed equity; **∼ variable** variable capital; **∼ versé** paid-in capital

capitale *f* (imprimerie) capital letter, upper case letter

capitalisation *f* capitalization; **∼ boursière** stock market capitalization; **∼ fiscale** tax capitalization; **∼ globale** total capitalization; **∼ des intérêts** capitalization of interest; **∼ minimale** thin capitalization

capitaliser *vt* capitalize, convert into capital

capitalisme *m* capitalism; **∼ d'affaires** merchant capitalism; **∼ d'état** state capitalism; **∼ industriel** industrial capitalism; **∼ de monopole** monopoly capitalism; **∼ de monopole d'État** state monopoly capitalism

capitaliste¹ *adj* capitalist, capitalistic

capitaliste² *mf* capitalist; **les ∼s** the capitalist class

capitalistique *adj* capital-intensive

capitation *f* capitation tax

capitaux *m pl* (fonds) capital, funds; **mouvements de ∼** capital movements; **marché des ∼** capital markets; **avoir besoin/manquer de ∼** need/lack capital; **∼ d'amorçage** seed capital, seed money; **∼ circulants** circulating capital; **∼ empruntés** borrowed capital; **∼ étrangers** foreign capital; **∼ fébriles** hot money; **∼ fixes** capital assets; **∼ flottants** hot money; **∼ de lancement** seed money; **∼ permanents** capital funds, permanent

capital; ∼ **propres** equity capital,
stockholders' equity; ∼ **roulants** circulating
capital; ∼ **spéculatifs** refugee capital, hot
money

capot m (Transp) (automobile) bonnet BrE,
hood AmE

capter vt (communication téléphonique) tap into;
(Média) (signal) pick up

caractère m character, nature; (en
imprimerie) typeface; (lettre, symbole) character;
en petits/gros ∼s in small/large print; ∼
approprié appropriateness; ∼ **distinctif**
distinctiveness; ∼ **d'effacement** delete
character; ∼ **d'espacement arrière**
backspace character; ∼ **frauduleux**
fraudulence; ∼ **gras** (en imprimerie) character
in bold type, boldface character; ∼ **interdit**
(en imprimerie) illegal character

caractéristique¹ adj characteristic

caractéristique² f (d'un produit) feature; ∼
additionnelle additional feature; ∼ **clé** key
feature; ∼ **essentielle** essential feature; ∼s
de l'obligation f pl bond features, bond
terms; ∼ **optionnelle** optional feature; ∼s
du poste job specification; ∼ **produit**
product feature; ∼s **du risque** description of
risk

carat m carat; **or 18** ∼s 18-carat gold

carburant m petrol BrE, gas AmE, gasoline
AmE

carence f (Droit) insolvency

car-ferry m ferry

cargaison f cargo, freight; (dans un camion)
lorryload BrE, truckload; (dans un train)
trainload; ∼ **d'aller** outward cargo; ∼ **en
douane** bonded cargo; ∼ **mixte** general
cargo; ∼ **de retour** return cargo; ∼
soumise aux droits de douane dutiable
cargo; ∼ **TECH** (**cargaison toxique,
explosive, corrosive, hasardeuse**) TECH
cargo (toxic, explosive, corrosive, hazardous
cargo)

cargo m freighter; ∼ **de divers** (navire)
general cargo ship; ∼ **de ligne régulière**
(navire) cargo liner; ∼ **de marchandises
diverses** (navire) general cargo ship; ∼
polyvalent (navire) omnicarrier

carnet m notebook; (groupe de tickets, bons)
book; ∼ **d'adresses** (livre) address book; ∼
d'agent de change bargain book; ∼ **ATA**
ATA carnet; ∼ **de chèques** chequebook BrE,
checkbook AmE; ∼ **de commandes** order
book; ∼ **de commandes fermes** final
orders; ∼ **de dépôt** deposit book, deposit
passbook; ∼ **d'échéances** bill diary; ∼ **de
quittances** receipt book; ∼ **TIR** (**carnet de
transport international routier**)
international customs transit document; ∼
de versement paying-in book; ∼ **de vol** log
book

carré¹, **e** adj square; **dix mètres** ∼s ten
square metres

carré² m square

carrière f career

carriériste¹ adj career-orientated, careerist

carriériste² mf careerist

carte f (document, pour écrire) card;
(géographique) map; (Info) board, card; **avoir** ∼
blanche have a free hand, have carte
blanche; **horaire/programme à la** ∼
personalized timetable/schedule; ∼
d'abonnement season ticket BrE,
commutation ticket AmE; ∼ **accélératrice**
accelerator card; ∼ **d'achat** charge card; ∼
bancaire bank card, debit card; ∼ **bleue**®
credit card; ∼ **consulaire** consular
declaration; ∼ **de crédit** credit card; ∼ **de
débarquement** landing card; ∼
d'échantillons sample card; ∼
d'embarquement boarding pass; ∼
d'entrée entrance card; ∼ **d'entreprise**
corporate card; ∼ **d'extension mémoire**
memory expansion board; ∼ **famille
nombreuse** family discount card; ∼ **de
fidélité** loyalty card; ∼ **de garantie**
warranty card; ∼ **d'identité** identity card;
∼ **d'identité bancaire** cheque card BrE,
banker's card, check card AmE; ∼
infographique computer map; ∼
magnétique magnetic card, smart card; ∼
mécanographique data card; ∼ **de
membre** membership card; ∼ **mère**
motherboard, mothercard; ∼ **nationale
d'identité** national identity card; ∼ **or** gold
card; ∼ **de paiement** direct debit card; ∼
perforée punch card, punched card; ∼ **de
pointage** clock card; ∼ **à puce** chip card,
smart card; ∼ **de retrait bancaire** cash
card; ∼ **de séjour** alien registration card
US, green card US, residence permit; ∼ **SIM**
SIM card; ∼ **de téléphone** phone card; ∼
vermeil senior citizen's railcard UK; ∼
verte (automobile) green card, certificate of
motor insurance; ∼ **de visite** visiting card;
∼ **de visite professionnelle** business card;
∼ **vitale** social insurance smart card

carte-adaptateur f (Info) adapter card

cartel m cartel; ∼ **de l'acier** steel cartel; ∼
des matières premières commodity cartel;
∼ **des prix** price cartel

carter m (Info) cover

carte-réponse f reply card

carton m (papier épais) cardboard BrE,
tagboard AmE; (boîte) cardboard box, carton;
∼ **contrecollé** pasteboard

cartonné, e adj (made of) cardboard; **boîte**
∼e cardboard box; **couverture** ∼e (de livre)
case-cover; **livre** ∼ hardback

cartouche f cartridge; ∼ **d'encre** ink
cartridge

cas m case; **au** ∼ **par** ∼ on a case by case
basis; **le** ∼ **de figure le plus pessimiste** the
worst-case projection; ∼ **limite** borderline
case; ∼ **qui a une incidence considérable**
high-impact case; **dans le** ∼ **présent** in this
case, in this instance; **en aucun** ∼ on no

account; **en ~ d'empêchement** if anything should crop up; **en ~ de non-distribution** if undelivered; **faire ~ de son avis** air one's views; **le ~ échéant** should the occasion arise; **étudier le ~ de qn** look into sb's case

case f (dans un formulaire) box; (Info) button; (boîte) box; **cocher la ~ correspondante** tick the appropriate box

casier m record; **avoir un ~** have a (police) record; **~ judiciaire** police record; **~ judiciaire vierge** clean record

casque m helmet; **~ de chantier** hard hat

casquer vi (infrml) foot the bill, cough up BrE (infrml); **faire ~** (infrml) bleed (infrml)

cassage des prix m price cutting, underselling

cassation f (d'un jugement) annulment, quashing

casse f (imprimerie) case

casser vt (prix) cut, undercut; (jugement) annul, quash; (monopole) break; **~ les prix** slash prices, undersell

cassette f cassette; **~ audio** audio cassette; **~ vidéo** video cassette

catalogage m cataloguing, online catalogue

catalogue m catalogue BrE, catalog AmE; **~s en ligne** brochureware; **~ de vente par correspondance** mail-order catalogue BrE, mail-order catalog AmE; **~ en ligne** e-catalogue, online catalogue

cataloguer vt (produits) catalogue BrE, catalog AmE

catalyseur m catalyst

catégorie f category, class; (niveau de responsabilité) grade; **de ~ supérieure** (hôtel) high-class; **~ de biens** class of property; **~ de coûts** type of costs; **~ d'emploi** class of employment; **~ d'entreprise** class of business; **~ d'imposition** tax category; **~ de risques** class of risk; **~ socio-professionnelle** socioprofessional group; **~ de tarif** rate class

catégoriquement adv (refuser) flatly

catégorisation f categorization

catégoriser vt categorize

CATIF abrév (▸**contrat à terme d'instrument financier**) financial futures contract

cause f (affaire) case; (raison, ensemble d'intérêts) cause; **à ~ de** because of, due to, owing to; **être en ~** (système, fait, organisme) be at issue; (personne) be involved; **pour ~ économique** for financial reasons; **pour ~ de maladie** because of illness; **les ~s du chômage** the causes of unemployment; **fermé pour ~ d'inventaire/de travaux** closed for stocktaking/renovation; **mettre en ~** question; **la ~ est entendue** (Droit) the case is closed; **~ déterminante** procuring cause; **~ de résiliation** cause of cancellation; **~ du sinistre** cause of loss

causer vt cause

causette f (Info) (sur Internet) chat; **séance de ~** chat session

caution f (Assur) bond; (argent versé) deposit; (Droit) bail; (document) bail bond, letter of indemnity; (garantie) guarantee, guaranty; **verser une ~** pay a deposit; **se porter ~ pour qn** stand surety ou guarantor for sb; **~ judiciaire** judicial bond; **~ en numéraire** surety in cash

cautionnement m security, surety; **~ pour avarie commune** general average deposit; **~ judiciaire** judicial bond; **~ perdu** forfeited security; **~ réciproque** cross guarantee

cautionner vt (soutenir) give one's support to; **~ qn** (se porter garant) stand surety for sb

CBA abrév (▸**coût et assurance**) CEI

CBV abrév (▸**Conseil des bourses de valeurs**) regulatory body of the Paris Stock Exchange

c/c abrév (▸**compte courant**) C/A (current account BrE, checking account AmE)

CCI abrév (▸**Certificats coopératifs d'investissement**) investment certificates reserved to cooperative and mutual companies

CDD abrév (▸**contrat à durée déterminée**) fixed-term contract

CDI abrév (▸**contrat à durée indéterminée**) permanent contract

CD-R m CD-R

CD-RW m CD-RW

CE abrév (▸**Communauté européenne**) EC (European Community); (▸**Conseil de l'Europe**) CE (Council of Europe); (▸**comité d'entreprise**) joint consultative committee, works committee UK

CEA abrév (▸**compte d'épargne en actions**) equity savings account; (▸**Commissariat à l'énergie atomique**) ≈ AERE (Atomic Energy Research Establishment)

CECA abrév (▸**Communauté européenne du charbon et de l'acier**) ECSC (European Coal and Steel Community)

cédant, e m,f assignor, cedant

céder ① vt (transférer) cede; (perdre) give up, shed; (vendre) sell; **~ qch à bail** lease sth; **~ la propriété** transfer ownership ② vi back down, give in

cédérom m CD-ROM

cédétiste mf member of the CFDT trade union

CEDEX abrév (▸**courrier d'entreprise à distribution exceptionnelle**) business mail service

cédi m (Com) cedi

CEEA abrév (▸**Communauté européenne de l'énergie atomique**) EAEC (European Atomic Energy Community)

cégétiste mf member of the CGT trade ⋯⋙

union

CEI *abrév* (▸**Communauté des États indépendants**) CIS (Commonwealth of Independent States)

ceinture: ~ **verte** *f* (autour d'une ville) green belt

CEL *abrév* (▸**compte épargne logement**) savings account (*for purchasing a property*)

célèbre *adj* famous, renowned

célébrité *f* (personne) celebrity; **la** ~ fame

célibataire *mf* (homme) single man, (femme) single woman

cellule *f* (Info, Transp) cell; ~ **de guidage** cell guide; ~ **de réflexion** think-tank (infrml)

CEN *abrév* (▸**Centre européen de normalisation**) European Committee for Standardization

censure *f* censorship

cent *m* hundred; **pour** ~ per cent

centile *m* percentile

centime *m* centime

central *m* (téléphone) exchange

centrale *f* power station; ~ **d'achat** central purchasing agency, (dans une entreprise) central purchasing department; ~ **électrique** power station; ~ **hydro-électrique** hydroelectric power station; ~ **nucléaire** nuclear plant, nuclear power station; ~ **syndicale** confederation of trade unions; ~ **thermique** thermal power station

centralisateur, -trice *adj* centralizing

centralisation *f* centralization

centraliser *vt* centralize

centre *m* centre BrE, center AmE ; **un grand** ~ **culturel/industriel/d'affaires** a large cultural/industrial/business centre; **c'est au** ~ **des discussions** it's at the centre *ou* heart of the discussions; ~ **d'accueil** reception centre; (pour touristes) visitor centre; ~ **d'activité** hub of activity; ~ **administratif** administrative centre; ~ **d'affaires** business centre; ~ **d'appel** call centre; ~ **d'autorisation** authorization centre; ~ **de bilan professionnel** assessment centre; ~ **de calcul** computer centre; ~ **commercial** shopping centre; ~ **de conférences** conference centre; ~ **des congrès** convention centre; ~ **de dégroupage** (navigation) break bulk centre; ~ **de détention** detention centre; ~ **de distribution** distribution centre; ~ **de documentation** resource centre; ~ **de documentation et d'information** learning resource centre; ~ **d'études économiques** centre for economic studies; **Centre européen de normalisation** European Committee for Standardization; **Centre européen pour la recherche nucléaire** European Organization for Nuclear Research; **Centre de formalités d'entreprise** *centre for registering new businesses*; ~ **de formation** training centre; ~ **de formation**

des apprentis vocational training centre; ~ **de gestion informatique** administrative data processing centre; ~ **de gravité** centre of gravity; ~ **de groupage** groupage depot; ~ **industriel** industrial centre; ~ **informatique** computer centre; **Centre international de contrôle du crédit** International Credit Control Centre; ~ **de loisirs** leisure centre; ~ **médico-social** health centre; ~ **opérationnel** operations centre; ~ **de presse** press room; ~ **régional** regional centre; ~ **de traitement à façon** service bureau; ~ **de traitement de texte** word-processing centre; ~ **de transit international** international gateway; ~ **de tri postal** sorting office

centre-ville *m* town centre BrE, town center AmE; (de grande ville) city centre BrE, city center AmE

cercle *m* circle; ~ **vicieux** vicious circle; ~ **vicieux du chômage/de la pauvreté** unemployment/poverty trap; ~ **de qualité** quality circle

CERN *abrév* (▸**Centre européen pour la recherche nucléaire**) European Organization for Nuclear Research

certain *adj* (indiscutable) certain; (date, prix) definite, fixed; (taux) fixed

certif. *abrév* (▸**certificat**) cert. (certificate)

certificat *m* (document, titre) certificate; ~ **attestant de qch** document certifying sth, certificate attesting (to) sth; ~ **attestant que** certificate showing that; ~ **d'acheminement** routing certificate; ~ **d'action** share certificate BrE, stock certificate AmE; ~ **d'agrément** certificate of registration; (navigation) ~ **d'aptitude** (navigation) certificate of competency; ~ **d'aptitude à la profession d'avocat, CAPA** *postgraduate legal qualification needed to practise as a solicitor or barrister*; ~ **d'aptitude professionnelle** *vocational training qualification*; ~ **d'assurance** certificate of insurance; ~ **d'audit** accounts certification; ~ **d'authenticité** certificate of authenticity; ~ **d'avarie commune** general average certificate; ~ **de bord** mate's receipt; ~ **de brevet** patent certificate; ~ **de circulation** movement certificate; ~ **de commerce international** international trading certificate; ~ **de contrôle** certificate of inspection; **Certificats coopératifs d'investissement** *investment certificates reserved to cooperative and mutual companies*; ~ **de débarquement** landing certificate; ~ **de décès** death certificate; ~ **de dédouanement d'entrée** jerque note; ~ **de dépôt** certificate of deposit, investment certificate; ~ **d'emprunt** loan certificate; ~ **d'emprunt cessible** transferable loan certificate; ~ **d'enregistrement** certificate of registration; ~ **d'entrepôt** (commercial) warehouse warrant; (port) dock warrant; ~ **d'épargne** savings certificate; ~

d'exemption, ∼ **d'exonération** certificate of exemption, exemption certificate; ∼ **d'expédition** (de marchandises) certificate of shipment; ∼ **d'expertise** survey certificate; ∼ **de fabrication** certificate of manufacture; ∼ **d'investissement** investment certificate; ∼ **médical** medical certificate; ∼ **numérique** digital certificate; ∼ **d'obligation** bond certificate, debenture bond; ∼ **d'occupation** certificate of occupancy; ∼ **d'option** warrant; **Certificats pétroliers** *oil company investment certificates exclusive to Total and Elf-Erap*; ∼ **de placement** investment certificate; ∼ **au porteur** bearer certificate; ∼ **de prêt** loan certificate; ∼ **de propriété** (Droit, Immob) certificate of ownership, land certificate; ∼ **de protection renforcée ou supplémentaire** supplementary protection certificate; ∼ **provisoire** interim certificate; ∼ **de qualité** certificate of quality, quality certificate; ∼ **du receveur général** receiver's certificate; ∼ **de travail** *document from a previous employer giving dates and nature of employment*; ∼ **d'utilisation** certificate of use; ∼ **d'utilité** utility certificate; ∼ **de validité d'un titre** (de propriété) opinion of title; ∼ **vétérinaire** veterinary certificate; ∼ **de vie** certificate of existence; ∼ **de visite** (d'un navire) certificate of survey; ∼ **de vote fiduciaire** voting trust certificate; ∼ **de vote groupé** voting trust certificate

certification *f* (procédure) auditing; (résultat) auditor's opinion; (d'un produit) acknowledgement, certification; (d'un document) authentication; (d'un acte notarié, d'une attestation officielle) acknowledgement; (d'une signature) witnessing, attestation

certifier *vt* (produit) certificate, guarantee; (document) authenticate; (signature) witness, attest; (avion) certificate; ∼ **conforme** notarize

certitude *f* certainty

CES *abrév* (▸**contrat d'emploi solidarité**) *part-time work for the young unemployed*

cessation *f* (de paiements) suspension; (de fonctions) termination; ∼ **d'activité** (d'une personne) retirement; (d'une entreprise) termination of business; ∼ **de commerce** winding-up; ∼ **de fonctions avec préavis** termination of employment with notice

cesser *vt* (activité, paiement) stop, cease; ∼ **de cotiser à qch** contract out of sth; ∼ **d'exister** (Fisc) cease to be extant; ∼ **ses activités** (entreprise) cease trading; ∼ **le travail** (définitivement) stop work; (à cause d'une grève) go on strike, walk out; **faire** ∼ put an end to; **les taux d'intérêt ne cessent d'augmenter/de baisser** interest rates keep (on) rising/falling

cessibilité *f* (de biens) assignability; (de traite, pension) negotiability

cessible *adj* (biens) assignable; (traite, pension) negotiable; (droits) transferable

cession *f* (Droit, Fin) assignment, transfer; (d'un brevet, d'une marque déposée) abandonment, assignment; (d'une créance) assignment; (d'un bien) abandonment; (d'un droit) assignment; **faire** ∼ **de** assign; ∼ **de droits/de titres/d'actifs** transfer of rights/of securities/of assets; ∼ **d'éléments d'actif** realization of assets; ∼ **horizontale** divestiture; ∼ **au pair** par delivery; ∼ **de portefeuille** portfolio transfer; ∼ **de valeurs mobilières** disposal of securities

cession-bail *f* leaseback

cessionnaire *mf* (Droit, Fin) assignee, transferee

cessure *f* (Bourse) break-out

c'est: ∼**-à-dire** *conj* (à l'écrit) i.e.; (à l'oral) that is to say

césure *f* (imprimerie) hyphenation

CETI *abrév* (▸**contrat d'échange de taux d'intérêts**) interest rate swap

cf *abrév* cf

CFAO *abrév* (**▸conception et fabrication assistées par ordinateur**) CAD/CAM (computer-aided design and computer-assisted manufacturing)

CFDT *abrév* (**Confédération française démocratique du travail**) *French trade union*

CFE *abrév* (**▸Centre de formalités d'entreprise**) *centre for registering new businesses*

CGT *abrév* (**▸Confédération générale du travail**) *French trades union*

chaînage *m* concatenation

chaîne *f* (de magasins, d'hôtels) chain; (de caractères, de données) string; (de télévision) channel; **travailler à la** ∼ work on the assembly line; ∼ **d'activités** business system; ∼ **affiliée** affiliated chain; ∼ **alimentaire** food chain; ∼ **d'approvisionnement** supply chain; ∼ **logistique** supply chain; ∼ **de montage** assembly line; ∼ **de production** production line

chaîner *vt* link

chaland¹, e *m,f* (client) regular customer

chaland² *m* barge

chalandage *m* ∼ **fiscal** treaty shopping; ∼ **d'opinion** opinion shopping

chaland-citerne *m* tank barge

chalandise *f* catchment area of a shop

chalutier *m* trawler

chambre *f* (dans un hotel) bedroom, room; (Droit) chambers; (Pol) chamber; **Chambre de commerce** Board of Trade UK, Chamber of Commerce; ∼ **de commerce française pour le Royaume-Uni** French Chamber of Commerce for the United Kingdom; ∼ **de compensation** clearing corporation US, clearing house; **Chambre de** ···⟩

compensation des instruments financiers de Paris clearing house for financial instruments in Paris; ∼ **à deux lits** twin room; ∼ **pour deux personnes** double room; ∼ **forte** strongroom; ∼ **frigorifique** cold storage; ∼ **froide** cold storage; ∼ **d'hôte** b&b, bed and breakfast; ∼ **individuelle** single room; **Chambre des métiers** Chamber of Trade; **Chambre des représentants** House of Representatives US

champ m field; ∼ **d'activité** field of activity, sphere of activity; ∼ **d'adresse** (Info) address field; ∼ **d'application de la couverture** (Assur) scope of coverage; ∼ **de données** (Info) data field; ∼ **de fond** (Info) background field; ∼ **d'imposition** (Fisc) field of taxation

chance f (occasion) opportunity; (possibilité) chance; (sort favorable) (good) luck; ∼ **sur le marché** break in the market; **avoir une bonne** ∼ **de** stand a good chance of; **ne pas avoir la moindre** ∼ not stand a chance

chancelier m chancellor; ∼ **de l'Échiquier** Chancellor of the Exchequer UK

change m (taux) exchange rate; (opération) foreign exchange; ∼ **à terme** forward exchange

changement m (de l'offre, de la demande) change; ∼ **d'adresse** change of address; ∼ **de carrière** career change; ∼ **de cours à terme** futures price change; ∼ **de date d'échéance** maturity transformation; ∼ **de ligne** line feed; ∼ **de ligne automatique** word wrap; ∼ **de marque** rebranding; ∼ **de page** page break; ∼ **de page obligatoire** hard page break; ∼ **de prix** price change; '∼ **de propriétaire**' 'under new management'

changer [1] vt change; ∼ **l'image d'un produit** restyle a product, repackage a product [2] vi change; (orientation) switch over; ∼ **d'avion/de train** change planes/trains; ∼ **d'avis** have second thoughts; ∼ **de direction** change direction; ∼ **de logement** move house; ∼ **de main** change hands; ∼ **de propriétaire** change hands

changeur m (personne) money changer; (machine) change machine

chantage m blackmail

chantier m construction site; **en** ∼ (bâtiment) under construction; (loi, document) in the process of being drafted; **on espère la mise en** ∼ **de nouveaux programmes** we're hoping that new programmes will be created; ∼ **de ferraille** scrap yard; ∼ **de matériaux de construction** contractor's yard, builder's yard; ∼ **naval** shipyard

chapardage m pilfering, grazing (jarg)

chapitre m (de rapport, budget) section; ∼ **du tarif** sectional rate

charbon m coal; ∼ **de bois** charcoal

charbonnier m (navire) coal carrier, collier

charge f burden, responsibility; (Droit) encumbrance; (Transp) load; **à** ∼ (personne) dependent; **avoir la** ∼ **de faire**, **avoir pour** ∼ **de faire** be responsible for doing; ∼ **financière** financial burden, interest charge; ∼ **fiscale** tax burden, tax charge; ∼ **incomplète** part load; ∼ **indirecte** indirect cost, indirect expense; ∼ **non-courante** nonrecurring charge; ∼ **payable d'avance** upfront cost; ∼ **à payer** accrued expense, accrued liability; ∼ **de la preuve** burden of proof; ∼ **de travail** workload; ∼ **utile** carrying capacity, payload; ∼ **utile réelle** (poids net) actual payload

chargé, e adj (véhicule) loaded; (lettre, colis) registered; (journée) busy, full; **être** ∼ **de** (projet) be in charge of; **trop** ∼ (véhicule, programme) overloaded; **avoir un casier judiciaire** ∼ have had several previous convictions

chargé: ∼ **d'affaires** (Pol) chargé d'affaires; ∼ **du marketing** marketing manager; ∼ **de mission** (Pol) official representative; ∼ **de prêts** lending officer, loan officer

chargement m (action) loading; (de marchandises) cargo, load; ∼ **et livraison** loading and delivery; **à** ∼ **automatique** (machine) self-loading; (Info) autoloading; ∼ **d'aller** outward cargo; ∼ **manuel** (Info) manual feed; ∼ **de retour** inward cargo

charger vt (marchandises) load; (Info) (programme) load

charges f pl charges, expenses; ∼ **associées** add-on costs; ∼ **courantes** running costs; ∼ **exceptionnelles** (bilan) exceptional expenses; ∼ **d'exploitation** operating costs, running expenses; ∼ **d'intérêts** interest charge, interest charges; ∼ **latentes** contingent expenses; ∼ **de main-d'œuvre directes** direct labour costs BrE, direct labor costs AmE; ∼ **prévues** estimated charges, estimated costs; ∼ **sociales** social security contributions BrE, welfare contributions AmE, payroll taxes

chargeur m (Transp) loading agent, shipper; (Info) (de disques) disk pack; ∼ **feuille à feuille** (machine) sheet feeder; ∼ **et transporteur** shipper and carrier

chariot m (de supermarché) trolley BrE, cart AmE; ∼ **à bagages** luggage trolley BrE, baggage cart AmE; ∼ **élévateur à fourche** fork-lift truck; ∼ **élévateur pour palettes** pallet truck

charognard m bottom fisher

charte f charter; ∼ **bancaire** bank charter; ∼ **constitutive** (d'une société) memorandum of association; ∼ **de création** copy platform; **Charte européenne de l'énergie** European Energy Charter; ∼ **graphique** (identité de l'entreprise) house style; ∼ **sociale** social charter; **Charte sociale européenne** European Social Charter

charte-partie *f* (maritime) charter party

charter *m* (avion) charter plane; (vol) charter flight; ~ **ouvert** open charter

chasseur de têtes *m* headhunter; **elle a été recrutée par un** ~ she was headhunted

chaudière *f* boiler; ~ **auxiliaire** auxiliary boiler

chaudronnier *m* boiler manufacturer

chaufferie *f* boiler room

chauffeur *m* driver; ~ **de camion** lorry driver BrE, truck driver, trucker

chavirer *vi* (navire) capsize, turn over

ch. de f. *abrév* (▸**chemin de fer**) railway BrE, railroad AmE

chécographe *m* cheque writer BrE, check writer AmE

chef *m* (Admin) chief, head, (Gestion) (supérieur) boss (infrml), chief, head manager; ~ **d'accusation** charge, count of indictment; ~ **des achats** chief buyer, purchasing manager; ~ **d'agence** branch office manager; ~ **d'atelier** line manager, supervisor; ~ **de bureau** office manager; ~ **de chantier** site foreman; ~ **de la circulation** (chemin de fer) traffic manager; ~ **comptable** chief accountant; ~ **de département** departmental head, division manager; ~ **d'entreprise** company manager, head of the company; ~ **d'équipe** team leader; ~ **d'établissement** plant manager; ~ **d'État** head of state; ~ **d'exploitation** operational manager, operations manager; ~ **de fabrication** production manager; ~ **de gare** stationmaster; ~ **de production** production manager; ~ **de produit** brand manager, product manager; ~ **de projet** project leader, project manager; ~ **de publicité** advertising manager; ~ **de rayon** department manager, departmental manager; (dans un grand magasin) section manager, department manager; ~ **de rédaction** copy chief; ~ **de service** department head, section head

chemin *m* (Info) path; ~ **d'accès** (Info) pathway; ~ **critique** critical path; ~ **de fer** railway BrE, railroad AmE; ~ **de papier** paper trail

cheminée *f* (d'un navire) funnel, smokestack; ~ **d'usine** smokestack

cheminot *m* railwayman BrE, railroad worker AmE

chemise *f* (pour documents) folder

chenal *m* (dans un cours d'eau) fairway

chèque *m* cheque BrE, check AmE; **faire un** ~ make out a cheque, write a cheque; ~ **bancaire** bank cheque; (tiré par une banque sur une autre) bank draft; ~ **barré** crossed cheque; ~ **en blanc** blank cheque; ~ **en bois** (infrml) bounced cheque, rubber cheque (infrml); ~ **en circulation** outstanding cheque; ~ **compensé** cleared cheque; ~ **à** encaisser uncashed cheque; ~ **falsifié** forged cheque; ~ **frappé d'opposition** stopped cheque; ~ **de guichet** counter cheque; ~ **d'intérêt** interest cheque; ~ **d'un montant de** cheque to the amount of; ~ **non-endossable** account payee cheque; ~ **oblitéré** cancelled cheque; ~ **par procuration** preauthorized cheque; ~ **payable à l'ordre de qn** cheque in favour of sb; ~ **périmé** stale cheque; ~ **au porteur** bearer cheque, cheque made out to cash; ~ **postdaté** postdated cheque; ~ **refusé** returned cheque; ~ **de règlement de salaire** pay cheque, salary cheque; ~ **sans provision** bounced cheque, not-sufficient-funds cheque, bad cheque; ~ **de voyage** traveller's cheque

chèque-cadeau *m* gift token, gift voucher

chèque-repas *m* luncheon voucher BrE, meal ticket AmE

chèque-restaurant *m* luncheon voucher BrE, meal ticket AmE

chéquier *m* chequebook BrE, checkbook AmE

cher, -ère *adj* (onéreux) expensive, dear; ~ **assez cher** underpriced; **peu** ~ cheap, inexpensive; **trop** ~ overpriced

chercher *vt* (personne, objet, appartement, emploi) look for; (approbation) seek; (Info) (piste) search; ~ **la contre-partie** (Bourse) seek a market; ~ **un emploi** look for a job; **'cherchons vendeuses'** 'sales assistants wanted'; ~ **à faire** try to do; **je cherche à vous joindre depuis ce matin** I've been trying to contact you since this morning; **aller** ~ **qn à l'aéroport** meet sb at the airport

chercheur, -euse *m,f* research worker, researcher; ~ **d'occasion** bargain hunter

cherté *f* (de produit, terrain) high cost; (de monnaie) high price; ~ **de la vie** high cost of living

chevalet *m* easel; ~ **à feuilles mobiles** flip chart

chevalier *m* (Fin) knight; ~ **blanc** white knight; ~ **d'industrie** wheeler-dealer (infrml); ~ **noir** black knight

cheval-vapeur *m* horsepower

chez *prép* (sur enveloppe) c/o, care of

chien *m* dog; ~ **de garde** watchdog; ~**s écrasés** (presse) *column made up of filler items*

chiffre *m* (symbole) figure; (numéro, nombre) number; (résultat) figure; (total) amount; **le** ~ **des dépenses** the total expenditure; ~ **global** total amount; ~ **sans précédent** (le plus haut) all-time high; **le** ~ **le plus bas jamais atteint** (prix, niveau, taux) all-time low; ~ **d'affaires** (résultats d'une société) turnover; ~ **d'affaires d'une agence de publicité** agency billing; ~ **d'affaires de l'exercice** annual turnover; ~ **d'affaires prévisionnel** forecast turnover; ~ **approximatif** approximate figure, ballpark figure (infrml); ~ ⋯⟩

décimal decimal number, decimal digit; ∼ **rond** round figure, round number; ∼ **de ventes** sales figures, sales

chiffrement *m* encryption

chiffrer: se ∼ **à** *v pron* amount to, come to; **être chiffré à** amount to

chiffres *m pl* statistics, figures; ∼ **parus aujourd'hui** figures out today; **en** ∼ **ronds** in round figures; **les** ∼ **de ce mois sont mauvais** this month's figures are bad; ∼ **du chômage** unemployment figures; ∼ **du commerce** (extérieur ou intérieur) trade figures; ∼ **corrigés** revised figures; ∼ **de l'emploi** employment figures; ∼ **officiels** official figures; ∼ **réels** actual figures; ∼ **de tirage** (d'un journal) circulation figures

chiffreur, -euse *m,f* cipher clerk

chiffrier *m* work sheet

chirographaire *adj* (créance, obligation) unsecured

choc *m* shock; ∼ **culturel** culture shock; ∼ **d'offre** supply shock, supply-side shock; ∼ **d'offre négatif** adverse supply shock; ∼ **pétrolier** oil crisis

choisir *vti* choose (**entre** between); **bien/mal** ∼ choose well/badly; ∼ **qn comme assistant** pick sb as an assistant

choix *m* (alternative) choice, option; (sélection) selection; (gamme) choice, range, selection; **au** ∼ **du vendeur** seller's option; **faire son** ∼ take one's pick; **avoir/ne pas avoir le** ∼ have a/no choice; **faire le bon/mauvais** ∼ make the right/wrong choice; **trois coloris au** ∼ a choice of three colours; **être libre de son** ∼ be free to choose; **de** ∼ (produit) choice, premium; (candidate) first-rate; **de premier** ∼ prime, top-grade; ∼ **du consommateur** consumer choice; ∼ **de marchandises** assortment of goods, choice of goods; ∼ **d'une marque** branding; ∼ **des médias** media selection; ∼ **optimal** best alternative; ∼ **des supports** media selection; ∼ **tacite** negative option (jarg); ∼ **des termes** (d'un contrat) wording

chômage *m* unemployment; **au** ∼ out of work, unemployed, on the dole UK (infrml); ∼ **en augmentation** rising unemployment; **500 ouvriers au** ∼ **technique** 500 workers laid off; **mettre au/en** ∼ **technique** lay off; ∼ **caché** concealed unemployment, hidden unemployment; ∼ **conjoncturel** cyclical unemployment; ∼ **cyclique** cyclical unemployment; ∼ **déclaré** registered unemployment; ∼ **déguisé** disguised unemployment; ∼ **entraîné par l'immigration** migration-fed unemployment; ∼ **à grande échelle** mass unemployment; ∼ **involontaire** involuntary unemployment; ∼ **de longue durée** long-term unemployment; ∼ **partiel** short-time working; ∼ **saisonnier** seasonal unemployment; ∼ **technique** layoffs; ∼ **volontaire** voluntary unemployment

chômer *vi* (être improductif) (personne, machine, capital) be idle; (être sans travail) (employé) be out of work; (usine, machine) stand idle; (industrie) be at a standstill; **nous ne chômons pas en ce moment** we're not short of work at the moment; **laisser** ∼ **les terres** leave the land fallow

chômeur, -euse *m,f* jobless person, unemployed person; **les** ∼**s** the jobless, the unemployed; **les** ∼**s inscrits à l'Agence nationale pour l'emploi** the registered unemployed UK; ∼ **de longue durée** long-term unemployed BrE, hard-core unemployed AmE

chronique *adj* (chômage, déficit) chronic

chroniqueur, -euse *m,f* (presse) columnist; (radio, TV) commentator

chronogramme *m* time chart

chronométrage *m* timing; (étude) time study; ∼ **des travaux administratifs** clerical work measurement

chronomètre *m* timer

Chronopost® *m* France express mail service

chronoval *m* (Bourse) *real-time stock market news service*, ≈ Regulatory News Service UK

chute *f* (baisse) drop, fall; ∼ **brutale** collapse; ∼ **rapide** fast decline; ∼ **du dollar** fall in the price of the dollar; ∼ **de la Bourse** fall on the stock market; ∼ **de 5%** 5% drop; **économie/prix/popularité en** ∼ plummeting economy/prices/popularity; **être en** ∼ **libre** be in freefall; ∼ **de tension** brownout US; ∼ **verticale** tailspin (infrml)

chuter *vi* (température, tension, prix) fall, drop; (ventes, production) fall; (actions, valeurs) fall; ∼ **de 10 euros** fall *ou* drop by 10 euros; **la livre a chuté de deux points (par rapport au dollar)** the pound has fallen two points (against the dollar); **faire** ∼ **les cours** bring prices down, cause prices to fall

CI *abrév* (▸**certificat d'investissement**) investment certificate; (▸**circuit intégré**) IC (integrated circuit)

ci-après *adv* below; **voir** ∼ see below

ciblage *m* (V&M) targeting; ∼ **négatif** negative targeting; ∼ **des prix** target pricing

cible *f* (Info, V&M) target; (public) target audience; ∼ **commerciale** marketing target; ∼ **publicitaire** advertising target

cibler *vt* (un public) target; **ils ont mal ciblé leur clientèle** they didn't target their market properly

ci-contre *adv* opposite

ci-dessous *adv* below; **voir** ∼ see below

ci-dessus *adv* above; **voir** ∼ see above

Cie *abrév* (▸**compagnie**) Co. (company); **et** ∼ *abrév* (▸**et compagnie**) and Co (and company)

CII *abrév* (▸**crédit d'impôt à l'investissement**) ITC (investment tax credit)

ci-inclus, e *adj* attached, enclosed

ci-joint, e *adj* attached, enclosed

circonscription *f* (Admin) division, district; ~ **électorale** electoral constituency BrE, electoral district AmE; ~ **judiciaire** jurisdiction

circonspection *f* caution

circonstance *f* circumstance, occasion; **en raison des** ~s under the circumstances; ~s **imprévues** unforeseen circumstances; ~s **particulières** special circumstances; **dans ces** ~s under the circumstances; **dans des** ~s **semblables** in similar circumstances; **en pareille** ~ in a situation like this; **en toute** ~ in any event; **pour la** ~ for the occasion; ~s **atténuantes** extenuating *ou* mitigating circumstances; ~s **matérielles** (Assur) material circumstance

circonstanciel, -elle *adj* incidental

circuit *m* circuit; (Info) circuit; ~ **de commandes** (V&M) channel for orders; ~ **commercial** (Com) trade channel; (V&M) marketing channel; ~ **de commercialisation**, ~ **de distribution** distribution network; ~ **fermé** closed circuit; ~ **intégré** integrated circuit; ~ **de vente** sales channel

circulaire *f* (Admin) circular; ~ **du conseil d'administration** directors' circular

circulation *f* (Banque, Econ) circulation; (Info) flow; (Média) readership; (de véhicules) traffic; **en** ~ (effets) in circulation; **mettre en** ~ put into circulation; **retirer de la** ~ withdraw from circulation; ~ **aérienne** air traffic; ~ **des données** (Info) data flow; ~ **de la main-d'œuvre** movement of labour BrE, movement of labor AmE; ~ **des marchandises** commodity flow; ~ **routière** road traffic

circuler *vi* (train, bus) run; (bateau) operate; (information, idée) circulate, go round; (marchandises, billets) circulate; **faire** ~ (information) circulate; (billets, action) put into circulation

citation *f* (Droit) citation, statement of claim; ~ **à comparaître** (adressée à un témoin) subpoena; (adressée à l'accusé) summons

cité *f* city; (plus petite) town; (ensemble de logements) housing estate, housing project AmE; ~ **ouvrière** workers' housing development

citer *vt* (Droit) cite; (accusé) summons; (témoin) subpoena; ~ **comme témoin** call as a witness; ~ **à comparaître** (accusé) summons; (témoin) subpoena

citerne *f* tank; ~ **de cargo** cargo tank; ~ **de stockage** storage tank

citoyen, -enne *m,f* citizen; ~ **de seconde classe** second-class citizen

citoyenneté *f* citizenship

clair, e *adj* (discours) straightforward; **en** ~

in plain language

clairvoyant, e *adj* far-seeing, far-sighted

clandestin, e *adj* (affaire) clandestine, secret; (travailleur, commerce) illegal

clarifier *vt* (problème) shed light on; (situation) clarify

classe *f* class; **de** ~ **mondiale** world-class; **de première** ~ first-class; **la** ~ **ouvrière** the working class; **les** ~s **sociales défavorisées** the underprivileged classes; ~ **d'actifs moins liquides** Tier Two assets; ~ **d'actifs plus liquides** Tier One assets; ~ **d'actions** class of shares, share class; ~ **affaires** (aviation) business class; ~ **dirigeante** ruling class; ~ **économique** (aviation) economy class; ~ **social** social class; ~ **touriste** economy class, tourist class

classement *m* (de documents) filing; (Admin) (rang) ranking, rating; ~ **d'avaries** (Assur, Transp) average statement; ~ **par matières** subject filing; ~ **standard du commerce de marchandises** standard freight trade classification

classer ① *vt* (attribuer un rang à) class, grade; (Droit) (dossier, affaire) close; (classifier) categorize, classify; (ranger) file, file away; **classé AAA** triple-A-rated; **classé par catégorie** (fruits, légumes) graded by size; **classé confidentiel** (dossier) classified ② **se classer** *v pron* (pays, entreprise) rank

classeur *m* (meuble) filing cabinet; (à anneaux) ring binder; (à compartiments) file

classification *f* classification; ~ **AAA** triple-A rating; ~ **des emplois** job classification; ~ **industrielle standard** standard industrial classification; ~ **des normes du commerce international** Standard International Trade Classification; ~ **des risques** (Assur) classification of risks; ~ **des tâches** work classification

classifier *vt* classify

clause *f* (Assur) clause; (Droit) clause, provision; ~ **d'abandon** waiver clause; ~ **d'abordage** (maritime) running down clause; ~ **abrogatoire** annulling clause; ~ **d'accélération** acceleration clause premium; ~ **additionnelle** additional clause; ~ **d'ajustabilité** adjustment clause; ~ **d'annulation** (contrat) cancellation clause; ~ **d'arbitrage** arbitration clause; ~ **attrayante** incentive; ~ **avarie** average clause; ~ **du bénéficiaire** beneficiary clause; ~ **bris** breakage clause; ~ **de catastrophe** disaster clause; ~ **de collision** collision clause; ~ **de couverture** hedge clause; ~ **de droits acquis** (Droit) grandfather clause; ~ **échappatoire** escape clause, let-out clause; ~ **d'évaluation** valuation clause; ~ **d'exclusion** exclusion clause; ~ **d'exonération** exemption clause; ~ **de franchise** deductible clause; ~ **d'habilitation** enabling clause; ~

⋯▸

d'insolvabilité insolvency clause; ∼ **de mobilité** mobility clause; ∼ **de négligence** neglect clause, negligence clause; (charte-partie) negligence clause; ∼ **de parité** parity clause; ∼ **pénale** penalty clause; ∼ **au porteur** (Bourse) bearer clause; ∼ **de post-acquisition** after-acquired clause; ∼ **de prolongation** continuation clause; ∼ **provisoire** draft clause; ∼ **de rachat** (Bourse) call feature; (Droit) buy-back clause; ∼ **de recours et de conservation** (Assur) sue and labour clause BrE, sue and labor clause AmE; ∼ **de régularisation** adjustment clause; ∼ **de renonciation** contracting-out clause; ∼ **de report** continuation clause; ∼ **résolutoire**, ∼ **de résiliation** cancellation clause, termination clause; ∼ **de la responsabilité civile professionnelle** errors and omissions clause; ∼ **de sauvegarde** (Assur) disaster clause; (Bourse) (dans un contrat) hedge clause; (Droit) escape clause; ∼ **de séquestre** (maritime) escrow clause; ∼ **sérieuse** bona fide clause; ∼ **de signature** attestation clause; ∼ **subrogatoire** subrogation clause; ∼ **de surenchère** escalation clause; ∼ **de survie** survivorship clause; ∼ **tout ou rien** all-or-nothing clause; ∼ **de transport** transit clause; ∼ **valeur agréée** (maritime) agreed valuation clause; ∼ **de la valeur vénale** market value clause; ∼ **de vétusté** obsolescence clause

clavier m (Info) keyboard; (plus petit) keypad; ∼ **numérique** digital keyboard; ∼ **personnalisé** customized keyboard; ∼ **programmable** soft keyboard; ∼ **de saisie** input keyboard

claviste mf (Info) keyboard operator, keyboarder

clé f key; (Info) key; ∼ **d'accès** (Info) key; ∼ **électronique de protection** (Info) dongle; ∼ **d'enregistrement** (Info) record key; ∼s **en main** (projet, usine) turnkey; ∼ **numérique de contrôle** (Info) check digit; ∼ **principale** (Info) master key; ∼ **de recherche** (Info) search key; ∼ **de voûte** (de l'économie) backbone, keystone

clerc m (Admin) clerk; ∼ **de notaire** notary's clerk

clic (Info) click m; **double** ∼ double click; **de** ∼s **et de briques** (Com, Info) clicks and mortar

client, e m,f (d'avocat) client; (de magasin) customer; (d'hôtel) guest, patron; ∼s (Compta) trade receivables; ∼ **difficile** difficult customer, problem customer; ∼ **important** big customer; ∼ **principal** main customer; **pays** ∼s client countries; ∼ **emprunteur** borrowing customer, borrower; ∼ **étranger** overseas customer; ∼ **éventuel** prospect, prospective customer; **le** ∼ **roi** consumer sovereignty; ∼ **sûr** blue-chip customer; ∼ **zappeur** (V&m) switcher, brand switcher

clientèle f (clients) customer base, customers; (commerce) custom, goodwill; **axé sur la** ∼ customer-orientated, customer-oriented; ∼ **privée conseillée** (Fin) advisory account; ∼ **privée gérée** (Fin) discretionary account

client-serveur adj (Info) (architecture) client-server

clignotant m (Ind) performance indicator; ∼ **économique** economic indicator

clignotement m ∼ **des indicateurs économiques** signalling BrE, signaling AmE

climat m atmosphere, background; ∼ **économique financier** economic financial climate; ∼ **économique favorable** favourable economic climate BrE, favorable economic climate AmE; ∼ **social** social climate

climatisation f air conditioning

clinique f (établissement) private hospital

cliquer vt click; ∼ **deux fois** double-click

cloison f (d'un bureau) partition; (d'un avion, d'un navire) bulkhead

cloisonnement m (Admin) (entre services) compartmentalization

cloisonner vt (Admin) (secteurs) compartmentalize; **non cloisonné** (bureau) open-plan

clone m clone

cloner vt clone

clore vt (séance, réunion) close (par with); (Info) (session) log off; **l'exercice clos le 31 décembre** the financial year which ended on 31 December

clos, e adj closed; (enveloppe) sealed

clôture f (Bourse) close; (de magasin, bureau) closing; (de débat) closure; **à la** ∼ at closing, at the close; **prix/stock de** ∼ closing price/stock; **achat/vente/opération après** ∼ after-hours buying/selling/trading; **valoir 10 euros en** ∼ close at 10 euros; ∼ **de compte** closing statement; ∼ **des comptes** accounts close-off; ∼ **à découvert** short closing; ∼ **de l'exercice** year end, year-end closing; ∼ **de marché** (Bourse) close of the market, market close; ∼ **à minuit** midnight deadline; ∼ **des offres** (Bourse) bid closing

clôturer vt (comptes) wind up; (séance) close

club m club; ∼ **d'actionnaires** subscription club; ∼ **des exportateurs** export club; ∼ **d'investissement** investment club; ∼ **de session** (Info) logging off; ∼ **de souscripteurs** subscription club

cluster m cluster

CM abrév (▶**Chambre des métiers**) professional association, Chamber of Trade

CNE abrév (▶**Caisse nationale d'épargne**) ≈ National Savings Bank

CNPF abrév (▶**Conseil national du patronat français**) national council of French employers, ≈ CBI (Confederation of British Industry)

coacquéreur m joint purchaser

coacquisition *f* joint purchase

coadministrateur, -trice *m,f* (Gestion) joint administrator; (Droit) joint trustee

coalition *f* (Pol) coalition

coassociation *f* joint partnership

coassocié, e *m,f* joint partner

coassurance *f* coinsurance

coassuré, e *adj* coinsured

coassurer *vt* co-insure

COB *abrév* (►**Commission des opérations de Bourse**) *French stock exchange watchdog*

cobol *m* (Info) COBOL

cocher *vt* tick (off) BrE, check (off) AmE; ~ **la case** (sur un formulaire) put a tick in the box BrE, check box AmE; put a check in the box AmE

co-commissaire *mf* joint auditor

cocontractant, e *m,f* contracting party

co-création *f* (Internet) co-creation

codage *m* coding, encoding; ~ **binaire** (Info) binary coding

code *m* code; ~ **d'arbitrage** (Bourse) code of arbitration; ~ **d'article courant** (Pol) standard object code; ~ **d'article de rapport** (Compta) reporting object code; ~ **d'autorisation** (Banque) authorization code, authorization number; ~ **à barres** bar code; ~ **bancaire de tri** (des chèques) bank code, sort code UK; ~ **de bonne conduite** code of practice; ~ **de caractères** (Info) code set; ~ **de commerce** (Droit) commercial code; ~ **de commerce uniforme** uniform commercial code; ~ **de compensation foncière** land compensation code; ~ **comptable** chart of accounts; ~ **de comptes** code of accounts; ~ **de conduite** code of conduct; ~ **machine** machine code; ~ **ONU** UN code; ~ **personnel** (Banque) personal identification number; ~ **postal** postcode BrE, zip code AmE; ~ **de responsabilité professionnelle** code of professional responsibility US; ~ **des usages** (Bourse) rules of fair practice, uniform practice code US; ~ **des valeurs** (Bourse) stock symbol

code-barre *m* bar code

co-débiteur, -trice *m,f* joint debtor; ~ **hypothécaire** co-mortgagor US

codéposant, e *m,f* (Brevets) joint applicant

codet *m* (Info) code element

codétenteur, -trice *m,f* joint holder

CODEVI *abrév* (►**compte pour le développement industriel**) industrial development savings account

codicille *m* (Droit) codicil

codification *f* codification; ~ **des comptes** classification of accounts

codifier *vt* (lois) codify; (comptes) classify; (usage) standardize

codirecteur, -trice *m,f* (administrateur) co-director, joint director; (responsable) co-manager, joint manager

codirection *f* joint management

coefficient *m* (Com) factor; (proportion) ratio; (pourcentage indéterminé) margin; (statistiques) coefficient; ~ **d'erreur** margin of error; ~ **de bénéfice brut** gross profit ratio; ~ **bêta** beta factor BrE, beta coefficient AmE; ~ **de capital** capital ratio; ~ **de capitalisation des résultats** price-earnings ratio; ~ **de conversion** conversion factor; ~ **de discrimination du marché** market discrimination coefficient; ~ **d'écart** coefficient of variation; ~ **d'employés** employee ratio; ~ **d'évaluation** assessment ratio; ~ **d'exploitation** working ratio; ~ **d'imposition** tax ratio; ~ **de liquidité** liquid ratio; ~ **de perte** loss ratio; ~ **de réserve** reserve rate, reserve ratio; ~ **de trésorerie** cash deposits ratio, cash ratio

coentrepreneur *m* joint venturer

coentreprise *f* joint venture; ~ **avec création de société commune** equity joint venture; ~ **sans création de société** contract joint venture

coéquation *f* (Admin) proportional assessment

coercitif, -ive *adj* coercive, compulsory

coffre *m* (de banque) safe deposit, safe-deposit box; (de voiture) boot BrE, trunk AmE; ~ **de nuit** night safe

coffre-fort *m* safe

cofinancement *m* cofinancing

cofinancer *vt* cofinance

cogérance *f* joint management

cogérant, e *m,f* joint manager

cogestion *f* joint management

cohabitation *f* joint occupancy

cohérence *f* (de raisonnement) coherence; (de programme) consistency; **manquer de** ~ be inconsistent

cohérent, e *adj* (logique) coherent; (homogène) consistent

cohéritier, -ière *m,f* joint heir

cohésion *f* cohesion

coin *m* corner; ~ **des bonnes affaires** bargain basement

coincer: se ~ *v pron* (partie d'une machine) jam

coïncider *vi* (événements) coincide; (chiffres) agree, concur; ~ **avec** coincide with

coinculpé, e *m,f* co-accused, codefendant

col *m* collar; ~ **blanc** white-collar worker; ~ **bleu** blue-collar worker

colis *m* package, parcel; ~ **en instance de livraison** parcels awaiting delivery; ~ **lourd** *m* (manutention) heavy load, heavy lift

colistier, -ière *m,f* (Pol) fellow candidate BrE, running mate AmE

collaborateur, -trice *m,f* (coauteur) collaborator; (collègue) colleague; (assistant) ····>

assistant; (personne qui contribue à un journal) contributor

collaboration f collaboration; (assistance) cooperation; **de ~** collaborative; **en ~ avec** in collaboration with; **~ technique** technical cooperation

collaborer vi (travailler) collaborate (**avec** with); **~ à** (journal, magazine) contribute to; (projet) collaborate on

collage m (publicité) paste-up

collecte f (de fonds) collection; **faire une ~** make a collection; **~ de bienfaisance** charity fundraising; **~ de données** (Info) data collection, data gathering; **~ électronique d'informations** electronic news gathering; **~ de fonds** fund-raising

collecter vt collect

collectif , -ive adj collective

collection f (de tableaux, de mode) collection; (d'échantillons) line; **~ de produits** product line

collectivement adv collectively

collectivisation f collectivization

collectiviser vt collectivize

collègue mf co-worker, colleague

coller vt (timbre) affix; (étiquette) affix, stick; (Info) paste

colleter: se ~ avec v pron (difficultés) grapple with

collision f collision

colloque m conference, symposium

collusion f collusion

colocataire mf cotenant

colocation f cotenancy

colonie f colony

colonne f (de chiffres, imprimerie) column; **~ créditrice, ~ des crédits** credit column; **~ débitrice, ~ des débits** debit column; **~ de droite** right-hand column; **~ de gauche** left-hand column; **~ Morris** advertising tower; **~ publicitaire** advertising tower

colporter vt (marchandises) hawk, peddle

colporteur, -euse m,f (vendeur) hawker, pedlar

com abrév (▸**commission**) com. (commission); (▸**comité**) board, com. (committee)

combat m battle, contest

combattre vt (inflation, crime) combat, fight

combinaison f (de coffre-fort) combination; (Info) (de bits) configuration; **~ d'écarts verticaux** (Bourse) box spread

combine f (inrfml) (intrigue) scam (infrml)

combiné, e adj combined, composite

combiner vt (réunir) combine; (action, stratégie) plan

combler vt (déficit, écart) make up; (manque, perte) make up for; **~ le déficit** close the gap, make up the deficit; **~ l'écart** bridge the gap, make up the difference

combustible m fuel; **~ fossile** fossil fuel; **~ lourd** heavy fuel; **~ non-fumigène** (pollution) smokeless fuel; **~ sans plomb** lead-free fuel

combustion f combustion; **~ spontanée** (des marchandises) spontaneous combustion

comité m board, committee; **être membre d'un ~** be on a committee, serve on a committee; **~ d'accueil** welcoming party, welcoming committee; **~ d'aide au développement** development aid committee; **~ d'audit** audit committee; **~ consultatif** advisory board, advisory committee; **~ de coordination** umbrella committee; **~ directeur** management committee; **~ d'entreprise** works council; **Comité européen des assurances** European Insurance Committee; **Comité européen de coopération juridique** European Committee on Legal Co-operation; **~ exécutif** executive committee; **~ de gestion** board of management, prudential committee US; **~ de grève** strike committee; **~ de l'immobilier** board of estate agents BrE, board of realtors AmE; **~ d'inspection** committee of inspection; **Comité international des normes de comptabilité** International Accounting Standards Committee; **~ régulateur** regulatory committee; **~ de surveillance** watchdog committee; **~ de vérification** Can audit committee

commandant m chief officer, master; **~ de bord** (d'un avion) captain

commande f (Com) order; (Info) command; **passer une ~ de qch à qn** place an order for sth with sb; **prendre/honorer/différer une ~** take/honour/postpone an order; **payable à la ~** cash with order; **fabriquer/travailler sur ~** make/work to order; **être en ~** be on order; **à ~ par effleurement** (Info) touch-activated; **à ~ vocale** (Info) voice-activated, voice-actuated; **~ annuelle** annual order; **~ en attente** back order, outstanding order; **~ automatique** automatic control; **~ de contrôle** control command; **~s en cours** orders on hand; **~ à crédit** credit order; **~ à distance** remote control; **~ d'essai** trial order; **~ d'exportation de marchandises** export of goods order; **~ ferme** firm order; **~ de flux** flow control; **~ globale** blanket order; **~ importante** large order; **~ intégrée** embedded command; **~s non satisfaites** unfilled orders; **~ numérique** (Fin) numerical control; **~ par correspondance** mail order; **~ provisoire** draft order; **~ par quantité** bulk order; **~ reçue** incoming order; **~ de remplacement** alternative order; **~ renouvelée** repeat order, repeat business; **~ de réservation** booking order; **~ en retard, ~ en souffrance** back order; **~s en suspens** backlog of orders; **~ urgente** rush order, urgent order

commandé, e adj (Info) remote-controlled; **~ par clavier** keyboard-operated; **~ par souris** mouse-driven

commandement m leadership; (Droit) summons, writ; **~ de saisie** (Droit) writ of attachment

commander vt (marchandises) order; (personnel) be in charge of, manage; **~ qch par correspondance** order sth by mail

commanditaire mf (bailleur de fonds) sleeping partner BrE, silent partner AmE; (sponsor) backer; (Droit) limited partner

commandité, e m,f general partner

commanditer vt (Droit, fin) (société) support, finance

commencement m beginning; **~ de preuve** (Droit) prima-facie evidence

commencer vi begin, start; **devoir ~ en février** (projet) be scheduled to begin in February; **~ à faire** begin to do, start doing

commentaire m (remarque) comment; (Media) commentary; **faire des ~s** comment; **~ sur image** (film) voice-over

commerçant¹, e adj businesslike; **peu ~** unbusinesslike

commerçant², e m,f shopkeeper BrE, storekeeper AmE; **les ~s** tradespeople; **~ inscrit à la TVA** VAT registered trader UK; **gros ~** large retailer

commerce m (activité) trade; (magasin) shop BrE, store AmE; (entreprise) business; **dans le ~** in the stores BrE, in the stores AmE; **tenir un ~** run a shop; **cinq mille mètres carrés de ~** five thousand square metres of business space; **faire du ~** be in business; **faire le ~ de** trade in; **~ affilié** related business; **~ alimentaire de détail** food retailing, retail food trade; **~ de billets de banque** banknote trading; **~ de cabotage** (maritime) coasting trade; **~ de la chaussure** shoe trade, footwear trade; **~ collaboratif** collaborative commerce, c-commerce; **~ de compensation** counter trade; **~ concurrentiel** competitive trading; **~ cyclique** cyclical trade; **~ de détail** retail trade; **~ dominical** Sunday trading; **~ d'échange** barter; **~ électronique** e-commerce; **~ en ligne** e-commerce; **~ équitable** fair trade; **~ avec l'Europe continentale** UK continental trade, cross-Channel trade; **~ extérieur** foreign trade; **~ familial** family business; **~ frontalier** cross-border trading; **~ de gros** wholesale trade; **~ d'importation** import trade; **~ intégré** one-stop shopping centre BrE, one-stop shopping center AmE; **~ intérieur** domestic trade, home trade; **~ international** international trade; **~ intracommunautaire** intra-Community trade, intra-EU trade; **~ mondial** world trade; **~ multinational** multinational trading; **~ parallèle** parallel trading; **~ de produits pharmaceutiques** pharmaceuticals trade; **~ de proximité** local shop BrE, neighborhood store AmE; (dans un village) village shop BrE, village store AmE; **~ réciproque** reciprocal trading; **~ spécialisé** niche trading; **~ des surplus** black trading; **~ à tempérament** tally trade; **~ à terme** futures trading, futures transaction; **~ traditionnel** over-the-counter retailing; **~ transfrontalier** cross-border trade; **~ trans-Manche** cross-Channel trade; **~ de troc** (international) barter trade, counter trade

commercer vi trade; **~ avec** trade with

commerciabilité f marketability

commercial¹, e adj commercial

commercial², e m,f salesperson

commercialement adv commercially

commercialisable adj marketable

commercialisation f marketing, commercialization

commercialiser vt market, commercialize

commis m (de bureau) clerk, office boy; (Bourse) waiter (jarg); **~ d'agent de change** stockbroker's assistant; **~ de magasin** shop assistant BrE, sales clerk AmE; **~ principal** chief clerk, senior clerk

commissaire m (membre d'une commission) commissioner; (membre d'un comité) committee member; **~ de bord** (d'un avion, d'un navire) purser; **~ aux comptes** auditor; **~ aux comptes indépendant** independent auditor; **~ aux faillites** ≈ Superintendent of Bankruptcy Can, ≈ Official Receiver UK

commissaire-priseur m auctioneer

Commissariat à l'énergie atomique m ≈ Atomic Energy Research Establishment

commission f (comité) commission; (réunion de personnes) board, committee; (pourcentage) commission; (course) errand; **faire une ~** run an errand; **être payé à la ~** be on commission; **prendre 5% de ~** take a 5% commission; **toucher 10% de ~ sur chaque transaction** get 10% commission on each transaction; **~ d'acceptation** acceptance fee; **~ d'acquisition** acquisition commission; **~ ad hoc** ad hoc committee; **~ d'affacturage** factorage; **~ d'agent** agent's commission; **~ d'aller-retour** (Bourse) round turn; **~ anti-monopole** antitrust commission; **~ d'arbitrage** arbitration committee, board of conciliation UK; **~ bancaire** banking commission; **~ des cartels** cartel commission; **~ de chef de file** management fee; **~ clandestine** kickback; **Commission des communautés européennes** Commission of the European Community; **~ des conflits sociaux** disputes committee; **~ consultative** advisory board, advisory committee; **~ de courtage** broker's commission, brokerage fee; **Commission sur l'énergie et l'environnement** Commission on Energy ⋯⋗

and the Environment; ~ **d'enquête** investigating committee, commission of inquiry, court of inquiry UK; **Commission européenne** European Commission; ~ **exécutive** executive committee; ~ **faible** soft commission; ~ **fixe**, ~ **forfaitaire** flat fee; ~ **de garantie** underwriting fee; ~ **de gestion** (Banque) agency fee; ~ **d'inspection** committee of inspection; **Commission intergouvernementale des migrations européennes** Intergovernmental Committee for European Migration; ~ **d'investissements** board of investment; ~ **de mise sur le marché** selling concession; ~ **mixte** joint committee; ~ **en nature** soft commission; **Commission des opérations de Bourse** *French stock exchange watchdog*; ~ **d'organisation** steering committee; ~ **paritaire** joint committee; ~ **paritaire consultative** joint consultative committee; ~ **de participation** participation fee; ~ **payable d'avance** front-end load; ~ **permanente** standing committee; ~ **sur prêt** procuration fee; ~ **de vente** sales commission

commissionnaire *m* (Com, Droit) agent, broker; ~ **en douane** customs broker; ~ **exportateur** export agent; ~ **de groupage** groupage operator; ~ **de transport international** international freight forwarder

commuable *adj* commutable

commuer *vt* (peine) commute; ~ **en** commute to

commun, e *adj* (volonté, intérêts) common; (projet, stratégie, biens) joint; **d'un ~ accord** by mutual agreement

communautaire *adj* (concernant la Communauté Européenne) (budget, droit) Community

communauté *f* community; ~ **de biens** community of goods; (Droit) joint estate; **Communauté des États indépendants** Commonwealth of Independent States; **Communauté européenne** European Community; **Communauté européenne du charbon et de l'acier** European Coal and Steel Community; **Communauté européenne des coopératives de consommateurs** European Community of Consumers' Co-operatives; **Communauté européenne de l'énergie atomique** European Atomic Energy Community; ~ **d'intérêts** community of interests; ~ **rurale** rural community; ~ **virtuelle** virtual community

commune *f* (Admin) commune

communicateur, -trice *m,f* communicator

communication *f* communication; (relations sociales) communications; (média) communications; (au téléphone) call; (lettre) letter, communication; (à une conférence)

paper; **être en ~ avec** (au téléphone) be on the line to, be talking to; (être en contact) be in communication with, be in touch with; **problème de ~** communication problem; **stratégie de ~** communications strategy; ~ **entre individus** interpersonal communication; **diplôme en ~** diploma in communications; **l'industrie de la ~** communications industry; **prix de la ~** cost of a call; ~ **de données** data communications; ~ **hiérarchique** formal communication; ~ **horizontale** horizontal communication; ~ **interne** internal communications; ~ **interurbaine** long-distance call; ~ **de masse** mass communication; ~ **non verbale** nonverbal communication; ~ **officieuse** unofficial communication, unoffical report; ~ **avec préavis** (au téléphone) person-to-person call; ~ **par satellite** satellite communication; ~ **en PCV** (au téléphone) reverse charge call BrE, collect call AmE; ~ **téléphonique** phone call, telephone call; ~ **verbale** verbal communication

communiqué *m* bulletin, communiqué; ~ **officiel** official statement; ~ **de presse** news release, press release

communiquer *vt* communicate

commutateur *m* switch; ~ **DIP** DIP switch

commutatif, -ive *adj* commutative

commutation *f* (Assur) commutation; (Info) switching; ~ **de messages** message switching

commuter *vt* (courant électrique) switch

compagnie *f* company, firm; **et ~** and company; ~ **aérienne** airline; ~ **aérienne domestique** domestic airline; ~ **des agents de change** *f* Institute of Stockbrokers; ~ **d'assurances** insurance company, insurer; ~ **de cars** coach company; (qui fait des voyages touristiques) tour operator; ~ **cédante** ceding company; ~ **à charte** chartered company; ~ **fiduciaire** trust company; ~ **financière** financial company; ~ **limitée** limited company UK; ~ **maritime** ferry company, ferry line; ~ **mixte** mixed activity holding company; ~ **mutuelle** mutual insurance company; ~ **mutuelle d'assurance** mutual insurance company; ~ **de navigation** shipping company, shipping line; ~ **pétrolière** oil company

comparabilité *f* comparability; ~ **des salaires** pay comparability

comparable *adj* comparable

comparaison *f* comparison; **en ~ avec** compared with; ~ **de rendement** yield comparison

comparaître *vi* (Droit) (personne) appear; ~ **devant** appear before, come before

comparatif, -ive *adj* comparative

comparer ⊡ *vt* compare; ~ **les prix** shop

around; ~ **à** compare to

2 **se comparer** *v pron* compare; ~ **avec** compare with

compartiment *m* compartment; ~ **moteur** (d'un navire) engine room

compartimenter *vt* compartmentalize

compatibilité *f* (entre des produits) compatibility; ~ **ascendante** (Info) upward compatibility; ~ **descendante** (Info) downward compatibility; ~ **avec l'environnement** environmental compatibility; ~ **du matériel** (Info) hardware compatibility; ~ **PC** PC-compatibility

compatibilité-produit *f* product compatibility

compatible *adj* compatible; ~ **avec** compatible with, consistent with; ~ **IBM®** IBM-compatible

compensation *f* compensation; (Assur) compensation; (d'un chèque) clearing; (Bourse) offset; **à titre de** ~ by way of compensation; ~ **aller** onward clearing; ~ **bancaire** bank clearing; ~ **de chèques** cheque clearing BrE, check clearing AmE; ~ **de couverture** offset; ~ **dollar contre dollar** dollar-for-dollar offset; ~ **des dommages** compensation for damage; ~ **financière** compensatory financial facility; ~ **fiscale** tax offset; ~ **interbancaire** bank clearing, clearing; ~ **journalière** (Fin) daily settlement; ~ **particulière** special clearing UK; ~ **des pertes** compensation for loss; ~ **sur place** (Banque) local clearing; ~ **triangulaire** (commerce international) triangular compensation

compensatoire *adj* compensating, compensatory

compensé, e *adj* (Banque) cleared

compenser **1** *vt* compensate for, make up for; (chèque) clear; (perte) offset, set off; ~ **une chute de la demande** compensate for a fall in demand; ~ **un débit par un crédit** set off a debit against a credit; ~ **les pertes** offset a loss

2 **se compenser** *v pron* balance each other out, balance out

compétence *f* (aptitude) ability; (dans un emploi, une activité) competence, (expertise) expertise; (professionnelle) qualification; **faire preuve de** ~ show ability; **faire la preuve de ses** ~**s** show one's ability *ou* competence; **manquer de** ~ lack competence; **avec une grande** ~ very competently; **faire appel aux** ~**s de qn** call on sb's expertise; **être dans les** ~**s de qn** be in sb's domain; **donner à qn les** ~ **pour faire qch** qualify sb to do sth; ~ **fiscale** tax jurisdiction; ~ **de gestion** management skills; ~ **de management** management competence; ~ **dans le service** service qualification; ~ **dans le travail** job competence; ~ **d'un tribunal** competence of court

compétent, e *adj* (apte) able; (qualifié) qualified; (administration, service) appropriate; ~ **à juger** (Droit) entitled to adjudicate; **tribunal** ~ court of competent jurisdiction

compétiteur, -trice *m,f* competitor

compétitif, -ive *adj* competitive; **très** ~ highly competitive

compétition *f* competition

compétitivité *f* competitiveness; ~ **des prix** price competitiveness

compilateur *m* compiler

compiler *vt* (recueil) compile

complément *m* complement; (Info) supplement; ~ **de salaire** extra pay

complémentaire *adj* complementary, supplementary

complet, -ète *adj* (hôtel) booked up, fully booked; (étude, liste, dossier, exposé) complete, comprehensive; (gamme) full, comprehensive

complètement *adv* completely

compléter *vt* (formulaire) complete, fill in; (formation, série) complete; (paiement) round off; (somme) top up; (connaissances) supplement

complexe¹ *adj* complex

complexe² *m* complex; ~ **immobilier** housing estate, housing project AmE; ~ **industriel** industrial complex, industrial estate BrE, industrial park AmE; ~ **de loisirs** entertainment complex; ~ **d'ordinateurs** computer network

complexité *f* (du marché) sophistication

complication *f* complication

compliquer *vt* complicate; ~ **la vie** complicate matters, complicate things; ~ **la vie en formalités** spin red tape (jarg)

comportement *m* (V&M) behaviour BrE, behavior AmE; ~ **d'achat** buying behaviour; ~ **du consommateur** consumer behaviour; ~ **des cours** price behaviour; ~ **informatif** cognitive behaviour; ~ **du produit** (marketing) product performance

comporter *vt* (risque) carry; (comprendre) comprise, include

composant, e *m,f* component; ~**s de conditionnement** packaging materials

composer *vt* (numéro) dial; (Droit) compound

composite *adj* composite

composition *f* (structure) composition; (typographie) typesetting; ~ **de l'actif** (Fin) asset mix; ~ **en devises** currency mix

composter *vt* (billet) punch

compréhension *f* understanding

comprendre *vt* (inclure) comprise, include; (intellectuellement) understand

compression *f* (de données) compression; (de salaire) compression, reduction; ~ **budgétaire** budget cut; ~ **de crédit** credit squeeze; ~ **de données** data compression; ~ **de personnel** staff cuts, staff reduction; ~ **du prix de revient** cost containment

comprimer *vt* (dépenses, demande, effectifs) ⋯▹

cut, reduce; (budget) cut

compris, e *adj* included; **être ~ dans** be
included in; **tout ~** all-in, inclusive; **y ~**
including; **non ~** extra; **TVA ~e/non ~e**
including/not including VAT

compromettre *vt* compromise; (situation)
jeopardize

compromis *m* compromise; **arriver à un ~**
come to/reach a compromise; **~ d'avaries**
average bond

comptabilisation *f* (Compta) posting; **~
en coûts standards** standard costing

comptabiliser *vt* (Compta) enter in the
books, post; **~ au journal** (Compta) journalize

comptabilité *f* (profession) accounting;
(tenue de livres) book-keeping; (ensemble des
comptes) accounts; **~ analytique** (de produit)
cost accounting; (d'entreprise) management
accounting; **~ analytique standardisée**
standard cost accounting; **~ assouplie**
creative accounting; **~ budgétaire**
budgeting; **~ de caisse** cash flow
accounting; **~ par centres de profits** profit
centre accounting BrE, profit center
accounting AmE; **~ client** receivable basis,
receivable method; **~ commerciale**
business accounting; **~ de coûts courants**
current cost accounting; **~ de coûts par
produit** product costing; **~ d'engagements**
accrual basis, accrual method; **~
d'entreprise** business accounting; **~
d'exercice** accrual basis, accrual method; **~
par fabrication** process costing; **~
financière** financial accounting; **~
générale** financial accounting; **~ par fonds**
fund accounting; **~ de gestion** managerial
ou management accounting; **~ indexée sur
le niveau général des prix** general price
level accounting; **~ industrielle**
management accounting; **~ informatisée**
computer accounting; **~ de magasin** store
accounting; **~ des matières premières**
materials accounting; **~ nationale** national
accounts; **~ en partie simple/double**
simple/double-entry accounting; **~ au prix
de remplacement** replacement costing; **~
publique** (règles) public accounts; (service)
public accounts office; **~ des sections**
responsibility accounting; **~ des stocks**
store accounting; **~ de trésorerie** cash flow
accounting; **~ de la valeur actuelle**
current value accounting

comptable *mf* accountant, accounting
officer; (d'une petite société) book-keeper

comptage *m* counting; **~ de la
circulation** (Transp) traffic count

comptant¹ *adv* cash; **payer ~** pay cash;
acheter une voiture ~ pay cash for a car

comptant² *m* (espèces) cash; **au ~** for cash;
~ à l'expédition cash on shipment

compte *m* (Com, Banque) account; **au ~ de**
to the order of; **avoir son ~ bancaire à** bank
with; **faire mettre qch sur le ~ de qn** charge

sth to sb's account; **pour ~** on account; **pour
le ~ de** on behalf of; **faire le ~ de** (dépenses,
recettes) work out; (personnes, objets) add up;
faire ses ~s do one's accounts; **tenir les ~s**
do the books, keep the accounts; **verser de
l'argent sur son ~** pay money into one's
account; **retirer de l'argent de son ~**
withdraw money from one's account; **avoir
un ~ chez** (commerçant, fournisseur) have an
account with; **être à son ~** be self-employed;
travailler à son ~ be self-employed; **se
mettre/s'établir à son ~** start up one's own
business, start up in business;

⬭ **compte a...** ~ **d'acceptations**
acceptance account; **~ d'achats à crédit**
charge account, credit account; **~ actif**
active account; **~ d'actif** asset account; **~
d'affectation des bénéfices** appropriation
account; **~ d'agios** agio account; **~
d'amortissement** depreciation account; **~
anonyme** numbered account; **~ arrêté**
settlement account; **~ d'attente** contra
account, suspense account; **~ d'avances**
loan account; **~ d'avances à montant fixe**
imprest account;

⬭ **b...** ~ **bancaire** bank account; **~ en
banque** bank account; **~ de bilan** balance
sheet; **~s de bilan** permanent account; **~
bloqué** blocked account;

⬭ **c...** ~ **de caisse** cash account; **~ de
charges** expense account; **~ chèques**
current account BrE, checking account AmE;
~ chèques postal ≈ Post Office Giro
account UK; **~ clients** (Compta) accounts
receivable, book debt; **~ compensatoire
cumulatif** cumulative offset account; **~ au
comptant** cash account; **~ courant** current
account BrE, checking account AmE; **~ de
courtage** brokerage account; **~ de
couverture** margin account; **~ créance**
trade debtors; **~ crédit** budget account;

⬭ **d...** ~ **débiteur** debit account; **~ de
dépôt** deposit account UK; **~ de dépôt de
droits douaniers** duty deposit account; **~
pour le développement industriel**
industrial development savings account; **~
en devises** foreign exchange account; **~
discrétionnaire** discretionary account; **~s
de divers** sundries account; **~ double** double
account;

⬭ **e...** ~ **d'épargne** savings account; **~
d'épargne en actions** equity savings
account; **~ d'épargne courant** current
savings account; **~ épargne logement**
savings account *(for purchasing a property)*; **~
d'épargne-placement** investment savings
account; **~ d'épargne à taux bonifié** bonus
savings account, premium savings account;
~s de l'état public accounts; **~
d'exploitation** operating account;

⬭ **f...** ~ **fiduciaire** fiduciary account; **~s de
fin d'exercice** final accounts; **~s
fournisseurs** (Compta) accounts payable,

payables AmE, creditors BrE; **~s frappés d'imposition** tax-assessed accounts;

(**g…**) **~ en garantie** assigned account; **~ gelé** frozen account; **~ géré** managed account; **~ de gestion de fonds** cash management account; **~ de grand livre** ledger account;

(**h…**) **~ hors bilan** memo account, memorandum account;

(**i…**) **~ d'immobilisations** capital account, capital asset account; **~ inactif** dormant account, inactive account; **~ à intérêt quotidien** daily interest account; **~ d'intermédiaire** nominee account;

(**j…**) **~ joint** joint account, joint bank account;

(**l…**) **~ en ligne** online account;

(**n…**) **~ numérique** numbered account;

(**o…**) **~ omnibus** catch-all account; **~ d'opérations de change** foreign exchange account; **~ ouvert** open account, open credit;

(**p…**) **~ particulier** private account; **~s à payer à la fin de l'exercice** payables at year-end AmE; **~s de pension de retraite** superannuation accounts; **~ de pertes et profits** profit and loss account *ou* statement; **~ de placement** investment account; **~ de position** position account; **~ à préavis** notice account; **~ de prêt hypothécaire** mortgage account; **~ prête-nom** nominee account; **~ prévisionnel d'exploitation** estimated trading account;

(**r…**) **~ rémunéré** interest-bearing account; **~ rendu** report; (d'une séance) minutes; **~ rendu de conférence** conference report; **~ rendu de contact** contact report; **~ rendu non-négociable** non-negotiable report of findings; **~ rendu de réunion** call report; **~ rendu de séance** minutes; **~s de résultats** profit and loss account, statement of income US; **~ de retour** banker's ticket; **~ de retraits** drawing account;

(**s…**) **~s semestriels** interim accounts; **~s sociaux audités** individual company audited accounts; **~ soldé** closed account; **~ à solde nul** zero-balance account; **~ sous-débité** undercharged account; **~ de souscripteur** underwriting account;

(**v…**) **~ de virement** transfer account; **~ à vue** demand account

compter [1] *vt* count (up)
[2] *vi* count; **à ~ de** as from; **~ comme personne à charge** count as a dependant; **~ sur** rely on, count on

compteur *m* metre BrE; meter AmE; **~ additif** (Info) adding counter

comptoir *m* (dans un magasin) counter; (succursale) branch; **~ de liquidation** clearing house

comté *m* (Admin) county

concaténation *f* (Info) concatenation

concédant, e *m,f* (Droit) grantor

concentration *f* concentration; **~ complète** aggregate concentration; **~ globale** aggregate concentration; **~ maximale admissible** (Envir) maximum allowable concentration

concentrer [1] *vt* concentrate, focus; **~ son attention sur** concentrate one's attention on, focus one's attention on
[2] **se concentrer** *v pron* concentrate, focus (**sur** on)

concept *m* concept; **~ de base** basic concept; **~ d'écoulement** flow concept; **~ publicitaire** advertising concept

concepteur, -trice *m,f* designer; **~ de moteurs** engine designer

concepteur-rédacteur *m* (publicité) copywriter

conception *f* design; (publicité) copywriting; **de ~ ergonomique** ergonomically-designed; **~ et agencement** (d'un magasin) design and layout; **~ assistée par ordinateur** computer-aided design; **~ de l'emballage** package design; **~ et fabrication assistées par ordinateur** computer-aided design and computer-aided manufacturing; **~ globale** unitary approach; **~ graphique** graphic design; **~ de produit** product design; **~ de programmes assistée par ordinateur** computer-aided software engineering, computer-assisted software engineering

concernant *prép* about, regarding

concerne: en ce qui ~ about, regarding; **en ce qui ~ votre lettre** with reference to your letter

concerté, e *adj* (plan, action) concerted

concession *f* (action, droit concédé) concession; (licence) licence BrE, license AmE; **de ~** concessional; **~ de crédit** granting of credit; **~ d'exploitation** operation lease; **~s mineures** minor concessions; **~s mutuelles** mutual concessions; **~ réciproque de licences** cross licensing

concessionnaire[1] *adj* concessionary; **être ~** (dans une grande surface) run a concession

concessionnaire[2] *mf* agent, dealer; **~ exclusif** sole agent; **~ d'une licence** licensee

concevoir *vt* (idée, plan) conceive; **~ l'inconcevable** think the unthinkable

conciliateur, -trice *m,f* conciliator, conciliation officer; **~ unique** single arbitrator

conciliation *f* (Droit) conciliation; **~ privée** individual conciliation; **~ prud'hommale** grievance arbitration

concilier *vt* (adversaires) conciliate; (des intérêts opposés) reconcile

concluant, e *adj* conclusive, decisive

conclure [1] *vt* (accord) reach; (contrat, transaction) conclude, finalize; (terminer) end, finish; (vente) close, make; **~ une affaire** *ou* ···⊁

c

un marché strike a bargain, strike a deal, close a deal; ∼ **sa plaidoirie** rest one's case
2 **se conclure** v pron come to an end
conclusion f conclusion; (d'un tribunal) finding
concomitant, e adj collateral, concomitant
concordance f account reconciliation; ∼ **bancaire** bank reconciliation
concordat m: ∼ **(judiciaire)** (accord) legal settlement, composition; (attestation) bankrupt's certificate
concordataire[1] adj (débiteur) certified; **procédure** ∼ composition proceedings
concordataire[2] mf certified bankrupt
concorder vi (chiffres) agree, be in agreement; **ne pas** ∼ be at variance
concours m (de circonstances) conjunction; (compétition) contest; (aide) help, assistance; (coopération) support; **prêter son** ∼ **à** help; ∼ **à court terme** short-term advance
concret, -ète adj (mesure, résultat) concrete
concrétiser 1 vt consolidate
2 **se concrétiser** v pron (projet) materialize, take shape
concubin, e m,f (Droit) common-law spouse, common-law husband/wife
concubinage m (Droit) cohabitation
concurrence f competition; **être en** ∼ **avec** be in competition with; **la** ∼ competitors; **jeu de la** ∼ free play of competition; ∼ **acharnée** bitter competition; ∼ **déloyale** unfair competition; ∼ **féroce** bitter competition; ∼ **libre** free competition; ∼ **loyale** fair competition
concurrencer vt (personne, entreprise) compete with; (produit, invention) pose a threat to; **être fortement concurrencé par** come up against fierce competition from; **marché fortement concurrencé** highly competitive market
concurrent, e m,f competitor; **être** ∼**s** be competitors, compete; ∼ **dangereux** tough competitor
concurrentiel, -elle adj competitive; **très** ∼ highly competitive; **avantage** ∼ competitive advantage
concussion f misappropriation of public funds, peculation (frml)
condamnation f (reproche) condemnation; (au tribunal) sentence; (inculpation) conviction
condamner vt (reprocher) condemn; (au tribunal) sentence; (inculper) convict; (porte, voie) condemn; ∼ **qn à une amende** fine sb, impose a fine on sb
condition f (état) condition; (stipulation) condition, term; **à** ∼ **de** provided that; **à la** ∼ **expresse que** on the stipulation that; **à** ∼ **que** provided that; **poser ses** ∼**s** set out one's terms; **satisfaire aux** ∼**s requises** meet the requirements, fulfil the necessary criteria; ∼ **d'admissibilité** eligibility

requirement; ∼ **d'éligibilité** eligibility requirement; ∼ **expresse** express condition; ∼ **d'obtention d'une licence** licensing requirement; ∼ **préalable** prerequisite, precondition; ∼ **de résidence** residence status; ∼ **résolutoire** condition subsequent US, resolutory condition; ∼ **sine qua non** causa sine qua non (frml); ∼ **tacite** implied condition; (d'un contrat) implied term
conditionnement m (action, matériaux d'emballage) packaging; ∼ **en gros** bulk package; ∼ **sous vide** vacuum packaging; ∼ **en vrac** bulk packaging
conditionner vt (emballer) package **(en in)**
conditions f pl (ensemble de circonstances) conditions; (d'un contrat) conditions, terms; (du marché) conditions; **aux** ∼ **habituelles** on the usual terms; ∼**s d'adhésion** membership conditions; ∼**s d'admission** admission requirements; ∼ **ambiantes** environmental conditions; ∼ **bancaires** bank requirements; ∼ **de carburant** fuel terms; ∼ **commerciales** business conditions; ∼ **contractuelles** conditions of contract, contractual conditions; ∼ **de crédit** credit requirements; ∼ **de déclaration** reporting requirements; ∼ **défavorables pour le commerce** adverse trading conditions; ∼ **économiques favorables** favourable economic conditions BrE, favorable economic conditions AmE; ∼ **d'embauche** conditions of employment; ∼ **d'émission d'une obligation** bond terms; ∼ **d'envoi** terms of shipment; ∼ **européennes** European terms; ∼ **de faveur** concessionary terms, concessional terms; ∼ **intéressantes** attractive terms; ∼ **de livraison des marchandises** cargo delivery terms; ∼ **de l'offre** conditions of tender, terms of tender; ∼ **de paiement** terms of payment; ∼ **de règlement** settlement discount; ∼ **de soumission** conditions of tender, terms of tender; ∼ **spéciales** (prix) special terms; ∼ **de travail** working conditions; ∼ **d'utilisation** conditions of use; ∼ **de vie** living conditions
conducteur, -trice m,f driver; ∼ **de camion** lorry driver BrE, truck driver; ∼ **de travaux** (sur un chantier) clerk of works
conduire vt (entreprise) manage, run; (véhicule) drive
conduite f (d'une entreprise) management, running; ∼ **contraire au code professionnel** unprofessional conduct
confection f (industrie) clothing industry; (vêtements) ready-to-wear clothes; (production) making
confectionné, e adj made, made up
confectionner vt make, make up
Confédération: ∼ **générale du travail** French trade union; ∼ **syndicale européenne** European Trade Union Confederation

conférence f (congrès) conference; (discours) lecture, talk; **faire une ~** deliver a lecture; **Conférence mondiale sur l'énergie** World Power Conference; **Conférence des Nations Unies sur le commerce et le développement** United Nations Conference on Trade and Development; **Conférence des Nations Unies sur l'environnement et le développement** United Nations Conference on the Environment and Development; **~ de presse** news conference, press conference; **~ au sommet** summit meeting, summit conference; **~ téléphonique** conference call, three-way call

conférencier, -ière m,f lecturer, speaker

conférer vt (privilège, droit, diplôme) confer; **~ un privilège à qn** confer a privilege on sb

confiance f confidence, trust; **avoir ~ en qn, faire ~ à qn** trust sb; **gagner/perdre la ~ de qn** win/lose sb's trust; **en toute ~** (acheter, prêter) with complete confidence; **~ de la clientèle** (dans les produits) customer confidence; **~ du marché** market confidence

confidentialité f confidentiality; **~ des données** data privacy BrE, data security AmE

confidentiel, -elle adj confidential

confier vt place in trust; **~ une cause à** brief; **~ qch à qn** (dire) confide sth to sb, tell sb sth in confidence; (mission, lettre) entrust sb with sth; (argent) entrust sth to sb

configurable adj (Info) configurable

configuration f (Com, Info) configuration; **~ de base** base configuration; **~ binaire** bit configuration; **~ nécessaire** system requirements

configurer vt configure, set up

confirmation f confirmation; **~ d'une commande, ~ d'un ordre** confirmation of order; **~ de réservation** booking confirmation

confirmer ⏹1 vt (vérifier) confirm; (commande, fait) confirm; (verdict) uphold; (intention, volonté) affirm, confirm; **confirmez par télex SVP** please telex your confirmation ⏹2 **se confirmer** v pron (rumeur) be confirmed; (témoignage) be corroborated

confiscation f confiscation, impounding

confisquer vt confiscate, impound

conflit m conflict, dispute; **en ~** in dispute; **~ de compétence** jurisdiction dispute; **~ des générations** generation gap; **~ d'intérêts** conflict of interest; **~ intersyndical** interunion dispute, demarcation dispute; **~ de loi** (droit international) conflict of law; **~ social** industrial dispute

conforme adj **être ~ à** (normes, règlement) comply with; (loi, tradition) be in keeping with; (modèle) conform to; **~ à l'échantillon** true to sample, up-to-sample

conformément adv: **~ à** according to; (réglementation) in compliance with; **~ à vos instructions** in accordance with your instructions; **~ à l'article 120** pursuant to article 120; **~ à la loi** in accordance with the law; **~ à la norme** according to the norm; **~ au programme** as scheduled

conformer ⏹1 vt (Compta) agree; **~ les écritures** agree the books ⏹2 **se conformer à** v pron conform to; (règle) abide by

conformité f compliance; **être en ~ avec** be in compliance with; **~ au contrat** contract compliance; **~ aux normes de l'UE** compliance with EU standards

confrère m colleague

confrontation f confrontation

confronter vt confront

congé m (arrêt de travail) leave; (vacances) holiday BrE, vacation AmE; **être en ~** be off work, be on leave; **avoir ~ le lundi** have Mondays off; **~ annuel** annual holiday BrE, annual leave, annual vacation AmE; **~ de maladie** sick leave; **~ de maternité** maternity leave; **~ de navigation** sea letter; **~ de paiement** (Fin) payment holiday; **~ parental** paternity leave; **~ spécial** leave of absence; **~s payés** paid leave

congédiement m dismissal

congédier vt dismiss, pay off

conglomérat m conglomerate; **~ financier** financial conglomerate

congrès m conference, convention; **~ commercial** business convention

congressiste mf conference delegate

conjecturer vt conjecture, speculate

conjoint¹, e adj joint

conjoint², e m,f spouse; **~ divorcé** divorced spouse; **~ de fait** common-law spouse; **~ au foyer** nonworking spouse; **~ survivant** surviving spouse

conjointement adv jointly; **~ et solidairement** jointly and severally; **~ avec** in conjunction with; **~ et solidairement responsable de** jointly and severally liable for

conjoncture f situation; **~ actuelle** current economic situation, current economic climate; **~ favorable** favourable business conditions BrE, favorable business conditions AmE; **~ du marché** market conditions; **~ mondiale** world economy, global economic situation; **~ politique** political climate

conjoncturel, -elle adj (situation, fluctuations) economic; (déficit, politique) short-term

conjoncturiste mf economic analyst

connaissance f knowledge; (personne) acquaintance; **faire la ~ de qn** make sb's acquaintance; **~ approfondie** (d'un problème) acute awareness; **~ des coûts** cost awareness; **~ d'office** judicial notice; **~ présumée des faits** constructive notice US

connaissances f pl (théoriques) knowledge; ⋯▷

(pratiques) experience; **avoir de bonnes ~ de** have a working knowledge of; **ayant des ~ en informatique** computer literate; **~ en informatique** computing experience, computer literacy; **~ non transférables** non-transferable knowledge, locked-in knowledge

connaissement *m* (Transp) bill of lading; **~ abrégé** short form (bill of lading); **~ embarqué** (maritime) shipped bill, shipped bill of lading; **~ d'entrée** inward bill of lading; **~ de l'expéditeur** forwarder's bill of lading; **~ de groupage** house bill of lading; **~ net** clean bill of lading; **~ nominatif** straight bill of lading; **~ périmé** stale bill of lading; **~ public** government bill of lading; **~ avec réserves** claused bill of lading

connaître *vt* know; (personne) be acquainted with, know; (faire l'expérience de) experience; **~ une croissance rapide** experience rapid growth; **faire ~** (faits) announce; (opinions) air

connecter [1] *vt* connect; (brancher) plug in; **être connecté** (Info) be on line; **ne pas être connecté** (Info) be off line; **mon PC est connecté à Internet** my PC is connected to the Internet [2] **se connecter** *v pron* (composant, élément) be connected (à to); (personne) log in, log on

connexion *f* connection; **~ permanente** (Internet) 'always on' connection

connu, e *adj* known; **aussi ~ sous le nom de** a.k.a., also known as; **~ de nom** known by name

consacrer *vt* (du temps, de l'argent) devote

conscience *f* consciousness; **prendre ~ de** become aware of; **faire prendre ~ de** raise awareness of; **~ des coûts** cost consciousness; **~ du marché** market awareness

conscient, e *adj* (au fait) aware

consécration *f* (d'un édifice) dedication

consécutif, -ive *adj* consecutive, subsequent; **~ à** resulting from, following

conseil *m* (avis) piece of advice; (réunion) committee, council; (personne) adviser, advisor, consultant; (avec avocat) counsel; (expertise) consultancy, consultancy work; **donner des ~s à** advise; **sur les ~s de** on the advice of; **~ d'administration** (d'une société) board of directors, executive board; (d'une organisation internationale) governing board; **Conseil d'affaires européen/ANASE** European/ASEAN Business Council; **~ d'arbitrage** board of arbitration, conciliation board; **Conseil des armateurs européens** European Shippers Council; **Conseil des bourses de valeurs** *regulatory body of the Paris Stock Exchange;* **~ de direction** board of directors, governing body, management board; **~ en direction** management consultant; **Conseil de l'Europe** Council of Europe; **~ général** ≈ county council UK; **~ en gestion d'entreprise** business

consultant, management consultant; **~ en informatique** computer consultant; **Conseil international du sucre** International Sugar Council; **~ juridique** legal advice; **~ des ministres** council of minister; **~ municipal** council; **~ national du patronat français** ≈ Confederation of British Industry; **Conseil des prud'hommes** ≈ industrial tribunal UK, labor court AmE; **~ en recrutement** recruitment consultant; **Conseil de sécurité de l'ONU** UN Security Council; **~ de surveillance** supervisory board; **~ syndical** trade union council

conseillé, e *adj* advisable

conseiller[1], **-ère** *m,f* adviser, advisor, consultant; (membre d'un conseil) councillor; **~ économique** economic adviser; **~ financier** financial adviser; **~ fiscal** tax adviser; **~ juridique** legal adviser; **~ municipal** town councillor; **~ d'orientation** careers adviser

conseiller[2] *vt* advise; (Droit) counsel; **~ qn sur qch** advise sb on sth

consensus *m* consensus

consentement *m* consent; **par ~ mutuel** by mutual consent; **~ implicite** implied consent; **~ et règlement** accord and satisfaction

consentir *vt* (permission, augmentation) grant; **~ à** consent to; **~ un prêt à qn** grant a loan to sb; **~ une remise à qn** give sb a discount; **~ un délai à qn** allow sb extra time

conséquence *f* consequence; **en ~ as a** result, consequently; **~ fiscale** tax incidence

conséquent, e *adj* (important) considerable, sizeable; (cohérent) consistent; **par ~ as a** result, consequently

conservateur[1], **-trice** *adj* conservative

conservateur[2] *m* (dans aliments) preservative

conservateur[3], **-trice** *m,f* conservative; **~ des hypothèques** registrar of mortgages; **~ de titres** (Bourse) custodian

conservation *f* (de titres) custody; (de matériel, bâtiments) maintenance; (de patrimoine) conservation; **~ d'actions** custody of shares

conservatisme *m* conservatism

conserver *vt* (Ind) preserve; (Info) keep

conserverie *f* (usine) cannery; (secteur) canning industry; **~ de viande** meat packing

conserves *f pl* preserved foods

considérable *adj* (demande) substantial; (prix) considerable, hefty (infrml)

considérablement *adv* significantly, substantially

considérants *m pl:* **les ~** (Droit) the whereas clauses

considération *f* consideration; **~ de prudence** prudential consideration

considéré, e *adj* (en question) under

consideration; **gérer les projets** ∼s manage the projects under consideration; **bien** ∼ highly regarded

considérer *vt* consider; ∼ **qn/qch comme ...** consider sb/sth to be ...

consignataire *mf* (Droit, Fin) depositary; (Com) consignee; ∼ **douanier** customs consignee; ∼ **de navires** ship's agent

consignateur, -trice *m,f* (Transp) consigner, shipper

consignation *f* (somme) deposit; (action) consignment; **en** ∼ (marchandises) on consignment

consigne *f* (lieu) left-luggage office BrE, baggage checkroom AmE; (somme) deposit; ∼ **automatique** left-luggage locker BrE, baggage locker AmE

consigné, e *adj* (bouteille, caisse) returnable; **non** ∼ nonreturnable

consigner *vt* (fait) record; (marchandises) consign; ∼ **qch par écrit** put sth down in writing

consœur *f* colleague

console *f* console

consolidation *f* (de résultats, bilan, bénéfices) consolidation; (de dette) funding; (de monnaie) strengthening; ∼ **du capital** capital consolidation; ∼ **initiale** initial funding; ∼ **par intégration totale** acquisition accounting

consolidé, e *adj* consolidated; **non** ∼ (Compta) nonconsolidated

consolider *vt* (résultat, bilan, bénéfices) consolidate, (dette) fund; (monnaie) strengthen; ∼ **un emprunt** fund a loan

consolidés *m pl* consols UK

consommables *m pl* (Com, Info) consumables

consommateur, -trice *m,f* consumer; ∼ **final** end consumer; ∼ **précoce** early adopter

consommation *f* consumption; **baisse/relance de la** ∼ drop/boost in consumption; ∼ **d'électricité** electricity consumption; ∼ **des ménages** household consumption, private consumption; ∼ **nationale** domestic consumption; ∼ **par tête** consumption per capita; ∼ **des services publics** public consumption

consommatique *f* consumer research

consommer *vt* (utiliser) consume; (accord) consummate; (combustible) consume

consortial, e *adj* (prêt) syndicated

consortialiser *vt*: ∼ **un prêt** syndicate a loan

consortium *m* consortium, syndicate; ∼ **bancaire** banking syndicate, consortium bank; ∼ **de banques** group banking; ∼ **de compagnies de ligne** (maritime) liner consortium

constant, e *adj* (stable) constant; (fréquent) constant; (continu) continuous; (investissement)

continuing; (préoccupation) ongoing; **être en baisse/hausse** ∼**e** be continually falling/rising

constante *f* constant; ∼ **annuelle d'hypothèque** annual mortgage constant

constatation *f* ascertainment; ∼ **d'une perte** (Compta) recognition of loss

constater *vt* (établir) ascertain; (observer) note; (transaction) recognize; ∼ **une perte/un profit** report a loss/a profit; ∼ **une amélioration** note an improvement

constituant¹, e *adj* (partie, élément) constituent

constituant² *m* (Droit) (de procuration, vente) settlor

constitué, e *adj* (institution) incorporated UK; (trust) constituted

constituer *vt* (problème) constitute, pose; (société) incorporate; (jury) empanel; (comité) appoint, set up; (stocks) build up; ∼ **une contrefaçon** constitute an infringement; ∼ **un quorum** constitute a quorum, form a quorum; **la nouvelle société constituée par l'actuelle direction** the new company formed by the existing management; **les chômeurs constituent 10% de la population active** unemployed people make up 10% of the working population

constitution *f* (d'un établissement) constitution, incorporation; (d'une société) formation; (principes fondamentaux) constitution; ∼ **d'une rente** settling of an annuity; ∼ **en société** incorporation; ∼ **en société par actions** incorporation; ∼ **de stocks** stockpiling

constitutionnel, -elle *adj* constitutional

constructeur, -trice *m,f* maker, manufacturer; ∼ **automobile** car manufacturer; ∼ **de navires** shipbuilder

constructeur-promoteur *m* property developer

construction *f* (édification) building; (production) manufacture, construction; (bâtiment) building; (secteur industriel) construction; ∼ **aéronautique/automobile** aircraft/car manufacturing; ∼ **électrique** electrical engineering; ∼ **ferroviaire** railway construction; ∼ **de moteurs** engine manufacture; ∼ **navale** naval construction, shipbuilding; ∼ **de routes** road building

construire *vt* (Ind) (bâtiment, pont, navire) build; (produire) manufacture, construct

construit, e *adj* built; ∼ **sur mesure** (immeuble) purpose-built

consul *m* consul; **Consul général** Consul General

consulage *m* consulage

consulat *m* consulate; **Consulat général** Consulate-General

consultant, e *m,f* adviser, advisor, consultant; ∼ **en gestion** management consultant; ∼ **en investissement**

investment consultant

consultatif, -ive *adj* (comité) advisory; (approche, méthode) consultative

consultation *f* consultation; (avec un avocat) counsel; (d'un fichier) inquiry, lookup; (avec un expert, d'un livre) consultation; **en ~ avec** in consultation with; **~ paritaire** joint consultation

consulter *vt* consult; **~ un avocat** seek legal advice, consult a lawyer; **~ qn sur qch** consult sb about sth; **à ~ sur place** (livre, journal) for reference use only

consumérisme *m* consumerism

consumériste *mf* consumerist

contact *m* contact; (publicité) exposure; **entrer en ~ avec** get in touch with, get in contact with; **mettre en ~** put in touch; **prendre ~ avec** make contact with, get in touch with; **garder le ~** keep in touch; **avoir des ~s à New York** have contacts in New York; **prise de ~** first meeting; **~ visuel** eye contact

contacter *vt* (personne, journal, organisme) contact; **~ qn au sujet de qch** contact sb about sth, get in touch with sb about sth

container *m* ▸conteneur

contamination *f* contamination, pollution

contaminé, e *adj* contaminated, polluted; **~/non ~** (Info) virus-infected/virus-free

contaminer *vt* contaminate, pollute

contenance *f* (Transp) capacity; **~ en vrac** bulk capacity

conteneur *m* (Transp) container; **mise en ~s** containerization; **~ à bestiaux** cattle container; **~ calorifique** heated container; **~ de collecte de verre usé** bottle bank; **~ découvert** open container; **~ frigorifique** refrigerated container; **~ hors-cotes** high cube; **~ isotherme** insulated container; **~ plat** gondola flat; **~ ventilé** (mechanically) ventilated container; **~ de vrac** bulk freight container, bulktainer

conteneur-citerne *m* bulk liquid container, tank container

conteneurisation *f* containerization

conteneurisé, e *adj* containerized

conteneuriser *vt* containerize

contenir *vt* (récipient) contain, hold; (Econ) (l'inflation) hold in check, keep down; **~ un rapport** (journal) carry a report; **~ des renseignements sur** carry information on

contenter: se ~ de *v pron* be satisfied with

contentieux *m* (litige) bone of contention; (département) legal department; (affaires) litigation

contenu *m* (d'un récipient) contents; (d'un document, d'un livre) subject matter, content; (de l'abrégé) content; (Info) (de site web) content; **~ indivisible** no explosion of the total contents

contestable *adj* (question) arguable, debatable; (allégation, fait) traversable

contestation *f* (Pol) protest (**de** against); (Droit) traverse; **prêter à ~** be questionable; **sans ~** beyond dispute

contester *vt* (succession, testament) contest; (droit) deny; (chiffre, décision) dispute; (impôt, projet) challenge; **je ne souhaite pas ~** (Droit) nolo contendere (frml)

contextuel, -elle *adj* (Info) context-sensitive

contigu, -uë *adj* adjoining, contiguous

continent *m* continent; **~ européen** continent of Europe

continental, e *adj* continental

contingent *m* (Econ) quota; **~ d'importation** import quota; **~ libre** unrestricted quota; **~ tarifaire** tariff quota

contingenté, e *adj* (produits) subject to quota

contingentement *m* quota fixing, quota system

contingenter *vt* establish quotas for, subject to quota

continu, e *adj* continuous, ongoing

continuer *vt* continue; **~ à courir** (Fin) run on; **~ à faire** continue doing, continue to do

continuité *f* (des méthodes) consistency, continuity; **~ de l'emploi** continuity of employment

contractant, e *m,f* contracting party, contractor

contracter *vt* (marché) conclude; (engagement) enter into; (dette) incur; **~ des dettes** incur debts; **~ un emprunt/une assurance** take out a loan/a policy

contraction *f* contraction; **~ des bénéfices** profit squeeze; **~ des cours** (Bourse) drop in prices; **~ de l'offre** fall in supplies

contraignant, e *adj* restricting

contraindre *vt* compel, force; **je me vois contraint de démissionner** I have no option but to resign; **~ à faire qch** compel sb to do sth, force sb to do sth; **~ par corps** (Droit) imprison sb for debt; **~ qn par saisie de biens** (Droit) distrain sb's property

contrainte *f* constraint; (Droit) duress; **sans ~** freely; **sous la ~** under duress; **~ par saisie de biens** distraint; **~ par corps** imprisonment for debt; **les ~s du marché** market constraints; **~ budgétaire/horaire** budget/time constraint

contraire¹ *adj* (avis, intérêts) conflicting; (effet, décision) opposite; **~ à** conflicting with, opposite to; **~ à la loi** against the law, unlawful; **sauf avis ~** unless otherwise informed/advised

contraire² *m* contrary, opposite; **au ~** on the contrary; **jusqu'à preuve du ~** until proved otherwise

contraste *m* contrast

contraster *vt* contrast; (Info) highlight

contrat *m* contract, agreement; **signer/ rompre un ~** sign/break a contract; **le ~ prévoit...** the contract provides for...; **sous ~ avec** under contract to; **s'engager par ~ à faire qch** contract to do sth; **être sous ~** be on a retainer; **~ d'abonnement** (Assur) floater US, floating policy; **~ d'achat à terme** forward purchase contract; **~ d'acquisition** purchase contract; **~ d'affrètement** charter contract; **~ d'agence** agency agreement; **~ d'assurance** insurance contract; **~ d'assurance maladie** health insurance policy; **~ d'assurance responsabilité civile** liability insuring agreement; **~ de bail** lease; **~ bilatéral** (propriété intellectuelle) reciprocal agreement; **~ de cession** deed of assignation; **~ clé en main** turnkey contract; **~ collectif** collective agreement; **~ de complaisance** sweetheart agreement; **~ conditionnel** conditional contract US; **~ de crédit** instalment contract BrE, installment plan AmE; **~ de crédit-bail** finance lease; **~ de crédit à la consommation** hire-purchase agreement; **~ à durée déterminée** fixed-term contract; **~ à durée indéterminée** permanent contract; **~ d'échange de taux d'intérêts** interest rate swap; **~ à échéance la plus courte** nearly contract; **~ écrit** written agreement; **~ d'embauche** employment contract; **~ d'emploi à l'essai** placement test; **~ d'emploi-solidarité** *part-time work for the young unemployed;* **~ d'exclusivité** sole agency agreement; **~ exécutoire** tying contract; **~ contre le faux et usage de faux** commercial forgery policy; **~ ferme et définitif** binding agreement; **~ foncier** land contract; **~ au forfait** lump-sum contract; **~ de franchisage** franchise; **~ de gage** bailment; **~ de garantie** underwriting agreement; **~ d'indemnisation** contract of indemnity; **~ initiative emploi** (government-funded) recruitment incentive; **~ irrévocable** binding agreement; **~ de location** lease agreement, rental agreement; **~ de location-acquisition** capital lease agreement; **~ de location-financement** direct financial leasing agreement; **~ de maintenance** service agreement, service contract; **~ de marchandises** commodity contract; **~ de mariage** marriage contract; **~ sur mesure** tailor-made contract; **~ non-exécutoire** unenforceable contract; **~ obligataire** bond indenture; **~ d'occupation partielle** limited occupancy agreement; **~ d'option** option contract, stock option; **~ d'option d'achat** call option; **~ d'option de vente** put option; **~ prénuptial** prenuptial agreement; **~ de prêt** loan agreement; **~ principal** prime contract; **~ public** government contract; **~ de rente** (Fisc) annuity contract; **~ de rente viagère** annuity policy; **~ de représentation exclusive** exclusive agency agreement; **~**

de revenus garantis guaranteed income contract; **~ de service** contract for services, service contract; **~ social** social contract; **~ de société** deed of partnership; **~ de sous-traitance** subcontract; **~ syndical** union contract; **~ tacite** implied contract; **~ à tempérament** instalment contract BrE, installment contract AmE; **~ à terme** forward contract, futures contract; **~ à terme d'instrument financier** financial futures contract; **~ à terme sur taux d'intérêt** interest rate contract, interest-rate futures contract; **~ terme-terme** forward-forward contract; **~ à titre gratuit** bare contract; **~ de travail** service contract AmE, employment contract; **~ de travail indépendant** freelance contract; **~ de vente à tempérament** instalment contract BrE, installment contract AmE; **~ de vente à terme** forward sales contract; **~ verbal** oral contract

contravention *f* (Droit) infringement, violation; **~ à la loi** infringement of the law

contre¹ *prép* against; **~ espèces** for cash; **~ paiement** against payment; **~ texte** (publicité) against text; **~ tous les risques** against all risks

contre² *m*: **le pour et le ~** the pros and cons

contre-accusation *f* (Droit) counter-charge

contre-analyse *f* check analysis

contre-assurance *f* reinsurance

contrebalancer *vt* compensate, counterbalance

contrebande *f* (activité) smuggling; (marchandises) contraband, smuggled goods; **cigarettes de ~** smuggled cigarettes; **faire de la ~ de qch** smuggle sth

contrecarrer *vt* (influence, décision) counteract; (projet) thwart

contrecoup *m* consequence, repercussions

contre-écriture *f* (Compta) contra-entry

contre-expertise *f* second opinion

contrefaçon *f* forgery, counterfeiting; (copie) counterfeit, copy

contrefacteur, -trice *m,f* forger, counterfeiter

contrefaire *vt* (pièce de monnaie, signature) counterfeit, forge

contremaître *m* foreman

contremarque *f* countermark

contre-offensive *f* counteroffensive

contre-offre *f* counteroffer

contre-OPA *f* counter-bid, counter-offer

contrepartie *f* counterpart, offset; **en ~** in compensation, in exchange; **moyennant ~** for a consideration; **~ conditionnelle** contingent consideration; **~ exclue** excluded consideration; **~s commerciales** commercial considerations

contrepartiste *mf* dealer in securities, ⋯▶

market maker

contre-passation f (écriture) contra entry

contre-passer vt (lettre de change) endorse back; (écriture) reverse; ~ **une écriture** reverse an entry; ~ **une hypothèque** reverse a mortgage

contre-performance f poor performance; **faire une** ~ underperform

contrepoids m counterbalance; (Econ) countervailing power

contre-proposition f counter-proposal, alternative proposal

contre-publicité f adverse publicity

contrer vt (attaque) counter

contreseing m countersignature

contresigner vt (document) countersign

contre-valeur f (Fin) exchange value

contrevenir vi: ~ **à** (ordre) contravene; (accord, loi, règle) infringe; ~ **à la loi** infringe the law

contribuable mf taxpayer; ~ **contrevenant** delinquent taxpayer; ~ **à faible revenu** low-income taxpayer; ~ **à revenu élevé** high-income taxpayer; ~ **à revenu moyen** middle-income taxpayer

contribuant adj: ~ **à** conducive to

contribuer vt contribute; ~ **à** (progrès, redressement) aid; (croissance) be conducive to; **qui contribue à** conducive to

contributeur, -trice m,f contributor

contribution f contribution; **les** ~**s directes** ≈ the Inland Revenue UK, ≈ the Internal Revenue US; ~**s foncières** land taxes BrE, property taxes AmE; ~ **incorporelle** intangible contribution; ~**s indirectes** excise, indirect taxes; ~ **du personnel** staff levy; ~ **politique** political contribution; ~ **privée** private contribution; ~**s directes** direct taxation, direct taxes; ~ **sociale généralisée** supplementary social security contribution (deducted at source)

contrôlabilité f auditability

contrôlable adj (situation, coût, variable) controllable; (pouvant être surveillé) which can be monitored; **exportations difficilement** ~**s** exports which are difficult to monitor

contrôle m (maîtrise) control; (vérification) check, inspection; (Compta) auditing; (Droit) regulation; (Fin) audit, auditing; (Ind) test; (d'un produit) inspection; (Info) check; ~ **d'une région/société** control of a region/company; **prendre/perdre le** ~ **de** take/lose control of; **prendre le** ~ **de** (Fin) take a controlling interest in; **reprendre le** ~ **de** regain control of; **sous** ~ under control; **sous le** ~ **de** under the control of; ~ **d'accès** (Info) access control; ~ **automatique** (Info) built-in check; ~ **des bagages** baggage check; ~ **budgétaire** budgetary control; ~ **de caisse** cash control; ~ **des changes** exchange control; ~ **de la circulation aérienne** air traffic control; ~ **de cohérence** consistency

check; ~ **comptable** accounting control; ~ **continu** continuous assessment, (Compta) continuous audit; ~ **du crédit** credit control; ~ **des dépenses publiques** control of public expenditure; ~ **douanier** customs control; ~ **de l'environnement** environmental control, pollution control; ~ **d'État** state control; ~ **après expédition** post-shipment inspection; ~ **de fabrication** manufacturing control; ~ **de flux** (Info) flow control; ~ **frontalier** border control, frontier control; ~ **de gestion** management audit, management control; ~ **d'identité** identity check; ~ **de l'immigration** immigration control; ~ **de l'inflation** control of inflation; ~ **limité** limited check; ~ **de l'offre** supply control; ~ **des opérations** operational control; ~ **de parité** (Info) parity check; ~ **partiel** limited check; ~ **des passeports** passport control; ~ **de la performance** performance monitoring; ~ **des points de vente** (marketing) retail audit; ~ **de la pollution atmosphérique** air pollution control; ~ **portuaire** port control; ~ **des prix** (par le producteur ou le distributeur) price control, price supervision, public pricing; ~ **de programmation** code check; ~ **de la qualité** quality assurance, quality control; ~ **de la qualité globale** total quality control; ~**s qualitatifs** qualitative controls; ~**s quantitatifs** quantitative controls; ~ **de risques** risk monitoring; ~ **de routine** routine check; ~ **des salaires** wage control; ~ **de sécurité** (d'un candidat, d'un visiteur) security check; ~**s sévères** tight controls; ~**-surprise** spot check; ~ **du trafic aérien** air traffic control; ~ **d'uniformité** consistency check; ~ **de validité** validity check; ~**s vétérinaires** veterinary controls

contrôler vt (déclaration d'impôt, billet) check; (entreprise, marché, prix) control; (résultat, témoignage) verify; (performance) monitor; (Compta) audit; (Droit) regulate; ~ **au hasard** spot-check; **non** ~ (Compta) unaudited; **contrôlé par souris** (Info) mouse-driven

contrôleur, -euse m,f inspector; (Fin) controller; (Fisc) inspector; ~ **adjoint** assistant controller; ~ **aérien** air-traffic controller; ~ **des comptes** auditor; ~ **des droits et taxes** tax inspector; ~ **financier** financial controller; ~ **de gestion** management controller; ~ **des prix** price supervisor; ~ **de la qualité** quality control inspector; ~ **des transports** transport controller

controverse f controversy; ~ **d'addition** (Econ) adding-up controversy

convaincre vt win over

convenable adj (solution, endroit) suitable; (somme, salaire, résultat) decent, reasonable

convenance f convenience; **à la** ~ **de qn** at sb's convenience; **pour** ~ **personnelle** for personal reasons

convenir vt (concéder) admit (que that); ~ **à**

(personne) suit; (circonstance, activité) be suitable for; ~ **de** (prix, conditions) agree on, agree upon; ~ **de faire** agree to do, decide to do; ~ **d'une entrevue** arrange an interview

convention *f* convention, agreement; ~ **d'arbitrage** arbitration agreement; ~ **collective** collective agreement, labour agreement BrE, labor agreement AmE; ~**s comptables** accounting conventions; ~ **de crédit** credit agreement; **Convention sur les droits d'auteur** Copyright Act; **Convention européenne sur les brevets** European Patent Convention; **Convention européenne des droits de l'homme** European Convention on Human Rights; ~ **fiscale** tax agreement, tax treaty; **Conventions de La Haye** The Hague Rules; ~ **internationale** international agreement; ~ **de non-concurrence** covenant not to compete; ~ **sur les nouvelles technologies** new technology agreement UK; ~ **de protection** protective covenant; ~ **salariale** wage agreement; ~ **à syndicat unique** single-union agreement UK, single-union deal UK; ~ **verbale** simple contract, verbal agreement

convention-cadre *f* outline agreement

conventionné, e *adj* (Admin) (clinique) registered; **tarifs ~s** charges approved by the Department of Health

conventionnel, -elle *adj* (clause) contractual

convenu, e *adj* (heure, endroit, montant) agreed; **avoir ~ de qch** be agreed on sth; **comme ~** as agreed, as per agreement

convergence *f* confluence, convergence; ~ **des technologies numériques** digital convergence

convergent, e *adj* confluent, convergent; **être ~s** converge

converger *vi* converge; **tous nos efforts doivent ~ vers un seul but** all of our efforts should be focused on one goal

conversationnel, -elle *adj* (Info) interactive

conversion *f* (de mesures, poids) conversion; (de titres, d'immeubles) conversion; (Info) (d'un mode à un autre) conversion; ~ **accélérée** (d'obligations) accelerated conversion; ~ **de devises** foreign currency conversion; ~ **de données** data conversion; ~ **de fichiers** file conversion; ~ **d'obligations** bond conversion

convertibilité *f* (Bourse, Fin) convertibility

convertible *adj* (Bourse, Fin) convertible; **non ~** nonconvertible

convertir *vt* (devises, prêt, dette) convert; (Info) (d'un mode à un autre) convert; (industrie, logements) convert; ~ **en espèces** change into cash, convert into cash

conviction *f* firm belief

convivial, e *adj* friendly; (Info) user-

friendly; **non ~** (Info) user-unfriendly

convivialité *f* (Info) user-friendliness

convocation *f* (d'une réunion) calling; ~ **au tribunal** summons

convoquer *vt* (réunion) call, convene; (Droit) (témoin) summon; **la réunion est convoquée pour le 12 juin** the meeting has been called *ou* convened for 12 June

convoyeur, -euse *m,f:* ~ **de fonds** security guard

coopérateur, -trice *m,f* (Ind) cooperator, joint operator; (associé) collaborator; (membre d'une coopérative) member of a cooperative

coopératif, -ive *adj* (société, banque) cooperative

coopération *f* cooperation; **apporter sa ~ à un projet** cooperate in a project; ~ **et concurrence** coopetition; **Coopération européenne en matière de science et de technologie** European Cooperation in Science and Technology, COST; ~ **industrielle** industrial cooperation; ~ **avec un pays tiers** (commerce international) third country cooperation; ~ **politique** political cooperation; ~ **technologique** technological cooperation

coopérative *f* cooperative, cooperative society; ~ **agricole** cooperative farm; ~ **de détaillants** retail coop, retail cooperative; ~ **ouvrière** workers' cooperative; ~ **de vente en gros** wholesale cooperative; (magasin) cooperative store

coopérer *vi* cooperate; ~ **à** cooperate on *ou* in

cooptation *f* co-option; **il a été admis par ~** he was coopted; **un membre par ~** a coopted member

coopter *vt* coopt

coordinateur¹, -trice *adj* coordinating

coordinateur², -trice *m,f* coordinator; ~ **des exportations** export coordinator

coordination *f* coordination; ~ **négociée** negotiated coordination

coordonné, e *adj* coordinated

coordonnées *f pl* personal details, particulars; ~ **bancaires** bank details

coordonner *vt* coordinate; (ressources) pool, coordinate

coparticipant, e *m,f* copartner

coparticipation *f* (Droit) copartnership; ~ **aux bénéfices** profit-sharing

copie *f* (Admin) facsimile, fax; (contrefaçon) copy; (Info) copy; **faire une ~ de sauvegarde** (Info) make a backup copy; ~ **antenne** (télévision) master; ~ **carbone** carbon copy; ~ **certifiée conforme** (Droit) certified copy; ~ **conforme** (Admin) (d'un document) certified copy, transcription; ~ **imprimée** hard copy; ~ **de sauvegarde** backup copy; ~ **de travail** (d'une déclaration d'impôt) working copy; ~ **type** specimen copy

copier *vt* copy, duplicate

copier-coller *m* (Info) copy-and-paste

copieur *m* copier, photocopier

coprocesseur *m* coprocessor

coproduit *m* co-product

copropriétaire *mf* co-owner, joint owner

copropriété *f* joint ownership, communal ownership; ~ **non solidaire** tenancy in severalty

copyright *m* (Brevets, Droit) copyright

coque *f* (d'un navire) hull; ~ **intérieure** (d'un navire, d'un avion) fuselage, skin

coquille *f* (imprimerie) typo, typographical error, misprint

corbeille *f* basket; (pour le courrier) tray; (Bourse) trading floor; ~ **des affaires en cours** pending tray; ~ **de rangement** filing basket

co-régulation *f* joint regulation

coresponsabilité *f* joint liability

corporation *f* corporation; (Admin) public body; (Droit) corporate body; ~ **acheteuse** corporate purchaser; ~ **bénéficiaire** corporate beneficiary; ~ **contrôlée** (Bourse) controlled company, controlled corporation; ~ **coopérative** cooperative corporation; ~ **dispensée** exempt corporation; ~ **dominante** (Bourse) controlling corporation; ~ **issue d'une fusion** amalgamated corporation; ~ **mère** (Bourse) parent corporation; ~ **mutuelle** (Assur) mutual corporation; ~ **de placement** (Bourse) investment corporation; ~ **de portefeuille** holding corporation

corporel, -elle *adj* (Droit) corporeal, tangible; **biens** ~**s** corporeal property

corps *m* (groupe) body; (profession) profession; (Info) (de lettre, d'email) body; ~ **d'ingénieurs/ de spécialistes** body of engineers/of specialists; **faire** ~ **avec** (groupe, profession) stand solidly behind; **prendre** ~ take shape; ~ **constitué** public body; ~ **du délit** corpus delicti; ~ **législatif** legislative body, legislature; ~ **de métier** trade association; ~ **professionnel** professional body

corpus *m* corpus

correct, e *adj* (sans erreur) correct; (honnête) fair

correctement *adv* correctly

correcteur, -trice *m,f* (d'épreuves) proofreader; (édition) editor; ~ **orthographique** (Info) spellcheck, spellchecker

correction *f* correction; ~ **à la baisse** downward correction; ~**s de fin d'exercice** year-end adjustments

corrélation *f* correlation, interrelation

corresp. *abrév* (▸**correspondance**) corr. (correspondence)

correspondance *f* (communication) correspondence; (lettres) mail, post BrE, correspondence; (Transp) connection; (par avion) connecting flight, connection; **être en** ~ **avec qn** correspond with sb; **faire des études par** ~ do a correspondence course; **être vendu par** ~ be available by mail order

correspondant[1], e *adj* (avantage, chiffre, emploi, période, reçu) corresponding; (étiquette, boulon) matching

correspondant[2], e *m,f* correspondent; ~ **à l'étranger** foreign correspondent; ~ **financier** financial correspondent; ~ **en valeurs du Trésor** reporting dealer

correspondre *vi* correspond; ~ **à** match, correspond to; ~ **à un poste inoccupé** fill a manpower gap

corriger *vt* (erreurs) correct; (Droit) amend; (Info) edit; ~ **des épreuves** proofread; ~ **à la hausse/baisse** (chiffres) round up/down; **corrigé en fonction des variations saisonnières** (chiffres) seasonally adjusted

corroborer *vt* confirm, corroborate

corrompre *vt* (policier, juge) bribe; (mœurs) corrupt

corrosion *f* corrosion

corruption *f* (avec de l'argent) bribery; (perversion) corruption; **affaire de** ~ bribery scandal; ~ **active** giving bribes; ~ **de fonctionnaire** graft (infrml), bribery of a public official; ~ **passive** taking bribes

cosignataire *mf* cosignatory

cosignature *f* joint signature

cosigner *vt* cosign

cosourçage *m* cosourcing

cotable *adj* quotable

cotation *f* (Fin, Assur) quotation; (Bourse, Fin) (valeur à l'origine) marking; ~ **assistée en continu** (Bourse) automated quotation; ~ **boursière** (Bourse) security rating; ~ **ferme** firm quote; ~ **sans intérêt** flat quotation; ~ **à l'ouverture** opening quotation; ~ **au-dessus du pair** premium quotation; ~ **suspendue** suspended trading; ~ **d'un taux d'intérêt** interest rate quotation

cote *f* (évaluation) rating; (Bourse) (valeur) quotation, quote; (des cours de Bourse) price list; **valeurs admises/inscrites à la** ~ listed securities; **actions hors** ~ unlisted securities; ~ **d'alerte** danger level; ~ **en Bourse** security rating; ~ **longue** (Bourse) long strike price; ~ **officielle** (Bourse) stock exchange list; ~ **de popularité** popularity rating

coté, e *adj*: ~ **en bourse** listed, quoted; **non** ~ (Bourse) unlisted, unquoted; ~ **à** listed at, quoted at, valued at

côte *f* shore

côté *m* side; ~ **du crédit** credit side; ~ **du débit** debit side

coter *vt* (au pair) list, quote; ~ **le stock** mark stock

cotisant, e *m,f* contributor

cotisation *f* contribution; (à un club) subscription; ~ **des adhérents** membership subscription; ~ **allocation familiale** family

benefit contribution; ∼ **arbitraire** arbitrary
assessment; ∼ **assurance maladie** health
insurance contribution; ∼ **au civil** civil
assessment; ∼**s d'employé** employee
pension contributions; ∼ **express** (Fisc)
walk-through assessment; ∼ **d'impôt**
assessed tax; ∼ **initiale** initial assessment;
∼**s de membre** membership dues; ∼
patronale employer's contribution; ∼**s pour
la retraite** superannuation contributions;
∼**s sociales** social security contributions;
∼ **syndicale** union dues

cotiser 1 *vt* contribute
2 *vi* (à un club) subscribe

cotitulaire *mf* joint holder; ∼**s avec droit
de survivance** joint tenants

couche *f* layer; (de société) stratum; ∼
d'ozone ozone layer; ∼**s sociales** social
strata

couchette *f* (dans un navire, un train)
couchette

coulage *m* leakage; ∼ **des nappes** oil
slick sinking; ∼ **et casse** leakage and
breakage

couler 1 *vt* (infrml) (société) bankrupt, bring
down
2 *vi* (société) go bankrupt

couleur *f* colour BrE, color AmE; ∼ **de fond**
background colour BrE; ∼ **du titre** (Immob)
colour of title BrE

couloir *m* (dans un bureau, un avion, un train)
aisle; ∼ **aérien** air corridor

coup *m* (affaire) deal; (choc) blow; (manœuvre)
move; **à** ∼**s de subventions** by means of
subsidies; **sous le** ∼ **d'un embargo** under an
embargo; **porter un** ∼ **(sévère) à** (personne,
organisation) deal sb/sth a (severe) blow; **ce fut
un** ∼ **dur pour l'économie** it was a great
blow to the economy; **tomber sous le** ∼
d'une condamnation be liable to conviction;
être sous le ∼ **d'une procédure
d'extradition** be facing extradition
proceedings; **donner un** ∼ **de collier** put
one's back into it; **tenter le** ∼ (infrml) have a
go (infrml), give it a try (infrml); **réussir son** ∼
(infrml) pull it off (infrml); **rater son** ∼ (infrml)
blow it (infrml); **à** ∼**s d'accordéon** (Econ)
stop-and-go; ∼ **de bélier** (infrml) cash flow
squeeze; ∼**s et blessures** (Droit) assault and
battery; ∼ **de bol** (infrml) lucky break; ∼ **de
chance** lucky break; ∼ **de fil** (infrml) (phone)
call; ∼ **de pot** (infrml) lucky break; ∼ **de
pouce publicitaire** plug (infrml); ∼ **de
téléphone** (phone) call

coup. *abrév* (▶**coupure**) (Bourse) subshare;
(billet de banque) denom. (denomination);
(▶**coupon**) c., CP (coupon)

coupable[1] *adj* guilty; ∼ **du délit d'outrage
à magistrat** in contempt of court

coupable[2] *mf* guilty party

coupe *f* cut; **annoncer une** ∼ **de 10% dans
le budget** announce a 10% cut in the budget;
∼ **claire** drastic cut; ∼ **sombre** cutback,

drastic cut; ∼ **transversale** cross section

coupe-feu *adj* fire-resistant, fireproof

couper *vt* cut; ∼ **les liens avec** sever links
with; ∼ **les vivres à qn** stop sb's allowance

couper-coller *m* (Info) cut and paste

couplé et perdu (Bourse) matched and
lost

coupon *m* (Fin, Bourse) coupon; ∼ **attaché**
(avec le dividende) cum dividend; ∼ **à court
terme** short coupon; ∼ **détaché** ex-coupon;
∼ **de dividende** dividend coupon; ∼ **échu**
matured coupon; ∼ **d'intérêt** interest
coupon; ∼ **obligataire** bond coupon; ∼ **au
porteur** bearer coupon

couponnage *m* couponing; ∼ **croisé**
(V&M) cross couponing

coupon-réponse *m* (vente par
correspondance) reply coupon

coupure *f* (Bourse) subshare; (billet de banque)
denomination; (presse) cutting BrE, clipping
AmE; ∼ **d'alimentation** power failure; ∼ **de
courant** blackout; ∼ **publicitaire**
commercial break

cour *f* (Droit) court; **la Cour** the Bench
(infrml); ∼ **d'appel** court of appeal BrE, court
of appeals AmE; ∼ **d'arbitrage** court of
arbitration; ∼ **d'assises** criminal court; ∼
de cassation (final) Court of Appeal; ∼ **de
la chancellerie** chancery; **Cour des
comptes** (UE) Court of Auditors; France
≈ National Audit Office UK; **Cour
Européenne** European Court; **Cour
Européenne des droits de l'homme**
European Court of Human Rights; **Cour
internationale de justice** International
Court of Justice; ∼ **de justice** court of law;
Cour de justice européenne European
Court of Justice; **Cour suprême** Supreme
Court; Angleterre et Pays de Galles the High
Court UK

courant[1]**, e** *adj* (pratique, erreur) common;
(mois, année) current; (procédure, fonctionnement)
usual; **votre courrier du 5** ∼ (frml) your letter
of 5th instant

courant[2] *m* (électrique) electrical current,
power; (tendance) trend; ∼ **de** abreast of,
up to date on; **tenir qn au** ∼ keep sb posted,
keep sb informed; **mettre qn au** ∼ bring sb
up to date; **dans le** ∼ **du mois/de l'année** in
the course of the month/of the year; ∼
alternatif alternating current; ∼ **continu**
direct current

courbe *f* curve; ∼ **d'accoutumance**
learning curve; ∼ **d'augmentation de
salaire** salary progression curve; ∼ **des
bénéfices** profit graph; ∼ **en cloche** bell
curve; ∼ **de demande** demand curve; ∼
d'indifférence indifference curve; ∼ **du
marché** market line; ∼ **d'offre inversée**
backward-bending supply curve; ∼ **de
rapport inversée** inverted yield curve,
negative yield curve; ∼ **de rendement** yield
curve; ∼ **de rentabilité** profit graph; ∼ **des** ⋯⋗

taux yield gap; ~ **de vie** (d'un produit) life cycle

courir ⟦1⟧ *vt* (risque) run; ~ **le risque de faire** run the risk of doing ⟦2⟧ *vi* (intérêts) accrue, run

courrier *m* (lettres) mail, post BrE; (une lettre) letter; **par retour de** ~ by return of post BrE, by return mail AmE; **par** ~ **ordinaire** by surface mail; ~ **à l'arrivée** incoming mail, incoming post BrE; ~ **au départ** outgoing mail; ~ **départ** out-tray; ~ **électronique** e-mail, electronic mail; ~ **d'entreprise à distribution exceptionnelle** *business mail service*; ~ **à expédier** outgoing mail; ~ **en gros** bulk mail; ~ **recommandé** registered mail; ~ **au tarif normal** first-class post BrE; ~ **à tarif réduit** second-class post BrE; ~ **urgent** urgent post BrE, urgent mail

cours *m* (d'une valeur mobilière) price, quotation; (de devises) rate; (session d'enseignement) class; (magistral) lecture; (stage) course; **suivre un** ~ do/take a course; **au** ~ **d'une certaine période** over a period of time; **au** ~ **de la Bourse** at the market price; **au** ~ **des dernières années** in recent years; **au** ~ **des négociations** during the negotiations, in the course of the negotiations; ~ **du marché** at market; **avoir un** ~ **faible** (Bourse) run low; **dans le** ~ in-the-money; **en** ~ (affaires) current; (négociations, réunion, travail) in progress; **en** ~ **de construction** under construction; **en** ~ **de discussion** under discussion; **en** ~ **de réalisation** (projet) in the pipeline; **en** ~ **de révision** under review; **en** ~ **de traitement** (commandes) in the pipeline; **en** ~ **de validité** (passeport) valid; ~ **d'achat** buying rate; (d'une devise) buying rate of exchange; ~ **acheteur et vendeur** bid-and-asked price, bid-and-offered price; ~ **des actions** stock quotation; ~ **avantageux** favourable exchange rate BrE, favorable exchange rate AmE; ~ **en baisse** falling price; ~ **bancaire** (du taux de change) bank selling rate; ~ **bas** low price; ~ **de base** basis price; ~ **après bourse** street price; ~ **des choses** trend of events; ~ **après clôture** price after hours; ~ **au comptant** spot price, spot rate; ~ **des denrées** commodity price; ~ **directeur** guide price; ~ **estimatif** valuation price; ~ **d'exercice de l'option d'achat** call's strike; ~ **d'exercice de l'option de vente** put's strike; ~ **extrêmes** high and low prices; ~ **inscrit à la cote officielle** quoted price; ~ **légal** legal tender; ~ **légal couvert** (de change) hedged tender; ~ **limite** price limit; ~ **de liquidation** final settlement price; ~ **du marché** current market price; ~ **minimal** minimum quote size; ~ **moyen** average price; ~ **normal des affaires** normal course of business; ~ **de l'obligation** bond price; ~ **de l'option d'achat** call option premium; ~ **de l'option de vente** put option premium; ~

d'ouverture opening price; ~ **plancher** bottom, bottom price; ~ **le plus bas** bottom price, lowest price; ~ **le plus haut** highest price, top price; ~ **pratiqué** ruling price; ~ **prédéterminé** predetermined price; ~ **des produits de base** primary commodity prices; ~ **de référence** mark; ~ **en repli** falling price; ~ **du soir** evening class; ~ **en vigueur** prevailing price, ruling price

course *f* errand; (compétition) race; **les** ~**s** shopping; **faire une** ~ run an errand; **ne plus être dans la** ~ be out of the running; ~ **d'essai** test drive

coursier, -ière *m,f* (de messagerie) courier; (d'une entreprise) messenger

court, e *adj* short; **être à** ~ **de** be low on, be short of; **à** ~ **d'argent** short of money; **à** ~ **d'une devise** short in a currency; **à** ~ **de liquidité** cash-strapped; **à** ~ **de personnel** short-handed, short-staffed; **à** ~ **terme** short-term; (obligation, dette) short-dated, short-term; **à** ~**e distance** short-haul; **à** ~**e échéance** short-term; **de** ~**e durée** short-lived, short-term; (répercussions) short-run

courtage *m* (Bourse) (activité) brokerage, broking; **faire le** ~ broker; ~ **d'assurance** insurance broking; ~ **d'obligations** bond dealings; ~ **réduit** discount brokerage

court-circuit *m* (électrique) short circuit

courtier, -ière *m,f* (Bourse) broker; ~ **d'affrètement** (navigation) chartering broker; ~ **d'affrètement maritime** shipper and carrier; ~ **associé** allied member; ~ **d'assurance** insurance broker; ~ **attitré** registrant; ~ **de Bourse** stockbroker; ~ **de change** bill broker, bill merchant; ~ **de détail** retail broker; ~ **en devises** foreign exchange broker, foreign exchange dealer; ~ **en douane** customs broker; ~ **d'escompte** bill broker, bill merchant; ~ **hypothécaire** mortgage broker; ~ **livreur** delivery broker; ~ **mandataire** agency broker; ~ **du marché primaire** primary market dealer; ~ **en matières premières** commodity broker; ~ **monétaire** money broker; ~ **obligataire** bond broker; ~ **d'options agréé** registered options broker; ~ **spéculateur** spectail; ~ **tous services** full-service broker; ~ **en valeurs** market maker, stockbroker; ~ **en valeurs mobilières** investment dealer; ~ **en valeurs de sociétés de logiciel** software broker

coussin *m* cushion; ~ **de devises** (Econ) monetary reserve

coût *m* cost; ~ **accessoire** additional cost, soft cost; ~ **d'achat** acquisition cost, purchase cost; ~ **d'achat des marchandises vendues** cost of sales; ~ **d'acquisition** acquisition cost; ~ **d'acquisition comptable** book cost; ~ **d'adaptation sociale** social adjustment cost; ~ **admissible d'un bien** eligible asset cost; ~ **affecté** applied cost; ~ **amorti**

depreciated cost, amortized cost; **~ et assurance** cost and insurance; **~, assurance, fret** cost, insurance and freight; **~s budgétaires** budgetary costs; **~ budgété** budgeted cost; **~ du capital** capital cost; **~ des capitaux** cost of funds; **~s en capital** capital costs; **~s à la clôture** closing costs; **~s de commercialisation** front-end costs; **~s conjoints** joint costs; **~ direct** direct cost, direct expense; **~ économique** economic cost; **~ effectif** actual cost, real cost; **~ d'emballage** packaging cost; **~ de l'emprunt** borrowing cost; **~s engagés** committed costs; **~ d'entrée** initial outlay, input cost; **~s essentiels** hard costs; **~ estimé** estimated cost; **~s d'exploitation** running costs; **~ de facture** invoice cost; **~ aux fins de l'impôt** tax cost; **~s en fin d'exercice** closing costs; **~ fixe** fixed cost; **~s fixes de fabrication** manufacturing overheads; **~ de fret** cost of freight; **~ et fret** cost and freight; **~ d'habitation** occupancy cost; **~ en hausse** rising cost; **~s d'investissement** capital costs; **~ limite** cost objective; **~ de location** (d'un bien) rental cost; **~ de main-d'œuvre** labour cost BrE, labor cost AmE; **~s maîtrisés** managed costs; **~ marginal** marginal cost; **~s opérationnels** operational costs, running costs; **~ d'opportunité** opportunity cost; **~ d'option** opportunity cost; **~ périphérique** soft cost; **~ permanent** continuing cost; **~ de portage** carrying cash, cost of carry; **~ du recouvrement** collection cost; **~ réel** actual cost, real cost; **~ de revient standard** standard cost; **~ de rupture de stock** stockout cost; **~ salarial** labour cost BrE, labor cost AmE, payroll cost; **~ social** social cost; **~ social du chômage** social cost of unemployment; **~ toujours valide** unexpired cost; **~ de transformation** conversion cost; **~ utile de base** relevant cost base; **~s variables** variable costs; **~ de la vie** cost of living

coûtant *adj*: **prix ~** cost price; **à prix ~** at cost price

coûter *vi* cost; **~ cher** be expensive; **ne pas ~ cher** be cheap, not cost a lot; **~ 100 euros** cost 100 euros; **~ son emploi à qn** cost sb his/her job; **qui coûte cher** costly, expensive

coûteux, -euse *adj* costly, expensive

coutume *f* custom, practice

coutumier, -ière *adj* customary

couturier *m* fashion designer

couvert, e *adj* (Assur, Bourse) covered; **~ par l'assurance** covered by insurance

couverture *f* (Assur) cover BrE, coverage AmE; (Bourse) hedging; (d'un magazine) front; (publicitaire) exposure; **faire une ~ croisée** (Bourse) cross-hedge; **~ par achat d'option** option-buying hedge; **~ par achat d'options de vente** put buying hedge; **~ par l'actif** asset coverage; **~ d'assurance** insurance cover BrE, insurance coverage AmE; **~ d'assurance au tiers** third-party insurance cover BrE, third-party insurance coverage AmE; **~ bancaire** bank reserve; **~ de change** foreign exchange hedge; **~ à court terme** short hedge; **~ des dividendes** dividend coverage; **~ d'un événement** news coverage; **~ des frais généraux** overheads recovery; **~ globale** blanket cover, blanket coverage; **~ contre l'inflation** hedge against inflation; **~ d'investissement** investment hedger; **~ longue** long hedge; **~ médiatique** media coverage, media exposure; **~ or** gold cover; **~ publicitaire** advertising coverage; **~ à terme** forward cover; **~ par vente d'option** option-selling hedge

couvrir ☐ *vt* cover; **~ les frais de** cover the cost of, defray the expenses of ☐ **se couvrir** *v pron* (Bourse) hedge

covariance *f* (statistiques) covariance

covoiturage *m* (Transp) car pooling

CP *abrév* (▸**Certificats pétroliers**) *oil company investment certificates exclusive to Total and Elf-Erap*

CPAO *abrév* (▸**conception de programmes assistée par ordinateur**) CASE (computer-aided software engineering, computer-assisted software engineering)

cr. *abrév* (▸**crédit**) Cr (credit)

crayon-lecteur *m* bar code scanner

créance *f* debt, claim; **~s** (Compta) accounts receivable, trade receivables; **~ due depuis** debt due from; **recouvrer une ~** collect a debt; **~ admissible** qualifying debt obligation; **~ commerciales** trading debts; **~ douteuse** bad debt, doubtful debt; **~ exigible** debt due; **~ financière** financial claim; **~ fiscales** tax claims; **~ en garantie** assigned account; **~ garantie** secured debt; **~ gelées** frozen receivables; **~ immobilisées** (bilan) frozen receivables; **~ irrévocable** bad debt; **~ légitime** legal claim; **~ litigieuse** contested claim; **~ prioritaire** senior debt; **~ privilégiées du fisc** liens for taxes; **~ à recouvrir** outstanding debt; **~ en retard** past-due claim

créancier, -ière *m,f* creditor; **assurance-vie ~ bénéficiaire** creditor rights life insurance; **~ garanti** secured creditor; **~ hypothécaire** mortgagee; **~ obligataire** bond creditor; **~ privilégié** preferential creditor, preferred creditor

créateur, -trice *m,f* (de produit) designer; **~ d'entreprises** venturer; **~ de marchés** market maker UK; **~ publicitaire** commercial designer

création *f* creation, making; **la ~ d'une société/d'un comité** the setting up of a company/of a committee; **il y aura des ~s d'emplois** new jobs will be created; **on va** ⋯▸

encourager les ~s d'entreprises they are going to encourage business start-ups; ~ **assistée par ordinateur** computer-aided design, computer-assisted design, design automation; ~ **commerciale** trade creation, trade development; ~ **d'entreprise** business creation, business start-up; ~ **de marché** market creation; ~ **d'une mode** trendsetting; ~ **de postes** job creation; ~ **de produit** product creation, product development; ~ **de réseaux** network building

créativité *f* creativeness, creativity; ~ **commerciale** creative marketing

crédibilité *f* credibility; ~ **au tiers** (relations publiques) third-party credibility (jarg)

crédit *m* credit; (somme allouée) funds; **accorder un ~ à qn** grant credit terms *ou* facilities to sb; **six mois de ~ gratuit** six month interest-free credit; **faire ~ à qn** give sb credit; **acheter qch à ~** buy sth on credit; **la colonne des débits et des ~s** the debit/credit side; **votre ~ est de 500 euros** you are 500 euros in credit; **porter une somme au ~ de qn** credit sb's account with a sum of money; **à ~** on hire purchase, on tick UK; **à votre ~** balance in your favour BrE, balance in your favor AmE; **donnant droit à un ~** creditable; **nous disposons d'un ~ de 10 000 euros** we have funds of 10,000 euros; **voter un ~** allocate funds; **nos ~s sont épuisés** we have run out of funds; **injecter des ~s supplémentaires** pump in additional funds *ou* money; **les ~s de la recherche/défense** research/defence funding *ou* budget; ~ **par acceptation** acceptance line of credit; ~ **d'achat** cash credit, purchase credit; ~ **acheteur** buyer credit; ~ **agricole** agricultural credit; ~ **autorisé** authorized credit, credit line, line of credit AmE; ~ **bancaire** bank credit; ~ **de base** basic credit allowance; ~**s bloqués** frozen credits; ~ **budgétaire** budgetary appropriation; ~ **de caisse** cash advance, cash credit; ~ **commercial** trade credit; ~ **de complaisance** accommodating credit; ~ **à la consommation** consumer lending, consumer credit; ~**s en cours** credit outstanding, outstanding credit; ~ **à court terme** short-term credit; ~ **de courtier** broker's loan; ~ **croisé** (Bourse) swap; (Fin) cross-currency swap; ~ **déductible** allowable credit; ~ **de dépenses en capital** capital expenditure vote; ~ **pour dépenses de fonctionnement** operating expenditure vote; ~ **documentaire** documentary credit, DOC credit; ~ **des droits et taxes** extended deferment; ~ **endossé** back-to-back loan; ~ **d'enlèvement** simple deferment; ~ **aux entreprises** commercial lending, corporate credit; ~ **pour études** study grant, training grant; ~ **pour éventualités** contingencies

vote; ~ **exceptionnel** backstop loan facility; ~ **à l'exportation** export credit, export loan; ~ **extraordinaire** nonrecurring appropriation; ~ **de face à face** back-to-back credit; ~ **foncier** land bank; ~ **foncier étalé** building loan agreement; ~ **fournisseur** supplier credit; ~ **garanti** secured credit; guaranteed facility; ~ **global** packaging credit; ~ **hypothécaire** mortgage loan; ~ **immobilier** home-buyer's loan, property loan; ~ **d'impôt** tax credit; ~ **d'impôt à l'investissement** investment tax credit; ~ **d'impôt aux petites entreprises pour capital de risque** small business venture capital tax credit; ~ **d'impôt remboursable** refundable tax credit; ~ **inutilisé** unused credit; ~ **librement négociable** (commerce international) freely negotiable credit; ~ **maximum** (pour fournisseur, client) high credit; ~**s nets du secteur public** net lending by the public sector; ~ **parlementaire** parliamentary appropriation, parliamentary vote; ~ **permanent** revolving credit; ~ **personnel** personal allowance UK, personal exemption US; ~ **ponctuel** spot credit; ~ **réglementaire** statutory appropriation; ~ **de relais** bridging advance, interim loan; ~ **remboursable payé d'avance** refundable prepaid credit; ~ **remboursable à terme** instalment credit BrE, installment credit AmE; ~ **renouvelable** revolving credit; ~ **de sécurité** swing line; ~ **de soutien** standby line of credit; ~ **à taux privilégié** soft loan; ~ **à taux révisable** roll-over credit, roll-over loan; ~ **à taux variable** roll-over credit facility; ~ **transférable** (Banque) transferable credit; (Compta) assignable credit; ~ **transitaire** transit credit

crédit-bail *m* leasing; ~ **de biens d'équipement** equipment leasing; ~ **financier** financial leasing

créditer *vt* credit; ~ **un compte de 100 euros** credit an account with 100 euros

créditeur, -trice *m,f* creditor; ~**s à court terme** short-term liabilities

crédit-rentier *m* annuitant

créer **1** *vt* (entreprise) set up, start up; (possibilités d'emploi, demande, marché) create; (produit) design, invent; (Info) generate; ~ **une provision pour dépréciation** (Compta) depreciate, write down; ~ **une sûreté sur un bien** (Fisc) create a charge on a property **2** **se créer** *v pron* **se ~ une clientèle** (médecin, notaire) build up a practice; **se ~ du travail** create work for oneself

créneau *m* (dans le marché) business opportunity, market gap; **trouver un ~ dans le marché** find a gap in the market; ~ **commercial** market niche, market opportunity; ~ **favorable** window of opportunity; ~ **horaire** time slot; ~ **porteur** niche

crénelage *m* (Info) aliasing

creux¹, -euse *adj* (heure) off-peak; (saison) off-peak, slack

creux² *m* (ralentissement d'activité) slack period; (sur un graphique) dip, trough; ~ **sans précédent** (du marché) all-time low

criée *f* auction; **à la** ~ open outcry

crime *m* crime; ~ **économique** economic crime; ~ **organisé** organized crime

criminalité *f* crime; ~ **d'affaires**, ~ **en col blanc** white-collar crime; ~ **informatique** computer crime

criminel, -elle *adj* criminal; **acte** ~ criminal act; **l'origine criminelle de l'accident ne fait pas de doute** there's no doubt that the accident was caused deliberately

crise *f* (Econ) crisis, slump; (pénurie) shortage; ~ **bancaire/boursière/pétrolière** banking/ stock market/oil crisis; ~ **agricole** crisis in the agricultural industry, farming crisis; **en (pleine)** ~ (secteur, pays) in (the middle of a) crisis; **en temps de** ~ in times of crisis; **ressentir les effets de/sortir de la** ~ feel the effects of/come out of the slump; ~ **de confiance** crisis of confidence; ~ **économique** economic crisis, recession; ~ **de l'emploi** job shortage; ~ **énergétique** energy crisis; ~ **du logement** housing shortage; ~ **de main-d'œuvre** shortage of labour; ~ **des opérations bancaires secondaires** fringe banking crisis; ~ **structurelle** structural crisis

critère *m* criterion; (du progrès de l'économie) yardstick; ~ **d'appréciation** yardstick; ~**s économiques** economic criteria; ~**s d'évaluation** standards; ~**s d'investissement** investment criteria; ~**s de qualité** quality standards; ~ **de recettes** revenue test; ~ **de recettes brutes** gross revenue requirement; ~ **de rentabilité** profit requirement, profitability requirement

critique *adj* critical

critiquer *vt* criticize

crochet *m* (imprimerie) square bracket; **entre** ~**s** in square brackets

croire *vt* believe; ~ **qn sur parole** take sb's word for it; **faire** ~ pretend; ~ **à** *or* **en** believe, believe in, have faith in

croisement *m* (Transp) junction; (carrefour) crossroads; ~**s d'actifs** (Fin) asset swap

croissance *f* (des bénéfices) growth; **à** ~ **rapide** fast-growing; **de** ~ **nulle** no-growth; **en** ~ **constante** ever-increasing; ~ **annuelle globale** compound annual growth; ~ **par autofinancement** internal expansion; ~ **du capital** capital growth; ~ **contraire** antagonistic growth; ~ **démographique nulle** zero population growth; ~ **économique** economic growth; ~ **effective** real growth; ~ **effective du PIB** real GDP growth; ~ **entraînée par les exportations** export-led growth; ~ **de**

l'entreprise corporate growth; ~ **équilibrée** balanced growth; ~ **exponentielle** exponential growth; ~ **horizontale** horizontal expansion; ~ **induite par la demande** demand-led growth; ~ **non-inflationniste soutenue** sustained non-inflationary growth; ~ **rapide** rapid growth; ~ **réelle** real growth; ~ **à un rythme soutenable** sustainable development, sustainable growth; ~ **verticale** vertical expansion; ~ **zéro** zero growth

croissant, e *adj* growing, increasing

croître *vi* grow, increase

cryptage *m* (Info) encryption

crypter *vt* (Info) encrypt

CSP *abrév* (▸**catégorie socio-professionnelle**) socioprofessional group

CU *abrév* (▸**charge utile**) PL (payload)

cubage *m* (volume) volume, cubic contents

cube *adj* cubic

cueillette *f* (ramassage de fruits, fleurs) picking; ~ **du coton/des pommes** cotton/ apple-picking; ~ **à la ferme** pick-your-own

cueillir *vt* pick

cuisine *f* (d'un avion, d'un navire) galley

cuivre *m* copper

cul-de-sac *m* (rue) cul-de-sac

culminer *vi* (inflation, chômage) reach its peak; **l'inflation a culminé à 5% en mai** inflation peaked at 5% in May

culture *f* (agriculture) farming, agriculture; (action de cultiver) cultivation; (végétal cultivé) crop; (ensemble d'idées) culture; ~ **céréalière** cereal crop; ~ **d'entreprise** corporate culture; ~ **d'exportation** export crop; ~ **extensive** extensive farming; ~ **informatique** (Info) computer literacy; ~ **intensive** intensive farming; ~ **de rapport** cash crop; ~ **de la vigne** vine growing

culturel, -elle *adj* cultural

cum. *abrév* (▸**cumulatif**) cum. (cumulative)

cumul *m* roll-up, running total; ~ **jusqu'à ce jour** total to date; ~ **de l'année** year to date; ~ **d'emploi** holding of several jobs; ~ **d'inscriptions** (Bourse) dual listing; ~ **de risques** accumulation of risk

cumulatif, -ive *adj* cumulative

cumulé, e *adj* (Compta) (intérêts) accrued; (dividendes, amortissements) accumulated; ~ **sur l'exercice en cours** year to date

cumuler *vt* (emplois) hold two jobs (concurrently)

cupidité *f* cupidity, greed

curatelle *f* administration

curateur, -trice *m,f* curator; (successions) administrator, trustee

curriculum vitae *m* curriculum vitae, resumé AmE

curseur *m* (Info) cursor, pointer

CV *abrév* (▸**curriculum vitae**) CV ····⟩

(curriculum vitae); (►**cheval-vapeur**) HP (horsepower)

CVP *abrév* (►**cycle de vie d'un produit**) PLC (product life cycle)

cyberacheteur, -euse *m,f* e-consumer

cybercafé *m* cybercafe

cybercriminalité *f* cybercrime

cyberculture *f* cyberculture

cyberespace *m* cyberspace

cybermagazine *m* e-zine

cybermercatique *f* electronic marketing

cybernétique *f* cybernetics

cyberpiratage *m* cyberpiracy

cyberpoint de vente *m* e-point-of-sale, electronic point of sale

cybertexte *m* cybertext

cycle *m* cycle; ∼ **comptable** accounting cycle; ∼ **de conversion de liquidités** cash conversion cycle; ∼ **de développement d'un produit** product cycle; ∼ **économique** business cycle, economic cycle; ∼ **d'exploitation** operating cycle; ∼ **de facturation** billing cycle; ∼ **long** (Econ) long wave; ∼ **de travail** work cycle; ∼ **de vie** life cycle; ∼ **de vie d'un produit** product cycle, product life cycle

cyclique *adj* cyclical; **non** ∼ noncyclical

cylindre *m* cylinder

cylindrée *f* (automobile) cubic capacity

Dd

D *abrév* (►**directeur**) director

DAB *abrév* (►**distributeur automatique de billets**) ACD (automatic cash dispenser)

dactylo *mf* typist; ∼ **intérimaire** temporary secretary

dactylographie *f* typing

dactylographié, e *adj* typewritten

dactylographier *vt* type, typewrite

danger *m* danger; **en** ∼ **de** in danger of; **mettre qch en** ∼ endanger sth

dans *prép* (lieu, état) in; (approximation) about, around; ∼ **les 30 euros/20%** about 30 euros/20%; **être** ∼ **les affaires/l'édition** be in business/publishing

DAP *abrév* (►**distributeur automatique de produits**) automatic vending machine

datation *f* (attribution d'une date) dating; (date attribuée) date

date *f* date; **à la** ∼ **d'échéance** at due date; **à une** ∼ **ultérieure** at a subsequent date, at some future date; **par** ∼ by date; **en** ∼ **du 7 février** of 7 February; **à/depuis cette** ∼ at/from that time; **jusqu'à une** ∼ **récente** until recently; ∼ **d'achèvement** completion date; ∼ **d'arrivée** (d'un envoi) arrival date; ∼ **d'attribution** (d'actions) date of grant; ∼ **de base** base date; ∼ **butoir** cutoff date; ∼ **de clôture** closing date; ∼ **de délivrance** date of grant; ∼ **de départ** departure date; (d'un navire) sailing date; ∼ **de dépôt** date of filing; ∼ **de distribution** release date; ∼ **d'échéance** due date, expiry date, maturity date; ∼ **d'écoulement de l'intérêt** interest roll-over date; ∼ **d'effet** (Assur) attachment date; (Com) effective date; ∼ **d'effet de couverture** commencement of cover BrE,

commencement of coverage AmE; ∼ **d'émission** date of issue, issue date; ∼ **d'enregistrement** date of registration, record date; ∼ **d'entrée en vigueur** effective date; ∼ **d'entrée en vigueur de l'intérêt** effective interest date; ∼ **d'exercice** (droit) exercise date; ∼ **d'expédition** day of shipment; ∼ **d'expiration** expiration date, expiry date, retention date; ∼ **d'expiration d'une obligation** (Res Hum) expiry of agreement; ∼ **de facture** date of invoice; ∼ **de levée** (d'une prime) date of exercise, exercise date; ∼ **limite** closing date, deadline, latest date; ∼ **limite de consommation** use-by date; ∼ **limite d'exercice** exercise deadline; ∼ **limite des offres** bid closing date; ∼ **limite de vente** (pour alimentation) sell-by date; ∼ **de vente** (pour alimentation) sell-by date; ∼ **de livraison** delivery date; ∼ **de mise sur le marché** offering date; ∼ **de mise en vente** (d'un imprimé) on-sale date AmE; ∼ **de naissance** date of birth; ∼ **de l'opération** transaction date; ∼ **de paiement** date of payment, payment date; ∼ **de parution** publication date, on-sale date AmE; ∼ **de péremption** expiry date; ∼ **prévue** target date; ∼ **de publication** publication date; ∼ **de réception des marchandises** receiving date; ∼ **de règlement** (Bourse) settlement date, value date; ∼ **de remboursement** redemption date; ∼ **de remboursement en espèces** cash refunding date; ∼ **de résiliation** cancelling date BrE, canceling date AmE; ∼ **de révision du taux** roll-over date; ∼ **de révision du taux d'intérêt** interest roll-over date; ∼ **de versement** date of payment

dater *vt* (document) date; **la circulaire est**

datée du... the circular is dated the ...; **~ et signer un chèque** date and sign a cheque; **document non daté** undated document; **à ~ du 31 juillet/de demain** as from 31 July/tomorrow

DAU *abrév* (▸**document administratif unique**) SAD (single administrative document)

db *abrév* (▸**décibel**) db (decibel)

D.E. *abrév* (▸**demandeur d'emploi**) job seeker

dealer *m* (Bourse) dealer (in securities)

débâcle *f* (de l'économie) collapse; (d'une monnaie) rout

déballage *m* (de marchandises) unpacking; (exposition) display

déballer *vt* (marchandises) unpack; (exposer) display

débardeur *m* docker BrE, longshoreman AmE

débarquement *m* (de passagers) disembarkation; (de marchandises) unloading, unshipment; **~ de l'avion** de-planing AmE, disembarkation

débarquer *vt* (personnes) disembark; (marchandises) unload

débarrasser: se ~ de *v pron* get rid of; **débarrassez-vous du travail en retard d'abord** get rid of the backlog first; **se ~ des déchets** dispose of waste

débat *m* discussion; **~ final** (Pol) adjournment debate UK

débats *m pl* (Droit) court proceedings, proceedings; **~ de conférence** conference proceedings

débattre *vt* (discuter) debate, discuss; (négocier) (prix, salaire) negotiate; **salaire à ~** salary negotiable; **à ~** or nearest offer

débauchage *m* (licenciement) laying off; (de personnel d'entreprises rivales) poaching

débaucher *vt* (licencier) lay off; (personnel d'entreprises rivales) poach

débenture *f* debenture; **~ bancaire** bank debenture

débit *m* (dans un relevé de compte) debit; (de production) capacity; (de chaîne de montage) output; (de magasin) turnover (of stock); (de restaurant) customer turnover; (Info) speed; **porter un achat au ~ de qn** charge a purchase to sb's account; **produit qui a un bon ~** product which sells well, product which has a good turnover rate; **~ binaire** (Info) bit rate; **~ net** net debit; **~ du terminal** (Info) terminal throughput; **~ de transfert des données** (Info) data transfer rate

débiter *vt* (compte) debit; **être débité de** (compte) be debited to *ou* from; **~ un compte de 100 euros** debit 100 euros to *ou* from an account; **~ le compte de qn** make an entry against sb

débiteur¹, -trice *adj* (compte, solde) debit; (entreprise) which is in debt; **pays ~** debtor

country; **il leur est ~ d'un million** he owes them a million

débiteur², -trice *m,f* debtor; **~ externe** external debtor; **~ fiscal** tax debtor; **~ hypothécaire** mortgager; **~ principal** principal debtor; **~ sans adresse** skip

déblocage *m* (de fonds) releasing; (de salaires) unfreezing; (de prix) deregulating

débloquer *vt* (compte bancaire) unblock; (salaires, prix) unfreeze; (négociation) break the deadlock in; (crédits, subvention) make available; (Info) unlock; **~ la situation** break the stalemate

débogage *m* (Info) debugging

déboguer *vt* (Info) debug

débogueur *m* (Info) debugger

déboisement *m* (de région) deforestation

débouché *m* (perspective d'avenir) opening, job opportunity; (pour déchets dangereux) outlet; (marché) outlet

débours *m* (Com) cash advance; (Compta) disbursement; **~ effectif** actual cash disbursement; **~ ou dépenses** outlays or expenses

déboursable *adj* disbursable

déboursement *m* paying out, disbursement; **~ bilatéral** bilateral disbursement

débourser *vt* pay out, disburse

débriefer *vt* debrief

débris *m pl* (ordures) rubbish; (d'édifice) ruins, remains; (d'avion) wreckage

débrouiller *vt* unscramble

début *m* start; **~ mars/1999** early in March/1999; **dès le ~** from the outset; **en ~ de carrière** at the start of one's career; **en être à ses ~s** be in its early stages; **~ de l'exercice** (Compta) beginning of the year; **~ de séance** opening

débuter *vi* (entreprise) start up

décaissement *m* cash disbursement, outward payment; **~ effectif** actual cash disbursement

décaisser *vt* (Fin) pay out; (Transp) uncrate

décalage *m* (écart) gap; (désaccord) discrepancy; (dans le temps) time lag; (avance) move forward; (retard) move back; (dans l'espace) shift; **souffrir du ~ horaire** (aviation) be jetlagged; **~ à droite** (Info) right shift; **~ fiscal** fiscal drag; **~ à gauche** (Info) left shift; **~ horaire** time lag; **~ d'impôts** shifting of taxes; **~ négatif de taux d'intérêt** negative interest rate gap; **~ du poids de l'impôt** shifting of the tax burden; **~ des salaires** wage lag

décaler *vt* (frais) stagger; (avancer une date, un départ) bring forward; (reculer) put back BrE, move back

décédé, e *adj* deceased

décennie *f* decade

décentralisation *f* decentralization; **~** ⋯⁝›

économique economic devolution

décentraliser vt decentralize

décerner vt (un prix) award; (Droit) (mandat) issue

décevant, e adj disappointing

décharge f (Envir) dumping ground, tip, dump; (Droit) acquittance; ~ **brute** open dump; ~ **contrôlée** landfill site; ~ **de déchets** waste dump; ~ **d'effluent** effluent discharge; ~ **d'importation** import release note; ~ **municipale** municipal dump; ~ **non contrôlée** indiscriminate dumping; ~ **partielle** partial release; ~ **sauvage** uncontrolled dumping site

déchargement m unloading, off-loading; ~ **et livraison** (des marchandises) landing and delivering

décharger 1 vt (marchandises) unload, off-load

2 **se décharger de** v pron se ~ **de qch** off-load sth (**sur qn** onto sb); **se ~ d'un paquet d'actions** unload stocks on the market

déchéance f (Assur, Droit) lapse; **tomber en ~** lapse; ~ **du terme** (Fin) event of default

déchet m waste product; ~ **de fabrication** (recyclage) waste product; ~ **de route** loss in transit; ~ **sous forme gazeuse** gaseous waste; ~ **toxique** toxic waste

déchets m pl waste; ~ **dangereux** dangerous waste; ~ **encombrants** bulky waste; ~ **de faible activité** low-level waste; ~ **de faible et moyenne activité** indeterminate waste; ~ **de forte activité** high-level waste; ~ **huileux** oil waste; ~ **industriels** industrial refuse, industrial waste; ~ **ménagers** domestic waste; ~ **nucléaires** nuclear waste; ~ **plastiques** plastic waste

déchetterie f waste disposal facility

déchiffrement m (de message codé) decoding; (Info) decryption

déchiffrer vt (texte codé) decode; (Info) decrypt

déchiffreur m (de message codé) decoder; ~ **de code-barres** bar code scanner

déchiqueteuse f paper shredder

décibel m decibel

décider 1 vt (prendre une décision) decide; (une affaire, une réclamation) adjudicate; ~ **du montant** (d'une indemnité) settle the figure; ~ **d'un prix** fix a price; ~ **d'une date** set a date

2 **se décider** v pron decide, make up one's mind; **se ~ pour** opt for, choose; **se ~ tout d'un coup** make a snap decision; **être décidé à faire** be determined to do, be intent on doing

décideur, -euse m,f decision maker; ~ **de politique** policymaker

décimale f decimal; ~ **codée binaire** binary-coded decimal; ~ **non condensée** zoned decimal

décimalisation f decimalization

décisif, -ive adj decisive

décision f decision; **prendre une ~** make a decision; ~ **d'achat** purchase decision; ~ **commerciale** business decision; ~ **de compromis** compromise decision; ~ **de dernière minute** last-minute decision; ~ **globale** global decision, decision package; ~ **interlocutoire** interlocutory decree; ~ **judiciaire**, ~ **de justice** court order; ~ **de principe** policy decision; ~ **prise à la majorité** majority decision; ~ **raisonnable** rational decision

décisionnel, -elle adj (système) decision-making; **processus** ~ decision-making process; **avoir un pouvoir** ~ have the power to make decisions

déclarant, e m,f (Fisc) taxpayer, taxfiler Canada; (Assur) person making a statement

déclaration f (officielle) declaration; (communication publique) statement; (Assur) claim; (Admin) notification; (Droit) statement; **faire une ~** make a statement; ~ **d'achat et de vente** purchase and sale statement; ~ **d'adjudication** declaration of adjudication; ~ **d'avarie** average claim; ~ **de chargement** cargo declaration; ~ **classifiée** (Fisc) classified return; ~ **commune** joint statement; ~ **conjointe d'intérêts** joint declaration of interest; ~ **de dédouanement d'entrée** inward clearing bill; ~ **de dividende** dividend declaration; ~ **en douane** customs declaration; ~ **en douane de navire** clearance of ship; ~ **douanière** customs declaration, customs entry; ~ **écrite** written declaration, written notice; ~ **écrite sous serment** affidavit; ~ **d'entrée en douane** bill of entry; ~ **de faillite** adjudication of bankruptcy; ~ **fausse** false statement; ~ **d'impôt** tax return; ~ **d'impôt sur le revenu** income-tax return; ~ **d'initié** insider report; ~ **d'intention** memorandum of intent; ~ **d'intérêts en commun** (dans une société commerciale) joint declaration of interest; ~ **officielle de vente** official notice of sale; ~ **d'origine certifiée** certified declaration of origin; ~ **avec remboursement** (Fisc) refund return; ~ **de revenus** income tax return; ~ **de sinistre** insurance claim; ~ **avec solde dû** debit return; ~ **sommaire** summary statement; ~ **sommaire de culpabilité** summary conviction; ~ **de sortie de douane** clearance outwards, entry outwards; ~ **sous serment** deposition, sworn statement; ~ **trompeuse** deceptive statement; ~ **de TVA** VAT return UK; ~ **avec versement** remittance return

déclarer vt (marchandises, revenus, employé) declare; (vol) report; (naissance, décès) register; (Droit) claim; ~ **qn insolvable** declare sb insolvent; ~ **catégoriquement** state categorically; ~ **illégal** outlaw; ~ **un**

montant claim an amount; ~ **nul** revoke; ~
par écrit (Droit) swear on affidavit; ~ **une**
perte/un profit report a loss/a profit; ~ **qn**
en faillite adjudicate sb bankrupt; ~ **à sa**
charge claim as a dependant; ~ **sous**
serment declare on oath

déclassement *m* (Envir, Ind)
decommissioning

déclasser *vt* (Envir, Ind) decommission;
(employé, concurrent, hôtel) downgrade

déclencher *vt* (crise) spark off, trigger;
(Gestion) activate; (Info) (opération) initiate

déclin *m* (Econ, Ind) decline; **en ~** (région)
depressed, in decline; ~ **rapide de la prime**
(Bourse) rapid premium decay

décliner *vi* (région) decline; **la construction**
ne cesse de ~ depuis… the building
industry has been in constant decline since…

décloisonnement *m*
decompartmentalization, opening up

décodage *m* decryption

décodeur *m* (Info) decoder; (pour télévision)
decoder

décollage *m* (Transp) takeoff

décoller *vi* (Transp) take off

décommander *vt* (commande, livraison)
cancel; (rendez-vous) call off, cancel

décomposer *vt* analyse BrE, analyze AmE,
break down

décompte *m* (relevé) detailed account,
breakdown; (déduction) deduction, discount;
(calcul) count; ~ **de prime** (Fin) premium
statement

décompter *vt* (déduire) deduct; (calculer)
(frais) work out; (votes) count

déconcentration *f* (de services administratifs)
decentralization; (Econ) demerger; ~**s**
transfrontières cross-border demergers

déconnecté, e *adj* (Info) inactive

déconnecter ⟦1⟧ *vt* (Info) disconnect
⟦2⟧ **se déconnecter** *v pron* (Info) log off,
log out

déconseillé, e *adj* (action) unadvisable; ~
aux enfants not recommended for children

déconseiller *vt* ~ **qch à qn** advise sb
against sth; ~ **à qn de faire qch** warn sb
against doing sth

décontaminer *vt* clean up, decontaminate

décote *f* (Bourse) below par rating,
undervalue; (actions) discount (**par** from);
(Fisc) tax rebate; (baisse) drop; **avec une ~** at
a discount; **avec une ~ de deux pour cent**
at a two per cent discount

découler *vi* (provenir) result; ~ **de** result
from, stem from

découper *vt* (territoire) divide up; ~ **un**
projet en tranches divide up a project into
phases/sections, chunk a project (jarg)

décourager *vt* (personne, épargne, initiative)
discourage

découvert *m* bank overdraft; **être à ~** be

in the red, be overdrawn; **accorder un ~ à**
qn allow sb an overdraft; **être à ~ sur**
contrat à terme be short in futures; **faire la**
chasse au ~ (jarg) squeeze the shorts (jarg);
~ **autorisé** authorized overdraft, credit
limit; ~ **bancaire** bank overdraft; ~ **en**
blanc unsecured overdraft

décrémenter *vt* decrement

décret *m* (Droit) decree; ~ **d'application**
statutory instrument; ~ **irrévocable** decree
absolute

décréter *vt* (loi) enact

décriminaliser *vt* decriminalize

décrire *vt* describe

décroissant *adj* (nombre, vitesse)
decreasing, falling; (pouvoir, fortune) declining;
par/en ordre ~ in descending order

décroître *vi* (inflation, chômage) go down;
(niveau) fall, drop; (influence) decline

décrutement *m* outplacement

décryptage *m* (Info) decryption

décupler *vt* increase tenfold

dédier *vt* (consacrer) dedicate; ~ **à** dedicate
to

dédit *m* (Fin) forfeit money, fine (*for breach*
of contract); ~ **de rupture de contrat**
penalty for breach of contract

dédomiciliation *f* dedomiciling

dédommagement *m* (Assur)
compensation, indemnity; **à titre de ~** in
compensation

dédommager *vt* (Assur) compensate; ~ **qn**
pour qch compensate sb for sth

dédouanage *m* customs clearance

dédouanement *m* customs clearance; ~
de chargement cargo clearance

dédouaner *vt* clear through customs;
dédouané ou non whether cleared through
customs or not; **non ~** uncleared

déductibilité *f* deductibility

déductible *adj* (du revenu imposable)
deductible; ~ **d'impôts** tax-deductible

déduction *f* deduction; (Fisc) deduction,
(tax) allowance; ~ **faite de** net of; **ne pas**
admettre une ~ disallow a deduction; ~
pour amortissement capital cost allowance;
~ **annuelle** yearly allowance; ~ **combinée**
combined total claim; ~ **complémentaire**
top-up deduction; ~ **pour dépenses**
deduction for expenses; ~ **discrétionnaire**
discretionary deduction; ~ **pour dons**
deduction for gifts; ~ **pour épuisement**
depletion allowance; ~ **fiscale** tax
deduction; ~ **pour frais de garde d'enfant**
deduction for childcare expenses; ~ **avant**
impôt allowance; ~ **d'impôt à l'emploi**
employment tax deduction; ~ **pour**
inventaire inventory allowance; ~ **pour**
pertes sur prêts deduction for loan losses; ⋯⋙

~ **aux petites entreprises** small business deduction; ~ **pour placements** investment allowance; ~ **de taxe immobilière** property tax allowance, property tax credit Can

déduire *vt* (soustraire) deduct; ~ **de** (somme) deduct from; (raisonnement) conclude from; ~ **un montant** deduct an amount; **tous frais déduits** after deduction of expenses

déduplication *f* merge and purge (jarg)

défaillance *f* (panne) breakdown; (mauvais fonctionnement) fault; ~ **matérielle** (Info) hardware failure

défaire ① *vt* undo; (accord) disaffirm
② **se défaire de** *v pron* (volontairement) get rid of; (à regret) part with

défaisance *f* (Fin) defeasance

défalquer *vt* (frais d'envoi) deduct; ~ **de** deduct from

défaut *m* (imperfection) flaw; (insuffisance) shortage; (absence) lack; (Droit) absence; (Info) default; **par** ~ by default; **à** ~ **de qch** if sth is not available; **à** ~ **de paiement immédiat** unless prompt payment is made; **à** ~ **de renseignements précis** in the absence of detailed information; ~ **d'acceptation** nonacceptance; ~ **d'acceptation de paiement** dishonour BrE, dishonor AmE; ~ **caché** latent defect; ~ **de comparution** (Droit) failure to appear; ~ **de se conformer** failure to comply; ~ **de fabrication** manufacturing fault; ~ **de livraison** non-delivery, failed delivery; ~ **de paiement** default of payment, nonpayment; ~ **de paiement de prêt** loan default; ~ **de provision** insufficient funds

défavorable *adj* (facteur, rapport, conditions) adverse; (prix, change) unfavourable BrE, unfavorable AmE; **être** ~ **à** go against; **émettre un avis** ~ give an unfavourable response

défectueux, -euse *adj* (matériel, article) faulty, defective

défendeur, -eresse *m,f* (procédure civile) defendant, respondent

défendre *vt* (Droit) defend; (accès, entrée) ban; (personne, intérêts) defend, stand up for

défense *f* defence BrE, defense AmE; **la** ~ (Droit) the defence BrE, the defense AmE; ~ **d'afficher** stick no bills; ~ **d'entrer** no trespassing; ~ **d'entrer sous peine de poursuites** trespassers will be prosecuted; ~ **de fumer** no smoking; ~ **des consommateurs** consumer protection; ~ **de l'environnement** nature conservation

défi *m* challenge; **lancer un** ~ **à qn** challenge sb; **relever le** ~ take up the challenge

déficience *f* deficiency; ~ **mentale ou physique** mental or physical impairment

déficient, e *adj* (insuffisant) (budget, contrôle, système) inadequate, deficient; (jugement) faulty

déficit *m* deficit; **avoir un** ~ run a deficit;

combler/enregistrer un ~ make up/show a deficit; ~ **accumulé** accumulated deficit; ~ **actuariel** (Assur) actuarial deficit, experience loss; ~ **de la balance commerciale** trade deficit; ~ **de la balance des paiements** balance of payments deficit; ~ **budgétaire** budgetary deficit; ~ **de caisse** cash deficit; ~ **exonéré** exempt deficit; ~ **extérieur** trade deficit; ~ **fédéral** federal deficit; ~ **financier** (Compta) fiscal deficit; (Fin) funding gap; ~ **net d'exploitation** net operating loss; ~ **réel** actual deficit; ~ **de trésorerie** cash deficit

déficitaire *adj* (budget) adverse; (activité, secteur) non-profit-making, nonprofit AmE; (entreprise) loss-making; (année) poor, bad

défier *vt* challenge

défiguration *f*: ~ **de titres** (Bourse) bad delivery

défilé *m* (suite de candidats, visiteurs) stream; ~ **de mode** fashion show

défilement *m* (Info) scrolling; ~ **vers le bas** scrolling down; ~ **vers le haut** scrolling up

défiler *vi* (Info) (vers le bas) scroll down; (vers le haut) scroll up

définir *vt* (loi, règle) define, specify; ~ **sa politique éditoriale** lay down firm editorial guidelines; ~ **des règles** set out rules, establish rules

définitif, -ive *adj* (accord, règlement, jugement) definitive; (comptes, rapport, résultat, choix, plan) definitive; (édition) final; (prix) set, fixed; (fermeture, arrêt) permanent; (échec, succès) conclusive; (refus) absolute; **rien de** ~ nothing definite

définition *f* definition; (Info) resolution; ~ **des objectifs/du marché** target/market specification; **écran à haute** ~ (Info) screen with high-resolution graphics; ~ **des articles** definition of items; ~ **de base** basic definition, core definition; ~ **des limites** definition of limits; ~ **de marché** market base; ~ **de la mission** mission statement; ~ **des objectifs** objective setting, target setting; ~ **de poste** job description

défiscalisation *f* exemption from tax

défiscalisé, e *adj* tax-free

défiscaliser *vt* exempt from tax

déflation *f* deflation

déforestation *f* deforestation

défraîchi, e *adj* soiled

défrayer *vt* (rembourser) ~ **qn** pay sb's expenses

défunt¹, e *adj* (personne) deceased; (parti, idéologie) defunct

défunt², e *m,f* deceased person

défusionner *vt* demerge; (Info) unbundle

dégagement *m* (Bourse) sell-off; (Fin) (de fonds de crédits) release

dégager ① *vt* (fonds, crédits) release;

(créneaux) create; ~ **sa responsabilité de** assume no responsibility for; ~ **des bénéfices** show a profit

2 se dégager v pron (d'une obligation, d'un contrat) back out; **se ~ de** back out of

dégâts m pl damage; **60 million d'euros de** ~ 60 million euros worth of damage; **faire des ~** (incendie) cause damage; ~ **aux biens loués** damage to rented property; ~ **causés par un incendie** fire damage, damage caused by a fire; ~ **des eaux** water damage; ~ **matériels** damage to property

dégeler vt (crédits) unfreeze

dégradation f (dégât provoqué) damage; (détérioration, usure) deterioration; (d'un immeuble) wear and tear; (de l'environnement) damage, destruction; **la ~ du pouvoir d'achat** the erosion in purchasing power; ~ **biologique** biodegradation; ~ **écologique** ecological damage; ~ **des performances** (Info) software rot; ~ **des sols** land degradation

dégrader vt (site, environment) damage; (confiance commerciale) erode

dégraissage m (licenciements) demanning, downsizing; ~ **d'actifs** (Fin) asset stripping; ~ **de main-d'œuvre** labour shedding BrE, labor shedding AmE, job cuts

dégraisser vt (entreprise) streamline; ~ **le personnel** trim the workforce

degré m (Celsius) degree Celsius; ~ **de certitude** (Assur) audit assurance; ~ **des dommages** extent of damage; ~ **Fahrenheit** degree Fahrenheit; ~ **d'incapacité** degree of disablement; ~ **d'invalidité** (Assur) degree of disablement; ~ **de risque** level of risk, degree of risk; (Bourse) degree of exposure; ~ **de solvabilité** credit rating; ~ **de volatilité du cours** (Bourse) price volatility

dégressif, -ive adj (impôt) graduated; **tarif** ~ tapered rates, tapered charges; ~ **sur le temps acheté** time discount

dégression f degression

dégrèvement m refund, relief; **avoir droit à un ~** (Fisc) be entitled to tax relief; ~ **sur biens commerciaux** relief on business assets; ~ **pour l'emploi précaire** interim relief; ~ **d'impôt** tax rebate, tax relief; ~ **total** full exemption

dégrever vt (Fisc) (contribuable) relieve the tax burden on; (Droit) (propriété) disencumber

dégriffé, e adj (vêtement de marque) marked-down; **veste ~e** marked-down designer jacket

dégringoler vi (prix, cours) plunge

dégroupage m unbundling; ~ **des marchandises** cargo disassembly

dégrouper vt demerger; (Info) unbundle; ~ **une livraison** break bulk

dégroupeur m break bulk agent

déhouillement m mining

déjeuner m lunch; **pause du ~** lunch

break; ~ **d'affaires** business lunch

déjouer vt (adversaire) defeat; (surveillance) evade

délabrement m (d'équipement) dilapidation; (des affaires, de l'économie) poor state

délai m (date limite) deadline; (période accordée) period of time; ~**s serrés** tight deadlines; **dans les ~s prescrits** within the prescribed time; **dans un ~ de** within a period of; **dans un ~ de sept jours** within a week; **dans les meilleurs ~s** as soon as possible; **respecter un ~** meet a deadline; **rester dans les ~s** meet the deadline; ~ **absolu** absolute limit; ~ **administratif** administration lag; ~ **d'attente** waiting period; ~ **de démarrage** (d'un produit nouveau) lead time; ~ **d'exécution** turnaround time; ~ **de fabrication** lead time; ~ **fixe** allowed time, standard time; ~ **de franchise** grace period; ~ **de grâce** grace period; ~ **d'identification** recognition lag; ~ **de livraison** delivery time, delivery turnaround; (de stock) lead time; ~ **de mise en œuvre** implementation lag; ~ **de mise sur le marché** time to market; ~ **de paiement** term of payment; ~ **de placement** (Bourse) period of digestion; ~ **de préavis** statutory notice; ~ **prescrit** prescribed time; ~ **de réaction** lag response; ~ **de recouvrement** debt recovery period; ~ **de redressement** turnaround time; ~ **de réflexion** (avant de signer un contrat) cooling-off period; ~ **de remboursement** repayment term; ~ **de rigueur** deadline

délaisser vt (Droit) (bien) relinquish; (activité) abandon

délégation f (de pouvoirs, fonctions) delegation; (de personnes) delegation (**à qn** to sb); ~ **d'autorisation** delegation of authorization; ~ **de créance** assignment of debt; ~ **de pouvoir** delegation of authority

délégué¹, e m,f delegate; ~ **en bourse** trader; ~ **commercial** trade representative; ~ **du personnel** staff representative; ~ **syndical** union representative

délégué², e adj (administrateur, directeur) acting; ~ **à qch** (adjoint, conseiller) responsible for sth

déléguer vt delegate; ~ **son autorité à** give vicarious authority to; **être délégué auprès de qch** be appointed as a delegate to sth

délibération f deliberation; ~**s** (Droit) proceedings

délit m (criminal) offence; ~ **d'abstention** (d'agir) nonfeasance; ~ **d'initié** (Fin) insider dealing, insider trading

délivraison f redelivery

délivrance f delivery; (d'un avis, certificat) issuance

délivrer vt (brevet) grant; (avis, certificat) issue; ~ **un mandat à qn** serve sb with a warrant

délocalisation f (d'entreprise) relocation

délocaliser vt (entreprise) relocate

déloyal, e adj (concurrence) unfair

demande f request; (de brevet) application; (devant un tribunal) petition; (pour un produit) call, demand; **à la ~** at the request of; **à la ~ générale** by popular request; **faire une ~** make a request; **faire une ~ d'adhésion** apply for membership; **faire une ~ auprès des autorités compétentes** make a request to the appropriate authority; **faire une ~ d'emploi** apply for a job, put in an application for a job; **faire une ~ par écrit** send a written request; **faire une ~ de prêt** apply for a loan; **faire une ~ de remboursement** make an expenses claim, claim expenses; **faire une ~ de souscription d'actions** apply for shares; **la ~ est pendante** application is pending; **sur ~** on demand; **~ accumulée** pent-up demand; **~ active** brisk demand; **~ en augmentation** growing demand; **~ de biens** demand for goods; **~ de brevet** patent application; **~ de brevet déposée** patent pending; **~ de crédit** loan request, loan application; **~ de dépôt de brevet** patent specifications; **~ de dommages et intérêts** claim for damages; **~ d'emploi** job application; **~ excédentaire** excess demand; **~ d'exemption personnelle** claim for personal exemption; **~ ferme** firm bid; **~ globale** aggregate demand, overall demand; **~ en hausse** growing demand; **~ d'indemnisation** claim for indemnification; **~ d'indemnité** compensation claim; **~ industrielle** industrial demand; **~ d'inscription à la cote** listing application; **~ d'introduction en bourse** application for quotation; **~ de main-d'œuvre** labour demand BrE, labor demand AmE; **~ du marché** market demand; **~ d'option** option demand; **~ de paiement** request for payment; **~ péremptoire** requirement; **~ de prêt** loan application; **~ en réduction de dommages-intérêts** mitigation of damages; **~ réglementaire** statutory requirement; **~ de remboursement** claim for refund; **~ de remboursement de frais de voyage** travel expense claim; **~ en retard** backlog demand

demander vt (conseil) seek; (honoraires) charge; (objet) ask for; (passeport, permis) apply for; (personne) call for; (en télécommunications) page; (taxi) order; **~ l'avis d'un expert** take expert advice; **~ des comptes à qn** call sb to account; **~ un conseil juridique** seek legal advice; **~ une déduction** claim a deduction; **~ des dommages et intérêts** claim damages; **~ le point de vue d'un spécialiste** ask for an expert opinion; **~ le remboursement de** (dette) call in; **~ des renseignements** make enquiries; **~ réparation** claim compensation

demandeur, -euse m,f (d'un brevet) applicant; (Droit) claimant; **~ d'emploi** job

seeker; **~ d'emploi de longue durée** long-term unemployed BrE, hard-core unemployed AmE

démantèlement m (Com) break-up; (Econ) dismantling; **~ de l'actif** (Fin) asset stripping

démanteler vt (Fin) wind down; (institution, frontières) dismantle; (marché) break up

démarcation f demarcation

démarchage m (vente) door-to-door selling; (prospection) canvassing; **~ par téléphone** (par un représentant) cold calling

démarche f (approche) approach; (tentative) step; **faire des ~s auprès de qn** approach sb; **les ~s nécessaires** the appropriate steps; **~ collective** joint representation

démarcher vt (vendre) sell door-to-door; (prospecter) canvass

démarcheur, -euse m,f (prospecteur) business canvasser; **~ à domicile** door-to-door salesman

démarque f markdown

démarqué, e adj marked down

démarrage m (d'entreprise) start-up; (de projet) start; **~ à froid** (Info) cold start

démarrer vt (entreprise) start up; (affaire) get off the ground; **faire ~ qn en qualité de** start sb off as

dématérialisation f dematerialization; **~ des transferts de fonds** truncation

dématérialisé, e adj dematerialized, paperless

démembrement m (Comm) break-up, dismemberment; **~ de l'actif/de dividendes** (Fin) asset/dividend stripping

démembrer vt (Comm) break up, dismember, carve up

déménagement m (changement de locaux) move; (enlèvement des meubles) removal; **~ en chaîne** chain migration; **société de ~** removal company

démenti m (Assur) disclaimer

demi-gros m wholesale direct to the public

démission f resignation; **donner sa ~** resign, hand in one's resignation

démissionner vi resign, hand in one's resignation

démo f demo, demo version

démocratie f democracy; **~ d'entreprise** industrial democracy

démocratique adj democratic

démodé, e adj old-fashioned, out of fashion; (idée, produit) outdated

démographie f demography

démolition f demolition

démonétisation f demonetization; **~ de l'or** gold demonetization

démonétiser vt demonetize

démonstrateur, -trice m,f demonstrator

démonstration f demonstration; **faire la**

~ **d'un appareil** demonstrate an appliance; **de** ~ (matériel) demonstration

démotivation f demotivation

démotiver vt demotivate

démutualisation f demutualization

démutualiser vt demutualize

dénationalisation f denationalization

dénationaliser vt denationalize

déni m denial; ~ **de justice flagrant** gross miscarriage of justice

deniers m pl money; **les** ~ **de l'État** public purse

dénombrement m census

dénomination f (de société) name

denrée f commodity; (aliment) foodstuff; ~**s de consommation courante** basic foodstuffs; ~ **périssables** perishables, nondurable goods; ~ **de première nécessité** essential foodstuffs; ~ **au taux zéro** (Fisc) zero-rated good

densité f density; ~ **de caractères** character density; ~ **de peuplement** population density

déontologie f (approved) code of practice; ~ **des affaires** business ethics

dépannage m (Info) troubleshooting

dépanneur, -euse m,f (Info) troubleshooter

dépanneuse f (Transp) recovery vehicle BrE, towtruck

dépareillé, e adj (service, ensemble) unmatched; (objet) odd, unmatched; **articles** ~**s** oddments

départ m departure; **de** ~ start-up; **dès le** ~ from the outset; **être avantagé dès le** ~ have a head start; **salaire de** ~ starting salary; ~ **en retraite** retirement; ~ **usine** ex factory, x-mill; ~ **volontaire à la retraite** voluntary retirement

département m department; ~ **commercial** sales department; ~ **gouvernemental** government department, Bureau US; ~ **d'outre-mer** overseas department

dépassé, e adj obsolete

dépassement m (Compta) overrun; ~ **de budget** overspending; ~ **des coûts** cost overrun; ~ **de risques** (Assur) passing of risk

dépasser vt (excéder) exceed; (montrer une supériorité sur) surpass; ~ **le cubage** (Transp) cube out

dépendances f pl (Assur) appurtenant structures

dépendant, e adj dependent

dépendre: ~ **de** vt (personne, économie) be dependent on; (être sous l'autorité de) come under the control of

dépens m pl costs

dépense f (Compta) expense; (Com) expenditure; ~**s** expenses; **faire des** ~**s**

incur expenses; ~**s acceptables** qualified expenditure; ~**s budgétaires** budget expenditure; ~**s en capital** capital expenditure; ~**s de consommation** consumer expenditure, consumer spending; ~**s courantes** running costs; ~**s en cours** current spending; ~**s déductibles** allowable expenses; ~**s effectives** actual expenditure; ~**s encourues** incurred expenses; ~**s engagées** incurred expenses; ~**s d'entreprise** business expenses, business expenditure; ~**s excessives** overspend; ~**s avant fabrication** preproduction expenditure; ~**s inutiles** wasteful expenditure; ~**s d'investissement** investment spending; ~**s des ménages** consumer spending; ~**s mineures** petty expenses; ~**s nationales brutes** gross national expenditure; ~**s publicitaires** advertising expenditure; ~**s publiques** public spending; ~**s sociales** social spending; ~**s en subventions** grants expenditures

dépenser vt spend; **ne pas** ~ **totalement** under-spend

dépensier, -ière m,f spendthrift

déperdition f (perte) loss; (baisse) decline; (affaiblissement) weakening; ~ **d'actif** wasting asset; ~ **naturelle** natural wastage

dépeuplement m depopulation

déphasé, e adj out of sync

déplacement m (Ind) relocation; (Pol) (des voix) shift; **être en** ~ be on a business trip; ~ **de bloc** (Info) block move; ~ **professionnel** business trip

déplacer ⟨1⟩ vt (Ind) relocate; (personnel) transfer

⟨2⟩ **se déplacer** v pron (pour affaires) travel

déplafonnement m (de cotisations) lifting of the ceiling

déplafonner vt (cotisations) lift the ceiling on

dépliant m brochure, pamphlet

déploiement m deployment

déployer vt deploy

dépolluer vt (plage, rivière) clean up

déport m discount; **avec un** ~ at a discount; ~ **de change** exchange discount

déposant, e m,f depositor; (de biens sous contrat) bailor; (d'un brevet) applicant; ~ **distinct** (Bourse) separate customer

déposer ⟨1⟩ vt (argent) deposit; ~ **de l'argent à la banque/sur son compte** deposit money in the bank/in one's account; (amendement) table; (marque, brevet, nom) register; (Info) drop; ~ **le bilan** file for bankruptcy; ~ **sa candidature** apply; (Pol) stand BrE, run; ~ **une demande** file a claim; ~ **une demande de** make an application for; ~ **une plainte** lodge a complaint; ~ **plainte contre qn** bring an accusation against sb; ~ **une réclamation** put in a claim; ~ **sous la** ⋯◊

foi du serment give evidence on oath; **non déposé** (marque, brevet, nom) unregistered
2 vi (Droit) give evidence

dépositaire mf (Com) dealer, agent; (Fin) depository; ~ **agréé** (Banque, Fin) approved depository; ~ **de biens** (Droit) bailee; ~ **exclusif** sole agent; ~ **intermédiaire agréé** (Bourse) authorized dealer

déposition f (Droit) evidence; ~ **sous serment** deposition, sworn statement; ~ **sur la foi d'autrui** hearsay; ~ **du témoin** statement of witness; ~ **volontaire** unsolicited testimony

dépositionner vt (V&M) deposition

déposséder vt dispossess; ~ **qn de qch** divest sb of sth, take sth away from sb

dépossession f divestiture

dépôt m (local) warehouse; (chemin de fer) railway yard BrE, railyard AmE; (succursale) outlet; (d'argent à la banque) deposit; (enregistrement) (de plainte, de candidature) filing; (de brevet, de marque) registration; (d'amendement) tabling; ~ **à** (Banque) deposit with; **en** ~ (Transp) on consignment; (fonds) on deposit; **en** ~ **fiduciaire** in escrow; ~ **bancaire** bank deposit; ~**s bancaires retraitables** bank demand deposits; ~ **de bilan** voluntary bankruptcy; ~ **de bonne foi** good-faith deposit; ~ **de candidature** application; ~ **en coffre** safe deposit; ~ **contrôlé de déchets** controlled dumping; ~**s en devises** currency deposits; ~ **de distribution** distribution depot; ~ **à échéance fixe** fixed-term deposit, term deposit; ~**s étrangers** foreign assets; ~ **en euromonnaie** Euromoney deposit; ~ **de garantie** deposit, retention money; ~**s de gros** wholesale deposits; ~**s portant intérêts** interest-bearing deposits; ~ **des signatures** signing authority; ~ **à taux variable** floating-rate deposit; ~ **à terme en eurodollars** Eurodollar time deposit; ~ **à vue** demand deposit, sight deposit

dépotage m (de conteneur) stripping

dépoter vt (conteneur) strip

dépouillement m analysis; ~ **de l'actif** asset stripping; ~ **des surplus** surplus stripping

dépouiller vt (examiner) go through; ~ **le courrier** open the mail; ~ **le scrutin** count the votes

dépourvu, e adj; ~ **de** (talent, qualities) devoid of, lacking in

dépréciation f depreciation; ~ **de l'actif** depreciation of assets, loss in value of assets; ~ **économique** (immobilier) economic depreciation; ~ **irrémédiable/non-irrémédiable** incurable/curable depreciation; ~ **d'une monnaie** currency depreciation

déprécier 1 vt (monnaie) depreciate; **non déprécié** (Compta) undepreciated
2 **se déprécier** v pron depreciate

déprédation f (Droit) embezzlement

dépression f (Econ) depression, slump

déprimé, e adj depressed; **non** ~ undepressed

déprogrammer vt (réunion) cancel; (Info) remove

DEPS abrév (▶**dernier entré, premier sorti**) LIFO (last in, first out)

député, e m,f (Pol) deputy, ≈ Member of Parliament UK, Congressman, Congresswoman US; ~ **du Parlement Européen** Euro MP, Member of the European Parliament

déqualification f (de la main d'œuvre) deskilling

dérapage m (augmentation) escalation; (perte de contrôle) sliding, drift; ~ **des prix** price escalation; ~ **des salaires** wage drift, earnings drift

déraper vi slip

déréglementation f (commerce international) deregulation; ~ **mondiale** global deregulation

dérégulation f deregulation

déréguler vt deregulate

dérive f (Econ) slide; ~ **budgétaire** budgetary slide; ~ **des salaires** earnings drift, wage drift

dérivé m (Ind) by-product; (Fin) derivative, wage drift

dernier, -ière adj last; (le plus récent) latest; ~ **entré, premier sorti** last in, first out; **de dernière minute** last-minute; **de** ~ **moment** last-minute; **à la dernière place** in last position; **en** ~ **ressort** as a last resort; ~ **avertissement** final warning; **dernière cotation** closing price; ~ **cours** closing price; ~ **cri** trendy UK (infrml); (matériel) state-of-the-art; ~ **délai** at the latest, deadline; **dernière enchère** closing bid; **dernière entrée** (dans une liste) tail; ~ **jour de cotation** last trading day; ~ **jour de notification** last notice day; ~ **jour de transaction** last trading day; **la dernière mode** the latest fashion; **dernière mise en vente** last sale; **dernière offre** closing bid; ~ **prix en premier** last in, first out price; **dernière quinzaine** (du mois) last half; **dernière réprimande** final warning; **dernières volontés** last will and testament

dernier-né, dernière-née m,f (d'une gamme de produits) latest addition

dérogation f (autorisation) special dispensation; (Compta) relief; (à une loi) infringement, derogation; **par** ~ notwithstanding; **par** ~ **aux dispositions de** (Droit) notwithstanding the provisions of

dérogatoire adj (Droit) derogatory; **clause** ~ derogation clause

déroulement m (Info) flow; ~ **de l'achat** buying process; ~ **de carrière** career development; ~ **des opérations** (Info) work flow; ~ **de programme** (Info) program flow

dérouler ⟨1⟩ *vt* unroll; ~ **le tapis rouge** roll out the red carpet

⟨2⟩ **se dérouler** *v pron* (réunion) take place; (négociations) proceed; **cela s'est déroulé comme prévu** it went as expected, it went as planned

dérouleur *m* holder; ~ **de bande** (Info) tape drive

déroutement *m* route diversion; ~ **frauduleux** (navigation) deviation fraud

derrick *m* derrick

désaccord *m* (divergence) disagreement; (entre des déclarations) discrepancy; (des comptes d'une société de courtage) break; **être en ~ conflit**, disagree; **être en ~ avec qn sur qch** disagree with sb about sth, be in disagreement with sb about sth

désactivé, e *adj* (Info) inactive

désaisonnalisé, e *adj* seasonally adjusted

désaisonnaliser *vt* adjust seasonally

désavantage *m* (inconvénient) drawback; (position) disadvantage; **présenter des ~s** have drawbacks; ~ **concurrentiel** competitive disadvantage

descendant, e *adj* (courbe) downward; (Info) downward

descriptif *m* (Brevets) (imprimé) specifications; **sur ~** on speculation, on spec (infrml); ~ **des marchandises à vendre** (publicité) trade description

description *f* description; ~ **de brevet** (imprimé) patent specifications; ~ **juridique** legal description; ~ **de poste** job description; ~ **de la propriété à vendre** particulars of sale; ~ **du risque** description of risk

déséconomie *f* diseconomy; ~ **d'échelle** diseconomy of scale; ~ **urbaine** agglomeration diseconomy

désélectionner *vt* deselect

désendettement *m* (partiel) reduction of the debt; (complet) clearing of debts; (Bourse, Fin) defeasance; ~ **de fait** in substance defeasance

désengagement *m* (Bourse) withdrawal; (Compta) decommitment

désengager: se ~ *v pron* withdraw, pull out

désépargne *f* dissaving

déséquilibre *m* imbalance; ~ **commercial** trade imbalance

désescalade *f* de-escalation

déshérence *f* escheat; **tomber en ~** escheat

déshérité, e *adj* underprivileged

design *m* (conception) design; (stylique) design; ~ **industriel/graphique** industrial/graphic design

désignation *f* (de brevet) designation; (d'une personne) appointment; (d'un immeuble) description

désigné, e *adj* designated; **personne ~e** nominee

designer *m* designer

désigner *vt* (Pol) nominate; (à un emploi) appoint; (choisir) choose, designate; (fixer) (date) choose, set; (lieu) name, choose; **avoir été désigné comme** have been designated as; ~ **qn comme son successeur** designate/name sb as a successor

désincitation *f* disincentive

désincorporation *f* disintegration

désindexation *f* deindexation

désindexer *vt* deindex

désindustrialisation *f* deindustrialization

désinflation *f* deflation, disinflation

désinformation *f* disinformation

désinstaller *vt* (Info) deinstall, uninstall

désintensification *f* deintensification; ~ **des cultures** (Envir) deintensified farming

désintéressement *m* (d'un individu) buyout; (de créanciers) paying off; ~ **pour endettement** (Bourse, Fin) leveraged buyout

désintéresser *vt* (un individu) buy out; (créanciers) pay off

désintermédiation *f* disintermediation

désinvestir *vi* disinvest; **on désinvestit dans la sidérurgie** investment in the steel industry is being cut

désinvestissement *m* disinvestment

désistement *m* (Droit) disclaimer; ~ **d'action** abandonment of action; ~ **d'un appel** withdrawal of an appeal

désister: se ~ *v pron* stand down; **se ~ d'un appel** discontinue an appeal

désolé, e *adj* sorry; ~ **de vous avoir fait attendre** sorry to keep you waiting

désolidariser: se ~ *v pron* break ranks (de with)

dessaisir *vt* (priver) ~ **qn de qch** (dossier) take sb off sth; (responsabilité) relieve sb of sth; (déposséder) ~ **qn de** (bien) divest sb of; ~ **un juge d'une affaire** remove a judge from a case

dessaisissement *m* (Droit) (dans une succession) divestment; (d'après la loi anti-trust) divestiture

desserrer *vt* (Econ) ease

dessin *m* design; ~ **assisté par ordinateur** computer-aided design, computer-assisted design; ~ **industriel** technical design

dessinateur, -trice *m,f* (concepteur) designer; ~ **industriel** (Ind) draughtsman BrE, draftsman AmE; ~ **de publicité** commercial designer, commercial artist

dessous *adv* below; **en ~ de** below; **les chèques en ~ de 20 euros** cheques for less than 20 euros

d

dessous-de-table *m* (pot-de-vin) bribe, undercover payment

dessus *prép* above; **avoir le ~** have the upper hand

déstabilisation *f* destabilization; **manœuvres de ~** destabilizing activities; **~ d'un opposant** unsettling of an adversary; **~ monétaire** monetary destabilization

déstabiliser *vt* (situation) destabilize

destinataire *mf* (de courrier) addressee; (Info) target; (Transp) consignee; **~ d'une offre** offeree

destination *f* destination; **à ~ de** bound for; **à ~ est/sud** (envoi de marchandises) eastbound/southbound

destiner *vt* aim; (Fin) earmark; **des mesures destinées à faire** measures aimed at doing; **produits destinés à l'exportation** goods for export; **~ qch à qn** (concevoir pour) design sth for sb; **être destiné à faire** (objet, système) be designed to do, be intended to do

déstockage *m* reduction of stocks

destruction *f* destruction; **~ involontaire** (Assur) involuntary conversion

désuétude *f* obsolescence; **tomber en ~** become obsolete; **~ calculée** built-in obsolescence, planned obsolescence

désutilité *f* (Econ) disutility

détail *m* (de facture) itemization; **faire le ~ de qch** itemize sth; **au ~** (V&M) retail; **de ~** (V&M) retail; **tous les ~s** (Com) full particulars; **~ technique** technicality

détaillant, e *m,f* retailer, retail trader; **~ affilié** affiliated retailer

détaillé, e *adj* (rapport, étude, réponse) comprehensive, detailed; (facture) itemized

détailler 1 *vt* (marchandises) retail; (facture) itemize

2 **se détailler** *v pron* (V&M) retail

détaxe *f* remission of charges

détaxé, e *adj* (marchandises) duty-free

détecteur *m* detector; **~ de faux billets/de virus** forged banknotes/virus detector

détendre *vt* (taux d'intérêt) ease

détenir *vt* (marché, actions) hold; (biens) own; **non détenu** (marché, actions) not held; **~ en garantie** hold as security

détente *f* (des taux d'intérêts) easing, slackening

détenteur, -trice *m,f* (de prêt, d'option) holder; **~ d'actions** equity holder; **~ de bon de souscription** warrant holder; **~ de carte** cardholder; **~ de droits d'auteur** royalty holder; **~ d'une licence** licence holder BrE, license holder AmE; **~ d'obligations** bondholder; **~ de redevances** royalty holder; **~ de titres** stockholder

détention *f* (Bourse) holding; (Transp) (navires) libelling BrE, libeling AmE; **en ~ préventive** (Droit) in custody; **placer en ~ préventive** remand in custody

détérioration *f* (déclin) deterioration; **~ de l'environnement** environmental damage; **~ matérielle** physical deterioration; **~ des prix** price deterioration; **~ du sol** soil degradation

détériorer: se ~ *v pron* deteriorate

déterminant, e *adj* decisive

détermination *f* determination; **~ de l'assiette d'imposition** (Fisc) assessment; **~ conjointe** codetermination; **~ du lieu de résidence** residence status; **~ des prix** price determination; **~ des prix à parité** parity pricing; **~ de la résidence** residence status; **~ des salaires entre initiés** insider wage setting

déterminer *vt* determine; (prix des options) shape; (motif, circonstances, cause) establish, determine; **~ l'équilibre** find the balance; **~ l'impôt à payer** assess tax; **~ l'origine d'un appel** trace a call; **~ le prix de** set the price of, price

détonateur *m* (Transp) detonator; (marchandises dangereuses) igniter

détournement *m* (de recettes, dividendes) misappropriation; (de fonds) embezzlement, misappropriation; **~ d'impôts** defraudation, tax fraud; **~ d'itinéraire** rerouting

détourner *vt* (fonds) embezzle, misappropriate

détriment: au ~ de to the detriment of

détritus *m pl* rubbish BrE, garbage AmE

détruire *vt* (Transp) write off

dette *f* debt; **avoir des ~s** be in debt; **faire des ~s** run up debts; **être couvert de ~s** be debtridden; **avoir 1000 euros de ~s** have debts of 1,000 euros; **~ due à** (personne, société) debt due to; **~ échue** le debt due by; **~ exigible** le debt due by; **~ active** outstanding debt; **~ actuarielle** actuarial liability; **~ brute** gross debt; **~s commerciales** business exposures liability; **~ consolidée** funded debt; **~ à court terme** (Compta) current liability; **~s et engagements** (Compta) claims and liabilities; **~s escomptables** eligible liability; **~ extérieure** external debt; **~ fiscale** tax liability; **~ flottante** floating debt, unfunded debt; **~ garantie** secured debt; **~ garantie par obligations** bonded debt; **~ par habitant** per capita debt; **~ hypothécaire** mortgage debt; **~ indépendante** self-supporting debt; **~ liquide** liquid debt; **~ à long terme** (Compta) long-term liability; **~ mezzanine** mezzanine debt; **~ nationale brute** gross national debt; **~ non garantie** unsecured debt; **~ obligataire** bonded debt; **~ publique** public debt; **~ recouvrable** recoverable debt; **~ testamentaire** testamentary debt

deux *adj* two; **à ~ niveaux** two-tier; **à ~ revenus** double-income; **tous les ~ jours** every other day

deuxième *adj* second; ~ **démarque** (vente au détail) second markdown, double reduction; ~ **mise sur le marché** secondary offering; ~ **rang** second best; ~ **semestre** second half of the year; ~ **société** second largest company; ~ **trimestre** second quarter

deuxièmement *adv* secondly

dévalorisation *f* (de monnaie) (action) devaluation; (résultat) depreciation; (de politique, diplôme) devaluation

dévaloriser ① *vt* (monnaie) devalue
② **se dévaloriser** *v pron* lose value

dévaluation *f* devaluation; ~ **monétaire** currency devaluation

dévaluer ① *vt* devalue
② **se dévaluer** *v pron* become devalued

devant *prép* in front of; **être ~ les tribunaux** (affaire) be sub judice

devanture *f* (façade de magasin) shop front; (vitrine) shop window

développé, e *adj* advanced

développement *m* (d'un produit) development; (d'entreprise, d'économie) development, expansion; (du chômage, des investissements) increase; **pays en voie de ~** developing nation; **l'entreprise a connu un fort ~ dans les années 90** the firm expanded greatly in the nineties; ~ **des affaires** business development; ~ **de carrière** career development; ~ **économique** economic development; ~ **du marché** market expansion; ~ **de la marque** brand development; ~ **organisationnel** organizational development; ~ **de produits nouveaux** new product development; ~ **régional** regional development; ~ **des ressources humaines** human resource development; ~ **de système** (Info) system development

développer ① *vt* develop; (ses activités) expand; (son entreprise) build up
② **se développer** *v pron* build up, develop

développeur, -euse *m,f* (Info) software developer

devenir *vi* become; ~ **caduc** (contrat) cease to have effect; ~ **effectif** come into effect, come into force

déverrouiller *vt* (Fin, Info) unlock

déversement *m* (de polluant) dumping; ~ **accidentel** spillage; ~ **de pétrole** oil spillage

déverser *vt* (Envir) dump

devis *m* quotation, quote; ~ **approximatif** rough estimate; ~ **estimatif** cost estimate, preliminary estimate; ~ **de participation** (V&M) lowball (jarg), underestimation; ~ **le plus récent** latest estimate

devise *f* (Fin) currency; ~ **apatride** (jarg) stateless currency; ~ **clé** key currency; ~ **comptable** reporting currency; ~ **contrôlée** managed currency; ~ **convertible** convertible currency; ~

étrangère foreign currency; ~ **d'exploitation** functional currency; ~ **faible** soft currency; ~ **flottante** fluctuating currency; ~ **forte** hard currency; ~ **d'intervention** intervention currency; ~ **de référence** reference currency; ~ **saine** sound currency; ~ **sous-évaluée** undervalued currency; ~ **surévaluée** overvalued currency

dévoiler *vt* (plans, propositions) unveil; ~ **ses intentions** show one's hand

devoir¹ *m* duty

devoir² *vt* (argent) owe; ~ **qch à qn** owe sth to sb, owe sb sth

dévolu, e *adj* (Fisc) passing; (à un bénéficiaire) vested; **être ~ à qn** (droit) be devolved on sb, be vested in sb

DG *abrév* (▸**directeur général**) CEO (chief executive officer) US, MD (managing director) UK

DGA *abrév* (▸**directeur général adjoint**) ADG (assistant director general)

DGAC *abrév* France (▸**Direction générale de l'aviation civile**) ≈ ATA (Air Transport Association) US, ≈ CAA (Civil Aviation Authority) UK

diagnostic *m* diagnosis; ~ **d'un expert** expert opinion; ~ **financier** financial analysis

diagramme *m* chart; ~ **circulaire** pie chart

dialogue *m* dialogue BrE, dialog AmE; **boîte de ~** dialog box

dicter *vt* (écrire, imposer) dictate; **mesures dictées par la conjoncture** measures dictated by the situation

dif. *abrév* (▸**différé**) def. (deferred)

diffamation *f* (par écrit) libel; (verbalement) slander; **poursuivre qn en ~** sue sb for libel

diffamatoire *adj* defamatory; (texte) libellous BrE, libelous AmE; (geste, parole) slanderous

diffamer *vt* defame; (par écrit) libel; (verbalement) slander

différé, e *adj* (action) deferred; (Info) off-line; **en ~** (Info) off-line; (Média) recorded

différence *f* difference, distinction; **faire la ~ entre** differentiate between, make a distinction between; ~ **de caisse** cash short; ~ **de conversion** translation difference; ~ **offert-demandé** (Bourse) turn; ~ **de prix** price differential

différenciation *f* (marketing) differentiation; ~ **des prix** differential pricing; ~ **de produits** product differentiation

différencier *vt* differentiate

différend *m* disagreement; (Droit) dispute

différentiel *m* (rendement) differential; ~ **de qualifications** skill differential; ~ **de taux** rate differential

différer ① *vt* (paiement, remboursement) defer; (réunion, decision) postpone; (Droit) adjourn; ~ ⋯╪

le paiement de l'impôt postpone tax
2 *vi* differ (**from** de)

difficile *adj* difficult, hard

difficulté *f* difficulty, trouble; **avoir des ∼s**
be in trouble; **avoir des ∼s de trésorerie**
have cash flow problems; **∼s indues** (Fisc)
undue hardship

diffuser *vt* broadcast

diffusion *f* (radio, télévision) broadcasting;
(presse) circulation, readership; **pour ∼
immédiate** (presse) for immediate release; **∼
de données** data broadcasting; **∼ de
l'information** information broadcasting

digital, e *adj* (Info) digital

digne *adj* (représentant, successeur) worthy; **∼
de confiance** trustworthy

dilapider *vt* (argent) squander; (énergie) waste

dilatoire *adj* evasive

diligence *f* diligence; **avoir de la ∼** be
diligent; **∼ des intermédiaires** procuring
cause; **∼ normale** due diligence

diligenter *vt* expedite, hasten

diluer *vt* (idée, politique) water down; (Fin)
(capitaux) dilute

dilution *f* dilution; **∼ de l'avoir** (Bourse)
equity dilution; **∼ des tarifs** (Transp) rate
dilution

dimanche *m* Sunday; **∼s et jours fériés
compris** Sundays and holidays included; **∼s
et jours fériés exceptés** Sundays and
holidays excepted

diminué, e *adj* reduced

diminuer 1 *vt* (taux, taxe, salaire) lower;
(dépenses) reduce
2 *vi* (facture, montant, chômage, taux, prix)
decrease; (demande) ease off; (ventes) tail off,
fall; **∼ progressivement** decrease gradually;
(prix) shade

diminution *f* decrease; **∼ d'impôt** tax
discounting; **∼ d'intérêt** interest rebate; **∼
de marge** margin shrinkage; **∼ de l'ozone**
ozone depletion; **∼ du risque** decrease of
risk; **∼ de valeur** decrease in value

dîner¹ *m* dinner; **∼ officiel** formal dinner

dîner² *vi* have dinner; **∼ dehors** eat out

dioxyde de soufre *m* sulphur dioxide

diplomatie *f* diplomacy; **la ∼** ≈ the
Diplomatic Service UK

diplôme *m* certificate, diploma; **∼
d'administration publique** Diploma in
Public Administration; **∼ d'études
commerciales** Diploma of Commerce; **∼
d'études universitaires générales**
*university diploma taken after two years of
study*; **∼ de gestion des entreprises**
Diploma in Industrial Management; **∼ en
sciences économiques** Diploma of
Economics; **∼ universitaire** university
degree; **∼ universitaire de technologie**
Diploma in Technology

diplômé¹, e *adj* qualified

diplômé², e *m,f* graduate; **∼ en
administration des entreprises** Bachelor
of Business Administration; **∼ de
l'université** university graduate

dircom *m* (infrml) communications director,
company spin doctor (infrml)

direct¹, e *adj* (contact, rapport, impôt) direct;
(accès, liaison) direct; (expérience, formation)
hands-on; (trajet) direct; **en ∼** (émission) live; **∼
ou présumé couvert** (Assur) direct or held
covered

direct² *m* (Média) spot coverage

directement *adv* directly; **être ∼
intéressé par** have a vested interest in; **∼
exploitable** (Info) machine-readable; **∼ lié à**
directly related to

directeur, -trice *m,f* manager;
(administrateur) director; (chef) head; **∼ des
achats** chief buyer; **∼ adjoint** assistant/
deputy manager; **∼ d'agence** branch
manager; **∼ de banque** bank manager; **∼
de bureau** office manager; **∼ de chantier**
site manager; **∼ clientèle** customer
relations manager; **∼ commercial** sales
manager; **∼ de comptabilité** chief
accountant, chief accounting officer; **∼ de
département** department head; **∼ du
développement** development manager; **∼
de division** division head; **∼ exécutif**
executive manager; **∼ de fabrication**
production manager; **∼ financier** chief
financial officer; **∼ général** (société anonyme
par actions) managing director UK, chief
executive officer US; **∼ général adjoint**
assistant director-general; **∼ informatique**
IT director, information systems manager; **∼
de journal** newspaper publisher; **∼ du
marketing** marketing director; **∼ du
personnel** personnel manager; **∼ de projet**
project manager; **∼ de la publication** chief
editor; **∼ régional** district manager; **∼ des
relations publiques** public relations officer;
∼ des ressources humaines director of
human resources; **∼ du service** department
head; **∼ du service après-ventes** after-
sales manager; **∼ de succursale** branch
office manager; **∼ technique** technical
director, production manager; **∼ des
transports** traffic manager; **∼ d'usine** plant
manager; **∼ des ventes** sales manager; **∼
de zone** area manager

direction *f* management; (bureau) manager's
office; **de ∼** managerial; **∼ de
l'aménagement du territoire** town and
country planning department; **∼ centrale**
headquarters; **∼ commerciale** sales
management; **∼ de la concurrence, de la
consommation et de la répression de
fraudes** ≈ Office of Fair Trading UK, ≈
Trading Standards Office US; **∼
d'entreprise** corporate management; **∼
générale** general management; (bureau) main
office; **Direction générale de l'aviation
civile** France Civil Aviation Authority UK, Air

Transport Association US; ~ **hiérarchique** line management; ~ **opérationnelle** operating management; ~ **par objectifs** management by objectives; ~ **du personnel** personnel management; ~ **de planning** planning department; ~ **des ressources humaines** human resources department; ~ **des salaires et des traitements** wage and salary administration; ~ **de service** departmental management; ~ **des ventes** sales management

directive f guideline; ~ **préliminaire** draft directive; ~ **de l'Union européenne** EU Directive

directoire m management board; ~ **interdépendant** interlocking directorate

directorial, e adj managerial

directrice f manageress

dirigeant¹, e adj managing

dirigeant², e m,f (d'une banque, d'une corporation) manager; ~ **de corporation** corporate manager; ~ **d'entreprise** business manager, company executive; ~ **opérationnel** line executive

diriger vt (usine, entreprise) run, manage; (parti, opération) lead; (réunion) conduct; ~ **les débats** be in the chair

dirigisme m (Econ) interventionism

dirigiste adj (Econ) interventionist

disaggio m (Bourse) discount

disciple mf follower

discompte m discount

discompter vt discount

discompteur m discounter

discontinuer vt (fonds) terminate

discours m speech; **faire un** ~ make a speech; ~ **programme** (Pol) keynote speech

discrétion f discretion; **à la** ~ **de** at the discretion of; **à notre** ~ at our discretion

discrétionnaire adj discretionary

discrimination f discrimination; ~ **s'appliquant à l'âge** age discrimination; ~ **entre hommes et femmes** sex discrimination; ~ **indirecte** indirect discrimination; ~ **inverse** reverse discrimination; ~ **masquée** indirect discrimination; ~ **positive** positive discrimination; ~ **pour motifs religieux** religious discrimination; ~ **de prix** price discrimination; ~ **raciale** racial discrimination

discriminer vt discriminate

disculper vt clear

discussion f discussion; **soumis à** ~ under discussion; ~ **approfondie** in-depth discussion

discutable adj (notion, question) debatable, arguable; (choix, méthode, procédé) controversial

discuter vt (contester) contest; (mesure, projet de loi) debate; (question, point) discuss; ~ **le budget** debate the budget; ~ **l'utilité/le**

bien-fondé de question the usefulness/the grounds for

dispacheur m (maritime) average adjuster

disparate adj (articles) odd

disparité f disparity

dispense f (Droit, Assur) exemption; (certificat) certificate of exemption

disperser: se ~ v pron (rassemblement) break up; **nous nous sommes trop dispersés** we spread ourselves too thinly

dispersion f (de rassemblement) dispersal; ~ **des logements** scattered site housing BrE, scattersite housing AmE; ~ **des risques** (Assur) distribution of risks

disponibilité f availability; ~**s** (Fin) liquid assets; ~ **des ressources** resource availability

disponible adj available, free; ~ **sans délai** available at short notice

disposé, e adj (prêt) ~ **à** willing to; **peu** ~ **à faire qch** reluctant to do sth

disposer vt (objets) arrange; ~ **de** dispose of; **ne pas** ~ **de fonds suffisants** have insufficient funds, be undercapitalized

dispositif m (mesures) operation; (appareil) device; ~ **d'alarme** warning device; ~ **antivol** antitheft device; ~ **câblé** (Info) hardware device; ~ **de déclenchement** trigger mechanism; ~ **financier** financial operation; ~ **de protection électronique** dongle; ~ **de réfrigération** cooling system

disposition f (arrangement) arrangement; (de salle) layout; (mesure) measure, arrangement; (d'une loi) provision; (tendance) tendency; (Assur, Droit) clause; ~**s particulières** special arrangements; ~**s fiscales/législatives** tax/legal measures; ~**s en cas d'imprévu** contingency arrangements; **mettre qch à la** ~ **de qn** put sth at sb's disposal; **à la** ~ **du public** for public use; **se tenir à la** ~ **de qn** be at sb's disposal; ~ **de l'année courante** current year disposition; ~ **contractuelle** contractual provision; ~ **fiscale** tax provision; ~ **obligatoire** mandatory provision; ~ **présumée** deemed disposition; ~ **de récupération** clawback; ~ **réputée** deemed disposition

disputé, e adj (marché) sought-after; (question, projet) controversial; (épreuve) keenly contested

disque m (Info) disk; ~ **compact** compact disk; ~ **compact interactif** compact disk interactive; ~ **double face** double-sided disk; ~ **dur** hard disk; ~ **d'initialisation** boot disk; ~ **monoface** single-sided disk; ~ **souple** diskette, floppy disk; ~ **de travail** scratch disk; ~ **virtuel** RAM disk, random access memory disk

disquette f (Info) diskette, floppy disk; ~ **double densité** double-density disk; ~ **d'installation** installation disk; ~ **protégée** copy-protected disk

d

dissimulation *f* (Droit) concealment; ~ **de pertes** (Bourse, Compta) concealment of losses

dissimuler *vt* (des faits, la vérité) conceal, cover up (à qn from sb); ~ **des informations** withhold information

dissolution *f* (du parlement) dissolution

dissuader *vt* ~ **qn de faire** dissuade sb from doing

distance *f* distance; **à** ~ (Info) (commande, accès, manipulation) remote

distancer *vt* leave behind

distant, e *adj* (Info) remote

distillation *f* distilling

distinctif, -ive *adj* distinctive

distinction *f* distinction; **faire une** ~ **entre** draw a distinction between, distinguish between

distinguer *vt* single out; ~ **entre** make a distinction between

distorsion *f* distortion; ~ **commerciale** trade distortion; ~ **du marché** market distortion, market failure

distribuer *vt* (information, produit) distribute; (crédits, tâches, rôles) allocate; (marketing) market

distributeur, -trice *m,f* (personne, société) distributor; ~ **automatique** vending machine; ~ **automatique de billets** automatic cash dispenser; ~ **automatique de produits** automatic vending machine; ~ **de crédit** credit grantor; ~ **d'eau** water supplier; ~ **exclusif** sole distributor; ~ **de monnaie** change dispenser

distribution *f* distribution; (secteur) retailing; ~ **alimentaire** food retailing; **grande** ~ volume retailing; ~ **d'actions** share allotment; ~ **par âge** age distribution; ~ **automatique** vending; ~ **d'échantillons gratuits** distribution of free samples, sampling; ~ **de montant global** lump-sum distribution; ~ **de plus-values** capital gains distribution; ~ **restreinte** limited distribution; ~ **des revenus** distribution of income; ~ **de la richesse** wealth distribution; ~ **du travail** allocation of work

dit *adv* a.k.a., also known as

div. *abrév* (▸**dividende**) div. (dividend)

divergence *f* (d'opinions, de résultats) divergence; **des** ~**s d'intérêts** divergences of interest; ~ **de points de vue** divergence of opinion; **avoir des** ~**s d'opinion avec qn** have a different point of view from sb, disagree with sb

diverger *vi* (opinions) diverge; (lois) differ

divers, e *adj* (varié) various, diverse; (plusieurs) various, several; (frais) miscellaneous; **dépenses** ~**es** sundries

diversification *f* diversification; ~ **de l'actif** asset diversification; ~ **des affaires** business diversification; ~ **de produits** product diversification

diversifié, e *adj* diversified

diversifier *vt* diversify; ~ **les risques** (Bourse) diversify risk

diversion *f* diversion; ~ **commerciale** trade diversion

diversité *f* diversity, variety

divertir *vt* entertain

divertissement *m* entertainment

dividende *m* dividend; **les** ~**s des actions** dividends from shares, share dividends; **verser/toucher des** ~**s** pay out/receive dividends; **avec** ~ cum dividend; ~ **par action** dividend per share; ~ **en actions** stock dividend US; ~ **annuel** annual dividend, yearly dividend; ~ **attaché** cum dividend; ~ **brut** gross dividend; ~ **en capital** capital dividend; ~ **cumulé** accrued dividend, accumulated dividend; ~ **déclaré** declared dividend; ~ **à découvert** times uncovered; ~ **détaché** ex-dividend; ~ **différé** scrip dividend; ~ **exceptionnel** capital bonus; ~ **exonéré d'impôt** tax-exempt dividend; ~ **fictif** unearned dividend; ~ **de filiale** subsidiary dividends; ~ **de fin d'exercice** year-end dividend; ~ **sur les gains en capital** capital gains dividend; ~ **illicite** illegal dividend US; ~ **de liquidation** liquidation dividend; ~ **majoré** grossed-up dividend; ~ **en nature** dividend in kind; ~ **sur obligations** liability dividend; ~ **passé** omitted dividend; ~ **à payer** accrued dividend, dividend payable; ~ **de portefeuille** portfolio dividend; ~ **prélevé sur le capital** capital dividend; ~ **à terme échu** dividend in arrears

divisé, e *adj* divided; ~ **par** divided by

diviser *vt* divide

division *f* (Com) (dans une entreprise) department, division; ~ **d'actions** (Bourse) share split, stock split AmE; ~ **administrative** administrative unit, organizational unit; ~ **en deux** two-way split; ~ **opérationnelle** operating division; ~ **du travail** division of labour BrE, division of labor AmE; ~ **du trésor public** tax jurisdiction, tax district UK

divulgation *f* (Droit) disclosure; ~ **exclusive** (Pol) exclusive distribution; ~ **sur le marché** market disclosure; ~ **restreinte** (Pol) limited distribution

divulguer *vt* (informations) leak; (secret) disclose; **ne pas** ~ conceal

dock *m* dock; ~ **fermé** enclosed dock

docker *m* docker BrE, longshoreman AmE

docteur *m* Doctor; ~ **en droit** Doctor of Law; ~ **en sciences économiques** Doctor of Economics

document *m* document; **avec** ~**s à l'appui** by means of documentary evidence; ~**s d'accompagnement** supporting material, backup material; ~**s contre acceptation** documents against acceptance; ~ **administratif unique** single administrative document; ~ **authentique** legal document;

~ de base master document, source document; **~ d'engagement** (Droit) commitment document; **~ d'exécution** artwork; **~s d'expédition** shipping documents; **~ expert** intelligent document; **~ financier prévisionnel** estimated financial report; **~ d'information** background paper; **~ joint** accompanying document; **~ justificatif** supporting data; **~s contre paiement** documents against payment; **~ de travail** working paper

documentaire *adj* (caractère, intérêt) documentary; **recherche ~** (Info) desk research; **à titre ~** for your information

documentaliste *mf* researcher

documentation *f* documentation, reference material; **~ publicitaire** sales literature

dol *m* (Droit) fraud; **~ d'assurance maritime** marine insurance fraud

dol. *abrév* (▶**dollar**) dol. (dollar)

dollar *m* dollar; **~ au comptant et à terme** dollar spot and forward; **~s constants** constant dollars US; **~s indexés** common dollars; **~s offshore** offshore dollars

dollarisation *f* dollarization

DOM *abrév* (▶**département d'outre-mer**) French overseas administrative department

domaine *m* (propriété) property, estate; (spécialité) field, domain; (Info) domain; **nom de ~** domain name; **dans le ~ public** in the public sphere; **tomber dans le ~ public** (œuvre) be out of copyright; **~ d'activité** field of endeavour BrE, field of endeavor AmE; **~ des affaires** business sector; **~ d'attributions** jurisdiction; **~ d'expertise** area of expertise; **~ financier** financial field; **~ d'imposition** field of taxation; **~ problématique** problem area; **~ public** public domain; **~ de responsabilité** area of responsibility; **~ technique** technical field

domestique *mf* servant

domicile *m* (d'une société) registered address; (d'une personne) domicile, place of abode; **~ à domicile** (vente) door-to-door, house-to-house; **~/dépôt** (Transp) house/depot; **~ d'imposition** tax domicile; **~ légal** legal residence

domiciliation *f* (Fin) domiciliation

domicilié, e *adj* domiciled

dominant, e *adj* dominant

dominer ① *vt* (marché, secteur) dominate; (un pays) rule; **~ la situation** be in control of the situation ② *vi* (être en tête) be in the lead; (prévaloir) (idée) prevail

dommage *m* (Assur) damage; **~ causé avec intention** malicious damage; **~ causé par un incendie** damage caused by fire; **~s aux biens loués** damage to rented property; **~s connus** known loss; **~s corporels** physical injury; **~s indirects** consequential damage; **~s et intérêts** damages; **~s et intérêts accessoires** incidental damages; **~s et intérêts compensatoires** compensatory damages; **~s et intérêts en réparation d'un préjudice moral** vindictive damages; **~ irréparable** irreparable damage; **~s aux marchandises en entrepôt** damage to goods in custody; **~ matériel** damage to property, property damage; **~s d'ordre physique** *m* physical injury; **~s partiels** partial loss; **~s peu importants** minor damage

domotique *f* home automation

DOM-TOM *abrév* (▶**départements et territoires d'outre-mer**) French overseas departments and territories

don *m* (Fisc) donation, gift; **~ de biens** (Droit) gift of property; **~ de charité** charitable donation; **~ net** outright gift; **~ promis** donation pledged; **~s spéciaux en argent** (Fisc) one-off cash gifts; **~ par testament** (Droit) gift by will

donataire *mf* (Fisc) donee

donateur, -trice *m, f* donor

donation *f* (Droit) donation, gift; **faire une ~ en faveur de qn** make a settlement on sb; **~ entre vifs** gift inter vivos

donnée *f* (élément d'information) fact; (élément chiffré) piece of data, data item; **~s** data; **en ~s brutes non corrigées** in unadjusted figures; **en ~s corrigées** in adjusted figures; **~s d'acceptation de saisie** entry acceptance data; **~s antérieures** emission data, historical data; **~s de base** source data; **~s brutes** raw data; **~s clés** key data; **~s comptables** accounting records; **~s de contrôle** control data; **~s corrigées des variations saisonnières** seasonally adjusted figures; **~s d'entrée** input data; **~s justificatives** supporting data; **~s de mouvement** transaction data; **~s non traitées** raw data; **~s de sortie** output data; **~s statistiques de référence** benchmark statistics; **~s type** sample data

donner ① *vt* give; **~ congé** give notice to quit; **~ un pourboire à** tip; **~ du pouvoir à** empower; **~ à qn le droit de faire qch** qualify sb to do sth, give sb the right to do sth; **donné spontanément** (informations) volunteer; **donné en garantie** (Droit) cautionary ② **se donner** *v pron* (s'imposer) **se ~ beaucoup de mal** go to a lot of trouble; (s'octroyer) **se ~ les moyens de faire** find the means to do

donneur *m* (Bourse) giver; **~ à bail** (Droit) lessor; **~ d'une licence** (Brevets) licensor; **~ d'option d'achat** giver for a call; **~ d'une option de vente** giver for a put

doper *vt* (ventes, marché, monnaie) boost, give a boost to

dormant, e *adj* (argent) inactive

d

DOS® *abrév* (**système d'exploitation à disques**) DOS® (disk operating system)

dose *f* dose; ~ **fatale** (pollution) lethal dose; ~ **de rayonnement** radiation dose

dossier *m* file, records; (sur une affaire) brief; (Droit) (documents) file; (affaire) case; (Info) file; **constituer un ~ sur qn/qch** build up a file on sb/sth; **faire un ~ de demande de prêt** make an application for a loan; **verser une pièce au ~** add information to the file; **classer le ~** close the case; **délégué chargé du ~ agricole** delegate responsible for agricultural affairs; ~ **d'audit** audit file, audit working papers; ~ **commercial** trade brief; ~ **de demande de subvention** application for subsidies; ~ **médical** medical record; ~ **personnel** personal records, case history; ~ **de presse** (imprimé) press kit; (publicité) background paper

dot *f* dowry

dotation *f* (Droit) endowment; (Compta, Fin) appropriation; ~ **aux amortissements** allowance for depreciation US, amortization expense; ~ **en facteurs de production** factor endowment; ~ **aux investissements** capital consumption allowance; ~ **en personnel** staffing

dotcom *f* dot-com

doter *vt* (accorder une somme à) ~ **qn de qch** allocate sth to sb; (fournir en équipement) ~ **qn/qch de** equip sb/sth with; **le projet est doté d'un million d'euros** the project has been allocated one million euros; **l'ordinateur est doté d'un nouveau système** the computer is equipped with a new system

douane *f* (service) customs; (taxe) duty; **agent des ~s** customs officer; **marchandises saisies par la ~** goods seized by customs; **zone/port sous ~** zone/port under the authority of the Customs and Excise; **bureau de ~** customs; **déclaration de ~** customs declaration; **passer des marchandises en ~** clear goods through customs; **payer les droits de ~** pay duty; **exempt de ~** duty-free

douanier, -ière *m,f* customs officer; ~ **affecté aux opérations d'import/export** shipping officer

double¹ *adj* double; **à ~ action** (Info) double-acting; ~ **assurance** (Assur) double insurance; ~ **clic** (Info) double click; ~ **commission** (Bourse) each way; ~ **couverture** (Assur) duplication of benefits; ~ **densité** (Info) double density; **à ~ effet** (Ind) double-acting; ~ **étalon** parallel standard; ~ **face** (Info) (disquette) two-sided; ~ **frappe** (Info) double strike; ~ **interligne** double space, double spacing; ~ **marché du travail** dual labour market BrE, dual labor market AmE; ~ **option** (Bourse) double option, put and call; ~ **page centrale** centrefold; ~ **réduction** double reduction; ~ **résidence** (Fisc) dual residence; ~ **taux de**

change dual exchange rate

double² *m* duplicate

double-cliquer *vi* (Info) double-click (**sur** on)

doubler ⓵ *vt* double
⓶ *vi* increase twofold

doublon *m* (faisant double emploi) duplication

doucher *vt* (infrml) (enthousiasme) dampen

doué, e *adj* gifted

douteux, -euse *adj* (affaire, individu, transaction) shady; (renseignement, authenticité) dubious; (résultat, succès) uncertain

douz. *abrév* (▸**douzaine**) doz. (dozen)

douzaine *f* dozen

doyen, -enne *m,f* (d'un pays) oldest citizen; (d'une organisation) most senior member

DP *abrév* (▸**documents contre paiement**) DAP (documents against payment)

DPA *abrév* (▸**dividende par action**) dividend per share; Can (▸**déduction pour amortissement**) CCA (capital cost allowance)

DR *abrév* (▸**délai de recouvrement**) debt recovery period

drachme *m* drachma

drainage *m* (du sol) drainage; ~ **des cerveaux** brain drain

drainer *vt* (sol) drain; (capitaux) siphon off (**vers** to)

dresser *vt* (monument, échafaudage) erect; (liste, contrat) draw up; ~ **un budget** draw up a budget, prepare a budget; ~ **les états financiers** prepare the financial statements; ~ **l'inventaire** take stock; ~ **l'ordre du jour** draw up the agenda

DRH *abrév* (▸**directeur des ressources humaines**) HR director, director of human resources; (▸**direction des ressources humaines**) HR department, human resources department

droit *m* (prérogative) right; (ensemble de lois) law; (redevance) fee; **avoir ~ à qch** be eligible for sth, be entitled to, qualify for sth; **ayant ~ à** eligible for; **ayant un ~ sur** (Fisc) beneficially interested in; **de ~** (Droit) de jure; **être en ~ de faire** be justified in doing; **faire ~ à** admit, allow; **faire ~ à une demande** (Droit) sustain a claim; **tous ~s réservés** all rights reserved, copyright reserved;

(droit a...) ~ **d'accès** access right; ~ **d'accise** excise duty; ~ **d'acconage** lighterage charge; ~ **acquis** (dans une entreprise) vested interest; ~ **d'acquisition** acquisition fee; ~ **d'action** (pour dettes) cause of action; ~s **d'adhésion** application fees, (Fisc) initiation fees; ~ **administratif** administrative law; ~ **des affaires** business law; ~ **d'affouage** estovers; ~ **ancien** old law; ~s **annuels de maintien d'un brevet** patent renewal fees; ~ **d'anticipation** anticipation; ~ **d'appel** right of appeal; ~s

d'auteur copyright, (Média) performing rights; (éditions) royalties;

(**b...**) ~ **de bail** leasehold; ~ **bancaire** banking law; ~**s de bassin** (navigation) dock charges; (port) dock dues; ~ **sur les biens transmis par décès** inheritance duty; ~ **au brevet** right to a patent;

(**c...**) ~ **de canal** (navigation) canal dues; ~ **au capital** capital interest; ~ **civil** civil law; ~**s civiques** civil rights; ~ **à la clientèle** goodwill; ~**s de codétermination** codetermination rights; ~ **commercial** commercial law; ~ **de compensation** (Banque) right of offset; ~**s compensatoires** (Imp/exp) countervailing duties; ~ **composé** (douane) compound duty; ~ **comptable** accounting law; ~**s conférés par qn** rights afforded by sb; ~ **à congé** holiday entitlement; ~**s consulaires** consulage; ~ **de conversion** (Bourse) conversion right; ~ **de courtage** brokerage fee; ~ **coutumier** common law;

(**d...**) ~ **dérogatoire** overriding interest; ~ **à des dommages-intérêts** right of recovery; ~**s de douane** customs (duty);

(**e...**) ~ **d'échange libre** free right of exchange; ~ **écrit** statute law; ~ **d'émission** emission fee; ~ **d'entrée** admission fee; (importation) import duty; ~ **des entreprises** corporate law; ~**s exclusifs d'exploitation** (de l'invention brevetée) patent rights; ~ **d'exécution** performing rights; ~ **d'exploitation** (Brevets) rental right; (Com) operating interest;

(**f...**) ~**s de fabrication** manufacturing rights; ~ **fiscal** fiscal law; ~**s fondamentaux** natural rights;

(**g...**) ~ **de gage** lien; ~**s de garde** custody charge; ~ **de grève** right to strike;

(**h...**) ~**s de l'homme** human rights;

(**i...**) ~ **incorporel** incorporeal right; ~ **d'indemnisation** right of recovery; ~ **à l'information** right to know; ~ **d'inscription** registration fee; ~**s d'inscription** tuition fees; ~ **d'interdire** prohibition right;

(**j...**) ~ **jurisprudentiel** case law;

(**m...**) ~**s miniers** mineral rights; ~ **mixte** (douane) compound duty; ~**s de mouillage** anchorage charges; ~ **de mutation** transfer tax; ~**s de mutation** inheritance tax UK;

(**o...**) ~**s d'objection** appraisal rights US;

(**p...**) ~**s particuliers de retrait** (Banque) special drawing rights; ~ **de passage** right of way; ~**s de port** harbour dues BrE, harbor dues AmE; ~ **positif** substantive law; ~ **de poursuite** stoppage in transit; ~ **de premier refus** right of first refusal; ~ **prescrit** specified right; ~ **prévu par la loi** statutory right UK; ~ **de priorité** priority right; ~ **privé** private law; ~ **de procédure** adjective law; ~ **proportionné**

commensurate charge; ~ **de propriété** proprietorship; ~**s de propriété** property rights; ~**s de propriété collectifs** common ownership; ~ **à la propriété industrielle** design right; ~**s de propriété intellectuelle** intellectual property rights; ~**s protecteurs** protective duties; ~ **public** public law;

(**r...**) ~ **de recours** right of appeal; ~ **de remboursement** right of redemption; ~ **de remorquage** (navigation) towage charges, towage dues; ~ **à réparation** right of recovery, right of redress; ~ **de réponse** right of reply; ~ **de reprise** right of resumption; ~ **de résidence** right of residence; ~ **de rétention bancaire** bank lien; ~ **de retour** right of return; ~**s de retransmission** broadcasting rights; ~**s des riverains** riparian rights;

(**s...**) ~ **de séjour** right of residence; ~ **de souscription** application right, subscription right; ~ **de souscription négociable** allotment letter UK; ~ **de souscription prioritaire** subscription privilege; ~ **spécifique** specific duty, specific tax; ~ **statutaire** lex scripta (frml) statutory right UK; ~**s de succession** inheritance tax UK, legacy tax US; ~ **des successions** succession law; **avec** ~ **de souscription** (Bourse) cum warrant; ~ **du survivant** right of survivorship; ~**s syndicaux** union rights;

(**t...**) ~ **du tenancier** tenant's right UK; ~ **de tenure à bail** leasehold interest; ~ **de timbre** stamp duty; ~ **de timbre sur les successions** probate duty; ~**s de tirage spéciaux** special drawing rights; ~ **au travail** right to work; ~ **du travail** employment law, labour law BrE, labor law AmE;

(**u...**) ~ **d'usufruit** beneficial interest; ~ **d'utilisation** licence BrE, license AmE; ~**s d'utilisation** (Banque) (de carte) cardholder fee;

(**v...**) ~ **sur la valeur globale de la succession** estate duty; ~ **de vote** right to vote, voting right

droite f (opposé à gauche) **la** ~ the right; (Pol) **de** ~ (parti, personne) right-wing

DTS abrév (▸**droits de tirage spéciaux**) SDR (special drawing rights)

dû[1] m due; (cotisation) dues; **payer son** ~ pay one's dues; ~ **30 euros** 30 euros outstanding

dû[2]**, due** adj (à payer) due; **les intérêts dus** the interest due; **en bonne et due forme** in due form

dûment adv duly; ~ **signé** duly signed

dumping m (Info) dumping

duopole m duopoly; ~ **local** spatial duopoly

duplex m duplex; ~ **intégral** (Info) full-duplex

duplicata m duplicate

duplicateur, -trice *adj* duplicatory

duplication *f* copying; ~ **de main-d'œuvre** double manning

dupliquer *vt* copy, duplicate

dur, e *adj* harsh, tough; **être ~ en affaires** drive a hard bargain

durabilité *f* sustainability

durable *adj* (bien, marchandise) durable; (amélioration, hausse) lasting; (déséquilibre, situation) long-standing; **développement ~** sustainable development

durcir ① *vt* (position) harden; ~ **sa politique en matière de** take a harder line on
② **se durcir** *v pron* (mouvement, conflit) intensify

durée *f* duration; (de temps) time span; (de séjour, de règne) length; (de contrat, de bail, de fonctions) term; (Bourse) term to maturity; (d'une option, d'un prêt, d'un emprunt) life; **pendant la ~ des stocks** while stocks last; **pour la ~ de** for the duration of; **pour une ~ déterminée/indéterminée** for a limited/unlimited period; ~ **d'actionnariat** holding period; ~ **aller-retour** round-trip time; ~ **de crédit initiale** original maturity; ~ **à échéance** term to maturity; ~ **d'exécution** execution time; ~ **de fonctionnement** operation time; ~ **forfaitaire** allowed time,

standard time; ~ **garantie** guaranteed term; ~ **d'option** option period; ~ **de perturbation** (Math) disturbance term; ~ **de réalisation** operation time; ~ **de service** length of service; ~ **de transport** transit time; ~ **d'utilisation de ressources** resource time; ~ **de validité d'un brevet** patent life; ~ **de vie** (Bourse) trading life; (V&M) (d'un produit) shelf life; ~ **de vie comptable** depreciable life; ~ **de vie utile** (d'un avoir) useful life

durement *adv* (critiquer) harshly; (affecter) badly; **être ~ touché** (économiquement) be badly hit

durer *vi* last; (conférence, festival) run; ~ **10 jours** last 10 days; ~ **du 6 au 10 mai** run from the 6th to the 10th of May

DUT *abrév* (▸**diplôme universitaire de technologie**) *vocational diploma in technology*

DVD *m* (Info) DVD; **lecteur ~** (sur ordinateur) DVD drive; (machine) DVD player

dynamique¹ *adj* (cadre) upwardly mobile; (croissance, caractère) dynamic

dynamique² *f* dynamics; ~ **industrielle** industrial dynamics; ~ **de marché** market dynamics

dysfonctionnement *m* (de système) malfunctioning

Ee

EAO *abrév* (▸**enseignement assisté par ordinateur**) CAL (computer-aided learning, computer-assisted learning)

e. à p *abrév* (▸**effet à payer**) bp (bill payable)

e. à r *abrév* (▸**effet à recevoir**) br (bill receivable)

eau *f* water; ~ **douce** fresh water; ~ **potable** drinking water; **les Eaux et Forêts** (Admin) ≈ Forestry Commission UK; **~x territoriales** territorial waters; **~x usées** sewage

ébauche *f* (dessin) preliminary sketch; (rapport, réforme) preliminary draft; (publicité) scamp (jarg); **être encore à l'état d'~** be still at a rough stage

ébaucher ① *vt* (programme, projet) draft
② **s'ébaucher** *v pron* (stratégie) begin to take shape; (négociations) start

EBE *abrév* (▸**excédent brut d'exploitation**) GM (gross margin)

e-business *m* e-business

écart *m* (Econ) gap; variance; (Bourse)

spread; (de taux, de revenus) differential; (de statistique) discrepancy; ~ **inflationniste/technologique** inflationary/technological gap; **creuser/réduire l'~** widen/narrow the gap; **rester à l'~ des négociations** keep out of the negociations; ~ **acheteur-vendeur** (Bourse) bid-offer spread; ~ **d'acquisition négatif** negative goodwill; ~ **d'acquisition positif** goodwill; ~ **d'ajustement** (Econ) adjustment gap; ~ **baissier** (Bourse) bear call spread; ~ **budgétaire** budget variance; ~ **de caisse** cash short; ~ **composite** (Banque) composite spread; ~ **de conversion** translation differential; ~ **de cours** (Bourse) quotation spread; ~ **des coûts** marketing marketing cost variance; ~ **entre les cours du comptant** spot rate spread; ~ **entre les cours du terme** forward rate spread; ~ **entre les taux d'intérêt** interest rate differential; ~ **favorable** (Compta) favourable variance BrE, favorable variance AmE; ~ **haussier** (Bourse) bull call spread; ~ **inférieur à zéro** (Bourse) zero-minus tick; ~ **maximal de cours**

(Bourse) maximum price fluctuation; ∼ **minimum de fluctuation** (Bourse) minimum price fluctuation; ∼ **monétaire** money spread; ∼ **moyen** (statistique) mean deviation; ∼ **net** (cours) net change; ∼ **d'option** option spread; ∼ **perpendiculaire** (Bourse) perpendicular spread; ∼ **de prix** price gap; ∼ **de réajustement** adjustment gap; ∼ **récessionniste** recessionary gap; ∼ **de rendement** efficiency variance, yield variance; ∼ **de rendement inverse** reverse yield gap; ∼**s de répartition** splitting spreads: ∼ **des salaires** pay differential, wage differential, ∼ **supérieur à zéro** (Bourse) zero-plus tick; ∼ **sur budget** budget variance; ∼ **sur stock** inventory shortage, inventory shrinkage; ∼ **de taux** rate differential; ∼ **type** (Fin), standard deviation; ∼ **vide** (Bourse) price gap

écarter ⓵ *vt* (possibilité) rule out; (concurrence) stave off; (d'une liste) exclude ⓶ **s'écarter** *v pron* (dévier) **s'∼ de** (direction, norme) deviate from, move away from; **s'∼ de son sujet** get sidetracked

échange *m* (Fin) exchange; (Econ) trade; **ils ne font pas d'∼ dans ce magasin** they don't exchange goods in this shop; **en ∼** in return; **faire un ∼** make an exchange, swap; **faire un ∼ de** exchange, swap; ∼ **d'idées** exchange of ideas; ∼ **d'actifs** asset swap; ∼ **de brevets** patent trading; ∼ **cambiste** treasury swap; ∼**s commerciaux** commerce, trade; ∼ **de contrats** exchange of contracts; ∼ **de créances** debt swap; ∼ **de devises** currency swap; ∼ **de données informatisées** electronic data interchange; ∼ **financier** swap; ∼ **financier à terme** forward swap; ∼**s aux frontières** cross-border trading; ∼ **d'informations commerciales** Trade Data Interchange; ∼ **de lettres** exchange of letters; ∼ **moteur** engine transplant (jarg); ∼**s d'options** options exchanges; ∼ **renouvelable** roller swap; ∼ **standard** replacement; ∼ **syndiqué** syndicated swap; ∼ **de taux d'intérêt** interest rate swap; ∼ **à terme** forward swap; ∼ **à terme de devises** currency swap; ∼ **de valeurs** exchange

échangeable *adj* (article) exchangeable

échanger ⓵ *vt* exchange (contre for); ∼ **une chose contre une autre** trade one thing for another; **'les articles ne sont ni échangés ni repris'** 'no exchanges or returns' ⓶ **s'échanger** *v pron* **s'∼ à** (Bourse) (actions) trade at

échantillon *m* sample; ∼ **commercial** commercial sample; ∼ **d'estimation** estimation sampling; ∼ **d'exploration** discovery sampling; ∼ **gratuit** free sample; ∼ **par quota** quota sample; ∼ **de population** statistical population, population sample; ∼ **représentatif** cross section; ∼ **segmental** (étude de marché) cluster sample;

∼ **statistique** statistical sampling; ∼ **type** representative sample, sample mean

échantillonnage *m* sampling; ∼ **d'activités** activity sampling; ∼ **aléatoire** random sampling; ∼ **par attributs** attribute sampling; ∼ **multiphase** multistage sampling; ∼ **multiple** block sampling, block testing; ∼ **séquentiel** sequential sampling; ∼ **systématique** systematic sampling; ∼ **par tranche** stratified sampling; ∼ **de variables** variables sampling

échantillonner *vtr* (Ind) take a sample of; (Info) sample

échappatoire *f* way out, joker US; ∼ **fiscale** tax loophole

échappement *m* (de gaz) (dispositif) exhaust; ∼ **accidentel** (pollution) accidental discharge

échapper *vi* (éviter) ∼ **à** (danger, constraintes) manage to avoid; (faillite) avoid, escape; ∼ **à l'attention** escape notice; ∼ **à une taxation** (légalement) be exempt from a tax, (illégalement) evade a tax; **l'erreur nous a échappé** we did not spot the mistake

échéance *f* (de dette, facture, quittance, traite) due date; (Banque) term; (Bourse) due date, expiry BrE, expiration AmE; (Com) deadline; (d'un effet, d'un billet) date; (Fin) maturity; **payer avant l'∼** pay before the due date; **payable à ∼** payable when due; **à trois mois d'∼** three months after date; ∼ **fin courant** due at the end of the month; **arriver à ∼** (traite, emprunt) fall due; (assurance, placement) mature; **billet à longue/courte ∼** long-/short-dated bill; ∼ **de contrat à terme** futures expiry date BrE, futures expiration date AmE; ∼ **décalée** mismatched maturity; ∼ **fixée** fixed maturity; ∼ **modifiée** modified accrual; ∼ **moyenne** (des titres) average maturity; ∼ **à terme** time bill; ∼ **d'une traite** currency of a bill

échéancier *m* (Banque) tickler file; (Bourse) bill diary; ∼ **de dette** maturity structure of debt; ∼ **d'effets** (Compta) bill book; ∼ **de paiement** schedule of repayments

échec *m* failure, setback; (Info) failure; **voué à l'échec** doomed to failure; ∼ **d'une société** company failure

échelle *f* scale; **à l'∼ internationale** on an international scale; **à l'∼ mondiale** globally, on a worldwide scale; **sur une grande ∼** on a large scale; **sur une petite ∼** on a small scale; ∼ **d'attitudes** (étude de marché) attitude scale; ∼ **de commission** scale of commission; ∼ **de cotation des emplois** job evaluation scale; ∼ **des effectifs** manning scale; ∼ **d'évaluation** rating scale; ∼ **de grandeur** ratio scale; ∼ **d'intervalle** interval scale; ∼ **mobile** sliding scale; ∼ **nominale** nominal scale; ∼ **d'offre** offering scale; ∼ **de participation** ladder of participation; ∼ **des prix** price range; ∼ ⋯▶

des promotions promotion ladder; ~ **des salaires** pay scale

échelon m (rang) grade; (niveau) level; **à l'~ international** at international level; **gravir les ~s de la hiérarchie** climb the promotion ladder

échelonnement m (de paiements) spreading out; (de congés, départs) staggering; ~ **brut** (Bourse) gross spread; ~ **des échéances** staggering maturities

échelonner vt (paiements, travail) spread; (congés) stagger

échoir vi (investissement) mature; (engagement) become due; **à** ~ (intérêts) accruing

échoué, e adj (discussions) failed

échouer vi (personne, tentative) fail; (négociations, relations) break down; **faire** ~ (plan) abort; (projets) defeat

échu, e adj (Com) overdue, past-due; (Bourse) matured; **non** ~ (Bourse) unmatured; ~ **et impayé** due and unpaid

éclairer vt (question, situation) clarify, throw light on

éclatement m (de parti, de communauté) break-up

éclateur m (Info) burster

école f school; ~ **classique** (Econ) classical economics; ~ **de commerce** business school; ~ **monétariste** (Econ) Currency School UK; ~ **Nationale d'Administration** French School of Public Management; ~ **privée** private school, public school UK; ~ **professionnelle** vocational school; ~ **publique** (système) state education UK, public education US; (lieu) state school UK, public school US; ~ **supérieure** college, polytechnic UK; ~ **supérieure de commerce** graduate school of business

e-collaboration f e-collaboration

écologie f ecology

écologique adj (équilibre, catastrophe) ecological; (produit) environmentally-friendly, green

écologiste[1] adj (candidat) green; (mesure) ecological

écologiste[2] mf (partisan) environmentalist; (chercheur) ecologist

e-commerce m e-commerce

économat m (fonction) bursarship; (bureau) bursar's office

économe[1] adj thrifty

économe[2] mf bursar

économétrique adj econometric

économie f (de pays, de région) economy; (science) economics; (somme économisée) saving; **faire une** ~ **de** save; ~ **d'abondance** economy of abundance; ~ **d'actionnariat** share economy; ~ **appliquée** applied economics; ~ **autarcique** self-sufficient economy; ~ **autofinancée** autoeconomy; ~ **autosuffisante** self-sufficient economy; ~ **de blocus** siege economy; ~ **de champ**

economy of scope; ~ **communale** communal economy; ~ **complexe** complex economy; ~ **de la connaissance** knowledge economy; ~ **développée** advanced economy; ~ **du développement** development economics; ~ **dimensionnelle** economy of size; ~ **dirigée** controlled economy; ~ **domestique** home economics; ~ **dominante** core economy; ~ **du droit** economics of law; ~ **d'échelle** economy of scale; ~ **d'échelle externe** external economy of scale; ~ **d'échelle financière** pecuniary economy of scale; ~ **à l'échelle humaine** human-scale economics; ~ **enclavée** enclave economy; ~ **de l'énergie** energy conservation; ~ **d'engorgement** agglomeration economy; ~ **d'entreposage** warehouse economy; ~ **d'entreprise** business economics; ~ **extérieure** external economy; ~ **externe financière** pecuniary external economy; ~ **fermée** closed economy; ~ **de filiales** branch economy; ~ **financière** financial economy; ~ **industrielle** industrial economics; ~ **de l'information** information economy; ~ **intérieure** internal economy; ~ **libérale** free market economy; ~ **de main-d'œuvre** labour-intensive economy BrE, labor-intensive economy AmE; ~ **manufacturière** manufacturing-based economy; ~ **de marché** free market economy; ~ **de marché contrôlée** controlled market economy; ~ **de marché intégrale** pure market economy; ~ **mature** mature economy; ~ **minéralière** mineral-based economy; ~ **mixte** mixed economy; ~ **mondiale** global economy, world economy; ~ **monétaire** monetary economics; ~ **de monoculture** one-crop economy; ~ **des mouvements** motion economy; ~ **nationale** national economy; ~ **néo-classique** new classical economics; ~ **normative** normative economics; ~ **numérique** digital economy; ~ **de l'occupation des sols** land economy; ~ **de l'offre** supply-side economics; ~ **organisationnelle** organizational economics; ~ **ouverte** open economy; ~ **parallèle** black economy; ~ **de partenariat** wider share ownership, stakeholder economy; ~ **de pénurie** shortage economy; ~ **planifiée** centrally-planned economy; ~ **de plein emploi** full employment economy; ~ **politique** political economy; ~ **rurale** rural economy; ~ **de services** service economy; ~ **sociale de marché** social market economy; ~ **souterraine** underground economy; ~ **de subsistance** subsistence economy; ~ **de succursale** branch economy; ~ **en surchauffe** overheated economy; ~ **de télétravail** networking economy; ~ **transactionnelle** transaction cost economics; ~ **des transferts** grants economics; ~ **des transports** transport economics; ~ **de troc** barter economy; ~ **urbaine** agglomeration economy, urban economics

économies *f pl* savings; **faire des ~ d'énergie** save energy; **~ contractuelles** contractual savings; **~ de pays à industrialisation récente** newly-industrialized economies

économique *adj* (peu coûteux) cheap, economical; (politique, crise) economic

économiquement *adv* economically

économiser *vt* (argent, énergie) save; (réduire ses dépenses) economize; **~ sur qch** economize on sth

économiseur *m* fuel-saving device; **~ d'écran** (Info) screen saver

économiste *mf* economist; **~ en chef** chief economist; **~ d'entreprise** business economist; **~ vulgaire** vulgar economist

écoproduit *m* environmentally-friendly product, clean product, green product

écosystème *m* ecosystem

écoulé, e *adj* (précédent) past; (épuisé) exhausted; (vendu) sold; **la semaine/saison ~e** the past week/season; **les stocks sont ~s** the stocks are exhausted; **la viande ~e était contaminée** the meat sold was contaminated

écoulement *m* (Com) distribution and sale; (Fin) (de billets) circulation

écouler ① *vt* (stock, produit) sell ② **s'écouler** *v pron* (produit) move, sell; **s'~ lentement** move slowly, sell slowly

écoute *f* (Média) audience; **heure de grande ~** (radio) peak listening time; (TV) prime time; **~ familiale** (radio, télévision) family audience

écran *m* (Info) screen; **~ d'aide** help screen; **~ couleur** colour display BrE, color display AmE; **~ d'ordinateur** computer screen; **~ principal** main screen; **~ publicitaire** (télévision, radio) commercial break; **~ tactile** touch(-sensitive) screen; **~ de télévision** television screen; **~ de terminal** monitor, terminal screen; **~ VGA** video graphics array card; **~ vidéo** video display

écrasement *m* (Info, Transp) crash; **~ de la tête** (Info) head crash (jarg)

écraser: s'~ *v pron* (avion) crash

écrémage *m* (sélection) creaming off; **~ du marché** (politique des prix) market skimming

écrémer *vt* (sélectionner) cream off

écrire *vt* write; **~ de nouveau** rewrite

écrit¹, e *adj* written; **par ~** in writing; **la presse ~e** print journalism; **épreuve ~e** written test

écrit² *m* (document) document; **l'~** the printed word; **l'~ diffamatoire** libel

écriture *f* (Compta), (inscription) entry, item; **~ d'annulation** reversing entry; **~ d'attente** suspense entry; **~ de clôture** closing entry; **~ de compensation** clearing entry, offsetting entry; **~ comptable** accounting entry; **~ de contre-passement** reserve entry; **~ de contrepartie** contra

entry; **~ au grand livre** ledger posting; **~ informatique** paperless entry; **~ pour mémoire** memo item, memorandum item; **~ multiple** compound entry; **~ non-réglée** outstanding entry; **~ originale** original entry; **~ passée au crédit** credit entry; **~ passée au débit** debit entry; **~ rectificative** adjusting entry, correcting entry

écritures *f pl* (Compta) accounts; **tenir les ~** keep the accounts; **~ extraordinaires** unusual items

écrivain *m* writer; **~ indépendant** freelance writer

ECU *abrév* (▶**unité monétaire européenne**) ECU (European Currency Unit)

éd. *abrév* (▶**édition**) ed. (edition)

e-démocratie *f* e-democracy

EDF *abrév* (**Électricité de France**) *French electricity company*

EDI *abrév* (▶**Échange de Données Informatisées**) EDI (electronic data interchange)

édicté, e *adj* enacted (**par** by)

édicter *vt* (peine, règle) decree; (loi, norme) enact

édit. *abrév* (▶**édition**) ed. (edition)

éditer *vt* (Info) edit; (livre) publish; (cassette, CD) release

éditeur, -trice *m,f* (de livre, de musique) publisher; (Info) editor; **~ d'écran** screen editor; **~ de ligne** line editor; **~ de logiciel** software house; **~ pleine page** full-screen editor; **~ de texte** text editor

édition *f* (Info) editing; (de livres) publishing; (de CD, de film) release; (un livre) edition; **~ commémorative** commemorative edition, anniversary publication; **~ électronique** electronic publishing; **~ graphique** graphical editing; **~ revue et corrigée** revised edition; **~ à tirage limité** limited edition

éditorial *m* editorial; **~ vendu à plusieurs journaux** syndicated column

effaçable *adj* (Info) (mémoire) erasable

effacement *m* (Info) (de texte, de mots) deletion; (de mémoire) blanking; **touche d'~** delete key

effacer *vt* (texte) delete; (bande) wipe; (mémoire) blank, erase; (écran) clear

effectif¹, -ive *adj* (aide, contrôle) real; (durée) actual; (contribution) effective; **devenir ~** come into effect

effectif² *m* workforce, labour force BrE, labor force AmE; **à ~ pléthorique** overstaffed

effectivement *adv* effectively

effectuer *vt* (paiement) make; (étude, enquête) conduct, carry out; (transaction) carry out; **~ des démarches** take steps; **~ un paiement** make a payment; **~ une vente** make a sale; **~ un versement** make a payment

e

effet *m* (conséquence) effect; (Fin) bill; **sous l'~ de la dévaluation** under the impact of devaluation; **~ secondaire** side effect; **avec ~ à compter du** with effect from; **avec ~ rétroactif** backdated; **avoir un ~ sur** affect; **les résultats sont en ~ excellents** the results are indeed excellent; **~ à l'acceptation** acceptance bill; **~ accepté** accepted bill; **~ d'annonce** (Pol) announcement effect; **~ avalisé** guaranteed bill; **~ bancaire** bank bill; **~ en cascade** (Econ) ripple effect; **~ en circulation** outstanding item; **~ de commerce** bill of exchange; **~ de complaisance** accommodation paper; **~ de contagion** (Econ) spread effect; **~ dissuasif** deterrent; **~ douteux** unsafe paper; **~ d'éloignement** alienation effect; **~ à encaisser** bill for collection, draft for collection; **~ escomptable** eligible bill; **~ escompté** discounted bill; **~ euro** euro effect; **~ d'éviction** (Econ, Fin) crowding out; **~ externe** (Econ) externality; **~ financier** finance paper, financial paper; **~ d'incitation** (Econ) incentive effect; **~ d'inertie** (Pol) inertial effect; **~ irréductible** (Envir) undepletable externality; **~ juridique** (Fisc) legal effect; **~ de levier** gearing BrE, leverage AmE; **~ de levier négatif** reverse gearing BrE, reverse leverage AmE; **~ libre** clean bill; **~ menace** (Econ) threat effect; **~ multiplicateur** (Econ) multiplier effect; **~ de nantissement** collateral bill; **~ négociable** negotiable instrument; **~ nocif** (Envir) harmful effect; **~ non-acceptable** ineligible paper; **~ payable à vue** bill payable at sight; **~ à payer** bill payable, note payable; **~ périmé** expired bill; **~ pervers du prix** (Econ) perverse price; **~ d'une police** (Assur) commencement of a policy; **~ au porteur** bearer bill; **~ de prix** price effect; **~ de rappel** (publicité) carry-over effect; **~ à recevoir** bill receivable, note receivable; **~ refusé** dishonoured bill BrE, dishonored bill AmE; **~ de règlement** settlement draft; **~ de remous** (Econ) backwash effect; **~ de retombées** (Econ) spillover effect; **~ rétroactif sur salaire** back pay; **~ de revenu** (Econ) income effect; **~ richesse** (Econ) wealth effect; **~ sans risque** (Bourse) risk-free debt instrument; **~ de serre** (Envir) greenhouse effect; **~ de substitution** substitution effect; **~ tiré** drawn bill

efficace *adj* (action, mesure, remède) effective; (personne, dispositif, machine) efficient

efficacement *adv* effectively

efficacité *f* (d'action) effectiveness; (de personne, machine) efficiency; **~ d'allocation** allocative efficiency; **~ de la direction** managerial effectiveness; **~ d'exploitation** operating efficiency; **~ publicitaire** advertising effectiveness; **~ technique** technical efficiency

efficience *f* efficiency; **~ des échanges** exchange efficiency; **~ maximale** maximum efficiency, top-level efficiency

efficient, e *adj* efficient

effleurement *m* light touch; **à ~** (Info) (clavier) touch-sensitive

effluent *m* effluent; **~ gazeux** exhaust gas, waste gas; **~ industriel** industrial waste

effondrement *m* (de prix, d'économie, des cours) collapse; **provoquer l'~ du prix plancher** cause the bottom to drop out of the market; **~ du marché** stock market collapse

effondrer: s'~ *v pron* (régime, prix, monnaie) collapse

effort *m* (physique, intellectuel) effort; (subvention) financial aid; (mise de fonds) investment, financial outlay; **représenter un gros ~ financier** represent a substantial outlay

effraction *f* (Droit) forcible entry; **~ informatique** hacking

effréné, e *adj* (concurrence, spéculation) frantic; (ambition, gaspillage) unbridled

égal, e *adj* equal; **augmentation/baisse ~e ou inférieure à 2%** rise/drop of 2% or less; **combattre à armes ~s** be on an equal footing

égaler *vt* equal, match

égalisation *f* (des revenus) levelling out; **~ des chances** bringing about equality of opportunity

égaliser ①*vt* equalize ② **s'égaliser** *v pron* (prix) even out

égalitarisme *m* egalitarianism; **~ spécifique** (Econ) specific egalitarianism

égalitariste *adj* egalitarian

égalité *f* equality; **~ des chances** equal opportunity; **~ des chances face à l'emploi** equal employment opportunities; **~ des droits des travailleurs** fair employment; **~ des salaires** equal pay

égard *m* consideration; **à cet ~** in this respect; **à bien des ~s** in many repects

e-gouvernement *m* e-government

éjecter *vt* eject

éjection *f* ejection

élaboration *f* (de projet) development; (de document) drafting; **~ de l'image** (V&M) imaging; **~ de programmes** (Info) programming; **~ des stratégies** strategy formulation; **~ des tarifs** rate setting, rate formulation

élaborer *vt* (plan, stratégie) develop

élan *m* momentum; **donner de l'~ à** (entreprise, réforme) give impetus to

élargir *vt* (activités) broaden; (moyens, secteur) expand; (débat) widen; (contacts, droit) extend; **~ son champ d'action** widen one's field of action

élargissement *m* (de réforme) extension; (de budget, d'activités) expansion; **~ de l'assiette fiscale** tax base broadening; **~ de la gamme** extension of the product

range, line extension; ~ **de l'UE**
enlargement of the EU

élasticité f (de l'offre, du marché, des prix)
elasticity; **à l'~ égale à 1** (Econ) unitary
elastic; ~ **des anticipants** elasticity of
expectations; ~ **d'anticipation** elasticity of
anticipation; ~ **d'arc** arc elasticity; ~ **de la
demande** elasticity of demand; ~ **de la
demande et de l'offre** elasticity of demand
and supply; ~ **de la demande par rapport
au revenu** income-elasticity of demand; ~
fiscale tax buoyancy, tax elasticity; ~
négative negative elasticity; ~ **de l'offre**
elasticity of supply; ~ **ponctuelle** point
elasticity; ~ **des prix** price elasticity, price
flexibility; ~ **de substitution** elasticity of
substitution; ~ **unitaire** unitary elasticity

élastique adj (demande) elastic; ~ **par
rapport au revenu** income-elastic

électeur, -trice m,f elector, voter; **les ~s**
the electorate; ~ **indécis** floating voter

élection f election; ~ **échelonnée**
staggered election; ~ **éliminatoire** runoff
election US; ~ **fédérale** federal election US;
~s législatives general election; ~ **locale**
local election; ~ **partielle** by-election UK,
off-year election US; **~s présidentielles**
presidential election

électronique[1] f electronics

électronique[2] adj electronic; **adresse ~**
e-mail address; **argent/commerce ~**
e-money/e-commerce

élément m (d'appareil) component;
(d'ensemble) element; (Info) item; ~ **d'actif**
asset; ~ **d'actif corporel** tangible asset; ~
d'actif couvert hedged asset; ~ **d'actif
national** domestic asset; ~ **d'activité**
activity element; ~ **d'activité
administrative** administrative activity
element; ~ **des administrations centrales**
central government item; ~ **d'arrêt** (Info)
stop bit; ~ **du capital** capital instrument; ~
au choix (Bourse) optional feature; ~
commun (dans une copropriété) common
element US; ~ **constitutif** component part;
~ **constitutif de l'impôt** tax component; ~
du coût cost factor; ~ **éligible** qualifying
item; ~ **encastré** fitment; ~ **exceptionnel**
extraordinary item; ~ **extraordinaire**
extraordinary item; ~ **de la loi** piece of
legislation; ~ **de passif couvert** hedged
liability; ~ **du passif-dépôts** deposit
liabilities; ~ **pondérateur** (Econ) balancing
item

élevage m (de bétail) livestock farming; ~
intensif intensive livestock farming; ~
industriel factory farming; ~ **piscicole** fish
farm; ~ **de volailles** poultry farm

élévateur m (manutention) elevator; ~ **à
godets** bucket elevator; ~ **de grain** grain
elevator

élevé, e adj high; **trop ~** too high

élève mf pupil, student; **~-programmeur**

trainee programmer

élever: s'~ à v pron (bénéfices,
investissements) come to; (offre, prix, chiffre d'affaire)
stand at; **la facture des réparations s' élève
à 750 euros** the repair bill comes to 750
euros

éleveur, -euse m,f stockbreeder; ~ **de
bovins/porcs** cattle/pig breeder

éligible adj eligible

élimination f (d'actifs) stripping; (de déchets)
disposal; ~ **d'actifs non rentables** asset
stripping; ~ **des déchets** waste disposal; ~
des ordures ménagères refuse disposal; ~
progressive phasing out

éliminatoire f (élection) runoff US

éliminer vt (candidat) eliminate; (déchets)
remove; ~ **à la présélection** screen out; ~
progressivement phase out

élire vt elect; ~ **qn au conseil
d'administration** elect sb to the board; ~
domicile take up residence; (Droit) elect a
domicile

élite f elite

éloigné, e adj (dans l'espace) distant; (dans le
passé) remote

éluder vt (impôt) evade

e-mail m e-mail, email; **envoyer un ~ à qn**
send sb an e-mail, e-mail sb

émancipation f emancipation

émarger ① vt (Admin) (document, circulaire)
sign
② vi ~ **à l'université** be on the payroll of
the university; ~ **à 10 000 euros** draw 10,000
euros

emballage m packaging; ~
biodégradable biodegradable packaging; ~
bulle blister packaging; ~ **en caisses** case
packaging; ~ **en carton** carton, cardboard
box; ~ **composite** composite packaging; ~
export-départ usine (livraison) ex works
export packing; ~ **familial** family-size pack;
~ **sous film rétractable** shrink-packaging,
shrink-wrapping; ~ **imperméable**
waterproof packaging; ~ **intermodal**
intermodal packaging; ~ **métallique** metal
packaging; ~ **primaire** primary package; ~
trompeur deceptive packaging

emballé, e adj (enveloppé) wrapped; (dans un
carton) packed

emballer vt (dans du papier) wrap (up); (dans
un carton) pack (up)

emballeur, -euse m,f packer; ~
d'exportations export packer

embarcadère m (dans un port) pier

embarcation f boat; ~ **de service** service
boat

embargo m embargo; **lever l'~** lift the
embargo; ~ **commercial** trade embargo

embarqué, e adj (Info) on-board; (Transp)
(connaissement) shipped on board; ~ **à bord**
shipped aboard

embarquement m (montée à bord) ⋯⋙

boarding; (prise à bord) embarkation; (départ)
departure

embarquer vt (prendre à bord) take aboard;
(cargaison) load; (passagers) board

embauche f appointment UK, hiring;
salaire d'~ starting salary; ~
préférentielle direct discrimination UK; ~
et renvoi hiring and firing

embaucher vt (personnel) hire, take on; ~
et renvoyer hire and fire

emboîtage m (manutention) nesting

emboîter vt (Info) nest

embouteillage m (en ville) traffic jam; (sur
autoroute) tailback; (de système) bottleneck

embranchement m (chemin de fer) branch
line; ~ **particulier** siding BrE

embrasser vt (carrière, profession) pursue

émergent, e adj emerging; **les marchés
~s** emerging markets

émetteur¹, -trice adj (Fin) issuing; **banque
émettrice** issuing bank

émetteur², -trice m,f (de chèque) drawer;
(Bourse) issuer; (Média) transmitter; ~ **de
cartes** card issuer; ~ **de cartes de crédit**
credit card issuer; ~ **de dette** liability
issuer; ~ **d'engagement** liability issuer

émettre vt (chèque) draw, write; (obligation)
issue, launch; (à la radio, télévision) broadcast;
~ **par adjudication** issue by tender; ~ **des
actions à l'escompte** issue shares at a
discount; ~ **des actions dans le public** go
public; ~ **un emprunt** float a loan, raise a
loan; ~ **une lettre de crédit** issue a letter of
credit; ~ **de nouveau reissue;** ~ **un nouvel
emprunt** refloat a loan; ~ **une objection**
make an objection, raise an objection; ~ **des
obligations** launch a bond issue; ~ **un signal
sonore** bleep

émeute f riot, civil commotion; **~s,
troubles de l'ordre public et grèves** riots,
civil commotions and strikes

e-migration f e-migration

éminent, e adj distinguished

émis, e adj (Fin, Bourse) issued; **non ~**
unissued; ~ **et en circulation** issued and
outstanding

émission f (d'emprunt) flotation; (d'actions)
issue; (Envir) emission; (Média) broadcast,
transmission; (programme) programme; **faire
une ~** (Média) broadcast; ~ **d'actions** stock
issue; ~ **d'actions aux ayants-droit** rights
issue; ~ **d'actions gratuites** bonus issue
UK, scrip issue; ~ **d'actions de numéraire**
share issue for cash; ~ **de bons** bond issue,
bond issue operation; ~ **de capital** equity
issue; ~ **de chèque sans provision**
cheque-kiting BrE, check-kiting AmE; ~ **de
chèques** cheque issue BrE, check issue AmE;
~ **de conversion** conversion issue; ~ **en
différé** prerecorded broadcast; ~ **à
diffusion restreinte** (Bourse) private issue;
~ **de dioxyde de carbone** carbon dioxide

emission; ~ **en direct** live broadcast, live
program AmE; ~ **sur l'euromarché des
capitaux** Eurocapital market issue; ~
d'euro-obligations Eurobond issue; ~
excédentaire overissue; ~ **fiduciaire**
fiduciary issue, note issue; ~ **garantie**
guaranteed issue; ~ **de gaz
d'échappement** exhaust emission; ~
globale (pollution) global emission; ~
hasardeuse sticky deal; ~ **initiale** primary
issue; ~ **à ligne ouverte** phone-in
programme BrE, phone-in program AmE; ~
locale (pollution) local emission; ~ **d'une
obligation à court terme** short-term note
issuance facility; ~ **d'une obligation
subordonnée** subordinated bond issue; ~
d'obligations bond issue, bond issue
operation; ~ **de polluants
atmosphériques** air pollution emission; ~
publique public issue; (titres) public
distribution; ~ **secondaire** junior issue US;
~ **sonore** noise emission; ~ **d'une
télécopie** fax transmission; ~ **de titres** (par
société commerciale) corporate issue; ~ **de
titres nationaux** domestic issue; ~ **de
valeurs d'État** government stock issue, tap
issue

emmagasinage m storage, warehousing

emmagasiner vt store

emménager vi move in; ~ **dans des
locaux plus grands** move to larger premises

émoluments m pl (salaire) remuneration;
(de notaire, d'huissier, d'avocat) fees

empan m span; ~ **visuo-manuel** (Admin)
eye-hand span; ~ **visuo-vocal** (Admin) eye-
voice span

empaquetage m packaging

empaqueter vt package

emparer: s'~ de v pron (nouveau produit,
actions) snap up

empattement m (Info) serif

empêchement m unforeseen difficulty;
avoir un ~ de dernière minute be detained
at the last minute; **en cas d'~** if anything
should crop up

empêcher vt prevent; (concurrence) block;
(croissance) hamper; ~ **d'exercer** (Bourse) bar;
(Info) inhibit; **pour ~ toute tentative d'OPA**
to stave off ou ward off any takeover attempt

emphatique adj emphatic

empiètement m encroachment (sur on)

empiéter vt encroach on; ~ **sur** (droits)
impinge on

empilage m stack; ~ **double** (conteneurs)
double stack

empiler vt stack; ~ **en doubles piles**
(conteneurs) double-stack

empirer vi deteriorate, get worse

empirique adj empirical

emplacement m site; ~ **imposé** (publicité)
appointed space; ~ **indéterminé** (presse) run
of paper; ~ **isolé** (presse) solus position; (dans

un magasin) island; ∼ **le long d'une route**
(pour un panneau publicitaire) roadside site; ∼ **de
premier choix** prime location; ∼ **de la
signature** letterfoot

emploi *m* (embauche) employment; (poste de
travail) job, situation; (utilisation) use; **être sans
∼** be out of work; ∼ **agricole** agricultural
job; ∼ **annexe** additional job, sideline; ∼ **de
bureau** clerical work; ∼ **civil** civilian
employment; ∼ **de départ** entry-level job; ∼
donnant droit à la retraite pensionable
employment; ∼ **dans la fonction publique**
public service employment; ∼ **de fonds** use
of funds; ∼ **intérimaire** (situation) temporary
job; ∼ **involontaire** involuntary
employment; ∼ **à mi-temps** part-time job,
part-time employment; ∼ **permanent**
permanent employment; ∼ **à plein temps**
full-time job, full-time employment; ∼**s
précédents** work history; ∼ **principal**
central occupation; ∼ **protégé** sheltered
employment; ∼ **sans avenir** dead-end job
BrE, blind-alley job AmE; ∼ **secondaire**
sideline job; ∼ **du secteur tertiaire** service
job; ∼**s successifs** employment record; ∼
temporaire temporary job; ∼ **du temps**
timetable; ∼ **à temps partiel** part-time
employment; ∼ **à vie** lifetime employment

employé, e *m,f* (travailleur) employee; ∼ **de
banque** bank clerk; ∼ **de bureau** office
worker; ∼ **aux écritures** accounts clerk; ∼
à l'essai probationary employee,
probationer; ∼ **de magasin** sales assistant,
shop assistant BrE, sales clerk AmE; ∼ **à mi-
temps** part-time employee; ∼ **modèle** model
worker; ∼ **occasionnel** casual worker; ∼ **à
plein temps** full-time employee, full-timer;
∼ **des postes** postal worker; ∼ **de
production** production worker; ∼
temporaire casual worker; ∼ **à temps
partiel** part-time employee, part-timer

employer *vt* (avoir à son service) employ;
(embaucher) hire; (utiliser) use; **être employé à
plein temps/à mi-temps** be employed full-
time/part-time; ∼ **la manière forte** use
strong-arm tactics

employeur, -euse *m,f* employer; ∼
désigné specified employer

emporter *vt* (position) take; ∼ **l'accord de
qn** get sb's agreement; **l'∼ sur** (équipe,
candidat) outperform; **∼ le morceau** (infrml)
swing a deal (infrml); **emporté et livré**
collected and delivered

empotage *m* (de conteneur) stuffing; ∼ **et
dépotage** stuffing and stripping

empoter *vt* (conteneur) stuff BrE, van AmE

emprise *f* expropriation

emprisonnement *m* imprisonment

emprunt *m* (action) borrowing; (somme) loan;
∼ **d'actions** share borrowing, stock
borrowing; ∼ **bancaire** bank loan; ∼
boursier securities borrowing; ∼ **de
cadres** executive leasing; ∼ **de capitaux**

étrangers borrowing abroad; ∼ **consolidé**
consolidation loan; ∼ **de conversion**
conversion loan; ∼ **à court terme** short-
term loan; ∼ **d'État** government loan, public
loan; ∼ **à faible intérêt** low-interest loan; ∼
de fonds externes borrowing of external
funds; ∼ **garanti** collateral loan, secured
loan; ∼ **gigogne** piggyback loan; ∼
hypothécaire mortgage loan; ∼
hypothécaire plafonné closed-end
mortgage; ∼ **indexé** index-tied loan, indexed
loan; ∼ **industriel** industrial loan; ∼
irrécouvrable loan loss; ∼ **lié** tied loan; ∼
municipal municipal bond US; ∼ **non-
garanti** unsecured loan; ∼ **obligataire** bond
issue, bond loan; ∼**-obligation** bond
liability, bond payable; ∼ **parallèle** parallel
loan; ∼ **à plus d'un an** long-term debt; ∼ **à
prime** premium loan; ∼ **public** public loan;
∼ **de redressement** rehabilitation import
loan; ∼ **à risques** nonaccruing loan; ∼
sans intérêt interest-free loan; ∼
subordonné subordinated loan; ∼ **à taux
fixe** fixed-rate loan; ∼ **à taux flottant**
floating-rate loan; ∼ **à taux nul** interest-free
loan; ∼ **à taux variable** floating-rate loan,
roll-over loan; ∼ **à terme** time loan; ∼ **de
titres** security borrowing

emprunter *vt* borrow; ∼ **à** borrow from; ∼
de l'argent borrow money; ∼ **à 10%** borrow
at 10%; ∼ **sur 15 ans à 5%** take out a loan
over 15 years at 5%; ∼ **de l'argent sur qch**
raise money on sth; ∼ **à court/long terme**
borrow short/long; ∼ **sur hypothèque**
borrow on mortgage; ∼ **à intérêt** borrow at
interest; ∼ **sans intérêt** borrow interest-free;
∼ **sur titres** borrow on securities; ∼ **à vue**
borrow at call

emprunteur, -euse *m,f* borrower; ∼ **de
premier ordre** premier borrower BrE, prime
borrower AmE; ∼ **public** sovereign borrower;
∼ **du secteur privé** private sector
borrower; ∼ **très solvable** premier
borrower BrE, prime borrower AmE

emprunt-logement *m* housing bond

émulateur *m* (Info) emulator; ∼ **de
terminal** terminal emulator

émulation *f* emulation

émuler *vt* emulate

émulsion *f* emulsion; ∼ **de pétrole brut**
crude oil emulsion

ENA *abrév* (▶**École Nationale
d'Administration**) French School of Public
Management

ENBAMM *abrév* (**entreprise non-
bancaire admise au marché monétaire**)
non-bank financial institution

encadrement *m* management; ∼ **du
crédit** credit control, credit squeeze; ∼
réduit lean management

encadrer *vt* (personnel) supervise; (Econ)
(crédit) restrict; (prix) control

encaissable *adj* (chèque) cashable; ∼ **par** ⋯⟶

anticipation retractable

encaisse f (disponibilités) cash in hand, cash balance; (sommes, valeurs) cash; ~ **fractionnaire** fractional cash reserve; ~ **or** bullion

encaissement m (Fin) (de cotisation) collection; (de chèque) cashing; (de dividende) receipt; **frais d'**~ transaction costs; ~ **par anticipation** retraction; ~ **de comptes clients** collection of accounts; ~ **d'un effet** collection of a bill; ~ **de primes** collection of premiums; ~ **d'une traite** collection of a bill; ~ **d'une tranche de prêt** drawdown

encaisser vt (chèque) cash; (paiement) collect; **non encaissé** uncashed/uncollected

encaisseur, -euse m,f (de cheque) payee; (de traite) collector; ~ **de loyers** rent collector

encan m auction; **être à l'**~ be up for auction; **mettre qch à l'**~ put sth up for auction

encart m insert; ~ **broché** (presse, édition) tip-in; ~ **dépliant** gatefold; ~ **publicitaire** promotional insert; ~ **à volets** gatefold

enceinte f (espace) (de tribunal) interior; (dans une cérémonie, fête) enclosure

enchaînement m (Info) concatenation; ~ **arrière** (Ind) backward linkage; ~ **avant** (Ind) forward linkage

enchère f (offre) bid; (activité) bidding; **faire une** ~ make a bid; **vente aux** ~s auction; **vendre qch aux** ~s sell sth by auction; ~ **à la criée** open-outcry auction market; ~ **électronique** e-bid; ~ **initiale** opening bid; ~ **au rabais** Dutch auction

enchérir vt (Bourse) bid; ~ **sur qn** outbid sb, bid more than sb; ~ **sur une offre/un prix** make a higher bid

enchérisseur, -euse m,f (Bourse) bidder

enclavé, e adj landlocked

enclos m enclosure; ~ **avec habitation** curtilage

encodage m (Info) encoding

encoder vt encode

encombrant, e adj (objet) bulky

encombrement m (Info) (en mémoire) storage requirements; (Transp) (circulation) traffic congestion, traffic jam; ~ **du marché** (Econ) glut on the market

encourageant, e adj encouraging

encouragement m encouragement; (incitation) incentive; ~ **à l'investissement** investment incentive; ~ **du personnel** staff incentivization; ~ **à la production** production incentive

encourager vt encourage; (idées nouvelles) promote; (soutien) stimulate; (motiver) incentivize; (paticipants) encourage

encourir vt incur; ~ **des dépenses** incur cost, incur expenses; ~ **des dettes** incur debts

encours m amount outstanding; ~ **de**

crédit outstanding credit; ~ **de la dette** outstanding debt; ~ **sous forme d'acceptation** acceptance liability; ~ **de pension minimum** minimum pension liability; ~ **de prêts** outstanding loans; ~ **des prêts hypothécaires** outstanding mortgage loans

encryptage m (Info) encryption

encrypter vt (Info) encrypt

enculturation f enculturation

endémique adj endemic

endetté, e adj (personne, entreprise) in debt; **être très** ~ be heavily in debt; **être** ~ **de 1 million d'euros** be 1 million euros in debt

endettement m debt; ~ **du consommateur** consumer debt, consumer leveraging

endetter [1] vt put into debt [2] **s'endetter** v pron get into debt (**auprès de** with)

endommagé, e adj damaged; **non** ~ undamaged; ~ **en cours de route** (Transp) damaged in transit; ~ **à l'origine** country-damaged

endos m (Banque) endorsement; ~ **conditionnel** qualified endorsement

endossataire mf (Banque) endorsee

endossement m (Banque) endorsement; ~ **en blanc** blank endorsement; ~ **de complaisance** accommodation endorsement

endosser vt (Fin) endorse; **non endossé** unendorsed; **endossé par la banque** bank-endorsed

endosseur m endorser; ~ **par complaisance** accommodation maker, accommodation party

endroit m (lieu) place; **à l'**~ **des travaux** ex works

endurance f staying power

énergie f energy, power; ~ **éolienne** wind power; ~ **hydro-électrique** hydroelectric power; ~ **marémotrice** tidal power; ~ **nouvelle** alternative energy; ~ **nucléaire** nuclear energy; ~ **solaire** solar power; ~ **de substitution** alternative energy; ~ **thermique** thermal energy; ~ **verte** green energy

enfant mf child; ~ **à charge** (Fisc) dependent child

enficher vt (Info) plug in

enfourchement m ~ **d'impôt** tax straddle

enfreindre vt (Droit) infringe, break; ~ **la loi** break the law

enfuir: s'~ v pron (Droit) abscond

engagement m commitment; (embauche) appointment; ~**s financiers** financial commitments; **prendre un** ~ make a commitment; **ne pas honorer/respecter ses** ~**s** fail to honour one's commitments; **sans** ~ **de votre** ~ with no obligation on your part; ~ **d'acheter** (Bourse) take-or-pay contract; ~ **actuariel** (Assur) actuarial liability; ~ **actuel** (Compta) undischarged commitment; ~ **antérieur** previous engagement; ~ **à la baisse** (Bourse) bear commitment; ~ **en cours** (Compta) outstanding commitment; ~ **de dépenses** (Econ) hypothecation; ~ **écrit** (Droit) bond; ~ **excédentaire** overcommitment; ~ **ferme** firm commitment; ~ **formel** (Droit) covenant; ~ **de fret** booking note; ~ **de garantie** (actions privilégiées) guarantee agreement; ~ **à la hausse** bull commitment; ~ **hypothécaire** mortgage commitment; ~ **d'hypothèque générale** general obligation bond US; ~ **d'investissement** capital commitment; ~ **obligataire moral** (Bourse) moral obligation bond; ~ **permanent** continuing commitment; ~ **du personnel** staff commitment

engager [1] *vt* (personnel) hire; ~ **des dépenses** incur expenses; ~ **des frais** incur cost; ~ **des poursuites** take legal action [2] **s'engager** *v pron* s'~ **à** commit oneself to; s'~ **à faire qch** undertake to do sth; s'~ **à payer** promise to pay; s'~ **par contrat** sign a contract, sign a legal agreement; s'~ **par contrat à faire qch** contract to do sth; s'~ **dans** embark on

engendrer *vt* (croissance) be conducive to; (confiance) breed

englober *vt* comprise

engorgement *m* (Econ) un ~ **du marché** a glut of products on the market

engorger *vt* (marché) glut

engrais *m* (agriculture) fertilizer; ~ **azoté** nitrogen fertilizer; ~ **chimique** chemical fertilizer

engrenage *m* (Transp) gears; ~ **planétaire** (Transp) planetary gear

enjeu *m* stake; l'~ **est très important** the stakes are high

enlèvement *m* removal; ~ **de l'excédent** surplus stripping; ~ **par route** collection on wheels

enlever *vt* remove; à ~ **à bord** ex ship

enliser: s'~ **dans** *v pron* get bogged down in

ennui *m* trouble; **avoir des ~s** have problems, be in trouble; **avoir des ~s avec le fisc** fall foul of the tax authorities

énoncé *m* statement; ~ **des clauses et conditions** statement of terms and conditions; ~ **des objectifs** statement of objectives

enquête *f* investigation, inquiry; (de marché) survey; **faire une ~** make enquiries; **ouvrir/mener une ~** set up/lead an investigation *ou* inquiry; **une ~ par téléphone** a telephone survey; l'~ **suit son cours** the investigation is continuing; ~ **administrative** public inquiry; ~ **sur les antécédents** background investigation; ~ **d'attitude** attitude survey; ~ **d'autorisation** licensing examination; ~ **auprès des consommateurs** consumer survey; ~ **sur les dépenses de consommation** consumer expenditure survey; ~ **sur les dépenses publiques** public expenditure survey; ~ **par échantillonnage** judgment sample; ~ **exhaustive** full-scale investigation; ~ **indépendante** independent inquiry; ~ **judiciaire** judicial inquiry; ~ **sans mandat** warrantless investigation; ~ **de motivations** motivational research; ~ **d'opinion** opinion survey; ~ **de police** police investigation; ~ **préliminaire** preliminary investigation; ~ **par sondage** sample survey; ~ **sur le terrain** field survey; ~ **tous azimuts** across-the-board investigation

enquêter *vt* investigate; (V&M) conduct a survey; ~ **sur** make investigations into; (crime) investigate

enquêteur, -trice *m,f* investigation officer; (étude de marché) interviewer, field investigator; ~ **sur le terrain** (étude de marché) field worker

enrayer *vt* (inflation) stamp out

enregistré, e *adj* recorded, on tape; **non ~** unrecorded; ~ **à l'avance** prerecorded; ~ **sur les livres** (Compta) in the books

enregistrement *m* (d'une société) registration, incorporation; (d'une commande) booking; (à l'aéroport) check-in; (Info) (de données) recording; (article de base de données) record; ~ **des archives** (Info) archival storage; ~ **de commande** (V&M) order entry; ~ **comptable** accounting entry; ~ **net** net register; ~ **quotidien des transactions** (Bourse) street book (jarg); ~ **de société** incorporation

enregistrer *vt* (gains) account for; (Compta) (somme, transaction) enter, post; (Bourse) record; (à l'aéroport) check in; ~ **un bénéfice** show a surplus; **faire ~** (Com) register; ~ **des gains** post gains, enter gains; ~ **une hausse** (à la Bourse) register a high; ~ **une perte** carry a loss; ~ **une perte de** show a loss of; ~ **une provision contre** (Compta) write off

enregistreur *m* recorder; ~ **à tambour** (Info) drum plotter

enrichi, e *adj* (Info) enhanced

enrichir: s'~ *v pron* get rich

enrichissement *m* (des tâches) enrichment; ~ **des emplois** job enrichment

ensachage *m* (des marchandises) bagging

enseigne *f* (V&M) trade sign; ~ **lumineuse** neon sign

enseignement *m* education; ~ **assisté par ordinateur** computer-aided learning, computer-assisted learning; ~ **secondaire** secondary education; ~ **supérieur** higher education

ensemble *m* (groupe) set; (de bureaux) complex; (de réformes) package; ~ **des attributions** role set; ~ **de biens mobiliers** ⋯⋗

set of chattels; ∼ **de données** (Info) data set; ∼ **d'états financiers** set of accounts; ∼ **des informations** coverage; ∼ **de logiciels** (Info) bundled software; ∼ **de marchandises** cargo mix; ∼ **de produits** product mix; ∼ **de produits financiers** financial package; ∼ **des risques** risk package; ∼ **des salaires versés** total payroll

ensuite *adv* afterwards

entamer *vt* (fonds) eat into; (projet) embark on; (réserves) draw on; ∼ **des poursuites** take legal action; ∼ **une procédure contre qn** bring a lawsuit against sb

entendre [1] *vt* (comprendre) understand [2] **s'entendre** *v pron* agree; **s'∼ avec qn** (sympathiser) get on with; (se mettre d'accord) agree

entente *f* understanding; ∼ **tacite** tacit understanding; **parvenir à une ∼** come to an understanding; ∼ **commerciale** trade arrangement; ∼ **illicite entre enchérisseurs** (vente aux enchères) knockout agreement; ∼ **sur les prix** pricing arrangement

entérinement *m* (d'une décision) ratification, confirmation

entériner *vt* (ratifier) ratify; (admettre) confirm

en-tête *m* (de lettre) heading; (Info) header; **papier à lettres à ∼** headed paper, headed stationery

entier, -ière *adj* complete

entièrement *adv* completely; ∼ **à charge** wholly dependent; ∼ **distribué** fully distributed; ∼ **et exclusivement** wholly and exclusively; ∼ **expertisé** fully valued; ∼ **réservé** booked up

entité *f* entity; ∼ **constituée** corporate entity; ∼ **juridique** legal entity; ∼ **soumise à l'audit** auditee

entraînement *m* drive; ∼ **d'embrayage** (Transp) clutch drive; ∼ **par ergots** (Info) tractor feed; ∼ **par friction** (Info) friction feed

entraîner *vt* (avoir pour conséquence) result in; (frais) involve

entrave *f* (gêne) hindrance; (Droit) constraint; ∼ **à la liberté du commerce** restraint of trade; ∼ **technique au commerce** technical barrier to trade

entraver *vt* obstruct; (contrat) interfere with

entre *prép* between; (parmi) among; ∼ **autres** among others, inter alia (frml); ∼ **états** (commerce) interstate US; ∼ **eux** inter se (frml); ∼ **les mains de** in the hands of; ∼ **les personnes présentes** inter praesentes (frml); ∼ **vifs** (Droit) inter vivos (frml)

entrée *f* (Admin) entry; (de fonds) inflow; (Info) input; ∼ **gratuite** free admission; ∼ **interdite** no admittance, no trespassing; ∼ **libre** (magasin) no obligation to buy; ∼ **de caisse** cash collection; ∼ **de capitaux**

capital inflow; ∼ **directe commerçant** direct trader input; ∼ **de données** data input; ∼ **en fonction** taking up office; ∼ **des fournisseurs** trade entrance; ∼ **de gamme** entry-level product; ∼ **de l'ordinateur** computer input; ∼ **du port** port access; ∼ **en possession anticipée** acceleration; ∼ **de service** tradesman's entrance; ∼ **en vigueur** entry into force

entrée/sortie *f* (Info) input/output

entremise *f* intervention; **par l'∼ de** through the agency of

entreposage *m* storage, warehousing; ∼ **frigorifique** cold storage; ∼ **en vrac** bulk storage

entreposer *vt* store

entrepôt *m* warehouse; **à prendre en ∼** ex-warehouse; **en ∼ sous douane** in bond; ∼ **de céréales** granary; ∼ **de données** data warehouse; ∼ **en douane** bonded warehouse; ∼ **frigorifique** cold storage plant, refrigerated warehouse; ∼ **des marchandises** goods depot; ∼ **de marchandises dangereuses** dangerous cargo compound; ∼ **de réception** reception depot; ∼ **de vente au détail** retail warehouse; ∼ **à vin** wine warehouse

entreprenant, e *adj* enterprising

entreprendre *vt* undertake; ∼ **de faire qch** undertake to do sth; ∼ **la production de qch** put sth into production

entrepreneur, -euse *m,f* (chef d'entreprise) entrepreneur; (de travaux) contractor; ∼ **général de transports** common carrier; ∼ **sur mesure** custom builder; ∼ **de remorquage** towage contractor; ∼ **de transports routiers** haulage contractor, haulier BrE, hauler AmE; ∼ **de travaux publics** civil engineering contractor

entrepreneurial, e *adj* entrepreneurial

entrepreneuriat *m* entrepreneurship

entreprise *f* (projet) undertaking, venture; (société) business, company, firm; **d'∼ à ∼** business-to-business; ∼ **absorbante** absorbing company; ∼ **acquise** acquired company; ∼ **agricole** farming business; ∼ **d'assurance** insurance business; ∼ **à but non lucratif** non-profitmaking company BrE, nonprofit enterprise AmE; ∼ **de camionnage** carrier, haulage company; ∼ **cible** target company; ∼ **cliente** client company, corporate customer; ∼ **commerciale** business concern, business enterprise; ∼ **commerciale risquée** business venture, commercial venture; ∼ **concurrentielle** competitive business; ∼ **cyclique** cyclical company; ∼ **diversifiée** diversified company; ∼ **dominante** dominant firm, core firm; ∼ **d'État** state enterprise; ∼ **familiale** family firm, family business; (à nombre d'actionnaires réduit) closed company BrE, closed corporation AmE; ∼ **financière** financial enterprise; ∼ **de gros**

bulk business; ~ **à haut risque** high-risk venture; ~ **hybride** clicks and mortar company, hybrid company; ~ **illimitée** unlimited company; ~ **industrielle lourde** heavy industrial plant; ~ **internationale** international venture, cross-border joint venture; ~ **Internet** Internet business; ~ **d'investissement** investment firm; ~ **leader** market leader; ~ **leader pour les coûts** cost leader; ~ **locale** local firm; ~ **de messageries** courier firm; ~ **à monopole syndical** preferential shop; ~ **multinationale** multinational company; ~ **nationale** domestic corporation; ~ **non constituée en société** unincorporated business; ~ **optimum** optimum firm; ~ **en participation** joint venture; ~ **périphérique** periphery firm; ~ **de premier ordre** blue-chip company; ~ **privée** private company, private enterprise; ~ **à propriétaire unique** sole proprietorship; ~ **publique** public enterprise; ~ **réglementée** regulated firm; ~ **risquée** wildcat venture; ~ **du secteur privé** private sector enterprise; ~ **du secteur public** public sector enterprise; ~ **semi-publique** semipublic enterprise; ~ **de services** service company; ~ **soutenue par l'État** government-sponsored enterprise; ~ **transnationale** transnational corporation; ~ **de transport public** common carrier; ~ **de transports routiers** haulage company, haulier BrE, trucking company AmE; ~ **de travaux sur commandes** job shop; ~ **unipersonnelle** sole trader; ~ **de vente par correspondance** mail-order business

entrer *vt* (Info) (données) enter, key in; ~ **en contact avec** come into contact with; ~ **dans le champ d'application de** fall within the scope of; ~ **dans le cours** move into the money; ~ **dans les détails** go into detail, get down to specifics; **faire** ~ admit; **faire** ~ **qn** show sb in; ~ **en jeu** come into play; ~ **en ligne de compte** be a factor; ~ **en liquidation** go into liquidation, go into receivership; ~ **en récession** enter recession; ~ **en relation avec** come into contact with; ~ **en vigueur** come into force, take effect; ~ **en vigueur à partir de** take effect from

entre-temps *adv* meanwhile

entretenir *vt* (bureau) maintain; (confiance) sustain; (relations, correspondance) maintain; (inflation) fuel; ~ **des relations commerciales à l'intérieur du Commonwealth** trade within the Commonwealth

entretien *m* (de matériel, de bâtiments) maintenance; (Info) servicing; (d'embauche) interview; **faire passer un** ~ **à** interview; ~, **réparation et révision** maintenance, repair and overhaul; ~ **de carrière** performance appraisal; ~ **de l'équipement** plant maintenance; ~ **d'évaluation** performance

appraisal interview; ~ **informel** informal interview; ~ **en profondeur** depth interview; ~ **de reconversion** retraining consultation; ~ **de routine** routine maintenance; ~ **total de l'équipement** total plant maintenance

entretoise *f* (Transp) spacer

entrevue *f* interview; ~ **de départ** exit interview; ~ **structurée** structured interview

énumération *f* enumeration

énumérer *vt* enumerate

envahir *vt* (marché) flood

enveloppe *f* (de lettre) envelope; (argent) pay packet BrE, pay check AmE; (Fin) envelope; ~ **matelassée** padded envelope; ~ **timbrée à vos nom et adresse** stamped addressed envelope BrE, self-addressed stamped envelope AmE; ~ **affranchie** stamped envelope; ~ **budgétaire** budget envelope; ~ **budgétaire pluriannuelle** multiyear resource envelope; ~ **de défense** defence envelope BrE, defense envelope AmE; ~ **de dépenses directes** direct spending envelope; ~ **de la dette publique** public debt envelope; ~ **à fenêtre** panel envelope, window envelope; ~ **globale** block grant UK; ~ **des services de l'État** services-to-government envelope

enveloppe-réponse *f* business reply envelope

envergure *f* (d'une entreprise) size; (de projet) scale; **sans** ~ (projet, débat) limited

environ *adv* (à peu près) about, around

environnement *m* environment; ~ **de l'entreprise** business environment; ~ **fiscal** tax environment; ~ **du marché** market environment

environnemental, e *adj* environmental; **audit** ~ environmental audit

environs *m pl* surroundings

envisager *vt* (projeter) plan; (imaginer) envisage; (entrevoir) foresee; ~ **des problèmes** foresee problems; ~ **la situation sous un jour pessimiste** take a gloomy view of the situation

envoi *m* (de marchandises) consignment; ~ **par avion** air mail; ~ **avec avis de réception** recorded delivery; ~ **de détail** (Transp) consignment of less than one carload; ~ **d'échantillons** sample mailing; ~ **de fonds** (Banque) remittance; ~ **mixte** (Transp) mixed consignment; ~ **en nombre** bulk mail; (Info) bus mailing; ~ **par la poste** mailing; ~ **de prospectus** mailing shot; ~ **publicitaire par la poste** mailing shot; ~ **recommandé** registered post BrE, certified mail AmE; ~ **par télécopie** facsimile transaction

envolée *f* (des prix, de monnaie) surge; ~ **du marché** bulge in the market

envoyé, e *m,f* (presse) correspondent; ~ ┅┅▷

permanent à l'étranger foreign correspondent; ∼ **spécial** special correspondent

envoyer *vt* (par la poste) post BrE, mail AmE; ∼ **une déclaration d'impôts** file a tax return; ∼ **qch par la poste** post sth, send sth by post BrE, mail sth AmE; ∼ **par télécopie** fax, send by fax; ∼ **qch par colis postal** send sth by parcel post; ∼ **qch par l'intermédiaire d'un agent** send sth via an agent; ∼ **qch en recommandé** send sth by registered post BrE, send sth by certified mail AmE; ∼ **sous pli discret** send under plain cover; ∼ **qn chercher qch** send sb for sth; ∼ **qch à temps** send sth in time

épargnant, e *m,f* investor, saver

épargne *f* savings, thrift US; ∼ **brute** gross savings; ∼ **des entreprises** corporate savings; ∼ **forcée** forced savings; ∼ **liquide** liquid savings; ∼ **mensuelle** monthly savings; ∼ **négative** negative saving; ∼ **obligatoire** compulsory saving; ∼ **des particuliers** personal savings

épargner *vt* save

épauler *vt* (personne) back up

épaves *f pl* (Transp) stranded goods

éphémère *adj* (produit, succès) short-lived

époque *f* period

épouse *f* spouse, wife; **et ∼** (Droit) et ux (frml); ∼ **séparée** estranged spouse

époux *m* husband, spouse; ∼ **divorcé** divorced spouse; ∼ **séparé** estranged spouse

épreuve *f* (Info) hard copy; (Média) proof; ∼ **de force** showdown, tug-of-war; ∼ **de vérité** acid test

EPROM *abrév* (▸**mémoire morte programmable électroniquement**) EPROM (electronically programmable read only memory)

épuisé, e *adj* (marchandise) out of stock; (livre) out of print; **être ∼** (fond) run out

épuisement *m* (Econ) depletion; (Fin) burnout; **jusqu'à ∼ des stocks** until stocks run out, while stocks last; ∼ **accumulé** (Compta, Fisc) accumulated depletion; ∼ **gagné** (Compta, Fisc) earned depletion

épuiser ⟦1⟧ *vt* exhaust
⟦2⟧ **s'épuiser** *v pron* (réserves, ressources) run out

épuration *f* (des eaux) purification

équation *f* equation; ∼ **comptable** accounting equation

équilibre *m* balance; (Econ) equilibrium; **en ∼** (budget) balanced; ∼ **autarcique** no-trade equilibrium; ∼ **de la balance des paiements** balance of payments equilibrium; ∼ **des forces** balance of power; ∼ **général du marché** general market equilibrium; ∼ **interne** internal balance; ∼ **du marché** market equilibrium; ∼ **partiel** partial equilibrium; ∼ **permanent** steady-state equilibrium; ∼

planétaire global balance; ∼ **de portefeuille** portfolio balance; ∼ **des pouvoirs** balance of power; ∼ **des recettes et des dépenses** equalization of revenue and expenditure

équilibré, e *adj* (budget) balanced; (personne) well-balanced; **être ∼** (Compta) balance

équilibrer ⟦1⟧ *vt* (budget) balance; (coûts, bénéfices) average out; ∼ **les comptes** agree the accounts
⟦2⟧ **s'équilibrer** *v pron* balance

équipage *m* crew; ∼ **d'un avion** (air)crew

équipe *f* team; (de travail posté) shift; **travailler en ∼** work as a team; (travail posté) work in shifts; ∼ **d'audit** audit group, audit team; ∼ **de chercheurs** research team; ∼ **de contrôle** audit group, audit team; ∼ **de débardeurs** stevedoring gang; ∼ **dédoublée** split shift; ∼ **de direction** management team; ∼ **d'entretien** maintenance crew; ∼ **de jour** day shift; ∼ **de nuit** night shift; ∼ **opérationnelle** operational staff; ∼ **de rédaction** editorial staff; ∼ **au sol** ground crew; ∼ **suppléante** relief shift; ∼ **tournante** relief shift, swing shift; ∼ **de travail posté** rotating shift; ∼ **de vente** sales force; ∼ **de vérification** audit group, audit team

équipement *m* accessories, equipment; (Info) hardware; ∼ **agricole/de bureau** farm/office equipment; **l'∼ de la région a coûté deux millions d'euros** improving the region's facilities cost two million euros; **∼s collectifs** public amenities

équiper *vt* (personne) fit out; (hôpital, bureau) equip; (pays, ville) equip; ∼ **de** provide with, equip with

équipier, -ière *m,f* team player

équitable *adj* equitable, fair; **commerce ∼** fair trade

équité *f* (Droit, Fin) equity; ∼ **fiscale** tax fairness; ∼ **horizontale/verticale** horizontal/vertical equity

équivalence *f* equivalence; ∼ **par anticipation** anticipation equivalence; ∼ **des charges fiscales** commensurate taxation; ∼ **de rendement** yield equivalence; ∼ **de valeur** (V&M) cash equivalence

équivalent¹, e *adj* equivalent; **à peu près ∼** roughly equivalent; **être ∼ à** correspond to *ou* with

équivalent² *m* equivalent; ∼ **en actions ordinaires** common shares equivalent BrE, common stock equivalent AmE; ∼ **clavier** (Info) keyboard equivalent; ∼ **de trésorerie** *m* cash equivalent

ergonome *m* ergonomist; ∼ **d'interface** (Info) interface ergonomist

ergonomie *f* (Admin) ergonomics, human engineering; ∼ **cognitive** cognitive ergonomics

ergonomique *adj* ergonomic

ériger *vt* erect

érosion *f* erosion; ~ **fiscale** tax erosion; ~ **monétaire** depreciation of the currency; ~ **du sol** soil erosion

erratum *m* erratum

erreur *f* error, mistake; (Info) error, fault; **faire une** ~ make a mistake; ~**s et omissions** errors and omissions; ~ **acceptable** permissible error; ~ **aléatoire** random error; ~ **de calcul** miscalculation, computational error; ~ **de classement** sequence error; ~ **de compensation** compensating error; ~ **de comptabilisation** posting error; ~ **comptable** accounting error; ~ **de date d'échéance** maturity mismatch; ~ **d'échantillon** sampling error; ~ **d'écriture** clerical error; (Compta) posting error; ~ **intermittente** soft error; ~ **d'inversion** transposition error; ~ **judiciaire** miscarriage of justice; ~ **de programmation** programming error; ~ **récurrente** hard error; ~ **type** standard error

erroné, e *adj* erroneous

E/S *abrév* (▶**entré/sortie**) I/O (input/output)

esc. *abrév* (▶**escompte**) disc. (discount)

escalade *f* (des prix) escalation

escale *f* (Transp) (aviation) stopover; **faire une** ~ stop over

escalier *m* (marches) stairs; ~ **roulant** escalator; ~ **de secours** fire escape, fire exit

escomptable *adj* bankable

escompte *m* (Com) discount; **à** ~ at a discount; ~ **de banque** banker's discount; ~ **de caisse** cash discount; ~ **d'effets de commerce** discounting of bills BrE, discounting of notes AmE; ~ **d'émission d'obligations** bond discount; ~ **d'obligation non amorti** unamortized bond discount; ~ **de première émission** original issue discount; ~ **sur ventes** sales discount

escompter *vt* discount

escorter *vt* accompany, escort

ESCP *abrév* (**École Supérieure de Commerce de Paris**) *Paris business school*

escroc *m* swindler, crook (infrml), embezzler

escroquer *vt* swindle, rip off (infrml)

escroquerie *f* swindle; (Droit) fraud; ~ **à l'assurance** fraudulent misrepresentation

escudo *m* escudo

e-sourcing *m* e-sourcing

espace *m* (place) space; (de mémoire) space; (zone) area; (intervalle) gap; ~ **bureau** office accommodation; ~ **disponible** (en mémoire, sur disque) available space; ~ **disque** disk space; ~ **habitable** floor space; ~ **perdu** (arrimage) broken stowage; ~ **publicitaire** advertising space; (radio, télévision) airtime; ~ **de travail** working area, workspace; ~ **de**

vente selling space; ~ **vital** living space

espacement *m* spacing; (Info) pitch; ~ **arrière** backspace

espèce *f* species; ~ **menacée** endangered species; ~ **en voie d'extinction** endangered species

espèces *f pl* (argent) cash; **en** ~ (paiement) in cash

espérance *f* hope; ~ **de vie** life expectancy; ~ **de vie d'un produit** product life expectancy

esperluette *f* (Info) ampersand

espionnage *m* espionage; ~ **industriel** industrial espionage

esprit *m* (caractéristique) spirit; (éthique) ethic; **conforme à/contraire à l'** ~ **de l'entreprise** in accordance with/contrary to the company ethic; ~ **commercial** commercialism; ~ **d'entreprise** entrepreneurship; ~ **d'équipe** team spirit

esquisse *f* (dessin) sketch; (de programme) outline

esquissé, e *adj* (Droit, Pol) drafted; ~ **dans ses grandes lignes** (Pol) broad-brush

esquisser ① *vt* (Droit, Pol) draft; (programme) outline, sketch out ② **s'esquisser** *v pron* **une solution commence à s'**~ a solution is taking shape

essai *m* (expérience) test; (expérimentation) trial; **coup d'**~ try; **période d'**~ trial period; (for employee) probationary period; **à l'**~ on approval; **faire des** ~**s** run trials; **prendre qn à l'**~ take sb on a trial basis; ~ **de fiabilité** reliability test; ~ **en laboratoire** (Info) alpha test; ~ **de marché** market testing; ~ **nucléaire** nuclear test; ~ **pilote** (Info) beta test; ~ **de programme** (Info) program testing; ~ **radio** air check; ~ **de réception** (V&M) acceptance trial; ~ **sur route** (Transp) test drive, test run; ~ **sur le terrain** (V&M) field testing; ~ **de transport** (distribution) test transit; ~ **de vente** (V&M) market testing; ~ **de vérification des performances** performance testing

essaimage *m* (Fin) spin-off

essaimer *vi* hive off, spin off

essayer *vt* (produit) test, try out

essence *f* petrol BrE, gas AmE; ~ **avion** aviation fuel; ~ **industrielle** industrial spirit; ~ **pour moteurs** motor spirit; ~ **sans plomb** unleaded petrol BrE, unleaded gas AmE; ~ **verte** green petrol

essentiel¹, -elle *adj* (différence, tâche) main, essential; **document/rôle/point** ~ key document/role/point

essentiel² *m* (chose principale) **c'est l'**~ that's the main thing; (objets indispensables) basics, essentials; (d'une conversation) gist; (partie la plus importante) bulk; **l'**~ **du revenu** the bulk of the revenue; **l'**~ the essentials, the basics

essentiellement *adv* primarily

essieu *m* axle; ∼ **de remorquage** towing dolly (jarg); ∼ **simple** dolly (jarg); ∼**x en tandem** *m pl* tandem axle

essor *m* boom, expansion; ∼ **économique** economic boom

essuyer *vt* (nettoyer) wipe; (rendre sec) dry; (pertes) suffer; ∼ **un revers** suffer a setback

estamper *vt* (monnaie) stamp; (infrml) (escroquer) swindle; **se faire** ∼ get ripped off (infrml)

estampille *f* (cachet, signature) stamp; (label) trademark

estampiller *vt* (document) stamp; (marchandise) mark

estaries *f pl* (navigation) laytime; ∼ **gagnées** all laytime saved; ∼ **moyennes** average laytime

estimatif, -ive *adj* (coût) estimated

estimation *f* (de coût) estimate; (valeur) valuation; (de dégâts) assessment; **faire une** ∼ **des besoins futurs** make an appraisal of future needs; ∼ **approximative** tentative estimate; (d'un bien immobilier) approximate valuation; ∼ **des coûts** cost estimate; ∼ **interne** in-house valuation; ∼ **monétaire du prix de revient d'un produit** product costing; ∼ **prudente** safe estimate; ∼ **de la valeur patrimoniale** net worth assessment; ∼ **des ventes** sales estimate

estime *f* respect, esteem; **avoir beaucoup d'**∼ **pour qn** have a high regard for sb

estimé, e *adj* (tableau, propriété) valued

estimer *vt* (prix) estimate; (marchandises, bien immobilier) value; (dégâts, besoins) assess; ∼ **nécessaire** deem necessary

estompé, e *adj* (Info) dimmed

estrope *f* (Transp) strop

estuaire *m* estuary; ∼ **à marée** tidal river estuary

établi, e *adj* established; (société) based; ∼ **depuis longtemps** long-established

établir **1** *vt* (compte) make up; (comité) form; (facture) make out; (fait, date) establish; (liste) draw up, make; (prix) ascertain; (record) set; (réputation) build up. ∼ **le bien-fondé d'une réclamation** substantiate a claim; ∼ **le bilan** (Bourse) find the balance; ∼ **un budget** draw up a budget, prepare a budget; ∼ **un chèque à l'ordre de qn** make a cheque payable to sb BrE, make out a cheque to sb BrE, raise a check to sb AmE; ∼ **une comptabilité de qch** (Compta) render an accounting for sth; ∼ **une cotisation d'impôt** assess tax; ∼ **une créance** prove a debt; ∼ **une liaison directe avec** establish a direct link with; ∼ **une liaison entre** establish a link between, link; ∼ **des liens avec** build links with; ∼ **une liste restreinte** draw up a shortlist; ∼ **l'ordre du jour** draw up the agenda; ∼ **le procès-verbal d'une réunion** take the minutes of a meeting, record a meeting

2 **s'établir** *v pron* (dans un nouvel emploi) settle; **s'**∼ **à son compte** set up one's own business

établissement *m* (entreprise, organisme) organization, establishment; (institué) institution; (bâtiments) premises; (usine) works; (cours) fixing; (d'un rapport) drawing up; (d'impôt, de taxe) introduction; ∼ **d'un budget** budgeting, budget preparation; ∼ **du budget d'investissement** capital budgeting; ∼ **commercial** commercial establishment, place of business; ∼ **du coût de production** production costing; ∼ **de crédit** credit institution, lending institution; ∼ **de cure** health farm; ∼ **de dossier** briefing; ∼ **d'enseignement** educational institution; ∼ **des états financiers** compilation of the financial statements; ∼ **fixe d'affaires** fixed place of business; ∼ **des frais** fixing of costs; ∼ **industriel** industrial plant; ∼ **membre d'une bourse** member corporation; ∼ **de la moyenne du revenu** income averaging; ∼ **national** state school; ∼ **d'objectifs** goal setting, target setting; ∼ **des plannings** planning; ∼ **principal** chief place of business; ∼ **des prix** (Bourse) fixing of costs; (V&M) price determination, pricing; ∼ **de réseaux** networking; ∼ **scolaire** educational institution, school

étain *m* tin

étalage *m* display, window display

étalagiste *mf* (décorateur) window dresser

étalement *m* (de paiements) spreading; (Bourse) spread trading; ∼ **sur les années précédentes** backward averaging; ∼ **des revenus** income spread; ∼ **des vacances** staggering of holidays BrE, staggering of vacations AmE

étaler *vt* (paiements, coûts) spread; (vacances, horaires) stagger

étalon *m* (poids et mesures) standard; (modèle) yardstick; ∼ **argent** silver standard; ∼ **de change or** gold exchange standard; ∼ **devise** currency standard; ∼ **dollar** dollar standard; ∼ **de lingots d'or** gold bullion standard; ∼ **marchandises** commodity standard; ∼ **de mesure** benchmark; ∼ **monétaire** monetary standard

étalon-or *m* gold standard

étanche *adj* watertight; ∼ **à l'air** airtight; ∼ **aux hydrocarbures** oiltight

étant: ∼ **donné les circonstances** given the circumstances; ∼ **entendu que** on the understanding that

étape *f* stage; **par** ∼**s** in stages; ∼ **de transition** stage of transition; ∼ **de la vérification** verification phase; ∼ **de vol** flight stage

état *m* (d'affaires, d'économie, de finances, de pays) state; (Compta) statement; (Droit) status; **à l'**∼ **de projet** in draft form; **en** ∼ **livrable** in a deliverable state; **en** ∼ **de navigabilité** (avion) airworthy; **en bon** ∼ in good repair, in good condition; **en l'~** as is; **en l'~ actuel de la législation** as the law stands at present; **en mauvais ~** in a bad state of repair, in bad condition; **être en ~ d'alerte** be on the alert; **être en ~ de cessation de paiement** be insolvent; **~ des achats et des ventes** purchase and sale statement; **~ annuel** annual return; **~ d'avancement des travaux** status report, progress report; **~ de banque** bank statement; **~ budgétaire** budgetary statement; **~ de caisse** cash statement; **~ civil** civil status, marital status; **~ consolidé** aggregate statement; **~ contractant** contracting state; **~ corporatif** corporate state; **~ de dédouanement** customs clearance status; **~ de droit** rule of law; **~ de l'économie** state of the economy; **~ financier** financial statement; **~s financiers** published accounts; **~ financier récapitulatif** financial summary; **~ financier semestriel** interim statements; **~ de flux de trésorerie** source and application of funds; **~ des frais** bill of costs; **~ membre** member state; **~ mensuel** monthly return; **~ de navigabilité** seaworthiness; **~ de non-croissance** stationary state economy, steady-state economy; **l'~ patron** the state as an employer; **~ de produits et de charges** statement of income and expenses; **~ providence** welfare state; **~ de rapprochement** reconciliation statement; **~ des rémunérations versées** pay statement; **~ des risques** risk position; **~s de service** credentials, service record; **~ stationnaire** stationary state economy, steady-state economy; **~ tampon** buffer state; **~ de la valeur ajoutée** value-added statement; **~ de variations de trésorerie** source and application of funds; **~ zéro** zero state

État *m* (nation) state, State; (gouvernement) state, government; **les ~s européens** the European States

étatique *adj* (contrôle, financement, gestion) state; **un système d'économie ~** a state-controlled economic system

étatisation *f* state control

étatiser *vt* (entreprise, économie, secteur) bring under state control

état-major *m* (Pol) administrative staff; (d'une société) top management

étayer *vt* (Econ) underpin

été *m* summer; **heure d'~** summer time UK, daylight-saving time US

éteindre *vt* (hypothèque) pay off; (Info) switch off, turn off

éteint, e *adj* (voyant) off

étendre *vt* (activités) expand; (Info) (mémoire) upgrade

étendu, e *adj* (effet) widespread

étendue *f* extent, scope; **~ du contrôle** audit coverage; **~ des dégâts** extent of

damage; **~ de garantie** underwriting spread; **~ de l'indemnité** measure of indemnity; **~ de la négociation** bargaining scope; **~ des responsabilités** span of control

éthique *f* code of ethics; **~ du travail** work ethic

ethnomercatique *f* ethnomarketing

étiquetage *m* labelling BrE, labeling AmE; **~ écologique** eco-labelling; **~ informatif** informative labelling BrE

étiquette *f* label, tag; **~ adhésive** stick-on label; **~ adresse** address label; **~ à bagages** baggage tag, luggage label; **~ de marchandises** cargo tag; **~ à œillet** tie-on label; **~ de prix** price sticker, price tag; **~ promotionnelle** shelf-talker (jarg), special offer ticket

étoffe *f* fabric, material; **avoir l'~ de** have the makings of

étranger¹, -ère *adj* (personne, lieu, langue, journal, capitaux) foreign; **~ au sujet** irrelevant

étranger², -ère *m,f* foreigner; **~ en situation irrégulière** illegal alien; **à l'~** abroad

étrave *f* (d'un navire) stem; **~ à bulbe** (d'un navire) bulbous bow

étroit, e *adj* narrow; (coopération, rapport) close

Ets *abrév* (▶**Établissements**) '**~ Baude**' (en façade) 'Baude'

ETTD *abrév* (▶**équipement terminal de traitement de données**) DTE (data terminal equipment)

étude *f* (recherche, observation) study; (enquête) survey; (d'avocat, notaire) (bureau) office; (charge) practice; **à l'~** under examination; **faire une ~ de** (projet, terrain, situation) survey; **une ~ portant sur** a study of; **~ d'aménagement des locaux** site planning; **~ d'avocats** law firm, law practice; **~ des besoins de la clientèle** customer research; **~ du budget** budget review; **~ de cas** case study; **~ de conception** design engineering; **~ de consommation** consumer research, consumer survey; **~ détaillée** in-depth study; **~ des écarts** gap study; **~ de faisabilité** feasibility study; **~ globale** global study; (Gestion) systems approach; **~ de l'impact** impact study; **~ des implantations** plant layout study; **~ d'investissement** investment review; **~ de marché** market research; **~ des méthodes** methods engineering, methods study; **~ de motivations** motivational research; **~ des mouvements** motion study; **~ multiclients** omnibus survey; **~ des périodes** time and motion study; **~ pilote** pilot study; **~ préalable** preliminary study, pilot study, feasibility survey; **~ prévisionnelle** forecast; **~ de produit** product analysis; **~ de projet** project appraisal; **~ de rappel** recall study; **~ de rentabilité** profitability ····>

analysis; ~ **témoin** sample study

études *f pl* studies; **faire des ~ d'ingénieur** study engineering; **faire des ~ de comptabilité** study accountancy; ~ **commerciales** business studies; ~ **économiques** economic research; ~ **de gestion** business studies; ~ **publicitaires** advertising research

étudiant, e *m,f* student; (avant la licence) undergraduate; ~ **étranger** foreign student

étudiant-chercheur *m* research student

étudier *vt* (question) investigate, look into; (langue, système) study; (dossier, situation) examine

euro *m* euro

euro- *préf* Euro-

eurocentrique *adj* eurocentric

eurocontrol *m* Eurocontrol

eurocrate *mf* Eurocrat

eurodevise *f* Eurocurrency

eurodollar *m* Eurodollar

euro-emprunt *m* Eurobond

eurofranc *m* Eurofranc

euroland *m* euroland

euromarché *m* Euromarket

euromonnaie *f* Eurocurrency, Euromoney

Euronet *m* Euronet

euro-obligation *f* Eurobond; ~ **à moyen terme** medium-term Euronote

europalette *f* Europallet

europapier commercial *m* Eurocommercial paper

Europe *f* Europe; ~ **continentale** continental Europe; ~ **de l'Est** Eastern Europe; ~ **occidentale** Western Europe; ~ **de l'Ouest** Western Europe

européen, -enne *adj* European

europhile *adj* Europhile

eurosceptique *mf* Eurorebel, Eurosceptic

eurotaux *m pl* Euro-rates

eurovaleur mobilière *f* Euro-security

évacuation *f* (de lieu) evacuation; ~ **des déchets** waste disposal

évaluateur, -trice *m,f* examiner

évaluation *f* (titres) valuation; (d'une situation, d'un choix) assessment; (du personnel) appraisal; (du dédommagement, de l'indemnité) assessment; (d'un travail) feedback; (Info) computation; ~ **a posteriori** a posteriori assessment, assessment with the benefit of hindsight; ~ **de l'apporteur** vendor rating; ~ **basée sur une activité** activity-based costing UK; ~ **de biens immobiliers** property valuation BrE, real estate appraisal AmE; ~ **boursière** market valuation; ~ **du capital humain** human asset accounting; ~ **des comptes** accounts appraisal; ~ **des coûts** costing; ~ **des coûts de systèmes** estimating systems costs; ~ **du crédit** credit rating, credit scoring; ~ **du cycle de vie** life cycle assessment; ~ **des dégâts** damage

appraisal, appraisal of damages; ~ **de la demande** demand assessment; ~ **des dépenses en capital** capital expenditure appraisal; ~ **du dommage** damage appraisal, appraisal of damage; ~ **douanière** customs valuation; ~ **de l'état des revenus** income test; ~ **financière** financial appraisal; ~ **des immobilisations** asset valuation, fixed asset assessment; ~ **d'impôts** tax assessment; ~ **interne** internal assessment; ~ **d'investissement** investment appraisal; ~ **d'investissement sur budget** capital investment appraisal; ~ **du marché** market appraisal, market evaluation; ~ **obligataire** bond valuation; ~ **d'origine** original assessment; ~ **des performances** performance appraisal; ~ **du personnel** staff appraisal; ~ **du point** point estimate; ~ **de poste** job appraisal, job review; ~ **des problèmes** problem assessment; ~ **de produit** product evaluation; ~ **de projet** project appraisal; ~ **prudente** conservative estimate; ~ **de la qualité** quality assessment; ~ **des réserves** stock inventory, stocktaking; ~ **des ressources** resource appraisal

évalué, e *adj* (risques, coûts, dégâts, besoins) assessed; (grandeur, durée) estimated; (propriété, patrimoine) ~ **à** valued at

évaluer *vt* (risques, coûts, dégâts, besoins) assess; (grandeur, durée) estimate; (propriété, patrimoine) value, appraise US; (Info) compute; ~ **le montant de la dette** assess the total debt; ~ **qch à 100 euros** value sth at 100 euros; ~ **les coûts de qch** cost sth

évasif, -ive *adj* (réponse) evasive

évasion *f* escape; ~ **de capitaux** capital flight; ~ **fiscale** tax avoidance, tax evasion; ~ **monétaire** capital flight

événement *m* event; ~ **d'actualité** current event; ~ **imprévu** contingency; ~ **médiatique** media event; ~ **postérieur à la date du bilan** subsequent event; ~ **sportif** sporting event

événementiel, -ielle *adj* factual; **marketing** ~ event marketing

éventail *m* range; ~ **de contrôle** span of control; ~ **des négociations** (Bourse) trading range; ~ **des prix** price range; ~ **des produits** product range; ~ **des produits en vente** product mix, sales mix; ~ **des salaires** wage spread

éventualité *f* (événement possible) eventuality; (hypothèse) possibility; ~ **peu probable** remote possibility

éventuel, -elle *adj* (possible) possible; (responsabilité, obligation) contingent, prospective; (client) potential, prospective

évidence *f* (fait) obvious fact; **se rendre à l'~** face the facts; **mettre en ~** (importance, faiblesse) highlight

évident, e *adj* evident, obvious

évincer *vt* (candidat, compétiteur) oust; (Droit)

(déposséder) evict

éviter *vt* (impôt, problème) avoid

évolué, e *adj* (Info) high-level

évoluer *vi* evolve; ~ **en parallèle** move in tandem; **qui peut** ~ (Info) upgradeable

évolutif, -ive *adj* (Info) upgradeable

évolution *f* (de la demande) development; (prix) change; (Econ) trend; (Info) growth; **l'**~ **d'une situation** the development of a situation; **l'**~ **du pouvoir d'achat** the fluctuations in buying power; **suivre l'**~ **du marché** track the market, follow the market trend; ~ **économique** economic trend; ~ **d'un investissement** investment history; ~ **du marché** market development; ~ **matérielle** (Info) hardware upgrade; ~ **des ventes** sales trend; ~ **de la situation économique** economic trend

évolutivité *f* (Info) upgradeability

exact, e *adj* (réponse, calcul) correct; (chiffres, prévision) accurate; (intention, but) express

exactement *adv* correctly

exactitude *f* accuracy

exagéré, e *adj* exaggerated

examen *m* (de cas, de dossier) examination; (de compte) inspection; (Droit) examination; (Fin) review; (de produit) inspection; **être en cours d'**~ (dossier, budget) be under review; (question, demande) be under consideration; (cas) be under investigation; **mettre qn en** ~ (Droit) interview sb under caution; ~ **annuel des ventes** annual sales review; ~ **approfondi** close examination; ~ **des besoins** needs test; ~ **du budget publicitaire** advertising budget review; ~ **des débouchés** market study; ~ **de la demande d'assurance** examination of proposal; ~ **d'entrée** entrance examination; ~ **financier** financial review; ~ **médical** medical examination; ~ **préliminaire** preliminary examination; ~ **de proposition** examination of proposal; ~ **public** public examination; ~ **des ressources** resource appraisal; ~ **de revenu** (Admin) means test, earnings test; ~ **de soumission** examination of proposal; ~ **systématique** across-the-board investigation, systematic investigation

examinateur, -trice *m,f* examiner

examiner *vt* (candidature) examine; (question) investigate, look into; (propriété) survey; ~ **de nouveau** re-examine; (cotisation) reconsider; ~ **les chiffres** look at the figures

ex-bon *m* ~ **de souscription** (Bourse) ex-warrant

ex-c *abrév* (▶**ex-coupon**) ex.cp. (ex-coupon)

excédent *m* surplus; (baux commerciaux) overage; **les** ~**s agricoles** agricultural surpluses; **l'**~ **des dépenses sur les recettes** excess of expenditure over receipts; **avoir un** ~ run a surplus; **en** ~ in surplus; **en** ~ **financier** in financial surplus; ~ **de**

l'actif sur le passif surplus of assets over liabilities; ~ **agricole** farm surplus; ~ **alimentaire** food surplus; ~ **d'argent** surplus money, excess money; ~ **de bagages** excess baggage; ~ **de la balance des paiements** balance of payments surplus; ~ **brut d'exploitation** gross margin; ~ **budgétaire** budget surplus; ~ **de caisse** cash surplus, excess cash; ~ **du commerce extérieur** foreign trade surplus; ~ **commercial** trade balance, trade surplus; ~ **commercial étranger** external trade surplus, foreign trade surplus; ~ **d'exportation** export surplus; ~ **financier** fiscal surplus; ~ **d'importation** import surplus; ~ **de main-d'œuvre** overmanning; ~ **net quotidien** net daily surplus; ~ **des opérations courantes** current account surplus BrE, checking account surplus AmE; ~ **de prix** premium; ~ **de production** production overrun; ~ **de réévaluation** appraisal increment; ~ **des sinistres** excess of loss; ~ **de trésorerie** cash surplus, excess cash

excédentaire *adj* in surplus; ~ **dans une devise donnée** long in a currency

excepté *prép* except; **tous les jours,** ~ **le jeudi** every day except Thursday

exception *f* exception; **à l'**~ **de** with the exception of; **faire une** ~ make an exception; ~ **culturelle** exclusion of cultural products from the Free Trade provisions of GATT; ~ **péremptoire** (Droit) demurrer

exceptionnel, -elle *adj* exceptional; (dépenses) below the line

excès *m* excess; **en** ~ (objects, substance) excess; **l'**~ **de la demande sur l'offre** excess of demand over supply; ~ **d'indemnisation** overcompensation; ~ **de pouvoir** (Droit) ultra vires action

excessif, -ive *adj* excessive, unreasonable

excessivement *adv* excessively

exclu¹, e *adj* (personne) excluded; (hypothèse, possibilité) ruled out

exclu², e *m,f* outcast; **les** ~**s** social outcasts; **les** ~**s de la croissance/du système** those excluded from economic growth/from the system

exclure *vt* (personne) exclude; (hypothèse, possibilité) rule out; ~ **d'avance** preclude; ~ **qn d'une société** bar sb from a company

exclusif, -ive *adj* (agent, concessionnaire) sole; (produit, procédé) exclusive; (droit, propriété, privilège) exclusive; (interview, document) exclusive; **représentation exclusive** sole agency

exclusion *f* exclusion; **à l'**~ **de** with the exception of; ~ **de garantie** exclusion clause, exemption clause; ~ **des risques d'entreprise** business risk exclusion; ~ **sociale** social exclusion; ~ **statutaire** statutory exclusion; ~ **par voie d'achats** (d'un actionnaire) buying out

e

exclusivement *adv* exclusively

exclusivisme *m* exclusivism

exclusivité *f* (presse) scoop; (médias) franchise; (droits) exclusive rights; **en ∼** (vendre, publier) exclusively; **acheter l'∼ d'une marque** buy the exclusive rights to a brand; **c'est une ∼ de notre entreprise** it's exclusive to our company

ex-conjoint, e *m,f* former spouse

ex-coupon *adj* ex-coupon

excursion *f* (tourisme) tour; **∼ en train** rail tour; **∼ avec guide** guided tour

excuse *f* apology

excuser: s'∼ *v pron* apologize; **s'∼ de** apologize for; **s'∼ de qch auprès de qn** apologize to sb for sth

ex-dividende *m* ex dividend

ex droit *m* (Droit) ex claim

exécutable *adj* (projet) practicable; (tâche) manageable; (Droit) executable; (Info) (programme) executable; **contrat non ∼** (Droit) naked contract

exécuter *vt* (contrat) implement; (ordre) fill; (travaux) perform; (programme) run; **faire ∼** (Droit) enforce; **∼ ou annuler** (Bourse) fill-or-kill; **∼ sous tension** (Info) boot, boot up

exécuteur, -trice *m,f* executor; (femme) executrix; **∼ testamentaire** estate executor

exécutif, -ive *adj* (comité, pouvoir) executive

exécution *f* (de travail, projet) execution; (d'un contrat) fulfilment; (de décision, plan, budget) implementation; (de décision, de commande) carrying out; (Droit) (d'une loi) administration; (de jugement) enforcement; (Fin) (d'ordre) carrying out; (Info) execution; **l'∼ du programme demandera deux ans** it will take two years to implement the programme; **travaux en cours d'∼** work in progress; **veiller à la bonne ∼ d'une tâche/ commande** see that a job is done well/an order is filled properly; **∼ en Bourse** buy-in; **∼ d'un débiteur** (Droit) distraint of property; **∼ de la livraison** delivery performance; **∼ de la politique** policy execution; **∼ pure et simple** (Droit) (d'un contrat) specific performance; **∼ de services** performance of services

exécutoire *adj* (jugement) enforceable; (pouvoir) executory

exemplaire *m* copy; **en deux ∼s** in duplicate; **en quatre ∼s** in quadruplicate; **en trois ∼s** in triplicate; **∼ d'archives** file copy; **∼ de presse** press copy; **∼ témoin** advance copy

exemple *m* example; (Info) (programme) sample; **par ∼** for example; **∼ type** textbook case

exempt, e *adj* exempt; **∼ de droit de douane** (marchandises) duty-free; **∼ d'erreur** error-free; **∼ d'impôts** tax-exempt

exempter *vt* exempt; **non exempté** nonexempt

exemption *f* exemption; **∼ de base** basic exemption; **∼ pour dividendes** dividend allowance; **∼ pour enfants à charge** exemption for dependent children; **∼ fiscale** tax exemption; **∼ maximale pour redevances** royalty exemption limit; **∼ personnelle** personal allowance UK, personal credit Canada, personal exemption US; **∼ statutaire** statutory exemption, statutory immunity; **∼ de la TVA** zero rating

ex-épouse *f* former spouse

ex-époux *m* former spouse

exercer ▯1▯ *vt* (droit, option) exercise; (contrôle, autorité, pression) exert; (métier) practise; **∼ le métier de professeur** work as a teacher; **∼ la profession de juriste** practise as a lawyer; **∼ une influence sur** have influence over; **∼ de la pression à la baisse sur le marché** raid the market; **∼ une pression sur** bring pressure to bear on ▯2▯ *vi* (travailler) work; (professionnel) practise

exercice *m* financial year, fiscal year; **∼ antérieur** prior period; **∼ anticipé** early exercise; **∼ anticipé d'un droit** anticipation; **∼ budgétaire** budget year; **∼ clos** financial year ended, fiscal year ended; **∼ clos à cette date** financial year then ended, fiscal year then ended; **∼ comptable** accounting period, accounting year; **∼ courant** current fiscal year; **∼ en cours** current year; **∼ écoulé** past year; **∼ d'évacuation** fire drill; **∼ de poursuites judiciaires** conduct of a law suit; **∼ social** trading year; **∼ suivant** upcoming fiscal year

exhaustif, -ive *adj* exhaustive; (rapport, étude) comprehensive

exigeant: demanding; **∼ une grande qualification** skill-intensive; **∼ beaucoup de personnes** people-intensive

exigence *f* requirement; **∼ des consommateurs** consumer requirement; **∼s de déclaration** reporting requirements; **∼ de dépôt initial** initial margin requirement; **∼ juridique** legal requirement; **∼ de publication** disclosure requirement; **∼ de rentabilité** profit requirement; **∼s de sécurité** safety requirements

exiger *vt* require, demand; **∼ qch de qn** require sth of sb

exigibilité *f* (d'impôt, de traite) payability; (de dette) repayability; **date d'∼ de la TVA** tax point; **∼ anticipée** (du remboursement d'un prêt) acceleration of maturity

exigible *adj* (impôt, traite, dette) payable, due; **∼ d'avance** (paiement) payable in advance; **créances ∼** debts due; **passif ∼** current liabilities; **TVA ∼** input tax

exil *m* exile; **∼ fiscal** tax exile

existant¹, e *adj* actual

existant² *m* (Transp) actuals; **∼ en caisse** (Compta) cash in hand

ex-navire *adv* ex-ship

exode *m* exodus; ∼ **des cerveaux** brain drain

exonération *f* exemption; ∼ **des gains en capital** capital gains exemption; ∼ **d'impôts** tax exemption, tax immunity; ∼ **mutuelle** (Assur) (à la suite de collision) knock-for-knock agreement; ∼ **statutaire** statutory exemption, statutory immunity

exonéré, e *adj* exempt; ∼ **d'impôts** tax-exempt

exonérer *vt* exempt

exorbitant, e *adj* exorbitant

expansion *f* expansion; ∼ **commerciale** business expansion; ∼ **économique** economic expansion; ∼ **de faible amplitude** boomlet

expansionnisme *m* expansionism

expansionniste *adj* expansionist

expatriation *f* (de personne) expatriation; l'∼ **de capitaux** the transfer of capital abroad

expatrié, e *m,f* expatriate

expectative *f* anticipation

expédier *vt* send, forward; (par la poste) post BrE, mail AmE; (Info) dispatch; (marchandises) dispatch; (par bateau) ship; ∼ **par avion** (lettre, colis) airmail; ∼ **par la poste** send by post BrE, send by mail AmE; ∼ **par le train** ship by rail

expéditeur, -trice *m,f* (de courrier) sender; (de marchandises) consigner, shipper

expédition *f* (envoi de lettres, de marchandises) dispatching, sending; (marchandises, expédiées) consignment, shipment; ∼ **en conteneur** containerized shipment; ∼ **groupée** forwarding in bulk; ∼ **ordinaire** customary dispatch; ∼ **en vrac** bulk shipment

expéditionnaire *mf* shipping clerk

expérience *f* (en laboratoire) experiment; (travail) experience; **ayant de l'∼** experienced; **faire l'∼ de** experience; ∼ **d'agence** (publicité) agency experience; ∼ **professionnelle** work experience; ∼ **de terrain** hands-on experience

expérimenté, e *adj* experienced

expert¹, e *adj* expert

expert² *m* expert; (Info) troubleshooter; (Assur) adjuster; ∼ **d'assurance** insurance adjuster; ∼ **cité comme témoin** (Droit) expert witness; ∼ **désigné par les tribunaux** official valuer; ∼ **en fiscalité** tax expert; ∼ **indépendant** (Assur) independent adjuster; ∼ **en marketing** marketing expert, marketeer

expert-comptable *m* certified accountant UK, certified public accountant US

expert-conseil *m* consultant

experticiel *m* (Info) knowledgeware

expertise *f* consultancy work; (Assur) appraisal, survey; (compétence) expertise; ∼

des avaries damage survey; ∼ **comptable** accountancy; ∼ **des dégâts** damage survey; ∼ **intermédiaire** intermediate survey; ∼ **quadriennale** quadriennal survey

expertiser *vt* value; ∼ **les dommages** appraise damages; ∼ **qch** (bijou, propriété) make a valuation of sth

expiration *f* (échéance) expiry BrE, expiration AmE; **arriver à ∼** expire; ∼ **d'affectation** (Compta) lapsing resources; ∼ **du bail** termination of tenancy; ∼ **du contrat à terme** (Bourse) futures expiry date BrE, futures expiration date AmE

expirer *vi* expire; ∼ **dans le cours** expire in-the-money; ∼ **sans valeur** expire worthless

explicite *adj* explicit

expliquer *vt* explain; (en démontrant) demonstrate

exploitable *adj* exploitable

exploitant, e *m,f* (Com) manager; (Transp) aircraft operator; ∼ **agricole** farmer; ∼ **individuel** sole trader

exploitation *f* (mise en valeur) (de mine) working; (de gisement) mining; (de forêt, terre) exploitation; (de ressources) use; (d'entreprise, ferme) running; (de brevet) use; (de réseau, liaison, aérienne) operation; (entreprise) ∼ **commerciale/industrielle** business/industrial concern; (traitement injuste) exploitation; **dépenses d'∼** operating expenses, running costs; **déficit d'∼** operating loss, trading loss; ∼ **agricole** farm; ∼ **à ciel ouvert** opencast mining BrE, strip mining AmE; ∼ **de données** data mining; ∼ **économique des ressources** economical use of resources; ∼ **forestière** logging; ∼ **intensive** (en agriculture) intensive farming; ∼ **mesurée des ressources** economical use of resources; ∼ **portuaire** port operation

exploiter *vt* (mine) work; (gisement, mineral, terre, forêt) exploit; (entreprise) run, operate; (réseau, ligne aérienne) operate; (brevet) use; (personnel) exploit; (ressources, marché) tap; ∼ **25 hectares** farm 25 hectares

explosif *m* explosive; ∼ **déflagrant** deflagrating explosive; ∼ **détonant** detonating explosive

explosion *f* explosion; ∼ **du contenu total** explosion of total contents; ∼ **démographique** population explosion; ∼ **des salaires** wage explosion

expomarché *m* trade mart

export *m* export; (Info) ∼ **de données** data export

exportateur¹, -trice *adj* exporting

exportateur², -trice *m,f* exporter; ∼ **net** net donator

exportation *f* export; ∼ **concessionnaire** concessional export; ∼ **envoyée par la poste** postal export; ∼ **indivisible** ⋯⋙

indivisible export; ∼ **invisible** invisible
export; ∼ **mondiale** world export; ∼
principale staple export; ∼ **subventionnée**
subsidized export; ∼ **visible** visible export

exporté, e *adj* exported

exporter ① *vt* (marchandises, capitaux)
export
② **s'exporter** *v pron* (produit) be exported;
s'∼ bien/mal be easy/difficult to export

exposant, e *m,f* exhibitor

exposé *m* statement; (oral) brief; ∼ **de**
l'invention disclosure of the invention

exposer *vt* (marchandises) display; ∼ **à**
(pression) expose to; ∼ **qch en détail** expose
sth in detail; ∼ **ses arguments** argue one's
case; **être exposé à un risque** face a risk

exposition *f* (salon professionnel) exhibition,
trade show; (d'objets à vendre) fair; (d'objets d'art)
exhibition, exhibit AmE; ∼ **agricole**
agricultural show; ∼ **d'artisanat** craft fair;
∼ **itinérante** travelling fair BrE, traveling
fair AmE; ∼ **réelle totale** (publicité) total
effective exposure; ∼ **aux risques** risk
exposure; ∼ **de taux d'intérêt** interest rate
exposure

exposition-vente *f* fair

exprès *adj* (courrier) special delivery;
envoyer qch en ∼ send sth special delivery

express *adj* (liaisons, transports) express

expression *f* expression; ∼ **de la**
politique policy formulation

exprimer *vt* (idée, opinion, remerciement)
express

expropriation *f* (de maison, d'immeuble)
compulsory purchase UK, condemnation US;
∼ **pour cause d'utilité publique**
compulsory purchase UK, condemnation US

exproprier *vt* (personne) dispossess; (maison,
terrain) put a compulsory purchase order on
UK, condemn US

expulser *vt* (locataire) evict; (immigré) deport

expulsion *f* (d'un bénéfice) voidance; (d'un
locataire) eviction; (d'un immigré) deportation; ∼
effective actual eviction; ∼ **de**
représailles retaliatory eviction

ex répartition *f* (Fin) ex allotment

extensible *adj* (Info) expandable,
upgradeable

extensif, -ive *adj* (culture) extensive; (sens)
wide; (signification, usage) extended

extension *f* (Info) extension, upgrading; ∼
de la gamme (V&M) brand extension; ∼
matérielle (Info) hardware upgrade; ∼
mémoire (Info) memory upgrade; ∼ **à des**
risques annexes (Assur) extended cover,
extended coverage

externalisation *f* outsourcing

externaliser *vt* outsource

externalité *f* (Econ) externality; ∼
spatiale (Econ) neighbourhood effect BrE,
neighborhood effect AmE

externe *adj* (extérieur) external; (recrutement)
outside

extinction *f* (d'un contrat) discharge; ∼
d'une action (en justice) extinction of an
action; ∼ **d'une instance** extinction of an
action; ∼ **d'un privilège** discharge of lien

extorquer *vt* (argent, promesse) extort

extra-budgétaire *adj* nonbudgetary

extracommunautaire *adj* non-EU

extraction *f* extraction; ∼ **de données**
data retrieval

extraire *vt* (charbon, minerai) extract

extrait *m* (document) extract; (d'un acte)
abstract; ∼ **de comptes** abstract of
accounts; ∼ **des comptes clients** accounts
receivable statement; ∼ **de minute** (tribunal)
abstract of record; ∼ **de naissance** birth
certificate; ∼ **d'un rapport officiel** abstract
of record; ∼ **du registre** extract from the
register

extranet *m* extranet

extraordinaire *adj* (dépenses, mesure,
assemblée) extraordinary

extraparlementaire *adj*
extraparliamentary

extra-plat *adj* slim-line, ultra-slim

extraterritorial, e *adj* offshore

Ff

FAB *abrév* (▶**franco à bord**) FOB (free on
board), FOS (free on ship, free on steamer)

fabricant *m* maker, manufacturer; ∼
automobile car manufacturer

fabrication *f* making; (pour le commerce)
manufacturing; **de ∼ française** French-
made; ∼ **assistée par ordinateur**

computer-aided manufacturing; ∼ **intégrée**
par ordinateur computer-integrated
manufacturing; ∼ **par lots** batch production;
∼ **pilote** pilot production; ∼ **en série** mass
production

fabrique *f* factory; ∼ **de papier** paper mill;
∼ **de produits chimiques** chemical works

fabriqué, e *adj* made; (industriellement) manufactured; ∼ **en France** made in France; ∼ **en grandes séries** (production) mass-produced; ∼ **sur commande** custom-made

fabriquer *vt* make; (industriellement) manufacture; ∼ **sur mesure** customize, make to measure

facile *adj* easy, simple; ∼ **à utiliser** user-friendly

facilitation *f* facilitation; (de trafic de marchandises) transport facilitation; ∼ **des échanges** trade facilitation

facilité *f* facility; ∼ **d'accès** easy access; ∼ **bancaire internationale** international banking facility; ∼ **de caisse** overdraft facility; ∼ **commerciale** trade facilitation; ∼ **de crédit** borrowing facility, credit facility; ∼ **d'émission d'achat** purchase issue facility; ∼ **d'émission garantie** issuance facility; ∼ **d'emprunt cessible** transferable loan facility; ∼ **de manutention** ease of handling; ∼ **d'organisation** organizational convenience; ∼ **de trésorerie** advance

faciliter *vt* facilitate

facilités *f pl* (possibilités) opportunities; (capacités) skills; ∼ **commerciales/ d'importation** commercial/import opportunities; ∼ **de caisse** overdraft facility; ∼ **à communiquer** communication skills; ∼ **en vol** in-flight facilities; ∼ **de paiement** easy terms; ∼ **de prêt** loan facility

façon *f* (manière) way; (production) making; ∼ **de penser** way of thinking; **de** ∼ **aléatoire** randomly; **de** ∼ **cohérente** consistently; **de** ∼ **pragmatique** pragmatically

façonner *vt* (objet artisanal) make; (pièce, outil) manufacture; (opinion) mould BrE, mold AmE

fac-similé *m* facsimile, fax

factage *m* (livraison) carriage, forwarding

facteur *m* (Econ) factor; (employé des postes) postman BrE, mailman AmE; ∼ **d'actualisation** (Assur) annuity due; (Fin) present value factor; ∼ **aléatoire** random factor; ∼ **d'attention** (publicité) attention factor; ∼ **de charge** (Transp) load factor; ∼ **commun de distinction** common distinguishing factor; ∼ **de contrainte** (V&M) constraining factor; ∼ **coût** cost factor; ∼ **décisif** decisive factor; ∼ **de déflation** deflator; ∼ **d'entrée** (Fin) input factor; ∼ **d'équilibre** (Econ) balancing item; ∼ **d'équivalence** (Fisc) pension adjustment; ∼ **humain** human factor; ∼ **de production** production factor, input; ∼ **risque** risk factor, element of risk; ∼ **saisonnier** seasonal factor; ∼ **de stabilisation** steadying factor; ∼ **stress** stress factor; ∼ **d'usure** wear factor

factice *adj* artificial

factieux, -ieuse *adj* factious

faction *f* faction

factorage *m* factoring

factoriel, -elle *adj* factorial; **analyse factorielle** factor analysis

factoring *m* factoring; ∼ **d'assurance** insurance factoring

factotum *m* handyman, odd-job man

facturation *f* billing, invoicing; ∼ **anticipée** prebilling; ∼ **des clients** customer billing; ∼ **électronique** electronic billing, e-billing, electronic invoice presentation; ∼ **globale** gross billing; ∼ **au temps passé** billing for the time spent

facture *f* bill, invoice; **une** ∼ **de 100 euros** an invoice for 100 euros; **faire une** ∼ make out an invoice; **régler une** ∼, **payer une** ∼ settle *ou* pay a bill; **suivant** ∼ as per invoice; ∼ **d'achat** purchase invoice; ∼ **d'avitaillement** (navigation) victualling bill BrE, victualing bill AmE; ∼ **certifiée** certified invoice; ∼ **commerciale** commercial invoice; ∼ **détaillée** itemized invoice; ∼ **de douane** customs invoice; ∼ **d'électricité** electricity bill BrE, hydro bill Can; ∼ **établie en devise indépendante** invoice in a third currency; ∼ **de l'étranger** foreign bill; ∼ **d'expédition** shipping invoice; ∼ **d'exportation** export invoice; ∼ **originale** original invoice; ∼ **pétrolière** oil bill; ∼ **pro forma** pro forma invoice; ∼ **provisoire** provisional invoice; ∼ **rectificative** corrected invoice; ∼ **valide** valid invoice

facturer *vt* invoice; ∼ **les coûts et charges** invoice cost and charges; ∼ **qch à qn** invoice sb for sth; **je ne vous ai pas facturé les pièces détachées** I haven't charged *or* invoiced you for the spare parts

facturier¹ *m* (livre) invoice book

facturier², -ière *m,f* (employé) invoice clerk

facultatif, -ive *adj* optional

faculté *f* (université) faculty; (aptitude) (intellectuelle) faculty; (physique) ability; (Droit) right; (**de faire** to do); (option) option; ∼ **d'achat et de revente** (Bourse) purchase and resale agreement; ∼ **d'adaptation** adaptability; ∼ **contributive** (Econ) taxation capacity; ∼ **de droit** law school; ∼ **de rachat** (Assur) commutation right; ∼ **de recours** (Droit) power of recourse

faible *adj* (intérêt, opérations) light; (marché, commerce) sluggish; (prix, somme) low, small; (rendement, revenu) low; (protection) weak; (demande) poor, weak; (quantité, différence) small; **à** ∼ **rendement** low-yielding; ∼ **niveau de vie** low standard of living

faiblement *adv* (augmenter) slightly; (qualifié) poorly; ∼ **peuplé** sparsely populated

faiblesse *f* weakness; (insuffisance) inadequacy; **être en position de** ∼ be in a weak position; **la** ∼ **de nos revenus** our low level of income; **la** ∼ **de la livre sterling** the weakness of the pound

faille *f* flaw; (Droit) loophole; ∼ **dans la législation** loophole in the law

failli[1], **e** *adj* bankrupt

failli[2], **e** *m,f* bankrupt; ~ **réhabilité** discharged bankrupt

faillibilité *f* fallibility

faillible *adj* fallible

faillite *f* bankruptcy; **au bord de la** ~ on the verge of bankruptcy; **être en** ~ (entreprise) be bankrupt; **faire** ~ go bankrupt; **se mettre en** ~ file for bankruptcy; ~ **de banque** bank failure; ~ **d'entreprise** bankruptcy, business failure; ~ **forcée** involuntary bankruptcy; ~ **frauduleuse** fraudulent bankruptcy

faire ⟦1⟧ *vt* make; (demande) send in; (enquête) hold; (liste) make, draw up; (offre) submit; (plan) draw up; (étude) conduct; (réclamation) file; ~ **avancer les choses** get things moving; ~ **suivre SVP** please forward; ~ **concurrence à** compete against, compete with; ~ **une découverte** make a discovery; ~ **défiler** (bande) advance; (écran) scroll; ~ **défiler vers le bas/haut** (Info) scroll down/up; ~ **face à** confront, face; ~ **naître** (confiance) breed; ~ **part de** (détails) announce; (griefs) air; ~ **part de qch à qn** advise sb of sth, inform sb of sth; ~ **part à qn que** advise sb that, inform sb that; ~ **partie intégrante de qch** be part and parcel of sth; ~ **de la réclame** advertise; **qui fait gagner du temps** time-saving

⟦2⟧ **se faire** *v pron* **se** ~ **avoir** (infml) be taken in; **se** ~ **domicilier** take up legal residence; **se** ~ **enregistrer** book in; **se** ~ **envoyer qch** send away for sth, send off for sth; **se** ~ **excuser** be excused; **se** ~ **rembourser** get a refund, get one's money back (obligations) cash in

faisable *adj* feasible, manageable

fait[1], **e** *adj* made; ~ **pour durer** made to last; ~ **à la main** handmade; ~ **en série** machine-made; ~ **sur mesure** (Com) custom-made, tailor-made; (Ind) made to measure

fait[2] *m* fact; **de** ~ de facto; **être au** ~ **de** be abreast of, be familiar with; **les** ~**s et les chiffres** facts and figures; ~ **établi** ascertained fact; ~ **d'être acceptable** adequacy; ~**s matériels d'une affaire** (Droit) achievements, res gestae (frml); ~ **pertinent** material fact

falsification *f* (de comptes) falsification; (de signature) forgery

falsifier *vt* (comptes) falsify; (signature) forge

familier, -ière *adj* familiar (à to)

famille *f* family; ~ **de caractères** (Info) font family; ~ **de fonds de placement** (Bourse) family of funds; ~ **immédiate** close family, immediate family; (Bourse) immediate family; ~ **monoparentale** single-parent family

F&A *abrév* (▸**fusions et acquisitions**) M&A (mergers and acquisitions)

FAO *abrév* (▸**fabrication assistée par ordinateur**) CAM (computer-aided

manufacture), computer-assisted manufacture

FAP *abrév* (▸**franc d'avarie particulière**) FPA (free of particular average); ~ **sauf** FPA unless

FAQ *abrév* (▸**franco à quai**) FOQ (free on quay); (▸**foire aux questions**) (Internet) FAQ (frequently asked questions)

fardeau *m* burden; ~ **fiscal** tax burden; ~ **de la dette** debt burden, burden of debt; ~ **de la preuve** burden of proof

fascicule *m* (brochure) booklet; ~ **horaire** working timetable

fatigue *f* tiredness, fatigue; ~ **de l'ajustement** adjustment fatigue

faute *f* error, mistake; (responsabilité) fault; (Droit) misdeed; ~ **de** in the absence of; ~ **de quoi** failing which; ~ **de détails** in the absence of detailed information; ~ **de renseignements** in the absence of any information; ~ **de copiste** clerical error; ~ **de frappe** typo; ~ **grave** gross misconduct; ~ **d'impression** misprint; ~ **non intentionnelle** mistake; ~ **professionnelle** professional misconduct

faux[1], **fausse** *adj* (chèque, document) forged; (déclaration) false; (passeport) false, forged; (billet) counterfeit; (résultat) wrong; **fausse alerte** false alarm; ~ **chèque** forged cheque BrE, forged check AmE; **fausse déclaration délibérée** wilful misrepresentation of facts; **fausse économie** false economy; **fausse écriture** fraudulent entry; ~ **frais** incidental allowances, incidental expenses; ~ **fret** (navigation) deadfreight; ~ **numéro** wrong number; ~ **pas** faux pas; ~ **serment** perjury; **fausse signature** forged signature; ~ **témoignage** (déposition) false evidence; (délit) perjury; ~ **témoin** false witness

faux[2] *m* (document) forgery; (objet, tableaux) fake

faveur *f* favour BrE, favor AmE; **faire/demander une** ~ **à qn** do/ask sb a favour; **les mesures en** ~ **de l'emploi** measures to promote employment

favorabilité *f* favourability BrE, favorability AmE

favorable *adj* (balance commerciale) positive; (conditions, taux d'échange, écart) favourable BrE, favorable AmE; ~ **à** (projet, suggestion) in favour of BrE, in favor of AmE

favori *m* (Info) bookmark, favourite; **liste de** ~**s** (Info) favourites, hot list

favoriser *vt* (personne, groupe) favour BrE, favor AmE; (emploi, relations) encourage, promote; ~ **l'efficacité** promote efficiency; **des mesures favorisant le développement** measures to promote *ou* encourage development

fax *m* (machine) fax machine; (document) facsimile, fax

fco *abrév* (▸**franco**) fco. (franco)

FDE *abrév* (▸**Fonds de développement**

européen) EDF (European Development Fund)

FEDER *abrév* (▸**Fonds européen de développement régional**) ERDF (European Regional Development Fund)

fédéral, e *adj* federal

fédéralisme *m* federalism; **~ fiscal** fiscal federalism, top-sided federalism

fédération *f* federation; **Fédération internationale des bourses de valeurs** International Federation of Stock Exchanges; **F~ internationale de documentation** International Federation for Documentation; **F~ internationale de la navigation** International Shipping Federation; **F~ internationale des producteurs agricoles** International Federation of Agricultural Producers; **F~ mondiale des associations des Nations Unies** World Federation of United Nations Associations; **F~ syndicale** trade union UK, labor union US; **~ syndicale mondiale** World Federation of Trade Unions

félicitations *f pl* congratulations (**pour** on; **à** to)

féliciter *vt* congratulate (**pour qch** on sth)

félin *m* (Bourse) strip bond, stripped bond

fémelot *m* (navigation) gudgeon

femme *f* woman; **~ active** working woman; **~ d'affaires** businesswoman; **~ mariée** married woman

fenêtre *f* (Info) (sur un écran) window; **~ active** active window; **~ d'alerte** alert box; **~ de contrôle** audit window; **~ de dialogue** dialogue box BrE, dialog box AmE

fente *f* (pour introduire une carte) slot

féodalisme *m* feudalism

fer *m* iron; **~ de lance** spearhead; **au ~ à droite** (Info) flush right, right-justified; **au ~ à gauche** (Info) flush left, left-justified

ferblanterie *f* tinware

férié, e *adj* **jour ~** public holiday BrE, bank holiday BrE, holiday AmE

ferme¹ *adj* (marché) buoyant, firm; (commande, engagement, prix, vente) firm

ferme² *f* farm; **~ laitière** dairy farm

fermé, e *adj* closed

fermer *vt* (compte) close; (entreprise, usine) close, shut; **~ définitivement** close down, shut down; **~ boutique** go out of business, shut up shop (infrml)

fermeté *f* (du marché) buoyancy

fermeture *f* (action) closing; (résultat) closure; (d'une usine) closure, shutdown; **~ annuelle** annual closure, annual holiday; **~ d'usine** factory closure, factory shut-down

ferraille *f* scrap metal

ferrailleur *m* scrap dealer

ferreux, -euse *adj* ferrous; **métaux non ~** nonferrous metals

ferroutage *m* road-rail transport BrE, piggyback traffic AmE (jarg)

fertiliser *vt* (champs) fertilize

festival *m* festival; **~ du cinéma** film festival

fête *f* holiday; **~ publique** bank holiday BrE, legal holiday AmE

feu *m* (combustion, incendie) fire; (lumière) light; (à un carrefour) traffic light; **~ vert** green light; **donner son ~ vert à qn** give sb the go-ahead

feuille *f* sheet; (publicité) leaflet; (formulaire) form; **à ~s mobiles** loose-leaf; **~ bamboche** (impression) badly imposed page; **~ de calcul électronique** (Info) spreadsheet; **~ de chou** (infrml) (presse) rag (infrml); **~ de couverture** (édition) base sheet; **~ d'impôts** (déclaration) tax return; (avis de débit) tax demand, tax statement; **~ de paie** payslip; **~ de pointage** tally sheet, time card; **~ de présence** time sheet; **~ de programmation** (Info) code sheet, work sheet; **~ de route** consignment note, waybill; **~ de tôle** tin plate; **~ de travail** (Compta) audit working papers, working papers

FF *abrév* (▸**franc français**) FF (French franc)

FG *abrév* (▸**frais généraux**) overhead charges, overheads

fiabilité *f* reliability; **~ du produit** product reliability

fiable *adj* reliable; **peu ~** unreliable

fibre *f* fibre BrE, fiber AmE; **~ optique** fibre optics BrE, fiber optics AmE; **~ synthétique** man-made fibre BrE, man-made fiber AmE; **~ de verre** fibreglass BrE, fiberglass AmE

FIBV *abrév* (▸**Fédération internationale des bourses de valeurs**) IFSE (International Federation of Stock Exchanges)

ficelles du métier *f pl* tricks of the trade

fichage *m* (Admin) filing system

fiche *f* index card, file card; **mettre qch sur ~** put sth on file; **mettre qn sur ~** put sb on file, put sb on one's books; **~ de client** customer card; **~ des communs** (Assur) aggregate liability index; **~ d'instructions de transport** transport instruction form; **~ d'inventaire** stock sheet; **~ d'ordre** trade ticket; **~ de paie** pay sheet, payslip BrE, pay bill AmE; **~ de poste** job card; **~ de prix de revient** job cost sheet; **~ de recherche** tracer; **~ de spécimen de signature** signature card; **~ de suivi** checklist; **~ technique** data sheet

fichier *m* (collection de fiches) card index; (meuble) filing cabinet; (Info) file; **~ actif** active file; **~ d'adresses** address file; **~ d'archives** archive file; **~ sur bande** tape file; **~ caché** hidden file; **~ de caractères** font file; **~ central** computer bank, data bank; **~ de consignation** log file; **~ en cours** active file; **~ créateur** father file; **~** ···>

de dessins drawing file; ~ **de données**
data file; ~ **informatique** computer file; ~
de mise à jour transaction file; ~ **des**
oppositions negative file; ~ **père** master
file; ~ **principal** main file, master file; ~
résultant output file; ~ **de sauvegarde**
backup file; ~ **séquentiel** batch file; ~ **de**
sortie output file; ~ **de stock** inventory
file; ~ **à traitement différé** spool file; ~ **de**
transactions transaction file; ~ **de travail**
scratch file; ~ **de tri** sort file; ~ **vidéo**
image file; ~ **de visualisation** display file

fictif, -ive adj fictitious; (Fin) (revenu)
notional; (profits) paper; (société) dummy

fidéicommis m (Droit) trusteeship; ~
complexe complex trust US; ~ **de**
concédant grantor trust; ~ **institué par**
testament testamentary trust; ~ **institué**
sans document formel involuntary trust
US; ~ **irrévocable** irrevocable trust; ~
entre vifs inter vivos trust

fidéicommissaire m,f (Droit) trustee

fidéjusseur m (Assur) surety; (Droit)
guarantor

fidèle adj (loyal) loyal (à to); (conforme)
faithful (à to); (Compta) true and fair

fidélisation f (publicité) continuous
promotion; ~ **du client** customer retention

fidélité f (de client, électeur) loyalty; (à une
promesse) faithfulness; (de récit, traduction)
accuracy; **carte de** ~ loyalty card; ~ **du**
consommateur consumer loyalty; ~ **à une**
marque brand loyalty

fiduciaire[1] adj (émission, circulation) fiduciary;
société ~ trust company

fiduciaire[2] mf trustee

fiduciairement adv fiduciarily

fiducie f (testaments et droits de succession)
trust; (Bourse) trustee status; ~
commerciale commercial trust; ~
d'employés employee trust; ~ **offshore**
offshore trust

figurer vi appear; ~ **en tête d'affiche** get
top billing

file f line; ~ **d'attente** queue BrE, line AmE;
(Info) queue; ~ **d'attente de travaux** job
queue

filer vi (s'éloigner) (infrml) leave; ~ **à**
l'anglaise take French leave (infrml)

filet m net ~ **de chargement** basket hitch;
~ **d'élingue** cargo net

filiale f (agence, grande surface, banque) branch;
(compagnie, firme) affiliated firm, subsidiary
(company); ~**s** registered offices; ~
bancaire bank subsidiary; ~ **étrangère**
foreign branch, foreign affiliate; ~ **en**
propriété exclusive wholly-owned
subsidiary

filière f (domaine d'activité) sector, field; (suite de
formalités) channels; (domaine d'études) course of
study; (opération clandestine) ring; **la** ~
administrative official administrative

channels; **suivre la** ~ **habituelle** follow the
usual career path

filigrane m watermark

fils m son; **Martin** ~ (entreprise) Martin junior

filtre m filter; ~ **Internet** (de censure)
censorware

fin f (de séance, de reunion) close, end; (de groupe
industriel, de société) break-up, end; **à cette** ~
with this in view; **de** ~ **d'année** year-end; **en**
~ **de compte** at the end of the day; **en** ~ **de**
journée at the end of the day; **mettre** ~ **à un**
contrat terminate a contract; ~ **juin** at the
end of June; ~ **courant** at the end of the
current month; **à des** ~**s comptables** for
book purposes; ~ **admise** specified purpose;
~ **de l'année d'imposition** end of the
taxation year; ~ **des émissions** (télévision)
close-down, ~ **d'exercice** year end; ~ **de**
fichier end of file; ~ **de message** end of
message; ~ **de mois** end of month; ~ **de**
non-recevoir demurrer; ~ **de séance**
(Bourse) close; ~ **de série** oddment, end-of-
line item; ~ **de trimestre** quarter end

final, e adj final

finalement adv eventually, finally

finalité f aim, objective

finance f finance; ~**s** finances; ~**s des**
collectivités locales local government
finance; ~ **d'entreprise** corporate finance;
~ **fédérale** federal finance US, revenue
sharing US; ~ **globale** outside finance; ~**s**
locales local finance; ~ **d'ouverture** front-
end finance; ~**s publiques** government
finance, public finance

financement m financing, funding; **le** ~
du projet ne sera pas facile financing the
project won't be easy; **disposant d'un** ~
suffisant adequately funded; **campagne de**
~ fundraising campaign; ~ **d'une**
acquisition acquisition financing; ~
d'actifs active financing; ~ **d'amorçage**
seed capital; ~ **d'apport** vendor finance; ~
de base core funding; ~ **de baux**
financiers (Banque) lease financing; ~ **par**
capital-risque venture-capital financing ou
funding; ~ **du commerce extérieur** trade
finance; ~ **des comptes clients** (Compta)
accounts receivable financing; ~ **conjoint**
cofinancing; ~ **par crédit relais** bridge
financing; ~ **du déficit** gap financing; ~ **du**
déficit budgétaire deficit financing; ~
déguisé backdoor financing; ~ **de**
démarrage start-up capital; ~ **externe**
external financing; ~ **sur fonds propres**
equity capital, equity financing; ~ **à forfait**
nonrecourse financing; ~ **de franchise**
franchise financing; ~ **garanti par l'actif**
asset-backed finance; ~ **global** block
funding; ~ **hors bilan** off-balance-sheet
financing; ~ **d'immobilisations** capital
funding; ~ **industriel** industrial finance; ~
initial front-end financing; ~ **à long terme**
long-term funding; ~ **non durable** soft

funding; ~ **obligataire** (Bourse) bond financing; ~ **officiel** official financing; ~ **des opérations commerciales** trade finance, trade financing; ~ **de projets** project financing; ~ **provisoire** interim financing; ~ **à recours limité** limited recourse financing; ~ **de redressement** turnaround; ~ **de remplacement** alternate funding, replacement capital; ~ **à rendement élevé** high-yield financing; ~ **reposant sur l'actif** asset-based financing; ~ **sans recours** nonrecourse finance, nonrecourse financing; ~ **véreux** backdoor financing

financer *vt* (projet) finance, fund, back; bankroll US; ~ **la différence** finance the difference; ~ **directement** finance directly; **financé par l'État** government-funded

financier¹, -ière *adj* financial

financier², -ière *m,f* financier; ~ **à risque** venture capitalist

fini, e *adj* (travail, tâche) completed, finished

finir ⓵ *vt* complete, finish; ~ **le travail** finish work, knock off (infrml) ⓶ *vi* finish, end; (contrat, bail) run out, expire; **il a fini directeur de la société** he ended up as company director; ~ **par être payant** finish in the money

FIO *abrév* (▸**fabrication intégrée par ordinateur**) CIM (computer-integrated manufacturing)

fioul *m* fuel oil

FIPA *abrév* (▸**Fédération internationale des producteurs agricoles**) IFAP (International Federation of Agricultural Producers)

firme *f* firm; ~ **affiliée** member firm; ~ **sous contrôle étranger** foreign-owned company; ~ **de courtiers** stock brokerage firm; ~ **dominante** core firm, dominant firm; ~ **étrangère** foreign firm; ~ **non-affiliée** nonmember firm; ~ **souple et mobile** flexible firm

fisc *m* ≈ Inland Revenue UK, ≈ Internal Revenue Service US

fiscal, e *adj* tax, fiscal; **l'appareil ~** the tax system

fiscaliste *mf* fiscalist, tax expert

fiscalité *f* (fait d'imposer) taxation; (système) tax system; ~ **excessive** overtaxation; ~ **latente passive** deferred tax liabilities; ~ **à taux zéro** zero rate taxation

fixage *m* (Fin) fixing

fixation *f* (de salaire, de taux, des conditions) setting; (de dédommagement) assessment; (de cours) pegging; ~ **administrative des prix** administered pricing; ~ **d'impôt** tax assessment; ~ **marginale du prix** marginal pricing; ~ **d'objectifs** goal setting; ~ **du point de base** basing point pricing; ~ **des prix** pricing; ~ **d'un prix de déclenchement** trigger pricing; ~ **d'un**

prix élevé premium pricing; ~ **des prix par anticipation** anticipatory pricing; ~ **des prix par une entreprise leader** price leadership; ~ **des prix par le jeu du marché** commodity pricing; ~ **des prix de transfert** (multinationales) transfer pricing; ~ **des tarifs** fare pricing

fixe *adj* (prix, taux) fixed; (tarif) flat; (poste, personnel, résidence) permanent

fixé, e *adj* (avec un rivet) riveted; (tarif) flat; ~ **au sol** (construction) affixed to land

fixer *vt* (date, endroit, objectif) set; (indemnité) determine; (prix) fix; (cours) peg; ~ **le prix de** fix the price of, price; ~ **la cotisation d'impôt** assess tax; ~ **une date** set a date; ~ **le montant** settle the figure; ~ **un prix forfaitaire** fix an all-inclusive price, set a price-point

fixeur *m*: ~ **de prix** price maker

flambage *m* (navigation) buckling

flambant *adj*: ~ **neuf** brand-new

flambée *f* (de violence) flare-up; (des cours) explosion; ~ **des prix** price escalation

flamber *vi* (prix) rocket; (cours) boom

flanquer *vt*: ~ **qn à la porte** (infrml) give sb the sack (infrml), throw sb out (infrml)

flash *m* flash; ~ **d'information** (TV, radio) news flash; ~ **publicitaire** advert BrE, commercial AmE

flèche *f* arrow; ~ **de défilement** scroll arrow; ~ **de retour arrière** back arrow; ~ **verticale** down arrow

fléchir *vi* (marché, monnaie) weaken; (demande, cours) fall, drop; (prix, tendance du marché) dip, fall

fléchissement *m* (de marché) weakening; (de prix, de demande, de cours) fall, drop; ~ **de la hausse** topping out

flexibilité *f* flexibility; ~ **des emplois** job flexibility; ~ **des horaires** flexitime; ~ **des prix** price flexibility; ~ **des salaires** wage flexibility; ~ **des tarifs** rate flexibility

flexible *adj* flexible; (heure, date) flexible, adjustable

florin *m* florin, guilder

florissant, e *adj* flourishing, thriving; **être ~** flourish, thrive

flot *m* flow; (de documents, de visiteurs) flood; (de clients) stream; **à ~** afloat

flottage *m* float; ~ **en amont** upstream float; ~ **en aval** downstream float

flottant¹, e *adj* (taux d'intérêt, capitaux, devise) floating; (Assur) (police) floating, open

flottant² *m* (Banque) bank float, debit float; (Bourse) floating stock, floating supply

flotte *f* fleet

flottement *m* (de monnaie) floating; ~ **impur** (Econ) dirty float; ~ **pur** clean float

fluctuation *f* fluctuation; ~ **des cours** price move; ~ **défavorable** adverse movement; ~ **journalières** *f pl* daily ⋯⋗

fluctuations, (Bourse) mark-to-the-market, marking-to-market; ~ **du niveau des prix** price level change; ~ **de prix** price fluctuation, (Bourse) price tick; ~ **saisonnière** seasonal swing; ~**s des taux de change** exchange rate movements

fluctuer vi (marché, cours) fluctuate

flux m (Fin) flow; **à ~ tendus** just-in-time; ~ **d'affaires** business stream; ~ **de capitaux** capital flow; ~ **commercial** trade flow; ~ **de données** data stream; ~ **de l'encaisse** cash flow; ~ **financier** financial flow, flow of funds; ~ **monétaire** flow of money; ~ **des revenus** income stream; ~ **de travail** work flow; ~ **de trésorerie** flow of funds; ~ **de trésorerie disponible** available cash flow

FME abrév (▶**Fonds monétaire européen**) EMF (European Monetary Fund)

FMEC abrév (▶**Fonds monétaire européen de coopération**) EMCF (European Monetary Cooperation Fund)

FMI abrév (▶**Fonds monétaire international**) IMF (International Monetary Fund)

focaliser vt (Media) (attention) focus; (efforts) concentrate; (V&M) target

foi f faith; **en ~ de quoi** (Droit) in witness whereof; ~ **aveugle** blind faith

foire f exhibition; ~ **de l'artisanat** craft fair; ~ **commerciale** trade fair, trade show; ~ **d'empoigne** rat race

fois f time; **cette ~-là** this time; **à la ~** at the same time; **une ~** once; **deux ~** twice; **vous pouvez régler en trois ~** you can pay in three instalments

foncier¹, -ière adj (impôt) land; (revenu) from land; **biens ~s** real esate; **propriétaire ~** landowner; **taxe foncière** property tax

foncier² m real estate; ~ **non bâti** vacant land; ~ **à perpétuité** freeholder

fonction f (Admin) post; (rôle) function; (Info) function; **entrer en ~s** take up one's post; **se démettre/être démis de ses ~s** resign/be dismissed from one's post; **dans le cadre de mes ~s** as part of my duties; **en ~ de** according to; **en ~ des informations à connaître** on a need-to-know basis; **avoir une ~ de** perform the office of; **de par ses ~s** by virtue of one's position, ex officio (frml); **en ~** in charge, in office; ~**s complémentaires** support activities; ~ **de consommation** (Econ) consumption function; ~ **consultative** advisory function, advisory work; ~ **de direction** managerial function; ~ **élevée** high office, important office; ~ **d'épargne** savings function; ~ **d'offre** (Econ) supply function; ~ **de production** (Econ) production function; ~ **programmable** (Info) programmable function; ~ **publique** civil service UK, public service; ~ **de recherche et remplacement** (Info) search and replace; ~ **de surprise** (Econ) surprise function; ~

d'utilité (Econ) utility function

fonctionnaire mf civil servant UK, public servant, public officer; ~ **boursier** floor official; ~ **de l'immigration** immigration officer; ~ **de l'ordre judiciaire** legal officer; ~ **titulaire** senior civil servant

fonctionnalité f functionality

fonctionnel, -elle adj functional

fonctionnement m (Admin) functioning; (Droit) machinery; **en ~** at work

fonctionner vi function, operate; ~ **en tandem** operate in tandem

fond m (d'un navire) bottom; ~ **de cale** bilge; ~ **de panier** (Info) motherboard, mothercard

fondamental, e adj fundamental

fondateur, -trice m,f (Droit) settlor UK; **groupe ~** founding group; **membre ~** founder member

fondation f (Droit, Fisc) foundation; (navigation) foundation; **Fondation européenne** European Foundation; ~ **privée** (Fisc) private foundation; ~ **publique** (Fisc) public foundation; ~ **d'utilité publique** (Fisc) charitable trust

fondé, e adj (réclamation) justifiable; (demande) legitimate; **non ~** (accusation) groundless; (confiance) misplaced; **être ~ à faire** be justified in doing; ~ **de pouvoir** (Droit) proxy, attorney US; (de société) authorized representative; (de banque) manager

fondement m basis; ~ **d'une action** cause of action

fonder vt (baser) base; (créer) establish; **'maison fondée en 1920'** 'established 1920'

fonderie f smelting works

fondre vt (métal) fuse; (minerai) smelt

fonds m (organisme) fund; (propriété) business; (capital) fund, funds; **un ~ d'épicerie** a grocery business; **recueillir des ~** raise money; **manquer de ~** be short of funds; **gérer/affecter des ~** manage/earmark funds; **mise de ~** capital outlay; **rentrer dans ses ~** recover outlay, recoup one's investment; **disposer des ~ nécessaires** have the necessary funds; **à ~ perdus** at a loss; **à ~ publics** publicly-funded; **avec ~ bancaires** bank-financed; **injecter des ~ dans** pump funds into; ~ **accumulés** accumulating fund; ~ **d'actions ordinaires** common shares fund BrE, common stock fund AmE; ~ **d'affectation spéciale** trust fund; **Fonds agricole européen** European Agricultural Fund; ~ **d'aide au développement** aid money; ~ **d'amortissement** sinking fund; ~ **d'arbitrage** hedge fund; ~ **autogénérés** self-generated funds; ~ **cadre** umbrella fund; ~ **de caisse** cash in hand; ~ **de capital et d'emprunt** capital fund; ~ **de cautionnement** guaranty fund; ~ **des changes** exchange fund; ~ **de cohésion** cohesion fund; ~ **de commerce** business (concern); ∼ **commercial** goodwill money; ∼ **commun de placement** unit trust UK, mutual fund US; ∼ **de compensation** equalization fund; ∼ **de consolidation** umbrella fund; ∼ **courants** general fund; ∼ **de courtage** broker fund UK; ∼ **de croissance** growth fund; **Fonds de développement européen** European Development Fund; ∼ **disponibles** available funds, liquid funds; ∼ **disponibles en banque** cash in bank; ∼ **de dividendes** dividend fund; ∼ **empruntés** borrowed funds; ∼ **d'escompte** discount market loan; ∼ **d'État** government security, government stock, ≈gilt UK; ∼ **à l'étranger** funds abroad; ∼ **de l'étranger** offshore funds; **Fonds européen de coopération monétaire** European Monetary Cooperation Fund; **Fonds européen de développement régional** European Regional Development Fund; ∼ **exceptionnels** Superfund US; ∼ **externes** external funds; ∼ **de garantie** (Bourse) compensation fund UK; ∼ **de garantie bancaire** bank insurance fund; ∼ **de garantie des salaires** national salary guarantee fund; ∼ **gelés** frozen assets; ∼ **géré en devises** managed currency fund; ∼ **hautement spéculatif** go-go fund; ∼ **indice** index fund; ∼ **indiciel** index fund; ∼ **insuffisants** insufficient funds; ∼ **d'investissement en actions** equity investment fund; ∼ **d'investissement à capital fixe** closed-end mutual fund US; ∼ **de liquidation** cleanup fund; ∼ **mis de côté** impound account; ∼ **mixtes** mixed funds; ∼ **monétaire** money-market fund US; **Fonds monétaire européen** European Monetary Fund; **Fonds monétaire européen de coopération** European Monetary Cooperation Fund; **Fonds monétaire international** International Monetary Fund; ∼ **mutuel d'entraide sociale** social consciousness mutual fund; ∼ **nets disponibles** net liquid funds; ∼ **non-agréés** unapproved funds; ∼ **obligataire** bond fund; ∼ **obligataire municipal** single-state municipal bond fund; ∼ **occultes** secret reserve; ∼ **périmés** lapsed funds; ∼ **de placement** investment trust; ∼ **prêtables** lendable funds; ∼ **de prévoyance** contingency fund, contingency reserve; ∼ **propres** equity capital, shareholders' equity; ∼ **publics** (Bourse) government stock, government securities; (recettes de l'État) government funds, federal funds US; ∼ **de rachat** purchase fund; ∼ **renouvelable** revolving fund; ∼ **de réserve** (d'une banque) bank reserve, rest fund; **Fonds de rétablissement du conseil de l'Europe** Council of Europe Resettlement Fund; ∼ **de retraite** pension fund; ∼ **de roulement** working capital; ∼ **sans frais** no-load fund US; ∼ **de sauvegarde** hedge fund; **Fonds social**

européen European Social Fund; ∼ **soutenu** hard money (jarg); ∼ **spéculatifs** performance fund, speculative fund; ∼ **de stabilisation** stabilization fund

fongibles *m pl* (Econ) fungibles

fonte *f* (d'un métal) fusion; (Info) font; ∼ **froide** (imprimerie) cold type

forage *m* drilling; ∼ **d'exploration** wildcat drilling; ∼ **d'exploration contrôlé** controlled wildcat drilling; ∼ **sauvage** wildcat drilling

force *f* strength; **avoir** ∼ **de loi** have statutory effect; ∼ **d'appui** (Pol) leverage; ∼ **contenue** pent-up energy; ∼ **financière** (Fin) financial strength; ∼ **de loi** (Droit) legal force; ∼ **majeure** force majeure; ∼**s du marché** market forces; ∼ **de vente** (V&M) sales force

forcé, e *adj* compulsory

forcer *vt* force; ∼ **qn à faire qch** force sb to do sth, oblige sb to do sth

forclusion *f* (Droit) foreclosure; ∼ **fiscale** tax foreclosure; ∼ **légale** statutory foreclosure

fordisme *m* (Econ) Fordism

forfait *m* (prix global) fixed rate, fixed price, flat rate; (montant) lump sum; (séjour) package; (offre promotionnelle) package; (abonnement) season ticket; **travailler/être payé au** ∼ work for/be paid a fixed rate; ∼ **hebdomadaire** weekly rate; **être au** ∼ (Fisc) be taxed for an estimated income; **à** ∼ at a flat price; (contrat) at an agreed price; ∼ **de port** carriage forward; ∼ **de sous-traitance** lump (infrml); ∼ **vol-croisière** fly-cruise

forfaitaire *adj* (prix) all-inclusive, fixed; **coût** ∼ inclusive cost; **tarif** ∼ flat fare *ou* price; **somme** ∼ lump sum; **indemnité** ∼ basic allowance

formaliser *vt* (idée) formalize

formalité *f* formality; ∼**s douanières** customs clearance, customs formalities; ∼**s douanières d'une cargaison** customs cargo clearance; ∼**s juridiques** legal formalities

format *m* (Info) format; (d'un document) format, size; ∼ **de l'écran** (Info) aspect ratio; ∼ **d'enregistrement** (Info) record format; ∼ **horizontal** (Info) (impression) landscape format; ∼ **vertical** (Info) portrait format

formatage *m* (Info) (de disque, disquette) formatting

formater *vt* (Info) (disque, disquette) format; **non formaté** unformatted

formateur[1], **-trice** *adj* (influence, rôle, élément) formative; **stage** ∼ training course

formateur[2], **-trice** *m,f* trainer; ∼ **à Internet** Web tutor, Internet tutor

formation *f* (instruction scolaire) education; (professionnelle) training; **en** ∼ (stagiaire, technicien) undergoing training, trainee; '∼ **assurée**' 'training provided'; **ayant une** ∼ **en** ⋯⟩

informatique computer literate, computerate; ∼ **par alternance** sandwich course; ∼ **des cadres** executive training; ∼ **continue** continuing professional education; ∼ **en dehors de l'entreprise** off-the-job training; ∼ **en entreprise** on-the-job training; ∼ **de formateurs** training of trainers; ∼ **générale** general training; ∼ **des jeunes** youth training; ∼ **en ligne** (Info) online training, e-training; ∼ **permanente** further education; ∼ **du personnel** staff training; ∼ **pratique** hands-on training; ∼ **professionnelle** vocational training; ∼ **programmée** (Info) computer-based training; ∼ **supérieure** advanced education, advanced training; ∼ **sur le tas** on-the-job training

forme f (procédé, condition) form; (configuration) shape; (de paiement, recrutement) method; **la ∼ de l'économie mondiale** the shape of the world economy; **en ∼ provisoire** in draft form; **pour la ∼** pro forma; **prendre la ∼ de** take the form of; ∼ **organisationnelle** organizational shape; ∼ **de propriété** ownership form US

former vt (comité) form; (nouvelle entreprise) establish, form; (à l'emploi) train; **non formé** (personnel) untrained; ∼ **un recours** (Droit) appeal

formidable adj tremendous

formulaire m (imprimé) form; **remplir un ∼** fill in a form, fill out a form; ∼ **commercial** business form; ∼ **de déclaration de sinistre** (Assur) claim form; ∼ **de demande de renseignements** enquiry form, inquiry form; ∼ **électronique** e-form; ∼ **d'inscription** application form; ∼ **normalisé** aligned form; ∼ **réglementaire** prescribed form; ∼ **sensible** (Fisc) sensitive form; ∼ **T** (Imp/Exp) T form; ∼ **de transfert** transfer; ∼ **de transit** transit form; ∼ **de versement** remittance return

formulation f (action) formulation; (chose formulée) wording; ∼ **de la politique** policy-making

formule f formula; ∼ **de calcul d'intérêt** interest formula; ∼ **de chèque** blank cheque BrE, blank check AmE; ∼ **de l'établissement du prix de l'option** (Bourse) option-pricing formula; ∼ **d'étalement** (Banque) averaging formula; ∼ **d'évaluation des options** (Bourse) option-pricing formula; ∼ **fiscale** tax form; ∼ **gravée** engraved form; ∼ **magique** golden formula; ∼ **de marketing** marketing mix; ∼ **de politesse** complimentary close; ∼ **au porteur** bearer form; ∼ **préférentielle** preferential form; ∼ **quinquennale** five-year formula; ∼ **à usage restreint** sensitive form

formuler vt (conditions) set out; (demande) formulate; (acte) draw up; ∼ **une demande de renseignements** make enquiries

fort, e adj (puissant, résistant) strong; (ample) (somme, majorité, réduction) large; (concentration, taux, inflation) high; (expansion, pénurie) great, marked; (croissance) strong; **à ∼ coefficient de main-d'œuvre** labour-intensive BrE, labor-intensive AmE; **à ∼ coefficient de recherche** (production) research-intensive; ∼ **coefficient d'arrimage** (marchandises) high stowage factor; **à ∼e image de marque** high-profile; **à ∼e intensité de capitaux** capital-intensive; **à ∼e intensité de connaissances** knowledge-intensive; **être en ∼e hausse** be booming; ∼**e augmentation** sharp rise; ∼**e baisse** sharp drop; ∼**e concurrence** tough competition; ∼**e demande** active demand, heavy demand; ∼**e expansion** boom; ∼**e hausse** boom, sharp rise; ∼**e progression** boom

fortement adv (baisser) sharply; (polluer) badly; **être ∼ présent** be strongly in evidence, be very much in evidence; ∼ **peuplé** densely-populated

forteresse f fortress; ∼ **Europe** (UE) fortress Europe

fortuit, e adj chance

fortune f fortune; **faire ∼** make a fortune, strike it rich (infrml); ∼ **de mer** (assurance) sea damage

fortuné, e adj well-to-do

forum m forum; ∼ **de discussion** newsgroup

fossé m gap; ∼ **numérique** (Info) digital divide; ∼ **entre les salaires** wage gap

fouille f (douane) search, examination; ∼ **au hasard** spot check; ∼ **incontestée** uncontested physical search; ∼ **et perquisition** search

fouiller vt search

fourche f fork; ∼ **à palettes** (manutention) pallet fork; ∼ **à rallonge** extension fork

fourchette f (de prix, température, fluctuation) range; (de revenus, d'âge) bracket; **dans une ∼ comprise entre 1000 et 200 euros** in a price range of 1,000 to 2,000 euros; ∼ **horaire** period; ∼ **des prix limites de transaction** (Bourse) trading range; ∼ **supérieure d'imposition** higher tax bracket; ∼ **de variation du cours** (Bourse) distribution area; ∼ **visée** target range

fourgon m goods wagon BrE, freight car AmE; ∼ **isotherme** insulated van; ∼ **postal** mail van BrE, mailcar AmE

fourguer vt (infrml) (marchandises) flog BrE (infrml), hustle AmE (infrml)

fourni, e adj (approvisionné) **bien/mal ∼** well-/ill-stocked (**en** with); ∼ **avec** supplied with; (Info) bundled with; **non ∼ par ailleurs** not otherwise provided

fournir [1] vt (marchandises) supply; (service) provide; (preuve) adduce, provide; ∼ **une assistance technique** provide technical assistance; ∼ **des directives à** brief; ∼ **des**

marchandises à crédit supply goods on credit; ∼ **un marché pour** provide a market for; ∼ **du personnel à** staff, resource; ∼ **des preuves à l'appui d'une demande** substantiate a claim; ∼ **un soutien technique** provide technical assistance **2** **se fournir** *v pron* (s'approvisionner) **se** ∼ **chez** buy from; (entreprise) get supplies from

fournisseur *m* (Com) provider, supplier; (détaillant) retailer; ∼ **habituel/principal** usual/prime supplier; ∼ **d'accès Internet** Internet access provider; ∼ **d'alimentation fine** purveyor of fine foods; ∼ **de contenus** (Info) content provider; ∼ **de crédit** credit grantor; ∼ **de matériaux** materials supplier; ∼ **de navires** ship's chandler; ∼ **d'ordinateurs** computer vendor; ∼ **de services d'application** (Info) application service provider; ∼ **de système** (Info) system-provider; ∼ **de vidéos sur Internet** Internet media provider

fourniture *f* (vente) supply; (équipement) equipment; ∼**s** (objets) materials; (choses fournies) supplies; ∼**s de bureau** office supplies; ∼**s consommables** factory supplies; ∼ **publique** public procurement; ∼**s au taux zéro** (Fisc) zero-rated supplies UK

foyer *m* (maison) home; (famille) household; (d'incendie) fire; ∼ **à caractère d'incendie** (Assur) hostile fire; ∼ **à faible revenu** low-income household; ∼ **fiscal** tax unit

FPP *abrév* (▸**frontière des possibilités de production**) (Econ) production possibility frontier

fraction *f* (partie) part; (Math) fraction; (Fin) portion; (Compta) fraction; ∼ **d'action** fractional share; ∼ **convenue** (Fisc) agreed portion; ∼ **inutilisée** (Fisc) unused part; ∼ **non amortie du coût** (Compta) undepreciated cost; ∼ **à risques** (Fisc) (de l'intérêt d'un commanditaire) at-risk amount

fractionnement *m* dividing up; ∼ **d'actions** (Banque) stock split AmE; ∼ **de portefeuille** (Bourse) portfolio split; ∼ **du revenu** (Fisc) income splitting

fractionner *vt* divide up; ∼ **un chargement/une livraison** break bulk; **livraison fractionnée** part shipment

fragile *adj* (sur les paquets) handle with care

fragmentation *f* fragmentation

fragmenter *vt* break up, chunk down (jarg)

frais *m pl* (Com) expenses; (pour un service commercial) charges; (pour un service professionnel) fees; (Droit) costs; (Compta) outgoings; (Fisc) expenses; **tous** ∼ **payés** all expenses paid; **rentrer dans ses** ∼ break even, recoup one's expenses; **faux** ∼ incidental costs; ∼ **annexes** fringe expenses; **à moindres** ∼ at very little cost; **partager les** ∼ share the cost; **faire les** ∼ **de qch** bear the brunt of sth; ∼ **à la charge de qn** costs taxable to sb; ∼ **fixes/variables** fixed/variable costs; ∼

moyens average costs; ∼ **mensuels** monthly expenses; **faire face à des** ∼ meet costs; **en être pour ses** ∼ be out of pocket;

frais a… ∼ **accessoires** incidental charges; ∼ **accumulés** accrued charges; ∼ **d'achat** original cost; ∼ **d'acquisition** acquisition cost; ∼ **d'adaptation** compliance costs; ∼ **administratifs** administrative costs; ∼ **admissibles** eligible expense; ∼ **d'agence** agency fees; ∼ **amortis** sunk cost; ∼ **d'annulation** cancellation fee; ∼ **anticipés** advanced charge; ∼ **d'assurance** insurance cost; ∼ **d'audit** audit costs;

b… ∼ **bancaires** bank charges; ∼ **du barème** scale charge; ∼ **de bureau à domicile** home office expenses;

c… ∼ **de camionnage** trucking charges; ∼ **de change** exchange charges; ∼ **de commercialisation** front-end costs, selling expenses; ∼ **commerciaux** sale charges; ∼ **de commission** load; ∼ **comptables** accounting fees; ∼ **de conservation** sue and labour charges BrE, sue and labor charges AmE; ∼ **consulaires** consulage; ∼ **de contentieux** legal charges; ∼ **de courtage** brokerage charges, commission; ∼ **de couverture** carrying cost;

d… ∼ **de débarquement** (dans un port) landing charge; ∼ **de déblaiement** costs of clearance of debris; ∼ **déductibles** (Fisc) allowable expense; ∼ **de démarrage** start-up costs; ∼ **et dépens** legal costs; ∼ **de déplacement** travel expenses; ∼ **de développement** development expenditure; ∼ **différés** deferred charge; ∼ **directs** direct cost; ∼ **de distribution** distribution costs; ∼ **divers** miscellaneous expenses; (voyage d'affaires) subsistence allowance; ∼ **pour droit d'accès** (Banque) standby charges; ∼ **pour droit d'usage** (Banque) standby charges;

e… ∼ **d'emballage et d'envoi non compris** exclusive of post and packing; ∼ **d'émission** flotation cost; ∼ **d'emprunt** cost of borrowing; ∼ **d'encaissement** collection charge; ∼ **d'engagement** liability cost; ∼ **engagés** incurred expenses; ∼ **engagés à l'extérieur** away from home expenses; ∼ **d'enlèvement** collection charge; ∼ **d'entreposage à l'exportation** export depot charges; ∼ **d'entreposage à l'importation** import depot charges; ∼ **d'entrepôt** warehouse charges; ∼ **d'entretien** maintenance charges; ∼ **d'envoi** dispatching charge; ∼ **d'escompte** discount charges; ∼ **d'essence** fuel expenses; ∼ **d'établissement** set-up costs; ∼ **d'étude de base** basic research cost; ∼ **d'expédition** dispatching charge; ∼ **d'expertise** consultancy fees; ∼ **d'exploitation** operating costs; ∼ **d'exploitation actuels** current expenditure; ∼ **d'extension** extension costs;

f… ∼ **de fabrication** manufacturing ⋯⋗

expenses; ∼ **financiers** finance charge; ∼ **fixes** fixed charges; ∼ **de fonctionnement** running costs, running expenses; ∼ **de fret** (navigation) cargo dues;

(**g...**) ∼ **de garde d'enfants** childcare expenses; ∼ **généraux** overheads; ∼ **généraux d'administration** administrative overheads; ∼ **généraux de fabrication** manufacturing overheads; ∼ **de gestion** handling charge; ∼ **de gestion de compte** bank charges, account charges;

(**h...**) ∼ **hors-site** off-site cost; ∼ **d'hospitalisation** hospital expenses;

(**i...**) ∼ **imputés** applied overhead; ∼ **indirects** indirect cost; ∼ **d'inscription** registration fee;

(**j...**) ∼ **de jouissance** (de propriété) carrying charge; ∼ **de justice** legal costs;

(**l...**) ∼ **de lancement** flotation cost; ∼ **de liquidation** closing-down costs; ∼ **de livraison** delivery charge; ∼ **de location** hire charges;

(**m...**) ∼ **de magasinage** storage charges; ∼ **de main-d'œuvre** labour costs, manpower costs; ∼ **de maintenance** maintenance charges; ∼ **de manutention des marchandises** cargo-handling charge; ∼ **médicaux** medical expenses; ∼ **de mise en conformité** compliance costs; ∼ **de mise à quai** wharfage charges; ∼ **de mise à terre** (dans un port) landing account; ∼ **de mission** (voyage d'affaires) business travel expenses; ∼ **de mouvement** (Banque) (à payer par le client) activity charge;

(**n...**) ∼ **de négociation** negotiation fee;

(**o...**) ∼ **d'option** option fee; ∼ **par opération** transaction cost;

(**p...**) ∼ **particuliers** particular charge; ∼ **de passage** throughput charge BrE, pass-through charge AmE; ∼ **à payer** accrued expenses; ∼ **payés d'avance** prepaid charges; ∼ **de personnel** personnel overheads; ∼ **personnels** personal expenses; ∼ **de placement** investment expense; ∼ **de port** port charge; ∼ **de port et d'emballage** postage and packing; ∼ **de portage** carrying charge; ∼ **de possession** carrying charge; ∼ **de premier établissement** promotion cost; ∼ **prioritaires** expense preference; ∼ **de procédure** cost of proceedings; ∼ **de production** capacity charge; ∼ **professionnels** business expenses; ∼ **progressifs** step cost; ∼ **de publicité** advertising costs;

(**r...**) ∼ **de recouvrement** collection cost; ∼ **de règlement** claims expenses; ∼ **relatifs à un emploi** employment expense; ∼ **de remorquage** towage dues; ∼ **de remplacement** cost of replacement; ∼ **reportés** deferred charge; ∼ **de représentation** entertainment allowance; ∼ **de réservation** booking fee; ∼ **de retrait**

back-end load; ∼ **rétroactifs** billback US; ∼ **de révision** audit costs;

(**s...**) ∼ **de scolarité** school fees; ∼ **de séjour** living expenses; ∼ **de service** service charge; ∼ **de subsistance** living expenses; ∼ **superflus** avoidable cost;

(**t...**) ∼ **de taxi** taxi fares; ∼ **de traitement** throughput charge BrE, pass-through charge AmE; ∼ **de transaction** transaction fee; ∼ **de transfert international** cable rate; ∼ **de transmission** transmission expenses; ∼ **de transport** transport charges; ∼ **de transport non compris** exclusive of transport charges; ∼ **de transport au pro rata** pro rata freight; ∼ **de trésorerie** finance costs;

(**u...**) ∼ **d'utilisation** (d'une carte) user fee;

(**v...**) ∼ **de vente** selling expenses; ∼ **de voyage** travel expenses

franc¹, franche *adj* (sans ambiguïté) absolute; (honnête) frank; (exempt de taxe) duty-free; (Assur) (gratuit) free; **jouer ∼ jeu** play fair; **parler ∼** be perfectly frank; **six jours ∼s** six clear days; ∼ **d'avarie grosse** free of general average; ∼ **d'avarie particulière** (assurance maritime) free of particular average; ∼ **d'avaries communes** free of general average; ∼ **de capture et de saisie** free of capture and seizure; ∼ **de port** carriage paid; ∼ **de réclamation pour accident signalé** free of claim for accident reported; ∼ **de sinistre pour l'accident constaté** free of claim for accident reported; ∼ **de toute avarie** free of all average; ∼ **de toute charge** free and clear US

franc² *m* franc; ∼ **or** French gold franc

franc-bord *m* (navigation) freeboard

franchement *adv* (parler, s'exprimer) frankly, openly; (répondre) candidly; (dire) frankly

franchir *vt* (seuil) cross; (distance) cover; ∼ **la barre des 10%** pass the 10% mark; ∼ **le pas** take the plunge; **l'entreprise a franchi un cap décisif en rachetant sa rivale** buying up its rival was an important turning point for the company

franchisage *m* franchising

franchise *f* (Assur) excess; (contrat) franchise; (exonération) exemption; **en ∼ douanière** (marchandises) duty-free; **envoyer qch en ∼ postale** send sth post-free; **ouvrir un magasin en ∼** open a franchise; ∼ **de bagages** baggage allowance; ∼ **bancaire** free banking; ∼ **douanière** exemption from customs duties; ∼ **fiscale** tax exemption; ∼ **obligatoire** compulsory deduction; ∼ **de poids** weight allowed free

franchisé, e *m,f* franchisee

franchiser *vt* franchise

franchiseur *m* franchisor

franc-jeu *m* fair play

franco *adv* free of charge; ∼ **allège** (navigation) free into barge; ∼ **à bord** free on board; ～ **assurance et transport** free insurance and carriage; ～ **chargement** free in; ～ **déchargement** free discharge, landed terms; ～ **gare** free on rail; ～ **de port** (lettre, colis) postage free; (marchandises) carriage-free; ～ **à port** (maritime) free in harbour BrE, free in harbor AmE; ～ **à quai** free on quay; ～ **transporteur** free carrier

frappe f (de monnaie) mintage; (Info) (sur clavier) typing, keying; **erreur de** ～ typing error, keying error; ～ **répétée** double strike

frapper vt strike; (touches) hit

fraude f fraud; ～ **d'assurance** insurance fraud; ～ **électorale** election rigging; ～ **étendue** long fraud; ～ **fiscale** tax evasion; ～ **informatique** computer fraud; ～ **maritime** maritime fraud

frauder vt defraud; (fisc) evade

fraudeur, -euse m,f defrauder; ～ **fiscal** tax evader

frauduleusement adv fraudulently

frayer vt: ～ **le chemin à qch** pave the way for sth

FRCE abrév (▶Fonds de rétablissement du conseil de l'Europe) CERF (Council of Europe Resettlement Fund)

fre abrév (▶facture) inv. (invoice)

free-lance[1] adj (journaliste, traducteur) freelance

free-lance[2] mf freelancer; **travailler en** ～ work freelance

frein m (de véhicule) brake; (entrave) restraints; ～**s à air comprimé** full air brakes; ～**s à l'investissement** investment restriction

freiner vt (faire ralentir) (véhicule, chute) slow down; (modérér) (l'inflation) curb; ～ **les coûts** control costs

freinte f loss; ～ **de route** (Transp) loss in transit; ～ **de stock** (Com) inventory shortage, inventory shrinkage

fréquence f (radio) frequency; (incidence répandue) frequency, high-incidence; ～ **de base** (Info) clock rate

fréquentation f attendance; (de magasin) footfall; ～ **à plein temps** full-time attendance

fret m (cargaison) freight; (coût) freight (charges); (location) chartering; **avion de** ～ cargo plane; **compagnie de** ～ freight company; ～ **et assurance payés** freight and insurance paid; ～ **aérien** air cargo, air freight; ～ **aller** cargo outward; ～, **assurance et frais d'expédition** freight, insurance and shipping charges; ～ **de charte-partie** charter party freight; ～ **de distance** distance freight; ～ **à forfait** lump-sum freight; ～ **au long cours** (maritime) ocean freight; ～ **payable à destination** freight forward; ～ **payé d'avance** freight prepaid; ～ **payé jusqu'à** (lieu désigné) freight paid to; ～ **de retour** back freight, cargo homeward, return freight; ～ **sec** dry freight;

～ **à temps** time freight; ～ **de transbordement** transshipment freight; ～ **et surestarie** freight and demurrage; ～ **à l'unité payante** (maritime) liner rate; ～ **sur le vide** (navigation) deadfreight

fréter vt (donner en location) charter out; (prendre en location) charter

fric m (infrml) bread (infrml), money

friperie f secondhand clothes shop UK, thrift shop US

friser vt (frôler) (insolence) border on; (catastrophe) be on the brink of; ～ **l'illégalité** sail close to the wind

front m (Pol) front; **sur le** ～ **de l'emploi** on the employment front

frontal[1], **e** adj (Info) front-end

frontal[2] m (Info) front-end computer

frontière[1] adj inv (ville, zone) border

frontière[2] f border, frontier; ～ **commune** common border; ～ **extérieure** (d'un pays) external border; ～ **fiscale** fiscal frontier; ～ **nationale** national border, national boundary; ～ **des possibilités de production** production possibility frontier

fruit m fruit; **récolter les** ～**s de ses efforts** reap the fruits of one's efforts; ～**s naturels** (Droit) emblements

FSE abrév (▶Fonds social européen) ESF (European Social Fund)

FSM abrév (▶Fédération syndicale mondiale) WFTU (World Federation of Trade Unions)

fuite f leak, leakage; ～ **de capitaux** flight of capital; ～ **de cerveaux** brain drain; ～ **devant la monnaie** flight from money; ～ **vers la qualité** flight to quality

fumeur, -euse m,f smoker; **zone** ～**s/non** ～**s** smoking/non-smoking area

fumoir m smoking room

fur: **au** ～ **et à mesure** as one goes along; **au** ～ **et à mesure de leur besoins** as and when they need it

fuseau m: ～ **horaire** time zone; **changer de** ～ **horaire** change time zones

fusion f (de sociétés) merger, amalgamation (**entre** between); **opérer une** ～ merge; ～**s et acquisitions** mergers and acquisitions; ～ **de capitaux** commingling of funds; ～ **conforme aux statuts** statutory merger; ～ **dans un conglomérat** conglomerate merger; ～ **avec une entreprise étrangère** foreign merger; ～ **avec un fichier d'adresses** mail merge; ～ **horizontale** horizontal merger; ～ **transnationale** cross-border merger; ～ **triangulaire** triangular merger; ～ **verticale** vertical merger

fusionnement m merger, amalgamation

fusionner vi (sociétés) merge, amalgamate; ～ **en** merge into

fût m cask, barrel

Gg

g *abrév* (▸**gramme**) g (gram)

G7 *abrév* (▸**Groupe des Sept**) G7

GAB *abrév* (▸**guichet automatique de banque**) ATM (automatic teller machine)

gabarit *m* (Ind, Info) (modèle) template; (de véhicule) size; **véhicule hors ~** oversize vehicle; **~ de surface** template

gâchage *m* (construction) mixing; **~ des prix** price cutting

gâcheur, -euse *m,f* spoiler (jarg)

gâchis *m* waste; **~ d'emploi** job wastage

gadget *m* gadget

gage *m* (chez l'usurier) pledge; (Banque) security; **prêter sur ~s** lend against security; **mettre qch en ~** pawn sth; **~ de second rang** junior lien

gages *m pl* pay, wages

gagnant¹, e *adj* winning

gagnant², e *m,f* winner

gagne-pain *m* livelihood

gagner *vt* (de l'argent) earn; (client) win; **~ sa vie** earn a living; **~ un salaire de** earn a salary of; **~ du terrain** gain ground; **~ en valeur** gain value; **~ 100 euros par jour** earn 100 euros a day, make 100 euros a day; **~ de l'argent rapidement** make money fast, earn a fast buck (infrml); **~ le gros lot** hit the jackpot; **~ qn à son point de vue** win sb over to one's point of view

gain *m* (profit en Bourse) gain; (profit) profit, gain; (économie) saving; **être en ~** (action) be gaining in value; **clôturer sur un ~ de 6 points** close 6 points up; **c'est un ~ de temps/d'argent considérable** it saves a considerable amount of time/money; **~ aléatoire** gain contingency; **~ en capital** capital gain; **~ en capital après impôt** net capital gain; **~ en capital immédiat** immediate capital gain; **~ en capital imposable** taxable capital gain; **~ en capital imposable admissible net** net eligible taxable capital gain; **~ en capital imposable net** net taxable capital gain; **~ en capital imposable net cumulatif** cumulative net taxable capital gain; **~ en capital imposé** taxed capital gain; **~ exceptionnel** windfall gain; **~ immobilier** real estate gain; **~ de mortalité** mortality gain; **~ net de trésorerie** net cash flow; **~ normal** ordinary gain; **~ ou perte à court terme** short-term gain or loss; **~ ou perte sur titres** paper profit or loss; **~ reconnu** recognized gain

gains *m pl* earnings; **faire des ~** make gains; **réaliser des ~** make gains, make

profits; **~ avant imposition** pre-tax earnings; **~ exonérés** exempt earnings; **~ à l'exportation** export earnings; **~ à l'importation** import earnings; **~ non-réalisés** unrealized gains; **~ d'opportunité** transfer earnings; **~ de productivité** productivity gains; **~ réalisés** realized gains

galée *f* (typographie) galley, galley proof

galerie *f* gallery; **~ marchande** shopping centre BrE, shopping mall AmE

galiote *f* (navire) galliot

gallon *m* gallon; **~ américain** *3,785 litres*, American gallon; **~ impérial** *4,546 litres*, imperial gallon

gamme *f* (de produits) line, range; **bas de ~** bottom of the range; **haut de ~** top of the range; (Info) high-end; **~ d'amortissement d'actif** (Compta, Fin) asset depreciation range; **~ étendue** wide range; **~ d'ordinateurs** computer range; **~ de prix** price range; **~ de produits** product line, product range, range of products

gap *m* (Bourse) price gap

GAP *abrév* (▸**gestion actif-passif**) ALM (assets and liabilities management)

garage *m* garage; (d'autobus) depot; **~ à deux voies** (d'un roulier) two-lane deck

garant, e *m,f* guarantor; (Assur) guarantee; **être le ~ d'un prêt** stand guarantor for a loan; **être le ~ de** (Assur) guarantee

garanti, e *adj* (Bourse) (émission) underwritten; (Econ) (prix, salaire) guaranteed; (dette, emprunt) secured, guaranteed

garantie *f* (Com) guarantee, warranty; (Fin) security; (Assur) cover; (Droit) guarantee; **~ du fabricant** manufacturer's guarantee; **sous ~** under guarantee; **en ~** (Fin) under security; **montant des ~s** (Assur) sum insured; **~s légales** legal guarantees; **~ annexe** extended cover; **~ anticipée** advance guaranty UK; **~ d'assurabilité** guaranteed insurability; **~ d'assurance** insurance cover BrE, insurance coverage AmE; **~ d'avarie commune** general average guarantee; **~ bancaire** bank guarantee; **~ bancaire globale** comprehensive bank guarantee; **~ de bonne exécution** performance guarantee; **~ de bonne fin** contract bond, performance bond; **~ de commerce extérieur** external trade guarantee; **~ de dépôt** (Assur) surety; **~ contre l'échouement** cover against stranding; **~ d'émission négociée** negotiated underwriting; **~ d'émission obligataire** bond underwriting; **~ d'émission renouvelable** revolving underwriting facility; **~ d'engagement ferme** firm commitment underwriting; **~ fidélité** fidelity guarantee; **~ fiduciaire** fiduciary bond; **~ générale** blanket bond; **~ générale de commerce** commercial blanket bond; **~ contre la hausse des prix** cost escalation cover; **~ implicite** implied warranty; **~ inassurable** uninsurable title; **~ invalidité** (Assur) disability annuity; **~ matérielle** (Banque) physical collateral; **~ du moins disant** bid bond; **~ d'option** (Bourse) option coverage; **~ de paiement** (Droit) payment bond; **~ de permis** (Droit) permit bond; **~ de prêt** loan guarantee; **~ de provisions** advance payment guarantee; **~ de la qualité marchande** warranty of merchantability; **~ des recettes** revenue guarantee; **~ de revenu** revenue guarantee; **~ responsabilité civile** third-party cover; **~ de soumission** bid security; **~ de stocks supplémentaires** supplementary stocks guarantee; **~ de taux plafond** interest rate capping; **~ de taux plancher** floor

garantir *vt* (product, service) guarantee, warrant; (prêt) secure; (Bourse) underwrite; **~ une dette par hypothèque** secure a debt by mortgage; **~ par nantissement** collateralize; **~ un placement** secure an investment

garçon *m* boy; **~ de courses** messenger boy

garde *f* (Droit) ward; (d'un enfant) custody; **~ conjointe** (d'un enfant) joint custody; **~ et surveillance** (d'un enfant) custody and control; **~ des valeurs** (Banque) safekeeping; **~ des valeurs actives** safekeeping of assets

garder *vt* (argent) keep; (en lieu sûr) safeguard; (Com) (stand) man; **~ qch présent à l'esprit** bear sth in mind; **~ en réserve** keep in reserve; **~ secret** keep secret, keep under wraps; **~ une trace écrite de** keep a note of; **parking gardé** staffed *ou* manned car park; **l'entrepôt est gardé** there is a security guard at the warehouse

gardien, -enne *m,f* (d'un enfant) custodian; (bureau, usine) guard, security guard; **~ de nuit** night watchman

gare *f* railway station BrE, railroad station AmE; **~ aéroglisseur** (navigation) hoverport; **~ de destination** (chemin de fer) receiving station; **~ d'expédition** (chemin de fer) forwarding station; **~ routière** (pour cars) bus station; (pour camions) haulage depot

garniture *f*; **~ du conteneur** container stuffing

gasohol *m* (Envir) green petrol

gas-oil *m* diesel (oil)

gaspillage *m* waste

gaspiller *vt* (ressources) squander, waste; (temps, argent, énergie) waste

GATT *abrév* (▸**Accord général sur les tarifs et le commerce**) GATT (General Agreement on Tariffs and Trade)

gauche *adj* left; **de ~** (Pol) left-wing

gauchisme *m* leftism

gauchissement *m* (d'un objet) bending; **~ oblique** (Transp) racking

gaz *m* gas; **~ brûlé** exhaust gas; **~ d'échappement** exhaust emissions; **~ à effet de serre** greenhouse gas; **~ de la mer du Nord** North Sea gas; **~ naturel** natural gas; **~ naturel liquéfié** liquefied natural gas; **~ de pétrole liquéfié** liquid petroleum gas; **~ toxique** noxious gas

gazoduc *m* gas pipeline

gazole *m* diesel (oil), gas oil

GDF *abrév* (**Gaz de France**) *French gas board*

gel *m* (Econ) freeze; **~ des prix** price freeze; **~ des salaires** pay freeze

gelé, e *adj* (prix, avoirs, négociations) frozen

geler *vt* (salaire, prix, compte, avoirs) freeze

gendarme *m* gendarme, policeman; **~ maritime** coastguard

gendarmerie *f* police force; (bureaux) police station; **~ maritime** coastguard

gêne *f* (pauvreté) financial difficulty

gêné, e *adj* (désargenté) in financial difficulty, short of money

gêner *vt* (progrès) hamper; **~ les négociations** get in the way of the negotiations

généralisé, e *adj* (Com) across-the-board; (processus, surproduction) general; (pessimisme, corruption) widespread

généraliser ① *vt* (impôt) make general ② *vi* generalize ③ *v pron* **se généraliser** (grève) spread; (phénomène, technique) become widespread

généralités *f pl* background information, overview

générateur *m* (Ind, Info) generator; **~ de recettes** revenue earner

génération *f* (personnes du même âge) generation; (stade de progrès technique) generation; (de profits) generation; (d'énergie) generation; **~ de troisième ~** third-generation; **~ du baby-boom** baby-boomers; **~ d'électricité** electricity generation; **~ d'états** (Info) report generation; **~ de programmes d'édition** (Info) report generation

générer *vt* (déchets, profits) generate; (confiance) breed, generate; (programme) generate

générique¹ *adj* (nom, caractère) generic

générique² *m* (Média) masthead

génie *m* (personne) genius, wizard; (science) engineering; **avoir le ~ de** be a wizard at (infrml); **~ biologique** bioengineering; **~ électrique** electrical engineering; **~ de la finance** (personne) financial wizard; **~ industriel** industrial engineering; **~** ⋯▸

g

informatique computer engineering; ~ **de l'informatique** (personne) computer wizard; ~ **logiciel** software engineering

géodistribution f (Info, Transp) global distribution system

geomarketing m geomarketing

géomercatique f geomarketing

géomètre m land surveyor; ~ **expert** chartered surveyor

géopolitique adj geopolitical

gérance f management; **mettre en** ~ (magasin, société) appoint a manager for; **prendre en** ~ take over the management of; **assurer la** ~ **de qch** manage sth; ~ **informatique** facilities management; ~ **libre** contract management; ~ **de portefeuille** portfolio management; ~ **salariée** salaried management

gérant, e m,f (de magasin, société) manager; ~ **général** general administrator; ~ **d'hôtel** hotel manager; ~ **de société** (à responsabilité limitée) managing director; ~ **de succursale** branch manager

gerbage m (manutention) stacking; ~ **du chargement** stacking of cargo; ~ **double** (conteneurs) double stack; (technique) double stacking; ~ **des marchandises** stacking of cargo

gerber vt stack; ~ **en doubles piles** (conteneurs) double-stack

gérer vt (entreprise, hôtel, magasin, projet) manage, run; (situation) handle; (franchise) exercise; ~ **de grosses sommes d'argent** handle large sums of money; ~ **par ordinateur** computerize; **géré par ordinateur** computer-controlled; **géré par le système central** (Info) host-driven

gestion f (administration d'entreprise, de comptes) management; (d'une propriété, d'un patrimoine) administration; (de situation, de crise, d'information) handling; (Info) management; **de** ~ managerial; ~ **de l'actif** asset management; ~ **actif-passif** asset and liability management; ~ **d'actions** management of shares; ~ **active** active management; ~ **d'agenda** calendar management; ~ **automatisée** computerized management; ~ **de bas en haut** bottom-up management; ~ **du bilan** asset and liability management; ~ **à bord** (d'un navire) shipboard management; ~ **des canaux de communication** channel management; ~ **de carrière** career management; ~ **cellulaire** divisional management; ~ **commerciale** market management; ~ **des comptes** account management; ~ **consultative** bottom-up management; ~ **de la contingence** contingency management; ~ **de couverture** hedge management; ~ **de créances** credit management; ~ **de déchets** waste management; ~ **par département** divisional management; ~ **du**

développement development management; ~ **de disque dur** hard disk management; ~ **de la distribution physique** physical distribution management; ~ **des documents essentiels** vital records management; ~ **de données** database management; ~ **des effectifs** manpower management; ~ **électronique** e-management; ~ **d'entreprise** business management, corporate governance; ~ **de fichiers** file management; ~ **des finances** financial administration, financial management; ~ **financière internationale** international financial management; ~ **fonctionnelle** (Admin) systems management; ~ **par fonctions** functional management, horizontal specialization; ~ **de fonds** fund management; ~ **immobilière** property management; ~ **des immobilisations** fixed asset management; ~ **de l'information** information management; ~ **informatisée** computerized management; ~ **des installations** facilities management; ~ **des marchandises** merchandise control; ~ **de la marque** brand management; ~ **des opérations** operations management; ~ **par ordinateur** computerized management; ~ **du passif** liability management; ~ **des performances** performance management; ~ **du personnel** personnel management; ~ **d'une petite entreprise** small business administration; ~ **de portefeuille** portfolio management; ~ **portuaire** port management; ~ **prévisionnelle des stocks** inventory planning; ~ **de processus industriel** process control; ~ **de produit** product management; ~ **du projet** project management; ~ **de la qualité** quality management; ~ **de réseau** networking; ~ **des ressources** resources management; ~ **des ressources humaines** human resource management; ~ **des risques** risk management; ~ **de la sécurité** safety management; ~ **de service** departmental management; ~ **des stocks** inventory management, stock control, stock management; ~ **du stress** stress management; ~ **systématisée** systems management; ~ **des tâches** task management; ~ **de taux** yield management; ~ **du temps de travail** time management; ~ **tenant compte des imprévus** contingency management; ~ **transactionnelle** transaction management; ~ **des travaux** job control; ~ **de trésorerie** cash management; ~ **d'usine** plant management; ~ **de la vente au détail** retail management; ~ **des ventes** sales management

gestionnaire mf (de service, de société) manager; (d'une propriété, d'un patrimoine) administrator; ~ **de l'actif** asset manager; ~ **de couverture** hedge manager; ~ **de la dette** liability manager, debt manager; ~ **de**

fait de facto manager; **~ de fonds** fund manager; **~ du passif** liability manager; **~ de portefeuille** portfolio manager; **~ des risques** risk manager

GIEE *abrév* (▶**Groupement d'intérêt économique européen**) EEIG (European Economic Interest Grouping)

gigaoctet *m* gigabyte

gisement *m* (Bourse) bond pool; (Ind) (de minerai) deposit; **~ de charbon** coal deposit; **~ de houille** coal deposit; **~ de pétrole** oil deposit; **~ pétrolifère** oil deposit

glissement *m* (évolution) (d'électorat, d'opinion) swing; (de prix) fall; **un ~ à droite** (Pol) a swing to the right; **~ de terrain** (Envir) landslide; **~ d'une tranche d'imposition à l'autre** bracket creep, tax-bracket creep

glisser ① *vi* (prix) slide, slip
② *vt* (Info) (icône) drag; **~ un mot en faveur de qn** put in a good word for sb

glisser-déposer *vt* (Info) drag and drop

global, e *adj* (revenu, somme, effectif) total; (croissance, résultat, coût) overall; (accord, plan, solution) global; (montant, valeur, demande) aggregate

globalement *adv* globally, overall

globalisation *f* globalization

globaliser *vt* globalize

globalité *f*: **considérer qch dans sa ~** consider sth in its entirety, consider sth as a whole

gloire *f* (renom) fame, glory; (mérite) credit

glossaire *m* glossary

GMT *abrév* (▶**heure de Greenwich**) GMT (Greenwich Mean Time)

Go *abrév* (▶**gigaoctet**) Gb (gigabyte)

gondole *f* (présentoir) gondola

gonflement *m* (de la note) padding

gonfler *vt* (chiffres, prix) inflate; (compte) swell

goulot *m* **~ d'étranglement** (Transp) bottleneck

gourmand, e *adj* (gastronomique) **repas ~** gourmet meal; **étape ~e** good eating place; (avide d'argent) greedy, grasping; **un courtier ~** a greedy broker; **~ en mémoire** (Info) memory-hungry (infrml)

goût *m* taste; (gré) liking; **~ de la propriété** acquisitiveness; **avoir le ~ du risque** like taking risks

gouvernement *m* government; **~ de coalition** coalition government; **~ donateur** donor government; **~ de l'entreprise** corporate governance; **~ étranger** foreign government; **~ fédéral** federal government

gouvernemental, e *adj* governmental; **non ~** non-governmental

gouverner *vt* govern

gouverneur *m* governor; **~ général** governor general

GPL *abrév* (▶**gaz de pétrole liquéfié**) LPG (liquid petroleum gas)

gradé *m* non-commissioned officer; **~ de banque** bank officer

gradin *m* (bancs) tier; (de stade) **les ~s** the terraces BrE, the bleachers AmE

gradué, e *adj* graduated; **règle ~e** ruler

graduel, -elle *adj* gradual

graduellement *adv* gradually

graisser *vt* grease; **~ la patte à qn** (infrml) grease sb's palm (infrml)

grammage *m* paper weight

gramme *m* gramme BrE, gram AmE

grand¹, e *adj* (dimension, quantité, nombre) large; (élevage, production) large-scale; **le ~ public** the general public; **~ public** (spectacle) popular; **à ~e échelle** (projet) large-scale; **produits de ~e consommation** staple goods; **de ~e envergure** (opération, projet, manifestation) large-scale; (réformes, mesures) far-reaching, wide-ranging; **en ~e banlieue** in the outer suburbs; **en ~e partie** largely, to a large extent; **en ~es quantités** in large quantities; **~e annonce** display advertisement; **~e banlieue** commuter belt UK; **~ capital** big investors; **~ compte** major account; **~ ensemble** housing complex; **~e entreprise** large company, large corporation; **~s pays industrialisés** First World, industrialized countries; **~e industrie** large-scale industry; **~e informatique** macrocomputing; **~e ligne** (chemin de fer) main line; **~ livre** (comptabilité générale) book of accounts, general ledger; **~ livre auxiliaire** subsidiary ledger; **~ livre auxiliaire des clients** customers' ledger; **~ livre auxiliaire des fournisseurs** accounts payable ledger; **~ livre des comptes fournisseurs** accounts payable ledger; **~ livre des ventes** sales ledger; **~ magasin** department store; **~e presse** national press; **~ réseau** wide area network; **~ risque** large exposure; **~e société** big company; **~e surface** supermarket, superstore; **~e surface spécialisée** specialist superstore; **~e valeur industrielle** blue-chip industrial

grand² *m* (pays) big power; (entreprise) leader, big name; **c'est un ~ de la publicité** he's big in advertising; **les ~s de l'automobile** major car manufacturers, top car manufacturers; **un ~ de la distribution** a major distributor, a leading distributor; **les cinqs ~s** the Big Five

grandeur *f* (taille) size; (importance) magnitude

grand-rue *f* high street BrE, main street AmE

graphe *m* graph

grapheur *m* (Info) graphics software

graphiciel *m* (Info) graphics software

graphique¹ *adj* graphic

graphique² *m* chart, graph; **faire un ~** plot a graph; **~ d'acheminement** flow chart; **~ des activités** activity chart; **~ à bandes** bar chart, bar graph; **~ camembert** pie ⋯⟩

chart; ∼ **de circulation** flow chart; ∼ **en
dents de scie** Z chart; ∼ **des étapes
critiques** milestone chart; ∼**s de gestion**
business graphics

graphique[3] f (Info, Média) (technique, art)
graphics

graphisme m (Info, Média) graphics; ∼
maison (identité de l'entreprise) house style

graphiste mf graphic designer

grappe f (Info) (de terminaux) cluster

grappin m (matériel de manutention) grab

gras, -se adj (Média) (caractère) bold

graticiel m (Info) freeware

gratifiant, e adj gratifying; (travail)
rewarding

gratification f bonus, incentive; ∼
collective (jarg) synthetic incentive

gratis adv free BrE, for free AmE

gratuit, e adj (échantillon, service) free; (crédit)
interest-free; (logement) rent-free; (appel,
numéro) Freefone® BrE, toll-free AmE; (autoroute)
free; **logiciel** ∼ freeware; **entrée** ∼**e** free
admission; **à titre** ∼ free of charge

gratuitement adv free BrE, for free AmE

grave adj (problème, accident, erreur) serious;
question ∼ big issue

gravure f (Média) lettering

gré m (goût) liking; (gratitude) **savoir** ∼ **à qn
de qch** be grateful to sb for sth; **de** ∼ **à** ∼
by mutual agreement, by mutual consent; **je
vous saurais** ∼ (frml) I should be much
obliged (frml)

gréeur m (dans un port) lasher, rigger

greffier, -ière m,f (d'un tribunal) clerk

grève f industrial action, strike; **en** ∼ on
strike; **faire** ∼ strike, take industrial action;
faire une ∼ **surprise** stage a walkout; ∼ **des
achats** boycott; ∼ **d'avertissement** token
strike; ∼ **des chemins de fer** rail strike; ∼
éclair hit-and-run strike, lightning strike; ∼
de la faim hunger strike; ∼ **générale** all-
out strike; ∼ **illicite** illegal strike; ∼ **légale**
legal strike; ∼ **perlée** go-slow BrE, slowdown
AmE; ∼ **avec préavis** official strike; ∼
revendicative protest strike; ∼ **sauvage**
unofficial strike, wildcat strike; ∼ **de
solidarité** sympathy strike; ∼ **symbolique**
token strike; ∼ **sur le tas** sit-down strike; ∼
par le travail work-in; ∼ **du zèle** work-to-
rule

grever vt (budget, économie) be a strain on;
grevé d'impôt crippled by taxes, burdened
with taxes; **l'entreprise est grevée de
charges** the company is crippling
overheads

gréviste mf striker

GRH abrév (▸gestion des ressources
humaines) HRM (human resource
management)

grief m grievance; **avoir un** ∼ **contre qn**
have a grievance against sb

griffe f (prêt-à-porter) label; ∼ **d'un grand
couturier** designer label

grille f (de prix, tarifs, salaires) scale; (sur écran)
grid; ∼ **d'échantillonnage** sampling grid;
∼ **de gestion** managerial grid; ∼ **de
produits** product group; ∼ **des salaires**
salary scale

grimper vi climb; ∼ **dans la hiérarchie**
climb the ladder; ∼ **en flèche** (infrml) (prix)
rocket (infrml), soar

gros[1]**, -se** adj big, large; **personne à** ∼
revenus high earner; **en** ∼**se quantité** in
bulk; ∼**se affaire** (contrat) big contract, big
business; (entreprise) big company; ∼
bénéfice big profit, killing (infrml); ∼
bonnets (infrml) brass (jarg), top brass (infrml);
∼ **budget** big budget, sizeable budget; ∼
calibre high-calibre BrE, high-caliber AmE; ∼
client big customer, major customer; ∼
dommages (maritime) hidden damage; ∼**se
entreprise** big company; ∼ **exportateur**
large-scale exporter; ∼ **importateur** large-
scale importer; ∼ **ordinateur** mainframe; ∼
producteur big producer; ∼**se quantité**
large quantity; ∼**se remise** hard discount;
∼ **revenus** upper income; ∼ **système**
mainframe; ∼ **titre** (presse, radio, télévision)
headline; ∼ **transporteur** (véhicule) high
loader; ∼ **utilisateur** heavy user; ∼
utilisateur industriel big industrial user

gros[2]**: en** ∼ adv (acheter, vendre) wholesale,
in bulk; (achat, vente) bulk, wholesale;
(commande) bulk

gros-porteur m (Transp) jumbo jet, heavy
jet

grosse f (Com) (douze douzaines) gross

grossiste f wholesaler; ∼ **affilié** affiliated
wholesaler

grouillot m (Bourse) blue button UK (jarg),
messenger

groupage m (Transp) consolidation; ∼ **par
conteneur** bulk unitization; ∼ **des frais**
combination of charges; ∼ **des
marchandises** cargo assembly; ∼ **des
tarifs** combination of rates

groupe m (de pays, de personnes, de sociétés)
group; (Info) cluster; ∼ **affilié** affiliate; ∼
d'audit audit group, audit team; ∼
bancaire banking group; **Groupe de la
Banque mondiale** World Bank Group; ∼
de bits (Info) packet; ∼ **cible** target group;
∼ **de clients liés** group of connected
clients; ∼ **concurrentiel** competing group;
∼ **de cotation** (Bourse) pit, pitch UK; **le** ∼
dirigeant the establishment; ∼ **de
discussion** forum; ∼ **de distribution** store
group; ∼ **électrogène de secours** standby
power plant; ∼ **d'éléments d'actif** (Compta,
Fin) group of assets; ∼ **d'emplois** job cluster;
∼ **d'étude** task force; ∼ **filiale** affiliated
group; ∼ **HLM** housing estate, housing
project AmE; ∼ **d'intérêt** interest group; ∼
d'intervention (Fin, Pol) task force; ∼

d'investisseurs investor group; ∼ **lié** related group; ∼ **de négociation** (Bourse) crowd; ∼ **non-concurrentiel** noncompeting group; ∼ **d'options** set of options; ∼ **de portefeuille financier** financial holding group; ∼ **de pression** lobby group, pressure group; ∼ **de pression agricole** farm lobby; ∼ **de produits** product group; ∼ **de référence** reference group; ∼ **de réflexion** think-tank; ∼ **de sociétés** group of companies; **Groupe des Sept** Group of Seven; ∼ **témoin** consumer panel; ∼ **de travail** working party; ∼ **d'utilisateurs** user group

groupement *m* (de pays, de personnes, de sociétés) group; (de ressources) pool; (Bourse) trading party; ∼ **d'acheteurs** buyer concentration; ∼ **aveugle** (Fin) blind pool; ∼ **bancaire** group of banks, bank group; **Groupement de coopération européen** European Cooperation Grouping; ∼ **d'entreprises** consortium, group of companies; ∼ **d'intérêt** interest group; ∼ **d'intérêt économique** association for developing economic interests; **Groupement d'intérêt économique européen** European Economic Interest Grouping; ∼ **professionnel** professional body

grouper *vt* (ressources, intérêts) pool; (commandes, livraisons) consolidate, group; (marchandises) bundle; (paquets) bulk

groupeur, -euse *m,f* consolidator, forwarding agent

grue *f* crane; ∼ **sur camion** lorry-mounted crane BrE, truck-mounted crane; ∼ **de déchargement** unloader crane; ∼ **portique** portal crane; ∼ **roulante** mobile crane

grumier *m* (navire) timber ship

grutier, -ière *m,f* crane driver, crane operator

guerre *f* war; ∼ **commerciale** trade war; ∼ **du Golfe** Gulf War; ∼ **des prix** price war; ∼ **des tarifs** tariff war

guetter *vt* be on the lookout for

gui *m* (d'un navire) boom

guichet *m* counter; (d'un théâtre) box office, ticket office, wicket US; ∼ **automatique** automatic teller machine; ∼ **automatique de banque** bank teller machine; '∼ **fermé**' (dans banque) 'position closed'; ∼ **unique** one-stop shop

guichetier, -ière *m,f* bank teller, teller; (dans un théâtre) ticket clerk

guide *m* (brochure, livre, personne) guide; ∼ **aérien** airline guide; ∼ **d'audit** auditing manual; ∼ **de contrôle** auditing manual; ∼ **de l'entreprise** employee handbook; ∼ **d'entretien** service handbook; ∼ **d'entrevue** interview guide; ∼ **gastronomique** good food guide; ∼ **de l'utilisateur** instructions, user manual

guillemets *m pl* (typographie) inverted commas

gulden *m* florin, guilder

Hh

h *abrév* (▸**heure**) h, hr (hour)

ha *abrév* (▸**hectare**) ha (hectare)

habileté *f* skill

habiliter *vt* authorize (**à faire** to do); **habilité à juger** entitled to adjudicate

habillage *m* (jarg) (typographie) run-around; ∼ **de bilan** (Compta) window-dressing

habillement *m* clothing industry

habiller *vt* dress; (fournir en vêtements) (recrue, personnel) provide with clothing; ∼ **le bilan** window-dress, massage the figures

habitant, e *m,f* inhabitant; **par** ∼ per capita

habitat *m* (milieu) habitat; (mode de logement) housing; ∼ **collectif** collective housing

habitation *f* (construction) house; (résidence) home; ∼**s en grappe** cluster housing; ∼ **à loyer modéré** council flat UK, public housing unit US

habitude *f* habit; ∼**s d'achat** buying habits, spending patterns; ∼**s des consommateurs** patterns of consumption, consumer patterns; ∼**s et accords d'industrie** custom and practice; ∼**s du métier** trade customs, trade practices

habituel, -elle *adj* usual

habituellement *adv* usually; ∼ **domicilié** ordinarily resident

halo *m* (V&M) halo

handicap *m* (infirmité) disability; (désavantage) handicap; **c'est un** ∼ **pour votre carrière** it's a handicap in your career; ∼ **physique/ mental** physical/mental disability

handicapé, e *m,f* disabled person; **les** ∼**s** the disabled

hangar *m* shed; (entrepôt) warehouse; ∼ **des exportations** export shed; ∼ **de transit** transit shed

harcèlement *m* harassment; ∼ ⋯⟩

psychologique psychological abuse; ~ **sexuel** sexual harassment

hardware m (Info) hardware

harmonisation f harmonization; ~ **comptable** accounting harmonization UK; ~ **fiscale** tax harmonization; ~ **juridique** legal harmonization; ~ **au niveau mondial** global harmonization; ~ **de la politique** policy harmonization; ~ **salariale** salary harmonization

harmoniser vt harmonize

hasard m chance; **au** ~ at random

hasardeux, -euse adj (peu sûr) risky; (dangereux) hazardous

hausse f (des prix, du chômage) increase, rise; (de monnaie, d'actions) appreciation, run-up; **forte/légère** ~ **des prix** sharp/slight increase in prices; ~ **saisonnière** seasonal increase; **une** ~ **de 10%/10 euros** a 10%/10 euro increase; **être en** ~ (prix) be rising; (marchandise) be going up in price; **subir une forte** ~ rocket, shoot up; **revoir à la** ~ revise upward; **en** ~ **de 14%** up 14%; **à la** ~ (Bourse) (marché, tendance) bullish; **jouer à la** ~ (Bourse) speculate on a rise; **valeur en** ~ (Bourse) rising security; ~ **brutale** spike; ~ **sans effet** dead rise; ~ **maximum** (Bourse) limit up; ~ **d'une monnaie** appreciation of a currency; ~ **des prix** rise in prices; ~ **du prix du pétrole** oil price increase; ~ **rapide** fast rise

haussier¹, -ière adj (Bourse) bullish, upward; **être** ~ be bullish

haussier² m bull; ~ **et baissier** bull and bear

haut¹ m top; **des** ~**s et des bas** ups and downs; ~ **de casse** upper case; ~ **de gamme** (produits) high-end, top-of-the-range; ~ **de gamme du marché** top end of the market; ~ **de gamme dans la série** top end of the range; **le** ~ **de la gamme** the top of the range

haut² adv high; (dans un texte) above; **comme indiqué plus** ~ as noted above; **voir plus** ~ see above; **en** ~ (de l'échelle) at the top end; ~ **placé** top-ranking

haut³, e adj high; **à** ~ **profil** (profession, compagnie) high-profile; **une décision prise en** ~ **lieu** a high-level decision; **trop** ~ (prix, devis) too high; ~ **commissariat** high commission; **Haute Cour (de Justice)** High Court of Justice; ~**e densité** high density; ~**e direction** top management; ~**e finance** high finance; ~ **fonctionnaire** top-ranking official; ~**s fourneaux** blast furnace; **en** ~ **lieu** in high places; ~ **lieu de** centre of; ~ **niveau sans précédent** all-time high; ~**e résolution** high-resolution; ~**e technologie** high-tech; ~ **risque** high-risk; ~**e saison** peak season; ~**e saison des importations** peak importing season; **très** ~**e fréquence** very high frequency; **très** ~**e résistance** extra strong

hautement adv highly; ~ **perfectionné** high-stream; ~ **qualifié** highly-skilled

hauteur f height; **une tour d'une** ~ **de 30m** a tower 30m high; **être à la** ~ be up to scratch (infrml); **être à la** ~ **de la situation** be equal to the situation; ~ **du châssis** (véhicule routier) frame height; ~ **de page** page depth

havre m haven

hebdomadaire adj weekly

hébergement m (commercial) accommodation BrE, accommodations AmE; (social) housing; (de site Internet) hosting

héberger vt (touriste) accommodate; (sans-abri) provide shelter for; (site Internet) host

hectare m hectare

hégémonie f hegemony

hélicoptère m helicopter

héliport m heliport

hélistation f helistop

hémorragie f (de capitaux, de devises) massive outflow; (de clients) exodus

héritage m (biens légués) inheritance; (abstrait) legacy

hériter vt inherit; ~ **qch de qn** inherit sth from sb

héritier, -ière m,f (Droit) heir, heiress; ~**s et ayants droit** heirs and assigns; ~ **légitime** rightful heir; ~ **testamentaire** devisee

hermétique adj (étanche aux gaz) airtight; (étanche aux liquides) watertight

hésitant, e adj hesitant

hétérogène adj heterogeneous

heure f hour, time; **à l'**~ **convenue** at the appointed time; **à une** ~ **déterminée** at a given time; **être à l'**~ be on time; **à 7** ~**s précises** at 7 o'clock sharp; **25 euros de l'**~ 25 euros per hour; ~**s d'affluence** peak period, peak time; ~**s annualisées** annualized hours; ~ **d'arrivée prévue** estimated time of arrival; ~**s de bourse** market hours, trading hours; ~**s de bureau** office hours; ~ **comptée double** double time; ~ **courante** (charte-partie) running hour; ~**s creuses** off-peak period; ~ **de départ prévue** estimated time of departure; ~ **d'écoute** (radio) listening time; (télévision) viewing time; ~ **d'été** daylight saving; ~**s du dernier jour** (Bourse) last-day hours; ~ **de fermeture** closing time; ~ **de grande écoute** (radio, télévision) prime time; ~ **de Greenwich** Greenwich Mean Time; **l'**~ **fixée** the appointed time; ~**s inemployées** idle time; ~ **légale française** French Standard Time; ~ **locale** local time; ~**s machines** (Info) computer time; ~**s de négociation** trading hours; ~**s normales** regular hours; ~**s d'ouverture** opening hours, business hours; (Banque) banking hours; ~ **de pointe** peak time; (de la circulation) rush hour; ~ **précise** (navigation) right time; ~**s récupérées** compensatory time; **~s supplémentaires** overtime; **~s de travail** working hours; **~ du triple sabbat** (Bourse) triple witching hour US; **~ universelle** universal time coordinated; **~s d'utilisation** service hours

heureux, -euse *adj* happy; **heureuse arrivée** safe arrival

heuristique *f* (Info) heuristics

hiérarchie *f* hierarchy; **en remontant la ~** up the line; **~ des besoins** hierarchy of needs; **~ de commandement** chain of command; **~ des effets** (marketing) hierarchy of effects; **~ des objectifs** hierarchy of objectives; **~ salariale** pay differential, wage spread

histogramme *m* bar chart, histogram

histoire *f* history; **~ de l'entreprise** business history

historique¹ *adj* historical

historique² *m* case history; (commercial) background paper; **~ d'un investissement** investment history

hiver *m* winter

HLM *abrév* (▶**habitation à loyer modéré**) council flat UK, public housing unit US

holding *m* holding company; **~ à activité mixte** mixed-activity holding company; **~ bancaire** bank holding company

homme *m* man; **l'~ de la rue** the man in the street; **~ actif** working man; **~ d'affaires** businessman; **~ de confiance** confidential clerk; **~ économique** economic man; **~ de loi** legal practitioner; **~ du métier** professional; **~ de paille** dummy; **~ de peine** handyman; **~ politique** politician; **~ de terrain** field operator; **~ à tout faire** handyman, odd-job man

homogène *adj* homogeneous

homologation *f* (d'un produit) approval; (Droit) homologation; **~ de testament** probate of will

homologue *mf* (personne) opposite number

homologuer *vt* (produit) approve; (testament) grant probate of

honnête *adj* honest; (juste) faire; (moyen) reasonable

honnêteté *f* honesty

honneur *m* honour BrE, honor AmE

honorable *adj* (compagnie, marque) venerable; (classement) creditable; (moyens financiers, nombre, proportion) sizable; (salaire) decent

honoraire *adj* honorary

honoraires *m pl* (professions libérales) fee; **~ annuels** annual fee; **~ d'avocat** legal fees; **~ comptables** accounting fees; **~ consulaires** consular fees; **~ dérogatoires** override; **~ d'encouragement** incentive fee; **~ éventuels** contingent fee; **~ d'expertise** survey fee; **~ d'expertise comptable** accounting fees; **~ de gestion** management fee; **~ non-remboursables** nonrefundable fee; **~ de recherche** finder's

fee; **~ supplémentaires** refresher UK

honorariat *m* honorary membership

honorer *vt* (chèque, lettre de change) honour BrE, honor AmE; (emprunt, effet) take up; (engagements, obligations) fulfil BrE, fulfill AmE, meet; **ne pas ~** dishonour BrE, dishonor AmE; **ne pas ~ ses échéances** default

honorifique *adj* honorary

hôpital *m* hospital; **~ public** public hospital

horaire¹ *adj* (salaire, rendement, débit, tarif) per hour; **tranche/plage ~** time-slot

horaire² *m* (emploi du temps) timetable, schedule; (de vols) schedule; (de trains, de bus) timetable BrE, schedule AmE; **~ d'exploitation** operating schedule; **à ~ variable** numerical flexibility UK; **~ d'été/d'hiver** summer/winter timetable; **être en avance sur l'~** (Transp) be ahead of schedule; **être en retard sur l'~** be running late; **les ~s de travail** working hours; **les ~s de cours** timetable of lessons; **avoir un ~ chargé** have a busy schedule; **~s aménagés** flexible working hours, flexitime; **~s à la carte** flexitime; **~s flexibles** flexible schedule; **~s libres** flexitime; **~ des trains** railway timetable BrE, railroad timetable AmE; **~s variables** gliding shift, gliding schedule

horizon *m* horizon; **~ temporel** (Econ) time span

horizontal, e *adj* horizontal

horloge-calendrier *f* clock-calendar

horloge-pointeuse *f* time clock

hors *prép* apart from; **~ de** outside; **être ~ de portée** be out of range; **être ~ d'usage** be out of order; **~ bilan** (Compta) off-balance-sheet; **~ bourse** after-hours, after-market; **~ du cadre légal** outside the legal framework, extra-legal; **~ EU** extra-EU; **~ de compétence** (Droit) ultra vires; **~ de la compétence de** (Droit) outside the reference of; **~ conférence** (maritime) no liner; **~ contingent** (Econ) above quota; **~ cote** (Bourse) (marché) off-the-board, over-the-counter US, curb US; (titres) unlisted, not quoted on the Stock Exchange; **~ du cours** (Bourse) out-of-the-money; **~ faute** (Assur) no fault; **~ impôts** net of taxes; **~ jeu** (Bourse) out-of-the-money; **~ ligne** (Info) off-line; **~ marché** (Bourse) away from the market; **~ média** below-the-line; **~ normes** (Transp) high cube; **~ saison** off season; **~ séance** (Bourse) after-hours, after-market; **~ série** custom-built; **~ service** out of order; **~ taxes** exclusive of tax, tax-free

hostile *adj* hostile (à to)

hôte *m* host; (Info) host; **~ payant** paying guest

hôtel *m* hotel; **~ d'aéroport** airport hotel; **~ de congrès** convention hotel; **~ international** international-standard hotel; **Hôtel de la Monnaie** French mint, ≈ Royal ⋯⊹

Mint UK; ~ **trois-étoiles** three-star hotel

hôtesse *f* (de société, magasin) receptionist; (d'exposition) hostess; (de train, bateau) stewardess; ~ **de l'air** flight attendant

houille *f* coal; ~ **blanche** white coal

houillère *f* coal mine

housse *f* (Info) cover, dust cover; (Transp) (pour palettes) snood

HS *abrév* (▸**heures supplémentaires**) OT (overtime)

huile *f* oil; ~ **de carter** (navigation) cargo oil; ~ **combustible** burning oil; ~ **résiduaire** waste oils

huis: à ~ clos in camera

huissier *m* (de justice) bailiff

huitième *m* eighth

humeur *f* mood

hybride *adj* hybrid; **entreprise** ~ clicks and mortar company (jarg), hybrid company

hydrocarbure *m* hydrocarbon

hydroélectrique *adj* hydroelectric

hydrofoil *m* hovercraft

hydroglisseur *m* hovercraft

hydromètre *m* hydrometer

hygiène *f* hygiene; ~ **de l'environnement** environmental hygiene; ~ **et sécurité du travail** health and safety; ~ **du travail** industrial hygiene, occupational health

hyperdocument *m* (Info) hyperdocument

hyperfréquence *f* very high frequency, micro-wave frequency

hyperinflation *f* hyperinflation, runaway inflation; ~ **de la monnaie** helicopter money

hyperlien *m* (Info) hotlink, hyperlink

hypermarché *m* hypermarket, superstore

hypertexte *m* (Info) hypertext

hypertextuel, -elle *adj* (Info) hypertext

hypothèque *f* mortgage; ~ **auto-amortissable** self-amortizing mortgage; ~ **sur bien loué** leasehold mortgage; ~ **sur biens meubles** chattel mortgage US; ~ **à capital croissant** growing-equity mortgage US; ~ **sans date limite** open-ended mortgage; ~ **de deuxième rang** second mortgage, junior mortgage US; ~ **fiduciaire** trust mortgage; ~ **garantie** guaranteed mortgage; ~ **garantie par nantissement** collateralized mortgage obligation; ~ **générale** blanket mortgage, general mortgage; ~ **immobilière** property mortgage; ~ **intégrante** wraparound mortgage; ~ **investie en actions** equity-linked mortgage; ~ **de premier rang** first mortgage; ~ **à règlements variables** flexible-payment mortgage; ~ **à remboursements fixes** fixed repayment mortgage, level-payment mortgage US; ~ **sous-jacente** underlying mortgage; ~ **à taux fixe** fixed-rate mortgage; ~ **à taux réglable** adjustable-rate mortgage

hypothéquer *vt* mortgage; ~ **l'avenir** mortgage one's future

hypothèse *f* assumption, hypothesis; **faire des ~s** speculate; ~ **alternative** alternative hypothesis; ~ **de la convergence** (Econ) convergence hypothesis; ~ **du cycle de vie** (Econ) life-cycle hypothesis; ~ **de l'écart de valeur** (Econ) value discrepancy hypothesis; ~ **optimiste** best-case scenario; ~ **pessimiste** worst-case scenario; ~ **de revenu absolu** absolute income hypothesis; ~ **du revenu relatif** relative income hypothesis; ~ **des salaires réels** real-wage hypothesis; ~ **de travail** working hypothesis; ~ **d'uniformité** uniformity assumption

hypothétique *adj* hypothetical

Ii

I *abrév* (▸**important indice du marché**, ▸**indice du marché principal**) MMI (Major Market Index)

IA *abrév* (▸**intelligence artificielle**) AI (artificial intelligence)

IAO *abrév* (▸**ingénierie assistée par ordinateur**) CAE (computer-aided engineering, computer-assisted engineering)

IATA *abrév* (▸**Association internationale des transports aériens**) IATA (International Air Transport Association)

ibid. *abrév* (▸**ibidem**) ibid. (ibidem)

ibidem *adv* ibidem

IC *abrév* (▸**intérêts courus**) AI (accrued interest)

icône *f* (Info) icon; **par ~** by icon

iconiser *vt* (Info) iconify

id. *abrév* (▸**idem**) id. (idem)

ID *abrév* (▸**identification**) ID (identification)

idée *f* idea; ~ **de base** basic concept; ~ **directrice** governing principle; ~ **dominante** governing principle; ~ **force** key idea; ~ **générale du marché** (Econ) feel of the market; ~ **de vente** (V&M) selling idea

idem *adj* idem

identifiable *adj* identifiable; (Fisc) ascertainable

identifiant *m* (Info) identifier

identificateur *m* (Info) identifier

identification *f* identification; ∼ **des besoins** need identification; ∼ **d'incident** (Info) problem determination, troubleshooting; ∼ **de la marque** (V&M) brand recognition

identité *f* identité; (similarité) similarity; ∼ **fondamentale** (Compta) accounting identity; ∼ **graphique** logo

IDP *abrév* (▸**indication de durée et de prix**) ADC (advice of duration and/or charge)

IEP *m* (▸**Institut d'Études Politiques**) institute of political science

IGF *abrév* (▸**impôt sur les grandes fortunes**) wealth tax

illégal, e *adj* illegal

illégalement *adv* illegally

illicite *adj* (acte, vente, profits, utilisation) illegal; (pratique) illegal, unlawful

illimité, e *adj* (Bourse) unlimited; (Envir) (ressources) infinite; ∼ **à la hausse** unlimited on the upside

illisible *adj* (document, écriture) illegible; (Info) unreadable

illusion *f* illusion; ∼ **inflationniste** inflation illusion; ∼ **monétaire** money illusion, price perception

illustration *f* illustration

illustré *m* illustrated magazine

illustrer *vt* illustrate

îlot *m* (V&M) gondola; (de vente) island

image *f* image, picture; **donner une** ∼ **fidèle de qch** present sth fairly; ∼ **de l'entreprise** corporate image; ∼ **fidèle** (Compta) true and fair view BrE, fair presentation AmE; ∼ **de fond** (Info) background picture; ∼ **globale** global image; ∼ **graphique** (Info) clip art; ∼ **de marque** (de l'entreprise) corporate image; (d'un produit) product image; (V&M) brand label; ∼ **rémanente** (publicité) afterimage

images *f pl* (Média) graphics

imagination *f* imagination, creative thinking

imbrication *f* (Info) nesting

imbriqué, e *adj* (Info) embedded, nested

imbriquer *vt* (Info) nest

IME *abrév* (▸**Institut monétaire européen**) EMI (European Monetary Institute)

imitation *f* copy

imiter *vt* (signature, billet) forge

immatériel, -elle *adj* (Fin) (actifs, valeurs) intangible

immatriculation *f* registration; (Fisc) registration; (d'une voiture) (car) registration;

∼ **des navires** registry of shipping

immatriculé, e *adj* registered; ∼ **au Canada** registered in Canada

immatriculer *vt* (personne, société) register; **faire** ∼ (véhicule) register BrE, license AmE

immédiat, e *adj* immediate; **dans l'**∼ in the short term

immeuble *m* block of flats BrE, apartment building AmE; (Droit) real asset; ∼ **de bureaux** office block BrE, office building; ∼ **commercial** office block BrE, office building; ∼ **en copropriété** block of individually owned flats BrE, condominium AmE; ∼ **à usage d'habitation** residential block BrE, apartment building AmE

immigration *f* immigration; ∼ **clandestine** illegal immigration

immigré, e *m,f* immigrant; ∼ **clandestin** illegal immigrant

immiscer: **s'**∼ **dans** *v pron* interfere in

immixtion *f* interference

immobilier *m* property BrE, real estate AmE; ∼ **acquis** property acquired; ∼ **commercial** commercial property; ∼ **de placement** investment property; ∼ **de rapport** rented property BrE, rental building AmE; ∼ **en viager** life estate

immobilisation *f* (arrêt) standstill, immobilization; (Fin) capital investment; ∼ **de capitaux** locking up of capital, immobilization of capital; ∼**s** capital assets, fixed assets; ∼ **amortissable** depreciable property; ∼ **corporelle** tangible asset, tangible fixed asset; ∼ **en cours** asset under construction; ∼ **défectible** wasting asset; ∼ **incorporelle** intangible asset, intangible fixed asset

immobilité *f* immobility; ∼ **en matière salariale** wage standstill

immunisation *f* immunization

immunité *f* immunity; ∼ **diplomatique** diplomatic immunity; ∼ **fiscale** tax immunity; ∼ **légale** legal immunity, statutory immunity

imp. *abrév* (▸**importation**) imp. (import)

impact *m* impact; ∼ **sur l'environnement** environmental impact; ∼ **visuel** visual impact

impair, e *adj* odd

imparfait, e *adj* flawed

impartial, e *adj* impartial

impasse *f* deadlock; **être dans une** ∼ have reached a deadlock; ∼ **budgétaire** deficit spending; ∼ **professionnelle** dead-end job BrE, blind-alley job AmE

impayé¹, e *adj* (facture) outstanding, unpaid

impayé² m unpaid bill

impenses *f pl* maintenance expenditures, upkeep

impératif, -ive *adj* mandatory

impératifs *m* requirement; ∼**s de la dette** ···⟶

debt obligations

imperfection f flaw

impérialisme m imperialism; ~ **capitaliste** capitalist imperialism

imperméable adj waterproof

implantation f (décharge) site development; (mise en place) setting up, establishment; (Ind) (d'une usine) siting, location; ~ **à l'étranger** foreign venture, foreign site; ~ **fonctionnelle** functional layout; ~ **d'usine** plant location

implanter [1] vt (Info) implement; (usine, entreprise) establish, locate; (agence) open; (hypermarché, grande surface) build

[2] **s'implanter** v pron (entreprise) establish itself; (usine) be built; **s'~ sur un marché** break into a market

implémentation f (Info) (de système) implementation

implémenter vt (Info) implement

implication f involvement; ~ **du personnel** involvement of employees, staff involvement

implicite adj (non formulé) implicit; (Bourse) implied; (Info) by default, defaulting

impliquer vt (faire participer) (personnel) involve; (mêler) (personne) implicate; (mettre en jeu) involve; (signifier) mean

impopulaire adj unpopular

import m import; ~ **de données** (Info) data import

importable adj importable

importance f (gravité) importance; (taille) size; (de dégâts) extent; ~ **d'un droit** magnitude of a right; ~ **relative** (Compta) materiality

important, e adj (rôle) major, important; (hausse, réduction) significant; (achat) large; (gain) substantial; (personne) high-powered; **peu ~** small; ~ **indice du marché** Major Market Index

importateur¹, -trice adj (pays) importing

importateur², -trice m,f importer; ~ **net** net receiver

importation f import, importation; ~**s communautaires** (UE) community imports; ~ **invisible** invisible import; ~ **parallèle** parallel import; ~ **temporaire** temporary importation; ~ **visible** visible import

importé, e adj (produit) imported

importer vt import

import-export m import-export

importun, e adj (publicité) intrusive; (visiteur) unwelcome; (intervention, visite) ill-timed; (question) awkward

imposable adj (personne) liable to tax; (revenu, bénéfice) taxable; **non ~** (personne) not liable to tax; (revenu, bénéfice) non-taxable

imposé, e adj taxed; ~ **à la source** taxed at source

imposer [1] vt (limite, sanctions, délai, restriction) impose; (loi, règlement) lay down; (pénalité) levy; (idée, point de vue) impose; (style, mode) set; (Fisc) (personne, produit) tax; ~ **une amende à qn** impose a fine on sb; ~ **des règles** lay down the rules; ~ **une taxe** raise a tax

[2] **s'imposer** v pron (choix, solution) be obvious; (prudence, mesure) be called for

imposition f taxation; ~ **arbitraire** arbitrary taxation; ~ **directe et indirecte** direct and indirect taxation; ~ **d'après le domicile** domicile taxation; ~ **multiple** multiple taxation; ~ **optimale** optimal taxation; ~ **présomptive** presumptive tax; ~ **régressive** regressive taxation

impossibilité f impossibility; **être dans l'~ de faire qch** be unable to do sth; ~ **d'exécuter un contrat** (Droit) frustration of contract

impossible adj impossible; ~ **à trafiquer** (Com) tamper-proof

impôt m tax; **l'~** taxation; **frappé d'~** taxed; **payer des ~s** pay tax; **payer ses ~s** pay one's taxes; **avant/après ~** before/after tax; ~ **direct/indirect** direct/indirect tax; ~ **progressif/proportionnel** progressive/proportional tax; **payer 5 000 euros d'~s** pay 5,000 euros in tax; ~ **accumulé** accrual tax; ~ **agricole** agricultural levy; ~ **de base** basic tax; ~ **sur les bénéfices** profits tax; ~ **sur les bénéfices exceptionnels** windfall-profit tax; ~ **de Bourse** transaction tax; ~ **sur le capital** capital tax; ~ **de capitation** capitation tax; ~ **sur le chiffre d'affaires** turnover tax; ~ **contesté** disputed tax; ~ **correctif** corrective subsidy, corrective tax; ~ **déduit** tax deduction; ~**s déduits** after-tax; ~ **dégressif** decreasing tax, degressive tax; ~ **déguisé** hidden tax, stealth tax; ~ **différé** deferred tax; ~ **sur les dividendes** dividend tax; ~ **sur les dons** gifts tax; ~ **éludé** defrauded tax; ~ **établi** assessed tax; ~ **de l'État** state tax; ~ **étranger** foreign tax; ~ **étranger accumulé** foreign accrual tax; ~ **excessif** overtax; ~**s excessifs** excessive taxation; ~ **exigible** tax payable; ~ **sur l'exploitation minière** mining tax; ~ **fédéral net** net federal tax; ~ **fictif** phantom tax; ~ **fixé** assessed tax; ~ **foncier** property tax; ~ **forfaitaire** basic-rate tax, flat-rate tax, standard-rate tax; ~ **sur la fortune** wealth tax; ~ **sur les gains exceptionnels** windfall tax; ~ **général sur le revenu** general income tax; ~ **sur les grandes fortunes** wealth tax; ~ **de guerre** war tax; ~**s irrécouvrables** uncollectable taxes; ~**s locaux** ≈ council tax UK, ≈ local taxes US; ~ **sur les mines** mining tax; ~ **minier** mining tax; ~ **moyen** average tax; ~ **municipal** local tax; ~ **négatif sur le revenu** negative income tax; ~ **payable par ailleurs** tax otherwise payable; ~ **à payer** tax liability, tax payable; ~ **programmé**

schedular tax; ~ **de progrès social** social development tax Canada; ~ **progressif** graduated tax, progressive tax; ~ **rajusté à payer** adjusted tax payable; ~ **de redressement** compensation tax; ~ **réduit** reduced tax; ~ **réellement versé** taxes actually paid; ~ **régressif** regressive tax; ~ **régulier** standard tax; ~ **de remplacement** replacement tax; ~ **reporté** deferred profit-sharing plan; ~ **répressif** repressive tax; ~ **retenu** tax deduction AmE; ~ **retenu à la source** source tax, withholding tax; ~ **sur le revenu** income tax; ~ **sur le revenu des corporations** corporate income tax; ~ **sur le revenu inversé** reverse income tax; ~ **sur le revenu de placements** investment income tax; ~ **sur le revenu reporté** deferred income tax; ~ **sur les revenus pétroliers** oil revenue tax, petroleum revenue tax; ~ **sur les sociétés** corporate tax; ~ **sinon exigible** tax otherwise payable; ~ **de sortie** output tax; ~ **à la source** source tax; ~ **sous-déclaré** underdeclared tax; ~ **spécifique** earmarked tax; ~ **sur les successions** inheritance tax, legacy tax AmE, succession duty, succession tax AmE; ~ **supplémentaire** incremental tax; ~ **par tête** capitation; ~ **sur le travail sélectif** selective employment tax; ~ **sur la valeur** ad valorem tax; ~ **sur les valeurs** securities tax; ~ **uniforme** flat tax, normal tax; ~ **unitaire** unit tax; ~ **par unité** per unit tax

impraticable *adj* (projet) unworkable, impractical

impression *f* (Info) printing; ~ **artistique** art print; ~ **du contenu de la mémoire** memory print-out; ~ **de droite à gauche** reverse printing; ~ **en gras** bold printing; ~ **au verso** (édition) backing up

impressionnant, e *adj* impressive; peu ~ unimpressive

impressionner *vt* impress

imprévisible *adj* unpredictable

imprévoyant, e *adj* short-sighted

imprévu¹, e *adj* unforeseen; dépenses ~es unforeseen expenses

imprévu² m (incident) hitch; ~ **de dernière minute** last-minute hitch; sauf ~ barring accidents

imprimante *f* printer; ~ **à cartes** credit-card imprinter; ~ **électrostatique** electrostatic printer; ~ **graphique** graphics printer; ~ **à impact** impact printer; ~ **à jet d'encre** ink-jet printer; ~ **à laser** laser printer; ~ **à série** serial printer; ~ **à tambour** drum printer

imprimé¹, e *adj* printed; ~ **en caractères gras** printed in bold type

imprimé² m (formulaire) form; ~s printed matter; ~s **publicitaires** junk mail; ~ **à remplir** blank form

imprimer *vt* (livres, journaux) print; (Info)
print (out); ~ **à la française** print in portrait; ~ **à l'italienne** print in landscape

imprimerie *f* (Ind) printing works

imprimeur *m* (directeur) printer; (ouvrier) print-worker, printer; ~ **éditeur** printer and publisher

improductif, -ive *adj* unproductive

impropre *adj* (usage, terme) incorrect; (inadapté) ~ **à la consommation** unfit for consumption; ~ **à faire** unfit to do

improviser *vt* improvise

improviste: à l'~ unexpectedly

impulsion *f* (force) impetus; (Ind) pulse; donner une (nouvelle) ~ à give fresh impetus to

imputable *adj* (Compta) chargeable; ~ **à** (erreur, accident) attributable to

imputation *f* (Compta) charging; (accusation) accusation; ~ **des charges** allocation of costs; ~ **d'un coût** cost application

imputer *vt* (attribuer) attribute; (Compta) charge; ~ **une dépense à un compte** charge an expense to an account; ~ **à l'exercice** charge off; ~ **qch à qn** attribute sth to sb

inabordable *adj* (service, produit) unaffordable; (prix, tarif) prohibitive

inachevé, e *adj* incomplete, unfinished

inactif, -ive *adj* (Fin) inactive; (Info) idle, inactive

inadapté, e *adj* (méthode, moyen) inappropriate; (outil) unsuitable; (système, loi) ill-adapted

inadéquat, e *adj* (système, moyen, réponse) inadequate; (structure, bâtiment) unsuitable

inadmissible *adj* (proposition) unacceptable; (erreur, situation) intolerable; (preuve) inadmissible

inadvertance: par ~ inadvertently

inaliénable *adj* (Droit) inalienable

inanimé, e *adj* (sans vie) lifeless

inapplicable *adj* (clause, traité) unenforceable; (réforme) unworkable

inappliqué, e *adj* (loi, réglementation) unenforced

inapte *adj* unfit; ~ **à faire qch** unfit to do sth; ~ **à qch** unfit for sth

inaptitude *f* unfitness; ~ **à qch/à faire qch** unfitness for sth/for doing sth; ~ **au travail** unfitness for work, unemployability

inassurable *adj* uninsurable

inattaquable *adj* (droit) unchallengeable; (argumentation, jugement) irrefutable; (Ind) (par la rouille) rust-proof

inattendu, e *adj* unforeseen

INC *abrév* (▶**Institut national de la consommation**) ≈ CA (Consumers' Association)

incapable *adj* (qui ne peut pas) (par nature) incapable; (temporairement) unable; (incompétent) incompetent; ~ **de faire** incapable of doing, unable to do

incapacitant, e *adj* incapacitating

incapacité *f* (impossibilité) inability; (incompétence) incompetence (**en matière de** as regards); (invalidité) disability; (Droit) incapacity; ~ **à faire** inability to do; ~ **civile** legal incapacity; ~ **de travailler** unfitness for work

incarcération *f* imprisonment

incendie *m* fire; ~ **et vol au tiers** third-party fire and theft; ~ **volontaire** arson

incertitude *f* uncertainty

incessant, e *adj* (soutien) continuing; (effort) unceasing; (changements) constant

incessible *adj* (Droit) untransferable

inchangé, e *adj* unaltered, unchanged

incidence *f* impact; (Econ) incidence; **avoir une ~ sur qch** have an impact on sth; ~ **budgétaire** budget incidence; ~ **comptable** accounting effect; ~ **fiscale** tax incidence; ~ **sur le profit** profit impact; ~ **statutaire** statutory incidence

incident *m* incident; **l'~ est clos** the matter is closed; ~ **machine** (Info) hardware failure; ~ **technique** technical hitch

incinérateur *m* incinerator

incinération *f* incineration

incitation *f* incentive; (Droit) (à enfreindre la loi) inducement; ~ **économique** economic incentive; ~ **fiscale** tax incentive; ~ **monétaire** monetary inducement; ~ **au rendement** productivity incentive; ~ **à la vente** sales incentive; ~ **à voyager** travel incentive

inciter *vt* encourage, incentivize; ~ **qn à faire qch** urge sb to do sth

inclure *vt* (joindre) (document, chèque) enclose; (prix, forfait) include

inclus, e *adj* (dans une lettre) enclosed; (dans un prix) included; **les taxes sont ~es dans le prix** the taxes are included in the price; **jusqu'à jeudi** ~ until Thursday inclusive BrE, through Thursday AmE

inclusion *f* inclusion

inclusivement *adv* inclusively; **jusqu'au 4 mai** ~ until 4 May inclusive BrE, through 4 May AmE

incomber: ~ **à** *vi* (responsabilité, faute) lie with; (tâche, dépense) fall to

incombustible *adj* fireproof

incomparable *adj* unparalleled

incompatible *adj* incompatible; **être ~ avec** conflict with

incompétence *f* incompetence; (Droit) incompetency

incompétent, e *adj* incompetent

incomplet, -ète *adj* incomplete; (Droit) inchoate

inconditionnel, -elle *adj* (contrat) absolute, unconditional; (Info) unconditional

inconnu, e *adj* not known; ~ **à cette adresse** unknown at this address

incontestable *adj* unquestionable; (contrat) unimpeachable

inconvenable *adj* unsuitable

inconvénient *m* drawback, disadvantage

inconvertibilité *f* (d'une devise) inconvertibility

inconvertible *adj* (devise) inconvertible

incopiable *adj* (Info) copy-protected

incorporation *f* incorporation

incorporé, e *adj* (micro, antenne, cellule) built-in

incorporel, -elle *adj* (Droit) (droits, biens) intangible

incorporer *vt* incorporate, integrate

incorrectement *adv* wrongly

incrémentiel, -elle *adj* incremental

incrimination *f* accusation

incriminer *vt* accuse

incroyable *adj* incredible; (hors du commun) staggering

incubateur *m* (Fin) (pour start-up) incubator

inculper *vt* (Droit) charge; **être inculpé de** be charged with

incursion *f* raid

indéchirable *adj* (matériau) tear-proof

indécis, e *adj* undecided

indécomposabilité *f* indecomposability

indemnisation *f* indemnity, compensation; ~ **des accidents du travail** workers' compensation; ~ **des dommages** reparation for damage; ~ **de maladie** sickness pay; ~ **pétrolière** petroleum compensation

indemniser *vt* indemnify, compensate; ~ **qn pour qch** compensate sb for sth; **se faire ~** receive compensation

indemnité *f* (dédommagement) indemnity, compensation; (protection sociale) allowance, benefit BrE; **verser des ~s** pay compensation; ~ **absolue** aggregate indemnity; ~ **en cas de perte** compensation fee; ~ **de cessation d'emploi** severance pay; ~ **de chômage** unemployment benefit BrE, unemployment compensation AmE; ~ **de déménagement** removal allowance; ~ **de départ** severance pay; (dans le cadre d'une OPA), golden parachute; ~ **de déplacement** travel allowance BrE, traveling allowance AmE; ~ **différée** deferred compensation; ~ **d'emploi régional** regional employment premium; ~ **équitable** just compensation; ~ **fixe** fixed benefits; ~ **de fonction** acting allowance; ~ **de frais accessoires** incidentals allowance; ~ **individuelle** personal allowance UK, personal credit Canada, personal exemption US; ~ **kilométrique** ≈mileage allowance; ~ **de licenciement** redundancy pay; (de personnel en surnombre) push money (infrml); ~ **de logement** housing allowance; ~ **de maladie** sickness benefit, sickness pay; ~

de manutention handling allowance; ~ **de maternité** maternity pay; ~ **non-imposable** tax-free allowance; ~ **pécuniaire** compensation money; ~ **quotidienne** daily allowance; ~ **de repas** meal allowance; ~ **de subsistance** subsistence allowance; ~ **de vie chère** cost-of-living allowance

indépendance f independence; ~ **des exercices** (Compta) accrual accounting

indépendant, e adj independent; (appartement, industrie) self-contained; (financièrement) self-supporting, self-sufficient; (Info) stand-alone; (travailleur) freelance; ~ **de** independent of

indéterminé, e adj indefinite

index m (Admin, Fin, Info) index

indexation f indexation, index-linking; (pour classer) indexing; ~ **légale** formal indexation; ~ **des salaires sur le coût de la vie** cost-of-living adjustment

indexé, e adj (Econ) index-linked; (Info) indexed

indexer vt (Econ) index-link, index; (Info) index

indicateur m indicator; (horaire) timetable; (de tendances) gauge BrE, gage AmE; ~ **de conjoncture** business indicator; ~ **économique** economic indicator; ~ **de marché** market indicator; ~ **principal de tendance** leading indicator; ~ **de prospérité** prosperity indicator

indicatif¹, -ive adj indicative; ~ **de** indicative of

indicatif² m (téléphone) dialling code BrE, dialing code AmE; (radio, télévision) jingle; ~ **d'appel** call sign; ~ **interurbain** area code; ~ **musical** theme tune; ~ **de pays** country code; ~ **de zone** area code

indication f indication; (instruction) instruction; (renseignement) information; **sauf** ~ **contraire** unless otherwise indicated; ~ **additionnelle** additional matter; ~ **de durée et de prix** advice of duration and/or charge; ~ **de provenance** indication of source; ~ **technique** (de reprise) technical sign

indice m (Econ, Fin) index; (signe) sign; (Info) index; ~ **des actions** share index, stock exchange price index; ~ **de base** economic base; (calcul de rapport) index basis; ~ **de base total** total base number; ~ **boursier** share index, stock price index; ~ **de charge** load factor; ~ **composé** composite index; ~ **composite** composite index; ~ **composite principal** composite leading index; ~ **du coût de la construction** construction cost index UK; ~ **du coût de la vie** cost-of-living index; ~ **de croissance** growth index; ~ **de diffusion** diffusion index; ~ **Dow-Jones** Dow-Jones index; ~ **de l'eurodollar** Eurodollar index; ~ **des grandes valeurs** index of leading indicators; ~ **d'inconfort**

discomfort index; ~ **des indicateurs à courte durée** index of shorter leading indicators; ~ **des indicateurs à longue durée** index of longer leading indicators; ~ **des indicateurs retardés d'activité** index of lagging indicators; ~ **des indicateurs simultanés** index of coincident indicators; ~ **d'intérêt** indication of interest; ~ **des marchandises** commodities index; ~ **du marché principal** Major Market Index; ~ **des matières premières** commodities index UK; ~ **mondial des bourses de valeurs** Capital International World Index; ~ **des obligations** bond index; ~ **pondéré** weighted index; ~ **pondéré des cours** price-weighted index; ~ **des prix** price index; ~ **des prix à la consommation** consumer price index; ~ **des prix de détail** retail price index; ~ **des prix de gros** wholesale price index; ~ **des prix à la production** producer price index; ~ **de rareté** scarcity index; ~ **de traitement** salary grade; ~ **d'utilité** revealed preference, util; ~ **des valeurs unitaires** unit value index; ~ **du volume** volume index

indigent, e m,f pauper; **les** ~ the destitute, the poor

indiquer vt set out; (prix) quote; (montant) claim; ~ **pour mention**, ~ **en passant** mention

indirect, e adj indirect; **de façon** ~**e** indirectly

indirectement adv indirectly

indiscutable adj indisputable, unquestionable

indispensable¹ adj (équipement, activité, employé) essential; (aide, élément) essential, vital; (précaution) necessary; **c'est** ~ it's essential

indispensable² m **l'**~ the essentials; **faire l'**~ do what is necessary

indisponibilité f unavailability

indisponible adj unavailable

individu m individual

individualisme m individualism

individuel, -elle adj individual; (chambre) single; (maison) detached

individuellement adv individually; ~ **mais non-conjointement** (Droit) severally but not jointly

indivisibilité f indivisibility

indivision f (Droit) joint ownership; (propriété louée) joint tenancy; **posséder qch en** ~ own sth jointly

indu m payment made in error, money not owed

induire vt (entraîner) lead to; (inciter) induce; ~ **en erreur** mislead

induit, e adj induced

industrialisation f industrialization

industrialisé, e adj industrialized

industrialiser ① vt industrialize ⇢

2 **s'industrialiser** *v pron* become industrialized

industrie *f* industry; ~ **aéronautique** aircraft industry; ~ **affaiblie** ailing industry, declining industry; ~ **agro-alimentaire** food processing industry, agrifood industry; ~ **alimentaire** food industry; ~ **artisanale** cottage industry; ~ **des assurances** insurance industry; ~ **de base** basic industry; ~ **du bâtiment** construction industry; ~ **de capitaux** capital-intensive industry; ~ **capitale** essential industry; ~ **cinématographique** film industry; ~ **clé** key industry; ~ **en croissance rapide** growth industry, sunrise industry; ~ **cyclique** cyclical industry; ~ **en déclin** ailing industry, declining industry; ~ **diversifiée** runaway industry; ~ **sans entraves** footloose industry; ~ **extractive** extractive industry, resource industry; ~ **figée** locked-in industry; ~ **à forte intensité de capitaux** capital-intensive industry; ~ **du gaz** gas industry; ~ **à haute technologie** high-technology industry; ~ **horlogère** watch trade; ~ **houillère** coal industry; ~ **intérieure** domestic industry; ~ **légère** light industry; ~ **locale** local industry; ~ **des loisirs** leisure industry; ~ **lourde** heavy industry; ~ **manufacturière** manufacturing industry, processing industry; ~ **mécanique légère** light engineering; ~ **minière** mining industry; ~ **naissante** infant industry; ~ **nationalisée** nationalized industry; ~ **nucléaire** nuclear industry; ~ **du papier** paper industry; ~ **du passé** sunset industry; ~ **patrimoniale** patrimonial industry; ~ **pétrolière** oil industry, petroleum industry; ~ **pharmaceutique** drug industry, pharmaceutical industry; ~ **plastique** plastics industry; ~ **primaire** primary industry; ~ **principale** key industry; ~ **réglementée** regulated industry; ~ **secondaire** nonbasic industry; ~ **du secteur primaire** primary industry; ~ **de service** service industry; ~ **du spectacle** entertainment industry; ~ **technologique** technology-based industry; ~ **textile** textile industry; ~ **du tissage** weaving trade; ~ **traditionnelle** smokestack industry; ~ **de transformation** processing industry; ~ **viticole** wine industry

industriel[1], **-elle** *adj* (titre, valeur) industrial

industriel[2], **-elle** *m,f* industrialist

inéchangeable *adj* unexchangeable

inéconomique *adj* uneconomic

inédit, e *adj* (livre, texte) unpublished; (procédé) totally new

inefficacité *f* inefficiency; ~ **sur le marché** inefficiency in the market

inefficience *f* inefficiency

inégalité *f* (disproportion) disparity (**entre** between); (iniquité) inequality (**devant** as regards); **l'~ des ressources** the disparity in resources

inélasticité *f* inelasticity; ~ **de la demande** inelasticity of demand; ~ **de l'offre** inelasticity of supply; ~ **des prix** price inelasticity

inemployé, e *adj* (capacité) idle; (capital) unemployed; (ressources) untapped

inépuisable *adj* inexhaustible, infinite

inertie *f* inertia; ~ **administrative** administrative inertia; ~ **industrielle** industrial inertia

inestimable *adj* (valeur) inestimable; (dommages) incalculable; (aide, service) invaluable; (œuvre d'art) priceless

inévitable *adj* inevitable, unavoidable

inévitablement *adv* inevitably

inexactitude *f* inaccuracy; (manque de ponctualité) unpunctuality

inexécution *f* (de travaux, d'une tâche) non-performance, nonexecution; ~ **du contrat** nonfulfilment of contract BrE, nonfulfillment of contract AmE

inexpliqué, e *adj* unexplained; **rester ~** remain unexplained, remain unaccounted for

inexploitable *adj* (mine) unworkable; (richesses) unexploitable; (documents) unusable; (données, fichiers) unprocessable

inexploité, e *adj* (ressources, marché, créneau) untapped, unexploited; (documents) unused; (données, fichiers) unprocessed

infaillible *adj* infallible, unfailing

infaisable *adj* infeasible, impossible

inférer *vt* infer, conclude (**de** from)

inférieur, e *adj* (en valeur) (coût, salaire, nombre) lower (**à** than); (de qualité moindre) inferior (**à** to); ~ **à la moyenne** below average; **un taux ~ à 3%** a rate of less than 3%, a rate lower than 3%; **un travail de qualité ~** a poor piece of work; ~ **au taux de base** France (Econ) off-prime; ~ **au taux préférentiel** Canada (Econ) off-prime

infiltration *f* (d'eau) seepage

infirmation *f* (d'un jugement) invalidation

infirmer *vt* (jugement) invalidate

inflation *f* inflation; **un taux d'~ de 2.5%** a 2.5% inflation rate; **forte/faible ~** high/low inflation; ~ **bouchon** bottleneck inflation; ~ **cachée** hidden inflation; ~ **contenue** suppressed inflation; ~ **par les coûts** cost-push inflation; ~ **déguisée** hidden inflation; ~ **par la demande** demand-pull inflation; ~ **dirigée** administered inflation; ~ **fiscale** taxflation; ~ **mondiale** world inflation; ~ **monétaire** monetary inflation; ~ **par les prix** price inflation; ~ **du prix de l'actif** asset price inflation; ~ **des prix de gros** wholesale price inflation; ~ **rampante** creeping inflation; ~ **réglementée** administered inflation; ~ **des salaires** wage inflation; ~ **par les salaires** wage-push inflation; ~ **sous-jacente** underlying inflation; ~ **structurelle** core inflation, structural inflation; ~ **structurelle des prix à la consommation** core consumer price inflation

inflationnisme *m* inflationism

inflationniste *adj* inflationary; **tensions/ pressions** ~**s** inflationary pressures

infliger *vt* (amende) impose; ~ **une sanction à** penalize

influence *f* influence; **avoir de l'**~ be influential; ~ **fiscale** tax influence; ~ **des marchés financiers** capital market influence; ~ **personnelle** personal influence

influencer *vt* influence; (économie, situation) affect

influent, e *adj* influential

influer: ~ **sur** *vt* (coûts) have an influence on

infographie *f* computer graphics; ~ **à adressage binaire** bit-mapped graphics

informaticien, -enne *m,f* computer expert

information *f* (renseignement) information; **une** ~ a piece of information; (Média) a news item; (Info) item of data; **traitement de l'**~ data processing; (Média) **les** ~**s** the news; **pour** ~ for your information, FYI; ~ **commerciale** market intelligence; ~ **comptable** reporting; ~**s confidentielles** confidential information; ~ **de contrôle** control information; ~ **contrôlée** managed news; ~ **économique** economic intelligence; ~**s économiques** economic news; ~ **erronée ou trompeuse** false or misleading information; ~ **financière** reporting; ~ **d'initié** inside information; ~ **à jour** up-to-date information; ~ **judiciaire** judicial inquiry; ~ **probante** audit evidence; ~**s de vol** flight information

informatique *f* (science) computer science, computing; (techniques) information technology, IT; ~ **de gestion** business computing; ~ **graphique** computer graphics; ~ **individuelle** personal computing, end-user computing; ~ **interactive** interactive computing; ~ **professionnelle** business computing; ~ **répartie** distributed computing

informatisation *f* computerization

informatisé, e *adj* computerized

informatiser *vt* computerize

informé *m* (Droit) **pour plus ample** ~ for further information

informel, -elle *adj* informal

informer ⟦1⟧ *vt* inform; ~ **qn de qch** inform sb of sth; ~ **qn que** inform sb that; **de source bien informée** from a reliable source

⟦2⟧ **s'informer** *v pron* keep oneself informed; (se mettre au courant) **s'**~ **de qch** inquire about sth; **je m'informe des prix avant d'acheter** I check the prices before I buy; **s'**~ **si l'avion a atterri** check whether

the plane has landed; **s'**~ **sur qn** make inquiries about sb

infraction *f* (Droit) offence; **commettre une** ~ commit an offence; **c'est une** ~ **à la loi/au règlement** it's a breach of the law/rules; ~ **fiscale** tax offence; ~ **à la loi** breach *ou* violation of the law; ~ **mineure** misdemeanour; ~ **pénale** criminal offence; ~ **aux règles de sécurité** safety breach *ou* violation

infrastructure *f* infrastructure; (équipement) facilities; ~ **hôtelière/de transport** hotel/transport facilities; **d'**~ infrastructural

infructueux, -euse *adj* (collaboration) unrewarding; (tentative) fruitless

ingénierie *f* engineering; ~ **assistée par ordinateur** computer-aided engineering, computer-assisted engineering; ~ **financière** financial engineering; ~ **informatique** computer engineering; ~ **inverse** reverse engineering; ~ **médicale** medical engineering; ~ **de pointe** advanced engineering

ingénieur *m* engineer; ~ **agronome** agricultural engineer; ~ **de chantier** site engineer; ~ **en chef** chief engineer; ~ **cogniticien** knowledge engineer; ~ **commercial** sales engineer; ~ **conseil** consultant engineer; ~ **des constructions navales** naval architect; ~ **électricien** electrical engineer; ~ **électronicien** electronic engineer; ~ **d'entretien** maintenance engineer; ~ **d'études** design engineer; ~ **expert** surveyor; ~ **du génie maritime** naval architect; ~ **informatique** computer engineer; ~ **logiciel** software engineer; ~ **maritime** marine engineer; ~ **de produit** product engineer; ~ **programmeur** software engineer; ~ **projet** project engineer; ~ **système** systems engineer

ingérable *adj* unmanageable

ingérence *f* (dans les affaires) interference

ingérer: **s'**~ **dans** *v pron* interfere in

inhospitalier, -ière *adj* inhospitable

initial, e *adj* (investissement) initial; (opération) opening; (coût, intérêt) initial; **versement** ~ first instalment, front-end payment

initiale *f* initial

initialisation *f* (Info) initialization

initialiser *vt* (Info) initialize

initiateur, -trice *m,f* (de projet) originator; (Pol) initiator

initiative *f* initiative; **à/sur l'**~ **de qn** at sb's initiative; **faire preuve d'**~ show initiative

initié, e *m,f* insider; (Fin) insider trader; ~ **à l'informatique** computer literate

injecter *vt* (capitaux) inject

injection *f* (Econ) injection; ~ **de capitaux** capital injection

injonction *f* (Droit) injunction; ~ **donnée** ⋯⟫

par un tribunal mandatory injunction; ∼ **provisoire** interim injunction

injuste *adj* unfair; ∼ **envers** unfair to

injustice *f* (Droit) injustice; **réparer une** ∼ right a wrong

injustifié, e *adj* unjustified

innocenter *vt* (excuser) clear; (Droit) prove innocent

innovateur¹, -trice *adj* innovative

innovateur², -trice *m,f* innovator

innovation *f* innovation; ∼ **de produit** product innovation; ∼ **technologique** technological innovation

innover *vi* (personne, entreprise) innovate; (équipement) break new ground

inobservation *f* failure to comply, noncompliance; ∼ **des conditions** nonobservance of conditions, noncompliance with the conditions

inoccupé, e *adj* (logement locatif) untenanted

inonder *vt* (marché) flood, swamp, glut

inopportun, e *adj* untimely

input *m* input, inputs; ∼ **de l'ordinateur** computer input

inscription *f* (de société) registration; ∼ **aux ASSEDIC** signing-on; ∼ **au budget** budgeting; ∼ **au cadastre** land registration; ∼ **comptable** accounting entry; ∼ **fausse ou trompeuse** false or deceptive entry; ∼ **gigogne** (Bourse) piggyback registration; ∼ **hypothécaire** registration of mortgage; ∼ **au registre foncier** land registration

inscrire ⟨1⟩ *vt* (Com) book in; (nom, rendez-vous) write down; ∼ **au barreau** call to the bar, admit to the bar US; ∼ **au budget** list in the budget; ∼ **des charges à payer** accrue previously unrecorded expenses; ∼ **à la cote** (Bourse) list; ∼ **à l'heure de sortie** book out; ∼ **des informations dans un registre** enter information onto a register; ∼ **des produits à recevoir** accrue previously unrecorded revenues; ∼ **au registre** record in the register

⟨2⟩ **s'inscrire** *v pron* sign up; **s'**∼ **au chômage** sign on

inscrit, e *adj* (Bourse) listed; ∼ **au compte de résultat** above the line; ∼ **à la cote** (Bourse) listed

INSEE *abrév* (▶**Institut national de la statistique et des études économiques**) ≈ CSO (Central Statistical Office) UK

insensible *adj* (sans réaction) unresponsive; ∼ **aux défaillances** (Info) fault-tolerant

insérer *vt* insert; ∼ **une annonce dans le journal** place *ou* run an ad in the paper; ∼ **une annonce pour un poste dans le journal** advertise a job in the paper; ∼ **qch dans un contrat** build sth into a contract

insertion *f* (d'annonce, de clause) insertion; (intégration) integration; ∼ **professionnelle** professional integration; ∼ **légale** (Droit) publication of a legal judgment in the press

insignifiant, e *adj* trifling

insister *vi* insist; ∼ **sur** stress, lay the emphasis on

insoluble *adj* insoluble

insolvabilité *f* insolvency

insolvable *adj* insolvent

inspecter *vt* inspect

inspecteur, -trice *m,f* inspector, supervisor AmE; ∼ **de banque** bank inspector, bank examiner US; ∼ **en chef** chief inspector; ∼ **des impôts** revenue officer, tax inspector; ∼ **maritime** marine superintendent; ∼ **des plaintes** claims inspector; ∼ **des services de santé** health inspector; ∼ **du travail** labour inspector BrE, labor inspector AmE, factory inspector

inspection *f* inspection; ∼**s renforcées** tight controls; ∼ **du dossier** (demande de brevet) inspection of files; ∼ **officielle des banques** bank inspection, bank examination US; ∼ **du personnel** staff inspection; **Inspection du travail** Health and Safety Inspectorate UK, labor inspectorate US

instabilité *f* instability; ∼ **du marché** market sensitivity

instable *adj* (Econ) (cours, prix, marché) unstable, volatile; (gouvernement) unstable

installation *f* facility, installation; ∼ **à bord** shipboard facility; ∼**s et agencements** fittings and fixtures; ∼ **de combustion** combustion plant; ∼ **défectueuse** faulty installation; ∼ **d'élimination des déchets** waste disposal facility; ∼ **fixe** (Ind) fixed plant; ∼ **flexible** (Ind) flexible plant; ∼ **de forage** oil rig; ∼**s industrielles** plant; ∼ **de loisirs** leisure facility; ∼ **en mer** offshore installation; ∼**s portuaires** harbour facilities BrE, harbor facilities AmE; ∼ **de secours** backup facility; ∼ **de stockage** (déchets) storage facility; ∼**s techniques** plant, production goods

installé, e *adj* (Info) installed

installer ⟨1⟩ *vt* (Info) set up, install BrE, instal AmE; ∼ **le siège de** headquarter AmE

⟨2⟩ **s'installer** *v pron* (dans une résidence, dans un pays) settle; (professionnellement) set oneself up in business; **s'**∼ **à son compte** set up one's own business

instance *f* (autorité) authority; (Droit) legal proceedings; **introduire une** ∼ institute legal proceedings; **affaire en** ∼ pending matter; **courrier en** ∼ mail awaiting attention; **en** ∼ (Droit) outstanding, pending; ∼ **d'arbitrage** (Droit, Ind) arbitration board; ∼**s dirigeantes** executive

instaurer *vt* (Info) set; (loi, taxe, contrôle) institute; (dialogue, quota, régime) impose

instinct *m* instinct; ∼ **de possession** acquisitive instinct, acquisitiveness

institué, e *adj* constituted

institut *m* institute; **Institut d'études**

politiques ≈ Centre for Political Studies; **Institut monétaire européen** European Monetary Institute; **Institut national de la consommation** ≈ Consumers' Association; **Institut national de la statistique et des études économiques** ≈ Central Statistical Office UK; **Institut des Nations Unies pour la formation et la recherche** United Nations Institute for Training and Research; **∼ des prêts à la consommation** consumer loan institute; **∼ de recherche agréé** approved research institute; **Institut de Recherche des Nations Unies pour le développement social** United Nations Research Institute for Social Development; **Institut Universitaire de Technologie** university institute of technology (*providing vocational training*)

institution *f* institution; **∼ bancaire** banking institution; **∼ centralisée** centralized institution; **∼ coopérative de crédit** cooperative credit institution; **∼ de crédit** lending institution; **∼ de dépôts** deposit institution, depository; **∼ économique** economic institution; **∼ financière** financial institution; **∼ financière désignée** specified financial institution; **∼ financière para-bancaire** nonbank bank; **∼ du marché monétaire** money-market institution

institutionnalisme *m* institutional economics

instruction *f* (Droit) preliminary investigation; (Info) command, instruction, statement; **pour toute ∼ complémentaire** for further instructions; **pour ∼s** for orders; **∼ d'arrêt** (Info) breakpoint instruction; **∼ effective** (Info) actual instruction; **∼s d'expédition** forwarding instructions; **∼ machine** (Info) instruction; **∼ de renvoi** (Info) breakpoint instruction

instruire *vt* (informer) **∼ qn de qch** inform sb of sth; **∼ une affaire** conduct an investigation

instruit, e *adj* educated

instrument *m* (Droit, Fin) instrument; **∼ créateur d'un fidéicommis** trust instrument; **∼ de dépôt** deposit instrument; **∼ dérivé** derivative instrument; **∼ d'emprunt cessible** transferable loan instrument; **∼ financier** financial instrument; **∼ financier dérivé** derivative; **∼ hors change** off-exchange instrument; **∼ du marché monétaire** money-market certificate; **∼ du marché monétaire à court terme** short-term money-market instrument; **∼ à moyen terme** medium-term instrument; **∼ négociable** marketable instrument, negotiable instrument

insuffisamment *adj* (pas assez) insufficiently; (mal) inadequately; **∼ ciblé** (public) untargeted; **∼ financé** underfunded

insuffisance *f* (pénurie) insufficiency,

shortage; (déficit) shortfall; **l'∼ de la demande/production** the shortfall in demand/production; **∼ actuarielle** actuarial deficit, experience loss; **∼ de capital** lack of capital, undercapitalization; **∼ d'effectifs** undermanning; **∼ de personnel** staff shortage; **∼ de provision** insufficient funds; **∼ des ressources** insufficiency of ressources

insuffisant, e *adj* (quantitativement) (nombre, rendement) insufficient; (qualitativement) (mesures, préparation) inadequate

int. *abrév* (▸**intérêt**) int. (interest)

intact, e *adj* intact, free of damage

intégral, e *adj* (version, texte) unabridged; (paiement, remboursement) full, in full

intégralement *adv* (payer, publier) in full

intégration *f* integration; **∼ en amont** backward integration; **∼ en aval** forward integration; **∼ économique** economic integration; **∼ à la sécurité sociale** integration with social security

intégré, e *adj* (incorporé) built-in; (circuit, logiciel) integrated; **∼ à** integrated into; **gestion ∼e** integrated project management; **traitement ∼ des données** integrated data processing

intégrer *vt* integrate; **∼ au revenu** add to income

intégrité *f* integrity; **∼ de données** (Info) data integrity

intelligence *f* intelligence; **∼ artificielle** artificial intelligence; **∼ économique** economic intelligence

intelligent, e *adj* intelligent

intendance *f* (service) administration; (de domaine) stewardship

intendant, e *m,f* (financier) paymaster; (Admin) comptroller; (biens immobiliers) bailiff, steward

intense *adj* intense

intensif, -ive *adj* intensive

intensification *f* intensification; **∼ de l'apport en capital** capital deepening

intensifié, e *adj* (activité) stepped-up

intensifier ⏹1 *vt* heighten; (effort) intensify; (échanges, production) step up, intensify ⏹2 **s'intensifier** *v pron* (concurrence) intensify

intensité *f* intensity; **industrie à forte ∼ capitalistique** capital-intensive industry; **∼ de la circulation** traffic flow; **∼ de l'utilisation des sols** land-use intensity

intenter *vt*: **∼ une action** take legal action; **∼ une action à qn** bring an action against sb; **∼ un procès à qn** bring an action against sb, take legal action against sb; **∼ un procès en diffamation** sue for libel; **∼ un procès en diffamation à qn** (pour texte injurieux) bring an action for libel against sb; (pour paroles injurieuses) bring an action for slander against sb; **∼ un procès en dommages-intérêts** file ⸱⸱⸱⸳

a claim for damages

intention *f* intention; **à l'~ de qn** aimed at sb; **avec ~ de nuire** maliciously; **avec une ~ frauduleuse** fraudulently; **avoir l'~ de faire** intend to do; **dans l'~ de faire** with a view to doing; **~ d'achat** intention to buy; **~s cachées** hidden agenda; **~ criminelle**, **~ délictueuse** (Droit) malicious intent

interactif, -ive *adj* (Info) interactive

interaction *f* interaction

interactivité *f* interactivity

interbancaire *adj* interbank

intercaler *vt* (insérer) insert; (Info) embed

interchangeabilité *f* interchangeability, commutability

interchangeable *adj* interchangeable, commutable; (Droit) fungible

interclassement *m* (Info) collation

interconnecter *vt* interconnect; (Info) network

interconnexion *f* interconnection; (Info) networking; **~ portuaire** port interchange; **~ de systèmes ouverts** (Info) open-systems interconnection

interdépendance *f* interdependence; **~ des stratégies** (Gestion) strategic interdependence

interdépendant, e *adj* interdependent

interdiction *f* (Droit) ban, prohibition; (de fonctionnaire) barring from office; **~ d'aliénation** restraint of alienation; **~ générale** blanket ban; **~ judiciaire** (Droit) declaration of legal incompetence; **~ d'opérations** (Bourse) cease-trading order

interdire *vt* ban, prohibit; **~ la vente de qch** ban the sale of sth

interentreprises *adj inv* inter-company; **commerce ~** business to business, B2B

intéressant, e *adj* (qui retient l'attention) interesting; (avantageux) advantageous; (offre, conditions, prix) attractive; **sembler ~** look promising

intéressé¹, e *adj* (concerné) concerned; (attiré) interested (par in); **les personnes ~es aux bénéfices** those with a share in the profits

intéressé², e *m,f* person concerned; **les ~s** the people concerned

intéressement *m* (Fin) financial involvement; (Ind) share of production plan; **~ aux bénéfices** profit-sharing; **~ par option de souscription d'actions** incentive stock option; **~ du personnel aux bénéfices** profit-sharing

intérêt *m* (attention) interest; (avantage, utilité) interest; (Fin, Bourse) interest; **avoir des ~s dans une affaire** have a share in a business; **à ~ non comptabilisé** nonaccrual; **avec ~** (Bourse) and interest; **avoir de l'~ sur des actions** have an equity interest; **prêt sans ~** interest-free loan; **payer des ~s** pay interest; **porter ~** bear interest; **susciter/éveiller l'~ de qn** arouse sb's interest; **manifester son ~ pour qch** express an interest in sth; **d'~ général/public** of general/public interest; **agir par ~** act out of self-interest; **~ sur arriérés** interest on arrears; **~ d'assurance** insurable interest; **~ bancaire** bank interest; **~ capitalisé** capitalized interest; **~ commercial** business interest, commercial interest; **~ complémentaire** additional interest; **~s composés** compound interest; **~ composé mensuellement** monthly compounding of interest; **~s en cours** running interest; **~s courus** accrued interest, interest accrued; **~s cumulés** accrued interest, cumulative interest; **~s débiteurs** debit interest; **~ sur les dépôts** deposit interest; **~ de deuxième rang** subordinated interest; **~ direct** (dans une corporation) direct equity; **~s échelonnés** graduated interest; **~ économique** economic benefit; **~ exonéré** exempt interest; **~ gagné** earned interest; **~ important** substantial interest; **~s imputés** imputed interest; **~ d'investissement à terme** forward investment return; **~ matériel** (dans une société) material interest; **~ minoritaire** minority interest, minority stake; **~s moratoires** postmaturity interest; **~ national** national interest; **~ obligataire** bond interest, interest on bonds; **~ quotidien** daily interest; **~ réel nul** zero real interest; **~s de retard** postmaturity interest; **~s simples** simple interest; **~s en souffrance** interest on arrears; **~ supplémentaire** add-on interest, extra interest; **~s versés** interest paid; **~ visuel** visual appeal

inter-États *adj inv* (loi) interstate US

interface *f* (Info) interface; **~ graphique** graphical interface; **~ parallèle** parallel interface; **~ technologie-marché** technology-and-market interface; **~ utilisateur** user interface

interfacer *vt* (Info) interface

interférence *f* interference

interfinancement *m* cross subsidization

interfonctionnement *m* (Info) interoperability

intergouvernemental, e *adj* (sommet) intergovernmental

intergroupal, e *adj* intergroup

intérieur, e *adj* (d'une organisation) (règlement) internal; (d'un pays) (marché, politique, consommation, vol, réseau) domestic, internal; **à l'~ de l'État** intrastate US

intérim *m* (période) interim; (travail temporaire) temporary work, temping; **par ~** (directeur) acting, ad interim (frml); **pendant l'~** in the interim; **travailler en ~** temp (infrml), do temporary work; **agence d'~** temporary employment agency; (de secrétariat) temping agency

intérimaire¹ *adj* (directeur) acting, interim

intérimaire² *mf* temporary worker, temp

interjeter *vt*: ~ **appel** appeal, lodge an appeal

interligne *m* (Info) line space; ~ **simple** single spacing; ~ **double** double spacing

interlocuteur, -trice *m,f* (dans une négociation) spokesperson, representative

intermédiaire¹ *adj* (entreprises, taux, situation) intermediate; (Info) midrange

intermédiaire² *m,f* go-between, intermediary; (Econ) middleman; **par l'**~ **de** through (the agency of); **sans** ~ (traiter) direct, without an intermediary; (vendre) direct, without a middleman; ~ **de Bourse** agency broker; ~ **des échanges** medium of exchange; ~ **entre courtiers** interdealer broker

intermédiation *f* intermediation; ~ **financière** financial intermediation; ~ **ratée** misintermediation

intermittent¹, e *adj* intermittent

intermittents: ~ **du spectacle** *m pl* casual show-business labor AmE, casual show-business labour BrE

intermodal, e *adj* (Transp) intermodal

internalisation *f* (Econ) internalizing

international, e *adj* international

internationalisation *f* internationalization

internationaliser *vt* internationalize

internaute *mf* (Info) Internet user, netsurfer

interne *adj* (système) internal; (Info) in-house; ~ **à** within; **en** ~ (travailler) in-house; **formation** ~ in-house training; **marché** ~ internal market

Internet *m* Internet; **avoir accès à** ~ (chez soi) be on the Internet; (au travail) have access to the Internet; ~ **haut débit** high speed Internet; ~ **mobile,** ~ **nomade** mobile Internet

interopérabilité *f* (Ind, Info) interoperability

interphone *m* intercom

interpolation *f* interpolation

interprétation *f* (version) interpretation; (de langues) interpreting; **donner une** ~ **peu rigoureuse de qch** give a loose interpretation of sth

interprète *mf* interpreter

interpréter *vt* interpret

interprofessionnel, -elle *adj* interprofessional

interpropriété *f* crossownership

interrogation *f* debriefing; (Info) inquiry, query

interrogatoire *m* (Droit) cross-examination

interrogeable *adj* which can be interrogated; ~ **à distance** (répondeur) with a remote-access facility

interroger *vt* (candidat) interview; (accusé) cross-examine; **50% des personnes interrogées** 50% of those questioned; **être interrogé comme témoin** be called as a witness

interrompre *vt* interrupt; (activité commerciale) suspend; (programme) abort, interrupt

interrupteur *m* (Info) button, switch; ~ **à bascule** toggle switch; ~ **à positions multiples** dual-in-line package switch

interruption *f* (arrêt) break; (fin) ending; (de programme) interruption; **après une** ~ **de trois mois** after a three-month break; **sans** ~ nonstop, continuously; ~ **des émissions** blackout; ~ **matérielle** (Info) hardware interrupt; ~ **publicitaire** (télévision) commercial break; ~ **du voyage** break in the journey

intersaison *f* (tourisme) low season; **sommet** ~ shoulder period

interurbain *adj* (appel) long-distance

intervalle *m* (dans l'espace) space; (dans le temps) interval; **dans l'**~ meanwhile; ~ **d'un demi-point** (Bourse) half a strike price interval

intervenant, e *m,f* (sur un marché) participant; (dans des négociations) player; (Bourse) operator, dealer

intervenir *vi* (avoir lieu) happen; (agir) intervene, step in; ~ **dans** intervene in; ~ **en Bourse pour son propre compte** trade for one's account

intervention *f* intervention; **prix d'**~ intervention price; **seuil d'**~ intervention threshold; ~ **après protêt** (droit commercial) act of honour BrE, act of honor AmE; ~ **de l'État** state intervention; ~ **minimale de l'État** minimal state intervention; ~ **d'un tiers** third-party intervention

interventionniste *adj* interventionist; **non** ~ non-interventionist

intervertir *vt* invert; (rôles) reverse

interview *f* interview; ~ **collective** group interview; ~ **dirigée** (étude de marché) directed interview; ~ **d'évaluation des performances** performance appraisal interview; ~ **par téléphone** (étude) telephone interviewing; ~ **en profondeur** in-depth interview

interviewé, e *m,f* interviewee

intervieweur, -euse *m,f* interviewer

intestat *adj* (succession) intestate; **mourir** ~ die intestate

intimidation *f* intimidation; ~ **injustifiée** unjustified threat

intitulé *m* (Compta) title; ~ **de colonne** column heading; ~ **de compte** account holder's name, title of an account; ~ **de crédit** budget heading; ~ **de l'emploi** generic job title

intra-communautaire *adj* (UE) intra-   ····⟩

community

intraministériel, -elle *adj*
intradepartmental

Intranet *m* (Info) Intranet

intransigeant, e *adj* uncompromising

intrapreneuriat *m* intrapreneurship

introduction *f* introduction; (Droit) (d'un
appel) institution; ~ **en Bourse** stock
exchange listing, flotation; ~ **à la cote**
stock exchange listing, flotation; ~ **de
données** data entry; ~ **d'instance**
institution of legal proceedings; ~
progressive phasing in; ~ **du système
métrique** metrication

introduire ⟦1⟧ *vt* (modifications, mesures, idée,
produit) introduce; (données) enter, input; ~
sur le marché (produit) bring out; ~
progressivement phase in; ~ **en Bourse**
(nouvelle émission) float; ~ **qch dans un
contrat** build sth into a contract
⟦2⟧ **s'introduire** *v pron* **s'**~ **dans le marché**
gain a toehold in the market; **s'**~ **en Bourse**
go public

intrus, e *m,f* intruder; **l'**~ the odd one out

intrusion *f* interference; ~ **illicite sur la
propriété d'autrui** unlawful trespass

inutilisable *adj* unusable

inutilisé, e *adj* unused

invalidation *f* (d'un accord, d'un document)
invalidation

invalider *vt* (document, vote) invalidate

invalidité *f* disability; (Droit) invalidity; ~
répétée recurrent disability

invendable *adj* unmarketable, unsaleable
BrE, unsalable AmE

invendu¹, e *adj* unsold

invendu² *m* unsold item; (édition) returned
book; ~s unsold goods, sales returns

inventaire *m* stocktaking BrE, inventory
AmE; **faire l'**~ do the stocktaking BrE, take
inventory AmE; **fermé pour cause d'**~ closed
for stocktaking; ~ **de clôture** ending
inventory; ~ **comptable** book inventory; ~
continu continuous inventory; ~ **des
effectifs** manpower audit, staff audit; ~
matériel materials accounting, store
accounting; ~ **permanent** continuous
stocktaking; ~ **physique** physical inventory;
~ **du prix d'exercice** closing inventory; ~
des produits frais fresh produce inventory;
~ **des réserves** stock inventory,
stocktaking; ~ **des stocks** stocktaking; ~
tournant perpetual inventory

inventer *vt* invent

inventeur, -trice *m,f* inventor

inventif, -ive *adj* (novateur) inventive

invention *f* invention; ~ **brevetable**
patentable invention; ~ **personnelle**
brainchild (infrml)

inventorier *vt* (marchandises) make out
a stocklist of BrE, make out an inventory
of AmE; (Droit) (succession) draw up an

inventory of

inverser *vt* (tendance) reverse; (Info) invert;
~ **une position** (Bourse) close a position,
liquidate a position; ~ **un swap** (Bourse)
reverse a swap; ~ **une transaction par
compensation** (Bourse) unwind a trade

inversion *f* inversion; (Info) case shift; ~
de la courbe des taux (Econ) yield-curve
inversion

investir *vt* invest (dans in); ~ **en actions/
obligations** invest in bonds/shares; ~ **en
Bourse** invest on the Stock Exchange; ~ **qn
de qch** vest sb with sth

investissement *m* investment (dans in);
~s capital expenditure; **susceptible d'**~
investible; ~ **actif** active investment; ~ **en
actions** equity investment; ~ **adapté** fit
investment; ~ **de base** expenditure base; ~
basé sur l'actif asset-based investment; ~
brut gross investment; ~s **à capacité
fiscale** tax-efficient investments; ~ **en
capital** capital investment; ~ **collectif** real
investment; ~ **commercial** trade
investments; ~ **à court terme** short-term
investment; ~s **de l'État** government
investment; ~ **d'exploitation** operational
investment; ~ **extraterritorial** offshore
investment; ~ **fiduciaire** fiduciary
investment; ~ **garanti par des actifs**
asset-backed investment; ~ **initial** initial
investment, seed money; ~ **intérieur net** net
domestic investment; ~ **involontaire**
unintended investment; ~ **légal** statutory
investment; ~ **licite** legal investment; ~s
nationaux domestic investments; ~ **de
portefeuille** portfolio investment; ~ **en
prêt** loan investment; ~ **de qualité** legal
investment; ~s **de rationalisation** capital
deepening; ~ **réel** actual investment; ~ **à
rendement fixe** straight investment; ~ **à
revenu fixe** fixed-income investment; ~
sain sound investment; ~s **des sociétés**
corporate investment; ~ **à taux variable**
floating-rate investment; ~s **à valeur
constante en dollars** dollar cost averaging

investisseur *m* investor; ~ **accrédité**
accredited investor; ~ **actif** active investor;
~ **en actions** equity investor; ~ **averti**
experienced investor; ~ **chevronné**
experienced investor; ~ **commercial**
corporate investor; ~ **à contre-tendance**
contrarian; ~ **institutionnel** institutional
investor

invisibles *m pl* (Econ) invisibles

invite *f* (Info) prompt; ~ **DOS** DOS prompt

inviter *vt* (suggestions) welcome

invoquer *vt* (loi) invoke; ~ **son ignorance**
plead ignorance

iota *m* iota

IPC *abrév* (▶**indice des prix à la
consommation**) CPI (consumer price index)

IRNUDS *abrév* (▶**Institut de Recherche
des Nations Unies pour le**

développement social) UNRISD (United Nations Research Institute for Social Development)

irréalisable *adj* unfeasible, unworkable

irrécouvrable *adj* (dette) irrecoverable

irréductible *adj* (personne, motivation) indomitable

irréfutable *adj* (réputation) irrefutable

irrégularité *f* irregularity

irrégulier, -ière *adj* unsteady; (résultats) erratic; (tendance) uneven

irrémédiable *adj* (perte, faute) irreparable; (déclin) irreversible; (situation) beyond remedy

irremplaçable *adj* irreplaceable

irréparable *adj* beyond repair, irreparable; **être ~** be a write-off (infrml)

irrésolu, e *adj* (problème, question) unresolved

irréversible *adj* (stratégie) irreversible

irrévocable *adj* (Droit) binding, irrevocable; (décision) irreversible

isocoût *m* isocost

isolation *f* insulation; **~ phonique/acoustique** soundproofing

isolationniste *adj* isolationist

isolé, e *adj* isolated

isoler *vt* (contre les intempéries) insulate; (politicien, ennemi) isolate

isoloir *m* polling booth, voting booth

isotherme *adj* insulated

issue *f* outcome; **~ positive** successful outcome; **~ probable** likely outcome

italique *f* italics; **en ~** in italics

itération *f* iteration

itinéraire *m* itinerary; **~ détourné** indirect route; **~ direct** direct route, through route; **~ à escales multiples** (navigation) multiport itinerary

IUT *abrév* (▸**Institut Universitaire de Technologie**) university institute of technology (*providing vocational training*)

Jj

jachère *f* (pratique) fallow; (terrain) fallow land; **en ~** lying fallow

jalon *m* milestone

jambe *f* (Bourse) (d'un écart) leg

jaquette *f* (d'un livre) dust jacket

jardinerie *f* garden centre BrE, garden center AmE

jargon *m* jargon; **~ juridique/publicitaire** legal/advertising jargon; **~ administratif** officialese; **~ Internet** netspeak; **~ journalistique** journalese

JAT *abrév* (▸**juste à temps**) JIT (just in time)

jauge *f* (pour mesurer) gauge; (capacité) capacity; (d'un navire) tonnage; **~ sous le pont** under-deck tonnage

jaugeage *m* (d'un navire) tonnage measurement

jaune *mf* (péj) blackleg BrE (pej), scab BrE (pej), strikebreaker

Java® *m* (Info) Java®

jetable *adj* disposable

jeter ⓵ *vt* throw; (Envir) dump; **~ les bases de** lay the foundations for; **~ un froid sur** put a damper on; **~ un œil** browse; **~ un œil à/sur** have a quick look at; **~ par-dessus bord** (Transp) jettison; **~ son argent par les fenêtres** (infrml) throw one's money about (infrml)

⓶ **se jeter** *v pron* (être jetable) be disposable

jeton *m* token; **~s de présence** director's fees

jeu *m* (partie) game; (interaction) interplay; (Bourse) gambling, speculation; (Info) (de caractères) set; **par ~x de** (Gen com) in sets of; **au ~** (Bourse) at-the-money; **en ~** at stake; (Bourse) in-the-money; **entrer en ~** (facteurs) come into play; **le libre ~ de la concurrence** the free play of competition; **~ à la baisse** strong bearish play; **~ d'entreprise** business game; **~ d'essai** testdeck; **~ à la hausse** strong bullish play; **~x d'hypothèses** what-if games (jarg); **~ de revendications** set of claims; **~ de rôles** (formation commerciale) role play, role-playing; **~ à somme négative/positive** negative/positive sum game; **~ à somme nulle** zero-sum game

jeu-concours *m* competition

jeune *adj* (en âge) young; (nouveau) new; **un ~ diplômé** a new graduate; **être ~ dans le métier** be new to the trade; **les ~s** young people; **~ cadre** junior executive; **~ cadre dynamique** young upwardly mobile professional, yuppie (infrml); **~ loup** up-and-coming executive; **~ pousse** (business) start-up; **~ prodige** whizz kid (infrml)

jingle *m* signature tune, jingle

J.J. *abrév* (Fin, Banque) (▸**au jour le jour**) (opération) overnight

jl *abrév* (▸**journal**) (Compta) db (daybook); (Média) mag (magazine)

JO *abrév* (▸**Journal officiel**) (UE) OJ ⋯▸

(Official Journal); (France) *French government publication outlining new legislation and ministerial decisions*

job *m* (infrml) (petit boulot) casual work; (pour les vacances) summer job; (travail rémunéré) job

jobber *m* (Bourse) market maker

joignable *adj* il n'est pas ∼ en ce moment he can't be contacted at the moment

joindre *vt* (notes, liste, document) append; (échantillon, CV) attach, enclose; (Info) (fichier) attach; ∼ qn par téléphone get sb on the phone

joint, e *adj* (à un courrier) enclosed; **pièce** ∼e (Info) attachment

joint-venture *m* joint venture; **signer un** ∼ sign a joint venture agreement

joker *m* (Info) wild card

jonction *f* connection, interface; ∼ **des appels** (Fisc) joinder of appeals

jouer **1** *vt* (rôle) perform, play; ∼ **le marché** play the market; ∼ **un rôle dans** play a part in **2** *vi* (spéculer) gamble, speculate; (facteurs) come into play; ∼ **à la bourse** gamble *ou* speculate on the stock exchange; ∼ **à la baisse** (Bourse) go a bear; ∼ **à la hausse** go a bull; ∼ **gros jeu** play for high stakes; (Bourse) take a flier; **laisser** ∼ **le marché** allow the free play of market forces

jouir *vi* ∼ **de** (droits, allocation, bonne réputation) enjoy

jouissance *f* (Droit) use; **avoir la** ∼ **de qch** have the use of sth; **avec** ∼ **au** payable on; ∼ **anticipée** anticipation; ∼ **immédiate** vacant possession, immediate possession; ∼ **tranquille** (d'un bien immobilier) quiet enjoyment

jour *m* day; (date) date; **être à** ∼ be up to date; **à ce** ∼ to date; **au** ∼ **le jour** on a day-to-day basis; (Fin, Banque) overnight; **de** ∼ **en jour** from day to day; **du** ∼ **au lendemain** (livraison) next-day; **être à** ∼ **de** (paiements) be up to date with, keep up with; **le** ∼ **même** (livraison) same-day; **par** ∼ per day; **tous les** ∼s daily, every day; **mettre à** ∼ update, bring up to date; **mise à** ∼ (données, application) updating; ∼s **après acceptation** days after acceptance; ∼ **d'assignation** (de l'option) assignment day; ∼s **d'attente** wait days; ∼ **de bourse** market day; ∼ **de chargement** loading date; ∼ **civil** calendar day; ∼ **de compensation** clearing day; ∼ **de congé** day off; ∼s **consécutifs** consecutive days; (Transp) running days; ∼ **courant** (charte-partie) running day; ∼ **courant de travail** (charte-partie) running working day; ∼ **creux** off-peak day; ∼ **de déclaration** (maritime) reporting day; ∼ **de départ** (d'un navire) sailing date; ∼ **d'échéance de la prime** due date of premium; ∼ **des élections** polling day; ∼ **de l'évaluation** valuation day; ∼ **de facturation** billing day; ∼ **férié** bank

holiday UK, legal holiday US, public holiday; ∼ **de fermeture avancée** early-closing day UK; ∼ **fixé** appointed day; ∼ **franc** clear day; ∼s **de franchise** days of grace; ∼ **de liquidation** account day; ∼ **de livraison** delivery day; ∼ **des opérations au compte de réserve** reservable day; ∼ **ouvrable** business day, working day BrE, workday AmE; ∼ **de paie** payday; ∼ **de règlement** settlement date, value date; ∼ **des reports** continuation day, preliminary day; ∼s **restant jusqu'à échéance** days to maturity; ∼s **restant jusqu'à livraison** days to delivery; ∼ **du terme** term day; ∼ **de transfert des biens** assignment day; ∼ **de travail** business day, working day BrE, workday AmE; ∼s **de valeur** float time; ∼s **de vue** days after sight

journal *m* (presse) newspaper; (comptabilité) account book; (Info) log; (d'un institut, d'une société) journal; (à la radio, télévision) news bulletin; ∼ **des achats** purchase book; ∼ **auxiliaire** special journal; ∼ **de banque** bankbook; ∼ **de bord** (navigation) ship's log; ∼ **économique** economic journal; ∼ **d'entreprise** house journal; ∼ **interne d'entreprise** house organ; ∼ **gratuit** free newspaper; ∼ **local** local newspaper; ∼ **de marche** computer log; ∼ **de mode** fashion magazine; ∼ **national** national newspaper; **Journal officiel** *French government publication outlining new legislation and ministerial decisions*; (UE) Official Journal; ∼ **petit format** tabloid, tabloid newspaper; ∼ **plein format** broadsheet; ∼ **professionnel** trade journal; ∼ **radio** (d'un navire) radio logbook; ∼ **réglementaire** (d'un navire) official logbook; ∼ **des rentrées de fonds** cash receipts journal; ∼ **sérieux** quality newspaper; ∼ **des sorties de caisse** cash payments journal; ∼ **des ventes** sales book, sales journal

journalier[1], **-ière** *adj* (travail, taux, variations) daily

journalier[2], **-ière** *m,f* casual labourer BrE, casual laborer AmE

journalisme *m* journalism; ∼ **à sensation** chequebook journalism BrE (pej), checkbook journalism AmE (pej)

journaliste *mf* journalist; ∼ **économique** economic affairs correspondent; ∼ **indépendant** (presse, radio, télévision) freelance journalist, freelance correspondent; ∼ **radio** radio journalist; ∼ **à sensation** muckraker (pej)

journée *f* day; ∼ **d'études** study day; ∼ **à tarif réduit** off-peak day; ∼s **de remplacement** lieu days

judiciaire *adj* (acte, institution) judicial; (aide) legal

judicieux, -euse *adj* advisable

juge *m* (Droit) judge; (dans un concours) judge, adjudicator; **être** ∼ **de** (concours) judge, adjudicate; ∼ **arbitre** judicial arbitrator; ∼ **compétent** magistrate entitled to adjudicate; ∼ **consulaire** judge in a commercial court; ∼ **d'instance** *or* **de paix** justice of the peace; ∼ **d'instruction** examining magistrate UK, committing magistrate US; ∼ **médiateur** trial examiner; ∼ **des référés** summary judge

jugement *m* (d'un tribunal) order of the court, ruling; (règlement d'une controverse) adjudication, judgment; ∼ **d'allure** performance rating; ∼ **avant dire** interlocutory decree; ∼ **compensatoire** deficiency judgment; ∼ **déclaratif de liquidation judiciaire** adjudication of bankruptcy order; ∼ **par défaut** default judgment; ∼ **entérinant un accord** consent decree; ∼ **gracieux** special case; ∼ **de valeur** value judgment

juger *vt* (Droit) judge, try; (réclamation) adjudicate; (candidats) judge; ∼ **nécessaire** deem necessary; ∼ **en référé** (Droit) hear a case in chambers; **être jugé par un jury** have a jury trial; **l'affaire est jugée** the case is closed

juguler *vt* (chômage) stamp out; (inflation) curb

jurer *vt* swear

juridiction *f* jurisdiction; **clause de** ∼ competence clause; **relever de la** ∼ **de** fall within the jurisdiction of; **hors/sous ma** ∼ within/outside my jurisdiction; ∼ **administrative** administrative tribunals; ∼ **d'arbitrage** court of arbitration; ∼ **compétente** court entitled to adjudicate; ∼ **fiscale** tax jurisdiction

juridique *adj* legal

juridiquement *adv* legally; ∼ **tenu** legally bound

juridisme *m* juridification

jurisprudence *f* case law, jurisprudence; **faire** ∼ set a legal precedent

juriste *mf* (qui pratique le droit) lawyer; (qui a étudié le droit) jurist, paralegal; ∼ **d'entreprise** corporate lawyer

jury *m* (Droit) jury, trial jury US; **président du** ∼ foreman of the jury; ∼ **ad hoc** special jury; ∼ **populaire** trial jury US; ∼ **de présélection** (de candidats) screening board;

∼ **de sélection** (de candidats) selection board, selection panel; ∼ **spécial** special jury

jusqu'à *prép* up to; ∼ **concurrence de** up to a maximum of; ∼ **nouvel ordre** until further notice; ∼ **preuve du contraire** in the absence of evidence to the contrary

jusqu'ici *adv* (Droit) heretofore

juste *adj* (estimation, prévision) correct; (raisonnement) accurate; (prix, salaire) fair; (Droit) equitable, fair; ∼ **à temps** just-in-time; ∼ **valeur marchande** fair market value

justesse *f* (d'un jugement) accuracy

justice *f* (principe) justice; (pouvoir) law, legal system; **aller en** ∼ go to court; **passer en** ∼ stand trial; **poursuivre en** ∼ sue; **être traduit en** ∼ be brought before the court; ∼ **fiscale entre générations** intergenerational equity; ∼ **de paix** court of petty session

justifiable *adj* justifiable

justificateur, -trice *adj* justificatory

justificatif¹, -ive *adj* (facture, document) supporting; **pièce justificative** documentary evidence, written proof

justificatif² *m* (document) written proof, documentary evidence; (Compta) voucher; ∼ **de caisse** petty cash voucher; ∼ **de compte créditeur** credit account voucher; ∼ **de domicile** proof of domicile; ∼ **de guichet automatique** automatic telling machine statement; ∼ **de paiement** receipt

justification *f* (action) justification; (preuve orale) explanation; (preuve écrite) documentary evidence; (de texte) justification; ∼ **de dette** proof of debt; ∼ **de livraison** proof of delivery; ∼ **de perte** proof of loss; ∼ **de titre** proof of title

justifié, e *adj* justified; **non** ∼ groundless; (texte) unjustified; ∼ **à droite/gauche** (texte) right-/left-justified

justifier ① *vt* (méthode, politique, décision) justify; (action, dépense, résultat) account for, justify; (affirmation) prove, substantiate; (opinion, droits) vindicate; (texte) justify; ∼ **à droite/gauche** (Info) justify to the right/left ② *vi* ∼ **de** (expérience professionnelle, connaissances) have; ∼ **de son identité** prove one's identity

Kk

kermesse *f* fête UK, bazaar

kérosène *m* kerosene

keynésianisme *m* Keynesian economics, Keynesianism; ∼ **abâtardi** bastard

Keynesianism; ∼ **militaire** military Keynesianism

keynésien, -enne *adj* Keynesian

kilo *m* (▸**kilogramme**) kilo (kilogram);

~-octet (Info) kilobyte

kilogramme *m* kilogramme BrE, kilogram AmE; **~ au centimètre carré** kilogramme per square centimetre BrE

kilométrage *m* ≈ mileage; **~ illimité** (location de voitures) ≈ unlimited mileage

kilomètre *m* kilometre BrE, kilometer AmE; **~-avion** aircraft kilometre; **~ carré** square kilometre; **~-heure** kilometres per hour; **~-passager** passenger-kilometre

kilowatt *m* kilowatt; **~-heure** kilowatt-hour

kiosque *m* (à journaux) kiosk

kiosquier, -ière *m,f* newsvendor

kit *m* kit; **vendu en ~** sold in kit form; **~ mains libres** (pour téléphone portable) (pour conducteur) hands-free kit; (pour piéton) hands-free headset

km au cent *abrév* (▶**kilomètres au cent**) ≈ mpg (miles per gallon)

km/h *abrév* (▶**kilomètre-heure**) km/h (kilometres per hour BrE, kilometers per hour AmE)

ko *abrév* (▶**kilo-octet**) kb (kilobyte)

kopeck *m* kopeck; **ça ne vaut pas un ~** it's not worth a penny

krach *m* crash; **le ~ de Wall Street** the Wall Street crash

kraft *m* **papier ~** brown paper; **enveloppe ~** manilla envelope

krone *f* krone

kurtose *m* kurtosis

kyrielle *f*: **une ~ de qch** a string of sth

label *m* label; **~ de qualité** quality label; **~ syndical** union label

laboratoire *m* laboratory; **~ d'idées** think tank; **~ de recherche** research laboratory

lacune *f* (dans un document) gap; (de projet, de système) deficiency; (Droit) loophole in the law

laine *f* wool; **~ mérinos** merino wool; **~ de verre** glass wool

lainier, -ière *adj* (industrie, commerce) wool; (région) wool-producing

laïque *adj* (enseignement) nondenominational

laisse *f* (partie de rivage) foreshore; **~ de basse mer** (maritime) low-water mark; **~ de haute mer** (maritime) high-water mark

laisser 1 *vt* leave; **~ un espace** leave a space; **~ de côté** put on the back burner, put to one side; **~ entendre à qn que** give sb to understand that; **~ entrer** admit; **~ flotter** float; **~ la question en suspens** leave the matter open; **~ tomber** drop; **tout ~ en plan** (infrml) drop everything; (personne) leave in the lurch (infrml)

2 **se laisser** *v pron* **se ~ corrompre** take bribes

laisser-faire *m* laissez-faire

laissez-passer *m* pass

lamanage *m* (maritime) boatage

lamaneur *m* lasher, rigger

lame *f* (Ind) blade; (Transp) blade

lancement *m* (d'un produit, d'une campagne, d'un entreprise) launch; (d'emprunt, d'émission) floating; (de fabrication) scheduling; (de système) booting; (d'un navire) launching; **~ d'un appel d'offres** opening of tenders; **~ automatique** (Info) autoboot, autostart; **~ d'une mode** trendsetting; **~ dans la presse** (publicité) press launch; **~ de tâche** (Info) task initiation; **~ test** pilot launch

lancer 1 *vt* (produit, campagne) launch; (entreprise) launch, start up; (Bourse) (emprunt, émission) float; (fabrication) launch, start; (programme) initiate; (système) activate, boot up; (prospectus) issue; **~ un appel** launch an appeal; **~ un appel d'offres** put out for tender; **~ une campagne nationale** (publicité) launch a national campaign; **~ un mandat** issue a warrant; **~ une mode** set a trend; **~ la mode de** start the fashion for, set the trend for; **~ un mot d'ordre de grève** call a strike; **~ une OPA contre une société** launch a takeover bid for a company, raid a company

2 **se lancer** *v pron* **se ~ dans de grosses dépenses** go to great expense; **se ~ dans les affaires** set up in business; **se ~ sur le marché** venture into the market

lanceur, -euse *m,f* (en affaires) promoter; **~ d'OPA** raider

langage *m* language; **~ commun** common language; **~ évolué** (Info) high-level language; **~ gestuel** body language; **~ informatique** computer language; **~ d'interrogation** (Info) query language; **~ objet** (Info) target language; **~ à objets** (Info) object-oriented language; **~ de programmation** programming language

langue *f* language; **~ d'arrivée or cible** target language; **~ commune** common language; **~ étrangère** foreign language; **~ source** source language

laps *m*: ～ **de temps** period of time; **dans le ～ de temps imparti** within the allotted time frame

large *adj* wide; **à ～ bande** (Info) broadband

largement *adv* widely; **～ diversifié** (gamme de produits) broadly diversified; **～ reconnu** widely recognized

largeur *f* (de zone) width; (d'un navire) beam; **～ de bande** bandwidth; **～ totale** overall width

larguer *vt* (du lest) jettison; **～ les amarres** unmoor

lat. *abrév* (▸**latitude**) lat. (latitude)

latent, e *adj* latent; (valeur, plus-value) underlying

latéral, e *adj* (mouvement) lateral

latex *m* latex

latitude *f* latitude; **laisser toute ～ à qn pour faire qch** give sb a free hand to do sth

lavage *m* washing; **～ au brut** (pétroliers) crude oil washing; **～ de cerveau** brainwashing

l/c *abrév* (▸**lettre de change**) B/E (bill of exchange)

L/C *abrév* (▸**lettre de crédit**) L/C (letter of credit)

leader *m* (Pol, V&M) leader; (éditorial) lead story, leading article UK; (produit) leader, market leader; **région/usine ～** foremost region/factory; **～ du marché** market leader; **～ naturel** natural leader; **～ né** born leader; **～ au niveau des prix** price leader; **～ d'opinion** opinion leader; **～ spontané** informal leader

leasing *m* leasing

lèche-vitrines *m* window-shopping; **faire du ～** be window-shopping, go window-shopping

lecteur¹ *m* (Info) reader; **～ de cartes** card reader; **～ de cassette** cassette player; **～ de codes barres** bar code reader, bar code scanner; **～ de disques** disk drive; **～ (de) DVD** DVD player; **～ par défaut** default drive; **～ de disquettes** floppy disk drive; **～ de documents** document reader; **～ d'étiquettes** tag reader; **～ laser** laser scanner; **～ optique** optical scanner; **～ série** serial reader; **～ de Zips®** Zip® drive

lecteur², -trice *m,f* (personne) reader

lectorat *m* (d'un journal) readership; **～ secondaire** pass-along readership (jarg)

lecture *f* reading; (Info) reading, scanning; **erreur de ～** (Info) read error

lecture/écriture *f* (Info) read/write

légal, e *adj* (activité, possession) lawful; (âge, définition, formalités, voies) legal; **monnaie ～e** legal tender; **domicile ～** official residence; **avoir une existence ～e** be legally recognized

légalement *adv* lawfully, legally; **～ contraignant** legally binding; **être ～ obligé de** be under a legal obligation to

légalisation *f* (d'une signature) attestation, authentication; (d'un contrat, d'un document) legalization

légaliser *vt* (pratique, activité) decriminalize; (contrat, document) legalize, notarize; (signature) attest, authenticate

légaliste *adj* legalistic

légalité *f* lawfulness, legality; **rester dans/ sortir de la ～** remain within/break the law

légataire *mf* devisee, legatee; **～ universel** sole legatee

légende *f* (Média) caption

léger, -ère *adj* (progrès, baisse, hausse, retard) slight

légèrement *adv* (baisser, augmenter) slightly; **～ inférieur à** a little under, slightly less than

légiférer *vi* bring in legislation, introduce legislation, legislate

Légion *f*: **la ～ d'honneur** the Legion of Honour

législateur, -trice *m,f* legislator

législatif, -ive *adj* legislative; **élections législatives** general election

législation *f* legislation; **faire passer une ～** bring in legislation, introduce legislation; **la ～ en vigueur** the laws in force; **selon la ～ française** under French legislation; **～ anti-évasion fiscale** anti-avoidance legislation; **～ anti-monopoles** antimonopoly laws; **～ antitrust** antitrust legislation; **～ douanière** tariff legislation; **～ nationale** national legislation; **～ relative à l'alimentation** food safety legislation; **～ relative au contrat de licence** licensing laws; **～ relative à la liquidation judiciaire** insolvency legislation; **～ relative à la protection des consommateurs** consumer protection legislation; **～ secondaire** piggyback legislation, secondary legislation; **～ sociale** welfare legislation; **～ sur les faillites** bankruptcy law, bankruptcy legislation; **～ du travail** employment law, labour laws BrE, labor laws AmE

légitime *adj* justifiable, legitimate; (propriétaire) rightful

legs *m* legacy; **faire un ～ à qn** leave a legacy to sb; **～ de biens immobiliers** devise; **～ de biens mobiliers** legacy

léguer *vt* leave, bequeath; (des biens immobiliers) devise

lendemain *m*: **le ～** the following day, the next day; **au ～ de** (guerre, élection) in the aftermath of

lent, e *adj* slow; **～ déclin** slow decline; **～e remontée** slow rise; **～ à répondre** slow to reply

LEP *abrév* (▸**livret d'épargne populaire**) savings book

lésiner *vt*: **～ sur** (finition, qualité) skimp on (infrml)

lésion *f* lesion; **～ corporelle** personal

⋯⟩

injury

lest *m* ballast; **~ d'eau** water ballast; **~ permanent** (navigation) permanent ballast

lettrage *m* (Média) lettering

lettre *f* (de l'alphabet) letter; (courrier) letter; (Bourse, Fin) bill; **à la ~** by the book; **~ datée du six** letter dated the sixth; **adresser une ~ à qn** write a letter to sb; **écrire une somme en toutes ~s** write an amount in full; **~ d'accompagnement** covering letter, cover letter AmE, accompanying letter; **~ d'accord du client** client agreement letter UK; **~ d'accord présumé** comfort letter; **~ d'accréditation** procuratory letter; **~ d'affaires** business letter; **~ d'approbation** award letter; **~ d'attribution** letter stock; **~ d'autorité** letter of authority; **~ d'aval** guarantee letter; **~ par avion** airmail letter; **~ d'avis** advice note, letter of advice; **~ de candidature** letter of application; **~ de change** bill of exchange; **~ de change garantie** backed bill of exchange; **~ de change négociable** negotiable bill of exchange; **~ de change de premier ordre** gilt-edged bill of exchange; **~ circulaire** circular; **~ commerciale** business letter; **~ de complaisance** facility letter; **~ de consentement** letter of consent; **~ de coopération** letter of cooperation; **~ de couverture** (Admin) covering letter; (Assur) cover note UK, binder US; **~ de crédit** letter of credit; **~ de déclaration d'intention** letter of intent; **~ de demande de renseignements** letter of enquiry; **~ de démission** letter of resignation; **~ d'engagement** letter of commitment; (Bourse) guarantee letter; **~ d'engagement d'audit** audit brief; **~ d'excuse** letter of apology; **~ d'exemption des droits de douane** bill of sufferance; **~ de garantie** (Banque) letter of indemnity; **~ de groupage aérien** house air waybill; **~ hypothécaire** letter of hypothecation; **~ d'information aux investisseurs** market letter US; **~ d'instruction** letter of direction; **~ d'intention** letter of intent; **~ d'introduction** covering letter; **~ de licenciement** letter of dismissal, redundancy letter BrE; **~ majuscule** capital letter, upper case letter; **~ minuscule** lower case letter; **~ de motivation** covering letter, cover letter AmE (*with a job application*); **~ négociable** negotiable bill; **~ de nomination** letter of appointment; **~s patentes** letters patent; **~ de procuration** procuratory letter; **~ publicitaire** sales letter; **~ de rappel** follow-up letter; **~ de réclamation** letter of complaint; **~ de recommandation** letter of recommendation; **~ recommandée** registered letter; **~ de remerciement** thank-you letter; **~ de renoncement** (Bourse) letter of renunciation; **~ en souffrance** unclaimed letter; **~ de souscription** (Fin) letter of application; **~ de soutien** (Compta) comfort letter; **~ de subordination** letter of subordination; **~ subrogatoire** letter of subrogation; **~ de transmission** (Admin) transmittal letter; **~ de transport aérien** air waybill; **~ de transport aérien de bout en bout** through air waybill; **~ de transport aérien groupé** master air waybill; **~ de transport maritime** sea waybill; **~ de voiture** (Transp) waybill, consignment note

leu *m* leu

lev *m* lev

levable *adj* (Bourse) exercisable

levage *m* (Transp) lift on-lift off, lo-lo

levé *m* survey; **~ aérien** aerial survey

levée *f* (Fin) (d'une option) exercise; (de la poste) collection; (d'un embargo, d'une peine) lifting; (de mesures, quotas) suspension; (de séance) close; **~ d'impôts** levy of taxes; **~ d'une nouvelle émission** (Bourse) takeup; **~ de l'option** exercise of an option, option exercise

lever *vt* (option, prime) exercise, take up; (courrier) collect; (embargo, sanction) lift, raise; (impôt) levy, raise; **~ des capitaux** raise capital; **~ la séance** adjourn the meeting; **~ une taxe** raise a tax

levier *m* lever; **effet de ~** gearing BrE, leverage AmE; **~ financier** financial gearing BrE, financial leverage AmE

LHT *abrév* (▸**longueur hors tout**) (Transp) LOA (length overall)

liaison *f* liaison; (Info) link; **en ~ avec** (travailler) in association with, in liaison with; **assurer la ~ avec qn** liaise with sb; **~ avec la clientèle** customer liaison; **~ de données** (Info) data link; **~ dans l'entreprise** channels of communication within the company; **~ ferroviaire** rail link; **~s fonctionnelles** functional relations; **~s hiérarchiques** line relations; **~ par modem** modem link; **~ numérique à débit asymétrique** (Info) asymmetric digital subscriber line; **~ train-avion** rail-air link

liasse *f* (de billets, de papiers) bundle; **~ fiscale** income tax return

lib. *abrév* (▸**libéré**) FP (fully paid)

libellé *m* (d'une lettre) terms, wording; **~ d'un crédit** vote wording; **~ d'une obligation** bond denomination

libeller *vt* (chèque) make out; **~ un chèque** write a cheque BrE, write a check AmE; **chèque libellé à l'ordre de qn** cheque made out to sb

libéral¹, e *adj* (parti, candidat) liberal; (économie, doctrine) free-market

libéral², e *m,f* (Pol) Liberal; (Econ) free marketeer

libéralisation *f* liberalization; **~ du commerce** trade liberalization

libéraliser *vt* liberalize

libéralisme *m* liberalism; ~ **économique** laissez-faire economy; ~ **social** social liberalism

libération *f* (d'engagement) release; (des prix) deregulation; (de dette) discharge; (d'échanges) freeing; (d'actions, de capital) paying up; ~ **des mouvements de capitaux** removal of control on capital flows; ~ **du fidéicommissaire** discharge of the trustee; ~ **d'hypothèque** discharge of mortgage; ~ **à la participation** (Fin) payment in full on allotment; ~ **partielle** partial release; ~ **des prix** price deregulation; ~ **sous caution** release of recognizance; ~ **des tarifs** lifting of tariff controls; ~ **à titre onéreux** (d'une obligation) accord and satisfaction; ~ **ou rachat** (Fisc) release or surrender

libéré, e *adj* (titre) freed up; (poste, lieu) vacant; (personne, entreprise) free; ~ **d'obligations** free from obligations

libérer 1 *vt* (prix) deregulate; (prisonnier) discharge, release; ~ **sous caution** release on bail
2 **se libérer** *v pron* (se rendre disponible) be free; **se** ~ **d'une dette** pay a debt

liberté *f* freedom, liberty; **en** ~ (prisonnier) discharged, released; **mettre en** ~ **provisoire sous caution** bail; ~ **d'action** freedom of action; ~ **d'association** freedom of association; ~ **de choix** freedom of choice; ~ **de circulation** freedom of movement; ~ **de concurrence** freedom of competition; ~ **de direction** right to manage; ~ **de dissociation** right to dissociate; ~ **économique** economic freedom; ~ **d'établissement** (Droit) freedom of establishment; ~**s publiques** civil rights; ~**s syndicales** trade union rights; ~ **du travail** (Droit) freedom of contract

libre *adj* free; ~ **de dettes** clean, clear of debts; ~ **à l'entrée** (import/export) uncustomed; ~ **d'hypothèque** (propriété) unmortgaged; **la ligne n'est pas** ~ (au téléphone) the number is engaged BrE *ou* busy; ~ **accès** open admissions; ~ **circulation** (des biens, des services) free movement; ~ **circulation de la main-d'œuvre** free movement of labour BrE, free movement of labor AmE; ~ **entreprise** free enterprise; ~ **immatriculation** (de navires) open registry; ~ **possession** (Droit) vacant possession

libre-échange *m* free trade; ~ **réciproque** (établissement des prix) fair trade

libre-service *m* self-service; ~ **bancaire** self-service banking

licence *f* (Droit, Brevets) licence BrE, license AmE; (diplôme) bachelor's degree; **produit sous** ~ licensed product; **fabriquer qch sous** ~ **japonaise** make sth under licence from a Japanese manufacturer; ~ **contractuelle** contract licence; ~ **de droit** law degree; ~ **d'enseignement** education *ou* teaching degree; ~ **exclusive** exclusive licence; ~

d'exportation export licence; ~ **de fabrication** manufacturing licence; ~ **globale** blanket licence, bulk license; ~ **d'homologation** certification mark; ~ **d'importation** import licence; ~ **informatique** computer software licence; ~ **obligatoire** (Brevets) compulsory licence; ~ **de prospection pétrolière** oil exploration licence; ~ **sur site** (Info) site licence; ~ **de surveillance** surveillance licence; ~ **temporaire d'exportation** temporary export licence; ~ **de vente** distribution licence

licencié¹, e *adj* (renvoyé) redundant; **être** ~ be made redundant

licencié², e *m,f* graduate; ~ **en dessin industriel** ≈ Bachelor of Industrial Design; ~ **en droit** law graduate, ≈ Bachelor of Laws; ~ **d'enseignement** teaching graduate, education graduate, Bachelor of Education; ~ **en études d'administration des entreprises** graduate in business administration, ≈ Bachelor of Science in Business Administration; ~ **en études commerciales** business studies graduate, ≈ Bachelor of Commerce; ~ **ès lettres** arts graduate, ≈ Bachelor of Arts; ~ **en sciences économiques** economics graduate, ≈ Bachelor of Economics; ~ **ès Sciences** science graduate, ≈ Bachelor of Science; ~ **en sciences des relations humaines** graduate in industrial relations, ≈ Bachelor of Science in Industrial Relations

licenciement *m* dismissal, redundancy; ~ **abusif** unfair dismissal; ~ **arbitraire** wrongful dismissal; ~ **collectif** collective dismissal UK, mass redundancy; ~ **justifié** fair dismissal; ~ **pour raisons économiques** economic redundancy; ~ **sec** compulsory redundancy (*without any compensation*); ~ **sommaire** summary dismissal

licencier *vt* (pour raisons économiques) make redundant; (pour faute) dismiss, fire (infrml); ~ **qn** terminate sb's employment, make sb redundant, lay sb off; (pour faute) dismiss sb, fire sb

lié, e *adj* (par contract) bound; (à un investissement, à une indexation) linked; ~ **à l'environnement** environmental; ~ **à l'épargne** savings-linked; ~ **juridiquement** legally bound

lien *m* connection, link; ~ **contractuel** contractual relationship; ~ **de parenté** relationship; ~**s en amont** backward linkage; ~**s en aval** forward linkage

lier *vt* (événements) link; (contrat) bind; **un contrat le lie à son entreprise** a contract binds him to his company; **notre avenir est lié à celui de l'Europe** our future is bound up with that of Europe; ~ **l'aide économique à des changements politiques** link economic aid to political change; ~ **juridiquement** legally bind

lieu *m* (d'événement) place, venue; **les ~x** the premises; **au ~ de** instead of; **avoir ~** take place; **~ du congrès** conference venue; **~ de destination** place of destination; **~ d'entrée** point of entry; **~ d'essai pilote** beta site; **~ d'immersion** (en mer) dumping ground; **~ de livraison** place of delivery; **~ d'origine** (Transp) place of origin; **~ de paiement** place of payment; **~x de pêche** fishing grounds; **~ de réception** place of acceptance; **~ de résidence** place of residence; **~ de réunion** venue; **~ de travail** workplace; **~ de vente** point of sale

lieudit *m* locality

lignage *m* (presse) linage, lineage

ligne *f* (de chiffres) row; (téléphonique) line; (compagnie, route) line; (service) service; (de produits) line; **en ~** (Info) online; **être en ~ avec** be through to; **rester en ~** hold the line; **par ~ familiale** per stirpes; **~ aérienne** airline; **~ aérienne intérieure** domestic airline; **~ aérienne internationale** international airline; **~ de base** (Info) baseline; **~ de code** (Info) code line; **~ de commande** (Info) command line; **~ commune** party line; **~ de comportement** behaviour line BrE, behavior line AmE; **~ de conduite** course of action; **~ continue** (d'un graphique) solid line; **~ de crédit** credit line; **~ de crédit ouverte par l'émission de titres à court** note issuance facility; **~ de crédit par acceptation** acceptance credit line; **~ de crédit renouvelable** revolving credit line; **~ de crédits croisés** swap credit line; **~ de découvert** credit line; **~ directe** direct line; (Info) hot line; **~ directrice** blueprint; (Brevets) reference line; **~ d'état** (Info) status line; **~ de fond** (d'un graphique) baseline; **~ à imprimer** print line; **~ interurbaine** trunk line; **~ maritime** shipping line; **~ de moindre résistance** line of least resistance; **~ multipoint** party line; **~ d'obligeance** (Assur) oblige line; **~ du parti** (Pol) party line; **~ pointillée** (impression) dotted line; (Info) dashed line; **~ de pont** (d'un navire) deck line; **~ principale** (chemin de fer) main line; **~ de production** flow line; **~ de produits** product line; **~ de programmation** code line; **~ régulière** scheduled service; **~ secondaire** (chemin de fer) branch line; **~ de sommets baissière** (Bourse) descending tops; **~ de sommets haussière** (Bourse) ascending tops; **~ de substitution** (Banque) backup line

limitation *f* (de pouvoir, liberté) restriction, limitation; (Droit) limit; (de prix, de taux d'intérêt) control; **~s budgétaires des prix** budget/ price control; **la ~ des armements** arms control, arms limitation; **~ du crédit** restriction of credit; **~ des dommages** damage limitation; **~ d'impôt** tax restriction; **~ du nombre de passagers** passenger control; **~ des pertes** loss limitation; **~s à la planification** planning restrictions; **~ de poids** weight limit; **~ des salaires** wage restraint; **~s de sous-traitance aux salariés** labour-only subcontracting BrE, labor-only sub-contracting AmE; **~s aux valorisations** (Bourse) valuation restrictions

limite *f* (d'un cours) limit; **âge ~** maximum age; **cas ~** borderline case; **date ~** deadline; **date ~ de vente** sell-by date; **hauteur/ largeur/poids ~** (Transp) maximum height/ width/weight; **~ à la baisse/hausse** (Fin) limit down/up; **~s** (d'un terrain) boundary; **dans la ~ de, dans les ~s de** within the limits of; **dans la ~ du possible** as far as possible; **dans la ~ de nos moyens** in so far as our means allow; **dans une certaine ~** up to a point, to a certain extent; **~ d'âge** age limit; **~ de construction** building line; **~ de crédit** credit ceiling, credit limit; **~ de dépenses** expenditure limit; **~ discrétionnaire** discretionary limit; **~ des disponibilités de trésorerie** cash limit; **~ d'émission** (de gaz polluant) emission limit; **~ d'emprise** position limit; **~ d'exonération de droits d'auteur** royalty exemption limit; **~ de financement externe** external financing limit; **~ de fluctuation** price fluctuation limit; **~ de fluctuation quotidienne** (Bourse) daily price limit; **~s fondamentales de la garantie** basic limits of liability; **~ de levée** (Bourse) exercise limit; **~ de prix** price limit; **~s de propriété** property line; **~ supérieure** upper limit; **~ de trésorerie** cash limit; **~ de variation des cours** fluctuation limit

limité, e *adj* (possibilités, intérêt) limited; (Droit) restricted; (ressources énergétiques) finite

limiter *vt* (dépenses, nombre) limit, restrict; **~ le nombre de** limit the number of; **cela limite nos possibilités** that rather limits our scope; **nous sommes limités dans le temps** our time is limited; **~ les dégâts** minimize the damage; **je limiterai mon intervention à une ou deux remarques** I'll restrict my speech to just one or two remarks

linéaire *m* (V&M) shelf space

liner *m* (avion) airliner; (navire) boat, liner

lingot *m* ingot; **~ d'or** gold ingot; **~s d'or** gold bullion

lingua franca *f* lingua franca

liquidateur, -trice *m,f* (Droit, Fin) liquidator, receiver

liquidation *f* (d'une société) liquidation, winding-up; (d'une dette) settlement, satisfaction; (du stock) clearance, clearance sale; **mettre une société en ~** put a company into liquidation *ou* receivership; **entrer en ~** go into receivership *ou* liquidation; **~ totale du stock** total clearance; **jour de ~** (Banque) settlement day; **~ en continu** (Bourse) continuous net settlement UK; **~ d'un contrat à terme**

avant maturité (Bourse) ringing out (jarg); ∼ **en espèces** cash settlement; ∼ **fictive quotidienne** (Bourse) settlement to the market; ∼ **de fin d'année** (Compta) yearly settlement; ∼ **de fin de mois** (Banque) monthly settlement; ∼ **forcée** (Droit) compulsory liquidation; ∼ **judiciaire** involuntary liquidation; ∼ **des positions** (Bourse) book squaring; ∼ **de sinistres** (Assur) runoff; ∼ **suivante** (Fin) succeeding account; ∼ **volontaire** (d'une société) voluntary liquidation, voluntary winding up

liquide¹ *adj* (Fin) liquid; **non** ∼ illiquid

liquide² *m* (espèces) cash, ready money; **payer en** ∼ pay cash

liquidé, e *adj* closed-out, liquidated

liquider *vt* (opération) close, sell off; (société) sell out, sell up; (biens) realize, sell off; (dette) clear, satisfy; (marchandises, stock) clear; (comptes) settle; ∼ **avant fermeture** (marchandises) closing-down sale BrE, close out AmE; ∼ **une opération** close a deal; ∼ **une position** (Bourse) close a position, liquidate a position

liquidité *f* (Fin) available cash, liquidity; **des** ∼**s** liquid assets; ∼ **bancaire** bank liquidity; ∼ **d'ouverture** front money, front-end money; ∼ **du secteur privé** private sector liquidity; ∼ **de la société** company liquidity; ∼**s et titres d'État** liquid assets and government securities

lire¹ *f* lira

lire² *vt* read; (Info) read, scan; ∼ **le téléscripteur** read the tape

lisible *adj* (écriture) legible; ∼ **par la machine** machine-readable

lissage *m* (technique de prévision) smoothing

lisser *vt* smooth

listage *m* (Gen com) listing; (Info) print-out; ∼ **informatique** computer print-out; ∼ **multiple** (immobilier) multiple listing US; ∼ **d'ordinateur** computer print-out

liste *f* list; (d'erreurs) catalogue BrE, catalog AmE; (de noms) list; **être sur** ∼ **d'attente** (Transp) be on standby; **faire une** ∼ make a list; **être sur** ∼ **rouge** be ex-directory BrE, be unlisted AmE; ∼ **d'adresses** mailing list; ∼ **agréée** approved list; ∼ **d'attente** waiting list; ∼ **des candidats** (Pol) list of candidates, slate US; ∼ **de colisage** packing list; ∼ **de commissions** shopping list; ∼ **de contrôle** check list; ∼ **de contrôle des commandes d'exportation** export order check list; ∼ **de correspondances** cross reference listing; ∼ **des cours** price quotation list; ∼ **de départs** (maritime) sailing schedule; ∼ **de diffusion** distribution list, mailing list; ∼ **électorale** electoral register; ∼ **immobilière** list US, listing; ∼ **d'investissement agréée** approved list; ∼ **noire** blacklist; ∼ **officielle des taux d'imposition** tax rate structure;

∼ **d'oppositions** (Banque) hot list, stop list; ∼ **ouverte** open listing; ∼ **partagée** split ticket US; ∼ **des passagers** passenger list, passenger manifest; ∼ **du personnel** payroll; ∼ **des priorités** list of priorities, hit list (infrml); ∼ **des prix** price list; ∼ **des produits** (Brevets) specification of goods; ∼ **restreinte** shortlist; ∼ **des services** (Brevets) specification of services; ∼ **de signets** (Info) favourites BrE, favorites AmE, hotlist; ∼ **de surveillance** watch list; ∼ **des valeurs les plus actives** (Bourse) most active list; ∼ **de vérification** checklist

lister *vt* (Info) list

listing *m* (Info) listing, computer print-out; ∼ **informatique** computer print-out; ∼**s pré-imprimés** continuous forms

litige *m* dispute; (Droit) litigation; **point de** ∼ bone of contention; (Droit) point at issue; **être en** ∼ (Droit) be involved in litigation; **les parties en** ∼ (Droit) the litigants; **régler un** ∼ settle a dispute

litispendance *f* (Droit) pendency

livr. *abrév* (▶livraison) D (delivery)

livrable *adj* deliverable; ∼ **à quai** ex quay, ex-wharf

livraison *f* delivery; ∼ **contre remboursement** cash on delivery; **payer à la** ∼ pay on delivery; **paiement à la** ∼ payment on delivery; **prendre** ∼ **de qch** take delivery of sth; ∼ **dès réception du paiement** cash before delivery; ∼ **droits non payés** delivered duty unpaid; ∼ **et re-livraison** delivery and redelivery; **faire une** ∼ **de** make delivery of; ∼ **franco de douane** delivered duty paid; ∼ **franco de douane à quai** delivered ex quay; ∼ **à la frontière** delivered at frontier; ∼ **au navire** delivered ex ship; ∼ **au comptant** spot delivery; ∼ **correcte** (Bourse) good delivery; ∼ **dans la journée** same-day delivery; ∼ **différée** delayed delivery; ∼ **directe** direct delivery; ∼ **à domicile** home delivery; ∼ **garantie** guaranteed delivery; ∼ **gratuite** free delivery; ∼ **au gré du vendeur** (Bourse) (dans un délai convenu) seller's option; ∼ **en gros** wholesale delivery; ∼ **groupée** consolidated delivery; ∼ **immédiate** immediate delivery; ∼ **matérielle** (Bourse) physical delivery; ∼ **multiple** multidelivery; ∼ **ordinaire** (Bourse) regular way delivery; ∼ **au pair** par delivery; ∼ **partielle** (Bourse) partial delivery, short delivery; ∼ **à quai** (navigation) delivered at docks; ∼ **par route** delivery on wheels; ∼ **tardive** late delivery; ∼ **à terme** (Bourse) forward delivery; ∼ **par voie ordinaire** (Bourse) regular way delivery

livre¹ *m* book; (Compta) book, ledger; (Pol) paper; ∼ **des acceptations** acceptance ledger; ∼ **d'achats** sold ledger; ∼ **des achats** purchase book; ∼ **de balance** balance book; ∼ **de banque** cashbook; ∼ **blanc** White Paper; ∼ **de bord** (d'un avion, ⋯⟩

d'un navire) official logbook; ∼ **de caisse** cashbook; ∼ **cartonné** (édition) hardback, hardback book; ∼ **des chèques** cheque register BrE, check register AmE; ∼ **à colonnes** columnar journal; ∼ **de comptes** analysis book, book of accounts, books; ∼ **des créditeurs** creditors' ledger; ∼ **des effets** (à payer et à recevoir) bill book; ∼ **d'entrepôt** (contrôle des stocks) warehouse book; ∼ **des fournisseurs** bought ledger; ∼ **à gros succès** (édition) best seller; ∼ **d'inventaire** inventory book; ∼ **journal général** (Compta) general journal; ∼ **d'or** visitors' book; ∼ **de paie** payroll; ∼ **de poche** (édition) paperback; ∼ **de rendement** yield book; ∼ **des ventes** (V&M) sales book

livre² f (monnaie) pound; (demi-kilo) half a kilo; (anglo-saxonne) pound; ∼ **irlandaise** punt; ∼ **maltaise** Maltese pound; ∼ **sterling** pound sterling; ∼ **verte** green pound

livré, e adj delivered

livrer vt (marchandises) deliver; (Bourse) make delivery of, tender; (presse) issue; **ne pas pouvoir** ∼ fail to deliver; **se faire** ∼ **qch** have sth delivered; **nous livrons à domicile** we do home deliveries; ∼ **qn** deliver sb's order; ∼ **à terme** tender

livret m booklet; ∼ **de compte** bankbook; ∼ **de compte d'épargne** savings book; ∼ **de dépôt** deposit book; ∼ **d'épargne populaire** savings book; ∼ **de marche** (chemin de fer) working timetable

livreur, -euse m,f delivery man, delivery woman

L.O.A. abrév (Fin) (▶**location avec option d'achat**) leasing

local¹, e adj (journal, industrie, autorités) local

local² m (Gen com) premises; **les locaux de l'usine** factory premises; **les locaux du journal/parti** the newspaper/party offices; ∼ **à bail** demised premises; ∼ **commercial** commercial premises; ∼ **homologué** approved premises; ∼ **professionnel** business premises

localisation f (lieu) location; (Info) localization; ∼ **défensive** (pétrolier) protective location; ∼ **de l'usine** plant location

localiser vt (repérer) locate; (panne) troubleshoot; (envoi) trace; (Info) localize

locataire mf tenant; ∼ **agricole** agricultural tenant; ∼ **à bail** lessee; ∼**s en commun** joint tenants; ∼ **débordant** sitting tenant BrE, holdover tenant AmE; ∼ **à vie** life tenant

location f hire; (par le locataire) let UK, tenancy; (par le propriétaire) letting, renting out; (de spectacle) booking, reservation; ∼ **commerciale** commercial letting UK; ∼ **en commun** tenancy in common; ∼ **de conteneurs** container leasing; ∼ **sous contrat** contract hire; ∼ **contractuelle** contract hire; ∼ **à durée indéterminée** tenancy at will; ∼ **d'équipement** plant hire;

∼ **fermière** farm tenancy; ∼ **foncière** land lease; ∼ **immobilière** let property; ∼ **indexée** leverage lease; ∼ **intégrale** tenancy by the entirety; ∼ **longue durée** contract hire; ∼ **de matériel** equipment leasing; ∼ **au mois** month-to-month tenancy; ∼ **avec option d'achat** leasing; ∼ **par téléphone** telephone booking; ∼ **de voitures** car hire BrE, auto rental AmE

location-acquisition f capital lease

location-vente f hire purchase BrE, installment plan AmE

lock-out m lockout

logement m (local d'habitation) accommodation BrE, accommodations AmE; (fait de loger) housing; (Info) slot; **le marché du** ∼ the housing market; **loi sur le** ∼ housing law; ∼ **pour cadres** executive-style housing; ∼ **de fonction** (appartement) company flat BrE, company apartment AmE; (maison) company house; ∼ **gratuit** free lodging; ∼ **à l'hôtel** hotel accommodation; ∼ **locatif** accommodation for rent; ∼ **partagé** shared accommodation; ∼ **plurifamilial** multifamily housing; ∼ **préfabriqué** prefabricated housing; ∼ **social** social housing, local authority housing GB, public housing US; ∼ **de vacances** holiday accommodation

loger vt accommodate, lodge

logiciel m (computer) software; ∼ **antivirus** antivirus software; ∼ **d'application** applications software; ∼ **d'audit** audit software; ∼ **de base** systems software; ∼ **de calcul fiscal** tax software; ∼ **de commande** driver; ∼ **de comptabilité** accounting software; ∼ **contributif** or **à contribution** shareware; ∼ **du domaine public** public domain software; ∼ **éducatif** educational software; ∼ **d'émulation** emulation software; ∼ **d'enseignement à distance** courseware; ∼ **de filtrage** filtering software, blocking software; ∼ **de gestion** business software; ∼ **de gestion des investissements** portfolio management software; ∼ **de gestion de réseau** networking software; ∼ **graphique** graphics software, drawing software; ∼ **gratuit** freeware; ∼ **de groupe (de travail)** groupware; ∼ **intégré** bundled software, integrated software; ∼ **maison** in-house software; ∼ **médiateur** middleware; ∼ **de navigation** web browser, browser software; ∼ **de pilotage** driver; ∼ **piloté par paramètres** parameter-driven software; ∼ **prêt à l'emploi** off-the-shelf software; ∼ **propre à un constructeur** proprietary software; ∼ **de reconnaissance vocale** speech recognition software; ∼ **de simulation financière** financial simulation software; ∼ **de télétexte** telesoftware; ∼ **de traitement de texte** word-processing software; ∼ **de transition** bridgeware, bridging software; ∼ **de vérification** audit software

logique[1] *adj* logical, consistent; **c'est** ~ it makes sense, it's logical

logique[2] *f* logic, consistency

logis *m* dwelling

logistique[1] *adj* logistical; **soutien** ~ logistical support

logistique[2] *f* logistics

logistiquement *adv* logistically

logo *m* logo

logotype *m* logo, logotype; ~ **de la société** company logo, company logotype

loi *f* law; (texte, législatif) act; **au regard de la** ~ in the eyes of the law; **ne pas observer la** ~ fail to observe the law; ~ **sur les administrations locales** local authority bill; ~ **amendée** amended act; ~**s anti-monopoles** antimonopoly laws, antimonopoly legislation; ~ **antitrust** antitrust legislation; ~**s de l'arrivage** packaging laws; ~ **sur les coalitions** combination acts UK; ~**s sur la concurrence** competition acts; ~ **des coûts croissants** law of increasing costs; ~ **des coûts d'opportunité croissants** increasing opportunity costs law; ~ **sur le crédit à la consommation** consumer credit act UK; ~ **de la demande réciproque** law of reciprocal demand; ~**s contre la diffamation** libel laws; ~**s économiques** economic laws; ~ **sur les faillites** bankruptcy act; ~ **de gestion financière** financial administration act; ~ **des grands nombres** law of large numbers; ~ **de l'impôt sur le revenu** income tax act; ~ **modifiée** amended act; ~ **de l'offre et de la demande** law of supply and demand; ~ **sur les opérations bancaires internationales** international banking act; ~ **du pavillon** law of the flag; ~ **du prix unique** one-price law; ~ **des proportions variables** law of variable proportions; ~ **sur la protection de l'emploi** Employment Protection Act UK; ~ **sur la protection des renseignements personnels** data protection act; ~ **sur les rapports patrons-ouvriers** Labor Management Relations Act US; ~ **sur le recouvrement provisoire de l'impôt** provisional collection of taxes act; ~ **du reflux** law of reflux; ~ **de réforme fiscale** tax reform act; ~**s relatives à l'arrivage** packaging laws; ~ **relative à l'avarie commune** (Assur) general average act; ~**s relatives à l'étiquetage** labelling laws BrE, labeling laws AmE; ~ **relative à la novation de créance** substitution law; ~**s relatives à l'octroi de licences** licensing laws; ~ **relative à la subrogation** substitution law; ~ **relative aux titres et valeurs mobilières** securities act; ~ **des rendements décroissants** law of diminishing returns; ~ **sur les salaires** wages act; ~ **sur la sécurité sociale** social security act; ~ **somptuaire** sumptuary law; ~ **de substitution** substitution law; ~ **sur les taux réels de prêt** truth in lending act; ~ **sur les taxes à l'importation** import duty act; ~ **de temporalisation** sunset act; ~ **sur la transparence du crédit** truth in lending law; ~ **de la valeur** law of value; ~ **sur les ventes de marchandises** sales of goods law

loi-cadre *f* outline law

loin *adv* (dans l'espace) a long way; (dans le temps) a long time ago; ~ **du but** wide of the mark (infrml); ~ **du marché** away from the market

loisir *m* leisure; **industrie/civilisation des** ~**s** leisure industry/society

long *adj* long; **à** ~ **terme** long-term; ~ **week-end** long weekend; **au** ~ **cours** (navire) ocean-going; ~ **coupon** (d'intérêts) long coupon; ~ **étranglement** *m* (Bourse) long strangle

long-courrier *m* (navire) ocean-going ship; (avion) long-haul aircraft

longitudinal, e *adj* longitudinal

longueur *f* length; (Info) (d'un enregistrement) size; **sur la même** ~ **d'onde** on the same wavelength; ~ **de mot** word length; ~ **totale** overall length

lot *m* (d'objets en vente) batch; (aux enchères) lot; (de terrain) plot; (à la loterie) prize; **gagner le gros** ~ hit the jackpot; ~ **d'articles divers** job lot; ~ **de fabrication** batch; ~ **fractionnaire** fractional lot, uneven lot; ~ **de marchandises composites** mixed bundling; ~ **régulier** round lot US (jarg)

loterie *f* lottery; ~ **nationale** national lottery

lotir *vt* (terrain) apportion, divide into plots

lotissement *m* housing estate; (terrain) plot; ~ **interne** inside lot

louage *m* hiring; ~ **de services** contract of employment

louer *vt* (embaucher) hire; (logement) (donner en location) let BrE, rent out; (prendre en location) rent; (véhicule, équipement) hire BrE, rent; (place) book; **à** ~ to let BrE, for rent AmE; ~ **à l'avance** book in advance; ~ **à bail** lease

loueur, -euse *m,f* (bailleur) lessor; (locataire d'un logement) letter, lessee; (de véhicule, d'équipement) hirer BrE, renter; ~ **de voitures** car rental firm

loup *m* (Bourse) stag

lourd, e *adj* (marché) sluggish, stale; (charge, impôt, perte) heavy

lourdement *adv* (taxé) heavily

loyal, e *adj* (personne) honest, trustworthy

loyauté *f* (d'une personne) honesty, trustworthiness

loyer *m* (de logement) rent; **hausse des** ~**s** rent increase; ~ **de l'argent** (Fin) interest rates; ~ **de base** base rent US; ~ **brut** gross rent; ~ **contractuel** contract rent; ~ **économique** economic rent; ~ **équitable** ⋯▷

fair rent; ~ **ferme** fixed rent; ~ **fixe** fixed rent; ~ **hebdomadaire** weekly rent; ~ **indexé** index lease; ~ **industriel** industrial rent; ~ **du marché** market rent; ~ **mensuel** monthly rent; ~ **modéré** fair market rent

lucratif, -ive adj (emploi, travail) lucrative; (opération) profitable

lugubre adj bleak

luminosité f (de l'écran) brightness

lundi m Monday; ~ **noir** (Bourse) Black Monday

lutte f battle, contest; ~ **antipollution** pollution control; ~ **biologique** biocontrol; ~ **des classes** class struggle; ~ **pour le pouvoir** power struggle

lutter vi fight; ~ **contre** (chômage, trafic de stupéfiants) combat, fight; ~ **pour** (survie d'une société) fight for

luxe m luxury; **de** ~ (marchandises) luxury

LV abrév (▸lieu de vente) POS (point of sale)

lycée m secondary school BrE, high school AmE; ~ **d'enseignement professionnel** m secondary school for vocational training; ~ **mixte** coeducational secondary school ou high school

Mm

M abrév (▸agrégats monétaires) M (monetary aggregates)

M. abrév (▸Monsieur) Mr

mâcher vt ~ **le travail à qn** spoon-feed sb

machine f machine; ~ **à adresser** addressing machine; ~ **à affranchir** franking machine BrE, stamping machine; ~ **de bureau** business machine; ~ **à calculer** adding machine, calculator; ~ **à calculer électronique** electronic calculator; ~ **à calculer à imprimante** printing calculator; ~ **de compilation** source computer; ~ **comptable** business machine; ~ **à écrire** typewriter; ~ **à écrire les chèques** cheque-writing machine BrE, check-writing machine AmE; ~ **à facturer** biller; ~ **de gestion** business machine

machine-outil f machine tool

machines f pl machinery

macrodéchet m macrowaste

macroéconomie f macroeconomics

macroéconomique adj macroeconomic

macroinformatique f macrocomputing

macro-ordinateur m mainframe

Madame f (sur une enveloppe, un document) Mrs; (en début de lettre) Dear Madam

Mademoiselle f (sur une enveloppe, un document) Miss; (en début de lettre) Dear Madam

magasin m (entrepôt) warehouse; (pour vendre) shop BrE, store AmE; ~ **de centre-ville** town-centre store; ~ **en dehors de la ville** out-of-town store; ~ **grand** department store; **une chaîne de** ~s a chain of shops BrE ou stores AmE; **tenir/prendre un** ~ run/open a shop ou store; ~ **de chaussures/d'alimentation** shoe/food shop ou store; **avoir qch en** ~ have sth in stock; **mettre qch en** ~ put sth in stock; ~ **de brocante** second-hand shop BrE, thrift shop AmE; ~ **discompte** discount store; ~ **de groupage** (conteneurs) container base BrE, container freight station AmE; ~ **indépendant** independent store; ~ **de prestige** flagship store; ~ **à prix unique** one-price store; ~ **de proximité** corner shop BrE, convenience store; ~ **à succursales multiples** chain store; ~ **d'usine** factory shop, factory outlet

magasinage m storage, warehousing

magasinier m storeman, warehouseman

magazine m magazine; ~ **de grande diffusion** (pour le grand public) consumer magazine; ~ **illustré** illustrated magazine; ~ **de luxe** glossy magazine

magistrat m magistrate; ~s **compétents** magistrates entitled to adjudicate

magnat m magnate, tycoon; ~ **de la finance/presse** financial/press magnate

magnétophone m tape recorder; ~ **à cassettes** cassette recorder

magnétoscope m video recorder

magnétothèque f tape library

magouille f (infrml) (procédé) fiddling; (résultat) trick; ~s **financières** financial sharp practice

mailing m mailshot, mailing; **faire un** ~ do a mailshot

main f hand; **fait** ~ (produit) handmade; **donner un coup de** ~ **à qn** give sb a hand; **mettre la dernière** ~ **à** put the finishing touches to; **à la** ~ manually, by hand; **en** ~ **tierce** in the hands of a third party; (Fin) in escrow; ~ **courante** daybook; ~ **invisible** (Econ) invisible hand; ~ **visible** (Econ) visible hand

main-d'œuvre f labour BrE, labor AmE, workforce; ~ **bon marché/qualifiée/**

immigrée cheap/skilled/immigrant labour; **coût de la** ~ labour costs; ~ **abstraite** abstract labour; ~ **concrète** concrete labour; ~ **contractuelle** contract labour; ~ **exploitée** sweated labour; ~ **improductive** unproductive labour; ~ **indirecte** indirect labour; ~ **locale** local labour; ~ **non déclarée** unregistered labour; ~ **non qualifiée** unskilled labour; ~ **productive** productive labour; ~ **de remplacement** replacement labour force; ~ **syndiquée** organized labour; ~ **temporaire** casual labour

maintenance f maintenance; ~ **préventive** preventative maintenance

mainteneur m: ~ **de marché** market maker UK

maintenir ⟦1⟧ vt (situation, équilibre) maintain; (les marges) hold; ~ **les prix** keep prices stable; **être maintenu dans ses fonctions** be kept on in one's post; ~ **à flot** (affaire) keep afloat; ~ **à jour** (dossiers) keep up to date; ~ **le marché** make a market; ~ **un profil bas** keep a low profile
⟦2⟧ **se maintenir** v pron (prix, pouvoir d'achat) remain stable; (monnaie) hold steady; **se** ~ **à la page** keep up to date; **se** ~ **au même niveau que** keep pace with, keep up with

maintien m maintaining; (Fisc) upkeep; ~ **artificiel** (des prix) valorization; ~ **des prix** price maintenance; ~ **du prix de revente** retail price maintenance

mairie f town hall

maison[1] adj (traducteur, rédacteur) in-house, in-company; (système) in-house; (fait par soi) homemade; (fait sur place) made on the premises; **notre formation/spécialiste** ~ our in-house training scheme/specialist

maison[2] f (société) establishment, firm; (bâtisse) house; ~ **d'acceptation** acceptance house; ~ **d'achat étrangère** foreign buying house; ~ **d'arbitrage** arbitrage house; ~ **bancaire** banking house; ~ **de commerce** business concern, commercial establishment; ~ **de commission** commission house; ~ **de courtage** brokerage firm, brokerage house; ~ **de couture** fashion house; ~ **de disque** label record company; ~ **d'édition** publishing house; ~ **d'exportation** export company; ~ **de gros** wholesale company, wholesale firm; ~ **individuelle** single-family house BrE, single-family home; ~ **jumelée** semi-detached house BrE, duplex AmE; ~ **mère** main branch; ~ **de santé** nursing home; ~ **témoin** show house; ~ **de titres** securities company; ~ **de vente par correspondance** mail-order company

maître m: ~ **d'hôtel** (dans restaurant) head waiter; (dans maison privée) porter; ~ **d'œuvre** prime contractor

maîtrise f (encadrement) middle management; (diplôme) Master's degree; (contrôle) control; ~ **des coûts** cost control; ~ **de gestion des**

entreprises ≈ MBA, ≈ Master of Business Administration; ~ **de sciences** ≈ MSc, ≈ Master of Science; ~ **en sciences économiques** ≈ MEcon, ≈ Master of Economics; ~ **technique** technical mastery

maîtriser vt (demande, inflation) contain; (dépenses, urbanisme) control; ~ **les coûts** keep costs under control

majeure f (Transp) (compagnie) major

majoration f overcharge; (hausse de prix) increase, mark-up; **une** ~ **de 2%** a 2% increase; **la** ~ **des cotisations** the increase in contributions; ~ **d'âge** (Assur) addition to age; ~ **de dividende** (Assur) dividend addition; ~ **des dividendes** (Bourse) dividend gross-up; ~ **de prix** increase in prices, rise in prices; ~ **de retard** (Fisc) penalty for late tax payment

majorer vt (prix) increase, mark up; ~ **une somme de 10 euros/15%** increase a sum by 10 euros/15%

majorité f (des voix, en âge) majority; ~ **absolue** absolute majority; ~ **innovatrice** (marketing) early majority (jarg); ~ **qualifiée** qualified majority; ~ **silencieuse** silent majority; ~ **simple** simple majority; ~ **tardive** (marketing) late majority (jarg)

majuscule f capital letter, upper case letter

mal adv badly; ~ **administrer** mismanage; ~ **appliquer** misapply; ~ **calculer** miscalculate; ~ **classer** misfile; ~ **gérer** mismanage; ~ **représenter** misrepresent; ~ **payé** low-paid, poorly paid

maladie f disease, illness; ~ **professionnelle** occupational disease ou illness; ~ **de la vache folle** mad cow disease

malaise m (état de crise) unrest; (en Bourse) uneasiness; ~ **des cadres** executive unrest; ~ **économique** economic malaise; ~ **social** industrial unrest, labour unrest BrE, labor unrest AmE

malentendu m misunderstanding

malfaçon f (défaut) defect; (mauvais travail) bad workmanship

malheureusement adv unfortunately

malhonnête adj dishonest

malle f trunk; ~ **diplomatique** Diplomatic Service Post, diplomatic bag

management m management; ~ **baladeur** management by walking around; ~ **directif** lead management; ~ **intuitif** intuitive management; ~ **participatif** multiple-management; ~ **de produits** product marketing management

manager[1] m manager

manager[2] vt (entreprise, équipe) manage

manageur m manager; ~ **de produits** product marketing manager

manche m (d'outil) handle; ~ **à balai** (Info) joystick

manchette f (journal) (banner) headline

mandat *m* (postal) postal order BrE, money order, postal note Aus; (charge) term of office; (d'un comité) terms of reference; (**Droit**) warrant; **toucher un ~** cash a money order; **exercer un ~** be in office; **~ d'arrêt** arrest warrant; **~ d'audit** audit engagement; **~ de banque** bank postbill; **~ de dépôt** committal order; **~ d'expulsion** expulsion order; **~ international** international money order; **~ postal** postal order BrE, money order; **~ de paiement international** international money draft; **~ de perquisition** search warrant; **~ spécial** special warrant

mandataire *m* (représentant) representative; (Droit) proxy, attorney US; (Gen com) authorized agent; (Info) proxy server; **~ spécial** attorney-in-fact US

mandat-carte *m* postal order (in the form of a postcard)

mandater *vt* (Admin, Banque) commission; (élire) appoint as one's representative; **~ des frais** pay expenses by money order

mandat-lettre *m* postal order

manette *f* lever; **~ de jeux** (Info) joystick

manier *vt* (objets, argent) handle; (fonds, affaires) manage; (langue vivante) use

manière *f* (façon) way; (style) style; **~ d'opérer** modus operandi; **c'est la ~ habituelle de procéder** it is standard practice; **de ~ prononcée** (monter, tomber) sharply; **employer la ~ forte** use strong-arm tactics

manifestation *f* (Pol) demonstration; **~ d'intérêt** indication of interest

manifeste¹ *adj* obvious; (signal) strong

manifeste² *m* (Transp) manifest; **~ d'entrée** clearance inwards; **~ de fret** freight manifest; **~ de marchandises** cargo manifest; **~ de marchandises pour conteneurs** container import cargo manifest; **~ des passagers** passenger manifest; **~ de sortie** clearance outwards; **~ de transfert** transfer manifest

manifester 1 *vt* (soutien, opposition, solidarité) show, demonstrate
2 *vi* demonstrate; **~ contre/en faveur de** demonstrate against/for
3 **se manifester** *v pron* (phénomène) appear; (candidat, témoin) come forward; (tendance) emerge; (signes, reprise) become apparent

manille *f* (manutention) clutch hook, shackle

manipulateur, -trice *m,f* (provocateur) manipulator

manipulation *f* (Fin, Bourse) rigging; (Info) manipulation; **~ de données** data handling; **~ de l'information** information handling; **~ de marchés** market rigging; **~ des prix** stock jobbery UK

manipuler *vt* (données, chiffres) massage; (opinion, presse, personne) manipulate; **~ les chiffres** massage the figures; **~ les cours à la hausse** kite; **~ le marché** rig the market; **~ les registres** (Compta) cook the books BrE, tamper with the books

mannequin *m* fashion model, model

manomètre *m* manometer; **~ pour pneus** tyre gauge BrE, tire gage AmE

manœuvre¹ *m* labourer BrE, laborer AmE, unskilled worker

manœuvre² *f* manoeuvre BrE, maneuver AmE; **~s dilatoires** delaying tactics; **~s frauduleuses** illegal practices

manquant, e *adj* (marchandises) missing; (personnel) absent; **~s** (marchandises) shortages; **~ à l'embarquement** (Transp) short-shipped

manque *m* (pénurie) lack, shortage; (Compta) shortfall; (de capital ou de fonds) absence; (de main-d'œuvre) shortage; **~ de communication** communication gap; **~ à gagner** shortfall in earnings; **~ de liquidités** liquidity crisis; **~ en magasin** out of stock; **~ de main-d'œuvre** undermanning; **~ de personnel** shortage of staff, staff shortages

manquement *m* (Droit) breach; **~ au devoir** breach of duty, dereliction of duty; **~ à la discipline** misconduct; **~ grave à la discipline** gross misconduct

manquer *vt* (occasion, rendez-vous) miss; **~ de** be lacking in, be short of; **~ de cohérence** lack consistency; **~ d'expérience** lack experience; **~ de personnel** be understaffed, be short-staffed; **~ à une règle** break a rule; **~ à son devoir** fail in one's duty

manuel¹, -elle *adj* (travailleur) manual

manuel² *m* handbook, manual; **~ du code des comptes** coding manual; **~ d'utilisation** instruction manual

manuellement *adv* manually

manufacturé, e *adj* manufactured

manuscrit¹, e *adj* handwritten

manuscrit² *m* manuscript

manutention *f* (des marchandises) handling; **~ des bagages** baggage handling; **~ horizontale** roll on/roll off; **~ verticale** lift on/lift off

manutentionnaire *m* warehouseman, packer

mappe *f* (Info) map, mapping

maquette *f* (publicité) visual, advanced layout

maquignonnage *m* (Ind, Pol) horse trading, sharp practice

maquillage *m* (de document) faking; (de chèque, de chiffres, de témoignage) falsification, falsifying; **~ du bilan, ~ des comptes** window-dressing

maquiller *vt* (document) fake; (chèques, chiffres, témoignage) falsify

maraîchage *m* market gardening BrE, truck farming AmE

maraîcher, -ère *m,f* market gardener BrE, truck farmer AmE

marasme *m* (Econ) stagnation, slump; **dans le ~** in the doldrums

marchand¹, e *adj* (secteur, trafic, économie) trade; (V&M) (produit, denrée) saleable, marketable; **qualité ~e** marketable quality; **prix ~** market *ou* ruling price; **valeur ~e** market value, commercial value; **compte ~** merchant account

marchand², e *m,f* (négociant) merchant, dealer; (commerçant) trader; **~ ambulant** pedlar, street trader BrE, street vendor AmE; **~ de biens** estate agent BrE, realtor AmE; **~ de fonds** estate agent BrE, realtor AmE; **~ de journaux** (dans la rue) news vendor; (magasin) newsagent; **~ de journaux-buraliste** newsagent and tobacconist; **~ de vins** wine merchant

marchandage *m* (tractations) bargaining, haggling; (sur le prix) haggling

marchander **1** *vt* (marchandises, prix) bargain over, haggle over; (rabais) haggle for **2** *vi* **~ avec qn** bargain with sb

marchandisage *m* merchandising

marchandise *f* commodity; **~s** goods, merchandise, commodities; **exporter/transporter des ~s** export/transport goods; **50 000 euros de ~s** 50,000 euros worth of goods; **~s en gros/au détail** wholesale/retail goods; **livrer/fournir la ~** deliver/provide the goods; **tromper qn sur la ~** swindle sb; **~s à l'arrivée** incoming goods; **~s commerciales** commercial cargo; **~s communautaires** Community goods; **~s consignées** returnable goods; **~s de consommation ou services** consumer goods or services; **~s de contrebande** contraband; **~s couvertes par un certificat** goods covered by warrant; **~s au cubage** measurement goods; **~s dangereuses** dangerous cargo, hazardous cargo; **~s à densité élevée** high-density freight; **~s détaxées** duty-free goods UK; **~ disponible** spot commodity; **~s diverses** general cargo; **~s diverses non-unitisées** break bulk, break bulk cargo; **~s emballées** package goods; **~s encombrantes** bulky cargo; **~s entreposées sous douane** bonded goods; **~s à l'essai** goods on approval; **~s exclues** (Transp) shut-out cargo; **~s à faible densité** low-density freight; **~s en gros** wholesale goods; **~s homogènes** homogeneous cargo; **~s hors taxes** duty-free goods UK; **~s importées** imported goods; **~s isolées** cargo in isolation; **~s légères** measurement freight; (cargaison) light cargo; **~s liquides** wet goods; **~s livrables à terme** future goods; **~s lourdes** deadweight cargo; **~s manquantes** missing cargo, short shipment; **~s mixtes** general merchandise; **~s non-conteneurisables** uncontainerable goods; **~s non-déclarées** unmanifested cargo; **~s périssables** perishables, nondurable goods; **~s physiques** actuals; **~s prohibées** prohibited goods; **~s de provenance étrangère** foreign goods, goods of foreign origin; **~s de qualité** quality goods; **~s à la réception** incoming goods; **~s à réexporter** goods for re-export; **~ réglementée** controlled commodity, regulated commodity; **~s reprises** returned goods; **~s retournées** returned goods; **~s sèches** dry cargo, dry freight; **~s sous douane** bonded cargo, bonded goods; **~s à terme** commodity futures; **~s vérifiées** ascertained goods; **~s volumineuses** bulky cargo; **~s en vrac** bulk cargo, loose cargo

marche *f* (de mécanisme) operation; (d'organisation) running; **en état de ~** in working order; **bonne ~ de l'entreprise/du projet** smooth running of the company/project; **en ~** under way; (Info) (machine) up (infrml); **faire ~ arrière** backtrack, back-pedal; **~ arrière** backtracking, back-pedalling BrE, back-pedaling AmE; **~ erratique** (Info) random walk; **~ d'essai** (Info) test drive

marché *m* (Fin, Econ) market; (lieu) marketplace; (contrat) bargain, deal; **mettre qch sur le ~** put sth on the market; **trouver de nouveaux ~s** find new outlets, find new markets; **retirer qch du ~** withdraw sth from the market; **nouveau ~** new technologies exchange; **~ financier/monétaire/de l'or** financial/money/gold market; **le ~ de l'automobile/de l'immobilier** the car/property market; **~ baissier/haussier** bearish/bullish market; **ouvrir un nouveau ~** open up a new market; **pénétrer un ~** break into a market; **un des plus grands ~s du monde** one of the largest marketplaces in the world; **~ porteur** buoyant market; **un ~ avantageux** a good deal; **conclure un ~ avec qn** strike a deal with sb; **bon/meilleur ~** (produit) cheap/cheaper; **vendre meilleur ~** sell cheaper; **faire des ~s à court terme** (Bourse) be short in futures; **faire des ~s à long terme** (Bourse) be long in futures; **faire mieux que le ~** outperform the market; **faire un ~ au comptant** (Bourse) bargain for cash; **faire un ~ à terme** (Bourse) bargain for account; **le ~ s'est effondré** the bottom has fallen out of the market; **~ conclu!** it's a deal! **le ~ est rompu** the deal is off;

⎛ **marché a...** ⎞ **~ accéléré** fast market; **~ des acceptations** acceptance market; **~ acheteur** buyer's market; **~ actif** brisk trading, swimming market; **~ des actions** equity market; **~ des adjudications** auction market; **~ ample** broad market; **~ animé** brisk market; **~ après bourse** evening trade; **~ arrivé à la maturité** mature market; **~ artificiellement soutenu** technical market; **~ des assurances** insurance market; **~ atone**   ⸱⸱⸱▸

shallow market;

b... ~ **à la baisse** bear market, buyer's market; ~ **en baisse** declining market; ~ **baissier sans issue** graveyard market; ~ **blanc** white market; ~ **bloqué** locked market; ~ **boursier** securities exchange, stock market;

c... ~ **des capitaux** capital market, financial market; ~ **captif** captive market; ~ **des certificats de dépôt** certificate of deposit market; ~ **des changes** currency market, foreign exchange market; ~ **cible** target market; ~ **ciblé sur les jeunes** teenage market; **Marché commun** Common Market; ~ **de compensation** clearing market; ~ **au comptant** cash market, spot market; ~ **conditionnel** contingent market; ~ **de la consommation** consumer market; ~ **des conteneurs** container market; ~ **continu** all-day trading; ~ **de contrats à terme** futures market; ~ **des contrats à terme sur indice** stock index futures market; ~ **à court terme** short market; ~ **du crédit** credit market, loan market; ~ **du crédit à la consommation** consumer credit market;

d... ~ **à découvert** short market; ~ **en déport** inverted market; ~ **des devises au comptant** spot currency market; ~ **des devises principales** major foreign exchange market; ~ **des disponibilités** liquid market; ~ **à double prime à court terme** short straddle; ~ **à double tendance** two-sided market; ~ **d'échanges croisés** swap market;

e... ~ **des effets acceptés** acceptance market; ~ **effondré** market whose bottom has dropped out; ~ **des émissions** issue market; ~ **de l'emploi** labour market BrE, labor market AmE; ~ **des emplois non déclarés** secondary labour market BrE, secondary labor market AmE; ~ **aux enchères** auction market; ~ **épuisé** sold-out market; ~ **d'escompte** discount market; ~ **étranger** foreign market, overseas market; ~ **étroit** narrow market, limited market; ~ **des euro-obligations** Eurobond market; ~ **des eurodevises** Eurocurrency market; ~ **de l'eurodollar** Eurodollar market; ~ **exploité** developed market; ~ **à l'exportation** export market;

f... ~ **des facteurs de production** factor market; ~ **falsifié** sophisticated market; ~ **favorable aux vendeurs** seller's market; ~ **ferme** firm deal; ~ **figé** locked market; **financier** financial market, financial marketplace; ~ **financier international** global financial market; ~ **financier à terme** financial futures market; ~ **à fort volume** broad market; ~ **fragmenté** fragmented market; ~ **du fret** freight market; ~ **du fret à terme** freight futures market; ~ **de futures et d'options de marchandises** commodity market;

g... ~ **de gré à gré** over-the-counter market US; ~ **gris** grey market BrE, gray market AmE; ~ **de gros** wholesale market;

h... ~ **à la hausse** bull market, seller's market; ~ **hésitant** hesitant market; ~ **non homogène** fragmented market; ~ **hors bourse** kerb market BrE, curb market AmE; after-hours market; ~ **hors cote** over-the-counter market US; ~ **hors séance** after-hours market; ~ **hypothécaire** mortgage market;

i... ~ **de l'immobilier** property market, real estate market; ~ **imparfait** imperfect market; ~ **indécis** sideways market; ~ **inégal** (commerce international) unequal trade; ~ **instable** sensitive market, unsettled market; ~ **interbancaire** interbank market; ~ **intérieur** domestic market, home market, internal market; ~ **intérieur des valeurs mobilières** domestic securities market; ~ **des intermédiaires** intercompany market; ~ **international des actions** International Equities Market; ~ **international des capitaux** International Equities Market; ~ **international des options** International Options Market; ~ **international du pétrole** International Petroleum Exchange UK; ~ **interne du travail** internal labour market BrE, internal labor market AmE; **Marché interprofessionnel européen** European Interprofessional Market; ~ **d'investissement agréé** designated investment exchange UK, recognized investment exchange; ~ **irrégulier** irregular market;

l... ~ **libre** free market, open market; ~ **de libre entreprise** free enterprise market; ~ **libre et ouvert** free and open market; ~ **liquide** liquid market; ~ **du logement** housing market;

m... ~ **manipulé** rigged market; ~ **manquant** missing market; ~ **marginal** fringe market; ~ **de matières premières** commodity market; ~ **des messageries** parcels market; ~ **des métaux** metal market; ~ **des métaux précieux** bullion market; ~ **à moitié au noir** semiblack market; ~ **mondial** world market; ~ **monétaire** money market; ~ **monétaire à court terme** short-term money market; ~ **monétaire de gros** wholesale money market; **Marché monétaire international** International Monetary Market US; ~ **monétaire national** domestic money market; ~ **morose** soft market; ~ **mort** graveyard market;

n... ~ **noir** black market;

o... ~ **obligataire** bond market; ~ **des obligations à taux fixe** straights market; ~ **de l'occasion** (marché de revente) second-hand market; ~ **officiel** controlled market, official market; ~ **des opérations de change à terme** forward exchange market; ~ **à options** options market; ~ **à options**

international International Options Market; **Marché des options négociables de Paris** Paris traded options exchange; ~ **des options sur obligations** bond options market; ~ **de l'or** gold market; ~ **ordonné** orderly market; ~ **orienté à la baisse** bear market, buyer's market; ~ **orienté à la hausse** bull market, bullish market, seller's market; ~ **ouvert 24 heures sur 24** twenty-four hour trading;

 p...   ~ **parallèle** grey market BrE, gray market AmE; ~ **parfait** perfect market; ~ **peu actif** soft market; ~ **en pleine maturité** mature market; ~ **des prêts aux entreprises** corporate lending market; ~ **à prime** cash bargain, option bargain; ~ **à primes international** International Options Market; ~ **privé** private contract; ~ **des produits de grande consommation** consumer market; ~ **public** public contract;

 r...   ~ **qui se raffermit** hardening market; ~ **réglementé** regulated market; ~ **de remplacement** replacement market; ~ **restreint** restricted market; ~ **qui se rétrécit** shrinking market; ~ **de la revente** resale market;

 s...   ~ **secondaire** secondary market; ~ **sensible** sensitive market; ~ **serré** tight market; ~ **des services** service contract; ~ **des services publics** public service contract;

 t...   ~ **technique** technical market; ~ **à terme** forward market; (contrat) settlement bargain; ~ **à terme de devises** forward exchange market; ~ **à terme d'instruments financiers** France financial futures market; ~ **à terme des matières premières** commodity futures market; ~ **à terme de titres financiers** financial futures market; ~ **à terme sur les valeurs de transport** freight futures market; ~ **-test** test market, pilot market; ~ **trafiqué à la hausse** rigged market; ~ **de transit** transit market; ~ **du travail** job market, labour market BrE, labor market AmE;

 u...   ~ **unique** (de l'UE) Single Market; **Marché unique européen** European Single Market;

 v...   ~ **des valeurs en espèces** bullion market; ~ **des valeurs mobilières** securities market; ~ **des valeurs de premier ordre** gilt-edged market, gilts market; ~ **des valeurs à revenu fixe** fixed income securities market; ~ **des valeurs de transport** freight market; ~ **vendeur** seller's market; ~ **de vente à la criée** outcry market; ~ **des voyages d'affaires** business travel market

marcher vi (affaires) do well; (travail) go well; ~ **avec son temps** keep abreast of the times; **faire** ~ **qch** get sth to work; **faire** ~ **l'affaire** run the show; **ça fait** ~ **les affaires** it's good for business; **comment marchent les affaires?** how is business?

marée f tide; ~ **basse** low tide; ~ **descendante** ebb tide; ~ **haute** high tide; ~ **de morte-eau** neap tide; ~ **noire** oil spill, oil spillage; ~ **de vive-eau** spring tide

marge f (écart) profit margin; (pourcentage) mark-up; (Bourse) margin, spread; (sur une page) margin; (latitude) scope; **avoir une faible** ~ (Gen com) have a small profit margin; **avoir plus de** ~ **de décision** have more scope for making decisions; **notre** ~ **d'action est faible** we have very little room for manoeuvre BrE ou maneuver AmE; **ne disposer d'aucune** ~ **d'initiative** have no scope to use one's initiative; ~ **de gauche/ de droite/du haut/du bas** left/right/top/ bottom margin; **laisser/tracer une** ~ leave /rule a margin; **certains pays craignent de rester en** ~ **de l'Europe** some countries are afraid they will remain on the periphery of Europe; **en** ~ **de la réunion, le président a déclaré** outside the meeting, the president said; **de** ~ marginal; **sur** ~ on margin; ~ **amont** upstream float; ~ **d'arbitrage** arbitrage margin UK; ~ **aval** downstream float; ~ **bancaire** banker's turn; ~ **bénéficiaire** profit margin; (d'un détaillant) margin, mark-up; ~ **bénéficiaire brute** gross profit margin; ~ **bénéficiaire nette** net profit margin; ~ **bénéficiaire du résultat net** bottom-line profit margin; ~ **brute** gross margin; ~ **brute d'autofinancement** cash flow; ~ **commerciale** return on sales; ~ **complémentaire** additional margin; ~ **d'un contrepartiste** (fourchette de prix) jobber's spread, jobber's turn; ~ **sur coûts variables** contribution margin, net contribution; ~ **de crédit** Can bank line, line of credit; ~ **de départ** original margin; ~ **de détail** retail margin; ~ **entre produits** intra-commodity spread; ~ **d'entretien** (transactions à terme) maintenance margin; ~ **d'erreur** margin of error; ~ **étroite** narrow margin; ~ **eurodollar** Eurodollar spread; ~ **d'exploitation** operating margin; ~ **de fluctuation** (taux de change) fluctuation band; ~ **de fond** (d'une page) back margin; ~ **de garantie** margin; ~ **initiale** initial margin, original margin; ~ **d'intérêt** interest margin, interest spread; ~ **de liberté** degree of freedom; ~ **de maintenance** maintenance margin; ~ **de manœuvre** room for manoeuvre BrE ou maneuver AmE; ~ **nette sur les intérêts** net interest margin; ~ **obligatoire** compulsory margin UK; ~ **opérationnelle** operating margin; ~ **des produits de base** intercommodity spread; ~ **de profit finale** bottom-line profit margin; ~ **de sécurité** safety margin; ~ **de solvabilité** solvency margin; ~ **supérieure** (d'une page) header, top margin; ~ **à terme** (commerce international) forward margin; ~ **de tolérance** tolerance margin; ~ **de variation** variation margin

margeur *m* margin stop

marginal, e *adj* (Econ) marginal; (coût) incremental

marginalement *adv* marginally

marginaliser *vt* marginalize

marginalisme *m* marginalism

marginaliste *m* (Econ) marginalist

marginaux *m pl* (relations publiques) peripherals

marier *vt* (vente aux enchères) marry up

marine *f* navy; ~ **marchande** merchant navy

maritime *adj* (trafic, fret, commerce) maritime; (compagnie, agent) shipping; (région) coastal

mark *m* mark; ~ **allemand** mark, Deutschmark

marketing *m* marketing; ~ **de bouche à oreille** word-of-mouth marketing; ~ **de comportement** performance marketing; ~ **de création** creative marketing; ~ **du créneau** niche marketing; ~ **de différenciation** differentiated marketing; ~ **dynamique** aggressive marketing; ~ **global** global marketing; ~ **interactif** interactive marketing; ~ **de la marque** brand marketing; ~ **de masse** mass marketing; ~ **mix** marketing mix; ~ **multiniveau** multilevel marketing; ~ **personnalisé** one-to-one marketing; ~ **de produit** product marketing; ~ **des produits de grande consommation** consumer marketing; ~ **des produits industriels** industrial marketing; ~ **de relance** remarketing; ~ **téléphonique** telemarketing; ~ **viral** viral marketing

market maker *m* market maker UK

marnage *m* (maritime) tidal range

marquage *m* branding, marking; (Info) highlighting; ~ **de la date de péremption** (sur marchandises) date marking

marque *f* (d'un produit) brand; (sur l'article) trademark, label; (de machine, de voiture) make; (contre un nom) tick BrE, check AmE; **des voitures de** ~ **japonaise** Japanese cars; **produits de** ~ branded goods; **invité de** ~ distinguished guest, VIP; **de** ~ **déposée** proprietary; ~ **d'acheteur** buyer's own brand; ~ **associée** (Brevets) associated mark; ~ **de certification** (Brevets) certification mark; ~ **combinée** (Brevets) composite mark; ~ **dénominative** (Brevets) work mark; ~ **déposée** registered trademark; ~ **de distributeur** distributor's brand name, store brand; ~ **d'essai** certification mark; ~ **du fabricant** producer's brand; ~ **de fabrique** (propriété intellectuelle) trademark; ~ **figurative** (Brevets) device mark; ~ **de fin de fichier** (Info) end-of-file mark; ~ **de franc-bord** (d'un navire) plimsoll line; ~ **générique** generic brand; ~ **grand public** consumer brand; ~ **d'homologation** (d'un véhicule) approval

mark; ~ **de jauge** (d'un navire) tonnage mark; ~ **notoire** well-known mark; ~ **de prestige** status symbol; ~ **propre** distributor's brand name; ~ **de qualité** (d'un produit) quality brand; ~ **réputée** name brand; ~ **de service** (Brevets) service mark; ~ **verbale** (Brevets) work mark

marqué, e *adj* (déclin, différence, prix) marked

marquer *vt* score; (marchandises) mark; ~ **un prix** (Compta) mark off

marqueur *m* (stylo) marker, marker pen

marteau *m* (d'un commissaire-priseur) gavel

mascaret *m* (d'une rivière) bore

masque *m* (Info) form; ~ **d'étrave** (Transp) (d'un roulier) bow visor

masquer *vt* hide

masse *f* (majorité) bulk; **les** ~**s** the masses; **les** ~**s laborieuses** the working masses; **de** ~ (culture) popular; ~ **brute** gross mass; ~ **brute réelle** actual gross weight; ~ **créancière** (maritime) amount to be made good; ~ **des créditeurs** body of creditors; ~ **critique** critical mass; ~ **de la faillite** bankruptcy estate; ~ **des fournisseurs** body of creditors; ~ **monétaire** money supply; ~ **salariale** payroll, wage bill; ~ **successorale** deceased estate

massif, -ive *adj* (quantité) huge; (publicité) massive; (licenciements) mass

mass média *m pl* mass media

mastodonte *m* (camion) juggernaut

mât *m* (d'un navire) mast; ~ **de charge** (d'un navire) cargo derrick

matelot *m* sailor, seaman; ~ **de pont** deck hand; ~ **qualifié** able seaman, able-bodied seaman

matérialiser *vi* materialize

matériau *m* material; ~ **de base** basic material; ~ **combustible** combustible material; ~**x de construction** building materials; ~**x en gros** bulk material; ~ **récupérable** recoverable material

matériel *m* (documents) material; (machines, outils) equipment; (Info) hardware; ~ **agricole** farm implements; ~ **audiovisuel** audiovisual aids, audiovisual equipment; ~ **de bureau** office equipment; ~ **complémentaire** add-on equipment; ~ **d'entretien** maintenance equipment; ~ **humain** labour power BrE, labor power AmE; ~ **de manutention** cargo-handling equipment; ~ **périphérique** peripheral equipment; ~ **publicitaire** publicity material; ~ **de publicité sur le lieu de vente** point-of-sale material; ~ **réservé** allocated material; ~ **roulant** (chemin de fer) rolling stock

matière *f* (sujet) matter, subject, subject matter; (substance) material; ~ **brute** raw material; ~ **explosive** explosive substance; ~ **imposable** taxable article; ~ **minérale** mineral resource; ~ **plastique** plastic; ~

première raw material, commodity; ~
première agricole soft commodity; ~
première au comptant spot commodity; ~
première contrôlée controlled commodity
UK; ~ **première directe** direct material; ~
première réglementée regulated
commodity; ~ **récupérable** (recyclage)
recoverable material

MATIF *abrév* France (▸**Marché à terme
d'instruments financiers**) financial futures
market, ≈ CBT US (Chicago Board of Trade),
≈ LIFFE UK (London International Financial
Futures Exchange)

matin *m* morning; **la réunion est le** ~ the
meeting is in the morning; **8 heures du** ~
8am; **le 3 au** ~ on the morning of the 3rd

matraquage *m*: ~ **publicitaire** burst
advertising

matrice *f* (Info) matrix

maturité *f* maturity; ~ **moyenne** average
maturity; **à** ~ (effet) at maturity

mauvais, e *adj* bad; **de** ~**e foi** (Droit) mala
fide (frml); ~ **achat** bad buy; ~**e
administration** mismanagement; ~**e
affaire** bad bargain, bad deal; ~
alignement misalignment; ~**e approche**
mishandling; ~ **calcul** miscalculation; ~**e
créance** bad debt; ~ **état de navigabilité**
(d'un navire) unseaworthiness; ~
fonctionnement (d'une machine) malfunction;
~**e gestion** mismanagement; ~**e nouvelle**
bad news; ~ **papier** (Banque) bad paper
(infrml); ~ **payeur** defaulter; ~**e réputation**
bad name, bad reputation; ~ **risque** bad
risk, unsound risk; ~ **travail** bad
workmanship; ~ **usage** misuse; ~**e
volonté** bad will, ill will

MAV *abrév* (▸**mercatique après-vente**)
after-sales marketing

maxi-discompte *m* hard discount

maxi-discompteur *m* hard discounter

maximal, e *adj* maximal, maximum

maximalisation *f* maximization; ~ **des
profits** profit maximization; ~ **des
recettes** revenue maximization

maximaliser *vt* maximize

maximin *m* maximin

maximiser *vt* maximize

maximum *adj* maximum

mazout *m* fuel oil; ~ **de soute** (d'un navire)
bunker fuel oil

MBA *abrév* (▸**marge brute
d'autofinancement**) cash flow

m-business *m* m-business

MCAC *abrév* (▸**Marché commun
d'Amérique centrale**) CACM (Central
American Common Market)

M.D.D. *abrév* (▸**marque de distributeur**)
distributor's brand name

mécanicien, -enne *m,f* machine operator,
mechanic

mécanique *f* mechanical engineering; ~

de précision precision engineering

mécanisation *f* mechanization; ~ **de la
manutention** mechanization of cargo
handling

mécanisé, e *adj* (Ind) (production)
mechanized

mécaniser *vt* mechanize

mécanisme *m* device, mechanism; ~ **de
coupe-circuit** circuit breaker mechanism
US; ~ **d'escompte** discount mechanism; ~
de garantie d'achat purchase underwriting
facility; ~ **d'indexation** pegging device; ~
du marché market mechanism; ~ **pour
minimiser les pertes** (Banque) stop-loss
rules; ~ **de mouvement en numéraire**
specie flow mechanism; ~ **de négociation**
negotiating machinery; ~ **des prix** price
mechanism; ~ **de taux de change**
exchange rate mechanism; ~ **de
transmission** transmission mechanism

mécanographe *m* punch card operator

mécénat *m* sponsorship; ~ **d'entreprise**
(publicité) corporate sponsorship

mécène *m* patron, sponsor

méconnu, e *adj* (valeur) unrecognized

mécontentement *m* dissatisfaction; ~
sur le lieu de travail discontent in the
workplace

MEDAF *abrév* (▸**modèle d'évaluation des
actifs financiers**) CAPM (capital asset
pricing model)

média *m* medium; ~ **éphémère** transient
medium

médiane *f* median

médias *m pl* media; **les** ~ the media; ~
classiques basic media, traditional media;
~ **publicitaires** advertising media

médiateur, -trice *m,f* arbitrator, mediator

médiation *f* arbitration, mediation

médiatique *adj* (succès, vedette, événement,
campagne) media

médiatiser *vt* (événement) give a lot of
media coverage to

médicament *m* drug, medicine; ~
générique generic drug; ~ **sans
ordonnance** over-the-counter medicine; ~
vendu sous marque proprietary drug

méfait *m* misdemeanour BrE, misdemeanor
AmE; ~ **prémédité** malicious mischief

méfiance *f* distrust, suspicion

méfiant, e *adj* suspicious, wary

mégabit *m* megabit

mégadimension *f* mammoth size

méga-octet *m* megabyte

meilleur, e *adj* (perspective) better, brighter;
~ **marché** cheaper; ~ **moyen pratique** best
practical means; **ou à** ~ **prix** (Bourse) or
better still; ~ **prix** best price; ~ **que la
moyenne** better than average; ~ **que prévu**
(résultat) better than expected; ~ **des cas**
best-case scenario; ~**e offre** best bid; ~**e** ⋯▷

option best alternative

mélange *m* mix; ~ **dosé** blending; ~ **de politiques** policy mix

membre *m* member; ~ **affilié** affiliate member; ~ **opérateur de la Bourse des valeurs** trading member; ~ **d'une chambre de compensation** clearing member; ~ **d'un comité** committee member, member of a committee; ~ **d'une commission** committee member; ~ **du conseil de surveillance** member of the supervisory board; ~ **du directoire** member of the board of management; ~ **d'équipage** (d'un avion, d'un navire) crew member; ~ **de l'équipe d'audit** audit officer; ~ **fondateur** founder member; ~ **de la haute société socialiste**; ~ **de non-compensation** nonclearing member; ~ **d'office** ex officio member; ~ **du Parlement Européen** (UE) Euro MP, Member of the European Parliament; ~ **à part entière** full member; ~ **du personnel** member of staff; ~ **du public** member of the public; ~ **spécifié** specified member; ~ **suppléant du directoire** deputy member of the board of management; ~ **d'un syndicat** union member

même *adj* same; ~ **langue** same language; **être du ~ avis (que)** agree (with); **de la ~ façon** in the same way; **être à ~ de faire** be in a position to do

mémoire[1] *m* (d'un compte) bill; (rapport) report; (Droit) memorandum, statement; ~ **descriptif** specifications; ~ **descriptif de brevet** patent specifications; ~ **de vente** prompt note

mémoire[2] *f* (d'une personne) memory; (Info) (storage) memory; ~ **d'accès rapide** cache memory, cache storage; ~ **additionnelle externe** add-on memory; ~ **d'archivage** archival storage; ~ **auxiliaire** archival storage; ~ **auxiliaire d'entrée/de sortie** bulk input/output; ~ **basse** low memory; ~ **à bulles** bubble memory; ~ **cache** cache memory; ~ **centrale** core memory; ~ **commune** global memory; ~ **d'expansion** expanded memory, extended memory; ~ **de grande capacité** bulk storage, mass memory; ~ **intermédiaire** buffer storage; ~ **interne** internal memory; ~ **magnétique** magnetic storage; ~ **de masse auxiliaire** auxiliary memory, auxiliary storage; ~ **morte** read only memory, ROM; ~ **morte programmable électroniquement** electronically programmable read only memory; ~ **d'ordinateur** computer memory; ~ **principale** core storage; ~ **réelle** real storage; ~ **de sauvegarde** backup memory; ~ **supplémentaire** add-on memory; ~ **tampon** buffer (storage); ~ **à tores** core storage, magnetic core; ~ **de travail** scratch pad, working storage; ~ **ultra-rapide** high-speed memory; ~ **vive** random access memory, RAM; ~ **vive dynamique** dynamic

random access memory

mémorandum *m* (note) memo, memorandum

mémorisation *f* (Info) storage; ~ **assistée** aided recall; ~ **de données** data storage

mémoriser *vt* memorize; (Info) (données) store

menace *f* threat; ~ **de grève** strike threat

menacé, e *adj* (population) at risk; (équilibre, économie) in jeopardy

ménage *m* (private) household; ~ **d'agriculteurs** agricultural household; ~ **sans enfants** childless couple

ménager *vt* (matériel, ressources) be careful with; (personne) handle carefully, deal carefully with; ~ **la chèvre et le chou** sit on the fence (infrml)

ménagère *f* housewife

mener *vt* (campagne) run, wage; (vente, commerce) conduct; (Gestion) (équipe) lead; (V&M) carry out; ~ **une affaire à bien** pull off a deal; ~ **une campagne négative** wage a negative campaign; ~ **qch à terme** follow sth through; ~ **la vie dure à qn** make things hard for sb; ~ **à** (baisse, échec) lead to; ~ **une enquête** hold an investigation

meneur, -euse *m,f* (chef) leader; **avoir des qualités de ~** have leadership qualities; ~ **mondial** world leader; **~s et traînards** (Bourse) leads and lags

mensualité *f* monthly instalment BrE, monthly installment AmE; **par ~s** in monthly instalments

mensuel[1], **-elle** *adj* monthly

mensuel[2] *m* monthly magazine

mensuel[3], **-elle** *m,f* employee who is paid *monthly*

mensuellement *adv* monthly

mentionné, e *adj* ~ **ci-dessous** as mentioned below; ~ **ci-dessus** as mentioned above; ~ **plus bas** as mentioned below; ~ **plus haut** as mentioned above

mentionner *vt* bring up, mention

menu *m* (dans un restaurant) menu; ~ **déroulant** (Info) pull-down menu; ~ **édition** edit menu; ~ **fichier** file menu; ~ **hiérarchique** hierarchical menu; ~ **principal** main menu; ~ **surgissant** pop-up menu

méprise *f* mistake

mer *f* sea; **en ~** (plate-forme) afloat, offshore

mercantile *adj* mercantile

mercantilisme *m* mercantilism

mercantiliste *adj* mercantilist

mercaphonie *f* phone marketing

mercaticien, -enne *m,f* marketing expert, marketer

mercatique *f* marketing; ~ **d'amont** upstream direct marketing; ~ **après-vente** after-sales marketing; ~ **associée** trade

marketing; ~ **d'aval** customer marketing; ~
écologique ecomarketing; ~ **électronique**
e-marketing; ~ **téléphonique** telephone
marketing, telemarketing

mercatis *adj* market-driven

merchandiser *m* merchandiser

merchandising *m* merchandising

merci *excl* thank you; ~ **de votre lettre**
thank you for your letter

méridien *m* meridian

méritocratie *f* meritocracy

Mesdames *f pl* ladies; ~ **et Messieurs**
ladies and gentlemen

Mesdemoiselles *f pl* ladies

mésoéconomie *f* mesoeconomy

message *m* message; (publicité) message;
transmettre/adresser un ~ give/send a
message (à to); **je peux laisser un** ~**?** can I
leave a message?; ~ **d'alerte** (Info) alert box;
~ **de bienvenue** welcome message; ~
brouillé scrambled message; ~ **codé** coded
message; ~s **contradictoires** mixed signals;
~ **de diagnostique** diagnostic message; ~
électronique electronic mail, e-mail; ~
d'entrée input message; ~ **d'erreur** error
message; ~ **d'erreur d'entrée/de sortie**
input/output error message; ~ **d'état** status
message; ~ **guide-opérateur** prompt; ~
d'intervention action code, action message;
~ **publicitaire** (TV, radio) commercial,
advertising message, spot; ~ **publicitaire à
la radio** radio commercial; ~ **publicitaire
télévisé** TV commercial; ~ **publiposté**
direct mail; ~ **téléphonique** telephone
message; ~ **texte** text message; ~ **SMS** text
message

messager[1], **-ère** *m,f* courier, messenger

messager[2] *m:* ~ **de poche** pager

messagerie *f* courier service; ~s
aériennes air freight service; ~
électronique e-mail, electronic mail; ~s
maritimes sea service; ~s **de presse** press
distribution service; ~ **vocale** voice mail

Messieurs *m pl* gentlemen

mesure *f* (initiative) measure; (évaluation)
measurement; ~ **économique/
administrative** economic/administrative
measure; **par** ~ **d'économie** as an economy
measure; **prendre des** ~s take measures,
take steps; ~ **de faveur** favour BrE; **dans la**
~ **où** in so far as BrE, insofar as AmE; **être en**
~ **de faire** be in a position to do; **par** ~
d'économie as an economy measure; **par** ~
préventive/de précaution as a preventive/
precautionary measure; **prendre la** ~ **de la
concurrence** weigh up the competition; **fait
sur** ~ (robe, costume) made-to-measure; **c'est
du sur** ~ (vêtement) it's made to measure, it's
custom tailored AmE; **agir avec** ~ behave in
a moderate way; **garder une juste** ~ keep a
sense of proportion; ~s **anti-
discriminatoires** (à l'embauche) positive

discrimination BrE, affirmative action AmE;
~s **d'arbitrage** arbitration proceedings; ~
de banc d'essai bench mark; ~ **de bien-
être économique** (économétrie) measure of
economic welfare; ~ **de capacité liquide**
liquid measure; ~ **de compensation**
countermeasure; ~ **de conservation** (Envir)
conservation measure; (Assur) (maritime) sue
and labour BrE, sue and labor AmE; ~ **de
contrôle** measure of control; ~ **de
cotisation** (Fisc) assessing action; ~ **de
degrés** degree measure; ~s **disciplinaires**
disciplinary measures; ~ **dissuasive**
deterrent; ~s **draconiennes** drastic
measures; ~ **d'exécution** (prise par le
Ministère) enforcement action; ~ **fiscale** tax
measure; ~ **fiscale d'incitation** tax
incentive; ~s **d'incitation économique**
deficit financing, pump priming; ~s **et
limites** (Immob) metes and bounds; ~ **de
mobilité géographique** mobility status; ~s
particulières pour l'emploi special
employment measures; ~ **par pieds-
planches** board measure; ~ **de
performances** performance measurement;
~ **de postcotisation** postassessing; ~ **de
précaution** precautionary measure; ~ **de
précotisation** preassessing; ~ **préventive**
precautionary measure, preventive measure;
~ **de la productivité** productivity
measurement; ~ **de la quantité** quantity
surveying; ~s **réglementaires** regulatory
measures; ~ **de relance** stimulative
measure; ~ **du rendement** performance
measurement; ~s **de représailles**
retaliatory measures; ~ **du revenu** income
measure; ~ **de sécurité** safety measure,
safety precaution; ~s **de sécurité contre
incendie** fire prevention measures; ~s **de
superficie** square measures; ~s **de
surface** square measures; ~ **du travail**
work measurement; ~ **du travail par
sondage** (étude de marché) activity sampling;
~s **d'urgence** emergency measures

mesurer *vt* measure; (risques, difficultés)
assess; ~ **le rendement de qn** measure sb's
performance

méta *m* white coal

métadonnées *f pl* (Info) metadata

métal *m* metal; ~ **affiné** refined metal; ~
jaune yellow metal; ~ **lourd** (pollution) heavy
metal; ~ **précieux** precious metal

métaldéhyde *m* white coal

métalliste *mf* metallist

métallo *m* (infrml) metalworker, steelworker

métallurgiste *mf* metallurgist; (ouvrier)
metalworker, steelworker

métamercatique *f* metamarketing

métamoteur *m:* ~ **de recherche** (Info)
meta search engine

métayer, -ère *m,f* tenant farmer GB,
sharecropper US

méthanier *m* LPG tanker

méthode *f* method, system; ~ **ABC** ABC method; ~ **d'achat au prix coûtant** purchase method; ~ **de l'achèvement des travaux** completed contract method; ~ **d'actualisation** present value method; ~ **d'alignement sur la concurrence** competitive-parity method; ~ **d'amortissement** amortization method, payback method; ~ **d'amortissement linéaire** straight-line method of depreciation; ~ **basée sur le pourcentage des ventes** percentage-of-sales method; ~ **du bénéfice brut** gross profit method; ~ **de la carotte et du bâton** carrot and stick approach; ~ **de la comptabilité d'exercice** accrual basis, accrual method; ~ **de la comptabilité de trésorerie** receivable basis, receivable method; ~ **comptable** accounting method, accounting procedure; ~ **comptable du passif** liability method; ~ **de consolidation par intégration globale** purchase method; ~ **du coût complet** absorption costing, full-cost method; ~ **des coûts directs** direct costing; ~ **des coûts marginaux** marginal costing; ~ **des coûts moyens** overall expenses method; ~ **du coût de revient standard** standard cost accounting, standard cost system; ~ **des coûts variables** contribution analysis; ~ **de croissance régulière** steady-growth method; ~ **des dépenses globales** overall expenses method; ~ **par échelles** daily balance interest calculation; ~ **de l'étude de cas** case study method; ~ **d'évaluation des stocks au prix coûtant** (inventaire) cost method; ~ **d'exploitation agricole** farming method; ~ **de financement préétablie** formula funding; ~ **de l'impôt exigible** flow-through basis, tax payable basis; ~ **de l'impôt reporté** deferred tax accounting; ~ **de l'indice-chaîne** chain index method; ~ **d'inventaire périodique** periodic inventory method; ~ **d'investissement préétablie** formula investing; ~ **manuelle** manual mode; ~ **de la mise en équivalence** equity method; ~ **des observations instantanées** random observation method; ~ **de paiement** method of payment; ~ **par paliers** daily balance interest calculation; ~ **à partie double** double-entry method; ~ **de pourcentage d'achèvement** percentage-of-completion method; ~ **de préparation** method of preparation; ~ **du prix d'achat** purchase price method; ~ **du prix de revient complet** absorption costing, full-cost pricing; ~ **progressive** progressive method, step by step method; ~ **de qualification par points** points-rating method; ~ **de recyclage** recycling method; ~ **de référence** (Fin) bench mark method; ~ **de réserve d'investissement** investment reserve system; ~ **statique** static method; ~ **temporelle** temporal method; ~ **de transfert de technologie**

(Econ) transfer of technology method; ~ **des unités de production** units-of-production method

metical *m* metical

méticuleusement *adv* meticulously, painstakingly

méticuleux, -euse *adj* meticulous, painstaking

métier *m* job, occupation; **ayant du** ~ experienced; ~**s analogues** allied trades; ~ **de base** core business; ~ **à tisser** (machine) weaving loom

métrage *m* ≈ yardage; ~ **carré** (d'un immeuble) square footage; ~ **de planche** board measure

mètre *m* (unité) metre BrE, meter AmE; (instrument) tape measure; **le** ~ **carré** (loyer) ≈ per square metre; ~ **de couturière** tape measure; ~ **cube** cubic metre; ~ **ruban** measuring tape

métro *m* (à Londres) underground; (à New York) subway; (à Montréal) metro

métropole *f* metropolis, metropolitan town

métropolitain, e *adj* metropolitan

mettre ⟦1⟧ *vt* place, put; ~ **l'accent sur** emphasize, place emphasis on; ~ **l'adresse sur** put the address on; ~ **une annonce** advertise; ~ **une annonce dans le journal** put an advert in the paper; ~ **en application** enforce, implement; ~ **en balance** weigh up; ~ **au banc d'essai** benchmark; ~ **au chômage partiel** (personnel) put on short-time working, stand off; ~ **au chômage technique** (personnel) lay off; ~ **les choses au point** get sth straight; ~ **en commun** (ressources) pool; ~ **en communication avec** connect, put through to; ~ **un compte à découvert** overdraw an account; ~ **un compte à jour** post up an account; ~ **en contact** bring together; (deux ou plusieurs personnes) put in touch; ~ **en conteneurs** containerize; ~ **à la corbeille** bin; (presse) spike; ~ **en corrélation** correlate; ~ **de côté** (de l'argent) put away, save; ~ **en danger** compromise, endanger; ~ **la dernière main à** put the finishing touches to; ~ **en détention préventive** remand in custody; ~ **à disposition** make available; ~ **en doute** query; ~ **à l'eau** (navire) launch; ~ **en eau** impound; ~ **un embargo sur** place an embargo on; ~ **une enchère** bid, put in a bid; ~ **à l'épreuve** put to the test; ~ **à l'essai** (machine, produit) test out; ~ **en évidence** (zone, caractère) highlight; ~ **à exécution** carry out, execute; ~ **en faillite** bankrupt; ~ **en fidéicommis** place in trust; ~ **en file d'attente** (programmes) queue; ~ **fin à** abolish, bring to an end; ~ **fin à une session** log off, log out; ~ **en fonction** (système) activate; ~ **en forme** (jarg) edit, format; (presse) edit, rewrite; ~ **en fourrière** impound; ~ **une histoire à la une** lead with a story; ~ **hors tension** turn off; ~ **un impôt**

sur qch impose a tax on sth, put a tax on sth; ~ **à l'index** blacklist; ~ **en jachère** (terre) set aside; ~ **à jour** update; ~ **en liberté provisoire sous caution** release on bail; ~ **en ligne** align BrE, aline AmE; ~ **en liquidation** put into receivership; ~ **en lumière** bring to light; ~ **en manchette** (presse) splash; ~ **en marche** activate, switch on; ~ **à la mode** bring into fashion; ~ **un nouveau produit à l'essai** carry out trials on a new product, test a new product; ~ **(en) œuvre** (brevet) work; (politique) carry out; (projet, plan, décision, article) implement; (Info) implement; ~ **en ordre** put in order; ~ **de l'ordre dans ses affaires** put one's affairs in order; ~ **par écrit** set down in writing; ~ **en péril** (emploi) compromise, jeopardize; ~ **un piquet de grève devant** picket; ~ **en place** put in place; (Info) install BrE, instal AmE; ~ **en place progressivement** phase in; ~ **au point** adjust, finalize, fine-tune; (projet) formulate; ~ **à la poste** (lettre) post BrE, mail AmE; ~ **en pratique** put into practice; ~ **en préretraite obligatoire** force into early retirement; ~ **la pression sur qn** put pressure on sb; ~ **en priorité** prioritize; ~ **au propre** write a fair copy of; ~ **qn en apprentissage chez qn** apprentice sb to sb; ~ **qn au courant de qch** brief sb on sth, update sb on sth; ~ **qn au courant de la situation** acquaint sb with the situation; ~ **qn à l'essai** give sb a trial; ~ **qn au pied du mur** corner sb, call sb's bluff; ~ **qn à la porte** (infrml) sack (infrml); ~ **une question à l'ordre du jour** put a question on the agenda; ~ **en relief** outline; ~ **à la retraite** pension off, retire; ~ **en route** set up; ~ **en service** (appareil, véhicule) bring into service; (autoroute, aerogare) open; ~ **son veto à** put a veto on, veto; ~ **sous forme de tableau** tabulate; ~ **sous tension** power up, turn on; ~ **en soute** bunker; ~ **sur liste noire** blacklist; ~ **sur le marché** release; ~ **sur ordinateur** computerize; ~ **une taxe sur qch** impose a tax on, put a tax on sth; ~ **à la terre** earth BrE, ground AmE; ~ **en tutelle** place under guardianship; ~ **en valeur** reclaim; ~ **en vente** put on the market, put up for sale; ~ **en vigueur** enforce, put into force; ~ **aux voix** (résolution) put to the vote; ~ **à zéro** zero $\boxed{2}$ **se mettre** *v pron* **se** ~ **à** (une tâche) begin, start; **se** ~ **d'accord** agree; **se** ~ **dans l'illégalité** fall foul of the law; **se** ~ **en évidence** come to the fore; **se** ~ **en grève** go on strike, take industrial action; **se** ~ **en grève de solidarité** strike in sympathy; **se** ~ **qn à dos** alienate sb; **se** ~ **à son compte** set up in business on one's own; **se** ~ **au travail** get down to work, start work

meunier, -ière *m,f* miller

meurtre *m* murder; ~ **avec préméditation** premeditated murder, murder one US (infrml)

mévente *f* slump in sales

micro *m* microphone

microcoupure *f* brownout US

microcrédit *m* microcredit

microdisquette *f* microdisk

microéconomie *f* microeconomics

micro-éditer *vt* desktop-publish

micro-édition *f* desktop publishing

micro-électronique *f* microelectronics

microfiche *f* microfiche

microfilm *m* microfilm

micro-informatique *f* microcomputing

micro-interrupteur *m* DIP switch

microlecteur *m* microfiche reader

micrologiciel *m* firmware

micromarketing *m* micromarketing

micronavigateur *m* micro browser

micro(-)ordinateur *m* microcomputer

micro-ordinateur *m* microcomputer

microplaquette *f* (micro)chip, die

microprocesseur *m* microprocessor

microprogramme *m* firmware, microprogram

mieux *adv* better; **il vaudrait** ~ **vendre maintenant** you'd be better-off selling now; **ou** ~ or better still; ~ **que la moyenne** better than average; ~ **que prévu** better than predicted; ~ **disant** (Bourse) highest bidder

migration *f* migration; ~**s alternantes** commuting, commutation AmE; ~ **circulaire** circular migration

mile *m* mile; ~ **carré** square mile; ~**s/ heure** miles per hour, mph; ~ **marin** (navigation) nautical mile

milice *f* militia; **une** ~ **ouvrière** a workers' militia; ~ **patronale** goon squad US (jarg); ~ **de quartier** local vigilante group

milieu *m* environment; **au** ~ (jarg) (Bourse) at-the-money; **au** ~ **du navire** midships; **de** ~ **de gamme** midrange; ~**x d'affaires** business circles, business community; ~ **aménagé** planned environment; ~ **constant** controlled atmosphere; ~**x financiers** financial circles; ~**x industriels** industrial circles; ~**x informatiques** computer circles, computer world; ~ **naturel** natural environment; ~ **du navire** midship

militant, e *m,f* activist, militant

millésime *m* (d'un vin) vintage

milliard *m* billion, thousand million BrE

milliardaire *mf* billionaire, multimillionaire

millième *m* (Fisc, Immob) millage rate US; ~ **d'un dollar** mill US

milligramme *m* milligram

millilitre *m* millilitre BrE, milliliter AmE

millimètre *m* millimetre BrE, millimeter AmE

million *m* million

millionnaire *mf* millionaire; ~ **en actions** paper millionaire

m

millirem *m* ~ **par heure** (radioactivité) millirem per hour

milliseconde *f* millisecond

min. *abrév* (▸**minimum**) min. (minimum)

mine *f* mine; ~ **de charbon** coal mine; ~ **d'or** gold mine; (source de richesse) money-spinner (infrml), cash cow (jarg)

miner *vt* erode

minerai *m* ore; ~ **argentifère** silver ore; ~ **argileux** clay ore; ~ **de cuivre** copper ore; ~ **d'étain** tin ore; ~ **de fer** iron ore; ~ **lourd** hard commodity; ~ **métallique** metalliferous ore; ~ **d'or** gold ore; ~ **de plomb** lead ore; ~ **de zinc** zinc ore

minéralier *m* (navigation) ore carrier

mineur, e *m,f* miner; (Droit) minor

mini *adj* mini; (Info) slim-line

miniaturisé, e *adj* miniaturized, subcompact

minibus *m* minibus; ~ **de transport en commun** public service minibus

minimal, e *adj* minimal

minimax *m* minimax

minimiser *vt* (risques) minimize; (résultats) soft-pedal (infrml)

minimum¹ *adj* (▸**min.**) minimum (min.)

minimum² *m* minimum amount; ~ **imposable** tax threshold; ~ **vieillesse** basic old age pension; ~ **vital** (salaire) minimum living wage

ministère *m* (au-Royaume-Uni, aux États-Unis) department; (ailleurs) ministry; ~ **des Affaires étrangères** ≈ Ministry of Foreign Affairs, ≈ Foreign and Commonwealth Office UK; ~ **des Affaires sociales** ≈ Department of Work and Pensions UK; ~ **du Commerce et de l'Industrie** ≈ Department of Trade and Industry UK; ~ **débiteur** debtor department; ~ **de la Défense nationale** ≈ Ministry of Defence UK, ≈ Department of Defense US; ~ **de l'Énergie** ≈ Department of Energy US; ~ **de l'Environnement** Department of the Environment, ≈ Department for the Environment, Food and Rural Affairs UK; ~ **des Finances** Ministry of Finance, ≈ Treasury UK, ≈ Treasury Department US; ~ **de la Justice** ≈ Ministry of Justice; ~ **public** (service) public prosecutor's office; (magistrat) prosecution, public prosecutor; ~ **du Tourisme** Ministry of Tourism, ≈ Department of Culture, Media and Sport UK; ~ **des Transports** ≈ Department for Transport, Local Government and the Regions UK; ~ **du Travail et de l'Emploi** ≈ Department for Education and Skills UK

ministre *mf* minister, Secretary of State UK, secretary US; ~ **des Affaires étrangères** ≈ Foreign Secretary UK, ≈ Secretary of State US, foreign minister; ~ **de la Défense nationale** ≈ Defence Minister UK, ≈ Defense Secretary US; ~ **délégué** deputy minister; ~

de l'Environnement Minister for the Environment; ~ **d'État** Secretary of State UK; ~ **des Finances** ≈ Chancellor of the Exchequer UK, ≈ Secretary of the Treasury US, Minister of Finance; ~ **de la Justice** ≈ Lord Chancellor UK, ≈ Attorney General US; ~ **titulaire d'un portefeuille** departmental minister

minoration *f* (de prix, de taux) reduction; (de biens) undervaluation; (Compta, Fisc) (de revenus) underreporting

minorer *vt* (prix, taux) reduce (**de** by); (biens) undervalue; (Compta, Fisc) (revenus) underreport

minorité *f* minority; ~ **ethnique** ethnic minority

minuscule *f* lower-case letter

minutage *m* timing

minuties *f pl* minutiae

miracle¹ miracle *m*; ~ **économique** economic miracle

miracle² *adj*: **un remède/une solution** ~ a miracle cure/solution; **un procédé/matériau** ~ a miraculous process/material; **une méthode** ~ a magic formula

mire *f* test card

miroir *m* mirror; **site** ~ (Info) mirror site

mis, e *adj* ~ **en attente** (Info) camp-on; **être** ~ **au chômage** be made redundant; ~ **en évidence** highlighted; ~ **à l'index** blacklisted; **être** ~ **en minorité** be outvoted; ~ **au point** perfected; **être** ~ **en règlement judiciaire** go into receivership

mise *f* (argent) outlay; ~ **en accusation** indictment; ~ **en administration judiciaire** placing in receivership; ~ **en application** (Droit) enforcement; (Info) implementation; ~ **en balles** (de marchandises) baling; ~ **à bord** lading; ~ **en bouteille** bottling; ~ **en cale sèche** (d'un navire) dry docking; ~ **au chômage partiel** short-time working; ~ **en commun** pool, pooling; ~ **en commun des risques** risk pooling; ~ **en conteneurs** containerization; ~ **au courant** briefing, update; ~ **en couverture** commencement of cover; ~ **en décharge** dumping; ~ **en demeure** enforcement order; ~ **en demeure avec garantie** injunction bond; ~ **en disponibilité** (d'un employé) secondment; ~ **à disposition de crédit** granting of credit; ~ **à disposition de main-d'œuvre** manpower aid; ~ **sur écoute téléphonique** telephone tapping, wiretapping; ~ **en évidence** (de texte) highlighting; ~ **en file d'attente** queueing; ~ **de fonds** capital outlay; ~ **en forme** (d'une disquette) formatting; ~ **en forme juridique** formalization; ~ **en fourrière** impounding; ~ **en gage** pledging; ~ **en garde** caution; ~ **à jour** update, updating; ~ **à jour des fichiers** (V&M) list maintenance; ~ **en liquidation** placing in receivership; ~ **en main tierce** escrow; ~

sur le marché market entry; ∼ **à niveau**
(Info) upgrade, upgrading; ∼ **en œuvre**
application; (d'un brevet) carrying-out; (d'un
article, plan) (Info) implementation; ∼ **en
œuvre du domaine public** public
development; ∼ **en œuvre de la politique**
policy execution; ∼ **sur ordinateur**
computerization; ∼ **en page** (de texte) page
layout, page setting; ∼ **en pension**
repurchase agreement; ∼ **en pension
inverse** reverse repurchase; ∼ **à pied** (de
personnel) lay-off; ∼ **en place progressive**
phasing in; ∼ **au point** adjustment,
formulation; (Info) fine-tuning; ∼ **au point
des objectifs** goal setting; ∼ **au point du
produit** product development; ∼ **au point
de programme** program testing; ∼ **à prix**
floor price; (ventes aux enchères) reserve price
BrE, upset price AmE; ∼ **à prix au point
mort** break-even pricing; ∼ **à prix
prévisionnelle** anticipatory pricing; ∼ **en
réseau** (Info) networking; ∼ **à la retraite
d'office** compulsory retirement BrE,
mandatory retirement AmE; ∼ **en route**
start; ∼ **en sac** (de marchandises) bagging; ∼
en service commissioning; ∼ **sous
tension** powering up; ∼ **à la terre** earthing
BrE, grounding AmE; ∼ **en valeur** reclaiming;
∼ **en vigueur** (d'une loi) enforcement

miser ① *vt* (argent) bet, gamble
② *vi* gamble; ∼ **sur la situation/qualité**
bank on the situation/quality; ∼ **sur un
événement** count on an event; ∼ **sur qn**
place all one's hopes in sb

mission *f* mission; (charge) assignment; ∼
commune joint assignment; ∼
diplomatique diplomatic mission; ∼
économique economic mission; ∼
d'enquête fact-finding mission; ∼
d'entreprise corporate mission; ∼ **à
l'étranger** foreign mission

mi-temps *m* (emploi) part-time job; (système)
part-time work; **un poste à** ∼ a part-time
job; **elle travaille à** ∼ she works part-time

mix *m* mix; ∼ **de produits** product mix; ∼
des produits en vente sales mix

mixage *m* (enregistrement) mix, mixing

mixte *adj* (cales) combined

Mlle *abrév* (▶**Mademoiselle**) Miss

Mme *abrév* (▶**Madame**) Mrs

MMI *abrév* (▶**Marché monétaire
international**) IMM (International Monetary
Market)

m/o *abrév* (▶**mon ordre**) m/o (my order)

Mo *abrév* (▶**méga-octet**) Mb (megabyte)

mobile¹ *adj* (personnel) mobile; **échelle** ∼
des salaires sliding salary scale; **téléphone**
∼ mobile phone; **téléphonie** ∼ mobile
communications, mobile telephony

mobile² *m* (motif) motive; (téléphone) mobile
(phone); ∼ **d'achat** purchasing motivator

mobilier¹, -ière *adj*: **biens** ∼s movable
property; **valeurs mobilières** securities;

plus-values mobilières capital gains (on the
sale of securities)

mobilier² *m* furniture; ∼ **de bureau** office
furniture; ∼ **domestique** household effects

mobilisation *f* liquidation; ∼ **de fonds**
capital raising, mobilization of capital

mobiliser *vt* (actif) liquidate; ∼ **des
capitaux** raise capital; ∼ **des fonds
extérieurs** raise external funds

mobilité *f* mobility; ∼ **fiscale** fiscal
mobility; ∼ **de la main-d'œuvre** labour
mobility BrE, labor mobility AmE; ∼
professionnelle job mobility; ∼ **du travail**
occupational mobility; ∼ **verticale** vertical
mobility

modalité *f* method, mode; ∼ **de paiement**
method of payment

modalités *f pl* (conditions) terms; (Fin) (d'une
émission) terms and conditions; (façon de
fonctionner) practical details; **les** ∼ **de
l'opération/l'unification** the practical details
of the operation/the unification process; ∼
de consolidation consolidation method; ∼
en dollars American terms; ∼ **de
financement** methods of funding; ∼ **de
paiement** terms of payment; ∼ **de
remboursement** terms of repayment

mode¹ *m* (façon) way, mode; (Info) mode; ∼
aide (Info) help mode; ∼ **bloc** (Info) block
mode; ∼ **brouillon** (Info) draft mode; ∼
continu (Info) burst mode; ∼
conversationnel, ∼ dialogué (Info)
conversational mode; ∼ **discontinu** (Info)
byte mode; ∼ **document** (Info) document
mode; ∼ **d'édition** (Info) edit mode; ∼
d'emploi instructions; ∼ **d'exploitation
normal** standard operating procedure; ∼ **de
fonctionnement** operating instructions; ∼
graphique (Info) graphics mode; ∼
d'imposition method of taxation; ∼
interactif (Info) interactive mode; ∼ **listage**
(Info) draft mode; ∼ **opératoire** modus
operandi; ∼ **de paiement** method of
payment; ∼ **de rémunération** wage system; ∼
∼ **réponse** (Info) answer mode; ∼ **texte**
(Info) text mode; ∼ **de transmission de
données par rafales** (Info) burst mode; ∼
de transport means of transport, mode of
transport; ∼ **de vie** way of life

mode² *f* fashion; **à la** ∼ in fashion; **qui crée
la** ∼ trendsetter; ∼ **passagère** fad

modelage *m* modelling BrE, modeling AmE; ∼
statistique statistical modelling BrE

modèle *m* design; (copie) model; (illustrations)
artwork; ∼ **comptable** accounting model; ∼
de consommation consumption pattern; ∼
de convention boilerplate; ∼ **de décision**
decision model; ∼ **déposé** registered design;
∼ **dynamique de gestion** dynamic
management model; ∼ **économique**
economic model; ∼ **économique à moyen
terme pour la communauté européenne**
(économétrie) Common Market Medium Term ⋯⋯➔

Model; ~ **de l'entreprise** company model, corporate model; ~ **d'évaluation des actifs financiers** capital asset pricing model; ~ **d'évaluation d'un prix** pricing model; ~s **d'exploitation** working patterns; ~ **de facture** specimen invoice; ~ **global** unitary model; ~ **de lettre** standard letter, specimen letter; ~ **de liaison ascendante** bottom-up linkage model; ~ **de liaison descendante** top-down linkage model; ~s **macroéconomiques comparatifs** linkage models; ~ **structure-conduite-performance** structure-conduct-performance model; ~ **structurel** structural model; ~ **d'utilité** utility model

modélisation f modelling BrE, modeling AmE; ~ **discrète** soft modelling BrE; ~ **de simulation** simulation modelling BrE

modéliser vt model

modem m modem; ~ **câble** cable modem; ~ **à connexion directe** direct-connect modem

modéré, e adj moderate, modest

modérément adv moderately, modestly

modérer vt contain, moderate

modernisation f modernization, revamping

moderniser vt modernize, revamp

modeste adj (investissement, budget, salaire) modest; (facture, coût) moderate

modification f alteration, modification; (Droit) amendment, revision; ~ **du capital** alteration of capital; ~ **de la clause d'attribution** (assurance-vie) change of beneficiary provision; ~ **du comportement** behaviour modification BrE, behavior modification AmE; ~ **comptable** accounting change; ~ **de la consommation** shift in consumption; ~ **d'itinéraire** change of itinerary, rerouting; ~ **provisoire** draft amendment

modifié, e adj altered, modified; (Droit) amended

modifier vt alter, modify; (Droit) amend, revise

modulation f modulation; ~ **de fréquence** frequency modulation

module m module; ~ **d'alarme** (navigation) automatic watch keeper; ~ **de décision** decision package; ~ **d'extension** (Info) plug-in

moduler vt modulate

moindre adj à un ~ **degré** to a lesser extent; ~ **coût** least-cost

moins[1] adv less; ~ **cher** cheaper; ~ **onéreux** cheaper

moins[2] m (signe) minus; ~ **net** net capital loss; ~ **sur titres** paper loss

moins[3] prép less; ~ **de** under; **un peu ~ de** (quantité, chiffre) a bit less than, a little under

moins-disant m (Bourse) lowest bidder, lowest tender

moins-perçu m underpaid sum

moins-value f capital loss

mois m month; **un ~ à l'avance** a month in advance; ~ **civil** calendar month; ~ **après date** months after date; ~ **d'échéance** expiry month; ~ **d'échéance le plus proche** nearest month; ~ **d'exercice** fiscal month; ~ **d'expiration** expiry month; ~ **de livraison** delivery month; (d'un contrat) contract month; ~ **de livraison du contrat** contract delivery month; ~ **de livraison immédiate** spot delivery month; ~ **prochain** next month; ~ **de transaction** months traded; ~ **à vue** months after sight

moitié f half; ~ **de vie** half-life

moment m moment; **à tout ~** at all times, constantly; **à un ~ donné** at a given moment, at some stage; **pour le ~** for the time being

mon adj my; ~ **compte** m/a, my account; ~ **ordre** my order

monde m world; **dans le ~ entier** all over the world; ~ **des affaires** business world, business community; ~ **anglophone/ francophone** English/French-speaking world; ~ **de la finance** financial world, world of finance; ~ **de la publicité** advertising world; ~ **du spectacle** show business

mondial, e adj world, worldwide

mondialement adv worldwide

mondialisation f (des marchés) globalization

mondialiser vt (marchés) globalize

MONEP abrév (▶**Marché des options négociables de Paris**) Paris traded options exchange, ≈ CBOE (Chicago Board Options Exchange), ≈ LIFFE (London International Financial Futures Exchange)

monétaire adj monetary

monétarisme m monetarism; ~ **global/ instantané** global/instant monetarism

monétariste adj monetarist

monétique f e-money

monétisation f monetization

monétiser vt monetize

moniteur m (dispositif, matériel) monitor; ~ **analogique** (matériel) analog monitor

monnaie f (unité monétaire) currency; (pièces de monnaie) coins; (pièces de faible valeur) change; ~ **forte/faible** strong/weak currency; **fausse** ~ forged ou counterfeit currency; **petite** or **menue** ~ small change; **faire de la ~** get some change; **faire de la ~ à qn** give sb some change; **frapper une** ~ strike coins ou a coinage; **ne pas rendre assez de** ~ **à qn** short-change sb; **menue** ~ petty cash; ~ **de banque** bank money; ~ **de base** basic currency; ~ **bloquée** blocked currency; ~ **centrale** centralized money; ~ **en circulation** active money; ~ **composite** composite currency; ~ **dominante** major currency; ~ **d'échange** circulating medium; ~ **électronique** e-cash; ~ **étrangère** foreign currency; ~ **euro** euro cash; ~ **externe** outside money; ~ **fiduciaire** credit money, fiat money US, fiduciary currency; ~ **forte** hard money; ~ **légale** legal tender; ~ **locale** local currency; ~ **marchandise** commodity money; ~ **nationale** national currency; ~ **principale** major currency; ~ **de règlement** settlement currency; ~ **de réserve** reserve currency; ~ **scripturale** bank money; ~ **de singe** (infrml) quasi-money; ~ **surévaluée** overvalued currency; ~ **unique** single currency; ~ **unique européenne** single European currency; ~ **verte** green currency

Monnaie f (Banque) Mint

monoéconomie f monoeconomics

monométalliste adj monometallic

monopole m monopoly; **avoir le quasi-~ du marché** have a stranglehold on the market; ~ **absolu** absolute monopoly; ~ **discriminatoire** discriminating monopoly; ~ **intégral** pure monopoly; ~ **en matière de brevets** patent monopoly; ~ **naturel** natural monopoly; ~ **partagé** shared monopoly, oligopoly; ~ **pur** pure monopoly; ~ **régional** local monopoly; ~ **syndical** closed shop

monopolisation f monopolization

monopoliser vt monopolize

monopoliste adj monopolistic

monorail m (chemin de fer) monorail

monospace m (Transp) multipurpose vehicle

monotone adj monotonous

monoxyde m monoxide; ~ **de carbone** carbon monoxide

Monsieur m (sur une enveloppe, un document) Mr; (en début de lettre) Dear Sir

monsieur tout-le-monde m the man in the street, John Doe AmE

montage m assembly; (Info) set-up; (publicité) paste-up; ~ **financier** financing package; ~ **financier à options multiples** multioption financing facility; ~ **préalable** (publicité) rough

montagne f mountain; ~ **de beurre/ viande** butter/meat mountain

montant m amount; (d'une facture) total amount; **un ~ global** a sum total; **le ~ des pertes/bénéfices** the total losses/profits; **le ~ du budget de la défense** the total defence budget; **le ~ du contrat** the total value of the contract; **pour un ~ de** (chèque, déficit, épargne) to the amount of; (marchandises, propriété) for a total of, amounting to; ~ **de l'adjudication** tender price; ~ **amortissable** depreciable amount; ~ **annuel de la rente** annual annuity amount; ~ **arrondi** round sum; ~ **attribué** designated amount; ~ **des avaries** amount of damage; ~ **de base** basic

amount; ~ **brut** gross amount; ~ **en capital** principal amount; ~ **de la communication téléphonique** call charge; ~ **compensatoire** compensatory amount; ~ **du contrat** contract value; ~ **convenu** agreed sum; ~ **cumulatif des immobilisations admissibles** cumulative eligible capital; ~ **cumulatif imputé** cumulative imputed amount; ~ **à découvert** uncovered amount; ~ **déductible** allowable deduction; ~ **déterminant** threshold amount; ~ **déterminé** specific amount; ~ **différé** deferred amount; ~ **du dommage** amount of damage; ~ **dû** amount due, invoice amount; ~ **échu** amount overdue; ~ **estimatif** estimated amount; ~ **étalé** averaging amount; ~ **éventuel** amount if any; ~ **des gains** earnings amount; ~ **garanti** amount secured; ~ **global** overall amount; ~ **impayé** amount outstanding; ~ **moyen** average amount; ~ **net de l'actif** net asset amount; ~ **net des emprunts** net borrowing; ~ **net des prêts** net lending; ~ **de l'offre** bid value; ~ **payable** amount payable; ~ **payable à terme** amount payable on settlement; ~ **payé par acomptes** amount paid by instalments BrE, amount paid by installments AmE; ~ **à payer** amount to pay; ~ **de redressement pour provision nette** net reserve adjustment amount; ~ **réel** actual amount; ~ **remboursable** amount repayable; ~ **reporté** amount brought forward; ~ **du sinistre** amount of loss; ~ **des sommes versées à la sécurité sociale** (bilan) total social charges; ~ **versé** amount paid out

montée f (Fin) rise; (de coûts, frais) increase; **la ~ du dollar** the rise in the dollar; **la brusque ~ du prix du pétrole** the surge ou sudden rise in oil prices; ~ **des enchères** bidding up; ~ **en flèche** (des prix) boom, jump; ~ **soudaine des dépenses** spending surge; ~ **en spirale** upward spiral

monter 1 vt (affaire, machine, système) set up; (campagne) mount
2 vi (prix) climb, rise; **faire ~** (prix, couts, monnaie) push up, force up; ~ **en flèche** escalate; (activité boursière) shoot up; (prix) soar; ~ **lentement** edge up; ~ **à nouveau** rise again
3 **se monter à** v pron: amount to; (charges, frais) add up to; **se ~ en** (s'équiper) get oneself set up with

montrer 1 vt show; ~ **une hausse des exportations** show a rise in exports
2 **se montrer** v pron **se ~ discret** keep a low profile; **se ~ à la hauteur** be up to scratch (infrml); **se ~ irréductible sur** adhere to, stick to

monument m monument; ~ **classé** listed building UK

moral¹, **e** adj ethical, moral; **personne ~e** (Droit) legal entity

moral² m (du personnel) morale

m

moratoire *m* moratorium (frml)

moratorium *m* moratorium, standstill agreement

morceler *vt* (terrain) break up, parcel up

morcellement *m* (action) (d'héritage, de terrain) dividing up; (résultat) division

morne *adj* (avenir, perspective) bleak

morose *adj* (marché) sluggish; (Bourse) bearish

morosité *f* (du marché) sluggishness

mortalité *f* mortality; ~ **infantile** infant mortality; ~ **présumée** expected mortality

morte-saison *f* off season, slack period

mot *m* word; **avoir son** ~ **à dire dans qch** have a say in sth; ~ **clé** key word; ~**s à la minute** words per minute; ~ **à la mode** buzz word; ~ **d'ordre** watchword; ~ **d'ordre de grève** strike call; ~ **de passe** password; ~ **du président** chairman's brief

moteur *m* engine, motor; (force) driving force; ~ **de croissance** engine of growth; ~ **d'exécution** (Info) runtime software; ~ **d'inférence** (Info) inference engine; ~ **de recherche** search engine

motif *m* (raison) motive; (d'opposition) grounds; (Info) pattern; ~ **de prévention** precautionary motive; ~ **de renvoi** grounds for dismissal; ~ **de résiliation** cause of cancellation

motion *f* motion; ~ **de censure** motion of censure

motivant, e *adj* motivational

motivateur *m* motivator

motivation *f* motivation; ~ **de l'actif** (économie monétaire) asset motive; ~ **d'équipe** team building; ~ **par les prix** price incentive; ~ **par le profit** profit motive

motivé, e *adj* (personne) motivated; (retard, décision) justifiable; ~ **par le profit** profit-motivated

motiver *vt* motivate

mouchard *m* (Info) cookie

mouillage *m* (Transp) (emplacement) anchorage; (manœuvre) anchoring; **être au** ~ lie *ou* ride at anchor

mourir *vi* die; ~ **intestat** die intestate

moutons *m pl* (Bourse) lambs (infrml)

mouvement *m* move, movement; (d'un compte) activity; **être dans le** ~ be in the swim (infrml), be up-to-date; ~**s de l'actif** asset turnover; ~ **anormal** (Bourse) (du cours d'une action, vers le haut ou vers le bas) break-out; ~ **à la baisse** bearish tendency, downward trend; ~ **brusque** sharp movement; ~ **comptable** account turnover; ~ **de compte** account activity; ~ **contraire** (de prix des obligations) adverse movement; ~ **du cours** price move; ~**s des cours** swings; ~**s de l'encaisse** cash flow; ~**s de fonds** flow of funds; ~ **à la hausse** bullish tendency, upward movement; ~ **d'imposition unique** single tax movement; ~ **des marchandises**

movement of freight; ~ **ouvrier** labour movement BrE, labor movement AmE; ~ **du personnel** staff turnover; ~ **planifié** disciplined movement; ~ **populaire** grass-roots movement; ~**s sociaux** industrial action; ~ **de solidarité** solidarity action; ~ **soudain** sharp movement; ~ **des stocks** stock turnover; ~ **syndical** trade union movement UK, labor union movement US; ~ **des taux d'intérêt** interest rate movement; ~**s de trésorerie** cash flow; ~**s de trésorerie annuels** annual cash flow; ~ **de virement automatique** direct deposit transaction Can

moyen¹, -enne *adj* average; **à** ~ **terme** (valeurs, planification) medium-term

moyen² *m* (de procéder, d'action, de production) means; (possibilité) way; (d'investigation, de paiement) method; ~ **audiovisuel** audiovisual aid; ~ **de communication** means of communication; ~ **de communication secrète** back-channel US; ~ **d'échange** medium of exchange; ~ **d'évaluation** yardstick; ~ **de paiement** (Com) means of payment; (Econ) medium of exchange; (Fin) payment device; ~ **de rachat** (Fin) medium of redemption; ~ **de souscription renouvelable** (Assur) revolving underwriting facility; ~ **terme** medium term; ~ **de transport** means of transport BrE, means of transportation AmE

moyennant *prép* for; ~ **un versement initial/20 euros par personne** for a down payment/20 euros a head; ~ **abonnement** on payment of a subscription; ~ **quelques modifications** with a few adjustments; ~ **contrepartie valable** (Droit) for good and valuable consideration

moyenne *f* average, mean; **être inférieur/ supérieur à la** ~ be below/above average; **des résultats faibles par rapport à la** ~ **européenne** poor results against *ou* compared with the European average; **en** ~ on average; **faire une** ~ average out, take an average; **faire une** ~ **à la baisse** average down; **faire une** ~ **à la hausse** average up; ~ **arithmétique** arithmetic mean; ~ **d'un compte** medium of account; ~ **de l'échantillon** sample mean; ~ **générale** general average; ~ **journalière** average equity; ~ **mobile** moving average; ~ **nationale** national average; ~ **pondérée** weighted average; ~ **tous secteurs confondus** all-sector average

moyens *m pl* (ressources financières) means; (soutien, matériel) resources; (compétences) ability; **manquer de** ~ lack the resources; **faute de** ~ through lack of money; **donner à qn les** ~ **de faire qch** give sb the means to do sth; **la ville a mis d'énormes** ~ **à notre disposition** the town put vast resources at our disposal; **avoir les** ~ **d'acheter qch** be able to afford to buy sth; **ne pas être doté de** ~ **de financement suffisants** be

underfunded; **~ d'action promotionnelle**
(publicité) promotional mix; **~ de**
communication means of communication;
~ financiers financial means; **~ légaux**
lawful means; **~ de paiement** means of
payment; **~ de production** means of
production; **~ de trésorerie** financial
means

moyeu *m* (Transp) hub

MP *abrév* (▸**mandat postal**) PO (postal
order) BrE, MO (money order) AmE

MTC *abrév* (▸**mécanisme de taux de**
change) ERM (exchange rate mechanism)

multicanaux *m pl* (Info) (stratégie,
distribution) multi-channel

multidevise *f* (Fin) multicurrency

multi-fonction *adj* multipurpose

multijuridictionnel, -elle *adj*
multijurisdictional

multilatéral, e *adj* multilateral

multimédia *adj* multimedia

multinationale *f* multinational company

multiple *adj* multiple

multiplet *m* byte

multiplicateur *m* multiplier; **~ de crédit**
credit multiplier, credit scoring; **~ de**
l'emploi employment multiplier; **~ des**
réserves bancaires deposit multiplier

multiplier ① *vt* (chiffres) multiply; (risques,
gains, rendement) increase; **~ les bénéfices par**
cinq/par cent increase profits fivefold/a
hundredfold; **~ les risques d'accident** make
the risk of accidents more likely

② **se multiplier** *v pron* (succursales) grow in
number; (difficultés, obstacles) increase

multipostage *m* bus mailing; **~ abusif**
spam, spamming

multiprocesseur *m* multiprocessor

multiprogrammation *f*
multiprogramming

multipropriété *f* time share, time sharing;
acheter un appartement en ~ buy a time-
share property

multiracial, e *adj* multiracial

multirisque *adj* (police d'assurance automobile)
comprehensive

multi-route *adj* multiroute

multistandard *adj* (Info) multistandard

multitraitement *m* (Info) multiprocessing

multi-utilisateur, -trice *m* multiuser

municipal, e *adj* (impôt, arrêté) local; (parc,
piscine) municipal; **conseil ~** (de petite ville)
town council; (de grande ville) city council

municipalité *f* (conseil) local council, local
government; (ville) municipality

mur *m* wall; **~ mitoyen** party wall

musique *f* music; **~ en vol** in-flight music

mutation *f* transfer; **~ de personnel** staff
transfer; **~ des structures** organizational
change

muter *vt* (un fonctionnaire) transfer

mutuelle *f* (Assur) mutual insurance
company

mystique *f* mystique

Nn

n *abrév* (▸**nominal**) n. (nominal)

N/A *abrév* (▸**numérique-analogique**) (Info)
D/A (digital-analog)

nantir *vt* (Droit) (emprunt) secure; (créancier)
give security; (bien, valeurs) pledge; **~ qn de**
provide sb with; (titre, pouvoirs) award to sb

nantissement *m* pledging (**sur** of); (Droit)
collateral security; **détenir en ~** hold in
pledge; **donner un bien en ~** supply
collateral; **~ pour acompte** security bond
for down payment; **~ de crédit** perfected
security; **~ hypothécaire** mortgage lien; **~**
de prêt lending securities; **~ d'un prêt par**
titres rehypothecation

nappe *f* (de mazout) slick; **~**
d'hydrocarbures/de pétrole hydrocarbon/
oil slick

narcodollars *m pl* narcodollars

NAS *abrév* (▸**numéro d'assurance**
sociale) SIN (social insurance number)

nat. *abrév* (▸**national**) nat. (national)

natif, -ive *m,f* native

nation *f* nation; **~ industrialisée**
industrial nation; **~ la plus favorisée**
most-favoured nation BrE, most-favored
nation AmE; **Nations Unies** United
Nations

national, e *adj* (produit, dette) national;
(marché) domestic; (grève, campagne) national,
nationwide

nationalisation *f* nationalization

nationaliser *vt* nationalize; **être**
nationalisé come under public ownership, be
nationalized

nature *f* nature; **en ~** (paiement) in kind; **~**
baissière (du marché) bearishness; **~ d'un** ···⊱

call call feature; **~ haussière** (du marché) bullishness; **~ de l'invention** nature of the invention; **~ des obligations** bond features

naufrage *m* shipwreck; **faire ~** (navire) be wrecked; (entreprise) collapse; **le ~ de l'économie** the collapse of the economy

navette *f* (vol) shuttle; (autobus) (bus) shuttle; **faire la ~** commute; **~ spatiale** space shuttle

navetteur, -euse *m,f* Bel commuter

navigabilité *f* (de bateau) seaworthiness; (d'avion) airworthiness

navigateur *m* (Info) browser

navigation *f* navigation; (trafic sur l'eau) shipping, navigation; (Info) browsing; **~ fluviale** river navigation; **~ sur lest** ballast sailing; **~ à vue** (Transp) window-guidance; (aviation) visual flight rules

naviguer *vi* (bateau) sail; (Info) browse; **en état de ~** seaworthy; **~ sur Internet** surf the Internet

navire *m* ship, vessel; **par ~** (Assur, Transp) any one bottom, any one vessel; **~ d'apport** feeder vessel; **~ charbonnier** coal carrier; **~ de charge** freighter; **~ collecteur** feeder vessel; **~ de commerce** merchant ship; **~ couvert** arrived ship; **~ dépollueur** oil clearance vessel; **~ à deux classes** two-class vessel; **~ de divers** general trader; **~ de forte stabilité** stiff vessel; **~ frigorifique** refrigerated ship; **~s inemployés** idle shipping; **~ inférieur aux normes** substandard ship; **~ de ligne** liner; **~ long-courrier** ocean-going vessel; **~ à manutention horizontale et verticale** roll on/roll off-lift on/lift off ship; **~ marchand** merchant ship, trading vessel; **~ sous pavillon national** flagship; **~ sous pavillon tiers** third flag carrier; **~ pétrolier** crude carrier; **~ polyvalent** multipurpose vessel; **~ porte-conteneurs** container ship; **~ roulier** roll-on-roll-off ship, ro-ro; **~ transbordeur** ferry boat; **~ de transport** freighter; **~ à vapeur** steamer, steamship

navire-citerne *m* tanker

navire-usine *m* factory ship

n° *abrév* (▸**numéro**) no. (number)

nécessaire *adj* necessary

nécessité *f* necessity; **de première ~** vital; **par ~** out of necessity; **~ urgente/ impérieuse** urgent/pressing need; **la ~ de faire** the need to do; **~s économiques/de gestion** economic/management demands; **~ de couverture** margin requirements

nécessiter *vt* necessitate, require

nécessiteux *m pl*: **les ~** the needy

négatif, -ive *adj* (non positif) negative; (néfaste) negative, adverse

négativement *adv* negatively

négligé, e *adj* (travail) careless, sloppy

négligemment *adv* negligently

négligence *f* (Droit) negligence; **par ~** through negligence; **douce ~** benign neglect; **~ coupable** criminal negligence; **~ professionnelle** professional negligence

négligent, e *adj* (travailleur) negligent, careless

négliger *vt* (travail, affaires) neglect; **~ de faire qch** omit to do sth

négoce *m* trading, trade; **faire du ~ avec** trade with; **~ d'entrée et sortie** (Bourse) in and out trading (jarg); **~ du frigorifique** reefer trade; **~ marginal** (Bourse) margin trading; **~ de titres sauvegardés** (Bourse) hedge trading; **~ du vin** wine trade

négociabilité *f* (Bourse) marketability, negotiability

négociable *adj* negotiable; (titres) marketable; **non ~** non-negotiable **~ en banque** bankable

négociant, e *m,f* dealer; (sur une grande échelle) wholesaler, wholesale dealer; (Bourse) trader; **~ en bloc de titres** block positioner; **~ exportateur** export merchant; **~ en laine** wool merchant; **~ en titres** dealer in securities, market maker; **~ en titres agréé** authorized dealer; **~ en valeurs** trader in securities; **~ en valeurs mobilières** investment dealer; **~ en vins** wine merchant

négociant-courtier *m* broker-dealer; **~ de parquet** floor trader

négociateur, -trice *m,f* negotiator; (Bourse) trader; **~ agréé** registered competitive trader; **~ de blocs d'actions** block stock trader; **~ individuel de parquet** floor trader; **~ d'obligations** bond trader; **~ d'options agréé** registered options trader; **~ de positions à long terme** position trader; **~ sur rompus de titres** odd-lot dealer; **~ unique** sole bargaining agent UK; **~ en valeurs mobilières** broker

négociation *f* (principe) bargaining, negotiation; (pourparlers) negotiations; **entrer en ~s** enter into negotiations; **la table de ~** the negotiating table; **~s avant l'ouverture** (Bourse) before-hours dealings; **~ d'actions** equity trading; **~ assistée par ordinateur** programme trading BrE, program trading AmE; **~ bidon** (jarg) blue-sky bargaining; **~ de blocs d'actions** (Bourse) volume trading; **~ par branche** company bargaining; **~ collective** collective bargaining; **~ collective sur le lieu de travail** workplace bargaining; **~s commerciales** trade talks; **~ continue** (Bourse) all-day trading; **~ des contrats de productivité** productivity bargaining; **~ à un cours inférieur** (Bourse) downtick, minus tick; **~ à un cours supérieur** (Bourse) plus tick, uptick; **~ individuelle** individual bargaining; **~ modèle** pattern bargaining (jarg); **~ d'obligations** (Bourse) bond trading; **~s**

paritaires joint negotiation; ~ **à plusieurs employeurs** multiemployer bargaining; ~**s salariales** wage talks; ~**s serrées** hard bargaining; ~ **à un seul niveau** single table bargaining UK; ~ **à terme** dealing for the settlement, dealing for the account; ~ **par tranches** fragmented bargaining

négocier ⟨1⟩ *vt* (emprunt, salaire, prix) negotiate (**avec** with); ~ **en bourse** deal; ~ **en position de force** negotiate from a position of strength; ~ **pour le compte de** trade under the name of; **négocié massivement** (Bourse) heavily traded ⟨2⟩ **se négocier** *v pron* be negotiated; **se** ~ **à** trade at

néo-capitalisme *m* late capitalism

néo-corporatisme *m* neo-corporatism

néo-fédéralisme *m* new federalism

nerveux, -euse *adj* (marché) nervous, jumpy

net¹, nette *adj* (changement, recul) marked; (baisse) sharp; (situation) clear-cut; (prix) net, all-inclusive; (après déductions) net; **prix/salaire** ~ net price/salary; **augmentation/perte nette** net increase/loss; ~ **d'impôt** net of tax; **créations nettes d'emplois** net job creation; **immigration nette** net immigration

net² *m* (Compta, Fin) (revenu) net income; (bénéfices) net earnings; **augmentation de 2% en** ~ net 2% increase; ~ **à payer** (fiche de paie) net payable

Net *m* (Info) **le** ~ the Net

netéconomie *f* (Info) neteconomy, e-economy

nétiquette *f* (Info) (sur Internet) netiquette

nettement *adv* (augmenter, se détériorer) markedly, significantly; (dire) clearly; (refuser) flatly

nettoyer *vt* clean up

neuf, neuve *adj* new; **tout** ~ brand-new; **'état ~'** 'as new'; **refaire à** ~ renovate completely

neurone *m* neurone; ~ **artificiel** (Info) artificial neurone

neutraliser *vt* cancel out, counteract

neutralité *f* neutrality; ~ **monétaire** neutrality of money

neutre *adj* neutral; **de** ~ **à baissier** (Bourse) neutral to bearish; **de** ~ **à haussier** (Bourse) neutral to bullish

NF *abrév* (▸**norme française**) French manufacturing standard

niche *f* market niche, niche; ~ **écologique** ecological niche; ~ **fiscale** (tax) loophole

nier *vt* (fait, signature) deny; (dette) repudiate

NIP *abrév* (▸**numéro d'identification personnel**) PIN (personal identification number); (Bourse) (▸**négociateur individuel de parquet**) floor trader, local (jarg)

niveau *m* level; (compétence) standard; **à un** ~ **record** record-high; **au** ~ **international** at international level, internationally; **au** ~ **régional** at regional level, regionally; **être au**

~ be up to standard; ~ **d'acidité** (pollution) acidity level; ~ **d'activité** activity ratio; ~ **d'aptitude** ability level; ~ **budgétaire** budget level; ~ **cadre** executive grade; ~ **de commandes** (V&M) level of orders; ~ **de concurrence réalisable** workable competition; ~ **de confiance** confidence level; ~ **de dépenses** level of expenditure; ~ **effectif du chômage** actual level of unemployment; ~ **des effectifs** manning levels, staffing levels; ~ **élevé** high standards; ~ **de fluctuation** degree of fluctuation; ~ **historique** all-time high; ~ **de l'indice des prix** price index level; ~ **d'investissement** level of investment; ~ **locatif** rental level; ~ **de marge initiale** initial margin level; ~ **maximum** peak level; ~ **de négociation** bargaining level; ~ **de notoriété** (V&M) awareness level; ~ **d'occupation** occupancy level; ~ **de prix** price level; ~ **de prix relatifs** relative price level; ~ **de qualification** ability level; ~ **record** all-time high, peak level; ~ **de risque** degree of risk; ~ **des salaires** wage level; ~ **sans précédent** all-time high; ~ **seuil** threshold level; ~ **sonore** noise level; ~ **de soutien** level of support; ~ **tarifaire** tariff level; ~ **de vie** standard of living; ~ **de vie bas** low standard of living; ~ **de vie élevé** high standard of living

nivellement *m* (des prix, des salaires) levelling out BrE, leveling out AmE; ~ **par le bas/haut** levelling down/up BrE

nocturne *f* (de magasin) late-night opening; ~ **le vendredi** late opening Friday

nœud *m* (Info) node

noir *m* black; **au** ~ (acheter, vendre) on the black market; (réparation, travaux) on the side; **travailler au** ~ moonlight, work on the side

nolisement *m* (navire, avion) chartering

noliser *vt* (navire, avion) charter

nom *m* name; **au** ~ **de** on behalf of; ~ **et adresse** name and address; **exercer sous le** ~ **de** do business as; ~ **de code** code name; ~ **commercial** trading name; ~ **d'un compte** title of an account; ~ **de document** document name; ~ **de domaine** domain name; ~ **d'emprunt** nominee name; ~ **d'hôte** (Info) host name; ~ **et prénoms** full name; ~ **de l'intermédiaire** nominee name; ~ **légal** legal name; ~ **de marque** brand name, household name; ~ **patronymique** surname; ~ **d'utilisateur** username

nombre *m* number; **en** ~ **pair** even-numbered; ~ **moyen d'exemplaires vendus** average number of copies sold; **le** ~ **croissant/décroissant** the increasing/decreasing number; ~ **d'actions émises** number of shares issued; ~ **de chômeurs en données non corrigées des variations saisonnières** seasonally unadjusted employment figures; ~ **entier** ⋯⋗

natural number; ∼ **indice** index number; ∼ **de lignes par page** page length; ∼ **de lignes d'une petite annonce** linage, lineage; ∼ **de salariés** number of employees

nomenclature *f* (des composants et des matières premières) bill of materials; (Info) nomenclature

nominal, e *adj* nominal

nominatif, -ive *adj* nominal; (action, titre) registered

nomination *f* (à un poste) appointment; ∼ **à la tête de** appointment as head of; **obtenir sa** ∼ be appointed

nommé, e *adj* designated; (à un poste) appointed

nommer *vt* designate; (à un poste) appoint

non-acceptation *f* (de titre) nonacceptance, dishonour

non-accepté, e *adj* unaccepted

non-adhésion *f* nonmembership

non-assujetti, e *adj* ∼ **à l'impôt** nontaxable; ∼ **à la TVA** zero-rated

non-bancable *adj* unbankable; (Assur) not negotiable

non-comparution *f* (Droit) nonappearance

non-comptabilisé, e *adj* off the books

non-concordance *f* (Compta) mismatch

non-confirmé, e *adj* (information, source) unconfirmed

non-conformité *f* (Droit) nonconformity

non-cumulatif, -ive *adj* (Bourse) noncumulative

non-divulgation *f* (Assur) nondisclosure; (Droit) concealment

non-élasticité *f*: ∼ **des prix** price inelasticity

non-exécution *f* nonfulfilment BrE, nonperformance, nonfulfillment AmE; ∼ **du contrat** nonfulfilment of contract BrE

non-fumeur *m* nonsmoker

non-garanti, e *adj* (Banque) unsecured

non-imposable *adj* nontaxable

non-imposé, e *adj* unassessed

non-inscrit¹, e *adj*: ∼ **à la cote** unlisted, unquoted

non-inscrit², e *m,f* (Fisc) unregistered person; (Pol) Independent

non-intervention *f* nonintervention

non-jouissance *f* absence of rights of owner

non-lieu *m* (Droit) dismissal (*of a charge*); **rendre un** ∼ dismiss a case for lack of evidence

non-livraison *f* failure to deliver

non-marketing *m* (publicité) demarketing

non-membre *m* nonmember

nonobstant *adv, prép* notwithstanding; ∼ **les autres dispositions** notwithstanding any other provision

non-paiement *m* nonpayment

non-remboursement *m* default

non-remplacement *m*: ∼ **des départs** (Econ, Ind) natural wastage

non-résident, e *m,f* nonresident

non-résiliation *f* (Droit) nonforfeiture

non-respect *m*: ∼ **de** (clause, accord) failure to comply with; ∼ **des conditions** nonobservance of conditions; ∼ **du contrat** nonfulfilment of contract BrE, nonfulfillment of contract AmE

non-responsabilité *f* (Droit) nonliability

non-ressortissant *m*: ∼ **de l'UE** non-EU national

non-vérification *f* (Compta) nonaudit

normalisation *f* (régularisation) normalization; (standardisation) standardization; ∼ **comptable** accounting standard setting; ∼ **quantitative** (Econ) variety reduction

normalisé, e *adj* standardized

normaliser *vt* (régulariser) normalize; (standardiser) standardize

normalité *f* normality BrE, normalcy AmE

normatif, -ive *adj* normative, prescriptive

norme *f* norm; (Droit, Info) standard; **être/ rester dans la** ∼ be/remain within the norm; **s'écarter de la** ∼ deviate from the norm; **revenir à la** ∼ return to normal; ∼ **AFNOR** *standard set by the French national standards authority*; ∼s **d'audit** audit standards, auditing standards; ∼s **commerciales** trading standards; ∼s **comptables** accounting standards, accounting conventions; ∼s **de déversement** dumping standards; ∼ **écologique** environmental standard; ∼ **d'émission** emission standard; ∼s **d'exploitation** licensing standards; ∼ **d'hygiène** hygiene standard; ∼ **industrielle** industry standard; ∼ **opérationnelle d'audit** Auditor's Operational Standard; ∼ **de prix de revient** cost standard; ∼ **de production** production standard; ∼ **d'un produit** product standard; ∼ **de pureté de l'air** ambient standard US; ∼s **de qualité** quality standards; ∼s **de qualité de l'environnement** environmental quality standards; ∼ **de rendement** performance standard; ∼s **de sécurité** safety standards; ∼s **techniques** technical standards

nos *abrév* (**numéros**) nos. (numbers)

notaire *m* lawyer, notary public, solicitor BrE

notation *f* (Bourse) rating; (Fin) rating; ∼ **exponentielle** exponential notation; ∼ **de la main-d'œuvre** workforce rating; ∼ **des résultats** performance rating; ∼ **d'une valeur** security rating

note *f* (facture) bill, check AmE; (évaluation) mark, grade; ∼ **d'hôtel/de restaurant** hotel/ restaurant bill; **payer** *or* **régler une** ∼ pay a bill *ou* check AmE; ∼ **en bas de page** footnote; ∼ **de chargement** (maritime) shipping note; ∼ **de couverture** (Assur) cover note UK, binder US; ∼ **de crédit** (Fin) credit note; ∼ **de débit** (Banque) debit memorandum US, debit note; ∼ **de frais** expense account; ∼ **d'honoraires** bill; ∼ **en marge** marginal note, side note; ∼ **de réservation de fret** (maritime) booking note; ∼ **de service** memo, memorandum

notice *f* (mode d'emploi) instructions; (exposé) note; ∼ **d'emballage** packing instruction; ∼ **d'entretien** service manual; ∼ **explicative** instructions, instruction leaflet; ∼ **de montage** assembly instructions

notification *f* notification; (Droit) notice; **avoir** *or* **recevoir** ∼ **de** be notified of; ∼ **d'exercice** (Bourse) exercise notice; ∼ **requise par la loi** legal notice

notifier *vt* notify; ∼ **qch à qn** notify sb of sth; (Droit) give sb notice of sth; **être notifié à qn** be made known to sb

notion *f* notion; ∼s (de science, langue) basic knowledge; **avoir des** ∼s **de** have a basic knowledge of

notoriété *f* (de produit) fame; (de personne) fame; ∼ **de la marque** (V&M) brand awareness, brand recognition; ∼ **d'un produit** (V&M) product awareness

notre *adj* our; ∼ **propre marque** our own make; ∼ **référence** our reference

nouveau, -elle *adj* new; ∼x **clients** new business; **de** ∼ once more; **nouvelles activités** new business; **nouvel affrètement** (maritime) new charter; **nouvel an** New Year; **nouvelle autorité de placement** New Investment Authority; **nouvel aval** re-endorsement; **nouvelle charte-partie** (maritime) new charter; **nouvelle cotisation** reassessment; **nouvelle droite** New Right; **nouvelle économie** new economy; **nouvelle édition** new edition; **nouvelle émission** new issue; **nouvel examen** re-examination; **nouvel examen d'une cotisation** reconsideration of an assessment; **nouvelle flambée des prix** resurgence in prices; **nouvelle inscription hypothécaire** rehypothecation; **nouvelle loi** new law; **nouvelle microéconomie** new microeconomics; **nouvelle offre** retendering; **nouvel ordre mondial** new world order; **nouvelle récolte** new crop; **nouvelles technologies** new technology; **nouvelles technologies de l'information et de la communication** new information and communications technologies

nouveauté *f* (originalité) novelty; (nouvelle idée) breakthrough, innovation; (objet nouveau) new product; (appareil, voiture) new model; ∼s fancy goods; ∼s **d'automne** (mode) autumn fashions

nouvelle *f* piece of news; ∼s news

nouvellement *adv* (publié) recently; (bâti) newly; ∼ **élu** newly-elected

novateur¹, -trice *adj* innovative

novateur², -trice *m,f* innovator

novation *f* novation

novice *mf* novice; **être un** ∼ be wet behind the ears (infrml)

noyau *m* (commerce international) hardcore; (Info) kernel; ∼ **dur** (groupe) hard core

n/réf *abrév* (▶**notre référence**) our ref. (our reference)

NTIC *abrév* (▶**nouvelles technologies de l'information et de la communication**) new information and communications technologies

nu, e *adj* (mur, pièce) bare

nuancer *vt* (vision des choses) modify; (avis) qualify; (propos) moderate; ∼ **son jugement** moderate one's stance

nucléaire *adj* nuclear

nue-propriété *f* (Droit) bare ownership

nuisance *f* nuisance; ∼s **acoustiques** noise pollution

nuisible *adj* (influence, effet) harmful; (déchets) dangerous; ∼ **à** detrimental to, harmful to; **non** ∼ **à l'environnement** environmentally-friendly

nuit *f* night; **d'une** ∼ (séjour) overnight

nul¹, nulle *adj* (Droit) null; ∼ **et non avenu** (Droit) null and void; **le contrat est** ∼ **en cas de fausse déclaration** the contract is void in the case of a false declaration

nul², nulle *pron* no one; ∼ **n'est censé ignorer la loi** ignorance of the law is no excuse

nullité *f* (Droit) nullity; **frapper de** ∼ render null and void

numération *f* number facts; ∼ **décimale** decimal notation

numérique *adj* (Info) (enregistrement, lecture, appareil photo) digital; (données, commande) numerical

numérique-analogique *adj* digital-analog

numérisation *f* (Info) digitization

numériser *vt* (Info) digitize

numériseur *m* scanner, digitizer

numéro *m* (nombre) number; (presse) issue; ∼ **d'abonné** customer's number; ∼ **d'annonce** (presse) box number; ∼ **antérieur** (édition) back issue; ∼ **d'appel** telephone number; ∼ **d'assurance sociale** social insurance number; ∼ **d'autorisation** authorization code; ∼ **de commande** order number; ∼ **de compte** account number; ∼ **de compte de versements** remittance account number; ∼ **couplé** (presse) combined issue; ∼ **d'enregistrement** registration number; ∼ **gratuit** Freefone number BrE, toll-free number AmE; ∼ **d'identification** ID number, identification number; ∼ **d'identification en code barres** bar-coded identification number; ∼ **d'identification personnel** personal identification number; ∼ **d'immatriculation** number plate BrE, license plate; ~ **d'inscription douanière** customs registered number; ~ **d'inscription à la TVA** VAT registration number UK; ~ **d'interclassement** collator number; ~ **intra** intra number; ~ **de licence d'exportation** export licence number BrE, export license number AmE; ~ **d'obligation** bond number; ~ **d'ordre** (Info) sequence number; ~ **de page** page number; ~ **de porte** (aéroport) gate number; ~ **de référence** reference number, reference; (presse) box number, reference number; ~ **de référence unique** unique reference number;

~ **de série** serial number; ~ **de succursale** branch number; ~ **de téléphone** telephone number; ~ **de train** train number; ~ **un mondial** world leader; ~ **UN** (Transp) UN number; ~ **vert** Freefone number BrE, toll-free number AmE; ~ **d'urgence** (Info) hotline; ~ **de vol** flight number

numérotation f numbering

numéroter vt number; ~ **consécutivement** number consecutively

nu-propriétaire m (Droit) bare owner

Oo

OAT abrév (▶**obligation assimilable du Trésor**) French government bond, French treasury bond

obéir vti ~ **à** obey; ~ **à une décision** comply with a decision

objecter vi object; ~ **à qn que** object to sb that

objectif¹, -ive adj impartial, objective; **vous n'êtes pas** ~ you're not being objective

objectif² m aim, goal; (Econ) (des entreprises) objective, target; **se donner qch pour** ~ set oneself something as an objective; **l'**~ **est double** there are two objectives; **nous avons pour** ~ **de faire** our objective is to do; ~ **d'arbitrage** hedging goal; ~**s d'une campagne publicitaire** advertising programme objectives BrE, advertising program objectives AmE; ~ **commercial** sales objective; ~ **à court terme** short-term objective; ~ **de couverture** hedging goal; ~ **de l'entreprise** company objective; ~ **immédiat** immediate aim; ~ **à long terme** long-term objective; ~ **de marché** market aim; ~ **de performance** performance target; ~ **de placement** investment objective; ~ **de production** production target; ~ **professionnel** career goal; ~ **de profit** profit target; ~ **de recherche** research objective; ~ **de vente** sales target

objection f objection; ~ **admise** (Droit) objection sustained; ~ **rejetée** (Droit) objection overruled; **faire une** ~ make an objection; **soulever des** ~**s** raise objections

objectivité f objectivity; **en toute** ~ objectively; (être jugé) on one's/its merits

objet m (chose) object; (but) aim, object; (d'un accord, d'un contrat, d'une réunion) subject; (d'une enquête) subject, focus; (d'une société) purpose; (en haut d'une lettre, d'un email) subject, re; **faire l'**~ **de** (enquête, critique) be the subject of;

(poursuite, lutte) be the object of; ~ **de collection** collectible; ~**s personnels** personal possessions; (Admin) personal effects; ~**s de valeur** valuables

obligataire¹ adj (marché, émission, rendement) bond

obligataire² mf (Bourse) bondholder; (Droit) obligee

obligation f (professionnelle) obligation, responsibility; (Fin, Bourse) bond, debenture; (Droit) obligation, binding agreement; **satisfaire à ses** ~**s** fulfil one's obligations ou duties; **manquer à ses** ~**s** fail in one's responsibilities; **sans** ~ **d'achat** with no obligation to buy; **avec** ~ **d'achat** with the obligation to buy; **sans** ~ **de votre part** with no obligation; **avoir des** ~**s envers qn** feel an obligation toward(s) sb; **contracter une** ~ **envers qn** (Droit) contract an obligation toward(s) sb; **s'acquitter d'une** ~ meet an obligation; **être dans l'**~ **de faire qch** be obliged to do sth; **être dans l'**~ **légale de** be under a legal obligation to;

⌐ **obligation a...** ⌐ ~ **d'acceptation** (Banque) acceptance duty; ~ **d'adaptation** (propriété intellectuelle) must match; ~ **alimentaire** (Droit) maintenance obligation; ~ **amortissable** callable bond, redeemable debenture; ~ **à un an** one year government bond, yearling BrE; ~ **assimilable du Trésor** French government bond; ~ **d'assurance** compulsory insurance; ~ **au-dessous du pair** discount bond; ~ **autorisée** authorized bond;

⌐ **b...** ⌐ ~ **bancaire** bank bond; ~ **à bon de souscription** bond with warrant; ~ **à bons de souscription en actions** bond cum warrant; ~ **à bons de souscription en actions rachetables** bond with redeemable share warrant; ~ **à bons de souscription d'obligations** bond with bond-buying warrant;

c... ~ **en circulation** bond outstanding; ~ **conditionnelle** contingent obligation; ~ **conjointe** joint bond; ~ **conjointe et solidaire** joint and several obligation; ~ **contractuelle** contractual obligation, contractual liability; ~ **contrôlée** managed bond; ~ **de conversion** redemption bond; ~ **convertible à bons de souscription en actions** convertible bond with share warrant; ~ **convertible à prime élevée** high-premium convertible debenture; ~ **à coupon zéro** zero-coupon bond; ~ **à coupons** coupon bond; ~ **à cours non limité** unlimited tax bond;

d... ~ **sur demande** on demand bond; ~ **démembrée** stripped bond, strip; ~ **de deuxième rang** second debenture; ~ **de développement industriel** industrial development bond; ~ **pour le développement de la petite entreprise** small business development bond;

e... ~ **à échéance** drawn bond; ~ **à échéance prorogeable** extendible bond; ~ **échéant par tranches** serial bond; ~ **émise au pair** parity bond; ~ **émise par une société privée** corporate bond; ~ **encaissable par anticipation** retractable bond; ~ **essentiellement nominative** fully registered bond; ~ **d'État** ≈gilt UK, government bond, state bond; ~ **en eurodollars** Eurodollar bond; ~ **éventuelle** contingent liabilities;

f... ~ **fiscale** tax liability;

g... ~ **garantie** secured debenture, warranty bond; ~ **de garantie** retention bond, salvage bond; ~ **garantie pour acompte** security bond for down payment; ~ **garantie par nantissement de titres** collateral trust bond;

h... ~ **à haut risque** junk bond; ~ **hypothécaire** mortgage bond;

i... ~ **immatriculée** registered bond; ~ **immobilière** property bond; ~ **implicite** implied obligation; ~ **indexée** indexed bond; ~ **d'information** disclosure requirement; ~ **à intérêt différé** deferred interest bond; ~ **à intérêt élevé** full coupon bond; ~ **à intérêts composés** compound interest bond;

j... ~ **juridique** legal obligation, perfect obligation;

l... ~ **légale** legal obligation; ~ **de limiter le dommage** mitigation of damages; ~ **à long terme émise par une collectivité** utility revenue bond; ~ **à lots** prize bond, Premium Bond UK;

m... ~ **à maturité courte** short coupon; ~ **morale** (Droit) imperfect obligation;

n... ~ **nantie** collateral trust bond; ~ **ne portant pas d'intérêt** passive bond; ~ **négociable** marketable bond; ~ **négociée bien en dessous du pair** deep discount

bond; ~ **nominative** registered bond; ~ **nominative à coupons** coupon registered bond; ~ **non convertible** straight bond; ~ **non-garantie** debenture, unsecured bond; ~ **non remboursable** noncallable bond;

o... ~ **officielle** public engagement;

p... ~ **de pacotille** junk bond; ~ **de paiement** payment commitment; ~ **à paiement anticipé** advance payment bond; ~ **participante** dividend bond, participating bond, profit-sharing bond; ~ **perpétuelle** perpetual bond; ~ **peu active** inactive bond; ~ **au porteur** bearer bond, bearer debenture; ~ **pourrie** junk bond; ~ **de premier ordre** high-grade bond; ~ **prévue par la loi** statutory obligation; ~ **à primes** premium bond; ~ **prioritaire** prior-lien bond; ~ **provisoire** provisional bond;

r... ~ **redditionnelle** accountability; ~ **remboursable** redeemable bond, redeemed debenture; ~ **remboursable au pair** par bond; ~ **remboursable à périodes déterminées** put bond; ~ **de rente** annuity bond; ~ **de réserve** confidentiality agreement; ~ **à revenu variable** variable rate income bond, variable rate income debenture; ~ **à revenu fixe** fixed rate bond;

s... ~ **sans bon de souscription** bond ex warrant; ~ **de société** corporate bond, corporate debenture; ~ **solidaire** joint liability; ~ **sous-jacente** underlying bond; ~ **sous-option** underlying bond; ~ **statutaire** statutory obligation; ~ **subordonnée** subordinated debenture;

t... ~ **à taux variable** floating-rate debenture; ~ **du Trésor** T-bond, Treasury bond;

v... ~ **vendue au-dessous du pair à l'émission** original issue discount bond; ~ **vendue avant l'émission** bond sold prior to issue

obligatoire *adj* compulsory, obligatory; (Droit) mandatory; (décision) binding

obligé, e *m,f* (Droit) obligor

obliger *vt* oblige; (Droit) bind; ~ **qn à faire qch** force sb to do sth; **être obligé de faire qch** to be obliged to do sth; (Droit) be bound to do sth; **un contrat oblige toutes les parties signataires** a contract is binding on all parties

OBSA *abrév* (►**obligation à bons de souscription en actions**) bond cum warrant

OBSAR *abrév* (►**obligation à bons de souscription en actions rachetables**) *bond with redeemable share warrants*

observateur, -trice *m,f* observer

observation *f* (remarque) comment, observation; (d'une règle, d'une politique) observance; **faire des ~s sur qch** comment on sth; ~ **fiscale** tax compliance; ~ **volontaire** voluntary compliance

observer *vt* remark; (loi) observe

OBSO *abrév* (▶**obligation à bons de souscription d'obligations**) bond with bond-buying warrant

obsolescence *f* obsolescence; ∼ **économique** economic obsolescence; ∼ **fonctionnelle** functional obsolescence; ∼ **programmée** (Ind, V&M) built-in obsolescence, planned obsolescence

obsolète *adj* obsolete

obstacle *m* obstacle; **contourner l'**∼ get around the obstacle; **se heurter à un** ∼ come up against an obstacle; **faire** ∼ **aux négociations/au développement** obstruct the negotiations/the development; ∼ **à la communication** communication barrier

obtenir *vt* (autorisation, consentement) get, obtain; (emploi) get; (total, somme) get, arrive at; (résultat) achieve; ∼ **la communication avec qn** get through to sb; ∼ **frauduleusement** obtain by fraud; ∼ **l'accord officiel de** gain formal approval from; ∼ **l'approbation de** have the approval of; ∼ **une augmentation de salaire** get a pay rise; ∼ **de bons résultats** get good results; ∼ **gain de cause** get justice; ∼ **une majorité sur** outvote; ∼ **de nouvelles commandes** secure new orders; ∼ **la permission par écrit** obtain permission in writing; ∼ **un prêt** take out a loan; ∼ **une réponse** get an answer; ∼ **son diplôme** qualify, graduate

obtention *f* (d'une autorisation) getting, obtaining; (de résultats) achievement; (d'un contrat) securing

OCBSA *abrév* (▶**obligation convertible à bons de souscription en actions**) *convertible bond with share warrant*

occasion *f* (objet usagé) secondhand buy, secondhand item; (bonne affaire) bargain; (chance) occasion, opportunity; **avoir l'**∼ **de** have the opportunity to; **donner à qn l'**∼ **de** give sb the opportunity to; **si l'**∼ **se présente** should the occasion arise; **le marché de l'**∼ the secondhand market; **acheter d'**∼ buy secondhand; ∼ **d'investissement** investment opportunity

occasionnel, -elle *adj* occasional; **de façon occasionnelle** occasionally

occasionner *vt* cause

occidentaliser ⓵ *vt* westernize ⓶ **s'occidentaliser** *v pron* become westernized

occulte *adj* secret, hidden; **réserves** ∼**s** slush fund, secret fund

occupant, e *m,f* (de maison) occupant, occupier

occupation *f* (de lieu) occupancy; (emploi) job, occupation; **grève avec** ∼ **des locaux** sit-down strike; **taux d'**∼ occupancy rate; ∼**s professionnelles** professional activities; ∼ **commerciale** commercial occupancy; ∼ **industrielle** industrial occupancy; ∼ **par le propriétaire** owner occupation; ∼ **des sols** (niveau local) land use

occupé, e *adj* (personne, vie) busy; (ligne téléphonique) engaged BrE, busy; (Info) busy; **être** ∼ **à faire** be engaged in doing; **ça sonne** ∼ it's busy *ou* engaged BrE; **'toutes nos lignes sont occupées, veuillez patienter'** 'all our lines are busy, please hold'

occuper ⓵ *vt* (espace) occupy; (exercer) (emploi) have; (poste, fonctions) have, hold; (employer) employ; ∼ **la sixième place du classement** be sixth in the ranking; **ceux qui occupent des emplois précaires** those who have no job security; ∼ **un créneau dans le marché** fill a gap in the market; ∼ **le devant de la scène** hold centre stage
⓶ **s'occuper de** *v pron* (affaire) run; (magasin) attend to; (projet) be in charge of; (d'une tâche) be engaged in; (clientèle) deal with

OCDE *abrév* (▶**Organisation de coopération et de développement économique**) OECD (Organization for Economic Cooperation and Development)

octet *m* byte

octroi *m* grant; ∼ **de crédit** granting of credit; ∼ **de dommages-intérêts** awarding of damages; ∼ **d'un emprunt** borrowing allocation; ∼ **de licence** licensing; ∼ **de subventions** subsidization

octroyer *vt* award, grant

ODPE *abrév* (▶**obligation pour le développement de la petite entreprise**) SBDB (small business development bond)

OECE *abrév* (▶**Organisation européenne de coopération économique**) OEEC (Organization for European Economic Cooperation)

œuvre *f* (travail) work; **être à l'**∼ be at work; **se mettre à l'**∼ get down to work; **mettre en** ∼ (programme, réforme) implement; **mise en** ∼ implementation; **tout mettre en** ∼ **pour faire (qch)** make every effort to do (sth); **être l'**∼ **de** be the work of; **faire** ∼ **durable** create a work of lasting significance; ∼ **accomplie** accomplishment; ∼ **de bienfaisance** charity; ∼ **caritative reconnue d'utilité publique** registered charity

œuvrer *vi* work, labour BrE, labor AmE

offensive *f* offensive; **lancer une** ∼ launch an offensive; ∼ **commerciale** sales offensive

offert, e *adj* offered

office *m* (Admin, Droit) (charge) office; **d'**∼ automatic, without consultation; **renvoi d'**∼ automatic discharge; **mise à la retraite d'**∼ forced *ou* compulsory retirement; **par les bons** ∼**s de qn** through the mediation of sb, through the good offices of sb; **commis** *or* **nommé d'**∼ (avocat) appointed by the court; ∼ **désigné** designated office; ∼ **élu** elected office; ∼ **européen des marques** Community Trade Mark Office; ∼ **du logement** accommodations bureau AmE; ∼ **récepteur** receiving office; ∼ **du tourisme** Tourist Board UK

officialiser *vt* formalize, make official

officiel, -elle *adj* official, formal

officiellement *adv* officially; (Droit) ex officio (frml)

officier *m* officer; ~ **d'intendance** catering officer; ~ **payeur** disburser; ~ **de service** duty officer; ~ **supérieur** senior officer; ~ **supérieur de la police des frontières** chief immigration officer

officieux, -euse *adj* off-the-record, unofficial

offrant *m* bidder, offerer; **vendre qch au plus** ~ sell sth to the highest bidder

offre *f* (proposition) offer, offering; (Econ) supply; (Fin, Bourse) (pour l'achat d'actions ou d'une participation) bid; (dans un appel d'offre) bid, tender; **recevoir/accepter une** ~ receive/ accept an offer; ~ **d'achat/de vente** offer to buy/sell; **répondre à une** ~ **d'emploi** reply to a job advertisement; **faire paraître une** ~ **d'emploi** advertise a job; **l'excédent de l'**~ surplus supply; **l'équilibre entre l'**~ **et la demande** the balance between supply and demand; **faire une** ~ make an offer, make a bid; **faire une** ~ **d'argent pour régler une dette** tender money in discharge of debt; **faire une** ~ **ferme** make a firm offer; (Bourse) make a firm bid; **faire une** ~ **pour** (marché) tender for; **lancer une** ~ **publique d'achat sur** make a takeover bid for; ~ **d'achat** tender offer, bid; ~ **d'achat d'actions** (pour employés) share scheme; ~ **d'acquisition** buyout proposal; ~ **auto-payante** (Fin) self-liquidator; (marketing) premium offer; ~ **de base** basic submission, basic tender; ~ **de biens** supply of goods; ~ **demandée** offer wanted; ~ **au détail** retail offer; ~ **en dollars** dollar bid; ~ **écrite** written offer; ~ **d'emploi** job offer; ~**s d'emploi** (dans le journal) appointments vacant, situations vacant BrE; ~**s d'emploi non satisfaites** unfilled vacancies; ~ **d'essai** trial offer; ~ **et acceptation** offer and acceptance; **l'**~ **et la demande** supply and demand; ~ **excédentaire** excess supply; ~ **ferme** firm offer, bona fide offer; ~ **fixe** fixed supply; ~ **flottante** floating supply; ~ **forfaitaire** fixed-price offering; ~ **globale** aggregate supply; ~ **indexée** leveraged bid; ~ **irrévocable** binding offer; ~ **de lancement** introductory offer; ~ **de main-d'œuvre** labour supply BrE, labor supply AmE; ~ **non concurrentielle** noncompetitive bid; ~ **originale** original bid; ~ **ouverte** open bid; ~ **plus interessante** better offer; ~ **plus avantageuse** better offer; ~ **la plus élevée** highest bid; ~ **de prix** price bid; ~ **promotionnelle** bargain offer; (publicité) special purchase; ~ **publique d'achat** takeover bid; ~ **publique d'échange** exchange offer; ~ **publique d'enchère** public invitation to bid; ~ **publique initiale** initial public offering; ~ **publique de vente** offer for sale, public offering; ~ **rampante** creeping tender; ~ **de répartition** split offering; ~ **de services** supply of services; ~ **spéciale** special offer, bargain offer; ~ **de valeur** value proposal; ~ **variable** soft offer; ~ **verbale** verbal offer

offrir ① *vt* (somme d'argent, choix, démission) offer; (difficultés) present; ~ **qch à qn** give sth to sb; ~ **ses services** offer one's services; ~ **sa démission** offer *ou* tender one's resignation; ~ **des conditions plus avantageuses** offer better terms; ~ **beaucoup de possibilités** offer considerable scope

② **s'offrir** *v pron* **pouvoir s'**~ **qch** be able to afford to buy sth

offshore *adj* (banque, centre, fonds, fiducie) offshore

OGM *abrév* (▸**organisme génétiquement modifié**) GMO (genetically modified organism)

OIT *abrév* (▸**Organisation internationale du travail**) ILO (International Labour Organization)

oléoduc *m* oil pipeline

oligopole *m* oligopoly; ~ **collusif** collusive oligopoly; ~ **local** spatial oligopoly

OM *abrév* (▸**organisation et méthodes**) O&M (organization and methods)

ombrage *m* (Info) shading

ombre *f* shadow

OMC *abrév* (▸**Organisation mondiale du commerce**) WTO (World Trade Organization)

OMCL *abrév* (▸**obligation la moins chère à livrer**) CTD (cheapest to deliver)

omettre *vt* omit, leave out; (par négligence) overlook; (Info) skip; ~ **de faire** fail to do, omit to do; ~ **les détails** (dans un rapport) skip the details; ~ **le paiement d'un dividende** pass a dividend

omission *f* omission; ~ **coupable** negligence; ~ **volontaire** wilful default

omnibus *m* (chemin de fer) slow train

OMS *abrév* (▸**Organisation mondiale de la santé**) WHO (World Health Organization)

once *f* ounce; ~ **liquide** fluid ounce; ~ **troy** (d'or) troy ounce

on-dit *m inv* **les** ~ hearsay

onéreux, -euse *adj* costly

ONG *abrév* (▸**organisation non-gouvernementale**) NGO (non-governmental organization)

ONU *abrév* (▸**Organisation des Nations Unies**) UN (United Nations), UNO (United Nations Organization)

OP *abrév* (▸**ordinateur personnel**) PC (personal computer)

OPA *abrév* (▸**offre publique d'achat**) TOB (takeover bid); ~ **négociée à l'amiable** agreed takeover; ~ **inamicale** hostile takeover bid; ~ **à rebours** reverse takeover; ⋯⋗

~ **sauvage** hostile takeover bid

OPCVM *abrév* (▶**organisme de placements collectifs en valeurs mobilières**) UCITS (undertakings for collective investment in transferables)

OPE *abrév* (▶**offre publique d'échange**) exchange offer

opéable *adj* raidable

OPEP *abrév* (▶**Organisation des pays exportateurs de pétrole**) OPEC (Organization of Petroleum Exporting Countries)

opérateur, -trice *m,f* operator; (Bourse) trader; ~ **en Bourse** stock exchange trader *ou* dealer; ~ **de conteneurs** container operator; ~ **en couverture** (Bourse) hedger; ~ **sur graphique** chartist; ~ **des groupages import** import groupage operator; ~ **de machine** machine operator; ~ **sur le marché monétaire** money-market trader; ~ **en obligations** bond trader; ~ **sur ordinateur** computer operator; ~ **principal du marché** bill broker, discount house; ~ **professionnel** professional trader; ~ **de saisie** keyboarder; ~ **télécom** telecommunications company; ~ **de terminal** terminal operator; ~ **d'usine** plant operator

opération *f* (Fin) (transaction) transaction; (arrangement) deal, operation; (Info) process; **faire une** ~ make a transaction; **faire des** ~**s symétriques** (Bourse) marry; ~ **d'achat** buy transaction; ~ **d'achat-vente compensée** matched sale-purchase transaction; ~ **sur actions** equity trading; ~ **d'arbitrage** arbitrage, arbitration transaction; ~ **d'arbitrage** arbitrage trading; ~ **d'assainissement** cleaning-up operation; ~ **au-dessous de ligne** below-the-line item; ~ **au-dessus de ligne** above-the-line item; ~ **bancaire** banking transaction; ~**s bancaires** banking; ~**s bancaires à distance** (par téléphone) telebanking; ~**s bancaires étrangères** foreign banking; ~**s bancaires en eurodevises** Eurobanking; ~**s bancaires fiduciaires** fiduciary banking; ~**s bancaires internationales** international banking transactions; ~**s bancaires sur le marché intérieur** home banking; ~**s de banque d'affaires** merchant banking; ~**s des banques commerciales** commercial banking; ~**s sur blocs d'actions** volume trading; ~**s en Bourse** trading operations; ~ **boursière** stock exchange transaction; ~**s boursières au pair** par trading; ~ **de caisse** cash transaction; ~ **de change** foreign exchange transaction *ou* deal; ~ **de change à terme** (échange de devises) forward exchange contract; ~ **commerciale** business transaction; ~**s commerciales compensées** matched trade; ~ **de compensation** (commerce international) barter transaction; ~ **comptable** account

transaction; ~ **au comptant** cash transaction; (Bourse) spot business; ~**s en compte courant** open-account business; ~ **conjointe** joint-venture company; (action) joint venture; ~ **de contre-achats** switch dealing (jarg); ~ **à un cours fictif** wash sale; ~ **de couverture** hedging; ~ **de couverture sûre** safe hedge; ~ **de couverture à terme** hedge, hedging; ~**s de crédit commercial** commercial lending; ~ **à la criée** open-outcry action; ~ **sur des devises** foreign exchange deal; ~**s en devises** forex trading; ~**s de dividendes** trading dividends; ~ **en dollars** dollar transaction; ~ **d'émission obligataire** bond issue operation; ~ **de face à face** back-to-back transaction; ~ **fictive** shell operation; ~ **fiduciaire** fiduciary operation; ~ **de financement quotidienne** day-to-day funding activity; ~ **immobilière** property deal; ~**s d'initiés** insider trading; ~ **intégrée** embedded option; ~**s interbancaires** interbank transactions; ~ **interdite** illegal operation; ~ **interne** in-house operation; ~ **liée** straddle; ~ **de liquidation** closing trade, closing transaction; ~ **machine** computer operation; ~**s sur marchandises** commodity trading; ~**s de marché** market operations; ~**s sur le marché hors cote** over-the-counter trading US; ~**s sur le marché monétaire** (commerce international) open-market trading; ~**s sur le marché à options** option bargains; ~ **mixte** spread, spreading; ~ **mixte à la baisse** bear spread, bearish spread; ~ **mixte à la hausse** bull spread, bullish spread; ~ **mixte horizontale** calendar spread, horizontal spread; ~ **mixte du papillon** butterfly spread; ~ **mixte sur options d'achat** call spread; ~ **mixte sur options avec dates d'échéance** calendar spread; ~ **mixte sur options avec dates d'échéance différentes** time spread, vertical spread; ~ **mixte sur options de vente** put spread; ~ **mixte symétrique** box spread; ~ **de nettoyage** cleaning-up operation; ~ **non valide** illegal operation; ~**s sur obligations** bond trading; ~ **de pleine concurrence** arm's-length transaction; ~**s portuaires** dock operations; ~ **de prêt** loan transaction; ~**s de prêt** loan transaction; ~ **de protection** hedging; ~ **de report** contango business UK; ~ **de soutien du cours de l'action** share support operation; ~ **à terme** forward operation; ~ **à terme sur les marchandises** commodity futures trading; ~ **sur titres** securities dealing, securities transaction; ~ **de trésorerie** cash operation, cash transaction; ~ **de troc** (commerce international) barter transaction; ~ **twist** (Econ) price twist; ~ **sur valeurs mobilières** securities transaction; ~**s sur valeurs de placement** investment banking US, merchant banking UK; ~ **vente-rachat** (jarg) (Fisc) quick flip

opérationnel, -elle *adj* operational

opérer [1] *vt* make; (restructuration) carry out; ~ **une retenue sur salaire** make a salary deduction; ~ **un retour** make a comeback; ~ **une saisie-arrêt** (Droit) issue a writ of attachment, garnish; ~ **une transaction** carry out a transaction, transact [2] *vi* (procéder) proceed; **comment allons-nous** ~? how are we going to proceed?

ophélimité *f* (Econ) Pareto optimality

opinion *f* opinion, view; **se faire une** ~ form an opinion; **'sans** ~**'** (dans un sondage) 'don't know'; ~ **défavorable** adverse opinion; ~ **publique** public opinion; ~ **avec réserve** qualified opinion; ~ **sans réserve** unqualified opinion

OPM *abrév* (▸**opérateur principal du marché**) bill broker, discount house

opportun, e *adj* advisable

opportunisme *m* opportunism

opportunité *f* (d'une décision, d'un événement) timeliness; (bien fondé) appropriateness; (occasion) opportunity; ~ **commerciale** business opportunity; ~ **sur un marché** break in the market

opposé, e *adj* (effets) adverse; ~ **à** alien to; ~ **au risque** (Econ) risk averse

opposer [1] *vt* (argument, résistance) put up; ~ **son refus à qn** refuse sb [2] **s'opposer à** *v pron* oppose; (proposition) object to; (développement, changement) stand in the way of; (contraster) contrast with; **s'**~ **à une évaluation** object to an assessment; **s'**~ **résolument à une décision** make a stand against a decision

opposition *f* opposition; (Droit) adverse claim; **être en** ~ **avec** be in opposition to; **faire** ~ **à** counter, oppose; **faire** ~ **à un chèque** stop a cheque BrE, stop a check AmE; **par** ~ **à** in contrast to; ~ **du débiteur** payment stopped; ~ **au paiement** payment stopped

opter *vi* opt; ~ **pour** opt for

optimal, e *adj* optimum

optimalité *f* optimality

optimisation *f* optimization; ~ **du profit** profit optimization; ~ **des revenus** revenue maximization

optimiser *vt* optimize; (machine) upgrade; ~ **la fonction objective** optimize the objective function

optimum[1] *adj* optimum

optimum[2] *m* optimum; ~ **de premier rang** (Bourse) first best

option *f* (choix) option; (accessoire) optional extra, optional feature; (Bourse) option, stock contract, privilege US; **à** ~ optional; **être en** ~ be an optional extra; **lever une option** (Bourse) take up an option; ~ **d'achat** call, buyer's option; (accord de contrat) binder; ~ **d'achat d'actions** share option, stock

option; ~ **d'achat dans le cours** in-the-money call option; ~ **d'achat couverte** covered call option; ~ **d'achat à découvert** naked call option, uncovered call; ~ **d'achat sur devises** currency call option; ~ **d'achat hors du cours** out-of-the-money call; ~ **d'achat au jeu**, ~ **d'achat au milieu** at-the-money call option; ~ **d'achat sur obligation** bond call option; ~ **d'achat de papillon long** long butterfly call; ~ **d'achat à parité** at-the-money call option; ~ **d'achat sans garantie** naked call; ~ **d'achat sur titres détenus** covered call UK; ~ **d'achat à trois mois** three-month call; ~ **d'achat vendue** written call; ~ **d'action à prime** incentive stock option; ~ **sur actions** stock option; ~ **de change** currency option, forex option; ~ **sur contrats à terme** futures option; ~ **cotée en Bourse** listed option; ~ **couplée** (d'achat et de vente) matched book; ~ **au cours** at-the-money option; ~ **à cours moyen** middle strike option; ~ **couverte** covered option; ~ **à découvert** naked option, uncovered option; ~ **par défaut** default option; ~ **sur devises** currency option, forex option; ~ **donnant lieu à un règlement en espèces** cash delivery option; ~ **du double** double option; ~ **du double pour livrer** put of more option; ~ **d'échange** swap option, swaption; ~ **à échéance dépassée** lapsed option; ~ **à échéance plus longue** longer-term option; ~ **écrite** written call; ~ **d'entrée sur le marché** market entry option; ~ **euro-américanisée** Americanized-European option; ~ **européenne** European option; ~ **expirée** lapsed option; ~ **hors du cours** out-of-the-money option; ~ **d'immobilisation** (prise de contrôle de société) lock-up option; ~ **d'indexation** stock index option; ~ **inscrite à la cote** exchange traded option, listed option; ~ **dans la monnaie** in-the-money option; ~ **de monnaies** currency linked; ~ **négociable** traded option; ~ **négociée de gré à gré** over-the-counter option US; ~ **d'obligation à long terme** long-term bond option; ~ **sur obligations** bond option; ~ **de paiement par anticipation** prepayment privilege; ~ **à parité** at-the-money option; ~ **à plus court terme** shorter-term option; ~ **à plus long terme** longer-term option; ~ **produire ou acheter** make-or-buy decision; ~ **de rachat** buy-back option; ~ **de reconduction** renewal option; ~ **rente viagère** annuity plan; ~ **de repli** fall-back option; ~ **à risques limités** (achat ou vente) stellage straddle option; ~ **de route** route option; ~ **sans garantie** naked option; ~ **de sortie** opting out; ~ **de souscripteurs d'actions sans impôt** qualifying stock option; ~ **à taux d'intérêt** interest rate option; ~ **sur titres** stock option; ~ **de titre fictif** phantom share option; ~ **sur valeurs mobilières** equity option; ~ **vendue**   ⸱⸱⸱▸

written option; ~ **de vente** putseller's option; ~ **de vente dans le cours** in-the-money put option; ~ **de vente à découvert** naked put option; ~ **de vente en dedans** in-the-money put option; ~ **de vente en dehors** out-of-the-money put; ~ **de vente garantie** qualifying stock option; ~ **de vente garantie par un dépôt en liquide** cash-secured put; ~ **de vente hors du cours** out-of-the-money put; ~ **de vente au jeu** at-the-money put option; ~ **de vente de papillon long** long butterfly put; ~ **de vente à parité** at-the-money put, at-the-money put option; ~ **de vente sans garantie** naked put; ~ **de vente sur devises** currency put option; ~ **de vente sur obligation** bond put option; ~ **de vente vendue** short put, written put

options *f pl* (Info) options, settings

optique *f* (point de vue) outlook; **changer d'~** change one's outlook *ou* perspective; **dans cette ~** from this perspective; ~ **de la direction générale** top management approach

OPV *abrév* (▸**offre publique de vente**) offer for sale, public offering

or *m* gold; ~ **d'importation** import gold; ~ **massif** solid gold; ~ **monétaire** gold bullion; ~ **noir** black gold

ORA *abrév* (▸**obligations remboursables en actions**) *bonds redeemable in shares*

orateur, -trice *m,f* speaker

ordinaire *adj* ordinary; (qualité, modèle) standard; (lecteur, consommateur) average, ordinary; (Bourse) (jarg) ordinary

ordinateur *m* computer; **mettre qch sur ~** put sth on the computer; ~ **analogique** digital computer; ~ **de bureau** desktop computer; ~ **de calcul** number cruncher; ~ **central** mainframe; ~ **cible** target computer; ~ **civil** commercial computer; ~ **de compilation** source computer; ~ **connecté** active computer; ~ **dédié** applications terminal; ~ **domestique** home computer; ~ **frontal** front-end computer; ~ **de gestion** business computer, business machine; ~ **individuel** personal computer; ~ **multimédia** multimedia computer; ~ **numérique** digital computer; ~ **personnel** personal computer; ~ **de poche** palm top, pocket computer; ~ **portable** laptop computer; ~ **professionnel** business computer, business machine; ~ **sans clavier** pen-based computer; ~ **satellite** peripheral computer, satellite computer; ~ **spécialisé** applications terminal; ~ **de traitement par lots** batch computer

ordinatique *f* computer science

ordinogramme *m* block diagram, flow chart

ordonnance *f* (Droit) court order, ruling; (d'un tribunal) order of the court; (pour médicament) prescription; ~ **de la cour** court

order; ~ **émanant du pouvoir exécutif** ministerial order; ~ **de libération** order of discharge; ~ **de mise en liquidation** winding-up order; ~ **de mise sous séquestre** receiving order; ~ **de paiement** dividend warrant; ~ **de saisie-arrêt** writ of attachment; ~ **du tribunal** court order

ordonnancement *m* (production) scheduling; ~ **de la production** production schedule

ordonner *vt* command; (Droit) enact, prescribe; (mettre en ordre) put in order

ordre *m* (commande) order; (Droit) court order; (Info) command, sequence; **être à l'~ du jour** be on the agenda; **par ~ alphabétique** in alphabetical order; **en ~ croissant/décroissant** in ascending/descending order; **par ~ de préférence** in order of preference; **par ~ d'importance** in order of importance; **par ~ de priorité** in order of priority; **un chèque à l'~ de** a cheque made payable to; **donner un ~ à qn** give sb an order; **agir sur ~ de qn** act on sb's orders; **travailler sous les ~s de qn** work under sb; **elle a 15 personnes sous ses ~s** she has 15 people (working) under her; **jusqu'à nouvel ~** until further notice; ~ **d'achat** (Banque, Bourse) order, buying order; ~ **d'achat obligatoire** compulsory purchase order UK; ~ **d'achat préalable** presale order; ~ **d'annulation** cancel order; ~ **annuel** annual order; ~ **d'arrimage** stowage order; ~ **en attente** resting order; ~ **des avocats** ≈ the American Bar Association US, ≈ the Bar UK; ~ **bivalent** alternative order; ~ **de cession de vente** sell-stop order; ~ **conditionnel** conditional market order UK; ~ **à cours limité** limited order; ~ **au cours du marché** market order; ~ **de courtier** broker's order UK; ~ **décroissant** decreasing order; ~ **d'écart** spread order; ~ **d'exécution** work order; ~ **d'expropriation** compulsory purchase order UK; ~ **de fabrication** job order, work order; ~ **de grandeur** order of magnitude; ~ **du jour** agenda; ~ **du jour provisoire** provisional agenda; ~ **lié** (Fin, Bourse) matched order, straddle; ~ **lié un contre un** one-to-one straddle; ~ **limité** limit order; ~ **limité inversé** stop-loss order; ~ **limite ou mieux** (Bourse) at or better; ~ **de liquidité croissante** increasing liquidity order; ~ **de liquidité décroissante** decreasing liquidity order; ~ **au mieux** market order; ~ **au mieux à la clôture** market order on the close; ~ **au mieux conditionnel** conditional market order UK; ~ **mixte** spread order; ~ **ouvert** open order; ~ **de paiement** payment order; ~ **de paiement international** international payment order; ~ **de paiement permanent** standing order UK; ~ **préalable à la vente** presale order; ~ **de rang** rank order; ~ **de reconduction** roll-over order; ~ **de recouvrement de**

créances debt collection order; ∼ **de
réexpédition** forwarding instructions; ∼ **de
report de position** roll-over order; ∼ **de
retrait négociable** negotiable order of
withdrawal; ∼ **à révocation** open order,
good-till-cancelled order; ∼ **semaine** week
order; ∼ **sous condition** contingency order;
∼ **de suspendre les paiements** stop-
payment order; ∼ **de transfert** transfer
order; ∼ **de transfert monétaire** money
transfer order; ∼ **valable tout le mois**
month order; ∼ **de vente** resting order; ∼
de vente stop sell-stop order; ∼ **de
virement** transfer order; ∼ **de virement
bancaire** banker's order

ordures *f pl* refuse BrE, garbage AmE; ∼
ménagères household refuse BrE

organe *m* (institution) organ; ∼ **consultatif**
advisory body; ∼ **de dépôt de titres** ≈
Depository Trust Company US

organigramme *m* flow chart, process
chart; ∼ **de données** data flow chart

organisateur, -trice *m,f* organizer; ∼ **de
transport combiné** combined transport
operator; ∼ **de voyages** (package) tour
operator

organisation *f* organization; **comité d'**∼
organizing committee; ∼ **d'aide aux
exportations** export facilitation
organization; **Organisation pour
l'alimentation et l'agriculture** Food and
Agriculture Organization; ∼ **autonome**
self-regulating organization; **Organisation
de l'aviation civile internationale**
International Civil Aviation Organization; ∼
des bureaux office management; ∼ **à
caractère éducatif** educational
organization; ∼ **caritative** charity; ∼
cellulaire (production) cell organization;
**Organisation pour la coopération
commerciale** Organization for Trade Cooperation; **Organisation de coopération et
de développement économique**
Organization for Economic Cooperation and
Development; **Organisation de défense
des consommateurs** ≈ Consumers'
Association; ∼ **des déplacements** journey
planning; ∼ **de l'entreprise** business
organization; ∼ **et méthodes** organization
and methods; **Organisation européenne
de brevets** European Patent Organization;
**Organisation européenne pour le
contrôle de qualité** European Organization
for Quality Control; **Organisation
européenne de coopération économique**
Organization for European Economic
Cooperation; **Organisation européenne de
transport** European Transport Organization;
∼ **hiérarchique** line organization; ∼
horizontale functional organization, staff
organization; ∼ **humanitaire** aid agency; ∼
indépendante self-regulatory organization;
∼ **industrielle** industrial organization; ∼
informelle (gestion) informal organization; ∼

internationale international organization;
**Organisation internationale de
normalisation** International Standards
Organization; **Organisation internationale
du sucre** International Sugar Organization;
Organisation internationale du travail
International Labour Organization BrE; ∼
des inventaires inventory planning; ∼ **en
matrices** matrix management; ∼ **mixte** line
and staff organization; **Organisation
mondiale du commerce** World Trade
Organization; **Organisation mondiale
pour la propriété intellectuelle** World
Intellectual Property Organization;
Organisation mondiale de la santé World
Health Organization; **Organisation des
Nations Unies** United Nations, United
Nations Organization; ∼ **non-
gouvernementale** non-governmental
organization; ∼ **des objectifs** goal
programming; ∼ **par secteurs d'activité**
functional organization; **Organisation des
pays exportateurs de pétrole**
Organization of Petroleum Exporting
Countries; ∼ **de la production** production
management; ∼ **professionnelle** trade
organization; ∼ **réglementaire relative à
une succession** (testaments) estate planning;
∼ **en réseau** network organization; ∼ **sans
but lucratif** nonprofit organization; ∼
scientifique scientific management; ∼
scientifique du travail scientific
management; ∼ **sur le terrain** (d'une société)
field organization; ∼ **du temps** time
management; ∼ **du trafic** (maritime) routing;
**Organisation du Traité de l'Atlantique
Nord** North Atlantic Treaty Organization; ∼
du travail work organization; ∼ **tripartite**
three-ply organization (jarg); ∼ **uniforme** flat
organization; **Organisation de l'unité
africaine** Organization of African Unity; ∼
des ventes sales management; ∼ **verticale**
line organization, vertical organization

organiser *vt* organize; (prêt) arrange;
(référendum) hold; (conférence) stage; ∼ **une
grève** stage a strike; ∼ **un stage de
formation** organize a training course; ∼ **le
trafic** route

organisme *m* organization; (de l'État)
agency, body; ∼ **autorégulateur** self-
regulatory organization; ∼ **bancaire de
crédit aux agriculteurs** agricultural bank;
∼ **de charité** charity; ∼ **consultatif**
advisory body; ∼ **de défense des
consommateurs** consumer organization; ∼
de défense des intérêts watchdog;
**Organisme européen de contrôle et
certification** European Organization for
Testing and Certification; **Organisme
européen pour la promotion du
commerce** European Trade Promotion
Organization; ∼ **intergouvernemental**
intergovernmental organization; ∼
municipal municipal body; ∼ **officiel** ⋯⋮

statutory body; ~ **de placement collectif** collective investment undertaking; ~ **de placements collectifs en valeurs mobilières** undertakings for collective investment in transferables; ~ **privé de formation** private training company; ~ **professionnel** professional body; ~ **public** government agency, public body; **Organisme de recherche spatiale européenne** European Space Research Organization; ~ **de réglementation** regulatory authority, regulatory body; ~ **régulateur des assurances-vie et des SICAV** ≈ Life Assurance and Unit Trust Regulatory Organization UK; ~ **du secteur public** public sector body; ~ **de services communs** common service agency; ~ **de services publics** public service body; ~ **spécialisé accrédité** recognized professional body; ~ **de tutelle** regulatory body; ~ **volontaire** voluntary body

oriental, e *adj* eastern

orientation *f* (conseil) guidance; (d'enquête, de politique, de recherche) direction; (tendance) trend; (ligne directrice) guidelines; ~ **à la baisse** downtrend; ~ **vers le client** customer orientation; ~ **à la hausse** uptrend; ~ **du marché** market trend; ~ **professionnelle** career guidance; ~ **vers le consommateur** consumer orientation

orienté, e *adj* orientated; **être** ~ **vers** be geared towards; ~ **à la baisse** (Bourse) bearish; ~ **vers la clientèle** customer-orientated; ~ **vers l'exportation** export-orientated; ~ **grand public** consumer-orientated; ~ **à la hausse** (Bourse) bullish; ~ **par le marché** market-orientated; ~ **vers la recherche** research-orientated

orienter *vt* (fonds publics) channel; (guider) direct, steer; (visiteur) direct; (conseiller) advise

original¹, e *adj* original

original² *m* original; **un** ~ **et trois copies** one top and three copies

origine *f* (d'un produit) origin

or-papier *m* paper gold

orphelin *m* (typographie) orphan

O.S. *abrév* (►ouvrier spécialisé) skilled worker

oscillation *f* swing; ~**s des cours** swings; ~**s du marché** ups and downs

osciller *vi* (cours) swing; (monnaie) fluctuate

OST *abrév* (►organisation scientifique du travail) scientific management

OTAN *abrév* (►Organisation du Traité de l'Atlantique Nord) NATO (North Atlantic Treaty Organization)

ôter *vt* take away; ~ **7 de 49** take 7 away from 49

OTV *abrév* (►obligation à taux variable) FRN (floating-rate note)

OUA *abrév* (►Organisation de l'unité africaine) OAU (Organization of African Unity)

ouï-dire *m* hearsay; **par** ~ by hearsay

outil *m* tool; ~ **industriel** industrial production capacity; ~ **logiciel** software tool; ~**s du métier** tools of the trade; ~ **pédagogique** teaching tool; ~ **de production** production tool; ~ **de programmation** programming aid; ~ **de vente** sales tool

outillage *m* tools; ~ **industriel** industrial equipment, plant

outiller *vt* equip

outilleur *m* toolmaker

outrage *m* insult; ~ **à magistrat** contempt of court

outre: en ~ *adv* further

outrepasser *vt* (fonctions, prérogatives) exceed; (limites, ordres) overstep

ouvert, e *adj* open; (Info) open-ended; (fichier) open; (question, série) open-ended; **être** ~ **aux idées nouvelles** be open to new ideas; ~ **sur l'extérieur** outward-looking; ~ **à l'achat** open-to-buy

ouverture *f* (d'un compte, d'un magasin) opening; (occasion) opportunity, window of opportunity; (Info) slot; (Pol) openness, transparency; (libéralisation) opening-up; (proposition) overture; **à l'~** (Bourse) at the opening; **capital/stock d'~** opening capital/stock; **faire des** ~**s à qn** make overtures to sb; **politique d'~** policy of openness *ou* transparency; ~ **automatique de session** (Info) auto login, auto logon; ~ **du concours** bid opening; ~ **des frontières** abolition of border controls, (commerciales) abolition of trade controls; ~ **des magasins le dimanche** Sunday trading; ~ **en nocturne** late-night opening; ~ **préventive** (Bourse) pre-emptive bid; ~ **de séance** opening; ~ **de tonnage** (d'un navire) tonnage opening

ouvrable *adj* (jour) working; **aux heures** ~**s** during working hours *ou* business hours

ouvrage *m* work; (livre) book; ~ **approuvé** approved project; ~ **d'intérêt général** trade book

ouvrier, -ière *m,f* worker; ~ **agricole** farm labourer BrE, farm laborer AmE; ~ **du bâtiment** construction worker; ~ **de l'équipe de jour** dayworker; ~ **de l'industrie automobile** car worker; ~ **membre du conseil d'administration** worker director; ~ **métallurgiste** metalworker; ~ **non-qualifié** unskilled worker; ~ **non-syndiqué** nonunion worker; ~ **payé à l'heure** hourly worker; ~ **de la production** production worker; ~ **qualifié** skilled worker; ~ **sans travail fixe** casual labourer BrE, casual laborer AmE; ~ **sidérurgiste** steelworker; ~ **spécialisé** semi-skilled worker; ~ **d'usine** factory hand

ouvrir *vt* open; '~ **ici**' 'open here'; ~ **un dossier** (Info) open a file; ~ **une session**

(Info) log in, log on; ~ **à la baisse** (Bourse) open a short position; ~ **un compte** open an account; ~ **un compte bancaire avec** open a bank account with; ~ **le courrier** open the mail; ~ **des crédits provisoires** grant interim supply; ~ **une écriture** (Compta) start an entry; ~ **à la hausse** (Bourse) open a long position; ~ **le marché à la concurrence** open the market up to competition; ~ **la**

porte à open the door to; ~ **une position** (Bourse) open a position; ~ **une position courte** (Bourse) open a short position; ~ **une position longue** (Bourse) open a long position; ~ **une souscription pour** invite subscriptions for; ~ **les transactions** open trading; ~ **la voie** break new ground; **ouvrant droit à pension** pensionable; **Ouvrez-moi** (Info) ReadMe document

Pp

p. *abrév* (▸**page**) pg. (page); (▸**poids**) wt (weight)

PAC *abrév* (▸**politique agricole commune**) CAP (Common Agricultural Policy)

pack *m* (lot) pack; (de téléphone) mobile phone package; ~ **de trois** tripack

PACS *m* (▸**pacte civil de solidarité**) (Droit) contract of civil union for same sex or mixed couples in France

pacte *m* accord, alliance; ~ **d'aide mutuelle** mutual aid pact; **Pacte de stabilité et croissance** Stability and Growth Pact

PAF *abrév* (▸**Police de l'air et des frontières**) border police

page *f* page; (Info) frame, page; **en première** ~ on the front page; **être à la** ~ keep up to date; ~ **d'accueil** (Info) home page; ~**s économiques** (presse) economic section; ~ **de garde** flyleaf; ~ **à l'italienne** landscape page; **Pages Jaunes**® (annuaire) Yellow Pages® UK; ~ **mal imposée** (imprimerie) badly imposed page; ~ **de publicité** (télévision, radio) commercial break; ~ **de titre** face page; ~ **sur la toile** (Info) web page

pagination *f* pagination

paginer *vt* (document) paginate

paie *f* pay; **toucher sa** ~ get paid; **faire la** ~ **des ouvriers** do the workers' payroll; **bulletin** *or* **feuille de** ~ payslip; **livre de** ~ payroll; ~ **de départ** payoff; ~ **hebdomadaire** weekly pay packet; ~ **tenant lieu de préavis** pay in lieu of notice

paiement *m* payment; (d'une dette) discharge; **faire** *or* **effectuer un** ~ make a payment; **mode** *or* **moyen de** ~ means *ou* method of payment; ~ **comptant** *or* **en espèces** cash payment; ~ **de la dette extérieure** payment of the foreign debt; ~ **contre documents** payment against documents; ~ **contre livraison** delivery versus payment; **en** ~ **de** in satisfaction of, in payment of; ~ **fait à** payment made to; ~**s d'achat à crédit** instalment payments BrE,

installment payments AmE; ~ **anticipé** advance payment; ~ **en arriérés** payment in arrears; ~ **d'assistance sociale** social assistance payment Can, social security payment UK; ~ **automatique** automatic withdrawal; ~ **d'avance en espèces** cash in advance; ~ **avant la livraison** cash before delivery; ~ **par avis de prélèvement** preauthorized payment; ~ **budgétaire** budget payment; ~ **par carte** credit card payment; ~ **par chèque** cheque payment BrE, check payment AmE; ~ **à la commande** cash with order; ~ **compensatoire** (Econ) deficiency payment; ~ **de complaisance** accommodation payment; ~ **pour le compte d'autrui** payment on behalf of others; ~ **contractuel** contract payment; ~ **sans contrepartie** nugatory payment; ~ **contre son gré** payment under protest; ~**s en cours** progress payments; ~ **à date due** payment in due course; ~ **déterminé** specific payment; ~ **différé** deferred payment; ~ **différentiel** deficiency payment; ~ **direct** direct payment; ~ **à dix jours de vue** ten days after sight pay; ~ **électronique** electronic payment; ~ **par étape** stage payment; ~ **en fonction des résultats** payment by results; ~ **au fur et à mesure** pay-as-you-go; ~ **incitatif** inducement payment; ~ **intégral** full payment, full settlement; ~ **d'intérêts supplémentaires** bonus interest payment; ~ **international** international payment; ~ **à la livraison** cash on delivery; ~ **locatif** rental payment; ~**s de loyer minimum** (loyer du capital) minimum lease payments; ~ **multilatéral** multilateral disbursement; ~ **en nature** payment in kind; ~ **partiel** part payment; ~ **de péréquation** equalization payment; ~ **rapide** prompt payment; ~ **reçu** inward payment; ~ **de redevances par anticipation** advance royalty payment; ~ **réel** actual cash disbursement; ~**s réguliers** regular payments; ~ **de rente** annuity

o
p

payment; ~ **sous réserve** payment under reserve; ~ **symbolique** token payment; ~ **tardif** late payment; ~**s de terminaison** (à la retraite) termination payments; ~ **en timbres-poste** postage stamp remittance; ~ **à titre de faveur** ex gratia payment; ~ **de transfert** transfer payment; ~ **en trop** overpayment; ~ **unique** single payment; ~ **par versements échelonnés** deferred payment; ~ **par virement bancaire** bank transfer, Bank Giro UK

pair¹, e adj (jour, chiffre) even

pair² m par, parity; **au ~** at par; **valeur au ~ par** value; **au-dessous/au-dessus du ~** below/above par; **vendre des actions au-dessous/au-dessus du ~** sell shares at a discount/at a premium; ~ **du change** mint par of exchange; ~ **métallique** mint par, mint par of exchange

palais m: ~ **des expositions** exhibition centre BrE, exhibition center AmE; ~ **de justice** court of law; **le Palais Brongniart** the Paris Stock Exchange

palan m (manutention) hoist; (matériel de levage) tackle; **sous ~** (navigation) below bridges; **sur ~** above bridges

palette f pallet; **mettre sur ~s** palletize; ~ **à ailes** winged pallet; ~ **de bois** wooden pallet; ~ **à montants** post pallet; ~ **principale** master pallet; ~ **à véhicules** (navigation) car pallet

palette-caisse f box pallet

palettiser vt (marchandises) palletize

palier m stage, level; **avancer par ~s** proceed by stages; **atteindre un ~** reach a plateau, level off; **l'inflation a atteint un ~** inflation has reached a plateau; **avancer par ~s** proceed by stages; ~ **en milieu de carrière** mid-career plateau; ~ **de résistance** resistance level; ~ **de revenu** income range; ~ **supérieur de revenu** upper income range

panachage m: ~ **à court terme** (Bourse) current blend

panamax m (navigation) Panamax vessel

panaméricain, e adj Pan-American

pancarte f sign

panel m (de spécialistes) panel; (échantillon) panel group; ~ **de consommateurs** consumer panel

paneuropéen, -enne adj Pan-European

panier m (Econ) basket; (Loisirs) package deal; ~ **de denrées** basket of goods; ~ **de devises** currency basket; ~ **de la ménagère** shopping basket; ~ **de produits** basket of products; ~ **de rebut** reject bin; ~ **de taux** basket of rates

panique f panic; **début de ~** moment of panic; **ventes ~s** panic selling; ~ **bancaire** run on the banks; ~ **financière** financial panic

paniquer vi panic

panne f (de véhicule, machine) breakdown; (de moteur, d'électricité) failure; (Info) fault; **en ~** out of action, out of order; (Info) down; **tomber en ~** break down; ~ **d'appareil** (bureau) equipment failure; ~ **d'électricité** blackout, power failure; ~ **machine** (Info) hardware failure; ~ **de machine** (usine) equipment failure; ~ **de secteur** blackout, power failure; ~ **système** (Info) system failure

panneau m (de commande) panel; (d'un navire) hatch; **par ~ et par jour** (maritime) per hatch per day; ~ **d'affichage** notice board BrE, bulletin board AmE; ~ **d'affichage portatif** poster site; ~ **avertisseur** warning sign; ~ **de commande** control panel; ~ **d'écoutille** (navigation) hatch covering; ~ **géant animé** spectacular (jarg); ~ **publicitaire** advertising hoarding BrE, billboard; ~ **de signalisation** traffic sign

panoplie f (de mesures, moyens) range; (d'objets) array; ~ **d'options** range of options

panorama m (radio, télévision) take-out US (jarg)

PAO abrév (▶**publication assistée par ordinateur**) DTP (desktop publishing)

paperasserie f (infrml) paperwork

papeterie f (commerce, articles) stationery; (usine) paper mill

papetier, -ière m,f (commerçant) stationer

papier m paper; (Info) form; **feuille de ~** sheet of paper; ~**s** documents, papers; ~ **d'affaires** trade paper; ~ **d'ambiance** (Média) background story; ~ **anticipant une obligation** bond anticipation note; ~ **avalisé par la banque** bank paper; ~ **bancable** bankable paper; ~ **baryté** baryta paper; ~ **bitumé** waterproof paper; ~ **brillant** glossy paper; ~ **buvard** blotting paper; ~ **calque** tracing paper; ~ **carbone** carbon paper; ~ **commercial** commercial paper; ~ **commercial de premier ordre** prime paper; ~ **en continu** continuous stationery; ~ **couché mat** art matt paper; ~ **d'emballage** wrapping paper; ~ **à en-tête** headed stationery, headed writing paper; ~ **eurocommercial** Eurocommercial paper; ~ **feuille à feuille** cut paper; ~ **financier** financial paper; ~ **glacé** glossy paper; ~**s d'identité** identity papers; ~ **informatique** computer paper; ~ **à lettres** writing paper; ~ **libre** plain plain paper; ~ **monétaire** money-market paper; ~ **ordre** order paper; ~ **par avion** airmail paper; ~ **à polycopier** manifold; ~ **recyclé** recycled paper; ~ **réglé** ruled paper; ~ **support** base sheet

papillon m (Assur) attachment; ~ **long** (Bourse) long butterfly

paquebot m ocean liner

paquet m (colis) package, parcel; (d'actions) parcel; (Info) packet; (journaux, lettres) bundle; (emballage commercial) pack, packet; ~

économique economy pack; ∼ **familial** family(-size) pack; ∼ **promotionnel** (publipostage) package; ∼ **de trois** tripack

paquetage *m* (arrimage des marchandises) baling

paradis *m*: ∼ **fiscal** tax haven

paradoxe *m* paradox; ∼ **de l'épargne** paradox of thrift; ∼ **de la valeur** (Econ) paradox of value, water and diamonds paradox; ∼ **du vote** paradox of voting

paraffine *f* paraffin; ∼ **dure** paraffin wax

paragraphe *m* paragraph; **décrit au** ∼ **1** referred to in paragraph 1; ∼ **passe-partout** (dans un contrat) boilerplate; ∼ **de tête** (presse) lead

paraître *vi* (publication) come out; (livre) be published, come out; **faire** ∼ (édition) issue; **faire** ∼ **une annonce pour** advertise for; **qui paraît tous les mois** published monthly

paralégal, e *adj* paralegal

parallèle *adj* parallel; (marché) unofficial; (Info) parallel; **en** ∼ in parallel; **en** ∼ **à** parallel to; **nos compétiteurs ont suivi une démarche** ∼ our competitors took similar steps; **traitement/imprimante** ∼ parallel processing/printer; **mener une activité** ∼ (comme dérivatif) have an activity as a sideline; (en fraude) have a sideline

parallèlement *adv*: ∼ **à** in parallel with

paralyser *vt* (industrie, économie) paralyse; (production) bring to a halt; **paralysé par une grève** strikebound

paramètre *m* parameter; ∼**s** (Info) settings; ∼ **d'évaluation d'option** option-pricing parameter; ∼ **temps** time component

parasite *m* (économétrie) noise, white noise; ∼**s** interference

paravent *m* screen

parc *m* (de biens d'équipement) stock; ∼ **d'activités**, ∼ **d'affaires** business park; ∼ **d'attractions** amusement park; ∼ **automobile** fleet of cars; ∼ **à bestiaux** stockyard; ∼ **de conteneurs** container pool; ∼ **européen de palettes** European pallet pool; ∼ **d'expositions** exhibition centre BrE, exhibition center AmE; ∼ **immobilier** housing stock; ∼ **locatif** housing stock; ∼ **à réservoirs de stockage** tank farm; ∼ **scientifique** science park; ∼ **de stationnement** car park BrE, parking lot AmE; ∼ **technologique** technology park; ∼ **à thème** theme park; ∼ **de véhicules** pool of vehicles; ∼ **de voitures** car pool

parcage *m* (de voitures) parking; ∼ **automatique** (Info) (des têtes de lecture, d'écriture) autopark

parcelle *f* (de terre) parcel

parcelliser *vt* (terrain) parcel out; (travail) break down into individual tasks; (opinion publique) divide

parcourir *vt* (Info) browse; (lettre, offres d'emploi) glance at, skim

parcours *m* (trajet) route; ∼ **professionnel** track record; ∼ **rapide** fast track

pardonner *vt* forgive; ∼ **qch à qn** forgive sb sth

pare-chocs *m* bumper BrE, buffer AmE

pare-feu *m* (Info) firewall

parent *m* parent; ∼**s proches** immediate family; ∼ **unique** single parent

parental, e *adj* parental

parenthèse *f* parenthesis; ∼**s** round brackets; **entre** ∼**s** in brackets

parfaire *vt* (formation) round off, complete; (technique, connaissance) perfect; (somme d'argent) make-up

pari *m* (activité) betting; (défi) gamble; ∼ **commercial** commercial gamble; **un** ∼ **sur l'avenir** a gamble on the future

parier *vt* (jouer) gamble; (aux courses) bet

parieur, -euse *m,f* (jouer) gambler; (aux courses) better BrE, bettor AmE

paritaire *adj* (comité) joint; (réunion) between labour and management; **commission** ∼ joint collective agreement committee

parité *f* (Info, Fin) parity; **à** ∼ at-the-money; **échelle/rapport de** ∼ parity sale/ratio; ∼ **de change** parity of exchange; ∼ **de conversion** conversion parity UK; ∼ **à crémaillère** crawling peg; ∼ **croisée** (exchange) cross rate; ∼ **glissante** sliding parity; ∼ **indexée optimale** optimal peg; ∼ **en légère baisse** sliding parity; ∼ **du pouvoir d'achat** purchasing power parity; ∼ **des taux** parity on rates

parjure *m* (Droit) perjury; **commettre un** ∼ commit perjury

parking *m* car park BrE, parking lot AmE; ∼ **courte durée** short-term car park; ∼ **à étages multiples** multistorey carpark; ∼ **relais** park and ride

parlement *m* parliament; **Parlement européen** European Parliament; ∼ **fédéral** Federal Parliament

parlementaire¹ *adj* parliamentary

parlementaire² *mf* member of Parliament

parler *vi* talk; ∼ **affaires** talk business; ∼ **boutique**, ∼ **boulot** (infml) talk shop (infml)

paroi *f*: ∼ **de cale** (navigation) wing

parquet *m* (de la Bourse) trading floor; **sur le** ∼ on the stock exchange

parrain *m* sponsor

parrainage *m* sponsorship; ∼ **de bienfaisance** charity sponsorship

parrainer *vt* sponsor

parraineur *m* sponsor

part *f* (de marché, de bénéfices) share; (Fisc) *unit on which the calculation of personal tax is based*; **avoir des** ∼**s dans une société** have shares in a company; **de la** ∼ **de** on behalf of; **faire la** ∼ **du feu** cut one's losses; **faire sa** ∼ **de travail** do one's share of the work; **la** ∼ **du lion** the lion's share; **pour ma** ∼ for my part; **à ~s égales** in equal parts; **sans obligation de votre ~** without obligation; **~ discrétionnaire** discretionary share; **~ éditeur** remit rate; **~ équitable** fair share; **~ de fiducie** trust unit; **~ de fondateur** founder's share; **~ fractionnaire** fractional share; **~ de marché** market share, share of the market; **~ de marché de la marque** brand share; **~ nette** net line; **~ d'un organisme de placement collectif** unit of a collective investment undertaking; **~ de responsabilité imputée à la victime dans l'accident** contributory negligence; **~ de responsabilité relative** (accidents) comparative negligence; **~ sociale** share; **~ souscrite** written line

partage m (répartition) sharing (**avec** with); (séparation) division, partition; (droit des successions) distribution; **~ d'actions cinq pour une** five-for-one split; **~ de données** data sharing; **~ de l'emploi** job share; **~ de fichiers** file sharing; **~ de poste** job share; **~ du pouvoir** power sharing; **~ des risques** risk sharing; **~ de temps** time sharing

partager vt share; **~ la différence** split the difference; **je partage votre avis** I agree with you; **~ proportionnellement** (finances) prorate

partance f: **en ~** (avion) about to take off; (navire) about to sail; (train, personne) about to leave; **être en ~ pour** (avion, navire, train, personne) be bound for

partenaire mf partner; **~ actif** active partner; **~ commercial** trading partner; **~ étranger** associated company abroad; **~s sociaux** unions and management

partenariat m partnership

parti m party; **le ~ écologiste** the Green Party; **~ politique** political party; **~ pris** bias

partial, e adj partial

partialité f bias; **~ de l'enquêteur** interviewer bias

participant¹, e adj participating

participant², e m,f participant; **~ à une conférence** conference delegate; **~ du marché** market participant

participatif, -ive adj participative

participation f involvement, participation; (Fin) share, interest; **avoir une ~ en actions** have an equity interest; **avoir des ~s dans une entreprise** have holdings in a company; **avoir une ~ de 45% dans une société** have a 45% stake ou interest in a company; **~ de l'assuré à l'assurance** coinsurance; **~ dans une banque** holding in a bank; **~ aux bénéfices** profit-sharing; **~ au capital** capital interest; **~s croisées** cross holdings between companies; **~ déterminante** working control; **~ différée aux bénéfices** deferred contribution plan; **~ directe** working interest; **~ électorale** voter

turnout; **~ des employés** worker participation, organicity; **~ des employés aux bénéfices** employee profit-sharing; **~ de la main-d'œuvre** labour force participation BrE, labor force participation AmE; **~ majoritaire** majority holding, majority stake, controlling interest; **~ minoritaire** minority holding, minority stake; **~ partielle** trust share; **~ permanente** permanent participation; **~ de police** policy dividend; **~ qualifiée** qualifying holding; **~ des travailleurs à la gestion** worker participation

participer vi participate; **~ à** play a part in; **~ à qch** (détenir une part) take a share in sth; **~ à un travail d'équipe** work as part of a team

particularité f detail

particulier¹, -ière adj (propre) particular; (personnel) (voiture, secrétaire) private; (investisseur) private individual; (spécifique) (rôle, droits, privilèges, statut) special

particulier² m private individual; **vente de ~ à ~** private sale; **~ admissible** eligible individual

partie f (portion) part; (dans un contrat) party; **tout ou ~** (Droit) wholly or in substantial part; **~ adverse** (litige) opposing party, adversary; **~ associée** related party; **~ ayant capacité à contracter** competent party; **~ caractérisante** (Brevets) characterizing portion; **~ contractante** contracting party; **~ convenue** agreed portion; **~ gagnante** prevailing party; **~ intégrante** (d'un contrat) integral part; **~ intéressée** interested party; **~ juridique** legal section; **~ lésée** injured party; **~ en litige** litigant; **~ par million** parts per million; **~ non utilisée** unused part; **~ plaignante** prosecution; **~ prenante dans une convention** party to an agreement; **~ requérante** claimant; **~ réservée d'une émission** preferential form; **~ souscrite** (Assur) written line

partiel, -elle adj partial; **chargement/paiement ~** part load/payment

partiellement adv partially; **~ déchargé** (un envoi) partially knocked down; **~ démonté** (Transp) semiknocked down; **~ libéré** (Bourse) partly paid

partir vi (s'en aller) go, leave; **~ en retraite** retire; **~ de zéro** start from scratch; **à ~ de** starting from, with effect from; **à ~ de 16 heures/du 5 février** from 4 o'clock/5 February (onwards); **à ~ de 100 euros** from 100 euros

partisan, e m,f supporter; **~ convaincu de** strong supporter of; **~ de l'inflation** inflationist

partition f (Info) (de mémoire) partition

partout adv (en tous lieux) everywhere; **~ dans le monde** worldwide

parution f publication

parvenir *vi* ~ **à** (solution, conclusion) reach; ~ **à un accord** come to an understanding, reach an agreement; ~ **à un accord avec** (ses fournisseurs) come to an arrangement with; **faire** ~ (lettre, document) send

pas *m* step; **donner le** ~ set the pace; **faire le premier** ~ make the first move; ~ **à pas** step-by-step; ~ **de siège** (Transp) seat pitch

pas-de-porte *m* (somme d'argent) key money

passage *m* switchover, transition; **le** ~ **à l'euro** the switchover to the euro; **clientèle de** ~ passing trade; ~ **automatique à la ligne** (Info) word wrap; ~ **imprimé en petits caractères** (dans un contrat) small print; ~ **à la ligne** (Info) line feed; ~ **en machine** (Info) machine run; ~ **de production** production run; ~ **d'une tranche d'imposition à une autre** tax-bracket creep

passager, -ère *m,f* (Transp) passenger; ~ **à destination de** passenger travelling to; ~ **en provenance de** passenger arriving from; ~ **clandestin** stowaway; ~**s à l'arrivée** inbound passengers

passant, e *m,f* passer-by

passation *f* (Compta) reversal, writing back; ~ **autoritaire de contrat** authoritative contracting; ~ **par pertes et profits** write off

passavant *m* (Imp/Exp) carnet, transire; ~ **général** general transire

passe *f* (navigation) fairway, narrows; ~ **de caisse** (Compta) cashier's error allowance

passé, e *adj* ~ **de mode** out of fashion

passeport *m* passport; **délivrer/renouveler un** ~ issue/renew a passport; **contrôle des** ~**s** passport control; ~ **valable** valid passport

passer *vt* (commande) place; (une écriture) pass; ~ **un accord** enter into an agreement; ~ **une annonce** advertise; ~ **en assises** have a jury trial; ~ **un avis d'appel d'offres** (publicité) advertise for bids; ~ **en charges** charge off; ~ **aux comptes de résultat** write off; ~ **un contrat avec** let out a contract to; ~ **un coup de fil à** (infrml) phone, call; ~ **au crible** screen; ~ **au crible la candidature de qn** screen sb for a job; ~ **une écriture dans le grand livre** enter an item in the ledger; ~ **l'éponge** wipe the slate clean; **faire** ~ pass; **faire** ~ **clandestinement** smuggle; **faire** ~ **en premier** prioritize; **faire** ~ **qch au premier plan** bring sth to front; ~ **outre** (à un veto) override; ~ **aux profits et pertes** write off; ~ **qch sous silence** pass sth over in silence; ~ **au secteur privé** (médecine) go private; ~ **sous presse** (édition, presse) go to press; ~ **par la voie hiérarchique** go through the proper channels

passerelle *f* gateway; (pour piloter) bridge; ~ **de débarquement** (maritime) bridge, gangway

passible *adj*: ~ **d'amende** liable to a fine; ~ **d'une pénalité** liable to a penalty; ~ **de**

poursuites actionable; ~ **de prosécution** liable to prosecution

passif¹, -ive *adj* passive; (affiche) passive; **mémoire passive** (Info) read-only memory

passif² *m* liabilities; ~ **à court terme** short-term debt; ~**-dépôts** deposit liabilities; ~ **éventuel** contingent liabilities; ~ **exigible** short-term debt, current liabilities; ~ **exigible à terme** fixed liabilities; ~ **national** domestic liabilities; ~ **de réserve** reserve liability; ~ **subordonné** subordinated liabilities

pastille *f* (Info) chip

pâte *f* (céramique) paste; ~ **à papier** paper pulp

patente *f* (permis) licence (*to exercise a trade or profession*); (taxe) business rates, franchise tax US; **payer** ~ be duly licensed; ~ **de santé** (navigation) bill of health; ~ **de santé nette** clean bill of health

patenté, e *adj* licensed

patient, e *m,f* patient; ~ **privé** private patient

patin *m* (manutention) skid

patrimoine *m* (d'une entreprise) assets; (d'un individu) estate, personal fortune; ~ **naturel** natural heritage

patron, -onne *m,f* (propriétaire) owner; (directeur, gérant) manager, boss (infrml); **être son propre** ~ be one's own boss; ~ **de paille** straw boss (infrml)

patronal, e *adj* (organisation, représentant) employers'; **cotisation** ~**e** employer's contribution

patronat *m* employers; ~ **et travailleurs** managers and workers

patronner *vt* sponsor; **patronné par l'État** government-sponsored

pause *f* (au travail) break UK; **faire une** ~ take a break; ~ **de midi** lunch break

pause-café *f* coffee break

pauvre *adj* poor; **être** ~ **en** (calories) be low in; ~ **en liquidité** cash-poor

pauvreté *f* hardship, poverty; ~ **absolue** absolute poverty

pavé *m* (presse) display; ~ **numérique** (Info) numeric keypad; ~ **publicitaire** display advertisement; ~ **de touches** (Info) keypad

pavillon *m* (navigation) flag; (d'exposition) pavilion; ~ **de complaisance** flag of convenience; ~ **étranger** foreign flag

pavois *m* (d'un navire) bulwark

payable *adj* payable; ~ **à l'avance** payable in advance; **le travail est** ~ **d'avance** the work must be paid for in advance; ~ **à la commande** cash with order; ~ **sur demande** payable on demand; ~ **à échéance** payable at maturity; ~ **à la livraison** cash on delivery; ~ **mensuellement à terme échu** payable monthly in arrears; ~ **à préavis** payable after notice; ~ **en six versements** payable in six instalments; ~ **à vue** payable ⋯✧

on presentation, payable at sight

payant, e *adj* (affaire, activité) profitable; (mesures) worthwhile; (efforts, stratégie) which pays off; **chaîne** ~**e** subsciption channel; **ce service est** ~ there is a charge for this service; **leur tactique a été** ~**e** their strategy paid off

payé, e *adj* paid; ~ **d'avance** prepaid; ~ **comptant à l'avance** cash in advance; ~ **à l'heure** paid by the hour; ~ **intégralement** fully paid; ~ **à la livraison** paid on delivery; ~ **à la pièce** paid by the piece; **non** ~ (Bourse) nil paid; (Fin) delinquent

payé-emporté *m* (Gen com) cash and carry

payer ⟨1⟩ *vt* pay; (fournisseur, artisan) settle up with; ~ **par chèque/carte de crédit** pay by cheque/credit card; ~ **à l'année** pay by the year; ~ **cash** (infrml) pay cash; ~ **et classer** (impôt sur les sociétés) pay and file; ~ **à l'échéance** pay when due, pay at due date; ~ **au comptant** pay cash; ~ **les dépenses de** defray the expenses of; ~ **la facture** settle the bill; **faire** ~ **qch à qn** charge sb for sth; ~ **le fret au volume** (maritime) pay for cargo by measurement; ~ **en liquide** pay cash; ~ **en nature** pay in kind; ~ **à l'ordre de** pay to the order of; ~ **qch au prix fort** pay over the odds for sth; ~ **qn au forfait** pay sb a flat rate; ~ **rubis sur l'ongle** pay on the line (jarg); ~ **à la semaine** pay by the week; ~ **par trimestre** pay by the quarter; ~ **par virement bancaire** pay by giro ⟨2⟩ *vi* (rapporter) (profession, activité) pay; **c'est un métier qui paie bien** it's a job that pays well

payeur, -euse *m,f* (client) payer; (trésorier) paymaster; **mauvais** ~ bad debtor

pays *m* country; **du** ~ (légumes) home-grown; ~ **d'accueil** host country; ~ **autonome** self-governing nation; ~ **bailleur de fonds** donor country; ~ **destinataire** country of destination; ~ **développé** developed country; **les** ~ **développés** the developed world; ~ **donateur** donor country; ~ **emprunteur** borrower country; ~ **exportateurs de pétrole** oil-exporting countries; ~ **à faible revenu modérément endetté** moderately indebted low-income country; ~ **à haut risque** country of ultimate risk; ~ **hôte** host country; ~ **industrialisé** industrialized country; ~ **limitrophe** neighbouring country BrE, neighboring country AmE; ~ **méditerranéens** Mediterranean bloc; ~ **membre** member country; ~ **moins avancé** developing country, less developed country; ~ **non producteur de pétrole** non-oil country; ~ **nouvellement industrialisé** newly industrialized country; **les** ~ **occidentaux** the Western World; ~ **d'origine** country of origin, home country; ~ **producteur de pétrole** oil-producing country; ~ **à revenu intermédiaire**

modérément endetté moderately indebted middle-income country; ~ **à revenu moyen et à fort endettement** heavily indebted middle-income country; ~ **scandinaves** Nordic countries; ~ **technologiquement avancé** advanced country; ~ **tiers** (commerce international) third country; ~ **du tiers-monde** Third World country; ~ **en voie de développement** developing country

paysage *m* landscape; **le** ~ **économique** the economic scene *ou* landscape; ~ **audiovisuel français** French radio and TV scene; ~ **informatique** computer environment

paysager, ère *adj* (Envir) environmental; (bureau) open-plan

PBR *abrév* (▸**prix de base rajusté**) ACB (adjusted cost base)

PC *m* (Info) PC; **pour** ~ PC-based

p.d. *abrév* (▸**port dû**) carr fwd (carriage forward), frt fwd (freight forward)

PDG *abrév* (▸**président-directeur général**) chairman and managing director BrE, chief executive officer AmE

péage *m* toll; **autoroute à** ~ toll motorway, turnpike US; **pont à** ~ tollbridge; **télévision à** ~ pay TV; ~ **automatique** automatic fare collection; ~ **d'autoroute** motorway toll; ~ **du tunnel** tunnel toll

peak *m*: ~ **arrière** (d'un navire) afterpeak; ~ **avant** (d'un navire) forepeak

peaufiner *vt* (système) refine; (contrat, travail) put the finishing touches to

pêche *f* fishing

pêcherie *f* fishery

pécuniaire *adj* financial

PEE *abrév* (▸**plan épargne entreprise**) company savings plan

peine *f* penalty; ~ **contractuelle** penalty clause; ~ **pécuniaire civile** civil penalty; ~ **de prison** prison sentence

PEL *abrév* (▸**plan d'épargne logement**) savings scheme entitling depositor to a cheap mortgage

pénalisation *f* penalty; ~ **fiscale** tax penalty; ~ **importante pour fausse déclaration** serious misdeclaration penalty UK; ~ **pour récidive** second or further occurrence penalty

pénaliser *vt* penalize

pénalité *f* penalty; ~ **fiscale** tax penalty; ~ **pour infraction** penalty for noncompliance; ~ **d'intérêt** interest penalty; ~ **pour première contravention** (Fisc) first occurrence penalty; ~ **pour récidive** (Fisc) second or further occurrence penalty; ~ **de remboursement anticipé** prepayment penalty; ~ **pour retrait anticipé** early-withdrawal penalty; ~ **de retrait de fonds** back-end load

pénétration *f* (publicité) penetration; ~ **commerciale** sales penetration; ~ **du**

marché market penetration

pénétrer *vt* penetrate, make inroads into; ~ **le marché** penetrate the market

péniche *f* barge

pensée *f* thought; (manière de penser) thinking; ~ **créatrice** creative thinking; ~ **latérale** lateral thinking; ~ **politique** political thinking

penser *vt* think

pension *f* pension; **toucher une** ~ draw a pension; **taux des prises en** ~ (Bourse) repurchase rate, repo rate; ~ **alimentaire** (Droit) alimony; ~ **anticipée** Bel early retirement annuity; ~ **complète** full board; ~ **différée** deferred retirement credit; ~ **d'invalidité** disablement pension; ~ **livrée** REPO AmE, repurchase agreement; ~ **non-contributive** noncontributory pension scheme; ~ **de retraite** retirement pay; ~ **de retraite anticipée** early retirement scheme; ~ **de reversion** reversion benefit; ~ **viagère** life annuity; ~ **de vieillesse** old age pension

pensionnaire *mf* paying guest

pensionné, e *m,f* pensioner

pénurie *f* shortage; ~ **de dollars** dollar gap; ~ **de logements** housing shortage; ~ **de main-d'œuvre** labour shortage BrE, labor shortage AmE; ~ **de matières premières** shortage of raw material; ~ **de moyens de paiement** liquidity famine; ~ **de pétrole** oil shortage

PEPS *abrév* (▶**premier entré, premier sorti**) FIFO (first in, first out)

percée *f* breakthrough; ~ **commerciale** commercial breakthrough, market breakthrough

percepteur, -trice *m,f* tax inspector; ~ **des droits de port** rates officer

perception *f* (Fisc) (bureau) tax office; (de l'impôt) collection; ~ **des deniers publics** collection of public money; ~ **des droits de douane** collection of customs duties; ~ **de l'impôt** tax collection; ~ **du prix** price perception; ~ **standard à l'exportation** standard export levy

percer *vi* break through; ~ **sur un marché** break into a market

percevoir *vt* (impôt) collect; (pension, loyer, indemnité) receive; (salaire) be paid, receive; ~ **un salaire horaire de** be paid a rate of; **être bien/mal** ~ be well/badly received

perdre *vt* (procès, élections) lose; ~ **la partie** (individu) go to the wall; ~ **son emploi** lose one's job; ~ **du terrain** lose ground; ~ **de la valeur** go down in value

perdu, e *adj* (emballage) nonreusable

perdurer *vi* last

père *m* father; **un** ~ **de famille** (jarg) blue-chip customer; **Dupont** ~ Dupont senior

péremption *f* (Droit) extinction; **date de** ~ use-by date; ~ **prévue** (Compta) estimated lapse

péremptoire *adj* (preuve, argument) conclusive

pérennité *f* sustainability

péréquation *f* (d'impôts, prix) equalization; (des pensions, salaires) adjustment; ~ **fiscale** tax equalization

perfectionné, e *adj* enhanced, improved

perfectionnement *m* (formation) training; (de système) improvement; (Info) enhancement; **stage de** ~ advanced training course; ~ **des cadres** executive development

perforage *m* puncturing

perforation *f* (opération) punching; (trou) hole; ~**s d'entraînement** feed holes

perforatrice *f* punch; ~ **de bande** tape punch; ~ **de cartes** card punch; ~ **à clavier** keypunch

performance *f* performance, result; ~ **de la société** company results; ~ **à l'exportation** export performance; ~ **du prix des actions** share price performance; ~ **supérieure** outperformance

performant, e *adj* (système) efficient; (action) performing; (employé, technique) effective; (entreprise) competitive; **un investissement** ~ a high-return investment

péricliter *vi* (entreprise) go under; (économie) be in decline

péril *m* danger, peril; (Assur) (maritime) peril; **les** ~**s de la mer** the perils of the sea; **tous** ~**s** (Assur) all-risk

périmé, e *adj* (passeport, billet) out-of-date; (idée, institution) outdated; **son passeport est** ~ his passport has expired

périmer: se ~ *v pron* (billet, passeport) expire; (idée, style) become obsolete

périmètre *m* perimeter; ~ **de consolidation** companies included within consolidation

période *f* period; (d'un prêt) term; **en** ~ **de crise** at a time of crisis; **en** ~ **électorale** at election time; **par** ~**s** periodically; **pendant la** ~ **d'essai** during the trial period; **en** ~ **creux** off-peak; **pendant la** ~ **précédant** (élections) in the run-up to; **pour la** ~ **considérée** for the period; ~ **d'accueil** orientation; ~ **d'admissibilité** qualifying period; ~ **d'amortissement de l'actif** asset depreciation range; ~ **applicable** relevant period; ~ **d'attente** waiting time; ~ **de base** base period; ~ **budgétaire** budgetary period; ~ **de chômage** period of unemployment; ~ **complémentaire** supplementary period; ~ **comptable** accounting period; ~ **de cotation obligatoire** mandatory quote period; ~ **de couverture** time on risk, cover period, coverage period AmE; ~ **creuse** slack period; ~ **de déclaration** reporting period; ~ **de détente** cooling-off period; ~ **de détention** holding period; ~ **avec droits** (Bourse) cum ···⟩

rights period; ~s **d'échéance** (Fin) maturity bands; ~ **d'essai** trial period; ~ **d'étalement du revenu** averaging period; ~ **ex-droits** (Bourse) ex-rights period; ~ **d'exclusion** excluded period; ~ **d'exonération** exempt period; ~ **de gains** earnings period; ~ **de garantie** (pendant laquelle on se porte garant pour qn) bail-out period; ~ **de gestation** gestation period; ~ **gratuite** (location) rent-free period; ~ **d'imposition** taxation period; ~ **de jouissance foncière** tenure in land; ~ **de latence** waiting period; ~ **de livraison** delivery period; ~ **de location** tenancy period; ~ **longue** (Econ) long period; ~ **de maintien** retention period; ~ **moyenne d'encaissement** average collection period; ~ **obligatoire d'affichage des prix** mandatory quote period; ~ **de l'option** option period; ~ **de paie** pay period; ~ **porteuse pour le marché** period of market growth; ~ **de programmation** time segment; ~ **de prospérité économique** economic boom; ~ **de qualification** qualifying period; ~ **de récupération** payback period; ~ **de référence** reference period; ~ **de réflexion** cooling-off period; ~ **de remboursement** payback period; ~ **de rodage** running in period; ~ **de transition** transitional period; ~ **de vacances** holiday period; ~ **de validité** validity period
périodique[1] *adj* periodic; (Compta) (rapport, résultats) interim
périodique[2] *m* magazine, periodical
périphérique[1] *adj* peripheral; (quartier) outlying; (Info) add-on, peripheral
périphérique[2] *m* (Info) peripheral, device; (route) ring road; ~ **d'entrée** input device; ~ **de sortie** output device; ~ **de stockage** storage device
péripole *m*: ~ **technologique** technology park
périssable *adj* perishable; denrées ~s perishables, perishable foodstuffs
permanence *f* (service) manned service; (local) manned office; (des méthodes comptables) consistency; ~ **de 9 à 11 heures** open 9am to 11am; ~ **téléphonique** hot line
permanent[1], e *adj* ongoing, permanent
permanent[2], e *m,f* (employé) permanent employee; (membre) permanent member; (de syndicat) union official
permettre [1] *vt* allow, authorize; ~ **à qn d'accéder à** give sb access to [2] **se permettre** *v pron* afford
permis[1], e *adj* (déduction) allowed
permis[2] *m* (d'exercer une activité) licence BrE, license AmE, permit; **qui ne nécessite pas de** ~ permit-free; ~ **de conduire** (document) driver's licence BrE, driver's license AmE; (examen) driving test; ~ **de conduire international** international driver's licence BrE; ~ **de conduire international pour**

transports routiers international road haulage permit; ~ **de construire** building permit AmE, planning permission BrE; ~ **de débarquement** landing permit; ~ **d'entrée** clearance inwards; ~ **multilatéral** (UE) multilateral permit; ~ **de séjour** residence permit; ~ **de séjour limité** temporary residence permit; ~ **de sortie** clearance outwards; ~ **spécifique individuel** specific individual licence BrE; ~ **de transbordement** transshipment delivery order; ~ **de travail** work permit
permutabilité *f* commutability
permutable *adj* commutable
permutation *f* (Info) swap
perpendiculaire *f* perpendicular
perpétuel, -elle *adj* (obligation) perpetual; (poste, secrétaire) permanent
perpétuité *f* perpetuity; **à** ~ in perpetuity
perquisition *f* search; ~ **à domicile** house search; ~ **et saisie** search and seizure
personnage *m* (personne importante) figure; **un** ~ **important** an influential figure; ~ **de marque** very important person, VIP
personnalisable *adj* customizable, tailorable
personnalisation *f* customization; (publicité) personalization
personnalisé, e *adj* customized
personnaliser *vt* customize, tailor
personne *f* (**cinquante euros par** ~ fifty euros per person; **un groupe de dix** ~s a group of ten people; **les** ~s **concernées** those concerned; **50% des** ~s **interrogées** 50% of those interviewed; ~ **apparentée** related person; ~ **à charge** dependant; ~ **civile** (Droit) artificial person; ~ **étrangère** nonmember; ~ **interrogée** (marketing) respondent; ~ **morale** legal entity; ~ **nommée** appointee; ~ **nommément désignée** named person; ~ **non déclarante** (Fisc) nonfiler; ~ **non déclarée** unregistered person; ~ **physique** (Droit) natural person; ~ **prospectable** prospect
personnel *m* personnel, staff; (d'usine) workforce; **faire partie du** ~ be on the payroll, be on the staff; ~ **administratif** administrative staff; ~ **de bureau** clerical staff; ~ **de contrôle** audit staff; ~ **de direction** managerial staff; ~ **d'encadrement** managerial staff; ~ **de fabrication** manufacturing workforce; ~ **financier de soutien** financial support staff; ~ **intérimaire** casual labour BrE, casual labor AmE; ~ **de maîtrise** supervisory staff; ~ **navigant commercial** (avion) cabin staff; ~ **non syndiqué** nonunion labour BrE, nonunion labor AmE; ~ **pléthorique** surplus staff; ~ **de production** manufacturing workforce; ~ **de réception** front-office personnel; ~ **réduit** skeleton staff; ~ **de révision** Bel audit staff; ~ **salarié** salaried

staff; ∼ **de service et de remplacement** indirect workers; ∼ **subalterne** down-the-line personnel; ∼ **de surveillance** supervisory staff; ∼ **de terrain** field staff; ∼ **titulaire** tenured staff; ∼ **de vente** sales personnel

personnellement *adv* personally; ∼ **responsable** (Droit) personally liable

perspective *f* prospect, outlook; ∼s **d'avenir** future prospects; ∼s **de carrière** career prospects; ∼s **commerciales** market prospects; ∼s **économiques** economic outlook; ∼s **du marché** market prospects; ∼ **de profit** profit outlook; ∼s **de travail** work prospects

persuasion *f* persuasion

perte *f* (fait d'égarer) loss; (fait de ne pouvoir garder) loss; (de capital) loss; (gaspillage) waste; **vendre à** ∼ sell at a loss; **c'est une** ∼ **de temps** it's a waste of time; ∼s **accumulées** accumulated deficit; ∼ **actuarielle** actuarial loss; ∼ **agricole** farm loss; ∼ **apparente** superficial loss; ∼ **sur des biens amortissables** loss on depreciable property; ∼ **d'un bien par confiscation** forfeiture; ∼s **et bénéfices de change** premium and discount on exchange; ∼ **en capital** capital loss; ∼ **en capital déductible** allowable capital loss; ∼ **en capital nette cumulative** (Fisc) cumulative net capital loss; ∼ **catastrophique** catastrophic loss; ∼ **censée totale** (Assur) constructive total loss; ∼ **de clientèle** attrition; ∼ **commerciale** business loss; ∼ **compensatoire** compensating loss UK; ∼ **comptable** book loss; ∼ **de conversion** (commerce international) translation loss; ∼ **courante** net operating loss; ∼ **sur créance** credit loss; ∼ **à découvert** uncovered hedge loss; ∼ **déductible au titre d'un placement d'entreprise** allowable business investment loss; ∼ **du droit à l'indemnité** loss of claim; ∼ **effective** actual loss; ∼ **d'embarcation** (navigation) craft loss; ∼ **exceptionnelle** windfall loss; ∼ **d'exploitation** business loss; ∼s **d'exploitation** trading losses; ∼ **finale** terminal loss; ∼ **fortuite** fortuitous loss; ∼s **indirectes** consequential loss; ∼ **d'information** (Info) dropout; ∼ **sur investissement** investment loss; ∼ **à long terme** long-term loss; ∼ **de marché** loss of market; ∼ **de mortalité** mortality loss; ∼ **nette** net loss; ∼ **non réalisée** unrealized loss; ∼ **normale** ordinary loss; ∼ **à l'origine** historical loss; ∼ **partielle ou totale** partial/total loss; ∼ **sur prêts** loan loss; ∼ **primitive d'acquisition** historical loss; ∼ **de la priorité** loss of priority; ∼s **et profits** profit and loss; ∼s **réalisées** realized losses; ∼ **de récolte** (agriculture) crop failure; ∼ **réelle sur prêts** actual loan loss experience; ∼ **de réinvestissement** reinvestment loss; ∼s **reportées** losses carried forward; ∼ **réprimée totale**

seulement constructive total loss only; ∼ **réputée totale** (sinistre d'assurance) constructive total loss; ∼ **de salaire** loss of pay; ∼ **de sauvetage** salvage loss; ∼ **sèche** clear loss; ∼ **sèche sur prêt** loan write-off; ∼ **simple** elementary loss; ∼s **subies** losses suffered; ∼ **au titre d'un placement d'entreprise** business investment loss; ∼ **totale** total loss; ∼ **totale effective** (Assur) actual total loss; ∼ **totale relative** (Assur) constructive total loss; ∼ **totale transigée** (Assur) arranged total loss; ∼ **sur transactions** (commerce international) transaction loss; ∼ **de valeur** decrease in value

perturbation *f* (d'un service, du marché) disruption

perturber *vt* (trafic, marché, réunion) disrupt

peser ⟦1⟧ *vt* weigh; ∼ **contre** (nouvelle loi) bring to bear against; ∼ **le pour et le contre** weigh up the pros and cons
⟦2⟧ *vi* (avoir un poids) weigh; (être lourd) be heavy; ∼ **sur qn** (menaces, soupçons, risques) hand over sb; (impôts, charges, contraintes) weigh sb down; ∼ **lourdement sur** rest heavily on

pesticide *m* pesticide

petit, e *adj* small; **de** ∼**e taille** small-scale; ∼ **actionnaire** private investor; ∼**e annonce** (journaux, magazines) ad (infrml), advert, advertisement; ∼**e annonce classée** classified advertisement; ∼ **boulot** menial job; ∼s **boulots** odd jobs; ∼**e caisse** petty cash; ∼ **capital** small investors; ∼s **caractères** (dans un contrat) small print; ∼ **commerçant** shopkeeper BrE, storekeeper AmE, trader; ∼**e coupure** small denomination; ∼ **cultivateur** (agriculture) smallholder; ∼ **employeur** small employer; ∼**e entreprise** small business; ∼**e entreprise commerciale qualifiable** qualifying small business corporation; **la** ∼**e épargne** small savings; ∼ **fonctionnaire** petty official; ∼ **fond** (édition) back margin; ∼ **gain rapide** quick flip; ∼**es et moyennes entreprises** small and medium-sized enterprises; ∼**es et moyennes industries** small and medium-sized manufacturing companies; ∼ **porteur** small shareholder; ∼s **prix** budget prices; **les** ∼s **salaires** the low-paid; ∼**e série** batch, short run

pétition *f* petition

P et P *abrév* (▸**pertes et profits**) P&L (profit and loss)

pétrin *m* (infrml) jam (infrml); **dans le** ∼ (infrml) in a jam (infrml)

pétrodevise *f* petrocurrency

pétrole *m* oil; ∼ **brut** crude oil; ∼ **carburant pour tracteurs** vapourizing oil BrE, vaporizing oil AmE

pétrolier[1], **-ière** *adj* (prix, industrie, marché) oil; (pays) oil-producing

pétrolier[2] *m* (navigation) oil tanker; ∼ **de ligne sans escales** (navigation) oil-bearing ⋯⟩

continuous liner

pétrolifère *adj* oil-bearing

pétro-obligation *f* petrobond

pharmaceutique *adj* pharmaceutical

phase *f* (dans les négociations) stage; (mise en œuvre d'un projet) phase; **être en ~ d'achèvement** be nearing completion, near completion; **~ d'alerte** (publicité) advance publicity; **~ clé** key stage; **~ de démarrage** start-up; **~ initiale** phase zero (jarg); **~ intermédiaire** intermediate stage; **~ d'introduction** introductory phase; **~ de lancement** (marketing) introductory phase; **~ préliminaire** draft stage; **~ de production** processing stage; **~ de récession** recessionary phase; **~ de traitement** computer run; **~ de vérification** verification phase

photocalque *m* blueprint

photocomposition *f* filmsetting BrE, photocomposition AmE

photocopie *f* photocopy, Xerox® AmE; **faire une ~ de** photocopy, Xerox® AmE

photocopier *vt* photocopy, Xerox® AmE

photocopieuse *f* photocopier

photographe *mf* photographer; **~ de presse** press photographer

photograveur, -euse *m,f* process engraver

photostyle *m* light pen, stylus

phrase *f* phrase; **~ d'appel** (presse) blurb

physiquement *adv* physically

PIB *abrév* (▶**produit intérieur brut**) GDP (gross domestic product); **~ d'équilibre** equilibrium GDP; **~ par habitant** GDP per capita

picorage *m* (Fin) cherry picking

pièce *f* (de monnaie) coin; (exemplaire) document; (composant) component; **10 euros la ~** 10 euros each *ou* apiece; **la ~ ci-jointe** the enclosed document; **travail à la ~** piecework; **travailler à la ~** be on piecework; **~ de caisse** cash voucher; **~ comptable** voucher; **~ détachée** spare part; **~s d'un dossier** case papers; **~s d'embarquement** shipping documents; **~ fiscale** tax voucher; **~ d'identité** identity papers; **~ jointe** enclosure; (Info) attachment; **~ justificative** supporting document; (Compta) voucher; **~ justificative de caisse** cash voucher; **~ justificative de virement de fonds** transfer of funds voucher; **~ de monnaie** coin; **~ en or** gold coin; **~ d'or** d'investissement investment gold coin; **~ de rechange** spare part; **~ de règlement bancaire** bank settlement voucher

pied *m* (mesure) foot; **sur le même ~** on the same footing; **~ carré** square foot; **~ cube** cubic feet; **~ de façade** front foot US

piège *m* trap; **~ de la liquidité** liquidity trap; **~ de la mobilité** mobility trap

pierre *f* (immobilier) property BrE, real estate

AmE; **investir dans la ~** invest in bricks and mortar; **~ d'achoppement** stumbling block; **~ angulaire** cornerstone

piéton, -onne *m,f* pedestrian; **rue piétonne** pedestrian street; **zone piétonne** pedestrian precinct BrE, pedestrian mall AmE

pige *f* (pour journalistes) fee; **travailler à la ~** do freelance work

pigiste *mf* freelance journalist

pignon *m* (petite roue) pinion

pile *f* (électrique) battery; (tas) stack; (numérotage des conteneurs) row; **~ auxiliaire** battery backup; **~ de conteneurs** container stack; **~ de secours** battery backup

pilier *m* (de l'économie) backbone, keystone

pillage *m* (Fin) corporate raiding; (de magasins) looting; (plagiat) plagiarism

pilotage *m* (gestion) (d'entreprise) running; (de négociations) leading; **comité de ~** steering committee

pilote[1] *adj* (étude, projet) pilot; (ferme, hôpital, école) experimental

pilote[2] *m* (automobile) driver; (de l'air) pilot; (navigation) pilot; (télévision, radio) pilot; (Info) driver; **~ automatique** autopilot; **~ d'écran** screen driver; **~ d'émission** (télévision) anchor; **~ d'impression** print driver; **~ de ligne** pilot; **~ de périphérique** device driver; **~ de souris** mouse driver

piloté, e *adj* (Info) driven; **~ par logiciel** software-driven; **~ par menus** menu-driven; **~ par ordinateur** computer-driven; **~ par souris** mouse-driven

piloter *vt* (voiture) drive; (avion, navire) pilot; (entreprise) run; (négociation) lead

pionnier, -ière *m,f* pioneer

pipeline *m* pipeline

piquet *m*: **~ de grève** picket line

piratage *m* piracy; **~ de films vidéo** video piracy; **~ informatique** computer hacking; **~ de logiciel** software piracy

pirate *m* pirate; **~ informatique** (computer) hacker

pirater *vt* (Info) hack, hack into

piraterie *f* (maritime) marine piracy

pire *m*: **le ~ des cas** worst-case scenario

pisciculture *f* fish farming

pistage *m* (Econ) tracking

piste *f* track; (aéroport) runway; **~ d'audit** audit trail; **~ de bande magnétique** channel; **~ de roulement** (aéroport) taxiway; **~ sonore** soundtrack

pistonner *vt*: **~ qn** (infrml) pull strings for sb, pull wires for sb AmE

pivot *m* (d'économie, de gouvernement) linchpin; **société ~** key firm

pixel *m* (Info) pixel, picture element

p.j. *abrév* (▶**pièce jointe**) enc, enclosure; (Info) attachment

PL *abrév* (▶**port en lourd**) (navigation) D/W

(deadweight)

placard *m* (affiche) bill; (imprimerie) galley; ∼ **publicitaire** large display advertisement; (pleine page) full-page advertisement

place *f* (espace) room, space; (position) position; (siège) seat; (emploi) job; **à la** ∼ **de** instead of, in lieu of; **en** ∼ (système, structures) in place; (dirigeant, parti, pouvoir) ruling; **mettre en** ∼ (stratégie) put in place; (marché, régime, réseau) establish, set up; (ligne téléphonique) install; **sur** ∼ on the spot; ∼ **bancaire** banking centre BrE, banking center AmE; ∼ **boursière** stock market; ∼ **extraterritoriale** (Fin) offshore place; ∼ **financière** financial market; ∼ **kilomètre utilisée** seat kilometres used BrE, seat kilometers used AmE; ∼ **du marché** marketplace; ∼ **mille** seat mile; ∼ **milles par heure-moteur** seat miles per engine hour; ∼ **publique** public

placement *m* (Fin) investment; **faire des** ∼**s** invest; **faire un** ∼ **immobilier** invest in property; **le** ∼ **des diplômés** finding jobs for graduates; ∼ **en actions** equity investment; ∼ **en actions ordinaires** common share investment BrE, common stock investment AmE; ∼ **admissible** qualified investment; ∼ **d'un bloc de contrôle** secondary-primary distribution; ∼ **éthique** ethical investment; ∼ **excessif** overplacing; ∼ **de fonds commun d'options** option mutual fund; ∼ **initial** (titres) primary distribution, primary offering; ∼ **de premier ordre** blue chip (investment); ∼ **sûr** safe investment; ∼ **en valeurs** investment in securities

placer [1] *vt* (Bourse, Fin) (investir) invest; (mettre en dépôt) deposit, put; (trouver un emploi pour) find a job for; ∼ **de l'argent en viager** invest in an annuity; ∼ **un dépôt** place a deposit; ∼ **qn comme apprenti chez qn** apprentice sb to sb; ∼ **qn dans une situation financière difficile** impose financial hardship on sb; ∼ **en report** lend; ∼ **ses petits copains** (infrml) get jobs for the boys (infrml); ∼ **sous administration judiciaire** put into receivership; ∼ **sous garde** (documents saisis) place in custody [2] **se placer** *v pron* take a position; **se** ∼ **à cheval** take a straddle position

placier *m* sales representative

plafond *m* (limite) upper limit, ceiling; **à concurrence d'un** ∼ **de** up to a maximum of; **crever le** ∼ break the ceiling; ∼ **des bénéfices retraite** pension earnings cap; ∼ **budgétaire** budget ceiling; ∼ **de crédit** credit limit; ∼ **des dépenses** expenditure limit; ∼ **des emprunts** borrowing limit; ∼ **d'hypothèque** mortgage ceiling; ∼ **maximal de la période d'amortissement** asset depreciation range; ∼ **d'un prêt** lending ceiling; ∼ **de prix** price ceiling; ∼ **sur les taux d'intérêt** interest rate ceiling

plafonnement *m* (de prix, de salaires) ceiling

(de on); (de dépenses) limitation; ∼ **des bénéfices** profit ceiling; ∼ **des salaires** wage ceiling

plafonner [1] *vt* (prix, salaire, production) put a ceiling on; **l'augmentation des salaires est plafonnée à 3%** wage increases are limited to a maximum of 3%; (taux d'intérêt) cap [2] *vi* (se stabiliser) level off (**à** at); (atteindre une limite) reach a ceiling

plage *f* (éventail) range; (tranche horaire) slot; ∼ **de prix** price range; ∼ **horaire** time slot

plagiat *m* plagiarism; ∼ **de brevets d'entreprise** corporate plagiarism

plaider [1] *vt* plead; ∼ **sa cause** argue one's case [2] *vi* plead, put in a plea; ∼ **coupable** plead guilty

plaideur, -euse *m,f* litigant

plaidoirie *f* plea

plaidoyer *m* pleading

plaignant, e *m,f* plaintiff

plaindre: se ∼ *v pron* complain

plainte *f* complaint; (droit pénal) complaint; **déposer une** ∼ **contre qn auprès de** lodge a complaint against sb with; ∼ **contre X** action against X, action against person or persons unknown

plaire *vi*: ∼ **à** appeal to

plan *m* (projet) plan, project; (Ind) (de machine, d'appareil) (schéma directeur) blueprint; (après construction) plan; **sur le** ∼ **international** at international level; ∼ **d'accession au logement** housing scheme; ∼ **d'accroissement de capital volontaire** voluntary accumulation plan; ∼ **d'achat d'actions** stock purchase plan; ∼ **d'action** action plan; ∼ **d'affaires** business plan; ∼ **d'aménagement d'une zone** zone improvement plan US, area development plan; ∼ **d'amortissement** amortization schedule; ∼ **annuel de vérification** annual audit plan UK; ∼ **d'assurance** insurance scheme; ∼ **d'audit** audit plan; ∼ **de base** ground plan; ∼ **budgétaire** budgetary planning; ∼ **de carrière** career path, career planning; ∼ **de charge** load plan; ∼ **de chargement** (d'un navire) cargo plan, stowage plan; ∼ **comptable** accounting plan, chart of accounts; ∼ **de désengagement** withdrawal plan; ∼ **de développement** business plan; ∼ **de développement pluriannuel** multiyear operational plan; ∼ **directeur** master plan; ∼ **de divisions** departmental plan; ∼ **d'économies sur la masse salariale** payroll savings plan; ∼ **d'encouragement** incentive plan; ∼ **d'ensemble** master plan; ∼ **d'entreprise** (d'une banque) business plan; ∼ **d'entreprise détaillé** in-depth business plan, detailed business plan; ∼ **d'épargne en actions** personal equity plan UK; ∼ **d'épargne-retraite** retirement savings plan; ∼ **d'exploitation** operating plan; ∼ **de** ⋯‣

financement financing plan; ~ **financier** financial planning; ~ **de formation** training scheme; ~ **de garantie de prêts** loan guarantee scheme; ~ **d'identification d'un produit** pack shot; ~ **d'intéressement aux bénéfices** profit-sharing scheme UK, profit-sharing plan US; ~ **d'intéressement des employés** share participation scheme, share scheme; ~ **d'investissement** investment plan; ~ **d'investissement pour cadres** executive option scheme; ~ **d'investissement en titres indexés** Indexed Security Investment Plan; ~ **à longue échéance** forward planning; ~ **de lot** plot plan US; ~ **de marché** (processus de planification) market planning; ~ **de masse** site plan; ~ **média** (V&M) media planning; ~ **d'occupation des sols** (local) land-use planning; ~ **opérationnel de l'année budgétaire** budget year operational plan; ~ **d'options sur titres** stock option plan; ~ **paquet** (V&M) pack shot; ~ **personnel de capitalisation** personal equity plan UK; ~ **de redressement** recovery plan; ~ **de relance** recovery scheme; ~ **de remboursement** redemption table; ~ **de retraite basée sur les primes d'assurance** benefit-based pension plan; ~ **de retraite financé par avance** advance-funded pension plan UK; ~ **de retraite professionnelle de l'employeur** employer's occupational pension scheme UK; ~ **de sauvetage d'hypothèque** mortgage rescue scheme UK; ~ **de secours** contingency plan; ~ **de site** (Info) site map; ~ **social** planned redundancy scheme; ~ **de souscription à des actions** stock option plan; ~ **stratégique** strategic planning; ~ **de travail** (work) schedule; ~ **de trésorerie** cash forecast; ~ **de vérification** audit work schedule

plancher m (Econ, Fin) floor, lower limit; **atteindre un** ~ (prix, cours) bottom out; ~ **des prix** price floor; ~ **des salaires** wage floor; ~ **des taux** rate floor

planificateur m planner; ~ **financier agréé** certified financial planner

planification f planning; ~ **administrative** business planning; ~ **de base** floor planning; ~ **des bénéfices** profit planning; ~ **des bureaux** office planning; ~ **d'entreprise** organization planning; ~ **du financement d'immobilisations** capital-funding planning; ~ **fiscale** tax planning; ~ **préliminaire** preplanning; ~ **de produit** product planning; ~ **des ressources humaines** human resource planning; ~ **stratégique de l'impôt** strategic tax planning; ~ **à terme** forward planning

planifier vt (production, semaine) plan; **non planifié** unscheduled; ~ **à court/long terme** draw up a short-/long-term plan; ~ **l'économie à moyen terme** draw up a

medium-term economic plan; **économie planifiée** planned economy

planigramme m planning

planning m (de travail) schedule; (Compta) planning; **respecter le** ~ keep to the schedule; ~ **des cabines** (navigation) cabin allocation; ~ **des charges** expenditure planning; ~ **de la production** production planning

plantage m (Info) crash

plantation f plantation; ~ **nationale** state-owned plantation

plaque f (de porte) nameplate; ~ **indicatrice** (Transp) data plate

plaquette f brochure; ~s (Compta) published accounts; ~ **publicitaire** advertising brochure

plastique m plastic; **sac en** ~ plastic bag; ~ **biodégradable** biodegradable plastic

plat, e adj flat

plateau m (niveau constant) plateau; **arriver à un** ~ (inflation) level off; ~ **de cargaison** (Transp) cargo tray

plate-forme f (pétrole) platform; (Info) (matérielle, logicielle) platform; (chemin de fer) flat car US; ~ **de changement** tail lift; ~ **de forage** oil platform, oil rig

plein, e adj full; **à** ~ **rendement** at full capacity; **au** ~ **d'avenir** up-and-coming; **de** ~ **droit** ex officio (frml); ~ **écran** full-screen; ~ **emploi** full employment; ~**e garantie** full cover; ~**e page** full-screen; ~ **propriétaire** freeholder; ~**e propriété** freehold property; ~ **tarif** full fare

plénier, -ière adj plenary; **séance** ~ plenary session

pléthore f (de marchandises) superabundance; ~ **de l'offre** oversupply

pli m (lettre) letter; ~ **urgent** urgent letter; **sous** ~ **cacheté** in a sealed envelope; **sous** ~ **séparé** under separate cover; ~ **accordéon** (publicité) accordion folding

pluie f rain; ~s **acides** acid rain

pluri-annuel, -elle adj multiyear

plus adv more; **au** ~ at the most; **avec** ~ **ou moins de** with varying degrees of; **en** ~ **de** in addition to; **le service est en** ~ service is extra; **au** ~ **tard** at the latest; ~ **bas** below; **de** ~ further; **de** ~ **en plus** increasingly; ~ **haut** above; ~ **ou moins** more or less; **le** ~ **tôt possible** as soon as possible, a.s.a.p.; **pour** ~ **de sûreté** to be on the safe side; **pour** ~ **amples renseignements** for further information; ~ **haut niveau** peak rate; ~ **offrant** highest bidder; ~ **petit dénominateur commun** lowest common denominator

plusieurs adj several; **à** ~ **étages** multistorey

plus-value f (bénéfice à la vente) capital gain; (accroissement de la valeur) increase in value; (excédent) surplus; ~ **absolue** absolute surplus value; ~ **de capital** capital appreciation; ~ **éventuelle** potential profit; ~ **foncière** unearned increment of land; ~ **imposable** taxable capital gain; ~ **de prime** unearned premium

PLV *abrév* (▸**publicité sur le lieu de vente**) point-of-sale advertising

PMA *abrév* (▸**pays moins avancé**) developing country

PME *abrév* (▸**petites et moyennes entreprises**) SME (small and medium-sized enterprises); ~ **existante** existing SME

PMI *abrév* (▸**petites et moyennes industries**) SMME (small and medium-sized manufacturing companies)

PNB *abrév* (▸**produit national brut**) GNP (gross national product)

pneu *m* tyre BrE, tire AmE

PNN *abrév* (▸**produit national net**) NNP (net national product)

p.o. *abrév* (▸**par ordre**) by order

pognon *m* (infrml) bread (infrml), dough US (infrml), money

poids *m* weight; de ~ forceful; **donner du ~ à** (argument) lend weight to; ~ **et capacité à charge complète** (conteneur) full loaded weight and capacity; ~ **ou cubage** (tarif) weight/measurement; ~ **brut** gross weight; ~ **de cargaison** weight of cargo; ~ **du commerce** avoirdupois; ~ **constaté** weight ascertained; ~ **constructeur** (véhicule) design weight; ~ **de la dette** debt burden; ~ **garanti** (gestion des stocks) weight guaranteed; ~ **de l'impôt** tax burden; ~ **juste** full weight; ~ **lourd** heavy goods vehicle, road haulage vehicle; ~ **média** media weight; ~ **et mesures** weights and measures; ~ **mort** dead load; ~ **des pertes** burden of losses; ~ **de la preuve** burden of proof; ~ **prévu** (véhicule routier) design weight; ~ **à sec** dry weight; ~ **spécifique** specific gravity; ~ **total en charge** (véhicule routier) gross vehicle weight; ~ **transitaire** shipper weight; ~ **à vide** weight when empty; ~ **à vide de la remorque** trailer unladen weight

poignée *f* handle

point *m* point; (Info) dot; (de l'ordre du jour) item; (dans un système de calcul) point; **du ~ de vue de l'emploi** on the employment front; **du ~ de vue ergonomique** ergonomically; **du ~ de vue historique** historically; **faire le ~ d'un compte** reconcile an account; **faire le ~** (de la situation) take stock of the situation; **mettre au ~** finalize; **un ~ de rencontre** a meeting point; **marquer/perdre des ~s** score/lose points; **être un bon ~ pour** be a plus point for; **être un mauvais ~ pour** be a black mark against; **un programme en trois ~s** a three-point plan; ~**s sur lesquels il convient de revenir** matters to be followed up; ~ **d'accès** (Transp) gateway, access port; ~ **d'ancrage soudé** (sur un navire) fixed lashing plate; ~ **d'appui** fulcrum; ~ **d'arrêt**

break point; ~ **bas** bottom, low; (d'un graphe, d'une courbe) trough; ~ **de base** basis point; ~ **butoir** cutoff point; ~ **central** (débat) focal point; focus group; ~ **chaud** hot spot, trouble spot; ~ **de combustion en degrés Celsius** flash point in degrees centigrade; ~ **de combustion en degrés Fahrenheit** flash point in degrees Fahrenheit; ~ **commun** mutual interest, mutual ground; ~ **de comparaison** baseline; ~ **de contrôle** checkpoint; ~ **critique** peril point; ~ **décisif** turning point; ~ **de départ** starting point, point of departure; ~ **de discussion** bargaining chip; ~**s divers** any other business; ~ **de droit** point of law; ~ **d'ébullition initial** initial boiling point; ~ **d'équilibre** break-even point; ~ **essentiel** key point; ~ **d'exportation** point of export; ~ **d'impact** ground zero; ~ **d'indice** index point; ~ **d'interruption** breakpoint; ~ **en litige** issue; ~ **mort** break-even point; ~ **noir** problem, problem area; (sur la route) blackspot; ~**s par pouce** (Info) dots per inch; ~ **de pourcentage** percentage point; ~ **de ralliement** rallying point; ~ **de référence** bench mark; ~ **de repère** (référence) bench mark; (dans l'espace) landmark; ~ **de reprise** (d'un programme) checkpoint; ~**s de suspension** suspension marks; ~ **de vente** sales outlet, point of sale; ~ **de vente électronique** electronic point of sale; ~ **de vente de services de détail** retail outlet; ~ **de vue** point of view, position, viewpoint

pointage *m* (vérification) checking; (Ind) (en entrant) clocking-in; (en sortant) clocking-off; **une feuille de ~** a time sheet; ~ **des emplacements disponibles** (publicité) available sites list

pointe *f* (niveau élevé) high; (Bourse) spike; de ~ (technologie, technique) advanced, state-of-the-art; (secteur, industrie) high-tech; (entreprise, spécialiste) leading; **une ~ de 20%** a 20% high; **aux heures de ~** during the rush hour, at peak time; ~ **de puissance** power surge; ~ **saisonnière** seasonal high

pointer *vi* (chargement, déchargement d'un navire) tally; ~ **à l'agence pour l'emploi** sign on at the unemployment office; (en arrivant) clock in, clock on; (en sortant) clock off, clock out

pointeur *m* (Info) pointer

pointillé *m* dotted line

point-virgule *m* semicolon

polarisation *f* polarization

pôle *m* pole; ~ **de croissance** growth pole; ~ **d'attractions** attraction centre

polémique *f* controversy

poli, e *adj* polite

police *f* police; (Info, Média) font; (Assur) (contrat) policy; ~ **d'abonnement** open policy; ~ **de l'Air et des Frontières** border police; ~ **annulable** voidable policy; ~ **d'assurance** insurance policy; ~ ⋯⋗

d'assurance hypothèque mortgage
insurance policy; ~ **d'assurance incendie
accidents risques divers** property and
casualty policy insuring agreement; ~
d'assurance maritime marine insurance
policy; ~ **d'assurance mixte** mixed policy;
~ **d'assurance sur la vie** life insurance
policy; ~ **d'assurance temporaire** term
insurance policy; ~ **d'assurance au tiers**
third-party insurance policy; ~
d'assurance tous risques comprehensive
insurance policy; ~ **d'assurance-vie
agréée** registered life insurance policy; ~
**d'assurance-vie indexée sur le cours
des valeurs boursières** equity-linked
policy; ~ **de base** master policy; ~ **de
caractères** font; ~ **contre catastrophe**
catastrophe policy; ~ **commerciale**
commercial form; ~ **évaluée** valued policy;
~ **flottante** floating policy; ~ **flotte** fleet
policy; ~ **forfaitaire** block policy; ~ **de fret**
freight policy; ~ **globale** blanket policy; ~
incendie normalisée standard fire policy
US; ~ **multirisque** comprehensive insurance
policy; ~ **non-évaluée** unvalued policy; ~
nulle void policy; ~ **ouverte** open cover; ~
avec participation aux bénéfices
participating policy; ~ **perte d'exploitation**
business interruption insurance; ~ **pertes
indirectes** consequential-loss policy;
(assurance de dommages) pay as cargo; ~ **au
porteur** policy to bearer; ~ **preuve de
l'intérêt assuré** policy proof of interest; ~
pour propriétaires d'entreprise business
owner's policy; ~ **provisoire** binder US,
provisional policy; ~ **de rente individuelle**
individual annuity policy; ~ **revenu
familial garanti** family income policy; ~
aux risques désignés named peril policy;
~ **sans effet légal** honour policy BrE,
honor policy AmE; ~ **tarifée** rated policy;
~ **à temps** time policy; ~ **à terme**
term policy; ~ **tous risques d'argent
et des valeurs** money and securities
broad-form policy; ~ **en valeur agréée**
valued policy; ~ **au voyage** voyage
policy

politique[1] *adj* political

politique[2] *f* (science, art) politics; (manière de
gouverner) policy; ~ **étrangère/intérieure/
agricole/sociale** foreign/domestic/
agricultural/social policy; **nouvelle ~ de
recrutement** new recruitment policy; **notre
~ des prix** our pricing policy; ~
d'acquisition acquisition policy; ~
agricole commune (UE) Common
Agricultural Policy; ~ **d'ajustement
structurel** structural adjustment policy; ~
anti-discriminatoire (à l'embauche) positive
discrimination BrE, affirmative action AmE; ~
de l'argent cher tight monetary policy; ~
d'argent facile easy money policy; ~
attentiste wait-and-see policy; ~ **du bâton**
policy of the big stick; ~ **budgétaire**

budgetary policy; ~ **commerciale** business
policy; ~ **comptable** accounting policy; ~
conjoncturelle stabilization policy; ~
contractuelle collective agreement policy;
~ **contractuelle en matière de salaires**
bargaining theory of wages; ~ **du coup de
force** power politics; ~ **des coups
d'accordéon** stop-go policy UK; ~ **de crédit**
credit policy; ~ **du crédit à bon marché**
cheap money policy; ~ **de défense du
consommateur** consumer policy; ~ **de
déficit budgétaire** compensatory fiscal
policy; ~ **démographique** population
policy; ~ **de développement** development
policy; ~ **dictée par les besoins de la
clientèle** client-led marketing policy; ~
**dictée par les besoins des
consommateurs** consumer-led marketing
policy; ~ **d'écrémage** (marketing) skimming
policy; ~ **de l'égalité des chances** Equal
Opportunity Policy UK; ~ **de l'emploi**
employment policy; ~ **d'encadrement du
crédit** tight monetary policy; ~
énergétique energy policy; ~ **d'entreprise**
business politics; ~ **de l'environnement**
environment policy, environmental policy; ~
d'expédients practical politics; ~
extérieure external government policy; ~
d'immobilisation fixed asset policy; ~
d'intimidation power politics; ~ **de la
main-d'œuvre** manpower policy; ~ **de
non-intervention** hands-off policy; ~ **des
organisations** organizational politics; ~ **du
parti** party line; ~ **des petits pas** (infrml)
gradualism; ~ **de la porte ouverte** open-
door policy; ~ **de prêt** lending policy; ~ **de
prise en compte globale** (Envir) bubble
policy; ~ **de prix différentiels** differential
pricing; ~ **de providence** popularism; ~
de prudence prudent policy; ~
règlementaire statutory policy UK; ~ **de
relance par le déficit budgétaire** deficit
spending policy; ~ **de resserrement
budgétaire** tight fiscal policy; ~ **de
resserrement des dépenses** tight fiscal
policy; ~ **salariale** incomes policy, wages
policy

politiquement *adv* politically

politiser *vt* politicize

polluant[1], e *adj* polluting; **peu ~** low-
polluting

polluant[2] *m* pollutant; ~ **atmosphérique**
air pollutant, atmospheric pollutant; ~ **des
eaux** water pollutant

pollué, e *adj* polluted

polluer *vt* pollute

pollueur, -euse *m,f* polluter

pollutaxe *f* tax on polluters

pollution *f* pollution; ~ **atmosphérique**
air pollution, atmospheric pollution; ~ **des
cours d'eau** river pollution; ~ **diffuse**
background pollution; ~ **des eaux** water
pollution; ~ **par les hydrocarbures** oil

pollution; ~ **du littoral** coastal pollution; ~ **marine** marine pollution; ~ **par les pluies acides** acid rain pollution; ~ **radioactive** radioactive pollution

polycopie f (procédé) duplicating; (feuille) duplicate

polycopier vt duplicate

polyculture f mixed farming

polyglotte adj multilingual

polygone m polygon; ~ **de fréquence** frequency polygon

polyvalence f multiskilling

polyvalent, e adj all-purpose

ponction f levy; **faire une** ~ **sur les réseves** tap the reserves; ~ **fiscale** tax levy

ponctionnement m: ~ **des réserves** (Econ) draining reserves

ponctionner vt (somme) levy; (réserves) tap

ponctualité f punctuality

ponctuel, -elle adj (chargement, paiement) prompt; (personne) punctual; (problème) isolated; (ciblé) selective; (limité) limited; **débrayages** ~s **dans une usine** selective stoppages in a factory

pondération f (Fin) weighting; (d'un portefeuille) indexing; (équilibrage) balancing; ~ **du risque** risk weighting

pondérer vt (Fin) weight; (équilibrer) balance

pont m (d'un navire) deck; (vacances) extended weekend; **faire le** ~ have an extended weekend; **faire un** ~ **d'or à qn** pay sb a fortune; **à** ~ **unique** (navire) single-deck; ~ **aérien** airlift; ~s **et chaussées** highways department; ~ **découvert** (d'un navire) open deck; ~ **inférieur** (d'un avion, navire) lower deck; ~ **à péage** toll bridge; ~ **promenade** (d'un navire) promenade deck; ~ **supérieur** (d'un navire) upper deck; ~ **terrestre** landbridge; ~ **wagons** (transbordeur) train ferry deck

pontée f (navigation) deck cargo, deck load; **en** ~ (cargaison) above deck

ponton m (maritime) pontoon

ponton-grue m (maritime) floating crane

pool m (de dactylos) pool; ~ **bancaire** consortium of banks

POP abrév (▶port payé) CPT (carriage paid to)

populaire adj popular

population f population; ~ **active** working ou active population; ~ **de droit** de jure population; ~ **de fait** de facto population

port m (avec installations portuaires) port; (pour accoster) harbour BrE, harbor AmE; (Info) port; ~ **et assurance payés jusqu'à** (lieu de destination) carriage and insurance paid to; ~ **payé jusqu'à** (lieu nommé de destination) carriage paid to; ~ **à** ~ port to port; ~ **d'accès** port; ~ **d'aéroglisseurs** hoverport; ~ **d'armement** port of registry;

~ **d'arrivée** port of arrival, port of entry; (navigation) destination port; ~ **d'attache** port of registry; ~ **autonome** self-governing port; ~ **de chargement** port of loading, shipping port; ~ **de commerce** trading port, commercial port; ~ **de conteneurs** container port; ~ **de déchargement** port of discharge; ~ **de destination** port of destination; ~ **dû** freight forward; ~ **et emballage** postage and packing; ~ **franc** free port; ~ **en lourd** dead weight; (d'un navire) deadweight tonnage; ~ **en lourd total** (d'un navire) deadweight all told; ~ **maritime** sea port, seaport; ~ **payé** (lettre) postage paid; (marchandises) carriage paid; ~ **de pêche** fishing port; ~ **de refuge** port of necessity; ~ **série** serial port

portabilité f (Info) portability

portable[1] adj (Info) laptop, portable

portable[2] m (ordinateur) laptop, laptop computer; (téléphone) mobile

portage m (Info) porting

portatif, -ive adj portable; (caméra) hand-held

porte f door; **mettre qn à la** ~ (infrml) sack sb, fire sb; ~ **coupe-feu** fire door; ~ **à dépôt** door-to-depot; ~ **d'embarquement** boarding gate; ~s **ouvertes** open day BrE, open house AmE

porte-à-porte m door-to-door selling; **faire du** ~ be a door-to-door salesperson

porte-barges m (navigation) barge carrier

porte-barils m barrel handler

porte-conteneurs m (navigation) container ship

portée f (étendue) scope; (effet) impact; **à la** ~ **de tous** accessible; **d'une** ~ **considérable** far-reaching; **être à** ~ **de main** (accessible) be within reach; (dans un endroit commode) be to hand; **c'est à la** ~ **de toutes les bourses** everybody can afford it; ~ **de commandement** chain of command; ~ **et fréquence** (publicité) reach and frequency; ~ **du plancher** (navigation) floor bearing; ~ **statistique** statistical spread

portefeuille m portfolio; **investissements de** ~ portfolio investments; ~ **d'actifs** asset portfolio; ~ **d'actions** stock portfolio; ~ **d'activités** business portfolio; ~ **effets de change** bill holding, bill portfolio; ~ **équilibré** balanced portfolio; ~ **hypothécaire** mortgage portfolio; ~ **d'investissement** investment portfolio; ~ **de marques** brand portfolio; ~ **de négociation** (d'un établissement) trading book; ~ **d'obligations** bond portfolio; ~ **des prêts** loan portfolio; ~ **de produits** product portfolio; ~ **de titres** securities portfolio; ~ **de valeurs portant intérêt** interest-bearing trading portfolio

porte-parole m spokesperson

porter [1] vt (initiales, titre) have; (sceau) bear; (Compta) post; (Droit) lay; (toast) propose; ~ ⋯⋗

son attention à turn one's attention to; ~ **au compte de charge**; ~ **un coup très dur à l'économie** throw a wrench into the economy; **porté au crédit de** (Fin) credited to; ~ **la date du 28 avril** be dated 28 April; ~ **au débit d'un compte** charge to an account; ~ **une écriture** post an entry; ~ **indûment préjudice** cause undue hardship; ~ **un intérêt de** bear an interest of; **portant intérêt** interest-bearing; ~ **plainte contre qn** bring an accusation against sb; ~ **en réduction sur** charge against; ~ **au revenu** add to income
[2] **porter sur** *vi* (mesure, accord) concern, apply to; (interdiction) apply to; **l'impôt porte sur les objets de luxe** the tax applies to luxury goods
[3] **se porter** *v pron* **se ~ aval pour qn** stand as guarantor for sb; **se ~ candidat à un poste** apply for a job; **se ~ caution pour qn** stand surety for sb; **se ~ garant de** answer for; **se ~ garant de qn** stand as guarantor for sb

porteur[1], **-euse** *adj* (marché) buoyant; (métier) booming; **être ~ d'intérêts** (compte) bear interest-bearing

porteur[2], **-euse** *m,f* (de titres d'une société) bearer; **au ~** (chèque, titre) bearer; ~ **d'actions** equity holder; ~ **de bonne foi** holder in due course; ~ **de carte** cardholder; ~ **de droits de souscription** rights holder; ~ **d'obligations** bondholder; ~ **d'obligations non garanties** debenture holder; ~ **de titres** security holder

portier *m* (concierge) porter; (d'un hôtel) commissionaire UK

portillon *m* barrier

portique *m* (manutention) gantry crane; ~ **pour colis lourds** heavy lifting beam; ~ **à conteneurs** portainer crane; ~ **sur pneus** travelift

portrait *m* (presse, édition) portrait; ~ **complet** (V&M) cross section

pose *f*: ~ **de tabulations** (Info) tab setting

poser *vt* affix; (une question) ask; ~ **sa candidature à une élection** stand for election; ~ **sa candidature pour un emploi** apply for a job

positif, -ive *adj* (effet, conséquence, rendement) positive; (réponse) affirmative; (entretien) constructive; (réaction) positive, favourable BrE, favorable AmE; (point) positive, plus; (image) positive

position *f* (situation) position; (dans la société) status; (sur une question) position, stance; (au classement) place, position; (Banque) balance; (Bourse) position; **être en ~ minoritaire/ majoritaire** be in the minority/majority; **être en ~ dominante sur le marché** be a market leader; **être en ~ créditrice/débitrice** (compte) be in credit/debit; **avoir une ~ longue sur contrat à terme** be long in futures; **déboucler une ~** close a position, liquidate a position; ~ **acheteur** (pour options)

bull position; ~ **acheteur initiale** open long position; ~ **acheteur sur options d'achat** call purchase, long call; ~ **acheteur sur options de vente** put purchase; ~ **anti-inflationniste** anti-inflationary stance; ~ **à la baisse** bear position; ~ **binaire** bit location; ~ **de choix** (sur le marché) prime position; ~ **de compensation** clearing position; (à découvert) value position; ~ **de compensation en compte** long value position; ~ **au comptant** spot position; ~ **du compte** account statement; ~ **d'un compte à découvert** short account position; ~ **concurrentielle** competitive position; ~ **courte** short position; ~ **courte sur contrat à terme** short futures position; ~ **courte sur option** short option position; ~ **couverte** bull position; ~ **de couverture** offset; ~ **à découvert** bear position; ~ **fermée** evened-out position; ~ **fiscale** tax position; ~ **de force** bargaining position; ~ **à la hausse** bull position; ~ **inflexible** tough stance; ~ **initiale** opening position; ~ **inverse** offset; ~ **isolée** island display; ~ **liquidée** closed position; ~ **longue** long position; ~ **de longue option d'achat** long call position; ~ **de longue option de vente** long put position; ~ **de marché** market position; ~ **mixte** spread position; ~ **au mouillage** (navigation) anchor position; ~ **de négociation** negotiating position; ~ **nette débitrice** exposed net asset position; ~ **nette à terme** net forward position; ~ **à l'ouverture** opening position; ~ **de place** (Bourse, Fin) open interest; ~ **de repli** fall-back position; ~ **à risque** risk position; ~ **sociale** social standing; ~ **de titres en garde** segregated free position; ~ **vendeur** bear position; ~ **vendeur sur option d'achat** short call position; ~ **vendeur sur option de vente** short put position

positionnement *m* positioning; ~ **dynamique** dynamic positioning; ~ **de la marque** brand positioning

positionner [1] *vt* position
[2] **se positionner** *v pron* position oneself

positivement *adv* positively

possédants *m pl*: **les ~** the wealthy

possession *f* (bien) possession; (de bien, maison, terres) ownership, possession; **être en ~ de** be in possession of; **entrer en/prendre ~ de qch** take possession of; (héritage) come into; ~ **d'actions** shareholding, stockholding; ~ **effective de terres** occupation; ~ **de fait** adverse possession; ~ **immédiate** immediate occupancy; ~ **sommaire** summary possession

possibilité *f* (occasion) opportunity; (solution) option; (éventualité) possibility; ~**s** (de personne) abilities; (d'appareil) potential uses; **dans la mesure de ses ~s** according to one's means; ~**s d'adaptation** adaptability; ~ **d'écoulement des excédents** vent for surplus; **~s d'emploi** job opportunities; **~ d'emprunt** borrowing power; **~s d'épargne** savings ratio; **~s offertes** facilities; **~ de rachat** buy-back option; **~ de virement** transferability

possible *adj* possible; **dès que ~** as soon as possible, a.s.a.p.; **tout est ~** the sky's the limit

postacheminement *m* on-carriage

postdaté, e *adj* postdated

postdater *vt* postdate

poste¹ *m* (emploi) post, position; (Ind) (période de travail) shift; (Fin, Compta) item; **un ~ de secrétaire/comptable** a position as a secretary/an accountant; **~ vacant, ~ à pourvoir** vacancy; **supprimer dix ~s** cut ten jobs; **suppression de ~s** job cuts; **trois ~s vacants/à pourvoir** three vacancies; **numéro de ~** (téléphone) extension number; **pourrais-je avoir le ~ 426?** could I have extension 426?; **travailler par ~s de huit heures** do eight-hour shifts; **~ d'actif** asset item; **~ auxiliaire** subpost office; **~ du bilan** balance sheet item; **~ de chalandage** (port) lighterage berth; **~ clients** trade creditors; **~ de commandement** position of authority; **~ de débutant** junior position; **~ de désarmement** (port) lay-up berth; **~ de direction** managerial position; **~ de douane** customs station; **~ douanier frontalier** frontier customs post; **~ fournisseurs** accounts payable; **~ à marchandises diverses** (port) general cargo berth; **~ opérationnel** line position; **~ de passif** liability item; **~ de péage** tollbooth; **~ de radio** radio; **~ de relève** relief shift, swing shift; **~ à temps partiel** part-time job; **~ de travail** workstation

poste² *f* (service) post BrE, mail AmE; **mettre qch à la ~** post sth BrE, mail sth; **par la ~** by post BrE; **~ aérienne** airmail; **~ restante** poste restante UK, general delivery US

poster *vt* (lettre) post BrE, mail AmE; (employé) assign to a shift

postévaluation *f* (Fisc) postassessing

postier, -ière *m,f* postal worker

postulant, e *m,f* applicant

postulat *m* premise; **~s comptables** accounting conventions

postuler **1** *vt* apply for
2 *vi* apply; **~ pour un emploi** apply for a job

pot *m* (réunion) (infrml) drinks party; **~ catalytique** catalytic converter; **~ de lancement** (infrml) (d'un livre) launch party

pot-de-vin *m* bribe, backhander, kickback; **toucher des pots-de-vin** take bribes

poteau *m* post; **~ indicateur** signpost; **~ télégraphique** telegraph pole

potentiel¹, -elle *adj* potential, prospective; (client) prospective

potentiel² *m* potential (**de** for); **avoir du ~** have potential; **~ de bénéfice** profit potential; **~ de croissance** growth potential; **~ de croissance de production** potential output, productive potential; **~ d'emprunt** borrowing potential; **~ d'expansion** development potential; **~ à la hausse** upside potential; **~ inemployé** surplus capacity; **~ du marché** market potential; **~ de production** production capacity, productive capacity; **~ de production utilisé** utilized capacity; **~ sous-utilisé** idle capacity, surplus capacity; **~ de vente** sales potential

potentiellement *adv* potentially

poulie *f* (manutention) block

pourboire *m* tip

pourcentage *m* (fraction) percentage; (rémunération) commission; **comme ~ de** as a percentage of; **être au ~** be on commission; **~ d'actions de priorité** preferred stock ratio; **~ d'augmentation** percentage increase; **~ du bénéfice net distribué en dividende** dividend payout ratio; **~ de clients perdus** attrition rate, churn rate; **~ déterminé** specified percentage; **~ d'exonération** exempt percentage; **~ de frais** expense ratio; **~ d'intérêt** percentage interest; **~ sur les recettes** back end (jarg); **~ de variation** percentage change

pourparlers *m pl* negotiations (**entre** between)

poursuite *f* (Droit) proceedings; (suite) continuation; **engager des ~ contre qn** take proceedings against sb; **abandonner les ~s** drop the charges; **la ~ d'un dialogue** the continuation of a dialogue; **~ contre assuré** defence of suit against insured BrE, defense of suit against insured AmE; **~s en diffamation** libel proceedings; **~ en dommages et intérêts** action for damages; **~s judiciaires** legal proceedings

poursuivre **1** *vt* (efforts, activité, tentative) continue; (négociations, objectif, travaux, carrière) pursue; (en justice) prosecute; **~ pour contrefaçon** prosecute for forgery; **~ pour diffamation** sue for libel; **~ pour dommages-intérêts** sue for damages; **~ pour faux** prosecute for forgery; **~ jusqu'au bout** follow sth through; **~ qn en justice** (en droit pénal) take legal action against sb; (en droit civil) sue sb; **~ ses études** continue one's studies; **~ ses remboursements hypothécaires** keep up payment on one's mortgage; **~ qn devant les tribunaux** (en droit pénal) take legal action against sb; (en droit civil) sue sb
2 **se poursuivre** *v pron* (continuer) continue

pourvoi *m* appeal

pourvoir **1** *vt* **~ un poste** fill a vacancy; **~ en personnel** man, staff; **pourvu en personnel** staffed; **~ en capital** *ou* **en fonds** capitalize

2 *vi* ~ **à** (besoins) cater for, provide for
3 **se pourvoir** *v pron*: **se** ~ **en appel** appeal, lodge an appeal

poussée *f* (augmentation de prix) sharp rise *ou* increase; (d'activité) upsurge; ~ **inflationniste** inflationary trend; ~ **récessionniste** contractionary pressure

pousser *vt* (produit) push; (acheteur) prompt; ~ **qn à bout** push sb to the limit; ~ **à la vente** hammer the market; ~ **à la baisse** (Bourse) bear; ~ **à la hausse** (Bourse) bull

poussière *f* dust; ~ **de charbon** coal dust

pouvoir *m* (puissance, autorité) power; **donner** ~ **à qn** (Droit) give sb a proxy; **au** ~ (gouvernement) in power; **avoir le** ~ **de** have the power to; **être au** ~ hold power; ~ **d'achat** spending power, purchasing power; ~ **d'achat courant** current purchasing power; ~ **d'achat discrétionnaire** discretionary spending power; ~ **d'un acheteur sur le marché** market power; ~ **administratif** administrative authority; ~ **budgétaire** budgetary power; ~ **compensatoire** countervailing power; ~ **de crédit commercial** commercial lending power; ~ **discrétionnaire** discretionary authority; ~ **d'emprunt des titres** borrowing power of securities; ~**s d'enquête** investigatory powers; ~**s d'exception** emergency powers; ~ **d'instruction** investigatory powers; ~ **judiciaire** judiciary; ~ **législatif** legislative power; ~ **de monopole** monopoly power; ~ **de négociation** bargaining power; ~ **policier** police power; ~ **de prêt** lending power; **les** ~**s publics** the authorities; ~ **de signer les documents financiers** financial signing authority; ~ **de vendre** power of sale

p.p. *abrév* (▸**port payé**) p.p. (postage paid); (▸**par procuration**) p.p, per pro. (frml) (per procurationem); (▸**pages**) pp. (pages); (▸**prépayé**) p.p. (prepaid)

PPA *abrév* (▸**parité du pouvoir d'achat**) PPP (purchasing power parity)

ppp *abrév* (▸**points par pouce**) dpi (dots per inch)

P.R. *abrév* (▸**parc relais**) park and ride

pragmatique *adj* pragmatic

pratique¹ *adj* (expérience, formation) hands-on; (renseignement, conseil, moyen) practical; (problème, détail) practical; (endroit) convenient; (appareil, objet) practical, handy; **avoir l'esprit** ~ be practical

pratique² *f* (application de principes) practice; (habitude) practice; (expérience) practical experience; **en** ~ in practice; **mettre qch en** ~ put sth into practice; **avoir une bonne** ~ **de l'anglais** have a good working knowledge of English; **une** ~ **courante/frauduleuse** a common/fraudulent practice; **manquer de** ~ lack experience; **avoir une longue** ~ **de** have many years' experience in; ~ **abusive** (du

vendeur) abusive practice; ~**s anticoncurrentielles** anticompetitive practices; ~ **des cinq pour cent** five per cent rule; ~**s commerciales** business practices, trade practices; ~**s commerciales déloyales** unfair trading practices; ~**s commerciales respectant la libre concurrence** fair business practices; ~**s comptables** accounting practices; ~**s déloyales** anticompetitive practices; ~ **de discrimination** discrimination; ~ **de fabrication sous licence** licensing; ~**s illégales** (commerce) illegal practices; ~ **d'investissement** investment practice; ~ **des prix magiques** odd-value pricing; ~ **de prix sauvage** predatory pricing; ~ **professionnelle** working practice; ~**s restrictives** (industrielles) restrictive practices

pratiquer *vt* (méthode) use; (politique) pursue; (taux d'intérêt) charge; (métier, langue) practise BrE, practice AmE; ~ **une déduction** make a deduction; ~ **un prix d'appel** set a price-point; **les prix pratiqués** the current prices

préalable *adj* (permission, avis) prior; (entretien, étude) preliminary; **conditions** ~**s** preconditions, prerequisites

préambule *m* preamble, precondition

préavis *m* notice; **donner 5 jours de** ~ give 5 days' notice; **délai de** ~ term of notice, notice period; **sans** ~ without notice; ~ **de clause de résiliation** notice of cancellation clause; ~ **de grève** notice of strike action; ~ **légal** legal notice; ~ **de licenciement** notice of dismissal; ~ **en règle** formal notice

pré-budgétaire *adj* pre-budget

précautionneux, -euse *adj* cautious

précédent¹, e *adj* previous

précédent² *m* precedent; **créer un** ~ create a precedent; **sans** ~ unprecedented

précéder *vt* precede

précis, e *adj* (personne) precise; (rapport, chiffre, donnée, calcul) accurate; (date) definite; (cas, motif, critère) specific; (moment, endroit) exact; (idée) clear, definite; **à deux heures** ~**es** at exactly 2 o'clock

précisé, e *adj* specified

préciser *vt* (programme, idées) clarify; (forme d'un contrat) formalize, qualify; (date, lieu, nombre) specify

précision *f* (détail) detail; (justesse) accuracy; (de rapport, de document) accuracy; ~ **à la seconde près** split-second timing; **pour plus de** ~**s contacter...** for further details, please contact...; ~**s sur la personne à charge** details of dependant

précité, e *adj* aforementioned, as mentioned above

précompte *m* deduction; ~ **de l'impôt** deduction of tax at source

précompter *vt* (cotisation) deduct (**sur** from)

préconditionner *vt* prepack, pre-package

préconiser *vt* advocate, recommend

prédateur, -trice *m,f* corporate raider, predator

prédécesseur *m* predecessor; **∼ en droit** legal predecessor

pré-défini, e *adj* preset, pre-defined

prédéterminé, e *adj* prearranged, predetermined

prédéterminer *vt* prearrange, predetermine

prédire *vt* foresee

prédominant, e *adj* prevailing

prédominer *vi* prevail

préemballé, e *adj* (marketing) prepackaged

prééminent, e *adj* pre-eminent

pré-enregistré, e *adj* prerecorded

préétablir *vt* pre-establish; (Fin) precompute

préévaluation *f* preassessing

préf. *abrév* (▸**préférence**) pref. (preference)

préfabriqué, e *adj* prefabricated

préférence *f* preference; **avoir une ∼ marquée pour qch** have a clear preference for sth; **donner la ∼ à** give preference to; **par ordre de ∼** in order of preference; **∼ du consommateur** consumer preference, consumer choice; **∼ pour la liquidité** liquidity preference; **∼ pour une marque** brand preference; **∼ révélée** revealed preference

préfigurer *vt* anticipate

préfinancement *m* bridge financing

préjudice *m* harm, damage; (perte) loss; **au ∼ de** to the detriment of; **porter ∼ à qn** harm sb; **porter ∼ à qch** damage sth; **sans ∼ de** (Droit) without prejudice to; **au ∼ de qn** to the detriment of sb; **∼ indu** undue hardship; **∼ irréparable** irreparable harm; **∼ matériel** material loss; **∼ moral** moral wrong; **∼ subi** losses suffered

préjudiciable *adj* prejudicial

préjugé *m* bias; **∼s sexistes** sex stereotyping; **avoir un ∼ en défaveur de qn/ qch** have a prejudice against sb/sth

prélèvement *m* (Fin) (opération) debiting, withdrawal; (sur emprunt) drawing; (Fisc) deduction, levy; **∼ agricole** agricultural levy; **∼ automatique** direct debit; **∼ compensatoire à l'exportation** compensatory levy; **∼ de la cotisation syndicale** check-off US; **∼ de droits** charges collect; **∼ forfaitaire** standard deduction, flat-rate withholding; **∼s obligatoires** compulsory tax and social security deductions; **∼ PAC** (UE) CAP levy; **∼ sur le salaire** payroll deduction; **∼ à la source** salary deduction; **∼ sur stocks** withdrawal from stocks

prélever *vt* (Fin) (sur compte bancaire) debit; (des fonds) withdraw; (argent, pourcentage) take; (Fisc) deduct, levy; **∼ sur** draw from; **∼ un**

intérêt charge interest

préliminaires *m pl* preliminaries; **∼ d'absorption** absorption approach

prématuré, e *adj* premature

préméditation *f* premeditation; **avec/sans ∼** (agir) with/without premeditation

premier, -ière *adj* first; **de ∼ ordre** top-rated; **de ∼ plan** front-running; (Info) foreground; **de ∼ rang** senior; **en ∼ lieu** in the first instance; **∼ entré, ∼ sorti** (évaluation des stocks) first in, first out; **être le ∼ à faire qch** take the lead in doing sth; **le ∼ janvier/ juin** the first of January/June; **de première classe** first-rate; **article ∼ du code pénal** first article of the penal code; **de première génération** first-generation; **le ∼ producteur de vin** the leading wine producer; **nos ∼s prix** (pour voyage) our cheapest holidays; (pour billets) our cheapest tickets; **∼ avertissement** verbal warning; **première classe** first class; **∼ clerc** head clerk, senior clerk; **première commande** original order; **∼ coupon** long coupon; **∼ cours** opening price; **première date de remboursement** first call date; **∼ détenteur des droits d'auteur** first owner of copyright; **première écriture** prime entry; **première édition matinale** (presse) early edition BrE, first edition BrE, bulldog edition AmE; **première émission publique** initial public offering AmE; **première épreuve** (publicité) pull; **∼ jour de notification** first notice day; **∼ jour des opérations** first dealing day; **∼ ministre** prime minister; **première mise de fonds** initial outlay; **première mouture** draft; **première offre** opening bid; **première page** title page; **∼ plan** foreground; **∼ privilège** first lien; **∼ projet** rough draft; **première qualité** premium grade; **première quinzaine** (du mois) first half; **∼ semestre** first half; **première sortie** (Transp) roll-out; **∼ trimestre** first quarter

prémisse *f* premise

premium *m* premium; **∼ de l'option d'achat** call option premium; **∼ de l'option de vente** put option premium

prémunir *v pron*: **se ∼ contre** provide against

prendre *vt* (associé, emploi) take; (abonnement, brevet) take out; (le pouvoir, le commandement) assume, take on; (marchandises) pick up; **∼ de l'âge** age; **∼ de l'avance** forge ahead; **∼ de l'avance petit à petit** edge ahead; **∼ un bon départ** get off to a flying start; **∼ une chambre** (dans un hôtel) book a room; **∼ en charge** assume responsibility for; **∼ des commandes** take orders; **∼ en compte** take into account; (Bourse) discount; **∼ congé** take leave; **∼ conscience de** realize; **∼ contact avec** get in touch *ou* contact with; **∼ le contrôle** take control; **∼ le contrôle administratif** (d'une société) take

····▸

administrative control; ～ **le contrôle de take over**; ～ **un créneau dans le marché** bridge a gap in the market; ～ **une décision** make a decision; ～ **un dépôt** take a deposit; ～ **les devants** take the lead; ～ **un échantillon** take a sample; ～ **effet** take effect; ～ **effet le…** take effect from…; ～ **ferme** (émission) underwrite; ～ **fin** come to an end; (contrat) cease to have effect; ～ **forme** (idée) take shape; ～ **les frais à sa charge** bear the costs; ～ **des garanties** obtain security; ～ **l'initiative** take the initiative; ～ **livraison** (Bourse) take delivery, take up; ～ **livraison de** accept delivery of; ～ **livraison des titres** take up stocks; ～ **des mesures** take steps; ～ **en note** take down; ～ **note de qch** make a note of sth; ～ **l'offensive** take the offensive; ～ **les paroles de qn pour argent comptant** take sb's word at face value; ～ **part à** take part in; ～ **parti pour qn** take sides with sb; ～ **une participation dans** acquire an interest in; ～ **une participation en actions dans** take an equity stake in; ～ **le passif à sa charge** take over liabilities; ～ **une position** take up a position; ～ **possession** take possession; ～ **qch en compte** or **en considération** take sth into account; ～ **qch en sténo** take sth down in shorthand; ～ **rendez-vous avec qn** make an appointment with sb; ～ **des renseignements sur qn** take up sb's references; ～ **une réservation** make a reservation; ～ **la responsabilité de qch** take responsibility for sth; ～ **du retard** fall behind schedule; ～ **sa retraite** retire; ～ **une retraite anticipée** take early retirement; ～ **un risque** take a risk; ～ **des risques** take a gamble; ～ **des sanctions contre qn** (Res Hum) take disciplinary action against sb; ～ **soin de** make a point of; ～ **la succession de** take over from; ～ **le taux** (Bourse) take the rate; ～ **un tournant** take a turn; ～ **toutes les mesures nécessaires** take such steps as are considered necessary; ～ **des vacances** take a holiday BrE, take a vacation AmE; ～ **de la valeur** (bien) appreciate; ～ **de la vitesse** gather speed; ～ **un weekend prolongé** take a long week-end

preneur, -euse *m,f* (acheteur) taker, buyer; (d'un chèque) payee; **trouver ~** (article) attract a buyer; (personne) find a buyer; ～ **à bail** lessee; ～**s d'offre** takers-in; ～ **de prix** price taker

prénom *m* first name, forename; ～ **usuel** usual first name

préoccuper *vt* (inquiéter) worry; (occuper) concern

préparateur, -trice *m,f* (en laboratoire) laboratory assistant; ～ **de copie** copy editor, sub

préparation *f* preparation; (d'un bilan) making up; ～ **du budget** budgeting; ～ **des budgets de trésorerie** cash budgeting; ～ **de copie** (composition) mark-up; ～ **des données** (Info) data preparation

préparer *vt* plan, prepare; ～ **un budget** budget; ～ **qch** (à l'avance) plan ahead for sth; ～ **qch pour qn** lay sth on for sb; ～ **le terrain pour qch** pave the way for sth

prépayé, e *adj* prepaid

prépension *f* Bel early retirement

prépensionné, e *m,f* Bel preretiree

préplacement *m* (Fin) pre-marketing

préposé, e *m,f* (employé) employee; ～ **à plein temps** full-time attendant; ～ **aux prêts** loan officer

pré-projet *m* draft project

préretraite *f* early retirement

préretraité, e *m,f* preretiree

prérogative *f* prerogative; ～**s de la direction** managerial prerogative

près *adv*: **à peu ~** in the region of

prescripteur, -trice *m,f* (V&M) (d'un produit) promoter, advocate

prescription *f* (Droit) statute of limitations, time bar

prescrire *vt* prescribe

prescrit, e *adj* prescribed; (Droit) time-barred

préséance *f* precedence; **avoir la ~ sur** take precedence over

présélection *f* (de candidats) shortlisting, screening

présélectionner *vt* (candidats) shortlist

présence *f* presence; (au travail) attendance; ～ **sur un marché** market presence

présentateur, -trice *m,f* (télévision) presenter, anchor; (du journal télévisé) newsreader BrE, newscastor AmE

présentation *f* (de personne) introduction; (de lettre, magazine) layout; (de carte, ticket) production; (d'une lettre de change) presentment; (Compta) layout; (véhicule) roll-out; (de produit) presentation; **sur ~** (Compta) on demand; (Fin) at sight; ～ **de bilan en compte** account form; ～ **budgétaire** budgetary submission; ～ **de collections** fashion show; ～ **des comptes annuels** reporting treatment; ～ **de documents** presentation of documents; ～ **erronée des faits** misrepresentation of the facts; ～ **horizontale** (bilan) account form; ～ **d'informations par voie de notes** note disclosure; ～ **visuelle** (Info) soft copy

présenter ⬚1 *vt* (personne) introduce; (marchandises) display; (faits, budget, conclusions, situation) present; (ticket, documents, pièce justificative) produce; (théorie, objections) set out; (risque, difficultés) present; (signes) show; (candidature) submit; (objectifs d'un projet) set forth; (rapport) present; (émission) present; ～ **un chèque au paiement** present a cheque for payment BrE, present a check for payment AmE; ～ **les conditions requises pour** be eligible for sth; ～ **un déficit** run a deficit; ～ **sur écran** display; ～ **un excédent** run a surplus; ～ **une facture pour remise** present a bill for discount; ~ **peu d'attrait pour les consommateurs** have little consumer appeal; ~ **une proposition** submit a proposal; ~ **ses excuses** apologize; ~ **qch sous un jour favorable** present sth in a favourable light; ~ **un solde de** show a balance of; ~ **une traite à l'acceptation** present a draft for acceptance

2 **se présenter** *v pron* (à un poste) apply in person; **se ~ aux élections** stand for election; **se ~ à l'enregistrement** check in; **se ~ à la réception** (hôtel) check in

présentoir *m* (meuble) display stand; ~ **géant** merchandiser; ~ **de gondole** shelf display; ~ **en vrac** dump bin

présérie *f* pilot run

préservation *f* (de site, bâtiment) conservation, preservation; (de l'environnement) conservation; ~ **financièrement rentable de l'environnement** economic conservation; ~ **du portefeuille** conservation of portfolio

préserver *vt* (patrimoine) preserve; (droit, intérêt, environment) protect

présidence *f* presidency

président, e *m,f* president; (de comité) chair, chairperson; ~ **adjoint** vice-president; ~ **du comité exécutif** chairman of the executive committee; ~ **du conseil** chairman of the board; ~ **du conseil d'administration** chairman of the administrative board; ~ **directeur général** chairman and managing director UK, managing director UK, chairman and chief executive US, chief executive officer US; ~ **du directoire** chairman of the board of management; ~ **élu** chairman elect; ~ **de la Haute Cour de Justice** ≈ Lord Chief Justice UK; ~ **d'honneur** honorary chairman, honorary president; ~ **de syndicat financier** syndicate manager; ~ **de tribunal** presiding judge

présider *vt* (réunion, commission) chair; (Droit) (cour) preside over

présidium *m* presidium

présomption *f* (d'innocence) (de of) presumption

presse *f* press; ~ **financière** financial press; ~ **à imprimer** (imprimerie) printing press; ~ **populaire** tabloid press; ~ **nationale** national press; ~ **parallèle** alternate press; ~ **à scandale** gutterpress; ~ **spécialisée** trade press

pressé, e *adj* in a hurry; **être ~ par le temps** be under time pressure

pressentir *vt* (sonder) approach; ~ **qn pour un emploi** approach sb about a job

pression *f* pressure; **faire ~ sur qn** put pressure on sb; **travailler sous ~** work under pressure; **faire/exercer des ~s sur qn** put pressure on sb; **groupe de ~** pressure group; ~ **de citerne** tank pressure; ~ **effective moyenne** mean effective pressure; ~ **fiscale** tax burden; ~ **à la hausse**

upward pressure; ~ **indirecte** leverage; ~ **inflationniste** inflationary pressure; ~ **morale** moral persuasion; ~ **sur les prix** price pressure; ~ **de service** working pressure

prestataire *m* (de l'aide sociale) benefit recipient, welfare recipient AmE; ~ **de services** service provider, service enterprise

prestation *f* (aide) benefit; (prêt, fourniture) provision (**de** of); (au travail) performance; (service) service; ~ **accessoire** accessorial service; ~ **d'assistance** welfare payment; ~ **d'assistance sociale** social security payment BrE, social assistance payment Can; ~**s bancaires** banking services; ~ **bénévole** ex gratia payment; ~ **en cas de maladie** sickness benefit; ~ **de décès** death benefit; ~ **d'entretien** maintenance fee; ~ **en espèces** cash benefit; ~ **de gestion** (de portefeuille) management fee; ~ **pour incapacité** disability annuity, disability benefit; ~**s maladie** health benefits; ~ **maladie réglementaire** statutory sick pay UK; ~ **en nature** allowance in kind; ~**s de préretraite** early retirement benefits; ~ **de service** provision of service; ~ **de service bancaire** bank service charge; ~**s sociales** Social Security benefits UK, welfare benefits; ~ **supplémentaire** supplementary assistance

prestigieux, -euse *adj* prestigious

prêt¹, e *adj* ready; ~ **à l'emploi** ready for use; ~ **pour l'expédition** ready for shipment; ~**, volontaire et capable** ready, willing and able

prêt² *m* (somme, prêtée) loan; (action) lending; **demander un ~** apply for a loan; **obtenir un ~** secure a loan; **un ~ de 5000 euros** a 5000-euro loan; **un ~ à 15%** a 15% loan; **faire un ~** take out a loan; **demande de ~** loan application;

prêt a... ~ **pour achat de titres** purpose loan; ~**s agricoles** agricultural lending; ~ **aux agriculteurs** farm loan; ~ **d'aide au développement** aid development loan; ~ **d'ajustement structurel** structural adjustment loan; ~ **d'amélioration de l'habitat** home improvement loan; ~**s en amont** upstream loans; ~ **d'amortissement** amortization loan; ~ **de l'argent emprunté** on-lending; ~ **d'assistance technique** technical assistance loan; ~ **au-dessus du pair** lending at a premium; ~ **automobile** car loan;

b... ~ **bancaire** bank loan; ~ **de banque** bank loan; ~ **bilatéral** bilateral loan; ~ **bonifié** soft loan; ~ **boursier** securities loan;

c... ~ **capitalisé à l'échéance** interest-only loan; ~ **certifié** truth in lending; ~ **commercial** commercial loan; ~ **aux conditions commerciales** hard loan; ~ ⤳

aux conditions du marché hard loan; ~
conjoint joint loan; ~ **consenti pour**
l'achat d'une maison home purchase loan;
~ **à la consommation** consumer loan; ~ **à**
la construction construction loan; ~ **de**
conversion conversion loan; ~s **en cours**
outstanding loans; ~ **de courtage** broker's
loan;

d... ~ **déguisé** backdoor lending;

e... ~ **entièrement productif** fully
performing loan; ~s **aux entreprises**
corporate lending; ~ **escompté** discounted
loan; ~ **d'État** government loan; ~
étudiant student loan;

f... ~ **de façade** fronting loan; ~ **fixe**
fixed loan; ~ **au fonds d'amortissement**
sinking fund loan; ~ **à forfait** nonrecourse
loan;

g... ~ **garanti** secured loan; ~ **garanti**
par l'État sovereign loan; ~ **géré** managed
loan; ~ **global** package mortgage, whole
loan;

h... ~ **d'honneur** loan on trust; ~
hypothécaire mortgage loan; ~
hypothécaire avec participation à la
plus-value shared-appreciation mortgage; ~
hypothécaire classique conventional
mortgage; ~ **hypothécaire à court terme**
à taux d'intérêt renégociable roll-over
mortgage; ~s **hypothécaires en cours**
outstanding mortgage loans; ~
hypothécaire de deuxième rang second
mortgage lending; ~ **hypothécaire investi**
en actions equity-linked mortgage; ~
hypothécaire de premier rang first
mortgage, first mortgage loan; ~
hypothécaire à remboursements
périodiques amortized mortgage loan; ~
hypothécaire résidentiel residential
mortgage loan; ~ **hypothécaire à taux**
réglable adjustable-rate mortgage; ~
hypothécaire variable adjustable mortgage
loan; ~ **sur hypothèque** mortgage loan;

i... ~ **immobilier** home purchase loan; ~
impayé outstanding loan; ~ **indexé** index-
tied loan; ~ **initial** front-end loan, start-up
loan; ~s **interbancaires** bank-to-bank
lending; ~ **à intérêt fixe** fixed interest loan;
~ **intermédiaire** pass-through loan; ~
irrécouvrable bad loan; ~ **irrévocable**
uncallable loan;

j... ~ **au jour le jour** day-to-day loan;

l... ~ **lié** tied loan; ~-**logement gigogne**
piggyback loan;

m... ~ **maritime** maritime loan; ~
minimum floor loan; ~ **à moyen terme**
medium-term loan; ~ **multidevises**
multicurrency loan;

n... ~ **sur nantissement** advance against
security; ~ **à la navigation** shipping loan;
~ **non garanti** unsecured loan; ~ **non**
productif nonproductive loan; ~ **non**
remboursé outstanding loan;

o... ~ **obligataire** debenture loan;

p ~s **par découvert** overdraft lending;
~s, **participations et avances** loans,
investments and advances; ~ **en**
participation participation loan; ~
personnel personal loan; ~ **personnel**
garanti secured personal loan; ~ **à prime**
lending at a premium; ~ **principal** senior
loan; ~ **de production** production loan; ~
progressif step-up loan;

q... ~ **de qualité** quality loan;

r... ~ **recouvré** loan recovery; ~
remboursable sur demande call loan; ~
remboursable en monnaie forte hard
loan; ~ **remboursable par versements**
instalment loan BrE, installment loan AmE; ~
à remboursement régulier constant-
payment loan UK; ~ **révocable** callable loan;
~ **à risque souverain** sovereign risk loan;

s... ~ **sans intérêt** interest-free loan; ~
sans recours nonrecourse loan; ~ **de**
secours aid loan; ~ **simple** straight loan;
~ **à une société** corporate loan; ~ **en**
souffrance noncurrent loan; ~ **soumis à**
fluctuations swing loan; ~ **de soutien**
standby loan;

t... ~ **à taux de base** prime rate loan; ~
à taux de financement plafonné cap rate
loan; ~ **à taux fixe** fixed-rate loan; ~ **à**
taux nul interest-free loan; ~ **à taux**
plafonné cap rate loan; ~ **à taux**
préférentiel Can prime rate loan; ~ **à taux**
révisable roll-over loan, roll-over loan; ~
à titre gratuit gratuitous loan; ~ **de titres**
securities loan; security lending;

v... ~ **sur la valeur nette d'une maison**
home equity loan; ~ **à vue** demand loan

prêt-à-monter m kit, flat-pack; **bureau en**
~ flat-packed desk, self-assembly desk

prêt-à-porter m (vêtements, secteur) ready-
to-wear; **acheter du** ~ buy clothes off the
peg

prêt-bail m leasing

prétendre ⟦1⟧ vt claim (**que** that)
⟦2⟧ vi ~ **à** claim; **à des indemnités** claim
damages

prétendu, e adj alleged

prête-nom m frontman; (société) dummy
company

prétention f (revendication) claim; **avoir des**
~s **à** or **sur qch** have a claim to sth; (dans un
entretien d'embauche) **quelles sont vos** ~s?
what are your salary expectations?

prêter vt (de l'argent) lend; ~ **à intérêt** lend
at interest; ~ **contre titre** lend against
security; ~ **sur gages** lend on security; ~ **de**
l'importance à attach importance to; ~ **sur**
nantissement lend on security ou collateral;
~ **en participation** syndicate a loan

prêteur, -euse m,f lender; ~ **de dernier**
ressort lender of last resort; ~ **sur gages**
pawnbroker; ~ **hypothécaire** mortgage

lender; ∿ **institutionnel** institutional
lender; ∿ **privé** private lender; ∿ **résiduel**
residual lender

prêt-relais *m* bridging loan

preuve *f* evidence, proof; **ayant fait ses ∿s**
experienced; **faire ses ∿s** win one's spurs; ∿
d'achat/de propriété proof of purchase/of
ownership; ∿ **d'audit** audit evidence; ∿
concluante conclusive evidence; ∿
contradictoire conflicting evidence; ∿ **de**
créance evidence of indebtedness; ∿ **écrite**
documentary evidence, written evidence; ∿
factuelle factual evidence; ∿ **indirecte**
circumstantial evidence; ∿ **irréfragable**
conclusive evidence; ∿ **matérielle** concrete
evidence; ∿ **péremptoire** conclusive
evidence; ∿ **du titre** evidence of title; ∿ **de**
l'utilisation evidence of use

prévaloir *vi* prevail (**sur** over; **contre**
against)

prévarication *f* (Droit) breach of trust

prévenir *vt* (donner un advertissement) warn;
(éviter) prevent

préventif, -ive *adj* preventive; **à titre ∿** as
a preventive measure

prévention *f* prevention; ∿ **des**
accidents accident prevention; ∿ **des**
fraudes fraud prevention; ∿ **du gaspillage**
waste prevention; ∿ **de sinistre** claims
prevention

prévisible *adj* foreseeable, predictable

prévision *f* (action de prévoir) forecasting;
(résultat) forecast, projection; **en ∿ d'une**
chute du cours in anticipation of a fall in
the price; ∿ **autoproductive** (Bourse) self-
fulfilling prophecy; ∿ **des bénéfices** profit
planning; ∿ **de bénéfices et de**
performances profit and performance
planning; ∿ **de caisse** cash forecast; ∿**s**
commerciales business forecasting; ∿ **de**
coûts cost forecast; ∿ **de la demande**
demand forecasting; ∿ **des dépenses**
d'investissement capital budgeting; ∿**s de**
dépenses publiques public spending plans;
∿**s détaillées** detailed forecasting; ∿**s**
économiques business forecasts; ∿ **des**
effectifs staff forecasting; ∿ **dans**
l'entreprise business forecasting; ∿**s sur**
l'environnement environmental forecasting;
∿**s financières** financial forecasts; (Fisc)
fiscal projections; ∿ **à long terme** long-
range forecast; ∿ **de main-d'œuvre**
manpower forecasting; ∿**s du marché**
market forecast; ∿**s normatives** normative
forecasting; ∿ **de programme** programme
forecast BrE, program forecast AmE; ∿**s**
rationnelles rational expectations; ∿ **des**
réponses (publicité) response projection; ∿
technologique technological forecasting; ∿
de trésorerie cash forecast; ∿ **de ventes**
sales projection, sales forecast

prévisionniste *mf* forecaster

prévisualiser *vt* preview

prévoir *vt* anticipate; ∿ **une baisse de**
cours be bearish; ∿ **des frais de** budget for;
∿ **une hausse de cours** be bullish; ∿ **une**
marge d'erreur allow for a margin of error

prévoyance *f* foresight; (Fin) contingency;
fonds de ∿ contingency fund; **manque de ∿**
lack of foresight; **organisme de ∿** provident
society; ∿ **inoffensive** (Pol) hold-harmless
provision (jarg); ∿ **pour pertes** (feuille de bilan,
inventaire comptable) loss contingency

prévu, e *adj* anticipated, expected; ∿ **par la**
loi statutory; ∿ **par réglement** prescribed;
comme ∿ according to plan, as scheduled;
être ∿ pour be scheduled for; **qui n'est pas**
∿ **par un texte de loi** nonstatutory

prière *f* (demande) request; ∿ **de faire suivre**
please forward; ∿ **d'insérer immédiatement**
for immediate release

primaire *adj* (secteur, industrie) primary

primauté *f* (Ind, Econ) leadership

prime *f* (récompense) bonus; (pour les prêts)
bonus, premium; (indemnité) allowance;
(subvention) subsidy; **à ∿** at a premium; **en ∿**
as a bonus; ∿ **absorbée** earned premium; ∿
d'achat call option price, call premium; ∿
acheteur buyer's option; ∿ **acquise** earned
premium; ∿ **additionnelle** additional
premium; ∿ **d'adieu** golden handshake; ∿
d'ancienneté seniority bonus; ∿ **annuelle**
annual premium; ∿ **en argent** cash bonus;
∿ **d'assurance** insurance premium; ∿
d'assurance automobile motor premium;
∿ **d'assurance-vie** life insurance premium;
∿ **pour bons et loyaux services** golden
handshake; ∿ **de célérité** (chargement/
déchargement) despatch money; ∿ **collective**
group bonus, group incentive; ∿
conditionnement (marketing) container
premium; ∿ **constante** level premium; ∿ **à**
la construction (navale) construction
subsidy; ∿ **de conversion** conversion
premium; ∿ **dégressive** premiums
reducing; ∿ **de départ** golden handshake; ∿
de dépôt deposit premium; ∿ **d'émission**
bond discount, share premium BrE, paid-in
surplus AmE; ∿ **d'émissions d'obligations**
bond premium; ∿ **d'encouragement**
incentive bonus; ∿ **à l'exportation** export
subsidy; ∿ **de fidélité** loyalty bonus; ∿ **de**
fin d'année Christmas bonus; ∿ **de fin de**
contrat terminal bonus; ∿ **fixe** fixed
premium; ∿ **forfaitaire** flat-rate bonus; ∿
d'heures supplémentaires overtime
premium; ∿ **de licenciement** redundancy
payment; ∿ **multirisque** combined
premium; ∿ **nivelée** level premium; ∿ **non**
hiérarchisée flat-rate bonus; ∿ **en options**
sur actions compensatory stock option UK;
∿ **payée d'avance** advance premium; ∿
de présence attendance bonus; ∿ **de**
production production bonus; ∿ **de**
productivité acceleration premium; ∿
provisionnelle deposit premium; ∿ **de**
recrutement golden hello, recruitment ····⟶

bonus; ~ de **régularisation** adjustment
premium; ~ de **remboursement**
redemption premium; ~ **de**
remboursement des obligations bond
redemption premium; ~ de **rendement**
production bonus; ~ de **rentabilité**
incentive pay; ~ de **réorientation**
redeployment premium; ~ de **risque** risk
premium, risk-related premium; ~ **salariale**
wage bonus; ~ **sur réserve capitalisée**
bonus reserve; ~ **sur taux d'intérêt**
interest rate subsidy; ~ **au temps** time
premium; ~ de **terme** term premium; ~ **en**
trop excess contribution; ~ **unique** single
premium; ~ **vendeur** seller's option; ~ **au**
vendeur push money; ~ **à la vente**
(publicité) push incentive

primeur f: avoir la ~ de **l'information** be
the first one to hear the news

principal[1], e *adj* principal, main; (hiérarchie)
senior; **principaux partenaires**
commerciaux main trading partners; ~
producteur major producer

principal[2] *m* (Admin) head clerk, senior
clerk; (Fin) principal amount; ~ **et intérêts**
principal and interest; ~ **d'une obligation**
bond principal

principalement *adv* principally

principe *m* principle; (Compta) convention;
en ~ in theory; par ~ on principle; ~ de
l'accélérateur acceleration principle; ~
d'ancienneté seniority principle; ~ **d'audit**
auditing principles; ~ de **compensation**
compensation principle; ~ de **la continuité**
de l'exploitation going-concern principle; ~
directeur guiding principle; ~ de **l'échelle**
des salaires wage-scale principle; ~
d'exclusion exclusion principle; ~
marginal d'attribution marginal principle
of allocation; ~ de **l'observation**
volontaire principle of voluntary
compliance; ~ de la **péréquation** principle
of equalization; ~ de **la permanence**
consistency principle; ~ **pollueur-payeur**
polluter pays principle; ~ **du prix de pleine**
concurrence arm's-length principle; ~ de
prudence conservatism principle, principle
of conservatism; ~ de **rattachement à**
l'exercice accrual concept

prioritaire *adj* priority; **être** ~ have
priority

priorité f priority; **avoir la** ~ **sur** take
precedence over, take priority over; **donner**
la ~ **à** give priority to; **prendre la** ~ **sur qch**
take priority over sth; **être une** ~ **absolue**,
être la ~ **numéro un** be the top priority; ~
absolue number one priority; ~ **antérieure**
earlier priority

prioritiser *vt* prioritize

prise f: ~ de **bénéfices** profit taking; ~ **en**
charge totale des soins médicaux
comprehensive health-care system; ~ **en**
compte de l'inflation allowance for

inflation; ~ de **contrôle** takeover; ~ **de**
contrôle adossée leveraged buyout; ~ **de**
contrôle convenue agreed takeover; ~ **de**
courant plug; ~ de **décision** decision
making; ~ **d'échantillon** sample drawing;
~ **d'effet du contrat d'assurance**
commencement of coverage; ~ **ferme** bought
deal, underwriting; ~ de **livraison** taking
delivery; ~ **en pension** repurchase
agreement, REPO AmE; ~ de **possession**
(d'un lieu) occupation

prisée f (Fin) pricing

priser *vt* (Fin) price

priseur *m* (Fin) pricer

privation f hardship; ~ de **liberté** (Droit)
constraint

privatisation f privatization

privatisé, e *adj* privatized

privatiser *vt* privatize

privé[1]**, e** *adj* private; (non officiel) (visite,
entretien, source) unoffical; ~ **de** deprived of

privé[2] *m*: (secteur économique) **le** ~ the private
sector

privilège *m* privilege; (Droit) lien; (immobilier)
licence BrE, license AmE; ~ **d'exemption de**
paiement skip-payment privilege; ~ **fiscal**
tax lien, tax privilege; ~ **général** general
lien; ~ **hypothécaire** mortgage lien; ~ **de**
pavillon (navigation) flag discrimination

privilégié, e *adj* (avantagé) privileged; (en
droit) privileged; (préféré) preferred; (traitement)
preferential; (liens, moment) special; (position)
privileged

prix *m* (coût, valeur) price; (récompense, honneur)
prize; (option) premium, price; **à** ~ **coûtant** at
cost; **à des** ~ **allant de** at prices ranging
from; **à** ~ **réduit** low-cost; **au** ~ **actuel** at
current prices; **au** ~ **de revient** at cost; **deux**
pour le ~ **d'un** buy one get one free; **en** ~
constants at constant prices; **faire baisser le**
~ beat the price down; **les** ~ **se sont**
inscrits en baisse prices have been marked
down; **soumis à des contrôles de** ~ subject
to price controls; ~ **en gare de départ** at
station price; **pour un** ~ **convenu** at an
agreed price;

⟨ **prix a...** ⟩ ~ **d'achat** purchase price; ~
achat garanti hypothécairement
purchase money mortgage; ~ **acheteur** bid
price; ~ **actualisé de l'action** discounted
share price; ~ **affiché** displayed price; ~
d'un aller-retour return fare BrE, round-trip
fare AmE; ~ **d'appel** loss-leader price,
reduced price; ~ **au-dessus du pair**
premium;

⟨ **b...** ⟩ ~ **en baisse** falling price; ~ de **base**
base price; ~ de **base approprié** (d'un bien)
relevant cost base; ~ de **base rajusté**
adjusted cost base; ~ **du billet** fare; (train)
train fare; ~ **du billet d'avion** air fare; ~
budgétaires budget prices;

⟨ **c...** ⟩ ~ de la **cabine** (navigation) cabin

charge; ∼ **cassé** (infrml) bargain price; ∼ **de catalogue** catalogue price BrE, catalog price AmE, list price; ∼ **de cession** transfer price; ∼ **cible** target price; ∼ **de clôture** shutdown price; ∼ **du commerce** high-street prices UK; ∼ **de la communication téléphonique** call charge; ∼ **de compensation du marché** market clearing price; ∼ **compétitif** competitive price; ∼ **comptable** accounting price; ∼ **au comptant** spot price; ∼ **de conclusion** (de transaction) closing cost; ∼ **concurrentiel** competitive price; ∼ **conseillé** recommended retail price; ∼ **à la consommation** consumer price; ∼ **constants** constant prices; ∼ **contractuel** contract price US; ∼ **contrôlé** pegged price; ∼ **coté** quoted price; ∼ **courant** current price; ∼ **coûtant** cost price;

d... ∼ **sur demande** prices on application; ∼ **demandé** (Bourse, Fin) asking price; (ventes aux enchères) reserve price BrE, upset price; ∼ **des denrées** commodity price; ∼ **départ quai** (livraison) ex-wharf price; ∼ **départ usine** price ex-works; ∼ **dernier entré, premier sorti** last in, first out price; ∼ **de déséquilibre** disequilibrium price; ∼ **directeur** price leader; ∼ **de discompte** discount price; ∼ **discriminatoires** price discrimination;

e... ∼ **élevé** high price, premium price; ∼ **d'émission** issue price; ∼ **d'émission obligataire** bond issuing price; ∼ **d'entrée** admission fee; ∼ **d'entrée en possession** acceptance price; ∼ **d'équilibre** equilibrium price; ∼ **estimatif** valuation price; ∼ **exceptionnel** bargain price; ∼ **excessif** excessive price; (Econ) overshooting price; ∼ **d'exercice** striking price; ∼ **d'exercice d'une option d'achat** call strike price; ∼ **d'exercice d'une option de vente** option strike price; ∼ **à l'exportation** export prices;

f... ∼ **de fabrique** manufacturer's price; ∼ **de facture** invoice price; ∼ **ferme** bona fide price; ∼ **à flot** (bourse de marchandises) afloat price; ∼ **forfaitaire** all-inclusive price, flat-rate price; ∼ **forfaitaire contractuel final** (contrats à terme) final contract settlement price; ∼ **fort** premium price;

g... ∼ **de gros** bulk price, wholesale price;

h... ∼ **homologué** probate price; ∼ **hors séance** after-hours price;

i... ∼ **immobiliers** house prices; ∼ **à l'importation** import price; ∼ **imposé** prescribed price; ∼ **indexé** pegged price; ∼ **initial** original cost; ∼ **intérieur américain** American selling price; ∼ **d'intervention** intervention price;

j... ∼ **justifié** justified price;

l... ∼ **de lancement** introductory price; ∼ **de levée** exercise price, strike price; ∼ **de levée à la baisse** bear strike price; ∼

de levée à la hausse bull strike price; ∼ **libellé en dollars** dollar price; ∼ **de location** rent, rental;

m... ∼ **majoré** premium price; ∼ **marchand** market price; ∼ **de marchandises** commodity price; ∼ **maximum** top price; ∼ **modiques** budget prices; ∼ **mondial** world price; ∼ **de monopole** monopoly price; ∼ **moyen** mid price, mean price; ∼ **moyen pratiqué** average market price;

o... ∼ **de l'offre** supply price; ∼ **d'option** option premium, option price; ∼ **de l'or** gold price; ∼ **ouvert** open price;

p... ∼ **au pair** parity price; ∼ **pervers** perverse price; ∼ **pour petits ordres** green stripe price; ∼ **peu flexible** sticky price; ∼ **des places** ticket price; ∼ **plafond** ceiling price, limit price; ∼ **plancher** floor price; ∼ **de pleine concurrence** arm's-length price; ∼ **le plus bas** lowest price; ∼ **le plus élevé** highest price; ∼ **à la production** producer price; ∼ **des produits de base** primary commodity prices; ∼ **promotionnels** budget prices, promotional prices; ∼ **psychologique** (V&M) psychological price, psychological pricing; ∼ **public** published price; (ventes) manufacturer's recommended price; ∼ **publicitaire** advertising price;

r... ∼ **réclame** bargain price; ∼ **recommandé par le fabricant** (ventes) manufacturer's recommended price; ∼ **record** peak ou record price; ∼ **réduit** bargain price, reduced price; ∼ **réel** actual price; ∼ **de référence** base price; ∼ **réglementé** controlled price; ∼ **relatif** relative price; ∼ **de rétrocession** buyback price; ∼ **de revient** cost price; ∼ **de revient calculé au plus juste** strict cost price; ∼ **de revient initial** prime cost, supplementary cost;

s... ∼ **sacrifié** mammoth reduction; ∼ **de seuil** threshold price; ∼ **de solde** sale price; ∼ **de soutien** (agriculture) support price; ∼ **standards** standard prices;

t... ∼ **à terme** future price, terminal price; ∼ **théorique** nominal price; ∼ **tout compris** all-inclusive price; ∼ **toutes taxes comprises** tax inclusive price, price including VAT UK; ∼ **de la transaction** trade price; ∼ **en trompe-l'œil** (V&M) odd price;

u... ∼ **unique** uniform price; ∼ **unitaire**, ∼ **à l'unité** unit price;

v... ∼ **variable** variable charge; ∼ **de vente** selling price; ∼ **de vente imposé** retail price maintenance; ∼ **virtuel** shadow price

proactif, -ive *adj* proactive

probabilité *f* likelihood, probability

probable *adj* likely, probable; **peu/fort peu** ∼ unlikely/highly unlikely

p

probant, e *adj* (preuve) conclusive; (argument, démonstration) convincing

probité *f* integrity; ∼ **de l'entreprise** corporate morality

problématique *adj* problematic

problème *m* problem, issue; **avoir beaucoup de** ∼**s** have a lot of trouble *ou* problems; **avoir des** ∼**s** be in trouble; ∼ **de la dette mondiale** world debt problem; ∼ **d'environnement** green issue; ∼**s humains** people-related problems; ∼ **majeur** big issue; ∼ **préoccupant** concern; ∼**s relatifs aux consommateurs** consumer issues; ∼**s sociaux** labour troubles BrE, labor troubles AmE

procédé *m* process; ∼ **analytique** analytic process; ∼ **comptable** accounting procedure; ∼ **de fabrication** production process; ∼ **industriel** industrial process; ∼ **original** (Brevets) original device

procéder *vi* proceed

procédural, e *adj* procedural

procédure *f* (Gen com, Ind) procedure; (Droit) procedure; ∼ **d'appel** appeals procedure; ∼ **d'arbitrage** arbitration proceedings; ∼ **en cas de conflit** dispute procedure; ∼ **de choix d'investissement** capital budgeting; ∼**s de clôture des comptes** cutoff procedures; ∼ **coercitive** enforcement procedure; ∼ **de commande** control procedure; ∼ **de conciliation** conciliation procedure; ∼ **de contrôle** auditing procedure; ∼ **courante** standing procedure; ∼ **de dépôt de plainte** complaints procedure; ∼ **disciplinaire** disciplinary procedure; ∼ **douanière** customs procedure; ∼ **électorale** voting procedure; ∼ **d'essai** testing procedure; ∼ **d'éviction** ejectment; ∼ **d'exercice** exercise procedure; ∼ **d'expropriation** (immobilier) dispossess proceedings; ∼ **de faillite** bankruptcy proceedings; ∼**s de fin d'exercice** cutoff procedures; ∼**s de gestion** management procedures; ∼**s d'inventaire** year-end procedures; ∼ **judiciaire** court procedure; ∼ **de licenciement** redundancy procedure; ∼ **normale à suivre** standard operating procedure; ∼ **prud'hommale** grievance procedure; ∼ **de réclamation** claims procedure; ∼ **de réclamation concernant les marchandises** cargo claims procedure; ∼**s de recouvrement de protection** jeopardy collection procedures

procédurier, -ière *adj* procedural

procès *m* (Droit) (civil) case, law suit; (pénal) trial; **faire un** ∼ **à qn** take sb to court; **perdre son** ∼ lose one's case; ∼ **à l'amiable** friendly suit; ∼ **civil** civil proceedings; ∼ **en diffamation** libel proceedings; ∼ **avec jury** jury trial

processeur *m* (Info) processor; ∼ **central** central processing unit, mainframe; ∼

d'entrée/de sortie input/output processor; ∼ **vectoriel** array processor

processus *m* process; ∼ **d'achat** buying process; ∼ **d'adoption** (d'enfant, de produit) adoption process; ∼ **d'autorisation** approval process; ∼ **de compensation** clearing process; ∼ **décisionnel** decision-making process; ∼ **de décision des ménages** household decision-making; ∼ **de prise de décision** decision-making process

procès-verbal *m* (compte rendu de réunion) minutes; (Droit) statement of offence BrE; **figurer au** ∼ appear in the minutes

prochain, e *adj* forthcoming, next; ∼ **exercice fiscal** upcoming fiscal year; ∼ **mois de livraison** (Bourse) spot delivery month

proche *adj* close, near; ∼ **admissible** (Fisc) qualified relation; ∼ **avenir** near future; ∼ **parent** (Admin) next of kin

procuration *f* (pouvoir) power of attorney; (pour une élection) proxy; **agir par** ∼ act by proxy; **avoir une** ∼ **sur un compte** have power of attorney over an account; **donner** ∼ **à qn** give sb power of attorney; **par** ∼ per procurationem; ∼ **autorisant le transfert d'actions** stock power; ∼ **en blanc** bearer proxy

procurer ① *vt* (argent, avantages) give; ∼ **qch à qn** give sb sth ② **se procurer** *v pron* obtain; **se** ∼ **de l'argent** raise funds, raise money; **se** ∼ **des capitaux** raise capital

procureur *m* prosecutor; ∼ **général** ≈ public prosecutor, Attorney General US; ∼ **de la République** ≈ Director of Public Prosecutions UK, French state prosecutor, ≈ district attorney US

producteur¹, -trice *adj* **pays** ∼ **de café/ pétrole** a coffee/oil-producing country

producteur², -trice *m,f* producer; ∼ **de fruits** fruit farmer; ∼ **de réserve** (Ind) swing producer

productif, -ive *adj* (travail, réunion) productive; (capital investissement) profitable; ∼ **d'intérêts** interest-bearing

production *f* (fait de produire) production; (quantité produite) output, production; ∼ **agricole** agricultural production; ∼ **à la chaîne** line production; ∼ **continue** continuous-flow production; ∼ **dans les délais impartis** just-in-time production; ∼ **à domicile** home production; ∼ **globale** aggregate output, aggregate production; ∼ **à grande échelle** large-scale production; ∼ **hâtive** (Fisc) (d'une déclaration) early filing; ∼ **intégrée par ordinateur** computer-integrated manufacturing; ∼ **en masse** mass production; ∼ **nationale** domestic output; ∼ **en petites séries** batch production; ∼ **tardive** (Fisc) (d'une déclaration) late filing; ∼ **d'usine** plant manufacturing

productivité *f* (rendement) productivity,

output

produire *vt* produce; (intérêts, perte) yield; (argent) bring in, generate; (des idées) generate; (preuve) adduce; **cette usine produit peu** this factory has a low output; **∼ une déclaration** file a return; **∼ en grandes séries** mass-produce; **∼ un revenu** generate income

produit¹, e *adj* produced, made; **∼ en France** made in France; **∼ en grandes séries** mass-produced; **∼ en série** mass-produced

produit² *m* commodity, product; (revenu) income; (bénéfice) profit; (Compta) revenue item; (d'une vente) proceeds; (d'un investissement) yield, return; **∼s** goods, commodities; **ce ∼ est en vente à un prix inférieur à sa vraie valeur** this product is underpriced; **∼ fictif ou moins-value** (Bourse) paper profit or loss; **∼s d'achat courant** convenience goods; **∼ agricole** agricultural product; **∼ agricole de base** agricultural commodity; **∼s agro-alimentaires** foodstuffs; **∼s alimentaires** foodstuffs; **∼ alimentaire industriel** processed food; **∼ d'appel** appeal product, sell up product, loss leader; **∼ d'appel bon marché** leader US, product leader; **∼ d'assurance** insurance product; **∼s d'assurance** insurance proceeds; **∼s audiovisuels** brown goods; **∼ en baisse** soft commodity; **∼ banal** homogeneous goods; **∼ bas de gamme** down-market product; **∼ de base** primary commodity; **∼ biologique** organic product; **∼s blancs** white goods; **∼ brut** (Fin) gross cash flow; **∼s bruts** crude goods; **∼s budgétés** budgeted income; **∼s et charges** revenue and expenses; **∼s chimiques** chemicals; **∼s chimiques dangereux** hazardous chemicals; **∼s de choc** impulse goods; **∼ compensatoire** compensating product; **∼s conditionnés** packaged goods; **∼ de consommation** consumer product; **∼s de consommation courante** convenience goods; **∼s de consommation durables** consumer durables; **∼ constaté d'avance** accrued income; **∼s dangereux à bord** dangerous goods on board; **∼ dérivé** by-product; **∼s divers de gestion courante** nonoperating revenue; **∼s à durée de vie moyenne** orange goods; **∼ écologique** clean product, environmentally-friendly product; **∼s entreposés en douanes** bonded goods; **∼s d'épicerie** dry goods; **∼ d'excellente qualité** high-quality product; **∼ d'exploitation commun** common revenue; **∼ de la ferme** farm produce; **∼ final** end product; **∼ financier** financial product; **∼s financiers** (Compta) income from interest; (compte de pertes et profits) interest earned; **∼s finis** final goods, final products; **∼ à forte rentabilité** cash cow product; **∼ à forte valeur ajoutée** high added-value product; **∼s frais** fresh food,

fresh goods; **∼s de grande consommation** convenience goods, red goods (jarg); **∼s de grande consommation à forte rotation** fast-moving consumer goods; **∼ grand public** consumer-oriented product; **∼ haut de gamme** up-market product; **∼ de l'impôt** tax proceeds; **∼ d'intérêts** interest income; **∼ intérieur brut** gross domestic product; **∼ intérieur brut au coût des facteurs** gross domestic product at factor cost; **∼ intérieur brut de l'État** gross state product; **∼ intérieur brut aux prix du marché** gross domestic product at market prices; **∼s intermédiaires** semifinished goods; **∼s jaunes** yellow goods (jarg); **∼s laitiers** dairy products; **∼ leader** brand leader, core product; **∼s libres** unbranded goods; **∼ lié** (V&M) complement; **∼s liés** joint products; **∼ locomotive** star product; **∼s manufacturés** manufactured goods; **∼ marginal du travail** marginal product of labour BrE, marginal product of labor AmE; **∼ national brut** gross national product; **∼ national net** net national product; **∼ nationaux** home products; **∼s pétroliers** mineral oil products; **∼s pharmaceutiques** pharmaceuticals; **∼ potentiel** potential output; **∼ pourvu d'un code barres** bar-coded product; **∼ de première catégorie** top-rank product; **∼ de privatisation** privatization proceeds; **∼ à recevoir** accrued asset, accrued revenue; **∼ de récupération** waste product; **∼ de remplacement** substitute product; **∼ de la revente** proceeds from resale; **∼ secondaire** nonbasic commodity; **∼s de services** tertiary products; **∼s soumis à l'accise** excisable goods; **∼s du tabac** tobacco products; **∼ tertiaire** staple commodity, tertiary product; **∼s d'utilisation finale** end use goods; **∼ vedette** star product; **∼ de la vente** sale proceeds; **∼ vert** environmentally-friendly product

profession *f* occupation; (libérale) profession; (manuelle) trade; **quelle est votre ∼** what's your occupation?; **sans ∼** unemployed; (femme au foyer) housewife; **exercer la ∼ d'architecte** be an architect by profession; **être comptable de ∼** be an accountant (by profession); **∼ bancaire** banking; **∼ comptable** accountancy; **∼ connexe** closely connected profession; **∼ de courtier en bourse** stockbroking

professionnalisation *f* professionalization

professionnalisme *m* professionalism

professionnel¹, -elle *adj* (qualification, catégorie, réussite, prétention) professional; (maladie) occupational; (enseignement, formation, baccalauréat) vocational; (exposition, salon) trade; (vie, milieu) working

professionnel², -elle *m,f* professional; **un ∼ du bâtiment** a person working in the ⋯⟩

building trade; **les ∼s de la santé** health professionals

profil m profile; **avoir le ∼ de l'emploi** have the right qualifications for the job; **le candidat n'a pas le ∼ requis pour le poste** this candidate is not suited to the job; **∼ d'acquisition** acquisition profile; **∼ de la clientèle** customer profile; **∼ de compétences** skills profile; **∼ du consommateur** (marketing) consumer profile; **∼ démographique** demographics; **∼ de l'emploi** job profile; **∼ de l'entreprise** company profile; **∼ du lectorat** (étude de marché) readership profile; **∼ d'un marché** market profile; **∼ du poste** job specification; **∼ des ressources** resource profile; **∼ de risque** risk profile; **∼ des salaires** wage contour; **∼ du salarié** employee profile; **∼ selon l'âge et les revenus** age-earnings profile; **∼ technique** technical profile; **∼ type** model profile; **∼ de l'utilisateur** user profile

profit m profit, gain; **vendre à ∼** sell at a profit; **tirer ∼ de qch** benefit from sth; **∼ exceptionnel** extraordinary gain; **∼ fictif** illusory profit; **∼ non matérialisé** paper profit; **∼ non réalisé** unrealized profit; **∼ sectoriel** segment profit

profitable adj (rentable) profitable

profiter vi **∼ de** (situation, vente, employé) take advantage of; **∼ à qn** be of benefit to sb, be to sb's advantage; **∼ d'une occasion pour faire** take advantage of an opportunity to do

profiteur, -euse m,f profiteer

profond, e adj deep; (problèmes) deep-seated

profondément adv (Bourse) (hors du cours) deeply, profoundly; **∼ ancré** (problèmes) deep-rooted, deep-seated

profondeur f depth; **en ∼** in depth; **∼ au quai** (navigation) depth alongside

pro forma adj pro forma

profusion f abundance, profusion

progiciel m (Info) software package; **∼ de comptabilité** accounting package ou software; **∼ de gestion intégré** ERP application

programmateur m timer; **∼ de vol** flight scheduler

programmation f programming; (production) scheduling; (Info) computer programming; **∼ économique** economic programming; **∼ horaire** timetable planning; **∼ d'itinéraires** route planning; **∼ linéaire** (économétrie) linear programming; **∼ par objets** object-orientated programming; **∼ de la production** production planning, production scheduling; **∼ progressive** forward scheduling; **∼ régressive** backward scheduling; **∼ systèmes** systems programming; **∼ des tâches** task scheduling

programme m (planning) programme BrE, program AmE; (Fin) schedule; (de placements)

programme BrE, schedule; (Info) program; **changement de ∼** change of plan; **avoir un ∼ très chargé** have a very busy schedule; **∼ d'action** action plan; **∼ d'aide** aid scheme, aid programme BrE; **∼ alimentaire mondial** World Food Programme BrE; **∼ d'analyse** analyser BrE, analyzer AmE; **∼ des annonces** advertising schedule; **∼ d'appel** calling program; **∼ d'application** applications program, applications software; **∼ d'assemblage** assembly programme BrE; **∼ d'audit annuel** annual audit plan UK; **∼ de base** core curriculum; **∼ chargé** busy schedule; **∼ de contrôle** audit programme BrE; (Info) control program; **∼ de dépenses directes** direct spending programme BrE; **∼ de développement** development planning; **∼ de diagnostic** diagnostic routine; **∼ en direct** (radio, télévision) live programme BrE; **∼ d'édition** (Info) editor; **∼ élargi** enriched programme BrE; **∼ d'entretien** maintenance schedule; **∼ d'études** (universitaire) curriculum; (scolaire) syllabus; **∼ d'exploitation** (Info) operating schedule; **∼ d'exploitation/de compilation** (Info) operating/compiling system; **∼ de fabrication** production schedule; **∼ des immobilisations** capital programme BrE; **∼ informatique** computer program; **∼ intensifié** extended programme BrE; **∼ d'interprétation** (Info) translator; **∼ d'interrogation** (Info) enquiry program, inquiry program; **∼ machine** (Info) computer program; **∼ de matériel roulant** rolling programme BrE; **∼ ministériel** departmental programme BrE; **∼ de mise à jour** maintenance schedule; **∼ de négoce** trading programme BrE; **∼ d'ordinateur** computer program; **∼ d'origine** source program; **∼ de participation boursière** share participation scheme; **∼ de participation directe** direct participation programme BrE; **∼ de primes de rendement** bonus scheme; **∼ prioritaire** foreground program; **∼ réglementaire** statutory programme BrE; **∼ de relance** restart program; **∼ de remboursements** schedule of repayments; **∼ de salaires au rendement** incentive wage plan; **∼ sans endettement** unleveraged programme BrE; **∼ secret** hidden agenda; **∼ tenant compte des imprévus** contingency planning; **∼ transportable** (Info) canned program; **∼ de travail** work schedule; **∼ utilitaire** utility, utility program; **∼ d'utilité publique** Community Programme UK; **∼ de vérification** audit programme BrE

programmer vt (Info) programme BrE, program AmE; (rendez-vous, réunion, visite) schedule; (travail, production) plan, schedule; **être programmé pour** (réunion) be scheduled for

programmeur, -euse m,f computer programmer; **∼ d'applications** applications programmer; ~ **système** systems programmer

progrès *m* progress; (de technique, recherche, science) advance; (de résultat, chiffre) increase; **les ~ de l'informatique** advances in computing; **afficher un ~ de 2%** show a 2% increase; **faire des ~** make progress; ~ **commercial** business development; ~ **technique** technical progress; ~ **technique incorporé** embodied technical progress; ~ **technique mis en application** embodied technical progress

progresser *vi* move ahead; (entreprise) make progress; (inflation, taux, indice, salaires) rise; (pouvoir d'achat) increase; (économie, marché, Bourse) improve; (enquête, négociations) make progress; ~ **lentement** make slow progress; **faire ~** (travail) advance

progressif, -ive *adj* progressive, gradual; (impôt, taux) progressive

progression *f* (de chômage, salaires, inflation, pouvoir d'achat) increase; **être en ~** (résultat) be up; **les ventes sont en ~ constante** sales are increasing steadily; **leur chiffre d'affaire est en ~ de 10%** their turnover is up by 10%

progressivement *adv* progressively

prohibitif, -ive *adj* prohibitive

prohibition *f* prohibition, ban; ~ **d'entrée/de sortie** import/export ban

projection *f* projection, forecast; ~ **catastrophe** worst-case projection; ~ **d'image de marque** image projection; ~ **des profits** profit projection, profit forecast

projet *m* (plan) plan; (travail en cours) project; (Admin) blueprint; (esquisse) draft; **réaliser un ~** carry out a plan; **le ~ prend du retard** the project is falling behind schedule; ~ **d'acte** draft; ~ **de budget** budget proposal; ~ **cadre** umbrella project; ~ **cahotique** rolling plan; ~ **commercial** business plan; ~ **de contrat** draft contract; ~ **et contrôle de la production** production planning and control; ~ **d'essai** pilot project; ~ **d'expédition** (Transp) project forwarding; ~ **financé par des bons** aid-financed project; ~ **de financement de grandes entreprises** corporate financing project; ~ **d'investissement** investment scheme; ~ **de loi** bill; ~ **de loi des finances** finance bill; ~ **de lotissement** housing project; ~ **de mise à l'étude** exposure draft; ~ **pilote** pilot scheme; ~ **réalisé** accomplishment; ~ **de réforme** reform package; ~ **de stabilisation monétaire** currency stabilization scheme

projeter *vt* plan, project

prolétariat *m* proletariat

prolétarisation *f* proletarianization

prolifération *f* spread, proliferation

prolongation *f* (de contrat, validité) extension; ~ **d'échéance** extended terms

prolongé, e *adj* prolonged

promesse *f* (Droit) agreement, commitment; **faire une ~ de vente** agree *ou* commit to sell; **honorer ses ~s** honour one's commitments; ~ **solidaire** binding promise; ~ **unique de vente** unique selling proposition

prometteur, -euse *adj* promising

promettre *vt* promise; ~ **qch à qn** promise sb sth

promoteur, -trice *m,f* property developer BrE, real estate developer AmE; ~ **commercial** commercial developer

promotion *f* (du personnel) promotion; (technique de vente) promotion; (article en réclame) special offer; **en ~** on special offer, on special AmE; **j'ai eu une ~** I have been promoted; ~ **par l'argument charitable** charity promotion; ~ **auprès des détaillants** trade promotion; ~ **des cadres** executive advancement, executive promotion; ~ **concertée** (fabricant et détaillant) tie-in promotion US; ~ **discrète** (de vente) soft sell; ~ **immobilière** property development BrE, real estate development AmE; ~ **jumelée** tie-in display US, tie-in promotion US; ~ **sur le lieu de vente** point-of-sale promotion; ~ **produit** brand promotion; ~ **rapide** fast tracking

promotion-cadeau *f* (publicité) gift promotion

promotionnel, -elle *adj* (campagne, vidéo, action, matériel) promotional; (budget) publicity; ~ **prix** ~ special offer

promotion-réseau *f* trade promotion

promouvoir *vt* promote; **être promu** be promoted

promulgation *f* (de loi) enactment

promulguer *vt* (loi) enact

prononcer [1] *vt* (discours) deliver; (condamnation, jugement) pass; ~ **une condamnation** pass a sentence; ~ **un jugement sous toutes réserves** reserve judgment; ~ **quelques mots de bienvenue** say a few words of welcome [2] **se prononcer** *v pron* **se ~ sur qch** give one's opinion on sth

pronostic *m* forecast; **faire des ~s** make forecasts; ~ **relatif au marché** market forecast

propager *vt* (rumeur) spread

propension *f* propensity; ~ **à consommer** propensity to consume; ~ **à épargner** propensity to save; ~ **marginale à investir** marginal propensity to invest

propice *adj* favourable BrE, favorable AmE

proportion *f* proportion; (Fin) (share) part; **comme ~** as a proportion of; **être hors de ~ avec** be out of proportion with; **dans une ~ de 6 contre 1** in a ratio of 6 to 1; ~ **de travailleurs handicapés** disabled quota

proportionalité *f* proportionality

proportionné, e *adj* commensurate

proportionnel, -elle *adj* proportional; (impôt) ad valorem (frml); **directement/ inversement ~ à** directly/inversely proportional to

proportionnellement *adv* proportionally

propos *m* remark; (intention) intention; **à ~ de votre travail** regarding *ou* about your work; **à ce ~** in this respect; **des ~** comments

proposé, e *adj* proposed

proposer *vt* offer, put forward; (emploi, situation) offer; **~ qn pour un poste** put sb forward for a job; **~ sa candidature** apply, put in an application; **~ ses services** offer one's services

proposition *f* proposal, proposition; (d'affaires) business proposal; **faire une ~ à qn** make an approach to sb; **~ alléchante** attractive offer; **~ fiscale** tax proposal

propre *adj* (à soi) own; (pas sale) clean; **~ à** appropriate for, characteristic of; **~ assurance** self-insurance; **~ à une unité** device-specific

propriétaire *mf* (de terres, bien immeuble, objet) owner; (d'hôtel, de restaurant) proprietor, owner; (de propriété louée) (male) landlord; (female) landlady; **~ pour compte** nominee; **~ exploitant** owner-operator; **~ gérant** owner-manager; **~ immatriculé** registered owner; **~ immobilier** property owner; **~ inscrit au registre du cadastre** registered proprietor; **~ légitime** rightful owner, true owner; **~ majoritaire** majority owner; **~ non occupant** nonoccupying owner; **~ d'obligations** bondowner; **~ occupant** owner-occupier; **~ d'origine** original owner; **~ de ranch** rancher; **~ terrien** landowner; **~ usufruitier** limited owner

propriété *f* (fait d'être propriétaire) ownership; (possession) property; **~ absolue** outright ownership; **~ à bail** leasehold property; **~ bénéficiaire** beneficial ownership; **~ conjointe** joint ownership; **~ d'État** state ownership; **~ foncière** land ownership; **~ foncière libre** freehold property; **~ foncière, habitations et biens immobiliers hérités** land, tenements, and hereditaments; **~ d'habitat** home ownership; **~ immobilière** immovable property; **~ indivise** (immobilier) joint tenancy, tenancy in severalty; **~ industrielle** patent rights, industrial property; **~ intellectuelle** intellectual property; **~ louée** leasehold property; **~ marginale** marginal property; **~ mobilière** personal property; **~ non grevée** unencumbered estate; **~ de petite entreprise** small business property; **~ privée** private property; **~ résiduelle** residuary estate; **~ saisie** distressed property

prorata *m* pro rata; **au ~** on a pro rata basis, pro rata (frml)

prorogation *f* (de session, assemblée) adjournment, deferment; (de prêt, bail) extension, renewal; (de passeport) renewal; **~ des délais** extension of time limits; **~ de délais pour les déclarations** (Fisc) extension for returns; **~ d'échéance** extended terms

proroger *vt* (date, échéance) defer; (réglementations) extend; (contrat, passeport) renew

proscrire *vt* ban, prohibit; (Droit) outlaw

prospect *m* prospect, prospective customer

prospecter *vt* prospect; (V&M) canvass

prospecteur, -trice *m,f* prospector

prospection *f* (Gen com) business development; (V&M) canvassing, prospecting; **~ à l'improviste** cold canvass; **~ des marchés** market exploration

prospective *f* (à long terme) forecasting

prospectus *m* brochure, flyer; (Bourse) prospectus; **~ d'admission** prospectus; **~ d'émission définitif** final prospectus; **~ modifié** amended prospectus; **~ provisoire** red-herring prospectus; **~ de vente** sales leaflet

prospère *adj* prosperous

prospérer *vi* flourish; (entreprise, personne) thrive

prospérité *f* prosperity; **~ d'après-guerre** postwar boom

protecteur, -trice *m,f* protector; **~ de chèque** cheque protector BrE, check protector AmE

protection *f* (Econ, Assur, Info) protection; **~ conférée par un brevet** patent protection; **~ du consommateur** consumer protection; **~ des données** data protection; **~ douanière** tariff protection; **~ de l'environnement** environmental protection; **~ fiscale** tax shield; **~ pleine et entière** full protection; **~ provisoire** provisional protection; **~ tarifaire** tariff protection

protectionnisme *m* protectionism; **~ commercial** trade protectionism

protégé, e *adj* protected; **~ contre la copie** copy-protected; **~ contre les pirates** (Info) hacker-proof (infrml); **~ en écriture** write-protected

protéger **1** *vt* protect; (Bourse) insulate; (Fisc) shield; **~ contre la copie** copy-protect; **~ les intérêts de** protect the interests of **2** **se protéger** *v pron* protect oneself; **se ~ contre** protect oneself against; **se ~ de qch** protect oneself from sth

protestation *f* outcry

protester **1** *vt* (Droit) (effet, billet) protest **2** *vi* protest (**contre** against)

protocole *m* protocol; (Info) protocol; **~ d'accord** draft agreement; **~ des affaires** business etiquette; **~ WAP** WAP

prototype *m* prototype; **faire un ~ de qch** prototype sth

prouvé, e *adj* well-tried

prouver *vt* prove, substantiate; ∼ **son identité** prove one's identity

provenance *f* origin; (de marchandises) country of origin; **en** ∼ **de** (marchandises, personne) from; ∼ **des fonds** sources of funds

provenir *vi* ∼ **de** (marchandise, capitaux, profit) come from; (situation, déséquilibre) stem from

provincial, e *adj* provincial

provision *f* (Gen com) stock, supply; (Fin) (acompte) deposit; (sur un compte en banque) credit; (arrhes) advance payment; (Compta) payment on account; **être sans** ∼ (chèque) bounce (infrml); **faire** ∼ **pour** make provision for; ∼**s pour amortissement** provision for depreciation; ∼ **en aval** downstream float; ∼ **pour créances irrécouvrables** bad debt provision; ∼**s de crédit** credit reserves; ∼ **pour épuisement** depletion reserve; ∼ **pour évaluation d'actifs** valuation allowance; ∼ **pour impôts différés** deferred tax liabilities; ∼ **pour inflation** allowance for inflation UK; ∼ **d'une lettre de change** bill cover; ∼ **mathématique** policy reserve; ∼ **pour moins-value** valuation allowance; ∼ **pour perte sur prêt** loan loss provision; ∼ **pour pertes sur risques de crédit** reserve for credit risk losses; ∼ **réglementaire** mandatory provision; ∼ **pour risques** provision for contingency; ∼**s pour sinistre à payer** reserve for unpaid claims; ∼ **transitoire** transitional provisions

provisoire *adj* (solution, installation, situation) temporary; (gérant) acting, temporary; (accord, bilan) provisional; (jugement) ad interim

provisoirement *adv* provisionally

provoquer *vt* (déclencher) cause, spark off; ∼ **la déflation** deflate

prudemment *adv* carefully, prudently

prudence *f* caution; **avec** ∼ prudently; **faire preuve de** ∼ show caution

prudent, e *adj* cautious, prudent; (évaluation, dépenses) conservative; **se montrer** ∼ **dans son analyse/ses prévisions** appear cautious in one's analysis/one's forecasts

prud'homal, e *adj* of an industrial tribunal BrE, of a labor relations board AmE

prud'homme *m* member of an industrial tribunal BrE, member of a labor relations board AmE; **conseil de** ∼ industrial tribunal BrE, labor relations board AmE

psychologie *f* psychology; ∼ **d'entreprise**, ∼ **d'organisation** organizational psychology; ∼ **du travail** industrial psychology

PTC *abrév* (▸**poids total en charge**) (véhicule routier) GVW (gross vehicle weight)

PTPE *abrév* (▸**perte au titre d'un placement d'entreprise**) BIL (business investment loss)

pub *f* (▸**publicité**) ad, advert; **faire de la** ∼ **pour un produit** advertise a product

public¹, -ique *adj* public; (entreprise) government-owned, public

public² *m* (tout le monde) public; (de spectacle, de conférence) audience; (lecteurs) readership; ∼ **bien informé** informed public; ∼ **captif** captive audience; **le** ∼ (relations publiques) the public; (secteur) the public sector

publication *f* (divulgation) disclosure; (magazine) magazine, publication; ∼**s** published information; **pour** ∼ **immédiate** (presse) for immediate release; ∼ **agricole** agricultural publication; ∼ **anniversaire** anniversary publication; ∼ **assistée par ordinateur** desktop publishing; ∼ **d'entreprise** house journal, house magazine; ∼ **trimestrielle** quarterly

publiciste *mf* advertising executive, adman (infrml)

publicitaire¹ *adj* (agence, budget) advertising; (campagne, espace, tarif) advertising; (objet, vente, voiture, jeu) promotional; **cadeau de** ∼ free gift

publicitaire² *m* advertising agency

publicité *f* (annonce) advert; (radio, TV) commercial; (métier) advertising (industry); **dans la** ∼ (travailler) in advertising; **faire de la** ∼ advertise; **faire de la** ∼ **pour un produit** advertise a product; ∼ **aérienne** aerial advertising; ∼ **par affichage** poster advertising; ∼ **d'amorçage** advance publicity; ∼ **anticyclique** anticyclic advertising; ∼ **par ballons** balloon advertising; ∼ **de bouche à oreille** word-of-mouth advertising; ∼ **bouche-trou** (presse) filler advertisement; ∼ **par cadeaux-primes** speciality advertising; ∼ **centrée sur une zone** zoned advertising; ∼ **au cinéma** cinema advertising; ∼ **collective** cooperative advertising; ∼ **comparative** comparative advertising; ∼ **de complément** accessory advertising; ∼ **sur comptoir** counter-advertising; ∼ **par correspondance** direct action advertising; ∼ **directe** direct mail advertising; ∼ **sur double page** double spread advertising; ∼ **d'entreprise à entreprise** business-to-business advertising; ∼ **du fabricant** producer advertising; ∼ **foncière** publication of sale of property; ∼ **grand public** consumer advertising; ∼ **groupée** cooperative advertising; ∼ **informative** informative advertising; ∼ **institutionnelle** corporate advertising; ∼ **intensive** heavy advertising; ∼ **de liaison** tie-in advertising US; ∼ **sur le lieu de vente** point-of-sale promotion; ∼ **médias** above the line; ∼ **mensongère** deceptive advertising; ∼ **mystère** teaser ad; ∼ **PLV** POS advertising; ∼**-presse** press advertising; ∼ **de produit** product advertising; ∼ **quart de page** quarter-page advertisement; ∼ **rédactionnelle** editorial advertising; (presse) reading notice (jarg); ∼ **subliminale** subliminal advertising; ∼ **tapageuse** stunt ⋯⟩

p

advertising

publier vt (édition) publish; (des gains) announce, report; (presse) issue; ~ **une déclaration** put out a statement; ~ **une offre d'emploi dans un journal** (publicité) advertise a job in the paper; **être publié** (un ouvrage) come out

publipostage m mailing; **faire un** ~ do a mailshot; ~ **direct** direct mail; ~ **frauduleux** mail fraud

publireportage m advertorial

puce f (Info) chip, microchip; ~ **électronique** silicon chip; ~ **mémoire** memory chip

puiser vt ~ **dans** raid; ~ **dans ses économies** draw on one's savings

puissance f power; ~ **d'achat** buying power; ~ **de calcul** computing power; ~ **en chevaux** horsepower; ~ **au frein** brake horsepower; ~ **des médias** power of media; ~ **nominale** nominal horsepower; ~ **réelle** effective horsepower

puissant, e adj powerful

puits m well; ~ **en exploitation** (de pétrole, etc) commercial well; ~ **en mer** offshore well; ~ **sous-marin** subsea well

punir vt discipline

pupitre m desk; ~ **de commande** (Info) control panel; ~ **de négociation** trading desk

pur, e adj (substance, laine) pure; (ligne, style) pure; ~ **et dur** hardline; ~**e économie de crédit** pure credit economy

purge f (d'une hypothèque) redemption; ~ **d'un privilège** (Droit) discharge of lien

purger vt (hypothèque) redeem

purification f purification

put m put; ~ **couvert** covered put

PV abrév (►**point de vente**) POS (point of sale)

PVD abrév (►**pays en voie de développement**) developing country

px abrév (►**prix**) pr. (price)

pyramidal, e adj pyramidal; **vente** ~**e** pyramid selling

pyramide f pyramid; ~ **des âges** age pyramid; ~ **financière** financial pyramid

Qq

QG abrév (►**contrôle de la qualité globale**) TQC (total quality control)

qté abrév (►**quantité**) qnty, qt. (quantity)

quai m (de gare, de métro) platform; (au port) wharf, quay; **à** ~ **ou non** (charte-partie) whether in berth or not; (navigation) berth no berth; **arriver à** ~ dock; **à prendre à** ~ ex-quay, ex-wharf; ~ **à domicile** pier to house; ~ **à quai** pier to pier, quay to quay; ~ **de chargement** charging wharf, loading dock; ~ **à conteneurs** (au port) container berth; ~ **de déchargement** (au port) discharging wharf; (chemin de fer) unloading platform; ~ **de la douane** sufferance wharf; ~ **à manutention horizontale** portal berth; ~ **mis à disposition** (au port) ready berth; ~ **polyvalent** (au port) multiproduct berth; ~ **réservé aux exportations** (au port) export berth; ~ **réservé aux importations** (au port) import berth

quaiage m quayage

qualification f (diplôme) qualification; (compétences) skills; (emploi) job title, qualification; **avoir les** ~**s nécessaires pour le poste** have the right qualifications for the job; ~ **des comptes** qualification; ~ **financière** financial reward; ~ **professionnelle véritable** genuine occupational qualification BrE, bona fide

occupational qualification; ~**s professionnelles** professional qualifications; ~ **du travail** job evaluation

qualifié, e adj (diplômé) qualified; (compétent) skilled; (emploi, poste) skilled; **non** ~ (personnel) unskilled; ~ **pour faire qch** qualified to do sth

qualifier vt qualify

qualitatif, -ive adj qualitative; **contrôle** ~ quality control

qualitativement adv qualitatively

qualité f (de produit) quality; (statut) status; (fonction) position; ~ **courante** fair average quality; ~ **conforme à l'échantillon** quality as per sample; **de** ~ **inférieure** substandard; **de** ~ **marchande** marketable; **de** ~ **suffisante** of acceptable quality; **de** ~ **supérieure** top-quality; **en sa** ~ **de représentant** in his capacity as a representative; ~**s de chef** leadership qualities; **gestion/assurance/maîtrise de la** ~ quality management/assurance/control; **nom, prénom et** ~ last name, first name, position; ~ **des bénéfices** quality of earnings; ~ **brouillon** (Info) draft quality; ~ **commerciale** fair average quality; ~ **courrier** letter quality; ~ **de l'eau** water quality; ~ **supérieure** top quality; ~ **de vie**

quality of life; ~ **de la vie active** quality of working life

qualiticien, -enne *m,f* quality controller

quant à *prép* in respect of, regarding

quantifier *vt* quantify

quantitatif, -ive *adj* quantitative

quantité *f* quantity, amount; **acheter en grande/petite** ~ buy in bulk/small quantities; **des** ~**s de** a lot of, masses of (infrml); ~ **autorisée** quantity permitted; ~ **d'équilibre** equilibrium quantity; ~ **optimale de commande** economic order quantity; ~ **optimale de réapprovisionnement** economic order quantity

quarantaine *f* (isolement) quarantine; (environ quarante) about forty

quart *m* quarter; (unité de mesure) quart

quartier *m* (d'une ville) area, district; **de** ~ (commerçant, médecin, cinéma) local; ~ **d'affaires** business district; ~ **commerçant** shopping area; ~**s déshérités** deprived areas; (à l'intérieur d'une ville) inner-city areas; ~ **général** headquarters; ~ **locatif** rentable area

quartile *m* quartile; ~ **inférieur** lower quartile; ~ **supérieur** upper quartile

quart-monde *m* fourth world

quasi- *préf* quasi-; ~**-certitude** likelihood; ~**-contrat** implied contract, quasi-contract; ~**-espèces** cash equivalent; ~**-fabricant** quasi-manufacturer; ~**-indépendance** quasi-independence; ~**-monnaie** near cash, near money; ~**-monopole** near monopoly; ~**-rente** quasi-rent; ~**-totalité** almost all, almost the whole of

quatrième *adj* fourth; ~ **âge** very old people; ~ **de couverture** back cover, fourth cover; ~ **marché** fourth market; ~ **trimestre** fourth quarter

quelconque *adj* (personne) dull, ordinary; (produit) second-rate

quelque *adj* some; (dans interrogation) any; ~**s** some, a few; ~**s euros** a few euros

question *f* (demande) question (**sur** about); (sujet à l'ordre du jour) item; (problème) issue, question; **répondre à/poser une** ~ answer/ask a question; **la** ~ **(du) nucléaire** the nuclear issue; **en** ~ at issue, in question; **remettre en** ~ reassess, reappraise; **c'est hors de** ~ it's out of the question; ~ **clé** key issue; ~ **de compétence** question of jurisdiction; ~ **controversée** vexed question; ~**s diverses** (figurant à l'ordre du jour) any other competent business; ~ **écologique** environmental issue; ~ **fermée**

(étude de marché) closed question; ~ **d'intérêt secondaire** side issue; ~ **d'opinion** matter of opinion; ~**s à l'ordre du jour** items on the agenda; ~ **ouverte** (étude de marché) open-ended question; ~**s en suspens** outstanding matters; ~ **très débattue** vexed question

questionnaire *m* questionnaire; **remplir un** ~ fill in *ou* out a questionnaire; ~ **à choix multiples** multiple choice questionnaire; ~ **directif** (étude de marché) closed questionnaire; ~ **non directif** (étude de marché) open-ended questionnaire

questionner *vt* question; ~ **discrètement** sound out

quêter *vt* (l'approbation de qn) seek

queue *f* line AmE, queue BrE; **faire la** ~ queue up BrE, stand in line, wait in line AmE; ~ **de portefeuille** (Assur) runoff

quinquennial, e *adj* (de cinq ans) five-year; **plan** ~ five-year plan

quintal *m* quintal

quinzaine *f* (environ quinze) about fifteen; (deux semaines) two weeks, fortnight BrE; ~ **commerciale** two-week sale

quittance *f* (reçu) receipt; (Droit) acquittance; ~ **de loyer/d'électricité** rent/electricity receipt; ~ **comptable** accountable receipt

quitter *vt* leave; (Info) quit; ~ **son travail** (définitivement) leave one's job; **ne quittez pas, s'il vous plaît** hold the line please

quitus *m* (de dette) full discharge, quietus; **donner** ~ **à qn** give quietus to sb; ~ **fiscal** ≈ tax certificate

quorum *m* quorum; **avoir atteint le** ~ have a quorum, be quorate

quota *m* quota; ~ **à l'importation** import quota; ~ **imposable** taxable quota; ~ **de ventes** sales quota

quote-part *f* share, portion; (Fin) percentage interest; ~ **du capital détenu** percentage of capital held; ~ **dans les résultats** share

quotidien¹, -enne *adj* (dépense, tâche) daily

quotidien² *m* daily, daily newspaper

quotidiennement *adv* daily

quotient *m* quotient; ~ **de réussite** achievement quotient

quotité *f* quota; (Bourse) trading unit; ~ **du contrat** contract size; ~ **imposable** taxable quota, taxable portion of income; ~ **minimale** minimum quote size UK; ~ **normale de transaction** normal trading unit

q

Rr

r. *abrév* (▸**recommandé**) regd. (registered); (▸**route**, ▸**rue**) Rd. (road)

rabais *m* discount, rebate; **obtenir un ~ de 20%/50 euros sur qch** get a 20%/50 euro discount on sth; **accorder un ~ à qn sur qch** give sb a discount on sth; **au ~** (achat, vente) at a discount; (acheter, vendre) at a discount, cheaply; **~ de gros** trade discount; **~ importants** deep discounts; **~ sur marchandise** merchandise allowance

rabatteur, -euse *m,f* (de clients) tout

rabattre *vt* (pourcentage, somme) knock off; (des clients) tout for

raccorder *vt* (Info) connect; **raccordé à** coupled with

raccourci *m* shortcut; **~ clavier** (Info) hot key, keyboard shortcut

raccourcir *vt* shorten

raccourcissement *m* (de programme) curtailment

raccrocher *vi* (téléphone) hang up

rachat *m* (de société) buyout; (de dette, de rente) redemption; (d'objet vendu) repurchase, buyback; **vente avec faculté de ~** sale with option of repurchase; **~ d'actions** buyback, share redemption; **~ d'entreprise** buyout; **~ d'entreprise financé par l'endettement** leveraged buyout; **~ d'une entreprise par ses employés** worker buyout; **~ d'une entreprise par des investisseurs** leveraged management buy-in; **~ d'une entreprise par ses salariés** ≈ management buyout; **~ modifié** modified rebuy (jarg); **~ d'office** buy-in; **~ de parts de gestionnaires** management buyout

rachetable *adj* (objet) repurchasable; (emprunt) callable; (dette) redeemable; **~ au gré du porteur** retractable

racheté, e *adj* (action) redeemed

racheter *vt* (entreprise) buyout; (objet vendu) buy back; (article semblable) buy another; (emprunt) recall, (dette, action) redeem; (enchères) buy in; **~ un emprunt obligataire** call bonds; **~ qch de moins cher** trade down

racheteur, -euse *m,f* buyer; **~ de sociétés** (par offre publique d'achat et offre publique d'échange) corporate raider

racine *f* (Info) root

racoler *vt* (des clients) tout for

radar *m* (navigation) radar

rade *f* (maritime) roads

radiation *f* (Brevets) (d'une inscription au registre) cancellation; (Compta) write-off; (Droit) (d'avocat) disbarring; **~ de la cote** delisting; **~ de dette** deletion of a debt; **~ d'une**

perte writing off a loss; **~ partielle** partial write-off

radical, e *adj* radical

radicalisme *m* radicalism; **~ économique** radical economics

radier *vt* delete; (Brevets) cancel; (Compta) (perte) write off; (Droit) (un avocat) disbar

radio *f* radio; **~ cellulaire/commerciale** cellular/commercial radio

radiodiffuser *vt* broadcast

radiodiffusion *f* broadcasting; **~ par satellite** satellite broadcasting

radiotéléphone *m* radiophone, radiotelephone

raffermi, e *adj* (Bourse) consolidated

raffermir ① *vt* consolidate ② **se raffermir** *v pron* (cours de la bourse) become steady, firm up, strengthen

raffinage *m* refining; (du pétrole) oil refining

raffiné, e *adj* (pétrole) refined

raffinement *m* (pétrole) refinement

raffinerie *f* refinery; **~ de pétrole** oil refinery

raffineur, -euse *m,f* refiner

rafraîchir *vt* refresh; (des bureaux) revamp

rafraîchissement *m* (des bureaux) revamping

raid *m* raid; (Bourse) bear raiding

raider *m* (Bourse) raider

rail *m* rail

raison *f* reason; **à ~ de** at a rate of; **en ~ de** by virtue of, on account of; **pour quelque ~ que ce soit** for any reason; **~s médicales** medical grounds; **pour des ~s d'opportunité** on grounds of expediency; **pour ~s de santé** on the grounds of ill health; **~ sociale** corporate name; **~ spécifiée** specified purpose

raisonnable *adj* reasonable; (consommation) moderate; (sensé) sensible

raisonnement *m* reasoning; **~ par déduction** deductive reasoning

rajeunir *vt* (une entreprise) rejuvenate; (secteur économique, système) modernize; (corps de métier) bring new blood into

rajeunissement *m* (d'une entreprise) rejuvenation; (de secteur économique, système) modernization

rajouter *vt* add

rajusté, e *adj* adjusted

rajustement *m* (de salaires) adjustment; **~ annuel** annual adjustment; **~ de taux d'intérêt** interest rate adjustment

rajuster *vt* adjust

ralentir ⓵ *vt* slow down; (Bourse) (activité) scale down ⓶ *vi* slow down ⓷ **se ralentir** *v pron* slow down

ralentissement *m* (d'activité) slowdown; ∼ **économique** economic slowdown, downturn in the economy

rallonge *f* (infrml) (de temps) extension; (d'argent) extra money

rallongé, e *adj* lengthened

RAM *f* (Info) RAM; ∼ **dynamique** dynamic RAM, DRAM

ramassage *m* collection; ∼ **et livraison** collection and delivery; ∼ **des ordures ménagères** refuse collection BrE, garbage collection AmE

ramasser *vt* collect

rame *f* (de papier) ream; (métro, train) train; ∼ **de wagons** rake of wagons

ramener *vt* (rapporter) bring back; (ordre, calme) restore; ∼ **qn dans une fourchette imposable** bring sb within the tax net; ∼ **l'inflation à 4%** reduce inflation to 4%; ∼ **les prix à leur niveau antérieur** restore prices to their previous level

rampe *f* (place) ramp; ∼ **d'accès** (d'autoroute) sliproad BrE, entrance ramp AmE; ∼ **d'accès réglable** (navigation) adjustable shore ramp; ∼ **d'appontement** (navigation) link span; ∼ **mécanique** (dans grands magasins) travelscator

rand *m* rand

rang *m* rank; ∼ **inférieur** lower rank; **de** ∼ **supérieur** top-flight; **arriver au 5ᵉ** ∼ **mondial des exportations de café** rank 5th in the world for coffee exports; **être au 3ᵉ** ∼ **mondial des exportateurs de coton** be the 3rd largest exporter of cotton in the world; **sur les** ∼**s pour** in the running for; **hypothèque de premier/deuxième** ∼ first/second mortgage; **obligation de premier/deuxième** ∼ senior/junior bond

rangée *f* (Info) array

ranimer *vt* revive

rapatriement *m* repatriation; ∼ **de bénéfices** repatriation of profits; ∼ **de capitaux détenus à l'étranger** repatriation of overseas funds

rapatrier *vt* (profits) repatriate; (données) retrieve

rapetisseur *m* (jarg) (Bourse) lowballer (jarg)

rapide¹ *adj* fast; (service) quick, speedy; (progrès, développement) rapid; (livraison, succès, amélioration, aggravation) quick, rapid; (réponse, décision) prompt

rapide² *m* (train) express (train), InterCity UK

rapidité *f* speed; ∼ **de changement** pace of change

rappel *m* (avis de facturation) reminder; (en publicité) follow-up; (Bourse) recall; **lettre de** ∼ reminder; **recevoir/envoyer un** ∼ receive/

send a reminder; **'dernier** ∼**'** 'final reminder'; ∼ **automatique** (par téléphone) automatic redialling BrE, automatic redialing AmE; ∼ **d'impôts** back tax; ∼ **de salaire** back pay

rappeler *vt* (à la bourse) recall; (au téléphone) call back, phone back; ∼ **un numéro de référence** quote a reference number

rapport *m* (lien) connection, link; (document) report; (rendement) return, yield; ∼ **officiel** official report; ∼ **confidentiel** confidential report; **rédiger un** ∼ prepare a report, draw up a report; **investissement d'un bon** ∼ investment that offers a good return; **produire un** ∼ **de 4%** produce a 4% return; ∼**s relations**; **par** ∼ **à** compared with, in relation to; **en** ∼ **étroit avec** in close touch with; **en** ∼ **indirect avec** indirectly related to; ∼ **financier utilisé comme prospectus** statement in lieu of prospectus UK; ∼ **annuel** annual report; ∼ **d'audit** audit report, auditor's report; ∼ **d'audit favorable** clean (audit); ∼ **d'avaries** damage report; ∼ **de bureau de douane** customs house report; ∼ **du capital à l'actif** capital-to-asset ratio; ∼ **capital-travail** capital-labour ratio BrE, capital-labor ratio AmE; ∼ **chiffre d'affaires-immobilisations** turnover ratio; ∼ **du commissionnaire aux comptes** audit report, auditor's report; ∼ **comptable** accounting report; ∼ **de conférence** (V&M) call report; ∼ **contractuel** (Droit) privity; ∼ **cours-bénéfice** price-earnings ratio; ∼ **coût-efficacité** cost-effectiveness; ∼ **coûts-avantages** cost-benefit analysis; ∼ **détaillé** detailed account; ∼ **dettes-actions** debt-equity ratio; ∼ **dividende-prix** dividend-price ratio; ∼ **documentaire** background paper; ∼ **d'évaluation** valuation report; ∼ **d'exercice** (audit) annual certificate, annual report; ∼ **d'expertise** survey report; (Assur) damage report, survey report; ∼ **financier** financial statement; ∼ **financier annuel détaillé** comprehensive annual financial report; ∼ **des flux financiers** application of funds statement; ∼ **de gestion financière** financial management report; ∼ **indiqué** indicated yield; ∼ **d'intervention** call report; ∼ **d'irrégularité** irregularity report; ∼ **maximum** maximum return; ∼ **de mer** ship's protest, voyage report; ∼ **moyen** (analyse de valeurs) mean return; ∼ **d'opération** trade report; ∼ **d'ouverture de compte** new-account report; ∼ **de parité** parity ratio; ∼ **parlementaire** government report; ∼ **passif-réserves** reserve-assets ratio; ∼ **plancher** floor return; ∼ **de prêt** loan yield; ∼ **prêt-garantie** loan value; ∼ **prêt-valeur** loan-to-value ratio; ∼ **profit sur ventes** profit/volume ratio; ∼ **qualité-prix** (marketing) quality-price ratio; ∼ **réservé** qualified report; ∼ **risque-bénéfice** risk-reward ratio; ∼ **sinistres-primes** burning cost, loss ratio; ∼ **de solvabilité** credit report; ∼ ⋯⟶

sommaire summary report; ~ **de synthèse** conspectus; ~ **valeur-poids** value-to-weight ratio

rapporter ① *vt* (intérêts) earn; (bénéfice) yield; ~ **un intérêt de** bear an interest of; ~ **ses conclusions** report one's conclusions

② *vi* (procurer un bénéfice) be profitable, be lucrative; (métier, investissement) be lucrative; **qui rapporte** (capital, avoirs) active

③ **se rapporter à** *v pron* relate to, pertain to

rapprochement *m* (comparaison) connection; (Banque) reconciliation; (Pol) rapprochement; **faire** *or* **établir un** ~ **entre** establish a connection between; ~ **bancaire** bank reconciliation; ~ **bancaire de contrôle** cutoff bank reconciliation; ~ **de comptes** account reconciliation, reconciliation of accounts

rapprocher *vt* (réunir) bring together; (comparer) compare; (Compta) reconcile

rare *adj* (matières premières, main-d'œuvre, produit) scarce

raréfaction *f* (pénurie) scarcity, growing shortage; ~ **de l'ozone** ozone depletion

rassemblement *m* (de personnes) gathering; ~ **de données** (Info) data collection, data gathering

rassembler *vt* (des personnes) gather together; (des informations, des preuves) collect; (Info) (données) gather

ratification *f* ratification (**de** of)

ratifié, e *adj* (traité, contrat) ratified

ratifier *vt* (un traité, un contrat) ratify; (cotisation) confirm

ratio *m* ratio; **à** ~ **d'endettement élevé** highly-geared; **le** ~ **de x à y** the ratio of x to y; ~ **d'actifs** asset coverage; ~ **d'actifs disponibles** quick assets ratio; ~ **administration-production** administration-production ratio; ~ **des bénéfices d'exploitation sur le capital employé** primary ratio; ~ **de capital** capital ratio; ~ **du capital de base** base capital ratio; ~ **de capital redressé** adjusted capital ratio; ~ **de capitalisation** capitalization ratio; ~ **comptable** accounting ratio; ~ **de corrélation** correlation ratio UK; ~ **cours-bénéfice** price-earnings ratio; ~ **coût-chiffre d'affaires** expense ratio; ~ **de couverture** hedge ratio; ~ **de couverture des dividendes** dividend coverage ratio; ~ **débiteur** debit ratio; ~ **des dépenses publiques sur le produit intérieur brut** public spending ratio; ~ **de la dette extérieure sur les exportations** ratio of external debt to exports; ~ **d'emprunt** borrowing ratio; ~ **d'endettement** debt ratio, gearing ratio BrE, leverage ratio AmE; ~ **épargne-revenus** savings-to-income ratio; ~ **fonds engagements** capital cover; ~ **du**

fonds de roulement current ratio, working-capital ratio; ~ **de gestion** management ratio; ~ **d'immobilisations et chiffre d'affaires** asset turnover; ~ **d'intensité de capital** capital-outlay ratio, capital-output ratio; ~ **de levier** gearing ratio BrE, leverage ratio AmE; ~ **de liquidité** current ratio, liquidity ratio; ~ **de placement** placement ratio; ~ **prêt sur valeur** loan-to-value ratio; ~ **du prix coûtant au prix de détail** cost ratio; ~ **de recouvrement** collection ratio; ~ **de rentabilité** profitability ratio; ~ **du résultat aux capitaux propres** net income to net worth ratio; ~ **de solvabilité** (établissements de crédit) solvency ratio; ~ **de versement** (marketing) payout ratio

rationalisation *f* (Ind) streamlining, rationalization; ~ **des choix budgétaires** programme budgeting BrE, program budgeting AmE

rationaliser *vt* rationalize, streamline

rationalité *f* rationality; ~ **limitée** bounded rationality

rationnement *m* rationing; ~ **des fonds** capital rationing

rationner *vt* (ressource, essence) ration; (population) impose rationing on

rattachement *m* (de territoire) unification; (de personne) **demander son** ~ **à** ask to be posted to; ~ **des charges et des produits** (bilans, coûts et revenus) matching principle US

rattacher *vt* (service, région) attach; (devise) link; (employé) post; ~ **des charges à un exercice** (Compta) apply expenses to a period; ~ **des produits à un exercice** (Compta) apply revenues to a period

rattrapage *m* (remise à jour) adjustment; (de retard) catching up; ~ **des salaires/prix** adjustment of wage rates/prices; ~ **du déséquilibre** adjustment of the imbalance; ~ **de la demande** catch-up demand; ~ **de salaire** make-up pay

rattraper ① *vt* (concurrent) catch up with; (temps perdu) make up for; (arriérés, déficit) make up; ~ **son retard** catch up

② **se rattraper** *v pron* (compenser le temps perdu) make up for lost time

rature *f* deletion; **sans** ~**s ni surcharges** without deletions or alterations

ravitaillement *m* (en carburant) refuelling BrE, refueling AmE; (aviation) catering; (provisions) supplies

ravitailler ① *vt* ~ **en carburant** refuel

② **se ravitailler** *v pron*: **se** ~ **en carburant** refuel

ravitailleur, -euse *m* (Transp) tender

rayé, e *adj* (navigation) expunged

rayer *vt* delete, cross out; ~ **qn de la liste** cross sb's name off the list; '~ **la mention inutile**' 'delete whichever does not apply'

rayon *m* (en grand magasin) department; (dans

un petit magasin) section; (étagère) shelf; **en ~** out on the shelves; **dans un ~ de 20 km** within a 20 km radius; **~ d'action** sphere of activity; **~ hommes** men's department; **~ laser** laser beam; **~ des soldes** bargain counter

rayonnage *m* shelf space

rayonnement *m* (radiation) radiation

RCB *abrév* (▸**rationalisation des choix budgétaires**) PPBS (planning, programming, budgeting system)

RCI *abrév* (▸**rentabilité des capitaux investis**) ROCE (return on capital employed)

réabonnement *m* renewal of a subscription

réabonner: se ~ *v pron* renew one's subscription

réacteur *m* reactor; **~ nucléaire** nuclear reactor; **~ thermique** thermal reactor

réactif, -ive *adj* reactive

réaction *f* reaction; (plus réfléchi) response; **en ~ à** in reaction to, in response to; **temps de ~** response time; **~ de l'acheteur** buyer response; **~ d'anticipation** anticipatory response; **~ en chaîne** knock-on effect; **~ des consommateurs** consumer response; **~ négative** negative feedback

réactionnaire *adj* reactionary

réadressable *adj* relocatable

réadressage *m* relocation

réaffectation *f* (de fonds) reallocation, reassignment; (de personne) redeployment

réaffecter *vt* (fonds) reallocate, reassign; (personne) redeploy, reassign

réaffirmer *vt* reaffirm

réagir *vi* react

réajustement *m* adjustment; **~ après inventaire** inventory valuation adjustment; **~ de pension** pension adjustment; **~ du prix de base** adjustment to cost base

réajuster *vt* adjust; **~ en baisse** adjust downwards; **~ en hausse** adjust upwards

réalisable *adj* (but) achievable; (projet) feasible; (innovation) workable; (Fin) realizable

réalisateur, -trice *m,f* (radio, télévision) director

réalisation *f* (chose réalisée) accomplishment, achievement; (d'étude) carrying out; (Fin) (d'un bénéfice) making; (télévision, radio) direction; **~ comparée aux projets** performance against objectives; **~ d'éléments d'actif** realization of assets

réaliser 1 *vt* realize, sell out; (obligations) cash in; (invention) carry out, make; (objectif) achieve; (télévision, radio) direct; (sondage, projet, tâche) carry out; (équilibre idéal) achieve; **~ des actifs** realize assets; **~ un bénéfice** make a profit, take a profit; **~ des économies** make savings; **~ des gains** make gains; **~ une plus-value** make a capital gain; **~ une première pénétration du marché** get a toehold in the market

2 **se réaliser** *v pron* come off, come to fruition

réaliste *adj* realistic

réalité *f* reality; **les ~s économiques** economic realities; **devenir (une) ~** become a reality; **~ des objectifs** goal congruence; **~ virtuelle** (Info) virtual reality

réaménagement *m* (d'une dette) rescheduling; (immobilier) redevelopment; (aviation) request for change; **~ des devises** currency reordering

réaménager *vt* (dette) reschedule; (immobilier) redevelop

réamorçage *m* (Info) rebooting

réamorcer *vt* (Info) reboot

réapprovisionner 1 *vt* (compte) top up, replenish; (magasin) restock

2 **se réapprovisionner** *v pron* replenish one's stocks, restock

réarmement *m* (navigation) ship conversion

réarrimage *m* (Transp) restowage

réassort *m* (activité) restocking; (marchandise) fresh stock

réassortir 1 *vt* (stock) replace

2 **se réassortir** *v pron* stock up (en on)

réassortisseur, -euse *m,f* shelf filler

réassurance *f* reinsurance; **~ effective** active reinsurance; **~ en excédent brut de sinistre** gross excess reinsurance policy; **~ en excédent de pertes** stop-loss reinsurance; **~ générale** treaty reinsurance; **~ de portefeuille** portfolio reinsurance

réattribution *f* reallowance

reboisement *m* reafforestation

rebut *m* rubbish BrE, garbage AmE; (lettre) dead letter; **mettre qch/qn au ~** put sth/sb on the scrapheap

recalculer *vt* recalculate

récapituler *vt* summarize

recensement *m* (des habitants) census; (inventaire) inventory; **faire un ~ de** make an inventory *ou* list of; **~ de l'activité économique** census of business; **~ de la population** population census

récent, e *adj* recent

recentrage *m* refocusing

récépissé *m* receipt; (de paiement) receipt, acknowledgement; **~ de dépôt** deposit receipt; **~ de documents** receipt for documents; **~ d'entrepôt** warehouse receipt, warehouse warrant; **~ d'un envoi** certificate of posting; **~ de livraison** delivery receipt; **~ du transitaire** forwarding agent's receipt; **~ de versement** deposit receipt

récepteur *m* (Envir) receptor; (radio, TV) receiver; **~ de papier** paper stacker; **~ téléphonique** telephone receiver

réceptif *m*: **~ précoce** (marketing) early adopter

réception *f* reception, front desk; **dès ~ de ⋯⋗**

r

on receipt of; **dès ~ de la facture** on receipt of invoice; **sur ~** on receipt; **~ et chargement des marchandises** (maritime) receiving and loading cargo; **~ favorable** acceptance; **~ des marchandises** receipt of goods; **~ officielle** function; **~ organisée pour le lancement d'un livre** launch party

réceptionnaire *mf* (dans un hôtel) receptionist; (Com) receiving clerk

réceptionner *vt* (livraison, marchandises) accept delivery of

réceptionniste *mf* receptionist

réceptivité *f* acceptance, receptiveness; **~ des consommateurs** consumer acceptance; **~ du marché** market receptiveness

récession *f* recession, slump; **une phase de ~ a** recessionary period; **~ conjuguée à l'inflation** slumpflation (jarg); **~ provoquée par l'inflation** infession (jarg)

récessionniste *adj* recessionary

recette *f* (Fin) takings; (Fisc) tax office, revenue office; (Econ) **~s** revenue; (Compta) receipts; **faire ~** be a success; **faire la ~** collect sums due; **les ~s et les dépenses** (Compta) receipts and expenses; **~s budgétaires** budgetary revenue; **~s au comptant** cash receipt; **~s courantes** current revenues; **~s effectives** actual takings; **~s effectuées** monies paid in; **~s en espèces** cash receipt; **~s fiscales** tax receipts, tax revenue; **~s d'honoraires** fee income; **~s liquides** cash inflow; **~ marginale** marginal revenue; **~s nettes en commun** net receipts pool; **~s nettes en vertu d'un crédit** vote-netted revenue; **~s non fiscales** nontax revenue; **~s obligataires** bond proceeds; **~ de primes** premium income; **~s de privatisation** privatization proceeds; **~s publicitaires** advertising revenue; **~s publicitaires par média** advertising revenue by media; **~ totale** total revenue; **~s à valoir sur le crédit** receipts credited to the fund, vote-netting revenue; **~s de ventes** sales revenue

recevabilité *f* acceptability; (Droit) (d'une demande, d'une action) admissibility

recevable *adj* (excuse, offre) acceptable; (Droit) (preuve, témoignage, recours) admissible

receveur, -euse *m,f* (Transp) warrantee; **~ des douanes** customs collector; **~ de l'enregistrement** (Droit) registrar of deeds; **~ des impôts** tax collector, tax officer; **~ municipal** rate collector; **~ des postes** postmaster

recevoir *vt* (invités) entertain, (lettre, paiement) receive; **à ~** (intérêts, comptes) receivable; **~ contre paiement** receive versus payment; **ne pas pouvoir ~** fail to receive; **~ un visa d'inspection favorable** pass inspection

rechange *m*: **de ~** (solution) alternative; (pièce) spare

RECHAR *abrév* (►reconversion charbon)

European Union scheme introduced in 1990 to help the revitalization of areas hit by coal pit closures

recharger *vt* (Info, Transp) reload

réchauffement *m* (Envir) warming; (de relations) improvement; **~ de la planète** global warming

recherche *f* (étude) research; (fait de chercher) search; (sur Internet) search, websearch; **être à la ~ de** be in search of; **faire une ~ de** search for; **personne à la ~ d'un emploi** job hunter, jobseeker; **~ active** action research; **~s sans applications immédiates** blue-sky research; **~ appliquée** applied research; (étude de marché) industrial research; **~ avancée** (sur Internet) advanced search; **~ des besoins des consommateurs** consumer research; **~ binaire** binary search; **~ de cadres** executive search; **~ commerciale** commercial research, marketing research; **~ et développement** research and development; **~ dichotomique** binary search; **~ documentaire** information retrieval; (étude de marché) desk research; **~ en économie** economic research; **~ d'emploi** job hunting, job search; **~ d'erreurs** tick-up; **~s éditées** published research; **~ expérimentale** applied research; **~ globale** global search; **~ d'informations** information retrieval; **~ sur Internet** websearch; **~ par mot clé** keyword search; **~ de motivations** motivational research; **~ d'objectifs** goal-seeking; **~ opérationnelle** operational research, operations research; **~ de produit** product research; **~ du profit** profit motive; **~ rapide** (Info) quick search; **~ scientifique** scientific research; **~ sur le terrain** (étude de marché) field research; **~ universitaire** academic research

recherché, e *adj* in demand, sought-after; **être ~ par les chasseurs de têtes** be headhunted; **être très ~** be in great demand

rechercher *vt* look for, search for; (de l'aide) seek; (cadres) headhunt, seek; **~ un marché** seek a market; **~ qch dans un fichier** search a file for sth

rechute *f* double dip (jarg)

récidive *f* second offence BrE, second offense AmE

récipiendaire *mf* recipient

réciproque *adj* reciprocal

réciproquement *adv* conversely, reciprocally

réclamation *f* complaint; (Assur) claim; **faire une ~** (se plaindre) make a complaint; (Assur) put in a claim; **lettre de ~** letter of complaint; **sur ~** on request; **~ acceptable** valid claim; **~ de l'assureur** insurer's claim; **~ concernant les marchandises** cargo claim; **~ en dommages-intérêts** (Droit) claim for damages; **~ faite par un tiers** third-party claim; **~s fiscales** tax claims; ~ **recevable** allowable claim; ~ **de rembroursement** repayment claim

réclamer [1] *vt* claim; ~ **un dédommagement** claim compensation; ~ **des dommages et intérêts** claim damages [2] *vi* (se plaindre) complain

reclassement *m* (de salaire) regrading; (d'employé) redeployment; ~ **en amont d'un prêt** upgrading of a loan; ~ **externe** outplacement

reclasser *vt* (employé) redeploy; (compte) reclassify

reclassification *f* (des comptes) reclassification; ~ **continue** (navigation) continuous survey

réclusion *f* (criminelle) imprisonment

récolte *f* (activité) harvest; (produits récoltés) crop; ~ **de céréales** grain crop; ~ **de rapport** cash crop

récolter *vt* harvest; (Fin) reap; ~ **les bénéfices** reap the benefits; ~ **les rémunérations** reap the rewards

recommandataire *mf* (Banque, Admin) referee (in case of need)

recommandation *f* recommendation; **faire des ~s à qn** make recommendations to sb; **sur les ~s de qn** on sb's recommendation; **avoir une ~ de qn** be recommended by sb; **lettre de ~** reference, testimonial; ~ **générale** blanket recommendation; ~**s professionnelles** (Compta, Fin) audit guide

recommandé¹, e *adj* (lettre, colis) registered; (produit) recommended; **sous pli ~** by registered post BrE *ou* mail

recommandé² *m* **envoyer qch en ~** send sth by registered post BrE *ou* mail

recommander *vt* (conseiller) recommend; (lettre) register

récompense *f* reward; **en ~ de** as a reward for; ~ **financière** financial reward

récompenser *vt* reward

recompiler *vt* (Info) recompile

réconcilier *vt* reconcile

reconditionnement *m* (V&M) repackaging

reconditionner *vt* (V&M) repackage

reconduction *f* renewal; (Fin) roll-over; ~ **tacite** tacit renewal

reconduire *vt* renew; (Fin) roll over

reconfiguration *f* reconfiguration

reconnaissance *f* (d'une obligation) recognition; (de dette) acknowledgement; (des syndicats) recognition; (en marketing) recognition; (d'erreurs, de torts) admission; (de mérites qualités) recognition; ~ **de dépôt** cash deposit acknowledgement; ~ **de dette** I owe you, acknowledgement of debt, due bill AmE; ~ **d'endettement** acknowledgement of indebtness; ~ **légale** legal recognition; ~ **mutuelle** (UE) mutual recognition; ~ **optique des caractères** optical character

recognition; ~ **de la parole** speech recognition; ~ **d'une perte** recognition of loss; ~ **vocale** voice recognition

reconnaître *vt* (identifier) recognize; (erreur, dette) acknowledge, admit; (syndicat, régime, diplôme, droit de grève) recognize; ~ **qn coupable/non coupable** (Droit) find sb guilty/not guilty

reconnu, e *adj* recognized

reconsidération *f* reconsideration; ~ **d'une évaluation** (Fisc) reconsideration of an assessment

reconsidérer *vt* reconsider

reconsigner *vt* (Transp) reconsign

reconstituer *vt* (Econ, Bourse) (société) reconstruct; (stock) rebuild, build up again; (Info) (fichier) rebuild

reconstitution *f* (Econ, Bourse) (de société) reconstruction; (de stock) rebuilding; (Info) rebuilding

reconstruire *vt* (édifice, ville) reconstruct; (machine, économie, pays) rebuild

reconversion *f* (devise) retranslation; (usine) reconversion; ~ **charbon** European Union scheme introduced in 1990 to help the revitalization of areas hit by coal pit closures

reconvertir *vt* (Econ, Info) reconvert

record¹ *adj* (année, prix, croissance, niveau) record; (récolte) bumper, record; **en temps ~** in record time

record² *m* record; **établir/détenir/battre un ~** to set/hold/break a record; ~ **absolu** all-time record; ~ **le plus élevé** all-time high; ~ **de vente** selling climax

recouper: se ~ *v pron* (résultats) add up; (versions, témoignages) tally

recours *m* (moyen) recourse; (moyen extrême) resort; (Admin) claim of recourse; (Droit) appeal; **avec ~** with recourse; **avoir ~ à** (remède, technique) have recourse to; (expédient, stratagème) resort to; (personne) turn to; (agence, expert) go to; **avoir ~ à la justice** take legal action; **déposer un ~ devant un tribunal** lodge an appeal; ~ **et conservation** sue and labour BrE, sue and labor AmE; **en dernier ~** as a last resort; ~ **en annulation** action for cancellation; ~ **bilatéral à l'arbitrage** bilateral reference; ~ **collectif en justice** class action; ~ **entre coassurés** cross liability; ~ **à l'impasse budgétaire** deficit financing; ~ **des tiers** third-party claim

recouvrable *adj* (Fin) (dette) recoverable; (impôt) collectable

recouvrement *m* (impôts, effets) collection; (de créances, de dettes) recovery, collection; **pour ~** for collection; ~ **de base** recovery of basis; ~ **complexe** advanced collection; ~ **de créances** debt collection; ~ **sur créance radiée** bad debt recovery; ~ **des dépenses** recovery of expenses; ~ **de l'impôt** tax collection; ~ **de prêt** loan recovery

recouvrer vt (dette) recover, collect

récrire vt (Info) rewrite

recrutement m recruitment; **entretien de ~** job interview; **~ et gestion des effectifs** human resource planning; **~ interne** internal search; **~ en ligne** e-cruitement; **~ du personnel** staffing, staff recruitment

recruter vt (personnel) recruit; **~ des cadres** headhunt

recruteur, -euse m,f recruitment consultant; (Bourse) canvasser

rectificatif, -ive adj (facture, compte) corrected, amended; **article ~** (Compta) correcting entry

rectification f (de chiffres) adjustment; (de contrat) rectification; (de cours) correction; **~ comptable** accounting adjustment

rectifier vt (cours) correct; (contrat) rectify; (Droit) amend; (chiffres, erreurs) adjust

recto m (d'une page) recto; **au recto** on the front; **~ verso** on both sides, recto verso

reçu¹, e adj received

reçu² m receipt; **~ d'action** stock receipt; **~ à l'appui** supporting receipt; **~ en blanc** blank receipt; **~ en bonne et due forme** formal receipt; **~ de caisse** till receipt; **~ de chargement** data freight receipt; **~ de dépôt** deposit receipt; **~ de livraison** delivery receipt; **~ officiel** official receipt

recueil m collection; (de documents) compendium; **~ de données** (Info) data collection, data gathering; **~ des lois** statute book UK

recueillir vt collect, gather; **~ des informations** gather information, gather intelligence

recul m (de la production, des ventes, des investissement) drop (**de** in), fall (**de** in); (du chômage) decline; (d'une date, d'une réunion) postponement; **~ du dollar** fall in the dollar; **être en ~** (ventes, exportations) be dropping, be falling; (tendance) be on the decline; **un ~ de 5%/10 points** a 5%/10 point drop; **avec le ~** with hindsight, in retrospect

reculer 1 vt (date, réunion) postpone, put back
2 vi (production, ventes, valeur boursière) drop, fall; (chômage, devise, valeur boursière) fall; **faire ~** (exportations) cause a fall in

récupérable adj (matériel) reusable, recyclable; (argent, créance) recoverable; (impôt) refundable; (heures de travail) which can be made up; (données) retrievable

récupérateur m salvage dealer; **~ de pétrole** oil recovery skimmer

récupération f (Fin, Compta) recovery; (Info) (de données) retrieval, recovery; (Envir) recycling; (des marchandises, des bagages) reclaiming; (d'heures perdues) making up; (du capital investi) payback; (de la TVA) refunding; **~ de l'amortissement** depreciation recapture;

~ de la déduction pour épuisement depletion recapture; **~ de l'énergie** (recyclage) energy recovery; **~ des frais** recovery of expenses; **~ de l'information** (Info) information retrieval; **~ primaire** (Fisc) primary recovery

récupérer vt (dette, argent) recover; (Info) (données, fichier) retrieve; (Envir) (pertes) recoup; (marchandises, bagages) reclaim; (heures perdues) make up; (TVA) get back; **~ ses débours** recoup one's expenditure

récusation f denial of opinion; (Droit) **~ de juré** challenging a juror; **droit de ~** right of challenge

recyclable adj (Envir) recyclable; **non ~** (Envir) nonrecyclable

recyclage m (Envir) recycling; (formation) retraining; **~ des déchets** waste recycling; **~ professionnel** vocational retraining

recycler vt (Envir) recycle; (employé) retrain

rédacteur, -trice m,f (presse) news editor; (édition) editor; **~ en chef** (journaux) editor; **~ en chef adjoint** (journaux) deputy editor; **~ de mode** fashion editor; **~ publicitaire** copywriter

rédaction f (d'un document) writing; (d'un contrat) drafting, drawing up; (presse) (le personnel) editorial staff; (les bureaux) editorial offices

reddition f rendering; **~ de comptes** rendering of accounts

redéfinir vt redefine

redéfinition f redefinition, redefining; (Info) remapping; **~ du contenu d'un poste** job regulation

redémarrage m (de l'économie) recovery, rally; (Info) restart; **~ automatique** autorestart; **~ soutenu** (Econ) sustained recovery

redémarrer vt (économie) rally, recover, take off again; (entreprise) relaunch itself; (Info) restart

redéploiement m redeployment

redéployer vt redeploy

redéposer vt (Banque) redeposit

redevance f (Droit) rental right; (droit d'exploitation) royalty; (Média) licence BrE, license AmE; (pour un service) fees; **~s d'émission** (Envir) emission charges; **~ fixe** fixed fee; **~ foncière** rent charge; **~ forfaitaire** flat-rate fee; **~ de pollution** pollution tax; **~ de télévision** television licence UK

rédigé, e adj (contrat) drafted

rédiger vt (un document) write; (contrat) draft, draw up; (chèque) make out, write

redimensionner vt (Info) maximize

redistribution f (de richesses) redistribution; (de tâches, de terres) reallocation; **~ des ressources** reallocation of resources; **~ des revenus** income redistribution

redondance *f* redundancy

redonner *vt* (donner à nouveau) give again; (rendre) give back; ~ **confiance à qn** bolster up sb's confidence

redoublé, e *adj* (activité, efforts) renewed

redressement *m* (du marché) recovery; (Bourse) rally, rallying; (Fisc, Compta) adjustment; ~ **affecté aux exercices antérieurs** prior period adjustment; ~ **pour amortissement** amortization adjustment; ~ **comptable** accounting adjustment; ~ **des comptes clients** adjustment of accounts receivable; ~ **économique** recovery; ~ **économique lié aux exportations** export-led economic recovery; ~ **d'entreprises** corporate turnaround; ~ **financier** gearing adjustment BrE, leverage adjustment AmE; ~ **fiscal** tax adjustment; ~ **du marché** market recovery; ~ **du taux d'endettement** gearing adjustment BrE, leverage adjustment AmE

redresser ① *vt* (bilan) right; (Compta) adjust; (entreprise) turn round BrE, turn around AmE; (marge de bénéfices) improve; (monnaie) aid the recovery of; (erreur) correct; (compte) adjust; ~ **l'équilibre** redress the balance ② **se redresser** *v pron* (Econ) rally, recover

réduction *f* (diminution) reduction, cut; (action de diminuer) reducing, cutting; (d'effectifs, de coûts) cutting, pruning; (de dépenses, production) cutting, reducing; (dans un magasin) discount, markdown; (pour étudiants, personnes âgées) concession; **faire une ~ de 5% à qn** give sb a 5% discount; ~ **étudiants/familles** concessions for students/families; ~ **de l'écart entre** narrowing the gap between; ~ **pour achat en gros** bulk discount; ~ **budgétaire** budget cut; ~ **de capital** reduction in capital; ~ **des coûts** cost reduction, cutback; ~ **du délai d'exécution** acceleration; ~ **d'effectifs** staff cuts, downsizing (jarg); ~ **d'emplois secondaires** reduction in force; ~ **générale** across-the-board cut; ~ **d'impôt** tax relief; ~ **sur le loyer** rent rebate; ~ **du nombre d'actions** stock split-down; ~ **du personnel** staff cutback, staff reduction; ~ **des prix** price cutting; ~ **du risque** risk minimizing; ~ **des tarifs** rate cutting; ~ **du taux d'escompte** fall in the bank rate; ~ **de valeur** impairment of value

réduire *vt* (chômage) reduce, bring down; (activité) scale down; (stocks, dépenses, coûts, impôts) reduce; (personnel) cut, shake out; (prix) reduce; (écart) narrow; ~ **de moitié** halve; ~ **peu à peu** (frais, commissions, capital) whittle down; ~ **la valeur** (Compta) write down; ~ **les frais de crédit** buy down; ~ **le personnel** trim the workforce; ~ **les pertes** cut one's losses; ~ **à la portion congrue** (Fin) put on short allowance.

réduit, e *adj* (vitesse, taux, cotisation) reduced, lower; (stock, nombre) limited; (format, version) reduced, scaled-down; (moyens, choix) limited; (main-d'œuvre) reduced, smaller; (délai) shorter; **à prix ~** cut-price, at a reduced price

rééchelonnement *m* rescheduling; ~ **de la dette** debt rescheduling

rééchelonner *vt* reschedule

réécouter *vt* (message) replay

réécrire *vt* rewrite

rééditer *vt* republish

réel, -elle *adj* (coût, cause) actual; (risque, revenu) real; (taux d'intérêt) effective; (Droit) real; **garantie réelle** pledge of real property

réélection *f* re-election

réembaucher *vt* re-employ, rehire

réémettre *vt* reissue

réemploi *m* re-employment, rehiring

réemployer *vt* re-employ, rehire

réescomptable *adj* rediscountable

réescompte *m* rediscount, rediscounting

réévaluation *f* (d'actifs, de monnaie) revaluation; (de patrimoine, d'impôts, d'intérêts) reassessment; ~ **légale** legal revaluation; ~ **monétaire** currency revaluation; ~ **des salaires** salary review

réévaluer *vt* (estimer à nouveau) reassess, reappraise; (Fin) (actifs, monnaie) revalue; (patrimoine, dépenses, emploi) reassess; (salaire, impôt, taux de crédit) revise

réexamen *m* re-examination; (de décision, candidature) reconsideration

réexaminer *vt* re-examine; (décision, candidature) reconsider; ~ **une évaluation** reconsider an assessment; ~ **les termes d'une transaction** (Bourse) clear the market (jarg)

réexécuter *vt* (programme) rerun

réexécution *f* (d'un programme) rerun

réexpédier *vt* (au destinataire) forward, redirect; (à l'expéditeur) return, send back

réexpédition *f* (au destinataire) forwarding, redirecting; (retour à l'expéditeur) returning to sender; **frais de ~** return postage

réexportateur, -trice *m,f* re-exporter

réexportation *f* re-export, re-exportation

réfaction *f* allowance

référence *f* (sur document) reference; (V&M) bench mark; (Info) label; **faire ~ à** refer to; **avoir d'excellentes ~s** have excellent references, have excellent testimonials; **année/période de ~** base year/period; **point de ~** reference point; **en ~ à** with reference to; ~ **notre télex** reference our telex; **par ~ à** by referral to, referring to; **votre ~** your reference; ~ **bancaire** banker's reference

référencer *vt* list, classify; (article) list, stock; (sur moteur de recherche) reference

référenciation *f* benchmarking

référendum *m* referendum

référer: se ~ à *v pron* refer to

refinancement *m* refinancing; ~ ····≫

d'obligations bond refunding

refinancer *vt* refinance

refléter *vt* reflect

réflexion *f* reflection; **à la ~** upon further consideration

refondre *vt* (dette) recast

reformater *vt* (Info) reformat

réforme *f* reform; **~ agraire/fiscale/ monétaire** land/tax/currency reform

réformer *vt* reform

refouler *vt* (candidat) reject; (avion) push back

refrain *m* (télévision) theme tune; **~ publicitaire** advertising jingle

refrapper *vt* (Info) re-enter, retype

réfrigéré, e *adj* refrigerated

refroidir *vt* (enthousiasme) dampen

refuge *m* haven; **~ fiscal** tax haven

réfugié, e *m,f* refugee; **~ politique** political refugee

refus *m* refusal; **~ d'acceptaion** (d'une traite) non-acceptance; **~ d'obtempérer** (à un ordre) noncompliance; **~ de reconnaissance** derecognition UK

refuser *vt* refuse; **~ d'accepter une traite** refuse acceptance of a draft; **~ une déduction** disallow a deduction; **~ pour défaut de provision** (chèque) bounce (infrml); **~ de mettre qn en liberté sous caution** refuse sb bail; **~ de payer un chèque** dishonour a cheque BrE, dishonor a check AmE

regarder ① *vt* look at; **~ les choses en face** face the facts
② *vi* (sans acheter) browse; **~ vers l'avenir** look ahead

régénérer *vt* (Envir) reclaim; (Info) refresh

régie *f* ≈ Customs & Excise UK; **~ d'État** (gestion) (par l'État) state control; (par la commune) local government control, local authority control UK; (entreprise) public corporation UK; (entreprise) public corporation UK, state-owned company; **~ directe** (gestion) direct management of a public service; (service) directly managed public service, state-run service; **~ de presse** press advertising agency; **~ publicitaire** advertising agency (selling advertising space only)

régime *m* (Admin) (organisation) scheme; (règlement) regulations; **~ d'assurances/de retraite** insurance/pension scheme; **~ des changes/d'échanges** exchange/trade regulations; **~ complémentaire** private pension scheme; **~ d'assurance maladie** medical care insurance plan; **~ commercial** trade regime; **~ complémentaire professionnel de prévoyance** supplementary company pension scheme; **~ de la communauté des biens** joint property agreement (for married couple); **~ douanier** customs arrangements; **~ enregistré d'épargne-retraite** registered retirement savings plan; **~ d'épargne** savings plan; **~ fiscal** tax system, taxation

system; **~ matrimonial** marriage settlement; **~ de participation des employés aux bénéfices** employee profit-sharing plan; **~ de pension d'employés** employee pension plan; **~ plein** full basis; **~ de préretraite** bridging pension scheme; **~ de prestations aux employés** employee benefit plan; **~ privé d'assurance maladie** private health care plan; **~ de redevances** royalty system; **~ de retraite agréé** registered pension plan; **~ de retraite basé sur les avantages salariaux** benefit-based pension plan; **~ de retraite entièrement financé par l'employeur** noncontributory pension plan; **~ de retraite indépendant** personal pension plan; **~ de retraite mixte** contributory pension plan; **~ de retraite proportionnel** graduated pension scheme; **~ de retraite sans capitalisation** unfunded pension scheme; **~ de la séparation des biens** agreement whereby each spouse retains ownership of his/her property; **~ de taux de change** exchange rate regime

région *f* area, region; (Info) (de mémoire) region; **les ~s les plus défavorisées** the most deprived areas; **~ centrale** core region; **~ en crise/en déclin** depressed region; **~ désignée** (Fisc) designated region; **~ à développer** development region; **~ viticole** wine-producing area

régional, e *adj* regional

régir *vt* govern

régisseur *m* (de domaine) estate manager; (immobilier) bailiff; (Admin) *person holding a concession to manage a public service*

registre *m* (cahier) log book, register; (Bourse) book; (Info) (d'un programme) register; **tenir un ~** keep a register; **être inscrit au ~ du commerce** be a registered company; **porter qch au ~** enter *ou* record sth in the register; **~ des actionnaires** shareholders' register, register of members; **~ des actions** stock register; **~ des Caisses Nationales d'Épargne** National Savings Register UK; **~ des chèques** cheque register BrE, check register AmE; **~ des commandes en attente** backlog order books; **~ du commerce** trade register, companies register; **~ du commerce européen** European Registry of Commerce; **~ de comptabilité** account book; **~ de comptage** tally register; **~ de contrôle de caisse** cash control record; **~ des créances** liability ledger; **~ des délibérations** (d'une société) minute book; **~ électoral** electoral register; **~ des engagements** commitment record; **~ d'état civil** register of births, marriages and deaths; **~ foncier** land registry, plat book US; **~ d'hôtel** hotel register; **~ d'immatriculation** shipping register; **~ du personnel** payroll; **~ de pointage** time book; **~ de la police** police records; **~ des ventes** sales record; **~ des visiteurs** (d'une entreprise) business visitors' memorandum

réglable *adj* (vitesse, hauteur) adjustable; (Fin) payable; ~ **en 6 mensualités** payable in 6 monthly instalments BrE

réglage *m* (de volume, de pression) adjustment; (de moteur) tuning; ~ **de l'affichage** (Info) display setting

réglé, e *adj* (Fisc) clean-assessed; ~ **par l'agent** (Transp) paid by agent; ~ **en espèces** settled in cash; **non** ~ **à l'échéance** past-due

règle *f* rule; **selon les** ~**s** according to the rules; **en** ~ (demande) formal; (papiers, comptes) in order; **se mettre en** ~ **avec le fisc** get one's tax affairs in order; **en** ~ **générale** as a rule; ~ **d'admissibilité** eligibility rule; ~ **anti-évitement** anti-avoidance rule; ~ **de calcul au prorata** apportionment rule; ~ **des cinq pour cent** five per cent rule; ~ **disciplinaire** disciplinary rule; ~ **majoritaire** majority rule; ~ **de mise en service** put-in-use rule; ~ **des neuf obligations** nine bond rule; ~ **d'or** golden rule; ~ **de priorité absolue** absolute priority rule; ~ **proportionnelle** average clause; ~ **de rattachement à l'exercice** accrual principle; ~ **de la vente à découvert** short-sale rule

règlement *m* (règle) rule; (règles) regulations; (des pertes) adjustment; (paiement) payment; (d'une dette) discharge, settlement; (d'un conflit) settlement; **c'est contraire au** ~ it's against the regulations; **effectuer un** ~ make a payment; **en** ~ **de** in settlement of; **en** ~ **partiel** in part payment; **être en** ~ **judiciaire** be in the hands of the receiver; **mode de** ~ method of payment; ~ **administratif** bylaw; ~ **à l'amiable** out-of-court settlement; ~ **anticipé** (Bourse) ringing out (jarg); ~ **d'assurance** insurance settlement; ~ **d'avaries** average adjustment; ~ **par avis de prélèvement** preauthorized payment; ~ **par carte** credit card payment; ~ **par chèque** cheque payment BrE, check payment AmE; ~ **de commande et de contrôle** command and control regulation; ~ **de comptes** settling of scores; ~ **en continu** continuous net settlement UK; ~ **de dettes** settlement of debts; ~ **disciplinaire** disciplinary rule; ~ **en espèces** cash settlement; ~ **intérieur** company regulations; ~ **intérieur de l'usine** works rules UK; ~ **judiciaire** legal settlement; ~ **livraison en continu** rolling settlement; ~ **mensuel** monthly instalment BrE, monthly installment AmE; ~ **de sécurité** safety regulations; ~ **de sinistre** claim settlement; ~ **syndical** union rules; ~ **à terme** settlement; ~**-type** pattern settlement; ~ **des ventes à terme** short-sale rule

réglementaire *adj* (format) prescribed; (procédure) statutory; (pouvoir) regulatory; **les textes** ~**s** rules and regulations

réglementation *f* regulation; ~ **des banques** banking regulation; ~ **des**

commandes order regulation; ~ **commerciale** trade regulations; ~ **comptable** accounting standard setting; ~ **des exportations** export regulations; ~ **foncière** land-use regulation; ~ **des importations** import regulations; ~ **de l'impôt sur le revenu** income tax regulations; ~ **de l'impôt sur le revenu à la source** PAYE remittances UK; ~ **privée** private ruling; ~ **des prix** price regulation; ~ **relative à la construction** building regulations; ~ **sanitaire** health regulations; ~ **stricte** tight controls; ~ **du tarif extérieur** overseas tariff regulations; ~ **des transactions** dealing restriction

réglementer *vt* regulate; **réglementé par l'État** government-regulated

régler *vt* (compte, dette) settle; (facture, montant, taxe) pay; (achats, travaux, fournitures) pay for; (différends) resolve; (créancier, fournisseur, notaire) pay; (ajuster) adjust; (Assur) adjust; (Bourse) settle; ~ **à l'amiable** (Droit) settle amicably; ~ **un compte** settle an account; ~ **un conflit** settle a dispute; ~ **un conflit par arbitrage** settle a dispute by arbitration; ~ **une dette à l'amiable** compound a debt; ~ **en espèces/par chèque** pay cash/by cheque; ~ **la note** settle the bill; ~ **des problèmes** troubleshoot; ~ **un sinistre** (Assur) adjust a claim; **compte non réglé** outstanding *ou* unpaid account

régleur, -euse *m,f* (Assur), adjuster; ~ **d'avaries communes** loss adjuster

règne *m* reign

régner *vi* prevail, reign

régresser *vi* (chômage, production) drop; (marché, industrie) decline; **faire** ~ **le chômage** push down unemployment

régressif, -ive *adj* regressive

régression *f* regression, decline; **être en** ~ be in decline; ~ **linéaire** (Compta, Fin) linear regression; ~ **multiple** (Compta, Fin) multiple regression

regret *m* regret; **avoir le** ~ **d'informer qn que** regret to inform sb that

regroupement *m* (de services, d'usines, de sociétés) grouping, consolidation; (fusion de sociétés) merger; (de comptes) consolidation; (d'intérêts, de ressources) pooling; ~ **d'actions** consolidation of shares; ~ **économique mondial** world economic grouping; ~ **régional** regional grouping

regrouper *vt* group together; (ressources, intérêts) pool; (amalgamer) merge; (services) consolidate, centralize; (comptes) consolidate; ~ **aux arrêts** (Bourse) gather in the stops

régularisation *f* (d'un compte bancaire) regularization; (Compta) adjustment; (Fin) equalization; (des cours) stabilization

régulariser *vt* (compte bancaire) put in order, regularize; (Compta) adjust; (Fin) (dividende) equalize; (cours, marché) stabilize

régularité *f* (au travail) punctuality; (Compta) ⋯⋗

conformity to accounting rules; (légalité) legality, correctness; (de production, progrès) steadiness

régulateur¹, -trice *adj* regulating; (Droit) regulatory; **jouer un rôle ~** act as a regulator; **avoir une influence régulatrice sur les prix** have a steadying influence on prices

régulateur², -trice *m,f* regulator; (aviation) despatcher, dispatcher; **~ de tension** voltage regulator

régulation *f* control; (aviation) despatching, dispatching; **~ de la circulation** traffic control; **~ employeur-employé** master-servant rule; **~ de processus** process control; **~ de production** production control; **~ du trafic** traffic control

réguler *vt* regulate; (Transp) (trafic) despatch, dispatch

régulier, -ière *adj* (versements, arrivages) regular; (client, lecteur) regular; (affaire, personne) above board; (Transp) (train, ligne, service) scheduled, regular; (demande, production) steady; (qualité, progrès) consistent; (papiers) in order; (épaisseur, surface) even

régulièrement *adv* (progresser) steadily; (expédier) regularly

réhabilitation *f* (réinsertion) rehabilitation; (Droit) rehabilitation; (de failli) discharge; (d'immeuble, de quartier) renovation; **~ de faillite** (Droit) discharge of bankruptcy

réhabiliter *vt* (personne, accusé) rehabilitate; (failli) discharge; (quartier, immeuble) renovate

rehausser *vt* enhance

REI *abrév* (▸**rachat d'une entreprise par des investisseurs**) LMBI (leveraged management buy-in)

réimplantation *f* resettlement

réimplanter *vt* resettle

réimposer *vt* reimpose

réincorporation *f* (de personnel) re-employment, re-engagement

réincorporer *vt* add back; (personnel) re-employ, re-engage

réinitialisation *f* (Info) rebooting, reset; **~ automatique** automatic reset

réinitialiser *vt* (Info) reboot, reset

réinjecter *vt* (capitaux) reinject

réintégration *f* reintegration; (réadmission à son travail) reinstatement; (Compta) reinstatement

réintégrer *vt* (rétablir) reintegrate; **~ qn (dans ses fonctions)** reinstate sb; **~ qn dans ses droits** restore sb's rights; (Compta) reinstate

réinvestir *vt* (bénéfices) plough back BrE, plow back AmE, reinvest

réinvestissement *m* reinvestment; **~ des dividendes** reinvestment of dividends

réitérer *vt* reiterate

rejet *m* (de proposition, réclamation, demande)

rejection; (Admin, Droit) (de plainte, charges, recours, résolution) dismissal; (déchets) dumping; (de motion, proposition, projet de loi) defeat; (industriel) discharge; (dans l'air, dans l'eau) effluent; **~ accidentel/intentionnel** (pollution) accidental/intentional discharge; **~s toxiques** toxic waste

rejeter *vt* (proposition, réclamation, théorie, conseil, candidature) reject; (Admin, Droit) (recours, plainte, charges, résolution) dismiss; (requête) deny; (demande) refuse; (déchets) dump; (motion, projet de loi) defeat; (déduction) disallow; (imprimé) spike; (décision) overrule

relâché, e *adj* (contrôle) slack

relâchement *m* relaxation

relâcher [1] *vt* (discipline, surveillance) relax [2] *vi* (navigation) put into port [3] **se relâcher** *v pron* (dans son travail) be slack; **~ la bride** slacken the reins

relais *m* **travail par ~** shift work; **prendre le ~ de qn** take over from sb; **passer le ~ à qn** hand over to sb; **credit-~**, **prêt-~** bridging loan

relance *f* (du client) follow-up; (Econ) boost; (d'industrie) revival; (d'inflation) rise; (par augmentation de la masse monétaire) reflation; (de négociations) reopening; (Info) rebooting, restart; **des mesures/une politique de ~** reflationary measures; **lettre de ~** (V&M) follow-up letter; (en cas de non-paiement) reminder; **entraîner la ~ de** (commerce) give a boost to; (inflation) lead to a rise in; **~ en route** (Info) autorestart

relancement *m* (d'une campagne, d'un projet) relaunch

relancer *vt* (client) follow up; (investissement, production) boost; (compagnie, campagne, projet) relaunch; (inflation) refuel; (économie) kick-start, boost; (créancier) chase up; (Info) (ordinateur) restart; (programme) reload; **~ un secteur affaibli** take up the slack (infrml)

relatif, -ive *adj* (majorité, importance, succès) relative; (valeur) comparative; (position, poids) relative; **~ à** relating to, relative to; **~ au commerce** trade-related

relation *f* (connaissance) acquaintance; (personne puissante) connection; (rapport) connection; **en ~ avec** in partnership with; **~s** (liens) relations; **avoir des ~s** have connections; **être/entrer en ~s avec qn** be/get in touch with sb; **être en ~ d'affaires avec qn** have business dealings with sb; **~ d'affaires** business acquaintance; **~s d'affaires** (avec une société) business relations; **~s avec les employés** employee relations; **~s avec la presse** press relations; **~s commerciales et exportations** Commercial Relations and Exports UK; **~s commerciales officielles** formal trade links; **~s directes patronat-employés** positive labour relations BrE, positive labor relations AmE; **~s entre groupes** intergroup relations; **~s**

extérieures foreign affairs, external relations; ~s **gouvernementales** government relations; ~s **humaines** human relations; ~s **humaines dans l'entreprise** industrial relations; ~s **publiques** public relations; ~ **qualifiée** (Fisc) qualified relation; ~ **rendement d'une valeur** (Bourse) security market line; ~s **syndicales** industrial relations; ~s **de travail** work relationship

relationnel¹, -elle n relational

relationnel² m interpersonal skills; **avoir un bon** ~ have good interpersonal skills

relativement adv comparatively, relatively; ~ **à** regarding, with reference to

relaxer vt acquit, discharge

relayer vt take over from, relieve

relevé m statement; **faire un** ~ **de compte** draw up a statement of account; ~ **bancaire** bank statement; ~ **de compensation** clearing report; ~ **de compte** account statement, statement of account; (Banque) bank statement; ~ **de compte de liquidation** broker's statement; ~ **de compte mensuel** monthly statement; ~ **de comptes** abstract of accounts; ~ **des comptes clients** accounts receivable statement; ~ **de courtage** brokerage statement; ~ **des effets émis** statement of instruments issued; ~ **d'erreurs** notice of default; ~ **de frais** expense account; ~ **général** (de comptes) general statement; ~ **des opérations avec solde** transaction balance report; ~ **d'opérations de courtage** brokerage statement; ~ **de la position nette** net position report; ~ **quotidien des opérations** daily activity report; ~ **quotidien de la situation** daily position statement; ~ **de solde de compensation** clearing balance statement

relever vt (défi) take up; (Fin) put up; (équipe) relieve; ~ **de la compétence de** come under the jurisdiction of; ~ **conformément à l'inflation** (prix) raise in line with inflation; ~ **un compteur** take a meter reading, read the meter

relié, e adj connected; **être** ~ **à** (Info) interface with; **livre** ~ hardback, hardcover

relier vt link, connect; (appareils) connect; (Info) (ordinateurs) link; (édition) bind

reliquat m (Compta) (de somme) remainder; (de compte) balance; (de dette) outstanding amount; (Bourse) overhang

relire vt re-read; (épreuves) proof-read; (bande) replay

remake m remake

remaniement m (de plan, de projet) modification; (d'équipe) reorganization; (Pol) reshuffle; ~ **de capital** reorganization of capital; ~ **de l'équipe dirigeante** management reshuffle; ~ **ministériel** cabinet reshuffle

remanier vt (plan, projet) modify, revise; (équipe) reorganize; (Pol) (cabinet, ministère) reshuffle

remarquable adj (qualité, produit) remarkable

remarque f remark, comment; **faire des** ~s comment

remarquer vt note, remark

remb. abrév (▸**remboursable**) red. (redeemable)

remballage m repacking

remballer vt repack

rembarquer vt re-embark

rembaucher vt re-hire, re-engage

rembobiner vt rewind

remboursable adj refundable; (empreint, dette, avance) repayable; (Bourse) redeemable; (obligation) noncallable, unredeemable; ~ **sur 15 ans** (emprunt) repayable over 15 years; ~ **sur demande** repayable on demand; ~ **par anticipation** callable

remboursé, e adj (Bourse, Compta) redeemed

remboursement m (de dette, d'emprunt) repayment; (par un commerçant) refund; (d'argent déboursé) reimbursement, refund; (de prêt) amortization; (d'une hypothèque) repayment, redemption; ~ **admissible** allowable refund; ~ **anticipé** anticipated repayment, redemption before due date; ~ **par déchéance du terme** repayment by acceleration; ~ **de dette** debt retirement; ~ **de la dette de l'État** public sector debt repayment; ~ **de la dette sociale** tax on income designed to offset the social security budget deficit; ~ **des droits de douane** drawback; ~ **échelonné sur 2 ans** repayment over 2 years; ~ **des emprunts** debt financing; ~ **final** payout; ~ **d'impôt** tax refund; ~ **d'une partie du principal** paydown; ~ **périodique** amortization payment; ~ **en tranches égales** level payment, level repayment; ~ **trimestriel** quarterly instalment BrE, quarterly installment AmE

rembourser vt (prix d'achat) refund; (emprunt, créancier) pay back, repay; (Bourse) (obligation) redeem, retire; (dette) pay off; **à** ~ outstanding; ~ **des obligations** (Bourse) call bonds; ~ **qch à qn** give sb a refund on sth; **se faire** ~ **qch** get a refund on sth; ~ **qch sur 5 ans** pay sth back over 5 years

remède m cure, remedy; **porter** ~ **à qch** find a cure/a remedy for sth

remédier vi: ~ **à** (déficit, défaillance, situation) remedy

remembrement m (de terrains) regrouping, assemblage

remercier vt (dire merci à) thank; (congédier) dismiss; **en vous remerciant d'avance** thanking you in anticipation; **je vous remercie** thank you; **nous vous remercions d'adresser votre courrier à** please address ····⟩

your letters to

reméré m **vente à** ~ sale with option of repurchase; **clause de** ~ repurchase clause

remettre vt (ajourner) postpone; (lettre, colis) deliver; (rapport) hand in, submit; ~ **en activité** reactivate; ~ **à neuf** refurbish, renovate; ~ **l'accent sur** re-emphasize; ~ **en bon état** (équipement) recondition; (bâtiment) restore; ~ **sa démission** hand in ou tender one's resignation; ~ **une dette** forgo a debt; ~ **en forme** (Info) reformat; ~ **à plus tard** postpone; ~ **qch à une huitaine** adjourn sth for a week; ~ **en valeur** (Envir) reclaim; ~ **à zéro** reset, zero

remise f (rabais) discount, rebate; (de peine, de dette) remittal; (d'un impôt) remission; (de marchandises) delivery; (de rapport) handing in, submission; **contre** ~ **des documents** on presentation of the documents; **faire une** ~ **de 50 euros/20%** give a 50 euro/20% discount; ~ **de fonds** remittance of funds; ~ **d'un effet à l'encaissement** remittance of a bill for collection; ~ **absolue** (Fin) unconditional remission; ~ **bancaire** bank remittance; ~ **de capital à la société mère** repatriation of capital; ~ **de cause** (Droit) adjournment (of hearing); ~ **de charges** (Fisc) remission of charges; ~ **en compensation** (Banque) onward clearing; ~ **de dette** debt forgiveness; ~ **de distribution** (V&M) distribution allowance; ~ **à l'encaissement** (Banque) remittance for collection; ~ **en état** rehabilitation; ~ **hypothécaire** mortgage discount; ~ **d'impôt** tax remission; ~ **de peine** remission (of sentence); ~ **à neuf** renovation; ~ **à plus tard** postponement; ~ **sur la quantité** bulk discount, quantity discount; ~ **totale** (Banque) payout; ~ **en valeur** (Envir) reclaiming; ~ **à zéro** (Info) reset

remisier m (Bourse) intermediate broker

remodelage m (Transp) lifting

remontée f (hausse) rise; **les cours du pétrole poursuivent leur** ~ oil prices continue to rise; ~ **de l'information** (indication) feedback

remonter vi (cours, monnaie) go up, rise again; ~ **dans les sondages** (Pol) move up in the opinion polls; ~ **à la troisième place** move up to third position; **le cours sont remontés de 20%** prices have gone up another 20%; **faire** ~ **le dollar** send the dollar up again; **faire** ~ **les cours** put prices up again; ~ **par rapport à la livre sterling** go up against the pound; ~ **jusqu'à l'origine de** trace back

remorquage m tow, towing

remorque f trailer; **être à la** ~ **de** trail behind; ~ **autochargeable** self-loading trailer; ~ **fourgon** box trailer; ~ **à timon** drawbar trailer

remorquer vt tow

remorqueur m (navigation) anchor-handling tug; ~ **pilote** pilotage tug; ~ **de sauvetage** anchor-handling salvage tug

rempaquetage m repacking

rempaqueter vt repack

remplaçant, e m,f (provisoire) substitute, replacement; (définitif) successor

remplacement m replacement; **faire des** ~**s** do temporary work, temp; **en** ~ **de qn/ qch** as a replacement for sb/sth; ~ **du revenu** income replacement

remplacer vt (succéder à) (méthode, technologie, personne) replace; (prendre provisoirement la place de) (collègue) stand in for, cover for; (changer) (pièce, matériel) replace; ~ **les membres du conseil d'administration** unseat the board

remplir vt (conditions) meet, fulfil; (rôle, mission, fonction) carry out; (obligations, objectifs) fulfil, carry out; (formulaire) complete, fill in, fill out; **à** ~ blank; ~ **les conditions** qualify for; ~ **une déclaration** prepare a return; ~ **ses obligations** meet one's obligations

remplissage m: **taux de** ~ (aviation) occupancy rate; ~ **truqué** (marketing) slack fill (jarg)

remporter vt win; ~ **un grand succès** be a great success, score a hit

remue-méninges m brainstorming

rémunérateur, -trice adj profitable, lucrative; **peu** ~ unprofitable

rémunération f pay, remuneration; (de compte) interest; (d'investissement) return; ~ **de l'affréteur** (navigation) charterer's pay dues; ~ **des cadres** executive remuneration; ~ **du capital** return on capital; ~**s commerciales** commercial considerations; ~**s et charges sociales** salaries, wages and fringe benefits; ~ **des heures supplémentaires** overtime pay; ~ **aux honoraires** fee system; ~ **occulte** secret payment; ~ **de service** service fee; ~ **totale du personnel** total wages and salaries

rémunéré, e adj (compte, placement) interest-bearing; (travail, service) paid; **bien/mal** ~ well-paid/badly-paid

rémunérer vt (personne) pay; (travail, service) pay for

renantissement m (Fin) remargining

renchérissement m (de marchandises, de main-d'œuvre) increase in price, rise in price; (de prix) increase; **un** ~ **de 16%** a 16% increase

rencontrer vt (personne) meet; (problème) encounter

rendement m (Fin) return; (de machine, de travailleur) output; (d'usine) output, throughput; (d'investissement, d'impôt) yield; **à** ~ **élevé** (Fin) high-return, high-yielding; ~ **au travail** job performance; ~ **de l'actif** asset return; ~ **des actifs** return on investment; ~ **de l'action** return on equity; ~ **des actions**

earnings yield; ∼ **actualisé** yield to maturity; ∼ **annuel** annual yield; ∼ **après impôt** after-tax yield; ∼ **d'un bon** bond yield; ∼ **boursier** dividend yield, earnings yield; ∼ **du capital investi** return on invested capital; ∼ **du combustible** fuel efficiency; ∼ **comptable** accounting return; ∼ **coupon** coupon yield; ∼ **courant** current return, current yield; ∼ **à l'échéance** yield to maturity; ∼ **économique** commercial efficiency, economic efficiency; ∼ **effectif** (d'un investissement) actual yield, effective yield; ∼ **énergétique** energy efficiency; ∼ **équitable** fair return; ∼ **équivalent sur obligation** bond equivalent yield; ∼ **factoriel** factor productivity; ∼ **global** compound yield, aggregate output; ∼ **à l'hectare** (agriculture) yield per acre; ∼ **horaire** output per hour; ∼ **de l'impôt** tax yield; ∼ **maximum** maximum efficiency, maximum output; ∼ **moyen** average yield; ∼ **par ouvrier** output per head; ∼ **de placement** investment yield; ∼ **portant intérêt** interest-bearing yield; ∼ **d'un prêt** loan yield

rendez-vous *m* appointment; **donner** ∼ **à qn** make an appointment with sb; **prendre** ∼ **avec qn** make an appointment with sb; **sur** ∼ **uniquement** by appointment only

rendre *vt* (article) return; (argent) pay back; (investissement) yield; (jugement) pass; ∼ **compte de** account for; ∼ **compte des résultats** report one's findings; ∼ **les coups** fight back; ∼ **exigible immédiatement** (dette) call in; ∼ **indépendant** (filiale) hive off; ∼ **un jugement en faveur de qn** give a ruling in favour of sb BrE, give a ruling in favor of sb AmE; ∼ **nul** make void; ∼ **nul et non avenu** abate, render null and void; ∼ **périmé** render obsolete; ∼ **service à** help, oblige; ∼ **supportable** alleviate; ∼ **un verdict de culpabilité** find sb guilty; ∼ **un verdict de non culpabilité** find sb not guilty; ∼ **visite à qn** call on sb, pay a visit to sb

rendu, e *adj* delivered; ∼ **à domicile** (marchandises) delivered domicile; ∼ **droits acquittés** delivered duty paid; ∼ **droits non acquittés** delivered duty unpaid; ∼ **à la frontière** delivered at frontier; ∼ **à quai** delivered at docks; ∼ **à quai droits acquittés** delivered ex quay

renégociation *f* renegotiation

renégocier *vt* renegotiate

renfermé, e *adj* locked in

renfermer *vt* lock in

renflouement *m* (d'une personne, d'une entreprise) bail-out, bailing out

renflouer *vt* (personne, entreprise) bail out

renforcé, e *adj* (équipe, monnaie) strengthened

renforcement *m* (d'équipe, d'effectif) strengthening; (d'activité) increase; (de sécurité) tightening

renforcer ▮**1**▮ *vt* (équipe, effectifs, monnaie) strengthen; (règlement, consignes) stiffen; (sécurité) tighten; ∼ **la confiance de** bolster the confidence of
▮**2**▮ **se renforcer** *v pron* (tendance) increase; (groupe, influence, secteur) grow stronger; (équipe, effectifs) grow

rengagement *m* (d'employé) re-employment, re-engagement

rengager *vt* re-employ, re-engage

renom *m* fame, renown; **de** ∼ (entreprise) renowned; **d'honnêteté/qualité** reputation for honesty, quality

renommée *f* (réputation) reputation; (célébrité) renown, fame

renommer *vt* (Info) (fichier) rename; (personne) reappoint

renoncer *vi* ∼ **à** give up, renounce; (projet, plainte) abandon; (Fisc) waive; (mandat, pouvoir) relinquish; (privilèges) waive; (poste, activité) give up; ∼ **à faire** abandon the idea of doing; ∼ **à une succession** relinquish an inheritance; ∼ **à toute prétention** abandon any claim

renonciation *f* abandonment; (Brevets) waiving; (Droit) disclaimer; (Fisc) waiver; ∼ **aux droits conférés par un brevet** surrender of a patent

renouvelable *adj* renewable; **non renouvelable** nonrenewable

renouvelé, e *adj* (bail) renewed

renouveler *vt* (stock, bail, passeport, abonnement, contrat) renew; (commande) repeat; (personnel, matériel, équipe) replace; (soutien) renew

renouvellement *m* (de stock, bail, contrat, soutien, passeport, abonnement) renewal; (d'une lettre de change) reissue; (d'équipe, de matériel) replacement; ∼ **d'hypothèque** renewal of mortgage

rénovation *f* renovation; (de projet, de procédure) revamping; (Pol) renewal; ∼ **urbaine** urban renewal; ∼ **de vieux quartiers** greenlining (jarg)

rénové, e *adj* reconditioned, renovated

rénover *vt* renovate; (projet, procédure) revamp; (petits travaux) refurbish

renseignement *m* piece of information; ∼**s** information; **des** ∼**s utiles** useful information; **'pour tous** ∼**s, s'adresser à...'** 'all enquiries to...'; **demander des** ∼**s à qn** ask sb for information; ∼**s commerciaux** status information; ∼**s d'initié** price-sensitive information; ∼**s de listage** listing particulars; ∼**s sur crédit** credit information; ∼**s téléphoniques** directory enquiries BrE, directory information AmE; ∼**s en vol** in-flight information

renseigner ▮**1**▮ *vt* ∼ **qn sur qch** inform sb about
▮**2**▮ **se renseigner** *v pron* find out, make enquiries

rentabilité *f* profitability; (profit) return; ····⟩

(d'une valeur) earnings performance; ~ **des actifs** return on investment; ~ **des capitaux investis** return on capital employed; ~ **des entreprises** corporate earning power; ~ **à la hausse** upside break-even; ~ **de produit** product profitability; ~ **des ventes** return on sales

rentable *adj* (méthode) profitable, cost-effective; **être** ~ pay back; **peu** ~ unprofitable

rente *f* (contrat, financier) annuity; (revenu personnel) private income; ~ **anticipée** early retirement annuity; ~ **conjointe au dernier survivant** joint and survivor annuity US; ~**s consolidées** consolidated annuities UK; ~ **en cours** current annuity; ~ **économique** economic rent; ~ **d'État** government stock *ou* bond, consols UK; ~ **d'invalidité** disability benefit; ~ **d'invalidité en remplacement de revenu** income replacement; ~ **à paiement différé** deferred payment annuity; ~**s et paiements différés** deferred benefits and payments; ~ **payable d'avance** annuity in advance; ~ **payable à terme échu** annuity in arrears; ~ **perpétuelle** perpetual annuity; ~ **réversible** reversionary annuity; ~ **de survie** reversionary annuity

rentier, -ière *m,f* person of independent means; ~ **viager** life annuitant

rentrée *f* (recettes) receipts; (revenu) income; (dans une caisse) takings; (recouvrement d'une dette) collection; ~ **d'argent** (Compta) cash inflow; ~ **sur créance radiée** (Compta, Fin) bad debt recovery; ~ **de fonds** (Compta) cash inflow, inflow of funds; ~**s de fonds** (Fin) cash receipt, cash streams

rentrer *vi* (argent, loyer, créance) come in; **faire** ~ **l'argent** get the money in; ~ **dans ses frais** break even

renversement *m* reversing; ~ **de la tendance** trend reversal

renvoi *m* (de personnel) dismissal, firing (infrml); (de marchandises) return; (d'un procès) adjournment; (à une instance inférieure) remand, remittal; (référence) reference; ~ **automatique d'un appel** (Info) call forwarding; ~ **pur et simple** (de personnel) summary dismissal; ~ **en révision** (Droit) writ of error

renvoyer *vt* (personnel) dismiss, fire (infrml); (marchandises) return; (procès) adjourn; ~ **l'ascenseur** return the favour BrE, logroll AmE; ~ **devant** refer to

réorganisation *f* reorganization; ~ **du capital** capital reorganization; ~ **de structure** structural adjustment

réorganiser *vt* reorganize

réorientation *f* redeployment

réorienter *vt* redeploy; (production) switch

répandu, e *adj* widespread

réparateur, -trice *m,f* engineer

réparation *f* (Assur) compensation; (Droit) (d'injustice) redress; (de tort, préjudice, dommage) compensation; (travaux) repair; ~ **du dommage** compensation for damage; ~ **d'immeuble** building repair; ~ **en justice** legal redress; ~ **légale** legal redress, redress; ~ **locative** tenant's repair

réparer *vt* repair; (erreurs) correct, redress; (faute, préjudice, dommage, perte) compensate for

réparti, e *adj* distributed; ~ **uniformément** evenly spread

repartir *vi* (Econ) pick up, recover; **faire** ~ (Econ) reflate; ~ **à la hausse** bounce up; ~ **à zéro** start again from scratch

répartir *vt* (somme, biens, objets) share out; (actions) apportion; (bénéfices) distribute; (tâches) divide up, share out; (Compta) apportion, allocate; (terrain, propriété) apportion; ~ **le risque** (Assur) spread the risk; ~ **les avaries** (maritime) apportion the average; ~ **au prorata** prorate

répartiteur *m* (Fisc) assessor; (aviation) despatcher, dispatcher; ~ **d'avaries** (Transp) (maritime) average adjuster

répartition *f* sharing out, distribution; (Bourse) allotment; (Compta) apportionment, allocation; (des risques) allocation, (aviation) despatching, dispatching; (de la charge) distribution; ~ **des actifs** asset allocation; ~ **par âge** age distribution; ~ **de bonus** allotment of bonus; ~ **de capital** distribution of capital; ~ **des charges** apportionment of costs; ~ **équitable** equitable distribution; ~ **immobilière** estate distribution; ~ **des pouvoirs** division of powers; ~ **au prorata** proration; ~ **des recettes** revenue allocation; ~ **des responsabilités** allocation of responsibilities; ~ **des ressources** resource allocation; ~ **du résultat** annual appropriation; ~ **du résultat net** distribution of net profit; ~ **du revenu** income distribution; ~ **du revenu national entre les facteurs de production** functional income distribution; ~ **des richesses** distribution of wealth; ~ **des risques** distribution of risks; ~ **des tâches** job assignment

repasser *vt* (Info) rerun

repenser *vti* (théorie, travail, organisation) rethink; (pratiques, système) take a fresh look at

repérage *m* (aviation) location (**de** of); ~ **de l'environnement** environmental scanning

répercussion *f* repercussion; (Fin) knock-on effect; ~ **sur les bénéfices** profit implication

répercuter ⬜**1** *vt* (transmettre) pass on; **la baisse de la TVA sera répercutée sur le tarif des tranports** the drop in VAT will be reflected in transport charges ⬜**2** **se répercuter** *v pron* (augmentation, baisse) be reflected in

repère *m* (aviation) landmark; (économique, boursier)

indicator, benchmark

répertoire *m* (carnet) notebook; (Info) directory, index; ~ **d'adresses** address book; ~ **de base** root directory; ~ **par défaut** default directory; ~ **de fichiers** file directory; ~ **opérationnel des métiers et des emplois** job bank

répéter *vt* repeat

repli *m* (du marché) downturn; (régression) fall; **le ~ du dollar/des valeurs/des exportations** the fall in the dollar/in share prices/in exports

réplique *f* (Droit) reply

répondant, e *m,f* (Fin) surety, guarantor; (Droit) bail

répondeur *m* answering machine, answerphone

répondre 1 *vt* answer, reply; (à une lettre) write back; ~ **par retour du courrier** reply by return; ~ **au téléphone** answer the phone 2 *vi* ~ **à** (besoins, conditions, exigences) meet; (demande) satisfy; ~ **aux attentes de qn** meet sb's expectations, come up to sb's expectations; ~ **à un besoin** fill a gap; ~ **aux besoins de** meet the needs of; ~ **à un objectif** meet a goal; ~ **à une prime** declare an option

réponse *f* answer, reply; (réaction) response; (Info) answer; **donner une ~** answer; **en ~ à** in response to; **en ~ à votre appel** further to your telephone call; **en ~ à votre lettre** further to your letter; ~ **affirmative** positive response; ~ **à un appel d'offre** competitive bid; ~ **du défendeur** answer; ~ **du demandeur** reply; ~ **directe** direct response

report *m* (de procès) adjournment; (de rendez-vous, réunion) postponement; (de jugement) deferment; (Compta) (d'écriture) posting; (de somme) carrying forward; (somme reportée) amount carried forward; **faire le ~ d'une somme** carry a sum forward; ~ **en amont** carry-back; ~ **en aval** carry-forward; ~ **d'échéance** extension of due date; ~ **de l'impôt sur le revenu** income tax deferral; ~ **négatif** negative carry; ~ **à nouveau** profit carried forward; ~ **d'une perte en amont** loss carry-back; ~ **d'une perte sur une année ultérieure** loss carry-forward; ~ **de position** roll-over, rolling in; ~ **de position à la baisse** roll-down, rolling down; ~ **d'une position d'une échéance sur une autre** switch trading; ~ **de position à la hausse** rolling up; ~ **rétrospectif** carry-back

reportage *m* (Media) (technique) reporting; (émission) report; ~ **financier** financial reporting

reporté, e *adj* (procès) adjourned; (rendez-vous, réunion) postponed; (jugement) deferred

reporter¹ *m* reporter; ~ **à la tâche** assignment man

reporter² *vt* (procès) adjourn; (rendez-vous,

réunion, décision) postpone, put back; (délai) extend; (titres) take in; (jugement) defer; (Compta) (calcul, somme, résultat) carry forward; (écriture) post; (Bourse) (position) carry over; ~ **une décision** postpone making a decision; ~ **la réunion de lundi à vendredi** postpone Monday's meeting until Friday; **à ~** (sur un bilan) carried forward; ~ **en arrière** carry down; ~ **sur un exercice ultérieur** carry forward; ~ **l'impôt** defer tax; ~ **un paiement** defer payment; ~ **qch jusqu'à la semaine prochaine** adjourn sth for a week; ~ **le remboursement d'une dette** defer a debt

repos *m* rest; **valeurs de tout ~** gilt-edged securities

reposer *vi* ~ **sur** be based on

repositionnement *m* (marketing) repositioning

reprendre 1 *vt* (article, invendus) take back; (discours) resume; (employé) re-employ, re-hire; ~ **le travail** go back to work 2 *vi* (Econ) (commerce, affaires) pick up; (negociations) resume; **les affaires ont du mal à ~** business is only picking up slowly; ~ **à sa charge** (dettes) take over 3 **se reprendre** (marché, valeur, titre) rally, pick up

représailles *f pl* reprisals, retaliation; **de ~** tit-for-tat; **en ~** in retaliation

représentant, e *m,f* (délégué) representative; ~ **de commerce** sales representative, sales rep (infrml); **le ~ d'OUP** the OUP representative; ~ **en vins/produits de beauté** representative for a wine merchant/a cosmetics firm; ~ **accrédité** authorized representative; ~ **agréé** registered representative; ~ **à la commission** commission representative; ~ **à l'étranger** overseas agent; ~ **exclusif** sole agent; ~ **en fret** freight sales representative UK; ~ **légal** legal representative; ~ **d'une marque de fabrique** trademark agent; ~ **multicarte** sales representative for several firms; ~ **du personnel** staff representative; ~ **au pourcentage** commission representative; ~ **régional** area sales representative, area salesperson; ~ **du service clientèle** customer-service representative

représentation *f* representation; (mandataires, délégation) representatives; **faire de la ~** be a sales representative; ~ **commerciale** (activité) commercial representation; (de voyageur de commerce) commercial travelling; ~**s graphiques** graphics; ~ **internationale** international representation; ~ **paritaire** joint representation; ~ **du personnel** worker representation; ~ **proportionnelle** proportional representation; ~ **par ratification** agency by ratification; ~ **régionale** (d'une chaîne de magasins) regional representation

r

représenter *vt* represent

répression *f* (Pol, Droit) suppression; ~ **des fraudes** fraud prevention; ~ **des fraudes maritimes** maritime fraud prevention

reprise *f* (de demande, production) increase; (de marchandise) return; (contre nouvel achat) trade-in, part-exchange; (d'entreprise, de commerce) takeover, acquisition; (de l'économie) rally, upturn; (du marché) recovery; (Droit) (de biens) repossession; (dans l'immobilier) key money; (de négociations) resumption; (Info) (d'un travail) recovery; (du traitement) rerun; **donner qch en** ~ trade sth in; **300 euros de** ~ 300 euro trade-in; **valeur de** ~ trade-in value, part-exchange value; ~ **des affaires** business recovery; ~ **après clôture** after-hours rally; ~ **après sinistre** (Info) disaster recovery; ~ **boursière** market recovery; ~ **économique** recovery; ~ **sur erreur** error recovery; ~ **à fort effet de levier** high-geared takeover BrE, high-leveraged takeover AmE; ~ **du marché obligataire** bond market rally; ~ **sur provisions** writing back; ~ **technique** technical rally; ~ **des transactions** (Bourse) resumption of trading *ou* dealing; ~ **du travail** return to work

reproduction *f* reproduction; (Info) copy; ~ **automatique** autoduplication; ~ **des bénéfices** duplication of benefits

reproduire *vt* copy; ~ **d'après l'original** copy from the original

reprogrammer *vt* (Info) reprogram

réprouver *vt* censure

répudiation *f* (loi de l'impôt sur le revenu) disclaimer

répudier *vt* disclaim

réputation *f* reputation; ~ **bien établie** proven track record; ~ **de solvabilité** credit rating, credit standing

requalifier *vt* (emploi) upgrade

requérant, e *m,f* (Droit) applicant, claimant

requête *f* request; ~ **sommaire** summary application; ~ **unilatérale** ex parte application (frml)

réquisitionner *vt* (Droit) levy

réquisitoire *m* statement of prosecution

RES *abrév* (▶**rachat d'une entreprise par ses salariés**) ≈ MBO (management buyout)

rescinder *vt* rescind

rescision *f* rescission

réseau *m* (Gen com, Info) network; ~ **bancaire** banking network; ~ **de chemin de fer** rail network, railway system BrE, railroad system AmE; ~ **commercial** sales network; ~ **de communication** communications network; ~ **de détaillants** retail network; ~ **de distribution** distribution network; ~ **de données** data network; ~ **d'eau** water system; ~ **d'entreprise** corporate network; ~ **étendu** wide area network; ~ **en étoile** star

network; ~ **d'information** information network; ~ **informatique** computer network; ~ **local** local area network; ~ **mondial** global network; ~ **de points de vente** network of sales outlets; ~ **routier** road network; ~ **de spécialistes** expert network; ~ **de succursales** branch network; ~ **de télévision** television network; ~ **de vente** sales network

réservation *f* booking, reservation; ~ **directe** direct booking; ~ **groupée** block booking

réserve *f* (provision) stock, (Banque) reserve; (restriction) reservation; (local de stockage) stockroom; (ventes aux enchères) reserve price BrE, upset price AmE; **de** ~ (Admin) backup; ~**s de pétrol** oil reserves; **avoir/garder qch en** ~ have/keep sth in store *ou* stock; **sans** ~ unreservedly, without reservation; **sous** ~ **de disponibilité/changement** subject to availability/change; ~ **bancaire** bank reserve; ~**s bancaires** bank capital; ~**s des banques de dépôts** banker's deposits UK; ~**s de bilan** balance sheet reserves; ~**s cachées** secret reserves; ~ **pour catastrophe** catastrophe reserve; ~**s en chambre forte** vault reserve US; ~**s de charbon** coal reserves; ~**s déclarées** disclosed reserves; ~ **pour dépassement des crédits législatifs** reserve for statutory overruns; ~**s en devises étrangères** foreign exchange reserves; ~ **d'emprunt** borrowed reserve; ~**s énergétiques** energy reserves; ~ **en espèces** cash reserve, vault cash; ~ **pour éventualités** contingency reserve; ~ **excédentaire** excess reserve, supplementary reserve; ~ **de fonds commun de placement** mutual-fund custodian; ~ **fractionnaire** fractional cash reserve, fractional reserve; ~ **générale** general reserves; ~ **globale visée par règlement** prescribed aggregate reserve; ~ **pour impôts sur le revenu reportés** deferred income tax reserve; ~ **légale** legal reserve, general reserves; ~ **de main-d'œuvre** labour pool BrE, labor pool AmE; ~ **métallique** stock of bullion; ~ **monétaire** monetary reserve, money reserve; ~ **naturelle nationale** national nature reserve; ~ **négative** negative reserve; ~ **obligatoire** bench mark reserve US, reserve deposit; ~ **obligatoire des régimes de retraite** pension plan liability reserve; ~**s obligatoires** required reserves, reserve requirements; ~**s d'or** gold reserves; ~ **primaire** primary reserve; ~ **prime d'émission** premium reserve; ~ **pour réclamations non réglées** (assurance-vie) reserve for unpaid claims; ~**s de réévaluation** revaluation reserves; ~ **pour sinistres** claims reserve; ~ **spéciales** (contributions à la Sécurité sociale) special provisions; ~ **totale prescrite** prescribed aggregate reserve; ~ **de trésorerie** cash

r

reserve; ~ **de valeur** store of value

réservé, e *adj* reserved; ~ **à l'administration** for office use only

réserver *vt* (chambre, billet) book, reserve; (Fin) earmark, ring-fence; (garder pour plus tard) set aside, save; (limiter) reserve, limit; ~ **à l'avance** book in advance; ~ **une chambre** book *ou* reserve a room; ~ **son jugement** reserve judgment

résidant, e *adj* resident

résidence *f* (Admin) place of residence; (maison) residence; (groupe d'immeubles) residential development, apartment complex AmE; **établir** ~ **en France** take up residence in France; ~ **distincte** separate residence; ~ **habituelle** permanent residence; ~ **légale** legal residence; ~ **principale** main residence; ~ **secondaire** second home; ~ **temporaire** temporary residence

résident, e *m,f* resident; ~ **contribuable** resident taxpayer; ~ **étranger** resident alien; ~ **en mémoire** (Info) memory resident; ~ **permanent** permanent resident; ~ **temporaire** temporary resident

résidentiel, -elle *adj* residential

résider *vi* reside (frml), live; ~ **et travailler** reside and work

résidu *m* (dépôt) residue; (détritus) waste; ~s **industriels** industrial waste

résignation *f* (Droit) (abandon) relinquishment

résiliable *adj* (contrat, bail) terminable; (Droit) voidable

résiliation *f* (d'un contrat) termination; ~ **d'un contrat de location** termination of tenancy

résilier *vt* (contrat) terminate

résistance *f* resistance; ~ **aux changement** resistance to change; ~ **des consommateurs** consumer resistance; ~ **du marché** market resistance; ~ **des matériaux** strength of materials

résister *vt* **résister à** (opposition) overcome; (changement, crise, grève) withstand; (concurrence) stand up to; (pression, influence) resist

résolu, e *adj* determined; **être** ~ **à faire qch** be determined to do sth

résolution *f* (d'un accord) cancellation; (motion) resolution; (décision) resolution; (Gestion) (solution) resolution, solution; **voter une** ~ pass a resolution; **prendre une** ~ make a resolution; ~ **budgétaire** budget resolution US; ~ **de conflit** dispute resolution; ~ **de contrat** frustration of contract; ~ **de problèmes** problem solving

résorbé, e *adj* (économétrie) absorbed

résorber ⓵ *vt* absorb; ~ **un surplus de véhicules d'occasion** absorb a used-car surplus

⓶ **se résorber** (excédent, déficit) be reduced; (chômage, inflation) be falling

résoudre *vt* (problème) resolve, solve

respect *m* (Droit) observance; (de conditions) compliance; (du règlement) observance; ~ **strict du contrat** strict adherence to the contract

respecter *vt* (personne, promesse) respect; (contrat) abide by, comply with; (disposition) comply with; (loi) observe; (engagement) honour BrE, honor AmE; **ne pas** ~ (contrat, règle) breach; ~ **les délais** meet the deadlines; ~ **le règlement** comply with the regulations

respectivement *adv* respectively

respectueux, -euse *adj* respectful; ~ **de l'environnement** environmentally-friendly

responsabiliser *vt* give a sense of responsability to

responsabilité *f* responsibility; (Droit) liability; ~ **civile** compulsory third-party insurance; (Droit) civil liability; ~ **collective** joint liability; ~ **commerciale** business liability; ~ **conjointe** joint liability; ~ **conjointe et solidaire** joint and several liability; ~ **contractuelle** contractual liability; ~ **délictuelle** tort liability; ~ **directe** direct liability; ~ **de la direction** accountability in management; ~ **du fabricant** product liability; ~ **fiscale** tax liability; ~ **globale** comprehensive responsibility; ~ **hiérarchique** line responsibility; ~ **objective** absolute liability; ~ **pleine et entière** full liability; ~ **professionnelle** professional indemnity, professional liability; ~ **des sociétés** corporate accountability; ~ **au tiers** third-party liability

responsable¹ *adj* responsible; (Droit) (civilement) liable; ~ **de** in charge of, accountable for; ~ **devant** answerable to; ~ **en droit** responsible in law; **être** ~ be in charge; **être** ~ **de** answer for, be answerable for; (entreprise, projet) be in charge of; ~ **légalement** responsible in law

responsable² *mf* person in charge; (gérant, directeur) manager; (chef de service) head; (Admin) official; (Pol) leader; ~ **des achats** head buyer, purchasing manager; ~ **administratif** administration officer; ~ **du budget** account manager; ~ **financier** financial director, financial manager; ~ **de la formation professionnelle** professional development manager; ~ **d'hôtel** hotel manager; ~ **opérationnel** line manager; ~ **de permanence** duty officer; ~ **régional** district officer, regional manager; ~ **des relations publiques** public relations officer; ~ **de la sécurité** safety officer; ~ **du service de distribution** (presse) circulation manager; ~ **du service de presse** press officer; ~ **des stocks** inventory controller, stock controller; ~ **des techniques commerciales** merchandiser; ~ **en titre** titular head; ~ **des transports** traffic superintendent; ~ **des ventes** sales manager

resserrement *m* tightening; ~ **des bénéfices** profit squeeze; ~ **des coûts** cost containment; ~ **du crédit à découvert** short squeeze (jarg); ~ **de la politique monétaire** snugging

resserrer *vt* tighten; ~ **les cordons de la bourse** tighten the purse strings

ressortissant, e *m,f* national; ~ **étranger** foreign national

ressource *f* resource; ~**s** (Compta) funds; (Fin) (argent) resources; **être sans** ~**s** have no means of support; ~ **en capital** capital resource; ~**s et emplois de capitaux** source and disposition of funds; ~ **énergétique** energy resource; ~**s humaines** human resources; ~ **minière** mineral resource; ~**s naturelles** natural resources; ~ **non renouvelable** nonrenewable resource; ~ **primaire** primary resource; ~ **renouvelable** renewable resource; ~ **réutilisable** recoverable reserve; ~ **de trésorerie** cash resource

restaurant *m* restaurant; ~ **d'entreprise** staff canteen; ~ **d'usine** works canteen

restaurateur, -trice *m,f* restaurateur; (propriétaire) restaurant owner

restauration *f* catering trade; (Info) reset; ~ **rapide** fast food; ~ **en vol** in-flight catering

restaurer *vt* (Info) undelete

reste *m* remainder; (d'une somme d'argent) balance; (Droit) residuum; **le** ~ **du monde** the rest of the world; ~ **à bord** (Transp) remain on board

rester *vi* remain, stay; ~ **dans les cours** (Bourse) stay in-the-money; ~ **dans la course** keep in step with one's competitors; ~ **dans la légalité** keep within the law; ~ **ferme** (sur un prix) stand firm; ~ **en grève** stay out; ~ **informé** stay informed; ~ **en relation avec** keep in touch with; ~ **en suspens** remain in suspense, stand over

restitution *f* (de droit, de qualité) restoration; (de bien, de terre) return, restitution (frml); ~ **de la garantie** return of guarantee; ~ **d'un trop-perçu** return of amount overpaid

restocker *vt* (V&M) replenish, restock

restreindre *vt* (dépenses) curb, cut back; (possibilités, choix) limit; (importations, subventions, droit) restrict

restrictif, -ive *adj* restrictive

restriction *f* restriction; ~**s commerciales/de crédit/budgétaires** trade/credit/budget restrictions; ~**s salariales** wage restraints; ~ **à la liberté du commerce** restraint of trade

restructuration *f* reorganization, restructuring; ~ **du capital** capital reorganization, recapitalization; ~ **industrielle** restructuring of industry; ~ **du travail** work restructuring

restructuré, e *adj* reorganized, restructured

restructurer *vt* reorganize, restructure

résultat *m* outcome, result; (d'une discussion) outcome; (Info) output; ~**s** (chiffre d'affaires) trading results, figures; (revenu) income; (bénéfice) profit; (gains) earnings; **être le** ~ **de** be the result of; **sans** ~ without success; **avoir pour** ~ **de faire** have the effect of doing; ~ **brut d'exploitation** gross operating profits; ~ **comptable** accounting income, accounting profit; ~ **courant** trading profits; ~ **effectif** actual outcome; ~ **de l'exercice** annual earnings; ~ **d'exploitation** operating profits; ~ **final** end result; ~ **financier** financial profit or loss; ~ **heureux** successful outcome; ~ **négatif** losses; ~ **net de l'exercice** distributable profit; ~ **net d'exploitation** net operating income; ~ **opérationnel** operating profits; ~ **positif** profits; ~ **probable** likely outcome; ~ **réel** actual earnings

résulter *vi* ~ **de** result from; **résultant de** resulting from

résumé *m* summary, résumé; ~ **des informations** news roundup; ~ **de la séance** summary of the proceedings; ~ **succinct** brief summary

résumer *vt* summarize

rétablir *vt* re-establish, restore; ~ **l'ordre public** restore law and order

rétablissement *m* re-establishment

retard *m* delay; **en** ~ **économique** (région) economically backward; **être en** ~ **dans ses paiements** be in arrears; **rattraper son** ~ catch up; **avoir du courrier/travail en** ~ have a backlog of mail/work

retarder *vt* (reporter) (une réunion) postpone, put off; (vol, projet) delay; (un paiement) defer; (mettre en retard) hold up

retenir *vt* (caution) retain; (somme, cotisation, impôt) deduct; (personne) detain; (table, chambre) reserve, book; (date) set; ~ **à l'avance** book in advance; ~ **l'impôt** deduct tax; ~ **une place** make a reservation; **être retenu** (pour un poste) be shortlisted

rétention *f* retention; (refus de communiquer) withholding (de of); ~ **d'information** (Droit) withholding of information

retenue *f* (prélèvement) deduction; (de crédit) containment; (sur salaire) stoppage; ~ **fiscale** tax withholding; ~ **de garantie** contract holdback; ~ **d'impôt** tax withholding; ~ **de l'impôt sur le revenu à la source** pay as you earn, PAYE UK, pay-as-you-go US; ~ **à la source** deduction at source

réticence *f* (Droit) nondisclosure

retirer **1** *vt* (offre, argent) withdraw; (marchandises) collect, pick up; ~ **du commerce** (article défectueux) recall; ~ **du marché** take off the market; ~ **progressivement** (Info) phase out
2 **se retirer** *v pron* pull out, withdraw; **se** ~ **des affaires** retire from business

retombées *f pl* (conséquences) effects, consequences; **avoir des ~ favorables sur** have a favourable effect on; **~ acides** acid deposit; **~ économiques** spin-off effect; **~ radioactives** radioactive fallout

retour *m* return; **~ à l'envoyeur** return to sender; **par ~ du courrier** by return of post; **~ de souscription** (avis) regret; **~ au tiroir** refer to drawer; **être de ~ dans une heure** be back within an hour; **~ sur les avantages acquis** giveback (jarg); **~ à l'emploi** return to work; **~ d'information** feedback; **~s et réfactions sur achats** purchase returns and allowances; **~ à vide** deadheading AmE

retournement *m* (de situation) reversal (**de** of), turnaround (**de** of); **~ à la baisse** downturn

retourner *vti* return; (la situation) reverse; **~ à la case départ** go back to square one; **~ à l'envoyeur** return to sender

retrait *m* (d'argent) withdrawal; (de commande, de dossier) collection; (de plainte) withdrawal; (de marchandises) collection; (d'article défectueux) recall; **faire un ~** make a withdrawal; **~ d'agrément** (d'un régime de retraite) deregistration; **~ d'argent à la caisse** cash-back (in shops); **~ automatique** automatic withdrawal; **~ des bagages** baggage reclaim area; **~ d'espèces** cash withdrawal; **~ de fonds** withdrawal of capital; **~ de l'investiture** deselection UK; **~ d'une opposition** withdrawal of an objection; **~ partiel** partial withdrawal

retraite *f* (pension) pension; (cessation d'activités) retirement; **~ anticipée** early retirement; **~ complémentaire de prévoyance** supplementary pension scheme; **~ constituée dans l'entreprise** internally funded pension; **~ de dette** retirement of debt; **~ différée** deferred retirement; **~ de l'État** state pension UK; **~ obligatoire** compulsory retirement BrE, mandatory retirement AmE; **~ professionnelle** occupational pension

retraité, e *m,f* retired person, retiree AmE

retraitement *m* (Envir) reprocessing

retraiter *vt* (Envir) reprocess

retrancher *vt* take away, deduct

retransmission *f* (Media) broadcast

rétrécissement *m* (de marché) shrinking; **~ de la demande** contraction of demand

rétribution *f* payment; **~ d'agence** (navigation) agency fee; **~ en nature** noncash rewards

rétroactif, -ive *adj* (effet, mesure) retroactive, retrospective; (augmentation) backdated; (loi) retrospective, ex post facto; **la loi n'a pas d'effet ~** the law cannot be applied retrospectively

rétroaction *f* feedback; **~ tous azimuts** 360 degree feedback; **~ positive** positive feedback

rétrocession *f* retrocession; **~ de fonds empruntés** on-lending

rétrogradation *f* (d'un employé) demotion, downgrading

rétroprojecteur *m* overhead projector

retrouver *vt* trace; (Info) retrieve

réunification *f* reunification

réunion *f* meeting; **être en ~** (personne) be in a meeting; (comité) be meeting; **~ des actionnaires** company meeting; **~ d'affaires** business meeting; **~ de comité/commission** committee meeting; **~ du conseil d'administration** board meeting; **~ extraordinaire** special meeting; **~ informelle** informal meeting; **~ de mise au point** debriefing; **~ de vendeurs** sales conference

réunir ① *vt* (personnes) bring together; **~ des fonds** raise funds; **~ en trust** trustify ② **se réunir** *v pron* (délégués, comité) meet; (sociétés) merge

réussi, e *adj* successful

réussir ① *vt* succeed; **~ à faire** manage to, succeed in doing; **~ un grand coup** make a scoop (infrml); **~ qch** make a go of sth ② *vi* (projet, personne, commerce) be successful

réussite *f* success; **~ constante** continued success

réutilisable *adj* reusable

réutiliser *vt* reuse

revalorisation *f* revalorization; (de salaire) adjustment

revaloriser *vt* (salaire) adjust; (emploi) upgrade

révélation *f* revelation, disclosure; **~ de l'actif** asset exposure

révéler ① *vt* disclose; **non révélé** (Fin) undisclosed ② **se révéler** *v pron* prove to be; **se ~ faux** prove wrong; **se ~ vrai** prove right

revendication *f* (réclamation) claim; (reconnaissance) claiming of responsibility; **mouvement de ~** protest action; **~ complémentaire** secondary action; **~ légitime** legal claim; **~ salariale** wage claim; **~ d'un tiers** third-party claim

revendiquer *vt* (droit, augmentation, égalité) demand; (action, attent) claim responsibility for; **~ 300 membres** claim to have 300 members

revendre ① *vt* resell; (vendre au détail) retail ② **se revendre** resell

revente *f* resale; **~ de titres** secondary distribution

revenu *m* (de personne) income, earnings; (de l'État) revenue; (d'une entreprise) revenue, income; **~ accumulé** accumulating income; **~ accumulé tiré de biens** accrual property income; **~ de l'actif** asset return; **~ agricole** farming income; **~ annuel** annual return; **~ après impôt** after-tax

⋯⫶

income; ∼ **brut** gross earnings, gross income; ∼ **compensatoire** compensating income UK; ∼ **déclaré en moins** understatement of income; ∼ **direct** basic income; ∼ **disponible** disposable income; ∼ **élevé** high return; ∼ **d'entreprise** business income; ∼ **estimé** estimated revenue; ∼s **de l'État** public revenue; ∼ **exonéré** exempt income; ∼ **familial** family income; ∼ **foncier** estate revenue; ∼ **garanti** guaranteed income; ∼ **par habitant** income per head, per capita income; ∼ **horaire moyen** average hourly earnings; ∼ **immobilier** estate income, property income; ∼ **imposable** taxable income; ∼ **locatif** rental income; ∼ **modeste** moderate income; ∼ **moyen** average income; ∼ **national brut** gross national income; ∼ **net** net income; ∼ **non pécunier** nonpecuniary returns; ∼ **personnel** personal income, private income; ∼ **personnel disponible** personal disposable income; ∼ **de portefeuille** income from securities; ∼ **potentiel** potential income; ∼ **des primes** premium income; ∼ **de production** production revenue; ∼ **de profession libérale** self-employment income; ∼ **de société** partnership income; ∼ **de source étrangère** foreign income; ∼ **sous-déclaré** understatement of income; ∼ **d'une succession** estate income; ∼ **total** total income, total revenue

reversement *m* payout

réversible *adj* (charte-partie) reversible; (Droit) reversionary

réversion *f* (Droit) reversion; **pension de** ∼ reversion benefit

revirement *m* turnabout; (vers la gauche/droite) swing

réviser *vt* (contrat, projection, prévision) revise; (Compta) audit; (prix, salaire) adjust, review; (stratégie, projet) review; (machine, voiture) service; ∼ **à la baisse/à la hausse** (prix) adjust downwards/upwards

réviseur *m* (Compta) auditor; ∼ **indépendant** independent auditor

révision *f* (de contrat) revision; (Compta) auditing; (de prix, de salaire) adjustment, review; (de stratégie) review, reappraisal; (de véhicule, machine) service; ∼ **analytique** systems-based audit; ∼ **annuelle** annual review; ∼ **à la baisse** downward revision; ∼ **comptable** audit; ∼ **de conformité** compliance audit; ∼ **externe** external audit, independent audit; ∼ **à la hausse** upvaluation, upward revision; ∼ **des prix** pricing review; ∼ **des tarifs** rates review

revitalisation *f* revitalization

revitaliser *vt* revitalize

révocable *adj* (contrat) revocable; (personne) dismissible

révocation *f* (de contrat) revocation; (de personne) dismissal

revoir *vt* (projet, méthode) review; (prévision, tarifs) revise; (prix) adjust; (prévision) revise; ∼ **à la baisse/à la hausse** revise downward/upward

révolution *f* revolution; ∼ **démographique** demographic transition, vital revolution; ∼ **industrielle** industrial revolution; ∼ **Internet** Internet revolution, e-revolution; ∼ **verte** green revolution

revue *f* journal, magazine; ∼ **agricole** agricultural publication; ∼ **analytique** accounts appraisal; ∼ **d'entreprise** house journal; ∼ **féminine** women's magazine; ∼ **illustrée** illustrated magazine; ∼ **en ligne** e-zine, cybermagazine; ∼ **de mode** fashion magazine; ∼ **professionnelle** trade journal

rez-de-chaussée *m* ground floor BrE, first floor AmE

rezonage *m* (immobilier) downzoning

rf. *abrév* (▶**référence**) ref. (reference)

RFC *abrév* (▶**requête formulée par le client**) (aviation) CR (change request), RFC (request for change)

rhétorique *f* rhetoric (**de** of)

riche *adj* rich, wealthy; ∼ **en liquidité** cash-rich; ∼ **en pétrole** oil-rich

richesse *f* wealth; ∼ **corporelle/incorporelle** tangible/intangible wealth

rigidité *f* rigidity; ∼ **des prix/salaires** price/wage rigidity

rigoureusement *adv* stringently

rigoureux, -euse *adj* stringent

risque *m* risk; **à** ∼ **élevé** high-risk; **à ses** ∼**s et périls** at one's own risk; **aux** ∼**s de l'acheteur** at buyer's risk; **aux** ∼**s du vendeur** at seller's risk; **aux** ∼**s et périls du propriétaire** at owner's risk; **aux** ∼**s et périls du transporteur** carrier's risk; **ne pas prendre de** ∼ play safe; **qui tient compte du** ∼ risk-orientated; **tous** ∼**s** (assurance) fully comprehensive; ∼ **d'accident** accident risk; ∼ **actuel** current risk; ∼ **aléatoire** unsystematic risk; ∼ **assumé en dernier ressort** ultimate risk; ∼ **assurable** insurable risk; ∼ **assuré** insured peril; ∼ **de base** basic risk; ∼ **calculé** calculated risk; ∼ **de catastrophe** catastrophe hazard, catastrophe risk; ∼ **commercial** business risk, commercial risk; ∼ **considérable** large risk; ∼ **constant** constant risk; ∼ **de contrepartie** credit risk; ∼ **de conversion** translation risk; ∼ **à cotisation et à prestations déterminées** target risk; ∼ **de décès** death risk; ∼ **de déchargement** unloading risk; ∼ **encouru** risk exposure; ∼ **envisageable** foreseeable risk; ∼ **global** aggregate risk; ∼ **de guerre** war risk; ∼ **de guerre uniquement** war risk only; ∼ **à la hausse** upside risk; ∼ **illimité** unbounded risk; ∼ **imminent** imminent peril; ∼ **important** large risk; ∼ **d'incendie** fire hazard; ∼ **d'incendie sur fret** fire risk on freight; ∼ **indirect** consequential loss; ∼

inhérent inherent risk; ~ **de litige** (arrhes) litigation risk; ~ **du marché** market risk; ~ **maritime** maritime risk; ~ **de masse** mass risk; ~ **ménager** domestic risk; ~ **de mer** sea risk; ~ **du métier** occupational hazard; ~ **moral** moral hazard; ~ **ouvert** open-ended risk; ~ **des parités croisées** (commerce international) cross-currency exposure; ~**s prévus** expected perils; ~ **privilégié** preferred risk; ~ **de recours au tiers** third-party risk; ~ **de retard** lag risk; ~ **sanitaire** health hazard; ~ **pour la sécurité** safety hazard; ~ **souverain** sovereign risk; ~ **statistique** statistical risk; ~ **à terme** time risk; ~ **au tiers** third-party risk; ~ **du transporteur** carrier's risk; ~ **ultime** ultimate risk; ~ **de vol** theft risk

risqué, e *adj* risky

ristourne *f* discount, rebate; ~ **de mise en rade** (Assur) lay-up return; ~ **de participation** (Assur) experience refund; ~ **sur quantité** (marchandises) volume rebate; ~ **pour résiliation** (Assur) cancelling return BrE, canceling return AmE

rivage *m* shore

rivaliser *vi* : ~ **avec** compete with

riverain, e *m,f* (de rue) resident

riveraineté *f* (Droit) riparian rights

robot *m* robot; ~ **de recherche** (Info) crawler

robotique *f* robotics

robotiser *vt* robotize

robuste *adj* robust

rocade *f* ring road

rogner *vi* : ~ **sur** (budget) cut down on; (économies) whittle away at

rôle *m* function, role; ~ **consultatif** advisory function; ~ **dominant en matière de prix** price leadership; ~ **d'équipage** articles of agreement, ship's articles; ~ **du gouvernement** government role

roll-over *m* roll-over

ro/lo *m* (navigation) ro/lo

ROME *abrév* (►répertoire opérationnel des métiers et des emplois) job bank

rompre *vt* (marché, traité) break; (négociations, relations) break off; ~ **un contrat** contract out of an agreement; ~ **les liens avec** sever links with

rompu *m* (Bourse) broken amount, broken lot; ~ **de titres** broken amount, broken lot, odd lot

rond-point *m* roundabout BrE, traffic circle AmE

rotation *f* turnover; (d'un navire) turnround BrE, turnaround AmE; ~ **de l'actif** asset turnover; ~ **des cultures** crop rotation; ~ **des éléments d'actif** asset turnover; ~ **du personnel** (de poste en poste) staff rotation; (dans une entreprise) staff turnover; ~ **des postes** job rotation; ~ **des stagiaires**

trainee turnover; ~ **des stocks** stock turnover, inventory turnover

rotonde *f* roundhouse

rouages *m pl* machinery; **les ~ du gouvernement** the wheels of government; ~ **administratifs** administrative machinery

rouble *m* rouble

roue *f* wheel

rouge *adj* red; **être dans le ~** be in the red; **sortir du ~** get out of the red

rouillé, e *adj* (personne, outil, voiture) rusty

roulage *m* haulage

rouleau *m* (cylindre) roll; (Ind) roller; ~ **compresseur** steamroller

roulement *m* (Fin) turnover; (de personnel) job rotation; **travailler par ~** work in shifts; **établir un ~** draw up a rota; ~ **en arrière** (options) rolling in; ~ **en avant** (options) rolling out; ~ **à la baisse** (options) rolling down; ~ **à la hausse** (options) rolling up

rouler *vt* (infrml) take in (infrml)

roulier *m* roll on/roll off ship

roupie *f* rupee

routage *m* (de journaux, de colis) sorting and mailing; (Info) routing

route *f* road; **en ~** en route; **faire fausse ~** be on the wrong track; ~ **commerciale** trade route; ~ **de desserte** accommodation road; ~ **directe** (navigation, aviation) direct route; ~ **maritime** sea route; ~ **principale** major road, trunk road; ~ **à utilisateurs multiples** multiuser route

router *vt* route

routeur *m* (Info) router

routier *m* lorry driver BrE, truck driver

routine *f* routine

royalties *f pl* royalties; ~ **dues par le concessionnaire d'un brevet** patent royalties

RSVP *abrév* (►répondez s'il vous plaît) RSVP (please reply)

RTP *abrév* (►réserve totale prescrite) PAR (prescribed aggregate reserve)

rubrique *f* section; (Compta) heading; (Média) column; ~ **économique** economic section; ~ **économique et financière** business pages

rue *f* street; **de la ~** (mode) high-street UK; ~ **à double sens** two-way street

ruée *f* rush; ~ **sur les banques** run on the banks; ~ **sur le dollar** run on the dollar, rush on the dollar; ~ **vers l'or** gold rush

ruiné, e *adj* bankrupt

ruiner *vt* (personne, société) bankrupt

rumeur *f* hearsay, rumour BrE, rumor AmE

runner *m* (Bourse) runner

rupteur *m* (Info) burster

rupture *f* (de contrat, de garantie) breach; (de négociations) breakdown; **en ~ de stock** out of stock; ~ **de contrat/de garantie** breach of ⋯›

contract/warranty; ~ **de stock** stock shortage

rusé, e *adj* (campagne de vente, personne) slick

Ss

SA *abrév* (►**société anonyme**) plc (public limited company) UK, limited company UK

saborder *vt* (navigation) scuttle

sacrifier *vt* (marchandise) give away, sell off at knockdown prices; (prix) slash; **prix sacrifiés** knockdown prices

saignée *f* (dans un budget) hole (**dans** in)

saigner *vt* bleed (infrml); ~ **qn à blanc** (infrml) bleed sb dry (infrml)

sain, e *adj* (concurrence) healthy; (économie) buoyant, healthy; (sans virus informatique) uninfected; (gestion, jugement) sound

saisie *f* (confiscation) (marchandises, drogue) seizure; (Droit) distraint of property; (de données) capture; **opérer une** ~ make a seizure; ~ **d'un bien hypothéqué** foreclosure; ~ **codée de données** coded data entry; ~ **directe** direct data entry; ~ **conservatoire** sequester of property; ~ **de données** data capture, keyboarding; ~ **d'écran** screen capture; ~ **d'hypothèque sans faculté de rachat** strict foreclosure

saisie-arrêt *f* (d'une créance) attachment, garnishment; ~ **sur salaire** withholding of wages

saisine *f* (Droit) submission of a case before a court

saisir *vt* (marchandises, drogue) seize; (biens mobiliers) distrain, attach; (hypothèque) foreclose; (données, entrées) key in; ~ **un bien hypothéqué** foreclose a mortgage; ~ **une créance** attach a debt; **faire** ~ (par ordre d'un tribunal) sell up; ~ **la justice d'une affaire** refer a matter to a court; **'affaire à ~'** 'amazing bargain'

saisissage *m* (Transp) lashing

saisisseur *m* (arrimeur) lasher

saison *f* season; **morte/basse** ~ slack season, off-season; **haute/pleine** ~ high/peak season; ~ **touristique** tourist season

saisonnalité *f* seasonality; ~ **de la demande** seasonality of demand

saisonnier¹, -ière *adj* seasonal; **données corrigées des variations saisonnières** seasonally adjusted figures

saisonnier², -ière *m,f* seasonal worker

salaire *m* pay, salary, wage(s); ~ **à débattre** salary to be negotiated; ~ **annuel** annual salary, annual wage; ~ **annuel**

rythme *m* pace; ~ **de facturation** billing cycle; ~ **de production** throughput

garanti guaranteed annual wage; ~ **d'appoint** supplementary income; ~ **et avantages complémentaires** remuneration package; ~ **de base avec commission** on-target earnings; ~ **de base** basic salary, base salary AmE; ~ **basé sur le rendement** payment by results UK; ~ **bonifié** premium pay; ~ **brut** gross pay; ~ **cotisable** pensionable earnings; ~ **de croissance** incremental payment; ~ **de départ** starting salary; ~ **différentiel** differential pay; ~ **élevé** high salary; ~ **d'embauche** starting salary; ~ **fixe** fixed salary; ~ **en fonction des résultats** payment by results; ~ **garanti** guaranteed wage; ~ **hebdomadaire** weekly wage packet; ~ **horaire** hourly wage; ~ **initial** starting salary, threshold rate AmE; ~ **lié aux bénéfices** profit-related pay; ~ **lié aux résultats** performance-related pay; ~ **mensuel** monthly salary, monthly wage; ~ **minimum garanti** guaranteed minimum wage, statutory minimum wage; ~ **minimum interprofessionnel de croissance** index-linked guaranteed minimum wage; ~ **minimum interprofessionnel garanti** guaranteed minimum wage; ~ **net** net pay, take-home pay; ~ **à la pièce** piece rate; ~ **plafond** earnings ceiling; ~ **réel** actual wage, real pay; ~ **au rendement** performance-related pay; ~ **du secteur public** public sector pay; ~ **selon l'ancienneté dans le poste** longevity pay; ~ **unique** single income

salariat *m* (ensemble des salariés) wage-earners; (mode de rémunération) (au mois) payment by salary; (à l'heure, la semaine) payment by wages

salarié¹, e *adj* employed

salarié², e *m,f* salaried employee, wage earner; **les** ~**s d'une entreprise** the employees on a company's payroll

salle *f* room; ~ **de bavardage** (Info) chatroom; ~ **des coffres** safe-deposit vault, safety vault; ~ **du conseil** boardroom; ~ **des cotations** (Bourse) boardroom; ~ **des dépêches** (Bourse) boardroom; ~ **d'embarquement** airport lounge, departure lounge; ~ **d'embarquement Classe Club** (aérien et maritime) executive lounge, club class lounge; ~ **d'exposition** showroom; ~ **des**

machines sans surveillance (production) unmanned machinery area; ~ **des marchés** (Bourse) trading room, dealing floor; ~ **d'opération** (Bourse) trading room; ~ **des ordinateurs** computer room; ~ **de projection** viewing room; ~ **de rédaction** (presse) newsroom; ~ **de stockage** storeroom; ~ **des ventes** auction room

salon *m* (pour professionnels) trade show, trade fair; (pour le public) fair, exhibition; ~ **de l'aéronautique** air show; ~ **de l'agriculture** agricultural show; ~ **d'essayage** fitting room; ~ **interprofessionnel** trade show; ~ **passagers** passenger lounge

salutaire *adj* beneficial

salutations *f pl* greetings; (dans formule de politesse) **sincères** ~ (à une personne nommée) yours sincerely; (à une personne non nommée) yours faithfully

sanction *f* (mesure) sanction; (pénalité) penalty; (approbation) sanction, approval; **~s économiques** economic sanctions; **prendre des ~s contre qn** (Admin) take disciplinary action against sb; (Econ) impose sanctions on sb; **lever les ~s** lift the sanctions; ~ **disciplinaire** (Admin) disciplinary measure

sanctionner *vt* (punir) punish; (loi, conduite) sanction; **compétences sanctionnées par un diplôme** skills recognized by a diploma

sans *prép* without; **avec et** ~ (Bourse) cum and ex; ~ **cesse** without respite; ~ **accès à la mer** landlocked; ~ **additifs** free of all additives; ~ **adresse** (maritime) free of address; ~ **appel** with no right of appeal; ~ **arôme artificiel** no artificial flavoring AmE, no artificial flavouring BrE; ~ **avaries** free of damage; ~ **bénéfice du sauvetage** (Assur) without benefit of salvage; ~ **but lucratif** non-profit-making BrE, nonprofit AmE; ~ **condition** unconditional; ~ **conditions** with no strings attached; ~ **conservateur** no preservatives; ~ **conservateur ni additif** no preservatives or additives; ~ **constituer de précédent** without prejudice; ~ **couverture suffisante** (Banque) insufficient funds; ~ **date** undated; ~ **déduction pour dépréciation** new for old; ~ **dettes** clean; ~ **droit** ex-rights; ~ **effet** no effects; ~ **égard à la responsabilité** (assurance, dommages) no fault; ~ **emballage** unpacked; ~ **emploi** jobless, out of work; ~ **endettement** clear of debts; ~ **engagement de notre part** without any liability on our part; ~ **engagement de votre part** without obligation; ~ **expérience** inexperienced, unfledged; ~ **faille** (soutien) continuing; ~ **fil** cordless; ~ **fioriture** with no extras, with no trimmings; ~ **fondement** unfounded; ~ **frais** without charge; ~ **garantie** without engagement; ~ **indication de prix** unpriced; ~ **intérêt** interest-free, ex-interest; ~ **liquidité** cash-strapped; ~ **locataire** untenanted; ~ **nom** (fichier) unnamed; ~ **objet** not applicable, n/a; ~ **ordonnance** (médicament) over-the-counter; ~ **papier** paperless; ~ **pareil** second to none; ~ **plomb** lead-free, unleaded; ~ **préavis** no advice, without prior notice; ~ **précédent** unprecedented; ~ **préjudice** without prejudice; ~ **preuves** unsupported; ~ **privilège** without privileges; ~ **problèmes** trouble-free; ~ **publicité** unadvertised; ~ **recours** without recourse; ~ **répit** (travail) without respite; ~ **réponse** unacknowledged; ~ **réserve** absolute, unconditional; ~ **restriction** uncurtailed; ~ **rival** unrivalled; ~ **scintillement** flicker-free; ~ **scrupules** unscrupulous; ~ **tenir compte de** irrespective of; ~ **travail** workless; ~ **valeur** valueless; ~ **valeur commerciale** no commercial value; ~ **valeur déclarée** no value declared; ~ **valeur douanière** no customs value; ~ **valeur nominale** no-par value

sans-abri *mf* homeless person; **les** ~ the homeless

sans-emploi *mf* unemployed person; **les** ~ the unemployed

sans-logis *mf* homeless person; **les** ~ the homeless

santé *f* health; ~ **publique** public health; ~ **sur le lieu de travail** occupational health

saper *vt* undermine

SARL *abrév* (▸**société à responsabilité limitée**) Inc. (incorporated company) US; Ltd (limited liability company) UK

sas *m* (canal) lock-chamber

satellite *m* satellite; **ville** ~ satellite town; ~ **de communication** communications satellite

satisfaction *f* satisfaction; **demander/obtenir** ~ seek/obtain satisfaction; ~ **du consommateur** consumer satisfaction; ~ **non financière** (jarg) nonfinancial reward

satisfaire *vt* (besoins) accommodate, satisfy; (demande) meet, keep up with; (revendication, exigences) meet; ~ **à** (désir) gratify; (normes, conditions) meet; (obligation, ambition) fulfil; ~ **au contrôle** pass inspection

satisfaisant, e *adj* satisfactory

satisfait, e *adj* satisfied; **être** ~ **de** be satisfied with

saturation *f* saturation; **arriver à** ~ reach saturation point; ~ **du marché** market saturation

saturer *vt* (marché) glut, saturate

sauf *prép* except; (navigation) excepted; ~ **avarie commune** (Assur) unless general; ~ **avis contraire** unless otherwise informed; ~ **causé par** unless caused by; ~ **dimanches et jours fériés** Sundays and holidays excepted; ~ **disposition contraire** unless otherwise provided; ~ **erreur** unless I'm mistaken; ~ **erreur ou omission** errors and omissions excepted; ~ **indication contraire** ⋯▸

S

unless otherwise stated

saut *m* skip; ∼ **de page** form feed; ∼ **de papier** (Info) paper throw

sauter *vt* (ligne, page, étape) skip; ∼ **les détails** skip the details; ∼ **un paiement** skip a payment

sauvage *adj* (vente) illegal, unauthorised; (urbanisation) uncontrolled; (concurrence) unfair; **affichage** ∼ fly posting; **OPA** ∼ hostile takeover bid

sauvegarde *f* safeguard; (Info) save; (avec diskette) backup; **fichier/disquette de** ∼ backup file/disk; ∼ **automatique** autosave; ∼ **fixe** timed backup

sauvegarder *vt* safeguard; (Info) (données) save; (sur diskette) back up

sauvetage *m* (d'entreprise) rescue; **plan de** ∼ rescue plan; (du navire et des biens) salvage

sauveteur *m* (d'entreprise) rescuer; (maritime) salvor

SAV *abrév* (▶**service après-vente**) after-sales service

savant *m* (scientifique) scientist

savoir *vt* know

savoir-faire *m* know-how; (professionnel) ability

SBF *abrév* (▶**Société des bourses françaises**) ≈ ISE (International Stock Exchange)

scalpage *m* day trading, scalping US (infrml)

scalper *m* day trader, scalper US (infrml)

scandale *m* scandal

scanner *vt* scan

scanneur *m* scanner; ∼ **de prix** price scanner

sceau *m* seal; ∼ **d'approbation** seal of approval; ∼ **légal** company seal

scellé, e *adj* sealed

scellés *m pl* seals; **sous** ∼ under seals; **apposer les** ∼ affix seals

schéma *m* (dessin) diagram; (points principaux) outline; (d'un projet) plan, outline; ∼ **d'activité économique** pattern of economic activity; ∼ **de consommation** consumption pattern; ∼ **de la demande** demand pattern; ∼ **directeur** development plan

schématique *adj* (de schéma) schematic; (simpifié) simplistic

sciences *f pl* sciences; ∼ **économiques** economics

scinder *vt* demerge

scission *f* demerger; ∼ **d'actif** divestment

score *m* score; ∼ **bêta de portefeuille** portfolio beta score

SCRA *abrév* (▶**système de compensation et de règlement automatisé**) ACSS (Automated Clearing Settlement System)

scrutation *f* (Info) scanning

scrutin *m* poll; (vote) ballot; **par voie de** ∼ by ballot; **premier tour de** ∼ first ballot; ∼ **secret** secret ballot

SCS *abrév* (▶**société en commandite simple**) limited partnership

séance *f* (parlementaire) assembly, session; (en publicité, de photos) shoot; **être en** ∼ be in session; (Pol) sit; **en début/fin de** ∼ (Bourse) at the opening/close of trading; ∼ **de bourse** trading session; ∼ **de clôture** closing session; ∼ **extraordinaire** extraordinary meeting; ∼ **d'information** briefing, briefing session; ∼ **de négociation** trading session; ∼ **plénière** plenary session; ∼ **des questions** (parlement) (parliamentary) question time UK; ∼ **de travail** working session, workshop

seau *m* pail

sécheresse *f* drought

second¹, e *adj* second; ∼ **marché** unlisted securities market UK, second market

second² *m* (adjoint) second in command; (marine) chief mate, first mate

secondaire *adj* (de moindre importance) minor, secondary; (école, enseignement) secondary

seconder *vt* assist

secouer *vt* shake up

secourir *vt* help

secours *m* help, assistance; **de** ∼ backup, standby; **les** ∼ (secouristes) rescue team; ∼ **d'urgence** first aid; **les premiers** ∼ first aid

secousse *f* (émotion) shock; ∼ **sur l'offre** supply-side shock

secret¹, -ète *adj* secret

secret² *m* (ce qui est caché) secret; (discrétion) secrecy; ∼ **commercial** trade secret; ∼ **professionnel** professional secrecy

secrétaire *mf* secretary; ∼ **de direction** personal assistant; ∼ **d'État** minister, Secretary of State UK; ∼ **général** (d'une société) general secretary; ∼ **par intérim** temporary secretary, temp; ∼ **privé** private secretary; ∼ **de rédaction** copy editor; (presse) chief sub-editor

secrétariat *m* secretary's office; (gouvernement) secretariat; **poste de** ∼ secretarial job; ∼ **d'État** State Secretariat

secteur *m* area, zone; (de représentation) territory, patch (infrml), sector; (de recherche) field; (d'activité) industry, sector; (Info) cluster, sector; **du** ∼ **privé** private-sector; ∼ **agricole** agricultural sector; ∼ **bancaire** banking industry; ∼ **de croissance** growth area, growth sector; ∼ **défectueux** (Info) bad sector; ∼ **électrique** electricity sector; ∼ **exportateur** export sector; ∼ **exposé** exposed sector; ∼ **financier** financial sector; ∼ **à fort coût de main-d'œuvre** labour-intensive industry BrE, labor-intensive industry AmE; ∼ **industriel** industrial sector; ∼ **des investissements** investment business; ∼ **nationalisé** nationalized sector; ∼ **primaire** primary sector; **le** ∼ **privé** the

private sector; ∼ **de production**
manufacturing sector; ∼ **public** public
sector; ∼ **du représentant** (publicité) agent's
territory; ∼ **à risque** exposed sector; ∼ **de
la santé** health care industry; ∼
secondaire secondary *ou* manufacturing
sector; ∼ **des services** service sector; ∼
tertiaire services, tertiary sector, service
industry; ∼ **de vente** sales area

section *f* (division) unit, department; (Admin)
section; (d'une organisation, d'un parti, d'un syndicat)
branch; (Media) section; (coupe) section; ∼
économie (presse) economic section; ∼
d'investissement (collectivités locales) capital
fund; ∼ **juridique** legal section; ∼
syndicale agency shop

sectoriel, -elle *adj* sectoral

sectorisation *f* divisionalization; ∼
logicielle soft sectoring

sectoriser *vt* sector, divide into sectors

Sécu *abrév* France (infrml) (▸**Sécurité
sociale**) *French national health and pensions
organization*, ≈ National Health Service UK

sécurisé, e *adj* (paiement, serveur) secure;
transaction ∼e (Info) secure transaction

sécurité *f* (contre les agressions) security;
(contre les accidents) safety; ∼ **de l'emploi** job
security; ∼ **informatique** computer
security; ∼ **routière** road safety; ∼ **sociale**
*French national health and pensions
organization*, ≈ National Health Service UK

segment *m* segment; ∼ **démographique/
géographique** demographic/geographic
segment; ∼ **de base** root segment; ∼ **ciblé**
target segment; ∼ **du marché** market
segment

segmentation *f* segmentation; (marketing)
clustering; ∼ **du marché** market
segmentation

segmenter *vt* (marché) segment

ségrégation *f* segregation; ∼
professionnelle occupational segregation

sélection *f* (action) selection; (choix) choice,
selection; **faire une première ∼** draw up a
shortlist; ∼ **adverse** adverse selection; ∼
aléatoire random selection; ∼ **de
portefeuille** portfolio selection

sélectionné, e *adj* selected; **être ∼ pour**
(avancement) be selected for

sélectionner *vt* (selon des critères) screen,
shortlist; (choisir) select; (Info) (mot, texte)
highlight

self-service *m* (restaurant) self-service; (sur
Internet) self-service economy

sellette *f* **sur la ∼** in the hot seat

selon *prép* according to; (normes, règlement) in
accordance with; ∼ **le calendrier** according
to schedule; ∼ **l'estimation la plus basse** at
the lowest estimate; ∼ **l'estimation la plus
élevée** at the highest estimate; ∼ **l'horaire**
according to schedule; ∼ **la loi** by law, by
statute; ∼ **la norme** according to the norm;

∼ **les normes de la compagnie** by the
company's standards; ∼ **le planning** as
scheduled, according to schedule; ∼ **le
programme** according to schedule; ∼ **les
termes du contrat** under the terms of the
contract

SEM *abrév* (▸**société à économie mixte**)
partially-privatized company, semi-public
company

semaine *f* week; **dans deux ∼s** in a
fortnight; **dans une ∼** within a week; **en ∼**
on weekdays, during the week; **une ∼ à
l'avance** a week in advance; ∼
commerciale trade week; ∼ **garantie**
guaranteed week; ∼ **record** (Bourse) bull
week; ∼ **de travail** working week BrE,
workweek AmE

semblable *adj* similar

semer *vt* (confusion, désordre) spread; ∼ **la
pagaille** wreak havoc, cause chaos

semestre *m* half year, six-monthly period

semestriel, -elle *adj* (dividende) half-yearly,
semiannual

semestriellement *adv* half-yearly

semi-conducteur *m* semiconductor

semi-durable *adj* semidurable

semi-fini, e *adj* semifinished

semi-industrialisé, e *adj* semi-
industrialized

séminaire *m* seminar

semi-remorque *m* (camion) articulated
lorry

sénat *m* senate

sens *m* (direction) way, direction; (d'un mot)
meaning; (intuition) sense; ∼ **des affaires**
business sense; ∼ **du commerce**
commercial acumen; ∼ **des
responsabilités** sense of responsibility

sensibilisation *f* awareness; **campagne
de ∼** awareness campaign

sensibiliser *vt* make aware; ∼ **le public à
un problème** increase public awareness of an
issue

sensibilité *f* awareness, sensitivity; ∼ **aux
coûts** cost awareness; ∼ **aux taux
d'intérêt** interest rate sensitivity

sensible *adj* sensitive (à to); (Info) (image,
zone) clickable; ∼ **au coût** (client) cost-
sensitive; ∼ **au marché** market-sensitive; ∼
aux prix price-sensitive

sentence *f* (décision) sentence; ∼ **arbitrale**
arbitral award; ∼ **arbitrale de protection**
protective award

sentier *m* path; ∼ **de croissance** growth
path

sentiment *m* feeling; ∼ **de bien-être**
feeling of well-being; (Pol) feelgood factor

SEO *abrév* (▸**sauf erreur ou omission**)
E&OE (errors and omissions excepted)

séparateur *m* (Info) separator; (de feuilles)
burster

S

séparation *f* (de la terre) severance; ~ **de biens** (Droit) matrimonial division of property; ~ **de corps/judiciaire** judicial separation; ~ **de fait** (Droit) de facto separation

séparé, e *adj* (distinct) separate

séparément *adv* separately

séquence *f* sequence; ~ **de classement** collating sequence; ~ **d'échappement** escape sequence; ~ **de touches** key sequence

séquentiel, -elle *adj* sequential

séquestration *f* sequestration

séquestre *m* sequestration; ~ **judiciaire** writ of sequestration

séquestrer *vt* (biens) sequester

série *f* (suite) series; (collection) set; (TV) series; (Info) set; **de** ~ standard model; (voiture) production model; **en** ~ (Info) serial; **fabriqué en** ~ mass-produced; **numéro de** ~ serial number; ~ **limitée** limited edition; **production en** ~ mass production; **numéro hors** ~ special issue; **par** ~**s de** in sets of; ~ **chronologique** seasonal variations; ~ **économique de fabrication** economic manufacturing quantity; ~ **de mesures** set *ou* series of measures; ~ **de négociations salariales** pay round, wage round; ~ **d'options** (Bourse) option series, series of options; ~ **de produits** product line

sériel, -elle *adj* serial

serment *m* oath; **déclarer sous** ~ swear on oath

serpent *m* snake; ~ **monétaire** (européen) (UE) snake

serré, e *adj* (délais, budget) tight; (contrôle, gestion) strict; (négociations) heated; (étude, analyse) close

serv. *abrév* (▸**service**) dept. (department)

serveur *m* (Info) server; ~ **de courrier électronique** email server; ~ **de fichiers** file server; ~ **télématique** bulletin board service, online data service

service *m* (section) department; (faveur) favour BrE, favor AmE; (d'une dette) servicing; (Info) service; **être au** ~ **de la société** serve the company; **être de** ~ be on duty; **pour** ~**s rendus** for services rendered;

service a...   ~**s accessoires** ancillary services; ~ **d'accueil** front-of-house jobs; ~ **des achats** procurement department, purchasing department; ~ **administratif** administration, administrative service; ~**s des administrations publiques** general government services; ~ **annuel de la dette** annual debt service UK; ~ **d'appel gratuit** Freefone number BrE, toll-free number AmE; ~ **d'appoint** (navigation) backup service; ~ **après-vente** after-sales service; ~**s d'assistance sociale** welfare department; ~ **d'assistance technique par téléphone** technical support hotline; ~ **assuré** manned

service; ~ **d'astreinte** standby duty; ~ **d'audit** auditing department; ~**s auxiliaires** ancillary operations;

b...   ~**s bancaires** bank facilities; ~**s bancaires commerciaux** commercial banking; ~**s bancaires de détail** retail banking; ~**s bancaires aux entreprises** corporate banking; ~**s bancaires de fiducie** fiduciary banking; ~**s bancaires de gros** wholesale banking; ~**s bancaires aux particuliers** personal banking services, private banking; ~ **bas de gamme** down-market service;

c...   ~ **de la caisse** cash department; ~ **du change** foreign exchange department; ~ **clientèle** customer services; ~ **des coffres** safe custody department; ~ **commercial** sales department; ~ **commun** joint service; ~ **de la comptabilité** accounting office, accounts department; ~ **conseil** consultancy service; ~**s de conseil** (interne) advisory services, management services; ~ **conseil au consommateur** consumer advisory service; ~ **conseil en placements** investment advisory service; ~ **du contentieux** legal department; ~ **des contributions** revenue department; ~ **de contrôle interne** compliance department; ~ **du crédit** (Banque) credit department; (Fin) loan department;

d...   ~ **de dépôt** deposit facility; ~ **de la dette** debt service; ~ **de la dette publique** public debt service; ~**s de direction** management services; ~ **de distribution** distribution service; ~ **de documentation** information service; ~ **des douanes** customs service, Customs and Excise department UK;

e...   ~**s d'état-major** management services; ~ **d'expédition** despatch department, dispatch department; ~**s d'expertise comptable** accountancy services;

f...   ~ **facturation** billing department US, invoicing department; ~ **ferroviaire** railway service BrE, railroad service AmE; ~**s financiers** financial services, financial services industry; ~**s fiscaux** revenue centre BrE, revenue center AmE; ~**s fonctionnels** management services;

g...   ~**s de garde** safekeeping; ~ **de gestion** administration; ~ **de gestion de portefeuille** portfolio management service; ~ **de groupage** cargo consolidation service, joint cargo service;

h...   ~ **haut de gamme** up-market service; ~ **d'hébergement** (Info) hosting service;

i...   ~**s industriels** industrial services; ~ **informatique** computer department; ~**s en informatique** computer services; ~ **d'intendance** ancillary operations; ~ **d'investissement** investment service;

j...   ~ **juridique** legal department; ~**s**

juridiques legal services;

(l...) ~ **en ligne** online service; ~ **de livraison** delivery service; ~ **de location de voitures** car hire service; ~ **logistique** support service;

(m...) ~ **des marchandises** goods department; ~ **marketing** marketing department;

(n...) ~ **non compris** (au restaurant, à l'hôtel) service not included;

(o...) ~ **des opérations** operations department;

(p...) ~ **payant** fee-based service; ~ **personnalisé** customized service; ~ **du personnel** personnel department, human resources department; ~ **de planification** planning department; ~**s professionnels** professional services; ~ **public** public utility; ~**s publics** public service;

(r...) ~ **de rédaction** copy department; ~ **de réexpédition anonyme** (Info) remailer; ~ **des règlements** settlements department; ~ **régleur** claims department; ~ **régulier** regular service, scheduled service; ~ **des relations publiques** public relations department; ~ **de remplacement** substitute product; ~ **de renseignements** advisory service; ~ **de renseignements de la police** police intelligence; ~ **de réseau à valeur ajoutée** value-added network service; ~ **des réservations** advance booking office, reservation counter; ~ **de routage** routes section;

(s...) ~**s de santé** health care services; ~**s de sécurité** security services; ~ **des sinistres** claims department; ~ **social** welfare department; ~**s de soutien** back office;

(t...) ~ **technique** engineering and design department; ~ **des titres** securities department; ~**s de transports** travel services;

(u...) ~ **d'urgence** emergency service;

(v...) ~ **des ventes** sales department; ~ **de virement automatique** automatic transfer service UK; ~ **en vol** in-flight service; ~ **voyageurs** passenger service; ~ **24 heures sur 24** round-the-clock service, around-the-clock service AmE

servir vt serve; ~ **les intérêts** service a loan; **pour** ~ **cet objectif** in furtherance of this goal

servitude f easement, encumbrance; ~ **implicite** implied easement; ~ **touristique** scenic easement; **immeuble sans** ~ building free from encumbrance

spécialiser: se ~ **dans** v pron specialize in

session f meeting; (parlementaire) session; **la** ~ **fut levée** the meeting broke up; ~ **ininterrompue** (Bourse) twenty-four-hour trading; ~ **parlementaire d'été** summer recess UK; ~ **de travail** working session

seuil m threshold; ~ **du bien-être** bliss point; ~ **de commande** reorder point; ~ **critique** critical level; ~ **de divergence** divergence threshold; ~ **d'enregistrement** registration threshold; ~ **d'importance relative** materiality level; ~ **d'imposition minimum** tax threshold; ~ **d'intervention** support level; ~ **de pauvreté** poverty line; ~ **de réajustement** adjustment limit; ~ **de réapprovisionnement** reorder point; ~ **de rentabilité** break-even point; ~ **de rentabilité à la hausse** upside break-even point; ~ **de revenu familial** family income threshold

seul, e adj (unique) only, sole; **en un** ~ **lieu** in any one location; **à** ~**e fin de faire** with the sole object of doing; ~ **dépositaire** sole agent; ~ **inventeur** sole inventor; ~ **propriétaire** sole owner

sévère adj harsh

sexisme m sex discrimination

SGF abrév (▸**système de gestion financière**) financial management system

shipchandler m ship's chandler

SICAF abrév (▸**société d'investissement à capital fermé ou fixe**) CEIC (closed-end investment company)

SICAV abrév (▸**société d'investissement à capital variable**) OEIC (open-end investment company), unit trust BrE, mutual fund AmE; ~ **éthique** ethical unit trust; ~ **en mines d'or** gold mutual fund; ~ **monétaire** money market fund; ~ **à plus-value maximum** maximum capital gains mutual fund

siège m (à la Chambre) seat; (d'entreprise) head office, registered office; (d'organisation) headquarters; **une entreprise dont le** ~ **est à Toronto** a Toronto-based company, a company with its head office in Toronto; ~ **bancaire** bank address; ~ **social** (d'un parti) headquarters; (d'une société) head office, registered office; ~ **à suspension** suspension seat

siéger vi (à la Chambre) sit; (tenir séance) be in session

SIG abrév (▸**système intégré de gestion**) MIS (management information system)

sigle m acronym

signal m signal; ~ **d'alarme** alarm signal, warning indicator; ~ **d'appel** (au téléphone) call-waiting service; ~ **d'arrêt** stop signal; ~ **de baisse** bearish signal information; ~ **de hausse** bullish signal information; ~ **sonore** beep; ~ **technique** technical sign

signalement m description

signaler vt (faire savoir) inform; (indiquer) indicate; **rien à** ~ nothing to report; (Info) flag

signataire mf (d'un contrat, d'un traité) signatory; **être** ~ **de** be a signatory to; ~ **autorisé** signing officer

signature f signature; ∼ **pour acceptation** signing and accounting; **avoir la** ∼ be authorized to sign; **pour** ∼ for signature; ∼ **collective** joint signature; ∼ **des contrats** exchange of contracts; ∼ **électronique** digital signature; ∼ **en fac-similé** facsimile signature; ∼ **non authentifiée** unauthenticated signature; ∼ **sans réserve** clean signature; ∼ **témoin** specimen signature; ∼ **d'une vente** completion of sale

signe m signal; (indication) sign; ∼ **de référence** reference sign

signé, e adj signed; **non** ∼ unsigned

signer vt (accord) sign; **à** ∼ for signature; ∼ **un contrat légal** sign a legal agreement; ∼ **les contrats** exchange contracts; ∼ **à la sortie** book out; ∼ **sur les pointillés** sign on the dotted line

significatif, -ive adj (recul, rôle, changement, conséquences) significant

signification f (portée) importance, significance; (Droit) notification; ∼ **statistique** statistical significance

signifier vt stand for; (indiquer) signify; (arrêt) notify; (avis) serve; ∼ **un acte judiciaire à qn** issue a writ against sb; ∼ **une assignation** enter a writ; ∼ **un avis contraire** serve counternotice

silo m silo; ∼ **à céréales** grain silo

SIM abrév (▸**système d'information de management**) MIS (management information system)

similitude f similarity

simplification f simplification; ∼ **des tâches** job simplification, work simplification

simplifié, e adj simplified

simplifier vt (instructions, mode opératoire) simplify; ∼ **les choses** simplify matters

simulation f simulation; ∼ **de gestion** management game; ∼ **par** or **sur ordinateur** computer simulation

simulé m computer simulation

simuler vt simulate

simultané¹, e adj simultaneous; (Info) full-duplex; **en** ∼ simultaneously

simultané² m simultaneous broadcast, simulcast

simultanées f pl (Fisc) concurrent returns

sinécure f sinecure

sinistre m (catastrophe) disaster; (perte) loss; (incendie) fire; (accident) accident; (dégâts) damage; (procédure) claim; ∼ **d'assurance** insurance claim; ∼ **au comptant** cash loss; ∼ **partiel** partial loss; ∼ **payé** or **réglé** claim paid; ∼ **tardif** belated claim

sinistré, e m,f disaster victim; (Assur) claimant

sis, e adj (juridique) located

site m site; (Info) site, website; **hors** ∼ off-site; **sur** ∼ in-house; ∼ **contaminé** contaminated site; ∼ **de décharge** dump site, landfill; ∼ **de décharge contrôlée** landfill site; ∼ **industriel** industrial estate BrE, industrial park AmE; ∼ **marchand** e-commerce site, retail site; ∼ **miroir** (Info) mirror site; ∼ **perso** (infrml) personal website; ∼ **de premier choix** (surtout en logement individuel) prime site; ∼ **touristique** tourist attraction; ∼ **vedette** (magasin, salle d'exposition, garage, hôtel) flagship site

situation f situation; (emploi) job, position; (emplacement) location; **avoir la** ∼ **bien en main** have the situation well in hand; **avoir une** ∼ have a job; **perdre sa** ∼ lose one's job; ∼ **de la caisse et de la dette** cash and debt position; **être dans une** ∼ **financière difficile** be in financial straits; ∼ **de banque** bank statement; ∼ **de blocage** standoff; ∼ **budgétaire** budgetary position; ∼ **de caisse** cash position; ∼ **de compte** (relevé) bank statement; ∼ **de l'économie** state of the economy; ∼ **économique** economic situation; ∼ **de l'emploi** employment situation; ∼ **épineuse** sticky situation; ∼ **de famille** marital status; ∼ **financière** financial situation; (d'une entreprise) financial standing; ∼ **fiscale** tax status; ∼ **hypothétique** hypothetical situation; ∼ **juridique** juridical position, legal standing; ∼ **nette** (Bourse) shareholders' equity; (Fin) net position; ∼ **nette du gouvernement** general government net worth; ∼ **politique** political situation; ∼ **à terme** forward position; ∼ **de trésorerie** cash position; (relevé) cash flow statement

situé, e adj located

situer vt (dans l'espace) locate; (dans le temps) place

slogan m (publicitaire) slogan, tagline; ∼ **publicitaire** advertising slogan, catch line

SM abrév (▸**système métrique**) metric system

SME abrév (▸**Système monétaire européen**) EMS (European Monetary System)

SMIC abrév (▸**salaire minimum inter-professionnel de croissance**) index-linked minimum wage

SMIG abrév (▸**salaire minimum inter-professionnel garanti**) guaranteed minimum wage, ≈ National Minimum Wage UK

SNCF abrév (▸**Société nationale des chemins de fer français**) French national railway company

social, e adj social

socialiste mf socialist

société f (communauté humaine) society; (entreprise) company, firm; **se monter en** ∼ set up in business; **fonder/constituer une** ∼ set up a company; ∼ **née d'une fusion** merger company;

⎯⎯⎯⎯⎯⎯⎯⎯⎯⎯⎯⎯⎯
(**société a...**) **la** ∼ **d'abondance** the

affluent society; ~ **absorbante** acquiring company, absorbing company; ~ **absorbée** acquired company, amalgamated company; ~ **acquise** purchased company; ~ **par actions** joint-stock company; ~ **affiliée** associate company, corporate affiliate; ~ **annexe** subsidiary company; ~ **anonyme** public limited company UK; ~ **apparentée** associate company, corporate affiliate; ~ **apporteuse** vendor company; ~ **d'assurance toutes branches** composite insurance company; ~ **d'assurances** insurance company; ~ **autoritaire** authoritarian society; ~ **auxiliaire** intermediary company;

(**b...**) ~ **de biens de grande consommation** consumer goods company; ~ **de bourse** brokerage firm, brokerage house; **Société des bourses françaises** ≈ International Stock Exchange;

(**c...**) ~ **à la campagne** greenfield site company UK; ~ **de capital-risque** venture capital company; ~ **à capital variable** open-end fund; ~ **captive** daughter company; ~ **cédante** transferor company; ~ **cessionnaire** transferee company; ~ **civile de placement immobilier** real estate investment trust US; ~ **cliente** corporate client, client firm; ~ **en commandite** limited partnership; ~ **en commandite par actions** public limited partnership; ~ **en commandite simple** limited partnership; ~ **commerciale** company, firm, trading company; ~ **commerciale de droit étranger** alien corporation; ~ **commerciale non cotée** unquoted trading company; ~ **de commercialisation des services** service provider; ~ **de compensation d'actions** options clearing corporation; ~ **concessionnaire** statutory company, consultancy firm; ~ **de conseil** consulting firm, consultancy firm; ~ **de conseil juridique** law firm; ~ **de consommation** consumer society; ~ **constituante** constituent company; ~ **constituée** incorporated company US; ~ **contrôlée par l'État** government-controlled corporation; ~ **coopérative** cooperative society; ~ **cotée en bourse** quoted company; ~ **de courtage** retail house; ~ **de crédit** finance house UK, loan company; ~ **de crédit-bail** leasing company;

(**d...**) ~ **déclarante** reporting corporation; ~ **dominante** controlling company;

(**e...**) ~ **à économie mixte** semi-public company; ~ **écran** shell company, shell corporation; ~ **émettrice** issuing company; ~ **enregistrée** incorporated company US; ~ **entièrement cotée** fully quoted company; ~ **exonérée d'impôts** tax-exempt corporation; ~ **d'exploitation en commun** joint-venture company; ~ **d'exportation** indent house;

(**f...**) ~ **de fait** de facto corporation; ~

fantôme bogus company; ~ **favorable à l'autorité** authoritarian society; ~ **fédérée** federated company; ~ **fermée** closely-held corporation; ~ **fictive** bogus company; (Fisc) shell company (jarg); ~ **de fiducie** trust company; ~ **filiale à cent pour cent** wholly-owned subsidiary; ~ **de financement** finance house UK, promotary company US; ~ **financière** financial company; ~ **financière de portefeuille** financial holding company; ~ **financière satellite** captive finance company; ~ **fondatrice** founding company;

(**g...**) la ~ **de gaspillage** the waste society; ~ **de gestion** asset management company; ~ **de gestion à capital fixe** closed-end management company UK;

(**h...**) ~ **de holding** holding company; ~ **holding bancaire** pure holding company;

(**i...**) ~ **immatriculée** registered company; ~ **immobilière** real estate company; ~ **d'import-export** import/export company, trading company; ~ **importante** big company; ~ **d'importation** trading company; ~ **imposable** taxable corporation; ~ **individuelle de portefeuille** personal holding company US; ~ **industrielle** manufacturing company; ~ **industrielle et commerciale** industrial and commercial company; ~ **industrielle de première qualité** blue-chip industrial; ~ **informatique** computer company; ~ **inscrite au registre du commerce** registered company; ~ **intégrée** integrated company; ~ **d'intérêt public** nationalized industry, public interest company; ~ **d'intérim** temping agency; ~ **intermédiaire** intermediary corporation, nominee company; ~ **d'investissement à capital fermé ou fixe** closed-end investment fund; ~ **d'investissement à capital variable** open-end investment trust; ~ **d'investissement et de crédit immobiliers** ≈ building society BrE, ≈ building and loan association AmE; ~ **d'investissement réglementée** regulated investment company; ~ **d'investissement de revenus** income investment company; ~ **d'investissement révocable** revocable trust;

(**l...**) ~ **de leasing** lease company; ~ **en logiciel** software company;

(**m...**) ~ **mandataire** agent corporation; ~ **membre** corporate member, member firm; ~ **mère** holding company; ~ **mère holding** holding company; ~ **mixte** joint venture, joint-venture company; ~ **multinationale** multinational corporation, multinational company; ~ **mutualiste** mutual corporation; ~ **mutuelle** (Assur) cooperative society, mutual benefit society; ~ **mutuelle de crédit** cooperative credit institution;

(**n...**) ~ **nationale** public corporation UK; **Société nationale des chemins de fer français** *French national railway company*; ⋯▸

~ **en nom collectif** partnership; ~ **à nombre d'actionnaires réduit** closely held corporation; ~ **non-inscrite à la cote** unlisted company; ~ **non-résidente** nonresident company;

(**p...**) ~ **en participation** joint equity venture company; ~ **pétrolière** oil company; ~ **de placement** investment company, investment firm; ~ **de placement à capital variable** open-end investment trust; ~ **plagiaire** me-too firm; ~ **point-com** dotcom; ~ **de portefeuilles** investment firm, holding company; ~ **de portefeuilles privée** private holding corporation; ~ **post-industrielle** post-industrial society; ~ **de premier ordre** blue-chip company; ~ **preneuse** purchasing company; ~ **de prêt hypothécaire** mortgage loan company; ~ **prête-nom** nominee company; ~ **de prévoyance** friendly society BrE, benefit society AmE; ~ **privée** privately-owned company; ~ **publique** public corporation UK;

(**r...**) ~ **de réassurance** reinsurance company; ~ **à responsabilité limitée** limited liability company UK, incorporated company US;

(**s...**) ~ **sans argent** cashless society; ~ **de secours mutuel** mutual benefit society; ~ **du secteur privé** private sector company; ~ **de services** service company; ~ **de services et de conseils en informatique** computer consultancy firm; ~ **de services d'ingénierie informatique** computer services company;

(**t...**) ~ **tiroir** off-the-shelf company; ~ **transnationale** transnational corporation; ~ **très fermée** closed company BrE, closed corporation AmE;

(**v...**) ~ **au vert** greenfield site company UK; ~ **vieillissante** grey society BrE, gray society AmE

société-sœur f sister company

socioculturel, -elle adj sociocultural

socio-économique adj socioeconomic

socio-professionel, -elle adj socioprofessional

SOFRES abrév (▸**Société française d'enquêtes par sondage**) French national institute for market research and opinion polls

soi pron en ~ per se

soi-disant adj so-called

soin m care; **avec** ~ carefully; ~**s** (traitement médical) treatment; **avoir/prendre** ~ **de faire** (s'appliquer) be careful to do; (s'assurer) make sure to do; **par les bons** ~**s de** through the good offices of; ~**s en clinique** private hospital treatment; ~**s gratuits** free medical treatment; ~**s et prévention** care and control; ~**s d'urgence** emergency care

sol m (terrain) soil; ~ **naturel** unspoilt land

solde m (d'un bilan, d'un compte) balance of account; (vente) sale; **faire le** ~ **d'un compte** settle an account; **à** ~ **nul** at a flat price; **'pour** ~ **de tout compte'** 'in full settlement'; **mettre des marchandises en** ~ sell goods at sale price BrE, put goods on sale AmE; ~**s** sale, clearance sale; ~ **accumulé** accumulated balance; ~ **bancaire** balance in bank; ~ **de caisse** cash balance; ~ **de caisse non dépensé** unspent cash balance; ~ **de clôture** closing balance; ~ **commercial** trade account; ~ **compensateur** compensating balance; ~ **comptable** account balance, balance of account; ~ **de compte d'attente** suspense balance; ~ **de compte bancaire** bank balance; ~ **de compte courant** current account balance BrE, checking account balance AmE; ~ **d'un compte du grand livre** ledger balance; ~ **des comptes** make-up (jarg); ~ **créditeur** balance due to creditor, credit balance; ~ **créditeur minimum** minimum balance, minimum credit balance; ~ **créditeur de votre compte** amount standing to your account; ~ **débiteur** debit balance; ~ **débiteur net des clients** customers' net debit balance; ~ **de dépôt** deposit balance; ~ **disponible** available balance; ~ **de dividende** (Bourse) final dividend; (Fin) liquidating dividend; ~ **dû** balance due; ~ **d'exploitation** operational balance; ~ **extérieur** trade balance; ~ **de facture** balance of invoice; ~ **de fin de saison** end-of-season sale; ~ **général** aggregate balance; ~ **d'hypothèque** final mortgage payment; ~ **impayé** outstanding balance; ~ **inemployé** (d'un crédit) unexpended balance; ~ **initial** opening balance; ~ **non grevé** unencumbered balance; ~ **non mouvementé** idle balance; ~ **non réclamé** unclaimed balance; ~ **non réparti** undistributed balance; ~ **d'ouverture** opening balance; ~ **quotidien à la fermeture** daily closing balance; ~ **à régler** balance due; ~ **à reporter** balance carried forward; ~ **de trésorerie** cash balance

solder **1** vt (marchandises) sell off; (compte) balance
2 **se solder par** v pron end in

soldeur, -euse m,f discount trader; (Fin) remainderman

solidaire adj (équipe, groupe) united; **se montrer** ~ **de qn** show solidarity with sb; (Droit) **un contrat** ~ a contract which is binding on all parties

solidairement adv jointly; ~ **responsable** severally liable; ~ **tenu** severally liable

solidarité f solidarity; **grève de** ~ sympathy strike

solide adj (réputation) strong; (société, personne) sound; **financièrement** ~ financially sound

solidement adv steadily

solidité f (de marché, monnaie) firmness

S

solliciter vt (entretien, avis) seek; (personne, organisation) approach; (client, électeur) canvas; **non sollicité** unsolicited

solution f (d'un problème) solution; ~ **clé en main** turnkey solution; ~ **de compromis** compromise solution; ~ **e-business** e-solution; ~ **de fortune** makeshift solution

solvabilité f (de débiteur) solvency; (de client, emprunteur) creditworthiness; **enquête de** ~ status enquiry

solvable adj (débiteur) solvent; (client, emprunteur) creditworthy

sombre adj bleak

sommaire m summary, synopsis; ~ **descriptif** executive summary; **Sommaire des facteurs d'intrant** m (Econ) Summary of Input Factors

sommation f (acte d'huissier) notice; ~ **de payer** notice to pay; ~ **de comparaître en justice** summons to appear in court

somme f (argent) sum; (quantité) amount; (total) sum total; ~ **en capital** principal sum; ~ **considérable** vast sum; ~ **de contrôle** checksum; ~ **due** amount due; ~ **exonérée** exempted sum; ~ **forfaitaire** lump sum; ~ **investie** amount invested; ~ **à investir** amount to be invested; ~ **nulle** zero sum; ~ **payable** amount payable; ~s **périodiques** periodic amounts; ~ **reportée** amount brought forward; ~ **totale** grand total, total sum; ~ **en toutes lettres** amount in full; ~ **versée** amount paid; ~s **versées** monies paid in; ~ **versée à l'avance** retainer; ~ **à verser** amount charged

sommelier, -ière m,f wine waiter

sommet m (rencontre) summit; (haut) top; ~ **économique** economic summit; ~ **de l'iceberg** tip of the iceberg; **du** ~ **à la base** top-down

son m sound

sonal m signature tune

sondage m poll, survey; ~ **aléatoire** random sampling; ~ **Gallup** (étude de marché) Gallup poll; ~ **d'opinion** (étude de marché) opinion poll, straw vote; ~ **par grappes** cluster sampling; ~ **par quota** quota sampling; ~ **par segments** (études de marché) cluster sampling; ~ **par téléphone** phone poll; ~ **en profondeur** depth polling

sonder vt (enquêter) (pour opinion) poll; (pour étude) survey; **36% de la population sondée** 36% of those polled

sonnerie f alarm; ~ **d'alarme** alarm bell

sophistication f sophistication

sophistiqué, e adj sophisticated

sorte f sort, kind; **de** ~ **que** so that

sortie f exit; (de fonds) outflow; (commercialisation) (de film, disque) release; (de livre) publication; (de collection) presentation; (de produit) launch; (Info) output; ~ **d'argent** cash outflow; ~ **de capitaux** capital outflow; ~ **de devises étrangères** foreign currency outflow; ~ **de données** data output; ~ **de fonds** cash outflow, outflow of funds; ~ **d'imprimante** print-out; ~ **imprimée** print-out; ~ **d'ordinateur** computer output; ~ **papier** hard copy; ~ **de pavillon** (navigation) flagging out; ~ **de secours** emergency exit, fire exit; ~ **de session** timeout; ~ **de trésorerie** cash outflow; ~ **usine** (livraison) ex mill

sortir [1] vt (un nouveau produit) bring out; (CD, film) release; (collection) present; (produire) turn out; (Info) output; ~ **d'affaire** bail out [2] vi (un nouveau produit) come out; (journal, périodique) be published; (Info) exit; ~ **dîner** eat out; ~ **de l'impasse** break the stalemate; ~ **du pays** flow out of the country; ~ **du tunnel** be out of the woods; ~ **de la chaîne/ des presses** come off the production line/ press

souche f (de carnet, de livret) stub, counterfoil; (Transp) passenger coupon; **par** ~ (Droit) (descente) per stirpes (frml)

souci m (soin) care, concern; **avoir des** ~s have problems; **se faire beaucoup de** ~ worry a lot; **avoir le** ~ **de la qualité** be quality-conscious; ~ **du client** customer care

soudoyer vt (infrml) bribe

soudoyeur m (infrml) intermediary in any form of political payoff or corruption

souffrance f **en** ~ (Compta) overdue, past-due; (projet, dossier) pending, awaiting attention; (colis non livré) awaiting delivery

souffrant, e adj ailing

souffrir vi suffer

soulager vt alleviate

soulever vt (question, sujet) bring up; (problème, difficulté) raise; (protestations, débats) give rise to

soulignement m (Info) underline, underscore

souligner vt (importance, situation) emphasize, underline; (Info) underline, underscore

soumettre [1] vt (pour approbation) submit; (article) contribute; (motion, proposition) propose; (opinion) deliver; ~ **à** refer to; ~ **à l'approbation** submit for approval; ~ **un différend à arbitrage** submit a dispute to arbitration; ~ **une proposition à un comité** put a suggestion before a committee [2] **se soumettre à** v pron (règlement) submit to; **se** ~ **à la loi** comply with the law

soumis, e adj subjected to; **être** ~ **à** be subjected to; ~ **à l'impôt** liable for tax, taxable; ~ **à un rabais** rebateable; ~ **aux réserves** reservable

soumission f (Fin) (achat) tender; **faire une** ~ **put up for tender, tender; **par voie de** ~ by tender; ~ **à un appel d'offres** tender; ~ **cachetée** sealed tender; ~ **concurrentielle** competitive tendering; ~ **contraignante**

···❯

binding tender; ~ **de couverture de contrat** tender to contract cover; ~ **obligatoire en vue d'adjudication** compulsory competitive tendering UK; ~ **des offres** bidding, submission of bids; ~ **ouverte** open tendering

soumissionnaire *mf* bidder; ~ **le moins disant** lowest bidder

soumissionner *vt* bid for, tender for

souple *adj* flexible

souplesse *f* adaptability, flexibility

sourçage *m* sourcing

source *f* source; **à la** ~ at source; **de** ~ **confidentielle** (presse) on lobby terms BrE, not for attribution AmE; ~ **d'emprunts** borrowing facility; ~ **d'énergie** source of energy; ~ **de financement** funding source; ~ **industrielle** industrial source; ~ **de pollution** pollution emitter; ~ **de revenus** source of income

sourceur, -euse *m,f* sourcing expert, sourcer

souriant, e *adj* (perspective) rosy

souris *f* (Info) mouse; **tapis/bouton de la** ~ mouse button/mat

sous *prép* under; ~ **l'angle de** in terms of; ~ **aucune condition** not on any terms; ~ **les auspices de** under the umbrella of; ~ **caution** on bail; ~ **forme provisoire** in draft form; ~ **forme de subvention** in grant form; ~ **forme de tableau** in tabulated form; ~ **garantie** under guarantee; ~ **la forme de** in the form of; ~ **la main** ready to hand; ~ **le pont** (navigation) below deck; ~ **pli cacheté** in a sealed envelope; ~ **pli séparé** under separate cover; ~ **réserve de** subject to; ~ **réserve d'approbation** subject to approval; ~ **réserve de changement** subject to change; ~ **réserve que** provided that; ~ **serment** under oath; ~ **60 jours** under 60 days; ~ **toutes réserves** without prejudice

sous-absorber *vt* underabsorb

sous-activité *f* subactivity

sous-affectation *f* suballotment

sous-affréter *vt* subcharter

sous-agent *m* subagent

sous-capacité *f* undercapacity

sous-chef *m* assistant manager

sous-compte *m* subsidiary account

sous-consommation *f* underconsumption

souscripteur, -trice *m,f* (Assur) policyholder; (de titres, emprunt) subscriber; ~ **d'action à découvert** uncovered writer; ~ **par complaisance** accommodation party; ~ **de soutien** standby underwriter

souscription *f* (Fin) (d'emprunt) subscription; ~ **d'un contrat d'assurance** taking out an insurance policy; ~ **à** application for; ~ **à des actions** subscription for shares; ~ **excédentaire** oversubscription; ~ **négociée** negotiated underwriting; ~

d'obligations bond underwriting; ~ **privilégiée** subscription privilege; ~ **surpassée** oversubscription

souscrire *vt* (assurance, abonnement, plan d'épargne) take out; (prêt) apply for; ~ **à** (à un accord de confidentialité des actions) subscribe to; ~ **un billet à ordre** make a promissory note; ~ **à une émission** subscribe to an issue; ~ **à un emprunt** apply for a loan, subscribe for a loan; ~ **à une police d'assurance** take out a policy

souscrit, e *adj* (Bourse) underwritten; **totalement** ~ (émission) fully distributed

sous-déclaration *f* underdeclaration

sous-développement *m* underdevelopment

sous-directeur, -trice *m,f* deputy manager

sous-effectif *m* undermanning

sous-emploi *m* underemployment

sous-employer *vt* (personnel, ressources) underemploy

sous-ensemble *m* subset

sous-entendre *vt* imply

sous-estimation *f* underestimation

sous-estimer *vt* underestimate

sous-évaluation *f* undervaluation

sous-évaluer *vt* underestimate

sous-fichier *m* subfile

sous-groupe *m* subgroup

sous-hypothèque *f* submortgage

sous-imposer *vt* undertax

sous-imposition *f* underassessment

sous-imputation *f* underabsorption; ~ **des frais généraux** underrecovery of overhead costs

sous-imputer *vt* underabsorb

sous-investissement *m* underinvestment

sous-licence *f* sublicence BrE, sublicense AmE

sous-locataire *mf* subtenant

sous-location *f* sublease, sublet

sous-officier *m* petty officer

sous-payer *vt* underpay

sous-production *f* underproduction

sous-produire *vt* underproduce

sous-produit *m* by-product

sous-programme *m* (Info) subprogram, subroutine

sous-répertoire *m* (Info) subdirectory

sous-représentation *f* (sur marché) underrepresentation

sous-représenter *vt* underrepresent

sous-rubrique *f* subentry

sous-secteur *m* subsector

soussigné, e *adj* **je** ~ **certifie que ...** I the undersigned hereby testify that ...; **je** ~ **déclare que ...** I the undersigned declare that ...

sous-titre *m* (presse) caption

sous-total *m* subtotal

soustracteur *m* subtractor; **~ de valeur** value subtractor

soustraire ⯈1 *vt* subtract
⯈2 **se soustraire à** *v pron* escape; (impôt) evade; **se ~ à la justice** abscond, escape justice

sous-traitance *f* contracting out, subcontracting

sous-traitant *m* subcontractor

sous-traiter *vt* subcontract

sous-utilisation *f* (des crédits) underrun

sous-utiliser *vt* (matériel, facilités) underuse

sous-valeur *f* negative goodwill

soutage *m* bunkering

soute *f* (navigation) bunker; **~ à bagages** (avion) belly hold; **~ permanente** (maritime) permanent bunker

soutenir *vt* (marché) hold; (pour défendre) back; (devise cours, économie) support; (prix) buy, sustain; (personne, projet, action, candidat) support, back; (comparaison) bear; (intérêt) sustain

soutenu, e *adj* (marché) buoyant; (intérêt) continuing; **~ par l'État** government-backed, government-supported

soutien *m* (financier, moral) support; (Info) support; **mesures de ~ à l'économie** measures to support the economy; **~ à l'encadrement** management support; **~ de famille** breadwinner; **~ financier** financial assistance, financial support; **~ du marché** market support; **~ des prix** pegging, price support; **~ au revenu** income support UK

soutirer *vt* **~ qch à qn** (argent) squeeze sth out of sb; **~ des renseignements à qn** wring information out of sb

souverain *m* sovereign

souveraineté *f* sovereignty; **~ du consommateur** consumer sovereignty

speaker, -erine *m,f* (radio, télévision) announcer

spécial, e *adj* special

spécialement *adv* especially

spécialisation *f* specialization; **~ des exercices** accrual accounting; **~ du poste** job specialization; **~ réussie** niche; **~ verticale** vertical specialization

spécialisé, e *adj* specialized

spécialiste *mf* specialist; **~ en débogage** (Info) troubleshooter; **~ de l'environnement** environmental expert; **~ du marché automobile** car market watcher; **~ en marketing** marketeer; **~ du matériel** hardware specialist; **~ en obligations** bond specialist; **~ des questions financières** financial expert; **~ des services de banque d'affaires** merchant banker UK, investment banker US

spécialité *f* speciality

spécification *f* specification; **~ de changement notifié** (aviation) specification change notice

spécificité *f* specificity; **~ de l'actif** asset specificity

spécifié, e *adj* specified; **personne ~e** (Fisc) specified person; **non ~ par ailleurs** not elsewhere specified, not otherwise specified

spécifier *vt* (date, heure) specify; (termes, conditions) specify, stipulate

spécifique *adj* specific; **~ à un pays** (aide) country-specific

spécimen *m* specimen copy; (presse, édition) presentation copy, press copy; **~ gratuit** complimentary copy; **~ de signature** (Banque) specimen signature

spéculateur, -trice *m,f* (Bourse) speculator; **~ à la baisse** bear speculator; **~ expérimenté** wolf (jarg); **~ habituel** trader; **~ à la hausse** bull speculator; **~ immobilier** property speculator; **~ sur la journée** scalper US (infrml); **~ en obligations** bond trader

spéculatif, -ive *adj* speculative

spéculation *f* (prix des actions) speculation; **~ à la baisse** bear speculation; **~ à la hausse** bull speculation; **~ à la journée** day trading

spéculer *vi* speculate; **~ à la baisse** bear, go a bear; **~ au comptant** bargain for cash; **~ à la hausse** bull, go a bull; **~ à terme** bargain for account

sphère *f* sphere; **~ d'activité/d'influence** sphere of activity/influence

spirale *f* spiral; **~ ascendante** upward spiral; **~ descendante** downward spiral; **~ inflationniste** spiralling inflation, inflationary spiral; **~ des salaires et des prix** wage-price spiral

spiritueux *m* spirit; **les ~** spirits, wet stock

sponsor *m* sponsor

sponsoring *m* sponsorship

sponsorisation *f* sponsorship

sponsoriser *vt* sponsor

spontané, e *adj* on spec (infrml), on speculation

spooling *m* (Info) spooling; **faire un ~** spool

sporadique *adj* sporadic

spot *m* (publicité) commercial; **~ publicitaire** advert, commercial; **~ radio/télévisé** radio/TV commercial

spouling *m* (Info) spooling

spread *m* (Bourse) spread; **~ baissier** bear spread, bearish spread; **~ calendaire** calendar spread; **~ haussier** bull spread, bullish spread; **~ vertical** price spread, vertical spread

SS *abrév* France (⯈**Sécurité sociale**) ≈ NHS UK (National Health Service)

S

SSCI *abrév* (▶**société de services et de conseils en informatique**) computer consultancy firm

SSII *abrév* (▶**société de services d'ingénierie informatique**) computer services company

stabilisation *f* stabilization; ~ **des prix** price stabilization

stabiliser ⬚1 *vt* (prix, marché, monnaie) stabilize
⬚2 **se stabiliser** *v pron* (tendance, graphique) flatten out; (prix, marché, chômage, taux) stabilize

stabilité *f* (d'un navire) stability; ~ **des prix** price stability

stable *adj* stable

stade *m* stage; **au ~ des épreuves** at proof stage

stage *m* (de formation) vocational training; (sur un lien de travail) work placement; **faire un ~ go** on a course; ~ **d'accueil** induction course; ~ **de direction d'entreprise** management training course; ~ **en entreprise** company placement, attachment; ~ **de formation sur le lieu de travail** in-service training; ~ **d'initiation** introductory course, induction course; ~ **de perfectionnement** advanced training course; ~ **de recyclage** retraining course; ~ **à temps complet** residential course

stagflation *f* stagflation

stagiaire *mf* trainee

stagnant, e *adj* stagnant

stagnation *f* stagnation

stagner *vi* stagnate

stand *m* (dans une foire, une exposition) stand

standard¹ *adj* (modèle) standard

standard² *m* standard; ~ **budgétaire** budget standard; ~ **d'égalité** equality standard; ~ **téléphonique** switchboard

standardisation *f* standardization

standardiser *vt* standardize

standardiste *mf* switchboard operator

standing *m* standard of living; **de (grand) ~** (appartement) luxury

starie *f* (maritime) layday

start-up *f* start-up

station *f* (de métro, de radio) station; (lieu de séjour) resort; ~ **balnéaire** seaside resort; ~ **d'épuration** purification plant; ~ **d'épuration des eaux usées** sewage treatment plant; ~ **de montagne** mountain resort; ~ **de taxis** taxi rank, taxi stand AmE; ~ **de traitement des déchets** waste treatment plant; ~ **de travail** workstation

stationnaire *adj* stationary, static

stationnement *m* car parking

station-service *f* petrol station BrE, gas station AmE

statique *adj* static

statisticien, -enne *m,f* statistician

statistique¹ *adj* statistical

statistique² *f* statistics; ~**s de banc d'essai** benchmark statistics; ~**s du chômage** unemployment statistics; **statistiques du commerce extérieur** foreign trade statistics; ~**s commerciales** trade returns; ~ **démographique** population statistics; ~**s de l'emploi** employment figures; ~**s non paramétriques** nonparametric statistics; ~**s officielles** official statistics, statistical returns; ~**s portuaires** port statistics; ~**s de publicité** advertising statistics; ~**s sur les ventes** sales returns

stature *f* (envergure) calibre BrE, caliber AmE

statut *m* status; (Info) status; ~ **de cadre** staff status; ~ **d'entreprise** corporate status UK; ~ **fiduciaire** trustee status; ~ **fiscal** tax status; ~ **des immigrés** migrant status; ~ **légal** legal status; ~ **socio-économique** socioeconomic status; ~ **temporaire** temporary status

statutaire *adj* statutory; **non ~** nonstatutory

statuts *m pl* (société à responsabilité limitée) articles of association; (société commerciale) articles of incorporation; ~ **et règlements** rules and regulations

Sté *abrév* (▶**société**) Co. (company)

stellage *m* put and call option

sténo *abrév* (infrml) (▶**sténographie**) shorthand, stenography

sténodactylo *mf* shorthand typist

sténographie *f* shorthand, stenography

stérile *adj* (discussion, travail) fruitless

stérilisation *f* sterilization

steward *m* flight attendant, steward

stimulant¹, e *adj* stimulating

stimulant² *m* booster; ~ **compétitif** (V&M) competitive stimulus; ~ **salarial** wage incentive

stimulation *f* stimulation; ~ **financière** financial incentive

stimuler *vt* (confiance, demande) stimulate; (efficacité) boost; ~ **les exportations** be a stimulus for exports

stipulation *f* (Droit) stipulation; (Assur) provision; ~**s d'un contrat** contract specifications; ~ **dérogatoire** derogatory stipulation

stipuler *vt* (condition) stipulate; (dans un acte, un contrat) lay down

stock *m* (en magasin) stock; **avoir qch en ~** have sth in stock; ~ **de base** baseload; ~ **comptable** book inventory; ~ **conjoncturel** cyclical stock; ~ **en cours** current stock; ~ **au début de l'exercice** opening inventory; ~ **de dépannage** safety bank; ~ **disponible** stock in hand; ~**s existants** goods on hand; ~ **de fabrication** manufacturing inventory; ~ **fermé** closed stock; ~ **en fin d'exercice** closing stock; ~ **de marchandises** merchandise inventory;

∼s marchands commercial stocks;
∼-option stock option, share option; **∼ outil** base stock; **∼ de précaution** safety stock; **∼ principal** staple stock; **∼ réel** actual stock BrE, actual inventory AmE; **∼ de régularisation** buffer stock; **∼ régulateur** buffer stock; **∼s reportés** carry-over stocks; **∼ de sécurité** safety stock; **∼ volé** hot stock (infml)

stockage m stocking; (accumulation excessive) stockpiling; (Info) storage; **unité/capacité de ∼** storage device/capacity; **∼ des archives** archive storage; **∼ commercial** commercial storage; **∼ de données** data storage; **∼ d'informations** information storage; **∼ en vrac** bulk storage

stocker vt stock; (à l'excès) stockpile; (Info) store

stockiste mf stockist UK, dealer US; **∼ attitré** appointed stockist ou dealer

store m awning

strangle m (Bourse) strangle; **∼ sur option à delta neutre** delta-neutral strangle

stratagème m scheme; **∼ frauduleux** (fraude fiscale) scheme

strate f stratum; **∼ de marché** market segment

stratège m strategist

stratégie f strategy; **∼ des affaires** business strategy; **∼ d'arbitrage inversée** reverse conversion; **∼ de bas prix** (marketing) penetration pricing; **∼ des cadres** executive manpower strategy; **∼ commerciale** business strategy; **∼ de communication** communication strategy; (publicité) copy strategy; **∼ concurrentielle** competitive strategy; **∼ de couverture** hedging strategy; **∼ de création** (publicité) creative strategy; **∼ de croissance** expansion strategy; **∼ de défense** defensive strategy; **∼ de différenciation** differentiation strategy UK; **∼ de diversification** diversification strategy; **∼ d'écart sur livraisons** interdelivery spread; **∼ d'écart sur matières premières** intercommodity spread; **∼ économique** economic strategy; **∼ économique de rechange** alternative economic strategy; **∼ d'ensemble** global strategy; **∼ d'entreprise** business strategy; **∼ d'expansion** expansion strategy; **∼ d'exploitation** operating strategy; **∼ de groupe** corporate strategy; **∼ d'imitation** me-too strategy; **∼ de marché** marketing strategy; **∼ de marque** brand strategy; **∼ de négociation** negotiation strategy; **∼ de participation** profit-taking strategy; **∼ de produit** product strategy; **∼ de profit** profit strategy; **∼ promotionnelle** promotional strategy; **∼ publicitaire** advertising tactics; **∼ réactive** reactive strategy; **∼ sectorielle** sectoral strategy; **∼ de segmentation** segmentation strategy UK; **∼ de survie** survival strategy

stratégique adj strategic

stratification f stratification; **∼ sociale** social stratification

structuration f structuring

structure f structure; **∼ arborescente** (Info) tree structure; **∼ d'autorité** authority structure; **∼ du capital** capital structure; **∼ commerciale** business organization; **∼ du conteneur** container frame; **∼ des coûts** cost structure; **∼ des crédits** vote structure; **∼ de données** data structure; **∼ de l'entreprise** company structure, corporate structure; **∼ fonctionnelle** line function; **∼ de gestion** management structure; **∼ hiérarchique** line organization; **∼ matricielle** matrix organization; **∼ organisationnelle** organization(al) structure

structuré, e adj structured; **non ∼** unstructured

structurer vt structure

studio m studio; **∼ de création** design studio

stupéfiant, e adj staggering

style m style; **de ∼ occidental** western-style; **∼ de direction** managerial style; **∼ de l'entreprise** house style; **∼ de gestion** management style; **∼ de vie** lifestyle

stylique f design

styliser vt stylize

styliste mf stylist

stylo m pen; **∼ à bille** ball point; **∼ optique** bar code reader

subalterne mf junior

subdivisé, e adj subdivided

subdivision f subdivision

subir vt (dommage) suffer; (dégâts, défaite) sustain, suffer; (transformations) undergo; **∼ une perte** take a loss; suffer loss; **∼ un préjudice** suffer loss; **∼ la pression de** come under pressure from; **∼ les effets de la concurrence/récession** be affected by competition/the recession

subjectif, -ive adj subjective

subordonné¹, e adj (dans une hiérarchie) subordinate

subordonné², e m,f (employé) subordinate

subordonner vt subordinate

subside m (de l'État, d'une association) grant; **∼s** (Bourse) subsidiary dividends

subsidiaire adj subsidiary

subsidiarité f subsidiarity

subsistance f subsistence; **moyens de ∼** means of support

substance f substance; **∼ biodégradable** biodegradable substance; **∼ radioactive** radioactive substance; **∼ toxique** dangerous substance, toxic substance

substantiellement adv substantially

substituer vt substitute; **∼ une chose à une autre** substitute one thing for another

S

substitut *m* substitute

substitution *f* substitution; ~ **d'importation** import substitution

subterfuge *m* ploy; ~ **fiscal** tax ploy

subvenir *vi* ~ **aux besoins de** meet the needs of, provide for

subvention *f* grant, subsidy; ~ **à l'agriculture** agricultural subsidy; ~ **de contrepartie** matching grant; ~ **corrective** corrective subsidy; ~ **démographique** demogrant; ~ **de l'État** government grant, state subsidy; ~ **d'exploitation** operating subsidy; ~ **à l'exportation** export subsidy; ~ **financière** grant-in-aid, proportionate grant; ~ **d'investissement** investment grant; ~ **proportionnelle** grant-in-aid, proportionate grant; ~ **pour la recherche** research grant; ~ **remboursable sous condition** forgivable loan; ~ **des salaires** wage subsidy; ~ **sans condition** unconditional grant; ~ **de soutien** sustaining grant; ~ **de soutien de taux** rate support grant UK

subventionné, e *adj* subsidized; **non ~** unsubsidized; ~ **par l'État** state-subsidized, state-aided

subventionnement *m* subsidization, featherbedding

subventionner *vt* (entreprise) subsidize, aid

succédané *m* ersatz, substitute product

succéder *vi* ~ **à** take over from

succès *m* success; **avoir du ~ de** be successful; **avec ~** successfully; ~ **d'estime** (théâtre) critical success; ~ **ininterrompu** continued success; ~ **de librairie** best seller

successeur *m* successor

successif, -ive *adj* consecutive, successive

succession *f* (série, suite) succession; (de patrimoine) inheritance, estate; (de biens) succession; **prendre la ~ de** succeed; ~ **ab intestat** intestacy; ~**s consécutives** quick successions; ~ **d'utilisation des sols** land-use succession; ~ **vacante** estate in abeyance

successivement *adv* successively

succursale *f* branch office; (d'une banque) agency, branch; **magasin à ~s multiples** chain store, multiple; ~ **bancaire** bank branch; ~ **à l'étranger** foreign branch; ~ **extraterritoriale** offshore banking unit; ~ **principale** main branch

sucre *m* sucre

suffisamment *adv* sufficiently; ~ **financé** adequately funded

suffisant, e *adj* adequate, sufficient

suffrage *m* (système) suffrage; (voix) vote; ~ **universel** universal suffrage

suggestion *f* suggestion; **faire une ~** make a suggestion

suite *f* (résultat) result; **les ~s** (d'un acte, d'une décision) consequences; (d'affaire, d'incident) repercussions; ~ **rapide** quick succession; ~

à in response to; **à la ~ de** in the wake of; ~ **à votre demande** with reference to your inquiry; **donner ~ à** (demande) follow up; (décision) act on; **faire ~ à** (lettre) act upon; ~ **à votre appel** further to your telephone call; ~ **à votre lettre** further to your letter, with reference to your letter; **prendre la ~ de qn** take over from sb

suivant¹, e *adj* following

suivant² *prép* (selon) according to; (en fonction de) depending on; ~ **avis de** as per advice from; ~ **l'ordre indiqué** in the order specified; ~ **relevé** as per statement

suivi *m* (de procédure, des dépenses) monitoring; (de commande) follow-up, tracking; **assurer le ~ d'un produit** ensure a continuous supply of a product; **faire le ~ de** (commandes) track; ~ **d'enquêtes** research survey; ~ **d'études de marché** research survey; ~ **de marché** middle office; ~ **de la production** progress control

suivisme *m* conformity; (Bourse) tailgating

suivre *vt* (se situer après) follow; (procédure, dépenses) monitor; (commande) track, follow up on; (progrès, procès, événements) follow; (conseil, règlement, exemple) follow; **à ~** continued, matters to be followed up; **comme suite à** as follows; ~ **le développement de quelque chose** keep track of sth; **faire ~** forward; **faire ~ son courrier** have one's mail forwarded; ~ **les fortunes** follow the fortunes; ~ **un modèle similaire** follow a similar pattern; ~ **le mouvement** go with the flow; ~ **la trace de** trace; ~ **la voie de** follow the path of

sujet¹, -ette *adj* ~ **à** liable to, subject to; ~ **à la casse** subject to breakage; ~ **à controverse** controversial; ~ **à discussion** open to debate

sujet² *m* matter; (de discours, d'exposition) subject; (problème) issue; **au ~ de** about, regarding, with reference to; ~ **doué** high achiever; ~ **peu doué** low achiever

super *m* (essence) four-star petrol BrE, premium-grade gasoline AmE; ~ **ordinateur** supercomputer

superbénéfice *m* surplus profit

supercarburant *m* four-star petrol BrE, premium-grade gasoline AmE

supercommission *f* overriding commission

superdividende *fm* surplus dividend

superficie *f* surface area; ~ **cultivée** cultivated area

superflu, e *adj* (inutile) unnecessary, unwanted; (de trop) superfluous

supérieur¹, e *adj* (employé) senior; ~ **à** above; **être ~ à** rank above; ~ **à la moyenne** above-average

supérieur², e *m,f* (chef) superior; **mon ~ hiérarchique** my immediate superior

supermarché *m* supermarket; ~ **de**

produits financiers financial supermarket; ∼ **à succursales multiples** supermarket chain UK

superpétrolier *m* supertanker

superpuissance *f* superpower

superstructure *f* superstructure

superviseur *m* supervisor; ∼ **de premier niveau** line supervisor

supplanter *vt* (personne) supersede

suppléant, e *m,f* replacement; (de juge) deputy

suppléer *vt* (temporairement) stand in for, deputize for; (définitivement) replace

supplément *m* extra; (paiement) additional charge, extra charge; (en voyage, à l'hôtel) supplement; (Transp) excess fare; **en** ∼ extra; ∼ **couleur** (presse) colour supplement BrE, color supplement AmE; ∼ **pour excédent de bagages** excess baggage charge; ∼ **d'impôt** additional tax; ∼ **publicitaire** advertising supplement; ∼ **de revenu garanti** guaranteed income supplement; ∼ **de salaire** additional pay

supplémentaire *adj* additional, extra; **accorder un délai** ∼ grant an extension of the deadline; **heures** ∼**s** overtime

support *m* (radio, TV) medium; ∼ **audiovisuel** audiovisual aid; ∼ **client** customer support; ∼ **papier** hard copy; ∼ **pédagogique** teaching aid; ∼ **publicitaire** advertising medium; ∼ **de stockage** storage medium; ∼ **supplémentaire** backup support; ∼ **technique** technical support; ∼ **visuel** visual aid

supporter *vt* (dépenses, frais, responsabilité) bear; ∼ **les conséquences** (de ses actions) suffer the consequences; ∼ **le coût de** bear the cost of; ∼ **les frais généraux** absorb overheads; ∼ **une perte** stand a loss; ∼ **des pertes** sustain losses

supports *m pl* media; ∼ **de communication** communication media; ∼ **comptables** accounting papers; ∼ **publicitaires** advertising media; ∼ **visuels** visuals

supposition *f* assumption; ∼ **éclairée** educated guess

suppression *f* (d'un impôt, d'une taxe) abolition; (d'un mot, d'une ligne) deletion; (de restrictions) lifting; (de monopole) breaking; (du chômage) elimination; ∼ **des barrières douanières** abolition of trade controls; ∼ **de la double imposition** double taxation relief; ∼ **d'emplois** job cuts, redundancies; ∼ **progressive** phasing out

supprimer *vt* (emploi) cut; (mot, ligne) delete; (impôt) abolish; (restrictions) lift; (chômage) eliminate; (aide, crédit) stop; (effet, cause) remove; ∼ **progressivement** phase out

supra *adv* supra

supranational, e *adj* supranational

suprématie *f* supremacy (**sur** over); ∼ **du**

droit rule of law

sur *prép* above

sûr, e *adj* (investissement, jugement) sound; (information, personne) reliable; (sans danger) safe; (garanti) certain; (convaincu) sure

surabondance *f* overabundance; ∼ **de l'offre** oversupply; ∼ **de personnel** overstaffing; ∼ **de pétrole** oil glut

suraccumulation *f* overaccumulation

suracheté, e *adj* overbought

suractivé, e *adj* overstimulated

suramélioration *f* overimprovement

surapprentissage *m* overlearning

surassuré, e *adj* overinsured

surbaissé, e *adj* slim-line

surbooké, e *adj* (transports aériens) overbooked

surcapacité *f* excess capacity, overcapacity

surcharge *f* (de véhicule) overloading; (excédent de poids) overload, excess load; (argent) penalty; (Compta) alteration, amendment; **en** ∼ (véhicule) overloaded; **ni** ∼**, ni rature** no addition, no correction; ∼ **de frais** extra expenses; ∼ **de travail** extra load of work; ∼ **sensorielle** sensory overload

surchauffe *f* overheating

surchauffeur *m* superheater

surcommission *f* overriding commission

surconsolidation *f* overfunding

surconsommation *f* overconsumption

surcoût *m* additional cost

surcroît *m* increase; ∼ **de travail** extra work; ∼ **de capacité** spare capacity

surdépendance *f* overdependence

surdoué, e *m,f* overachiever; ∼ **de l'informatique** computer wizard

sureffectif *m* overmanning, overstaffing; **en** ∼ overstaffed

surémission *f* overissue

suremploi *m* overemployment

surenchère *f* higher bid; **faire une** ∼ make a higher bid

surenchérir *vi* (vente aux enchères) bid higher; ∼ **sur qn** bid higher than sb, outbid sb; ∼ **sur une offre** make a higher bid, top a bid (infrml)

surendettement *m* overindebtedness

suréquiper *vt* overequip; ∼ **en personnel** overman, overstaff

surestaries *f pl* demurrage

surestimer *vt* overestimate

sûreté *f* (Bourse) security interest; (Fin) surety; ∼ **sur un bien** charge upon a property

surévaluation *f* overvaluation; ∼ **d'actif** watered stock

surévalué, e *adj* (Fin) overvalued; (claim) exaggerated

surévaluer *vt* overvalue

surexploitation *f* overexploitation

surf *m* (Info) browsing, surfing

surface *f* surface; **~ d'appui** (rampe d'accès) bearing surface; **~ au sol** floor space; **~ de stockage** storage area; **~ totale des sols** (d'un immeuble) net leasable area; **~ de vente** (dans un magasin) sales area

surfacturation *f* extra-billing

surfer *vi* **~ sur Internet** surf the Internet

surfourniture *f* overprovision

surfrappe *f* strikeover

surfret *m* extra freight

surimposition *f* excessive taxation, overtax

surintendant *m* superintendent; **~ des assurances** Superintendent of Insurance; **~ des faillites** Superintendent of Bankruptcy

surmenage *m* overwork

surmonter *vt* (récession) weather; (obstacle, crise, problème) overcome

surmortalité *f* excess mortality

surmultiplication *f* overdrive

surnombre *m* **en ~** (objet) surplus; (employé) redundant; (personnel) excess; (marchandises) surplus

surnuméraire *adj* supernumerary

suroffre *f* higher offer, better offer

surpaiement *m* overpayment

surpasser *vt* surpass

surpâturage *m* overgrazing

surplus *m* surplus; **être en ~** be in surplus; **~ acquis** acquired surplus US; **~ de capital en main** capital surplus on hand; **~ du consommateur** consumer's surplus; **~ désigné** designated surplus; **~ disponible** unappropriated surplus; **~ exonéré** exempt surplus; **~ de main-d'œuvre** overmanning; **~ net** net surplus; **~ du producteur** producer's surplus

surproduction *f* overproduction

surproduire *vt* overproduce

surremplissage *m* overstuffing

surreprésentation *f* (surmarché) overrepresentation

surreprésenter *vt* overrepresent

surréservation *f* overbooking

sursalaire *m* extra pay

sursis *m* (de paiement) deferment; (Droit) suspended sentence; **~ simple** simple deferment

sursouscrit, e *adj* oversubscribed

surtare *f* extra tare

surtarifé, e *adj* overpriced

surtaxe *f* surcharge; (impôts) overtaxation; (somme à payer) surtax; **~ pour combustibles** (maritime) fuel surcharge; **~ des corporations** corporate surtax; **~ d'encombrement** congestion surcharge; **~ postale** additional postage; **~ progressive** surtax at graduated rates

surtension *f* power surge

surtout *adv* especially

survaleur *f* goodwill

surveillance *f* (de travail) supervision; (sécurité) surveillance; (de prix) monitoring; (de production) control; **~ de la bourse** surveillance department of exchanges; **~ des établissements de crédit** supervision of credit institutions; **~ de la production** production control

surveillant, e *m,f* supervisor; **~ d'entrepôt** warehouse keeper

surveiller *vt* watch; (prix) monitor, supervise; (équipe) supervise; (taux, marché) monitor; **~ de près** keep a close watch on; **~ ses arrières** watch one's back

survendu, e *adj* oversold

survie *f* survival; (Droit) survivorship

survivre *vi* survive

survol *m* (Info) browsing

survoler *vt* (Info) browse

susceptible *adj* **~ de** capable of; **~ d'application industrielle** open to *ou* suitable for industrial application; **~ d'interprétations diverses** open to several interpretations

susciter *vt* (intérêt, soupçon) give rise to

susdit, e *adj* aforementioned

susmentionné, e *adj* aforementioned, as mentioned above

susnommé, e *adj* above-named

suspendre *vt* (autorisation) suspend; (procédure de faillite) stop; **~ les cotations** suspend trading; **~ le paiement d'un chèque** stop a cheque BrE, stop a check AmE; **~ les transactions** suspend trading

suspens *m* **en ~** (dossier) pending; (problème) outstanding; (projet) in abeyance

suspension *f* suspension; (d'une action) abatement; (de séance) adjournment; (d'un employé) suspension; **~ des affaires** business interruption; **~ d'affrètement** (maritime) off hire; **~ d'appel** stay of appeal; **~ de droits** duty suspension; **~ d'intérêt** cessation of interest UK; **~ de paiement des primes** cessation of payment of premiums; **~ des transactions** halt of trading, trading halt

SVN *abrév* (▸**sans valeur nominale**) NPV (no-par value)

swap *m* (Bourse) swap; **~ simple** plain vanilla swap

switch *m* switch trading

sylviculture *f* forestry

sylvo-agriculture *f* agro-forestry

symbole *m* symbol; **~ monétaire** currency symbol; **~ de pointage** ticker symbol

symbolique *adj* symbolic

symétrie *f* symmetry

symétrique *adj* (relation) symmetric

synchrone *adj* synchronous

synchronisation *f* synchronization

syndic *m* (d'immeuble) property manager, managing agent; **~ de faillite** trustee in bankruptcy, official receiver

syndicalisation *f* unionization

syndicalisé, e *adj* unionized

syndicalisme *m* trade unionism

syndicaliste *mf* union activist

syndicat *m* trade union UK, labor union US; **les ~s et le patronat** unions and management; **~s affiliés** affiliated trade unions; **~ de banque** banking syndicate; **~ de distribution** distribution syndicate; **~ d'émission** underwriting syndicate; **~ d'employés** nonmanual union; **~ d'enchères** tender panel; **~ d'entreprise** enterprise union; **~ exerçant un monopole de l'embauche** closed union; **~ financier** syndicate; **~ de garantie** purchase group; **~ général** general union; **~ indépendant** independent trade union; **~ d'initiative** tourist information office; **~ maison** company union; **~ de métier** craft union; **~ d'ouvriers qualifiés** skilled union UK; **~ patronal** employers' association; **~ du personnel de production** blue-collar union; **~ de placement** distributing syndicate; **~ de prise ferme** underwriting syndicate; **~ de producteurs** producers' association; **~ professionnel** occupational union UK; **~ regroupant les adhérents par métier** vertical union; **~ regroupant les adhérents par niveau** horizontal union

syndicataire *mf* (Assur, Fin) underwriter

syndication *f* syndication

syndiqué, e *m,f* union member; (Fin) (prêts, titres) syndicated

syndiquer **1** *vt* unionize
2 se syndiquer *v pron* (ouvrier, personnel) join a union

syndrome *m* syndrome; **~ des bâtiments insalubres** sick building syndrome

synergie *f* synergy

syntaxe *f* syntax

synthèse *f* synthesis; (resumé) summary

synthétique *adj* synthetic

systématique *adj* (contrôle, recherche, classification) systematic

systématiquement *adv* systematically

systématiser *vt* systematize

système *m* system; (plan, méthode) scheme; (hi-fi, informatique) set-up, system;

(**système a...**) **~ d'accueil des idées** (du personnel) suggestion scheme; **~ d'administration financière** system of financial administration; **~ d'aide à la décision** decision support system; **~ d'amortissement dégressif** declining balance method, reducing balance method; **~ d'analyse des tendances assisté par ordinateur** computerized market timing system; **~ d'appel d'offres** competitive bidding; **~ d'assurance maladie** health insurance scheme; **~ d'attribution de codes comptables** coding system; **~ d'autoévaluation** self-assessing system; **~ autonome** stand-alone system; **~ d'avance de fonds à plafond** imprest system;

(**b...**) **~ bancaire** banking system; **~ de banque à succursales** branch banking system; **~ de bons** voucher system; **~ budgétaire** budget system;

(**c...**) **~ carrousel** circuit working; **~ centralisé de cotation** consolidated quotation system; **~ centre périphérie** centre periphery system BrE, center periphery system AmE; **~ de classement** filing system; **~ de classification des emplois** job evaluation scheme; **~ de communication interréseau** gateway; **~ de compensation** clearing system; **~ de compensation des actionnaires** Investors' Compensation Scheme UK; **~ de compensation de chèques** cheque-clearing system BrE, check-clearing system AmE; **~ de compensation et de règlement automatisé** Automated Clearing Settlement System; **~ de comptabilité sur ordinateur** computerized accounting system; **~ comptable** accounting system; **~ comptable auxiliaire** subsidiary accounting system; **~ comptable électronique** electronic accounting system; **~ connecté** online system; **~ de contrôle de la circulation aérienne** air traffic control system; **~ de cotation automatisé** screen-based quotation system, Stock Exchange Automated Quotation UK; **~ de cotation électronique** computer-assisted trading system; **~ de crédits d'impôt** tax credit system; **~ à la criée** open-outcry system;

(**d...**) **~ décentralisé** distributed system; **~ de déductions sociales** (pour les dons aux institutions caritatives) payroll deduction scheme; **~ dégressif** tapering; **~ démontable** (véhicules routiers) demountable system; **~ duplex** duplex computer;

(**e...**) **~ d'économie mixte** mixed economic system; **~ économique** economic system; **~ économique national** domestic economy, domestic system; **~ énergétique** energy system; **~ de l'entreprise privée** private enterprise system; **~ d'évaluation des risques** risk asset system, risk-based banking standards; **~ d'évaluation de la solvabilité** credit rating system; **~ d'exploitation** operating system; **~ d'exploitation à disques** disk operating system; **~ d'exploitation des entrées/sorties** basic input/output operating system;

(**f...**) **~ de fabrication** manufacturing system; **~ financier** financial system; **~ fiscal** tax system, taxation system;

(**g...**) **~ de garantie** backup system; **~ généralisé des tarifs et préférences** generalized system of tariffs and preferences; **~ de gestion** management system; **~ de** ⋯⋗

s

gestion de bases de données database management system; ~ **de gestion de caisse** cash management system; ~ **de gestion financière** financial management system; ~ **de gestion informatisé** management information system; ~ **de gestion des secteurs de dépenses** policy and expenditure management system; ~ **de gestion de trafic maritime** vessel traffic management system; ~ **de gestion de trésorerie** cash management system;

(**h...**) ~ **d'heures annualisées** annualized hours system;

(**i...**) ~ **de l'impôt progressif sur le revenu** progressive income tax system; ~ **d'indemnité de maladie** sick-pay scheme UK; ~ **d'indexation** pegging system; ~ **d'information** information system; ~ **d'information de marketing** marketing information system; ~ **informatique** computer system, information system; ~ **informatique embarqué** (navigation) loadmate; ~ **insensible aux défaillances**, ~ **insensible aux pannes** (Info) fault-tolerant system; ~ **intégré de gestion** (Info) integrated management system, management information system; ~ **interactif** (Info) interactive system; ~ **d'interaction économique** business system;

(**j...**) ~ **judiciaire** judiciary; ~ **juridique** legal system;

(**l...**) ~ **de libre entreprise** free enterprise system; ~ **en ligne** (Info) online system; ~ **de livraison** delivery system; ~ **de livraison agréé** approved delivery facility UK;

(**m...**) ~ **maison** (Info) in-house system; ~ **majoritaire** majority rule; ~ **de marché** market system; ~ **métrique** metric system; ~ **de mise en commun** (fonds commun) pooling system; **Système monétaire européen** European Monetary System; ~ **monétaire international** international monetary system; ~ **monétaire mondial** world monetary system; ~ **multi-utilisateur** (Info) multiuser system;

(**o...**) ~ **d'option sur les bénéfices** (avantages des employés) share option scheme; ~ **d'organisation** organization behaviour BrE, organization behavior AmE;

(**p...**) ~ **de paiement** payment system; ~ **de paiement sans argent** (par carte de crédit) cashless payment system; ~ **de partage des bénéfices** (avantage aux employés) profit-

sharing scheme UK, profit-sharing plan US; ~ **de partage du travail** job share scheme; ~ **de participation** employee stock ownership plan US; ~ **de participation financière** financial participation scheme UK; ~ **de planification avancée** (Info) Advanced Planning System; ~ **de planning, de budget et de programmation** planning, programming, budgeting system; ~ **politique** political system; ~ **de préférences généralisé** generalized system of preferences; ~ **de primes d'encouragement** incentive scheme; ~ **privé d'assurance maladie** private health scheme UK; ~ **de prix** price system; ~ **de production au large** (maritime) floating production system; ~ **de protection par programme informatique** (Bourse) program trading;

(**q...**) ~ **de quotas** quota system; ~ **des quotes-parts** (tarifs aériens) proration;

(**r...**) ~ **de recherche documentaire** information retrieval system; ~ **de règlement bancaire** bank settlement system; ~ **de règlement des chèques** cheque payment system BrE, check payment system AmE; ~ **réglementaire** regulatory system; ~ **de rémunération** salary scheme; ~ **de repérage** tracking system; ~ **de réservation** reservation system; ~ **de retenue de l'impôt à la source** (Fisc) pay-as-you-earn, PAYE UK, pay-as-you-go AmE; ~ **de retraite** funded pension plan US; ~ **de retraite par accumulation** funded pension plan US; ~ **de retraite professionnelle** occupational pension scheme UK; ~ **routier** road network;

(**s...**) ~ **des salaires** wage system; ~ **social** social system; ~ **de sonorisation** PA system, public address system; ~ **de soumission** competitive bidding;

(**t...**) ~ **de télévirement** electronic funds transfer system; ~ **de traitement de texte** word-processing system; ~ **de transaction inter-marchés** Intermarket Trading System US; ~ **de transactions automatisées** computer trading US; ~ **de transfert** (aéroport) people mover; ~ **de transport** transportation system; ~ **de transport combiné** intermodal transport system; ~ **de travail à la pièce** piecework system;

(**v...**) ~ **de virements bancaires** banking transfer system

Tt

t. *abrév* (Fin) (▸**titre**) security; (▸**tare**) t.
(tare); (▸**tonne**) t. (ton, tonne)

T4M *abrév* (▸**taux moyen mensuel du
marché monétaire**) average monthly
money market rate

tabac *m* tobacco

table *f* table; ~ **agrégée** aggregate table; ~
d'allocation des fichiers (Info) file
allocation table; ~ **de change** (Bourse) desk;
~ **de conférence** conference table; ~ **de
décision** (Info) decision table; ~
d'invalidité disability percentage table; ~
des matières table of contents; ~ **des
négociations** bargaining table, negotiating
table; ~ **de référence** lookup table; ~
ronde round table (talks)

tableau *m* (présentation graphique) table; (d'une
situation) picture; (liste) régister, roll AmE;
(affichant des renseignements) board; (Info) array;
~ **d'affichage** notice board BrE, bulletin
board AmE; ~ **d'affichage électronique**
electronic indicator board; ~ **de bord**
management chart; ~ **comptable** financial
statement; ~ **de concordance**
reconciliation table; ~ **de cotation**
quotation board; ~ **de données** array; ~
d'échanges inter-industriels input/output
table; ~ **économique d'ensemble** financial
balance; ~ **électronique** spreadsheet
program; ~ **électronique de cotations**
screen-based quotation system, Stock
Exchange Alternative Trading Service UK; ~
à feuilles mobiles flip chart; ~ **de
financement** source and applications of
funds statement; ~ **de financement
consolidé** consolidated cash flow statement;
~ **des opérations financières** flow-of-
funds table; ~ **de remboursement**
redemption table; ~ **de service** (Admin)
duty roster; ~ **des tarifs** scale of charges; ~
de ventilation spreadsheet

tabler *vi* ~ **sur** bank on

tableur *m* (Info) spreadsheet

tabloïd *adj* (jarg) (presse) tabloid

tabulation *f* (horizontale, verticale) tabulation;
faire une ~ tab

tâche *f* task; **à la** ~ at piece rate

tacite *adj* tacit

tactile *adj* (Info) (écran) touch-sensitive

tactique *f* tactics *pl*; **changer de** ~ change
tactics; ~ **concurrentielle** competitive
tactics

taille *f* size; **entreprise de** ~ **moyenne**
medium-sized company; **de grande/petite** ~
large/small; **de** ~ (problème, enjeu)

considerable, sizable; (question) very
important; ~ **au-dessous** next size down; ~
des lots batch size; ~ **normale du marché**
normal market size BrE; ~ **d'une
organisation** organizational size; ~
standard standard size, basic size; ~s **tout-
venant** random sizes

taire *vt* withhold

talent *m* (aptitude) talent

talon *m* (de carnet, de registre) stub; (Bourse)
talon; ~ **de chèque** cheque stub BrE, check
stub AmE

TAM *abrév* (▸**taux annuel monétaire**)
annual monetary rate

tambour *m* (Info) drum; ~ **en
contreplaqué** plywood drum

tampon *m* (à estampiller) rubber stamp; (Info)
buffer; **apposer un** ~ **sur un document**
stamp a document; ~ **encreur** ink pad; ~
d'entrée (dans un nouveau pays) entry stamp

tantième *m* percentage; (Gestion) fee

TAO *abrév* (▸**traduction assistée par
ordinateur**) CAT (computer-aided
translation, computer-assisted translation)

taper *vt* (dactylographier) type; **tapé à la
machine** typewritten

tapis *m* carpet; ~ **roulant** (pour les personnes)
moving pavement BrE, travolator AmE; (pour
objets) conveyor belt; ~ **de souris** mouse
mat

taquet *m* (arrêt) stop; ~ **de tabulation**
tabulator

tarage *m* taring

tare *f* tare, tare weight; ~ **brute** gross tare
weight; ~ **nette** net tare weight; ~ **d'usage**
customary tare

tarif *m* rate; (liste des prix) price list; (prix)
current price; (Transp) fare; (de consultant) fee;
~ **normal/réduit/spécial** (Transp) normal/
reduced/special fare; ~ **normal/économique**
(postes) first-class/second-class rate; ~ **de nuit**
(téléphone) off-peak rate, night-time rate; **le** ~
en vigueur the going rate; **payer plein** ~ pay
full price; (Transp) pay full fare; ~
d'abonnement subscription fee; ~
d'affranchissement postage; ~ **aller-
retour** round-trip rate; ~ **à la boîte** (Transp)
box rate; ~ **de bout en bout** through
charge; ~ **charge complète** carload rate; ~
en classe économique economy fare; ~
commun joint fare, joint rate; ~ **commun
compensatoire** compensating common
tariff; ~ **complet** full rate; ~
concurrentiel competitive rate; ~ **à
déterminer** rate to be agreed; ~ **direct** ⋯⟩

through rate; ~ **discriminatoire** price discrimination; ~ **douanier** customs tariff; ~ **douanier communautaire** (UE) common customs tariff; ~ **extérieur commun** common external tariff; ~ **familles** family fare; ~ **fixe** flat rate; ~ **forfaitaire** inclusive rate, fixed rate; (Transp) through charge, through rate; ~ **fret à perte** (distribution) under cost freight rate; ~ **global** blanket rate; ~ **de groupage** groupage rate; ~ **groupé** consolidated rate; ~ **de groupe** blanket rate; ~ **des importations** import tariff; ~ **intérieur** domestic rate; ~ **au kilo excédant le poids pivot** (aviation) overpivot area; ~ **lent** third-class rate US; ~ **à la ligne** (presse) linage, lineage; ~ **marchandises** freight tariff; ~ **marchandises demandé** required freight rate; ~ **marchandises diverses** general cargo rate; ~ **minimum** minimum charge; ~ **non dégressif** flat rate; ~ **non répertorié** (Transp) rate not reported; ~ **normal** normal rate; ~ **passagers** passenger tariff; ~ **à perte** rate below cost; ~ **par poids** weight charge; ~ **préférentiel** commodity rate; ~ **promotionnel** bargain rate; ~ **publicitaire** advertising rates, adrate; ~ **de recouvrement** collection tariff; ~ **réduit** reduced rate, concessionary rate; (Transp) reduced fare; ~ **réduit aux heures creuses** off-peak charges; ~ **et réglementations extérieurs** overseas tariff and regulations; ~ **séparant coûts variables et coûts fixes** two-part tariff; ~ **par wagon** (chemin de fer) carload rate

tarifaire adj (accord, barrière, politique) tariff

tarification f (Gen com) pricing, price-setting; (Fin, fisc) tarification; ~ **en charge maximum** peak-load pricing; ~ **envisagée** prospective rating; ~ **en fonction du marché** market pricing; ~ **de pointe** peak-load pricing; ~ **de prestige** prestige pricing; ~ **sauvage** predatory pricing; ~ **selon la statistique** experience rating; ~ **à l'unité** unit pricing

tas m **formation sur le ~** on-the-job training; **former qn sur le ~** train sb on the job; **grève sur le ~** sit-down strike

taux m rate; ~ **fixe/mensuel/moyen** fixed/ monthly/average rate; ~ **de chômage/ criminalité** unemployment/crime rate; **obligations à ~ variable** variable-rate bonds; **à ~ fixe** at a flat rate; **au ~ annuel** at an annual rate; **au ~ de** at; **au ~ standard** standard-rated; **faire grimper les ~ d'intérêts** push interest rates up; **faire monter les ~ artificiellement** push rates up artificially, kite;

(**taux a...**) ~ **d'absentéisme** absentee rate; ~ **d'absorption** absorption rate; ~ **d'accroissement** rate of increase; ~ **acheteur** buyer's rate; ~ **d'action préférentiel** preferred stock ratio; ~ **d'activité** activity rate; ~ **d'actualisation**

hurdle rate of return; ~ **actuariel** yield to maturity; ~ **actuel** current rate; ~ **d'amortissement** rate of depreciation; ~ **annuel** annual rate; ~ **annuel corrigé des variations saisonnières** seasonally adjusted annual rate; ~ **annuel monétaire** annual monetary rate; ~ **d'argent au jour le jour** call money rate, daily money rate; ~ **d'attrition** churn rate; ~ **d'augmentation** rate of increase; ~ **en augmentation** rising interest rate;

(**b...**) ~ **bancaire moyen** average interest rate; ~ **de base** base rate UK, prime rate US; ~ **de base bancaire** bank base rate; ~ **de bénéfice au chiffre d'affaires** return on sales; ~ **bonifié** preferential interest rate; ~ **de bons du Trésor** Treasury bill rate; ~ **brut** gross rate;

(**c...**) ~ **de change** exchange rate, rate of exchange; ~ **de change acheteur** buying rate; ~ **de change artificiel** artificial exchange rate; ~ **de change en données corrigées des changes** trade-weighted exchange rate; ~ **de change effectif** effective exchange rate; ~ **de change pondéré en fonction des échanges commerciaux** trade-weighted exchange rate; ~ **de change réservé aux touristes** tourist exchange rate; ~ **de change de soutien** pegged rate of exchange; ~ **de change spécial appliqué au commerce** special commercial exchange rate; ~ **de change à terme** forward exchange rate; ~ **cible** target rate; ~ **de clientèle** (V&M) switching-in rate; ~ **de commission** commission rate; ~ **composé** compound rate; ~ **de comptant** spot rate; ~ **contractuel du prêt** contractual loan rate; ~ **de conversion** conversion rate; ~ **de courtage** brokerage commission rate; ~ **de couverture** cover ratio; ~ **de couverture de la dette** debt coverage ratio; ~ **de couverture du dividende** dividend cover; ~ **de couverture des frais financiers fixes** fixed-charge coverage; ~ **de crédit variable** variable lending rate; ~ **de croissance** growth rate; ~ **de croissance économique** economic growth rate; ~ **de croissance économique soutenable** sustainable economic growth rate; ~ **de croissance garantie** guaranteed growth rate; ~ **de croissance prévu** anticipated growth rate;

(**d...**) ~ **de déclin** rate of decay; ~ **dégressif** decreasing rate; ~ **de dégrèvement** rate of relief; ~ **demandé** rate asked; ~ **de départs** quit rate; ~ **de départs naturels** attrition rate; ~ **de dépendance** dependency ratio; ~ **de déport** backwardation rate; ~ **de dépréciation** rate of decay; ~ **de diffusion** (production) diffusion rate; ~ **directeur** key rate; ~ **des disponibilités** liquid ratio; ~ **disponible** liquid ratio;

e... ~ **d'échecs** failure rate; ~ **effectif global** annualized percentage rate; ~ **d'emprunt** borrowing ratio; ~ **d'emprunt à terme** forward borrowing rate; ~ **d'encadrement** management ratio; ~ **d'endettement** gearing ratio BrE, leverage ratio AmE; ~ **d'endettement élevé** high gearing BrE, high leverage AmE; ~ **d'épargne bonifié** bonus savings rate; ~ **d'épargne des ménages** savings ratio; ~ **d'érosion** attrition rate; ~ **d'erreurs** error rate; ~ **d'escompte** discount rate, rate of discount; ~ **de l'escompte** bank lending rate, bank rate; ~ **d'escompte bancaire** bank discount rate; ~ **d'escompte interne** internal rate of discount; ~ **d'escompte du marché** market rate of discount; ~ **d'escompte social** social rate of discount; ~ **excédentaire** rate of surplus value; ~ **d'exploitation** rate of exploitation; ~ **des exportations** export figures;

f... ~ **favorable** favourable rate BrE, favorable rate AmE; ~ **de financement** financing rate; ~ **de financement à court terme** short-date financing rate; ~ **fixe de l'impôt** fixed tax rate; ~ **flottant** floating rate, variable rate;

g... ~ **de gain** switching-in rate; ~ **général des matières premières** general commodity rate; ~ **glissant** gliding rate; ~ **global de fertilité** (Econ) total fertility rate;

h... ~ **horaire** hourly rate; ~ **hors banque** open-market rate, private rate of discount;

i... ~ **d'imposition** rate of taxation, tax rate; ~ **d'imposition de base des corporations** basic corporate tax rate; ~ **d'imposition prévu par la loi** statutory tax rate; ~ **de l'impôt foncier** residential tax rate; ~ **de l'impôt sur le revenu** income tax rate; ~ **d'inclusion** (des gains et des pertes en capital) inclusion rate; ~ **incrémental de dépenses en capital** incremental capital-output ratio; ~ **d'inflation** inflation rate; ~ **d'inflation apparent** headline rate; ~ **d'inflation sous-jacente** underlying inflation rate; ~ **de l'inflation structurelle** core inflation rate; ~ **interbancaire** interbank exchange rate, interbank rate; ~ **interbancaire offert à Paris** Paris Interbank Offered Rate; ~ **interbancaire proposé** interbank offered rate; ~ **d'intérêt en baisse** declining interest rate; ~ **d'intérêt bancaire** banking interest; ~ **d'intérêt de base** prime rate of interest; ~ **d'intérêt bonifié** bonus rate of interest; ~ **d'intérêt brut** pure interest rate; ~ **d'intérêt composé** compound annual rate UK; ~ **d'intérêt comptable** accounting rate of interest; ~ **d'intérêt de compte d'épargne bancaire** banker's deposit rate; ~ **d'intérêt à la consommation** consumption rate of interest UK; ~ **d'intérêt contractuel** coupon rate; ~ **d'intérêt à**

court terme short-term interest rate; ~ **d'intérêt créditeur** deposit rate; ~ **d'intérêt des dépôts bancaires** bank deposit rates; ~ **d'intérêt des emprunts** borrowing rate; ~ **d'intérêt en hausse** rising interest rate; ~ **d'intérêt du marché** market rate of interest; ~ **d'intérêt mélangé** blended rate; ~ **d'intérêt net de toutes charges** interest rate net of all charges; ~ **d'intérêt nominal** coupon rate, nominal interest rate; ~ **d'intérêt obligataire** bond rate; ~ **d'intérêt plafond** cap rate; ~ **d'intérêt préférentiel** Canada prime rate of interest; ~ **d'intérêt d'un prêt à vue** call loan rate; ~ **d'intérêt propre** own rate of interest; ~ **d'intérêt variable** variable interest rate; ~ **internationaux de liquidité** international liquidity ratios;

l... ~ **de liquidation du contrat à terme** futures liquidation rate; ~ **de liquidation d'opération à terme** futures liquidation rate; ~ **de liquidité** liquidity ratio; ~ **de liquidité immédiate** acid-test ratio, quick ratio; ~ **de liquidités** liquid assets ratio; ~ **locatif** rental rate;

m... ~ **du marché au comptant** cash market rates; ~ **du marché monétaire** money-market rate; ~ **de marché obligataire** bond market rate; ~ **de marge brute** return on sales; ~ **marginal** marginal rate; ~ **marginal d'impôt** marginal tax rate; ~ **marginal de substitution** marginal rate of substitution; ~ **marginal de transformation** marginal rate of transformation; ~ **mobile** gliding rate; ~ **de mortalité** death rate; ~ **moyen mensuel du marché monétaire** average monthly money market rate; ~ **moyen pondéré** average weighted rate; ~ **mystère** teaser rate;

n... ~ **de natalité** birth rate; ~ **naturel de chômage** natural rate of unemployment; ~ **naturel de croissance** warranted rate of growth; ~ **naturel d'emploi** natural rate of employment; ~ **naturel d'intérêt** natural rate of interest; ~ **net** net rate; ~ **nominal** nominal yield; ~ **nominal d'emprunt** nominal loan rate; ~ **non rajustable** nonadjustable rate; ~ **nul d'imposition** zero rate of tax;

o... ~ **d'obligation** liability rate; ~ **officiel d'escompte** minimum lending rate UK; ~ **de l'offre interbancaire de Londres** London Interbank Bid Rate; ~ **pour les opérations à terme** forward rate; ~ **optimal de pollution** optimal level of pollution; ~ **de l'option d'achat** call rate; ~ **de l'option de vente** put rate;

p... ~ **de participation** participation rate; ~ **de pénalisation** penalty rate; ~ **de pénétration** (marketing) penetration rate; ~ **de perte de clientèle** switching-out rate; ~ **pivot** central rate; ~ **plafond** ceiling rate; ~ **plafond de l'impôt** ceiling tax rate; ~ ····}

plancher floor rate; ∼ **préférentiel** preferential rate; ∼ **de prélèvement fiscal** tax burden; ∼ **prescrit** prescribed rate; ∼ **de prêt** lending rate; ∼ **de prêt contractuel** contractual loan rate; ∼ **de prêt hypothécaire** mortgage rate; ∼ **de prêt à vue** call loan rate; ∼ **de prise en pension** repo rate; ∼ **privé de l'escompte** private rate of discount; ∼ **privilégié** concessionary rate, preferred rate; ∼ **de production** production rate;

(**r...**) ∼ **de rachat** (marketing) repeat rate; ∼ **de réescompte** rediscount rate; ∼ **de remplissage** load factor; ∼ **de rémunération** salary rate; ∼ **de rendement** (d'actions) rate of return; (de la production) capacity ratio; ∼ **de rendement du capital différentiel** incremental capital-output ratio; ∼ **de rendement comptable** accounting rate of return; ∼ **de rendement minimal** hurdle rate; ∼ **de rendement moyen** average yield; ∼ **de rendement sur le capital employé** rate of return on capital employed; ∼ **révisable annuellement** *interest rate subject to modification every year*; ∼ **de roulement** rate of rolling;

(**s...**) ∼ **de salaire horaire** base pay rate; ∼ **de solvabilité** solvency ratio; ∼ **statutaire d'imposition** statutory tax rate; ∼ **de syndicalisation** level of union membership;

(**t...**) ∼ **à terme** forward rate; ∼ **à terme à la hausse** cap;

(**u...**) ∼ **uniforme** blanket rate, flat rate; ∼ **uniforme de salaire** flat rate of pay; ∼ **d'utilisation de la main-d'œuvre** capacity ratio; ∼ **d'utilisation d'un quai** berth user rate;

(**v...**) ∼ **vendeur** seller's rate; ∼ **en vigueur** going rate;

(**z...**) ∼ **zéro** (TVA) zero-rated

taxation *f* (Fisc) taxation; **la** ∼ **de l'épargne** the taxing of savings; ∼ **à la valeur** valuation charge; ∼ **au volume** volume charge; ∼ **zéro** zero rating

taxe *f* (Econ, Fisc) tax; (Imp/Exp) duty, levy; (Droit) taxation; **une** ∼ **de 5%** a 5% tax; **la** ∼ **sur le tabac** tobacco tax, tax on tobacco; **hors** ∼ exclusive of tax; **toutes** ∼**s comprises** inclusive of tax; **soumis à la** ∼ taxable; (Imp/Exp) dutiable; ∼ **sur les achats** purchase tax; ∼ **d'aéroport** airport tax; ∼ **d'affaires** business tax; ∼ **annuelle** renewal fee; ∼ **d'apprentissage** training tax; ∼ **sur les articles de luxe** luxury tax; ∼ **sur le capital** capital tax; ∼ **sur les carburants** fuel tax, petroleum revenue tax; ∼ **compensatrice** compensation tax; ∼ **de consommation** consumption tax; ∼ **sur la consommation** commodity tax, expenditure tax; ∼ **de débarquement** (port) port tax; ∼ **sur les dépenses du consommateur** expenditure tax; ∼ **directe** direct tax; ∼ **à**

l'exportation export tax; ∼ **fixe** fixed duty; ∼ **forfaitaire** flat-rate tax; ∼ **sur un facteur de production** factor tax; ∼ **sur la formation professionnelle** continuing education tax; ∼ **franche** open tax; ∼ **d'habitation** property tax, ≈ council tax UK; ∼ **immobilière** property tax; ∼ **à l'importation** import duty; ∼ **passager** passenger dues; (maritime) passenger toll; ∼ **postale** postage due; ∼ **de prestation de service** goods and services tax; ∼ **professionnelle** business tax, *local tax on business activity*; ∼ **de séjour** tourist tax, visitor's tax; ∼ **de succession** transfer tax; ∼ **superposée** superimposed tax; ∼ **de transport** transport tax; ∼ **sur le transport aérien** air transportation tax; ∼ **à la valeur** value surcharge; ∼ **sur la valeur** ad valorem tax (frml); ∼ **sur la valeur ajoutée** value-added tax UK; ∼ **sur les ventes** sales tax

taxer *vt* impose a tax

taxi *m* taxi

TBB *abrév* (▸**taux de base bancaire**) bank base rate

tech. *abrév* (▸**technicien**) technical assistant

technicien, -ienne *m,f* technician, technical assistant; (expert) technical expert (de in); (réparateur) engineer; ∼ **d'entretien** maintenance engineer; ∼ **de hardware** hardware specialist; ∼ **informatique** computer engineer, computer technician; ∼ **de maintenance** service engineer; ∼ **de surface** cleaner

technico-commercial, e *m,f* commercial engineer, sales engineer

technique¹ *adj* technical

technique² *f* (méthode) technique; (Econ, Ind) technology; ∼ **de l'appât** (destinée à tromper le client) bait and switch advertising US; ∼ **d'audit** auditing technique; ∼ **du budget base zéro** zero-base budgeting, ZBB; ∼ **de contrôle** audit technique; ∼ **courante** standard technique; ∼ **des enchères** bidding technique; ∼ **de gestion** management technique; ∼ **informatique** computer technology; ∼ **de pointe** advanced engineering; ∼ **du prix d'appel** (marketing) loss pricing

technocratique *adj* technocratic

technologie *f* technology; **les nouvelles** ∼**s** the new technologies; ∼ **adaptée** appropriate technology; ∼ **appropriée** appropriate technology; ∼ **de bureau** office technology; ∼ **de communication** communications technology; ∼ **complémentaire** incremental technology; ∼ **douce** alternative technology, soft technology; ∼ **écologique** clean technology; ∼ **énergétique** energy technology; ∼ **idoine** appropriate technology; ∼ **de l'information** information technology; ∼ **informatique** computer technology; ∼ **non**

polluante clean technology; ∼ **de pointe** advanced technology, hi tech, high technology; ∼ **propre** clean technology; ∼ **de remplacement** replacement technology

technologique *adj* technological

technopole *m* centre of excellence in advanced research and technology

technopôle *m* high-tech business zone

TEI *abrév* (▸**traitement électronique de l'information**) EDP (electronic data processing)

tél. *abrév* (▸**téléphone**) tel. (telephone)

télé *abrév* (▸**télévision**) TV (television)

téléachat *m* teleshopping

télé-assistance *f* remote support

téléautographie *f* telewriting

Télécarte® *f* phone card

téléchargeable *adj* (Info) downloadable

télécharger *vt* (Info) download; upload

télécom *adj* (réseau, satellite) telecommunications

télécommande *f* remote control

télécommandé, e *adj* remote-controlled

télécommunications *f pl* telecommunications; ∼ **numériques sans fil** cordless digital telecommunications

télécommuniquer *vt* telecommunicate

télécoms *m pl* telecommunications

téléconférence *f* (vidéoconférence) teleconference; (audioconférence) conference call; ∼ **informatisée** computer conferencing

téléconseiller, -ère *m,f* call centre agent, hotliner

téléconsultation *f* (Info) remote access

télécopie *f* facsimile, fax

télécopier *vt* fax

télécopieur *m* fax machine

tel écran, tel écrit *adj* WYSIWYG (jarg), what you see is what you get

télédémarchage *m* telephone canvassing

télédiffusion *f* broadcasting

téléenregistrement *m* telerecording

télé-enseignement *m* distance learning

télégramme *m* telegram, cable

télégraphier *vt* cable

télé-impression *f* remote printing

téléimprimeur *m* tape machine BrE, ticker AmE, teleprinter BrE, teletypewriter AmE

télélogiciel *m* (Info) telesoftware

télémaintenance *f* (Info) remote maintenance

télémarché *m* telemarket

télémarketing *m* telemarketing, telephone marketing

télématique *f* (Info) telematics

télémercaticien, -ienne *m,f* telemarketer

télémercatique *f* telemarketing, telephone marketing

télémessage *m* telemessage

téléopérateur, -trice *m,f* call centre agent

télépaiement *m* electronic payment

téléphone *m* phone, telephone; **au** ∼ (parler) on the phone; (réservation) over the telephone; **le** ∼ **arabe** the grapevine; ∼ **automatique** direct dialling BrE, direct dialing AmE; ∼ **automatique international** international subscriber dialling BrE; ∼ **cellulaire** cellphone; ∼ **à cartes** cardphone; ∼ **à clavier** touch-tone phone; ∼ **Internet** Internet phone; ∼ **mobile** mobile phone; ∼ **portable** mobile phone; ∼ **à poussoirs** Can key telephone set; ∼ **public** pay phone BrE, pay station AmE; ∼ **rouge** hot line; ∼ **sans fil** cordless phone; ∼ **à touches** touch-tone phone; ∼ **de voiture** car phone

téléphoner *vi* phone; ∼ **à** phone, telephone; ∼ **en PCV** make a reverse charge call BrE, call collect AmE

téléphonie *f* telephony; ∼ **mobile** mobile communications

téléphonique *adj* telephonic

téléscripteur *m* teleprinter BrE, teletypewriter AmE

téléspectateur, -trice *m,f* (television) viewer; ∼ **assidu** heavy viewer

Télétel® *m* France *Viewdata service operated by France Telecom,* ≈ Prestel® UK

Télétex® *m* Teletex®

télétexte *m* teletext UK

télétraitement *m* remote processing, teleprocessing; ∼ **par lots** remote batch processing

télétravail *m* telecommuting

télétravailleur, -euse *m,f* teleworker

Télétype® *m* Teletype®

télévendeur, -euse *m,f* telesales operator *ou* agent

télévente *f* telesales

télévirement *m* electronic funds transfer; ∼ **au point de vente** electronic funds transfer at point of sale

télévirer *vt* transfer by wire

téléviser *vt* broadcast, televise

télévision *f* television; ∼ **câblée/par câble** cable television; ∼ **payante**, ∼ **à péage** pay TV; ∼ **par satellite** satellite television

télévisuel, -elle *adj* televisual

télex *m* telex

telle entrée, telle sortie garbage in, garbage out

témoignage *m* (déposition) evidence, testimony; (compte rendu) account; **en** ∼ **de quoi** in witness whereof; ∼ **contradictoire** conflicting evidence

témoigner *vi* testify, give evidence; ∼ **en faveur de/contre** give evidence in favour of/against

t

témoin *m* witness; (marketing direct) control; ~ **à charge** witness for the prosecution; ~ **défaillant** defaulting witness; ~ **de la défense** witness for the defence BrE, witness for the defense AmE; ~ **oculaire** eye witness

tempérament *m* **à** ~ (Fin) in *or* by instalments BrE, in *or* by installments AmE; **acheter à** ~ buy on the installment plan AmE, buy on credit

température *f* temperature; ~ **ambiante** room temperature; ~ **minimale** minimum temperature

temporaire *adj* temporary; (accord, travail) interim

temporairement *adv* provisionally, temporarily

temps *m* (durée) time; (météo) weather; **à** ~ **partiel** part-time; **à** ~ **plein** full-time; **en** ~ **opportun** at the appropriate time; **être dans les** ~ be on schedule; **qui prend beaucoup de** ~ time-consuming; ~ **d'accès** access time; ~ **d'accès à l'information** retrieval time; ~ **d'accès moyen** average access time; ~ **d'antenne** airtime; ~ **d'arrêt** (Info) down time; ~ **de connexion** (Info) connection time; ~ **forts** highlights; ~ **d'inactivité** (Info) idle time; (plan) lead time; ~ **de latence** reaction time; ~ **libre** spare time; ~ **machine** (Info) computer time; ~ **mort** (Com) slack period; (Info) idle time; ~ **publicitaire** advertising time; ~ **de réaction** reaction time; ~ **réel** real time; ~ **de référence** standard time; ~ **de réponse** (administration) lag, response time; ~ **de rotation** turnaround time; **Temps universel** universal time coordinated; ~ **de vol** flight time; ~ **de vol réel** airborne time

tendance *f* tendency, trend; **avoir** ~ **à** tend to; **le marché a** ~ **à se stabiliser** the market is becoming more stable; **la** ~ **reste à l'expansion** the trend is still toward(s) growth; **la** ~ **s'est inversée** the trend has been reversed; ~ **à la baisse** downward trend; (Bourse) bearish movement, downtrend; ~ **de base** basic trend; ~ **de la circulation** traffic trend; ~ **commerciale** business trend; ~ **du cours** price trend; ~ **dominante** major trend; ~ **économique** economic trend; ~ **du flux des commandes** (publipostage) order flow pattern; ~ **à la hausse** upward trend; (Bourse) bullish movement, uptrend; (du marché) buoyancy; ~ **à la hausse des salaires** earnings drift, wage drift; ~ **inflationniste** inflationary trend; ~ **à long terme** long-term trend; ~ **du marché** market trend; ~ **marginale à importer** marginal propensity to import; ~ **moyenne de la consommation** average propensity to consume; ~ **moyenne à économiser** average propensity to save; ~ **sous-jacente** underlying trend; ~ **tarifaire** rate trend

tendre ① *vt* (présenter) ~ **qch à qn** hold sth out to sb; (un piège) set

② *vi* ~ **à/vers** (viser) strive for; (se rapprocher) (valeur) approach; (zéro) tend to

tendu, e *adj* (marché) nervous; (relations, réunion) tense

teneur[1] *m* maker; ~ **de marché** market maker UK; ~ **de marché agréé** (actions) registered equity market maker; ~ **de marché éléctronique** e-market maker

teneur[2] *f* content; (d'un rapport, discours) import; (Ind) assay; **à faible** ~ **en alcool** low-alcohol; ~ **en alcool insuffisante** under proof

tenir ① *vt* (stand) man; ~ **une boulangerie** run a bakery; ~ **serrée la bride de la politique monétaire** tighten the monetary reins; ~ **compte de qch** take sth into account; ~ **les cordons de la bourse** (infrml) hold the purse strings (infrml); ~ **le bon filon** (infrml) strike it rich (infrml); ~ **le marché** make a market; ~ **qn au courant** keep sb informed; ~ **qn au courant de** (événements) keep sb up to date with, keep sb abreast of; ~ **qn responsable de qch** hold sb responsible for sth

② *vi* (durer) last; ~ **bon** hold one's ground, stand firm; ~ **bon en sachant que** stand firm in the belief that

tension *f* tension; ~ **due au travail** work-related stress; ~ **nerveuse** stress

tentative *f* endeavour BrE, endeavor AmE; ~ **d'offre publique d'achat** takeover attempt; ~ **d'OPA surprise** dawn raid; ~ **de prise de contrôle sauvage** hostile takeover bid

tenu, e *adj* ~ **par la loi** legally bound; **être** ~ **de faire** be under an obligation to do, be bound to do; ~ **de payer des dommages et intérêts** be liable for damages

tenue *f* (Fin) performance; **bonne/mauvais** ~ **d'une action** good/poor performance of a share; **la bonne** ~ **de dollar** the steadiness of the dollar; ~ **des barèmes d'imposition** asset; (immobilier) run of schedule; ~ **de compte** account operation; ~ **des livres comptables** book-keeping

tenure *f* (droit commercial et immobilier) holding; ~ **à bail** leasehold

terme *m* (mot) terme; (fin) end; (période de temps) term; ~**s** (d'un accord) terms; (date de paiement du loyer) due date; **au** ~ **de** at the end of; **en** ~**s absolus** in absolute terms; **selon les** ~**s du contrat** under the terms of the contract; **en** ~**s de pourcentage** in percentage terms; **en** ~**s réels** in real terms; **en** ~**s relatifs** in relative terms; **à** ~ **future**; **à court/long** ~ short/long-term; **à** ~ **moyen** (Bourse) medium-dated; ~ **à** ~ (Bourse) forward-forward; **achat/vente à** ~ forward buying/selling; **payer son** ~ (location) pay one's rent; **mettre un** ~ **à** put an end to; **toucher à son** ~ come to an end; **mener qch à** ~ see sth through to the end; **arriver à** ~ come to an end; (période, délai, contrat) expire; **trouver un moyen** ~ (équilibre) find a happy

medium; (compromis) find a compromise; ~ **à
la mode** buzz word; ~ **commercial
international** international commercial
term; ~**s et conditions** terms and
conditions; ~**s de l'échange** terms of trade;
~ **d'échéance** term of payment; ~**s
factoriels de l'échange** factorial terms of
trade; ~ **locatif** rental term; ~**s précisés**
(d'un contrat) express terms; ~ **de rigueur**
strict time limit

terminal *m* (Info) terminal, visual display
unit; (Transp) passenger terminal, terminal;
~ **acier** steel terminal; ~ **d'aéroglisseurs**
hoverport; ~ **autonome** (Info) smart
terminal; ~ **à conteneurs** (maritime)
container terminal; ~ **d'édition** (Info) report
terminal; ~ **de fret** freight terminal; ~
frigo (Transp) (navigation) cold store terminal;
~ **graphique** (Info) graphic display terminal;
~ **informatique** computer terminal; ~
intérieur onshore terminal; ~ **de paiement
électronique** electronic payment terminal;
~ **passif** (Info) dumb terminal; ~ **pétrolier**
oil terminal; ~ **plein écran** (Info) full-screen
terminal; ~ **point de vente** point-of-sale
terminal

terminé, e *adj* completed

terminer ①︎ *vt* end, finish; **le dollar a
terminé la semaine à 1.2 euro** the dollar
ended the week at 1,2 euro; ~ **premier** finish
first; **l'indice a terminé en baisse/hausse**
(Fin) the index closed lower/higher; ~ **en
hausse de 12 points à 1821** close twelve
points up at 1821; ~ **dans le cours** finish in
the money; ~ **les émissions** close down; ~
une session (Info) log out, log off
②︎ **se terminer** *v pron* finish

terrain *m* (parcelle) plot of land; **céder/
gagner du** ~ give/gain ground; **préparer le**
~ pave the way; **travail sur le** ~ work in the
field; **recherches sur le** ~ fieldwork; **trouver
un** ~ **d'entente** find common ground; **être
en** ~ **connu** be on familiar territory; **être en**
~ **sûr** be on solid ground; ~ **à bâtir** building
plot; ~ **entourant la maison d'habitation**
curtilage; ~ **non bâti** undeveloped plot,
vacant lot AmE; ~ **non constructible** plot
not suitable for development; ~ **pétrolifère**
oil field; ~ **remis en valeur** reclaimed area;
~ **vague** wasteland

terre *f* land; **à** ~ onshore; ~ **agricole**
farmland; ~ **agricole occupée par le
propriétaire** owner-occupied farmland; ~
améliorée improved land; ~ **blanche** white
land (jarg); ~**s cultivées** farmland; ~**s
inondables** flood plain; ~**s en jachère**
fallow land; ~ **vague** waste ground BrE,
empty lot AmE; ~ **vierge** raw land

terre-plein *m* (Transp) open storage; (port)
standage area

terrestre *adj* terrestrial

territoire *m* territory; ~ **de vente** (zone)
sales territory, trading area

territorial, e *adj* (d'un État) territorial; (d'une
région) regional

test *m* test; ~ **d'admissibilité** eligibility
test; ~ **alpha** alpha test; ~ **anonyme**
(marketing) blind test; ~ **d'aptitude** aptitude
test; ~ **assisté par ordinateur** computer-
aided test; ~**s assistés par ordinateur**
computer-aided testing, computer-assisted
testing; ~ **aveugle** (marketing) blind test; ~
comparatif comparison test; ~ **de concept**
concept test; ~ **de conformité** compliance
test; ~ **de consommation** consumer test;
~ **d'évaluation des performances** (Info)
benchmark test; ~ **intégré** built-in test; ~
de marché test marketing; ~ **de
mémorisation assistée** (étude de marché)
aided recall test; ~ **de niveau** achievement
test; ~ **d'observation** observation test; ~
sur un panel (étude de marché) panel testing;
~ **pilote** beta test; ~ **de produit** product
testing; ~ **psychométrique** psychometric
test; ~ **publicitaire** advertising test; ~ **de
rentabilité** profit test; ~ **de sélection**
selection test; ~ **statistique** statistical test;
~ **de vente** (sur une région) market test

testamentaire *adj* (lettre) testamentary;
donation ~ bequest, legacy; **exécuteur** ~
executor

testateur *m* testator

testatrice *f* testatrix

testé, e *adj* tested; (Droit) testate

tester ①︎ *vt* test
②︎ *vi* (Droit) make a will

testeur, -euse *m,f* tester

testimonial, -e *adj* testimonial

tête *f* head; **par** ~ per head, per capita; **20
euros par** ~ 20 euros a head *ou* per person;
le PNB par ~ the per capita GNP; **être à la**
~ be top of the list; (d'élection, de sondage) be
in the lead; **être à la** ~ **d'une entreprise** be
at the head of a company; ~ **fixe** (Transp)
fixed head; ~ **de lecture/d'écriture** (Info)
read/write head; ~ **de ligne** (Transp)
railhead; ~ **de liste minimale** (Ind)
minimum list heading UK

texte *m* text; (presse) copy; **le** ~ **d'un
contrat** the wording of a contract; ~**s
d'application** (UE) secondary legislation; ~
d'écran soft copy; ~ **intégral** text in full; ~
législatif legal enactment; ~ **de loi** (proposé)
bill; (promulgé) act; ~ **de présentation** blurb
(jarg); ~ **promulgué** legal enactment; ~
publicitaire advertising copy; ~
publicitaire obligatoire mandatory copy

textile *m* textiles; **le** ~ (industrie) the textile
industry; ~**s artificiels/synthétiques**
artificial/man-made fibres

texto *m* text message; **envoyer un** ~ **à qn**
text sb

textuellement *adv* verbatim

TGD *abrév* (▸**transport à grande
distance**) long-range transport

TGV *abrév* (▶**train à grande vitesse**) TGV, high-speed train

théâtre *m* (de débat) topic, subject; (de discours) theme; (genre) theatre BrE, theater AmE

thème *m* theme; ∼ **musical** (télévision) theme tune; ∼ **publicitaire** advertising theme

théonomie *f* theonomy

théorème *m* theorem; ∼ **de la baignoire** bathtub theorem; ∼ **d'équivalence de Ricardo** Ricardo invariance principle; ∼ **du péage** turnpike theorem; ∼ **de la surcapacité** excess capacity theorem

théoricien, -enne *m,f* theoretician, theorist; ∼ **d'option** option theorist

théorie *f* theory; ∼ **catastrophe** catastrophe theory; ∼ **du chaos** chaos theory; ∼ **des coûts comparatifs** theory of comparative costs; ∼ **économique** economic theory; ∼ **évolutionniste** (de firme) evolutionary theory; ∼ **de l'information** information theory; ∼ **des jeux** game theory; ∼ **de l'organisation** organization(al) theory; ∼ **des probabilités** probability theory; ∼ **des salaires** wage theory

théorique *adj* theoretical

thermomètre *m* thermometer; ∼ **publicitaire** advertising thermometer

thésauriser ① *vt* (argent, richesses) hoard ② *vi* hoard money

THS *abrév* (▶**transaction hors séance**) THS transaction

TIC *abrév* (▶**taux d'intérêt comptable**) ARI (accounting rate of interest)

ticket *m* ticket; ∼ **de caisse** till receipt BrE, sales slip AmE

ticket-repas *m* luncheon voucher BrE, meal ticket AmE

ticket-restaurant® *m* luncheon voucher BrE, meal ticket AmE

tiers[1], **tierce** *adj* third; **tierce personne** (Droit) third party; **tierce collision** collision coverage, collision insurance; ∼ **monde** Third World

tiers[2] *m* (fraction) third; (personne) outsider; (Droit) third party; **assurance au** ∼ third party insurance; ∼ **payant** direct payment by insurance (for medical care); ∼ **provisionnel** tax payment (*equal to one third of annual tax*)

timbre *m* postage stamp; ∼ **d'endos** endorsement stamp; ∼ **fiscal** revenue stamp; ∼ **de quittance** receipt stamp

timbre-poste *m* postage stamp

timbre-prime *m* trading stamp

timbre-taxe *m* postage-due stamp

TIOP *abrév* (▶**taux interbancaire offert à Paris**) PIBOR (Paris Interbank Offered Rate)

TIOT *abrév* (▶**taux interbancaire offert à Tokyo**) TIBOR (Tokyo Interbank Offered Rate)

TIR *abrév* (▶**transport international routier**) *convention on the contract for the international carriage of goods by road*

tirage *m* (d'un effet, d'un chèque) drawing; (Info) hard copy; (presse) circulation; (d'un livre) print run; (impression, réimpression) impression; ∼ **à découvert** kiting; ∼ **au sort** draw

tiré, e *m,f* (au sort) drawee; (Fin) drawee; (d'une traite) acceptor

tire-au-flanc *m* (infrml) shirker, skiver BrE (infrml)

tirer ① *vt* (chèque, conclusion) draw; (information) extract; (livre, texte) print; (exemplaire, épreuve) run off; ∼ **avantage de** benefit from; ∼ **beaucoup de profit de** (des biens) make a good deal by; ∼ **le bon numéro** spot the winner; ∼ **à découvert** overdraw; ∼ **les ficelles pour qn** (infrml) pull strings for sb (infrml), pull wires for sb AmE (infrml); ∼ **parti de** make full use of; ∼ **des plans** draw up *ou* make plans; ∼ **profit de** benefit from; ∼ **la sonnette d'alarme** blow the whistle (infrml); **journal tiré à 10 mille exemplaires** newspaper with a circulation of ten thousand; ∼ **une traite en l'air** kite ② **se tirer** *v pron* **se** ∼ **d'affaire** get out of trouble

tiret *m* dash; ∼ **court** en dash; ∼ **long** em dash

tireur, -euse *m,f* (de chèque) drawer; (d'un effet) maker

titre *m* (Droit) deed; (Fin) (valeur) security; (rang) title; (imprimé) headline; (de chapitre) heading; (de livre, film) title; (de revue, de périodique) title; **à** ∼ **consultatif** in an advisory capacity; **à** ∼ **de précaution** as a precautionary measure; **à** ∼ **provisoire** on a provisional basis **à** ∼ **gracieux** ex gratia (frml); **à** ∼ **comparatif/expérimental** by way of a comparison/an experiment; **à** ∼ **honoraire** in an honorary capacity; **à** ∼ **d'information** for your information; **à** ∼ **officiel/non officiel** in an official/unofficial capacity; **à** ∼ **onéreux** for a consideration; **en** ∼ (directeur) titular; **les** ∼**s de l'actualité** news headlines; ∼ **acquis sur marge** margin security; ∼ **d'action** share certificate BrE, stock certificate AmE; ∼ **appelé au remboursement** called security; ∼ **assurable** insurable title; ∼ **bêta** beta stock UK, beta US; ∼ **avec bons de souscription** stock with subscription rights; ∼ **commercial** (détail) commercial bill AmE, trade bill; ∼ **du compte** title of an account; ∼ **du compte de placement** investment account security; ∼ **constitutif de propriété sur la marchandise** title to the goods; ∼ **contestable** defective title; ∼ **convertible** convertible security; ∼ **court neutre garanti** neutral covered short; ∼ **de créance** credit instrument; (pour le créancier) certificate of indebtedness; ∼ **de créance**

hypothécaire mortgage-backed security; ∼ **de créance principale** primary instrument of indebtedness; ∼ **de créances** proof of debt; ∼ **démembré** stripped security; ∼ **déposé en garantie** collateral security; ∼ **déprécié** wallflower (jarg); ∼ **détenu** security holding; ∼ **détenu sans profit** stale bull (jarg); ∼ **de deuxième ordre** second-class paper; ∼ **avec droit de vote** voting security; ∼ **d'emprunt** (pour l'emprunteur) debt security; ∼ **essentiellement nominatif** fully registered security; ∼ **d'État** government bond, government stock; ∼ **fictif** phantom share; ∼ **flamboyant** (presse) streamer; ∼ **de fonction** job title; ∼ **garanti** guaranteed security; ∼ **du gouvernement fédéral américain** US federal government paper; ∼ **de hors-cote** over-the-counter US; ∼ **hors marché** municipal bond US; ∼ **imparfait** defective title; ∼ **incontestable** clear title US; ∼ **indexé** indexed security; ∼ **d'investissement** security; ∼ **irréfragable** clear title US; ∼ **irréfutable** absolute title, clear title US; ∼ **du jour au lendemain** overnight security; ∼ **long neutre garanti** neutral covered long; ∼ **mutilé** mutilated security; ∼ **négociable** marketable title, merchantable title AmE; ∼ **nominatif** registered security; ∼ **non négociable** nonmerchantable title AmE; ∼ **d'obligataire** obligation bond; ∼ **d'une option couverte** covered option securities; ∼ **participatif** participating security; ∼ **de participation** equity investment, participation certificate; ∼ **de placement** (Banque) investment account security; (Bourse) marketable bond; ∼ **portant intérêt** interest-bearing security; ∼ **au porteur** bearer certificate, bearer security; ∼ **pouvant faire l'objet d'options** option eligible security; ∼ **préférentiel** prior-lien bond; ∼ **de prêt** loan certificate; ∼ **prioritaire** senior security; ∼ **privilégié** senior security; ∼ **privilégié à taux variable** adjustable-rate preferred stock; ∼ **de propriété** proof of ownership; (Droit) title deed; ∼ **de propriété inscrit au registre du cadastre** registered title; ∼ **de propriété invalide** bad title; ∼ **de propriété sur la marchandise** title to the goods; ∼ **de référence** bellwether (jarg); ∼ **avec rétrocession immédiate** pass-through security; ∼ **subordonné à durée indéterminée** subordinated perpetual bond; ∼ **subordonné remboursable** subordinated redeemable bond; ∼ **transporté en gage** pledge security; ∼ **transporté en nantissement** pledge security; ∼ **trou d'air** air pocket stock (jarg); ∼ **universel de paiement** universal payment order

titres *m pl* (actions) securities, stocks; (documents) paper qualifications; **faire les gros ∼ des journaux** hit the headlines; ∼ **de**
l'actualité (presse, radio, télévision) news headline; ∼ **admis à la cote officielle** quoted securities; ∼ **avec certification informatique** book-entry securities; ∼ **de chemin de fer** railway securities BrE, railroad securities AmE; ∼ **en compte** securities long; ∼ **cotés** listed securities; ∼ **à découvert** securities short; ∼ **demandés** securities wanted; ∼ **détenus en fiducie** securities held in trust; ∼ **empruntés** borrowed stock; ∼ **d'État** government securities; ∼ **exonérés d'impôts** tax-exempt securities; ∼ **formant rompus** broken amount, broken lot; ∼ **frappés d'opposition** stopped bonds; ∼ **garantis par actif financier** asset-backed securities; ∼ **garantis par le nantissement du matériel** equipment trust bond; ∼ **négociables** negotiable securities; ∼ **non achetés** floating securities; ∼ **non remboursables** noncallable securities; ∼ **non rémunérés** non-interest-bearing securities; **Titres participatifs à bons de souscription de titres participatifs** *equity loans with equity loans warrants*; **Titres participatifs convertibles en certificats d'investissement privilégiés** *equity loans convertible into preference investment certificates*; ∼ **partiellement payés** partly paid up shares; ∼ **en pension** pawned stock; ∼ **de placement** marketable securities; ∼ **de propriété** muniments, muniments of title; **Titres subordonnés remboursables avec bons de souscription d'obligations remboursables en actions** *subordinated redeemable notes with warrants that can be converted into bonds or shares*; ∼ **très liquides** near cash (jarg); ∼ **vendus en pension livrée** securities sold under repurchase agreement

titrisation *f* (Fin, Bourse) securitization

titriser *vt* (Fin, Bourse) securitize

titulaire¹ *adj* permanent; (enseignant) tenured

titulaire² *mf* (d'un poste) incumbent; (Bourse) (option) buyer, (option) holder; ∼ **du brevet** *m* patent proprietor; ∼ **de carte** *m* cardholder; ∼ **d'un compte** *m* account holder; ∼ **d'un compte courant** *m* current account holder BrE; ∼ **contractant** *m* contracting holder; ∼ **d'une licence** *m* (propriété intellectuelle) licensee; ∼ **d'un passeport** *m* passport holder

titularisation *f* permanent appointment

titulariser *vt* (Admin) (agent, personnel) give permanent status to; (enseignant) grant tenure to; **être titularisé** be confirmed in post, get a permanent contract; (enseignant) get tenure

TJJ *abrév* (▸**taux d'argent au jour le jour**) call money rate, daily money rate

TMI *abrév* (▸**tendance marginale à importer**) MPI (marginal propensity to   ⸱⸱⸱▷

import)

TMM *abrév* (▶**taux du marché monétaire**) money-market rate

TMMMM *abrév* (▶**taux moyen mensuel du marché monétaire**) average monthly money market table

TMO *abrév* (▶**taux de marché obligataire**) bond market rate

TMP *abrév* (▶**taux moyen pondéré**) average weighted rate

TMS *abrév* (▶**trouble musculo-squelettique**) RSI (repetitive strain injury)

TOF *abrév* (▶**tableau des opérations financières**) flow-of-funds table

Toile *f* (Info) web; **sur la ~** on the web; **centre d'appel sur la ~** web call centre BrE, web call center AmE; **~ mondiale** World Wide Web

toilettes *f pl* toilet BrE, rest room AmE

tolérable *adj* (attente, situation) tolerable, bearable; (comportement, retard) tolerable

tolérance *f* tolerance; **~ de pannes** (Info) fault-tolerant; **~ à l'importation** import allowance; **~ maximale** absolute limit

tolérant, e *adj* tolerant; **~ à l'acide** acid-resistant

tollé *m* outcry; **~ général** public outcry

tombée *f* (Média) copy deadline

tomber *vi* (valeur, prix) fall; **faire ~** (prix) bring down; (obstacle) remove; (barrières) break down; **~ d'accord** agree; **~ au-dessous du plancher** bottom out; **~ dans le champ d'application de** fall within the scope of; **~ en deçà d'un objectif** undershoot a target; **~ en désuétude** fall into abeyance; **~ à l'eau** (projet) fall through; **~ en panne** (machine) break down; (Info) crash; **~ sous le coup de la loi** fall foul of the law

tonalité *f* dialling tone BrE, dial tone AmE

toner *m* toner

tonnage *m* (d'un navire) tonnage; **~ brut** gross tonnage; **~ brut complet** (train) gross train weight; **~ de cargaison** cargo tonnage; **~ cube** cubic tonnage; **~ désarmé** (navigation) idle tonnage; **~ de jauge** register tonnage; **~ en lourd** deadweight tonnage; **~ sous pavillon national** (navires) national flag tonnage

tonne *f* (1000 kilos) (metric) ton, tonne; **~ connaissement** bill of lading ton; **~ courte américaine** American short ton; **~ d'encombrement** measurement ton; **~ (d')équivalent pétrole** ton (of) oil-equivalent; **~ forte** gross ton, long ton; **~ de jauge** registered ton; **~ de jauge brute** gross register ton; **~ de jauge nette** net register ton; **~ kilométrique** tonne kilometre BrE, ton kilometer AmE; **~ métrique** metric ton; **~ par mile** ton mile, tonne mile

tonneau *m* barrel, cask; **~ d'affrètement** shipping ton

tonnelet *m* keg

tonnellerie *f* cooperage

topographie *f* (Info) map; **~ de mémoire** storage map

tore *m* (Info) core; **~ magnétique** magnetic core

tort *m* (faute) fault; (préjudice) wrong; (erreur) mistake; **à ~** wrongly; **avoir ~** be wrong; **avoir ~ de faire** be wrong to do; **porter ~ à qn/qch** harm sb/sth; **demander réparation d'un ~** demand compensation for a wrong

total¹, e *adj* (contrôle, retrait) complete, total; (revenu, qualité, prix, surface, budget) total; (hauteur, nombre) full

total² *m* total; **faire le ~ des dépenses** add up the expenditure; **cela fait 350 euros au ~** altogether that comes to 350 euros; **~ de l'actif** asset value, total assets; **~ par activité** activity total; **~ annuel mobile** moving annual total; **~ du budgétaire** total budgetary; **~ de contrôle** checksum; **~ des créditeurs** total liabilities; **~ cumulé** total to date; **~ cumulé de l'année** year to date; **~ de la dette publique** total public debt; **~ des emprunts et dettes** total liabilities; **~ des feuilles de paie** total payroll; **~ des fonds fournis** total funds provided; **~ des fonds imputés** total funds applied; **~ général** grand total; **~ du non-budgétaire** total nonbudgetary; **~ partiel** subtotal; **~ des prévisions** total estimates

totalisateur *m* (Info) accumulator

totalisation *f* totalling

totaliser *vt* (faire le total de) add up; (atteindre le total de) total, have a total of; **~ 7 000 euros** have a total of 7 000 euros

totalité *f* entirety; **~ des dépenses publiques** total public spending; **dans sa ~** in its entirety; **en ~** wholly, entirely; **en ou presque** wholly or in substantial part

touche *f* touch; (de clavier) key; **sur la ~** on the touchline; **d'activation** hot key; **~ d'aide** help key; **~ barre oblique inverse** backslash key; **~ de commande de curseur** arrow key; **~ de contrôle** control key; **~ de direction** arrow key; **~ d'échappement** escape key; **~ à effleurement** touch key; **~ Entrée** enter key; **~ de fonction** function key; **~ majuscule** shift key; **~ morte** dead key; **~ option** dead key; **~ rapide** hot key; **~ de remise à zéro** reset button; **~ Retour** enter key; **~ souris** mouse button, mouse key

toucher *vt* (chèque) cash; (prime) collect; (cours le plus bas) hit, record; (région, secteur, pays, groupe) affect; **~ des allocations** receive benefit UK, be on welfare US; **~ le cours offert** hit the bid; **~ un mot à qn au sujet de qch** have a word with sb about sth; **~ des pots-de-vin** be on the take (infrml), take bribes; **~ une retraite** get *ou* draw a pension; **~ un salaire de** earn a salary of

toujours *adv* always; **~ en vigueur** (contrat)

unexpired

tour¹ *m* tour; **à ~ de rôle** in rotation; **faire un ~ d'horizon de la situation** survey the situation

tour² *f* tower; **~ de contrôle** (aéroport, port maritime) air traffic control; **~ d'habitation** high rise, tower block

tourisme *m* tourism; **agence/bureau de ~** tourist agency/office; **~ blanc** skiing holidays; **~ bleu** seaside holidays; **~ étranger** foreign tourism

touriste *mf* tourist; **~ étranger** foreign tourist

tournant *m* turning point; **marquer un ~** mark a turning point

tournée *f* tour; **en ~** (théâtre) on tour; **~ électorale** election tour; **~ de présentation** road show; **~ de promotion** promotional tour; **~ publicitaire** advertising tour

tourner *vi* turn, veer; **~ bien** go well; **~ mal** go wrong, turn out badly; **~ au ralenti** tick over; **~ à plein régime** go full steam; **~ autour de** (prix) be in the region of, be around; **tournez s'il vous plaît** (en bas de page) please turn over; **tourné vers l'action** action-oriented; **tourné vers l'avenir** forward-looking; **tourné vers le commerce** business-orientated

tournure *f* turn; **prendre ~** take shape, shape up; **prendre mauvaise ~** go wrong, take a turn for the worse; **prendre bonne ~** take a turn for the better, get better; **~ des événements** turn of events

tour-opérateur *m* tour operator

toxicité *f* toxicity

toxicologique *adj* toxicological

toxique *adj* toxic

TPBSTP *abrév* (►**Titres participatifs à bons de souscription de titres participatifs**) equity loans with equity loans warrants

TPCCIP *abrév* (►**Titres participatifs convertibles en certificats d'investissement privilégiés**) equity loans convertible into preference investment certificates

TPE *abrév* (►**terminal de paiement électronique**) EPT (electronic payment terminal); (►**très petite entreprise**) very small business

TPS *abrév* (►**taxe de prestation de service**) GST (goods and services tax)

TPV *abrév* (►**terminal point de vente**) POST (point-of-sale terminal)

TRA *abrév* (►**taux révisable annuellement**) interest rate subject to modification every year

traçabilité *f* traceability

trace *f* trace

tracer *vt* (graphique) plot; **~ une courbe** chart; **~ une voie nouvelle** break new ground

traceur *m* (Info) plotting pen; **~ de courbes** graph plotter; **~ à tambour** drum plotter

trackball *m* (Info) trackball

tracker *m* tracker fund

tract *m* flier, flyer

tractage *m* (aviation) towing

tracteur *m* (routier) tractive unit; **~ de terminal** (ports) tugmaster

tradition *f* tradition

traditionnel, -elle *adj* traditional; **entreprise traditionnelle** traditional company; (sans présence sur Internet) bricks and mortar company

traducteur, -trice *m,f* translator

traduction *f* translation; **~ assistée par ordinateur** computer-aided translation; **~ automatique** machine translation; **~ simultanée** simultaneous translation

traduire ⊞ *vt* (langues) translate; (Droit) **qn en justice** bring sb to justice
② **se traduire** *v pron* **~ par** (crise, instabilité) result in; **se ~ par un échec** result in failure

trafic *m* traffic; (commerce illégal) trafficking; (d'armes) dealing; (Info) traffic; **faire du ~ de qch** traffic/deal in sth; **~ aérien** air traffic; **~ de drogue** drug trafficking; **~ ferroviaire** rail traffic; **~ international** international traffic; **~ de marchandises** freight traffic; **~ maritime** maritime shipping; **~ de poids lourds** heavy goods traffic; **~ portuaire** port throughput, port traffic; **~ de remplissage** (marchandises) filler traffic; **~ réservé** booked traffic; **~ sur pneus** rubber-tyred traffic BrE, rubber-tired traffic AmE; **~ à tarif voyageurs** passenger-rated traffic; **~ de terminal** terminal traffic; **~ de transit** transit traffic

trafiquant, e *m,f* (de drogue) trafficker; (d'armes) dealer

trafiquer *vt* traffic, deal

trafiqueur *m* (Bourse) scalper US (infrml)

train *m* train; (de réformes) package; **~ bloc de conteneurs** freightliner BrE; **~ direct** through train; **~ électrique** electric train; **~ ferry** train ferry; **~ à grande vitesse** high-speed train; **~ de marchandises** goods train BrE, freight train AmE; **~ roulant à vide** deadhead AmE (infrml); **~ routier** drawbar combination, road train Australia, triback; **~ de voyageurs** passenger train

traînard *f* (infrml) (Bourse) laggard

traîne *f* **être à la ~** fall behind

traîner *vi* **~ derrière** lag behind; **~ en justice** take sb to court

traite *f* (Fin) draft, bill; (versement) instalment BrE, installment AmE; **tirer/escompter une ~** draw/discount a draft; **donner avis d'une ~** advise a draft; **~ à l'acceptation** acceptance bill; **~ acceptée** accepted draft; ····⊱

~ **en l'air** (jarg) kite (jarg); ~ **avisée** advised bill; ~ **bancaire** bank draft BrE, cashier's check AmE; ~ **de complaisance** accommodation draft, convenience bill; ~ **à courte échéance** short bill; ~ **en devises** currency draft; ~ **documentaire** documentary draft; ~ **à échéance** usance bill; ~ **impayée** dishonoured bill of exchange BrE, dishonored bill of exchange AmE; ~ **induite** induced draft; ~ **nantie par des titres** stock draft; ~ **à payer** bill payable; ~ **à recevoir** bill receivable; ~ **à vue** sight draft

traité *m* treaty; ~ **commercial** trade agreement; ~ **commercial bilatéral** (commerce international) bilateral trade treaty; ~ **de coopération relatif aux brevets d'invention** (propriété intellectuelle) Patent Cooperation Treaty; ~ **de réassurance** stop-loss reinsurance; **Traité de Rome** Treaty of Rome; **Traité de l'Union européenne** European Union Treaty

traitement *m* (de personne) treatment; (manière d'aborder, de régler) handling; (de chèque, brevet, demande) processing; (d'une plainte, d'un dossier) handling; (salaire) salary; (Info) processing; ~ **en arrière-plan** background processing; ~ **automatique des données** automatic data processing; ~ **de base** basic rate; ~ **biologique** biological treatment; ~ **communautaire** (de marchandises) Community treatment; ~ **comptable** accounting treatment; ~ **concurrent** concurrent processing; ~ **décentralisé** distributed computing; ~ **des déchets** waste treatment; ~ **des denrées alimentaires** food processing; ~ **différé** batch processing; ~ **différé des entrées/ sorties** spooling; ~ **en direct des opérations bancaires** online banking; ~ **des données** data processing; ~ **des eaux** water treatment; ~ **des eaux usées** wastewater treatment; ~ **électronique de l'information** electronic data processing; ~ **des entrées** inward processing; ~ **des erreurs** error control; ~ **de faveur** preferential treatment; ~ **fiscal** tax treatment; ~ **de fond** background processing; ~ **de l'information** information handling; ~ **informatique** computer processing; ~ **interactif** interactive processing; ~ **par lots** batch job, batch processing; ~ **de messages** message handling; ~ **de mouvements** transaction processing; ~ **multitâche** multitasking; ~ **multitravail** multijobbing; ~ **de la nation la plus favorisée** (commerce international) most-favoured nation treatment BrE, most-favored nation treatment AmE; ~ **non-prioritaire** background processing; ~ **par ordinateur** computer processing; ~ **par paquets** batch processing; ~ **en parallèle** parallel processing; ~ **de la parole** speech processing; ~ **du personnel** payroll; ~

préliminaire pretreatment; ~**s et salaires** salaries and wages; ~ **en série** serial processing; ~ **simultané** concurrent processing; ~ **en simultanéité** parallel processing; ~ **en tâche de fond** background processing; ~ **de texte** word processing; ~ **transactionnel** transaction processing; ~ **vocal** speech processing

traiter ① *vt* (problème, dossier) deal with; (bois, textile, récoltes) treat; (Info) (données, information) process; ② *vi* negotiate, do a deal; ~ **avec qn** negotiate with sb, deal with sb

trajet *m* (voyage) journey; (parcours) route; ~**s journaliers** commuting, commutation BrE; ~ **direct** direct route; ~ **à escales multiples** (routier) multiple drop; ~ **d'essai** test drive; ~ **fixe** fixed route; ~ **de retour** (expédition) back haul; ~ **à la zone de travail** travel-to-work area

trame *f* (Info) raster; (de télécommunication) frame

tranche *f* band; (d'imposition) bracket; (d'un graphique) segment; ~ **d'âge** (étude de marché) age bracket, age group; ~ **d'âge du consommateur** consumer age group; ~ **de crédit** credit rating; ~ **horaire** time band; ~ **horaire de fin de soirée** late night slot, late fringe US (jarg); ~ **horizontale de cellule** (porte-conteneurs) slot; ~ **d'imposition** tax band, tax bracket; ~ **inférieure de revenus** lower income bracket; ~ **matinale** (jarg) (Média) early fringe (jarg); ~ **mezzanine** mezzanine bracket; ~ **moyenne du marché** middle range of the market; ~ **moyenne de revenus** middle income bracket; ~ **de la nuit** (Média) late night; ~ **de revenu** income band, income bracket; (étude de marché) income group; ~ **de salaires** wage bracket; ~ **supérieure de revenus** higher income bracket

trancher *vi* (arbitrer) arbitrate

transaction *f* (commerciale) transaction, deal; (en Bourse) transaction, deal, trade; ~**s** trading; **faire une** ~ make a transaction; ~ **d'achat** bought deal; ~ **aller et retour** bed and breakfast deal (jarg); ~**s automatisées** computer trading, US paperless trading; ~ **à la baisse** bear operation, bear transaction; ~ **sur bloc de titres** block trade; ~ **de clôture** closing trade, closing transaction; ~ **commerciale** business transaction, business deal; ~ **complexe** complex transaction UK; ~ **au comptant** (Bourse) spot transaction; (Compta) cash deal; ~ **sur contrat à terme** futures transaction; ~ **croisée** crossed trade; ~ **en devises** foreign currency transaction; ~ **à l'échelon de cotation inférieur** zero-minus tick; ~ **à l'échelon de cotation supérieur** zero-plus tick; ~ **expédiée** bundled deal; ~ **fictive** sham trading; ~ **financière transfrontalière** cross-border financial transaction; ~ **à la hausse** bull operation, bull transaction; ~**s**

hors bourse after-hours dealing, after-hours trading; ~ **hors corbeille** ex-pit transaction; ~ **hors parquet** upstairs market; ~ **hors séance** THS transaction; ~ **d'initié** insider dealing, insider trading; ~ **inverse** opposite transaction; ~ **sans lien de dépendance** arm's-length transaction; ~ **nette de frais** net transaction; ~ **au pair** par trading; ~ **au prix du marché** arm's-length transaction; ~ **programmée par ordinateur** programme trade BrE, program trade AmE; ~ **sans risque** risk-free transaction; ~ **sur rompu** odd lot transaction; ~ **à terme** forward transaction; ~ **transfrontières** cross-border transaction; ~s **24h/24** twenty-four hour trading

transactionnel, -elle *adj* transactional

transbordement *m* (de marchandises) transshipment; (de passagers) transfer; ~ **direct** direct transhipment; ~ **de véhicule** vehicle transhipment

transborder *vt* (marchandises) transship; (passagers) transfer

transbordeur *m* ferry; ~ **de passagers et véhicules** passenger-vehicle ferry

transcoder *vt* transcode

transcodeur *m* transcoder

transcripteur *m* transcriber

transcription *f* transcription

transcrire *vt* transcribe

transducteur *m* transducer

transeuropéen, -enne *adj* transeuropean

transférabilité *f* (des données) import-export

transférable *adj* transferable; **non** ~ nontransferable

transférer *vt* (société) relocate; (propriété) assign, convey; (fonds) transfer; (Info) dump; ~ **par endossement** transfer by endorsement

transfert *m* transfer; (de société, d'usine) relocation; (de propriété) assignment, conveyance; ~ **d'actif** transfer of assets; ~ **d'actions** legal transfer, share transfer; ~ **d'appel** call forwarding; ~ **d'argent** money transfer; ~ **d'argent immédiat** immediate money transfer; ~ **de bloc** block move, block transfer; ~ **de données** data transfer; ~ **électronique de fonds** electronic funds transfer; ~ **entre dépôts** interdepot transfer; ~ **entre frontières** (de déchets dangereux) cross-frontier transfer; ~ **aux entreprises** transfer to business; ~ **de fonds** cash transfer, funds transfer; ~ **d'information** information transfer; ~ **interne** (Bourse) internalization; ~ **légal** (de valeurs) legal transfer; ~ **libre d'impôt** roll-over; ~ **de marchandises** cargo transfer; ~ **par courrier** mail transfer; ~ **pécuniaire** cash transfer; ~ **de personnel** staff transfer; ~ **de portefeuille** portfolio transfer; ~ **de prime** premium transfer; ~

social (Banque) payment transfer; ~ **de technologie** technology transfer; ~ **télégraphique** telegraphic transfer; ~ **de vote** crossover vote US

transformation *f* (Gen com) change; (radicale) transformation; (de locaux) alteration, conversion; (acier, produit agricole, textile) processing; **travaux de** ~ alterations; ~ **de créances en participation** debt-equity swap; ~ **des déchets** waste processing; ~ **de la monnaie en marchandises** commodification of money

transformer ⟩1⟩ *vt* (Gen com) change; (profondément) transform; (locaux) carry out alterations to, convert; (acier, produit agricole, textile) process ⟩2⟩ **se transformer** *v pron* change

transfrontalier, -ière *adj* cross-border, transfrontier

transgénique *adj* genetically modified, transgenic

transiger *vi* compromise; ~ **sur une dette** compound a debt

transit *m* transit; **en** ~ in transit; ~ **communautaire** (marchandises à l'intérieur de l'UE) Community transit; ~ **contrôlé** controlled transit; ~ **de marchandises** cargo transit

transitaire *mf* forwarding agent

transitionnel, -elle *adj* transitional

translatable *adj* (Info) relocatable

translation *f* (Info) relocation

transmanche *adj* cross-Channel

transmetteur, -trice *adj* (fil) transmitting

transmettre *vt* (message, signaux, données) transmit; (pouvoir, direction) hand over; (information, savoir, ordre) pass on

transmis, e *adj* (Fisc) passing

transmissible *adj* (Droit) transferable

transmission *f* (communication) transmission, passing on; (de signaux, de données) transmission; (de propriété) conveyance; ~ **de capital** capital transfer; ~ **de données** data communications; ~ **de l'information par voie hiérarchique** formal communication; ~ **d'octets en série** byte mode; ~ **simultanée** (radio-télévision) simultaneous broadcast; ~ **de titres au porteur ordinaire** regular way delivery; ~ **unidirectionnelle** (Info) simplex

transnational, e *adj* cross-border, transnational

transpalette *m* pallet truck; (manutention) hand pallet-transporter

transparence *f* transparency; (Fin) visibility; (Pol) openness, transparency; ~ **bancaire en matière de prêts** (commercial) truth in lending; ~ **financière** financial visibility; ~ **fiscale** tax transparency; ~ **de l'information** transparency of information (jarg); ~ **du marché** market transparency; ~ **à trente jours** thirty-day visible supply

transparent¹, e *adj* transparent

transparent² *m* overhead transparency

transport *m* transport, transportation AmE; ~ **aérien** air freight, air transport; ~ **de bout à bout** through shipment; ~ **par chemin de fer** rail freight; ~ **de colis lourds** (navigation) belship; ~ **collectif rapide** mass rapid transit; ~ **combiné** combined transport, intermodal transport; ~**s en commun** public transport, public transportation AmE; ~ **par conteneurs** container transport; ~ **ferroviaire** rail transport; ~ **à grande distance** long-range transport; ~ **international** international carriage, international traffic; ~ **international routier** *convention on the contract for the international carriage of goods by road*; ~ **de marchandises** conveyance of goods, freight transport; ~ **maritime** sea transport; ~ **maritime à la demande** tramping; ~ **multimodal** combined transport, multimodal transport; ~ **de nuit** night trunk; ~ **privé du client** customer's own transport; ~ **routier** haulage, motor freight, road transport; ~**s routiers** road haulage; ~ **par service rapide** expressage; ~ **par terre** land carriage; ~ **terrestre** ground transportation, land carriage; ~ **thermorégulé** temperature-controlled transport; ~ **par voie d'eau** water transportation

transportable *adj* transportable

transporter *vt* (Transp) transport; (Fin) (créance) transfer; ~ **par avion** transport by air; **transporté par mer** (marchandises) seaborne

transporteur *m* (entreprise) carrier; ~ **aérien** air carrier; ~ **à bande** conveyor belt; ~ **de colis lourds** (navigation) heavy lift ship; ~ **pour compte propre** industrial carrier; ~ **contractuel** contract carrier; ~ **destinataire** receiving carrier; ~ **direct** through transport operator; ~ **de données** data carrier; ~ **émetteur** issuing carrier; ~ **de GNL** liquefied natural gas carrier; ~ **de GPL** liquid petroleum gas carrier; ~ **intégral** integrator; ~ **intérieur** (entreprise) inland carrier; ~ **interligne** (aviation) interline carrier; ~ **livrant** delivering carrier; ~ **maritime** sea carrier; ~ **mixte** (navigation) combi carrier; ~ **multimodal** multimodal transport operator; ~ **participant** participating carrier; ~ **principal** principal carrier; ~ **de produits** (navigation) product tanker; ~ **réel** actual carrier; ~ **routier** forwarding company, freight forwarder; ~ **substitué** actual carrier; ~ **de voitures** car transporter; ~ **en vrac** (navigation) bulk carrier

transposer *vt* transpose

transposition *f* (Droit) transposal

transversal, e *adj* transverse

travail *m* work; (manuel) labour BrE, labor AmE; (métier, tâche) job; **à ~ égal, salaire égal** same job, same pay; ~ **en cours** work in progress; **être en plein ~** be up to one's neck in work (infrml); **qui facilite le ~** labour-saving BrE; ~ **en souffrance** outstanding work, work pending; ~ **administratif** administrative work, paperwork; ~ **d'audit** audit activity UK; ~ **bénévole** voluntary work; ~ **de bureau** clerical work, office work; ~ **clandestin** moonlighting; ~ **en colis volant** (manutention) union purchase; ~ **compté** measured daywork; ~ **en continu** continuous labour BrE; ~ **à domicile** work at home, outwork; ~ **à domicile par réseau informatique** telecommuting; ~ **d'équipe** teamwork; ~ **par équipes** shift work; ~ **à forfait** contract work; ~ **de groupe** group working; ~ **à l'heure** time work; ~ **indépendant** self-employment; ~ **intermittent** casual work; ~ **de jour** daywork; ~ **à la journée** measured daywork; ~ **manuel** manual work; ~ **matérialisé** materialized labour BrE; ~ **à mi-temps** part-time employment; ~ **moyen d'une journée** average day's work, fair day's work; ~ **nécessaire** indispensable labour BrE; ~ **au noir** moonlighting; ~ **non déclaré** secondary employment; ~ **de nuit** night work; ~ **occasionnel** casual work; ~ **pénible** slog (infrml); ~ **à la pièce** piecework; ~ **posté** shift work; ~ **préparatoire** groundwork; ~ **de prospection** missionary work; ~ **par relais** shift work; ~ **en réseau** homework, networking; ~ **en retard** work backlog; ~ **temporaire** casual work, temporary work; ~ **à temps partiel** part-time employment; ~ **d'urgence** rush job

travailler *vi* work; ~ **d'arrache-pied** work flat out; ~ **en association avec** work in partnership with; ~ **de concert** work together; ~ **côte à côte avec qn** work alongside sb; ~ **dur** graft (infrml), labour BrE, labor AmE; ~ **ensemble** work together; ~ **par équipes** work in shifts; ~ **en étroite collaboration avec** work closely with; ~ **en free-lance** work freelance; ~ **pour gagner sa vie** work for a living; ~ **à horaire réduit** be on short time; ~ **en indépendant** work freelance; ~ **à mi-temps** work part-time; ~ **au noir** moonlight; ~ **à plein temps** work full-time; ~ **selon un horaire strictement minuté** work to a very tight schedule; ~ **sous pression** work under pressure; ~ **sur** work on; ~ **à temps partiel** work part-time; ~ **pendant ses vacances** do holiday work BrE, do vacation work; ~ **un week-end sur deux** work alternate weekends

travailleur, -euse *m,f* worker; ~ **à la chaîne** assembly line worker, production worker; ~**s atypiques** atypical workers; ~ **clandestin** undocumented worker; ~ **à domicile** homeworker; ~ **étranger** foreign worker; ~ **frontalier** frontier worker; ~

handicapé disabled worker; ~ **immigré** guestworker, immigrant worker; ~ **indépendant** self-employed person; ~ **intermittent** casual worker; ~ **itinérant** mobile worker; ~ **manuel** manual worker; ~ **à mi-temps** part-time worker, part-timer; ~ **migrant** migrant worker; ~ **mobile** mobile worker; ~ **au noir** moonlighter; ~ **occasionnel** occasional worker; ~ **payé à l'heure** hourly worker; ~**s périphériques** peripheral workers; ~ **posté** shift worker; ~ **social** social worker; ~**s sous contrat à court terme** short-term workers; ~ **temporaire** casual worker; ~ **à temps partiel** part-time worker, part-timer; ~ **volontaire pour le développement** volunteer development worker

travaux *m pl* (sur route) road works; (en chantier) work; ~ **de construction** construction work, building work; ~ **d'aménagement** (de bâtiment) alterations; (d'un site) redevelopment; ~ **de conférence** conference proceedings; ~ **en cours** work-in-progress BrE, work-in-process AmE; ~ **de fin d'exercice** year-end adjustment; ~ **menus** odd jobs; ~ **publics** public works; ~ **de transformation** alterations

traversée *f* (de mer, de pays) crossing; **la ~ du désert** (pour une entreprise) a difficult period

traverser *vt* (frontière) cross

traversier *m* Can ferry boat

trémie *f* hopper tank; (récipient) hopper

Trésor *m*: **le ~ Public** public revenue department, ≈ the Treasury

trésorerie *f* (ressources disponibles) funds; (somme en liquide) cash; (comptabilité) accounts; (le Trésor public) revenue office; (en Grande-Bretagne) the Treasury; **besoins de ~** cash requirements; **difficultés de ~** cash flow problems; **état/gestion prévisions de ~** cash flow statement/management forecast; **sorties de ~** cash outflows; ~ **zéro** zero fund

trésorier, -ière *m,f* treasurer; (Admin) paymaster; ~ **d'entreprise** corporate treasurer; ~ **de société** corporate treasurer

treuil *m* winch

tri *m* sort, sorting; (Info) sort; (de candidats) selection; **faire le ~ de** sort; ~ **des déchets** waste sorting; ~ **numérique** digital sort

triade *f* triad

triangle *m*: **le ~ d'or** the golden triangle

triangulaire *adj* triangular

triangulation *f* triangulation

tribord *m* (navigation) starboard

tribunal *m* (Droit) court; **aller devant les tribunaux** (affaire) go before the court, go to trial; (personne) go to court; **le ~ est en cours d'audience** court is now in session; ~ **d'arbitrage** arbitration tribunal; ~ **civil** ≈ county court; ~ **de commerce** bankruptcy court; ~ **compétent** court of competent jurisdiction; ~ **des faillites** bankruptcy

court; ~ **de grande instance** higher level court (dealing with cases of a fairly serious nature) ≈ county court UK; (de l'Union européenne) Court of First Instance; ~ **d'instance** small claims court; ~ **réglant les litiges douaniers** customs court US; ~ **des successions et des tutelles** probate court; ~ **du travail** Canada labour court BrE, labor court AmE

tributaire *adj* ~ **des clients** customer-driven

trieur, -euse *m,f* sorter

trimestre *m* quarter; **chaque ~** every quarter; ~ **civil** calendar quarter; ~ **d'exercice** fiscal quarter

trimestrialité *f* quarterly instalment BrE

trimestriel, -elle *adj* (presse) quarterly

trimestriellement *adv* quarterly

triple *adj* triple; **à ~ expansion** (Transp) triple-expansion; **en ~ exemplaire** (courrier, facture) in triplicate; ~ **exemption d'impôt** triple tax exempt; ~ **réduction** triple reduction

tripler ① *vt* (somme, quantité) treble ② *vi* (prix) treble, increase threefold

tripotages *m pl* (Bourse) (des cours) manipulation

troc *m* barter; **faire un ~** barter; **commerce du ~** barter trade

trois *adj* three; **à ~ hélices** triple-screw; **à ~ mois** three-month

troisième *adj* third; **de ~ classe** (place) third-class; ~ **de couverture** inside back cover; **de ~ ordre** third-rate; ~ **âge** third age; ~ **monnaie** third currency; ~ **trimestre** third quarter; ~ **voie** market socialism, third way

troisièmement *adv* thirdly

tromper ① *vt* mislead ② **se tromper** *v pron* make a mistake, be mistaken, be wrong; **se ~ dans les chiffres** get the figures wrong

tromperie *f* fraud; ~ **sur la charte-partie** charter party fraud; ~ **sur le connaissement** bill of lading fraud

trompeur, -euse *adj* misleading

tronçon *m* section; ~ **de vol** flight stage

tronquer *vt* (Info) truncate

trop-perçu *m* amount overpaid; (Fisc) overpayment of tax; **remboursement d'un ~** tax refund

troquer *vt* barter; ~ **une chose contre une autre** trade one thing for another

trottoir *m* pavement; ~ **de chargement** (véhicules) loading platform; ~ **roulant** moving pavement BrE, travolator AmE

trouble *m* (insécurité) unrest; **de graves ~s ont éclaté** serious disturbances have broken out; **réprimer des ~s** quell unrest; ~ **musculo-squelettique** repetitive strain injury

trousse *f* case; (contenu) kit; ~ **de premiers secours** first-aid kit; ~ **de réparation** repair kit

trouvaille *f* (découverte) find; (idée originale) innovation; (publicité) gimmick; ~ **publicitaire** advertising gimmick

trouver ⟦1⟧ *vt* find; ~ **un débouché pour** market; ~ **le juste milieu** strike a balance; ~ **à redire à** find fault with; ~ **un second souffle** get a second wind
⟦2⟧ **se trouver** *v pron* se ~ **à court de** run short of

truc *m* gimmick; ~ **publicitaire** (infrml) advertising gimmick

truquage *m* (des comptes) falsification; ~ **du bilan** (Compta) window-dressing

truquer *vt* (comptes) falsify; (élections) rig, fix; (dossier, déclaration) doctor

trust *m* trust; ~**s d'actifs disponibles** ready assets trusts

TSDI *abrév* (▶**titre subordonné à durée indéterminée**) subordinated perpetual bond

TSR *abrév* (▶**titre subordonné remboursable**) subordinated redeemable bond

TSVP *abrév* (▶**tournez s'il vous plaît**) PTO (please turn over)

TTA *abrév* (▶**taxe sur le transport aérien**) ATT (air transportation tax)

TTC *abrév* (▶**toutes taxes comprises**) inclusive of tax

TU *abrév* (▶**Temps universel**) UTC (universal time coordinated)

tube *m* tube; ~ **à rayons cathodiques** cathode ray tube

tunnel *m* tunnel; ~ **sous la Manche** Channel Tunnel

turbine *f* turbine; ~ **BP** low-pressure turbine; ~ **haute pression** high-pressure turbine; ~ **à vapeur** steam turbine

turbo-électrique *adj* turbo-electric

tutelle *f* (Admin) supervision; (Droit) guardianship; **autorité de** ~ supervision authority; **organisme de** ~ parent body; **être placé sous** ~ **administrative** be placed under administrative supervision

tuteur, -trice *m,f* (Droit) guardian; (Admin) administrator

tuyau *m* (infrml) (information) tip; ~ **boursier** stock tip

TVA *abrév* (▶**taxe sur la valeur ajoutée**) VAT (value-added tax) UK

type *m* (sorte) type; ~ **d'activité économique** pattern of economic activity; ~ **d'assurance** class of insurance; ~ **de construction** class of construction; ~ **de données** (Info) data type; ~ **d'écart** (Bourse) (stratégie d'option) backspread; ~ **de paiement** payment method

typiquement *adj* typically

typographe *mf* typographer

typologie *f* typology; (V&M) cluster analysis

Uu

UC *abrév* CPU (central processing unit)

UCE *abrév* (▶**unité de compte européenne**) EUA (European unit of account)

UE *abrév* (▶**Union européenne**) EU (European Union)

UEM *abrév* (▶**Union économique et monétaire**) EMU (Economic and Monetary Union)

UEP *abrév* (▶**Union européenne des paiements**) EPU (European Payments Union)

UER *abrév* (▶**Union européenne de radiodiffusion**) EBU (European Broadcasting Union)

UIT *abrév* (▶**Union internationale des télécommunications**) ITU (International Telecommunications Union)

ultérieur, e *adj* (date) later; (développement, réunion) subsequent; **à une date** ~**e** at a later date

ultérieurement *adv* at a later date

ultimatum *m* ultimatum; **lancer un** ~ **à, envoyer un** ~ **à** issue an ultimatum to, present an ultimatum to

ultime *adj* (avertissement, délai) final; (appel, concession) final, last; (but) ultimate; **consommateur** ~ end user, final user

ultra-confidentiel, ielle *adj* top-secret

ultramoderne *adj* (technique, système, matériel) state-of-the-art

ultrarapide *adj* high-speed

UME *abrév* (▶**Union monétaire européenne**) EMU (European Monetary Union)

unanime *adj* unanimous

unanimement *adv* unanimously

unanimité *f* unanimity; **à l'**~ (voter, adopter) unanimously; **prendre une décision à l'**~ reach a unanimous decision

une *f*: **la** ~ (presse) the front page; **être à la**

~ be front-page news

UNEDIC *abrév* (▸**Union nationale pour l'emploi dans l'industrie et le commerce**) ≈ Unemployment Benefit Office UK

uni, e *adj* united; (d'un teint) plain, self-coloured BrE, self-colored AmE; **~ par les liens du sang** connected by blood relationship

unicité *f* uniqueness; **~ du brevet européen** unity of European patent

unidirectionnel, -elle *adj* one-way

unification *f* (d'un pays) unification; (de poids et mesures) standardization; (d'un prêt) consolidation; **~ étrangère** foreign merger

unifier *vt* (parti politique, pays) unify; (poids, mesures) standardize

uniforme¹ *adj* steady, uniform; **tarif ~** flat rate

uniforme² *m* uniform

uniformisation *f* standardization; **~ des salaires** standardization of salaries

uniformiser *vt* standardize

uniformité *f* uniformity

unilatéral, e *adj* unilateral

unilatéralement *adv* unilaterally

union *f* (alliance) union; (association) association; (Pol) alliance; **~ de producteurs/consommateurs** producers'/consumers' association; **~ douanière** customs union; **~ économique** economic union; **Union économique et monétaire** Economic and Monetary Union; **Union européenne** European Union; **Union européenne des paiements** European Payments Union; **Union européenne de radiodiffusion** European Broadcasting Union; **Union internationale des télécommunications** International Telecommunications Union; **~ libre** common-law marriage; **~ monétaire** monetary union; **Union monétaire européenne** European Monetary Union; **Union nationale pour l'emploi dans l'industrie et le commerce** ≈ Unemployment Benefit Office UK; **~ patronale** employers' association

unipersonnel, -elle *adj* **entreprise/société unipersonnelle** one-man/one-woman business, sole proprietorship

unique *adj* (seul) only; (pour tous) single; (remarquable) unique; **marché/monnaie ~** single market/currency; **tarif ~** flat rate; **propriétaire ~** sole owner; **à prix ~** one-price; **à salaire ~** single-income; **~ inventeur** sole inventor

unir ① *vt* (combiner) combine; (rassembler) (pays, territoire, intérêts, personnes) unite ② **s'unir** *v pron* unite; **s'~ pour faire** unite to do

unitaire *adj* (prix, coût) unit; (stratégie, campagne) common

unité *f* (élément) unit; (cohésion) unity; (étalon) unit; (Math) unit; (Info) device; **à l'~ de chargement** (tarification) freight all kinds; **prix à l'~** unit price; **10 euros l'~** 10 euros each, 10 euros apiece; **~ d'affichage** display unit; **~ agricole** agricultural unit; **~ de bande magnétique** tape unit; **~ de base** basic unit; **~ boursière** trading unit; **~ centrale** central processing unit, processor; **~ de charge** unit load; **~ de compte** unit of account; **~ de compte étrangère** foreign currency unit; **~ de compte européenne** European unit of account; **~ de décision** decision unit; **~ de disque** disk drive; **~ de disque dur** hard disk drive; **~ de disquette** floppy disk drive; **~ d'élevage** stockkeeping unit; **~ d'entrée** input device; **~ de fabrication** manufacturing unit; **~ implicite** default device; **~ d'invention** unity of invention; **~ de mémoire de masse** bulk storage; **~ minimale de transaction** unit of trading; **~ monétaire** currency unit, monetary unit; **~ monétaire européenne** European Currency Unit; **~ de négociation** bargaining unit; **~ périphérique** peripheral (device); **~ de production** production plant, production unit; **~ de saisie** data entry terminal; **~ salariale** wage unit; **~ de stockage** storage facility; **~ de traitement** computer run; **~ de transaction** trading unit; **~ de transport** transport unit

univers *m* universe; **l'~ d'une enquête** (marketing, publicité) the total field of a survey

universel, -elle *adj* (ordinateur, appareil) all-purpose, general purpose; (suffrage, principe, système) universal

universitaire *adj* (honneur) academic; (ville) university

université *f* university

urbain, e *adj* urban

urbanisation *f* urbanization; **~ excessive** overurbanization

urbaniser *vt* urbanize

urbanisme *m* town planning BrE, city planning AmE

urbaniste *mf* town planner BrE, city planner AmE

urgence *f* (cas urgent) emergency; (caractère) urgency; **d'~** (agir, se réunir) immediately, as a matter of urgency

urgent, e *adj* urgent; **quelque chose d'~** a matter of urgency; **il est ~ de prendre des mesures** steps must be taken immediately

urne *f* ballot box; **se rendre aux ~s** go to the polls

usage *m* (utilisation) use; (coutume) custom; (pratique professionnelle) practice; **à ~ général** general purpose; **à ~s multiples** multipurpose; **à ~ commercial/industriel/personnel** for commercial/industrial/personal use; **à l'~ de qn** for the use of sb; **d'~** usual, customary; **conformément aux** ⋯⟩

u

~s in accordance with custom; **hors d'~** out of order; **précautions d'~** usual precautions; **~ abusif** misuse; **~ antérieur** prior use; **~s commerciaux** business practices; **~ non conforme** nonconforming use; **~ du port** custom of port; **~ pratique** practical use; **~ public** public use

usagé, e *adj* (déjà utilisé) used; (usé) worn

usager *m* (d'une route, d'un moyen de transport) user; **~ des chemins de fer** rail user

usance *f* (Fin) usance; **à ~ de trente jours** at thirty days' usance

usine *f* factory, plant; **~ de base** baseload power station; **~ center** factory shop, factory outlet; **~ de composants** component factory; **~ de construction mécanique** engineering works; **~ d'essai** testing plant; **~ existante** existing plant; **~ à gaz** gasworks; **~ d'incinération** incineration plant; **~ et matériels** plant and machinery; **~ de montage** assembly plant; **~ de papeterie** paper mill; **~ de pièces détachées** component factory; **~ de production** plant, production plant; **~ de retraitement** reprocessing plant; **~ en service** existing plant; **~ sidérurgique** ironworks; **~ thermique** thermal power station; **~ de traitement** processing plant; **~ de traitement des déchets** waste treatment plant; **~ transplantée** transplant factory

usine-pilote *f* pilot plant, pilot factory

usufruit *m* (Droit) usufruct, life interest, beneficial ownership; **avoir/garder l'~ de qch** have/retain the usufruct of sth

usufruitier, -ière *m,f* life tenant, beneficial occupant *ou* owner

usuraire *adj* usurious

usure *f* wear and tear; (rente) usury; **~ normale** (du matériel) normal wear and tear

usurier, -ière *m,f* usurer, loan shark (infrml)

usurpation *f* (Droit) encroachment

usurper *vt* (Droit) (les droits de qn) encroach upon

util *m* (Econ) revealed preference, util

utile *adj* useful; **~ à qn** useful to sb

utilement *adv* (combattre, intervenir) effectively; (se référer) profitably

utilisable *adj* (objet, déchets) usable; **fonds ~ sans restrictions** expendable fund

utilisateur, -trice *m,f* (d'une machine) user; **conçu en pensant à l'~** user-orientated, user-oriented; **~ comme armateur** (d'un navire) disponent owner; **~ final** (Info) end-user; **~ inscrit au registre** registered user

utilisation *f* use; (de ressources) utilization; **une nouvelle ~ d'un produit** a new use for a product; **d'~ facile** user-friendly; **~ abusive d'informations privilégiées** unfair use of inside information; (Bourse) frontrunning; **~ en alternance** alternating use; **~ anormale** (d'un outil) abnormal use; **~ à bonne fin** (Imp/Exp) completion of end use UK; **~ des capacités** capacity utilization; **~ du capital** capital utilization; **~ collective de fichier** file sharing; **~ du conteneur** (seul conteneur) container use, container utilization; **~ des conteneurs** container use, container utilization; **~ excessive** overuse; **~ de la flotte** fleet utilization; **~ finale** end use; **~ des fonds** (Bourse) application of funds; (Compta) application of funds; **~ non-agricole** nonagricultural use; **~ du parc automobile** fleet utilization; **~ la plus rentable** (Immob) highest and best use AmE; **~ du potentiel industriel** industrial capacity utilization; **~ du potentiel de production** capacity utilization; **~ préexistante** pre-existing use; **~ des remorques** trailer utilization

utiliser *vt* use; (ressource, avantage, compétence, potentiel) make use of, use; **bien ~** make good use of

utilitaire¹ *adj* (conception) utilitarian; (rôle, enseignement) practical; (objet) functional; (véhicule) utility, commercial

utilitaire² *m* (Info) utility; (véhicule) utility vehicle, commercial vehicle; **~ de sauvegarde** (Info) backup utility

utilitarisme *m* utilitarianism

utilité *f* (caractère utile) usefulness; (utilisation) use; (Econ) utility; **~ de lieu** place utility; **~ marginale** marginal significance, marginal utility; **~ marginale privée** private marginal benefit; **~ ordinale** ordinal utility; **~ primordiale** cardinal utility; **~ publique** (Droit) public benefit

Vv

vacance *f* vacancy; **~ de poste** job vacancy; **~ du pouvoir** power vacuum

vacances *f pl* holiday BrE, vacation AmE; **être/partir en ~** be/go on holiday BrE *ou*

vacation AmE; **~ fiscales** tax holiday; **~ parlementaires** parliamentary recess; **~ de succession** (Droit) abeyance of succession

vacancier, -ière *m,f* holiday-maker BrE,

vacationer AmE, vacationist AmE

vacant, e *adj* (emploi, poste) vacant; (logement) vacant, empty; **succession ~e** estate in abeyance

vacation *f* (Droit) recess UK vacations

vaccination *f* vaccination

vacciner *vt* vaccinate

vache *f* cow; **~ à lait** cash cow

vague *f* wave; **être au creux de la ~** (personne, entreprise) be at a low ebb; **~ d'achats** buying surge

vaisseau *m* (navire) vessel; **~ auxiliaire** (navire) auxiliary

val. *abrév* (▶**valeur**) security, stock

valable *adj* (excuse, passeport) valid; (solution) viable, valid; **non ~** invalid; (Bourse) invalid not held

valant *adj* worth; **~ 10 livres** worth £10

valeur *f* (Bourse) security, stock; (prix) value, worth; (effet de commerce) bill of exchange; (Compta) asset; **~s** securities, stock, stock and shares; **avoir de la ~** be valuable; **prendre/perdre de la ~** go up/down in value; **vendre qch en dessous de sa ~** sell sth for less than its worth *ou* value; **mettre un terrain en ~** develop a plot of land; **attirer des candidats de ~** attract high-calibre candidates; **~ légale** legal validity; **date de ~** (Banque) value date; **ceci n'a pas ~ d'engagement** this does not constitute a commitment; **les ~s minières** mining shares/stock/securities; **le marché/la Bourse des ~s** the stock market; **~s disponibles/ immobilisées** (Compta) liquid/fixed assets; **à la ~ nominale** at face value, at par; **à sa pleine ~** fully valued; **de ~** valuable; **sur la ~** (Banque) ad valorem (frml);

valeur a... **~ d'accroche** (publicité) attention value; **~ de l'acquisition** acquisition value; **~ de l'actif** asset value, capital value; **~ de l'actif net** net asset value; **~ de l'actif par action** asset value per share; **~ actualisée** present value; **~ actualisée nette** net present value; **~ actuelle** current value; **~ affective** affection value; **~ agréée** agreed value; **~ agricole** agricultural stock, agricultural paper US; **~ ajoutée** added value; **~s alpha** alpha stock; **~ amortie** written-down value; **~ à amortir** depreciable amount; **~ de l'argent** value of money; **~ arrivant à échéance** maturing value; **~ autorisée** authorized stock;

b... **~ en baisse** bearish stock, declining share; **~s bancaires** bank shares; **~ bêta** beta share, beta stock; **~ boursière** trading security; **~s brûlantes** (jarg) hot stock (jarg);

c... **~ de caisse** cash value; **~ du capital** capital value; **~ capitalisée** capitalized value; **~ à certificat endommagé** mutilated security; **~ comptable** (d'une action) book value; **~ comptable brute** gross book value; **~**

comptable globale nette aggregate book value; **~ comptable d'investissement** book value of investment; **~ comptable nette** net book value; **~ comptable du patrimoine** balance sheet value of shares; **~s en compte** securities long; **~ du compte de placement** investment account security; **~ du contrat** contract value; **~ contributive** contributory value; **~ convertible** convertible security; **~ convertible à coupon zéro** zero-coupon convertible security; **~ corporelle** tangible asset; **~ à la cote** quote value; **~ cotée en bourse** listed security, quoted security; **~ à coupon zéro** zero-coupon security; **~ au cours du marché** current market value; **~s à cours non limité** unlimited securities; **~ à court terme** short-term security; **~ critique** critical value; **~ de croissance** growth stock, performance stock; **~ croissante** growth in value; **~ cumulative** cumulative security; **~s cycliques** cycle stock, cyclical fluctuation;

d... **~ déclarée en douane** declared value for customs; **~ déclarée pour le transport** declared value for carriage; **~s à découvert** securities short; **~s défensives** defensive securities; **~ delta** delta stock UK; **~s demandées** securities wanted; **~ détenue** security holding; **~s disponibles** available assets, liquid assets; **~ de dollar** dollar value; **~ en douane par kilo brut** customs value per gross kilogramme BrE, customs value per gross kilogram AmE; **~ en douane par livre brute** customs value per gross pound;

e... **~ d'échange** exchange value; **~ à échéance** maturity value; **~ économique** economic value; **~ effective au comptant** actual cash value; **~ égale** equal value; **~ émise en robinet continu** (jarg) tap (jarg); **~ d'emprunt** loan value; **~ à l'encaissement** value for collection; **~ d'une entreprise prospère** going-concern value; **~ équitable** fair value; **~ en espèces** value in cash; **~ estimée** estimated value; **~ d'État** government stock; **~ étrangère** foreign security; **~ d'excédent** rate of exploitation, surplus value; **~ externe** (Econ) extremum (frml); **~ externe pondérée en fonction des échanges commerciaux** trade-weighted external value; **~ extrinsèque** extrinsic value;

f... **~ de la facture** invoice value; **~ fixe** locked-in value; **~ de fonds de portefeuille** blue-chip security; **~ des fonds propres** capital value; **~s fréquemment négociées** active securities;

g... **~ garantie** guaranteed security; **~ garantie par hypothèque** mortgage-backed security; **~s garanties par le gouvernement** government-backed securities; **~ de grande qualité** gilt-edged stock; **~ de gré à gré** tap (jarg);

V

(h...) ~ **en hausse** rising share, bullish stock; ~**s en hausse** highs;

(i...) ~ **des immobilisations incorporelles** intangible asset worth; ~**s immobilisées** fixed assets; ~ **imposable** taxable value; ~ **imputée** imputed value; ~ **incorporelle** intangible asset; ~ **indexée de premier choix** index-linked gilt; ~ **industrielle** industrial share, industrial security; ~ **industrielle de premier ordre** blue-chip industrial; ~**s des industries de haute technologie** high-tech stock; ~ **inscrite à la cote** listed security, quoted security; ~ **intérieure actuelle** current domestic value; ~ **intrinsèque** intrinsic value, value in use; ~ **d'inventaire** stocktaking value; ~ **d'inventaire des titres détenus** (bilan) balance sheet value of shares;

(j...) ~ **jour** same-day value;

(l...) ~ **de liquidation** break-up value, liquidating value; ~ **liquidative** cash-in value; ~ **livrable** deliverable security; ~ **locative** (Fin) leasehold value; (Fisc) rental value; ~ **à long terme** lockaway (jarg), long-term security;

(m...) ~ **marchande** market value, sale value; ~ **marchande actuelle** (d'un bien) current market value; ~ **marchande contre valeur comptant réelle** market value versus actual cash value; ~ **du marché** market value; ~**s du marché monétaire à court terme** short-term money-market instrument; ~ **matérielle** tangible asset; ~ **mixte** blended value; ~ **mobilière** security; ~ **mobilière de participation** shareholding; ~**s mobilières négociables** negotiable securities; ~ **moindre** undervalue; ~ **moyenne** mean value;

(n...) ~ **nantie** pledged security; ~ **négociée** trading security; ~ **nette** net value, net worth; ~**s nettes** net assets; ~ **nette du déficit** deficit net worth; ~ **nominale** face value, par value; ~ **nominative** registered security; ~ **non-cotée** unlisted security, unquoted security; ~ **de nouveauté** novelty value;

(o...) ~ **objective** objective value; ~ **obligataire** bond capital, bond denomination; ~ **originale de la police** value as in original policy;

(p...) ~ **au pair** par value; ~ **au pair d'une devise** par value of currency; ~ **patrimoniale nette** net asset value; ~ **perçue** perceived value; ~**s pétrolières** oil shares; ~ **de père de famille** (jarg) blue chip; ~ **peu active** delta stock UK, cabinet security US; ~ **de placement** investment account security; ~**s de placement** marketable securities; ~**s au plus haut** highs; ~ **d'un point** value of one point; ~ **de pointage** tick size (infrml); ~ **de la police d'origine** value as in original policy;

~**s en portefeuille** securities in portfolio; ~**s au porteur** bearer stock; ~ **de premier ordre** blue chip, gilt-edged security; ~ **principale** principal value; ~ **privilégiée à taux variable** floating-rate preferred share; ~ **au prix coûtant** value at cost; ~ **publicitaire** advertising value;

(r...) ~ **de rachat** surrender value; ~ **de rachat au comptant** cash surrender value; ~ **rachetée** called security; ~ **de rareté** scarcity value; ~ **réalisable estimative** estimated realizable value; ~ **de réalisation nette** equity, equity value; ~ **de reconstruction** reproduction cost; ~ **reçue en pension** note purchased under resale agreement; ~ **réelle de l'argent** real money (jarg); ~ **réelle nette** tangible net worth; ~ **de référence** (de l'indicateur de tendance) barometer stock; ~ **refuge** safe investment, secure investment; ~ **de remplacement** replacement value, actual cash value; ~ **renfermée** (actions attribuées au personnel) locked-in value; ~ **de reprise** trade-in allowance; ~ **résiduelle** residual value; ~ **résiduelle de liquidation** salvage value, winding-up value; ~ **de revente** resale value; ~ **à revenu fixe** fixed income security; ~ **de réversion** reversionary value; ~ **risquée** risky asset;

(s...) ~**s sans certificat** book-entry securities; ~ **de seconde catégorie** junior security US; ~ **de seuil** (Info) threshold value; ~ **de société de crédit** finance company paper; ~ **en solde en fin de journée** overnight security; ~ **sous-jacente** underlying security; ~**s de spéculation** floating securities; ~ **spéculative d'une société surendettée** stub equity; ~ **sûre** blue chip; ~ **de surtaxe** surcharge value;

(t...) ~ **tangible** tangible asset; ~ **à taux fixe** fixed-rate security; ~ **à taux variable** floating-rate security; ~ **temporelle** time value; ~**-temps** time value; ~ **à terme** forward security, short-term security; ~ **des transactions obligataires** bond turnover; ~**s très actives** active securities; ~**s très liquides** active securities; ~**s du Trésor** Treasury bill bonds US, government obligations US;

(u...) ~ **unitaire** unit value; ~ **d'usage** use value, value in use;

(v...) ~ **vedette** glamour stock BrE, glamor stock AmE, leader, leading stock; ~ **vénale** market value, sale value; ~ **venant à échéance** maturing security, maturing value; ~**s vedettes et titres à la traîne** leaders and laggards; ~ **en vogue** high-flier, high-flying stock;

(y...) ~ **yo-yo** (jarg) yo-yo stock (jarg)

valeurisation f (Banque) securitization

validation f validation; (d'un acte) authentication; (d'un testament) probate

valide *adj* (contrat, laissez-passer, passeport) valid; **non** ∼ invalid

valider *vt* validate; (acte) authenticate; (testament) probate; (**Info**) enable

validité *f* validity

valise *f* case, suitcase BrE; **faire/défaire ses** ∼**s** pack/unpack; ∼ **diplomatique** diplomatic bag BrE, diplomatic pouch AmE

valoir *vt* be worth; **à** ∼ paid in advance; **une somme à** ∼, **un à** ∼ a payment on account; **faire** ∼ **ses droits** put in a claim; **faire** ∼ (argent) put to work; (terrain) develop; (droit) assert; (intention) make known; (mérite, nécessité) point out; **faire** ∼ **une exception** enter a plea; ∼ **la peine** be worthwhile; ∼ **très cher** command a very high price; **valant 10 euros** worth 10 euros

valorisation *f* (d'un produit) valorization; (**Fin**) valuation; (d'un terrain) development; ∼ **à leur coût total** (des produits) full costing; ∼ **des stocks** stock valuation

valoriser *vt* (produit) valorize, promote; (région) develop; (capital) put to work

valuation *f*: ∼ **de l'apporteur** vendor rating

VAN *abrév* (▸**valeur actuelle nette**) NPV (net present value)

vanter *vt* praise

vapeur¹ *m* steamer; ∼ **à hélices** screw steamer; ∼ **à turbine** turbine steamship

vapeur² *f* steam

vaquer *vi* ∼ **à ses occupations** go about one's business

variabilité *f* variability

variable¹ *adj* (modifiable) adjustable; (fluctuant) variable; **à taux** ∼ at variable rates; **prêt à taux** ∼ variable-rate loan

variable² *f* variable; ∼ **aléatoire** random variable; ∼ **auxiliaire** (économétrie) dummy variable; ∼ **du but** goal variable; ∼ **décalée** lagged variable; ∼ **exogène** (économétrie) exogenous variable; ∼ **indicateur** indicator variable; ∼ **locale** (Info) local variable

variance *f* variance; ∼ **de l'échantillon** sampling variance; ∼ **des sorties** output variance

variation *f* (d'un cours, d'un prix) fluctuation, variation; **en données corrigées des** ∼**s saisonnières** seasonally adjusted; **connaître de fortes** ∼**s** fluctuate considerably; ∼ **aléatoire** random variation, random walk; ∼ **boursière** trading variation; ∼ **conjoncturelle** cyclic variation; ∼ **de cours minimale** minimum price fluctuation; ∼**s à court terme** short-term fluctuations; ∼**s cycliques** cyclical variations; ∼ **maximale des cours autorisée** maximum price fluctuation; ∼ **négative de trésorerie** negative cash flow; ∼ **nette** net change; ∼ **positive de trésorerie** positive cash flow; ∼ **de prix** price fluctuation, price variation;

∼**s saisonnières** seasonal variations

varié, e *adj* diverse, varied

varier *vi* vary

variété *f* variety

variomètre *m* variometer

vaste *adj* (secteur, réseau) vast; (marché) huge; (projet, entreprise) massive; (campagne) extensive; (débat) wide ranging; ∼ **gamme** wide-ranging

vecteur *m* (Math) vector; (support) vehicle

vedette *f* star; (navigation) cutter; (navire) motor launch; **avoir la** ∼ hold the stage; **produit** ∼ leading product, big seller

véga *m* vega

véhicule *m* vehicle; ∼ **articulé** articulated vehicle; ∼ **automobile** motor vehicle; ∼ **à bagages** baggage vehicle; ∼ **de communication** (publicité) advertising vehicle; ∼ **composé** built-up vehicle; ∼ **construit sur commande** purpose-built vehicle; ∼ **industriel** industrial vehicle; ∼ **de location sans chauffeur** self-drive hire vehicle, self-drive rental vehicle; ∼ **à moteur à essence** petrol engine vehicle BrE, gasoline engine vehicle AmE; ∼ **d'occasion** second-hand vehicle, used vehicle; ∼ **passager** passenger vehicle; ∼ **ravitailleur** tender vehicle; ∼ **routier à moteur diesel** diesel-engined road vehicle BrE; ∼ **simple** rigid vehicle; ∼ **de tourisme** passenger vehicle; ∼ **de transport public** public service vehicle; ∼ **utilitaire** commercial vehicle, utility vehicle

veille *f* (garde) watch; ∼ **à la concurrence** competitive intelligence; ∼ **économique** economic intelligence; ∼ **technologique** technology watch

veilleur *m* watchman; ∼ **de nuit** night watchman

veine *f* (infrml) (chance) luck

vélin *m* vellum

vélocité *f* velocity

vendable *adj* saleable BrE, salable AmE

vendange *f* (récolte) wine harvest

vendeur, -euse *m,f* (dans un magasin) salesperson, shop assistant BrE, sales clerk AmE; (responsable des ventes) salesperson, salesman, saleswoman; (d'options) grantor, option seller; (dans une transaction) seller; (**Droit**) vendor; ∼ **de bateaux** yacht broker; ∼ **de call couvert** covered writer; ∼ **de choc** (infrml) advertising agent; ∼ **à commission** commission salesperson; ∼ **à découvert** bear, short seller; ∼ **de double option** straddle seller, straddle writer; ∼ **d'espace publicitaire** advertising space seller; ∼ **ferme** firm seller; ∼ **de médias** media seller; ∼ **d'option** option seller, option writer; ∼ **d'option d'achat à découvert** uncovered call writer; ∼ **d'option à découvert** naked writer, uncovered writer; ∼ **d'options d'achat** call option writer; ∼ ···⊱

d'options d'achat partiellement à découvert ratio writer; ~ **d'options sur devises** currency options seller, currency options writer; ~ **d'options de vente** put option writer; ~ **par correspondance** inertia salesperson; ~ **régional** area salesperson; ~ **d'un straddle** straddle seller, straddle writer; ~ **de temps** (publicité, radio, télévision) time seller

vendre 1 *vt* sell; ~ **au-dessous du prix normal** (titres, valeurs) scalp (infrml); ~ **à la clôture** sell on close; ~ **à la commission** sell on commission; ~ **au comptant** sell spot; ~ **un contrat** short a contract; ~ **au cours du marché** sell at market; ~ **à couvert** sell for delivery; ~ **à crédit** sell on credit; ~ **à découvert** sell a bear, sell short; ~ **au détail** retail; ~ **aux enchères** auction, auction off, sell by auction; ~ **de gré à gré** sell by private treaty; ~ **en gros** sell in bulk; ~ **une idée à qn** sell sb an idea; ~ **en masse** (Bourse) unwind a trade; ~ **meilleur marché que ses concurrents** undersell one's competitors; ~ **moins cher que** (concurrent) undercut; ~ **une option** write a stock option; ~ **une option à découvert** write a naked option; ~ **une option en face de** write against; ~ **à perte** take a loss; ~ **qch à la casse** sell sth for scrap; ~ **en reprise** trade in; ~ **à terme** sell on credit; **vendu ou repris** (marchandises) on sale or return

2 **se vendre** *v pron* sell; **se** ~ **mal** (article) undersell, sell badly; **ne pas savoir se** ~ (personne) undersell oneself

venir *vi* come; ~ **de** come from; **à** ~ forthcoming; ~ **en aide à** come to the rescue of; ~ **à échéance** come to maturity; ~ **à la rescousse de** come to the rescue of; ~ **en tête** come top

vent *m* wind; **être dans le** ~ be abreast of things

vente *f* (transaction) sale; (activité) selling, sales; **en** ~ for sale; **en** ~ **libre** freely available; (médicament) available without prescription, available over the counter; **équipe/ technique/surface de** ~ sales team/ technique/area; **directeur/service des** ~s sales manager/department; **avoir l'expérience de la** ~ have sales experience; ~ **avec possibilité d'échanger** sale or exchange; **faire une** ~ make a sale; **mettre qch en** ~ put sth up for sale; ~ **agressive** hard sell; ~ **anticipée** anticipated sale; ~ **par appartements** asset stripping; ~ **d'appel** impulse sale; ~ **d'argenté** in-the-money put; ~ **attrape-nigaud** bait and switch selling US; ~ **par autorité de justice** judicial foreclosure, judicial sale; ~ **avant imposition** tax selling; ~ **à la baisse** bear sale; ~ **bien arrosée** wet sell (jarg); ~ **à la boule de neige** pyramid selling; ~ **d'un call à découvert** naked call, uncovered call; ~ **sur catalogue** mail order; ~ **pour cause d'inventaire**

stocktaking sale; ~ **pour cessation de commerce** winding-up sale; ~ **de charité** (d'objets d'occasion) charity sale, jumble sale BrE, rummage sale AmE; ~ **de choc** impulse sale; ~ **sous condition** conditional sale, conditional sales agreement; ~ **par correspondance** mail-order business, mail-order selling; ~ **couplée** tie-in sale US; ~ **à couvert** sale for delivery; ~ **couverte** covered option writing; ~ **à crédit** credit sale, hire purchase BrE; ~ **à la criée** auction sale; ~ **à découvert** bear sale, short selling; ~ **à découvert protégée** hedged short sale; ~ **définitive** absolute sale; ~ **en dépôt** consignment sale; ~ **au détail** retailing; (profession) retail trade; ~ **directe** (résultat) direct sale; (technique) face-to-face selling, direct selling; ~ **en distributeurs automatiques** automatic selling; ~ **par distributeur automatique** automatic merchandising; ~ **à domicile** door-to-door selling; ~ **d'un écart papillon** short butterfly; ~ **aux enchères** auction sale; ~ **par ensembles** pure bundling; ~ **d'espace** (publicité) space selling; ~ **à l'essai** sale on approval; ~ **expérimentale** market test, sales test; ~**s à l'exportation** export sales; ~ **facile** quick sale; ~ **fictive** sham trading; ~ **fictive d'obligations** bear hug takeover; ~ **forcée** (technique) hard sell, pressure selling; (sans commande préalable) inertia selling; ~ **forcée de marchandises** forced sale of stock; ~ **à forfait** forfaiting; ~ **en gros** wholesale, wholesaling; (profession) wholesale trade; ~ **groupée** (marketing), banded offer, banded pack; ~ **hors magasin** nonstore retailing; ~**s imposables** taxable sales; ~ **indirecte** backselling; ~ **irrévocable** absolute sale; ~ **judiciaire** judicial foreclosure, judicial sale; ~ **jumelée** (marketing) banded offer, banded pack, composite package; ~ **en ligne** e-tail, e-tailing; ~ **de liquidation** closing-down sale, final clearance sale; ~ **liquidative** closing sale transaction; ~ **pour livraison** sale for delivery; ~ **et location d'une immobilisation** sale and leaseback; ~ **par lots** pure bundling; ~**s sur le marché intérieur** domestic sales, home sales; ~ **de médias** media selling, media sales; ~**s mensuelles** monthly sales; ~ **par des méthodes de persuasion** soft sell; ~ **nécrophage** scavenger sale (infrml); ~**s nettes** net sales; ~**s d'obligations** bond sales; ~ **d'option couverte** covered put, covered short; ~ **d'une option de vente** short put; ~ **d'options d'achat** call writing; ~ **d'options couvertes** covered option writing; ~ **personnelle** (marketing) personal selling; ~ **à perte** dumping, loss leader pricing; ~ **sur plans** (Immob) sale on plans, presale; ~ **au plus haut** selling climax; ~ **en porte-à-porte** door-to-door selling; ~**s prévues** anticipated sales; ~ **à prix imposé** price maintenance; ~ **à prix sacrifié** leader pricing, loss leader pricing; ~ **promotionnelle** promotional sale; ~ **publique** public sale; ~ **pyramidale** pyramid selling; ~ **au rabais** discount sale, discount selling; **~rachat de titres** (Bourse) quick flip; **~s record** record sales; **~s de renouvellement** repeat sales; **~s répétées** repeat sales; ~ **par réseau coopté** multilevel marketing; ~ **sous réserve d'arrivée en bon état** sale subject to safe arrival; ~ **sur saisie** foreclosure sale; ~ **par soumission** sale by tender; ~ **de straddle** short straddle; ~ **de strangle** short strangle; **~s taxables** taxable sales; ~ **par téléphone** telephone sales, teleselling; ~ **à tempérament** instalment sale BrE, installment sale AmE; ~ **à terme** sale for the account; ~ **à un tiers** third-party sale; ~ **de valeurs à revenu fixe** bond washing; ~ **par voie d'adjudication** sale by tender

ventilation f (de coûts, frais, comptes) breakdown; (Compta) allocation, apportionment; (Info) (d'une zone de données) exploding; ~ **des charges** breakdown of expenses; ~ **des coûts** cost apportionment; ~ **de la paie** payroll distribution; ~ **en pourcentage** percentage distribution

ventiler vt ventilate; (coûts, frais, comptes) break down; (Compta) allocate, apportion; (Info) (zone de données) explode; ~ **les charges entre certains comptes** allocate ou apportion costs to certain accounts

vépéciste m mail-order company

verbal, e adj verbal

verbalement adv verbally; **s'engager ~** make a verbal commitment

verdict m verdict; **rendre un ~** return ou announce a verdict; ~ **rendu à la majorité** majority verdict

vérifiable adj verifiable; (Compta) auditable

vérificabilité f (Compta) auditability

vérificateur, -trice m,f (Compta) auditor; ~ **des crédits** credit controller; ~ **externe** external auditor, independent auditor; ~ **financier supérieur** senior financial auditor; ~ **indépendant** independent auditor; ~ **interne** internal auditor; ~ **d'orthographe** spellchecker, spellcheck

vérification f checking; (Compta) audit; (Info) check; ~ **de l'efficacité des ventes** sales effectiveness test; ~ **analytique** Can analytical audit, systems-based audit; ~ **du bilan** (balance sheet) audit; ~ **cachée** undercover audit; ~ **comptable** verification of accounts; audit; ~ **continue** continuous audit; ~ **dissimulée** undercover audit; ~ **douanière** customs check, customs examination; ~ **externe** external audit, independent audit; ~ **fiscale** tax audit; ~ **illimitée** unlimited checking; ~ **interne** administrative audit, internal audit; ~ **du logiciel comptable** application control; ~ **a posteriori** postaudit; ~ **sur place** field

audit; ~ **préalable** preaudit; ~ **de premier palier** prime range audit; ~ **de routine** routine control; ~ **par sondages** sample audit, test audit; ~ **des stocks** stock control

vérifier vt check, verify; (comptes) audit; **qui n'a pas été vérifié** unverified; **non ~** unchecked, unverified; (Compta) unaudited

véritable adj (réel) real, actual; (cuir) genuine, real; (or, argent) real; (Droit) bona fide

verrou m lock; ~ **de sécurité** (Info) keylock; ~ **tournant** (fixation des conteneurs) twistlock

verrouillage m (de conteneurs) locking; ~ **d'enregistrement** record locking

verrouiller vt lock in; (clavier, enregistrement) lock

vers prép (en direction de) to, toward(s); (approximativement) about, around; ~ **le bas** downward, downwards; ~ **le haut** upward, upwards; ~ **le milieu de l'année** midyear, towards the middle of the year

versé, e adj (somme) paid

versement m (en plusieurs fois) instalment BrE, installment AmE; (action) payment; (dépôt) deposit; **faire un ~** make a payment; **faire un ~ sur son compte** pay money into one's account; **par ~s** in instalments; ~ **annuel** annual payment, annual instalment; ~ **bilatéral** bilateral disbursement; ~ **différé d'annuités** deferred group annuity; **~s échelonnés** instalment payments; ~ **fixe** fixed instalment; **~s de garantie** guarantee payments; ~ **hypothécaire** mortgage payment; ~ **illégal** illegal payoff; ~ **d'impôt** remittance of tax; ~ **initial** front-end payment; ~ **d'intérêt** interest payment; ~ **libératoire** final instalment; ~ **net** net remittance; ~ **postal** payment by post, postal remittance; ~ **de rente** annuity instalment; ~ **de souscription** allotment money, application money; ~ **d'une tranche de prêt** drawdown; ~ **trimestriel** quarterly instalment

verser vt (de l'argent) pay; ~ **un acompte** make a down payment; ~ **à la baisse** buy down; ~ **de l'argent sur son compte** pay money into one's account

version f version; (modèle) model, version; ~ **actualisée** revised version; ~ **avancée** advanced version; ~ **bêta** beta version; ~ **de logiciel** (software) version, (software) release; ~ **révisée** (édition) revised version

verso m (d'une page) back, verso; **voir au ~** see overleaf

vert, e adj (Envir) green

vertical, e adj vertical

verticalement adv vertically

Verts m pl: **les ~** the Greens

vertu f (qualité) quality virtue; **en ~ de** by virtue of; **en ~ de l'article 120** pursuant to article 120; **en ~ de la loi** in accordance with the law, in compliance with the law

vestiges *m pl* remains

veto *m* veto; **mettre** *or* **opposer son** ∼ **à qch** veto sth; **droit de** ∼ right of veto

veuve *f* (typographie) widow

VHF *abrév* (▸**très haute fréquence**) VHF (very high frequency)

via *prép* via

viabilisation *f* land improvement; ∼ **foncière** land development

viabiliser *vt* (terrain) develop

viabilité *f* viability; ∼ **économique** economic viability

viable *adj* (projet) viable

vice *m* defect; ∼ **caché** latent defect; ∼ **du consentement** duress; ∼ **de forme** irregularity

vice-président, e *m,f* vice-president; ∼ **directeur général** executive vice-president

vice versa *adv* vice versa

vicier *vt* (acte) invalidate; (marchandises) taint

victoire *f* victory; ∼ **dans un fauteuil** runaway victory, walkaway AmE

vidage *m* turnout; (Info) dump; ∼ **d'écran** screen dump; ∼ **de mémoire** memory dump, storage dump; ∼ **de mémoire sur imprimante** memory print-out; ∼ **de mouvements** change dump; ∼ **de transfert sur disque** dump, dumping

vidange *f* (de cuve) emptying; (d'un vehicule) oil change; ∼ **des eaux usées** sewage disposal, wastewater disposal

vide¹ *adj* (caisse, bouteille) empty; (écran) blank

vide² *m* (Transp) ullage; **à** ∼ empty; **camion à** ∼ truck with no return load; **emballage sous** ∼ vacuum packing; **laisser/créer/ combler un** ∼ leave/create/fill a vacuum; ∼ **juridique** gap in the law

vidéo *f* (média) video; ∼**s à la demande** video-on-demand; ∼ **inverse** reverse video; ∼ **promotionnelle** promotional video

vidéoachat *m* videoshopping

vidéocassette *f* video cassette

vidéoconférence *f* (séance) video conference; (technique) video conferencing

vidéodisque *m* video disk

vidéographie *f* video graphics; ∼ **interactive** videotex®

vide-ordures *m* rubbish chute BrE, garbage chute AmE

vidéosurveillance *f* videosurveillance

vidéotex® *m* videotex®

videotexte *m* videotext

vidéothèque *f* video library

vider *vt* (tiroir, boîte) empty; (Info) clear, dump

vie *f* life; **à** ∼ for life; **dans la** ∼ **politique** in the public sphere; **la** ∼ **d'entreprise** corporate life; **coût/niveau de** ∼ cost/ standard of living; ∼ **active** working life; ∼ **économique** economic life; ∼ **entière à primes temporaires** limited payment life insurance US; ∼ **privée** private life, privacy; ∼ **d'un produit** product life

vieillir *vi* age, grow old

vieillissement *m* obsolescence; ∼ **programmé** built-in obsolescence; ∼ **technologique** technological obsolescence

vierge *adj* (feuille, papier) blank; (disquette) blank; (terrain) virgin

vignette *f* (ayant valeur légale) stamp; (d'une marque de fabrique) label; (automobile) tax disc BrE, tax disk AmE; (poids lourd) road-fund licence BrE, road-fund license AmE; (Info) clip art

vignoble *m* vineyard

vigoureux, -euse *adj* sharp, vigorous

vigueur *f* (du marché) strength; **en** ∼ (régime, tarif, conditions) current; (loi, règlement) in force, applicable; **entrer en** ∼ come into play; **être en** ∼ (loi, mesure) be in force

ville *f* town; (plus grande) city; ∼ **d'accueil** host city; ∼ **moteur** generative city; ∼ **nouvelle** new town UK; ∼ **parasite** parasitic city; ∼ **satellite** satellite town; ∼ **test** test town

ville-dortoir *f* dormitory suburb BrE, bedroom community AmE

violation *f* breach, violation; (d'un brevet) infringement; **en** ∼ **de** in breach of, in violation of; ∼ **de contrat** breach of contract; ∼ **d'un droit** offence, violation of a law; ∼ **de propriété** trespassing, unlawful trespass; ∼ **du secret** breach of confidentiality

violence *f* brutality, violence; ∼ **familiale** family violence

violer *vt* (brevet) infringe, violate; (traité) violate; ∼ **la loi** break the law; ∼ **une propriété privée** trespass on private property

virage *m* (changement de direction) change of direction; ∼ **à 180 degrés** U-turn BrE, flip-flop AmE

viral, e *adj* viral; **marketing** ∼ viral marketing

virement *m* (de fonds) transfer; ∼ **automatique** bank transfer, direct deposit Can ; ∼ **par avion** airmail transfer; ∼ **bancaire** bank transfer; ∼ **direct de fonds** direct fund transfer; ∼ **entre crédits** intervote transfer; ∼ **interbancaire** interbank transfer; ∼ **en nature** in-kind transfer; ∼ **télégraphique** cable transfer

virer ① *vt* (de l'argent) transfer; (employé) fire (infrml), sack BrE (infrml); **être viré** (infrml) get the sack (infrml)
② *vi* (à droite, à gauche) swing

virgule *f* (nombre décimal) decimal point; (typographie) comma

virt *abrév* (▸**virement**) (de fonds) tr. (transfer)

virtuel, -elle *adj* virtual; **argent/porte-monnaie** ∼ e-money/e-wallet; **communauté virtuelle** virtual community

virus *m* virus; ~ **informatique** computer virus

visa *m* (passeport) visa; ~ **accordé pour deux entrées** double-entry visa; ~ **accordé pour une entrée** single-entry visa; ~ **de certification** certification mark; ~ **en cours de validité** working visa; ~ **d'entrée** entrance visa, entry visa; ~ **permanent** multientry visa, multiple-entry visa; ~ **de signification** service mark; ~ **touristique** tourist visa; ~ **de transit** visa

vis-à-vis *prép* (à l'égard de) ~ **de** in relation to

viscosité *f* (Econ) viscosity; ~ **de la demande** viscous demand; ~ **de l'offre** viscous supply

visée *f* (objectif) aim; (dessein) design; ~ **de couverture** hedging goal

viser *vt* (loi, campagne) be aimed at, target; (marché, poste, objectif) aim for, aim at; (Admin) (document) stamp; (passeport) visa BrE, put a visa in; **les employés visés par la décision** the employees affected by the ruling, the employees to whom the ruling applies; **visé à l'alinéa 1** referred to in paragraph 1; **visé par règlement** prescribed

visibilité *f* (V&M) visibility

visible *adj* (Econ) visible

visibles *m pl* visibles

visière *f* visor; ~ **d'étrave** (d'un roulier) bow visor

vision *f* vision; ~ **du monde** view of the world

visiophone *m* videophone

visite *f* (de la police) search; (customs) examination; (tourisme) tour; **en** ~ visiting; ~ **d'affaires** business call; ~ **domiciliaire** house search; ~ **éclair** flying visit; ~ **à l'étranger** foreign trip, foreign visit; ~ **impromptue** (par un vendeur) cold call; ~ **d'inspection** inspection, visitation; ~ **des machines** (d'un navire) machinery survey; ~ **médicale** check-up, medical examination; ~ **périodique** periodical survey; ~ **de représentant** sales call

visiter *vt* visit; (maison à vendre) view, look round; (tourisme) go round; (navire) survey; **faire** ~ **l'usine à qn** show sb round the factory BrE, show sb around the factory AmE

visiteur, -euse *m,f* visitor; (représentant) representative, rep (infrml); (de site Internet) visitor; ~ **avec permis de séjour d'étudiant** visitor with a student visa; ~ **étranger** overseas visitor; ~ **médicale** medical rep; ~ **en pharmacie** pharmaceuticals rep, drugs reps

visualisation *f* visual display

visualiser *vt* display, view

visuel¹, -elle *adj* visual

visuel² *m* (Info) visual display unit

vite *adv* fast; **aussi** ~ **que possible** as quickly as possible

vitesse *f* rate, speed; ~ **d'ajustement** (des prix) adjustment speed; ~ **d'alimentation** feed rate; ~ **appropriée** (d'un navire) convenient speed; ~ **de calcul** (Info) computing speed; ~ **de circulation monétaire** velocity of money; ~ **de frappe** typing speed; ~ **d'impression** printing speed; ~ **de rotation** turnover rate; ~ **de traitement des documents** (Info) document rate; ~ **de transfert** (Info) transfer rate; ~ **de transmission de données** (Info) data rate

viticulteur, -trice *m,f* wine grower, viticulturalist

viticulture *f* wine growing, viticulture

vitrine *f* shop window, window; ~ **virtuelle** electronic storefront, cyberstorefront

vivre *vi* live; ~ **de l'aide sociale** receive benefit UK, be on welfare AmE; ~ **au-dessus de ses moyens** live beyond one's means

VL *abrév* (▸**voiture-lit**) sleeper, sleeping car

vocation *f* (de personne) calling, vocation; (d'institution) purpose; **à** ~ **générale** general purpose; (compte) all-purpose; ~ **de la société** corporate mission

vogue *f* fashion, vogue; **en** ~ in fashion, in vogue

voie *f* (chemin) way; (moyen, intermédiaire) channel; (chaussée) carriageway, lane; (chemin de fer) line, track; **en** ~ (chemin de fer) on track; **être sur la bonne/mauvaise** ~ be on the right/wrong track; **par** ~ **de terre** by surface mail; **par la** ~ **de** via; **sur/dans la** ~ **de** on the road to; **montrer la** ~ lead the way; **ouvrir la** ~ **à** pave the way for; **les travaux sont en bonne** ~ work is progressing well; ~ **d'accès** (aux données) path; ~ **aérienne** airway; ~ **analogique** analog channel; ~ **d'arrêt** bay; ~ **de chargement** siding BrE, sidetrack AmE; ~ **de circulation** traffic lane; ~ **de communication** channel of communication; ~ **d'embranchement** branch line; ~ **ferrée** railway line BrE, railroad track AmE; ~ **fluviale** inland waterway; ~ **de garage** siding BrE, sidetrack AmE; ~ **hiérarchique** line of command; ~ **navigable** inland waterway; ~ **de navigation** shipping lane; ~ **privée** private road; ~ **publique** public highway; ~ **de raccordement** (d'usine) siding; ~ **rapide** (de route) fast lane; ~ **de retour** reverse channel; ~ **de terre** surface mail; ~ **de triage** siding BrE, sidetrack AmE

voir *vt* see; ~ **autrement** take a different view; ~ **au dos** (édition) see overleaf; **en** ~ **de toutes les couleurs** (infrml) have a lot of trouble; ~ **le tiré** (Banque) refer to acceptor; ~ **le tireur** (Banque) refer to drawer

voisinage *m* neighbourhood BrE, neighborhood AmE

voiture *f* car, automobile AmE; (chemin de fer) coach BrE, car AmE; ~ **avec la conduite à droite** right-hand drive car; ~ **de fonction** ⠵

company car; ~ **de location** hire car, rental car; ~ **d'occasion** second-hand car; ~ **de société** company car

voiture-lit *f* sleeper, sleeping car

voix *f* vote; ~ **consultative** advisory voice; ~ **contre** opposing vote

vol[1] *abrév* (▸**volume**) vol. (volume)

vol[2] *m* (délit) robbery, theft; (par avion) flight; **le ~ pour Paris** the Paris flight; ~ **affrété** charter flight; ~ **d'arrivée** incoming flight; ~ **avec effraction** burglary; ~ **camionné** truck service; ~ **charter** charter flight; ~ **en classe économique** economy flight; ~ **de correspondance** connecting flight; ~ **domestique** domestic flight, internal flight; ~ **à l'étalage** shoplifting; ~ **d'inauguration** inaugural flight; ~ **intérieur** domestic flight, internal flight; ~ **interligne** interchange flight; ~ **qualifié** grand larceny US; ~ **régulier** scheduled flight; ~ **retardé** delayed flight; ~ **de retour** return flight, incoming flight; ~ **sans escale** nonstop flight

volant *m* (de carnet de tickets, de chèques) leaf, tear-off portion; (réserve) margin, reserve; ~ **de sécurité** safety margin, reserve fund; ~ **de trésorerie** cash reserve

volatile *adj* volatile

volatilité *f* volatility; ~ **historique** historical volatility; ~ **implicite** implied volatility

voler [1] *vt* (quelqu'un) rob; (quelque chose) steal; ~ **de l'argent dans la caisse** rob the till; ~ **qch à qn** steal sth from sb [2] *vi* (par avion) fly

volet *m*: **trier sur le ~** cherry-pick

voleur, -euse *m,f* robber, thief

volontaire *mf* volunteer

volte-face *f* turnaround, turnround; **faire ~** do a U-turn BrE, do a flip-flop AmE

volume *m* volume; (d'un fichier) size; **à ~ élevé** high-volume; ~ **d'affaires** amount of business, volume of business; ~ **balle** (d'un navire) bale space; ~ **des commandes** volume of orders; ~ **d'échanges** volume of trade, trade flow; ~ **des échanges commerciaux** trade volume; ~ **d'effets à recevoir** receivables turnover; ~ **des exportations** volume of exports, amount exported; ~ **important** high volume; ~ **non indiqué** volume deleted; ~ **des opérations** (Bourse) volume of trading; ~ **perdu** (Transp) waste cube; ~ **de production** output volume, production volume; ~ **quotidien** (Bourse) daily volume; ~ **des transactions** (Bourse) trading volume; ~ **des transactions effacé** (Bourse) volume deleted; ~ **des transactions sur obligations** bond turnover; ~ **de ventes** sales volume; ~ **des ventes au détail** volume of retail sales

volumineux, -euse *adj* bulky, voluminous

vorace *adj* acquisitive

votant, e *m,f* voter

vote *m* vote; ~ **d'un budget** voting on a budget; ~ **d'une loi** passing of a bill; ~ **à l'aveuglette** bullet vote; ~ **à bulletin secret** blanket ballot US, secret ballot; ~ **par correspondance** postal vote; ~ **à mains levées** vote by show of hands; ~ **majoritaire** majority vote; ~ **à la majorité** majority rule voting; ~ **à la majorité qualifiée** qualified majority vote; ~ **par procuration** proxy vote, vote by proxy; ~ **de protestation** protest vote; ~ **réglementaire** statutory vote; ~ **statutaire** statutory voting; ~ **utile** tactical vote

voter *vt* (budget) vote; (loi) pass; ~ **des crédits provisoires** vote interim supply; ~ **la dotation totale** vote full supply; ~ **au scrutin** ballot, vote by ballot; ~ **la totalité des crédits** vote full supply; ~ **à l'unanimité** unanimously accept

vouloir *vt* (exiger) want; (désirer) wish; (dans formule de politesse) **veuillez accepter nos excuses** please accept our apologies; **veuillez agréer, Madame/Monsieur, l'expression de mes sentiments distingués** (à personne nommée) Yours sincerely; (à personne non nommée) Yours faithfully; **veuillez m'excuser** I'm sorry, please excuse me; ~ **dire** mean; (abréviation, initiale) stand for

voyage *m* voyage; ~**s de groupe** group travel; **les ~s en avion** air travel; ~**s de nuit** overnight travel; ~**s à tarif réduit** discount travel; ~**s tous frais payés** subsidized travel; ~ **d'affaires** business trip; ~ **d'aller** outward voyage; ~ **d'essai** shakedown (infrml); ~ **d'études** field trip, study trip; ~ **d'études sur le terrain** field trip; ~ **à forfait** inclusive tour, package tour; ~ **gratuit** free trip; ~ **inaugural** maiden voyage; ~ **international de courte distance** short international voyage; ~ **organisé** package holiday BrE, package vacation AmE; ~ **professionnel** business trip; ~ **de retour** homeward voyage; ~ **par voiture tout compris** all-inclusive motor tour

voyager *vt* travel; ~ **en bateau** sail

voyageur, -euse *m,f* traveller BrE, traveler AmE; (train, autobus) passenger; ~ **par avion** air traveller BrE; ~ **de commerce** travelling salesperson BrE; ~ **représentant placier** commercial traveller BrE; ~ **représentant placier régional** area salesman, area salesperson; ~ **en transit** transit passenger

voyagiste *mf* tour operator

voyant *m* light; ~ **lumineux** signal light

V-P *abrév* (▸**vice-président**) VP (vice-president)

VPC *abrév* (▸**vente par correspondance**) MO (mail order)

vrac *m* (articles à transporter) bulk; ~ **liquide** wet bulk cargo; ~ **sec** dry bulk cargo; **en ~**

in bulk

vraquier *m* bulk carrier; ~ **porte-conteneurs** bulk container ship

V/réf. *abrév* (▸**votre référence**) yr ref. (your reference)

VRP *abrév* (▸**voyageur représentant placier**) commercial traveller BrE, commercial traveler AmE; ~ **régional**

area salesperson

vue *f* sight; **à** ~ at sight; **en** ~ **de faire** with a view to doing; **très en** ~ (profession) high-profile; ~ **en coupe** cross section; ~ **à court terme** short-termism; ~ **d'ensemble** overall view, conspectus; ~ **générale** general view, conspectus; ~ **du marché** market view

vulnérable *adj* vulnerable

Ww

wagon *m* wagon BrE, car AmE; ~ **découvert** gondola; ~ **de marchandises couvert** goods truck BrE, boxcar AmE; ~ **plat** flat car US, gondola; ~ **à plate-forme surbaissée** low loader; ~ **porte-conteneurs** container car US; ~ **postal** mail van BrE, mailcar AmE; ~ **pour transport d'automobiles** car transporter; ~ **voyageurs** (passenger) carriage

wagon-citerne *m* tank wagon BrE, tank car AmE

wagon-lit *m* sleeper, sleeping car

wagon-restaurant *m* dining car, restaurant car

WAP *adj* (terminal, technologie) WAP; **téléphone** ~ WAP phone

warrant *m* (Bourse) bond warrant; (Droit) warrant; **avec** ~ cum warrant; ~ **à l'achat** call warrant; ~ **agricole** agricultural warrant; ~ **couvert** covered warrant; ~ **à la vente** put warrant

warrantage *m* warrant discounting

web *m* **le** ~ the web; **page/serveur/site/espace** ~ web page/server/site/space

webcam *f* webcam

webcamé, e *m,f* (infrml) cyberholic (infrml)

webmaster *m* webmaster

webmestre *m* webmaster

webtrotteur *m* web reporter, cyber-reporter

WL *abrév* (▸**wagon-lit**) sleeper, sleeping car

Xx

xénophobe[1] *adj* xenophobic

xénophobe[2] *mf* xenophobe

xérographique *adj* xerographic

xième *adj* nth; **pour la** ~ **fois** for the nth time

XML *m* (Info) XML, extensible Mark-up Language

Zz

ZAC *abrév* (▸**zone d'aménagement concerté**) EZ (enterprise zone)

ZAD *abrév* (▸**zone d'aménagement différé**) future development zone

zappeur, -euse *adj* **client** ~ (brand)

switcher, fickle customer

zapping *m* (infrml) brand switching

zèle *m* zeal

zéro *m* zero, nought BrE; **tout reprendre à** ~ start all over again; **budget base** ~ zero ⋯⬦

base budgeting; **croissance** ~ zero growth; ~ **défaut** zero defect

zinc *m* zinc

zip *m* (Info) zip; **fichier** ~ zip file

Zip® *m* **disquette/lecteur** ~ Zip® disk/drive

zipper *vt* (Info) zip

zonage *m* zoning; ~ **du gaz et du pétrole** oil and gas lottery; ~ **de lieu** spot zoning

zonation *f* banding

zone *f* area, zone; (Info) field; (de mémoire) area, zone; ~ **d'accueil** reception area; ~ **d'activité économique** enterprise zone; ~ **d'alerte** alert box; ~ **d'aménagement concerté** enterprise zone; ~ **d'aménagement différé** future development zone; ~ **d'aménagement rural** rural development area UK; ~ **d'aménagement urbain** urban development area; ~ **d'appel** catchment area; ~ **d'arrimage** stowage area; ~ **d'assistance** assisted area; ~ **d'attraction** catchment area; ~ **de chalandise** catchment area; (dans un magasin) trading area; ~ **de chargement des camions** lorry reception area BrE, truck reception area; ~ **cible** target zone; ~ **cible de change** exchange rate target zone; ~ **commerçante** shopping precinct BrE, shopping mall; ~ **commerciale** retail park; ~ **de comptes négociables** transferable account area; ~ **en crise** depressed area; ~ **critique** problem area; (test statistique) critical region; ~ **en déclin** depressed area; ~ **défavorisée** disadvantaged *ou* poor area; ~ **destinataire** target field; ~ **de développement rural** rural development area; ~ **à développer** development area; ~ **de dialogue** dialogue box BrE, dialog box AmE; ~ **de diffusion** (publicité) advertising zone; ~ **dollar** dollar area; ~ **écologiquement fragile** environmentally-sensitive zone; ~ **économique européenne** European economic area; ~ **économique spéciale** special economic zone; ~ **d'enregistrement** (Transp) reception area; ~ **d'entreprise** enterprise zone; ~ **euro** euro zone, euro area; ~ **à faible population** sparsely populated area;

~ **franche** free zone; ~ **géographique** geographical area; ~ **habitée** built-up area; ~ **industrielle** industrial estate BrE, industrial park; ~ **industrielle en déclin** declining industrial area; ~ **industrielle nouvelle** greenfield site; ~ **interdite** off-limits area; ~ **de liberté** zone of freedom; ~ **de libre-échange** free-trade area, free-trade zone; ~ **de ligne de charge** (navigation) load line zone; ~ **limitée** restricted area; ~ **du marché primaire** primary market area; ~ **de mémoire** (Info) storage area; ~ **métropolitaine** metropolitan area; ~ **monétaire** currency zone; ~ **monétaire optimale** optimum currency area; ~ **de navigation** trading limit; ~ **de navigation côtière** inshore traffic zone; ~ **de non-libre-échange** Non Free Trade Zone; ~ **de numérisation** (Info) scan area; ~ **peu peuplée** sparsely populated area; ~ **piétonne** pedestrian precinct BrE, pedestrian area; ~ **portuaire franche** (maritime) free port zone; ~ **de recrutement de la main-d'œuvre** recruiting area; ~ **de récupération des bagages** baggage reclaim area; ~ **réglementée** (aviation) restricted area; ~ **de responsabilité** jurisdiction; ~ **rurale** rural area; ~ **de salaire** wage zone; ~ **sinistrée** depressed area; ~ **de stabilité** stability zone; ~ **de stationnement interdit** no parking area; ~ **sterling** sterling area, sterling zone; ~ **tampon** buffer area, buffer zone; ~ **de tarification européenne** European zone charge; ~ **test** test area; ~ **de travail** working area; ~ **très fortement peuplée** densely populated area; ~ **troisième âge** grey belt BrE (jarg), gray belt AmE (jarg); ~ **à urbaniser** development area, development zone; ~ **à urbaniser en priorité** priority development zone; ~ **à vitesse limitée** restricted speed area; ~ **vulnérable** sensitive zone

zoom *m* (Info) zooming, zoom; **faire un** ~ **avant/arrière** zoom in/out

ZUP *abrév* (▶**zone à urbaniser en priorité**) priority development zone

● ●

Correspondence/Correspondance

Présentation d'une lettre commerciale

- en-tête/adresse de l'expéditeur
- raison sociale

Watchdog Technologies

Unit 7 Harwell Trading Park
London SE1 2JF
Tel: + 44 (0) 20 7132 4186 **Fax**: + 44 (0) 20 0745 8765
email: pbrandon@watchdogtechs.co.uk

EH/PB/33 ····· ■ *référence*

19 January 2002 ····· ■ *date*

Gabriel Kent
Head of Purchasing
Forest Security
15 The Avenue ····· ■ *destinataire*
Canterbury
CT3 9DN

Dear Mr Kent ····· ■ *formule d'appel*

Catalogue request ····· ■ *objet*

Thank you for your interest in our new range of security products. I have pleasure in enclosing our current catalogue as well as a price list and order form.

If you would like a demonstration of the new models in the Z500 alarm series I would be happy to arrange for our representative to call on you at your convenience. Full technical specifications for all our products can be found on our website at **www.watchdogtech.co.uk**

I would like to take this opportunity to draw your attention to the range of discounts currently on offer on orders placed before 1 March 2002. Please do not hesitate to contact me for any further information.

Yours sincerely ····· ■ *formule de politesse*

J. Murphy ····· ■ *signature*

John Murphy ····· ■ *nom de l'expéditeur*

Sales Manager ····· ■ *désignation*

enc. ····· ■ *pièce(s) jointe(s)*

Head office: Watchdog Technologies
Unit 7 Harwell Trading Park London SE1 2JF
Registered in England: 750 63941
Vat no: 635 0895 41

- corps de la lettre
- *Numéro d'inscription au registre du commerce* ■

Correspondence/Correspondance

How to lay out a business letter

company registration number ■   *date* ■

company name ■

Etablissements Renard

Siège social: Zone Industrielle Gustave Eiffel
38250 Saint-Egrève

letterhead/
sender's address ■

Société Anonyme au capital de 50 millions d'€
Registre du commerce 38C 87
Téléphone: 03 76 75 43 21   Télécopie: 03 76 75 88 47

Saint-Egrève, le 23 mai 2002

addressee ■

Madame Annick Deschamps
"Electrolux"
25, Rue du Lavoir
38740 VINAY

reference ■   Référence 05-02 VLS

subject ■   Objet: envoi de tarifs

salutation ■   Madame,

En réponse à votre lettre du 16 courant, j'ai le plaisir
de vous informer que nous pouvons vous fournir des pièces
de rechange pour toutes les grandes marques d'appareils
électro-ménagers fabriqués au cours des quinze dernières
années. Nos prix, joints en annexe, sont donnés hors TVA
et port non compris. Si vous décidez de commander, il est
impératif que vous nous indiquiez, outre la marque, le
nom et le numéro de série de votre appareil.

body of ■
the letter

Dès réception de votre commande, nous ferons le
nécessaire pour que les pièces vous parviennent
rapidement. Si vous en avez besoin de façon très urgente,
nous pouvons vous les faire livrer par coursier (le port
étant à votre charge).

complimentary ■
close

Dans l'espoir que ces précisions répondront à votre
attente, je vous prie d'agréer, Madame, l'expression de
mes sentiments distingués.

signature ■

sender's name ■   Jean-Michel Brun

organizational ■   Directeur Commercial
role

enclosures ■   P.J. tarif des pièces détachées robots ménagers.

La présentation d'une lettre d'affaires en anglais

La présentation la plus courante pour une lettre d'affaires est d'aligner le corps du texte à gauche à partir de la marge et de laisser un double interligne entre chaque paragraphe. Il est de plus en plus courant d'omettre la ponctuation pour les dates, les adresses et les formules de salutation en début et en fin de lettre.

En-tête/adresse de l'expéditeur

La majorité des entreprises utilisent du papier à en-tête avec le nom de la société, le logo et les coordonnées présentées au centre de la page ou en haut à droite. Si le papier utilisé n'a pas d'en-tête, l'adresse complète doit être écrite en haut à droite de la page. En Grande-Bretagne, on inscrit le code postal sur une ligne séparée, en-dessous du nom de la ville. Aux Etats-Unis on inscrit le 'ZIP code' juste après le nom de l'État.

Références

La référence indique le code de classement de la lettre ainsi que des informations telles que le numéro de client ou de commande. On la trouve soit à gauche de la lettre avant les coordonnées du destinataire ou sous la date à droite. Elle est souvent indiquée par l'abréviation *Your ref:/Our ref:*

Date

En Grande-Bretagne, on écrit la date dans l'ordre jour/mois/année sans virgule après le jour: *22 February 2002*. Les Américains préfèrent l'ordre mois/jour/année, avec une virgule après le jour: *February 22, 2002*.

Adresse du destinataire

Les coordonnées du destinataire doivent être données dans leur intégralité et préciser le poste occupé ou la fonction de la personne concernée.

Formule d'appel

La formule d'appel d'usage pour une lettre d'affaires est *Dear*.
- *Dear Sir or Madam* (si vous connaissez le titre ou la fonction de la personne mais ignorez s'il s'agit d'un homme ou d'une femme)
- *Dear Sirs* (si vous vous adressez à l'entreprise)
- *Dear Mr Dixon/Mrs Dixon* (si vous connaissez le nom de la personne)
- *Dear Ms Dixon* (*Ms* est utilisé par les femmes mariées et célibataires indifféremment. On l'utilise toujours suivi du nom de famille)
- *Dear Paul/Dear Martha* (pour les amis et collègues)

Objet

L'objet de la lettre est donné brièvement sous la formule d'appel et avant le corps de la lettre elle-même. Il est présenté en caractères gras, en majuscules ou souligné.

Formule de politesse

Si vous avez utilisé le nom du destinataire en début de lettre:
- *Yours sincerely*

Si vous ne connaissez pas le nom du destinataire:
- *Yours faithfully*

À un collègue ou à une connaissance:
- *Best wishes/Yours/Regards*

L'usage américain préfère *Sincerely yours* ou simplement *Sincerely*.

The layout of a French business letter

Letterhead/sender's address

Most companies have headed stationery with their full company name, logo and contact details which are displayed at the top of the page or at the top left-hand side of the page. When not using pre-printed stationery it is customary for the sender to type their details at the top left-hand side of the page. In French addresses the name of the town is written in capitals preceded by the post code on the same line eg: *44350 GUERANDE*

Addressee

The addressee's full address is given on the right-hand side of the page or beneath the letterhead. The name of the company is preceded by *Messieurs* if it is a family name: eg. *Messieurs Durtal & Cie*. The addressee's full title or organizational role is included in the address.

Date

The date in French is usually placed on the right-hand side of the page above or below the addressee's address. It is always given in the form: town, day/month/year: *Paris, le 12 juillet 2002; Lille, 1er avril 2002*

Reference

The reference line is usually placed on the left-hand side of the page opposite or below the addressee's details. It may take the form *N/réf:/V/réf:* or *Notre réf:/Votre réf:*

Subject

The subject of the letter is given succinctly before the opening salutation e.g.:
Objet: votre commande 456-8900

Salutation

The standard formulas for formal correspondence are:
- *Madame/Monsieur*
- *Mademoiselle* (There is no equivalent for the English Ms. If unsure of marital status use *Madame*)
- *Messieurs* (to a company or institution)
- *Mesdames*
- *Maître/Cher Maître* (to a lawyer)
- *Monsieur le Maire/ Madame le Consul* etc. to a prominent person

Complimentary close

Complimentary closes in French are lengthier than their British counterparts and some examples are listed below. It is always necessary to insert the title used in the salutation into the closing formula.
- *Dans l'attente de votre réponse , je vous prie d'agréer, Madame/Monsieur, l'expression de mes salutations distinguées*
- *Veuillez croire, Madame/Monsieur, à l'assurance de mes salutations distinguées* or *les meilleures*
- *Recevez, Madame/Monsieur, l'expression de ma considération distinguée*
- *Je vous prie d'agréer, Monsieur/Madame, l'expression de mes sentiments distingués* or *les meilleurs*

To a colleague or close personal contact:
- *Cordialement/Bien amicalement/Amitiés*

Expressions utiles

As requested I am forwarding you a [price list, catalogue]

As stated in your letter of [date] concerning...

Thank you for your letter of [date] concerning/requesting...

Thank you for sending me a [catalogue, price list, brochure]

Thank you for your enquiry of [date] concerning...

Further to our telephone conversation of [date]...

I am sorry to inform you that...

I am writing to confirm our telephone conversation of [date]

I am writing to enquire whether...

I am writing to express my dissatisfaction with...

I am writing to inform you that...

I am pleased to inform you that...

In reply to your letter/enquiry of [date]

I refer to your letter of [date] concerning...

I wish to draw your attention to...

I wish to inform you that..

I would be grateful if you could forward me a [price list/catalogue]

Please find enclosed ...

With reference to your letter/order of [date]

Formules de politesse

I look forward to hearing from you

I look forward to your response

I would be most grateful if you would look into this matter as soon as possible

I trust that you will give this matter your urgent attention

Please do not hesitate to contact me should you require any further information

Please let me know as soon as possible what action you propose to take

Abréviations d'usage

asap (as soon as possible)—dès que possible

bcc (blind carbon copy)—copie invisible

by return of post—par retour du courrier

c (circa)—env. (environ)

cc (carbon copy)—copie carbone

certified true copy—copie certifiée conforme

c/o (care of)—aux bons soins de, chez

confidential—confidentiel

draft—avant-projet

enc(s)., encl(s). (enclosure(s))— PJ (pièce(s) jointe(s))

FAO (for the attention of)— à l'attention de

FYI (for your information)—à titre d'information

incl. (including)—compris

N/A (not applicable)—sans objet

please forward—prière de faire suivre

pp. (per procurationem)—pp (par procuration)

printed matter—imprimés

private—privé

ps (postscriptum)—ps (post scriptum)

PTO (please turn over)—TSVP (tournez s'il vous plaît)

re—concernant

recd (received)—reçu

registered—recommandé avec accusé de réception

SAE (stamped addressed envelope)— enveloppe timbrée (à votre/son/ mon nom)

TBC (to be confirmed)—à confirmer

under separate cover—sous pli séparé

without prejudice—sans préjudice

Useful phrases

J'ai bien reçu votre [catalogue, réponse] et je vous en remercie

J'ai bien reçu votre lettre du [date] concernant...

Je vous remercie de votre lettre et de vos suggestions concernant...

Pour faire suite à notre conversation téléphonique du [date]...

Suite à notre entretien téléphonique de ce jour, je vous envoie ...

Je vous remercie par avance de bien vouloir me faire parvenir [un catalogue, un dossier de candidature] à l'adresse ci-dessus

Je vous serais reconnaissant de bien vouloir m'envoyer...

Comme vous le précisez dans votre lettre/fax du [date]...

Je vous informe par la présente de mon intention de...

Je me permets de porter à votre connaissance les faits suivants

J'attire/Je me permets d'attirer votre attention [sur le fait que, sur]...

Je vous prie de trouver ci-joint...

Closures

Merci de me dire ce que vous comptez faire pour remédier à ce problème

Je vous demande de remédier à cette situation dans les meilleurs délais

Je vous prie de bien vouloir me répondre par retour du courrier

N'hésitez surtout pas à me contacter pour tout renseignement complémentaire

Written conventions and abbreviations

à confirmer—TBC (to be confirmed)

à l'attention de—FAO (for the attention of)

AR (accusé de réception)—acknowledgement of receipt

à titre d'information—FYI (for your information)

aux bons soins de—c/o (care of)

avant-projet—draft

cc (copie carbone)—cc (carbon copy)

copie certifiée conforme—certified true copy

chez—c/o (care of)

confidentiel—confidential

copie invisible—bcc (blind carbon copy)

dès que possible—ASAP (as soon as possible)

enveloppe timbrée (à votre/son/mon nom)—SAE (stamped addressed envelope)

env. (environ)—c (circa)

exp. (expéditeur)—sender

imprimés—printed matter

incl. (inclus)—included

par retour du courrier—by return of post

PJ (pièce(s) jointe(s))—enc.(s), encl(s).

prière de faire suivre—please forward

privé—private

ps (post scriptum)—ps (post-scriptum)

pp (par procuration)—pp. (per procurationem)

recommandé avec accusé de réception—registered

sans objet— N/A (not applicable)

sous pli séparé—under separate cover

sans préjudice—without prejudice

TSVP (tournez s'il vous plaît)—PTO (please turn over)

Demande de renseignements

Herriot Consulting

18 Robert Adam Place   Tel: +44 (0) 131 339 8896
Edinburgh EH15 6YF   Fax: +44 (0) 131 339 8810

The Conference Manager
The Craiglochart Hotel
George Grove
GLASGOW G3 6DD

12th August 2002

Dear Sir or Madam

I am currently organizing a two-day residential staff-training event for
40 staff from our Scottish offices. In addition to accommodation and meals,
our requirements would include a fully equipped conference room, and four
syndicate rooms suitable for workshop sessions.

I would be very grateful if you would forward me information on your
conference facilities and details of availability for early November.

I look forward to hearing from you.

E. Ashford-Leigh

Edward Ashford-Leigh

Professional Development Manager

Demande d'échantillons

THE FRANK COMPANY

22 BLOOMING PLACE   TEL: 020-8669 7868
LONDON SW12   FAX: 020-8669 7866

The Sales Director
June Office Supplies
55 Dewey Road
Wolverhampton WV12 HRR

5 June 2002

Dear Sir/Madam,

Thank you for sending us your brochures. We are particularly interested in the Dol-
lis range, which would complement our existing stock.

We would be grateful if you could send us samples of the whole range promptly, as
we are hoping to place an order soon for the autumn.

Thanking you in advance,

Yours faithfully,

T Jones

Mr T Jones
Manager

Request for information

Julie Collins
Service des reproductions
Sandford Publishing Co.
Dalton Street
Wantage OX12 6DP
Grande-Bretagne
Tel/fax: +44 1235 764092

Service des Archives du film
Centre National de la Cinématographie

le 13 février 2002

Madame, Monsieur,

Sandford Publishing Co s'apprête à publier un ouvrage sur l'urbanisme dans le cinéma européen. Les auteurs souhaitant insérer un certain nombre de clichés appartenant à vos archives, je vous serais très reconnaissante de bien vouloir me faire parvenir une documentation sur les modalités et les coûts de reproduction.

Veuillez agréer, Madame, Monsieur, l'expression de ma considération distinguée.

Julie Collins

Request for samples

le 18 avril 2002

Ateliers Bordoni
Siège social:
2, impasse du Parc
50760 Barfleur
Registre du Commerce 71 F 34
Téléphone/Fax: 02 45 45 22 34/5
email: bordoni@Ateliersbarfleur.com

> Filatures Fouquet
> 185 route de Nantes
> 49300 Cholet

Madame, Monsieur,

J'ai bien reçu votre catalogue et je vous en remercie, mais avant de passer ma commande, je souhaiterais recevoir un lot d'échantillons des tissus qui figurent de la page 254 à la page 256, réf. TAF.10/54/5/6.

Je vous remercie de votre compréhension et vous adresse, Madame, Monsieur, mes salutations distinguées.

G. Bordoni
Propriétaire

Lettre promotionnelle

Fashion Statements

Wallace Road, Ellon, Aberdeenshire AB32 5BY

Tel: 01224 497214 Fax: 01224 497234

February 2002

Dear Mrs Evans

As one of our most valued customers, I wanted to make sure that you would have the opportunity to select your orders from the advance copy of our new Spring-Summer catalogue which I enclose.

More Choice

As you will see from our catalogue, we have more women's styles in more sizes than ever before, with a greater range of fittings to suit all our customers.

Top quality

We pride ourselves on the quality of our goods and will ensure that your order reaches you within 28 days in perfect condition. Our customer care team is on hand to deal with queries on our customer hotline and if you are not completely satisfied with your order they will arrange for an immediate refund.

Post your completed order form today, or call our team on **01224 445382** to enjoy next season's fashions today.

Faith Pickett

Faith Pickett
Customer Care Manager

Commande

BUTLERS OF BATH LTD

Garrard Street Mall, BathBA7 2JD
Tel: 01225 678 9865 Fax: 01225 678 9800

Joseph Hayes
Sales Manager, New Textiles Express
Bexford Way
Thatcham
RG18 2WS

21 March 2002

Dear Sir

Following our discussion last week I am pleased to confirm my order for an initial batch of 20 Harlequin bed linen sets at a unit price of £13.99.

A purchase order form is enclosed which takes into account a 10% trade discount. I would be grateful if you could send me confirmation of receipt of the order and dispatch details.

I look forward to hearing from you.

Yours faithfully

Amy Peterson

Amy Peterson
Manager

Sales promotion

France V.P.C.
Route de Londres
93100 Montreuil-sous-Bois

Monsieur et Madame Roux
34 rue Victor Hugo
31300 Toulouse

le 1er mars 2002

Chère Madame, cher Monsieur,

Bientôt la belle saison, il est temps de songer à s'habiller pour les vacances ! Et c'est justement le moment pour nous de vous présenter notre nouveau catalogue printemps-été. Cette année encore, nous nous plaçons résolument sous le signe du choix, de la qualité et des services, comme en témoignent nos nouveautés.

Plus de choix et de qualité :
- Nouvelle collection enfant : désormais toute la famille peut trouver son bonheur chez V.P.C., grâce à notre ligne de vêtements enfants solides, faciles d'entretien, et surtout qui plaisent à nos bambins !
- Gamme d'articles de sport étendue pour vos activités sportives des vacances : voyez notamment nos nouvelles pages vélo. Tous les cycles sont garantis deux ans.

Plus de services :
- De nouvelles fiches d'informations figurent sur les pages électroménager, pour vous permettre de mieux choisir vos appareils. Mieux informés, vous pouvez mieux acheter.
- Commande par Internet : l'informatique au service de notre clientèle. La commande devient plus facile et plus rapide.
- Livraisons plus rapides : la garantie de recevoir vos articles en 48h.

De plus, pour vous, chers clients, V.P.C. baisse ses prix de 20% sur la collection hiver toujours disponible, vous accorde une remise de 100 F sur votre premier achat dans le catalogue printemps-été (offre valable jusqu'au 15 avril 2002).

Nous vous remercions de votre fidélité et de votre confiance ! Cordialement,

France V.P.C.

Placing an order

Matignon et Cie.
34, avenue Gambetta
03000 Moulins
Tél: 04 54 78 56 22
Télécopie: 04 54 78 56 23

Monsieur Marc Poujol
Directeur commercial
Mobilier Moderne
62, avenue du Parc
45000 Orléans
Orléans, le 4 juillet 2002

Objet: commande

Monsieur,

Suite à notre conversation téléphonique, je vous confirme la commande suivante:

Article	Référence	Quantité	Prix unitaire
siège 'dactylo ergonomique'	Réf: SDE/423	2	126,00€
poste de travail 130x90 cm	Réf: PDT/452	3	224,56€

Le règlement sera effectué au comptant comme convenu à réception de la facture.

Je vous prie de bien vouloir me confirmer cette commande par retour du courrier et de me faire connaître la date de livraison des meubles.

Veuillez croire, Monsieur, à l'assurance de mes salutations distinguées,

Daniel Schwinger

Daniel Schwinger
Directeur des achats

Facture

Art Decoratif

224 Haversham Road, Reading, Berkshire, RG32 5SE

VAT No 280 268690

Item	Quantity	Unit Price	£
gilt mirror (Regency)	10	£27.90	270.90
lampshade code 02345	7	£10	70.00
rug 120x75 code 0346	5	£62.45	312.25
		Carriage	18.75
		Total excluding VAT	671.90
		VAT @ 17.5 %	117.58
		Total including VAT	789.48

Charges are payable when this invoice is issued. The account is therefore due for settlement

---

The Round Place

2 Nighend High, Bristol, BS9 0UI
Tel: 0117 66900   Fax: 0117 55450

Famous Gourmet   4 June 2002
399 Old Green Road
Bristol
BS12 8TY

Dear Sirs,

Invoice no. B54/56/HP

We would be glad if you would amend your recent invoice (copy enclosed).

The quantities of the last three items are incorrect, since they refer to "24 dozen" instead of the correct quantity of "14 dozen" in each case. In addition to this, our agreed discount of 4% has not been allowed.

Please check your records and issue a revised invoice, which we will then be happy to pay within the agreed time.

Yours faithfully,

M R Edwardson

M. R Edwardson
Chief Supplies Officer

Encl.

. . . .

Invoice

Editions Verbatim

27, rue Pierre Maurois
75009 Paris
tél/fax 01 56 47 87 90/1

Désignation	Qté	Prix unitaire	€ (euro)
manuels 'Marché conclu'	10	5,75	57,50
coffret audio	1	48,50	48,50
CD-ROM	1	26,00	26,00
cassette VHS 'Voyage d'affaires'	1	18,50	18,50

total hors taxe:	150,50
TVA 18,2%	27,39
TTC	177,89

Pour paiement intégral à la date prévue par les parties.

"La Maison du Sous-Vêtement"

15, rue Magenta
42000 Saint-Etienne
Tél.: 04 77 42 17 82

le 12 septembre 2002
USINES LOIRETEXTILE
Confection - Vente en gros
Z.I. des Epis
42319 Roanne CEDEX

Référence commande n° 00/08/30-ZDX

Messieurs,

J'ai bien reçu votre livraison, mais je me vois dans l'obligation
de vous retourner le colis, les tailles des articles ne
correspondant pas à celles indiquées sur le bon de commande.

Je vous saurais gré de bien vouloir corriger votre erreur et de me
faire parvenir les articles conformes à ma commande dans les plus
brefs délais.

Veuillez agréer, Messieurs, l'expression de ma considération
distinguée.

A. Hébert
Gérant

Relevé de compte

RBS Stationery Supplies

Unit 2, Maltby Way
Swindon
SN4 7JT
Tel: 0870 674 532
Fax: 0870 674 453

Customer No. BH/345/29

Date	INVOICE AND STATEMENT OF ACCOUNT	Amount
	Balance brought forward as at 06 Jul 01	132.95
20 Jul 01	Payment – thank you	132.95CR
25 Jul 01	25 x boxes A4 laser printer paper @4.99	124.75
25 Jul 01	2 x RBS toner @11.99	23.98
25 Jul 01	Carriage	7.00
Payments and transactions received after 06 Aug 01 are not shown		
PAYMENT IS DUE WITHIN 10 DAYS OF RECEIPT *For details of how to pay, please see over*		£155.73

Head Office: 45 Glebe Rd, Swindon SN4 5 KT
Registered in England: 679 4289
Vat no: 562 9832 43

Reçu

Date *4 February* 20 *02*   No. 5450
Customer's Name *Mr Charles*
Address *97 Lyon Terrace, Chichester*

Stock No.	Description of Article Sold		Amount	
B78-54	*Leather briefcase*	£	*95—*	*00*
	10% discount	£	*(9—*	*50)*
		£	*85—*	*50*
	Paid in full – cheque			

Thank you for your custom
McCarthy's Limited — 50 Kingsgate, Chichester Tel: 643876

Statement of Account

Musique d'Ailleurs

3, rue Victor Jara
75011 Paris
tél/fax 01 40 39 27 62/3

Médiathèque Municipale
52 rue de la République   Nº d'abonné YL 33209
59162 Marpent

Date	Désignation	Montant €	Date de paiement
7/02/02	Coffret 3 CD Amérique Latine	30,00	30/01/02
7/03/02	Coffret 3 CD Moyen-Orient	30,00	27/02/02
8/04/02	Coffret 3 CD Europe de l'Est	30,00	
	Montant dû	30,00	

Si vous réglez votre facture par prélèvement automatique, votre compte sera débité
le 30 de ce mois. Pour tout paiement par Carte Bleue, chèque bancaire ou Compte
Chèque Postal voir au verso.

Receipt

Date	10.10.02		**Nº 7350**
Nom	Mme Vernoux		
Adresse	10 rue du Petit Pont		
	18000 Bourges		

Référence:	Description		Montant €
BX 543	bicyclette VTT Eclair		320 00
	escompte 5%		16 00
		Total	304 00
	Paiement effectué par		
	CCP 36-841		

Avec nos remerciements
La Maison du Tout Terrain   Place de la Gare   18000 Bourges   Tel 02.48.36.24.02

Télécopie

Cantata Publishing

55 Mill St
Liverpool L12 GH
Tel: +44 (0)151 234 8970
Fax: +44 (0)151-235-8744

FACSIMILE NUMBER:+ 44 (0)151-4497-8744

Message for: Peter Evans
Address: Boom Books, The Market Place
Marville
M33 7GH
Fax number: 0377-624-994
From: Mary Dunn
Date: 14 June 2002

Number of pages including this one: 2

Thank you for confirming that you will be able to exhibit at the New Age Book Fair on 12 June 2002. I have reserved a room on a bed and breakfast basis at the Consort Hotel which is close to our venue (see attached plan) from the 11 July –14 July inclusive.

We will need to receive all your promotional material, samples, books and posters by the 2 July at the very latest so that stands can be prepared on 11 July.

Can you confirm that the arrangements above are acceptable. If you require any further details, don't hesitate to get in touch.

Look forward to meeting you again on 11 July.

Mary Dunn

Promotions Coordinator

Note de service

Memorandum

```
To:        All staff
From:      F. Farnes, Expenses administrator
CC:        Head of Finance
Date:      3/3/2002
Subject:   Expense claims
```

Staff are reminded that all expense claims must be submitted by 14 March 2002 in time to be processed before the end of this financial year. Reimbursement of late claims will be delayed.

Fax

. . . .

L.C. INFORMATIQUE

12, RUE CLAUDE BERNARD
86000 POITIERS
N° de téléphone: 05 49 41 54 67
N° de télécopie: 05 49 41 22 82

TRANSMISSION PAR TELECOPIE

Date: 12 août 2002

Veuillez remettre ce document à : Jean Briant

Numéro de télécopie : 00 44 705 82 31 54

De la part de : Stéphanie Langlois

Nombre de pages (y compris cette page) : 1

Message : Prière de me faire parvenir de toute urgence, par
Chronopost si possible, l'original de vos billets d'avion et de
train pour que je puisse procéder à votre remboursement.

J'aurai aussi besoin de vos notes d'hôtel et de restaurant, mais
c'est moins urgent.

Merci, et amitiés,

Langlois

S. Langlois

**Si vous ne recevez pas ce document au complet, veuillez nous en aviser le plus rapidement
possible par t l phone ou t l copie.**

Memorandum

NOTE DE SERVICE

Le 05/06/2002

Pour des raisons de sécurité, il est rappelé au
personnel que l'accès aux locaux est strictement
interdit du vendredi 22h00 au lundi 6h00, sauf
autorisation spéciale délivrée par M. Fabre.

La direction

Le courrier électronique

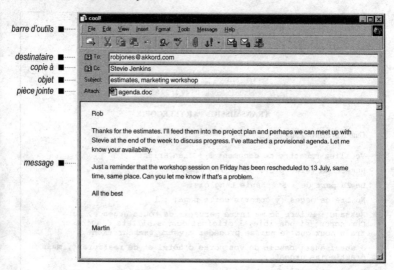

barre d'outils ■

destinataire ■

copie à ■

objet ■

pièce jointe ■

To: robjones@akkord.com
Cc: Stevie Jenkins
Subject: estimates, marketing workshop
Attach: agenda.doc

Rob

Thanks for the estimates. I'll feed them into the project plan and perhaps we can meet up with Stevie at the end of the week to discuss progress. I've attached a provisional agenda. Let me know your availability.

message ■

Just a reminder that the workshop session on Friday has been rescheduled to 13 July, same time, same place. Can you let me know if that's a problem.

All the best

Martin

to be on email	être connecté	to receive an attachment	recevoir une pièce jointe/une annexe
an email	un message électronique, un e-mail	to open an attachment	ouvrir une pièce jointe/une annexe
an email address	une adresse électronique	to save a message on the desktop/hard disk	enregistrer un message sur le bureau/le disque dur
an at sign	un arobase	to delete a message	effacer/supprimer un message
an address book	un carnet d'adresses		
a distribution list	une liste de diffusion	an inbox	une boîte de réception
to send an email	envoyer un e-mail	an outbox	une boîte d'envoi
to receive an email	recevoir un e-mail	freemail	un service de courrier électronique gratuit
to forward an email	faire suivre un message		
to copy somebody in, to cc somebody	envoyer un message en copie à quelqu'un	snail mail	le courrier postal
c.c. (carbon copy)	copie	to send/get spam	envoyer/recevoir des messages non sollicités
b.c.c. (blind carbon copy)	copie invisible		
a file	un fichier	spamming	le multipostage abusif, la publicité rebut par courrier électronique
a signature file	un fichier signature		
an emoticon, a smiley	une frimousse/un souriant/un smiley	a mail bomb	une bombe (électronique)
to attach a file	envoyer une pièce jointe/une annexe	a modem	un modem

Correspondence/Correspondance

. . . .

Using email

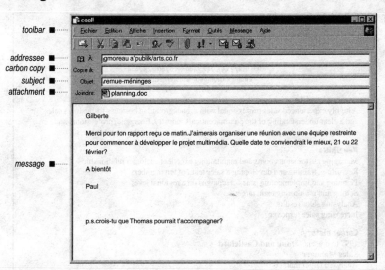

- toolbar
- addressee
- carbon copy
- subject
- attachment

À gmoreau'a'publik/arts.co.fr

Copie à:

Objet: remue-méninges

Joindre: planning.doc

- message

> Gilberte
>
> Merci pour ton rapport reçu ce matin. J'aimerais organiser une réunion avec une équipe restreinte pour commencer à développer le projet multimédia. Quelle date te conviendrait le mieux, 21 ou 22 février?
>
> A bientôt
>
> Paul
>
> p.s. crois-tu que Thomas pourrait t'accompagner?

être connecté	to be on email	ouvrir une pièce jointe/une annexe	to open an attachment
un message électronique, un e-mail	an email	enregistrer un message sur le bureau/le disque dur	to save a message on the desktop/hard disk
une adresse électronique	an email address		
un arobase	an at sign	effacer/supprimer un message	to delete a message
un carnet d'adresses	an address book	une boîte de réception	an inbox
une liste de diffusion	a distribution list	une boîte d'envoi	an outbox
envoyer un e-mail	to send an email	un service de courrier électronique gratuit	freemail
recevoir un e-mail	to receive an email		
faire suivre un message	to forward an email	le courrier postal	snail mail
envoyer un message en copie à quelqu'un	to copy somebody in, to cc somebody	envoyer/recevoir des messages non sollicités	to send/get spam
copie	c.c. (carbon copy)	le multi-postage abusif, la publicité rebut par courrier électronique	spamming
copie invisible	b.c.c. (blind carbon copy)		
un fichier	a file	une bombe électronique	a mail bomb
un fichier signature	a signature file		
une frimousse, un souriant, un smiley	an emoticon, a smiley	un modem	a modem
envoyer une pièce jointe/une annexe	to attach a file		
recevoir /une pièce jointe/une annexe	to receive an attachment		

Curriculum vitae: cadre britannique

Madeleine Thompson
132 Albert Road, Brighton, BN1 7RF

Tel: 01273 455 942 Mobile: 0780 273 7414
Email: mthompson@fasternet.co.uk

Personal profile
A highly experienced sales professional with a background in business-to-business sales and a clear understanding of the pharmaceuticals industry. Energetic, professional and self-motivated with a proven ability to exceed targets and develop new business.

Key Skills
Managing customer accounts and maintaining excellent customer relationships
Recruiting, training and developing a sales team of ten members
Planning and implementing sales campaigns on a regional level
Setting and monitoring team targets
Analysing sales results
Increasing sales turnover

Career history
1997 to present **Dunn and Castleford**
Sales Manager
Analysed target markets
Formulated long-term sales strategy
Negotiated major sales contracts worth in excess of £2 million over five years with national companies including The Drugstore chain, Chemco, and the High Street chemist chain Scotts
Managed major client accounts
Built up a sales team of ten and created an in-house training programme

1994-1997 **Trent Pharmaceuticals**
Sales Associate
Travelled throughout the South West revitalizing sales networks and establishing new contacts
Won Salesperson of the Year Award 1996
Produced quarterly sales analysis for head office

1992-1994 **Pharmwares**
Telesales Administrator
Responsible for running a telesales unit of five staff
Presented company products and services to prospective clients
Handled complaints and enquiries
Updated customer databases

Education and Training
1993-1994 London Business Institute - Postgraduate Diploma in Retail Marketing
1990-1993 Brighton College - Diploma in Sales and Marketing
Currently working towards a certificate in e-customer relationship management by open learning

Personal Details
Date of birth: 22 March 1972
Driving Licence: Full UK licence
Interests: horse-riding, travel, chess
References: Available on request

Curriculum vitae: French executive

Frédéric Malmaison

38 rue de la Glacière
75013 Paris

Juriste

Parcours professionnel

1994 à ce jour: **responsable du service juridique** chez **Bernier et Milleaux**, Paris, entreprise de services juridiques, financiers et comptables (350 personnes en France, plus 3 filiales en Europe)
- assuré la préparation de dossiers juridiques de fusion d'entreprises et de création de filiales
- assuré la liaison entre avocats d'affaires et ministères de l'industrie et du commerce

Réalisations marquantes:
- réorganisation et uniformisation de la gestion juridique des différentes filiales du groupe
- développement d'un projet de quatrième filiale en Italie

1989-1994 **assistance juridique** chez **ATTM**, Bruxelles
(Assurances des transports terrestres et maritimes)

- négociations de contrats de transport et d'affrètement
- suivi instruction des sinistres
- élaboration d'un programme de formation interne du personnel

1987-1988 stage de trois mois à la **Commission Européenne**

- préparation de dossiers visant à l'uniformisation des systèmes d'assurances pour les entreprises des pays membres

Formation

1988 Diplôme de la Chambre de Commerce de Bruxelles
1987 Cours d'anglais des affaires, Chambre de Commerce de Londres
1986 DESS Droit des Affaires, Université de Paris I
1985 Maîtrise de Droit Européen, mention 'très bien', Université de Paris I

Divers

37 ans, marié, un enfant
trilingue français, anglais, néerlandais
vidéaste amateur
pratique du hockey sur glace
références disponibles sur demande

Curriculum Vitae

Curriculum vitae: jeune diplômé

Curriculum Vitae *(sidebar)*

Alexander Joseph

23 Nevis Close
Carlisle
CL13 7HK
Tel: 01228 677 453

Personal profile

A hard-working, self-motivated and enthusiastic Information Technology graduate
with a keen interest in the Internet and the digital economy. A good problem-solver
with an ability to work well as part of a team.

Career objectives

I am looking for a position where I could further develop my strong IT skills in a
business environment.

Education and training

1998-2002 **University of Aberdeen**
BSc Honours Computing Science (2:1)
1991-1998 **Carlisle Community College**
Obtained three 'A' levels (maths, physics, information technology) at grade A and
seven 'O' levels including English
Programming languages: HTML,C, C++, Java,VRML, Oracle Forms 4
Environments: Microsoft Windows 98 & NT, Sun Solaris

Work experience

2001-2002 Weekend work as cashier and customer advisor - Buildit Discount Store,
Carlisle
2001 Summer employment as junior programmer in a local software house writing
browser-enabled customer billing and stock control software.

Achievements

Represented my university in the triathlon at the National Student Games 2000
Chair of the University Debating Society 2001
Editorial assistant on the student newspaper

Personal details

Date of birth: 14 December 1979
Full UK driving licence
Interests: athletics, music, travel
References: available on request

Curriculum vitae: French graduate

Marie Baudin
57 rue de la Victoire
18 000 Bourges
Tél 02 47 50 19 51

née le 28 avril 1978

Mon ambition
exprimer mes compétences au sein d'une équipe dynamique pour contribuer au succès
de projets d'entreprise.

Formation
2000: Certificat d'études commerciales et de marketing
Stevenson University College, Edimbourg, Ecosse
1999: cours de 4 semaines d'anglais intensif à IAL, Oxford
1998: Ecole régionale des Beaux-Arts d'Orléans, section photographie
1996: Bac B, mention bien, Lycée Albert Marcoeur, Bourges

Expérience professionnelle
2000: remplacement de trois mois comme assistante du directeur du marketing chez
'Tourist Publications' à Edimbourg:
- publicité produits
- suivi de la création: planning, exécutions, maquettes
- gestion des freelances

1999: stage d'un mois non rémunéré chez 'Tourist Publications'
- publicité photo
- coordination édition-marketing

Divers
bilingue français, italien
anglais courant
bonne connaissance de l'outil informatique, en particulier sur Macintosh

Curriculum Vitae

La présentation d'un curriculum vitae en anglais

En règle générale, un curriculum vitae ne doit pas excéder deux pages. Il doit également être concis et bien présenté. Il est coutume de ne pas s'exprimer à la première personne du singulier dans la description de son parcours professionnel et de ses compétences. Les informations d'ordre personnel telles que le nom de jeune fille et la nationalité ne sont plus systématiquement mentionnées sauf si elles ont un rapport direct avec l'emploi concerné.

Le style de présentation le plus courant est le CV par ordre chronologique en commençant par l'expérience professionnelle la plus récente.

Qualités personnelles/personal profile

Cette section permet de 'vendre' des qualités personnelles ainsi que des aptitudes difficiles à insérer ailleurs. Vous pouvez y mentionner vos aspirations avec une phrase du type:
I am looking for a position as a…/ I am looking for a role where…
Certains termes et expressions accrochent plus que d'autres:
an established track record in [sales, retail]
proven administrative/staff management skills
articulate
able to work to deadlines
creative
dynamic
efficient
energetic
enthusiastic
experienced
flexible
highly motivated
innovative
organized
people-oriented
reliable
self-motivated
team-player
versatile

Compétences essentielles/key skills

Cette section du CV permet au candidat de fournir des détails sur les compétences acquises au cours de sa formation et de sa carrière. Les expressions ci-dessous peuvent vous être utiles:
a detailed knowledge of [financial planning, project management]
good analytical and problem-solving skills
good communications skills
team leadership skills
strategic thinking
commercial awareness
administrative experience
bookkeeping skills
good telephone manner
staff management experience
keyboard skills (60 wpm)
shorthand
conversational/reading knowledge of German
fluent Italian
good written/spoken Spanish
proficient in using spreadsheets/ Excel/PowerPoint

Curriculum Vitae

Parcours professionnel/career history

Dans la description de vos réalisations il est recommandé d'utiliser des participes passés en omettant le sujet 'I'. Verbes utiles:

analysed
coordinated
created
delivered
designed
directed
evaluated
facilitated
headed
identified
implemented
launched
liaised
maintained
managed
monitored
organized
planned
prepared
produced
provided
researched
reorganized
resolved

Vous pouvez souligner l'importance de votre contribution dans les différents postes occupés en choisissant des expressions positives telles que:

achieved [increase/improvement]
completed [the project on time and within budget]
drove forward [the implementation of]
exceeded [targets/objectives]
increased [profits/turnover/sales]
improved [efficiency/information flow]

maximized [impact/productivity]
negotiated [contract/deal]
pioneered [technique/system]
reduced [wastage/costs]
resolved [conflict, difficulty]
secured [contracts/customers]
upgraded [system/procedure]
streamlined [process/procedure]
successfully [delivered/implemented/completed/negotiated]
won [contract/tender]

The presentation of a French curriculum vitae

A curriculum vitae should not generally exceed two pages in length and should be clearly laid out and succinctly worded. It is standard practice to avoid the use of the first person when describing one's career outline and skills. Personal details such as marital status, maiden name and nationality are now often omitted in a British curriculum vitae except where they have a direct bearing on the job for which one is applying. However, in France they are still often given. It is common for French job advertisements to specify a handwritten letter (*lettre manuscrite*) and a photograph. Advertisements for professional positions rarely give any indication of salary and a candidate is asked to state their current salary (*rémunération actuelle*) or their desired salary (*prétentions*).

The most common style of presentation is the chronological CV with experience listed in reverse order, starting with the most recent or current position.

Personal profile/qualités personnelles

The candidate has the opportunity in an opening statement to 'sell' the personal qualities and aptitudes which might not be evident elsewhere in the CV. It may be appropriate to state your career aspirations here with a phrase such as : *Je recherche un poste de.../ Je cherche un poste où mon rôle serait de...* Useful phrases might include:
    expérience confirmée de la gestion du personnel

administrateur chevronné
connaissance approfondie de
aptitude à communiquer
créatif
dynamique
efficace
énergique
enthousiaste
expérimenté
souplesse d'esprit
très motivé
esprit d'innovation
sens de l'organisation
bon relationnel
fiable
très motivé
esprit d'équipe
polyvalent

Key skills/compétences essentielles

The applicant will wish to provide details of general competencies acquired over the course of their education, training or career. Useful phrases could include:
    esprit d'analyse et aptitude à résoudre les problèmes
    communicateur
    aptitude à conduire une équipe
    aptitude à l'élaboration de stratégie
    esprit commercial
    expérience de l'administration
    expertise en comptabilité
    sachant répondre au téléphone
    expérience de la gestion du personnel
    vitesse de frappe (60 mpm)
    connaissance de la sténographie
    allemand parlé/lu
    italien courant
    bonne maîtrise de l'espagnol écrit/oral

Career history/parcours professionnel

When listing one's achievements it is usual to employ action verbs in the past tense without the subject pronoun 'Je'. Useful verbs might include:

  créé
  livré
  conçu
  dirigé
  évalué
  facilité
  mené
  identifié
  mis en place
  lancé
  travaillé en liaison avec
  assuré l'entretien de
  contrôlé
  organisé
  planifié
  préparé
  produit
  fourni
  recherché
  réorganisé
  résolu

You can stress the benefits you have brought to the companies you have worked for with positive phrases such as:

  augmenté
  amélioré
  mené à terme [le projet dans les limites du budget imparti]
  accéléré [la mise en place de]
  dépassé [les objectifs]
  augmenté [les bénéfices/le chiffre d'affaires/les ventes]
  accru [l'efficacité/la circulation de l'information]
  maximisé [l'impact/la productivité]

négocié [un contrat/un marché]
mis au point [une technique/un système]
réduit [pertes/coûts]
résolu [un conflit/une difficulté]
fidélisé [contractants/clients]
perfectionné [système/ procédure]
simplifié [procédé/procédure)]
réussi à [fournir/instaurer]
mené/négocié avec succès
emporté [contrat/offre]

Curriculum Vitae

Lettre de motivation

17 Roslyn Terrace,
London
NW2 3SQ

15th October 2002

Ms R. Klein,
Travis Consulting Group
44 Commercial Way
LONDON
E14 5BH

Dear Ms Klein,

Principal Consultant, E-business Strategy

I should like to apply for the above post, advertised in today's Sunday Times and have pleasure in enclosing my curriculum vitae for your attention.

MBA-qualified, I am a highly experienced information systems strategy consultant and have worked with a range of blue-chip clients, primarily in the financial services and retail sectors. In my most recent role, with Herriot Consulting, I have successfully led the development of a new e-business practice.

I am now seeking an opportunity to fulfil my career aspirations with a major management consultancy, such as TCG, which has recognised the enormous potential of the e-business revolution. I believe I can offer TCG a combination of technical understanding, business insight and entrepreneurial flair.

I would be delighted to discuss this opportunity further with you at a future interview and look forward to hearing from you.

Yours sincerely,

Jane Penner

Jane Penner

enc

Expressions utiles

I am writing in response to your advertisement in [publication] of [date]

I wish to enquire about the vacancy for a [job title]

I should like to apply for the post of [job title] advertised in [publication] of [date]

As you will see from the enclosed CV...

Please find enclosed a copy of my curriculum vitae/résumé (AmE)

Formules de politesse

Thank you for considering this application

I should be pleased to attend an interview

Please do not hesitate to contact me on the above number if you should require any further information

I look forward to hearing from you

I look forward to discussing this position further with you at a future interview

Covering letter for a job application

Simon PULVAR
15, impasse des mimosas
38000 GRENOBLE
Tel: 04 56 78 39 31

Monsieur le Directeur des Ressources humaines
Groupe TOPCONSEIL
78, avenue Jules Ferry
78000 VERSAILLES

Grenoble, le 6 juin 2002

Objet: annonce no.TC 564

Monsieur,

Votre annonce parue dans Le Figaro du 4 juin concernant un poste de consultant en nouvelles technologies a retenu mon attention. Je pense que mes compétences et mon expérience professionnelle sont paticulièrement bien adaptées au poste que vous désirez pourvoir.

Comme l'indique le CV ci-joint, je suis diplômé d'une grande école de gestion et je possède trois ans d'expérience en conseil acquise chez CONSULTICA. À ce titre, j'ai assuré de nombreuses missions de conseil en stratégie e-business, y compris deux missions dans la succursale de CONSULTICA à Londres.

Je recherche l'opportunité de valoriser mes atouts au sein d'une équipe pluridisciplinaire et de participer au développement du cabinet en Europe. Je pense pouvoir apporter à votre équipe une compétence technique alliée à un excellent relationnel.

Je vous remercie de l'attention que vous voudrez bien apporter à ma candidature et dans l'attente de votre réponse, je vous prie d'agréer, Monsieur, l'expression de mes sentiments distingués.

S Pulvar

Simon Pulvar

PJ: curriculum vitae

Useful phrases

Je vous adresse ma candidature suite à votre annonce parue dans [publication] du [date]

En réponse à votre annonce parue le [date] dans [publication], je vous adresse mon CV

Suite à votre annonce parue dans [publication] du [date], je me permets de vous adresser ma candidature pour le poste de…

Le CV ci-joint vous permettra de mesurer l'évolution de ma carrière

Vous trouverez ci-joint un CV qui vous donnera plus de précisions sur mon parcours professionnel

Closing formulas

Je me tiens à votre disposition pour un entretien au cours duquel nous pourrions discuter du poste à pourvoir

Je souhaiterais vivement vous rencontrer afin que nous puissions discuter plus en détail des attributions de ce poste

Espérant vous rencontrer très prochainement, je vous prie de croire, Monsieur/Madame, à l'expression de mes salutations distinguées

Je me tiens à votre disposition pour toute information complémentaire concernant ma candidature

Infos pratiques: comment téléphoner

Au Royaume-Uni

Pour téléphoner au sein du Royaume-Uni, composez l'indicatif régional suivi du numéro de téléphone de la personne que vous cherchez à joindre. Si l'indicatif, est le même que celui de la région où vous vous trouvez, il n'est pas nécessaire de le composer.

Pour les appels internationaux, composez le code d'accès au réseau international:

- 00 + l'indicatif du pays appelé + l'indicatif régional + le numéro de téléphone de la personne que vous souhaitez appeler.

Si l'indicatif régional de la personne que vous appelez commence par un 0, il ne faut pas le composer.

Aux États-Unis

Aux États-Unis, les numéros de téléphone sont composés d'un indicatif régional à trois chiffres suivi d'un numéro à sept chiffres. Si vous faites un appel local il ne faut pas composer l'indicatif. Pour les appels nationaux, il faut composer le:

- 1 + l'indicatif à trois chiffres + le numéro à 7 chiffres.

Pour les appels internationaux, composez le code d'accès au réseau international:

- 011 + l'indicatif du pays appelé + l'indicatif régional + le numéro de la personne que vous souhaitez appeler.

Si l'indicatif régional de la personne que vous appelez commence par un 0, il ne faut pas le composer.

Au téléphone ...

En anglais, on donne les numéros de téléphone chiffre par chiffre. Pour le 0208 549 44 53, on dira:

- oh two oh eight, five four nine, double four, five three.

Vocabulaire utile

Le téléphone et les appels téléphoniques

the handset, the receiver	le combiné
the keypad	les touches
the telephone cord	le fil du téléphone
to pick up the phone	décrocher
to hang up	raccrocher
a telephone call	un appel téléphonique/un coup de téléphone
to make a phone call	passer/donner un coup de téléphone
a telephone number	un numéro de téléphone
an extension (phone)	un téléphone/un poste supplémentaire
an extension (number)	un numéro de poste
the dialling tone	la tonalité
the tone (in a recorded message)	le bip sonore/le signal sonore
to dial the number	composer le numéro
to dial 999/911	composer le 999/911
the area/country code	l'indicatif d'une ville/d'un pays
the operator	l'opérateur
the switchboard	le standard
the switchboard operator	le/la standardiste
a digital phone, a tone-dialling phone	un téléphone à fréquence vocale
a cordless phone	un téléphone sans fil
an answering machine	un répondeur
voice mail	une messagerie vocale
a telephone directory	un annuaire
a phone book	un annuaire, un bottin®
the Yellow Pages®	les Pages Jaunes®
a business/residential number	un numéro professionnel/personnel
a Freefone number (GB), a toll-free number (US)	un numéro vert, un numéro d'appel gratuit
the emergency services number (999 in the UK and 911 in the US)	le numéro d'appel d'urgence

Practical information: how to phone

Within Metropolitan France

Metropolitan France is divided into five telephone calling zones and all French numbers consist of ten digits. The first two digits correspond to the various zones:

- all numbers for Paris/Île-de-France are prefixed by 01;
- all numbers for the North-West are prefixed by 02;
- all numbers for the North-East are prefixed by 03;
- all numbers for the South-East (including Corsica) are prefixed by 04;
- and finally, all numbers for the South-West are prefixed by 05.

To the overseas departments

Wait for the dialling tone:
- dial 0 + the area code + the number (six digits).

To overseas territories and foreign countries

Wait for the dialling tone, dial 00. On hearing the new dialling tone, dial the area code (for overseas territories) or the country code and area code plus the number. When calling a foreign country or when calling France from abroad, the initial 0 of the area code is dropped.

On the phone...

In French, telephone numbers are given using double figures e.g. for 01 34 67 62 12 you say:

- zéro-un trente-quatre soixante-sept soixante-deux douze.

Useful vocabulary

The phone and the calling procedures

décrocher	to pick up the phone
raccrocher	to hang up
le combiné	the receiver, the handset
un numéro de téléphone	a phone number
un numéro de poste	an extension number
composer le numéro	to dial the number
la tonalité	the dialling tone
l'indicatif (téléphonique) d'une ville/d'un pays	the area/country code
un correspondant	a correspondent
un opérateur	an operator
un téléphone sans fil	a cordless phone
un téléphone à fréquence vocale	a digital phone, a tone-dialling phone
un répondeur	a telephone answering machine
un bip sonore	a tone (on recorded message)
une messagerie vocale	voice mail
un annuaire	a telephone directory
un bottin®	a phone book
les Pages Jaunes®	the Yellow Pages®
les pages blanches	the phone book
les numéros d'appel d'urgence	the emergency telephone numbers (15 for emergency medical assistance, 17 for the police and 18 for the fire brigade)
un numéro vert	a Freefone number (GB), a toll-free phone number (US)
c'est occupé/ça sonne occupé	it's engaged/ the line is engaged
ça ne répond pas	there's no answer

Common phrases used on the phone

Allô ?	Hello!
Ne quittez pas	Hold the line please
Veuillez patienter	Hold the line please

it's engaged/the line is engaged	c'est occupé/ça sonne occupé
there's no answer	ça ne répond pas
to leave a message on the answerphone	laisser un message sur le répondeur

Expressions utiles pour téléphoner

Hello!	Allô ?
It's Rebecca Major	(C'est) Rebecca Major à l'appareil
May I speak to … ?	Est-ce que je pourrais parler à …?
Who's calling, please?	C'est de la part de qui?
It's Louise speaking	C'est Louise à l'appareil
Speaking!	C'est moi !
One moment please	Un instant je vous prie
Hold the line please	Ne quittez pas
I'll put you through (ie to their extension)	Je vous le/la passe
I'll put him/her on	Je vous le/la passe
I'll put you on hold	Ne quittez pas/Merci de patienter un instant
Mr Fowler cannot come to the phone at the moment	M. Fowler ne peut pas vous parler maintenant
May I take/leave a message?	Puis-je prendre/laisser un message ?
I'll call back later	Je rappellerai plus tard
Please leave your message after the tone	Merci de laisser un message après le bip

Quand vous n'êtes pas chez vous

a phone booth, a phone box	une cabine (téléphonique)
a payphone	un téléphone public
a coin-operated phone	un téléphone à pièces
a cardphone	un Publiphone, un téléphone à carte
a phonecard	une Télécarte
a phone credit card, a phone chargecard	une carte de téléphone (pour faire facturer ses appels sur sa propre ligne)
a cell phone, a cellular phone	un téléphone cellulaire

a car phone	un téléphone de voiture
a pager	un pager/un bip

La téléphonie mobile

a mobile, a mobile phone	un portable, un téléphone portable, un mobile
mobile telephony	la téléphonie mobile
an Internet phone	un téléphone Internet
a WAP phone	un téléphone WAP
a call alert	un avis d'appel
call credit	le crédit prépayé
call charges	le coût des appels
a mobile phone package	un pack téléphone mobile
a hands-free headset	un casque mains-libres
a hands-free kit	un kit mains libres
a phone charger	un chargeur
a text alert	une alerte texte
a ringtone	une sonnerie
vibrate setting	un vibreur
an SMS message	un message SMS
a text message	un message texte, un texto
text sb	envoyer un message texte à qn
a network	un réseau
a prepaid mobile phone voucher	une carte téléphonique prépayée (pour téléphone portable)

Fonctions et services spéciaux

fault reporting	les dérangements
directory enquiries, directory assistance	les renseignements (téléphoniques)
to be ex-directory	être sur liste rouge
to make a reverse charge call to somebody, to call somebody collect	téléphoner à quelqu'un en PCV
three-way calling	la conversation à trois
call waiting	le signal d'appel
call diversion	le transfert d'appel
caller display	la présentation du numéro
last number redial	le rappel du dernier numéro

Je vous le/la passe	I'll put you on to him/her
C'est de la part de qui ?	Who's calling please?
Puis-je lui transmettre un message ?	May I take a message?
Un instant, je vous prie	One moment, please
Est-ce que je pourrais parler à …	May I speak to …
Je rappellerai plus tard	I'll call back later
C'est personnel	It's a personal call
Monsieur Hallé est en ligne	Mr Hallé is on the phone
(C'est) Lise à l'appareil	It's Lise (speaking)
Puis-je parler à Claire, s'il vous plaît?	May I speak to Claire, please?
C'est moi !	Speaking!

When you are not at home

une cabine (téléphonique)	a phone booth, a phone box
un téléphone à pièces	a coin-operated payphone
un Publiphone/ téléphone à carte	a cardphone
une Télécarte	a phonecard
un Point-phone	a coin-operated payphone available for public use in restaurants, hotels, etc.
un téléphone de voiture	a car phone
un pager, un bip	a pager

Mobile telephony

un téléphone portable, un portable	a mobile phone, a mobile
la téléphonie mobile	mobile telephony
un téléphone Internet	an Internet phone
le WAP	WAP
un téléphone WAP	a WAP phone
un avis d'appel	a call alert
l'identification de l'appelant	caller identification
le coût des appels	call charges
un pack téléphone mobile	a mobile phone package
un casque mains-libres	a hands-free headset
un kit mains libres	a hands-free kit
un chargeur	a phone charger
une alerte texte	a text alert

une sonnerie	a ringtone
la touche de navigation	cursor key
un vibreur	vibrate setting
un message SMS	an SMS message
un message texte, un texto (infrml)	a text message
envoyer un message texte à qn	text sb
un réseau	a network

Some of the services offered by France Telecom

les dérangements	fault reporting
les renseignements (téléphoniques)	directory enquiries, directory assistance
être sur liste rouge	to be ex-directory
l'annuaire électronique	electronic directory on Minitel or on the Internet
téléphoner à quelqu'un en PCV	to make a reverse charge call to somebody or to call somebody collect
la conversation à trois	three-way calling
le signal d'appel	call waiting
la facturation détaillée	itemized billing
le transfert d'appel	call diversion
le Mémo-appel	the reminder call
un Minitel	a terminal linking phone users to databases

Countries/Les pays

Country/ Pays	Inhabitant/ Habitant	Official language(s)/ Langue(s) officielle(s)	Currency/ Devise
Afghanistan *Afghanistan m*	Afgan *Afghan m*	Pushtu/Dari *pushtou/dari*	afghani *afghani m*
Albania *Albanie f*	Albanian *Albanais m*	Albanian *albanais*	lek *lek m*
Algeria *Algérie f*	Algerian *Algérien m*	Arabic/French *arabe/français*	dinar *dinar m*
Andorra *Andorre f*	Andorran *Andorran m*	Catalan/French/Spanish *catalan/français/ espagnol*	euro *euro m*
Angola *Angola m*	Angolan *Angolais m*	Portuguese *angolais*	kwanza *kwanza m*
Antigua and Barbuda *Antigua f*	Antiguan/Barbudian *d'Antigua*	English *anglais*	East Caribbean *dollar antillais m*
Argentina *Argentine f*	Argentinian/Agentine *Argentin m*	Spanish *espagnol*	peso *peso m*
Armenia *Arménie f*	Armenian *Arménien m*	Armenian *arménien*	dram *dram m*
Australia *Australie f*	Australian *Australien m*	English *anglais*	Australian dollar *dollar australien m*
Austria *Autriche f*	Austrian *Autrichien m*	German *allemand*	euro *euro m*
Azerbaijan *Azerbaïdjan m*	Azeri/Azerbaijani *Azéri/Azerbaïdjanais m*	Azeri/Russian *azéri/russe*	manat *manat m*
Bahamas *Bahamas f pl*	Bahamian *des Bahamas*	English *anglais*	Bahamian dollar *dollar des Bahamas m*
Bahrain *Bahreïn m*	Bahraini *Bahreïni m*	Arabic *arabe*	Bahrain dinar *dinar de Bahreïn m*
Bangladesh *Bangladesh m*	Bangladeshi *Bangladeshi/ Bangladais m*	Bengali *bengali*	taka *taka m*
Barbados *Barbade f*	Barbadian *Barbadien m*	English *anglais*	Barbados dollar *dollar de Barbade m*
Belarus *Biélorussie f*	Belarussian *Biélorusse mf*	Belarussian *biélorusse*	Belarussion rouble *rouble biélorusse m*
Belgium *Belgique f*	Belgian *Belge mf*	French/flemish *français/flamand*	euro *euro m*
Belize *Bélize m*	Belizean *Bélizien m*	English/Spanish/Creole *anglais/espagnol/créole*	Belize dollar *dollar de Bélize m*
Benin *Bénin m*	Beninese *Béninois m*	French *français*	C.F.A. franc *franc CFA m*
Bermuda *Bermudes f pl*	Bermudan/Bermudian *Bermudien m*	English *anglais*	dollar *dollar m*
Bhutan *Bhoutan m*	Bhutanese/Bhutani *Bhoutanais m*	Dzongka *dzongka*	ngultrum/Indian rupee *ngultrum m/roupie indienne f*

Countries

Country/ Pays	Inhabitant/ Habitant	Official language(s)/ Langue(s) officielle(s)	Currency/ Devise
Bolivia *Bolivie f*	Bolivian *Bolivien m*	Spanish, Quechua, Aymara *espagnol, quechua, aymara*	boliviano *boliviano m*
Bosnia-Herzogovina *Bosnie-Herzégovine f*	Bosnian *Bosniaque mf* *Bosnien m*	Serbian, Croatian, Bosnian *serbe, croate, bosnien*	convertible marka *marka convertible m*
Botswana *Botswana m*	Botswanan *du Botswana*	English/Setswana *anglais, tswana*	pula *pula m*
Brazil *Brésil m*	Brazilian *Brésilien m*	Portuguese *portugais*	cruzeiro *cruzeiro m*
Brunei *Brunei m*	Brunei/Bruneian *du Brunei*	Malay/English *malais/anglais*	Brunei dollar *dollar du Brunei m*
Bulgaria *Bulgarie f*	Bulgarian *Bulgare mf*	Bulgarian *bulgare*	lev *lev m*
Burkina Faso *Burkina Faso m*	Burkinabe *du Burkina Faso*	French/Mossi *français/mossi*	C.F.A. franc *franc CFA m*
Burma *Birmanie f*	Burmese *Birman m*	Burmese *birman*	kyat *kyat m*
Burundi *Burundi m*	Burundian *Burundais m*	Kirundi/French *kirundi/français*	Burundi franc *franc du Burundi m*
Cambodia *Cambodge m*	Cambodian *Cambodgien m*	Khmer *khmer*	riel *riel m*
Cameroon *Cameroun m*	Cameroonian *Camerounais m*	French/English *français/anglais*	C.F.A. franc *franc CFA m*
Canada *Canada m*	Canadian *Canadien m*	English/French *anglais/français*	Canadian dollar *dollar canadien m*
Central African Republic *République centrafricaine f*	from the Central African Republic *de la République centrafricaine*	French/Sangho *français/sangho*	C.F.A. franc *franc CFA m*
Chad *Tchad m*	Chadian *Tchadien m*	Arabic/French *arabe/français*	C.F.A. franc *franc CFA m*
Chile *Chili m*	Chilean *Chilien m*	Spanish *espagnol*	Chilean peso *peso chilien m*
China *Chine f*	Chinese *Chinois m*	Mandarin/Chinese *mandarin/chinois*	yuan *yuan m*
Colombia *Colombie f*	Colombian *Colombien m*	Spanish *espagnol*	Columbian peso *peso colombien m*
Comoros *Comores f pl*	Comorian/Comoran *Comorien m*	French/Arabic *français/arabe*	Comorian franc *franc comorien m*
Congo (Democratic Republic of The) *Congo m (République démocratique du)*	Congolese *Congolais m*	French/Lingala *français/lingala*	Congolese franc *franc congolais m*
Congo (Republic of The) *Congo m (République du)*	Congolese *Congolais m*	French *français*	C.F.A. franc *franc CFA m*
Costa Rica *Costa Rica m*	Costa Rican *Costarican m*	Spanish *espagnol*	colón *colón m*
Côte d'Ivoire *Côte d'Ivoire f*	Ivorian *Ivoirien m*	French *français*	C.F.A. franc *franc CFA m*

Country/ Pays	Inhabitant/ Habitant	Official language(s)/ Langue(s) officielle(s)	Currency/ Devise
Croatia *Croatie f*	Croat/Croatian *Croate mf*	Croatian *croate*	kuna *kuna m*
Cuba *Cuba f*	Cuban *Cubain m*	Spanish *espagnol*	Cuban peso *peso cubain m*
Cyprus *Chypre f*	Cypriot *Cypriote/Chypriote*	Greek/Turkish *grec/turc*	Cyprus pound *livre chypriote f*
Czech Republic *République tchèque f*	Czech *Tchèque mf*	Czech *tchèque*	koruna *couronne f*
Denmark *Danemark m*	Dane *Danois m*	Danish *danois*	Danish krone *krone danoise f*
Djibouti *Djibouti m*	Djibuti/Djibutian *Djiboutien m*	Arabic/French *arabe/français*	Djibouti franc *franc de Djibouti m*
Dominica *Dominique f*	Dominican *Dominiquais m*	English *anglais*	East Caribbean *dollar antillais m*
Dominican Republic *République dominicaine f*	Dominican *Dominicain m*	Spanish *espagnol*	Dominican peso *peso dominicain m*
Ecuador *Équateur m*	Ecuadorian/Ecuadoran *Équatorien m*	Spanish *espagnol*	sucre *sucre m*
Egypt *Égypte f*	Egyptian *Égyptien m*	Arabic *arabe*	Egyptian pound *livre égyptienne f*
El Salvador *Salvador m*	Salvadoran/Salvadorean *Salvadorien m*	Spanish *espagnol*	colón *colón m*
England *Angleterre f*	Englishman/-woman *Anglais m*	English *anglais*	Sterling pound *livre sterling f*
Equatorial Guinea *Guinée équatoriale f*	Equatorial Guinean *Guinéen équatorial m*	Spanish *espagnol*	C.F.A. franc *franc CFA m*
Estonia *Estonie f*	Estonian *Estonien m*	Estonian *estonien*	kroon *kroon f*
Ethiopia *Éthiopie f*	Ethiopian *Éthiopien m*	Amharic *amharic*	birr *birr m*
Fiji *Fidji f pl*	Fijian *Fidjien m*	English *anglais*	Fijian dollar *dollar fidjien m*
Finland *Finlande f*	Finn *Finlandais m*	Finnish *finlandais*	euro *euro m*
France *France f*	Frenchman/woman *Français m*	French *français*	euro *euro m*
French Guiana *Guyane f*	French Guianese *Guyanais m*	French *français*	euro *euro m*
French Polynesia *Polynésie française f*	French Polynesian *polynésien*	French/Tahitian *français/tahitien*	CFP franc *franc CFP m*
Gabon *Gabon m*	Gabonese *Gabonais m*	French *français*	C.F.A. franc *franc CFA m*
Gambia *Gambie f*	Gambian *Gambien m*	English *anglais*	dalasi *dalasi m*
Georgia *Géorgie f*	Georgian *Géorgien m*	Georgian *géorgien*	lari *lari m*

Countries

Country/ Pays	Inhabitant/ Habitant	Official language(s)/ Langue(s) officielle(s)	Currency/ Devise
Germany *Allemagne f*	German *Allemand m*	German *allemand*	euro *euro m*
Ghana *Ghana m*	Ghanaian *Ghanéen m*	English *anglais*	cedi *cédi m*
Greece *Grèce f*	Greek *Grec m*	Greek *grec*	euro *euro m*
Grenada *Grenade f*	Grenadian *Grenadin m*	English *anglais*	East Caribbean *dollar antillais m*
Guadeloupe *Guadeloupe f*	Guadeloupian *Guadaloupéen m*	French *français*	euro *euro m*
Guatemala *Guatémala m*	Guatemalan *Guatémaltèque mf*	Spanish *espagnol*	quetzal *quetzal m*
Guinea *Guinée f*	Guinean *Guinéen m*	French *français*	Guinean franc *franc guinéen f*
Guinea-Bissau *Guinée-Bissau f*	from Guinea-Bissau *de Guinée-Bissau*	Portuguese *portugais*	C.F.A. Franc *franc C.F.A. m*
Guyana *Guyane f*	Guyanese/Guyanan *Guyanais m*	English *anglais*	Guyana dollar *dollar guyanais m*
Haiti *Haïti m*	Haitian *Haïtien m*	French *français*	gourde *gourde f*
Honduras *Honduras m*	Honduran *Hondurien m*	Spanish *espagnol*	lempira *lempira m*
Hong Kong *Hong Kong f*	from Hong Kong *de Hong Kong*	English *anglais*	Hong Kong dollar *dollar de Hong Kong m*
Hungary *Hongrie f*	Hungarian *Hongrois m*	Hungarian *hongrois*	forint *forint m*
Iceland *Islande f*	Icelander *Islandais m*	Icelandic *islandais*	krona *krona f*
India *Inde f*	Indian *Indien m*	Hindi/English *hindi/anglais*	Indian rupee *roupie indienne f*
Indonesia *Indonésie f*	Indonesian *Indonésien m*	Indonesia *indonésien*	Indonesian rupiah *roupie indonésienne f*
Iran *Iran m*	Iranian *Iranien m*	Iranian *iranien*	Iranian rial *rial iranien m*
Iraq (also Irak) *Iraq (ou Irak) m*	Iraqi/Iraki *Iraquien/Irakien m*	Arabic *arabe*	Iraqi dinar/Iraki dinar *dinar iraquien mf/ dinar irakien m*
Israel *Israël m*	Israeli *Israélien m*	Hebrew/Arabic *hébreu/larabe*	New Israeli shekel *nouveau shekel israélien m*
Italy *Italie f*	Italian *Italien m*	Italian *italien*	euro *euro m*
Jamaica *Jamaïque f*	Jamaican *Jamaïcain m*	English *anglais*	Jamica dollar *dollar jamaïcain m*
Japan *Japon m*	Japanese *Japonais m*	Japanese *japonais*	yen *yen m*
Jordan *Jordanie f*	Jordanian *Jordanien m*	Arabic *arabe*	Jordan dinar *dinar jordanien m*

Country/ Pays	Inhabitant/ Habitant	Official language(s)/ Langue(s) officielle(s)	Currency/ Devise
Kazakhstan *Kazakhstan m*	Kazakh/Kazak *Kazakh mf*	Kazakh/Russian *kazakh/russe*	kazakhstani tenge *tenge kazakh m*
Kenya *Kenya m*	Kenyan *Kenyan m*	Swahili/English *swahili/anglais*	kenyan shilling *shilling kenyan m*
Korea, South *Corée du Sud f*	South Korean *Sud-Coréen m*	Korean *coréen*	won *won m*
Kuwait *Koweït m*	Kuwaiti *Koweïtien m*	Arabic *arabe*	Kuwaiti dinar *dinar koweïtien m*
Kyrgyzstan *Kirghizstan m*	Kyrgyz *du Kirghizstan*	Kyrgyz *kirghiz*	som *som m*
Laos *Laos m*	Laotian *Laotien m*	Lao *laotien*	kip *kip m*
Latvia *Lettonie f*	Latvian *Letton m*	Latvian *letton*	lats *lats m*
Lebanon *Liban m*	Lebanese *Libanais m*	Arabic *arabe*	Lebanese pound *livre libanaise f*
Lesotho *Lesotho m*	Mosotho/Basotho *du Lesotho*	Sesotho/English *sotho/anglais*	loti *loti m*
Liberia *Libéria m*	Liberian *Libérien m*	English *anglais*	Liberian dollar *dollar libérien m*
Libya *Libye f*	Libyan *Libyen m*	Arabic *arabe*	Libyan dinar *dinar libyen m*
Liechtenstein *Liechtenstein m*	Liechtensteiner *du Liechtenstein*	German *allemand*	Swiss franc *franc suisse m*
Lithuania *Lituanie f*	Lithuanian *Lituanien m*	Lithuanian *lituanien*	litas *litas m*
Luxembourg *Luxembourg m*	Luxemburger *Luxembourgeois m*	French/German *français/allemand*	euro *euro m*
Macedonia *Macédoine f*	Macedonian *Macédonien m*	Macedonian *macédonien*	denar *denar m*
Madagascar *Madagascar f*	Madagascan *Malgache mf*	Malagasy/French *malgache/français*	Malagasy franc *franc malgache m*
Malawi *Malawi m*	Malawian *Malawien m*	Chichewa/English *chichewa/anglais*	Malawian kwacha *kwacha malawien m*
Malaysia *Malaisie f*	Malaysian/Malay *Malaisien m*	Malay *malais*	Malaysian ringgit *ringgit malaisien m*
Maldives *Maldives f pl*	Maldivian *des Maldives*	Dhivehi *divehi*	rufiyaa *rufiyaa m*
Mali *Mali m*	Malian *Malien m*	French *français*	C.F.A. franc *franc CFA m*
Malta *Malte f*	Maltese *Maltais m*	Maltese/English *maltais/anglais*	Maltese pound *livre maltaise f*
Martinique *Martinique f*	Martiniquais *Martiniquais m*	French *français*	euro *euro m*
Mauritania *Mauritanie f*	Mauritanian *Mauritanien m*	Arabic/French *arabe/français*	ouguiya *ouguiya m*
Mauritius *Île Maurice f*	Mauritian *Mauricien m*	English/French *anglais/français*	Mauritian rupee *roupie mauricienne f*

Country/ Pays	Inhabitant/ Habitant	Official language(s)/ Langue(s) officielle(s)	Currency/ Devise
Mayotte *Mayotte f*	Mahorais *Mahorais m*	French *français*	euro *euro m*
Mexico *Mexique m*	Mexican *Mexicain m*	Spanish *espagnol*	Mexican peso *peso mexicain m*
Micronesia (Federated States of) *Micronésie f (États fédérés de)*	Micronesian *micronésien m*	English *anglais*	us dollar *dollar m*
Moldova *Moldavie f*	Moldovan *Moldave mf*	Moldovan/Romanian *moldave/roumain*	leu *leu m*
Monaco *Monaco m*	Monegasque *Monégasque mf*	French *français*	euro *euro m*
Mongolia *Mongolie f*	Mongolian *Mongol m*	Khalkha/Mongol *khalkha/mongol*	tugrik *tugrik m*
Montenegro *Monténégro m*	Montenegrin *Monténégrin m*	Serbian *serbe*	dinar *dinar m*
Morocco *Maroc m*	Moroccan *Marocain m*	Arabic/French *arabe/français*	dirham *dirham m*
Mozambique *Mozambique m*	Mozambican *Mozambican m*	Portuguese *portugais*	metical *metical m*
Myanmar *Birmanie f*	Burmese *Birman m*	Burmese *birman*	kyat *kyat m*
Namibia *Namibie f*	Namibian *Namibien m*	English/Afrikaans *anglais/afrikaans*	Namibian dollar *dollar namibien m*
Nepal *Népal m*	Nepalese/Nepali *Népalais m*	Nepali *népalais*	Nepali rupee *roupie népalaise f*
Netherlands, The *Pays Bas, Les m pl*	Dutchman/-woman Netherlander *Hollandais/ Néerlandais m*	Dutch *hollandais/ néerlandais*	euro *euro m*
New Caledonia *Nouvelle Calédonie f*	New Caledonian *Néo-Calédonien m*	French *français*	C.F.P franc *franc CFP m*
New Zealand *Nouvelle-Zélande f*	New Zealander *Néo-Zélandais m*	English/Maori *anglais/maori*	New Zealand dollar *dollar néo-zélandais m*
Nicaragua *Nicaragua m*	Nicaraguan *Nicaraguayen m*	Spanish *espagnol*	cordoba *cordoba f*
Niger *Niger m*	Nigerian *Nigérien m*	French *français*	C.F.A. franc *franc CFA m*
Nigeria *Nigéria m*	Nigerian *Nigérien m*	English *anglais*	naira *naira m*
Northern Ireland *Irlande du Nord f*	Irishman/-woman *Irlandais m*	Irish Gaelic/English *gaélique irlandais/ anglais*	Sterling pound *livre sterling f*
Norway *Norvège f*	Norwegian *Norvégien m*	Norwegian *norvégien*	Norwegian krone *krone norvégienne f*
Oman *Oman m*	Omani *Omanais m*	Arabic *arabe*	Omani rial *rial omanais m*
Pakistan *Pakistan m*	Pakistani *Pakistanais m*	Urdu/English *ourdi/anglais*	Pakistan rupee *roupie pakistanaise f*

Country/ Pays	Inhabitant/ Habitant	Official language(s)/ Langue(s) officielle(s)	Currency/ Devise
Panama *Panama m*	**Panamanian** *Panaméen m*	**Spanish** *espagnol*	**balboa** *balboa m*
Papua New Guinea *Papouasie-Nouvelle Guinée f*	**from Papua New Guinea, Papuan** *de Papouasie-Nouvelle Guinée*	**English/Motu** *anglais/motu*	**kina** *kina m*
Paraguay *Paraguay m*	**Paraguayan** *Paraguayen m*	**Spanish** *espagnol*	**guarani** *guarani m*
Peru *Pérou m*	**Peruvian** *Péruvien m*	**Spanish/Quechua** *espagnol/quechua*	**nuevo sol** *nuevo sol m*
Philippines *Philippines f pl*	**Philippine/Filipino** *Philippin m*	**Pilipino/English** *philippin/anglais*	**Philippine peso** *peso philippin m*
Poland *Pologne f*	**Pole** *Polonais m*	**Polish** *polonais*	**zloty** *zloty m*
Portugal *Portugal m*	**Portuguese** *Portugais m*	**portuguese** *portugais*	**euro** *euro m*
Puerto Rico *Porto Rico m*	**Puerto Rican** *Portoricain m*	**Spanish/English** *espagnol/anglais*	**U.S. dollar** *dollar US m*
Qatar *Qatar m*	**Qatari** *du Qatar*	**Arabic** *arabe*	**Quatar riyal** *riyal du Quatar m*
Republic of Ireland (also Eire) *République d'Irlande f*	**Irishman/-woman** *Irlandais m*	**Irish Gaelic/English** *gaélique irlandais/ anglais*	**euro** *euro m*
Reunion *Réunion f*	**Reunionese** *Réunionnais m*	**french** *français*	**euro** *euro m*
Romania/Rumania *Roumanie f*	**Romanian/Rumanian** *Roumain m*	**Romanian** *roumain*	**Romanian leu** *leu roumain m*
Russia (Russian federation) *Russie f (Fédération de Russie)*	**Russian** *Russe mf*	**Russian** *russe*	**rouble** *rouble/ruble m*
Rwanda *Ruanda/Rwanda m*	**Rwandese** *Ruandais/Rwandais m*	**French/English/Kinyarwanda** *français/anglais kinyaruandais*	**Rwanda franc** *franc ruandais m franc rwandais m*
Saint Lucia *Sainte-Lucie f*	**Saint Lucian** *de Sainte-Lucie*	**English** *anglais*	**East Caribbean dollar** *dollar antillais m*
Saint Pierre and Miguelon *Saint-Pierre-et Miquelon f*	**Saint Pierre Islander/ Miguelon Islander** *Saint-Pierrais m/ Miquelonnais m*	**French** *français*	**euro** *euro m*
Saint Vincent and the Grenadines *Saint-Vincent et les Grenadines m pl*	**Vincentian** *de Saint-Vincent*	**English** *anglais*	**East Caribbean dollar** *dollar antillais m*
San Marino *Saint-Marin m*	**San Marinese** *de Saint-Marin*	**Italian** *italien*	**euro** *euro m*
Saudi Arabia *Arabie Saoudite f*	**Saudi/Saudi Arabian** *Saoudien m*	**Arabic** *arabe*	**Saudi Arabian riyal** *riyal d'Arabie m*

Country/ Pays	Inhabitant/ Habitant	Official language(s)/ Langue(s) officielle(s)	Currency/ Devise
Scotland *Écosse f*	Scot, Scotsman/-woman *Écossais m*	English *anglais*	Sterling pound *livre sterling f*
Senegal *Sénégal m*	Senegalese *Sénégalais m*	French *français*	C.F.A. franc *franc CFA m*
Seychelles *Seychelles f pl*	Seychellois/Seselwa *des Seychelles*	English/French/Creole *anglais/français/créole*	Seychelles rupee *roupie des Seychelles f*
Sierra Leone *Sierra Léone m*	Sierra Leonean *Sierra Léonais m*	English *anglais*	leone *leone m*
Singapore *Singapour m*	Singaporean *Singapourien m*	Chinese/Malay Tamil/English *chinois/malais tamoul/ anglais*	Singapore dollar *dollar de Singapour m*
Slovakia (Slovak Republic) *Slovaquie f (République Slovaque)*	Slovak *Slovaque mf*	Slovak *slovaque*	Slovak koruna *koruna slovaque f*
Slovenia *Slovénie f*	Slovenian/Slovene *Slovène mf*	Slovene *slovène*	tolar *tolar m*
Somalia *Somalie f*	Somali/Somalian *Somalien m*	Somali/Arabic *somali/anglais*	Somali shilling *shilling somalien m*
South Africa *Afrique du Sud f*	South African *Sud-Africain m*	Afrikaans/English *afrikaans/anglais*	rand *rand m*
Spain *Espagne f*	Spaniard *Espagnol m*	Spanish *espagnol*	euro *euro m*
Sri Lanka *Sri Lanka m*	Sri Lankan *Sri-Lankais m*	Sinhalese/Tamil/English *cingalais/tamoul/anglais*	Sri Lanka rupee *roupie cingalaise f*
Sudan *Soudan m*	Sudanese *Soudanais m*	Arabic *arabe*	Sudanese dinar *dinar soudanais m*
Suriname *Surinam m*	Surinamese *Surinamais m*	Dutch *hollandais/néerlandais*	Suriname guilder *florin du Surinam m*
Swaziland *Swaziland m*	Swazi *Swazi m*	Siswati/English *siswati/anglais*	lilangeni *lilangeni m*
Sweden *Suède f*	Swede *Suédois m*	Swedish *suédois*	Swedish krona *krone suédoise f*
Switzerland *Suisse f*	Swiss *Suisse mf*	French/German/Italian *français/allemand/italian*	Swiss franc *franc suisse m*
Syria *Syrie f*	Syrian *Syrien m*	Arabic *arabe*	Syrian pound *livre syrienne f*
Taiwan *Taïwan m*	Taiwanese *Taïwanais m*	Mandarin/Chinese *mandarin/chinois*	Taiwan dollar *dollar de Taïwan m*
Tadjikistan *Tadjikistan m*	Tajik *Tadjik mf*	Tajik *tadjik*	rouble *rouble/ruble m*
Tanzania *Tanzanie f*	Tanzanian *Tanzanien m*	Swahili/English *swahili/anglais*	Tanzanian shilling *shilling tanzanien m*
Thailand *Thaïlande f*	Thai *Thaïlandais m*	Thai *thaï*	baht *baht m*
Togo *Togo m*	Togolese *Togolais m*	French *français*	C.F.A. franc *franc CFA m*
Trinidad and Tobago *Trinité-et-Tobago f*	Trinidadian/Tobagoan/ Tobagodian *Trinidadien m/ de la Trinité*	English *anglais*	Trinidad and Tobago dollar *dollar de Trinité-et- Tobago m*

Country/ Pays	Inhabitant/ Habitant	Official language(s)/ Languel(s) officiellel(s)	Currency/ Devise
Tunisia *Tunisie f*	**Tunisian** *Tunisien m*	**Arabic** *arabe*	**Tunisian dinar** *dinar tunisien m*
Turkey *Turquie f*	**Turk** *Turc m*	**Turkish** *turc*	**Turkish lira** *lire turque f*
Turkmenistan *Turkménistan m*	**Turkmen** *Turkmène mf*	**Turkmen** *turkmène*	**manat** *manat m*
Uganda *Ouganda m*	**Ugandan** *Ougandais m*	**Swahili/English** *swahili/anglais*	**Uganda shilling** *shilling ougandais m*
Ukraine *Ukraine f*	**Ukrainian** *Ukrainien m*	**Ukrainian** *ukrainien*	**hryvna** *hrivna m*
United Arab Emirates *Émirats Arabes Unis m pl*	**from the United Arab Emirates** *des Émirats Arabes Unis*	**Arabic** *arabe*	**dirham** *dirham m*
United Kingdom *Royaume-Uni m*	**Briton** *Britannique mf*	**English** *anglais*	**Sterling pound** *livre sterling f*
United States of America *États-Unis d'Amérique m pl*	**American** *Américain m*	**English** *anglais*	**dollar** *dollar m*
Uruguay *Uruguay m*	**Uruguayan** *Uruguayen m*	**Spanish** *espagnol*	**peso** *peso m*
Uzbekistan *Ouzbékistan m*	**Uzbek** *Ouzbek m*	**Uzbek** *ouzbek*	**Uzbekistani som** *som d'Ouzbékistan m*
Vanuatu *Vanuatu m*	**Ni-Vanuatu** *Ni-Vanuatu*	**French/English** *français/anglais*	**vatu** *vatu m*
Venezuela *Vénézuela m*	**Venezuelan** *Vénézuélien m*	**Spanish** *espagnol*	**bolivar** *bolivar m*
Vietnam *Viêt Nam m*	**Vietnamese** *Vietnamien m*	**Vietnamese** *vietnamien*	**dông** *dông m*
Wales *Pays de Galles m*	**Welshman/-woman** *Gallois m*	**English/Welsh** *anglais/gallois*	**Sterling pound** *livre sterling f*
Wallis and Futuna *Wallis et Futuna*	**Wallisian/Futunan** *wallisien/futunien m*	**French/Wallisian** *français/wallisien*	**CFP franc** *franc CFP m*
Yemen *Yémen m*	**Yemeni** *Yéménite mf*	**Arabic** *arabe*	**Yemeni rial** *rial yéménite m*
Yugoslavia (Federal Republic of) *Yougoslavie f (République fédérale de)*	**Yugoslav** *Yougoslave mf*	**Serbian** *serbe*	**Yugoslav dinar** *dinar yougoslave m*
Zambia *Zambie f*	**Zambian** *Zambien m*	**English** *anglais*	**kwacha** *kwacha m*
Zimbabwe *Zimbabwe m*	**Zimbabwean** *Zimbabwéen m*	**English** *anglais*	**Zimbabwe dollar** *dollar du Zimbabwe m*

The euro

On 1 January 2002 France, along with the eleven other European countries that make up the euro zone, replaced its national currency with euro notes and coinage. This single currency is valid across the twelve euro zone member countries.

The basic unit of currency is the euro (€) which is divided into 100 cents. There are seven notes with values of 5, 10, 20, 50, 100, 200 and 500 euros and eight coins with values of 1, 2, 5, 10, 20, 50 cents, 1 euro and 2 euros. The design of the euro notes is uniform throughout the euro zone. All the coins have a common face denoting the value and a national face indicating where they were produced.

One euro is worth approximately 60 pence and £1 is worth approximately 1.66 euro, subject to foreign exchange fluctuations.

The exchange rates for sterling and euros are not fixed and will vary just as the pound did against the currencies the euro replaces. The official conversion rate between the French franc and the euro is fixed at the rate: 1 euro = 6.55957 F. As a rule of thumb to convert figures in francs into an approximate number of euros, take the figure in francs, add half as much again and divide that total by ten.

euros	francs
1	6.56
2	13.12
5	32.80
10	65.60
20	131.19
50	327.98
100	655.96
200	1311.91
500	3279.79

francs	euros
1	0.15
2	0.30
5	0.76
10	1.52
20	3.05
50	7.62
100	15.24
200	30.49
500	76.22

Aa

A1 *adj* de première qualité, parfait

A3 *n* format A3 *m*

A4 *n* format A4 *m*

AA *abbr* (▸**average adjuster**) dispacheur *m*, répartiteur d'avaries *m*

AAA: ∼ **bond** *n* obligation notée AAA *f*; ∼ **rating** *n* classification AAA *f*

AAD *abbr* (**at a discount**) (Stock) avec une décote, à escompte

AAG *abbr* (▸**Area Advisory Group**) UK *groupe consultatif de zone visant à développer les marchés étrangers vers lesquels les sociétés britanniques veulent exporter*

AAR *abbr* (▸**against all risks**) tous risques contre tous les risques

abandon *vt* (plan, trial, person, hope) abandonner; (claim, idea, right) renoncer à; (goods in customs) délaisser; (option) abandonner; ∼ **any claim** renoncer à toute prétention; ∼ **ship** abandonner le navire

abandonee *n* (Ins) abandonnataire *mf*

abandonment *n* renonciation *f*; (marine insurance) abandon *m*; (Patents) cession *f*; (of right) renonciation *f*; (of complaint) retrait *m*; (of option) abandon *m*; ∼ **of action** désistement d'action *m*

abate *vt* (taxes, prices) baisser, réduire; (sentence) remettre; (writ) annuler, rendre nul et non avenu; (Tax) annuler

abatement *n* (Acc) réduction *f*; (of price) rabais *m*, remise *f*, réduction *f*; (Law) (of action) arrêt *m*, suspension *f*; (Tax) annulation *f*, dégrèvement *m*

abbreviate *vt* abréger, raccourcir

abbreviation *n* abréviation *f*

ABC analysis *n* analyse ABC *f*

ABCC *abbr* (▸**Association of British Chambers of Commerce**) *association des chambres de commerce britanniques*

abeyance *n*: in ∼ (issue, matter) en souffrance, en suspens; (in property law) inappliqué; **fall into** ∼ tomber en désuétude

abide: ∼ **by** *vt* (result) assumer, accepter; (rule, decision) respecter, se conformer à; (statement) maintenir; (agreement) se conformer à, se soumettre à

ability *n* (competence) capacité *f*, compétence *f*, savoir-faire *m*; (talent) talent *m*; ∼ **to do** capacité de faire, aptitude à faire; **to the best of one's** ∼ de son mieux; ∼ **level** *n* (of student) niveau d'aptitude *m*; (of worker, applicant) niveau de qualification *m*; ∼ **to pay** (of employer) capacité de paiement *f*; (Law) solvabilité *f*; (Tax) capacité contributive *f*; ∼ **to repay** capacité de remboursement *f*

able *adj* compétent; **be** ∼ **to do** pouvoir faire; (have acquired a skill) savoir faire; **be** ∼ **to afford to buy sth** avoir les moyens d'acheter qch, pouvoir s'offrir qch; ∼ **to work** apte au travail

abnormal *adj* anormal

aboard ① *adv* à bord ② *prep* à bord de (ship, plane); dans (coach, train); ∼ **ship** à bord

abolish *vt* (right, law, penalty) abolir; (service, subsidy) supprimer

abolition *n* (of right, law, penalty) abolition *f*; (of service, subsidy) suppression *f*; ∼ **of trade controls** suppression des barrières douanières *f*

abort ① *vt* (program) abandonner, interrompre; (mission, trial, launch) interrompre ② *vi* (program) s'arrêter

about¹ *adv* (approximately) environ, à peu près

about² *prep* (concerning) concernant, en ce qui concerne, au sujet de

above¹ *adj* (earlier in the text) mentionné ci-dessus, mentionné plus haut, susmentionné

above² *adv* ci-dessus, plus haut; (in letter) ci-dessus; **as** ∼ comme ci-dessus

above³ *prep* au-dessus de; **be** ∼ **average** être au-dessus de la moyenne, être supérieur à la moyenne; ∼ **the line** (Acc) au-dessus de la ligne, inscrit au compte de résultat; (S&M) au-dessus de la ligne; ∼ **market price** au-dessus du cours; ∼ **the norm** au-dessus de la norme; ∼ **quota** au-dessus du quota, hors contingent

above: ∼-**average** *adj* au-dessus de la moyenne, supérieur à la moyenne; ∼ **board** *adj* (action, deal) correct, régulier/-ière; (person) honnête, loyal, régulier/-ière; (Law) correct; ∼-**mentioned** *adj* mentionné ci-dessus, mentionné plus haut, susmentionné; ∼-**named** *adj* susnommé

above-the-line¹ *n* (Acc, Bank) compte créditeur *m*; (in advertising) publicité média *f*

above-the-line² *adj* (advertising, expenditure, promotion) média *inv*

abreast *adv*: ∼ **of** au courant de; **be** ∼ **of** (latest developments) se tenir au courant de, suivre; **be** ∼ **of things** être dans le vent; **keep** ∼ **of** se tenir au courant de; **keep** ∼ **of the times** marcher avec son temps

abroad *adv* à l'étranger

abrogate *vt* abroger

abrogation *n* abrogation *f*

abscond *vi* s'enfuir, se soustraire à la justice

absence n (being elsewhere) absence f,
éloignement m; (lack) défaut m, manque m;
(Law) défaut m; **in sb's ~** en l'absence de qn;
in the ~ of (news) faute de; **in the ~ of
detailed information** faute de détails, à
défaut de renseignements précis; **in the ~ of
evidence to the contrary** jusqu'à preuve du
contraire; **~ of consideration** absence de
contrepartie f; (Fin) défaut de provision m; **~
without leave** absence non justifiée f,
absence non motivée f

absent adj absent; **be ~ due to sickness**
être absent pour cause de maladie

absentee n absent/-e m/f; (habitually)
absentéiste mf; **~ ballot** n AmE vote par
correspondance m; **~ owner** n propriétaire
absentéiste mf

absenteeism n absentéisme m

absolute adj (certainty, discretion, right, power)
absolu; (in contracts) inconditionnel/-elle, sans
réserve; (court order, decree) définitif/-ive; **in ~
terms** en termes absolus; **~ advantage** n
avantage absolu m; **~ liability** n
responsabilité objective f; **~ limit** n
tolérance maximale f; (within prescribed time-
limits) délai absolu m; **~ majority** n majorité
absolue f; **~ monopoly** n monopole absolu
m; **~ priority rule** n règle de priorité
absolue f; **~ sale** n vente définitive f, vente
irrévocable f; **~ title** n (to property) titre
irréfutable m

absorb vt (costs, profits, business) absorber;
(shock, impact) amortir; (staff, management)
recruter; (stock, surplus) résorber; **~
overheads** supporter les frais généraux

absorbed adj assimilé; (in cost accounting)
affecté, pris en charge par l'entreprise,
résorbé; (company securities) absorbé

absorption n (of business, company, costs,
profit) absorption f; (of shock, impact)
amortissement m; (Transp) absorption f; **~
costing** n méthode du coût complet f,
méthode du coût de revient complet f; **~ rate**
n taux d'absorption m

absorptive capacity n capacité
d'absorption f

abstain vi (in vote, election) s'abstenir

abstention n abstention f

abstract n (summary of document) abrégé m,
résumé m; (Law) extrait m; (Patents) abrégé
m, résumé m; **~ labor** AmE, **~ labour** BrE n
travail abstrait m; (workers) main-d'œuvre
abstraite f; **~ of accounts** extrait de
comptes m, relevé de comptes m; **~ of
record** extrait d'un rapport officiel m; **~ of
title** extrait du répertoire des mutations de
propriété m

ABT abbr (▸**American Board of Trade**)
bureau américain du commerce

ABTA abbr (▸**Association of British
Travel Agents**) *association des agents de
voyage britanniques*

abundance n abondance f

abundant adj abondant

abuse¹ n (of system, patent) abus m; **~ of
confidence** abus de confiance m; **~ of
power** abus de pouvoir m; **~ of rights** abus
de droits m; **~ of trust** abus de confiance m

abuse² vt (privilege, power, trust) abuser

abusive practice n pratique abusive f

a/c abbr (▸**account**) compte m

academic adj (career, post, work, text)
universitaire

ACAS abbr UK (▸**Advisory, Conciliation
and Arbitration Service**) *service consultatif
d'arbitrage et de conciliation*

ACC abbr (▸**American Chamber of
Commerce**) *chambre américaine de
commerce*

accede: ~ to vt (request, post) accéder à;
(agreement) adhérer à

accelerable guarantee n UK garantie
remboursable par anticipation f

accelerate vti accélérer

accelerated adj (training course) accéléré; **~
capital cost allowance** n déduction pour
amortissement accéléré f; **~ cost recovery
system** n amortissement accéléré m,
amortissement dégressif m; **~ depreciation**
n amortissement accéléré m, amortissement
dégressif m; **~ learning** n apprentissage
accéléré m; **~ purchase** n achat accéléré m;
~ redemption n remboursement anticipé
m; **~ repayment** n remboursement anticipé
m

acceleration n (in rate) accélération f; (in
real estate deals) accélération f, prise de
possession anticipée f; **~ clause** n (for
mortgages) clause accélératrice f; **~ of
maturity** demande de remboursement
anticipé f, exigibilité anticipée f; **~
premium** n (HRM) prime de rendement f;
(Ind) prime de productivité f; **~ principle** n
principe de l'accélérateur m

accelerator n (in investment) accélérateur m;
~ principle n principe de l'accélérateur m

accent n accent m; **place the ~ on quality**
mettre l'accent sur la qualité

accept vt (credit card, call, bid, tender) accepter;
(task, role, function) assumer; **~ delivery of**
prendre livraison de, réceptionner; **~ no
liability** sans recours; **~ on presentation**
accepter à vue

acceptability n (of candidate, idea, suggestion)
admissibilité f; (of offer) recevabilité f; (Econ)
(of money) pouvoir libératoire m

acceptable adj acceptable; **of ~ quality**
de qualité acceptable; **~ use policy** n
(Comp) principes d'utilisation acceptable m pl

acceptance n (of goods) réception f; (of
offer, invitation) acceptation f; (of plan, proposal)
approbation f; (assent) consentement m; (of bill
of exchange) acceptation f; (of contract)
acceptation f, agrément m, consentement m;
(of product, brand) acceptation f, accueil

favorable m; (Acc, Bank) acceptation f; **gain ~** gagner l'approbation; **letter of ~** lettre d'acceptation f; **refuse ~** refuser d'accepter; **~ account** n compte d'acceptations m; **~ against documents** acceptation contre documents f; **~ bank** n banque d'acceptation f; **~ bill** n effet à l'acceptation m, traite à l'acceptation f; **~ certificate** n attestation de prise en charge f; **~ credit** n crédit par acceptation m; **~ fee** n commission d'acceptation f; **~ house** n banque d'acceptation f, maison d'acceptation f; **~ ledger** n livre des acceptations m; **~ liability** n encours sous forme d'acceptation m; **~ line of credit** n crédit par acceptation m, ligne de crédit par acceptation f; **~ market** n marché des acceptations m, marché des effets acceptés m; **~ price** prix d'entrée en possession m; **~ register** n livre des acceptations m; **~ slip** n bordereau d'acceptation m; **~ test** n, **~ trial** n essai de réception m

accepted adj accepté; (written on bill) bon pour acceptation; **~ bill** n effet accepté m; **~ draft** n traite acceptée f

accepting adj (banker) acceptant; **~ bank** n banque d'acceptation f

acceptor n (of bill) accepteur m, tiré m

access¹ n accès m, point d'accès m; **give sb ~ to** permettre à qn d'accéder à; **have ~ to information** avoir accès à l'information; **~ control** n contrôle d'accès m; **~ differential** n différentiel d'accès m; **~ provider** n (Comp) fournisseur d'accès m; **~ right** n droit d'accès m; **~ time** n temps d'accès m

access² vt (database, information, machine) accéder à, avoir accès à

accessibility n (of information) accessibilité f; (of public places) facilité d'accès f

accessible adj (file, information) accessible; (widely available) à la portée de tous; (person) accessible, disponible; (place) accessible; (price) abordable; **easily ~** d'accès facile

accession n accession f

accessories n pl accessoires m pl

accessory¹ adj accessoire

accessory² n (complementary item) accessoire m; (Law) complice mf; **~ advertising** n publicité de complément f

accident n accident m; **have an ~** avoir un accident; **~ at sea** accident en mer m; **~ and health insurance** n US assurance-accidents et maladies f; **~ insurance** n assurance contre les accidents f, assurance-accidents f; **~ insurer** n assureur accidents m; **~ prevention** n prévention des accidents f; **~ risk** n risque d'accident m

accidental discharge n rejet accidentel m, échappement accidentel m

accommodate vt (need, request) satisfaire; (provide room for) accueillir, héberger; (contain) contenir; **~ sb with a loan** consentir un prêt à qn; **~ sb with sth** (service, item) fournir qch

à qn

accommodating credit n crédit de complaisance m

accommodation n (Bank, Fin) crédit m, prêt m; (compromise) adaptation f, arrangement m, compromis m; (offices) bureaux m pl; (lodging) hébergement m, logement m; **take ~** contracter un crédit, contracter un emprunt, faire un emprunt; **~ acceptance** n acceptation par complaisance f; **~ address** n BrE boîte aux lettres f; **~ agency** n agence de logement f; **~ allowance** n indemnité de logement f; **~ bill** n billet de complaisance m, effet de complaisance m; **~ draft** n traite de complaisance f; **~ endorsement** n endossement de complaisance m; **~ maker** n (Fin) endosseur par complaisance m, souscripteur par complaisance m; **~ note** n, **~ paper** n billet de complaisance m, effet de complaisance m; **~ payment** n paiement de complaisance m

accommodations n pl AmE logement m, hébergement m

accompany vt accompagner, escorter; **accompanied by** accompagné de, accompagné par

accompanying: ~ document n document joint m, pièce jointe f; **~ letter** n lettre d'accompagnement f

accomplish vt accomplir

accomplishment n (of task) accomplissement m, exécution f, réalisation f; (thing accomplished) projet réalisé m, réussite f; (skill) talent m

accord n accord m, convention f; (treaty) traité m, pacte m

accordance: in ~ with (standards, regulations) conformément à, selon; **in ~ with the law** en vertu de la loi; **in ~ with your instructions** conformément à vos instructions; **be in ~ with** être conforme à

according: ~ to conformément à, d'après, selon, suivant; **~ to the norm** conformément à la norme, selon la norme; **~ to plan** comme prévu; **~ to schedule** comme prévu

accordingly adv en conséquence

account¹ n (bill) facture f, note f; (money held in the bank) compte m; (credit arrangement) compte m; (description) compte rendu m; (S&M) (advertising client) budget m; (Stock) UK *règlement à la bourse de Londres,* règlement mensuel m; **~ of** pour le compte de; **on ~** (as downpayment) en acompte; **on no ~** en aucun cas; **on ~ of** en raison de, à cause de; **~ payee** (on cheque) chèque non-endossable m; **rendering of ~s** reddition de comptes f; **call sb to ~** demander des comptes à qn; **give an ~ of** faire un compte rendu de; **take ~ of** tenir compte de; **take sth into ~** prendre qch en compte, tenir compte de qch, prendre qch en considération; **put sth on one's ~, charge sth to one's ~** mettre qch sur son compte; **settle an ~** régler un compte; (in hotel) régler une note; **set up on one's own** ~ se mettre à son compte; ~ **balance** n solde m, solde comptable m; ~ **book** n journal m, livre de comptes m, registre de comptabilité m; ~ **current** n compte de mandataire m; ~ **day** n jour de liquidation m; ~ **executive** n (advertising) responsable d'agence mf; (finance) responsable de budget mf; (brokerage firm) *responsable de la gestion du compte d'un client, courtier m;* ~ **form** n présentation de bilan en compte f, (balance sheet) présentation horizontale f; ~ **holder** n titulaire d'un compte mf; ~ **manager** n (Bank) directeur/-trice des comptes m/f; (finance) responsable de budget mf; (advertising) chef de publicité m, chef de publicité d'agence m; ~ **market** n marché à terme m; ~ **name** n intitulé de compte m, nom d'un compte m; ~ **number** n numéro de compte m; ~ **statement** n relevé de compte m; (amount) position du compte f; (securities) avis de compte m, relevé de compte m; ~ **transaction** n opération comptable f, transaction f

account²: ~ **for** vt (enter in accounts) comptabiliser; (expenses) justifier, rendre compte de; (record) enregistrer; (represent) représenter; (explain) expliquer

accountability n responsabilité f; (Acc) obligation fiduciaire f, obligation redditionnelle f; ~ **in management** responsabilisation des cadres supérieurs f

accountable adj responsable; ~ **for** responsable de; **be** ~ **to sb** être responsable devant qn; ~ **advance** n avance à justifier f; ~ **receipt** n quittance comptable f

accountancy n (profession) profession comptable f; (bookkeeping) comptabilité f, expertise comptable f; **study** ~ faire des études de comptabilité; ~ **services** n pl services d'expertise comptable m pl

accountant n comptable mf, expert-comptable m

Accountant General n chef comptable m, directeur/-trice de comptabilité m/f

accounting n comptabilité f; ~ **adjustment** n rectification comptable f, redressement comptable m; ~ **analysis** n analyse comptable f; ~ **balance of payments** n balance des paiements comptables f; ~ **control** n contrôle comptable m, contrôle interne m; ~ **costs** n pl frais comptables m pl; ~ **cycle** n cycle comptable m; ~ **data** n pl données comptables f pl; (published by companies) informations financières f pl; ~ **department** n service de la comptabilité m; ~ **entry** n inscription comptable f; ~ **error** n erreur comptable f; ~ **fees** n pl frais comptables m pl, honoraires comptables m pl; ~ **firm** n cabinet d'expertise comptable m, cabinet d'experts-comptables m; ~ **income** n (net profit) bénéfice comptable m, résultat

comptable m; (revenue) chiffre d'affaires m; ~ **method** n méthode comptable f; ~ **model** n modèle comptable m; ~ **package** n logiciel de comptabilité m, progiciel de comptabilité m; ~ **period** n exercice comptable m, exercice financier m; ~ **practice** n cabinet d'expertise comptable m, cabinet d'experts-comptables m; ~ **practices** n pl pratiques comptables f pl; ~ **profit** n bénéfice comptable m, résultat comptable m; ~ **rate of interest** n taux d'intérêt comptable m; ~ **rate of return** n taux de rendement comptable m; ~ **ratio** n ratio comptable m; ~ **records** n pl données comptables f pl, livres comptables m pl; ~ **return** n rendement comptable m; ~ **software** n logiciel de comptabilité m, progiciel de comptabilité m; ~ **standards** n pl normes comptables f pl; ~ **system** n système comptable m, système de comptabilité m; ~ **year** n exercice comptable m, exercice financier m

accounts n pl (records) comptes m pl, comptabilité f; (department) service de la comptabilité m; **keep the** ~ tenir les comptes, tenir la comptabilité; ~ **appraisal** n revue analytique f, évaluation des comptes f; ~ **certification** n approbation de comptes f, certificat d'audit m; ~ **department** n service de la comptabilité m, services comptables m pl; ~ **payable** n pl comptes créditeurs m pl, comptes fournisseurs m pl; ~ **receivable** n pl comptes clients m pl, créances f pl, débiteurs m pl

accredit vt (guarantee) garantir; (institution, qualification) agréer; (representative, official) accréditer, agréer

accreditation n (of institution, qualification) agrément m; (of representative, official) accréditation f, agrément m

accredited adj (institution, body, qualification) agréé; (representative, official) accrédité, agréé

accretion n accroissement m; (Stock) ajustement de la valeur de l'obligation m

accrual n accumulation f; ~ **accounting** n comptabilité d'engagements f; ~ **basis** n comptabilité d'engagements f, comptabilité d'exercice f; ~ **date** n date de paiement des intérêts courus m; ~ **method** n comptabilité d'engagements f, comptabilité d'exercice f; ~ **of interest** accumulation d'intérêts f; ~ **principle** n principe de rattachement à l'exercice m; ~ **tax** n impôt accumulé m

accruals n pl (Acc, Bank) compte de régularisation m; (Fin) accumulation f, compte de régularisation m; (of interest, cost, revenue) accumulation f; **the** ~ **of wages** les charges salariales constatées f pl

accrue vi (expense, interest, revenue) courir, s'accroître, s'accumuler; (Fin) s'accumuler; **previously unrecorded expenses** inscrire des charges à payer

accrued adj cumulé; (wealth) amassé;

~ **asset** n produit à recevoir m; ~ **charges** n pl charges constatées d'avance f pl, frais accumulés m pl; ~ **compound interest** n intérêts composés courus m pl; ~ **credit** n produit constaté d'avance m; ~ **dividend** n dividende cumulé m; ~ **expense** n charge constatée par régularisation f, charge à payer f; ~ **expenses** n pl frais à payer m pl; ~ **income** n produit constaté d'avance m, revenu à recevoir m; ~ **interest** n intérêts courus m pl, intérêts cumulés m pl; ~ **interest payable** n intérêts courus à payer m pl; ~ **interest receivable** n intérêts courus à recevoir m pl; ~ **liability** n charge à payer f; ~ **revenue** n produit constaté par régularisation m, produit à recevoir m

accruing adj (expenses, revenue) afférent; (interests) à échoir

acct abbr (▸**account**) compte m

accumulate ①① vt (debt) accumuler; (wealth) amasser; (information) rassembler ②② vi (debt, interest) s'accumuler

accumulated adj (dividends, depreciation) cumulé; ~ **balance** n solde accumulé m; ~ **deficit** n (Acc) pertes accumulées f pl; (Tax) déficit accumulé m; ~ **dividend** n dividende cumulé m; ~ **profits** n pl (on balance sheet) report à nouveau m; ~ **surplus** n bénéfice accumulé m; ~ **total** n cumul m

accumulation n accumulation f; (of capital, wealth, interest) accroissement m; ~ **of risk** cumul de risques m

accumulator n accumulateur m, totalisateur m

accuracy n (of report, document, statement) précision f; (of figures, data) exactitude f; (of judgement) justesse f

accurate adj (description) fidèle; (figures, estimate) exact; (judgement) juste; (report, aim) précis

accusation n accusation f, incrimination f, plainte f; **make/refute an** ~ porter/réfuter une accusation

accuse vt accuser, incriminer; **stand** ~**d of sth** être accusé de qch

accused n **the** ~ l'accusé/-e m/f

ACD abbr (▸**automated cash dispenser**, ▸**automatic cash dispenser**) DAB m (distributeur automatique de billets)

ACE abbr (▸**Amex Commodities Exchange**) (Stock) Bourse de commerce de l'Amex f

ACH abbr (▸**Automated Clearing House**) chambre de compensation automatisée f

achievable adj réalisable

achieve vt (growth, level, objective) arriver à, atteindre; (result) obtenir, réaliser; (consensus) arriver à; (goal, ambition) réaliser

achievement n (of goal, ambition) réalisation f; (accomplishment) réussite f; ~ **quotient** n quotient de réussite m; ~ **test** n test de niveau m

achiever n personne qui réussit f; **high** ~ sujet doué m

acid: ~ **pollution** n dépôts acides m pl; ~ **rain** n pluies acides f pl; ~ **test** n épreuve de vérité f; ~**-test ratio** n ratio de liquidité immédiate m, taux de liquidité immédiate m

acknowledge vt (debt, claim) reconnaître; (arrival) prendre note de; (fact) admettre; (mistake) reconnaître; ~ **receipt by letter** accuser réception par courrier; ~ **receipt of** (letter, cheque, mail, goods) accuser réception de; ~ **one's sources** citer ses sources; **an** ~**d expert** un expert incontesté

acknowledgement n reconnaissance f; (on document) signature f; (of payment) quittance f, reçu m, récépissé m; (of request for goods, services) confirmation f; (Law, S&M) certification f, reconnaissance f; ~ **of debt** reconnaissance de dette f; ~ **of order** accusé de réception d'une commande m; ~ **of receipt** accusé de réception m; (Fin) récépissé m

acquaint vt: ~ **sb with sth** avertir qn de qch, aviser qn de qch; ~ **sb with the situation** mettre qn au courant de la situation; **be** ~**ed with** (news) être au courant de; (person) connaître

acquaintance n connaissance f, relation f; **make sb's** ~ faire la connaissance de qn; **business** ~**s** des relations d'affaires f pl

acquire vt (goods, property, shares, company) acquérir, acheter; (skill, experience) acquérir; (information) obtenir; (reputation) se faire; ~ **an interest in** prendre une participation dans

acquired adj acquis; ~ **company** n entreprise acquise f; ~ **share** n US action rachetée f; ~ **surplus** n US surplus acquis m

acquiring: ~ **authority** n administration acquéreuse f; ~ **company** n acquéreur m

acquisition n achat m, acquisition f; ~ **accounting** n comptabilité par coûts historiques f; (method of consolidation) consolidation par intégration totale f; ~ **of assets** acquisition d'immobilisations f; ~ **cost** n coût d'achat m, coût d'acquisition m; ~ **financing** n financement d'une acquisition m; ~ **policy** n politique d'acquisition f; ~ **price** n prix d'achat m; ~ **of shareholdings** acquisition d'actions f; ~ **of stock** acquisition d'actions f; ~ **value** n valeur de l'acquisition f

acquisitive adj (company) possédant une politique agressive de rachat; (person, society) attaché aux biens de consommation, âpre au gain; ~ **instinct** cupidité f, instinct de possession m

acquisitiveness n goût de la propriété m, soif de possession f

acquit vt (debt, duty) s'acquitter de; (accused) acquitter; **he** ~**ted himself well in the meeting** la réunion s'est bien passée pour lui

acquittal n (of the accused, of a debt) acquittement m

acquittance *n* (confirmation of payment) décharge *f*, quittance *f*

acronym *n* acronyme *m*, sigle *m*

across: ~ **the board** *adv* de façon systématique, systématiquement; ~ **the counter** *adv* sans intermédiaire

across-the-board *adj* général, systématique; (changes) de bas en haut, général; ~ **cut** *n* (in prices, wages, taxes) réduction générale *f*; ~ **increase** *n* (in prices, wages, taxes) augmentation globale *f*, augmentation générale *f*; ~ **investigation** *n* enquête tous azimuts *f*, examen systématique *m*

ACSS *abbr* (▶**Automated Clearing Settlement System**) SCRA *m* (système de compensation et de règlement automatisé)

act[1] *n* acte *m*, action *f*; (Law) acte *m*; (Pol) acte *m*, loi *f*; ~ **of acknowledgement** (Law) acte de reconnaissance *m*, acte récognitif *m*; ~ **of bankruptcy** acte de faillite *m*, acte de mise en faillite *m*; ~ **of cession** acte de cession *m*; ~ **of God** catastrophe naturelle *f*

act[2] *vi* agir; ~ **as** servir de; ~ **in good faith** agir de bonne foi; ~ **in one's official capacity** agir dans l'exercice de ses fonctions; ~ **on sb's behalf** agir au nom de qn, agir pour le compte de qn; ~ **on**, ~ **upon** *vt* (advice, suggestion) se conformer à, suivre; (decision) donner suite à; (order) exécuter

Act: ~ **of Congress** *n* loi votée par le Congrès *f*; ~ **of Parliament** *n* loi votée par le Parlement *f*

acting *adj* intérimaire, par intérim, provisoire; ~ **director** *n* directeur/-trice par intérim *m/f*; ~ **partner** *n* associé/-e commandité/-e *m/f*

action *n* action *f*; (to deal with a situation) mesures *f pl*; (Law) action *f*, poursuites *f pl*, procès *m*; **take** ~ agir, prendre des mesures; **put a plan into** ~ mettre un projet à exécution; **be out of** ~ (machine) être en panne; (telephone) être en dérangement; **take legal** ~ avoir recours à la justice, entamer des poursuites, intenter une action; **take legal** ~ **against sb** intenter un procès à qn; ~ **against X** action contre X *f*, plainte contre X *f*; ~ **for cancellation** recours en annulation *m*; ~ **committee** *n* comité d'action *m*; ~ **for damages** action en dommages-intérêts *f*, poursuite en dommages et intérêts *f*; ~ **group** *n* groupe de pression *m*; ~ **for libel** procès en diffamation *m*; ~ **in rem** action réelle *f*; ~ **plan** *n* plan d'action *m*, programme d'action *m*

actionable *adj* (claim) recevable; (remark, offence, allegation) passible de poursuites

activate *vt* (Comp) lancer, mettre en marche; (mechanism, button, switch) actionner, activer; (contingency plan, procedure) déclencher

activated *adj* activé

active *adj* (person) actif/-ive; (Comp) actif/-ive, connecté; (capital, assets) productif/-ive, qui rapporte; (Stock) (market) animé; **be** ~ (law) être en vigueur; **be** ~ **in doing** s'employer activement à faire; **play an** ~ **role in sth** jouer un rôle actif dans qch; **take an** ~ **interest in** s'intéresser activement à; **in** ~ **employment** en activité; ~ **account** *n* compte actif *m*; ~ **bond** *n* US *catégorie d'obligations faisant l'objet de forts volumes de transactions à la bourse de New York*, obligation à revenu fixe *f*; ~ **business** *n* entreprise qui marche bien *f*; ~ **capital** *n* capital actif *m*; ~ **dealings** *n pl* (Stock) marché animé *m*; ~ **demand** *n* demande importante *f*, forte demande *f*; ~ **file** *n* (Comp) fichier actif *m*, fichier en cours *m*; ~ **financing** *n* financement d'actifs *m*; ~ **investment** *n* investissement actif *m*, placement actif *m*; ~ **investor** *n* investisseur actif *m*; ~ **management** *n* gestion active *f*; ~ **market** *n* marché animé *m*; ~ **money** *n* monnaie circulante *f*, monnaie en circulation *f*; ~ **partner** *n* partenaire actif *m*, commandité/-e *m/f*; ~ **population** *n* population active *f*; ~ **securities** *n pl* valeurs fréquemment négociées *f pl*, valeurs très actives *f pl*, valeurs très liquides *f pl*; ~ **shares** *n pl* actions fréquemment négociées *f pl*; ~ **trader** *n* commerçant en exercice *m*; ~ **trading** *n* marché animé *m*

actively *adv* activement; ~ **traded** UK (Stock) activement négocié

activist *n* activiste *mf*, militant/-e *m/f*

activity *n* activité *f*; (of account) activité *f*, mouvement *m*; **business/sales** ~ les affaires/les ventes *f pl*; **business activities** activités professionelles *f pl*; ~ **analysis** *n* analyse d'activité *f*; ~**-based costing** *n* évaluation basée sur une activité *f*; ~ **coding** *n* (Acc) codage par activités *m*; ~ **rate** *n* taux d'activité *m*; ~ **ratio** *n* niveau d'activité *m*

actual *adj* (figures) réel/-elle; (commodity) effectif/-ive, existant, réel/-elle; ~ **level of unemployment** niveau effectif du chômage *m*; ~ **amount** *n* (of outlay, expenditure) montant réel *m*; ~ **cash value** *n* valeur de remplacement *f*, valeur effective au comptant *f*; ~ **cost** *n* coût réel *m*, coût réellement engagé *m*; (Tax) coût effectif *m*, coût réel *m*; ~ **deficit** *n* déficit réel *m*; ~ **earnings** *n pl* revenu réel *m*, résultat réel *m*; ~ **expenditure** *n* dépense effective *f*, dépense réelle *f*; ~ **investment** *n* UK investissement réel *m*; ~ **loss** *n* perte effective *f*, perte subie *f*; ~ **outcome** *n* résultat effectif *m*; ~ **price** *n* prix réel *m*; ~ **quotation** *n* (Stock) cours effectif *m*; ~ **stock** *n* UK stock réel *m*; ~ **takings** *n pl* recettes effectives *f pl*; ~ **tax rate** *n* taux d'imposition réel *m*; ~ **total loss** *n* (Ins) perte totale effective *f*; ~ **yield** *n* (of bond, investment) rendement effectif *m*

actuality *n* réalité *f*

actualize *vt* (represent realistically) actualiser; (make real) réaliser

actuals *n pl* (physical commodity) biens physiques *m pl*, marchandises physiques *f pl*; (freight market) existant *m*; **this month's ~** les chiffres réels pour le mois *m pl*

actuarial *adj* actuariel/-ielle; **~ deficit** *n* déficit actuariel *m*, insuffisance actuarielle *f*; **~ liability** *n* dette actuarielle *f*, engagement actuariel *m*; **~ loss** *n* déficit actuariel *m*

actuary *n* actuaire *mf*

ACV *abbr* (▸**actual cash value**) valeur de remplacement *f*, valeur effective au comptant *f*

ad *n* (infrml) annonce *f*, annonce publicitaire *f*; (TV, radio) pub *f* (infrml), spot (publicitaire) *m* (infrml); (in newspapers, magazines) petite annonce *f*; **~ button** *n* (on website) bouton publicitaire *m*; **~ server** *n* (Comp) serveur publicitaire *m*; **~ space** *n* espace publicitaire *m*; **~ view** *n* (on website) impression *f*

A/D *abbr* (**after date**) à/c (à compter de); (Comp) (**analog-digital**) analogique-numérique

adapt ① *vt* adapter
② *vi* s'adapter

adaptability *n* (of product, machine, system) adaptabilité *f*, possibilités d'adaptation *f pl*; (of person) faculté d'adaptation *f*; (of technology, procedure, project) souplesse *f*

adaptable *adj* adaptable

adaptation *n* adaptation *f*

adaptive: ~ control *n* contrôle adaptatif *m*, contrôle souple *m*; **~ expectations** *n pl* espoirs d'adaptation *m pl*

adaptor *n* (Comp) adaptateur *m*

add *vt* (Gen Comm) ajouter, rajouter; (column of figures) totaliser; (figures) additionner, totaliser; **~ back** (sum) réincorporer, réintégrer; **~ in** inclure; **~ on** ajouter; **~ to** (increase) ajouter à, augmenter; **~ together** additionner; (figures) additionner, totaliser; **~ up** ① *vt* (bill, column of figures) totaliser; ② *vi* (figures, results) se recouper; **~ up to** s'élever à

added value *n* valeur ajoutée *f*

addendum *n pl* **-da** addenda *m*, annexe *f*; (Law) additif *m*

adding *n* addition *f*; **~ machine** *n* machine à calculer *f*

addition *n* (new asset) achat *m*, acquisition *f*; (to fixed assets) addition *f*, augmentation *f*; (Math) addition *f*; (text amendment) addition *f*, ajout *m*; **in ~ to** en plus de; **no ~, no correction** ni surcharge, ni rature

additional *adj* supplémentaire; **~ charge** *n* supplément *m*; **~ clause** *n* avenant *m*, clause additionnelle *f*; **~ conditions** *n pl* conditions complémentaires *f pl*, conditions supplémentaires *f pl*; **~ feature** *n* caractéristique additionnelle *f*; **~ interest** *n* intérêt complémentaire *m*; **~ labor** AmE, **~**

labour BrE *n* apport de main-d'œuvre *m*; **~ pay** *n* supplément de salaire *m*; **~ postage** *n* surtaxe postale *f*; **~ premium** *n* prime additionnelle *f*; **~ security** *n* (Ins) garantie supplémentaire *f*; **~ tax** *n* supplément d'impôt *m*; **~ worker hypothesis** *n* hypothèse de l'employé supplémentaire *f*

additive *n* additif *m*

add-on[1] *adj* (Gen Comm) supplémentaire; (Comp) (memory) complémentaire, d'appoint; (software) complémentaire; **on an ~ basis** avec supplément

add-on[2] *n* (Bank) ajout *m*; (Comp) produit supplémentaire *m*, extension *f*

add-on: ~ costs *n pl* charges associées *f pl*, charges supplémentaires *f pl*; **~ equipment** *n* périphériques *m pl*; **~ interest** *n* intérêt supplémentaire *m*

address[1] *n* (talk, speech) allocution *f*, discours *m*; (of person, company, building) adresse *f*; (Comp) adresse *f*; **~ bar** *n* (Comp) barre d'adresses *f*; **~ book** *n* carnet d'adresses *m*, répertoire d'adresses *m*; **~ label** *n* étiquette-adresse *f*

address[2] *vt* (parcel, envelope) mettre l'adresse sur; (person, meeting, group) s'adresser à; (speech, talk) adresser; (issue, problem) aborder; (Law) adresser; **~ oneself to** (issue, problem) s'attaquer à; (task) se mettre à; **~ your complaints to** adressez vos réclamations à

addressable *adj* adressable

addressee *n* destinataire *mf*

addresser *n* expéditeur/-trice *m/f*

addressing *n* adressage *m*

adduce *vt* (proof, reason) apporter, fournir

adequacy *n* (of report, explanation) adéquation *f*; (of description) à-propos *m*; (of person) compétence *f*; **~ of coverage** (Ins) adéquation de couverture *f*

adequate *adj* (funds, supply, explanation) adéquat, suffisant; (technique) adapté; (work, performance) correct; **be ~** (be suitable) convenir; (suffice) suffire

adequately *adj* suffisamment; **~ funded** suffisamment financé

ADG *abbr* (▸**assistant director general**) DGA *mf* (directeur/-trice général/-e adjoint/-e)

adhere: ~ to *vt* (contract) se montrer irréductible sur; (principle) adhérer à, être attaché à

adhesive *adj* adhésif/-ive; **~ label** *n* étiquette adhésive *f*; **~ tape** *n* ruban adhésif *m*

ad hoc *adj* (committee, decision, alliance) ad hoc, temporaire

ad idem *adv* (fml) en parfait accord

ad interim *adj* (fml) par intérim; (judgement) provisoire

adjoining *adj* avoisinant, contigu/-uë; (room, building) attenant

adjourn ① *vt* (meeting) remettre, reporter; ⋯▸

(case, trial) ajourner, remettre, reporter; ~ **the meeting** lever la séance; ~ **sentence** ajourner une sentence; (close session) lever la séance; (Law) suspendre la séance

adjournment *n* (Law) ajournement *m*, prorogation *f*; (of decision) remise *f*; (of meeting) ajournement *m*, suspension *f*; ~ **debate** *n* UK (Pol) débat final *m*

adjudge *vt* (decree) déclarer; (award) accorder, allouer; ~ **damages** accorder des dommages-intérêts, allouer des dommages-intérêts

adjudicate *vt* (claim) adjuger, examiner, juger; (dispute) régler; (contest) juger, être juge de; (prize) décerner; ~ **sb bankrupt** déclarer qn en faillite; ~ **on** se prononcer sur

adjudication *n* jugement *m*; (Law) arrêt *m*, décision *f*, jugement *m*; ~ **of bankruptcy** déclaration de faillite *f*, jugement déclaratif de faillite *m*

adjudicator *n* arbitre *m*, juge *m*

adjunct *n* accessoire *m*; (person) subalterne *mf*

adjust ① *vt* (Acc) ajuster, rectifier, répartir; (Bank) rectifier; (Ins) (average) répartir; (price, amount, timetable, tax) ajuster, réajuster; (price, salary) rajuster, revoir, réajuster, réviser; (wages) rajuster, revaloriser; (terms) mettre au point; (mechanism, component, level) ajuster, mettre au point; (figures, error) rectifier; ~ **a claim** (Ins) régler un sinistre ② *vi* s'adapter; ~ **to** s'adapter à; ~ **downwards** (prices) réviser à la baisse; ~ **upwards** (prices) réviser à la hausse

adjustable *adj* (mortgage rate, timetable, policy) variable; (appliance, position, speed) réglable; (hours, rate) flexible; ~**-rate mortgage** *n* hypothèque à taux variable *f*; ~**-rate preferred stock** *n* action de priorité à taux variable *f*, titre privilégié à taux variable *m*

adjusted *adj* rajusté; ~ **capital ratio** *n* ratio de capital redressé *m*; ~ **claim** *n* indemnité réajustée *f*; ~ **income** *n* (Tax) revenu rajusté *m*; ~ **selling price** *n* prix de vente rajusté *m*; ~ **tax payable** *n* impôt rajusté à payer *m*; ~ **taxable income** *n* revenu imposable modifié *m*

adjuster *n* (Ins) expert *m*, responsable du règlement des sinistres *mf*

adjusting entry *n* écriture de correction *f*, écriture de redressement *f*

adjustment *n* ajustement *m*, rajustement *m*, réajustement *m*; (in accrual accounting) redressement *m*, régularisation *f*; (of statistics, error) correction *f*, rectification *f*; (of prices, rates, charges) ajustement *m*, réajustement *m*, révision *f*; (of wages) rajustement *m*, revalorisation *f*; (Bank) rectification *f*; (of appliance, position, speed) ajustage *m*, mise au point *f*, réglage *m*; (to situation) adaptation *f*;

(Ins) répartition *f*; (of loss) règlement *m*; (Tax) rajustement *m*, réajustement *m*; ~ **account** *n* compte de régularisation *m*; ~ **bond** *n* *obligation de transition émise par une société en situation de faillite*; ~ **clause** *n* (Ins) clause d'ajustabilité *f*, clause de régularisation *f*; ~ **to cost base** (Tax) réajustement du prix de base *m*; ~ **fatigue** *n* fatigue de l'ajustement *f*; ~ **limit** *n* (Tax) seuil de réajustement *m*; ~ **premium** *n* (Ins) prime de régularisation *f*; (Tax) réajustement du prix de base *m*

adman *n pl* **-men** (infrml) publiciste *m*, publicitaire *m*

admass *adj* (culture, society) de grande consommation, de masse

admin *n* (work) administration *f*; (department) service administratif *m*; (management) administration *f*, gestion *f*

administer *vt* administrer, gérer

administered: ~ **price** *n* prix imposé *m*, prix réglementé *m*; ~ **pricing** *n* fixation administrative des prix *f*, fixation conventionnelle des prix *f*

administration *n* (work) administration *f*; (department) service administratif *m*; (management) administration *f*, gestion *f*; (of company, funds) gestion *f*; (of estate, inheritance) curatelle *f*, gestion *f*; (of act) application *f*, exécution *f*; (government) administration *f*; ~ **costs** *n pl* frais d'administration *m pl*, frais de gestion *m pl*; ~ **expenses** *n pl* frais d'administration *m pl*, frais de gestion *m pl*; ~ **lag** *n* délai administratif *m*; ~ **officer** *n* agent administratif *m*; ~ **order** *n* ordonnance instituant l'administration judiciaire *f*

administrative *adj* administratif/-ive; ~ **assistant** *n* adjoint/-e administratif/ive *m/f*; ~ **audit** *n* audit interne *m*; ~ **authority** *n* pouvoir administratif *m*; ~ **board** *n* conseil d'administration *m*; ~ **charge** *n* frais administratifs *m pl*, frais d'administration *m pl*; ~ **costs** *n pl* frais administratifs *m pl*, frais de gestion *m pl*; ~ **expense** *n* frais administratifs *m pl*, frais de gestion *m pl*; ~ **law** *n* droit administratif *m*; ~ **officer** *n* agent d'administration *m*; ~ **overheads** *n pl* frais généraux d'administration *m pl*; ~ **staff** *n pl* personnel administratif *m*; ~ **work** *n* travail administratif *m*

administrator *n* (Admin) administrateur/ -trice *m/f*; (Fin) administrateur judiciaire *m*; (of estate) curateur *m*; (Law) administrateur *m*; (of inheritance) administrateur judiciaire *m*

admissibility *n* (Law) recevabilité *f*

admissible *adj* (document) valable; (evidence, claim) admissible, recevable; (Patents) (claim) autorisé

admission *n* (entry) admission *f*, entrée *f*; (at customs) admission en franchise officielle *f*; (of a crime) aveu *m*; **gain** ~ se faire admettre; **refuse sb** ~ refuser l'entrée à qn; **by his**

own ~ de son propre aveu; ~ **fee** n droit
d'entrée m, prix d'entrée m; ~ **to listing** UK,
~ **to quotation** admission à la cote f; ~ **of
securities** admission de valeurs mobilières f
admit vt (acknowledge) admettre, avouer,
reconnaître; (claim) faire droit à; (let in) faire
entrer, laisser entrer; (new partner) admettre,
coopter; ~ **one is wrong** avouer qu'on est
dans son tort; ~ **to the bar** US (Law) inscrire
au barreau
admittance n accès m, admission f; **no ~**
entrée interdite
adopt vt (procedures, resolution) adopter,
approuver; (single currency, idea, bill,
recommendation) adopter; (method) adopter,
choisir; (child, product) adopter
adoption n (of procedures, resolution) adoption
f; (of single currency, idea, bill, recommendation)
adoption f; (of a method) choix m; ~ **process**
n (of child, product) processus d'adoption m
ADP abbr (▶**automatic data processing**)
traitement automatique des données m
ADR abbr (▶**American depositary
receipt**) certificat américain d'actions
étrangères
adrate n tarif publicitaire m
adrift adj (Transp) à la dérive
ADSL abbr (**assymetric digital
subscriber line**) RNA m (raccordement
numérique assymétrique)
adult n adulte mf; ~ **fare** n plein tarif m; ~
population n population adulte f
adulterate vt falsifier
adulteration n falsification f
ad valorem adj (frml) ad valorem,
proportionnel/-elle, sur la valeur
advance¹ n (increase) hausse f; (payment)
acompte m; (Bank) facilité de trésorerie f;
(down payment) acompte m, arrhes f pl; (on
salary) avance f; (in technology) avance f, percée
f, progrès m; (loan) avance f; (of civilization, in
science) progrès m; (of prices) progression f,
augmentation f; **make an ~** (of money) faire
une avance; **in ~** (book, reserve, notify) à
l'avance; (pay, decide, thank) à l'avance,
d'avance; **5,000 euros in ~** 5 000 euros
d'avance, 5 000 euros d'acompte; **make an ~
payment** verser des arrhes; ~ **account** n
compte d'avances m; ~ **against goods**
avance sur marchandises f; ~ **against
security** avance sur nantissement f, prêt sur
nantissement m; ~ **billing** n facturation par
anticipation f; ~ **booking** n réservation
faite à l'avance f; ~ **copy** n (publishing)
exemplaire en prépublication m, exemplaire
témoin m; ~ **freight** n avance sur le fret f,
fret payé d'avance m; ~ **notice** n préavis m;
~ **on goods** avance sur marchandises f; ~
on salary avance sur salaire f; ~ **payment**
n (in full) paiement anticipé m, paiement par
anticipation m; (down payment) acompte m,
arrhes f pl; ~ **publicity** n publicité
d'amorçage f; ~ **selling** n UK vente

anticipée f
advance² ① vt (career, knowledge) faire
avancer, faire progresser; (work) faire
progresser; (loan) accorder, consentir; (cause)
promouvoir; (theory) avancer
② vi (person, society, civilization) faire des
progrès; (work) progresser
advanced adj (stage, state, idea) avancé,
développé; (research) poussé; (level) élevé;
(software, system) sophistiqué, évolué; (Mgmnt,
Pol) évolué; ~ **country** n pays industrialisé
m, pays technologiquement avancé m; ~
economy n économie développée f; ~
engineering n ingénierie de pointe f; ~
search n (on Internet) recherche avancée f; ~
technology n technologie de pointe f; ~
training n, ~ **training course** n stage de
perfectionnement m
Advanced level n UK ≈ baccalauréat m
advancement n (promotion) avancement m,
promotion f; (Econ, Pol) essor m
advances received n pl avances reçues
sur commandes en cours f pl
advantage n avantage m; **have an ~ over
sb/sth** avoir un avantage sur qn/qch; **give sb
an ~ over sb** donner à qn un avantage par
rapport à qn; **put sb at an ~** avantager qn;
be to sb's ~ profiter à qn; **take ~ of** (service,
offer, facility) profiter de; (situation, person) tirer
profit de; **take ~ of an opportunity to do**
profiter d'une occasion pour faire
advantageous adj avantageux/-euse;
(lucrative) intéressant, profitable
adversary n adversaire mf, partie adverse f
adverse adj (budget) déficitaire;
(consequences, influence, effect) négatif/-ive;
(reaction, factor, conditions) défavorable; ~
balance of trade n balance commerciale
défavorable f, balance commerciale
déficitaire f; ~ **claim** n (Law) opposition f; ~
movement n (in price of bonds) fluctuation
défavorable f, mouvement contraire m; ~
opinion n avis défavorable m, opinion
défavorable f; ~ **selection** n sélection
adverse f; ~ **trading conditions** n pl
conditions défavorables pour le commerce
f pl; ~ **weather** n temps défavorable m
adversely affected adj affecté
négativement
advert n (on radio) pub f (infrml), publicité f,
spot publicitaire m; (in newspaper, magazine)
annonce f, annonce publicitaire f; (in personal
column) petite annonce f
advertise ① vt (house, car) mettre une
annonce pour vendre, passer une annonce
pour; (product, service) faire de la publicité
pour, faire de la réclame pour; (price, rate)
annoncer; ~ **a job in the paper** insérer une
annonce pour un poste dans le journal
② vi (for product, service) faire de la publicité,
faire de la réclame; (for staff) passer une
annonce; (in newspaper, magazine) mettre une
annonce; ~ **for** faire paraître une annonce

pour; ~ **for bids** passer un avis d'appel d'offres; **as advertised on television** vu à la télévision

advertisement n (on TV, radio) publicité f, pub f (infrml), spot publicitaire m; (in newspaper, magazine) annonce f, annonce publicitaire f; (in personal column) petite annonce f

advertiser n annonceur m

advertising n publicité f, pub f (infrml); **tobacco** ~ la publicité pour le tabac; **radio** ~ la publicité à la radio; **work in** ~ travailler dans la publicité; ~ **agency** n agence de publicité f; ~ **appeal** n axe publicitaire m, thème publicitaire m; ~ **appropriation** n, ~ **budget** n budget de la publicité m; ~ **campaign** n campagne de publicité f; ~ **channel** n canal publicitaire m; ~ **code** n code publicitaire m; ~ **concept** n axe publicitaire m, concept publicitaire m; ~ **consultant** n conseil en publicité m; ~ **copy** n texte publicitaire m; ~ **coverage** n couverture publicitaire f; ~ **department** n (of magazine) service publicité m; ~ **director** n chef du service publicité m, directeur/-trice de la publicité m/f; ~ **effectiveness** n efficacité publicitaire f, ~ **executive** n publicitaire mf; ~ **expenditure** n dépense de publicité f, dépense publicitaire f; ~ **gimmick** n astuce publicitaire f, truc publicitaire m (infrml); ~ **industry** n publicité f, pub f (infrml); ~ **jingle** n jingle m, sonal m; ~ **manager** n chef de publicité m, directeur/-trice de la publicité m/f; ~ **material** n matériel publicitaire m; ~ **media** n pl supports publicitaires m pl, médias publicitaires m pl; ~ **medium** n canal publicitaire m, support publicitaire m; ~ **message** n message publicitaire m; ~ **overkill** n excès de publicité m; ~ **policy** n politique publicitaire f; ~ **potential** n potentiel publicitaire m; ~ **rates** n pl tarifs publicitaires m pl; ~ **revenue** n recettes publicitaires f pl, rentrées publicitaires f pl; ~ **slogan** n slogan publicitaire m; ~ **space** n espace publicitaire m; ~ **space buyer** n acheteur d'espace publicitaire m; ~ **space seller** n vendeur d'espace publicitaire m; ~ **tactics** n pl stratégie publicitaire f; ~ **technique** n technique publicitaire f; ~ **text** n texte publicitaire m; ~ **time** n temps publicitaire m; ~ **tour** n tournée publicitaire f; ~ **turnover** n chiffre d'affaires publicitaires m; ~ **value** n valeur publicitaire f; ~ **vehicle** n véhicule de communication m; ~ **weapon** n arme publicitaire f; ~ **world** n monde de la publicité m

Advertising Standards Authority n UK ≈ Bureau de vérification de la publicité m

advertorial n publireportage m

advice n (suggestions) conseils m pl; (notification) avis m; **give sb** ~ **about sth** donner des conseils à qn à propos de qch; **get expert/legal** ~ consulter un expert/un

avocat; **take** ~ **from sb about** demander conseil à qn à propos de; **take sb's** ~ suivre les conseils de qn; **do sth against sb's** ~ faire qch malgré les recommandations de qn; **on the** ~ **of** sur les conseils de; ~ **note** n lettre d'avis f; ~ **of arrival** n avis d'arrivée m; ~ **of delivery** n avis de livraison m

advisable adj recommandé, conseillé; **if you think it** ~ si vous le jugez bon

advise vt (inform) aviser, informer; (recommend) recommander; (give advice to) conseiller, donner des conseils à; ~ **sb on sth** conseiller qn sur qch; ~ **sb of sth** faire part de qch à qn, informer qn de qch; ~ **sb that** faire part à qn que, informer qn que; ~ **sb to do** conseiller à qn de faire; ~ **sb against doing** déconseiller à qn de faire; ~ **a draft** donner avis d'une traite

advised bill n traite avisée f

adviser, advisor n conseil m, conseiller/-ère m/f, consultant/-e m/f; **act as a scientific** ~ **to the committee** avoir un rôle de conseiller scientifique auprès du comité

advisory adj (role) consultatif/-ive; **in an** ~ **capacity** à titre consultatif; ~ **account** n (Fin) clientèle privée conseillée f; ~ **board** n comité consultatif m; (Pol) commission consultative f; ~ **body** n organisme consultatif m; ~ **committee** n comité consultatif m, commission consultative f; (for rescheduling of debt) comité de restructuration m; ~ **function** n fonction consultative f, rôle consultatif m; ~ **services** n pl services de conseil m pl

Advisory, Conciliation and Arbitration Service n UK service consultatif d'arbitrage et de conciliation

advocate vt préconiser, recommander

aerial: ~ **advertising** n publicité aérienne f; ~ **survey** n levé aérien m

aerodrome n BrE aérodrome m

aeroplane n BrE avion m

aerosol n (can) bombe aérosol f; (system) aérosol m

aerospace adj aérospatial

AF abbr (▸**advance freight**) fret payé d'avance m

affairs n pl affaires f pl; **state of** ~ situation f; **put one's** ~ **in order** mettre de l'ordre dans ses affaires

affect vt (concern) concerner; (influence) avoir un effet sur, influencer; (business, earnings) avoir un effet sur, avoir une incidence sur; (unemployed people, small businesses, low earners) toucher; (supply of money) affecter

affidavit n affidavit m, attestation f, déclaration écrite sous serment f

affiliate[1] n (organization) groupe affilié m; (member, person) affilié/-e m/f; ~ **company** n filiale f, société affiliée f; ~ **program** AmE, ~ **programme** BrE n programme d'affiliation m

affiliate[2] [1] vt affilier; ~ **oneself to**

s'affilier à

2 *vi* ~ **to** s'affilier à

affiliated *adj* affilié; ~ **to** affilié à; ~ **bank** *n* banque affiliée *f*; ~ **company** *n* société associée *f*, filiale *f*; ~ **firm** *n* filiale *f*; ~ **trade unions** *n pl* syndicats affiliés *m pl*

affiliation *n* affiliation *f*

affinity: ~ **card** *n* carte de parenté par alliance *f*; ~ **marketing** *n* marketing par affinité *m*

affirmative *adj* (reply, statement) affirmatif/ -ive; ~ **action** *n* AmE discrimination positive *f*, mesures anti-discriminatoires *f pl*

affix *vt* (label) attacher, coller; (notice, poster) afficher, poser; (signature, seal) apposer; (stamp) coller

affixed *adj* (attached, enclosed) ci-joint

affluence *n* abondance *f*, richesse *f*

affluent *adj* (person) aisé, riche; **the ~ society** la société d'abondance *f*

afford *vt* (pay for) avoir les moyens d'acheter; (time) disposer de; **we can't ~ to lose** nous ne pouvons pas nous permettre de perdre

affordable *adj* (price) abordable; (item, product) (d'un prix) abordable

affreightment *n* affrètement *m*

AFL-CIO *abbr* (▸**American Federation of Labor and Congress of Industrial Organizations**) *confédération générale américaine du travail*

afloat *adj* (business, company) à flot; (at sea) en mer; **keep ~** (business) se maintenir à flot; ~ **price** *n* prix à bord *m*, prix à flot *m*

aforementioned *adj* précité, susdit, susmentionné

AFT *abbr* (▸**automatic funds transfer**) virement automatique *m*, virement automatique de fonds *m*

after *prep* après; **six months ~ date** à six mois d'échéance, à six mois de date; ~ **sight** de vue; ~**-acquired clause** *n* clause de post-acquisition *f*; ~**-hours** *adj* (Stock) hors bourse, hors séance; ~**-hours market** *n* marché hors bourse *m*, marché hors séance *m*; ~**-hours trading** *n* transactions hors bourse *f pl*, transactions hors séance *f pl*; ~ **market** *n* marché secondaire *m*; ~**-sales** *adj* après-vente; (revenue) généré par le premier achat; ~**-sales service** *n* service après-vente *m*; ~**-tax** *adj* après impôts, net d'impôt; ~**-tax capital gain** *n* gain en capital après impôt *m*, gain en capital net *m*; ~**-tax dividend** *n* dividende après impôt *m*; ~**-tax profit** *n* bénéfices après impôts *m pl*; ~**-tax rate of return** *n* taux de rendement après-impôts *m*; ~**-tax yield** *n* rendement après impôt *m*, rendement net *m*

after-effect *n* répercussion *f*, suite *f*

afterimage *n* image rémanente *f*

aftermath *n* conséquences *f pl*; **in the ~ of** à la suite de

afterwards *adv* après; (in a sequence) ensuite

AG *abbr* (Acc) (▸**Accountant General**) chef comptable *m*, directeur/-trice de comptabilité *m/f*; (UK) (▸**Agent General**) représentant général *m*

against *prep* contre; ~ **all risks** (Ins) tous risques, contre tous les risques; ~ **documents** contre documents; **it is ~ our policy to grant discounts** il est contraire à notre politique d'accorder des remises; ~ **the law** contraire à la loi; ~ **payment** contre paiement

age[1] *n* âge *m*; ~ **at entry** âge à l'entrée *m*; ~ **at expiry** âge à terme *m*; ~ **bracket** *n* tranche d'âge *f*; ~ **discrimination** *n* discrimination en matière d'âge *f*, discrimination s'appliquant à l'âge *f*; ~ **distribution** *n* distribution par âge *f*, répartition par âge *f*; ~ **exemption** *n* exemption en raison d'âge *f*; ~ **group** *n* tranche d'âge *f*; ~ **limit** *n* limite d'âge *f*, âge limite *m*

age[2] 1 *vt* (accounts) classer par ancienneté, classer par antériorité; ~ **inventories** classer le stock par date d'entrée

2 *vi* prendre de l'âge, vieillir

ageing population *n* BrE population vieillissante *f*

ageism *n* BrE âgisme *m*

agency *n* (Gen Comm, Admin) agence *f*, bureau *m*; (Bank) succursale *f*; (organization, body, trust institution) organisme *m*; (means) opération *f*; (company) agence *f*, bureau *m*; (representing firm) concessionnaire *m*; (intermediary) intermédiaire *mf*; (Stock) intermédiation *f*; **through the ~ of** par l'intermédiaire de; **have sole ~ for a product range** avoir la représentation exclusive d'une gamme de produits; ~ **account** *n* compte agence *m*; ~ **agreement** *n* contrat d'agence *m*, contrat de représentation *m*; ~ **billing** *n* (Media) chiffre d'affaires d'une agence de publicité *m*; ~ **cost** *n* UK (Stock) frais d'agence *m pl*, frais de courtage *m pl*; ~ **fee** *n* (Gen Comm) frais d'agence *m pl*; (Bank) commission de gestion *f*; ~ **fund** *n* (Gen Comm) commission de gestion *f*; (Law) fonds en fidéicommis *m pl*; ~ **staff** *n pl* personnel intérimaire *m*

agenda *n* ordre du jour *m*, programme *m*; **be on the ~** être à l'ordre du jour; **draw up an ~** établir un ordre du jour

agent *n* (Gen Comm) agent *m*, commissionnaire *mf*, représentant/-e *m/f*; (Fin) courtier *m*; (Ind) délégué/-e syndical/-e *m/f*; (S&M) mandataire *mf*, représentant/-e *m/f*

Agent General *n* UK représentant général *m*

agglomeration *n* agglomération *f*

aggregate[1] *adj* (amount, value) global, total

aggregate[2] *n* (Econ) agrégat *m*, ensemble *m*; (Math) ensemble *m*, total *m*; ~ **balance** *n* ⋯▸

solde général *m*; ~ **book value** *n* (Acc)
valeur comptable globale nette *f*; ~ **demand**
n demande globale *f*; ~ **demand-aggregate**
supply *n pl* demande et offre globale *f*,
demande globale-offre globale *f*; ~ **income** *n*
revenu global *m*; ~ **output** *n* aggrégat de la
production *m*, production globale *f*,
rendement global *m*; ~ **risk** *n* risque global
m; ~ **supply** *n* offre globale *f*

aggregate³ *vt* réunir; (data, orders)
regrouper

aggressive *adj* (marketing, person, policy, sales)
agressif/-ive; ~ **investment** *n*
investissement agressif *m*; ~ **marketing** *n*
marketing dynamique *m*; ~ **pricing** *n*
politique de prix agressive *f*

aging population *n* AmE ▸**ageing**
population BrE

agio *n* agio *m*; ~ **account** *n* compte d'agios
m

agiotage *n* agiotage *m*

agism *n* AmE ▸**ageism** BrE

AGM *abbr* (▸**annual general meeting**)
assemblée générale annuelle *f*

AGNP *abbr* (▸**augmented GNP**) PNBA *m*
(PNB augmenté)

agora *n* agorot *m*

agree [1] *vt* (date, venue, terms, method, fee) se
mettre d'accord sur, convenir de; (candidate,
plan, change) se mettre d'accord sur; (minutes)
approuver; ~ **the accounts** équilibrer les
comptes; ~ **the books** accorder les écritures,
approuver les comptes; ~ **to do** (arrange)
convenir de faire, se mettre d'accord pour
faire; (consent) accepter de faire
[2] *vi* (consent) donner son accord; (figures,
statements) concorder, coïncider; (share opinion)
être d'accord, être du même avis; ~ **on**
(prices, terms) convenir de; ~ **to** (discount)
consentir à; (project, plan) donner son adhésion
à; (terms) accepter; ~ **upon** (price, terms)
convenir de; ~ **with** (person) être du même
avis que; (figures, report, proposal) approuver

agreed *adj* (time, place, terms, total) convenu;
as ~ comme convenu; **at an** ~ **price**
(contract) pour un prix convenu, à forfait; **be**
~ **on sth** être d'accord sur qch; ~ **price** *n*
prix convenu *m*; ~ **sum** *n* forfait *m*, montant
convenu *m*; ~ **takeover** *n* OPA amicale *f*,
OPA négociée à l'amiable *f*; ~ **valuation**
clause *n* clause valeur agréée *f*; ~ **value** *n*
valeur agréée *f*

agreement *n* accord *m*, (contract) contrat *m*,
convention *f*; **as per** ~ comme convenu; **be**
in ~ (tally) concorder; **be in** ~ **with sb** être
d'accord avec qn; **enter into an** ~ passer un
accord, passer un contrat; **reach an** ~
parvenir à un accord; **under the terms of the**
~ selon les termes du contrat; ~ **of sale**
contrat de vente *m*; ~ **of service** contrat de
travail *m*

agribusiness *n* agro-industries *f pl*,
agrobusiness *m*

agricultural¹ *adj* agricole; ~ **bank** *n*
banque agricole *f*; ~ **building** *n* bâtiment
agricole *m*; ~ **credit** *n* crédit agricole *m*; ~
engineer *n* ingénieur agronome *m*; ~
export subsidy *n* subvention à l'exportation
agricole *f*; ~ **insurance** *n* assurance
agricole *f*; ~ **job** *n* emploi agricole *m*; ~
land *n* terre agricole *f*; ~ **loan** *n* prêt
agricole *m*; ~ **policy** *n* politique agricole *f*;
~ **price support** *n* soutien des prix
agricoles *m*; ~ **produce** *n* produits agricoles
m pl; ~ **production** *n* production agricole *f*;
~ **sector** *n* secteur agricole *m*; ~ **show** *n*
exposition agricole *f*, salon de l'agriculture
m; ~ **subsidy** *n* subvention agricole *f*,
subvention à l'agriculture *f*; ~ **unit** *n* unité
d'exploitation agricole *f*

agriculture *n* agriculture *f*

agriculturist *n* agriculteur/-trice *m/f*

agrifood industry *n* industrie agro-
alimentaire *f*

agrifoodstuffs *n pl* agro-alimentaire *m*,
produits agro-alimentaires *m pl*

agriscience *n* agrotechnologie *f*

agrochemical *n* produit agrochimique *m*

agro-forestry *n* agroforesterie *f*

agro-industry *n* agro-industrie *f*

agronomist *n* agronome *m*

agronomy *n* agronomie *f*

aground *adv* run ~ échouer

agt *abbr* (▸**agent**) agent *m*,
commissionnaire *mf*, représentant/-e *m/f*

ahead *adv* get ~ progresser; (in career)
réussir; get ~ **of a competitor** prendre de
l'avance sur un concurrent; **plan** ~ prévoir;
plan ~ **for sth** préparer qch, prévoir qch; **be**
~ **of the field** devancer les autres; **be** ~ **of**
sb (in ranking, rating) avoir un avantage sur qn;
~ **of schedule** en avance sur le calendrier
établi, en avance sur les prévisions

AI *abbr* (▸**accrued interest**) IC *m pl*
(intérêts courus); (▸**artificial intelligence**)
IA *f* (intelligence artificielle)

aid¹ *n* (help) aide *f*; (Comp) assistance *f*;
(equipment) aide *f*; **in** ~ **of** au profit de; **with**
the ~ **of** à l'aide de; **come to sb's** ~ venir
en aide à qn; ~ **in kind** *n* aide en nature *f*;
~ **loan** *n* prêt de secours *m*; ~ **money** *n*
fonds d'aide au développement *m*; ~ **money**
program AmE, ~ **programme** *n* BrE
programme d'aide *m*

aid² *vt* aider; (company) subventionner;
(development) apporter une aide à, soutenir;
(person) assister, venir en aide à; (financially)
aider, secourir; ~ **and abet** être le complice
de

AIDA *abbr* (S&M) (**attention, interest,**
desire, action) AIDA *m* (attention, intérêt,
désir, action)

aide *n* assistant/-e *m/f*; ~**-memoire** *n* aide-
mémoire *m inv*

aided recall *n* mémorisation assistée *f*;

∼ test n test de mémorisation assistée m

ailing adj (person) souffrant; (company) mal en point; **∼ economy** n économie qui périclite f; **∼ industry** n industrie en déclin f

aim[1] n but m, objectif m, objet m; (Mgmnt, S&M) finalité f

aim[2] vt (criticism, product, programme) destiner; **∼ at** viser; **∼ to do** (try) s'efforcer de faire; (intend) avoir l'intention de faire; **∼ high** viser haut

AIM abbr (▸**Alternative Investment Market**) place boursière londonienne pour nouvelles entreprises

air[1] n air m; **by ∼** par avion; **∼ bag** n airbag m; **∼ bill** n lettre de transport aérien f; **∼ cargo** n fret aérien m; **∼ carrier** n transporteur aérien m; **∼ conditioning** n air conditionné m, climatisation f; **∼ consignment note** n lettre de transport aérien f; **∼ corridor** n couloir aérien m; **∼ fare** n prix du billet d'avion m; **∼ freight** n fret aérien m, transport aérien m; **∼ freighter** n avion-cargo m; **∼ hostess** n hôtesse de l'air f; **∼ pollution** n pollution atmosphérique f; **∼ show** n salon de l'aéronautique m; **∼ terminal** n aérogare f; **∼ traffic** n circulation aérienne f, trafic aérien m; **∼ traffic control** n (activity) contrôle de la circulation aérienne m, contrôle du trafic aérien m; (building) tour de contrôle f; **∼-traffic controller** n aiguilleur du ciel m, contrôleur aérien m; **∼ transport** n transport aérien m; **∼ transport insurance** n assurance transport aérien f; **∼ travel** n voyages en avion m pl; **∼ traveler** AmE, **∼ traveller** BrE n voyageur par avion m; **∼ waybill** n lettre de transport aérien f

air[2] vt (idea, proposal) avancer, exprimer, mettre sur le tapis; (opinion, view) afficher, faire connaître, faire part de; **∼ one's opinions**, **∼ one's views** faire connaître ses idées, faire cas de son avis

airborne adj en vol; **∼ time** n temps de vol réel m

airbus n airbus m

air-conditioned adj climatisé

aircraft n inv pl avion m, aéronef m; **∼ charter agreement** n contrat d'affrètement aérien m; **∼ industry** n industrie aéronautique f; **∼ operator** n exploitant m

aircrew n équipage d'un avion m

airdrome n AmE ▸**aerodrome** BrE

airlift n pont aérien m

airliner n avion de ligne m

airmail[1] n poste aérienne f; **by ∼** par avion; **∼ envelope** n aérogramme m; **∼ letter** n lettre par avion f

airmail[2] vt (letter) expédier par avion

airplane n AmE avion m

airport n aéroport m; **∼ advertising** n publicité d'aéroport f; **∼ hotel** n hôtel d'aéroport m; **∼ lounge** n salle d'embarquement f; **∼ security** n contrôles de sécurité dans les aéroports m pl; **∼ tax** n taxe d'aéroport f

airtight adj (container, seal) hermétique, étanche (à l'air)

airtime n (time of broadcast) heure d'émission f; (for advertising) espace publicitaire m, temps d'antenne m; (slot on radio, TV) créneau horaire m, temps d'antenne m

airway n (route) voie aérienne f

airworthiness n navigabilité f; **∼ certification** n certification f

airworthy adj en état de navigation

aisle n (in cinema, shop) allée f; (in train, aeroplane) couloir m

a.k.a. abbr (▸**also known as**) alias, aussi connu sous le nom de

alarm n (as warning) alarme f, alerte f; (in clock) sonnerie f; **∼ bell** n sonnerie d'alarme f; **∼ call** n réveil par téléphone m; **∼ signal** n signal d'alarme m

aleatory adj (Ins) (contract) aléatoire

alert n alerte f; **be on the ∼** être en état d'alerte; **to be on the ∼ for** être à l'affût de; **give the ∼** donner l'alerte

A level n UK ≈ baccalauréat m

algorithm n algorithme m

alias[1] adv alias

alias[2] n pseudonyme m; (Comp) alias m

aliasing n (Comp) crènelage m

alien[1] adj étranger/-ère; **∼ from** éloigné de, étranger/-ère à; **∼ to** contraire à, opposé à

alien[2] n étranger/-ère m/f; **∼ registration card** n US carte de séjour f

alienable adj aliénable

alienate vt (Gen Comm) (colleague, person) écarter; (Law) (person) aliéner

alienation n (Law) aliénation f; **∼ effect** n effet d'éloignement m

alienee n aliénataire mf

align vt BrE aligner; **∼ oneself with** s'aligner sur

alignment n alignement m

alimony n aliments m pl

aline AmE ▸**align** BrE

aliquot adj (parts) aliquote

all-day trading n marché continu m

allegation n allégation f

alleged adj prétendu, allégué

all-employee option scheme n UK programme d'options ouvert à tous les employés m

alleviate vt (problem) rendre supportable, soulager; (crisis, stress, unemployment) réduire

alliance n alliance f, union f

allied adj (subject, issue, sector) connexe; (Pol) allié; **∼ industries** n pl industries connexes f pl; **∼ trades** n pl métiers analogues m pl

all-in adj (price) net/nette, tout compris

all-inclusive adj (price) forfaitaire, tout ⋯⋗

compris; (rate) net/nette, tout compris

all-loss *adj* (Ins) tous risques

allocate *vt* (money, duties, funds, resources) affecter, allouer, attribuer; (work) assigner; (share out) distribuer, répartir; (contract) adjuger; (Acc) ventiler; **~ costs to certain accounts** ventiler les charges entre certains comptes

allocation *n* (of funds) affectation *f*; (of name, role) attribution *f*; (of resources) affectation *f*, allocation *f*; (of money, duties) affectation *f*, attribution *f*; (of contract) adjudication *f*; (Acc) ventilation *f*, répartition *f*; (Law) ventilation *f*; (Stock) répartition *f*; **~ of costs** imputation des charges *f*, répartition des coûts *f*; **~ of earnings** répartition des revenus *f*; **~ to the lowest tenderer** adjudication au soumissionnaire le moins offrant *f*; **~ of responsibilities** répartition des responsabilités *f*; **~ by tender** allocation par appel d'offre *f*, répartition par voie d'adjudication *f*; **~ of work** distribution du travail *f*

allonge *n* (Bank) allonge *f*

all-or-nothing clause *n* clause tout ou rien *f*

allot *vt* (Acc, Admin) affecter; (money, resources) accorder, allouer, attribuer; (time) consacrer; (task, role) assigner, répartir; (Bank) consentir; (Stock) (shares) attribuer, répartir

allotment *n* (of money, resources) attribution *f*, allocation *f*; (of tasks, roles) répartition *f*; (Acc, Admin) affectation *f*; (Fin) attribution *f*; (Stock) (of shares) répartition *f*; (Transp) (shipping) délégation de solde *f*; **~ money** *n* versement de souscription *m*; **~ price** *n* prix de souscription *m*

allotted share *n* (Stock) action attribuée *f*

all-out *adj* (effort) maximum; **~ strike** *n* grève générale *f*

allow *vt* (action, change) autoriser; (claim) agréer, faire droit à; (money, resources) accorder; (person, organization) permettre; (allocate) prévoir, allouer; **~ sb a discount** consentir une remise à qn; **~ sb to do** autoriser qn à faire; **~ sb £8,000 in damages** accorder à qn 8 000 livres sterling de dommages et intérêts; **~ for** (delay, leakage, wastage) tenir compte de; **~ for a margin of error** prévoir une marge d'erreur

allowable *adj* (permissible) admissible; (Law) légitime; (Tax) déductible; **~ claim** *n* réclamation admissible *f*, réclamation recevable *f*; **~ credit** *n* crédit déductible *m*; **~ deduction** *n* montant déductible *m*; **~ expense** *n* frais fiscalement déductibles *m pl*

allowance *n* (Gen Comm) (sum of money) allocation *f*; (for travel, accommodation) indemnité *f*; (discount) rabais *m*, remise *f*, réduction *f*, franchise *f*; (tolerance) marge de tolérance *f*; (welfare payment) allocation *f*; (for damaged or lost goods) réfaction *f*; (Acc)

réduction *f*; (Tax) abattement fiscal *m*, déduction avant impôt *f*; (Transp) franchise *f*; **make an ~ on** (discount) accorder une remise sur; **make ~ for** (Acc) défalquer; **make ~s for sth** tenir compte de qch; **~ for bad debts** provision pour créances douteuses *f*; **~ for depreciation** US dotation aux amortissements *f*; **~ for exchange fluctuations** provision pour fluctuations du change *f*; **~ for inflation** UK prise en compte de l'inflation *f*, provision pour inflation *f*; **~ in kind** avantage en nature *m*, prestation en nature *f*; **~ for living expenses** allocation de subsistance *f*; **~ for loss** réfaction *f*; **~ for personal expenses** allocation pour frais personnels *f*; **~ for travelling expenses** allocation pour frais de déplacement *f*

allowed *adj* (deduction) admis, permis; **~ time** *n* délai fixe *m*

all-purpose *adj* (statement) à vocation générale; (device) polyvalent, universel/-elle

all-risk *adj* (Ins) tous risques; (policy) tous périls

all-round *adj* (fee, price) tout compris

all-sector average *n* moyenne tous secteurs confondus *f*

all-time: **~ high** *n* niveau historique *m*, niveau sans précédent *m*, record absolu *m*; (Stock) niveau record *m*; **~ low** *n* le chiffre le plus bas jamais atteint; (Stock) creux sans précédent *m*; **~ record** *n* record absolu *m*

ally *vt* allier; **be allied with** être allié avec, être allié à

ALM *abbr* (▶**assets and liabilities management**) GAP *f* (gestion actif-passif), gestion du bilan *f*

alongside *adv* (Transp) à quai

alpha: **~ share** *n* action fréquemment négociée *f*; **~ stock** *n* valeurs alpha *f pl*

alphabetical *adj* alphabétique; **in ~ order** par ordre alphabétique

alphanumeric *adj* alphanumérique

alpha test¹ *n* essai en laboratoire *m*, test alpha *m*

alpha test ² *vt* tester en laboratoire

also: **~ known as** alias, aussi connu sous le nom de

alt. *abbr* (▶**altered**) changé, modifié

alter *vt* changer, modifier

alteration *n* modification *f*; **~ of capital** modification du capital *f*

alterations *n pl* travaux de transformation *m pl*

altered *adj* changé, modifié

alternate¹ *adj* (by turns) alternatif/-ive, alterné; (successive) en alternance; **on ~ days** tous les deux jours

alternate² *n* remplaçant/-e *m/f*, suppléant/-e *m/f*; **~ funding** *n* financement de remplacement *m*; **~ press** *n* (Media) presse parallèle *f*

alternate³ *vt* alterner

alternative¹ *adj* (other) autre, de rechange; (product) de remplacement; **~ economic strategy** stratégie économique de rechange

alternative² *n* alternative *f*, option *f*; (from several) choix *m*, possibilité *f*; **there is no ~** il n'y a pas d'alternative; **have no ~** ne pas avoir le choix

alternative: ~ cost *n* coût d'opportunité *m*; **~ energy** *n* énergie de substitution *f*, énergie nouvelle *f*; **~ hypothesis** *n* hypothèse alternative *f*; **~ order** *n* commande de remplacement *f*; **~ proposal** *n* contre-proposition *f*; **~ solution** *n* contre-solution *f*; **~ technology** *n* technologie de remplacement *f*, technologie douce *f*

Alternative Investment market *n* UK *place boursière londonienne pour nouvelles entreprises*

altruism *n* altruisme *m*

aluminium BrE, **aluminum** AmE *n* aluminium *m*

always *adv* toujours

always-on connection *n* (Comp) (cable) connexion permanente câble *f*; (ADSL) connexion permanente ADSL *f*

am *abbr* (**ante meridiem**) **at 2 ~** à deux heures du matin

amalgamate *vti* fusionner

amalgamated: ~ bank *n* banque issue d'une fusion *f*; **~ corporation** *n* corporation fusionnée *f*, corporation issue d'une fusion *f*

amalgamation *n* fusion *f*; (Stock) fusion *f*, fusionnement *m*; **~ agreement** *n* accord de fusion *m*

amass *vt* (money, property, goods) amasser

amateur¹ *adj* amateur

amateur² *n* amateur *m*

ambassador *n* ambassadeur *m*

ambient *adj* (temperature, noise) ambiant; **~ quality standard** *n* (of air) norme relative à la qualité *f*; **~ standard** *n* US (of air quality) norme de pureté de l'air *f*

ambition *n* ambition *f*

ambitious *adj* (person, plan) ambitieux/-ieuse

amend *vt* corriger, modifier, revoir; (Law) amender, (Patents) modifier, revoir; (Pol) amender, modifier, revoir

amended *adj* modifié; **~ act** *n* loi amendée *f*, loi modifiée *f*, loi révisée *f*; **~ prospectus** *n* (Stock) prospectus modifié *m*

amendment *n* modification *f*, révision *f*, (Law) amendement *m*

amenities *n pl* (of hotel, locality) équipements *m pl*; (of house) installations *f pl*; **public ~** équipements collectifs *m pl*

American¹ *adj* américain

American² *n* Américain/-e *m/f*

American: ~ Board of Trade *n* bureau américain du commerce; **~ Chamber of Commerce** *n* chambre américaine de commerce; **~ depositary receipt** *n* certificat américain d'actions étrangères; **~ Federation of Labor and Congress of Industrial Organizations** *n* confédération générale américaine du travail; **~ National Standards Institute** *n* association américaine de normalisation; **~ selling price** *n* prix intérieur américain *m*; **~ Stock Exchange** *n* la bourse de New York secondaire où sont listées les valeurs qui n'apparaissent pas au New York Stock Exchange; **~ terms** *n pl* modalités en dollars *f pl*

AMEX *abbr* (▸**American Stock Exchange**) *la deuxième bourse de New York où sont listées les valeurs qui n'apparaissent pas au New York Stock Exchange*, AMEX *f*

Amex Commodities Exchange *n* bourse de commerce de l'Amex *f*

amicable *adj* (manner) plaisant; (person) aimable, amical; (solution) à l'amiable; **come to an ~ agreement with sb** arriver à un accord à l'amiable avec qn; **~ settlement** *n* arrangement à l'amiable *m*

amicably *adv* à l'amiable

amortizable *adj* amortissable

amortization *n* amortissement *m*; (of loan) amortissement *m*, remboursement *m*; **~ adjustment** *n* redressement pour amortissement *m*; **~ expense** *n* dotation aux amortissements *f*; **~ fund** *n* fonds d'amortissement *m*; **~ loan** *n* prêt d'amortissement *m*; **~ of a loan** *n* amortissement d'un emprunt *m*; **~ payment** *n* remboursement périodique *m*; **~ reserve** *n* provision pour amortissements *f*; **~ schedule** *n* plan d'amortissement *m*

amortize *vt* amortir

amortized: ~ cost *n* coût amorti *m*, coût amortissable *m*; **~ value** *n* valeur comptable nette *f*

amortizement *n* amortissement *m*

amount¹ *n* (of goods) quantité *f*; (of people, objects) nombre *m*; (sum of money) somme *f*; (Fin) chiffre *m*, nombre *m*; (total of bill, expenses, damages) montant *m*; **up to the ~ of** jusqu'à un plafond de; **unpaid bills to the ~ of £10,000** des factures impayées qui s'élèvent à 10 000 livres sterling; **a cheque in the ~ of**, **a cheque to the ~ of** un chèque d'un montant de; **for an undisclosed ~** pour une somme non dévoilée; **~ brought forward** montant reporté *m*, somme reportée *f*; **~ of business** volume d'affaires *m*; (Stock) volume des transactions *m*; **~ carried forward** report à nouveau *m*; **~ charged** montant à payer *m*, somme à verser *f*; **~ due** montant dû *m*; **~ invested** somme investie *f*; **~ outstanding** montant impayé *m*, solde *m*; **~ overdue** montant échu *m*; **~ overpaid** trop-perçu *m*; **~ paid** montant ····⊱

versé *m*, somme versée *f*; ~ **paid out** montant versé *m*; ~ **to pay** montant à payer *m*; ~ **payable** montant payable *m*, somme payable *f*; ~ **repayable** montant remboursable *m*

amount²: ~ **to** *vt* (add up to) s'élever à, se chiffrer à, être chiffré à; (be equivalent to) équivaloir à, revenir à

ampersand *n* esperluette *f*

AMT *abbr* (▸**amount**) (of goods) quantité *f*; (of people) nombre *m*; (sum of money) somme *f*; (Fin) chiffre *m*, nombre *m*; (total of bill, expenses, damages) montant *m*

AMTRAK *n* US *société nationale des chemins de fer américains*

amusement: ~ **industry** *n* (leisure) industrie des loisirs *f*; (performing arts) industrie du spectacle *f*; ~ **park** *n* parc d'attractions *m*

analog *adj* analogique; ~**-digital** *adj* analogique-numérique

analogical *adj* analogique

analyse *vt* BrE analyser

analysis *n* analyse *f*; (account, report) analyse *f*, dépouillement *m*; **in the final** ~ en fin de compte; ~ **book** *n* (Acc) livre de comptes *m*; ~ **of cost variances** analyse des écarts de coûts *f*; ~ **of costs by nature** répartition par nature des charges d'exploitation *f*

analyst *n* analyste *mf*

analytic *adj* analytique; ~ **accounting** *n* comptabilité analytique *f*; ~ **process** *n* processus analytique *m*, procédé analytique *m*

analytical *adj* analytique; ~ **auditing** *n* audit analytique *m*, contrôle des comptes analytique *m*

analyze *vt* AmE ▸**analyse** BrE

anarchism *n* anarchisme *m*

ancestor *n* ancêtre *mf*

anchor *n* (Media) présentateur/-trice *m/f*; (Transp) ancre *f*

anchorage *n* ancrage *m*, mouillage *m*; ~ **charges** *n pl* droits de mouillage *m pl*

ancillary *adj* (costs) accessoire; (service, operation, department) auxiliaire; ~ **operations** *n pl* (Gen Comm) services auxiliaires *m pl*; (Mgmnt) services d'intendance *m pl*; ~ **services** *n pl* services accessoires *m pl*; ~ **staff** *n pl* personnel auxiliaire *m*

anecdotal *adj* (evidence) anecdotique

angel *n* commanditaire *mf*

angle *n* (Gen Comm, Math) angle *m*; (point of view) point de vue *m*; **from every** ~ sous tous les angles; **seen from this** ~ sous cet angle

Anglo-French *adj* anglo-français

annex AmE ▸**annexe** BrE

annexe¹ *n* BrE (of building, document) annexe *f*

annexe² *vt* (territory, land, country) annexer

annexed *adj* (Law) ci-inclus, ci-joint

anniversary *n* anniversaire *m*

annotate *vt* annoter

announce *vt* annoncer; (details) faire connaître, faire part de; (profit, figures) enregistrer, publier

announcement *n* annonce *f*; (Admin) (written) avis *m*; **make an** ~ faire une annonce; ~ **of sale** avis de vente *m*

announcer *n* annonceur/-euse *m/f*; (on radio) présentateur/-trice *m/f*; (on TV) speaker/-erine *m/f*

annual *adj* annuel/-elle; **at an** ~ **rate** au taux annuel; **on an** ~ **basis** annuellement; ~ **abstract of statistics** *n* rapport annuel de statistiques économiques *m*; ~ **accounts** *n pl* comptes annuels *m pl*, comptes sociaux *m pl*; ~ **adjustment** *n* rajustement annuel *m*; ~ **basis** (statistics) base annuelle *f*; ~ **cash flow** *n* marge brute d'autofinancement annuelle *f*, mouvements de trésorerie annuels *m pl*; ~ **certificate** *n* rapport annuel des commissaires aux comptes *m*, rapport d'exercice *m*; ~ **depreciation** *n* amortissement annuel *m*; ~ **depreciation charge** *n* dotation annuelle aux amortissements *f*; ~ **dividend** *n* dividende annuel *m*; ~ **earnings** *n pl* (Acc, Tax) résultat de l'exercice *m*; ~ **fee** *n* honoraires annuels *m pl*; ~ **general meeting** *n* BrE assemblée générale annuelle *f*; ~ **holiday** *n* BrE congé annuel *m*; ~ **installment** AmE, ~ **instalment** BrE *n* annuité *f*, versement annuel *m*; ~ **leave** *n* congé annuel *m*; ~ **meeting** *n* assemblée générale annuelle *f*; ~ **meeting of shareholders** *n* assemblée ordinaire annuelle des actionnaires *f*; ~ **net cash inflow** *n* autofinancement net annuel *m*; ~ **net profit** *n* bénéfice de l'exercice *m*, bénéfice net annuel *m*; ~ **percentage rate** *n* taux annualisé *m*, taux d'intérêt annuel *m*, taux effectif global *m*; ~ **premium** *n* (Ins) prime annuelle *f*; ~ **rate** *n* taux annuel *m*; ~ **report** *n* rapport annuel *m*, rapport d'exercice *m*; ~ **review** *n* révision annuelle *f*; ~ **salary** *n* salaire annuel *m*; ~ **salary review** *n* révision annuelle des salaires *f*; ~ **sales conference** *n* conférence annuelle de la force de vente *f*; ~ **turnover** *n* chiffre d'affaires de l'exercice *m*; ~ **vacation** *n* AmE congé annuel *m*; ~ **wage** *n* salaire annuel *m*; ~ **yield** *n* rendement annuel *m*

annualize *vt* annualiser

annualized *adj* calculé annuellement, présenté par année; ~ **hours** *n pl* heures annualisées *f pl*; ~ **hours system** *n* système d'heures annualisées *m*; ~ **percentage rate** *n* taux annualisé *m*, taux d'intérêt annuel *m*; ~ **rate** *n* (of interest) taux pour un an *m*

annually *adv* (cost, earn, yield, produce) annuellement, par an; (take place, occur, organize) tous les ans

annuitant *n* (life annuity) crédit-rentier *m*, rentier *m*

annuity *n* annuité *f*; (Ins) rente *f*; ~ **in**

advance *n* rente payable d'avance *f*; ~ **in arrears** *n* rente payable à terme échu *f*; ~ **assurance** *n* assurance de rente *f*; ~ **bond** *n* obligation de rente *f*; ~ **fund** *n* rente *f*; ~ **income** *n* revenu de rente *m*; ~ **insurance** *n* assurance-vie avec option rente viagère *f*; ~ **plan** *n* option rente viagère *f*; ~ **policy** *n* contrat de rente viagère *m*; ~ **in reversion** *n* rente réversible *f*

annul *vt* (Law) abolir, abroger; (contract) annuler, résilier; (decision, judgement) annuler, casser

annulling *adj* qui annule

annulment *n* (of contract) annulation *f*, résiliation *f*; (Law) abolition *f*, abrogation *f*; (of decision, judgement) annulation *f*, cassation *f*

anomaly *n* anomalie *f*

anonymity *n* anonymat *m*

anonymous *adj* anonyme; **remain ~** garder l'anonymat

Ansaphone® *n* répondeur (téléphonique) *m*

ANSI *abbr* (▸**American National Standards Institute**) *association américaine de normalisation*, ≈ AFNOR *f*

answer[1] *n* réponse *f*; **get an ~** obtenir une réponse; **in ~ to your letter** suite à votre lettre; **there's no ~** (on telephone) ça ne répond pas

answer[2] [1] *vt* (person, call, letter, need, question) répondre à; (Law) (charge) répondre de; ~ **the door** aller *or* venir ouvrir la porte; ~ **the phone** répondre au téléphone
[2] *vi* donner une réponse; ~ **to sb for sth** répondre de qch à qn; ~ **for** (person) se porter garant de; (action, behaviour) répondre de; (safety) répondre de, être responsable de

answerable *adj* **be ~ to sb** être responsable devant qn; **be ~ for** (decision, action) être responsable de; **they are ~ to no-one** ils n'ont de comptes à rendre à personne

answerback code *n* indicatif *m*

answering machine *n* répondeur (téléphonique) *m*

answerphone *n* répondeur (téléphonique) *m*

antagonistic *adj* antagoniste

ante- *pref* avant

antedate *vt* (document, cheque) antidater; (event) précéder

antedated *adj* antidaté

antedating *n* antidatation *f*

antialiasing *n* (Comp) anticrènelage *m*

anti-avoidance legislation *n* législation anti-évasion fiscale *f*

anticipate *vt* (bill, debt) anticiper; (later work, development) préfigurer; (problem, delay) prévoir, s'attendre à; (reaction, need, result, demand) anticiper; **as anticipated** comme prévu

anticipated *adj* attendu, prévu; ~ **demand** *n* demande escomptée *f*, demande prévue *f*; ~ **growth rate** *n* taux de

croissance prévu *m*; ~ **profit** *n* bénéfices prévus *m pl*; ~ **repayment** *n* remboursement anticipé *m*; ~ **sale** *n* (Stock) vente anticipée *f*; ~ **sales** *n pl* ventes prévues *f pl*

anticipation *n* (Gen Comm) attente *f*; (of profits, income) anticipation *f*, expectative *f*, jouissance anticipée *f*; (Econ) anticipation *f*, prévision *f*; (Law, Prop) droit d'anticipation *m*, exercice anticipé d'un droit *m*; **thanking you in ~** en vous remerciant d'avance; **in ~ of a fall in the price** en prévision d'une chute du cours; **in ~ of your reply** dans l'attente de votre réponse

anticipatory *adj* **take ~ action** prendre des mesures par anticipation; ~ **breach of contract** *n* rupture anticipée de contrat *f*; ~ **pricing** *n* anticipation des prix *f*, fixation des prix par anticipation *f*

anticompetitive *adj* anticoncurrentiel/-ielle; ~ **practices** *n pl* pratiques anticoncurrentielles *f pl*, pratiques déloyales *f pl*

anticyclical *adj* (Econ) anticyclique, conjoncturel/-elle

antidumping *n* antidumping *m*; ~ **agreement** *n* accord antidumping *m*

anti-inflation *adj* (policy, programme) anti-inflationniste; ~ **stance** *n* attitude anti-inflationniste *f*, position anti-inflationniste *f*

anti-inflationary *adj* anti-inflationniste

antimonopoly legislation *n pl* lois anti-monopoles *f pl*, législation anti-monopoles *f*

anti-strike ballot *n* vote contre la grève *m*

antitheft device *n* antivol *m*

antitrust *adj* antitrust; ~ **commission** *n* commission anti-monopole *f*; ~ **law** *n* loi antitrust *f*

antivirus software *n* logiciel antivirus *m*

any: ~ **other business** points divers *m pl*

AO *abbr* (**account of**) pour le compte de

AOB *abbr* (**any other business**) points divers *m pl*

AOCB *abbr* (**any other competent business**) autres questions à l'ordre du jour *f pl*, questions diverses *f pl*

AON clause *n* (▸**all-or-nothing clause**) (Stock) clause tout ou rien *f*

APACS *abbr* UK (▸**Association for Payment Clearing Services**) *Association de services de compensation des paiements f*

apartment *n* AmE appartement *m*; ~ **building** *n* AmE immeuble *m*

API *abbr* UK (**alternative participation instrument**) instrument de participation différent *m*; (▸**application program interface**) IPA *f* (interface de programmation d'applications)

apiece *adv* (for each person) chacun/-e *m/f*; (for each item) (la) pièce

apologize vi présenter ses excuses, s'excuser; ~ **for** s'excuser de; ~ **to sb for sth** faire ses excuses à qn pour qch, s'excuser de qch auprès de qn

apology n excuse f; **make an** ~ s'excuser; **offer an** ~ présenter ses excuses; **send one's apologies** envoyer ses excuses

apparatus n (equipment) appareil m; (organization) machine f

apparel n habillement m

apparent adj (seeming) apparent; (clear) évident; **become** ~ **that** devenir évident que; ~ **authority** n (Law) mandat apparent m; ~ **good order of goods** bon état apparent des marchandises m

appeal[1] n (of plan, product, idea) attrait m; (to public) appel m; (Law) appel m; ~ **court** n cour d'appel f; ~ **for funds** n appel de fonds m; ~ **proceedings** n pl procédure d'appel f; ~ **product** n produit d'appel m; ~ **for tenders** n appel d'offres m

appeal[2] vi (Law) faire appel; ~ **against a judgement** appeler d'un jugement, faire appel d'une décision; ~ **for funds** faire un appel de fonds; ~ **for tenders** faire un appel d'offres; ~ **to** (attract) attirer, plaire à; (advertising, broadcasting) s'adresser à; (product, flavour, colour) plaire à

appeals: ~ **court** n cour d'appel f; ~ **procedure** n procédure d'appel f

appear vi (become visible) apparaître; (arrive) arriver; (be printed, published) paraître; (be listed, recorded) figurer, paraître; (come before a court) comparaître; ~ **to be/do** avoir l'air d'être/de faire; ~ **before the court** comparaître devant le tribunal

appellate court n cour d'appel f

append vt joindre; (document) annexer, joindre; (signature) apposer

appended adj ci-inclus, ci-joint

appendix n annexe f, appendice m

applet n (Comp) appliquette f, microprogramme m, applet m

appliance n appareil m

applicable adj (argument) valable; (rule, requirement) en vigueur; ~ **to** applicable à; **be** ~ **to** s'appliquer à; **not** ~ ne s'applique pas, non-applicable; **if** ~ le cas échéant

applicant n candidat/-e m/f; (for licence, visa, asylum, grant) demandeur/-euse m/f; (for trademark) déposant/-e m/f; (for job) candidat/-e m/f, postulant/-e m/f; (Law) demandeur m, requérant m; (for shares) souscripteur m

application n (for job, licence) candidature f, demande f; (for grant, visa, asylum) demande f; (of idea) application f; (of technique) mise en œuvre f; (Comp) application f; (Law) application f; (Patents) demande f; (Stock) (for shares) demande de souscription f; **make a job** ~ poser sa candidature à un poste; **fill out a job** ~ remplir un formulaire de candidature; **letter of** ~ lettre de candidature f; **make an**

~ **for** (asylum, passport, transfer grant, registration) déposer une demande de; ~ **for admission** (to the stock exchange) demande d'admission f; ~ **form** n (for credit card, passport, loan) formulaire de demande m; (for job) formulaire de candidature m; (for membership, course) formulaire d'inscription m; (for educational institution) dossier d'inscription m; ~ **of funds** emplois m pl, utilisation des fonds f; ~ **for listing** demande d'inscription à la cote f; ~ **money** n versement de souscription m; ~ **program interface** n interface de programmation d'applications f; ~ **for quotation** demande d'introduction en bourse f; ~ **right** n droit de souscription m; ~ **server** n (Comput) serveur d'applications m; ~ **service provider** n fournisseur de services d'application m; ~ **for shares** demande de souscription d'actions f, souscription d'actions f; ~**s software** n logiciel d'application m, programme d'application m

applied: ~ **cost** n coût affecté m, coût imputé m, coût réparti m; ~ **economics** n + sing v économie appliquée f; ~ **overhead** n frais généraux imputés m pl; ~ **research** n recherche appliquée f

apply [1] vt (principle, rule, method) appliquer; (sum, rent) imputer; ~ **revenue to a period** rattacher des produits à un exercice [2] vi (for a job) faire une demande, proposer sa candidature; (penalty, law) être en vigueur; ~ **to sth** (be applicable) être applicable à; ~ **to do** demander à faire; ~ **to sb for sth** s'adresser à qn pour obtenir qch; ~ **in person** se présenter; ~ **in writing to...** envoyez votre candidature par lettre manuscrite à ...; ~ **at the office** adressez-vous au bureau; ~ **for** (passport, licence, grant, patent) demander; ~ **for a job** se porter candidat à un poste, poser sa candidature pour un emploi; ~ **for a loan** faire une demande de prêt, souscrire à un emprunt; ~ **for membership** faire une demande d'adhésion; ~ **for shares** faire une demande de souscription d'actions

appoint vt (date) fixer; (person) désigner, nommer; (committee) constituer; (place) désigner; (new staff) engager; ~ **sb to a position** nommer qn à un poste

appointed adj (agent, chairman) attitré, nommé; **at the** ~ **time** à l'heure convenue; ~ **day** n jour fixé m; ~ **stockist** n stockiste attitré m

appointee n (executive) personne nommée f; (junior) candidat/-e retenu/-e m/f

appointive adj AmE obtenu par nomination

appointment n (job) poste m; (nomination) désignation f, nomination f; (meeting, consultation) rendez-vous m; **by** ~ **only** sur rendez-vous uniquement; **keep an** ~ aller à un rendez-vous; **make an** ~ **with sb** prendre rendez-vous avec qn; **take up an** ~ **as director** prendre ses fonctions comme directeur

appointments vacant n pl offres d'emploi f pl

apportion vt (**Acc**) ventiler; (costs) affecter; (land, property) lotir, partager, répartir; (**Stock**) (shares) répartir; (blame) répartir; ~ **the average** (**Ins**) (marine) répartir les avaries

apportionment n (**Acc**) affectation f, répartition f, ventilation f; (**Patents**) répartition f; (**Prop**) lotissement m, partage m; (of property expenses) affectation f, répartition f; ~ **of costs** affectation des frais f, répartition des charges f, ventilation des coûts f; ~ **of funds** allocation des fonds f

appraisal n estimation f, évaluation f; (by expert) expertise f; (of job performance) évaluation f; (**Prop**) estimation f, évaluation f; **make an** ~ **of** évaluer; ~ **of damage** n expertise des dommages f; ~ **report** n rapport d'expertise m

appraise vt (**Gen Comm**) juger; (**Fin**) estimer, évaluer; (project, job performance, employee) évaluer; ~ **damages** expertiser les dommages, faire une évaluation des dégâts

appraised value n valeur estimative f, valeur estimée f

appraisee n (**HRM**) personne évaluée f

appraisement n estimation f

appraiser n (**Fin, Insur, Prop**) expert m; (**HRM**) personne responsable de l'évaluation f

appreciable adj appréciable

appreciate ① vt (realize) se rendre compte de, être conscient de; (advice, help) apprécier ② vi (asset) augmenter en valeur, prendre de la valeur; (value) monter

appreciated surplus n plus-value f

appreciation n (**Acc, Prop, Tax**), accroissement de la valeur m, plus-value f; (of currency, share) hausse f; (gratitude) remerciement m; (awareness) compréhension f; ~ **in value** valorisation f

apprentice¹ n élève mf; (in crafts) apprenti/ -e m/f

apprentice²: ~ **sb to sb** mettre qn en apprentissage chez qn, placer qn comme apprenti chez qn; **be** ~**d to sb** être en apprentissage chez qn

apprenticeship n apprentissage m

appro n: **on** ~ (infrml) à l'essai

approach¹ n (method) approche f, méthode f; (proposal) proposition f; (overture) démarche f; **make approaches to sb** faire des démarches auprès de qn

approach² vt contacter; ~ **sb about sth** contacter qn au sujet de qch

appropriate¹ adj (suitable) approprié; (department, authority) compétent; ~ **for sth** convenant à qch, propre à qch; **be** ~ **for** convenir à

appropriate² vt (funds, resources) affecter; (resources) affecter; (**Fin, Law**) (for own use) s'approprier

appropriateness n applicabilité f, à-propos m

appropriation n (**Acc, Econ**) (of funds) affectation f, dotation f; (of resources) affectation f, allocation f; (**Law**) (of funds) appropriation f; (budget, fund) budget m; ~ **account** n compte d'affectation des bénéfices m; ~ **of advertising** n budget de la publicité m; ~**s for contingencies** n pl provisions pour éventualités f pl; ~ **control** n contrôle des crédits m; ~ **of income** n affectation des bénéfices f

Appropriation Act UK, **Appropriation Bill** US n loi de finances f, projet de loi de finances m

approval n (**Gen Comm**) approbation f, assentiment m; (of accounts) approbation f; (of loan) autorisation f; (of contract, request) agrément m; (of machine, product, process) homologation f; **for** ~ pour approbation; **give one's** ~ **to** donner son approbation à; **have the** ~ **of** obtenir l'approbation de; **on** ~ à l'essai; **subject to sb's** ~ soumis à l'approbation de qn; ~**s procedure** procédure d'approbation f

approve vt (**Admin**) approuver; (loan) autoriser; (action, accounts, minutes) approuver; (contract, request) agréer; (decision, document, plan) approuver, homologuer, ratifier; (**Ins, Tax**) agréer; (**Pol**) approuver; ~ **of** apprécier

approved adj (**Gen Comm**) agréé, approuvé; (decision, document) ratifié; (**Admin**) approuvé; (**Bank**) autorisé; (**Ins**) (marine) agréé, approuvé; (**Tax**) agréé; ~ **code of practice** n déontologie f; ~ **list** n liste agréée f; ~ **premises** n pl locaux homologués m pl; ~ **price** n prix approuvé m; ~ **share** n action approuvée f

approx. abbr (▸**approximately**) approximativement, environ

approximate¹ adj approximatif/-ive; ~ **figure** n, ~ **number** n chiffre approximatif m; ~ **price** n prix approximatif m

approximate² ① vt (be close to) approcher de; (resemble) ressembler à ② vi ~ **to** (come close to) approcher de; (resemble) ressembler à

approximately adv approximativement, environ

approximation n approximation f; (of international policies) rapprochement m

appurtenant adj accessoire, annexe

APR abbr (▸**annual percentage rate**, ▸**annualized percentage rate**) taux annualisé m, taux d'intérêt annuel m

apron n (at airport) aire de stationnement f

aptitude n aptitude f; ~ **test** n test d'aptitude m

AR abbr (**Ins**) (**all risks**) tous risques

arbiter n (**Law**) arbitre m, médiateur/-trice m/f

arbitrage n arbitrage m, opération ···❭

d'arbitrage *f*; ~ **bonds** *n pl* US obligations d'arbitrage *f pl*; ~ **dealer** *n* arbitragiste *mf*; ~ **house** *n* maison d'arbitrage *f*; ~ **stocks** *n pl* actions d'arbitrage *f pl*; ~ **trader** *n* arbitragiste *mf*; ~ **trading** *n* arbitrage *m*, opérations d'arbitrage *f pl*

arbitrageur *n* arbitragiste *mf*

arbitral *adj* arbitral; ~ **award** *n* sentence arbitrale *f*

arbitrary *adj* (income, result, taxation) arbitraire

arbitrate *vi* arbitrer, trancher

arbitration *n* arbitrage *m*, médiation *f*; **go to** ~ aller aux prud'hommes; (refer a case to arbitration) soumettre une affaire à l'arbitrage; ~ **agreement** *n* convention d'arbitrage *f*; ~ **award** *n* sentence arbitrale *f*; ~ **board** *n* commission d'arbitrage *f*, instance d'arbitrage *f*; ~ **clause** *n* clause compromissoire *f*, clause d'arbitrage *f*; ~ **committee** *n* commission d'arbitrage *f*; ~ **proceedings** *n pl* mesures d'arbitrage *f pl*, procédure d'arbitrage *f*; ~ **transaction** *n* opération d'arbitrage *f*; ~ **tribunal** *n* tribunal d'arbitrage *m*

arbitrator *n* arbitre *m*, médiateur/-trice *m/f*

arcade *n* (for shopping) galerie marchande *f*

architect *n* architecte *mf*

architecture *n* architecture *f*

archive[1] *n* archive *f*; ~ **file** *n* fichier d'archives *m*; ~ **storage** *n* stockage des archives *m*

archive[2] *vt* archiver

archiving *n* archivage *m*

archivist *n* archiviste *mf*

area *n* (Econ) région *f*; (surface) superficie *f*; (in town) quartier *m*; (of knowledge) champ *m*, domaine *m*; (of operation, specialization) domaine *m*, secteur *m*; (designated space) zone *f*; (Pol) région *f*; **in the London** ~ dans la région de Londres; ~ **of doubt/concern** sujet de doute/d'inquiétude *m*; ~ **code** *n* (telephone) indicatif de zone *m*, indicatif interurbain *m*; ~ **of expertise** domaine d'expertise *m*, domaine de spécialisation *m*; ~ **manager** *n* directeur/-trice régional/-e *m/f*, chef de région *m*; ~ **of responsibility** domaine de responsabilité *m*; ~ **salesperson** *n* voyageur représentant placier régional *m*, vendeur/-euse régional/-e *m/f*, représentant/-e régional/-e *m/f*

Area Advisory Group *n* UK *groupe consultatif de zone visant à développer les marchés étrangers vers lesquels les sociétés britanniques veulent exporter*

arguable *adj* contestable

argue [1] *vt* discuter (de); ~ **the point** débattre la question; ~ **one's case** exposer ses arguments, plaider sa cause; ~ **the case for** exposer les raisons en faveur de; ~ **that** soutenir que

[2] *vi* (put one's case) argumenter; ~ **in favour**

of parler en faveur de; ~ **in favour of/ against doing** exposer les raisons pour faire/ ne pas faire

ARI *abbr* (▸**accounting rate of interest**) TIC *m* (taux d'intérêt comptable)

arithmetic *n* (subject) arithmétique *f*; (calculations) calcul *m*; ~ **mean** *n* moyenne arithmétique *f*; ~ **progression** *n* progression arithmétique *f*

arm *n* (Econ) bras *m*

arm's-length *adj* non privilégié, sans lien de dépendance; ~ **competition** *n* concurrence libre *f*; ~ **price** *n* prix de pleine concurrence *m*; ~ **transaction** *n* transaction au prix du marché *f*

around *adv* (approximately) environ; (with time) vers

around-the-clock *adj* (service) 24 heures sur 24

arrange *vt* (meeting, event, schedule) organiser; (date, price, appointment) fixer; (loan, mortgage) accorder; ~ **an interview** convenir d'un entretien

arrangement *n* (layout) disposition *f*; (agreement) accord *m*; (plan) dispositions *f pl*; **price by** ~ prix à débattre; **come to an** ~ **with** parvenir à un accord avec; **financial/ security** ~**s** mesures financières/de sécurité *f pl*; **make** ~**s** prendre des mesures; **make** ~**s to do** s'arranger pour faire; **make** ~**s for doing** prendre des dispositions pour faire; **under the** ~ selon l'accord; ~ **fee** *n* (Bank) commission de montage *f*, frais de montage *m pl*

arranger *n* (Fin) organisateur/-trice *m/f*

array *n* (of figures, data) tableau *m*; (of measures, incentives) panoplie *f*; ~ **of products** gamme de produits *f*, éventail de produits *m*

arrearage *n* (Fin) arriéré *m*, arrérages *m pl*, dettes *f pl*; (Stock) arriéré *m*

arrears *n pl* (money owed) arriéré *m*, arrérages *m pl*; (in wages) rappel *m*; **be in** ~ être en retard dans ses paiements; **fall into** ~ s'arriérer; **mortgage** ~ arriérés de crédit-logement *m pl*; **rent** ~ arrérages de loyer *m pl*; ~ **of interest** arriéré d'intérêts *m*

arrest[1] *n* (Law) arrestation *f*; (Ins) (marine) arrestation *f*; **be under** ~ être en état d'arrestation

arrest[2] *vt* (Law) arrêter

arrival *n* arrivée *f*

arrive *vi* arriver

arson *n* incendie volontaire *m*

art *n* art *m*; ~ **board** *n* (advertising) carton couché *m*; ~ **department** *n* (advertising) service création *m*; ~ **designer** *n* (advertising) graphiste *mf*; ~ **of the possible** (Pol) art du compromis *m*

article *n* (Gen Comm) article *m*; (Law) article *m*, clause *f*; (Media) article *m*; (Comp) (in newsgroups) article (de forum) *m*

articled clerk *n* UK avocat/-e stagiaire *m/f*

articles: ~ **of agreement** n pl (Transp) rôle d'équipage m; ~ **of association** n pl statuts m pl; ~ **of incorporation** n pl statuts m pl

articulated: ~ **lorry** n semi-remorque m; ~ **vehicle** n véhicule articulé m

artificial adj artificiel/-ielle, factice; ~ **barrier to entry** n (Econ) barrière non-tarifaire à l'importation f; ~ **exchange rate** n taux de change artificiel m; ~ **intelligence** n intelligence artificielle f

Arts Council n UK organisme public britannique de promotion des arts

artwork n illustrations f pl; (in advertising) document m

A/S abbr (Bank) (**at sight**) sur présentation, à vue; (**after sight**) de vue

ASA abbr (UK) (▸**Advertising Standards Authority**) ≈ BVP m (Bureau de vérification de la publicité)

a.s.a.p. abbr (**as soon as possible**) aussitôt que possible, dans les meilleurs délais, dès que possible, le plus tôt possible

ascending: in ~ **order** en ordre croissant

ascertain vt (fact) constater, vérifier; (price, truth) établir

ascertainable adj (group, person) identifiable

ascertained: ~ **fact** n fait établi m; ~ **goods** n pl marchandises vérifiées f pl

ASCII abbr (**American Standard Code for Information Interchange**) (Comp) ASCII m

ascots n pl UK ascots m pl

ascribe vt ~ **sth to sb** attribuer qch à qn

ASE abbr (▸**American Stock Exchange**) la deuxième bourse de New York où sont listées les valeurs qui n'apparaissent pas au New York Stock Exchange

A share n action ordinaire sans droit de vote f

Asia n Asie f

Asian adj asiatique; ~ **American** n Americain/-e d'origine asiatique m/f; ~ **Briton** n Britannique originaire du sous-continent indien m

ask ① vt demander à ② vi demander

asked price n (Prop) prix demandé m; (Stock) cours vendeur m

asking price n prix de départ m

ASP abbr (▸**application service provider**) FSA m (fournisseur de services d'application)

aspect n aspect m

assay[1] n essai m; ~ **mark** n (on gold and silver) marque d'essai f

assay[2] vt (metals) analyser, essayer

assembling n (Ind) montage m

assembly n (Admin) réunion f; (Ind) montage m; (Pol) (body) assemblée f; (meeting) réunion f, séance f; ~ **line** n chaîne de montage f; ~ **line worker** n travailleur/-euse à la chaîne m/f; ~ **plant** n usine de montage f

assent n consentement m; (of parliament) assentiment m

assert vt affirmer

assertion n affirmation f, assertion f

assertiveness training n entraînement à la prise de parole m

assess vt (loss, damage) estimer; (person, work) estimer, évaluer; (Mgmnt) évaluer; (Tax) (person) imposer; ~ **tax** déterminer l'impôt à payer, fixer la cotisation d'impôt; **be** ~**ed for tax** être imposé

assessed: ~ **income** n revenu imposé m; ~ **tax** n cotisation d'impôt f, impôt fixé m, impôt établi m

assessment n (evaluation) appréciation f; (of tax) détermination de l'assiette d'imposition f; (of compensation, damage) estimation f, fixation f, évaluation f; (HRM) évaluation f; (Tax) cotisation f, imposition f; ~ **center** AmE, ~ **centre** BrE n centre d'évaluation m, centre de bilan professionnel m

assessor n (Ins) (marine) expert m; (Tax) répartiteur m

asset n (Acc, Fin) élément d'actif m; (fixed) immobilisation f; (Econ) actif m; (strong point) atout m; (Stock) actif m; ~**-backed investment** n investissement garanti par des actifs m; ~**-based financing** n financement reposant sur l'actif m; ~ **coverage** n (Acc) ratio d'actifs m; (Stock) couverture par l'actif f; ~ **management** n gestion de l'actif f; ~ **management company** n (Fin) société de gestion f; ~ **manager** n gestionnaire de l'actif mf; ~ **mix** n composition de l'actif f; ~ **price inflation** n inflation du prix de l'actif f; ~ **sale** n cession d'actifs f; ~ **stripping** n (Acc) cannibalisation f, démantèlement de l'actif m; (Econ) dégraissage d'actifs m; ~ **swap** n croisement d'actifs m, échange d'actifs m; ~ **turnover** n mouvements de l'actif m pl, rotation de l'actif f; ~ **valuation** n évaluation des immobilisations f; ~ **value** n total de l'actif m, valeur de l'actif f

assets n pl (Gen Comm, Stock) actif m; (Acc, Fin) biens m pl; (of company) patrimoine m; ~ **and drawbacks** avantages et inconvénients m pl; ~ **held abroad** avoirs à l'étranger m pl; ~ **and liabilities management** n gestion actif-passif f; ~ **and liabilities statement** n bilan m

assign vt (Acc) (costs) imputer; (role, value, responsibility) attribuer; (time, date, place) fixer; (Law) céder, faire cession de, transférer, transmettre; ~ **a task to sb** affecter qn à une tâche; ~ **sb to do** désigner qn pour faire

assignable adj cessible, transférable; ~ **credit** n crédit transférable m

assignee n (Acc, Law Patents) cessionnaire m/f; ~ **in bankruptcy** syndic de faillite m

assignment n (mission) mission f; (diplomatic, military) poste m; (Acc) (of receivables) cession f; (of money) allocation f; (task) mission f; (of role, responsibility) attribution f; (Law) cession f, transfert m; (Patents) cession f; (Prop) transfert m; (Stock) assignation f; **be sent on an ∼** être envoyé en mission; **∼ of advertising expenditure** n allocation du budget publicitaire f; **∼ day** n (Stock) jour de transfert des biens m; (options) jour d'assignation m; **∼ of lease** n cession de bail f; **∼ notice** n (Stock) avis d'assignation m, avis de transfert m

assignor n cédant m

assimilation n assimilation f

assistance n aide f, assistance f

assistant n adjoint/-e m/f, assistant/-e m/f, auxiliaire mf; **∼ controller** n (shipping) contrôleur adjoint m; **∼ director** n directeur/-trice adjoint/-e m/f; **∼ director general** n directeur/-trice général/-e adjoint/-e m/f; **∼ head of section** n adjoint/-e du chef de section m/f, chef d'unité adjoint m; **∼ manager** n directeur/-trice adjoint/-e m/f, sous-directeur/-trice m/f; **∼ to manager** n adjoint/-e m/f

assisted area n région assistée f, zone d'assistance f

associate¹ n associé/-e m/f; **∼ company** n société affiliée f, société apparentée f; **∼ editor** n rédacteur/-trice d'édition m/f; **∼ member** n membre associé m

associate² [1] vt associer; **∼ sth with** associer qch à [2] vi **∼ with** (person, group) fréquenter; (company, partner) s'associer avec, s'associer à

associated adj associé; **be ∼ with** être associé à; **∼ account** n compte associé m; **∼ company** n filiale f, société affiliée f, société associée f; **∼ corporations** n pl corporations associées f pl; **∼ person** n UK (Stock) associé/-e m/f

Associated Press n US les presses associées

association n (body, group) association f, société f; **in ∼ with** en association avec; (between people, organizations) relations f pl; (between ideas) association f; **a close ∼** une étroite association; **∼ bargaining** n négociation avec association patronale f, négociation collective f; **∼ subscription** n cotisation à une association f

Association: ∼ of British Chambers of Commerce n association des chambres de commerce britanniques; **∼ of British Travel Agents** n association des agents de voyage britanniques; **∼ for Payment Clearing Services** n UK Association de services de compensation des paiements f

assortment n (of products, sizes, colours) assortiment m; (of people) mélange m; **in an ∼ of colours** dans différents coloris; **∼ of goods** assortiment de produits m, choix de marchandises m

asst abbr (▸**assistant**) adjoint/-e m/f, assistant/-e m/f, auxiliaire mf

assume vt (suppose) supposer; (commitment) assumer; (risk, power) assumer, prendre; **∼ no responsibility for** dégager sa responsabilité de (frml); **∼ responsibility for** prendre en charge

assumption n hypothèse f, supposition f

assurance n assurance f

assured adj assuré; **the ∼ n** (Ins) l'assuré/-e m/f

assurer n assureur m

asylum n asile m

asymmetry n asymétrie f

asynchronous adj asynchrone

at prep (Fin) au taux de; **as ∼** (with date) au; **∼ sign** n (Comp) arobase m

ATA abbr US (**Air Transport Association**) association de transport aérien des États-Unis, ≈ DGAC f (Direction générale de l'aviation civile)

ATC abbr (▸**air traffic control**) (activity) contrôle du trafic aérien m; (building) tour de contrôle f

ATM abbr (▸**automated teller machine**) GAB m (guichet automatique de banque); **∼ card** n carte de retrait f

atmosphere n (Econ, Pol) climat m; (Envir) atmosphère f

ATS abbr (Bank) (UK) (**automatic transfer service**) service de virement automatique m

attach vt (Gen Comm) attacher; (document) joindre, envoyer en pièce jointe; **∼ importance to** attacher de l'importance à, prêter de l'importance à

attaché n attaché/-e m/f

attached adj ci-inclus, ci-joint

attachment n (in email) pièce jointe f, annexe f; (Acc, Bank) effet m; (Fin, Law, Tax) effet m, papillon m

attend vt (meeting) assister à; **∼ to** (customer, problem) s'occuper de

attendance n (Gen Comm) fréquentation f; (presence) présence f; **trade fair ∼ is falling** la fréquentation des salons est en baisse; **∼ fees** n pl jetons de présence m pl; **∼ record** n taux de présence m

attention n attention f; **attract/hold sb's ∼** attirer/retenir l'attention de qn; **for the ∼ of** à l'attention de; **∼ value** n (advertising) valeur d'accroche f

attest vt (declare) attester, certifier; (authenticate) légaliser; **∼ to** (prove) témoigner de; (affirm) attester

attestation n (Law) attestation f; (of signature) certification f, légalisation f

at-the-money: ∼ call option n option d'achat au jeu f, option d'achat à parité f; **∼ put option** n option de vente au jeu f, option de vente à parité f

attitude n attitude f; ~ **survey** n enquête d'opinion f

attorney n US (representative) mandataire mf, représentant/-e m/f; ~**-at-law** n US avocat/-e m/f

Attorney General n US ≈ ministre de la Justice mf; UK ≈ procureur de la République m

attract vt (Gen Comm) (person, buyer, investment, criticism) attirer; (Fin) (interest) comporter; ~ **new business** attirer de nouveaux contrats; ~ **sb's attention** attirer l'attention de qn

attractive¹ adj (for investors) attractif/-ive, attrayant; (idea, plan) séduisant, attrayant; ~ **offer** n proposition alléchante f; ~ **terms** n pl conditions intéressantes f pl

attributable adj: ~ **to** imputable à

attribute¹ n (Gen Comm) attribut m, caractéristique f; ~ **sampling** n (in auditing) échantillon représentatif m; (in statistics) échantillonnage d'attribut m, échantillonnage de distribution m; (in market research) échantillonnage par attributs m

attribute² vt attribuer; ~ **sth to sb** attribuer qch à qn, imputer qch à qn; **attributed to** attribué à

attribution n attribution f; **not for** ~ AmE (Media, Pol) de source confidentielle, de source officieuse; ~ **rules** n pl (Tax) règles d'attribution f pl

attrition n (S&M) perte de clientèle f; ~ **rate** n pourcentage de clients perdus m, taux d'érosion m

atypical adj atypique

auction¹ n vente aux enchères f, adjudication f; (Stock) vente aux enchères f; **at** ~ aux enchères; **for sale by** ~ en vente aux enchères; ~ **house** n société de commissaires-priseurs f; ~ **market** n marché aux enchères m, marché des adjudications m; ~ **room** n salle des ventes f; ~ **rate** n (of foreign exchange) taux d'adjudication m; ~ **sale** n vente aux enchères f; ~ **site** n (on Internet) site de vente aux enchères m

auction² vt vendre aux enchères; ~ **off** vendre aux enchères

auctioneer n commissaire-priseur m

audience n public m; (for the press) lectorat m; (in advertising) audience f; ~ **measurement** n audimétrie f

audio adj audio; ~ **cassette** n cassette audio f; ~ **tape** n bande magnétique audio f

audiotyping n audiotypie f

audiovisual adj audiovisuel/-elle; ~ **aid** n support audiovisuel m

audit¹ n audit m, vérification f; (of balance sheet) vérification du bilan f; (of tax returns) vérification comptable f; ~ **activity** n UK activité d'audit f, travail d'audit m; ~ **committee** n comité d'audit m, comité de vérification m; ~ **file** n dossier d'audit m; ~ **group** n équipe d'audit f, équipe de contrôle f; ~ **officer** n agent de vérification m, membre de l'équipe d'audit m; ~ **report** n rapport d'audit m, rapport du commissaire aux comptes m; ~ **software** n logiciel d'audit m; ~ **team** n équipe de contrôle f, équipe de vérification f; ~ **trail** n piste d'audit f, piste de révision f

audit² vt auditer, contrôler, réviser

auditable adj vérifiable

Audit Bureau of Circulation n ≈ Office de justification de la diffusion m

audited statement n état comptable vérifié m

auditee n entité soumise à l'audit f

auditing n audit m, certification f, contrôle m, vérification f; ~ **department** n service d'audit m; (within company) service d'audit interne m; ~ **procedure** n procédure de contrôle f

auditor n auditeur m, commissaire aux comptes m; ~**'s report** n rapport d'audit m, rapport du commissaire aux comptes m

augment vt accroître, augmenter

augmentation n augmentation f

augmented GNP n PNB augmenté m

AUP abbr (Comp) (▶**acceptable use policy**) principes d'utilisation acceptable m pl

austerity n austérité f

autarky n autarcie f

authenticate vt (signature) certifier; (Law) légaliser, valider; (Comp) authentifier

authentication n (Comp) authentification f, (of signature) certification f, (Law) légalisation f, validation f

authoring adj (Comp) (package, software) de rédaction

authority n (person, power) autorité f; (Law) autorisation f, mandat m, pouvoir m; ~ **to buy** autorisation d'achat f; **have** ~ **over** avoir de l'ascendant sur; **have the** ~ **to do** avoir toute autorité pour faire; **give sb (the)** ~ **to do** donner à qn l'autorité de faire; **an** ~ **on** une autorité/un expert en matière de; **the authorities** les autorités f pl, les pouvoirs publics m pl

authorization n (Gen Comm) autorisation f, permis m; (Fin) ordonnance f; (Law) autorisation f, pouvoir m; (consent) agrément m; ~ **code** n, ~ **number** n code d'autorisation m, numéro d'autorisation m

authorize vt autoriser; ~ **sb to do** autoriser qn à faire

authorized adj (payment, version, visit, signatory) autorisé; (agency, distributor) agréé; **be** ~ **to sign** avoir la signature; ~ **expenditure to the amount of** dépenses autorisées jusqu'à un plafond de f pl; ~ **agent** n agent fondé de pouvoir m, mandataire mf; ~ **bond** n obligation autorisée f; ~ **capital** n capital ⸺⸽

nominal *m*, capital social *m*; ∼ **capital share** *n* capital social autorisé *m*; ∼ **capital stock** *n* capital social autorisé *m*; ∼ **credit** *n* crédit autorisé *m*; ∼ **dealer** *n* (Stock) dépositaire intermédiaire agréé *m*, négociant en titres agréé *m*; (S&M) distributeur agréé *m*, concessionnaire *mf*; ∼ **person** *n* personne autorisée *f*; ∼ **representative** *n* représentant accrédité *m*, mandataire *mf*; ∼ **share** *n* capital autorisé *m*, valeur autorisée *f*; ∼ **share capital** *n* capital actions autorisé *m*, capital autorisé *m*; ∼ **stock** *n* capital autorisé *m*, valeur autorisée *f*

auto *n* AmE voiture *f*; ∼ **rental** *n* AmE location de voitures *f*

autobank *n* guichet automatique *m*; ∼ **card** *n* carte de guichet automatique *f*

autoeconomy *n* économie autofinancée *f*

autofinancing *n* autofinancement *m*

automate *vt* automatiser

automated *adj* automatisé; ∼ **cash dispenser** *n* distributeur automatique de billets *m*; ∼ **quotation** *n* cotation assistée en continu *f*; ∼ **teller machine** *n* guichet automatique de banque *m*

Automated: ∼ **Clearing House** *n* chambre de compensation automatisée *f*; ∼ **Clearing Settlement System** *n* système de compensation et de règlement automatisé *m*

automatic *adj* automatique; ∼ **cash dispenser** *n* billetterie automatique *f*, distributeur de billets *m*; ∼ **check-off** *n* US prélèvement automatique des cotisations syndicales *m*; ∼ **data processing** *n* traitement automatique des données *m*; ∼ **funds transfer** *n* virement automatique *m*, virement automatique de fonds *m*; ∼ **reinvestment** *n* plan d'épargne avec capitalisation *m*, réinvestissement automatique *m*; ∼ **teller machine** *n* guichet automatique de banque *m*; ∼ **transfer** *n* virement automatique *m*; ∼ **updating** *n* mise à jour automatique *f*; ∼ **withdrawal** *n* retrait automatique *m*

automatically *adv* automatiquement

automation *n* automatisation *f*

automobile *n* AmE voiture *f*; ∼ **insurance** *n* assurance automobile *f*; ∼ **liability insurance** *n* US assurance automobile contre la responsabilité civile *f*

automotive *adj* automobile

autonomous *adj* autonome; ∼ **expenditure** *n* (Econ) dépenses autonomes *f pl*; ∼ **work group** *n* groupe de travail autonome *m*

autonomy *n* autonomie *f*

autopilot *n* pilote automatique *m*

autoresponder *n* (Comp) autorépondeur *m*

autosave *n* (Comp) sauvegarde automatique *f*

aux. *abbr* (▸**auxiliary**) auxiliaire *mf*

auxiliary[1] *adj* auxiliaire

auxiliary[2] *n* auxiliaire *mf*

av. *abbr* (▸**average**) moyenne *f*

availability *n* disponibilité *f*; (Media) temps d'antenne disponible *m*; ∼ **thesis** *n* (Econ) thèse des disponibilités *f*

available *adj* disponible; ∼ **at short notice** disponible sans délai; **make sth ∼ to sb** mettre qch à la disposition de qn; ∼ **assets** *n pl* valeurs disponibles *f pl*; ∼ **balance** *n* solde disponible *m*; ∼ **cash** *n* disponibilités *f pl*, liquidité *f*; ∼ **cash flow** *n* bénéfice disponible *m*, flux de trésorerie disponible *m*; ∼ **funds** *n pl* disponibilités *f pl*, fonds disponibles *m pl*; ∼ **space** *n* espace disponible *m*

avails *n pl* (Bank, Fin) produit *m*

avant-garde *adj* d'avant-garde

avatar *n* (Comp) avatar *m*

avdp. *abbr* (▸**avoirdupois**) avoirdupois *m*

average[1] *adj* moyen/-enne; ∼ **number of copies sold** nombre moyen d'exemplaires vendus

average[2] *n* moyenne *f*; (Stock) indice boursier *m*; **take an ∼** prendre une moyenne; **work out an ∼** faire une moyenne; **with ∼** (Ins) (marine) avec avaries

average[3]: ∼ **down** [1] *vt* (Stock) acheter par échelons de baisse; [2] *vi* (Stock) faire une moyenne à la baisse; ∼ **out** [1] *vt* équilibrer [2] *vi* (cost, profit) faire une moyenne; **their pay averages out at €60 per hour** ils gagnent en moyenne 60€ de l'heure; ∼ **up** [1] *vt* (Stock) acheter par échelons de hausse [2] *vi* (Stock) faire une moyenne à la hausse

average: ∼ **access time** *n* (Comp) temps moyen d'accès *m*; ∼ **adjuster** *n* (Ins) (marine) dispacheur *m*, répartiteur d'avaries *m*; ∼ **adjustment** *n* (Ins) règlement d'avaries *m*; ∼ **amount** *n* montant moyen *m*; ∼ **balance** *n* solde moyen *m*; ∼ **bond** *n* (Ins) compromis d'avaries *m*; ∼ **claim** *n* (Ins) action d'avarie *f*, déclaration d'avarie *f*; ∼ **cost** *n* (Acc) coût moyen *m*; ∼ **costs** *n pl* frais moyens *m pl*; ∼ **daily balance** *n* moyenne des soldes quotidiens *f*; ∼ **income** *n* revenu moyen *m*; ∼ **incremental cost** *n* coût marginal moyen *m*; ∼ **interest rate** *n* taux bancaire moyen *m*; ∼ **life** *n* durée de vie moyenne *f*; ∼ **market price** *n* prix courant *m*, prix du marché *m*; ∼ **net income** *n* revenu net moyen *m*; ∼ **pay** *n* salaire moyen *m*; ∼ **premium** *n* (Ins) prime moyenne *f*; ∼ **price** *n* (Stock) cours moyen *m*; ∼ **rate** *n* taux moyen *m*; ∼ **revenue** *n* chiffre d'affaires moyen *m*, recettes moyennes *f pl*; ∼ **unit cost** *n* coût unitaire moyen *m*; ∼ **wage** *n* salaire moyen *m*; ∼ **working week** *n* BrE, ∼ **workweek** *n* AmE semaine de travail moyenne *f*; ∼ **yield** *n* rendement moyen *m*

averager *n* (Stock) faiseur de moyennes *m*

averaging: ∼ **amount** *n* montant

d'étalement m; ~ **formula** n formule
d'étalement f; ~ **period** n période
d'étalement du revenu f

aviation n aviation f; ~ **fuel** n kérosène
aviation m; ~ **insurance** n assurance-
aviation f; ~ **risk** n risque de transport
aérien m

avoid vt éviter; (tax) éluder, éviter; (Transp)
annuler, éviter

avoidable adj évitable; ~ **cost** n coût
évitable m, frais superflus m pl

avoidance n (Ins, Transp) annulation f; ~
clause n clause résolutoire f

avoirdupois n avoirdupoids m

award¹ n (prize) prix m; (grant) bourse f; (Law)
attribution f; (of a contract) adjudication f; (of
grant, prize) attribution f; **an ~ of damages**
des dommages-intérêts m pl

award² vt (contract) adjuger, octroyer,
attribuer; (increase) accorder; (grant) attribuer;
(prize) décerner; ~ **damages** accorder des
dommages-intérêts

awarder n adjudicateur/-trice m/f

aware adj conscient

awareness n conscience f; **increase public
~ of sth** sensibiliser le public à qch; ~
campaign n campagne de sensibilisation f;
~ **level** n (of brand) niveau de notoriété m

awash adj: ~ **with cash** regorgeant de
liquidités

away from home expenses n pl frais
de déplacement m pl

awning n store m

ax¹ AmE, **axe¹** BrE n get the ~ (infrml)
(person) se faire virer (infrml); (project) être
abandonné

ax² AmE, **axe²** BrE vt (jobs, funding)
supprimer; (plan, projet) abandonner; (worker)
virer (infrml)

axis n axe m; **on the x ~** sur l'axe des x

axle n axe m

AZERTY keyboard n clavier AZERTY m

Bb

B2A abbr (▶**business-to-administration**)
transactions entre une entreprise et une
administration f pl, (commerce) B2A m

B2B abbr (▶**business-to-business**)
commerce interentreprises m, (commerce)
B2B m; ~ **sector** le secteur du commerce
interentreprises m; ~ **applications** les
applications dans le secteur du commerce
interentreprises f pl; ~ **e-commerce** n
commerce électronique interentreprises m;
~ **e-hub** n place de marché électronique
collaborative f; ~ **transactions** n pl
transactions interentreprises f pl

B2B2C abbr (▶**business-to-business-to-
consumer**) commerce interentreprises
orienté client m, (commerce) B2B2C m

B2C abbr (▶**business-to-consumer**)
commerce de professionnel à particulier m,
(commerce) B2C m; ~ **e-commerce** n
commerce électronique grand public m

B2G abbr (▶**business-to-government**)
échanges entre une entreprise et un
gouvernement m pl, (commerce) B2G m

BA abbr (**Bachelor of Arts**) (degree) ≈
licence de lettres f

BAA abbr (▶**British Airports Authority**)
administration des aéroports britanniques

baby: ~ **bond** n US obligation inférieure à
$100; ~ **boom** n baby-boom m; ~ **boomer** n
personne née pendant les années du baby-

boom f; ~**boomers** n pl génération du
baby-boom f

bachelor's degree n licence f

back¹ adv be ~ **within an hour** être de
retour dans une heure; **go ~ to square one**
retourner à la case départ; **go ~ and forth**
faire la navette; **be ~ in control** avoir repris
les commandes; **get one's money ~** se faire
rembourser

back² vt (loan) garantir; (candidate) soutenir;
(project) commanditer, financer, avaliser; ~
down céder; ~ **down from** (confrontation)
chercher à éviter; ~ **down on** (proposal)
reconsidérer; ~ **off** se dégager, se retirer; ~
out se désister, reculer; ~ **out of** (contract,
deal) revenir sur, se dégager de, se retirer de;
(obligation) se soustraire à; ~ **up** (file, data)
sauvegarder; (claim) soutenir, confirmer;
(person) soutenir

back: ~**-channel** n US (Pol) moyen de
communication secrète m; ~ **cover** n
(Media) quatrième de couverture f; ~ **end** n
(Media) pourcentage sur les recettes m; ~
interest n arriéré d'intérêts m; ~ **issue** n
ancien numéro m; ~ **load** n chargement de
retour m; ~ **office** n (Admin) arrière-guichet
m, service administratif m, activités de
gestion et de logistique f pl; (Stock) service de
post-marché m; ~ **order** n commande en
attente f, commande en souffrance f; ~ **pay**
n rappel de salaire m, rappel de traitement ⋯⟩

m; ~ **payment** *n* arrérages *m pl*, arriéré *m*;
~**-pedaling** AmE, ~**-pedalling** BrE *n* marche
arrière *f*; ~ **rent** *n* arriéré de loyer *m*; ~ **tax**
n arriéré d'impôts *m*, rappel d'impôts *m*;
~**-to-back loan** *n* crédit endossé *m*

backbench *n* UK (Pol) banc des membres
sans portefeuille *m*; ~ **MP** *n* député/-e
ordinaire *m/f*

backbencher *n* UK (Pol) député/-e
ordinaire *m/f*

backbone *n* (of economy) clé de voûte *f*,
pilier *m*; (Comp) dorsale *f*

back burner *n* put sth on the ~ mettre
qch en veilleuse

backdate *vt* (cheque, contract) antidater

backdated *adj* antidaté; **be** ~ **to 1ˢᵗ April**
être antidaté avec effet rétroactif au 1ᵉʳ avril

backdating *n* antidatation *f*

backdoor: ~ **financing** *n* financement
déguisé *m*, financement véreux *m*; ~
lending *n* crédit de soutien *m*, prêt déguisé
m; ~ **operation** *n* opération d'arrière-
boutique *f*

backdrop *n* (to situation, event) toile de fond *f*

backed bill of exchange *n* lettre de
change avalisée *f*, lettre de change garantie *f*

backer *n* bailleur de fonds *m*,
commanditaire *mf*; (of bill) avaliseur *m*

background *n* (Econ) climat *m*; (training)
formation *f*; (of event, situation) contexte *m*,
climat *m*; **be in the** ~ être au second plan;
push sth into the ~ reléguer qch au second
plan; **give the** ~ **to sth** mettre qch en
contexte; ~ **check** *n* étude *f*; ~ **color** AmE,
~ **colour** BrE *n* couleur de fond *f*; ~
information *n* généralités *f pl*, notions
générales *f pl*; ~ **investigation** *n* (of applicant)
enquête sur les antécédents *f*; ~ **paper** *n*
document d'information *m*; ~ **pollution** *n*
pollution de fond *f*; ~ **processing** *n* (Comp)
traitement en arrière-plan *m*, traitement
non-prioritaire *m*; US (background check) étude
f; ~ **reading** *n* lectures complémentaires
f pl; ~ **task** *n* tâche non prioritaire *f*

backhander *n* (infrml) pot-de-vin *m*

backing *n* appui *m*, soutien *m*; (of currency)
garantie *f*; (financial) soutien financier *m*

backlog *n* (of orders) accumulation *f*; (of
payments, work, rent) arriéré *m*; **clear one's** ~
liquider le travail en retard; ~ **demand** *n*
demandes non exécutées *f pl*; ~ **order** *n*
commande en attente *f*; ~ **of orders**
commandes en suspens *f pl*; ~ **of payments**
arriéré de paiements *m*; ~ **of work** travail
en retard *m*

backselling *n* vente indirecte *f*

backslash *n* barre oblique inverse *f*,
antislash *m*

backspace¹ *n* (Comp) retour arrière *m*

backspace² *vi* (Comp) faire un retour
arrière

backspread *n* (Stock) type d'écart *m*

backstop *n* (Ind) protection *f*; ~ **loan
facility** *n* (Fin) crédit exceptionnel *m*

backtrack *vi* (from plan, promise) faire
marche arrière

backtracking *n* marche arrière *f*

backup¹ *adj* (supplies) de réserve,
supplémentaire; (plan) de secours; (Comp) (disk,
version) de sauvegarde

backup² *n* (support) appui *m*, soutien *m*;
(Comp) (help) assistance technique *f*; (copy)
sauvegarde *f*; (Fin) appui *m*

backup: ~ **copy** *n* (of file, data) copie de
sauvegarde *f*; ~ **facility** *n* (Gen Comm, Comp)
(installations) installation de secours *f*; ~ **file** *n*
fichier de sauvegarde *m*; ~ **line** *n* (Bank)
ligne de substitution *f*; ~ **material** *n*
documentation *f*; ~ **support** *n* (Stock)
support supplémentaire *m*; ~ **system** *n* (Gen
Comm) système de secours *m*; (Stock) (for
options) système de garantie *m*

backward: ~ **averaging** *n* (of income)
étalement sur les années précédentes *m*; ~
integration *n* intégration en amont *f*,
intégration en arrière *f*; ~ **linkage** *n*
enchaînement arrière *m*, liens en amont
m pl; ~ **scheduling** *n* programmation
régressive *f*

backwardation *n* UK déport *m*, report *m*;
~ **business** *n* activité de report *f*; ~ **rate** *n*
taux de déport *m*

backward-looking *adj* passéiste

backwash effect *n* effet d'osmose *m*,
effet de remous *m*

backyard *n* not in my ~ attitude de celui
qui est un faveur d'un projet à condition que
celui-ci ne soit pas effectué près de chez lui

bad: ~ **bargain** *n* mauvaise affaire *f*; ~
break *n* (infrml) manque de pot *m* (infrml); ~
buy *n* mauvais achat *m*; ~ **check** AmE, ~
cheque BrE *n* chèque en bois *m* (infrml),
chèque sans provision *m*; ~ **deal** *n*
mauvaise affaire *f*; ~ **debt** *n* créance
irrécouvrable *f*, mauvaise créance *f*; ~ **debt
provision** *n* provision pour créances
irrécouvrables *f*; ~ **debt recovery** *n*
recouvrement sur créance radiée *m*; ~
debtor *n* débiteur douteux *m*; ~ **delivery** *n*
(Stock) défiguration de titres *f*; ~
investment *n* placement qui ne rapporte pas
m; ~ **loan** *n* prêt irrécouvrable *m*; ~ **loan
provision** *n* provision pour prêts
irrécouvrables *f*; ~ **luck** *n* manque de
chance *m*; ~ **management** *n* mauvaise
administration *f*, mauvaise gestion *f*; ~
name *n* mauvaise réputation *f*; ~ **news** *n*
mauvaise nouvelle *f*; ~ **paper** *n* (Bank)
mauvais papier *m*; ~ **reputation** *n*
mauvaise réputation *f*; ~ **risk** *n* mauvais
risque *m*; ~ **will** *n* mauvaise volonté *f*; ~
workmanship *n* mauvais travail *m*

badly *adv* (not well) mal; (disrupt, affect)
sérieusement; (damaged) gravement; ~ **in
debt** criblé de dettes; ~ **paid** mal payé; **go** ~

(meeting, exam, interview) mal se passer; **do ~** (company, candidate) obtenir de mauvais résultats; **be ~ hit** (company) être durement touché

baggage n bagages m pl; **~ allowance** n franchise de bagages f; **~ cart** n AmE chariot à bagages m; **~ check** n (document) bulletin de consigne m; (for security) contrôle des bagages m; **~ handling** n manutention des bagages f; **~ locker** n AmE consigne automatique f; **~ reclaim area** n réception des bagages f; **~ tag** n étiquette à bagages f; **~ trolley** n BrE chariot à bagages m

bagman n pl **-men** (pej) (Gen Comm) voyageur représentant placier m; (Fin) US racheteur m

bail¹ n (guarantor) répondant m; (money) caution f, garantie f; **on ~** sous caution; **release sb on ~ of £10,000** libérer qn contre une caution de 10 000 livres sterling; **~ bond** n caution f

bail² vt (Law) mettre en liberté provisoire sous caution; **~ out** (Fin) (company) renflouer; (person) tirer d'affaire; (Law) mettre en liberté provisoire sous caution

bailee n dépositaire mf, dépositaire de biens mf

bailiff n (Law) huissier m; (on estate, farm) intendant/-e m/f, régisseur m

bailment n dépôt m; (Law) contrat de gage m

bailor n déposant m

bail-out n (of company) renflouement m

bait n (S&M) appât m; **~ advertising** n US annonce attrape-nigaud f; **~ and switch advertising** n US technique de l'appât f

bal. abbr (▶balance) (of account) solde m

balance¹ n équilibre m; (Acc, Bank, Fin) solde m; (of budget) équilibre m; **the ~** (sum outstanding) le restant (de la somme) m; **~ in your favor** AmE, **~ in your favour** BrE à votre crédit; **~ of account** n solde m, solde de compte m; **~ brought down** n solde reporté m, solde à reporter m; **~ brought forward** n solde reporté m, solde à nouveau m, solde à reporter m; **~ carried forward** n solde reporté m, solde à reporter m; **~ due** n solde dû m, solde à régler m; **~ due to creditor** n solde créditeur m; **~ due to debitor** n solde débiteur m; **~ in bank** n solde bancaire m; **~ of invoice** n solde de facture m; **~ item** n (Acc) poste du bilan m; **~ on current account** n balance de compte courant f, balance des opérations courantes f; **~ of payments** n balance des paiements f; **~ of payments deficit** n déficit de la balance des paiements m; **~ of payments surplus** n excédent de la balance des paiements m; **~ of power** n (between states) équilibre des forces m; (in government) équilibre des pouvoirs m; **~ sheet** n bilan m, bilan d'inventaire m; **~ of trade** n balance commerciale f, balance du commerce extérieur f

balance² [1] vt (Acc) (budget, economy) équilibrer; (account) arrêter; (positive with negative factors) contrebalancer, équilibrer; **~ the books** arrêter les comptes; **~ the cash** faire la caisse

[2] vi (Acc) s'équilibrer, être équilibré; **~ out**, **~ each other out** (benefits and drawbacks, factors) se compenser

balanced adj (view, discussion, schedule) équilibré; (report) objectif/-ive; (decision) réfléchi; (books) équilibré; **~ budget** n budget équilibré m; **~ growth** n croissance équilibrée f; **~ portfolio** n portefeuille équilibré m

balancing item n (Acc) écriture de contrepartie f

bale n (Transp) balle f

baling n (Transp) mise en balles f, paquetage m

ballast n lest m

balloon n (Bank) versement final m; **~ interest** n (Stock) (on loan) retard d'intérêt m; **~ loan** n prêt avec versement final supérieur; **~ payment** n (Stock) intérêt accumulé payable à la maturité d'une obligation

ballot¹ n (process) scrutin m; (vote) vote m; (Transp) (shipping) ballot m; **by ~** au scrutin; **secret ~** scrutin secret m; **strike ~** vote pour décider d'une grève m; **take a ~** procéder à un vote; **~ box** n urne f; **~ paper** n bulletin de vote m

ballot² [1] vt consulter (par vote) [2] vi voter au scrutin

ballpark figure n (infml) chiffre approximatif m

ban¹ n embargo m, interdiction f; (Law) défense f, interdiction f; **a ~ on overtime** une interdiction de faire des heures supplémentaires

ban² vt interdire, défendre, proscrire; **~ sb from doing** interdire à qn de faire

band n (range) tranche f; (Tax) tranche f; **~ advertising** n bandeau publicitaire m

b&b abbr (▶bed and breakfast) ≈ chambre d'hôte f

banded lot n, **banded offer** n, **banded pack** n (different products) vente jumelée f; (same product) vente groupée f

banding n (HRM) zonation f; (Tax) assiette fiscale f

bandwagon n jump on the **~** prendre le train en marche; **~ effect** n effet Panurge m

bandwidth n (radio) largeur de bande f; (Comp) bande passante f

bank¹ n banque f; **~ acceptance** n acceptation de banque f; **~ account** n compte bancaire m, compte en banque m; **~ advance** n avance bancaire f, facilité de caisse f; **~ annuities** n pl rente perpétuelle f; **~ balance** n solde en banque m, solde de compte bancaire m; **~ base rate** n taux de base bancaire m; **~ bill** n (document) chèque ⋯⟶

bancaire *m*, effet bancaire *m*; (currency, note) AmE billet de banque *m*; ~ **bond** *n* obligation bancaire *f*; ~ **branch** *n* succursale de banque *f*; ~ **card** *n* carte bancaire *f*; ~ **certificate** *n* bon de caisse *m*, certificat bancaire *m*; ~ **charges** *n pl* frais bancaires *m pl*, frais de gestion de compte *m pl*; ~ **check** AmE, ~ **cheque** BrE *n* chèque bancaire *m*; ~ **clearing** *n* compensation bancaire *f*, compensation interbancaire *f*; ~ **clerk** *n* employé/-e de banque *m/f*; ~ **code** *n* code bancaire de tri *m*; ~ **commission** *n* commission bancaire *f*, frais bancaires *m pl*; ~ **credit** *n* crédit bancaire *m*; ~ **credit transfer** *n* virement automatique de fonds *m*; ~ **deposit** *n* dépôt bancaire *m*, dépôt en banque *m*; ~ **deposit rates** *n pl* taux d'intérêt des dépôts bancaires *m*; ~ **details** *n pl* coordonnées bancaires *f pl*; ~ **draft** *n* chèque bancaire *m*, effet bancaire *m*, traite bancaire *f*; ~ **group** *n* groupe bancaire *m*; ~ **guarantee** *n* caution bancaire *f*, garantie bancaire *f*; ~ **guaranty** *n* caution bancaire *f*; ~ **holding company** *n* holding bancaire *m*; ~ **holiday** *n* BrE jour férié *m*; ~ **of issue** *n* banque d'émission *f*; ~ **lending** *n* prêts bancaires *m pl*; ~ **lending rate** *n* taux de l'escompte *m*; ~ **loan** *n* emprunt bancaire *m*; ~ **manager** *n* directeur/-trice d'agence *m/f*, directeur/-trice de banque *m/f*; ~ **money** *n* monnaie de banque *f*, monnaie scripturale *f*; ~ **overdraft** *n* découvert *m*, découvert bancaire *m*; ~ **paper** *n* papier avalisé par la banque *m*; ~ **rate** *n* taux de base bancaire *m*, taux de l'escompte *m*; ~ **reserve** *n* couverture bancaire *f*, fonds de réserve *m*; ~ **return** *n* situation de banque *f*; ~ **securities** *n pl* valeurs de banque *f pl*; ~ **sort code** *n* UK code bancaire de tri *m*; ~ **statement** *n* (of bank's finances) situation de banque *f*, état de banque *m*; (of customer account) relevé de compte *m*; ~ **subsidiary** *n* filiale bancaire *f*; ~ **teller** *n* guichetier/-ière *m/f*; ~**-to-bank lending** *n* prêts interbancaires *m pl*; ~ **transfer** *n* virement automatique de fonds *m*, virement bancaire *m*

bank² *vt* (cheque, money) déposer à la banque; ~ **on** tabler sur; ~ **with** avoir son compte bancaire à

Bank: ~ **of England** *n* banque d'Angleterre; ~ **for International Settlements** *n* Banque des Règlements Internationaux *f*; ~ **Giro** *n* UK paiement par virement bancaire *m*

bankable *adj* bancable, escomptable, négociable en banque; ~ **assets** *n pl* actif bancable *m*; ~ **bill** *n* effet bancable *m*; ~ **paper** *n* papier bancable *m*

bankassurance *n* bancassurance *f*

bankbook *n* (for customers) livret de compte *m*

banker *n* banquier/-ière *m/f*; ~**'s acceptance** *n* acceptation de banque *f*, effet

bancaire *m*; ~**'s card** *n* carte d'identité bancaire *f*; ~**'s check** AmE, ~**'s cheque** BrE *n* chèque de banque *m*; ~**'s deposits** *n pl* UK réserves des banques de dépôt *f pl*; ~**'s discount** *n* escompte de banque *m*; ~**'s draft** *n* chèque de banque *m*; ~**'s order** *n* ordre de virement bancaire *m*; ~**'s reference** *n* référence bancaire *f*

banking *n* (business, activity) opérations bancaires *f pl*; (profession) banque *f*; ~ **account** *n* compte bancaire *m*, compte en banque *m*; ~ **activity** *n* activité du secteur bancaire *f*; ~ **business** *n* activité bancaire *f*, commerce de banque *m*; ~ **charges** *n pl* frais de banque *m pl*; ~ **community** *n* banquiers *m pl*; ~ **group** *n* groupe bancaire *m*; ~ **hours** *n pl* heures d'ouverture de la banque *f pl*; ~ **house** *n* maison bancaire *f*; ~ **industry** *n*, ~ **sector** *n* secteur bancaire *m*; ~ **services** *n pl* prestations bancaires *f pl*; ~ **transaction** *n* opération bancaire *f*

banknote *n* BrE billet de banque *m*

bankroll¹ *n* US fonds *m pl*, ressource monétaire *f*

bankroll² *vt* financer

bankrupt¹ *adj* failli, ruiné

bankrupt² *n* failli/-e *m/f*

bankrupt³ *vt* mettre en faillite, ruiner

bankruptcy *n* faillite *f*; **on the verge of** ~ au bord de la faillite; ~ **act** *n* loi sur les faillites *f*; ~ **committee** *n* administration de la faillite *f*; ~ **court** *n* tribunal de commerce *m*, tribunal des faillites *m*; ~ **estate** *n* actif de la faillite *m*, masse de la faillite *f*; ~ **legislation** *n* législation sur les faillites *f*; ~ **notice** *n* avis de faillite *m*; ~ **proceedings** *n pl* procédure de faillite *f*

banner *n* banderole *f*, bannière *f*; (on Internet) bandeau (publicitaire) *m*, bannière (publicitaire) *f*; ~ **campaign** *n* campagne publicitaire sur Internet utilisant les bannières *f*; ~ **headline** *n* gros titre *m*, manchette *f*, titre en caractères d'affiche *m*; ~ **year** *n* année exceptionnelle *f*

bar¹ *abbr* (▶**barrel**) (for petroleum) baril *m*; (for food, wine) fût *m*, tonneau *m*

bar² *n* empêchement *m*, obstacle *m*; **be a** ~ **to** constituer un obstacle à; ~ **chart** *n* histogramme *m*; ~ **code** *n* code (à) barres *m*; ~ **code reader** *n*, ~ **code scanner** *n* crayon optique *m*, lecteur de codes barres *m*; ~ **graph** *n* histogramme *m*; ~ **graphics** *n pl* AmE code (à) barres *m*

bar³ *vt* (person) exclure; (activity) défendre, interdire; ~ **sb from a company** exclure qn d'une société; ~ **sb from doing** interdire à qn de faire

Bar *n* UK ≈ barreau *m*, ≈ ordre des avocats *m*

bare *adj* (Ins) non-assuré, nu; ~ **contract** *n* contrat à titre gratuit *m*; ~ **owner** *n* (Prop) nu-propriétaire *m*; ~ **property** *n* (Prop) nue-propriété *f*; ~ **version** *n* (Comp) version brute *f*, version sans options *f*

bargain¹ *n* (item at low price) article en réclame *m*, article en solde *m*; (good buy) bonne affaire *f*; (contract) marché *m*; (Stock) transaction *f*; **strike a** ~ conclure un marché; **drive a hard** ~ négocier ferme; **into the** ~ par-dessus le marché; **keep one's side of the** ~ teinr sa part du marché; ~ **basement** *n* (in store) coin des bonnes affaires *m*; ~ **book** *n* (Stock) carnet d'agent de change *m*; ~ **hunter** *n* personne à l'affût d'une bonne affaire *f*; (Stock) chercheur de marchés avantageux *m*, investisseur à la recherche d'une bonne affaire *m*; ~ **offer** *n* offre promotionnelle *f*, offre spéciale *f*; ~ **price** *n* prix exceptionnel *m*, prix réduit *m*, prix soldé *m*; ~ **rate** *n* tarif promotionnel *m*; ~ **sale** *n* soldes *m pl*

bargain² *vi* (over price) marchander; (over terms) négocier; ~ **for** (increase, terms) négocier; ~ **for a lower price** marchander un prix plus bas; ~ **for account** (Stock) faire un marché à terme, spéculer à terme; ~ **with sb** (haggle) marchander avec qn; (negotiate) négocier avec qn; ~ **on sth** (expect) s'attendre à qch

bargainee *n* acheteur/-euse *m/f*, preneur/-euse *m/f*

bargainer *n* négociateur/-trice *m/f*

bargaining *n* (discussion) négociation *f*; (haggling) marchandage *m*; ~ **agent** *n* agent négociateur *m*; ~ **chip** *n* atout dans les négociations *m*; ~ **position** *n* position de négociation *f*; ~ **power** *n* pouvoir de négociation *m*; ~ **table** *n* table de négociations *f*; ~ **unit** *n* unité de négociation *f*

barge *n* chaland *m*, péniche *f*

barometer *n* (of trends) baromètre *m*; ~ **stock** *n* valeur de référence *f*

barrel *n* (for petroleum) baril *m*; (for wine, food) fût *m*, tonneau *m*; ~**s per day** barils par jour *m pl*

barrier *n* (Econ) barrière *f*, obstacle *m*; **break down** ~**s** supprimer les barrières; ~ **to entry** (Imp/Exp) barrière d'entrée *f*; ~ **to exit** barrière de sortie *f*; ~ **to trade** barrière commerciale *f*, entrave au commerce *f*

barrister *n* UK (Law) avocat/-e *m/f*

barter¹ *n* troc *m*, échange *m*; ~ **agreement** *n* accord de compensation *m*, accord de troc *m*; ~ **trade** *n* commerce d'échanges compensés *m*, commerce de troc *m*, compensation *f*; ~ **transaction** *n* opération de compensation *f*, opération de troc *f*

barter² 1 *vt* troquer
2 *vi* faire du troc

base¹ *n* (basis) base *f*; (of worker) base (de travail) *f*; **steal a** ~ **on sb** devancer qn; **touch** ~ **with sb** prendre contact avec qn; ~ **amount** *n* (Tax) montant de base *m*; ~ **capital** *n* capital de base *m*; ~ **lending rate** *n* UK taux de base *m*; ~ **pay** *n* AmE salaire de

base *m*; ~ **period** *n* (Tax) période de base *f*; ~ **price** *n* prix de base *m*, prix de référence *m*; ~ **product** *n* produit de base *m*; ~ **rate** *n* UK taux de base *m*; ~ **stock** *n* stock-outil *m*; ~ **year** *n* année de base *f*, année de référence *f*

base² *vt* (assumption, decision, calculation) baser, fonder; (company, offices) baser; ~ **sth on** baser qch sur, fonder qch sur

based *adj* **be** ~ **in Rome** (person) être basé à Rome; (company) avoir son siège à Rome, être basé à Rome

baseline *n* (standard) point de comparaison *m*; (of diagram) ligne de fond *f*, ligne zéro *f*; (in advertising) signature *f*; ~ **costs** *n pl* coûts de base *m pl*

baseload *n* stock de base *m*, stock minimal *m*; ~ **power station** *n* centrale en charge de base *f*, usine de base *f*

basic *adj* (before additions) de base; (facilities, supplies, services) de base; (knowledge, rule, education) élémentaire; (research, problem, principle) fondamental; ~ **amount** *n* montant de base *m*; ~ **assumption** *n* hypothèse de base *f*; ~ **books** *n pl* (Fin) livres de base *m pl*; ~ **commodity** *n* produit de base *m*; ~ **concept** *n* concept de base *m*, idée de base *f*; ~ **consumer products** *n pl* produits de consommation courante *m pl*; ~ **earnings per share** *n pl* bénéfice non-dilué par action *m*; ~ **exemption** *n* (Tax) exemption de base *f*; ~ **foodstuffs** *n pl* alimentation de base *f*, denrées alimentaires de base *f pl*; ~ **income** *n* revenu direct *m*; ~ **industry** *n* industrie de base *f*, industrie extractive *f*; ~ **material** *n* matériau de base *m*; ~ **media** *n pl* médias classiques *m pl*; ~ **needs** *n pl* besoins fondamentaux *m pl*; ~ **pay** *n* salaire de base *m*; ~ **premium** *n* prime essentielle *f*; ~ **price** *n* prix de base *m*; ~ **rate** *n* traitement de base *m*; ~**-rate tax** *n* impôt forfaitaire *m*; ~ **salary** *n* salaire de base *m*; ~ **tax** *n* impôt de base *m*; ~ **trend** *n* tendance de base *f*, tendance fondamentale *f*; ~ **unit** *n* unité de base *f*; ~ **wage** *n* salaire de base *m*

basics *n pl* **the** ~ l'essentiel *m*; **go back to** ~ revoir les principes fondamentaux; **get down to** ~ aborder l'essentiel

basin *n* (harbour) bassin *m*

basis *n* base *f*, fondement *m*; (Stock) base *f*; **on the** ~ **of** sur la base de; **on the** ~ **that** en partant du principe que; **serve as the** ~ **for sth** servir de base à qch; ~ **of assessment** (Tax) assiette de l'impôt *f*, assiette fiscale *f*; ~ **of calculation** base de calcul *f*; ~ **for discussion** base de discussion *f*; ~ **for taxation** assiette de l'impôt *f*, assiette fiscale *f*; ~ **point** *n* (Fin) point de base *m*

basket *n* panier *m*; ~ **of currencies** panier de devises *m*, panier de monnaies *m*; ~ **of goods** assortiment de denrées *m*, panier de denrées *m*; ~ **purchase** *n* achat à un prix forfaitaire *m*, achat à un prix ⸱⸱⸱⸳

global m

batch n (Gen Comm, Comp) (group of items) lot m; (Ind) lot de fabrication m, petite série f; (of invoices) paquet m; (of letters) liasse f, paquet m; (S&M) (of goods) lot m; ~ **control** n contrôle par lots m; ~ **file** n fichier de commandes m, fichier séquentiel m; ~ **job** n traitement par lots m; ~ **processing** n traitement par lots m; ~ **production** n fabrication par lots f, production par lots f; ~ **size** n taille des lots f

battery n (automobile) batterie f; (for torch, radio) pile f; ~ **backup** n (Comp) alimentation auxiliaire f

battle¹ n combat m, lutte f

battle²: ~ **for** vt (contract) se bagarrer pour (infrml), se disputer; (existence) lutter pour; (share in the market) se battre pour

baud n baud m

bay n (rail) quai subsidiaire m, voie d'arrêt f

bazaar n vente de charité f

BBC abbr (▶British Broadcasting Corporation) compagnie de télévision et de radio nationale britannique, BBC f

BB Certificate n déclaration d'admission en douane d'un navire

BBS abbr (▶bulletin board system) messagerie f, tableau d'affichage électronique m

bcc abbr (blind carbon copy) copie invisible f

BCC abbr (▶British Chamber of Commerce) chambre de commerce britannique

BCom abbr (Bachelor of Commerce) (degree) licence en études commerciales f; (person) ≈ licencié/-e en études commerciales m/f

b/d abbr (▶balance brought down) solde reporté m, solde à reporter m; (▶barrels per day) barils par jour m pl

B/Dft abbr (▶bank draft) chèque bancaire m, traite bancaire f

BE abbr (▶Bank of England) banque d'Angleterre f

B/E abbr (▶bill of exchange) l/c f (lettre de change)

beaching n (shipping) échouage m

beacon n balise f

beam vt (message) envoyer (à partir d'un assistant personnel numérique)

bear¹ n (Stock) baissier m, spéculateur à la baisse m, vendeur à découvert m; **sell a** ~ vendre à découvert; ~ **account** n position vendeur f, position à découvert f, position à la baisse f; ~ **campaign** n spéculation à la baisse f; ~ **covering** n rachat des vendeurs à découvert m; ~ **hug** n (corporate takeover) rachat d'une société m; ~ **market** n marché baissier m; ~ **operation** n transaction à la baisse f; ~ **operator** n acheteur à la baisse m, baissier m, spéculateur à la baisse m; ~

position n position vendeur f, position à découvert f, position à la baisse f; ~ **raid** n attaque des baissiers f; ~ **sale** n vente à découvert f, vente à la baisse f; ~ **speculation** n spéculation à la baisse f; ~ **speculator** n spéculateur à la baisse m; ~ **transaction** n transaction à la baisse f

bear² ⊡ vt (burden, responsibility) supporter; (market, prices, shares) chercher à faire baisser; (interest) rapporter; ~ **the cost of** supporter le coût de, supporter les frais de; ~ **the costs** prendre les frais à sa charge, supporter les coûts; ~ **the date May 11**ᵗʰ porter la date du 11 mai; ~ **an interest of** rapporter un intérêt de; ~ **the risk of** courir le risque de, prendre le risque de; ~ **sth in mind** garder qch présent à l'esprit

⊡ vi jouer à la baisse

bearer n porteur m; ~ **bill** n effet au porteur m; ~ **bond** n obligation au porteur f; ~ **certificate** n certificat au porteur m, titre au porteur m; ~ **check** AmE, ~ **cheque** BrE n chèque au porteur m, chèque payable au porteur m; ~ **clause** n clause au porteur f; ~ **debenture** n obligation au porteur f; ~ **instrument** n instrument au porteur m; ~ **proxy** n procuration en blanc f, ~ **security** n titre au porteur m; ~ **share** n action au porteur f; ~ **stock** n action au porteur f, valeurs au porteur f pl; ~ **warrant** n bon de souscription au porteur m

bearish adj baissier/-ière, en baisse, orienté à la baisse; **be** ~ être baissier/-ière; ~ **market** n marché baissier m, marché à la baisse m; ~ **movement** n tendance baissière f, tendance la baisse f; ~ **stock** n valeur en baisse f; ~ **tendency** n tendance baissière f, tendance à la baisse f

bearishness n (of market) pessimisme m

beat vt (person) devancer; (rush, crowds) éviter; ~ **the price down** faire baisser le prix; ~ **sb down to £500** faire descendre qn à 500 livres sterling; ~ **off** (competition) repousser

Beaufort scale n échelle de Beaufort f

BEcon abbr (Bachelor of Economics) (degree) licence en sciences économiques f; (person) ≈ licencié/-e en sciences économiques m/f

bed n get into ~ with (infrml) (group, lobby, company) s'associer à, faire son lit avec (infrml); ~ **and breakfast** n ≈ chambre d'hôte f; ~ **and breakfast deal** n (Stock) transaction aller et retour f

BEd abbr (Bachelor of Education) (degree) ≈ licence d'enseignement f; (person) ≈ licencié/-e d'enseignement m/f

bedroom n chambre f; ~ **community** n AmE ville-dortoir f

before prep avant; ~ **due date** anticipé, avant l'échéance; ~ **maturity** avant l'échéance; ~**hours** adj (Stock) avant bourse; ~**hours dealings** n pl négociations avant l'ouverture f pl, transactions avant-bourse *f pl*; **~-tax** *adj* avant impôt

begin ① *vt* commencer, se mettre à; **~
doing** commencer à faire; **~ to do**
commencer à faire; **~ work** se mettre au
travail, commencer à travailler
② *vi* commencer

beginning *n* début *m*; **~ inventory** *n* stock
au début de l'exercice *m*, stock d'ouverture
m; **~ of the year** *n* début de l'exercice *m*

behalf *n*: **on ~ of** (act, speak, sign, accept) au
nom de; (phone, write) de la part de

behavior *n* AmE ►**behaviour** BrE

behavioral science *n* AmE
►**behavioural science** BrE

behaviour *n* BrE comportement *m*

behavioural science *n* BrE science du
comportement *f*

belated *adj* tardif/-ive; **~ claim** *n* (Ins)
déclaration de sinistre tardif *f*, sinistre tardif
m

belief *n* conviction *f*; **to the best of my ~** à
ma connaissance; **contrary to popular ~**
contrairement à ce qu'on pense; **it is my ~
that…** je suis convaincu que…

believe *vti* croire; **~ in sth** croire à qch; **~
in sb** avoir confiance en qn

bell *n* BrE (infrml) coup de fil *m* (infrml), coup de
téléphone *m*; **~s and whistles** *n pl* (infrml)
(Gen Comm, Comp) options *f pl*; **~ curve** *n*
courbe en cloche *f*

bellwether *n* cours d'action indicateur *m*,
titre de référence *m*

belong: **~ to** *vt* (be sb's property) appartenir
à; (union) appartenir à; (club, library) être inscrit
à

below[1] *adv* (later in text) ci-dessous; **as ~**
comme ci-dessous; **see ~** voir ci-dessous

below[2] *prep* au-dessous de, en-dessous de;
~ the 5% mark au-dessous de la barre de
5%; **~ the line** (Acc, Fin) au-dessous de la
ligne; **~ market price** au-dessous du cours;
~ the norm au-dessous de la norme; **~ par**
au-dessous du pair; **~ quota** au-dessous du
quota

below-average *adj* au-dessous de la
moyenne, inférieur à la moyenne

below-the-line[1] *n* publicité hors-media *f*

below-the-line[2] *adj* (advertising, costs,
promotion) hors-média

below-the-line: **~ item** *n* article de
dessous de ligne *m*, opération au-dessous de
ligne *f*; **~ revenue** *n* produit exceptionnel *m*

Bench *n* (infrml) (Law) Cour *f*, Tribunal *m*

benchmark[1] *n* (Gen Comm) jalon *m*, point
de repère *m*, point de référence *m*; (Comp)
test d'évaluation *m*, test des performances *m*;
~ method *n* méthode de référence *f*; **~
reserve** *n* US réserve obligatoire *f*; **~
statistics** *n pl* données statistiques de base *f
pl*, données statistiques de référence *f pl*; **~
test** *n* test d'évaluation des performances *m*

benchmark[2] *vt* évaluer les performances

de

benchmarking *n* référenciation *f*,
benchmarking *m*

beneficial *adj* avantageux/-euse; (result,
outcome) favorable; (change) salutaire; **~
interest** *n* (Law) droit d'usufruit *m*; (Tax)
droit de bénéficiaire *m*; **~ owner** *n* (Law)
ayant droit économique *m*, usufruitier/-ière
m/f; (Stock, Tax) propriétaire *mf*; **~
ownership** *n* (Law) usufruit *m*; (Stock)
propriété *f*; (Tax) propriété bénéficiaire *f*

beneficiary *n* bénéficiaire *mf*; **~ under a
trust** bénéficiaire d'une fiducie *mf*; **~ clause**
n clause du bénéficiaire *f*

benefit[1] *n* (profit) bénéfice *m*, profit *m*; (perk)
avantage *m*; (social payment) allocation *f*,
prestation *f*; (Ins) (from plans) prestation *f*;
(advantage) avantage *m*, bénéfice *m*; (Tax)
allocation *f*, avantage *m*; (gala performance)
soirée de bienfaisance *f*; **be of ~ to sb**
profiter à qn; **be on ~** BrE toucher des
allocations; **reap the ~s of sth** récolter les
bénéfices de qch; **feel the ~ of** ressentir
l'effet favorable de; **for the ~ of sb** à
l'intention de qn; **give sb the ~ of the doubt**
accorder le bénéfice du doute à qn; **~ in
kind** *n* avantage en espèces *m*, avantage en
nature *m*; **~ society** *n* AmE association de
secours mutuel *f*, société de prévoyance *f*

benefit[2] ① *vt* profiter à
② *vi* bénéficier, profiter; **~ from** tirer
avantage de, tirer profit de

benefits *n pl* (in job package) avantages
sociaux *m pl*

benevolent[1] *adj* (organization, trust, fund) de
bienfaisance

benign neglect *n* douce négligence *f*

bequeath *vt* léguer

bequest *n* legs *m*

berth *n* (in ship, train) place couchée *f*,
couchette *f*; (for vessel) mouillage *f*

berthing *n* (of ships) accostage *m*

best: **~ alternative** *n* meilleure option *f*;
~-before date *n* date limite de
consommation *f*; **~ bid** *n* meilleure offre *f*;
~ bidder *n* mieux disant *m*; **~-case
scenario** *n* hypothèse optimiste *f*, meilleur
des cas *m*; **~ practice** *n* meilleures
pratiques *f pl*; **~ price** *n* meilleur prix *m*,
prix le plus avantageux *m*; **~ seller** *n* (book)
livre à succès *m*, best-seller *m*; (product, line)
best-seller *m*, article de grande vente *m*;
~-selling *adj* (product) à grand succès; (author)
à succès

best-of-breed *adj* **~ solution** meilleure
solution de sa catégorie *f*, solution best-of-
breed *f*

bet[1] *n* (gamble) pari *m*; **make a ~** parier,
faire un pari; **be a safe ~**, **be a good ~** être
une valeur sûre; **your best ~ is to do** le
mieux pour vous c'est de faire; **my ~ is
that…** moi je pense que…

bet² *vt* (Gen Comm) parier; (Fin) miser

beta *n* US (Stock) action bêta *f*, titre bêta *m*, valeur bêta *f*; ~ **coefficient** *n* AmE, ~ **factor** *n* BrE coefficient bêta *m*, facteur bêta *m*; ~ **share** *n* action bêta *f*, titre bêta *f*, valeur bêta *f*; ~ **stock** *n* action bêta *f*, titre bêta *m*, valeur bêta *f*; ~ **version** *n* version bêta *f*

beta test¹ *n* bêta test *m*, essai pilote *m*

beta test² *vt* tester la version bêta de

better¹ *adj* meilleur; ~ **than average** meilleur que la moyenne, mieux que la moyenne; ~ **than expected** mieux que prévu; ~ **than predicted** mieux que prévu; ~**-off** plus riche; **you'd be ~-off selling now** il vaudrait mieux vendre maintenant; ~ **offer** *n* offre plus intéressante *f*, suroffre *f*

better² *adv* mieux; **at or ~** (Stock) à la limite ou mieux; **or ~ still** ou mieux

better³ *vt* (own performance, rating) améliorer; (rival, competitor) faire mieux que; ~ **sb's offer** offrir un meilleur prix que qn

betterment *n* amélioration *f*, plus-value *f*; ~ **tax** *n* impôt sur les plus-values *m*

betting *n* (activity) paris *m pl*; (odds) cote *f*

beyond *prep* (after a certain point, place) au-delà de; ~ **repair** irréparable; ~ **one's means/resources/ability** au-dessus de ses moyens/ressources/capacités

b/g *abbr* (▶**bonded goods**) marchandises entreposées sous douane *f pl*

BHC *abbr* (▶**British High Commission**) haut-comité britannique *m*

bhp *abbr* (▶**brake horsepower**) puissance au frein *f*

biannual *adj* semestriel/-ielle

bias¹ *n* parti pris *m*, préjugé *m*

bias² *vt* (person, decision) influer sur; ~ **sb against/in favour of** prévenir qn contre/en faveur de

biased BrE, **biassed** AmE *adj* (decision, judge) partial; **be ~** (report) manquer d'objectivité; **be ~ against/in favour of** avoir un préjugé défavorable/favorable envers

bid¹ *n* offre *f*, offre d'achat *f*; (at auction) enchère *f*; (for contract) soumission *f*; (for company) offre *f*, offre d'achat *f*; **make a ~**, **put in a ~** faire une offre; (at auction) faire une enchère; (for contract, tender) soumissionner; ~ **bond** *n* (Gen Comm) garantie du moins disant *f*; (Stock) caution de participation à une adjudication *f*; ~ **closing** *n* clôture des offres *f*; ~ **opening** *n* ouverture du concours *f*; ~ **price** *n* prix acheteur *m*, prix d'achat *m*; ~ **vehicle** *n* moyen d'effectuer une offre *m*

bid² ① *vt* (money) offrir
② *vi* (for company) faire une offre; (for contract, project) soumissionner; (at auction) enchérir, faire une offre; ~ **for sth** (Gen Comm) faire une offre pour; (contract) soumissionner pour; (at auction) mettre une enchère sur; ~ **up** faire

une offre, offrir; ~ **up the price for** faire monter le prix de

bidder *n* (in tender offer) soumissionnaire *mf*; (at auction) enchérisseur/-euse *m/f*

bidding *n* (at sale) enchère *f*; (submission of bids) soumission des offres *f*; (S&M) enchère *f*; ~ **requirements** *n pl* conditions nécessaires pour concourir *f pl*; ~ **up** *n* montée des enchères *f*

BIDS *abbr* (**British Institute of Dealers in Securities**) *institut britannique des courtiers de valeurs*

biennial *adj* biennal, bisannuel/-elle

big *adj* (change, decision, difference, event, building) grand; **be ~ in pharmaceuticals** être connu dans l'industrie pharmaceutique; **be ~ business** (product, sector) rapporter gros; **earn ~ money** (infrml) gagner gros; **hit the ~ time** (infrml) réussir; **make it ~** (infrml) avoir du succès; ~ **budget** *n* gros budget *m*; ~ **business** *n* (sector) grandes entreprises *f pl*; ~ **company** *n* grande société *f*; ~ **customer** *n* client important *m*; ~ **employer** *n* gros employeur *m*; ~ **exporter** *n* gros exportateur *m*; ~ **idea** *n* (S&M) idée force *f*; ~ **importer** *n* gros importateur *m*; ~ **investors** *n pl* grand capital *m*; ~ **name** *n* (company) entreprise réputée *f*; (brand) marque réputée *f*; ~ **producer** *n* gros producteur *m*; ~ **ticket item** *n* article cher *m*; (white goods) gros appareil électro-ménager *m*; ~ **wheel** (infrml) gros bonnet *m* (infrml), magnat *m*

bilateral *adj* bilatéral; ~ **aid** *n* aide bilatérale *f*; ~ **contract** *n* contrat bilatéral *m*; ~ **loan** *n* prêt bilatéral *m*; ~ **trade agreement** *n* accord commercial bilatéral *m*

bilateralism *n* bilatéralisme *m*

bilge *n* bouchain *m*, fond de cale *m*

bill¹ *n* (promissory note) effet *m*, traite *f*; (account) facture *f*, note *f*; BrE (account in hotel) note *f*; (in restaurant) addition *f*; (Ins) effet *m*; (Law) projet de loi *m*; (poster) affiche *f*, placard *m*; (Stock) lettre *f*, effet *m*, traite *f*; (banknote) AmE billet (de banque) *m*; **a ~ for €800** une facture de 800€; **telephone ~** facture de téléphone *f*, note de téléphone *f*; ~ **book** *n* livre des effets *m*, échéancier d'effets *m*; ~ **broker** *n* courtier d'escompte *m*, courtier de change *m*; ~ **of costs** *n* état des frais *m*; ~ **diary** *n* carnet d'échéances *m*, échéancier *m*; ~ **for discount** *n* effet à l'escompte *m*; ~ **of entry** *n* (customs) déclaration d'entrée en douane *f*; ~ **of exchange** *n* effet de commerce *m*, lettre de change *f*, traite *f*; ~ **of freight** *n* lettre de voiture *f*; ~ **of health** *n* (Imp/Exp) patente *f*; ~ **of lading** *n* (freight) connaissement *m*; ~ **market** *n* marché de l'escompte *m*; ~ **of materials** *n* (production) cahier des charges *m*, nomenclature *f*; ~ **posting** *n* affichage *m*; ~ **receivable** *n* effet à recevoir *m*, traite à recevoir *f*; ~ **of sale** *n* acte de vente *m*; ~ **of sight** *n* déclaration provisoire d'importation *f*; ～ **sticking** *n* affichage *m*; ～ **of store** *n* autorisation de réimportation *f*

bill² *vt* (request payment) facturer; (in advertising) annoncer; ～ **sb for sth** facturer qch à qn; **they ～ us for repairs** ils nous facturent les réparations

billback *n* US frais rétroactifs *m pl*

billboard *n* panneau d'affichage *m*, panneau publicitaire *m*

billing *n* (of customers) facturation *f*; (advertising) volume global des contrats billing *m*; **get top ～** figurer en tête d'affiche; ～ **department** *n* US service facturation *m*

billion *n* (one thousand million) milliard *m*; (one million million) BrE billion *m*

billionaire *n* milliardaire *mf*

BIM *abbr* (**British Institute of Management**) *institut britannique de gestion*

bimetallic *adj* bimétallique

bimonthly *adj* (every two months) bimestriel/ -ielle; (twice a month) bimensuel/-elle

bin *vt* mettre à la corbeille

binary *adj* binaire

bind *vt* (commit) engager; (document, book) relier; ～ **sb to do** contraindre qn à faire; **be bound by** (law, rule, constraint) être tenu par

binder *n* (file) classeur *m*; (insurance contract) US lettre de couverture *f*, police provisoire *f*

binding *adj* (decision) irrévocable; (contract, procedure) qui engage, qui lie; **the contract is ～** le contrat vous engage; ～ **agreement** *n* contrat irrévocable *m*, contrat qui engage *m*; ～ **offer** *n* offre irrévocable *f*; ～ **promise** *n* promesse solidaire *f*; ～ **tender** *n* soumission contraignante *f*

binomial¹ *adj* binomial

binomial² *n* binôme *m*

biodegradable *adj* biodégradable

bioeconomics *n* + *sing v* bioéconomie *f*

bioengineering *n* bioingénierie *f*, génie biologique *m*

biometrics *n* + *sing v* biométrie *f*

biotechnology *n* biotechnologie *f*

biotope *n* biotope *m*

birth *n* naissance *f*; ～ **certificate** *n* extrait de naissance *m*; ～ **rate** *n* taux de natalité *m*

BIS *abbr* (▸**Bank for International Settlements**) BRI *f* (Banque des Règlements Internationaux)

bit *n* bit *m*; ～ **rate** *n* débit binaire *m*; ～**s per inch** *n pl* bits par pouce *m pl*; ～**s per second** *n pl* bits par seconde *m pl*

bitter *adj* (rivalry, opposition) farouche; (argument) violent; (blow) dur; (disappointment) cruel/-elle; ～ **competition** concurrence acharnée *f*, concurrence féroce *f*

biweekly *adj* (every two weeks) bimensuel/ -elle; (twice a week) bihebdomadaire

bk *abbr* (▸**bank**) banque *f*

bkcy *abbr* (▸**bankruptcy**) faillite *f*

bkg *abbr* (▸**banking**) opérations bancaires *f pl*

bkpt *abbr* (▸**bankrupt**) failli/-e *m/f*

B/L *abbr* (▸**bill of lading**) connt *m* (connaissement)

black¹ *n* (Fin) **be in the ～** être créditeur/ -trice; **stay in the ～** maintenir un solde créditeur

black² *vt* boycotter

black: ～ **books** *n pl* (takeover bids) livres noirs *m pl*; ～ **box** *n* boîte noire *f*; ～ **economy** *n* économie parallèle *f*, économie souterraine *f*; ～ **gold** *n* pétrole *m*

Black: ～ **Friday** *n* vendredi noir *m*; ～ **Monday** *n* lundi noir *m*

blacking *n* boycottage *m*

blackleg *n* UK briseur/-euse de grève *m/f*, jaune *mf*

blacklist¹ *n* liste noire *f*

blacklist² *vt* mettre sur la liste noire, mettre à l'index

blacklisted *adj* mis à l'index

blackmail¹ *n* chantage *m*

blackmail² *vt* faire chanter

blackmailer *n* maître-chanteur *m*

black market *n* marché noir *m*; **buy/sell on the ～** acheter/vendre au noir; **the ～ in pirated software** le marché noir du logiciel piraté

black marketeer *n* personne qui vend au marché noir *f*

blackout *n* (of electrical supply) coupure de courant *f*, panne d'électricité *f*; (on TV, radio) interruption des émissions *f*

blank¹ *adj* (form) vierge, à remplir; (disk) vierge; (screen) vide; (paper) blanc/blanche

blank² *n* blanc *m*; **fill in the ～s** remplir les blancs; **draw a ～** faire chou blanc (infml)

blank³ *vt* effacer, supprimer

blank: ～ **check** AmE, ～ **cheque** BrE *n* chèque en blanc *m*; ～ **endorsement** *n* endossement en blanc *m*; ～ **form** *n* formulaire vierge *m*; ～ **order** *n* commande dont le montant n'est pas spécifié; ～ **signature** *n* blanc-seing *m*

blanket: ～ **agreement** *n* accord global *m*; ～ **amount** *n* somme globale *f*; ～ **ballot** *n* US vote à bulletin secret *m*; ～ **ban** *n* interdiction générale *f*; ～ **bond** *n* (Ins) garantie générale *f*; (Stock) contrat général *m*; ～ **clause** *n* clause de condition générale *f*; ～ **contract** *n* contrat global *m*; ～ **cover** *n* couverture globale *f*; ～ **coverage** *n* couverture globale *f*; ～ **insurance** *n* assurance globale *f*; ～ **licence** BrE, ～ **license** AmE *n* licence globale *f*, licence générale *f*; ～ **order** *n* commande globale *f*; ～ **policy** *n* contrat global *m*, police globale *f*; ～ **rate** *n* (Gen Comm) tarif global *m*, tarif uniforme *m*; (Acc) taux uniforme *m*; ～ **recommendation** *n* recommandation générale *f*; ～ **statement** *n* bilan général *m*

bleak adj (outlook) sombre

bleed vt faire casquer (infrml), saigner (infrml); ~ **sb dry** (infrml) saigner qn à blanc (infrml)

bleeding edge adj (research, technology) trop innovateur/-trice

blighted area n (of city) quartier vétuste m

blight notice n avertissement tardif m

blind: ~-**alley job** n AmE emploi sans avenir m; ~ **faith** n foi aveugle f; ~ **test** n blind-test m, test aveugle m; ~ **testing** n tests aveugles m pl

blister packaging n emballage blister m, emballage bulle m

blitz¹ n (S&M) campagne de marketing intensive f

blitz² vt (group, target market) bombarder

BLK CAR abbr (▶**bulk carrier**) transporteur en vrac m, vraquier m

bloatware n (Comp) logiciel gonflé m (qui comporte trop de fonctionnalités)

bloc n bloc m

block¹ n (section) bloc m; (of currency) bloc m; (of shares) paquet m; (larger) bloc m; (Stock) inconvertibilité f; ~ **averaging** n établissement d'une moyenne m; ~ **booking** n (at hotel, for travel) réservation groupée f; (for theatre) location groupée f; ~ **diagram** n ordinogramme m, organigramme m, schéma fonctionnel m; ~ **of flats** n BrE immeuble m; ~ **funding** n (Acc, Fin, Tax) (public sector) financement global m; ~ **grant** n UK (Admin) enveloppe globale f; (Pol) dotation globale de fonctionnement f; ~ **purchase** n achat en bloc m, achat groupé m; ~ **of shares** n bloc d'actions m; ~ **stock trader** n négociateur de blocs d'actions m; ~ **trade** n transaction sur bloc de titres f; ~ **vote** n vote groupé m

block² vt (account, currency, credit, funds, competition) bloquer; (vote, bill) bloquer, faire opposition à; (progress, advance) faire obstacle à

blockade n blocus m

blockbuster n (film) superproduction f

blocked: ~ **account** n compte bloqué m; ~ **currency** n monnaie bloquée f

blocker n force d'inertie f

blocking software n (Comp) logiciel de filtrage m

blow¹ n coup m; **be a** ~ **to sb/sth** être un coup pour qn/porté à qch

blow² vt (infrml) (money) claquer (infrml)

blowout n AmE article de détail vendu rapidement très bon marché

blue vt BrE (infrml) claquer (infrml)

blue: ~ **chip** n valeur de fonds de portefeuille f, valeur de premier ordre f, valeur sûre f; ~-**chip company** n société de premier ordre f; ~-**chip customer** n client de premier ordre m; ~-**chip security** n, ~-**chip stock** n valeur de fonds de portefeuille f, valeur de premier ordre f, valeur sûre f; ~-**collar union** n syndicat du

personnel de production m; ~-**collar worker** n col bleu m, travailleur manuel m; ~-**sky research** n recherches sans applications immédiates f pl

Blue laws n pl US législation d'inspiration puritaine sur le repos dominical et qui limite les activités le dimanche

blueprint n (Gen Comm) plan m, projet m; (design) bleu m

Bluetooth n Bluetooth m, normes relatives à l'interopérabilité de téléphones portables, PC et assistants personnels numériques

blunder n gaffe f (infrml); **make a** ~ gaffer (infrml)

blurb n (on book cover) texte de présentation m; (S&M) baratin publicitaire m

BN abbr (▶**billion**) (one thousand million) milliard m; (one million million) BrE billion m

BO abbr (▶**branch office**) (regional) succursale f, agence régionale f, bureau régional m; (local) agence de quartier f, agence locale f

board¹ n (committee) comité m, conseil m, commission f; (hardware) carte f; **be on the** ~, **sit on the** ~ **of directors** siéger au conseil d'administration; ~ **of conciliation** n UK commission d'arbitrage f; ~ **control** n contrôle du conseil d'administration m; ~ **of directors** n conseil d'administration m, conseil de direction m; ~ **of inquiry** n commission d'enquête f; ~ **of management** n comité de gestion m, directoire m; ~ **meeting** n réunion du conseil d'administration f

board² vt embarquer

boarding n embarquement m; ~ **card** n carte d'embarquement f; ~ **gate** n porte d'embarquement f; ~ **pass** n carte d'embarquement f

boardroom n (room) salle du conseil f; (members of the board) direction f

boat n bateau m

boatload n cargaison f

bodily injury n blessure corporelle f

body n (organization) organisme m; (of letter, email) corps m; ~ **of evidence** faisceau de preuves m; ~ **language** n langage corporel m; ~ **of laws** recueil de lois m; ~ **shop** n atelier de carrosserie m

B of E (▶**Bank of England**) banque d'Angleterre

bogie n (rail) bogie m

BOGOF abbr (**buy one, get one free**) deux pour le prix d'un

bogus adj (document, invoice) faux/fausse; (claim) bidon inv; ~ **company** n société fantôme f, société fictive f

bold adj (printing) gras/grasse; ~ **type** n caractères gras m pl

boldface character n caractère gras m

bolster vt soutenir; ~ **the confidence of** renforcer la confiance de; ~ **up sb's**

confidence redonner confiance à qn

bona fide adj sérieux/-ieuse, véritable; ~ **offer** n offre sérieuse f; ~ **price** n prix ferme m; ~ **purchaser** n acheteur/-euse de bonne foi m/f

bona fides n (Law) bonne foi f

bond n (of agreement) contrat m, engagement m; (Fin) obligation f; (certificate) bon m, titre m; (Ins) caution f; (guarantee) engagement écrit m; (link) lien m; (Stock) obligation f; (short-term) bon m; (sterling) obligation f; **in ~** (Imp/Exp) en entrepôt sous douane; **put sth in ~** entreposer qch en douane; **forge/strengthen a ~** créer/resserrer des liens; ~ **broker** n courtier en obligations m; ~ **capital** n capital obligations m, valeur obligataire f; ~ **certificate** n certificat d'obligation m; ~ **conversion** n conversion d'obligations f, conversion de bons f; ~ **creditor** n créancier obligataire m; ~ **dealer** n courtier en obligations m; ~ **debt** n dette obligataire f; ~ **discount** n escompte d'émission d'obligations m, prime d'émission f; ~ **financing** n financement par obligation m; ~ **fund** n fonds obligataire m; ~ **holdings** n pl avoirs en obligations m pl, obligations en portefeuille f pl; ~ **index** n indice des obligations m; ~ **interest** n intérêt sur obligation m; ~ **issue** n émission d'obligations f, émission de bons f; ~ **loan** n emprunt obligataire m; ~ **market** n marché obligataire m; ~ **number** n numéro d'obligation m; ~ **price** n cours de l'obligation m; ~ **rating** n évaluation d'une obligation f; ~ **sales** n pl ventes d'obligations f pl; ~ **sinking fund** n fonds pour amortissement des obligations m; ~ **switching** n arbitrage d'obligations m; ~ **trader** n négociateur d'obligations m, opérateur en obligations m, spéculateur en obligations m; ~ **trading** n négociation d'obligations f, opérations sur obligations f pl; ~ **underwriting** n garantie d'émission obligataire f; ~ **washing** n vente de valeurs à revenu fixe f; ~ **yield** n rendement d'un bon m, rendement de l'obligation m

bonded: ~ **cargo** n marchandises entreposées sous douane f pl; ~ **goods** n pl marchandises entreposées sous douane f pl, marchandises sous douane f pl; ~ **warehouse** n entrepôt en douane m

bondholder n obligataire mf, porteur d'obligations m

bone of contention n contentieux m

bonus n (Fin, Stock) dividende exceptionnel m; (for staff) prime f; ~ **issue** n UK émission d'actions gratuites f; ~ **payment** n (for staff) prime f; (Stock) dividende exceptionnel m; ~ **scheme** n (for effort) programme de primes d'encouragement m; (for productivity) programme de primes de rendement m; ~ **stock** n action donnée en prime f, action gratuite f

book¹ n (Gen Comm) livre m; (of tickets, vouchers, cheques, stamps) carnet m; (ledger) registre m; (Acc) livre m, livre de comptabilité m; (Bank) livret de compte m; (Fin) livre de comptabilité m; **for ~ purposes** à des fins comptables; **do things by the ~** suivre le règlement; ~ **of accounts** n grand livre m, livre de comptes m; ~ **cost** n coût d'acquisition comptable m; ~ **debt** n compte clients m, compte créance m; ~ **depreciation** n amortissement comptable m; ~ **entry** n écriture comptable f; ~ **inventory** n inventaire comptable m, stock comptable m; ~-**keeper** n aide-comptable mf, comptable mf; ~-**keeping** n comptabilité f, tenue des comptes f; ~ **loss** n perte comptable f; ~ **profit** n bénéfice comptable m; ~ **squaring** n (Stock) liquidation des positions f; ~ **token** n chèque-livre m; ~ **value** n valeur comptable f

book² ① vt (Gen Comm, Leis) (room, table, seat) réserver, retenir; (Transp) (ticket, seat) réserver; (trip, holiday) faire les réservations pour; (Acc) comptabiliser; (order) enregistrer; ~ **sth to sb's account** mettre qch sur le compte de qn; ~ **an activity to a code** assigner un code à une activité ② vi réserver; ~ **in advance** réserver à l'avance; ~ **in** ① vt (person) inscrire ② vi (check in) (at hotel, offices) se présenter à la réception; (reserve a room) réserver une chambre; ~ **out** ① vt (person) inscrire à la sortie ② vi signer à la sortie, signer en partant; (at hotel) quitter sa chambre; ~ **up** réserver; **be fully ~ed up** (hotel) être complet/-ète; **I'm fully ~ed up this week** je suis pris tous les jours cette semaine

booked up adj complet/-ète, entièrement réservé

booking n (of orders) enregistrement m; (travel and tourism, theatre, advertising space) réservation f; ~ **confirmation** n confirmation de réservation f; ~ **fee** n frais d'agence m pl, frais de réservation m pl; ~ **office** n (Leis) bureau de location m, bureau des réservations m; (Transp) guichet m; ~ **system** n (S&M) plan de réservation m

booklet n brochure f, livret m

bookmark¹ n (for website) signet m

bookmark² vt (website) marquer d'un signet, mettre dans la liste des favoris

books n pl (Acc) livre de comptes m, registres m pl, écritures f pl; **in the ~** enregistré sur les livres; **off the ~** non-comptabilisé; **keep the ~** tenir les comptes; **be on an agency's ~** être inscrit dans les fichiers d'une agence

boom¹ n (Econ) boom m, période de prospérité f; (in prices) flambée f, montée en flèche f; (in trade) forte hausse f; (of sector) essor m, forte expansion f; (in sales) forte progression f; (in orders) surcroît m, vague f; ⋯⧫

~ **industry/sector** industrie/secteur en pleine expansion; ~ **period** période de forte croissance; ~ **and bust economy** économie en dents de scie

boom² *vi* (exports, prices) flamber, monter en flèche, être en forte hausse; (industry, sector) être en plein essor; **business is** ~**ing** les affaires vont bien; **computer sales are** ~**ing** les ventes d'ordinateurs connaissent une forte progression

boomlet *n* expansion de faible amplitude *f*

boost¹ *n* relance *f*; **give sth a** ~ (Gen Comm) stimuler; (economy) relancer; (product) faire du battage pour

boost² *vt* (Gen Comm) stimuler; (demand, exports) accroître, développer; (economy) relancer; (sales) doper, relancer; (investment) encourager; (capacity, value, number, profit) augmenter; (S&M) (product) faire la promotion de, promouvoir

boot¹ *n* BrE (Transp) coffre *m*

boot² *vt* (Comp) amorcer, lancer; ~ **out** (infrml) (person) virer (infrml); ~ **up** (computer) amorcer, lancer

boot disk *n* disque d'initialisation *m*

bootup *n* amorçage *m*, lancement *m*

BOP *abbr* (▶**balance of payments**) balance des paiements *f*

border *n* frontière *f*; ~ **control** *n* contrôle aux frontières *m*; ~ **police** *n* ≈ Police de l'Air et des Frontières *f*; ~ **trade** *n* commerce frontalier *m*; ~ **worker** *n* frontalier/-ière *m/f*

bordereau *n pl* -**aux** bordereau *m*

borderline case *n* cas-limite *m*

borough *n* municipalité *f*; (in London) arrondissement *m*

borrow ① *vt* emprunter; ~ **money** emprunter de l'argent
② *vi* emprunter; ~ **at call** emprunter à vue; ~ **interest-free** emprunter sans intérêt; ~ **long** emprunter à long terme; ~ **on securities** emprunter sur titres; ~ **short** emprunter à court terme; ~ **against** (income) emprunter en fonction de; ~ **from** emprunter à

borrowed: ~ **capital** *n* capitaux empruntés *m pl*; ~ **funds** *n pl* emprunts *m pl*, fonds empruntés *m pl*; ~ **money** *n* argent emprunté *m*

borrower *n* emprunteur/-euse *m/f*

borrowing *n* emprunt *m*; ~ **abroad** emprunt de capitaux étrangers *m*; ~ **by banks** emprunts bancaires *m pl*; ~ **bank** *n* banque de crédit *f*; ~ **capacity** *n* capacité d'endettement *f*; ~ **ceiling** *n* plafond des emprunts *m*; ~ **cost** *n* coût de l'emprunt *m*; ~ **facility** *n* facilité de crédit *f*; ~ **fee** *n* frais *m pl*; ~ **limit** *n* plafond des emprunts *m*; ~ **power** *n* capacité d'emprunt *f*, capacité de crédit *f*; ~ **rate** *n* taux d'intérêt des emprunts *m*; ~ **requirement** *n* besoins de crédit *m pl*

boss *n* (infrml) chef *m*; **be one's own** ~ être son propre patron

Boston Matrix *n* (Mgmnt) matrice du Boston Consulting Group *f*, matrice BCG *f*

bottle *n* bouteille *f*; ~ **bank** *n* réceptacle à verre *m*

bottleneck *n* goulot d'étranglement *m*; (in traffic) bouchon *m*, embouteillage *m*

bottom¹ *n* (Gen Comm) (of container) fond *m*; (of page list) bas *m*; (Fin) plancher *m*; (of organization) bas *m*, base *f*; (Econ) creux *m*, point bas *m*, plancher *m*; (Stock) cours plancher *m*, plancher *m*; (Transp) (of ship) fond *m*; ~ **end of the range** bas de gamme *m*; **the** ~ **has dropped out of the market, the** ~ **has fallen out of the market** le marché s'est effondré; **be at the** ~ **of the heap** être au bas de l'échelle; ~ **price** *n* cours le plus bas *m*; (Stock) cours plancher *m*

bottom²: ~ **out** *vi* (Econ) atteindre son niveau plancher; (market, prices, graph) atteindre son niveau le plus bas

bottom line *n* (Acc) résultat net *m*; **the** ~ **line is that ...** la vérité c'est que ...; **the department is overstaffed, that's the** ~ le service est en sureffectif, c'est ça le vrai problème; **they only care about the** ~ ils ne s'intéressent qu'aux bénéfices; ~ **profit** *n* (Acc) bénéfices nets *m pl*, résultat net *m*

bottom-of-the-range *adj* bas de gamme

bottomry bond *n* contrat à la grosse aventure *m*

bottom-up *adj* (Gen Comm) en partant de la base; (Comp) ascendant, de bas en haut; ~ **management** *n* gestion consultative *f*, gestion de bas en haut *f*; ~ **planning** *n* planification pyramidale *f*

bought: ~ **book** *n* (Acc) livre des achats *m*, livre des fournisseurs *m*; ~ **contract** *n* bordereau d'achat *m*; ~ **deal** *n* prise ferme *f*, transaction d'achat *f*; ~ **journal** *n*, ~ **ledger** *n* livre des achats *m*, livre des fournisseurs *m*; ~ **note** *n* bordereau d'achat *m*

bounce ① *vt* (cheque) refuser pour défaut de provision, refuser pour non-provision; (email) renvoyer à l'expéditeur
② *vi* (cheque) être sans provision; (email) revenir à l'expéditeur; ~ **back** (currency, prices) remonter; ~ **up** (price) repartir à la hausse

bounced check AmE, **bounced cheque** BrE *n* chèque en bois *m* (infrml), chèque sans provision *m*

bound *adj* ~ **for** à destination de

boundary *n* frontière *f*, limites *f pl*; ~ **constraint** *n* contrainte de limite *f*

bounty *n* (to employees) prime *f*, subvention *f*

bows *n pl* (shipping) avant *m*

box¹ *n* (carton) boîte *f*; (larger) caisse *f*; (on form) case; (Comp) (infrml) ordinateur *m*, machine *f*;

tick the ~ cocher la case; **think outside the** ~ considérer la question sous un autre angle; ~ **number** n (in newspaper) numéro d'annonce m, numéro de référence m; ~ **office** n guichet de vente des billets m; (theatre) bureau de location m; ~ **office hit** n succès au box office m; ~ **office takings** n pl recette f; ~ **pallet** n palette-caisse f

box²: ~ **up** vt mettre en caisse, encaisser

boxcar n AmE wagon de marchandises couvert m

boycott¹ n boycottage m, boycott m

boycott² vt boycotter

b.p. abbr (**bill payable**) b. à p. m (billet à payer)

BPA abbr (**British Ports Association**) association des ports britanniques

bpi abbr (▸**bits per inch**) bpp m pl (bits par pouce)

BPR abbr (▸**business process re-engineering**) reengineering m, reconfiguration f

bps abbr (▸**bits per second**) bps m pl (bits par seconde)

b.r. abbr (▸**bill receivable**) b. à r. m (billet à recevoir)

bracket n (category) classe f, groupe m; (of prices, taxes) fourchette f, tranche f; ~ **creep** n (Tax) glissement d'une tranche d'imposition à l'autre m

brainchild n (infrml) idée personnelle f, invention personnelle f

brain drain n exode des cerveaux m, fuite de cerveaux f

brainstorm vi faire du brainstorming

brainstorming n brainstorming m, remue-méninges m

brake n frein m; **put a** ~ **on sth** freiner qch

branch n (Gen Comm) (local office) agence f, filiale f; (of bank) agence f, succursale f; (of credit institution, shop) succursale f; ~ **bank** n banque à succursales f; ~ **banking** n activité bancaire par succursales f; ~ **line** n (Transp) ligne secondaire f; ~ **manager** n (of bank) directeur/-trice d'agence m/f; (of shop) directeur/-trice de succursale m/f; (of company) directeur/-trice de filiale m/f; ~ **network** n réseau de succursales m; ~ **office** n (regional) agence f, bureau régional m, succursale f; (local office) agence de quartier f, agence locale f, succursale f

brand n marque f; ~ **acceptance** n accueil réservé à la marque m; ~ **advertising** n publicité produit f; ~ **association** n association de la marque f; ~ **awareness** n notoriété de la marque f; ~ **building** n création de marque f; ~ **development** n développement de la marque m; ~ **familiarity** n connaissance de la marque f; ~ **identification** n identification de la marque f; ~ **identity** n identité de marque f; ~ **image** n image de marque f; ~ **label** n

image de marque f; ~ **leader** n marque de tête f, produit leader m; ~ **loyalty** n fidélité à une marque f; ~ **management** n gestion de la marque f; ~ **manager** n chef de marque m, chef de produit m; ~ **marketing** n marketing de la marque m; ~ **name** n marque de fabrique f, nom de marque m; ~ **name product** n produit de marque m; ~ **name recall** n mémorisation de la marque f, mémo-marque f; ~ **portfolio** n portefeuille de marques m; ~ **positioning** n positionnement de la marque m; ~ **preference** n préférence pour une marque f; ~ **promotion** n promotion produit f; ~ **recognition** n identification de la marque f; ~ **share** n part de marché de la marque f; ~ **strategy** n stratégie de la marque f; ~ **switching** n changement de marque m

branded goods n pl articles de marque m pl

branding n marquage m

brand-new adj flambant neuf/neuve, tout neuf/toute neuve

breach¹ n (Law) (of rights, of law and order) atteinte f; (of the law) contravention f; (of rules and regulations) infraction f; (of agreement) rupture f; (of copyright, privilege) violation f; (by failure to comply) manquement m; **be in breach of** (Law) enfreindre; (agreement) violer; ~ **of confidentiality** n violation du secret professionnel f; ~ **of contract** n rupture de contrat f; ~ **of duty** n manquement au devoir m; ~ **of professional etiquette** n faute professionnelle f; ~ **of secrecy** n violation du secret f; ~ **of trust** n abus de confiance m, prévarication f; ~ **of warranty** n rupture de garantie f

breach² vt (contract, rule) ne pas respecter; (treaty) violer; ~ **the law** enfreindre la loi, violer la loi

bread n (infrml) fric m (infrml), argent m; ~**-and-butter** n gagne-pain m; ~**-and-butter line** n (infrml) gamme qui rapporte à l'entreprise de quoi se maintenir à flot f

breadth n (of market) ampleur f; (of experience, knowledge) étendue f; (of vision, opinion, mind) largeur f

breadwinner n soutien de famille m

break¹ n (pause) pause f; (with tradition, past) rupture f; (in supplies) rupture f; (in share prices) effondrement m; ~ **in the market** opportunité sur un marché f, percée dans un marché f; **lucky** ~ chance f, veine f; ~ **bulk cargo** n (shipping) cargaison fractionnée f; ~**-even analysis** n analyse de rentabilité f; ~**-even level of income** n niveau de revenu équilibré m, seuil de rentabilité m; ~**-even point** n point d'équilibre m, point mort m, seuil de rentabilité m; ~**-even pricing** n fixation des prix au niveau du point mort f, mise à prix au point mort f; ~**-even quantity** n (Econ) point mort en quantité m; (Ind, Mgmnt) point mort m

b

break² ⟦1⟧ *vt* (contract) rompre; (ties, links) rompre; (strike) briser; (record) battre; (monopoly) casser; (news) révéler, annoncer; (conditions, terms, embargo) ne pas respecter; (ruin financially) ruiner; ~ **bulk** dégrouper un chargement, dégrouper une livraison; ~ **the ceiling** crever le plafond; ~ **the law** enfreindre la loi, violer la loi; ~ **new ground** ouvrir la voie, tracer une voie nouvelle; ~ **the news** annoncer la nouvelle; ~ **ranks** se désolidariser; ~ **a rule** manquer à une règle; ~ **the stalemate** débloquer la situation, sortir de l'impasse; ~ **one's word/promise** manquer à sa parole/promesse; ~ **away from** (organization) rompre avec; ~ **down** ⟦1⟧ *vt* (costs, expenses) ventiler; (data, findings) décomposer; (opposition, resistance) vaincre ⟦2⟧ *vi* (equipment, vehicle) tomber en panne; (negotiations, relations) échouer; (system) s'effondrer; (communications) cesser; ~ **even** atteindre le point mort, atteindre le seuil de rentabilité, rentrer dans ses frais; ~ **into** (market) percer sur, s'implanter sur; (savings) entamer; ~ **off** (negotiations, ties, contact) rompre; ~ **up** ⟦1⟧ *vt* (Law, Prop) (estate, land) morceller; (empire) démembrer ⟦2⟧ *vi* (alliance, consortium) éclater; (meeting) prendre fin, se terminer; (group) se disperser, se séparer

breakage clause *n* (Ins) clause bris *f*

breakaway union *n* syndicat dissident *m*

breakdown *n* (of costs, figures, budget) ventilation *f*; (of argument) décomposition *f*; (of vehicle, equipment) panne *f*; (of communications, negotiations) rupture *f*; (of plan, project) échec *m*; (of alliance) éclatement *m*; (for analysis) répartition *f*; (S&M) segmentation *f*; ~ **of expenses** ventilation des charges *f*; **a ~ of customers by age** une répartition des clients par tranche d'âge

breakthrough *n* (in science) percée *f*; (Ind) innovation *f*; (in negotiations) progrès *m*

break-up *n* (of company, association) démantèlement *m*, démembrement *m*; (of meeting) fin *f*; (of group, party) éclatement *m*; (of alliance, relationship) rupture *f*; ~ **value** *n* valeur de liquidation *f*

breed *vt* engendrer, faire naître, générer

bribe¹ *n* pot-de-vin *m*, dessous-de-table *m*; **giving ~s** corruption active *f*; **taking ~s** corruption passive *f*

bribe² *vt* acheter, corrompre, soudoyer

bribery *n* corruption *f*

bricks and mortar *adj* (company, firm) traditionnel/-elle

bricks to clicks *n* passage d'une société traditionnelle sur Internet

bridge *vt* (two eras) enjamber; ~ **the gap** boucher le trou, combler l'écart; ~ **a gap in the market** occuper un créneau dans le marché; ~ **the gap between two cultures** effectuer un rapprochement entre deux cultures

bridge: ~ **financing** *n* financement par crédit relais *m*, préfinancement *m*; ~ **loan** *n* AmE ▸**bridging loan** BrE

bridging *n* relais *m*; ~ **advance** *n*, ~ **facility** *n*, ~ **loan** BrE *n* crédit-relais *m*

brief¹ *n* (case, file) dossier *m*; (remit) attributions *f pl*; (assignment) mission *f*; (Law) affaire *f*, dossier *m*; (instructions) directives *f pl*; **it is her ~ to do** sa tâche consiste à faire; **fall within/exceed sb's ~** faire partie de/dépasser les attributions de qn; **work to a ~** suivre des directives

brief² *vt* (give instructions to) briefer, fournir des directives à; (bring up to date) mettre au courant; (Law) (case) établir le dossier de; (lawyer) confier une cause à; ~ **sb on sth** mettre qn au courant de qch

briefing *n* briefing *m*, séance d'information *f*; ~ **session** *n* briefing *m*, séance d'information *f*

bright *adj* (future, prospects, outlook) brillant

bring *vt* amener; ~ **into operation** (plan) réaliser; ~ **a lawsuit against sb** entamer une procédure contre qn, intenter une action en justice contre qn; ~ **an action against sb** intenter un procès à qn; ~ **off a deal** mener une affaire à bien; ~ **out on strike** amener à la grève; ~ **pressure to bear on sb** faire pression sur qn; ~ **sb up to date on sth** mettre qn au courant de qch; ~ **sth up to strength** compléter l'effectif de qch; ~ **to bear against** (Law) peser contre; ~ **to an end** mettre fin à; ~ **to light** mettre en lumière; ~ **under control** (inflation, unemployment) maîtriser; ~ **sth up to date** actualiser qch, mettre qch à jour; ~ **about** (change, reform) provoquer; (settlement) amener; (success, failure) entraîner; ~ **back** ramener; ~ **down** (inflation, expenditure) réduire; (rate, level, price) faire baisser; ~ **forward** (meeting) avancer; (Acc) reporter; ~ **in** (amount, interest, money) rapporter; (expert, consultant) faire appel à; (measures) introduire; ~ **in legislation** faire passer une législation, légiférer; ~ **out** (product) lancer; (Stock) (new issue) introduire sur le marché, émettre; (version, new model, edition) sortir; ~ **together** mettre en contact, réunir; ~ **up** (subject) aborder, soulever

brisk *adj* actif/-ive, animé; ~ **demand** *n* demande active *f*, demande vive *f*; ~ **market** *n* marché animé *m*; ~ **trading** *n* marché actif *m*, marché animé *m*

Britain *n* Grande-Bretagne *n*

British *adj* britannique; ~ **Airports Authority** *n* autorité aéroportuaire britannique; ~ **Broadcasting Corporation** *n* compagnie de télévision et de radio nationale britannique; ~ **Chamber of Commerce** *n* chambre de commerce britannique; ~ **High Commission** *n* haut-comité britannique *m*; ~ **Standard Time** *n* heure légale britannique; ~ **Standards Institution** *n* association britannique de normalisation, ≈

Association française de normalisation f; ~ **Standards Specification** n *spécification standardisée britannique*, ≈ norme de l'Association française de normalisation f; ~ **Summer Time** n *heure d'été en Grande-Bretagne*; ~ **Technical Education Certificate** n ≈ baccalauréat professionnel m

broadband¹ *adj* (television, radio, network, connection) à large bande; ~ **Internet** n Internet (à) haut débit m

broadband² n (for television, radio) diffusion en larges bandes de fréquence f; (Comp) large bande f

broad-brush *adj* esquissé dans ses grandes lignes

broadcast¹ n (television, radio) émission f

broadcast² ① vt (on radio) diffuser, radiodiffuser; (on television) diffuser, téléviser ② vi (person) faire une émission

broadcasting n (on radio) diffusion f, radiodiffusion f; (on television) diffusion f, télédiffusion f; ~ **rights** n pl droits de retransmission m pl

broaden vt (outlook, horizons, client base) élargir; (experience, scope, appeal) étendre

broadly *adv* (agree, conform, correspond) en gros; (similar, compatible) globalement; ~ **speaking** en général; ~ **diversified** (range of products) largement diversifié, très diversifié

broadsheet n journal grand format m

brochure n brochure f, dépliant m, prospectus m

brochureware n (Comp) catalogues en ligne m pl

broken: ~ **amount** n, ~ **lot** n (Stock) rompu m, rompu de titres m, titres formant rompus m pl; ~ **lots** n pl (S&M) articles dépareillés m pl, fins de série f pl

broker¹ n (Gen Comm) commissionnaire mf, intermédiaire mf; (Stock) courtier m, courtier en valeurs mobilières m, négociateur en valeurs mobilières m; ~ **fund** n capital de courtage m, fonds de courtage m; ~**'s commission** n commission de courtage f; ~**'s loan** n crédit de courtier m, prêt de courtage m

broker² ① vt (deal) négocier ② vi faire le courtage

brokerage n courtage m; ~ **account** n compte de courtage m; ~ **commission** n, ~ **fee** n commission de courtage f, courtage m; ~ **firm** n, ~ **house** n maison de courtage f, société de bourse f

brokering n courtage m

broking n courtage m; ~ **house** n maison de courtage f

brown: ~ **book** n UK (jarg) (Pol) livre brun m; ~ **goods** n pl produits bruns m pl

brownout n US baisse de courant f, baisse de tension f, chute de courant f

browse ① vt (Comp) (document, database)

parcourir, survoler; ~ **the Internet** naviguer sur Internet ② vi (in a shop window) regarder; ~ **through** (book, document) feuilleter

browser n (Comp) navigateur m; ~ **interface** n interface de navigation f

browsing n (on Internet) navigation f

brush: ~ **up on** vt (skill) repasser, réviser, se remettre à

B/S *abbr* (▸**balance sheet**) bilan m

BSc *abbr* (**Bachelor of Science**) (degree) ≈ licence de sciences f; (person) licencié/-e en sciences m/f

BSCP *abbr* (**British Standard Code of Practice**) *code référentiel des standards de qualité en Grande-Bretagne*

B-share n UK *action ordinaire avec droit de vote*

BSI *abbr* UK (▸**British Standards Institution**) *association britannique de normalisation*, ≈ AFNOR f

BSS *abbr* (▸**British Standards Specification**) ≈ norme AFNOR f

BST *abbr* (▸**British Summer Time**) *heure d'été en Grande-Bretagne*

BTEC *abbr* (▸**British Technical Education Certificate**) ≈ baccalauréat professionel m

bubble n (Stock) projet sans valeur m, bulle f; **the bursting of the dot-com** ~ l'éclatement de la bulle dot-com

bubblewrap¹ n film à bulles m, emballage bulle m

bubblewrap² vt emballer dans du film à bulles

buck¹ n US (infrml) dollar m; **make a fast** ~, **make a quick** ~ (infrml) se faire du fric facilement (infrml); **pass the** ~ refiler la responsabilité à quelqu'un d'autre

buck² vt (market) aller à l'encontre de; ~ **the trend** aller à l'encontre de la tendance générale; ~ **the system** lutter contre l'ordre établi

bucket shop n (Fin) bureau de courtier marron m; (Leis) agence de voyages à prix réduits f

buck-passing n transfert de responsabilités m

budget¹ *adj* (Acc, Fin) budgétaire; (inexpensive) économique

budget² n budget m; **be over** ~ avoir dépasse le budget; **go over** ~ dépasser le budget; **stay within** ~ ne pas dépasser le budget; **operate on a tight** ~ avoir un budget serré

budget³ ① vt budgétiser, inscrire au budget ② vi préparer un budget, établir un budget; ~ **for** budgétiser, inscrire au budget, prévoir des frais de

budget: ~ **account** n (Fin) compte crédit m; ~ **analysis** n analyse budgétaire f; ⋯▷

~ appropriation n affectation budgétaire f, allocation des fonds f; **~ ceiling** n plafond budgétaire m; **~ constraint** n contrainte budgétaire f; **~ control** n contrôle budgétaire m; **~ cut** n compression budgétaire f, restriction des dépenses f; **~ cutting** n compression budgétaire f; **~ day** n UK jour de la présentation du Budget m; **~ deficit** n déficit budgétaire m; **~ expenditure** n dépense budgétaire f; **~ forecasts** n pl prévisions budgétaires f pl; **~ heading** n poste budgétaire m; **~ period** n période budgétaire f; **~ planning** n planification du budget f; **~ prices** n pl petits prix m pl, prix promotionnels m pl; **~ reduction** n compression budgétaire f, restriction budgétaire f; **~ resolution** n US (Pol) résolution budgétaire f; **~ surplus** n excédent budgétaire m; **~ variance** n écart budgétaire m; **~ year** n exercice budgétaire m

Budget n UK Budget m; **~ speech** n UK discours de présentation du Budget m

budgetary adj budgétaire; **~ accounts** n pl comptes du budget m pl; **~ control** n contrôle budgétaire m; **~ cut** n compression budgétaire f, réduction budgétaire f; **~ deficit** n déficit budgétaire m; **~ expenditure** n (governmental) dépenses budgétaires f pl; **~ policy** n politique budgétaire f; **~ spending** n dépenses budgétaires f pl; **~ surplus** n excédent budgétaire m

budgeted: **~ cost** n coût budgété m, coût standard m; **~ income** n revenu budgété m; **~ profit** n bénéfice budgété m

budgeting n (Acc, Fin) budgétisation f, comptabilité budgétaire f

buffer: **~ state** n état tampon m; **~ stock** n stock de régularisation m, stock régulateur m; **~ zone** n zone tampon f

bug n (Comp) (in program) bogue m, bug m; (fault) défaut m

build vt (housing, offices) bâtir, construire; (team) former, bâtir; (career, fortune) bâtir; (empire) fonder; (relationship) établir; **~ links with** établir des liens avec; **~ sth into a contract** (clause, guarantee, provision) insérer qch dans un contrat; **~ up** (business) développer; (profile, picture) établir; (reputation) bâtir, établir; (production) augmenter, accroître

building n (offices, flats) immeuble m; (sector, structure) bâtiment m; (work) construction f; **~ and loan association** n AmE ≈ société d'investissement et de crédit immobiliers f; **~ materials** n pl matériaux de construction m pl; **~ permit** n AmE permis de construire m; **~ plot** n terrain à bâtir m; **~ and public works** n le bâtiment et les travaux publics; **~ regulations** n pl réglementation relative à la construction f; **~ society** n BrE ≈ société d'investissement et de crédit immobiliers f

build quality n qualité de construction f

built adj (Prop) construit

built-in adj incorporé, intégré; **~-in check** n (Comp) contrôle automatique m; **~-in obsolescence** n (of product) obsolescence planifiée f, vieillissement programmé m; **~-in stabilizer** n (Econ) mécanisme automatique de stabilisation m

built-up area n agglomération urbaine f

bulge n (Econ) brève montée des prix f, envol de courte durée m; (in statistics) poussée f; **demographic ~** poussée démographique f

bulk n (volume) grosse quantité f, volume m; (Transp) (items to be carried) vrac m; **in ~** (transport) en vrac; (buy, sell) en gros; **the ~ of** (imports, applications, research) la majeure partie de; (workers, voters) la plupart de; (workforce) le plus gros de; **~ business** n entreprise de gros f; **~ buyer** n acheteur en gros m; **~ buying** n achat en gros m; **~ carrier** n transporteur en vrac m, vraquier m; **~ commodity** n marchandises en vrac f pl; **~ discount** n remise sur la quantité f; **~ email** n publipostage électronique sauvage m; **~ freight container** n conteneur de vrac m; **~ goods** n pl marchandises en vrac f pl; **~ orders** n pl commandes en gros f pl, commandes par quantité f pl; **~ price** n prix de gros m; **~ purchaser** n acheteur en gros m; **~ sale** n vente en gros f; **~ shipment** n expédition en vrac f; **~ storage** n entreposage en vrac m; **~ transport** n transport en vrac m

bulk-buy vt (individual) acheter en grosses quantités; (company) acheter en gros

bulkhead n cloison f

bulktainer n conteneur de vrac m

bulky adj encombrant, volumineux/-euse

bull¹ n (Stock) acheteur à la hausse m, haussier m, spéculateur à la hausse m; **~ account** n position acheteur f, position couverte f, position à la hausse f; **~ buying** n achat à la hausse m, spéculation à la hausse f; **~ campaign** n spéculation à la hausse f; **~ market** n marché haussier m, marché orienté à la hausse m, marché à la hausse m; **~ operation** n transaction à la hausse f; **~ operator** n acheteur à la hausse m, haussier m, spéculateur à la hausse m; **~ position** n position acheteur f, position couverte f, position à la hausse f; **~ purchase** n achat à la hausse m, position couverte f; **~ speculation** n spéculation à la hausse f; **~ speculator** n spéculateur à la hausse m; **~ transaction** n transaction à la hausse f

bull² vt (prices, shares) pousser à la hausse; **~ the market** spéculer à la hausse

bulldog bond n UK obligation sterling émise par une société étrangère

bullet n (Bank) emprunt remboursable in fine m

bulletin n (statement, report) bulletin m,

b

communiqué m; (on TV) journal m; (news) informations f pl; ~ **board** n AmE panneau d'affichage m; (Comp) messagerie électronique f, tableau d'affichage électronique m; ~ **board system** n messagerie électronique f, tableau d'affichage électronique m

bullet point n puce f

bullion n (Bank) encaisse-or f; ~ **market** n marché des métaux précieux m

bullish adj en hausse, haussier/-ière, à la hausse; be ~ être haussier/-ière; ~ **market** n marché haussier m, marché à la hausse m; ~ **movement** n tendance haussière f, tendance à la hausse f; ~ **stock** n valeur en hausse f; ~ **tendency** n tendance haussière f, tendance à la hausse f

bullishness n (of market) ambiance à la hausse f, nature haussière f

bulwark n (Transp) (shipping) pavois m

bumboat n bateau à provisions m

bumper[1] adj (crop, sales) record inv; (edition) exceptionnel/-elle; ~ **year** n année exceptionnelle f

bumper[2] n BrE (on car) pare-chocs m

bundle[1] n (of papers, notes) liasse f; (Transp) ballot m, paquet m; (Comp) logiciels groupés m pl, bundle m

bundle[2] vt grouper

bundled adj come ~ with être vendu avec; ~ **deal** n (Stock) transaction expédiée f; ~ **software** n ensemble de logiciels (fourni à l'achat d'un ordinateur) m, bundle m

bundling n (S&M) groupage m

bunker n (shipping) soute f

bunkering n (Transp) soutage m

buoyancy n (of market) fermeté f, tendance à la hausse f

buoyant adj actif/-ive, animé; (economy) en expansion, robuste; (prices) soutenu; (profits, sales, currency) ferme, soutenu

burden n (of responsibility) charge f, fardeau m; (Pol) fardeau m; (Tax) valeur comptable f; (weight) poids m; ~ **center** AmE, ~ **centre** BrE n centre de coût m, section homogène f; ~ **of losses** poids des pertes m; ~ **of proof** charge de la preuve f

bureau n agence f, bureau m; ~ **de change** n bureau de change m

Bureau n US département gouvernemental m, service gouvernemental m; ~ **of Labour Statistics** n institut statistique de l'emploi

bureaucracy n bureaucratie f

bureaucrat n bureaucrate mf

bureaucratic adj bureaucratique

bureaucratization n bureaucratisation f

burglar alarm n sonnerie d'alarme f

burglary n cambriolage m; (Law) vol avec effraction m

burn vt (cash, capital) dépenser; (CD) graver; ~ **out** s'user, s'épuiser

burnout n (exhaustion) surmenage m, épuisement m; (Tax) épuisement m

burn rate n taux d'érosion du capital m

bursar n économe m

burst: ~ **advertising** n matraquage publicitaire m; ~ **campaign** n campagne de matraquage f

bus n (Transp) autobus m; (Comp) bus m; ~ **company** n compagnie de cars f; ~ **station** n gare routière f

business n (duties) activités f pl, occupations f pl; (firm) entreprise f; (trade, commerce) affaires f pl, commerce m; be in ~ être dans les affaires; set up in ~ s'établir à son compte; do ~ faire des affaires; do ~ with sb traiter avec qn, faire des affaires avec qn; be in the insurance ~ travailler dans les assurances; lose ~ perdre de la clientèle; ~ has trebled notre chiffre d'affaires a triplé; we need their ~ nous avons besoin de leur clientèle; we get a lot of ~ from Japan nous avons beaucoup de clients japanais; put sb out of ~ obliger qn à cesser leurs activités; any other ~ autres questions à l'ordre du jour f pl, questions diverses f pl; be on a ~ trip être en déplacement; go about one's ~ vaquer à ses occupations; go out of ~ faire faillite; ~ is picking up les affaires reprennent; ~ is slack les affaires ne marchent pas; on ~ (travel) pour affaires; talk ~ parler affaires; get down to ~ passer aux choses sérieuses; make it one's ~ to do se charger de faire;

business a... ~ **account** n compte d'affaires m; ~ **accounting** n comptabilité d'entreprise f; ~ **acquaintance** n relation d'affaires f; ~ **activity** n affaires f pl; ~ **acumen** n sens aigu des affaires m; ~ **address** n (of person) adresse au bureau f; (of company) adresse commerciale f, adresse professionnelle f; ~ **administration** n administration commerciale f; ~ **agent** n agent d'affaires m; (Ind) US délégué/-e syndical/-e m/f; ~ **angel** n business angel m, investisseur privé providentiel m; ~ **assets** n pl actif commercial m; ~ **associate** n associé/-e m/f;

c... ~ **call** n (phone call) communication d'affaires f; (visit) visite d'affaires f; ~ **card** n carte de visite (professionnelle) f; ~ **center** AmE, ~ **centre** BrE n centre d'affaires m; (in airport) bureau de services de secrétariat m; ~ **charges** n pl frais d'administration m pl, frais professionnels m pl; ~ **circles** n pl milieux d'affaires m pl; ~ **class** n (Transp) classe affaires f, classe club f; ~ **college** n école de commerce f; ~ **community** n monde des affaires m; ~ **computing** n informatique de gestion f, informatique professionnelle f; ~ **concern** n entreprise commerciale f, firme f, fonds de commerce m; ~ **conditions** n pl conditions commerciales f pl, conjoncture f; ~ **consultancy** n cabinet de conseil en gestion d'entreprise m; ⋯▶

~ **consultant** n conseil en gestion d'entreprise m, conseiller/-ère en gestion d'entreprise m/f; ~ **continuity** n continuité des affaires f; ~ **continuity plan** n plan de continuité des affaires m; ~ **corporation** n entreprise commerciale f, société commerciale f; ~ **creation** n création d'entreprise f; ~ **cycle** n cycle économique m;

(**d...**) ~ **day** n jour de travail m; (for shop) jour ouvrable m; ~ **deal** n affaire f; ~ **dealings** n pl opérations commerciales f pl; ~ **decision** n décision commerciale f; ~ **development** n développement commercial m, prospection f; ~ **development manager** n directeur/-trice du développement m/f;

(**e...**) ~ **economics** n + sing v économie d'entreprise f; ~ **economist** n économiste d'entreprise mf; ~ **environment** n (Econ) conjoncture f; ~ **ethics** n pl déontologie f, déontologie des affaires f; ~ **etiquette** n protocole des affaires m; ~ **expansion** n expansion commerciale f; ~ **expenses** n pl (operating costs) frais d'exploitation m pl; (professional outlay) frais professionnels m pl; ~ **experience** n expérience professionnelle f;

(**f...**) ~ **failure** n faillite (d'entreprise) f; ~ **finance** n gestion financière des entreprises f; ~ **forecasting** n prévisions commerciales f pl; ~ **forecasts** n pl prévisions économiques f pl;

(**g...**) ~ **game** n jeu de simulation de gestion d'entreprise m; ~ **goods** n pl biens de production m pl; ~ **growth** n croissance des affaires f;

(**h...**) ~ **hours** n pl (of shop) heures d'ouverture f pl; (of office) heures de bureau f pl; ~ **house** n maison de commerce f;

(**i...**) ~ **indicator** n indicateur de conjoncture m; ~ **intelligence** n veille économique f; ~ **interest** n intérêt commercial m; ~ **interruption insurance** n assurance contre les pertes d'exploitation f;

(**l...**) ~ **law** n droit commercial m; ~ **lease** n bail commercial m; ~ **letter** n lettre commerciale f; ~ **liability** n responsabilité commerciale f; ~ **loan** n prêt à l'entreprise m; ~ **loss** n perte commerciale f, perte d'exploitation f; ~ **lunch** n déjeuner d'affaires m;

(**m...**) ~ **management** n administration d'entreprise f, gestion d'entreprise f, management m; ~ **manager** n chef d'entreprise m, dirigeant/-e d'entreprise m/f; (Media) directeur/-trice commercial/-e m/f; ~ **meeting** n réunion d'affaires f; ~ **model** n business model m;

(**n...**) ~ **name** n raison sociale f;

(**o...**) ~ **opportunity** n créneau m, opportunité commerciale f;

(**p...**) ~ **package** n logiciel de gestion m; ~ **pages** n pl (of newspaper) rubrique économique et financière f; ~ **park** n parc d'activités m, parc d'affaires m; ~ **plan** n projet commercial m, business plan m; ~ **planning** n (on-going) planification de projet f, planification d'activités f; (for new business) préparation d'un projet commercial f, préparation d'un business plan f; ~ **policy** n politique commerciale f; ~ **portfolio** n portefeuille d'activités m; ~ **practices** n pl pratiques commerciales f pl, usages commerciaux m pl; ~ **premises** n pl locaux commerciaux m pl; ~ **process re-engineering** n reengineering m, reconfiguration f; ~ **profits** n pl bénéfices industriels et commerciaux m pl; ~ **proposition** n proposition f;

(**r...**) ~ **recovery** n reprise des affaires f; ~ **reply card** n carte-réponse f; ~ **reply envelope** n enveloppe-réponse f; ~ **reply service** n service de préaffranchissement d'enveloppes-réponses m; ~ **risk** n risque commercial m;

(**s...**) ~ **school** n école de commerce f; ~ **sector** n domaine des affaires m; ~ **sense** n sens des affaires m; ~ **services** n pl services aux entreprises m pl; ~ **slowdown** n ralentissement économique m; ~ **software** n logiciel de gestion m; ~ **space** n locaux à usage commercial m pl; ~ **start-up** n création d'entreprise f; ~ **strategist** n spécialiste en stratégies commerciales mf; ~ **strategy** n stratégie commerciale f; ~ **stream** n flux d'affaires m; ~ **studies** n pl études commerciales f pl, études de gestion f pl;

(**t...**) ~ **tax** n taxe d'affaires f, taxe professionnelle f; ~ **transaction** n opération commerciale f, transaction commerciale f; ~ **travel** n voyages d'affaires m pl; ~ **trip** n déplacement professionnel m, voyage d'affaires m;

(**v...**) ~ **venture** n entreprise commerciale f, aventure commerciale f;

(**w...**) ~ **world** n monde des affaires m, monde du commerce m;

(**y...**) ~ **year** n exercice m

businesslike adj sérieux/-ieuse, efficace

businessman n pl -men homme d'affaires m

business-orientated adj axé sur les affaires, tourné vers le commerce

business-to-administration n (sector) transactions entre une entreprise et une administration f pl

business-to-business n commerce interentreprises m; **the** ~ **sector** le secteur du commerce interentreprises; ~ **applications** les applications dans le secteur du commerce interentreprises

business-to-business-to-consumer n commerce interentreprises orienté client m

business-to-consumer n commerce de professionnel à particulier m; ~ **e-commerce** n commerce électronique grand public m

business-to-government *n* échanges entre une entreprise et un gouvernement *f pl*

businesswoman *n pl* **-women** femme d'affaires *f*

busy *adj* (person) occupé; (day, week) chargé; (town) animé; (telephone) occupé; (machine) en service; **the busiest time of year** la période la plus active de l'année; ∼ **schedule** *n* programme chargé *m*; ∼ **signal** *n*, ∼ **tone** *n* tonalité 'occupé' *f*

butter mountain *n* montagne de beurre *f*

button *n* (Comp) bouton *m*; (switch) interrupteur *m*

buy[1] *n* acquisition *f*; **a good/bad** ∼ une bonne/mauvaise affaire *f*

buy[2] *vti* acheter; ∼ **sth at a reduced price** acheter qch au rabais; ∼ **the book** (Stock) acheter l'inventaire; ∼ **a bull** spéculer; ∼ **for the account** acheter en liquidation; ∼ **on approval** acheter à l'essai; ∼ **on bid** acheter aux enchères; ∼ **on the black market** acheter au marché noir; ∼ **on close** (Stock) acheter à la clôture; ∼ **on credit** acheter à crédit; ∼ **on a fall** acheter à la baisse; ∼ **on hire purchase** BrE, ∼ **on the installment plan** AmE acheter à tempérament; ∼ **on margin** acheter à terme en versant un dépôt de garantie; ∼ **on a rise** acheter à la hausse; ∼ **on tick** BrE (infrml) acheter à crédit; ∼ **sth on credit** faire un achat à crédit; ∼ **sth on spec** (infrml) effectuer un achat spéculatif; ∼ **some time** gagner du temps; ∼ **back** racheter; ∼ **down** (Bank) réduire les frais de crédit; ∼ **forward** acheter à terme; ∼ **in** (stock up on) racheter, s'approvisionner en; (Stock) exécuter; ∼ **into** (idea, plan) approuver sans réserve; ∼ **out** désintéresser; ∼ **over** soudoyer; ∼ **up** (property, shares) acheter

buy-back *n* rachat d'actions *m*; ∼

agreement *n* accord de rachat *m*; ∼ **clause** *n* clause de rachat *f*; ∼ **option** *n* option de rachat *f*, possibilité de rachat *f*

buyer *n* acheteur/-euse *m/f*; (Stock) acheteur/-euse *m/f*, détenteur/-trice *m/f*, titulaire *mf*; **at** ∼**'s risk** aux risques de l'acheteur; ∼ **credit** *n* crédit acheteur *m*; ∼ **response** *n* réaction de l'acheteur *f*; ∼**'s market** *n* marché acheteur *m*, marché à la baisse *m*; ∼**'s option** *n* option d'achat *f*, prime acheteur *f*; ∼**'s rate** *n* taux acheteur *m*, cours acheteur *m*

buy-in *n* (Stock) exécution en Bourse *f*, rachat d'office *m*

buying *n* achat *m*; ∼ **behavior** AmE, ∼ **behaviour** BrE *n* comportement d'achat *m*; ∼ **commission** *n* commission d'achat *f*; ∼ **habits** *n pl* habitudes d'achat *f pl*; ∼ **hedge** *n* couverture d'une position acheteur *f*; ∼ **house** *n* centrale d'achat pour indépendants *f*; ∼**-in price** *n* (EU) prix de rachat *m*; ∼ **order** *n* ordre d'achat *m*; ∼ **power** *n* pouvoir d'achat *m*; ∼ **price** *n* prix d'achat *m*; ∼ **rate** *n* (Bank) cours acheteur *m*, taux de change acheteur *m*; ∼ **surge** *n* vague d'achats *f*

buyout *n* (Fin) désintéressement *m*; (Stock) achat *m*, acquisition *f*, rachat d'entreprise *m*

buzzer *n* (Comms) interphone *m*

buzz word *n* (infrml) mot à la mode *m*, terme branché *m* (infrml)

bye-law *n* ▶bylaw

by-election *n* UK (Pol) élection partielle *f*

bylaw *n* règlement administratif *m*; (from local authority) arrêté municipal *m*

by-product *n* dérivé *m*, produit dérivé *m*

byte *n* octet *m*

Cc

C2C *abbr* (▶**consumer-to-consumer**) commerce entre particuliers *m*, transactions de consommateur à consommateur *f pl*, commerce C2C *m*

CA *abbr* (Acc) UK (▶**certified accountant**, ▶**chartered accountant**) expert-comptable *m*

C/A *abbr* (▶**capital account**) compte de capital *m*; (▶**credit account**, ▶**current account**) c/c *m* (compte courant)

CAA *abbr* UK (▶**Civil Aviation Authority**) ≈ DGAC *f* (Direction générale de l'aviation civile)

CAB *abbr* UK (▶**Citizens Advice Bureau**)

bureau d'aide et de conseil aux citoyens

cabin *n* (on ship, aircraft) cabine *f*; ∼ **staff** *n* personnel de bord *m*, personnel navigant commercial *m*

cabinet *n* (Pol) cabinet *m*, conseil des ministres *m*; ∼ **reshuffle** *n* remaniement ministériel *m*

cable[1] *n* câble *m*; ∼ **modem** *n* modem câble *m*; ∼ **program** AmE, ∼ **programme** *n* BrE émission sur chaîne câblée *f*; ∼ **television** *n* télévision par câble *f*; ∼ **television company** *n* câblo-opérateur *m*

cable[2] *vt* (Comms) câbler, télégraphier

cabotage *n* cabotage *m*

cache memory *n* antémémoire *f*

CAD *abbr* (▶**computer-aided design**, ▶**computer-assisted design**) CAO *f* (conception assistée par ordinateur); (▶**cash against documents**) comptant contre documents *m*

cadastre *n* cadastre *m*

CAD/CAM *abbr* (▶**computer-aided design and computer-aided manufacturing**, ▶**computer-assisted design and computer-assisted manufacturing**) CFAO *f* (conception et fabrication assistées par ordinateur)

cadre *n* cadres *m pl*; (Pol) pouvoir exécutif *m*

CAL *abbr* (▶**computer-aided learning**, ▶**computer-assisted learning**) EAO *m* (enseignement assisté par ordinateur)

calculable *adj* calculable

calculate *vt* calculer

calculated risk *n* risque calculé *m*

calculating machine *n* machine à calculer *f*

calculation *n* calcul *m*; **make a ∼** faire un calcul; **according to my ∼s** d'après mes calculs

calculator *n* calculatrice *f*, calculette *f*

calendar *n* calendrier *m*; **∼ day** *n* jour civil *m*; (in a contract) jour du calendrier *m*; **∼ month** *n* mois civil *m*; (in a contract) mois du calendrier *m*; **∼ year** *n* année civile *f*

caliber AmE, **calibre** BrE *n* calibre *m*

call¹ *n* appel *m*, communication *f*, coup de fil *m* (infrml), coup de téléphone *m*; (Fin) appel *m*; (demand) demande *f*; (Stock) call *m*, option d'achat *f*; (summons) appel *m*; (request) appel *m*; (visit) visite *f*; **give sb a ∼** appeler qn; **make a ∼** appeler, téléphoner; **at ∼** (Fin) à vue; (Stock) au remboursement; **∼ account** *n* compte bancaire à vue *m*; **∼ box** *n* cabine téléphonique *f*; **∼ buyer** *n* acheteur d'un call *m*; **∼ center** AmE, **∼ centre** BrE *n* centre d'appel *m*; **∼ center agent** AmE, **∼ centre agent** BrE opérateur/-trice de centre d'appel *m/f*, téléopérateur/-trice *m/f*; **∼ charge** *n* montant de la communication téléphonique *m*, prix de la communication téléphonique *m*; **∼ date** *n* date de remboursement par anticipation *f*; **∼ diversion** *n* transfert d'appel *m*; **∼ for bids**, **∼ for tenders** *n* appel d'offres *m*; **∼ for papers** *n* appel à communications *m*; **∼ loan** *n* (Bank) prêt au jour le jour *m*, prêt remboursable sur demande *m*; (Stock) prêt à vue *m*; **∼ money** *n* emprunt au jour le jour *m*, emprunt remboursable sur demande *m*; **∼ notice** *n* avis de rachat *m*; **∼ option** *n* contrat d'option d'achat *m*, option d'achat *f*; **∼ option price** *n* prime d'achat *f*; **∼ premium** *n* prime d'achat *f*, prix d'option d'achat *m*; **∼ price** *n* prix d'exercice *m*, prix de rachat *m*; **∼ protection** *n* garantie contre le risque de remboursement anticipé *f*; **∼ provision** *n*

provision pour le prix d'un rachat; **∼ purchase** *n* achat d'une option d'achat *m*, long call *m*, position acheteur sur options d'achat *f*; **∼ queuing** *n* mise en file d'attente des appels *f*; **∼ rate** *n* (interest rates) taux au jour le jour *m*; (of stock, shares) taux de l'option d'achat *m*; **∼ sign** *n* (Transp) indicatif d'appel *m*; **∼ spread** *n* opération mixte sur options d'achat *f*; **∼ waiting** *n* (on telephone) signal d'appel *m*

call² *vt* (telephone) appeler; (summon) convoquer; (Bank) appeler au remboursement; (Comp) appeler; (meeting) organiser; **∼ sb as a witness** citer qn comme témoin; **∼ bonds** racheter un emprunt obligataire, rembourser des obligations; **∼ collect** AmE téléphoner en PCV; **∼ sb collect** AmE appeler qn en PCV, téléphoner à qn en PCV; **∼ sb to account** demander des comptes à qn; **∼ sb for interview** convoquer qn pour un entretien; **∼ sb toll-free** AmE appeler qn par numéro vert; **∼ a strike** appeler à la grève, lancer un mot d'ordre de grève; **∼ sb to the bar** (Law) inscrire qn au barreau; **∼ back** (Comms) rappeler; **∼ for** demander; **∼ in** (debt) demander le remboursement de; **∼ in on** rendre visite à; **∼ off** (deal) interrompre; (meeting) annuler; **∼ off a strike** annuler un ordre de grève; **∼ on** visiter; **∼ out** (members) lancer un ordre de grève à; **∼ up** (Comms) appeler

CALL *abbr* (▶**computer-aided language learning**, ▶**computer-assisted language learning**) apprentissage des langues assisté par ordinateur *m*

callable *adj* rachetable, remboursable; **∼ bond** *n* obligation amortie *f*, obligation remboursable *f*; **∼ capital** *n* capital exigible *m*; **∼ loan** *n* prêt révocable *m*; **∼ preferred stock** *n* US obligation remboursable par anticipation *f*

callback *n* (on Internet) option de routage d'un appel sur un agent *f*, callback *m*

called: **∼-away** *adj* (bonds) dont le remboursement est demandé; **∼ security** *n* titre rappelé au remboursement *m*, valeur rachetée *f*; **∼-up capital** *n* capital appelé *m*

caller *n* (Comms) personne qui appelle *f*; (visitor) visiteur/-euse *m/f*; **∼ display** *n* affichage du numéro *m*

calling *n* vocation *f*

call-through *n* (on Internet) liaison directe via la voix par téléphonie IP *f*

CAM *abbr* (▶**computer-aided manufacture**, ▶**computer-aided manufacturing**, ▶**computer-assisted manufacture**, ▶**computer-assisted manufacturing**) FAO *f* (fabrication assistée par ordinateur)

cambist *n* cambiste *mf*

camera: **in ∼** *adj* (meeting) à huis clos

camera-ready *adj* final, prêt pour la

reproduction; ∼ **copy** n copie prête à la reproduction f

campaign n campagne f

Canadian: ∼ **English** n (language) anglais du Canada m; ∼ **French** n (language) français du Canada m

canal n canal m

can bank n conteneur de boîtes de conserve à recycler m

cancel ☐1 vt (event, flight, booking, order) annuler; (appointment) décommander; (Comp) annuler; (contract, policy) résilier; (cheque) mettre opposition à; (debt) annuler; (Patents) radier

☐2 vi se décommander; ∼ **out** (effect, gain, trend) neutraliser; (figures, arguments) s'annuler

cancellation n (of order, project, shares) annulation f; (Patents) radiation f; ∼ **clause** n clause d'annulation f, clause de résiliation f; ∼ **fee** n frais d'annulation m pl; ∼ **notice** n avis d'annulation m, avis de résolution m

cancelled: ∼ **cheque** n BrE chèque oblitéré m, chèque payé m; ∼ **share** n BrE action annulée f

C&E abbr UK (▶**Customs & Excise**) administration des douanes britanniques f, régie f

C&F abbr (▶**cost and freight**) C&F (coût et fret)

C&I abbr (▶**cost and insurance**) C&A (coût et assurance)

candidacy n candidature f

candidate n candidat/-e m/f; **this** ∼ **is not suited to the job** le candidat n'a pas le profil requis pour le poste; **the successful** ∼ le candidat retenu

candidature n candidature f

canton n canton m

canvass vt (Gen Comm) (area) prospecter; (for a survey) sonder; ∼ **opinions on sth** sonder l'opinion au sujet de qch; ∼ **sb for their support** solliciter le soutien de qn

canvasser n (S&M) démarcheur/-euse m/f, placier-ière m/f; (Pol) agent électoral m

canvassing n (S&M) démarchage m, prospection f

cap¹ abbr (Acc) (▶**capital**) capital m; (▶**capital letter**) (lettre) majuscule f

cap² n (Gen Comm) plafond m; (Acc) restriction f; (Bank) taux plafond m; (Econ) garantie de taux plafond f, taux à terme à la hausse m; ∼ **rate** n (for interest) taux d'intérêt plafond m, taux plafond m

cap³ vt (interest rate, budget) plafonner

CAP abbr (▶**Common Agricultural Policy**) PAC f (politique agricole commune)

capability n (aptitude) aptitude f; (potential strength) capacité f; (capacity) capacité f

capable adj capable; ∼ **of doing sth** (able) capable de faire qch; (liable) susceptible de faire qch

capacity n (rate of production) débit m, rendement m; (of container) contenance f, capacité f; (personal, professional) aptitude f, capacité f, compétence f; (of building) capacité d'accueil f; (Transp) contenance f; **in the** ∼ **of** en qualité de; **in an advisory** ∼ à titre consultatif; ∼ **to work** aptitude à travailler f; ∼ **utilization** n utilisation des capacités f, utilisation du potentiel de production f; ∼ **utilization rate** n taux d'utilisation des capacités m, taux d'utilisation du potentiel de production m

capital n (Acc) capital m; (letter) (lettre) majuscule f; (Econ, Fin) capital m, capitaux m pl; **in** ∼**s** en majuscules; **make** ∼ **out of sth** tirer profit de qch; ∼ **account** n (Acc) compte de capital m; (Bank) compte d'immobilisations m; ∼ **aid** n aide financière en capital f; ∼ **allotment** n affectation pour dépenses en capital f; ∼ **allowance** n (Acc) déduction fiscale pour amortissement f; (Tax) déduction fiscale pour investissement f; ∼ **appreciation** n plus-value de capital f; ∼ **assets** n pl (Econ) actif immobilisé m, capitaux fixes m pl; (investment) immobilisations financières f pl; ∼ **base** n capital de base m; (Stock) capital social m; ∼ **bonus** n dividende exceptionnel m; (Stock) actions gratuites f pl; ∼ **budget** n budget d'investissement m; ∼ **budgeting** n budgétisation des immobilisations f; ∼ **contribution** n apport m, apport de capital m; ∼ **cost** n coût d'immobilisation m; ∼ **costs** n pl (Econ, Fin) coûts d'investissement m pl, coûts en capital m pl; ∼ **cover** n (Bank) ratio fonds engagements m, ratio fonds propres m; ∼ **deepening** n (Econ) augmentation de capital f, intensification de l'apport en capital f, investissements de rationalisation m pl; ∼ **expenditure** n dépenses en capital f pl, mise de fonds f, investissements m pl; ∼ **expenditure budget** n budget des investissements m; ∼ **financing** n financement d'immobilisations m; ∼ **flight** n fuite de caitaux f; ∼ **flow** n flux de capitaux m; ∼ **funding** n financement d'immobilisations m; ∼ **gain** n gain en capital m, plus-value f; ∼ **gains allowance** n abattement sur les plus-values m; ∼ **gains tax** n impôt sur les plus-values m; ∼ **goods** n pl biens d'équipement m pl; ∼ **growth** n (Stock) croissance du capital f; ∼ **increase** n augmentation de capital f; ∼ **inflow** n afflux de capitaux m, afflux de fonds m, entrée de capitaux f; ∼ **injection** n injection de capitaux f; ∼ **invested** n capital investi m; ∼ **investment** n immobilisation f, investissement de capitaux m; ∼ **leverage** n levier financier m; ∼ **loss** n moins-value f; ∼ **market** n marché des capitaux m; ∼ **outflow** n fuite de capitaux f, sortie de capitaux f; ∼ **outlay** n (Fin) mise de fonds f; ∼ **profit** n plus-value f, plus-value sur la réalisation d'actifs immobilisés f; ····⟩

~ property n bien en immobilisation m; **~ requirements** n pl besoins en capitaux m pl; **~ reserves** n pl réserves f pl; **~ resource** n ressource en capital f; **~ risk** n risque de capital m; **~ shares** n pl actions donnant droit aux plus-values f pl; **~ stock** n capital actions m, capital social m; **~ strategy** n stratégie d'investissement f; **~ structure** n structure du capital f, répartition des capitaux f; **~ sum** n capital m; **~ transaction** n opération sur le capital f; **~ transfer** n transmission de capital f; **~ transfer tax** n UK droits de mutation m pl; **~ utilization** n utilisation du capital f; **~ value** n valeur de l'actif f, valeur du capital f

capital-intensive adj (Gen Comm) capitalistique; (Econ) à forte proportion de capital

capitalism n capitalisme m

capitalist¹ adj capitaliste

capitalist² n capitaliste mf

capitalization n capitalisation f; **~ bond** n obligation de capitalisation f; **~ of interest** n capitalisation des intérêts f; **~ issue** n attribution d'actions gratuites f; **~ rate** n taux de capitalisation m; **~ shares** n pl actions gratuites f pl

capitalize vt (Acc) activiser; (Econ, Stock) avoir recours à la capitalisation boursière; (estimate value of sth) capitaliser; (provide with capital) pourvoir de capital; **~ on** tirer profit de

capitalized value n valeur capitalisée f

capitation n impôt par tête m; **~ tax** n capitation f

capsize vi chavirer

captain n (of aircraft) commandant de bord m; (ship's officer) capitaine m, commandant m; **~ of industry** n capitaine d'industrie m

caption n légende f, (for TV, film) sous-titre m

captive: **~ audience** n public captif m; **~ market** n marché captif m

capture¹ n (of data) saisie f

capture² vt (data) saisir; (market) s'emparer de, accaparer

car n voiture f, **~ allowance** n indemnité de déplacement f; **~ ferry** n car-ferry m; **~ hire** n BrE location de voitures f; **~ industry** n industrie automobile f; **~ loan** n prêt automobile m; **~ manufacturer** n constructeur automobile m, fabricant automobile m; **~ park** n BrE parc de stationnement m, parking m; **~ parking** n stationnement m; **~ pool** n (fleet) parc de voitures m; **~ pooling** n covoiturage m; **~ registration** n immatriculation f; **~ rental** n location de voitures f; **~ rental firm** n loueur de voitures m; **~ worker** n ouvrier de l'industrie automobile m

CAR abbr UK (▸compound annual rate) taux annuel composé m, taux d'intérêt composé m

carat n carat m

carbon copy n copie carbone f

card n (for correspondence) carte f; (cardboard) carton m; **~-carrying member** n membre adhérent m; **~ file** n, **~ index** n fichier m; **~ issuer** n (Bank) émetteur/-trice de cartes m/f; **~ reader** n lecteur de cartes m; **~ swipe** n lecteur de carte magnétique m

cardboard n BrE carton m; **~ box** n carton m

cardholder n titulaire de carte mf, détenteur/-trice de carte m/f

care n attention f, soin m; **take ~ of** (arrangements, details) s'occuper de; (shop, valuables) garder; **'~ of'** (on mail) 'aux bons soins de', 'chez'

career n carrière f; **it's a good ~ move for him/her** c'est un pas en avant dans son évolution professionnelle; **~ break** n interruption de carrière f; **~ change** n changement de carrière m; **~ development** n développement de carrière m; **~ expectations** n pl attentes professionnelles f pl; **~ goals** n pl objectifs professionnels m pl; **~ guidance** n orientation professionnelle f; **~ ladder** n échelle professionnelle f; **~ path** n plan de carrière m; **~ planning** n plan de carrière m; **~ prospects** n pl perspectives de carrière f pl

Career Development Loan n UK prêt de développement de carrière m

careerist¹ adj carriériste

careerist² n (pej) arriviste mf

career-orientated adj carriériste

careers: **~ adviser** n conseiller/-ère d'orientation professionnelle m/f; **~ office** n service d'orientation professionnelle m; **~ officer** n conseiller/-ère d'orientation professionnelle m/f

carefully adv prudemment

cargo n cargaison f, chargement m, marchandises f pl; **~ aircraft** n avion-cargo m; **~ boat** n cargo m; **~ capacity** n capacité de chargement f, capacité utile f; **~ declaration** n déclaration de chargement f; **~ dues** n pl (shipping) frais de fret m pl; **~ handler** n manutentionnaire m; **~-handling charge** n frais de manutention des marchandises m pl; **~ homeward** n fret de retour m; **~ insurance** n assurance sur facultés f; **~ liner** n cargo mixte m; **~ outward** n fret aller m; **~ plane** n avion-cargo m; **~ transfer** n transfert de marchandises m; **~ vessel** n cargo m

carnet n autorisation d'importation temporaire f

carr: **~ fwd** abbr (▸carriage forward) p.d. (port dû); **~ pd** abbr (▸carriage paid) p.p. (port payé)

carriage n (transportation) factage m, transport m; (fee) frais de port m pl; (for rail travel) wagon voyageurs m; **~ charge** n frais de port *m pl*; ∼ **expenses** *n pl* frais de port *m pl*; ∼ **forward** *n* port dû *m*; ∼**-free** *adv* franco de port; ∼ **paid** *adv* port payé

carried: ∼ **down** *adj* (on balance sheet) à reporter; ∼ **forward** *adj* (in bookkeeping) à reporter

carrier *n* (aviation) transporteur aérien *m*; (road) camionneur *m*, entreprise de transports routiers *f*; ∼**'s risk** aux risques et périls du transporteur

carrot *n* use the ∼ **and stick method** utiliser la méthode de la carotte et du bâton

carry *vt* (risk, warning) comporter; (goods) transporter; (penalty, fine) être passible de; (advertisement) publier; (model, product line) vendre; (Fin) comptabiliser, enregistrer; ∼ **a loss** enregistrer une perte; ∼ **a report** (newspaper) contenir un rapport; ∼ **back** (Acc) reporter en amont, reporter en arrière; ∼ **down** (Acc) reporter, reporter en avant; ∼ **forward** (Acc) reporter prospectivement, reporter sur un exercice ultérieur; ∼ **on** (business) diriger, faire marcher; ∼ **on doing** continuer à faire; ∼ **out** (audit) effectuer; (instruction, order) exécuter; (plans, policies) mettre en œuvre, mettre en pratique, mettre à exécution; (duties) remplir; (invention) réaliser; (research, survey) mener; ∼ **out a trial on a new product** mettre un nouveau produit à l'essai; ∼ **over** (balance, debt) reporter

carry: ∼**-back** *n* application à une année antérieure *f*, report en amont *m*, report sur les exercices précédents *m*, report sur une année antérieure *m*; ∼**-forward** *n* report en aval *m*, report sur les exercices suivants *m*; ∼**-over** *n* report *m*; ∼**-over business** *n* report sur l'exercice suivant *m*; ∼**-over effect** *n* effet de rappel *m*, effet de rémanence *m*; ∼**-over loss** *n* déficit reportable sur les années suivantes *m*; ∼**-over stocks** *n pl* stocks de report *m pl*, stocks reportés *m pl*

carrying: ∼ **capacity** *n* capacité de charge *f*, charge utile *f*, jauge *f*, tonnage *m*; ∼ **charge** *n* (Stock) frais de couverture *m pl*, frais de portage *m pl*

cart *n* AmE chariot *m*

cartage *n* camionnage *m*, factage *m*

cartel *n* cartel *m*

carton *n* carton *m*, emballage en carton *m*

cascading style sheets *n pl* (Comp) feuilles de style en cascade *f pl*

case *n* (instance) cas *m*; (situation) cas *m*; (Law) affaire *f*, cas *m*, procès *m*; (luggage) valise *f*; (print) casse *f*; (crate, chest) caisse *f*; **in** ∼ au cas où; **in** ∼ **of** en cas de; **in this** ∼ dans le cas présent; **a** ∼ **in point** un cas d'espèce, un example typique; **on a** ∼ **by** ∼ **basis** au cas par cas; **in 8 out of 10** ∼**s** 8 fois sur 10; **be a** ∼ **of doing** s'agir de faire; **argue the** ∼ **for sth** donner des arguments en faveur de; **there is a strong** ∼ **for doing/not doing** il y a de bonnes raisons pour faire/ne pas faire;

the ∼ **is closed** (Gen Comm, Law) l'affaire est entendue; ∼ **file** *n* dossier *m*; ∼ **for the defence** BrE, ∼ **for the defense** AmE la défense *f*; ∼ **for the prosecution** accusation *f*; ∼ **history** *n* dossier personnel *m*, historique *m*; ∼ **law** *n* jurisprudence *f*, ∼ **notes** *n* dossier *m*; ∼ **papers** *n pl* pièces d'un dossier *f pl*; ∼ **study** *n* étude de cas *f*; ∼ **study method** *n* méthode de l'étude de cas *f*

CASE *abbr* (▸**computer-aided software engineering**, ▸**computer-assisted software engineering**) CPAO *f* (conception de programmes assistée par ordinateur)

case-sensitive *adj* (Comp) sensible à la casse

cash¹ *n* (Acc) caisse *f*, disponibilités *f pl*; (funds in cash or at disposal of cashier) encaisse *f*; (funds available for a particular use) fonds *m pl*; (liquid capital of organization) trésorerie *f*; (amount available immediately) liquidités *f pl*; (available capital) disponibilités *f pl*, liquide *m*; (notes, coins) argent liquide *m*, espèces *f pl*; (currency) monnaie *f*; (legal tender) argent *m*; (money paid at time of purchase) argent comptant *m*, comptant *m*; **pay in** ∼ (not cheque) payer en espèces, payer en liquide; (not credit) payer comptant; **buy sth for** ∼ acheter qch au comptant; ∼ **before delivery** paiement avant la livraison *m*; **for** ∼ comptant, contre espèces; **have** ∼ **flow problems** avoir des difficultés de trésorerie; **have** ∼ **in hand** avoir de l'argent disponible, avoir de l'argent en caisse; **500 dollars** ∼ **in hand** 500 dollars en liquide; **discount for** ∼ remise pour paiement comptant *f*; ∼ **against documents** comptant contre documents; ∼ **in advance** payé comptant à l'avance; ∼ **on delivery** livraison contre remboursement, paiement à la livraison; ∼ **on shipment** comptant à l'expédition; ∼ **with order** paiement à la commande *m*, payable à la commande; ∼ **account** *n* compte au comptant *m*, compte de caisse *m*; ∼ **accounting** *n* comptabilité base caisse *f*; ∼ **advance** *n* avance de trésorerie *f*, crédit de caisse *m*, débours *m*; ∼ **assets** *n pl* actif liquide *m*; ∼ **balance** *n* solde de caisse *m*, solde de trésorerie *m*; ∼ **benefit** *n* avantage supplémentaire *m*; (Ins) prestation en espèces *f*; ∼ **bonus** *n* prime en argent *f*; ∼ **box** *n* caisse *f*; ∼ **budget** *n* budget de trésorerie *m*; ∼ **buyer** *n* acheteur/-euse au comptant *m/f*; ∼ **card** *n* carte de retrait bancaire *f*; ∼ **certificate** *n* bon de caisse *m*; ∼ **collection** *n* entrée de caisse *f*; ∼ **contribution** *n* apport en espèces *m*; ∼ **control** *n* contrôle de caisse *m*; ∼ **cow** *n* vache à lait *f*; ∼ **credit** *n* crédit d'achat *m*, crédit de caisse *m*; ∼ **crop** *n* culture commerciale *f*, culture de rapport *f*; ∼ **deal** *n* transaction au comptant *f*; ∼ **deficit** *n* déficit de caisse *m*, déficit de trésorerie *m*; ∼ **department** *n* service de la caisse *m*; ∼ **deposits ratio** *n* coefficient de trésorerie *m*; ⋯⧫

∼ **desk** n caisse f; ∼ **discount** n escompte de caisse m; ∼ **dispenser** n, ∼**-dispensing machine** n distributeur automatique de billets m; ∼ **dividend** n dividende en espèces m; ∼ **economy** n économie du sans facture f; ∼ **flow** n (Acc) cash-flow m, marge brute d'autofinancement f, mouvements de trésorerie m pl; ∼ **flow accounting** n comptabilité de caisse f, comptabilité de trésorerie f; ∼ **flow problem** n problème de liquidité m, problème de trésorerie m; ∼ **holdings** n pl disponibilités f pl; ∼ **inflow** n recette liquide f, rentrée d'argent f; ∼ **in hand** n argent en caisse m, fonds de caisse m; ∼ **limit** n (Econ) limite de trésorerie f, plafond des dépenses m; ∼ **management** n gestion de trésorerie f; ∼ **market** n (Stock) marché au comptant m; ∼ **office** n caisse f, trésorerie f; ∼ **outflow** n décaissement m, sortie d'argent f; ∼ **payment** n paiement comptant m; ∼ **point** n distributeur automatique de billets m; ∼**-poor** adj pauvre en liquidité; ∼ **price** n prix au comptant m; ∼ **purchase** n achat au comptant m; ∼ **register** n caisse f, caisse enregistreuse f; ∼ **reserve** n (Bank) réserve en espèces f; (Acc) réserve de trésorerie f; ∼**-rich** adj riche en liquidité; ∼**-settled** adj réglé en espèces; ∼ **settlement** n règlement en espèces m; ∼**-strapped** adj sans liquidité; ∼ **surplus** n excédent de trésorerie m, excédent de caisse m; ∼ **transaction** n (Gen Comm) opération au comptant f; (Acc) opération de caisse f, opération de trésorerie f; ∼ **value** n valeur de caisse f; ∼ **withdrawal** n retrait d'espèces m

cash² vt (Bank) (cheque) encaisser, toucher; ∼ **in** (bonds) réaliser, se faire rembourser; ∼ **in on** (demand) exploiter, profiter de, tirer profit de; ∼ **up** faire la caisse

cashable adj encaissable, payable à vue

cash-and-carry n libre-service de vente en gros m

cashbook n livre de banque m, livre de caisse m

cashier n caissier/-ière m/f; ∼**'s check** AmE, ∼**'s cheque** BrE n traite bancaire f

cashless society n société sans argent f

casino n casino m

cask n fût m, tonneau m

cassette n cassette f; ∼ **player** n lecteur de cassettes m; ∼ **recorder** n magnétophone à cassettes m; ∼ **tape** n cassette audio f

casual: ∼ **contract** n contrat temporaire m; ∼ **labor** n AmE ▸**casual labour** BrE; ∼ **laborer** n AmE ▸**casual labourer** BrE; ∼ **labour** n BrE personnel intérimaire m; (manual) main-d'œuvre occasionnelle f, main-d'œuvre temporaire f; ∼ **labourer** n BrE intérimaire m/f; (on building site) ouvrier/-ière temporaire (sans travail fixe) m/f; (on farm) journalier/-ière m/f; ∼ **work** n, travail occasionnel m, travail temporaire m; ∼

worker n employé/-e temporaire m/f, travailleur/-euse temporaire m/f

casualization n précarisation f; ∼ **of labour** précarisation de l'emploi

casualize vt précariser

casualty insurance n US assurance dommages f

CAT abbr (▸**computer-aided translation**, ▸**computer-assisted translation**) TAO f (traduction assistée par ordinateur); (▸**computer-aided testing**, ▸**computer-assisted testing**) TAO m pl (tests assistés par ordinateur)

catalog AmE, **catalogue** BrE n catalogue m; **buy from a** ∼ acheter sur catalogue; ∼ **price** n prix catalogue m, prix de catalogue m; ∼ **store** n magasin de vente sur catalogue m, avec disponibilité immédiate de la marchandise

catalyst n catalyseur m

catalytic converter n pot catalytique m

catastrophe n catastrophe f; ∼ **policy** n (Ins) police contre catastrophe f; ∼ **theory** n théorie catastrophe f

catch¹ n (drawback) piège m; ∼**-22 situation** n situation inextricable f; ∼**-all clause** n clause couvrant tous les cas de figure f; ∼ **line** n slogan publicitaire m; ∼**-up demand** n rattrapage de la demande m; ∼**-up effect** n effet de rattrapage m

catch² vt (competitor) rattraper; ∼ **up** (in one's work) rattraper son retard; (in competative terms) regagner du terrain; ∼ **up on** (news) se remettre au courant de; ∼ **up with sb**, ∼ **sb up** rattraper qn

catchment area n (S&M) zone d'appel f, zone d'attraction f, zone de chalandise f

catchword n slogan m

categorization n catégorisation f

categorize vt (Gen Comm) catégoriser, classer; (Admin) classer

category n catégorie f

cater: ∼ **for** vt (guests) préparer des repas pour; (needs) pourvoir à, s'adresser à, satisfaire; ∼ **to** vt (person, viewer, client) s'adresser à

catering n (Leis) restauration f; (Transp) armement m, ravitaillement m; ∼ **trade** n restauration f

CATS abbr (Stock) (▸**computer-assisted trading system**) système de cotation électronique m

cats and dogs n pl (Stock) actions et obligations de valeur douteuse f pl

cattle n bétail m; ∼ **container** n conteneur à bestiaux m; ∼ **truck** n bétaillère f

cause¹ n (Law) action f; (Pol) cause f; (reason) cause f; ∼**s of unemployment** causes du chômage; **with good** ∼ pour cause, à juste titre; **without good** ∼ sans motif valable; **there is** ∼ **for alarm/optimism** il y a des raisons de s'inquiéter/d'être optimiste; **give**

∼ for concern susciter des inquiétudes; **show ∼** (Law) exposer ses raisons

cause² vt (problem, damage) causer, occasionner; (delay, chaos, reaction) provoquer; **∼ sb concern** préoccuper qn; **∼ trouble** créer des problèmes

caution n (wariness) circonspection f; (care) prudence f; (Law) avertissement m; **err on the side of ∼** pécher par excès de prudence; **throw ∼ to the winds** oublier toute prudence; **a word of ∼** un conseil; **∼ money** n (Gen Comm) caution f, dépôt de garantie m; (Law) caution f, cautionnement m

cautionary adj (Law) donné en garantie

cautious adj prudent, précautionneux/ -euse

caveat n mise en garde f; (Law) notification d'opposition f

caveat emptor aux risques de l'acheteur

caveat venditor aux risques du vendeur

CBI abbr (▸**Confederation of British Industry**) ≈ CNPF m (Conseil national du patronat français)

CBO abbr US (**Congressional Budget Office**) Commission des finances f, Bureau du budget du Congrès m

CBT abbr (▸**computer-based training**) EAO m (enseignement assisté par ordinateur)

cc abbr (▸**carbon copy**) copie carbone f; (▸**continuation clause**) clause de prolongation f, clause de report f

CC abbr (▸**Chamber of Commerce**) Chambre de commerce f; UK (▸**county council**) ≈ conseil général m

c-commerce n commerce collaboratif m

CCTV abbr (▸**closed-circuit television**) télévision en circuit fermé f

cd abbr (Acc) (▸**carried down**) à reporter

CD abbr (▸**certificate of deposit**) CD m (certificat de dépôt); (▸**compact disc**) CD m, disque compact m; (▸**customs declaration**) déclaration en douane f

CD-I abbr (▸**compact disc interactive**) CD-I m, disque compact interactif m

CD-R abbr (▸**compact disc recordable**) CD-R m, disque compact enregistrable m

CD-ROM abbr (▸**compact disc read-only memory**) CD-ROM m, cédérom m

CD-RW abbr (▸**compact disc rewritable**) CD-RW m, disque compact réinscriptible m

CE abbr (▸**Council of Europe**) CE m (Conseil de l'Europe)

cease ① vt cesser; **∼ to have effect** (contract) arriver à échéance, devenir caduc/ caduque, prendre fin; **∼ trading** cesser ses activités
② vi prendre fin

cedant n cédant m

cede vt céder

cedi n cédi m

ceding company n compagnie cédante f

ceiling n plafond m; **∼ price** n prix plafond m; **∼ rate** n taux plafond m

cell n (Comms) cellule f

cellphone n téléphone cellulaire m, téléphone portatif m

censor vt censurer

censorship n censure f

censorware n (on Internet) logiciel de filtrage m, filtre Internet m

censure vt (criticize) critiquer, réprouver

census n recensement m

cent n (fraction of dollar) cent m; (fraction of euro) cent m, centime m

center n AmE ▸**centre** BrE

centerfold n AmE ▸**centrefold** BrE

centime n centime m

central adj (feature, message, role) principal; (district, area) central; (Pol) central; **∼ bank** n banque centrale f; **∼ business district** n centre d'affaires d'une ville m, quartier central d'affaires m; **∼ buying** n achat dans une centrale d'achats m; **∼ government** n administration centrale f; **∼ planning** n planification centralisée f; **∼ processing unit** n unité centrale f; **∼ purchasing department** n centrale d'achat f; **∼ reservation system** n système de réservation central m

Central: **∼ European Time** n heure de l'Europe centrale f; **∼ Office of Information** n UK Bureau central de l'information m; **∼ Register** n UK registre central des firmes autorisées; **∼ Standard Time** n US heure normale des états du centre des États-Unis f; **∼ Statistical Office** n UK ≈ Institut national de la statistique et des études économiques m, INSEE m

centralization n centralisation f

centralize vt centraliser

centralized adj centralisé

centrally: **∼-financed program** AmE, **∼-financed programme** BrE n (Acc) programme financé par l'administration centrale m; **∼-planned economy** n économie planifiée f

centre¹ n BrE centre m; **∼ spread** n BrE (Media) double page centrale f

centre²: **∼ on** vt BrE tourner autour de

centrefold n BrE double page centrale f, vraie double f

CEO abbr US (▸**chief executive officer**) PDG m (président-directeur général)

certain adj certain, sûr

certainty n certitude f

certificate¹ n (Gen Comm, Patents) certificat m; (diploma) diplôme m; (Acc) rapport m; (Admin) acte m, certificat m; (Fin) certificat m, titre m; **∼ of deposit** bon de caisse m, certificat de dépôt m; **∼ of exemption** (Tax) certificat d'exemption m, certificat d'exonération m; **∼ of health** certificat ⋯⟶

médical de bonne santé *m*; ~ **of incorporation** (Law) acte constitutif d'une personne morale *m*; ~ **of insurance** attestation d'assurance *f*, certificat d'assurance *m*; ~ **of origin** certificat d'origine *m*; ~ **of origin and consignment** certificat d'origine et d'expédition *m*; ~ **of ownership** certificat de propriété *m*, titre de propriété *m*; ~ **of posting** récépissé d'un envoi *m*; ~ **of quality** certificat de qualité *m*; ~ **of registration** (of intellectual property) certificat d'enregistrement *m*; (Tax) certificat d'agrément *m*; ~ **of shipment** certificat d'expédition *m*; ~ **of title** titre de propriété *m*; ~ **of use** (Prop) certificat d'utilisation *m*; ~ **of value** UK (Imp/Exp) attestation de valeur *f*

certificate² *vt* (product) certifier

certification *n* (Gen Comm, Law) authentification *f*, certification *f*; (Ind, Patents) certification *f*, homologation *f*; (Tax) attestation *f*, certificat *m*; ~ **authority** *n* (Comp) autorité de certification *f*

certified: ~ **accountant** *n* UK expert-comptable *m*; ~ **accounts** *n pl* comptes certifiés *m pl*; ~ **copy** *n* copie conforme *f*; ~ **declaration of origin** *n* déclaration d'origine certifiée *f*; ~ **invoice** *n* facture certifiée *f*; ~ **mail** *n* AmE, ~ **post** BrE *n* courrier recommandé *m*; ~ **public accountant** *n* US expert-comptable *m*; ~ **true copy** *n* copie certifiée conforme *f*

certify *vt* (diploma) viser; (goods) guarantir; (authenticate) authentifier

certifying officer *n* agent certificateur *m*

cessation *n* cessation *f*; ~ **of interest** UK (Bank) suspension d'intérêt *f*; ~ **of payment of premiums** (Ins) cessation de paiement des primes *f*

cession *n* (Gen Comm) abandon *m*; (Law) cession *f*

CET *abbr* (▸**Central European Time**) heure de l'Europe centrale *f*

CF *abbr* (▸**carriage forward**) p.d. (port dû); (▸**carried forward**) à reporter

CFB *abbr* (**central freight bureau**) bureau central de transport *m*

CFC *abbr* (▸**chlorofluorocarbon**) CFC *m* (chlorofluorocarbone)

CFE UK (▸**college of further education**) centre d'enseignement postscolaire *m*

CFO *abbr* (▸**chief financial officer**) directeur financier *m*, responsable financier *m*

CGA *abbr* (**color/graphics adaptor**, ▸**colour/graphics adaptor**) CGA *m*, adaptateur graphique couleur *m*

CGI *abbr* (**Common Gateway Interface**) (Comp) (protocole) CGI *m*

chain *n* chaîne *f*; ~ **bank** *n* US banque à succursales multiples *f*; ~ **of command** *n* hiérarchie *f*; ~ **of distribution** *n* circuit de distribution *m*; ~ **of events** *n* série d'événements *f*; ~ **of production** *n* chaîne de production *f*; ~ **reaction** *n* réaction en chaîne *f*; ~ **store** *n* grand magasin *m*

chair¹ *n* président *m*; **be in the** ~ diriger les débats

chair² *vt* (meeting) présider

chairman *n* président *m*; (of company) président du conseil (d'administration) *m*; ~ **of the board** président du conseil *m*; ~ **of the board of directors** président-directeur général *m*; ~ **of the board of management** président du directoire *m*, président-directeur général *m*; ~ **and chief executive** US président-directeur général *m*; ~ **and managing director** UK président-directeur général *m*

chairmanship *n* présidence *f*

chairperson *n* président/présidente *m/f*

chairwoman *n* présidente *f*

challenge¹ *n* défi *m*; (Law) contestation *f*; **issue a** ~ lancer un défi; **take up a** ~ relever un défi; **face a** ~ affronter une épreuve

challenge² *vt* (person) défier; (authority, statement) contester; (stimulate) stimuler; (Law) (witness) récuser

challenger *n* challenger *m*

chamber *n* chambre *f*

Chamber: ~ **of Commerce** *n* Chambre de commerce *f*; ~ **of Trade** *n* Chambre des métiers *f*

chambers *n pl* (Law) cabinet *m*

chance *adj* (meeting, remark) fortuit

Chancellor of the Exchequer *n* UK Chancelier de l'Échiquier *m*, *le ministre des finances britannique*

chancery *n* cour de la chancellerie *f*

change¹ *n* (by replacement) changement *m*; (by adjustment) modification *f*; (in demand or supply) changement *m*; (money) monnaie *f*; (in price) variation *f*, évolution *f*; **a** ~ **for the better/worse** un changement en mieux/pire; **make a** ~ **in sth** changer qch; **make** ~**s in** (text) apporter des changements à; (company) faire des changements dans; **have you got** ~ **for 100 euros?** est-ce que vous pouvez me changer un billet de cent euros?; ~ **of address** changement d'adresse *m*; ~ **of itinerary** modification d'itinéraire *f*; ~ **management** *n* gestion du changement *f*; ~ **of ownership** *n* (Gen Comm) changement de propriétaire *m*; (Admin, Law) mutation *f*; ~ **of plan** changement de programme *m*

change² ① *vt* changer; (in shop) échanger; ~ **X for Y** remplacer X par Y; ~ **money** changer de l'argent; ~ **hands** (money, goods or businesses) changer de main, changer de propriétaire; ~ **sth into cash** convertir qch en espèces

② *vi* changer, se transformer

changeover n transition f

channel[1] n voie f; (Comms) canal m, voie f; (on TV) chaîne f; **go through the proper ~s** passer par la voie hiérarchique; **~ of communication** voie de communication f; **~ of distribution** canal de distribution m; **~ of sales** circuit de vente m

channel[2] n (funds into project) canaliser; **~ off** (funds, resources) affecter

Channel Tunnel n tunnel sous la Manche m

chaos theory n théorie du chaos f

chapel n UK (of trade union) section f

CHAPS abbr US (▶**Clearing House Automatic Payments System**) Chambre de compensation interbancaire internationale f

chapter n (of organization) section f

character n (printing) caractère m; **~ set** n police de caractères f; **~ string** n chaîne de caractères f

characteristic[1] adj caractéristique; **~ of** propre à

characteristic[2] n caractéristique f; (of person) trait de caractère m

charge[1] n (Acc) débit m; (Fin) charge f; (cost, debt) frais m pl, prix m; (Law) chef d'accusation m, chef d'inculpation m; **bring ~s** porter plainte; **take ~** prendre les choses en main; **at no ~** gratis, gratuit, gratuitement; **at no extra ~** sans supplément; **there is no ~** c'est gratuit; **additional ~** supplément m; **delivery ~** frais de livraison mpl; **be in ~** être délégué, être préposé, être responsable; **be in ~ of** s'occuper de, être chargé de, être responsable de; **the person in ~** le/la responsable m/f; **in ~ of** responsable de; **without ~** gratis, gratuitement, sans frais; **~ account** n compte d'achats à crédit m; **~-back** n US réimputation f; **~ buyer** n BrE acheteur/-euse à crédit m/f; **~ card** n carte d'achat f; **~ hand** n chef d'équipe m; **~ upon a property** n sûreté sur un bien f

charge[2] vt (fee) demander, faire payer; (Law) inculper; (S&M) (client, user, customer) faire payer; **~ interest** prélever un intérêt; **how much do you ~?** combien est-ce que vous prenez?; **~ against** déduire de, imputer à, porter en réduction sur; **~ to** (expenses) imputer à; **~ an expense to an account** imputer une dépense à un compte; **~ sth to sb's account** faire mettre qch sur le compte de qn; **~ to an account** porter au débit d'un compte

chargeable adj (to an account) imputable; **~ expenses** n pl frais facturables m pl; **~ staff** n pl personnel à charge m; **~ to tax** imposable, soumis à l'impôt

charges n pl (Gen Comm) charges f pl, frais m pl; (Acc, Fin) charges f pl

charitable: **~ donation** n don à une œuvre de charité m; **~ foundation** n fondation de charité f; **~ organization** n œuvre de bienfaisance f, organisation caritative f; **~ purposes** n pl fins charitables f pl; **~ trust** n fondation d'utilité publique f

charity n œuvre de bienfaisance f, organisation caritative f; **~ fundraising** n collecte de bienfaisance f; **~ sale** n vente de charité f

chart[1] n diagramme m, graphique m

chart[2] vt (record) enregistrer; (plot) tracer la courbe de

charter[1] n (licence) charte f; (of rights) charte f; (of company) statuts m pl; (of vehicles) affrètement m, charter m; **~ flight** n vol charter m, vol affrété m; **~ party** n charte-partie f; **~ plane** n (avion) charter m

charter[2] vt (Law) accorder une charte à; (vehicle) affréter, noliser

chartered: **~ accountant** n UK expert-comptable m; **~ aircraft** n avion affrété m, avion charter m; **~ bank** n US banque à charte f; **~ company** n compagnie à charte f; **~ flight** n vol charter m, vol affrété m; **~ life underwriter** n US (Ins) agent d'assurance-vie agréé m; **~ plane** n (avion) charter m

charterer n affréteur m, chargeur m

chartering n affrètement m, nolisement m; **~ agent** n agent d'affrètement m; **~ broker** n courtier d'affrètement m

chartism n analyse chartiste f

chartist n chartiste mf, conjoncturiste mf, opérateur sur graphique m

chat n (on Internet) causette f, chat m, bavardage m

chatroom n salle de causette f, salle de bavardage f, salon de bavardage m

chattel n bien meuble m; **~ mortgage** n US hypothèque sur biens meubles f

cheap n bon marché inv, pas cher/chère, économique

cheaper adj meilleur marché, moins cher

cheat[1] n (person) tricheur/-euse m/f; (trick, short-cut) astuce f

cheat[2] [1] vt (person, company) tromper; **~ sb out of** dépouiller qn de [2] vi tricher

check[1] n (Bank) AmE chèque m; (verfication) contrôle m, test m, vérification f; (bill) AmE (account in hotel) note f; (in restaurant) addition f; (restraint) frein m; **~ in the amount of** AmE chèque d'un montant de; **~ in favor of sb** AmE chèque payable à l'ordre de qn; **place a ~ on** mettre un frein à; **keep a ~ on** surveiller; **raise a ~ to sb** AmE établir un chèque à l'ordre de qn; **pick up the ~** payer l'addition; **~ box** n AmE case à cocher f; **~ card** n AmE carte d'identité bancaire f; **~ clearing** n AmE compensation de chèques f; **~-clearing system** n AmE système de ····>

compensation de chèques *m*; ∼ **counterfoil** *n* AmE talon de chèque *m*; ∼ **list** *n* check-list *f*, liste de contrôle *f*; ∼ **payment** *n* AmE paiement par chèque *m*, règlement par chèque *m*; ∼ **stub** *n* AmE talon de chèque *m*; ∼**-up** *n* (medical) visite médicale *f*

check² *vt* (tick) AmE cocher; (verify) contrôler, vérifier; (curb) (increase, growth, progress) freiner; (prices, rise, inflation) contrôler; ∼ **for** (problem) dépister; (flow, sign) chercher; ∼ **in** *vt* (luggage) enregistrer; *vi* (at airport) se présenter à l'enregistrement; (at hotel) se présenter à la réception; ∼ **off** cocher; ∼ **on** (person) surveiller; (progress) vérifier; ∼ **over**, ∼ **through** vérifier; ∼ **out** (of hotel) quitter sa chambre; ∼ **up** vérifier; ∼ **up on sth** vérifier qch

checkbook *n* AmE carnet de chèques *m*, chéquier *m*

checker *n* (HRM) manutentionnaire *mf*, pointeur *m*; (S&M) AmE caissier/-ière *m/f*

check-in *n* (Transp) enregistrement *m*

checking *n* vérification *f*; ∼ **account** *n* AmE compte courant *m*; ∼ **account holder** *n* AmE titulaire d'un compte courant *mf*

checklist *n* fiche de suivi *f*, check-liste *f*

checkout *n* caisse *f*; ∼ **assistant** *n* BrE, ∼ **clerk** *n* AmE caissier/-ière *m/f*

checkpoint *n* (Comp, Transp) point de contrôle *m*

checksum *n* (Comp) somme de contrôle *f*, total de contrôle *m*

chemical *n* produit chimique *m*; ∼ **fertilizer** *n* engrais chimique *m*; ∼ **tanker** *n* (shipping) chimiquier *m*; ∼ **works** *n inv pl* fabrique de produits chimiques *f*

cheque *n* BrE chèque *m*; ∼ **in favour of sb** (Bank) chèque payable à l'ordre de qn; ∼ **made to cash** chèque payable au porteur; ∼ **to the amount of** chèque d'un montant de; **make a** ∼ **payable to sb** établir un chèque à l'ordre de qn; **make out a** ∼ faire un chèque; **make out a** ∼ **to sb** établir un chèque à l'ordre de qn; ∼ **card** *n* carte d'identité bancaire *f*; ∼ **clearing** *n* compensation de chèques *f*; ∼**-clearing system** *n* système de compensation de chèques *m*; ∼ **counterfoil** *n* talon de chèque *m*; ∼ **payment** *n* paiement par chèque *m*, règlement par chèque *m*; ∼ **stub** *n* talon de chèque *m*

chequebook *n* BrE carnet de chèques *m*, chéquier *m*; ∼ **journalism** *n* BrE journalisme à sensation *m*

cherry-pick *vt* trier sur le volet

cherry picker *n nouvelle société point com proposant des activités en ligne à des prix inférieurs à ceux proposés par des entreprises de clics et de briques*

chief *n* chef *m*; ∼ **accountant** *n* chef comptable *m*, directeur/-trice de comptabilité *m/f*; ∼ **accounting officer** *n* chef comptable *m*, directeur/-trice de comptabilité *m/f*; ∼

buyer *n* chef du service achats *m*, directeur/-trice des achats *m/f*, responsable des achats *mf*; ∼ **clerk** *n* chef de bureau *m*; ∼ **economist** *n* économiste en chef *mf*; ∼ **executive** *n* directeur général *m*; ∼ **executive officer** *n* US président-directeur général *m*; ∼ **financial officer** *n* directeur/-trice financier/-ière *m/f*, responsable financier/-ière *m/f*; ∼ **inspector** *n* inspecteur/-trice en chef *m/f*; ∼ **operating officer** *n* chef de service *m*; ∼ **value** *n* valeur principale *f*

child *n pl* **-dren** enfant *m*; ∼ **benefit** *n* UK allocations familiales *f pl*; ∼ **tax credit** *n* UK crédit d'impôt pour enfants *m*

childcare *n pl* structures d'accueil pour les enfants d'âge préscolaire *f pl*; ∼ **expenses** *n pl* frais de garde d'enfants *m pl*; ∼ **facilities** *n pl* crèche *f*

child-centered AmE, **child-centred** BrE *adj* centré sur l'enfant

childless couple *n* ménage sans enfants *m*

Chinese wall *n pl* (Stock) muraille de Chine *f*

chip *n* (Comp) puce *f*; ∼ **card** *n* carte à mémoire *f*, carte à puce *f*

CHIPS *abbr* US (▶**Clearing House Interbank Payments System**) Chambre de compensation interbancaire internationale *f*

chlorofluorocarbon *n* chlorofluorocarbone *m*

choice¹ *adj* de premier choix, de première qualité

choice² *n* choix *m*; **make a** ∼ faire un choix, choisir; **have the** ∼ avoir le choix; ∼ **of goods** choix de marchandises

choose *vti* choisir

chose *n* (Law) chose *f*, objet *m*; ∼ **in action** *n* droit incorporel *m*

Christian name *n* BrE prénom *m*

Christmas bonus *n* prime de fin d'année *f*

churn¹ *n* (S&M) attrition *f*; ∼ **index** *n* indice de fidélité du client *m*; ∼ **rate** *n* taux d'attrition *m*, pourcentage de clients perdus *m*

churn² *vt* (Bank, Stock) faire tourner; ∼ **out** (goods) produire en série

churning *n* (Fin, S&M) escroquerie *f*

CI *abbr* (▶**chief inspector**) inspecteur/-trice en chef *m*

CIF *abbr* (▶**cost, insurance and freight**) CAF (coût, assurance, fret)

CIF&C *abbr* (▶**cost, insurance, freight and commission**) coût, assurance, fret et commission

CIF&I *abbr* (▶**cost, insurance, freight and interest**) coût, assurance, fret et intérêt

CIFC&I *abbr* (▶**cost, insurance, freight, commission and interest**) coût, assurance, fret, commission et intérêt

CIFI&E *abbr* (▸**cost, insurance, freight, interest and exchange**) coût, assurance, fret, intérêt et change

CIM *abbr* (▸**computer-integrated manufacture,** ▸**computer-integrated manufacturing**) FIO *f* (fabrication intégrée par ordinateur)

CIO *abbr* (**chief information officer**) directeur/-trice informatique *m/f*, responsable des systèmes informatique *mf*

CIP *abbr* (**carriage and insurance paid to**) port et assurance payés jusqu'à

circle *n* (political, business) cercle *m*, milieu *m*; **in business ~s** dans les milieux d'affaires

circuit *n* (Comp) circuit *m*; (Law) circonscription *f*; **~ breaker mechanism** *n* US (Stock) mécanisme de coupe-circuit *m*

circular *n* (Comms) circulaire *f*, prospectus *m*

circulate *vt* (information, news) propager; (list, document) diffuser

circulating: ~ capital *n* capitaux roulants *m pl*, fonds de roulement *m*; **~ medium** *n* monnaie d'échange *f*

circulation *n* (Bank, Econ) circulation *f*; (of newspapers) diffusion *f*, tirage *m*; **in ~** en circulation; **'for ~ to'** (on document) 'transmettre à'; **~ department** *n* (print) service de la diffusion *m*, service des ventes *m*; **~ figures** *n pl* chiffres de tirage *m pl*; **~ manager** *n* directeur/-trice du service des ventes *m/f*, responsable du service de distribution *mf*

circumstance *n* circonstance *f*

circumstances *n pl* (state of affairs) circonstances *f pl*; (situation in life) situation *f*; **in similar ~** dans des circonstances semblables; **under the ~** dans ces circonstances; **due to ~ beyond our control** pour des raisons indépendantes de notre volonté

circumstantial evidence *n* preuve indirecte *f*

CIS *abbr* (▸**Commonwealth of Independent States**) CEI *f* (Communauté des États indépendants)

citation *n* (Law) citation *f*

cite *vt* (Law) citer

citizen *n* (Law) habitant/-e *m/f*; (Pol) citoyen/-enne *m/f*, habitant/-e *m/f*

Citizens Advice Bureau *n* UK *bureau d'aide et de conseil aux citoyens*

citizenship *n* citoyenneté *f*

city *n* (grande) ville *f*; **~ center** *n* AmE, **~ centre** *n* BrE centre-ville *m*; **~ planner** *n* AmE urbaniste *mf*; **~ planning** *n* AmE urbanisme *m*

City *n* UK **the ~** *le centre des affaires à Londres*, la City *f*

civil *adj* (Gen Comm, Law) civil; **~ action** *n* action civile *f*; **~ aviation** *n* aviation civile *f*; **~ commotion** *n* émeute *f*; **~ law** *n* droit civil *m*; **~ liability** *n* responsabilité civile *f*; **~ proceedings** *n pl* procès civil *m*; **~ rights** *n pl* droits civils *m pl*, droits civiques *m pl*; **~ rights act** *n* US (Law) loi de 1964 sur les droits civiques *f*; **~ servant** *n* fonctionnaire *mf*; **~ service** *n* Administration *f*, fonction publique *f*; **~ status** *n* (Law) état civil *m*

Civil: ~ Aviation Authority *n* UK autorité *de l'aviation civile*, ≈ Direction générale de l'aviation civile *f*; **~ Service Commission** *n* ≈ Commission de la fonction publique *f*

claim[1] *n* (assertion) affirmation *f*; (Acc, Fin) créance *f*; (by trade union) revendication syndicale *f*; (demand) réclamation *f*; (Ins) (for damages, refund) demande de remboursement *f*; (for incident, accident) déclaration de sinistre *f*, sinistre *m*; (Law) revendication *f*, réclamation *f*; (Patents) revendication *f*; (Tax) réclamation *f*; (for benefit) demande d'allocation *f*; **make a ~** (Ins) faire une demande d'indemnisation; (for benefit) faire une demande d'allocation; **put in a ~** (Ins) faire une déclaration de sinistre; **entertain a ~** faire droit à une réclamation; **have a prior ~** avoir un droit de priorité; **advertising ~** argument publicitaire *m*; **travel ~** demande de remboursement de frais de voyage *f*; **~ for damages** demande de dommages et intérêts *f*; **~ for indemnification** (Ins) demande d'indemnisation *f*; **~ for refund** demande de remboursement *f*; **~ form** *n* (Ins) formulaire de déclaration de sinistre *m*; **~ payment** *n*, **~ settlement** *n* (Ins) règlement de sinistre *m*

claim[2] *vt* (assert one's right to) revendiquer; (Law) (contend) déclarer, prétendre; (demand) revendiquer, réclamer; (benefit) faire une demande de; **~ compensation** demander réparation; **~ damages** demander des dommages et intérêts; **~ expenses** faire une demande de remboursement de frais; **~ back** se faire rembourser

claimant *n* (Law) demandeur/-eresse *m/f*, partie requérante *f*, requérant *m*; (Wel) (for benefit) demandeur/-euse *m/f*; **the ~** (Ins) l'assuré *m*, le sinistré *m*

claims: ~ adjuster *n* inspecteur régleur *m*; **~ department** *n* (Ins) service des sinistres *m*; **~ and liabilities** *n pl* (Acc) dettes et engagements *m pl*; **~ manager** *n* chef du service des réclamations *m*; **~ procedure** *n* procédure de réclamation *f*

clandestine *adj* clandestin

clarify *vt* clarifier, éclairer; **a clarifying statement** une mise au point

class[1] *n* classe *f*; (Patents, Stock) catégorie *f*, classe *f*; (Transp) classe *f*; (group of students) classe *f*; (lesson, lecture) cours *m*; **be in a ~ of one's own** être hors catégorie; **travel first/second ~** voyager en première/deuxième classe; **~ of shares** (Stock) classe d'actions *f*; **~ struggle** *n* lutte des classes *f*

class² *vt* classer

classic *adj* classique; ~ **example** *n* exemple-type *m*

classification *n* classification *f*; ~ **of accounts** (Acc) codification des comptes *f*; ~ **of risks** (Ins) classification des risques *f*

classified *adj* (document, information) confidentiel/-ielle; ~ **ad** *n* (infrml) annonce classée *f*, petite annonce *f*; ~ **advert** *n*, ~ **advertisement** *n* annonce classée *f*, petite annonce *f*

classify *vt* (Gen Comm) classifier; (restrict access to) classer, classer confidentiel, classer secret

clause *n* clause *f*, disposition *f*; (in policy) avenant *m*, clause *f*; (of contract) article *m*, clause *f*

claw: ~ **back** *vt* (Tax) récupérer; (investment) récupérer

clawback *n* (Fin) récupération *f*; (Tax) (of capital gains tax relief) disposition de récupération *f*

clean¹ *adj* (not dirty) propre; (driving licence) vierge; (reputation) sans taches; (Acc) sans dettes; (car) non-polluant; **come** ~ dire la vérité; ~ **bill of health** *n* patente de santé nette *f*; ~ **bill of lading** *n* connaissement net *m*, connaissement sans réserves *m*; ~ **fuel** *n* biocarburant *m*; ~ **product** *n* produit écologique *m*, écoproduit *m*; ~ **record** *n* (Law) casier judiciaire vierge *m*; ~ **technology** *n* technologie non-polluante *f*, technologie propre *f*

clean²: ~ **up** *vt* nettoyer

cleaning-up operation *n* opération de nettoyage *f*

clear¹ *n* be in the ~ (free of suspicion) être lavé de tout soupçon; (safe) être hors de danger

clear² *adj* (instruction, description) clair; (lack, need, sign) évident; (gain, profit) net *inv*; (day, week) entier/-ière; **be** ~ **of** (debt) être libre de; (blame) être exempt de; (suspicion) être lavé de; **make** ~ préciser; **make one's views** ~ exprimer clairement ses opinions

clear³ ☐ *vt* (cheque, funds) compenser; (wipe out, erase) effacer; (debt) liquider, s'acquitter de; (mortgage) purger; (loan) liquider, rembourser; (profit) faire, rapporter; (accused person) disculper, innocenter; (transhipment) apurer; (request, proposal) approuver; (employee) mener une enquête administrative sur; (Comp) (screen, data) effacer; ~ **30,000 euros** faire un bénéfice de 30 000 euros; ~ **sth with sb** obtenir l'accord de qn pour qch; ~ **customs** passer à la douane; ~ **one's name/ reputation** blanchir son nom/sa réputation; ~ **the way for** (development) ouvrir la voie pour; (person) laisser la place à ☐ *vi* (cheque) être compensé; ~ **up** (problem, difficulty) résoudre; (misunderstanding) dissiper

clear: ~ **days** *n pl* (shipping) jours francs *m pl*; ~ **loss** *n* perte sèche *f*; ~ **profit** *n*

bénéfice net *m*; ~ **title** *n* US (Law) titre irréfutable *m*

clearance *n* (at customs) dédouanement *m*, formalités douanières *f pl*; (S&M) liquidation *f*, soldes *m pl*; ~ **inwards** déclaration d'entrée en douane *f*, manifeste d'entrée *m*; ~ **outwards** déclaration de sortie de douane *f*, manifeste de sortie *m*; ~ **sale** *n* (total) liquidation *f*; (partial) soldes *m pl*

clear-cut *adj* (category, plan, idea, example) précis; (distinction) net/nette; (issue, problem) clair

clearer *n* banque de dépôt *f*

clearing *n* (Bank) compensation interbancaire *f*, clearing *m*; (of account) liquidation *f*; (of cheque) compensation *f*; (of debt) acquittement *m*; ~ **account** *n* compte de clearing *m*; ~ **bank** *n* banque de dépôt *f*; ~ **center** AmE, ~ **centre** BrE *n* centre de compensation *m*; ~ **day** *n* jour de compensation *m*; ~ **house** *n* (Bank) chambre de compensation *f*; (Stock) comptoir de liquidation *m*; ~ **system** *n* système de compensation *m*

Clearing: ~ **House Automatic Payments System** *n* US Chambre de compensation interbancaire internationale *f*; ~ **House Interbank Payments System** *n* US Chambre de compensation interbancaire internationale *f*

clerical: ~ **error** *n* (Acc) erreur d'écriture *f*; ~ **staff** *n* personnel de bureau *m*, personnel de secrétariat *m*; ~ **work** *n* travail de bureau *m*, travail de secrétariat *m*; ~ **worker** *n* employé/-e de bureau *mf*

clerk *n* commis *m*, employé/-e de bureau *m/f*; (Law) clerc *m*, greffier *m*; ~ **of works** conducteur de travaux *m*

click: ~ **payment** *n* paiement au clic *m*; ~ **rate** *n* taux de clics *m*; ~**s and bricks** *adj*, ~**s and mortar** *adj* (company) de clics et de brique(s), de clics et de mortier, hybride

click¹ *n* (Comp) clic *m*

click² *vi* (Comp) cliquer

clickable *adj* (Comp) cliquable, sensible

clickstream *n* séquence de requêtes *f*, parcours (effectué par un internaute) *m*

click-through *n* clic (avec téléchargement complet) *m*, lien cliqué *m*; ~ **rate** *n* taux de clics *m*

client *n* client/-e *m/f*; ~ **account** *n* compte client *m*; ~ **base** *n* base de clientèle *f*; ~ **group** *n* segment de clientèle *m*; ~**-led marketing policy** *n* politique dictée par les besoins de la clientèle *f*

clientele *n* clientèle *f*

clients *n pl* clientèle *f*

client-server *adj* (architecture, model) client-serveur

client-side *adj* (Comp) côté-client

climb ☐ *vt* ~ **the ladder** grimper dans la hiérarchie

2 *vi* (Gen Comm) augmenter; (price, currency) monter; (unemployment) grimper, s'accroître; ∼ **down** revenir sur sa décision; ∼ **down over sth** céder sur

climb-down *n* reculade *f*

clinch *vt* (loan, funding, market) décrocher; ∼ **a deal** conclure un affaire; (Pol) conclure un accord; **what** ∼**ed it was...** ce qui a été décisif c'est...

clip art *n* clipart *m*; **a piece of** ∼ une image clipart

clipboard *n* presse-papier *m*

clipping *n* (from newspaper) coupure *f*, coupure de presse *f*

cloakroom *n* (for baggage) consigne *f*; (for coats) vestiaire *m*

clock: ∼ **in** *vi* pointer en arrivant; ∼ **off** *vi* pointer en sortant; ∼ **on** *vi* pointer en arrivant; ∼ **out** *vi* pointer en sortant

clocking-in *n* pointage *m*

clone¹ *n* clone *m*

clone² *vt* cloner

close¹ *adj* (scrutiny, examination) minutieux/-ieuse; (cooperation, relationship) proche, étroit; **in** ∼ **touch with** en rapport étroit avec

close² *n* clôture *f*; **at the** ∼ (Stock) en clôture, à la clôture

close³ *vt* (Gen Comm) fermer; (session, sale) clôturer, conclure; (Acc) arrêter; (Comp) (file) fermer; (session) terminer; (Stock) liquider; ∼ **a deal** liquider une opération; ∼ **the gap** combler le déficit; ∼ **the meeting** lever la séance; ∼ **a position** (Fin) inverser une position; (Stock) (options on currency futures) liquider une position; ∼ **down 1** *vt* (business, factory) fermer définitivement **2** *vi* (business, shop) fermer définitivement; (radio, television) terminer les émissions; ∼ **out** (goods) liquider avant fermeture

close: ∼ **company** *n* BrE, ∼ **corporation** *n* AmE compagnie proche *f*; ∼**-down** *n* (in broadcasting) fin des émissions *f*; ∼ **of the market** clôture du marché *f*

closed *adj* fermé; ∼**-out** *adj* liquidé; ∼ **account** *n* (Fin) compte clos *m*, compte soldé *m*; ∼**-circuit television** *n* télévision en circuit fermé *f*; ∼ **economy** *n* économie fermée *f*; ∼**-end investment company** *n* société d'investissement à capital fermé *f*, société d'investissement à capital fixe *f*; ∼**-end investment trust** *n* (Fin) société de gestion de portefeuille à capital non-variable *f*; ∼**-end mortgage** *n* emprunt hypothécaire plafonné *m*; ∼ **position** *n* (Fin) position non-dénouée *f*; (Stock) position liquidée *f*, position non-dénouée *f*; ∼ **question** *n* question fermée *f*; ∼ **season** *n* (Media) période creuse *f*; ∼ **shop** *n* monopole syndical *m*; ∼ **stock** *n* (S&M) article sans suite *m*, stock fermé *m*; ∼ **union** *n* syndicat exerçant un monopole de l'embauche *m*

closing *n* (Gen Comm) clôture *f*; (Prop) conclusion *f*; (Stock) clôture *f*; ∼ **of the accounts** (Acc) arrêt des comptes *m*; **at** ∼ (Stock) en clôture, à la clôture; ∼ **balance** *n* solde de clôture *m*; ∼ **bid** *n* dernière enchère *f*, dernière offre *f*; ∼ **date** *n* date limite *f*, dernier délai *m*; ∼ **entry** *n* écriture de clôture *f*; ∼ **price** *n* (Stock) cours de clôture *m*, dernier cours *m*, dernière cotation *f*; ∼ **quotation** *n* (Stock) cours de clôture *m*, dernière cotation *f*; ∼ **session** *n* (Stock) séance de clôture *f*; ∼ **stock** *n* stock en fin d'exercice *m*, stock final *m*; ∼ **time** *n* heure de fermeture *f*

closure *n* clôture *f*

clothing *n* vêtements *m pl*; ∼ **business** *n*, ∼ **industry** *n* confection *f*

clout *n* (infrml) influence *f*; **carry a great deal of** ∼ avoir beaucoup d'influence

club¹ *n* club *m*; ∼ **class** *n* classe affaires *f*, classe club *f*

club²: ∼ **together** *vi* cotiser

cluster *n* groupe *m*; ∼ **analysis** *n* analyse par segments *f*, typologie *f*; ∼ **of countries** *groupe de pays partageant certaines caractéristiques*; ∼ **sample** *n* échantillon segmental *m*; ∼ **sampling** *n* sondage par grappes *m*, sondage par segments *m*

clustering *n* (S&M) segmentation *f*

CM *abbr* (▶**content management**) (Comp) gestion du contenu (de sites) *f*; (▶**configuration management**) gestion de la configuration *f*

cmdty *abbr* (▶**commodity**) marchandise *f*, produit *m*; (food, product) denrée *f*; (raw material) matière première *f*, produit de base *m*

CN *abbr* (▶**credit note**) note de crédit *f*; (▶**cover note**) (Ins) lettre de couverture *f*, police provisoire *f*

cnee *abbr* (▶**consignee**) dépositaire *mf*, destinataire *mf*

c/o *abbr* (▶**care of**) aux bons soins de, chez; (▶**certificate of origin**) certificat d'origine *m*

Co. *abbr* (▶**company**) Cie *f* (compagnie), Sté *f* (société); **Smith and** ∼ Smith et Cie

co-accused *n* coïnculpé/-e *m/f*

coach *n* car *m*, autocar *m*; (rail) voiture *f*; ∼ **company** *n* compagnie de cars *f*; ∼ **station** *n* gare routière *f*

coal *n* charbon *m*, houille *f*; ∼**-fired power station** *n* usine thermique à houille *f*; ∼ **industry** *n* industrie houillère *f*, industrie minière *f*; ∼ **mine** *n* charbonnage *m*, houillère *f*, mine de charbon *f*; ∼ **mining** *n* charbonnage *m*

coalition *n* coalition *f*; ∼ **government** *n* gouvernement de coalition *m*

coastal pollution *n* pollution des côtes *f*, pollution du littoral *f*

coaster *n* (vessel) navire cargo sans ligne régulière *m*

coastguard *n* (organization) gendarmerie ····⟶

maritime f; (person) garde-côte m

coasting n cabotage m

co-branding n (S&M) co-griffage m, alliance de marques f, co-branding m

co-browsing n (Comp) co-navigation f

cobweb n (Econ) modèle d'analyse cobweb m

co-creation n (on website) co-création f, enrichissement du contenu d'un site par l'internaute

COD abbr (▶**cash on delivery**) livraison contre remboursement f, paiement à la livraison m

code¹ n (dialling) code m, indicatif m; (post) code postal m; (Comp) code m; (Law) code m; **area/country ∼ code** indicatif de zone/pays; **∼ of advertising practice** code de pratique publicitaire m; **∼ of conduct** code de conduite m; **∼ of ethics** déontologie f, éthique f; **∼ name** n nom de code m; **∼ of practice** code de bonne conduite m, déontologie f; **∼ of professional responsibility** US code de responsabilité professionnelle m

code² vt coder

coded adj codé; **∼ data entry** n saisie codée de données f; **∼ message** n message codé m

codefendant n (Law) coïnculpé/-e m/f

codetermination n codétermination f, détermination conjointe f

codicil n codicille m

codification n codification f

codify vt (Law) codifier; (procedure) faire un code de

coding n (Comms) codage m; (Comp) codage m, programmation f; **∼ error** n (Comp) erreur de programmation f

co-director n codirecteur/-trice m/f

coefficient n coefficient m

coerce vt exercer des pressions sur

coercion n coercition f

coercive adj coercitif/-ive

cofferdam n (shipping) cofferdam m, maille sèche f

cofinance vt cofinancer

cofinancing n cofinancement m, financement conjoint m

cognition n (knowledge) connaissance f

cognitive: ∼ behavior AmE, **∼ behaviour** BrE n comportement informatif m; **∼ dissonance** n dissonance cognitive f

coherence n cohérence f

coherency n cohérence f

coherent adj cohérent

cohesion n cohésion f; **∼ fund** n (EU) fonds de cohésion m

COI abbr UK (▶**Central Office of Information**) service d'information gouvernemental m

coin n pièce (de monnaie) f

coinage n monnaie f

coincide vi coïncider; **∼ with** coïncider avec

coinsurance n coassurance f

coinsured adj coassuré

coinsurer n coassureur m

cold: ∼ boot n (Comp) démarrage à froid m; **∼ call** n visite impromptue f; **∼ calling** n démarchage par téléphone m; **∼ canvass** n prospection à l'improviste f; **∼ sell** n vente sans préavis f; **∼ storage** n chambre frigorifique f, chambre froide f; **∼ store** n entrepôt frigorifique m

collaborate vi collaborer, coopérer

collaboration n collaboration f, coopération f

collaborative adj collaboratif/-ive; (action, approach) collaboratif/-ive, de collaboration; (project, task) en collaboration; **∼ e-marketplace** n place de marché électronique collaborative f

collaborator n collaborateur/-trice m/f

collapse¹ n (in prices) chute brutale f, dégringolade f (infrml); (of economy, market, currency, bank system, regime) effondrement m; (of company) faillite f; (of deal, talks) échec m

collapse² vi (economy, market, currency, bank, regime, system) s'effondrer; (company) faire faillite; (deal, talks) échouer

collate vt collationner

collateral¹ adj (Gen Comm) (phenomenon) concomitant; (Fin) subsidiaire; (Math) parallèle

collateral² n gage m, nantissement m

collateral: ∼ acceptance n acceptation de cautionnement f; **∼ bill** n effet de nantissement m; **∼ loan** n emprunt garanti m, prêt garanti m; **∼ security** n nantissement m, titre déposé en garantie m; **∼ trust bond** n obligation garantie par nantissement de titres f, obligation nantie f

collateralize vt garantir par nantissement

collation n collation f

colleague n collègue mf; (among lawyers) (male) confrère m; (female) consœur f

collect vt (person) aller chercher, passer prendre; (keys, paperwork, item) récupérer, passer prendre; (as as hobby) collectionner, faire collection de; (debt) recouvrer; (payment, rent) encaisser; (tax, fine) percevoir; (statistics, information) rassembler, recueillir; (premium) ramasser, toucher; (take away) ramasser; (mail, post) faire la levée de; **∼ sums due** faire la recette

collectable¹ adj be **∼** être prisé

collectable² n objet de collection m

collect call n AmE appel en PCV m; **make a ∼ call** appeler en PCV, téléphoner en PCV

collecting bank n banque de recouvrement f

collection n (Acc) (of money, rent) encaissement m; (of debts) recouvrement m; (Tax) levée f, perception f, recouvrement m; (of facts, information) rassemblement m; (of mail) levée f; (sum collected) collecte f; (set of items) collection f; ~ **and delivery** ramassage et livraison; **for** ~ (security) pour recouvrement m; **make a** ~ faire une collecte; ~ **agent** n (Tax) agent de recouvrement m; ~ **of a bill** (bill of exchange) encaissement d'un effet m, encaissement d'une traite m; ~ **charge** n (for debt) frais d'encaissement m pl, frais de recouvrement m pl; (Transp) frais d'enlèvement m pl; ~ **of customs duties** perception des droits de douane f; ~ **of debts** recouvrement de dettes m; ~ **period** n (of debts) période moyenne de recouvrement f; ~ **of premiums** encaissement de primes m

collective¹ adj collectif/-ive

collective² n entreprise collective f

collective: ~ **bargaining** n négociation collective f; ~ **bargaining agreement** n accord patronat-syndicats m, convention collective f; ~ **good** n bien public m; ~ **insurance** n (Ins) assurance collective f; ~ **pay agreement** n accord collectif sur les salaires m

collectively adv collectivement

collectivism n collectivisme m

collectivization n collectivisation f

collectivize vt collectiviser

collector n receveur m; (of rent, debt) encaisseur m; (of art, antiques etc.) collectionneur/-euse m/f; ~ **of taxes** receveur des impôts m

college n (place of higher education) établissement d'enseignement supérieur m; (university) université f, faculté f; (specialist establishment) école f; **business/secretarial** ~ école de commerce/de secrétariat f; **go to** ~, **be at** ~, **be in** ~ AmE faire des études supérieures; ~ **education** n études supérieures f pl; ~ **of further education** UK centre d'enseignement postscolaire m; ~ **student** n étudiant/-e m/f

colliery n houillère f, mine f

collision n collision f; ~ **clause** n clause de collision f; ~ **damage waiver** n (Ins) prime collision sans franchise f; ~ **insurance** n tierce collision f

collusion n collusion f

co-locate vt (Comp) co-localiser

co-location n (Comp) co-localisation f

colon n colon m

colony n colonie f

color n AmE ▸colour BrE

color/graphics adaptor n AmE ▸colour/graphics adaptor BrE

colour n BrE couleur f; ~ **copier** n photocopieuse couleur f; ~ **display** n (Comp) affichage couleur m; ~ **printer** n imprimante couleur f; ~ **supplement** n supplément couleur m

colour/graphics adaptor n BrE adaptateur graphique couleur m

column n (in table) colonne f; (of print) colonne f; (regular article) rubrique f; ~ **heading** n intitulé de colonne m; ~ **inch** n millimètre colonne m

columnist n chroniqueur/-euse m/f, journaliste mf

com. abbr (▸commission) (payment) commission f; (order) commande f; (warrant) mandat m, (fee) commission f, pourcentage m; (Stock) courtage m, droit de courtage m, frais de courtage m pl; (▸committee) com (comité)

co-manager n codirecteur/-trice m/f

Companies: ~ **Act** n UK loi sur les sociétés f; ~ **Registration Office** n ≈ RCS m (Registre du commerce et des services)

combat vt combattre, lutter contre

combination n (Gen Comm) association f, coalition f, combinaison f; (Math) combinaison f; ~ **carrier** n pétrolier-minéralier m; ~ **charge** n, ~ **rate** n tarif groupé m

combine¹ n association f, cartel m, corporation f

combine² vt associer, combiner; ~ **with** combiner avec

combined: ~ **amount** n (Tax) montant global m; ~ **issue** n (of periodical) numéro couplé m; ~ **premium** n prime multirisque f; ~ **ticket** n billet combiné m; ~ **transport** n transport combiné m, transport multimodal m; ~ **transport operation** n opération de transport combiné f; ~ **transport operator** n entrepreneur de transport combiné m

come vt arriver, venir; ~ **along** (progress) faire des progrès; ~ **before** (court) comparaître devant; ~ **forward** se présenter; ~ **from** provenir de, venir de; ~ **to** (total) se chiffrer à; ~ **off** (plan) réussir, se réaliser; ~ **out** (publication) paraître, sortir, être publié; ~ **up** (issue) être soulevé; (question) se poser; ~ **up with** (idea) proposer; (money, solution) trouver

comeback n (return) rentrée f, come-back m; **make a** ~ (person) faire une rentrée, opérer un retour; (style, object) revenir à la mode; (redress) recours m; **have no** ~ n'avoir aucun recours

COMEX abbr US COMEX f bourse des matières premières de New-York

comfort letter n (Acc) lettre de soutien f; (Fin) lettre d'accord présumé f

comma n virgule f

command¹ n (Gen Comm) commandement m, ordre m; (Comp) commande f, instruction f; **be in** ~ **of** commander; **have a good** ~ **of Spanish** avoir une bonne maîtrise de l'espagnol; ~ **economy** n économie planifiée ⋯⋫

f; ~ **file** *n* (Comp) fichier de commande *m*

command² *vt* (order) ordonner à; (have at one's disposal) disposer de; (inspire) inspirer; ~ **a very high price** valoir très cher

commencement *n* commencement *m*; ~ **of cover** *n* (Ins) mise en couverture *f*; ~ **of a policy** *n* (Ins) effet d'une police *m*

commensurate *adj* proportionné

comment¹ *n* commentaire *m*, observation *f*, remarque *f*

comment² *vi* faire des commentaires, faire des observations, faire des remarques; ~ **on sth/sb** faire des commentaires sur qn/qch; ~ **on a document** commenter un document

commentary *n* commentaire *m*

commerce *n* affaires *f pl*, commerce *m*; ~ **site** *n* (on Internet) site marchand *m*

commercial¹ *adj* commercial; **no** ~ **value** sans valeur commerciale

commercial² *n* (on TV, radio) publicité *f*, pub *f* (infrml), spot publicitaire *m*

commercial: ~ **activity** *n* activité commerciale *f*; ~ **advantage** *n* avantage commercial *m*; ~ **analysis** *n* analyse commerciale *f*; ~ **art** *n* arts graphiques *m pl*; ~ **artist** *n* créateur publicitaire *m*, dessinateur de publicité *m*, graphiste *mf*; ~ **bank** *n* banque de dépôt *f*; ~ **bill** *n* AmE titre commercial *m*; ~ **break** *n* page de publicité *f*, publicité *f*; ~ **broker** *n* US courtier en immobilier commercial *m*; ~ **center** AmE, ~ **centre** BrE *n* centre commercial *m*; ~ **concern** *n* entreprise commerciale *f*; ~ **contract** *n* contrat commercial *m*; ~ **credit insurance** *n* US (Ins) assurance crédit commercial *f*; ~ **designer** *n* (in advertising) créateur publicitaire *m*, dessinateur de publicité *m*, graphiste *mf*; ~ **developer** *n* promoteur commercial *m*; ~ **development** *n* développement commercial *m*; ~ **dock** *n* port de commerce *m*; ~ **interest** *n* intérêt commercial *m*; ~ **law** *n* droit commercial *m*; ~ **lease** *n* bail commercial *m*; ~ **lending** *n* crédit aux entreprises *m*, opérations de crédit commercial *f pl*, prêts commerciaux *m pl*; ~ **letting** *n* UK location commerciale *f*; ~ **loan** *n* prêt commercial *m*; ~ **manager** *n* cadre commercial *m*, directeur commercial *m*; ~ **paper** *n* (Gen Comm) effet de commerce *m*, papier commercial *m*; (short-term instrument) billet de trésorerie *m*; ~ **policy** *n* politique commerciale *f*; ~ **port** *n* port de commerce *m*; ~ **premises** *n pl* locaux commerciaux *m pl*; ~ **property** *n* immobilier commercial *m*; ~ **radio** *n* radio commerciale *f*; ~ **radio station** *n* station de radio commerciale *f*; ~ **risk** *n* risque commercial *m*; ~ **risk analysis** *n* analyse des risques commerciaux *f*; ~ **sample** *n* échantillon commercial *m*; ~ **stocks** *n pl* stocks marchands *m pl*; ~ **strategy** *n* stratégie commerciale *f*; ~ **targets** *n pl* objectifs commerciaux *m pl*; ~ **television** *n* télévision commerciale *f*; ~

traveler AmE, ~ **traveller** BrE *n* représentant de commerce *m*, voyageur de commerce *m*, voyageur représentant placier *m*, VRP *m*; ~ **treaty** *n* accord commercial *m*; ~ **vehicle** *n* utilitaire *m*, véhicule utilitaire *m*; ~ **venture** *n* entreprise commerciale *f*; ~ **world** *n* monde du commerce *m*

commercialism *n* (pej) mercantilisme *m*; (profit-making) esprit commercial *m*

commercialization *n* commercialisation *f*

commercialize *vt* commercialiser

commercially *adv* commercialement; ~ **available** *adj* disponible dans le commerce; ~ **sensitive** *adj* confidentiel/-ielle; ~ **viable** rentable

commingling *n* (Stock) (securities, trust banking) *mélange des titres des clients avec les titres détenus par la société*; ~ **of funds** (Law) fusion de capitaux *f*

commissary *n* US intendance *f*

commission¹ *n* (payment) commission *f*; (order) commande *f*; (warrant) mandat *m*; (fee) commission *f*, pourcentage *m*; (Stock) courtage *m*, frais de courtage *m pl*; **get 2%** ~ toucher une commission de 2%; **charge 5%** ~ prendre 5% de commission; **work to** ~ travailler sur commande; **on a** ~ **basis** à la commission; ~ **agent** *n* agent *m*, commissionnaire *mf*, courtier *m*; ~ **broker** *n* US courtier à la commission *m*; ~ **for acceptance** *n* commission d'acceptation *f*; ~ **house** *n* maison de commission *f*, maison de courtage *f*; ~ **of inquiry** *n* commission d'enquête *f*; ~ **merchant** *n*, ~ **salesman** *n* agent *m*, commissionnaire *m*, courtier *m*, vendeur à commission *m*; ~ **salesperson** *n* agent *m*, commissionnaire *mf*, courtier *m*, vendeur/-euse à commission *m/f*

commission² *vt* (empower) mandater; (order) commander; (Transp) mettre en service

commissionaire *n* UK (of hotel) portier *m*

commissioner *n* commissaire *m*

Commissioner: ~ **of Customs and Excise** *n* UK commissionnaire chargé du recouvrement des droits de douane *m*; ~ **of Inland Revenue** *n* UK ≈ Percepteur des impôts *m*

commissioning *n* (Transp) mise en service *f*

commit *vt* (money, time) consacrer; (crime, error) commettre; ~ **to paper** consigner (par écrit); ~ **forgery** se rendre coupable d'un faux; ~ **perjury** se perjurer; ~ **oneself to** s'engager à; **it doesn't** ~ **you to anything** cela ne vous engage à rien

commitment *n* (promise, pledge) engagement *m*, promesse *f*; (obligation) engagement *m*, obligation *f*; **have a strong** ~ **to sth** être très attaché à qch; **meet one's** ~**s** honorer ses engagements; ~ **fee** *n* (Law) commission d'engagement *f*, commission sur le montant d'un prêt non-utilisé *f*

committed costs *n pl* coûts engagés *m pl*

committee *n* comité *m*; (to report, inquire) commission *f*; (Pol) comité *m*, commission *f*; **be on a** ∼ être membre d'un comité; **in** ∼ en comité; ∼ **of inquiry** *n* commission d'enquête *f*; ∼ **meeting** *n* réunion de comité *f*, réunion de commission *f*; ∼ **member** *n* (Gen Comm) membre d'un comité *m*; (reporting, inquiring) membre d'une commission *m*

commodities *n pl* marchandises *f pl*; ∼ **index** *n* UK indice des marchandises *m*, indice des matières premières *m*; ∼ **trading** *n* opérations sur marchandises *f pl*

Commodities Exchange *n* US bourse *des matières premières de New-York*, ≈ Bourse des marchandises *f*, ≈ Bourse du commerce *f*

commodity *n* marchandise *f*; (consumer good) article *m*, produit *m*; (food, product) denrée *f*; (raw material) matière première *f*, produit de base *m*; ∼ **broker** *n* courtier en marchandises *m*, courtier en matières premières *m*; ∼ **credit** *n* crédits commerciaux *m pl*; ∼ **currency** *n* monnaie marchandise *f*; ∼ **exchange** *n* US bourse de marchandises *f*; ∼ **futures** *n pl* (Fin) contrat à terme de marchandises *m*, contrats à terme sur matières premières *m pl*; ∼ **futures market** *n* marché à terme des matières premières *m*; ∼ **futures trading** *n* opération à terme sur les marchandises *f*; ∼ **market** *n* bourse de commerce *f*, bourse de marchandises *f*, marché de matières premières *m*; ∼ **price** *n* cours des denrées *m*, prix de marchandises *m*, prix des denrées *m*; ∼ **pricing** *n* fixation des prix par le jeu du marché *f*; ∼ **rate** *n* tarif préférentiel *m*; ∼ **tax** *n* taxe sur la consommation *f*; ∼ **trading** *n* opérations sur marchandises *f pl*

common *adj* (frequent) courant, fréquent; (shared) commun; **in** ∼ **use** d'un usage courant; **be** ∼ **among** (people, group) être répandu chez; **by** ∼ **agreement** d'un commun accord; **be** ∼ **knowledge** être de notoriété publique; **in** ∼ en commun; **hold sth in** ∼ (Law) posséder qch en commun; ∼ **average** *n* (Ins) avarie commune *f*; ∼ **carrier** *n* (Ind, Transp) entrepreneur général de transports *m*, transporteur *m*; ∼ **cost** *n* charge commune *f*; ∼ **currency** *n* monnaie unique *f*; ∼ **customs tariff** *n* tarif douanier communautaire *m*; ∼ **denominator** *n* dénominateur commun *m*; ∼ **directive** *n* directive commune *f*; ∼ **dividend** *n* dividende ordinaire *m*, dividende sur actions ordinaires *m*; ∼ **equity** *n* action ordinaire *f*, capital actions ordinaire *m*; ∼ **language** *n* langue commune *f*; ∼ **law** *n* droit coutumier *m*; ∼**-law marriage** *n* concubinage *m*; ∼**-law spouse** *n* concubin/-e *m/f*, conjoint/-e de fait *m/f*; ∼ **par value** *n* valeur nominale commune *f*; ∼ **policy** *n* politique commune *f*; ∼ **pricing** *n* entente illicite en matière de prix *f*; ∼ **revenue** *n* produit d'exploitation commun *m*; ∼ **share** *n* action ordinaire *f*; ∼ **share certificate** *n* certificat d'actions ordinaires *m*; ∼ **share dividend** *n* BrE dividende ordinaire *m*, dividende sur actions ordinaires *m*; ∼ **shareholder** *n* actionnaire ordinaire *mf*; ∼ **stock** *n* AmE action ordinaire *f*

Common: ∼ **Agricultural Policy** *n* politique agricole commune *f*; ∼ **Market** *n* Marché commun *m*

commonality *n* standardisation *f*

Commons *n pl* UK (Pol) **the** ∼ les Communes *f pl*

Commonwealth *n* Commonwealth *m*; ∼ **of Independent States** *n* Communauté des États indépendants *f*

comms *abbr* (▸**communications**) communication *f*

communal *adj* (shared) commun, (of or within a community) communautaire; ∼ **ownership** *n* copropriété *f*

commune *n* commune *f*

communicate *vt* (idea) communiquer, (instruction, order, information) transmettre

communication *n* (of information) transmission *f*; (fax, letter) communication *f*; (contact) communication *f*; **a lack of** ∼ un manque de communication *m*; **be in** ∼ **with sb** être en communication avec qn; **the lines of** ∼ les voies de communications *f pl*; ∼ **barrier** *n* obstacle à la communication *m*; ∼ **gap** *n* manque de communication *m*; ∼ **media** *n pl* supports de communication *m pl*, moyens de communication *m pl*, médias *m pl*; ∼ **network** *n* réseau de transmission *m*; ∼ **skills** *n pl* aptitudes à la communication *f pl*, facilités à communiquer *f pl*; ∼ **strategy** *n* stratégie de communication *f*; ∼ **technology** *n* technologie de communication *f*

communications *n pl* (Comms) communication *f*; (roads, railways) moyens de communication *m pl*; ∼ **channel** *n* canal de communication *m*; ∼ **director** *n* directeur/ -trice de la communication *m/f*, dircom *m* (infrml); ∼ **network** *n* réseau de communication *m*; ∼ **satellite** *n* satellite de communication *m*

communicator *n* **be a good** ∼ avoir le sens de la communication

communiqué *n* communiqué *m*

communism *n* communisme *m*

communist *adj* communiste

community[1] *adj* communautaire

community[2] *n* (Gen Comm, Comp) communauté *f*

Community *adj* (EU) communautaire; ∼ **aid** *n* aide communautaire *f*; ∼ **budget** *n* Budget communautaire *m*, Budget de la Communauté *m*; ∼ **goods** *n pl* marchandises communautaires *f pl*

community: ~ **action** n action collective f, action communautaire f; ~ **of goods** n communauté de biens f; ~ **property** n US (Law) bien en communauté m; ~ **spirit** n esprit communautaire m

communize vt (land) collectiviser

commutability n interchangeabilité f, permutabilité f; (Law) commuabilité f

commutable adj interchangeable, permutable; (Law) commuable

commutate vt commuter

commutation n (Ins, Law) commutation f; (Transp) AmE migrations alternantes f pl, trajets journaliers m pl; ~ **right** n (Ins) faculté de rachat f; ~ **ticket** n AmE carte d'abonnement f

commutative adj (Law) commutatif/-ive

commute ① vt convertir, échanger; (Law) commuer
② vi (Transp) faire la navette

commuter n (Transp) navetteur/-euse m/f; (aircraft) avion de transport régional m; ~ **airline** n compagnie de transport régional f; ~ **belt** n UK grande banlieue f

commuting n migrations alternantes f pl, trajets journaliers m pl

co-mortgagor n US co-débiteur/-trice hypothécaire m/f

compact n (verbal agreement) entente f; (written agreement) accord m, contrat m; (Law) convention f; ~ **disc** n disque compact m; ~ **disc interactive** n disque compact interactif m; ~ **disc read-only memory** n CD-ROM m, cédérom m; ~ **disc recordable** n CD-R m, disque compact enregistrable m; ~ **disc rewritable** n CD-RW m, disque compact réinscriptible m

company n compagnie f, entreprise f, firme f, société f; ~ **accounts** n pl comptes sociaux m pl; ~ **attorney** n AmE conseiller/ -ère juridique d'une entreprise m/f; (business law expert) juriste d'entreprise mf; ~ **benefits** n pl avantages annexes m pl, avantages sociaux m pl; ~ **car** n voiture de fonction f; ~ **credit card** n carte de crédit professionnelle f; ~ **director** n chef d'entreprise m; ~ **executive** n cadre d'entreprise m, dirigeant/-e d'entreprise m/f; ~ **flotation** n lancement d'entreprise m; ~ **law** n droit des sociétés m; ~ **lawyer** n BrE conseiller/-ère juridique d'une entreprise m/f; (business law expert) juriste d'entreprise mf; ~-**level agreement** n accord au niveau d'une société m; ~ **logo** n logo de la société m; ~ **manager** n chef d'entreprise m; ~ **meeting** n assemblée des actionnaires f, réunion des actionnaires f; ~ **name** n (Law) raison sociale f; ~ **pension scheme** n régime de retraite de l'entreprise m; ~ **philosophy** n philosophie de l'entreprise f; ~ **policy** n politique de l'entreprise f; ~ **profile** n profil de l'entreprise m; ~ **results** n pl performances de la société f pl, résultats

de la société m pl; ~ **seal** n (Law) sceau légal m; ~ **secretary** n UK secrétaire général/-e m/f; ~ **strategy** n stratégie de l'entreprise f; ~ **structure** n structure de l'entreprise f; ~ **tax** n impôt sur les sociétés m; ~ **union** n syndicat maison m

comparability n comparabilité f; (of pay) harmonisation f, alignement m

comparable adj comparable; ~ **to,** ~ **with** comparable à

comparative adj (value, method, study) comparatif/-ive; (relative) relatif/-ive; ~ **advantage** n avantage comparatif m; ~ **advertising** n publicité comparative f

comparatively adv relativement

compare vti comparer; ~ **to** comparer à; ~ **with** comparer avec; ~d **with** par rapport à

comparison n comparaison f; ~ **shopping** n achat réfléchi comparatif m; ~ **site** n (on Internet) moteur de comparaison de prix m; ~ **test** n test comparatif m

compartment n compartiment m

compartmentalization n cloisonnement m

compartmentalize vt compartimenter, cloisonner

compatibility n compatibilité f

compatible adj compatible; ~ **with** compatible avec

compel vt contraindre; ~ **sb to do sth** contraindre qn à faire qch

compensate vt compenser; (pay) rémunérer; (Law) dédommager, indemniser; ~ **for** compenser; ~ **for a fall in demand** compenser une chute de la demande; ~ **sb for sth** dédommager qn pour qch, indemniser qn pour qch

compensating adj compensatoire; ~ **balance** n solde compensateur m; ~ **error** n erreur de compensation f

compensation n (Gen Comm) indemnisation f, rémunération f; (payment) rémunération f; (Econ) compensation f; (Ins) compensation f, dédommagement m; (Law) indemnisation f, indemnité f; (Tax) compensation f, dédommagement m; **in** ~ en contrepartie; **by way of** ~ **for** en compensation de; ~ **agreement** n accord de compensation m; ~ **claim** n demande d'indemnité f; ~ **for damage** n compensation des dommages f; ~ **for loss** n compensation des pertes f; ~ **fund** n UK (Stock) caisse de garantie f, fond de garantie m; ~ **settlement** n (Law) accord d'indemnisation f; ~ **stocks** n pl UK (Stock) actions de compensation f pl

compensatory adj compensatoire; ~ **damages** n pl (Law) dommages-intérêts compensatoires m pl; ~ **fiscal policy** n politique de déficit budgétaire f

compete vi (for prominence, prize, job)

rivaliser; (companies) se faire concurrence; ~
against , ~ **with** concurrencer, faire
concurrence à, être en concurrence avec;
**they were competing for the same job/
client** ils se disputaient le même emploi/
client

competence n aptitude f, capacité f,
compétence f; (Law) compétence f; **have the
~ to do** avoir la compétence voulue pour
faire; ~ **of a court** compétence d'un
tribunal f

competent adj (capable) compétent; (trained)
qualified; (work) honorable; (Law) compétent;
~ **party** n (Law) partie ayant capacité à
contracter f

competing adj rival, concurrent; (product)
concurrentiel/-ielle

competition n concurrence f; **be in ~
with** être en concurrence avec; **in close ~** en
concurrence étroite

Competition Commission n UK ≈
Commission de la concurrence f

competitive adj (company, price) compétitif/
-ive; (product) concurrentiel/-ielle; **have a ~
advantage over sb** avoir un avantage
concurrentiel sur qn; ~ **advertising** n
publicité concurrentielle f; ~ **bid** n réponse
à un appel d'offres f, soumission f; ~
bidding n système d'appel d'offres m,
système de soumission m; ~ **disadvantage**
n désavantage concurrentiel m; ~ **edge** n
avantage concurrentiel m; ~ **intelligence** n
veille à la concurrence f; ~ **position** n
position concurrentielle f; ~ **positioning** n
positionnement concurrentiel m; ~ **price** n
prix compétitif m, prix concurrentiel m; ~
pricing n fixation des prix à des niveaux
compétitifs f; ~ **strategy** n stratégie
concurrentielle f; ~ **tactics** n pl tactique
concurrentielle f; ~ **tendering** n soumission
concurrentielle f

competitiveness n compétitivité f

competitor n concurrent/-e m/f; **be ~s**
être concurrents; ~ **analysis** n analyse des
concurrents f

compilation n (Acc) établissement des
états financiers m

compile vt (book, report) rédiger; (list, index)
dresser; (facts, evidence) rassembler; (Comp)
compiler

complain vi se plaindre; ~ **to sb** se
plaindre à qn; (officially) se plaindre auprès de
qn

complaint n réclamation f; (civil action)
demande introductive d'instance f; (criminal
law) plainte f; **make a ~** se plaindre; **have
cause for ~** avoir lieu de se plaindre; **there
have been ~s of discrimination** on s'est
plaint de discrimination; **in case of ~** en cas
de réclamation

complaints procedure n procédure de
réclamation f; (Law) procédure de dépôt de
plainte f

complement n (Acc, Gen Comm)
complément m; (S&M) produit lié m

complementary adj complémentaire

complete¹ adj (finished) achevé; (whole)
complet/-ète, entier/-ière, total; ~ **audit** n
audit complet m

complete² vt (finish) achever, finir,
terminer; (make whole) compléter

completed adj (finished) achevé, fini,
terminé; (Law) (in contracts) accompli

completely adv complètement,
entièrement

completeness n (of accounting data,
information) intégralité f

completion n (of work) achèvement m; **near
~** être en phase d'achèvement; ~ **date** n
date d'achèvement f; ~ **of sale** n signature
d'une vente f

complex¹ adj complexe

complex² n (of buildings) complexe m,
ensemble m; **sports/leisure ~** complexe
sportif/de loisirs m

compliance n (Gen Comm) conformité f,
consentement m; (Law) conformité f,
observation f; ~ **costs** n pl (Acc) coûts de
soumission m pl, frais de mise en conformité
m pl; (Admin) frais d'adaptation m pl, frais
d'administration m pl; **be in ~ with** être en
conformité avec; **in ~ with** conformément à;
in ~ with the law en vertu de la loi; ~ **test**
n test de conformité m

complicate vt compliquer; ~ **matters**, ~
things compliquer la vie

complication n complication f

complimentary adj (free) gratuit, à titre
gracieux; (review, article, comment) flatteur/-euse;
~ **close** n formule de politesse f; ~ **copy** n
spécimen gratuit m; ~ **subscription** n
abonnement gratuit m

compliments n pl compliments m pl; ~
slip n carte avec les compliments de
l'expéditeur f

comply: ~ **with** vt (request) accéder à;
(rules) obéir à, respecter; (directives, orders,
criteria, standards) se conformer à; ~ **with the
law** se soumettre à la loi; ~ **with the
regulations** respecter le règlement; **failure to
~ with the rules** non-respect des règles

component¹ adj composant, constituant

component² n (Gen Comm) composant m,
composante f, élément m; (Ind) composant m,
pièce f

component: ~ **factory** n usine de
composants f, usine de pièces détachées f; ~
part n (of system) composant m, composante f,
élément constitutif m; (Ind) composant m

composed: ~ **of** composé de

composite adj combiné, composite; ~
commodity n (Econ) produit composite m;
~ **currency** n monnaie composite f; ~
index n (Econ, Fin) indice composite m,
indice composé m; ~ **insurance** n (Ins)

assurance avec participation aux bénéfices *f*; ~ **rate** *n* taux composite *m*; ~ **spread** *n* (Bank) écart composite *m*; ~ **yield** *n* rendement composite *m*

composition *n* (agreement) compromis *m*; (make-up) composition *f*; (with creditor) accommodement *m*, arrangement *m*

compound¹ *adj* composé; ~ **annual rate** *n* UK taux annuel composé *m*, taux d'intérêt composé *m*; ~ **duty** *n* (customs) droit composé *m*, droit mixte *m*; ~ **entry** *n* (Acc) écriture multiple *f*; ~ **growth rate** *n* taux de croissance global *m*; ~ **interest** *n* intérêt composé *m*, intérêts composés *m pl*; ~ **journal entry** *n* écriture du journal multiple *f*; ~ **rate** *n* taux composé *m*; ~ **yield** *n* rendement global *m*

compound² *vt* (worsen) aggraver; (Law) composer, transiger; ~ **a debt** régler une dette à l'amiable, transiger sur une dette

comprehensive *adj* (measures) d'ensemble; (coverage, range, training) complet/-ète; (report, review, answer) complet/-ète, détaillé, exhaustif/-ive; (Ins) multirisque; ~ **agreement** *n* accord d'ensemble *m*; ~ **budget** *n* budget directeur *m*, budget général *m*; ~ **insurance** *n* assurance tous risques *f*; ~ **insurance policy** *n* police d'assurance tous risques *f*, police multirisque *f*; ~ **liability insurance** *n* assurance responsabilité civile générale *f*; ~ **responsibility** *n* responsabilité globale *f*; ~ **tax reform** *n* réforme fiscale globale *f*

compress *vt* (file, data, salary) comprimer

compression *n* (of data, salary) compression *f*

comprise *vt* comporter, comprendre, inclure; **be ~d of** être composé de

compromise¹ *n* compromis *m*; **reach a ~** arriver à un compromis; **agree to a ~** accepter un compromis; ~ **agreement** *n* accord de compromis *m*; ~ **solution** *n* solution de compromis *f*

compromise² [1] *vt* (person) compromettre; (project, principles, negotiations) compromettre, mettre en danger; ~ **oneself** se compromettre
[2] *vi* accepter un compromis, transiger

comptroller *n* (Acc) contrôleur/-euse de gestion *m/f*; (Admin) intendant/-e *m/f*; (Fin) contrôleur/-euse *m/f*

Comptroller General *n* US Président de la cour des comptes *m*

compulsive buying *n* achat impulsif *m*

compulsory *adj* (power, authority) coercitif/-ive; (regulation) obligatoire; ~ **arbitration** *n* UK arbitrage d'office *m*, arbitrage obligatoire *m*; ~ **competitive tendering** *n* UK soumission obligatoire en vue d'adjudication *f*; ~ **deduction** *n* franchise obligatoire *f*, prélèvement obligatoire *m*; ~ **licence** BrE, **license** AmE *n* licence obligatoire *f*; ~ **liquidation** *n* liquidation forcée *f*; ~

purchase *n* expropriation *f*; ~ **purchase order** *n* UK ordre d'achat obligatoire *m*, ordre d'expropriation *m*; ~ **redundancy** *n* licenciement sec *m*; ~ **retirement** *n* BrE mise à la retraite d'office *f*, retraite obligatoire *f*

computation *n* calcul *m*

compute *vt* calculer

computer *n* ordinateur *m*; ~ **age** *n* l'ère de l'informatique *f*; ~**-aided** *adj* assisté par ordinateur; ~**-aided design** *n* conception assistée par ordinateur *f*, création assistée par ordinateur *f*; ~**-aided design and computer-aided manufacturing** *n* conception et fabrication assistées par ordinateur *f*; ~**-aided language learning** *n* apprentissage des langues assisté par ordinateur *m*; ~**-aided learning** *n* enseignement assisté par ordinateur *m*; ~**-aided manufacture** *n*, ~**-aided manufacturing** *n* fabrication assistée par ordinateur *f*; ~**-aided software engineering** *n* conception de programmes assistée par ordinateur *f*; ~**-aided testing** *n* test assisté par ordinateur *m*; ~**-aided translation** *n* traduction assistée par ordinateur *f*; ~**-animation** *n* imagerie de synthèse *f*; ~**-assisted** *adj* assisté par ordinateur; ~**-assisted design** *n* conception assistée par ordinateur *f*, création assistée par ordinateur *f*; ~**-assisted design and computer-assisted manufacturing** *n* conception et fabrication assistées par ordinateur *f*; ~**-assisted language learning** *n* apprentissage des langues assisté par ordinateur *m*; ~**-assisted learning** *n* enseignement assisté par ordinateur *m*; ~**-assisted manufacture** *n*, ~**-assisted manufacturing** *n* fabrication assistée par ordinateur *f*; ~**-assisted software engineering** *n* conception de programmes assistée par ordinateur *f*; ~**-assisted testing** *n* tests assistés par ordinateur *m pl*; ~**-assisted trading system** *n* système de cotation électronique *m*; ~**-assisted translation** *n* traduction assistée par ordinateur *f*; ~**-based** *adj* informatisé; ~**-based training** *n* enseignement assisté par ordinateur *m*; ~ **center** AmE, ~ **centre** BrE *n* centre informatique *m*; ~ **code** *n* code machine *m*; ~ **company** *n* société informatique *f*; ~ **conferencing** *n* téléconférence informatisée *f*; ~ **consultancy firm** *n* société de services et de conseils en informatique *f*, SSCI *f*; ~ **consultant** *n* conseil en informatique *m*; ~**-controlled** *adj* géré par ordinateur; ~ **department** *n* service informatique *m*; ~ **engineer** *n* informaticien/-ienne *m/f*; ~ **engineering** *n* ingénierie informatique *f*; ~ **expert** *n* informaticien/-ienne *m/f*; ~ **file** *n* fichier informatique *m*; ~ **fraud** *n* fraude informatique *f*; ~ **graphics** *n pl* infographie *f*; ~ **graphics expert** *n* infographiste *mf*; ~ **hacker** *n* pirate informatique *m*; ~ **hacking** *n* piratage informatique *m*; ~**-integrated manufacture** *n*, ~**-integrated manufacturing** *n* fabrication intégrée par ordinateur *f*, production intégrée par ordinateur *f*; ~ **literacy** *n* connaissances en informatique *f pl*, maîtrise de l'outil informatique *f*; ~**-literate** *adj* ayant des connaissances en informatique, ayant une bonne connaissance de l'outil informatique; ~ **network** *n* réseau informatique *m*; ~**-operated** *adj* géré par ordinateur; ~ **operator** *n* opérateur sur ordinateur *m*; ~ **package** *n* logiciel informatique *m*, progiciel *m*; ~ **print-out** *n* sortie sur papier *f*; (on continuous sheets) listing *m*; ~ **processing** *n* traitement informatique *m*, traitement par ordinateur *m*; ~ **program** *n* programme (informatique) *m*; ~ **programmer** *n* programmeur *m*; ~ **programming** *n* programmation *f*; ~ **room** *n* salle des ordinateurs *f*; ~ **science** *n* informatique *f*; ~ **scientist** *n* informaticien/-ienne *m*|*f*; ~ **screen** *n* écran d'ordinateur *m*; ~ **security** *n* sécurité informatique *f*; ~ **services** *n pl* services en informatique *m pl*; ~ **services company** *n* société de services d'ingénierie informatique *f*, SSII *f*; ~ **simulation** *n* simulation sur ordinateur *f*, simulé *m*; ~ **software** *n* logiciel *m*; ~ **system** *n* système informatique *m*; ~ **technology** *n* technologie informatique *f*; ~**-telephony integration** *n* couplage téléphonie-informatique *m*; ~ **terminal** *n* terminal d'ordinateur *m*; ~ **trading** *n* US système de transactions automatisées *m*; ~ **vendor** *n* constructeur d'ordinateurs *m*, fournisseur d'ordinateurs *m*

computerization *n* (of information) mise sur ordinateur *f*; (of system, workplace) automatisation *f*, informatisation *f*; (processing) traitement par ordinateur *m*

computerize *vt* (information) traiter par ordinateur; (system, process, workplace) automatiser, informatiser

computerized *adj* automatisé, informatisé; **become** ~ s'informatiser

computing *n* informatique *f*; ~ **center** *n* AmE, ~ **centre** *n* BrE centre informatique *m*; ~ **company** *n* société informatique *f*; ~ **power** *n* puissance de calcul *f*

con *n* (infrml) escroquerie *f*, arnaque *f* (infrml); ~ **artist** *n* escroc *m*; ~ **trick** *n* escroquerie *f*, duperie *f*

conceal *vt* (information) ne pas divulguer; (object, truth) cacher, dissimuler

concealed: ~ **assets** *n pl* actif latent *m*; ~ **unemployment** *n* chômage caché *m*

concealment *n* dissimulation *f*, non-divulgation *f*

conceive *vt* concevoir

concentrate ⬛1 *vt* concentrer; **be ~d in**

the hands of (power, ownership, resources) être concentré dans les mains de
⬛2 *vi* se concentrer; ~ **on** se concentrer sur; ~ **one's attention on** concentrer son attention sur; ~ **one's resources on doing** employer ses ressources à faire

concentrated *adj* (effort) intense

concentration *n* concentration *f*; ~ **of industry** concentration industrielle *f*

concept *n* concept *m*; ~ **test** *n* test de concept *m*

conceptual *adj* conceptuel/-elle; ~ **framework** *n* cadre conceptuel *m*

concern[1] *n* (business organization) affaire *f*, entreprise *f*, firme *f*, maison *f*; (share) intérêt *m*; (worry) inquiétude *f*; (preoccupation) problème préoccupant *m*

concern[2] *vt* (worry) inquiéter; (affect) concerner

concerned *adj* intéressé

concerning *prep* concernant, en ce qui concerne

concerted *adj* (action, campaign) concerté; ~ **effort** *n* effort concerté *m*

concession *n* (reduction) remise *f*, réduction *f*, tarif réduit *m*; (distribution right) concession *f*; (Acc) réduction *f*; (Law) concession *f*; (Prop) réduction *f*; (Tax) abattement fiscal *m*, allègement *m*

concessionaire *n* concessionnaire *mf*

concessional *adj* avantageux/-euse, favorable

concessionary[1] *adj* concessionnaire, à prix réduit; ~ **rate** *n* taux privilégié *m*; (Leis) tarif réduit *m*

concessionary[2] *n* concessionnaire *mf*

concessioner *n* concessionnaire *mf*

conciliate *vt* apaiser, concilier; (Law) concilier

conciliation *n* conciliation *f*; ~ **board** *n* commission d'arbitrage *f*

conciliator *n* conciliateur/-trice *m*|*f*

conclude *vt* conclure, finir, terminer; ~ **from** déduire de, inférer de

concluded *adj* fini

conclusion *n* (of agreement, inquiry, report) conclusion *f*; (of contract) passation *f*

conclusive *adj* concluant, probant, péremptoire; ~ **evidence** *n* preuve concluante *f*, preuve péremptoire *f*

concomitant *adj* concomitant

concrete[1] *adj* (data, facts) concret/-ète; ~ **evidence** *n* preuve matérielle *f*

concur *vi* (agree) s'entendre, être d'accord; (coincide) arriver en même temps, coïncider; (tally) concorder; ~ **to do** (combine) contribuer à faire

concurrent *adj* simultané

condemn *vt* condamner

condemnation *n* condamnation *f*; (Prop) condamnation *f*, expropriation pour cause ⤙⤍

d'utilité publique *f*

condition¹ *n* (stipulation) condition *f*; (state) état *m*; **fulfil the ∼s** remplir les conditions; **on ∼ that** à condition que; **it is a ∼ of the contract that ...** le contrat stipule que ...; **be in good/bad ∼** être en bon/mauvais état

condition² *vt* déterminer

conditional *adj* conditionnel/-elle; **make sth ∼ on** faire dépendre qch de; **∼ clause** *n* clause conditionnelle *f*; **∼ endorsement** *n* (Fin) endossement conditionnel *m*; **∼ sale** *n* vente sous condition *f*; **∼ sales agreement** *n* vente sous condition *f*

conditions *n pl* (circumstances) circonstances *f pl*, conditions *f pl*; (terms of contract) conditions *f pl*; **living/working ∼** conditions de vie/de travail *f pl*; **under present ∼** dans les conditions actuelles; **∼ of carriage** conditions de transport *f pl*; **∼ of contract** conditions contractuelles *f pl*, conditions d'un contrat *f pl*; **∼ of employment**, **∼ of service** conditions d'embauche *f pl*; **∼ of sale** conditions de vente *f pl*; **∼ of use** conditions d'utilisation *f pl*

condominium *n* AmE immeuble en copropriété *m*

conducive *adj*: **∼ to** favorable à, favorisant, qui contribue à; **be ∼ to** (growth) contribuer à, favoriser

conduct¹ *n* conduite *f*, comportement *m*

conduct² *vt* (business, campaign, inquiry, meeting) conduire, mener; (manage, carry out) diriger; (poll, survey) effectuer, faire; **∼ the investigation** (Gen Comm) mener l'enquête; (Law) instruire

confederation *n* confédération *f*

Confederation of British Industry *n* UK ≈ Conseil national du patronat français *m*

confer *vt* (right) accorder, conférer; (degree) conférer; **∼ a privilege on sb** conférer un privilège à qn

conference *n* conférence *f*, réunion *f*; (convention) colloque *m*, congrès *m*; (Pol) assemblée *f*, congrès *m*; **∼ call** *n* conférence téléphonique *f*, téléconférence *f*; **∼ delegate** *n* congressiste *mf*, délégué/-e *m/f*; **∼ proceedings** *n pl* actes de conférence *m pl*; **∼ report** *n* compte rendu de la conférence *m*; **∼ table** *n* table de conférence *f*; **∼ venue** *n* lieu du congrès *m*

confession *n* aveu *m*; **make a ∼** faire un aveu

confide [1] *vt* confier; **∼ sth to sb** confier qch à qn
[2] *vi* **∼ in sb** se confier à qn

confidence *n* (faith) confiance *f*; (certainty) certitude *f*; (self-assurance) assurance *f*, confiance en soi *f*; **lack ∼** manquer d'assurance; **in ∼** en secret; **take sb into one's ∼** se confier à qn; **have ∼ in sb/sth** avoir confiance en qn/qch; **∼ level** *n* niveau

de confiance *m*; **∼ man** *n* escroc *m*; **∼ trick** *n* abus de confiance *m*, escroquerie *f*; **∼ trickster** *n* escroc *m*

confidential *adj* confidentiel/-ielle; **∼ information** *n* informations confidentielles *f pl*; **∼ secretary** *n* secrétaire privé *m*

confidentiality *n* confidentialité *f*; **∼ agreement** *n* accord de confidentialité *m*

configuration *n* configuration *f*; **∼ control** *n*, **∼ management** *n* gestion de la configuration *f*

configure *vt* configurer

confirm *vt* (details, information, fact) confirmer, corroborer; (decree) entériner, homologuer; (assessment) ratifier; **∼ receipt of** accuser réception de; **be ∼ed** se confirmer

confirmation *n* (of plans) confirmation *f*, ratification *f*; (Law) ratification *f*; (of decision) confirmation *f*, entérinement *m*; (Stock) avis d'exécution *m*, avis d'opéré *m*; **∼ notice** *n* avis d'exécution *m*, avis de confirmation *m*; **∼ of order** (S&M) confirmation d'une commande *f*; **∼ of renewal** (Ins) confirmation de renouvellement *f*

confirmed: **∼ credit** *n* crédit confirmé *m*; **∼ letter of credit** *n* lettre de crédit confirmée *f*

confirming house *n* agence spécialisée dans la mise en contact d'exportateurs et d'acheteurs

confiscate *vt* confisquer

confiscation *n* confiscation *f*, saisie *f*

conflict¹ *n* conflit *m*; **be in ∼ with sb/sth** être en conflit avec qn/qch; **have a ∼ of loyalties** être déchiré par des loyautés contradictoires; **∼ of interest** conflit d'intérêts *m*; **∼ resolution** *n* résolution des conflits *f*

conflict² *vi* (ideas, views) être en contradiction; (events) être incompatibles

conflicting *adj* contraire; **∼ evidence** *n* (Law) preuve contradictoire *f*; (testimony) témoignage contradictoire *m*; **∼ interest** *n* intérêt personnel opposé et divergent *m*

conform *vi* se conformer; **∼ to** (standards) se conformer à, être en conformité avec; (Law) se conformer à

conformed copy *n* (of legal document) copie conforme *f*

conformity *n* accord *m*, conformité *f*, ressemblance *f*; **in ∼ with** conformément à; **∼ to accounting rules** régularité *f*

confront *vt* affronter, confronter, faire face à

confrontation *n* affrontement *m*, confrontation *f*

congestion *n* encombrement *m*; (on telephone lines) saturation *f*; **∼ surcharge** *n* (Transp) taxe d'encombrement *f*

conglomerate *n* conglomérat *m*; **∼ merger** *n* fusion dans un conglomérat *f*

congress *n* congrès *m*

Congressional adj US (Pol) du Congrès

congressman n pl -men US (Pol) ≈ député m

congresswoman n pl -women US (Pol) ≈ députée f

congruence n conformité f

congruent adj conforme; ~ **with** conforme à

conjecture vi conjecturer

conjunction n (of circumstances) concours m; **in ~ with** conjointement avec

connect vt (Gen Comm, Comp) connecter, raccorder; (Comms) mettre en communication avec, relier

connected adj (event, matter, idea) lié; (road, town) relié; (Comp) connecté; **be ~ to the Internet** être connecté à Internet; **everything ~ with advertising** tout se qui se rapporte à la publicité

connecting adj (room) attenant; ~ **carrier** n transporteur qui assure la correspondance m; ~ **flight** n correspondance f, vol de correspondance m

connection n (logical link) rapport m; (personal tie, link) lien m; (acquaintance, contact) relation f; (Transp) correspondance f; (Comp) (to Internet) connexion f; (to network, services) raccordement m; **in ~ with** au sujet de, à propos de; **make the ~ between** faire le rapprochement entre; **have a ~ with** avoir un rapport avec; **have close ~s with** (company, area, town) avoir des liens étroits avec; **miss one's ~** (Transp) râter sa correspondance; **Internet ~** connexion à Internet; **have ~s in publishing** avoir des relations dans l'édition; **a bad ~** (on phone line) une mauvaise ligne; **get a ~** (Comms) avoir une ligne; ~ **charge** n (Comms) taxe de raccordement f; ~ **time** n (Comp) temps de connexion m

connectivity n (Comp) connectivité f

conscious adj conscient; ~ **of** conscient de

consciousness n conscience f

consecutive adj consécutif/-ive, successif/-ive

consensus n accord général m, consensus m; **a broad ~** un large consensus; **reach a ~** parvenir à un consensus; **what's the ~?** quelle est l'opinion générale?; ~ **agreement** n accord consensuel m; ~ **politics** n politique de consensus f

consent¹ n assentiment m, consentement m; **by mutual ~** d'un commun accord

consent² vi consentir; ~ **to** consentir à

consequence n conséquence f; **as a ~** en conséquence, par conséquent; **in ~** en conséquence, par conséquent

consequential: ~ **damage** n (Ins) dommages indirects m pl; ~ **damages** n pl dommages-intérêts indirects m pl; ~ **loss** n pertes indirectes f pl, risque indirect m

consequently adv en conséquence, par conséquent

conservation n (of heritage) conservation f; (of natural environment) protection f, préservation f

conservationist n écologiste mf

conservatism n conservatisme m

conservative¹ adj (spending, attitude) prudent; (Pol) conservateur/-trice; ~ **estimate** n évaluation prudente f

conservative² n (Pol) conservateur/-trice m/f

Conservative Party n UK parti conservateur m

conserve vt (cash, stocks) économiser; (environment) protéger

consgt abbr (►**consignation**) consignation f, envoi m, expédition f

consider **1** vt (offer) étudier; (facts, proposal, alternative, options) étudier, considérer; (evidence, problem, case) examiner; (risk, cost, difficulty) prendre en considération; (envisage) envisager; ~ **whether** (decide) décider si; ~ **how** réfléchir à la façon dont; **all things ~ed** tout compte fait **2** vi réfléchir

considerable adj (Gen Comm) considérable, non-négligeable; (debt, demand) considérable

considerably adv considérablement

consideration n considération f; (Law) (contract) contrepartie f; (money) rémunération f, rétribution f; **give ~ to** réfléchir à; **upon further ~** à la réflexion; **after careful ~** après mûre réflexion; **take sth into ~** prendre qch en considération; **be under ~** (idea) être à l'étude; **she is under ~ for the job** on est en train d'étudier sa candidature; **for a small ~** moyennant une petite somme en contrepartie

considered adj (answer, views) réfléchi

consign vt envoyer, expédier

consignation n envoi m, expédition f

consignee n dépositaire mf, destinataire mf

consignment n (sending) envoi m, expédition f; **on ~** en consignation, en dépôt; ~ **note** n bordereau d'expédition m, feuille de route f, lettre de voiture f

consignor n (goods) livraison f, lot m; (sender) expéditeur/-trice m/f

consist: ~ **of** vt consister en, comprendre

consistency n (Gen Comm) cohérence f, logique f; (of procedures) continuité f, permanence f; (of quality, achievement) qualité suivie f; ~ **check** n contrôle d'uniformité m, contrôle de cohérence m

consistent adj (growth, quality) regulier/-ière; (attempt, criticism, demands) répété; (argument, position) cohérent, conséquent, logique; (in methods) conséquent, logique; ~ **with** compatible avec, en accord avec

c

consistently adv de façon cohérente

consolidate vt (Econ) renforcer; (funds, loan) consolider; (companies) fusionner; (knowledge) renforcer; (position) concrétiser, consolider, raffermir; (resources) réunir, consolider; (orders) grouper; (Transp) grouper

consolidated adj (Gen Comm) consolidé, raffermi, renforcé; (Acc, Bank, Fin) consolidé; (Econ) consolidé, renforcé; ~ **accounts** n pl comptes consolidés m pl; ~ **annuities** n pl UK fonds consolidés m pl, rentes consolidées f pl; ~ **cash-flow statement** n (Acc) tableau de financement consolidé m; ~ **fund** n UK fonds d'amortissement de la dette publique m; ~ **net profit** n bénéfice net consolidé m; ~ **rate** n (Transp) tarif groupé m; ~ **stock** n UK fonds consolidés m pl, rentes consolidées f pl

consolidation n (Acc) (of accounts) consolidation f; (of loan) consolidation f; (of holdings) consolidation f, fusion f; (of knowledge) renforcement m; (of orders) groupage m; (Transp) groupage m, groupement m; (of shares) regroupement m

consolidator n (Transp) groupeur m

consols n pl UK fonds consolidés m pl

consortium n pl **-tia** (Gen Comm) consortium m, groupe m, groupement d'entreprises m; (Bank, Fin) consortium m; ~ **bank** n consortium bancaire m

conspectus n vue d'ensemble f, vue générale f

conspicuous consumption n consommation ostentatoire f

constant[1] adj (regular) constant; (ever-present) permanent; (incessant) incessant

constant[2] n (Comp, Math) constante f

constant: ~ **capital** n (Econ) capital fixe m; ~ **dollars** n pl US dollars constants m pl; ~ **prices** n pl prix constants m pl

constantly adv constamment

constituent[1] adj composant, constituant; ~ **company** n (Stock) société constituante f

constituent[2] n (Pol) électeur/-trice m/f

constitute vt (problem, threat) constituer; (body, committee) créer; (percentage) constituer

constituted adj (Gen Comm) établi; (Law) (trust) constitué, institué

constitution n (establishment) constitution f; (Pol) constitution f, statuts m pl

constitutional adj constitutionnel/-elle

constr abbr (▶**construction**) construction f

constrain vt contraindre; ~ **sb to do sth** contraindre qn à faire qch

constraining factor n facteur de contrainte m

constraint n contrainte f; **put a** ~ **on sb** imposer une contrainte à qn; **under** ~ sous la contrainte; **you are under no** ~ vous n'êtes en rien obligé

construct vt construire

constructed adj construit

construction n construction f; **under** ~ en cours de construction; ~ **industry** n industrie du bâtiment f, bâtiment m; ~ **worker** n ouvrier/-ière du bâtiment m/f

constructive adj constructif/-ive; ~ **discharge** n AmE, ~ **dismissal** BrE n démission forcée f, démission provoquée f

consul n consul m

consulate n consulat m

Consulate-General n Consul général m, Consulat général m

consult vt consulter; ~ **sb about sth** consulter qn au sujet de qch

consultancy n (discipline) conseil m; (firm) cabinet-conseil m, société de conseil f

consultant n conseil m, conseiller/-ère m/f, consultant/-e m/f; **tax** ~ conseiller fiscal m; **management** ~ conseil en gestion m, consultant en gestion m

consultation n consultation f; **in** ~ **with** en consultation avec

consultative adj consultatif/-ive; **in a** ~ **capacity** à titre consultatif; ~ **body** n organisme consultatif m; ~ **committee** n comité consultatif m, commission consultative f

consulting firm n cabinet d'experts m, société de conseil f, cabinet-conseil m

consumables n pl consommables m pl

consume vt (use) consommer

consumer n consommateur/-trice m/f; ~ **acceptance** n acceptation par les consommateurs f, réceptivité des consommateurs f; ~ **advertising** n publicité grand public f; ~ **advisory service** n service de conseil au consommateur m; ~ **banking** n services bancaires au consommateur m pl; ~ **behavior** AmE, ~ **behaviour** BrE n comportement du consommateur m; ~ **benefit** n bénéfice au consommateur m; ~ **brand** n marque grand public f; ~ **brands** n pl produits de grande consommation m pl; ~ **choice** n choix du consommateur m, préférence du consommateur f; ~ **credit** n crédit à la consommation m; ~ **demand** n demande des consommateurs f; ~ **durables** n pl biens de consommation durables m pl; ~ **expectations** n pl attentes du consommateur f pl; ~ **expenditure** n dépenses de consommation f pl; ~ **goods** n pl biens de consommation m pl; ~ **group** n association de consommateurs f; ~ **habits** n pl habitudes de consommation f pl; ~**-led** adj dicté par les besoins du consommateur; ~ **lending** n crédit à la consommation m; ~ **loan** n prêt personnel m, prêt à la consommation m; ~ **loyalty** n fidélité du consommateur f; ~ **magazine** n revue du consommateur f; ~ **market** n marché des produits de grande consommation m; ~ **marketing** n marketing des produits de

grande consommation *m*; ~ **needs** *n pl*
besoins des consommateurs *m pl*; ~
organization *n* organisme de défense des
consommateurs *m*; ~ **panel** *n* groupe témoin
m, panel de consommateurs *m*; ~ **patterns**
n pl habitudes des consommateurs *f pl*; ~
preference *n* préférence du consommateur
f; ~ **price** *n* prix à la consommation *m*; ~
price index *n* indice des prix à la
consommation *m*; ~ **products** *n pl* produits
de consommation courante *m pl*; ~ **profile** *n*
profil du consommateur *m*; ~ **protection** *n*
défense des intérêts du consommateur *f*,
protection du consommateur *f*; ~ **relations**
manager *n* chef du service consommateurs
m, directeur/-trice du service clientèle *m/f*; ~
research *n* étude de la consommation *f*,
étude de marché *f*; ~ **resistance** *n*
résistance des consommateurs *f*; ~
response *n* réaction des consommateurs *f*;
~ **satisfaction** *n* satisfaction du
consommateur *f*; ~ **society** *n* société de
consommation *f*; ~ **spending** *n*
consommation *f*, dépenses de consommation
f pl; ~ **survey** *n* enquête auprès des
consommateurs *f*; ~ **test** *n* test de
consommation *m*; ~**-to-consumer**
commerce *n* commerce entre particuliers
m, transactions de consommateur à
consommateur *f pl*; ~ **trends** *n pl* tendances
de la consommation *f pl*; ~ **watchdog** *n*
organisme chargé de défendre les intérêts des
consommateurs

consumerism *n* consumérisme *m*

Consumers': ~ **Advisory Council** *n* US
commission consultative des consommateurs;
~ **Association** *n* UK ≈ Association de
défense du consommateur *f*, ≈ Institut
national de la consommation *m*

consummate *vt* consommer, parfaire

consumption *n* consommation *f*; ~
goods *n pl* biens de consommation *m pl*; ~
pattern *n* schéma de consommation *m*

contact¹ *n* contact *m*; (professional
acquaintance) contact *m*; (general acquaintance)
connaissance *f*, relation *f*; **come into** ~ **with**
entrer en contact avec, entrer en relation
avec; **get in** ~ **with** prendre contact avec;
make ~ se mettre en contact; **be in close** ~
être en rapports constants; **put sb in** ~ **with**
mettre qn en rapport avec

contact² *vt* contacter; ~ **sb about sth**
contacter qn au sujet de qch

contain *vt* (amount) contenir; (demand, inflation)
contenir, maîtriser; (costs) limiter

container *n* conteneur *m*, container *m*; ~
berth *n* poste à quai pour navires porte-
conteneurs *m*; ~ **car** *n* US (rail) wagon porte-
conteneurs *m*; ~ **depot** *n* aire de stockage
des conteneurs *m*; ~ **dock** *n* dock pour la
manutention des conteneurs *m*; ~ **load** *n*
conteneur complet *m*; ~ **port** *n* port de
conteneurs *m*; ~ **ship** *n* navire porte-

conteneurs *m*; ~ **transport** *n* transport par
conteneurs *m*; ~ **yard** *n* dépôt de conteneurs
m

containerization *n* conteneurisation *f*,
mise en conteneur(s) *f*

containerize *vt* conteneuriser, mettre en
conteneur(s)

containerized *adj* conteneurisé

containment *n* (of credit) retenue *f*

contaminate *vt* (Gen Comm) contaminer;
(environment) polluer

contaminated *adj* contaminé; (environment)
pollué

contamination *n* (Gen Comm)
contamination *f*; (of environment) pollution *f*

contango *n* UK report *m*; ~ **day** *n* UK jour
des reports *m*

cont'd *abbr* (▶**continued**) à suivre

contempt of court *n* outrage à la cour
m; **be in** ~ être coupable du délit d'outrage à
la cour

content *n* (Gen Comm) contenu *m*; (of
website) contenu *m*; ~ **developer** *n*
développeur-concepteur web *m*, développeur-
concepteur de contenu *m*; ~ **management**
n gestion de contenu *f*; ~ **manager** *n*
directeur/-trice de contenu *m/f*; ~ **provider**
n fournisseur de contenu *m*

contention *n* (dispute) dispute *f*, désaccord
m; (opinion) assertion *f*; **matter of** ~ sujet de
dispute *m*; **my** ~ **is ...** je soutiens que ...

contents *n pl* (of container) contenu *m*; (of file,
document) contenu *m*; (Ins) biens mobiliers *m*
pl; **list of** ~, **table of** ~ table des matières *f*

contentware *n* (Comp) logiciel de gestion
de contenu web *m*

contest¹ *n* (competition) concours *m*; (struggle)
lutte *f*

contest² *vt* (will, clause) attaquer, contester;
(decision) contester; ~ **an election** se
présenter à une élection

contested *adj* (market) disputé; ~ **claim** *n*
(Fin) créance litigieuse *f*

context *n* contexte *m*, cadre *m*; **in the** ~ **of**
dans le cadre de

context-sensitive *adj* (Comp)
contextuel/-elle; ~ **help** *n* (software) aide
contextuelle *f*

contiguous *adj* contigu

continent *n* continent *m*; ~ **of Europe**
continent européen *m*

Continent *n* Europe continentale *f*

continental *adj* continental; ~ **trade** *n*
(with Europe) commerce trans-Manche *m*

contingencies vote *n* (Fin) crédit pour
éventualités *m*

contingency *n* imprévu *m*, éventualité *f*,
événement imprévu *m*; **build 5% for**
contingencies into the estimate inclure 5%
pour les frais éventuels dans le devis; **add**
£2,000 for contingencies ajouter 2 000 livres ···❯

sterling pour parer aux frais éventuels; ~ **clause** n clause pour imprévus f; ~ **fund** n (personal budgets) caisse de prévoyance f, fonds de prévoyance m; ~ **order** n (Stock) ordre sous condition m; ~ **payments** n pl (budgeting) charges imprévues f pl; ~ **plan** n plan d'urgence m, plan de secours m; ~ **planning** n planification tenant compte des imprévus f; ~ **reserve** n fonds de réserve m

contingent adj fortuit, imprévu, éventuel/-elle; ~ **asset** n (Acc) actif potentiel m, actif éventuel m; ~ **budget** n (Fin) budget conjoncturel m; ~ **claim** n (Acc, Fin) réclamation potentielle f; ~ **consideration** n contrepartie conditionnelle f; ~ **expenses** n pl dépenses imprévues f pl; ~ **liabilities** n pl (Acc) engagements éventuels m pl; (Fin, Law) dette éventuelle f; ~ **order** n (Stock) ordre lié m

continuation n (of situation, process) continuation f; (resumption) reprise f; (Fin) report m; ~ **clause** n (Ins) clause de prolongation f, clause de report f; ~ **day** n (Stock) jour des reports m

continue ① vt (Gen Comm) continuer; (programme, studies, inquiry) poursuivre; ~ **doing** continuer à faire; ~ **to do** continuer à faire ② vi continuer; ~ **with** continuer, poursuivre

continued adj 'to be ~' 'à suivre'; ~ **overleaf** suite à la page suivante; ~ **on p21** suite (à la) page 21; ~ **success** n (of person, company, product) réussite constante f, succès permanent m

continuing adj (trend) continuel/-elle; (interest) soutenu; (investment) constant; (support) incessant, sans faille

continuity n continuité f; **provide ~ of services** assurer la continuité des services

continuous adj continu; ~ **assessment** n contrôle continu m; ~ **audit** n audit en continu, contrôle continu m, vérification continue f; ~ **budget** n budget perpétuel m; ~ **inventory** n inventaire continu m, inventaire permanent m; ~ **market** n (Stock) marché en continu m; ~ **process** n (Ind) procédé de fabrication en continu m; ~ **production** n production en continu f; ~ **stocktaking** n inventaire permanent m; ~ **survey** n enquête permanente f; ~ **variable** n variable continue f

contra¹ n (Acc) contrepartie f, écriture de compensation f; ~ **account** n compte d'attente m, compte de régularisation m; ~ **entry** n écriture de compensation f, écriture de contrepartie f

contra² vt contre-passer

contraband¹ adj de contrebande

contraband² n (activity) contrebande f; (goods) marchandises de contrebande f pl

contract¹ n contrat m; **be on a ~** être sous contrat; **be under ~ with** être sous contrat avec; **be under ~ to do** être tenu par contrat

de faire; **put work out to ~** donner un travail en sous-traitance; **award a ~ to** octroyer un contrat à; **secure a ~** obtenir un contrat; **enter into a ~ with** passer un contrat avec; **by private ~** de gré à gré, à l'amiable; ~ **agreement** n accord contractuel m; ~ **bargaining** n négociations salariales f pl; ~ **of employment** contrat d'emploi m; ~ **for services** contrat de services m; ~ **for the sale of goods** contrat de vente de biens m; ~ **joint venture** n joint-venture sans création de société m; ~ **labor** AmE, ~ **labour** BrE n main-d'œuvre contractuelle f; ~ **negotiations** n pl négociation du contrat f; ~ **note** n (Stock) bordereau d'achat m, bordereau de vente m; ~ **party** n (Law) partie contractante f; ~ **price** n US (Tax) (instalment sale) prix contractuel m, prix forfaitaire m; ~ **of sale** n contrat de vente m; ~ **specifications** n pl stipulations contractuelles f pl; ~ **work** n travail à forfait m; ~ **worker** n contractuel/-elle m/f

contract² ① vt (debt, loan) contracter; ~ **to do sth** s'engager par contrat à faire qch; **be ~ed to do** être tenu par contrat de faire ② vi (market) se rétrécir, se réduire; (economy) être en recul; ~ **in** s'engager; ~ **into** (scheme, plan) souscrire à; ~ **out** ① vt (maintenance, work) donner en sous-traitance ② vi (opt out) renoncer par contrat, se dégager; ~ **out of sth** (scheme) se retirer de, cesser de cotiser à; ~ **out of an arrangement** rompre un contrat

contracting n (Econ) embauche f; ~ **out** n sous-traitance f; ~**-out clause** n clause de renonciation f; ~ **party** n contractant m, partie contractante f

contraction n contraction f, rétrécissement m; ~ **of demand** rétrécissement de la demande m

contractionary pressure n poussée récessionniste f

contractor n (supplier of labour) entrepreneur m; (Ind) (supplier) entrepreneur m; (Law) (party to contract) contractant m; (Prop) (party to contract) contractant m; (supplier of building services) entrepreneur m; (contract worker) contractuel/-elle m/f; **chief ~, prime ~** maître d'œuvre m

contracts manager n directeur/-trice chargé/-e des contrats m/f

contractual adj contractuel/-elle; ~ **clause** n clause conventionnelle f; ~ **liability** n responsabilité contractuelle f; ~ **obligation** n obligation contractuelle f; ~ **payment** n paiement forfaitaire m; ~ **relationship** n lien contractuel m, relation contractuelle f

contractually adv contractuellement; **be ~ bound to do** être obligé par contrat de faire

contrary n contraire m; **on the ~** au

contraire; be a ∼ to être contraire à; ∼ to rumours contrairement à la rumeur; ∼ to expectations contre toute attente

contrast n contraste m; in ∼ to par contraste avec; be a ∼ to présenter un contraste avec; by ∼ par contre

contravene vt contrevenir à, enfreindre

contribute vt contribuer; (article) soumettre; (ideas, experience) apporter; (Ins) cotiser; ∼ to (newspaper, magazine) collaborer à

contributed capital n capital d'apport m

contribution n (to pension fund) cotisation f; (financial) apport m; (personal) contribution f; (Ins) cotisation f; contribution f; ∼ of capital (Fin) apport de capital m; make a ∼ (of capital) faire un apport; make a ∼ to apporter une contribution à

contributor n (Econ) contributeur m; (Media) collaborateur/-trice m/f; (Tax) cotisant m; (to charity) donateur/-trice m/f; ∼ of capital bailleur de fonds m

contributory adj (Law) accessoire; be a ∼ cause être partiellement responsable; be a ∼ factor in sth contribuer à qch; ∼ negligence n faute de la victime f; ∼ pension fund n caisse de retraite avec cotisation salariale f; ∼ pension plan n, ∼ pension scheme n régime de retraite mixte m, système de retraite par répartition m

control¹ n (Gen Comm) contrôle m; (of operation, investigation, project) direction f; (S&M) (in direct marketing) témoin m; (Comp) commande f; be in ∼ of (problem) maîtriser; (operation, investigation, project) diriger; take ∼ of (situation) prendre en main; (operation, investigation, project) prendre la direction de; (company) prendre le contrôle de; be under sb's ∼ être sous le contrôle de, être sous la direction de; be under ∼ être maîtrisé; let sth get out of ∼ perdre le contrôle de qch; keep costs under ∼ maîtriser les coûts; ∼ account n compte de contrôle m; ∼ block n (Stock) bloc de contrôle m; ∼ character n caractère de commande m; ∼ freak n (infrml) personne qui veut tout contrôler f; ∼ panel n (Gen Comm) tableau de bord m; (Comp) panneau de commande m; ∼ stock n actions de contrôle f pl

control² vt (inflation) juguler, maîtriser; (situation, organization, prices, wages, market) contrôler; (project, investigation, operation) diriger; (problem) maîtriser; (trade, imports, exports) réglementer; (Fin, Stock) (company) être majoritaire dans; ∼ costs freiner les coûts, maîtriser les coûts

controlled: ∼ atmosphere n milieu constant m; ∼ commodity n UK marchandise réglementée f, matière première contrôlée f; ∼ corporation n corporation contrôlée f; ∼ economy n économie dirigée f; ∼ market n marché officiel m; ∼ price n prix réglementé m; ∼ rate n (in currency

exchange) taux de change réglementé m

controller n (Acc) (governmental) contrôleur de gestion m, contrôleur financier m; (Fin) contrôleur m, vérificateur m

controlling: ∼ account n compte collectif m; ∼ company n société dominante f; ∼ corporation n corporation dominante f; ∼ interest n participation majoritaire f; ∼ shareholder n actionnaire majoritaire mf

controversial adj (open to discussion) discutable; (criticized) controversé, sujet à controverse

controversy n controverse f, polémique f

convene 1 vt (group) convoquer 2 vi se réunir

convenience n convenance f; at your ∼ quand cela vous conviendra, à votre convenance (frml); at your earliest ∼ dès qu'il vous sera possible; ∼ bill n traite de complaisance f; ∼ flag n pavillon de complaisance m; ∼ food n aliment prêt à cuire m, aliment tout préparé m; ∼ goods n pl, ∼ products n pl produits de consommation courante m pl; ∼ shop n BrE, ∼ store n AmE magasin de proximité m

convening n convocation f

convenor n responsable de section mf

convention n (Acc) principe m; (Law) convention f; (conference) colloque m, congrès m; (Pol) congrès m; ∼ center AmE, ∼ centre BrE n centre de congrès m; ∼ hotel n hôtel recevant des congrès m; ∼ participant n congressiste mf, délégué-e m/f; (Pol) congressiste mf

converge vi (ideas, activities) converger, être convergent

convergence n (of opinions, results, of futures price) convergence f; (Comp, Comms) convergence f; ∼ hypothesis n hypothèse de la convergence f

convergent adj convergent

conversational mode n (Comp) mode conversationnel m, mode dialogué m

conversely adv inversement

conversion n (of currency, measures, assets) conversion f; (of raw materials) transformation f; ∼ algorithm n règle de conversion f; ∼ cost n coût de transformation m; ∼ factor n (Stock) facteur de conversion m; ∼ issue n émission de conversion f; ∼ loan n emprunt de conversion m, prêt de conversion m; ∼ rate n (Fin, S&M) taux de conversion m

convert vt (currency) convertir; ∼ into capital capitaliser; ∼ into cash convertir en espèces

convertibility n convertibilité f

convertible adj convertible; ∼ bond n obligation convertible f; ∼ currency n devise convertible f; ∼ security n titre convertible m, valeur convertible f; ∼ share n action convertible f; ∼ stock n action convertible f

convey vt (property) céder, transférer, transmettre; (goods, passengers) acheminer, transporter; (order, message, information) transmettre

conveyance n (of property) cession f, transfert m; (Transp) acheminement m, transport m; ∼ **of goods** transport de marchandises m

conveyor belt n tapis roulant m

convict vt condamner; ∼ **sb of doing** déclarer qn coupable d'avoir fait

conviction n (Law) condamnation f; (belief) conviction f; ∼ **on fraud charges** condamnation pour fraude

convince vt (gain credibility of) convaincre; (persuade) persuader; ∼ **sb to do** persuader qn de faire

convincing adj (proof, evidence, theory) convaincant; (lead, victory) indiscutable

convincingly adv (argue, prove, claim) de façon convaincante; (win, beat) de façon indiscutable

convocation n convocation f

convoke vt convoquer

COO abbr (▸**chief operating officer**) chef de service m; (▸**country of origin**) pays d'origine m

cookie n (Comp) mouchard m, cookie m

cooling-off period n (before signing contract) délai de réflexion m; (in dispute) période de détente f

coop n coopé f (infml); (Prop) US partage de commission m; ∼ **advertising** n publicité collective f, publicité groupée f

cooperate vi coopérer

cooperation n coopération f; **in close** ∼ **with** en étroite coopération avec; **with the** ∼ **of** avec la coopération de, avec le concours de; ∼ **agreement** n accord de coopération m

cooperative n coopérative f, coopérative de vente en gros f; ∼ **advertising** n publicité collective f; ∼ **credit institution** n société mutuelle de crédit f; ∼ **farm** n coopérative agricole f; ∼ **society** n coopérative f, société coopérative f, société mutuelle f

coopetition n coopération et concurrence f

coopt vt coopter

coordinate vt coordonner

coordinated adj coordonné

coordinating adj (service, department, office) coordinateur/-trice; (committee, body) de coordination

coordination n coordination f

coordinator n coordinateur/-trice m/f

co-owner n copropriétaire mf

co-ownership n copropriété f

copier n (office equipment) photocopieuse f

copper n cuivre m; ∼ **ore** n minerai de cuivre m

coppers n pl (Stock) valeurs cuprifères f pl

coprocessor n (Comp) coprocesseur m

co-product n coproduit m

copy[1] n (duplicate) copie f, reproduction f; (counterfeit article) contrefaçon f, copie f, imitation f; (of newspaper, magazine) exemplaire m, numéro m; (text as opposed to title) texte m; (journalistic, advertising text) copie f; ∼ **appeal** n attrait du message m, axe publicitaire du message m; ∼ **chief** n chef de conception m, chef de rédaction m; ∼ **deadline** n date limite de la remise d'un texte f; ∼ **department** n service de rédaction m; ∼ **editor** n (print) préparateur/-trice de copie m/f, réviseur m, secrétaire de rédaction mf; ∼ **protection** n (of software) protection contre la copie f

copy[2] vt copier; ∼ **from the original** reproduire d'après l'original, s'inspirer de l'original; ∼ **sth to sb** envoyer une copie de qch à qn

copying n (process) duplication f, reprographie f

copy-protect vt protéger contre la copie

copy-protected adj protégé contre la copie

copyright n (on data, software) copyright m, droits d'auteur m pl; ∼ **reserved** tous droits réservés; **in** ∼ protégé par copyright; **be out of** ∼ être tombé dans le domaine public; ∼ **material** n œuvre protégée conformément à la loi sur la propriété littéraire et artistique

copywriter n concepteur-rédacteur m, rédacteur/-trice publicitaire m/f

copywriting n conception f

cordless adj (telephone) sans fil

core[1] adj (activity) principal; (issue, concept) fondamental

core[2] n cœur m, essentiel m, fond m

core: ∼ **audience** n cœur de cible m; ∼ **business** n activité principale f; ∼ **curriculum** n programme de base m; ∼ **firm** n entreprise dominante f, firme dominante f; ∼ **hours** n pl plages horaires fixes f pl; ∼ **inflation** n inflation structurelle f; ∼ **product** n produit leader m; ∼ **region** n région centrale f; ∼ **skills** n pl compétences de base f pl; ∼ **time** n plage horaire fixe f

corner[1] n monopole m; **have a** ∼ **in** avoir le monopole de; **cut** ∼**s** (financially) faire des économies; (in procedures) simplifier les choses; ∼ **shop** BrE n, ∼ **store** AmE n magasin de proximité m

corner[2] vt (market) accaparer; ∼ **sb** mettre qn au pied du mur

cornerer n accapareur m

cornerstone n pierre angulaire f

corp. abbr (▸**corporation**) corporation f, société commerciale f

corpographics n + sing v gestion des profils d'entreprises f

corporate adj (responsibility, spending, decision) collectif/-ive; (funds, clients) d'une société;

~ **advertising** *n* publicité institutionnelle *f;*
~ **affiliate** *n* filiale *f,* société affiliée *f;* ~
asset *n* élément d'actif *m;* ~ **banking** *n*
services bancaires aux entreprises *m pl;* ~
body *n* (Law) personne morale *f;* ~ **bond** *n*
US (Stock) (local) obligation municipale *f;*
(private) obligation émise par une société
privée *f;* ~ **campaign** *n* (S&M) campagne
institutionnelle *f;* ~ **client** *n* entreprise
cliente *f,* société cliente *f;* ~ **credit** *n* crédit
aux entreprises *m;* ~ **credit card** *n* carte de
crédit professionnelle *f;* ~ **culture** *n* culture
d'entreprise *f;* ~ **customer** *n* entreprise
cliente *f,* société cliente *f;* ~ **database** *n*
base de données d'entreprise *f;* ~ **debt**
securities *n pl* bons de caisse *m pl;* ~
earnings *n pl* bénéfices de l'entreprise *m pl;*
~ **executive** *n* dirigeant/-e de société *m/f;*
~ **finance** *n* finance d'entreprise *f;* ~
financing *n* financement des sociétés *m;* ~
governance *n* gouvernance des entreprises *f;*
~ **growth** *n* croissance de l'entreprise *f;* ~
hospitality *n* invitations de prestige *f pl*
(*pour clients établis et clients éventuels*); ~
identity *n* identité d'entreprise *f;* ~ **image**
n image de l'entreprise, image de marque *f;*
~ **insider** *n* membre initié d'une société *m;*
~ **investment** *n* investissements des
sociétés *m pl;* ~ **investor** *n* UK investisseur
commercial *m;* ~ **issue** *n* (Fin) émission de
titres *f;* ~ **law** *n* droit des entreprises *m,*
droit des sociétés *m;* ~ **lawyer** *n* (expert)
juriste d'entreprise *mf;* (in a firm) avocat/-e
d'entreprise *m/f,* juriste d'entreprise *mf;* ~
lending *n* prêts aux entreprises *m pl;* ~
loan *n* prêt à une société *m;* (Stock)
obligation du secteur privé *f;* ~
management *n* direction d'entreprise *f;* ~
member *n* (Stock) société membre *f;* ~
model *n* modèle de l'entreprise *m;* ~ **name**
n raison sociale *f;* ~ **network** *n* réseau
d'entreprise *m;* ~ **planning** *n* planification
de l'entreprise *f;* ~ **policy** *n* politique de
l'entreprise *f;* ~ **raider** *n* prédateur *m,*
racheteur de société *m;* ~ **raiding** *n* (Fin)
rachat d'une société *m;* (Stock) pillage *m,*
rachat d'une société *m;* ~ **spending** *n*
dépenses des entreprises *f pl;* ~
sponsorship *n* mécénat d'entreprise *m;* ~
state *n* état corporatif *m;* ~ **status** *n* UK
statut d'entreprise *m;* ~ **strategy** *n* stratégie
de l'entreprise *f;* ~ **structure** *n* structure de
l'entreprise *f;* ~ **tax** *n* impôt sur les sociétés
m; ~ **treasurer** *n* trésorier/-ière d'entreprise
m/f; ~ **turnaround** *n* redressement
d'entreprises *m;* ~ **venture capital** *n*
capital-risque pratiqué par des filiales
spécialisées des grandes entreprises

corporation *n* corporation *f,* société
commerciale *f;* ~ **tax** *n* BrE impôt sur les
sociétés *m*

corporatism *n* corporatisme *m*

corporeal *adj* corporel/-elle; ~
hereditaments *n pl* (Law) biens corporels

transmissibles par héritage *m pl*

corportal *n* (Comp) portail corporatif *m,*
portail d'entreprise *m*

correct¹ *adj* (answer) exact, bon/bonne;
(figure) exact; (decision, method, order, number)
bon/bonne; **the ~ time** l'heure exacte; **that is**
~ c'est exact

correct² *vt* (errors) corriger, rectifier;
(spellings, proofs, text) corriger

corrected invoice *n* facture rectificative
f

correcting entry *n* (Acc) écriture
d'extourne *f,* écriture de correction *f*

correction *n* (of error) correction *f,*
rectification *f;* (of text, spelling) correction *f;*
(Stock) correction *f*

corrective *adj* (measure) de redressement,
correctif/-ive; ~ **action** *n* correction *f*

correctly *adv* correctement, exactement

correlate *vt* mettre en corrélation

correlation *n* corrélation *f*

correspond *vi* (exchange letters)
correspondre; ~ **to** (be equivalent)
correspondre à, être équivalent à; ~ **with** (be
similar) correspondre à, être équivalent à; (by
letter) correspondre avec

correspondence *n* (letter writing)
correspondance *f;* (mail received) courrier *m;*
be in ~ with correspondre avec; **enter into**
~ **with** engager une correspondance avec

correspondent *n* (letter writer)
correspondant/-e *m/f;* (Bank, Fin)
correspondant/-e *m/f;* (Media) correspondant/
-e *m/f,* envoyé/-e *m/f,* journaliste *mf;* ~ **bank**
n banque correspondante *f*

corresponding *adj* (equivalent)
correspondant

corroborate *vt* corroborer

corrupt *vt* corrompre

corruption *n* corruption *f*

cosign *vt* cosigner

cosignatory *n* cosignataire *mf*

co-sourcing *n* co-sourçage *m*

cost¹ *n* coût *m;* **at ~** au prix de revient, à
prix coûtant; **at a ~ of 500 dollars** au prix
de 500 dollars; **at your ~** à vos frais; **at no**
extra ~ sans frais supplémentaires; ~ **and**
freight coût et fret; ~ **and insurance** coût et
assurance; ~**, insurance and freight** coût,
assurance, fret; ~**, insurance, freight and**
commission coût, assurance, fret et
commission; ~**, insurance, freight,**
commission and exchange coût, assurance,
fret, commission et change; ~**, insurance,**
freight and interest coût, assurance, fret et
intérêt; ~ **accountant** *n* analyste des coûts
mf; ~ **accounting** *n* comptabilité analytique
f; ~ **allocation** *n* affectation des charges *f,*
ventilation des coûts *f;* ~ **analysis** *n* analyse
des coûts *f;* ~ **apportionment** *n* répartition
des charges *f,* ventilation des coûts *f;* ~
awareness *n* connaissance des coûts *f;* ┈┊

~ **base** n (Tax) prix de base m; ~**-benefit analysis** n analyse coûts-avantages f, analyse coûts-rendements f, rapport coûts-avantages m; ~ **of borrowing** n frais d'emprunt m pl; ~ **center** AmE, ~ **centre** BrE n centre de coût m; ~ **of compliance** n coût de mise en conformité m; ~ **control** n maîtrise des coûts f; ~**-cutting** n réduction des frais f; ~**-effective** adj rentable; ~**-effectiveness** n rapport coût-efficacité m, rentabilité f; ~**-effectiveness analysis** n analyse de rentabilité f, analyse du rapport coût-efficacité f; ~ **estimate** n estimation des coûts f; ~ **factor** n facteur coût m, élément du coût m; ~ **forecast** n prévision de coûts f; ~ **of freight** n coût de fret m; ~ **of living** n coût de la vie m; ~**-of-living adjustment** n US indexation des salaires f; ~**-of-living allowance** n indemnité de vie chère f; ~**-of-living index** n indice du coût de la vie m; ~ **method** n (Acc) (for intercorporate investments) comptabilisation à la valeur d'acquisition f, (inventory) méthode d'évaluation des stocks au prix coûtant f; ~ **minimization** n minimisation des coûts f; ~ **overrun** n dépassement des coûts m; ~ **price** n (for consumer) prix d'achat m, prix coûtant m; (for producer) prix de revient m; ~**-push inflation** n inflation par les coûts f; ~ **ratio** n ratio du prix coûtant au prix de détail m; ~ **of replacement** n frais de remplacement m pl; ~ **of sales** n coût de la production vendue m; ~ **structure** n structure des coûts f; ~ **variance** n écart de prix m

cost² vt coûter; (project) calculer le coût de; (product) calculer le prix; **the project was ~ed at £2 million** le coût du projet a été évalué à 2 millions de livres sterling; **that decision ~ him his job** cette décision lui a coûté son travail; **it ~ us the contract/election** cela nous a fait perdre le contrat/les élections

costing n (Gen Comm) évaluation des coûts f; (Acc) établissement des prix de revient m

costings n pl (projected figures) évaluation des coûts f

costly adj (action) qui coûte cher; (materials, error) coûteux/-euse

costs n pl (Econ, Fin) coûts m pl, dépens m pl; (Law) dépens m pl, frais m pl; **labour/transport/legal ~** frais de main-d'œuvre/transport/justice m pl; **production ~** coûts de production m pl; **cover ~** couvrir les frais; **pay ~** (Law) être condamné aux dépens; **be awarded ~** (Law) se voir accorder le remboursement des frais

cotenancy n colocation f

cotenant n colocataire mf

cottage industry n industrie artisanale f

cotton n coton m

couchette n couchette f

cough: ~ **up** vi BrE (infrml) casquer (infrml)

council n (Admin) UK ≈ municipalité f; (local government) conseil municipal m; (meeting) conseil m; ~ **flat** n UK habitation à loyer modéré f, HLM f; ~ **tax** n UK ≈ impôts locaux m pl

councillor n conseiller/-ère m/f

Council: ~ **of Europe** n Conseil de l'Europe m; ~ **of Ministers** n (EU) Conseil des ministres m; ~ **of State** n (Pol) Conseil d'État m

counsel¹ n (advisor) conseiller/-ère m/f; (advice) conseil m, consultation f; (lawyer) avocat/-e m/f; ~ **for the prosecution** UK avocat/-e général/-e m/f

counsel² vt (recommend) conseiller, recommander; (give advice to) conseiller

counsellor n conseiller/-ère m/f

count¹ vt compter; (votes) décompter; ~ **against** jouer contre; ~ **on** compter sur; ~ **up** compter

count² n décompte m; (at election) dépouillement du scrutin m; (level) taux m; (point) point m; **keep ~ of** tenir compte de; **at the last ~** au dernier décompte; **you are wrong on both ~s** vous avez tort sur les deux points; ~ **of indictment** n (Law) chef d'accusation m, chef d'inculpation m

counter¹ n (Bank) caisse f, comptoir m, guichet m; (service point) (in shop) caisse f, comptoir m; (in supermarket) caisse f; (section of shop) rayon m; ~ **check** AmE, ~ **cheque** BrE n chèque de guichet m; ~ **staff** n caissiers/-ières m pl/f pl; ~ **trade** n commerce de compensation m, commerce de troc m

counter² vt (accusation, claim) répondre à; (trend) s'opposer à; (effect) neutraliser; (increase, inflation) enrayer

counteract vt (balance) compenser; (thwart) contrecarrer; (effects) neutraliser; (influence, decision) contrer

counter-argument n contre-argument m

counter-attack n contre-attaque f

counter-attraction n attraction concurrente f

counterbalance vt contrebalancer

counter-bid n surenchère f

counterclaim n (Law) demande reconventionnelle f

counterfeit¹ adj contrefait; ~ **money** fausse monnaie f

counterfeit² n contrefaçon f

counterfeit³ vt contrefaire

counterfeiter n contrefacteur/-trice m/f, faussaire mf

counterfeiting n contrefaçon f

counterfoil n talon m, souche f

counter-inflationary adj anti-inflationniste

countermand vt décommander

counter-measure n contre-mesure f, mesure de compensation f

counter-move n mouvement contraire m

counter-offer n contre-offre f

counterpart n (equivalent) contrepartie f; (of person) homologue mf; (of document) double m

counter-productive adj contre-productif/-ive

countersign vt contresigner

countervailing duties n pl (Imp/Exp) droits compensatoires m pl

counting n comptage m; ~ **of votes** dépouillement du scrutin m

country n pays m; ~ **of destination** pays destinataire m; ~ **of origin** provenance f, pays d'origine m

county n UK comté m, ≈ département m; ~ **council** n UK ≈ conseil général m; ~ **court** tribunal civil m, tribunal d'instance m; ~ **seat** n AmE, ~ **town** n BrE chef-lieu de comté m

County Hall n UK siège du conseil de comté

coupled: ~ **with** ajouté à

coupon n (Fin, Stock) coupon m; (voucher) bon m, coupon m; (money-off voucher) bon de réduction m; ~ **bond** n obligation à coupons f

courier n coursier m; ~ **firm** n entreprise de messageries f; ~ **service** n messagerie (rapide) f

course n (progress) cours m; (for training) stage m; **in the** ~ **of negotiations** au cours des négociations; **be on** ~ **for** (vehicle) être en route pour; (person, company) aller vers; **change** ~ changer de direction; **go off** ~ faire fausse route; **the economy is back on** ~ l'économie s'est restabilisée; **stay the** ~ tenir bon, tenir le coup (infrml); **go on a** ~ faire un stage; **be on a** ~ suivre un cours; **in due** ~ en temps utile; ~ **of action** parti m, ligne de conduite f; ~ **material** n support de cours m; ~ **of study** programme m; (at university) cursus m

courseware n (Comp) didacticiel m, logiciel d'enseignement à distance m

court n cour f, tribunal m; ~ **of inquiry** n UK commission d'enquête f; ~ **of law** n cour de justice f, palais de justice m; ~ **order** n décision judiciaire f

Court: ~ **of Appeal** n cour d'appel f, ≈ Cour de cassation f; ~ **of Auditors** n Cour des comptes f; ~ **of First Instance** n tribunal de grande instance m, tribunal de première instance m; ~ **of Justice** n Cour de justice f

covenant n contrat m, convention f

covenantor n contractant m, partie contractante f

cover¹ n (Ins) BrE couverture f; (Stock) couverture f, garantie f; **under separate** ~ sous pli séparé; ~ **letter** n AmE lettre d'accompagnement f, lettre explicative f; (for job application) lettre de motivation f; ~ **note** n (Ins) lettre de couverture f, police provisoire f

cover² vt (conceal) cacher; (seal over) couvrir; (loss) absorber, couvrir; (payments) couvrir, faire face à; (Ins, Stock) couvrir; ~ **the cost of** couvrir les frais de; ~ **up** cacher, dissimuler

coverage n (in media) couverture f; (Ins) AmE couverture f; (in book, article, programme) traitement m; **give a lot of media** ~ **to** médiatiser; **television** ~ couverture par la télévision; **live** ~ émission en direct f; ~ **ratio** n (Ins) rapport entre le sinistre et la protection m

covered adj (Ins, Stock) couvert; **be** ~ avoir des garanties; ~ **by insurance** couvert par l'assurance; ~ **long** n (Stock) achat d'option couverte m; ~ **option** n (Stock) option couverte f; ~ **position** n UK (Stock) (options) position couverte f; ~ **short** n vente d'option couverte f

covering letter n lettre d'accompagnement f, lettre explicative f; (for job application) lettre de motivation f

co-worker n collègue mf

CPA abbr US (▸**certified public accountant**) expert-comptable m; (▸**critical path analysis**) analyse du chemin critique f

CPC n (**cost per click**) coût par clic m

CPFR abbr (**collaborative planning, forecasting and replenishment**) gestion collaborative des prévisions et des approvisionnements f

CPI abbr (▸**consumer price index**) IPC m (indice des prix à la consommation)

CPM abbr (▸**critical path method**) méthode du chemin critique f; (**cost per mille**) (S&M) coût au mille m; (Comp) coût pour mille pages vues m

CPT abbr (**carriage paid to**) port payé jusqu'à

CPU abbr (▸**central processing unit**) UC f (unité centrale)

cr abbr (▸**credit**) cr. (crédit); (▸**creditor**) créditeur m

cracker n (Comp) pirate informatique m, fouineur/-euse m/f

craftsman n artisan m

crane n grue f; ~ **operator** n grutier m

crash¹ n (Comp) plantage m (infrml); (Stock) krach m; (Transp) accident m

crash² vi (Comp) planter (infrml), tomber en panne; (prices, economic activity) s'effondrer; (Transp) avoir un accident

crate n caisse f

crawler n (Comp) robot de recherche m

cream: ~ **off** vt (money, profits) prélever, écrémer; (illegally) détourner

create vt (demand) créer; (agency) créer, fonder; (opportunities) créer; (product, precedent, market) créer; (problem) poser

creation n création f

creative¹ adj (person, solution, use) ⋯

créatif/-ive; (process, act) créateur/-trice

creative² n (advertising) créatif/-ive m/f

creative: ~ **accounting** n comptabilité assouplie f, comptabilité créative f; ~ **strategy** n (advertising) stratégie de création f; ~ **thinking** n imagination f, pensée créatrice f

creativity n créativité f

credentials n pl (service record) états de service m pl; (identification) pièce d'identité f

credibility n crédibilité f

credit¹ n (Fin) crédit m; (approval) mérite m; (credence) crédit m; **on** ~ à crédit; **give sb three months'** ~ accorder un crédit de trois mois à qn; **my** ~ **is good** j'ai une réputation de bon payeur; **be 200 dollars in** ~ avoir un crédit de 200 dollars; **get the** ~ **for sth** se voir attribuer le mérite de qch; **get the** ~ **for doing** se voir attribuer le mérite d'avoir fait; **take** ~ **for sth** s'attribuer le mérite de qch; **take** ~ **for doing** s'attribuer le mérite d'avoir fait; **have sth to one's** ~ (achievement) avoir qch à son actif; **gain** ~ acquérir du crédit; **place** ~ **in sth** ajouter foi à qch; ~ **account** n compte d'achats à crédit m; ~ **advisor** n conseiller en crédit m; ~ **agency** n agence d'évaluation de la solvabilité f; ~ **agreement** n accord de crédit m; ~ **balance** n solde créditeur m; ~ **bureau** n (Fin) agence de notation f, agence de rating f, bureau de cotation m; ~ **card** n carte de crédit f; ~ **card booking** n location par carte de crédit f; ~**-card imprinter** n imprimante à cartes de crédit f; ~ **card issuer** n émetteur de cartes de crédit m; ~ **card payment** n paiement par carte de crédit m, règlement par carte de crédit m; ~ **card transaction** n opération sur carte de crédit f; ~ **ceiling** n découvert autorisé m, limite de crédit f; ~ **conditions** n pl conditions de crédit f pl; ~ **control** n contrôle du crédit m, encadrement du crédit m; ~ **controller** n vérificateur des crédits m; ~ **counsellor** n conseiller/-ère en crédit m/f; ~ **crunch** n reserrement du crédit m; ~ **department** n (Bank) service du crédit m; ~ **entry** n (Acc) écriture passée au crédit f; ~ **facility** n facilité de crédit f; ~ **freeze** n gel des crédits m; ~ **guarantee** n caution f; ~ **history** n antécédents en matière de crédit m pl; ~ **information** n renseignements sur le crédit m pl; ~ **institution** n établissement de crédit m; ~ **insurance** n assurance crédit f; ~ **limit** n découvert autorisé m, limite de crédit f; ~ **line** n autorisation de crédit f, ligne de crédit f; ~ **loss** n créance irrécouvrable f; ~ **management** n gestion de créances f; ~ **money** m monnaie fiduciaire f; ~ **note** n note de crédit f; ~ **policy** n politique de crédit f; ~ **rating** n degré de solvabilité m, réputation de solvabilité f; ~ **reference agency** n agence de notation f, agence de rating f, bureau de cotation m; ~

requirements n pl conditions de crédit f pl; ~ **restriction** n encadrement du crédit m; ~ **risk** n (Fin) risque de contrepartie m; (S&M) risque de crédit m; ~ **sale** n vente à crédit f; ~ **side** pl (Acc) côté du crédit m; ~ **slip** n bulletin de versement m; ~ **squeeze** n encadrement du crédit m, restriction du crédit f; ~ **standing** n réputation de solvabilité f; ~ **transfer** n virement m; ~ **union** n caisse de crédit f, caisse populaire f; ~ **voucher** n bon de remboursement m

credit² vt (account) créditer; ~**ed to** (Fin) porté au crédit de; ~ **sth to sb's account** porter qch au crédit de qn; ~ **sb with sth** (achievement) attribuer qch à qn

creditor n (Fin) créancier/-ière m/f, prêteur m; ~ **country** n pays créancier m

creditworthiness n solvabilité f

creditworthy adj solvable

creeping inflation n inflation larvée f, inflation rampante f

crew n équipage m; ~ **member** n membre de l'équipage m

crime n crime m, délit m

criminal¹ adj criminel/-elle

criminal² n criminel/-elle m/f

criminal: ~ **case** n affaire f; ~ **charges** n pl charges f pl; ~ **conviction** n condamnation f; ~ **justice** n justice pénale f; ~ **law** n droit pénal m; ~ **negligence** n faute grave f; ~ **offence** n délit m, infraction pénale f; ~ **record** n casier judiciaire m

crisis n crise f; (Econ) crise f, récession f; **cash** ~ crise de trésorerie; **energy** ~ crise d'énergie; ~ **of confidence** crise de confiance; **be in** ~ être en crise; **reach** ~ **point** atteindre un point critique; **be at** ~ **level** être à un niveau critique; ~ **management** n gestion des crises f

criterion n pl -ia critère m

critic n (reviewer, analyst) critique m/f; (detractor) détracteur/-trice m/f

critical adj (crucial) critique, décisif/-ive; (disapproving) critique; **be** ~ **to the future of sth** être critique pour assurer l'avenir de qch; **take a** ~ **look at sth** examiner qch d'un œil critique; ~ **level** n seuil critique m; ~ **mass** n masse critique f; ~ **path** n chemin critique m; ~ **path analysis** n analyse du chemin critique f; ~ **path method** n méthode du chemin critique f

criticize vt critiquer

CRM abbr (▸**customer relationship management**) GRC f (gestion de la relation client)

CRO abbr (▸**Companies Registration Office**) ≈ RCS m (Registre du commerce et des services)

crony n (petit/-e) copain/copine m/f

cronyism n copinage m, népotisme m

crook n (infrml) escroc m

crop¹ n culture f; (harvest) récolte f; **export/ cereal ~** culture d'exportation/céréalière; **~ failure** n perte de récolte f

crop²: **~ up** vi (problem, subject) surgir; (opportunity) se présenter

cropper n: **come a ~** (infrml) se casser la figure (infrml)

cross¹ n (Stock) transaction dont l'achat et la vente sont assurés par le même courtier; **~ check** AmE n chèque barré m; **~ default** n défaut croisé m; **~ hedging** n (Stock) couverture croisée f; **~ liability** n (Ins) recours entre coassurés m, responsabilité croisée f; **~ licensing** n concession réciproque de licences f; **~ merchandising** n UK présentation de produits complémentaires côte à côte; **~ reference** n renvoi m; **~ section** n coupe transversale f, profil m, vue en coupe f; (of population) échantillon représentatif m; **~ selling** n (between companies) vente croisée f; (sale of additional items) vente par association f, vente de produits complémentaires à un premier achat f; **~ subsidy** n aide d'interfinancement f

cross² vt (cheque) barrer; (frontier) traverser; **~ a picket line** traverser un cordon de grévistes; **~ off, ~ out** rayer, barrer

cross-border adj transnational, transfrontalier/-ière; **~ payment** n paiement transfrontalier m; **~ trade** n commerce transfrontalier m

cross-Channel trade n commerce trans-Manche m

cross-check¹ n recoupement m

cross-check² [1] vt vérifier par recoupement
[2] vi faire des recoupements

cross-cutting adj (multi-disciplinary) pluri-disciplinaire; (between departments) inter-départmental, inter-services

crossed check AmE, **crossed cheque** BrE n chèque barré m

cross-hedge vt (Stock) faire une couverture croisée

cross-ownership n interpropriété f

crossposting n (Comp) envoi multiple m

cross-sell vt **~ a product** vendre un produit complémentaire à un premier achat

crowd¹ n (Stock) groupe de négociation m

crowd²: **~ out** vt (borrowers, investors) évincer

crown jewels n pl (infrml) joyaux de la couronne m pl, entreprises faisant partie du patrimoine national

CRP abbr (**continuous replenishment programme**) programme de réassortiment continu m

crude adj (estimate) approximatif/-ive; (material, product) brut; **~ carrier** n navire pétrolier m; **~ goods** n pl produits bruts m pl; **~ oil** n pétrole brut m

cruzeiro n cruzeiro m

CS abbr (▸**civil service**) Administration f, fonction publique f; (▸**continuous stocktaking**) inventaire permanent m

CSC abbr (▸**Civil Service Commission**) ≈ Commission de la fonction publique f

CSO abbr UK (▸**Central Statistical Office**) ≈ INSEE m (Institut national de la statistique et des études économiques)

CSP abbr (**commerce service provider**) fournisseur de services de commerce m

CST abbr (US) (▸**Central Standard Time**) heure normale des états du centre des États-Unis f

CTI abbr (▸**computer-telephony integration**) CTI m (couplage téléphonie-Internet)

CTR abbr (▸**click-through rate**) taux de clics m

CTT abbr (▸**capital transfer tax**) droits de mutation m pl

cu abbr (▸**cubic**) cube

cubage n (Transp) (volume) cubage m

cubic adj cube; **~ capacity** n cylindrée f; **~ centimeter** AmE, **~ centimetre** BrE n centimètre cube m; **~ meter** AmE, **~ metre** BrE n mètre cube m; **~ tonnage** n (of a ship) tonnage cube m

cul-de-sac n cul-de-sac m

culminate: **~ in** vt aboutir à, se solder par

culpable adj coupable

cultivate vt (land, person) cultiver

cultivation n (agricultural) culture f; **under ~** en culture

cultural adj culturel/-elle; **~ center** AmE, **~ centre** BrE n centre culturel m; **~ revolution** n révolution culturelle f

culture n culture f; **~ shock** n choc culturel m

cum prep (Stock) avec; **~ dividend** avec dividende; **~ rights** avec droits

cum. abbr (▸**cumulative**) cum. (cumulatif)

cumulative adj (dividends, interest) cumulatif/-ive; **~ liability** n (Ins) responsabilité cumulative f; **~ net capital loss** n perte en capital nette cumulative f; **~ preference share** n BrE action de priorité cumulative f

cupidity n cupidité f

curator n (in bankruptcy) curateur m

Curb n (infrml) la deuxième bourse de New York où sont listées les valeurs qui n'apparaissent pas au New York Stock Exchange

curb market n US (Stock) marché hors bourse m

currency n devise f, monnaie f; **gain ~** (idea, belief) se répandre; **~ accounts** n pl (Fin) tranche de crédit f; **~ basket** n panier de devises m; **~ of a bill** (Acc) échéance ⋯⇨

d'une traite f; ~ **board** n institut qui émet une monnaie nationale convertible à taux fixe uniquement en contrepartie d'une devise de réserve détenue par la banque centrale avec laquelle elle est à parité; ~ **deposits** n pl dépôts en devises m pl; ~ **convertor** n convertisseur de devises m; ~ **devaluation** n dévaluation monétaire f; ~ **futures** n pl contrat à termes de change m, contrat à termes de devises m; ~ **futures market** n marché à terme de devises m; ~ **holdings** n pl avoirs en devises m pl; ~ **market** n marché des changes m; ~ **restriction** n restriction monétaire f; ~ **standard** n étalon devise m; ~ **swap** n swap de devises m; ~ **unit** n unité monétaire f; ~ **zone** n zone monétaire f

current[1] adj (research, work, developments) en cours; (situation, policy, exchange rate) actuel/-elle; **at ~ prices** au prix actuel

current[2] n (electric) courant m, courant électrique m; (trend) tendance f; **a ~ of opinion** un courant d'opinion

current: ~ **account** n BrE compte courant m; ~ **account balance** n BrE solde de compte courant m; ~ **account customer** n, ~ **account holder** n BrE titulaire d'un compte courant mf; ~ **affairs** n pl l'actualité f; ~ **assets** n pl actif circulant m; ~ **business year** n exercice en cours m; ~ **cost** n (Acc) coût courant m, coût de remplacement m; ~ **cost accounting** n comptabilité aux coûts de remplacement f, comptabilité de coûts courants f; ~ **cost basis** n (Acc) base de prix de revient actuel f; ~ **economic trend** n conjoncture actuelle f; ~ **events** n pl l'actualité f; ~ **expenditure** n frais d'exploitation actuels m pl; ~ **fiscal year** n exercice courant m; ~ **holdings** n pl (Stock) participations actuelles f pl; ~ **liability** n dette à court terme f; ~ **market value** n valeur marchande actuelle f; ~ **operating profit** n (Acc) bénéfice d'exploitation actuel m; ~ **price** n (Econ) prix courant m; (Fin) prix courant m, tarif m; ~ **spending** n dépenses courantes f pl, dépenses en cours f pl; ~ **stock** n stock en cours m; ~ **value** n valeur actuelle f; ~ **value accounting** n comptabilité de la valeur actuelle f; ~ **year** n année en cours f, exercice en cours m; ~ **yield** n rendement actuel m

currently adv actuellement

curriculum n programme d'études m; ~ **vitae** n curriculum vitae m

cursor n curseur m

curtailment n (of service, expenditure) réduction f; (of talks, holiday) interruption f; (of freedom) limitation f

curtain-sided trailer n remorque à ridelles f

curve n courbe f

custodian n (Law) gardien m; (Stock)

conservateur de titres m, dépositaire mf

custody n (of child) garde f; (Stock) conservation f; **in ~** (Law) en détention

custom n usage m; (clientele) achalandage m, clientèle f; (Law) coutume f; ~ **and practice** (HRM) habitudes et accords d'industrie f pl

customary adj habituel/-elle, coutumier/-ière

custom builder n entrepreneur sur mesure m

custom-designed adj personnalisé

customer n client/-e m/f; ~ **account** n (Fin) compte client m; ~ **awareness** n mémorisation f; ~ **base** n clientèle f; ~ **billing** n facturation des clients f; ~ **card** n fiche de client f; ~ **care** n attention portée aux besoins de la clientèle f, souci du client m; ~ **careline** n service d'assistance téléphonique m; ~ **confidence** n confiance de la clientèle f; ~**-facing** adj en relation directe avec les clients; ~ **liaison** n liaison avec la clientèle f; ~ **needs** n pl besoins de la clientèle m pl; ~**-orientated** adj axé sur la clientèle, orienté vers la clientèle; ~ **profile** n profil de la clientèle m; ~ **relationship management** n gestion de la relation client f; ~ **relations manager** n directeur/-trice des relations avec la clientèle m/f; ~ **research** n (market research) étude des besoins de la clientèle f; ~ **service** n service clientèle m; ~ **service manager** n resonsable du service clientèle mf; ~ **service representative** n représentant/-e du service clientèle m/f; ~ **retention** n fidélisation du client f; ~ **support** n support client m

customers n pl clientèle f

customizable adj personnalisable

customize vt (hardware, software, service) personnaliser; (production) fabriquer sur mesure, personnaliser

customized adj (service, solution) personnalisé, à la carte

custom-made adj fabriqué sur commande, fait sur mesure

customs n pl douane f; **go through ~** passer à la douane; **no ~ value** sans valeur douanière; ~ **arrangements** n pl régime douanier m; ~ **barrier** n barrière douanière f; ~ **broker** n courtier en douane m; ~ **check** n vérification douanière f; ~ **clearance** n dédouanement m; ~ **declaration** n déclaration en douane f; ~ **duty** n droits de douane m pl; ~ **formalities** n pl formalités douanières f pl; ~ **inspection** n contrôle douanier m; ~ **invoice** n facture de douane f; ~ **officer** n agent en douane m, douanier/-ière m; ~ **procedure** n procédure douanière f; ~ **regulations** n pl règlements douaniers m pl; ~ **tariff** n tarif douanier m; ~ **union** n union douanière f; ~ **valuation** n évaluation douanière f

Customs: ~ **and Excise** n UK administration des douanes f, régie f; ~ **and Excise Department** n UK service des douanes m

cut n (share) part f; (reduction) réduction f; (in prices, rates) baisse f; **a** ~ **of the profits** une part des bénéfices; **job** ~**s** suppressions d'emplois f pl; **price** ~ réduction f; **interest rate** ~ baisse du taux d'intérêt f

cut² vt (budget) comprimer; (price, rate) baisser; (cost, expenditure, inflation, staff) réduire; (size) diminuer; (working week) réduire; (Comp) (text) couper; (Tax) alléger; ~ **and paste** couper-coller; ~ **one's losses** réduire les pertes; ~ **back** vt (production, spending staffing levels) réduire; (expansion) limiter; vi faire des économies; ~ **down on** (consumption, spending, numbers, time) réduire; ~ **sb in** mettre qn dans le coup (infrml); ~ **sb in on a deal** mettre qn dans le coup (infrml); ~ **off** (financial aid) suspendre; (grant, allowance) supprimer; (phone, power) couper

cutback n réduction des coûts f; ~**s in production** réductions de la production; ~**s in defence spending** réductions dans le budget de la défense

cutoff n limite f; ~ **date** n date butoir f; ~ **point** n (capital budgeting) point butoir m; (Fin, Tax) plafond m

cut-price¹ adj à prix réduit

cut-price² adv (offer, sell) à prix réduit

cutthroat competition n concurrence acharnée f, concurrence féroce f

cutting n (from newspaper) coupure f; ~ **and pasting** (Comp) coupé-collé m

cutting-edge¹ adj d'avant-garde

cutting-edge² n avant-garde f; **be at the** ~ **of technology** être à l'avant-garde de la technologie

CV abbr (▸**curriculum vitae**) CV m (curriculum vitae)

CVC abbr (▸**corporate venture capital**) capital-risque pratiqué par les filiales spécialisées des grandes entreprises

CWO abbr (▸**cash with order**) paiement à la commande m

cyberauction n vente aux enchères en ligne f

cybercafé n cybercafé m

cybercitizen n webcitoyen/-enne m/f, cybercitoyen/-enne mf

cyberconsumer n cyberconsommateur/-trice m/f

cybercrime n cybercriminalité f

cybercriminal n cybercriminel/-elle m/f

cyberculture n cyberculture f

cyberholic n cyberdépendant/-e m/f, webcamé/-e m/f (infrml)

cybermagazine n cybermagazine m

cybermall n cybermarché m, galerie marchande électronique f

cybermarketing n cybermarketing m

cybernetics n +sing v cybernétique f

cyberpiracy n cyberpiratage m

cybershopping n achats en ligne m pl

cyberspace n cyberspace m

cyberspeak n cyberjargon m

cybersquatter n cybersquatter m

cybersquatting n cybersquat m, accaparement des noms de domaine m

cyberstorefront n vitrine virtuelle f

cybersurfer n internaute mf

cyberterrorist n cyberterroriste mf

cybrarian n cyberdocumentaliste mf

cycle n cycle m; ~ **stock** n (Stock) valeurs cycliques f pl

cyclical adj cyclique; ~ **demand** n demande cyclique f; ~ **fluctuation** n (in commodity prices) valeurs cycliques f pl; ~ **trade** n commerce cyclique m; ~ **unemployment** n chômage conjoncturel m, chômage cyclique m; ~ **variations** n pl variations cycliques f pl

cyclic variation n (Econ) variation conjoncturelle f

Dd

D/A abbr (▸**deposit account**) compte de dépôt m, compte sur livret m; (▸**digital-nalog**) N/A (numérique-analogique); (▸**documents against acceptance**) documents contre acceptation m pl; (**days after acceptance**) jours après acceptation m pl; (Law) US (▸**district attorney**) ≈ procureur de la République m

DAF abbr (▸**delivered at frontier**) livraison à la frontière f

daily¹ adj (wage, rate) journalier/-ière; (routine, visit, delivery, event) quotidien/-ienne

daily² adv quotidiennement, tous les jours

daily³ n (newspaper) quotidien m

daily: ~ **activity report** n relevé quotidien des opérations m; ~ **allowance** n (Ins) ···᠅

indemnité journalière *f*; ∼ **closing balance** *n* solde quotidien à la fermeture *m*; ∼ **interest** *n* intérêt quotidien *m*; ∼ **interest savings account** *n* compte d'épargne à intérêt quotidien *m*; ∼ **newspaper** *n* quotidien *m*; ∼ **settlement** *n* (Stock) liquidation fictive quotidienne *f*; ∼ **volume** *n* (Stock) volume quotidien *m*

dairy *n* (company) société laitière *f*; (shop) crémerie *f*; ∼ **farm** *n* ferme laitière *f*; ∼ **products** *n pl* produits laitiers *m pl*

damage *n* (to goods, property) dégâts *m pl*; (Ins) dommage *m*, dégâts *m pl*; (Law) dommage *m*; (to company, reputation) atteinte *f*; (to ship, shipment) avarie *f*, dommage *m*; ∼ **caused by fire** dégâts causés par un incendie *m pl*; ∼ **limitation** *n* limitation des dommages *f*, limitation des dégâts *f*; ∼ **report** *n* rapport d'expertise *m*; (on ship, cargo) rapport d'avaries *m*; ∼ **to property** dégâts matériels *m pl*

damaged *adj* (cargo, goods) avarié; ∼ **in transit** avarié en cours de route

damages *n pl* dommages et intérêts *m pl*, dommages-intérêts *m pl*

dampen *vt* (growth) freiner, étouffer; (enthusiasm) refroidir

danger *n* danger *m*; **in** ∼ **of** en danger de; ∼ **money** *n* prime de risque *f*

dangerous *adj* dangereux/-euse; ∼ **cargo** *n* marchandises dangereuses *f pl*; ∼ **goods** *n pl* produits dangereux *m pl*; ∼ **substance** *n* substance toxique *f*; ∼ **waste** *n* déchets dangereux *m pl*

DAP *abbr* (▸**documents against payment**) DP (documents contre paiement)

dash *n* (typography) tiret *m*, tiret cadratin *m*

dashed line *n* ligne de pointillés *f*

data *n* (Gen Comm) données *f pl*, informations *f pl*; (Comp) données *f pl*; ∼ **bank** *n* banque de données *f*; ∼ **capture** *n* saisie de données *f*; ∼ **collection** *n* collecte de données *f*, rassemblement de données *m*; ∼ **communications** *n pl* communication de données *f*, transmission de données *f*; ∼ **compression** *n* compression de données *f*; ∼ **dictionary** *n* dictionnaire de données *m*; ∼ **entry** *n* introduction de données *f*, saisie de données *f*; ∼ **entry keyboarder** *n* opérateur/-trice de saisie de données *m/f*; ∼ **entry terminal** *n* unité de saisie *f*; ∼ **file** *n* fichier de données *m*; ∼ **flow** *n* circulation des données *f*; ∼ **flow chart** *n* organigramme de données *m*; ∼ **gathering** *n* collecte de données *f*, rassemblement de données *m*; ∼ **handling** *n* manipulation de données *f*; ∼ **input** *n* entrée de données *f*, saisie de données *f*; ∼ **loss** *n* perte de données *f*; ∼ **management** *n* gestion de données *f*; ∼ **medium** *n* support de données *m*; ∼ **mining** *n* exploitation de données *f*; ∼ **output** *n* sortie de données *f*; ∼ **plate** *n* (on container) plaque indicatrice *f*; ∼ **privacy** *n*

BrE confidentialité des données *f*; ∼ **processing** *n* informatique *f*, traitement des données *m*; ∼ **protection** *n* protection des données *f*; ∼ **protection act** *n* UK directive sur la protection des données personnelles *f*; ∼ **retrieval** *n* extraction de données *f*; ∼ **security** *n* (Gen Comm) sécurité des données *f*; (privacy) AmE confidentialité des données *f*; ∼ **sharing** *n* partage de données *m*; ∼ **storage** *n* stockage de données *m*; ∼ **stream** *n* flux de données *m*; ∼ **transfer** *n* transfert de données *m*; ∼ **transfer rate** *n* taux de transfert des données *m*; ∼ **warehouse** *n* entrepôt de données *m*

database *n* base de données *f*; ∼ **management** *n* gestion de données *f*; ∼ **management system** *n* système de gestion de bases de données *m*

datamart *n* entrepôt de données spécialisées *m*

date *n* (day of the year) date *f*; (of bill) échéance *f*; **at a later** ∼ ultérieurement; ∼ **as postmark** pour la date se référer au cachet de la poste; **keep up to** ∼ se tenir au courant; **keep sth up to** ∼ (filing) maintenir à jour; **keep up to** ∼ **with** se tenir au courant de; **be up to** ∼ (document) être à jour; **bring up to** ∼ (equipment) moderniser; (records) mettre à jour; (person) mettre au courant; **to** ∼ à ce jour; ∼ **of filing** (Patents) date de dépôt *f*; ∼ **of grant** (Patents) date de délivrance *f*; ∼ **of invoice** date de facture *f*; ∼ **of issue** date d'émission *f*; ∼ **marking** *n* (S&M) marquage de la date de péremption *m*; ∼ **of maturity** (Stock) date d'échéance *f*; ∼ **of payment** date de paiement *f*, date de versement *f*; ∼ **of registration** (Patents) date d'enregistrement *f*

daughter company *n* société captive *f*

dawn raid *n* (Fin) tentative d'OPA surprise *f*

day *n* jour *m*; **every** ∼ tous les jours; **every other** ∼ tous les deux jours; **from** ∼ **to day** de jour en jour; **give the employees a** ∼ **off** accorder une journée de congé aux employés; **on a** ∼**-to-day basis** au jour le jour; ∼ **laborer** AmE, ∼ **labourer** BrE *n* journalier/-ière *m/f*; ∼ **loan** *n* prêt au jour le jour *m*; ∼ **off** *n* jour de congé *m*; ∼ **order** *n* (Stock) ordre valable ce jour *m*; ∼ **release** *n* formation en alternance *f*; ∼ **shift** *n* équipe de jour *f*; ∼**-to-day** *adj* quotidien/-ienne; ∼**-to-day loan** *n* prêt au jour le jour *m*; ∼**-to-day money** *n* argent au jour le jour *m*; ∼ **trader** *n* scalper *m*, spéculateur à la journée *m*; ∼ **trading** *n* scalpage *m*, spéculation à la journée *f*

daybook *n* journal *m*, main courante *f*

daylight saving *n* heure d'été *f*

daywork *n* travail de jour *m*

dayworker *n* ouvrier/-ière de l'équipe de jour *m/f*

db *abbr* (▸**daybook**) jl (journal); (**decibel**)

db *m* (décibel); (▸**debenture**) obl. *f* (obligation)

Dbk *abbr* (▸**drawback**) remboursement des droits de douane *m*

DBMS *abbr* (▸**database management system**) SGBD *m* (système de gestion de bases de données)

DCF *abbr* (▸**discounted cash flow**) valeur actualisée nette *f*

dd *abbr* (▸**due date**) date d'échéance *f*, échéance *f*; (▸**delivered**) (Gen Comm) livré; (Transp) rendu

DD *abbr* (▸**direct debit**) prélèvement automatique *m*; (▸**demand draft**) traite à vue *f*; (▸**delivered at docks**) livraison à quai *f*

DDP *abbr* (▸**delivered duty paid**) livraison franco de douane, rendu droits acquittés

DDU *abbr* (▸**delivered duty unpaid**) rendu droits non-acquittés

dead: ∼ **account** *n* compte inactif *m*; ∼**-end job** *n* BrE emploi sans avenir *m*; ∼ **letter** *n* lettre mise au rebut *f*; ∼ **load** *n* poids mort *m*; ∼ **stock** *n* (S&M) invendus *m pl*; ∼ **weight** *n* port en lourd *m*, tonnage en lourd *m*; ∼ **weight capacity** *n* port en lourd *m*, tonnage en lourd *m*; ∼ **weight cargo** *n* marchandises lourdes *f pl*; ∼ **weight tonnage** *n* tonnage de port en lourd *m*

deadfreight *n* faux fret *m*, fret sur le vide *m*

deadheading *n* AmE (Transp) retour à vide *m*

deadline *n* délai *m*, date limite *f*; **meet a** ∼ respecter un délai; **miss a** ∼ dépasser les délais; **work to tight** ∼**s** travailler dans des délais très serrés; **the** ∼ **for applications is the 20ᵗʰ** les candidatures doivent être déposées avant le 20

deadlock *n* impasse *f*; **reach** ∼ aboutir à une impasse; **break the** ∼ sortir de l'impasse

deal¹ *n* affaire *f*, marché *m*; (S&M) vente *f*; **clinch a** ∼ conclure un marché, conclure une affaire; **the** ∼ **is off** l'affaire est annulée, le marché est rompu; **do a** ∼, **make a** ∼ conclure un marché, faire une affaire; **it's a** ∼! marché conclu!; **a good** ∼ une bonne affaire; **a cash/credit** ∼ une vente au comptant/à crédit

deal² *vi* (on stock exchange) faire des opérations boursières, négocier en bourse; ∼ **in** (commodity, product) faire le commerce de; ∼ **with** (arrangement, crisis, customer) s'occuper de; (person, company) traiter avec; ∼ **with the mail** ouvrir le courrier

dealer *n* (Fin) agent *m*; (S&M) (supplier, stockist) fournisseur *m*, négociant *m*, marchand *m*; (for specific make, product) concessionnaire *mf*; (Stock) négociant *m*, opérateur *m*; (trafficker) trafiquant *m*; **authorized** ∼ dépositaire agréé *m*; **exclusive**

∼ dépositaire exclusif *m*; ∼ **in securities** contrepartiste *mf*, dealer *m*, négociant en titres *m*

dealership *n* concession *f*

dealing *n* (S&M) vente *f*; (in drugs) trafic *m*; (Stock) opérations *f pl*; **share** ∼ transactions boursières *f pl*; ∼ **is slow on the London Stock Exchange** la Bourse de Londres est calme; **when** ∼ **resumes** quand les transactions reprendront; ∼ **floor** *n* parquet *m*, salle des marchés *f*

dealings *n pl* (relationships) rapports *m pl*; (Stock) opérations *f pl*, transactions *f pl*; ∼ **for the account** *n pl* (Fin) opérations de liquidation *f pl*, opérations à terme *f pl*

dear *adj* (expensive) cher/chère, coûteux/-euse

death *n* mort *f*, décès *m*; ∼ **benefit** *n* (Ins) capital décès *m*, prestation de décès *f*; ∼ **certificate** *n* acte de décès *m*; ∼ **duties** *n pl* droits de succession *m pl*, impôt sur les successions *m*; ∼ **rate** *n* taux de mortalité *m*; ∼ **tax** *n* AmE droits de succession *m pl*, impôt sur les successions *m*

debasement *n* (of currency) dépréciation *f*

debatable *adj* contestable

debate *vt* discuter de, débattre de

debenture *n* (Stock) obligation *f*, obligation non-garantie *f*; ∼ **bond** *n* certificat d'obligation *m*; ∼ **capital** *n* capital obligations *m*; ∼ **holder** *n* obligataire *mf*, porteur d'obligations non garanties *m*; ∼ **loan** *n* prêt obligataire *m*; ∼ **stock** *n* obligations non-garanties *f pl*

debit¹ *n* débit *m*; ∼ **account** *n* compte débiteur *m*; ∼ **balance** *n* solde débiteur *m*; ∼ **card** *n* carte bancaire *f*; ∼ **column** *n* colonne des débits *f*; ∼ **entry** *n* écriture passée au débit *f*; ∼ **interest** *n* intérêts débiteurs *m pl*; ∼ **memorandum** *n* US note de débit *f*; ∼ **note** *n* note de débit *f*; ∼ **side** *n* côté du débit *m*

debit² *vt* (account) débiter; **be** ∼ **to** (account) être débité de

debrief *vt* débriefer

debriefing *n* compte rendu *m*, debriefing *m*

debt *n* (Gen Comm) (amount owed) dette *f*; (owing of money) endettement *m*; (Acc) créance *f*; (Econ) endettement *m*; ∼ **due by** dette exigible le, dette échue le; ∼ **due from** créance due depuis; ∼ **due to** dette due à; **get into** ∼ s'endetter; **run up a** ∼ faire des dettes; **be in** ∼ **to** devoir de l'argent à; **pay off one's** ∼**s** rembourser ses dettes; ∼ **burden** *n* poids de la dette *m*; ∼ **charges** *n pl* frais rattachés à une dette *m pl*; ∼ **collection** *n* recouvrement de créances *m*, recouvrement de dettes *m*; ∼ **collection agency** *n* bureau de recouvrement de créances *m*; ∼ **collection order** *n* ordre de recouvrement de créances *m*; ∼ **collector** *n* agent de recouvrement de créances *m*; ∼ **consolidation** *n* consolidation de la dette *f*; ∼ **financing** *n* financement par emprunt ⋯⭢

bancaire *m*; ~ **forgiveness** *n* remise de
dette *f*; ~ **instrument** *n* titre de créance *m*;
~ **management** *n* gestion des dettes *f*; ~
ratio *n* ratio d'endettement *m*; ~ **recovery**
period *n* délai de recouvrement *m*; ~ **relief**
n allègement de la dette *m*; ~ **rescheduling**
n rééchelonnement de la dette *m*; ~
restructuring *n* rééchelonnement de la dette
m; ~ **service** *n* (Acc) service de la dette *m*

debtor *n* débiteur/-trice *m/f*

debug *vt* (Comp) déboguer

decade *n* décennie *f*; **in the ~ to 1999** dans
les dix années qui ont précédé 1999

deceased *adj* décédé, défunt; ~ **estate** *n*
masse successorale *f*; ~ **person** *n* défunt/-e
m/f, personne décédée *f*

decelerate *vi* (growth) ralentir

deceleration *n* ralentissement *m*

decent *adj* convenable

decentralization *n* décentralisation *f*

decentralize *vt* décentraliser

decentralized *adj* décentralisé; ~
management *n* gestion décentralisée *f*; ~
market economy *n* économie de marché
décentralisée *f*

deceptive *adj* trompeur/-euse; ~
advertising *n* publicité mensongère *f*

decide **1** *vt* (matter, dispute) régler; (outcome,
fate) décider de; ~ **to do** décider de faire;
(after much reflection) se décider à faire; ~
when/where décider quand/où
2 *vi* décider, prendre une décision; ~
against (plan, idea) ne pas adopter; (candidate)
rejeter; ~ **against doing** décider de ne pas
faire; ~ **between** faire un choix entre; ~ **in**
favour of (candidate) choisir; (plaintiff) se
prononcer pour; ~ **on** (choose) se décider
pour; (date) fixer; (candidate) choisir

decimal *adj* décimal; **calculate to two ~**
places calculer à deux décimales; ~ **point** *n*
virgule *f*

decimalization *n* (of currency)
décimalisation *f*; (of number) conversion en
fraction décimale *f*

decimalize *vt* (currency) décimaliser; (Math)
transposer dans le système décimal

decision *n* décision *f*; **make a ~, take a ~**
prendre une décision; ~ **maker** *n* décideur
m; ~ **making** *n* prise de décision *f*;
~**-making process** *n* processus de prise de
décision *m*, processus décisionnel *m*; ~
model *n* modèle de décision *m*; ~ **process**
n processus de la décision *m*; ~ **support**
system *n* système décisionnel *m*; ~ **table** *n*
table de décision *f*; ~ **tree** *n* arbre de
décision *m*

decisive *adj* (argument) concluant; (factor,
influence) décisif/-ive; (Law) concluant

deck *n* (on ship) pont *m*

declaration *n* déclaration *f*; ~ **of**
dividend déclaration de dividende *f*; ~ **of**
origin déclaration d'origine *f*; ~ **of income**

déclaration de revenus *f*

declare *vt* (to customs officer) déclarer; (on tax
return) déclarer; ~ **on oath** déclarer sous
serment; **'nothing to ~'** 'rien à déclarer'

declared: ~ **dividend** *n* dividende
déclaré *m*; ~ **value for customs** *n* valeur
déclarée en douane *f*

declassify *vt* (Gen Comm) (document) rendre
accessible; (Pol) déclassifier

decline[1] *n* déclin *m*; (in employment, demand,
trade, output, prices, support) baisse *f*; (Ind) déclin
m; **be in ~** (industry, economy) être en déclin;
(trade, support, demand) être en baisse; **fall into**
~ tomber en déclin; **on the ~** en déclin

decline[2] *vi* (support) être en baisse; (number,
rate, sales, demand, price) baisser; (trade) ralentir

declining *adj* (sector, influence) en déclin; ~
balance depreciation *n* amortissement
dégressif *m*; ~ **industrial area** *n* zone
industrielle en déclin *f*; ~ **industry** *n*
industrie en déclin *f*; ~ **inflation rate** *n*
taux d'inflation en baisse; ~ **interest rate** *n*
taux d'intérêt en baisse *m*; ~ **market** *n*
marché en baisse *m*; ~ **share** *n* action en
baisse *f*, action qui fléchit *f*

decoder *n* décodeur *m*

decommission *vt* (industrial or nuclear plant)
déclasser, démanteler

decommissioning *n* (of industrial or nuclear
plant) déclassement *m*, démantèlement *m*

decompartmentalization *n*
décloisonnement *m*

decompartmentalize *vt* décloisonner

decompress *vt* (data) décompresser

decompression *n* (of data) décompression
f

decrease[1] *n* diminution *f*; (in price) baisse *f*;
~ **in spending** baisse de la consommation *f*;
~ **in value** diminution de valeur *f*, perte de
valeur *f*; ~ **of risk** (Ins) diminution du
risque *f*

decrease[2] **1** *vt* diminuer, réduire
2 *vi* (Econ) (population, size, weight) diminuer;
(price, rate, popularity) baisser

decreasing *adj* (population, size, amount)
décroissant; (price) en baisse; ~ **order** *n*
ordre décroissant *m*; ~ **rate** *n* taux dégressif
m; ~ **tax** *n* impôt dégressif *m*

decree[1] *n* (Law) ordonnance *f*

decree[2] *vt* (Law) ordonner, édicter

decrement *vt* (Comp) décrémenter

decriminalize *vt* décriminaliser, légaliser

decrypt *vt* déchiffrer, décoder

decryption *n* déchiffrement *m*, décodage *m*

dedicated *adj* (hardware) dédié, spécialisé;
(for specific purpose) spécialisé

dedomiciling *n* dédomiciliation *f*

deduce *vt* déduire

deduct *vt* (sum, expenses) déduire; ~ **tax at**
source prélever l'impôt à la source

deductible *adj* déductible; ~ **clause** *n*

deduction ···▷ deflationary gap·····

(Ins) clause de franchise *f*

deduction *n* (on wages) retenue *f*; (Tax) prélèvement *m*; (on bill, price) déduction *f*; **make a ~ from** opérer une déduction sur, opérer une retenue sur; (Tax) faire un prélèvement sur; **after ~s** une fois les retenues effectuées; **~ at source** retenue à la source *f*

deed *n* (Law) acte *m*, acte authentique *m*, (Prop) acte de propriété *m*; **~ of assignation** acte de cession *m*, contrat de cession *m*; **~ of covenant** UK acte de donation *m*; **~ of partnership** acte d'association *m*, contrat de société *m*; **~ poll** *n* acte unilatéral *m*; **~ of trust** acte de fiducie *m*, acte de fidéicommis *m*

deem *vt* considérer, estimer; **~ necessary** estimer nécessaire, juger nécessaire

deemed *adj* considéré, jugé

deep: **~ discount bond** *n* obligation négociée en dessous du pair *f*, obligation à escompte important *f*; **~-rooted**, **~-seated** *adj* (habit) profondément ancré, (problem, belief) profondément enraciné; (loyalty) profond; **~-sea shipping lane** *n* route de navigation en eau profonde *f*

deeply *adv* profondément

deepwater harbor AmE, **deepwater harbour** BrE *n* port en eau profonde *m*

def. *abbr* (▶**deferred**) (Acc) à reporter

de facto *adv* de facto, de fait; **~ corporation** *n* société de fait *f*

defalcation *n* détournement *m*

defamation *n* diffamation *f*

defamatory *adj* diffamatoire

defame *vt* calomnier, diffamer

default¹ *adj* (Gen Comm, Comp) (font, homepage, setting, value) par défaut

default² *n* (on debt, fine) non-paiement *m*; (on loan, mortgage) non-remboursement *m*; (Law) non-comparution *f*; **by ~** par défaut; **in ~ of** en l'absence de

default³ *vi* ne pas honorer ses échéances; **~ on** (payments) ne pas effectuer; (loan) ne pas régler; (fine) ne pas payer; (promise) ne pas tenir

default: **~ interest** *n* arriéré d'intérêts *m*, intérêt sur arriérés *m*; **~ judgement** *n* jugement par défaut *m*; **~ option** *n* option par défaut *f*; **~ of payment** *n* défaut de paiement *m*

defaulter *n* (non-payer) personne qui n'acquitte pas ses dettes *f*; (non-attender) partie défaillante *f*

defaulting witness *n* témoin défaillant *m*

defeasance *n* (Fin) défaisance *f*, désendettement *m*; (Law) (action) annulation *f*, abrogation *f*

defeat¹ *n* (in contest, election) défaite *f*; (of proposal, bill) rejet *m*; **suffer a ~** essuyer une défaite

defeat² *vt* (attempt, plan, takeover) faire échouer; (candidate, opposition) battre

defect *n* défaut *m*; (minor) imperfection *f*; (in construction, machine) malfaçon *f*, vice *m*; **structural ~** vice de construction *m*

defective *adj* défectueux/-euse; **~ title** *n* titre contestable *m*, titre imparfait *m*

defence *n* BrE défense *f*; **the ~** (Law) la défense *f*; **~ lawyer** *n* UK avocat/-e de la défense *m/f*

defend *vt* (person, interest) défendre

defendant *n* défendeur/-eresse *m/f*; (in assize court) accusé/-e *m/f*; (on appeal) intimé/-e *m/f*; (in criminal case) prévenu/-e *m/f*

defense *n* AmE ▶**defence** BrE

Defense Secretary *n* US ≈ ministre de la Défense nationale *mf*

defer *vt* (decision, plan, publication, trip) reporter; (meeting) ajourner, reporter; (payment) différer, reporter; (judgement) suspendre, reporter; **~ a debt** reporter le remboursement d'une dette; **~ a payment** reporter un paiement; **~ tax** reporter l'impôt

deferment *n* (of meeting) ajournement *m*, report *m*; (of decision, journey, publication, plan) report *m*; (Law) prorogation *f*; **~ of a debt** sursis de paiement d'une dette *m*

deferral *n* (Tax) report *m*

deferred *adj* (tax, taxation, revenue) reporté; (closure, purchase, departure) différé; **~ amount** *n* montant différé *m*; **~ annuity** *n* rente différée *f*, rente à paiement différé *f*; **~ billing** *n* facturation différée *f*; **~ credit** *n* revenu reporté *m*; **~ futures** *n pl* contrats à terme différés *m pl*; **~ income** *n* revenu reporté *m*; **~ income tax** *n* impôt sur le revenu reporté *m*; **~ interest bond** *n* obligation à intérêt différé *f*; **~ payment** *n* (in instalments) paiement par versements échelonnés *m*; (credit) paiement différé *m*; **~ sale** *n* vente à tempérament *f*, vente à crédit *f*; **~ share** *n* action à dividende différé *f*; **~ stock** *n* action à dividende différé *f*

deficiency *n* (Gen Comm) défaut *m*, manque *m*; (Fin) insuffisance *f*; (Tax) déficit *m*; **~ judgement** *n* jugement compensatoire *m*

deficient *adj* (flawed) déficient; (inadequate) insuffisant

deficit *n* (Gen Comm, Acc) déficit *m*; **make up the ~** combler le déficit; **in ~** en déficit, déficitaire; **~ balance of payments** balance des paiements déficitaire *f*; **~ spending** *n* financement par l'emprunt *m*, impasse budgétaire *f*

define *vt* définir

definition *n* définition *f*

deflate *vt* (prices) faire baisser; **~ the economy** pratiquer une politique déflationniste, ralentir l'économie

deflated *adj* (earnings) à la baisse

deflation *n* déflation *f*, désinflation *f*

deflationary *adj* déflationniste; **~ gap** *n* ···▷

écart déflationniste *m*, écart récessionniste *m*; ~ **pressures** *n pl* pressions déflationnistes *f pl*

deforestation *n* déboisement *m*, déforestation *f*

defraud *vt* (person) escroquer; (tax authority) frauder; ~ **sb of sth** escroquer qch à qn

defraudation *n* détournement d'impôts *m*

defrauded tax *n* impôt éludé *m*

defray *vt* couvrir, rembourser; ~ **the cost of** couvrir les frais de

defunct *adj* (organisation) défunt; (practice) révolu; ~ **company** *n* société dissoute *f*

degree *n* (measure) degré *m*; (qualification) diplôme universitaire *m*; **have a ~** être diplômé; **to such a ~ that** à un tel point que; **to some ~** dans une certaine mesure; **to a lesser ~** dans une moindre mesure; **a ~ of autonomy** une certaine autonomie; ~ **of risk** niveau de risque *m*

degression *n* dégression *f*

degressive *adj* dégressif/-ive; ~ **tax** *n* impôt dégressif *m*

dehire *vt* AmE licencier

dehiring *n* AmE licenciement *m*

deindustrialization *n* désindustrialisation *f*

deinstall *vt* (Comp) désinstaller

deintensified farming *n* désintensification des cultures *f*

de jure *adv* de droit, de jure

delay *n* (slowness) retard *m*; (time lapse) délai *m*; **without further ~** sans plus tarder

delayed: ~ **delivery** *n* livraison différée *f*; ~ **flight** *n* vol retardé *m*

delayering *n* réduction du nombre de niveaux hiérarchiques *f*

delaying tactics *n pl* manœuvres dilatoires *f pl*

delegate¹ *n* délégué/-e *m/f*

delegate² *vt* (powers, responsibilities) déléguer

delegation *n* (of people, power) délégation *f*; ~ **of authority** délégation de pouvoir *f*

delete *vt* (Gen Comm) supprimer; (score out) barrer, rayer; (from list) radier; (debt) abandonner, annuler; (Comp) effacer, supprimer; ~ **where not applicable** rayer les mentions inutiles

delete key *n* touche effacement *f*

deletion *n* (Gen Comm, Comp) suppression *f*; (from list) radiation *f*; ~ **of a debt** abandon d'une dette *m*, radiation d'une dette *f*

delinquency *n* (Acc) (amount) montant d'un compte douteux *m*; (Fin) (non-payment) défaut de paiement *m*

delinquent *adj* (Fin) non-payé, échu

delisting *n* (Stock) radiation de la cote *f*

deliver ⚀ *vt* (goods) livrer; (service) fournir; (speech) prononcer; (opinion) soumettre; (shares) livrer; (ultimatum, decision) donner; (verdict, ruling) rendre; (message, note) remettre; (work,

document, report) rendre; ~ **a lecture** faire une conférence; (at university) faire cours; **have sth ~ed** faire livrer qch

⚁ *vi* (live up to one's promises) tenir ses engagements

deliverable¹ *adj* livrable; **in a ~ state** en état livrable

deliverable² *n* livrable *m*

deliverables: ~ **bills** *n pl* bons livrables *m pl*; ~ **security** *n* valeur livrable *f*

delivered *adj* (Gen Comm) livré; (Transp) rendu; ~ **at docks** rendu à quai; ~ **at frontier** rendu à la frontière; ~ **domicile** rendu à domicile; ~ **duty paid** livraison franco de douane; ~ **duty unpaid** livraison droits non payés, rendu droits non acquittés

delivery *n* (Gen Comm) (of goods) livraison *f*; (of passport, receipt, shares) délivrance *f*; (handing over) remise *f*; **take ~ of sth** prendre livraison de qch; **on ~** à la livraison; ~ **versus payment** (Stock) paiement contre livraison; ~ **charge** *n* frais de livraison *m pl*; ~ **date** *n* date de livraison *f*; ~ **deadline** *n* date limite de livraison *f*; ~ **man** *n* livreur *m*; ~ **note** *n* bon de livraison *m*; ~ **notice** *n* avis de livraison *m*; ~ **receipt** *n* reçu de livraison *m*, récépissé de livraison *m*; ~ **service** *n* service de livraison *m*; ~ **slip** *n* (Stock) avis de livraison *m*; ~ **time** *n* délai de livraison *m*; ~ **turnround** *n* délai de livraison *m*; ~ **van** *n* fourgonnette de livraison *f*; ~ **woman** *n* livreuse *f*

delta *n* (Fin, Stock) delta *m*; ~ **stock** *n* (Stock) UK valeur delta *f*

de luxe *adj* de luxe

dely *abbr* (▶**delivery**) (Gen Comm) livr. (livraison); (of passport, receipt) délivrance *f*

de-man ⚀ *vt* dégraisser
⚁ *vi* réduire la main-d'œuvre

demand¹ *n* (request) demande *f*; (Econ, S&M) demande *f*; (Tax) demande formelle *f*; (pressure) exigences *f pl*; **be in great ~** (skill, staff) être très recherché; **in ~** (skill, jobs) recherché; **on ~** (Gen Comm) à la demande; (Acc, fin) sur demande, sur présentation, à vue; **final ~** (for payment) dernier avertissement *m*; **make ~s on sb's finances** entamer les finances de qn; **I have many ~s on my time** je suis très pris; **make ~s of sb** exiger beaucoup de qn; **there is no ~ for this product** cet article ne se vend pas; **by popular ~** à la demande générale; ~ **aggregation** *n* regroupement de la demande *m*; ~ **aggregator** *n* regroupeur de demandes *m*; ~ **curve** *n* courbe de demande *f*; ~ **deposit** *n* dépôt à vue *m*; ~ **draft** *n* prélèvement automatique *m*, traite à vue *f*; ~ **factor** *n* facteur de demande *m*; ~ **function** *n* fonction de la demande *f*; ~ **for goods** demande de biens *f*; ~ **for money** (Econ) demande de monnaie *f*; ~ **forecasting** *n* prévision de la demande *f*; ~-**led** *adj* stimulé par la demande; ~-**led growth** *n* croissance induite par la demande f; ~ **loan** n prêt à vue m; ~ **money** n argent au jour le jour m; ~ **note** n billet à ordre payable à vue m; ~ **price** n prix selon la demande m; **~pull inflation** n inflation par la demande f

demand² vt demander; (forcefully) exiger; (in dispute) revendiquer; (Tax) exiger; (skill, patience, payment, attention) exiger; ~ **sth from sb** exiger qch à qn

demanning n dégraissage m

demarcation n (trade unions) démarcation f; ~ **dispute** n UK conflit d'identité m

demarketing n non-marketing m

demerge vt défusionner, dégrouper, scinder

demerger n (of companies) déconcentration f, scission f

demise charter party n (Transp) charte-partie à temps f

demised premises n pl locaux à bail m pl

demo n (infrml) démo f (infrml); ~ **disk** n disquette de démonstration f; ~ **version** n version de démonstration f

democracy n démocratie f

democratic adj démocratique

democratically adv démocratiquement

demographic¹ adj (data, profile, segment) démographique

demographic² n segment démographique m

demographics n + sing v profil démographique m

demography n démographie f

demolition n démolition f

demonetization n démonétisation f

demonetize vt démonétiser

demonstrate [1] vt (by table, graph) expliquer; (machine, product) faire la démonstration de; (theory) démontrer; (skill) montrer; (support) manifester; **this ~s the principle that...** cela démontre le principe selon lequel...; ~ **how to do** montrer comment faire
[2] vi (Pol) manifester

demonstration n (Pol) manifestation f; (of machine, theory) démonstration f

demoralize vt démoraliser

demote vt rétrograder

demotion n rétrogradation f

demotivate vt démotiver

demotivation n démotivation f

demutualize vi démutualiser

denationalization n dénationalisation f

denationalize vt dénationaliser

denial of service attack n (Comp) attaque par déni de service f

denominate vt (Fin) libeller

denomination n (of coins) valeur f; (of notes) coupure f; **high/low ~ banknote** grosse/petite coupure f

denominator n dénominateur m

densely-populated adj fortement peuplé

density n densité f

deny vt (entitlement, accusation) contester, nier; (rumour, report) démentir; ~ **sb sth** refuser qch à qn; ~ **sb access to sth** refuser à qn l'accès à qch

department n (in company) service m; (district) département m; (in store) rayon m; (Pol) ministère m; ~ **head** n chef de service m, directeur/-trice du service m/f; ~ **manager** n chef de service m; (in store) chef de rayon m; ~ **store** n grand magasin m; ~ **store chain** n chaîne de grands magasins f

Department: ~ **of Commerce** n US ≈ ministère du Commerce m; ~ **of Defense** n US ≈ ministère de la Défense nationale m; ~ **of Education** n US ≈ ministère de l'Éducation nationale m; ~ **for Education and Skills** n UK ministère de l'Education et de l'Emploi m; ~ **of Energy** n US ministère de l'Énergie m; ~ **of Transport, Local Government and the Regions** n UK ministère du Transport, de l'Administration locale et des Régions m; ~ **of Health** n UK ≈ ministère de la Santé m; ~ **of Health and Human Services** n US ≈ ministère de la Santé m; ~ **of Industry** n US ≈ ministère de l'Industrie m; ~ **of Labor** n US ≈ ministère du Travail m; ~ **of Trade and Industry** n UK ministère du Commerce et de l'Industrie m; ~ **of Work and Pensions** n UK ≈ ministère des Affaires sociales m

departmental: ~ **head** n chef de service m; (in shop) chef de rayon m; ~ **management** n direction de service f, gestion de service f; ~ **manager** n chef de service m; (in shop) chef de rayon m

departmentalization n cloisonnement m, départementalisation f

departmentalize vt cloisonner

departure n (Transp) départ m; (from job) départ m; (from tradition, policy) rupture f; **a ~ from the norm** un écart par rapport à la norme; **a ~ from the past** une rupture avec le passé; **a ~ from the rules** un manquement au règlement; ~ **gate** n porte de départ f; ~ **lounge** n salle d'embarquement f

depend: ~ **on** vt (be determined by) dépendre de; (rely on) compter sur

dependant n personne à charge f; ~ **tax credit** n crédit pour personne à charge m

dependency n dépendance f; ~ **on sth** dépendance vis-à-vis de; ~ **culture** n culture de dépendance f, société d'assistés f

dependent adj (child, person) à charge; (Tax) dépendant; **be ~ on** dépendre de

de-planing n AmE débarquement de l'avion m

deplete vt réduire, diminuer

depletion n (of resources) amortissement m; ⋯⋗

(of stocks, funds) baisse *f*, diminution *f*

deploy *vt* (resources) déployer; (team, staff) affecter

deployment *n* déploiement *m*; (of team) affectation *f*

depolarize *vt* (parties) rapprocher; (discussion, talks) débloquer

depopulation *n* dépeuplement *m*

deport *vt* (immigrant) expulser

deportation *n* expulsion *f*

deposit¹ *n* (Acc) acompte *m*, caution *f*; (Bank) dépôt *m*; (as security) caution *f*, cautionnement *m*; (down payment on goods, room) arrhes *f pl*, acompte *m*; (in hire purchase) versement initial *m*; (of minerals) gisement *m*; (Patents) dépôt *m*; **make a ~** effectuer un dépôt; **on ~** en dépôt; **put down a ~ on sth** effectuer un versement initial pour qch; **leave a ~ on sth** verser des arrhes pour qch, verser un acompte pour qch; **~ account** *n* UK compte de dépôt *m*, compte sur livret *m*; **~ bank** *n* banque de dépôt *f*; **~ book** *n* livret de dépôt *m*; **~ insurance** *n* US garantie des dépôts à terme (par l'État) *f*; **~ interest** *n* intérêt sur les dépôts *m*; **~ note** *n* bordereau de dépôt *m*; **~ rate** *n* taux d'intérêt créditeur *m*; **~ slip** *n* bordereau de dépôt, bordereau de versement *m*

deposit² *vt* (into bank) verser, déposer; **~ money into an account** verser de l'argent sur un compte, déposer de l'argent sur un compte

depositary *n* banque de dépôt *f*

deposition *n* déposition sous serment *f*, témoignage en justice consigné par écrit *m*

depositor *n* déposant/-e *m/f*

depository *n* (Fin) banque de dépôt *f*; (for goods) dépôt *m*; (for furniture) garde-meubles *m*

depot *n* (Transp) gare *f*; (for storage) dépôt *m*, garage *m*; **~ charges** *n pl* frais d'entrepôt *m pl*

depreciable: **~ asset** *n* actif amortissable *m*; **~ cost** *n* coût amortissable *m*; **~ property** *n* biens amortissables *m pl*

depreciate ⟨1⟩ *vt* (Acc) amortir; (currency) déprécier, dévaloriser; (investment, assets) amortir
⟨2⟩ *vi* se déprécier, se dévaloriser

depreciated cost *n* coût amorti *m*

depreciation *n* (writing off of investment, asset) amortissement *m*; (of currency) dépréciation *f*, dévalorisation *f*; (Fin, Prop) (loss of value) dépréciation *f*, moins-value *f*; **~ allowance** *n* dotation aux amortissements *f*; **~ of fixed assets** dotations aux amortissements *f pl*; **~ reserve** *n* provision pour dépréciation *f*; **~ schedule** *n* plan d'amortissement *m*

depressed *adj* (prices, profits, wages) en baisse; **~ area** *n* zone en crise *f*, zone en déclin *f*; **~ region** *n* région en crise *f*, région en déclin *f*

depression *n* crise économique *f*,

dépression *f*, récession *f*

depressive *adj* (effect, policy) dépressif/-ive

deprive: **~ of** *vt* (assets, funds) priver de; (right, privilege) déposséder de

deprived *adj* (person, area) démuni; **~ of** privé de

dept. *abbr* (▶**department**) serv. (service)

depth *n* (Gen Comm) profondeur *f*; (of recession, crisis) gravité *f*; (of knowledge) étendue *f*; **in ~** en profondeur; **~ alongside** *n* profondeur au quai *f*; **~ analysis** *n* analyse en profondeur *f*; **~ interview** *n* entretien en profondeur *m*

deputy *n* (aide) adjoint/-e *m/f*; (replacement) remplaçant/-e *m/f*; **act as a ~ for sb** remplacer qn; **~ chairman** *n* vice-président/-e *m/f*; **~ chief executive** *n* directeur/-trice général/-e adjoint/-e *m/f*; **~ director** *n* directeur/-trice adjoint/-e *m/f*, sous-directeur/-trice *m*; **~ editor** *n* rédacteur/-trice en chef adjoint/-e *m/f*; **~ leader** *n* UK (Pol) ≈ vice-président/-e *m/f*; **~ manager** *n* directeur/-trice adjoint/-e *m/f*, sous-directeur/-trice *m/f*; **~ managing director** *n* directeur/-trice général/-e adjoint/-e *m/f*; **~ minister** *n* ministre délégué/-e *m/f*, sous-ministre *mf*

Deputy Speaker *n* UK (Pol) vice-président/-e des communes *m/f*

derecognition *n* UK (of trade union) refus de reconnaissance *m*

deregulate *vt* (trade, market) dérégler; (prices) libérer

deregulation *n* (international trade) déréglementation *f*; (Pol) déréglementation *f*, dérégulation *f*

dereliction of duty *n* manquement au devoir *m*

derivative *n* (Stock) instrument financier dérivé *m*, dérivé *m*; **~ product** *n* produit dérivé *m*

derivatives: **~ market** *n* marché des instruments dérivés *m*; **~ trader** *n* trader en produits dérivés *m*

derived demand *n* demande dérivée *f*

derogation *n* atteinte *f*, dérogation *f*

derrick *n* mât de charge *m*

describe *vt* décrire

description *n* (Gen Comm) description *f*; (Patents, Prop) description *f*; (S&M) description *f*, désignation *f*

descriptive *adj* descriptif/-ive; **~ labeling** AmE, **~ labelling** BrE *n* étiquetage donnant des informations détaillées sur le produit

deselect *vt* (Comp) désélectionner, supprimer; UK (Pol) (candidate) retirer l'investiture de

deselection *n* UK (Pol) retrait de l'investiture *m*

desertification *n* désertification *f*

design¹ *n* (sketch) conception *f*, projet *m*;

(idea, conception) conception *f*; (Patents) dessin *m*, modèle *m*; (style, appearance) design *m*; (fashion) stylisme *m*; (pattern) motif *m*; (model, object) modèle *m*; (item of clothing) création *f*; **study ∼** étudier le design; **the new season's ∼s** les nouvelles créations de la saison; **∼ agency** *n* agence de design *f*; **∼ automation** *n* conception assistée par ordinateur *f*; **∼ and layout** (of store) la conception et l'agencement; **∼ department** *n* bureau de design *m*; **∼ fault** *n* vice caché *m*, faute de conception *f*; **∼ office** *n* bureau d'étude *m*, bureau de design *m*, bureau de dessin *m*; **∼ right** *n* (Law) droit à la propriété industrielle *m*; **∼ specification** *n* spécification *f*; **∼ team** *n* équipe des concepteurs *f*

design² *vt* (building, equipment) faire les plans de, dessiner; (garment) créer; (plan, course) concevoir; **be ∼ed for** (made for) être conçu pour; (intended for) être destiné à

designate *vt* désigner, nommer

designated *adj* désigné, nommé; **∼ amount** *n* (Tax) montant attribué *m*; **∼ beneficiary** *n* (Tax) bénéficiaire assimilé *m*, bénéficiaire étranger *m*; **∼ income** *n* (trust) revenu de distribution *m*; **∼ shareholder** *n* (Tax) actionnaire déterminé *m*

designation *n* (Patents) désignation *f*

designer *n* concepteur/-trice *m/f*, designer *m*; (in fashion) couturier/-ière *m/f*; (in publishing) maquettiste *mf*; **∼ clothing** *n* vêtements griffés *m pl*; **∼ label** *n* griffe *f*

Designs Registry *n* UK *registre des œuvres ou modèles créés et déposés*

desk *n* bureau *m*; (trading position) table de change *f*; **∼ research** *n* recherche documentaire *f*; **∼ trader** *n* négociateur aux pupitres *m*

deskilling *n* (of workforce) déqualification *f*

desktop *n* (Comp) (on screen) bureau *m*; **∼ computer** *n* ordinateur de bureau *m*; **∼-publish** *vt* micro-éditer; **∼ publishing** *n* micro-édition *f*, publication assistée par ordinateur *f*

despatch ▸dispatch

despatcher *n* ▸dispatcher

despatching *n* ▸dispatching

destabilize *vt* déstabiliser

destination *n* destination *f*; **∼ airport** *n* aéroport d'arrivée *m*; **∼ marketing** *n* marketing de destination *m*; **∼ port** *n* port d'arrivée *m*

destitute *adj* démuni; **the ∼ n pl** les démunis *m pl*

destruction *n* destruction *f*

destructive *adj* destructeur/-trice; **be ∼ to** être nuisible à; **∼ competition** *n* concurrence sauvage *f*

detail *n* détail *m*; **in ∼** en détail; **a point of ∼** un point de détail

detailed *adj* détaillé; **∼ account** *n*

décompte *m*, rapport détaillé *m*

details *n pl* (information) détails *mpl*, renseignements *m pl*; (personal contact information) coordonnées *f pl*; **go into ∼** entrer dans les détails; **for further ∼** pour de plus amples renseignements

detain *vt* (delay) retenir; (place in custody) placer en détention

detention *n* (of ship, cargo) saisie *f*; (Law) détention *f*

deter *vt* dissuader, décourager; **∼ sb from doing** dissuader qn de faire

deteriorate *vi* (situation, relationship, substance) se détériorer; (economy, market, sales) décliner; (area, work) se dégrader

deterioration *n* détérioration *f*

determination *n* (Law) décision judiciaire *f*; (Tax) décision *f*, détermination *f*; (of price) fixation *f*; (of policy, conditions) détermination *f*

determine *vt* (find out) déterminer; (decide on) déterminer, fixer

deterrent *n* moyen de dissuasion *m*; **∼ effect** *n* effet dissuasif *m*

detour *n* détour *m*

detriment *n*: **to the ∼ of** au détriment de, au préjudice de

de-unionization *n* UK désyndicalisation *f*

Deutschmark *n* deutschemark *m*

devalorization *n* dévalorisation *f*

devaluation *n* dévaluation *f*

devalue *vt* dévaluer

develop **1** *vt* (business, argument, market) développer; (plan, theory) concevoir, élaborer; (skill, knowledge) acquérir; (technique, procedure) mettre au point; (ties, links) établir; (system, software) développer; (land) mettre en valeur; (property) viabiliser **2** *vi* (business, area, region) se développer; (skills) s'améliorer; (problem) s'aggraver; (relationship) se développer; **∼ into** devenir

developed: **∼ country** *n* pays développé *m*; **∼ market** *n* marché exploité *m*; **∼ world** *n* pays développés *m pl*

developer *n* (of property) promoteur *m*; (Comp) développeur/-euse *m/f*

developing *adj* (area, sector, community) en expansion; **∼ country** *n* pays en voie de développement *m*

development *n* (Gen Comm) développement *m*; (Econ) développement *m*, expansion *f*, industrialisation *f*; (of prototype, new model, of product) développement *m*; (discovery) découverte *f*; (of land) mise en valeur *f*; (of site) aménagement *m*; (new event) changement *m*; **the latest ∼s** les dernières nouvelles *f pl*; **recent ∼s in Italy** les derniers événements en Italie; **await ∼s** attendre la suite des événements; **∼ aid** *n* aide au développement *f*; **∼ area** *n* UK zone à développer *f*; **∼ assistance** *n* assistance au développement *f*; **∼ costs** *n pl* coûts de développement *m pl*; **∼ director** *n* ⋯❯

administrateur/-trice chargé/-e du développement *m*/*f*; ~ **expenditure** *n* frais de développement *m pl*; ~ **management** *n* gestion du développement *f*; ~ **manager** *n* directeur/-trice du développement *m*/*f*; ~ **plan** *n* projet de développement *m*; ~ **planning** *n* planification à long terme *f*; ~ **policy** *n* politique de développement *f*; ~ **potential** *n* potentiel d'expansion *m*, potentiel de développement *m*; ~ **program** AmE, ~ **programme** BrE *n* (Pol) programme de développement *m*; ~ **project** *n* projet de développement *m*; ~ **region** *n* région à développer *f*; ~ **stage** *n* phase de développement *f*; ~ **zone** *n* UK zone à urbaniser *f*

developmental *adj* du développement

deviation *n* (Law) dérogation *f*; (Math) écart *m*, déviation *f*

device *n* (Gen Comm, Ind) dispositif *m*, appareil *m*; (Comp) périphérique *m*, unité *f*; ~ **driver** *n* pilote de périphérique *m*; ~ **mark** *n* (Patents) marque figurative *f*

devise¹ *n* (Law) legs *m*, legs de biens immobiliers *m*

devise² *vt* (Law) léguer

devisee *n* (Law) héritier/-ière testamentaire *m*/*f*, légataire *mf*

devote *vt* consacrer

dft *abbr* (▸**draft**) (Bank, Fin) traite *f*

DFT *abbr* (▸**direct fund transfer**) virement direct de fonds *m*

D-G *abbr* (▸**director-general**) DG *m*/*f* (directeur/-trice général/-e)

DHTML *abbr* (**Dynamic HyperText Mark-up Language**) DHTML *m*

DI *abbr* US (▸**Department of Industry**) ≈ ministère de l'Industrie *m*

diagnosis *n* diagnostic *m*

diagnostic¹ *adj* diagnostique; (disk, program) de diagnostic

diagnostic² *n* diagnostic *m*

diagnostics *n pl* diagnostic *m*

diagonal spread *n* (Stock) écart diagonal *m*

diagram *n* schéma *m*

dial *vt* composer; ~ **a number** composer un numéro, faire un numéro; ~ **up** établir la liaison avec

dialing AmE ▸**dialling** BrE

dialling: ~ **code** *n* BrE indicatif *m*; ~ **tone** *n* BrE tonalité *f*

dialog *n* AmE ▸**dialogue** BrE

dialogue *n* BrE dialogue *m*; ~ **box** *n* BrE fenêtre de dialogue *f*

dial tone *n* AmE tonalité *f*

dial-up: ~ **access** *n* (Comp, comms) accès par ligne commutée *m*; ~ **connection** *n* (Comp, comms) connexion par ligne téléphonique *f*

diamond investment trust *n* fonds d'investissement diamantaire *m*

diary *n* agenda *m*; **put sth in one's** ~ noter qch dans son agenda; **my** ~ **is full** je suis très pris

dictate *vt* dicter

dictionary *n* dictionnaire *m*

die *vi* mourir; ~ **intestate** mourir intestat

diesel oil *n* gas-oil *m*, gazole *m*

differ *vi* différer

difference *n* (dissimilarity) différence *f*; (disagreement) différend *m*; **make up the** ~ combler l'écart, rajouter la différence; **settle one's** ~**s** régler ses différends; **a** ~ **of opinion** une divergence d'opinion; ~**s within sth** divergences dans qch

differences *n pl* (Stock) soldes *m pl*

differential *n* différentiel *m*, écart *m*; ~ **analysis** *n* analyse différentielle *f*, analyse modulée *f*; ~ **pay** *n* salaire différentiel *m*, écart des salaires *m*; ~ **price** *n* prix différentiel *m*; ~ **pricing** *n* fixation de prix différentiels *f*; (S&M) différenciation des prix *f*; ~ **wage** *n* écart des salaires *m*

differentiate *vt* différencier; ~ **between** faire la différence entre

differentiated: ~ **goods** *n pl* produits différenciés *m pl*; ~ **marketing** *n* marketing de différenciation *m*; ~ **products** *n pl* produits différenciés *m pl*

differentiation *n* différenciation *f*; **product** ~ différenciation du produit *f*

differentiator *n* élément de différenciation *m*

difficult *adj* difficile

difficulty *n* difficulté *f*; **have** ~ **(in) doing sth** avoir du mal à faire qch; **run into difficulties** se heurter à des difficultés

diffusion diffusion *f*

dig *vt* ~ **one's heels in** (infrml) se braquer; ~ **into** (past) fouiller dans; ~ **out** (information, document) dénicher (infrml); ~ **up** (information, facts) dénicher (infrml)

digerati *n pl* cyberélite *f*, cyber-intellectuels *m pl*

digit *n* chiffre *m*; **a three-**~ **number** un nombre à trois chiffres

digital *adj* numérique; ~**-analog** *adj* numérique-analogique; ~ **audiotape** *n* cassette audionumérique *f*; ~ **cash** *n* argent électronique *m*; ~ **certificate** *n* certificat électronique *m*; ~ **convergence** *n* convergence numérique *f*; ~ **divide** *n* fossé numérique *m*, fracture numérique *f*; ~ **economy** *n* économie numérique *f*; ~ **marketplace** *n* place de marché électronique *f*; ~ **signature** *n* signature électronique *f*

digitization *n* numérisation *f*

digitize *vt* numériser

dilution *n* dilution *f*; ~ **of equity** (Stock) dilution de l'avoir des actionnaires *f*, dilution du bénéfice par action *f*; ∼ **of labor** AmE, **of labour** BrE adjonction de main-d'œuvre non qualifiée *f*

dime *n* US pièce de dix cents *f*

diminish 1 *vt* (resources, quantity, popularity) diminuer; (strength, influence, authority) amoindrir
2 *vi* (numbers, influence, authority) diminuer; (strength, influence, authority) s'amoindrir

diminishing *adj* (number) de moins en moins élevé; (funds, resources) de moins en moins important; (influence) de moins en moins fort

diminishing returns rendements décroissants *m pl*; **law of** ∼ loi des rendements décroissants *f*; ∼ **to scale** rendements d'échelle décroissants *m pl*

dinar *n* dinar *m*

dining car *n* wagon-restaurant *m*

dinkie *n* (▸**double income no kids**) *homme ou femme qui vit en couple sans enfants avec deux revenus*

dip[1] *n* (in profits, sales, rates) baisse *f*

dip[2] *vi* (profits) fléchir; (price, value, rate) baisser, descendre

Dip. *abbr* (▸**diploma**) diplôme *m*

DipCom *abbr* (▸**Diploma of Commerce**) diplôme d'études commerciales *m*

diploma *n* diplôme *m*; **a** ∼ **in management** un diplôme de gestion; **have a** ∼ être diplômé

diplomacy *n* diplomatie *f*

Diploma: ∼ **of Commerce** *n* diplôme d'études commerciales *m*; ∼ **in Industrial Management** *n* diplôme de gestion des entreprises *m*; ∼ **in Public Administration** *n* diplôme d'administration publique *m*

diplomatic *adj* (relations, passport, immunity) diplomatique; (remark) plein de tact; ∼ **bag** *n* BrE, ∼ **pouch** *n* AmE valise diplomatique *f*; ∼ **corps** *n* corps diplomatique *m*

Diplomatic Service *n* UK ≈ diplomatie *f*

dir. *abbr* (▸**direct**) direct

direct[1] *adj* (route, appeal, approach, control, impact) direct; (person) franc/franche; **be** ∼ **with sb** être franc/franche avec qn

direct[2] *adv* (speak, deal) directement; **fly** ∼ prendre un vol direct

direct[3] *vt* (company, project, economy, organization) diriger; (campaign) cibler; (appeal, remark) adresser; (funds) affecter; (Media) (show, film, documentary) réaliser; ∼ **sb to do** (instruct) ordonner à qn de faire; **a campaign** ∼**ed at teenagers** une campagne qui vise les adolescents, une campagne qui cible les adolescents

direct: ∼ **access** *n* (Comp) accès direct *m*; ∼ **action advertising** *n* publicité directe *f*, publicité par correspondance *f*, publicité par coupon-réponse *f*; ∼ **bill of lading** *n* connaissement direct *m*; ∼ **call** *n* appel automatique *m*; ∼ **clearer** *n* membre

adhérent *m*; ∼ **clearing member** *n* membre adhérent *m*; ∼ **cost** *n* charge directe *f*, coût direct *m*; ∼ **costing** *n* méthode des coûts directs *f*; ∼ **debit** *n* prélèvement automatique *m*, prélèvement autorisé *m*; ∼ **dialing** AmE, ∼ **dialling** BrE *n* téléphone automatique *m*; ∼ **financial leasing agreement** *n* contrat de location-financement *m*; ∼ **flight** *n* vol direct *m*; ∼ **fund transfer** *n* virement direct de fonds *m*; ∼ **liability** *n* responsabilité directe *f*; ∼ **line** *n* ligne directe *f*; ∼ **mail** *n* publicité directe *f*, publipostage *m*; ∼ **mailing** *n* publicité directe *f*, publipostage *m*; ∼ **mail shot** *n* mailing *m*; ∼ **marketing** *n* marketing direct *m*; ∼ **overhead** *n* charge directe de structure *f*; ∼ **payment** *n* (Econ) (grants) paiement direct *m*; ∼ **report** *n* (HRM) subordonné/-e direct/-e *m/f*; ∼ **response advertising** *n* publicité à réponse directe *f*, publicité par correspondance *f*, publicité par coupon-réponse *f*; ∼ **route** *n* (Transp) itinéraire direct *m*; ∼ **sale** *n* vente directe *f*; ∼ **selling** *n* vente directe *f*; ∼ **taxation** *n* imposition directe *f*, contributions directes *f pl*; ∼ **transhipment** *n* transbordement direct *m*; ∼ **yield** *n* (Stock) rendement direct *m*

directed: ∼ **interview** *n* interview dirigée *f*; ∼ **verdict** *n* *verdict recommandé au jury par le juge*

direction *n* (taken by company, career) orientation *f*; (route) direction *f*; (of interest rates) orientation *f*, tendance *f*; (Media) (of film, show, documentary) réalisation *f*; (Mgmnt) direction *f*; (instruction) instruction *f*; **a change of** ∼ un changement d'orientation; **lack** ∼ (person) manquer d'objectifs; **under the** ∼ **of** sous la direction de; **a step in the right** ∼ un pas dans la bonne direction; ∼ **finder** *n* (Transp) radiogoniomètre *m*

directions *n pl* (instructions) instructions *f pl*; (for route) indications *f pl*; ∼ **for use** mode d'emploi *m*; **ask for** ∼**s** demander son chemin; **give sb** ∼**s** donner des indications à qn

directive *n* directive *f*

directly *adv* directement; ∼ **related to** directement lié à; ∼ **responsible to** directement responsable vis-à-vis de

director *n* (of company, organization) directeur/-trice *m/f*, dirigeant/-e *m/f*; (board member) administrateur/-trice *m/f*; (of project, investigation) responsable *mf*; (Media) réalisateur/-trice *m/f*; ∼**-general** *n* directeur général *m*, président-directeur général *m*; ∼ **of communications** *n* directeur/-trice des communications *m/f*, dircom *m* (infml); ∼ **of public relations** *n* chef du service des relations publiques *m*, directeur/-trice des relations publiques *m/f*

directorate *n* conseil d'administration *m*

Director of Public Prosecutions *n* ⋯⋗

UK ≈ procureur de la République *m*

directors': ～ **fees** *n pl* jetons de présence *m pl*; ～ **report** *n* rapport annuel *m*; ～ **shares** *n* actions réservées aux membres du conseil d'administration *f pl*

directorship *n* (of organization, institution) direction *f*; (in company) poste d'administrateur *m*; **hold a** ～ occuper le poste d'administrateur

directory *n* (Gen Comm, Comp) répertoire *m*; (telephone listings) annuaire *m*; ～ **assistance** *n* AmE, ～ **enquiries** *n pl* BrE, ～ **information** *n* AmE (service *m* des) renseignements *m pl*

dirham *n* dirham *m*

dirty *adj* (contest) déloyal; ～ **bill of lading** *n* connaissement avec réserves *m*, connaissement brut *m*; ～ **float** *n* flottement impur *m*; ～ **tricks campaign** *n* campagne diffamatoire *f*

disability *n* invalidité *f*; (of employee) handicap *m*; ～ **benefit** *n* prestation pour incapacité *f*, rente d'invalidité *f*; ～ **cover** *n* assurance invalidité *f*; ～ **insurance** *n* assurance incapacité *f*, assurance invalidité *f*

disable *vt* (option) désactiver

disabled *adj* (person) handicapé; (Comp) (option) désactivé; ～ **workers** *n pl* travailleurs handicapés *m pl*

disablement *n* invalidité *f*; ～ **pension** *n* pension d'invalidité *f*

disadvantage *n* inconvénient *m*, désavantage *m*; **be at a** ～ être désavantagé; **put sb at a** ～ désavantager qn

disadvantaged *adj* désavantagé

disadvantageous *adj* désavantageux/ -euse, défavorable

disaffirm *vt* défaire, dénoncer

disagio *n* courtage *m*

disagree *vi* (person) ne pas être d'accord, être en désaccord; (facts, accounts) ne pas concorder; ～ **with** (plan, proposal) s'opposer à; (person) ne pas être d'accord avec

disagreement *n* (dispute, argument) différend *m*; (difference of opinion) désaccord *m*; **be in** ～ **with sb** être en désaccord avec qn; **there was** ～ **over the method** il y a eu un désaccord sur le choix de méthode

disallow *vt* ne pas accepter, rejeter

disappointing *adj* décevant

disarm *vti* désarmer

disarmament *n* désarmement *m*

disaster *n* catastrophe *f*; (long-term) désastre *m*; **financial** ～ désastre financier; **be heading for** ～ courir à la catastrophe; ～ **clause** *n* (Ins) clause de catastrophe *f*, clause de sauvegarde *f*; ～ **recovery** *n* reprise d'activités après un sinistre *f*

disastrous *adj* (results, consequences) désastreux/-euse

disastrously *adv* (turn out, end) d'une

manière désastreuse; **go** ～ **wrong** tourner à la catastrophe

disbursable *adj* déboursable

disburse *vt* débourser

disbursement *n* (sum) débours *m*; (act) déboursement *m*

disc. *abbr* (▸**discount**) discompte *m*, esc. (escompte)

discharge¹ *n* (repayment) acquittement *m*, paiement *m*, règlement *m*; (of bankrupt) réhabilitation *f*; (of contract) accomplissement *m*; (of prisoner) libération *f*; (of waste) déversement *m*; **in the** ～ **of one's duties** dans l'exercice de ses fonctions; ～ **at sea** rejet en mer *m*; ～ **of bankruptcy** réhabilitation de faillite *f*; ～ **in bankruptcy** réhabilitation du failli *f*; ～ **of mortgage** libération d'hypothèque *f*; ～ **port** port de déchargement *m*

discharge² *vt* (bill) acquitter; (debt) acquitter, régler; (employee) renvoyer; (obligation) remplir, accomplir; (bankrupt) réhabiliter; (prisoner) libérer; (cargo) décharger; (duty) s'acquitter de; (waste) décharger; (liquid waste) déverser; ～ **one's responsibilities** assumer ses responsabilités

discharging *n* (unloading) déchargement *m*

disciplinary *adj* disciplinaire; ～ **measures** *n pl* mesures disciplinaires *f pl*; ～ **procedure** *n* procédure disciplinaire *f*

discipline¹ *n* discipline *f*

discipline² *vt* discipliner, prendre des sanctions contre

disciplined *adj* (person, manner) discipliné; (approach) méthodique; ～ **movement** *n* (Transp) mouvement planifié *m*

disclaim *vt* répudier

disclaimer *n* (Gen Comm) démenti *m*; (Ins) démenti *m*, renonciation à un droit *f*; (Law) désistement *m*, renonciation *f*; **issue a** ～ publier un démenti

disclose *vt* divulguer, révéler

disclosed reserves *n pl* réserves déclarées *f pl*

disclosure *n* (Gen Comm) révélation *f*; (publication) publication *f*; (Stock) publication *f*; ～ **of information** divulgation d'information *f*; ～ **requirement** *n* obligation d'information *f*; (Stock) exigence de publication *f*

discomfort index *n* (Econ) indice d'inconfort *m*

disconnect ① *vt* (appliance) débrancher; (telephone, electricity) couper ② *vi* (Comp) se déconnecter

discontinue *vt* (service) supprimer; (production) arrêter; ～**d line** fin de série *f*

discount¹ *n* (on papers, bills) escompte *m*; (between currencies) déport *m*; (on price, goods) réduction *f*, rabais *m*, remise *f*; (on shares) décote *f*; **at a** ～ (Fin) avec un déport, à escompte; (Stock) avec une décote, à escompte; **buy sth at a** ～ acheter qch au rabais; **at a two per cent** ~ avec une décote de deux pour cent; **give sb a** ~ consentir une remise à qn; ~ **for cash** escompte de caisse *m* (pour paiement au comptant); ~ **bill** *n* billet à escompte *m*; ~ **bond** *n* obligation au-dessous du pair *f*, obligation à escompte *f*; ~ **broker** *n* courtier exécutant *m*; ~ **card** *n* carte de réduction *f*; ~ **center** AmE, ~ **centre** BrE *n* magasin discompte *m*, magasin discount *m*; ~ **charges** *n pl* frais d'escompte *m pl*; ~ **house** *n* magasin discompte *m*, magasin discount *m*; ~ **market** *n* (Fin) marché d'escompte *m*; ~ **price** *n* prix discompte *m*, prix discompté *m*; ~ **rate** *n* taux d'escompte *m*; ~ **sale** *n* vente au rabais *f*; ~ **selling** *n* vente au rabais *f*; ~ **shop** *n* BrE, ~ **store** *n* magasin discompte *m*, magasin discount *m*; ~ **travel** *n* voyages à tarif réduit *m pl*; ~ **window** *n* AmE prises en pension *f pl*; ~ **yield** *n* (Stock) *rendement d'une valeur vendue en dessous du pair*

discount[2] *vt* (Bank) (bill) escompter; (sum of money) faire une remise de; (goods) solder; (Acc) actualiser; (idea, claim) écarter; (advice, recommendations) ne pas tenir compte de

discounted: ~ **bill** *n* effet escompté *m*; ~ **bond** *n* obligation au-dessous du pair *f*, obligation à escompte *f*; ~ **cash flow** *n* valeur actualisée nette *f*; ~ **loan** *n* prêt escompté *m*; ~ **present value** *n* valeur actualisée *f*; ~ **share price** *n* prix actualisé de l'action *m*

discounter *n* discompteur *m*

discounting *n* (Acc) actualisation *f*; ~ **of bills** *n* BrE, ~ **of notes** *n* AmE escompte d'effets de commerce *m*

discourage *vt* décourager

discovery *n* découverte *f*; (Law) communication de pièces *f*

discrepancy *n* désaccord *m*, écart *m*

discrete *adj* (Gen Comm) distinct; ~ **variable** *n* variable discrète *f*

discretion *n* discrétion *f*; **at our** ~ à notre discrétion; **at the** ~ **of** au bon vouloir de, à la discrétion de; **use one's** ~ agir à sa discrétion; **leave sth to sb's** ~ laisser qch à la discrétion de qn

discretionary *adj* discrétionnaire; ~ **account** *n* clientèle privée gérée *f*, compte discrétionnaire *m*; ~ **authority** *n* pouvoir discrétionnaire *m*; ~ **cost** *n* coût discrétionnaire *m*; ~ **limit** *n* limite discrétionnaire *f*; ~ **policy** *n* politique discrétionnaire *f*; ~ **share** *n* part discrétionnaire *f*; ~ **spending power** *n* pouvoir d'achat discrétionnaire *m*

discriminate *vt* discriminer; ~ **against** établir une discrimination envers; ~ **in favour of** établir une discrimination en faveur de

discrimination *n* discrimination *f*; **no** ~ **factor** facteur de non-discrimination *m*; **racial/sexual** ~ discrimination raciale/

sexuelle *f*

discuss *vt* discuter de; (in writing) examiner

discussion *n* discussion *f*; (in public) débat *m*; **under** ~ en cours de discussion, soumis à discussion; **bring sth up for** ~ (topic) à discuter; ~ **document** *n*, ~ **paper** *n* avant-projet *m*; ~ **group** *n* forum de discussion *m*; ~ **thread** *n* (Comp) fil de discussion *m*

diseconomy *n* déséconomie *f*; ~ **of scale** déséconomie d'échelle *f*

disembark *vti* débarquer

disembarkation *n* débarquement *m*

disequilibrium *n* déséquilibre *m*

dishonest *adj* malhonnête

dishonor *n* AmE ▶**dishonour** BrE

dishonored AmE ▶**dishonoured** BrE

dishonour[1] *n* BrE (Bank) défaut d'acceptation de paiement *m*

dishonour[2] *vt* BrE (cheque) ne pas honorer

dishonoured: ~ **bill** *n* BrE effet refusé *m*; ~ **bill of exchange** *n* BrE traite impayée *f*; ~ **cheque** *n* BrE chèque impayé *m*

disincentive *n* désincitation *f*; **act as a** ~ **to do** ne pas inciter à faire

disinflation *n* désinflation *f*

disinformation *n* désinformation *f*

disintegration *n* (Gen Comm) désintégration *f*; (Econ, Pol) désincorporation *f*

disintermediate [1] *vt* procéder à une désintermédiation de [2] *vi* procéder à une désintermédiation

disintermediation *n* désintermédiation *f*

disinvest *vi* désinvestir

disinvestment *n* désinvestissement *m*

disk *n* disque *m*; **on** ~ sur disque; ~ **drive** *n* lecteur de disques *m*, unité de disques *f*; ~ **operating system** *n* (Comp) système d'exploitation à disques *m*; ~ **space** *n* espace disque *m*

diskette *n* disquette *f*, disque souple *m*

dismantle *vt* (organization, system) démanteler; (equipment) démonter

dismantling *n* (of barriers, system, organization) démantèlement *m*; (of equipment) démontage *m*

dismiss *vt* (employee) licencier, renvoyer; (Law) (appeal, claim) rejeter; (suggestion) écarter; (possibility) exclure; **the case was** ~**ed** il y a eu non-lieu

dismissal *n* (of employee) licenciement *m*, renvoi *m*; (Law) (of appeal, claim) rejet *m*

disparity *n* disparité *f*, écart *m*

dispatch[1] *n* expédition *f*, envoi *m*; ~ **bay** *n* quai de chargement *m*; ~ **department** *n* service d'expédition *m*; ~ **note** *n* bordereau d'expédition *m*

dispatch[2] *vt* (goods) acheminer, expédier; (problem) régler; (work) expédier

dispatcher *n* expéditeur/-trice *m/f*

dispatching n acheminement m, expédition f

dispensation n dispense f

displacement n (of staff, workers) déplacement m; ~ **loaded** n, ~ **tonnage** n déplacement en charge m

display¹ n (Comp) affichage m, visualisation f; (screen) écran m; (of small goods) étalage m; (of large goods, equipment) exposition f; (for decoration, viewing) exposition f; (sign) panneau d'affichage m; **be on** ~ être exposé; ~ **advertisement** n grande annonce f; ~ **monitor** n écran de visualisation m; ~ **stand** n (for books, goods) présentoir m; ~ **window** n vitrine f

display² vt (Comp) afficher, visualiser; (price, details) afficher; (goods) présenter, exposer; **the** ~**ed price** le prix affiché

disposable adj (packaging, product) jetable; ~ **funds** n pl fonds disponibles m pl, disponibilités f pl; ~ **goods** n pl biens de consommation non durables m pl; ~ **income** n revenu disponible m

disposables n pl articles jetables m pl

disposal n (Fin, Law, Stock) cession f; (Tax) disposition f; (sale) vente f; **be at the** ~ **of sb** être à la disposition de qn; **have sth at one's** ~ avoir qch à sa disposition; **place sth at sb's** ~ mettre qch à la disposition de qn; **all the means at my** ~ tous les moyens dont je dispose; ~ **facility** n déchetterie f; ~ **value** n valeur de cession f

dispose: ~ **of** vt (stock) écouler; (assets, securities) céder; (property, goods) vendre; (waste) se débarrasser de; (evidence) détruire

dispossess vt (Law) déposséder; (Prop) déposséder, exproprier

dispute¹ n conflit m, désaccord m; ~ **procedure** n procédure de règlement des conflits f; ~ **resolution** n résolution de conflit f

dispute² vt (claim, will) contester

disruption n (to supply) interruption f; (to service, plans) perturbation f

dissaving n désépargne f

disseminate vt (ideas, views) propager; (information, details) diffuser

dissemination n (of ideas, views) propagation f; (of information) diffusion f

dissolution n (of partnership, parliament) dissolution f

dissolve vt (partnership, parliament) dissoudre

distance learning n apprentissage à distance m, télé-enseignement m

distilling n distillation f

distinction n (difference) différence f, distinction f; (outstanding quality) distinction f; **make a** ~ **between** distinguer entre, faire la différence entre; **with** ~ avec mérite

distinctive adj distinctif/-ive

distinctiveness n caractère distinctif m

distinguish vt distinguer

distinguished adj remarquable, éminent

distort vt (figures) fausser; (facts) dénaturer; (truth) déformer

distortion n (of price, figures) distorsion f; (of fact, truth) déformation f

distraint n saisie f, saisie-exécution f

distribute vt (load, burden, task) répartir; (goods, supplies, money, information) distribuer

distributed: ~ **computing** n informatique répartie f; ~ **database** n base de données répartie f

distribution n (of wealth, capital) répartition f; (of money, information, resources) distribution f; (of estate) partage m, répartition f; (by manufacturer, supplier) distribution f; (Stock) placement m; (of load) répartition f; (in statistics) repartition f; ~ **allowance** n (S&M) remise de distribution f; ~ **area** n (Stock) fourchette de variation du cours f; ~ **center** AmE, ~ **centre** BrE n centre de distribution m; ~ **chain** n chaîne de distribution f; ~ **channel** n canal de distribution m; ~ **costs** n pl frais de distribution m pl; ~ **depot** n dépôt de distribution m; ~ **list** n liste de distribution f; ~ **manager** n chef de la distribution m; ~ **network** n circuit de commercialisation m, circuit de distribution m, réseau de distribution m; ~ **of risks** n répartition des risques f; ~ **of wealth** n répartition des richesses f

distributor n distributeur m

district n (in town) quartier m; (administrative sector) district m; (region) région f; ~ **attorney** n US ≈ procureur de la République m; ~ **court** n US tribunal fédéral de première instance m; ~ **manager** n directeur/-trice régional/-e m/f

District Council n UK (Admin) conseil de district

disutility n désutilité f

div. abbr (▸**dividend**) div. (dividende)

diverge vi (exchange rates, opinions) diverger

divergence n (of opinions, results, futures, price) divergence f; ~ **indicator** n (Econ) (EU) indicateur de divergence m

divergent adj (views, reasoning) divergent; ~ **thinking** n avis divergent m

diverse adj différent, varié

diversification n diversification f; ~ **strategy** n stratégie de diversification f

diversified company n entreprise diversifiée f

diversify 1 vt diversifier; ~ **risk** diversifier les risques

2 vi se diversifier; ~ **into cosmetics** se diversifier en fabriquant des produits de beauté

diversity n diversité f

divest vt ~ **sb of sth** dépouiller qn de qch; ~ **oneself of** se défaire de

divestiture n dessaisissement m,

dépossession *f*

divestment *n* scission d'actif *f*

divide *vt* diviser; ~ **into plots** lotir; ~ **up** partager

divided *adj* (society, body) divisé; (interests, opinions) divergent; **be ~ on an issue** être divisé sur une question

dividend *n* (Fin) dividende *m*; (advantage, bonus) avantage *m*; **pay ~s** rapporter; ~ **announcement** *n* déclaration de dividende *f*; ~ **bond** *n* obligation participante *f*; ~ **cover** *n* taux de couverture du dividende *m*; ~ **income** *n* revenu de dividende *m*; ~ **net** *n* dividende net *m*; ~ **payable** *n* dividende à payer *m*; ~ **per share** *n* dividende par action *m*; ~ **reinvestment** *n* réinvestissement des dividendes *m*; ~ **tax** *n* impôt sur les dividendes *m*; ~ **warrant** *n* ordonnance de paiement *f*; ~ **yield** *n* rendement boursier *m*, rendement des actions *m*

division *n* (branch, sector) division *f*; (department) service *m*; (of market) segmentation *f*; (sharing) répartition *f*; (of several items) distribution *f*; **sales ~** service des ventes *m*; ~ **head** *n* chef de secteur *m*, chef de division *m*; ~ **of labor** AmE, ~ **of labour** BrE division du travail *f*; ~ **manager** *n* chef de division *m*, chef de département *m*; ~ **sign** *n* signe de division *m*

divisional: ~ **head** *n* chef de division *m*, chef de département *m*; ~ **management** *n* gestion cellulaire *f*, gestion par département *f*; ~ **manager** *n* chef de division *m*, chef de secteur *m*

divisionalization *n* sectorisation *f*

DIY *abbr* (▸**do-it-yourself**) bricolage *m*

DLO *abbr* (**Dead Letter Office**) bureau des rebuts *m*

D/N *abbr* (▸**debit note**) note de débit *f*

DNS *abbr* (▸**domain name system**) système d'adressage par domaines *m*

DOC credit *n* (▸**documentary credit**) crédit documentaire *m*

dock *n* (Transp) bassin *m*, dock *m*; UK (Law) banc des accusés *m*; ~ **charges** *n pl* droits de bassin *m pl*; ~ **dues** *n pl* droits de bassin *m pl*; ~ **operations** *n pl* opérations portuaires *f pl*; ~ **warrant** *n* certificat d'entrepôt *m*

docker *n* BrE docker *m*, débardeur *m*

docking *n* amarrage *m*

docks *n pl* docks *m pl*

doctor *n* médecin *m*

doctorate *n* doctorat *m*

document¹ *n* document *m*; **identity/ insurance ~s** papiers d'identité/d'assurance *m pl*; ~ **feeder** *n* dispositif d'alimentation de document *m*; ~ **format** *n* format de document *m*; ~ **holder** *n* classeur *m*; ~ **reader** *n* lecteur de documents *m*; ~ **retrieval system** *n* système de recherche

documentaire *m*; ~ **wallet** *n* chemise (en carton) *f*

document² *vt* (claim, case) documenter; (describe) décrire

documentary¹ *adj* documentaire

documentary² *n* documentaire *m*

documentary: ~ **credit** *n* crédit documentaire *m*; ~ **draft** *n* traite documentaire *f*; ~ **evidence** *n* preuve documentaire, preuve écrite *f*; ~ **fraud** *n* fraude documentaire *f*

documentation *n* documentation *f*

documents: ~ **against acceptance** *n pl* documents contre acceptation *m pl*; ~ **against payment** *n pl* documents contre paiement *m pl*; ~ **of title** *n pl* titre de propriété *m*

DOD *abbr* US (▸**Department of Defense**) ≈ ministère de la Défense nationale *m*

DOE *abbr* US (▸**Department of Energy**) ministère de l'Énergie *m*

dog *n* (S&M) poids mort *m*; ~ **fund** *n* fonds d'investissement peu performant *m*

DOH *abbr* UK (▸**Department of Health**) ≈ ministère de la Santé *m*

DOI *abbr* US (▸**Department of Industry**) ministère de l'Industrie *m*

do-it-yourself *n* bricolage *m*

dol. *abbr* (▸**dollar**) dol. (dollar)

doldrums: **in the ~** dans le marasme

dole¹ *n* BrE (infrml) allocation chômage *f*, indemnité de chômage *f*; **on the ~** au chômage; ~ **office** *n* bureau d'aide sociale *m*

dole²: ~ **out** *vt* distribuer

dollar *n* dollar *m*; ~ **area** *n* zone dollar *f*; ~ **bid** *n* (options) offre en dollars *f*; ~ **drain** *n* déficit en dollars du commerce extérieur des États-Unis; ~ **gap** *n* pénurie de dollars *f*; ~ **premium** *n* (options) prime en dollars *f*; ~ **rate** *n* taux du dollar *m*; ~ **sign** *n* symbole du dollar *m*; ~ **standard** *n* étalon dollar *m*; ~ **transaction** *n* opération en dollars *f*; ~ **value** *n* (Stock) valeur de dollar *f*

domain *n* (Comp, Math) domaine *m*; ~ **name** *n* nom de domaine *m*; ~ **name system** *n* système d'adressage par domaines *m*

domestic *adj* (Econ) intérieur, national; (Transp) intérieur; ~ **agreement** *n* UK accord interne *m*; ~ **airline** *n* ligne aérienne intérieure *f*; ~ **business** *n* affaires intérieures *f pl*; ~ **consumption** *n* (of country) consommation intérieure *f*; (of household) consommation ménagère *f*; ~ **demand** *n* demande intérieure *f*; ~ **economy** *n* système économique national *m*; ~ **flight** *n* vol intérieur *m*; ~ **industry** *n* industrie intérieure *f*; ~ **investments** *n pl* investissements nationaux *m pl*; ~ **issue** *n* (Stock) émission de titres nationaux *f*; ~ **market** *n* marché intérieur *m*; ~ **money market** *n* marché monétaire national *m*; ⋯⟶

∼ **output** n production nationale f; ∼ **sales** n pl ventes sur le marché intérieur f pl; ∼ **trade** n commerce intérieur m; ∼ **waste** n déchets ménagers m pl

domicile n (Law) domicile m

domiciled adj domicilié

dominant adj dominant; ∼ **firm** n entreprise dominante f, firme dominante f; ∼ **position** n position dominante f

dominate vt (market) dominer

donate vt faire un don de

donated: ∼ **stock** n action rendue gracieusement à la société; ∼ **surplus** n (Stock) crédit au bénéfice de l'actionnaire provenant d'une donation d'actions

donation n don m

donee n (Tax) donataire mf

dong n dōng m

dongle n (Comp) clé électronique de protection f, dongle m

donor n donateur/-trice m/f; ∼ **aid** n aide au développement f; ∼ **country** n pays bailleur de fonds m, pays donateur m

don't know n (in a survey) sans opinion mf

doomwatcher n prophète de malheur m

door n ∼s open at (for exhibition, conference) ouverture à; **open the** ∼ **to sth** ouvrir la voie à qch; **get a foot in the** ∼ mettre un pied dans la place; **this will open** ∼s **for us** cela va nous ouvrir des portes; **sell** ∼ **to** ∼ vendre à domicile

door-to-door adj (service, delivery) porte à porte, à domicile; ∼ **salesman** n démarcheur à domicile m; ∼ **selling** n démarchage m, porte à porte m, vente à domicile f

dormant: ∼ **account** n compte inactif m; ∼ **balance** n solde inactif mf

dormitory suburb n BrE ville-dortoir f

DOS® abbr (Comp) (▶**disk operating system**) DOS® m (système d'exploitation à disques)

dossier n dossier m

dot n point m; ∼**-matrix printer** n imprimante matricielle f

dot-com¹ adj (era, revolution) Internet; (millionaire) de l'Internet; (shares) de sociétés point com, de dot-coms

dot-com² n société point com f, point com f, dot-com f

dot-corp n dot-corp f, grande société s'ouvrant à Internet

dots per inch n pl (typeface) points par pouce m pl

dotted line n pointillé m

double¹ vt (amount, price) doubler; (number) multiplier par deux

double² adj double; **be in** ∼ **figures** (inflation, growth) franchir la barre de 10%; **have** ∼ **standards** faire deux poids deux mesures; ∼ **income no kids** homme ou femme vivant en couple sans enfants avec deux revenus

double: ∼ **account** n compte double m; ∼ **declining balance** n amortissement dégressif double m; ∼**-density disk** n disquette double densité f; ∼**-digit inflation** n inflation à deux chiffres f; ∼ **dip** n rechute f; ∼**-entry accounting** n, ∼**-entry bookkeeping** n comptabilité en partie double f; ∼ **insurance** n assurance cumulative f, double assurance f; ∼ **manning** n duplication de main-d'œuvre f; ∼ **room** n chambre double f, chambre pour deux personnes f; ∼**-sided disk** n disque double face m; ∼ **space** n double interligne m; ∼ **spacing** n double interligne m; ∼ **spread** n publicité sur double page f; ∼ **taxation** n double imposition f; ∼ **time** n (pay) heure comptée double f

double-book vi surbooker

double-check vt vérifier à nouveau

double-click¹ n double clic m

double-click² vi double-cliquer, cliquer deux fois

double-income adj (family, household) à deux revenus

doubtful adj (past, activity) douteux/-euse; (future, result, argument, evidence) incertain; (person) sceptique; ∼ **debt** n créance douteuse f; ∼ **debtors** n pl débiteurs douteux m pl

dowager n (Law) douairière f

dower n (Law) douaire m

Dow Jones n US (Fin) Dow Jones m; ∼ **average** n indice Dow Jones m; ∼ **index** n indice Dow Jones m; ∼ **industrial average** n indice Dow Jones des 30 valeurs boursières les plus importantes m

down¹ adj **be** ∼ (Econ) être en baisse; (Comp) être en panne

down² vt ∼ **tools** cesser le travail; (strike) se mettre en grève

down: ∼ **arrow** n (on keyboard) flèche verticale f; ∼**-market** adj bas de gamme; ∼**-market product** n produit bas de gamme m; ∼**-market service** n service bas de gamme m; ∼ **payment** n acompte m; ∼ **time** n (Comp, Ind) durée d'immobilisation f, temps mort m

downgrade vt (job) déclasser; (employee) rétrograder; (task, occupation) dévaloriser

downgrading n (of employee) rétrogradation f; (of job) déclassement m; (of task, occupation) dévalorisation f

downhill adv: **go** ∼ (business) aller mal, péricliter

download¹ n téléchargement m

download² vt télécharger

downloadable adj téléchargeable

downscale vt déclasser

downshift vi choisir un mode de vie moins lucratif mais moins stressant

downshifter n personne qui choisit un

mode de vie moins lucratif mais moins stressant

downside *n* n inconvénient *m*, désavantage *m*; **on the ~** côté désavantages; **~ risk** *n* évaluation du risque de baisse *f*

downsize¹ *n* compression de personnel *f*

downsize² *vt* (workforce) dégraisser

downsizing *n* dégraissage *m*, réduction d'effectifs *f*

downstream *adv* en aval; **~ industry** *n* industrie en aval *f*

downswing *n* baisse *f*, ralentissement *m*, repli *m*

downtrend *n* tendance à la baisse *f*

downturn *n* (Econ) déclin *m*; (in profits, consumer spending) baisse *f*; (Stock) (in the market) repli *m*

downward: ~ communication *n* (Mgmnt) communication avec la base *f*; **~ compatibility** *n* compatibilité descendante *f*; **~ movement** *n* (Stock) mouvement vers le bas *m*, tendance à la baisse *f*; **~ pressure** *n* (on currency, interest rates) pression inflationniste *f*; **~ revision** *n* révision à la baisse *f*; **~ spiral** *n* (in wages, prices) descente en spirale *f*, spirale descendante *f*; **~ trend** *n* (Stock) mouvement à la baisse *m*, tendance baissière *f*

downwards *adv* vers le bas, à la baisse

downzoning *n* (Prop) rezonage *m*

dowry *n* dot *f*

doz. *abbr* (▸**dozen**) douz. (douzaine)

dozen *n* douzaine *f*

DP *abbr* (▸**documents against payment**) DP (documents contre paiement)

dpi *abbr* (▸**dots per inch**) (Comp) ppp *m pl* (points par pouce)

DPP *abbr* UK (Law) (▸**Director of Public Prosecutions**) ≈ procureur de la République *m*

DPR *abbr* (▸**director of public relations**) chef du service des relations publiques *m*, directeur/-trice des relations publiques *m/f*

Dr *abbr* (▸**Doctor**) Dr (docteur)

drachma *n* drachme *m*

draft¹ *n* (Bank) traite *f*; (of contract, document) première ébauche *f*, avant-projet *m*; (Fin) traite *f*; (of letter, speech) brouillon *m*; (Law) projet d'acte *m*; **make a ~ on a bank** tirer sur une banque; **~ agreement** *n* protocole d'accord *m*; **~ amendment** *n* amendement provisoire *m*; **~ budget** *n* projet de budget *m*; **~ clause** *n* clause provisoire *f*; **~ contract** *n* projet de contrat *m*; **~ directive** *n* avant-projet de directive *m*, directive préliminaire *f*; **~ project** *n* avant-projet *m*, pré-projet *m*; **~ prospectus** *n* (Stock) projet de prospectus *m*; **~ report** *n* avant-projet de rapport *m*; **~ resolution** *n* projet de résolution *m*; **~ ruling** *n* décision préliminaire *f*; **~ stage** *n* phase provisoire *f*, phase préliminaire *f*

draft² *vt* (report) rédiger, établir; (plan) esquisser, dresser; (contract) rédiger, dresser

drag *vt* (Comp) faire glisser, déplacer

drag and drop *n* glisser-déposer *m*

dragon *n* (Econ) dragon *m*

drain *n* (of people, money, skills, resources) hémorragie *f*; **be a ~ on** (funds, profits, resources) représenter une ponction sur

draining reserves *n pl* ponctionnement des réserves *m*

DRAM *abbr* (▸**dynamic random access memory**) (Comp) RAM dynamique *f*

drastic *adj* (policy, move) draconien/-ienne; (reduction) drastique; (effect) catastrophique; **~ cut** *n* coupe sombre *f*; **~ measures** *n* mesures draconiennes *f pl*

draw¹ *n* (act of drawing) tirage au sort *m*; (lottery) loterie *f*; (attraction) attraction *f*

draw² *vt* (cheque, bill) tirer; (money) retirer; (stock) entamer; (benefit, allowance) percevoir; (pension, wages) toucher; (Law, Pol) rédiger; **~ a check** AmE, **~ a cheque** BrE faire un chèque, émettre un chèque; **~ a distinction between** faire une distinction entre; **~ from** prélever sur; **~ on** (skills, strength) exploiter; (reserves) puiser dans; **~ on one's savings** puiser dans ses économies; **~ up** (plan, will) faire; (report) rédiger, établir; (list, shortlist) dresser; (Law) rédiger; (white paper) dresser, rédiger; (proposal, criteria) établir; **~ up the agenda** dresser l'ordre du jour, établir l'ordre du jour; **~ up a statement of account** faire un relevé de compte

drawback *n* désavantage *m*, inconvénient *m*; (Imp/Exp) remboursement des droits de douane *m*

drawdown *n* (Bank) encaissement d'une tranche de prêt *m*, tirage *m*

drawee *n* tiré *m*

drawer *n* souscripteur *m*, tireur *m*

drawing *n* (of cheque, draft) tirage *m*; (on loan) prélèvement *m*; (illustration) dessin *m*; **~ account** *n* compte de retraits *m*; **~ board** *n* tableau *m*; **~ facility** *n* (Bank) mécanisme de tirage *m*; **~ officer** *n* agent tireur *m*; **~ software** *n* logiciel graphique *m*; **~ up** *n* (of report) rédaction *f*, établissement *m*

drawn: ~ bill *n* effet tiré *m*; **~ bond** *n* obligation à échéance *f*

dress-down Friday *n* port d'une tenue *plus décontractée au travail le vendredi*

drill down¹ *n* (Comp) recherche approfondie *f*

drill down² *vi* (Comp) faire une recherche approfondie

drive¹ *n* (Comp) lecteur *m*, unité *f*; (campaign, effort) campagne *f*; **have a sales ~** faire une campagne de vente

drive² ① *vt* pousser; **~ sb to do** pousser qn à faire; **~ sb hard** surcharger qn de travail, surmener qn; **~ a hard bargain** négocier ferme, négocier serré

···⊱

2 *vi* conduire; **~ down** (price, rate, unemployment) faire baisser; **~ up** (price, rate, unemployment) faire monter

driven *adj* (person) motivé; **~ by** (a certain factor) imposé par, provoqué par

driver *n* (of vehicle) conducteur/-trice *m/f*; (professional) chauffeur *m*; (Comp) (software) gestionnaire de périphérique *m*; (Mgmnt) (motivating factor) force motrice *f*; **~'s licence** BrE, **~'s license** AmE *n* permis de conduire *m*

Driver and Vehicle Licensing Agency *n* UK *centre d'émission des permis de conduire et des vignettes automobiles*

drivetime *n* heure de pointe *f*

driving *n* (Transp) conduite *f*; **be in the ~ seat** être aux commandes, tenir les rênes; **~ force** *n* moteur *m*; **~ test** *n* examen du permis de conduire *m*

drop¹ *n* (Econ) (in demand, inflation) baisse *f*; (in spending) chute *f*; (in price, orders, shares) chute *f*; **there has been a sharp ~ in unemployment** on constate une forte baisse du nombre de chômeurs

drop² **1** *vt* (idea, plan) renoncer à; (charges, claim) retirer; (price) baisser; (Comp) déposer; **~ everything** tout laisser en plan (infrml) **2** *vi* (prices, inflation, level) baisser; **~ out** (from project, bidding) se retirer; (from university course) abandonner ses études

drop-down menu *n* menu déroulant *m*

drought *n* sécheresse *f*

drug *n* (medicinal) médicament *m*; (narcotic) drogue *f*; **~ industry** *n* industrie pharmaceutique *f*; **~ trafficking** *n* trafic de drogue *m*

drum *n* (barrel) bidon *m*

drummer *n* AmE (infrml) voyageur de commerce *m*, représentant *m*

dry *adj* sec/sèche; **~ bulk cargo** *n* vrac sec *m*; **~ cargo** *n* marchandises sèches *f pl*; **~ dock** *n* bassin de radoub *m*, cale sèche *f*; **~ goods** *n pl* produits d'épicerie *m pl*; **~ measure** *n* mesure pour produits secs *f*; **~ weight** *n* poids à sec *m*

DTI *abbr* UK (▸**Department of Trade and Industry**) ministère du Commerce et de l'Industrie *m*

DTP *abbr* (▸**desktop publishing**) PAO *f* (publication assistée par ordinateur)

dual *adj* double; **~ exchange rate** *n* double taux de change *m*; **~ job holding** *n* cumul d'emplois *m*; **~ listing** *n* (Stock) cumul d'inscriptions *m*; **~ residence** *n* double résidence *f*; **~ responsibility** *n* (EU) cumul de responsabilités *m*; **~ sourcing** *n* approvisionnement auprès de deux sources *m*

dud *adj* (infrml) (fake) faux/fausse; (useless) nul/nulle (infrml); **~ banknote** *n* faux billet *m*; **~ check** AmE, **~ cheque** BrE *n* (infrml) chèque en bois *m* (infrml), chèque sans provision *m*

due *adj* (amount, sum) dû/due; **interest ~** les intérêts dus; **be/fall ~** arriver/venir à échéance; **at ~ date** à la date d'échéance; **fall ~ on the 16th** devoir être payé le 16; **be ~ for completion** devoir être achevé; **be ~ to do** devoir faire; **after ~ consideration** après mûre réflexion; **in ~ course** en temps utile; **in ~ form** (Law) en bonne et due forme; **~ bill** *n* AmE reconnaissance de dette *f*; **~ capital** *n* capital échu *m*; **~ date** *n* date d'échéance *f*, échéance *f*; **~ date of premium** *n* (Ins) jour d'échéance de la prime *m*; **~ date of renewal** *n* (Ins) date limite pour le renouvellement *f*; **~ diligence** *n* diligence normale *f*

dues *n pl* cotisation *f*, cotisation syndicale *f*

duly *adv* (Law) dûment; (as arranged) comme prévu; **~ signed** dûment signé

dummy *n* homme de paille *m*, prête-nom *f*

dump¹ *n* (Comp) (data transfer) vidage de mémoire sur disque *m*; **~ bin** *n* présentoir en vrac *m*; **~ site** *n* site de décharge *m*

dump² *vt* (waste at sea) déverser; (refuse) jeter; (chemicals, sewage) déverser; (Comp) vider

dumping *n* (Fin, Gen Comm) dumping *m*; (of waste) décharge *f*; (Stock) vente à perte *f*; **~ ground** *n* décharge *f*

dun *vt* (debtor) relancer

duopoly *n* duopole *m*

dup. *abbr* (▸**duplicate**) (Gen Comm) double *m*; (Law) duplicata *m*

duplex *n* AmE (apartment) duplex *m*; (house) maison jumelée *f*

duplicate¹ *adj* (cheque, receipt) en duplicata; **a ~ key** un double de clé

duplicate² *n* (Gen Comm) double *m*; (Law) duplicata *m*

duplicate³ *vt* copier; (work) refaire (inutilement)

duplication *n* (copying) reproduction *f*; (of work, effort) répétition *f* (inutile); **~ of benefits** *n* (Ins) double couverture *f*, reproduction des bénéfices *f*

durable *adj* (material) résistant; (equipment) solide; **~ household goods** *n pl* biens d'équipement ménager *m pl*, biens de consommation durables *m pl*

durables *n pl* biens durables *m pl*

duration *n* durée *f*; **for the ~ of** pour la durée de; **~ of guaranty** durée de la garantie *f*

duress *n* (Law) contrainte *f*, vice du consentement *m*; **do sth under ~** faire qch sous la contrainte

Dutch auction enchère au rabais *f*, enchère décroissante *f*

dutiable: **~ cargo** *n* cargaison soumise aux droits de douane *f*; **~ goods** *n pl* biens taxables *m pl*

duties *n pl* fonctions *f pl*, responsabilités *f pl*; **take up one's ~** entrer en fonctions; **carry out one's ~** remplir ses fonctions

duty *n* (Law) devoir *m*; (Tax) taxe *f*; (work, shift) service *m*; **have a ~ to do** avoir le devoir de faire; **do one's ~** accomplir son devoir; **customs ~** droits de douane *m pl*; **pay ~ on sth** payer des droits de douane sur; **be on ~** être de service; **be off ~** ne pas être de service, être libre; **~ officer** *n* officier de service *m*, officier de permanence *m*; **~ suspension** *n* suspension de droits *f*

duty-free *adj* hors taxes, détaxé, exempt de droit de douane; **~-free allowance** *n* UK quantités autorisées de produits hors taxe *f pl*; **~-free goods** *n pl* UK marchandises détaxées *f pl*, marchandises hors taxes *f pl*; **~-free shop** *n* UK boutique hors taxes *f*

DVD *abbr* (**digital versatile disc**) DVD *m*; **~-audio** *n* DVD-audio *m*; **~ drive** *n* lecteur DVD *m*; **~ player** *n* lecteur DVD *m*; **~-video** *n* DVD-vidéo *m*

DVLA *abbr* UK (►**Driver and Vehicle Licensing Agency**) *centre d'émission des permis de conduire et des vignettes automobiles*

D/W *abbr* (**dead weight**) PL (port en lourd); (►**dock warrant**) warrant *m*, bulletin de dépôt *m*

DWC *abbr* (**deadweight capacity**) PL (port en lourd) *m*

dwelling *n* (Prop) logement *m*; (Tax) domicile *m*

dwindle *vi* (demand) diminuer

DWT *abbr* (**deadweight tonnage**) PL *m* (port en lourd)

dynamic *adj* (growth, personality) dynamique; (Comp) dynamique; **~ management model** *n* modèle dynamique de gestion *m*; **~ positioning** *n* positionnement dynamique *m*; **~ programming** *n* programmation dynamique *f*; **~ RAM** *n* (Comp) RAM dynamique *f*, mémoire vive dynamique *f*; **~ web page** *n* page web dynamique *f*

dynamism *n* dynamisme *m*

dysfunction *n* dysfonctionnement *m*

dysfunctional *adj* dysfonctionnel/-elle

Ee

e-administration *n* administration en ligne *f*, administration électronique *f*

EAEC *abbr* (►**European Atomic Energy Community**) CEEA *f* (Communauté européenne de l'énergie atomique)

EAI *abbr* (**enterprise application integration**) intégration des applications d'entreprise *f*, EAI *m*

early[1] *adj* (attempt, draft) premier/-ière **at the earliest** au plus tôt; **at an ~ date** (soon) très bientôt, prochainement; **at the earliest possible opportunity** le plus tôt possible; **the earliest I can manage is Friday** je ne peux rien faire avant vendredi; **in ~ trading** (Stock) en début de séance; **~ adopter** *n* (S&M) consommateur précoce *m*, réceptif précoce *m*; **~ edition** *n* BrE édition du matin *f*; **~ exercise** *n* (Stock) (options) exercice anticipé *m*; **~ redemption** *n* rachat anticipé *m*; **~ retirement** *n* retraite anticipée *f*, préretraite *f*; **~ retirement pension** *n* préretraite *f*; **~ retirement scheme** *n* plan de retraite anticipée *m*; **~-withdrawal penalty** *n* pénalité pour retrait anticipé *f*

early[2] *adv* (in good time) tôt; **as ~ as possible** aussitôt que possible; **~ next year** au début de l'année prochaine

earmark *vt* (funds, resources) réserver, désigner; (person, site) désigner

earmarked *adj* **be ~ for** (promotion) être

sélectionné pour; **~ check** AmE, **~ cheque** BrE *n* chèque réservé *m*

earmarking *n* (of resources) affectation *f*, allocation *f*; (of public funds) affectation *f*

earn *vt* (interest) produire, rapporter; (reputation) acquérir; (income) gagner; **~ a fast buck** (infrml) gagner de l'argent rapidement, se faire rapidement du fric (infrml); **~ a living** gagner sa vie; **~ one's keep** gagner sa vie; **~ a salary of** gagner un salaire de, toucher un salaire de; **~ 40K** gagner 40 000 livres sterling; **~ £100 a week** gagner 100 livres sterling par semaine; **~ sb's respect** se faire respecter par qn

earned: **~ income** *n* revenus professionnels *m pl*; **~ interest** *n* intérêt rapporté *m*; **~ surplus** *n* bénéfices non-distribués *m pl*

earner *n* (person) salarié/-e *m/f*; **a nice little ~** (infrml) une belle petite source de revenus

earnest money *n* (Prop, Stock) arrhes *f pl*

earning: **~ capacity** *n*, **~ power** *n* capacité de gain *f*, rentabilité *f*; **~ streams** *n pl* rentrées d'argent *f pl*

earnings *n pl* (of person) salaire *m*, revenu *m*; (of company) profits *m pl*, gains *m pl*; (from shares) rendement *m*; **~ ceiling** *n* salaire plafond *m*; **~ drift** *n* dérapage des salaires *m*, dérive des salaires *f*; **~ forecast** *n* prévision de bénéfices *f*; **~ per share** *n pl* ⋯►

bénéfice par action *m*; ∼ **performance** *n* (of a stock) rentabilité *f*; ∼ **report** *n* rapport financier *m*; ∼ **yield** *n* (Fin) rendement *m*; (Stock) rendement des actions *m*

earphones *n pl* écouteurs *m pl*

Easdaq *abbr* (**European Association of Securities Dealers Automated Quotation**) Easdaq *m*, *marché européen des valeurs technologiques*

ease¹ *n* facilité *f*; ∼ **of handling** facilité de manutention *f*

ease² **1** *vt* (credit controls) desserrer; (economic policy) détendre; (crisis, shortage, problem) atténuer; (burden) alléger; (congestion, restrictions) réduire; (development, transition) faciliter

2 *vi* (problem) s'atténuer; (situation) se détendre; ∼ **off** (demand, congestion) diminuer

easement *n* (Prop) servitude *f*

easing *n* (of credit control, restrictions) détente *f*

Eastern: ∼ **bloc** *n* bloc de l'Est *m*; ∼-**bloc country** *n* pays du bloc de l'Est *m*; ∼ **Europe** *n* Europe de l'Est *f*; ∼ **European Time** *n* heure de l'Europe de l'Est *f*; ∼ **Standard Time** *n* US heure de l'Est *f*

easy *adj* facile; ∼ **to do** facile à faire; **make things easier** faciliter les choses; **take the** ∼ **way out** choisir la solution de facilité; ∼ **market** *n* marché en légère baisse *m*; ∼ **money** *n* (Econ) argent facile *m*; ∼ **option** *n* solution de facilité *f*; ∼ **payment** *n* facilité de paiement *f*; ∼ **terms** *n pl* facilités de paiement *f pl*

eat: ∼ **into** *vt* (savings, reserves) entamer; ∼ **out** *vi* (in restaurant) aller au restaurant

e-auction *n* vente aux enchères en ligne *f*

e-bank *n* banque en ligne *f*, banque sur Internet *f*

e-banking *n* banque en ligne *f*, banque sur Internet *f*

ebb¹ *n* **business is at a low** ∼ les affaires marchent mal; ∼ **tide** *n* marée descendante *f*

ebb² *vi* (support) décliner

e-bid *n* enchère électronique *f*

e-bill *n* facture électronique *f*

e-billing *n* facturation électronique *f*

EBITDA *abbr* (**earnings before interest, tax, depreciation, and amortization**) EBE *m* (excédent brut d'exploitation)

e-book *n* livre électronique *m*

EBRD *abbr* (▸**European Bank for Reconstruction and Development**) BERD *f* (Banque européenne pour la reconstruction et le développement)

e-broker *n* courtier en ligne *m*

e-brokering *n* courtage en ligne *m*, e-courtage *m*

e-business *n* commerce électronique *m*, e-business *m*, cyberbusiness *m*; ∼ **facilitator** *n* facilitateur/-trice de commerce électronique *m/f*; ∼ **strategist** *n* stratège en

commerce électronique *m*

EC *abbr* (▸**European Community**) CE *f* (Communauté européenne)

e-card *n* carte virtuelle *f*

e-cash *n* argent électronique *m*, argent virtuel *m*

ECB *abbr* (▸**European Central Bank**) Banque centrale européenne *f*

echelon *n* échelon *m*

ECOFIN *abbr* (▸**European Community Finance Ministers**) ministres des finances de la communauté européenne *m/f pl*

ecolabeling AmE, **ecolabelling** BrE *n* étiquetage écologique *m*

e-collaboration *n* e-collaboration *f*

ecological *adj* écologique; ∼ **damage** *n* dégradation écologique *f*

ecologically *adj* écologiquement; ∼ **sound** qui ne nuit pas à l'environnement

ecology *n* écologie *f*; ∼ **lobby** *n* lobby écologiste *m*

ecomarketing *n* marketing écologique *m*

e-commerce *n* commerce électronique *m*, commerce en ligne *m*; ∼ **hub** *n* place de marché collaborative *f*; ∼ **site** *n* site marchand *m*; ∼ **solution** *n* solution de commerce électronique *f*, e-solution *f*; ∼ **strategist** *n* stratège en commerce électronique *m*

e-community *n* communauté virtuelle *f*, communauté en ligne *f*

econometric *adj* économétrique

econometrician *n* économétricien/-ienne *m/f*

econometrics *n* +*sing v* économétrie *f*

economic *adj* économique; (profitable) rentable; ∼ **activity** *n* activité économique *f*; ∼ **advancement** *n* développement économique *m*; ∼ **adviser** *n* conseiller/-ère économique *m/f*; ∼ **analysis** *n* analyse économique *f*; ∼ **analyst** *n* (Stock) conjoncturiste *m/f*; ∼ **benefit** *n* avantage économique *m*; ∼ **climate** *n*, ∼ **conditions** *n pl* conjoncture *f*; ∼ **crisis** *n* crise économique *f*; ∼ **cycle** *n* cycle économique *m*; ∼ **data** *n* données économiques *f pl*; ∼ **efficiency** *n* rendement économique *m*; ∼ **forecast** *n* prévisions économiques *f pl*; ∼ **forecasting** *n* prévisions économiques *f pl*; ∼ **growth** *n* croissance économique *f*; ∼ **growth rate** *n* taux de croissance économique *m*, ∼ **indicator** *n* indicateur économique *m*, clignotant économique *m*; ∼ **institution** *n* institution économique *f*; ∼ **intelligence** *n* information économique *f*; ∼ **migrant** *n* migrant/-e *m/f*; ∼ **model** *n* modèle économique *m*; ∼ **and monetary union** *n* union économique et monétaire *f*; ∼ **news** *n* informations économiques *f pl*; ∼ **outlook** *n* perspectives économiques *f pl*; ∼ **performance** *n* résultats économiques *m pl*; ∼ **planning** *n* planification économique *f*; ∼

policy n politique économique f; ~
recovery n redressement de l'économie m,
reprise économique f; ~ **sanctions** n pl
sanctions économiques f pl; ~ **situation** n
conjoncture f; ~ **slowdown** n
ralentissement économique m; ~ **strategy** n
stratégie économique f; ~ **summit** n sommet
économique m; ~ **theory** n théorie
économique f; ~ **trend** n conjoncture
économique f, tendance économique f; ~
union n union économique f; ~ **welfare** n
bien-être économique m

economical adj économique; (person)
économe; ~ **use of resources** n
exploitation mesurée des ressources f,
exploitation économique des ressources f

economically adv économiquement; (run,
operate) de façon économique; ~ **backward** en
retard économique; ~ **viable**
économiquement viable

economics n +sing v (as subject of study)
sciences économiques f pl; (science) économie
f; (financial aspects) aspects économiques
m pl

economism n économisme m

economist n économiste mf

economize vi économiser, faire des
économies; ~ **on** économiser sur, faire des
économies de

economy n économie f; ~ **of abundance**
n économie d'abondance f; ~ **brand** n
marque économique f; ~ **class** n classe
touriste f, classe économique f; ~**class
flight** n vol en classe économique m; ~ **fare**
n tarif en classe économique m; ~ **flight** n
vol en classe économique m; ~ **pack** n
paquet économique m; ~ **of scale** n
économie d'échelle f; ~ **of scope** n
polyvalence de la production f, économie de
champ f; ~ **size** n taille économique f

economy-wide adj touchant l'ensemble
de l'économie

e-consumer n cyberconsommateur/-trice
m/f

eco-product n écoproduit m

ecosystem n écosystème m

e-coupon n bon de réduction électronique
m

ECP abbr (▸**Eurocommercial paper**) (Fin)
europapier commercial m; (Stock) billet de
trésorerie euro m, papier eurocommercial m

ECR abbr (▸**efficient consumer
response**) ROC f (réponse optimale au
consommateur)

e-CRM abbr (▸**electronic customer
relationship management**) gestion
électronique de la relation client f

e-cruitment n recrutement en ligne m

ECSC abbr (▸**European Coal and Steel
Community**) CECA f (Communauté
européenne du charbon et de l'acier)

ECU abbr (▸**European Currency Unit**)

ECU f (unité monétaire européenne)

ED abbr (▸**Eurodollar**) eurodollar m

e-democracy n e-démocratie f

EDF abbr (▸**European Development
Fund**) FDE m (Fonds de développement
européen)

edge¹ n: have the ~ on sb, have the ~
over sb avoir l'avantage sur qn; have a
slight ~ avoir une légère avance

edge²: ~ **ahead** vi prendre de l'avance
petit à petit; ~ **up** vi monter lentement,
progresser lentement

EDI abbr (▸**electronic data interchange**)
EDI m (échange de données informatisé)

edict n décret m; **issue an** ~ faire paraître
un décret

edit vt (assemble, arrange) éditer; (correct)
corriger, réviser; (newspaper) être le
rédacteur/la rédactrice en chef de

editing n (of papers, data) édition f; (for
publication) mise au point f, révision f; (Media)
rédaction f, (programme) émission f

edition n (book, newspaper, journal) édition f

editor n (software) programme d'édition m; (of
book, manuscript) correcteur/-trice m/f,
rédacteur/-trice m/f; (of newspaper) rédacteur/
-trice en chef m/f; (in radio, TV) realisateur/
-trice m/f; (in publishing) directeur/-trice de la
rédaction m/f; (of series) directeur/-trice de la
publication m/f

editorial n (in newspaper, magazine) éditorial
m; ~ **advertising** n publicité rédactionnelle
f; ~ **staff** n équipe de rédaction f; ~ **writer**
n éditorialiste mf

editorialist n éditorialiste mf

editorship n rédaction f

EDP abbr (▸**electronic data processing**)
TEI m (traitement électronique de
l'information)

educated adj (person) instruit; ~ **guess** n
supposition éclairée f

education n (system) enseignement m;
(training) éducation f

educational: ~ **background** n
formation f; ~ **establishment** n, ~
institution n établissement scolaire m,
établissement éducatif m; ~ **software** n
didacticiel m, logiciel éducatif m

edutainment n logiciel ludo-pédagogique
m

EEA abbr (▸**European economic area**)
zone économique européenne f

effect¹ n effet m; **in** ~ en effet; **with** ~ **from**
avec effet à compter du, à partir de; **to good**
~ avec succès; **have the** ~ **of doing** avoir
pour effet de faire; **come into** ~ (act,
regulation, rule) entrer en vigueur; **take** ~ (law,
rule) entrer en vigueur; (price increase) prendre
effet

effect² vt (reform, reduction, repair) effectuer;
(settlement) parvenir à

effective *adj* efficace; (actual) réel/réelle; **be ~** (rule) être en vigueur; **become ~** (rule) entrer en vigueur; **~ control** *n* (Fin) contrôle de fait *m*; **~ date** *n* date d'effet *f*, date d'entrée en vigueur *f*; **~ demand** *n* demande effective *f*; **~ rate** *n* (Acc) taux réel *m*; **~ tax rate** *n* taux d'imposition effectif *m*; **~ yield** *n* rendement effectif *m*

effectively *adv* (work, compete, communicate) efficacement; (demonstrate, show) avec force

effectiveness *n* efficacité *f*

efficiency *n* efficacité *f*; (of machine) rendement *m*, performance *f*; **~ agreement** *n* UK accord de rendement *m*; **~ drive** *n* campagne d'efficacité *f*; **~ ratio** *n* ratio d'efficience *m*; **~ variance** *n* écart de rendement *m*

efficient *adj* (person, method) efficace; (machine) performant; **be 50% ~** avoir un rendement de 50%; **~ consumer response** *n* réponse optimale au consommateur *f*

effluent *n* effluent *m*; **~ discharge** *n* décharge d'effluent *f*

EFL *abbr* (▶**English as a Foreign Language**) anglais langue étrangère *m*

e-form *n* formulaire électronique *m*

EFT *abbr* (▶**electronic funds transfer**) transfert électronique de fonds *m*, télévirement *m*

EFTA *abbr* (▶**European Free Trade Association**) AELE *f* (Association européenne de libre-échange)

EFTPOS *abbr* (▶**electronic funds transfer at point of sale**) transfert électronique de fonds au point de vente *m*

e.g. *abbr* (**exempli gratia**, **for example**) ex. (par exemple)

egalitarian *adj* égalitarien/-ienne

egalitarianism *n* égalitarisme *m*

EGM *abbr* (▶**extraordinary general meeting**) AGE *f* (assemblée générale extraordinaire)

ego-surf *vi* (infrml) égosurfer, *surfer sur le web à la recherche d'informations sur soi-même*

e-government *n* administration électronique *f*, administration en ligne *f*

EIB *abbr* (▶**European Investment Bank**) BEI *f* (Banque européenne d'investissement)

e-integration *n* intégration e-business *f*

EIP *abbr* (▶**electronic invoice presentation**) facturation électronique *f*; (▶**enterprise information portal**) portail d'entreprise *m*

eject *vt* éjecter

ejectment *n* (Law, Prop) action en revendication de biens *f*, procédure d'éviction *f*

e-journal *n* revue en ligne *f*

e-lancer *n* cybertravailleur/-euse indépendant/-e *m/f*, e-lance *mf*

elapse *vi* s'écouler; **~d time** temps écoulé *m*

elastic *adj* élastique; **~ demand** *n* demande élastique *f*; **~ supply** *n* offre élastique *f*

elasticity *n* (Econ) élasticité *f*; **~ of demand and supply** élasticité de la demande et de l'offre *f*; **~ of substitution** élasticité de substitution *f*; **~ of supply** élasticité de l'offre *f*

e-learning *n* apprentissage en ligne *m*

elect *vt* (course of action) choisir; (Pol) choisir, élire; **~ sb to the board** élire qn au conseil d'administration

elected office *n* office élu *m*

election *n* élection *f*; (Tax) choix *m*; **in the ~, at the ~** aux élections; **win/lose an ~** gagner/perdre aux élections; **~ campaign** *n* campagne électorale *f*; **~ manifesto** *n* programme électoral *m*; **~ results** *n pl* résultats du scrutin *m pl*

elective *adj* obtenu par nomination

elector *n* électeur/-trice *m/f*

electoral register *n*, **electoral roll** *n* liste électorale *f*

electorate *n* électeurs *m pl*

electrical *adj* électrique; **~ appliance** *n* appareil électrique *m*; **~ current** *n* courant électrique *m*; **~ engineer** *n* ingénieur électricien *m*; **~ engineering** *n* génie électrique *m*

electricity *n* électricité *f*, courant (électrique) *m*; **~ bill** *n* BrE facture d'électricité *f*; **~ consumption** *n* consommation d'électricité *f*; **~ generation** *n* génération d'électricité *f*

electronic *adj* électronique; **~ billing** *n* facturation électronique *f*; **~ bill presentment** *n* facturation électronique *f*; **~ business** *n* commerce électronique *m*, commerce en ligne *m*, e-business *m*; **~ business facilitator** *n* facilitateur/-trice de commerce électronique *m/f*; **~ catalogue** *n* catalogue en ligne *m*; **~ certificate** *n* certificat numérique *m*, certificat électronique *m*; **~ commerce** *n* commerce électronique *m*, commerce en ligne *m*, e-commerce *m*; **~ coupon** *n* bon de réduction électronique *m*; **~ customer relationship management** *n* gestion électronique de la relation client *f*; **~ data interchange** *n* échange de données informatisé *m*; **~ data processing** *n* traitement électronique des données *m*; **~ directory** *n* annuaire électronique *m*; **~ engineer** *n* ingénieur électronicien *m*; **~ form** *n* formulaire électronique *m*; **~ funds transfer** *n* transfert électronique de fonds *m*; **~ funds transfer at point of sale** *n* transfert électronique de fonds au point de vente *m*, télévirement au point de vente *m*; **~ government** *n* administration en ligne *f*; **~ invoice presentation** *n* facturation électronique f; ∼ **mail** n courrier électronique m; ∼ **marketing** n cybermercatique f, marketing en ligne m; ∼ **messaging** n messagerie électronique f; ∼ **money** n monétique f, argent électronique m; ∼ **news gathering** n collecte électronique d'informations f, reportage électronique m; ∼ **order form** n bon de commande électronique m; ∼ **payment** n paiement électronique m, télépaiement m; ∼ **payment terminal** n terminal de paiement électronique m; ∼ **personal organizer** n (diary) agenda électronique m; (pocket PC) ordinateur de poche m; ∼ **point of sale** n point de vente électronique m; ∼ **publishing** n éditique f, édition électronique f; ∼ **shopping** n achats en ligne m pl; ∼ **shopping basket** n panier (virtuel) m; ∼ **shopping cart** n caddie® (virtuel) m; ∼ **signature** n signature électronique f; ∼ **storefront** n vitrine virtuelle f

electronics n + sing v électronique f

element n (constituent part) élément m; (factor) facteur m; **human/time** ∼ facteur humain/temps m; **an** ∼ **of danger** une part de danger; ∼ **of risk** facteur risque m

elevator n AmE ascenseur m; ∼ **pitch** (to introduce oneself) bref exposé sur soi-même m; (in venture capital) résumé d'un business plan pour la création d'une start-up destiné à un capital-risqueur

eligibility n droit m, admissibilité f; (for election) éligibilité f; ∼ **for tax relief** droit à un allègement d'impôts m; ∼ **requirement** n condition d'admissibilité f; ∼ **test** n test d'admissibilité m

eligible adj (Gen Comm) admissible; (Bank) bancable; (to vote) éligible; **be** ∼ (applicant, candidate) présenter les conditions requises; **be** ∼ **for** (subsidy, benefit, allowance, grant) avoir droit à; **be** ∼ **to do** être en droit de faire; ∼ **bill** n effet escomptable m; ∼ **expense** n frais admissibles m pl; ∼ **paper** n effet bancable m

eliminate vt éliminer

elite n élite f

email¹, e-mail¹ n (medium) courrier électronique m, courriel m; (message) e-mail m, message électronique m; (on letterhead, business card) mél m; **be on** ∼ avoir une adresse électronique; **send sb an** ∼ envoyer un message électronique à qn, envoyer un e-mail à qn; ∼ **account** n compte de courrier électronique m; ∼ **address** n adresse électronique f; ∼ **bomb** n bombe électronique f; ∼ **box** n boîte aux lettres électronique f; ∼ **message** n e-mail m, message électronique m; ∼ **server** n serveur de courrier électronique m

email², e-mail² vtr ∼ **sb** envoyer un e-mail à qn; ∼ **sth** envoyer qch par courrier électronique; ∼ **sth to sb** envoyer qch à qn par courrier électronique

e-mall n centre commercial virtuel m, galerie marchande virtuelle f

emancipation n émancipation f

e-marketing n cybermercatique f, marketing en ligne m

e-market maker n teneur de marché électronique m

e-marketplace n place de marché électronique f

embargo n embargo m; ∼ **trade** ∼ embargo commercial m; **impose an** ∼ **on** mettre l'embargo sur; **lift an** ∼ lever l'embargo

embark vt embarquer; ∼ **on** (course of action) s'engager dans

embarkation n embarquement m; ∼ **card** n carte d'embarquement f

embassy n ambassade f

embezzle vt (funds) détourner

embezzlement n détournement m

embezzler n escroc m

embodiment n (Prop) incorporation f

e-merchant n cybermarchand m

emergency n urgence f; **in an** ∼, **in case of** ∼ en cas d'urgence; ∼ **aid** n aide d'urgence f; ∼ **call** n appel d'urgence m; ∼ **exit** n sortie de secours f; ∼ **landing** n atterrissage forcé m; ∼ **measures** n pl mesures d'urgence f pl; ∼ **powers** n pl pouvoirs d'exception m pl; ∼ **service** n service d'urgence m

emerging adj (market, nation) émergent

EMF abbr (▶**European Monetary Fund**) FME m (Fonds monétaire européen)

e-migration n migration sur Internet f, e-migration f

e-minister n UK (Pol) ministre chargé de la promotion et de la législation des nouveaux médias

emission n (of gases) émission f; ∼ **standard** n norme d'émission f

e-money n monétique f, argent électronique m

emoticon n (Comp) frimousse f, binette f Can

empanel vt (Law) constituer

emphasis n accent m; **place** ∼ **on** mettre l'accent sur

emphasize vt mettre l'accent sur; ∼ **that** insister sur le fait que

emphatic adj emphatique

empirical adj empirique

employ vt (method) employer, utiliser; (person) employer

employable adj apte au travail

employed adj (person) qui a un emploi; (waged) salarié; (capital) investi; **be** ∼ être employé; **the** ∼ n pl les actifs m pl; ∼ **taxpayer** n contribuable salarié m

employee n employé/-e m/f, salarié/-e m/f; ∼ **association** n association d'employés f; ⋯⋗

~ benefits *n pl* avantages en nature *m pl*, avantages sociaux *m pl*; **~ buyout** *n* rachat de l'entreprise par les salariés *m*; **~ contributions** *n pl* contributions des salariés *f pl*, cotisation salariale *f*; **~ handbook** *n* guide de l'entreprise *m*; **~ involvement** *n* UK participation *f*, cogestion *f*; **~ pension plan** *n* régime de retraite pour employés *m*; **~ profile** *n* profil du salarié *m*; **~ profit sharing** *n* participation des employés aux bénéfices *f*; **~ profit sharing plan** *n* régime de participation des employés aux bénéfices *m*; **~ relations** *n pl* relations avec les employés *f pl*, relations ouvrières *f pl*; **~ self-service** *n* (Admin, Comp) libre service pour employés *m*; **~ shareholding scheme** *n* actionnariat des salariés *m*; **~ stock option plan** *n* plan d'option d'achat d'actions *m*, plan de souscription à des actions *m*

employer *n* employeur *m*; **~s** *n pl* (collectively) patronat *m*

employers': **~ association** *n* union patronale *f*; **~ contribution** (to social security charges) cotisation patronale *f*; **~ liability insurance** *n* assurance responsabilité civile de l'employeur *f*

employment *n* (working) emploi *m*; (job) travail *m*, emploi *m*; **seek ~** chercher du travail, chercher un emploi; **be in ~** avoir un emploi, travailler; **people in ~** les actifs *m pl*; **take up ~** commencer un travail; **~ agency** *n*, **~ bureau** *n* agence de placement *f*, bureau de placement *m*; **~ contract** *n* contrat de travail *m*; **~ consultant** *n* conseil en recrutement *m*; **~ figures** *n pl* chiffres de l'emploi *m pl*, statistiques de l'emploi *f pl*; **~ growth** *n* croissance de l'emploi *f*; **~ law** *n* droit du travail *m*; **~ protection law** *n* loi sur la protection du travail *f*; **~ record** *n* expérience professionnelle *f*; **~ tax** *n* taxe sur l'emploi *f*; **~ tax credit** *n* crédit d'impôt d'emploi *m*

Employment: **~ Act** *n* loi sur le travail; **~ Protection Act** *n* UK loi sur la protection de l'emploi *f*; **~ Service** *n* UK ≈ Agence nationale pour l'emploi *f*

emporium *n* grand magasin *m*

empower *vt* responsabiliser, donner du pouvoir à; **~ sb to do** autoriser qn à faire

empowerment *n* responsabilisation *f*

empty¹ *adj* vide

empty² *vt* vider

empty nesters *n pl* (infrml) (in the housing market) ménage sans enfants *m*

EMS *abbr* (▸**European Monetary System**) SME *m* (Système monétaire européen)

EMU *abbr* (Econ) (▸**Economic and Monetary Union**) UEM *f* (Union économique et monétaire); (▸**European Monetary Union**) UME *f* (Union monétaire européenne)

emulate *vt* (Gen Comm, Comp) émuler

enable *vt* (allow) permettre; (promote) faciliter, favoriser; **~ sb to do** (allow) permettre à qn de faire; (give opportunity) donner à qn la possibilité de faire

enabler *n* facilitateur *m*, facilitateur/-trice *m/f*

enabling clause *n* clause d'habilitation *f*

enact *vt* (Law) promulguer

enactment *n* (Law) promulgation *f*

enc. *abbr* (▸**enclosed**) ci-inclus, ci-joint; (▸**enclosure**) PJ *f* (pièce jointe)

encash *vt* encaisser

encashable *adj* encaissable

encashment *n* encaissement *m*

encl. *abbr* (▸**enclosed**) ci-inclus, ci-joint; (▸**enclosure**) PJ *f* (pièce jointe)

enclave economy *n* économie enclavée *f*

enclose *vt* (document) joindre; (include) inclure

enclosed *adj* ci-inclus, ci-joint, joint; **please find ~** veuillez trouver ci-joint

enclosure *n* pièce jointe *f*

encode *vt* (Gen Comm) coder, chiffrer; (Comp) encoder

encoding *n* encodage *m*, codage *m*

encompass *vt* inclure, comprendre

encounter *vt* (problem) rencontrer; (setback) essuyer; (resistance) se heurter à

encourage *vt* (provide support) encourager; (boost, foster) stimuler; **~ sb to do** encourager qn à faire

encouragement *n* encouragement *m*

encouraging *adj* encourageant

encroachment *n* (Law) empiètement *m*, usurpation *f*

encroach: **~ on**, **~ upon** *vt* empiéter sur, usurper

encrypt *vt* encrypter

encryption *n* chiffrement *m*, cryptage *m*

enculturation *n* enculturation *f*

encumbered: **~ with** (debts) grevé de

encumbrance *n* (Law, Pol) charge *f*, servitude *f*; (to freedom, movement) entrave *f*

end¹ *n* (conclusion, finish) fin *f*; (aim, goal) but *m*; **at the ~ of the day** en fin de compte; **at the ~ of June** fin juin; **come to an ~** (event) prendre fin, se terminer; **put an ~ to** mettre fin à, mettre un terme à; **a means to an ~** un moyen d'arriver à ses fins; **an ~ in itself** une fin en soi; **~ consumer** *n* consommateur final *m*; **~-of-line goods** *n pl* fins de série *f pl*; **~ of financial year** *n* fin de l'exercice *f*; **~-of-month account** *n* liquidation de fin de mois *f*; **~ product** *n* produit final *m*; **~ result** *n* résultat final *m*; **~-of-season sale** *n* solde de fin de saison *m*; **~ to end** *adj* de bout en bout; **~ use goods** *n pl* produits d'utilisation finale *m pl*; **~-user** *n* utilisateur final *m*

end² [1] *vt* (meeting, debate) conclure, mettre fin à; (search, strike, rumour) mettre fin à [2] *vi* finir; (contract, agreement) expirer; **~ in**

(failure, victory) se terminer par

endanger *vt* mettre en danger

endeavor[1] AmE, **endeavour**[1] BrE *n* tentative *f*; **make every** ∼ **to do** faire tout son possible pour faire

endeavor[2] AmE, **endeavour**[2] BrE *vt* ∼ **to do** faire tout son possible pour faire; (succeed) réussir à faire

endemic *adj* endémique

ending balance *n* (Acc) solde de clôture *m*

endogenous variable *n* variable endogène *f*

endorse *vt* (action, decision) approuver; (cheque, warrant) endosser; (claim, candidate) appuyer, soutenir; (opinion) souscrire à; (promote) promouvoir, faire la promotion de

endorsee *n* (Acc) cessionnaire *mf*

endorsement *n* (Bank) endos *m*, endossement *m*; (of action, decision) approbation *f*, sanction *f*; (of candidate) appui *m*, soutien *m*; (product promotion) promotion *f*

endorser *n* endosseur *m*

endorsor *n* endosseur *m*

endowment *n* dotation *f*; ∼ **insurance** *n* assurance à capital différé *f*; ∼ **mortgage** *n* hypothèque liée à une assurance en cas de vie *f*; ∼ **policy** *n* assurance à capital différé *f*

energy *n* énergie *f*; ∼ **conservation** *n* économie de l'énergie *f*; ∼ **crisis** *n* crise énergétique *f*; ∼ **efficiency** *n* rendement économique *m*; ∼ **policy** *n* politique énergétique *f*; ∼ **source** *n* source de l'énergie *f*; ∼ **supply** *n* alimentation en énergie *f*, alimentation énergétique *f*

energy-efficient *adj* (machine) d'un bon rendement énergétique

enforce *vt* (one's rights) faire valoir; (policy, decision) appliquer, mettre en application, mettre en vigueur; (ruling) faire observer; (contract) faire exécuter; (payment) exiger; (discipline) imposer

enforceable *adj* (rule, law) applicable; (verdict, ruling) exécutoire; **be** ∼ (Law) avoir pouvoir exécutoire

enforced *adj* obligatoire, forcé

enforcement *n* (Law) exécution *f*, mise en application *f*, mise en vigueur *f*; ∼ **order** *n* mise en demeure *f*; ∼ **procedure** *n* procédure coercitive *f*

enfranchise *vt* accorder le droit de vote à

engage *vt* (staff) engager; (lawyer) prendre

engaged *adj* (telephone line) occupé; **be** ∼ **in** (activity) être occupé à; **be** ∼ **in discussions/negotiations** être en discussion/négociations; **be** ∼ **in doing** être occupé à faire; ∼ **tone** *n* BrE tonalité 'occupé' *f*

engagement *n* (promise) engagement *m*; (meeting) rendez-vous *m*; **without** ∼ sans garantie; **official/social** ∼ obligation officielle/sociale *f*; ∼ **diary** *n* agenda *m*; ∼ **manager** *n* responsable de mission *mf*

engine *n* moteur *m*

engineer *n* (graduate) ingénieur *m*; (repairer) réparateur *m*, technicien/-ienne *m/f*

engineering *n* (subject) ingénierie *f*; (industry) industrie mécanique *f*; ∼ **consultant** *n* ingénieur-conseil *m*; ∼ **department** *n* département d'ingénierie *m*; ∼ **firm** *n* (consultancy) bureau d'étude *m*; (factory) entreprise de construction mécanique *f*; ∼ **industry** *n* industrie mécanique *f*; ∼ **manager** *n* directeur/-trice technique *m/f*; ∼ **process** *n* procédé de fabrication *m*; ∼ **works** *n pl* usine de construction mécanique *f*

English *n* (language) anglais *m*; ∼ **as a Foreign Language** *n* anglais langue étrangère *m*; ∼**-speaking** *adj* anglophone

enhance *vt* (purchasing power) rehausser; (value) augmenter; (salary, pension) majorer; (prospects, status, reputation) améliorer; (rights, power) accroître; (attributes, qualities) mettre en valeur

enhanced *adj* (quality, features) amélioré; (yield) plus élevé

enhancement *n* (of reputation, prospects) amélioration *f*; (of power, privileges) accroissement *m*; (of salary, pension) majoration *f*; (of attributes, qualities) mise en valeur *f*; (of value) augmentation *f*

enjoin *vt* (obedience) imposer; (discretion, caution) prescrire

enjoy *vt* aimer; (benefits, reputation) jouir de

enlarged: ∼ **copy** *n* agrandissement *m*; ∼ **edition** *n* édition augmentée *f*

enlargement *n* (of photo, text) agrandissement *m*; (of EU) élargissement *m*

enquiry *n* (question, query) demande de renseignements *f*; (investigation) enquête *f*; **make enquiries** (ask for information) demander des renseignements; (investigate) faire une enquête; **'with reference to your** ∼**'** (by letter) 'en réponse à votre courrier'; (by phone) 'suite à votre appel téléphonique'; **'all enquiries to ...'** 'pour tous renseignements s'adresser à ...'; **hold an** ∼ mener une enquête; **launch/ open an** ∼ ouvrir une enquête; ∼ **desk** *n* bureau de renseignements *m*; ∼ **office** *n* bureau de renseignements *m*

enrol BrE, **enroll** AmE [1] *vt* inscrire [2] *vi* s'inscrire; ∼ **on a course** s'inscrire à un cours

enrollment AmE, **enrolment** BrE *n* inscription *f*

en route *adv* en route

ensue *vi* s'ensuivre; ∼ **from** résulter de

enter [1] *vt* (phase, firm, profession) entrer dans; (on form, list) inscrire; (data) entrer, introduire, saisir; ∼ **an appeal** faire appel; ∼ **information onto a register** inscrire des informations dans un registre; ∼ **an item in the ledger** passer une écriture dans le grand livre; ∼ **the market** arriver sur le marché; ····⫸

~ **a plea** faire valoir une exception; ~ **(a) recession** entrer en récession; ~ **a writ** signifier une assignation

[2] *vi* entrer; ~ **for** (enrol) s'inscrire à; ~ **into** (correspondence) entrer en; (negotiations, debate) entamer; (explanations) se lancer dans; (deal, alliance) conclure; ~ **into an agreement** passer un accord; ~ **into a contract with** passer un contrat avec; ~ **into force** entrer en vigueur

entered in *adj* (Imp/Exp) déclaré entré

enterprise *n* (company) entreprise *f*, entreprise commerciale *f*; (initiative) esprit d'entreprise *m*; ~ **allowance** *n* UK aide à la création d'une entreprise *f*; ~ **culture** *n* culture entrepreneuriale *f*; ~ **information portal** *n* portail d'entreprise *m*; ~ **resource planning** *n* planification des resources d'entreprise *f*; ~ **resource planning application** *n* progiciel de gestion intégré *m*; ~ **zone** *n* zone d'activité économique *f*, zone d'aménagement concerté *f*

enterpriser *n* entrepreneur/-euse *m/f*

enterprising *adj* entreprenant

entertain *vt* (divert) amuser, divertir; (play host to) recevoir

entertainment *n* divertissement *m*; ~ **allowance** *n* frais de représentation *m pl*; ~ **complex** *n* complexe de loisirs *m*; ~ **expense** *n* frais de représentation *m pl*

entirety *n* totalité *f*; **in its** ~ dans sa totalité

entitle *vt* autoriser; ~ **sb to do** autoriser qn à faire

entitled *adj* autorisé; ~ **to adjudicate** (Law) compétent à juger, habilité à juger

entitlement *n* droit *m*

entity *n* (Law) entité *f*

entrance *n* (to building, premises) entrée *f*; ~ **examination** *n* concours d'entrée *m*, examen d'entrée *m*; ~ **fee** *n* droit d'entrée *m*; ~ **requirements** *n pl* diplômes requis *m pl*; ~ **ticket** *n* billet d'entrée *m*; ~ **visa** *n* visa d'entrée *m*

entrepôt *n* entrepôt *m*

entrepreneur *n* entrepreneur/-euse *m/f*

entrepreneurial *adj* entrepreneurial

entrepreneurship *n* (concept) entrepreneuriat *m*; (business flair) esprit d'entreprise *m*

entrust *vt*: ~ **sb with sth** confier qch à qn

entry *n* (access) entrée *f*; (Acc) écriture *f*; (in register, diary, log) entrée *f*; (Fin) écriture *f*; (Imp/Exp) déclaration douanière *f*; (Stock) (into market) entrée *f*; (for quiz, competition) réponse *f*; ~ **inwards** déclaration d'entrée en douane *f*; ~ **outwards** déclaration de sortie de douane *f*; **make an** ~ **against sb** (Acc) débiter le compte de qn; **make an** ~ **in a ledger** passer une écriture; **gain** ~ **to** (building) s'introduire dans; (computer file) accéder à; ~ **barrier** *n* barrière d'entrée *f*; ~ **into force** entrée en vigueur *f*; ~ **fee** *n* droit d'entrée *m*; ~ **form**

n fiche d'inscription *f*; ~-**level job** *n* emploi de départ *m*; ~-**level product** *n* produit entrée de gamme *m*; ~ **permit** *n* (Gen Comm) autorisation d'accès *f*; (visa) visa d'entrée *m*; ~ **price** (Stock) (futures) cours de la transaction *m*; ~ **stamp** *n* (Imp/Exp) tampon d'entrée *m*; ~ **visa** *n* visa d'entrée *m*

enumerate *vt* énumérer

enumeration *n* énumération *f*

envelope *n* (stationery) enveloppe *f*; (Fin) enveloppe budgétaire *f*; **push the** ~ innover, faire œuvre nouvelle; ~ **curve** *n* (Econ) courbe d'enveloppe *f*

environment *n* (Comp, Envir) environnement *m*; ~ **policy** *n* politique de l'environnement *f*

environmental *adj* (concern) lié à l'environnement; (effect) sur l'environnement; ~ **accounting** *n* comptabilité écologique *f*; ~ **audit** *n* audit environnemental *m*; ~ **control** *n* protection de l'environnement *f*; ~ **damage** *n* atteinte à l'environnement *f*; ~ **disaster** *n* catastrophe écologique *f*; ~ **goods** *n pl* éco-produits *m pl*; ~ **impact** *n* impact sur l'environnement *m*; ~ **issue** *n* problème écologique *m*; ~ **law** *n* droit de l'environnement *m*; ~ **lobby group** *n* groupe de pression écologique *m*; ~ **policy** *n* politique de l'environnement *f*; ~ **pressure group** *n* groupe de pression écologique *m*; ~ **problem** *n* problème écologique *m*; ~ **protection** *n* protection de l'environnement *f*; ~ **protection agency** *n* agence pour la protection de l'environnement *f*; ~ **standard** *n* norme écologique *f*; ~ **tax** *n* écotaxe *f*

Environmental Health Officer *n* UK responsable de l'hygiène publique *mf*

environmentalism *n* écologisme *m*, environnementalisme *m*

environmentalist *n* écologiste *mf*

environmentally: ~-**aware** *adj* respectueux/-euse de l'environnement; ~-**friendly** *adj* qui respecte l'environnement; ~-**friendly product** *n* éco-produit *m*, produit écologique *m*; ~ **sound** *adj* qui ne nuit pas à l'environnement

envisage *vt* envisager, prévoir

envision *vt* envisager

EO *abbr* (►**executive officer**) cadre supérieur *m*

EOC *abbr* UK (►**Equal Opportunities Commission**) *commission pour l'égalité des chances pour l'emploi*

EP *abbr* (►**European Parliament**) Parlement européen *m*

EPA *abbr* (Envir) (►**environmental protection agency**) agence pour la protection de l'environnement *f*; UK (►**Employment Protection Act**) loi sur la protection de l'emploi *f*

EPO *abbr* (►**European Patent Organization**) Organisation européenne des brevets *f*

EPOS *abbr* (►**electronic point of sale**) point de vente électronique *m*

e-procurement *n* approvisionnement en ligne *m*, e-procurement *m*

EPS *abbr* (►**earnings per share**) BPA *m* (bénéfice par action)

equal¹ *adj* égal; **all things being ~** toutes choses égales, toutes choses étant égales; **in ~ proportions** à parts égales; **on ~ terms** (compete) à armes égales; (judge, place) sur un pied d'égalité; **~ and opposite** égaux et opposés; **be ~ to** (task) être à la hauteur de; **feel ~ to doing** se sentir à même de faire

equal² *n* égal/-e *m/f*; **be the ~ of** être l'égal de

equal³ *vt* (Math) égaler; (match) égaler

equal: ~ opportunities *n pl* égalité des chances *f*; **~ opportunities employer** *n* employeur respectant l'égalité des chances *m*; **~ opportunity** *n* égalité des chances *f*; **~ pay** *n* égalité des salaires *f*, égalité salariale *f*

Equal: ~ Credit Opportunity Act *n* US *loi protégeant contre toute forme de discrimination dans l'octroi de crédit*; **~ Employment Opportunity Commission** *n* US *commission pour l'égalité des chances pour l'emploi*; **~ Opportunities Commission** *n* UK *commission pour l'égalité des chances pour l'emploi*; **~ Opportunity Policy** *n* UK politique de l'égalité des chances *f*; **~ Pay Act** *n* UK loi sur l'égalité des salaires *f*; **~ Pay Directive** *n* (EU) Directive d'égalité des salaires *f*

equality *n* égalité *f*; **~ of opportunity** égalité des chances *f*

equalization *n* (Tax) péréquation *f*; **~ fund** *n* fonds de compensation *m*, fonds de régularisation *m*; **~ payment** *n* paiement de péréquation *m*

equalize *vt* égaliser

equation *n* équation *f*

equilibrium *n* équilibre *m*; **in ~** en équilibre; **~ GNP** *n* PIB d'équilibre *m*; **~ price** *n* prix d'équilibre *m*

equipment *n* (office, electrical) matériel *m*; (industrial, military) équipement *m*; **~ failure** *n* panne *f*; **~ leasing** *n* location de matériel *f*

equitable *adj* équitable, juste

equity *n* (Acc) capitaux propres *m pl*, fonds propres *m pl*; (Bank) valeur de réalisation nette *f*, valeur de réalisation réelle *f*; (investment in a company) participation *f*; (Law, Prop) équité *f*; (Stock) actif net *m*, actions *f pl*; **have an ~ interest** avoir une participation en actions; **take an ~ stake in** prendre une participation en actions dans; **~ capital** *n* capitaux propres *m pl*, fonds propres *m pl*; **~ dilution** *n* dilution de l'avoir des actionnaires *f*; **~ financing** *n* financement sur fonds propres *m*; **~ funds** *n pl* capitaux propres *m pl*, fonds propres *m pl*; **~**

investment *n* placement en actions *m*; **~ issue** *n* émission de capital *f*; **~ joint venture** *n* joint-venture avec création de société commune *m*; **~-linked policy** *n* police d'assurance-vie indexée sur le cours des valeurs boursières *f*; **~ market** *n* marché des actions *m*; **~ method** *n* méthode de la mise en équivalence *f*; **~ ownership** *n* (Stock) participation *f*; **~ savings account** *n* compte d'épargne en actions *m*; **~ share** *n* action de participation *f*; **~ trading** *n* négociation d'actions *f*, opération sur actions *f*; **~ value** *n* valeur de réalisation nette *f*, valeur nette *f*; **~ warrant** *n* bon de souscription d'actions *m*

equivalence *n* équivalence *f*

equivalent *n* équivalent; **be ~ to** être équivalent à, équivaloir à

ERA *abbr* (►**exchange rate agreement**) accord sur les taux de change *m*

eradicate *vt* mettre fin à, supprimer

erase *vt* effacer

ERC *abbr* (►**European Registry of Commerce**) Registre du commerce européen *m*

e-recruitment *n* recrutement en ligne *m*

erect *vt* (customs barriers) dresser, ériger

e-revolution *n* révolution Internet *f*

ergonomic *adj* ergonomique

ergonomically-designed *adj* de conception ergonomique

ergonomics *n* + *sing v* ergonomie *f*

ergonomist *n* ergonome *mf*

ERM *abbr* (►**exchange rate mechanism**) MTC *m* (mécanisme de taux de change)

erode *vt* (business confidence, power) saper, miner

erosion *n* (of land, of an option's premium, of power, of confidence) érosion *f*

ERP *abbr* (►**enterprise resource planning**) planification des ressources d'entreprise *f*; **~ application** *n* progiciel de gestion intégré *m*

err *vi* se tromper

errand *n* commission *f*, course *f*

erratic *adj* irrégulier/-ière

erratum *n pl* -ta erratum *m*

erroneous *adj* erroné

error *n* erreur *f*; **make an ~** faire une erreur; **by ~, in ~** par erreur; **human ~** erreur humaine *f*; **~ of judgement** erreur de jugement *f*; **~ message** *n* message d'erreur *m*; **~ report** *n* rapport d'erreurs *m*

errors and omissions *n pl* erreurs et omissions *f pl*

ersatz *n* succédané *m*

ESA *abbr* (►**European Space Agency**) ASE *f* (Agence spatiale européenne)

escalate ① *vt* (problem, effort) intensifier ② *vi* (prices) monter en flèche; (conflict, tension) s'intensifier

escalation n (intensification) intensification f;
(of prices, inflation rate) montée en flèche f; ~
clause n clause contre l'augmentation de
prix f, clause de surenchère f

escalator n escalier roulant m; ~ **clause**
n clause de sauvegarde f

escape: ~ **clause** n clause de sauvegarde
f, clause dérogatoire f; ~ **key** n touche
d'échappement f

escort vt (visitor) accompagner, escorter

escrow n mise en main tierce f; **in** ~ en
dépôt fiduciaire; ~ **account** n compte de
mise en main tierce m; ~ **agreement** n
contrat de dépôt m

escudo n escudo m

ESF abbr (▶**European Social Fund**) FSE m
(Fonds social européen)

e-solution n solution de commerce
électronique f, e-solution f

e-sourcing n approvisionnement en ligne
m, e-sourçage m

esp. abbr (▶**especially**) (on purpose)
spécialement; (above all) surtout

especially adv (on purpose) spécialement;
(above all) surtout

espionage n espionnage m

essential¹ adj (role, feature, element)
essentiel/-ielle; (maintenance, ingredient, reading)
indispensable; (services) de base

essential² n (item) objet indispensable m;
(quality) qualité essentielle f; **the ~s** l'essentiel
m

essential: ~ **feature** n (Patents)
caractéristique essentielle f; ~ **foodstuffs**
n pl denrées de première nécessité f pl; ~
industry n industrie capitale f

est. abbr (▶**established**) fondé, établi

EST abbr US (▶**Eastern Standard Time**)
heure de l'Est f

establish vt (company) fonder, établir; (fact,
guilt, ownership, guidelines, date) établir; (cause)
déterminer; ~ **a direct link with** établir une
liaison directe avec

established adj fondé, établi

establishment n (of business) fondation f,
établissement m; (of rule, law) institution f;
(organization) établissement m; (Stock) maison f

Establishment n UK classe dirigeante f

estate n (assets) biens m pl; (Prop) (manor)
domaine m, propriété f; (housing development)
(large) cité f; (small) lotissement m; (council
owned) cité HLM f; (Tax) succession f; ~
agency n BrE agence immobilière f; ~
agent n BrE (person) agent immobilier m; ~
agents n pl BrE (shop) agence immobilière f;
~ **of bankrupt** n actif du failli m; ~ **duty** n
droit sur la valeur globale de la succession
m; ~ **executor** n exécuteur testamentaire
m; ~ **in reversion** n biens grevés d'une
reversion m pl; ~ **income** n revenu d'une
succession m, revenu immobilier m; ~
manager n (Fin, Law) administrateur de

biens m; (Prop) (steward) régisseur m; ~ **tax** n
US droits de succession m pl

estimate¹ n (statistics) estimation f,
évaluation f; (Tax) montant estimatif m;
(quote) devis m; **at a rough** ~ très
approximativement; **at a conservative** ~
sans exagération; **at the highest** ~ selon
l'estimation la plus élevée; **at the lowest** ~
selon l'estimation la plus basse; **put in an** ~
for sth établir un devis pour qch

estimate² vt (Gen Comm) estimer, évaluer;
(Fin) estimer

estimated: ~ **amount** n (Tax) montant
estimatif m; ~ **arrival time** n heure
d'arrivée prévue f; ~ **cost** n coût estimé m;
~ **deductions** n pl déductions estimatives f
pl; ~ **time of arrival** n heure d'arrivée
prévue f; ~ **time of departure** n heure de
départ prévue f; ~ **value** n valeur estimative
f, valeur estimée f

estimates n pl (budget) prévisions
budgétaires f pl; ~ **of expenditure** n pl
(Fin) budget des dépenses m

estimation n (judgement) avis m, opinion f;
(esteem) estime f; (evaluation) évaluation f; **in
my** ~ à mon avis; ~ **sampling** n
échantillon d'estimation m

estimator n responsable de l'évaluation du
prix de revient mf

estoppel n (Law) interdiction faite aux
parties de revenir sur une déclaration

estuary n estuaire m

ETA abbr (▶**estimated time of arrival**)
heure d'arrivée prévue f

e-tail n vente en ligne f, cybervente f

e-tailer n vendeur/-euse en ligne m/f,
cybervendeur/-euse m/f

ETD abbr (▶**estimated time of departure**)
heure de départ prévue f

ethical adj (problem, objection) moral; ~ **code**
n code déontologique m; ~ **investment** n
placement éthique m; ~ **unit trust** n SICAV
éthique f

ethics n + sing éthique f; **professional** ~
déontologie f

ethnic adj ethnique; ~ **minority** n
minorité ethnique f; ~ **monitoring** n
surveillance des origines du personnel f

ethnomarketing n ethnomercatique f

e-ticketing n billeterie électronique f

etiquette n protocole m

e-trader n vendeur/-euse en ligne m/f,
cybervendeur/-euse m/f

e-trading n vente en ligne f, cybervente f

e-trainer n formateur/-trice en ligne m/f,
e-formateur/-trice m/f

e-training n formation en ligne f

EU abbr (▶**European Union**) UE f (Union
européenne); ~ **Directive** n directive de
l'Union européenne f, directive européenne f

euro n euro m; ~ **area** n zone euro f;

~ **cash** n monnaie euro f; ~ **effect** n effet euro m; ~ **zone** n zone euro f

Euro- pref euro-

Eurobanking n opérations bancaires en eurodevises f pl

Eurobond n (Bank) euro-emprunt m; (Stock) euro-obligation f

eurocentric adj eurocentrique

Eurocommercial paper n europapier commercial m; (money market) billet de trésorerie euro m

Eurocurrency n eurodevise f, euromonnaie f

Eurodollar n eurodollar m

Euro Fer n (▶Association of European Steel Producers) association des producteurs européens d'acier

euroland n euroland m

Euromarket n euromarché m

Euromoney n eurodevise f, euromonnaie f; ~ **deposit** n dépôt en euromonnaie m

Euro MP abbr député/-e du Parlement Européen m/f

Europe n Europe f

European[1] adj européen/-éenne

European[2] n Européen/-éenne m/f

European: ~ **Atomic Energy Community** n Communauté européenne de l'énergie atomique f; ~ **Bank for Reconstruction and Development** n Banque européenne pour la reconstruction et le développement f; ~ **Central Bank** n Banque centrale européenne f; ~ **Coal and Steel Community** n Communauté européenne du charbon et de l'acier f; ~ **Commission** n Commission européenne f; ~ **Community** n Communauté européenne f; ~ **Community Finance Ministers** n pl ministres des finances de la communauté européenne mf pl; ~ **Convention on Human Rights** n Convention européenne des droits de l'homme f; ~ **Court of Justice** n Cour de justice européenne f; ~ **Currency Unit** n unité monétaire européenne f; ~ **Development Fund** n Fonds de développement européen m; ~ **economic area** n zone économique européenne f; ~ **Free Trade Association** n Association européenne de libre-échange f; ~ **Investment Bank** n Banque européenne d'investissement f; ~ **Member of Parliament** n député/-e du Parlement Européen m/f; ~ **Monetary Agreement** n Accord monétaire européen m; ~ **Monetary Fund** n Fonds monétaire européen m; ~ **Monetary System** n Système monétaire européen m; ~ **Monetary Union** n Union monétaire européenne f; ~ **MP** n député/-e du Parlement Européen m/f; ~ **Nuclear Energy Authority** n Autorité européenne de l'énergie nucléaire f; ~ **option** n option européenne f; ~ **Options Exchange** n

Bourse d'options européenne f; ~ **Organization for Nuclear Research** n Centre européen pour la recherche nucléaire m; ~ **Parliament** n Parlement européen m; ~ **patent** n brevet européen m; ~ **Patent Organization** n Organisation européenne de brevets f; ~ **Registry of Commerce** n Registre du commerce européen m; ~ **Social Charter** n Charte sociale européenne f; ~ **Social Fund** n Fonds social européen m; ~ **Space Agency** n Agence spatiale européenne f; ~ **Union** n Union européenne f

Europhile n europhile mf

Eurorates n pl eurotaux m pl

Eurosceptic n eurosceptique mf

evade vt (question, problem) éluder; (responsibility) fuir; ~ **taxes** se rendre coupable d'évasion fiscale

evaluate vt (situation, performance, method, results) évaluer; (progress) mesurer; (person, application) évaluer

evaluation n évaluation f; **performance** ~ évaluation de performances f

evasive adj (action) dilatoire; (reply) évasif/-ive

even[1] adj (number) pair; ~**-numbered** adj en nombre pair

even[2]: ~ **out** ⎡1⎤ vt (prices) égaliser; (burden, distribution) répartir ⎡2⎤ vi (prices) s'égaliser; (differences, inequalities) s'atténuer; ~ **up** vt équilibrer

evened-out position n position fermée f

evening class n cours du soir m

evenly adj (apply) uniformément; (share, divide) en parts égales; (distributed) équitablement; ~ **spread** adj réparti uniformément

event n événement m; **the course of** ~s les circonstances; **in any** ~, **at all** ~s de toute façon; **in the** ~ en l'occurrence; **in the** ~ **of** en cas de; **in either** ~ en tout cas; ~ **marketing** n marketing événementiel m

eventuality n éventualité f

eventually adv finalement

eventuate vi se concrétiser

ever-changing adj qui évolue sans cesse

evergreen n crédit permanent non-confirmé m

ever-increasing adj (demand) en croissance constante

ever-present adj toujours présent

evict vt expulser

eviction n (of tenant) expulsion f; ~ **order** n arrêté d'expulsion m

evidence n (proof) preuves f pl; (testimony) témoignage m; (testimony in court) déposition f; **be in** ~ être fortement présent; **give** ~ déposer, témoigner; **give** ~ **for/against** témoigner en faveur de/contre; **show** ~ **of** faire preuve de; **there is** ~ **to suggest that** il ⋯⋗

y a de bonnes raisons de penser que; **there is no ~ that** rien ne prouve que; **all the ~ suggests that** tout indique que

evident *adj* évident; **(Law)** probant

evolution *n* évolution *f*

evolve *vi* évoluer

e-wallet *n* portefeuille électronique *m*, porte-monnaie électronique *m*

ex *adv* **(Stock)** ex, sans

ex. *abbr* (▸**exchange**) **(Bank)** change *m*; **(Econ)** change *m*, échange *m*; (▸**excluding**) excepté, à l'exception de; (▸**example**) exemple *m*; (▸**extra**) extra *m*, supplément *m*

exact *vt* exiger

exacting *adj* exigeant

exaggerated *adj* exagéré; **(insurance claim)** surévalué

ex allotment *n* **(Fin)** ex répartition *f*

exam *n* examen *m*; **sit/pass an ~** passer/réussir un examen; **~ results** *n pl* résultats d'examen *m pl*

examination *n* **(test)** examen *m*; **(inspection)** examen *m*; **(by customs)** fouille *f*, visite *f*; **(Law)** examen *m*; **(of witness)** interrogatoire *m*; **on ~** après examen; **under ~** **(matter, technique)** à l'étude; **sit/pass an ~** passer/réussir un examen

examine *vt* **(application, facts document)** examiner; **(problem, issue)** étudier; **(accounts)** visiter; **(luggage)** fouiller; **(witness)** interroger

examiner *n* examinateur/-trice *m/f*

example *n* exemple *m*; **for ~** par exemple

exceed *vt* **(threshold, limit)** dépasser; **(authority)** outrepasser; **(be higher than, more than)** être supérieur à; **~ expectations** dépasser toute attente

except *prep* excepté, sauf, à l'exception de

excepted *adj* sauf; **Fridays and holidays ~** sauf vendredis et jours fériés

exception *n* **(special case)** exception *f*; **(Ins)** exclusion *f*; **make an ~** faire une exception; **with the ~ of** à l'exception de; **with some ~s** à quelques exceptions

exceptional *adj* **(case, circumstances)** exceptionnel/-elle

excess¹ *adj* **~ speed/weight** excès de vitesse/poids *m*

excess² *n* excès *m*; **(Ins)** franchise *f*; **in ~ of** supérieur à; **be in ~ of** excéder, dépasser; **~ amount** *n* excédent *m*; **~ baggage** *n* excédent de bagages *m*; **~ baggage charge** *n* supplément pour excédent de bagages *m*; **~ capacity** *n* capacité excédentaire *f*, capacité inutilisée *f*, surcapacité *f*; **~ cash** *n* **(Acc)** excédent de caisse *m*, excédent de trésorerie *m*; **~ demand** *n* demande excédentaire *f*; **~ fare** *n* supplément *m*; **~ insurance** *n* assurance complémentaire *f*; **~ postage** *n* surtaxe postale *f*; **~ profits** *n pl* bénéfices exceptionnels *m pl*, superbénéfices *m pl*; **~ profits tax** *n* impôt sur les bénéfices exceptionnels *m*; **~ reserve** *n* réserve

excédentaire *f*; **~ supply** *n* offre excédentaire *f*

excessive *adj* abusif/-ive, excessif/-ive; **~ taxation** *n* impôts excessifs *m pl*, surimposition *f*

excessively *adj* excessivement

exch. *abbr* (▸**exchange**) **(Gen Comm)** échange *m*; **(Bank)** change *m*; **(Econ)** change *m*, échange *m*; **(Stock)** bourse *f*, change *m*

Exch. *abbr* (▸**Exchequer**) Échiquier *m*

exchange¹ *n* **(Gen Comm)** échange *m*; **(Bank)** change *m*; **(telephone)** central (téléphonique) *m*, échange *m*; **(of currency, money)** change *m*, échange *m*; **(Fin)** change *m*; **(Stock)** bourse *f*, change *m*; **(visit)** échange *m*; **in ~** en contrepartie; **in ~ for** en échange de; **~ of contracts** signature des contrats *f*, échange de contrats *m*; **~ control** *n* contrôle des changes *m*; **~ delivery settlement price** *n* cours de liquidation *m*; **~ differences** *n pl* différences de change *f pl*; **~ discount** *n* **(Stock)** déport de change *m*; **~ fund** *n* **(Stock)** fonds des changes *m*; **~ of information** échange d'information *m*; **~ office** *n* bureau de change *m*; **~ rate** *n* taux de change *m*; **~ rate agreement** *n* accord sur les taux de change *m*; **~ rate fluctuations** *n pl* fluctuations des taux de change *f pl*; **~ rate mechanism** *n* **(EU)** mécanisme de taux de change *m*; **~ risk** *n* risque de change *m*; **~ of securities** échange de titres *m*; **~ value** *n* valeur d'échange *f*

exchange² *vt* **(information, views)** échanger; **~ contracts** signer les contrats; **~ one thing for another** échanger quelque chose contre quelque chose d'autre

Exchequer *n* Échiquier *m*

excisable goods *n pl* biens passibles de droits *m pl*, produits soumis à l'accise *m pl*

excise *n* contributions indirectes *f pl*; **~ bond** *n* acquis à caution *m*; **~ duty** *n* contributions indirectes *f pl*, droit d'accise *m*; **~ tax** *n* excise *f*, accise *f*, impôt indirect *m*

exciseman *n* employé des contributions indirectes *m*

excl. *abbr* (▸**excluding**, ▸**exclusive of**) excepté, à l'exception de

ex claim *n* **(Law)** ex droit *m*

exclude *vt* exclure

excluded *adj* exclu

excluding *prep* excepté, à l'exception de, à l'exclusion de

exclusion *n* exclusion *f*; **to the ~ of** à l'exclusion de; **~ clause** *n* clause d'exclusion *f*, exclusion de garantie *f*; **~ principle** *n* principe d'exclusion *m*

exclusive *adj* **(story, report)** exclusif/-ive; **(luxurious)** de luxe; **~ of** excepté, à l'exception de, à l'exclusion de; **~ of tax** hors taxes; **~ of post and packing** frais d'emballage et d'envoi non compris; **have ~ use of sth** avoir l'usage exclusif de qch; **~ agency**

agreement *n* contrat d'agence exclusive *m*, contrat de représentation exclusive *m*; ∼ **agency listing** *n* contrat d'exclusivité *m*; ∼ **interview** *n* interview en exclusivité *f*; ∼ **licence** BrE, ∼ **license** AmE *n* licence exclusive *f*; ∼ **monopoly** *n* monopole exclusif *m*; ∼ **right** *n* droit exclusif *m*; ∼ **selling rights** *n pl* droits de vente exclusifs *m pl*; ∼ **taxation** *n* imposition exclusive *f*

exclusively *adv* exclusivement

exclusivism *n* exclusivisme *m*

ex-coupon *adj, adv* ex-coupon

exculpatory *adj* qui disculpe, qui innocente

excursion fare *n* tarif excursion *m*

excuse[1] *n* excuse *f*

excuse[2] *vt* (exempt) dispenser, exempter; (justify) justifier

ex-directory *adj* BrE (number) sur la liste rouge; **be** ∼ être sur la liste rouge

ex-div. *abbr* (▶**ex-dividend**) (Stock) ex-dividende, coupon détaché

ex-dividend *adj, adv* (Stock) ex-dividende, coupon détaché

ex docks *adj, adv* franco à quai; ∼ **price** *n* prix franco à quai *m*

exec. *abbr* (▶**executive**) cadre *m*; (▶**executor**) exécuteur *m*, exécuteur testamentaire *m*

execute *vt* (order, piece of work) réaliser; (project, plan) mettre à exécution; (purpose, sb's wishes) accomplir; (contract, document) valider; (deed, will) exécuter; (Comp) exécuter; (Stock) exécuter

executed contract *n* contrat exécuté *m*, contrat validé *m*

execution *n* (of plan, policy) exécution *f*; (Law) (of contract) exécution *f*, validation *f*; (Stock) exécution *f*

executive[1] *adj* exécutif/-ive

executive[2] *n* (person) cadre *m*; (board, committee) instances dirigeantes *f pl*

executive: ∼ **advancement** *n* promotion des cadres *f*; ∼ **assistant** *n* adjoint exécutif *m*, cadre adjoint *m*; ∼ **board** *n* conseil d'administration *m*; ∼ **class** *n* classe affaires *f*, classe club *f*; ∼ **committee** *n* comité exécutif *m*; (of a union) commission exécutive *f*; (decision-making) comité de direction *m*; ∼ **development** *n* perfectionnement des cadres *m*; ∼ **director** *n* directeur/-trice exécutif/-ive *m/f*; ∼ **grade** *n* niveau cadre *m*; ∼ **information system** *n* système d'aide à la décision *m*; ∼ **lounge** *n* salle d'embarquement classe club *f*, salon classe club *m*; ∼ **manager** *n* directeur/-trice exécutif/-ive *m/f*; ∼ **officer** *n* cadre supérieur *m*; ∼ **option scheme** *n* plan d'investissement pour cadres *m*; ∼ **perks** *n pl* avantages complémentaires du personnel d'encadrement *m pl*; ∼ **promotion** *n* promotion des cadres *f*; ∼ **recruitment**

agency *n* agence pour le recrutement des cadres *f*; ∼ **search** *n* assistance au recrutement de cadres *f*; ∼ **search firm** *n* cabinet de recrutement de cadres *m*; ∼ **secretary** *n* secrétaire de direction *mf*; ∼ **share option scheme** *n* plan d'investissement en actions pour cadres *m*; ∼ **stress** *n* le stress des cadres *m*; ∼ **summary** *n* descriptif sommaire *m*; ∼ **vice president** *n* vice-président directeur général *m*

executor *n* (Law) exécuteur testamentaire *m*

executory *adj* exécutoire

executrix *n* (Law) exécutrice testamentaire *f*

ex-employee *n* ancien/-ienne employé/-e *m/f*

exempt[1] *adj* exempt, exonéré; ∼ **income** *n* revenu exonéré *m*; ∼ **interest** *n* intérêt exonéré *m*; ∼ **period** *n* période d'exonération *f*; ∼ **surplus** *n* surplus exonéré *m*

exempt[2] *vt* exempter, exonérer

exemption *n* exemption *f*, exonération *f*; **tax** ∼ dégrèvement d'impôts *m*; ∼ **clause** *n* clause d'exonération *f*, exclusion de garantie *f*

exercisable *adj* (options) levable

exercise[1] *n* (task) exercice *m*; (of duties, powers, rights) exercice *m*; (operation) opération *f*; **marketing** ∼ opération de marketing *f*; **PR** ∼ campagne de relations publiques *f*; ∼ **of an option** (Stock) levée de l'option *f*; ∼ **price** *n* (Stock) prix d'exercice *m*, prix de levée *m*; ∼ **of undue authority** abus d'autorité *m*

exercise[2] *vt* (right, power) exercer, faire valoir; (franchise) gérer; (Stock) (option) lever; (caution, restraint) faire preuve de

exert *vt* (effect, pressure, influence) exercer

ex factory *adj, adv* départ usine

ex gratia *adj* (payment) à titre gracieux

exhaust *vt* (resources) épuiser

exhaust emissions *n pl* gaz d'échappement *m pl*

exhaustive *adj* exhaustif/-ive

exhibit[1] *n* objet exposé *m*; (artwork) œuvre exposée *f*; (exhibition) AmE exposition *f*; **on** ∼ exposé

exhibit[2] *vt* (goods) exposer

exhibition *n* exposition *f*; ∼ **center** AmE, ∼ **centre** BrE *n* palais des expositions *m*; ∼ **room** *n* salle d'exposition *f*; ∼ **stand** *n* stand (d'exposition) *m*

existing *adj* (customer, market) actuel/-elle, existant

exit[1] *n* sortie *f*; ∼ **barrier** *n* barrière de sortie *f*; ∼ **price** *n* (Stock) prix de sortie *m*; ∼ **strategy** *n* (of backer, investor) stratégie de sortie *f*; ∼ **visa** *n* visa de sortie *m*

exit[2] *vi* sortir

ex mill *adj, adv* départ usine, sortie usine; ~ **price** *n* prix départ usine *m*

ex officio[1] *adv* de par ses fonctions, officiellement

ex officio[2] *adj* (member) de droit

exorbitant *adj* abusif/-ive, exorbitant

exp. *abbr* (▶**export**) exportation *f*

expand [1] *vt* (activity, business, network, range) développer, élargir, étendre; (production, sales, workforce) accroître; (knowledge) élargir; (premises) agrandir [2] *vi* (activity, business, sector, town) se développer; (production, sales) s'accroître; (market, economy) être en pleine expansion; ~ **into Europe** s'implanter sur le marché européen

expandable *adj* (hardware, software) extensible, évolutif/-ive

expansion *n* (of company, trade, business, range, production) développement *m*; (of market, town, economy) expansion *f*; (of sales) progression *f*; (of borrowing, population, workforce) accroissement *m*; (of premises) agrandissement *m*; ~ **into Europe** implantation sur le marché européen *f*; ~ **card** *n* (Comp) carte d'extension *f*; ~ **of demand** accroissement de la demande *m*; ~ **strategy** *n* stratégie d'expansion *f*, stratégie de croissance *f*

expansionary *adj* (policy) expansionniste

ex parte *adj* (Law) ex parte, unilatéral

expatriate *n* expatrié/-e *m/f*

expect *vt* s'attendre à

expectation *n* (hope) attente *f*, anticipation *f*; (assumption, forecast) prévision *f*; **in ~ of** en prévision de; **against all ~s** à l'encontre des prévisions générales; **beyond all ~** au-delà de toute attente; **live up to/fail to live up to sb's ~s** répondre à/ne pas répondre à l'attente de qn

expected *adj* (result, outcome) attendu, prévu; (date) prévu

expediency *n* convenance *f*

expedite *vt* (speed up) accélérer; (finish) expédier; (send) expédier

expendable *adj* non réutilisable; ~ **goods** *n pl* biens non durables *m pl*

expendables *n pl* consommables *m pl*

expenditure *n* dépense *f*, dépenses *f pl*; ~ **limit** *n* limite de dépenses *f*, plafond des dépenses *m*

expense *n* (Acc) (expenditure) dépense *f*; (amount spent) dépenses *f pl*; (cost) frais *m pl*; (on income statement) charge *f*; **go to great ~** se lancer dans de grosses dépenses; **go to the ~ of** faire la dépense de; **at one's own ~** à ses propres frais; **at the ~ of** (safety, health) au détriment de; (jobs) au risque de perdre; **at sb's ~** aux dépens de qn; ~ **account** *n* frais de représentation *m pl*; ~ **allowance** *n* (Tax) allocation pour frais *f*; ~ **budget** *n* budget des dépenses *m*; ~ **center** AmE, ~ **centre** BrE *n* (Acc) centre de coûts *m*; ~ **item** *n* (Acc)

dépense *f*

expenses *n pl* (spending) dépenses *f pl*, frais *m pl*; (Acc, Fin) charges *f pl*; **allowable ~** frais déductibles *m pl*; **entertainment ~** frais de représentation *m pl*; **legal ~** frais de justice *m pl*; **all ~ paid** tous frais payés; **cover sb's ~** prendre à sa charge les frais de qn; **get one's ~ paid** se faire rembourser ses frais; ~ **incurred** *n pl* frais encourus *m pl*

expensive *adj* cher/chère, coûteux/-euse

experience[1] *n* expérience *f*; **from ~, by ~** d'expérience; **from my own ~** d'après mon expérience; **have ~ in computers** avoir de l'expérience en informatique; ~ **curve** *n* courbe d'expérience *f*; ~ **loss** *n* (Fin, Ins) déficit actuariel *m*

experience[2] *vt* connaître; ~ **rapid growth** connaître une croissance rapide

experienced *adj* expérimenté, ayant de l'expérience

experiment *n* expérience *f*; **carry out an ~** faire une expérience; **by way of ~** à titre d'expérience

expert[1] *adj* **take ~ advice, get an ~ opinion** demander l'avis d'un expert; **be ~ at doing** être expert dans l'art de faire

expert[2] *n* spécialiste *mf*, expert *m*; **marketing ~** spécialiste de marketing; **be an ~ in** être spécialiste en

expert: ~ **knowledge** *n* savoir de spécialiste *m*; ~ **system** *n* système expert *m*; ~ **valuation** *n* expertise *f*; ~ **witness** *n* expert cité comme témoin *m*

expertise *n* compétences *f pl*; (highly specialized) expertise *f*; ~ **in** compétences dans le domaine de; **have the ~ to do** avoir les compétences requises pour faire

expiration *n* AmE expiration *f*, échéance *f*; (Stock) échéance *f*; ~ **date** *n* (of credit card, permit) date d'expiration *f*; (of contract) terme *m*; (of loan) date d'échéance *f*

expire *vi* (loan) arriver à échéance; (offer, contract, document) expirer; (period) arriver à terme; **my passport has ~d** mon passeport est périmé; ~**d bill** *n* effet périmé *m*; ~**d policy** *n* police échue *f*

expiry *n* BrE expiration *f*, échéance *f*; (Stock) échéance *f*; ~ **date** *n* (of credit card, permit) date d'expiration *f*; (of contract) terme *m*; (of loan) date d'échéance *f*; (on perishable item) date de péremption *f*

explain *vti* expliquer

explicit *adj* explicite

exploit *vt* exploiter

exploitation *n* exploitation *f*

explosion *n* (of prices) flambée *f*; (of group, movement) essor *m*; **population ~** explosion démographique *f*

explosive[1] *adj* explosif/-ive

explosive[2] *n* explosif *m*

exponent *n* exposant *m*

exponential *adj* exponentiel/-ielle

export *n* exportation *f*; ∼ **agent** *n* commissionnaire exportateur *m*; ∼ **ban** *n* interdiction d'exporter *f*, embargo sur les exportations *m*; ∼ **company** *n* société d'exportation *f*; ∼ **control** *n* contrôle des exportations *m*; ∼ **credit** *n* crédit à l'exportation *m*; ∼ **director** *n* directeur/ -trice des exportations *m/f*, directeur/-trice export *m/f*; ∼ **duty** *n* droit d'exportation *m*, droit de sortie *m*; ∼ **earnings** *n pl* bénéfices à l'exportation *m pl*; ∼ **figures** *n pl* taux des exportations *m*; ∼ **finance** *n* financement à l'exportation *m*; ∼ **firm** *n* maison d'exportation *f*; ∼ **of goods order** *n* commande d'exportation de marchandises *f*; ∼ **house** *n* maison d'exportation *f*; ∼ **invoice** *n* facture d'exportation *f*; ∼**-led growth** *n* croissance entraînée par les exportations *f*; ∼ **licence,** BrE, ∼ **license** AmE *n* licence d'exportation *f*; ∼ **manager** *n* directeur/-trice des exportations *m/f*, directeur/-trice export *m/f*; ∼ **market** *n* marché à l'exportation *m*; ∼ **marketing manager** *n* directeur/-trice marketing des exportations *m/f*; ∼**-orientated** *adj* orienté vers l'exportation *f*; ∼ **permit** *n* autorisation d'exporter *f*; ∼ **prices** *n pl* prix à l'exportation *m pl*; ∼ **promotion** *n* promotion des exportations *f*; ∼ **regulations** *n pl* réglementation des exportations *f*; ∼ **sales** *n pl* ventes à l'exportation *f pl*; ∼ **sales manager** *n* responsable des ventes à l'exportation *mf*; ∼ **sector** *n* secteur exportateur *m*; ∼ **subsidy** *n* prime à l'exportation *f*; ∼ **surplus** *n* excédent d'exportation *m*; ∼ **tax** *n* taxe à l'exportation *f*; ∼ **trade** *n* commerce d'exportation *m*; ∼ **turnover** *n* chiffre d'affaires à l'exportation *m*

exportation *n* exportation *f*

exported *adj* exporté

exporter *n* exportateur/-trice *m/f*; (country) pays exportateur *m*

exporting *adj* exportateur/-trice

expose *vt* exposer; ∼ **to** (pressures, effect, influence) exposer à

exposed: ∼ **net asset position** *n* position nette débitrice *f*; ∼ **net liability position** *n* compte rendu de passif net *m*

exposition *n* (Stock) risque *m*

exposure *n* (Fin, Ins) risque *m*; (advertising) couverture médiatique *f*; (visibility) visibilité *f*

express[1] *adj* (intent) précis; (order, instruction, promise) formel/-elle

express[2] *n* (transportation service) express *m*

express[3] *vt* exprimer

express: ∼ **authority** *n* autorisation expresse *f*; ∼ **condition** *n* condition expresse *f*; ∼ **contract** *n* contrat explicite *m*; ∼ **delivery** *n* envoi exprès *m*; ∼ **mail service** *n* courrier express *m*, courrier exprès *m*; ∼ **terms** *n pl* (of contract) termes précisés *m pl*; ∼ **warranty** *n* garantie

expresse *f*

expressway *n* autoroute *f*

expropriation *n* emprise *f pl*

expunged *adj* rayé

ex quay *adj, adv* livrable à quai; **delivered** ∼ rendu à quai

ex-rights *adj, adv* (Stock) droit détaché, ex-droit, sans droit

ex ship *adj, adv* départ navire

extend *vt* (loan) accorder, consentir; (clientele, knowledge) élargir; (visit, visa) prolonger; (idea, business) développer; (power) étendre; (research, study) approfondir; (scope, range) élargir, étendre; (rules, time limit, contract, loan) proroger; ∼ **a deadline** accorder un délai supplémentaire

extendable *adj* (contract, visa, lease) renouvelable

extended: ∼ **cover** *n* (Ins) extension à des risques annexes *f*, garantie annexe *f*; ∼ **terms** *n pl* (Bank) prorogation d'échéance *f*

extendible bond *n* (Stock) obligation à échéance prorogeable *f*

extension *n* (telephone number) (numéro de) poste *m*; (extra telephone) poste supplémentaire *m*; (of contract, visa, loan) prorogation *f*; (of time) délai supplémentaire *m*; (of powers, scheme) extension *f*; (of business, idea) développement *m*; (Comp) extension *f*

extensive *adj* (range, network, programme) vaste; (list) long/longue; (testing, investigation) approfondi; (operations, changes, developments) de grande envergure; (training, consultation) complet/-ète

extent *n* étendue *f*

extenuating circumstances *n pl* circonstances atténuantes *f pl*

external *adj* (outer) extérieur; (trade) extérieur; (examiner) externe; (force, influence) extérieur; ∼ **audit** *n* audit externe *m*, contrôle externe *m*; ∼ **auditor** *n* auditeur indépendant *m*, commissaire aux comptes indépendant *m*; ∼ **balance** *n* équilibre de la balance des paiements *m*; ∼ **borrowings** *n pl* emprunts extérieurs *m pl*; ∼ **call** *n* (outgoing) appel vers l'extérieur *m*; (in-coming) appel de l'extérieur *m*; ∼ **debt** *n* dette extérieure *f*; ∼ **economy** *n* économie extérieure *f*; ∼ **financing** *n* financement externe *m*; ∼ **market** *n* marché extérieur *m*, marché étranger *m*; ∼ **relations** *n pl* relations extérieures *f pl*

externality *n* effet externe *m*, externalité *f*

externalize *vt* externer

extort *vt* extorquer

extra[1] *adj* supplémentaire; **delivery is** ∼ la livraison est en supplément

extra[2] *n* (charge) supplément *m*; (feature) option *f*

extra: ∼ **charge** *n* supplément *m*; ∼ **freight** *n* surfret *m*; ∼ **interest** *n* intérêt supplémentaire *m*; ∼ **pay** *n* sursalaire *m*, ⋯⋙

⋯⋙

supplément de salaire *m*; ~ **postage** *n* affranchissement supplémentaire *m*

extract[1] *n* extrait *m*

extract[2] *vt* (information, minerals, energy resources) extraire

extraction *n* (of oil, gas) extraction *f*

extractive industries *n pl* industries minières *f pl*

extranet *n* extranet *m*

extraordinary *adj* extraordinaire; ~ **charge** *n* (Acc) charge exceptionnelle *f*; ~ **expenses** *n pl* (Acc) frais extraordinaires *m pl*; ~ **general meeting** *n* assemblée générale extraordinaire *f*; ~ **item** *n* (revenue) profit exceptionnel *m*; (Tax) élément exceptionnel *m*; ~ **meeting** *n* assemblée extraordinaire *f*

extrapolate *vt* extrapoler

extrapolation *n* extrapolation *f*

extreme[1] *adj* extrême; ~ **hardship** *n* situation financière extrêmement difficile *f*

extreme[2] *n* extrême *m*; **carry sth to** ~**s** pousser qch à l'extrême

extremely *adv* extrêmement

extrinsic *adj* (motivation, factor, advantage, value) extrinsèque

EXW *abbr* (►**ex works**) départ usine

ex warehouse *adj, adv* départ d'entrepôt

ex-warrant *n* (Stock) bon de souscription détaché *m*, ex-bon de souscription *m*

ex-wharf price *n* prix départ quai *m*

ex works *adj, adv* départ usine

eye *n* **in the** ~**s of the law** aux yeux de la loi; **see** ~ **to** ~ **with sb on** partager le point de vue de qn au sujet de; **catch sb's** ~ attirer l'attention de qn; **be up to one's** ~**s in work** être submergé de travail; **be up to one's** ~**s in debt** être endetté jusqu'au cou; **with an** ~ **to doing** en vue de faire; ~**-catching** *adj* (headline, advert) accrocheur/-euse; ~ **contact** *n* échange de regards *m*; ~ **witness** *n* témoin oculaire *m*

eyeball *n* (infrml) (on Internet) visiteur (d'un site web) *m*

eyes only *adj* AmE confidentiel/-ielle

EZ *abbr* (►**enterprise zone**) ZAC *f* (zone d'aménagement concerté)

e-zine *n* cybermagazine *m*, revue en ligne *f*

Ff

FAA *abbr* US (►**Federal Aviation Administration**) *administration fédérale de l'aviation*

fabric *n* étoffe *f*

fabricate *vt* (goods) fabriquer; (evidence, excuse) fabriquer de toutes pièces

face[1] *n* **change the** ~ **of** (industry, landscape) changer le visage de; **the changing** ~ **of Europe** la face changeante de l'Europe; **lose/save** ~ perdre/sauver la face; **in the** ~ **of** face à; ~ **up** à l'endroit; ~ **down** à l'envers

face[2] *vt* (criticism, attacks, future, problem) faire face à; (choice) être contraint de faire; (ruin, redundancy) se trouver menacé de; (fine, penalty) risquer; **be** ~**d with** se trouver confronté à; ~ **the facts** regarder les choses en face; ~ **a risk** être exposé à un risque; ~ **up to** (problem, responsibility) faire face à; (somebody) affronter

face-time *n* contact direct *m*

face-to-face[1] *adj* ~ **discussion**, ~ **meeting** face-à-face *m inv*; ~ **selling** vente directe *f*

face-to-face[2] *adv* (speak) en personne; (meet) en face-à-face

face value *n* (Stock) valeur nominale *f*; **at** ~ (Gen Comm) au premier abord; (Stock) à la valeur nominale

facilitate *vt* (change, progress, talks, choice) faciliter; (growth) favoriser

facilitation *n* (of goods traffic) facilitation *f*; (of trade procedures) assouplissement *m*; (of meeting, talks) facilitation *f*

facilitator *n* faciliteur *m*, facilitateur/-trice *m/f*

facilities *n pl* installation *f*, équipement *m*; ~ **management** *n* (Comp) infogérance *f*, gestion des informations *f*; (of infrastructure) gestion des installations *f*

facility *n* (feature) fonction *f*; (building) installation *f*, complexe *m*; (arrangements) facilités *f pl*

facing *n* (S&M) linéaire *m*, surface de présentation *f*

facsimile *n* (document) fac-similé *m*, télécopie *f*; (hardware) fax *m*, télécopieur *m*

fact *n* fait *m*; ~**s and figures** les faits et les chiffres; **due to the** ~ **that** étant donné que; **in** ~ en fait; **the** ~ **remains that** toujours est-il que; **the** ~ **of the matter is that** le fait est que; ~**-finding committee** *n* commission d'enquête *f*; ~**-finding mission** *n* enquête *f*, mission d'enquête *f*

faction *n* faction *f*

factor *n* (element, aspect) facteur *m*; (Fin)

(agent) agent *m*; (of commodities) commissionnaire *m*; (Math) coefficient *m*, facteur *m*, indice *m*; **deciding** ∼ facteur décisif *m*; **human** ∼ élément humain *m*; **plus** ∼ atout *m*; **unknown** ∼ inconnue *f*; **be a** ∼ entrer en ligne de compte; **rise by a** ∼ **of** ten être multiplié par dix; ∼ **analysis** *n* analyse factorielle *f*

factorage *n* commission d'affacturage *f*

factorial *adj* factoriel/-ielle

factoring *n* (of debts) affacturage *m*; (by agent) courtage *m*; ∼ **company** *n* société d'affacturage *f*

factory *n* usine *f*; ∼ **farming** *n* élevage industriel *m*; ∼ **floor** *n* atelier *m*; ∼ **gate price** *n* prix sortie d'usine *m*; ∼ **hand** *n* ouvrier/-ière d'usine *m/f*; ∼ **inspector** *n* inspecteur/-trice du travail *m/f*; ∼ **outlet** *n* magasin d'usine *m*; ∼ **outlet centre** *n* centre de magasins d'usine *m*; ∼ **shop** *n* magasin d'usine *m*; ∼ **supplies** *n pl* fournitures consommables *f pl*

factual *adj* (account) basé sur des faits; (information) factuel/-elle; ∼ **error** *n* erreur sur les faits *f*; ∼ **evidence** *n* preuve factuelle *f*

faculty *n* faculté *f*

fad *n* mode passagère *f*

fail¹ *n* échec *m*; **without** ∼ sans faute; ∼**-safe** *adj* (device, system) à sécurité intégrée; ∼**-soft** *adj* à dégradation progressive

fail² ☐**1** *vt* (candidate) refuser; (test, exam) échouer à, rater (infrml); ∼ **in one's attempt to do** échouer dans sa tentative de faire; ∼ **in one's duty** manquer à son devoir; ∼ **to do** (omit) manquer de faire; (be unable) ne pas réussir à faire; ∼ **to deliver** (Stock) (securities) ne pas pouvoir livrer; ∼ **to observe the law** ne pas observer la loi
☐**2** *vi* (bank) faire faillite; (hardware) tomber en panne; (company) faire faillite, échouer; (candidate, attempt, plan) échouer; (crop, harvest) être mauvais

failed *adj* (attempt, project) raté (infrml); ∼ **delivery** *n* (Stock) défaut *m*, défaut de livraison *m*

failure *n* (of equipment) panne *f*, défaillance *f*; (of company, scheme) échec *m*; ∼ **in payment** défaut de paiement *m*; ∼ **rate** *n* taux d'échecs *m*; ∼ **to accept** refus *m*; ∼ **to agree** absence d'accord *f*; ∼ **to appear** (Law) non-comparution *f*; ∼ **to comply** (Law) inobservation *f*; ∼ **to deliver** non-livraison *f*

fair¹ *adj* juste, équitable

fair² *n* (exhibition) salon *m*, foire *f*; **book** ∼ salon du livre *m*, foire du livre *f*

fair: ∼ **average quality** *n* qualité commerciale *f*; ∼ **business practices** *n pl* pratiques commerciales loyales *f pl*, pratiques commerciales respectant la libre concurrence *f pl*; ∼ **competition** *n* concurrence loyale *f*; ∼ **employment** *n* égalité des droits des travailleurs *f*; ∼

market price *n* prix équitable *m*; ∼ **market rent** *n* loyer modéré *m*; ∼ **market value** *n* juste valeur marchande *f*; ∼ **play** *n* fair-play *m*, franc-jeu *m*; ∼ **rate of return** *n* (Acc, Fin) rendement équitable *m*; (Stock) rendement raisonnable *m*; ∼ **rent** *n* loyer équitable *m*; ∼ **rental value** *n* juste valeur locative *f*; ∼ **sample** *n* échantillon représentatif *m*; ∼ **share** *n* part équitable *f*; ∼ **trade** *n* commerce équitable *m*; US régime des prix imposés *m*; ∼ **trading** *n* pratiques commerciales loyales *f pl*

faith *n* confiance *f*; **have** ∼ **in sb** avoir confiance en qn; **have** ∼ **in** (method, technology) avoir confiance dans; **in good** ∼ en toute bonne foi

faithful *adj* (copy) exact, fidèle; (loyal) fidèle

faithfulness *n* fidélité *f*

fake¹ *adj* faux/fausse

fake² *n* faux *m*

fake³ *vt* (falsify a document) maquiller; (election) truquer; (results) falsifier; (illness) feindre; (signature, document) contrefaire

faking *n* (Gen Comm) maquillage *m*

fall¹ *n* (Econ) chute *f*; (in price) baisse *f*, chute *f*; AmE (autumn) automne *m*; ∼ **of currency** baisse de la monnaie *f*; ∼ **in the bank rate** réduction du taux d'escompte *f*; ∼ **in foreign exchange reserves** baisse des réserves en devises *f*; ∼ **from power** chute *f*; ∼ **from grace** disgrâce *f*; ∼ **in supplies** contraction de l'offre *f*; ∼ **in value** baisse de valeur *f*, dépréciation *f*

fall² *vi* (price) chuter; (Stock) baisser, chuter; ∼ **behind schedule** prendre du retard; ∼ **foul of the law** tomber sous le coup de la loi; ∼ **foul of sb** se brouiller avec qn; ∼ **foul of the tax authorities** avoir des ennuis avec le fisc; ∼ **in value** (Stock) baisser; ∼ **short of** (expectations, target) être inférieur à; ∼ **within the scope of** (Law) entrer dans le champ d'application de; ∼ **apart** (plan, negotiations) tomber à l'eau; ∼ **away** (numbers, bookings) diminuer; ∼ **back on** avoir recours à; ∼ **behind** prendre du retard; ∼ **behind with** (payments) être en retard avec; ∼ **down** (plan, building) s'effondrer; ∼ **off** (numbers, takings, sales, attendance, output) diminuer; (enthusiasm, quality) baisser; (interest) tomber; (curve on a graph) décroître; ∼ **in with** (proposal) accepter; ∼ **through** (plan, project) tomber à l'eau (infrml)

fall-back *n* plan de secours *m*; ∼ **option** *n* option de repli *f*; ∼ **position** *n* position de repli *f*

fallen angel *n* (Stock) ange déchu *m*

fallibility *n* faillibilité *f*

fallible *adj* faillible

falling-off *n* baisse *f*, diminution *f*

falling: ∼ **price** *n* (Gen Comm) prix en baisse *m*; (Stock) cours en baisse *m*, cours en repli *m*; ∼ **trend** *n* tendance baissière *f*

fallout n (consequences) conséquences f pl, retombées f pl

fallow adj en jachère

false adj (name, address, banknote) faux/fausse; (allegation, rumour) faux/fausse; (idea, information, impression) faux/fausse; ~ **accounting** n faux en écriture m; ~ **advertising claim** n annonce mensongère f; ~ **alarm** n fausse alerte f; ~ **economy** n fausse économie f; ~ **or misleading information** information erronée ou trompeuse f; ~ **return** n (Tax) fausse déclaration f; ~ **statement** n fausse déclaration f; ~ **witness** n faux témoin m

falsification n (alteration) falsification f; (distortion) déformation f

falsify vt (alter) falsifier; (distort) déformer

falter vi chanceler

familiar adj familier/-ière; **be** ~ **with** bien connaître

family n famille f; ~ **allowance** n allocation familiale f; ~ **audience** n écoute familiale f; ~ **brand** n marque générale f; ~ **business** n commerce familial m; ~ **circumstances** n pl situation de famille f; ~**-friendly** adj (policy) en faveur de la famille; ~ **hour** n heure de grande écoute f; ~ **income** n revenu familial m; ~**-size pack** n emballage familial m, paquet familial m

famous adj (person) célèbre; (company, university, product) réputé

fancy goods n pl nouveautés f pl

FAO abbr (▸**Food and Agriculture Organization**) Organisation des nations unies pour l'Alimentation et l'Agriculture f

FAQ abbr (▸**free alongside quay**) FAQ (franco à quai); (Comp) (**frequently asked questions**) FAQ f (foire aux questions), questions courantes f pl

far adv ~ **and away** de loin; **by** ~ de loin; **in so** ~ **as** dans la mesure où; **so** ~ jusqu'ici; ~**-flung** adj (network) vaste; ~**-reaching** adj (consequences) d'une portée considérable; ~**-sighted** adj avisé

fare n tarif m; ~ **pricing** n fixation des tarifs f; ~ **war** n guerre des tarifs f

farm[1] n ~ **equipment** n équipement agricole m; ~ **gate price** n prix reçu par les producteurs m; ~ **laborer** AmE, ~ **labourer** BrE n ouvrier/-ière agricole m/f; ~ **loan** n prêt agricole m; ~ **lobby** n groupe de pression agricole m; ~ **produce** n produits de la ferme m pl; ~ **shop** n UK boutique dans une exploitation agricole qui vend les produits de la ferme; ~ **subsidy** n subvention aux agriculteurs f; ~ **surplus** n excédent agricole m

farm[2] vt (land) cultiver, exploiter; ~ **out** (work) externaliser, sous-traiter

farmer n agriculteur m; **pig** ~ éleveur/-euse de porcs m/f

farmhand n ouvrier/-ière agricole m/f

farming n agriculture f; **pig/sheep** ~ élevage de porcs/moutons m; ~ **business** n exploitation agricole f; ~ **subsidy** n subvention à l'agriculture f

farmland n terre agricole f, terres cultivées f pl

FAS abbr (▸**free alongside ship**) FLB (franco le long du bord)

fascism n fascisme m

fashion n mode f; **women's** ~**s** vêtements pour femmes m pl; **in** ~ en vogue, à la mode; **out of** ~ démodé, passé de mode; **set the** ~ **for** lancer la mode de; ~ **designer** n couturier m; ~ **editor** n rédacteur/-trice de mode m/f; ~ **goods** n pl articles de mode m pl; ~ **house** n maison de couture f; ~ **magazine** n journal de mode m, revue de mode f; ~ **model** n mannequin m; ~ **parade** n défilé de mode m; ~ **show** n présentation de collections f

fast adj rapide; ~ **decline** n (Stock) (currency expectations) chute rapide f; ~ **food** n restauration rapide f, fast-food m; ~ **lane** n voie rapide f; ~ **market** n marché accéléré m; ~**-moving article** n article à forte rotation m, article à grand débit m; ~**-moving consumer goods** n pl produits de grande consommation à forte rotation m pl; ~ **rise** n (Stock) (currency expectation) hausse rapide f; ~ **track** n promotion accélérée f; ~ **tracking** n promotion accélérée f

fatal: ~ **accident** n accident mortel m; ~ **error** n (Comp) erreur fatale f

fat cat n (infrml) PDG surpayé m

father of the chapel n UK secrétaire de section m

fault[1] n (blame) faute f; (in system, machine) défaut m; (electrical) panne f; **no** ~ (insurance) sans égard à la responsabilité; ~**-tolerant system** (Comp) système insensible aux défaillances m, système insensible aux pannes m

fault[2] vt prendre en défaut, trouver des défauts à; ~ **sb for doing** reprocher à qn d'avoir fait

faultless adj irréprochable

faulty adj défectueux/-euse

favor AmE ▸**favour** BrE

favorable adj AmE ▸**favourable** BrE

favorite n AmE ▸**favourite** BrE

favour[1] n BrE service m; **do sb a** ~ rendre un service à qn; **as a special** ~ à titre de service exceptionnel; **be in** ~ **of** être pour, approuver; **vote in** ~ **of** voter pour; **speak in** ~ **of** soutenir; **be in sb's** ~ être avantageux pour qn; **work in sb's** ~ avantager qn

favour[2] vt BrE (choice, method, solution) être pour; (course of action) être partisan de; (change, growth, development) favoriser; ~ **sb** montrer une préférence pour qn; (unfairly) favoriser qn

favourable adj BrE (conditions, reply, reaction)

favorable; (report, result, sign) bon/bonne; **have a ~ reception** être bien reçu; **~ balance of trade** *n* balance commerciale excédentaire *f*; **~ economic conditions** *n pl* conditions économiques favorables *f pl*, conjoncture favorable *f*; **~ exchange** *n* cours avantageux *m*; **~ rate** *n* taux favorable *m*; **~ variance** *n* écart favorable *m*

favourite *n* BrE (Comp) favori *m*

fax¹ *n* (equipment) fax *m*, télécopieur *m*; (document) fax *m*, télécopie *f*

fax² *vt* (document) télécopier, faxer; (person) envoyer une télécopie à, envoyer un fax à

FBD *abbr* (▸**freeboard**) (shipping) franc-bord *m*

f/c *abbr* (▸**for cash**) comptant, contre espèces

FCC *abbr* (▸**French Chamber of Commerce**) Chambre de commerce française *f*

fco. *abbr* (▸**franco**) fco (franco)

FCO *abbr* UK (▸**Foreign and Commonwealth Office**) ministère des Affaires étrangères et du Commonwealth *m*

fd *abbr* (▸**free discharge**) franco déchargement; (▸**free domicile**) franco domicile

F/d *abbr* (▸**free dock**) FAQ (franco à quai)

FDA *abbr* US (▸**Food and Drug Administration**) *organisme gouvernemental de contrôle alimentaire et pharmaceutique*

feasibility *n* faisabilité *f*; **the ~ of doing** la possibilité de faire; **~ study** *n*, **~ survey** *n* étude de faisabilité *f*

feasible *adj* faisable, réalisable

featherbedding *n* maintien d'emplois non-productifs *m* (pour éviter les licenciements)

feature¹ *n* (distinctive trait) caractéristique *f*; (in newspaper) article de fond *m*; (aspect) aspect *m*; (Patents) caractéristique *f*; (function, facility) fonction *f*, **~ film** *n* long métrage *m*

feature² *vt* (depict) représenter; (present) présenter

fed. *abbr* (▸**federal**) féd. (fédéral)

Fed *n* US **the ~** (infrml) *banque centrale des États-Unis*, Réserve Fédérale *f*; **~ funds** *n pl* US fonds de la Réserve Fédérale *m*

federal *adj* fédéral; **~ deficit** *n* US déficit budgétaire fédéral *m*; **~ election** *n* US élection fédérale *f*; **~ finance** *n* US financement fédéral *m*; (government's system of handling money) finance fédérale *f*; (revenue sharing) redistribution partielle des recettes de l'État *f*; **~ funds** *n pl* US (public money) fonds publics *m pl*; (same-day money) argent au jour le jour *m*; **~ government** *n* gouvernement fédéral *m*; **~ government bond** *n* US bon du Trésor à long terme *m*, obligation du gouvernement fédéral *f*

Federal: **~ Aviation Administration** *n* US *administration fédérale de l'aviation*; **~**

funds *n pl* US fonds de la Réserve Fédérale *m pl*; **~ Parliament** *n* parlement fédéral *m*; **~ Reserve** *n* US Réserve Fédérale *f*; **~ Reserve Bank** *n* US Banque de la Réserve Fédérale *f*, Banque fédérale américaine de réserve *f*; **~ Reserve Board** *n* US *conseil d'administration de la Réserve Fédérale*; **~ Savings and Loan Insurance Corporation** *n* US *caisse nationale d'assurance de l'épargne et des prêts*; **~ Trade Commission** *n* US *commission fédérale du commerce*

federalism *n* fédéralisme *m*

federated company *n* société fédérée *f*

federation *n* fédération *f*

fee *n* (administrative) frais *m pl*; (for professional services) honoraires *m pl*; (membership dues) cotisation *f*; (for admission) droit d'entrée *m*; (Stock) frais *m pl*, royalties *f pl*; **charge a ~ income** *n* recettes d'honoraires *f pl*; **~ system** *n* rémunération par honoraires *f*

feed¹ *n* (Comp) alimentation *f*

feed² *vt* (machine) alimenter

feedback *n* feedback *m*, information en retour *f*, rétroaction *f*; **360-degree ~** évaluation tous azimuts *f*, rétroaction tous azimuts *f*

feedstuffs *n pl* aliments pour bétail *m pl*

feel¹ *n* (atmosphere) atmosphère *f*; (understanding) ~ **of the market** idée générale du marché *f*; **get a ~ for sth** s'habituer à qch

feel² *vt* (effects, consequences) ressentir; (unease, pride) éprouver, ressentir; **~ the pinch** (infrml) être à court d'argent

feelers *n pl*: **put out ~** tâter le marché, lancer un ballon d'essai

feel-good factor *n* sentiment de bien-être *m*

fence: **sit on the ~** (infrml) ne pas prendre position

fend: **~ off** *vt* (question) écarter, éluder; (takeover bid) repousser

ferry *n* ferry *m*; **~ company** *n*, **~ line** *n* compagnie maritime *f*

fertilize *vt* fertiliser

fertilizer *n* engrais *m*

fetch *vt* (collect) aller chercher; (sell for) se vendre à; (be worth) valoir; **~ a good price** rapporter un bon prix

FF *abbr* (▸**French franc**) FF (franc français)

FFA *abbr* (▸**free from alongside**) FLB (franco le long du bord)

FGA *abbr* (▸**free of general average**) FAC (franc d'avaries communes)

fiat money *n* US monnaie fiduciaire *f*

fiber *n* AmE ▸**fibre** BrE

fiberboard *n* AmE ▸**fibreboard** BrE

fiberglass *n* AmE ▸**fibreglass** BrE

fibre *n* BrE fibre *f*; **~ optic cable** *n* câble à fibre optique *m*; **~ optics** *n pl* +*sing v* BrE ⋯⟩

fibre optique *f*

fibreboard *n* BrE carton dur *m*

fibreglass *n* BrE fibre de verre *f*

FIC *abbr* (▶**free insurance and carriage**) franco assurance et transport

fictitious *adj* fictif/-ive

fiddle[1] *n* (infrml) combine *f*

fiddle[2] *vt* (infrml) (paperwork, tax return) truquer (infrml), maquiller (infrml); (figures) traficoter (infrml)

fidelity *n* fidélité *f*; **~ insurance** *n* assurance détournement et vol *f*

fiduciary *n* (Law) fiduciaire *mf*, représentant/-e *m/f*; **~ account** *n* compte fiduciaire *m*; **~ bond** *n* garantie fiduciaire *f*; **~ investment** *n* investissement fiduciaire *m*; **~ issue** *n* émission fiduciaire *f*

field *n* (Gen Comm) (area, sector) domaine *m*; (Comp) champ *m*, zone *f*; (Ind) domaine *m*, secteur *m*; **lead the ~** être en tête; **test sth in the ~** faire des essais de qch sur le terrain; **work in the ~** travailler sur le terrain; **~ of activity** branche d'activité *f*, champ d'activité *m*; **~ audit** *n* audit sur place *m*; **~ of interest** domaine d'intérêt *m*; **~ investigator** *n* enquêteur/-trice sur le terrain *m/f*; **~ operator** *n* homme de terrain *m*; **~ research** *n* recherche sur le terrain *f*; **~ sales manager** *n* directeur/-trice des ventes-clientèle *m/f*; **~ search** *n* (Comp) recherche par champ *f*; **~ service engineer** *n* ingénieur technico-commercial de terrain *m*; **~ staff** *n* personnel de terrain *m*; **~ study** *n* études sur le terrain *f pl*; **~ survey** *n* enquête sur le terrain *f*; **~ testing** *n* essai sur le terrain *m*; **~ trip** *n* (for one day) sortie éducative *f*; (for several days) voyage d'étude *m*; **~ work** *n* travail de terrain *m*; **~ worker** *n* (S&M) enquêteur/-trice sur le terrain *m/f*

fierce *adj* (competition) acharné

FIFO *abbr* (▶**first in, first out**) PEPS (premier entré, premier sorti)

fifty-fifty[1] *adj* **have a ~ chance (of success)** avoir une chance sur deux (de réussir)

fifty-fifty[2] *adv* (share) moitié-moitié; **go ~ on sth** partager qch moitié-moitié, partager qch fifty-fifty (infrml)

fight *vt* (problem) lutter contre; (campaign) mener; (election) disputer; (Law) (case, cause) défendre; **~ a losing battle against** se battre en pure perte contre; **~ back** rendre les coups; **~ for** lutter pour; **~ off** (criticism, takeover, bid, challenger) rejeter

figurative device *n* (Patents) marque combinée *f*

figure[1] *n* (number) chiffre *m*; (drawing) figure *f*; **a five ~ sum** un montant de cinq chiffres

figure[2] *vt* figurer; **~ out** (answer, reason) trouver; **~ out why/who** chercher à comprendre pourquoi/qui

figures *n pl* (data) chiffres *m pl*, données

f pl; **~ adjusted for seasonal variations** données corrigées en fonction des variations saisonnières; **in round ~** en chiffres ronds; **~ out today** chiffres parus aujourd'hui *m pl*; **go into double ~** (inflation rate) passer la barre des 10%

fih *abbr* (▶**free in harbor**, ▶**free in harbour**) franco à port

file[1] *n* (records) dossier *m*; (Comp) fichier *m*; (ring binder) classeur *m*; (cardboard wallet) chemise *f*; **~ compression** *n* (Comp) compression de fichiers *f*; **~ copy** *n* exemplaire d'archives *m*; **~ directory** *n* répertoire de fichiers *m*; **~ extension** *n* extension de fichier *f*; **~ format** *n* format de fichier *m*; **~ management** *n* gestion de fichiers *f*; **~ menu** *n* menu fichier *m*; **~ protection** *n* protection de fichiers *f*; **~ server** *n* serveur de fichiers *m*; **~ sharing** *n* partage de fichiers *m*

file[2] [1] *vt* (invoice, letter, document) archiver, classer; (submit) soumettre; (Law) (claim, application, request) déposer; **~ sth away** classer; **~ an application** faire acte de candidature; **~ a claim** (Ins) déposer une demande, faire une demande; **~ a claim for damages** intenter un procès en dommages-intérêts; **~ a lawsuit** engager des poursuites judiciaires, intenter un procès; **~ a tax return** envoyer une déclaration d'impôts [2] *vi* **~ for bankruptcy** déposer le bilan; **~ for divorce** demander le divorce

filing *n* (clerical duty) classement *m*; (of application) dépôt *m*, enregistrement *m*; (of a return) production *f*; **~ cabinet** *n* classeur (à tiroirs) *m*; **~ card** *n* fiche *f*; **~ clerk** *n* employé/-e de bureau chargé/-e du classement *m/f*; **~ system** *n* système de classement *m*

fill *vt* (order) exécuter; **~ a gap** répondre à un besoin; **~ a vacancy** pourvoir un poste; **~ the vacuum** combler le vide; **~ in** (date, detail) donner; (form) remplir; **~ sb in** mettre qn au courant; **~ sb in on sth** mettre qn au courant de qch; **~ in for sb** remplacer qn; **~ out** (form, box) remplir

filler *n* bouche-trou *m*; **~ advertisement** *n* publicité bouche-trou *f*

fill-in *n* remplaçant/-e *m/f*

film *n* film *m*; **~ advertising** *n* publicité cinématographique *f*; **~ festival** *n* festival du cinéma *m*; **~ industry** *n* industrie cinématographique *f*; **~-maker** *n* cinéaste *mf*, réalisateur/-trice *m/f*; **~-making** *n* cinéma *m*; **~ rights** *n pl* droits cinématographiques *m pl*; **~ script** *n* scénario *m*; **~ test** *n* bout d'essai *m*

filter *n* (Gen Comm, Comp) filtre *m*

filtering software *n* logiciel de filtrage *m*

final *adj* final; (answer, decision) définitif/-ive; (judgement) irrévocable; **the decision is ~** la décision est sans appel; **she has the ~ say** c'est à elle de décider; **~ acceptance** *n* acceptation définitive f; ~ **accounts** n pl comptes de fin d'exercice m pl; ~ **balance** n balance de clôture f; ~ **check-in** n contrôle d'embarquement m; ~ **demand** n demande finale f; ~ **dividend** n solde de dividende m; ~ **goods** n pl produits finis m pl; ~ **installment** AmE, ~ **instalment** BrE n versement libératoire m; ~ **invoice** n facture définitive f; ~ **mortgage payment** n solde d'hypothèque m; ~ **orders** n pl carnet de commandes fermes m; ~ **proof** n (Media) bon à tirer m; ~ **warning** n dernier avertissement m

finalize vt (deal, purchase, contract) conclure; (team) boucler; (timetable, route, date) fixer; (plan, decision) arrêter; (report) finaliser

finally adv finalement

finance¹ n (banking, money markets) finance f; (funds) fonds m pl; (credit) crédit m; **0%** ~ crédit gratuit; ~ **act** n UK loi de finances f; ~ **bill** n (Pol) projet de loi des finances m; ~ **committee** n comité des finances m; ~ **company** n, ~ **house** n UK société de crédit f, société de financement f; ~ **lease** n contrat de crédit-bail m; ~ **minister** n ministre des Finances mf; ~ **paper** n effet financier m, papier de financement m

finance² vt financer

finances n pl finances f pl; (of company, country) situation financière f

financial adj financier/-ière; **be in** ~ **difficulty** avoir des difficultés financières; ~ **accounting** n comptabilité de gestion f; ~ **administration** n gestion des finances f; ~ **advertising** n publicité financière f; ~ **advisor** n conseiller/-ère financier/-ière m/f; ~ **agent** n conseiller/-ère financier/-ière m/f; ~ **aid** n aide financière f; ~ **analysis** n analyse financière f, diagnostic financier m; ~ **analyst** n analyste financier/-ière m/f; ~ **appraisal** n évaluation financière f; ~ **assistance** n aide financière f, soutien financier m; ~ **backer** n bailleur de fonds m, commanditaire m; ~ **backing** n soutien financier m; ~ **burden** n charge financière f; ~ **capital** n capital financier m; ~ **center** AmE, ~ **centre** BrE n centre financier m; ~ **circles** n pl milieux financiers m pl; ~ **climate** n climat financier m; ~ **control** n contrôle financier m; ~ **difficulty** n gêne f; ~ **director** n directeur/-trice financier/-ière m/f, responsable financier/-ière m/f; ~ **disclosure** n divulgation financière f; ~ **firm** n (Fin) société financière f; ~ **flow** n flux financier m; ~ **forecasts** n pl prévisions financières f pl; ~ **future** n contrat à terme normalisé m; ~ **futures market** n marché à terme d'instruments financiers m; ~ **history** n antécédents financiers m pl; ~ **incentive** n stimulation financière f; ~ **institution** n institution financière f; ~ **instrument** n instrument financier m; ~ **intermediary** n intermédiaire financier m; ~ **involvement**

n intéressement m; ~ **leverage** n effet de levier financier m; ~ **management** n gestion des finances f; ~ **management system** n système de gestion financière m; ~ **manager** n directeur/-trice financier/-ière m/f; ~ **market** n marché financier m, place financière f; ~ **marketplace** n marché financier m; ~ **package** n ensemble de produits financiers m; ~ **paper** n effet financier m, papier financier m; ~ **period** n exercice comptable m; ~ **planning** n plan financier m, planning financier m; ~ **policy** n politique financière f; ~ **position** n situation financière f; ~ **reporting** n reporting financier m; ~ **requirements** n pl besoins financiers m pl; ~ **review** n examen financier m; ~ **risk** n risque financier m; ~ **sector** n secteur financier m; ~ **services** n pl services financiers m pl; ~ **services industry** n secteur des services financiers m, services financiers m pl; ~ **situation** n situation financière f; ~ **stability** n stabilité financière f; ~ **standing** n situation financière f; ~ **statement** n état financier m; ~ **strategy** n stratégie financière f; ~ **summary** n état financier récapitulatif m; ~ **support** n soutien financier m; ~ **world** n monde de la finance m; ~ **year** n exercice comptable m, exercice financier m; (Tax) année budgétaire f

Financial: ~ **Statement and Budget Report** n état financier et rapport budgétaire; ~ **Times Industrial Ordinary Share Index** n UK indice des actions industrielles ordinaires du Financial Times; ~ **Times Stock Exchange index** n UK indice FTSE m

financially adj financièrement; ~ **sound** adj financièrement solide

financier n financier m

financing n financement m; ~ **adjustment** n ajustement multiplicateur m; ~ **facility** n mécanisme de financement m; ~ **package** n montage financier m; ~ **plan** n plan de financement m

find¹ n trouvaille f, découverte f

find ² **1** vt trouver; ~ **fault with** trouver à redire à; ~ **sb guilty** reconnaître qn coupable; ~ **sb not guilty** reconnaître qn non coupable
2 vi ~ **for/against sb** se prononcer en faveur de/contre qn; ~ **out** (discover) découvrir; (establish) établir

finder's fee n commission de démarcheur f; (S&M) US honoraires (de recherche) m pl

finding n conclusion f, décision f

findings n pl conclusions f pl

fine¹ n amende f; **liable to a** ~ passible d'amende

fine² adv **cut it a bit** ~ être un peu juste, être trop juste

fine³ vt condamner à une amende; ~ **sb 600 euros** condamner qn à une amende de 600 euros

fine-tune *vt* (program) mettre au point; (economy) régler avec précision

fine-tuning *n* (of program) mise au point *f*; (of demand) gestion macroéconomique *f*, réglage *m*

finger *n* (Comp) finger *m*, *utilitaire qui peut donner des informations concernant un internaute*

finish ① *vt* finir, terminer; ~ **work** finir le travail
② *vi* finir, se terminer; ~ **in the money** finir par être payant, terminer dans le cours

finished goods *n pl* produits finis *m pl*

finite *adj* (resources) limité, non renouvelable

FIO *abbr* (▸**free in and out**) BAB (bord à bord)

fire¹ *n* incendie *m*; ~ **door** *n* porte coupe-feu *f*; ~ **drill** *n* exercice d'évacuation *m*; ~ **escape** *n* escalier de secours *m*; ~ **exit** *n* sortie de secours *f*; ~ **hazard** *n* risque d'incendie *m*; ~ **prevention** *n* mesures de sécurité contre l'incendie *f pl*; ~ **regulations** *n pl* règlements en matière d'incendie *m pl*

fire² *vt* (employee) licencier, renvoyer

fireproof *adj* ignifugé

fire-resistant *adj* ignifugé

firewall *n* (Comp) pare-feu *m*

firing *n* (of staff) licenciement *m*, renvoi *m*

firm¹ *adj* (order, market) ferme; (base, basis, foundation) solide

firm² *n* entreprise *f*, firme *f*, société *f*; (of lawyers, architects, accountants) cabinet *m*; (Stock) maison *f*; **haulage** ~ entreprise de transports *f*; **law** ~ cabinet juridique *m*; ~ **of consultants** cabinet de conseil *m*; **security** ~ société de surveillance *f*

firm³ *vi* (currency, prices) se raffermir; (market, shares) se stabiliser; ~ **up** (deal, details) se confirmer; ~ **sth up** (arrangements) confirmer

firm: ~ **belief** *n* conviction *f*; ~ **bid** *n* (Stock) demande ferme *f*; ~ **buyer** *n* acheteur ferme *m*; ~ **commitment** *n* engagement ferme *m*; ~ **deal** *n* marché ferme *m*; ~ **offer** *n* offre ferme *f*; ~ **order** *n* commande ferme *f*; ~ **seller** *n* vendeur ferme *m*

firmness *n* (of market, shares) fermeté *f*, solidité *f*

firmware *n* (Comp) micrologiciel *m*, microprogramme *m*

first *adj* premier/-ière; ~ **in, first out** premier entré, premier sorti; ~ **class** *n* (Transp) première (classe) *f*; ~**-class mail** *n*, ~**-class post** BrE *n* courrier au tarif normal *m*; ~**-class stamp** *n* timbre au tarif normal *m*; ~**-class ticket** *n* billet de première classe *m*; ~ **edition** *n* BrE (of newspaper) édition du matin *f*; ~ **generation** *n* première génération *f*; ~ **half** *n* (of year) premier semestre *m*; (of month) première quinzaine *f*; ~**-line management** *n*

maîtrise *f*; ~ **mortgage** *n* hypothèque de premier rang *f*; ~ **mover advantage** *n* avantage au premier entrant sur un marché *m*; ~ **name** *n* prénom *m*; ~ **preference share** *n* action privilégiée de premier rang *f*; ~ **preferred stock** *n* action privilégiée de premier rang *f*; ~ **principles** *n pl* principes premiers *m pl*; ~ **projections** *n pl* prévisions financières *f pl*; ~ **quarter** *n* premier trimestre *m*; ~**-rate** *adj* de première classe; ~**-time buyer** *n* personne qui achète sa première maison *f*

First World *n* grands pays industrialisés *m pl*

fiscal *adj* fiscal, budgétaire; ~ **agent** *n* agent financier *m*; ~ **barrier** *n* barrière fiscale *f*; ~ **deficit** *n* déficit budgétaire *m*; ~ **law** *n* droit fiscal *m*; ~ **period** *n* exercice financier *m*; ~ **policy** *n* politique budgétaire *f*, politique fiscale *f*; ~ **projections** *n pl* prévisions financières *f pl*; ~ **quarter** *n* trimestre d'exercice *m*; ~ **surplus** *n* excédent financier *m*; ~ **year** *n* exercice comptable *m*

fiscalist *n* fiscaliste *mf*

fishery *n* pêcherie *f*

fish: ~ **farm** *n* élevage piscicole *m*; ~ **farming** *n* pisciculture *f*

fishing *n* pêche *f*; ~ **grounds** *n pl* lieux de pêche *m pl*; ~ **port** *n* port de pêche *m*

fit¹ *adj* be ~ **for** (worthy) être digne de; (job) être capable de faire; (role) être capable de remplir

fit² *n* (Mgmnt) adaptation *f*; **market** ~ adaptation au marché

fit³ *vt* (requirements) remplir; ~ **out** (office) équiper; (ship) armer

fitness *n* (of staff) adaptation *f*

fitting out *n* (of ship) armement *m*

fitting room *n* salon d'essayage *m*

fittings and fixtures *n pl* (Prop) installations et agencements *f pl*

five: ~**-pound note** *n* UK billet de cinq livres *m*; ~**-year plan** *n* plan quinquennal *m*

fix *vt* (date, time, venue, limit) fixer; (meeting, visit) arranger; (problem) régler; (equipment) réparer; (contest, election) truquer; ~ **the price of** fixer le prix de; ~ **quotas** établir des quotas; ~ **on** (choose) choisir; ~ **up** organiser, arranger; ~ **up an interview** convenir d'une entrevue

fixed *adj* (price, rate, income, order, idea) fixe; (interval) régulier/-ière; (aim) arrêté; ~ **annuity** *n* rente fixe *f*; ~ **assets** *n pl* actif immobilisé *m*, immobilisations *f pl*, valeurs immobilisées *f pl*; ~ **capital** *n* capital fixe *m*, capital immobilisé *m*; ~ **charge** *n* charge fixe *f*, frais fixes *m pl*; ~ **charges** *n pl* frais fixes *m pl*; ~ **cost** *n* charge fixe *f*; ~ **costs** *n pl* frais fixes *m pl*; ~ **deposit** *n* dépôt à terme *m*; ~ **duty** *n* taxe fixe *f*; ~ **exchange rate** *n* taux de change fixe *m*; ~ **fee** *n* redevance fixe *f*; ~ **income** *n* revenu fixe *m*;

~ income security n (Stock) valeur à revenu fixe f; **~-interest loan** n prêt à intérêt fixe m; **~ overheads** n pl frais généraux fixes m pl; **~ premium** n prime fixe f, prime forfaitaire f; **~ price** n (package, deal) forfait m; (S&M) prix fixe m; **~-price contract** n contrat à prix fixe m; **~ rate** n taux fixe m; **~-rate bond** n (Stock) bon à taux fixe m, obligation à taux fixe f; **~-rate financing** n financement à taux fixe m; **~-rate loan** n emprunt à taux fixe m, prêt à taux fixe m; **~-rate mortgage** n hypothèque à taux fixe f; **~ rent** n loyer ferme m, loyer fixe m; **~ supply** n offre fixe f; **~-term contract** n contrat à durée déterminée m; **~-term loan** n prêt à durée fixe m

fixing n (of prices) fixage m, fixing m, établissement m; **~ of costs** établissement des frais m, établissement des prix m

fixture n (Prop) agencement m

fixtures and fittings n pl (Acc) reprise f; (Prop) installations et agencements f pl

flag¹ n (Comp) drapeau m, indicateur m; (Transp) pavillon m; **~ of convenience** pavillon de complaisance m

flag² ① vt (Gen Comm, Comp) indiquer, signaler; (highlight on screen) sélectionner ② vi (interest) faiblir; (currency) être en baisse; (morale) baisser

flagging adj (demand, economy) en baisse

flagship: ~ product n produit vedette m; **~ site** n site vedette m; **~ store** n magasin de prestige m

flame¹ n (on Internet) message électronique agressif m; **~ war** n guerre d'insultes (sur Internet) f

flame² vt (on Internet) envoyer des messages électroniques agressifs à, flinguer (infrml)

flamer n (on Internet) internaute qui envoie des messages agressifs mf, flingueur m (infrml)

flaming n (on Internet) envoi de messages électroniques agressifs m

flare: ~ up vi (anger, trouble) éclater

flat¹ adj (dull) plat, terne; (unchanged) fixe, fixé; (market) calme, stable; (spending, profits) stagnant; (refusal, denial) catégorique; **at a ~ price** à forfait, à solde nul; **at a ~ rate** (Stock) (buy, sell) à taux fixe

flat² n BrE (apartment) appartement m

flat³ adv turn sth down **~** refuser qch tout net; work **~** out (person) travailler d'arrache-pied; (factory) travailler à plein rendement

flat: ~-bed n véhicule articulé à plate-forme m; **~ bond** n obligation sans intérêt f; **~ fee** n forfait m; (Bank) commission fixe f; **~ grant** n aide pécuniaire uniforme f; **~ rate** n tarif fixe m, tarif non-dégressif m; (Tax) taux uniforme m; **~-rate** adj forfaitaire; **~-rate bonus** n prime forfaitaire f, prime non hiérarchisée f; **~-rate fee** redevance forfaitaire f; **~ rate of pay** n taux uniforme de salaire m; **~-rate price** n prix forfaitaire

m; **~-rate service** n service forfaitaire m; **~-rate subscription** n abonnement à forfait m; **~-rate tax** n impôt forfaitaire m; **~ sum** n forfait m; **~ tax** impôt uniforme m

flatly adv (deny) catégoriquement

flatten vi (curve) s'aplatir; **~ out** se stabiliser

flaunt vt étaler

flaw n défaut m, imperfection f; (Law) (in contract) vice de forme m

flawed adj défectueux/-euse, imparfait

fleet n (of ships, aircraft) flotte f; **~ of cars** parc automobile m; **~ manager** n (of cars) directeur/-trice du parc automobile m/f; (of ships, aircraft) directeur/-trice de la flotte m/f

flexibility n flexibilité f, souplesse f; **~ of time** flexibilité des horaires f

flexible adj flexible, souple; **~ budget** n budget variable m; **~ exchange rate** n taux de change flexible m; **~ learning** n formation à la carte f; **~-payment mortgage** n hypothèque à règlements variables f; **~ time** n flexibilité des horaires f; **~ working hours** n pl horaires à la carte m pl, horaires souples m pl

flexitime n horaires à la carte m pl, horaires souples m pl

flexprice n prix flexible m

flier n ▸flyer

flight n vol m; **the ~ to/from Brussels** le vol à destination de/en provenance de Bruxelles; **~ attendant** n (female) hôtesse de l'air f; (male) steward m; **~ of capital** n fuite de capitaux f; **~ information** n informations de vol f pl; **~ number** n numéro de vol m; **~ ticket** n coupon de vol m; **~ time** n temps de vol m; **~ to quality** (Stock) fuite vers la qualité f

flip chart n tableau de conférence m

float¹ n US (Bank) effets en circulation qui n'ont pas encore été encaissés m pl; **~ time** jours de valeur m pl; (cash in till) fonds de caisse m; (Stock) actions d'une entreprise en circulation f pl

float² ① vt (currency) flotter; (shares, securities) introduire en Bourse; (company) lancer en Bourse; (loan) lancer, émettre; (idea, suggestion) lancer ② vi (rate) fluctuer

floater n (Ins) US contrat d'abonnement m, garantie à tous endroits f, police flottante f; (Stock) US obligation à taux variable f

floating n (of bond issues, stock) émission f; **~ assets** n pl actif circulant m; **~ capital** n fonds de roulement m pl; **~ currency** n devise flottante f; **~ debt** n dette flottante f; **~ dock** n dock flottant m; **~ exchange rate** n taux de change flottant m; **~ interest rate** n taux d'intérêt flottant m; **~-point number** n nombre en virgule flottante m; **~ palette** n (Comp) palette flottante f; **~ policy** n contrat d'abonnement m, police ⋯▸

d'abonnement f, police flottante f; ~ **rate** n taux flottant m, taux variable m; ~**-rate loan** n emprunt à taux flottant m, emprunt à taux variable m; ~ **rate note** n bon à taux flottant m; ~**-rate security** n valeur à taux flottant f, valeur à taux variable f; ~ **voter** n électeur/-trice indécis/-e m/f

flood ¹ n (of people) flot m; (of complaints, applications) déluge m

flood ² vt (market) inonder

floor n (lowest price) taux plancher m, plancher m; (of building) étage m; (of room) plancher m; (of stock exchange) parquet m; ~ **broker** n courtier membre du parquet m; ~ **display** n présentoir au sol m; ~ **manager** n chef de rayon m; ~ **plan** n (of rooms) plan d'étage m; ~ **price** n prix plancher m; ~ **rate** n (Stock) taux plancher m; ~ **space** n espace habitable m, surface au sol f; ~ **trader** n négociant courtier de parquet m

flooring n (Bank) planification de base f

flop n (infrml) fiasco m; (film) navet m (infrml); **be a** ~ (scheme, project) être un fiasco; (show, film) faire un four (infrml)

floppy n disquette f; ~ **disk** n disquette f; ~ **disk drive** n lecteur de disquettes m

florin n florin m, gulden m

flotation n (of loan) lancement m; (of company) introduction en Bourse f; (of shares, stock) émission f, introduction en Bourse f; (of currency) flottement m

flourish vi (business, competition) prospérer

flourishing adj (sector, industry) florissant; (business, town) prospère

flow ¹ n (of funds) flux m; (of data) circulation f, flot m; (of operations) déroulement m; (of money) flux m; (of orders) afflux m; (of people) flot m; (of goods or passenger traffic) flux m; **go with the** ~ suivre le mouvement; ~ **chart** n organigramme m; ~ **control** n commande de flux f, contrôle de flux m; ~ **of funds** flux de trésorerie m, flux financier m; ~ **of money** flux monétaire m; ~**-of-funds account** n compte des flux financiers m; ~**-of-funds table** n tableau des opérations financières m; ~ **of orders** afflux de commandes m

flow ² vi (capital, money) affluer; ~ **out** (money) sortir

fluctuate vi fluctuer, varier; (price of shares, rate of exchange) fluctuer

fluctuating adj (mood, rate) fluctuant; ~ **currency** n devise flottante f

fluctuation n fluctuation f; ~ **limit** n (Stock) limite de variation des cours f, écart maximal de cours m

flurry n (Fin) accès de fièvre m; ~ **of activity** (Stock) agitation f, accès de fièvre m; ~ **of buying** vague d'achats f; ~ **of interest** mouvement d'intérêt m

flutter n: **have a** ~ UK (infrml) (gamble) parier; (on stock market) boursicoter

flux n flux m

fly vi voler

flyer n (advertisement) prospectus m, tract m; (speculative transaction) spéculation au hasard f

flying: ~ **pickets** n pl piquets de grève m pl; ~ **visit** n visite éclair f

flyleaf n page de garde f

fly posting n affichage sauvage m

fly tipping n décharge illégale f

FM abbr (▸**frequency modulation**) FM f (modulation de fréquence)

FMCG abbr (▸**fast-moving consumer goods**) produits de grande consommation à forte rotation m pl

FOB abbr (▸**free on board**) FAB (franco à bord)

FOC abbr (▸**free of charge**) franco, gratis

focal point n (of discussion) point central m; **act as a** ~ **for discussion** constituer le point central de la discussion

focus ¹ n point focal m; **lack** ~ manquer d'objectifs clairs; **the** ~ **will be on quality** l'accent sera mis sur la qualité; ~ **group** n groupe de discussion m; (S&M) groupe-témoin m

focus ² vt concentrer, focaliser; ~ **on**, ~ **upon** se concentrer sur; ~ **one's attention on** concentrer son attention sur

fold ⓵ vt plier
⓶ vi (business) fermer, faire faillite

folder n (cardboard) chemise f; (ringbinder) classeur m

follow ⓵ vt (person, advice, curve) suivre; (career) poursuivre; ~ **sb up** suivre qn; ~ **the fortunes** (Ins) (re-insurance) suivre les fortunes; ~ **the path of** suivre la voie de; ~ **a similar pattern** suivre un modèle similaire; ~ **suit** faire pareil
⓶ vi (in time) suivre; (in logical sequence) s'ensuivre; **as** ~**s** comme suit; **it** ~**s that** il s'ensuit que; ~ **through** (project, scheme) mener qch à terme; (idea, argument) aller jusqu'au bout de; ~ **up** (request, suggestion, wish) donner suite à, assurer le suivi de; (claim) suivre

follower n disciple m

follow-on n suite f

follow-up n (to event) suite f; (by letter) rappel m; (to defaulter) relance f, suivi m; ~ **letter** n lettre de rappel f, lettre de relance f; ~ **study** n étude de suivi f; ~ **visit** n visite de contrôle f; ~ **work** n travail complémentaire m

font n (typography) fonte f; (Comp) police de caractères f

food n alimentation f; ~ **aid** n aide alimentaire f; ~ **chain** n chaîne alimentaire f; ~ **processing** n traitement des denrées alimentaires m; ~**-processing industry** n agro-alimentaire m; ~ **retailing** n commerce alimentaire de détail m; ~ **store** n magasin d'alimentation m; ~ **surplus** n pl **-ses** excédent alimentaire m

Food: ~ **and Agriculture Organization** *n* Organisation des Nations unies pour l'Alimentation et l'Agriculture, OAA *f*; ~ **and Drug Administration** *n* US *organisme gouvernemental de contrôle alimentaire et pharmaceutique*

foodstuff *n* denrée alimentaire *f*, aliment *m*; ~**s** denrées alimentaires *f pl*

footer *n* (of document) bas de page *m*, pied de page *m*

footfall *n* (of shop) fréquentation *f*

footing *n* US addition *f*; **on the same** ~ sur le même pied; **be on an equal** ~ **with** être sur un pied d'égalité avec; **put something on a legal** ~ légaliser qch

footnote *n* note en bas de page *f*

Footsie *abbr* UK (▶**Financial Times Stock Exchange index**) indice Footsie *m*

FOQ *abbr* (▶**free on quay**) FAQ (franco à quai)

f.o.r. *abbr* (▶**free on rail**) franco gare, franco sur rail, franco wagon

forbid *vt* défendre

force¹ *n* force *f*; **be in** ~ être en vigueur; **come into** ~ entrer en vigueur; ~ **majeure** *n* force majeure *f*

force² *vt* contraindre, forcer; ~ **sb into early retirement** mettre qn en préretraite obligatoire; ~ **the issue** brusquer les choses; ~ **sb to do sth** obliger qn à faire qch; ~ **down** (interest rates) faire baisser; (prices, wages) faire diminuer; (inflation, demand) réduire; ~ **through** (measure, legislation) faire adopter; ~ **up** faire augmenter

forced: ~ **currency** *n* cours forcé *m*; ~ **landing** *n* atterrissage forcé *m*; ~ **sale** *n* vente forcée *f*; ~ **savings** *n pl* épargne forcée *f*

forceful *adj* (speech, defence) vigoureux/ -euse; (person) énergique (removal, eviction) forcé

forcible entry *adj* (by police) perquisition *f*; (by thief) effraction *f*

forecast *n* prévisions *f pl*

forecaster *n* prévisionniste *m*

forecasting *n* prévision *f*; (long term) prospective *f*; **market** ~ prévisions du marché *f pl*

foreclose *vt* saisir; ~ **a mortgage** saisir un bien hypothéqué; ~ **on** (person) forclore; (loan, mortgage) saisir

foreclosure *n* (action) forclusion *f*; ~ **of mortgage** saisie *f*, saisie d'un bien hypothéqué *f*; ~ **sale** *n* vente sur saisie *f*

forefront *n*: **at the** ~ **of** (research) à la pointe de

forego *vt* renoncer à; ~ **a debt** remettre une dette

foreground¹ *adj* de premier plan

foreground² *n* premier plan *m*

foreign *adj* étranger/-ère; ~ **account** *n* compte à l'étranger *m*; ~ **affairs** *n pl*

affaires étrangères *f pl*; ~ **agent** *n* agent à l'étranger *m*; ~ **aid** *n* aide étrangère *f*, aide à l'étranger *f*; ~ **assets** *n pl* avoirs extérieurs *m pl*, avoirs étrangers *m pl*; ~ **bank** *n* banque étrangère *f*; ~ **bond** *n* obligation étrangère *f*; ~ **borrowing** *n* emprunts étrangers *m pl*; ~ **company** *n* société étrangère *f*; ~ **competitor** *n* concurrent/-e étranger/-ère *m/f*; ~ **controlled** *adj* sous contrôle étranger; ~ **correspondent** *n* envoyé permanent à l'étranger *m*; ~ **currency** *n* devise étrangère *f*; ~ **currency transaction** *n* transaction en devises *f*; ~ **currency translation** *n* conversion de devises *f*; ~ **demand** *n* demande étrangère *f*; ~ **editor** *n* (Media) chef du service étranger *m*; ~ **exchange** *n* (currency) devises *f pl*; (action) change *m*, opération de change *f*; ~ **exchange dealer** *n* cambiste *mf*; ~ **exchange department** *n* service du change *m*; ~ **exchange earner** *n* personne rémunérée en devises étrangères *f*; ~ **exchange hedge** *n* couverture de change *f*; ~ **exchange holdings** *n pl* avoirs en devises *m pl*; ~ **exchange market** *n* marché des changes *m*; ~ **exchange office** *n* bureau de change *m*; ~ **exchange rate** *n* taux de change *m*; ~ **exchange reserves** *n pl* réserves de change *f pl*, réserves en devises étrangères *f pl*; ~ **exchange trader** *n* cambiste *mf*; ~ **firm** *n* entreprise étrangère *f*; ~ **flag** *n* pavillon étranger *m*; ~**-going vessel** *n* long-courrier *m*; ~ **government** *n* gouvernement étranger *m*; ~ **income** *n* revenu de source étrangère *m*; ~ **investment** *n* investissement à l'étranger *m*; ~ **language** *n* langue étrangère *f*; ~ **market** *n* marché étranger *m*, marché extérieur *m*; ~ **minister** *n* ministre des Affaires étrangères *mf*; ~ **money order** *n* mandat de l'étranger *m*; ~ **national** *n* ressortissant/-e étranger/-ère *m/f*; ~**-owned** *adj* sous contrôle étranger; ~**-owned company** *n* firme sous contrôle étranger *f*; ~ **sales** *n pl* vente à l'étranger *f*; ~ **security** *n* valeur de société étrangère *f*; ~ **share** *n* action de société étrangère *f*; ~ **stock** *n* action de société étrangère *f*; ~ **student** *n* étudiant/-e étranger/-ère *m/f*; ~ **trade** *n* commerce extérieur *m*; ~ **worker** *n* travailleur/-euse étranger/-ère *m/f*

Foreign: ~ **and Commonwealth Office** *n* UK ministère des Affaires étrangères et du Commonwealth *m*; ~ **Secretary** *n* UK ≈ ministre des Affaires étrangères *mf*

foreigner *n* étranger/-ère *m/f*

foreman *n pl* **-men** chef d'équipe *m*, contremaître *m*

forename *n* prénom *m*

foresee *vt* prédire

foreseeable *adj* prévisible; **in the** ~ **future** dans un avenir prévisible

forestry *n* sylviculture *f*

forex n (▸**foreign exchange**) (currency) devises f pl; (transaction) change m

forfeit vt perdre, être privé de; (voluntarily) renoncer à

forfeited security n (Ins) cautionnement perdu m

forfeiture n (of assets) confiscation f; ~ **of property** perte d'un bien par confiscation f; ~ **of right** déchéance d'un droit (pour inexécution d'une obligation) f

forge 1 vt (counterfeit) contrefaire; (alter) falsifier; (alliance) forger; (identity) établir; (plan) élaborer; ~ **a link with** établir un lien avec 2 vi ~ **ahead** (company, industry) être en plein essor; ~ **ahead with** (plan) aller de l'avant dans

forged adj faux/fausse; ~ **check** AmE, ~ **cheque** BrE n chèque falsifié m

forger n contrefacteur/-trice m/f

forgery n (of banknotes, signature) contrefaçon f; (false signature) contrefaçon f, falsification f; (fake document, artwork) faux m

forgivable loan n subvention remboursable sous condition f

forgive vt (debt) annuler; (act) pardonner; (person) pardonner à; ~ **sb sth** pardonner qch à qn

forgiveness n ~ **of debt** annulation de dettes f; ~ **of tax** remise d'impôt f, remise gracieuse d'impôt f

fork-lift truck n chariot élévateur à fourche m

form[1] n (printed) formulaire m; **in the ~ of** sous la forme de; ~ **letter** n lettre-type f

form[2] 1 vt (committee, alliance) former, établir; (new business) créer; (ideas, attitude) former; (subsidiary) créer; ~ **a partnership** s'associer; ~ **part of** faire partie de; ~ **the basis of** constituer la base de 2 vi se former

formal adj officiel/-ielle; ~ **agreement**, ~ **arrangement** n accord officiel m; ~ **communication** n communication hiérarchique f, transmission de l'information par voie hiérarchique f; ~ **dinner** n dîner officiel m; ~ **dress** n tenue de soirée f; ~ **economy** n économie officiellement répertoriée f; ~ **indexation** n indexation légale f; ~ **notice** n préavis en règle m; ~ **qualification** n qualification reconnue f; ~ **receipt** n reçu en bonne et due forme m; ~ **training** n formation professionnelle f

formality n formalité f; **customs formalities** formalités de douane f pl; **dispense with the formalities** se dispenser de formalités

formalization n mise en forme juridique f

formalize vt formaliser, officialiser

format[1] n format m

format[2] vt (disk) formater

formation n (of corporation) constitution f

formative adj formateur/-trice

formatting n (of disk) formatage m

former adj (employer, employee, client) ancien/-ienne; (first of two) premier/-ière

formula n pl -**lae** formule f; ~ **funding** n méthode de financement préétablie f

formulate vt (policy, idea, design, reply, charge) formuler; (rules, principles, strategy) élaborer

formulation n (of policy, idea, design, reply, charge) formulation f; (of rules, principles, strategy) élaboration f

forthcoming adj prochain, à venir

fortnight n quinze jours m pl, deux semaines f pl; **a ~ tomorrow** dans deux semaines; **the first ~ in June** la première quinzaine de juin

fortnightly[1] adj bimensuel/-elle

fortnightly[2] adv toutes les deux semaines

fortuitous adj fortuit; ~ **loss** n (Ins) perte fortuite f

fortune n (wealth) fortune f; (luck) chance f; **make a ~** faire fortune; **have the good ~ to do** avoir la chance de faire

forum n pl -**s**, **fora** forum m

forward[1] adv à l'avant

forward[2] vt (dispatch) expédier; (send on) faire suivre, réexpédier

forward: ~ **averaging** n (of income) étalement m; ~ **buying** n (Stock) achat à terme m; ~ **contract** n contrat à terme m; ~ **cover** n couverture à terme f; ~ **delivery** n livraison à terme f; ~ **exchange** n change à terme m; ~ **exchange market** n marché des opérations de change à terme m; ~ **exchange rate** n taux de change à terme m; ~ **facing** adj en relation directe avec le client; ~ **integration** n intégration en aval, intégration en avant f; ~ **market** n marché à terme m; ~ **operation** n (Stock) opération à terme f; ~ **planning** n planification à terme f; ~ **position** n position à terme f, situation à terme f; ~ **pricing** n établissement des prix à terme m; ~ **purchase contract** n contrat d'achat à terme m; ~ **rate** n cours à terme m, taux pour les opérations à terme m; ~ **sales contract** n contrat de vente à terme m; ~ **scheduling** n programmation progressive f; ~ **security** n valeur à terme f; ~ **slash** n barre oblique f; ~ **swap** n échange financier à terme m; ~ **transaction** n transaction à terme f

forwarder n (sender) expéditeur/-trice m/f; (carrier) expéditeur m, transitaire mf; ~'**s bill of lading** connaissement de l'expéditeur m; ~'**s certificate of receipt** attestation de prise en charge du transitaire f

forwarding n (of mail) expédition f; (of freight) transport m; ~ **address** n adresse de réexpédition f; ~ **agency** n bureau de transitaires m; ~ **agent** n (S&M) transitaire mf; (Transp) commissionnaire de transport m, groupeur m, transitaire mf; ~ **in bulk**

expédition groupée f; ~ **charges** n pl frais d'expédition m pl; ~ **company** n commissionnaire de transport m, transitaire mf; ~ **instructions** n pl instructions d'expédition f pl; ~ **station** n gare d'expédition f

forward-looking adj (person, project) tourné vers l'avenir

FOS abbr (▸free on ship) FAB (franco à bord)

fossil fuel n combustible fossile m

foster vt (environment, relationship) favoriser; (activity, image) promouvoir; (attitude) encourager

foul: ~ **bill of health** n patente de santé brute f; ~ **bill of lading** n connaissement brut m

foundation n fondation f; **lay the** ~**s for** jeter les fondements de; **without** ~ (of rumour) sans fondement; **there is no** ~ **in the report that...** il n'y a aucun fondement dans le rapport selon lequel...

founder[1] n fondateur/-trice m/f; ~ **member** n membre fondateur m

founder[2] vi (project) être en difficultés; (career, plans, negotiations) être compromis; ~ **on sth** être compromis par qch

founding company n société fondatrice f

fourth-generation adj de quatrième génération

FP abbr (▸fully paid) lib., payé intégralement

FPA abbr (Ins) (▸free of particular average) FAP (franc d'avarie particulière)

fraction n fraction f

fractionalize vt fractionner

fractional: ~ **lot** n lot fractionnaire m; ~ **share** n (Stock) fraction d'action f, parts fractionnaires f pl

fragile adj fragile

fragmentation n (of disk, market) fragmentation f

fragmented: ~ **bargaining** n négociation par tranches f; ~ **market** n marché fragmenté m, marché non-homogène m

frame n (Comp) (window) cadre m; ~ **of mind** humeur f; ~ **of reference** cadre de référence m

framework n (of institution, system) cadre m; **in the** ~ **of** dans le cadre de; ~ **document** n document de cadrage m; ~ **talks** n pl réunion de cadrage f

franc n franc m

franchise n franchise f; ~ **agreement** n accord de franchise m; ~ **tax** n US patente f

franchised dealer n UK concessionnaire titulaire d'une franchise mf

franchisee n franchisé/-e m/f

franchising n franchisage m, franchise f

franchisor n franchiseur m

franco adv franco

Franco-English adj franco-britannique, franco-anglais

frank vt (letter, parcel) affranchir

franking machine n BrE machine à affranchir f

fraud n fraude f; **computer** ~ fraude informatique f; **credit card** ~ fraude sur cartes de crédit f; ~ **prevention** n répression des fraudes f

Fraud Squad n UK brigade de la répression des fraudes

fraudulence n caractère frauduleux m

fraudulent adj (practice, use) frauduleux/ -euse; (cheque, signature) falsifié; (statement) faux/fausse; (claim) indu; (earnings) illicite; ~ **bankruptcy** n banqueroute frauduleuse f, faillite frauduleuse f; ~ **entry** n fausse écriture f; ~ **misrepresentation** n fausse déclaration intentionnelle f

fraudulently adv frauduleusement

FRB abbr US (▸Federal Reserve Board) conseil d'administration de la Réserve fédérale

free[1] adj (available) disponible, libre; (unrestricted) libre; (not requiring payment) gratuit; ~ **of address** sans adresse; ~ **of all additives** sans additifs; ~ **of all average** franc de toute avarie; ~ **of all taxation** exempt de tout impôt; ~ **alongside quay** franco le long du quai, franco à quai; ~ **alongside ship** franco le long du bord, ~ **of charge** gratuit; ~ **of damage** intact; (Ins) sans avaries; ~ **dock** (Transp) franco à quai; ~ **domicile** (Transp) franco domicile; ~ **from alongside** franco le long du bord; ~ **of general average** franc d'avarie grosse, franc d'avaries communes; ~ **in harbor** AmE, ~ **in harbour** BrE franco à port; ~ **in and out** bord à bord; ~ **insurance and carriage** franco assurance et transport; ~ **on aircraft** franco à bord aéroport; ~ **on board** franco à bord; ~ **on quay** franco à quai; ~ **on rail** franco gare, franco sur rail; ~ **on ship** franco à bord; ~ **on wharf** franco à quai; ~ **of particular average** (Ins) franc d'avarie particulière

free[2] adv gratuitement, gratis

free[3] vt (funds, capital) débloquer; (staff) libérer; ~ **sb up** libérer qn

free: ~ **baggage allowance** n BrE franchise de bagages f; ~ **capital** n disponibilités f pl; ~ **circulation** n libre circulation f; ~ **competition** n concurrence libre f; ~ **delivery** n livraison gratuite f; ~ **discharge** franco déchargement; ~ **economy** n économie libérale f; ~ **enterprise** n libre entreprise f; ~ **enterprise economy** n économie de libre entreprise f; ~**-for-all** n (infrml) foire d'empoigne f; ~ **gift** n prime f, cadeau m; ~ **luggage allowance** n AmE franchise de bagages f; ~ **market** n marché libre m; ~ **market economy** n économie de marché f, ⇢

économie libérale *f*; ~ **market price** *n* prix du marché libre *m*; ~ **movement** *n* (of goods and services) libre circulation *f*; ~ **movement of capital** *n* libre circulation des capitaux *f*; ~ **movement of labor** AmE, ~ **movement of labour** BrE *n* libre circulation de la main-d'œuvre *f*; ~ **newspaper** *n* journal gratuit *m*; ~ **and open market** *n* marché libre et ouvert *m*; ~ **paper** *n* journal gratuit *m*; ~ **port** *n* port entrepôt *m*, port franc *m*; ~**-rein leadership** *n* autorité qui s'exerce en douceur *f*; ~ **sample** *n* échantillon gratuit *m*; ~ **trade** *n* libre-échange *m*; ~**-trade agreement** *n* accord de libre-échange *m*; ~**-trade area** *n*, ~**-trade zone** *n* zone de libre-échange *f*, zone franche *f*; ~ **trial** *n* essai gratuit *m*; ~ **trial period** *n* période d'essai gratuit *f*

freebie *n* (infml) cadeau publicitaire *m*

freeboard *n* franc-bord *m*

freedom *n* (immunity) exemption *f*; (liberty) liberté *f*; ~ **of action** liberté d'action *f*; ~ **of association** liberté d'association *f*; ~ **of choice** liberté de choix *f*; ~ **of competition** liberté de concurrence *f*; ~ **of establishment** (Pol) (in EU) liberté d'établissement *f*; ~ **of movement** liberté de circulation *f*

Freedom of Information Act *n* US *loi sur la liberté de l'information*

freed up *adj* (security) libéré

Freefone® *n* UK service d'appel gratuit *m*; ~ **number** *n* UK ≈ numéro vert *m*

freehold *n* pleine propriété *f*, propriété foncière libre *f*; ~ **owner** *n* plein propriétaire *m*; ~ **property** *n* pleine propriété *f*, propriété foncière libre *f*

freeholder *n* propriétaire foncier à perpétuité *mf*

freelance¹ *adj* free-lance, indépendant

freelance² *n* free-lance *mf*, travailleur/-euse indépendant/-e *m/f*

freelance: ~ **contract** *n* contrat de travail indépendant *m*; ~ **journalist** *n* journaliste indépendant/-e *m/f*, journaliste payé/-e à la pige *m/f*, pigiste *mf*; ~ **worker** *n* free-lance *mf*, travailleur/-euse indépendant/-e *m/f*; ~ **writer** *n* pigiste *mf*, écrivain indépendant *m*

freelancer *n* free-lance *mf*, travailleur/-euse indépendant/-e *m/f*

freely *adv* librement; ~ **available** (accessible to all) ouvert à tous; (easy to find) d'un accès facile; ~ **negotiable credit** *n* crédit librement négociable *m*

Freepost® *n* UK port payé *m*

freesheet *n* journal gratuit *m*

freestanding *adj* autonome

freeware *n* logiciel gratuit *m*, graticiel *m*

freeway *n* AmE autoroute *f*

freeze¹ *n* (of credits, assets) gel *m*; (of rents, wages, prices) blocage *m*, gel *m*

freeze² **1** *vt* (credit, assets) geler; (rents, wages, prices) bloquer, geler; ~ **an account** bloquer un compte

2 *vi* (Comp) se bloquer; ~ **out** (competitor) supplanter

freezing *n* (of credit, assets) gel *m*; (of rents, wages, prices) blocage *m*, gel *m*

freight *n* cargaison *f*, fret *m*, marchandises *f pl*; ~ **forward** fret payable à destination *m*, port dû *m*; ~ **and insurance paid** fret et assurance payés *m pl*; ~ **prepaid** fret payé à l'expédition *m*, port payé *m*; ~ **car** AmE fourgon *m*; ~ **container** *n* conteneur de fret *m*; ~ **costs** *n pl* frais de transport *m pl*; ~ **forwarder** *n* transitaire *mf*, transporteur routier *m*; ~ **insurance** *n* assurance du fret *f*; ~ **manifest** *n* manifeste de fret *m*; ~ **note** *n* lettre de voiture *f*; ~ **policy** *n* (marine) police de fret *f*; ~ **rate** *n* tarif de fret *m*; ~ **terminal** *n* terminal de fret *m*; ~ **traffic** *n* trafic marchandises *m*; ~ **train** *n* train de marchandises *m*; ~ **transport** *n* transport de marchandises *m*; ~ **yard** *n* gare de marchandises *f*

freighter *n* (aircraft) avion-cargo *m*; (ship) cargo *m*, navire de charge *m*

French: ~ **Chamber of Commerce** *n* Chambre de commerce française *f*; ~ **franc** *n* franc français *m*; ~**-speaking world** *n* monde francophone *m*, francophonie *f*

frequency *n* fréquence *f*; ~ **curve** *n* courbe de fréquence *f*; ~ **distribution** *n* distribution des fréquences *f*, répartition de fréquence *f*; ~ **modulation** *n* modulation de fréquence *f*

frequent *adj* (event, visit, change) fréquent; (common, usual) courant

fresh: ~ **food** *n*, ~ **goods** *n pl* produits frais *m pl*; ~ **water** *n* eau douce *f*

friction *n* désaccord *m*

frictionless *adj* (commerce, economy) sans friction

friendly *adj* (person, attitude) amical; (nation, government) ami *inv*; (settlement) à l'amiable; **be on ~ terms with** être en bons termes avec; ~ **agreement** *n* accord à l'amiable *m*; ~ **society** *n* BrE société de prévoyance *f*, mutuelle *f*; ~ **suit** *n* procès à l'amiable *m*; ~ **takeover** *n* prise de contrôle amicale *f*

fringe: ~ **benefit** *n* complément de salaire *m*; ~ **benefits** *n pl* (HRM) (car, free lunches etc.) avantages en nature *m pl*, (health insurance, pension plan etc.) avantages sociaux *m pl*; ~ **market** *n* marché marginal *m*; ~ **meeting** *n* réunion en marge *f*

frisk *vt* fouiller

from *prep* (Transp) en provenance de

front *n* (Media) couverture *f*; (person) animateur/-trice *m/f*; **be ~-page news** être à la une; ~ **desk** *n* réception *f*; ~**-end** *n* (Comp) interface utilisateur *f*; ~**-end computer** *n* ordinateur frontal *m*; ~**-end costs** *n pl* frais de commercialisation *m pl*;

~-end financing n financement initial m; **~-end loading** n méthode de prélèvement des frais d'achat sur les premiers versements f; **~-end loan** n prêt initial m; **~-line employees** n pl personnel sur le terrain m; **~-line management** n maîtrise f; **~ money** n (Fin) liquidité d'ouverture f; **~-of-house jobs** n pl postes d'accueil m pl; **~ office** n (reception area) réception f; (Stock) salle des marchés f; (in commerce and services sectors) activités en relation directe avec le client f pl; **~-office application** n application de guichet f; **~-office personnel** n personnel de réception m

frontage n façade f

frontier n frontière f; **~ control** n contrôle aux frontières m, contrôle frontalier m

frozen adj bloqué, gelé; **~ account** n compte gelé m; **~ assets** n pl actif gelé m, fonds gelés m pl; **~ credits** n pl crédits gelés m pl; **~ foods** n pl surgelés m pl

frt abbr (▶freight) cargaison f, fret m, marchandises f pl; **~ fwd** (▶freight forward) fret payable à destination m; **~ ppd** (▶freight prepaid) fret payé à l'expédition m, p.p. (port payé)

fruit: **~ farmer** n producteur/-trice de fruits m/f; **~ farming** n culture fruitière f

fruition n: **come to ~** se réaliser

fruitless adj vain

frustration n frustration f; **~ of contract** n (Law) résolution de contrat f

FTA abbr (▶free-trade agreement) accord de libre-échange m

FT Index n UK (▶Financial Times Industrial Ordinary Share Index) indice des actions industrielles ordinaires du Financial Times

FTP abbr (file transfer protocol) protocole de transfert de fichiers m

FTSE abbr UK (▶Financial Times Stock Exchange index) indice FTSE m, le FTSE, ≈ l'indice CAC40 m

FTZ abbr (▶free-trade zone) zone de libre-échange f, zone franche f

FUD abbr (fear, uncertainty and doubt) **~ attack** n stratégie commerciale qui consiste à mettre en doute la compatibilité future de logiciels concurrents

fuel¹ n carburant m; **~ efficiency** n rendement du combustible m; **~ oil** n fioul m, mazout m; **~ tax** n taxe sur les carburants f

fuel² vt (inflation) alimenter, entretenir; (suspicion) susciter; (fears) aggraver

fulcrum n pivot m, point d'appui m

fulfil BrE, **fulfill** AmE vt (commitment, obligation) s'acquitter de; (obligations) honorer; (ambition) réaliser; (promise) tenir; (need) répondre à; (conditions, contract, role, duty) remplir

fulfillment AmE, **fulfilment** BrE n (of ambition) réalisation f; (of role, duty, obligation) accomplissement m; (of contract, plan) exécution f; (in commercial transaction) gestion optimale de la commande f, suivi de la commande jusqu'à la livraison m

full adj plein; **at ~ capacity** (machinery) à plein rendement, à plein régime; **be in ~ swing** battre son plein; **in ~ settlement** pour solde de tout compte; **~ loaded weight and capacity** (of container) poids et capacité à charge complète; **~ board** n pension complète f; **~ container load** n conteneur complet m; **~-cost pricing** n méthode du prix de revient complet f; **~ costing** n méthode de capitalisation du coût entier f; **~ cover** n (Ins) couverture totale f; **~ coverage** n (Ins) couverture totale f; **~ disclosure** n divulgation complète f; **~ employment** n plein emploi m; **~ exemption** n (Tax) dégrèvement total m; **~ fare** n plein tarif m; **~ liability** n responsabilité pleine et entière f; **~ member** n membre à part entière m; **~ name** n nom et prénom(s) m; **~-page advertisement** n placard publicitaire m; **~ particulars** n pl tous les détails m pl; **~ quotation** n cotation complète f; **~ rate** n tarif complet m; **~-scale investigation** n enquête exhaustive f; **~-screen** adj plein écran m, pleine page f; **~-service agency** n agence de publicité globale f; **~ session** n assemblée plénière f; **~ share** n action entière f; **~ taxation year** n année complète d'imposition f; **~ text** n texte intégral m; **~-text search** n (Comp) recherche en texte intégral f; **~-time** adj à temps complet, à temps plein; **~-time employment** n emploi à plein temps m; **~-timer** n employé/-e à plein temps m/f

fully: **~ booked** adj complet/-ète; **~ comprehensive** adj tous risques; **~ comprehensive insurance policy** n police d'assurance tous risques f; **~ paid** adj payé intégralement; **~-paid policy** n police payée intégralement f; **~-paid share** n action entièrement libérée f; **~ registered bond** n obligation essentiellement nominative f; **~ registered security** n titre essentiellement nominatif m

function¹ n (Math, Comp) fonction f; (party) réception officielle f; (feature) fonction f; (role) fonction f, rôle m; **as a ~ of** en fonction de

function² vi fonctionner; **~ as sth** (object) faire fonction de qch, servir de qch; (person) jouer le rôle de qch

functional adj (practical) fonctionnel/-elle; (operational) opérationnel/-elle; **~ analysis** n analyse fonctionnelle f; **~ approach** n démarche fonctionnelle f; **~ costing** n attribution des charges par fonction f; **~ currency** n devise d'exploitation f; **~ financing** n financement fonctionnel m; **~ layout** n implantation fonctionnelle f; **~ management** n gestion par fonctions f; **~ organization** n organisation fonctionnelle f, ⋯⟶

organisation horizontale *f*, organisation par secteurs d'activité *f*; ~ **relations** *n pl* liaisons fonctionnelles *f pl*; ~ **responsibility** *n* responsabilité fonctionnelle *f*

functionality *n* (Gen Comm, Comp) fonctionnalité *f*

functioning *n* fonctionnement *m*

fund¹ *n* caisse *f*, fonds *m*; ~ **appropriation** *n* (governmental) crédit créant un fond *m*; ~ **management** *n* gestion de fonds *f*; ~ **manager** *n* gestionnaire de fonds *mf*; ~**-raiser** *n* (person) collecteur/-trice de fonds *m/f*; (dinner) dîner organisé pour collecter des fonds *m*; (gala) gala organisé pour collecter des fonds *m*; ~**-raising** *n* appel de fonds *m*, collecte de fonds *f*

fund² *vt* (debt, loan) consolider; (project) financer

fundamental *adj* fondamental; ~ **analysis** *n* analyse fondamentale *f*; ~ **equilibrium** *n* équilibre fondamental *m*

funded: ~ **debt** *n* dette consolidée *f*; ~ **property** *n* biens en rente *m pl*

funding *n* financement *m*; (of debt) consolidation *f*; ~ **agency** *n* société de financement *f*; ~ **gap** *n* déficit financier *m*

funds *n pl* fonds *m pl*; **no** ~ défaut de provision *m*; ~ **abroad** *n pl* fonds à l'étranger *m pl*; ~ **transfer** *n* transfert de fonds *m*

fungible *adj* (person, goods) interchangeable; ~ **asset** *n* actif fongible *m*

fungibles *n pl* fongibles *m pl*

funnel *vt* (efforts, energy, aid) canaliser; (resources) affecter; ~ **funds into doing** débloquer des crédits pour faire

furlough *n* AmE (laying off of staff) mise en chômage temporaire *f*; (leave of absence) autorisation de congé *f*

furniture *n* mobilier *m*

further¹ *adv* de plus, en outre; ~ **to your letter** suite à votre lettre; ~ **to your telephone call** suite à votre appel

further² *vt* (idea) promouvoir; (chances) augmenter; (plan, career) faire avancer; (cause) servir

further: ~ **education** *n* ≈ enseignement professionnel *m*; ~ **information** *n* de plus amples renseignements *m pl*

furtherance *n* (of aim, objective) poursuite *f*; **in** ~ **of this goal** pour servir cet objectif

fuse ⟦1⟧ *vt* (ideas) faire fusionner ⟦2⟧ *vi* (ideas) fusionner

fusion *n* (of ideas, images, parties) fusion *f*

future¹ *adj* (prospects, development, plan) futur, d'avenir; **at some** ~ **date** à une date ultérieure

future² *n* avenir *m*; **in** ~ à l'avenir; **in the** ~ à l'avenir; **in the near** ~ dans un proche avenir; **have a bright** ~ avoir un bel avenir; **have no** ~ ne pas avoir d'avenir; **see into the** ~ lire l'avenir; **cars of the** ~ les voitures de demain

future: ~ **development zone** *n* zone d'aménagement différé *f*, ZAD *f*; ~ **goods** *n pl* marchandises livrables à terme *f pl*; ~ **orders** *n pl* commandes futures *f pl*; ~ **price** *n* (Stock) cours à terme *m*, prix à terme *m*; ~ **prospect** *n* perspectives d'avenir *f pl*; ~ **trends** *n pl* tendances futures *f pl*

future-proof¹ *adj* protégé contre l'obsolescence

future-proof² *vt* protéger contre l'obsolescence

futures *n pl* opérations à terme *f pl*; ~ **contract** *n* contrat à terme *m*, contrat à terme d'instrument financier *m*; ~ **market** *n* marché à terme *m*; ~ **position** *n* position à terme *f*; ~ **sales** *n pl* ventes à découvert *f pl*; ~ **trader** *n* opérateur sur les contrats à terme *m*; ~ **trading** *n* transactions sur les contrats à terme *f pl*

futurologist *n* futurologiste *mf*

futurology *n* futurologie *f*

fuzzy *adj* confus; (distinction) flou; ~ **loan** *n* prêt aux termes mal définis *m*; ~ **logic** *n* logique floue *f*

fwdr *abbr* (▸**forwarder**) expéditeur/-trice *m/f*, transitaire *mf*

FX *abbr* (▸**foreign exchange**) (transaction) change *m*; (currency) devises *f pl*; ~ **option** *n* option de change *f*, option sur devises *f*

FY *abbr* (▸**financial year**, ▸**fiscal year**) exercice comptable *m*, exercice financier *m*

FYI *abbr* (▸**for your information**) à titre d'information

Gg

G: **3G** *abbr* (▸**third generation**) 3G *f* (troisième génération); ~ **mobile telephony** téléphonie mobile de troisième génération *f*

G2B *abbr* (▸**government-to-business**) transactions gouvernement-entreprise *f pl*, transactions G2B *f pl*; ~ **portal/service**

portail/service gouvernement-entreprise *m*,
portail/service G2B *m*

G2C *abbr* (▸**government-to-citizen**)
transactions gouvernement-citoyen *f pl*,
transactions G2C *f pl*; ~ **portal/service**
portail/service gouvernement-citoyen *m*,
portail/service G2C *m*

G7 *abbr* (▸**Group of Seven**) G7 *m* (Groupe
des Sept)

GA *abbr* (▸**General Assembly**) AG *f*
(assemblée générale); (▸**general average**)
(Ins) a.c. (avarie commune); (Math) moyenne
générale *f*

GAB *abbr* (▸**general arrangements to
borrow**) AGE *m pl* (accords généraux
d'emprunt)

gadget *n* gadget *m*

gage *n*, *vt* AmE ▸**gauge** BrE

gagging order *n* UK interdiction de
rapporter les débats *f*

gag order *n* US interdiction de rapporter
les débats *f*

gain¹ *n* (advantage) gain *m*; (profit) gain *m*,
profit *m*; (increase) augmentation *f*; (in status,
knowledge) acquis *m*; **make** ~**s** faire des gains,
réaliser des gains; (shares, currency) être en
hausse; **show a five point** ~ (Stock) réaliser
une hausse de cinq points; **losses and** ~**s**
pertes et profits; ~**s in productivity** des gains
de productivité *m pl*; **make significant** ~**s in
a market** réaliser des progrès considérables
sur un marché

gain² [1] *vt* gagner; ~ **control of** prendre
le contrôle de; ~ **experience** acquérir de
l'expérience; ~ **approval from** obtenir
l'accord de; ~ **ground** gagner du terrain; ~
momentum (trend) s'accélérer; ~ **a toehold in
the market** s'introduire dans le marché; ~
value gagner de la valeur
[2] *vi* (Stock) (increase in value) se valoriser,
être en hausse; ~ **in popularity** gagner en
popularité; ~ **in value** gagner de la valeur

gainer *n* (Stock) valeur en hausse *f*

gainful *adj* (business) rentable; (occupation)
rémunérateur/-trice, lucratif/-ive; ~
employment *n* activité rémunérée *f*

gallery *n* galerie *f*

galley proof *n* galée *f*, placard *m*

galloping inflation *n* spirale
inflationniste *f*

Gallup poll *n* sondage Gallup *m*

gamble¹ *n* (risk) pari *m*; **take a** ~ prendre
des risques; **the** ~ **paid off** le pari a réussi

gamble² [1] *vt* miser
[2] *vi* (Gen Comm) miser; (on horses, cards)
parier; ~ **on the stock exchange** jouer à la
bourse; (as amateur) boursicoter; ~ **everything
on sth** tout miser sur qch; **we hadn't** ~**d on
a recession** nous n'avions pas prévu une
récession

gambling *n* jeu *m*

game *n* jeu *m*; ~ **plan** *n* plan d'action *m*,

stratégie *f*; ~ **theory** *n* théorie des jeux *f*

gamesmanship *n* art de gagner par des
astuces *m*

gameware *n* ludiciel *m*, logiciel de jeu *m*

gaming *n* jeu *m*

gamma *n* (Stock) gamma *m*; ~ **stock** *n* UK
action gamma *f*, action peu active *f*

gangway *n* passerelle de débarquement *f*

Gantt chart *n* diagramme de Gantt *m*

GAO *abbr* US (▸**General Accounting
Office**) ≈ Cour des comptes *f*

gap *n* (space) espace *m*; (deficit) déficit *m*;
(disparity) écart *m*; (in text) blanc *m*, trou *m*; (in
time) intervalle *f*; (in records, knowledge) lacune *f*;
(in market, timetable) créneau *m*; **look for a** ~ **in
the market** chercher un créneau sur le
marché; **fill a** ~ **in the market** répondre à un
besoin réel du marché; **the** ~ **between the
rich and the poor** l'écart entre les riches et
les pauvres; **close the** ~ supprimer l'écart;
training/technology ~ insuffisance en
matière de formation/technologie *f*; ~
financing *n* crédit relais *m*; ~ **loan** *n* prêt-
relais *m*; ~ **year** *n* année sabbatique *f* (*avant
d'entrer à l'université*)

garbage *n* (Comp) informations parasites *f
pl*; (rubbish) AmE déchets *m pl*, détritus *m pl*,
ordures *f pl*; ~ **in, garbage out** (Comp) telle
entrée, telle sortie

garnish *vt* opérer une saisie-arrêt sur,
pratiquer une saisie-arrêt sur

garnishee *n* tiers saisi *m*

garnishment *n* saisie-arrêt *f*

gas¹ *abbr* AmE (▸**gasoline**) carburant *m*,
essence *f*

gas² *n* gaz *m*; ~ **company** *n* compagnie du
gaz *f*; ~ **oil** *n* gas-oil *m*, gazole *m*; ~
pipeline *n* gazoduc *m*; ~ **station** *n* AmE
station-service *f*

gasoline *n* AmE carburant *m*, essence *f*

gasworks *n pl* usine à gaz *f*

gate *n* (attendance) nombre de spectateurs *m*;
(takings) recette *f*; (for flight) porte *f*; ~ **number**
n (aviation) numéro de porte *m*

gatefold *n* encart à volets *m*

gateway *n* (door) entrée *f*; (Comp) passerelle
f; (Transp) centre de transit international *m*;
(aviation) porte d'entrée *f*

gather [1] *vt* (data, information, evidence)
recueillir; ~ **that** déduire que; ~
intelligence recueillir des informations; ~
speed (vehicle) prendre de la vitesse; (trend,
movement) gagner du terrain
[2] *vi* (people) se rassembler; ~ **in** (papers,
objects) ramasser; (money) recueillir

gathering *n* (meeting) assemblée *f*

GATT *abbr* (▸**General Agreement on
Tariffs and Trade**) GATT *m* (Accord
général sur les tarifs et le commerce)

gauge¹ *n* BrE (of trends) indicateur *m*; (means
of judging) moyen de juger *m*; (instrument) ⋯⟶

jauge *f*

gauge² *vt* BrE (measure) calculer, mesurer; (estimate) évaluer

GAW *abbr* US (▸**guaranteed annual wage**) SMIG *m* (salaire minimum interprofessionnel garanti)

gazelle *n* petite entreprise en pleine croissance *f*

gazump *vt* UK *revenir sur un accord avec qn pour vendre à plus offrant*

gazumping *n* UK acceptation d'une suroffre *f*, fait de rompre une promesse de vente pour une offre plus élevée

Gb *abbr* (▸**gigabyte**) Go *m* (gigaoctet)

GCSE *abbr* UK (**General Certificate of Secondary Education**) certificat d'études secondaires *m*

GDP *abbr* (▸**gross domestic product**) PIB *m* (produit intérieur brut); ~ **per capita** *n* PIB par habitant *m*; ~ **per head** *n* PIB par habitant *m*

gds *abbr* (▸**goods**) (Gen Comm, Ind) articles *m pl*, produits *m pl*; (Econ) biens *m pl*

gear *vt* ~ **sth towards sb** adresser qch à qn; **be** ~**ed towards sb** s'adresser à, être orienté vers; **be** ~**ed towards doing** être destiné à faire; ~ **up** se préparer à; **be** ~**ed up for** être prêt pour; **be** ~**ed up to do** être prêt pour faire

gearing *n* BrE effet d'endettement *m*, effet de levier *m*; ~ **adjustment** *n* BrE redressement du taux d'endettement *m*; ~ **ratio** *n* BrE ratio d'endettement *m*, ratio de levier *m*

gender *n* sexe *m*; ~ **bias** *n*, ~ **discrimination** *n* discrimination sexuelle *f*, sexisme *m*; ~ **gap** *n* fossé entre les sexes *m*

general *adj* général; **in** ~ (usually) en général; (mostly, overall) dans l'ensemble; **give sb a** ~ **idea** donner une idée d'ensemble à qn; ~ **acceptance** *n* (document) acceptation sans réserve *f*, ~ **agent** *n* agent général *m*, représentant général *m*; ~ **arrangements to borrow** *n* accords généraux d'emprunt *m pl*; ~ **authorization** *n* autorisation générale *f*, ~ **average** *n* (Ins) avarie commune *f*; ~ **cargo** *n* cargaison mixte *f*; ~ **contractor** *n* entrepreneur *m*; ~ **creditor** *n* créancier non-garanti *m*; ~ **election** *n* élections législatives *f pl*; ~ **expenses** *n pl* frais généraux *m pl*; ~ **fund** *n* fonds courants *m pl*; ~ **governmental expenditure** *n* dépenses publiques *f pl*; ~ **journal** *n* livre-journal général *m*; ~ **ledger** *n* (Acc) grand livre *m*; ~ **liability insurance** *n* garantie générale d'assurance de responsabilité civile *f*; ~ **management** *n* direction générale *f*; ~ **manager** *n* directeur/-trice général/-e *m/f*; ~ **meeting** *n* assemblée générale *f*; ~ **meeting of shareholders** *n* assemblée générale des actionnaires *f*; ~ **obligation bond** *n* US obligation des collectivités locales garantie *f*; ~ **partner** *n* associé/-e général/e *m/f*,

commandité/-e *m/f*; ~ **policy committee** *n* commission de politique générale *f*; ~ **price level accounting** *n* comptabilité indexée sur le niveau général des prix *f*; ~ **public** *n* grand public *m*; ~**-purpose** *adj* à usage général; ~ **reserves** *n pl* réserve générale *f*, réserve légale *f*; ~ **secretary** *n* (of union) secrétaire général *m*; ~ **statement** *n* relevé général *m*; ~ **store** *n* bazar *m* (*qui fait aussi épicerie*); ~ **strike** *n* grève générale *f*; ~ **warranty deed** *n* US (Prop) acte notarié de garantie générale *m*

General: ~ **Accounting Office** *n* US ≈ Cour des comptes *f*; ~ **Agreement on Tariffs and Trade** *n* Accord général sur les tarifs et le commerce *m*; ~ **Agreement to Borrow** *n* Accord général d'emprunt *m*; ~ **Assembly** *n* assemblée générale *f*; ~ **Executive Manager** *n* Secrétaire général *m*

generalist *n* généraliste *mf*

generalize *vi* généraliser

generalized *adj* généralisé

generally *adv* (accepted, recognized, regarded) dans l'ensemble, en général; ~ **available** disponible pour le grand public; ~ **speaking** en général

generate *vt* (sales, data, graphics) produire; (waste, power, profit) générer; (employment) créer; (loss, publicity) entraîner; (interest, ideas) susciter; ~ **income** produire un revenu

generating station *n* centrale électrique *f*

generation *n* (of income, data) production *f*, (in product development, society) génération *f*; (of employment) création *f*; **third-**~ **mobile phone** téléphone portable de troisième génération *m*; ~ **gap** *n* conflit des générations *m*

generic *adj* générique; ~ **appeal** *n* appel publicitaire générique *m*; ~ **brand** *n* marque générique *f*; ~ **job title** *n* intitulé du poste *m*; ~ **market** *n* marché générique *m*; ~ **name** *n* nom générique *m*; ~ **product** *n* produit générique *m*; ~ **search** *n* (on Internet) recherche simple *f*

genetically modified *adj* transgénique, génétiquement modifié

genius *n* génie *m*

gentleman's agreement *n* accord à l'amiable *m*, gentleman's agreement *m*

gentlemen *n pl* (form of address) Messieurs *m pl*

gentrification *n* UK embourgeoisement *m*

genuine *adj* (buyer) serieux/-ieuse; (interest, effort) sincère; (bargain, motive) vrai; (authentic) authentique, véritable; ~ **article** *n* article authentique *m*

geocentric *adj* géocentrique

geodemographic *adj* géodémographique

geodemography *n* géodémographie *f*

geographic *adj* géographique; ~ **segment** *n* segment géographique *m*

geographical *adj* géographique

geography *n* géographie *f*

geomarketing *n* géomarketing *m*, géomercatique *f*

geometric *adj* géométrique; ~ **mean** *n* moyenne géométrique *f*; ~ **progression** *n* progression géométrique *f*

geopolitical *adj* géopolitique

gerrymander *vi* pratiquer le charcutage électoral

gerrymandering *n* charcutage électoral *m*

gestation period *n* période de gestation *f*

get ⓵ *vt* (obtain) obtenir; (receive) recevoir; (fetch) chercher; (earn) gagner, toucher ⓶ *vi* (become) devenir; ~ **in touch with** contacter; ~ **in touch with sb about sth** contacter qn au sujet de qch; ~ **into sb's good books** s'attirer les bonnes grâces de qn; ~ **onto sb** (infml) contacter qn; ~ **paid** se faire payer; ~ **worse** empirer; ~ **across** ⓵ *vt* (message) faire passer; ⓶ *vi* (message) passer; ~ **around** (news, rumour) circuler; ~ **back** (recover) recouvrer; ~ **one's money back** se faire rembourser; ~ **behind** prendre du retard; ~ **behind sth** (project, venture, campaign) soutenir; ~ **by** (cope) se débrouiller; ~ **by without sth** s'en tirer sans qch; ~ **over** (message) faire passer; ~ **round** (problem, law) contourner; ~ **through** (exam) réussir; (spend) dépenser; (consume) consommer; ~ **through to sb** (on telephone) avoir qn au téléphone, joindre qn; ~ **together** *vt* (people, staff) réunir; *vi* (people) se réunir

ghost site *n* (Comp) site fantôme *m*

GIF *abbr* (**Graphics Interchange Format**) (format) GIF *m*

gift *n* (present) cadeau *m*, (Tax) don *m*; ~ **by will** don par testament *m*; ~ **deed** *n* acte de donation *m*; ~ **promotion** *n* promotion-cadeau *f*; ~ **of property** don de biens *m*; ~ **token** *n*, ~ **voucher** *n* chèque-cadeau *m*; ~**s tax** *n* impôt sur les donations *m*

gigabyte *n* gigaoctet *m*

GIGO *abbr* (▶**garbage in, garbage out**) telle entrée, telle sortie

gilt *n* UK (government stock) fonds d'État *m*, obligation d'État *f*; (high-class securities) valeur de premier ordre *f*; ~**-edged bill of exchange** *n* lettre de change de premier ordre *f*; ~**-edged security** *n*, ~**-edged stock** *n* valeur de premier ordre *f*

gilts *n pl* UK (government issue) obligations d'État *f pl*; (high-class securities) valeurs de premier ordre *f pl*; ~ **market** *n* marché des valeurs de premier ordre *m*

gimmick *n* truc *m*; **advertising** ~ truc publicitaire *m*

Ginnie Mae *n* US (infml) société de prêt hypothécaire immobilier *f*

giro *n* virement *m*; (at post office) virement postal *m*; ~ **payment** *n*, ~ **transfer** *n* (Bank) virement bancaire *m*

gist *n* essentiel *m*

give *vt* donner; (offer) offrir; (hand over) remettre; (grant) accorder, donner; **given the circumstances** étant donné les circonstances; ~ **away** donner; (sample, ticket) distribuer; ~ **back** rendre; (in industrial relations) revenir sur les avantages acquis; ~ **in** céder; ~ **up** *vt* (claim, idea) renoncer à; (free time) consacrer; (job) quitter; (points) céder; ~ **up doing** cesser de faire, arrêter de faire; *vi* abandonner; ~ **way** céder; ~ **way to** (pressure, demand) céder à; (person) laisser la place à

give-away *n* cadeau publicitaire *m*; ~ **magazine** *n* magazine gratuit *m*, revue gratuite *f*

giveback *n* (in industrial relations) retour sur les avantages acquis *m*

given name *n* AmE prénom *m*

giver *n* (Stock) acheteur *m*; ~ **for a call** (Stock) acheteur d'une option d'achat *m*, donneur d'option d'achat *m*; ~ **for a put** (Stock) donneur d'une option de vente *m*; ~ **for a put and call** (Stock) donneur de double option *m*

glamor AmE ▶**glamour** BrE

glamour: ~ **issue** *n* BrE émission d'une valeur vedette *f*; ~ **stock** *n* BrE valeur vedette *f*

glasnost *n* glasnost *f*

glass ceiling *n* niveau professionnel que la discrimination empêche certains groupes sociaux de dépasser

gliding rate *n* taux glissant *m*, taux mobile *m*

glitch *n* problème technique *m*

global *adj* (comprehensive) global; (worldwide) mondial; ~ **bank** *n* banque universelle *f*; ~ **corporation** *n* transnationale *f*, multinationale *f*; ~ **deregulation** *n* déréglementation mondiale *f*; ~ **distribution system** *n* système mondial de distribution *m*; ~ **economy** *n* économie mondiale *f*; ~ **financial market** *n* place financière internationale *f*; ~ **image** *n* image globale *f*; ~ **marketing** *n* marketing global *m*; ~ **network** *n* réseau mondial *m*; ~ **player** *n* acteur planétaire *m*; ~ **search** *n* (of document, data) recherche globale *f*; ~ **search and replace** *n* fonction recherche et remplacement automatiques *f*; ~ **strategy** *n* stratégie d'ensemble *f*; ~ **warming** *n* réchauffement de l'atmosphère *m*

globalization *n* mondialisation *f*, globalisation *f*

globalize *vt* mondialiser, globaliser

globally *adv* (universally) globalement; (worldwide) mondialement, à l'échelle mondiale

glocal *adj* glocal

glocalization *n* glocalisation *f*

gloom *n* pessimisme *m*; **economic** ~ morosité économique *f*

glossary *n* glossaire *m*

glossy *adj* (brochure, catalogue) de luxe; ∼ **magazine** *n* magazine illustré de luxe *m*

glut¹ *n* surabondance *f*, ∼ **on the market** encombrement du marché *m*

glut² *vt* (economy, market) inonder, saturer

GM *abbr* (▸**genetically modified**) transgénique, génétiquement modifié; (▸**gross margin**) EBE *m* (excédent brut d'exploitation), marge brute *f*

GMO *n* (**genetically modified organism**) OGM *m* (organisme génétiquement modifié)

GMT *abbr* (▸**Greenwich Mean Time**) TU *m* (temps universel)

GNI *abbr* (▸**gross national income**) revenu national brut *m*

GNMA *abbr* US (▸**Government National Mortgage Association**) société de prêt hypothécaire immobilier *f*

GNP *abbr* (▸**gross national product**) PNB *m* (produit national brut)

go¹ *n* make a ∼ of sth réussir qch; give sth a ∼ essayer qch

go² ① *vt* ∼ **a bear** spéculer à la baisse ② *vi* aller; ∼ **well** marcher, bien se passer; ∼ **back to square one** retourner à la case départ; ∼ **bankrupt** faire faillite; ∼ **against sb** (decision, vote) être défavorable à qn, aller contre qn; ∼ **ahead** (take place) avoir lieu; ∼ **ahead with sth** (project) mettre qch en route; ∼ **back on** (promise) revenir sur; ∼ **before** (court) comparaître devant; ∼ **down** (price, standard, level) baisser; ∼ **over** (details) passer en revue; (accounts, figures) vérifier; (work, facts) revoir; ∼ **through** (contract) étudier; (mail, files) parcourir; ∼ **under** (company) couler (infrml), faire faillite; ∼ **up** (share, price, level) augmenter

go-ahead *n* give sb the ∼ donner le feu vert à qn; get the ∼ recevoir le feu vert

goal *n* objectif *m*; set/meet ∼s fixer/ atteindre des objectifs; ∼ **congruence** *n* harmonisation des objectifs *f*, ∼ **programming** *n* organisation des objectifs *f*, ∼ **setting** *n* fixation d'objectifs *f*, établissement d'objectifs *m*

go-between *n* intermédiaire *mf*

G-O bond *abbr* US (▸**general obligation bond**) (municipal bond) obligation des collectivités locales garantie *f*

go-go fund *n* fonds hautement spéculatif *m*

GOH *abbr* (▸**goods on hand**) stocks existants *m pl*

going: ∼ **concern** *n* entreprise prospère *f*, affaire qui marche *f*, ∼**-concern principle** *n* principe de la continuité de l'exploitation *m*; ∼**-concern value** *n* valeur de l'entreprise en continuité d'exploitation *f*, ∼ **price** *n* prix actuel *m*; ∼ **rate** *n* (price) prix actuel *m*; (wage, rate of pay) tarif en vigueur *m*; (percentage) taux en vigueur *m*; ∼ **short** *adj* (sale) à découvert

gold *n* or *m*; ∼ **bullion** *n* lingots d'or *m pl*; ∼ **bullion standard** *n* étalon de lingots d'or *m*; ∼ **coin** *n* pièce en or *f*, ∼ **cover** *n* couverture or *f*, ∼ **currency** *n* monnaie en or *f*, ∼ **exchange standard** *n* étalon de change or *m*, étalon-or de change *m*; ∼ **fixing** *n* fixing *m*; ∼ **market** *n* marché de l'or *m*; ∼ **mine** *n* (Ind) mine d'or *f*, (source of revenue) mine d'or *f*, ∼**-mining company** *n* société d'extraction de l'or *f*, ∼ **ore** *n* minerai d'or *m*; ∼ **price** *n* prix de l'or *m*; ∼ **reserves** *n pl* réserves d'or *f pl*; ∼ **rush** *n* ruée vers l'or *f*, ∼ **standard** *n* étalon-or *m*

golden: ∼ **age** *n* âge d'or *m*; ∼ **formula** *n* UK formule magique *f*, ∼ **handcuffs** *n pl* contrat lucratif offert à un cadre s'il s'engage à travailler pour une période déterminée; ∼ **handshake** *n* prime de départ *f*, ∼ **hello** *n* prime de recrutement *f*, ∼ **parachute** *n* indemnité de départ *f* (dans le cadre d'une OPA); ∼ **rule** *n* règle d'or *f*, ∼ **share** *n* action préférentielle *f*, action spécifique *f*, ∼ **triangle** *n* triangle d'or *m*

gondola *n* (shop fitting) gondole *f*, (rail) wagon découvert *m*

good¹ *adj* (Gen Comm) bon/bonne; (debt) bon/bonne, certain; (investment, securities) sûr; in ∼ working order en bon état de fonctionnement; make ∼ (repair) réparer; (succeed) faire de l'argent

good² *n* bien *m*; for the ∼ of the firm pour le bien de la société; be £3,000 to the ∼ avoir 3 000 livres sterling à son crédit

good: ∼ **bargain** *n* bonne affaire *f*, ∼ **credit risk** *n* bon risque de crédit *m*; ∼ **faith** *n* bonne foi *f*, in ∼ faith de bonne foi; ∼**-faith deposit** *n* dépôt de bonne foi *m*; ∼ **housekeeping** *n* bonne gestion *f*, ∼ **luck** *n* chance *f*, ∼ **news** *n pl* bonnes nouvelles *f pl*; ∼ **return** *n* (on investment) bon rendement *m*; ∼ **risk** *n* bon risque *m*; ∼ **title** *n* bon titre *m*, bon titre de propriété *m*

goods *n pl* marchandises *f pl*; (property) biens *m pl*; (Ind) articles *m pl*, produits *m pl*; (Transp) fret *m*, marchandises *f pl*; ∼ **and chattels** *n pl* biens meubles *m pl*; ∼ **depot** *n* entrepôt *m*; ∼ **of foreign origin** *n pl* marchandises de provenance étrangère *f pl*; ∼ **on approval** *n pl* marchandises à l'essai *f pl*; ∼ **on hand** *n pl* stocks existants *m pl*; ∼ **train** *n* BrE train de marchandises *m*; ∼ **truck** *n* BrE wagon de marchandises couvert *m*; ∼ **wagon** *n* BrE fourgon *m*

goodwill *n* (Fin) écart d'acquisition *m*, goodwill *m*, survaleur *f*, (clients) clientèle *f*, droit à la clientèle *m*; ∼ **money** *n* (Gen Comm) fonds commercial *m*; (Acc) fonds de commerce *m*

GOP *abbr* US (infrml) (▸**Grand Old Party**) parti républicain *m*

go-slow *n* BrE grève perlée *f*

govern *vt* (sale, manufacture, use) régir; (country) gouverner; (actions, decision) déterminer; (flow, speed, output) régler

governance n gouvernance f

governing: ∼ **board** n conseil d'administration m; ∼ **body** n conseil de direction m; ∼ **principle** n idée directrice f, idée dominante f

government n (Pol) administration f, gouvernement m; (management) gestion f; ∼ **accounting** n comptabilité publique f; ∼ **agency** n agence gouvernementale f, organisme public m; ∼ **annuity** n rente sur l'État f; ∼ **assistance** n aide gouvernementale f; ∼**-backed** adj soutenu par l'État; ∼ **bond** n bon du Trésor m, obligation d'État f; ∼ **broker** n agent du trésor m; ∼ **contract** n contrat d'État m, contrat public m; ∼ **contractor** n entreprise privée travaillant sous contrat pour l'État; ∼ **defence appropriations** BrE, ∼ **defense appropriations** AmE n pl budget de la défense m; ∼ **department** n département gouvernemental m, ministère m; ∼ **finance** n finances publiques f pl; ∼**-financed** adj financé par l'État, subventionné par les pouvoirs publics; ∼**-funded** adj financé par l'État, subventionné par les pouvoirs publics; ∼ **grant** n subvention de l'État f; ∼ **intervention** n intervention de l'État f; ∼ **loan** n emprunt d'État m, prêt d'État m; ∼ **obligations** n pl US bons du Trésor m pl; ∼**-owned** adj (company) public/-que; ∼ **policy** n politique gouvernementale f; ∼ **relations** n pl relations gouvernementales f pl; ∼ **securities** n pl US bons du Trésor m pl, titres d'État m pl; ∼**-sponsored** adj (project) patronné par l'État; ∼ **stock** n titre d'État m, valeur d'État f; ∼**-supported** adj (project) soutenu par l'État; ∼**-to-business** adj (portal, services) gouvernement-entreprise, G2B; ∼**-to-citizen** adj (portal, services) gouvernement-citoyen, G2C; ∼**-to-government** adj d'État à État

governmental adj gouvernemental; ∼ **accounting** n comptabilité publique f

Government National Mortgage Association n US société de prêt hypothécaire immobilier f

governor n gouverneur m; ∼ **general** n gouverneur général m

govt abbr (▶**government**) administration f, gouvernement m

GP abbr (▶**general purpose**) à usage général

GPRS abbr (**General Packet Radio Service**) (protocole) GPRS m

grab vt (attention) attirer; (opportunity) saisir

grabber hand n (Comp) main de saisie f

grace n **grant sb three days'** ∼ accorder un délai de trois jours à qn; ∼ **days** n pl jours de franchise m pl, jours de grâce m pl; ∼ **period** n délai de franchise m, délai de grâce m

grade¹ n catégorie f; (on salary scale) indice

m, échelon m; (rank) échelon m; (quality of product) catégorie f, qualité f; (size of product) calibre m; **make the** ∼ (person) être à la hauteur; ∼ **creep** n augmentation rampante f; ∼ **crossing** n traverse f; ∼ **drift** n dérapage catégoriel m

grade² vt classer; (by quality) classer; (by size) calibrer, classer

grading n classification f; (by size) calibrage m; ∼ **structure** n (of staff) structure hiérarchique f

gradual adj graduel/-elle, progressif/-ive

gradualism n politique des petits pas f (infrml), réformisme m

gradually adv graduellement, progressivement

graduate¹ n licencié/-e m/f; ∼ **recruitment** n recrutement de jeunes diplômés m; ∼ **school of business** n école supérieure de commerce f; ∼ **trainee** n stagiaire diplomé/-e m/f; ∼ **training programme** n programme de formation pour jeunes diplômés m

graduate² vi US (from school) obtenir le baccalauréat; UK (from university) obtenir sa licence, obtenir son diplôme

graduated adj (container) gradué; (rising) progressif/-ive; (falling) dégressif/-ive; **in** ∼ **stages** graduellement, progressivement; ∼ **income tax** n impôt progressif sur le revenu m; ∼ **interest** n intérêts échelonnés m pl; ∼ **payments** n pl paiements échelonnés m pl; ∼ **pension scheme** n régime de retraite proportionnel m; ∼ **tax** n impôt progressif m; ∼ **wage** n salaire modulé m

graft¹ n (infrml) (work) travail m; (corruption) corruption de fonctionnaire f; (bribe) pot-de-vin m; **hard** ∼ n boulot acharné m (infrml)

graft² ① vt (official) corrompre ② vi travailler dur

grain n (commodity) céréales f pl; ∼ **crop** n récolte de céréales f; ∼ **exchange** n bourse aux grains f; ∼ **prices** n pl prix des céréales m

granary n entrepôt de céréales m

grand n BrE (infrml) mille livres sterling f pl; ∼ **jury** n US jury d'accusation m; ∼ **larceny** n US vol qualifié m; ∼ **total** n somme totale f, total général m

grandfather clause n clause d'antériorité f, clause de droits acquis f

Grand Old Party n US (infrml) parti républicain m

granny bond n UK (infrml) bon du Trésor indexé m

grant¹ n (funding) subvention f; (of property) cession f; (Patents) attribution f, délivrance f; (for student) bourse f; **in** ∼ **form** sous forme de subvention; ∼**-in-aid** n subvention de l'État f

grant² vt (credit) accorder, allouer; (loan, overdraft) consentir; (concessions) accorder, octroyer; (request) accéder à; (will) homologuer, ⋯❯

valider; (licence) attribuer, délivrer; (tenancy) accorder; (option) consentir; **~ credit** accorder un crédit; **~ extended credit** accorder un crédit de longue durée; **~ interim supply** accorder des fournitures intérimaires, ouvrir des crédits provisoires; **~ a licence** BrE, **~ a license** AmE (for premises, trade) accorder une licence; **~ a loan to sb** accorder un prêt à qn, consentir un prêt à qn; **~ sb permission to do** autoriser qn à faire

grant-aided *adj* subventionné par l'État

grantee *n* bénéficiaire *mf*

grantor *n* (Law, Prop) concédant *m*; (Stock) vendeur *m*

granularity *n* granularité *f*

grapevine *n* téléphone arabe *m*; **hear sth on the ~** entendre qch par le téléphone arabe

graph *n* graphe *m*, graphique *m*; **~ paper** *n* papier quadrillé *m*

graphic *adj* graphique; **~ design** *n* conception graphique *f*; **~ designer** *n* graphiste *mf*; **~ display** *n* affichage graphique *m*; **~ display terminal** *n* terminal graphique *m*

graphically illustrated *adj* illustré à grand renfort de détails

graphics *n pl* graphiques *m pl*, graphisme *m*; (TV, film) images *f pl*; **computer ~** infographie *f*; **~-based browser** *n* navigateur graphique *m*; **~ card** *n* carte graphique *f*; **~ file** *n* fichier graphique *m*; **~ format** *n* format graphique *m*; **~ software** *n* logiciel graphique *m*

grapple: **~ with** *vt* (difficulty) se colleter avec; **~ with a problem** être aux prises avec un problème

grasping *adj* âpre au gain

grass-roots *n pl* **the ~** la base *f*; **~ movement** *n* mouvement populaire *m*; **~ promotion** *n* (S&M) promotion locale *f*; **~ support** *n* appui populaire *m*

gratify *vt* (desire) satisfaire

gratis¹ *adj* gratuit

gratis² *adv* gratis, gratuitement

gratuitous *adj* gratuit; **~ loan** *n* (Fin) prêt à titre gratuit *m*

gratuity *n* (tip) pourboire *m*

graveyard: **~ market** *n* (Stock) marché baissier sans issue *m*, marché mort *m*; **~ shift** *n* équipe de nuit *f*

gray: **~ area** *n* AmE ▸**grey area** BrE; **~ economy** *n* AmE ▸**grey economy** BrE; **~ market** *n* AmE ▸**grey market** BrE

grazing *n* (pilfering) chapardage *m*

grease *vt* graisser; **~ sb's palm** (infrml) graisser la patte à qn (infrml)

greed *n* cupidité *f*

greedy *adj* âpre au gain

green *adj* (candidate, issue, policy) écologiste; (product, marketing) écologique; **~ belt** *n*

ceinture verte *f*; **~ card** *n* US carte de séjour *f*; **~ currency** *n* monnaie verte *f*; **~ energy** *n* énergie verte *f*; **~ issue** *n* problème écologique *m*; **~ labelling scheme** AmE, **~ labelling scheme** BrE *n* programme d'étiquetage des produits écologiques *m*; **~ light** *n* feu vert *m*; **~ lobby** *n* lobby écologiste *m*; **~ marketing** *n* marketing vert *m*, marketing écologique *m*; **~ pound** *n* livre verte *f*; **~ revolution** *n* révolution verte *f*

Green: **~ Paper** *n* UK avant-projet de loi *m*; **~ Party** *n* parti écologiste *m*, Verts *m pl*

greenback *n* US (infrml) dollar *m*

greenfield site *n* (industrial development) nouvelle zone industrielle *f*; (empty land) terrain vierge *m*

greenhouse: **~ effect** *n* effet de serre *m*; **~ gas** *n* gaz à effet de serre *m*

greening *n* écologisation *f*; (of public opinion) prise de conscience écologiste *f*

greenlining *n* rénovation de vieux quartiers *f*

greenmail *n* US chantage financier *m* (*avec revente à une société d'actions achetées lors d'un raid*)

Greens *n pl* (Pol) Verts *m pl*

Greenwich Mean Time *n* temps universel *m*

greetings *n pl* compliments *m pl*, salutations *f pl*

grey: **~ area** *n* BrE zone floue *f*; **~ economy** *n* BrE économie parallèle *f*; **~ market** *n* BrE marché gris *m*, marché parallèle *m*

grid *n* grille *f*

grievance *n* griefs *m pl*; **have a ~ against sb** avoirs des griefs contre qn, avoir un grief contre qn; **air one's ~s** exposer ses griefs; **~ committee** *n* commission d'arbitrage *f*; **~ procedure** *n* instance prud'hommale *f*

gross¹ *adj* (Acc) brut

gross² *n* grosse *f*

gross³ *vt* faire un bénéfice brut de; **~ up** (interest, profits) calculer le montant brut de

gross: **~ amount** *n* montant brut *m*; **~ assets** *n pl* actif brut *m*; **~ book value** *n* valeur comptable brute *f*; **~ cash flow** *n* résultat brut d'exploitation *m*, marge brute d'autofinancement *f*; **~ cost** *n* coût brut *m*; **~ debt** *n* dette brute *f*; **~ dividend** *n* dividende brut *m*; **~ dividend yield** *n* rendement boursier brut *m*, rendement de dividende brut *m*, rendement des actions brut *m*; **~ domestic product** *n* produit intérieur brut *m*; **~ earnings** *n pl* revenu brut *m*; **~ federal debt** *n* US *dette nationale brute de l'État fédéral*; **~ income** *n* revenu brut *m*; **~ investment** *n* investissement brut *m*; **~ investment revenue** *n* revenu brut de placements *m*; **~ leasable area** *n* surface commerciale utile *f*; **~ margin** *n* marge brute *f*; **~ misconduct** *n* faute grave *f*; ~ **national debt** *n* dette nationale brute *f*; ~ **national expenditure** *n* dépenses nationales brutes *f pl*; ~ **national income** *n* revenu national brut *m*; ~ **national product** *n* produit national brut *m*; ~ **negligence** *n* faute lourde *f*; ~ **pay** *n* salaire brut *m*; ~ **profit** *n* bénéfice brut *m*; ~ **profit margin** *n* marge bénéficiaire brute *f*; ~ **rent** *n* loyer brut *m*; ~ **revenue** *n* revenu brut *m*; ~ **sales** *n* revenu brut *m*; ~ **savings** *n pl* épargne brute *f*; ~ **social product** *n* produit social brut *m*; ~ **spread** *n* marge brute *f*, échelonnement brut *m*; ~ **ton** *n* (maritime) tonne forte *f*; ~ **tonnage** *n* tonnage brut *m*; ~**-up** *n* majoration *f*; ~ **wage** *n* salaire brut *m*; ~ **weight** *n* poids brut *m*; ~ **yield** *n* rendement brut *m*

grossed-up dividend *n* dividende majoré *m*

grossing up *vt* majoration *f*

ground *n* on the ~ (in situ) sur le terrain; **on neutral** ~ en terrain neutre; **be thick/thin on the** ~ ne pas être légion *inv*; **gain** ~ gagner du terrain; **lose** ~ perdre du terrain; **stand one's** ~ tenir bon; **yield** ~ **to** céder du terrain devant; **go over the same** ~ se répéter; **break new** ~ innover; **be on dangerous** ~ être dans une position délicate; **prepare the** ~ **for sth** ouvrir la voie à qch; **run sth into the** ~ (business) laisser péricliter; **get off the** ~ (business, project) démarrer; ~ **control** *n* contrôle au sol *m*; ~ **crew** *n* équipe au sol *f*; ~ **floor** *n* BrE (street-level) rez-de-chaussée *m*; AmE (first floor) premier étage *m*; ~ **lease** *n* bail à terrain *m*; ~ **level** *n* rez-de-chaussée *m*; ~ **plan** *n* plan de base *m*; ~ **rent** *n* loyer foncier *m*; ~ **rules** *n pl* règles de base *f pl*

grounding *n* have a good ~ in sth avoir de bonnes bases en qch

groundless *adj* non fondé, non justifié; **prove to be** ~ s'avérer sans fondement

grounds *n pl* motif *m*; (Law) motif *m*; (for opposition, revocation) motifs *m pl*; ~ **for** (appeal, arrest, criticism, hope) motifs *m pl*; **have** ~ **for complaint** avoir des motifs de se plaindre; ~ **for dismissal** motifs de renvoi *m pl*; ~ **for doing** motifs pour faire; **have** ~ **to do** avoir des raisons pour faire; **on the** ~ **that** en raison du fait que; **on the** ~ **of** (cost, price, size) en raison de; **on** ~ **of expediency** pour des raisons d'opportunité; **on the** ~ **of ill health** pour raisons de santé

groundwork *n* travail préparatoire *m*; **do the** ~ faire le travail préparatoire; **lay the** ~ **for** jeter les bases de

group¹ *n* groupe *m*; ~ **accounts** *n pl* comptes consolidés *m pl*; ~ **advertising** *n* publicité collective *f*; ~ **of assets** *n* groupe d'éléments d'actif *m*; ~ **banking** *n* consortium de banques *m*, syndicat de banques *m*; ~ **buying** *n* achats groupés *m pl*; ~ **buying site** *n* (on Internet) site d'achats

groupés *m*; ~ **of companies** *n* groupe de sociétés *m*, groupement d'entreprises *m*; ~ **contract** *n* contrat collectif *m*; ~ **credit insurance** *n* US assurance crédit collective *f*; ~ **dynamics** *n pl* dynamique de groupe *f*; ~ **health insurance** *n* US assurance collective contre la maladie *f*; ~ **insurance** *n* assurance collective *f*; ~ **leader** *n* accompagnateur/-trice *m/f*, animateur/-trice de groupe *m/f*; ~ **profit** *n* bénéfice consolidé *m*; ~ **travel** *n* voyages de groupe *m pl*; ~ **working** *n* travail de groupe *m*

group² *vt* grouper; ~ **together** grouper

groupage *n* groupage *m*; ~ **agent** *n* groupeur *m*; ~ **depot** *n* centre de groupage *m*

Group: ~ **Executive Board** *n* bureau exécutif du consortium *m*, bureau exécutif du groupe *m*; ~ **of Seven** *n* Groupe des Sept *m*

grouping *n* groupage *m*

groupware *n* (Comp) synergiciel *m*, logiciel de groupe *m*

grow ⬚1 *vt* (Ind) produire; ~ **the business** (increase revenue) augmenter le chiffre d'affaires; (expand) développer l'entreprise ⬚2 *vi* (deficit, spending, market share) augmenter; (business, company) prospérer; (economy) être en expansion; (pressure, influence) devenir plus fort; (support, problem) devenir plus important; (list) s'allonger; ~ **in popularity** devenir plus populaire; ~ **old** vieillir

growing *adj* (number, demand, amount) croissant; (pressure, opposition, optimism) grandissant

growth *n* croissance *f*, évolution *f*; (of market, industry) croissance *f*, expansion *f*; (of sales, profits, income) progression *f*; ~ **accounting** *n* comptabilité de croissance *f*; ~ **area** *n* secteur en expansion *m*; ~ **curve** *n* courbe de croissance *f*; ~ **fund** *n* fonds de croissance *m*; ~ **index** *n* indice de croissance *m*; ~ **industry** *n* industrie en croissance rapide *f*; ~ **path** *n* sentier de croissance *m*; ~ **potential** *n* potentiel de croissance *m*; ~ **rate** *n* taux de croissance *m*; ~ **stock** *n* valeur de croissance *f*; ~ **strategy** *n* stratégie de croissance *f*

gr.wt. *abbr* (▶**gross weight**) poids brut *m*

GSM *abbr* (**Global System for Mobile**) GSM *m*

GT *abbr* (▶**gross tonnage**) tonnage brut *m*

guarantee¹ *n* (of debts, liabilities) garantie *f*; (for goods) garantie *f*; (pledge) garantie *f*, caution *f*; (cash, security) caution *f*; (of bill) aval *m*; **under** ~ sous garantie; **carry a three-year** ~ avoir une garantie de trois ans; **give sth as a** ~ (money) donner qch en caution; (object) donner qch en gage; ~ **letter** *n* lettre d'aval *f*, lettre d'engagement *f*; ~ **liability** *n* obligation de garantie *f*; ~ **of signature** *n* certification de signature *f*

guarantee² *vt* (bill of exchange) avaliser; (cheque) cautionner, garantir; (assure) ⋯❯

g

garantir, assurer; (goods) garantir; (loan) se porter garant de, garantir

guaranteed adj garanti; ~ **annual wage** n US salaire minimum interprofessionnel garanti m; ~ **bill** n billet garanti m, effet avalisé m; ~ **bond** n obligation garantie f; ~ **delivery** n livraison garantie f; ~ **facility** n crédit garanti m; ~ **income** n revenu garanti m; ~ **investment** n placement garanti m; ~ **letter of credit** n lettre de crédit garantie f; ~ **loan** n prêt garanti m; ~ **minimum wage** n salaire minimum interprofessionnel garanti m, SMIG m; ~ **price** n prix garanti m; ~ **security** n titre garanti m, valeur garantie f; ~ **share** n action garantie à dividende garanti f pl; ~ **stock** n actions à dividende garanti f pl; ~ **wage** n salaire garanti m

guarantor n (Gen Comm) garant m; (Bank) avaliseur m; (Law) fidéjusseur m; **stand ~ for sb** se porter garant de qn

guaranty n (of debt) caution f, garantie f; (Ins) guarantie f; (to undertake obligation) garantie f; (Law) caution f, garantie f; ~ **bond** n bon de cautionnement m; ~ **fund** n fonds de cautionnement m; ~ **savings bank** n caisse d'épargne f

guard[1] n gardien/-ienne m/f; **be under ~** (premises) être surveillé, être sous surveillance

guard[2]: ~ **against** vt se prémunir contre

guardian n tuteur m

guess[1] n supposition f, conjecture f; **make a ~, have a ~** deviner

guess[2] vt deviner

guesstimate[1] n (infrml) calcul approximatif f, estimation au jugé f

guesstimate[2] vt calculer approximativement

guest n (of hotel) client/-e m/f; (at conference, at home, on TV) invité/-e m/f; ~ **book** n (Gen Comm, Comp) livre d'or m; ~ **list** n liste des invités f; ~ **speaker** n invité/-e d'honneur m/f

guestworker n travailleur/-euse immigré/-e m/f

GUI n (**graphical user interface**) interface utilisateur graphique f

guidance n (advice) conseils m pl; (leadership) direction f

guide n (manual) guide m, manuel m; (person) guide m; ~ **price** n (EU) cours directeur m

guided interview n entretien dirigé m

guideline n (Admin) directive f; (advice) conseil m; **draw up a set of ~s** établir des directives

guiding principle n principe directeur m

guild n corporation f, corps de métier m

guilty adj coupable; **be ~ of** être coupable de; **be found ~/not ~** être reconnu coupable/déclaré non coupable; ~ **party** n coupable mf

Gulf: ~ **Plus** n prix au départ du Golfe m; ~ **War** n guerre du Golfe f

gunslinger n (Fin) spéculateur/-trice m/f

guru n gourou m; **management ~** gourou du management m

gutterpress n presse à scandale f, presse à sensation f

Hh

habeas corpus n habeas corpus m

hack vt pirater; ~ **into** pirater

hacker n pirate informatique m

hacker-proof adj protégé contre les pirates

hacking n piratage informatique m

hacktivist n piractiviste m, pirate informatique engagé dans une lutte politique

haggle vi marchander; ~ **with sb** marchander avec qn; ~ **about**, ~ **over** (price) discuter du prix, marchander sur

haggling n marchandage m

half[1] adj ~ **a litre, a ~-litre** un demi-litre; **two and a ~ pages** deux pages et demie; **two and a ~ percent** deux et demi pour cent; ~ **a dozen** une demi-douzaine; **a ~ circle** un demi-cercle; **be on ~ time**

travailler à mi-temps

half[2] n (one of two parts) moitié f; (fraction) demi m; **two and a ~** deux et demi; **reduce sth by a ~** réduire qch de moitié

half: ~ **board** n demi-pension f; ~ **day** n demi-journée f; ~ **fare** n demi-tarif m; ~ **measure** n demi-mesure f; ~ **monthly** adj bimensuel/-elle; ~ **pay** n demi-salaire m; ~**time** adj (work, post) à mi-temps; (Fin) (profits, figures) semestriel/-ielle; ~ **year** n semestre m

half-price[1] adj à moitié prix

half-price[2] adv à moitié prix

halfway[1] adj **reach the ~ point, reach the ~ stage** avoir terminé la moitié du travail; **the ~ stage** la mi-étape

halfway[2] adv **be ~ through doing** avoir à

moitié fini de faire; **meet sb** ~ faire un compromis avec qn, couper la poire en deux (infrml)

half-yearly[1] adj (bond, statement, meeting) semestriel/-ielle; ~**yearly dividend** n dividende semestriel m

half-yearly[2] adv (pay) semestriellement

halo n halo m; ~ **effect** n effet de halo m

halt n arrêt m; (temporary) suspension f; ~ **of trading** arrêt des opérations m, suspension des transactions f

halve vt (reduce) réduire de moitié; (divide) diviser en deux

hammer[1] n **go under the** ~ être vendu aux enchères

hammer[2] vt (criticize) critiquer; (person) déclarer insolvable; ~ **home** (point) bien insister sur; ~ **the market** pousser à la vente; ~ **prices** casser les prix; ~ **out** (agreement) parvenir à; (contract) réussir à conclure

hammer price n prix bradé après faillite m

hamper vt (growth, progress) entraver, gêner; (person) handicaper

hand[1] n (assistance) coup de main m; **lend sb a** ~ donner un coup de main à qn; **have a** ~ **in** (project, decision) prendre part à; **'by** ~' (on letter) 'par porteur'; **deliver sth by** ~ remettre qch en mains propres; **made by** ~ fait à la main, fait main; **in** ~ (funds, money) disponible en caisse; **have time in** ~ avoir du temps devant soi; **the matter in** ~ l'affaire en cours; **the work is in** ~ les travaux sont en cours; **stock in** ~ marchandises en magasin; **take sth in** ~ (problem) s'occuper de; (situation) prendre en main; **be in sb's** ~**s** être entre les mains de qn; **place sth in sb's** ~**s** (matter) remettre qch entre les mains de qn; **in good** ~**s** en bonnes mains; **play into sb's** ~**s** jouer le jeu de qn; **on** ~ (available) disponible; **keep sth to** ~ garder qch sous la main; **change** ~**s** changer de mains; **out of** ~ (reject, condemn) d'emblée; **get out of** ~ (expenditure, inflation) déraper; **have the upper** ~ avoir l'avantage; **turn one's** ~ **to** s'essayer à; **go** ~ **in** ~ **with** aller de pair avec; **in the** ~**s of a third party** en main tierce; **our** ~**s are tied** nous avons les mains liées; ~ **baggage** n, ~ **luggage** n bagage à main m

hand[2] vt ~ **sb sth** donner qch à qn; ~ **back** rendre; ~ **in** (key, equipment) rendre; (form, report, application) rendre, remettre; ~ **in one's resignation**, ~ **in one's notice** donner sa démission; ~ **out** (leaflets, samples) distribuer; ~ **over** (business, company) céder; (power) transmettre; ~ **over to sb** passer le relais à qn

handbill n prospectus m

handbook n manuel m; **training/user's** ~ manuel de formation/de l'utilisateur m; **staff** ~ guide de l'entreprise m

hand-held adj (device) portatif/-ive;

(computer) de poche

handicapped adj handicapé; ~ **person** n handicapé/-e m/f

handle vt (objects) manier, manipuler; (grievance, case, negotiations) traiter; (situation, crisis) faire face à; (complaints, enquiries, sale, account, client) s'occuper de; (orders, waste) traiter; ~ **with care** à manier avec précaution, fragile; ~ **large sums of money** gérer de grosses sommes d'argent

handling n (of goods) manutention f; (of case, matter, theme) façon de traiter f; (of process, business) gestion f; ~ **charge** n (for processing order) frais de gestion m pl; (for goods) frais de manutention m pl

handmade adj fait à la main

handout n (leaflet) prospectus m; (document) document m; (single sheet) feuille f; (payment) subvention f

handover n (of property, power) transfert m; (of product) remise f, ~ **date** n date de mise à disposition f

handpick vt (person) trier sur le volet

handset m combiné m

hands-free adj mains libres; ~ **headset** n (for phone) micro-casque m, casque mains libres m; ~ **kit** n (for car) kit mains libres m

hands-off adj (style, approach) non interventionniste; (manager) qui pratique la délégation du pouvoir; ~ **policy** n politique de non-intervention f

hands-on adj (control) direct; (manager) de terrain; (approach) pratique; ~ **experience** n expérience de terrain f; ~ **session** n discussion en prise directe f; ~ **training** n formation pratique f

handwritten adj manuscrit

handy adj (guide, book) utile; (tool, size, device) pratique; (well-located) bien situé

handyman n homme à tout faire m

hang vi (computer) se bloquer; ~ **up** (on phone) raccrocher

Hang Seng index n indice Hang Seng m

harbor AmE, **harbour** BrE n port m; ~ **authority** n autorité portuaire f; ~ **dues** n pl droits de port m pl; ~ **facilities** n pl installations portuaires f pl; ~ **master** n capitaine de port m

hard[1] adj (evidence, proof) solide; (data, facts) concret/-ète; (difficult) difficile; (negotiations) serré; (rigid) solide; **make things** ~ **for sb** mener la vie dure à qn; **take a** ~ **line** adopter une attitude ferme; ~ **and fast rules** règles absolues f pl; ~ **bargaining** n négociations serrées f pl; ~ **cash** n espèces f pl; ~ **copy** n sortie papier f, tirage m; ~ **core** n (group of people) noyau dur m; ~**-core unemployed** n pl AmE chômeurs de longue durée m pl; ~ **costs** n pl coûts essentiels m pl; ~ **currency** n devise forte f; ~ **discount** n grosse remise f; ~ **disk** n disque dur m; ~ **disk drive** n unité de disque dur f; ~ **goods** ⋯▷

n pl biens d'équipement *m pl*; ~ **hat** *n* casque (de chantier) *m*; ~**-hit** *adj* durement touché; ~ **landing** *n* atterrissage brutal *m*; ~ **loan** *n* prêt aux conditions du marché *m*; ~ **news** nouvelles sérieuses *f pl*; ~ **sell** *n* vente agressive *f*; ~ **sell tactics** *n pl* politique de promotion agressive *f*; ~ **selling** *n* vente agressive *f*

hard² *adv* (work) dur; (think) sérieusement; **be** ~ **hit** (person, sector, industry) être durement frappé; **try** ~ faire beaucoup d'efforts; **be** ~ **pressed to do** avoir du mal à faire

hardback book *n* livre relié *m*, livre emboîté *m*

hardball *n* (infrml) **play** ~ employer la manière forte

hardcover book *n* livre relié *m*, livre emboîté *m*

hard-earned *adj* (cash, money) durement gagné; (position) durement obtenu

harden *vi* (market, currency) se raffermir; (prices) être en hausse

hardening market *n* marché qui se raffermit *m*

hard-fought *adj* (contest, election) âprement disputé

hard-hitting *adj* (report, speech) sans concessions

hardline *adj* (Pol) (socialist, reformer) pur et dur; (measure, policy) très ferme

hardliner *n* pur et dur *m*, jusqu'au-boutiste *mf*

hard-nosed *adj* (infrml) impitoyable

hardship *n* privations *f pl*

hardware *n* (Comp) hardware *m*, matériel (informatique) *m*; ~ **failure** *n* incident machine *m*, panne machine *f*; ~ **firm** *n* constructeur d'ordinateurs *m*; ~ **requirements** *n pl* configuration matérielle *f*; ~ **security** *n* sécurité du matériel *f*; ~ **shop** *n* quincaillerie *f*; ~ **specialist** *n* technicien/-ienne de hardware *m/f*; ~ **upgrade** *n* amélioration matérielle *f*

harmful effect *n* (of chemical, process) effet nocif *m*; (of allegation, behaviour) effet nuisible *m*

harmonization *n* harmonisation *f*; ~ **process** *n* processus d'harmonisation *m*

harmonize *vt* (laws, taxes) harmoniser

harsh *adj* (competition) dur, sévère, âpre; (measures) strict, sévère; (penalty) sévère

hash *n* dièse *m*; ~ **key** *n* touche dièse *f*

hasten *vt* (departure, decline, end) précipiter; (destruction, ageing) accélérer

haulage *n* transport routier *m*, roulage *m*; ~ **company** *n* entreprise de transports routiers *f*; ~ **contractor** *n* entrepreneur de transports *m*, entrepreneur de transports routiers *m*, transporteur *m*; ~ **depot** *n* gare routière *f*

hauler *n* AmE (company) entreprise de transports routiers *f*, camionneur *m*; (owner) transporteur *m*; (driver) routier *m*

haulier *n* BrE (company) entreprise de transports routiers *f*, camionneur *m*; (owner) transporteur *m*; (driver) routier *m*

have *vt* avoir

haven *n* havre *m*, refuge *m*; **tax** ~ paradis fiscal *m*

havoc *n* **cause** ~ tout mettre sens dessus sessous; **cause** ~ **with** (plans, schedule) chambouler

hawk *vt* colporter

hawker *n* colporteur *m*, marchand ambulant *m*

hazard¹ *n* risque *m*, danger *m*; **be a health** ~ constituer un risque pour la santé; **the** ~**s of sth** les risques que constitue qch

hazard² *vt* (opinion, explanation) hasarder; ~ **a guess** hasarder une idée

hazardous *adj* dangereux/-euse; ~ **cargo** *n* marchandises dangereuses *f pl*; ~ **chemical** *n* produit chimique dangereux *m*; ~ **substance** *n* substance dangereuse *f*, substance nocive *f*

hazchem *abbr* (▸**hazardous chemical**) produit chimique dangereux *m*

hdlg *abbr* (▸**handling**) (of goods) manutention *f*

HDML *abbrev* (**Handheld Device Mark-up Language**) HDML *m*

head¹ *n* (of section, department) chef *m*, directeur/-trice *m/f*; (of office, organization) directeur/-trice *m/f*, responsable *mf*; **at the** ~ **of** (page, list) en haut de; **be at the** ~ **of** (team, group) être à la tête de; **be promoted over the** ~ **of sb** obtenir une promotion qui revenait de droit à qn; **be in over one's** ~ être complètement dépassé; **have a good** ~ **for figures/business** être doué pour le calcul/les affaires; **be above sb's** ~ dépasser qn; **a** ~, **per** ~ par personne; **have a** ~ **start** avoir une longueur d'avance, être avantagé dès le départ; ~ **accountant** *n* chef comptable *m*; ~ **buyer** *n* chef du service achats *m*, directeur des achats *m*; ~ **clerk** *n* (Admin) chef de bureau *m*; (Law) premier clerc *m*, principal *m*; ~ **count** *n* comptage du nombre de personnes présentes *m*; ~ **of department** *n* (in company) chef de service *m*; (in store) chef de rayon *m*; ~ **foreman** *n pl* **-men** chef d'atelier *m*; ~ **lease** *n* bail initial *m*; ~ **of the legal department** *n* chef du département juridique *m*; ~ **office** *n* siège social *m*; ~ **of the personnel department** *n* directeur/-trice des ressources humaines *m/f*, directeur/-trice du personnel *m/f*; ~ **and shoulders curve** *n* courbe en profil de buste *f*; ~ **of state** *n* chef d'État *m*

head² *vt* (firm, team, delegation) être à la tête de; (inquiry, investigation) mener; (column, list, queue) être en tête de; ~ **for** (disaster, bankruptcy) courir à; **be** ~**ing for a fall** courir à l'échec; ~ **off** (question) éluder; (complaint, revolt) éviter; ~ **up** (team, department) diriger

headed *adj* (paper, stationery) à en-tête

header *n* (of document) en-tête *m*

headhunt ① *vt* recruter; **be ~ed** être recherché par les chasseurs de têtes ② *vi* recruter des cadres

headhunter *n* chasseur de têtes *m*

heading *n* (on letter) en-tête *m*; (of balance sheet) chapitre *m*; (in budget) poste *m*; (of subject area, topic) rubrique *f*; (main title) titre *m*

headline *n* gros titre *m*; **~ rate** *n* taux d'inflation apparent *m*

headphones *n pl* écouteurs *m pl*

headquarter *vt* AmE (company) installer le siège de

headquarters *n pl* siège social *m*

heads *n pl* (in newspaper) gros titres *m pl*; **~ of agreement** *n pl* principes fondamentaux *m pl*

headway *n*: **make ~** faire des progrès

health *n* santé *f*; **~ benefits** *n pl* prestations maladie *f pl*; **~ care** *n* services de santé *m pl*; **~ center** AmE, **~ centre** *n* centre médico-social *m*; **~ check** *n* bilan de santé *m*; **~ club** *n* club de remise en forme *m*; **~ education** *n* enseignement de l'hygiène *m*; **~ farm** *n* établissement de cure *m*; **~ foods** *n pl* aliments macrobiotiques *m pl*, aliments naturels *m pl*; **~ hazard** *n* risque pour la santé *m*, risque sanitaire *m*; **~ insurance** *n* assurance maladie *f*; **~ insurance scheme** *n* régime d'assurance maladie *m*; **~ officer** *n* inspecteur/-trice des services de santé *m/f*; **~ record** *n* dossier médical *m*; **~ risk** *n* risque pour la santé *m*, risque sanitaire *m*; **~ and safety** *n* hygiène et sécurité du travail *f*; **~ sector** *n* secteur de la santé *m*, secteur sanitaire *m*

Health: ~ Authority *n* UK administration régionale de la santé publique *f*; **~ and Safety Executive** *n* UK ≈ Inspection du travail *f*

healthy *adj* (competition, economy, market) sain; (profit) excellent

hear *vt* entendre; (news, rumour) apprendre; (speech, lecture) écouter; (case, evidence) entendre; **~ a case in chambers** juger en chambre du conseil, juger en référé; **~ from** recevoir des nouvelles de; **I'm waiting to ~ from Accounts** j'attends une réponse du service comptabilité; **~ of** entendre parler de

hearing *n* (Law) audience *f*, audition *f*

hearsay *n* on-dit *m*, ouï-dire *m*; (Law) déposition sur la foi d'autrui *f*; **based on ~** fondé sur des 'on-dit'

heavily *adv* (taxed, indebted) lourdement, fortement; (invest) fortement; (lose) beaucoup; **be ~ subsidised** bénéficier de beaucoup de subventions; **~ traded** activement négocié; **borrow ~** faire de gros emprunts

heavy *adj* (penalty, fine) sévère; (cuts, criticism) fort; (goods, weight) lourd; (loss, debt) lourd; (charge, investment) important; **have a ~ workload** avoir beaucoup de travail; **~**

~ advertising *n* publicité intensive *f*; **~ demand** *n* demande considérable *f*, forte demande *f*; **~ duty** *adj* (strong) à haute résistance; (for industrial use) à usage industriel; **~ engineering** *n* industrie lourde *f*; **~ goods traffic** *n* trafic de poids lourds *m*; **~ goods vehicle** *n* poids lourd *m*; **~ industrial plant** *n* entreprise industrielle lourde *f*; **~ industry** *n* industrie lourde *f*; **~ share** *n* action lourde *f*, action à prix élevé *f*; **~ user** *n* gros utilisateur/-trice *m/f*; **~ viewer** *n* téléspectateur/-trice assidu/-e *m/f*

hedge¹ *n* arbitrage *m*, couverture *f*, opération de couverture à terme *f*; **~ clause** *n* clause de couverture *f*; **~ cost** *n* coût de couverture *m*, frais de couverture *m pl*; **~ fund** *n* fonds d'arbitrage *m*, fonds de sauvegarde *m*; **~ management** *n* gestion de couverture *f*; **~ manager** *n* gestionnaire de couverture *mf*; **~ strategy** *n* stratégie de couverture *f*

hedge² ① *vt* (risk) couvrir; **~ one's bets** se couvrir ② *vi* se couvrir

hedged: ~ asset *n* élément d'actif couvert *m*; **~ liability** *n* élément de passif couvert *m*

hedger *n* opérateur en couverture *m*

hedging *n* couverture *f*, opération de couverture *f*, opération de couverture à terme *f*; **~ operations** *n pl* arbitrage en couverture de risques *m*, compensations des risques de change *f pl*, opérations de couverture à terme *f pl*

hefty *adj* (price, profit, debt) considérable

hegemony *n* hégémonie *f*

height *n* hauteur *f*; **at the ~ of the season** en pleine saison; **at the ~ of the crisis** au plus fort de la crise; **be at the ~ of one's career** être au sommet de sa carrière

heighten *vt* (tension, fear) intensifier; (effect) accentuer; **~ sb's awareness of sth** sensibiliser qn à qch

heir *n* héritier *m*; **to be ~ to sth** hériter de qch

heiress *n* héritière *f*

heirs and assigns *n pl* (in deeds, wills) héritiers et ayants droit *m pl*

held: not ~ *adj* (Stock) non détenu, non valable

helicopter *n* hélicoptère *m*; **~ money** *n* augmentation rapide de la masse monétaire *f*; **~ view** *n* vue d'ensemble *f*

heliport *n* héliport *m*

help¹ *n* aide *f*; **be of ~ to sb** rendre service à qn; **with the ~ of sth/sb** à l'aide de qch/avec l'aide de qn; **come to sb's ~** venir à l'aide de qn, venir au secours de qn; **we need professional ~** nous devons consulter un professionnel; **~ desk** *n* service d'assistance *m*; **~ key** *n* touche d'aide *f*; **~ mode** *n* mode aide *m*

help² ① *vt* aider; (in crisis) secourir; ┄┄▷

(situation, problem) améliorer; ~ **sb to do** aider qn à faire; ~ **to do** (contribute) contribuer à faire

2 *vi* aider; ~ **along** (process, talks, project) faire avancer; (person) donner un coup de main à; ~ **out** (Gen Comm) donner un coup de main à; (Fin) dépanner

helpline *n* service d'assistance (téléphonique) *m*

hereby *adv*: **I the undersigned ~ testify that...** (Law) j'atteste par la présente que..., je soussigné certifie que...; **I ~ declare that...** je déclare par la présente que...; **I ~ promise that...** je, soussigné, promets que...

herein *adv* ci-inclus, ci-joint

hereto *adv* à ceci, à cela

hereunder *adv* ci-dessous

herewith *adv* ci-inclus, ci-joint

Her: ~ **Majesty's Customs** *n* UK *douanes britanniques*; ~ **Majesty's Customs and Excise** *n* UK *administration britannique des douanes et des contributions indirectes*, régie *f*; ~ **Majesty's Government** *n* UK *le gouvernement de sa Majesté*; ~ **Majesty's Stationery Office** *n* UK ≈ Imprimerie nationale *f*

hesiflation *n croissance hésitante dans un contexte d'inflation élevée*

hesitant *adj* hésitant; ~ **market** *n* marché hésitant *m*

heterogeneous *adj* hétérogène

heuristic *adj* heuristique

heuristics *n pl +sing v* heuristique *f*

HGV *abbr* (▶**heavy goods vehicle**) PL *m*, poids lourd *m*

hidden: ~ **agenda** *n* intentions cachées *f pl*, programme secret *m*; ~ **asset** *n* actif latent *m*; ~ **defect** *n* vice caché *m*; ~ **inflation** *n* inflation cachée *f*, inflation déguisée *f*; ~ **reserves** *n pl* réserves occultes *f pl*, réserves secrètes *f pl*; ~ **tax** *n* impôt déguisé *m*; ~ **unemployment** *n* chômage caché *m*, chômage déguisé *m*

hide *vt* cacher

hierarchical *adj* hiérarchique

hierarchy *n* hiérarchie *f*; ~ **of effects** hiérarchie des effets *f*; ~ **of needs** hiérarchie des besoins *f*; ~ **of objectives** hiérarchie des objectifs *f*

high[1] *adj* (number, ratio, wage) élevé; (futures price) plafond, élevé

high[2] *n* **a record ~, an all-time ~** un niveau record; **reach a new ~** atteindre un niveau record

high: ~ **achiever** *n* (person) sujet doué *m*; ~ **added-value product** *n* produit à forte valeur ajoutée *m*; ~ **availability** *n* haute disponibilité *f*; ~ **commission** *n* haut commissariat *m*; ~ **cube** *n* (Transp) conteneur hors normes *m*; ~**-density disk** *n* disquette à haute densité *f*; ~**-density freight** *n* marchandises à densité élevée *f pl*;

~**-end** *adj* (equipment, system) haut de gamme; ~**-end goods** *n pl* articles haut de gamme *m pl*; ~ **earner** *n* personne à gros revenus *f*; ~ **finance** *n* haute finance *f*; ~**-flier** *n* personne ambitieuse *f*; (in civil service) haut fonctionnaire *m*; ~**-flying stock** *n* valeur en vogue *f*, valeur volatile *f*; ~**-geared takeover** *n* BrE rachat d'entreprise financé par un fort endettement *m*, reprise à fort effet de levier *f*; ~**-grade bond** *n* obligation de premier ordre *f*, obligation de première qualité *f*; ~**-income** *adj* à revenus élevés; ~**-involvement** *adj* à forte participation du consommateur; ~**-level** *adj* (talks, meeting) à haut niveau; (official) de haut niveau; ~**-level decision** *n* décision prise à haut niveau *f*; ~**-level language** *n* (Comp) langage de haut niveau *m*; ~ **office** *n* fonction élevée *f*; ~**-powered** *adj* (person) important; ~**-pressure selling** *n* vente agressive *f*; ~ **price** *n* prix élevé *m*; ~**-profile** *adj* (company) à haut profil; (job, person) bien en vue; (product) à forte image de marque; ~**-quality product** *n* produit d'excellente qualité *m*; ~ **rate of investment** *n* taux d'investissement élevé *m*; ~**-resolution** *adj* haute résolution, à haute résolution; ~ **return** *n* revenu élevé *m*; ~**-return** *adj* (shares, investment) à rendement élevé; ~ **rise** *n* tour d'habitation *f*; ~**-risk** *adj* à haut risque, à risque élevé; ~**-risk venture** *n* entreprise à haut risque *f*; ~ **season** *n* haute saison *f*; ~ **speed** *adj* (connection, link, network) (à) haut débit; ~**-speed Internet** *n* Internet haut débit *m*; ~**-speed train** *n* train à grande vitesse *m*; ~**-spending** *adj* dépensier/-ière; ~ **standard of living** *n* niveau de vie élevé *m*; ~ **standards** *n pl* niveau élevé *m*; ~**-stream** *adj* hautement perfectionné, technologiquement avancé; ~**-stream industry** *n* industrie artisanale *f*; ~ **street** *n* BrE rue principale *f*, grand-rue *f*; ~**-street** *adj* UK (fashion) de la rue; ~**-street bank** *n* UK grande banque de dépôt *f*; ~**-street prices** *n pl* prix du commerce *m pl*; ~**-street shop** *n* commerce (de centre-ville) *m*, appartenant à une chaîne; ~**-street spending** *n* UK dépenses de grande consommation *f pl*; ~**-street retailer** *n* magasin appartenant à une chaîne *m*; ~**-tech stock** *n* valeurs des industries de haute technologie *f pl*, valeurs haute-technologie *f pl*; ~**-tech** *adj* (industry, company) de pointe; (equipment, office) ultramoderne; (system) à la pointe de la technologie; ~ **technology** *n* technologie de pointe *f*; ~**-technology industry** *n* industrie à haute technologie *f*; ~**-up** *adj* (official) très haut placé; (post) de haut rang; ~ **volume** *n* volume important *m*; ~**-volume** *adj* à volume élevé; ~**-yield** *adj* à rendement élevé; ~**-yield financing** *n* financement à rendement élevé *m*; ~**-yielding** *adj* à haut rendement, à rendement élevé

High Court n UK Cour suprême f
higher: ~ **education** n enseignement
supérieur m; ~ **income bracket** n tranche
supérieure de revenus f
Higher: ~ **National Certificate** n UK
*certificat national d'études techniques
supérieures*, ≈ BTS m; ~ **National Diploma**
n UK *diplôme national d'études techniques
supérieures*
highest: ~ **bid** n offre la plus élevée f; ~
bidder n (at auction) plus offrant m; (in tender)
mieux disant m; ~ **price** n (Gen Comm) prix
le plus élevé m; (Stock) cours le plus haut m;
~ **tender** n mieux disant m; ~ **tenderer** n
mieux disant m
highlight¹ n (of show, event) point culminant
m; (of exhibition) clou m; (of week, evening) point
fort m
highlight² vt (Comp) (word-processed text, menu
option) sélectionner; (with pen) surligner;
(differences, similarities) souligner
highlighter n (pen) surligneur m
highlights n pl (on TV) résumé m; (of week,
year) temps forts m pl
highly adv extrêmement; **speak/think ~ of
sb** dire/penser beaucoup de bien de qn; ~
competitive adj (environment, market) très
compétitif/-ive, très concurrentiel/-ielle;
~-paid adj très bien payé; **~-placed** adj
haut placé; **~-priced** adj de grand prix,
cher/chère; **~-skilled** adj hautement
qualifié; **~-trained** adj parfaitement
entraîné
hike¹ n hausse f, augmentation f; **wage/
price** ~ hausse des salaires/prix
hike² vt (price) augmenter, majorer
hinder vt gêner
hindrance n entrave f
hinge: ~ **on** vt dépendre de
hint n conseil m, tuyau m (infrml)
hinterland n arrière-pays m
hire¹ n (of tool, car) location f; **for ~** à louer;
on ~ en location; **car ~** location de voitures;
~ **car** n voiture de location f; ~ **charge** n
coût de la location m; ~ **company** n, ~
firm n agence de location f
hire² 1 vt (staff) embaucher, engager; (tool,
car) louer
2 vi embaucher; ~ **and fire** embaucher et
renvoyer; ~ **out** louer
hire purchase BrE vente à crédit f, vente à
tempérament f, location-vente f; **on ~** (buy) à
crédit; ~ **agreement** n accord d'achat à
crédit m
hirer n loueur m
hiring n (of staff) embauche f; (of tool, car)
location f; ~ **and firing** embauche et renvoi
m
histogram n histogramme m
historical adj (accounts, records) historique;
~ **cost** n coût historique m; ~ **loss** n perte
primitive d'acquisition f, perte à l'origine f;

~ **trade** n commerce historique m
historically adv du point de vue
historique; (in the past) dans le passé, par le
passé
history n histoire f; (on Internet) historique
(de requêtes) m; **they have a ~ of strikes** ils
ont connu de nombreuses grèves
hit¹ n (success) succès m; (on Internet) (match,
occurrence) résultat (d'une recherche) m, page
trouvée f; (visit to site) accès m, connexion f,
visite f; **be a ~** avoir un succès fou; **be a ~
with sb** avoir beaucoup de succès auprès de
qn; ~ **counter** n compteur de visites m,
compteur d'accès m
hit² vt (affect) affecter, toucher; (reach)
atteindre; (Comp) frapper; ~ **the bid**
enchérir, toucher le cours offert; ~ **the
bricks** AmE faire grève; ~ **the headlines**
faire la une (infrml), faire les gros titres des
journaux; ~ **the jackpot** gagner le gros lot;
~ **the market** (product) arriver sur le marché;
~ **on a solution** trouver une solution; ~ **a
problem** rencontrer un problème; **small
businesses will be the hardest ~** ce sont les
petites entreprises qui seront les plus
touchées; **inflation has ~ 9%** le taux
d'inflation a atteint 9%
hit-and-run strike n grève éclair f
hi-tech adj ▸high-tech
hit-or-miss adj (method) empirique
hive: ~ **off** vt (company) essaimer, séparer
HMC abbr UK (▸**Her Majesty's Customs**)
douanes britanniques
HMC&E abbr UK (▸**Her Majesty's
Customs and Excise**) *administration
britannique des douanes et des contributions
indirectes f*, régie f
HMG abbr UK (▸**Her Majesty's
Government**) *le gouvernement de Sa Majesté*
HMSO abbr UK (▸**Her Majesty's
Stationery Office**) ≈ Imprimerie nationale
f
HNC abbr UK (▸**Higher National
Certificate**) *certificat national d'études
techniques supérieures*, ≈ BTS m
HND abbr UK (▸**Higher National Diploma**)
*diplôme national d'études techniques
supérieures*
hoard vt (money) thésauriser; (supplies)
stocker; (food) amasser
hoarding n panneau d'affichage m, panneau
publicitaire m
hold¹ n (of aircraft, ship) cale f; **get ~ of** (item)
se procurer; (details, information) découvrir; **get
~ of sb** (by phone) joindre qn; **on
~** (on the phone) en attente; **put sb on ~** faire
patienter qn; **put a call on ~** mettre un
appel en attente; **put a project/plan on ~**
laisser un projet/des projets en suspens; **have
a ~ over sb** avoir de l'emprise sur qn
hold² 1 vt tenir; (permit, card, job, position,
degree) avoir; (contain) contenir; (inquiry) mener; ⋯⟶

(margins) maintenir; (ballot, election, referendum) organiser; (bonds, shares) détenir; (market) détenir, soutenir; (attention, interest) retenir; (meeting, talks) organiser, tenir; (exhibition, show) monter, organiser; (interview) faire passer; (record) détenir; (mortgage) avoir; (opinion) avoir; **be held** (event) avoir lieu; **~ as security** détenir en garantie; **~ funds for a check** AmE, **~ funds for a cheque** BrE bloquer les fonds pour un chèque; **~ in check** (prices) contenir, maîtriser; **~ the line** (on phone) rester en ligne, patienter; **can you ~ the line please** ne quittez pas s'il vous plaît; **~ one's ground** tenir bon; **~ a position** (Stock) avoir une situation; **~ power** être au pouvoir; **~ the purse strings** tenir les cordons de la bourse; **~ sb responsible for sth** tenir qn responsable de qch; **~ the stage** avoir la vedette
[2] *vi* (offer, theory) tenir, rester valable; (on the phone) patienter, rester en ligne; **~ back** *vt* (payment) différer; (information) cacher; *vi* ne pas s'engager; **~ down** (costs, inflation, rate, number) limiter; (job) garder; **~ off** (creditor) faire patienter; (postpone) remettre à plus tard; **~ on** (on phone) patienter; (wait) attendre; **~ onto** (shares) garder; (power, lead, title) conserver; **~ out** (stocks, supplies) durer; **~ out for** insister pour obtenir; **~ over** (postpone) ajourner; **~ up** *vt* (delay) retarder; *vi* (share price) se maintenir; (currency) se maintenir, résister; (theory, argument) tenir

holdback *n* (deduction) prélèvement *m*; (Prop) retenue *f*

holder *n* (of record, ticket, key) détenteur/-trice *m/f*; (of passport, degree, post) titulaire *mf*; (of shares) porteur/-euse *m/f*, détenteur/-trice *m/f*; **~ for value** (of bill of exchange) détenteur contre valeur *m*; **~ in due course** (Law) porteur de bonne foi *m*; **~ of record** (of securities, shares) porteur/-euse *m/f*

holding *n* (Law) tenure *f*; (of securities, shares) détention *f*; **~ company** *n* holding *m*, société de holding *f*; **~ corporation** *n* corporation de portefeuille *f*; **~ gain** *n* plus-value *f*; **~ pattern** *n* (Fin, Stock) actionnariat à tendance normale *m*; **~ period** *n* (Stock) durée d'actionnariat *f*, période de détention *f*

holdings *n pl* avoirs *m pl*, participations *f pl*; **have ~ in a company** avoir des participations dans une entreprise

holdover *n* **~ effect** *n* effet de rémanence *m*; **~ tenant** *n* locataire sur les lieux *mf*

hold-up *n* retard *m*

holiday *n* BrE congé *m*, vacances *f pl*; **do ~ work** travailler pendant ses vacances; **go on ~, take a ~** prendre des vacances; **on ~** en congé, en vacances; **~ accommodation** *n* logement de vacances *m*; **~ entitlement** *n* droit au congé *m*; **~ leave** *n* congé annuel *m*; **~-maker** *n* vacancier/-ière *m/f*; **~ pay** *n* congés payés *m pl*; **~ period** *n*, **~ season** *n* période des vacances *f*

holidays *n pl* BrE vacances *f pl*; **~ with pay** congés payés *m pl*

home *n* (house) maison *f*; (household) foyer *m*; **~ address** *n* adresse personnelle *f*; (on form) domicile *m*; **~ affairs** *n pl* (Pol) affaires intérieures *f pl*; **~ automation** *n* domotique *f*; **~ banking** *n* banque à domicile *f*; **~ business** *n* entreprise à domicile *f*; **home buying** *n* accession à la propriété *f*; **~ computer** *n* ordinateur *m*; **~ consumption** *n* (Econ) consommation intérieure *f*; **~ country** *n* pays d'origine *m*; **~ equity loan** *n* prêt sur la valeur nette d'une maison *m*; **~ improvement** *n* amélioration de l'habitat *f*; **~ improvement loan** *n* prêt destiné à l'amélioration de l'habitat *m*; **~ insurance** *n* assurance habitation *f*; **~ loan** *n* prêt immobilier *m*; **~ market** *n* marché intérieur *m*; **~ office** *n* bureau à domicile *m*; **~ page** *n* page d'accueil *f*; (of individual) page personnelle *f*, page perso *f* (infrml); **~ products** *n pl* produits nationaux *m pl*; **~ purchase loan** *n* prêt immobilier *m*; **~ sales** *n pl* (Econ) ventes sur le marché intérieur *f pl*; **~ shopping** *n* téléachat *m*; **~ trade** *n* commerce intérieur *m*; **~ work** *n* travail à domicile *m*; **~ worker** *n* travailleur/-euse à domicile *m/f*; **~ working** *n* travail à domicile *m*

home-grown *adj* du pays, local

homeless *adj* sans abri; **the ~ n pl** les sans-abri *m pl*, les sans-logis *m pl*; **~ person** *n* sans-abri *mf*, sans-logis *m*

homeowner *n* propriétaire *mf*

homeowners': **~ association** *n* association des propriétaires *f*; **~ policy** *n* assurance habitation *f*

home ownership *n* fait d'être propriétaire de son logement *m*; **~ is rising** de plus en plus de gens sont propriétaires de leur logement

homestead *n* US propriété *f*

homeward *adv* (cargo, freight, journey) de retour

homogeneous *adj* homogène

homologation *n* homologation *f*

honest *adj* honnête, loyal; **~ broker** *n* médiateur/-trice *m/f*

honesty *n* honnêteté *f*

honor *n*, *vt* AmE ▶**honour** BrE

honorarium *n* honoraires *m pl*

honorary *adj* (member) honoraire, sur la base du bénévolat; (rank) honorifique; **in an ~ capacity** à titre bénévole; **~ chairman** *n* président/-e d'honneur *m/f*; **~ membership** *n* honorariat *m*; **~ president** *n* président/-e d'honneur *m/f*

honour[1] *n* BrE honneur *m*

honour[2] *vt* BrE (cheque, signature) honorer; (agreement) remplir; (promise, commitment) tenir

hook up *vt* connecter, raccorder

hopper *n* (receptacle) trémie *f*

horizon *n* horizon *m*; **on the ~** en vue; **within a five year ~** en l'espace de cinq ans; **broaden one's ~** élargir ses horizons; **open up new ~** ouvrir de nouveaux horizons; **~ analysis** *n* analyse de la situation *f*

horizontal *adj* horizontal; **~ amalgamation** *n* fusion horizontale *f*; **~ analysis** *n* analyse à travers plusieurs exercices *f*; **~ balance sheet** *n* bilan en forme de compte *m*; **~ business combination** *n* concentration horizontale *f*; **~ communication** *n* communication horizontale *f*; **~ equity** *n* avoir horizontal *m*, équité horizontale *f*; **~ expansion** *n* croissance horizontale *f*, développement horizontal *m*; **~ integration** *n* intégration horizontale *f*; **~ merger** *n* fusion horizontale *f*; **~ portal** *n* (Comp) portail horizontal *m*; **~ specialization** *n* gestion par fonctions *f*; **~ spread** *n* opération mixte horizontale *f*

horse trading *n* maquignonnage *m*

hospital *n* hôpital *m*; **~ care insurance plan** *n* régime d'assurance-hospitalisation *m*; **~ expenses** *n pl* frais d'hospitalisation *m pl*

host¹ *n* (Gen Comm, Comp) hôte *m*; **play ~ to sb/sth** accueillir qn/qch; **~ city** *n* ville d'accueil *f*; **~ country** *n* pays d'accueil *m*; **~ name** *n* nom d'hôte *m*, adresse Internet *f*

host² *vt* (Comp) (website) héberger; (event) accueillir

hosted site *n* (Comp) site hébergé *m*

hostile takeover bid *n* OPA hostile *f*, offre publique d'achat hostile *f*, tentative de prise de contrôle inamicale *f*, tentative de prise de contrôle sauvage *f*

hosting *n* (Comp) hébergement *m*

hot *adj* (newly issued) neuf/neuve, tout chaud; (stolen) (infrml) volé; **in the ~ seat** sur la sellette; **~ bills** *n pl* billets neufs *m pl*; **~ issue** *n* US émission brûlante *f*, émission très attendue *f*; **~ key** *n* (Comp) raccourci clavier *m*; **~ list** *n* (Bank) liste d'oppositions *f*; (Comp) liste de signets *f*, liste de favoris *f*; **~ money** *n* capitaux flottants *m pl*, capitaux fébriles *m pl*; **~ stock** *n* action nouvellement émise et très demandée *f*

hotel *n* hôtel *m*; **~ accommodation** (Gen Comm) logement à l'hôtel *m*; (room) chambre d'hôtel *f*; **~ chain** *n* chaîne hôtelière *f*; **~ industry** *n* industrie hôtelière *f*; **~ manager** *n* gérant/-e d'hôtel *m/f*; **~ proprietor** *n* propriétaire d'hôtel *mf*; **~ register** *n* registre de l'hôtel *m*; **~ trade** *n* hôtellerie *f*

hotelier *n* hôtelier/-ière *m/f*

hot line *n* (between heads of government) téléphone rouge *m*; (phone service) permanence téléphonique *f*, hotline *f*

hotliner *n* téléconseiller/-ère *m/f*

hotlink *n* hyperlien *m*

hotspot *n* (Comp) zone cliquable *f*, zone

hour *n* heure *f*; **be paid by the ~** être payé à l'heure; **100 dollars per ~** 100 dollars (de) l'heure; **a 35 ~ week** une semaine de 35 heures

hourly *adj* horaire; **~ rate** *n* taux horaire *m*; **~ wage** *n* salaire horaire *m*; **~ worker** *n* ouvrier/-ière payé/-e à l'heure *m/f*, travailleur/-euse payé/-e à l'heure *m/f*

hours of business *n pl* (of shop) heures d'ouverture *f pl*; (of office) heures de bureau *f pl*

house *n* maison *f*; **sell ~-to-house** vendre à domicile; **~ account** *n* (Stock) compte maison *m*; **~ bill of lading** *n* connaissement de groupage *m*; **~ brand** *n* marque de distributeur *m*; **~-building** *n* bâtiment *m*; **~ journal** *n*, **~ magazine** *n*, **~ organ** *n* revue d'entreprise *f*; **~ prices** *n pl* prix immobiliers *m pl*; **~ purchase** *n* achat de maison *m*; **~ search** *n* (by police) perquisition à domicile *f*, visite domiciliaire *f*; **~ style** *n* style de l'entreprise *m*, style maison *m*; **~-to-house selling** *n* démarchage *m*

House: ~ of Commons *n* UK Chambre des communes *f*; **~ of Lords** *n* UK Chambre des lords *f*; **~ of Representatives** *n* US Chambre des représentants *f*; **the ~** *n* UK la Chambre des communes, le Parlement britannique

household *n* ménage *m*; **~ appliance** *n* appareil ménager *m*; **~ commodity** *n* article de ménage *m*; **~ consumption** *n* consommation des ménages *f*; **~ durables** *n pl* biens ménagers durables *m pl*; **~ name** *n* nom de marque *m*; **~ policy** *n* assurance multirisque habitation *f*; **~ waste** *n* ordures ménagères *f pl*

householder *n* habitant/-e *m/f*; (owner) propriétaire *mf*; (tenant) locataire *mf*

Houses of Parliament *n pl* UK Parlement britannique *m*

housing *n* logement *m*; **~ allowance** *n* indemnité de logement *f*; **~ benefit** *n* UK allocation logement *f*; **~ bond** *n* emprunt-logement *m*; **~ development** *n*, **~ estate** *n* BrE (large) cité *f*; (small) lotissement *m*; **~ industry** *n* bâtiment *m*; **~ market** *n* marché du logement *m*; **~ project** *n* (planned) projet de lotissement *m*; AmE (housing estate) cité *f*; (small) lotissement *m*; **~ shortage** *n* pénurie de logements *f*; **~ stock** *n* parc immobilier *m*; **~ subsidy** *n* aide au logement *f*

hover: ~ around *vi* (prices) osciller autour de

HP *abbr* BrE (▸hire purchase) vente à crédit *f*, vente à tempérament *f*, location-vente *f*; (horsepower) CV *m* (cheval-vapeur)

HQ *abbr* (▸headquarters) quartier général *m*; (of company) siège social *m*

HR *abbr* (▸human resources) RH *f pl* (ressources humaines)

HRD *abbr* (▸**human resource development**) développement des ressources humaines *m*

HRM *abbr* (▸**human resource management**) GRH *f* (gestion des ressources humaines)

HRP *abbr* (▸**human resource planning**) planification des ressources humaines *f*, le recrutement et la gestion des ressources humaines *f*

HSE *abbr* UK (▸**Health and Safety Executive**) ≈ *Inspection du Travail*

HTML *abbr* (**Hypertext Mark-up Language**) HTML *m*; ~ **editor** *n* éditeur HTML *m*; ~ **file** *n* fichier HTML *m*

hub *n* (Gen Comm, Transp) centre *m*, moyeu *m*, pivot *m*; (Comp) concentrateur *m*, hub *m*; ~ **of activity** centre d'activité *m*

huckster *n* (S&M) vendeur baratineur *m*; AmE (advertising) publicitaire *mf*

huge *adj* (success) énorme; (premises) vaste; (debts, profits, sum) gros/grosse; (redundancies) massif/-ive

hull *n* coque *f*

human *adj* humain; ~ **asset accounting** *n* évaluation du capital humain *f*; ~ **capital** *n* capital humain *m*; ~ **engineering** *n* ergonomie *f*, ~-**machine interface** *n* interface utilisateur *f*; ~ **resource** *n* ressource humaine *f*; ~ **resource accounting** *n* évaluation des ressources humaines *f*; ~ **resource administration** *n* administration des ressources humaines *f*; ~ **resource development** *n* développement des ressources humaines *m*; ~ **resource management** *n* gestion des ressources humaines *f*; ~ **resource planning** *n* planification des ressources humaines *f*, le recrutement et la gestion des effectifs; ~ **resources** *n pl* personnel *m*, ressources

humaines *f pl*; ~ **rights** *n pl* droits de l'homme *m pl*

humanocentric *adj* humanocentrique

hurdle *n* obstacle *m*; ~ **rate** *n* (expenditure) taux de rendement minimal *m*

hush money *n* (infrml) pot-de-vin *m*; **to pay sb** ~ acheter le silence de qn

hustle *vt* (sell) fourguer (infrml)

hybrid *adj* hybride; ~ **auction** *n* adjudication hybride *f*, enchère hybride *f*; ~ **company** *n* société de clics et de briques *f*, société de clics et de mortier *f*, société hybride *f*; ~ **computer** *n* ordinateur hybride *m*

hydroelectric *adj* (energy, power, scheme) hydro-électrique; ~ **power station** *n* centrale hydro-électrique *f*

hydrofoil *n* hydroptère *m*

hype[1] *n* battage publicitaire *m*, campagne publicitaire agressive *f*

hype[2] *vt* faire du battage publicitaire pour

hyperdocument *n* hyperdocument *m*

hyperinflation *n* hyperinflation *f*

hyperlink *n* hyperlien *m*

hypermarket *n* grande surface *f*, hypermarché *m*

hypermedia *n* hypermédia *m*; ~ **document** *n* document hypermédia *m*

hypertext *n* hypertexte *m*; ~ **link** *n* lien hypertexte *m*

hyperword *n* hypermot *m*

hypothesis *n* hypothèse *f*; ~ **testing** *n* essai d'hypothèse *m*

hypothetical *adj* hypothétique; ~ **conditions** *n pl* conditions hypothétiques *f pl*; ~ **question** *n* question hypothétique *f*; ~ **situation** *n* situation hypothétique *f*

Ii

i *abbr* (▸**interest**) intérêt *m*, intérêts *m pl*

IAP *abbr* (▸**Internet access provider**) FAI *m* (fournisseur d'accès Internet)

IATA *abbr* (▸**International Air Transport Association**) IATA *f* (Association internationale des transports aériens)

IB *abbr* (▸**in bond**) en entrepôt sous douane

IBEC *abbr* (▸**International Bank for Economic Cooperation**) Banque internationale pour la coopération économique *f*

IBRD *abbr* (▸**International Bank for Reconstruction and Development**) BIRD *f*

(Banque internationale pour la reconstruction et le développement)

ICAO *abbr* (▸**International Civil Aviation Organization**) OACI *f* (Organisation de l'aviation civile internationale)

ICAs *abbr* (▸**International Commodity Agreements**) accords internationaux sur les matières premières *m pl*

ICJ *abbr* (▸**International Court of Justice**) Cour internationale de justice *f*

icon *n* icône *f*

iconify *vt* (Comp) iconiser, iconifier

ICT *abbr* (**information and**

communications technology) technologie de l'information et de la communication f

ID[1] *abbr* (▸**identification**) identification f; (▸**import duty**) droit d'entrée m, taxe à l'importation f; ∼ **number** n numéro d'identification m

ID[2] n carte d'identité f

IDA *abbr* (▸**International Development Association**) Association internationale pour le développement f

IDD *abbr* (▸**international direct dialing**) appel international automatique m

ideal *adj* idéal; ∼ **capacity** n capacité maximale f, capacité théorique f

ideas: ∼ **man** n pl **-men** concepteur m; ∼ **woman** n pl **-men** conceptrice f

identification n identification f; (proof of identity) pièce d'identité f

identifier n (Comp) identificateur m; (unique code) identifiant m

identity n identité f; ∼ **card** n carte d'identité f

idle *adj* (hardware) inactif/-ive; (worker) au chômage; (factory, machinery, plant) arrêté; (ship) désarmé, inemployé; (speculation) oiseux/-euse; (port, dock) à l'arrêt; ∼ **balance** n solde non-mouvementé m; ∼ **capacity** n capacité inutilisée f, potentiel sous-utilisé m; ∼ **cash** n argent oisif m; ∼ **money** n argent improductif m, argent qui dort m; ∼ **shipping** n navires désarmés m pl, navires inemployés m pl; ∼ **time** n (Comp) temps mort m, temps d'inactivité m; (HRM) heures inemployées f pl

iDTV *abbr* (▸**interactive digital television**) télévision numérique interactive f

i.e. *abbr* (**id est**, **that is to say**) c-à-d (c'est-à-dire)

IFA *abbr* (▸**independent financial advisor**) conseiller/-ère financier/-ière indépendant/-e m/f

IFAP *abbr* (**International Federation of Agricultural Producers**) FIPA f (Fédération internationale des producteurs agricoles)

ignore *vt* (person) ignorer; (advice) ne pas suivre; (rule, law) ne pas respecter; (letter) ne pas répondre à; (mistake, behaviour) passer sur; (information, fact, remark) ne pas tenir compte de; (Law) (claim) rejeter

illegal *adj* illégal; ∼ **alien** n étranger/-ère en situation irrégulière m/f; ∼ **dividend** n US dividende illicite m; ∼ **immigrant** n immigré/-e clandestin/-e m/f; ∼ **immigration** n immigration clandestine f; ∼ **practices** n pl manœuvres frauduleuses f pl, pratiques illégales f pl; ∼ **strike** n grève illicite f

illegally *adv* illégalement

illiquid[1] *adj* en brèche de trésorerie, non-liquide; ∼ **assets** n pl actif non-disponible m

illusory profit n profit fictif m, profit illusoire m

illustrate *vt* (book, point) illustrer; ∼ **how** illustrer la façon dont

illustrated *adj* illustré

illustration n (example, picture) illustration f; **by way of** ∼ à titre d'exemple

ill will n mauvaise volonté f

ILO *abbr* (▸**International Labour Organization**) OIT f (Organisation internationale du travail)

IM *abbr* (▸**instant messaging**) messagerie instantanée f

image n image f; (of company, product) image de marque f; ∼ **advertising** n publicité institutionnelle f; ∼**-conscious** *adj* conscient de son image de marque; ∼**-maker** n professionnel/-elle de l'image m/f; ∼ **processing** n traitement de l'image m; ∼ **projection** n projection d'image de marque f

imaging n (Comp) imagerie f

IMB *abbr* (▸**International Maritime Bureau**) Bureau maritime international m

imbalance n déséquilibre m; ∼ **of trade** déséquilibre commercial m

IMC *abbr* (▸**International Maritime Committee**) Comité maritime international m

IMF *abbr* (▸**International Monetary Fund**) FMI m (Fonds monétaire international)

IMM *abbr* (▸**International Monetary Market**) MMI m (Marché monétaire international)

immediate *adj* (effect, reaction) immédiat; (concern, goal) premier/-ière; (problem, crisis) urgent; **for** ∼ **attention** urgent; ∼ **access** n accès immédiat m; ∼ **aim** n objectif immédiat m; ∼ **delivery** n livraison immédiate f; ∼ **family** n famille immédiate f, parents proches m pl; ∼ **possession** n (of property) jouissance immédiate f

immigrant n immigré/-e m/f; ∼ **worker** n travailleur/-euse immigré/-e m/f

immigration n immigration f; ∼ **control** n contrôle de l'immigration m; ∼ **officer** n agent du service de l'immigration m; ∼ **policy** n politique de l'immigration f

imminent *adj* (danger, arrival) imminent; ∼ **peril** n (Ins) risque imminent m

immovable: ∼ **estate** n bien immobilier m; ∼ **property** n propriété immobilière f

immovables n pl biens immeubles m pl

immunity n immunité f; **be granted** ∼ se voir accorder l'immunité

imp. *abbr* (▸**import**, ▸**importation**) imp. (importation)

impact[1] n effet m, impact m; **have an** ∼ **on** avoir un impact sur; ∼ **effect** n effet d'impact m; ∼ **multiplier** n multiplicateur d'impact m; ∼ **study** n étude de l'impact f

impact[2] *vt* avoir un impact sur; ∼ **on** avoir ⋯⟩

un impact sur

impair *vt* (purchasing power) affaiblir, diminuer; (capital) diminuer; (performance) affecter; (efficiency, progress, productivity) diminuer, affecter

impairment *n* (Tax) déficience *f*; **~ of value** (of security) baisse de valeur *f*, réduction de valeur *f*

impartial *adj* (advice, decision, inquiry) impartial; (account, report) objectif/-ive

impasse *n* impasse *f*; **reach an ~** aboutir à une impasse

imperfect *adj* (goods) défectueux/-euse; **~ competition** *n* concurrence imparfaite *f*; **~ market** *n* marché imparfait *m*; **~ obligation** *n* obligation morale *f*

imperialism *n* impérialisme *m*

impetus *n* (trigger) impulsion *f*, incitation *f*; (momentum) élan *m*; **gain/lose ~** prendre/ perdre de l'élan

impinge: ~ on *vt* (rights) empiéter sur

implement *vt* (Comp) implémenter; (article, plan) réaliser; (contract, decision) exécuter, mettre en œuvre

implementation *n* implémentation *f*; (of article, plan) mise en œuvre *f*; (of contract) exécution *f*, mise en œuvre *f*; **~ lag** *n* délai de mise en œuvre *m*; **~ schedule** *n* calendrier d'exécution *f*

implications *n pl* conséquences *f pl*, répercussions *f pl*

implicit *adj* implicite; **~ cost** *n* coût implicite *m*

implied¹ *adj* implicite, tacite; **~ condition** *n* condition tacite *f*; **~ consent** *n* consentement implicite *m*; **~ contract** *n* contrat tacite *m*; **~ terms** *n pl* conditions implicites *f pl*; **~ warranty** *n* garantie implicite *f*

imply *vt* (insinuate) insinuer; (lead to believe) laisser entendre; (indicate, mean) impliquer; **~ that** impliquer que; (term, word) laisser supposer; **as their name implies** comme leur nom le laisse supposer

import¹ *n* importation *f*; **~ allowance** *n* tolérance à l'importation *f*; **~ ban** *n* interdiction d'importation *f*; **~ controls** *n pl* contrôles à l'importation *m pl*; **~ credit** *n* lettre de créance à l'importation *f*; **~ duty** *n* (tax) droit d'entrée *m*, taxe à l'importation *f*; **~ earnings** *n pl* gains à l'importation *m pl*; **~-export** *n* import-export *m*; **~ licence** BrE, **~ license** *n* AmE licence d'importation *f*; **~ licensing** *n* autorisation d'importation *f*; **~ manager** *n* directeur/-trice des importations *m/f*; **~ permit** *n* autorisation d'importer *f*; **~ price** *n* prix à l'importation *m*; **~ quota** *n* contingent d'importation *m*, quota à l'importation *m*; **~ regulations** *n pl* réglementation des importations *f*; **~ surplus** *n* excédent d'importation *m*; **~ tax** *n* taxe à l'importation *f*

import² *vt* (Imp/Exp) (goods) importer; (Comp) (data) importer

important *adj* important; **very ~ person** personnage de marque *m*; **~ office** *n* fonction élevée *f*

importation *n* importation *f*

imported *adj* importé; **~ goods** *n pl* marchandises importées *f pl*

importer *n* importateur/-trice *m/f*; (country) pays importateur *m*

importing *adj* importateur/-trice

impose *vt* (burden, condition) imposer; (fine, penalty) infliger; (limit, restriction, law) imposer; **~ extreme hardship on sb** placer qn dans une situation financière extrêmement difficile; **~ a tax on** mettre un impôt sur

imposition *n* (of burden, law, limit, restriction) imposition *f*; (tax) impôt *m*, taxe *f*

impound *vt* (goods) confisquer; (documents) saisir; (vehicle) mettre en fourrière; (ship) mettre en eau

impoverished *adj* appauvri

impress [1] *vt* impressionner [2] *vi* faire bonne impression

impression *n* (idea) impression *f*; (of book, newspaper) impression *f*, tirage *m*; (in Internet advertising) impression *f*; **make an ~ on** impressionner

impressive *adj* (growth, increase) impressionnant

imprest *n* avance temporaire *f*; **~ account** *n* compte d'avances à montant fixe *m*

imprinter *n* imprimante à cartes *f*

imprisonment *n* emprisonnement *m*, incarcération *f*

improper *adj* (irregular) irrégulier/-ière; (use) abusif/-ive, impropre

improve [1] *vt* (qualitatively) améliorer; (productivity, output, profits) accroître; **~ one's chances of doing** augmenter ses chances de faire [2] *vi* s'améliorer; **~ on** (productivity, profits) augmenter; (offer) renchérir sur; (score, rating) améliorer

improved *adj* (efficiency, conditions) amélioré; (access) facilité; (offer) meilleur

improvement *n* (in quality, condition) amélioration *f*; (in system, equipment) perfectionnement *m*; (progress) progrès *m pl*; (to property) aménagements *m pl*; **there is room for ~** on pourrait faire mieux

improvements *n pl* améliorations *f pl*

impulse *m* impulsion *f*; **act on ~** céder à une impulsion; **~ buy** *n* achat impulsif *m*, achat spontané *m*; **~ buyer** *n* acheteur/-euse impulsif/-ive *m/f*; **~ buying** *n* achat d'impulsion *m*, achat impulsif *m*; **~ purchase** *n* achat impulsif *m*

impute *vt* imputer, attribuer

imputed: ~ cost *n* frais imputés *m pl*; **~ income** *n* revenu implicite *m*, revenu imputé m; ~ **interest** n intérêts imputés m pl; ~ **value** n valeur imputée f

inability n incapacité f; ~ **to work** incapacité de travailler

inaccuracy n (of figures, calculation) inexactitude f

inaccurate adj (information, data) inexact; (statement, account) contenant des inexactitudes

inactive adj (Comp) déconnecté, inactif/-ive; (bill) dormant, inactif/-ive; (asset) dormant, inactif/-ive, peu actif/-ive; (market) calme; ~ **account** n compte inactif m; ~ **asset** n actif dormant m, avoir inactif m; ~ **bond** n obligation inactive f, obligation peu active f; ~ **stock** n action dormante f, action inactive f

inadvertently adv par inadvertance

inalienable adj (right) inaliénable

inapplicable adj inapplicable

inaugural adj (meeting, session) inaugural; ~ **flight** n vol d'inauguration m

inbound: ~ **flight** n vol d'arrivée m; ~ **passengers** n pl passagers à l'arrivée m pl

in-box n (for e-mail) boîte de réception f

Inc. abbr US (▸**incorporated company**) (in company name) ≈ SARL f (société à responsabilité limitée)

incapacity n incapacité f

incentive n (extra pay) prime f, gratification f; (encouragement) incitation f; (Tax) encouragement m, incitation f; ~ **bonus** n prime d'encouragement f; ~ **fee** n honoraires d'encouragement m pl; ~ **plan** n plan d'encouragement m; ~ **scheme** n système de primes d'encouragement m; ~ **wage** n salaire au rendement m

incentivize vt encourager, inciter

incestuous share dealing n commerce incestueux d'actions m

inchoate adj (document) incomplet/-ète

incidence n (effect) incidence f; (frequency) fréquence f; **the high/low** ~ **of** le taux élevé/le faible taux de

incidental adj (outlay) accessoire; (detail, fact) secondaire; ~ **charges** n pl frais accessoires m pl; ~ **damages** n pl dommages-intérêts accessoires m pl; ~ **expenses** n pl faux frais m pl

incidentals n pl faux frais m pl; ~ **allowance** n indemnité de frais accessoires f

incineration n (of waste) incinération f; ~ **plant** n usine d'incinération f

incinerator n incinérateur m

incl. abbr (▸**included**, ▸**inclusive**) compris, inclus; (▸**including**) compris, y compris

include vt inclure; (with a list of items) comprendre

included adj compris

including prep y compris; **up to and** ~ **Friday** jusqu'à vendredi inclus; ~ **service** service compris

inclusion n inclusion f

inclusive¹ adj (price) forfaitaire; **the 7ᵗʰ to the 12ᵗʰ** ~ du 7 au 12 inclus; **the price** ~ **of delivery** le prix, livraison comprise; ~ **terms** n pl prix tout compris m

inclusivism n (Gen Comm, Pol) politique de non-exclusion f

income n revenu m, revenus m pl; **be on an** ~ **of** gagner; **low-**~ **householders** ménages à bas revenus m pl; ~ **accounts** n pl comptes de recettes et dépenses m pl; ~ **band** n tranche de revenu f; ~ **bond** n obligation à revenu variable f; ~ **bracket** n tranche de revenu f; ~ **debenture** n obligation à revenu variable f; ~ **differential** n différentiel de revenu m; ~ **distribution** n répartition du revenu f; ~ **effect** n effet de revenu m; ~ **from interest** produits financiers m pl; ~ **from securities** produits des immobilisations financières m pl, revenu de portefeuille m; ~ **from services** prestations de services f pl; ~ **group** n tranche de revenu f; ~ **per head** n revenu par habitant m; ~ **statement** n compte de pertes et profits m, compte de résultat m; ~ **stream** n flux des revenus m; ~ **support** n UK ≈ revenu minimum d'insertion m; ~ **target** n objectif de revenu m; ~ **tax** n impôt sur le revenu m; ~ **tax bracket** n tranche d'imposition f; ~ **tax inspector** n inspecteur/-trice des impôts m/f; ~ **tax rate** n taux de l'impôt sur le revenu m; ~ **tax refund** n remboursement de l'impôt sur le revenu m; ~ **tax regulations** n pl règlements de l'impôt sur le revenu m pl; ~ **tax return** n déclaration fiscale f, déclaration de revenus f; (form) feuille d'impôts f; ~ **test** n évaluation de l'état des revenus f; ~**-tested supplement** n complément proportionnel aux ressources m

incomes policy n politique salariale f

incoming adj (president, chairman) nouveau/-elle; ~ **call** n appel de l'extérieur m; ~ **data** n pl données en entrée f pl; ~ **flight** n vol d'arrivée m; ~ **goods** n pl marchandises à l'arrivée f pl, marchandises à la réception f pl; ~ **mail** n courrier du jour m, courrier à l'arrivée m; ~ **order** n commande reçue f; ~ **post** n BrE courrier du jour m, courrier à l'arrivée m

incomings n pl rentrées f pl, recettes f pl

in-company adj (expert) maison; (training) interne

incompatible adj incompatible

incompetence n incompétence f

incompetent adj incompétent; ~ **work** n mauvais travail m

incomplete adj inachevé, incomplet/-ète

incontestable adj incontestable; ~ **clause** n clause d'incontestabilité f, clause incontestable f

incontrovertible adj (evidence, proof, sign) indéniable; (argument) irréfutable

inconvenience[1] n (drawback) inconvénient m; (trouble) dérangement m

inconvenience[2] vt déranger

inconvenient adj incommode; (time) inopportun

inconvertible money n argent inconvertible m

incorporate [1] vt (company) constituer; (include) incorporer [2] vi (merge) fusionner; (form a company) se constituer en société commerciale

incorporated adj (included) incorporé; UK (institution, company) constitué; ~ **company** n US société constituée f, société enregistrée f

incorporation n (of company) constitution en société f, constitution en société par actions f

incorporeal adj incorporel/-elle; ~ **hereditaments** n pl biens incorporels transmissibles par héritage m pl; ~ **property** n bien incorporel m

incorrect adj incorrect

increase[1] n augmentation f; (in price) augmentation f, hausse f; (in business) développement m, accroissement m; (in wages) augmentation f; (in prices) majoration f; (in demand, supply); croissance f; (in crime, support, unemployment) accroissement m; **be on the** ~ être en progression; ~ **in value** plus-value f

increase[2] [1] vt augmenter; ~ **the supply** accroître l'offre, augmenter l'offre [2] vi (sales, output, demand, supply, taxes, inflation) augmenter; (workload) s'accroître; (rate) monter; ~ **by** (amount, percentage) augmenter de; ~ **in value** augmenter en valeur; ~ **from ... to ...** passer de ... à ...; ~ **tenfold** décupler; ~ **twofold** doubler

increased value n plus-value f

increasing adj croissant; **with** ~ **frequency** de plus en plus fréquemment

increasingly adv de plus en plus

increment[1] n (on salary) augmentation (automatique) f; (Comp) incrément m

increment[2] vt (salary) augmenter automatiquement; (Comp) incrémenter

incremental adj (cost) marginal; ~ **analysis** n analyse marginale f; ~ **cash flow** n marge brute d'autofinancement marginale f; ~ **payment** n salaire de croissance m; ~ **scale** n échelle de croissance des salaires f; ~ **spending** n augmentation des dépenses f; ~ **tax** n impôt supplémentaire m

incubator n (Fin) incubateur m

incumbent n titulaire mf

incur vt (debts) contracter, encourir; (losses) subir; (penalty, risk) encourir; ~ **cost(s)** encourir des dépenses; ~ **expenses** encourir des dépenses, engager des frais

incurred: ~ **costs** n pl frais encouru m pl; ~ **expenses** n pl dépenses encourues

f pl, dépenses engagées f pl, frais encourus m pl

indebted adj (country, company) endetté; **be** ~ **to sb** (grateful) être redevable à qn

indebtedness n endettement m

indefinite adj (amount, number) indéterminé; (plan, idea, answer) vague; (duties) imprécis; (delay, strike, period) illimité; (ban) pour une durée indéterminée; ~ **laytime** n staries non-définies f pl

indemnify vt indemniser

indemnity n (compensation) dédommagement m, indemnité f; (safeguard) garantie f, assurance f; ~ **fund** n caisse de solidarité patronale f

indent n (in printing) alinéa m; (order) commande f; ~ **house** n société d'exportation f

indentation n (in printing) alinéa m

indenture n contract synallagmatique m

independence n indépendance f

independent adj indépendant; (self-governing) autonome; ~ **of** indépendant de; ~ **audit** n audit externe m, contrôle externe m; ~ **auditor** n auditeur indépendant m, commissaire aux comptes indépendant m; ~ **expert** n expert indépendant m; ~ **financial advisor** n conseiller/-ère financier/-ière indépendant/-e m/f; ~ **inquiry** n enquête autonome f, enquête indépendante f; ~ **local radio** n radio locale indépendante f; ~ **retailer** n détaillant indépendant m; ~ **school** n école libre f; ~ **store** n magasin indépendant m; ~ **trade union** n syndicat indépendant m; ~ **variable** n variable indépendante f

Independent n (Pol) non-inscrit m

in-depth adj approfondi; ~ **analysis** n analyse approfondie f; ~ **discussion** n discussion approfondie f; ~ **guide** n guide détaillé m; ~ **interview** n interview en profondeur f; ~ **study** n étude détaillée f

index[1] n pl **-dices** (in publication) index m; (Comp) index m; (Econ, Fin) index m, indice m; (Stock) (average) indice m, indice boursier m; **share** ~, **stock** ~ indice boursier m; ~ **basis** n indice de base m; ~ **card** n fiche f; ~**-card file** n fichier m; ~ **figure** n (number) indice m; ~ **fund** n fonds indice m, fonds indiciel m; ~ **futures** n pl contrats à terme indexés m pl; ~ **lease** n loyer indexé m; ~**-linked** adj indexé; ~**-linked guaranteed minimum wage** n salaire minimum interprofessionnel de croissance m, SMIC m; ~**-linked stock** n UK actions indexées f pl; ~ **linking** n indexation sur le coût de la vie f; ~ **number** n indice m; ~ **option** n option d'indexation f, option de mise sur indice f; ~ **options** n pl options sur indice f pl; ~ **point** n point d'indice m; ~ **price** n prix de l'indice m

index[2] vt (data, information) classer, cataloguer; (Econ, Fin) indexer; ~ **sth to inflation** indexer qch sur l'inflation

indexation n indexation f

indexed adj indexé; ∼ **bond** n obligation indexée f; ∼ **life insurance** n assurance-vie indexée f; ∼ **loan** n emprunt indexé m, prêt indexé m; ∼ **security** n titre indexé m

indexing n indexation f; (of portfolio) indexation f, pondération f

indicated yield n rapport indiqué m, rendement indiqué m

indication n indication f; **be an** ∼ **of** indiquer; **give sb an** ∼ **of sth** donner une idée de qch à qn; **all the** ∼**s are that ...** tout porte à croire que ...; ∼ **of interest** n indice d'intérêt m, manifestation d'intérêt f; ∼ **of source** n indication de provenance f

indicative adj indicatif/-ive; ∼ **of** indicatif/ -ive de; ∼ **planning** n planification indicative f

indicator n indicateur m; (in econometrics) clignotant m; ∼ **variable** n variable indicateur f

indict vt inculper

indictment n mise en accusation f

indifference n indifférence f; ∼ **curve** n courbe d'indifférence f

indirect adj indirect; ∼ **advertising** n publicité indirecte f; ∼ **costs** n pl frais indirects m pl; ∼ **discrimination** n discrimination indirecte f, discrimination masquée f; ∼ **expense** n charge indirecte f, coût indirect m, frais indirects m pl; ∼ **labor** AmE, ∼ **labour** BrE n main-d'œuvre indirecte f; ∼ **tax** n impôt indirect m; ∼ **taxation** n imposition indirecte f; ∼ **taxes** n pl contributions indirectes f pl; ∼ **workers** n pl personnel de service et de remplacement m

indirectly adv indirectement; ∼ **related to** en rapport indirect avec

indiscountable adj inescomptable

indiscriminate adj (generalized) sans distinction; ∼ **dumping** n décharge non contrôlée f

individual¹ adj individuel/-elle; (personalized, made-to-measure) à la carte, personnalisé

individual² n (person) individu m

individual: ∼ **bargaining** n négociation individuelle f; ∼ **consumer** n consommateur individuel m; ∼ **firm** n entreprise individuelle f; ∼ **investor** n investisseur individuel m; ∼ **licence** BrE, ∼ **license** AmE n licence individuelle f; ∼ **rights** n pl droits individuels m pl

individualism n individualisme m

individualization n personnalisation f

individually adv individuellement

indivisibility n indivisibilité f

indivisible adj indivisible; ∼ **export** n exportation indivisible f; ∼ **load** n masse indivisible f

indorse vt ▸endorse

indorsee n ▸endorsee

indorsement n ▸endorsement

indorser n ▸endorser

indorsor n ▸endorsor

induce vt persuader, inciter

induced draft n traite induite f

inducement n (bribe) pot-de-vin m; (Law) incitation f; **financial** ∼ avantage pécuniaire m; **be an** ∼ **to sth** encourager qch

induction n (of new employee) accueil m, intégration f; ∼ **course** n stage d'accueil et d'orientation m

industrial adj industriel/-ielle; ∼ **accident** n accident du travail m; ∼ **action** n action revendicative f; (strike) grève f; ∼ **activity** n activité industrielle f; ∼ **arbitration** n arbitrage en matière de conflits du travail m; ∼ **base** n base industrielle f; ∼ **center** AmE, ∼ **centre** BrE n centre industriel m; ∼ **complex** n complexe industriel m; ∼ **concentration** n concentration industrielle f; ∼ **conflict** n conflit du travail m, conflit social m; ∼ **country** n pays industrialisé m; ∼ **democracy** n démocratie industrielle f; ∼ **designer** m concepteur/-trice industriel/ -ielle m/f; ∼ **discharge** n (into river) rejet industriel m; ∼ **disease** n maladie professionnelle f; ∼ **dispute** n conflit du travail m, conflit social m; ∼ **economics** n pl +sing v économie industrielle f; ∼ **engineering** n génie industriel m; ∼ **equipment** n matériel m; ∼ **espionage** n espionnage industriel m; ∼ **estate** n BrE zone industrielle f; ∼ **incident** n incident au travail m; ∼ **injury** n accident du travail m; ∼ **marketing** n marketing des produits industriels m; ∼ **organization** n organisation industrielle f; ∼ **park** n AmE zone industrielle f; ∼ **process** n processus industriel m, procédé industriel m; ∼ **production** n production industrielle f; ∼ **products** n pl produits industriels m pl; ∼ **psychologist** n psychologue d'entreprise mf; ∼ **relations** n pl (between management and union) relations patronat-syndicats f pl; (between management and workers) relations humaines dans l'entreprise f pl; ∼ **research** n (market research) enquête sur les produits industriels f, recherche appliquée f; ∼ **revolution** n révolution industrielle f; ∼ **safety** n prévention des accidents du travail f; ∼ **shares** m pl valeurs industrielles f pl; ∼ **site** n site industriel m; ∼ **strife** n conflit social m; ∼ **tribunal** n UK ≈ Conseil des prud'hommes m; ∼ **union** n syndicat ouvrier m; ∼ **unrest** n malaise social m; ∼ **vehicle** n véhicule industriel m; ∼ **waste** n déchets industriels m pl; (liquid) effluent industriel m

industrialist n industriel m

industrialization n industrialisation f

industrialized adj industrialisé

industry n industrie f; **light/heavy ~** industrie légère/lourde; **the coal ~** l'industrie du charbon; **the advertising/ publishing ~** la publicité/l'édition; **~ portal** n portail vertical m, portail professionnel m; **~ standard** norme industrielle f; **~-wide agreement** convention généralisée à tout le secteur f

inefficiency n (of person) incompétence f; (of machine, method) inefficacité f

inelastic adj inélastique; **~ demand** n demande inélastique f; **~ supply** n offre inélastique f

inelasticity n inélasticité f; **~ of demand** inélasticité de la demande f; **~ of supply** inélasticité de l'offre f

inequality n inégalité f

inertia n inertie f; **~ selling** n vente forcée f, vente par correspondance f

inertial: ~ effect n effet d'inertie m; **~ inflation** n inflation sous-jacente f

inevitable adj inévitable

inevitably adv inévitablement

inexhaustible adj inépuisable

inexpensive adj peu cher/chère

infant: ~ industry n industrie naissante f; **~ mortality** n mortalité infantile f

infect vt (Comp) infecter

inferior adj (position) inférieur; (item, product) de qualité inférieure; **~ goods** n pl produits de qualité inférieure m pl

infession n récession provoquée par l'inflation f

infinite adj illimité; (resources) inépuisable

inflate vt (economy) relancer; (price) faire monter, gonfler

inflated adj (price) gonflé; (currency) inflationniste

inflation n inflation f; **~ accounting** n comptabilité d'inflation f; **~-proof** adj protégé contre les effets de l'inflation; **~ rate** n taux d'inflation m

inflationary adj inflationniste; **~ expectations** n pl anticipations inflationnistes f pl; **~ gap** n écart inflationniste m; **~ pressure** n pression inflationniste f; **~ spiral** n spirale inflationniste f; **~ trend** n tendance inflationniste f

inflationist n partisan de l'inflation m

in-flight: ~ catering n restauration en vol f; **~ entertainment** n distractions en vol f pl; **~ magazine** n revue de la compagnie aérienne f; **~ service** n service en vol m

inflow n entrée f; **~ of funds** rentrée de fonds f

influence[1] n influence f; **have ~ over** avoir de l'ascendant sur, exercer une influence sur; **~ peddling** n trafic d'influence m

influence[2] vt (result, decision, plan, choice,

costs) influer sur; (person) influencer

influential adj influent; **be ~** avoir de l'influence

info abbr (►**information**) renseignements m pl, informations f pl; **~-have** n (infrml) info-riche mf; **~-have-not** n (infrml) info-pauvre mf; **~-poor** adj info-pauvre; **~-rich** adj info-riche

infomediary n infomédiaire m

infomercial n documentaire publicitaire m

inform vt aviser, informer; (warn) avertir; **I regret to ~ you that...** j'ai le regret de vous informer que...; **I am pleased to ~ you that...** j'ai le plaisir de vous informer que...

informal adj (visit) privé; (person) sans façons; (interview, discussion) informel/-elle; (announcement, request) officieux/-ieuse; **~ agreement** n, **~ arrangement** n accord officieux m; **~ meeting** n réunion informelle f

informality n (of meeting) caractère informel m; (of person) simplicité f

informant n (source of information) informateur/-trice m/f; (informer) indicateur/-trice m/f

information n renseignements m pl, informations f pl; US (Comms) renseignements m pl; **call ~** appeler les renseignements; **for further ~** pour de plus amples renseignements; **a piece of ~** un renseignement m; **'for ~'** 'à titre de renseignement', 'pour information'; **for your ~** à titre d'information; **~ architect** n architecte de l'information mf; **~ brokering** n courtage d'informations m; **~ bureau** n, **~ desk** n bureau de renseignements m; **~ economy** n économie de l'information f; **~ flow** n flux de l'information m; **~ handling** n traitement des informations m; **~ highway** n autoroute de l'information f; **~ management** n gestion de l'information f; **~ network** n réseau informatique m; **~ office** n bureau de renseignements m; **~ officer** n (PR person) préposé à l'information m; (IT person) agent d'information m; **~ pack** n documentation f; **~ processing** n informatique f, traitement de l'information m; **~ retrieval** n recherche documentaire f; **~ revolution** n révolution de l'information; **~ retrieval system** n système de recherche documentaire m; **~ storage** n stockage d'informations m; **~ system** n système d'information m; **~ technology** n informatique f; **~ transfer** n transfert d'information m; **~ warfare** n guerre de l'information f; (on the web) cyberguerre f

informative adj (book, leaflet) riche en renseignements; (speaker) savant; (trip, day) instructif/-ive; **~ advertising** n publicité informative f; **~ content** n contenu informationnel m; **~ labeling** AmE, **~ labelling** BrE n étiquetage informatif m

informed adj (debate, choice, opinion) fondé;

(decision, argument) bien informé; (person) averti, informé; **~ about** au courant de; **keep sb ~** tenir qn au courant; **~ public** n public bien informé m, public averti m

infotainment n information-spectacle f

infotech n technologie de l'information f, informatique f

infrastructural adj (expenditure, investment) d'infrastructure

infrastructure n infrastructure f

infringe vt (rule, ban, law) enfreindre, contrevenir à; (agreement, secrecy, right) violer; (patent) commettre une contrefaçon de; (rights, copyright) ne pas respecter; **~ the law** contrevenir à la loi, enfreindre la loi

infringement n (of rule) contravention f, infraction f; (of agreement, secrecy, right) violation f; (of patent, trademark) contrefaçon f, violation f; **~ of the law** contravention à la loi f, infraction à la loi f

infringer n contrefacteur/-trice m/f

ingenuity n ingéniosité f

ingot n lingot m

inhabitant n habitant/-e m/f

inherent adj inhérent; **~ to** inhérent à, propre à

inherit vt (money, property) hériter de; (title) succéder à; **~ sth from sb** (money, property) hériter qch de qn

inheritance n (act, right, property) héritage m, succession f; **~ duty** n droit sur les biens transmis par décès m; **~ tax** n UK droits de succession m pl

inherited adj (wealth, debt) hérité; **~ property** n bien reçu en héritage m

inhibit vt (Law) interdire; (progress, choice, activity) entraver

inhibitor n (Mgmnt) force d'inertie f

in-house adj (service, worker) interne; (magazine) d'entreprise; (translator) maison, interne; **~ operation** n opération interne f; **~ software** n logiciel maison m; **~ system** n système interne m, système maison m; **~ training** n formation dans l'entreprise f

initial¹ adj (interest, cost, investment) initial; **in the ~ stages** dans un premier temps

initial² n initiale f

initial: **~ assessment** n (Tax) (of a return) cotisation initiale f; **~ capital** n capital d'apport m, capital initial m; **~ expenditure** n dépense initiale f; **~ funding** n consolidation initiale f; **~ inventory** n stock au début de l'exercice m, stock d'ouverture m, stock à l'ouverture de l'exercice m; **~ letter** n initiale f; **~ margin** n marge initiale f; **~ outlay** n mise de fonds initiale f; **~ public offering** n offre publique initiale f, première émission publique f

initialization n initialisation f

initialize vt initialiser

initiate vt (software) lancer; (talks) amorcer;

(plan, project) mettre en œuvre; (improvements, reorganization) entreprendre

initiative n initiative f; **take the ~** prendre l'initiative; **show ~** faire preuve d'initiative; **on one's own ~** de son propre chef

initiator n initiateur/-trice m/f

inject vt (money, capital) injecter; (new ideas) apporter

injection n (of funds) injection f

injunction n injonction f; **ask for an ~** faire une requête en injonction

injured party n partie lésée f

injury n (physical) blessure f; (to reputation) atteinte f; (Law) préjudice m, dommage m

ink n encre f; **~-jet printer** n imprimante à jet d'encre f

inland n (not coastal) intérieur; (domestic) intérieur; **~ carrier** n transporteur intérieur m; **~ haulage** n acheminement intérieur m; **~ trade** n commerce intérieur m; **~ waterway** n voie fluviale f, voie navigable f

Inland Revenue n (UK) service des impôts britannique, Fisc m

inner: **~ city** n centre-ville m; **~-city areas** n pl quartiers déshérités (du centre-ville) m pl

innovate vi innover

innovation n (introducing something new) innovation f; (something new) nouveauté f; **make ~s in sth** apporter des innovations à qch; **~ center** AmE, **~ centre** n BrE centre d'innovation m

innovative adj innovateur/-trice, novateur/-trice

innovator n innovateur/-trice m/f, novateur/-trice m/f

inoperative clause n clause inopérante f

inplacement n remplacement interne m

input¹ n (data) données d'entrée f pl; (putting in data) entrée f; (resource) facteur de production m; (money) apport m; (contribution) contribution f; **~ cost** n (Acc) coût d'entrée m; **~ device** n (Comp) périphérique d'entrée m; **~ message** n message d'entrée m

input² vt (data) entrer, introduire, saisir

input/output n entrée/sortie f; **~ processor** n processeur d'entrée/sortie m; **~ table** n tableau d'entrées/sorties m

inputs n pl input m, moyens de production m pl

inquire vi se renseigner; **~ about sth** se renseigner sur qch; **~ into sth** se renseigner sur qch; **'~ at the office'** 'adressez-vous au bureau'; **'~ within'** 's'adresser ici'

inquiry n (request) demande de renseignements f; (Comp) consultation f, interrogation f; (investigation) enquête f; **~ desk** n bureau de renseignements m; **~ form** n formulaire de demande de renseignements m; **~ office** n bureau de renseignements m; **~ terminal** n poste ⋯⟶

d'interrogation-réponse *f*

inroads *n pl*: **make ~ into** (market) pénétrer; (lead) réduire; (savings) entamer

insert¹ *n* (Media) encart *m*

insert² *vt* insérer

in-service training *n* formation continue *f*

inset *n* encart *m*

inside *n* our sources on the ~ nos informateurs qui sont dans la place; **a person on the ~** un initié/une initiée *m/f*

inside: **~ back cover** *n* troisième de couverture *f*; **~ front cover** *n* deuxième de couverture *f*; **~ information** *n* informations privilégiées *f pl*

insider *n* initié/-e *m/f*; **~ dealing** *n* délit d'initié *m*; **~ report** *n* déclaration d'initié *f*; **~ trading** *n* délit d'initié *m*

insofar *adv*: **~ as** dans la mesure où; **~ as is possible** dans la mesure du possible

insoluble *adj* insoluble

insolvency *n* insolvabilité *f*, **~ clause** *n* clause d'insolvabilité *f*; **~ legislation** *n* législation sur la faillite *f*

insolvent *adj* insolvable

insource *vt* internaliser

insourcing *n* internalisation *f*

inspect *vt* (premises) inspecter; (passport, tickets, accounts) contrôler, examiner; (luggage) visiter

inspection *n* (of passports, tickets, accounts) contrôle *m*, examen *m*; (of premises) inspection *f*; (visit) visite d'inspection *f*

inspector *n* (Gen Comm) inspecteur/-trice *m/f*; (Transp) contrôleur/-euse *m/f*; (Imp/Exp) visiteur *m*; **~ of taxes** *n* UK inspecteur/-trice des contributions directes *m/f*

inspectorate *n* (inspectors) inspection *f*, corps des inspecteurs *m*; (function) inspectorat *m*

instal ▸install

install *vt* (network) mettre en place; (software, peripherals, system) installer

installation *n* (Gen Comm, Comp) installation *f*; **computer/military ~** installation informatique/militaire *f*; **~ diskette** *n* disquette d'installation *f*

installment *n* AmE ▸instalment BrE

installment plan *n* AmE contrat de vente à tempérament *m*, contrat de vente à crédit *m*; **buy sth on the ~** acheter qch à tempérament, acheter qch à crédit

instalment *n* BrE (partial payment) versement *m*, acompte *m*; **in ~s** par versements, à tempérament; **pay for sth in ~s** payer qch en plusieurs versements; **monthly ~** mensualité *f*; **~ base** *n* base de crédit *f*; **~ contract** *n* contrat de vente à tempérament *m*; **~ credit** *n* BrE crédit échelonné *m*; **~ loan** *n* prêt remboursable par versements *m*, prêt à tempérament *m*; **~ payments** *n pl*

paiements d'achat à crédit *m pl*, versements échelonnés *m pl*; **~ repayment schedule** *n* calendrier de remboursement par versements *m*; **~ sale** *n* vente à tempérament *f*

instance *n* (example) exemple *m*; (case) cas *m*; **in the first ~** en premier lieu; **in this ~** dans le cas présent; **for ~** par exemple; **at the ~ of** à la demande de

instant messaging *n* (Comp) messagerie instantanée *f*

institute¹ *n* institut *m*

institute² *vt* (scheme) établir; (custom, rule, prize) instituer, instaurer; (inquiry) ouvrir; (Law) (action) intenter; **~ proceedings** entamer des poursuites; **~ an appeal** (Tax) interjeter appel

institution *n* (body, organization) institution *f*; (of change) introduction *f*; (of body, rule, prize) institution *f*; (of appeal, of legal proceedings) introduction *f*

institutional *adj* (structure, reform) institutionnel/-elle; **~ advertising** *n* publicité institutionnelle *f*; **~ investor** *n* investisseur institutionnel *m*; **~ lender** *n* prêteur institutionnel *m*

institutionalize *vt* (practice, system) institutionnaliser, donner un caractère officiel à; **become ~d** prendre un caractère officiel

in-store *adj* (consultant, advisor) dans le magasin; **~ promotion** *n* promotion sur le lieu de vente *f*

instruction *n* instruction *f*; **~ book** *n* guide d'utilisation *m*, guide de l'utilisateur *m*; **~ leaflet** *n* mode d'emploi *m*, notice explicative *f*; **~ manual** *n* guide d'utilisation *m*, guide de l'utilisateur *m*

instructions *n pl* instructions *f pl*; (book) guide de l'utilisateur *m*, manuel d'utilisation *m*; (on how to use something) mode d'emploi *m*, notice explicative *f*; (orders) instructions *f pl*; **for further ~** pour toute instruction complémentaire; **be under ~ to do** être chargé de faire; **give sb ~ to do** donner l'ordre à qn de faire

instructive *adj* instructif/-ive

instrument *n* (Gen Comm) instrument *m*; (Acc) effet *m*; (Bank, Fin) effet *m*, instrument *m*; (Law) acte juridique *m*, effet *m*, instrument *m*; (Stock) instrument *m*; (Tax) effet *m*

instrumental *adj* (capital) productif/-ive; **be ~ in sth** contribuer à qch; **be ~ in doing** contribuer à faire

instrumentality *n* US instrumentalité *f*

insufficient *adj* insuffisant; **have ~ resources** ne pas avoir assez de ressources; **~ funds** *n pl* défaut de provision *m*, fonds insuffisants *m pl*

insufficiently *adv* pas assez; (paid, protected, understood) mal; **~ stamped** *adj* pas suffisamment affranchi

insulate *vt* (Stock) couvrir, isoler, protéger

insulated *adj* (Transp) isotherme
insurable *adj* assurable; ~ **interest** *n*
intérêt assurable *m*; ~ **risk** *n* risque
assurable *m*; ~ **title** *n* titre assurable *m*; ~
value *n* valeur assurable *f*
insurance *n* assurance *f*; **take out** ~
s'assurer, souscrire une assurance; **take out**
~ **against** s'assurer contre, souscrire une
assurance contre; **work in** ~ travailler dans
les assurances; ~ **agency** *n* cabinet
d'assurances *m*; ~ **agent** *n* agent
d'assurances *m*; ~ **broker** *n* courtier
d'assurances *m*; ~ **broking** *n* courtage
d'assurances *m*; ~ **certificate** *n* attestation
d'assurance *f*; ~ **claim** *n* déclaration de
sinistre *f*; ~ **company** *n* compagnie
d'assurances *f*, société d'assurances *f*; ~
contract *n* contrat d'assurance *m*; ~ **cover**
n, ~ **coverage** *n* AmE couverture
d'assurance *f*, garantie d'assurance *f*; ~ **firm**
n cabinet d'assurances *m*; ~ **industry** *n*
industrie des assurances *f*; ~ **plan** *n* plan
d'assurance *m*, régime d'assurance *m*; ~
policy *n* police d'assurance *f*; ~ **premium** *n*
prime d'assurance *f*; ~ **scheme** *n* plan
d'assurance *m*, régime d'assurance *m*; ~
settlement *n* règlement d'assurance *m*; ~
underwriter *n* assureur *m*
insure *vt* (Ins) assurer; ~ **oneself against**
fire s'assurer contre l'incendie; ~ **oneself**
against risk (Ins) s'assurer contre un risque;
~ **oneself against delays** se garantir contre
les retards
insured *adj* assuré; **the** ~ l'assuré/-e *m/f*;
~ **account** *n* compte assuré *m*; ~ **party** *n*
assuré/-e *m/f*; ~ **peril** *n* risque assuré *m*; ~
value *n* montant de l'assurance *m*
insurer *n* assureur *m*, compagnie
d'assurances *f*; ~**'s claim** *n* réclamation de
l'assureur *f*
insurgent *adj* insurgé
int. *abbr* (▶**interest**) (in business, venture)
intérêts *m pl*, participation *f*; (on borrowings,
savings) int. (intérêt)
intake *n* (of new employees) admission *f*; (of
new orders) arrivée *f*; (year group) promotion *f*;
the new ~ (into job, training) les nouvelles
recrues *f pl*
intangible *adj* incorporel/-elle; ~ **asset** *n*
(Acc) actif incorporel *m*, immobilisation
incorporelle *f*, valeur incorporelle *f*; (Fin) actif
immatériel *m*, immobilisation incorporelle *f*;
~ **factor** *n* impondérable *m*; ~ **property** *n*
actif incorporel *m*; ~ **value** *n* valeur
incorporelle *f*; ~ **wealth** *n* biens intangibles
m pl, richesse incorporelle *f*
integral *adj* intégrant; ~ **to** intrinsèque à;
~ **part** *n* partie intégrante *f*
integrate *vt* incorporer, intégrer
integrated *adj* (system, service, scheme)
intégré; ~ **into** intégré à; ~ **circuit** *n* circuit
intégré *m*; ~ **company** *n* société intégrée *f*;
~ **management system** *n* système intégré

de gestion *m*; ~ **project management** *n*
gestion intégrée de projet *f*; ~ **services**
digital network *n pl* réseau numérique à
intégration de services *m*; ~ **software** *n*
logiciel intégré *m*
integration *n* intégration *f*
integrity *n* intégrité *f*
intellectual *adj* intellectuel/-elle; ~
capital capital intellectuel *m*; ~ **property** *n*
propriété intellectuelle *f*; ~ **property rights**
n pl droits de propriété intellectuelle *m pl*
intelligent *adj* intelligent; ~ **agent** *n*
(Comp) agent intelligent *m*; ~ **terminal** *n*
terminal intelligent *m*
intensification *n* intensification *f*
intensify [1] *vt* (effort) intensifier
[2] *vi* (competition) s'intensifier
intensive *adj* intensif/-ive; **capital-**~
capitalistique, à forte intensité de capitaux;
energy-~ à forte consommation en énergie;
~ **farming** *n* agriculture intensive *f*; ~
production *n* exploitation intensive *f*; ~
training *n* formation accélérée *f*
intention *n* intention *f*; **with the** ~ **of**
doing dans l'intention de faire; **the** ~ **is to**
do l'objectif est de faire; **with the best of** ~**s**
avec les meilleures intentions du monde
intentional *adj* intentionnel/-elle; ~
discharge *n* (pollution) rejet intentionnel *m*
intent *adj*: ~ **on** décidé à, résolu à
interactive *adj* (Gen Comm) interactif/-ive;
(Comp) interactif/-ive, conversationnel/-elle;
~ **computing** *n* informatique interactive *f*;
~ **digital television** *n* télévision numérique
interactive *f*; ~ **marketing** *n* marketing
interactif *m*; ~ **mode** *n* mode conversationnel
m, mode interactif *m*; ~ **processing** *n*
traitement interactif *m*; ~ **web page** *n* page
web dynamique *f*; ~ **website** *n* site web
dynamique *m*
interactivity *n* interactivité *f*
inter alia *adv* entre autres
interbank *adj* interbancaire; ~ **exchange**
rate *n* taux interbancaire *m*; ~ **market** *n*
marché interbancaire *m*; ~ **rate** *n* taux
interbancaire *m*; ~ **transactions** *n pl*
opérations interbancaires *f pl*; ~ **transfer** *n*
virement interbancaire *m*
intercept interview *n* entretien
spontané *m*
intercom *n* interphone *m*
intercommunity *adj*
intercommunautaire; ~ **trade** *n* (EU)
commerce intercommunautaire *m*
intercompany *adj* interentreprises; ~
comparison *n* comparaison interentreprises
f; ~ **market** *n* marché des intermédiaires *m*;
~ **profits** *n pl* bénéfices inter-sociétés *m pl*
interconnection *n* interconnexion *f*
intercontinental *adj* intercontinental
interdepartmental *adj*
interdépartemental, interministériel/-ielle; ⋯⟩

~ **settlement** n règlement interministériel m
interdependence n interdépendance f
interdependent adj interdépendant
interest n (enthusiasm, curiosity) intérêt m;
(accrued monies) intérêts m pl; (on borrowings,
savings) intérêt m; (in business, venture) intérêts
m pl, participation f; (hobby, pastime) centre
d'intérêt m; **simple/compound** ~ intérêts
simples/composés m pl; **account paying/not
paying** ~ compte rémunéré/non rémunéré
m; **business** ~s intérêts commerciaux m pl;
tobacco ~s intérêts dans le tabac m pl; **a
majority/minority** ~ une participation
majoritaire/minoritaire f; **receive** ~ **at 2%**
toucher un intérêt de 2%; **earn** ~ rapporter
des intérêts; **an account which earns 3%** ~
un compte qui rapporte 3% d'intérêt; **declare
one's** ~s faire état de ses participations; **in
the** ~s **of** (to promote) dans l'intérêt de; (out of
concern for) par souci de; **act in sb's** ~s agir
dans l'intérêt de qn; **look after one's own**
~s veiller sur ses propres intérêts; **have a
vested** ~ **in** être directement concerné par;
have an ~ **in** (sector, field, pastime) s'intéresser
à; **we've had** ~ **from venture capitalists** des
capital-risqueurs ont manifesté leur intérêt;
take an ~ **in** s'intéresser à; ~ **accrued** n
intérêts courus m pl, intérêts cumulés m pl;
~**-bearing** adj portant intérêt, productif
d'intérêts; ~**-bearing deposits** n pl dépôts
portant intérêts m pl; ~**-bearing liabilities**
n pl emprunts portant intérêts m pl;
~**-bearing security** n titre portant intérêt
m; ~ **charge** n (on loan) charges d'intérêts f
pl; (on statement) charge financière f; ~
coupon n coupon d'intérêt m; ~ **earned** n
(profit and loss account) produits financiers m pl;
~**-free** adj (credit) sans intérêt; ~**-free
deposit** n dépôt sans intérêt m; ~**-free loan**
n emprunt sans intérêt m; ~ **group** n
association f, groupe d'intérêt m, groupement
d'intérêt m; ~ **income** n produit d'intérêts
m; ~ **on arrears** n intérêt sur arriérés m; ~
on bonds n intérêt sur obligation m; ~
~**-only loan** n prêt capitalisé à l'échéance
m; ~ **payment** n versement d'intérêt m; ~
penalty n pénalité d'intérêt f; ~ **rate** n taux
d'intérêt m; ~ **rate adjustment** n
rajustement du taux d'intérêt m; ~ **rate
capping** n garantie de taux plafond f; ~
rate ceiling n plafond sur les taux d'intérêt
m; ~ **rate future** n (Fin, Stock) contrat à
terme sur taux d'intérêt m; ~ **rate
movement** n mouvement des taux d'intérêt
m; ~ **received** n intérêt perçu m; ~ **relief**
n abattement fiscal sur les intérêts versés m;
~ **rate risk** n risque de taux d'intérêt m; ~
spread n marge d'intérêt f; ~ **rate swap** n
swap de taux d'intérêt m
interested adj intéressé; **be** ~ **in**
s'intéresser à; **be** ~ **in doing** s'intéresser à
faire; ~ **party** n partie intéressée f; (Law)
ayant droit m, partie intéressée f
interface¹ n interface f; ~ **ergonomist** n

ergonome d'interface mf
interface² **1** vt connecter, relier
2 vi être connecté, être relié; ~ **with** être
connecté à, être relié à
interfere vi (intervene) intervenir; ~ **in**
intervenir dans, s'immiscer dans, s'ingérer
dans; ~ **with** (activity, right, freedom) empiéter
sur
interference n ingérence f, intervention f;
(electronic) parasites f pl
interfirm comparison n comparaison
interentreprises f
intergovernmental adj (organization,
summit) intergouvernemental
intergroup adj intergroupal; ~ **relations**
n pl rapports entre groupes m pl, relations
entre groupes f pl
interim¹ adj (post, employee) intérimaire;
(report, job) provisoire, temporaire; (payment,
interest) intermédiaire; (measure, arrangement)
provisoire
interim² n intérim m; **in the** ~ entre-temps
interim: ~ **accounts** n pl comptes de mi-
année m pl, comptes semestriels m pl; ~
agreement n accord provisoire m; ~ **audit**
n audit de mi-année m, audit intérimaire m;
~ **balance sheet** n bilan provisoire m; ~
certificate n (Stock) certificat provisoire m;
~ **dividend** n acompte sur dividende m,
dividende intérimaire m; ~ **financing** n
financement intérimaire m, financement
provisoire m; ~ **injunction** n injonction
provisoire f; ~ **loan** n crédit-relais m; ~
profits n pl résultats sémestriels m pl; ~
relief n dégrèvement pour emploi précaire
m; ~ **report** n rapport périodique m,
comptes semestriels m pl; ~ **statements** n
pl bilan de mi-année m, état financier
semestriel m
interlocking: ~ **directorates** n pl
directions croisées f pl; ~ **directorship** n
administration de liaison f
interlocutory decree n décision
interlocutoire f
Intermarket Trading System n US
système commercial inter-marchés m,
système de transaction inter-marchés m
intermediary¹ adj intermédiaire; ~
goods n pl demi-produits m pl
intermediary² n intermédiaire mf
intermediate adj (stage, step)
intermédiaire; (level) moyen/-enne; ~ **broker**
n remisier m; ~ **credit** n crédit à moyen
terme m; ~ **financing** n financement
intermédiaire m; ~ **loan** n prêt à moyen
terme m; ~ **technology** n technologie
intermédiaire f; ~**-term credit** n crédit à
moyen terme m
intermediation n intermédiation f
intermittent adj intermittent
intermodal adj (container, packaging)
intermodal; ~ **transport** n transport

combiné *m*; ~ **transport system** *n* système de transport combiné *m*

internal *adj* (dispute, problem, mail, phone line) interne; (candidate, appointment) interne à l'entreprise; ~ **assessment** *n* évaluation interne *f*; ~ **audit** *n* audit interne *m*; ~ **check** *n* contrôle interne *m*; ~ **communication** *n* communication interne *f*; ~ **debt** *n* dette publique *f*; ~ **economy** *n* économie intérieure *f*; ~ **financing** *n* autofinancement *m*, financement interne *m*; ~ **flight** *n* vol domestique *m*, vol intérieur *m*; ~ **market** *n* marché intérieur *m*; ~ **memorandum** *n* note de service *f*; ~ **policy** *n* politique intérieure *f*; ~ **rate of return** *n* taux de rentabilité interne *m*

internalizing *n* internalisation *f*

Internal Revenue Service *n* US *service des impôts américain*, Fisc *m*

international *adj* international; **at** ~ **level** au niveau international, sur le plan international; **on an** ~ **scale** à l'échelle internationale; ~ **affairs** *n pl* affaires internationales *f pl*; ~ **agreement** *n* accord international *m*, convention internationale *f*; ~ **airport** *n* aéroport international *m*; ~ **banking** *n* opérations bancaires internationales *f pl*; ~ **banking facility** *n* facilité bancaire internationale *f*, opérations bancaires internationales *f pl*; ~ **call** *n* appel international *m*; ~ **carriage** *n* transport international *m*; ~ **customs transit document** *n* carnet TIR *m*, carnet de transport international routier *m*; ~ **direct dialing** AmE, ~ **direct dialling** BrE *n* appel international automatique *m*; ~ **economic cooperation** *n* coopération économique internationale *f*; ~ **money draft** *n* mandat de paiement international *m*; ~ **money order** *n* mandat international *m*; ~ **organization** *n* organisation internationale *f*; ~ **payment order** *n* ordre de paiement international *m*; ~**-standard hotel** *n* hôtel international *m*; ~ **relations** *n pl +sing v* relations internationales *f pl*; ~ **standards** *n pl* normes internationales *f pl*; ~ **subscriber dialing** AmE, ~ **subscriber dialling** BrE *n* téléphone automatique international *m*; ~ **trade** *n* commerce international *m*; ~ **travel** *n* déplacements internationaux *m pl*

International: ~ **Air Transport Association** *n* Association internationale des transports aériens *f*; ~ **Bank for Economic Cooperation** *n* Banque internationale pour la coopération économique *f*; ~ **Bank for Reconstruction and Development** *n* Banque internationale pour la reconstruction et le développement *f*; ~ **Civil Aviation Organization** *n* Organisation de l'aviation civile internationale *f*; ~ **Commodity Agreements** *n pl* accords internationaux sur les matières premières *m pl*; ~ **Court of**

Justice *n* Cour internationale de justice *f*; ~ **Development Association** *n* Association internationale pour le développement *f*; ~ **Labour Organization** *n* Organisation internationale du travail *f*; ~ **Longshoremen's Association** *n* US *association internationale des débardeurs*; ~ **Maritime Bureau** *n* Bureau maritime international *m*; ~ **Maritime Committee** *n* Comité maritime international *m*; ~ **Monetary Fund** *n* Fonds monétaire international *m*; ~ **Monetary Market** *n* Marché monétaire international *m*; ~ **Options Market** *n* marché international des options *m*; ~ **Petroleum Exchange** *n* UK bourse internationale des produits pétroliers *f*; ~ **Road Transport Union** *n* Syndicat international des transporteurs routiers *m*; ~ **Shipping Federation** *n* Fédération internationale de la navigation *f*; ~ **Standards Organization** *n* Organisation internationale de normalisation *f*; ~ **Statistical Institute** *n* Institut international des statistiques; ~ **Stock Exchange** *n* UK Bourse de Londres *f*, ≈ Société des bourses françaises *f*; ~ **Trade Organization** *n Organisation internationale du commerce*; ~ **Transport Workers' Federation** *n* Fédération internationale des ouvriers du transport *f*

internationalism *n* internationalisme *m*

internationalization *n* internationalisation *f*

internationalize *vt* internationaliser

Internet *n* Internet *m*; **on the** ~ sur Internet; **be connected to the** ~ être connecté à Internet; **find sth on the** ~ trouver qch sur Internet; ~ **access** *n* accès à Internet *m*; ~ **access provider** *n* fournisseur d'accès Internet *m*; ~ **account** *n* compte Internet *m*; ~ **address** *n* adresse Internet *f*; ~ **advertising** *n* publicité sur Internet *f*, publicité en ligne *f*; ~ **auction** *n* vente aux enchères en ligne *f*; ~**-aware** *adj* (person) ayant une bonne maîtrise de l'outil web; ~ **bank** *n* banque en ligne *f*, banque sur Internet; ~ **banking** *n* banque en ligne *f*, banque sur Internet *f*; ~ **billing** *n* facturation en ligne *f*; ~ **business** *n* société point com *f*, entreprise Internet *f*; ~ **café** *n* cybercafé *m*; ~ **chat** *n* bavardage en temps réel *m*, chat *m*, IRC *m*; ~ **commerce** *n* commerce électronique *m*, commerce en ligne *m*; ~ **commerce site** *n* site marchand *m*; ~ **company** *n* société point com *f*, point com *f*, dot-com *f*; ~ **conferencing** *n* visioconférence sur Internet *f*; ~ **connection** *n* connexion à Internet *f*; ~**-enabled** *adj* (phone) Internet; (application) web; ~ **host** *n* hôte Internet *m*; ~ **hosting** *n* hébergement de sites web *m*; ~ **hosting service** *n* service d'hébergement de sites web *m*; ~ **marketing** *n* cybermarketing *m*, marketing en ligne *m*; ~ **marketplace** *n* ⋯⟩

place de marché électronique f; ∼ **media
provider** n fournisseur de vidéos sur
Internet m; ∼ **phone** n téléphone Internet
m; ∼ **presence** n présence sur Internet f; ∼
presence provider n fournisseur d'espace
web m; ∼ **protocol** n protocole Internet m;
∼ **publishing** n édition en ligne f, édition
sur Internet f; ∼ **Relay Chat** n bavardage
en temps réel m, chat m, IRC m; ∼
revolution n révolution Internet f; ∼
search n recherche sur Internet f; ∼
security n sécurité sur Internet f; ∼ **server**
n serveur Internet m; ∼ **service provider** n
fournisseur d'accès Internet m; ∼ **shopping**
n achats en ligne m pl, achats sur Internet m
pl; ∼ **site** n site Internet m; ∼ **start-up** n
jeune pousse f, start-up f; ∼ **storefront** n
vitrine virtuelle f; ∼ **telephone** n téléphone
Internet m; ∼ **telephony** n téléphonie sur
Internet f; ∼ **transaction** n transaction sur
Internet f; ∼ **use** n utilisation d'Internet f;
∼ **user** n internaute mf

internetworking n interconnection de
réseaux f

interoperability n interfonctionnement
m; (Comp) interopérabilité f

interpersonal skills n pl relationnel m;
have good ∼ avoir un bon relationnel

interplay n interaction f

interpolation n interpolation f

interpret ⓵ vt interpréter
⓶ vi faire l'interprète

interpretation n interprétation f; **give a
loose** ∼ **of sth** donner une interprétation
peu rigoureuse de qch; **place an** ∼ **on sth**
donner une interprétation à qch

interpreter n interprète mf

interpreting n interprétation f

interrelation n corrélation f

interrogatories n pl (Law) questions
écrites échangées entre parties ou adressées
aux témoins

interrupt vt (person, event) interrompre;
(supply) couper

interruption n interruption f; ∼
marketing n marketing d'interruption m,
techniques de diffusion d'informations
commerciales visant à forcer le destinataire à
recevoir le message en l'absence d'une
demande de sa part

interstate adj US entre états, inter-état

interstitial advertisement n (on
Internet) publicité interstitielle f

interval n intervalle m; **at four-weekly** ∼s
toutes les quatre semaines; **at two-hour** ∼s à
deux heures d'intervalle

intervene vi intervenir

intervention n (EU) intervention f; ∼
currency n (EU) devise d'intervention f; ∼
price n (EU) prix d'intervention m

interventionist[1] adj (EU)
interventionniste

interventionist[2] n (EU) interventionniste
mf

interview[1] n entretien m; (Media) interview
f; **be called for an** ∼ être convoqué à un
entretien; **job** ∼ entretien; **radio** ∼ interview
à la radio

interview[2] vt (candidate) faire passer un
entretien à; (Media) interviewer

interviewee n (for job) candidat/-e m/f;
(Media) interviewé/-e m/f; (for survey) personne
interrogée f

interviewer n (for job) personne faisant
passer l'entretien f; (Media) intervieweur/
-euse m/f; (market research) enquêteur/-trice m/
f; ∼ **bias** n partialité de l'enquêteur f

inter vivos adv entre vifs; ∼ **trust** n
fidéicommis entre vifs m

intestacy n succession ab intestat f

intestate adj ab intestat, intestat

in-the-money adj argenté, dans le cours,
en jeu

intimidation n intimidation f

intra-Community adj
intracommunautaire; ∼ **trade** n (EU)
commerce intracommunautaire m

intradepartmental adj intraministériel/
-ielle

intra-EU adj intracommunautaire; ∼ **trade**
n commerce intracommunautaire m

intranet n intranet m

intrapreneur n intrepreneur m

intrapreneurship n intrepreneuriat m

intrastate adj US à l'intérieur de l'état

intra vires adj statutaire

in-tray n corbeille arrivée f

intrinsic adj intrinsèque

introduce vt (person) présenter; (changes)
introduire; (product) lancer; (law, system);
mettre en place; (Pol) (bill, proposal) présenter;
∼ **legislation** faire passer une législation,
légiférer

introduction n (to book, speech)
introduction f; (of law, system, reform)
introduction f; (of new shares) introduction f,
introduction à la cote f; (of bill, proposal)
présentation f

introductory adj (paragraph, speech,
comments) préliminaire; ∼ **offer** n offre de
lancement f; ∼ **price** n prix de lancement m

intrusive adj importun

intuitive management n management
intuitif m

inure vt habituer, endurcir; **be** ∼**d to sth**
être habitué à qch, être endurci à qch

inv. abbr (▸**invoice**) fre (facture)

invalid adj (conclusion, argument) sans
fondement; (contract, will) nul/nulle; (claim) non
valable; (ticket, passport) périmé

invalidate vt (ballot) annuler, invalider;
(contract) annuler; (deed) vicier; (judgement)
casser, infirmer; (will, election) invalider

invalidation *n* (of ballot) annulation *f*, invalidation *f*; (of contract) annulation *f*; (of judgement) cassation *f*, infirmation *f*; (of will, election) invalidation *f*

invaluable *adj* inestimable

invent *vt* inventer

invention *n* invention *f*

inventive *adj* inventif/-ive

inventor *n* inventeur/-rice *m/f*

inventory¹ *n* (list) inventaire *m*; AmE (stock) stocks *m pl*; ~ **allowance** *n* déduction pour inventaire *f*; ~ **book** *n* livre d'inventaire *m*; ~ **certificate** *n* attestation d'inventaire *f*; ~ **control** *n* AmE gestion des stocks *f*; ~ **controller** *n* responsable des stocks *mf*; ~ **costing** *n* inventaire *m*; ~ **financing** *n* financement de stocks *m*; ~ **item** *n* unité en stock *f*; ~ **management** *n* gestion des stocks *f*; ~ **planning** *n* gestion prévisionnelle des stocks *f*; ~ **pricing** *n* valorisation des stocks *f*; ~ **turnover** *n* rotation des stocks *f*; ~ **valuation** *n* valorisation des stocks *f*

inventory² *vt* inventorier

inverse¹ *adj* inverse

inverse² *n* contraire *m*, inverse *m*

inversely *adv* inversement

inversion *n* inversion *f*

invert *vt* inverser, intervertir

inverted: ~ **commas** *n pl* guillemets *m pl*; ~ **market** *n* marché en déport *m*; ~ **scale** *n* échelle inversée *f*; ~ **yield curve** *n* courbe de rapport inversée *f*, courbe des taux inversée *f*

invest [1] *vt* (money) investir, placer; (time, energy, resources) consacrer; ~ **sb with** (authority, power) investir qn de [2] *vi* (Acc, Bank), investir; (Fin, Stock) faire des placements, investir; ~ **in an annuity** placer de l'argent en viager; ~ **in bonds** investir en obligations; ~ **in property** faire un placement immobilier; ~ **in shares** investir en actions, investir en valeurs; ~ **in new equipment** investir des capitaux dans du nouveau matériel

investee *n entreprise dans laquelle on investit*

investigate *vt* (situation) examiner, étudier; (crime) enquêter sur; (person) faire une enquête sur; (market, sector) sonder; (possibility, report) étudier

investigating committee *n* commission d'enquête *f*

investigation *n* (study) étude *f*, enquête *f*, examen *m*; (of crime) enquête *f*; **make** ~**s into** enquêter sur; **be under** ~ faire l'objet d'une enquête; **the matter under** ~ la question à l'étude

investigative *adj* (mission, journalist) d'investigation; ~ **approach** *n* (to field audits) approche par l'enquête *f*

investigatory: ~ **commission** *n*

commission d'enquête *f*; ~ **powers** *n pl* pouvoirs d'enquête *m pl*, pouvoirs d'instruction *m pl*

investment *n* (Fin, Stock) investissement *m*, placement *m*; (Acc, Bank) investissement *m*; ~ **in shares** placement en valeurs *m*; ~ **in equipment** investissement de capitaux dans le matériel; ~ **abroad** *n* investissement à l'étranger *m*; ~ **account** *n* compte de placement *m*; ~ **activity** *n* activité d'investissement *f*; ~ **advice** *n* conseils en investissements *m pl*; ~ **adviser,** ~ **advisor** *n* conseiller/-ère en placements *m/f*; ~ **allowance** *n* déduction pour placements *f*; ~ **analysis** *n* analyse d'investissements *f*, étude de rentabilité *f*; ~ **analyst** *n* analyste de placements *mf*; ~ **bank** *n* US banque d'affaires *f*, banque d'investissement *f*; ~ **banker** *n* US banquier/-ière d'affaires *m/f*, banquier/-ière d'investissement *m/f*, spécialiste des services de banque d'affaires *mf*, spécialiste des services de banque d'investissement *mf*; ~ **banking** *n* US opérations sur valeurs de placement *f pl*; ~ **business** *n* secteur des investissements *m*; ~ **company** *n* société d'investissement *f*, société de placement *f*, société de portefeuilles *f*; ~ **consultant** *n* conseiller/-ère en placements *m/f*, consultant/-e en investissement *m/f*; ~ **contract** *n* contrat d'investissement *m*; ~ **fund** *n* société d'investissement *f*; ~ **goods** *n pl* (Fin) biens d'investissement *m pl*; (S&M) biens d'équipement *m pl*; ~ **grade** *n* classe d'investissement *f*; ~**-grade** *adj* US de premier ordre, de qualité supérieure; ~ **incentive** *n* encouragement à l'investissement *m*; ~ **income** *n* revenu d'investissements *m*, revenu de placements *m*; ~ **loss** *n* perte sur investissement *f*; ~ **management** *n* gestion d'investissements *f*; ~ **mix** *n* stratégie des investissements *f*; ~ **opportunity** *n* occasion d'investissement *f*; ~ **portfolio** *n* portefeuille d'investissement *m*; ~ **property** *n* immobilier de placement *m*; ~ **revenue** *n* revenu de placements *m*; ~ **savings account** *n* compte d'épargne-placement *m*; ~ **tax credit** *n* crédit d'impôt à l'investissement *m*; ~ **trust** *n* fonds commun de placement *m*, fonds de placement *m*; ~ **yield** *n* rendement de placement *m*

investor *n* investisseur/-euse *m/f*; (in savings scheme) épargnant/-e *m/f*; (in shares) actionnaire *mf*

invisible *adj* (asset) invisible; ~ **balance** *n* balance des invisibles *f*; ~ **earnings** *n pl* gains invisibles *m pl*; ~ **export** *n* exportation invisible *f*; ~ **import** *n* importation invisible *f*; ~ **trade** *n* commerce d'invisibles *m*

invisibles *n pl* invisibles *m pl*

invitation *n* invitation *f*; **receive an** ~ **to do** être invité à faire; ~ **to bid** appel d'offres *m*; ~ **to tender** appel d'offres *m*

invite vt (person) inviter; (comments, suggestions) solliciter; ~ **subscriptions for** ouvrir une souscription pour; ~ **sb for an interview** convoquer qn pour un entretien

invoice[1] n facture f; ~ **amount** n montant de la facture m; ~ **clerk** n facturier/-ière m/f; ~ **price** n prix de facture m; ~ **value** n valeur de la facture f

invoice[2] vt (company, person, goods) facturer; ~ **sb for sth** facturer qch à qn; **be ~d** recevoir une facture

invoicing n facturation f; ~ **amount** n montant dû m; ~ **department** n service facturation m

invoke vt (law, penalty) invoquer

involuntary adj involontaire; ~ **bankruptcy** n faillite forcée f, faillite prononcée à la demande des créanciers f

involve vt (effort, travel) impliquer, nécessiter; (problems, risk) entraîner; (expenses) entraîner, impliquer; (person) faire participer; (implicate) impliquer; (affect) concerner, impliquer; ~ **doing** impliquer de faire, nécessiter; **be ~d in** (project, enterprise) participer à, être engagé dans; (scandal) être mêlé à; **be ~d in doing** s'occuper de faire; **get ~d** s'engager; **get ~d with/in sth** se trouver engagé dans qch; ~ **oneself in** prendre part à

involvement n (participation) participation f; (commitment) engagement m; (links, ties) liens m pl, relations f pl

inward: ~ **bill of lading** n connaissement d'entrée m; **~-bound** adj de retour; ~ **cargo** n chargement de retour m; ~ **charges** n pl frais à l'entrée m pl; ~ **investment** n (from overseas) investissement étranger m; ~ **investor** n (from overseas) investisseur/-euse étranger/-ère mf; **~-looking** adj replié sur soi-même; ~ **payment** n encaissement m, paiement reçu m

I/O abbr (▸**input/output**) E/S (entrée/sortie)

IOM abbr (▸**International Options Market**) marché international des options m

IOU abbr (▸**I owe you**) reconnaissance de dette f

IP abbr (▸**Internet protocol**) protocole IP m; ~ **address** n adresse IP f; ~ **telephony** n téléphonie IP f, téléphonie via Internet f

IPD abbr (**interest, profit and dividends**) revenu en provenance de l'étranger m

IPO abbr (▸**initial public offering**) offre publique initiale f, première émission publique f; (▸**international payment order**) ordre de paiement international m

ipso facto adv ipso facto

IR abbr (▸**industrial relations**) relations humaines dans l'entreprise f pl, relations professionnelles f pl; (between unions and management) relations patronat/syndicats f pl; UK (▸**Inland Revenue**) service des impôts britannique; Fisc m

IRC abbr (▸**Internet Relay Chat**) bavardage en temps réel m, chat m, IRC m

iron[1] n fer m; ~ **ore** n minerai de fer m

iron[2]: ~ **out** vt (difficulty, problem) aplanir

ironworks n pl usine sidérurgique f

IRR abbr (▸**internal rate of return**) taux de rentabilité interne m

irrecoverable debt n créance irrécouvrable f

irreducible adj (minimum) irréductible

irrefutable adj irréfutable; (Law) (assumption, claim, evidence) irréfragable

irregular adj irrégulier/-ière; ~ **market** n marché irrégulier m

irregularity n anomalie f, irrégularité f; (Law) vice de forme m

irrelevant adj étranger/-ère au sujet; **be ~ to sth** n'avoir aucun rapport avec qch

irreparable adj irréparable; ~ **damage** n dommage irréparable m; ~ **harm** n préjudice irréparable m

irreplaceable adj irremplaçable

irrespective adj: ~ **of** sans tenir compte de

irreversible adj (decision, verdict) irrévocable; (process) irréversible

irrevocable adj irrévocable; ~ **credit** n crédit irrévocable m; ~ **letter of credit** n lettre de crédit irrévocable f

IRS abbr US (▸**Internal Revenue Service**) service des impôts américain Fisc m

ISA abbr UK (**Individual Savings Account**) compte épargne individuel m (dont les revenus ne sont pas imposables)

ISD abbr (▸**international subscriber dialing**) téléphone automatique international m

ISDN abbr (▸**integrated services digital network**) RNIS m (réseau numérique à intégration de services)

ISE abbr (▸**International Stock Exchange**) ≈ SBF f (Société des bourses françaises)

ISI abbr UK (▸**International Statistical Institute**) Institut international des statistiques

island n (in shop) îlot m

ISO abbr (▸**International Standards Organization**) Organisation internationale de normalisation f

isocost n isocoût m

isolate vt isoler

isolated adj isolé

isolationist[1] adj isolationniste

isolationist[2] n isolationniste mf

isoproduct curve n courbe isoquante f

isoquant n isoquant m

ISP abbr (▸**Internet Service Provider**) FAI m (fournisseur d'accès Internet)

issuance n (Tax) délivrance f; ~ **facility** n

facilité d'émission garantie *f*

issue¹ *n* (topic of discussion) problème *m*, question *f*, sujet *m*; (action of issuing, shares issued) émission *f*; (magazine) numéro *m*; (outcome) résultat *m*; (descendants) descendance en ligne directe *f*; **the contract at ~** le contrat dont il s'agit, le contrat en question; **~ date** *n* date d'émission *f*; **~ market** *n* marché des émissions *m*; **~ premium** *n* prime d'émission *f*; **~ price** *n* prix d'émission *m*

issue² *vt* (cheque, shares, bond, banknote) émettre; (statement, ultimatum) délivrer; (magazine, newspaper) faire paraître; (prospectus) lancer; (Stock) émettre; **~ by tender** émettre par adjudication; **~ a letter of credit** émettre une lettre de crédit; **~ shares at a discount** émettre des actions à l'escompte; **~ a warrant** lancer un mandat; **~ a writ against sb** assigner qn en justice; **~ from** résulter de

issued: ~ capital *n* capital émis *m*; **~ share capital** *n* capital souscrit *m*

issuer *n* émetteur/-trice *m/f*

issuing¹ *adj* (Bank, Fin, Stock) émetteur/ -trice; **~ authority** *n* (of passport) autorité compétente (pour délivrer) *f*, **~ bank** *n* banque émettrice *f*; **~ company** *n* société émettrice *f*; **~ house** *n* banque de placement *f*, établissement responsable de l'émission *m*

IT *abbr* (▸**information technology**) informatique *f*, technologie de l'information *f*; UK (▸**industrial tribunal**) ≈ Conseil des

prud'hommes *m*

italic *adj* italique

italics *n pl* (typography) italique *m*; **in ~** en italique(s)

item *n* (Acc) (entry) article *m*, poste *m*, écriture *f*; (for sale) article *m*; (on agenda) point *m*, question *f*; (Comp) (on menu) élément *m*; **~ approved for inclusion** question dont l'inclusion a été approuvée *f*; **~s in the estimates** postes du budget des dépenses *m pl*; **~s on the agenda** questions à l'ordre du jour *f pl*

itemization *n* (of bill, invoice) détail *m*

itemize *vt* détailler

itemized *adj* (bill, billing, invoice) détaillé; **~ deductions** *n pl* (Tax) déduction des frais réels *f*, **~ pay statement** *n* bulletin de salaire analytique *m*

iteration *n* itération *f*

itinerary *n* itinéraire *m*, route *f*

ITM *abbr* (▸**in-the-money**) argenté, dans le cours, en jeu

ITO *abbr* (▸**International Trade Organization**) *organisation internationale du commerce*

ITV *abbr* UK (**Independent Television**) *chaîne de télévision indépendante diffusant des programmes régionaux*

iv *abbr* (▸**increased value**) plus-value *f*; (▸**invoice value**) valeur de la facture *f*

J/A *abbr* (▸**joint account**) compte joint *m*

jack: ~ up *vt* (infrml) (price) augmenter

jacket *n* (of book) jaquette *f*

jackpot *n* cagnotte *f*; **hit the ~** (win) gagner le gros lot; (be successful) faire un tabac (infrml)

jam¹ *n* (of equiment) blocage *m*; (difficult situation) (infrml) pétrin *m* (infrml); **in a ~** dans le pétrin

jam² *vi* se coincer, se bloquer

japanization *n* japanisation *f*

jargon *n* jargon *m*

Java *n* (Comp) Java *m*

jawbone *vt* US faire pression sur

J curve *n* courbe en J *f*

JDI *abbr* (▸**joint declaration of interest**) déclaration conjointe d'intérêts *f*

jeopardize *vt* (future, survival, chances) mettre en péril; (career, situation, job, plans) compromettre

jerque note *n* certificat de dédouanement d'entrée *m*

jet *n* jet *m*

jetfoil *n* hydroglisseur *m*

jetlagged *adj*: **be ~** souffrir du décalage horaire

jettison *vt* jeter par-dessus bord

Jiffy bag® *n* enveloppe matelassée *f*

jingle *n* jingle *m*

JIT *abbr* (▸**just-in-time**) JAT (juste à temps), à flux tendus

jitters *n pl* (Econ, stock) courant de nervosité *f*; **have the ~** être nerveux/-euse

jittery *adj* nerveux/-euse

jnr *abbr* (▸**junior**) (employee, post) subalterne; (son) fils *m*; (young) jeune

job *n* travail *m*; (specific project of individual) tâche *f*; (in company) projet *m*, travail *m*; (order) commande *f*; (employment) emploi *m*, travail *m*, métier *m*; (role, function) fonction *f*; (post) poste *m*; **look for/get a ~** chercher/trouver un emploi; **a secretarial ~** un poste de   ⋯⋯

secrétaire; **have a ~ as** être employé comme, avoir un poste de; **be out of a ~** être sans emploi, être au chômage; **hold two ~s** cumuler; **have the ~ of doing** avoir la tâche de faire; **learn on the ~** apprendre sur le tas; **do a good/poor ~** faire du bon/mauvais travail; **have a hard ~ doing** avoir du mal à faire; **give sth up as a bad ~** laisser tomber qch; **get ~s for the boys** (infrml) placer ses petits copains (infrml); **~ action** n action revendicative f, grève f; **~ advertisement** n offre d'emploi f; **~ analysis** n analyse des tâches f, analyse par poste de travail f; **~ application** n candidature f, demande d'emploi f; **~ appraisal** n entretien de carrière m; **~-approval rating** n indice de satisfaction m; **~ assignment** n affectation des tâches f, répartition des tâches f; **~ breakdown** n décomposition des tâches f; **~ cluster** n groupe d'emplois m; **~ control** n gestion des travaux f; **~ costing** n évaluation du coût d'un poste f; **~ creation** n création d'emplois f; **~ creation scheme** n plan de création d'emplois m; **~ description** n profil de poste m; **~ evaluation** n évaluation de l'emploi f, évaluation de poste f; **~ expectations** n pl perspectives de carrière f pl; **~ flexibility** n flexibilité des emplois f; **~ freeze** n gel de l'emploi m; **~ hopping** n changement fréquent d'emplois m; **~ hunt** vi chercher un emploi; **~ hunter** n demandeur/-euse d'emploi m/f, personne à la recherche d'un emploi m/f; **~ hunting** n recherche d'un emploi f; **~ interview** n entretien d'embauche m; **~ lot** n lot d'articles divers m; **~ market** n marché du travail m; **~ mobility** n mobilité professionnelle f; **~ offer** n offre d'emploi f; **~ opening** n emploi vacant m, possibilitié d'emploi f; **~ opportunity** n débouché m, possibilité d'emploi f; (imminent vacancy) poste qui se libère m; **~ order** n ordre de fabrication m; **~ order costing** n estimation du prix de revient par commande f; **~ performance** n rendement au travail m; **~ placement** n placement m; **~ profile** n profil de poste m; **~ prospects** n pl perspectives de carrière f pl; **~ queue** n (Comp) file d'attente de travaux f; **~-related injury** n blessure liée à l'exercice d'une profession f; **~ requirements** n pl exigences du poste f pl; **~ review** n évaluation de l'emploi f; **~ rotation** n rotation des postes f, roulement m; **~ satisfaction** n satisfaction au travail f; **~ search** n recherche d'un emploi f; **~ security** n sécurité de l'emploi f; **~ seeker** n demandeur/-euse d'emploi m/f; **~-share** n poste partagé m; **~ share scheme** n système de partage du travail m; **~ sharing** n partage de l'emploi m, partage du travail m; **~ specification** n profil de poste m; **~ splitting** n partage de poste m; **~ stream** n (Comp) flux de travaux m; **~ study** n analyse de poste f; **~ title** n qualification f, titre de

fonction m; **~ vacancy** n poste à pourvoir m

Jobcentre n UK bureau des services nationaux de l'emploi m, ≈ Agence nationale pour l'emploi f

jobless adj (total) des sans-emploi; (figures) du chômage; **the ~** les chômeurs m pl, les sans-emploi m pl; **~ person** n chômeur m, sans-emploi m; **~ rate** n taux de chômage m

jockey n (jarg) responsable de la gestion d'un investissement mf

join vt (meet up with) rejoindre; (firm) entrer dans; (organization, board, team) devenir membre de; (partner, colleague) s'associer à; (list) ajouter son nom à; (queue) se mettre dans; (club) adhérer à; (class, group) s'inscrire à; **~ a union** se syndiquer; **~ forces with sb** (merge) s'allier à qn; (collaborate) collaborer avec qn; **~ in** participer; **~ in sth** (talks, activity, campaign) participer à, prendre part à; **~ together** (companies) s'associer

joined adj AmE (document) en annexe

joint adj (communiqué, measures, procedure) commun; (responsibility, financing) conjoint; (talks) multilatéral; (winner) ex æquo; **~ account** n compte joint m; **~ action** n (Law) action collective f; **~ applicant** n (Patents) codéposant/-e m/f; **~ assignment** n mission commune f; **~ auditor** n co-commissaire m, commissaire aux comptes coresponsable m; **~ author** n co-auteur m; **~ authorization** n autorisation conjointe f; **~ bank account** n compte joint m; **~ bond** n obligation co-émise f, obligation conjointe f; **~ committee** n commission mixte f, commission paritaire f; **~ company** n société mixte f; **~ consultation** n consultation bilatérale f; **~ consultative committee** n comité d'entreprise m, commission paritaire consultative f; **~ container service** n service conteneur commun m; **~ contract** n contrat collectif m; **~ costs** n pl coûts conjoints m pl; **~ custody** n garde partagée f; **~ debtor** n co-débiteur/-trice m/f; **~ declaration of interest** n déclaration conjointe d'intérêts f; **~ director** n codirecteur/-trice m/f; **~ equity venture company** n joint-venture m, société en participation f; **~ estate** n biens communs m pl, communauté de biens f; **~ guarantee** n caution solidaire f; **~ heir** n cohéritier/-ière m/f; **~ holder** n codétenteur/-trice m/f, cotitulaire mf; **~ insurance** n assurance conjointe f, responsabilité conjointe f; **~ liability** n responsabilité collective f, responsabilité conjointe f; **~ management** n cogestion f, cogérance f; **~ manager** n codirecteur/-trice m/f, cogérant/-e m/f; **~ occupancy** n cohabitation f; **~ operator** n coopérateur/-trice m/f; **~ owner** n copropriétaire mf; **~ ownership** n copropriété f; **~ partnership** n co-association f; **~ products** n pl produits liés m pl; **~ regulation** n co-régulation f; **~ representation** n démarche collective f;

~ and several liability n responsabilité conjointe et solidaire f; **~ and several obligation** n obligation conjointe et solidaire f; **~ signature** n (Bank) signature collective f; (Gen Comm, Law) cosignature f; **~ statement** n déclaration commune f; **~-stock company** n société par actions f; **~ tenancy** n co-location f; **~ venture** n (Econ, Fin) coentreprise f, joint-venture m; (company) entreprise conjointe f, société d'exploitation en commun f; (collaborative action) collaboration f, coentreprise f; **~-venture bank** n pl banque en participation f; **~-venture company** n coentreprise f, joint-venture m, société en participation f; **~-venture investment bank** n, **~-venture merchant bank** n banque d'affaires en participation f, banque d'investissement en participation f; **~ working party** n groupe de travail paritaire m

jointly adv conjointement, ensemble; **~ owned** être **~ owned by** être la copropriété de; **~ and severally liable for** conjointement et solidairement responsable de

joker n US (Law) clause ambiguë f, échappatoire f

jot: ~ down vt noter

journal n (Acc) journal m; (periodical) revue f; (newspaper) journal m, revue f; **~ entry** n (Acc) écriture comptable f

journalism n journalisme m

journalist n journaliste mf

journalize vt (Acc) comptabiliser au journal

journey n voyage m; (short) trajet m; **make a ~** faire un voyage; **~ planner** n information pour les voyageurs f; **~ planning** n organisation des déplacements f; **~ time** n durée du trajet f; (by plane) durée du vol f

joystick n (Comp) manche à balai m, manette de jeux f

JP abbr (▸**justice of the peace**) juge de paix m

JPEG abbr (**Joint Photographic Experts Group**) format JPEG m

jr abbr (▸**junior**) (employee, post) subalterne; (son) fils m; (young) jeune

judge¹ n juge m

judge² ⬚1⬚ vt (Gen Comm, Law) juger; (competition, contest) faire partie du jury de; (estimate) estimer; (forsee) prévoir; (consider) juger, estimer ⬚2⬚ vi **as far as one can ~** autant qu'on puisse en juger; **judging by, judging from** à en juger par

judgement n (Gen Comm) jugement m, discernement m; (Law) arrêt m, décision f, jugement m; (opinion) avis m; **pass/give ~** prononcer/rendre un jugement; **in my ~** à mon avis; **reserve ~** réserver son jugement; **an error of ~** une erreur de jugement f; **do sth against one's better ~** faire qch en

sachant que l'on fait une erreur; **go against one's ~** aller à l'encontre de sa propre conscience; **sit in ~ over** juger; **~ creditor** n US créancier titulaire d'un jugement exécutoire pour le montant d'un crédit; **~ debtor** n US débiteur contre lequel un jugement a été obtenu; **~ sample** n enquête par échantillonnage f

judicial adj judiciaire; **~ affairs** n pl affaires judiciaires f pl; **~ notice** n connaissance d'office f; **~ proceedings** n pl poursuites judiciaires f pl; **~ sale** n vente judiciaire f, vente par autorité de justice f; **~ separation** n séparation de corps f, séparation judiciaire f

judiciary n pouvoir judiciaire m, système judiciaire m

juggernaut n poids lourd m, avec remorque ou semi-remorque

jumble sale n BrE vente de charité f

jumbo n (Transp) gros-porteur m, jumbo-jet m; **~ certificate of deposit** n certificat de très grand dépôt; **~ jet** n gros-porteur m, jumbo-jet m; **~ loan** n prêt d'une très grande somme m; **~ pack** n paquet géant m

jump¹ n (in prices) flambée f, montée en flèche f; (leap, transition) bond m; **make the ~ from secretary to PA** passer de secrétaire à secrétaire de direction

jump² ⬚1⬚ vt **~ the queue** resquiller; **~ the gun** anticiper ⬚2⬚ vi (prices, profits) monter en flèche; **~ to conclusions** tirer des conclusions hâtives; **~ at** (opportunity) saisir; (offer, suggestion) accepter avec enthousiasme

jumpy adj (market, person) nerveux/-euse

juncture n point m; **at this ~** à ce moment

junior¹ adj (son) fils; (young) jeune; (post, rank, position) subalterne; **be ~ to sb** (younger) être plus jeune que qn; (lower-ranking) occuper un poste inférieur à qn

junior² n (employee) subalterne mf, subordonné/-e m/f

junior: ~ counsel n UK avocat/-e subordonné/-e à l'avocat principal m/f; **~ creditor** n créancier non-prioritaire m; **~ debt** n dette de deuxième rang f; **~ issue** n US émission secondaire f; **~ manager** n jeune cadre m; **~ partner** n associé/-e minoritaire m/f; **~ position** n poste de débutant m; **~ security** n US valeur de second rang f, valeur de seconde catégorie f; **~ share** n action de dividende f, action de seconde catégorie f

junk n (poor quality goods) camelote f (infrml); **~ bond** n obligation spéculative à haut risque f, obligation pourrie f; **~ e-mail** n publicité rebut (par courrier électronique) f, pourriel m Can; **~ food** n nourriture industrielle f; **~ mail** n imprimés publicitaires m pl, prospectus m pl

junket¹ n voyage aux frais de la princesse m (infrml)

junket² *vi* voyager aux frais de la princesse (infrml)
juridical: ~ **person** *n* personne morale *f*; ~ **position** *n* situation juridique *f*
jurisdiction *n* (Law) circonscription judiciaire *f*, compétence *f*, juridiction *f*; (Admin) compétence *f*; **come under the** ~ **of** (Admin) relever de la compétence de; (Law) relever de la juridiction de; ~ **dispute** *n* conflit de compétence *m*
jurisdictional strike *n* grève provoquée par un conflit d'attributions syndicales
jurisprudence *n* droit *m*, jurisprudence *f*
juror *n* juré *m*
jury *n* jury *m*; ~ **trial** procès avec jury *m*; **have a** ~ **trial** passer en assises, être jugé par un jury
just *adj* (decision, cause, person) juste; (complaint, demand) justifié; (claim, criticism) légitime; (Law) (claim) fondé; (request) valable; ~ **compensation** *n* indemnité juste *f*, indemnité équitable *f*; ~ **price** *n* juste prix *m*
justice *n* justice *f*; **get** ~ obtenir gain de cause; ~ **ministry** *n* ≈ ministère de la Justice *m*; ~ **of the peace** *n* juge de paix *m*
justices *n pl* justices *f pl*
justifiable *adj* (which can be justified) justifiable; (Law) légitime
justification *n* justification *f*
justified *adj* (Gen Comm) justifié; (Comp) justifié; **be** ~ **in doing** être en droit de faire, être fondé à faire; ~ **price** *n* cours justifié *m*, prix justifié *m*
justify *vt* (action, policy, increase, opinion) justifié; (text) justifier
just-in-time *adj* (distribution, production, purchasing) juste à temps, à flux tendus
JV *abbr* (▶**joint venture**) (Econ, Fin) coentreprise *f*, joint-venture *m*; (collaborative action) collaboration *f*, coentreprise *f*
JWP *abbr* (▶**joint working party**) groupe de travail paritaire *m*

Kk

K *abbr* (infrml) (▶**thousand**) mille; **earn 40**~ gagner 40 000 livres sterling
kangaroo: ~ **court** *n* tribunal irrégulier *m*; ~ **ticket** *n* US (infrml) (Pol) liste kangourou *f*
kb *abbr* (▶**kilobyte**) ko *m* (kilo-octet)
KBS *abbr* (▶**knowledge-based system**) système expert *m*
KC *abbr* (UK) (▶**King's Counsel**) avocat de la Couronne
keen *adj* (price) défiant toute compétition; (competition, rivalry) intense; (demand) fort; (debate) animé; (interest) vif/vive; (supporter, campaigner) enthousiaste; (applicant, candidate) motivé; **be** ~ **on** (plan, project) tenir à; **be** ~ **on doing** tenir à faire; **I'm not very** ~ je ne suis pas très chaud (infrml)
keep¹ *n* (maintenance) pension *f*; **earn one's** ~ (person) gagner de quoi vivre; (branch, business) être viable
keep² *vt* (retain) garder; (store) mettre, ranger; (brand, product) avoir, vendre; (support financially) faire vivre, entretenir; (appointment) se rendre à; (promise) tenir; (shop, restaurant) tenir; (accounts, list, diary) tenir; (Comp) (file) conserver; ~ **back** (money) retenir; (information, fact) cacher; ~ **down** (number, costs, expenditure) limiter; (prices, wages, unemployment) limiter l'augmentation de; (inflation) maîtriser, juguler; ~ **to** (timetable, agenda, plan) respecter,

s'en tenir à; (rules) respecter; ~ **up** (person) suivre; (business, rival, competitor) rester à la hauteur; ~ **sth up** (correspondence) entretenir; (tradition) maintenir; ~ **up the pressure** continuer à faire pression; ~ **up with** (competitor) se maintenir au même niveau que; (developments) se tenir au courant de; (demand) faire face à; (standards) maintenir; (inflation, prices, fashion) suivre; ~ **up with one's payment** régler ses paiements à l'échéance
keeping: **in** ~ **with** en accord avec
keg *n* barillet *m*, tonnelet *m*
kerb: ~ **market** *n* marché hors bourse *m*, second marché *m*; ~ **weight** *n* (of vehicle) poids en ordre de marche *m*
key¹ *adj* (crucial) clé *inv*
key² *n* (to door) clé *f*; (Comp) clé *f*, clé d'accès *f*; (on keyboard) touche *f*
key³ *vt* (data, text) entrer, saisir; ~ **in** (data, text) entrer, saisir
key: ~ **account** *n* compte clé *m*; ~ **account management** *n* gestion de comptes clés *f*; ~ **currency** *n* devise clé *f*, monnaie clé *f*; ~ **data** *n pl* données clés *f pl*; ~ **driver** *n* facteur clé d'influence *m*; ~ **feature** *n* caractéristique clé *f*; ~ **industry** *n* industrie clé *f*; ~ **issue** *n* question clé *f*; ~ **money** *n* pas de porte *m*, reprise *f*; ~ **point** *n* point essentiel *m*; ~ **post** *n* poste clé *m*; ~ **rate** *n* taux directeur *m*; ~ **sequence** *n*

séquence de touches f; ~ **stage** n phase clé f; ~ **word** n mot clé m; ~ **worker** n travailleur/-euse occupant un poste clé m/f

keyboard n clavier m; ~ **shortcut** n raccourci clavier m

keyboarder n opérateur/-trice de saisie m/f, claviste mf

Keynesian adj keynésien/-ienne; ~ **economics** n + sing v keynésianisme m; ~ **policy** n politique keynésienne f

keynote speaker n intervenant/-e principal/-e m/f

keypad n pavé numérique m

keystone n (of economy) clé de voûte f, pilier m

keystroke n frappe f

keyword n mot clé m; ~ **search** n recherche par mot clé f

kickback n dessous-de-table m, pot-de-vin m

kick-start vt (economy) relancer

kill vt tuer

killer application n (Comp) application à grand succès f, application vedette f

killing n (infrml) bénéfice énorme m, gros bénéfice m; **make a** ~ faire un bénéfice énorme, faire un gros bénéfice

kilobyte n kilo-octet m

kilometer AmE, **kilometre** BrE n kilomètre m; ~**s per hour** v kilomètre/heure m

kilowatt n kilowatt m; ~**-hour** n kilowatt-heure m

kind n: **in** ~ (benefit, payment) en nature

King's Counsel n UK avocat de la Couronne

kinked demand curve n courbe de demande coudée f

kip n kip m

kite[1] n (infrml) (Law) avocat/-e commis/-e d'office m/f; (Stock) billet de complaisance m, cerf-volant m, traite en l'air f (infrml); **fly a** ~ lancer un ballon d'essai

kite[2] vi (Stock) faire monter les taux artificiellement, manipuler les cours à la hausse

kiting n tirage à découvert m

knock[1] n (misfortune) coup m; ~**-for-knock** adj (Ins) mutuel, à torts partagés; ~**-for-knock agreement** n (Ins) exonération mutuelle f; ~**-on effect** n réaction en chaîne f

knock[2]: ~ **back** vt (infrml) (offer) refuser; ~

down (goods at auction) adjuger; (price) (by retailer) baisser; (by buyer) faire baisser; ~ **off** vi (infrml) (stop work) finir le travail; ~ **out** vt (infrml) débiter

knockdown price n prix sacrifié m; **at** ~**s** à des prix imbattables

knocker n (infrml) (S&M) démarcheur m

knocking copy n publicité comparative dénigrante f

knockoffs n pl (infrml) (fashion) articles démarqués m pl

knockout: ~ **agreement** n entente illicite entre enchérisseurs f; ~ **competition** n compétition avec épreuves éliminatoires f

know[1] n be in the ~ **about** être au courant de

know[2] vt (have knowledge generally) savoir; (person, fact, information) connaître, savoir; ~ **one's customer** bien connaître son client

know-bot n robot de recherche de connaissances m

know-how n (infrml) savoir-faire m

knowledge n (overall wisdom) connaissances f pl; (of specific field) connaissance f; **have** ~ **of** avoir connaissance de; **have a working** ~ **of** avoir de bonnes connaissances en, avoir une bonne connaissance de; **bring sth to sb's** ~ porter qch à la connaissance de qn; **it has come to my** ~ **that** ... j'ai appris que ...; **without sb's** ~ à l'insu de qn; **to the best of my** ~ à ma connaissance; ~ **base** n base de connaissances f; ~**-based system** n système expert m; ~ **economy** n économie de la connaissance f; ~ **engineer** n ingénieur-cogniticien m, ingénieur de la connaissance m; ~ **engineering** n cognitique f; ~ **management** n gestion des connaissances f; ~ **sharing** n partage du savoir m; ~ **worker** n travailleur/-euse intellectuel/-elle m/f

knowledgeable adj bien informé

knowledgeware n (Comp) experticiel m, logiciel de système expert m

known adj connu; **not** ~ inconnu; ~ **by name** connu de nom; ~ **loss** n (Ins) dommages connus m pl

krona n krona f

krone n krone f

Krugerrand n krugerrand m

kudos n gloire f

kuna n kuna m

kurtosis n kurtose m

Ll

L/A *abbr* (▶**letter of authority**) lettre d'autorité *f*

lab *n* laboratoire *m*

label¹ *n* (tag, sticker) étiquette *f*; (brand) label *m*, marque *f*; (of designer) griffe *f*; (on diagram) légende *f*; (**Comp**) label *m*; (record company) label *m*; ~ **clause** *n* préambule *m*

label² *vt* (goods) étiqueter; (diagram) mettre des légendes sur

labeling AmE, **labelling** BrE *n* étiquetage *m*; ~ **laws** *n pl* lois relatives à l'étiquetage *f pl*

labor *n* AmE ▶**labour** BrE

laboratory *n* laboratoire *m*

laborer *n* AmE ▶**labourer** BrE

laboring class *n* AmE ▶**labouring class** BrE

labour¹ *n* BrE (workers) main-d'œuvre *f*; (work) travail *m*; **withdraw one's** ~ se mettre en grève; ~ **agreement** *n* accord patronat-syndicats *m*, convention collective *f*; ~ **clause** *n* clause concernant les salariés *f*; ~ **contract** *n* contrat de travail *m*; ~ **cost** *n* coût de main-d'œuvre *m*, coût salarial *m*; ~ **demand** *n* demande de main-d'œuvre *f*; ~ **dispute** *n* conflit du travail *m*; ~ **force** *n* (**Econ**) population active *f*; (within a firm) effectif *m*, main-d'œuvre *f*; **~-intensive** *adj* BrE (sector) à fort coefficient de main-d'œuvre; **~-intensive industry** *n* industrie à fort coefficient de main-d'œuvre *f*; ~ **law** *n* droit du travail *m*, droit social *m*; ~ **laws** *n pl* législation du travail *f*; ~ **legislation** *n* législation de l'emploi *f*; ~ **market** *n* marché de l'emploi *m*, marché du travail *m*; ~ **mobility** *n* mobilité de la main-d'œuvre *f*; ~ **movement** *n* mouvement ouvrier *m*; ~ **pool** *n* bassin d'emploi *m*, réserve de main-d'œuvre *f*; ~ **power** *n* capital humain *m*; ~ **relations** *n pl* relations sociales *f pl*; **~-saving** *adj* BrE qui facilite le travail; **~-saving device** *n* appareil électro-ménager *m*; ~ **shortage** *n* pénurie de main-d'œuvre *f*; ~ **supply** *n* offre de main-d'œuvre *f*; ~ **theory of value** *n* théorie de la valeur travail *f*; ~ **turnover** *n* rotation du personnel *m*; ~ **union** *n* syndicat *m*; ~ **unrest** *n* malaise social *m*

labour² *vi* BrE travailler dur

labourer *n* BrE ouvrier/-ière *m/f*; (on building site) ouvrier/-ière du bâtiment *m/f*, manœuvre *m*; **farm** ~ ouvrier/-ière agricole *m/f*

labouring class *n* BrE classe ouvrière *f*

Labour Party *n* UK (**Pol**) parti travailliste *m*

laches *n pl* négligence *f*, négligence coupable *f*

lack¹ *n* manque *m*; **through** ~ **of**, **for** ~ **of** par manque de

lack² ⓵ *vt* (confidence, support) manquer de; ~ **consistency** manquer de cohérence; ~ **experience** manquer d'expérience ⓶ *vi* **be** ~**ing** manquer; **be** ~**ing in** manquer de; **be** ~**ing in consistency** manquer de cohérence

ladder *n* échelle *f*; **career** ~ échelle professionnelle *f*; **work one's way up the** ~ gravir les échelons, **be at the top/bottom of the** ~ être au bas/au sommet de l'échelle

lade *vt* charger

laden *adj* chargé; **fully** ~ en pleine charge; ~ **in bulk** chargé en vrac

ladies *n pl* (form of address) Mesdames *f pl*; ~ **and gentlemen** Mesdames et Messieurs *m pl*

lading *n* chargement *m*, mise à bord *f*

lag¹ *n* (lapse) décalage *m*; (delay) retard *m*; (response time) temps de réponse *m*; ~ **risk** *n* (**Bank**) risque de retard *m*

lag² *vi* être en retard, être à la traîne; ~ **behind** (competitor) être en retard sur

laggard *n* (marketing) conservateur/-trice *m/f*; (**Stock**) traînard/-e *m/f* (infrml)

lagging indicator *n* indicateur retardé d'activité *m*

laid-up *adj* (ship) désarmé; ~ **tonnage** *n* navires désarmés *m pl*

laissez-faire *n* laisser-faire *m*; ~ **economy** *n* libéralisme économique *m*, économie de laisser-faire *f*

lame duck *n* canard boiteux *m*

LAN *abbr* (▶**local area network**) réseau local *m*

land¹ *n* (farmland) terre *f*; (**Law, Prop**) terrain *m*; (country) pays *m*; **building** ~ terrain à bâtir *m*; ~ **act** *loi relative à l'évaluation des indemnités d'expropriation*; ~ **bank** *n* banque de crédit foncier *f*; ~ **carriage** *n* transport par terre *m*, transport terrestre *m*; ~ **certificate** *n* certificat de propriété *m*; ~ **developer** *n* promoteur *m*; ~ **development** *n* viabilisation foncière *f*; ~ **economy** *n* économie de l'occupation des sols *f*; ~ **improvement** *n* viabilisation de terrain *f*; ~ **lease** *n* location foncière *f*; ~ **office** *n* administration des domaines *f*; ~ **owner** *n* propriétaire foncier *m*; ~ **ownership** *n* propriété foncière *f*; ~ **reform** *n* (agricultural) réforme agraire *f*; ~ **register** *n* BrE cadastre *m*; ~ **registration** *n* inscription au cadastre *f*; ~ **registry** *n* bureau du cadastre *m*;

~ rent n revenu foncier m; **~ tax** n impôt foncier m; **~ use** n (local level) occupation des sols f; (national) aménagement du territoire m; **~-value tax** n (Tax) impôt sur la valeur cadastrale m

land² **1** vt (aircraft) poser; (passengers) débarquer; (cargo) décharger; (job, contract) (infrml) décrocher (infrml)
2 vi (aircraft) se poser; **~ up doing** (infrml) finir par faire

landbridge n pont terrestre m

landed: **~ cost** n prix à quai m; **~ property** n bien-fonds m; **~ terms** n pl franco déchargement

landfill site n site de décharge contrôlée m

landing n (in plane) atterrissage m; (from ship) débarquement m; **~ card** n carte de débarquement f; **~ certificate** n certificat de débarquement m; **~ charge** n frais de débarquement m pl, frais de mise à terre m pl; **~ officer** n UK (shipping) employé/-e de débarquement m/f; **~ order** n autorisation de déchargement f; **~ permit** n permis de débarquement m; **~ stage** n débarcadère m, quai de déchargement m

landlocked adj sans accès à la mer, enclavé

landlord n propriétaire m

landmark n point de repère m; **~ decision** décision qui fait date f; **~ event** événement décisif m

landowner n propriétaire terrien m

landscape¹ adj (document) à l'italienne, horizontal; **~ format** n, **~ mode** n format horizontal m, format à l'italienne m; **~ page** n page à l'italienne f

landscape² vt (wasteland, office) aménager

lane n voie f

language n (of a nation) langue f; (system) langage m; **in plain ~** en clair; **~ barrier** n obstacle de la langue m; **~ course** n cours de langue m

lapse¹ n (error) faute f, erreur f; (shortcoming) défaillance f; (policy termination) abandon m, déchéance f; (of contract) expiration f; (of legal right) déchéance f; (interval) intervalle m; **~ of time** laps de temps m

lapse² vi (patent, right, law) tomber en désuétude; (contract, policy, membership) expirer; (insurance cover, subscription) prendre fin; **~ into** (jargon) tomber dans

lapsed adj (contract) périmé; (patent, policy) caduc/-uque

lapsing n (Acc) péremption prévue f; **~ appropriation** n annulation de crédits f

laptop¹ adj portable; **~ computer** n ordinateur portable m

laptop² n portable m

larceny n vol m

large adj (big) grand; (range, choice, number) grand; (sum, amount) important, gros/grosse; (percentage, population) fort; (purchase) grand, important; (customer, supplier) important; **in ~ quantities** en grandes quantités; **on a ~ scale** sur une grande échelle; **to a ~ extent** en grande partie; **~ employer** n gros employeur m; **~ exposure** n grand risque m; **~ order** n commande importante f; **~ producer** n gros producteur m; **~ quantity** n grosse quantité f; **~ risk** n risque considérable m; **~-scale** adj à grande échelle; **~-scale exporter** n gros exportateur m; **~-scale farming** n exploitation à grande échelle f; **~-scale importer** n gros importateur m; **~-scale industry** n grande industrie f; **~-scale integration** n intégration à grande échelle f; **~-scale model** n (Econ) macro-modèle économique m; **~-scale production** n production à grande échelle f; **~-scale redundancies** n pl licenciements à grande échelle mpl

largely adv en grande partie

laser n laser m; **~ beam** n rayon laser m; **~ pointer** n pointeur laser m; **~ printer** n imprimante à laser f; **~ scanner** n scanner m, scanneur m

last¹ adj dernier/-ière; **as a ~ resort** en dernier ressort; **in ~ position** à la dernière place

last² n le dernier/la dernière m/f; **~ in, first out** dernier entré, premier sorti

last³ adv **come ~** arriver en dernière place; **be placed ~** être classé dernier/-ière

last⁴ vi (situation) durer; (person) tenir

last: **~-day hours** n pl (Stock) heures du dernier jour f pl; **~ day of trading** n dernier jour de transaction m; **~-ditch** adj désespéré, ultime; **~ half** n (of month) dernière quinzaine f; **~-minute** adj (cancellation, change) de dernière minute; **~ notice day** n (Fin) dernier jour de notification m; **~ number redial** n fonction bis f; **~ resort** n dernier ressort m; **~ sale** n (Stock) dernière mise en vente f; **~ trading day** n dernier jour de cotation m, dernier jour de transaction m

late¹ adj (arrival, implementation) tardif/-ive; **be ~ for** (appointment, meeting) être en retard pour; **be ~ with one's payments** avoir des arriérés; **in ~ May** (à la) fin mai; **at this ~ stage** à ce stade avancé

late² adv (arrive, start, finish) en retard; (work, close) tard

late: **~ adopter** n utilisateur/-trice tardif/ -ive m/f; **~ delivery** n livraison tardive f; **~ entrant** concurrent/-e tardif/-ive m/f; **~ filing** n (of returns) production tardive f; **~ fringe** n US (in broadcasting) créneau après les heures de grande écoute m, tranche horaire de fin de soirée f; **~ night** n (broadcasting) créneau après les heures de grande écoute m, tranche de la nuit f; **~-night opening** n ouverture en nocturne f; **~ payment** n paiement tardif m

latency *n* latence *f*

lateness *n* retard *m*

latent defect *n* défaut caché *m*, vice caché *m*

later *adj* (date, development) ultérieur

lateral *adj* (movement) latéral; ∼ **integration** *n* intégration horizontale *f*, intégration latérale *f*; ∼ **thinking** *n* pensée latérale *f*

latest *adj* (edition, developments) dernier/-ière; **the ∼ fashion** la dernière mode *f*; **at the ∼** au plus tard, dernier délai; ∼ **addition** *n* (to product range) dernier-né *m*; ∼ **date** *n* date limite *f*; ∼ **estimate** *n* devis le plus récent *m*

latex *n* latex *m*

latitude *n* latitude *f*

latter¹ *adj* dernier/-ière

latter² *n* ce dernier/cette dernière *m/f*

launch¹ *n* lancement *m*; ∼ **party** *n* réception *f* (organisée pour le lancement d'un produit)

launch² *vt* (shares) émettre; (product) lancer, lancer sur le marché; (ship) lancer, mettre à l'eau; (campaign, career, company, project) lancer; (investigation) ouvrir; (computer program) lancer; (plan) mettre en action; ∼ **an appeal** (to public) lancer un appel; ∼ **a bond issue** émettre des obligations; ∼ **a national campaign** lancer une campagne nationale; ∼ **sth on the market** lancer qch sur le marché; ∼ **a takeover bid for a company** lancer une OPA contre une société

launching *n* lancement *m*

launder *vt* (money) blanchir

laundering *n* (of money) blanchiment *m*

laundry list *n* liste détaillée des priorités *f*

law *n* (academic discipline) droit *m*; (rule, body of rules) loi *f*; (principle) loi *f*; **be against the ∼** être interdit; **break/obey the ∼** enfreindre/ respecter la loi; **study ∼** faire son droit; **by ∼** conformément à la loi; **a ∼ against** une loi interdisant; **the bill became ∼** le projet de loi a été adopté; **as the ∼ stands at present** en l'état actuel de la législation; **in the eyes of the ∼** au regard de la loi, en vertu de la loi; **keep within the ∼** rester dans la légalité; **under European ∼** d'après la loi européenne; ∼**-abiding** *adj* respectueux/-euse des lois; ∼ **of comparative advantage** loi de l'avantage comparatif *f*; ∼**court** *n* tribunal *m*; ∼ **of diminishing marginal utility** loi de l'utilité marginale décroissante *f*; ∼ **of diminishing returns** loi des rendements décroissants *f*; ∼ **firm** *n*, ∼ **practice** *n* cabinet d'avocats *m*; ∼ **school** *n* faculté de droit *f*; ∼ **of supply and demand** loi de l'offre et de la demande *f*

lawful *adj* légal; ∼ **means** *n pl* moyens légaux *m pl*

lawfully *adv* légalement

lawfulness *n* légalité *f*

lawsuit *n* procès *m*; **bring a ∼ against sb** intenter un procès à qn

lawyer *n* avocat/-e *m/f*

lay¹ *adj* non initié, profane; ∼ **members** *n pl* (Law) assesseurs non juristes *m pl*; ∼ **official** *n* délégué/-e syndical/-e *m/f*; ∼ **person** *n* profane *mf*

lay² *vt* (charge, accusation) porter; (plans) préparer; (foundations) poser; (put forward) soumettre; ∼ **the basis for** jeter les bases de; ∼ **claim to** avoir des prétentions à, revendiquer; ∼ **down the rules** imposer des règles; ∼ **the emphasis on** insister sur; ∼ **the ground for sth** préparer le terrain pour qch; ∼ **a proposal before a committee** soumettre une proposition à une commission; ∼ **sth on for sb** préparer qch pour qn; ∼ **down** (laws) imposer, stipuler, établir; ∼ **off** (permanently) licencier; (temporarily) mettre en chômage technique; ∼ **out** (amount, sum) dépenser

layday *n* jour de planche *m*, starie *f*

layer *n* couche *f*

laying off *n* (permanently) licenciement *m*; (temporarily) mise en chômage technique *f*

lay off *n* (temporary) mise en chômage technique *f*; (permanent) licenciement *m*; ∼ **pay** *n* prime de licenciement *f*

layout *n* (of shop, building) agencement *m*; (of report, article) présentation *f*; (of page, magazine, word-processed document) mise en page *f*; (of town, estate) plan *m*; (of furniture) disposition *f*

laytime *n* temps de planche *m*; **all ∼ saved** (shipping) estaries gagnées *f pl*

LBO *abbr* (▸**leveraged buyout**) rachat d'entreprise financé par l'endettement *m*

L/C *abbr* (▸**letter of credit**) L/C (lettre de crédit)

LCCI *abbr* (▸**London Chamber of Commerce & Industry**) Chambre de commerce et d'industrie de Londres *f*

LCD *abbr* (▸**lowest common denominator**) plus petit dénominateur commun *m*

ld *abbr* (▸**load**) charge *f*

ldg *abbr* (▸**loading**) chargement *m*; ∼ **& dly** (**loading and delivery**) chargement et livraison

lead¹ *n* (main story) article de tête *m*; (competitive advantage) avance *f*; (initiative) initiative *f*; **be in the ∼** être en tête, mener; **go into the ∼** passer en tête; **have a 10 point ∼** avoir 10 points d'avance; **take the ∼** (get ahead) prendre les devants; (take the initiative) prendre l'initiative; **take the ∼ in doing sth** être le premier à faire qch; **follow sb's ∼** suivre l'exemple de qn; **give the ∼** donner l'exemple; ∼ **bank** *n* banque chef de file *f*; ∼ **contractor** *n* (in building) maître d'œuvre *m*; ∼ **management** *n* management directif *m*; ∼ **story** *n* article qui fait la une *m*, leader *m*; ∼ **time** *n* délai de mise en œuvre *m*; (of stock) délai de réapprovisionnement *m*; (in delivery) délai de livraison *m*; (in production) délai de fabrication *m*; (of plan) délai de réalisation *m*, délai de suite *m*, temps de latence *m*; (of new product) délai de démarrage *m*, délai de mise en production *m*; **~-time delay** *n* retard d'introduction *m*

lead² **1** *vt* (guide, escort) mener; (team, strike, investigation proceedings) mener; (research) diriger; (cause) **~ sb to do** amener qn à faire; **~ the world** être au premier rang mondial; **~ the market** être le numéro un du marché; **~ the way in biotechnology** être le numéro un de la biotechnologie **2** *vi* (be ahead) être en tête; (go first) prendre l'initiative; **~ for the defence** UK, **~ for the defense** US être l'avocat principal de la défense; **~ with a story** mettre une histoire à la une; **~ to** (difficulties, discovery, accident) entraîner; **~ up to** précéder

leader *n* (of team, group) chef *m*, dirigeant/-e *m/f*, leader *m*; (of project, operation) directeur/-trice *m/f*; (of strike) meneur/-euse *m/f*; (Ins) apériteur *m*, assureur principal *m*; UK (Law) avocat/-e principal/-e *m/f*; BrE (editorial) leader *m*; (Pol) chef d'État *m*; (in market) leader *m*; US (loss leader) produit d'appel *m*; (Stock) valeur vedette *f*; **~ application** (Comp) application vedette *f*; **~ pricing** *n* vente à perte *f*, vente à prix sacrifié *f*; **~ writer** *n* éditorialiste *mf*

leaders and laggards *n pl* valeurs vedettes et titres à la traîne *m pl*

leadership *n* commandement *m*, direction *f*; **the ~** la direction *f*, les dirigeants *m pl*; **under the ~ of** sous la direction de; **during his/her ~** pendant son mandat; **have ~ qualities** avoir des qualités de leader, avoir des qualités de chef

lead-free *adj* sans plomb; **~ petrol** *n* essence sans plomb *f*

leading *adj* (lawyer, consultant) éminent; (make, brand) dominant; (position) de premier plan; (role) principal; **a ~ player** un acteur majeur; **play a ~ role in** jouer un rôle majeur dans; **a ~ software house** un des éditeurs de logiciel les plus importants; **~ article** *n* UK article qui fait la une *m*, leader *m*; **~ indicator** *n* indicateur avancé de tendance *m*; **~ industries** *n pl* industries de pointe *f pl*; **~ line** *n* articles en réclame *m pl*; **~ stock** *n* valeur vedette *f*; **~ underwriter** *n* apériteur *m*

leading-edge *n* avant-garde *f*; **be at the ~ of technology** être à la pointe de la technologie; **~ technology/technique** technologie/technique de pointe *f*

leads and lags *n pl* meneurs et traînards *m pl*

leaf *n* (of cheque book) volant *m*; (of paper) feuille *f*; (page) page *f*

league *n* catégorie *f*, classe *f*; **be out of**

one's **~** ne pas faire le poids; **be top of the export ~** être en tête de liste des exportateurs; **~ table** *n* classement *m*

leak¹ *n* (of substance, information) fuite *f*

leak² **1** *vt* (substance) répandre; (information) divulguer **2** *vi* fuire

leakage *n* fuite *f*

lean *adj* (company) dégraissé; **~ management** *n* encadrement réduit *m*; **~ production** *n* production à flux tendus *f*; **~ workforce** *n* main-d'œuvre réduite *f*, main-d'œuvre dégraissée *f*; **~ year** *n* année de vaches maigres *f*, année difficile *f*

lean-back medium *n* (Media) médium passif *m*

lean-forward medium *n* (Media) médium interactif *m*

leaning *n* tendance *f*; **a ~ towards** une tendance à

leap¹ *n* (in prices, demand) bond *m*; **~ year** *n* année bissextile *f*

leap²: **~ up** *vi* (prices, profits, shares) faire un bond

leapfrog *vt* (rival, competitor) devancer

learn *vt* (facts, language) apprendre; (skill) acquérir; **~ the ropes** acquérir de l'expérience

learning *n* apprentissage *m*; **~ curve** *n* courbe d'apprentissage *f*

lease¹ *n* bail *m*, contrat de bail *m*; **take out a ~ on a flat** prendre un appartement à bail; **~ agreement** *n* contrat de location *m*; **~ company** *n* société de leasing *f*; **~-lend** *n* prêt-bail *m*; **~ option** *n* bail avec option d'achat *m*; **~ term** *n* durée de bail *f*

lease² *vt* (property) louer à bail; (car) louer; **~ out** (property) louer à bail

leaseback *n* cession-bail *f*

leased *adj* loué à bail; **~ line** *n* ligne louée *f*, ligne spécialisée *f*

leasehold *n* (contract) droit de bail *m*; **~ mortgage** *n* hypothèque sur bien loué *f*; **~ property** *n* propriété louée *f*, propriété à bail *f*

leaseholder *n* locataire à bail *mf*

leasing *n* crédit-bail *m*, leasing *m*; **~ agreement** *n* contrat de crédit-bail *m*; **~ company** *n*, **~ corporation** *n* société de crédit-bail *f*

least: **~-cost** *n* moindre coût *m*; **~-cost planning** *n* planification à moindre coût *f*; **~-favored regions** AmE, **~-favoured regions** BrE *n pl* régions les plus défavorisées *f pl*

leather goods *n pl* articles en cuir *m pl*, maroquinerie *f*

leave¹ *n* congé *m*; **be on ~** être en congé; **~ of absence** congé spécial *m*

leave² **1** *vt* (let remain, leave behind) laisser; (job, place) quitter; (money, property) laisser, ···⊱

léguer; ~ **sb in the lurch** (infrml) laisser qn en plan (infrml); ~ **the matter open** laisser la question en suspens; ~ **sth up to sb** laisser qch à qn; ~ **it up to sb to do** laisser à qn le soin de faire

2 vi partir, s'en aller; ~ **behind** (competition) distancer; **get left behind** se laisser distancer; ~ **out** oublier; (deliberately) omettre, exclure

lecture n (public talk) conférence f; (at university) cours m

lecturer n (speaker) conférencier/-ière m/f; (at university) UK enseignant/-e (du supérieur) m/f; US chargé de cours m

LED abbr (▸**light-emitting diode**) DEL f (diode électroluminescente)

ledger n grand livre m; ~ **account** n compte de grand livre m; ~ **balance** n solde d'un compte du grand livre m

left[1] adj gauche

left[2] n gauche f

left[3] adv à gauche

left: ~**-of-center** AmE, ~**-of-centre** BrE adj (Pol) centre-gauche; ~ **column** n colonne de gauche f; ~**-hand** adj de gauche; ~**-hand column** n colonne de gauche f; ~**-hand drive automobile** n AmE, ~**-hand drive car** n BrE voiture avec la conduite à gauche f; ~**-luggage locker** n BrE consigne automatique f; ~**-luggage office** n BrE consigne f; ~**-wing** adj (Pol) de gauche

left-click vi cliquer en appuyant sur le bouton gauche de la souris

leftism n gauchisme m

left-justify vt justifier à gauche

legacy n héritage m, legs m; ~ **application** n application héritée f; ~ **currency** n (EU) ancienne monnaie nationale f; ~ **data** n données existantes f pl; ~ **duty** n BrE droits de succession m pl, impôt sur les successions m; ~ **software** n logiciel hérité du passé m; ~ **system** n système informatique hérité du passé m; ~ **tax** n AmE droits de succession m pl, impôt sur les successions m

legal adj (error, investigation, power) judiciaire; (owner, claim) légitime; (recognized by law) légal; (relating to law) juridique; ~ **action** n action en justice f; ~ **advice** n conseil juridique m; ~ **adviser**, ~ **advisor** n avocat-conseil m, avocate-conseil f, conseiller/-ère juridique m/f; ~ **aid** n aide juridique f; ~ **charges** n pl frais de justice m pl; ~ **claim** n créance légitime f, revendication légitime f; ~ **costs** n pl (awarded by the court) frais et dépens m pl; ~ **department** n (for complaints) service du contentieux m; (for legal queries) service juridique m; ~ **document** n acte authentique m; ~ **effect** n effet juridique m; ~ **entity** n entité juridique f, personne morale f; ~ **expenses** n pl frais de justice m pl; ~ **fees** n pl honoraires d'avocat m pl; ~ **force** n force de loi f; ~ **formalities** n pl formalités juridiques f pl, formalités légales f

pl; ~ **framework** n cadre juridique m; ~ **harmonization** n (EU) harmonisation du droit f, harmonisation juridique f; ~ **holiday** n AmE jour férié m; ~ **immunity** n immunité légale f; ~ **liability** n responsabilité légale f; ~ **name** n nom légal m; ~ **notice** n notification requise par la loi f, préavis légal m; ~ **obligation** n obligation juridique f, obligation légale f; ~ **opinion** n avis de droit m, avis motivé d'un avocat m, avis juridique m; ~ **person** n personne morale f; ~ **practitioner** n homme de loi m; ~ **proceedings** n pl action en justice f, poursuites judiciaires f pl, procès m; ~ **redress** n réparation en justice f, réparation légale f; ~ **representative** n représentant légal m; ~ **requirement** n condition légale requise f, obligation légale f; ~ **residence** n domicile légal m; ~ **right** n droit légal m, droit reconnu légalement m; ~ **separation** n séparation légale f; ~ **services** n pl services juridiques m pl; ~ **settlement** n règlement judiciaire m; ~ **standing** n situation juridique f; ~ **status** n statut légal m; ~ **system** n système juridique m

legalistic adj légaliste

legality n légalité f

legalization n légalisation f

legalize vt légaliser

legally adv (valid, void) juridiquement; (work, buy, import, sell) légalement; (act) conformément à la loi; ~ **binding** adj (agreement) qui engage; ~ **bound** adj tenu par la loi

legal tender n cours légal m, monnaie légale f; **be** ~ avoir cours légal

legatee n légataire mf

legislate vi légiférer

legislation n loi f, législation f

legislative adj législatif/-ive; ~ **body** n corps législatif m; ~ **power** n pouvoir législatif m

legislator n législateur/-trice m/f

legislature n corps législatif m

leisure n (spare time) temps libre m, loisirs m pl; (activities) loisirs m pl; ~ **center** AmE, ~ **centre** BrE n centre de loisirs m; ~ **facilities** n pl installations de loisirs f pl; ~ **industry** n industrie des loisirs f; ~ **time** n temps libre m

lend 1 vt (money, item) prêter; (confer) conférer; ~ **weight to** (argument) donner du poids à; ~ **one's name to** prêter son nom à; ~ **support to sb** soutenir qn; ~ **one's support to a venture** prêter son concours à une entreprise

2 vi ~ **against security** prêter contre titre, prêter sur nantissement; ~ **on security** prêter sur gage, prêter sur nantissement

lendable adj prêtable

lender n prêteur/-euse m/f; ~ **of last resort** prêteur/-euse de dernier ressort m/f

lending n prêt m; ~ **business** n opérations

de prêt *f pl*; **∼ ceiling** *n* plafond de crédit *m*; **∼ institution** *n* institution de crédit *f*, institution de prêt *f*, établissement de crédit *m*; **∼ limit** *n* plafond d'endettement *m*; **∼ policy** *n* politique de prêt *f*; **∼ rate** *n* taux de prêt *m*

length *n* (measurement) longueur *f*; (duration) durée *f*; **be 15cm in ∼** faire 15 cm de long; durée de service *f*; **at ∼** (for a long time) longuement; **go to great ∼s to do sth** se donner beaucoup de mal pour faire qch; **go to the ∼s of doing** aller jusqu'à faire; **∼ of service** ancienneté *f*

lengthen ⚊1⚊ *vt* (list, waiting time, working hours) allonger; (stay, visit) prolonger ⚊2⚊ *vi* (queue, list) s'allonger; (visit) se prolonger

less¹ *adv* moins; **∼ and ∼** de moins en moins

less² *prep* moins; **∼ 5% discount** moins 5% de remise; **£3,000 ∼ tax** 3 000 livres sterling avant impôts

lessee *n* locataire à bail *mf*, preneur à bail *m*

lesser *adj* moindre; **to a ∼ extent** à un moindre degré

lessor *n* bailleur/-eresse *m/f*

let¹ *n* UK location *f*

let² *vt* (rent) BrE louer; (allow) laisser, **∼ sb do sth** laisser qn faire qch; **∼ out a contract to** passer un contrat avec; **'to ∼'** BrE 'à louer'

let-out *n* (infrml) échappatoire *f*, **∼ clause** *n* (Law) clause dérogatoire *f*

letter *n* (item of mail) lettre *f*; (of accommodation) loueur *m*; **to the ∼** à la lettre; **∼ of advice** *n* lettre d'avis *f*; **∼ of allotment** *n* (stock exchange) avis d'attribution d'actions *m*; **∼ of apology** *n* lettre d'excuse *f*; **∼ of application** *n* (from investor) lettre de souscription *f*; (from candidate) lettre de candidature *f*; **∼ of appointment** *n* lettre de nomination *f*; **∼ of assignment** *n* avis de cession *m*; **∼ of attorney** *n* procuration *f*; **∼ of authority** *n* lettre d'autorité *f*; **∼ of comfort** *n* lettre d'accord *f*; **∼ of consent** *n* lettre de consentement *f*; **∼ of credit** *n* lettre de crédit *f*; **∼ of indemnity** *n* caution *f*, lettre de garantie *f*; **∼ of inquiry** *n* lettre de demande de renseignements *f*; **∼ of intent** *n* lettre de déclaration d'intention *f*, lettre d'intention *f*; **∼ of introduction** *n* lettre d'introduction *f*, lettre de recommandation *f*; **∼ of recommendation** *n* lettre de recommandation *f*; **∼ of resignation** *n* lettre de démission *f*

lettering *n* caractères *m pl*

letters patent *n pl* lettres patentes *f pl*

letting *n* (of an apartment) location *f*; **∼ agency** *n* agence de location *f*

level¹ *adj* (stable) stable; **be ∼** (competitors, rivals) être à égalité; **remain ∼** (growth, figures) rester stable; **compete on a ∼ playing field** être sur un pied d'égalité

level² *n* (amount) niveau *m*; (of spending) montant *m*; (of satisfaction, anxiety) degré *m*; (of unemployment, crime) taux *m*; (percentage) taux *m*; (rank) niveau *m*, échelon *m*; (plane) plan *m*; (standard, quality) qualité *f*; **on a practical ∼** sur le plan pratique; **at a regional/national ∼** au plan régional/national; **at managerial ∼** au niveau de la direction; **∼ of quality** qualité *f*; **∼ of service** qualité du service *f*; **come down to sb's ∼** se mettre au niveau de qn; **be on the ∼** (infrml) être réglo (infrml); **∼ of expenditure** niveau de dépenses *m*; **∼ of investment** niveau d'investissement *m*; **∼ of orders** niveau de commandes *m*; **∼ repayment** *n* remboursement en tranches égales *m*; **∼ of support** niveau de soutien *m*

level³ *vt* **∼ criticism at** critiquer; **∼ off, ∼ out** (number, quantity, amount, growth, prices) se stabiliser; **∼ with sb** être honnête avec qn

level-headed *adj* (person, analysis) calme

leveling AmE, **levelling** BrE *n* nivellement *m*; **∼-off** *n* stabilisation *f*; **∼-out** *n* nivellement *m*

lever *n* levier financier *m*

leverage¹ *n* (Fin) AmE effet d'endettement *m*, effet de levier *m*; (Pol) force d'appui *f*, pression indirecte *f*; **∼ adjustment** *n* redressement du taux d'endettement *m*, redressement financier *m*; **∼ ratio** *n* ratio d'endettement *m*, ratio de levier *m*, taux d'endettement *m*

leverage²: **∼ up** *vi* augmenter le ratio d'endettement

leveraged: ∼ bid *n* (Stock) offre indexée *f*; **∼ buyout** *n* rachat d'entreprise financé par l'endettement *m*; **∼ company** *n* entreprise fortement endettée *f*; **∼ lease** *n* location endettée *f*; **∼ management buy-in** *n* rachat d'une entreprise par des investisseurs *m*; **∼ management buyout** *n* rachat d'une entreprise par ses salariés *m*; **∼ stock** *n* actions achetées à crédit *f pl*, valeur de croissance *f*

levy¹ *n* (act) perception *f*; (tax, duty) impôt *m*, taxe *f*; **import ∼** taxe à l'importation *f*; **agricultural ∼** prélèvement agricole *m*; **∼ of taxes** prélèvement d'impôts *m*

levy² *vt* (Law) réquisitionner, saisir; (Tax) lever, percevoir, prélever; (fine) imposer; **∼ a tax on sb/sth** prélever une taxe sur qn/qch

levying *n* levée *f*; **∼ of taxes** prélèvement d'impôts *m*

lh *abbr* (Acc, Fin) (▶**last half**) dernière quinzaine *f*

L/I *abbr* (▶**letter of indemnity**) lettre de garantie *f*

liabilities *n pl* (Gen Comm) dettes *f pl*; (on balance sheet) passif *m*; **meet one's ∼** faire face à ses engagements financiers

liability *n* (Fin) charge *f*; (responsibility) responsabilité *f*; (burden) handicap *m*; **without any ∼ on our part** sans engagement de notre part; **accept ∼ for sth** accepter la ⋯▶

responsabilitié de qch; **to deny ∼ for**
décliner toute responsabilité en ce qui
concerne; **∼ cost** n (Stock) coût d'obligation
m, frais d'engagement m pl; **∼ for tax**
assujettissement à l'impôt m; **∼ insurance**
n assurance responsabilité civile f; **∼ item** n
poste de passif m; **∼ ledger** n registre des
créances m; **∼ management** n gestion du
passif f; **∼ no-fault automobile insurance**
n US assurance responsabilité civile
automobile sans égard au responsable f

liable adj (Law) responsable; **be ∼ for duty**
être assujetti à des droits; **be ∼ for damages**
être tenu de payer des dommages et intérêts;
be ∼ for tax (person, business) être imposable;
(goods, property) être soumis à l'impôt; **∼ to**
sujet/-ette à; **be ∼ to do** (person) être sujet à
faire; (thing) être susceptible de faire; **be ∼ to
a fine** être passible d'amende; **be ∼ to a
penalty** être passible d'une pénalité; **be ∼ to
prosecution** être passible de prosécution; **be
held ∼ for sth** être tenu responsable de qch;
the contract is ∼ to changes le contrat peut
faire l'objet de modifications

liaise vi travailler en liaison; **∼ with**
travailler en liaison avec

liaison n liaison f; **in ∼ with** en liaison
avec; **∼ committee** n comité de liaison m

libel¹ n (Law) diffamation f; (publication) écrit
diffamatoire m; **∼ laws** n pl lois contre la
diffamation f pl; **∼ proceedings** n pl
poursuites en diffamation f pl, procès en
diffamation m

libel² vt diffamer

libelous AmE, **libellous** BrE adj
diffamatoire

liberal adj libéral

Liberal n libéral m

liberalism n libéralisme m

liberalization n libéralisation f; **∼ of
trade** libéralisation du commerce f

liberalize vt libéraliser

liberty n liberté f; **at ∼** en liberté

LIBID abbr (▸**London Interbank Bid
Rate**) taux d'emprunt interbancaire de
Londres m

LIBOR abbr (▸**London Interbank Offered
Rate**) TIOL m (taux interbancaire offert à
Londres)

library n bibliothèque f

licence n BrE (permission) autorisation f; (to
make, sell, use product) licence f; (for TV)
redevance f; (Patents) licence f; (for driver, gun,
hunting) permis m; **under ∼** sous licence; **∼
holder** n détenteur/-trice d'une licence m

licensable adj (Imp/Exp) nécessitant une
licence

license¹ n AmE ▸**licence** BrE

license² vt (authorize) autoriser; (vehicle) faire
immatriculer; (gun, equipment) obtenir un
permis pour; **∼ sb to do** autoriser qn à faire

licensed adj autorisé; (Law, Patents)

breveté, patenté; (production) sous licence;
(dealer) agréé; (vehicle) en règle; (TV, gun)
déclaré; (club) qui a une licence de débit de
boissons; (pilot, operator) breveté; **∼ premises**
n pl débit de boissons m

licensee n titulaire d'une licence mf

licensing n (Admin) autorisation f; (granting
of manufacture rights) octroi de licence m;
(practice) pratique de fabrication sous licence
f; **∼ agreement** n accord de cession de
licence m; **∼ laws** n pl lois relatives à
l'octroi de licences f pl; (for alcohol sales) lois
réglementant la vente des boissons
alcoolisées f pl

licensor n (Patents) organisme délivrant les
licences m

LICOM abbr (▸**London Interbank
Currency Options Market**) marché
interbancaire des options sur devises de
Londres m

lien n droit de rétention m

lieu n: **in ∼ of** au lieu de, à la place de; **∼
days** n pl journées de remplacement f pl

life¹ adj (member, membership, peerage) à vie;
(ban) définitif/-ive

life² n vie f; (validity of policy, contract) durée f;
(of equipment) durée de vie f; **a job for ∼** un
emploi à vie; **working/private ∼** vie
professionnelle/personnelle f

life: ∼ annuitant n rentier viager m; **∼
assurance** n BrE assurance-vie f; **∼
assurance policy** n BrE police d'assurance-
vie f; **∼ assurer** n assureur-vie m; **∼ cycle**
n cycle de vie m; **∼ estate** n immobilier en
viager m; **∼ event** n événement de la vie m;
∼ expectancy n (of machine) durée probable
de vie f; (of person) espérance de vie f; **∼
insurance** n assurance-vie f; **∼ insurance
company** n compagnie d'assurance-vie f; **∼
insurance policy** n police d'assurance sur
la vie f; **∼ insurance premium** n prime
d'assurance-vie f; **∼ insurer** n assureur-vie
m; **∼ interest** n (Law) usufruit m; **∼
savings** n pl épargne d'une vie f; **∼
tenancy** n bail à vie m, usufruit m

lifeless adj (Stock) inanimé

lifestyle n style de vie m, mode de vie m; **∼
concept** n concept des styles de vie m; **∼
product** n produit ciblé pour un mode de vie
m; **∼ segmentation** m segmentation des
styles de vie f

lifetime n (Comp, Stock) durée de vie f; (of
person) vie f

LIFFE abbr (▸**London International
Financial Futures Exchange**) ≈ MATIF m
(Marché à terme d'instruments financiers)

LIFO abbr (▸**last in, first out**) DEPS
(dernier entré, premier sorti)

lift¹ n BrE ascenseur m

lift² vt (ban, sanctions) lever; (control, restriction)
abolir, supprimer; AmE (mortgage) purger

lifting n (of ban, sanction), levée f; (of control,

restriction) suppression *f*

light¹ *adj* (interest) faible; **trading is ~** le volume de transactions est faible

light² *n* **bring to ~** révéler; **shed new ~ on sth** éclairer qch d'un jour nouveau; **in the ~ of** compte tenu de; **see sth in a different ~** voir qch sous un jour différent

light: **~-emitting diode** *n* diode électroluminescente *f*; **~ engineering** *n* industrie mécanique légère *f*; **~ industry** *n* industrie légère *f*; **~ pen** *n* photostyle *m*, crayon optique *m*

lightning strike *n* grève surprise *f*, grève éclair *f*

likelihood *n* probabilité *f*

likely *adj* probable; (explanation) plausible; (candidate) prometteur/-euse; (customer, client) potentiel/-ielle; **be ~ to fail** risquer d'échouer; **be ~ to succeed** avoir des chances de réussir; **~ outcome** *n* issue probable *f*, résultat probable *m*

limit¹ *n* (boundary) limite *f*; (of costs, prices) limite *f*; (restriction) limitation *f*; (Stock) limite *f*, ordre à cours limité *m*; **set a ~ on** limiter; **within ~s** dans une certaine mesure; **~ order** *n* ordre limité *m*, ordre à cours limité *m*; **~ price** *n* prix plafond *m*

limit² *vt* limiter; **~ the number of** limiter le nombre de; **be ~ed to doing** se limiter à faire; **~ oneself to** se limiter à

limitation *n* limitation *f*, limite *f*

limited *adj* limité; (choice, range) restreint, limité; **~ audit** *n* audit restreint *m*; **~ company** *n* UK compagnie limitée *f*, société anonyme *f*; **~ edition** *n* édition à tirage limité *f*; **~ liability company** *n* BrE société à responsabilité limitée *f*; **~ market** *n* marché étroit *m*; **~ order** *n* ordre à cours limité *m*; **~ owner** *n* propriétaire usufruitier *m*; **~ partner** *n* associé/-e commanditaire *m/f*, commandiraire *mf*; **~ partnership** *n* société en commandite *f*; **~ policy** *n* police limitée *f*; **~ term** *n* durée limitée *f*

limiting *adj* restrictif/-ive

line *n* (mark) ligne *f*; (Comms, Comp) ligne *f*; (stance) position *f*; AmE (queue) file d'attente *f*, queue *f*; (HRM) (workers) opérationnels *m pl*; (of products) gamme *f*, ligne *f*; (Transp) (route) ligne *f*; (track) voie *f*; (field of work) métier *m*; (of text) ligne *f*; **the official ~** la position officielle; **bring into ~** réaligner; **be in ~ with** (trend, policy, requirement) être en accord avec; (inflation) être proportionnel à; (expectations) être conforme à; **increase/fall in ~ with** augmenter/baisser proportionnellement à; **vary in ~ with** varier parallèlement à; **wait in ~** faire la queue; **be in ~ for promotion** avoir des chances d'être promu; **be in ~ for the post of** être bien placé pour obtenir le poste de; **have a ~ on** avoir des informations sur; **give sb a ~ on** donner un tuyau à qn sur; **fall into ~ with** être d'accord avec; **be on the right ~s** être sur la bonne voie; **~**

assistant *n* attaché/-e opérationnel/-elle *m/f*; **~ of attack** *n* angle d'attaque *m*; **~ authority** *n* autorité hiérarchique *f*; **~ of command** *n* voie hiérarchique *f*; **~ of credit** *n* autorisation de crédit *f*, crédit autorisé *m*; **~ executive** *n* dirigeant/-e opérationnel/-elle *m/f*; **~ extension** *n* élargissement de la gamme *m*; **~ management** *n* (managers) responsables opérationnels *m pl*; (system) direction hiérarchique *f*; **~ manager** *n* directeur/ -trice hiérarchique *m/f*, responsable opérationnel/-elle *m/f*; **~ organization** *n* organisation hiérarchique *f*, organisation verticale *f*; **~ production** *n* production à la chaîne *f*; **~ and staff organization** *n* organisation mixte *f*, structure mixte *f*; **~ supervisor** *n* agent de maîtrise *m*, contremaître *m*, superviseur de premier niveau *m*; **~ of work** métier *m*

lineage *n* (Media) tarif à la ligne *m*

linear *adj* linéaire; **~ measure** *n* mesure linéaire *f*; **~ program** AmE, **~ programme** BrE (Econ) *n* programme linéaire *m*; **~ programming** *n* programmation linéaire *f*; **~ regression** *n* régression linéaire *f*; **~ relationship** *n* relation linéaire *f*; **~ responsibility** *n* responsabilité hiérarchique *f*

liner *n* liner *m*, navire de ligne *m*

link¹ *n* (in trade) relation *f*; (historical, friendly) lien *m*; (between facts, events) rapport *m*; (Comp) liaison *f*; (on web page) lien *m*; (Media, Transp) liaison *f*; **~ page** *n* page de lien *f*; **~ word** *n* (Comp) hypermot *m*

link² *vt* (Comp) connecter; (physically) relier; (establish a connection) lier; (TV, radio) établir une liaison entre; (Stock) lier; **~ sth to sth** (Gen Comm) lier qch à qch, établir un lien entre qch et qch; (index) indexer qch sur qch; **~ sth to inflation** indexer qch sur l'inflation; **~ up** s'associer; **~ up with** s'associer avec

linkage *n* liaison *f*, lien *m*; (in international relations) association *f*; **~ models** *n pl* modèles macro-économiques comparatifs *m pl*

linked *adj* lié; (Stock) indexé

lion's share *n* part du lion *f*

liquid¹ *adj* liquide; (funds) liquide

liquid² *n* liquide *m*

liquid: **~ assets** *n pl* actif disponible *m*, disponibilités *f pl*, liquidités *f pl*; **~ capital** *n* capital liquide *m*; **~ debt** *n* dette liquide *f*; **~ funds** *n pl* disponibilités *f pl*, fonds disponibles *m pl*; **~ measure** *n* mesure de capacité liquide *f*; **~ petroleum gas** *n* gaz de pétrole liquéfié *m*; **~ ratio** *n* taux de liquidité *m*, taux des disponibilités *m*, taux disponible *m*; **~ savings** *n pl* épargne liquide *f*; **~ securities** *n* valeurs liquides *f pl*

liquidate **1** *vt* (capital) mobiliser; (debt) liquider, amortir; (assets, stock, company)

liquider
2 *vi* entrer en liquidation
liquidated *adj* (options) liquidé; ~
damages *n pl* dommages-intérêts liquidés *m*
pl; ~ **debt** *n* dette amortie *f*
liquidation *n* (of company, stock) liquidation
f; (of capital) mobilisation *f*; (of debt)
remboursement *m*; **go into voluntary** ~
déposer son bilan; ~ **dividend** *n* dividende
de liquidation *m*
liquidator *n* liquidateur *m*
liquidities *n pl* liquidités *f pl*
liquidity *n* liquidité *f*; ~ **crisis** *n* manque
de liquidités *m*; ~ **preference** *n* préférence
pour la liquidité *f*; ~ **problems** *n pl*
problèmes de liquidité *m pl*; ~ **ratio** *n*
coefficient de liquidité *m*; ~ **squeeze** *n*
compression des liquidités *f*
liquidization *n* liquidation *f*
lira *n* lire *f*
list¹ *n* liste *f*; **make a** ~ faire une liste; **draw
up a** ~ dresser une liste; ~ **administrator**
n gestionnaire de listes de diffusion *mf*; ~
broker *n* courtier en fichiers *m*; ~
brokering *n* courtage en fichiers *m*; ~ **price**
n prix catalogue *m*, prix au catalogue *m*
list² *vt* faire la liste de; (Comp) lister; (Stock)
coter, inscrire à la cote
listed *adj* (on stock exchange) coté en bourse,
inscrit à la cote; ~ **at** coté à; ~ **company** *n*
société cotée en bourse *f*; ~ **security** *n*
valeur cotée en bourse *f*, valeur inscrite à la
cote *f*; ~ **share** *n* action cotée *f*, action
inscrite à la cote officielle *f*
listeners' habits *n pl* habitudes d'écoute
f pl
listening time *n* heure d'écoute *f*
listing *n* (Comp) listage *m*, listing *m*; (Fin)
inscription *f*; (on stock exchange) cotation *f*; ~
application *n* demande d'inscription à la
cote *f*; ~ **requirements** *n pl* conditions
requises pour la cotation *f pl*
listless *adj* (market, trading) sans ressort
literature *n* (S&M) documentation *f*; **sales**
~ brochures publicitaires *f pl*,
documentation publicitaire *f*; ~ **search** *n*
recherche documentaire *f*
litigant *n* plaideur/-euse *m/f*, partie en litige
f
litigate 1 *vt* contester
2 *vi* plaider
litigation *n* litige *m*
live¹ *adj* en direct; ~ **broadcast** *n* émission
en direct *f*; ~ **program** AmE, ~ **programme**
BrE *n* émission en direct *f*
live² *vi* vivre; ~ **beyond one's means** vivre
au-dessus de ses moyens; ~ **off**, ~ **on**
(interest, profits) vivre de; (wage) vivre de; ~
with (situation, consequences) accepter; ~ **up to**
(standards) être fidèle à; (expectations) répondre
à; (reputation) mériter
lively *adj* (stock market) animé, actif/-ive;

(campaign) percutant; (account, style) vivant;
(place) animé
livestock *n* bétail *m*
living *n* vie *f*; **work for a** ~ travailler pour
gagner sa vie; **make a** ~ gagner sa vie; ~
conditions *n pl* conditions de vie *f pl*; ~
expenses *n pl* frais de séjour *m pl*; ~
space *n* espace vital *m*; ~ **standards** *n pl*
niveau de vie *m*; ~ **wage** *n* minimum vital
m
LLB *abbr* (▸**Bachelor of Laws**) (degree) ≈
licence de droit *f*
LLD *abbr* (▸**Doctor of Laws**) docteur en
droit *m*
Lloyd's: ~ **Agent** *n* agent de la Lloyds *m*;
~ **List** *n publication quotidienne du Lloyd's
indiquant les mouvements de navire*; ~
member *n* assureur Lloyd's *m*; ~ **Register**
n registre du Lloyd's *m*; ~ **Underwriting
Agents' Association** *n association des
agents souscripteurs du Lloyd's*
LMBI *abbr* (▸**leveraged management
buy-in**) REI *m* (rachat d'une entreprise par
des investisseurs)
LMBO *abbr* (▸**leveraged management
buyout**) RES *m* (rachat d'une entreprise par
ses salariés)
LM curve *n* courbe LM *f*
LME *abbr* (▸**London Metal Exchange**)
Bourse des métaux de Londres *f*
load¹ *n* (on vehicle) chargement *m*; (on plane,
ship) cargaison *f*; (workload) travail *m*, tâche *f*;
(weight) charge *f*; ~ **factor** *n* (in manufacturing)
facteur de charge *m*; (Transp) coefficient de
remplissage *m*; (for airline) taux de remplissage
m; ~ **line** *n* (Transp) ligne de charge *f*
load² *vt* (Transp) charger; (software) charger;
(Ins) (premium) majorer
loading *n* (Transp) chargement *m*; (Comp)
chargement *m*; (Ins) majoration *f*; ~ **agent** *n*
chargeur *m*; ~ **bay** *n* aire de chargement *f*;
~ **dock** *n* quai de chargement *m*
loan *n* (money borrowed) emprunt *m*; (money
lent) prêt *m*; **make a** ~ **to sb** accorder un prêt
à qn, consentir un prêt à qn; ~ **account** *n*
compte d'avances *m*, compte de prêts *m*; ~
agreement *n* contrat de prêt *m*; ~
application *n* demande de prêt *f*; ~ **capital**
n capital d'emprunt *m*; (Stock) capital
obligations *m*; ~ **company** *n* société de
crédit *f*; ~ **department** *n* service du crédit
m; ~ **exposure** *n* risque du crédit *m*; ~ **fee**
n commission de montage *f*, frais de montage
m pl; ~ **holder** *n* détenteur/-trice d'un prêt
m/f; ~ **insurance** *n* assurance de crédit *f*; ~
loss *n* perte sur prêts *f*; ~ **market** *n*
marché du crédit *m*; ~ **recipient** *n*
bénéficiaire d'un prêt *mf*; ~ **recovery** *n*
recouvrement de prêt *m*; ~ **repayment** *n*
remboursement de prêt *m*; ~ **repayment
schedule** *n* calendrier de remboursement de
l'emprunt *m*; ~ **shark** *n* (infrml) usurier *m*; ~
stock *n* capital obligations *m*, obligations

f pl; ~ **value** *n* (Bank) rapport prêt-garantie *m*; (amount lent) valeur du prêt *f*; ~ **write-off** *n* perte sèche sur prêt *f*; ~ **yield** *n* rapport de prêt *m*, rendement d'un prêt *m*

lobby¹ *n* lobby *m*; **on ~ terms** BrE de source confidentielle, de source officieuse; ~ **group** *n* (Pol) groupe de pression *m*, lobby *m*

lobby² 1 *vt* exercer une pression sur 2 *vi* ~ **for sth** faire pression pour obtenir qch

lobbying *n* lobbying *m*

lobbyist *n* lobbyiste *mf*

local¹ *adj* local; (Admin, Pol) municipal

local² *n* (Stock) négociateur individuel de parquet *m*

local: ~ **agreement** *n* accord local *m*; ~ **area network** *n* réseau local *m*; ~ **authority** *n* autorités locales *f pl*, ≈ municipalité *f*; ~ **authority bill** *n* obligation d'administration locale ou régionale *f*; ~ **authority bond** *n* bon d'administration locale *m*, obligation d'administration locale ou régionale *f*; ~ **call** *n* appel local *m*; ~ **council** *n* ≈ municipalité *f*; ~ **currency** *n* monnaie locale *f*; ~ **election** *n* élection locale *f*; ~ **government** *n* autorités locales *f pl*, ≈ municipalité *f*; ~ **government finance** *n* finances des collectivités locales *f pl*; ~ **labor** *n* ▸**local labour** BrE; ~ **labor market** *n* AmE ▸**local labour market** BrE; ~ **labour** *n* BrE main-d'œuvre locale *f*; ~ **labour market** *n* BrE marché du travail régional *m*; ~ **link** *n* (Comp) lien hypertexte *m*; ~ **loop** *n* (Comp) boucle locale *f*; ~ **monopoly** *n* monopole régional *m*; ~ **newspaper** *n* journal local *m*; ~ **services** *n pl* services de proximité *m pl*; ~ **shop** *n* BrE, ~ **store** *n* AmE magasin de proximité *m*; ~ **tax** *n* (of council) impôt municipal *m*; (of area, country) taxe locale *f*; ~ **time** *n* heure locale *f*

locality *n* (local area) région *f*

localization *n* (Comp) localisation *f*

localize *vt* (pinpoint) localiser; (restrict) restreindre; (Pol) décentraliser; (Comp) localiser

locally *adv* localement; (buy, produce, recruit) sur place

locate *vt* (factory) implanter; (business) établir; (building) construire; (problem, fault) localiser; (find) retrouver

located *adj* situé

location *n* endroit *m*; (exact site) emplacement *m*; ~**-independent working** *n* télétravail *m*

lock *vt* (file) verrouiller; ~ **in** (customer) rendre captif/-ive; ~ **in a rate** bloquer un cours; ~ **up** (funds, capital) bloquer

lockaway *n* (Stock) valeur à long terme *f*

lock-in *n* (S&M) accord exclusif *m*

lockout *n* lock-out *m*, grève patronale *f*

lock-up *n* (garage) garage *m*, (séparé du domicile)

loco price *n* prix sur place *m*

lodge 1 *vt* (person) loger; (money, valuables) déposer; ~ **an appeal** interjeter appel; ~ **a complaint** déposer une plainte 2 *vi* se loger

log¹ *n* (record) journal *m*, registre *m*; (Comp, Tax) journal *m*; (Transp) journal *m*; (of plane) carnet de vol *m*; (of ship) livre de bord *m*; ~ **book** *n* (Transp) ≈ carte grise *f*; ~ **file** *n* (Comp) fichier de consignation *m*

log² *vt* (record) enregistrer, noter; ~ **in** ouvrir une session, se connecter; ~ **off** terminer une session, se déconnecter; ~ **on** ouvrir une session, se connecter; ~ **out** terminer une session, se déconnecter

logging *n* exploitation forestière *f*

logic *n* logique *f*; ~ **bomb** *n* bombe logique *f*

logical *adj* logique

logistic *adj* logistique; ~ **cycle** *n* cycle logistique *m*; ~ **process** *n* processus logistique *m*

logistical *adj* logistique

logistically *adv* logistiquement

logistics *n* +*sing v* logistique *f*

log jam *n* blocage *m*

logo *n* logo *m*

logroll *vi* US renvoyer l'ascenseur

logrolling *n* US (Pol) trafic de faveurs *m*

Lombard rate *n* taux Lombard *m*

London: ~ **Chamber of Commerce & Industry** *n* Chambre de commerce et d'industrie de Londres *f*; ~ **Futures and Options Exchange** *n* bourse des marchés à terme et options de Londres *f*; ~ **Interbank Bid Rate** *n* taux d'emprunt interbancaire de Londres *m*; ~ **Interbank Currency Options Market** *n* marché interbancaire des options sur devises de Londres *m*; ~ **Interbank Offered Rate** *n* taux interbancaire offert à Londres *m*; ~ **International Financial Futures Exchange** *n* UK bourse des options de Londres *f*, ≈ Marché des options négociables de Paris *m*; ~ **Metal Exchange** *n* Bourse des métaux de Londres *f*; ~ **Options Clearing House** *n* UK ≈ Société de compensation des marchés conditionnels *f*; ~ **School of Economics** *n* UK École Supérieure d'Économie de Londres *f*; ~ **Stock Exchange** *n* Bourse de Londres *f*; ~ **Traded Options Market** *n* Bourse des options négociables de Londres *f*; ~ **weighting** *n* UK indemnité de résidence à Londres *f*; ~ **Chamber of Commerce & Industry** *n* Chambre de commerce et d'industrie de Londres *f*

long¹ *adj* long/longue; **be ~ in futures** avoir une position longue sur contrat à terme; **in the ~ term** à long terme; **it's a ~ shot** c'est risqué, c'est un coup à tenter; **take the** ⋯⟩

~**view** avoir une vision à long terme; **by a ~ way** de loin; **take a ~ time** (person) mettre longtemps; (task) prendre longtemps

long² *adv* (a long time) longtemps; **go ~** (Stock) prendre une position longue; **borrow ~** (Stock) emprunter à long terme

long³ *n* (Stock) long *m*, obligation à plus de 15 ans *f*

long: **~ bond** *n* bon à longue échéance *m*, obligation à long terme *f*; **~ call** *n* long call *m*, position acheteur sur options d'achat *f*; **~ call position** *n* (Stock) position de longue option d'achat *f*; **~-dated** *adj* (bill) à longue échéance, à long terme; **~-distance call** *n* (national) communication interurbaine *f*; (abroad) communication internationale *f*; **~-distance lorry driver** *n* routier *m*; **~-established** *adj* établi depuis longtemps; **~ futures position** *n* (Stock) (options) position longue sur contrat à terme *f*; **~-haul** *adj* long-courrier; **~-haul aircraft** *n* long-courrier *m*; **~ hedge** *n* couverture longue *f*, long hedge *m*, longue couverture *f*; **~ lease** *n* bail à long terme *m*; **~ position** *n* position acheteur *f*, position longue *f*; **~ put** *n* long put *m*, position acheteur sur options de vente *f*; **~-range** *adj* (plan, forecast) à long terme; **~-range planning** *n* planification à long terme *f*; **~-standing** *adj* (arrangement, rivalry, grievance) de longue date; **~-term** *adj* (placement, contract) à long terme; **~-term bond** *n* obligation à long terme *f*; **~-term debt** *n* dette à long terme *f*; **~-term financing** *n* financement à long terme *m*; **~-term gain** *n* plus-value à long terme *f*; **~-term loan** *n* prêt à long terme *m*; **~-term objective** *n* objectif à long terme *m*; **~-term planning** *n* planification à long terme *f*; **~-term security** *n* valeur à long terme *f*; **~-term trend** *n* tendance à long terme *f*; **~-term unemployed** *n* BrE chômeur/-euse de longue durée *m/f*; **~-term unemployment** *n* chômage de longue durée *m*; **~-time** *adj* de longue date; **~ ton** *n* tonne forte *f*

longevity pay *n* salaire selon l'ancienneté *m*

longshoreman *n* AmE docker *m*, débardeur *m*

look¹ *n* (glance) **have a ~ through** (document, file) parcourir; **have a ~ at** (briefly) jeter un coup d'œil à, jeter un coup d'œil sur; (closely) examiner soigneusement; (style) look *m* (infrml), style *m*; **create a new ~ for** relooker (infrml), transformer

look² **1** *vt* regarder; **~ who/how** regarder qui/comment
2 *vi* regarder; **~ promising** sembler intéressant; **~ after** (customer, business, finances) s'occuper de; **~ ahead** regarder vers l'avenir; **~ at** (figures) examiner; (problem, effect, options, plans) étudier; **be ~ing at bankruptcy** être au bord de la faillite; **~ for** chercher; **~ forward to** attendre avec

impatience; **~ into** étudier, examiner; (make enquiries) se renseigner sur; **~ out** se méfier, faire attention; **~ out for sb/sth** (hunt) être à l'affût de qch; **~ over** (document, contract) parcourir; (in detail) examiner; **~ round** visiter; **~ through** (archives, files) consulter; (notes, report) parcourir; **~ to** (person) se tourner vers; **~ up** **1** *vt* (person) passer voir; (details, phone number) chercher
2 *vi* (business) aller mieux; (situation) s'améliorer; (market) reprendre

lookout *n*: **be on the ~ for** guetter, être à l'affût de

lookup *n* consultation *f*; **~ table** *n* table de référence *f*

loop *n* boucle *f*; **local ~** boucle locale *f*; **be in the ~** (infrml) être dans le coup (infrml); **be out of the ~** (infrml) ne pas être dans le coup (infrml)

loophole *n* faille *f*, lacune *f*; **~ in the law** faille dans la législation *f*

loose: **~ cargo** *n* chargement en vrac *m*; **~ change** *n* monnaie *f*; **~-leaf** *adj* à feuilles mobiles

lorry *n* BrE camion *m*; **~ driver** *n* BrE chauffeur de camion *m*, routier *m*, camionneur *m*

lorryload *n* BrE cargaison *f*

lose **1** *vt* (case, elections) perdre; (order, customer) perdre; **~ control of** perdre le contrôle de; **~ ground** perdre du terrain; **~ one's job** perdre son emploi
2 *vi* perdre; **~ out** être perdant; **~ out on** (chance, bargain) rater; (deal) perdre dans

loss *n* perte *f*; (Ins) perte *f*, sinistre *m*; (deficit) déficit *m*; **take a ~** subir une perte; **trade at a ~** vendre à perte; **make a ~** (company) enregistrer une perte; **~ of income**, **~ of earnings** manque à gagner *m*; **with the ~ of 200 jobs** avec la suppression de 200 emplois; **cut one's ~es** arrêter les dégâts (infrml); **~ adjuster** *n* régleur d'avaries communes *m*; (Ins) expert en assurances *m*; **~ carry-back** *n* report d'une perte en amont *m*; **~ carry-forward** *n* report d'une perte sur une année ultérieure *m*; **~ of claim** perte du droit à l'indemnité *f*; **~ contingency** prévoyance pour pertes *f*; **~ of custom** baisse de clientèle *f*; **~ leader** *n* article vendu à perte *m*; (marketing) article d'appel *m*, produit d'appel *m*; **~ leader pricing** *n* vente à perte *f*, vente à prix sacrifié *f*; **~ limitation** *n* limitation des pertes *f*; **~-maker** *n* *n* article générateur de pertes *m*; **~-making** *adj* (product) vendu à perte; (company) déficitaire; **~-of-income insurance** *n* (personal) assurance perte de revenu *f*; **~ of pay** perte de salaire *f*; **~ pricing** *n* technique du prix d'appel *f*; **~ provision** *n* provision pour risques et changes *f*; **~ ratio** *n* coefficient de perte *m*; (Ins) rapport sinistres-primes *f*

losses *n pl* pertes *f pl*; **~ carried forward** *n pl* pertes reportées *f pl*, report des pertes *m;* ~ **suffered** *n pl* pertes subies *f pl,* préjudice subi *m*

lot *n* (of goods, in auction) lot *m;* (land) parcelle *f;* (of shares) paquet *m*

lottery *n* loterie *f;* ~ **winnings** *n pl* gains de loterie *m pl*

love money *n* argent emprunté aux amis ou aux proches lors de la création d'une start-up

low[1] *adj* (income, rate) faible; (price, wage) bas/basse, faible; (quality) inférieur; (futures price) bas/basse; **be** ~ **on** manquer de, être à court de; **the** ~**-paid** *n pl* les petits salaires *m pl*

low[2] *n* niveau bas *m,* point bas *m;* **sink to a** ~ (share, currency) atteindre son niveau le plus bas; **the stock market closed at a record** ~ la bourse a été clôturée à son niveau le plus bas; **hit a** ~ (economy) être dans le creux de la vague

low: ~ **achiever** *n* sujet peu doué *m;* ~**-budget** *adj* à petit budget; ~**-cost** *adj* à prix réduit; ~**-cost loan** *n* prêt à faible taux *m;* ~**-end** *adj* bas de gamme; ~ **end of the market** *n* bas de gamme du marché *m;* ~ **end of the range** *n* bas de gamme *m;* ~**-geared capital** *n* BrE capital à faible taux d'endettement *m;* ~ **gearing ratio** *n* BrE ratio d'endettement bas *m;* ~**-grade** *adj* de qualité inférieure; ~**-hanging fruit** *n* gains faciles *m pl;* ~**-income household** *n* foyer à faible revenu *m;* ~**-income taxpayer** *n* contribuable à faible revenu *mf;* ~**-level** *adj* (meeting, talks) informel/-elle; ~**-interest loan** *n* emprunt à faible intérêt *m,* prêt à faible intérêt *m;* ~**-key** *adj* discret/-ète; ~**-level waste** *n* déchets de faible activité *m pl;* ~ **leverage ratio** *n* AmE ratio d'endettement bas *m;* ~ **loader** *n* remorque à plate-forme surbaissée *f;* ~**-paid** *adj* (job) mal payé; ~ **pay** *n* bas salaire *m;* ~**-polluting** *adj* peu polluant; ~ **price** *n* (Stock) (currency futures) bas prix *m,* cours bas *m;* ~**-priced** *adj* à bas prix; ~**-profile** *adj* discret/-ète, à profil bas; (product) à profil bas; ~ **season** *n* basse saison *f;* ~ **standard of living** *n* faible niveau de vie *m,* niveau de vie bas *m;* ~**-tech** *adj* traditionnel/-elle; ~ **tide** *n* marée basse *f;* ~**-yielding** *adj* à faible rendement

lower *vt* (price, standard) baisser; (barriers) supprimer, abolir; (limit) abaisser

lower: ~ **case** *n* bas de casse *m,* minuscules *f pl;* ~**-case letter** *n* minuscule *f;* ~ **income bracket** *n* tranche inférieure de revenus *f;* ~ **limit** *n* plancher *m;* ~ **price** *n* prix plus bas *m,* prix réduit *m;* ~ **quartile** *n* quartile premier *m,* quartile inférieur *m*

lowering *n* (of rate, price, standard) baisse *f;* (of

age limit) abaissement *m;* (of barriers) suppression *f,* abolition *f;* ~ **of taxation** *n* diminution des impôts *f*

lowest: ~ **bidder** *n* moins-disant *m;* (Stock) soumissionnaire le moins disant *m;* ~ **common denominator** *n* plus petit dénominateur commun *m;* ~ **price** *n* (Stock) cours le plus bas *m,* prix le plus bas *m;* ~ **tender** *n* moins-disant *m;* ~ **tenderer** *n* moins-disant *m*

loyalty *n* fidélité *f;* **customer** ~ fidélité de la clientèle; **retain the** ~ **of** (client, customer) fidéliser; ~ **bonus** *n* prime de fidélité *f;* ~ **card** *n* carte de fidélité *f*

LPG *abbr* (▸**liquid petroleum gas**) GPL *m* (gaz de pétrole liquéfié)

LSE *abbr* UK (▸**London School of Economics**) École Supérieure d'Économie de Londres *f;* (▸**London Stock Exchange**) Bourse de Londres *f*

Ltd *abbr* UK (▸**limited liability company**) SARL *f* (société à responsabilité limitée)

LTOM *abbr* (▸**London Traded Options Market**) Bourse des options négociables de Londres

luck *n* chance *f;* **try one's** ~ tenter sa chance

lucky *adj* **be** ~ avoir de la chance; ~ **break** *n* coup de chance *m*

lucrative *adj* lucratif/-ive

luddite *n* luddite *m,* réactionnaire *mf*

luggage *n* bagages *m pl;* ~ **label** *n* étiquette à bagages *f;* ~ **trolley** *n* BrE chariot à bagages *m*

lull *n* accalmie *f*

lump: ~ **sum** *n* (total amount) somme globale *f;* (life insurance) somme forfaitaire *f;* ~**-sum contract** *n* contrat au forfait *m;* ~**-sum freight** *n* fret à forfait *m;* ~**-sum price** *n* prix forfaitaire *m;* ~ **sum payment** *n* versement unique *m;* ~**-sum purchase** *n* achat à montant global *m*

luncheon voucher *n* BrE ticket-repas *m,* ticket-restaurant® *m*

lurk *vi* (in a newsgroup) observer, faire le badaud (infrml)

lurker *n* (in a newsgroup) cyberbadaud *m,* observateur/-trice anonyme *m/f*

luxury[1] *adj* de luxe

luxury[2] *n* luxe *m*

luxury: ~ **goods** *n pl* biens de luxe *m pl,* articles de luxe *m pl;* ~ **tax** *n* taxe sur les articles de luxe *f*

LV *abbr* BrE (▸**luncheon voucher**) ticket-repas *m,* ticket-restaurant® *m*

Mm

Maastricht Summit n Sommet de Maastricht m

machine n machine f; ~**-aided translation** n, ~**-assisted translation** n traduction assistée par ordinateur f; ~ **code** n code machine m; ~**-made** adj fait en série, produit en série; ~ **operator** n opérateur/-trice de machine m/f; ~ **shop** n atelier m; ~ **tool** n machine-outil f; ~ **translation** n traduction automatique f, traduction assitée par ordinateur f

machine-readable adj (data, bar codes) directement exploitable; **in** ~ **form** directement exploitable

machinery n (in factory) machines f pl; (Admin) rouages administratifs m pl; (Econ) mécanisme m, rouages m pl; (Law) fonctionnement m, rouages m pl; (shipping) machines f pl

macro[1] n (Comp) macro f

macro-[2] pref macro-

macrocomputing n macroinformatique f

macroeconomic adj macroéconomique

macroeconomics n + sing v macroéconomie f

macroenvironment n macroenvironnement m

macromarketing n macromarketing m

macrosegment n macrosegment m

macrosegmentation n macrosegmentation f

made adj fabriqué, fait, produit; ~ **in France, French-**~ fabriqué en France; ~ **to last** fait pour durer; ~ **to measure** fait sur mesure; ~ **to order** fait sur commande

made bill n effet tiré à l'étranger m

magazine n magazine m, revue f

magic quadrilateral n carré magique m

magistrate n magistrat/-e m/f (non professionnel/-elle)

magistrates' court n tribunal d'instance m

magnate n magnat m; **newspaper** ~ magnat de la presse m

magnetic adj magnétique; ~ **card** n carte magnétique f; ~ **disk** n disque magnétique m; ~ **tape** n bande magnétique f

magnitude n grandeur f; (of problems, crisis) ampleur f; **an order of** ~ un ordre de grandeur; ~ **of a right** (Law) importance d'un droit f

maiden: ~ **name** n nom de jeune fille m; ~ **voyage** n premier voyage m, voyage inaugural m

mail[1] n (letters) courrier m; (service) poste f; (email) courrier électronique m; (email item) e-mail m; **through the** ~ par la poste; **buy sth by** ~ **order** acheter qch par correspondance; **open the** ~ dépouiller le courrier, ouvrir le courrier; ~ **bomb** n colis piégé m; (Comp) bombe électronique f; ~ **carrier** n AmE facteur/-trice m/f; ~ **management** n gestion du courrier électronique f; ~ **merge** n publipostage m; ~ **order** n vente par correspondance f; ~**-order business** n maison de vente par correspondance f; ~**-order catalog** AmE, ~**-order catalogue** BrE n catalogue de vente par correspondance m; ~**-order company** n, ~**-order firm** n maison de vente par correspondance f; ~**-order selling** n vente par correspondance f; ~ **room** n (service du) courrier m; ~ **server** n serveur de courrier électronique m

mail[2] vt AmE (letter) envoyer, expédier

mailbox n AmE (for delivery) boîte à lettres f; (for posting) boîte aux lettres f; (Comp) boîte à lettres électronique f, boîte aux lettres électronique f

mailing n (advertising) mailing m, publipostage m; (dispatch) envoi par la poste m; ~ **address** n adresse postale f; ~ **card** n carte-réponse f; ~ **list** n (of clients) fichier-clientèle m, liste d'adresses f; (distribution list) liste de diffusion f; ~ **list software** n gestionnaire de liste de diffusion mf

mailman n AmE facteur m

mailshot n mailing m, publipostage m; **do a** ~ faire un mailing, faire un publipostage

main adj principal; ~ **branch** n maison mère f; (Bank) succursale principale f; ~ **building** n bâtiment principal m; ~ **line** n (rail) grande ligne f; ~ **menu** n menu principal m; ~ **office** n siège social m; ~ **residence** n résidence principale f; ~ **street** n AmE grand-rue f; ~ **trading partners** n pl principaux partenaires commerciaux m pl

mainframe n ordinateur central m

mainline adj (railway station) de grandes lignes

mainly adv surtout, principalement

mains n pl BrE alimentation secteur f; ~ **adaptor** n BrE adaptateur secteur m

mainstay n pilier m; **be the** ~ **of the economy** être le pilier de l'économie

mainstream adj (dominant) principal; (traditional) traditionnel/-elle; ~ **economics** n + sing v théorie économique dominante f

maintain vt (control, contact, prices, value,

standards) maintenir; (office) assurer, entretenir; (good relations) entretenir, maintenir; (machine) entretenir; (advantage) conserver, garder; (assert) affirmer

maintenance *n* entretien *m*, maintenance *f*; (Law) (for spouse, child) pension alimentaire *f*; ∼ **charges** *n pl* frais d'entretien *m pl*, frais de maintenance *m pl*; ∼ **contract** *n* contrat d'entretien *m*, contrat de maintenance *m*; ∼ **crew** *n* équipe d'entretien *f*; ∼ **department** *n* service d'entretien *m*; ∼ **engineer** *n* ingénieur d'entretien *m*, technicien/-ienne d'entretien *m/f*; ∼ **equipment** *n* matériel d'entretien *m*; ∼ **expenses** *n pl* frais d'entretien *m pl*, frais de maintenance *m pl*; ∼ **fee** *n* (for account) frais de tenue de compte *m pl*; (Prop) prestation d'entretien *f*; ∼ **payment** *n* pension alimentaire *f*; ∼ **personnel** *n pl* personnel d'entretien *m*; ∼ **schedule** *n* programme d'entretien *m*, programme de mise à jour *m*; ∼ **staff** *n pl* personnel d'entretien *m*

major *adj* (main) principal; (change, client, company, decision) important; (difference, effect, role, work) majeur; (influence, significance) capital; ∼ **account** *n* grand compte *m*; ∼ **currency** *n* monnaie dominante *f*, monnaie principale *f*; ∼ **producer** *n* gros producteur *m*, principal producteur *m*; ∼ **road** *n* route principale *f*; ∼ **trend** *n* tendance dominante *f*

majority *n* majorité *f*; be in a ∼, be in the ∼ être en majorité; **working** ∼ majorité suffisante; **overwhelming** ∼ majorité écrasante; **by a** ∼ **of four to one** avec une majorité de quatre contre un; ∼ **decision** *n* décision prise à la majorité *f*; ∼ **holding** *n*, ∼ **interest** *n* participation majoritaire *f*; ∼ **interest partner** *n* associé/-e majoritaire *m/f*; ∼ **ownership** *n* participation majoritaire *f*; ∼ **rule** *n* gouvernement par la majorité *m*; ∼ **rule voting** *n* vote à la majorité *m*; ∼ **shareholder** *n* actionnaire majoritaire *mf*; ∼ **shareholding** *n* actionnariat majoritaire *m*, participation majoritaire *f*; ∼ **stake** *n* participation majoritaire *f*; ∼ **stockholder** *n* actionnaire majoritaire *mf*; ∼ **verdict** *n* verdict rendu à la majorité *m*; ∼ **view** *n* opinion de la majorité *f*; ∼ **vote** *n* vote majoritaire *m*

make[1] *n* marque *f*

make[2] *vt* faire; (car) construire; (offer) faire; (goods, equipment) fabriquer; (garments, foodstuffs) confectionner; (sale) conclure; (invention) réaliser; ∼ **an advance payment** verser un acompte; ∼ **an appointment with sb** prendre un rendez-vous avec qn; ∼ **an approach to sb** faire une proposition à qn; ∼ **a bid** faire une enchère; ∼ **a deal** conclure un marché; ∼ **forecasts** faire des pronostics; ∼ **money** faire de l'argent; ∼ **a profit/loss** faire un gain/une perte; ∼ **a sale** faire une vente; ∼ **£100 a week** gagner 100 livres sterling par semaine; ∼ **good** *vt* (damage, omission, loss)

réparer; (lost time) rattraper; (deficit, shortfall) combler; *vi* (succeed) réussir; ∼ **out** (cheque) libeller; (invoice) établir; (list) dresser, faire, établir; ∼ **over** (Law) transférer, céder; ∼ **up** (accounts) arrêter, établir; (deficit, shortfall, loss) combler; (list) dresser, établir; (garment) confectionner; (sale, loss) combler; ∼ **up for** (compensate) compenser; (deficit, loss) combler; ∼ **up for lost time** rattraper le temps perdu, rattraper son retard; ∼ **up for a mistake** compenser une erreur; **be made up of** être composé de, être constitué de; ∼ **up one's accounts** arrêter ses comptes; ∼ **up the difference** (financially) faire l'appoint

make-or-break *adj* (decision) qui passe ou qui casse; **it's a** ∼ **situation** ça passe ou ça casse

maker *n* (of cars, machinery) constructeur *m*; (of goods, equipment) fabricant *m*; (Law) (of note) rédigeur *m*, tireur *m*

makeshift *adj* improvisé; ∼ **solution** *n* solution de fortune *f*

make-up *n* (Fin) solde des comptes *m*; ∼ **pay** *n* rattrapage de salaire *m*

making *n* (of profit) réalisation *f*; (of clothes) confection *f*; (of machinery) construction *f*; (of goods) fabrication *f*; (of programme) réalisation *f*; **have the** ∼**s of a managing director** avoir l'étoffe d'un PDG; ∼ **up** *n* (for losses) compensation *f*; (of balance sheet) préparation *f*; ∼**-up price** *n* ajustement des prix *m*, cours de compensation *m*, cours de liquidation *m*

maladministration *n* (Admin, Mgmnt) mauvaise gestion *f*; (Law) malversations *f pl*

malfunction[1] *n* (poor operation) mauvais fonctionnement *m*; (breakdown) défaillance *f*

malfunction[2] *vi* mal fonctionner

malicious *adj* (allegation) calomnieux/-ieuse; **with** ∼ **intent** avec l'intention de nuire; ∼ **damage** *n* dommage causé avec intention *m*; ∼ **prosecution** *n* poursuites abusives *f pl*

maliciously *adv* avec l'intention de nuire, avec préméditation

malingerer *n* tire-au-flanc *m*

malingering *n* absentéisme injustifié *m*

mall *n* galerie marchande *f*; (out of town) centre commercial *m*

malleable capital *n* capitaux malléables *m pl*

malpractice *n* faute professionnelle *f*, négligence professionnelle *f*; **administrative** ∼ malversations *f pl*; **electoral** ∼ fraude électorale *f*

Maltese pound *n* livre maltaise *f*

mammoth *adj* énorme; **on a** ∼ **scale** sur une échelle gigantesque; ∼ **reduction** *n* prix sacrifié *m*

man[1] *n* the ∼ **in the street** l'homme de la rue *m*, monsieur tout-le-monde *m*

man[2] *vt* (factory, office) fournir du personnel à, pourvoir en personnel; (machine) assurer la manœuvre de; (exhibition stand) assurer

⋯❭

l'accueil de, assurer la permanence de; **lines are ~ned 24 hours a day** il y a une permanence téléphonique

manage ⊡ *vt* (business, shop, hotel, time, money) gérer; (company, bank, project, team) diriger; (change) gérer; **~ to do** réussir à faire ⊡ *vi* (succeed) réussir

manageable *adj* (size, quantity) maniable; (problem, issue) maîtrisable; (feasible) faisable; (level) raisonnable

managed: ~ bond *n* obligation contrôlée *f*; **~ costs** *n pl* coûts maîtrisés *m pl*; **~ currency** *n* devise contrôlée *f*, devise à haute puissance *f*; **~ economy** *n* économie planifiée *f*, économie dirigée *f*; **~ loan** *n* prêt géré *m*; **~ trade** *n* commerce planifié *m*

management *n* (of business, company, hotel) gestion *f*, management *m*; (of shop, estate, economy, personnel) gestion *f*; (on behalf of owner) gérance *f*; (discipline, techniques) gestion *f*, management *m*; (managerial staff) direction *f*; **senior ~** cadres dirigeants *m pl*, haute direction *f*; **middle ~** cadres moyens *m pl*; **~ and unions** la direction et les syndicats, les partenaires sociaux; **account/waste ~** gestion des comptes/déchets; **~ accountancy** *n* comptabilité analytique *f*, comptabilité de gestion *f*; **~ accountant** *n* contrôleur/-euse de gestion *m/f*, responsable de comptabilité analytique *mf*; **~ accounting** *n* comptabilité analytique *f*, comptabilité de gestion *f*; **~ accounts** *n pl* comptes analytiques *m pl*; **~ audit** *n* audit de direction *m*, audit de management *m*; **~ board** *n* conseil de direction *m*, directoire *m*; **~ buy-in** *n* apport de gestion *m*; **~ buyout** *n* rachat d'une entreprise par ses salariés *m*; **~ of change** *n* gestion du changement *f*; **~ chart** *n* tableau de bord *m*; **~ committee** *n* comité directeur *m*, comité de direction *m*; **~ consultancy** *n* cabinet de conseil en gestion *m*, cabinet de conseil en management *m*; **~ consultant** *n* conseil en gestion *m*, conseil en management *m*, conseiller/-ère en gestion *m/f*, conseiller/-ère en management *m/f*; **~ contract** *n* contrat du management *m*; **~ control** *n* contrôle de gestion *m*; **~ by exception** *n* gestion par exception *f*; **~ expenses** *n* frais de gestion *m pl*; **~ fee** *n* frais de gestion *m pl*; (in real estate) honoraires de gestion *m pl*; **~ game** *n* jeu de simulation de gestion *m*; **~ information system** *n* système intégré de gestion *m*; **~ by objectives** *n* direction par objectifs *f*; **~ reshuffle** *n* remaniement de l'équipe dirigeante *m*; **~ resource planning** *n* planification des ressources de fabrication *f*; **~ of shares** *n* gestion d'actions *f*; **~ skills** *n pl* compétences en gestion *f pl*; **~ staff** *n* personnel d'encadrement *m*, personnel dirigeant *m*; **~ structure** *n* structure de gestion *f*; **~ style** *n* style de gestion *m*, style directorial *m*, style managérial *m*; **~ system** *n* système de gestion *m*; **~ team** *n* équipe de direction *f*; **~ technique** *n* technique de gestion *f*; **~ theory** *n* théorie de la gestion *f*; **~ tool** outil de gestion *m*; **~ trainee** *n* cadre stagiaire *m*, apprenti manager *m*; **~ training** *n* (course) stage de direction d'entreprise *m*; (concept) formation des cadres *f*; **~ by walking about** *n* management baladeur *m*

manager *n* (of business, company, bank, hotel) directeur/-trice *m/f*; (of pub, shop, restaurant) gérant/-e *m/f*, manager *m*; (executive) cadre *m*; (department head) chef de service *m*; **~s and workers** patronat et travailleurs; **~'s office** *n* bureau du directeur *m*, direction *f*

manageress *n* (of company) directrice *f*; (of shop, hotel, restaurant) gérante *f*

managerial *adj* de direction, de gestion; (experience) en gestion; (training) des cadres; (problem) d'encadrement; **at ~ level** au niveau de la direction; **~ accounting** *n* comptabilité analytique *f*, comptabilité de gestion *f*; **~ effectiveness** *n* efficacité de la direction *f*; **~ position** *n* poste de direction *m*; **~ skills** *n pl* compétences en matière de gestion *f pl*; **~ staff** *n pl* cadres *m pl*, personnel d'encadrement *m*; **~ structure** *n* hiérarchie *f*; **~ style** *n* style de direction *m*

managing *adj* dirigeant; **~ agent** *n* gérant/-e *m/f*; **~ director** *n* président-directeur général *m*/presidente-directrice générale *f*; **~ owner** *n* (Transp) armateur-gérant *m*; **~ partner** *n* associé/-e gérant/-e *m/f*; **~ underwriter** *n* apériteur *m*

manat *n* manat *m*

M&A *abbr* (▸**mergers and acquisitions**) F&A *f pl* (fusions et acquisitions)

mandarin *n* mandarin *m*

mandate *n* (Fin, Law, Pol) mandat *m*

mandatory *adj* obligatoire; **~ accounting plans** *n pl* plans comptables obligatoires *m pl*; **~ copy** *n* (advertising) texte publicitaire obligatoire *m*; **~ injunction** *n* injonction donnée par un tribunal *f*; **~ quote period** *n* période de cotation obligatoire *f*; **~ retirement** *n* AmE mise à la retraite d'office *f*, retraite obligatoire *f*

man-day *n* homme-jour *m*

maneuver AmE ▸**manoeuvre** BrE

man-hour *n* heure de travail *f*

manifest *n* manifeste *m*; **~ of cargo** manifeste de marchandises *m*

manilla envelope *n* enveloppe en papier kraft *f*

manipulate *vt* (person, situation, opinion) manipuler; (facts, data) falsifier; **~ the figures** manipuler les chiffres; **~ the market** agir sur le marché

manipulation *n* manipulation *f*; (of market) tripotages *m pl*

manipulator *n* manipulateur/-trice *m/f*; (of market) agioteur *m*, manipulateur/-trice *m/f*

man-made *adj* artificiel/-ielle, synthétique;

~ **fiber** AmE, ~ **fibre** BrE n fibre synthétique f

manned service n permanence f, service assuré m

manning n effectifs m pl; ~ **level** n niveau des effectifs m

manoeuvre¹ n BrE manœuvre f; **have room for** ~ avoir une marge de manœuvre

manoeuvre² vt (person, vehicle) manœuvrer; ~ **sb into doing** manœuvrer qn pour qu'il fasse

manpower n main-d'œuvre f; ~ **audit** n inventaire des effectifs m; ~ **costs** n pl frais de personnel m pl; ~ **management** n gestion des effectifs f; ~ **planning** n planification des ressources humaines f, le recrutement et la gestion des effectifs; ~ **policy** n politique de la main-d'œuvre f; ~ **requirements** n pl besoins en main-d'œuvre m pl; ~ **shortage** n pénurie de main-d'œuvre f

manual¹ adj manuel/-elle

manual² n manuel m

manual: ~ **feed** n chargement manuel m; ~ **labor** n AmE, ~ **labour** BrE travailleurs manuels m pl; ~ **worker** n ouvrier/-ière m/f, travailleur/-euse manuel/-elle m/f

manually adv manuellement, à la main

manufacture vt (Ind) fabriquer; (evidence, excuse) fabriquer de toutes pièces; ~ **sth under licence** BrE, ~ **sth under license** AmE fabriquer qch sous licence

manufactured adj fabriqué, manufacturé; ~ **goods** n pl produits manufacturés m pl

manufacturer n fabricant m; (of cars) constructeur m; ~'s **guarantee** n garantie du fabricant f; ~'s **recommended price** n prix public m, prix recommandé par le fabriquant m; ~'s **suggested retail price** n prix de vente recommandé par le fabricant m

manufactures n pl produits manufacturés m pl

manufacturing n fabrication f; (of cars) construction f; ~ **activity** n activité manufacturière f; ~ **base** n base industrielle f; ~**based economy** n économie manufacturière f; ~ **capacity** n capacité de production f; ~ **company** n société industrielle f; ~ **costs** n pl coûts de fabrication m pl; ~ **industry** n industrie de transformation f, industrie manufacturière f; ~ **process** n processus de fabrication m; ~ **profits** n pl bénéfices de fabrication m pl; ~ **rights** n pl droits de fabrication m pl; ~ **sector** n secteur de production m, secteur industriel m

man-year n homme-année f

map¹ n (Gen Comm) carte f; (of town) plan m; (Comp) topogramme m, topographie f

map²: ~ **out** vt (policy) établir les grandes lignes de; (strategy) élaborer, mettre au point; (schedule) planifier; **her future is all** ~**ped out**

son avenir est tout tracé

mapping n mappage m

margin n (allowance) marge f; (profit) marge bénéficiaire f; (between rates of interest) écart m; (on page) marge f; (Stock) couverture f, dépôt m, marge f; (paid by client) couverture f; ~ **on** sur marge, à découvert; **allow a** ~ **for error** prévoir une marge d'erreur; **profit/safety** ~ marge bénéficiaire/de sécurité; **high/low** ~ forte/faible marge; ~ **account** n compte de couverture m, compte à marge m; ~ **buying** n achat marginal m, achat à découvert m; ~ **call** n appel de marge m; ~ **deposit** n dépôt de couverture m, dépôt de marge m; ~ **of error** n marge d'erreur f; ~ **purchase** n achat marginal m, achat à découvert m; ~ **requirement** n couverture obligatoire f; ~ **security** n titre acquis sur marge m; ~ **trading** n négoce marginal m, transactions sur marge f pl

marginal adj marginal; ~ **account** n compte marginal m; ~ **analysis** n analyse marginale f; ~ **case** n cas limite m; ~ **cost** n coût marginal m; ~ **cost pricing** n fixation des prix en fonction du coût marginal f; ~ **costing** n comptabilité marginale f, méthode des coûts marginaux f; ~ **note** n note en marge f, note marginale f; ~ **pricing** n fixation marginale du prix f; ~ **product** n produit marginal m; ~ **productivity** n productivité marginale f; ~ **profit** n bénéfice marginal m; ~ **propensity to consume** n propension marginale à consommer f; ~ **propensity to save** n propension marginale à épargner f; ~ **rate** n taux marginal m; ~ **return on capital** n rendement marginal sur le capital m; ~ **utility** n utilité marginale f

marginalism n marginalisme m

marginalize vt marginaliser

marginally adv marginalement

margining agreement n accord de garantie m

marine adj maritime; ~ **engineer** n ingénieur maritime m; ~ **insurance** n assurance maritime f; ~ **insurance policy** n police d'assurance maritime f; ~ **pollution** n pollution marine f; ~ **risk analyst** n analyste des risques maritimes mf; ~ **underwriter** n assureur maritime m

marital status n situation de famille f, état civil m

maritime adj maritime; ~ **canal** n canal maritime m; ~ **law** n droit maritime m; ~ **lien** n privilège maritime m; ~ **loan** n prêt maritime m; ~ **risk** n risque maritime m; ~ **shipping** n trafic maritime m; ~ **terminal** n terminal maritime m; ~ **trade** n commerce maritime m

mark¹ n (Deutschmark) mark allemand m; (Law, Patents) marque f; (Stock) cours de référence m; **go over the 10 dollar** ~ franchir la barre des dix dollars;

⋯▸

~-to-the-market n (Stock) fluctuations journalières f pl

mark² vt (indicate, label) marquer; **~ stock** (Stock) coter les valeurs; **~ down** (price) baisser; (product) baisser le prix de, démarquer; **~ out** (single out) distinguer; (select) désigner; **~ time** piétiner; **~ up** (price) majorer

markdown n (of goods) démarque f; (in price) rabais m, remise f, réduction f

marked adj (increase, decline, difference) marqué; **~ check** AmE, **~ cheque** BrE n chèque marqué m; **~ price** n prix marqué m

marker n (pen) marqueur m; (tag) repère m

market¹ n (S&M) marché m; (stock market) Bourse f; (trading structure) marché m; (for sale of produce, goods) marché m; **the youth ~** les adolescents m pl; **the job/property ~** le marché du travail/de l'immobilier m; **buyer's/seller's ~** marché favorable à l'acheteur/au vendeur m; **home ~, domestic ~** marché intérieur m; **flower/fish ~** marché aux fleurs m/halle aux poissons f; **at the ~** (Stock) au mieux; **at the ~ price** (Stock) au cours de la Bourse; **come onto the ~** arriver sur le marché; **make a ~** (Gen Comm) conclure une affaire; (Stock) se porter contrepartiste, tenir le marché; **on the ~** (goods, property) en vente; **put sth on the ~** mettre qch sur le marché; **find a ~ for sth** trouver un débouché pour qch; **be in the ~ for** chercher à acquérir; **play the ~** spéculer;

(**market a...**) **~ acceptance** n acceptation du produit par le marché f; **~ acces** n accès aux marchés m; **~ adjustment** n ajustement du marché m; **~ aim** n objectif de marché m; **~ analysis** n (S&M) étude de marché f; (Stock) analyse de marché f; **~ analyst** n (Stock) analyste-marché mf, conjoncturiste mf; **~ appeal** n attrait commercial m; **~ appraisal** n évaluation du marché f; **~ area** n segment du marché m, zone de chalandise f; **~ awareness** n conscience du marché f;

(**b...**) **~ base** n définition de marché f; **~ behaviour** AmE **~ behaviour** BrE n comportement du marché m;

(**c...**) **~ capitalization** n capitalisation boursière f; **~ close** n clôture du marché f; **~ comparison approach** n alignement sur les prix du marché m; **~ conditions** n pl conjoncture du marché f; **~ confidence** n confiance du marché f; **~ creation** n création de marché f;

(**d...**) **~ dealing** n activités sur un marché f pl; **~ demand** n demande du marché f; **~ development** n évolution du marché f; **~ disclosure** n divulgation sur le marché f; **~-driven** adj mercatisé, à l'écoute du marché;

(**e...**) **~ economy** n économie de marché f; **~ entry** n mise sur le marché f; **~ equilibrium** n équilibre du marché m; **~ evaluation** n évaluation du marché f; **~

expansion n développement du marché m; **~ exploration** n prospection des marchés f; **~ exposure** n exposition sur le marché f;

(**f...**) **~ fit** n adaptation au marché f, adaptation à la clientèle f; **~ fluctuations** n pl fluctuations du marché f pl; **~ forces** n pl forces du marché f pl; **~ forecast** n pronostic relatif au marché m, prévisions du marché f pl; **~ fragmentation** n fragmentation du marché f;

(**g...**) **~ gap** n créneau m; **~ growth** n croissance du marché f;

(**h...**) **~ hours** n pl heures de bourse f pl, heures de négociation f pl;

(**i...**) **~ index** n indice boursier m; **~ indicator** n indicateur de marché m; **~ intelligence** n information commerciale f;

(**l...**) **~ leader** n (company) leader du marché m, numéro un m; (product) produit vedette m; **~ leadership** n (S&M) position de numéro un f; **~ line** n courbe du marché f;

(**m...**) **~ maker** n teneur de marché m, contrepartiste mf, courtier en valeurs m; **~ management** n gestion commerciale f;

(**n...**) **~ niche** n créneau m, créneau commercial m, niche f;

(**o...**) **~ objective** n cible f; **~ of one** n marché exclusif m; **~ opening** n créneau m; **~ operations** n pl opérations de marché f pl; **~ opportunity** n créneau m, créneau commercial m; **~ order** n (Stock) ordre au cours du marché m, ordre au mieux m; **~-orientated** adj orienté par le marché;

(**p...**) **~ penetration** n pénétration du marché f; **~ plan** n plan de marché m; **~ position** n (Stock) (on currency) position de marché f; **~ positioning** n positionnement sur le marché m; **~ potential** n (of product) potentiel sur le marché m; (of market) potentiel du marché m; **~ presence** n présence sur un marché f; **~ price** n (S&M) prix du marché m, prix marchand m; (Stock) cours de la Bourse m; (last price) cours du marché m, prix du marché m; **~ pricing** n tarification en fonction du marché f; **~ profile** n profil du marché m; **~ prospects** n pl perspectives de marché f pl; **~ psychology** n psychologie du marché f;

(**r...**) **~ rate** n taux du marché m; **~ rate of interest** n taux d'intérêt du marché m; **~ receptiveness** n réceptivité du marché f; **~ recovery** n redressement du marché m; (Stock) reprise boursière f; **~ report** n (S&M) étude de marché f; (Stock) bulletin de la Bourse m; **~ research** n (Stock) analyse des marchés f; (S&M) étude de marché f; **~ research company** société d'études de marché f; **~ reasearcher** n chargé/-e d'études de marché m/f; **~ resistance** n résistance du marché f; **~ rigging** n manipulation de marchés f;

(**s...**) **~ saturation** n saturation du marché f; **~ sector** n secteur de marché m;

~ **segment** n segment du marché m, strate de marché f; ~ **segmentation** n segmentation du marché f; ~ **share** n part de marché f; ~ **skimming** (S&M) écrémage du marché m; ~ **slump** n dégringolade du marché f; ~ **socialism** n (Pol) troisième voie f; ~ **spoiler** n (on Internet) tueur du marché m; ~ **study** n étude de marché f; ~ **survey** n étude de marché f;

(t...) ~ **test** n test de marché m, test de vente m; ~ **testing** n essai de marché m, essai de vente m; ~ **trend** n tendance du marché f

(v...) ~ **valuation** n (Stock) évaluation boursière f; ~ **value** n (on balance sheets) valeur actuelle f; (Fin) valeur marchande f; (Ins, Prop) valeur du marché f; (S&M) valeur marchande f; (Stock) prix du marché m, valeur marchande f; ~ **view** n aperçu du marché m, vue du marché f

market² vt commercialiser; ~ **oneself** se vendre

marketability n (Stock) négociabilité f; (of product) possibilité de commercialisation f

marketable adj (in demand) commercialisable; (fit for sale) de qualité marchande, vendable; (shares) négociable; ~ **bond** n obligation négociable f, titre de placement m; ~ **instrument** n instrument négociable m; ~ **securities** n pl titres de placement m pl, valeurs de placement f pl; ~ **title** n titre négociable m; ~ **value** n valeur marchande f

marketeer n spécialiste en marketing mf, mercaticien/-ienne m/f

marketing n (of product) commercialisation f; (field) marketing m, mercatique f; ~ **agreement** n accord marketing m; ~ **appropriation** n dotations budgétaires affectées au marketing f pl; ~ **authorization** n autorisation de mise sur le marché f; ~ **budget** n budget de marketing m; ~ **campaign** n campagne commerciale f; ~ **company** n société de marketing f; ~ **concept** n concept marketing m; ~ **consultant** n conseiller/-ère commercial/-e m/f, mercaticien/-ienne m/f; ~ **cost** n coûts marketing m pl; ~ **department** n service marketing m; ~ **director** n directeur/-trice commercial/-e m/f, directeur/-trice du marketing m/f; ~ **expert** n mercaticien/-ienne m/f; ~ **information system** n système d'information de marketing m; ~ **manager** n directeur/-trice commercial/-e m/f, directeur/-trice du marketing m/f; ~ **mix** n formule de marketing f, marketing-mix m; ~ **model** n modèle marketing m; ~ **plan** n plan marketing m; ~ **policy** n politique de marketing f; ~ **research** n recherche commerciale f; ~ **strategy** n stratégie commerciale f, stratégie de marché f, stratégie marketing f; ~ **team** n équipe commerciale f; ~ **technique** n technique commerciale f; ~ **tool** n outil de marketing m

marketplace n place de marché f; (on Internet) place de marché virtuelle f, place de marché électronique f

markka n markka m

mark-up n (in printing) préparation de copie f; (increase) augmentation f; (retailer's margin) marge bénéficiaire f; ~ **language** n langage de balisage m; ~ **inflation** n inflation administrée f; ~ **tag** n balise f

mart n centre commercial m

Marxism n marxisme m

Marxist adj marxiste

mask vt (advertising) cacher; (Fin) (loss) dissimuler

mass adj (audience, movement, tourism) de masse; (protest, exodus) massif/-ive; ~ **appeal** n succès de masse m; ~ **communication** n communication de masse f; ~ **consumption** n consommation de masse f; ~ **distribution** n grande distribution f; ~ **email** n (concept) courrier électronique rebut m; (mail item) message réseau m, message électronique non sollicité m; ~ **mailing** n mailing m, publipostage m; ~ **market** n marché grand public m; ~**-marketed** adj (goods) destiné au grand public; ~ **marketing** n marketing de masse m; ~ **media** n mass-média m pl, médias m pl; ~ **redundancy** n licenciement collectif m; ~ **risk** n (Ins) risque de masse m; ~ **transit system** n AmE transports en commun m pl; ~ **unemployment** n chômage de masse m

massage vt ~ **the figures** (Gen Comm) manipuler les chiffres; (Acc, Stock) habiller le bilan

masses: the ~ n pl les masses f pl

massive adj (increase, cut) massif/-ive; (amount, debt, error) énorme; (majority, victory) écrasant; (programme, campaign) de grande envergure

mass-produce vt fabriquer en série

mass-produced adj fabriqué en série, produit en grandes séries

mass production n fabrication en série f

mast n (Comms) antenne f

master n (shipping) capitaine m, commandant m; ~ **budget** n budget principal m; ~ **copy** n original m; ~ **disk** n disque d'exploitation m; ~ **document** n document de base m, document maître m; ~ **file** n (Comp) fichier maître m, fichier principal m; ~ **key** n passe-partout m, clé principale f; ~ **lease** n bail maître m; ~ **owner** n (Transp) armateur m, patron m; ~ **plan** n plan d'ensemble m; ~ **policy** n US police de base f; ~ **tape** n bande mère f

mastermind vt (project, event, operation) organiser, diriger

Master: ~ **of Business Administration** n ≈ maîtrise de gestion des entreprises f; ~ **of Commerce** n ≈ maîtrise en sciences ⋯⟩

économiques *f*; ∼ **of Economics** *n* ≈ maîtrise en sciences économiques *f*; ∼ **of Science** *n* ≈ maîtrise de sciences *f*

masthead *n* (Media) ours *m*

MAT *abbr* (▸**machine-assisted translation**) TAO *f* (traduction assistée par ordinateur)

match¹ *n* (in web search) résultat *m*, réponse pertinente *f*, occurrence *f*

match² *vt* (description, results) correspondre à; (demand, expectations) répondre à; (success, record, achievement) égaler; ∼ **up to** (person) être à l'égal de; (expectations) répondre à; (reputation) être à la hauteur de

matched: ∼ **order** *n* ordre lié *m*; ∼ **securities** *n pl* ordres couplés *m pl*; ∼ **trade** *n* opérations commerciales compensées *f pl*

material¹ *adj* (benefit, change, damage, effect) matériel/-ielle; (cause, comfort, success, possessions) matériel/-ielle; **be** ∼ **to sth** se rapporter à qch; **in** ∼ **terms** sur le plan matériel

material² *n* (substance) matière *f*; (fabric) tissu *m*, étoffe *f*; (information) documentation *f*; (content) sujet *m*, contenu *m*; **be executive** ∼ avoir l'étoffe d'un cadre; **promotional** ∼ documentation publicitaire *f*; **collect** ∼ **on** se documenter sur

material: ∼ **fact** *n* fait pertinent *m*; ∼ **good** *n* bien matériel *m*; ∼ **interest** *n* (in company) intérêt matériel *m*

materialism *n* matérialisme *m*

materialize *vi* (offer, plan, threat) se concrétiser; (event) se réaliser, avoir lieu; (idea) prendre forme

materials *n pl* (substances, natural resources) matériaux *m pl*; (equipment) matériel *m*; **raw** ∼ matières premières *f pl*; ∼ **accounting** *n* comptabilité des matières premières *f*

maternity: ∼ **allowance** *n* allocation de maternité *f*; ∼ **benefit** *n* allocation de maternité *f*; ∼ **leave** *n* congé de maternité *m*; ∼ **pay** *n* indemnité de maternité *f*

matrix *n* matrice *f*; ∼ **analysis** *n* analyse matricielle *f*; ∼ **management** *n* organisation en matrices *f*; ∼ **organization** *n* structure matricielle *f*

matter¹ *n* (of specific nature) affaire *f*; (question) question *f*; (on list, agenda) point *m*; (content of publication) contenu *m*; **advertising** ∼ publicité *f*; **business** ∼s les affaires *f pl*; **money** ∼s les questions d'argent *f pl*; ∼s **arising** points non inscrits à l'ordre du jour; **the** ∼ **in hand**, **the** ∼ **under discussion** l'affaire en question; **it's a** ∼ **of time** c'est une question de temps; **it's a** ∼ **of doing** il s'agit de faire; **it's a** ∼ **of opinion** c'est une question d'opinion; **it's a** ∼ **of urgency** c'est urgent; **as a** ∼ **of routine** automatiquement

matter² *vi* avoir de l'importance

mature¹ *adj* (bill) échu; (policy) arrivé à échéance; (company) en pleine maturité; ∼ **economy** *n* (Econ) économie mature *f*; ∼ **market** *n* (S&M) marché arrivé à maturité *m*; (Stock) marché en pleine maturité *m*

mature² *vi* (bill) échoir; (policy) venir à échéance

matured *adj* (bond, coupon) arrivé à échéance, échu

maturing security *n* valeur arrivant à échéance *f*

maturity *n* (Fin) échéance *f*; (of person) maturité *f*; **at** ∼ à l'échéance, à maturité; **come to** ∼ arriver à échéance; ∼ **date** *n* date d'échéance *f*; ∼ **value** *n* valeur à échéance *f*

max. *abbr* (▸**maximal**, ▸**maximum**) max. (maximal, maximum)

maximal *adj* maximal

maximization *n* optimisation *f*; (Acc) maximalisation *f*

maximize *vt* (impact, profit, loss, advantage, sales) maximiser, maximaliser, (Comp) (window) agrandir; ∼ **one's potential** utiliser à fond toutes ses capacités

maximum¹ *adj* maximal, maximum

maximum² *n* maximum *m*; **a** ∼ **of 50 applicants** 50 candidats au maximum; **at a** ∼ au maximum; **do sth to the** ∼ faire qch à fond; **up to a** ∼ **of** jusqu'à un maximum de

maximum: ∼ **capacity** *n* (Ind) capacité maximale *f*; ∼ **efficiency** *n* rendement maximal *m*, rendement maximum *m*; ∼ **likelihood estimator** *n* estimateur de probabilité maximale *m*; ∼ **load** *n* charge limite *f*, charge maximale *f*; ∼ **market spread** *n* écart maximal hauts-bas *m*; ∼ **output** *n* rendement maximum *m*; ∼ **price** *n* prix maximum *m*; ∼ **rate** *n* taux plafond *m*; ∼ **return** *n* rapport maximum *m*, rendement maximum *m*

Mb *abbr* (▸**megabyte**) Mo *m* (méga-octet)

MBA *abbr* (▸**Master of Business Administration**) (diploma) ≈ maîtrise de gestion des entreprises *f*

m-banking *n* m-banking *m*, *transactions bancaires effectuées par téléphone ou terminal mobile*

MBO *abbr* (▸**management buyout**) RES *m* (rachat d'une entreprise par ses salariés)

MBS *abbr* (▸**mortgage-backed security**) titre de créance hypothécaire *m*, valeur garantie par hypothèque *f*

m-business *n* commerce électronique via le téléphone mobile *m*

MBWA *abbr* (▸**management by walking about**) management baladeur *m*

MCA *abbr* (▸**monetary compensatory account**) montant compensatoire monétaire *m*

MCom *abbr* (▸**Master of Commerce**) ≈ maîtrise en sciences économiques *f*

mature¹ *adj* (bill) échu; (policy) arrivé à

MD *abbr* (▸**managing director**) PDG *m* (président-directeur général)

meal *n* repas *m*; ∼ **allowance** *n* indemnité de repas *f*; ∼ **ticket** *n* AmE ticket-repas *m*, ticket-restaurant® *m*

mean¹ *adj* moyen/-enne

mean² *n* moyenne *f*

mean³ *vt* (signify, imply) vouloir dire; (entail) entraîner; **be meant for sb** être destiné à qn; **to** ∼ **to do** avoir l'intention de faire

mean: ∼ **cost** *n* coût moyen *m*; ∼ **deviation** *n* écart moyen *m*, écart type *m*; ∼ **effective pressure** *n* pression effective moyenne *f*; ∼ **price** *n* prix moyen *m*; ∼ **return** *n* rapport moyen *m*, rendement moyen *m*; ∼ **time** *n* temps moyen *m*; ∼ **time between failures** *n* temps moyen de bon fonctionnement *m*; ∼ **value** *n* valeur moyenne *f*

means *n pl* (way, method) moyen *m*, moyens *m pl*; (resources) moyens *m pl*, revenus *m pl*; **a** ∼ **of doing** un moyen de faire; **as a** ∼ **of** en tant que moyen de; **have the** ∼ **to do** avoir les moyens de faire; **by** ∼ **of** au moyen de; ∼ **of communication** moyen de communication *m*; ∼ **of payment** moyens de paiement *m pl*; ∼ **of transport** moyen de transport *m*

means test *n* examen de ressources *m*

means-test *vt* (person) soumettre à un examen de ressources

means-tested *adj* (benefit, grant) dépendant des ressources

measure¹ *n* (step) mesure *f*; (unit) unité de mesure *f*; (criterion) critère *m*; **economy** ∼ mesure d'économie; **take** ∼**s** prendre des mesures; ∼**s aimed at doing** mesures destinées à faire; **as a preventive** ∼ à titre préventif; **as a precautionary** ∼ par précaution; **as a temporary** ∼ provisoirement; **be a** ∼ **of** donner une idée de; **use something as a** ∼ **of** utiliser qch pour mesurer; **beyond** ∼ énormément; **a small** ∼ **of support** un soutien limité; ∼ **of economic welfare** mesure de bien-être économique *f*

measure² *vt* mesurer; ∼ **sb's performance** mesurer le rendement de qn; ∼ **up** (person) avoir les qualités requises; (product) être de qualité; ∼ **up to** être à la hauteur de (expectations); soutenir la comparaison avec (achievement)

measurement *n* (dimension) dimension *f*; (measuring) mesure *f*; (Transp) (nautical) jaugeage *m*; (volume) cubage *m*; ∼ **goods** *n pl* marchandises au cubage *f pl*; ∼ **ton** *n* tonne d'encombrement *f*

mechanic *n* mécanicien/-ienne *m/f*

mechanical engineering *n* mécanique *f*

mechanism *n* mécanisme *m*

mechanization *n* mécanisation *f*

mechanize *vt* mécaniser

mechanized *adj* mécanisé

MEcon *abbr* (▸**Master of Economics**) ≈ maîtrise en sciences économiques *f*

media¹ *adj* (personality) médiatique; (report, interest, influence, attention) des médias; (group) de médias

media² *n* **the** ∼ les médias *m pl*, les supports de communication *m pl*

media: ∼ **analysis** *n* analyse des médias *f*; ∼ **analyst** *n* analyste des médias *mf*; ∼ **buyer** *n* acheteur/-euse de médias *m/f*, acheteur/-euse d'espaces publicitaires *m/f*; ∼ **buying** *n* (advertising) achat de médias *m*; ∼ **consultant** *n* conseil en communications *m*; ∼ **coverage** *n* couverture médiatique *f*, médiatisation *f*; ∼ **event** *n* événement médiatique *m*; ∼ **fatigue** *n* désintérêt des médias *m*; ∼ **fragmentation** *n* (advertising) segmentation des médias *f*; ∼ **mix** *n* mix média *m*; ∼ **plan** *n* plan média *m*; ∼ **planner** *n* chargé d'études média *m*, médiaplanneur *m*; ∼ **planning** *n* média planning *m*, plan média *m*; ∼ **schedule** *n* calendrier de campagne *m*, plan média *m*; ∼ **selection** *n* choix des médias *m*, choix des supports *m*; ∼ **selling** *n* vente de médias *f*; ∼ **streaming** *n* transmission multimédia en continu *f*; ∼ **studies** *n pl* la communication et le journalisme; ∼ **vehicle** *n* support publicitaire *m*

median¹ *adj* (point, line) médian; (price, sum, value) moyen/-enne

median² *n* médiane *f*

mediate [1] *vt* (settlement) négocier; (dispute) arbitrer [2] *vi* intervenir comme médiateur, agir en médiateur; ∼ **between** arbitrer entre, agir en médiateur entre

mediation *n* médiation *f*; **through the** ∼ **of** par l'entremise de

mediator *n* médiateur/-trice *m/f*

medical¹ *adj* médical

medical² *n* visite médicale *f*, examen médical *m*

medical: ∼ **assistance** *n* assistance médicale *f*; ∼ **care insurance plan** *n* régime d'assurance maladie *m*; ∼ **costs** *n pl* frais médicaux *m pl*; ∼ **examination** *n* examen médical *m*, visite médicale *f*; ∼ **grounds** *n pl* raisons médicales *f pl*; ∼ **insurance** *n* assurance maladie *f*; ∼ **officer** *n* médecin du travail *m*

medicine *n* médicament *m*

medium¹ *adj* moyen/-enne; **in the** ∼ **term** à moyen terme

medium² *n pl* **-dia** (Comms) moyen de communication *m*, moyen d'expression *m*, média *m*; (mid-point) milieu *m*; (means) moyen *m*, intermédiaire *m*; **advertising** ∼ support publicitaire *m*; **the happy** ∼ le juste milieu; **through the** ∼ **of** par l'intermédiaire de

m

medium: ~**-dated** adj à moyen terme, à terme moyen; ~ **of exchange** moyen d'échange m; ~ **of redemption** moyen de rachat m; ~**-sized** adj de taille moyenne; **in the** ~ **term** à moyen terme; ~**-term** adj à moyen terme; ~**-term instrument** n instrument à moyen terme m; ~**-term loan** n prêt à moyen terme m

meet vt (person) rencontrer; (get to know) faire la connaissance de; (conditions) remplir; (loss) compenser; (bills) payer; (debts, overheads) couvrir; (criteria, standards) satisfaire à; (demand, order) satisfaire; (deadline) respecter; (requirements) répondre à; (targets) réaliser, atteindre; (challenge) se montrer à la hauteur de; ~ **costs** faire face à des frais; ~ **the demands** faire face aux demandes; ~ **a goal** répondre à un objectif; ~ **the needs of** répondre aux besoins de; ~ **one's obligations**, ~ **one's commitments** remplir ses obligations; **go to** ~ **sb at the station** aller chercher qn à la gare, aller attendre qn à la gare; ~ **with** (person) rencontrer; (difficulties, opposition, criticism, success) rencontrer; (failure) subir; (approval, praise) être accueilli avec

meeting n (official) réunion f; (coming together) rencontre f; **be in a** ~ être en réunion

megabit n mégabit m

megabucks n pl (infrml) millions de dollars m pl

megabyte n méga-octet m

megacorporation n très grande entreprise f

megastore n mégastore m

meltdown n economic ~ implosion de l'économie f

member n (of company, club, group, committee) membre m; (of trade union) syndiqué/-e m/f; **be a** ~ **of** être membre de; ~ **bank** n AmE banque affiliée f; ~ **of the board** administrateur/-trice m/f; ~ **of the board of management** membre du directoire m; ~ **firm** n société de bourse f; ~ **of staff** n employé/-e m/f; ~ **state** n (EU) État-Membre m; ~ **of a syndicate** syndicataire m/f

Member: ~ **of Congress** n US membre du Congrès m; ~ **of the European Parliament** n député/-e du Parlement Européen m/f; ~ **of the House of Representatives** n US membre de la Chambre des représentants m; ~ **of Parliament** n UK ≈ député/-e m/f; ~ **of the Scottish Parliament** n UK député/-e du Parlement écossais m/f; ~ **of the Welsh Assembly** n UK membre de l'Assemblée galloise m

membership n (belonging) adhésion f; (fee) cotisation f; (people) membres m pl; ~ **of the EU** adhésion à l'UE; **apply for** ~ faire une demande d'adhésion; ~ **card** n carte de membre f; ~ **dues** n pl cotisations (de membre) f pl

memo n note de service f; ~ **pad** n bloc-notes m

memorandum n pl **-da** (Admin) (message) note de service f; (Pol) mémorandum m; (Law) mémoire m, mémorandum m; ~ **account** n (Acc) compte hors bilan m, compte pour mémoire m; ~ **of agreement** n protocole d'accord m; ~ **and articles** n pl statuts m pl; ~ **of association** n acte constitutif de société m, statuts m pl; ~ **of intent** n déclaration d'intention f

memorize vt mémoriser

memory n mémoire f; ~ **bank** n bloc de mémoire m; ~ **chip** n puce mémoire f; ~**-hungry** adj (Comp) gourmand en mémoire; ~ **upgrade** n extension mémoire f

menial adj (role, position) subalterne; ~ **job** n petit boulot m

mention vt (allude to) faire mention de; (name, person) citer; (service, quality) mentionner; **as** ~**ed above** mentionné ci-dessus, mentionné plus haut; **as** ~**ed below** mentionné ci-dessous, mentionné plus bas

mentor n (HRM) mentor m

mentoring n (HRM) mentorat m

menu n menu m; ~ **bar** n barre des menus f; ~ **item** n élément de menu m

menu-driven adj piloté par menus

MEP abbr (▶**Member of the European Parliament**) député/-e du Parlement Européen m/f

mercantile adj mercantile; ~ **agency** n agence commerciale f; ~ **bank** n banque de commerce f; ~ **exchange** n bourse de commerce f, bourse de marchandises f; ~ **law** n droit commercial m; ~ **marine** n marine marchande f

mercantilism n mercantilisme m

merchandise n marchandises f pl; ~ **broker** n courtier en marchandises m; ~ **control** n gestion des marchandises f

merchandiser n (display stand) présentoir m; (person) responsable des techniques marchandes mf, merchandiser mf

merchandising n (S&M) commercialisation f, marchandisage m, merchandising m; ~ **director** n directeur/ -trice commercial/-e m/f, directeur/-trice de merchandising m/f; ~ **service** n service de merchandising m

merchant n (small trader) marchand/-e m/f; (selling in bulk) négociant m; (retailer) détaillant m; **wine** ~ négociant en vins m; ~ **account** n compte marchand m; ~ **bank** n UK banque d'affaires f; ~ **banker** n UK banquier/-ière d'affaires m/f; ~ **banking** n (profession) banque d'affaires f; (activity) opérations de banque d'affaires f pl; ~ **marine** n, ~ **navy** n marine marchande f; ~ **services provider** n fournisseur de comptes marchands m; ~ **ship** n navire de commerce m, navire marchand m; ~ **shipping** n navires de commerce *m pl*; ∼ **site** *n* (on Internet) site marchand *m*; ∼ **vessel** *n* navire de commerce *m*, navire marchand *m*

merchantable *adj* commercialisable, vendable; ∼ **quality** *n* qualité marchande *f*; ∼ **title** *n* AmE titre négociable *m*

merge¹ *n* (of document, computer file) fusion *f*; ∼ **and purge** *n* déduplication *f*

merge² ① *vt* (files, stock, companies) fusionner ② *vi* (companies) fusionner

merger *n* fusion *f*; ∼ **arbitrage** *n* arbitrage de fusion *m*; ∼ **company** *n* société née d'une fusion *f*

mergers and acquisitions *n pl* fusions et acquisitions *f pl*

meridian *n* méridien *m*

merit¹ *n* mérite *m*, valeur *f*; **have** ∼ avoir des mérites; **judge something on its own** ∼**s** juger qch de façon objective; ∼ **bad** *n* mal tutélaire *m*; ∼ **good** *n* bien tutélaire *m*; ∼ **increase** *n*, ∼ **raise** *n* AmE, ∼ **rise** *n* BrE (as incentive) prime d'encouragement *f*; (for productivity) prime de rendement *f*

merit² *vt* mériter

meritocracy *n* méritocratie *f*

mesoeconomy *n* mésoéconomie *f*

message *n* message *m*; **telephone** ∼ message téléphonique *m*; **take a** ∼ prendre un message; **get one's** ∼ **across** faire passer son message; ∼ **body** *n* corps de message *m*; ∼ **handling** *n* traitement de messages *m*; ∼ **header** *n* en-tête de message *m*; ∼ **switching** *n* commutation de messages *f*; ∼ **retrieval** *n* récupération de messages *f*; ∼ **window** *n* boite de dialogue *f*

messaging *n* messagerie électronique *f*

messenger *n* (in office) commissionnaire *mf*, coursier *m*; (Law) commissionnaire *mf*; **motorcycle** ∼ coursier à moto *m*

metadata *n pl* métadonnées *f pl*

metal *n* métal *m*; ∼ **market** *n* marché des métaux *m*

metaling AmE, **metalling** BrE *n* (Law, Ins) clause de doublage *f*

metallist *n* métalliste *mf*

metallurgist *n* métallurgiste *mf*

metamarketing *n* metamercatique *f*

metasearch *n* métarecherche *f*

meta search engine *n* métamoteur de recherche *m*

meter *n* (device) compteur *m*

meterage *n* AmE comptage *m*

metered mail *n* US courrier affranchi à la machine *m*

metering *n* comptage *m*, mesurage au compteur *m*

method *n* méthode *f*; (of taxation, treatment) mode *m*; ∼ **of depreciation** méthode de l'amortissement linéaire *m*; ∼ **of payment** modalité de paiement *f*, mode de paiement *m*

methodology *n* méthodologie *f*

methods: ∼ **engineering** *n* étude des méthodes *f*; ∼ **study** *n* étude des méthodes *f*

meticulous *adj* méticuleux/-euse

meticulously *adv* méticuleusement

me-too: ∼ **firm** *n* société plagiaire *f*; ∼ **product** *n* produit tactique *m*; ∼ **strategy** *n* stratégie d'imitation *f*

metric *adj* métrique; **go** ∼ adopter le système métrique; ∼ **system** *n* système métrique *m*

metrication *n* introduction du système métrique *f*

metrics *n + sing v* métrique *f*

metro *n* métro *m*

metropolis *n* métropole *f*

metropolitan *adj* métropolitain; ∼ **area** *n* agglomération *f*, zone métropolitaine *f*; ∼ **town** *n* métropole *f*

mezzanine: ∼ **bracket** *n* (Stock) souscripteurs de second rang *m pl*, tranche mezzanine *f*; ∼ **finance** *n* financement mezzanine *m*; ∼ **funding** *n* financement mezzanine *m*; ∼ **level** *n* niveau mezzanine *m*

mfd *abbr* (▸**manufactured**) fabriqué, manufacturé

MFN *abbr* (▸**most-favored nation** AmE, ▸**most-favoured nation** BrE) nation la plus favorisée *f*

mfrs *abbr* (**manufacturers**) fabricants *m pl*

micro *n* micro *m*

microbusiness *n* très petite entreprise *f* *avec moins de 10 employés*

microchip *n* microplaquette *f*, puce *f*

microcomputer *n* micro-ordinateur *m*

microcomputing *n* micro-informatique *f*

microeconomic *adj* microéconomique

microeconomics *n + sing v* microéconomie *f*

microedit *n* microédit *m*

microelectronics *n + sing v* micro-électronique *f*

microfiche *n* microfiche *f*; ∼ **reader** *n* lecteur de microfiches *m*

microfilm *n* microfilm *m*

micromarketing *n* micromarketing *m*

micro-marketplace *n* micromarché *m*

micropayment *n* micropaiement *m*

microphone *n* micro *m*, microphone *m*

microprocessor *n* microprocesseur *m*

microproduction *n* micro-production *f*

microprogram *n* microprogramme *m*

microsecond *n* microseconde *f*

microsegment *n* microsegment *m*

microsegmentation *n* microsegmentation *f*

microtransaction *n* microtransaction *f*

mid- *pref* **in the** ∼**-1990's** au milieu des années 90; ∼**-morning/afternoon** au milieu du matin/de l'après-midi *m*; ∼**-June** (à la) ⋯⊹

mi-juin; **in ~-career** à mi-chemin de ma/sa/
votre *etc* carrière

mid-career plateau *n* palier en milieu
de carrière *m*

middle¹ *adj* (size) moyen/-enne; (position) du
milieu, intermédiaire; **follow a ~ course**
adopter une position intermédiaire; **a ~ way**
un juste milieu

middle² *n* milieu *m*; **be in the ~ of doing
sth** être en train de faire; **split sth down the
~** (work, bill) partager qch en deux

middle: ~ class *n* bourgeoisie *f*; **~
income bracket** *n* tranche moyenne de
revenus *f*; **~-income taxpayer** *n*
contribuable à revenu moyen *mf*; **~
management** *n* cadres moyens *m pl*,
maîtrise *f*; **~ manager** *n* cadre moyen *m*; **~
office** *n* suivi de marché *m*; **~ price** *n*
(Stock) cours moyen *m*; **~ range of the
market** *n* tranche moyenne du marché *f*; **~
strike option** *n* option à cours moyen *f*; **~
strike price** *n* cours d'exercice moyen *m*

middleman *n* intermédiaire *mf*; **act as a
~** servir d'intermédiaire

middleware *n* (Comp) logiciel médiateur *m*

midnight deadline *n* clôture à minuit *f*

mid price *n* (Stock) cours moyen *m*, prix
moyen *m*

midrange *adj* de milieu de gamme,
intermédiaire

midweek¹ *n* milieu de la semaine *m*; **in ~**
en milieu de semaine

midweek² *adv* en milieu de semaine

midyear *adv* vers le milieu de l'année

migrant *n* migrant/-e *m/f*; **~ labor** AmE, **~
labour** BrE *n* (foreign) main-d'œuvre immigrée
f; (mobile within country) main-d'œuvre migrante
f; **~ worker** *n* travailleur/-euse migrant/-e
m/f

migration *n* (Econ) migration *f*; (of data)
transfert *m*; **~-fed unemployment** *n*
chômage entraîné par l'immigration *m*

mile *n* 1609 mètres, mile *m*

mileage *n* ≈ kilométrage *m*; **~ allowance**
n ≈ indemnité kilométrique *f*

miles: ~ per gallon *n pl* miles par gallon,
≈ kilomètres au cent *m pl*; **~ per hour** *n pl*
miles/heure *m pl*

milestone *n* étape *f*; **~ chart** *n* graphique
des étapes critiques *m*

militant *n* militant/-e *m/f*

military industrial complex *n*
complexe militaro-industriel *m*

milk¹ *n* lait *m*; **~ products** *n pl* produits
laitiers *m pl*; **~ round** *n* UK *recrutement
annuel des étudiants universitaires par les
grandes entreprises*

milk² *vt* (opportunity, situation) exploiter

mill *n* (Ind) (factory) fabrique *f*; **cotton ~**
filature *f*; **paper ~** papeterie *f*

milliard *n* milliard *m*

million *n* million *m*

millionaire *n* millionnaire *mf*

min. *abbr* (▸**minimum**) min. (minimum)

mind map® *n* schéma heuristique *m*, mind
map® *m*

mindset *n* façon de penser *f*

mine¹ *n* mine *f*

mine²: ~ for *vt* (minerals) extraire

miner *n* mineur *m*

mineral *n* (for extraction) minerai *m*; **~
industry** *n* industrie minière *f*; **~ oil
products** *n pl* produits pétroliers *m pl*; **~
resource** *n* ressource minérale *f*; **~ rights**
n pl droits miniers *m pl*

mini *adj* mini

miniaturize *vt* miniaturiser

mini-budget *n* mini-budget *m*

minibus *n* minibus *m*

minicomputer *n* mini-ordinateur *m*

minimal *adj* minimal

minimax *n* minimax *m*; **~ strategy** *n*
stratégie minimax *f*

minimize *vt* (incidence, significance) minimiser;
(risk, impact, cost, damage) réduire au maximum;
(Comp) (window) réduire

minimum¹ *adj* minimum

minimum² *n* minimum *mf*; **at the ~** au
minimum; **bare ~** strict minimum; **reduce
something to a ~** réduire qch au maximum;
keep sth to a ~ maintenir qch à un
minimum; **do the absolute ~** faire le strict
minimum

minimum: ~ amount *n* minimum *m*; **~
balance** *n* solde créditeur minimum *m*,
solde minimal *m*; **~ bill of lading** *n*
connaissement minimum *m*; **~ lending rate**
n UK taux officiel d'escompte *m*; **~ living
wage** *n* minimum vital *m*; **~ margin** *n*
(options) marge minimale *f*, marge minimum *f*;
~ payment *n* paiement minimum *m*; **~
quality standards** *n pl* critères de qualité
minima *m pl*; **~ temperature** *n*
température minimale *f*; **~ wage** *n* salaire
minimum *m*

mining *n* exploitation minière *f*; **~
company** *n* compagnie minière *f*; **~
industry** *n* industrie minière *f*; **~ shares**
n pl valeurs minières *f pl*

minister *n* ministre *mf*, secrétaire d'État *mf*

ministerial *adj* ministériel/-ielle; **~ order**
n arrêté ministériel *m*

ministry *n* ministère *m*

Ministry of Defence *n* UK ≈ ministère
de la Défense nationale *m*

minor¹ *adj* mineur; **~ league** *adj* (company,
player) de deuxième ordre

minor² *n* (Law) mineur/-e *m/f*

minority *n* minorité *f*; **be in the ~** être en
minorité; **be in a ~ of one** être le seul/la
seule à penser ça; **~ government** *n*
gouvernement minoritaire *m*; **~ holding** *n*,

~ **interest** n (Fin) participation minoritaire f; ~ **investment** n investissement minoritaire m; ~ **rule** n gouvernement par la minorité m; ~ **share** n action minoritaire f; ~ **shareholder** n actionnaire minoritaire mf; ~ **shareholding** n action minoritaire f, participation minoritaire f; ~ **stake** n intérêt minoritaire m, participation minoritaire f

mint¹ n hôtel m de la Monnaie f

mint² vt (coins) frapper

minus¹ n (symbol) moins m; ~ **factor** facteur négatif m; ~ **sign** n (Math) moins m, signe moins m

minus² prep moins

minute vt (comment, decision) prendre note de; (meeting) rédiger le procès-verbal de, rédiger le compte rendu de

minute book n registre des délibérations m

minutes n pl (of meeting) procès-verbal m, compte rendu m

MIP abbr (▸**marine insurance policy**) police d'assurance maritime f

mirror site n (Comp) site miroir m

MIS abbr (▸**management information system**) SIG m (système intégré de gestion); (▸**marketing information system**) SIM m (système d'information de marketing)

misaligned adj mal aligné

misalignment n mauvais alignement m

misapply vt mal appliquer

misapprehension n malentendu m; **be labouring under a** ~ se tromper

misappropriate vt détourner

misappropriation n (of money, funds) détournement m; (Law) concussion f

misc. abbr (▸**miscellaneous**) divers

miscalculate vt (amount, total) mal calculer; (risk, response) mal évaluer

miscalculation n (Math) erreur de calcul f; (poor judgement) mauvais calcul m

miscarriage of justice n erreur judiciaire f

miscellaneous adj divers; ~ **expenses** n pl frais divers m pl

miscoding n erreur de programmation f

misconduct n faute grave f, manquement à la discipline m

misdeed n méfait m

misdemeanor AmE, **misdemeanour** BrE n délit mineur m, méfait m

misfeasance n méfait m

misfile vt mal classer

misguided adj (strategy, attempt) peu judicieux/-ieuse

mishandle vt (meeting, operation) mal conduire; (case, problem) mal traiter; (person) ne pas savoir comment s'y prendre avec

misintermediation n intermédiation

ratée f

mislead vt (unintentionally) induire en erreur; (deliberately) tromper

misleading adj (information) trompeur/-euse; (claim, statement) mensonger/-ère; ~ **advertising** n publicité mensongère f

mismanage vt (economy, funds) mal administrer; (company, project) mal gérer

mismanagement n (of economy, funds) mauvaise administration f; (of company, project) mauvaise gestion f

mismatch n (Acc) décalage m, non concordance f; (of concepts, views) disparité f

mispricing n évaluation erronée du prix f

misprint n faute d'impression f, coquille f

misread vt (situation) mal interpréter; (sentence, word) mal lire

misrepresent vt (fact) déformer, dénaturer; (views, intentions) déformer; (person) présenter sous un faux jour

misrepresentation n (of person) représentation erronée f; (of facts, opinion) déformation f; (Law) déclaration inexacte f

miss vt (meeting, event, train, connection) rater; (deadline) dépasser; (sales target) ne pas réaliser; (chance, opportunity) laisser passer; (notice the absence of) remarquer la disparition de; **she** ~**ed her colleagues** ses collègues lui manquaient; ~ **out** (line, page) sauter; (person, fact) omettre; ~ **out on** (bargain, chance) laisser passer

mis-sell vt (pension, policy) vendre avec abus de confiance

mis-selling n vente avec abus de confiance f

missing adj (thing) qui manque; (vehicle, person) disparu

mission n mission f; ~ **critical** adj essentiel/-ielle; (system) vital; ~ **statement** n déclaration de mission f, définition de la mission f

missionary: ~ **salesperson** n prospecteur/-trice m/f; ~ **selling** n ventes de prospection f pl

mistake n (in calculation, judgement, procedure) erreur f; (in text, spelling) faute f; **make a** ~ faire une erreur, se tromper; (in spelling, typing) faire une faute; **by** ~ par erreur

mistaken adj (idea, conclusion) erroné; **be** ~ avoir tort, se tromper

mistime vt (intervention, comment) mal calculer; ~ **a product launch** mal choisir son moment pour lancer un produit

misunderstanding n malentendu m

misuse¹ n (poor use) mauvais usage m; (excessive use) usage abusif m; ~ **of funds** détournement de fonds m

misuse² vt (power) abuser de; (money, resources) mal employer; (funds) détourner

mitigating circumstances n pl circonstances atténuantes f pl

m

mitigation *n* (minimising) atténuation *f*; (of sentence) réduction *f*; **in ~ of sb's actions** à la décharge de qn; **~ of damages** demande en réduction de dommages-intérêts *f*

mix¹ *n* mélange *m*; (recording) mixage *m*; (S&M) mix *m*, mix de produits *m*

mix² **1** *vt* (combine) mélanger; (make) préparer; (concrete) malaxer
2 *vi* (socialize) être sociable; **~ with** fréquenter

mixed *adj* (varied) varié; (of both genders) mixte; (reaction, reception) mitigé; **experience ~ fortunes** connaître un succès mitigé; **~ bundling** *n* groupage *m*; **~ consignment** *n* envoi mixte *m*; **~ cost** *n* coût semi-variable *m*, coûts mixtes *m pl*; **~ economy** *n* économie mixte *f*; **~ farming** *n* polyculture *f*; **~ funds** *n pl* fonds mixtes *m pl*; **~ policy** *n* police d'assurance mixte *f*; **~ results** *n pl* résultats mitigés *m pl*; **~ signals** *n pl* messages contradictoires *m pl*

mixing *n* (combining) mélange *m*; (of sound) mixage *m*

MLM *abbr* (▸**multilevel marketing**) marketing multiniveau *m*, vente par réseau coopté *f*

MLR *abbr* UK (▸**minimum lending rate**) taux officiel d'escompte *m*

MMDA *abbr* US (▸**money-market deposit account**) compte de dépôt du marché monétaire *m*

MMF *abbr* US (▸**money-market fund**) fonds investi au marché monétaire *m*, fonds monétaire *m*

MMMF *abbr* US (▸**money-market mutual fund**) fonds commun de placement du marché monétaire *m*

MO *abbr* (▸**mail order**) VPC *f* (vente par correspondance); (▸**money order**) MP *m* (mandat postal); (▸**modus operandi**) manière d'opérer *f*, mode opératoire *m*; (▸**medical officer**) médecin du travail *m*

mobile¹ *adj* mobile

mobile² *n* (telephone) portable *m*, téléphone portable *m*

mobile: ~ communications *n pl* téléphonie mobile *f*; **~ home** *n* mobile home *m*; **~ Internet** *n* Internet mobile *m*; **~ payment** *n* paiement mobile *m*; **~ phone** *n*, **~ telephone** *n* téléphone mobile *m*, téléphone portable *m*; **~ telephony** *n* téléphonie mobile *f*; **~ worker** *n* travailleur/-euse itinérant/-e *m/f*, travailleur/-euse mobile *m/f*

mobility *n* mobilité *f*; **~ clause** *n* clause de mobilité *f*; **~ of labor** AmE, **~ of labour** BrE *n* mobilité de la main-d'œuvre *f*

mobilize *vt* mobiliser

MOD *abbr* UK (▸**Ministry of Defence**) ≈ ministère de la Défense *m*; (▸**movies-on-demand**) films à la demande *m pl*

mode *n* type *m*; (Comp, Math) mode *m*; **~ of**

funding type de financement *m*; **~ of leadership** style de direction *m*; **~ of life** mode de vie *m*; **~ of production** méthode de production *f*; **~ of transport** moyen de transport *m*

model¹ *n* (version of product, template) modèle *m*; (Math, Comp) modèle *m*; (scale version) maquette *f*; (for fashions) mannequin *m*; **~ factory** *n* usine modèle *f*; **~ profile** *n* profil type *m*; **~ worker** *n* employé/-e modèle *m/f*

model² *vt* (Math, Comp) modéliser

modeling AmE, **modelling** BrE *n* (Math, Comp) modélisation *f*

modem *n* modem *m*; **~ link** *n* liaison par modem *f*

moderate¹ *adj* (not extreme) modéré; (average) moyen/-enne; **~ income** *n* revenu modeste *m*, revenu moyen *m*

moderate² *n* (Pol) modéré/-e *m/f*

moderate³ *vt* modérer

moderated *adj* (mailing list, chat) modéré

moderately *adv* (in moderation) modérément; (averagely) moyennement; **~ good** *adj* assez bon; **~ priced** *adj* de milieu de gamme; **~ well** *adv* assez bien

moderator *n* (of group, meeting) animateur/-trice *m/f*; (of newsgroup) modérateur *m*

modern *adj* moderne

modernization *n* modernisation *f*

modernize *vt* moderniser

modest *adj* modeste; (sum, salary) modique; **shares show a ~ gain** les actions ont accusé une hausse modérée

modification *n* modification *f*; **make ~s to, carry out ~s to** apporter des modifications à

modified *adj* modifié; **~ net premium** *n* prime nette modifiée *f*; **~ rebuy** *n* rachat modifié *m*

modify *vt* (change) modifier, apporter des modifications à; (moderate) modérer

modular *adj* modulaire; **~ housing** *n* US logement modulaire *m*; **~ production** *n* fabrication modulaire *f*

modularity *n* modularité *f*

modulate *vt* moduler

modulation *n* modulation *f*

module *n* module *m*

modus operandi *n* manière d'opérer *f*, mode opératoire *m*

mold AmE ▸**mould** BrE

mom-and-pop store *n* AmE commerce familial *m*

moment *n* moment *m*; **at a given ~** à un moment donné; **at a given ~ in the future** dans l'avenir, à un moment donné dans le futur; **at the ~** en ce moment

momentum *n* élan *m*; **gain/lose ~** prendre/perdre de l'élan

monetarism *n* monétarisme *m*

monetarist¹ *adj* monétariste

monetarist² *n* monétariste *mf*

monetary *adj* monétaire; ~ **authorities** *n pl* autorités monétaires *f pl*; ~ **base** *n* base monétaire *f*; ~ **compensatory amount** *n* (EU) montant compensatoire monétaire *m*; ~ **economics** *n pl* + *sing v* économie monétaire *f*; ~ **item** *n* (on balance sheets) actif monétaire *m*; ~ **policy** *n* politique monétaire *f*; ~ **reserve** *n* (Bank) réserve monétaire *f*, (Econ) coussin de devises *m*, réserve monétaire *f*; ~ **restriction** *n* restriction monétaire *f*; ~ **standard** *n* étalon monétaire *m*; ~ **union** *n* union monétaire *f*; ~ **unit** *n* unité monétaire *f*

monetization *n* monétisation *f*

monetize *vt* monétiser

money *n* argent *m*; (Econ, Fin) argent *m*, capitaux *m pl*, monnaie *f*; (salary) salaire *m*; **earn good** ~ bien gagner sa vie; **make** ~ gagner de l'argent; **put up** ~ **for a project** investir de l'argent dans un projet; **raise** ~ trouver des capitaux; **get one's** ~ **back** (be refunded) se faire rembourser; (on loan, investment) rentrer dans ses fonds; **get one's** ~ **worth** en avoir pour son argent; ~ **at call** *n* ayant au jour le jour *m*; ~**-back coupon** *n* bon de remboursement *m*; ~**-back guarantee** *n* garantie de remboursement *f*; ~**-back offer** *n* offre de remboursement *f*; ~ **broker** *n* courtier monétaire *m*; ~ **income** *n* revenu nominal *m*; ~ **laundering** *n* blanchiment de capitaux *m*; ~ **lender** *n* prêteur/-euse sur gages *m/f*; ~ **management** *n* gestion financière *f*; ~ **market** *n* marché monétaire *m*; ~**-market deposit account** *n* US compte de dépôt du marché monétaire *m*; ~**-market fund** *n* US fonds investi au marché monétaire *m*, fonds monétaire *m*; ~**-market institution** *n* institution du marché monétaire *f*; ~**-market instrument** *n* instrument du marché monétaire *m*; ~**-market mutual fund** *n* US fonds commun de placement du marché monétaire *m*; ~**-market paper** *n* instrument du marché monétaire *m*, papier monétaire *m*; ~**-market rate** *n* taux du marché monétaire *m*; ~**-market returns** *n pl* rendements du marché monétaire *m pl*, revenu du marché monétaire *m*; ~**-market savings account** *n* US compte de dépôts monétaires *m*; ~**-market trader** *n* opérateur/-trice sur le marché monétaire *m/f*; ~ **matters** *n pl* affaires d'argent *f pl*; ~ **multiplier** *n* multiplicateur monétaire *m*; ~**-off voucher** *n* bon de réduction *m*; ~ **order** *n* mandat *m*, mandat postal *m*; ~ **reserve** *n* réserve monétaire *f*; ~ **restraint** *n* restriction monétaire *f*; ~**-spinner** *n* activité lucrative *f*, mine d'or *f*; ~ **supply** *n* masse monétaire *f*; ~ **up front** *n* argent devant soi *m*

moneymaker *n* (person) brasseur de capitaux *m*; (product) article qui rapporte beaucoup *m*

monies *n pl* fonds *m pl*, capitaux *m pl*; ~

paid in *n pl* recettes effectuées *f pl*, sommes versées *f pl*; ~ **paid out** *n pl* versements effectués *m pl*

monitor¹ *n* moniteur *m*, écran *m*

monitor² *vt* (rate, results) surveiller, contrôler; (progress, person, order, case) suivre

monitoring *n* surveillance *f*, (of progress, person, order, case) suivi *m*

monochrome *adj* monochrome

monoeconomics *n* + *sing v* monoéconomie *f*

monogram *n* monogramme *m*

monometallism *n* monométallisme *m*

monopolistic *adj* (control, market, competition) monopolistique

monopolization *n* monopolisation *f*

monopolize *vt* monopoliser

monopoly *n* monopole *m*; **have a** ~ **on** avoir le monopole de, détenir le monopole de; **end sb's** ~ mettre fin au monopole de qn; **state** ~ monopole d'État *m*; ~ **power** *n* pouvoir de monopole *m*; ~ **price** *n* prix de monopole *m*

monorail *n* monorail *m*

monotonous *adj* monotone

month *n* mois *m*

monthly¹ *adj* mensuel/-elle; **in** ~ **installments** AmE, **in** ~ **instalments** BrE par mensualités

monthly² *adv* (pay, earn) mensuellement, au mois; (happen, visit) tous les mois, une fois par mois

monthly³ *n* (magazine) mensuel *m*

monthly: ~ **compounding of interest** *n* intérêt composé mensuellement *m*; ~ **expenses** *n pl* frais mensuels *m pl*; ~ **installment** AmE, ~ **instalment** BrE *n* mensualité *f*, règlement mensuel *m*; ~ **investment plan** *n* plan d'investissement mensuel *m*; ~ **magazine** *n* mensuel *m*; ~ **rate note** *n* bon à taux mensuel *m*; ~ **rent** *n* loyer au mois *m*, loyer mensuel *m*; ~ **return** *n* état mensuel *m*; ~ **salary** *n* salaire mensuel *m*; ~ **sales** *n pl* ventes mensuelles *f pl*; ~ **savings** *n* (of employee) épargne mensuelle *f*; ~ **statement** *n* (for credit card, bank account) relevé de compte mensuel *m*; ~ **tenancy** *n* location au mois *f*; ~ **wage** *n* salaire mensuel *m*

months traded *n pl* (Stock) mois de transaction *m pl*

moonlight *vi* travailler au noir

moonlight economy *n* économie souterraine *f*

moonlighter *n* travailleur/-euse au noir *m/f*

moonlighting *n* travail au noir *m*

moral *adj* moral; ~ **persuasion** *n* pression morale *f*

morale *n* moral *m*; **raise** ~ remonter le moral; ~ **is low** le moral est bas

moratorium *n pl* **-ia** moratoire *m*

morphological analysis *n* analyse morphologique *f*

mortality *n* mortalité *f*; ~ **table** *n* (Ins) table de mortalité *f*

mortg. *abbr* (▶**mortgage**) hyp. (hypothèque)

mortgage¹ *n* (Fin) hypothèque *f*; (in house-buying) emprunt-logement *m*; **apply for a** ~ faire une demande d'emprunt-logement; **take out a** ~ faire un emprunt-logement; **pay off a** ~, **clear a** ~ rembourser un emprunt-logement, purger une hypothèque; ~ **account** *n* compte de prêt hypothécaire *m*; ~ **arrears** *n pl* arriérés d'emprunt-logement *m pl*; ~**-backed certificate** *n* certificat garanti par hypothèque *m*; ~**-backed security** *n* titre de créance hypothécaire *m*, valeur garantie par hypothèque *f*; ~ **banker** *n* US banquier hypothécaire *m*; ~ **bond** *n* US obligation hypothécaire *f*; ~ **broker** *n* US courtier hypothécaire *m*; ~ **ceiling** *n* plafond d'hypothèque *m*; ~ **company** *n* société de prêt hypothécaire *f*; ~ **credit association** *n* association de crédit hypothécaire *f*; ~ **debt** *n* dette hypothécaire *f*; ~ **discount** *n* remise hypothécaire *f*; ~ **insurance policy** *n* (personal) police d'assurance hypothèque *f*; ~ **lender** *n* prêteur hypothécaire *m*; ~ **life insurance** *n* US assurance-vie liée à l'hypothèque *f*; ~ **loan** *n* prêt hypothécaire *m*, prêt sur hypothèque *m*; ~ **loan company** *n* société de prêt hypothécaire *f*; ~ **loan corporation** *n* société de prêt hypothécaire *f*; ~ **market** *n* marché hypothécaire *m*; ~ **payment** *n* versement hypothécaire *m*; ~ **rate** *n* taux de prêt hypothécaire *m*; ~ **relief** *n* allègement d'un prêt hypothécaire *m*; ~ **repayment** *n* remboursement d'un prêt hypothécaire *m*; ~ **statement** *n* état de compte de prêt hypothécaire *m*

mortgage² *vt* hypothéquer; **the house is** ~**d** la maison est hypothéquée

mortgagee *n* créancier/-ière hypothécaire *m/f*

mortgager *n* débiteur/-trice hypothécaire *m/f*

most: ~ **active list** *n* liste des valeurs les plus actives *f*; ~**-favored nation** *n* AmE, ~**-favoured nation** *n* BrE nation la plus favorisée *f*; ~**-favoured nation clause** *n* BrE clause de la nation la plus favorisée *f*; ~**-favoured nation trading status** *n* BrE statut de nation la plus favorisée *m*

mothball *vt* mettre en sommeil; (plant) fermer provisoirement

motherboard *n* carte mère *f*

motion *n* (movement) mouvement *m*; (Admin, Pol) motion *f*; **set sth in** ~ mettre qch en route; **set the wheels in** ~ mettre les choses en route; **table/second the** ~ déposer/appuyer la motion; **carry/reject the** ~

adopter/rejecter la motion; ~ **of censure** *n* motion de censure *f*; ~ **economy** *n* économie des mouvements *f*; ~ **picture** *n* AmE film *m*; ~ **picture advertising** *n* AmE publicité cinématographique *f*; ~ **picture industry** *n* AmE industrie cinématographique *f*; ~ **pictures** *n pl* AmE cinéma *m*; ~ **study** *n* étude des mouvements *f*

motivate *vt* motiver; ~ **oneself** se motiver

motivated *adj* motivé

motivation *n* motivation *f*

motivational *adj* motivant; ~ **analysis** *n* analyse de motivation *f*; ~ **research** *n* étude de motivations *f*; ~ **study** *n* étude de motivations *f*

motivator *n* (incentive) mobile *m*, motivation *f*; (person) élément moteur *m*; **team** ~ moteur de l'équipe *m*

motive *n* motif *m*; (Ins, Law) mobile *m*

motor *n* moteur *m*; ~ **fleet** *n* parc automobile *m*; ~ **insurance** *n* assurance automobile *f*; ~ **mileage allowance** *n* UK ≈ indemnité kilométrique *f*; ~ **show** *n* salon de l'automobile *m*; ~ **vehicle** *n* véhicule automobile *m*, véhicule à moteur *m*; ~ **vehicle insurance** *n* assurance automobile *f*; ~ **vessel** *n* navire à moteur *m*

motorcar *n* BrE voiture *f*

motorway *n* BrE autoroute *f*

mould¹ *n* BrE moule *m*; **break the** ~ innover; **cast in the same** ~ **as** coulé dans le même moule que

mould² *vt* BrE (public opinion) façonner

mount *vt* (campaign, exhibition) monter; (Fin) (raid) lancer; ~ **a takeover bid for a company** lancer une OPA contre une société; ~ **a challenge to** lancer un défi à; ~ **up** (debts, price) monter; (number) augmenter

mountain *n* montagne *f*; **butter** ~ montagne de beurre *f*

mounting *adj* (pressure, tension, problems) croissant; (debts) de plus en plus important; (bills) de plus en plus élevé

mouse *n* souris *f*; ~ **button** *n* bouton de la souris *m*; ~**-driven** *adj* commandé par souris; ~ **mat** *n* tapis de souris *m*; ~ **pointer** *n* pointeur de la souris *m*

movable property *n* biens meubles *m pl*, biens mobiliers *m pl*

movables *n pl* biens meubles *m pl*, biens mobiliers *m pl*

move¹ *n* (change of residence, house) déménagement *m*; (of business) transfert *m*; (change of job) changement d'emploi *m*; (step) démarche *f*, manœuvre *f*; (in currency) fluctuation *f*; (Stock) mouvement *m*; **make the first** ~ faire le premier pas; **a good/bad** ~ une bonne/mauvaise idée; **make the** ~ **from sales to management** passer des ventes à la direction

move² **1** *vt* (change position of) déplacer; (sell) vendre, écouler; (motion, amendment) proposer; (employee, staff) muter; (offices, HQ) transférer; (possessions, furniture) déménager; ∼ **sb to do** (prompt) amener qn à faire; ∼ **house** déménager

2 *vi* (change location) déménager; (sell, be sold) se vendre; (take steps) agir; (progress) avancer, progresser; **get things moving** faire avancer les choses; ∼ **in tandem** évoluer en parallèle; ∼ **into the money** entrer dans le cours; ∼ **to larger premises** emménager dans des locaux plus grands; ∼ **ahead** (shares) progresser; ∼ **in** emménager; (intervene) intervenir; ∼ **in on** (market, company) lancer une opération sur; ∼ **into** se diversifier dans; ∼ **on** (problem, question) intervenir sur; ∼ **out** déménager; ∼ **together** (currencies) fluctuer, varier simultanément; ∼ **up** (employee) être promu; (profits, rates, prices) augmenter

movement *n* mouvement *m*; (in prices) fluctuation *f*; (Pol, Stock) mouvement *m*; ∼ **certificate** *n* certificat de circulation *m*; ∼ **of freight** mouvement des marchandises *m*, transport de marchandises *m*; ∼ **of labor** AmE, ∼ **of labour** BrE circulation de la main-d'œuvre *f*

mover and shaker *n* animateur/-trice *m/f*, homme d'action/femme d'action *m/f*

movie *n* AmE film *m*; ∼**-making** *n* cinéma *m*; ∼ **theater** *n* AmE cinéma *m*

movies-on-demand *n pl* films à la demande *m pl*

moving: ∼ **average** *n* moyenne mobile *f*; ∼ **pavement** *n* BrE tapis roulant *m*, trottoir roulant *m*; ∼ **van** *n* camion de déménagement *m*

MP3 *abbr* (**MPEG1 Audio Layer 3**) (format) MP3 *m*; ∼ **file** *n* fichier MP3 *m*; ∼ **player** *n* baladeur MP3 *m*

MPC *abbr* (▸**marginal propensity to consume**) propension marginale à consommer *f*

MPEG *abbr* (**moving pictures expert group**) (format) MPEG *m*

mpg *abbr* (▸**miles per gallon**) *miles par gallon*, ≈ km au cent (kilomètres au cent)

mph *abbr* (▸**miles per hour**) miles/heure *m pl*

MPS *abbr* (▸**marginal propensity to save**) propension marginale à épargner *f*

MRA *abbr* (▸**multiple regression analysis**) analyse de régression multiple *f*

MRP *abbr* (▸**manufacturer's recommended price**) prix recommandé par le fabricant *m*; (**Manufacturing Resource Planning**) planification des ressources de fabrication *f*

m/s *abbr* (▸**months after sight**) mois à vue *m*

MS *abbr* (▸**member state**) État-Membre *m*

MSc *abbr* (▸**Master of Science**) ≈ maîtrise de sciences *f*

MSP *abbr* (▸**member of the Scottish Parliament**) député/-e du parlement écossais

m/f

MSRP *abbr* (▸**manufacturer's suggested retail price**) prix de vente recommandé par le fabricant *m*

MT *abbr* (▸**machine translation**) traduction automatique *f*, traduction assistée par ordinateur *f*; (▸**mean time**) temps moyen *m*; (▸**minimum temperature**) température minimale *f*

MTBF *abbr* (▸**mean time between failures**) temps moyen de bon fonctionnement *m*

MTL *abbr* (▸**medium-term loan**) prêt à moyen terme *m*

m-trading *n* m-trading *m*, *négoce de valeurs mobilières par téléphone ou terminal mobile*

M/U *adj* (▸**making-up price**) cours de compensation *m*

multi-access *adj* (application, portal, solution) multi-accès

multicasting *n* multidiffusion *f*

multichannel *adj* (strategy, distribution, retailing) multicanaux

multicollinearity *n* (Econ) multicorrélation *f*; (in statistics) multicolinéarité *f*

multicurrency *n* multidevise *f*; ∼ **loan** *n* emprunt en plusieurs monnaies *m*, prêt multidevises *m*

multidelivery *n* livraison multiple *f*

multidisciplinary *adj* pluridisciplinaire

multiemployer bargaining *n* négociation avec association patronale *f*, négociation collective *f*

multientry visa *n* visa multi-transit *m*, visa permanent *m*

multijobbing *n* traitement multitravail *m*

multijurisdictional *adj* multijuridictionnel/-elle

multilateral *adj* multilatéral; ∼ **agency** *n* agence multilatérale *f*; ∼ **agreement** *n* accord multilatéral *m*; ∼ **aid** *n* aide multilatérale *f*; ∼ **development bank** *n* banque multilatérale de développement *f*; ∼ **donors** *n pl* donateurs multilatéraux *m pl*; ∼ **permit** *n* (EU) permis multilatéral *m*; ∼ **trade agreement** *n* accord commercial multilatéral *m*

multilateralism *n* multilatéralisme *m*

Multilateral Trade Organization *n* organisation mondiale du commerce *f*

multilevel *adj* (analysis) à plusieurs niveaux; (Comp) multiniveaux *inv*; ∼ **marketing** *n* marketing à niveaux multiples *m*, vente par réseau coopté *f*

multilingual *adj* polyglotte

multimedia *adj* (advertising, computer) multimédia

multimillionaire *n* milliardaire *mf*

multimillion pound deal *n* transaction de plusieurs millions libellés en livres

⋯⋗

sterling *f*

multimodal *adj* multimodal; ∼ **transport** *n* transport multimodal *m*; ∼ **transport service** *n* service de transport multimodal *m*

multinational[1] *adj* multinational

multinational[2] *n* multinationale *f*

multinational: ∼ **bank** *n* banque multinationale *f*; ∼ **company** *n*, ∼ **corporation** *n* multinationale *f*, société multinationale *f*; ∼ **trading** *n* commerce multinational *m*

multinationally *adv* de façon multinationale

multioption: ∼ **facility** *n* (Stock) montage financier à options multiples *m*; ∼ **financing facility** *n* facilité de financement multi-options *f*

multipack *n* emballage multiple *m*

multiperil insurance *n* assurance combinée *f*, assurance tous risques *f*

multi-platform *adj* à plate-forme multiple

multiple[1] *adj* multiple

multiple[2] *n* (Math) multiple *m*; (shop) magasin à succursales multiples *m*

multiple: ∼ **buyer** *n* acheteur/-euse multiple *m/f*; ∼ **choice** *adj* (survey, question) à choix multiple; ∼ **drop** *n* (road haulage) trajet à escales multiples *m*; ∼**-entry visa** *n* visa multi-transit *m*, visa permanent *m*; ∼ **exchange rate** *n* taux de change multiple *m*; ∼ **management** *n* management participatif *m*; ∼ **ownership** *n* multipropriété *f*; ∼ **regression** *n* régression multiple *f*; ∼ **regression analysis** *n* analyse de régression multiple *f*; ∼ **shop** *n*, ∼ **store** *n* magasin à succursales multiples *m*; ∼ **taxation** *n* imposition multiple *f*; ∼**-unit residential building** *n* immeuble résidentiel à logements multiples *m*

multiplication *n* multiplication *f*; ∼ **sign** *n* signe de multiplication *m*

multiplier *n* multiplicateur *m*; ∼ **effect** *n* (Econ) effet multiplicateur *m*; ∼ **principle** *n* principe multiplicateur *m*

multiply ⃞1 *vt* multiplier ⃞2 *vi* se multiplier

multiprocessing *n* multitraitement *m*

multiprocessor *n* multiprocesseur *m*

multiprogramming *n* multiprogrammation *f*

multipurpose *adj* (peripheral, software) à usages multiples; (tool, gadget) multi-fonction, à usages multiples; ∼ **vessel** *n* navire polyvalent *m*

multiracial *adj* multiracial

multirisk insurance *n* assurance combinée *f*, assurance multirisque *f*

multiskilling *n* polyvalence *f*

multistage sampling *n* échantillonnage

multiphase *m*

multistorey *adj* à plusieurs étages; ∼ **carpark** *n* parking à étages *m*

multitasking *n* traitement multitâche *m*

multiunion: ∼ **bargaining** *n* UK négociation plurisyndicale *f*; ∼ **plant** *n* usine à syndicats multiples *f*

multiuser *n* multiutilisateur *m*; ∼ **licence** BrE, ∼ **license** AmE *n* licence multiutilisateur *m*; ∼ **system** *n* système multiutilisateur *m*

multivariate analysis *n* analyse à variantes multiples *f*

multiyear *adj* pluriannuel/-elle; ∼ **operational plan** *n* plan de développement pluriannuel *m*; ∼ **rescheduling agreement** *n* accord de rééchelonnement pluriannuel *m*; ∼ **restructuring agreement** *n* accord de restructuration pluriannuel *m*; ∼ **spending envelope** *n* enveloppe pluriannuelle de dépenses *f*

municipal *adj* municipal; ∼ **bond** *n* US obligation municipale *f*; ∼ **bond offering** *n* US offre d'obligations municipales *f*; ∼ **notes** *n pl* US emprunts des municipalités locales *m pl*; ∼ **revenue bond** *n* US obligation municipale à revenu *f*

municipality *n* ≈ municipalité *f*

muniments *n pl* titres de propriété *m pl*; ∼ **of title** titres de propriété *m pl*

mutual *adj* (common) commun; (reciprocal) mutuel/-elle, réciproque; **it's to our** ∼ **advantage** c'est dans notre intérêt commun; **by** ∼ **agreement** avec l'accord des parties, d'un commun accord, de gré à gré; **by** ∼ **consent** (Law) de gré à gré, à l'amiable; (by general agreement) d'un commun accord, par consentement mutuel; ∼ **aid pact** *n* pacte d'aide mutuelle *m*; ∼ **benefit** *n* avantage réciproque *m*; ∼ **benefit society** *n* société de secours mutuel *f*, société mutuelle *f*; ∼ **border** *n* frontière commune *f*; ∼ **corporation** *n* corporation mutuelle *f*, société mutualiste *f*; ∼ **fund** *n* fonds commun de placement *m*; (open-ended) société d'investissement à capital variable *f*; ∼ **insurance company** *n* compagnie mutuelle d'assurance *f*, mutuelle *f*; ∼ **insurer** *n* assureur mutuel *m*; ∼ **recognition** *n* reconnaissance mutuelle *f*; ∼ **savings bank** *n* US caisse de crédit mutuelle *f*

mutuality *n* accord d'information mutuelle *m*; ∼ **of contract** (Law) principe de la réciprocité contractuelle *m*

mutually *adv* mutuellement; ∼ **acceptable** *adj* acceptable pour les deux parties; ∼ **agreed** *adj* fixé d'un commun accord

mystery shopper *n* client mystère *m*

mystique *n* mystique *f*

Nn

n. *abbr* (▸**nominal**) en titre, n (nominal)

n/a *abbr* (▸**no-account**) pas de compte; (**not applicable**) ne s'applique pas, non applicable; (**no advice**) sans préavis

NAFA *abbr* (▸**net acquisition of financial assets**) acquisition nette d'actifs financiers *f*

NAFTA *abbr* (▸**North American Free Trade Area**) ALENA *m* (Accord de libre-échange nord-américain)

naked: ∼ **call** *n* option d'achat sans garantie *f*, option d'achat à découvert *f*; ∼ **call option** *n* option d'achat découverte *f*, option d'achat à découvert *f*; ∼ **put** *n* option de vente sans garantie *f*, option de vente à découvert *f*; ∼ **put option** *n* option de vente découverte *f*, option de vente à découvert *f*; ∼ **writer** *n* vendeur/-euse d'option à découvert *m/f*

name¹ *n* (of person) nom *m*; (of bank) dénomination *f*; (of firm) raison sociale *f*; (of publication) titre *m*; (reputation) réputation *f*; ∼ **of an account** intitulé de compte *m*, nom d'un compte *m*; **first** ∼ prénom *m*; **full** ∼ nom et prénom(s) *m pl*; **last** ∼ nom de famille *m*; ∼ **and address** nom et adresse; **be a big** ∼ **in marketing** être une société importante dans le monde du marketing; **lend one's** ∼ **to, put one's** ∼ **to** apposer son nom à; **make a** ∼ **for oneself as** se faire un nom en tant que; ∼ **brand** *n* marque réputée *f*; ∼ **day** *n* deuxième jour de liquidation *m*, veille de la liquidation *f*

name² *vt* (call) nommer; (appoint) nommer; (cite) citer; (place, time) indiquer; (date, price) fixer; (source) révéler; (successor) nommer; ∼ **and shame** dénoncer publiquement

named: ∼ **client** *n* client/-e nommément désigné/-e *m/f*; ∼ **person** *n* personne nommément désignée *f*

nameplate *n* plaque *f*

names *n pl* (control of interbank money market) dénominations *f pl*

nanny: ∼ **software** *n* logiciel de filtrage *m*; ∼ **state** *n* (infml) État-hyperprotecteur *m*

narcodollars *n pl* narcodollars *m pl*

narrow¹ *adj* (space, gap) étroit; (range, choice) restreint; (margin, majority) faible; (vision, understanding) limité; (definition, market) étroit; **have a** ∼ **lead** avoir une légère avance

narrow² ⊡ *vt* (gap, deficit, margin) réduire; (choice, range, options) limiter; ⊡ *vi* (choice, range, options) se limiter; (gap, deficit, margin) se réduire; ∼ **down** (options, websearch, list) restreindre

narrowing inflation gap *n* écart d'inflation en diminution *m*

NASA *abbr* US (▸**National Aeronautics and Space Administration**) NASA *f*

NASDAQ *abbr* US (▸**National Association of Securities Dealers Automated Quotations**) Nasdaq *m*, *marché américain des valeurs technologiques*

national¹ *adj* (of the nation) national; (nationwide) national, à l'échelon national

national² *n* (person) ressortissant/-e *m/f*; (newspaper) grand quotidien *m*

national: ∼ **agency** *n* agence nationale *f*; ∼ **airline** *n* compagnie aérienne nationale *f*; ∼ **average** *n* moyenne nationale *f*; ∼ **currency** *n* monnaie nationale *f*; ∼ **debt** *n* dette publique *f*; ∼ **economy** *n* économie nationale *f*; ∼ **grid** *n* UK réseau national haute tension *m*; ∼ **identity card** *n* carte nationale d'identité *f*; ∼ **income** *n* produit social *m*; ∼ **interest** *n* intérêt national *m*; ∼ **lottery** *n* loterie nationale *f*; ∼ **minimum wage** *n* ≈ salaire minimum interprofessionnel de croissance *m*, SMIC *m*; ∼ **newspaper** *n* journal national *m*; ∼ **press** *n* grande presse *f*, presse nationale *f*; ∼ **quota** *n* quota national *m*; ∼ **sales tax** *n* US taxe de vente nationale *f*; ∼ **trend** *n* tendance nationale *f*; ∼ **wealth** *n* richesse nationale *f*

National: ∼ **Aeronautics and Space Administration** *n* US NASA *f*; ∼ **Association of Securities Dealers Automated Quotations** *n* US Nasdaq *m*, *marché américain des valeurs technologiques*; ∼ **Bureau of Standards** *n* US *association américaine de normalisation*, ≈ AFNOR *f*; ∼ **Contingency Fund** *n* Fonds national de prévoyance *m*; ∼ **Curriculum** *n* UK cursus national *m*; ∼ **Futures Association** *n* US *société nationale des opérations à terme*; ∼ **Health Service** *n* UK services de santé britanniques *m pl*, ≈ Sécurité sociale *f*; ∼ **Insurance** *n* UK *sécurité sociale britannique*; ∼ **Insurance contributions** *n pl* cotisations à la sécurité sociale *f pl*; ∼ **Insurance number** *n* numéro de sécurité sociale *m*; ∼ **Savings Certificate** *n* UK bon d'épargne *m*

nationalism *n* nationalisme *m*

nationality *n* nationalité *f*

nationalization *n* nationalisation *f*

nationalize *vt* nationaliser

nationalized *adj* nationalisé; ∼ **industry** *n* industrie nationalisée *f*, société d'intérêt public *f*; ∼ **sector** *n* secteur nationalisé *m*

nationally *adv* (at national level) à l'échelon ⋯▸

national; (nationwide) sur l'ensemble du pays; (known, available) dans tout le pays

nationhood *n* nationalité *f*

nationless *adj* apatride

nationwide¹ *adj* (scheme, strike) sur l'ensemble du territoire; (campaign) national; (survey, poll) à l'échelle nationale

nationwide² *adv* (distribute, deliver, travel) à travers tout le pays, sur l'ensemble du territoire

native¹ *adj* (local) du pays

native² *n* be a ~ of être originaire de

native: ~ **English speaker** *n* anglophone *mf*; ~ **French speaker** *n* francophone *mf*; ~ **industry** *n* industrie locale *f*

NATO *abbr* (▸**North Atlantic Treaty Organization**) OTAN *f* (Organisation du Traité de l'Atlantique Nord)

natural *adj* naturel/-elle; ~ **business year** *n* année fiscale *f*; ~ **environment** *n* milieu naturel *m*; ~ **gas** *n* gaz naturel *m*; ~ **heritage** *n* patrimoine naturel *m*; ~ **increase** *n* accroissement naturel *m*; ~ **leader** *n* leader naturel *m*; ~ **monopoly** *n* monopole naturel *m*; ~ **number** *n* entier naturel *m*, nombre entier *m*; ~ **person** *n* personne morale *f*, personne physique *f*; ~ **price** *n* prix naturel *m*; ~ **rate of growth** *n* taux de croissance naturel *m*; ~ **rate of interest** *n* taux naturel d'intérêt *m*; ~ **resource** *n* ressource naturelle *f*; ~ **rights** *n pl* droits fondamentaux *m pl*, droits naturels *m pl*; ~ **wastage** *n* non-remplacement des départs *m*

nature *n* (natural world) nature *f*; (character) caractère *m*, nature *f*; ~ **conservation** *n* défense de l'environnement *f*, protection de la nature *f*

nautical mile *n* mile marin *m*, mile nautique *m*

NAV *abbr* (▸**net asset value**) valeur de l'actif net *f*, valeur patrimoniale nette *f*

naval: ~ **architect** *n* architecte naval/-e *m/f*, ingénieur du génie maritime *m*; ~ **construction** *n* construction navale *f*; ~ **constructor** *n* constructeur de navires *m*

navigate *vi* naviguer; ~ **on the web** naviguer sur Internet

navigation *n* navigation *f*; ~ **aid** *n* (Comp) aide à la navigation *f*; ~ **bar** *n* (Comp) barre de navigation *f*; ~ **laws** *n pl* Code maritime *m*, droit maritime *m*

NCD *abbr* (▸**negotiable certificate of deposit**) CDN *m* (certificat de dépôt négociable)

NCR *abbr* (▸**net cash requirements**) besoins en capital net *m pl*, besoins nets de trésorerie *m pl*

n.c.v. *abbr* (▸**no commercial value**) sans valeur commerciale; (▸**no customs value**) sans valeur douanière

ND *abbr* (**no discount**) pas de rabais

near¹ *adj* proche; **in the** ~ **future** dans un avenir proche; ~ **cash** *n* quasi-monnaie *f*, titres très liquides *m pl*; ~ **future** *n* proche avenir *m*; ~ **money** *n* quasi-monnaie *f*

near² *vt* ~ **completion** (project, phase) toucher à sa fin; ~ **retirement** prendre bientôt sa retraite; ~ **the end of** (tax year, season) approcher de la fin de

nearby *adj* proche; (Fin) (contract) rapproché

necessary *adj* nécessaire; ~ **labor** AmE, ~ **labour** BrE *n* travail nécessaire *m*

necessitate *vt* nécessiter

necessity *n* (item) article essentiel *m*; (need) nécessité *f*; (necessary measure) impératif *m*; **be a** ~ être indispensable; **bare necessities** minimum nécessaire *m*; **the** ~ **of doing** la nécessité de faire; **out of** ~ par nécessité; **of** ~ nécessairement; **if the** ~ **arises** si le besoin se fait sentir

need¹ *n* (want, requirement) besoin *m*; (necessity) nécessité *f*; (poverty) besoin *m*; **be in** ~ **of** avoir besoin de; **be in** ~ **of repair** avoir besoin d'être réparé; **for all your software** ~s pour tous vos besoins en logiciel; **the** ~ **for closer cooperation** la nécessité d'une plus grande collaboration; **without the** ~ **for checks** sans que des contrôles soit nécessaires; **operate on a** ~ **to know basis** ne divulguer les informations qu'aux personnes strictement concernées; ~ **identification** *n* identification des besoins *f*

need² *vt* (require) avoir besoin de; ~ **to do** avoir besoin de faire

needs *n pl* besoins *m pl*; **manpower** ~ besoins en main-d'œuvre *m pl*; **energy** ~ besoins en énergie *m pl*; ~ **based** *adj* fondé sur les besoins; ~ **analysis** *n* analyse des besoins *f*; ~ **test** *n* examen des besoins *m*

needy *adj* (sector, organization) sans ressources; (person) nécessiteux/-euse; **the** ~ *n pl* les nécessiteux *m pl*

negate *vt* (advantage, effect, work) réduire à néant

negative¹ *adj* négatif/-ive; (effect, influence) néfaste; (bank balance) débiteur/-trice

negative² *n* réponse négative *f*

negative: ~ **amortization** *n* amortissement négatif *m*; ~ **carry** *n* report négatif *m*; ~ **cash flow** *n* cash-flow négatif *m*, marge brute d'autofinancement négative *f*, variation négative de trésorerie *f*; ~ **elasticity** *n* élasticité négative *f*; ~ **feedback** *n* réaction négative *f*; ~ **financing** *n* financement négatif *m*; ~ **income tax** *n* impôt négatif sur le revenu *m*; ~ **interest** *n* intérêt négatif *m*; ~ **investment** *n* investissement négatif *m*; ~ **net worth** *n* valeur nette déficitaire *f*, valeur nette négative *f*

negatively *adv* négativement

neglect¹ *n* (lack of care) négligence *f*; (lack of interest) indifférence *f*; (of equipment, property) manque d'entretien *m*

neglect² *vt* (work, problem) négliger; (sector, economy) se désintéresser de; (offer, opportunity) ignorer; ~ **to do** négliger de faire; ~ **to mention** omettre de mentionner

neglect clause *n* clause de négligence *f*

neglected *adj* (poorly maintained) mal entretenu; (overlooked) négligé; (uncared for) négligé

negligence *n* (Law) négligence *f*, omission coupable *f*; ~ **clause** *n* clause de négligence *f*

negligently *adv* négligemment, par négligence

negligible *adj* négligeable

negotiability *n* négociabilité *f*

negotiable *adj* négociable; ~ **bill** *n* lettre de change négociable *f*, lettre négociable *f*; ~ **bill of exchange** *n* lettre de change négociable *f*; ~ **certificate of deposit** *n* certificat de dépôt négociable *m*; ~ **instrument** *n* effet négociable *m*, instrument négociable *m*; ~ **order of withdrawal** *n* ordre de retrait de fonds négociable *m*; ~ **securities** *n pl* titres négociables *m pl*, valeurs mobilières cessibles *f pl*

negotiate *vt* (settlement, bond, contract, loan) négocier; (problem) résoudre; (difficulty) surmonter; **'to be ~d'** 'à négocier'

negotiated: ~ **market price** *n* prix de marché négocié *m*; ~ **price** *n* prix négocié *m*; ~ **settlement** *n* accord négocié *m*; ~ **underwriting** *n* garantie d'émission négociée *f*, souscription négociée *f*

negotiating: ~ **position** *n* position de négociation *f*; ~ **session** *n* séance de négociations *f*; ~ **table** *n* table des négociations *f*

negotiation *n* négociation *f*; **be open to** ~ être négociable; **be up for** ~ être à négocier; **be under** ~ être en cours de négociations; ~ **fee** *n* frais de négociation *m pl*; ~ **strategy** *n* stratégie de négociation *f*

negotiations *n pl* négociations *f pl*, pourparlers *m pl*; **pay** ~ négociations salariales *f pl*; **during the** ~ au cours des négociations; **enter into** ~ entrer en négociations; **break off** ~ rompre les négociations

negotiator *n* négociateur/-trice *m/f*; UK (Prop) agent immobilier *m*

neighborhood *n* AmE ▸neighbourhood BrE

neighboring *adj* AmE ▸neighbouring BrE

neighbourhood *n* BrE (district) quartier *m*; (vicinity) voisinage *m*; **in the** ~ **of 100 people** environ 100 personnes; ~ **shop** *n* BrE commerce de proximité *m*

neighbouring BrE *adj* voisin; ~ **country** *n* pays limitrophe *m*

neon sign *n* enseigne lumineuse *f*

nepotism *n* népotisme *m*

nerve center AmE, **nerve centre** BrE *n* centre névralgique *m*

NES *abbr* (**not elsewhere specified**) non précisé par ailleurs, non spécifié par ailleurs

nest *vt* imbriquer

nested *adj* (data) imbriqué

nest egg *n* magot *m*

nesting *n* (of data) imbrication *f* (infrml)

net¹ *adj* net/nette; ~ **of** déduction faite de; ~ **of taxes** (income tax) hors impôts; (Imp/Exp) hors taxes; ~ **acquisition of financial assets** *n* acquisition nette d'actifs financiers *f*; ~ **acquisitions** *n pl* acquisitions nettes *f pl*; ~ **asset value** *n* valeur de l'actif net *f*, valeur patrimoniale nette *f*; ~ **assets** *n pl* actif net *m*; ~ **base capital** *n* capital de base net *m*; ~ **book value** *n* valeur comptable nette *f*; ~ **borrowing** *n* montant net des emprunts *m*; ~ **capital expenditure** *n* dépenses nettes d'investissement *f pl*, mise de fonds nette *f*; ~ **capital spending** *n* dépenses nettes d'investissement *f pl*, mise de fonds nette *f*; ~ **cash flow** *n* gain net de trésorerie *m*; ~ **cash requirements** *n pl* besoins en capital net *m pl*, besoins nets de trésorerie *m pl*; ~ **change** *n* variation nette *f*, écart net *m*; ~ **cost** *n* coût net *m*; ~ **credit** *n* crédit net *m*; ~ **current assets** *n pl* actif circulant net *m*, fonds de roulement net *m*; ~ **debit** *n* débit net *m*; ~ **dividend** *n* dividende net *m*; ~ **earnings** *n pl* bénéfices nets *m pl*; ~ **earnings per share** *n* bénéfice net par action *m*; ~ **equity** *n* capitaux propres *m pl*, patrimoine *m*; ~ **estate** *n* US valeur nette du bien *f*; ~ **federal tax** *n* impôt fédéral net *m*; ~ **forward position** *n* position nette à terme *f*; ~ **gain** *n* gain net *m*; ~ **income** *n* bénéfice net *m*, revenu net *m*, résultat net *m*; ~ **interest income** *n* revenu net des intérêts *m*; ~ **interest yield** *n* (investment) rendement net des intérêts *m*; ~ **lending** *n* montant net des prêts *m*; ~ **listing** *n* liste nette *f*; ~ **loss** *n* perte nette *f*; ~ **margin** *n* marge nette *f*; ~ **national product** *n* produit national net *m*; ~ **output** *n* production nette *f*; ~ **pay** *n* salaire net *m*; ~ **premium** *n* prime nette *f*; ~ **present value** *n* valeur actuelle nette *f*; ~ **proceeds** *n pl* produit net *m*; ~ **profit** *n* bénéfice net *m*; ~ **profit for the current year** *n* bénéfice net de l'exercice *m*, résultat net *m*; ~ **profit margin** *n* marge bénéficiaire nette *f*; ~ **purchases** *n pl* achats nets *m pl*; ~ **rate** *n* taux net *m*; ~ **realizable value** *n* valeur réalisable nette *f*; ~ **receipts** *n pl* recettes nettes *f pl*; ~ **recorded assets** *n pl* actif comptabilisé net *m*; ~ **register** *n* enregistrement net *m*; ~ **registered tonnage** *n* tonnage de jauge net *m*; ~ **remittance** *n* versement net *m*; ~ **rental income** *n* revenu de location net *m*; ~ **sales** *n pl* ventes nettes *f pl*; ~ **surplus** *n* surplus net *m*; ~ **tangible assets per share** *n pl* actif corporel net par action *m*, ⋯▸

n

actif réel net par action m; ~ **tare weight** n
tare nette f; ~ **taxable capital gain** n gain
en capital imposable net m; ~ **tonnage** n
tonnage net m; ~ **trading surplus** n résultat
brut d'exploitation m; ~ **value** n valeur
nette f; ~ **weight** n poids net m; ~ **working
capital** n fonds de roulement net m; ~
worth n valeur nette f, valeur patrimoniale
f; ~ **worth assessment** n estimation de la
valeur patrimoniale f; ~ **yield** n rendement
net m

net² vt (Fin) établir la valeur nette de; (person,
company) faire une bénéfice de; (sale, deal)
rapporter; ~ **a profit of 800 dollars** faire un
bénéfice de 800 dollars

net³, **Net** n (Comp) Net m, Internet m; ~
access n accès à Internet m

netbrowser n navigateur m

netcasting n diffusion sur la Toile f

net economy n netéconomie f

net generation n génération Internet f

netiquette n nétiquette f

netizen n internaute mf

netrepreneur n entreprenaute mf,
entrepreneur/-euse sur Internet m/f

netspeak n jargon d'Internet m

netsurf vi surfer sur Internet

netsurfer n surfeur/-euse m/f

netsurfing n surf sur Internet m

network¹ n réseau m; **computer/telephone**
~ réseau informatique/téléphonique; **rail/
road** ~ réseau ferroviaire/routier; **television**
~ réseau de télévision; ~ **administrator** n
administrateur/-trice de réseau m/f; ~
analysis n analyse de réseau f; ~ **architect**
n architecte réseau mf; ~ **architecture** n
architecture de réseau f; ~ **computer** n
ordinateur de réseau m; ~ **diagram** n
diagramme de réseau m; ~ **engineer** n
ingénieur réseau m; ~ **manager** n chef de
réseau m; ~ **marketing** n vente en réseau
par cooptation f; ~ **of sales outlets** n
réseau de points de vente m; ~
organization n organisation en réseau f; ~
traffic n trafic de réseau m; ~ **television** n
US chaîne de télévision nationale f

network² **1** vt (Comp) mettre en réseau
2 vi établir un réseau de contacts

networked vi (computer, workstation) en
réseau

networker n télétravailleur/-euse m/f

networking n (Comp) mise en réseau f;
(teleworking) travail à domicile m; (making
contacts) exploitation des contacts d'affaires f;
~ **economy** n (HRM) économie du
télétravail f; (Comp) économie à base de
réseaux informatiques f; ~ **software** n
logiciel de gestion de réseau m

neural network n réseau neuronal m

neurolinguistic programming n
programmation neuro-linguistique f

neutral adj neutre

neutrality n neutralité f

new adj nouveau/-elle; (brand new) neuf/
neuve; ~ **for old** du vieux au neuf; '**under** ~
management', '**under** ~ **ownership**'
'changement de propriétaire'; '**as** ~' 'état
neuf'; ~ **business** n (customers) nouveaux
clients m pl; (contracts) nouveaux contrats
m pl; (trade) nouvelles activités f pl; ~
economics n néo-keynésianisme m; ~
economy n nouvelle économie f; ~ **edition**
n nouvelle édition f; ~ **federalism** n US
néo-fédéralisme m; ~ **information and
communications technologies** n pl
nouvelles technologies de l'information et de
la communication f pl; ~ **issue** n (Stock)
nouvelle émission f; ~ **money** n (restructuring
of loans) crédit de restructuration m; ~
product development n développement de
produits nouveaux m; ~ **share** n action
nouvelle f; ~ **technology** n nouvelles
technologies f pl; ~ **town** n UK ville nouvelle
f; ~ **wave** n nouvelle vague f

newbie n (infrml) novice d'Internet mf

newcomer n (to sector, market) nouveau
venu m/nouvelle venue f

New: ~ **Left** n nouvelle gauche radicale f;
~ **Right** n nouvelle droite f; ~ **York Curb
Exchange** n US Marché hors cote de New
York m; ~ **York Futures Exchange** n US
Marché des transactions à terme de New
York m, Marché à terme de New-York m; ~
York Mercantile Exchange n US marché à
terme de produits pétroliers et de platine de
New York; ~ **York Stock Exchange** n
Bourse de New York f

new-look adj (model, product) nouvelle
version inv; (edition) remanié; (team) nouveau/
nouvelle

newly: ~**-elected** adj nouvellement élu;
~ **industrialized country** n pays
nouvellement industrialisé m; ~**-privatized**
adj privatisé de fraiche date

news n (Gen Comm) informations f pl,
nouvelles f pl; (current affairs, new events)
actualités f pl, informations f pl; (TV bulletin)
journal m, informations f pl; ~ **of her
resignation** la nouvelle de sa démission;
break the ~ annoncer la nouvelle; **an item
of** ~ une nouvelle; **be in the** ~, **make the** ~
défrayer la chronique; **that's good/bad** ~
c'est une bonne/mauvaise nouvelle; ~
agency n agence de presse f; ~ **analyst** n
commentateur/-trice m/f; ~ **bulletin** n
bulletin d'informations m; ~ **conference** n
conférence de presse f; ~ **coverage** n
couverture médiatique f; ~ **editor** n
rédacteur/-trice m/f; ~ **flash** n flash
d'information m, flash info m; ~ **headlines**
n pl titres de l'actualité m pl; ~ **item** n sujet
d'actualité m, information f; ~ **posting** n (in
a newsgroup) article (de forum) m, contribution
f; ~ **release** n communiqué de presse m; ~
report n reportage m; ~ **roundup** n
informations en bref f pl, résumé des

informations m; ~ **server** n serveur de nouvelles m; ~ **service** n (agency) agence de presse f; ~ **sheet** n bulletin m; ~ **vendor** n marchand/-e de journaux m/f

newsagent n marchand/-e de journaux m/f

newscaster n présentateur/-trice du journal télévisé m/f

newsfeed n alimentation en nouvelles Usenet f

newsgroup n forum de discussion m

newsletter n bulletin m, circulaire f; (on e-mail) lettre d'information f, newsletter f

news-on-demand n actualités à la demande f pl

newspaper n journal m; ~ **advertising** n publicité-presse f; ~ **publisher** n directeur/-trice de journal m/f, directeur/-trice de publication m/f; ~ **syndicate** n US agence de vente de reportages pour la presse

newsroom n (salle de) rédaction f

next adj (in the future) prochain; (on list, in series) suivant; (adjacent) voisin; **the ~ size up/down** la taille au-dessus/en-dessous; **this time ~ week** d'ici une semaine; ~ **day** n lendemain m; **~-day** adj (delivery) en 24 heures; ~ **generation** adj (software, release, computer, product) (de) nouvelle génération

NF abbr (**no funds**) défaut de provision m

NFA abbr US (▸**National Futures Association**) société nationale des opérations à terme

NGO abbr (▸**non-governmental organization**) ONG f (organisation non-gouvernementale)

NHS abbr UK (▸**National Health Service**) services de santé britanniques m pl, ≈ SS f (Sécurité sociale)

NI abbr UK (▸**National Insurance**) sécurité sociale britannique

NIC abbr UK (▸**newly industrialized country**) NPI m (nouveau pays industrialisé)

niche n créneau m, créneau porteur m, niche f; ~ **bank** n banque créneau f; ~ **market** n marché spécialisé m, marché de niche m; ~ **marketing** n marketing ciblé m, marketing du créneau m; ~ **player** n acteur sur un segment de marché spécialisé m; ~ **trading** n commerce spécialisé m

NICT abbr (▸**new information and communications technology**) NTIC f pl (nouvelles technologies de l'information et de la communication)

night n nuit f; **work ~s** travailler de nuit; **be on ~s** être de nuit; ~ **safe** n coffre de nuit m; ~ **shift** n (team) équipe de nuit f; (work) poste de nuit m; ~ **watchman** n gardien de nuit m, veilleur m; ~ **work** n travail de nuit m

Nikkei: ~ **average** n indice Nikkei m; ~ **index** n indice Nikkei m

nil n (on forms) néant m; ~ **paid** capital non-appelé m, non-payé; ~ **profit** n bénéfice nul m

NIMBY abbr (▸**not in my backyard**) phénomène NIMBY m, attitude de celui qui est en faveur d'un projet à condition que celui-ci ne soit pas effectué près de chez lui

nine bond rule n règle des neuf obligations f, règlement de neuf garanties m

ninety-nine-year lease n bail emphytéotique m

NLP n (▸**neurolinguistic programming**) PNL f (programmation neuro-linguistique)

n.n.p. abbr (▸**net national product**) PNN m (produit national net)

no. abbr (▸**number**) n° (numéro)

no-claims bonus n UK bonus pour non sinistre m

node n (Comp) nœud m

no-fault adj (Ins) hors faute, sans égard à la responsabilité

no-frills adj (version, model) sans fioritures, dépouillé

no-growth adj de croissance nulle, de croissance zéro

noise n bruit m; (Comp) bruit m; (interference) parasites m pl; ~ **level** n niveau sonore m; ~ **pollution** n nuisances acoustiques f pl

no-load fund n US fonds sans frais m

nominal adj (in name only) nominal; (fee, sum) minimal; (fine, penalty) symbolique; (rent) dérisoire; ~ **assets** n pl actif fictif m; ~ **capital** n capital pourvu dans les statuts m; ~ **damages** n pl dommages-intérêts symboliques m pl; ~ **GDP** n PIB nominal m; ~ **growth** n croissance nominale f; ~ **income** n revenu nominal m; ~ **interest rate** n taux d'intérêt nominal m; ~ **ledger** n grand livre m; ~ **price** n prix théorique m; ~ **quotation** n cotation nominale f, cours estimé m; ~ **value** n valeur nominale f; ~ **wage** n salaire nominal m; ~ **yield** n rendement nominal m; (of fixed-income security) coupon m

nominate vt (appoint) nommer, désigner; (propose) proposer; ~ **sb for a post** proposer qn pour un poste; ~ **sb to do** désigner qn pour faire

nomination n (appointment) nomination f; (as candidate) proposition de candidat f

nominee n personne désignée f; (Bank) propriétaire pour compte m/f; (for post, role) candidat/-e désigné/-e m/f; ~ **account** n compte d'intermédiaire m, compte prête-nom m; ~ **company** n société intermédiaire f, société prête-nom f; ~ **shareholder** n actionnaire intermédiaire m/f, actionnaire-paravent m/f

nonacceptance n non-acceptation f; (of bill, note) défaut d'acceptation m

nonaccruing loan n emprunt à risques m

nonaffiliated adj autonome, non affilié

no-name adj (product) sans nom

nonappearance n non-comparution f

nonapproved adj non-approuvé

non assignable adj inaliénable

non-attendance n absence f

non-availability n pénurie f

non-available adj non disponible

nonbank bank n institution financière para-bancaire f

nonbasic: ~ **commodity** n produit non essentiel m, produit secondaire m; ~ **industry** n industrie secondaire f

non-biodegradable adj nonbiodégradable

nonbudgetary adj extra-budgétaire, non budgétaire

non-business income n bénéfices non commerciaux m pl

noncallable adj non rachetable, non remboursable; ~ **bond** n obligation non remboursable f; ~ **securities** n pl titres non remboursables m pl

noncash: ~ **item** n poste hors caisse m; ~ **payment** n paiement non financier m; ~ **rewards** n pl paiement en nature m, rétribution en nature f

nonclassified adj (document, report) non confidentiel/-ielle

nonclearing: ~ **item** n effet non admis à la compensation m, instrument non compensable m; ~ **member** n membre de non-compensation m, membre non compensant m

non-commercial adj (event, activity) à but non lucratif

noncommittal adj (reply, person) évasif/-ive

noncommunication n non-communication f

noncompeting group n groupe non concurrentiel m

non-completion n (of work) non-achèvement m; (of contract) non-exécution f

noncompliance n (with law) inobservation f; (with order) refus d'obtempérer m

noncompulsory adj facultatif/-ive

nonconformist adj non conformiste

nonconformity n non-conformité f

nonconsolidated adj non consolidé

noncontestability clause n clause de non-contestabilité f

noncontributory: ~ **pension fund** n caisse de retraite sans cotisation salariale f; ~ **pension plan** n, ~ **pension scheme** n régime de retraite entièrement financé par l'employeur m

nonconvertible adj (bond) non convertible

non-cooperation n refus de coopération m

noncumulative adj non cumulatif/-ive; ~ **preferred stock** n action à dividende prioritaire non cumulative f

noncurrent asset n actif à long terme m

noncyclical adj non cyclique

nondeductibility n (Tax) (of employer contributions) non-déductibilité f

non-delivery n (of goods) non-livraison f, défaut de livraison m; (of post) non-remise f

nondisclosure n non-divulgation f; ~ **agreement** n accord de non-divulgation m

nondiscretionary trust n holding sans mandat de gestion

nondurable goods n pl biens de consommation non durables m pl; (foodstuffs) denrées périssables f pl

nonencashable deposit n dépôt non encaissable m

nonenforceable adj non exécutoire

nonessential adj non essentiel/-ielle

non-EU national n non-ressortissant/-e de l'UE m/f

nonexecution n inexécution f, non-exécution f

nonexecutive adj non dirigeant; ~ **director** n administrateur/-trice externe m/f, administrateur/-trice non dirigeant/-e m/f

nonexempt adj non-exempté

nonfeasance n délit d'abstention m

nonforfeiture n non-résiliation f

nonfulfillment AmE, **nonfulfilment** BrE n non-exécution f; ~ **of contract** inexécution du contrat f, non-exécution du contrat f

nonfungible goods n pl biens non fongibles m pl

non-governmental organization n organisation non gouvernementale f

non-interest-bearing: ~ **deposit** n dépôt non productif d'intérêt m, dépôt non-rémunéré m; ~ **securities** n pl titres non rémunérés m pl, valeurs ne portant pas intérêt f pl

nonintervention n non-intervention f

noninvolvement n non-engagement m

nonliability n absence de responsabilité f, non-responsabilité f; ~ **company** n société en non-responsabilité f

nonlinear adj non linéaire; ~ **pricing** n tarification non linéaire f

non-listed adj (Stock) non coté

nonmandatory adj (guidelines) facultatif/-ive, n'ayant pas un caractère obligatoire

nonmanufacturing sector n secteur non manufacturier m

nonmarketable instrument n instrument non-négociable m

nonmarket sector n secteur non marchand m

nonmember n non-membre m, personne étrangère f; **open to** ~**s** ouvert au public; ~ **bank** n AmE banque non affiliée f, banque non-membre f; ~ **country** n pays non-membre m; ~ **firm** n firme non affiliée f, établissement non membre m

nonmembership *n* non-adhésion *f*

nonmerchantable title *n* AmE titre non négociable *m*

nonmetropolitan *adj* non-métropolitain

non-negotiable: ~ **bill of lading** *n* connaissement non négociable *m*; ~ **instrument** effet non négociable *m*, instrument non-négociable *m*

nonobservance *n* (of rules, contract)) inobservation *f*; ~ **of conditions** *n* inobservation des conditions *f*, non-respect des conditions *m*

nonparticipating share *n* action non participative *f*

nonpayment *n* non-paiement *m*; (of bill, note) défaut de paiement *m*

nonpecuniary returns *n pl* revenu non pécuniaire *m*

nonperformance *n* non-exécution *f*

nonperforming *adj* non productif/-ive; ~ **assets** *n* avoirs non productifs *m pl*; ~ **credit** *n* avoir non productif *m*; ~ **loan** *n* prêt non productif *m*

nonproductive *adj* non productif/-ive

nonprofessional behavior AmE, **nonprofessional behaviour** BrE *n* comportement non conforme aux règles de la profession *m*

non-profit *adj* AmE ▶**non-profit-making** BrE

non-profit-making *adj* BrE sans but lucratif, à but non lucratif; ~ **enterprise** *n* entreprise à but non-lucratif *f*; ~ **organization** *n* entreprise sans but lucratif *f*

nonpublic information *n* US informations non communiquées au public *f pl*

nonqualifying: ~ **share** *n* action non admissible *f*; ~ **stock option** *n* option de titres non statutaire

non-quoted *adj* (Stock) non coté

non-receipt *n* non-réception *f*

nonrecourse: ~ **finance** *n* financement sans recours *m*, financement à forfait *m*; ~ **loan** *n* prêt sans recours *m*, prêt à forfait *m*

non-recoverable *adj* irrécouvrable

nonrecurring: ~ **appropriation** *n* crédit extraordinaire *m*; ~ **charge** (annual) charge non courante *f*; ~ **expenses** *n pl* dépenses exceptionelles *f pl*

nonrecyclable *adj* non recyclable

nonrefundable *adj* non remboursable; ~ **deposit** *n* acompte non remboursable *m*; ~ **fee** *n* honoraires non remboursables *m pl*

nonrenewable *adj* non renouvelable; ~ **resource** *n* ressource non renouvelable *f*

nonresident¹ *adj* non résident

nonresident² *n* non-résident/-e *m/f*

nonresident: ~ **bank** *n* banque étrangère *f*; ~ **company** *n* société non résidente *f*, société étrangère *f*; ~ **tax** *n* impôt des non-résidents *m*

nonreusable *adj* perdu

nonroutine decisions *n pl* décisions exceptionnelles *f pl*

non-sale *n* non-vente *f*

nonscheduled *adj* non planifié

non-smoking *adj* non-fumeur *inv*

non-standard *adj* non standard

nonstarter *n* be a ~ (person) être hors-course; (plan, idea) être voué à l'échec

nonstatutory *adj* non statutaire, qui n'est pas prévu par un texte de loi

nonsterling area *n* zone non sterling *f*

nonstop¹ *adj* (flight) sans escale; (train) direct; (work, pressure) incessant; (service) permanent; (coverage) non-stop

nonstop² *adv* (work) sans arrêt; (fly) sans escale

nonstore retailing *n* vente hors magasin *f*

nontariff barrier *n* barrière non douanière *f*, barrière non tarifaire *f*

non-taxable *adj* non imposable

non-taxpayer *n* personne non imposable *f*

non-tax revenue *n* recettes non fiscales *f pl*

nontradeables *n pl* biens non marchands *m pl*

nontransferable *adj* (ticket, vote) transférable; ~ **debentures** *n pl* obligations nominatives *f pl*

nonunion: ~ **firm** *n* société sans représentation syndicale *f*; ~ **labor** AmE, ~ **labour** BrE *n* main-d'œuvre non syndiquée *f*; ~ **worker** *n* ouvrier/-ière non syndiqué/-e *m/f*

nonutilized *adj* (line of credit) non utilisé

nonvariable *adj* non variable

nonverbal communication *n* communication non verbale *f*

nonvoting share *n*, **nonvoting stock** *n* action sans droit de vote *f*

nop *abbr* (**not otherwise provided**) non fourni par ailleurs, non prévu par ailleurs

no-par stock *n* action non pair *f*

no-par-value *adj* sans valeur nominale; ~ **share** *n* action sans valeur nominale *f*

norm *n* norme *f*; **above/below the** ~ au-dessus/en dessous de la norme

normal¹ *adj* (place, time) habituel/-elle; (amount, size, price, service) normal; **in** ~ **circumstances** en temps normal; **in the** ~ **course of events** si tout va bien; **as** ~ comme d'habitude

normal² *n* normale *f*; **above/below** ~ au-dessus/en dessous de la norme; **get back to** ~ revenir à la normale

normal: ~ **capacity** *n* capacité de production normale *f*; ~ **conditions** *n pl* ⋯⋗

conditions normales *f pl*; ~ **course of business** *n* cours normal des affaires *m*; ~ **distribution** *n* distribution normale *f*; ~ **market size** *n* BrE quotité normale *f*; ~ **retirement age** *n* âge normal de départ à la retraite *m*; ~ **tax** *n* impôt uniforme *m*; ~ **trading unit** *n* quotité normale de transaction *f*; ~ **wear and tear** *n* usure normale *f*

normalcy AmE, **normality** BrE *n* normalité *f*; **return to** ~ revenir à la normale

normative *adj* selon les normes; (in statistics) normatif/-ive; ~ **economics** *n* économie normative *f*; ~ **forecasting** *n* prévisions normatives *f pl*

North: ~ **American Free Trade Area** *n* Accord de libre-échange nord-américain *m*; ~ **Atlantic Treaty Organization** *n* Organisation du Traité de l'Atlantique Nord *f*; ~ **Sea gas** *n* gaz de la mer du Nord *m*

nosedive *vi* (shares) être en chute libre, baisser rapidement

no-show *n* (for booking, flight) non-présentation *f*

no-smoking *adj* non-fumeur *inv*; ~ **area** *n* zone non-fumeur *f*

no-strike: ~ **agreement** *n* accord de non-recours à la grève *m*; ~ **clause** *n* clause de non-recours à la grève *f*

nostro account *n* compte nostro *m*

notarize *vt* certifier conforme, légaliser

notary public *n* notaire *m*

note¹ *n* (written record) note *f*; (short letter) mot *m*; (bankable) billet *m*; (Acc, Fin) bordereau *m*; (promise to pay) billet *m*, effet *m*; **keep a** ~ **of** garder une trace écrite de; **make a** ~ **of sth** prendre note de qch; **make a promissory** ~ souscrire un billet à ordre; **take** ~**s** prendre des notes; ~ **issue** *n* émission fiduciaire *f*; ~ **payable** *n* effet à payer *m*; ~ **receivable** *n* effet à recevoir *m*, traite à recevoir *f*; ~**s to the accounts** *n pl* annexe à porter sur les comptes *f*

note² *vt* (observe) constater, remarquer; (write down) noter

notebook *n* (pad) carnet *m*; (Comp) ordinateur de poche *m*

notepad *n* (paper) bloc-notes *m*; (Comp) ardoise électronique *f*

notepaper *n* papier à lettres *m*

notice¹ *n* (Admin, Law) avis *m*; (Gen Comm, Bank) (advance warning) préavis *m*; (advertisement) annonce *f*, avis *m*; (sign) pancarte *f*; (poster) affiche *f*; **give sb** ~ **that/serve** ~ **on sb that** aviser qn que; (of dismissal, resignation) **hand in one's** ~ donner sa démission; **give sb** ~ congédier qn; **give** ~ (tenant) donner son préavis; **at short** ~ au pied levé; **do sth at two days'** ~ faire qch dans un délai de deux jours; **until further** ~ jusqu'à nouvel ordre; **without prior** ~ sans préavis; **give sb** ~ **of sth** aviser qn de qch;

give five days' ~ donner cinq jours de préavis; **require two months'** ~ exiger deux mois de préavis; **take** ~ **of** faire attention à; **bring sth to sb's** ~ porter qch à l'attention de qn; **escape sb's** ~ échapper à l'attention de qn; ~ **account** *n* compte à préavis *m*; ~ **of assessment** (Tax) avis de cotisation *m*; ~ **of assignment** (currency options) avis d'assignation *m*, avis d'assignation de levée *m*, avis de transfert *m*; ~ **board** *n* panneau d'affichage *m*; ~ **of call** (Stock) avis de rachat *m*; ~ **of cancellation** (Stock) avis de résolution *m*; ~ **of dishonor** AmE, ~ **of dishonour** BrE avis de refus *m*; ~ **of intention** avertissement préalable *m*, préavis *m*; ~ **of objection** avis d'opposition *m*; ~ **of original assessment** avis de cotisation originale *m*; ~ **period** *n* délai de préavis *m*; ~ **of revocation** avis de révocation *m*; ~ **of shipment** avis d'expédition *m*; ~ **of withdrawal** *n* avis de retrait *m*; ~ **to pay** avis de l'avoir à payer *m*; ~ **to quit** (Prop) avis de congé *m*

notice² *vt* remarquer, s'apercevoir de

notification *n* (Admin, Law, Tax) notification *f*; (formal announcement) avis *m*; **receive written** ~ **of** recevoir notification écrite de; **receive** ~ **that** être avisé que

notify *vt* notifier; ~ **sb of sth** aviser qn de qch, informer qn de qch

notional *adj* (saving, charge, profit, loan) fictif/-ive; ~ **rent** *n* loyer notionnel *m*

no-trade equilibrium *n* équilibre autarcique *m*

notwithstanding *adv* malgré, en dépit de; ~ **the provisions of** par dérogation aux clauses de

nought *n* zéro *m*

novation *n* novation *f*

novelty *n* nouveauté *f*; ~ **value** *n* valeur de nouveauté *f*

NOW *abbr* (▸**negotiable order of withdrawal**) ordre de retrait de fonds négociable *m*; ~ **account** *n* US compte-chèques rémunéré *m*

no-win *adj* (situation) de perdant; (Law) **take the case on a** ~, **no fee basis** ne réclamer ses honoraires qu'en cas de gain de cause

np *abbr* (▸**net proceeds**) produit net *m*

NPE *abbr* (**non-profit enterprise**) entreprise à but non lucratif *f*

NPV *abbr* (▸**net present value**) VAN *f* (valeur actuelle nette); (Stock) (▸**no-par value**) SVN (sans valeur nominale)

NRT *abbr* (▸**net registered tonnage**) tonnage de jauge net *m*

NRV *abbr* (▸**net realizable value**) valeur réalisable nette *f*

NSA *abbr* (▸**nonsterling area**) zone non sterling *f*

n.s.f. *abbr* (**not sufficient funds**) fonds insuffisants *m pl*, insuffisance de provision *f*

Nt *abbr* (**net terms**) bord à bord

NTB *abbr* (▸**nontariff barrier**) barrière non douanière *f*

nuance¹ *n* nuance *f*

nuance² *vt* nuancer

nuclear *adj* nucléaire; ∼ **energy** *n* énergie nucléaire *f*; ∼ **industry** *n* industrie nucléaire *f*; ∼ **power station** *n* centrale nucléaire *f*; ∼ **reactor** *n* réacteur nucléaire *m*; ∼ **waste** *n* déchets nucléaires *m pl*

nugatory *adj* (without value) sans valeur; (not valid) non valable; ∼ **payment** *n* paiement sans contrepartie *m*

nuisance *n* (Law) nuisance *f*, tort causé à autrui *m*

null *adj* nul/nulle; ∼ **and void** nul et non avenu; **render** ∼ **and void** annuler, invalider; ∼ **hypothesis** *n* hypothèse nulle *f*

nullification *n* annulation *f*

number¹ *n* (of page, building, telephone, on list) numéro *m*; (written digit) chiffre *m*; (figure)

nombre *m*; (quantity, amount) nombre *m*, quantité *f*; ∼ **crunching** *n* calcul *m*; ∼ **of employees** *n* nombre de salariés *m*; ∼ **one priority** *n* priorité absolue *f*; ∼ **plate** *n* BrE numéro d'immatriculation *m*, plaque minéralogique *f*

number² *vt* (allocate a number to) numéroter; (include) compter

numbered account *n* compte anonyme *m*, compte numérique *m*

numbering *n* numérotation *f*

numeric *adj* numérique; ∼ **keypad** *n* pavé numérique *m*

NVD *abbr* (**no value declared**) sans valeur déclarée

NYFE *abbr* US (▸**New York Futures Exchange**) Marché des transactions à terme de New York *m*, Marché à terme de New York *m*

NYSE *abbr* US (▸**New York Stock Exchange**) Bourse de New York *f*

Oo

o/a *abbr* (**on account of**) en raison de, à cause de; (▸**overall**) total

OAP *abbr* BrE (▸**old age pensioner**) retraité/-e *m/f*

OAS *abbr* (**Organization of American States**) Organisation des états américains *f*

oath *n* serment *m*; **under** ∼ sous serment; **take the** ∼, **swear an** ∼ prêter serment

obey *vt* (person, command) obéir à; (law) obéir à, respecter, se conformer à; (summons, order) obtempérer à; (instructions) observer, se conformer à

object¹ *n* (item) objet *m*; (aim) but *m*, objet *m*, objectif *m*; (of debate, meeting) objectif *m*; **money is no** ∼ l'argent n'est pas un problème

object² *vi* objecter, soulever des objections; ∼ **to** (proposal, action, law) s'opposer à; (delay, inconvenience) se plaindre de; ∼ **to doing** se refuser à faire

objection *n* objection *f*; **make an** ∼ faire une objection; **make an** ∼ **to** marquer son opposition à; ∼ **overruled** objection rejetée; ∼ **sustained** objection admise

objective¹ *adj* objectif/-ive

objective² *n* objectif *m*; **set an** ∼ fixer un objectif; **meet an** ∼, **achieve an** ∼ atteindre un objectif, réaliser un objectif; **our** ∼ **is to do** nous avons pour objectif de faire

objective: ∼ **indicators** *n pl* indicateurs d'objectif *m pl*; ∼ **setting** *n* définition des

objectifs *f*; ∼ **value** *n* valeur objective *f*

obligate *vt* contraindre

obligated: **be** ∼ **to do sth** être dans l'obligation de faire qch, être obligé de faire qch

obligation *n* obligation *f*; (personal) engagement *m*; (duty) devoir *m*; **be under a legal** ∼ **to do** être dans l'obligation légale de faire; **be under an** ∼ **to do** être tenu de faire; **be under no** ∼ **to do** ne pas être dans l'obligation de faire; **without** ∼ sans engagement de votre part; **meet or fulfil ones** ∼**s** faire honneur à ses obligations, tenir ses engagements

obligatory *adj* obligatoire

oblige *vt* (do favour) rendre service à; (compel) obliger, contraindre; ∼ **sb to do sth** contraindre qn à faire qch, obliger qn à faire qch

obligee *n* créancier/-ière *m/f*, obligataire *mf*

obligor *n* obligé/-e *m/f*

OBS *abbr* (▸**off-balance-sheet**) hors bilan

observance *n* (of rule) respect *m*

observation *n* observation *f*; (comment) remarque *f*

observe *vt* (rule, law) observer, respecter; (notice) observer, remarquer

observer *n* observateur/-trice *m/f*

obsolescence *n* obsolescence *f*, vieillissement *m*; **built-in** ∼, **planned** ∼ ⋯⟩

obsolescence planifiée *f*

obsolete *adj* dépassé, périmé

obstacle *n* obstacle *m*

obstruct *vt* (traffic, road) bloquer; (progress) entraver, gêner; (plan) faire obstacle à

obtain 1 *vt* obtenir; (for oneself) se procurer; ~ **sth by fraud** obtenir qch frauduleusement; ~ **permission in writing** obtenir la permission par écrit; ~ **security** prendre des garanties
2 *vi* (system, method) avoir cours, prévaloir; (rule) être en vigueur

obtainable *adj* disponible

obtainment *n* obtention *f*

OBU *abbr* (▸**offshore banking unit**) succursale extraterritoriale *f*, succursale offshore *f*

obvious *adj* évident

OC *abbr* (▸**overcharge**) majoration *f*, surcharge *f*; (excess taken) trop-perçu *m*; (▸**open charter**) affrètement ouvert *m*, charter ouvert *m*; (▸**open cover**) police ouverte *f*

occasion *n* (circumstance) occasion *f*, circonstance *f*; **on a previous** ~ précédemment; **on a similar** ~ dans des circonstances semblables; **on one** ~ une fois; **should the** ~ **arise** le cas échéant, si l'occasion se présente; **on** ~ de temps en temps, à l'occasion; **special** ~ grande occasion *f*

occasional *adj* (expense, worker) occasionnel/-elle; (event) qui a lieu de temps en temps; (occurrence) qui se produit de temps en temps

occupancy *n* occupation *f*; ~ **cost** *n* coût d'occupation *m*; ~ **level** *n* niveau d'occupation *m*

occupant *n* (of post) titulaire *mf*; (Law, Prop) occupant/-e *m/f*

occupation *n* (trade) métier *m*; (profession) profession *f*; (protest action) occupation des locaux *f*; (Law) occupation *f*; (of property) prise de possession *f*

occupational *adj* (activity, group, training) professionnel/-elle; ~ **accident** *n* accident du travail *m*; ~ **disease** *n* maladie professionnelle *f*; ~ **hazard** *n* risque du métier *m*; ~ **health** *n* médécine du travail *f*; ~ **illness** *n* maladie professionnelle *f*; ~ **mobility** *n* mobilité professionnelle *f*; ~ **pension** *n* retraite professionnelle *f*; ~ **pension plan** *n* UK régime de retraite professionnel *m*; ~ **pension scheme** *n* UK régime de retraite professionnel *m*

occupier *n* occupant/-e *m/f*

occupy *vt* (position) remplir; (property) occuper; (time) prendre; (day, hour, week) durer; (person) occuper

occurrence *n* (instance) occurrence *f*; (event) fait *m*; **be a regular** ~ se produire régulièrement

ocean *n* océan *m*; ~ **bill of lading** *n* connaissement à ordre *m*; ~ **freight** *n* fret au long cours *m*; ~**-going passenger ship** *n* paquebot *m*; ~**-going** vessel *n* long-courrier *m*, navire au long cours *m*

OCR *abbr* (▸**optical character recognition**) ROC *f* (reconnaissance optique des caractères)

O/D *abbr* (▸**overdraft**) découvert *m*; (▸**overdrawn**) à découvert

odd *adj* (miscellaneous) disparate; (number) impair; (one of pair) dépareillé; **the** ~ **one out** l'intrus *m*; ~ **change** *n* monnaie *f*; ~**-job man** *n* homme à tout faire *m*; ~ **jobs** *n pl* petits boulots *m pl*; ~ **lot** *n* (Stock) quotité inférieure *f*, rompu de titres *m*; (of goods) lot dépareillé *m*; ~ **size** *n* taille peu courante *f*; ~**-value pricing** *n* pratique des prix magiques *f*

oddment *n* (not matching) article dépareillé *m*; (reduced) article en solde *m*

oddments *n pl* fins de série *f pl*

OECD *abbr* (▸**Organization for Economic Cooperation and Development**) OCDE *f* (Organisation de coopération et de développement économique)

OEIC *abbr* (▸**open-end investment company**) SICAV *f* (société d'investissement à capital variable)

off *adj* be ~ (cancelled) être annulé; (switched off) être éteint; **be** ~ **sick** être malade; (Admin, HRM) être absent pour cause de maladie, être en congé de maladie; **have Mondays** ~ ne pas travailler le lundi; **take time** ~ prendre un congé; **get time** ~ (briefly) obtenir la permission de s'absenter; **get 10%** ~ obtenir une remise de 10%; **5%** ~ 5% de remise

off-balance-sheet *adj* hors bilan; ~ **commitments** *n pl* engagements hors bilan *m pl*; ~ **financing** *n* financement hors bilan *m*

offence *n* (Law) délit *m*, infraction *f*; (insult) offense *f*; **commit an** ~ commettre une infraction; **cause** ~ **to sb** offenser qn

offer¹ *n* offre *f*; (discount, promotion) promotion *f*; **job** ~ offre d'emploi *f*; **make an** ~ faire une offre; **on** ~ (for sale) en vente; (reduced) en réclame, en promotion; **be under** ~ avoir fait l'objet d'une proposition; **or nearest** ~ à débattre; **open to** ~s ouvert à toutes propositions; ~s **in the region of £6,000** prix 6 000 livres sterling, à débattre; **a better** ~ une offre plus intéressante; **it's my best** ~ c'est mon dernier mot; ~ **for sale** *n* offre publique de vente *f*; ~ **price** *n* cours vendeur *m*; (Stock) cours vendeur *m*, prix offert *m*

offer² *vt* offrir, proposer; (advice) donner; (job) proposer; ~ **to do** se proposer pour faire; ~ **considerable scope** offrir beaucoup de possibilités; ~ **one's services** proposer ses services, ∼ **goods for sale** mettre des marchandises en vente; ∼ **sb a job** proposer un poste à qn; **she has a lot to** ∼ **the project** elle peut beaucoup apporter au projet

offered *adj* (Stock) offert, vendeur

offeree *n* destinataire d'une offre *mf*

offerer *n* offrant *m*

offering *n* (of new shares) nouvelle émission *f*; ∼ **price** *n* (Stock) prix d'offre *m*

office *n* bureau *m*; (of lawyer, doctor, professional) cabinet *m*; (department) service *m*; (position, role) fonction *f*; **be in** ∼, **hold** ∼ (political party) être au pouvoir; (minister) avoir un portefeuille; (president, mayor) être en fonction; **stand for** ∼, **run for** ∼ se présenter aux élections; **for** ∼ **use only** réservé à l'administration; ∼ **accommodation** *n* bureaux *m pl*, espace bureau *m*; ∼ **automation** *n* bureautique *f*; ∼ **block** *n*, ∼ **building** *n* immeuble de bureaux *m*; ∼ **equipment** *n* matériel de bureau *m*, équipement de bureau *m*; ∼ **hours** *n pl* heures de bureau *f pl*; ∼ **job** *n* travail de bureau *m*; ∼ **manager** *n* chef de bureau *m*, directeur/-trice de bureau *m/f*; ∼ **premises** *n pl*, ∼ **space** *n* bureaux *m pl*, locaux commerciaux *m pl*; ∼ **staff** *n pl* personnel de bureau *m*; ∼ **suite** *n* (Comp) ensemble d'applications bureautiques *m*; ∼ **supplies** *n pl* fournitures de bureau *f pl*; ∼ **technology** *n* bureautique *f*; ∼ **work** *n* travail de bureau *m*; ∼ **worker** *n* employé/-e de bureau *m/f*

Office: ∼ **of Fair Trading** *n* UK ≈ Direction de la concurrence, de la consommation et de la répression des fraudes *f*; ∼ **of International Trade** *n* Bureau de commerce international *m*; ∼ **of Population Censuses and Surveys** *n* UK *bureau des recensements et enquêtes de population*

officer *n* responsable *mf*, dirigeant/-e *m/f*; (in government) fonctionnaire *mf*; (in committee, union) membre du comité directeur *m*; **information/personnel** ∼ responsable de la communication/du personnel *mf*

official[1] *adj* officiel/-ielle

official[2] *n* (of police, customs) agent *m*; (of central, local government) fonctionnaire *mf*; (of union) permanent/-e *m/f*

official: ∼ **action** *n* UK action revendicative *f*; (strike) grève officielle *f*; ∼ **document** *n* document officiel *m*; ∼ **exchange rate** *n* taux de change officiel *m*; ∼ **figures** *n pl* chiffres officiels *m pl*; ∼ **list** *n* (Stock) cote boursière *f*, cote officielle *f*; ∼ **market** *n* marché officiel *m*; ∼ **quotation** *n* cotation officielle *f*; ∼ **rate** *n* taux officiel d'escompte *m*; ∼ **receiver** *n* administrateur judiciaire *m*; ∼ **statement** *n* communiqué officiel *m*; ∼ **strike** *n* grève avec préavis *f*, grève officielle *f*

officialese *n* jargon administratif *m*

officially *adv* officiellement

off-licence *n* BrE magasin de vins et de spiritueux *m*

off-limits *adj* interdit; ∼ **area** *n* zone interdite *f*

offline, off-line[1] *adj* (Comp) (equipment, system) autonome; (processing) en différé; (storage) non connecté; (not connected to the Internet) hors connexion; ∼ **browser** *n* aspirateur Web *m*

offline, off-line[2] *adv* (read, write, work) hors connexion; **go** ∼ se déconnecter

off-load *vt* (responsibility, work) se décharger de; (freight) décharger; (goods, stock) écouler

off-loading *n* (of freight) déchargement *m*; (of stock) écoulement *m*

off-peak *adj* en période creuse; ∼ **call** *n* appel (téléphonique) aux heures de tarif réduit *m*; ∼ **charges** *n pl* tarif réduit aux heures creuses *m*; ∼ **day** *n* jour creux *m*; ∼ **fare** *n* tarif réduit *m*; ∼ **season** *n* basse saison *f*

off-prime *adj* inférieur au taux de base

off season *n* basse saison *f*

off-season *adj* hors saison

offset[1] *n* (Acc, Fin) contrepartie *f*; (Stock) compensation *f*, compensation de couverture *f*

offset[2] *vt* compenser; ∼ **a debit against a credit** compenser un débit par un crédit; ∼ **a loss** compenser les pertes

offsetting: ∼ **entry** *n* écriture de compensation *f*; ∼ **transaction** *n* opération compensatrice *f*, opération de compensation *f*

offshore[1] *adj* (Fin) offshore, extraterritorial; (at sea) en mer

offshore[2] *adv* (Fin) offshore; (at sea) en mer

offshore: ∼ **bank** *n* banque offshore *f*; ∼ **banking** *n* banque offshore *f*; ∼ **banking unit** *n* succursale extraterritoriale *f*, succursale offshore *f*; ∼ **center** AmE, ∼ **centre** BrE *n* centre offshore *m*, place extraterritoriale *f*; ∼ **funds** *n pl* fonds offshore *m pl*; ∼ **installation** *n* installation en mer *f*, installation offshore *f*; ∼ **investment** *n* investissement extraterritorial *m*; ∼ **oilfield** *n* champ pétrolifère en mer *m*; ∼ **trust** *n* acte fiduciaire établi outre-mer *m*, fiducie offshore *f*

off-the-board *adj* (Stock) hors cote

off-the-peg[1] *adj* (garment) de prêt-à-porter; ∼ **fashions** le prêt-à-porter

off-the-peg[2] *adv* (buy) du prêt-à-porter

off-the-record *adj* officieux/-ieuse

off-the-shelf: ∼ **company** *n* société tiroir *f*; ∼ **goods** *n pl* marchandises disponibles en magasin *f pl*; ∼ **software** *n* logiciel fixe *m*, logiciel prêt à l'usage *m*

OFT *abbr* UK (►**Office of Fair Trading**) ≈ Direction de la concurrence, de la consommation et de la répression des fraudes *f*

OGM *abbr* (▸**ordinary general meeting**) AGO *f* (assemblée générale ordinaire)

OHMS *abbr* UK (▸**On Her Majesty's Service**) au service de sa Majesté

oil *n* pétrole *m*; **∼-bearing** *adj* pétrolifère; **∼ company** *n* compagnie pétrolière *f*; **∼ crisis** *n* choc pétrolier *m*; **∼ deposit** *n* gisement de pétrole *m*; **∼-exporting countries** *n pl* pays exportateurs de pétrole *m pl*; **∼ field** *n* terrain pétrolifère *m*; **∼ glut** *n* surabondance de pétrole *f*; **∼-importing country** *n* pays importateur de pétrole *m*; **∼ industry** *n* industrie pétrolière *f*; **∼ pipeline** *n* oléoduc *m*; **∼ platform** *n* plate-forme de forage *f*, plate-forme pétrolière *f*; **∼ price rise** *n* augmentation du prix du pétrole *f*, hausse du prix du pétrole *f*; **∼-producing country** *n* pays producteur de pétrole *m*; **∼ refinery** *n* raffinerie de pétrole *f*; **∼ revenue tax** *n* impôt sur les revenus pétroliers *m*; **∼-rich** *adj* (country) riche en pétrole; **∼ rig** *n* plate-forme de forage *f*; **∼ shares** *n pl* valeurs pétrolières *f pl*; **∼ shortage** *n* pénurie de pétrole *f*; **∼ slick** *n* nappe de pétrole *f*; **∼ spill** *n* déversement de pétrole *m*, marée noire *f*; **∼ tanker** *n* pétrolier *m*; **∼ terminal** *n* terminal pétrolier *m*

OIT *abbr* (▸**Office of International Trade**) Bureau de commerce international *m*

old *adj* (not new) vieux/vieille; (former) ancien/-ienne; **∼ age pension** *n* BrE pension de retraite *f*; **∼ age pensioner** *n* BrE retraité/-e *m/f*; **∼ economy** *n* ancienne économie *f*, vieille économie *f*; **∼-fashioned** *adj* démodé

oligopoly *n* monopole partagé *m*, oligopole *m*

oligopsony *n* oligopsone *f*

OM *abbr* (▸**options market**) marché à options *m*

ombudsman *n pl* **-men** (Pol) médiateur/-trice *m/f*; (Stock) arbitre *m*

omission *n* omission *f*; (from list, group) absence *f*

omit *vt* omettre; **∼ to do sth** négliger de faire qch

omitted dividend *n* dividende omis *m*, dividende passé *m*

omnibus survey *n* étude multiclients *f*

on-board *adj* à bord; (computer) embarqué; **∼ entertainment** *n* animation à bord *f*

oncosts *n pl* frais généraux *m pl*

one-man business *n* entreprise unipersonelle *f*

one-off[1] *adj* (offer, event) exceptionnel/-elle; (example) peu courant; (design, idea, experiment, order) unique; (agreement) unilatéral/-e

one-off[2] *n* **be a ∼** (issue, magazine) être un numéro spécial; (design, order, item) être unique; **it was a ∼** (of event) ça ne se reproduira plus

one-price store *n* magasin à prix unique *m*

onerous *adj* (responsibility, task, workload) lourd

one-stop shop *n* guichet unique *m*

one-stop shopping *n* achats regroupés *m pl*; **∼ center** AmE, **∼ centre** BrE *n* centre commercial *m*

one-time buyer *n* acheteur occasionnel *m*

one-to-one marketing *n* marketing personnalisé *m*

one-way *adj* (Comp) unidirectionnel/-elle; **∼ ticket** *n* AmE aller simple *m*

one-woman business *n* entreprise unipersonelle *f*

ongoing *adj* (activity, research, work) en cours; (concern) constant; (process) continu

on-lending *n* (Fin) prêt de l'argent emprunté *m*, rétrocession de fonds empruntés *f*

online, on-line[1] *adj* (on the Internet: help, service, ordering, bank, retailer) en ligne; **be ∼** (user) être connecté; (Comp) (access) direct; (mode) connecté; (processing) en direct

online, on-line[2] *adv* (search, shop, bank, buy) en ligne; **go ∼** se connecter

online, on-line: **∼ access** *n* accès en ligne *m*; **∼ advertisement** *n* publicité en ligne *f*; **∼ advertising** *n* publicité en ligne *f*; **∼ auction** *n* vente aux enchères en ligne *f*; **∼ banking** *n* banque en ligne *f*, banque sur Internet *f*; **∼ bookstore** *n* cyberlibrairie *f*, librairie en ligne *f*; **∼ business** *n* business en ligne *m*; **∼ catalogue** *n* catalogue électronique *m*; **∼ community** *n* communauté virtuelle *f*; **∼ customer** *n* cyberconsommateur/-trice en ligne *m/f*, consommateur/-trice en ligne *m/f*; **∼ government** *n* administration en ligne *f*; **∼ journal** *n* revue en ligne *f*, revue sur Internet *f*; **∼ learning** *n* apprentissage en ligne *m*, formation en ligne *f*; **∼ marketplace** *n* place de marché électronique *f*; **∼ order form** *n* bon de commande électronique *m*; **∼ payment** *n* paiement en ligne *m*; **∼ procurement** *n* approvisionnement électronique *m*; **∼ purchase** *n* achat en ligne *m*; **∼ recruitment** *n* recrutement en ligne *m*; **∼ sale** *n* vente en ligne *f*; **∼ selling** *n* vente en ligne *f*; **∼ service provider** *n* prestataire de services en ligne *m*; **∼ shop** *n* boutique en ligne *f*, cyberboutique *f*; **∼ shopper** *n* cyberconsommateur/-trice *m/f*, consommateur/-trice en ligne *m/f*; **∼ shopping** *n* achats en ligne *m pl*; **∼ trainer** *n* e-formateur/-trice *m/f*, formateur/-trice à Internet *m/f*; **∼ training** *n* formation en ligne *f*, formation sur Internet *f*

ono *abbr* (**or nearest offer**) à débattre

on-sale date *n* AmE date de mise en vente *f*

on-screen *adj* (help) sur l'écran

onset *n* début *m*

onshore *adj* (installation) début à terre *m*;

~ terminal n terminal intérieur m

on-target earnings n pl salaire de base plus commission m

on-the-job training n formation dans l'entreprise f, formation sur le tas f

on-the-spot adj (fine) sur les lieux de l'infraction; (advice, quotation) immédiat

onward: ~ clearing n compensation-aller f, remise en compensation f; **~ flight** n vol de correspondance m

OP abbr (Ins) (▶**open policy**) police d'abonnement f, police flottante f

OPEC abbr (▶**Organization of Petroleum Exporting Countries**) OPEP f (Organisation des pays exportateurs de pétrole)

open¹ adj (not closed) ouvert; (job) libre, vacant; (access, competition) ouvert à tous; (hearing, session) public/-ique; (candid) franc/ franche; (blatant) non dissimulé, manifeste; (question) non résolu; (file, document) ouvert; **~ to debate** sujet à discussion; **~ to several interpretations** susceptible d'interprétations diverses; **be ~ to offers/suggestions** être ouvert aux offres/suggestions; **have an ~ mind about** réserver son jugement sur; **leave the date ~** laisser la date en suspens

open² 1 vt (letter, packet) ouvrir; (attachment, file, document) ouvrir; (discussions, negotiations) entamer; (company, branch) ouvrir; **~ an account** ouvrir un compte; **~ a bank account with** ouvrir un compte bancaire à; **~ a file** ouvrir un dossier; **~ the mail** dépouiller le courrier, ouvrir le courrier; **~ the market up to competition** ouvrir le marché à la concurrence; **~ a position** ouvrir une position; **~ trading** ouvrir les transactions
2 vi (shop, bank) ouvrir; (meeting, discussion) commencer; (speak first) ouvrir le débat

open: ~ account n compte ouvert m; **~-account business** n opérations en compte courant f pl; **~ admissions** n pl libre accès m; **~ bid** n offre ouverte f; **~ charter** n affrètement ouvert m, charter ouvert m; **~ check** AmE, **~ cheque** BrE n chèque non-barré m, chèque ouvert m; **~ contract** n (Stock) position ouverte f; **~ cover** n (Ins) police ouverte f; **~ credit** n compte ouvert m; **~ day** n BrE journée portes ouvertes f; **~-door policy** n politique de la porte ouverte f; **~ economy** n économie ouverte f; **~-end fund** n société d'investissement à capital variable f, société de placement à capital variable f, société à capital variable f; **~-end investment company** n société d'investissement à capital variable f; **~-end investment trust** n société d'investissement à capital variable f; **~-end mortgage** n créance hypothécaire à taux d'intérêt variable f; **~-ended agreement** n convention à finalité variable f; **~-ended contract** n contrat modifiable m; **~-ended flight reservation** n

réservation de vol ouverte f; **~-ended interview** n entretien non-directif m; **~-ended mortgage** n hypothèque sans date limite f; **~-ended position** n position ouverte f; **~-ended question** n question ouverte f; **~-ended questionnaire** n questionnaire non-directif m; **~-ended risk** n (Stock) risque ouvert m; **~ government** n politique de transparence f; **~ house** n AmE journée portes ouvertes f; **~ learning** n formation à la carte ouverte à tous f par correspondance, sur Internet et dans des centres spécialisés; **~ market** n marché libre m; (Econ) marché monétaire m; **~-market operations** n pl opérations sur le marché monétaire f pl; **~-market rate** n taux hors banque m; **~-market trading** n opérations sur le marché monétaire f pl; **~ network** n réseau ouvert m; **~-plan** adj non cloisonné; **~-plan office** n bureau paysager m; **~ policy** n police d'abonnement f, police flottante f; **~ position** n position ouverte f; **~ price** n prix ouvert m; **~ shop** n (policy) appartenance non obligatoire à un syndicat f; **~ space** n (within a developed area) aire ouverte f; **~ system** n système ouvert m; **~-systems interconnection** n interconnexion de systèmes ouverts f; **~ tendering** n soumission ouverte f; **~ ticket** n billet open m; **~ union** n syndicat ouvert m

opening¹ adj (Stock) (trade) initial; (speech, statement) préliminaire

opening² n (start) début m; (gap) ouverture f; (of meeting) début de séance m, ouverture de séance f; (of shop) ouverture f; (in market) débouché m, créneau m; (job vacancy) poste (vacant) m; (in field, sector) possibilité de travail f; (of show) première f; **at the ~** (Stock) à l'ouverture; **late ~ Friday** nocturne le vendredi f; **there is an ~ for a secretary** il y a un poste (vacant) de secrétaire

opening: ~ balance n solde d'ouverture m, solde initial m; **~ bank** n banque de placement f; **~ bid** n enchère initiale f, première offre f; **~ hours** n pl heures d'ouverture f pl; **~ inventory** n stock au début de l'exercice m, stock d'ouverture m; **~ price** n (Stock) cours d'ouverture m, premier cours m; **~ of tenders** n lancement d'un appel d'offres m; **~ up** n décloisonnement m

openness n transparence f

operand n opérateur m

operate 1 vt (equipment) faire marcher; (policy) pratiquer; (ban) mettre en vigueur; (business) gérer, diriger; (scheme, service) avoir
2 vi (function) fonctionner, marcher; (take effect) entrer en vigueur; **~ out of, ~ from** (offices, town, country) avoir comme base d'operations

operating: ~ account n compte d'exploitation m; **~ budget** n budget d'exploitation m; **~ capacity** n capacité de fonctionnement f; **~ costs** n pl charges ·····▸

d'exploitation *f pl*, frais d'exploitation *m pl*; ~ **cycle** *n* cycle d'exploitation *m*; ~ **expenditure** *n*, ~ **expenses** *n pl* charges d'exploitation *f pl*, frais d'exploitation *m pl*; ~ **gearing** *n* BrE effet de levier de l'exploitation *m*; ~ **income** *n* bénéfice d'exploitation *m*; ~ **instructions** *n pl* mode de fonctionnement *m*; ~ **interest** *n* droit d'exploitation *m*; ~ **leverage** *n* AmE effet de levier de l'exploitation *m*; ~ **loss** *n* perte d'exploitation *f*; ~ **margin** *n* marge d'exploitation *f*; ~ **profit** *n* bénéfice d'exploitation *m*, résultat des opérations *m*; ~ **schedule** *n* programme d'exploitation *m*; ~ **system** *n* (Comp) système d'exploitation *m*

operation *n* (undertaking) opération *f*; (working) fonctionnement *m*; (Comp) opération *f*; (use of equipment) opération *f*; (Fin) opération *f*; (business activities) activités *f pl*; **our Danish ~** nos activités au Danemark; **be in ~** (equipment) être en service; (rule) être en vigueur; **come into ~** (regulation) entrer en vigueur

operational *adj* opérationnel/-elle; ~ **analysis** *n* analyse d'opérations *f*; ~ **budget** *n* budget d'exploitation *m*; ~ **control** *n* contrôle des opérations *m*; ~ **costs** *n pl* frais d'exploitation *m pl*, coûts opérationnels *m pl*; ~ **manager** *n* chef d'exploitation *m*, directeur/-trice des opérations *m/f*; ~ **planning** *n* planification des opérations *f*; ~ **requirements** *n pl* conditions de fonctionnement *f pl*; ~ **research** *n* recherche opérationnelle *f*; ~ **staff** *n* équipe opérationnelle *f*

operations *n pl* activités *f pl*, opérations *f pl*; ~ **analysis** *n* analyse des tâches *f*, analyse du travail *f*; ~ **breakdown** *n* décomposition des tâches *f*; ~ **management** *n* gestion des opérations *f*; ~ **manager** *n* chef d'exploitation *m*, directeur/-trice des opérations *m/f*; ~ **research** *n* recherche opérationnelle *f*

operative¹ *adj* (rule, law, system) en vigueur; (word) qui compte

operative² *n* agent *m*, employé/-e *m/f*; (manual) ouvrier/-ière *m/f*; (of machine) opérateur/-trice *m/f*

operator *n* (of equipment) opérateur/-trice *m/f*; (switchboard worker) standardiste *m/f*; (switchboard) standard *m*; **place a call through the ~** passer par le standard

opinion *n* avis *m*, opinion *f*; **in her ~** à son avis; **legal ~** avis juridique *m*; **personal/ public ~** opinion personnelle/publique *f*; **get a second ~** demander un autre avis; **have a high/poor ~ of sb/sth** avoir une bonne/ mauvaise opinion de qn/qch; ~ **is divided** les opinions sont partagées; ~ **leader** *n* leader d'opinion *m*; ~ **measurement** *n* sondage d'opinion *m*; ~ **poll** *n* sondage d'opinion *m*; ~ **shopping** *n* chalandage d'opinion *m*; ~ **survey** *n* enquête d'opinion *f*; ~ **of title** *n*

certificat de validité d'un titre *m*

opportunism *n* opportunisme *m*

opportunistic behavior AmE, **opportunistic behaviour** BrE *n* comportement opportuniste *m*

opportunity *n* (occasion) occasion *f*; (chance, possibility) possibilité *f*; **give sb the ~ to** donner à qn l'occasion de; **have the ~ to do** avoir l'occasion de faire; **at the earliest ~** à la première occasion; **training/career opportunities** possibilités de formation/de carrière *f pl*; **investment ~** possibilité d'investissement *f*; ~ **cost** *n* coût d'opportunité *m*, coût de substitution *m*

oppose *vt* s'opposer à; **be ~d** être contre; **be ~d to doing** être contre l'idée de faire

opposing *adj* (rival) adverse; ~ **vote** *n* voix contre *f*

opposite¹ *adj* opposé; (effect, direction, approach) inverse, contraire; (page) ci-contre; ~ **number** *n* homologue *mf*

opposite² *n* contraire *m*

opposition *n* opposition *f*; **put up ~ against** faire opposition à; **meet with strong ~ from sb** rencontrer une forte opposition de la part de qn

opt: ~ **for** *vt* opter pour; ~ **out** *vi* décider de ne pas participer; (school, hospital) renoncer au contrôle de l'État; ~ **out of** (undertaking, project) ne pas participer à; (pension scheme) ne pas cotiser à

optical *adj* optique; ~ **character recognition** *n* reconnaissance optique des caractères *f*; ~ **pen** *n* crayon optique *m*, photostyle *m*; ~ **scanner** *n* lecteur optique *m*; ~ **wand** *n* crayon-lecteur optique *m*

optimal *adj* optimal, optimum

optimistic *adj* optimiste; **be ~ about** être optimiste quant à; **be ~ that** avoir grand espoir que

optimization *n* optimisation *f*

optimize *vt* optimiser

optimum *adj* optimum, optimal

opt-in email *n* e-mail opt-in *m*, *diffusion de courrier électronique aux personnes qui ont clairement exprimé leur volonté de recevoir de la publicité*

opt-in marketing *n* permission marketing *m*, marketing de permission *m*

option *n* (something chosen) option *f*; (possibility of choosing) choix *m*; (Comp, Fin, Stock) option *f*; **easy ~, soft ~** solution facile *f*; **keep one's ~s open** ne pas s'engager; **consider one's ~s** considérer ses options; **have first ~** avoir priorité d'option; **have the ~ of doing sth** pouvoir choisir de faire qch; **take up an ~, exercise an ~** (Stock) lever une option; ~ **bargains** *n pl* opérations sur le marché à options *f pl*; ~ **buyer** *n* acheteur/ -euse d'option *m/f*; ~ **class** *n* catégorie d'options *f*, classe d'options *f*; ~ **contract** *n* contrat d'option *m*, option *f*; ~ **exercise** *n* levée de l'option *f*; ~ **fee** *n* frais d'option *m* *pl*; ~ **holder** *n* détenteur/-trice d'options *m/f*, titulaire *mf*; ~ **premium** *n* prime *f*, prix d'option *m*; ~ **price** *n* prime *f*, prix d'option *m*; ~**-pricing formula** *n* formule d'évaluation des options *f*, formule de l'établissement du prix de l'option *f*; ~ **seller** *n* vendeur/-euse d'option *m/f*; ~ **trading** marché des options *m*; ~ **spread** *n* écart d'option *m*; ~ **writer** *n* vendeur/-euse d'option *m/f*

optional *adj* facultatif/-ive; ~ **character** *n* (Comp) caractère spécial *m*; ~ **extras** *n pl* accessoires en option *m pl*; ~ **features** *n pl* options *f pl*; ~ **item** *n* (Fin) poste facultatif *m*

options: ~ **market** *n* marché à options *m*; ~ **on currency futures** *n pl* options sur contrat à terme sur devises *f pl*, options sur contrats à terme *f pl*

OR *abbr* (▸**operational research**) RO *f* (recherche opérationnelle)

oral contract *n* contrat verbal *m*, convention verbale *f*

orange goods *n pl* produits à durée de vie moyenne *m pl*

order¹ *n* (for goods and services) commande *f*; (command) ordre *m*; (Fin) ordonnance *f*; (Law) (from courts) arrêt *m*, ordonnance *f*, ordre *m*; (Stock) (to buy) ordre d'achat *m*; (to sell) ordre de vente *m*; (sequence) ordre *m*; **call a meeting to** ~ déclarer la séance ouverte; **be in working** ~ être en état de marche; **be out of** ~ (machine) être en panne; (phone) être en dérangement; **by** ~ par ordre *m*; **be in alphabetical** ~ être dans l'ordre alphabétique; **put in alphabetical** ~ mettre par ordre alphabétique; **put sth in** ~ (files, records) classer; **put one's affairs in** ~ mettre de l'ordre dans ses affaires; **in** ~ **of importance** par ordre d'importance; **in** ~ **of priority** par ordre de priorité; **the parts are on** ~ les pièces ont été commandées; **place an** ~ passer une commande; **place an** ~ **for sth** commander qch; **cash with** ~ payable à la commande; **on** ~ en commande; **rush/ repeat** ~ commande urgente/renouvelée; **telephone** ~ commande par téléphone; **made to** ~ fait sur commande; **to the** ~ **of** (Bank) à l'ordre de; **of the** ~ **of 20%** de l'ordre de 20%

order² *vt* (goods) commander; (taxi) demander; (inquiry, investigation) ordonner; ~ **sb to do** ordonner à qn de faire

order: ~ **bill of lading** *n* connaissement à ordre *m*; ~ **book** *n* carnet de commandes *m*; ~ **card** *n* carte-réponse *f*; ~ **of the court** *n* arrêt *m*, ordonnance *f*, ordre *m*; ~ **entry** *n* enregistrement de commande *m*; ~ **flow pattern** *n* tendance du flux des commandes *f*; ~ **form** *n* bon de commande *m*; ~ **of magnitude** *n* ordre de grandeur *m*; ~ **number** *n* numéro de commande *m*; ~ **to**

pay *n* (Acc) mandat *m*, ordre de paiement *m*

orderly market *n* marché ordonné *m*

ordinance *n* US arrêté municipal *m*, ordonnance *f*

ordinary *adj* ordinaire; ~ **account** *n* compte ordinaire *m*; ~ **annuity** *n* rente ordinaire *f*; ~ **gain** *n* gain normal *m*; ~ **general meeting** *n* assemblée générale ordinaire *f*; ~ **income** *n* revenu normal *m*; ~ **interest** *n* intérêt ordinaire *m*, intérêt simple *m*; ~ **loss** *n* perte normale *f*; ~ **share** *n* BrE action ordinaire *f*; ~ **shareholder** *n* actionnaire ordinaire *mf*; ~ **stockholder** *n* actionnaire ordinaire *mf*; ~ **ticket** *n* billet plein-tarif *m*

organic *adj* (produce) biologique; (meat) provenant de bétail élevé biologiquement; (system, unit, whole) intégré; (development, law) organique; ~ **farming** *n* agriculture biologique *f*; ~ **foodstuffs** *n pl* aliments biologiques *m pl*; ~ **growth** *n* croissance organique *f*

organiser *n* (Admin) (person) organisateur/ -trice *m/f*; (diary) agenda *m*; (electronic) agenda électronique *m*

organization *n* (group, body) organisation *f*; (voluntary body) association *f*; (statutory body) organisme *m*; (arrangement) organisation *f*; **government** ~ organisme gouvernemental *m*; **voluntary** ~ association de bénévoles *f*; ~ **behavior** AmE, ~ **behaviour** BrE *n* (HRM, Mgmnt) comportement organisationnel *m*, comportement de l'individu dans l'organisation *m*; ~ **chart** *n* organigramme *m*; ~ **cost** *n* frais de premier établissement *m pl*; ~ **culture** *n* culture de l'organisation *f*; ~ **development** *n* développement organisationnel *m*; ~ **and methods** *n pl* l'organisation et les méthodes *f pl*; ~ **planning** *n* planification d'entreprise *f*; ~ **structure** *n* structure de l'organisation *f*; ~ **theory** *n* théorie de l'organisation *f*, théorie organisationnelle *f*

organizational *adj* (role, skill) d'organisateur/-trice; ~ **behavior** AmE, ~ **behaviour** BrE *n* (HRM, Mgmnt) comportement organisationnel *m*, comportement de l'individu dans l'organisation *m*; ~ **change** *n* changement organisationnel *m*, mutation des structures *f*; ~ **development** *n* développement organisationnel *m*; ~ **effectiveness** *n* efficacité organisatrice *f*; ~ **fit** *n* adaptation organisationnelle *f*; ~ **psychology** *n* psychologie des organisations *f*; ~ **size** *n* taille d'une organisation *f*; ~ **structure** *n* structure de l'organisation *f*; ~ **theory** *n* théorie de l'organisation *f*, théorie organisationnelle *f*; ~ **unit** *n* division administrative *f*

Organization: ~ **for Economic Cooperation and Development** *n* Organisation de coopération et de ⋯

développement économique *f*; ~ **of Petroleum Exporting Countries** *n* Organisation des pays exportateurs de pétrole *f*

organize *vt* organiser; (workers) syndiquer

organized: ~ **crime** *n* crime organisé *m*; ~ **labor** AmE, ~ **labour** BrE *n* main-d'œuvre syndiquée *f*

organizing committee *n* comité d'organisation *m*

orientation *n* (for newcomer) cours d'introduction *m*; (Pol) orientation *f*

oriented *adj* orienté; **customer-**~ orienté vers le client; **export-**~ orienté vers l'exportation; **profit-**~ **company** société à but lucratif

origin *n* (of goods) provenance *f*; (of person, idea, custom) origine *f*; **country of** ~ pays d'origine; **of unknown** ~ d'origine inconnue

original¹ *adj* (first) originel/-elle; (new, innovative) original; (not copied) original; (receipt) original, d'origine

original² *n* original *m*

original: ~ **bid** *n* offre originale *f*; ~ **capital** capital d'origine *m*; ~ **cost** *n* frais d'achat *m pl*, prix initial *m*; ~ **device** *n* procédé original *m*; ~ **document** *n* original *m*; ~ **entry** *n* (Acc) écriture originale *f*; ~ **equipment manufacturing** *n* fabrication de matériel original *f*; ~ **invoice** *n* facture originale *f*; ~ **margin** *n* marge de départ *f*, marge initiale *f*; ~ **maturity** *n* durée de crédit initiale *f*; ~ **order** *n* première commande *f*; ~ **owner** *n* propriétaire d'origine *mf*

originate: ~ **from** *vt* (goods) provenir de; (proposal) émaner de

originator *n* initiateur/-trice *m/f*; (of letter) expéditeur/-trice *m/f*

o.s. *abbr* (**out of stock**) épuisé

OSI *abbr* (▶**open-systems interconnection**) ISO *f* (interconnexion de systèmes ouverts)

OSP *abbr* (▶**online service provider**) prestataire de services en ligne *m*

OT *abbr* (▶**overtime**) HS *f pl* (heures supplémentaires)

OTC *abbr* (▶**over-the-counter**) (Stock) US hors cote; (medication) sans ordonnance; ~ **market** *n* US marché de gré à gré *m*, marché hors cote *m*

OTCM *abbr* US (▶**over-the-counter market**) marché de gré à gré *m*, marché hors cote *m*

OTE *abbr* (▶**on-target-earnings**) salaire de base plus commission *m*

other *adj* autre; **in** ~ **respects** à d'autres égards; ~ **assets** *n pl* autres éléments d'actif *m pl*; ~ **income** *n* autre revenu *m*, autres produits *m pl*, produits divers *m pl*; ~ **liabilities** *n pl* autres dettes *f pl*; ~ **receivables** *n pl* (assets) autres comptes

financiers *m pl*

otherwise *adv* par ailleurs; **not** ~ **provided** non fourni par ailleurs, non prévu par ailleurs; **not** ~ **specified** non spécifié par ailleurs; **unless** ~ **agreed** sauf avis contraire; **unless** ~ **required** sauf indication contraire; **unless** ~ **specified** sauf stipulation contraire

OTM *abbr* (▶**out-of-the-money**) en dehors, hors du cours, hors-jeu

our ref. *abbr* (▶**our reference**) n/réf

our reference *n* notre référence *f*

oust *vt* (from job) évincer

out¹ *adv* **be** ~ (absent) être sorti; (strikers) être en grève; (published) publié; **to be** ~ **to do** (determined) être bien décidé à faire; **be** ~ **in one's calculations** se tromper dans ses calculs

out² *prep* (in ratios) **8** ~ **of 10 consumers** 8 consommateurs sur 10; (lacking) **be** ~ **of paper** ne plus avoir de papier

outage *n* panne *f*

outbid *vt* surenchérir sur

out-box *n* (for email) boîte d'envoi *f*

outcome *n* résultat *m*

outcry *n* protestations *f pl*; ~ **market** *n* marché de vente à la criée *m*

outdated *adj* (idea) dépassé; (product) démodé

outdo *vt* surpasser

outdoor advertising *n* publicité extérieure *f*

outflow *n* sortie *f*; ~ **of funds** sortie de fonds *f*

outgoing *adj* (president, chairperson) sortant; ~ **call** *n* appel au départ *m*, appel vers l'extérieur *m*; ~ **mail** *n* courrier au départ *m*, courrier à expédier *m*

outgoings *n pl* débours *m pl*, sorties *f pl*

outlaw *vt* déclarer illégal, interdire

outlay *n* dépenses *f pl*, débours *m pl*; **capital** ~ dépenses d'investissement *f pl*; **initial** ~ mise de fonds initiale *f*; ~**s or expenses** débours ou dépenses *m pl*; ~ **creep** *n* dérapage *m*

outlet *n* (market) débouché *m*; (point of sale) point de vente *m*; **retail** ~, **sales** ~ point de vente *m*; ~ **store** *n* point de vente *m*

outline¹ *n* idée *f*, bref exposé *m*; (structured) plan *m*, schéma *m*; **give a brief** ~ **of a plan** présenter un projet dans ses grandes lignes

outline² *vt* (aims, reasons) exposer brièvement; (plan) donner un aperçu de; (situation) exposer dans ses grandes lignes

outlook *n* (future prospects) perspectives *f pl*; (attitude) conception *f*; **the** ~ **is bleak/bright** les perpectives sont sombres/excellentes

outmaneuver AmE, **outmanoeuvre** BrE *vt* déjouer les plans de

out-of-court settlement *n* règlement à l'amiable *m*

out-of-favor stock AmE, **out-of-favour stock** BrE *n* titre boudé *m*

out-of-pocket expenses *n pl* débours *m pl*

out-of-the-money *adj* (Stock) en dehors, hors du cours, hors-jeu; ∼ **call** *n* option d'achat en dehors *f*, option d'achat hors du cours *f*; ∼ **option** *n* option en dehors *f*, option hors du cours *f*, option hors la monnaie *f*, option out-of-the-money *f*; ∼ **put** *n* option de vente en dehors *f*, option de vente hors du cours *f*

out-of-town: ∼ **retail development** *n* parc d'activités commerciales *m* (en dehors de la ville), lotissement commercial *m*; ∼ **store** *n* grande surface en dehors de la ville *f*

outpace *vt* dépasser

outperform *vt* l'emporter sur; ∼ **the market** faire mieux que le marché

outplacement *n* replacement externe *m*, reclassement (à l'extérieur de l'entreprise) *m*, décrutement *m*; ∼ **agency** *n* cabinet de placement *m*

output[1] *n* (Comp) résultat *m*, sortie *f*; (Econ) chiffre d'affaires *m*, output *m*; (of factory) production *f*, productivité *f*; (of machine) rendement *m*; ∼ **bonus** *n* prime de rendement *f*; ∼ **data** *n* données de sortie *f pl*; ∼ **device** *n* périphérique de sortie *m*; ∼ **tax** *n* impôt de sortie *m*; ∼ **volume** *n* volume de production *m*

output[2] *vt* (data, text) sortir

outright[1] *adj* (control, majority) absolu; (sale, owner, purchase) inconditionnel/-elle; (ban, refusal) catégorique; (favourite, winner, win) incontesté

outright[2] *adv* (ban, refuse) catégoriquement; (win) sans contestation possible; (sell, buy) comptant

outright: ∼ **gift** *n* don net *m*; ∼ **loss** *n* perte sèche *f*; ∼ **ownership** *n* propriété absolue *f*

outsell *vt* (retailer) vendre plus que; (product) se vendre mieux que

outset *n* at the ∼ au début; from the ∼ dès le début

outside[1] *adj* (line) extérieur; (call) de l'extérieur; (commitment, interests) en dehors du travail; (influence, world) extérieur; (help) de l'extérieur; (opinion) impartial; **an ∼ chance** une faible chance; **get an ∼ opinion** consulter une personne extérieure à l'entreprise

outside[2] *n* extérieur *m*; **bring in a consultant from (the)** ∼ faire venir un consultant de l'extérieur; **at the ∼** au maximum

outside[3] *prep* **it is** ∼ **my remit** ce n'est pas dans mes attributions; ∼ **the reference of** hors de la compétence de; ∼ **office hours** en dehors des heures de bureau

outside: ∼ **director** *n* administrateur/ -trice externe *m/f*; ∼ **finance** *n* finance globale *f*; ∼ **money** *n* monnaie externe *f*

outsider *n* personne extérieure *f*; ∼ **broker** *n* courtier non membre *m*

outsource *vt* externaliser

outsourcing *n* externalisation *f*, approvisionnement à l'extérieur *m*

outstanding *adj* (performance, achievement) exceptionnel/-elle; (example, feature) remarquable; (unresolved) en suspens; (bill) impayé; (work) inachevé; (account) impayé; (issue, question) qui n'a pas été résolu; **the ∼ amount** le restant de la somme *m*, l'arriéré *m*; ∼ **item** effet en circulation *m*; ∼ **advance** *n* (Acc) avance en cours *f*; ∼ **balance** *n* solde impayé *m*; ∼ **commitment** *n* engagement en cours *m*; ∼ **credit** *n* crédits en cours *m pl*, encours de crédit *m*; ∼ **debt** *n* créance à recouvrir *f*, dette active *f*, encours de la dette *m*; ∼ **loan** *n* prêt impayé *m*, prêt non remboursé *m*; ∼ **loans** *n pl* encours de prêts *m pl*, prêts en cours *m pl*; ∼ **matters** *n pl* questions en suspens *f pl*; ∼ **order** *n* commande en attente *f*; ∼ **shares** *n pl* actions en circulation *f pl*

out-tray *n* corbeille départ *f*

outvote *vt* obtenir une majorité sur; **be ∼ed** être mis en minorité

outward: ∼ **cargo** *n* cargaison d'aller *f*; ∼ **voyage** *n* aller *m*

outward-looking *adj* (approach) ouvert sur l'extérieur

outweigh *vt* prévaloir sur

outwork *n* travail à domicile *m*

outworker *n* travailleur/-euse à domicile *m/f*

over[1] *adj* (finished) fini, terminé; **get sth ∼ with** en finir avec qch

over[2] *prep* ∼ **the last decade** depuis les dix dernières années; ∼ **the last year** depuis un an; ∼ **one year** sur un an; ∼ **a period of time** au cours d'une certaine période; ∼ **the telephone** au téléphone; ∼ **the years** avec le temps; **be spread ∼ several weeks** s'échelonner sur plusieurs semaines

overaccumulation *n* suraccumulation *f*

overage *n* surplus *m*; (Prop) excédent *m*

overall[1] *adj* (expenditure, figures, increase, trend, value) global; (cost, measurement, length, responsibility) total; (control, impression, standard) général; (effect) d'ensemble; (majority) absolu; ∼ **rate of return** *n* taux de rentabilité *m*

overall[2] *adv* globalement

overbook *vi* surréserver

overbooked *adj* surréservé, surbooké

overbooking *n* surréservation *f*, surbooking *m*

overbought *adj* (Stock) suracheté

overcapacity *n* surcapacité *f*

overcapitalization *n* surcapitalization *f*

overcapitalized *adj* surcapitalisé

O

overcautious *adj* excessivement prudent

overcharge[1] *n* majoration *f*, surcharge *f*; (excess amount taken) trop-perçu *m*

overcharge[2] **1** *vt* faire trop payer **2** *vi* faire payer au prix fort; ~ **by £100** faire payer 100 livres sterling de trop

overcommit *vt* ~ **the company** (with assignments) prendre trop d'engagements pour l'entreprise; (financially) prendre trop d'engagements financiers pour l'entreprise; **be ~ted** (with assignments) avoir trop d'engagements; (financially) avoir trop d'engagements financiers

overcommitment *n* (Fin) engagement excédentaire *m*

overconsumption *n* surconsommation *f*

overdependence *n* surdépendance *f*

overdraft *n* découvert *m*; **have an ~** être à découvert; **take out an ~** obtenir un découvert; **agreed ~** découvert autorisé *m*; ~ **facility** *n* (Acc) facilité de caisse *f*; (Bank) autorisation de découvert *f*

overdraw *vt* ~ **an account** mettre un compte à découvert

overdrawn *adj* (account) à découvert; **be ~ by £800** avoir un découvert de 800 livres sterling; **go ~** se mettre à découvert

overdue *adj* (bill, account) impayé; (interest, debt) arriéré; (work) en retard; ~ **payment** *n* arriéré *m*

overemployment *n* suremploi *m*

overestimate *vt* surestimer

overexploitation *n* surexploitation *f*

overextend: ~ **oneself** *v refl* avoir des engagements au-dessus de ses moyens

overextended *adj* **be ~** avoir des engagements au-dessus de ses moyens

overhaul[1] *n* (of system) remise en état *f*, restructuration *f*; (of machine) révision *f*

overhaul[2] *vt* (system, procedures) restructurer; (equipment) réviser

overhead: ~ **charges** *n pl* frais généraux *m pl*; ~ **projector** *n* rétroprojecteur *m*

overheads *n pl* frais généraux *m pl*; ~ **recovery** *n* couverture des frais généraux *f*

overheated *adj* (Econ) surchauffé; ~ **economy** *n* économie en surchauffe *f*

overheating *n* (Econ) surchauffe *f*

overindebted *adj* surendetté

overindebtedness *n* surendettement *m*

overinsured *adj* surassuré

overissue *n* surémission *f*

overkill *n* matraquage *m*; **media/ advertising ~** matraquage médiatique/ publicitaire *m*

overland transport *n* transport terrestre *m*

overlook *vt* (detail, mistake) ne pas voir; (effect, fact, problem, need) ignorer; (candidate) ne pas considérer; ~ **the fact that** négliger le fait que

overmanned *adj* (plant, factory) en sureffectif, au personnel pléthorique; **be ~** être en sureffectif

overmanning *n* sureffectif *m*, effectif pléthorique *m*; **reduce ~** réduire les effectifs

overnight[1] *adj* (journey, flight) de nuit; (success, change) immédiat

overnight[2] *adv* (travel) de nuit; (change) du jour au lendemain

overnight: ~ **money** *n* argent au jour le jour *m*; ~ **travel** *n* voyages de nuit *m pl*

overpaid *adj* surpayé

overpay *vt* (employee) surpayer

overpayment *n* (Acc, Fin) paiement en trop *m*, surpaiement *m*; (Tax) trop-perçu *m*

overprice *vt* vendre trop cher

overpriced *adj* trop cher/-ère; (market) gonflé

overproduce *vt* surproduire

overproduction *n* surproduction *f*

overqualified *adj* surqualifié

overrate *vt* (person, product, value) surestimer; (Tax) surtaxer

overreach: ~ **oneself** *v refl* se fixer des objectifs trop ambitieux

overreact *vi* réagir de façon excessive

override *vt* (take precedence) l'emporter sur; (law, order) annuler; (opinion, consideration) passer outre à

overriding *adj* (trend, factor, consideration) dérogatoire; ~ **commission** *n* supercommission *f*, surcommission *f*; ~ **interest** *n* droit dérogatoire *m*

overrule *vt* (decision) annuler; (plan, conclusion, objection) rejeter; (person) l'emporter sur la décision de

overrun[1] *n* (Econ) dépassement *m*; (Ind) (in production) excédent de production *m*; ~ **cost** *n* surcoût *m*, dépassement du budget *m*

overrun[2] *vi* (project, presentation) dépasser le délai prévu

overseas[1] *adj* (investor, visit, student) étranger/-ère; (travel, investment) à l'étranger

overseas[2] *adv* à l'étranger

overseas: ~ **aid** *n* aide extérieure *f*; ~ **assets** *n pl* actif détenu à l'étranger *m*, avoirs extérieurs *m pl*; ~ **branch** *n* succursale à l'étranger *f*; ~ **customer** *n* client/-e étranger/-ère *m/f*; ~ **department** *n* (of France) département d'Outre-Mer *m*; ~ **tourism** *n* tourisme étranger *m*; ~ **tourist** *n* touriste étranger/-ère *m/f*; ~ **trade** *n* commerce extérieur *m*

Overseas Development Administration *n* UK ≈ Organisme du développement outre-mer *m*

oversee *vt* superviser, surveiller

overseer *n* chef d'équipe *m*, contremaître *m*

oversell *vt* (exaggerate the virtues of) trop vanter; (Econ) (product, commodity) vendre plus qu'on ne peut livrer; (Stock) survendre

overshoot *vt* (target, total) dépasser

oversight *n* erreur *f*, omission *f*

oversold *adj* survendu; (market) saturé

overspend *n* (Acc) dépense en trop *f*; (in public spending) dépassement budgétaire *m*

overspending *n* dépense excessive *f*; (in public spending) dépassement budgétaire *m*, dépassement de budget *m*

overstaffed *adj* en sureffectif, au personnel pléthorique; **be ~** être en sureffectif

overstaffing *n* sureffectif *m*, personnel pléthorique *m*; **reduce ~** réduire les sureffectifs

overstep *vt* (limits, bounds) surpasser; **~ the mark** dépasser les bornes

oversubscribed *adj* (Stock) sursouscrit

oversubscription *n* sursouscription *f*

oversupply *n* surabondance de l'offre *f*

overtaxation *n* fiscalité excessive *f*

over-the-counter *adj* (Stock) US hors cote; (medication) sans ordonnance; **~ market** *n* US marché de gré à gré *m*, marché hors cote *m*; **~ retailing** *n* commerce traditionnel *m*; **~ trading** *n* (Stock) US opérations sur le marché hors cote *f pl*

overtime *n* heures supplémentaires *f pl*; **work ~** faire des heures supplémentaires; **~ ban** *n* boycott des heures supplémentaires *m*; **~ hours** *n pl* heures supplémentaires *f pl*; **~ pay** *n* rémunération des heures supplémentaires *f*

overtrading *n* (Econ) *mauvaise maîtrise de son activité commerciale*

overuse¹ *n* abus *m*, utilisation excessive *f*

overuse² *vi* (service, substance) abuser de; (equipment) trop se servir de

overvaluation *n* surévaluation *f*

overvalue *vt* surévaluer

overvalued *adj* surévalué

overview *n* vue d'ensemble *f*

overwhelm *vt* accabler

overworked *adj* surmené

owe *vt* devoir; **~ sth to sb** devoir qch à qn

owing¹ *adj* à payer, dû; **how much is ~ to you?** combien est-ce qu'on vous doit?; **300 euros are still ~** il y a encore 300 euros à payer; **the amount ~** le montant à payer, le montant dû

owing² *prep* **~ to** en raison de

own¹ *adj* propre

own² *vt* avoir, posséder; (shop, business, house, car) être le propriétaire de

own brand *n* marque de distributeur *f*; **~ product** *n* produit à marque de distributeur *m*

owner *n* propriétaire *mf*; (Patents) titulaire *mf*; (in shipping) armateur *m*; **at ~'s risk** aux risques et périls du propriétaire; **~-manager** *n* propriétaire-gérant/-e *m/f*; **~ occupation** *n* occupation par le propriétaire *f*; **~-occupied home** *n* logement occupé par le propriétaire *m*; **~-occupier** *n* propriétaire-occupant/-e *m/f*; **~-operator** *n* propriétaire-exploitant/-e *m/f*

ownership *n* propriété *f*; (of land) possession *f*; **come under public ~** être nationalisé; **bring under public ~** nationaliser; **share ~** participation dans le capital d'une société *f*; **property ~** propriété immobilière *f*; **~ form** *n* US forme de propriété *f*

own-label *adj* marque de distributeur; **~ product** *n* produit à marque de distributeur *m*

ozone *n* ozone *m*; **~ depletion** *n* diminution de l'ozone *f*, raréfaction de l'ozone *f*; **~-friendly** *adj* qui protège la couche d'ozone; **~ layer** *n* couche d'ozone *f*

o
p

Pp

p *abbr* (▸**pence**) pence *m*

P-1 *abbr* (▸**prime paper**) papier commercial de premier ordre *m*

P2P *abbr* (▸**peer-to-peer**) poste à poste, d'égal à égal; (▸**path-to-profitability**) *voie menant à la rentabilité que doit suivre une start-up en phase de lancement et de croissance*

p.a. *abbr* (▸**per annum**) p.a. (par an); (▸**particular average**) avarie particulière *f*, avarie partielle *f*

PA *abbr* (▸**power of attorney**) procuration *f*; (▸**personal assistant**) (assistant) assistant/-e de direction *m/f*; (secretary) secrétaire de direction *mf*; (▸**public address system**) système de sonorisation *m*

PABX *abbr* (▸**Private Automatic Branch eXchange**) autocommutateur privé *m*

pace *n* (of trend, activity) rythme *m*; (speed) vitesse *f*; **~ of change** rapidité du changement *f*; **keep ~ with** (competitors) se maintenir au même niveau que; (change, events) arriver à suivre; **set the ~** donner le ⸱⸱⸱⸥

pas; **gather** ~ (process) prendre de l'ampleur; **step up/slow down the** ~ accélérer/ralentir le rythme

pacesetter n (company) société leader f

pacify vt apaiser

pack¹ n (box) paquet m; (sachet) sachet m; ~ **shot** n (advertising) plan-paquet m

pack² ①vt emballer; (for sale, display) conditionner; (committee) rendre favorable à ses vues

②vi (person) faire ses valises

package¹ n (parcel) colis m, paquet m; (for retail) paquet m, emballage m; (Comp) progiciel m; (of grants, incentives, proposals, reforms) ensemble m; (items sold as one) lot m; (combined pay and perks) salaire et avantages complémentaires m pl, contrat global m; **accounting** ~ progiciel comptable m; **aid** ~ ensemble de mesures d'assistance m; ~ **of financial services** ensemble de services financiers m; ~ **code** n code emballage m; ~ **deal** n contrat global m; (holiday) forfait m; ~ **design** n conception de l'emballage f; ~ **goods** n pl marchandises emballées f pl; ~ **holiday** n BrE voyage organisé m, forfait m; ~ **store** n AmE magasin de vins et de spiritueux m; ~ **tour** n BrE voyage organisé m, forfait m; ~ **tour operator** n voyagiste m, tour-opérateur m; ~ **vacation** n AmE voyage organisé m, forfait m

package² vt (goods, produce) emballer; (for sale, display, merchandising) conditionner; (design, proposal, project) présenter; (performer, personality) présenter

packaged goods n pl produits conditionnés m pl

packaging n emballage m; (for display, sales, merchandising) conditionnement m; (of company, policy) image publique f; ~ **cost** n coût d'emballage m; ~ **credit** n crédit global m; ~ **materials** n pl composants de conditionnement m pl

packer n emballeur/-euse m/f, conditionneur/-euse m/f

packet n (Gen Comm) paquet m; (Comp) groupe de bits m, paquet m

packing n emballage m, conditionnement m; ~ **slip** n note de livraison f; ~ **case** n caisse f; ~ **list** n bordereau de colisage m, liste de colisage f

pad¹ n bloc m

pad²: ~ **out** vt (report, speech) étoffer

padded envelope n enveloppe matelassée f

padding n rembourrage m

page¹ n page f; ~ **break** n saut de page m; ~ **layout** n mise en page f; ~ **length** n nombre de lignes par page m; ~ **number** n numéro de page m; ~ **setting** n mise en page f; ~ **traffic** n UK estimation du nombre de lecteurs d'une publication; ~ **view** n (on Internet) impression f

page² vt (on pager) biper

pagejacking n (on Internet) pratique consistant à incorporer à son propre site des pages d'un site bien référencé pour obtenir un meilleur positionnement dans les résultats des moteurs de recherche

pager n pager m, messager de poche m, bip m

paginate vt paginer

pagination n pagination f

paid adj (amount, dividend) payé, versé; (person, work) payé, rémunéré; **be** ~ **a rate of** percevoir un salaire horaire de; ~ **by the hour** payé à l'heure; ~ **by the piece** payé à la pièce; ~ **hourly** payé à l'heure; ~ **in advance** payé d'avance; ~ **on delivery** paiement à la livraison, payé à la livraison; ~ **piece rate** payé à la pièce; **poorly** ~ mal payé; ~ **holiday** n BrE congés payés m pl; ~**-in capital** n capital d'apport m, capital versé m; ~ **instrument** n acquit m; ~ **leave** n congés payés m pl; ~**-out capital** n capital remboursé m; ~**-up addition** n (Ins) bonification d'assurance libérée f; ~**-up capital** n capital libéré m; ~**-up member** n UK adhérent/-e m/f, (of union) syndiqué/-e à jour avec ses cotisations m/f; ~**-up shares** n pl actions libérées f pl; ~**-up vacation** n AmE congés payés m pl

painstaking adj méticuleux/-euse

painstakingly adv méticuleusement

PAL abbr (▶**program adjustment loan** AmE, ▶**programme adjustment loan** BrE) prêt-programme d'ajustement m; (▶**phase alternation line**) (TV) PAL m

pallet n palette f

palletize vt palettiser

palm¹ n **grease sb's** ~ (infml) graisser la patte à qn (infml)

palm² vt ~ **sth off as** faire passer qch pour; ~ **sth off on sb** refiler qch à qn (infml)

palmtop n ordinateur de poche m

pamphlet n dépliant m, brochure f

Pan American Standards Commission n US association panaméricaine de normalisation

P&L abbr (▶**profit and loss**) P et P (pertes et profits); ~ **account** n compte de pertes et profits m, comptes de résultats m pl

p&p abbr (▶**postage and packing**) frais de port et d'emballage m pl, port et emballage m pl

P&S abbr (▶**purchase and sale statement**) état des achats et des ventes m

panel n (sign, board) panneau m, tableau m; (for market research) panel m; (of experts, judges) comité m; ~ **envelope** n enveloppe à fenêtre f; ~ **member** n (S&M) panéliste mf; ~ **research** recherche par panel f; ~ **testing** n test sur un panel m

pan-European adj paneuropéen/-éenne

panic¹ n panique f; ~ **buying** n achats de

précaution (sous l'effet de la panique) *m pl*; ~ **reaction** *n* réaction de panique *f*; ~ **selling** *n* (Stock) vente précipitée d'actions (sous l'effet de la panique) *f*; ~**-stricken** *adj* frappé de panique

panic² ⃞1 *vt* paniquer, affoler
⃞2 *vi* paniquer

paper *n* papier *m*; (report) rapport *m*; (document) document *m*; (lecture, academic report) communication *f*; (Fin) effet *m*, papier *m*; (newspaper) journal *m*; (government publication) livre *m*; **get sth down on** ~ mettre qch par écrit; **present a** ~ **on sth** présenter une communication sur qch; **show one's** ~**s** présenter ses papiers; **it's a good idea on** ~ c'est une bonne idée en théorie; **it's not worth the** ~ **it's written on** ça ne vaut pas absolument rien; ~ **bag** sac en papier *m*; ~ **feed** *n* alimentation papier *f*; ~ **gold** *n* or-papier *m*; ~ **industry** *n* industrie du papier *f*, papeterie *f*; ~ **loss** *n* (Gen Comm) perte théorique *f*; (Stock) moins non réalisé sur titres *m*, moins sur titres *m*; ~ **mill** *n* fabrique de papier *f*, papeterie *f*; ~ **millionaire** *n* millionnaire en actions *m/f*; ~ **money** *n* monnaie fiduciaire *f*; ~ **profit** *n* (Acc) profit non matérialisé *m*; (Fin) bénéfice non réalisé *m*, bénéfice théorique *m*; ~ **pusher** *n* gratte-papier *m inv* (péj); ~ **qualifications** *n pl* diplômes *m pl*, titres *m pl*; ~ **shredder** *n* déchiqueteuse *f*; ~ **weight** *n* (measurement) grammage *m*

paperback *n* livre de poche *m*; ~ **book** *n* livre de poche *m*

paperboard *n* tableau de papier *m*

paperclip *n* trombone *m*

paperless *adj* (certificates of deposit) dématérialisé; (office) électronique; ~ **entry** *n* écriture informatique *f*; ~ **trading** *n* transactions informatisées *f pl*

paperwork *n* (Admin) travail administratif *m*; (documentation) documents *m pl*

par *n* pair *m*; **above** ~ au-dessus du pair; **at** ~ au pair, à la valeur nominale; **below** ~ au-dessous du pair; **be on a** ~ **with sth** être comparable à qch; **be on a** ~ **with sb** être l'égal de qn; ~ **bond** *n* obligation remboursable au pair *f*; ~ **stock** *n* action à valeur nominale *f*; ~ **trading** *n* opérations boursières au pair *f pl*, transaction au pair *f*; ~ **value** *n* parité *f*, valeur au pair *f*, valeur nominale *f*; ~ **value of currency** *n* valeur au pair d'une devise *f*; ~ **value share** *n* action à valeur nominale *f*; ~ **value stock** *n* action à valeur nominale *f*

PAR *abbr* (▸**prescribed aggregate reserve**) réserve globale visée par règlement *f*

paradigm *n* paradigme *m*

paradox *n* paradoxe *m*

paragraph *n* paragraphe *m*; **start a new** ~ aller à la ligne

paralegal¹ *adj* paralégal

paralegal² *n* juriste *mf*

parallel¹ *adj* parallèle; ~ **to** parallèlement à; **develop along** ~ **lines** évoluer de manière analogue; ~ **access** *n* accès en parallèle *m*; ~ **currency** *n* monnaie parallèle *f*; ~ **import** *n* importation parallèle *f*; ~ **interface** *n* interface parallèle *f*; ~ **loan** *n* emprunt parallèle *m*, prêt parallèle *m*; ~ **pricing** *n* tarification parallèle *f*; ~ **processing** *n* traitement en parallèle *m*, traitement en simultanéité *m*; ~ **trading** *n* commerce parallèle *m*

parallel² *n* (comparison) parallèle *m*; (Math) parallèle *f*; **in** ~ en parallèle; **to establish/ draw a** ~ **between** établir/faire un parallèle entre; **be on a** ~ **with** être comparable à; **without a** ~ sans parallèle

parameter *n* paramètre *m*; **set** ~**s** fixer les paramètres; **fall within certain** ~**s** ne pas dépasser certains paramètres

parametric *adj* paramétrique

parcel¹ *n* colis *m*, paquet *m*; (of land) parcelle *f*; (of shares) paquet *m*; ~**s awaiting delivery** colis en instance de livraison *m pl*; ~ **post** *n* service de colis postaux *m*, service de messageries *m*; ~**s van** *n* camion de messageries *m*

parcel²: ~ **out** *vt* morceler; ~ **up** *vt* (land) morceler; (goods) emballer

parceling AmE, **parcelling** BrE: ~ **out** *n* (of land) morcellement *m*; ~ **up** *n* (of land) morcellement *m*; (of goods) emballage *m*

pare: ~ **down** *vt* réduire

parent *n* parent *m*; (Comp) père *m*; (Law) parent *m*; ~ **bank** *n* banque mère *f*; ~ **company** *n* société mère *f*; ~ **company dividend** *n* dividende de la société mère *m*; ~ **corporation** *n* corporation mère *f*; ~ **dividends** *n pl* dividendes de la société mère *m pl*

parental *adj* parental; ~ **leave** *n* congé parental *m*

parenthesis *n pl* -**theses** parenthèse *f*; **in parentheses** entre parenthèses

Pareto's law *n* loi de Pareto *f*

Paris Interbank Offered Rate *n* taux interbancaire offert à Paris *m*

parity *n* parité *f*; (Stock) pair *m*; ~ **bond** *n* obligation émise au pair *f*; ~ **clause** *n* (Ins) clause de parité *f*; ~ **of exchange** parité de change *f*; ~ **price** *n* prix au pair *m*; ~ **pricing** *n* détermination des prix à parité *f*; ~ **ratio** *n* rapport de parité *m*; ~ **value** *n* valeur au pair *f*

park¹ *n* parc *m*; **business** ~ parc d'activités *m*, parc d'affaires *m*; **industrial/science** ~ parc industriel/scientifique *m*

park² ⃞1 *vt* garer
⃞2 *vi* se garer

park and ride *n* parking relais *m*

parking *n* stationnement *m*; (area) parking *m*; **no** ~ **area, no** ~ **zone** zone de   ···▸

P

stationnement interdit *f*; ~ **lot** *n* AmE
parking *m*; ~ **ticket** *n* (fine) procès-verbal *m*
parliament *n* parlement *m*; **get into** ~ UK
se faire élire député
parliamentary *adj* parlementaire; ~
appropriation *n* crédit parlementaire *m*; ~
private secretary *n* UK *parlementaire
attaché à un ministre*; ~ **procedure** *n*
procédure parlementaire *f*; ~ **vote** *n* (Fin)
crédit parlementaire *m*
part *n* (fraction of whole) partie *f*; (proportion)
proportion *f*; (component) pièce *f*; **be** ~ **of** faire
partie de; **be** ~ **and parcel of sth** faire partie
intégrante de qch; **for my** ~ pour ma part; **in**
~ **payment** en règlement partiel; **on the** ~
of sb de la part de qn; **play a** ~ **in sth**
participer à qch, jouer un rôle dans qch; **take**
~ **in** participer à, prendre part à; ~**s and
labour** pièces et main-d'œuvre; **spare** ~**s**
pièces détachées *f pl*; ~ **exchange** reprise
f; ~ **load** *n* charge incomplète *f*, chargement
partiel *m*; ~ **owner** *n* copropriétaire *mf*; ~
ownership *n* copropriété *f*; ~ **payment** *n*
paiement partiel *m*, règlement partiel *m*; ~
shipment *n* expédition partielle *f*
partial *adj* (biased) partial; (incomplete)
partiel/-ielle; ~ **basis** *n* (Fin) base partielle *f*;
(of bill) acceptation partielle *f*; ~
consideration *n* (Acc) paiement partiel *m*;
~ **delivery** *n* livraison partielle *f*; ~ **loss** *n*
(Ins) dommages partiels *m pl*, perte partielle
f, sinistre partiel *m*; ~ **release** *n* (Law) (of
property) décharge partielle *f*, libération
partielle *f*; ~ **withdrawal** *n* retrait partiel
m; ~ **write-off** *n* (Acc) radiation partielle *f*
partially *adv* (in part) partiellement; (unfairly)
avec partialité; ~**-privatized company** *n*
société à économie mixte *f*
partial/total loss *n* perte partielle ou
totale *f*
participant *n* participant/-e *m/f*
participate *vi* participer; ~ **in** participer à
participating *adj* participant; ~ **bond** *n*
obligation participante *f*; ~ **carrier** *n*
transporteur participant *m*; ~ **interest** *n*
intérêt de participation *m*, participation *f*; ~
preference share *n* action préférentielle *f*;
~ **preferred stock** *n* AmE action
préférentielle *f*; ~ **security** *n* titre de
participation *m*, titre participatif *m*
participation *n* participation *f*; **worker** ~
participation des ouvriers *f*; ~ **agreement** *n*
accord de participation *m*; ~ **loan** *n* crédit
syndical *m*, prêt participant *m*; ~ **rate** *n*
taux de participation *m*
participative *adj* participatif/-ive; ~
management *n* direction participative *f*
particular[1] *adj* (specific) particulier/-ière;
(demanding) exigeant
particular[2] *n* (detail) détail *m*; **in every** ~
dans tous les détails; **in several** ~**s** à plus
d'un titre; **in** ~ en particulier; ~ **average** *n*
avarie particulière *f*, avarie partielle *f*

particulars *n pl* (information) détails *m pl*;
(name and address) coordonnées *f pl*; (description)
description *f*; ~ **of sale** *n pl* description de
la propriété à vendre *f*
partition *n* (in office) cloison *f*; (Law, Prop)
morcellement de terrain *m*, partage *m*
partly *adv* partiellement; ~**-finished
goods** *n pl* biens semi-finis *m pl*; ~ **paid**
adj (shares) partiellement libéré; ~ **paid up
shares** *n pl* actions non entièrement
libérées *f pl*
partner *n* (in business) associé/-e *m/f*; (Econ,
Pol) partenaire *mf*; **active** ~ associé/-e
gérant/-e *m/f*; **general** ~ commandité/-e *m/f*;
junior ~ associé/-e minoritaire *m/f*; **limited**
~ commanditaire *mf*; **managing** ~ associé/-e
gérant/-e *m/f*; **senior** ~ associé/-e majoritaire
m/f, associé/-e principal/-e *m/f*; **working** ~
commandité/-e *m/f*
partnership *n* (Gen Comm) association *f*;
(firm) société en nom collectif *f*; (alliance)
partenariat *m*; **be in** ~ **with** être associé
avec; **go into** ~ **with** s'associer avec; **limited**
~, **special** ~ société en commandite simple
f; **professional** ~, **non-trading** ~ société non
commerciale *f*; **take sb into** ~ prendre qn
pour associé/-e; ~ **income** *n* revenu de
société *m*; ~ **share** *n* part d'associé *f*, part
sociale *f*
part-time[1] *adj* à temps partiel
part-time[2] *adv* (work) à temps partiel
part-time: ~ **employee** *n* employé/-e à
temps partiel *m/f*; ~ **employment** *n* travail
à temps partiel *m*; ~ **job** *n* poste à temps
partiel *m*; ~ **work** *n* travail à temps partiel
m; ~ **worker** *n* travailleur/-euse à temps
partiel *m/f*
part-timer *n* employé/-e à temps partiel *m/f*
party *n* (in contract) partie *f*; (group) groupe *m*;
(Pol) parti *m*; (social event) fête *f*; (social evening)
soirée *f*; (formal event) réception *f*;
contracting/defaulting/opposing ~ partie
contractante/défaillante/adverse *f*; **be a** ~ **to
negotiations** être partie prenante dans une
négociation; **become** ~ **to a contract** être
l'une des parties contractantes; ~ **line** *n*
(Comms) ligne commune *f*; (Pol) ligne du parti
f; ~ **ticket** *n* billet collectif *m*; ~ **to an
agreement** partie prenante dans une
convention *f*; ~ **to a contract** partie
contractante *f*
pass[1] *n* laisser-passer *m*; (for travel) carte
d'abonnement *f*
pass[2] *vt* (Acc) (entry) passer; (budget) faire
adopter, faire voter; (bill, invoice, loan)
approuver; (dividend) omettre le paiement de;
(judgement, verdict) prononcer; (resolution, motion,
bill) adopter; (candidate) admettre; (test, exam)
réussir; ~ **sth for press** donner qch à tirer;
'~ **for press**' 'bon à tirer'; ~ **inspection**
satisfaire au contrôle; ~ **sentence** prononcer
une condamnation; ~ **sth over in silence**
passer qch sous silence; **he was** ~**ed over in**

favour of another candidate on lui a préféré un autre candidat; ~ **through customs** passer la douane; ~ **off** (goods) faire passer; ~ **sth off as** faire passer qch pour; ~ **on** (message) transmettre; (cost) répercuter; ~ **up** (opportunity) laisser passer

passbook n livret de banque m, livret de compte m

passenger n (in car, boat, plane) passager/ -ère m/f; (in train, coach, metro) voyageur/-euse m/f; ~ **aircraft** n avion passagers m; ~ **control** n limitation du nombre de passagers f; ~ **coupon** n souche f; ~ **ferry** n ferry m; ~ **list** n liste des passagers f; ~ **lounge** n salon d'attente m; ~ **manifest** n liste des passagers m, manifeste des passagers m; ~ **ship** n paquebot m; ~ **terminal** n aérogare f, terminal m; ~ **throughput** n capacité de traitement des passagers f; ~ **train** n train de voyageurs m; ~ **vehicle** n véhicule de tourisme m

passer-by n passant/-e m/f

passing trade n clients de passage m pl

passive adj passif/-ive; ~ **bond** n obligation ne portant pas d'intérêt f; ~ **income** n revenu de placements m; ~ **investor** n investisseur passif m

passport n passeport m; ~ **control** n contrôle des passeports m; ~ **holder** n titulaire d'un passeport mf

password n mot de passe m; ~ **protected** adj protégé par un mot de passe

past-due adj non réglé à l'échéance; ~ **claim** n créance en retard f

paste vt (Comp) coller

paste-up n collage m, montage m

past year n (Acc) exercice écoulé m

pat. abbr (▸patent) brevet m

patch n (area covered by rep) secteur m, territoire m; (Comp) rustine f, correction de programme informatique f; **go through a bad** ~ traverser une mauvaise passe (infml)

patchy adj (quality, result) inégal; (performance) de qualité inégale; (knowledge) incomplet/-ète

patent n brevet m; ~ **pending** brevet dont l'homologation est en cours m, brevet déposé m; **hold/take out a** ~ détenir/obtenir un brevet; ~ **agent** n agent en brevets d'invention m; ~ **application** n demande de brevet f; ~ **certificate** n certificat de brevet m; ~ **engineer** n ingénieur-conseil en brevets industriels m; ~ **protection** n protection conférée par un brevet f; ~ **rights** n pl droits exclusifs d'exploitation m pl, propriété industrielle f; ~ **royalties** n pl royalties dues par le concessionnaire d'un brevet f pl; ~ **trading** n échange de brevets m

patentable adj brevetable, qui peut être breveté

Patent Office n UK Office des Brevets

paternalism n paternalisme m

paternity leave n congé de paternité m

path n (means) chemin m, route f; (option) voie f; (Comp) branche f, chemin m; **the** ~ **of least resistance** le chemin de la facilité; ~-**to-profitability** n voie menant à la rentabilité que doit suivre une start-up en phase de lancement et de croissance

pathfinder prospectus n (Stock) prospectus provisoire m

pathway n (Comp) chemin d'accès m

pat. pend. abbr (▸patent pending) brevet dont l'homologation est en cours m, brevet déposé m

patronage n (financial support) apport commercial m; (custom) clientèle f; (support) patronage m; ~ **of the arts** mécénat m

pattern n (motif, design) motif m, dessin m; (example, model) modèle m; (of tendency consumption) tendance f; (Comp) configuration f; **buying** ~s, **spending** ~s habitudes d'achat f; **working** ~s l'organisation du travail f; **follow a set** ~ se dérouler toujours de la même façon; **set the** ~ **for sth** déterminer le modèle de qch; **the** ~ **of events** l'enchaînement des événements m; ~ **of behaviour** mode de comportement m; ~ **book** n catalogue d'échantillons m; ~ **settlement** n (Econ) accord-type m; (HRM) règlement-type m

pauper n indigent/-e m/f

pave vt ~ **the way for sth** préparer le terrain pour qch

pawn[1] n (as security) gage m; **in** ~ au mont-de-piété

pawn[2] vt mettre au mont-de-piété

pawnbroker n prêteur/-euse sur gages m/f

pawned stock n titres en pension m pl

pawnshop n bureau de prêteur sur gages m, mont-de-piété m

pay[1] n salaire m, traitement m; **the** ~ **is good** c'est bien payé; ~-**as-you-earn** n UK (Tax) retenue de l'impôt sur le revenu à la source m; ~-**as-you-go** n US système de retenue à la source m; (S&M) paiement au fur et à mesure m; ~ **bill** n AmE bulletin de salaire m; ~ **check** AmE, ~ **cheque** BrE n chèque de salaire m; ~ **claim** n revendication salariale f; ~ **comparability** n comparabilité des salaires f; ~ **and conditions** n pl le salaire et les conditions de travail; ~ **cut** n réduction de salaire f; ~ **differential** n écart des salaires m; ~ **freeze** n gel des salaires m; ~-**in slip** n AmE bordereau de versement m; ~ **packet** n BrE (envelope) enveloppe de paie f; (wage) paie f; ~ **period** n période de paie f; ~ **phone** n BrE téléphone public m; ~ **policy** n politique salariale f; ~ **review** n révision des salaires f; ~ **rise** n augmentation de salaire f; ~ **round** n série de négociations salariales f; ~ **scale** n échelle des salaires f; ~ **statement** n état des rémunérations versées m; ~ **talks** n pl négociations salariales f pl; ~ **TV** n ⸺⸽

télévision à péage *f*, télévision payante *f*

pay² **1** *vt* (person, price, sum) payer; (employee) rémunérer; (make financial settlement) régler, payer; (instalment) effectuer; (fee) acquitter, régler; (yield, accrue interest) rapporter; ∼ **the bill** payer la facture, payer la note, régler la facture, régler la note; ∼ **a call on sb** rendre visite à qn; ∼ **cash** payer au comptant, payer cash, payer en espèces, payer en liquide; ∼ **a debt in full** acquitter une dette intégralement; ∼ **a deposit** verser des arrhes, verser un acompte; ∼ **duty** payer des taxes; ∼ **interest** payer des intérêts; ∼ **an invoice** régler une facture; ∼ **money into an account** approvisionner un compte; ∼ **sb a flat rate** payer qn au forfait; ∼ **sth into an account** verser qch sur un compte; ∼ **a visit to sb** rendre visite à qn; ∼ **attention to** faire attention à

2 *vi* (bring profit) rapporter; ∼ **for** payer; ∼ **by giro** payer par virement bancaire; ∼ **by the quarter** payer par trimestre, payer trimestriellement; ∼ **by the week** payer à la semaine; ∼ **by the year** payer à l'année; ∼ **in cash** payer au comptant, payer cash, payer en espèces, payer en liquide; ∼ **in kind** payer en nature; ∼ **in specie** payer en espèces; ∼ **on account** verser un acompte; ∼ **over the odds for sth** payer qch au prix fort; ∼ **to the order of** payer à l'ordre de; ∼ **back** **1** *vt* (debt) régler, rembourser; (loan) rembourser, amortir; (creditor) désintéresser, rembourser **2** *vi* être rentable; ∼ **down** (sum) verser un acompte de; ∼ **in** (money) verser; (cheque) déposer; ∼ **off** **1** *vt* (debt) régler, rembourser; (loan) rembourser, amortir; (mortgage) purger; (creditor) désintéresser, rembourser; (worker) licencier, congédier **2** *vi* (plan, work, strategy) se révéler payant; ∼ **out** (sum) dépenser, débourser; ∼ **up** payer

payable *adj* (amount, interest) à payer; **be** ∼ (amount, instalment, debt) être payable; ∼ **after notice** payable à préavis; ∼ **at maturity** payable à échéance; ∼ **at sight** payable sur demande, payable à vue; **be** ∼ **by sb** être à la charge de qn; ∼ **in advance** exigible d'avance, payable à l'avance; ∼ **in instalments** payable en plusieurs versements; ∼ **on demand** payable sur demande, payable à vue; ∼ **on presentation** payable sur demande, payable à vue; **cheque** ∼ **to** chèque libellé à l'ordre de; **write a cheque** ∼ **to** faire un chèque (libellé) à l'ordre de

payables at year-end *n pl* AmE comptes à payer à la fin de l'exercice *m pl*

payback *n* (of loan) remboursement *m*; (of investment) récupération du capital investi *f*, rentabilisation d'un investissement *f*; ∼ **method** *n* méthode d'amortissement *f*; ∼ **period** *n* (for loan) période de remboursement *f*; (of investment) delai de récupération du capital investi *m*; ∼ **provisions** *n pl* provisions d'amortissement *f pl*

payday *n* jour de paie *m*; (on Stock Exchange) jour de liquidation *m*

pay dirt *n* **hit** ∼, **strike** ∼ (infrml) trouver un bon filon

paydown *n* (Stock) remboursement d'une partie du principal *m*

PAYE *abbr* AmE (▸**payables at year-end**) CAPAFE *m pl* (comptes à payer à la fin de l'exercice); UK (▸**pay as you earn**) retenue de l'impôt sur le revenu à la source *f*

payee *n* bénéficiaire *mf*, preneur *m*

payer *n* (Gen Comm) payeur/-euse *m/f*; (of cheque) tireur *m*

paying *n* paiement *m*; ∼ **agent** *n* agent payeur *m*; ∼ **bank** *n* banque payeuse *f*; ∼ **banker** *n* banquier payeur *m*; ∼ **concern** *n* entreprise rentable *f*; ∼ **guest** *n* hôte payant *m*, pensionnaire *mf*; ∼ **in** *n* versement *m*; ∼**-in book** *n* carnet de versement *m*; ∼**-in slip** BrE *n* bordereau de versement *m*; ∼ **proposition** *n* affaire rentable *f*

payload *n* charge utile *f*

paymaster *n* (of wages) agent payeur *m*

payment *n* (sum of money) paiement *m*; (into account, of instalment) versement *m*; (to creditor) remboursement *m*; (hire purchase instalment) traite *f*; (in settlement) règlement *m*; **keep up** ∼ **on one's mortgage** poursuivre ses remboursements hypothécaires; ∼ **made to** paiement fait à; **make a** ∼ effectuer un paiement, faire un versement; **make a down** ∼ verser des arrhes, verser un acompte; **in** ∼ **for my order** en règlement de ma commande; **on** ∼ **of 200 dollars** moyennant 200 dollars; ∼ **on receipt of invoice** paiement sur réception de facture, paiement dès réception de facture; **fall behind with one's** ∼**s** avoir des arriérés; ∼ **authorization** *n* autorisation de prélèvement *f*; ∼ **bond** *n* (Law) garantie de paiement *f*; ∼ **by results** salaire au rendement *m*; ∼ **commitment** *n* obligation de paiement *f*; ∼ **date** *n* date de paiement *f*; ∼ **guarantee** *n* garantie de paiement *f*; ∼ **holiday** *n* (Bank, Fin) congé de paiement *m*; ∼ **in advance** paiement anticipé *m*, paiement en avance *m*; ∼ **in arrears** paiement en arriérés *m*; ∼ **in full** paiement intégral *m*; ∼ **in full on allotment** libération de la participation *f*; ∼ **in kind** paiement en nature *m*; ∼ **method** *n* méthode de paiement *f*; ∼ **on account** provision *f*, acompte *m*; ∼ **order** *n* mandat *m*, ordre de paiement *m*; ∼ **requisition** *n* demande de paiement *f*; ∼ **stopped** *n* opposition au paiement *f*; ∼ **transfer** *n* (Bank) transfert social *m*; ∼ **type** *n* méthode de paiement *f*

payoff *n* (Gen Comm) bénéfice *m*, gains *m pl*; (on an investment) rapport *m*

payola *n* US (infrml) pot-de-vin *m*

payout *n* (Bank) remise totale *f*; (marketing) versement *m*

pay-per-click *n* (on Internet) paiement par

clic *m*

pay-per-lead *n* (on Internet) *rémunération établie en fonction du nombre de visiteurs qui s'inscrivent sur le site partenaire*

pay-per-view *n* (on Internet) paiement par séance *m*

payroll *n* (all employees) ensemble du personnel *m*; (staff list) liste du personnel *f*; (total wage bill) masse salariale *f*; **be on the ~** faire partie du personnel

payslip *n* BrE bulletin de paie *m*, bulletin de salaire *m*

PBR *abbr* (▶**payment by results**) salaire au rendement *m*

PBS *abbr* US (▶**Public Broadcasting System**) *services de radio-télévision publics*

pc *abbr* (▶**petty cash**) menue monnaie *f*, petite caisse *f*; (▶**piece**) pièce *f*; (▶**per cent**) p. cent (pour cent)

PC *abbr* (▶**personal computer**) ordinateur (individuel) *m*, PC *m*; **~-compatible** *adj* compatible PC; **~-based** *adj* (software, service) pour PC; **~-compatibility** *n* compatibilité PC *f*

pd *abbr* (▶**postdated**) postdaté; (▶**paid**) (amount, dividend) acquitté, payé, versé

PDA *abbr* (▶**personal digital assistant**) assistant numérique personnel *m*, PDA *m*

PDF *abbr* (**portable document format**) format PDF *m*

PDO *abbr* (EU) (▶**protected designation of origin**) AOP *f* (appellation d'origine protégée)

peak¹ *n* (highest level) maximum *m*, niveau record *m*; (on graph) sommet *m*; (of achievement, career) apogée *f*; **~ level** *n* niveau maximum *m*, niveau record *m*; **~ period** *n* (for traffic) heures d'affluence *f pl*, heures de pointe *f pl*; (for holidays) haute saison *f*; **~ price** *n* prix maximum *m*, prix record *m*; **~ rate** *n* (for telephone calls) tarif en heures pleines *m*; **~ season** *n* haute saison *f*; **~ time** *n* (television) heure de grande écoute *f*, prime time *m*; **~ time advertising** *n* publicité au prime time *f*

peak² *vi* atteindre son maximum, atteindre son niveau record

peculation *n* détournement *m*, concussion *f*

pecuniary *adj* pécuniaire

peddle *vt* (goods) colporter

pedestrian *n* piéton/-onne *m/f*; **~ precinct** *n* zone piétonnière *f*

pedestrianization *n* création d'une zone piétonnière *f*

pedestrianize *vt* transformer en zone piétonnière

peer *n* pair *m*; **~ review** *n* examen par les pairs *m*

peer-to-peer *adj* (network) poste à poste, d'égal à égal

peg *vt* (rate, price, currency) indexer; (stabilize) stabiliser

pegged: **~ exchange rate** *n* taux de change indexé *m*; **~ price** *n* prix indexé *m*; **~ rate of exchange** *n* taux de change indexé *m*

pegging *n* soutien des prix *m*, stabilisation *f*; **~ device** *n* mécanisme d'indexation *m*

penalize *vt* pénaliser

penalty *n* (fine) amende *f*; (Law) peine *f*, pénalité *f*, sanction *f*; **~ clause** *n* clause pénale *f*; **~ for breach of contract** dédit de rupture de contrat *m*; **~ for late tax payment** majoration de retard *f*; **~ for noncompliance** pénalité pour infraction *f*; **~ rate** *n* taux de pénalisation *m*

pen-based computer *n* ardoise électronique *f*

pence *n* UK (unit of currency) penny *m*; **fifty ~** cinquante pence; **a ten ~ piece** une pièce de dix pence

pending *adj* (deal, matter) en attente, en souffrance; (case, charge, claim) en instance; **~ business** *n* affaires en cours *f pl*; **~ tray** *n* corbeille des affaires en cours *f*

penetrate *vti* pénétrer; **~ the market** pénétrer le marché

penetration *n* pénétration *f*; **~ pricing** *n* (Gen Comm) fixation du prix d'appel *f*; (S&M) politique de prix de pénétration par la base *f*; **~ rate** *n* taux de pénétration *m*

penny *n* (UK currency unit) penny *m*; (US currency unit) cent *m*; **by ~ numbers** par petits lots, en petites quantités; **not a ~ more** pas un centime de plus; **~ shares** *n pl* UK actions peu chères *f pl*; **~ stocks** *n pl* US actions cotées en cents *f pl*

pension¹ *n* (from the State) pension *f*, retraite de vieillesse *f*; (from company) retraite *f*; **~ charges** *n pl* primes de retraite *f pl*; **~ contributions** *n pl* cotisations à un régime de retraite *f pl*; **~ costs** *n pl* primes de retraite *f pl*; **~ fund** *n* caisse de retraite *f*, fonds de retraite *m*; **~-holder** *n* pensionné/-e *m/f*; **~ income** *n* revenu de pension *m*; **~ liabilities** *n pl* engagements de retraite *m pl*; **~ plan** *n* régime de retraite *m*; **~ scheme** *n* régime de retraite *m*

pension²: **~ off** *vt* mettre à la retraite

pensionable *adj* (post, service) donnant droit à une pension; **~ age** *n* âge de la retraite *m*; **~ earnings** *n pl* salaire cotisable *m*

pent-up: **~ demand** *n* demande accumulée *f*; **~ energy** *n* force contenue *f*

PEP *abbr* UK (▶**personal equity plan**) plan d'épargne en actions *m*, plan personnel de capitalisation *m*

peppercorn rent *n* loyer nominal *m*, loyer symbolique *m*

per *prep* par; **~ annum** par an; **as ~ previous order** conformément à la

commande précédente; **as ∼ statement**
suivant relevé; **as ∼ invoice** suivant facture;
∼ cent pour cent; **∼ day** (output) journalier/
-ière; **a rate of 100 euros ∼ hour** un tarif de
100 euros l'heure; **pay 50 dollars ∼ hour**
payer 50 dollars de l'heure; **∼ head** par
personne; **∼ procurationem** par ordre de,
par procuration; **∼ se** en soi; **∼ share**
(Stock) par action; **∼ share earnings** *n pl*
bénéfices par action *m pl*

PER *abbr* (▶**price-earnings ratio**) CCR *m*
(coefficient de capitalisation des résultats)

per capita *adj, adv* par habitant; **∼ debt**
n dette par habitant *f*; **∼ GDP** *n* PIB par
habitant *m*; **∼ income** *n* revenu par
habitant *m*

perceived *adj* (value, risk, quality) perçu

percentage *n* pourcentage *m*; **as a ∼ of**
comme pourcentage de; **in ∼ terms** en
termes de pourcentage; **get a ∼ on** toucher
un pourcentage sur; **∼ of product price
spent on promotion** (advertising) budget-
promotion *m*; **∼ of capital held** quote-part
du capital détenu *f*; **∼ change** *n*
pourcentage de variation *m*; **∼-of-
completion method** *n* méthode de
pourcentage d'achèvement *f*; **∼ distribution**
n ventilation en pourcentage *f*; **∼ interest** *n*
(in income or property of a trust) pourcentage
d'intérêt *m*, quote-part *f*; **∼ point** *n* point de
pourcentage *m*; **∼-of-sales method** *n*
méthode basée sur le pourcentage des ventes
f

percentile *n* centile *m*; **∼ ranking** *n*
classement par pourcentage *m*

perception *n* (Gen Comm, Tax) perception
f

perceptual *adj* perceptuel/-elle

perfect[1] *adj* parfait; (candidate, choice, solution,
opportunity, place) idéal **∼ competition** *n*
concurrence parfaite *f*; **∼ hedge** *n* (Stock)
couverture parfaite *f*; **∼ market** *n* marché
parfait *m*; **∼ monopoly** *n* monopole absolu
m, monopole parfait *m*; **∼ price
discrimination** *n* discrimination parfaite
par les prix *f*; **∼ substitute** *n* succédané
parfait *m*

perfect[2] *vt* perfectionner

perform [1] *vt* (task) exécuter; (duties,
function) remplir
[2] *vi* **∼ well** (company, department) avoir de
bons résultats; (security, currency) être à la
hausse; **∼ badly** (currency, share) baisser;
(company) afficher des pertes, avoir de
mauvais résultats

performance *n* (of company) résultats *m pl*;
(of work) exécution *f*; (at work) performance *f*;
(of contractual duty) exécution *f*; (of duties)
exercice *m*; (in marketing) performance *f*; (of
shares, options) performance *f*, rendement *m*;
(economic, political record) performances *f pl*; **∼
of services** exécution de services *f*,
prestation de services *f*; **∼ against**

objectives *n* réalisations comparées aux
projets *f pl*; **∼ appraisal** *n* évaluation des
performances *f*; **∼ bond** *n* garantie de bonne
fin *f*; **∼ budgeting** *n* rationalisation des
choix budgétaires *f*; **∼ evaluation** *n*
évaluation des performances *f*, évaluation des
résultats *f*; **∼ guarantee** *n* garantie de
bonne exécution *f*, garantie de bonne fin *f*; **∼
indicator** *n* clignotant *m*, indicateur de
performance *m*; **∼ management** *n* gestion
des performances *f*; **∼ marketing** *n*
marketing de comportement *m*; **∼
measurement** *n* mesure de performances *f*,
mesure du rendement *f*; **∼ monitoring** *n*
contrôle de la performance *m*; **∼ rating** *n*
(Fin, HRM) jugement d'allure *m*; **∼-related
indicator** *n* indicateur de performance *m*;
∼-related pay *n* salaire au rendement *m*,
salaire lié aux résultats *m*; **∼ review** *n*
évaluation des performances *f*; **∼ stock**
valeur de croissance *f*; **∼ target** *n* objectif de
performance *m*; **∼ test** *n* test de
performances *m*; **∼ testing** *n* essai de
vérification des performances *m*

performing: **∼ rights** *n pl* droits
d'auteur *m pl*; **∼ loan** *n* prêt productif *m*

peril *n* péril *m*, risque *m*; **∼ point** *n* point
critique *m*

perimeter advertising *n* publicité
périphérique *f*

period *n* (of time) période *f*; (era) époque *f*;
(fixed dates, deadline) délai *m*; **for the ∼** pour la
période considérée; **within a ∼ of** dans un
délai de; **∼ cost** *n* frais encourus pendant
une période donnée *m pl*; **∼ of grace** délai
de grâce *m*; (Patents) délai supplémentaire *m*;
∼ of payment délai de paiement *m*, terme
d'échéance *m*

periodic *adj* périodique

periodical[1] *adj* périodique

periodical[2] *n* périodique *m*

peripheral[1] *adj* périphérique

peripheral[2] *n* (Comp) périphérique *m*; **∼
device** *n* unité périphérique *f*

perishable *adj* (food) périssable; **∼ goods**
n pl denrées périssables *f pl*

perishables *n pl* denrées périssables *f pl*

perjury *n* faux témoignage *m*; **commit ∼**
faire un faux témoignage

perk *n* (infml) avantage *m*; **be a ∼ of the job**
faire partie des avantages du métier

permanent *adj* permanent; (closure, shutdown) définitif/-ive; **∼ account** *n* comptes de
bilan *m pl*; **∼ address** *n* adresse habituelle
f; **∼ appointment** *n* titularisation *f*; **∼
contract** *n* contrat à durée indéterminée *m*;
∼ employment *n* emploi permanent *m*; **∼
financing** *n* financement permanent *m*; **∼
income-bearing share** *n* obligation non
amortissable des sociétés d'investissement et
de crédit immobilier *f*; **∼ residence** *n*
résidence habituelle *f*; **∼ resident** *n*
résident/-e permanent/-e *m/f*; **∼ staff** *n*

personnel ayant un contrat à durée indéterminée *m*

permissible *adj* (error) acceptable, tolérable; (level, limit, conduct) admissible

permission *n* autorisation *f*; ∼ **marketing** *n* marketing de permission *m*, permission marketing *m*

permit¹ *n* autorisation *f*, permis *m*; **building** ∼ permis de construire *m*; **entry** ∼ visa d'entrée *m*; **work** ∼ permis de travail *m*; ∼ **bond** *n* garantie de permis *f*

permit² ⓵ *vt* autoriser; ∼ **sb to do** autoriser qn à faire
⓶ *vi* permettre; **weather permitting** si le temps le permet; **time permitting** à condition d'avoir assez de temps

permitted *adj* autorisé

permutation *n* permutation *f*

perpendicular spread *n* écart perpendiculaire *m*

perpetual *adj* perpétuel/-elle; ∼ **bond** *n* obligation perpétuelle *f*; ∼ **inventory** *n* inventaire permanent *m*; ∼ **lease** *n* bail perpétuel *m*, bail à vie *m*; ∼ **preferred share** *n* action privilégiée perpétuelle *f*

perpetuity *n* perpétuité *f*; **in** ∼ à perpétuité

per pro. *abbr* (frml) (▸**per procurationem**) p.p. (par procuration)

person *n* personne *f*; ∼**-day** personne-jour *m*; ∼**-hour** *n* heure de travail *f*; ∼**-job fit** *n* ajustement de la personne à son poste *m*; ∼**-to-person call** *n* AmE communication avec préavis *f*; ∼**-year** *n* personne-année *f*

persona *n* personne physique *f*

personal *adj* personnel/-elle; (service) personnalisé; ∼ **accident insurance** *n* assurance individuelle contre les accidents *f*; ∼ **ad** *n* petite annonce *f*; ∼ **allowance** *n* (Bank) UK crédit personnel *m*, indemnité individuelle *f*; (Tax) UK abattement fiscal personnel *m*; ∼ **assistant** *n* (assistant) assistant/-e de direction *m/f*; (secretary) secrétaire de direction *mf*; ∼ **banking services** *n pl* services bancaires aux particuliers *m pl*; ∼ **benefit** *n* avantage personnel *m*; ∼ **call** *n* communication privée *f*; ∼ **computer** *n* ordinateur (individuel) *m*, PC *m*; ∼ **details** *n pl* coordonnées *f pl*; ∼ **digital assistant** *n* assistant personnel numérique *m*; ∼ **disposable income** *n* revenu disponible des particuliers *m*, revenu personnel disponible *m*; ∼ **effects** *n pl* effets personnels *m pl*; ∼ **equity plan** *n* UK plan d'épargne en actions *m*, plan personnel de capitalisation *m*; ∼ **estate** *n* bien immobilier personnel *m*; ∼ **exemption** *n* US (Bank) crédit personnel *m*, indemnité individuelle *f*; (Tax) abattement fiscal personnel *m*; ∼ **expenses** *n pl* frais personnels *m pl*; ∼ **financial planning software** *n* logiciel de planification financière personnelle *m*; ∼ **growth** *n* autodéveloppement *m*, développement

personnel *m*; ∼ **holding company** *n* US société individuelle de portefeuille *f*; ∼ **identification number** *n* code personnel *m*, code confidentiel *m*; ∼ **injury** *n* (Law) lésion corporelle *f*; ∼ **liability** *n* responsabilité personnelle *f*; ∼ **living expenses** *n pl* frais de subsistance *m pl*; ∼ **loan** *n* prêt personnel *m*, prêt à la consommation *m*; ∼ **particulars** *n pl* coordonnées *f pl*; ∼ **pension plan** *n*, ∼ **pension scheme** *n* UK plan d'épargne-retraite individuel *m*; ∼ **property** *n* biens personnels *m pl*; ∼ **savings** *n pl* épargne des particuliers *f*; ∼ **secretary** *n* secrétaire de direction *mf*; ∼ **selling** *n* vente personnelle *f*; ∼ **share** *n* (Stock) action nominative *f*; ∼ **web page** *n* page personnelle *f*, page perso *f* (infrml)

personality *n* (temperament) caractère *m*; (celebrity) personnalité *f*

personalization *n* personnalisation *f*

personalize personnaliser

personalized *adj* personnalisé; ∼ **check** AmE, ∼ **cheque** BrE *n* chèque personnalisé *m*

personally *adv* personnellement; ∼ **liable** *adj*, ∼ **responsible** *adj* personnellement responsable

personalty *n* bien mobilier personnel *m*, bien meuble *m*

personnel *n* personnel *m*, ressources humaines *f pl*; ∼ **department** *n* direction des ressources humaines *f*, service du personnel *m*; ∼ **director** *n* chef du personnel *m*, directeur/-trice des ressources humaines *m/f*; ∼ **file** *n* dossier personnel *m*; ∼ **management** *n* gestion du personnel *f*, gestion des ressources humaines *f*; ∼ **manager** *n* chef du personnel *m*, directeur/-trice des ressources humaines *m/f*; ∼ **overheads** *n pl* frais de personnel *m pl*; ∼ **policy** *n* politique du personnel *f*; ∼ **rating** *n* appréciation du personnel *f*, notation du personnel *f*

persuasion *n* persuasion *f*

PERT *n* (▸**programme evaluation and review technique**) méthode PERT *f*; ∼ **chart** *n* diagramme PERT *m*

pertain: ∼ **to** *vt* se rapporter à; ∼**ing to** se rapportant à

pertinence tree *n* arbre de pertinence *m*

perverse price *n* effet pervers du prix *m*, prix pervers *m*

peseta *n* peseta *f*

peso *n* peso *m*

pessimistic *adj* pessimiste

peter: ∼ **out** *vi* disparaître peu à peu

petition¹ *n* pétition *f*; (Law) demande *f*, requête *f*; **a** ∼ **protesting against/calling for sth** une pétition protestant contre/réclamant qch; ∼ **in bankruptcy** *n* demande de déclaration de faillite *f*

petition² *vt* solliciter; ∼ **for** demander

petitioner *n* (signatory) pétitionnaire *mf*;   ⋯▸

(Law) requérant/-e *m/f*

petrobond *n* pétro-obligation *f*

petrocurrency *n* pétrodevise *f*

petrodollar *n* pétrodollar *m*

petrol *n* BrE carburant *m*, essence *f*; ~ **engine vehicle** *n* BrE véhicule à moteur à essence *m*; ~ **station** *n* BrE station-service *f*

petroleum *n* pétrole *m*; ~ **exporting country** *n* pays exportateur de pétrole *m*; ~ **industry** *n* industrie pétrolière *f*; ~ **product** *n* produit pétrolier *m*; ~ **revenue tax** *n* impôt sur les revenus pétroliers *m*

petty: ~ **cash** *n* petite caisse *f*, menue monnaie *f*; ~ **cash book** *n* livre de caisse *m*; ~ **official** *n* petit fonctionnaire *m*

pfennig *n* pfennig *m*

PFI *abbr* (▸**private finance initiative**) projet PFI *m*, *projet de partenariat public-privé ou les dépenses en capital et la prestation de services sont prises en charge par l'entité privée*

pg. *abbr* (▸**page**) p. (page)

PG *abbr* (▸**paying guest**) hôte payant *m*, pensionnaire *mf*

PGI *abbr* (**protected geographic indication**) IGP *f* (indication géographique de provenance)

phantom *adj* (income, share, stock, tax) fictif/-ive

pharmaceutical *adj* pharmaceutique; ~ **industry** *n* industrie pharmaceutique *f*; ~ **product** *n* produit pharmaceutique *m*

pharmaceuticals *n pl* produits pharmaceutiques *m pl*

phase¹ *n* phase *f*; **go through a difficult ~** traverser une phase difficile; **the first ~ of the work** la première phase des travaux; (in construction) la première tranche des travaux; **be in ~ with** être en harmonie avec; **be out of ~ with** ne pas être en harmonie avec; ~ **alternation line** *n* (TV) PAL *m*; ~ **zero** *n* phase initiale *f*

phase²: ~ **in** *vt* (technology, service, system) mettre en place progressivement; (new technique, way of working) introduire progressivement; ~ **out** *vt* (technology, service, system) supprimer progressivement; (product) retirer progressivement

phasing: ~ **in** *n* introduction progressive *f*, mise en place progressive *f*; ~ **out** *n* suppression progressive *f*

PHC *abbr* US (▸**personal holding company**) société individuelle de portefeuille *f*

PhD *abbr* (**Doctor of Philosophy**) doctorat *m*

phone¹ *n* téléphone *m*; **on the ~** au téléphone; **make a ~ call** passer un coup de fil (infrml), téléphoner; ~ **book** *n* annuaire téléphonique *m*; ~ **call** *n* coup de fil *m* (infrml); (Admin) communication téléphonique *f*; ~ **card** *n* Télécarte® *f*, carte de téléphone *f*;

~-**in** *n* émission à ligne ouverte *f*; ~ **link** *n* liaison téléphonique *f*; ~ **number** *n* numéro de téléphone *m*; ~ **voucher** *n* carte téléphonique prépayée *f*

phone² [1] *vt* appeler, téléphoner à, passer un coup de fil à (infrml) [2] *vi* téléphoner; ~ **back** rappeler

photocomposition *n* AmE photocomposition *f*

photocopiable *adj* photocopiable

photocopier *n* photocopieuse *f*

photocopy¹ *n* photocopie *f*

photocopy² *vt* faire une photocopie de, photocopier

phreak *n* pirate de téléphone *m*

phreaking *n* piratage de lignes téléphoniques *m*

physical: ~ **assets** *n pl* actif corporel *m*, biens corporels *m pl*; ~ **collateral** *n* garantie matérielle *f*; ~ **commodity** *n* denrée *f*, matière première *f*; ~ **depreciation** *n* dépréciation matérielle *f*; ~ **deterioration** *n* détérioration matérielle *f*; ~ **distribution management** *n* gestion de la distribution physique *f*; ~ **examination** *n* (of object) contrôle physique *m*; (of person) visite médicale *f*; ~ **inventory** *n* inventaire physique *m*; ~ **market** *n* marché au comptant *m*; ~ **quality of life index** *n* indice de la qualité matérielle de vie *m*

physically *adv* physiquement

piastre *n* piastre *f*

pibs *abbr* (▸**permanent income-bearing share**) obligation non amortissable des sociétés d'investissement et de crédit immobilier *f*

pick¹ *n* (choice) choix *m*; **take one's ~** choisir; **the ~ of the bunch** le/la meilleur/-e du lot

pick² *vt* (select) choisir; ~ **out** choisir; (single out) repérer; (recognize) reconnaître; ~ **up** [1] (TV and radio) capter; (cargo) prendre; (skill) développer; (language) apprendre; ~ **up the tab** (infrml) régler la note [2] *vi* (economy) repartir; (trade, market, business) reprendre

picket¹ *n* piquet de grève *m*; (individual) gréviste *mf*; ~ **line** *n* piquet de grève *m*

picket² [1] *vt* (factory) mettre un piquet de grève devant [2] *vi* organiser un piquet de grève

picketing *n* piquets de grève *m pl*

pick-up *n* (Media) communiqué *m*; ~ **bond** *n* obligation qui reprend *f*; ~ **cost** *n* frais de ramassage *m pl*; ~ **service** *n* service de ramassage *m*

pictogram *n* pictogramme *m*

picture *n* image *f*; (overall view) situation *f*; (description) description *f*; (painting) tableau *m*; (Media) image *f*; (photograph) photo *f*; **be in the ~ about** être au courant de; **put/keep sb in the ~** mettre/tenir qn au courant; **paint a**

p

gloomy ∼ of sth donner une image sombre de; **take a** ∼ **of sth** prendre une photo de qch

piece *n* (coin, item) pièce *f*; **at** ∼ **rate** à la tâche; **by the** ∼ à la pièce, au détail; ∼ **of advice** conseil *m*; ∼ **of information** information *f*; ∼ **of legislation** loi *f*; ∼ **rate** *n* salaire aux pièces *m*, salaire à la pièce *m*; ∼ **wage** salaire à la pièce *m*

piecework *n* travail à la pièce *m*; ∼ **system** *n* système de travail à la pièce *m*

pieceworker *n* ouvrier/-ière payé/-e à la pièce *m/f*

pie chart *n* camembert *m* (infrml), graphique circulaire *m*

PIF *abbr* (▶**purchase issue facility**) facilité d'émission d'achat *f*

piggyback *n* (Transp) ferroutage *m*; ∼ **legislation** *n* (Law) législation secondaire *f*; ∼ **loan** *n* (Fin) emprunt gigogne *m*

PIK bond *n* (**payment-in-kind bond**) caution garantissant le paiement en nature de la main-d'œuvre *f*

piker *n* boursicoteur *m*, petit joueur *m*

pilot¹ *adj* pilote

pilot² *n* (broadcast) émission pilote *f*; (aviation, shipping) pilote *m*

pilot: ∼ **boat** *n* bateau-pilote *m*; ∼ **launch** *n* lancement-test *m*; ∼ **plan** *n* plan pilote *m*; ∼ **production** *n* fabrication pilote *f*, présérie *f*; ∼ **project** *n* projet d'essai *m*; ∼ **run** *n* présérie *f*; ∼ **scheme** *n* projet pilote *m*; ∼ **study** *n* étude pilote *f*; ∼ **survey** *n* enquête pilote *f*

PIN *abbr* (▶**personal identification number**) NIP *m* (numéro d'identification personnel), CPI *m* (code personnel d'identité)

pink: ∼ **pound** *n* pouvoir d'achat de la communauté homosexuelle *m*; ∼ **slip** *n* AmE (infrml) lettre de licenciement *f*, lettre de renvoi *f*

pioneer¹ *n* pionnier/-ière *m/f*; ∼ **product** *n* innovation *f*

pioneer² *vt* innover

pipeline *n* pipeline *m*; (for oil) oléoduc *m*; (for gas) gazoduc *m*; **be in the** ∼ (order) être en cours de traitement; (project) être en cours de réalisation

piracy *n* (Comp, Media) piratage *m*

pirate *vt* pirater; ∼**d software** logiciel piraté *m*; ∼**d version** version illégale *f*

pirate: ∼ **radio** *n* radio pirate *f*; ∼ **video** *n* cassette vidéo pirate *f*

pit *n* corbeille *f*; **trading** ∼ corbeille *f*, parquet de la Bourse *m*

pitch¹ *n* (of idea) présentation *f*, soumission *f*; (site for trader) emplacement *m*; **sales** ∼ argument de vente *m*, boniment de vente *m*; **make a** ∼ **for** faire une soumission pour

pitch² *vt* (product) promouvoir; (campaign, speech) adapter; (idea) présenter, soumettre; ∼

for a contract faire une soumission pour un contrat; **a service** ∼**ed at young people** un service qui vise les jeunes; ∼ **in** mettre la main à la pâte (infrml); ∼ **in with a suggestion** apporter une contribution

pitfall *n* inconvénient *m*

pixel *n* pixel *m*

pkg *abbr* (▶**package**) (parcel) colis *m*, paquet *m*; (for retail) paquet *m*, emballage *m*; (Comp) progiciel *m*; (of grants, incentives, deals, proposals, reforms) ensemble *m*; (items sold as one) lot *m*; (▶**packaging**) emballage *m*; (for sale, display, merchandising) conditionnement *m*

PKI *abbr* (▶**public key infrastructure**) infrastructure à clé publique *f*

pkt. *abbr* (▶**packet**) paquet *m*

place¹ *n* endroit *m*; (seat, space) place *f*; (on list, in league) place *f*; (job) poste *m*, emploi *m*; **take** ∼ avoir lieu; **put sth in** ∼ (system, scheme) mettre qch en place; ∼ **of birth** lieu de naissance *m*; ∼ **of business** établissement commercial *m*; ∼ **of delivery** *n* lieu de livraison *m*; ∼ **of employment** lieu de travail *m*; ∼ **of residence** domicile *m*; ∼ **of work** lieu de travail *m*

place² *vt* (article, item, person) mettre; (order, contract) passer; (advert) insérer; ∼ **a deposit** (Stock) placer un dépôt; ∼ **an embargo on** mettre un embargo sur; ∼ **emphasis on** mettre l'accent sur; ∼ **a hold on an account** bloquer un compte; ∼ **in custody** placer sous garde; ∼ **in trust** confier, mettre en fidéicommis; ∼ **a question on the agenda** mettre une question à l'ordre du jour; ∼ **sb in charge of a project** confier un projet à qn

placement *n* (training period) stage *m*; (of bonds) placement *m*; (of product) placement *m*

placing *n* (of stock, loan) placement *m*

plaintiff *n* demandeur/-eresse *m/f*, plaignant/-e *m/f*

plan¹ *n* (project) plan *m*, projet *m*; (map, diagram) plan *m*; ∼ **B** plan de repli *m*; **have a** ∼ **to do** projeter de faire; **make** ∼**s** faire des projets; **draw up a** ∼ faire un plan; **go according to** ∼ se passer comme prévu; ∼**s for the future** projets d'avenir; ∼ **of action** plan d'action

plan² *vt* (design) concevoir; (schedule, meeting, operation) organiser, préparer; (day) organiser; (week) planifier; (system, future, economy, production) planifier; (career) faire un plan de; (visit) projeter; (new development) prévoir; (report, speech) faire le plan de; ∼ **ahead for sth** préparer qch; ∼ **to do** projeter de faire; (intend) avoir l'intention de faire; ∼ **for** prévoir; ∼ **out** (strategy, policy) définir, arrêter; (expenditure, production, week) planifier; (itinerary) arrêter

plane *n* avion *m*

plank *n* (of campaign, programme) point *m*; **form the** ∼ **of** être la pierre angulaire de

planned *adj* (growth, change) planifié; (sale, ···⟩

development, merger) prévu; ~ **economy** n économie planifiée f; ~ **obsolescence** n obsolescence programmée f

planning n planification f, planning m; ~ **approval** n permis de construire m; ~ **authority** n responsables de l'aménagement du territoire m pl; ~ **commission** n commission de la planification et de l'urbanisme f; ~ **department** n (in office, company) service de planification m, service planning m; (in town planning) commission d'urbanisme f; ~ **permission** n BrE permis de construire m; ~, **programming, budgeting** n US planification, programmation, budgétisation f pl; ~, **programming, budgeting system** n rationalisation des choix budgétaires f; ~ **regulations** m pl règlements d'urbanisme m pl; ~ **restrictions** n pl prescriptions urbanistiques f pl

plant n (fixed assets) installations industrielles f pl, installations techniques f pl; (equipment) matériel m, équipement m; (factory) unité de production f, usine f; ~ **bargaining** n négociation au niveau local f; ~ **capacity** n capacité de l'usine f; ~ **hire** n location d'équipement f; ~ **and machinery** n pl usine et matériels f; ~ **maintenance** n entretien de l'équipement m; ~ **management** n gestion d'usine f; ~ **manager** n directeur/-trice d'usine m/f

plastic[1] adj (bag, component) en plastique; (industry) des plastiques; ~ **money** n cartes de crédit f pl

plastic[2] n (substance) matière plastique f, plastique m; (credit cards) cartes de crédit f pl

plastics n matières plastiques f pl

plat book n US registre foncier m

platform n (Comp, Ind) plate-forme f; (Transp) quai m

play[1] n jeu m; **come into** ~ (factor) entrer en jeu

play[2] vt jouer; ~ **around with ideas/figures** jongler avec des idées/chiffres; ~ **it by ear** improviser; ~ **the market** boursicoter; ~ **a part in**, ~ **a role in** jouer un rôle dans, participer à; ~ **safe** ne pas prendre de risques; ~ **down** minimiser; ~ **X off against Y** créer une concurrence entre X et Y; ~ **on** exploiter; ~ **up** vt (benefits, advantages) mettre l'accent sur; vi (equipment) faire des siennes (infrml)

player n acteur m; **key/major** ~ acteur principal/majeur m

plc abbr UK (▶**public limited company**) SA f (société anonyme)

PLC abbr (▶**product life cycle**) CVP m (cycle de vie d'un produit)

plea-bargaining n (Law) négociations entre accusation et défense, l'accusé plaidant coupable pour un délit moins grave pour réduire les charges

plead [1] vt (case) plaider; ~ **ignorance**

prétexter l'ignorance
[2] vi (Law) ~ **guilty/not guilty** plaider coupable/non coupable

pleading n plaidoirie f, plaidoyer m

please adv s'il vous plaît; ~ **accept our apologies** veuillez accepter nos excuses; ~ **forward** (on mail) faire suivre SVP, prière de faire suivre; ~ **let us have your prices** veuillez nous indiquer vos prix; ~ **let us know which date suits you** veuillez nous indiquer la date qui vous convient; ~ **turn over** tournez s'il vous plaît

pledge n (promise) engagement m, promesse f; (security) gage m, nantissement m

pledged security n valeur nantie f

pledging n mise en gage f, nantissement m

plenary adj (session, discussion) plénier/-ière f

plot[1] n (conspiracy) complot m; (of land) terrain m, parcelle f; **building** ~ terrain à bâtir m

plot[2] vt (on a graph) tracer point par point; ~ **the progress of sth** tracer la courbe de progression de qch

plough back vt BrE réinvestir

ploughback n BrE autofinancement m, bénéfice réinvesti m

plowback n AmE ▶**ploughback** BrE

plow: ~ **back** vt AmE ▶**plough back** BrE

PLR abbr (▶**public lending right**) droit perçu par un auteur sur le prêt de ses ouvrages en bibliothèque

plug[1] n (Comp, Comms) fiche f; (on appliance) prise (de courant) f; (advertising) (infrml) pub f (infrml); **give sth a** ~ (infrml) faire de la pub pour qch (infrml); **pull the** ~ (Stock) cesser de soutenir un cours; **pull the** ~ **on** (project) retirer son soutien à

plug[2] vt (promote) (infrml) faire de la pub pour (infrml); ~ **in** brancher

plug-and-play n (Comp) plug-and-play m, équipement prêt à l'emploi m

plug-in n (Comp) module complémentaire m, plug-in m inv

plummet vi (share price, profits, sales) s'effondrer; (value) baisser brusquement; (standards, popularity) tomber à zéro

plunge[1] n dégringolade f, chute f; **a** ~ **in share prices** une chute du prix des actions; **take the** ~ se jeter à l'eau

plunge[2] vi dégringoler, chuter

pluralism n pluralisme m

plus[1] adj (Math) positif/-ive; **200** ~ plus de 200; **the** ~ **side** le côté positif; **on the** ~ **side** (Acc) à l'actif du compte; ~ **factor**, ~ **point** atout m

plus[2] n (advantage) avantage m, plus m

plus[3] prep plus

plus[4] conj et

plus sign n signe plus m

pm abbr (**post meridiem**) après-midi; **at 2** ~ à quatorze heures, à deux heures de l'après-midi

PM *abbr* (▶**prime minister**) Premier ministre *m*

PN *abbr* (▶**promissory note**) billet à ordre *m*

PNG *abbr* (**portable network graphics**) format PNG *m*

PO *abbr* BrE (▶**postal order**) MP *m* (mandat postal); (▶**post office**) b. de p. (bureau de poste); ∼ **box** *n* BP *f* (boîte postale)

poach *vt* (staff) débaucher; (ideas, information) s'approprier

poaching *n* (of staff) débauchage *m*; (of ideas, information) appropriation *f*

pocket¹ *n* (of consumer) poche *f*, porte-monnaie *m*; **be out of** ∼ en être pour ses frais; **prices to suit every** ∼ des prix à la portée de toutes les bourses; ∼ **calculator** *n* calculatrice de poche *f*, calculette *f*; ∼ **computer** *n* ordinateur de poche *m*; ∼ **money** *n* argent de poche *m*

pocket² *vt* (money, profits) empocher

POD *abbr* (▶**proof of delivery**) justification de livraison *f*; (▶**place of delivery**) lieu de livraison *m*; (▶**paid on delivery**) paiement à la livraison *m*, payé à la livraison

point¹ *n* (for discussion) point *m*; (stage) stade *m*; (Math) point *m*; (decimal point) virgule *f*; (on index of share prices) point *m*; **make a** ∼ **of doing** prendre soin de faire; **make a** ∼ faire une remarque; **make the** ∼ **that** faire remarquer que; **this proves my** ∼ cela confirme ce que je viens de dire; ∼ **by point** point par point; **a four-**∼ **plan** un plan en quatre points; **at this** ∼ **in my career** à ce stade de ma carrière; **the FT 100 was up/down 12** ∼**s** l'indice FT 100 a gagné/perdu 12 points; ∼ **of departure** *n* point de départ *m*; ∼ **of entry** *n* lieu d'entrée *m*; ∼ **estimate** *n* (Math) évaluation du point *f*; ∼ **of export** *n* point d'exportation *m*; ∼ **of law** *n* point de droit *m*; ∼ **of order** *n* point d'ordre *m*; ∼ **of origin** *n* lieu d'origine *m*; ∼ **price** *n* (Stock) (options) prix du point *m*; ∼ **of purchase** *n* lieu d'achat *m*; ∼ **of sale** *n* point de vente *m*; ∼**-of-sale advertising** *n* publicité sur le lieu de vente *f*; ∼**-of-sale material** *n* matériel de publicité sur le lieu de vente *m*; ∼**-of-sale promotion** *n* publicité sur le lieu de vente *f*; ∼**-of-sale terminal** *n* terminal point de vente *m*; ∼ **of view** *n* point de vue *m*

point² *vi* ∼ **and click** (Comp) pointer-cliquer; ∼ **to** (cite) indiquer; (suggest) sembler indiquer; (with finger, pointer) désigner; (emphasize) souligner; (with cursor) mettre le pointeur sur, pointer sur

pointer *n* (Comp) pointeur *m*; (indication) indicateur *m*; (hint, tip) tuyau *m*

points rating *n* (HRM) barème par points *m*; ∼ **method**, ∼ **system** *n* méthode de qualification par points *f*

poison pill *n* (Fin) pilule empoisonnée *f*

polarization *n* polarisation *f*

pole position *n* **be in** ∼ être à la meilleure place

police *n* police *f*; ∼ **force** *n* police *f*; ∼ **record** *n* casier judiciaire *m*

policy *n* politique *f*; (Ins) (type of cover) contrat *m*; (document) police *f*; **make** ∼ formuler la politique; **company/government** ∼ politique de l'entreprise/du gouvernement; **have a** ∼ **of doing** avoir politique de faire; **it is our** ∼ **to do** nous avons pour politique de faire; **take out a** ∼ contracter une assurance; ∼ **decision** *n* décision de principe *f*; ∼ **formulation** *n* élaboration de la politique *f*; ∼ **harmonization** *n* harmonisation de la politique *f*; ∼ **statement** *n* déclaration de principe *f*; ∼ **unit** *n* comité de conseillers politiques *m*

policyholder *n* assuré/-e *m/f*, souscripteur *m*

policymaker *n* décideur *m*

policymaking *n* décisions *f pl*

polite *adj* aimable, poli

political *adj* politique; ∼ **affairs** *n pl* affaires politiques *f pl*; ∼ **change** *n* changement politique *m*; ∼ **climate** *n* climat politique *m*, conjoncture politique *f*; ∼ **cooperation** *n* coopération politique *f*; ∼ **donation** *n* don en soutien aux activités politiques *m*; ∼ **economy** *n* économie politique *f*; ∼ **group** *n* groupe politique *m*; ∼ **issue** *n* question politique *f*; ∼ **party** *n* parti politique *m*; ∼ **refugee** *n* réfugié/-e politique *m/f*; ∼ **stability** *n* stabilité politique *f*; ∼ **system** *n* système politique *m*; ∼ **union** *n* union politique *f*

politically *adv* politiquement; ∼ **correct** *adj* politiquement correct

politician *n* homme politique *m*, femme politique *f*

politicize *vt* politiser

poll¹ *n* (vote casting) scrutin *m*; (election) élection *f*; (survey) sondage *m*; **carry out a** ∼ (S&M) effectuer un sondage; **a** ∼ **of students** un sondage effectué auprès des étudiants; **take a** ∼ **on** procéder à un vote sur; **get 65% of the** ∼ obtenir 65% des suffrages exprimés

poll² *vt* (votes) obtenir; (person) sonder l'opinion de, interroger

polling *n* (Comp) interrogation *f*; (vote) vote *m*; (turnout) participation électorale *f*; (of opinion) sondage *m*; ∼ **booth** *n* isoloir *m*; ∼ **company** *n* institut de sondage *m*; ∼ **day** *n* jour des élections *m*; ∼ **station** *n* bureau de vote *m*

pollutant *n* polluant *m*

pollute *vt* polluer, contaminer

polluted *adj* pollué, contaminé

polluter *n* pollueur *m*; ∼ **pays principle** *n* principe pollueur-payeur *m*

pollution *n* pollution *f*; ∼ **charge** *n* redevance de pollution *f*; ∼ **control** *n* ····÷

contrôle de l'environnement m, lutte antipollution f; ~ **tax** n ecotaxe f

pool¹ n (of money, resources) pool m; (of experts) équipe f; (of experience, skills) réservoir m; (of labour) réserve f; (consortium) US pool m; (monopoly) US trust m; **car ~** n parc automobile m; ~ **of vehicles** parc de véhicules m

pool² vt (resources) mettre en commun

pooling n mise en commun f; **car ~** covoiturage m; ~ **arrangements** n pl dispositifs de mise en commun des ressources m pl; ~ **of interests** n US absorption f, fusion f

poor adj (family, person, country) pauvre; (demand, chance) faible; (quality) inférieur; (work, performance) mauvais, médiocre; ~ **service** n service médiocre m

popular adj (support, enthusiasm) du public; (generally liked) populaire; (entertainment) grand public inv; (fashionable) en vogue; **by ~ request, by ~ demand** à la demande générale; **have ~ appeal** avoir du succès auprès du public; **the ~ press** la presse populaire; **the ~ view of, the ~ perception of** l'opinion générale sur

popularism n politique de providence f

popularity n popularité f; **lose ~** perdre de sa popularité; **gain ~** gagner en popularité; ~ **rating** n cote de popularité f

population n population f; ~ **census** n recensement de la population m; ~ **density** n densité de la population f; ~ **explosion** n explosion démographique f; ~ **statistics** n pl statistiques démographiques f pl; ~ **trends** n pl tendances démographiques f pl

pop-up menu n menu contextuel m, menu déroulant m

port¹ n (Transp) port m; (Comp) port m; **make ~ arriver au port;** ~ **to ~** port à port; ~ **of arrival** n port d'arrivée m; ~ **charge** n frais de port m pl; ~ **control** n contrôle portuaire m; ~ **of destination** n port de destination m; ~ **of discharge** n port de déchargement m; ~ **dues** n pl droits de port m pl; ~ **of entry** n port d'arrivée m; ~ **facilities** n pl installations portuaires f pl; ~ **of loading** n port de chargement m; ~ **of registry** n port d'armement m, port d'attache m; ~ **of shipment** n port de charge m; ~ **tariff** n tarif portuaire m; ~ **tax** n taxe de débarquement f; ~ **traffic** n trafic portuaire m

port² vt (Comp) transporter (d'un système à un autre)

portability n portabilité f

portable¹ adj portatif/-ive; (Comp) (software, hardware) portable

portable² n (Comp) portable m

portal n (Comp) portail m; **horizontal/ vertical ~** portail horizontal/vertical m

portfolio n (Pol, Stock) portefeuille m; ~

career n carrière mosaïque f; ~ **dividend** n dividende de portefeuille m; ~ **income** n revenu de placements m; ~ **insurance** n assurance de portefeuille f; ~ **investment** n investissement de portefeuille m; ~ **management** n gestion de portefeuille f; ~ **manager** n gestionnaire de portefeuille mf; ~ **selection** n sélection de portefeuille f; ~ **split** n fractionnement de portefeuille m; ~ **switching** n arbitrage de portefeuille m; ~ **trade** n transactions de portefeuille f pl; ~ **transfer** n cession de portefeuille f, transfert de portefeuille m

porting n (Comp) portage m

portion n (of dividend, amount) fraction f, partie f; (share of money, items, blame) part f; (of market) segment m

portrait n (Comp, Media) portrait m; ~ **format** n format portrait m

POS abbr (▶**point of sale**) PV m (point de vente); ~ **advertising** n publicité sur le lieu de vente f; ~ **promotion** n publicité sur le lieu de vente f; ~ **terminal** n terminal point de vente m

pose vt (problem, threat) poser; (risk) constituer; (challenge) présenter

position¹ n (point of view) position f, point de vue m; (situation) position f; (job) poste m; (Stock) position f; (service counter) guichet m; ~ **of authority/responsibility** poste de commandement/responsabilité m; **be in a ~ to do** être en mesure de faire; **be in a difficult ~** se trouver dans une situation difficile; **be in a good ~ to do** être bien placé pour faire; **be in a strong ~** être en position de force; ~ **closed** (Gen Comm, Bank) guichet fermé m; **take a ~** (Stock) se placer; **take a long ~** (Stock) aller loin, prendre une position longue; **carry over a ~** (Stock) reporter une position; **close one's ~** (Stock) liquider sa position; ~ **account** n compte de position m; ~ **paper** n déclaration de politique générale f; ~ **trader** n négociateur/-trice de positions à long terme m/f; ~ **trading** n négociation sur positions à long terme f, position trading f

position² vt positionner; ~ **oneself** se positionner

positioning n positionnement m

positive¹ adj positif/-ive; (good, advantage) réel/réelle; (proof, identification) formel/-elle; **be ~ that** être sûr que; **think ~** voir les choses de façon positive; ~ **action** n BrE (in recruiting) discrimination positive f; ~ **cash flow** n cash-flow positif m, marge brute d'autofinancement positive f; ~ **confirmation** n confirmation positive f; ~ **correlation** n corrélation positive f; ~ **discrimination** n BrE discrimination positive f; ~ **feedback** n réaction positive f, rétroaction positive f; ~ **gearing** n BrE effet de levier positif m; ~ **leverage** n AmE effet de levier positif m; ~ **response** n réponse affirmative *f*; ~ **thinking** *n* façon positive de voir les choses *f*

positive² *n* in the ~ à la forme affirmative

positively *adv* positivement

possess *vt* (property, goods, quality) posséder; (power, advantage) avoir

possession *n* possession *f*; be in ~ of être en possession de; get ~ of acquérir; be in ~ (tenant) occuper les lieux

possibilism *n* politique du possible *f*

possibility *n* possibilité *f*

post¹ *n* (letters) BrE courrier *m*; (service) BrE poste *f*; (job) poste *m*; **through the** ~ par la poste; **put sth in the** ~ poster qch, mettre qch à la poste; **hold a** ~ occuper un poste; **take up a** ~ prendre un poste; ~ **office** *n* bureau de poste *m*; ~ **office box** *n* boîte postale *f*; ~ **office savings bank** *n* caisse d'épargne de la poste

post² *vt* BrE (letter) expédier, poster; (Acc) comptabiliser, porter, porter sur un compte; (Comp) (article) poster, afficher; (notice) afficher; (employee) affecter; (team) affecter, muter; (Stock) (deficit, gain) enregistrer; ~ **an entry** (Acc) porter une écriture; ~ **a margin** afficher une marge; ~ **off** mettre à la poste; ~ **on** faire suivre; ~ **up** (notice) afficher; ~ **up an account** mettre un compte à jour

POST *abbr* (▸**point-of-sale terminal**) TPV *m* (terminal point de vente)

postage *n* (charges, rates) tarifs postaux *m pl*; (cost) tarif d'affranchissement *m*; ~ **included** port compris; ~ **paid** port payé *m*; ~-**due stamp** *n* timbre-taxe *m*; ~ **meter** *n* AmE machine à affranchir *f*; ~ **and packing** *n pl* frais de port et d'emballage *m pl*, le port et l'emballage; ~ **rates** *n pl* tarifs postaux *m pl*; ~ **stamp** *n* timbre *m*, timbre-poste *m*

postal *adj* (zone, district) postal; ~ **address** *n* adresse postale *f*; ~ **ballot** *n* BrE vote par correspondance *m*; ~ **checking account** *n* US compte courant postal *m*; ~ **code** *n* BrE code postal *m*; ~ **order** *n* BrE mandat *m*; ~ **service** *n* service postal *m*; ~ **vote** *n* vote par correspondance *m*; ~ **worker** *n* employé/-e des postes *m/f*

post-bankruptcy *adj* après faillite

postbox *n* BrE boîte aux lettres *f*

postcard *n* carte postale *f*

postcode *n* BrE code postal *m*

postdate *vt* postdater

postdated *adj* postdaté

posted price *n* prix public *m*

post-election *adj* post-électoral

poster *n* affiche *f*; ~ **advertising** *n* publicité par affichage *f*; ~ **campaign** *n* campagne d'affichage *f*

postgraduate *n* ≈ étudiant/-e du troisième cycle *m/f*

post-industrial society *n* société post-industrielle *f*

posting *n* (Acc) comptabilisation *f*; (of notice) affichage *m*; (job) affectation *f*

Post-it® *n* feuillet adhésif repositionnable *m*

postman *n* BrE facteur *m*

postmark *n* cachet de la poste *m*; date as ~ le cachet de la poste faisant foi

postmaster *n* (for email) administrateur/-trice de courrier électronique *m/f*

post-paid *adv* port payé

postpone *vt* remettre, reporter; ~ **tax** différer le paiement de l'impôt

postponement *n* report *m*, renvoi *m*

postscript *n* post-scriptum *m*

postwar *adj* d'après-guerre; ~ **boom** *n* prospérité d'après-guerre *f*; ~ **period** *n* période d'après-guerre *f*

potential¹ *adj* potentiel/-ielle

potential² *n* potentiel *m*; have ~ avoir du potentiel, être prometteur; the ~ to do les qualités nécessaires pour faire; human/sales ~ potential humain/de vente *m*; fulfil one's ~ montrer de quoi on est capable

potential: ~ **buyer** *n* acheteur/-euse potentiel/-ielle *m/f*; ~ **income** *n* revenu potentiel *m*; ~ **investor** *n* investisseur potentiel *m*, investisseur éventuel *m*; ~ **output** *n* potentiel de croissance de production *m*, produit potentiel *m*; ~ **profit** *n* plus-value éventuelle *f*, profit potentiel *m*

potentially *adv* potentiellement

pound *n* (currency) livre *f*; ~ **sterling** *n* livre sterling *f*

poverty *n* pauvreté *f*; ~ **line** *n* seuil de pauvreté *m*; ~ **trap** *n* cercle vicieux de la pauvreté *m*

power¹ *n* (electrical) courant *m*; (energy) énergie *f*; (Pol) pouvoir *m*; (country) puissance *f*; (control) pouvoir *m*; (strength) puissance *f*; (influence) influence *f*; (capability) pouvoir *m*; (authority) attributions *f pl*; (Math) puissance *f*; be in ~ être au pouvoir; come to ~ accéder au pouvoir; it is in my ~ to do il est en mon pouvoir de faire; do everything in one's ~ faire tout ce qui est en son pouvoir; I have no ~ over how the money is spent je n'ai aucune influence sur la façon dont l'argent est dépensé; the courts have the ~ to do il est dans les attributions de la justice de faire; ten to the ~ of three dix puissance trois; ~s of persuasion pouvoir de persuasion *m*; ~ of attorney *n* procuration *f*; ~ failure *n* panne d'électricité *f*; ~ politics *n pl* politique d'intimidation *f*; ~ of recourse *n* droit de recours *m*, faculté de recours *f*; ~ of sale *n* pouvoir de vente *m*; ~ station *n* centrale électrique *f*; ~ struggle *n* lutte pour le pouvoir *f*; ~ user *n* (Comp) utilisateur/-trice averti/-e *m/f*

power² *vt* faire marcher

powerful *adj* puissant

pp. *abbr* (▸**prepaid**) payé d'avance, prépayé

p.p. *abbr* (▸**post-paid**, ▸**postage paid**) p.p. ⋯⊱

(port payé); (▶**per procurationem**) p.p. (par procuration)

PPB *abbr* (▶**planning, programming, budgeting**) planification, programmation, budgétisation

PPBS *abbr* (▶**planning, programming, budgeting system**) rationalisation des choix budgétaires *f*

PPI *abbr* (▶**producer price index**) indice des prix à la production *m*

PPP *abbr* (▶**purchasing power parity**) PPA *f* (parité du pouvoir d'achat); (▶**profit and performance planning**) prévision de bénéfices et de performances *f*; UK (▶**public-private partnership**) partenariat entre l'État et le secteur privé *m*, partenariat public-privé *m*

PPS *abbr* UK (▶**parliamentary private secretary**) *parlementaire attaché à un ministre*

PQLI *abbr* (▶**physical quality of life index**) indice de la qualité matérielle de vie *m*

PR *abbr* (▶**proportional representation**) RP *f* (représentation proportionnelle); (▶**public relations**) RP *f pl* (relations publiques); ∼ **agency** *n* agence de relations publiques *f*; ∼ **consultant** *n* conseil en relations publiques *m*, conseil en communication *m*

PRA *abbr* (▶**purchase and resale agreement**) (Stock) accord de prise en pension *m*

practicability *n* viabilité *f*

practicable *adj* (proposal, plan) réalisable

practical *adj* pratique; (plan) réalisable; ∼ **politics** *n pl* politique d'expédients *f*; ∼ **use** *n* usage pratique *m*

practice *n* (not theory) pratique *f*; (procedure) pratique *f*, usage *m*; (custom) coutume *f*; (office of professional person) cabinet *m*; **accounting** ∼**s** pratiques comptables; **be in** ∼ (professional person) exercer; **set up in** ∼, **go into** ∼ (lawyer) s'établir en tant que juriste; **in** ∼ en pratique; **put sth into** ∼ mettre qch en pratique; **it is standard/common** ∼ il est d'usage/courant de faire; **the** ∼ **of doing** la coutume selon laquelle on fait; **to have had** ∼ **in sth** avoir de l'expérience en qch

practise ① *vt* (method) utiliser; (medicine) exercer; (tradition) pratiquer; ∼ **law** exercer la profession de juriste
② *vi* s'exercer

practising *adj* (lawyer) en exercice

pragmatic *adj* pragmatique

pragmatically *adv* de façon pragmatique

preamble *n* préambule *m*

prearrange *vt* prédéterminer

prearranged *adj* fixé à l'avance

preauthorized: ∼ **check** AmE, ∼ **cheque** BrE *n* chèque par procuration *m*, chèque préautorisé *m*; ∼ **payment** *n*

paiement par avis de prélèvement *m*

prebilling *n* facturation anticipée *f*

pre-budget *adj* pré-budgétaire

precaution *n* précaution *f*; **as a** ∼ par précaution; **take** ∼**s** prendre des précautions; **take the** ∼ **of doing** prendre la précaution de faire

precautionary *adj* préventif/-ive; **as a** ∼ **measure** par mesure de précaution; ∼ **saving** *n* épargne de précaution *f*

precede *vt* précéder

precedence *n* (in priority) priorité *f*; (in rank) préséance *f*; **take** ∼ **over** avoir la priorité sur, avoir la préséance sur

preceding *adj* précédent

precinct *n* (pedestrian zone) zone piétonne *f*; US (Admin) quartier *m*; **shopping** ∼ zone commerçante *f*; (covered) galerie marchande *f*

precious metal *n* métal précieux *m*

precision engineering *n* mécanique de précision *f*

preclude *vt* exclure; ∼ **sb from doing** empêcher qn de faire

precondition *n* condition requise *f*, condition nécessaire *f*

predate *vt* (cheque) antidater; (exist before) être antérieur à

predated *adj* (cheque) antidaté

predator *n* prédateur *m*

predatory: ∼ **competition** *n* concurrence déloyale *f*, concurrence sauvage *f*; ∼ **pricing** *n* pratique de prix sauvage *f*

predecessor *n* prédécesseur *m*

predetermine *vt* déterminer d'avance

predetermined *adj* déterminé d'avance

predict *vt* prévoir, prédire

predictable *adj* prévisible

predicted *adj* prévu

prediction *n* prévision *f*

predictive text input *n* (Comp, Comms) écriture prédictive *f*

pre-eminent *adj* (leading) dominant; (distinguished) éminent

pre-empt *vt* (anticipate) anticiper; (thwart) contrecarrer

pre-emption right *n* droit de préemption *m*

pre-emptive: ∼ **bid** *n* ouverture préventive *f*; ∼ **right** *n* droit de préemption *m*

pre-emptor *n* acquéreur *m*

pre-existing *adj* préexistant; ∼ **use** *n* utilisation préexistante *f*

prefabricated *adj* préfabriqué

prefer *vt* préférer; ∼ **charges** porter plainte; ∼ **charges against sb** engager des poursuites contre qn

preference *n* préférence *f*; **in** ∼ **to** de préférence à; **give** ∼ **to** donner la préférence à; ∼ **bond** *n* obligation privilégiée *f*;

∼ dividend n BrE dividende sur actions privilégiées m; **∼ rate** n taux préférentiel m; **∼ settings** n pl (Comp) ensemble de préférences personnelles m; **∼ share** n BrE action privilégiée f, action à dividende prioritaire f

preferential adj (tariff, terms, trade) préférentiel/-ielle; (debt, payment) privilégié; **∼ claim** n (Fin) créance privilégiée f; **∼ creditor** n créancier/-ière privilégié/-e m/f; **∼ interest rate** n taux bonifié m; **∼ rate** n taux préférentiel m; **∼ treatment** n traitement de faveur m

preferred adj (option, solution, method) préféré; **∼ beneficiary** n bénéficiaire privilégié/-e m/f; **∼ candidate** n candidat/-e prioritaire m/f; **∼ creditor** n créancier/-ière privilégié/-e m/f; **∼ dividend** n AmE dividende sur actions privilégiées m; **∼ dividend coverage** n couverture du dividende privilégié par le bénéfice f; **∼ position** n (Media) emplacement privilégié m; **∼ rate** n taux privilégié m; **∼ risk** n (Ins) risque privilégié m; **∼ stock** n AmE action privilégiée f, action à dividende prioritaire f

prefinancing credit n crédit de préfinancement m

prejudice n (damage) préjudice m; (bias) préjugé m; **without ∼** sans préjudice

prejudicial adj préjudiciable

preliminary adj préliminaire; **∼ to** préalable à; **∼ estimate** n devis estimatif m; **∼ examination** n examen préliminaire m; **∼ expenses** n pl frais d'établissement m pl; **∼ hearing** n (Law) audience préliminaire f; **∼ investigation** n enquête préliminaire f, instruction f; **∼ prospectus** n prospectus préliminaire m; **∼ ruling** n décision préliminaire f

premature adj prématuré

premise n prémisse f; **on the ∼ that** en supposant que

premises n pl locaux m pl; **business ∼** locaux commerciaux m pl; **office ∼** bureaux m pl; **factory ∼** usine f; **on the ∼** sur les lieux; **off the ∼** à l'extérieur; **leave the ∼** quitter les lieux

premium n (Bank, Fin, Ins) prime f; (Law) prime f; (on a lease) reprise f; (in advertising) prime f; (supplement) supplément m; (Stock) prime f, prix d'option m, prix au-dessus du pair m; (futures market) excédent de prix m, prime f; (of option) prime f; **be at a ∼** être très recherché; **time is at a ∼** le temps est très précieux; **sell at a ∼** (Stock) vendre à prime; (bond, share) vendre au-dessus du pair; **put a high ∼ on** mettre qch au tout premier plan; **∼ bond** n obligation à primes f; **∼ grade** n première qualité f; **∼-grade** adj de première qualité; **∼ loan** n emprunt à prime m; **∼ offer** n offre spéciale f; **∼ price** n prix élevé m; **∼ pricing** n fixation d'un prix élevé f; **∼ product** n produit de prestige m; **∼**

quotation n cotation au-dessus de la valeur nominale f, cotation au-dessus du pair f; **∼ rate** n taux de prime m; **∼ rate call** n communication à tarif normal f; **∼ rent** n surloyer m; **∼ reserve** n réserve prime d'émission f; **∼ statement** n (Fin) décompte de prime m

Premium Bonds n pl UK obligations à lots f pl

prenuptial agreement n, **prenuptial contract** n contrat prénuptial m

pre-owned adj d'occasion

prepackaged adj préemballé

prepacked adj préconditionné

prepaid adj payé d'avance; **carriage ∼** port payé; **∼ charges** n pl frais payés d'avance m pl; **∼ envelope** n enveloppe préaffranchie f; **∼ expenses** n pl charges payées d'avance f pl; **∼ interest** n intérêt payé d'avance m

preparation n préparation f; **∼s** préparatifs m pl; **make ∼s for** faire les préparatifs de; **in ∼ for** en vue de

prepare vt préparer; **∼ for** se préparer à; **∼ to do** se préparer à faire

prepay vt payer d'avance, régler d'avance

prepayment n paiement d'avance m, paiement par anticipation m

preplanning n planification préliminaire f

preproduction expenditure n dépense avant fabrication f

prerecord vt préenregistrer

prerecorded adj (programme) en différé, préenregistré

prerequisite[1] adj préalable

prerequisite[2] n condition préalable f

prerogative n prérogative f

prescribe vt prescrire

prescribed adj déterminé par règlement, prescrit; **within ∼ limits**, **within the ∼ time** dans les délais prescrits; **∼ aggregate reserve** n réserve globale visée par règlement f; **∼ contract** n contrat prescrit m; **∼ price** n prix imposé m; **∼ rate** n taux prescrit m; **∼ share** n (Stock) action visée par règlement f; **∼ time** n délai prescrit m

prescription n (remedy) remède m; (for medicine) ordonnance f

present[1] adj (current) actuel/-elle; (attending) présent; **at the ∼ time** actuellement; **in the ∼ state of affairs** les choses étant ce qu'elles sont, étant donné les circonstances; **∼ value factor** n facteur d'actualisation m; **∼ value method** n méthode d'actualisation f

present[2] n (gift) cadeau m; (now) présent m; **in the ∼** au présent

present[3] vt (report, figures, plan, documents) présenter; (problem, risk, challenge) présenter; (opportunity) offrir; (evidence) fournir; (award, certificate) remettre; (portray) présenter, représenter; (introduce) présenter; **∼ a bill for discount** présenter un effet à l'escompte, ⋯⟩

présenter une facture pour remise; ~ **a bill for reception** présenter une facture pour réception; ~ **a cheque for payment** BrE, ~ **a check for payment** AmE présenter un chèque au paiement; ~ **a draft for acceptance** présenter une traite à l'acceptation; ~ **sth fairly** donner une image fidèle de qch; **be** ~**ed with a choice/dilemma** se trouver face à un choix/dilemme

presentation *n* (of plan, bill, report, petition) présentation *f*; (verbal report, speech) exposé *m*; (portrayal) représentation *f*; **to give a ~ on** faire un exposé sur; **have good ~ skills** avoir le sens de la communication; ~ **copy** *n* spécimen *m*; ~ **package** *n*, ~ **software** *n* progiciel de présentation assistée par ordinateur *m*

presenter *n* présentateur/-trice *m/f*

preservation *n* protection *f*, préservation *f*

preservative *n* conservateur *m*; **no** ~**s** sans conservateur; **no** ~**s or additives** sans conservateur ni additif

preserve *vt* protéger, préserver; (food) conserver

preserved foods *n pl* conserves *f pl*

preset *adj* pré-défini

preside: ~ **over** *vt* (meeting) présider; (change, activity) présider à

presidency *n* présidence *f*

president *n* (of meeting) président/-e *m/f*; (of company) président-directeur général *m*

President *n* président/-e *m/f*

presidential *adj* (term, government) présidentiel/-ielle; (race, candidate) à la présidence; (office, policy) du président; ~ **election** *n* élections présidentielles *f pl*

presiding judge *n* président de tribunal *m*

presidium *n* présidium *m*

press[1] *n* presse *f*; **go to ~** passer sous presse; **get a good/bad ~** avoir bonne/ mauvaise presse; **pass sth for ~** donner le bon à tirer à qch; ~ **advertisement** *n* annonce par voie de presse *f*; ~ **advertising** *n* publicité-presse *f*; ~ **agency** *n* agence de presse *f*; ~ **agent** *n* attaché/-e de presse *m/f*; ~ **campaign** *n* campagne de presse *f*; ~ **clipping** *n* coupure de journal *f*, coupure de presse *f*; ~ **conference** *n* conférence de presse *f*; ~ **coverage** *n* couverture de presse *f*; ~ **cutting** *n* coupure de journal *f*, coupure de presse *f*; ~ **kit** *n* dossier de presse *m*; ~ **launch** *n* lancement dans la presse *m*; ~ **office** *n* service de presse *m*; ~ **officer** *n* responsable du service de presse *mf*; ~ **pack** *n* dossier de presse *m*; ~ **photographer** *n* photographe de presse *mf*; ~ **release** *n* communiqué de presse *m*; ~ **report** *n* reportage *m*; ~ **run** *n* tirage *m*

press[2] *vt* (button) appuyer sur; (point) insister sur; (matter, issue) mettre en avant; ~ **sb to do**

presser qn de faire; ~ **sb into doing** forcer qn à faire; ~ **the point** insister; ~ **for** (change, support) faire pression pour obtenir; ~ **on** passer à la suite; ~ **on with** (reform, plan) faire avancer

pressure[1] *n* pression *f*; **be under ~** être sous pression; **come under ~ from** subir la pression de; **work under ~** travailler sous pression; **exert ~ on** exercer une pression sur; **put ~ on sb to do** faire pression sur qn pour qu'il/elle fasse; **they are under ~ to sign** on fait pression sur eux pour qu'ils signent; **do sth under ~** faire qch sous la contrainte; **financial ~** contraintes financières *f pl*; ~ **group** *n* groupe de pression *m*; ~ **selling** *n* vente forcée *f*

pressure[2] *vt* (person) faire pression sur; ~ **sb into doing** contraindre qn à faire

prestige *n* prestige *m*; ~ **advertising** *n* publicité de prestige *f*; ~ **pricing** *n* tarification de prestige *f*; ~ **product** *n* produit de prestige *m*, produit de luxe *m*

prestigious *adj* prestigieux/-ieuse

presume *vt* (suppose) supposer, présumer; (presuppose) présupposer

presumption *n* présomption *f*

pre-tax *adj* avant impôts *inv*; ~ **earnings** *n pl* gains avant impôts *m pl*; ~ **profits** *n pl* bénéfice avant impôts *m*; ~ **rate of return** *n* taux de rendement avant impôts *m*; ~ **yield** *n* rendement brut *m*

prevail *vi* (win) prévaloir; (be usual) prédominer

prevailing *adj* (attitude, idea) prévalent; (conditions, situation, trend) actuel/-elle; (rate, price) en vigueur, du marché; (style, fasion) en vogue; ~ **market price** *n* (Gen Comm) prix courant du marché *m*; (Stock) cours du marché *m*; ~ **party** *n* (Law) partie gagnante *f*

prevent *vt* empêcher; (damage, conflict) éviter; ~ **sb/sth from doing** empêcher qn/qch de faire

prevention *n* prévention *f*, **accident ~** prévention des accidents *f*

preventive *adj* préventif/-ive; **as a ~ measure** à titre préventif

preview *vt* présenter; (Comp) prévisualiser

previous *adj* (day, meeting, page) précédent; (further back in time) antérieur; (Admin) (experience, consent, agreement) préalable; **have a ~ engagement** être déjà pris; ~ **history** *n* antécédents *m pl*

previously *adv* (before) auparavant, avant; (already) déjà

price[1] *n* prix *m*; (Stock) cours *m*; (quotation) cote *f*; (of a security) cours *m*; **at ~** à prix; ~**s and incomes policy** *n* politique des prix et des revenus *f*; ~**s on application** prix sur demande; **at ~s ranging from** à des prix allant de; ~**s can go down as well as up** (Stock) les cours peuvent aussi bien baisser que monter; **go up/down in ~** (goods, products) augmenter/baisser; **set a high ~ on** (loyalty, hard work) attacher beaucoup de prix à; **~ agreement** n accord sur les prix m; **~ bid** n (Stock) offre de prix f; **~ bracket** n fourchette de prix f; **~ ceiling** n plafond de prix m; **~ change** n changement de prix m, variation de prix f; **~ competitiveness** n compétitivité des prix f; **~ control** n contrôle des prix m, politique des prix f; **~ cut** n baisse de prix f, rabais m, réduction des prix f; **~ cutting** n réduction des prix f; **~ deregulation** n libération des prix f; **~ determination** n détermination des prix f, fixation des prix f, établissement des prix m; **~ differential** n écart de prix m; **~ discrimination** n tarif discriminatoire m; **~-earnings ratio** n (Stock) coefficient de capitalisation des résultats m, rapport cours-bénéfice m, ratio cours-bénéfice m; **~ effect** n effet de prix m; **~ escalation** n flambée des prix f; **~ ex-works** n prix départ usine m; **~-fixing** n (by government) contrôle des prix m; (Law) accord sur les prix m, entente illicite sur les prix f; (by shopkeeper) fixation des prix f; **~ floor** n plancher des prix m; **~ fluctuation** n variation de prix f; **~ for the account** cours à terme m; **~ freeze** n blocage des prix m, gel des prix m; **~ gap** n écart de prix m; **~ increase** n augmentation de(s) prix f; **~ index** n indice des prix m; **~ inelasticity** n inélasticité des prix f; **~ inflation** n inflation par les prix f; **~ label** n étiquette f, **~ level** n niveau de prix m; **~ level change** n fluctuation du niveau des prix f; **~ limit** n limite de prix f; (Stock) cours limite m; **~ list** n liste des prix f, tarif m; **~ maintenance** n maintien des prix m, vente à prix imposé f; **~ mechanism** n mécanisme des prix m; **~ offered** n prix offert m; (Stock) cours vendeur m, prix offert m; **~s policy** n politique des prix f; **~-performance ratio** n rapport prix-performance m; **~ pressure** n pression sur les prix f; **~ protection** n (Stock) (futures) protection du cours f; **~ quotation list** n liste des cours f; **~ range** n fourchette de prix f, gamme de prix f; **~ reduction** n réduction de(s) prix f; **~ regulation** n réglementation des prix f; **~ restrictions** n pl contrôle des prix m; **~ rigging** n manipulation des prix f; **~ ring** n cartel de vendeurs m; **~ rise** n augmentation des prix f, hausse des prix f; **~ scale** n échelle des prix f; **~ scanner** n scanneur de prix m; **~ schedule** n barème des prix m, tarif m; **~ sensitivity** n élasticité-prix f; **~ setting** n détermination des prix f, fixation des prix f; **~ spread** n (Stock) opération mixte verticale f, spread vertical m; **~ stability** n stabilité des prix f; **~ sticker** n étiquette de prix f; **~ structure** n structure de prix f; **~ swing** n variation de prix f; **~ tag** n (label) étiquette de prix f; (cost) prix m; **~ ticket** n étiquette de prix f; **~ undercutting** n gâchage m; **~ variation** n variation de prix

f; **~ war** n guerre des prix f

price² vt (determine price of) fixer le prix de; (mark the price) marquer le prix de; (estimate the value of) évaluer; **be competitively ~d** être à un prix compétitif; **~ oneself out of a market** perdre un marché en pratiquant des prix trop élevés; **~ up** augmenter le prix de

pricey adj (infrml) coûteux/-euse

pricing n fixation des prix f, tarification f; **~ arrangement** n entente sur les prix f; **~ down** n baisse du prix f; **~ model** n modèle d'évaluation d'un prix m; **~ policy** n politique des prix f; **~ review** n révision des prix f; **~ strategy** n politique des prix f; **~ up** n augmentation du prix f, hausse du prix f

prima facie evidence n (Law) commencement de preuve m, preuve prima facie f

primarily adv essentiellement

primary adj (initial) premier/-ière; (main) principal; **of ~ importance** de première importance; **~ activities** n pl activités du secteur primaire f pl, services primaires m pl; **~ capital** n capital bancaire m, valeur de premier choix f; **~ commodity** n produit de base m; **~ dealer** n spécialiste en valeurs du Trésor mf; **~ deficit** n déficit effectif m; **~ distribution** n (of new issue) placement initial m; **~ industry** n industrie du secteur primaire f, industrie primaire f; **~ issue** n (Stock) émission initiale f; **~ market** n marché primaire m; **~ market dealer** n courtier du marché primaire m; **~ offering** n (of new issue) placement initial m; **~ product** n produit de base m; **~ reserve** n réserve primaire f; **~ resource** n ressource primaire f; **~ sector** n secteur primaire m

prime¹ adj (land) de premier ordre; (property) exceptionnel/-elle; (produce) de premier choix; (factor, aim, target) principal; (example) excellent; (cause, reason) principal, fondamental; **of ~ quality** de première qualité; **in ~ condition** en parfait état

prime² n **be in its ~** être à son apogée; **be past its ~** avoir connu des jours meilleurs; **be past one's ~** avoir passé son heure de gloire

prime³ vt (brief) mettre au courant, briefer; (prepare) préparer

prime: ~ borrower n US emprunteur de premier ordre m, emprunteur très solvable m; **~ contractor** n maître d'œuvre m; **~ cost** n prix de revient initial m; **~ entry** n première écriture f; **~ lending rate** n US taux de base m; **~ location** n emplacement de premier choix m; **~ minister** n Premier ministre m; **~ mover** n moteur principal m; **~ paper** n papier commercial de premier ordre m; **~ position** n (in the market) position de choix f; **~ rate of interest** n taux d'intérêt de base m; **~ rate loan** n prêt accordé au taux de base m; **~ site** n site de ⸱⸱⸱▹

premier choix *m*; ~ **time** *n* heure de grande
écoute *f*, prime time *m*
principal¹ *adj* principal
principal² *n* (Admin) chef de section *m*;
(client) donneur d'ordres *m*; (lawyer's client)
commettant/-e *m/f*, mandant/-e *m/f*; (interest-
bearing sum) capital *m*; (debt before interest)
principal *m*
principal: ~ **accounting system** *n* (Acc)
système comptable principal *m*; ~ **amount** *n*
montant en capital *m*, principal *m*; ~ **assets**
n pl actif principal *m*; ~ **business** *n*
activité principale *f*; ~ **customer** *n* client/-e
principal/-e *m/f*; ~ **debtor** *n* débiteur/-trice
principal/-e *m/f*; ~ **place of business** *n*
siège social *m*; ~ **residence** *n* résidence
principale *f*; ~ **stockholder** *n* actionnaire
principal/-e *m/f*; ~ **sum** *n* somme en capital
f; ~ **value** *n* valeur principale *f*
principally *adv* principalement
principle *n* principe *m*; **in** ~ en principe;
on ~ par principe
print¹ *n* (typeface) caractères *m pl*; **fine** ~,
small ~ petits caractères *m pl*; **in** ~
disponible; **out of** ~ épuisé; **read the fine** ~,
read the small ~ lire tous les détails; **read
the small** ~ **of a contract** éplucher un
contrat
print² *vt* imprimer; ~ **off** (copy) tirer; ~ **out**
(document) sortir sur imprimante
print: ~ **journalism** *n* presse écrite *f*; ~
media *n* médias de presse écrite *m pl*;
~**-out** sortie (papier) *f*, sortie sur
imprimante *f*; (perforated list) listing *m*; ~
preview *n* (Comp) aperçu avant impression
m; ~ **run** *n* tirage *m*
printed *adj* imprimé; **the** ~ **word** l'écrit *m*;
~ **form** *n* imprimé *m*; ~ **matter** *n* BrE
imprimés *m pl*
printer *n* (Comp) imprimante *f*; (person)
imprimeur *m*; **at the** ~**'s** à l'imprimerie
printing *n* (Comp, Media) impression *f*; ~
press *n* presse à imprimer *f*; ~ **works** *n*
imprimerie *f*
prior¹ *adj* (experience, engagement) préalable;
have ~ **claim to** avoir (un) droit de priorité
sur; ~ **judicial authorization** *n*
autorisation judiciaire préalable *f*; ~**-lien
bond** *n* obligation prioritaire *f*, titre
préférentiel *m*; ~ **notice** *n* préavis *m*; ~
patent *n* brevet antérieur *m*; ~ **period** *n*
(Acc) exercice antérieur *m*; ~**-preferred
stock** *n* action préférentielle *f*, action
superprivilégiée *f*
prior² *prep* ~ **to** avant
prioritize *vt* donner la priorité à
priority¹ *adj* prioritaire
priority² *n* priorité *f*; **give** ~ **to** accorder la
priorité à; **have** ~ **over, take** ~ **over** avoir
la priorité sur; **get one's priorities right**
définir correctement l'ordre de ses priorités
priority: ~ **allocation** *n* (Stock)

adjudication prioritaire *f*, affectation de
priorité *f*; ~ **mail** *n* US courrier urgent *m*; ~
payment instrument *n* instrument de
paiement privilégié *m*; ~ **right** *n* droit de
priorité *m*; ~ **share** *n* action prioritaire *f*
privacy *n* vie privée *f*; ~ **laws** *n pl lois
relatives aux atteintes à la vie privée*; ~
policy *n* politique de protection des données
personnelles *f*; ~ **statement** *n* déclaration
de confidentialité *f*
private *adj* (not state-run) privé; (not for the
general public) privé; (secret, personal) privé; (not
associated with the company) personnel/-elle; (on
envelope) confidentiel; **by** ~ **contract** de gré à
gré, à l'amiable; **go** ~ (for medicine, education)
passer au secteur privé; ~ **account** *n*
compte particulier *m*; ~ **arrangement** *n*
accord à l'amiable; ~ **attorney** *n* fondé de
pouvoir *m*; ~ **bank** *n* banque privée *f*; ~
banking *n* services bancaires aux
particuliers *m pl*; ~ **brand** *n* marque de
distributeur *f*; ~ **buyer** *n* particulier *m*; ~
company *n* société fermée *f*, société privée *f*,
société à responsabilité limitée *f*; ~
consumption *n* consommation des ménages
f, ~ **contract** *n* contrat sous seing privé *m*,
marché privé *m*; ~ **cost** *n* (Econ) coût privé
m, coût social *m*; ~ **enterprise** *n* entreprise
privée *f*, libre entreprise *f*; ~ **finance
initiative** *n* projet PFI *m*, projet de
*partenariat public-privé ou les dépenses en
capital et la prestation de services sont prises
en charge par l'entité privée*; ~ **good** *n* bien
privé *m*; ~ **health scheme** *n* UK système
privé d'assurance maladie *m*; ~ **hearing** *n*
audience à huis clos *f*; ~ **hospital** *n* clinique
privée *f*; ~ **household** *n* ménage *m*; ~
income *n* revenu personnel *m*; ~
individual *n* particulier *m*; ~ **institution** *n*
institution privée *f*; ~ **investment** *n*
investissement du secteur privé *m*; ~
investor *n* investisseur privé *m*, petit
actionnaire *m*; ~ **lender** *n* prêteur privé *m*;
~ **lesson** *n* cours particulier *m*; ~ **limited
company** *n* UK société à responsabilité
limitée *f*; ~ **means** *n pl* moyens privés *m pl*;
~ **offering** *n* émission à diffusion restreinte
f; ~ **office** *n* bureau privé *m*; ~ **patient** *n*
patient/-e privé/-e *m/f*; ~ **property** *n*
propriété privée *f*; ~ **school** *n* école libre *f*,
école privée *f*; ~ **secretary** *n* secrétaire
particulier/-ière *mf*; ~ **sector** *n* secteur
privé *m*; ~ **sector borrower** *n* emprunteur
du secteur privé *m*; ~ **sector company** *n*
société du secteur privé *f*; ~ **sector
investment** *n* investissement du secteur
privé *m*; ~ **terms** *n pl* accords privés *m pl*,
conditions convenues *f pl*; ~ **tuition** *n* cours
particuliers *m pl*
privately: ~ **financed** *adj*, ~ **funded**
adj à financement privé; ~ **owned
company** *n* société privée *f*
privatization *n* privatisation *f*; ~
proceeds *n pl* produit de privatisation *m*,

recettes de privatisation *f pl*; ∼ **program**
AmE, ∼ **programme** BrE *n* programme de
privatisations *m*

privatize *vt* privatiser

privatized *adj* privatisé

privilege *n* (advantage, honour) privilège *m*;
US (Stock) option *f*; **without** ∼**s** sans
privilège

privileged *adj* (Fin) protégé; (Law) privilégié

prize *n* prix *m*

pro¹ *n* (professional) pro *m* (infrml),
professionnel/-elle *m/f*; (advantage) **the** ∼**s
and cons** le pour et le contre

pro² *pref* be ∼**-democracy/-change** être
pour la démocratie/le changement; ∼**-strike
ballot** *n* vote pour la grève *m*

PRO *abbr* (▸**public relations officer**)
responsable des relations publiques *mf*

proactive *adj* proactif/-ive

probability *n* (in statistics) probabilité *f*; (of
desirable event) chances *f pl*; (of unwelcome event)
risques *m pl*; (likely result) probabilité *f*; **the** ∼
of winning les chances de gagner; **the** ∼ **of
losing** les risques de perdre; **the** ∼ **of sth
happening** les chances que qch se passe; ∼
sample *n* échantillon probabiliste *m*; ∼
theory *n* théorie des probabilités *f*

probable *adj* probable

probate¹ *n* (Law) validation *f*, homologation
f; **grant** ∼ **of a will** homologuer un
testament, valider un testament; ∼ **court** *n*
tribunal des successions *m*; ∼ **price** *n*
(Stock) prix homologué *m*

probate² *vt* valider, homologuer

probationary period *n* période d'essai *f*

probationer *n* employé/-e à l'essai *m/f*

probation period *n* période d'essai *f*

probe¹ *n* enquête *f*; ∼ **into sth** enquête sur
qn

probe² *vt* (matter, causes) enquêter sur

problem *n* problème *m*; **cause a** ∼,
present a ∼ poser un problème; ∼ **analysis**
n analyse de problèmes *f*; ∼ **area** *n* domaine
problématique *m*, zone critique *f*; ∼
assessment *n* évaluation des problèmes *f*;
∼ **child** *n* (S&M) dilemme *m*, point
d'interrogation *m*; ∼ **customer** *n* (S&M)
client/-e difficile *m/f*; ∼ **loan** *n* emprunt à
risque *m*; ∼ **solver** *n* analyste *mf*; ∼
solving *n* résolution de problèmes *f*

problematic *adj* problématique

procedural *adj* (delay, detail, error, change) de
procédure; ∼ **agreement** *n* accord de
procédure *f*; ∼ **issue** *n* question de
procédure *f*

procedure *n* procédure *f*; **follow a** ∼
suivre une procédure; **complaints** ∼
procédure de réclamation *f*

proceed *vi* (project, work) avancer; (talks, trial,
interview) se poursuivre, se dérouler; ∼
according to plan se dérouler comme prévu;

∼ **to** (item, issue) passer à; ∼ **to do**
entreprendre de faire; ∼ **with** (sale, idea, plan)
poursuivre; (ballot) procéder à

proceedings *n pl* (Law) poursuites
judiciaires *f pl*, procédure *f*; (debate) débats
m pl, délibérations *f pl*; (meeting) réunion *f*;
(report, record) rapport *m*; (of conference) actes
m pl; **disciplinary** ∼ poursuites disciplinaires
f pl; **institute** ∼ engager des poursuites

proceeds *n pl* produit *m*; ∼ **of sales** *n*
produit de la vente *m*

process¹ *n* (on-going action) processus *m*;
(method) procédé *m*; (Comp) processus *m*,
traitement *m*; (lawsuit) procès *m*; **in** ∼ en
cours; **recruitment** ∼ processus de
recrutement *m*; **manufacturing** ∼ procédé de
fabrication *m*; **be in the** ∼ **of doing** être en
train de faire; **by due** ∼ **of law** par voie
légale; ∼ **analysis** *n* analyse des méthodes *f*;
∼ **chart** *n* organigramme *m*; ∼ **control** *n*
automatisme industriel *m*, gestion de
processus industriel *f*, régulation de
processus *f*; ∼ **costing** *n* comptabilisation
par processus *f*, comptabilité par fabrication
f; ∼ **engineering** *n* processus de fabrication
en continu *m*

process² *vt* (cheque, application, data, claim)
traiter; (order) exécuter, traiter; (waste, food)
traiter; (raw materials) transformer

processed food *n* produit alimentaire
industriel *m*

processing *n* (of cheque, application, data,
claim) traitement *m*; (of order) exécution *f*,
traitement *m*; (of food, raw material)
transformation *f*; **order** ∼ exécution des
ordres *f*; ∼ **fee** *n* droit d'administration *m*;
∼ **industry** *n* industrie de transformation *f*,
industrie manufacturière *f*; ∼ **plant** *n* usine
de traitement *f*; ∼ **stage** *n* phase de
production *f*

processor *n* processeur *m*

procuratory letter *n* lettre
d'accréditation *f*, lettre de procuration *f*

procure *vt* procurer; (for oneself) se procurer

procurement *n* (Gen Comm) obtention *f*; (of
goods, equipment) approvisionnement *m*; ∼
agent *n* acheteur/-euse *m/f*; ∼ **cost** *n* coût
de passation de commande *m*; ∼
department *n* achats *m pl*, service des
achats *m*; ∼ **manager** *n* chef
d'approvisionnement *m*

produce¹ *n* denrées alimentaires *f pl*,
produits agricoles *m pl*

produce² *vt* (cars, equipment) fabriquer;
(results) donner; (returns, interest, profits)
rapporter; (example, evidence, proof) fournir,
apporter; (documents, report) produire; (leaflet,
brochure) éditer; (reaction, change) provoquer;
(package, solution, argument, timetable) mettre au
point; (film, programme) produire

producer *n* (of produce, food) producteur *m*;
(of machinery, goods) fabricant *m*; (in TV, radio)
producteur/-trice *m/f*; ∼ **advertising** *n* ⸱⸱⸱➤

publicité du fabricant f; ∼ **price** n prix à la production m; ∼ **price index** n indice des prix à la production m; ∼'s **brand** n marque du fabricant f; ∼'s **goods** n pl biens de production m pl

product n produit m; end ∼ résultat final m; (Ind) produit final m; ∼ **acceptance** n acceptation d'un produit f; ∼ **adaptation** n adaptation du produit f; ∼ **advertising** n publicité de produit f; ∼ **analysis** n analyse de produit f; ∼ **assortment** n éventail de produits m; ∼ **bundling** n groupage de produits m; ∼ **compatibility** n compatibilité-produit f; ∼ **cost** n coût du produit m; ∼ **costing** n estimation du prix de revient d'un produit f; ∼ **cycle** n cycle de développement d'un produit m, cycle de vie d'un produit m; ∼ **data sheet** n fiche technique f, fiche de données techniques f; ∼ **design** n conception de produit f; ∼ **development** n mise au point du produit f; ∼ **differentiation** n différenciation de produits f; ∼ **diversification** n diversification de produits f; ∼ **evaluation** n évaluation de produit f; ∼ **feature** n caractéristique produit f; ∼ **image** n image de marque f; ∼ **information sheet** n fiche technique f, fiche de données techniques f; ∼ **knowledge** n connaissance du produit f; ∼ **launch** n lancement de produit m; ∼ **leader** n produit d'appel bon marché m; ∼ **liability** n responsabilité du fabricant f; ∼ **liability insurance** n assurance responsabilité produits f; ∼ **licence** BrE, ∼ **license** AmE autorisation de mise sur le marché f; ∼ **life cycle** n cycle de vie d'un produit m; ∼ **life expectancy** n durée de vie probable d'un produit f; ∼ **line** n gamme de produits f, ligne de produits f; ∼ **management** n gestion de produits f; ∼ **manager** n chef de produit m, directeur/-trice de produit m/f; ∼ **marketing** n commercialisation f, marketing de produit m; ∼ **mix** n ensemble de produits m, mix de produits m; ∼ **performance** n caractéristiques du produit f pl, comportement du produit m; ∼ **placement** n placement de produit m; ∼ **planning** n planification de produit f; ∼ **portfolio** n portefeuille de produits m; ∼ **positioning** n positionnement d'un produit m; ∼ **profile** n profil du produit m; ∼ **profitability** n rentabilité de produit f; ∼ **promotion** n communication du produit f; ∼ **range** n gamme de produits f, éventail des produits m; ∼ **research** n recherche de produit f, étude de produit f; ∼ **safety** n sécurité du produit f; ∼ **testing** n test de produit m

production n (of crop, foodstuff, material) production f; (of car, goods, equipment) fabrication f; (output) production f; (of document, report, ticket) présentation f; (in TV, film-making) production f; (show, film) production f; **go into** ∼ être fabriqué; **go out of** ∼ ne plus être

fabriqué; **on** ∼ **of documents** sur présentation de documents; **put sth into** ∼ entreprendre la production de; ∼ **bonus** n prime de production f, prime de rendement f; ∼ **capacity** n capacité de production f, potentiel de production m; ∼ **company** n société de production f; ∼ **control** n gestion de la production f; ∼ **cost** n coût de production m; ∼ **engineering** n organisation de la production f; ∼ **goods** n pl biens de production m pl; ∼ **line** n chaîne de production f; ∼ **line work** n travail à la chaîne m; ∼ **line worker** n travailleur/-euse à la chaîne m/f; ∼ **management** n gestion de la production f; ∼ **manager** n chef de production m, directeur/-trice de la production m/f; ∼ **planning** n programmation de la production f; ∼ **plant** n unité de production f, usine de production f; ∼ **process** n (activity) processus de production m; (method) procédé de fabrication m; ∼ **rate** n taux de production m; ∼ **schedule** n programme de fabrication m; ∼ **standard** n norme de production f; ∼ **target** n objectif de production m; ∼ **technique** n technique de production f; ∼ **time** n temps de production m; ∼ **unit** n unité de production f; ∼ **worker** n ouvrier/ -ière de production m/f; (on production line) travailleur/-euse à la chaîne m/f

productive adj (factory, industry, land, workforce) productif/-ive; (capacity, sector) productif/-ive; (experience, discussion, collaboration) fructueux/-euse; ∼ **capital** n capitaux productifs m pl; ∼ **potential** n potentiel de croissance de production m, potentiel de production m

productivity n productivité f; ∼ **agreement** n, ∼ **deal** n accord de productivité m; ∼ **drive** n campagne de productivité f; ∼ **gains** n pl gains de productivité m pl; ∼ **measurement** n mesure de la productivité f; ∼ **tool** n (Comp) logiciel de productivité m

pro-family adj (measures) en faveur de la famille

profession n profession f; (law, medicine) profession libérale f; **the legal/medical** ∼ (practitioners) le corps judiciaire/médical; **be an architect by** ∼ être architecte de métier

professional[1] adj professionnel/-elle; **take** ∼ **advice** consulter un professionnel

professional[2] n professionnel/-elle m/f

professional: ∼ **body** n groupement professionnel m; ∼ **ethics** n pl déontologie f; ∼ **fee** n honoraire m; ∼ **income** n revenu de profession libérale m; ∼ **indemnity** n responsabilité professionnelle f; ∼ **liability** n responsabilité professionnelle f; ∼ **liability insurance** n assurance de responsabilité professionnelle f; ∼ **portal** n portail vertical m; ∼ **secrecy** n secret professionnel m; ∼ **services** n pl services professionnels m pl;

~ staff n AmE cadres m pl; **~ status** n statut professionnel m; **~ worker** n AmE travailleur/-euse intellectuel/-elle m/f

professionalism n professionnalisme m

proficiency n (practical) compétence f; (academic) niveau m; **~ in doing** compétence à faire; **~ level** niveau de compétence m; **~ test** test de niveau m

proficient adj compétent

profile n (of business, competitor, market) profil m; **keep a low ~** adopter un profil bas, se montrer discret/-ète; **have a high ~** être très en vue

profiling n (S&M) classification selon le profil comportemental f, profiling m

profit n bénéfice m, profit m; **~ and loss** pertes et profit; **operate at a ~** être rentable; **move into ~** devenir rentable, devenir bénéficiaire; **sell sth at a ~** vendre qch à profit, vendre qch avec un bénéfice; **at a ~ of** pour un bénéfice de; **make a ~** réaliser un bénéfice, faire un bénéfice; **take a ~** réaliser un bénéfice; **~ before tax** n bénéfices avant impôts m pl; **~ carried forward** n report à nouveau m; **~ ceiling** n plafonnement des bénéfices m; **~ center** AmE, **~ centre** BrE n (Acc) centre de profit m; **~ center accounting** AmE, **~ centre accounting** BrE n comptabilité par centres de profits f; **~ forecast** n prévisions de bénéfices f; **~ and loss account**, **~ and loss statement** n compte de pertes et profits m; **~-making enterprise** n (commercial, not charitable) entreprise à but lucratif f; (viable company) entreprise rentable f; **~ margin** n marge bénéficiaire f; **~ maximization** n maximisation des bénéfices f; **~ motive** n recherche du profit f; **~ optimization** n optimisation du profit f; **~ and performance planning** prévision de bénéfices et de performances f; **~ planning** n planification des bénéfices f; **~ potential** n potentiel de bénéfice m; **~ projection** n projection des profits f; **~-related pay** n salaire lié aux bénéfices m; **~-sharing** n intéressement aux bénéfices m, participation aux bénéfices f; **~-sharing bond** n obligation participante f; **~-sharing plan** US, **~-sharing scheme** UK n plan d'intéressement aux bénéfices m, plan de participation aux bénéfices m, système de partage des bénéfices m; **~ squeeze** n contraction des bénéfices f; **~ taking** n prise de bénéfices f; **~ target** n objectif de profit m; **~ test** n test de rentabilité m; **~ warning** (Fin, Stock) alerte sur les résultats futurs f

profitability n rentabilité f; **~ analysis** n analyse de rentabilité f, étude de rentabilité f; **~ ratio** n ratio de rentabilité m

profitable adj rentable

profitably adv (usefully) utilement; (sell) à profit, avec bénéfice; (trade) à profit; (invest) avec profit

profiteer n profiteur/-euse m/f

profiteering n réalisation de bénéfices excessifs f

profits tax n impôt sur les bénéfices m

pro forma adj pour la forme, pro forma; **~ invoice** n facture pro forma f

profound adj profond

profoundly adv profondément

profusion n profusion f

prognosis n pl **-ses** pronostic m

prognostication n pronostic m

program[1] n (Comp) programme m; (on TV, radio) AmE émission f; (schedule, scheme) AmE programme m

program[2] vt AmE programmer

programme[1] n BrE (broadcast) émission f; (schedule) programme m; (Mgmnt) programme m; (scheme) programme m; **draw up a ~** arrêter un programme; **training/research ~** programme de formation/de recherche; **~ adjustment loan** n prêt-programme d'ajustement m; **~ budgeting** n rationalisation des choix budgétaires f; **~ deal** n contrat de programme m; **~ evaluation plan** n plan d'évaluation de programme m; **~ evaluation and review technique** n méthode PERT f; **~ manager** n (HRM) chef de projet m; (Comp) gestionnaire de programmes mf; **~ package** n progiciel m; **~ structure** n structure de programme f; **~ trading** n négociation assistée par ordinateur f

programme[2] vt BrE programmer

programmed: **~ learning** n enseignement programmé m; **~ management** n direction par programmes f, gestion programmée f

programmer n BrE programmeur/-euse m/f

programming n programmation f; **~ aid** n outils de programmation m pl; **~ language** n langage de programmation m

progress[1] n progrès m; (of person, event, inquiry) progression f; (of situation, career) évolution f; **in ~** en cours; **make ~** progresser, faire des progrès; **make quick ~** avancer à pas de géant; **~ board** n (chart) tableau de planning m; **~ chaser** n responsable du suivi d'un projet mf; **~ control** n suivi de la production m; **~ payments** n pl paiements en cours m pl; **~ report** n compte rendu sur l'état d'avancement des travaux m

progress[2] vi (work, research) progresser; (person) faire des progrès

progressive adj (gradual) progressif/-ive; (radical) progressiste; **~ scale** n barème progressif m, échelle progressive f; **~ tax** n impôt progressif m

progressively adv progressivement

prohibit vt (forbid) interdire; (make impossible) empêcher; **~ sb from doing** interdire à qn de ···▶

faire

prohibited goods n pl marchandises prohibées f pl

prohibition n interdiction f; ~ **notice** n avis d'interdiction m

prohibitive adj prohibitif/-ive

project[1] n projet m; (state housing) US cité HLM f; (smaller) lotissement HLM m; ~ **agent** n agent de projet m, assistant/-e du chef de projet m/f; ~ **analysis** n étude de projet f, évaluation de projet f; ~ **appraisal** n étude de projet f, évaluation de projet f; ~ **approval** n approbation de projet f; ~ **assessment** n étude de projet f, évaluation de projet f; ~ **engineer** n ingénieur projet m; ~ **financing** n financement de projets m; ~ **leader** n chef de projet m; ~ **management** n gestion de projet f, management de projet m; ~ **manager** n chef de projet m, directeur/-trice de projet m/f; ~ **outline** n avant-projet m; ~ **plan** n plan de projet m; ~ **planning** n planification de projet f; ~ **sponsor** n promoteur de projet m

project[2] vt (estimate) prévoir; ~ **a new image** donner une nouvelle image

projected adj (planned) projeté; (estimated) prévu; ~ **benefit obligation** n obligation anticipée de nouvelles mesures sociales f; ~ **growth** n croissance prévue f

projection n prévision f, projection f

projector n projecteur m

proliferate vi proliférer

proliferation n prolifération f

prolong vt prolonger

prolonged adj prolongé

prominent adj (person, position, feature) important; **play a ~ role in** jouer un rôle de premier plan dans

promise[1] n promesse f; **keep a ~** tenir une promesse; **go back on a ~** revenir sur sa promesse

promise[2] vt promettre; ~ **to pay** s'engager à payer; ~ **to sell** faire une promesse de vente

promising adj prometteur/-euse; (person) qui promet

promissory note n billet à ordre m

promo n (infrml) promo f (infrml)

promotary company n US société de financement f

promote vt (encourage) encourager, promouvoir; (foster) favoriser; (move up in rank) promouvoir; (publicize) faire de la publicité pour; (market) promouvoir; **be ~d** (employee) avoir une promotion, être promu

promoter n promoteur/-trice m/f

promotion n (of personnel) avancement m, promotion f; (of product, service) promotion f; (Stock) (of company) lancement m; **get a ~**, **gain a ~** être promu; **be in line for ~** avoir des chances d'être promu; **her ~ to manager** sa promotion au poste de directrice; **apply**

for ~ demander une promotion; ~ **cost** n frais de premier établissement m pl; ~ **ladder** n échelle des promotions f; ~ **mix** n moyens d'action promotionnelle m pl; ~ **prospects** n pl perspectives d'avenir f pl

promotional adj promotionnel/-elle; ~ **allowance** n, ~ **budget** n budget de la publicité m; ~ **campaign** n campagne de promotion f, campagne promotionnelle f; ~ **exercise** n campagne promotionnelle f; ~ **literature** n documentation publicitaire f; ~ **material** n matériel de promotion m; ~ **mix** n moyens d'action promotionnelle m pl; ~ **price** n prix promotionnel m; ~ **sample** n échantillon promotionnel m; ~ **site** n site promotionnel m; ~ **video** n vidéo publicitaire f

promotions: ~ **manager** n directeur/-trice de la publicité m/f; ~ **team** n équipe promotionnelle f

prompt[1] adj (reply, result, attention, service) rapide; **be ~ to do** être prompt à faire

prompt[2] n (Comp) (on command line) invite f; (instructions) message guide-opérateur m

prompt[3] vt (give rise to) provoquer; ~ **sb to do sth** inciter qn à faire qch, pousser qn à faire qch

prompt: ~ **note** n rappel de paiement m; ~ **payment** n paiement rapide m

promptly adv rapidement

proof n (evidence) preuve f; (of book, publication) épreuve f; **have ~ that** pouvoir prouver que; ~ **of debt** n justification de dette f, titre de créances m; ~ **of delivery** n justification de livraison f; ~ **of identity** n pièce d'identité f; ~ **of ownership** n titre de propriété m; ~ **of postage** n certificat d'expédition m; ~ **of purchase** n justificatif d'achat m; ~ **of title** n justification de titre f, titre de propriété m

proofread vt corriger les épreuves de

proofreader n correcteur/-trice d'épreuves m/f

propagate vt propager

prop: ~ **up** vt (currency, company, economy) soutenir

propensity n propension f; ~ **to consume** propension à consommer f; ~ **to save** propension à épargner f

property n (real estate) immobilier m; (house) propriété f; (land) terrain m; (belongings) biens m pl, propriété f; ~ **bond** n obligation immobilière f; ~ **company** n société immobilière f; ~ **developer** n promoteur immobilier m; ~ **development** n promotion immobilière f; ~ **development project** n projet de promotion immobilière m; ~ **held in joint names** n propriété indivise f; ~ **income** n revenu de biens m, revenu immobilier m; ~ **insurance** n assurance dommages matériels f; ~ **investment company** n société d'investissement immobilière f; ~ **loan** n prêt immobilier m; ~ **management** n gestion immobilière f;

p

~ **market** n marché de l'immobilier m; ~ **owner** n propriétaire immobilier/-ière m/f; ~ **register** n cadastre m; ~ **rights** n pl droits de propriété m pl; ~ **speculator** n spéculateur immobilier m; ~ **tax** n taxe immobilière f; ~ **valuation** n BrE évaluation de biens immobiliers f, évaluation immobilière f

proportion n proportion f; ~**s** (measurements) dimensions f pl, proportions f pl; **as a** ~ **of** comme pourcentage de, comme proportion de; **in** ~ **to** par rapport à; **the** ~ **of X to Y** le pourcentage de X par rapport à Y; **in equal** ~**s** à parts égales

proportional adj proportionnel/-elle; ~ **to** proportionnel/-elle à; ~ **income tax** n impôt proportionnel sur le revenu m; ~ **rate** n tarif proportionnel m; ~ **representation** n (Pol) représentation proportionnelle f; ~ **tax** n impôt proportionnel m

proportionality n proportionnalité f

proportionally adv proportionnellement

proportionate adj proportionnel/-elle

proportionately adv proportionnellement

proposal n proposition f; (Ins) proposition d'assurance f; **our** ~ **still stands** notre proposition reste valable; **make a** ~ faire une proposition, avancer une proposition; **a** ~ **for doing** une proposition visant à faire

propose vt (course of action, change, rule, person) proposer; (motion) présenter, soumettre; ~ **doing** proposer de faire

proposed adj (action, reform) envisagé

proposer n (of motion) auteur m; (of member) parrain/marraine m/f; (Ins) contractant m, souscripteur m; **the** ~ **of the motion** l'auteur de la proposition

proposition n (suggestion) proposition f; **make/put forward a** ~ faire/avancer une proposition; **a** ~ **for doing** une proposition visant à faire; **an economic** ~, **a paying** ~ une affaire rentable

proprietary adj (having a trade name) de marque; (privately owned) privé; (rights, duties) de propriétaire; ~ **brand** n marque déposée f; ~ **company** n société de holding f, société mère f; ~ **drug** n médicament vendu sous marque m; ~ **goods** n pl articles de marque m pl; ~ **name** n marque déposée f; ~ **rights** n pl droits de propriété m pl; ~ **software** n logiciel propre à un constructeur m, logiciel propriétaire m; ~ **system** n système breveté m, système exclusif constructeur m

proprietor n (of business) propriétaire mf; (Patents) titulaire mf; (of intellectual property) propriétaire mf

proprietorship n (owning) possession f; (Law) droit de propriété m; **under her** ~ pendant qu'elle est/était propriétaire

pro rata[1] adj proportionnel/-elle; **on a** ~ **basis** au prorata

pro rata[2] adv au prorata

prorate vt diviser de façon proportionnelle, répartir au prorata

prosecute vt poursuivre (en justice)

prosecuting attorney n US avocat/-e général/-e m/f; (public official) procureur m

prosecution n (legal action) poursuites f pl; (lawyers acting for the state) ministère public m; **liable to** ~ passible de poursuites

prospect[1] n (potential buyer) client/-e potentiel/-ielle m/f, client/-e éventuel/-elle m/f, prospect m; (expectation) espoir m, **there is some/little** ~ **of improvement** il y a espoir/ peu d'espoir que cela s'améliore; **face the** ~ **of/of doing** faire face à la perspective de/de faire; **career** ~**s** perspectives de carrière f pl; **future** ~**s** perspectives d'avenir f pl

prospect[2] [1] vt (region, market) prospecter [2] vi prospecter; ~ **for** (oil, minerals) prospecter pour trouver

prospecting n prospection f

prospective adj potentiel/-ielle, éventuel/ -elle; ~ **buyer** n acheteur/-euse potentiel/ -ielle m/f; ~ **customer** n client/-e potentiel/ -ielle m/f, client/-e éventuel/-elle m/f, prospect m

prospector n prospecteur/-trice m/f

prospectus n prospectus m; (Stock) prospectus (d'émission) m

prosperity n prospérité f

prosperous adj prospère, riche

protect [1] vt (keep safe) protéger; (consumer, rights, interests) défendre; (privacy) préserver; ~ **the interests of** protéger les intérêts de; ~**ed designation of origin** n appellation d'origine protégée f [2] v refl ~ **oneself** se protéger; ~ **oneself against** (risk) se protéger contre; ~ **oneself from sth** se protéger de qch

protection n protection f; **consumer** ~ protection du consommateur f, défense des intérêts du consommateur f

protectionism n protectionnisme m

protective adj (measures, clothing) de protection, (tarif, duty) protecteur/-trice, protectionniste

pro tem[1] adj provisoire

pro tem[2] adv provisoirement

protest[1] n (disapproval) protestation f; (complaint) réclamation f; (shipping) déclaration d'avaries f; **make a** ~ protester; **without** ~ sans protester; **in** ~ **at sth** pour protester contre qch; **lodge a** ~ faire une réclamation; (Law) déposer plainte; ~ **strike** n grève revendicative f; ~ **vote** n vote de protestation m

protest[2] vi protester

protocol n protocole m

prototype[1] n prototype m

prototype[2] vt faire un prototype de

prototyping n prototypage m

prove [1] vt prouver; **it remains to be** ····>

proven il reste à prouver; ~ **a point** montrer qu'on a raison; **events ~d us right/wrong** les événements nous ont donné raison/tort; ~ **one's identity** prouver son identité

2 *vi* ~ **right** s'avérer vrai, se révéler vrai; ~ **wrong** s'avérer faux, se révéler faux; ~ **to be difficult** se révéler difficile

proven *adj* confirmé; ~ **track record** réputation bien établie *f*; **have a ~ track record in consultancy** être un consultant confirmé

provide **1** *vt* (goods) fournir; (service) assurer; (advice) donner; (answer, support) apporter; (evidence, opportunity) fournir; ~ **a loan** consentir un prêt; ~ **sb with a loan** accorder un prêt à qn, consentir un prêt à qn; ~ **technical assistance** fournir une assistance technique

2 *vi* (stipulate) prévoir; ~ **that** (document, contract) prévoir que; ~ **against** se prémunir contre; ~ **against a risk** s'assurer contre un risque; ~ **for** (eventuality, contingency) envisager; (person) subvenir aux besoins de; **be well ~d for** être à l'abri du besoin

provided *conj* ~ **that** à condition que

provident fund *n* caisse de prévoyance *f*

provider *n* (of goods, equipment, materials) fournisseur *m*; (of service) prestataire *m*

providing *conj* à condition que

provincial *adj* provincial

provision *n* (in agreement, treaty) clause *f*; (of bill, act) disposition *f*, stipulation *f*; (supplying) fourniture *f*; (of service) prestation *f*; (Tax) disposition *f*; (reserve) provision *f*; (Fin) réserve *f*; **make ~ for** prévoir; **under the ~s of** aux termes de; **with the ~ that** à la condition que; **within the ~s of the treaty** dans le cadre du traité; ~ **for bad debts** (supply) provision pour créances douteuses *f*; ~ **for contingency** provision pour risques *f*; ~ **of services** prestation de services *f*

provisional *adj* provisoire; ~ **acceptance** *n* acceptation provisoire *f*; ~ **bond** *n* obligation provisoire *f*; ~ **invoice** *n* facture provisoire *f*; ~ **policy** *n* police provisoire *f*

provisionally *adv* provisoirement, temporairement

proviso *n* condition *f*, stipulation *f*; (Law) clause conditionnelle *f*; **with the ~ that** à condition que + *subjunctive*

proxy *n* (powers) procuration *f*; (person) mandataire *mf*; ~ **fight** *n* (Stock) *bataille de procurations*; ~ **server** *n* (Comp) serveur mandataire *m*; ~ **statement** *n* déclaration de procuration *f*, procuration *f*; ~ **vote** *n* vote par procuration *m*

PRP *abbr* (▶**profit-related pay**) salaire lié aux bénéfices *m*; (▶**performance-related pay**) salaire au rendement *m*, salaire lié aux résultats *m*

PRT *abbr* (▶**petroleum revenue tax**) impôt

sur les revenus pétroliers *m*

prudent *adj* prudent

prudential *adj* prudent; US (in local administration) administratif/-ive; ~ **committee** *n* US comité de gestion *m*

prudently *adv* avec prudence, prudemment

prune *vt* (staff) dégraisser, (costs, expenses) diminuer, réduire

pruning *n* diminution *f*, réduction *f*; ~ **of staff** dégraissage *m*

PSBR *abbr* UK (▶**public sector borrowing requirement**) besoins de financement du secteur public *m pl*

PSV *abbr* (▶**public service vehicle**) véhicule de transport en commun *m*

psychographic *adj* psychographique

psychographics *n + sing v* segmentation du marché en fonction de critères psychologiques

psychological *adj* psychologique; ~ **price** *n* prix psychologique *m*; ~ **profile** *n* profil psychologique *m*; ~ **test** *n* test psychologique *m*

psychology *n* psychologie *f*

psychometrics *n +sing v* psychométrie *f*

psychometric test *n* test psychométrique *m*

public[1] *adj* public/-ique; (amenity, library) municipal; (support, disquiet) général; (duty, spirit) civique; **in ~** en public; **be in the ~ interest** être dans l'intérêt public; **it is ~ knowledge that...** il est de notoriété publique que...; **make sth ~** publier; **at ~ expense** aux frais du contribuable; **go ~** (Stock) être introduit en bourse; **in the ~ sphere** dans le domaine public; **come into ~ ownership, come under ~ ownership** être nationalisé; **be in the ~ eye** être exposé à l'opinion publique

public[2] *n* public *m*; **the general ~, the ~ at large** le grand public *m*

public: ~ **access** *n* (to information) accès du public *m*; ~ **accounts** *n pl* comptes de l'État *m pl*, comptes publics *m pl*; ~ **address system** *n* système de sonorisation *m*; ~ **administration** *n* administration publique *f*; ~ **body** *n* corporation *f*, organisme public *m*, établissement public *m*; ~ **company** *n* société anonyme *f*; ~ **consumption** *n* consommation des services publics *f*; ~ **contract** *n* marché public *m*; ~ **corporation** *n* UK régie d'État *f*; ~ **debt** *n* dette publique *f*; ~ **distribution** *n* (Stock) émission publique *f*; ~ **domain** *n* domaine public *m*; ~ **domain software** *n* logiciel du domaine public *m*; ~ **expenditure** *n* dépenses publiques *f pl*; ~ **finance** *n* finances publiques *f pl*; ~ **funds** *n pl* fonds publics *m pl*; ~ **good** *n* bien public *m*, bien social *m*; ~ **health** *n* santé publique *f*; ~ **holiday** *n* fête légale *f*, jour férié *m*; ~ **image** *n* (S&M) image de marque *f*; ~ **interest company** *n* industrie nationalisée f, société d'intérêt public f; ~ **investor** n investisseur public m; ~ **issue** n émission publique f; ~ **lending right** n droit perçu par un auteur sur le prêt de ses ouvrages en bibliothèque; ~ **limited company** n UK société anonyme f; ~ **limited partnership** n société en commandite f, société en commandite par actions f; ~ **loan** n emprunt d'État m; ~ **money** n fonds publics m pl, deniers publics m pl; ~ **offering** n offre publique de vente f; ~ **opinion** n opinion publique f; ~ **ownership** n propriété publique f; ~**-private partnership** n UK partenariat entre l'État et le secteur privé m, partenariat public-privé m; ~ **procurement** n achats publics m pl, fourniture publique f, marchés publics m pl; ~ **prosecutor** n procureur général m; ~ **purse** n le Trésor Public m; ~ **records** n pl archives de l'État f pl; ~ **relations** n pl relations publiques f pl; ~ **relations agency** n agence de relations publiques f; ~ **relations consultant** n conseil en relations publiques m, conseil en communication m; ~ **relations department** n service des relations publiques m; ~ **relations exercise** n opération de relations publiques f; ~ **relations officer** n responsable des relations publiques mf; ~ **revenue** n revenus de l'État m pl, revenus publics m pl; ~ **sale** n vente aux enchères f; ~ **school** n UK (fee-paying) école libre f, école privée f; US (non fee-paying) école publique f; ~ **sector** n secteur public m; ~ **sector body** n organisme du secteur public m; ~ **sector borrowing requirement** n UK besoins de financement du secteur public m pl; ~ **sector deficit** n déficit du secteur public m; ~ **sector enterprise** n entreprise du secteur public f; ~ **sector pay** n salaire du secteur public m; ~ **service** n fonction publique f, services publics m pl; ~ **service body** n organisme de services publics m; ~ **service contract** n marché des services publics m; ~ **service corporation** n US service public non-étatisé m; ~ **service employment** n emploi dans la fonction publique m; ~ **service vehicle** n véhicule de transport en commun m; ~ **spending** n dépenses publiques f pl; ~ **transport** n transports en commun m pl; ~ **transport system** n BrE transports en commun m pl; ~ **utility** n service public m; ~ **works** n pl travaux publics m pl

publication n publication f; ~ **date** n date de parution f, date de publication f

Public Broadcasting System n US services publics de radio-télévision

publicity n publicité f; ~ **agency** n agence de publicité; ~ **budget** n budget publicitaire m; ~ **campaign** n campagne publicitaire f; ~ **department** n service de publicité m; ~ **expenses** n pl dépenses publicitaires f pl; ~ **manager** n chef de publicité m; ~ **machine** n machine publicitaire f; ~

material n matériel publicitaire m; ~ **photograph** n photo publicitaire f; ~ **stunt** n coup publicitaire m

publicize vt (product, event) faire de la publicité pour; (issue) attirer l'attention du public sur, sensibiliser l'opinion publique au sujet de; (make public) rendre public

publicly adv (state, announce) publiquement; ~**-funded** adj à fonds publics; ~ **listed company** n société cotée en bourse f; ~ **owned company** n entreprise publique f; ~ **traded share** n action cotée en bourse f

publish vt (book, article) publier; (newspaper, magazine) éditer; (accounts, figures) publier

published: ~ **accounts** n pl comptes publics m pl; ~ **charge** n tarif publié m; ~ **price** n prix public m

publisher n (person) éditeur/-trice m/f; (company) maison d'édition f

publishing n (business) édition f; (publication of book) publication f; ~ **company** n, ~ **firm** n, ~ **house** n maison d'édition f

pull[1] n (attraction) attrait m; **exert a** ~ **over** exercer une influence sur; **have the** ~ **to do** avoir le bras suffisamment long pour faire; ~**-down menu** n menu déroulant m; ~ **technology** n recherche individuelle f

pull[2] vt (customers, audience) attirer; ~ **the rug out from under sb** couper l'herbe sous les pieds de qn; ~ **strings for sb** BrE (infrml), ~ **wires for sb** AmE (infrml) pistonner qn (infrml); ~ **in** (customers, crowds, tourists) attirer; (money) rapporter; ~ **off** (coup) réaliser; (win, victory) décrocher; ~ **off a deal** conclure un marché, mener une affaire à bien; ~ **out** (withdraw) se retirer; ~ **out of** (talks, deal) se retirer de

pump vt ~ **funds into** injecter des fonds dans

pump prices n pl prix à la pompe m

pump priming n politique de soutien f, mesures d'incitation économique f pl

punch: ~ **in** vt (data) introduire; (code) taper

punctuality n ponctualité f

punitive adj (measures, action, damages) punitif/-ive

punt n (currency) livre irlandaise f; (Stock) boursicotage m

punter n (better) parieur/-ieuse m/f; (customer) (infrml) client/-e m/f; (Stock) boursicoteur/-euse m/f

purchase[1] n achat m; **make a** ~ faire un achat; **cash** ~ achat au comptant m; ~ **acquisition** n (Fin) reprise f; ~ **of assets** n achat de valeurs m; ~ **book** n journal des achats m, livre des achats m; ~ **contract** n contrat d'achat m; (Stock) bordereau d'achat m; ~ **cost** n (Acc) (of assets) coût d'achat m; ~ **credit** n crédit d'achat m; ~ **diary** n relevé d'achat journalier m; ~ **for settlement** n (Stock) achat pour liquidation ⋯▷

m, achat à terme m; ~ **fund** n fonds de rachat m; ~ **group** n syndicat de garantie m; ~ **invoice** n facture d'achat f; ~ **issue facility** n facilité d'émission d'achat f; ~ **ledger** n livre des achats m, registre des achats m; ~ **method** n (Acc) méthode d'achat au prix coûtant f, méthode de consolidation par intégration globale f; ~ **note** n bordereau d'achat m; ~ **order** n bon de commande m; ~ **price** n prix d'achat m; ~ **price method** n méthode du prix d'achat f; ~ **and resale agreement** n accord de prise en pension m, faculté d'achat et de revente f; ~ **and sale statement** n état des achats et des ventes m; ~ **tax** n taxe sur les achats f; ~ **underwriting facility** n mécanisme de garantie d'achat m

purchase² vt acheter; ~ **sth from sb** acheter qch à qn

purchaser n acheteur/-euse m/f, acquéreur/-euse m/f; ~ **behaviour** n comportement d'achat m

purchases n pl achats m pl; ~ **journal** n journal des achats m; ~ **ledger** n journal des achats m

purchasing n achat m, approvisionnement m; ~ **agent** n acheteur/-euse m/f; ~ **company** n société preneuse f; ~ **costs** n pl frais d'achat m pl; ~ **department** n achats m pl, service des achats m; ~ **hedge** n couverture longue f, long hedge m; ~ **manager** n chef des achats m; ~ **motivator** n mobile d'achat m; ~ **power** n pouvoir d'achat m; ~ **power parity** n parité du pouvoir d'achat f

pure adj pur; ~ **competition** n concurrence pure f; ~ **credit economy** n pure économie de crédit f, économie totalement fondée sur le crédit f; ~ **inflation** n inflation pure f; ~ **interest** n intérêt brut m; ~ **interest rate** n taux d'intérêt brut m; ~ **market economy** n économie de marché intégrale f; ~ **monopoly** n monopole intégral m, monopole pur m; ~ **play** adj (company) à activité unique; ~ **player** n société à activité unique f; (on Internet) société point-com f, dotcom f, société dont l'activité se déroule exclusivement sur Internet; ~ **profit** n bénéfice net m

purpose n (aim) but m, objet m; (use) usage m; **for the ~ of doing** dans le but de faire; **for business ~s** pour les affaires; **on ~** exprès; **lack ~** être indécis; **to no ~** inutilement; ~ **loan** n prêt pour achat de titres m

purpose-built adj construit sur mesure, fabriqué sur demande

pursuant adj ~ **to** conformément à, en vertu de

pursue vt (policy) mener; (ambition, aim) poursuivre; (excellence) rechercher; ~ **a career in** faire carrière dans

purveyor n fournisseur m

push¹ n (campaign) campagne f; (stimulus)

impulsion f; **sales ~** campagne de promotion des ventes; **a ~ for** une campagne en faveur de; **give sth/sb a ~** encourager qch/qn; **give sth a ~ in the right direction** faire avancer qch dans la bonne direction; **at a ~** (infrml) s'il le faut; ~ **incentive** n (sales) prime à la vente f; ~ **media** n média de diffusion m; ~ **money** n prime au vendeur f; ~ **technology** n distribution personnalisée f, distribution sélective f

push² vt pousser; (product) faire de la promotion pour; (policy, theory) promouvoir; ~ **sb to the limit** pousser qn à bout; ~ **sb into bankruptcy** acculer qn à la faillite; ~ **one's luck** forcer sa chance; ~ **ahead with** (plans) persévérer dans; ~ **back** (date, meeting) repousser; ~ **down** (price, rate) faire chuter; ~ **for** (action, change) faire pression en faveur de; ~ **forward** (idea, proposal) faire valoir; ~ **oneself forward** se mettre en avant; ~ **through** (deal) faire passer; (bill) faire voter; ~ **up** (price, rate) faire monter

put¹ n option de vente f, put m; ~ **bond** n obligation remboursable à périodes déterminées f; ~ **broker** n courtier en options non-agréé m; ~ **and call** n double option f, options de vente et d'achat f pl, stellage m; ~ **exercise price** n prix de levée de l'option de vente m; ~ **option** n contrat d'option de vente m, option de vente f, prix d'option de vente m; ~ **premium** n prime de vente f, prix d'option de vente m; ~ **price** n prix de revente m; ~ **rate** n taux de l'option de vente m; ~ **spread** n opération mixte sur options de vente f; ~ **strike** n prix d'exercice d'une option de vente m, prix de levée de l'option de vente m; ~ **warrant** n warrant à la vente m

put² vt mettre; ~ **an advert in the paper** mettre une annonce dans le journal; ~ **a check in the box** AmE, ~ **a tick in the box** BrE cocher la case; ~ **a damper on** jeter un froid sur; ~ **an embargo on** mettre un embargo sur; ~ **the final touches to,** ~ **the finishing touches to** mettre la dernière main à; ~ **forward a proposal** soumettre une proposition; ~ **in an application for a job** faire une demande d'emploi, poser sa candidature à un poste; ~ **in a claim** faire une réclamation; (Law) faire valoir ses droits; ~ **sb/sth in danger** mettre qn/qch en danger; ~ **in a good word for sb** glisser un mot en faveur de qn; ~ **in place** mettre en place; ~ **in a plea** plaider; ~ **sth in position** mettre qch en place; ~ **sb in touch with** mettre qn en contact avec, mettre qn en relation avec; ~ **into effect** (policy) mettre en vigueur; ~ **sth into execution** mettre qch à exécution; ~ **sth into force** mettre qch en vigueur; ~ **sth into order** mettre qch en ordre; ~ **sth into practice** mettre qch en pratique; ~ **into receivership** mettre en liquidation, placer sous administration judiciaire; ~ **it another way** autrement dit; ~ **money down** verser des arrhes, verser un acompte; ~ **out a statement** publier une déclaration; ~ **a question on the agenda** mettre une question à l'ordre du jour; ~ **sb in the picture** mettre qn au courant; ~ **sth down in writing** consigner qch par écrit; ~ **sth in the window** (highlight) présenter qch sous un jour favorable; ~ **sth on record** consigner qch par écrit; ~ **a suggestion before a committee** soumettre une proposition à un comité; ~ **sth up for sale** mettre qch en vente; ~ **about** (rumour, story) faire circuler; **it is being** ~ **about that...** le bruit court que...; ~ **across** (message, idea, point of view) communiquer; ~ **aside** (funds, money) mettre de côté; ~ **back** (meeting, departure) remettre, repousser; ~ **by** (funds, money) mettre de côté; ~ **down** (write down) écrire, mettre par écrit; ~ **down a deposit** verser des arrhes; ~ **forward** (idea, name) avancer; (plan, proposal, suggestion) soumettre; (opinion) émettre; ~ **oneself forward for a post** se présenter pour un poste; ~ **sb forward** présenter la candidature de qn; ~ **sb forward for a job** proposer qn pour un poste; ~ **in** (request, claim) faire; (sum, amount) contribuer ~ **in an application for** (visa, passport) faire une demande de; (job) poser sa candidature pour; ~ **in a lot of work** se donner beaucoup de mal; ~ **off** (dissuade) dissuader; (meeting, event) remettre à plus tard; (departure) retarder; ~ **off making a decision** retarder le moment de prendre une décision; ~ **on** (show, exhibition)

monter; (connect on the phone) passer; **I'll** ~ **him on** je vous le passe; ~ **out** (report, warning) publier; ~ **out a statement** faire une déclaration; (subcontract) donner en soutraitance; ~ **through** (bill, plan, measure) faire passer; (call, caller) passer; **I'll** ~ **you through to her** je vous la passe; ~ **together** (team, consortium) former; (list) dresser, établir; (newsletter, leaflet) rédiger; (portfolio, file) constituer; (case) constituer; (argument) construire; (presentation, video) préparer, faire; ~ **up** (price, rate) augmenter; (finance, capital, funding) fournir; (notice, sign) mettre; (list) afficher; (building) construire; ~ **sb up for** (leader, chairperson) proposer qn comme; (promotion, post) proposer qn pour

put's strike n cours d'exercice de l'option de vente m

p.v. abbr (▸**par value**) parité f, valeur au pair f, valeur nominale f

pyramid¹ n pyramide f; **age/wage** ~ pyramide des âges/salaires

pyramid² **1** vt structurer en holdings **2** vi (Stock) acheter des titres sur gains précédents

pyramidal adj pyramidal

pyramid selling n vente pyramidale f; ~ **scheme** n système pyramidal m

PYT abbr (▸**payment**) (sum of money) paiement m; (into account) versement m; (instalment) versement m

Qq

QA abbr (▸**quality assurance**) assurance de la qualité f, contrôle de la qualité m

QC abbr (▸**quality control**) contrôle de la qualité m; UK (▸**Queen's Counsel**) avocat de la Couronne

qnty abbr (▸**quantity**) qté (quantité)

qt. abbr (▸**quantity**) qté (quantité)

qtr abbr (▸**quarter**) quart m

quadripartite agreement n accord quadripartite m

qualification n (training, experience) qualification f; (degree, diploma) diplôme m; (modifying condition) condition f, réserve f; (suitability) capacité f, compétence f; (attribute) qualité f; (eligibility) droit m; (Acc) qualification des comptes f; **have the right** ~**s for the job** avoir le profil de l'emploi, avoir les qualifications nécessaires pour le poste; **my only** ~ **is that ...** ma seule réserve est que ...; **without** ~ sans réserve; ~ **of opinion** n

réserve apportée à un rapport d'audit f; ~ **period** n (Gen Comm) période de qualification f; (for benefit) période d'admissibilité f; ~ **shares** n pl actions statutaires f pl

qualified adj (suitable) compétent, qualifié; (trained) diplômé, qualifié; (praise, success) nuancé, mitigé; **be** ~ **to do sth** (Gen Comm) être qualifié pour faire qch; (on paper) avoir les titres requis pour faire qch; ~ **acceptance** n acceptation conditionnelle f, acceptation restreinte f; ~ **accountant** n commissaire aux comptes m, expert-comptable m; ~ **approval** n approbation modérée f; ~ **borrowing** n emprunts de référence m pl; ~ **endorsement** n, ~ **indorsement** n endos conditionnel m; ~ **investment** n placement admissible m; ~ **majority** n majorité qualifiée f; ~ **offer** n offre conditionnelle f; ~ **report** n (Acc) rapport réservé m

qualify **1** vt (statement, approval, opinion) ⋯⊱

nuancer; **~ sb to do sth** (confer the right) autoriser qn à faire qch, donner à qn le droit de faire qch; (equip with skills) donner à qn les compétences pour faire qch

2 *vi* (trainee, student) obtenir son diplôme; (meet criteria) remplir les conditions requises; **~ for** (holiday pay, aid, benefit) avoir droit à

qualifying *adj* (exam, stage) de qualification; **~ annuity** annuité conditionnelle *f*; **~ period** *n* (Gen Comm) période de qualification *f*; (Ins) période admissible *f*; **~ share** *n* action qui donne un droit d'entrée au conseil d'administration *f*; **~ shares** *n pl* actions statutaires *f pl*

qualitative *adj* qualitatif/-ive; **~ analysis** *n* analyse qualitative *f*; **~ approach** *n* approche qualitative *f*; **~ research** *n* recherche qualitative *f*

qualitatively *adv* qualitativement

quality¹ *adj* de qualité

quality² *n* qualité *f*

quality: **~ assessment** *n* évaluation de la qualité *f*; **~ asset** *n* avoir de qualité *m*; **~ assurance** assurance de la qualité *f*, contrôle de la qualité *m*; **~ brand** *n* marque de qualité *f*; **~ certificate** *n* certificat de qualité *m*; **~ circle** *n* cercle de qualité *m*; **~ control** *n* contrôle de la qualité *m*; **~ controller** *n* qualiticien/-ienne *m/f*; **~ engineer** *n* ingénieur qualité *m*; **~ goods** *n pl* marchandises de qualité *f pl*; **~ label** *n* label de qualité *m*; **~ of life** *n* qualité de vie *f*; **~ loan** *n* prêt de qualité *m*; **~ management** *n* gestion de la qualité *f*; **~ market** *n* marché de qualité *m*; **~ newspaper** *n* journal de qualité *m*; **~-price ratio** *n* rapport qualité-prix *m*; **~ standards** *n pl* critères de qualité *m pl*, normes de qualité *f pl*; **~ of working life** *n* qualité de la vie active *f*, qualité de la vie professionnelle *f*

quantifiable *adj* facile à évaluer

quantification *n* approche quantitative *f*

quantify *vt* quantifier

quantitative *adj* quantitatif/-ive; **~ analysis** *n* analyse quantitative *f*; **~ controls** *n pl* contrôles quantitatifs *m pl*; **~ methodology** *n* méthodologie quantitative *f*; **~ research** *n* (market research) recherche quantitative *f*; **~ restriction** *n* restriction quantitative *f*

quantity *n* quantité *f*; **in large quantities** en grande quantité; **discount for ~** remise sur quantité *f*; **unknown ~** inconnue *f*; **~ buyer** *n* acheteur/-euse en gros *m/f*; **~ discount** *n* remise sur la quantité *f*, remise sur volume *f*; **~ surveying** *n* métrage *m*; **~ surveyor** *n* métreur/-euse *m/f*

quarantine *n* quarantaine *f*

quarter *n* (of year) trimestre *m*; (one-fourth) quart *m*; **every ~** chaque trimestre, tous les trimestres; **~ end** *n* fin de trimestre *f*

quarterly¹ *adj* (magazine) trimestriel/-ielle

quarterly² *adv* trimestriellement

quarterly³ *n* (Media) publication trimestrielle *f*

quarterly: **~ dividend** *n* dividende trimestriel *m*; **~ installment** AmE, **~ instalment** *n* BrE versement trimestriel *m*; (Tax) acompte trimestriel *m*; **~ rate bond** *n* bon à taux trimestriel *m*

quartile deviation *n* déviation quartile *f*

quash *vt* (decision, proposal) rejeter; (order, verdict) annuler, casser

quashing *n* (of decision, proposal) rejet *m*; (Law) (of order) annulation *f*; (of verdict) annulation *f*, cassation *f*

quasi- *pref* quasi-; **~-contract** *n* quasi-contrat *m*; **~-money** *n* quasi-monnaie *f*

quay *n* quai *m*

quayage *n* droits de quai *m pl*, quaiage *m*

Queen's Counsel *n* UK *avocat de la Couronne*

query¹ *n* (Comp) interrogation *f*, requête *f*; (question) question *f*; **~ language** *n* langage d'interrogation *m*; **~ mode** *n* mode d'interrogation *m*; **~ window** *n* (for search) fenêtre de requête *f*, champ de requête *m*

query² *vt* (cast doubt) mettre en doute; (question) interroger

question¹ *n* (query) question *f*; (problem) problème *m*; (issue) question *f*; **in ~** en question

question² *vt* (interrogate) questionner; (cast doubt on tactics, motives) mettre en doute; (Law) contester; **~ sb about sth** questionner qn à propos de qch

questionable *adj* (debatable) discutable; (dubious) douteux/-euse

question mark *n* point d'interrogation *m*; (product) dilemme *m*, point d'interrogation *m*; **a ~ mark hangs over his/the plant's future** l'incertitude plane sur son avenir/sur l'avenir de l'usine; **there is a ~ over his competence** on s'interroge quant à sa compétence

questionnaire *n* questionnaire *m*

queue¹ *n* (line of people) BrE file d'attente *f*, queue *f*; (Comp) file d'attente *f*; **~ jumper** *n* BrE resquilleur/-euse *m/f*

queue² **1** *vt* mettre en file d'attente **2** *vi* BrE faire la queue; **~ up** BrE faire la queue

queueing *n* (Comp) mise en file d'attente *f*; **~ system** *n* file d'attente *f*

quick *adj* rapide; **~ assets** *n pl* actif disponible *m*, actif réalisable *m*; **~ fix** *n* solution à court terme *f*; (to case, affair) bouclage rapide *m*; **~ ratio** *n* ratio de liquidité immédiate *m*; **~ returns** *n pl* (Fin) rentrées de fonds rapides *f pl*; **~ sale** *n* vente facile *f*; **~ win** *n* gain rapide *m*

quid *n* BrE (infrml) livre sterling *f*

quid pro quo n (fml) contrepartie f

quiet adj (market, business) calme; **keep sth ~** ne pas divulguer qch

quirk n (anomaly) anomalie f; (deviation) écart m, variation f

quit ⓵ vt (job) démissionner de; (profession) quitter; (Comp) (application) sortir de ⓶ vi (stop) arrêter; (resign) démissionner; (Comp) quitter

quitclaim n renonciation à un droit f

quit rate n taux de départs m

quondam adj (fml) ancien/-ienne

quorum n quorum m; **have a ~** avoir atteint le quorum

quota n (prescribed number) quota m; (share) part f; **~ fixing** n contingentement m; **~ sample** n échantillon par quota m; **~ sampling** n sondage par quota m; **~ system** n contingentement m, système de quotas m

quotable adj (Stock) cotable

quotation n (Fin) cote f, cours m; (estimate) devis m; (Ins) cotation f; (Stock) cotation f, cote f, cours m; **~ board** n tableau de cotation m

quote[1] n (estimate) devis m; (Stock) cote f, cours m; **~ value** n valeur à la cote f

quote[2] vt (price, cost) indiquer; (Stock) (at par) coter; **~ a reference number** rappeler un numéro de référence; **they ~d us £200 for the repairs** dans leur devis ils ont demandé 200 livres sterling pour la réparation; **~ for** (work, service) établir un devis pour

quoted adj (Stock) coté, coté en bourse; **~ at** coté à; **~ company** n société cotée en bourse f; **~ price** n cours inscrit à la cote officielle m, prix coté m; **~ securities** n pl titres admis à la cote officielle m pl, valeurs cotées f pl; **~ security** n valeur cotée en bourse f, valeur inscrite à la cote f; **~ share** n action cotée f, action inscrite à la cote officielle f

quotient n quotient m

qv abbr (**quod vide**) voir

QWERTY keyboard n clavier QWERTY m

Rr

R/A abbr (▸**refer to acceptor**) voir le tiré

racial discrimination n discrimination raciale f

rack: ~ up vi (profit) réaliser; (success) remporter; (sales) totaliser

racket n (infml) (swindle) escroquerie f; **the drugs ~** le trafic des stupéfiants m; **be in on the ~** être dans le coup (infml)

racketeer n racketteur m

racketeering n racket m

radical adj radical

radio n radio f; **on the ~** à la radio; **~ advertising** n publicité radiophonique f; **~ audience** n auditeurs m pl; **~ broadcast** n émission de radio f, émission radiophonique f; **~ broadcasting** n diffusion radiophonique f; **~ commercial** n message publicitaire à la radio m; **~ program** AmE, **~ programme** BrE n émission de radio f, émission radiophonique f; **~ station** n station de radio f

raft n (of policies, measures) ensemble m

rag n (infml) (newspaper) canard m (infml); **~ trade** n (infml) confection f

raid[1] n (Stock) raid m; (by customs, police) rafle f

raid[2] vt (fund, reserves) entamer; **~ a company** lancer une OPA contre une société;

~ the market (Stock) attaquer le marché, exercer une pression à la baisse sur le marché

raidable adj (Stock) opéable

raider n prédateur m, raider m

rail n chemin de fer m; **by ~** par chemin de fer, par rail; **~-air link** n liaison train-avion f; **~ freight** n transport par chemin de fer m; **~ link** n liaison ferroviaire f; **~ network** n réseau ferroviaire m; **~ service** n service ferroviaire m; **~ shipment** n expédition par chemin de fer f; **~ strike** n grève des cheminots f, grève des chemins de fer f; **~ system** n réseau de chemins de fer m, réseau ferroviaire m; **~ terminal** n gare f; **~ ticket** n billet de train m; **~ timetable** n horaire des trains m; **~ traffic** n trafic ferroviaire m; **~ transport** n transport ferroviaire m; **~ user** n usager du chemin de fer m

railroad n AmE chemin de fer m; **~ bill** n lettre de voiture ferroviaire f; **~ consignment note** n AmE lettre de voiture ferroviaire f; **~ line** n voie ferrée f; **~ service** n service ferroviaire m; **~ station** n gare f; **~ system** n réseau de chemin de fer m, réseau ferroviaire m; **~ timetable** n horaire des trains m; **~ track** n voie ferrée f; **~ worker** n cheminot m

railway n BrE chemin de fer m; **use the** ∼ voyager en train; ∼ **bill** n lettre de voiture ferroviaire f; ∼ **consignment note** n lettre de voiture ferroviaire f; ∼ **line** n voie ferrée f; ∼ **service** n service ferroviaire m; ∼ **station** n gare f; ∼ **system** n réseau de chemin de fer m, réseau ferroviaire m; ∼ **timetable** n horaire des trains m; ∼ **track** n voie ferrée f; ∼ **worker** n cheminot m

railyard n AmE dépôt m

raise¹ n AmE (pay increase) augmentation f

raise² vt (ban, embargo) lever; (price, offer, salary, value, rate) augmenter; (invoice) rédiger; (doubts, fears, suspicion) faire naître; (problem, issue) soulever; (age limit) reculer; ∼ **the alarm** donner l'alarme; ∼ **awareness of** faire prendre conscience de; ∼ **the bidding** (at auction) monter l'enchère; ∼ **capital** mobiliser des capitaux, se procurer des capitaux; ∼ **a check** AmE faire un chèque; ∼ **finance** réunir des fonds, se procurer de l'argent, se procurer des capitaux; ∼ **external funds** mobiliser des fonds extérieurs; ∼ **in line with inflation** (price, benefit, salary) relever conformément à l'inflation; ∼ **a loan** émettre un emprunt; ∼ **money** réunir des fonds, se procurer de l'argent; ∼ **money on sth** emprunter de l'argent sur qch; ∼ **a question** poser une question; ∼ **an objection** émettre une objection; ∼ **a tax** imposer une taxe, lever une taxe; ∼ **one's sights** augmenter ses prétentions

raising n (of embargo) levée f; (of price, value, salary) augmentation f; (Tax) levée f; ∼ **of capital** mobilisation de capitaux f; ∼ **of funds** mobilisation de fonds f

rake: ∼ **in** vt (money, profits) amasser; ∼ **it in** (infrml) remuer l'argent à la pelle (infrml)

rake-off n (infrml) pourcentage m, commission f; **get a** ∼ toucher un pourcentage, toucher une commission

rally¹ n (of market, shares) reprise f, redressement m; **stage a** ∼ (price, currency) remonter

rally² ① vt (support, supporters) rassembler; (public opinion) rallier
② vi (market, shares) reprendre, se redresser; (currency, price) remonter

rallying n (of market, shares) redressement m, reprise f; (of prices, rates) remontée f; ∼ **point** n point de ralliement m

RAM abbr (▸random access memory) mémoire RAM f, mémoire vive f

ramp¹ n (swindle) (infrml) majoration exorbitante des prix f; (for vehicle) rampe f; (for loading) plate-forme de chargement f

ramp²: ∼ **up** vt (infrml) (production, prices) augmenter

rand n rand m

R&D abbr (▸research and development) R&D f (recherche et développement); ∼ **expenditures** n pl dépenses de R&D f pl

random¹ adj (fait) au hasard, aléatoire; **on a** ∼ **basis** au hasard

random² n **at** ∼ au hasard

random: ∼ **access** n accès direct m; ∼ **access memory** n mémoire RAM f, mémoire vive f; ∼ **check** n contrôle fait au hasard m; (statistics) contrôle par sondage m, contrôle par sélection aléatoire m; ∼ **error** n erreur aléatoire f; ∼ **number** n nombre aléatoire m; ∼**-number generator** n générateur de nombres aléatoires m; ∼ **observation method** n méthode des observations instantanées f; ∼ **sample** n échantillon aléatoire m; ∼ **sampling** n sondage aléatoire m, échantillonnage aléatoire m; ∼ **selection** n sélection aléatoire f; ∼ **variable** n variable aléatoire f; ∼ **variation** n variation aléatoire f; ∼ **walk theory** n théorie des variations aléatoires f

randomization n procédé de répartition aléatoire m

randomize vt randomiser

randomly adv au hasard, de façon aléatoire

range¹ n (of people, abilities, opinions) variété f; (of salaries, incentives) éventail m; (of issues) série f; (scope) étendue f; (of products, colours, prices) gamme f; (of options, activities) éventail m, choix m; (Math) échelle f; (Stock) (futures market) fourchette f, écart maximal hauts-bas m; (Tax) tranche de revenu f; **be out of** ∼ être hors de portée; **price/salary** ∼ éventail de prix/des salaires; **age** ∼ tranche d'âge f; **in the** ∼ **of 15-20%** dans les 15 à 20%; **in the 200-300 dollar** ∼ entre 200 et 300 dollars; **in a wide** ∼ **of prices** à tous les prix; ∼ **of products** gamme de produits f

range² vi (vary) varier; ∼ **from x to y** aller de x à y

rank¹ n rang m; **the** ∼ **and file** la base f; **pull** ∼ abuser de son rang; ∼ **order** n ordre de rang m

rank² ① vt classer
② vi se classer; ∼ **among** être classé parmi; **be** ∼**ed first** être classé en première place; ∼ **above** être supérieur à; ∼ **after** (Stock) être primé par; ∼ **below** être inférieur à

ranking n classement m; **improve one's** ∼ monter dans le classement

rapid adj rapide; ∼ **growth** n croissance rapide f; ∼ **transit system** n réseau express régional m

rapidly adv rapidement

rapprochement n rapprochement m

ratchet effect n effet de cliquet m

rate¹ n (number of occurrences) taux m; **birth** ∼ taux de natalité; (price, charge) tarif m; (Fin) (price) cours m; (charge for work) tarif m; (of currency) cours m; (speed) cadence f; (of work, production) rythme m, cadence f; (percentage) taux m; **at a** ∼ **of** à raison de; **at a fast** ∼ rapidement; **take the** ∼ (Stock) prendre le taux, reporter; **at the** ∼ **of** au rythme de, à la cadence de; ∼ **to be agreed** tarif à déterminer; **going** ∼ tarif courant *m*; ∼ **of absenteeism** taux d'absentéisme *m*; ∼ **of adoption** (S&M) taux d'adoption *m*; ∼ **asked** *n* (Stock) taux demandé *m*; ∼ **capping** *n* plafonnement des impôts locaux *m*; ∼ **ceiling** *n* plafond des taux *m*; ∼ **cutting** *n* réduction des tarifs *f*; ∼ **of decay** taux de déclin *m*, taux de dépréciation *m*; ∼ **of depreciation** taux d'amortissement *m*; ∼ **of discount** taux d'escompte *m*; ∼ **of exchange** taux de change *m*; ∼ **of exploitation** taux d'exploitation *m*, valeur d'excédent *f*; ∼ **fixing** *n* (of prices) fixation des prix *f*; (of charges) fixation des tarifs *f*; ∼ **for the job** salaire proposé pour l'emploi *m*; ∼ **of increase** taux d'accroissement *m*, taux d'augmentation *m*; ∼ **of inflation** taux d'inflation *m*; ∼ **of interest** taux d'intérêt *m*; ∼ **of relief** (Tax) taux de dégrèvement *m*; ∼ **resetting** refixation de taux *f*; ∼ **of return** rentabilité *f*, taux de rendement *m*; ∼ **of return on capital employed** taux de rendement des capitaux investis *m*, taux de rendement sur le capital employé *m*; ∼ **of surplus value** taux de la valeur excédentaire *m*; ∼ **tart** *n* BrE (infrml) (Fin) *personne qui change d'emprunt-logement ou de compte d'épargne à chaque fois qu'une offre à un taux plus avantageux se présente*; ∼ **of tax**, ∼ **of taxation** taux d'imposition *m*, taux d'impôt *m*; ∼ **of transfer** (Comp) taux de transfert *m*; ∼ **of turnover** vitesse de rotation *f*; ∼ **variance** *n* écart sur taux *m*; ∼ **war** *n* guerre des tarifs *f*

rate² *vt* (Fin, Stock) (company) noter; (evaluate) classer, évaluer; (deserve) mériter

rateable *adj* (value) imposable

rated *adj* (Fin) coté; **not** ∼ pas coté; ∼ **policy** *n* (Ins) police tarifée *f*

ratepayer *n* contribuable *mf*

rates *n pl* UK (local tax) ≈ impôts locaux *m pl*; (amount charged) tarifs *m pl*; ∼ **review** *n* révision des tarifs *f*; ∼ **structure** *n* structure tarifaire *f*

ratification *n* (of treaty) ratification *f*; (Law) validation *f*

ratify *vt* (treaty) ratifier; (Law) valider

rating *n* (Stock) notation *f*; (assessment) évaluation *f*, appréciation *f*; (rank, position) classement *m*, notation *f*; (in the polls) cote *f*; **achieve a good** ∼ être bien classé; **approval** ∼ indice de satisfaction *m*; **credit** ∼ réputation de solvabilité *f*; **market** ∼ cours en bourse *m*; **popularity** ∼ cote de popularité *f*; **share** ∼ cote en bourse *f*; ∼ **agency** *n* agence d'évaluation financière *f*, agence de notation *f*; ∼ **scale** *n* échelle d'évaluation *f*

ratings *n pl* (Media) indice d'écoute *m*, audimat® *m*

ratio *n* rapport *m*; (Fin, Stock) ratio *m*; (Math) ratio *m*; **the** ∼ **of x to y** le ratio de x à y; **in a** ∼ **of 5:7** dans une proportion de 5 à 7; **in**

inverse/direct ∼ **to** en raison inverse/directe de; ∼ **analysis** *n* analyse de rapport *f*; ∼ **call spread** *n* écart vertical sur ratio d'options de vente *m*; ∼ **put spread** *n* (options) écart vertical sur ratio d'options d'achat *m*

ration *vt* rationner

rational *adj* (argument, decision) rationnel/ -elle; (person) raisonnable; ∼ **expectations** *n pl* anticipations rationnelles *f pl*, prévisions rationnelles *f pl*; ∼ **management** *n* gestion rationnelle *f*

rationale *n* (reasons) raisons *m pl*; (logic) logique *f*; **the** ∼ **for doing** les raisons de faire; **the** ∼ **behind sth** la logique de qch

rationalization *n* rationalisation *f*; ∼ **program** AmE, ∼ **programme** BrE *n* programme de rationalisation *m*

rationalize *vt* (company, industry) rationaliser; (justify) justifier

rationing *n* rationnement *m*

rat race *n* foire d'empoigne *f*

raw *adj* (Comp, Math) brut, non traité; ∼ **data** *n* données brutes *f pl*; ∼ **land** *n* terre vierge *f*; ∼ **material** *n* matière brute *f*, matière première *f*

rcvd *abbr* (▸**received**) pour acquit, reçu

RD *abbr* (**refer to drawer**) voir le tireur; (▸**reserve deposit**) dépôt de couverture bancaire *m*, réserve obligatoire *f*

RDB *abbr* (▸**relational database**) BDR *f* (base de données relationnelles)

re *prep* (about) au sujet de, concernant, en ce qui concerne; (in letterhead, email) 'objet'; ∼ **your letter** suite à votre lettre

reach¹ *n* (audience) audience cumulée *f*; (of campaign, advert) portée *f*; **be within** ∼ être à portée de main; **be out of** ∼ être hors de portée; **put sth within/beyond sb's** ∼ mettre qch à la/hors de la portée de qn

reach² *vt* (deal, settlement) conclure; (place) arriver à, atteindre; (peak, level, age limit) atteindre; (decision, compromise, conclusion) arriver à; (audience) toucher; (contact) joindre; ∼ **an accommodation with sb** arriver à un compromis avec qn; ∼ **an agreement** parvenir à un accord; ∼ **a deal** conclure un marché, conclure une affaire; ∼ **saturation point** arriver à saturation; ∼ **a total of** atteindre un total de

reachback *n* (Tax) arriéré *m*

react *vi* réagir; ∼ **to** réagir à

reaction *n* réaction *f*; ∼ **time** *n* temps de latence *m*, temps de réaction *m*

reactionary¹ *adj* réactionnaire

reactionary² *n* réactionnaire *mf*

read *vt* (Gen Comm, Comp) lire; ∼ **law** faire son droit; ∼ **the tape** (Stock) lire le téléscripteur; ∼ **out** lire à haute voix; ∼ **over**, ∼ **through** lire; (a second time) relire; ∼ **up on** étudier à fond

readable *adj* lisible

reader n lecteur/-trice m/f

readership n lecteurs m pl, lectorat m

reading n lecture f

readjust vt (salary, forecast) réajuster

readjustment n réajustement m

read notification n (Comp) accusé de lecture m, confirmation de lecture f

read-only memory n mémoire morte f

readvertise ① vt (post, item) refaire paraître une annonce pour ② vi refaire paraître une annonce

readvertisement n deuxième annonce f

ready adj (prepared) prêt; (easily available) à portée de main; ~ **for shipment** prêt pour l'expédition; ~ **to hand** sous la main; ~ **to do** prêt à faire; ~ **assets trusts** n pl trusts d'actifs disponibles m pl; ~ **cash** n, ~ **money** n (Fin) argent liquide m, liquide m; ~ **reckoner** n barème de calculs m; ~-**to-wear** adj prêt-à-porter

ready-made adj (Gen Comm) tout-fait; ~ **clothing** prêt-à-porter m

reaffirm vt réaffirmer

reafforestation n reboisement m

real adj réel/réelle; **in ~ terms** en termes réels; ~ **agreement** n (Law) bail m; ~ **cost** n coût réel m; ~ **earnings** n pl revenu réel m; ~ **estate** n biens immobiliers m pl; ~ **estate agency** n US agence immobilière f; ~ **estate appraisal** n US évaluation de biens immobiliers f, évaluation immobilière f; ~ **estate business** n (sector) l'immobilier m; ~ **estate company** n société immobilière f; ~ **estate fund** n US fonds de placement en biens immobiliers m; ~ **estate investment trust** n US fonds de placements immobiliers m, société civile de placement immobilier f; ~ **estate market** n marché de l'immobilier m; ~ **estate register** n, ~ **estate registry** n US cadastre m; ~ **growth** n croissance effective f, croissance réelle f; ~ **income** n revenu réel m; ~ **interest rate** n taux d'intérêt réel m; ~ **investment** n (for hospitals, schools) investissement collectif m; ~ **rate of return** n taux de rendement réel m; ~ **wage** n salaire réel m

realign vt (Fin, Pol) (currency, stance) réaligner; (views) redéfinir

realignment n (Fin, Pol) (of currency, stance) réalignement m; (of views) redéfinition f

realism n réalisme m

realistic adj réaliste

realizable adj réalisable; ~ **assets** n pl actif réalisable m

realization n (Fin) réalisation f, liquidation f; (of goal, plan) réalisation f; (awareness) prise de conscience f; ~ **of assets** réalisation d'éléments d'actif f

realize vt (Fin) (profit, goal, plan, dream) réaliser; (become aware of) prendre conscience de, se rendre compte de; ~ **assets** réaliser des actifs, liquider des actifs; ~ **one's potential**

développer ses capacités; (fetch a certain price) rapporter; **the sale ~d £300,000** la vente a rapporté 300 000 livres sterling

realized: ~ **gains** n pl gains réalisés m pl; ~ **losses** n pl pertes réalisées f pl

reallocate vt (person, funds) réaffecter; (resources, tasks) redistribuer, réattribuer

reallocation n (of person, funds) réaffectation f; (of tasks, resources) redistribution f, réattribution f

reallowance n (Stock) réattribution f

realpolitik n realpolitik f

real time n (Acc, Comp, Econ) temps réel m; **in ~** en temps réel; ~ **chat** n bavardage en temps réel m; ~ **transmission** n transmission en temps réel f

realtor n AmE agent immobilier m

reap vt (profits) récolter; ~ **the benefits**, ~ **the rewards** récolter les bénéfices

reapply vi reposer sa candidature; ~ **for a job** reposer sa candidature à un poste

reappoint vt renommer

reappointment n renouvellement de nomination m

reappraisal n (of policy, issue) réexamen m; (of work) réévaluation f

reappraise vt (policy, issue) réexaminer; (work) réévaluer

reason n raison f; **for any ~** pour quelque raison que ce soit; **without good ~** sans raison valable; **for ~s of time** pour des raisons de temps; **for health ~s** pour raisons de santé; **by ~ of** en raison de; **the ~ given is that** la raison invoquée est que; **have good ~ to do** avoir tout lieu de faire; **all the more ~ to do** raison de plus pour faire; **with good ~** à juste titre; **within ~** dans la limite du raisonnable; **it stands to ~ that...** il va sans dire que...

reasonable adj (person, claim, expense) raisonnable; (moderately priced) abordable, raisonnable; (justified) légitime; **beyond ~ doubt** sans aucun doute possible

reasoned adj (argument, approach) raisonné

reasoning n raisonnement m

reassess vt (Tax) (person) fixer une nouvelle cotisation pour; (tax) recalculer; (Law) (damages) réévaluer; (problem, situation) réexaminer, reconsidérer; (policy) réexaminer, revoir

reassessment n (Tax) nouvelle cotisation f; (Law) (of damages) réévaluation f; (of situation) réexamen m; (of policy) réexamen m, révision f

reassign vt réaffecter

reassignment n réaffectation f

reassurance n (security) assurance f; (Ins) réassurance f; (comfort) réconfort m

reassure vt (comfort) rassurer; (Ins) réassurer; ~ **sb about sth** rassurer qn sur qch

rebate n (of interest) bonification f; (refund)

remboursement *m*; (on goods) remise *f*, rabais *m*; (Tax) dégrèvement *m*

reboot *vt* réamorcer

rebrand *vt* changer la marque de

rebranding *n* changement de marque *m*

rebuild *vt* (building, business) reconstruire

recalculate *vt* recalculer

recall¹ *n* (of faulty goods) rappel *m*; (of option) rachetée *f*, rappel *m*; (of brand name) mémorisation *f*; ~ **rate** *n* taux de mémorisation *m*; ~ **test** *n* test de mémorisation *m*, test de rappel *m*

recall² *vt* (faulty goods) rappeler; (option) racheter, rappeler; (person) rappeler

recapitalization *n* restructuration du capital *f*, recapitalisation *f*

recapitalize *vt* (company) recapitaliser, restructurer le capital de

recapture *vt* (market) reprendre

recast *vt* (debt, organization) refondre; (text) remanier; (argument, phrase) reformuler

recede *vi* (prices) baisser; (threat) s'éloigner; (prospect, possibility) s'estomper

receipt¹ *n* reçu *m*, récépissé *m*; (Stock) reçu *m*; (act of receiving) réception *f*; (from till) ticket de caisse *m*; (on receipt of delivery) accusé de réception *m*; **be in ~ of** (letter, payment) avoir reçu; (income, benefits) recevoir; **on ~** (of goods, document) sur réception; **on ~ of** dès réception de; **acknowledge ~ of sth** accuser réception de qch; **within 7 days of ~** à 7 jours de la réception; ~ **book** *n* carnet de quittances *m*; ~ **for payment** quittance *f*; ~ **of goods** (cargo) réception des marchandises *f*; ~ **stamp** *n* timbre de quittance *m*

receipt² *vt* (invoice) acquitter

receipts *n pl* recettes *f pl*, rentrées *f pl*

receivable¹ *adj* **accounts ~** comptes clients *m pl*, créances *f pl*; ~ **basis** *n* comptabilité client *f*, comptabilité de trésorerie *f*

receivable² *n* (Acc, Fin) créance *f*

receivables *n pl* (Acc, Fin) comptes clients *m pl*, créances *f pl*; ~ **turnover** *n* (Fin) volume d'effets à recevoir *m*

receive *vt* recevoir; (goods) réceptionner; ~ **benefit** UK toucher des allocations; ~ **financial help** bénéficier d'une aide financière; ~ **notice of** recevoir notification de; ~ **versus payment** recevoir contre paiement; **be positively ~d, be well ~d** être bien reçu, être bien accueilli

received *adj* (on invoice) pour acquit, reçu; (idea) reçu

receiver *n* (on telephone) combiné *m*; (in bankruptcy) liquidateur *m*, administrateur judiciaire *m*; (of mail) destinataire *mf*; (of delivery, goods) réceptionnaire *mf*; **pick up the ~** décrocher; **put down the ~** raccrocher; **be in the hands of the ~** être en règlement judiciaire; ~ **and manager** (in bankruptcy) administrateur judiciaire *m*, syndic de faillite *m*

receivership *n* mise en administration judiciaire *f*, mise en liquidation *f*; **go into ~** être mis en règlement judiciaire, être placé sous administration judiciaire; **be in ~** être en liquidation

recent *adj* récent; **in ~ years** au cours des dernières années

reception *n* (desk) accueil *m*; (in offices, hotel) réception *f*; (response) accueil *m*, réception *f*; (party) réception *f*; **get a good ~** être bien accueilli, être bien reçu; ~ **area** *n* accueil *m*, réception *f*

receptionist *n* réceptionniste *mf*

receptiveness *n* réceptivité *f*

recession *n* crise économique *f*, récession *f*; **be in ~** être en récession; **go into ~** entrer dans la récession

recessionary *adj* récessionniste; ~ **gap** *n* écart déflationniste *m*, écart récessionniste *m*; ~ **phase** *n* phase de récession *f*

recipient *n* (Gen Comm, Fin) bénéficiaire *mf*; (of allowance) allocataire *mf*; (of mail) destinataire *mf*

reciprocal *adj* réciproque; ~ **agreement** *n* accord bilatéral *m*; ~ **buying** *n* compensation *f*; ~ **taxation agreement** *n* accord de réciprocité fiscale *m*; ~ **trading** *n* commerce réciproque *m*; ~ **trading agreements** *n pl* accords commerciaux de réciprocité *m pl*

reciprocally *adv* réciproquement

reciprocate ① *vt* rendre, donner en retour; ~ **a service** rendre le même service; ~ **an entry** (Acc) passer une écriture en conformité ② *vi* rendre la pareille

reciprocity *n* réciprocité *f*

reckon *vt* calculer; ~ **up** calculer

reckoning *n* (Acc) calcul *m*, compte *m*; (approximate calculation) estimation *f*; **by my ~** d'après mes estimations

reclaim *vt* (land) mettre en valeur; (luggage, possessions, money) récupérer

reclaimed area *n* terrain remis en valeur *m*

reclaiming *n* (of land) mise en valeur *f*; (of cargo, possessions, luggage) récupération *f*

reclassification *n* reclassement *m*, reclassification *f*

reclassify *vt* reclasser

recognition *n* (Gen Comm) reconnaissance *f*; (of trade union) reconnaissance *f*; (Law) confirmation *f*, reconnaissance *f*; (identification) identification *f*; **brand ~** identification de la marque *f*; **win ~ for** être reconnu pour; **in ~ of** en reconnaissance de

recognize *vt* (identify, acknowledge) reconnaître; (Acc) (transaction) constater; (trade union) reconnaître; ~ **a loss** (Acc) constater une perte

recognized *adj* (union, body, party) reconnu; ⋯⋯

~ investment exchange n (Stock) marché d'investissement agréé m

recommend vt (commend) recommander; (advise) conseiller, recommander

recommendation n recommandation f; **letter of ~** lettre de recommandation f

recommended retail price n prix conseillé m

recompile vt recompiler

reconcile vt (Acc, Bank) (accounting statements) rapprocher; (people) réconcilier; (ideas, views) concilier

reconciliation n (of accounting statements) concordance f, rapprochement m; (of people) reconciliation f, (of views) conciliation f; **~ account** n compte collectif m; **~ of accounts** n rapprochement de comptes m; **~ statement** n (Acc) état de concordance m, état de rapprochement m; **~ table** n (Acc) tableau de concordance m

recondition vt remettre à neuf, rénover

reconditioned adj remis à neuf, rénové

reconditioning n remise à neuf f, rénovation f

reconfiguration n reconfiguration f

reconfigure vt reconfigurer

reconsider ① vt réexaminer ② vi (change one's mind) changer d'avis; (think harder) repenser

reconstruct vt (finances, company) reconstituer; (economy, building) reconstruire

reconstruction n (of company) reconstitution f, reconstruction f; (of economy, building) reconstruction f

recontract n contrat définitif m

record¹ n (account) compte rendu m; (of proceedings, in court) procès-verbal m; (file) dossier m; **personnel/medical ~** dossier personnel/médical; (archive material) archives f pl; **employment ~** antécédents professionnels m pl; (reputation) réputation f; **have a good/poor ~ on safety** avoir une bonne/mauvaise réputation en ce qui concerne la sécurité; (criminal past) casier judiciaire m; (Comp) (in database) enregistrement m; (best performance) record m; **set/hold the ~** établir/détenir le record; **keep a ~ of** noter; **put sth on ~** consigner qch par écrit; **have no ~ of** n'avoir aucune trace de; **in ~ time** en temps record; **say sth off the ~** dire qch en privé; **be on ~ as stating that** avoir déclaré officiellement que; **set the ~ straight** mettre les choses au clair; **reach a ~ high** atteindre un niveau record; **be at a ~ low** avoir atteint son niveau le plus bas; **for the ~** pour mémoire; **~ card** n fiche f; **~ company** n maison de disque f; **~ keeper** n archiviste mf; **~ office** n (Admin) bureau des archives m; (Law) greffe m; **~ results** n pl résultats record m pl; **~ sales** n pl ventes record f pl; **~ year** n année record f

record² vt (detail, information) noter; (for official purposes) enregistrer; (on tape, equipment) enregistrer; (Stock) (high, low) enregistrer; **~ a meeting** établir le procès-verbal d'une réunion

record-breaking adj record inv, qui bat tous les records

recorded adj (message) enregistré; (broadcast) en différé

recorded delivery n envoi recommandé m; **send sth ~** envoyer qch en recommandé

recording n enregistrement m

records n pl (Acc) registres m pl; (Admin) dossiers m pl; (historical files) archives f pl; **our ~ show that ...** d'après nos dossiers...

recoup vt (money) récupérer; (losses) compenser; **~ one's costs** rentrer dans ses frais

recourse n recours m; **have ~ to** avoir recours à; **with ~** avec recours; **without ~ to** sans recours à; **~ loan** n emprunt de recours m

recover ① vt (debt) recouvrer; (losses) compenser; (data, property) récupérer; (assets) recouvrer, récupérer; **~ one's investment** rentrer dans ses fonds ② vi (market, economy) se redresser; (shares, currency) remonter; (business) reprendre, repartir; (sales) reprendre, remonter

recoverable adj (Fin) recouvrable; (Ind) récupérable; **~ debt** n dette recouvrable f; **~ material** n matière récupérable f

recovery n (of expenses, debt) recouvrement m; (of assets) recouvrement m, récupération f; (of data, property) récupération f; (return to normal) reprise f; (of shares, currency, prices) remontée f; (Econ) redressement économique m, reprise f; (of market) redressement m, reprise f; **business ~** reprise des affaires f; **stock market ~** remontée de la Bourse f; **~ plan** n (for ailing business) plan de redressement m; (after major incident) plan de secours m; **~ scheme** n plan de relance m; **~ vehicle** n BrE dépanneuse f

recpt abbr (▶receipt) (Gen Comm) reçu m, récépissé m; (Bank, Fin Stock) reçu m

recreation n (leisure) loisirs m pl; **~ area** n salle de récréation f

recruit¹ n recrue f

recruit² vt recruter

recruiting: ~ office n bureau de recrutement m; **~ officer** n recruteur/-euse m/f

recruitment n recrutement m; **~ and selection** le recrutement et la sélection; **~ agency** n cabinet de recrutement m; **~ bonus** n prime de recrutement f; **~ consultant** n conseil en recrutement m; **~ drive** n campagne de recrutement f; **~ manager** n directeur/-trice du recrutement m/f

rectification n rectification f

rectify *vt* rectifier

recto *n* recto *m*

recur *vi* (event, error) se reproduire; (problem) réapparaître; (opportunity) se représenter

recurrent *n* récurrent

recyclable *adj* recyclable

recycle *vt* (waste) recycler; (Fin) (profits, revenue) réinvestir

recycled paper *n* papier recyclé *m*

recycling *n* recyclage *m*; ~ **of waste** recyclage des déchets *m*

red¹ *adj* rouge

red² *n* **be in the** ~ (individual) être à découvert; (company) être en déficit; **go into the** ~ (individual) avoir un découvert; (company) avoir un déficit

red: ~ **clause** *n* (Bank) clause rouge *f*; ~ **goods** *n pl* produits de grande consommation *m pl*; ~ **herring** *n* US (Stock) prospectus provisoire *m*; (diversion) faux problème *m*; ~ **tape** *n* (Admin) excès de formalités administratives *m*

redeem *vt* (Acc) rembourser; (buy back) racheter; (loan, debt) amortir, rembourser; (mortgage) purger; (Stock) (bond) amortir, rembourser

redeemable *adj* (before maturity, in advance) amortissable, rachetable, remboursable; ~ **bond** *n* obligation amortissable *f*, obligation rachetable *f*, obligation remboursable *f*; ~ **preference share** *n* action de priorité amortissable *f*, action privilégiée amortissable *f*; ~ **stock** *n* actions rachetables *f pl*, actions remboursables *f pl*

redeemed *adj* (bond) amorti, remboursé; (share) racheté; (mortgage) purgé

redemption *n* (buying back) rachat *m*; (Fin) (of bond, loan, debt) amortissement *m*, remboursement *m*; (of mortgage) purge *f*; ~ **before due date** (Fin) remboursement anticipé *m*, remboursement avant la date d'échéance *m*; ~ **bond** *n* obligation de conversion *f*; ~ **call** *n* (Stock) appel au rachat *m*; ~ **clause** *n* clause de réméré *f*; ~ **date** *n* date de remboursement *f*, date de règlement *f*; ~ **fee** *n* frais de rachat *m pl*; ~ **fund** *n* fonds d'amortissement *m*; ~ **premium** *n* prime de remboursement *f*; ~ **price** *n* prix de rachat *m*; ~ **table** *n* (Acc) tableau de remboursement *m*; ~ **value** *n* valeur de rachat *f*; ~ **yield** *n* rendement sur remboursement *m*, taux actuariel *m*

redeploy *vt* (staff) réaffecter; (resources) redéployer

redeployment *n* (of staff) réaffectation *f*; (of resources) redéploiement *m*

redevelop *vt* réaménager

redevelopment *n* réaménagement *m*; ~ **plan** *n* programme de réaménagement *m*

redirect *vt* (mail) faire suivre

rediscount *n* réescompte *m*

rediscountable *adj* réescomptable

rediscounter *n* réescompteur *m*

rediscounting *n* réescompte *m*

redistribute *vt* redistribuer

redistribution *n* redistribution *f*

redlining *n* refus d'accorder des prêts hypothécaires dans certains quartiers

redraft *vt* rédiger à nouveau

redress¹ *n* réparation *f*, réparation légale *f*; **seek** ~ demander réparation; **we have no (means of)** ~ nous n'avons aucun recours

redress² *vt* (errors) réparer; (situation) redresser; ~ **the balance** rétablir l'équilibre

reduce *vt* (consumption, investment) réduire; (inflation) freiner; (production) ralentir; (staff, total, impact, number, unemployment) réduire; (price, rate, cost) baisser; (workforce) comprimer; (taxation) alléger

reduced *adj* réduit; (at sale price) en solde, soldé; **be** ~ être en solde; **be** ~ **from 100 euros to 80 euros** être vendu 80 euros au lieu de 100 euros; **buy at a** ~ **price** acheter à prix réduit; ~ **fare** *n* tarif réduit *m*; ~ **lead time** *n* diminution du temps de réalisation *f*; ~ **price** *n* prix réduit *m*; ~ **rate** *n* taux réduit *m*; ~ **tax** *n* impôt réduit *m*

reduction *n* (Gen Comm) réduction *f*; (in price) réduction *f*, rabais *m*; (of workforce, salary) compression *f*; (Tax) allègement *m*; ~ **in the number of working hours** réduction du temps de travail *f*; ~ **in capital** (Stock) réduction de capital *f*; ~ **in value** (of asset) moins-value *f*, dépréciation *f*

redundancy *n* (dismissal of employee) licenciement *m*; (Comp) redondance *f*; ~ **check** *n* (Comp) contrôle par redondance *m*; ~ **letter** *n* lettre de licenciement *f*; ~ **pay** *n* indemnité de licenciement *f*, prime de licenciement *f*; ~ **payment** *n* indemnité de licenciement *f*, prime de licenciement *f*; ~ **plan**, ~ **programme** *n* plan social *m*

redundant *adj* (building, machinery) inutilisé; (superfluous) en surnombre, superflu; (dismissed) licencié; **be made** ~ être licencié, être mis au chômage; **make** ~ licencier, mettre au chômage

re-elect *vt* réélire

re-election *n* réélection *f*; **be up for** ~ se présenter pour un nouveau mandat; **stand for** ~ se représenter

re-embark *vti* rembarquer

re-embarkation *n* rembarquement *m*

re-employ *vt* (person) réembaucher; (method, product) réemployer

re-employment *n* réembauche *f*

re-endorsement *n* (Bank) nouvel aval *m*

re-engage *vt* réengager

re-engagement *n* réengagement *m*

re-engineer *vt* reconfigurer

re-engineering *n* reconfiguration *f*

re-enter *vt* (data) réintroduire; (country) revenir dans, entrer à nouveau dans

re-establish vt rétablir

re-establishment n rétablissement m

re-evaluate vt réévaluer

re-evaluation n réévaluation f

re-examination n nouvel examen m, réexamen m

re-examine vt examiner de nouveau, réexaminer

re-export[1] n réexportation f

re-export[2] vt réexporter

re-exportation n réexportation f

re-exporter n réexportateur/-trice m/f

ref. abbr (▶**reference**) réf. (référence)

refer [1] vt (decision, matter, problem) renvoyer; (Law) (case) déférer; ~ **sth back to sb** (decision, matter) renvoyer qch à qn; ~ **sb to** (department, person) renvoyer qn à; ~ **sth to arbitration** soumettre qch à l'arbitrage [2] vi ~ **to** (letter, document) se référer à; (notes) consulter; (event, issue, person) faire allusion à, parler de; (footnote, date, brochure, price list) se reporter à, se référer à; ~ **back to sth** revenir sur qch; ~ **to acceptor** voir le tiré; ~ **to drawer** voir le tireur

referee n personne pouvant fournir des références f; **act as a** ~ **for sb** fournir des références sur qn; ~ **in case of need** n (Bank) recommandataire mf

reference[1] n (on letter) référence f; (of employee) références f pl; (allusion) allusion f; **make** ~ **to** faire allusion à; **by** ~ **to** par rapport à; **have excellent** ~**s** avoir d'excellentes références; **take up sb's** ~**s** prendre des renseignements sur qn; **write sb a** ~ fournir des références à qn; **with** ~ **to** en ce qui concerne, quant à; **with** ~ **to your enquiry** comme suite à votre demande; **with** ~ **to your letter** suite à votre lettre; **without** ~ **to sb** sans consulter qn; **without** ~ **to sth** sans tenir compte de qch; **your** ~ (on letter) votre référence

reference[2] prep au sujet de, concernant

reference[3] vt (on search engine) référencer

reference: ~ **bank** n banque de référence f; ~ **book** n ouvrage de référence m; ~ **currency** n devise de référence f; ~ **cycle** n cycle de référence m; ~ **group** n groupe de référence m; ~ **level** n niveau de référence m; ~ **material** n documentation f; ~ **number** n numéro de référence m; ~ **point** n point de repère m

referencing n (on search engine) référencement m

referendum n référendum m; **hold a** ~ organiser un référendum

referral n (of matter, problem) renvoi m; ~ **to the committee is required** il est nécessaire de soumettre l'affaire au comité; **by** ~ **to** par référence à

referring: ~ **to** par référence à

refinance vt refinancer

refinance credit n crédit de

refinancement m

refinancing n refinancement m; ~ **risk** n risque de refinancement m

refine vt (raw material) raffiner; (websearch) affiner; (theory) peaufiner

refinery n raffinerie f

refit[1] n (of premises) rééquipement m, rénovation f; (of ship) réarmement m

refit[2] vt (premises) rééquiper, rénover; (ship) réarmer

reflate vt (economy) relancer

reflation n relance f

reflationary adj (measures) de relance

reflect vt (sb's opinion) refléter; ~ **well/badly on sb** faire honneur/tort à qn; **be** ~**ed in** se traduire par

refloat vt (company) renflouer; ~ **a loan** émettre un nouvel emprunt

refocus vi se recentrer

refocusing n recentrage m

reform[1] n réforme f; ~ **package** n projet de réforme m; ~ **program** AmE n, ~ **programme** BrE n programme de réformes m

reform[2] vt réformer

reformat vt (disk) reformater

refrain: ~ **from** vt s'abstenir de

refresh vt (computer screen) rafraîchir; (update memory) régénérer; (in websearch) actualiser

refresher n UK (Law) honoraires supplémentaires m pl; ~ **course** n cours de recyclage m

refresh rate n (Comp) vitesse de régénération f

refrigerated adj réfrigéré; ~ **container** n conteneur frigorifique m; ~ **lorry** n BrE, ~ **truck** n camion frigorifique m; ~ **warehouse** n entrepôt frigorifique m

refrigeration n réfrigération f

refuel [1] vt (vehicle) ravitailler en carburant; (inflation) relancer [2] vi se ravitailler en carburant

refueling AmE, **refuelling** BrE n ravitaillement m

refugee n réfugié/-e m/f; ~ **capital** n capitaux spéculatifs m pl

refund[1] n (Gen Comm, Stock, Tax) remboursement m; **full** ~ remboursement intégral m; **get a** ~ se faire rembourser

refund[2] vt rembourser

refundable adj remboursable; ~ **deposit** n acompte remboursable m; ~ **tax credit** n crédit d'impôt remboursable m

refurbish vt rénover

refurbishment n rénovation f

refusal n refus m; ~ **to do** refus de faire; **have first** ~ **of sth** avoir le droit de préemption sur qch; **give sb first** ~**of sth** offrir qch à qn en premier; **meet with a** ~ se heurter à un refus; ~ **rate** n taux de refus m

refuse¹ *n* BrE déchets *m pl*, ordures *f pl*; ~ **collection** *n* ramassage des ordures ménagères *m*; ~ **dump** *n* dépôt d'ordures *m*, décharge *f*

refuse² ⟦1⟧ *vt* refuser; ~ **to do** refuser de faire; ~ **sb sth** refuser qch à qn; ~ **acceptance of a draft** refuser d'accepter une traite; ~ **sb bail** refuser de mettre qn en liberté sous caution
⟦2⟧ *vi* refuser

regard¹ *n* (esteem) estime *f*; **have a high** ~ **for sb** avoir beaucoup d'estime pour qn; **as** ~**s, with** ~ **to** concernant, en ce qui concerne

regard² *vt* considérer

regarding *prep* concernant

regardless *prep* ~ **of cost/age** sans tenir compte du prix/de l'âge; ~ **of the weather/ outcome** quel que soit le temps/le résultat

regime *n* régime *m*

region *n* région *f*; **in the** ~ **of** environ, à peu près

regional *adj* régional; ~ **agreement** *n* accord régional *m*; ~ **airline** *n* compagnie de transport régional *f*; ~ **center** AmE, ~ **centre** BrE *n* centre régional *m*; ~ **development** *n* développement régional *m*; ~ **economics** *n + sing v* économie régionale *f*; ~ **manager** *n* chef de région *m*, responsable régional/-e *m/f*; ~ **market** *n* marché régional *m*; ~ **office** *n* bureau régional *m*; ~ **organization** *n* organisation par région *f*; ~ **trend** *n* tendance régionale *f*; ~ **wage bargaining** *n* négociation salariale au plan régional *f*

register¹ *n* registre *m*; **keep a** ~ tenir un registre; ~ **of companies** *n* registre du commerce *m*; ~ **of members** *n* registre des actionnaires *m*; ~ **office** *n* bureau de l'état civil *m*; ~ **tonnage** *n* tonnage de jauge *m*

register² ⟦1⟧ *vt* (Admin) (organization, dealer, practitioner) agréer; (company) faire enregistrer; (vehicle) faire immatriculer; (letter) recommander; (pension scheme) agréer; (business name) enregistrer; (loss, gain) enregistrer; (speed, temperature) indiquer; (birth, death) déclarer; ~ **a high** (on stock market) enregistrer une hausse
⟦2⟧ *vi* (for course) s'inscrire; (at hotel) se présenter à la réception; (for online service) s'abonner; ~ **for** (course) s'inscrire à; (share issue) souscrire à; ~ **with** (agency) s'inscrire à; (online service provider) s'abonner à

registered *adj* (Admin) (scheme, practitioner) agréé; (letter) recommandé; (vessel, vehicle) immatriculé; **the** ~ **unemployed** les chômeurs recensés; ~ **address** *n* adresse du siège social *f*; ~ **applicant for work** *n* demandeur/-euse d'emploi *m/f*; ~ **baggage** *n* bagages enregistrés *m pl*; ~ **bond** *n* obligation immatriculée *f*, obligation nominative *f*; ~ **charity** *n* ≈ œuvre caritative reconnue d'utilité publique *f*; ~

company *n* société inscrite au registre du commerce *f*; ~ **design** *n* modèle déposé *m*; ~ **mail** *n* envoi recommandé *m*; ~ **mark** *n* marque déposée *f*; ~ **name** *n* nom déposé *m*; ~ **office** *n* siège social *m*; ~ **offices** *n pl* (branches of company) filiales *f pl*; ~ **options broker** *n* courtier d'options agréé *m*; ~ **options trader** *n* négociateur d'options agréé *m*; ~ **owner** *n* (of bond) propriétaire immatriculé/-e *m/f*; (of vehicle) propriétaire *mf*; ~ **post** *n* envoi recommandé *m*; ~ **proprietor** *n* (Prop) propriétaire inscrit/-e au registre du cadastre *m/f*; ~ **representative** *n* représentant/-e agréé/-e *m/f*; ~ **security** *n* titre nominatif *m*, valeur nominative *f*; ~ **share** *n* action nominative *f*; ~ **shareholder** *n* actionnaire inscrit/-e *m/f*; ~ **title** *n* titre de propriété inscrit au registre du cadastre *m*; ~ **ton** *n* tonne de jauge *f*; ~ **trademark** *n* marque déposée *f*; ~ **user** *n* utilisateur/-trice disposant d'une licence *m/f*

registrar *n* (Admin) officier de l'état civil *m*; ~ **of deeds** *n* receveur de l'enregistrement *m*; ~ **of transfers** *n* agent comptable des transferts *m*; ~**'s office** *n* bureau de l'état civil *m*

registration *n* (Gen Comm, Admin) enregistrement *m*; (for course) inscription *f*; (for online services) abonnement *m*; (of birth, death, marriage) déclaration *f*; (of company name) inscription *f*; (accreditation) agrément *m*; (Law, Patents) enregistrement *m*, inscription *f*; (Prop) inscription *f*; (of vehicle) immatriculation *f*; (of luggage) enregistrement *m*; ~ **deadline** *n* date limite de clôture des inscriptions *f*; ~ **fee** *n* frais d'inscription *m pl*; ~ **number** *n* (Gen Comm) numéro d'enregistrement *m*; (of vehicle) numéro d'immatriculation *m*; ~ **office** *n* bureau d'enregistrement *m*; ~ **plate** *n* plaque minéralogique *f*, plaque d'immatriculation *f*

registry *n* (action) enregistrement *m*, inscription *f*; (office) bureau de l'enregistrement *m*; ~ **of deeds** bureau d'enregistrement des actes *m*; ~ **office** *n* (Admin) bureau de l'enregistrement *m*; (for civil ceremonies, records) bureau de l'état civil *m*; ~ **of shipping** immatriculation des navires *f*

regression *n* régression *f*; ~ **analysis** *n* analyse de régression *f*

regressive *adj* (effect) régressif/-ive; (measure, policy) rétrograde; ~ **supply** *n* offre régressive *f*; ~ **tax** *n* impôt régressif *m*; ~ **taxation** *n* imposition régressive *f*

regret¹ *n* regret *m*; (Stock) retour de souscription *m*; **send one's** ~**s** envoyer ses excuses; **to our** ~ à notre grand regret

regret² *vt* regretter; ~ **to inform sb that** avoir le regret d'informer qn que

regretfully *adv* malheureusement

regroup ⟦1⟧ *vt* regrouper
⟦2⟧ *vi* se regrouper

regular *adj* (fixed) régulier/-ière; **on a ~ basis** de façon régulière; (usual, habitual) habituel/-elle; (standard) normal; **~ customer** *n* client/-e habituel/-elle *m/f*; **~ expenditure** *n* dépense régulière *f*; **~ hours** *n pl* heures normales *f pl*; **~ income** *n* revenu régulier *m*; **~ meeting** *n* réunion normale *f*; **~ payments** *n pl* paiements réguliers *m pl*; **~ service** *n* service régulier *m*

regularly *adv* régulièrement

regulate *vt* (flow) régler; (industry, market) réglementer; (money supply) contrôler; (use) réglementer; (activity, tendancy) réguler; (machine) régler; (Law) réglementer

regulated: **~ agreement** *n* UK accord réglementé *m*; **~ commodity** *n* marchandise réglementée *f*, matière première réglementée *f*; **~ economy** *n* économie dirigée *f*; **~ firm** *n* entreprise réglementée *f*; **~ industry** *n* industrie réglementée *f*; **~ market** *n* marché réglementé *m*

regulation *n* (rule) règlement *m*; (of flow) règlement *m*; (of industry, market) réglementation *f*; (of money supply) contrôle *m*; (Law) réglementation *f*; (Tax) règlement *m*; **under the ~s** selon la réglementation; **meet the ~** se conformer à la réglementation; **contrary to the ~s** contrairement au règlement; **safety/fire ~s** consignes de sécurité/en cas d'incendie *f pl*; **building ~s** normes de construction *f pl*; **a set of ~s** une réglementation; **EU ~s** réglementation communautaire *f*; **~ authority** autorité de régulation *f*

regulator *n* (body) organisme de réglementation *m*, organisme de contrôle *m*; (person) régulateur/-trice *m/f*

regulatory *adj* régulateur/-trice; (height, weight, length) réglementaire; **~ agency** *n* agence de tutelle *f*; **~ authority** *n*, **~ body** *n* autorité de régulation *f*, organisme de réglementation *m*; **~ committee** *n* comité régulateur *m*; **~ framework** *n* cadre réglementaire *m*; **~ measures** *n pl* mesures de réglementation *f pl*; **~ system** *n* système réglementaire *m*

rehabilitate *vt* (reputation, company, official) réhabiliter; (area, building) réhabiliter

rehabilitation *n* (of reputation, company, official) réhabilitation *f*; (into the community) réinsertion *f*; (of area, building) réhabilitation *f*

rehire *vt* réembaucher

reign[1] *n* règne *m*

reign[2] *vi* régner

reimage *vt* changer l'image de, relooker

reimburse *vt* rembourser

reimbursement *n* remboursement *m*

reimport *vt* réimporter

reimportation *n* réimportation *f*

reimpose *vt* réimposer

rein *n* give free **~ to** donner libre cours à; **slacken the ~s** relâcher les rênes; **take up/**

hold the **~s** prendre/tenir les rênes

reinforce *vt* renforcer

reinforcement *n* renforcement *m*

reinfusion *n* réinjection *f*

reinstate *vt* (employee) réintégrer, rétablir dans ses fonctions; (service, law) rétablir

reinstatement *n* (of employee) réintégration *f*; (of service, law) rétablissement *m*

reinsurance *n* réassurance *f*; **~ company** *n* compagnie de réassurance *f*

reinsure *vt* réassurer

reinsurer *n* réassureur *m*

reintermediation *n* réintermédiation *f*

reinvest *vt* réinvestir

reinvestment *n* réinvestissement *m*; **~ rate** *n* taux de réinvestissement *m*

reinvoice *vt* refacturer

reinvoicing *n* refacturation *f*

reissue[1] *n* (of bill of exchange) renouvellement *m*; (of securities, stocks) nouvelle émission *f*; (of book) réédition *f*

reissue[2] *vt* (bill of exchange) renouveler; (securities, stocks) réémettre, émettre de nouveau; (book) rééditer

reiterate *vi* réitérer

reject[1] *n* (in production) article de rebut *m*; (for sale) article de deuxième choix *m*; **~ shop** *n* boutique spécialisée dans la vente de la marchandise de deuxième choix *f*

reject[2] *vt* (idea, proposal, advice, initiative, offer) rejeter; (applicant, candidate) refuser; (accusation, claim) démentir

rejection *n* (of idea, proposal, offer) rejet *m*; (of applicant) refus *m*; **~ letter** *n* lettre de refus *f*; **~ rate** *n* (Gen Comm) taux de refus *m*; (Ind) taux de rebut *m*

rejuvenate *vt* moderniser, rajeunir

rejuvenation *n* modernisation *f*, rajeunissement *m*

related *adj* (person) apparenté; (matter, subject) connexe; (information, evidence, event) lié; (similar) similaire; **~ business** *n* (Tax) activité commerciale complémentaire *f*, commerce affilié *m*; **~ party** *n* partie associée *f*

relation *n* (connection) rapport *m*, relation *f*; (family member) parent/-e *m/f*; **in ~ to** par rapport à

relational database *n* base de données relationnelles *f*

relations *n pl* relations *f pl*; **business ~** relations professionnelles *f pl*; **~ analysis** *n* analyse relationnelle *f*

relationship *n* (rapport) relations *f pl*; (connection) rapport *m*; **have a good ~ with** avoir de bonnes relations avec; **working ~**, **business ~** relations professionnelles *f pl*; **~ marketing** *n* marketing relationnel *m*

relative *adj* relatif/-ive; **in ~ terms** en termes relatifs; **~ to** relatif à; **~ error** *n* erreur relative *f*; **~ income hypothesis** *n* hypothèse du revenu relatif *f*; ~ **market share** *n* part de marché relative *f*; ~ **price** *n* prix relatif *m*; ~ **price level** *n* niveau de prix relatifs *m*; ~ **surplus value** *n* plus-value relative *f*

relatively *adv* relativement

relativities *n pl* relativités *f pl*

relaunch¹ *n* relancement *m*

relaunch² *vt* relancer

relax *vt* (rule, policy) assouplir

relaxation *n* (of rule, law, policy) assouplissement *m*

release¹ *n* (version of document, software) version *f*, révision *f*; (of cheque) libération *f*; (of product) lancement *m*, mise sur le marché *f*; (of record, film) sortie *f*; (from prison) libération *f*; (discharge document) décharge *f*; (announcement) communiqué *m*; **new** ~ (video, CD, film) dernière nouveauté *f*; ~ **date** *n* (for product) date de mise sur le marché *f*; (for shares allocated to employees) date de distribution *f*, date de libération *f*; ~ **for shipment** autorisation de sortie *f*; ~ **to market** *n* mise sur le marché *f*

release² *vt* (product) lancer, mettre sur le marché; (information) communiquer; (from prison) libérer; (record, film) faire sortir; (document) faire paraître; (report, list) publier; ~ **on bail** libérer sous caution; ~ **sb from sth** (promise, obligation) dégager qn de qch; ~ **sb from a debt** faire la remise d'une dette à qn

relevance *n* pertinence *f*, intérêt *m*; (in websearch) pertinence *f*; ~ **score** *n* score de pertinence *m*

relevant *adj* (year, period) en question; (experience) préalable; (fact, point, remark) pertinent; (information) utile; **be ~ to** avoir rapport à; ~ **authority** *n* autorité compétente *f*

reliability *n* fiabilité *f*; ~ **test** *n* essai de fiabilité *m*

reliable *adj* (equipment) fiable; (person, witness) fiable, digne de confiance; (information, source) sûr; (firm, employee) sérieux/-ieuse

reliance *n* dépendance *f*; ~ **on** dépendance vis-à-vis de

relief *n* (help) secours *m*, aide *f*; (from threat, anxiety) soulagement *m*; (replacement) relève *f*; US (welfare benefits) aides sociales *f pl*; (alleviation of debts, overheads) allègement *m*; (Tax) dégrèvement *m*, allègement *m*; **debt** ~ allègement des dettes *m*; ~ **fund** *n* fonds d'aide *m*; (in crisis) fonds de secours *m*; ~ **on business assets** *n* (Tax) dégrèvement sur biens commerciaux *m*; ~ **sailing** *n* navire supplémentaire *m*; ~ **shift** *n* équipe de relève *f*; ~ **work** *n* travail humanitaire *m*

relieve *vt* (take over from) relever; ~ **sb of a job** relever qn de son poste; ~ **sb of a duty** décharger qn d'une obligation

relinquish *vt* (power, freedom) renoncer à; (responsibility) délaisser; (privilege, claim, right)

renoncer à; ~ **an inheritance** renoncer à une succession

reload *vt* (software) recharger; (vehicle, ship, cargo) recharger

relocate **1** *vt* (employee) muter; (company) déplacer, délocaliser **2** *vi* (company) déménager, délocaliser; (employee) être muté

relocation *n* (of employee) mutation *f*; (of company) déplacement *m*, délocalisation *f*; ~ **allowance** *n* prime de relogement *f*; ~ **package** *n* indemnités de déménagement *f pl*

reluctant *adj* (reply, person) peu enthousiaste; (agreement, promise) à contre-cœur; **be ~ to do sth** être peu disposé à faire qch

rely: ~ **on** *vt* (count on) compter sur; (depend on) dépendre de

remailer *n* service de réexpédition anonyme *m*, remailer *m*

remain *vi* rester

remainder¹ *n* reste *m*; (remaining people) les autres *m pl*

remainder² *vt* solder

remainders *n pl* invendus soldés *m pl*

remand *vt* (case) ajourner, renvoyer; ~ **in custody** mettre en détention préventive

remargining *n* (Fin) renantissement *m*

remark¹ *n* remarque *f*

remark² *vt* observer, remarquer

remarket *vt* recommercialiser

remarketing *n* marketing de relance *m*

remedy¹ *n* remède *m*, solution *f*; (Law) recours *m*

remedy² *vt* (situation) remédier à

reminder *n* rappel *m*; **a ~ that** un rappel du fait que; **a ~ to sb to do** un rappel à qn lui demandant de faire; **be a ~ of sth, serve as a ~ of sth** rapeller qch; **letter of ~** lettre de rappel *f*

remission *n* remise *f*; ~ **of charges** détaxe *f*, remise de charges *f*; ~ **of tax** remise d'impôt *f*

remit¹ *n* attributions *f pl*; **be outside sb's ~** ne pas être dans les attributions de qn; **exceed one's ~** aller au-delà de ses attributions

remit² *vt* (sentence, debt) remettre; (case) renvoyer; (money) envoyer; (postpone) différer

remittal *n* (of sentence, debt) remise *f*

remittance *n* (payment) règlement *m*, paiement *m*; (sending) versement *m*, envoi de fonds *m*; ~ **account** *n* compte de remise non soldé *m*; ~ **advice** *n* avis de remise à l'encaissement *m*; ~ **slip** *n* bordereau de paiement *m*

remote *adj* (Comp) (server, terminal) distant, éloigné; ~ **access** *n* (Comp) accès à distance *m*, téléconsultation *f*; ~ **control** *n* commande à distance *f*, télécommande *f*; (unit) ⋯⃗

télécommande *f*; ∼-**controlled** *adj*
télécommandé; ∼ **payment** *n* télépaiement
m, paiement électronique *m*; ∼ **possibility** *n*
éventualité peu probable *f*; ∼ **processing** *n*
télétraitement *m*

removal *n* (of goods, restriction) enlèvement *m*;
(of tax, threat, tariff barrier) suppression *f*; (to new
premises) déménagement *m*; (of employee, official)
renvoi *m*; ∼ **allowance** *n* indemnité de
déménagement *f*; ∼ **expenses** *n pl* frais de
déménagement *m pl*; ∼ **van** *n* camion de
déménagement *m*

remove *vt* (object) enlever; (goods, restriction)
enlever; (tariff barrier, tax, threat, paragraph, word)
supprimer; (obstacle, difficulty) écarter; (doubt)
chasser; (employee, official) renvoyer; ∼ **sb's**
name from a list rayer qn d'une liste; ∼ **sb**
from office démettre qn de ses fonctions

remunerate *vt* rémunérer

remuneration *n* rémunération *f*; ∼
package *n* le salaire et les avantages
complémentaires

remunerative *adj* rémunérateur/-trice

render *vt* (account) remettre; (statement)
présenter; (service) rendre; ∼ **null and void**
invalider, rendre nul et non avenu; ∼
obsolete rendre désuet, rendre périmé; **for**
services ∼**ed** pour services rendus; **as per**
account ∼**ed** suivant compte remis

renege *vi* se rétracter; ∼ **on an agreement**
revenir sur un accord

renegotiate *vti* renégocier

renegotiation *n* renégociation *f*

renew *vt* (Fin) (contract, passport, efforts, credit)
renouveler; (negotiations) reprendre; (agreement)
reconduire; ∼ **one's subscription** se
réabonner

renewable *adj* renouvelable; ∼ **resource**
n ressource renouvelable *f*

renewal *n* (of contract, report, credit, passport,
lease) renouvellement *m*; (of agreement)
reconduction *f*; (of interest) regain *m*; ∼
notice *n* avis de renouvellement *m*; ∼
option *n* (Prop) option de reconduction *f*; ∼
of a subscription réabonnement *m*

renounce *vt* renoncer à

renovate *vt* (equipment) remettre à neuf;
(building) rénover

renovated *adj* (equipment) remis à neuf;
(building) rénové

renovation *n* (of equipment) remise à neuf *f*;
(of building) rénovation *f*; ∼**s** travaux de
rénovation *m pl*

renown *n* célébrité *f*, renommée *f*

renowned *adj* célèbre, de renom; ∼ **for**
célèbre pour

rent¹ *n* (on apartment, office) loyer *m*; **for** ∼ à
louer; ∼ **allowance** *n* aide locative *f*; ∼
collector *n* encaisseur de loyers *m*, receveur
des loyers *m*; ∼ **freeze** *n* gel des loyers *m*; ∼
increase *n* augmentation de loyer *f*; ∼ **per**
calendar month *n* BrE loyer mensuel *m*; ∼

rebate *n* remboursement de loyer *m*,
réduction sur le loyer *f*; ∼ **receipt** *n*
quittance de loyer *f*

rent² ⟨**1**⟩ *vt* louer
⟨**2**⟩ *vi* (tenant) être locataire; **to** ∼ à louer; ∼
out louer

rental *n* (act) location *f*; (sum paid) (for
apartment, office) loyer *m*; (for car) location *f*; (for
equipment) prix de location *m*; ∼ **agreement**
n contrat de location *m*; ∼ **charge** *n* (for
equipment) prix de location *m*; (for car) location
f; ∼ **cost** *n* (of property) montant du loyer *m*,
montant locatif *m*; ∼ **equipment** *n* matériel
de location *m*; ∼ **income** *n* revenu de
location *m*, revenu locatif *m*; ∼ **period** *n*
période de location *f*; ∼ **rate** *n* taux locatif
m; ∼ **right** *n* (Law, Patents) droit
d'exploitation *m*; ∼ **term** *n* terme locatif *m*;
∼ **value** *n* valeur locative *f*

rented *adj* (car) de location; (flat, room) loué

renter *n* (tenant) locataire *mf*; (owner) loueur/
-euse *m/f*, bailleur/-eresse *m/f*

rent-free¹ *adj* exempt de loyer, gratuit

rent-free² *adv* sans payer de loyer

rentier *n* rentier *m*

renting *n* location *f*; ∼ **out** *n* location *f*

reopen *vti* rouvrir

reorder¹ *n* nouvelle commande *f*; ∼ **form** *n*
bon de commande de réassortiment *m*; ∼
point *n* seuil de réapprovisionnement *m*

reorder² ⟨**1**⟩ *vt* commander à nouveau
⟨**2**⟩ *vi* passer une nouvelle commande

reorganization *n* (of finances)
restructuration *f*; (of company) restructuration
f, réorganisation *f*; ∼ **of capital**
remaniement de capital *m*

reorganize *vt* (company) restructurer,
réorganiser; (finances) restructurer

rep *n* (S&M) représentant/-e (de commerce)
m/f

repack *vt* remballer

repackage *vt* (goods, pay offer)
reconditionner; (personality, client) moderniser
l'image publique de, relooker; (product line)
remettre au goût du jour, relooker; (rewrap)
reconditionner

repackaging *n* (of personality, client)
modernisation de l'image publique *f*,
relookage *m*; (of product) remise au goût du
jour *f*, relookage *m*; (for display, sale)
reconditionnement *m*

repacking *n* remballage *m*

repair¹ *n* réparation *f*; **in good** ∼ en bon
état; **beyond** ∼ irréparable; **carry out** ∼**s**
effectuer des réparations; ∼ **shop** *n* atelier
de réparation *m*

repair² *vt* réparer

reparation *n* (Law) réparation *f*; ∼ **for**
damage indemnisation des dommages *f*; ∼
for loss dédommagement d'une perte *m*;
make ∼ **for sth** réparer qch; **obtain** ∼ **for**
obtenir réparation pour

repatriate *vt* (profits, person, funds) rapatrier

repatriation *n* (of profits, person, funds) rapatriement *m*

repay *vt* (loan) rembourser; (debt) rembourser, s'acquitter de

repayable *adj* remboursable; **~ on demand** remboursable sur demande

repayment *n* remboursement *m*; **~ over 2 years** remboursement échelonné sur 2 ans; **~ claim** *n* demande de remboursement *f*; **~ mortgage** *n* emprunt hypothécaire à remboursement *m*; **~ options** *n pl* formules de remboursement *f pl*; **~ schedule** *n* calendrier de remboursement *m*, échéancier (de remboursements) *m*; **~ term** *n* délai de remboursement *m*

repeal *vt* abroger, annuler

repeat¹ *n* répétition *f*

repeat² *vt* répéter; **~ed warnings** avertissements répétés *m pl*

repeat: **~ business** *n* commande renouvelée *f*; **~ buying** *n* achats répétés *m pl*; **~ demand** *n* demande renouvelée *f*; **~ order** *n* commande renouvelée *f*; **~ purchase** *n* achat renouvelé *m*; **~ rate** *n* taux de rachat *m*; **~ sales** *n pl* ventes de renouvellement *f pl*, ventes répétées *f pl*

repercussions *n pl* répercussions *f pl*

repetitive strain injury *n* trouble musculo-squelettique *m*

replace *vt* (substitute) remplacer; (put back) remettre; **~ the receiver** raccrocher

replacement *n* (person) remplaçant/-e *m/f*; (item) remplacement *m*; (putting back) remise en place *f*; **~ bond** *n* obligation de remplacement *f*; **~ capital** *n* financement de remplacement *m*; **~ cost** *n* coût de remplacement *m*; **~ investment** *n* provision pour dépréciation *f*; **~ market** *n* marché de remplacement *m*; **~ part** *n* pièce de rechange *f*; **~ price** *n* prix de remplacement *m*; **~ ratio** *n* taux de remplacement *m*; **~ value** *n* valeur de remplacement *f*

replenish *vt* (account) réapprovisionner; (shelves) restocker; **~ one's stocks** se réapprovisionner

reply¹ *n* réponse *f*; **in ~ to** en réponse à; **~ coupon** *n* coupon-réponse *m*; **~ paid** *adj* réponse payée *f*; **~-paid card** *n* carte-réponse payée *f*

reply² *vi* répondre; **~ by return** répondre par retour du courrier; **~ to** répondre à

REPO *abbr* AmE (▶**repurchase agreement**) (Fin) contrat de vente à réméré *m*; (Stock) prise en pension *f*, mise en pension *f*, pension livrée *f*

repo market *n* AmE (Stock) marché des prises en pension *m*

report¹ *n* rapport *m*; (account of meeting, debate) compte rendu *m*, procès-verbal *m*; (Media) reportage *m*; **draw up a ~** rédiger un rapport; **give a ~** faire un rapport; **accident**

~ constat d'accident *m*; **annual ~** rapport annuel *m*; **~ card** *n* AmE (HRM) évaluation *f*; **~ generation** *n* génération d'états *f*

report² **1** *vt* (problem, fault, fact) signaler; (death, theft, damage, accident) déclarer, signaler; (news story, event) faire un reportage sur; (colleague, employee) signaler; (earnings, losses, profits) enregistrer, annoncer; **~ a loss** constater une perte, déclarer une perte; **~ a profit** constater un profit, déclarer un profit; **~ one's conclusions** rapporter ses conclusions; **~ one's findings** rendre compte des résultats; **as ~ed** comme annoncé; **the company is ~ed to be in trouble** la société aurait des difficultés; **it is ~ed that** il paraît que; **~ a drop in sales** (company) enregistrer une baisse du chiffre d'affaires; (accountant, finance director) annoncer une baisse des ventes; **nothing to ~** rien à signaler **2** *vi* (present findings) faire un rapport; (Media) faire un reportage; **~ on sth** faire un compte rendu sur; (committee) rendre son rapport sur; (Media) faire un reportage sur; **~ back** (return) revenir; (call in) se présenter; **~ back to sb** (committee, team) présenter un rapport à qn; **~ to** (office, reception) se présenter à; (committee) faire son compte rendu à; (line-manager, superior) rendre des comptes à, être sous les ordres de

reporter *n* reporter *m*

reporting *n* (of fact, event) compte rendu *m*; (Acc) information comptable *f*, information financière *f*; (Media) reportages *m pl*; **~ currency** *n* devise comptable *f*; **~ dealer** *n* correspondant en valeurs du Trésor *m*; **~ of income** *n* déclaration de revenu *f*; **~ period** *n* (Tax) période de déclaration *f*; **~ requirements** *n pl* (Tax) conditions de déclaration *f pl*; **~ restrictions** *n pl* UK interdiction de rapporter les débats *f*; **~ standards** *n pl* normes de présentation de l'information *f pl*; **~ system** *n* (Acc) système d'information comptable *m*

reposition *vt* (brand, item) repositionner

repositioning *n* repositionnement *m*

repository *n* dépôt *m*

repossess *vt* (house) saisir; (goods) reprendre possession de, saisir

repossession *n* saisie immobilière *f*; **~ order** *n* ordre de saisie immobilière *m*

represent *vt* (act on behalf of) représenter; (present) présenter; (exemplify) représenter

representation *n* (Gen Comm, Pol) représentation *f*; (Law) déclaration *f*; **make ~s to sb** (request) faire des démarches auprès de qn; (complain) se plaindre auprès de qn

representative¹ *adj* représentatif/-ive, typique; **~ sample** *n* échantillon type *m*

representative² *n* (Gen Comm) représentant/-e *m/f*; (Law, Patents) mandataire *mf*

Representative n US député/-e m/f

repressive adj répressif/-ive

reprocess vt retraiter

reprocessing n retraitement m; ~ **plant** n usine de retraitement f

reproduction n reproduction f; (copy) copie f; ~ **rate** n taux de reproduction m

reprogram vt (Comp) reprogrammer

reprographics n + sing v reprographie f

republish vt rééditer

repudiate vt (industrial action) refuser de prendre part à; (contract, obligation) refuser d'honorer; (accusation) rejeter

repurchase n (Gen Comm) rachat m; (of debt) prise de contrôle f; ~ **agreement** n AmE (Fin) contrat de vente à réméré m; (Stock) mise en pension f, pension livrée f, prise en pension f; ~ **market** n (Stock) marché des prises en pension m; ~ **rate** n taux des prises en pension f

repurchased share n action autodétenue f

reputable adj (company, lawyer) de bonne réputation; ~ **brand** n marque réputée f

reputation n réputation f; **have a good/ bad** ~ avoir bonne/mauvaise réputation; **live up to one's** ~ être à la hauteur de sa réputation; **by** ~ de réputation

request[1] n demande f, requête f; (on Internet) requête f; ~ **for payment** demande de paiement f; **at the** ~ **of** à la demande de; **make a** ~ faire une demande; **make a** ~ **to the appropriate authority** faire une demande auprès des autorités compétentes; **on** ~ sur demande

request[2] vt demander; **as** ~ed (in letter) conformément à votre demande; ~ **access to** demander l'accès à; ~ **for proposal** n demande de propositions f

require vt (need) avoir besoin de; (demand) exiger; (action, investment) nécessiter; ~ **sth of sb** exiger qch de qn; ~ **that** exiger que; **be** ~d **by law** être exigé par la loi

required adj exigé; **by the** ~ **date** avant la date exigée, dans les délais prescrits; **meet the** ~ **conditions** satisfaire aux conditions requises; ~ **action** n action nécessaire f; ~ **rate of return** n taux de rendement requis m; ~ **reserves** n pl (Bank) réserves obligatoires f pl

requirement n (demand) exigence f; (Tax) demande péremptoire f, exigence f; (need) besoin m; (obligation) obligation f; (criteria) condition f; **legal** ~ obligation légale f; **cash** ~s besoins en trésorerie m pl; **market** ~s besoins du marché m pl; **performance** ~s critères de performance m pl; **meet sb's** ~s satisfaire les besoins de qn; **meet the** ~s remplir les conditions; **fulfil the membership** ~s remplir les conditions d'adhésion; **the** ~ **to do** l'obligation de faire; **there is a** ~ **that you do** vous êtes tenu de faire

requisite adj exigé, requis

rerouting n (Transp) modification d'itinéraire f

rerun[1] n (Comp) reprise f

rerun[2] vt (program) relancer; (film) repasser; (test, trials, election) refaire

resale n revente f; **'not for** ~**'** 'ne peut être vendu'; ~ **price** n prix de revente m; ~ **price maintenance** n maintien du prix de revente m; ~ **value** n valeur de revente f

reschedule vt (debt) rééchelonner; (event, meeting) changer la date de; (change the time of) changer l'heure de

rescheduling n (of debt) rééchelonnement m

rescind vt (judgement) rescinder, casser; (contract) résilier; (agreement, decision) annuler; (law) abroger

rescission n (of judgement) rescision f, cassation f; (of contract) résiliation f; (of agreement, decision) annulation f; (of law) abrogation f

rescue[1] n sauvetage m; **come to the** ~ **of** venir en aide à, venir à la rescousse de; ~ **operation** n opération de sauvetage f; ~ **package** n (Fin) plan de sauvetage m

rescue[2] vt (company) porter secours à; (industry, economy) venir à l'aide de; (factory) éviter la fermeture de

research[1] n recherche f; (market research) enquête f, étude f; **do some** ~ faire des recherches; ~ **shows that...** les études montrent que...; ~ **budget** n budget de recherche m; ~ **department** n bureau d'étude m, service de recherche m; ~ **and development** n recherche f et développement m; ~ **director** n directeur/ -trice de la recherche m/f; ~ **grant** n subvention pour la recherche f; ~ **laboratory** n laboratoire de recherches m; ~ **program** AmE, ~ **programme** BrE n programme de recherche m; ~ **student** n étudiant/-e qui fait de la recherche m/f; ~ **survey** n (market research) suivi d'enquêtes m, suivi d'études de marché m; ~ **team** n équipe de chercheurs f; ~ **worker** n chercheur/-euse m/f

research[2] vt (field) faire des recherches dans; (topic) faire des recherches sur; (book, article) préparer; (Media) se documenter sur; (S&M) (demand, attitudes) faire une étude sur

researcher n (for newspaper, TV) documentaliste m/f; (in market research, at university) chercheur/-euse m/f

resell vt revendre

reseller n revendeur/-euse m/f

reservation n (of hotel room, ticket, seat) réservation f; (doubt) réserve f; **make a** ~ (at hotel) réserver une chambre; (Transp) retenir une place; **express** ~s **about** émettre des réserves au sujet de; **have** ~s **about** avoir des doutes sur; **without** ~ (unequivocally) sans réserve; (without prior booking) sans réservation; **∼ counter**, **∼ desk** n service des réservations m; **∼ form** n confirmation de réservation f; **∼ system** n système de réservation m

reservations n pl bureau des réservations m

reserve¹ n (supply, stock) réserve f; (at auction sale) mise à prix f, prix minimum m; (Tax) réserve f; (doubt) réserve f; **keep in ∼** garder en réserve; **build up/hold ∼s** constituer/ détenir des réserves; **without ∼** sans réserve; **∼ account** n compte de réserve m; **∼ assets** n pl actif de réserve m; **∼ currency** n monnaie de réserve f; **∼ deposit** n dépôt de couverture bancaire m, réserve obligatoire f; **∼ for bad debts** provision pour créances douteuses f; **∼ for unpaid claims** (Ins) provisions pour sinistre à payer f pl; **∼ fund** n caisse de prévoyance f; **∼ liability** n passif de réserve m; **∼ price** n BrE (at auction sale) mise à prix f, prix minimum m; **∼ ratio** n (Bank) coefficient de réserve m; **∼ requirements** n pl (Bank) réserves obligatoires f pl; **∼ stock** n stock de réserve m

reserve² vt réserver; **∼ judgment** réserver son jugement; **∼ the right to do** se réserver le droit de faire

reserved adj réservé

reserves n pl réserves f pl; **draw on one's ∼s** puiser dans ses réserves; **gold/oil ∼s** réserves d'or/de pétrole

reset vt (clock, counter) remettre à zéro; (computer) réinitialiser

resettle ① vt (company) réimplanter ② vi se réimplanter

resettlement n (of company) réimplantation f

reshape vt (industry, company) restructurer, réorganizer; (policy) réviser

reship vt réexpédier

reshipping n réexpédition f

reshuffle¹ n remaniement m; **management ∼** remaniement de l'équipe dirigeante m; **cabinet ∼** remaniement ministériel m

reshuffle² vt (board, ministers) remanier

reside vi résider

residence n résidence f; **take up ∼** élire domicile; **legal ∼** domicile légal m; **∼ permit** n permis de séjour m

residency n (Bank) (of depositor) statut résidentiel m; (Law) droit de séjour m

resident¹ adj résidant

resident² n résident/-e m/f; **be ∼ in the UK** résider au Royaume-Uni

resident: ∼ alien n résident/-e étranger/ -ère m/f; **∼ bank** n banque résidente f; **∼ population** n population résidente f; **∼ taxpayer** n (Tax) résident/-e contribuable m/f

residential adj résidentiel/-ielle; **∼ accommodation** n logements m pl; **∼ course** n stage à temps complet en internat m; **∼ mortgage** n (Bank) prêt hypothécaire résidentiel m, prêt hypothécaire à l'habitation m; **∼ occupancy building** n immeuble d'habitation m; **∼ tax rate** n taux de l'impôt foncier m

residual adj résiduel/-elle; **∼ error** n erreur résiduelle f; **∼ lender** n prêteur/-euse résiduel/-elle m/f; **∼ value** n valeur résiduelle f

residue n résidu m; (Fin) actif net m; (Law) (of estate) reliquat m

resign ① vt (post, job) démissionner de ② vi démissionner

resignation n démission f; **hand in one's ∼** démissionner; **offer one's ∼** présenter sa démission; **∼ letter** n lettre de démission f

resilience n (of economy) ressort m, résistance f; (of character) résistance f

resistance n résistance f; **consumer ∼** résistance du consommateur f; **meet with ∼** se heurter à une résistance; **∼ level** n (Stock) niveau de résistance m, palier de résistance m

resize vt (Comp) (window) redimensionner

reskill vt recycler

reskilling n recyclage m

resolution n (of screen) définition f; (decision, determination) décision f, résolution f; (decree) résolution f; **pass a ∼** voter une résolution

resolve¹ n décision f, résolution f

resolve² vt (differences) régler; (problem) résoudre, **∼ that** décider que; **∼ to do** résoudre de faire

resource¹ n (facility, service) ressource f; (tool) outil m; **training ∼** outil pédagogique m; **∼ aggregation** n agrégation des ressources f; **∼ allocation** n allocation des ressources f, répartition des ressources f; **∼ appraisal** n examen des ressources m; **∼ industry** n industrie extractive f; **∼ sharing** n partage de ressources m

resource² vt (Fin) (department, organization) affecter les ressources nécessaires à; (HRM) (provide staff) trouver du personnel pour

resources n pl ressources f pl; **put more ∼ into** (project) (Fin) investir davantage dans; (HRM) affecter du personnel supplémentaire à; **∼ management** n gestion des ressources f

respect¹ n (esteem) respect m, estime f; **in this ∼** à cet égard, à ce propos; **in some/all ∼s** à certains/tous égards; **in ∼ of** (as regards) pour ce qui est de; (for) pour; **with ∼ to** par rapport à

respect² vt respecter

respectable adj (person) respectable; convenable; (performance, piece of work) honorable; (amount, sum) respectable

respectively adv respectivement

respite n (break) répit m; (Law) sursis m; **grant a ∼ for payment** surseoir au ⋯⟋

paiement; **without** ~ sans répit

respondent n (Law) défendeur/-eresse m/f; (in survey) personne interrogée f

response n (answer) réponse f; (reaction) réaction f; **in** ~ **to** en réponse à, suite à; **meet with a good** ~ être bien reçu; ~ **projection** n prévision des réponses f; ~ **rate** n taux de réponse m

responsibility n (Gen Comm) responsabilité f; (Econ) charge f; **take** ~ **for sth** prendre la responsabilité de qch; **have a** ~ **to sb/sth** avoir une responsabilité envers qn/quant à qch; **deny** ~, **disclaim** ~ décliner tout responsabilité; **claim** ~ **for** revendiquer; ~ **accounting** comptabilité des sections f; ~ **center** AmE, ~ **centre** BrE n centre de responsabilité m

responsible adj (person, firm) responsable; (job) à responsabilités; ~ **in law** (Law) responsable en droit; **be** ~ **for sth** (culpable) être responsable de qch; (in charge of) être chargé de; **be** ~ **to sb** être responsable devant qn; **hold sb** ~ tenir qn pour responsable

responsive adj qui réagit rapidement; (organization) dynamique; **be** ~ **to the needs of** être sensible aux besoins de

rest¹ n (remainder) reste m; (other people) les autres m pl; (break, relaxation) repos m; ~ **account** n, ~ **fund** n (Stock) fonds de réserve m; ~ **room** n AmE toilettes f pl

rest² ⟨1⟩ vt ~ **one's case** (Law) conclure son plaidoyer
⟨2⟩ vi se reposer; ~ **on** (depend) reposer sur; ~ **with** (decision) être entre les mains de

restart¹ n (of system) redémarrage m, relance f; (of economy) redémarrage m; ~ **program** n programme de relance m

restart² vt (system) redémarrer, relancer; (economy) redémarrer

restate vt (problem) reformuler; (intention) réaffirmer; (theory) exposer de nouveau; ~ **that** réaffirmer que; ~ **the case for doing** réaffirmer la nécessité de faire

restock vt (shop) réapprovisionner, réassortir; (shelves) regarnir, réapprovisionner

restore vt (give back) rendre, restituer; (repair) restaurer; (Comp) (window) redimensionner; (file, directory, text) restaurer; (right, custom) rétablir; ~ **law and order** rétablir l'ordre public

restraint n (moderation) modération f; (restriction) restriction f; **show** ~ faire preuve de modération; **pay** ~, **wage** ~ contrôle des salaires m; **price** ~ contrôle des prix m; **credit** ~ encadrement du crédit m; ~ **of trade** n entrave à la liberté du commerce f

restrict vt (numbers) limiter; (rights) limiter, restreindre; (use, activity, choice, growth) limiter; (freedom) restreindre; (access, membership) limiter; ~ **sth to sb** réserver qch à qn; ~ **oneself to** se limiter à

restricted adj (number, group) restreint, limité; (service, rights) réduit, limité; (document, report) secret/-ète; ~ **access** n accès réservé m; ~ **account** n compte de marge en débit m, compte limité m; ~ **area** n zone à accès réservé f; ~ **credit** n crédit restreint m; ~ **market** n marché restreint m; ~ **surplus** n AmE réserves indisponibles f pl

restriction n (rule) restriction f; (limit) limitation f; **impose** ~**s on** imposer des mesures de restriction sur; **currency** ~**s** contrôle des devises m; **speed/weight** ~**s** limitations de vitesse/poids f pl; ~ **of credit** n limitation du crédit f

restrictive adj restrictif/-ive; ~ **monetary policy** n (Econ) politique monétaire restrictive f; ~ **practices** n pl (by trade unions) pratiques restrictives f pl; (Econ, Law) entraves à la liberté du commerce f pl, atteintes à la libre concurrence f pl

restructure vt restructurer

restructured adj restructuré; ~ **loan** n prêt restructuré m

restructuring n restructuration f

restyle vt relooker, restyler

resubmit vt (plan, proposal) soumettre à nouveau

result¹ n résultat m; **as a** ~ en conséquence, par conséquent; **as a** ~ **of** par suite de, à la suite de; **with the** ~ **that** de sorte que; **get a** ~ obtenir des résultats

result²: ~ **from** vt résulter de; ~ **in** vt aboutir à, entraîner

results n pl (trading figures, of tests) résultats m pl; **get** ~ obtenir de bons résultats

resume ⟨1⟩ vt (work, talks) reprendre; ~ **doing** se remettre à faire
⟨2⟩ vi reprendre

résumé n (summary) résumé m; AmE (CV) curriculum vitae m

resurgence n (of economy) reprise f; (of currency) remontée f; ~ **of interest** regain d'intérêt m; ~ **in prices** nouvelle flambée des prix f

retail¹ n vente au détail f

retail² ⟨1⟩ vt vendre au détail, détailler
⟨2⟩ vi se vendre au détail, se détailler; ~ **at 300 euros** se vendre au détail à 300 euros

retail³ adv (sell) au détail

retail: ~ **bank** n banque commerciale f, banque de réseau f; ~ **banking** n banque de détail f, services bancaires de détail m pl; ~ **broker** n courtier de détail m; ~ **business** n commerce de détail m; ~ **center** AmE, ~ **centre** BrE n centre commercial m; ~ **chain** n chaîne de détail f, (group of shops) chaîne de magasins f; ~ **cooperative** n coopérative de détaillants f; ~ **deposit** n dépôt de détail m; ~ **deposits** n pl dépôts bancaires m pl; ~ **floorspace** n surface consacrée à la vente au détail f; ~ **food business** n commerce alimentaire de détail m; ~ **giant** n géant de la distribution *m*; ~ **investor** *n* épargnant/-e *m/f*; ~ **management** *n* gestion de la vente au détail *f*; ~ **margin** *n* marge de détail *f*; ~ **network** *n* réseau de détaillants *m*; ~ **offer** *n* offre au détail *f*; ~ **outlet** *n* point de vente de services de détail *m*; ~ **park** *n* parc d'activitiés commerciales *m*, zone commerciale *f*; ~ **price** *n* prix de détail *m*; ~ **price index** *n* indice des prix de détail *m*; ~ **price maintenance** *n* prix de vente imposé *m*; ~ **sale** *n* vente au détail *f*; ~ **sales analysis** *n* analyse des ventes au détail *f*; ~ **sector** *n* détail *m*; ~ **site** *n* (on web) site marchand *m*; ~ **trade** *n* commerce de détail *m*, détail *m*; ~ **trader** *n* détaillant/-e *m/f*; ~ **warehouse** *n* entrepôt de vente au détail *m*

retailer *n* détaillant/-e *m/f*, fournisseur *m*; ~ **cooperative** *n* groupe de détaillants *m*; ~ **margin** *n* marge du détaillant *f*

retailing *n* vente au détail *f*

retain *vt* (shares) garder, retenir; (control, support) garder; (lawyer) engager; ~ **sb's services** s'attacher les services de qn

retained: ~ **earnings** *n pl* bénéfices non distribués *m pl*, bénéfices non répartis *m pl*; ~ **profits** *n pl* bénéfices non distribués *m pl*, bénéfices non répartis *m pl*

retainer *n* (Law) provision *f*; (Fin) somme versée à l'avance *f*; (Prop) loyer réduit *m*, *permettant de conserver son logement en cas d'absence*; **be on a** ~ être sous contrat

retaliation *n* représailles *f pl*; **in** ~ **(for)** en représailles (de)

retaliatory measures *n pl* mesures de rétorsion *f pl*, mesures de représailles *f pl*

retendering *n* nouvelle offre *f*

retention *n* maintien *m*, conservation *f*; **customer** ~ fidélisation du client *f*; **have problems with staff** ~ avoir du mal à garder ses employés; ~ **date** *n* date d'expiration *f*; ~ **money** *n* dépôt de garantie *m*; ~ **on wages** *n* retenue sur salaire *f*

rethink ① *vt* repenser ② *vi* revoir la question

retire ① *vt* (employee) mettre à la retraite; (Stock) (bond, stock) rembourser ② *vi* (employee) prendre sa retraite; (official) se retirer; ~ **from business** se retirer des affaires

retired person *n* retraité/-e *m/f*

retirement *n* retraite *f*; **go into** ~ partir en retraite; **take early** ~ prendre une retraite anticipée; **come out of** ~ reprendre ses activités; ~ **age** *n* âge de la retraite *m*; ~ **annuity policy** *n* UK *police d'assurance qui fournit une rente viagère à l'âge de la retraite*; ~ **of debt** *n* retraite de dette *f*; ~ **fund** *n* caisse de retraite *f*; ~ **income** *n* revenu de retraite *m*; ~ **pension** *n* pension de retraite *f*; ~ **plan** *n* régime de retraite *m*; ~ **relief** *n* UK allègement de retraite *m*; ~ **savings plan** *n* plan d'épargne-retraite *m*; ~

scheme *n* régime de retraite *m*

retractable: ~ **bond** *n* obligation encaissable par anticipation *f*; ~ **share** *n* action rachetable au gré du porteur *f*

retraction *n* (of offer, statement) rétraction *f*

retraining *n* recyclage *m*; ~ **course** *n* stage de recyclage *m*

retrench *vt* (costs) réduire

retrenchment *n* (of costs) réduction *f*

retrieval *n* (Comp) (of data) extraction *f*; (of lost data, item) récupération *f*; (of money) recouvrement *m*; ~ **time** *n* (Comp) temps d'accès à l'information *m*

retrieve *vt* (Comp) (data, file) extraire; (lost data, item) récupérer

retroactive *adj* rétroactif/-ive *f*; ~ **pay rise** *n* rappel de salaire *m*

retrogress *vi* régresser

retrogression *n* régression *f*

retrospective *adj* (effect, claim, rebate) rétroactif/-ive

return[1] *n* (coming back) retour *m*; (sending back) renvoi *m*; (of lost, stolen goods) restitution *f*; (yield on investment) rendement *m*, rapport *m*; (unsold item, book) invendu *m*; (returned item) rendu *m*; (on capital) rendement *m*, rémunération *f*; **quick** ~ profit rapide *m*; (statement) état *m*, rapport *m*; ~ **expenses** — état de frais *m*; **tax** ~ déclaration d'impôt *f*, feuille d'impôt *f*; (paying back) remboursement *m*; (Comp) retour *m*; **by** ~ **of post** par retour du courrier; **in** ~ **for** en échange de; ~ **address** *n* adresse de l'expéditeur *f*; ~ **of amount overpaid** restitution d'un trop-perçu *f*; ~ **cargo** *n* cargaison de retour *f*; ~ **fare** *n* BrE prix d'un aller-retour *m*; ~ **flight** *n* (homeward bound) vol de retour *m*; (two-way flight) vol aller-retour *m*; ~ **freight** *n* fret de retour *m*; ~ **of income** déclaration de revenus *f*; ~ **journey** *n* (round trip) aller-retour *m*; (homeward trip) retour *m*; ~ **load** *n* chargement de retour *m*; ~ **on assets** (Acc, Fin) rendement de l'actif *m*, taux de rentabilité des actifs utilisés *m*; ~ **on book value** retour sur valeur comptable *m*; ~ **on capital** rendement du capital *m*; ~ **on capital employed** rentabilité des capitaux investis *f*; ~ **on equity** rendement des capitaux propres *m*, rendement des fonds propres *m*; ~ **on invested capital** rendement du capital investi *m*; ~ **on investment** rendement des actifs *m*, rendement des investissements *m*, rentabilité d'investissements *f*, rentabilité des actifs *f*, taux de rentabilité d'un investissement *m*; ~ **on net assets** rendement de l'actif net *m*; ~ **on net assets employed** rendement de l'actif net employé *m*, taux de rentabilité des actifs nets utilisés *m*; ~ **on real estate** revenu immobilier *m*; ~ **on sales** marge commerciale *f*, taux de marge brute *m*; ~ **ticket** *n* BrE billet aller-retour *m*, aller-retour ⋯⟶

m inv; **∼ to work** (after unemployment, break) retour à l'emploi *m*; (after strike) reprise du travail *f*

return² **1** *vt* (give back) rendre; (send back) renvoyer; (bring back) rapporter; (put back) remettre; (lost, stolen item) restituer; (loan) rembourser; (**Bank**) (cheque) refuser; (bill) contrepasser; (verdict) retourner; (**Tax**) (income) déclarer; (**Fin**) (profit, loss) enregistrer; (**Pol**) (candidate) élire; **∼ sb's call** rappeler qn **2** *vi* (come back) revenir; (go back) retourner; **∼ to profit** refaire des bénéfices; '**∼ to sender'** 'retour à l'expéditeur'

returnable *adj* (bottle) consigné; **∼ by 22 March** à rendre avant le 22 mars

returned: **∼ check** AmE, **∼ cheque** BrE *n* chèque refusé *m*, chèque retourné *m*; **∼ goods** *n pl* invendus *m pl*, marchandises de retour *f pl*

returns *n pl* (unsold goods) invendus *m pl*; (income, receipts) recettes *f pl*, rentrées *f pl*; (results) chiffre d'affaires *m*; (statistics) statistiques *f pl*; **election ∼** résultats des élections *m pl*; **∼ to scale** *n pl* rendements d'échelle *m pl*

reunification *n* réunification *f*

reusable *adj* réutilisable *f*

reuse¹ *n* réutilisation *f*

reuse² *vt* réutiliser

revalorization *n* revalorisation *f*

revaluation *n* réévaluation *f*; **∼ of assets** réévaluation des actifs *f*; **∼ of exchange rate** réévaluation du taux de change *f*; **∼ reserves** *n pl* réserves de réévaluation *f pl*

revalue *vt* (assets) réévaluer

revamp¹ *n* (of company) modernisation *f*; (of premises) rénovation *f*, transformation *f*; (of product, image) rajeunissement *m*

revamp² *vt* (company) moderniser, (premises) rénover, transformer; (image) rajeunir; (system) réorganiser

revamped *adj* (offices) retapé (infrml), transformé; (system, management) réorganisé, modernisé

revenue *n* (**Gen Comm**) revenu *m*; (**Tax**) impôts *m pl*; (from sales) recettes *f pl*; (turnover) chiffre d'affaires *m*; **advertising/current ∼s** recettes publicitaires/courantes *f pl*; **oil ∼s** revenus pétroliers *m pl*; **operating ∼s** résultat *m*, produit(s) d'exploitation *m* (*pl*); **∼ allocation** *n* (**Gen Comm**) répartition des recettes *f*; (**Tax**) attribution des recettes *f*; **∼ center** AmE, **∼ centre** BrE *n* services fiscaux *m pl*; **∼ curve** *n* courbe de recettes *f*; **∼ department** *n* US service des contributions *m*; **∼ earner** *n* générateur de recettes *m*; **∼ economy** *n* économie collectiviste *f*; **∼ and expenses** *n pl* (**Acc**) produits et charges *m pl*; **∼ guarantee** *n* (**Tax**) garantie de revenu *f*, garantie des recettes *f*; **∼ loss** *n* (**Acc**) perte courante *f*, perte d'exploitation *f*; **∼ office** *n* (**Tax**) bureau des contributions *m*; **∼ officer** *n*

(**Tax**) inspecteur/-trice des impôts *m/f*

reversal *n* (of trend, method) inversion *f*; (of policy, role) renversement *m*; (**Law**) annulation *f*; **∼ of fortune** revers de fortune *m*; (**Acc**, **Fin**) contre-passation *f*

reverse¹ *adj* (effect, trend, tendancy) contraire; (direction) opposé; **in ∼ order** en commençant par le dernier

reverse² *n* (opposite) contraire *m*; (of banknote) verso *m*; (of coin) revers *m*; (setback) revers *m*; (backwards motion) marche arrière *f*; **the same process but in ∼** le même procédé mais en sens inverse

reverse³ *vt* (**Acc**) (entry) contre-passer; (trend) inverser; (**Law**) (judgement) annuler; **∼ the charges** BrE téléphoner en PCV

reverse: **∼ auction** *n* vente aux enchères inversée *f*, vente aux enchères initiée par le client *f*; **∼ discrimination** *n* discrimination inverse *f*; **∼ engineer** *vt* désassembler; **∼ engineering** *n* désassemblage *m*, ingénierie inverse *f*; **∼ gearing** *n* BrE, **∼ leverage** *n* AmE effet de levier négatif *m*; **∼ repurchase** *n* mise en pension inverse *f*; **∼ repurchase agreement** *n* contrat de vente à réméré *m*; **∼ split** *n* regroupement d'actions *m*; **∼ takeover** *n* OPA à rebours *f*, contre-OPA *f*; **∼ video** *n* vidéo inverse *f*; **∼ yield gap** *n* courbe des taux inversée *f*, écart de rendement inverse *m*

reverse charge call *n* BrE appel en PCV *m*; **make a ∼ to sb** appeler qn en PCV

reversible *adj* réversible

reversing *n* (**Acc**, **Fin**) contre-passation *f*; **∼ entry** *n* écriture de contre-passation *f*

reversionary: **∼ annuity** *n* rente réversible *f*; **∼ bonus** *n* bonus réversible *m*; **∼ value** *n* valeur de réversion *f*

review¹ *n* révision *f*; (meeting) réunion d'évaluation *f*; (critical assessment) critique *f*; **set up a ∼** établir une révision; **be subject to ∼** (decision) pouvoir être reconsidéré; **salaries come up for ∼ next month** les salaires seront révisés le mois prochain; **be under ∼** (practices, policies) être réexaminé; (pay, terms) être révisé; **salary/policy ∼** révision des salaires/de la politique; **progress ∼** réunion de bilan *f*, réunion d'évaluation *f*; **keep sth under ∼** réviser qch régulièrement; **∼ board** *n* comité de révision *m*; **∼ body** *n* organisme de révision salariale *m*; **∼ document** *n* document de révision *m*; **∼ meeting** *n* réunion d'évaluation *f*, réunion de synthèse *f*; **∼ process** *n* processus de révision *m*

review² *vt* (situation, events, facts) réexaminer; (policy, case) réviser; (progress, performance) passer en revue; (document) réviser

revise *vt* (proposal, estimate, plan, forecast) réviser, modifier; (text) réviser; (position) revenir sur; (bring up to date) actualiser; **∼ downward** revoir à la baisse; **∼ upward** revoir à la hausse

revised: ~ **edition** n édition revue et corrigée f; ~ **figures** n pl chiffres corrigés m pl; ~ **net income** n revenu net révisé m; ~ **version** n version actualisée f, version révisée f

revision n révision f

revitalization n revitalisation f

revitalize vt (economy) donner un coup de fouet à, relancer; (company) faire redémarrer

revival n (of economy) reprise f; ~ **of interest** regain d'intérêt m

revive **1** vt (career, economy, movement) relancer; (proposal, plan) remettre à l'ordre du jour; (debate) relancer; (hopes) ranimer; ~ **interest in sth** susciter un regain d'intérêt pour qch
2 vi (economy, market) reprendre; (interest, enthusiasm) renaître

revocable adj révocable; ~ **credit** n crédit révocable m; ~ **trust** n société d'investissement révocable f

revocation n (of order, promise) révocation f; (of law) abrogation f; (of contract) annulation f; (of licence, permission) retrait m

revoke vt (order, promise) révoquer; (law) abroger; (contract) annuler; (licence, permission) annuler

revolution n révolution f; **bring about a ~ in sth** révolutionner qch

revolutionary adj révolutionnaire

revolutionize vt révolutionner

revolving: ~ **charge account** n accord de paiement différé renouvelable m; ~ **credit** n crédit permanent m, crédit renouvelable m, crédit revolving m; ~ **credit line** n ligne de crédit renouvelable f

reward¹ n récompense f; **as a ~ for** en récompense de; ~ **card** n carte de fidélité f

reward² vt récompenser; ~ **sb for sth** récompenser qn de qch

rewarding adj (job) gratifiant; (experience) enrichissant; (financially) rémunérateur/-trice

rewind vt (cassette, tape) rembobiner

rewritable adj (Comp) réinscriptible

rewrite vt (write again) réécrire; (re-work) remanier

RFP abbr (▶request for proposal) demande de propositions f

rhetoric n rhétorique f

rial n rial m

rich adj riche; **get ~** s'enrichir; **the ~** n pl les riches m pl

rid adj **get ~ of** se débarrasser de

rider n (proviso) correctif m; (to document) annexe f; (to contract, policy) avenant m

RIE abbr (▶recognized investment exchange) marché d'investissement agréé m

riel n riel m

rig vt (election, competition, result) truquer; ~ **the market** manipuler le marché

rigged market n marché manipulé m

rigging n (of election, competition, result) truquage m; (of market) manipulation f

right¹ adj (not left) droit, de droite; (fair, just) juste; (choice, decision, direction, answer, word) bon/bonne; (time) exact; **be ~** avoir raison; **get one's facts right** être sûr de ce qu'on avance; **when the time is ~** quand le moment sera venu; **the ~ equipment/model** le matériel/modèle qui convient, le matériel/modèle approprié; **be in the ~ place at the ~ time** être là où il faut au bon moment; **put sth ~** (mistake) corriger; (situation) arranger; **set sb ~** détromper qn; **the ~ product at the ~ time** le bon produit au bon moment; **be on the ~ track** être sur la bonne voie

right² n droit m; **have the ~ to do** avoir le droit de faire; **have a ~ to sth** avoir droit à qch; **give sb the ~ to do** accorder à qn le droit de faire, autoriser qn à faire; **with no ~ of appeal** sans appel; **be within one's ~s** être dans son droit

right³ adv (turn, go) à droite; **see sb ~** (infrml) (financially) dépanner qn

right⁴ vt (balance, wrong) redresser

right: ~ **of appeal** droit d'appel m, droit de recours m; ~ **column** colonne de droite f; ~ **of combination** droit syndical m; ~ **of entry** (Gen Comm) droit d'entrée m, (Prop) droit de prendre possession m; ~ **of establishment** droit d'établissement m; ~ **of first refusal** droit de premier refus m; ~ **of interest in a share** droit afférent à une action m; ~ **of offset** droit de compensation m; ~ **of recovery** droit d'indemnisation m, droit à des dommages-intérêts m, droit à réparation m; ~ **of redemption** droit de remboursement m; ~ **of redress** droit à réparation m; ~ **of reply** droit de réponse m; ~ **of residence** droit de résidence m, droit de séjour m; ~ **of return** droit de retour m; ~ **to associate** liberté d'association f; ~ **to know** droit à l'information m; ~ **to strike** droit de grève m; ~ **to vote** droit de vote m; ~ **to work** droit au travail m; ~ **of way** droit de passage m

right-click vi cliquer en appuyant sur le bouton droit de la souris

rightful adj (heir, owner, claim) légitime

right-justified adj justifié à droite

right-justify vt justifier à droite

rights n pl (Law, Patents) droits m pl; **all ~ reserved** tous droits réservés; **have sole ~ to sth** avoir l'exclusivité de qch; **property/publishing/manufacturing ~** droits de propriété/de publication/de production m pl; ~ **of conversion** n pl droits de conversion m pl; ~ **of exchange** n pl droits d'échange m pl; ~ **holder** n porteur de droits de souscription m; ~ **issue** n (Stock) émission de droits préférentiels de souscription f

right-sizing n dégraissage m, réduction ⋯⟶

d'effectifs *f*

right-wing *adj* (Pol) de droite

ring¹ *n* (network) réseau *m*; (Fin) syndicat *m*; (Comms) coup de fil *m* (infrml); **give sb a ~** passer un coup de fil à qn; **~ road** *n* périphérique *m*, rocade *f*

ring² 1 *vt* (telephoner) appeler 2 *vi* appeler, téléphoner; **~ off** *vi* raccrocher; **~ up** 1 *vt* (person) appeler; (losses) enregistrer 2 *vi* téléphoner

ring-fence *vt* (fund, grant) réserver

ring-fencing *n* affectation spéciale de fonds publics *f*

ringing out *n* liquidation d'un contrat à terme avant maturité *f*, règlement anticipé *m*

ringtone *n* sonnerie *f*

ripple effect *n* effet en cascade *m*

rise¹ *n* augmentation *f*; (in prices, sales) hausse *f*, augmentation *f*; (in quality, standard) amélioration *f*; (of sector, phenomenon) essor *m*; (in rate, tax) relèvement *m*, augmentation *f*; (pay increase) augmentation (de salaire) *f*; **~ in prices** hausse des prix *f*, augmentation des prix *f*; **give ~ to** (speculation, rumours) donner lieu à; (resentment, dissatisfaction) susciter; (problems) causer; (redundancies, expansion, disruption) entraîner; **be on the ~** (prices) être en hausse; (inflation, accidents, bankruptcies, unemployment) être en augmentation; **~ to fame** accession à la gloire *f*

rise² *vi* (rate, percentage) monter; (tension) monter; (price, cost, sales, unemployment, inflation) augmenter; (committee, parliament) lever la séance; **~ by 5%** augmenter de 5%; **~ to** (position, rank) accéder à; **~ to fame** atteindre la célébrité; **~ to a challenge** relever un défi; **~ through the ranks** gravir tous les échelons

rising *adj* (inflation, prices) en hausse; (wages, sales, demand) en augmentation; (optimism, dissatisfaction) croissant; **~ cost** *n* coût en augmentation *m*, coût en hausse *m*; **~ interest rate** *n* taux d'intérêt en hausse *m*, taux d'intérêt en augmentation *m*; **~ star** *n* (S&M) produit d'avenir *m*; **~ tendency** *n* (of market) tendance à la hausse *f*; **~ trend** *n* tendance à la hausse *f*; **~ unemployment** *n* chômage en augmentation *m*, chômage en hausse *m*

risk¹ *n* risque *m*; **at ~** menacé, en danger; **at owner's ~** aux risques du propriétaire; **at one's own ~** à ses risques et périls; **at sender's ~** aux risques de l'expéditeur; **spread the ~** répartir le risque; **take a ~** prendre un risque; **be a good/bad ~** être un bon/mauvais risque; **run the ~ of doing** courir le risque de faire; **put sth at ~** mettre qch en danger; **there is no ~ to health/the public** il n'y a aucun danger pour la santé/ pour le public; **~ analysis** *n* analyse des risques *f*; **~ arbitrage** *n* arbitrage des risques *m*; **~ assessment** *n* appréciation

des risques *f*; **~ averse** *adj* opposé au risque; **~ aversion** *n* aversion pour le risque *f*; **~-based premium** *n* assurance à la prime de risque *f*; **~-bearing capital** *n* (Fin) financement par capital-risque *m*; **~ capital** *n* capital-risque *m*, capital à risque *m*; **~ exposure** *n* (Acc) exposition aux risques *f*, risque encouru *m*; **~ factor** *n* facteur de risque *m*; **~-free** *adj* sans risque; **~ management** *n* (Fin, Ins) gestion des risques *f*; (Stock) gestion du risque *f*; **~ manager** *n* (Ins) gestionnaire des risques *mf*; **~ minimizing** *n* réduction du risque *f*; **~ monitoring** *n* contrôle de risques *m*; **~ package** *n* ensemble des risques *m*; **~ pooling** *n* mise en commun des risques *f*; **~ position** *n* position à risque *f*, état des risques *m*; **~ premium** *n* prime de risque *f*; **~ profile** *n* profil de risque *m*; **~-related premium** *n* prime de risque *f*; **~-reward ratio** *n* rapport risque-bénéfice *m*; **~ sharing** *n* partage de risque *m*, partage des risques *m*; **~ weighting** *n* pondération du risque *f*

risk² *vt* (Gen Comm) risquer; (health) compromettre; **~ doing** courir le risque de faire

riskless *adj* sans risque, sûr

risks: all ~ tous risques; **all ~ cover** *n* couverture tous risques *f*; **all ~ insurance** *n* assurance tous risques *f*

risky *adj* hasardeux/-euse, risqué

rival¹ *adj* (bid, business) rival; (claim) opposé; **~ good** *n* bien de la concurrence *m*

rival² *n* concurrent/-e *m/f*, rival/-e *m/f*

rival³ *vt* (equal) égaler; (compete favourably with) rivaliser avec; **~ sth in popularity** rivaliser de popularité avec qch

rivalry *n* rivalité *f*

river *n* fleuve *m*, rivière *f*; **~ bus** *n* bateau-bus *m*; **~ pollution** *n* pollution des cours d'eau *f*

riyal *n* riyal *m*

ROA *abbr* (▶return on assets) rendement des fonds propres *m*

road *n* route *f*; (in built-up area) rue *f*; **be on the ~** (sales rep) être en déplacement, être en voyage d'affaires; (of car) **£19,000 on the ~** 19 000 livres sterling clés en main; **reach the end of the ~** déboucher sur une impasse; **be on the ~ to success** être sur la voie du succès; **~ building** *n* construction de routes *f*; **~-fund licence** BrE, **~-fund license** AmE *n* ≈ vignette *f*; **~ haulage** *n* transports routiers *m pl*; **~ haulage vehicle** *n* poids lourd *m*; **~ network** *n* réseau routier *m*; **~-rail transport** *n* BrE ferroutage *m*; **~ safety** *n* sécurité routière *f*; **~ show** *n* tournée de présentation *f*; **~ sign** *n* panneau de signalisation *m*; **~ tax** *n* UK taxe routière *f*; **~ tax disc** *n* UK ≈ vignette *f*; **~ toll** *n* péage *m*; **~ traffic** *n* circulation routière *f*; **~ transport** *n* transport routier *m*;

~ works *n pl* travaux *m pl*

roadworthy *adj* **be ~** être en état de rouler

rob *vt* (person) voler; (shop) dévaliser; **~ sb of sth** (steal) voler qch à qn; (deprive) priver qn de qch; **~ the till** voler de l'argent dans la caisse

robber *n* voleur/-euse *m/f*

robbery *n* vol *m*

robot *n* robot *m*

robotics *n + sing v* robotique *f*

robust *adj* robuste, solide

ROC *abbr* (▸**return on capital**) rendement du capital *m*

ROCE *abbr* (▸**return on capital employed**) RCI *m* (rentabilité des capitaux investis)

rock *vt* (government, organization) ébranler; **~ the boat** semer la pagaille

rock bottom *n* point le plus bas *m*; **hit ~** toucher le fond; **be at ~** être au plus bas; **~ price** *n* prix plancher *m*

rocket *vi* (price, profit, value) monter en flèche

rocks *n pl* **be on the ~** être en faillite

ROE *abbr* (▸**return on equity**) rendement des capitaux propres *m*, rendement des fonds propres *m*

ROI *abbr* (▸**return on investment**) TRI *m* (taux de rentabilité d'un investissement), rendement des investissements *m*

ROIC *abbr* (▸**return on invested capital**) rendement du capital investi *m*

role *n* rôle *m*; **~ conflict** *n* conflit des rôles *m*; **~ model** *n* modèle *m*; **~ play**, **~-playing** *n* jeu de rôle *m*

roll¹ *n* (list, register) liste *f*; **~-back** *n* baisse des prix *f*; **~-down** *n* (Stock) baisse des prix imposée *f*, report de position à la baisse *m*; **~ on/roll off** *n* (system) roulage *m*, manutention horizontale *f*; **~ on/roll off ship** *n* roulier *m*; **~-out** *n* (of vehicle) présentation *f*; (of product) lancement *m*; **~-over** *n* (Bank, Fin) reconduction *f*, roll-over *m*; (Stock) reconduction *f*, report de position *m*; (Tax) roulement *m*, transfert libre d'impôt *m*; **~-over credit** *n* crédit à taux révisable *m*, prêt à taux révisable *m*; **~-over credit facility** *n* crédit à taux variable *m*, prêt à taux variable *m*; **~-over loan** *n* prêt à taux révisable *m*; **~-over order** *n* ordre de reconduction *m*, ordre de report de position *m*; **~-over relief** *n* (Tax) dégrèvement roll-over *m*

roll²: **~ back** *vt* (prices) faire baisser; **~ out** *vt* (vehicle) présenter; (product) lancer; **~ over** *vt* (debt, loan) reconduire; (interest rates) renouveler

rolling: **~ down** *n* (Stock) (options) report de position à la baisse *m*, roulement à la baisse *m*; **~ in** *n* (Stock) (options) report de position *m*, roulement en arrière *m*; **~ news** *n* informations en continu *f pl*; **~ options positions** *n pl* (Stock) positions de

roulement variable *f pl*; **~ out** *n* (options) roulement en avant *m*; **~ rate** *n* (Fin, Stock) taux variable *m*; **~-rate note** *n* (Fin, Stock) obligation à taux variable *f*; **~ settlement** *n* règlement graduel *m*; **~ stock** *n* matériel roulant *m*; **~ strikes** *n pl* grèves tournantes *f pl*; **~ up** *n* report de position à la hausse *m*, roulement à la hausse *m*

ROM *abbr* (▸**read only memory**) mémoire ROM *f*, mémoire morte *f*

room *n* pièce *f*; (in hotel) chambre *f*; (for meeting, teaching) salle *f*; (office) bureau *m*; **~ service** *n* service des chambres *m*; **~ temperature** *n* température ambiante *f*

RORCE *abbr* (▸**rate of return on capital employed**) (Econ, Fin) taux de rendement des capitaux investis *m*, taux de rendement sur le capital employé *m*

ro/ro *abbr* (▸**roll on/roll off**) roulage *m*, manutention horizontale *f*; **~ ship** *n* roulier *m*

roster *n* tableau de service *m*

rosy *adj* (prospects) souriant

rotate *vt* (stocks) opérer une rotation de; (staff) faire un roulement de

rotating shift *n* équipe de travail posté *f*

rotation *n* rotation *f*; **job/stock ~** rotation des postes/stocks *f*; **in ~** à tour de rôle; **~ clause** *n* clause de rotation *f*

rouble *n* rouble *m*

rough¹ *n* (sketch, design) ébauche *f*; (in advertising) montage préalable *m*; **a ~ idea**, **a ~ guess** une idée approximative; **a ~ draft** brouillon *m*, premier projet *m*; **~ estimate** *n* (of costs) devis approximatif *m*; **~ guide** *n* approximation *f*

rough²: **~ out** *vt* ébaucher, esquisser

roughly *adv* (calculate, sketch, indicate) grossièrement; (equal, equivalent) à peu près; **~ 10%** à peu près 10%

round¹ *adj* rond; **in ~ figures** en chiffres ronds

round² *n* (Econ) négociations commerciales *f pl*, round *m*; **the first ~ of budget talks** le premier round du débat budgétaire; **~ of negotiations** négociations *f pl*; **pay ~** négociations salariales *f pl*

round³: **~ down** *vt* (number) arrondir au chiffre inférieur; **~ off** *vt* (number, figure) arrondir; (meeting) compléter; **~ up** *vt* (number) arrondir

round: **~ brackets** *n pl* parenthèses *f pl*; **~ charter party** *n* contrat d'affrètement aller-retour *m*; **~ figure** *n* chiffre rond *m*; **~ lot** *n* US (Gen Comm) lot régulier *m*; (Stock) lot régulier *m*, quotité *f*; **~ number** *n* chiffre rond *m*; **~ robin** *n* (petition) pétition *f*; (circular) circulaire *f*; **~ sum** *n* montant arrondi *m*, somme en chiffres ronds *f*; **~ table** *n* table ronde *f*; **~ trip** *n* aller-retour *m*; **~-trip fare** *n* AmE prix d'un aller-retour *m*; **~-trip rate** *n* tarif aller-retour *m*; **~-trip ticket** *n* AmE ⋯⟩

billet aller-retour *m*; **~-trip time** *n* durée aller-retour *f*; **~ turn** *n* (Stock) commission d'aller-retour *f*

rounding error *n* erreur d'arrondi *f*

round-the-clock *adj* (service) 24 heures sur 24

round-up *n* (summary) résumé *m*

route¹ *n* route *f*; **~ analysis** *n* analyse de route *f*; **~ capacity** *n* capacité de route *f*; **~ diversion** *n* déroutement *m*; **~ planning** *n* programmation d'itinéraires *f*

route² *vt* (Comp, Transp) acheminer

router *n* (Comp) routeur *m*

routine¹ *adj* (matter, enquiry) de routine

routine² *n* routine *f*; (Comp) sous-programme *m*; **as a matter of ~** systématiquement

routine: ~ check *n* contrôle de routine *m*; **~ control** *n* vérification de routine *f*; **~ duties** *n pl* affaires courantes *f pl*; **~ maintenance** *n* entretien de routine *m*, entretien courant *m*

routing *n* (Comp, Transp) acheminement *m*, routage *m*

row *n* (of figures) ligne *f*; (of people, objects) rang *m*, rangée *f*; (of houses) rangée *f*

Royal: ~ Exchange *n* UK bourse de commerce de Londres; **~ Mint** *n* UK ≈ Hôtel de la Monnaie *m*

royalties *n pl* droits d'auteur *m pl*, royalties *f pl*

royalty *n* (to author, composer) droits d'auteur *m pl*; (to landowner, patentee) redevance *f*

RPI *abbr* (▸**retail price index**) indice des prix de détail *m*

RPM *abbr* (▸**resale price maintenance**) prix de vente imposé *m*

RRP *abbr* (▸**recommended retail price**) prix conseillé *m*

RRR *abbr* (▸**real rate of return**) taux de rendement réel *m*

RSI *abbr* (▸**repetitive strain injury**) TMS *m* (trouble musculo-squelettique)

RTM *abbr* (▸**release to market**) mise sur le marché *f*

rubber *n* (material) caoutchouc *m*; **~ band** *n* élastique *m*; **~ check** AmE, **~ cheque** BrE *n* (infrml) chèque en bois *m* (infrml), chèque sans provision *m*

rubber stamp *n* tampon *m*

rubber-stamp *vt* (document) tamponner; (decision) entériner sans discuter

rubbish *n* BrE déchets *m pl*, détritus *m pl*; (household) ordures *f pl*

ruin¹ *n* ruine *f*; **face ~, be on the brink of ~** être au bord de la ruine

ruin² *vt* (person, company, career) ruiner

rule¹ *n* (principle) règle *f*; **as a ~** en règle générale; **be against the ~s** être contraire au règlement; **break/bend the ~s** violer/contourner le

règlement, violer/contourner les règles; **it is a ~ that** il est de règle que; **~ book** *n* règlement *m*; **~ of law** suprématie du droit *f*, état de droit *m*; **~ of thumb** méthode empirique *f*; **~s of fair practice** code des usages *m*, règles de pratiques équitables *f pl*; **~s and regulations** statuts et règlements *m pl*

rule²: ~ out *vt* exclure, écarter

ruling *n* décision *f*, jugement *m*, ordonnance *f*; **give a ~** rendre une décision; **give a ~ in favor of sb** AmE, **give a ~ in favour of sb** BrE rendre un jugement en faveur de qn; **~ class** *n* classe dirigeante *f*

ruling price *n* cours en vigueur *m*, cours pratiqué *m*; **at ~s** aux tarifs en vigueur

rumor AmE, **rumour** BrE *n* bruit *m*, rumeur *f*; **~ has it that** le bruit court que; **start a ~** faire courir un bruit

run¹ *n* (Fin, Stock) ruée *f*; (series of goods produced) série *f*; (series of books printed) tirage *m*; **~ on the banks** panique bancaire *f*, ruée sur les banques *f*; **~ on the dollar** ruée sur le dollar *f*; **~ time** *n* (Gen Comm) délai d'exécution *m*; (Comp) (of program) durée de l'exécution *f*

run² **1** *vt* (company) diriger, gérer; (hotel) gérer; (event, workshop, course) organiser; (machinery) faire fonctionner; **~ an ad in the paper** insérer une annonce dans le journal, mettre une annonce dans le journal; **~ a concession** (in store) être concessionnaire; **~ a check on sb** se renseigner sur qn; (vet) vérifier les antécédents de qn; **~ a deficit** avoir un déficit, présenter un déficit; **~ an errand** faire une commission, faire une course; **~ the show** (infrml) faire marcher l'affaire; **~ a surplus** avoir un excédent, présenter un excédent

2 *vi* (last) durer; (Fin) (interest) courir; **~ aground** (ship) s'échouer; **~ foul of the tax authorities** avoir des ennuis avec l'administration fiscale; **~ low** (stocks) s'épuiser; (Stock) avoir un cours faible; **~ short of** se trouver à court de; **~ smoothly** bien fonctionner; **~ down** *vt* (production, reserves, operations) réduire; (disparage) d'énigrer; *vi* (reserves, stocks) s'épuiser; (company, industry) s'essouffler; **~ into** (opposition, problem) rencontrer, se heurter à; **~ into debt** s'endetter; **~ off** (print) tirer; **~ on** (meeting) se prolonger; **~ out** (supplies, resources) s'épuiser; (lease, passport) expirer; **~ out of** ne plus avoir de; **~ over, ~ through** (arrangements, details) passer en revue; **~ sth through the computer** passer qch dans l'ordinateur; **~ up** (bill) accumuler; **~ up a debt** s'endetter; **~ up a deficit** accumuler un déficit

runaway: ~ costs *n pl* dépenses incontrôlables *f pl*; **~ industry** *n* industrie diversifiée *f*; **~ inflation** *n* hyperinflation *f*, inflation galopante *f*, spirale inflationniste *f*; **~ shop** *n* (HRM, Ind) atelier fugitif *m*;

~ victory *n* victoire éclatante *f*

runner *n* (Gen Comm) messager/-ère *m/f*; (Stock) coursier/-ière *m/f*

running *n* (of company, business) gestion *f*, direction *f*; (of equipment) fonctionnement *m*; (Comp) (of program) exécution *f*; (of workshop) animation *f*; (of meeting) conduite *f*; **be in/out of the ~** être/ne plus être dans la course; **be in the ~ for** (post, promotion) être sur les rangs pour; **~ costs** *n pl*, **~ expenses** *n pl* (Gen Comm) dépenses courantes *f pl*; (Acc) charges d'exploitation *f pl*, dépenses de fonctionnement *f pl*; (of machine) frais de fonctionnement *m pl*; (of vehicle) frais d'entretien *m pl*; **~ interest** *n* (Bank) intérêts en cours *m pl*; **~ total** *n* cumul *m*

run-of-the-mill *adj* banal, quelconque

run-up *n* (Stock) hausse *f*; **in the ~ to** (event, elections) pendant la période précédant

runway *n* piste *f*

rupee *n* roupie *f*

rupiah *n* rupiah *f*

rural *adj* rural; **~ area** *n* zone rurale *f*; **~ community** *n* communauté rurale *f*; **~ delivery service** *n* US service de livraisons gratuites en zone rurale *m*; **~ development area** *n* UK zone d'aménagement rural *f*; **~ economy** *n* économie rurale *f*; **~ sector** *n* secteur agricole *m*

rush *vt* (task) expédier; (person) bousculer; **~ sth to sb** envoyer qch à qn d'urgence; **~ into a decision** prendre une décision précipitamment; **~ out** (report, document) préparer en vitesse; (product) sortir rapidement; **~ through** (order, request) traiter en priorité

rush: **~ hour** *n* heure de pointe *f*; **~ job** *n* travail d'urgence *m*; **~ on the dollar** *n* ruée sur le dollar *f*; **~ order** *n* commande urgente *f*

rusty *adj* (metal, person) rouillé

ryal *n* rial *m*

Ss

s.a.a.r. *abbr* (▶**seasonally adjusted annual rate**) taux annuel corrigé des variations saisonnières *m*

sack[1] *n* **get the ~** (infrml) être renvoyé, être viré (infrml); **give sb the ~** (infrml) mettre qn à la porte (infrml)

sack[2] *vt* BrE (infrml) (employee) renvoyer, virer (infrml)

sacking *n* (infrml) licenciement *m*

sacrifice *vt* (Ins) sacrifier; (goods) vendre à perte, sacrifier

s.a.e *abbr* UK (▶**stamped addressed envelope**) enveloppe timbrée à mon/son/votre adresse *f*

safe[1] *adj* (method, product) sans danger; (place, environment) sûr; (tactic, policy, decision) prudent; **be ~** (valuables, files) être en lieu sûr; (reputation, job, firm) ne pas être menacé; **a ~ bet** une valeur sûre; **as ~ as houses** sans risque; **play ~** être prudent; **be in ~ hands** être en bonnes mains; **to be on the ~ side** par précaution; **he's a ~ pair of hands** il est prudent

safe[2] *n* (Bank) coffre-fort *m*

safe: **~ asset** *n* actif sûr *m*; **~ deposit** *n* dépôt en coffre *m*; **~-deposit box** *n* coffre *m*; **~ estimate** *n* estimation prudente *f*; **~ hedge** *n* couverture sûre *f*, opération de couverture sûre *f*; **~ investment** *n* placement sûr *m*; **~ working load** *n* charge admissible de fonctionnement *f*

safeguard[1] *n* (Gen Comm) garantie *f*; (Law) (clause) sauvegarde *f*

safeguard[2] *vt* (Gen Comm) protéger; (assets) sauvegarder; (secret) garder; **~ against sth** se protéger contre qch

safekeeping *n* (Bank) garde des valeurs *f*; **entrust sth to sb's ~** confier qch à la garde de qn; **~ of assets** garde des valeurs actives *f*

safety *n* sécurité *f*; **~ bank** *n* stock de dépannage *m*; **~ belt** *n* ceinture de sécurité *f*; **~-deposit box** *n* coffre *m*; **~ hazard** *n* risque pour la sécurité *m*; **~ limits** *n pl* limites imposées par les normes de sécurité *f pl*; **~ management** *n* gestion de la sécurité *f*; **~ margin** *n* marge de sécurité *f*; **~ measure** *n* mesure de sécurité *f*; **~ net** *n* filet de sécurité *m*; **~ officer** *n* responsable de la sécurité *mf*; **~ precaution** *n* mesure de sécurité *f*; **~ record** *n* résultats en matière de sécurité *m pl*; **~ regulations** *n pl* règles de sécurité *f pl*; **~ requirements** *n pl* (for products) exigences de sécurité *f pl*; **~ standards** *n pl* normes de sécurité *f pl*; **~ stock** *n* stock de précaution *m*, stock tampon *m*

sag[1] *n* (Stock) fléchissement *m*

sag[2] *vi* (Stock) fléchir

sagging *adj* (profits, sales) en baisse

sail *vi* voyager en bateau; **~ close to the wind** friser l'illégalité; **~ through** gagner ⋯⟩

facilement; **he ∼ed through the interview** il s'en est bien tiré à l'entretien (infrml)

sailing *n* navigation *f*; (departure) départ *m*; ∼ **date** *n* date de départ *f*

sailor *n* marin *m*

salable *adj* AmE ▸**saleable** BrE

salaried: ∼ **employee** *n* salarié/-e *m/f*; ∼ **staff** *n* personnel salarié *m*

salaries: ∼ **and wages** *n pl* traitements et salaires *m pl*; ∼**, wages and fringe benefits** *n pl* salaires et charges sociales *m pl*

salary *n* salaire *m*; ∼ **to be negotiated** salaire à débattre; ∼ **base** *n* base salariale *f*; ∼ **check** AmE, ∼ **cheque** BrE *n* chèque de salaire *m*; ∼ **deduction** *n* retenue à la source *f*; ∼ **earner** *n* salarié/-e *m/f*; ∼ **increase** *n* augmentation de salaire *f*; ∼ **range** *n* éventail de salaires *m*; ∼ **rate** *n* taux de rémunération *m*; ∼ **review** *n* révision des salaires *f*, réévaluation des salaires *f*; ∼ **scale** *n* grille des salaires *f*; ∼ **structure** *n* structure des salaires *f*

sale *n* (act of selling) vente *f*; (at reduced prices) solde *m*; **for** ∼ à vendre; **offer sth for** ∼, **put sth up for** ∼ mettre qch en vente; **go on** ∼ être mis en vente; **have a** ∼ faire des soldes; **buy sth in a** ∼ acheter qch en solde; **make a** ∼ réaliser une vente, faire une vente; **on** ∼ en vente; (reduced) AmE en solde; **on** ∼ **or return** vendu avec possibilité de retour des invendus; ∼ **or exchange** vente avec possibilité d'échanger la marchandise; ∼ **agreement** *n* contrat de vente *m*; ∼ **by auction** *n* vente aux enchères *f*, vente à la criée *f*; ∼ **by tender** *n* vente par soumission *f*, vente par voie d'adjudication *f*; ∼ **commission** *n* commission de vente *f*; ∼ **for the account** *n* vente à terme *f*; ∼ **for delivery** *n* vente pour livraison *f*, vente à couvert *f*; ∼ **goods** *n pl* marchandises soldées *f pl*; ∼ **item** *n* article en solde *m*; ∼ **and leaseback** *n* cession-bail *f*; ∼ **on approval** *n* vente à l'essai *f*; ∼ **price** *n* (selling price) prix de vente *m*; (reduced price) prix soldé *m*; ∼ **proceeds** *n pl* produit de la vente *m*; ∼ **room** *n* salle des ventes *m*, hôtel des ventes *m*; ∼ **value** *n* valeur marchande *f*

saleable *adj* BrE vendable

sales *n pl* (act of selling) ventes *f pl*; (turnover) chiffre d'affaires *m*; (as a career) vente *f*; (department) service des ventes *m*; **work in** ∼ travailler dans la vente; ∼ **account** *n* compte de ventes *m*; ∼ **activity** *n* ventes *f pl*; ∼ **analysis** *n* analyse des ventes *f*; ∼ **analyst** *n* analyste commercial/-e *m/f*, analyste des ventes *mf*; ∼ **appeal** *n* attraction commerciale *f*, attrait commercial *m*; ∼ **area** *n* (in store) surface de vente *f*; (territory) secteur de vente *m*, territoire de vente *m*; ∼ **assistant** *n* vendeur/-euse *m/f*; ∼ **audit** *n* audit de vente *m*; ∼ **book** *n* journal des ventes *m*, livre des ventes *m*; ∼

budget *n* budget commercial *m*; ∼ **call** *n* visite de représentant *f*; ∼ **campaign** *n* campagne de vente *f*; ∼ **charge** *n* (Stock) commission d'achat *f*; ∼ **clerk** *n* AmE vendeur/-euse *m/f*; ∼ **commission** *n* commission (de vente) *f*; ∼ **conference** *n* conférence de la force de vente *f*, réunion de l'équipe de vente *f*; ∼ **contract** *n* contrat de vente *m*; ∼ **coverage** *n* couverture du marché *f*; ∼ **department** *n* service commercial *m*, service des ventes *m*; ∼ **director** *n* directeur/-trice commercial/-e *m/f*; ∼ **discount** *n* escompte sur ventes *m*; ∼ **drive** *n* animation des ventes *f*, campagne de vente *f*; ∼ **engineer** *n* ingénieur commercial *m*, technico-commercial/-e *m/f*; ∼ **executive** *n* cadre commercial *m*; ∼ **figures** *n pl* chiffre des ventes *m*, chiffre d'affaires *m*; ∼ **floor** *n* surface de vente *f*; ∼ **force** *n* force de vente *f*, équipe de vente *f*; ∼ **force automation** *n* automatisation des forces de vente *f*; ∼ **forecast** *n* prévisions de ventes *f pl*; ∼ **goal** *n* objectif de vente *m*; ∼ **incentive** *n* (for salesperson) incitation à la vente *f*; (for the buyer) offre promotionnelle *f*; ∼ **invoice** *n* facture de vente *f*; ∼ **leaflet** *n* prospectus de vente *m*; ∼ **ledger** *n* grand livre des ventes *m*, grand livre des comptes clients *m*; ∼ **letter** *n* lettre publicitaire *f*; ∼ **literature** *n* documentation publicitaire *f*; ∼ **management** *n* direction commerciale *f*, direction des ventes *f*; ∼ **manager** *n* directeur/-trice commercial/-e *m/f*, directeur/-trice des ventes *m/f*; ∼ **maximization** *n* maximisation des recettes *f*, optimisation des revenus *f*; ∼ **meeting** *n* réunion de représentants *f*; ∼ **mix** *n* mix des produits en vente *m*, éventail des produits en vente *m*; ∼ **network** *n* réseau de vente *m*; ∼ **objective** *n* objectif commercial *m*; ∼ **offensive** *n* offensive commerciale *f*; ∼ **office** *n* agence commerciale *f*; ∼ **opportunity** *n* créneau commercial *m*; ∼ **outlet** *n* point de vente *m*; ∼ **personnel** *n* personnel de vente *m*; ∼ **pitch** *n* arguments de vente *m pl*, baratin commercial *m* (infrml); ∼ **planning** *n* planification des ventes *f*; ∼ **policy** *n* politique de vente *f*; ∼ **portfolio** *n* argumentaire *m*; ∼ **potential** *n* potentiel de vente *m*; ∼ **presentation** *n* argumentaire de vente *m*; ∼ **projection** *n* prévision de ventes *f*; ∼ **promotion** *n* promotion des ventes *f*; ∼ **promotion agency** *n* agence de promotion des ventes *f*; ∼ **promotion manager** *n* directeur/-trice de la promotion des ventes *m/f*; ∼ **quota** *n* quota de ventes *m*; ∼ **ratio** *n* ratio des ventes *m*; ∼ **receipt** *n* reçu *m*; ∼ **record** *n* registre des ventes *m*; ∼ **rep** *n* (infrml) agent commercial *m*, représentant/-e *m/f*; ∼ **representative** *n* agent commercial *m*, représentant/-e *m/f*; ∼ **returns** *n pl* (revenues) recettes *f pl*; (statistics) statistiques sur les ventes *f pl*; (unsold items) invendus *m pl*; ∼ **revenue** *n* chiffre d'affaires *m*, recettes de ventes *f pl*; ∼ **slip** *n* (from cash register) ticket de caisse *m*; ∼ **slump** *n* mévente *f*; ∼ **staff** *n* équipe commerciale *f*, commerciaux *m pl*; ∼ **talk** *n* argumentaire de vente *m*; ∼ **target** *n* objectif de vente *m*; ∼ **tax** *n* US taxe à l'achat *f*; (on business turnover) impôt sur le chiffre d'affaires *m*; ∼ **team** *n* équipe de vente *f*, équipe commerciale *f*; ∼ **technique** *n* technique de vente *f*; ∼ **territory** *n* territoire de vente *m*; ∼ **test** *n* vente expérimentale *f*; ∼ **type lease** *n* location-vente *f*; ∼ **volume** *n* volume des ventes *m*

salesagent *n* agent commercial *m*

salesman *n* (door-to-door) représentant *m*; (in shop) vendeur *m*

salesmanship *n* art de la vente *m*

salesperson *n* (door-to-door) représentant/-e *m/f*; (in shop) vendeur/-euse *m/f*

saleswoman *n* (door-to-door) représentante *f*; (in shop) vendeuse *f*

salvage *n* (of vessel) sauvetage *m*; (of goods) récupération *f*; ∼ **agreement** *n* contrat de sauvetage *m*; ∼ **value** *n* (Econ) valeur résiduelle de liquidation *f*

salvor *n* sauveteur *m*

same *adj* même; **in the ∼ terms** de la même façon; **in the ∼ way** de la même façon; ∼ **job, same pay** à travail égal, salaire égal

same-day *adj* (repair, servicing) effectué dans la journée; ∼ **delivery** *n* livraison dans la journée *f*; ∼ **value** *n* (Bank) valeur jour *f*

sample¹ *n* (Gen Comm, Comp, Math) échantillon *m*; (of people, population) panel *m*; **take a ∼** prendre un échantillon; **true to ∼** conforme à l'échantillon; **correspond to ∼** être conforme à l'échantillon; ∼ **audit** *n* vérification par sondages *f*; ∼ **book** *n* catalogue d'échantillons *m*; ∼ **card** *n* carte d'échantillons *f*; ∼ **data** *n* données type *f pl*; ∼ **mailing** *n* envoi d'échantillons *m*; ∼ **study** *n* (market research) étude témoin *f*; ∼ **survey** *n* sondage *m*

sample² *vt* (food, produce) goûter; (product) essayer; (market, public opinion) sonder

sampler *n* échantillonneur/-euse *m/f*

sampling *n* échantillonnage *m*; ∼ **deviation** *n* écart type de l'échantillon *m*; ∼ **error** *n* erreur d'échantillonnage *f*; ∼ **offer** *n* offre d'essai *f*

sanction¹ *n* (penalty, punishment) sanction *f*; (authorization) autorisation *f*, sanction *f*; **economic/trade ∼s** sanctions économiques/ commerciales *f pl*; **impose ∼s on** prendre des sanctions contre; **powers of ∼** pouvoirs de sanction *m pl*

sanction² *vt* (give permission) autoriser; (approve) sanctionner

sanctions busting *n* violation de l'embargo *f*

sandwich course *n* formation en alternance *f*

sanity check *n* do a ∼ on sth (document,

report) (infrml) vérifier si qch tient la route (infrml)

s.a.s.e. *abbr* US (▸**self-addressed stamped envelope**) enveloppe timbrée à mon/son/votre adresse *f*

satellite *n* satellite *m*; ∼ **broadcasting** *n* radiodiffusion par satellite *f*; ∼ **communication** *n* communication par satellite *f*; ∼ **computer** *n* ordinateur satellite *m*; ∼ **dish** *n* antenne parabolique *f*, parabole *f*; ∼ **operator** *n* satello-opérateur *m*; ∼ **technology** *n* technologie satellite *f*; ∼ **television** *n* télévision par satellite *f*; ∼ **town** *n* ville satellite *f*

satisfaction *n* (Gen Comm) satisfaction *f*; (Fin) (of debt) liquidation *f*; **in ∼ of** en paiement de, en règlement de; **job ∼** satisfaction professionnelle *f*; ∼ **index** *n*, ∼ **rating** *n* taux de satisfaction *m*

satisfactory *adj* satisfaisant; **be less than ∼** être loin d'être satisfaisant

satisfied *adj* (content) satisfait; (convinced) convaincu; **be ∼ with** (make do) se contenter de; (be pleased) être satisfait de

satisfy *vt* (debt) liquider; (demand) répondre à, satisfaire à; (requirement) satisfaire; (obligation) s'acquitter de; (convince) convaincre

saturate *vt* (market) saturer; ∼**d market** marché saturé

saturation *n* (of market) saturation *f*; ∼ **advertising** *n* publicité de saturation *f*; ∼ **campaign** *n* campagne de saturation *f*

saturation point *n* point de saturation *m*; **reach ∼** être saturé

save ⟨**1**⟩ *vt* (put aside) mettre de côté; (money) épargner, mettre de côté; (economize on) économiser, faire des économies de; (time) gagner; (collect) collectionner; (Comp) (file, data) sauvegarder

⟨**2**⟩ *vi* faire des économies, mettre de l'argent de côté; ∼ **up** faire des économies; ∼ **up for sth** mettre de l'argent de côté pour s'acheter qch

save-as-you-earn *n* UK plan d'épargne national par prélèvements automatiques sur salaire *m*

saver *n* épargnant/-e *m/f*

saving *n* (reduction) économie *f*; (accumulation of funds) épargne *f*; (conservation) économie *f*; **a 10% ∼** une économie de 10%; **energy ∼** économies d'énergie *f pl*

savings *n pl* économies *f pl*; **live off one's ∼** vivre de ses économies; **make ∼** faire des économies; ∼ **account** *n* compte d'épargne *m*, dépôt à terme *m*; ∼ **account passbook** *n* livret de compte d'épargne *m*; ∼ **and loan association** *n* US société d'investissement et d'épargne logement *f*; ∼ **bank** *n* caisse d'épargne *f*; ∼ **bond** *n* US bon d'épargne *m*; ∼ **book** *n* livret de compte d'épargne *m*; ∼ **certificate** *n* bon d'épargne *m*; ∼ **deposit** *n* compte d'épargne *m*; ∼**-linked** *adj* lié à l'épargne; ∼ **plan** *n* plan d'épargne *m*;

⋯⋗

S

~ stamp n timbre d'épargne m; **~-to-income ratio** n ratio épargne-revenus m

say n have a **~ in sth** avoir son mot à dire dans qch; **have a ~ in choosing sth** avoir son mot à dire sur le choix de qch; **have no ~ in the matter** ne pas avoir voix au chapitre; **have the final ~** avoir le dernier mot

SAYE abbr UK (▸**save-as-you-earn**) plan d'épargne national par prélèvements automatiques sur salaire

SBA abbr (▸**small business administration**) (Gen Comm) administration des petites entreprises f; (in an individual case) gestion d'une petite entreprise f

SBU abbr (▸**strategic business unit**) unité d'activité stratégique f

scab n (pej) briseur de grève m, jaune mf (péj)

scalability n extensibilité f

scalable adj évolutif/-ive

scale¹ n (extent: of disaster, damage) étendue f; (scope: of crisis, project, research, recession) ampleur f; (of change, support) degré m; (for charging, assessing) échelle f; (of map, model) échelle f; **on a large/small ~** à grande/petite échelle; **on a reduced ~** à échelle réduite; **on a worldwide ~** à l'échelle mondiale; **on a ~ of 1-20** sur une échelle allant de 1 à 20; **to ~** à échelle; **pay ~, wage ~** échelle des salaires f; **value ~** échelle des valeurs f; **tax ~** barème d'imposition m; **~ charge** n frais du barème m pl; **~ of charges** n tableau des tarifs m; **~ model** n maquette f; **~ rate** n prix de barème m

scale²: **~ down** vt (production) ralentir; (costs, exports, activity, involvement, expenditure) réduire; **~ up** (activity) augmenter; (drawing) augmenter l'échelle

scalp¹ n US (infrml) (profit) petit profit m; (on securities) opération de scalpage f

scalp² vt US (tickets) vendre au-dessous du prix normal; (securities) spéculer sur

scalper n US (Stock) scalper m, spéculateur sur la journée m

scalping n US (Stock) scalpage m, scalping m

scam n (infrml) escroquerie f

scan vt (Comp) (document, image) numériser, scanner

scandal n scandale m; **the Collins ~** l'affaire Collins

scanner n (Comp) numériseur m, scanneur m

scant adj (reward) maigre; (information) insuffisant; **pay ~ attention to** ne faire guère attention à; **~ coverage** n couverture médiocre f

scarce adj (information, resources) limité; (natural resource) peu abondant, rare; (commodity) rare

scarcity n pénurie f; **~ value** n valeur de

rareté f

scatter diagram n, **scatter graph** n diagramme de dispersion m

SCE abbr (▸**supply chain execution**) exécution de la chaîne logistique f

scenario n scénario m; **nightmare ~** scénario catastrophe m

scepticism n BrE scepticisme m

schedule¹ n (of work, tasks) programme m, calendrier m; (programme of events) calendrier m; (timetable) (Gen Comm) emploi du temps m; (Transp) horaire m; (of prices, tarifs) barème m, liste f; (Tax) barème d'imposition m; (inventory) inventaire m; (Law) (annexe) annexe f; (projection) prévisions f pl; **be ahead of/behind ~** (project) être en avance/en retard sur le programme prévu; (train) être à l'heure/être en retard; **according to ~** comme prévu; **draw up a ~** établir un programme; **work to a ~** travailler selon un programme; **fall behind ~** prendre du retard sur le programme; **keep to a ~** suivre un programme; **finish on ~** finir dans les délais prévus; **arrive on ~** (train) arriver à l'heure; **full ~, busy ~** programme chargé, emploi du temps chargé; **tight ~** programme serré; **train ~** horaire des trains m; **work ~** programme de travail; **fit sb/sth into one's ~** intégrer qn/qch dans son programme; **as per the attached ~** conformément à liste ci-jointe

schedule² vt (event, trip) programmer; (activity) prévoir

scheduled adj (Transp) régulier/-ière; **as ~** comme prévu; **be ~ for** être programmé pour, être prévu pour; **be ~ to begin in 2004** devoir commencer en 2004, être prévu pour 2004; **~ flight** n vol régulier m; **~ price** n prix selon le tarif m; **~ service** n ligne régulière f, service régulier m

scheduling n programmation f

scheme n (Admin) (system) programme m, système m; (design) plan m; (plan) plan m

schilling n schilling m

scholarship n bourse d'études f

school n école f; **~-leaver** UK jeune à la fin de ses études secondaires

science n science f; **~ and technology** la science et la technologie; **~ park** n parc scientifique m

scientific adj scientifique; **~ management** n organisation scientifique du travail f; **~ research** n recherche scientifique f

scientist n savant m

SCM abbr (▸**supply chain management**) gestion de la chaîne logistique f

scoop¹ n (Media) exclusivité f; **get a ~** avoir une exclusivité

scoop² vt (contract, prize) décrocher

scope n (of plan) envergure f; (of study, inquiry) portée f; (of knowledge) étendue f; (of measures, damage, problem) ampleur *f*; (possibility) possibilité *f*; (**Patents**) (of claims) portée *f*, étendue *f*; **fall within/outside the ~ of the study** rentrer dans/sortir du champ de l'étude; **broaden the ~ of the inquiry** élargir le champ de l'enquête; **extend the ~ one's activities** élargir le champ de ses activités; **~ for research/expansion** possibilités de recherche/d'expansion; **~ for sb to do** possibilités pour qn de faire; **~ creep** *n* (**Admin**) débordement *m*; **~ of agreement** portée de la convention *f*; **~ of coverage** (**Ins**) étendue de la garantie *f*

score[1] *n* (mark) score *m*; **on that ~** à cet égard

score[2] [1] *vt* (point) marquer; (victory, success) remporter

[2] *vi* **~ well**, **~ highly** obtenir un bon résultat

SCP *abbr* (▸**structure-conduct-performance**) structure-conduite-performance; **~ model** *n* modèle structure-conduite-performance *m*

scrap[1] *n* (metal) feraille *f*; **be consigned to the ~ heap** être mis au rebut; **sell sth for ~** vendre qch à la casse; **~ dealer** *n* ferrailleur *m*; **~ metal** *n* ferraille *f*; **~ paper** *n* brouillon *m*; **~ yard** *n* chantier de ferraille *m*, casse *f*

scrap[2] *vt* (idea, project) abandonner, laisser tomber

scrape: **~ by** *vi* se débrouiller; **~ through** [1] *vt* (test) réussir de justesse [2] *vi* s'en tirer de justesse; **~ together** *vt* (capital, funds) réussir à réunir

scratch[1] *n* (**Comp**) brouillon *m*; **come up to ~** (infrml) se montrer à la hauteur; **start from ~** partir de zéro; **bring sth up to ~** amener qch au niveau requis; **~ disk** *n* (**Comp**) disque de travail *m*; **~ pad** *n* bloc-notes *m*; **~ file** *n* fichier de travail *m*

scratch[2]: **~ out** *vt* rayer

screen[1] *n* (Gen Comm, Comp) écran *m*; (office partition) cloison *f*; **~ advertising** *n* publicité cinématographique *f*; **~-based** *adj* (training, dealing) sur écran; **~ capture** *n* capture d'écran *f*; **~ copy** *n* recopie d'écran *f*; **~ dump** *n* capture d'écran *f*; **~ editor** *n* éditeur d'écran *m*; **~ saver** *n* économiseur d'écran *m*; **~ test** *n* bout d'essai *m*, essai filmé *m*

screen[2] *vt* (candidate, applicant) examiner le cas de; (application) examiner; (vet for security purposes) mener une enquête de sécurité sur; (event, programme) diffuser; (film) projeter; **~ out** (candidate) éliminer à la présélection; (data, calls, information) filtrer

screening *n* (of candidates) présélection *f*; (of data, information, calls) filtrage *m*; (of programme, event) diffusion *f*; (of film) projection *f*; **~ board** *n* jury de présélection *m*; **~ process** *n* présélection *f*

scrimp *vi* économiser; **~ and save**

économiser sur tout; **~ on** lésiner sur

scrip *n* (**Fin**) titre *m*; (certificate) certificat d'actions provisoire *m*; **~ dividend** *n* dividende différé *m*; **~ issue** *n* émission d'actions gratuites *f*

scroll *vt* (image, text) faire défiler; **~ down** faire défiler vers le bas; **~ up** faire défiler vers le haut

scroll: **~ arrow** *n* flèche de défilement *f*; **~ bar** *n* barre de défilement *f*

scrolling *n* défilement *m*; **~ down** *n* défilement vers le bas *m*; **~ up** *n* défilement vers le haut *m*

scrutiny *n* examen *m*; **avoid ~** échapper aux contrôles; **come under ~** être examiné; **stand up to ~** résister à l'examen

S curve *n* courbe en S *f*

SDR *abbr* (▸**special drawing rights**) (**Bank**) droits de tirage spéciaux *m pl*

sea *n* mer *f*; **at ~** en mer; **~ carrier** *n* transporteur maritime *m*; **~ change** *n* changement radical *m*; **~ port** *n* port de mer *m*, port maritime *m*; **~ risk** *n* risque de mer *m*; **~ route** *n* route maritime *f*; **~ transport** *n* transport maritime *m*; **~ waybill** *n* lettre de transport maritime *f*

SEA *abbr* (▸**Single European Act**) AUE *m* (Acte unique européen)

seagoing trade *n* commerce maritime *m*

seal[1] *n* (on document) cachet *m*, sceau *m*; (of company) cachet *m*; (**Law**) (on door) scellés *m pl*; **~ of approval** (**Admin**) homologation *f*, sceau d'approbation *m*; **give one's ~ of approval to sth** approuver qch; **customs ~** plomb de douane *m*; **~ of quality** label de qualité *f*

seal[2] *vt* (letter) cacheter; **~ off** fermer

sealed *adj* (package, door) scellé; (envelope) cacheté; **in a ~ envelope** sous pli cacheté; **~ tender** *n* soumission cachetée *f*

sealing wax *n* cire à cacheter *f*

seamless *adj* homogène

SEAQ *abbr* (▸**Stock Exchange Automated Quotation**) *système de cotation des valeurs automatisé*

SEAQI *abbr* (▸**Stock Exchange Automated Quotation International**) *système international de cotation des valeurs étrangères automatisé*

search[1] *n* (Gen Comm, Comp) recherche *f*; (of property, possessions) fouille *f*; (**Law**) (of premises) perquisition *f*; **be in ~ of** être à la recherche de; **carry out a ~** (Gen Comm, Comp) effectuer une recherche; **carry out a ~ of** (files) examiner; (premises) fouiller; (**Law**) perquisitionner; **~ and seizure** *n* perquisition et saisie *f*; **~ engine** *n* (**Comp**) moteur de recherche *m*; **~ history** *n* (**Comp**) historique de requêtes *m*; **~ results** *n pl* (**Comp**) résultats d'une recherche *m pl*; **~ tool** *n* (**Comp**) outil de recherche *m*; **~ warrant** *n* mandat de perquisition *m*

search[2] *vt* (**Comp**) (file, document) rechercher ···⟩

S

dans; (Imp/Exp) (ship, vehicle) fouiller, visiter; (Law) (premises, offices) perquisitionner; **~ a file for sth** rechercher qch dans un fichier; **~ and replace** recherche et remplacement; **~ for** chercher; **~ out** rechercher; **~ through** (files, records) examiner

season n saison f; off **~** basse saison f, morte saison f; **~ ticket** n BrE carte d'abonnement f; **~ ticket holder** n BrE abonné/-e m/f

seasonal adj saisonnier/-ière; **~ adjustments** n pl (statistics) variations saisonnières f pl; **~ factor** n facteur saisonnier m; **~ fluctuations** n pl variations saisonnières f pl; **~ labor** AmE, **labour** BrE n travailleurs saisonniers m pl; **~ swings** n pl variations saisonnières f pl; **~ unemployment** n chômage saisonnier m; **~ variations** n pl variations saisonnières f pl; **~ worker** n saisonnier/-ière m/f

seasonally adv (vary, change, adapt) selon la saison; **~ adjusted** adj corrigé en fonction des variations saisonnières, désaisonnalisé; **~ adjusted annual rate** n taux annuel corrigé des variations saisonnières m; **~ adjusted figures** n pl données corrigées des variations saisonnières f pl, données désaisonnalisées f pl

seasoned adj (campaigner) expérimenté; (leader) chevronné; **~ loan** n obligation émise depuis plus de trois mois f

seat n place f; (in Parliament) siège m; **~ belt** n ceinture de sécurité f

SEAT abbr UK (▸Stock Exchange Alternative Trading Service) tableau électronique de cotations m

SEC abbr (▸Securities and Exchange Commission) ≈ COB f (Commission des opérations de Bourse)

SECAL abbr (▸sector adjustment loan) emprunt de redressement sectoriel m

second¹ n (ordinal number) deuxième mf; second/-e m/f; (defective item) article à défaut m, article de qualité inférieure m; **have ~ thoughts** avoir des doutes; **on ~ thoughts** à la réflexion

second² vt (motion, resolution) appuyer; (Admin) (employee) détacher

second: **~-class mail** n courrier à tarif réduit m; **~-class paper** n titre de deuxième ordre m; **~-class post** n courrier à tarif réduit m; **~ debenture** n obligation de deuxième rang f; **~ generation** n deuxième génération f; **~-generation product** n produit de deuxième génération m; **~-grade** adj de qualité inférieure; **~ half of the year** n deuxième semestre m; **~-hand** adj d'occasion; **~-hand car** n voiture d'occasion f; **~-hand market** n (trade in used goods) marché de l'occasion m; **~-hand value** n valeur à la revente f; **~ home** n résidence secondaire f; **~ market** n second marché m; **~ mortgage** n

hypothèque de deuxième rang f; **~ quarter** n deuxième trimestre m; **~-rate** adj de qualité inférieure; **~ reading** n (of bill, directive) seconde lecture f; **~ to none** adj sans pareil

secondary adj secondaire; **~ action** n revendication complémentaire f; **~ activities** n pl activités du secteur secondaire f pl, services secondaires m pl; **~ bank** n banque d'affaires f; **~ boycott** n boycott complémentaire m; **~ claim** n (Acc) créance de deuxième rang f; **~ creditor** n créancier/-ière de deuxième rang m/f; **~ distribution** n (Stock) revente de titres f; **~ education** n enseignement secondaire m; **~ employment** n travail non déclaré m; **~ income** n revenu accessoire m; **~ labor market** AmE, **~ labour market** BrE n marché des emplois non déclarés m; **~ legislation** n (EU) législation secondaire f, textes d'application m pl; **~ market** n marché secondaire m; **~ offering** n (Stock) deuxième mise sur le marché f, offres sur deuxième marché f pl; **~ picketing** n mise en place d'un piquet de grève de solidarité f; **~ sector** n secteur secondaire m

second-guess vt (reaction, thoughts) anticiper; (person) anticiper les actions de

secondly adv deuxièmement

secondment n détachement m; **on ~ to** en détachement à

secrecy n secret m

secret¹ adj secret/-ète

secret² n secret m; **it's an open ~ that...** tout le monde sait que...

secret: **~ ballot** n vote à bulletin secret m; **~ reserve** n fonds occultes m pl, caisse noire f; **~ reserves** n pl (Acc) réserves cachées f pl, réserves latentes f pl

secretarial: **~ skills** n pl compétences en matière de secrétariat f pl; **~ staff** n personnel de secrétariat m

secretary n (Admin) secrétaire mf; (Pol) US ministre mf; **~'s office** n (Admin) secrétariat m

Secretary: **~ of State** n (Pol) UK ministre mf; US ≈ ministre des Affaires étrangères mf; **~ of the Treasury** n US ≈ ministre des Finances mf

section n (in shop, library) rayon m; (chapter) chapitre m; (passage) passage m; (Law) (of act) article m; (in newspaper) rubrique f; (of population, group) tranche f; (department) service m

sector¹ n (of economy) secteur m; (of disk) secteur m; **work in the insurance/sales ~** travailler dans les assurances/la vente; **public/private ~** secteur public/privé; **~ adjustment loan** n emprunt de redressement sectoriel m; **~ analysis** n analyse sectorielle f; **~ investment and maintenance loan** n prêt d'investissement et d'entretien sectoriel m; **~-specific aid** n aide spécifique à un secteur *f*

sector² *vt* (Comp) (disk) sectoriser

sectoral *adj* (interests, strategy) sectoriel/-ielle

secular trend *n* tendance à long terme *f*

secure¹ *adj* (income) stable; (foundation) solide; (position) assuré; (investment) sûr; (phone line, transaction, server) sécurisé; (job) assuré; ~ **electronic transaction** *n* transaction électronique sécurisée *f*; ~ **payment** *n* paiement sécurisé *m*

secure² *vt* (obtain) obtenir; (debt, loan) garantir; (Stock) (price) garantir, s'assurer de; ~ **a debt by mortgage** garantir une dette par hypothèque; ~ **an investment** garantir un placement; ~ **new orders** obtenir de nouvelles commandes

secured *adj* garanti; ~ **advance** *n* avance garantie *f*, avance sur garantie *f*; ~ **bond** *n* obligation garantie *f*; ~ **credit** *n* crédit garanti *m*; ~ **creditor** *n* créancier/-ière garanti/-e *m/f*; ~ **debenture** *n* obligation garantie *f*; ~ **debt** *n* créance garantie *f*, dette garantie *f*; ~ **loan** *n* emprunt garanti *m*, prêt garanti *m*; ~ **personal loan** *n* prêt personnel garanti *m*

Secure Sockets Layer *n* protocole SSL *m*

securities *n pl* (Stock) titres *m pl*, valeurs *f pl*; ~ **account** *n* (Bank) compte de dépôt de titres *m*; ~ **analysis** *n* analyse financière *f*; ~ **borrowing** *n* emprunt boursier *m*; ~ **business** *n* activités boursières *f pl*, opérations boursières *f pl*; ~ **company** *n* maison de titres *f*; ~ **dealing** *n* opération sur titres *f*, opération sur valeurs mobilières *f*; ~ **department** *n* service des titres *m*; ~ **exchange** *n* Bourse *f*, marché boursier *m*; ~ **firm** *n* maison de titres *f*; ~ **listing** *n* cote boursière *f*, cote officielle *f*; ~ **loan** *n* prêt boursier *m*, prêt de titres *m*; ~ **long** *n pl* titres en compte *m pl*, valeurs en compte *f pl*; ~ **market** *n* marché de valeurs mobilières *m*; ~ **portfolio** *n* portefeuille de titres *m*; ~ **short** *n pl* titres à découvert *m pl*, valeurs à découvert *f pl*; ~ **tax** *n* impôt sur le revenu des valeurs mobilières *m*; ~ **transaction** *n* opération sur titres *f*, opération sur valeurs mobilières *f*

Securities and Exchange Commission *n* US ≈ Commission des opérations de Bourse *f*

securitization *n* titrisation *f*

securitize *vt* titriser

security *n* (Admin) sécurité *f*; (Bank) gage *m*, garantie *f*; (Comp) sécurité *f*; (Fin, Ins) (pledge) cautionnement *m*, garantie *f*; (safety) sécurité *f*; (Stock) titre *m*, valeur *f*; **job** ~ sécurité de l'emploi *f*; **have** ~ **of tenure** (employee) être titularisé; **be a** ~ **risk** être susceptible de compromettre la sécurité; **stand** ~ **for sb** se porter garant de qn; **leave sth as** ~ laisser qch en garantie; **lend on** ~ prêter sur gage; ~ **breach** *n* (of safety) manquement aux

règles de la sécurité *m*; (of official secrecy) atteinte à la sûreté nationale *f*; (of industrial secrecy) violation du secret professionnel *f*; ~ **check** *n* contrôle de sécurité *m*; ~ **clearance** *n* habilitation sécuritaire *f*; ~ **copy** *n* copie de sauvegarde *f*; ~ **dealer** *n* négociant en titres *m*; ~ **guard** *n* gardien/-ienne *m/f*; ~ **holder** *n* porteur de titres *m*, porteur de valeurs *m*; ~ **interest** *n* sûreté *f*; ~ **leak** *n* fuite *f*; ~ **margin** *n* marge de sécurité *f*; ~ **measure** *n* mesure de sécurité *f*; ~ **rating** *n* (Stock) cotation boursière *f*, cote en Bourse *f*, notation *f*; ~ **risk** *n* personne susceptible de compromettre la sécurité d'une société *f*; ~ **services** *n pl* services de sécurité *m pl*

see *vti* voir; ~ **over** voir au dos, voir au verso; ~ **overleaf** voir au dos, voir au verso

seedbed *n* (for new businesses) pépinière d'entreprises *f*

seed capital *n*, **seed money** *n* capitaux d'amorçage *m pl*, capitaux de lancement *m pl*, investissement initial *m*

seek *vt* (advice, help, permission) demander; (agreement, solution, means) chercher; (employment) chercher; (person) rechercher; ~ **to do** chercher à faire; ~ **a job** chercher un emploi; ~ **legal advice** consulter un conseiller juridique; ~ **a market** (Stock) chercher la contre-partie, rechercher un marché; ~ **redress** demander réparation; ~ **sb's approval** chercher à obtenir l'approbation de qn

segment¹ *n* (Comp) (of file, program) segment *m*; (in pie chart) tranche *f*; (of market) segment *m*; ~ **information** *n* informations segmentaires *f pl*; ~ **margin** *n* bénéfice sectoriel *m*; ~ **profit** *n* profit sectoriel *m*

segment² *vt* (market) segmenter

segmental reporting *n* analyse par secteur d'activité *f*

segmentation *n* segmentation *f*; ~ **strategy** *n* stratégie de segmentation *f*

segregate *vt* séparer

segregated *adj* isolé, séparé

segregation *n* ségrégation *f*, séparation *f*; (of funds) affectation à des fins spéciales *f*

select¹ *adj* (group, client) privilégié; (area, hotel, restaurant) chic *inv*

select² *vt* choisir, sélectionner

select committee *n* UK (Pol) commission d'enquête *f*

selected *adj* (candidate, object, option) selectionné; (products, ingredients) de premier choix; **in** ~ **countries/shops** dans certains pays/magasins

selection *n* (choosing) sélection *f*, choix *m*; (assortment) sélection *f*; **make a** ~ faire une sélection; (purchaser, judge) faire un choix; ~ **board** *n* jury de sélection *m*; ~ **marketing** *n* marketing selectif *m*; ~ **method** *n* méthode de sélection *f*

S

selective adj sélectif/-ive; (biased)
tendancieux/-ieuse; ~ **distribution** n
distribution sélective f; ~ **hedge** n (Stock)
couverture sélective f; ~ **marketing** n
marketing sélectif m

self: ~-**actualization** n autoréalisation f;
~-**addressed envelope** n enveloppe à
mon/son/votre adresse f; ~-**addressed
stamped envelope** n AmE enveloppe
timbrée à mon/son/votre adresse f;
~-**adhesive** adj auto-adhésif/-ive,
autocollant; ~-**adjusting** adj
autorégulateur/-trice; ~-**appointed** adj
autonommé; ~-**appraisal** n autocritique f;
~-**assessment** n auto-évaluation f; UK (Tax)
auto-évaluation fiscale f; ~-**catering** adj
(accommodation) meublé; (holiday) en location;
~-**contained** adj indépendant; ~-**drive
hire vehicle** n véhicule de location sans
chauffeur m; ~-**employed person** n
travailleur/-euse indépendant/-e m/f;
~-**employment** n travail indépendant m;
~-**employment income** n revenu d'un
travail indépendant m; ~-**financing** n
autofinancement m; ~-**financing** adj
autofinancé; ~-**fulfilling prophecy** n
prédiction qui s'accomplit d'elle-même f;
~-**funded** adj autofinancé; ~-**generated**
adj autogénéré; ~-**generated funds** n pl
fonds autogénérés m pl; ~-**governing** adj
autonome; ~-**government** n autonomie f;
~-**help** n auto-assistance f; ~-**insurance** n
auto-assurance f; ~-**interest** n intérêt
personnel m; ~-**liquidating** adj auto-
amortissable; ~-**liquidator** n (advertising)
offre auto-payante f; ~-**made man** n self-
made man m; ~-**management** n
autogestion f; ~-**motivated** adj très motivé;
~-**motivation** n automotivation f;
~-**regulating organization** n UK
organisation autonome f, organisme auto-
réglementé m; ~-**regulation** n
autoréglementation f; ~-**regulatory** adj
autorégulateur/-trice; ~-**restraint** n retenue
f; ~-**service** n libre-service m, self-service
m; ~-**service application** n (Comp)
application en libre service f; ~-**service
banking** n (Bank) libre-service bancaire m;
~-**service economy** n économie du self-
service f, économie du libre-service f;
~-**starter** n personne ambitieuse et
indépendante f; ~-**stick note** n feuillet
adhésif repositionnable m; ~-**sufficiency** n
autosuffisance f; ~-**sufficient** adj
autosuffisant, indépendant; ~-**supporting**
adj indépendant; ~-**supporting debt** n
dette indépendante f; ~-**taught** adj
autodidacte

sell 1 vt (goods, product) vendre; (idea, image)
faire accepter, vendre; ~ **sth to sb** vendre
qch qn; ~ **sth for 1,000 dollars** vendre qch
1 000 dollars; ~ **oneself** se vendre, se mettre
en valeur
2 vi vendre; (product, goods) se vendre; ~ **at
£10 each** se vendre 10 livres sterling la

pièce; ~ **at auction** vendre aux enchères; ~
at market (Stock) vendre au cours du
marché; ~ **by auction** vendre aux enchères;
~ **by private treaty** vendre de gré à gré; '~
by March 2005' 'date limite de vente mars
2005'; ~ **for the account** (Stock) vendre à
terme; ~ **for delivery** (Stock) vendre à
couvert; ~ **for the settlement** (Stock) vendre
à terme; ~ **in bulk** vendre en gros; ~ **on
close** (Stock) vendre à la clôture; ~ **on
commission** vendre à la commission; ~ **on
credit** vendre à crédit, vendre à terme; ~ **on
trust** fournir des marchandises à crédit; ~
short (Stock) vendre à découvert; ~ **spot**
(Stock) vendre au comptant; **be sold on sb/
sth** (infrml) être emballé par qn/qch; **you've
been sold** (infrml) tu t'es fait avoir (infrml); ~
back (Gen Comm, Stock) revendre; ~ **down**
(prices) faire baisser; ~ **forward** (Stock)
vendre à terme; ~ **off** (stock, goods) liquider;
(in the sales) solder; ~ **on** revendre; ~ **out** vt
(Fin) (shares, interest, in a firm) vendre; vi (goods,
items) se vendre; (show, concert) afficher
complet; (Fin, Stock) vendre ses parts; (betray
one's ideals) retourner sa veste; **we've sold out
of printers** toutes les imprimantes ont été
vendues, nous n'avons plus d'imprimantes;
~ **up** vt (business, property) vendre; vi vendre
tout; **they've sold up** ils ont tout vendu

sell: ~-**by date** n date limite de vente f;
~-**off** n (Stock) dégagement m; ~-**side** adj
(application, system) destinée à la vente au
client final; ~-**up product** n produit d'appel
m

seller n vendeur/-euse m/f; **at ~ 's risk** aux
risques du vendeur; **be a good/bad ~**
(product) se vendre bien/mal; ~**'s market** n
marché vendeur m, marché à la hausse m;
~**'s option** n prime vendeur f; ~**'s rate** n
(Acc) taux vendeur m; (Bank) cours vendeur
m

selling n vente f; ~ **agent** n (Stock) agent
de placement m; ~ **concession** n (Stock)
commission de mise sur le marché f,
concession de vente f; ~ **expenses** n pl
(Acc) frais de commercialisation m pl, frais
de vente m pl; ~ **hedge** n (Stock) couverture
de vente f, short hedge m; ~ **point** n (of
product, service) argument de vente m; ~
policy n politique de vente f; ~ **price** n
prix de vente m; ~ **rate** n (Stock) cours
vendeur m; ~ **short** n vente à découvert f;
~ **space** n espace de vente m, surface de
vente f

sellout n (of stock) liquidation f; (betrayal)
revirement m; **be a ~** (show) jouer à guichets
fermés; **the CD-ROMs were a ~** les cédéroms
se sont très bien vendus

semiannual adj semestriel/-ielle

semicolon n point-virgule m

semi-detached house n BrE maison
jumelée f

semidurable adj (goods) semi-durable

semifinished: ~ **goods** n pl produits
intermédiaires m pl; ~ **product** n produit
semi-fini m

semifixed cost n coût semi-fixe m

seminar n séminaire m

semiprivate bank n banque semi-privée f

semiprocessed products n pl demi-
produits m pl

semipublic company n société semi-
publique f, société à économie mixte f

semipublic enterprise n entreprise
semi-publique f, entreprise à économie mixte
f

semiskilled adj (worker) spécialisé; ~
labor AmE, ~ **labour** BrE n main-d'œuvre
spécialisée f, ouvriers spécialisés m pl

semitrailer n semi-remorque f

semivariable: ~ **costs** n pl charges
semi-variables f pl; ~ **expense** n coût semi-
variable m

senate n US (Pol) sénat m

send vt (data, email, information, letter, document)
envoyer; ~ **away for sth** commander qch par
correspondance; ~ **by fax** envoyer par fax,
envoyer par télécopie; ~ **by mail,** ~ **by post**
envoyer par la poste, expédier par la poste;
~ **sb for sth** envoyer qn chercher qch; ~ **sth**
by certified mail AmE envoyer qch en
recommandé; ~ **sth by parcel post** envoyer
qch par colis postal; ~ **sth by registered**
post BrE envoyer qch en recommandé; ~
under plain cover envoyer sous pli discret;
~ **a written request** faire une demande par
écrit; ~ **back** (letter, goods) renvoyer; ~ **in**
(form, order) envoyer; (request) faire; (person)
faire entrer; ~ **in one's application** poser sa
candidature; ~ **off** envoyer; ~ **off for sth**
commander qch par correspondance; ~ **on**
(mail, letter) faire suivre; (document, memo)
transmettre; ~ **out** (letter, brochure) envoyer;
~ **round** (memo) faire circuler

sender n (Comms) expéditeur/-trice m/f

senior[1] adj (in age) aîné; (in rank) principal,
supérieur; **be** ~ (longer-serving) avoir de
l'ancienneté

senior[2] n (superior) supérieur/-e m/f; (older
person) aîné/-e m/f

senior: ~ **citizen** n personne âgée f; ~
civil servant n fonctionnaire titulaire mf; ~
clerk n chef de bureau m; ~ **debt** n créance
prioritaire f; ~ **executive** n cadre supérieur
m; ~ **loan** n prêt principal m; ~
management n direction f, cadres
supérieurs m pl; ~ **manager** n cadre
supérieur m; ~ **officer** n (Admin) haut
fonctionnaire m; ~ **partner** n associé/-e
principal/-e m/f, associé/-e majoritaire m/f;
~**-ranking official** n (civil servant) haut
fonctionnaire m; (Mgmnt) cadre supérieur m,
dirigeant/-e m/f; ~ **security** n titre
prioritaire m, titre privilégié m

seniority n ancienneté f; ~ **bonus** n prime

d'ancienneté f; ~ **principle** n principe
d'ancienneté m

sense n sens m; (feeling) sentiment m; ~ **of**
responsibility sens des responsabilités m; **it**
makes ~ c'est logique

sensitive adj (market) instable, sensible;
(information, document) confidentiel/-ielle;
(problem, issue) délicat

sensitivity analysis n analyse de
sensibilité f

sensitize vt sensibiliser

sentence[1] n (Law) condamnation f

sentence[2] vt (Law) condamner

separate adj with singular noun (own:
character, identity, facility) propre; (distinct: issue,
problem, event) autre; (not attached: component,
piece, organization) à part; with plural noun
(different) différent; (not related) distinct; **under**
~ **cover** sous pli séparé

sequence n (order) ordre m; (of problems)
succession f; (Comp) séquence f; **a** ~ **of**
events une succession d'événements; **in**
chronological ~ par ordre chronologique; ~
number n numéro d'ordre m

sequential adj séquentiel/-ielle; ~
analysis n analyse séquentielle f; ~
number n numéro d'ordre m; ~ **sampling**
n échantillonnage successif m,
échantillonnage séquentiel m

sequestration n séquestration f

sequestrator n administrateur séquestre
m

serial: ~ **access** n (Comp) accès
séquentiel m; ~ **bond** n obligation échéant
en série f, obligation échéant par tranches f;
~ **correlation** n corrélation sérielle f; ~
number n numéro de série m; ~ **port** n port
série m; ~ **printer** n imprimante série f; ~
processing n traitement série m

series n série f

serious adj (issue, discussion, offer, doubt)
sérieux/-ieuse; (condition, accident, situation,
matter, error, problem) grave; (attempt, concern)
réel/réelle; **be** ~ **about sth** prendre qch au
sérieux; **be** ~ **about doing** avoir vraiment
l'intention de faire

Serious Fraud Office n UK service de
répression des fraudes m

SERPS abbr UK (▶**State Earnings Related**
Pension Scheme) régime de retraite étatique
basé sur le salaire

serve [1] vt (community, area) desservir;
(market, customer) servir; ~ **the company** être
au service de la société; ~ **counternotice**
(Law) signifier un avis contraire; ~ **a**
purpose être utile; ~ **the purpose** faire
l'affaire; ~ **sb with a warrant** délivrer un
mandat à qn; ~ **a summons on sb** citer qn à
comparaître; ~ **notice of sth on sb** signifier
qch à qn

[2] vi (in shop) servir; (in restaurant) faire le
service; (in role, job) exercer ses fonctions;

⸱⸱⸱✦

S

~ **as** (intermediary, reminder) servir de; ~ **on a committee** être membre d'un comité; **it ~s to show that** cela sert à montrer que

server n (Comp) serveur m; ~ **side** adj côté serveur

service¹ n (office, department) service m; (work done, facility) service m; (overhaul) révision f; (Law) (of writ, demand, notice) signification f; (Transp) (route) ligne f; ~ **not included** service non compris m; **at sb's** ~, **in sb's** ~ au service de qn; **get good/bad** ~ être bien/mal servi; **be of** ~ **to sb** rendre service à qn, être utile à qn; **take sth out of** ~ retirer qch du service; **run a** ~ assurer un service; **train/coach** ~ service de trains/cars m; ~ **agreement** n contrat de maintenance m; ~ **bureau** n (Comp) centre de traitement à façon m; ~ **card** n (Comp) carte à bande magnétique f; (Bank) carte de retrait f; ~ **charge** n (Gen Comm) frais d'administration m pl; (Bank) frais de gestion de compte m pl; (on property) charges locatives fpl; (in restaurant) service m; ~ **company** n société de services f; ~ **contract** n contrat de maintenance m; ~ **delivery** n prestation de services f; ~ **economy** n économie de services f; ~ **engineer** n technicien/-ienne de maintenance m/f; ~ **enterprise** n entreprise de services f, prestataire de services m; ~ **fee** n rémunération de service f; ~ **handbook** n guide d'entretien m; ~ **history** n états de service m pl; ~ **industry** n (company) industrie de service(s) f, (sector) secteur tertiaire m; ~ **jobs** n pl emplois du secteur tertiaire m pl; ~ **manual** n guide d'entretien m; ~ **provider** n (Gen Comm) prestataire de services m, société de commercialisation des services f, (Comp) fournisseur d'accès m; ~ **record** n états de service m pl; ~ **sector** n secteur des services m; ~ **sector job** n emploi du tertiaire m, emploi de service m; ~ **station** n station-service f

service² vt (vehicle) faire la révision de; (equipment) entretenir; (debt) servir, payer les intérêts de; (market) servir

Service Level Agreement n contrat de niveau de service (qui formalise les droits et les devoirs du fournisseur et du client)

services n pl (Gen Comm) services f pl, prestations f pl; (Econ) secteur tertiaire m, services m pl; **for** ~ **rendered** pour services rendus

servicing n (of equipment) entretien m; (of car) révision f; (of debt) service m

session n (Comp) session f; (Pol) session f; (Law) séance f; (Stock) séance f; (meeting) réunion f; **trading** ~ séance de bourse f; **be in** ~ être en séance

set¹ adj (time, place, price) fixe; (task, rule, procedure) bien déterminé; (formula) tout fait; **be** ~ **in one's ways** avoir ses habitudes; **be** ~ **on sth** tenir absolument à qch; **be** ~ **on doing** tenir absolument à faire

set² n (of data, values, rules, instructions) série f; (of tools) jeu m; (of objects) série f; (batch) lot m; **in** ~**s of 20** par lots de 20

set³ vt (value, price, date, place, target) fixer; (fashion, trend) lancer; (precedent, record) établir; ~ **about** (work) se mettre à; ~ **about doing** commencer à faire; ~ **about the business of doing** commencer à faire; ~ **aside** (area, time) réserver; (money, stock) mettre de côté; (decision, request, verdict) rejeter; (judgement) casser; ~ **down** (rules, criteria) fixer; ~ **sth down in writing** mettre qch par écrit; ~ **forth** (findings, facts) exposer; (argument, case) présenter; ~ **off** (Acc) (loss) compenser; ~ **sth off against profits** déduire qch des bénéfices; ~ **off a debit against a credit** compenser un débit par un crédit; ~ **out** (display) exposer, présenter; (conclusions, ideas, proposal) présenter; (terms, objections) formuler; ~ **out to do** (report, documentary, book) avoir pour but de faire; (person) chercher à faire; ~ **up** (business) créer; (scheme, initiative) lancer; (deal) négocier; (financial operation) monter; (committee) constituer; (Comp) (install) installer; ~ **up in business** se lancer dans les affaires; ~ **up on one's own account**, ~ **up in business on one's own** se mettre à son compte; ~ **oneself up as a gardener** se mettre à son compte comme jardinier

set: ~ **of accounts** ensemble d'états financiers m; ~ **of bills of lading** jeu de connaissements m; ~ **of measures** série de mesures f; ~ **of options** (Stock) groupe d'options m; ~ **of rules** règlement m; ~ **theory** théorie des ensembles f

SET abbr ▸**secure electronic transaction** transaction électronique sécurisée f

setback n revers m; (on stock market) recul m; **suffer a** ~ essuyer un revers; **it is a** ~ **to our hopes of winning the contract** cela compromet nos chances de remporter le contrat

settings n pl (Comp) options f pl, paramètres m pl

setting-up costs n pl frais d'établissement m pl

settle ⬜1 vt (transaction, question, business, problem) régler; (bill, debt) payer, régler; ~ **an account** régler un compte; ~ **a dispute** régler un conflit; ~ **a dispute by arbitration** régler un conflit par arbitrage; ~ **the figure** décider du montant, fixer le montant; ~ **old scores** régler des comptes; ~ **one's affairs** mettre de l'ordre dans ses affaires ⬜2 vi (in job, residence, country) s'installer, s'établir; ~ **amicably** régler à l'amiable; ~ **in cash** régler au comptant, régler en espèces; ~ **out of court** parvenir à un règlement à l'amiable

settlement n (of debt, dispute, issue) règlement m, (payment) règlement m, paiement m; (Stock) règlement à terme m; (agreement) accord m; **come to an amicable** ~

s'arranger à l'amiable; **reach a** ~ arriver à un accord; **in** ~ (of a debt) en règlement; **make a** ~ **on sb** faire une donation en faveur de qn; ~ **account** n compte arrêté m; ~ **of account** n arrêté de compte m; ~ **bargain** n (Stock) marché à terme m; ~ **currency** n monnaie de règlement f; ~ **date** n date de règlement f, jour de règlement m; ~ **day** n jour de règlement m; ~ **of debts** règlement de dettes m; ~ **discount** n conditions de règlement f pl; ~ **draft** n effet de règlement m; ~ **market** n marché à terme m; ~ **per contra** n compensation f; ~ **price** n cours de compensation m; ~ **to the market** liquidation fictive quotidienne f; ~ **transaction** n transaction à terme f

settlements department n service des règlements m

settlor n UK (Law) donateur/-trice m/f

set-up n (system, organisation) organisation f, système m; (Comp) installation f; ~ **CD-ROM** n cédérom d'installation m; ~ **costs** n pl frais d'établissement m pl; ~ **fee** n (Bank) frais de montage m pl, commission de montage f; ~ **program** n (Comp) programme d'installation m

sever vt (contact, communication) couper; ~ **links with** rompre les liens avec

severally adv ~ **but not jointly** individuellement mais non conjointement; ~ **liable** adj solidairement responsable

severance n (separation) rupture f, séparation f; (redundancy) licenciement m; ~ **pay** n indemnité de licenciement f

sewage n eaux usées f pl; ~ **treatment** n traitement des eaux usées m; ~ **treatment plant** n station d'épuration des eaux usées f

sew: ~ **up** vt (deal) conclure; (market) dominer

sex n (gender) sexe m; ~ **discrimination** n discrimination sexuelle f; ~ **stereotyping** n préjugés sexistes m pl

sexual adj sexuel/-elle; ~ **discrimination** n discrimination sexuelle f; ~ **harassment** n harcèlement sexuel m

sexy adj (infrml) (image, product, campaign) accrocheur/-euse

SFA abbr (▶**sales force automation**) automatisation des forces de vente f

SFO abbr UK (▶**Serious Fraud Office**) service de répression des fraudes m

SGML abbr (**Standard Generalized Mark-up Language**) SGML m

shade vt (amount, quantity) diminuer progressivement

shadow[1] n ombre f; **cast a** ~ **over** jeter une ombre sur; ~ **cabinet** n UK (Pol) cabinet fantôme m; ~ **economy** n économie souterraine f, économie parallèle f; ~ **price** n prix virtuel m

shadow[2] vt (currency) s'aligner sur

shady adj louche, douteux/-euse

shake vt (confidence, market, belief) ébranler; ~ **off** (image, reputation) se débarasser de; ~ **out** (staff) réduire; ~ **up** (person) secouer; (company, department) réorganiser

shakedown n (infrml) AmE (swindle) chantage m, racket m (infrml); (staff cuts) dégraissage m, réduction du personnel f; (reorganization) réorganisation f

shake-out n (Econ) resserrement du marché intervenant après une période d'inflation; (staff cuts) dégraissage m, réduction du personnel f

shake-up n réorganisation f; (Pol) remaniement m

shaky adj (regime, situation, company) branlant, chancelant; (position) instable; (evidence, argument) peu solide; (start) mal assuré; **be on** ~ **ground** être peu sûr de soi

shallow market n marché peu actif m

shape[1] n (outline, condition) forme f; (character) forme f; (structure) structure f; **be in/out of** ~ être/ne pas être en forme; **be in good/bad** ~ (person, economy) se porter bien/mal; **take** ~ (plan, idea) prendre forme, se concrétiser; **the likely** ~ **of sth** la forme que prendra qch; **the changing** ~ **of the EU** l'évolution de l'UE; **the new** ~ **of the firm** la nouvelle structure de l'entreprise; **lick sth into** ~ (infrml) (proposal, report) mettre qch au point, donner le dernier tour de main à

shape[2] vt (policy) formuler; (person, public opinion, course of events) influencer; (price, future) déterminer; ~ **up** (project, plans) prendre tournure; (come up to scratch) être à la hauteur; **she's shaping up well** elle s'en sort bien; **how are things shaping up at head office?** quelle tournure prennent les choses au siège?; **be shaping up to** be être en train de devenir

share[1] n (portion, fraction) part f; (Stock) (publicly-held) action f, titre m; **have a** ~ **in a business** avoir une participation dans une affaire, avoir des intérêts dans une affaire; **take a** ~ **in sth** participer à qch; **have a half** ~ **in sth** posséder la moitié de qch; **do one's** ~ **of sth** faire sa part de qch; **bear one's** ~ **of the cost** participer aux frais; **go** ~s **with sb** partager les frais avec qn; ~ **allotment** n distribution d'actions f; ~ **capital** n capital actions m, capital social m; ~ **certificate** n BrE certificat d'action m, titre d'action m; ~ **class** n classe d'actions f; ~ **dividend** n dividende d'actions m; ~ **economy** n économie d'actionnariat f; ~ **index** n indice boursier m, indice des actions m; ~ **issue** n émission d'actions f; ~ **issue for cash** n émission d'actions de numéraire f; ~ **of the market** n part de marché f; ~ **option** n option d'achat d'actions f; (as perk for senior staff) stock-option f; ~ **option scheme** n plan de participation par achat d'actions m; ~ **ownership** n actionnariat m; ~ **participation scheme** n (for employees) plan d'intéressement des employés m; ~ **portfolio** ··⟶

S

n portefeuille (d'actions) *m*; ∼ **premium** *n* BrE prime d'émission *f*; ∼ **price** *n* prix des actions *m*; ∼ **price performance** *n* performance du prix des actions *f*; ∼ **redemption** *n* rachat d'actions *m*; ∼ **register** *n* registre des actions *m*; ∼ **split** *n* division d'actions *f*; ∼ **transfer** *n* transfert d'actions *m*

share² *vt* partager; (profits, work) répartir; ∼ **in** prendre part à; ∼ **out** distribuer, partager

shared *adj* (office, facilities) commun; (experience, interest) commun, partagé; ∼ **accommodation** *n* logement partagé *m*; ∼-**cost program** AmE, ∼-**cost programme** BrE *n* (Pol) programme à frais partagés *m*; ∼ **database** *n* (Comp) base commune de données *f*; ∼ **monopoly** *n* monopole partagé *m*, oligopole *m*; ∼ **ownership** *n* copropriété *f*

shareholder *n* actionnaire *mf*

shareholders': ∼ **equity** *n* (Stock) capital social *m*, fonds propres *m pl*; ∼ **meeting** *n* assemblée des actionnaires *f*

shareholding *n* (Stock) (concept) actionnariat *m*, possession d'actions *f*; (share) valeur mobilière de participation *f*; (stake) participation *f*; **minor/major** ∼ participation minoritaire/majoritaire *f*

shares *n pl* actions *f pl*; ∼ **authorized** *n pl* actions déclarées *f pl*, capital nominal *m*; ∼ **outstanding** *n pl* actions en circulation *f pl*, actions émises *f pl*

shareware *n* (Comp) logiciel contributif *m*, contribuciel *m*, partagiciel *m*

shark *n* (Fin) requin *m*; ∼ **repellents** *n pl* (Fin) (in takeovers) antirequins *m pl*; ∼ **watcher** *n* (Stock) détecteur de requin *m*

sharp¹ *adj* (fall, change) fort, brutal; (negotiator, business person) malin/maligne (pej)

sharp² *adv* (stop) net; **at 7 o'clock** ∼ à 7 heures précises

sharp: ∼ **drop** *n* forte baisse *f*; ∼ **movement** *n* mouvement brusque *m*, mouvement soudain *m*; ∼ **operator** *n* escroc *m*, filou *m*; ∼ **practice** *n* maquignonnage *m*; ∼ **rally** *n* reprise vigoureuse *f*; ∼ **rise** *n* forte augmentation *f*, forte hausse *f*

sharply *adv* (change, rise, fall) brutalement, brusquement

shed *vt* (workers) licencier; (Stock) (points) céder; ∼ **light on** (point, issue) clarifier; ∼ **jobs**, ∼ **staff** supprimer des emplois

sheet *n* (of paper) feuille *f*; ∼ **feeder** *n* chargeur feuille à feuille *m*

shekel *n* shekel *m*

shelf *n* étagère *f*; (in shop) rayon *m*; ∼ **display** *n* présentoir de gondole *m*; ∼ **filler** *n* (in store) réassortisseur/-euse *m/f*; ∼ **life** *n* (of product) durée de vie *f*; ∼ **price** *n* (of product) prix sur linéaire *m*; ∼ **registration** *n* US (Stock) enregistrement d'émissions de titres à date indéterminée *m*; ∼ **space** *n*

linéaire *m*, rayonnage *m*

shelfware *n* (Comp) logiciel prêt à l'usage *m*, logiciel fixe *m*

shell¹: ∼ **company** *n* (Tax) société écran *f*; ∼ **operation** *n* (Stock) opération fictive *f*

shell²: 1 *vt* (sum) débourser 2 *vi* (infrml) casquer (infrml)

shelter¹ *n* (from tax) abri *m*

shelter² *vt* abriter

sheltered industries *n pl* industries protégées de la concurrence étrangère *f pl*

shelve *vt* (stock) mettre sur les rayons; (plan, project) mettre en suspens

shelving *n* rayonnage *m*

shield *vt* protéger

shift¹ *n* (workers) équipe *f*, poste *m*; (work session) période de travail posté *f*; (change) changement *m*; (sudden change) revirement *m*; (Comp) (on keyboard) décalage *m*, shift *m*; (in demand or supply curve) modification *f*; (in emphasis) déplacement *m*; **work** ∼**s, be on** ∼**s** faire un travail posté; **work an 8 hour** ∼ faire les trois-huit; **work in** ∼**s** travailler par équipes, se relayer; **be on day/night** ∼ être de jour/nuit; **the day/night** ∼ l'équipe de jour/nuit; **a** ∼ **in public opinion** un retournement de l'opinion publique; ∼ **differential** *n* écart de rémunération (entre certains postes) *m*; ∼ **in consumption** modification de la consommation *f*; ∼ **key** touche majuscule *f*; ∼ **work** travail par équipes *m*, travail posté *m*; ∼ **worker** travailleur/-euse qui fait un travail posté *m/f*

shift² 1 *vt* (transfer) transférer; (sell) écouler; (responsibility) rejeter; ∼ **attention away from sth** détourner l'attention de qch 2 *vi* (goods) se vendre; (opinion, attitude) se modifier; **they won't** ∼ ils ne veulent pas changer d'avis

shill bidder *n* complice qui fait monter les enchères *mf*

ship¹ *n* vaisseau *m*; ∼-**broker** *n* courtier maritime *m*; ∼'s **survey** *n* visite du navire *f*; ∼'s **husband** *n* armateur-gérant *m*; ∼'s **log** *n* journal de bord *m*; ∼'s **manifest** *n* manifeste *m*; ∼'s **papers** *n pl* documents de bord *m pl*; ∼'s **protest** *n* rapport de mer *m*

ship² *vt* (cargo, freight) charger; (send) expédier; (send by sea) expédier par mer; ∼ **by rail** expédier par le train

shipbuilder *n* constructeur de navires *m*

shipbuilding *n* construction navale *f*

shipment *n* envoi *m*, expédition *f*

shipowner *n* armateur *m*

shipper *n* chargeur *m*; (charterer) affréteur *m*; (dispatcher) expéditeur *m*; ∼ **and carrier** chargeur et transporteur *m*, courtier d'affrètement maritime *m*

shipping *n* (sea traffic) navigation *f*; (sending) expédition *f*; (loading) chargement *m*; ∼ **address** *n* adresse du destinataire *f*; ∼ **agency** *n* agence maritime *f*; ∼ **agent** *n*

agent maritime *m*; (forwarder) transitaire *m*; ∼
broker *n* courtier maritime *m*; ∼ **business**
n affaires maritimes *f pl*; ∼ **charges** *n pl*
frais d'expédition *m pl*; ∼ **clerk** *n*
expéditionnaire *mf*; ∼ **company** *n* (by sea)
compagnie de navigation *f*; (by road)
entreprise de transport routier *f*; ∼ **costs**
n pl frais d'expédition *m pl*; ∼ **documents**
n pl (Imp/Exp) documents d'expédition *m pl*;
(Transp) documents de transport maritime
m pl; ∼ **and forwarding agent** *n* agent
maritime-transitaire *m*, chargeur transitaire
m; ∼ **instructions** *n pl* instructions
d'expédition *f pl*; ∼ **invoice** *n* facture
d'expédition *f*, facture de transport *f*; ∼ **lane**
n voie de navigation *f*; ∼ **line** *n* compagnie
de navigation *f*, ligne maritime *f*; ∼ **note** *n*
note de chargement *f*; ∼ **office** *n* (dispatch
department) bureau d'expédition *m*; (Transp)
agence maritime *f*; ∼ **port** *n* port de
chargement *m*; ∼ **register** *n* registre
d'immatriculation *m*; ∼ **terms** *n pl*
conditions du contrat de transport *f pl*; ∼
trade *n* armement *m*

shirker *n* (infrml) tire-au-flanc *m*

shock *n* choc *m*; ∼ **inflation** *n* inflation
induite par les chocs externes *f*

shockwave *n* remous *m pl*; **send** ∼**s**
throught the market provoquer des remous à
la Bourse

shoot¹ *n* (photo session) séance *f*; (film)
tournage *m*

shoot²: ∼ **up** *vi* (prices, rates) monter en
flèche

shop¹ *n* BrE magasin *m*; (small) boutique *f*;
(advertising agency) boîte *f* (jarg); ∼ **assistant** *n*
BrE vendeur/-euse *m/f*; ∼ **floor** *n* (place)
atelier *m*; (workers) ouvriers *m pl*;
∼**-floor agreement** *n* UK accord avec la
base *m*; ∼**-floor bargaining** *n* UK
négociation avec la base *f*; ∼ **steward** *n*
délégué/-e d'atelier *m/f*, délégué/-e syndical/-e
m/f; ∼ **window** *n* vitrine *f*

shop² *vi* faire ses courses; ∼ **at Maximart**
faire ses courses chez Maximart; ∼ **around**
bien chercher; (for the best price) comparer les
prix; (for the best interest rate) comparer les taux
d'intérêt

shopaholic *n* (infrml) accro du shopping *mf*
(infrml)

shopbot *n* (Comp) moteur de comparaison
de prix *m*, assistant d'achat en ligne *m*

shopfront *n* devanture de magasin *f*

shopkeeper *n* BrE commerçant/-e *m/f*;
small ∼ petit/-e commerçant/-e *m/f*

shoplifter *n* voleur/-euse à l'étalage *m/f*

shoplifting *n* vol à l'étalage *m*

shopper *n* client/-e *m/f*

shopping *n* courses *f pl*; **go** ∼ faire les
courses; ∼ **bag** *n* sac à provisions *m*; ∼
basket *n* (Gen Comm, Comp) panier *m*; ∼
cart *n* (Gen Comm, Comp) panier *m*, caddie®

m; ∼ **center** *n* AmE, ∼ **centre** *n* BrE centre
commercial *m*; ∼ **list** *n* liste (de
commissions) *f*; ∼ **mall** *n* centre commercial
m, galerie marchande *f*; ∼ **precinct** *n* BrE
(indoor) galerie marchande *f*; (open-air) zone
commerçante piétonnière *f*

shore up *vt* (economy, regime) soutenir

short¹ *adj* (not tall) court; (scarce) difficile à
trouver; ∼ **of** à court de; ∼ **of money** gêné, à
court d'argent; **just** ∼ **of 20,000 euros** pas
loin de 20 000 euros; **I'm** ∼ **of books** il me
manque des livres; **be** ∼ **on** manquer de; **be**
on ∼ **time** être en chômage partiel; **be** ∼ **in**
futures (Stock) faire des marchés à court
terme, être à découvert sur contrat à terme;
be ∼**-staffed** manquer de personnel; **be in** ∼
supply être difficile à trouver; **in the** ∼ **term**
dans l'immédiat; **time is getting** ∼ le temps
presse

short² *n* (Stock) vente à découvert *f*, short *f*;
(government stock) bon d'État à court terme *m*;
(futures market) marché à court terme *m*

short³ *adv* **run** ∼ **of** se trouver à court de;
go ∼ (Stock) vendre à découvert; **sell** ∼
(Stock) vendre à découvert; **fall** ∼ **of** (target)
ne pas atteindre; (forecast) être inférieur à;
(expectations) ne pas répondre à

short: ∼ **account** *n* compte à découvert
m; ∼ **bill** *n* traite à courte échéance *f*; ∼
closing *n* clôture à découvert *f*; ∼ **covering**
n rachat pour couvrir un découvert *m*;
∼**-dated** *adj* (Stock) à court terme, à
échéance proche; ∼ **delivery** *n* livraison
partielle *f*; ∼ **futures position** *n* cours à
court terme *m*, position courte sur contrat à
terme *f*; ∼**-handed** *adj* à court de main-
d'œuvre; ∼**-haul** *adj* (Transp) à courte
distance; ∼ **haul carrier** *n* court-courrier *m*;
∼ **hedge** *n* couverture courte *f*, couverture
à court terme *f*; ∼**-lived** *adj* de courte durée,
éphémère; ∼ **market** *n* marché à court
terme *m*, marché à découvert *m*; ∼ **position**
n (Stock) position courte *f*, position vendeur
f, position à découvert *f*; ∼**-range** *adj*
(forecast) à court terme; ∼**-range planning** *n*
planification à court terme *f*; ∼ **run** *n*
(production period) petite série *f*; ∼ **sale** *n* vente
à découvert *f*; ∼ **seller** *n* (Stock) vendeur/
-euse à découvert *m/f*; ∼ **selling** *n* (Stock)
vente à découvert *f*; ∼**-sighted** *adj* (policy,
decision) à courte vue; ∼**-staffed** *adj* à court
de personnel; ∼**-term** *adj* à court terme;
(Stock) (bond, debt) à court terme, à courte
échéance; ∼**-term advance** *n* concours à
court terme *m*; ∼**-term bond** *n* obligation à
court terme *f*; ∼**-term contract** *n* contrat à
court terme *m*; ∼**-term credit** *n* crédit à
court terme *m*; ∼**-term debt** *n* dette à court
terme *f*, passif exigible *m*, passif à court
terme *m*; ∼**-term deposit** *n* dépôt à court
terme *m*; ∼**-term fluctuations** *n pl*
variations à court terme *f pl*; ∼**-term**
interest rate *n* taux d'intérêt à court terme
m; ∼**-term investment assets** *n pl* actif ⋯▷

investi à court terme *m*; **∼-term investment portfolio** *n* portefeuille d'investissement à court terme *m*; **∼-term liabilities** *n pl* créditeurs à court terme *m pl*, emprunts et dettes à courte terme *m pl*; **∼-term loan** *n* emprunt à court terme *m*; **∼-term money market** *n* marché monétaire à court terme *m*; **∼-term objective** *n* objectif à court-terme *m*; **∼-term planning** *n* planification à court terme *f*, **∼-term security** *n* valeur à court terme *f*, valeur à terme *f*; **∼-term workers** *n pl* travailleurs sous contrat à court terme *m pl*; **∼-time working** *n* chômage partiel *m*

shortage *n* pénurie *f*, manque *m*; (chronic) crise *f*; **∼ of staff** manque de personnel *m*; **∼s of** une pénurie de, un manque de; **there is no ∼ of candidates** les candidats ne manquent pas; **job/housing/labour ∼** crise de l'emploi/du logement/de la main-d'œuvre

short-change *vt* (give too little money) ne pas rendre assez de monnaie à; (swindle) escroquer, rouler (infrml)

short-circuit *vti* court-circuiter

shortcoming *n* défaut *m*

shorten *vt* raccourcir; **∼ the working week** réduire le temps de travail

shortening *n* réduction *f*; **∼ of the working week** réduction du temps de travail

shortfall *n* insuffisance *f*, manque *m*; (Acc, Fin) déficit *m*; **∼ in earnings** manque à gagner *m*; **make up the ∼** combler le déficit

shorthand *n* sténographie *f*; **∼ typist** *n* sténodactylo *mf*

shorthanded *adj* à court de main-d'œuvre, à court de personnel

shortlist¹ *n* liste restreinte *f*

shortlist² *vt* sélectionner, établir une liste restreinte de; **be ∼ed** être retenu

shorts *n pl* UK (Stock) bons du Trésor à court terme *m pl*

shoulder *vt* (burden, cost, expense) assumer supporter; (risk, responsibility) endosser

shoulder period *n* intersaison *f*

show¹ *n* (trade fair) salon *m*; (entertainment) spectacle *m*; **be on ∼** être exposé; **∼ business** *n* monde du spectacle *m*, le show-business; **∼ flat** *n* appartement témoin *m*; **∼ house** *n* maison témoin *f*

show² ⌊1⌋ *vt* (ticket, voucher, passport) présenter; (products) exposer; (fashion collection) présenter; (prove, demonstrate) démontrer, prouver; **∼ a balance of** présenter un solde de; **∼ a loss of** enregistrer une perte de; **∼ one's hand** dévoiler ses intentions; **∼ a rise in exports** montrer une hausse des exportations; **∼ sb around the factory** faire visiter l'usine à qn; **∼ a surplus** enregistrer un bénéfice

⌊2⌋ *vi* (be noticeable) se voir; (turn up) (infrml) se montrer (infrml); (film) passer; **∼ in** (visitor) faire entrer; **∼ out** (visitor) reconduire; **∼ up** ⌊1⌋

vt (reveal) révéler

⌊2⌋ *vi* se révéler, se manifester

showcase¹ *n* (in shop) vitrine *f*; (to promote new ideas, products) vitrine *f*

showcase² *vt* (new product) présenter

showdown *n* confrontation *f*

showpiece *n* (of collection) joyau *m*, clou *m*

showroom *n* magasin d'exposition *m*

shredder *n* déchiqueteuse *f*

shrink *vi* (profit margin) diminuer; (economy, sales) être en recul; (profits, funds, stocks) s'amenuiser; (exports, market) se contracter

shrinkage *n* (theft) vol à l'étalage *m*; (of economy, trade) recul *m*; (of profit margin) diminution *f*

shrinking market *n* marché qui se rétrécit *m*

shrink-wrap *vt* emballer sous film plastique (thermo-rétractable)

shrink-wrapping *n* emballage sous film plastique (thermo-rétractable) *m*

shunter *n* (Stock) arbitragiste de place en place *mf*

shut ⌊1⌋ *vt* fermer

⌊2⌋ *vi* (business, office, factory) fermer; **∼ down** ⌊1⌋ *vt* (business, factory) fermer; (service) arrêter; (machinery) arrêter; (appliance) éteindre ⌊2⌋ *vi* (business, factory) fermer; (appliance) s'éteindre; **∼ off** (area, zone) interdire l'accès à; **∼ up** fermer; **∼ up shop** (infrml) fermer boutique

shutdown *n* (Comp) arrêt *m*, fermeture *f*; (of machine) arrêt *m*; (of factory, business) fermeture *f*; **∼ price** *n* (Stock) prix de clôture *m*

shutter *n* (on storefront) rideau de fer *m*; **put up the ∼s** (infrml) fermer boutique

shuttle *n* (flight, bus) navette *f*; **∼ service** *n* service de navette *m*

sick *adj* malade; **be off ∼** être absent pour cause de maladie; **∼ building syndrome** *n* syndrome des bâtiments insalubres *m*; **∼ leave** *n* congé de maladie *m*; **∼ note** *n* certificat médical *m*; **∼ pay** *n* indemnité de maladie *f* (*versée par l'employeur*)

sickness: **∼ benefit** *n* (welfare payment) prestations maladie *f pl*; **∼ insurance** *n* assurance maladie *f*; **∼ insurance premium** *n* prime d'assurance maladie *f*

side¹ *n* (faction, group) camp *m*, côté *m*; **take ∼** prendre position; **time is on our ∼** le temps travaille pour nous; **be on the sales ∼** faire partie du service commercial; **to be on the safe ∼** pour être sûr; **do something on the ∼** (illegally) faire qch au noir

side²**: ∼ with** *vt* (person) se mettre du côté de

side: **∼ effect** *n* effet secondaire *m*; **∼ issue** *n* question d'intérêt secondaire *f*

sideline¹ *n* activité secondaire *f*

sideline² *vt* mettre sur la touche

sidestep *vt* (question, problem) esquiver

sidetracked *adj* **get ∼** s'écarter de

son sujet

siding n BrE voie de garage f

siege economy n économie de blocus f, économie de siège f

sight n vue f; **at ~** sur présentation, à vue; **at ~ draft** AmE traite à vue f; **months after ~** mois à vue; **~ unseen** sur description; **lose ~ of sth** perdre qch de vue; **set one's ~s on sth** viser qch; **raise/lower one's ~s** viser plus haut/bas; **have one's ~s firmly fixed on sth** se fixer qch pour but; **~ bill** n traite à vue f; **~ deposit** n dépôt à vue m; **~ draft** n traite à vue f

sign¹ n (indication) signe m; (plus or minus) signe m; (by the roadside) panneau m; (outside a shop) enseigne f

sign² ① vt (contract, letter, document) signer; **~ a legal agreement** s'engager par contrat, signer un contrat légal; **~ on the dotted line** signer sur les pointillés
② vi signer; **~ away** (right) renoncer à qch par écrit; **~ for** (parcel, key) signer un reçu pour; **~ in** signer le registre en arrivant; **~ off** (authorize: form, claim) approuver; (letter) terminer; **~ on** s'inscrire au chômage; **~ out** signer le registre au départ; **~ up** s'inscrire

signal¹ n (indication) signe m; **send out mixed ~s** envoyer des messages contradictoires; **send a ~ to sb that** indiquer à qn que; **be a ~ that** indiquer que

signal² vt (willingness, reluctance, support) indiquer; (end, start) marquer

signaling AmE, **signalling** BrE n (Econ) clignotement des indicateurs économiques m

signatory n signataire mf; **be a ~ to** être signataire de

signature n (Comp, Comms) signature f; **for ~** pour signature, à signer; **put one's ~ to** apposer sa signature à; **~ loan** n prêt personnel m; **~ tune** n indicatif m; **~ file** n fichier signature m

signed adj signé

significant adj (meaningful) significatif/-ive; (substantial) considérable; (important) important

significantly adv considérablement

signify vt (indicate) signifier; (imply) impliquer; (show, display) exprimer

signpost¹ n panneau indicateur m

signpost² vt indiquer

silent adj silencieux/-ieuse; **~ majority** n majorité silencieuse f; **~ partner** n AmE associé/-e commanditaire m/f, commanditaire mf

silicon chip n puce électronique f

silver n (metal) argent m; **~ standard** n étalon argent m; **~ surfer** n (Comp) internaute senior mf

SIM card n carte SIM f

similar adj semblable

similarity n ressemblance f; (Patents) similitude f

simple adj simple; **~ contract** n convention verbale f; **~ fraction** n fraction simple f; **~ interest** n intérêts simples m pl; **~ yield** n (Stock) rendement simple m

simplified adj simplifié

simplify vt simplifier; **~ matters** simplifier les choses

simulate vt (Gen Comm, Comp) simuler

simulation n (Gen Comm, Comp) simulation f; **~ model** n modèle de simulation m; **~ modeling** AmE, **~ modelling** n BrE modélisation de simulation f

simulcast n diffusion simultanée f, simultané m

simultaneous adj simultané; **~ broadcast** n diffusion simultanée f, simultané m; **~ payments clause** n clause de paiements équivalents f; **~ translation** n traduction simultanée f

Sincerely: ~ yours AmE (letter ending) je vous prie d'agréer, Madame/Monsieur, l'expression de mes sentiments les meilleurs, veuillez agréer, Madame/Monsieur, mes salutations distinguées

sinecure n sinécure f

single¹ adj (sole) seul; (unmarried) célibataire; (room) individuel/-elle, pour une personne; **inflation is in ~ figures** le taux d'inflation est inférieur à 10%

single² n (ticket, fare) aller simple m; (room) chambre pour une personne f, chambre individuelle f

single³: ~ out vt choisir, désigner

single: ~ administrative document n (EU) document administratif unique m; **~-berth cabin** n cabine pour une personne f; **~ capacity** n (Stock) capacité simple f, capacité unique f; **~-capacity trading** n (Stock) activité réservée f, transactions en capacité unique f pl; **~ commission** n commission unique f; **~-contract finance** n financement contractuel unique m; **~ currency** n monnaie unique f; **~-employer bargaining** n UK négociation avec employeur unique f; **~-entry book-keeping** n comptabilité en partie simple f; **~-entry visa** n visa accordé pour une entrée m; **~ European currency** n monnaie unique européenne f; **~-family home** n AmE, **~-family house** BrE n maison unifamiliale f; **~ income** n salaire unique m; **~ labor market** AmE, **~ labour market** BrE n marché unique du travail m; **~ man** n célibataire m; **~ manning** n (Transp) conduite à un seul agent f; **~ parent** n parent unique m; **~-parent family** n famille monoparentale f; **~ payment** n paiement unique m; **~ person** n célibataire mf, personne seule f; **~ person's allowance** n (Tax) abattement pour personnes seules m; **~ premium** n prime unique f; **~-premium deferred annuity** n annuité différée à prime unique f; **~-premium life insurance** n ⟶

assurance-vie à prime unique *f;* ~ **room** *n* chambre individuelle *f,* chambre pour une personne *f;* ~**-room supplement** *n* supplément pour chambre individuelle *m;* ~ **sourcing** *n* approvisionnement auprès d'une source unique *m;* ~ **spacing** *n* interligne simple *m;* ~ **status** *n* statut unique *m;* ~ **table bargaining** *n* UK négociation à un seul niveau *f;* ~ **ticket** *n* BrE aller simple *m;* ~**-union agreement** *n* UK accord syndical unique *m,* convention à syndicat unique *f;* ~**-user licence** BrE, ~**-user license** AmE *n* (Comp) licence individuelle d'utilisation *f;* ~ **woman** *n* célibataire *f*

Single: ~ **European Act** *n* Acte unique européen *m;* ~ **European Market** *n* Marché unique européen *m;* ~ **Market** *n* marché unique *m*

singly *adv* (separately) séparément; (one by one) un à un; (alone) individuellement

sink 1 *vt* (debt) amortir; (company) faire couler; ~ **money into a project** investir de l'argent dans un projet
2 *vi* (ship) couler; (company) couler; (profits, productivity) baisser; **the project/product sank without trace** on n'a plus entendu parler du projet/produit

sinking: ~ **fund** *n* fonds d'amortissement *m;* ~ **fund loan** *n* prêt au fonds d'amortissement *m*

siphon: ~ **off** *vt* (money) détourner

sister: ~ **company** *n* société-sœur *f;* ~ **ship** *n* sister-ship *m*

sit *vi* (Pol) (Parliament, committee) siéger; ~ **tight** ne pas bouger; ~ **on the board** siéger au conseil d'administration; ~ **on a committee** faire partie d'un comité; ~ **in** assister; ~ **in on a meeting** assister à une réunion; ~ **on** (infrml) (report, application form) garder sous le coude (infrml)

sit: ~**-down strike** *n* grève sur le tas *f;* ~**-in** *n* manifestation avec occupation des locaux *f,* sit-in *m;* ~**-in strike** *n* grève sur le tas *f*

site *n* (Comp) site *m;* (of building, town) emplacement *m;* (for building work) chantier *m;* ~ **directory** *n* (Comp) répertoire de sites *m,* annuaire de sites *m;* ~ **engineer** *n* ingénieur de chantier *m;* ~ **foreman** *n* chef de chantier *m;* ~ **manager** *n* directeur/-trice de chantier *m/f;* ~ **map** *n* (on website) plan de site *m;* (in construction) plan de masse *m;* ~ **planning** *n* étude d'aménagement des locaux *f;* ~ **referencing** *n,* ~ **registration** *n* (Comp) référencement *m*

siting *n* implantation *f,* emplacement *m*

sitrep *abbr* (▸**situation report**) rapport de situation *m*

sits. vac. *abbr* BrE (▸**situations vacant**) offres d'emploi *f pl,* postes à pourvoir *m pl*

sitting tenant *n* BrE locataire dans les lieux *mf*

situation *n* (circumstances) situation *f;* (job)

situation *f,* emploi *m;* **have the ~ well in hand** avoir la situation bien en main; **save the ~** sauver la situation; **in an interview/ conflict ~** lors d'un entretien/conflit; **in a social ~** en société; **the staffing ~ is worsening** la crise du recrutement s'aggrave; **the current economic ~** la conjoncture actuelle; ~ **report** *n* rapport de situation *m*

situational marketing *n* mercatique de situation *f*

situations vacant *n pl* BrE offres d'emploi *f pl,* postes à pourvoir *m pl*

six monthly periods *n pl* semestres *m pl*

size¹ *n* taille *f;* (measurements) dimensions *f pl;* (of structure, building) grandeur *f;* (of population, audience) importance *f;* (of problem, project, task) ampleur *f;* (Comp) (of file) taille *f;* (of font) corps *m,* taille *f;* (of clothing) taille *f;* (of shoes) pointure *f*

size² *vt* (Comp) (window) dimensionner; ~ **up** *vt* (person) juger; (situation) évaluer; (problem, difficulty) mesurer

sizeable *adj* (sum, amounts, demand, debt) assez important; (budget) gros/grosse; (proportion) non négligeable

skeleton: ~ **contract** *n* contrat type *m;* ~ **service** *n* service de permanence *m;* ~ **staff** *n* personnel réduit *m*

sketch¹ *n* esquisse *f*

sketch² *vt* (plan, outline) ébaucher; (draw) esquisser

skew *vt* (result, survey) fausser; (deliberately bias) déformer

skewed *adj* (research, result) faussé; (deliberately biased) déformé; ~ **frequency curve** *n* courbe de fréquence embrochée *f*

skill *n* (intellectual flair) habileté *f;* (acquired ability) compétence *f;* (innate ability) aptitude *f;* (talent) talent *m;* ~ **at doing,** ~ **in doing** talent à faire; ~ **at sth,** ~ **in sth** compétence en qch; ~ **differential** *n* différentiel de qualifications *m;* ~ **level** *n* niveau de compétence *m;* ~ **sharing** *n* échange d'expériences *m*

skilled *adj* (work) qualifié; **be ~ as...** avoir des talents de...; ~ **labor** AmE, ~ **labour** BrE *n* main-d'œuvre qualifiée *f;* ~ **worker** *n* ouvrier/-ière qualifié/-e *m/f*

skill-intensive *adj* exigeant une grande compétence

skills *n pl* (abilities) capacités *f pl;* (training) connaissances *f pl;* **her ~ as a negotiator** ses talents de négociatrice; **computer/book- keeping ~** connaissances en informatique/ comptabilité *f pl;* ~ **analysis** *n* (HRM) analyse de qualification *f;* ~ **shortage** *n* manque de main-d'œuvre qualifiée *m*

skim *vt* écrémer

skimming *n* écrémage *f;* (Tax) fraude fiscale *f*

skimp: ~ **on** *vt* (infrml) (food, material) lésiner sur

skip¹ *n* (for waste) benne *f*; (Comp) saut *m*; (Bank) débiteur/-trice sans adresse *m/f*; **~-payment privilege** *n* privilège d'exemption de paiement *m*

skip² *vt* (meeting, lunch, page, chapter) sauter; **~ the details** omettre les détails, sauter les détails; **~ a payment** sauter un paiement

sky *n* **the ~'s the limit** tout est possible

skyrocket *vi* monter en flèche

SLA *abbr* (▸**Service Level Agreement**) contrat de niveau de service *m qui formalise les droits et les devoirs du fournisseur et du client*

slack¹ *adj* (control) relâché; (demand) calme; (season) creux/creuse; (worker) négligent; (work) négligé; **grow ~** se relâcher; **trading is ~** le marché est peu actif; **business is ~** les affaires tournent au ralenti

slack² *n* (in business climate) marasme *m*; (drop in trade, sales) ralentissement *m*; (in schedule, timetable) marge *f*; **take up the ~** (in economy) relancer un secteur affaibli

slack³: ~ off *vi* (business, demand, sales) ralentir

slack: ~ fill *n* remplissage truqué *m*; **~ period** *n* période creuse *f*

slacken ⟦1⟧ *vt* (pace) réduire ⟦2⟧ *vi* (recovery, business, demand, sales) ralentir

slackening *n* (of discipline) relâchement *m*; (of economy, trade, speed, demand) ralentissement *m*

slander¹ *n* (Law) diffamation orale *f*; **sue sb for ~** intenter un procès en diffamation à qn; **~ action** *n* procès en diffamation *m*

slander² *vt* diffamer

slanderous *adj* diffamatoire

slant¹ *n* (perspective) point de vue *m*; (bias) tendance *f*; **with a European ~** d'un point de vue européen; **give a new ~ on sth** offrir un angle nouveau sur

slant² *vt* (information, facts) présenter avec parti pris

slanted *adj* tendancieux/-ieuse

slapdash *adj* (work) bâclé (infrml)

slash¹ *n* (in typography) barre oblique *f*; (reduction) réduction *f*; **a 15% price ~** une réduction de prix de 15%

slash² *vt* (price) sacrifier; (amount, cost, expenditure, size) réduire considérablement; **~ 10% off the price** réduire le prix de 10%

slate *n* US (Pol) liste des candidats *f*

slaughter¹ *n* abattage *m*

slaughter² *vt* abattre

slaughterhouse *n* abattoir *m*

sleaze *n* (Pol) corruption *f*

sleeper *n* (HRM) bailleur de fonds *m*; (Transp) voiture-lit *f*, wagon-lit *m*; (unexpectedly successful product) succès à retardement *m*

sleeping: ~ beauty *n* (Stock) société opéable *f*; **~ car** *n* voiture-lit *f*, wagon-lit *m*; **~ economy** *n* avoirs dormants *m pl*; **~**

partner *n* BrE associé/-e commanditaire *m/f*, commanditaire *mf*

slice *n* part *f*; **~ of the market** (Econ, S&M) part de marché *f*

slick¹ *adj* (presentation, production, campaign, performance) habile; (deal, operation) mené rondement; (salesperson) habile, malin/-igne (péj)

slick² *n* (of oil) nappe *f*

slide *vi* (price) glisser

slider *n* (Comp) ascenseur *m*

slide projector *n* projecteur de diapositives *m*

sliding: ~ parity *n* parité en légère baisse *f*, parité glissante *f*; **~ scale** *n* échelle mobile *f*; **~ wage scale** *n* échelle mobile des salaires *f*

slight *adj* léger/-ère

slightly *adv* légèrement; **~ less than** légèrement inférieur à

slim: ~ down *vt* (workforce) dégraisser

slim-line *adj* (flat) ultra-plat; (small) mini

slip¹ *n* (form) bordereau *m*; **withdrawal/ deposit ~** bordereau de retrait/de versement *m*; **credit card ~** facturette *m/f*, reçu de carte de crédit *m*

slip² *vi* (price) glisser; (Stock) baisser, déraper; (quality, standard) baisser; **~ back** (prices, profits) reculer, baisser; **~ up** (infrml) faire une erreur, faire une gaffe (infrml)

slippage *n* (in output, production) dérapage *m*; (in schedule) retard *m*

slogan *n* (advertising) slogan *m*

slope *n* pente *f*

slot¹ *n* (for card, coin, ticket) fente *f*; (for letters) ouverture *f*; (in timetable, schedule) créneau *m*

slot²: ~ in *vt* (coin, ticket) insérer; (into schedule, meeting) trouver un créneau pour; (person) placer

slow¹ *adj* lent; **~ to reply** lent à répondre; **business is ~** les affaires tournent au ralenti; **~ decline** *n* (Stock) baisse lente *f*, lent déclin *m*; **~ rise** *n* (Stock) hausse lente *f*, lente remontée *f*; **~ train** *n* omnibus *m*

slow²: ~ down *vi* (Econ) se ralentir

slowdown *n* (Econ) ralentissement *m*; AmE (industrial action) grève perlée *f*; **a ~ in demand** un ralentissement de la demande

sluggish *adj* (Stock) faible, morose; (market) lourd, stagnant; **~ trading on the London Stock Exchange** journée morose à la Bourse de Londres

sluice-gate price *n* (EU) *prix minimum à l'importation pour les produits agricoles non communautaires*

slump *n* (Bank, Econ) crise *f*, récession *f*, marasme *m*; (in prices, profits, shares) effondrement *m*; (in popularity) chute *f*; (in support) baisse *f*; **experience a ~** (market) s'effondrer; **retail ~** effondrement de la vente au détail; **share ~** effondrement des valeurs ⋯⋯⫶

boursières; ∼ **in sales** mévente *f*

slumpflation *n* récession conjuguée à l'inflation *f*

slush fund *n* caisse noire *f*

SMA *abbr* (Stock) (**Secondary Market Association**) Association du marché secondaire *f*

small *adj* petit; (purchase) faible, peu important; **read the** ∼ **print of a contract** éplucher un contrat; **on a** ∼ **scale** sur une petite échelle; ∼ **ad** *n pl* petite annonce *f*; ∼ **business** *n* petite entreprise *f*; ∼ **business administration** *n* (Gen Comm) administration des petites entreprises *f*; (in an individual case) gestion d'une petite entreprise *f*; ∼ **change** *n* (Gen Comm) petite monnaie *f*; (Pol) (infrml) concessions mineures *f pl*; ∼ **claims court** *n* tribunal d'instance *m*; ∼ **denomination** *n* petite coupure *f*; ∼ **employer** *n* petit employeur *m*; ∼ **firm** *n* petite entreprise *f*; ∼ **investor** *n* petit épargnant *m*; ∼ **investors** *n pl* petit capital *m*; ∼ **and medium-sized companies** *n pl* petites et moyennes entreprises *f pl*; ∼ **and medium-sized enterprises** *n pl* petites et moyennes entreprises *f pl*; ∼ **and medium-sized manufacturing companies** *n pl* petites et moyennes industries *f pl*; ∼ **print** *n* (in contract) passage imprimé en petits caractères *m*, petits caractères *m pl*; ∼**-scale** *adj* (company, business) de petite taille; ∼ **speculator** *n* boursicoteur/-euse *m/f*; ∼ **trader** *n* petit commerçant *m*

smallholder *n* petit exploitant *m*

smart *adj* (clever) intelligent, futé; (elegant) élégant, chic *inv*; **the** ∼ **money is on ABC shares** les actions ABC sont un bon investissement; ∼ **card** *n* carte à puce *f*; ∼ **card reader** *n* lecteur de cartes à puce *m*; ∼ **money** *n* (Fin) réserve d'argent *f* (*pour réaliser un investissement intéressant*); ∼ **terminal** *n* terminal intelligent *m*

SME *abbr* (▶**small and medium-sized enterprises**) PME *f pl* (petites et moyennes entreprises)

smiley *n* (Comp) frimousse *f*, binette *f* Can

SMME *abbr* (▶**small and medium-sized manufacturing companies**) PMI *f pl* (petites et moyennes industries)

smokestack *n* (Ind) cheminée d'usine *f*; ∼ **industry** *n* industrie traditionnelle *f*

smoking *n* ∼ **is prohibited** il est interdit de fumer; **no** ∼ défense de fumer; ∼ **room** *n* fumoir *m*

smooth *vt* (Math) lisser; ∼ **out** (difficulty, surface) aplanir

smoothing *n* (Math) lissage *m*

smooth running *n* (of machine, business) bon fonctionnement *m*

SMS message *n* message SMS *m*, message texte *m*

smuggle *vt* (drugs, arms) faire du trafic de;

(person, message, item) faire passer clandestinement; ∼ **sth through customs** faire passer qch en contrebande à la douane, faire passer qch en fraude à la douane

smuggling *n* contrebande *f*; **drugs/arms** ∼ trafic de drogue/d'armes *m*

S/N *abbr* (▶**shipping note**) note de chargement *f*

snag *n* inconvénient *m*, problème *m*

snail mail *n* poste traditionnelle *f*

snake *n* (Econ) (EU) serpent *m*, serpent monétaire *m*

snap[1]: ∼ **decision** *n* décision rapide *f*; ∼ **strike** *n* grève surprise *f*

snap[2]: ∼ **up** *vt* (opportunity) saisir; (goods, products, shares) s'emparer de; ∼ **up a bargain** faire une affaire

snatch *vt* (opportunity) saisir; ∼ **up a bargain** faire une affaire

sneak preview *n* avant-première *f*

SNIG *abbr* (▶**sustained non-inflationary growth**) croissance non-inflationniste soutenue *f*

snip *n* (infrml) bonne affaire *f*; **it's a** ∼ **at that price** à ce prix-là, c'est donné

snowball *vi* faire boule de neige

Snr *abbr* (▶**senior**) (in age) aîné; (in rank) principal, supérieur

snugging *n* (Econ, Fin, Pol) resserrement de la politique monétaire *m*

s.o. *abbr* UK (▶**standing order**) virement automatique *m*, ordre de paiement permanent *m*; (Stock) (▶**seller's option**) livraison au gré du vendeur *f*

SO *abbr* (▶**senior officer**) haut fonctionnaire *m*

soar *vi* (profits, prices) monter en flèche; ∼ **above**, ∼ **beyond** dépasser; ∼ **to** (level, sum, figure) atteindre

soaring *adj* (prices) en forte hausse; (popularity) croissant; (profits, inflation, consumer demand) en forte progression

social *adj* social; ∼ **accounting** *n* comptabilité des charges sociales ou comptes publics *f*; ∼ **adjustment cost** *n* coût d'adaptation sociale *m*; ∼ **analysis** *n* analyse sociale *f*; ∼ **benefits** *n pl* avantages sociaux *m pl*; ∼ **capital** *n* capital social *m*; ∼ **category** *n* catégorie sociale *f*; ∼ **charter** *n* (EU) charte sociale *f*; ∼ **class** *n* catégorie sociale *f*, classe *f*; ∼ **compact** *n* contrat social *m*; ∼ **contract** *n* contrat social *m*; ∼ **cost** *n* coût social *m*; ∼ **democracy** *n* social-démocratie *f*; ∼ **good** *n* bien public *m*, bien social *m*; ∼ **insurance** *n* US assurance sociale *f*; ∼ **insurance number** *n* US numéro d'assurance sociale *m*; ∼ **outcast** *n* paria *m*; ∼ **overhead capital** *n* capital social *m*; ∼ **ownership** *n* démocratie d'entreprise *f*, propriété publique *f*; ∼ **policy** *n* politique sociale *f*; ∼ **product** *n* produit social *m*, revenu national *m*; ∼ **profit** *n*

analyse coût-rendement *f*, profit social *m*; ~
secretary *n* secrétaire social/-e *m/f*; ~
security *n* aide sociale *f*; ~ **security
benefits** *n pl* allocations de la sécurité
sociale *f pl*, prestations de la sécurité sociale
f pl; ~ **security contributions** *n pl*
cotisations sociales *f pl*; ~ **security
payment** *n* BrE paiement d'assistance sociale
m, prestation d'assistance sociale *f*; ~
spending *n* dépenses sociales *f pl*; ~
standing *n* position sociale *f*; ~ **status** *n*
standing *m*; ~ **strata** *n pl* couches sociales
f pl; ~ **studies** *n pl* sciences humaines *f pl*;
~ **system** *n* système social *m*; ~ **welfare** *n*
protection sociale *f*; ~ **work** *n* assistance
sociale *f*; ~ **worker** *n* assistant/-e social/-e
m/f, travailleur/-euse social/-e *m/f*

socialism *n* socialisme *m*

socialist *adj* socialiste; ~ **economy** *n*
économie socialiste *f*

socialization *n* socialisation *f*

sociocultural *adj* socioculturel/-elle

sociodemographic *adj* (profile, data,
segment) socio-démographique

socioeconomic *adj* socio-économique

sociometric *adj* sociométrique

socioprofessional *adj*
socioprofessionnel/-elle; ~ **group** *n* catégorie
socioprofessionnelle *f*

SOD *abbr* (▸**software only dealer**)
spécialiste de logiciels *mf*

soft *adj* (demand) faible; (prices) instable à la
baisse; (Pol) modéré; (target) vulnérable;
choose the ~ **option** choisir la facilité; ~
budget *n* budget en baisse *m*; ~ **copy** *n*
(Comp) affichage sur écran *m*, visualisation
sur écran *f*; ~ **cost** *n* coût accessoire *m*, coût
périphérique *m*; ~**-cover book** *n* livre de
poche *m*; ~ **currency** *n* devise faible *f*; ~
drink *n* boisson non alcoolisée *f*; ~ **funding**
n (temporary) financement non durable *m*; (low-
interest) fonds publics à taux favorable *m pl*;
~ **furnishings** *n pl* tapis et tissus
d'ameublement *m pl*; ~ **goods** *n pl*
(perishables) biens de consommation non
durables *m pl*; ~ **landing** *n* atterrissage en
douceur *m*; ~ **loan** *n* prêt bonifié *m*, crédit à
taux privilégié *m*; ~ **market** *n* (unstable and
declining) marché en baisse *m*; (stagnant)
marché morose *m*, marché peu actif *m*; ~
modeling AmE, ~ **modelling** BrE *n* (Econ)
modélisation discrète *f*; ~ **offer** *n* offre
variable *f*; ~ **sell** *n* promotion discrète *f*; ~
spot *n* point faible *m*; ~ **technology** *n*
technologie douce *f*

soften: ~ **up** *vt* (client) baratiner (infrml)

soft-pedal *vt* minimiser

software *n* (Comp) logiciel *m*; ~
application *n* application logicielle *f*; ~
broker *n* courtier en logiciel *m*, courtier en
valeurs de sociétés de logiciel *m*; ~
company *n* (software only) éditeur de logiciel
m, fabricant de logiciel *m*; (software and

services) société de services et d'ingénierie en
informatique *f*; ~ **and computer services
company** *n* société de services et
d'ingénierie en informatique *f*; ~
developer *n* développeur/-euse *m/f*;
~**-driven** *adj* piloté par logiciel; ~
engineer *n* ingénieur informaticien *m*; ~
engineering *n* génie logiciel *m*; ~ **house** *n*
(software only) éditeur de logiciel *m*, fabricant
de logiciel *m*; (software and services) société de
services et d'ingénierie en informatique *f*; ~
language *n* langage de programmation *m*; ~
library *n* logithèque *f*; ~ **only dealer** *n*
spécialiste de logiciels *mf*; ~ **package** *n*
progiciel *m*; ~ **piracy** *n* piratage de
logiciel *m*; ~ **release** *n* version de logiciel
f

SOHO *abbr* (**small office, home office**)
(small business) TPE *f* (très petite entreprise);
(individual) travailleur/-euse en solo à domicile
m/f

soiled *adj* (goods) défraîchi

sol *n* sol *m*

solar power *n* énergie solaire *f*

sold: ~ **daybook** *n* journal des ventes *m*;
~ **ledger** *n* livre des ventes *m*

sole *adj* exclusif/-ive; (single) seul, unique;
with the ~ **object of doing** avec pour
objectif de faire, à seule fin de faire; ~
agency *n* représentation exclusive *f*; ~
agency contract *n* contrat d'exclusivité *m*;
~ **agent** *n* agent exclusif *m*, concessionnaire
exclusif/-ive *m/f*; ~ **bargaining agent** *n* UK
négociateur/-trice unique *m/f*; ~ **bargaining
rights** *n pl* UK droits à position de
négociateur unique *m pl*; ~ **dealer** *n* (S&M)
concessionnaire exclusif/-ive *m/f*; ~ **of
exchange** *n* (Bank) seule de change *f*; ~
inventor *n* (Patents) seul inventeur *m*,
unique inventeur *m*; ~ **legatee** *n* légataire
universel/-elle *m/f*; ~ **owner** *n* unique
propriétaire *mf*; ~ **proprietor** *n* (business)
entreprise individuelle *f*, entreprise
unipersonnelle *f*; (owner) propriétaire unique
mf; ~ **proprietorship** *n* (legal ownership) droit
de propriété *m*; (business) entreprise
individuelle *f*, entreprise à propriétaire
unique *f*; ~ **right** *n* droit exclusif *m*; ~
supplier *n* fournisseur exclusif *m*; ~ **trader**
n (person) exploitant/-e individuel/-elle *m/f*;
(company) entreprise individuelle *f*, entreprise
unipersonnelle *f*

solicit *vt* (information, help, money) solliciter;
(business, orders) rechercher

solicitation *n* US (S&M) démarchage *m*

solicitor *n* UK (Law) (for court work) ≈ avocat/
-e *m/f*; (for oaths, conveyancing) ≈ notaire *m*; US
(chief law officer) chargé/-e des affaires
juridiques auprès de la municipalité *m/f*; US
(S&M) démarcheur/-euse *m/f*

solid *adj* (foundation, basis, evidence, information)
solide; (investment) sûr; (advice, worker) sérieux/
-ieuse; **be on** ~ **ground** être en terrain sûr; ⋯▸

~ **gold** n or massif m; ~ **line** n (on graph) ligne continue f

solidarity n solidarité f; **do sth out of** ~ **with sb** faire qch par solidarité envers qn; ~ **action** n mouvement de solidarité m

solo adv go ~ faire cavalier seul

solus adj isolé; ~ **position** n emplacement isolé m

solution n (to problem) solution f; (Patents) solution f; **the** ~ **to the problem** la solution du problème; **find a** ~ **to sth** trouver une solution à qch

solve vt (problem) résoudre; (crisis, poverty, unemployment) trouver une solution à

solvency n solvabilité f; ~ **margin** n marge de solvabilité f; ~ **ratio** n (Acc) taux de solvabilité m; (Fin) (with credit institution) ratio de solvabilité m

solvent adj solvable

soon adv bientôt; **as** ~ **as possible** dès que possible, dans les meilleurs délais

s.o.p. abbr (▶**standard operating procedure**) (of equipment) mode d'exploitation normal m; (local rules) procédure normale à suivre f

sophisticated adj (equipment, technology) sophistiqué, perfectionné; (person, taste) raffiné; (public) averti; (trendy) chic inv

sophistication n (of equipment, technology) sophistication f; (of market) complexité f; (of person, taste) raffinement m; (of public) caractère averti m; (trendiness) chic m

sop: ~ **up** vt (debt) absorber

sorry adj désolé; **I'm** ~ veuillez m'excuser; **I'm terribly** ~ je suis vraiment désolé, je suis navré; **be** ~ **that/if** être désolé que/si; ~ **to have kept you waiting** désolé de vous avoir fait attendre

sort¹ n (type) genre m, sorte f; (Comp) tri m; ~ **code** n (Bank) code d'agence m; ~ **file** n (Comp) fichier de tri m; ~ **key** n (Comp) critère de tri m

sort² vt (classify) classer; (applications, letters, goods) trier; ~ **X from Y** séparer X de Y; ~ **out** (problem) régler; (details, arrangements) s'occuper de; (replacement, stand-in) trouver; (finances, paperwork, affairs) mettre de l'ordre dans

sorter n trieur/-euse m/f

sought-after adj recherché

sound¹ adj (idea) bon/bonne; (structure, argument, knowledge) solide; (decision) sensé; (judgement, business, management) sain; (investment) sûr; ~ **advice** bon conseil m; **that makes** ~ **political sense** d'un point de vue politique, c'est très sensé; **on a** ~ **footing** sur des bases saines; **have a** ~ **grasp of sth** avoir une bonne compréhension de qch

sound² n son m; ~ **card** n (Comp) carte son f; ~ **check** n contrôle du son m; ~ **currency** n devise saine f; ~ **effects** n pl bruitage m

sound³ ① vt (warning) donner; ~ **the alarm** donner l'alarme; ~ **a note of caution** lancer un appel à la prudence

② vi sembler; ~ **out** vt (person) sonder, interroger

sounding board n personne sur qui on peut tester ses idées; **use sb as a** ~ tester ses idées sur qn

soundtrack n bande sonore f

source¹ n source f; **at** ~ (deduction, tax relief) à la source; ~ **address** n adresse émettrice f; ~ **of capital** base du capital f; ~ **code** n code source m; ~ **data** n données de base f pl; ~ **disk** n disque source m; ~ **document** n document de base m; ~ **file** n fichier source m; ~ **of funds** ressource de financements f; ~ **of income** source de revenus f

source² vt (new products) se procurer, sourcer

sourcer n sourceur/-euse m/f

sourcing n approvisionnement m, sourçage m; ~ **expert** n sourceur/-euse m/f

sovereign n (Pol) souverain/-e m/f; ~ **borrower** n emprunteur public m; ~ **loan** n prêt garanti par l'État m

SPA abbr (▶**subject to particular average**) (Ins) assujetti à l'avarie particulière

space n (Comms, Comp, Media) espace m; **advertising** ~ espace publicitaire m, emplacement publicitaire m; ~ **bar** n barre d'espacement f; ~ **broker** n courtier en publicité m; ~ **buyer** n acheteur/-euse d'espace m/f; ~ **buying** n achat d'espace m; ~ **rates** n pl tarifs d'espace m pl; tarifs d'insertion m pl; ~ **seller** n vendeur/-euse d'espace m/f; ~ **selling** n vente d'espace f

spaceman economy n économie du gaspillage et de l'irresponsabilité

spam¹ n multi-postage abusif m, publicité rebut par courrier électronique f, spam m

spam² vt ~ **sb** innonder qn de publicité rebut (par courrier électronique)

spamdexing n (Comp) référencement abusif de site m (pour obtenir le meilleur positionnement de son site dans les résultats du moteur de recherche)

spammer n auteur d'un multi-postage abusif m, expéditeur de courrier rebut (par courrier électronique) m, spammer m

spamming n multi-postage abusif m, envoi de publicité rebut (par courrier électronique) m, spamming m

span n (of time) durée f; **the** ~ **of her career** la durée de sa carrière; **over a** ~ **of six months** sur six mois; **a short** ~ **of time** une courte période; ~ **of control** attributions f pl, étendue des responsabilités f

spare¹ adj (available) disponible; (replacement) de rechange; (copy) en plus; (ticket) de trop; **a** ~ **moment** un moment de libre; ~ **capacity**

n (Econ, Ind) capacité inutilisée *f*, potentiel inemployé *m*; (Transp) surcroît de capacité *m*; ~ **cash** *n* argent en trop *m*; ~ **part** *n* pièce de rechange *f*; ~ **time** *n* temps libre *m*

spare² *vt* se passer de

spares *n pl* pièces détachées *f pl*

spark: ~ **off** *vt* (criticism, discussion, debate) déclencher, provoquer

sparsely populated *adj* peu peuplé, à faible population

spate *n* vague *f*

speaker *n* (lecturer, delegate) conférencier/-ière *m/f*; (in publice place) orateur *m*; (one of several in debate, meeting) intervenant/-e *m/f*

spearhead¹ *n* (of campaign) fer de lance *m*

spearhead² *vt* (campaign, reform) mener

spec *abbr* (►**specification**) (of design, product) spécification *f*; **built to sb's** ~ fabriqué selon les spécifications de qn, fabriqué selon le cahier des charges de qn; **job** ~ profil de poste *m*; **on** ~ (buy) sur descriptif; (apply, turn up) à tout hasard; ~ **sheet** *n* fiche technique *f*

special¹ *adj* (event, occasion, visitor, announcement) spécial; (deal, package, rate) spécial; (particular) particulier/-ière *m/f*; (powers, envoy, commission) spécial; **by** ~ **delivery** en exprès

special² *n* offre spéciale *f*, promotion *f*; **on** ~ en promotion

special: ~ **accounts** *n pl* (Acc) comptes spéciaux *m pl*; ~ **arrangements** *n pl* dispositions particulières *f pl*; ~ **assessment** *n* (Tax) évaluation spéciale *f*; ~ **case** *n* cas particulier *m*; (Law) jugement gracieux *m*, jugement gracieux sur requête *m*; ~ **circumstances** *n pl* circonstances particulières *f pl*; ~ **clearing** *n* UK (Bank) compensation particulière *f*; ~ **commissioner** *n* UK (Tax) commissaire spécial *m*; ~ **correspondent** *n* (Media) envoyé/-e spécial/e *m/f*; ~ **delivery** *n* (Comms) service exprès *m*; ~ **deposit** *n* (Bank) réserves obligatoires *f pl*; ~ **drawing rights** *n pl* (Bank) droits de tirage spéciaux *m pl*; ~ **endorsement** *n* (Bank) endossement spécial *m*; ~ **meeting** *n* assemblée extraordinaire *f*, réunion extraordinaire *f*; ~ **offer** *n* (S&M) offre spéciale *f*, promotion *f*; ~ **partner** *n* associé/-e commanditaire *m/f*, associé/-e en participation *m/f*; ~ **pleading** *n* argumentation spéciale *f*; ~ **purchase** *n* offre promotionnelle *f*; ~**-purpose allotment** *n* (Fin) affectation à but spécial *f*; ~ **relationship** *n* lien privilégié *m*; ~ **reserve** *n* (Acc) réserve spéciale *f*; ~ **situation** *n* situation particulière *f*; ~ **tax rate** *n* taux d'imposition spécial *m*; ~ **terms** *n pl* conditions spéciales *f pl*; ~ **terms for the trade** tarif spécial pour les membres de la profession *m*

specialist *n* spécialiste *mf*, expert *m*; US (Stock) spécialiste de la valeur *m/f*; **a** ~ **in**

mobile telephony un spécialiste de la téléphonie mobile; ~ **information** *n* informations spécialisées *f pl*; ~ **knowledge** *n* connaissances spécialisées *f pl*; ~ **shop** *n* magasin spécialisé *m*; ~ **staff** *n* personnel spécialisé *m*; ~ **work** *n* travail de spécialiste *m*

speciality *n* spécialité *f*; ~ **advertising** *n* publicité par cadeaux-primes *f*; ~ **goods** *n* articles de marque *m pl*; ~ **selling** *n* vente à domicile *f*; ~ **store** *n* magasin spécialisé *m*

specialization *n* spécialisation *f*

specialize *vi* se spécialiser; ~ **in** se spécialiser dans

specialized *adj* spécialisé

specialty *n* ►**speciality** BrE

specie *n* espèces *f pl*; **in** ~ (payment) en espèces

specific *adj* (particular) précis; (unique) spécifique; ~ **to sb/sth** spécifique à qn/qch; ~ **amount** *n* montant déterminé *m*; ~ **duty** *n* (Imp/Exp, Tax) droit spécifique *m*; ~ **payment** *n* paiement déterminé *m*; ~ **performance** *n* (Law) exécution intégrale du contrat par décision de justice *f*, exécution pure et simple *f*; ~ **provisions** *n* (Bank) provisions spécifiques *f pl*; ~ **tax** *n* droit spécifique *m*; ~ **training** *n* formation spécifique *f*

specifically *adv* (state, refer) explicitement; (designed) spécifiquement

specification *n* (of design) spécification *f*; (Law) stipulation *f*; ~**s of a car/computer** les caractéristiques d'une voiture/d'un ordinateur; **built to sb's** ~**s** construit selon les spécifications de qn, construit selon le cahier des charges de qn; **job** ~ profil de poste *m*; ~ **of goods** (Patents) liste des produits *f*; ~ **of services** (Patents) liste des services *f*; ~ **sheet** *n* fiche technique *f*

specifics *n pl* (Gen Comm) détails *m pl*; (Bank) provisions spécifiques *f pl*; **get down to** ~ entrer dans les détails

specified *adj* précisé, spécifié; **at the** ~ **tenor** à l'échéance prescrite; ~ **employer** *n* (Tax) employeur désigné *m*; ~ **financial institution** *n* (Fin, Tax) institution financière désignée *f*; ~ **load** *n* charge prescrite *f*; ~ **member** *n* (Tax) associé/-e déterminé/-e *m/f*, membre spécifié *m*; ~ **percentage** *n* (Tax) pourcentage déterminé *m*; ~ **person** *n* (Tax) personne apparentée *f*, personne spécifiée *f*; ~ **property** *n* (Tax) bien désigné *m*; ~ **purpose** *n* (Tax) fin admise *f*, raison spécifiée *f*

specify *vt* (person) préciser; (rules, contract, law) stipuler; **unless otherwise specified** sauf indication contraire; **not elsewhere specified** non dénommé ailleurs

specimen *n* échantillon *m*; ~ **charge** *n* (Law) chef d'accusation typique *m*; ~ **copy** *n* copie type *f*, spécimen *m*; ~ **invoice** *n* modèle de facture *m*; ~ **signature** *n* ⇢

signature témoin *f*, spécimen de signature *m*

speculate *vi* (Gen Comm, Stock) spéculer; ~ **on a rise/fall** spéculer à la hausse/baisse

speculation *n* (Gen Comm, Stock) spéculation *f*

speculative *adj* (Gen Comm, Stock) spéculatif/-ive; ~ **application** *n* candidature spontanée *f*; ~ **demand** *n* demande spéculative *f*; ~ **fund** *n* fonds spéculatifs *m pl*; ~ **stock** *n* valeur spéculative *f*; ~ **trading** *n* opérations spéculatives *f pl*

speculator *n* spéculateur/-trice *m/f*; **small-time** ~ boursicoteur/-euse *m/f*

speech *n* (oration) discours *m*; **make a** ~ faire un discours; ~ **recognition** *n* reconnaissance vocale *f*; ~ **recognition software** *n* logiciel de reconnaissance vocale *m*

speed¹ *n* (Gen Comm) vitesse *f*; (Comp) débit *m*, vitesse *f*; (Econ) vitesse *f*; **two-/three-~** à deux/trois vitesses

speed²: ~ **up** *vti* accélérer

speeding-up *n* accélération *f*

speedy *adj* rapide

spell *vt* (word) écrire; (out loud) épeler; ~ **out** *vt* (explain) expliquer point par point

spellcheck¹ *n* (Comp) correcteur orthographique *m*

spellcheck² *vt* effectuer une correction orthographique sur

spellchecker *n* (Comp) correcteur orthographique *m*

spend¹ *n* dépenses *f pl*; **advertising** ~ dépenses publicitaires *f pl*

spend² **1** *vt* (time) passer, consacrer; (money) dépenser; ~ **money on rent/raw materials** dépenser de l'argent en loyer/matières premières; ~ **money on one's home/family** dépenser de l'argent pour sa maison/famille
2 *vi* dépenser

spender *n* **be a big** ~ être dépensier/-ière

spending *n* dépenses *f pl*; ~ **on training** dépenses de formation *f pl*; **defence** ~ dépenses de défense *f pl*, dépenses militaires *f pl*; **credit card** ~ achats sur carte de crédit *m pl*; **government** ~, **public** ~ dépense publique *f*; **go on a** ~ **spree** faire des folies (infrml); ~ **authority** *n* autorisation de dépenser *f*; ~ **cuts** *n pl* restrictions budgétaires *f pl*; ~ **level** *n* niveau de dépenses *m*; ~ **money** *n* (available funds) argent disponible *m*; (for personal use) argent de poche *m*; ~ **patterns** *n pl* habitudes d'achat *f pl*; ~ **power** *n* pouvoir d'achat *m*; ~ **surge** *n* montée soudaine des dépenses *f*; ~ **targets** *n pl* prévisions de dépenses *f pl*

spendthrift *n* dépensier/-ière *m/f*

sphere *n* domaine *m*, sphère *f*; ~ **of activity** champ d'activité *m*, sphère *f*; ~ **of influence** sphère d'influence *f*

spike¹ *n* (Stock) hausse brutale *f*; (on graph) pointe *f*

spike² *vt* (idea, plan) mettre à la corbeille, rejeter

spill: ~ **over** *vi* (effect) se répandre

spillage *n* (Envir, Ind) déversement accidentel *m*

spillover *n* (Econ) retombées *f pl*; ~ **effect** *n* effet d'entraînement *m*, effet de retombées *m*

spin¹ *n* (pej) *façon de présenter une affaire aux médias et à l'opinion publique*; **what's their** ~ **on the crisis?** comment présentent-ils la crise?; **put a new** ~ **on sth** présenter qch sous un nouvel angle; **government** ~ manipulation des médias et le l'opinion par le gouvernement; ~ **doctor** *n* consultant/-e en communications *m/f*; ~ **doctoring** *n* manipulation des médias et de l'opinion publique *f*; ~**-off effect** *n* retombées *f pl*, effet secondaire *m*

spin²: ~ **off** **1** *vt* (subsidiary) créer par essaimage
2 *vi* essaimer

spin-off *n* (process) essaimage *m*; (secondary product) sous-produit *m*, produit dérivé *m*; (benefit) retombée favorable *f*; **a TV** ~ **from the film** une adaptation télévisée du film; ~ **effect** *n* retombées *f pl*, effet secondaire *m*

spiral¹ *n* (Econ) spirale *f*

spiral² *vi* (prices, roles, costs) monter en flèche

spiralling inflation *n* spirale inflationniste *f*

splash¹ *n* **make a** ~ (new product) faire sensation; ~ **screen** *n* (on Internet) écran graphique *m* (*qui s'affiche pendant le téléchargement d'une application*)

splash² *vt* (Media) mettre en manchette; ~ **out** *vi* (infrml) faire des folies (infrml); ~ **out on sth** s'offrir qch

splinter: ~ **group** *n* groupe séparatiste *m*; ~ **union** *n* syndicat dissident *m*

split¹ *n* (in group, movement) scission *f*, rupture *f*; (sharing out) partage *m*; **a three-way** ~ un partage en trois; ~ **decision** *n* décision partagée *f*; ~ **offering** *n* (Stock) offre de répartition *f*; ~ **rating** *n* (Fin) classement divergent *m*; ~ **screen** *n* écran divisé *m*, split screen *m*; ~**-second timing** *n* précision à la seconde près *f*; ~ **shift** *n* poste fractionné *m*; ~ **site** *adj* (plant, shop) dont les locaux sont dispersés; ~ **ticket** *n* US (Pol) liste partagée *f*

split² **1** *vt* (share, divide) partager; (movement, group) provoquer une scission dans; ~ **sth four ways** partager qch en quatre; **be** ~ **on an issue** être divisé/partagé sur une question; ~ **the difference** couper la poire en deux, partager la différence
2 *vi* (movement, consortium) se diviser; ~ **off** se séparer; ~ **off from** se séparer de; ~ **up**

1 *vt* (profits, tasks, money) partager, répartir
2 *vi* (meeting) se disperser; (alliance,

consortium) éclater

spoilage *n* déchet *m*

spoiler *n* (Media) article destiné à couper les effets de la concurrence *m*; ~ **campaign** *n* campagne publicitaire destinée à couper les effets de la concurrence *f*

spoilt ballot paper *n* (blank) bulletin blanc *m*; (defaced) bulletin nul *m*

spokesperson *n* porte-parole *m inv*

sponsor[1] *n* (of event, team) sponsor *m*; (of candidate, protégé); parrain/marraine *m*/*f*; (of programme) commanditaire *mf*, sponsor *m*; (patron) mécène *m*; (Fin) (guarantor) garant *m*; **act as ~ for sb** (Fin) être le garant de qn; ~ **demand** *n* (Econ) demande d'option *f*

sponsor[2] *vt* (student, studies, project) financer; (event, team) sponsoriser; (foundation, protegé, candidate, charity) parrainer

sponsorship *n* (Fin) (of event, team) sponsoring *m*; (of film, programme) parrainage *m*; (of arts, culture) patronage *m*, mécénat *m*; (of candidate, protegé) parrainage *m*; **seek ~ for sth** chercher des sponsors pour qch; **corporate ~** (of charity, arts, research) mécénat d'entreprise *m*; ~ **agreement** *n*, ~ **deal** *n* contrat de sponsoring *m*

sporadic *adj* sporadique

spot[1] *adj* (Stock) au comptant

spot[2] *n* (in advertising) spot publicitaire *m*; **on the ~** sur place

spot: ~ **business** *n* opération au comptant *f*, ~ **cash** *n* argent liquide *m*; ~ **charter** *n* affrètement spot *m*; ~ **check** *n* (quality) contrôle-surprise *m*; (customs) fouille au hasard *f*, ~ **commodity** *n* (Stock) marchandise disponible *f*, matière première au comptant *f*, ~ **credit** *n* crédit ponctuel *m*; ~ **currency market** *n* marché des devises au comptant *m*; ~ **delivery** *n* (Stock) livraison immédiate *f*; ~ **exchange rate** *n* cours des changes au comptant *m*; ~ **goods** *n pl* marchandises disponibles immédiatement *f pl*; ~ **market** *n* (Stock) marché au comptant *m*; ~ **position** *n* disponibilité *f*, position au comptant *f*, ~ **price** *n* (Stock) (commodities) prix sur place *m*, spot *m*; (currencies) cours au comptant *m*; ~ **quotation** *n* (Stock) cotation du disponible *f*; ~ **rate** *n* (Stock) cours au comptant *m*; ~ **transaction** *n* (Stock) transaction au comptant *f*

spot-check *vt* (randomly) effectuer un contrôle surprise sur; (Ind) (for quality) sonder

spotlight *n* **be under the ~**, **be in the ~** (person) être sur la sellette; (issue, event) faire la une *f*; **turn the ~ on sb/sth** attirer l'attention sur qn/qch

spouse *n* époux/épouse *m*/*f*; (Law) conjoint/conjointe *m*/*f*

spread[1] *n* (of news, information) diffusion *f*; (of knowledge, expertise) généralisation *f*; (of services, products) éventail *m*; (Math) étalement *m*;

(proliferation in a particular area) prolifération *f*; (Bank) marge *f*; (Stock) marge *f*; (of options) opération mixte *f*, spread *m*; **double page ~** page double *f*; ~ **effect** *n* (Econ) effet d'osmose *m*, effet de contagion *m*; ~ **order** *n* (Stock) ordre d'écart *m*, ordre mixte *m*; ~ **position** *n* (Stock) position mixte *f*; ~ **risk** *n* (Stock) risque lié à la marge *m*; ~ **trading** *n* (Stock) (currency market) étalement *m*

spread[2] [1] *vt* (repayments, consultations, meetings, course) échelonner, étaler; (Ins) (risks) répartir; (rumour) faire courir
[2] *vi* (news) se répandre; (panic) se propager; (rumour) courir, circuler; (crisis) s'étendre

spreading *n* (Fin) (of costs) ventilation *f*; (Stock) opération de spread *m*, opération mixte *f*; ~ **agreement** *n* (Stock) accord d'échelonnement *m*

spreadsheet *n* (chart) feuille de calcul *f*; (Comp) (software) tableur *m*; ~ **program** *n* tableur *m*

spree *n* **go on a spending ~** faire des folies (infrml)

spyware *n* logiciel espion *m*, *programme dissimulé qui transmet des données à une régie publicitaire*

SQC *abbr* (▶**statistical quality control**) contrôle statistique de qualité *m*

squander *vt* (money, resources, time) gaspiller

squandering *n* gaspillage *m*

square[1] *n* (Gen Comm, Math) carré *m*; ~ **brackets** *n pl* crochets *m pl*; ~ **footage** *n* (of building) métrage carré *m*; ~ **kilometer** AmE, ~ **kilometre** BrE *n* kilomètre carré *m*; ~ **measures** *n pl* mesures de superficie *f pl*

square[2]: ~ **up** *vi* régler ses comptes; ~ **with** *vt* (facts, evidence) correspondre à, cadrer avec

squatter *n* squatter *m*; ~**'s rights** *n pl* droits de l'occupant de fait *m pl*, droits de l'occupant sans titre *m pl*

squeeze[1] *n* reserrement *m*; ~ **and freeze** *n* gel des salaires et des prix *m*; ~ **credit** *n* encadrement du crédit *m*, reserrement du crédit *m*; **wage ~** reserrement des salaires *m*; **feel the ~** être gêné financièrement, avoir de la peine à joindre les deux bouts

squeeze[2] *vt* (prices) bloquer; ~ **the shorts** (jarg) (Stock) faire la chasse au découvert; ~ **sth out of sb** soutirer qch à qn; ~ **sb out of the market** pousser qn hors du marché

SRO *abbr* UK (▶**self-regulating organization**) organisation autonome *f*, organisme auto-réglementé *m*

SSA *abbr* (▶**standard spending assessment**) évaluation standard des dépenses *f*

SSL *abbr* (▶**secure sockets layer**) protocole SSL *m*

SSP *abbr* (▶**storage services provider**) hébergeur de données en ligne *m*

stability *n* (Econ, Pol), stabilité *f*; ~ **zone** *n* ⋯⋫

zone de stabilité *f*

stabilization *n* stabilisation *f*; ~ **fund** *n* (Tax) fonds de stabilisation *m*; ~ **loan** *n* emprunt de valorisation *m*; ~ **policy** *n* (Econ) politique conjoncturelle *f*

stabilize ① *vt* (Econ) stabiliser ② *vi* (Econ) se stabiliser

stabilized price *n* prix stabilisé *m*

stable *adj* stable; (share, market) ferme; ~ **equilibrium** *n* équilibre stable *m*

stack¹ *n* (pile) pile *f*, empilage *m*; (Comp) pile *f*

stack² *vt* empiler; (cargo) gerber

stacking *n* (cargo handling) gerbage *m*

staff¹ *n* personnel *m*; ~ **and line** structure staff and line *f*; ~ **appraisal** *n* appréciation du personnel *f*, évaluation du personnel *f*; ~ **assistant** *n* attaché/-e fonctionnel/-elle *m/f*; ~ **association** *n* association du personnel *f*; ~ **audit** *n* inventaire des effectifs *m*; ~ **canteen** *n* restaurant d'entreprise *m*; ~ **commitment** *n* engagement du personnel *m*; ~ **cost** *n* charges de personnel *f pl*; ~ **cutback** *n* compression de personnel *f*, réduction du personnel *f*; ~ **development** *n* la formation et le perfectionnement du personnel; ~ **discount** *n* rabais accordé au personnel *m*; ~ **management** *n* gestion du personnel *f*; ~ **mobility** *n* mobilité du personnel *f*; ~ **organization** *n* organisation fonctionnelle *f*, organisation horizontale *f*; ~ **planning** *n* planification des effectifs *f*; ~ **reduction** *n* compression de personnel *f*, réduction du personnel *f*; ~ **representative** *n* délégué/-e du personnel *m/f*; ~ **resourcing** *n* le recrutement et la gestion des effectifs; ~ **shortage** *n* manque de personnel *m*; ~ **status** *n* statut de cadre *m*; ~ **training** *n* formation du personnel *f*; ~ **transfer** *n* mutation de personnel *f*, transfert de personnel *m*; ~ **turnover** *n* rotation du personnel *f*, turnover *m*; ~ **welfare fund** *n* caisse de solidarité du personnel *f*

staff² *vt* (office) pourvoir en personnel; ~ **up** *vi* recruter du personnel

staffer *n* membre du personnel *m*

staffing *n* recrutement (du personnel) *m*; ~ **levels** *n pl* niveau des effectifs *m*; ~ **problems** *n pl* problèmes de recrutement *m pl*

stag *n* (Stock) loup *m*

stage¹ *n* (of career, life) stade *m*; (of project, process) phase *f*; (of journey, talks) étape *f*; (platform) estrade *f*; **at some** ~ à un moment donné; **in** ~**s** par étapes; **the project is still in its early** ~**s** le projet est encore à ses débuts; **in easy** ~**s** par petites étapes; **be at the half-way** ~ être à mi-chemin; **go through a difficult** ~ traverser une période difficile; **at this** ~ (for now) pour l'instant; (at this point) à ce stade; ~ **payment** *n* (Fin) paiement par étape *m*

stage² *vt* (event, conference) organiser; (fake)

simuler; ~ **a go-slow** organiser une grève perlée; ~ **a strike** organiser une grève; ~ **a walkout** faire une grève surprise

staged agreement *n* UK accord progressif *m*

stagflation *n* (Econ) stagflation *f*

stagger *vt* (appointments, visits) espacer; (holidays, journeys, payments) échelonner, étaler

staggered *adj* (payments, holidays) échelonné, étalé; ~ **board of directors** *n* conseil d'administration tournant *m*; ~ **hours** *n pl* horaires décalés *m pl*

staggering¹ *adj* (amount, difference) prodigieux/-ieuse *m*; (feat, change) stupéfiant; (news, information) incroyable

staggering² *n* échelonnement *m*, étalement *m*

staggering: ~ **maturities** *n pl* (Stock) échelonnement des échéances *m*; ~ **of vacations** *n* AmE, ~ **of holidays** *n* BrE étalement des vacances *m*, échelonnement des vacances *m*

stagnant *adj* (Econ) stagnant

stagnate *vi* (Econ) stagner, être dans le marasme

stagnation *n* (Econ) stagnation *f*, marasme *m*

stake¹ *n* (amount risked) enjeu *m*; (Fin, Stock) participation *f*; **at** ~ (matter) en jeu; **the** ~**s are high** l'enjeu est très important; **play for high** ~**s** jouer gros jeu; **raise the** ~**s** monter la mise; **there is a lot at** ~ l'enjeu est considérable; **put sth at** ~ mettre qch en jeu; **have a 10%** ~ avoir une participation de 10%

stake² *vt* (Fin) miser; (reputation) risquer

stakeholder *n* personne ayant une participation dans l'affaire *f*, partie prenante *f*; **be a** ~ avoir une participation, être partie prenante; ~ **economy** *n* économie participative *f*, économie d'actionnariat *f*; ~ **pension** *n* UK *système de retraite complémentaire destiné aux travailleurs indépendants et aux personnes à faibles revenus sans retraite professionnelle*

stale *adj* (Stock) (market) lourd

stalemate *n* impasse *f*; **have reached a** ~ être dans une impasse

stamp¹ *n* (postal) timbre *m*; (marking device) tampon *m*; (sticker) vignette *f*; ~ **duty** *n*, ~ **tax** *n* droit de timbre *m*

stamp² *vt* (card, form) tamponner; (date, name) apposer au tampon; (passport, document) viser; ~ **out** (abuse, inflation) enrayer, juguler

stamped addressed envelope *n* BrE enveloppe timbrée à mon/son/votre adresse *f*

stampede *n* (of investors) débandade *f*

stance *n* (on issue) position *f*; **take a** ~, **adopt a** ~ adopter un position

stand¹ *n* (for advertising) panneau d'affichage *m*; (at exhibition) stand *m*; **make a** ~ **against a decision** s'opposer résolument à une

décision; **take a ~ on** prendre position sur
stand² ⟦1⟧ *vt* (be liable) **~ to lose sth**
risquer de perdre qch; **~ to win sth** pouvoir
gagner qch; **~ the cost of** supporter le coût
de; **~ a good chance of** avoir une bonne
chance de; **~ a loss** supporter une perte; **not
~ a chance** ne pas avoir la moindre chance;
~ one's ground ne pas bouger, tenir bon; **~
surety for sb** se porter garant de qn,
cautionner qn

⟦2⟧ *vi* (be a candidate) se présenter; (offer,
proposal, agreement) rester valable; **~ as
guarantor for sb** se porter garant de qn; **~ at
a discount** être au-dessous de sa valeur
nominale; **~ at a premium** être au-dessus de
sa valeur nominale; **~ firm** ne pas bouger,
tenir bon; **~ firm in the belief that** tenir bon
en sachant que; **~ for election** poser sa
candidature à une élection, se présenter aux
élections; **~ in line** faire la queue; **~ in the
way of progress** faire obstacle au progrès; **~
at** (amount, balance, total) s'élever à, se situer à;
~ back prendre du recul; **~ back from**
prendre du recul par rapport à; **~ by** (person)
soutenir; (view, offer, decision) s'en tenir à;
(actions) assumer; **~ down** (candidate) se
désister; **~ for** (initials) signifier, vouloir dire;
~ in for remplacer; **~ off** (employees) mettre
en chômage technique; **~ out** être
remarquable; **~ out for** (pay rise, better
conditions) revendiquer; **~ over** (item on agenda)
rester en suspens; **~ up** (argument, theory)
tenir debout; **~ up for** (person, interest)
défendre; **~ up to** (opponent) résister,
affronter; **it won't ~ up to close scrutiny**
cela ne résistera pas à un examen
approfondi; **~ up to wear** faire beaucoup
d'usage

stand-alone *adj* autonome
standard¹ *adj* (model, equipment, rate, pay)
standard; (quality) ordinaire; (image)
traditionnel/-elle; **it is ~ practice to do** il est
d'usage de faire; **become ~, become ~
practice** se généraliser
standard² *n* (quality level) niveau *m*; (official
specification) norme *f*; (required level) niveau
requis *m*; (yardstick, measurement) étalon *m*; **~s
of service** la qualité du service; **safety ~s**
normes de sécurité *f pl*; **hygiene ~s** normes
d'hygiène *f pl*; **comply with EU ~s** être
conforme aux normes de l'UE; **be up to ~**
(person) avoir le niveau requis; (goods, products)
être confrome aux normes; **set the ~**
imposer le modèle à suivre; **this model
includes ABS as ~** ce modèle est équipé en
série de freins ABS; **gold ~** étalon or *m*
standard: **~ agreement** *n* contrat
standard *m*, contrat type *m*; **~ class** UK
(Transp) seconde classe *f*; **~ commodity** *n*
(Stock) bien étalon *m*; **~ contract** *n* contrat
standard *m*, contrat type *m*; **~ cost** *n* (Gen
Comm) coût de revient standard *m*, coût
standard *m*, prix de revient standard *m*; (Acc)
coût standard *m*; **~ cost accounting** *n*

comptabilité analytique standardisée *f*; **~
costing** *n* comptabilisation en coûts
standards *f*, méthode des coûts standards *f*; **~
costs** *n pl* coûts standards *m pl*; **~
deduction** *n* (Tax) déduction forfaitaire *f*,
prélèvement forfaitaire *m*; **~ design** *adj*
(Ind) de série; **~ deviation** *n* (statistics) écart
type *m*; **~ of equalization** *n* norme de
péréquation *f*; **~ error** *n* erreur type *f*; **~
grade** *n* niveau de référence *m*; **~ letter** *n*
lettre type *f*; **~ of living** *n* niveau de vie *m*;
~ operating procedure *n* (for equipment)
mode d'exploitation normal *m*; (local rules)
procédure normale à suivre *f*; **~ policy** *n*
(Ins) police type *f*; **~ price** *n* prix standard
m; **~-rated** (Tax) *adj* aux taux standard;
~-rate tax *n* impôt forfaitaire *m*, impôt à
taux standard *m*; **~ return** *n* (ticket) aller-
retour plein-tarif *m*; **~ size** *n* format
standard *m*; **~ spending assessment** *n*
évaluation standard des dépenses *f*; **~ time**
n (Gen Comm) temps de référence *m*, temps
standard *m*; (HRM) durée forfaitaire *f*, délai
fixe *m*
standardization *n* normalisation *f*,
standardisation *f*; **~ agreement** *n* accord de
normalisation *m*; **~ of salaries**
uniformisation des salaires *f*
standardize *vt* normaliser, standardiser,
uniformiser
standardized *adj* normalisé, standardisé
standby¹ *adj* (equipment) de secours
standby² *n* (person) remplaçant/-e *m/f*;
(Transp) stand-by *m*; **be on ~** être prêt à
intervenir; (passenger) être en stand-by;
(equipment) être en veille
standby: **~ agreement** *n* accord stand-by
m; **~ credit** *n* crédit de soutien *m*, crédit
stand-by *m*; **~ facility** *n* crédit de soutien *m*;
~ line of credit *n* crédit de soutien *m*; **~
loan** *n* prêt de soutien *m*; **~ passenger** *n*
(Transp) passager/-ère en stand-by *m/f*,
passager/-ère en attente *m/f*; **~ ticket** *n*
billet stand-by *m*
stand-in *n* remplaçant/-e *m/f*
standing: **~ advance** *n* (Bank) avance
permanente *f*; **~ committee** *n* (Pol)
commission permanente *f*; **~ down** *n* (HRM)
mise à pied *f*; **~ order** *n* UK (Bank) ordre de
paiement permanent *m*, virement
automatique *m*
standoff *n* (deadlock) impasse *f*
standstill *n* **be at a ~** (factory, rail network,
port) être au point mort; **come to a ~** (work,
production) s'arrêter; (talks) aboutir à une
impasse; **bring sth to a ~** (city, port, rail
services, factory) paralyser; **~ agreement** *n*
(Fin) accord moratoire *m*, moratorium *m*
staple¹ *adj* (product, industry, food) de base;
(crop) principal
staple² *n* (product) produit de base *m*, article
de base *m*; (food) aliment de base *m*; (crop)
culture principale *f*; (fastener) agrafe *f*

staple³ *vt* agrafer

staple: ~ **commodity** *n* produit tertiaire *m*; ~ **export** *n* exportation principale *f*; ~ **stock** *n* stock de base *m*

stapler *n* agrafeuse *f*

star *n* (S&M) vedette *f*; ~ **product** *n* produit vedette *m*, produit locomotive *m*

start¹ *n* (beginning) début *m*; (of machine, peripheral) démarrage *m*, mise en route *f*; **get off to a flying** ~ (business, project) prendre un bon départ; **make a** ~ **on sth** commencer à faire qch; **make a fresh** ~ recommencer à zéro; **give sb a** ~ **in business** aider qn à démarrer dans les affaires

start² 1 *vt* (activity) commencer; (machinery) mettre en marche; (car) faire démarrer; (firm, company) créer; (rumour) être à l'origine de; (quarrel) déclencher; ~ **doing** commencer à faire; ~ **to do** commencer à faire; ~ **an entry** (Acc) ouvrir une écriture; ~ **by doing** commencer par faire; ~ **from scratch** partir de zéro; ~ **in business** se lancer dans les affaires; ~ **a fashion** lancer une mode; ~ **a fashion for** lancer la mode de; ~ **sb off as** faire démarrer qn en qualité de; ~ **work** se mettre au travail

2 *vi* (Gen Comm) commencer; ~ **out** (person) débuter; ~ **over** recommencer à zéro; ~ **up** *vt* (firm, company) créer; *vi* (Gen Comm) commencer; (Econ) démarrer; (campaign, business) démarrer; ~ **up in business** se lancer dans les affaires

starting: ~ **point** *n* point de départ *m*; ~ **price** *n* (Stock) cours initial *m*; ~ **salary** *n* salaire d'embauche *m*, salaire de départ *m*

start-up *n* (company) start-up *f*, jeune pousse *f*; ~ **capital** *n* capital d'apport *m*, capital initial *m*, mise de fonds initiale *f*, financement de démarrage *m*; ~ **costs** *n pl* frais d'établissement *m pl*, frais de démarrage *m pl*; ~ **financing** *n* financement de lancement *m*; ~ **loan** *n* prêt initial *m*; ~ **phase** *n* phase de démarrage *f*

state¹ *n* (condition, situation) état *m*; (Pol) État *m*; **in a** ~ **of neglect** à l'abandon; **in a good/ bad** ~ en bon/mauvais état; **in a bad** ~ **of repair** en mauvais état; ~ **of alert/crisis** état d'alerte/de crise; ~ **of affairs** *n* situation *f*; ~ **aid** *n* aide de l'État *f*; ~**-aided** *adj*, ~**-funded** *adj* subventionné par l'État; ~**-of-the-art** *adj* (Comp) avancé, de pointe; (equipment, technology) de pointe, à la pointe du progrès; ~ **bond** *n* (Stock) obligation d'État *f*; ~ **control** *n* contrôle d'État *m*, contrôle étatique *m*; ~ **of the economy** situation économique *f*, état de l'économie *m*; ~ **education** *n* UK école publique *f*; ~ **enterprise** *n* entreprise d'État *f*, entreprise publique *f*; ~**-owned** *adj* étatique; ~ **ownership** *n* propriété d'État *f*; ~ **pension** *n* UK retraite de l'État *f*; ~**-run** *adj* (company, factory) géré par l'État; ~ **school** *n* UK école publique *f*; ~ **sector** *n* secteur public *m*; ~

subsidy *n* subvention de l'État *f*; ~ **tax** *n* impôt de l'État *m*

state² *vt* (fact, truth, opinion) exposer; (size, quantity, date, terms) spécifier, préciser; (age, job, income) indiquer; ~ **that** déclarer que; ~ **one's case** exposer son cas; ~ **categorically** déclarer catégoriquement; ~ **the obvious** énoncer une évidence

stated: ~ **capital** *n* (Acc) capital social *m*; ~ **value** *n* valeur comptable *f*

State Earnings Related Pension Scheme *n* UK *régime de retraite étatique basé sur le salaire*

stateless *adj* (Admin, Pol) apatride

statement *n* (declaration of views) déclaration *f*; (Acc) état *m*; (Comms, Media) communiqué *m*; (Comp) instruction *f*; (Bank) relevé de compte *m*; (Law) déclaration *f*; **make a** ~ (Gen Comm) faire une déclaration; (Law) faire une déposition; **financial** ~ état des comptes *m*, état financier *m*; ~ **of account** relève de compte *m*; ~ **of affairs** (Bank) (in bankruptcy) bilan de liquidation *m*; ~ **of assets and liabilities** bilan *m*; ~ **of earnings** US état des résultats *m*; ~ **of expenses** état de frais *m*; ~ **of fact** exposé des faits *m*; ~ **of financial position** bilan *m*; ~ **of income** US comptes de résultats *m pl*; ~ **of income and expenses** état de produits et de charges *m*; ~ **of intent** déclaration d'intention *f*; ~ **of objectives** énoncé des objectifs *m*; ~ **of terms and conditions** énoncé des clauses et conditions *m*

Statement of Revenue and Expenditure *n* état des recettes et dépenses *m*

static *adj* (output, price) stationnaire, statique

station *n* (Transp) gare *f*; (on radio) station de radio *f*; ~ **break** *n* (Media) page de publicité *f*

stationary *adj* (prices) stable; (queue, vehicle) à l'arrêt; (traffic) bloqué

stationery *n* papeterie *f*

statistic *n* statistique *f*

statistical *adj* statistique; ~ **modeling** AmE, ~ **modelling** BrE *n* modelage statistique *m*; ~ **quality control** *n* contrôle statistique de qualité *m*; ~ **returns** *n pl* résultats statistiques *m pl*, statistiques officielles *f pl*; ~ **risk** *n* risque statistique *m*; ~ **sampling** *n* échantillonnage statistique *m*, échantillonnage aléatoire *m*; ~ **significance** *n* signification statistique *f*; ~ **software** *n* logiciel statistique *m*; ~ **spread** *n* étalement statistique *m*

statistically significant *adj* statistiquement significatif/-ive

statistician *n* statisticien/-ienne *m/f*

statistics *n pl* +*sing* v statistique *f*

status *n* (Admin, Law) statut *m*; (prestige) prestige *m*; (Comp) statut *m*, état *m*; (social position) position *f*; **credit** ~ solvabilité *f*, situation financière *f*; **employment** ∼ situation professionnelle *f*; **financial** ∼ état financier *m*; **legal** ∼ statut légal *m*; **professional** ∼ statut professionnel *m*; **social** ∼ standing *m*; ≈ **bar** *n* (Comp) barre d'état *f*; ∼ **information** *n* renseignements commerciaux *m pl*; ∼ **inquiry** *n* (Fin) enquête sur la situation financière *f*; ∼ **line** *n* (Comp) ligne d'état *f*; ∼ **message** *n* (Comp) message d'état *m*; ∼ **quo** *n* status quo *m*; ∼ **report** *n* (Fin) rapport sur la solvabilité *m*; (Mgmnt) état d'avancement des travaux *m*; ∼ **seeker** *n personne qui a soif d'être socialement reconnue*; ∼ **symbol** *n* marque de prestige *f*

statute *n* (Law) loi *f*, statut *m*; **by** ∼ selon la loi; ∼ **book** *n* UK (Law) code *m*, recueil des lois *m*; ∼ **law** *n* (Law) droit écrit *m*

statutes of limitation of action *n pl* lois fixant la prescription d'une action en justice *f pl*

statutory *adj* légal, prévu par la loi, réglementaire, statutaire; **have** ∼ **effect** avoir force de loi; ∼ **accounts** *n pl* (Acc) comptes sociaux *m pl*, comptes statutaires *m pl*; ∼ **allocation** *n* (Pol) affectation réglementaire *f*; ∼ **appropriation** *n* (Pol) crédit réglementaire *m*; ∼ **audit** *n* audit légal *m*; ∼ **authority** *n* (Pol) autorité réglementaire *f*; ∼ **body** *n* (Law) organisme assurant un service public *m*, organisme officiel *m*; ∼ **books** *n pl* (Law) registres statutaires *m pl*; ∼ **company** *n* société concessionnaire *f*; ∼ **expenditure** *n* dépense réglementaire *f*; ∼ **holiday** *n* jour férié *m*; ∼ **instrument** *n* (Law) décret d'application *m*; ∼ **meeting** *n* assemblée statutaire *f*, **merger** *n* fusion conforme aux statuts *f*, fusion légale *f*; ∼ **minimum wage** *n* salaire minimum garanti *m*, ≈ salaire minimum interprofessionnel de croissance *m*, SMIC *m*; ∼ **notice** *n* (Law) délai de préavis légal *m*; ∼ **obligation** *n* (Law) obligation légale *f*, obligation prévue par la loi *f*, obligation statutaire *f*; ∼ **power** *n* pouvoir statutaire *m*; ∼ **report** *n* rapport présenté lors de la création d'une société; ∼ **requirement** *n* (Pol) demande réglementaire *f*; ∼ **right** *n* UK (Law) droit prévu par la loi *m*, droit statutaire *m*; ∼ **sick pay** *n* UK prestations maladie réglementaires *f pl versées par l'employeur*

stave: ∼ **off** *vt* (threat) écarter; (bankruptcy, defeat, crisis) éviter

stay[1] *n* (visit, trip) séjour *m*; (reprieve) répit *m*; ∼ **of appeal** *n* (Law) suspension d'appel *f*

stay[2] *vi* rester; ∼ **in the money** (Stock) rester dans le cours; ∼ **informed** rester informé; ∼ **out** (on strike) rester en grève

staying power *n* endurance *f*

Std *abbr* (▶**standard**) étalon *m*

STD *abbr* BrE (**subscriber trunk dialling**) (Comms) automatique (interurbain) *m*

steadily *adv* régulièrement

steady[1] *adj* (growth, rate) uniforme, régulier/-ière; (gradual) progressif/-ive; (job, income) fixe; **hold** ∼ (share, price, rate) se maintenir; ∼ **state economy** *n* état de non-croissance *m*, état stationnaire *m*

steady[2] *vi* (prices, rates) se stabiliser; (share price) se maintenir

steadying factor *n* facteur de stabilisation *m*

steal *vi* voler; ∼ **sth from sb** voler qch à qn

stealth tax *n* impôt déguisé *m*

steamroller *vt* (opposition) briser; ∼ **a project/bill through** user de son influence pour faire passer un projet/projet de loi

steel *n* acier *m*

steelworker *n* sidérurgiste *mf*

steelworks *n pl* aciérie *f*

steep *adj* (rise, fall, increase) fort; (recession) profond; (price) exorbitant; (bill) salé (infrml)

steeply *adv* (rise) en flèche; (drop, fall) fortement

steering *n* (Law, Prop) direction *f*; ∼ **committee** *n* (Gen Comm) commission d'organisation *f*; (for rescheduling of debt) comité de restructuration *m*; ∼ **group** *n* groupe de pilotage *m*

stem *vt* (crisis, increase) enrayer; (inflation, unemployment) juguler, enrayer; (tide, flow) enrayer; ∼ **from** provenir de, résulter de

stenographer *n* sténographe *mf*

stenography *n* sténo *f*, sténographie *f*

step[1] *n* (action taken) démarche *f*; (move) pas *m*; (measure) mesure *f*; **keep in** ∼ **with one's competitors** se maintenir au niveau de ses concurrents; **be one** ∼ **ahead of sb** avoir une longueur d'avance sur qn; **take the** ∼ **of doing** prendre l'initiative de faire; **take** ∼**s (to do)** prendre des mesures (pour faire); **take such** ∼**s as are considered necessary** faire les démarches nécessaires et appropriées; ∼ **cost** *n* (Fin) frais progressifs *m pl*; ∼ **transaction** *n* (Tax) opération en série *f*; ∼**-up loan** *n* prêt progressif *m*

step[2]: ∼ **back (from)** *vi* prendre du recul (par rapport à); ∼ **down** *vi* se retirer; (Pol) se désister; ∼ **forward** *vi* s'avancer; ∼ **in** *vi* intervenir; ∼ **up** *vt* (production) augmenter; (efforts, action, campaign) intensifier; (security, surveillance) renforcer

step-by-step *adj* (description, guide) détaillé; (policy, plan) progressif/-ive

stepped-up *adj* (activity) intensifié; (output) accru, augmenté; (pace) accéléré

sterilization *n* (Fin) stérilisation *f*

sterling *n* sterling *m*; ∼ **area** *n* zone sterling *f*; ∼ **balance** *n* balance sterling *f*; ∼ **commercial paper** *n* billet de trésorerie en livres sterling *m*; ∼ **warrant into gilt edged stock** *n* UK bon de souscription d'obligations d'État *m*; ∼ **zone** *n* zone sterling *f*

stevedore *n* docker *m*, arrimeur *m*

steward *n* (of estate, club) intendant *m*; (Transp) steward *m*

stewardship *n* (leadership) direction *f*; (Admin) gestion *f*

stg *abbr* (▶**sterling**) ster. (sterling)

stick *vt* coller; ∼ **no bills** défense d'afficher; ∼ **to** (facts, plan) s'en tenir à; (principles, brand) rester fidèle à; ∼ **up for** (infrml) (workers, rights) défendre

sticker *n* autocollant *m*

stickiness *n* (of website) pouvoir de rétention sur ses visiteurs *m*

sticking point *n* point de désaccord *m*

stick-on label *n* étiquette adhésive *f*

sticky *adj* (situation, problem) difficile; (website) accrocheur/-euse; ∼ **deal** *n* (Stock) émission hasardeuse *f*; ∼ **note** *n* feuillet adhésif (repositionnable) *m*; ∼ **price** *n* prix peu flexible *m*; ∼ **tape** *n* ruban adhésif *m*

stiff *adj* (Econ) (competition) rude, serré; (warning, penalty) sévère; (opposition) fort; (price) élevé; (task) difficile; (rules) rigide

stiffen *vt* (law, rule) renforcer

stimulate *vt* (confidence, support, demand) encourager, stimuler

stimulating *adj* (competition, discussion) stimulant

stimulative measure *n* (Econ) mesure de relance *f*

stimulus *n* (incentive) stimulant *m*; (boost) impulsion *f*; **be a** ∼ **for exports** stimuler les exportations; **the** ∼ **of competition** le stimulant de la concurrence

stipulate *vt* stipuler

stipulation *n* stipulation *f*; **on the** ∼ **that** à la condition expresse que

stock¹ *n* (in shop, warehouse) stock *m*; (supply, reserves) stock *m*; (of capital goods) parc *m*; (Fin) (capital) ensemble des actions d'une société *m*, ensemble du capital d'une société *m*; (Stock) valeur *f*, titre *m*; (in company) action *f*; (reputation, esteem) cote *f*; **in** ∼ (S&M) (in shop) en magasin; (in warehouse) en stock; **on the** ∼ **exchange** en bourse; **be out of** ∼ (goods) être épuisé; (shop, company) être en rupture de stock; **build up/run down** ∼**s** restocker/ déstocker; **lay in** ∼**s of** s'approvisionner en; **her** ∼ **has risen** sa cote a monté; ∼**s and shares** valeurs mobilières *f pl*; **government** ∼ titres d'État *m pl*, fonds d'État *m pl*; **oil** ∼ valeurs pétrolières *f pl*; ∼ **arbitrage** *n* (Stock) arbitrage de portefeuille *m*, arbitrage sur actions *m*; ∼ **brokerage firm** *n* (Stock) firme de courtiers *f*, maison de courtage *f*; ∼ **certificate** *n* US (Stock) certificat d'action *m*, certificat d'investissement *m*; ∼ **check** *n* contrôle de stocks *m*, vérification des stocks *f*; (Bank) traite à vue *f*; ∼ **clearance** *n* liquidation de stocks *f*; ∼ **company** *n* société anonyme *f*; ∼ **contract** *n* (Stock) contrat d'option *m*, option *f*; ∼ **control** *n* BrE contrôle des stocks *m*, gestion des stocks *f*; ∼

controller *n* responsable des stocks *mf*; ∼ **corporation** *n* US société anonyme par actions *f*; ∼ **dividend** *n* US dividende en actions *m*, dividende-actions *m*; ∼ **draft** *n* traite nantie par des titres *f*; ∼ **exchange** *n* (Stock) bourse de valeurs (mobilières) *f*, marché des valeurs *m*; ∼ **exchange list** *n* cote boursière *f*, cote officielle *f*; ∼ **exchange price index** *n* indice boursier *m*, indice des actions *m*, indice des cours des actions *m*; ∼ **exchange quotation** *n* cours en Bourse *m*; ∼ **exchange transaction** *n* opération boursière *f*, opération de Bourse *f*; ∼ **in hand** *n* stock disponible *m*; ∼ **index future** *n* contrat à terme sur indice *m*, contrat à terme sur indice boursier *m*; ∼ **index futures market** *n* marché des contrats à terme sur indice *m*; ∼ **index option** *n* option d'indexation *f*, option de mise sur indice *f*; ∼ **indexes and averages** *n pl* indices boursiers *m pl*; ∼ **issue** *n* (Stock) émission d'actions *f*; ∼ **line** *n* (S&M) article référencé *m*, article suivi *m*; ∼ **list** *n* (Gen Comm) liste des marchandises en stock *f*; (Stock) cours de la Bourse *m*; ∼ **management** *n* (S&M) gestion des stocks *f*; ∼ **market** *n* Bourse *f*, marché boursier *m*; ∼ **market capitalization** *n* capitalisation boursière *f*; ∼ **market collapse** *n* effondrement du marché *m*; ∼ **market cycle** *n* cycle du marché *m*; ∼ **market index** *n* indice boursier *m*; ∼ **market price index** *n* indice boursier *m*; ∼ **option** *n* option d'achat d'actions *f*, option sur actions *f*; (as a perk for senior staff) stock-option *f*; ∼ **ownership** *n* actionnariat *m*; ∼ **portfolio** *n* portefeuille d'actions *m*; ∼ **price index** *n* indice boursier *m*; ∼ **purchase plan** *n* plan d'achat d'actions *m*; ∼ **purchase warrant** *n* bon de souscription d'actions *m*; ∼ **quotation** *n* cours des actions *m*; ∼ **register** *n* registre des actions *m*; ∼ **rotation** *n* (S&M) rotation des stocks *f*; ∼ **sheet** *n* fiche d'inventaire *f*; ∼ **shortage** *n* rupture de stock *f*; ∼ **split** *n* AmE division d'actions *f*, fractionnement d'actions *m*; ∼ **swap** *n* échange d'actions *m*; ∼ **turnover** *n* mouvement des stocks *m*, rotation des stocks *f*; ∼ **valuation** *n* (Gen Comm) valorisation des stocks *f*; (Acc) inventaire *m*, évaluation des stocks *f*; ∼ **watcher** *n* (Stock) service de surveillance des titres *m*; ∼ **yield** *n* rendement d'une action *m*

stock² *vt* (have available) avoir en stock; (habitually sell, supply) avoir, vendre; (replenish) (shop) approvisionner; (shelves) garnir; ∼ **up on** s'approvisionner en

stockbroker *n* agent de change *m*, courtier en Bourse *m*

stockbroking *n* commerce des valeurs en Bourse *m*

Stock: ∼ **Exchange** *n* Bourse *f*; ∼ **Exchange Alternative Trading Service** *n* UK tableau électronique de cotations *m*; ∼

Exchange Automated Quotation *n*
système de cotation des valeurs automatisé; ∼
Exchange Automated Quotation
International *n système international de*
cotation des valeurs étrangères automatisé; ∼
Market *n* Bourse des valeurs *f*
stockholder *n* actionnaire *mf*
stockholders' equity *n* capitaux propres
m pl
stockholding *n* possession d'actions *f*
stockist *n* UK (S&M) fournisseur *m*
stocklist *n* inventaire *m*; **make à** ∼ **of**
inventorier
stockman *n* AmE magasinier *m*
stockout *n* rupture de stock *f*; ∼ **cost** *n*
coût de rupture de stock *m*
stockpile[1] *n* réserves *f pl*, stock *m*
stockpile[2] *vt* stocker, faire des stocks de
stockpiling *n* stockage *m*
stocks *n pl* (supplies) stocks *m pl*; (Stock)
titres *m pl*; (Acc, Ind) inventaire *m*, stocks
m pl; **while** ∼ **last** pendant la durée des
stocks, jusqu'à épuisement des stocks
stocktake *vi* faire un inventaire, dresser
un inventaire
stocktaking *n* inventaire des stocks *m*; ∼
sale *n* vente pour cause d'inventaire *f*
stop[1] *n* arrêt *m*; (Transp) (of ship, plane)
escale *f*; **be at a** ∼ (production) être arrêté;
bring sth to a ∼ arrêter qch; **come to a** ∼
s'arrêter; **put a** ∼ **to** mettre fin à; ∼**-go**
cycle of inflation *n* cycle d'inflation en
sinusoïde *m*; ∼**-go policy** *n* UK politique de
l'escarpolette *f*, politique des coups
d'accordéon *f*; ∼**-loss** *n* (Stock) ordre stop *m*;
∼**-loss order** *n* (Stock) ordre limité inversé
m, ordre stop *m*; ∼**-loss reinsurance** *n*
réassurance en excédent de pertes *f*; ∼**-loss**
rules *n pl* (Bank) mécanisme pour minimiser
les pertes *m*; ∼ **order** *n* ordre stop *m*;
∼**-payment order** *n* (Bank) ordre de
suspendre les paiements *m*; ∼ **time** *n* (Comp)
temps d'arrêt *m*
stop[2] [1] *vt* (cease) arrêter; (process, equipment,
activity, vehicle) arrêter; (payment, work,
proceedings) suspendre; (event) empêcher
d'avoir lieu; ∼ **doing** arrêter de faire; ∼ **to**
do s'arrêter pour faire; ∼ **sb from doing**
empêcher qn de faire; ∼ **bidding** (at auction
sale) s'arrêter; ∼ **a check** AmE, ∼ **a cheque**
BrE (Bank) faire opposition à un chèque; ∼
sb's allowance couper les vivres à qn; ∼ **a**
stock (Stock) *accepter de remettre une*
transaction dont on a garanti le prix; ∼ **£80**
out of sb's pay retenir 80 livres sterling sur
le salaire de qn; ∼ **work** arrêter de travailler,
cesser le travail; ∼ **working** cesser le travail
[2] *vi* s'arrêter; ∼ **over in Milan** faire une
halte à Milan; (on plane journey) faire escale à
Milan
stopgap *n* bouche-trou *m*; ∼ **measure** *n*
mesure provisoire *f*

stopover *n* (Transp) escale *f*
stoppage *n* (from wages) retenue *f*; (strike)
arrêt de travail *m*, grève *f*
stopped: ∼ **bonds** *n pl* titres frappés
d'opposition *m pl*; ∼ **check** AmE, ∼ **cheque**
BrE *n* chèque frappé d'opposition *m*; ∼ **stock**
n (Stock) transaction à prix garanti remise à
plus tard *f*
storage *n* (in warehouse, depot) entreposage *m*,
emmagasinage *m*, stockage *m*; (of furniture)
entreposage *m*; (of documents, archives)
conservation *f*; (Comp) (action) mémorisation *f*,
stockage *m*; (place) mémoire *f*; **put sth into** ∼
(goods) entreposer; (furniture) mettre au garde-
meuble; ∼ **allocation** *n* (Comp) affectation
de la mémoire *f*; ∼ **area** *n* (Gen Comm) aire
de stockage *f*, surface de stockage *f*; (Comp)
zone de mémoire *f*; ∼ **capacity** *n* capacité
de stockage *f*; ∼ **charges** *n pl* frais de
magasinage *m pl*; ∼ **device** *n* (Comp)
périphérique de stockage *m*; ∼ **facility** *n*
unité de stockage *f*; (for toxic waste) installation
de stockage *f*; ∼ **medium** *n* (Comp) support
de stockage *m*; ∼ **services provider** *n*
hébergeur de données en ligne *m*; ∼ **tank** *n*
citerne de stockage *f*
store[1] *n* (warehouse) magasin *m*; AmE (shop)
magasin *m*; (Comp) mémoire *f*; ∼
accounting *n* comptabilité des stocks *f*,
inventaire matériel *m*; ∼ **audit** *n*
vérification des stocks *f*; ∼ **brand** *n* marque
de distributeur *f*; ∼ **card** *n* carte de crédit
(d'un grand magasin) *f*; ∼ **group** *n* groupe
de distribution *m*; ∼ **promotion** *n* ventes
promotionnelles *f pl*
store[2] *vt* (data) stocker; (goods) emmagasiner,
entreposer, stocker
storefront *n* devanture *f*; ∼ **site** *n* (Comp)
vitrine virtuelle *f*
storehouse *n* entrepôt *m*, magasin *m*
storekeeper *n* AmE commerçant/-e *m/f*,
petit commerçant *m*; UK (in warehouse)
magasinier *m*
storeman *n pl* **-men** magasinier *m*
storeroom *n* magasin *m*
stores *n pl* (supplies) provisions *f pl*;
(warehouse) magasin *m*
storyboard *n* (S&M) scénarimage *m*, storyboard *m*
stow *vt* (cargo) arrimer
stowage *n* arrimage *m*
straddle *n* (Stock) opération liée *f*, ordre lié
m, straddle *m*; ∼ **buyer** *n* acheteur/-euse d'un
straddle *m/f*, acheteur/-euse de double option
m/f; ∼ **combination** *n* combinaison de
straddle *f*; ∼ **seller** *n* vendeur/-euse d'un
straddle *m/f*, vendeur/-euse de double option
m/f
straight *adj* (person) honnête; (answer) clair;
(advice) sûre; (choice) simple; (denial, refusal,
rejection) catégorique; (swap) simple; **set**
matters ∼ mettre les choses au clair; **be** ∼ ┄╏

S

with sb jouer franc jeu avec qn; **set the record** ~ établir la vérité; **be** ~ (debt-free) être quitte; ~ **bill of lading** n connaissement nominatif m; ~ **bond** n obligation non convertible f; ~ **life insurance policy** n police d'assurance-vie entière f; ~-**line depreciation** n amortissement linéaire m; ~ **loan** n prêt simple m

straighten: ~ **out** vt (problem, misunderstanding) tirer au clair; (economy, company, situation) redresser

straightforward adj (simple) simple; (honest) franc/franche

straightforwardness n franchise f

strained adj (relationship) tendu

stranded goods n pl (Ins) épaves f pl

strangle n (Stock) strangle m

stranglehold n mainmise f; **have a** ~ **on** avoir la mainmise sur; **have a** ~ **on the market** avoir le quasi-monopole du marché

strapline n signature f

strategic adj stratégique; ~ **alliance** n alliance stratégique f; ~ **business unit** n unité d'activité stratégique f; ~ **fit** n adaptation stratégique f; ~ **interdependence** n interdépendance des stratégies f; ~ **issue** n question de stratégie f; ~ **management accounting** n comptabilité de gestion stratégique f; ~ **overview** n aperçu stratégique m; ~ **partnership** n partenariat stratégique m; ~ **plan** n plan stratégique m; ~ **planning** n planification stratégique f; ~ **withdrawal** n (from market) repli stratégique m

strategist n stratège m

strategy n stratégie f; ~ **formulation** n élaboration des stratégies f; ~ **implementation** n application des stratégies f

stratum n pl -**ta** couche f

straw poll n sondage d'opinion m

stream n (of people) flot m; (of orders, products) afflux m; **data** ~ flux de données m; **earnings** ~ rentrées d'argent f pl; **come on** ~ (oil platform, factory) commencer la production, entrer en service; **go against the** ~ aller à contre-courant

streamer n (Media) manchette f; (Comp) dévideur m

streaming n (Comp) streaming m

streamline vt rationaliser

streamlining n rationalisation f

street n rue f; ~ **broker** n (Stock) coulissier m; ~ **dealings** n pl (Stock) transactions hors bourse f pl; ~ **price** n (Stock) cours après bourse m; ~ **trader** n BrE, ~ **vendor** n AmE colporteur m, marchand ambulant m

strength n force f; (of market) vigueur f; (of currency) fermeté f; (of materials) résistance f; (of case, claim) solidité f; (of argument) force f;

(asset) qualité f; **economic** ~ puissance économique f; **be in a position of** ~ être en position de force; **be below** ~ (team) ne pas être au complet; **be at full** ~ (team) être au complet; **bring the team up to** ~ compléter l'équipe; **gain** ~ (currency) se raffermir; **go from** ~ **to** ~ se porter de mieux en mieux

strengthen [1] vt consolider, renforcer; (team, claim) renforcer; (economy, currency) raffermir, consolider

[2] vi (currency, economy) se raffermir

strengthened adj renforcé

strengthening n (of currency) consolidation f, renforcement m; (of bond) consolidation f

stress[1] n stress m, tension f; **suffer from** ~, **be under** ~ être stressé; **lay the** ~ **on** (emphasize) mettre l'accent sur; **the** ~ **placed on quality** l'insistance sur la qualité; ~ **factor** n facteur stress m; ~ **management** n gestion du stress f; ~-**related** adj (illness) dû au stress

stress[2] vt insister sur; ~ **out** (person) stresser

stressed adj stressé; **feel** ~ se sentir stressé

stress-free adj antistress inv

stressful adj stressant

strict adj (order, instruction) formel/-elle; (deadline, limit) strict; (person, rule) strict, sévère; ~ **adherence to the contract** respect strict du contrat m; **on the** ~ **understanding that...** à condition expresse que...; **in the strictest confidence** à titre strictement confidentiel; ~ **cost price** n prix de revient calculé au plus juste m; ~ **time limit** n terme de rigueur m

strike[1] n grève f; **come out on** ~ UK, **go on** ~ se mettre en grève; **be on** ~ être en grève, faire grève; ~ **action** n grève revendicative f; ~ **call** n mot d'ordre de grève m; ~ **committee** n comité de grève m; ~-**free agreement** n accord de non-recours à la grève m; ~ **fund** n caisse syndicale de grève f; ~ **pay** n allocation aux grévistes f; ~ **price** n (Stock) prix de levée m; (on Eurodollar futures) prix d'exercice m; ~ **rate** n taux de réussite m; ~ **threat** n menace de grève f; ~ **yield** n (Stock) (interest rate futures) rendement à la levée m

strike[2] [1] vt (key) frapper; ~ **a balance** trouver le juste milieu; ~ **a bargain**, ~ **a deal** conclure un marché, conclure une affaire; ~ **it rich** (infrml) faire fortune; ~ **sth from the record** rayer qch du compte rendu; ~ **up a relationship with** établir des rapports avec

[2] vi cesser le travail, faire grève; ~ **off** (professional) radier; ~ **sb off the list** rayer qn de la liste

strikebound adj paralysé par la grève

strikebreaker n briseur/-euse de grève m/f

striker n gréviste m/f

striking price *n* (Stock) prix d'exercice *m*

stringent *adj* (market) tendu; (measures, programme, standard, testing) rigoureux/-euse

stringently *adv* rigoureusement

strings *n pl* no ∼ **attached** sans conditions

strip *n* (Stock) obligation démembrée *f*, obligation à coupon zéro *f*, obligation à coupons détachés *f*; ∼ **bond** *n* (Stock) félin *m*, obligation démembrée *f*, obligation à coupon zéro *f*, obligation à coupons détachés *f*; ∼ **development** *n* développement en bande *m*; ∼ **mining** *n* AmE exploitation à ciel ouvert *f*

strong *adj* (currency) fort, ferme; (market) ferme; (indication) manifeste; (reputation, evidence) solide; (competitor) sérieux/-ieuse; (candidate) bon/bonne; (measures, action) sévère; (criticism, opposition) vif/vive; (view) arrêté; **use ∼-arm tactics** utiliser la manière forte

strongroom *n* chambre forte *f*

structural *adj* structurel/-elle; ∼ **adjustment** *n* ajustement structurel *m*, réorganisation de structure *f*; ∼ **adjustment facility** *n* facilité d'ajustement structurel *f*; ∼ **adjustment loan** *n* crédit d'ajustement structurel *m*; ∼ **change** *n* changement de structure *m*; ∼ **crisis** *n* (EU) crise structurelle *f*; ∼ **deficit** *n* déficit structurel *m*; ∼ **engineering** *n* ponts et chaussées *m pl*; ∼ **funds** *n pl* (EU) fonds structurels *m pl*; ∼ **inflation** *n* inflation structurelle *f*; ∼ **model** *n* modèle structurel *m*; ∼ **unemployment** *n* chômage structurel *m*

structure[1] *n* structure *f*; ∼**-conduct-performance model** *n* modèle structure-conduite-performance *m*; ∼ **of the market** structure du marché *f*

structure[2] *vt* structurer

structured *adj* structuré; ∼ **interview** *n* entrevue structurée *f*; ∼ **programming** *n* programmation structurée *f*

structuring *n* structuration *f*

stub *n* (of cheque, ticket book) talon *m*; ∼ **equity** *n* (Stock) valeur spéculative d'une société surendettée *f*

stuck *adj* (in a fix) coincé

student *n* (at school) élève *mf*; (in higher education) étudiant/-e *m/f*; ∼ **loan** *n* prêt bancaire pour étudiants *m*

studies *n pl* études *f pl*

studio *n* studio *m*

study[1] *n* étude *f*; ∼ **day** *n* journée d'études *f*; ∼ **group** *n* groupe de travail *m*; ∼ **trip** *n* voyage d'études *m*

study[2] *vt* étudier; ∼ **accountancy** faire des études de comptabilité; ∼ **engineering** faire des études d'ingénieur

stuff *vt* (container) empoter

stuffer *n* (Media) encart publicitaire *m*

stumbling block *n* pierre d'achoppement *f*

stump: ∼ **up** *vi* BrE (infrml) casquer (infrml)

stunt[1] *n* (to gain attention) coup monté *m*; **publicity** ∼ coup de publicité *m*; ∼ **advertising** *n* publicité tapageuse *f*

stunt[2] (economic growth, progress, development) retarder, ralentir

style *n* style *m*; ∼ **sheet** *n* (Comp) feuille de style *f*

stylist *n* (in fashion) styliste *mf*; (in advertising, industry) concepteur/-trice *m/f*

stylize *vt* styliser

stylus *n* (Comp) (pen-based device) crayon optique *m*, photostyle *m*; (for PDA) stylet *m*

stymied *adj* (thwarted) coincé

sub[1] *n* BrE (advance) avance *f*; (on a newspaper) secrétaire de rédaction *mf*; (in printing) préparateur/-trice de copie *m/f*

sub[2] *vt* (in printing) corriger

subactivity *n* sous-activité *f*

subagent *n* sous-agent *m*

subcommittee *n* sous-comité *m*

subcontract[1] *n* contrat de sous-traitance *m*

subcontract[2] *vt* sous-traiter

subcontracting *n* sous-traitance *f*

subcontractor *n* sous-traitant *m*

subdirectory *n* (Comp) sous-répertoire *m*

subdivide *vt* subdiviser

subdivision *n* subdivision *f*

subedit *vt* corriger

subeditor *n* (on newspaper) secrétaire de rédaction *mf*; (in printing) préparateur/-trice de copie *m/f*

subentry *n* (Comp) sous-rubrique *f*

subfile *n* sous-fichier *m*

subgroup *n* sous-groupe *m*

subheading *n* sous-titre *m*

subject[1] *n* (topic) sujet *m*; (area of study, research) sujet *m*; (at school, college) matière *f*; (of email, memo) objet *m*; (person, citizen) sujet *m*; (focus) objet *m*; **be the ∼ of an enquiry** faire l'objet d'une enquête; ∼ **filing** *n* classement par matières *m*; ∼ **matter** *n* sujet *m*; ∼ **search** *n* recherche thématique *f*

subject[2]: ∼ **to** *prep* sujet/-ette à; (alteration, approval) sous réserve de; (constrained) assujetti à; (Tax) assujetti à; (law, rule) soumis à; ∼ **to approval** sous réserve d'approbation; ∼ **to availability** (goods) dans la limite des stocks disponibles; (flights, tickets) dans la limite des places disponibles; ∼ **to breakage** (Ins) sujet à la casse; ∼ **to change** sous réserve de changement; ∼ **to particular average** assujetti à l'avarie particulière; ∼ **to price controls** soumis à des contrôles de prix; ∼ **to quota** contingenté; ∼ **to taxation** imposable

subjected: be ∼ **to** être soumis à

subjective *adj* subjectif/-ive

sub judice *adj* (case) devant les tribunaux

sublease *n* sous-location *f*

S

subleasing n sous-location f

sublessee n sous-locataire mf

sublet¹ n sous-location f

sublet² vt (property) sous-louer; (work) sous-traiter

subletter n sous-locataire mf

subletting n sous-location f

subliminal advertising n publicité subliminale f

submanager n sous-directeur/-trice m/f

submission n (of document, application, report) soumission f; (report) rapport m; (proposal) soumission f, proposition f; ~ **of bids** soumission des offres f; ~ **for deletion of debts** demande de radiation de dettes f

submit vt (bid, claim) faire; (resignation, bill) présenter; (reports, accounts, plan, document) soumettre; ~ **a dispute to arbitration** soumettre un différend à arbitrage; ~ **an application for a job** faire une demande d'emploi; ~ **for approval** soumettre à l'approbation; ~ **a proposal** présenter une proposition; ~ **a statement of one's affairs** (Fin) déposer son bilan

suboffice n filiale f, succursale f

suboptimization n sous-optimisation f

subordinate¹ adj (rank, position) subalterne; (issue, matter) secondaire; ~ **debt** n dette de second rang f, dette subordonnée f, dette à court terme f

subordinate² n subordonné/-e m/f

subordinate³ vt subordonner

subordinated: ~ **assets** n pl actif subordonné m; ~ **debenture** n obligation subordonnée f; ~ **debt** n dette de rang inférieur f, dette subordonnée f; ~ **liabilities** n pl emprunts et dettes subordonnés m pl, passif subordonné m; ~ **loan** n emprunt subordonné m

subordination n subordination f; ~ **agreement** n accord de subordination m; ~ **interest** n intérêt de subordination m

subpoena¹ n assignation à comparaître f, citation à comparaître f

subpoena² vt citer, citer à comparaître

subprogram n sous-programme m

subrogation clause n clause subrogatoire f

subroutine n (Comp) sous-programme m

subscribe ⟦1⟧ vt (sum, amount) souscrire ⟦2⟧ vi (Media) s'abonner; (sign) apposer sa signature; (Stock) (for shares) souscrire; ~ **for a loan** souscrire à un emprunt; ~ **to** (theory, belief) souscrire à; (view) partager; (periodical, cable TV, Internet service) être abonné à; (fund) donner de l'argent à; ~ **to an issue** (Stock) souscrire à une émission

subscribed capital n capital souscrit m

subscriber n (Comms, Comp, Media) abonné/-e m/f; (Stock) souscripteur m

subscript n indice m

subscription n (fee for magazine, cable TV, Internet service) abonnement m; (Stock) souscription f; (club membership fee) cotisation f; (to fund) don m; **take out a** ~ prendre un abonnement; ~ **for shares** n souscription d'actions f; ~ **form** n bulletin de souscription m; ~**-free ISP** n fournisseur d'accès Internet gratuit m; ~ **price** n prix de souscription m; ~ **ratio** n taux de souscription m; ~ **receivable** n capital non souscrit m; ~ **right** n droit de souscription m; ~ **warrant** n bon de souscription m

subsector n sous-secteur m

subsequent adj (in the past) ultérieur; (in the future) à venir; ~ **to** résultant de; **at a** ~ **date** à une date ultérieure

subset n sous-ensemble m

subsidiarity n subsidiarité f

subsidiary¹ adj auxiliaire, subsidiaire

subsidiary² n (company) filiale f; **banking/insurance** ~ filiale d'une banque/d'une compagnie d'assurances

subsidiary: ~ **account** n sous-compte m; ~ **accounting record** n registre comptable auxiliaire m; ~ **company** n filiale f; ~ **dividends** n pl dividende de filiale m, subsides m pl; ~ **firm** n filiale f; ~ **ledger** n grand livre auxiliaire m

subsidize vt subventionner

subsidized adj (export prices, funds) subventionné

subsidy n subvention f

subsistence n subsistance f; ~ **allowance** n indemnité de subsistance f; ~ **crops** n pl cultures vivrières de base f pl; ~ **economy** n économie de subsistance f; ~ **farming** n agriculture de subsistance f; ~ **level** n niveau minimum pour vivre m; ~ **wage** n minimum vital m

substance n substance f

substandard adj de qualité inférieure

substantial adj (proportion, percentage, majority) appréciable; (sum, amount, fee, quantity) important; (loss) considérable; (change, difference, rise, fall, risk) considérable; (damages) substantiel/-ielle; (proof) solide; ~ **interest** n (Bank) intérêt important m; ~ **risk** n (Stock) risque substantiel m

substantially adv (change, increase, fall) considérablement; (better, lower, faster) nettement

substantiate vt (allegation, statement) justifier, prouver; ~ **a claim** fournir des preuves à l'appui d'une demande, établir le bien-fondé d'une réclamation

substantive adj (decision, change) important; (progress) considérable; ~ **agreement** n accord de base m, accord de fond m; ~ **law** n droit positif m

substitute¹ n (person) remplaçant/-e m/f; (product) produit de substitution m, succédané *m;* **there is no** ∼ **for...** rien ne remplace...; ∼ **product** *n* produit de substitution *m,* succédané *m*

substitute² *vt* substituer; ∼ **one thing for another** substituer une chose à une autre

substitution *n* substitution *f;* ∼ **effect** *n* (Econ) effet de substitution *m;* ∼ **law** *n* (Law) droit relatif à la novation de créance *m*

substructure *n* infrastructure *f*

subtenancy *n* sous-location *f*

subtenant *n* sous-locataire *mf*

subtotal *n* (Acc) total partiel *m;* (Math) sous-total *m*

subtract *vt* soustraire

suburb *n* banlieue *f*

suburbs *n pl* banlieue *f;* **in the outer** ∼ en grande banlieue

subway *n* métro *m*

succeed *vi* réussir

succeeding *adj* (in the past) suivant; (in the future) à venir

success *n* succès *m,* réussite *f;* **be a** ∼ (person) réussir; (product, film) être un grand succès, avoir un succès retentissant; **make a** ∼ **of** (business venture) faire un succès de; (career) réussir; **be a** ∼ **in business/ advertising** réussir en affaires/dans la publicité; **be a** ∼ **as a** (lawyer, consultant) avoir du succès comme; ∼ **story** *n* réussite *f*

successful *adj* (attempt, effort) qui réussit; (mission, partnership) réussi; (company) prospère; (policy, measure) efficace; (campaign) couronné de succès; (book, film, writer) à succès; (career) brillant; **be** ∼ réussir; **be** ∼ **in doing, be** ∼ **at doing** réussir à faire; ∼ **bidder** *n* adjudicataire *mf;* ∼ **outcome** *n* issue positive *f,* résultat heureux *m;* ∼ **tenderer** *n* adjudicataire *mf*

succession *n* (series) série *f,* succession *f;* (Law) succession *f;* ∼ **duty** *n* droits de succession *m pl,* impôt sur les successions *m;* ∼ **law** *n* droit des successions *m,* droit successoral *m;* ∼ **tax** *n* AmE droits de succession *m pl,* impôt sur les successions *m*

successive *adj* (day, week, year, attempt) consécutif/-ive, successif/-ive

successor *n* successeur *m*

sue ① *vt* (Law) intenter un procès à, poursuivre en justice; ∼ **sb for damages** poursuivre qn pour dommages-intérêts; ∼ **sb for libel** intenter un procès en diffamation à qn, poursuivre qn pour diffamation ② *vi* intenter un procès; ∼ **for damages** intenter un procès pour obtenir des dommages-intérêts

suffer ① *vt* (delay, damage) subir; ∼ **the consequences** supporter les conséquences; ∼ **loss** (Law) subir un préjudice, subir une perte; ∼ **a setback** essuyer un revers ② *vi* souffrir

sufficient *adj* (people, items, time) assez de, suffisament de; (amount, number, quality) suffisant; **not** ∼ **funds** (Bank) fonds insuffisants *m pl,* insuffisance de provision *f;* **be quite** ∼ suffire largement

suffrage *n* (Pol) suffrage *m*

suggest *vt* (put forward, recommend) suggérer; (indicate) sembler indiquer; (evoke) évoquer

suggested retail price *n* prix au détail conseillé *m*

suggestion *n* suggestion *f;* **make a** ∼ faire une suggestion; **at sb's** ∼ sur le conseil de qn; **there is no** ∼ **of fraud** rien ne laisse suggérer qu'il y a eu fraude; ∼ **box** *n* boîte à idées *f*

suit¹ *n* (Law) procès *m,* action *f;* (manager) (infrml) cadre *m*

suit² *vt* (be convenient, appropriate) convenir à

suitable *adj* (moment, conditions) propice; (employment, accommodation) adéquat; (time, place, day) qui convient; (candidate) apte

suitor *n* (in takeovers) candidat (au rachat d'une société) *m,* prétendant *m*

sulfur *n* AmE ▸**sulphur** BrE

sulphur: ∼ **dioxide** *n* BrE (acid rain) dioxyde de soufre *m;* ∼ **emission** *n* BrE émission sulfureuse *f*

sum¹ *n* (amount) somme *f;* (calculation) calcul *m;* **get the** ∼**s wrong** se tromper dans ses calculs; **advanced** ∼ (Bank) avance *f;* **assured** ∼ (Bank) capital assuré *m*

sum:² ∼ **up** ① *vt* (argument, case) résumer; (situation) apprécier; (person) se faire une idée de ② *vi* récapituler

summarize *vt* résumer; (speech) récapituler

summary¹ *adj* sommaire

summary² *n* abrégé *m,* résumé *m,* sommaire *m;* ∼ **of the proceedings** résumé de la séance *m;* ∼ **application** *n* requête sommaire *f;* ∼ **dismissal** *n* licenciement sommaire *m,* renvoi pur et simple *m;* ∼ **judge** *n* juge des référés *m;* ∼ **report** *n* rapport sommaire *m;* ∼ **statement** *n* déclaration sommaire *f;* ∼ **table** *n* tableau récapitulatif *m*

summit *n* (Pol) sommet *m;* ∼ **conference** *n* conférence au sommet *f;* ∼ **meeting** *n* réunion au sommet *f,* sommet *m*

summon *vt* (member, shareholder) convoquer

summons¹ *n* (Law) assignation *f,* citation *f*

summons² *vt* (Law) citer, citer à comparaître

Sunday *n* dimanche *m;* ∼ **trading** *n* commerce dominical *m*

sundries *n pl* (Acc) (goods) articles divers *m pl;* (in budget) divers *m pl*

sundry *adj* divers; ∼ **accounts** *n pl* comptes de divers *m pl;* ∼ **articles** *n pl* articles divers *m pl;* ∼ **expenses** *n pl* frais divers *m pl*

sunk cost *n* coût irrécupérable *m,* frais ····⟩

S

amortis *m pl*

sunrise industry *n* industrie en croissance rapide *f*

sunset: ~ **act** *n* (Law, Pol) loi de temporalisation *f*; ~ **industry** *n* industrie en déclin *f*; ~ **provision** *n* (Law) clause-couperet *f*, disposition légale stipulant une date d'expiration *f*

sunshine law *n* US *législation américaine imposant la transparence aux organismes publics*

superannuate *vt* mettre à la retraite

superannuation *n* pension de retraite *f*; ~ **fund** *n* caisse de retraite *f*; ~ **scheme** *n* régime de retraite *m*

supercomputer *n* super-ordinateur *m*

superficial *adj* superficiel/-ielle; ~ **loss** *n* perte apparente *f*

superhighway *n* AmE autoroute *f*

supermarket *n* supermarché *m*

supernumerary *adj* surnuméraire

superpower *n* superpuissance *f*

supersaver *n* (S&M) article en promotion *m*; **this week's** ~ l'affaire de la semaine *f*

superscript *n* (typography) exposant *m*

supersede *vt* remplacer, supplanter

superstore *n* (supermarket) hypermarché *m*, grande surface *f*; (specialist outlet) grande surface *f*; **furniture** ~ grande surface de l'ameublement *f*

supertanker *n* superpétrolier *m*

supervise *vt* (monitor) contrôler, surveiller; (HRM, Mgmnt) surveiller

supervision *n* (Gen Comm) supervision *f*, surveillance *f*; (monitoring) contrôle *m*; (HRM, Mgmnt) maîtrise *f*; ~ **of credit institutions** (Fin) surveillance des établissements de crédit *f*

supervisor *n* (HRM) agent de maîtrise *m*, surveillant/-e *m/f*; (among blue collar workers) chef d'atelier *m*, chef d'équipe *m*; (among white collar workers) chef de service *m*

supervisory *adj* (duty, role, work) de surveillance; **in a** ~ **capacity** à titre de surveillant; ~ **board** *n* conseil de surveillance *m*; ~ **management** *n* maîtrise *f*; ~ **personnel** *n* personnel de maîtrise *m*, personnel de surveillance *m*

supplement[1] *n* (to income, work) complément *m*; (extra charge) supplément *m*; (for traveller) supplément *m*; (in publication, newspaper) supplément *m*; **first class/flight** ~ supplément de première classe/de vol *m*; **as a** ~ en complément

supplement[2] *vt* augmenter

supplemental: ~ **agreement** *n* accord supplémentaire *m*; ~ **budget** *n* additif budgétaire *m*; ~ **technology** *n* technologie complémentaire *f*, technologie incrémentielle *f*

Supplementaries *n pl* (Fin, Pol) budget

des dépenses supplémentaires *m*

supplementary *adj* (details, sum, information) complémentaire; (jobs, problems, reasons, tax, costs) supplémentaire; ~ **assistance** *n* (Fin) aide complémentaire *f*; ~ **cost** *n* (Fin) prix coûtant *m*, prix de revient initial *m*; ~ **entry** *n* (Acc, Fin) écriture complémentaire *f*; ~ **estimates** *n pl* (Fin) crédits supplémentaires *m pl*; ~ **pension scheme** *n* retraite complémentaire (de prévoyance) *f*; ~ **period** *n* (Tax) période complémentaire *f*; ~ **reserve** *n* (Bank) réserve excédentaire *f*, réserve supplémentaire *f*

supplemented *adj* augmenté

supplier *n* fournisseur *m*; ~ **credit** *n* crédit fournisseur *m*

supplies *n pl* (equipment) matériel *m*; (small items) fournitures *f pl*; (food and essentials) réserves *f pl*; **office** ~ fournitures de bureau *f pl*

supply[1] *n* (stocks) réserves *f pl*, stock *m*; (act of providing) fourniture *f*, approvisionnement *m*; (of power, water, gas) alimentation *f*; **be in short/plentiful** ~ être facile/difficile à obtenir; **lay in a** ~ **of** s'approvisionner en; **have a** ~ **of sth** avoir qch en stock; ~ **and demand** l'offre et la demande; ~ **chain** *n* chaîne logistique *f*, chaîne d'approvisionnement *f*; ~ **chain automation** *n* automatisation de la chaîne logistique *f*; ~ **chain execution** *n* exécution de la chaîne logistique *f*; ~ **chain management** *n* gestion de la chaîne logistique *f*, gestion de la chaîne d'approvisionnement *f*; ~ **curve** *n* courbe de l'offre *f*; ~ **function** *n* fonction d'offre *f*; ~ **of goods** *n* offre de biens *f*; ~ **price** *n* prix de l'offre *m*; ~ **shock** *n* choc d'offre *m*, choc sur l'offre *m*; ~**-side economics** *n* + *sing v* économie de l'offre *f*

supply[2] *vt* (services, goods, information) fournir; (factory) approvisionner; (shop, retailer) fournir; (demand, need) répondre à; (requirement, needs) répondre à; ~ **sb with sth** fournir qch à qn; ~ **collateral** donner un bien en nantissement; ~ **goods on credit**, ~ **goods on trust** fournir des marchandises à crédit

support[1] *n* (moral) soutien *m*, appui *m*, (financial) soutien financier *m*, appui financier *m*; (assistance) assistance *f*, aide *f*; **have sb's** ~ avoir le soutien de qn, avoir l'appui de qn; **give sb/sth one's** ~ apporter son soutien à qn/qch; **get** ~ **from sb/sth** obtenir le soutien de qn/qch; **speak in** ~ **of** parler en faveur de; **a collection in** ~ **of refugees** une collecte au profit des réfugiés; **means of** ~ (Fin) moyens de subsistance *m pl*; **have considerable public** ~ bénéficier du soutien d'une grande partie de la population; **the project has little** ~ il y a peu de gens en faveur du projet; ~ **activities** *n pl* (Gen Comm, Comp, Mgmnt) fonctions complémentaires *f pl*; ~ **hotline** *n* service d'assistance technique par téléphone *m*;

~ **level** n (Econ) seuil d'intervention m; ~ **price** n (Econ) (EU) prix de soutien m; ~ **service** n service logistique m; ~ **staff** n personnel d'assistance technique m; ~ **system** n réseau de soutien m

support² vt (person, plan, reform, team, undertaking) soutenir; (decision) approuver; (application) appuyer; (dependent) avoir à charge, faire vivre; (claim, theory, argument) confirmer; (Econ) (currency, price) soutenir; (Comp) (file format, printer) permettre l'utilisation de

supported adj (Comp) (with maintenance) dont la maintenance est assurée; (with IT backup) pris en charge par le service informatique

supporter n partisan/-e m/f

supporting: ~ **data** n données justificatives f pl; ~ **document** n (Gen Comm) document annexe m, (Law) pièce justificative f; ~ **purchases** n pl achats de soutien m pl; ~ **receipt** n reçu à l'appui m

suppress vt (truth) dissimuler; (criticism, scandal) étouffer; (Comp) (remove) supprimer; (report, information) supprimer

suppressed inflation n inflation contenue f

supra adv supra

supranational adj supranational

Supreme Court n Cour suprême f

surcharge n (extra charge) supplément m; (Tax) surtaxe f; ~ **value** n valeur de surtaxe f

surety n (sum of money) caution f; (person) garant m; **stand ~ for sb** se porter garant de qn; ~ **in cash** caution en numéraire f

surf vt (Web, Net) surfer sur; ~ **the Internet** surfer sur Internet

surface n surface f; **by ~ mail** par courrier ordinaire, par voie de terre; ~ **area** n superficie f

surfer n (Comp) surfeur/-euse m/f

surfing n (Comp) surf (sur Internet) m

surge¹ n (in inflation, unemployment) hausse f; (in prices, shares) flambée f; (in demand, imports, borrowing) accroissement m

surge² vi (prices, profits, shares, demand) monter en flèche

surname n nom de famille m

surpass vt (be bigger, better) surpasser; (target) dépasser; ~ **expectations** dépasser les attentes

surplus n (Acc) plus-value f; (Econ) surplus m; **in ~** en excédent, excédentaire; **be in ~** être en surplus; ~ **of assets over liabilities** excédent de l'actif sur le passif m; ~ **capacity** n potentiel inemployé m, potentiel sous-utilisé m; ~ **dividend** n superdividende m; ~ **reserves** n pl réserves à des fins spécifiques f pl; ~ **value** n (Acc) approche des excédents f, valeur d'excédent f; (Econ) plus-value relative f

surprise function n (Econ) fonction de surprise f

surrender n (of document) remise f; (Ins) (of policy) rachat m; (Tax) abandon m; **for ~** (Stock) (of a security) pour remise; **on ~ of documents** contre remise de documents; ~ **charge** n (Ins) frais de rachat m pl; ~ **of a patent** abandon d'un brevet m; ~ **value** n valeur de rachat f

surrender² vt (insurance policy) racheter; (lease) céder; (documents, passport) remettre

surroundings n pl environs m pl

surtax n surtaxe f

surveillance n (Gen Comm, Law) surveillance f

survey¹ n (Gen Comm) enquête f; (by questioning) sondage m; (study) étude f; (Prop) expertise f; (Tax, Transp) (inspection visit) visite f; **carry out a ~** faire une enquête; (by questioning) faire un sondage, effectuer un sondage; (Prop) faire une expertise; **a ~ of 1,000 students** un sondage parmi 1 000 étudiants; ~ **fee** n honoraires d'expertise m pl; ~ **report** n rapport d'expertise m

survey² vt (Gen Comm) faire une étude de; (Prop) faire une expertise de; (Transp) visiter; ~ **the situation** faire un tour d'horizon de la situation

surveyor n (marine engineer) expert maritime m; (of property) expert m; (of land) géomètre expert m

survival n survie f; ~ **of the fittest** la survie des plus forts; ~ **strategy** n stratégie de survie f

survive vi survivre

survivor policy n (Ins) assurance-vie sur deux têtes f

survivorship n survie f; ~ **account** n (Bank) compte de survie m; ~ **clause** n US clause de survie f; ~ **insurance** n assurance de survie f

suspend vt (talks, hearing, trade) suspendre; (authorization, meeting) interrompre; ~ **trading** (Stock) suspendre les cotations, suspendre les transactions

suspended sentence n condamnation avec sursis f

suspense: ~ **account** n compte d'attente m; ~ **entry** n écriture d'attente f

suspension n (of aid, hostilities) cessation f; (of worker) suspension f; (of meeting, services) interruption f; (of payment, talks, quotas) suspension f

suspensive condition n (Law) condition suspensive f

sustain vt (growth) soutenir, appuyer; (confidence) entretenir; (loss, injury) subir; ~ **a claim** admettre le bien-fondé d'une réclamation; ~ **losses** (Acc) supporter des pertes

sustainability n (of development) durabilité f; (of growth rate) viabilité f

sustainable adj (forestry) durable; (resource) renouvelable; ~ **development** n (Econ,

⋯▹

Envir) développement durable m; ~
economic growth rate n taux de
croissance économique viable m; ~ **growth**
n croissance à un rythme viable f
sustained adj soutenu; ~ **non-**
inflationary growth n croissance non-
inflationniste soutenue f; ~ **resurgence** n
(of growth) redémarrage soutenu m
swamp vt (offices, town) envahir; (market)
inonder
swap¹ n (Gen com) échange m; (Fin) échange
financier m; (Stock) swap m, échange
financier m; (on interest rate instrument) crédit
croisé m; ~ **credit line** n, ~ **line of credit**
n (Fin) ligne de crédits croisés f; ~ **market** n
(Stock) marché d'échanges croisés m, marché
des swaps m; ~ **option** n (Fin) option
d'échange f; (Stock) option sur swap f
swap² vt échanger; ~ sth for sth échanger
qch contre qch; ~ **places** changer de place;
~ **sth around** permuter; ~ **sth over**
permuter
swatch n échantillon m
sway vt (outcome, person) influencer
swear vt (loyalty) jurer; ~ **on affidavit**
déclarer par écrit, déclarer sous serment; ~
sb to secrecy faire jurer le secret à qn; ~ **to**
do jurer de faire
sweated: ~ **goods** n pl marchandises
produites par une main-d'œuvre exploitée; ~
labor AmE, ~ **labour** BrE n main-d'œuvre
exploitée f
sweat equity n apport en main-d'œuvre m
(de la part d'un capital-risqueur moyennant
une part des bénéfices)
sweatshop n atelier où l'on exploite le
personnel m, bagne m (infrml)
sweeping adj (changes, reforms) radical;
(losses, cuts) considérable; (measures) d'une
portée considérable; (statement) trop général
sweetener n (infrml) incitation f, (illegal) pot-
de-vin m
sweetheart: ~ **agreement** n, ~
contract n contrat de complaisance m; (no-
strike deal) contrat de non-recours à la grève m
swell vt (accounts, coffers, figures) gonfler
swim n be in the ~ (infrml) être dans le
mouvement
swimming market n marché actif m
swindle¹ n escroquerie f
swindle² vt escroquer; ~ **sb out of sth**
soutirer qch à qn, escroquer qch à qn
swindler n escroc m
swing¹ n oscillation f; (of market, economy)
fluctuation f; (in activity) variation f; (Pol) (in
opinion, voting) revirement m; (Stock) variation
f; ~ **credits** n pl crédit-relais entre
partenaires commerciaux m; ~ **line** n crédit
de sécurité m; ~ **loan** n prêt soumis à
fluctuations m; ~ **shift** n poste de relève m,
équipe tournante f; ~ **voter** n électeur
girouette m (infrml)

swing² ① vt (decision, vote) influencer; ~ **a**
deal (infrml) emporter une affaire; ~ **it for sb**
arranger ça pour qn
② vi osciller, virer; (Pol) virer
swingeing adj (cuts, measures) drastique
swings n pl mouvements des cours m pl,
oscillations des cours f pl
swipe vt (credit card) faire passer dans un
lecteur de carte magnétique
swipe card n carte à mémoire f
switch¹ n (device) commutateur m,
interrupteur m; ~ **dealing** n opération de
contre-achats f; ~ **selling** n UK vente forcée
d'articles plus chers que ceux en promotion; ~
trading n switch m
switch² ① vt (support) reporter; (brand, place,
company, supplier, bank) changer de; (bank
account) transférer; (production) réorienter
② vi (change) ~ **from X to Y** changer de X à
Y; ~ **between X and Y** alterner entre X et Y;
~ **off** (appliance, light) éteindre; (engine)
mettre à l'arrêt; (appliance, light) allumer; ~ **on** (engine)
over changer; (shift workers) permuter; ~ **over**
to passer à; ~ **round** alterner, changer; (shift
workers) permuter
switchboard n standard m; ~ **operator** n
standardiste mf
switcher n consommateur qui change de
marque m, client zappeur m (infrml)
switching n (Gen Comm) changement m;
(Comms, Comp) commutation f; (Stock)
arbitrage de portefeuille m; ~ **cost** n coût de
sortie m, coûts entraînés par un changement
de fournisseur m pl; ~**in rate** n taux de
clientèle m, taux de gain m; ~**out rate** n
taux de perte de clientèle m
switchover n passage m; **the** ~ **to the**
euro le passage à l'euro
swop n échange m
SWOT abbr (**strengths, weaknesses,**
opportunities and threats) forces,
faiblesses, opportunités et menaces; ~
analysis n analyse des forces, des faiblesses,
des opportunités et des menaces f
syllabus n programme (d'études) m
symbiotic marketing n marketing
symbiotique m
symbol n symbole m
symbolic adj symbolique; **be** ~ **of**
symboliser
symmetric adj symétrique
symmetry n symétrie f
sympathetic: ~ **action** n action de
soutien f; ~ **strike** n grève de solidarité f
sympathy n go out in ~ **with** (strikers) se
mettre en grève par solidarité avec; ~
action n mouvement de solidarité m; ~
strike n grève de solidarité f
symposium n colloque m
sync n be in/out of ~ **with** être en phase/
être déphasé par rapport à

synchronization *n* synchronisation *f*
synchronous *adj* (Comp) synchrone
syndicate¹ *n* (of banks, companies)
consortium *m*; (of people) syndicat *m*; (Media)
syndicat de distribution *m*; (Stock) syndicat
m, syndicat d'émission *m*, syndicat de
placement *m*; **financial** ~ syndicat financier
m; **banking** ~ consortium bancaire *m*; **crime**
~ syndicat du crime *m*; **drugs** ~ cartel de la
drogue *m*; **be a member of a** ~ (individual)
être syndicataire; (company, bank) être membre
d'un consortium; ~ **manager** *n* (Fin)
président de syndicat financier *m*
syndicate² *vt* (workers) syndiquer; (banks)
regrouper au sein d'un consortium; ~ **a loan**
consortialiser un prêt, prêter en
participation; (newspaper column, website content)
vendre par l'intermédiaire d'un syndicat de
distribution
syndicated: ~ **loan** *n* prêt en
participation *m*; ~ **swap** *n* échange
syndiqué *m*
syndication *n* (Bank, Fin) syndication *f*; (of
newspaper column, website content) vente par
l'intermédiaire d'un syndicat de distribution
f
synergism *n* synergie *f*
synergy *n* synergie *f*
synopsis *n* résumé *m*, sommaire *m*
syntax *n* (Comp) syntaxe *f*; ~ **error** *n* faute
de syntaxe *f*
synthesis *n* synthèse *f*
synthetic *adj* synthétique; ~ **bond** *n*
(Stock) obligation synthétique *f*; ~ **long call**
n (Stock) achat d'un call synthétique *m*, achat
d'une option d'achat *m*; ~ **long put** *n* (Stock)
achat d'un put synthétique *m*, achat d'une

option de vente *m*

system *n* (of administration) système *m*; (Comp)
système *m*; (method) méthode *f*; (network)
réseau *m*; ~ **administrator** *n*
administrateur/-trice système *m/f*; ~ **design**
n conception de système *f*; ~ **development**
n développement de système *m*; ~ **disk** *n*
disque système *m*; ~ **error** *n* erreur système
f; ~ **failure** *n* panne du système *f*; ~ **file** *n*
fichier système *m*; ~**-provider** *n* fournisseur
de système *m*; ~ **requirements** *n pl*
configuration nécessaire *f*; ~ **software** *n*
logiciel système *m*
systematic *adj* systématique; ~ **cost
basis** *n* base de coût systématique *f*; ~ **risk**
n risque systématique *m*; ~ **sampling** *n*
échantillonnage systématique *m*; ~
withdrawal plan *n* plan de retrait
systématique *m*
systematize *vt* systématiser
systems: ~ **analysis** *n* analyse des
systèmes *f*; ~ **analyst** *n* analyste de
systèmes *mf*; ~ **architect** *n* (Comp)
ingénieur architecte système *m*; ~**-based
audit** *n* audit analytique *m*, contrôle des
comptes analytique *m*; ~ **design** *n*
conception de systèmes *f*; ~ **engineer** *n*
ingénieur système *m*; ~ **management** *n*
(Comp, Mgmnt) direction systématisée *f*,
gestion systématisée *f*; ~ **planning** *n*
planification des systèmes *f*; ~ **and
procedures** *n pl* méthodes administratives *f*
pl; ~ **programmer** *n* programmeur/-euse
système *m/f*; ~ **programming** *n*
programmation systèmes *f*; ~ **software** *n*
logiciel de base *m*, logiciel d'exploitation *m*;
~ **theory** *n* théorie des systèmes *f*

Tt

TA *abbr* (▶**transactional analysis**) analyse
transactionnelle *f*
tab¹ *n* (Comp) tabulation *f*; (in hotel) note *f*; (in
restaurant) addition *f*; (for service, supply) facture
f; (on file) onglet *m*; **pick up the** ~ (Gen
Comm) payer la facture; (in hotel) payer la
note; (in restaurant) payer l'addition; **set** ~**s**
placer des marques de tabulation; **keep** ~**s
on sth** avoir l'œil sur qch; **keep** ~**s on sb**
tenir qn à l'œil; ~ **setting** *n* (Comp) pose de
tabulations *f*
tab² *vi* faire une tabulation, tabuler
table¹ *n* (in document) table *f*, tableau *m*; **on
the** ~ (proposal) sur la table des négociations;
the offer is still on the ~ l'offre tient bon; ~

of contents table des matières *f*; ~ **of par
values** table de parités *f*
table² *vt* (postpone) ajourner; (amendment)
déposer; (motion) soumettre
tabloid¹ *adj* demi-format, tabloïd(e)
tabloid² *n* quotidien populaire *m*; ~ **press**
n presse populaire *f*
tabular *adj* tabulaire
tabulate *vt* (results, data) mettre sous forme
de tableau; **in** ~**d form** sous forme de tableau
tachograph *n* tachygraphe *m*
tacit *adj* implicite, tacite; **by** ~ **agreement**
par accord tacite; ~ **renewal** *n* reconduction
tacite *f*
tackle *vt* (problem) aborder; (task) s'attaquer ···ϟ

à; (person) parler à; (in confrontation) prendre qn de front; ~ **sb about sth** parler à qn de qch

TACs *abbr* (▸**total allowable catches**) (Envir) prises totales autorisées *f pl*

tactic *n* tactique *f*; ~**s** tactique *f*; **delaying** ~**s** tactique dilatoire *f*; **change** ~**s** changer de tactique

tactical *adj* tactique; ~ **plan** *n* plan tactique *m*; ~ **planning** *n* plan tactique *m*

tag¹ *n* (on cargo, goods) étiquette *f*; (Comp) balise *f*

tag² *vt* (goods) étiqueter; (Comp) baliser

tagline *n* slogan *m*

tail¹ *n* (of list) dernière entrée *f*; (treasury auctions, underwriting) suivi *m*; ~ **end** (final part) fin *f*; ~ **lift** *n* plate-forme de chargement *f*

tail²: ~ **away**, ~ **off** *vi* diminuer, décroître

tailgating *n* (Stock) suivisme *m*

tailor *vt* (clothing) façonner; (adapt) adapter; ~ **sth to** (need, requirement, person) adapter qch à; ~ **sth for** (user, market) concevoir qch pour; ~**ed to meet specific needs** adapté à des besoins spécifiques

tailorable *adj* (product) personnalisable

tailored *adj* (product, solution) personnalisé; ~ **to** adapté à

tailoring *n* (of product) personnalisation *f*

tailor-made *adj* fait sur mesure, personnalisé; ~ **contract** *n* contrat sur mesure *m*

tailspin *n* dégringolade *f*, chute verticale *f*; **be in a** ~ être en dégringolade, être en chute libre

taka *n* taka *m*

take¹ *n* (takings) recette *f*; (share) part *f*; **be on the** ~ (infrml) toucher des pots-de-vin; **what's your** ~ **on the merger?** (infrml) que pensez-vous de la fusion?

take² *vt* (hold, contain) pouvoir contenir; (partner) prendre; (view, attitude, measures) adopter; (job) accepter; (profit) prendre; (course) suivre; (test) passer; (credit card, cheque) accepter; ~ **aboard** (cargo, passengers) embarquer; ~ **action** agir, faire des démarches; ~ **administrative control** prendre le contrôle administratif; ~ **a bath** (infrml) boire la tasse (infrml), vendre à perte; ~ **bribes** accepter des pots-de-vin, se laisser corrompre; ~ **control** prendre le contrôle; ~ **delivery** (Gen Comm, Stock) prendre livraison; ~ **effect** entrer en vigueur, prendre effet; ~ **effect from** (date) entrer en vigueur à partir de, prendre effet à partir de; ~ **expert advice** demander l'avis d'un expert; ~ **a day off** prendre une journée de congé; ~ **an extra day off** (between a national holiday and a weekend) faire le pont; ~ **industrial action** se mettre en grève; ~ **into consideration** considérer, tenir compte de; ~ **leave of** prendre congé de; ~ **legal advice** consulter un avocat; ~ **measures** (against employee) prendre des mesures, prendre des

sanctions; ~ **off the market** retirer du marché; ~ **the offensive** prendre l'offensive; ~ **on extra work** accepter du travail supplémentaire; ~ **orders** prendre des commandes; ~ **part in** prendre part à; ~ **possession** prendre possession; ~ **sb to court** faire un procès à qn, poursuivre qn en justice; ~ **sb's word for it** croire qn sur parole; ~ **7 away from 49** ôter 7 de 49; ~ **sides with sb** prendre parti pour qn; ~ **stock** (of goods) dresser l'inventaire; (of progress) faire le point; ~ **away** (deduct) soustraire, enlever; ~ **back** (employee, goods) reprendre; (statement, claim) retirer; ~ **down** (make note of) noter; ~ **in** (cheat) rouler (infrml); (Stock) (stock) reporter; **be taken in** se faire avoir; ~ **off** (plane) décoller; (idea, fashion) prendre; (product, campaign) marcher; (sales) décoller; ~ **on** (work, job, task) accepter; (responsibility) assumer, prendre; (staff) embaucher, engager; (cargo) prendre; ~ **out** (subscription, patent) prendre; (insurance policy) souscrire; ~ **out a loan** contracter un crédit, contracter un emprunt, faire un prêt; ~ **out a policy** contracter une police d'assurance, souscrire une police d'assurance; ~ **over** (buy out) racheter; (company) prendre le contrôle de; (debts) reprendre à sa charge; (issue) absorber; ~ **over liabilities** prendre le passif à sa charge; ~ **over from** prendre la succession de, remplacer, succéder à; ~ **place** avoir lieu; ~ **up** (loan, bill) honorer; (challenge) relever; (offer, invitation) accepter; (Stock) (option) lever; (shares) prendre livraison de; (benefit) toucher; ~ **up legal residence** se faire domicilier; ~ **up a position** adopter une position, prendre une position

take-home pay *n* salaire net *m*

takeoff *n* décollage *m*

takeover *n* (Econ, Fin) prise de contrôle *f*, rachat *m*; **be a target for a** ~ être opéable; ~ **attempt** *n* tentative d'OPA *f*, tentative d'offre publique d'achat *f*; ~ **bid** *n* offre publique d'achat *f*

taker *n* preneur *m*; ~ **for a put and call** *n* (Stock) donneur de stellage *m*; ~ **of a rate** *n* (Stock) receveur de la prime *m*

takers-in *n pl* (Stock) preneurs d'offre *m pl*

take-up *n* (for offer, benefit, rebate) demande *f*; (Stock) levée d'une nouvelle émission *f*; **100%** ~ **of shares** (Stock) émission d'actions souscrite à 100%; ~ **rate** *n* taux de souscription *m*, taux de réclamation *m*; **an increase in the** ~ **of shares** une augmentation du pourcentage d'actions vendues

takings *n pl* recette *f*

talk¹ *n* exposé *m*; **give a** ~ **about** faire un exposé sur

talk² **1** *vt* ~ **business** parler affaires; ~ **shop** (infrml) parler boutique; **we're talking 10% minimum** il faut compter 10% au minimum

2 *vi* parler; ~ **about sth/about doing sth** parler de qch/de faire qch; ~ **to sb about sth** parler à qn de qch, parler à qn au sujet de qch; **we're talking about major clients** il s'agit de clients importants; ~ **over** (plan, idea) discuter de, parler de; ~ **round** (subject) tourner autour de; ~ **sb round** faire changer d'avis à qn; ~ **up** (product, candidate) vanter les mérites de

talks *n pl* discussions *f pl*; (negotiations) négociations *f pl*; (between countries, groups) conférence *f*; **pay/trade** ~ négociations salariales/commerciales *f pl*

talktime *n* (Comms) autonomie en appel *f*; **one hour's free** ~ une heure de communication gratuite

tally¹ *n* (record) compte *m*; (total) nombre total *m*; **keep** ~ **of** tenir compte de; ~ **clerk** *n* pointeur *m*; ~ **register** *n* registre de comptage *m*; ~ **roll** *n* bande de contrôle *f*; ~ **sheet** *n* feuille de pointage *f*; ~ **trade** *n* commerce à tempérament *m*

tally² **1** *vt* pointer
2 *vi* concorder, s'accorder

talon *n* (Stock) talon *m*

tamper: ~ **with** *vt* (equipment) manipuler en douce, trafiquer; (evidence, records, files) falsifier, trafiquer

tamper-proof *adj* impossible à trafiquer

tandem *n* tandem *m*; **in** ~ en tandem; ~ **account** *n* (Bank) compte en tandem *m*

tangible *adj* tangible, réel/-elle; (Law) corporel/-elle; ~ **asset** *n* (Acc, Fin) immobilisation corporelle *f*, valeur matérielle *f*, valeur tangible *f*, élément d'actif corporel *m*; ~ **fixed asset** *n* immobilisation corporelle *f*; ~ **net worth** *n* valeur réelle nette *f*; ~ **personal property** *n* bien matériel personnel *m*; ~ **wealth** *n* biens tangibles *m pl*, richesse corporelle *f*

tank *n* citerne *f*; (for fuel) réservoir *m*; **fill the** ~ (of vehicle) faire le plein; ~ **car** *n* AmE wagon-citerne *m*; ~ **container** *n* conteneur-citerne *m*; ~ **farm** *n* dépôt pétrolier *m*, parc à réservoirs de stockage *m*; ~ **truck** *n* AmE camion-citerne *m*

tanker *n* (shipping) bateau-citerne *m*, navire-citerne *m*; ~ **lorry** *n* BrE camion-citerne *m*

tap¹ *n* (Stock) valeur de gré à gré *f*, valeur émise en robinet continu *f* (jarg); **on** ~ disponible; ~ **bill** *n* bon émis en robinet continu *m*, effet placé de gré à gré *m*; ~ **issue** *n* (Stock) émission de valeurs d'État *f*; ~ **stocks** *n pl* UK (Stock) valeurs d'État *f pl*

tap² *vt* (resources, market) exploiter; ~ **the market for** (Stock) faire appel au marché pour; ~ **in** (key in) introduire, saisir

tape¹ *n* (Comms, Comp, Media) (medium) bande *f*; (cassette) cassette *f*; (recording) enregistrement *m*; (for sticking) ruban adhésif *m*; **on** ~ (recorded) enregistré; ~ **measure** *n* mètre *m*; ~ **recorder** *n* magnétophone *m*; ~ **recording** *n* enregistrement *m*

tape² *vt* (record) enregistrer; (stick) coller avec du ruban adhésif

taper *vt* (tax relief) effiler; ~ **off** diminuer, se réduire

tapering *adj* (rate, charge) dégressif/-ive

tare *n* tare *f*; ~ **weight** *n* poids à vide *m*, tare *f*

target¹ *n* (goal, aim) objectif *m*; (Media, S&M) (customer, audience) cible *f*; (Comp) cible *f*, destinataire *mf*; **be on** ~ réaliser ses objectifs; **meet one's sales** ~s atteindre ses objectifs de vente; **set a** ~ fixer un objectif; **miss a** ~ ne pas atteindre un objectif; **be the** ~ **of** (criticism, inquiry) faire l'objet de; ~ **audience** *n* cible *f*; ~ **buyer** *n* acheteur cible *m*; ~ **company** *n* entreprise cible *f*; ~ **computer** *n* ordinateur cible *m*; ~ **consumer** *n* consommateur cible *m*; ~ **cost** *n* coût cible *m*; ~ **date** *n* date prévue *f*; ~ **field** *n* (Comp) zone destinataire *f*; ~ **group** *n* groupe cible *m*; ~ **market** *n* marché cible *m*; ~ **price** *n* prix cible *m*; ~ **pricing** *n* ciblage des prix *m*; ~ **range** *n* (Econ, Fin) fourchette visée *f*; ~ **rate** *n* (Stock) taux cible *m*, taux de référence *m*; ~ **segment** *n* segment ciblé *m*; ~ **setting** *n* fixation des objectifs *f*, établissement d'objectifs *m*; ~ **zone** *n* (Econ, Fin) zone cible *f*

target² *vt* cibler, viser

targeting *n* (pinpointing) ciblage *m*; (setting goals) fixation des objectifs *f*

tariff *n* (price, rate) tarif *m*; (price list) tarif *m*, barème des prix *m*; (Imp/Exp) tarif douanier *m*; ~ **barrier** *n* barrière douanière *f*, barrière tarifaire *f*; ~ **legislation** *n* législation douanière *f*; ~ **level** *n* niveau tarifaire *m*; ~ **protection** *n* protection douanière *f*, protection tarifaire *f*; ~ **quota** *n* contingent tarifaire *m*; ~ **rate** *n* taux tarifaire *m*; ~ **reform** *n* réforme des tarifs douaniers *f*; ~ **schedule** *n* barème des tarifs *m*; ~ **wall** *n* barrière tarifaire *f*; ~ **war** *n* guerre des tarifs *f*

tarification *n* (EU) tarification *f*

task *n* tâche *f*; **take sb to** ~ **for sth** réprimander qn pour qch; ~ **force** *n* groupe de travail *m*; ~ **management** *n* gestion des tâches *f*; ~ **scheduling** *n* programmation des tâches *f*; ~ **setting** *n* fixation d'objectifs de travail *f*; ~ **work** *n* travail aux pièces *m*

taskbar *n* (Comp) barre des tâches *f*

taste *n* goût *m*; **develop a** ~ **for** prendre goût à; **suit all** ~s convenir à tous les goûts

tax¹ *n* (on income) impôt *m*; (on goods, sales, service) taxe *f*; **before** ~ brut; **after** ~ après déduction des impôts; **liable for** ~ imposable; **pay** ~ **on one's earnings** être imposé sur ce que l'on gagne; **put a** ~ **on** (earnings, funds) imposer, mettre un impôt sur; (goods) mettre une taxe sur;

(tax a...) ~ **abatement** *n* abattement d'impôt *m*, allègement fiscale *m*; ~ **adjustment** *n* ajustement d'impôt *m*, ⋯⊱

redressement fiscal *m*; ∼ **administration** *n* administration fiscale *f*; ∼ **advantage** *n* avantage fiscal *m*, bénéfice fiscal *m*; ∼ **advisor** *n* conseiller/-ère fiscal/-e *m/f*; ∼ **allowance** *n* abattement fiscal *m*; ∼ **arrears** *n pl* arriéré d'impôt *m*; ∼ **assessment** *n* imposition *f*, évaluation d'impôts *f*; ∼ **assistance** *n* aide fiscale *f*; ∼ **audit** *n* vérification fiscale *f*; ∼ **authorities** *n pl* administration fiscale *f*; ∼ **avoidance** *n* évasion fiscale *f*;

(b...) ∼ **band** *n* tranche d'imposition *f*; ∼ **barrier** *n* barrière fiscale *f*; ∼ **base** *n* assiette de l'impôt *f*, assiette fiscale *f*, base d'imposition *f*; ∼ **base broadening** *n* élargissement de l'assiette de l'impôt *m*, élargissement de l'assiette fiscale *m*; ∼ **benefit** *n* bénéfice fiscal *m*; ∼ **bracket** *n* tranche d'imposition *f*; ∼ **break** *n* avantage fiscal *m*, réduction d'impôt *f*; ∼ **buoyancy** *n* élasticité fiscale *f*; ∼ **burden** *n* charge fiscale *f*, poids de l'impôt *m*, pression fiscale *f*, taux de prélèvement fiscal *m*;

(c...) ∼ **claims** *n pl* créances fiscales *f pl*, réclamations fiscales *f pl*; ∼ **code** *n* code des impôts *m*; ∼ **collection** *n* perception de l'impôt *f*, recouvrement de l'impôt *m*; ∼ **collector** *n* percepteur *m*; ∼ **on company cars** *n* taxe sur les véhicules de société *f*; ∼ **concession** *n* avoir fiscal *m*; ∼ **consultant** *n* conseiller/-ère fiscal/-e *m/f*; ∼ **cost** *n* coût de l'impôt *m*; ∼ **credit** *n* (Econ) crédit d'impôt *m*; (Tax) avoir fiscal *m*; ∼ **cut** *n* réduction d'impôt *f*;

(d...) ∼ **debtor** *n* débiteur/-trice fiscal/-e *m/f*; ∼**-deductible** *adj* déductible des impôts; ∼ **deduction** *n* abattement fiscal *m*, déduction fiscale *f*; (at source) retenue d'impôt *f*; ∼ **deferral** *n* report de l'impôt *m*; ∼ **demand** *n* avis d'imposition *m*; ∼ **disc** BrE, ∼ **disk** AmE *n* vignette (automobile) *f*; ∼ **district** *n* UK division du trésor public *f*; ∼ **dodge** *n* combine pour éviter l'impôt *f*; ∼ **dodger** *n* fraudeur/-euse fiscal/-e *m/f*; ∼ **dodging** *n* fraude fiscale *f*;

(e...) ∼**-efficient investments** *n pl* UK investissements à capacité fiscale *m pl*; ∼ **equalization account** *n* compte de péréquation des impôts *m*; ∼ **equalization scheme** *n* système de péréquation des impôts *m*; ∼ **evader** *n* fraudeur/-euse fiscal/-e *m/f*; ∼ **evasion** *n* fraude fiscale *f*, évasion fiscale *f*; ∼**-exempt** *adj* (goods) exonéré de taxes; (income) exonéré d'impôts, non imposable; ∼**-exempt corporation** *n* corporation exonérée d'impôt *f*; ∼**-exempt securities** *n* titres exonérés d'impôts *m pl*; ∼**-exempt special savings account** *n* UK compte spécial d'épargne exonéré d'impôts *m*; ∼ **exemption** *n* exonération d'impôts *f*; ∼ **exile** *n* (state) exil fiscal *m*; (person) personne fuyant le fisc *f*; ∼ **expert** *n* expert en fiscalité *m*, fiscaliste *mf*;

(f...) ∼ **form** *n* feuille d'impôts *f*, déclaration

d'impôts *f*; ∼ **fraud** *n* fraude fiscale *f*;

∼**-free** *adj* (goods) exonéré de taxes; (income) exonéré d'impôts, non imposable; ∼**-free allowance** *n* indemnité non imposable *f*; ∼**-free shop** *n* boutique hors taxes *f*;

(g...) ∼ **guidelines** *n pl* directives fiscales *f pl*;

(h...) ∼ **harmonization** *n* harmonisation fiscale *f*; ∼ **haven** *n* paradis fiscal *m*; ∼ **holiday** *n* période d'exonération fiscale *f*;

(i...) ∼ **incentive** *n* avantage fiscal *m*; ∼ **inspector** *n* inspecteur/-trice des impôts *m/f*, percepteur *m*; ∼ **installment** AmE, ∼ **instalment** BrE *n* acompte provisionnel *m*;

(l...) ∼ **law** *n* droit fiscal *m*; ∼ **liability** *n* (amount to pay) dette fiscale *f*, impôt à payer *m*, obligation fiscale *f*; (duty, obligation) assujettissement à l'impôt *m*; ∼ **loophole** *n* échappatoire fiscale *f*;

(o...) ∼ **office** *n* perception *f*; ∼ **officer** *n* agent de l'impôt *m*; ∼ **offset** *n* compensation fiscale *f*;

(p...) ∼**-paid income** *n* revenu libéré d'impôt *m*; ∼ **package** *n* ensemble de mesures fiscales *m*; ∼ **payable** *n* impôt exigible *m*, impôt à payer *m*; ∼ **period** *n* période d'imposition *f*; ∼ **planning** *n* planification fiscale *f*; ∼ **policy** *n* politique fiscale *f*; ∼ **proceeds** *n pl* produit de l'impôt *m*; ∼ **proposal** *n* proposition fiscale *f*; ∼ **provisions** *n pl* provisions pour impôts *f pl*;

(r...) ∼ **rate** *n* taux d'imposition *m*, taux d'impôt *m*; ∼ **rate schedule** *n* barème d'imposition *m*, liste officielle des taux d'imposition *f*; ∼ **ratio** *n* coefficient d'imposition *m*; ∼ **rebate** *n* dégrèvement fiscal *m*; ∼ **record** *n* dossier d'impôt *m*; ∼ **reduction** *n* réduction d'impôt *f*; ∼ **reform** *n* réforme de la fiscalité *f*; ∼ **refund** *n* remboursement d'impôt *m*, remboursement sur impôt *m*; ∼ **relief** *n* allègement fiscal *m*, dégrèvement *m*, réduction d'impôt *f*; ∼ **remission** *n* remise d'impôt *f*; ∼ **return** *n* (Tax) (declaration) déclaration d'impôt sur le revenu *f*; (form) feuille d'impôts *f*; ∼ **revenue** *n* recettes fiscales *f pl*;

(s...) ∼ **schedule** *n* barème d'imposition *m*; ∼ **shelter** *n* abri fiscal *m*; ∼ **shield** *n* protection fiscale *f*; ∼ **software** *n* logiciel de calcul fiscal *m*; ∼ **status** *n* situation fiscale *f*, statut fiscal *m*; ∼ **system** *n* fiscalité *f*, régime fiscal *m*, système fiscal *m*;

(t...) ∼ **take** *n* ponction fiscale *f*; ∼ **threshold** *n* minimum imposable *m*, seuil d'imposition minimum *m*;

(u...) ∼ **umbrella** *n* ombrelle fiscale *f*; ∼ **unit** *n* (Econ, Tax) foyer fiscal *m*;

(w...) ∼ **write-off** *n* dépense déductible de l'impôt sur les sociétés *f*, perte sèche de l'impôt *f*;

(y...) ∼ **year** *n* (Gen Comm) année fiscale *f*; (Tax) exercice *m*; ∼ **yield** *n* rendement de l'impôt *m*

tax² vt (person) imposer; (earnings, profits) taxer; ~ **a vehicle** payer la vignette; **be ~ed at a higher rate** être soumis à un taux d'imposition plus élevé; **be ~ed at a rate of 20%** (person) être imposé au taux de 20%; (sum, income, profit) être taxé à 20%

taxable adj imposable, soumis à l'impôt; ~ **allowance** n allocation imposable f; ~ **allowances and benefits** n pl allocations et avantages imposables m pl; ~ **benefit** n avantage imposable m, bénéfice imposable m; ~ **capital** n capital imposable m; ~ **capital gain** n gain en capital imposable m, plus-value imposable f; ~ **dividend** n dividende imposable m; ~ **income** n revenu imposable m; ~ **profit** n bénéfice imposable m; ~ **quota** n quota imposable m, quotité imposable f; ~ **sales** n pl ventes imposables f pl, ventes taxables f pl; ~ **value** n valeur imposable f; ~ **year** n année d'imposition f

taxation n (imposition of tax) imposition f, taxation f, impôts m pl; (revenue) impôts m pl, contributions f pl; ~ **authorities** n pl administration fiscale f; ~ **office** n perception f; ~ **officer** n agent de l'impôt m; ~ **period** n période d'imposition f; ~ **system** n fiscalité f, régime fiscal m, système fiscal m; ~ **year** n année d'imposition f, année fiscale f, exercice m

taxed adj assujetti à l'impôt, imposé; ~ **at source** imposé à la source; ~ **capital gain** n gain en capital imposé m, plus-value imposée f

taxflation n (Econ, Tax) inflation fiscale f

taxi n taxi m; ~ **rank** n BrE, ~ **stand** n AmE station de taxis f

taxman n pl **-men** (official) inspecteur des impôts m, percepteur m; (tax authorities) (infrml) fisc m

taxpayer n contribuable mf

T-bill n (▸Treasury bill) bon du Trésor à court terme m

T-bond n (▸Treasury bond) bon du Trésor à long terme m, obligation du Trésor f

TDI abbr (**Trade Data Interchange**) échange d'informations commerciales m

team¹ n équipe f; **work well as a** ~ faire un bon travail d'équipe; **management** ~ équipe de direction f; ~ **briefing** n briefing d'équipe m; ~ **building** n développement d'équipe m, motivation d'équipe f; ~ **leader** n chef d'équipe m; ~ **member** n équipier/-ière m/f, membre de l'équipe m; ~ **spirit** n esprit d'équipe m; ~ **theory** n théorie des équipes f

team²: ~ **up** vi (people) faire équipe; (companies, groups) s'associer; ~ **up with** faire équipe avec, s'associer avec

team player n **be a** ~ avoir l'esprit d'équipe

teamster n AmE chauffeur de camion m, routier m

teamwork n travail d'équipe m

tear-off: ~ **coupon** n bulletin de commande détachable m; ~ **portion** n volant m

teaser n aguiche f; ~ **ad** n publicité mystère f; ~ **campaign** n campagne teasing f; ~ **rate** n (Fin) taux mystère m

teasing n (S&M) aguichage m

TEC abbr UK (▸**Training and Enterprise Council**) organisme gérant des programmes de formation professionnelle en entreprises

techMARK n UK (Stock) marché spécialisé dans les valeurs de haute technologie

technical adj technique; ~ **analysis** n (Stock) analyse technique f; ~ **assistance** n assistance technique f; ~ **cooperation** n collaboration technique f; ~ **data** n pl données techniques f pl; ~ **director** n directeur/-trice technique m/f; ~ **hitch** n incident technique m; ~ **manager** n directeur/-trice technique m/f; ~ **market** n (Stock) marché artificiellement soutenu m, marché technique m; ~ **mastery** n maîtrise technique f; ~ **point** n (Law) question de procédure f, vice de forme m; ~ **progress** n progrès technique m; ~ **salesman** n technico-commercial m; ~ **saleswoman** n technico-commerciale f; ~ **sign** n (Stock) indication technique f, signal technique m; ~ **staff** n techniciens m pl; ~ **standards** n pl normes techniques f pl; ~ **support** n assistance technique f

technicality n détail technique m; (Law) question de procédure f, vice de forme m

technique n technique f; **marketing** ~s techniques de marketing f pl

technological adj technologique; ~ **change** n changement technologique m; ~ **edge** n avance technologique f; ~ **forecast** n prévision technologique f; ~ **forecasting** n prévision technologique f; ~ **gap** n fossé technologique m; ~ **innovation** n innovation technologique f

technologically adv (backward, sophisticated) sur le plan technologique; ~ **advanced** adj à l'avant-garde technologique

technology n technologie f; **new technologies** nouvelles technologies f pl; ~**-and-market interface** n interface technologie-marché f; ~**-based industry** n industrie technologique f; ~ **park** n parc technologique m, péripole technologique m; ~ **stocks** n pl valeurs technologiques (de la nouvelle économie) f pl; ~ **transfer** n transfert de technologie m, transfert technologique m; ~ **watch** n veille technologique f

teething troubles n pl difficultés initiales f pl

tel. abbr (▸**telephone**) tél. (téléphone); ~ **no.** abbr (▸**telephone number**) n° tél. (numéro de téléphone)

telco n AmE (infrml) (▸**telephone company**) opérateur télécom m

telebanking n opérations bancaires à distance f pl

telecanvassing n télédémarchage m

telecommunication network n réseau de télécommunications m

telecommunications n + sing v or pl v télécommunications f pl; ~ **company** n opérateur télécom m; ~ **industry** n industrie des télécommunications f; ~ **network** n réseau de télécommunications m; ~ **satellite** n satellite de télécommunications m

telecommute vi faire du télétravail

telecommuter n télétravailleur/-euse m/f

telecommuting n télétravail m

telecoms n télécommunications f pl, télécoms m pl

teleconference n téléconférence f

teleconferencing n téléconférence f

telecottage n cybercentre m, centre informatique public m

telegraphic adj télégraphique

telelearning n apprentissage à distance m; (on Internet) apprentissage en ligne m

telemarketeer n télémercaticien/-ienne m/f

telemarketing n marketing téléphonique m, télémarketing m, télémercatique f

telematics n +sing v télématique f

teleordering n commande par ordinateur f

telepayment n paiement électronique m, télépaiement m

telephone¹ n téléphone m; **on the** ~, **over the** ~ au téléphone; **be on the** ~ (speaking) être au téléphone; (connected) avoir le téléphone; ~ **banking** n opérations bancaires effectuées par téléphone f pl, banque en direct par téléphone f; ~ **bill** n note de téléphone f; ~ **book** n annuaire téléphonique m; ~ **booking** n réservation par téléphone f; (theatre) location par téléphone f; ~ **booth** n AmE, ~ **box** n BrE cabine téléphonique f; ~ **call** n appel téléphonique m, communication téléphonique f; ~ **canvassing** n télédémarchage m, prospection téléphonique f; ~ **company** n opérateur télécom m; ~ **conversation** n conversation téléphonique f; ~ **directory** n annuaire téléphonique m; ~ **exchange** n centrale téléphonique f; ~ **extension** n poste m; ~ **interviewing** n (research) interview par téléphone f; ~ **line** n ligne de téléphone f; ~ **message** n message téléphonique m; ~ **number** n numéro de téléphone m; ~ **operator** n standardiste mf; ~ **order** n commande téléphonique f; ~ **poll** n sondage téléphonique m; ~ **sales** n + sing v télévente f, vente par téléphone f; ~ **selling** n télévente f, vente par téléphone f; ~ **subscriber** n abonné/-e au téléphone m/f; ~

survey n enquête téléphonique f; ~ **tapping** n mise sur écoute téléphonique f

telephone² **1** vt (person) téléphoner à; (instructions, order) téléphoner **2** vi téléphoner, appeler

telephony n téléphonie f

teleprinter n BrE téléscripteur m

teleprocessing n télétraitement m

telesales n + sing v télévente f, vente par téléphone f; ~ **agent** n télévendeur/-euse m/f, téléacteur/-trice m/f

teleselling n télévente f, vente par téléphone f

teleshopping n téléachat m

Teletex® n UK Télétex® m, vidéographie diffusée f

teletext n télétexte m

teletraining n formation à distance f; (on Internet) formation en ligne f, e-formation f

televise vt téléviser

television n (medium) télévision f; (set) téléviseur m, poste de télévision m; **on** ~ à la télévision; ~ **advertising** n publicité télévisée f; ~ **broadcast** n émission de télévision f; ~ **campaign** n campagne télévisuelle f; ~ **channel** n chaîne de télévision f; ~ **commercial** n message publicitaire télévisé m; ~ **journalist** n journaliste de télévision mf; ~ **licence** n UK redevance de télévision f; ~ **network** n réseau de télévision m; ~ **news** n journal télévisé m; ~ **program** AmE, ~ **programme** BrE n émission de télévision f; ~ **screen** n écran de télévision m; ~ **set** n téléviseur m, poste de télévision m; ~ **support** n support TV m; ~ **viewer** n téléspectateur/-trice m/f

televisual adj télévisuel/-elle

telework n télétravail m

teleworker n télétravailleur/-euse m/f

teleworking n télétravail m

telex¹ n télex m

telex² vt télexer

teller n caissier/-ière m/f, guichetier/-ière m/f

telly n BrE (infrml) télé f (infrml)

temp¹ n (infrml) intérimaire mf

temp² vi travailler en intérim

temperature n température f

temping n intérim m; ~ **agency** n agence d'intérim f

template n gabarit m

temporarily adv temporairement

temporary¹ adj provisoire, temporaire

temporary² n intérimaire mf

temporary: ~ **employment** n emploi intérimaire m, emploi temporaire m; ~ **job** n emploi intérimaire m, emploi temporaire m; ~ **residence** n résidence temporaire f; ~ **residence permit** n, ~ **residence visa** n permis de séjour limité m; ~ **resident** n résident/-e temporaire *m/f*; ~ **secretary** *n* secrétaire intérimaire *mf*; ~ **status** *n* statut temporaire *m*; ~ **work** *n* travail temporaire *m*; ~ **worker** *n* intérimaire *mf*

tenancy *n* (apartment, flat) location *f*; (lease) bail *m*; **a six month** ~ un bail de six mois; ~ **agreement** *n* bail *m*; ~ **period** *n* période de location *f*

tenant *n* (Prop) locataire *mf*; ~ **farmer** *n* métayer/-ère *m/f*

tend **1** *vt* (shop) s'occuper de
2 *vi* ~ **to** (customer, guest) s'occuper de; ~ **to do** avoir tendance à faire; ~ **towards** (value, figure, zero) tendre vers; ~ **upwards/downwards** avoir tendance à monter/baisser

tendency *n* tendance *f*; **have a** ~ **to do** avoir tendance à faire; **there is a** ~ **for customers to complain** les clients ont tendance à se plaindre

tender¹ *n* (bid) offre *f*, soumission *f*; (Stock) offre d'achat *f*; **by** ~ par voie d'adjudication, par soumission; **sealed** ~ soumission cachetée *f*; ~ **by private contract** adjudication de gré à gré *f*; **invite** ~**s** faire un appel d'offres; **make a** ~ **for a contract** faire une soumission pour un contrat; **put work/a contract out to** ~ mettre un ouvrage/contrat en adjudication, faire un appel d'offres pour un ouvrage/contrat; ~ **documents** *n pl* (Fin, Stock) enchère *f*; ~ **offer** *n* soumission *f*; (Stock) offre d'achat *f*; ~ **price** *n* montant de l'adjudication *m*; ~ **to contract** *n* soumission d'offre *f*

tender² **1** *vt* (money) offrir; (apology, thanks) présenter; ~ **money in discharge of debt** (Law) faire une offre d'argent pour régler une dette; ~ **one's resignation** donner sa démission
2 *vi* (bid) soumissionner, faire une soumission; ~ **for a contract** faire une soumission pour un contrat; ~ **for the construction of sth** soumissionner la construction de qch; **offer a contract for** ~ faire un appel d'offres pour un contrat; **invitation to** ~ appel d'offres *m*

tenderer *n* soumissionnaire *mf*; **successful** ~ adjudicataire *mf*

tendering *n* soumission *f*; **by** ~ par voie d'adjudication; **open** ~ appel d'offres ouvert *m*

tenement *n* immeuble *m*

tenor *n* (Fin) échéance *f*; (words of deed) teneur *f*

tentative *adj* (offer, conclusion, booking) provisoire; ~ **agenda** *n* ordre du jour provisoire *m*; ~ **estimate** *n* estimation approximative *f*; ~ **plan** *n* avant-projet *m*

tenure *n* (period of office) fonction *f*; (Law) bail *m*; **have** ~ être titulaire de son poste; **security of** ~ sécurité de l'emploi *f*

tenured *adj* titulaire; ~ **post** *n* poste de titulaire *m*; ~ **staff** *n* personnel titulaire *m*

term *n* (time period) période *f*, terme *m*;

(duration) durée *f*; (limit) terme *m*; (payment date) échéance *f*; (period before deadline) délai *m*; (word) terme *m*; (stipulation) condition *f*; (at school, university) trimestre *m*; **set a** ~ **to sth** mettre un terme à qch; **at** ~ (Fin) à échéance; ~ **day** *n* jour du terme *m*; ~ **deposit** *n* dépôt à terme *m*; ~ **draft** *n* lettre de change *f*; ~ **insurance** *n* assurance-vie couvrant une période prédéterminée *f*, assurance-vie temporaire *f*; ~ **insurance policy** *n* police d'assurance-vie temporaire *f*; ~ **of limitation** *n* délai de prescription *m*; ~ **loan** *n* prêt à terme *m*; ~ **of office** *n* (Gen Comm) *période pendant laquelle on exerce une fonction*; (Pol) mandat *m*; ~ **policy** *n* police à terme *f*; ~ **purchase** *n* achat à crédit *m*; ~ **sale** *n* vente à crédit *f*

terminable *adj* (contract) résiliable

terminal¹ *adj* (stage, point, phase) terminal; (decline) irréversible

terminal² *n* (Comp) poste de travail *m*, terminal *m*; (Transp) (for bus, train) terminus *m*; (aviation) aérogare *f*; **ferry** ~ gare maritime *f*

terminal: ~ **bonus** *n* bonus réversible *m*, prime de fin de contrat *f*; ~ **charges** *n pl* (Fin) taxes terminales *f pl*; ~ **emulator** *n* émulateur de terminal *m*; ~ **loss** *n* perte finale *f*; ~ **market** *n* (Stock) marché à terme *m*; ~ **price** *n* (Stock) cours du livrable *m*, prix à terme *m*

terminate **1** *vt* (discussion, arrangement) mettre fin à, terminer; (agreement) annuler; (contract, policy) résilier; ~ **one's appointment** donner sa démission; ~ **sb's employment** licencier qn
2 *vi* (contract, agreement) se terminer; (employment contract, employment) prendre fin

termination *n* (of contract, policy) résiliation *f*; ~ **benefits** *n pl* indemnités de départ *f pl*; ~ **of business** *n* cessation d'activité *f*; ~ **clause** *n* clause de résiliation *f*; ~ **of employment** *n* licenciement *m*, cessation de fonctions *f*; ~ **of employment with notice** *n* cessation de fonctions avec préavis *f*; ~ **of tenancy** *n* résiliation d'un contrat de location *f*

terminology *n* terminologie *f*

terms *n pl* (of role) attributions *f pl*; (Bank) modalités *f pl*; (of agreement) termes *m pl*; (of contract) conditions *f pl*; (of will) dispositions *f pl*; **come to** ~ parvenir à un accord; **in** ~ **of** (as expressed by) en fonction de; (from the point of view of) du point de vue de; **not on any** ~ sous aucune condition; **under the** ~ **of the contract** aux termes du contrat, selon les termes du contrat; **be on good/bad** ~ **with sb** être en bons/mauvais termes avec qn; **be on first-name** ~ **with sb** appeler qn par son prénom; **easy** ~ facilités de paiement *f pl*; **inclusive** ~ prix net *m*, prix tout compris *m*; **name one's** ~ fixer ses conditions; ~ **and conditions** (of payment) modalités de paiement *f pl*; (of arrangement) modalités *f pl*; ⋯▸

t

(of policy) termes et conditions *m pl*; (of issue) modalités *f pl*; ~ **and conditions of employment** clauses et conditions d'emploi *f pl*; ~ **of credit** conditions de crédit *f pl*; ~ **of payment** conditions de paiement *f pl*, modalités de paiement *f pl*; ~ **of reference** (of role, committee) attributions *f pl*, mandat *m*; ~ **of sale** conditions de vente *f pl*; ~ **of shipment** conditions d'envoi *f pl*; ~ **of tender** conditions de l'offre *f pl*, conditions de soumission *f pl*; ~ **of trade** termes de l'échange *m pl*

terrestrial *adj* terrestre

territorial waters *n pl* eaux territoriales *f pl*

territory *n* (of salesperson) secteur *m*, territoire *m*; **be on familiar** ~ être sur son terrain; **go with the** ~ (infrml) faire partie du boulot (infrml); ~ **manager** *n* chef de région *m*

tertiary *adj* tertaire; ~ **activities** *n pl* activités du secteur tertiaire *f pl*, services tertiaires *m pl*; ~ **education** *n* enseignement supérieur *m*; ~ **product** *n* produit tertiaire *m*; ~ **sector** *n* secteur tertiaire *m*

TESSA *abbr* UK (▸**tax-exempt special savings account**) compte d'épargne exonéré d'impôts *m*

test[1] *n* (of person, abilities) épreuve *f*; (exam) épreuve *f*; (Comp) (trial) essai *m*, test *m*; (of quality) contrôle *m*; (of system, machine) essai *m*; **put sb/sth to the** ~ mettre qn/qch à l'épreuve; **stand the** ~ **of time** résister à l'épreuve du temps; **intelligence/personality** ~ test d'aptitude/de personnalité; **undergo** ~**s** (product) subir des essais; ~ **area** *n* zone test *f*; ~ **audit** *n* contrôle par sondages *m*, vérification par sondages *f*; ~ **bench** *n* banc d'essai *m*; ~ **case** *n* (Law) procès qui fait jurisprudence *m*; ~ **drive** *n* essai sur route *m*; ~ **mailing** *n* publipostage-test *m*; ~ **market** *n* marché témoin *m*, marché test *m*; ~ **marketing** *n* test de marché *m*, tests de marché *m pl*; ~ **problem** *n* problème test *m*; ~ **run** *n* (of system, machine) essai *m*; (of car) essai sur route *m*; ~ **town** *n* ville test *f*

test[2] *vt* essayer, tester; ~**-drive** (car) essayer; ~ **out** (equipment) mettre à l'essai; (theory) tester

testamentary *adj* testamentaire

testate *adj* testé

testbed *n* banc d'essai *m*

testee *n* personne qui subit un test

tester *n* (person) testeur/-euse *m/f*; (sample) échantillon *m*

testify *vi* témoigner; ~ **that** attester que; ~ **to sth** attester qch

testimonial *n* référence *f*; **have excellent** ~**s** avoir d'excellentes références; ~ **advertisement** *n* testimonial *m*

testimony *n* témoignage *m*

testing *n* (trials, sampling) essai *m*; (of skills) évaluation *f*; ~ **plant** *n* usine d'essai *f*; ~ **procedure** *n* procédure d'essai *f*

test-market *vt* tester sur le marché

text[1] *n* texte *m*; ~**-based browser** *n* navigateur textuel *m*, navigateur non graphique *m*; ~ **editing** *n* édition de texte *f*; ~ **editor** *n* (Comp) éditeur de texte *m*; ~ **in full** *n* texte intégral *m*; ~ **message** *n* message texte *m*, message SMS *m*, texto *m* (infrml); ~ **mode** *n* mode texte *m*; ~ **processing** *n* traitement de texte *m*

text[2] *vt* envoyer un message texte à

textbook *n* manuel *m*; ~ **case** *n*, ~ **example** *n* exemple modèle *m*, exemple typique *m*; ~ **operation** *n* opération menée dans les règles de l'art *f*

textile *n* textile *m*; ~ **industry** *n* industrie textile *f*

textiles *n pl* textiles *m pl*

TGWU *abbr* UK (▸**Transport and General Workers' Union**) syndicat des transports et des travailleurs confédérés *m*

thank *vt* remercier; ~ **sb for sth** remercier qn de qch, remercier qn pour qch; ~**ing you in advance**, ~**ing you in anticipation** en vous remerciant d'avance, en vous remerciant par avance

thank-you letter *n* lettre de remerciement *f*

theater AmE, **theatre** BrE *n* théâtre *m*

theft *n* vol *m*; ~ **risk** *n* (Ins) risque de vol *m*

theft-proof *adj* inviolable

theme *n* thème *m*; ~ **park** *n* parc d'attractions *m*, parc de loisirs à thème *m*; ~ **tune** *n* indicatif *m*

theoretical *adj* théorique; ~ **capacity** *n* capacité théorique *f*; ~ **income** *n* revenu théorique *m*

theory *n* théorie *f*; **in** ~ en principe; ~ **of comparative costs** théorie des coûts comparatifs *f*

thermal *adj* (Ind) thermique; ~ **energy** *n* énergie thermique *f*; ~ **power station** *n* centrale thermique *f*; ~ **reactor** *n* réacteur thermique *m*

thief *n* voleur/-euse *m/f*

thin *adj* (evidence) insuffisant; (excuse) peu convaincant; ~ **capitalization** *n* capitalisation minimale *f*; ~ **market** *n* marché étroit *m*; ~ **trading** *n* (Stock) marché calme *m*

think [1] *vt* penser; ~ **the unthinkable** concevoir l'inconcevable [2] *vi* penser; (before acting, speaking) réfléchir

thinking *n* (reasoning) façon de penser *f*; **current** ~ **is that** la tendance actuelle de l'opinion est que; **to my way of** ~ à mon avis

think tank *n* groupe de réflexion *m*, laboratoire d'idées *m*

third[1] *adj* troisième

third² *n* (fraction) tiers *m*; (in order) troisième *mf*

third³ *adv* (finish, come) troisième, en troisième position

third: ~ **age** *n* troisième âge *m*; ~ **class** *n* (Transp) troisième classe *f*; ~**-class** *adj* (Transp) de troisième classe; ~**-class degree** *n* UK (education) licence sans mention *f*; ~**-class mail** *n* US tarif lent *m*; ~ **country** *n* (Econ) (international trade) pays tiers *m*; ~**-generation** *adj* de troisième génération; ~**-generation computer** *n* ordinateur de troisième génération *m*; ~ **party** *n* tierce personne *f*, tiers *m*; ~**-party credibility** *n* (public relations) crédibilité au tiers *f*; ~**-party effect** *n* effet d'entraînement *m*, effet de retombées *m*; ~**-party fire and theft** *n* assurance responsabilité civile contre l'incendie et le vol *f*, incendie et vol au tiers *m*; ~**-party insurance** *n* assurance au tiers *f*; ~**-party insurance cover** *n* BrE, ~**-party insurance coverage** *n* AmE couverture d'assurance au tiers *f*; ~**-party insurance policy** *n* police d'assurance au tiers *f*; ~**-party intervention** *n* intervention d'un tiers *f*; ~**-party liability** *n* responsabilité au tiers *f*; ~**-party risk** *n* risque au tiers *m*, risque de recours au tiers *m*; ~**-party sale** *n* vente à un tiers *f*; ~ **person** *n* tierce personne *f*, tiers *m*; ~ **quarter** *n* troisième trimestre *m*; ~**-rate** *adj* (company, hotel, book) de troisième ordre; (service, work) médiocre; ~ **way** *n* (Pol) troisième voie *f*

thirdly *adv* troisièmement

Third World *n* tiers monde *m*; ~ **country** *n* pays du tiers monde *m*

Thirty Share index *n* indice des principales valeurs industrielles *m*

thought *n* (idea) idée *f*; (consideration) considération *f*; (reflection) pensée *f*; **give ~ to** considérer; **give serious ~ to** (issue) bien réfléchir à; **have second ~s** changer d'avis; **after much ~** après mûre réflexion; **what are your ~s on...?** que pensez-vous de...?; ~ **leadership** *n* pensée innovatrice *f*

thousand million *n* milliard *m*

thrash: ~ **out** *vt* (solution, compromise) arriver à; (issue) discuter à fond de; (plan) réussir à élaborer

thread *n* (Comp) fil de discussion *m*

threat *n* menace *f*; ~ **effect** *n* effet menace *m*

three: ~**-martini lunch** *n* AmE (infrml) repas d'affaires bien arrosé *m*; ~**-month call** *n* (Stock) option d'achat à trois mois *f*; ~**-months' rate** *n* (Fin) taux de trois mois *m*; ~ **quarters** *n pl* trois-quarts *m pl*; ~**-shift system** *n* trois-huit *m pl*; ~**-star hotel** *n* hôtel trois étoiles *m*; ~**-way calling** *n* conversation à trois *f*; ~**-way split** *n* division en trois *f*

threshold *n* seuil *m*; **tax ~** seuil d'imposition minimum *m*, minimum imposable *m*; ~ **agreement** *n* accord sur le salaire initial *m*; ~ **amount** *n* (Tax) montant déterminant *m*; ~ **level** *n* niveau seuil *m*; ~ **point** *n* (Stock) seuil *m*; ~ **population** *n* (Econ) population-seuil *f*; ~ **price** *n* prix de seuil *m*; ~ **rate** *n* salaire de départ *m*, salaire initial *m*; ~ **value** *n* valeur de seuil *f*; ~ **worker** *n* travailleur/-euse au salaire initial *m/f*

thrift *n* épargne *f*; ~ **institution** *n* US banque d'épargne *f*, caisse d'épargne *f*; ~ **shop** *n* friperie *f*, magasin de brocante *m*

thrifty *adj* (person) économe

thrive *vi* prospérer, être florissant

thriving *adj* (industry, company) florissant; (person) prospère

through *adj* (finished) fini; **be ~ to** être en communication avec, être en ligne avec; **be ~ to the next round** être sélectionné pour le deuxième tour; ~ **bill of lading** *n* (shipping) connaissement direct *m*; ~ **charge** *n* tarif direct *m*, tarif forfaitaire *m*; ~ **rate** *n* tarif direct *m*, tarif forfaitaire *m*; ~ **route** *n* itinéraire direct *m*; ~ **shipment** *n* transport de bout à bout *m*; ~ **ticketing** *n* billetterie intégrée *f*; ~ **train** *n* train direct *m*

throughput *n* capacité de traitement *f*; (of machine) débit *m*, rendement *m*; (of plant) rythme de production *m*

throughway *n* AmE autoroute *f*

throw *vt* ~ **light on** éclairer; ~ **the book at sb** accabler qn d'accusations; ~ **one's money about** (infrml) jeter son argent par les fenêtres (infrml); ~ **money at a project** (infrml) claquer de l'argent dans un projet (infrml); ~ **a wrench into the economy** (infrml) porter un coup très dur à l'économie; ~ **away** jeter; ~ **in** (add) ajouter; (give free) faire cadeau de; ~ **out** (dispose of) jeter; (from club, body) renvoyer; (application, case, plan) rejeter; ~ **sb out** (infrml) flanquer qn à la porte (infrml); ~ **up** (problem, obstacle) créer; (fact) faire apparaître

THS transaction *n* (Stock) transaction hors séance *f*, THS *f*

thumb index *n* répertoire à onglets *m*

TIC *abbr* (▸**take into consideration**) tenir compte de

tick¹ *n* (mark) coche *f*; (Stock) tick *m*, écart maximum des cours du marché *m*; **on ~** BrE à crédit; **put a ~ in the box** cocher la case; ~ **box** *n* case à cocher *f*; ~ **size** *n* échelon minimum de cotation *m*

tick² *vt* (on list) cocher; ~ **the box** BrE cocher la case; ~ **off** cocher; ~ **over** (business, factory) tourner au ralenti

ticker *n* téléscripteur *m*; ~ **tape** *n* bande de téléscripteur *f*

ticket *n* (for theatre) billet *m*; (Transp) (for train, plane) billet *m*; (for bus, subway) ticket *m*; (Pol) US liste *f*; (Stock) fiche *f*; ~ **agency** *n* (for travel) agence de voyages *f*; (for theatre, concerts) agence de spectacles *f*; ~ **collector** ···⊱

n contrôleur/-euse *m*/*f*; ~ **day** *n* UK (Stock) deuxième jour de liquidation *m*; ~ **holder** *n* personne munie d'un billet *f*; ~ **machine** *n* distributeur de billets *m*; ~ **office** *n* bureau de vente des billets *m*; (window) guichet *m*; (at theatre) billetterie *f*; ~ **sales** *n* vente de billets *f*; ~ **tout** *n* revendeur/-euse de billets (au marché noir) *m*/*f*

ticketing *n* billetterie *f*

tickler file *n* (Bank) échéancier *m*

tidal: ~ **dock** *n* bassin d'échouage *m*, bassin de marée *m*; ~ **power** *n* énergie marémotrice *f*

tide *vt* ~ **sb over** (help out) dépanner qn

tie¹ *n* (constraining factor) contrainte *f*; (bond) lien *m*; **strengthen/sever** ~**s with** resserrer/ rompre les liens avec; ~**-in** *n* (connection) rapport *m*; (S&M) *article lié à une émission ou à un film*; ~**-in advertising** *n* publicité de liaison *f*; ~**-in display** *n* promotion jumelée *f*; ~**-in promotion** *n* (manufacturer and retailer) promotion concertée *f*; (of two products) promotion jumelée *f*; ~**-in sale** *n* vente couplée *f*

tie² *vt* (link) associer; **my hands are tied** j'ai les mains liées; ~ **in with** (concur) concorder avec; (be connected) être en rapport avec; ~ **sb/sth to sth** associer qn/qch à qch; **be tied to** (inflation, rate) être indexé sur; (company) être sous contrat à; (constraint, force) être soumis à; **be tied to doing sth** être dans l'obligation de faire qch; ~ **sb down to a price/time** arriver à soutirer un prix/une heure à qn; ~ **up** (capital) immobiliser; (details) régler; (deal) conclure; **be tied up (with sb)** être pris (avec qn); ~ **up the loose ends** régler les derniers détails

tied: ~ **aid** *n* aide liée *f*; ~ **cottage** *n* UK logement de fonction *m*; ~ **house** *n* UK (pub) débit de boissons lié à une brasserie *m*; (company property) logement de fonction *m*; ~ **loan** *n* emprunt lié *m*, prêt lié *m*

tiger: ~ **economy** *n* économie des tigres asiatiques *f*; ~ **team** *n* US équipe d'experts *f*

tight *adj* (security) strict; (deadline, budget) serré; (discipline, controls) rigoureux/-euse; (competition) serré; ~ **fiscal policy** *n* politique de resserrement budgétaire *f*, politique fiscale serrée *f*; ~ **market** *n* marché serré *m*, marché étroit *m*; ~ **money** *n* argent rare *m*, argent cher *m*; ~ **monetary policy** *n* politique d'encadrement du crédit *f*; ~ **schedule** *n* emploi du temps serré *m*

tighten *vt* (regulations) renforcer; (credit controls) resserrer; ~ **the purse strings** serrer les cordons de la bourse; ~ **up** (security) renforcer, resserrer; ~ **up on** renforcer la réglementation en matière de

till *n* caisse *f*; ~ **money** *n* encaisse *f*; ~ **receipt** *n* ticket de caisse *m*

tilt *vt* ~ **the balance** faire pencher la balance

time¹ *n* (hour of the day) heure *f*; (continuum,

duration) temps *m*; (occasion) fois *f*; **at a given** ~ à une heure déterminée; **at some** ~ **in the future** dans l'avenir; **be under** ~ **pressure** travailler sous pression; **for the** ~ **being** pour le moment; ~ **is of the essence** la vitesse s'impose; **this** ~ **last year** l'année dernière à la même époque; **within the allotted** ~ **frame** dans les temps impartis; **at all** ~**s** à tout moment; **keep up with the** ~**s, move with the** ~**s** être à la page; ~**s are hard** les temps sont durs; ~ **after sight** *n* délai de vue *m*; ~ **band** *n* plage horaire *f*, tranche horaire *f*; ~ **bar** *n* (Law) prescription *f*; ~**-barred** *adj* (Law) prescrit; ~ **bargain** *n* (Stock) marché à terme *m*; ~ **bill** *n* échéance à terme *f*; ~ **buyer** *n* (Media, S&M) acheteur/-euse de temps *m*/*f*; ~ **card** *n* feuille de pointage *f*; ~ **clock** *n* horloge pointeuse *f*; ~ **component** *n* paramètre temps *m*; ~ **constraint** *n* contrainte horaire *f*; ~**-consuming** *adj* qui prend beaucoup de temps; ~ **deposit** *n* dépôt à terme *m*; ~ **frame** délai *m*; ~ **and a half** *n* une fois et demie le tarif normal *f*; ~ **horizon** *n* (Mgmnt) échéance *f*; ~ **lag** *n* (Econ) décalage *m*, retard *m*; (between time zones) décalage horaire *m*; ~ **limit** *n* délai *m*; ~ **loan** *n* emprunt à terme *m*; ~ **management** *n* gestion du temps de travail *f*, organisation du temps *f*; ~ **and methods study** *n* étude des temps et des méthodes *f*; ~ **and motion study** *n* étude des périodes *f*, étude des temps et des mouvements *f*; ~ **off work** *n* absence ponctuelle *f*; (leave) congé *m*; ~ **policy** *n* police à temps *f*; ~ **premium** *n* (Stock) prime au temps *f*; ~ **rate** *n* salaire horaire *m*; ~**-saving** *adj* (device, procedure) qui fait gagner du temps; ~ **segment** *n* (advertising) période de programmation *f*; ~ **seller** *n* (Media, S&M) vendeur/-euse de temps *m*/*f*; ~**-served** *adj* qualifié; ~ **share** *n* multipropriété *f*; ~**-share developer** *n* promoteur de programmes en multipropriété *m*; ~**-share property** *n* multipropriété *f*; ~ **sharing** *n* (Comp) partage de temps *m*, temps partagé *m*; (HRM) temps partagé *m*, travail en simultanéité *m*; (Prop) multipropriété *f*; ~ **sheet** *n* feuille de présence *f*; ~ **slot** *n* (Media) (on radio, TV) créneau horaire *m*; ~ **span** *n* durée *f*; ~ **spread** *n* (Stock) opération mixte horizontale *f*, spread calendaire *m*, spread horizontal *m*; ~ **to market** *n* délai de mise sur le marché *m*; ~ **value** *n* (Stock) (options) valeur temporelle *f*, valeur-temps *f*; ~ **work** *n* travail à l'heure *m*; ~ **zone** *n* fuseau horaire *m*

time² *vt* (appointment, meeting, visit) fixer; (measure accurately) chronométrer; (judge) calculer

timeliness *n* opportunité *f*

timely *adj* opportun

time off *n* (free time) temps libre *m*; (leave) congé *m*; **take some** ~ prendre un congé; **ask for** ~ demander un congé; **take** ~ **to do**

sth (briefly) s'absenter pour faire qch

times *n pl* (multiplication) fois *f pl*; **nine ~ out of ten** neuf fois sur dix; **~ fixed charges** *n pl* (Acc) charges fixes à terme *f pl*; **~ uncovered** *n* (Fin) dividende à découvert *m*

timescale *n* délai *m*; **set a ~** fixer un délai; **within a two-month ~** dans un délai de deux mois; **do sth within the allotted ~** faire qch dans le délai prescrit; **work to tight ~s** travailler dans des délais très serrés; **over a six-month ~** sur une période de six mois

timetable¹ *n* (for work, at college) emploi du temps *m*; (schedule of project, talks) calendrier *m*; (Transp) horaire *m*; **train ~** horaire des trains *m*

timetable² *vt* (fix day) fixer la date de; (fix time) fixer l'heure de; (series of events) établir un calendrier de; **the workshop is ~d for Monday** l'atelier est fixé à lundi

timing *n* (duration) durée *f*; (of two events) synchronisation *f*; (of project) calendrier *m*; (precise) minutage *m*; (choice of time) choix du moment *m*; **the ~ of the election** la date choisie pour l'élection; **the ~ of the merger was unfortunate** le moment choisi pour la fusion était inopportun

tin *n* (Ind) étain *m*; **~ plate** *n* feuille de tôle *f*; **~ shares** *n pl* valeurs stannifères *f pl*

TINA *abbr* (▶there is no alternative) aucune alternative n'est possible, il n'y a pas d'alternative

tip¹ *n* (Envir) décharge *f*; (advice) conseil *m*, tuyau *m* (infrml); (gratuity) pourboire *m*; **~ of the iceberg** sommet de l'iceberg *m*

tip² *vt* (porter, waiter) donner un pourboire à; **~ the scales** faire pencher la balance

tip-off *n* (infrml) tuyau *m* (infrml)

tipper lorry BrE *n*, **tipper truck** AmE *n* camion à benne basculante *m*, camion-benne *m*

tipping *n* (Envir) dépôt de déchets *m*

tit-for-tat *adj* en représailles

title *n* (of book, film) titre *m*; (of report, document, job) intitulé *m*; (right to own) droit *m*; (magazine) titre *m*; (of invention) titre *m*; (rank) titre *m*; **~ of an account** intitulé de compte *m*; **~ deed** *n* titre de propriété *m*; **~ page** *n* première page *f*; **~ to the goods** titre constitutif de propriété sur la marchandise *m*

titular *adj* titulaire; **~ head** *n* responsable en titre *mf*

TM *abbr* (▶trademark) marque de fabrique *f*

TOB *abbr* (▶takeover bid) OPA *f* (offre publique d'achat)

tobacco *n* tabac *m*; **~ products** *n pl* produits du tabac *m pl*

TOE *abbr* (ton oil equivalent) TEP *f* (tonne équivalent pétrole)

toehold *n* **get a ~ in the market** réaliser une première pénétration du marché; **~ purchase** *n* achat précaire *m*

toes *n pl* **go ~ up** (infrml) faire faillite

token *n* (Gen Comm, Comp) jeton *m*; (promotional voucher) point *m*; **~ money** *n* monnaie fiduciaire *f*; **~ payment** *n* paiement symbolique *m*; **~ stoppage** *n* arrêt de travail symbolique *m*; **~ strike** *n* grève d'avertissement *f*, grève symbolique *f*

told *adj* **all ~** tout compris

tolerance *n* tolérance *f*

toll *n* (number of cases, incidents) nombre *m*; (Comms) AmE coût d'une communication téléphonique *m*; (Transp) péage d'autoroute *m*; **accident ~** nombre d'accidentés; **take a heavy ~** (on industry, environment) causer beaucoup de dégâts; **take a heavy ~ of bankruptcies** provoquer un lourd bilan de faillites; **take its ~ on sb** mettre qn à rude épreuve; **~ bridge** *n* pont à péage *m*; **~ call** *n* AmE communication interurbaine *f*; **~-free call** *n* AmE appel gratuit *m*, appel interurbain gratuit *m*; **~-free number** *n* AmE numéro d'appel gratuit *m*, numéro vert *m*; **~ motorway** *n* BrE autoroute à péage *f*

tollbooth *n* poste de péage *m*

tombstone *n* (Stock) avis d'émission publié dans la presse *m*; **~ ad** *n* plaquette publicitaire *f*

tomorrow *adv* demain; **~ week** demain en huit; **first thing ~** dès demain

ton *n* tonne *f*

tone: ~ down *vt* atténuer

toner *n* (for photocopier) encre *f*, toner *m*

tonnage *n* jauge *f*, tonnage *m*; **~ dues** *n pl* taxes de tonnage *f pl*

tonne *n* tonne *f*

tool¹ *n* (Gen Comm, Comp) outil *m*; **~s of the trade** *n pl* outils du métier *m pl*; **~ bar** *n* (Comp) barre d'outils *f*

tool²: **~ up** *vt* (factory, workshop) outiller

toolmaker *n* outilleur *m*

top¹ *adj* (best) meilleur; (leading) plus grand; (concern) majeur; (priority) absolu; **~ executive** cadre supérieur; **one of the ~ jobs** un des postes les plus prestigieux; **be in the ~ five** être dans les cinq premiers; **in the ~ left-hand corner** en haut à gauche; **pay the ~ price for sth** (consumer) acheter qch au prix fort; **pay ~ prices** (dealer, trader) offrir les meilleurs prix

top² *n* (of organization) sommet *m*; **at the ~ end** (of a scale) en haut; **be/stay on ~** avoir/ garder le dessus; **get on ~ of inflation** maîtriser l'inflation; **be on ~ of one's job** dominer son travail; **come out on ~** l'emporter; **~ end of the market** haut de gamme du marché *m*; **~ end of the range** haut de gamme dans la série *m*; **be at the ~ of one's profession** être tout en haut de l'échelle; **the ~ of the line** le haut de la gamme; **~ of the tree** (infrml) (status) le plus élevé; **~ brass** *n* (infrml) gros bonnets *m pl* (infrml); **~-class** *adj* de premier ordre;

⋯⟩

~ **copy** n (of document, invoice) original m; ~-**down** adj (design) de haut en bas; (management) directif/-ive, du sommet à la base; ~-**down linkage model** n modèle de liaison descendante m; ~ **executive** n cadre supérieur m; ~-**flight** adj de premier ordre; ~-**heavy** adj (business, company, capital structure) mal équilibré, trop lourd du haut; ~ **of the league** n leader m; ~-**level decision** n décision prise au plus haut niveau f; ~-**level efficiency** n efficience maximale f; ~-**level talks** n pl discussions au plus haut niveau f pl; ~ **management** n cadres supérieurs m pl, haute direction f; ~ **margin** n marge supérieure f; ~ **price** n (Stock) cours le plus haut m; ~ **prices** n pl prix maximums m pl; ~ **quality** n meilleure qualité f, qualité supérieure f; ~-**quality** adj de qualité supérieure; ~-**of-the-range** adj (model, product) haut de gamme; ~-**ranking** adj haut placé; ~-**ranking official** n haut/-e fonctionnaire m/f; ~-**rank product** n produit de première catégorie m, produit de première qualité m; ~-**rated** adj de premier ordre; ~ **rate of tax** n taux plafond d'imposition m; ~-**secret** adj ultra-secret; ~-**selling** adj (product) qui se vend très bien; (overall) qui se vend le mieux

top³ vt (sum, total) dépasser; (poll, survey) être en tête de; (surpass) dépasser; ~ **the list** être en tête de liste; **sales** ~**ped 3 million dollars** les ventes ont dépassé 3 millions de dollars; ~ **out** (reach highest level) plafonner; ~ **up** UK (Gen Comm) compléter; (savings) faire l'appoint à

topping: ~ **out** n plafonnement m; (Stock) fléchissement de la hausse m; ~-**up clause** n (Bank) condition au plus haut f

top-up: ~ **card** n carte téléphonique prépayée f; ~ **loan** n prêt complémentaire m

tort n délit m; ~ **liability** n responsabilité délictuelle f, responsabilité extracontractuelle f

total¹ adj total; (effect) global

total² n total m; **in** ~ au total; **it comes to a** ~ **of 4,000 euros** cela fait 4 000 euros en tout

total³ vt (add up) additionner, totaliser; (come to, reach) s'élever à, se monter à

total: ~ **allowable catches** n pl (fishing) prises totales autorisées f pl; ~ **amount** n (of bill) montant m; ~ **assets** n pl total de l'actif m; ~ **capitalization** n capitalisation globale f; ~ **cost** n coût total m; ~ **effective exposure** n (in advertising) exposition réelle totale f; ~ **estimates** n pl total des prévisions m/f; ~ **income** n revenu total m; ~ **liabilities** n pl total des créditeurs m, total des emprunts et dettes m; ~ **loss** n perte totale f; ~ **net flow** n flux net total m; ~ **net redemption** n (Bank) remboursement total net m; ~ **public debt** n dette publique globale f, dette publique totale f, total de la

dette publique m; ~ **public spending** n dépenses publiques globales f pl, totalité des dépenses publiques f; ~ **quality control** n contrôle de la qualité totale m; ~ **quality management** n gestion de la qualité totale f; ~ **revenue** n recette totale f, revenu total m; ~ **social charges** n pl montant des sommes versées à la sécurité sociale m; ~ **sum** n somme totale f; ~ **to date** n cumul jusqu'à ce jour m, total cumulé m; ~ **votes cast** n pl total de suffrages exprimés m; ~ **wages and salaries** n montant de la masse salariale m

totalize vt (numbers, amount) totaliser

totalling n totalisation f

tot: ~ **up** vt (numbers, amounts) additionner; ~ **up to** s'élever à

touch¹ n (Stock) touche f; **keep in** ~ **with** rester en relation avec; **get in** ~ **with sb** se mettre en contact avec qn; **lose** ~ **with sb** perdre contact avec qn; **put sb in** ~ **with** mettre qn en contact avec; **I'll be in** ~ je vous contacterai; **be out of** ~ (dated) ne pas être dans le coup (infrml); **lose one's** ~ perdre la main

touch² vt (reach) atteindre; ~ **off** (argument, disturbance) déclencher

touch: ~-**and-go** adj (risky) hasardeux/-euse, très risqué; ~ **pad** n (Comp) touchpad m; ~ **screen** n (Comp) écran tactile m; ~-**sensitive** adj (screen) tactile; (key) à effleurement

touchline n: **on the** ~ sur la touche

touchpad n (Comp) touchpad m

touch-type vi taper au toucher

tough adj (conditions) dur; (law, measure, policy) strict, sévère; (situation, decision, task) difficile; (challenge) redoutable; **have a** ~ **time** traverser une période difficile; ~ **competition** n forte concurrence f; ~ **competitor** n concurrent/-e dangereux/-euse m/f; ~ **stance** n position inflexible f

tough²: ~ **out** vt (crisis) surmonter; (recession) faire face à; ~ **it out** tenir le coup (infrml)

tour n (trip) excursion f; (by inspectors, team) tournée f; (of building) visite f; ~ **operator**, ~ **organizer** n voyagiste m, tour-opérateur m; ~ **of inspection** tournée d'inspection f

tourism n tourisme m

tourist n touriste mf; ~ **attraction** n site touristique m; ~ **class** n classe touriste f; ~ **information bureau** n, ~ **information office** n, ~ **office** n syndicat d'initiative m; ~ **season** n saison touristique f; ~ **tax** n taxe de séjour f; ~ **trade** n tourisme m; ~ **visa** n visa de tourisme m

Tourist Board n UK office du tourisme m

tout¹ n (for custom) racoleur/-euse m/f; (ticket seller) revendeur/-euse de billets au marché noir m/f

tout² vi (for custom) accoster des clients,

racoler; **∼ for trade** accoster des clients

tow¹ *n* remorquage *m*; **on ∼** en remorque

tow² *vt* remorquer

towage charges *n pl* frais de remorquage *m pl*

towboat *n* remorqueur *m*

tower block *n* tour d'habitation *f*

towing *n* remorquage *m*, tractage *m*

town *n* ville *f*; **out of ∼** (shop) en dehors de la ville; **∼ center** AmE, **∼ centre** BrE *n* centre-ville *m*; **∼ councillor** *n* conseiller/ -ère municipal/-e *m/f*; **∼ and country planning** *n* UK aménagement du territoire *m*; **∼ hall** *n* mairie *f*; **∼ planner** *n* BrE urbaniste *mf*; **∼ planning** *n* BrE urbanisme *m*

towtruck *n* AmE dépanneuse *f*

toxic *adj* toxique; **∼ effect** *n* effet toxique *m*; **∼ waste** *n* déchets toxiques *m pl*

toxicity *n* toxicité *f*

TP *abbr* (▸**third party**) tierce personne *f*, tiers *m*

TQC *abbr* (▸**total quality control**) contrôle de la qualité totale *m*

TQM *abbr* (▸**total quality management**) gestion de la qualité totale *f*

trace *vt* (follow trail) suivre la trace de; (locate) retrouver; (fault, malfunction) dépister; (Transp) localiser; (development, growth) faire l'historique de; **∼ sth back to** faire remonter qch jusqu'à; **∼ a call** déterminer l'origine d'un appel; **∼ a payment** trouver une trace d'un paiement

traceability *n* traçabilité *f*

traceable *adj* traçable; **be ∼ to** provenir de

track¹ *n* (Transp) voie *f*; **be on ∼** (talks, negotiations) se dérouler comme prévu; (project) progresser comme prévu; **be on the right ∼** être sur la bonne voie; **be on the wrong ∼** faire fausse route; **keep ∼ of** (events, developments) se tenir au courant de; (person, client) tenir à jour les détails concernant; (order) suivre; **lose ∼ of** (file, document, person) perdre la trace de

track² *vt* (earnings, expenditure, outlay) faire le suivi de; (developments, events) suivre, se tenir au courant de; (customer) tenir à jour les détails concernant; (order) suivre, suivre le parcours de; **∼ down** retrouver

trackball *n* boule de commande *f*

tracker fund *n* (Fin, Stock) tracker *m*, fonds indiciel *m*

tracking *n* (of sales, costs, order, expenses) suivi *m*; **∼ system** *n* système de suivi *m*, système de repérage *m*

track record (of company) antécédents *m pl*; (of employee) antécédents professionnels *m pl*; **have a proven ∼ in marketing** avoir une expérience confirmée en marketing

tradable *adj* (product) marchand; **∼**

promissory note *n* bon à ordre négociable *m*; **∼ Treasury bond** *n* bon du Trésor négociable *m*

trade¹ *n* commerce *m*; (Econ) commerce *m*, échanges commerciaux *m pl*; (job) métier *m*; (sector of activity) industrie *f*; (swap) échange *m*, troc *m*; **do ∼ with sb** faire du commerce avec qn; **do good ∼** faire de bonnes affaires; **the pharmaceutical ∼** l'industrie pharmaceutique; **∼ is good** les affaires marchent bien; **be in the pharmaceuticals ∼** travailler dans l'industrie pharmaceutique

trade² **1** *vt* (exchange) échanger, troquer; **∼ one thing for another** échanger une chose contre une autre

2 *vi* (countries, companies) avoir des relations commerciales; (Stock) négocier; **∼ as** faire du commerce sous le nom de; **∼ at** (Stock) se négocier, coter; **∼ at a profit/loss** vendre à profit/perte; **∼ for one's account** intervenir en Bourse pour son propre compte; **∼ in** (commodity) faire le commerce de; (item, product) vendre; **∼ in stocks and bonds** être opérateur en Bourse; **∼ under the name of** (Stock) négocier pour le compte de; **∼ with sb** faire du commerce avec, avoir des relations commerciales avec; **∼ down** acheter quelque chose de moins cher; **∼ in** (old model) vendre en reprise; **∼ off** faire un compromis; **∼ sth off against sth** peser le pour et le contre entre qch et qch; **∼ on** (image, name) exploiter; **∼ up** acheter quelque chose de plus cher

trade: **∼ acceptance** *n* acceptation commerciale *f*; **∼ account** *n* solde commercial *m*; **∼ agreement** *n* accord commercial *m*, traité commercial *m*; **∼ association** *n* association professionnelle *f*; **∼ balance** *n* balance commerciale *f*, balance du commerce extérieur *f*, excédent commercial *m*, solde extérieur *m*; **∼ barrier** *n* barrière douanière *f*; **∼ bill** *n* titre commercial *m*; **∼ book** *n* ouvrage d'intérêt général *m*; **∼ channel** *n* circuit commercial *m*; **∼ credit** *n* crédit commercial *m*; **∼ creditor** *n* fournisseur *m*; **∼ creditors** *n pl* BrE comptes clients *m pl*, poste clients *m*; **∼ cycle** *n* cycle économique *m*; **∼ date** *n* (Stock) date de l'opération *f*; **∼ deficit** *n* déficit de la balance commerciale *m*, déficit extérieur *m*; **∼ description** *n* descriptif des marchandises à vendre *m*; **∼ directory** *n* annuaire du commerce *m*; **∼ discount** *n* (on volume) rabais de gros *m*; (to trader, dealer) remise professionnelle *f*; **∼ embargo** *n* embargo commercial *m*; **∼ exhibition** *n* (for professionals) salon professionnel *m*; (public) foire commerciale *f*; **∼ facilitation** *n* facilitation des échanges *f*; **∼ fair** *n* (for professionals) salon professionnel *m*; (public) foire commerciale *f*; **∼ figures** *n pl* (domestic, overseas trade) chiffres de commerce *m pl*; (of company) chiffre d'affaires *m*; **∼ financing** *n* ⋯⟩

t

financement des opérations commerciales m,
financement du commerce extérieur m; ~
flow n (international) flux commercial m,
volume d'échanges m; ~ **gap** n déséquilibre
commercial m; ~ **imbalance** n déséquilibre
commercial m; **~-in** n reprise f; **~-in price**
n prix avec reprise m; **~-in value** n valeur
de reprise f; ~ **journal** n revue
professionnelle f; ~ **liberalization**
libéralisation des échanges f; ~ **magazine** n
revue professionnelle f; ~ **mart** n
expomarché m; ~ **mission** n mission
commerciale f; ~ **name** n marque f, marque
de fabrique f; **~-off** n (between two things)
compromis m; (exchange) échange m; ~
organization n organisation professionnelle
f; ~ **paper** n (Fin) effet de commerce m;
(publication) revue professionnelle f; ~
paperback n livre broché de qualité
supérieure au livre de poche; ~ **policy** n
politique commerciale f; ~ **practices** n pl
pratiques commerciales f pl, pratiques et
conventions du secteur f pl; ~ **press** n
presse spécialisée f; ~ **price** n prix
marchand m; ~ **promotion** n promotion
auprès des détaillants f, promotion-réseau f;
~ **register** n registre du commerce m; ~
regulations n pl réglementation
commerciale f; ~ **relations** n pl relations
économiques f pl; ~ **representative** n
délégué/-e commercial/-e m/f; ~ **restriction**
n restriction commerciale f, restriction du
commerce f; ~ **returns** n pl statistiques
commerciales f pl; ~ **route** n route
commerciale f; ~ **sanctions** n pl sanctions
commerciales f pl; ~ **secret** n secret
commercial m; ~ **show** n salon
interprofessionnel m; ~ **strategy** n stratégie
commerciale f; ~ **surplus** n excédent
commercial m; ~ **talks** n pl négociations
commerciales f pl; ~ **terms** n pl conditions
de vente f pl; ~ **ticket** n (Stock) fiche d'ordre
f; ~ **union** n UK syndicat m; ~ **union act** n
UK loi sur les syndicats f; ~ **union dues**
n pl UK cotisation syndicale f; ~ **union**
membership n adhésion à un syndicat f; ~
union movement n UK mouvement syndical
m; ~ **union representative** n UK délégué/-e
syndical/-e m/f; ~ **unionism** n UK
syndicalisme m; ~ **volume** n volume des
échanges commerciaux m; ~ **war** n guerre
commerciale f; ~ **week** n semaine
commerciale f

Trade: ~ **Descriptions Act** n UK loi
protégeant les consommateurs contre la
publicité mensongère; **~s Union Congress** n
UK confédération des syndicats britanniques

traded option n option négociable f

trademark n (Law, Patents, S&M) marque f,
marque de fabrique f; **registered ~** marque
déposée f

trader n (shopkeeper) commerçant/-e m/f; (in
consumer goods) marchand/-e m/f; (large-scale)
négociant/-e m/f; (Stock) opérateur/-trice m/f

tradesman n commerçant m

tradespeople n pl commerçants m pl

trading n (Econ, S&M) commerce m, négoce
m; (business) activité commerciale f,
commerce m; (Stock) transactions
(boursières) f pl; ~ **is quiet/heavy** (Stock) la
Bourse est calme/agitée; ~ **in wine** négoce du
vin m; ~ **account** n compte d'exploitation
m; ~ **activity** n (Stock) activité du marché f;
~ **area** n secteur de vente m; (S&M)
territoire de vente m; ~ **authorization** n
autorisation d'exercer un commerce f; ~
bloc n bloc commercial m; ~ **company** n
entreprise commerciale f; (Imp/Exp) société
d'import-export f, société d'importation f; ~
day n (Fin) séance (boursière) f; ~ **debts**
n pl créances f pl, créances commerciales f
pl; ~ **desk** n pupitre de négociation m; ~
dividends n pl dividendes négociés m pl,
opérations de dividendes f pl; ~ **estate** n
zone industrielle f; ~ **floor** n corbeille f,
parquet m; ~ **halt** n arrêt des opérations m,
suspension des transactions f; ~ **hours** n pl
heures de bourse f pl, heures de négociation
f pl; ~ **income** n revenu brut m; ~ **losses**
n pl pertes d'exploitation f pl; ~ **name** n
nom commercial m; ~ **operations** n pl
opérations en Bourse f pl; ~ **partner** n
partenaire commercial m; ~ **pattern** n
tendance du marché f; ~ **pit** n corbeille f,
parquet m; ~ **port** n port de commerce m; ~
portfolio n portefeuille d'actions m; ~ **post**
n (Stock) poste de négociation f; ~ **range** n
(commodities, securities) fourchette des prix
limites de transaction f, éventail des
négociations m; ~ **results** n pl (of company)
chiffre d'affaires m; ~ **room** n salle de
marché f; ~ **security** n valeur boursière f,
valeur négociée f; ~ **session** n séance de
bourse f, séance de négociation f; ~
standards n pl normes commerciales f pl;
~ **volume** n volume des opérations m,
volume des transactions m; ~ **year** n
exercice m, exercice social m

Trading Standards Office n UK
direction de la concurrence et de la protection
du consommateur f

tradition n tradition f

traditional adj traditionnel/-elle

traffic[1] n (on the streets) circulation f;
(vehicle/vessel movements) trafic m; (dealing)
trafic m; (Comms, Comp) trafic m; **air/freight**
~ trafic aérien/de frêt; ~ **builder** n (in
advertising) article d'appel m; ~ **congestion** n
embouteillage m, encombrement m; ~ **count**
n (in advertising) comptage de la circulation m;
~ **density** n (Transp) densité de la
circulation f; (Comms, Comp) densité du trafic
f; ~ **flow** n (Transp) intensité de la
circulation f; (Comms, Comp) intensité du
trafic f; ~ **jam** n embouteillage m; ~
manager n (on website) responsable du trafic
mf; ~ **planning** n (in advertising) gestion des
flux de travail f; ~ **sign** n panneau de

signalisation m; ~ **time** n (in advertising) heure de grande écoute f

traffic²: ~ **in** vt (arms, explosives, drugs) faire le commerce de

trafficker n trafiquant/-e m/f

trail vt (broadcast) annoncer

trailblazing adj (firm, industry) innovateur/-trice

trailer n (on television, in cinema) bande-annonce f; (Transp) remorque f

train¹ n train m; **a** ~ **of events** une série d'événements; ~ **fare** n prix du billet m; ~ **service** n service ferroviaire m; ~ **station** n BrE gare f; ~ **strike** n grève des chemins de fer f; ~ **ticket** n billet de train m

train² [1] vt former; ~ **sb for sth** former qn pour qch; **she's** ~**ing as an engineer, she's** ~**ing to be an engineer** elle fait des études d'ingénieur
[2] vi suivre une formation, étudier; ~ **up** (employee) former

trained adj (worker, staff) qualifié; (professional) diplômé; **highly** ~ hautement qualifié

trainee n stagiaire mf; ~ **manager** n cadre en formation m/f; ~ **solicitor** n UK avocat/-e stagiaire m, cadre stagiaire m

traineeship n poste de stagiaire m

trainer n formateur/-trice m/f

training n formation f; **staff** ~ formation du personnel; **receive computer** ~ suivre une formation en informatique; '~ **will be given'** (in advert) 'formation assurée'; ~ **center** AmE, ~ **centre** BrE n centre de formation m; ~ **course** n stage de formation professionnelle m; ~ **needs** n pl besoins en formation m pl; ~ **needs analysis** n analyse des besoins en formation f; ~ **officer** n directeur/-trice de formation m/f, responsable de la formation professionnelle mf; ~ **pack** n dossier de formation m; ~ **program** AmE, ~ **programme** BrE n programme de formation m; ~ **scheme** n plan de formation m; ~ **within industry** n formation dans l'entreprise f

Training and Enterprise Council n UK *organisme gérant des programmes de formation professionnelle en entreprise*

trainload n cargaison f

transact vt (sale, contract) négocier; ~ **business with sb** traiter avec qn, faire des affaires avec qn

transaction n (Gen Comm, Fin) transaction f; (sale) transaction f, (Bank) transaction f, opération f; (Stock) opération f; **make a** ~ faire une opération, faire une transaction; **the** ~ **of business** les relations d'affaires f pl; ~**s with clients** la relation clientèle f; ~ **cost** n (Bank) frais par opération m pl; ~ **costs** n pl frais de transaction m pl; ~ **data** n données de mouvement f pl; ~ **date** n date de l'opération f; ~ **fee** n frais de transaction m pl; ~ **file** n fichier de transactions m,

fichier mouvements m; ~ **management** n gestion transactionnelle f; ~ **processing** n traitement de mouvements m, traitement transactionnel m; ~ **risk** n risque d'opération en Bourse m; ~ **status** n état d'avancement des opérations m; ~ **tax** n impôt de Bourse m

transactional adj transactionnel/-elle; ~ **analysis** n analyse transactionnelle f; ~ **site** n (Comp) site transactionnel m

transcode vt transcoder

transcoder n transcodeur m

transcribe vt transcrire

transcript n copie conforme f

transcription n transcription f

transeuropean adj (network, trade) transeuropéen/-éenne

transfer¹ n (of funds) virement m, transfert m, transfert de fonds m; (of data, goods, skills, information, responsibilities) transfert m; (of employee) transfert m; (of civil servant) mutation f; (Patents) transfert m; (Prop) cession f; (Stock) virement m, transfert m; (document) autorisation de virement f, formulaire de transfert m; (Transp) transfert m; ~ **account** n compte de virement m; ~ **of assets** n transfert d'actif m; ~ **charge call** n appel en PCV m; ~ **deed** n (Law, Prop) acte de cession m, acte de translation m; (Stock) feuille de transfert f; ~ **desk** n (Transp) bureau de transit m; ~ **earnings** n pl gains d'opportunité m pl; ~ **fee** n montant du transfert m; ~ **income** n revenu de transfert m; ~ **order** n (Bank) ordre de transfert m, ordre de virement m; ~ **passenger** n voyageur/-euse en transit m/f; ~ **payment** n paiement de transfert m; ~ **price** n prix de cession m, prix de cession interne m; ~ **pricing** n fixation de prix de cession interne f; ~ **rate** n (Comp) taux de transfert m, vitesse de transfert f; ~ **register** n (Stock) registre des transferts m; ~ **of technology** n transfert de technologie m

transfer² [1] vt (office, employee) transférer; (civil servant) muter; (data) transférer; (debt) transporter; (funds) transférer, virer; (recopy) reporter; (Comms) (call) faire passer; (property, power) céder; ~ **by endorsement** transférer par endossement; ~ **the charges** téléphoner en PCV m; ~ **ownership** céder la propriété; **I'll** ~ **you to our after-sales service** je vous passe le service après-vente
[2] vi (office, employee) être transféré; (civil servant) être muté; (change aircraft) changer d'avion; (change train) changer de train

transferable adj (property, right, asset) cessible; (Stock) négociable, transférable; (skill, right) transmissible; **not** ~ (Stock) non transférable; ~ **credit** n crédit transférable m; ~ **loan certificate** n certificat d'emprunt cessible m, certificat de prêt transférable m; ~ **loan instrument** n instrument d'emprunt cessible m, instrument de prêt transférable ⸱⸱⸱⸵

m; ∼ **securities** n pl valeurs mobilières f pl, valeurs transférables f pl

transferee n cessionnaire mf; ∼ **company** n société cessionnaire f

transferor n (Law) cédant/-e m/f; (Stock) vendeur/-euse m/f; ∼ **company** n société cédante f

transferred share n action transférée f

transferrer n (Law) cédant/-e m/f

transform vt transformer

transformation industry n industrie de transformation f

transfrontier adj transfrontalier/-ière

tranship vt ▸transship

transhipment n ▸transshipment

transient adj temporaire; ∼ **medium** n média éphémère m; ∼ **population** n population de passage f; ∼ **worker** n travailleur/-euse migrant/-e m/f

transit n transit m; **in** ∼ en transit; ∼ **bond note** n acquit de transit m; ∼ **credit** n crédit transitaire m; ∼ **document** n document de transit m; ∼ **lounge** n salle de transit f; ∼ **market** n marché de transit m; ∼ **passenger** n voyageur/-euse en transit m/f; ∼ **rights** n pl droits de transit m pl; ∼ **time** n durée de transport f; ∼ **trade** n commerce transitaire m; ∼ **traffic** n trafic de transit m

transition n transition f; ∼ **period** n période transitoire f

transitional adj transitionnel/-elle; ∼ **period** n période de transition f; ∼ **relief** n (Tax) allègement transitoire m

transitory adj (phase, stage) transitoire; ∼ **income** n revenu transitoire m

translate vt (text, words) traduire; (measurement, currency) convertir

translation n (of text, words) traduction f; (of measurement, currency) conversion f; ∼ **agency** n agence de traduction f; ∼ **differential** n écart de conversion m; ∼ **rate** n taux de conversion m; ∼ **risk** n risque de conversion m

translator n (Comp) programme de traduction m; (person) traducteur/-trice m/f

transmission n (of data) transmission f; (Media) (broadcast) émission f

transmit vt transmettre

transmittal letter n lettre de transmission f, lettre d'accompagnement f

transmitter n (Comms) émetteur m

transnational adj transnational; ∼ **corporation** n entreprise transnationale f, société transnationale f

transparency n transparence f; ∼ **of information** transparence de l'information f

transparent adj (person, plans, process, decision-making) transparent

transplant vt transplanter

transplant factory n usine transplantée f

transport[1] n transport m; (vehicle) voiture m; **air/rail** ∼ transport aérien/ferroviaire; ∼ **advertising** n publicité dans les moyens de transport f; ∼ **agent** n transitaire mf; ∼ **company** n entreprise de transport f; ∼ **costs** n pl frais de transport m pl; ∼ **document** n (shipping) document de transport m; ∼ **facilities** n pl moyens de transport m pl; ∼ **insurance** n assurance contre les risques de transport f; ∼ **mode** n mode de transport m, moyen de transport m; ∼ **secretary** n ministre des transports m/f; ∼ **services** n pl services de transport m pl; ∼ **tax** n taxe de transport f; ∼ **unit** n unité de transport f

transport[2] vt transporter; ∼ **by air** transporter par avion

transportable adj transportable

Transport and General Workers' Union n UK syndicat des transports et des travailleurs confédérés m

transportation n transport m; ∼ **advertising** n publicité dans les moyens de transport f; ∼ **document** n document de transport m; ∼ **expenses** n pl frais de transport m pl; ∼ **services** n services de transport m pl; ∼ **system** n système de transport m

transposal n (Law, Pol) (EU) transposition f

transpose vt intervertir

transposition n interversion f; ∼ **error** n erreur d'interversion f

transship vt transborder

transshipment n transbordement m; ∼ **bill of lading** n connaissement de transbordement m

travel[1] n voyages m pl; **business/overseas** ∼ voyages d'affaires/à l'étranger; **the work involves** ∼ le travail exige des déplacements; ∼ **agency** n agence de voyages f; ∼ **agent** n agent de voyage m; ∼ **allowance** n indemnité de déplacement f; ∼ **card** n carte de transport f; ∼ **claim** n demande de remboursement de frais de déplacement f; ∼ **document** n document de voyage m; ∼ **expense claim** n demande de remboursement de frais de déplacement f; ∼ **expenses** n pl frais de déplacement m pl; ∼ **insurance** n assurance voyage f; ∼ **restriction** n restriction de voyage f; ∼ **services** n pl services de transports m pl; ∼ **voucher** n bon de voyage m

travel[2] [1] vt (country, distance, area) parcourir [2] vi voyager; ∼ **abroad** aller à l'étranger; ∼ **to France** aller en France

traveler n AmE ▸traveller BrE

traveling n AmE ▸travelling BrE

traveller n BrE voyageur/-euse m/f; ∼**'s cheque** n BrE chèque de voyage m

travelling n BrE voyages m pl; ∼ **allowance** n indemnité de déplacement f;

~ expenses n pl frais de déplacement m pl;
~ salesman n voyageur de commerce m; **~
salesperson** n voyageur/-euse de commerce
m/f; **~ saleswoman** n voyageuse de
commerce f

traverse vt (Law) contester

travolator n AmE tapis roulant m, trottoir
roulant m

trawler n chalutier m

treasurer n trésorier/-ière m/f; **company ~**
directeur/-trice, financier/-ière m/f; **~ check**
AmE, **~ cheque** BrE n chèque bancaire m;
~'s report n rapport financier m

Treasury n UK ≈ ministère des Finances m;
~ bill n US bon du Trésor à court terme m;
~ bill futures n contrat à terme de bons du
Trésor m; **~ bill rate** n taux de bons du
Trésor m; **~ bill tender** n UK adjudication
de bons du Trésor f; **~ Board** n Conseil du
Trésor m; **~ bond** n US bon du Trésor à long
terme m, obligation du Trésor f; **~
Department** n US ≈ ministère des Finances
m; **~ model** n prévisions économiques f pl;
~ note n billet de trésorerie m; **~ stock** n
US actions rachetées par la société f pl; **~
swap** n échange cambiste m

treat vt traiter; **~ oneself to sth** (infrml)
s'offrir qch

treaty n traité m; **enter into a ~ with**
conclure un traité avec; **for sale by private
~** à vendre de gré à gré; **~ reinsurance** n
réassurance générale f; **~ shopping** n (Tax)
chalandage fiscal m

treble adj triple

tree diagram n arbre m, arborescence f

tremendous adj formidable

trend n (Econ) tendance f, évolution f;
(fashion) mode f; **set a ~** lancer une mode;
follow a ~ suivre la mode; **the ~ towards
smaller families** la tendance en faveur des
familles moins nombreuses; **an upward/
downward ~** une tendance à la hausse/
baisse; **a ~ towards doing** une tendance à
faire; **a ~ away from** un désintérêt pour; **~
analysis** n analyse de tendance f; **~ analyst**
n prospectiviste mf; **~ of events** cours des
choses m, tournure des événements f; **~
reversal** n renversement de la tendance m

trendsetter n innovateur/-trice m/f,
personne qui crée la mode f; **be a ~** lancer
des modes

trendsetting n création d'une mode f,
lancement d'une mode m

trendy adj UK (infrml) branché (infrml), à la
mode

trespass vi s'introduire illégalement; **~ on
private property** entrer sans autorisation
dans une propriété privée; (Law) violer une
propriété privée

trespasser n intrus/-e m/f

trespassing n (Law) violation de propriété
f; **'no ~'** 'défense d'entrer', 'propriété privée'

trial n (Gen Comm, Ind, S&M) essai m; (Law)
procès m; (of drug, product, process) test m; **give
sb a ~** mettre qn à l'essai; **stand ~** (Law)
passer en jugement; **be on ~** (Law) être jugé;
go on ~ passer en jugement; **go to ~** (case)
être jugé; **take sth on ~** prendre qch à
l'essai; **carry out ~s** effectuer des essais,
effectuer des tests; **by ~ and error** par
expérience; **~ attorney** n US avocat/-e m/f;
~ examiner n juge médiateur m; **~ jury** n
US jury m; **~ lawyer** n US avocat/-e m/f; **~
offer** n offre d'essai f; **~ period** n période
d'essai f; **~ run** n (Gen Comm) essai m; (of
car) essai sur route m; **~ subscriber** n
abonné/-e à l'essai m/f; **~ subscription** n
abonnement à l'essai m

triangular adj (agreement, merger)
triangulaire

triangulation n triangulation f

tri-band adj tri-bande

tribunal n tribunal m; **~ of enquiry** n
commission d'enquête f

trick n (secret) astuce f; **the ~s of the trade**
les ficelles du métier f pl

trickle¹ n (of orders, funds) petite quantité f;
~ down theory n théorie selon laquelle la
richesse de quelques-uns apporte des bénéfices
à toutes les couches sociales

trickle²: ~ back vi (customers, clients)
retourner lentement; **~ in** vi (offers, letters)
arriver au compte-gouttes

trifling adj insignifiant

trigger¹ n déclencheur m; **act as a ~ for
sth** déclencher qch; **~ mechanism** n
dispositif de déclenchement m; **~ point** n
point de déclenchement m; **~ price** n prix
minimum à l'importation m; **~ pricing** n
fixation d'un prix de déclenchement f

trigger² vt déclencher

trim vt (reduce) réduire; **~ the workforce**
dégraisser le personnel, réduire le personnel

trimmings n pl garnitures f pl; **with no ~**
sans fioritures

tripack n lot de trois m, paquet de trois m

tripartism n concentration tripartite f

triple vt tripler

triple-A bond n obligation notée AAA f

triple-A-rated adj (customer) classé AAA

triple-A rating n classification AAA f

triplicate n **in ~** (document) en trois
exemplaires

trouble¹ n (problem) problèmes m pl;
(breakdown) panne f; (personal) ennuis m pl;
(difficulties) difficultés f pl; (effort) peine f; **be in
~** (company) avoir des difficultés; (person)
avoir des ennuis, avoir des problèmes; **get
out of ~** se tirer d'affaire; **go to a lot of ~**
se donner beaucoup de mal; **have a lot of ~**
avoir beaucoup de problèmes; **have ~ doing**
avoir du mal à faire; **take the ~ to do** se
donner la peine de faire; **be more ~ than it's
worth** donner plus de mal qu'il en vaut la ⋯⟶

peine; ~ **spot** n point noir m

trouble² vt déranger

trouble-free adj be ~ (vehicle, device) marcher sans problèmes

troublemaker n fauteur/-trice de troubles m/f

troubleshoot vi (Gen Comm) intervenir pour régler des problèmes; (locate a fault) localiser une panne

troubleshooter n (technician) expert m; (in business, industry) consultant/-e en gestion des entreprises m/f, redresseur d'entreprises m

troubleshooting n (fault diagnosis) dépannage m; (in an organization) intervention pour règler les problèmes f; (by consultants) redressement d'entreprises m

trough¹ n (of graph, curve) creux m, point bas m

trough² vi atteindre son point le plus bas

troy: ~ **ounce** n once troy f; ~ **weight** n poids troy m

truck n camion m; ~ **driver** n chauffeur de camion m, routier m; ~ **farmer** n AmE maraîcher m; ~ **farming** n AmE maraîchage m; ~ **service** n vol camionné m

truckage n camionnage m

trucker n chauffeur de camion m, routier m

trucking n vol camionné m; ~ **bill of lading** n lettre de voiture f; ~ **charges** n pl frais de camionnage m pl; ~ **company** n entreprise de camionnage f, entreprise de transport routier f

truckload n cargaison f

true adj vrai; (loyal) fidèle; ~ **copy** n (of document) copie conforme f; ~ **and fair** adj (audit) fidèle; ~ **and fair view** n BrE image fidèle f; ~ **lease** n bail conforme m; ~ **owner** n propriétaire légitime m/f; ~ **to sample** adj conforme à l'échantillon

trump card n atout m; **play one's** ~ jouer son atout

truncate vt tronquer

trunk n AmE (of car) coffre m; ~ **call** n UK communication interurbaine f, communication à longue distance f; ~ **road** n route principale f

trust¹ n (group of companies) trust m; (faith) confiance f; (Law) fidéicommis m; (Bank) fiducie f; **a position of** ~ un poste de confiance; **put one's** ~ **in** se fier à; **have complete** ~ **in** avoir une confiance absolue en; **I'll take it on** ~ je vous crois sur parole; ~ **account** n compte en fiducie m; ~ **agreement** n convention de fiducie f; ~ **company** n compagnie fiduciaire f, société de fiducie f; ~ **deed** n acte de fidéicommis m; ~ **fund** n fonds en fidéicommis m pl; ~ **instrument** n instrument créateur d'un fidéicommis m; ~ **mortgage** n hypothèque fiduciaire f; ~ **share** n participation partielle f; ~ **unit** n (Stock) part de fiducie f

trust² vt (believe) se fier à; (rely on) faire confiance à

trustbuster n US fonctionnaire fédéral chargé de l'application des lois antitrust

trustbusting n US (infml) action antitrust f

trusted third party n tierce partie de confiance f, tiers de confiance m

trustee n (of company) administrateur/-trice m/f; (Bank) syndic m; (Law) fiduciaire m/f; curateur m; ~ **in bankruptcy** syndic de faillite m

trusteeship n fidéicommis m

trustify vt réunir en trust

trustworthiness n honnêteté f, loyauté f

trustworthy adj (employee, company) sérieux/-ieuse; (person) digne de confiance, loyal; (account, source) fiable

truth n vérité f; ~ **in lending** n (Bank) transparence bancaire en matière de prêts f

truthfulness n sincérité f

try¹ n essai m; **have a** ~ essayer; **give sth a** ~ essayer qch

try² **1** vt essayer; (person) prendre à l'essai; (Law) (case, suspect) juger
2 vi (attempt) essayer; (ask) demander

TTC abbr (►**tender to contract**) soumission d'offre f

T-test n test t m

TTP abbr (►**trusted third party**) tierce partie de confiance f, tiers de confiance m

TU abbr UK (►**trade union**) syndicat m

TUC abbr UK (►**Trades Union Congress**) confédération des syndicats britanniques

tug n remorqueur m; ~**-of-war** n épreuve de force f

tugrik n tugrik m

tuition n cours m pl; ~ **fees** n pl frais pédagogiques m pl

tumble vi (cost, price, share, currency) chuter

tuning n (of business procedures) réglage m

tunnel n (Econ) tunnel m

turf war n guerre des territoires f

turn¹ n (in rotation) tour m; **the** ~ **of events** la tournure des événements f; (Stock) différence offert-demandé f, écart m; ~ **for the better** amélioration f; ~ **for the worse** aggravation f; **take a** ~ **for the better** (person, situation) s'améliorer; **take a** ~ **for the worse** (situation) se dégrader

turn² **1** vt (Gen Comm) tourner; ~ **sth into** convertir qch en; ~ **one's attention to** porter son attention à
2 vi tourner; ~ **to sb/sth** tourner vers qn/qch; ~ **around** vt (economy, situation, company) redresser; (factory, party) redresser la situation de; vi (business, company) se redresser; ~ **away** (candidate, applicant) refuser; ~ **away business** refuser des clients; ~ **down** vt (offer, request, proposal) rejeter; **they** ~**ed him down for the job** ils lui ont refusé le poste; vi (sales)

chuter; ～ **in** (profit) réaliser, rapporter;
(submit) soumettre; ～ **in a good performance**
(company) avoir de bons résultats; ～ **off**
éteindre; ～ **on** allumer, mettre en marche;
～ **out** *vt* (produce) fabriquer, produire; (train)
former; *vi* (end) ～ **out well/badly** bien/mal se
terminer; ～ **out to be** se révéler, s'avérer; **it**
～**s out that...** il s'avère que...; ～ **out to vote**
aller voter; ～ **over** (Fin) (sum) faire un chiffre
d'affaires de; ～ **round** (company) redresser;
the company has ～ed itself round
l'entreprise s'est redressée; ～ **up** (opportunity,
job) se présenter

turnabout *n* revirement *m*

turnaround *n* AmE ▸**turnround** BrE

turning point *n* point décisif *m*

turnkey *adj* (system, project) clés en main; ～
contract *n* contrat clés en main *m*; ～
solution *n* solution clés en main *f*

turnout *n* (in election) participation *f*

turnover *n* (volume of business) chiffre
d'affaires *m*; (of stock) rotation *f*; (of staff)
rotation *f*, turnover *m*; ～ **rate** *n* vitesse de
rotation *f*; ～ **ratio** *n* rapport chiffre
d'affaires-immobilisations *m*; ～ **tax** *n* impôt
sur le chiffre d'affaires *m*

turnpike *n* AmE autoroute à péage *f*

turnround *n* BrE (Fin) redressement *m*; (in a
trend) volte-face *f*, revirement *m*; (of ship)
rotation *f*; ～ **time** BrE (Transp) durée de
rotation *f*

TV *abbr* (▸**television**) télé *f* (infrml); ～
advertising *n* publicité télévisée *f*; ～
campaign *n* campagne publicitaire télévisée
f; ～ **commercial** *n* message publicitaire
télévisé *m*; ～ **network** *n* réseau de
télévision *m*; ～ **screen** *n* écran télé *m*

tweak *vt* améliorer, mettre au point,
peaufiner

twenty-four hour trading *n* (Stock)
marché ouvert 24 heures sur 24 *m*,
transactions 24h/24 *f pl*

twilight shift *n* BrE équipe de nuit *f*

twin room *n* chambre à deux lits *f*

twisting *n* (Fin) escroquerie *f*

two: ～**-digit inflation** *n* inflation à deux
chiffres *f*; ～**-tier** *adj* (structure, system) à deux
niveaux; (society, health service) à deux vitesses;
～**-way agreement** *n* accord bilatéral *m*;
～**-way split** *n* division en deux *f*; ～**-way
variance analysis** *n* analyse de variance à
deux sens *f*

tx. *abbr* (▸**telex**) télex *m*

txt msg *abbr* (▸**text message**) texto *m*
(infrml)

tycoon *n* magnat *m*

type[1] *n* (kind, sort) type *m*, genre *m*; (model,
make) marque *f*; (typography) caractères *m pl*; **in
bold** ～ en caractères gras; **in large/small** ～
en gros/petits caractères; ～ **of costs**
catégorie de coûts *f*

type[2] *vt* taper (à la machine); ～ **in** (word,
password) taper; (data) saisir, entrer; ～ **up**
(letter, report) taper

typeface *n* police de caractères *f*

typesetting *n* composition *f*

typewriter *n* machine à écrire *f*

typewritten *adj* dactylographié (frml), tapé
à la machine

typically *adv* typiquement

typify *vt* être caractéristique de

typing *n* dactylographie *f*; ～ **error** *n*
faute de frappe *f*; ～ **speed** *n* vitesse de
frappe *f*

typist *n* dactylographe *mf*, dactylo *mf*

typo *n* (infrml) coquille *f* (infrml)

Uu

UAWB *abbr* (▸**universal air waybill**)
LTAU *f* (lettre de transport aérien
universelle)

UKAEA *abbr* (▸**United Kingdom Atomic
Energy Authority**) agence de l'énergie
atomique du Royaume-Uni

ult. *abbr* (▸**ultimo**) du mois dernier

ultimate[1] *adj* (origin, cause) premier/-ière;
(decision, aim, effect, result) ultime; (loser, winner,
beneficiary) au bout du compte; (achievement,
sucess, power, responsibility) suprême; (consumer)
final; (product, car, holiday) dernier cri *inv*; ～
risk *n* (Bank) risque assumé en dernier

ressort *m*, risque ultime *m*

ultimate[2] *n* **the** ～ **in** le nec plus ultra de

ultimatum *n pl* **-ta** ultimatum *m*; **give sb
an** ～ donner un ultimatum à qn

ultimo *adv* (frml) du mois dernier

ultra-portable *adj* (laptop, device) ultra-
portable

ultra vires[1] *adj* **be** ～ (company) être en
dehors des statuts; (action, declaration)
constituer un excès de pouvoir; (contract) être
contraire aux statuts (de la société)

ultra vires[2] *adv* **act** ～ commettre un excès
de pouvoir

ultra vires: ~ **activities** n pl actes
effectués en dehors des statuts m pl; ~
borrowing n emprunt hors compétences m

umbrella n **under the** ~ **of** (protection) sous
la protection de; (authority) sous l'égide de; ~
committee n comité de coordination m; ~
fund n fonds cadre m, fonds de consolidation
m, fonds de coordination m; ~ **project** n
projet cadre m

UMTS abbr (**Universal Mobile Telephone
Service**) norme UMTS f, UMTS m

UN abbr (▸**United Nations**) ONU f
(Organisation des Nations Unies); ~
Security Council n Conseil de sécurité de
l'ONU m

UNA abbr (▸**United Nations Association**)
ANU f (Association des Nations Unies)

unabridged adj intégral

unacceptable adj (suggestion, idea)
inacceptable; (situation, behaviour) inadmissable

unaccepted adj non accepté

unaccompanied baggage n bagages
non accompagnés m pl

unaccounted adj **be** ~ **for** (be missing)
manquer; **be** ~ **for in the balance sheet**
(amount, item) ne pas apparaître dans le bilan

unaccounted-for adj inexpliqué

unacknowledged adj (letter, communication)
resté sans réponse; (contribution) non reconnu

unadjusted adj (data, statistics) brut; **in** ~
figures en données brutes non corrigées

unadvertised adj (not disclosed) sans
publicité

unadvisable adj déconseillé

unaffiliated adj (union) non affilié

unallocated adj disponible, non affecté

unallotted adj (shares) non attribué

unaltered adj inchangé; **remain** ~ rester
le/la même

unamortized adj (debt, discount) non amorti

unanimity n unanimité f

unanimous adj (decision) unanime; **be** ~ **in
doing** faire qch à l'unanimité

unanimously adv (approve, condemn)
unanimement; (vote) à l'unanimité; ~
accepted voté à l'unanimité

unanswered adj (call) resté sans réponse;
(letter, query) sans réponse

unanticipated adj imprévu

unappropriated adj non affecté; (profits)
non distribué

unapproved adj non approuvé; (dealer) non
agréé; ~ **funds** n pl fonds non agréés m pl

unassailable adj (conclusion, hypothesis)
irréfutable; (position) invulnérable

unassessed adj (revenue, income) non
imposé

unassignable adj (property, right)
inaliénable, incessible

unassured adj inassuré, non assuré

unattainable adj inaccessible

unaudited adj non audité, non vérifié

unauthenticated adj (document, signature)
non authentifié

unauthorized adj (expenditure, person) non
autorisé; ~ **access** n accès non autorisé m;
~ **shares** n pl actions non autorisées f pl

unavailability n (of person) indisponibilité f

unavailable adj non disponible,
indisponible; **be** ~ (person) ne pas être
disponible

unavoidable adj inévitable

unavoidably adv **be** ~ **absent** ne pas
pouvoir être présent; **be** ~ **detained** avoir
un empêchement

unbacked adj (account) non soldé

unbalanced adj (biased) partial; (uneven,
unstable) mal équilibré; ~ **growth** n
croissance mal équilibrée f

unbiased adj (advice, person, report)
impartial; **be** ~ (person) ne pas avoir de parti
pris

unblock vt (funds, grant, loan, prices)
débloquer, dégager

unbounded risk n risque illimité m

unbranded goods n pl produits libres
m pl, produits sans marque m pl

unbundle vt (goods) dégrouper; (group,
company) défusionner

unbundling n (of goods) dégroupage m; (of
group, company) défusionnement m

unbusinesslike adj (person) peu
commerçant; (conduct) contraire à la pratique
commerciale, irrégulier/-ière

uncallable adj non appelable

uncalled capital n capital non appelé m

uncashed check AmE, **uncashed
cheque** BrE n chèque non encaissé m

uncertainty n incertitude f

unchanged adj inchangé; **remain** ~ rester
le/la même

uncheck vt AmE (**Comp**) (box, option)
désactiver

unchecked[1] adj (figures) non vérifié;
(development) incontrôlé

unchecked[2] adv (spread, grow) de manière
incontrôlée

unchecked: ~ **baggage** n bagages non
enregistrés m pl; ~ **inflationary economy**
n économie inflationniste non contrôlée f

unclaimed: ~ **balance** n solde non
réclamé m; ~ **deposit** n dépôt non réclamé
m; ~ **letter** n lettre en souffrance f; ~ **right**
n droit non revendiqué m

uncleared adj (cheque) non compensé;
(Imp/Exp) (goods) non dédouané

uncollectable adj (Tax) non recouvrable,
irrécouvrable; ~ **account** n créance
irrécouvrable f, mauvaise créance f; ~ **taxes**
n pl impôts irrécouvrables m pl

uncollected adj (mail, property) non réclamé;

(welfare benefit) non réclamé; (tax) non perçu

uncommitted *adj* (voter, person) non engagé; (resources) non engagé; **~ funds** *n* fonds non engagés *m pl*

uncompromising *adj* (person, stance) intransigeant; (system) inflexible

unconditional *adj* (Law) inconditionnel/ -elle, sans condition, sans réserve; (offer, credit, withdrawal) sans condition; **~ acceptance** *n* acceptation inconditionnelle *f*

unconditionally *adv* (promise, lend) sans condition

unconfirmed *adj* (news, rumour, details) non confirmé; **~ credit** *n* crédit révocable *m*

unconsidered *adj* (comment) irréfléchi; (area, sector) négligé

uncontrollable *adj* (inflation, growth, spread) irrésistible, qui ne peut pas être contenu; **~ expenditures** *n pl* (Fin) dépenses incompressibles *f pl*

unconverted *adj* non converti

uncorrected *adj* non corrigé, non redressé

uncorroborated *adj* non corroboré; (Law) **~ evidence** *n* preuve par présomption *f*

uncounted *adj* non compté

uncovered: **~ advance** *n* avance à découvert *f*; **~ amount** *n* montant à découvert *m*; **~ balance** *n* découvert *m*; **~ bear** *n* baissier à découvert *m*; **~ call** *n* (Stock) option d'achat découverte *f*, option d'achat à découvert *f*; **~ option** *n* (Stock) option à découvert *f*; **~ put** *n* (Stock) option de vente découverte *f*, option de vente à découvert *f*

uncrossed check AmE, **uncrossed cheque** BrE *n* chèque non barré *m*

uncurbed *adj* (rivalry, competitiveness) effréné

uncurtailed *adj* (competition, rights) sans restriction

undamaged *adj* non endommagé

undamped *adj* (demand) soutenu

undated *adj* sans date

undecided *adj* (person, voter) indécis; (outcome) incertain

undelete *vt* restaurer

undeniable *adj* (advantage, benefit) indéniable

undependable *adj* peu fiable

undepreciated *adj* non amorti, non déprécié; **~ capital cost** *n* fraction non amortie du coût en capital *f*; **~ cost** *n* fraction non amortie du coût *f*

undepressed *adj* (Stock) non déprimé

under *prep* (less than) inférieur à, moins de; (beneath) sous; (according to) selon; (subordinate to) sous; **a little ~** légèrement inférieur à, un peu moins de; **~ the law/clause 21** selon la loi/l'article 21; **I have ten staff ~ me** j'ai 10 employés sous mes ordres

underabsorb *vt* sous-absorber, sous-imputer

underabsorption *n* (of costs) sous-absorption *f*, sous-imputation *f*

underachieve *vi* (person) ne pas obtenir les résultats dont il/elle est capable

underassess *vt* (Tax) sous-imposer; (Acc) sous-évaluer

underassessment *n* (Tax) sous-imposition *f*; (Acc) sous-évaluation *f*

underbid **1** *vt* faire une soumission plus avantageuse que **2** *vi* offrir des conditions plus avantageuses

undercapacity *n* sous-capacité *f*

undercapitalized *adj* sous-capitalisé; **be ~** ne pas disposer de fonds suffisants

undercharge *vt* (person) ne pas faire payer assez à; **he ~d me** il m'a fait payer moins cher qu'il n'aurait dû

undercharged account *n* compte insuffisamment débité *m*, compte sous-débité *m*

underclass *n* classe sous-prolétariat *f*

underconsumption *n* sous-consommation *f*

undercover *adj* (activity) clandestin; **~ audit** *n* audit anonyme *m*, vérification anonyme *f*; **~ payment** *n* dessous-de-table *m*

undercut *vt* (competitor) vendre moins cher que; (price) casser

undercutting *n* vente à des prix qui défient la concurrence *f*

underdeclared tax *n* impôt sous-déclaré *m*

underdeveloped country *n* pays en voie de développement *m*, pays sous-développé *m*

underdevelopment *n* sous-développement *m*

underemployed *adj* (person) sous-employé; (equipment, resource) sous-utilisé

underemployment *n* (of staff) sous-emploi *m*; (of resources, equipment) sous-utilisation *f*

underequipped *adj* sous-équipé

underestimate *vt* sous-estimer

underestimation *n* sous-estimation *f*

underfinanced *adj* insuffisamment financé, qui n'a pas de fonds suffisants

underfunded *adj* insuffisamment financé; **be ~** ne pas être doté de moyens de financement suffisants

undergo *vt* (change, alteration) subir; (training) suivre; **be ~ing repairs/training** être en réparation/formation

undergraduate *n* étudiant/-e *m/f* (*de premier ou deuxième cycle*)

underground[1] *adj* (secret) clandestin; (below ground) souterrain

underground[2] *n* (Transp) métro *m*

underground: **~ economy** *n* économie informelle *f*, économie souterraine *f*; **~ network** *n* (Transp) réseau de métro *m*; **~ train** *n* rame de métro *f*

u

underhand *adj* sournois
underinsure *vt* sous-assurer
underinsured *adj* sous-assuré
underinvest *vi* sous-investir
underinvestment *n* sous-investissement *m*
underline *vt* (text, point, issue) souligner
underling *n* subalterne *mf*
underlining *n* soulignement *m*
underlying *adj* (problem, issue) sous-jacent; (claim, liability) prioritaire; ~ **asset** *n* actif sous-jacent *m*, sous-jacent *m*; ~ **debt** *n* dette sous-jacente *f*; ~ **inflation** *n* inflation sous-jacente *f*; ~ **inflation rate** *n* taux d'inflation sous-jacente *m*; ~ **net assets** *n pl* actif net sous-jacent *m*; ~ **rate** *n* taux sous-jacent *m*; ~ **tendency** *n* tendance profonde *f*; ~ **trend** *n* tendance sous-jacente *f*
undermanned *adj* à court de main-d'œuvre; **be** ~ manquer de personnel
undermanning *n* (Gen Comm) sous-effectif *m*; (in labour force) manque de main-d'œuvre *m*; (of white-collar staff) manque de personnel *m*
undermentioned *adj* mentionné ci-dessous
undermine *vt* (authority, principle) saper; (organization, confidence, position) ébranler
underpaid *adj* sous-payé, sous-rémunéré
underpay *vt* sous-payer, sous-rémunérer
underperform *vi* (share) faire une contre-performance; (company) être peu rentable
underperforming *adj* (department, company) peu rentable; (share, fund) peu performant
underpin *vt* (economy, power, currency) étayer
underpopulated *adj* sous-peuplé
underprice *vt* mettre un prix trop bas à
underpriced *adj* (item, goods) vendu au-dessous de sa valeur; **this product is** ~ ce produit est en vente à un prix inférieur à sa vraie valeur
underprivileged *adj* (person, area) déshérité
underproduce *vt* sous-produire
underproduction *n* sous-production *f*
underquote *vt* (competitor) faire un prix plus avantageux que
underrate *vt* sous-estimer
underrated *adj* sous-estimé
underrecovery: ~ **of overhead costs** *n* sous-imputation des frais généraux *f*
underreport *vt* (revenue) minorer
underreporting *n* (of revenue) minoration *f*
underrepresent *vt* sous-représenter
underrepresentation *n* sous-représentation *f*
underscore *vt* souligner
under-secretary *n* sous-secrétaire *mf*
undersell ⟦1⟧ *vt* (rival) vendre moins cher que, vendre meilleur marché que; ~ **oneself** ne pas savoir se vendre; ~ **one's**

competitors vendre meilleur marché que ses concurrents
⟦2⟧ *vi* (goods) se vendre mal
underselling *n* cassage des prix *m*
undersigned *n* soussigné/-e *m/f*; **I the** ~ **declare that...** je soussigné déclare que...
underspend ⟦1⟧ *vt* (budget) sous-employer; (money, funds) ne pas dépenser totalement
⟦2⟧ *vi* dépenser moins que les crédits disponibles
underspending *n* dépenses inférieures aux crédits disponibles *f pl*
understaffed *adj* qui manque de personnel; **be** ~ manquer de personnel
understaffing *n* manque de personnel *m*, manque d'effectif *m*
understand *vt* comprendre; **give sb to** ~ **that** laisser entendre à qn que
understanding *n* (mutual arrangement) entente *f*; (grasp of subject) compréhension *f*; **come to an** ~ arriver à un accord, parvenir à un accord; ~ **with sb** s'entendre avec qn; **on the** ~ **that** étant entendu que; **on that** ~ sur cette base
understate *vt* (cost, risk, quantity, severity) minimiser
undersubscribed *adj* (issue) non-souscrit, non couvert
undertake *vt* entreprendre; ~ **to do sth** s'engager à faire qch
undertaking *n* (agreement) garantie *f*, promesse *f*; (venture) entreprise *f*; **joint** ~ joint-venture *m*; **give sb an** ~ **to do** promettre à qn de faire; **give a written** ~ s'engager par écrit
undertax *vt* (Tax) sous-imposer
undertaxation *n* sous-imposition *f*
under the counter *adv* (buy, trade, sell) clandestinement
under-the-counter *adj* (trade, goods) illicite; ~ **payment** *n* dessous-de-table *m*
underuse *vt* (person) sous-employer; (resource, facility) sous-utiliser; (land) sous-exploiter
underutilize *vt* (person) sous-employer; (resource, facility) sous-utiliser; (land) sous-exploiter
undervaluation *n* (of service, asset, currency) sous-évaluation *f*; (of person) sous-estimation *f*
undervalue *vt* (asset, service, currency) sous-évaluer; (person) sous-estimer
undervalued *adj* (asset, service, goods, currency) sous-évalué; (person) sous-estimé
underwrite *vt* (project) financer; (loss, cost) prendre en charge; (flotation, issue) garantir, souscrire; (risk) assurer, souscrire; (loan) garantir; (policy) réassurer, souscrire; (decision) donner son accord à; (proposal) soutenir
underwriter *n* (marine) assureur maritime *m*; (of loan) garant *m*; (of securities issue) syndicataire *m*; (Ins) réassureur *m*; (of policy)

souscripteur m; **leading ~** (Fin) chef de file m
underwriting n (of loan) garantie f; (Stock) prise ferme f; (of risk, policy) souscription f; **~ account** compte de souscripteur m; **~ agreement** n contrat de garantie m, contrat de prise ferme m; **~ contract** n (Fin) contrat de garantie m; **~ fee** n commission de garantie f, commission de placement f; **~ syndicate** n syndicat d'émission m, syndicat de prise ferme m
underwritten adj garanti, souscrit
undischarged adj (debt, fine) non acquitté, non soldé; (cargo) non déchargé; **~ bankrupt** failli non réhabilité m; **~ commitment** n engagement actuel m, engagement en cours m
undisclosed adj (amount, quantity) non révélé
undisposed of adj (stock, goods) non écoulé, non vendu
undistributable: ~ capital n capital non distribuable m; **~ reserves** n pl BrE réserves indisponibles f pl
undistributed: ~ allotment n affectation non répartie f; **~ balance** n solde non réparti m; **~ income** n bénéfices non répartis m pl; **~ profits** n pl bénéfices non distribués m pl
undivided: ~ interest n intérêt non réparti m; **~ profits** n pl bénéfices non distribués m pl; **~ property** n biens indivisibles m pl
undo vt (work, effort) détruire; (Comp) annuler
undocumented adj non documenté; **~ worker** n travailleur/-euse clandestin/-e m/f
undue adj (use, effort) excessif/-ive; **~ hardship** n (Tax) difficultés indues f pl, préjudice indu m; **~ influence** n abus d'influence m, intimidation f
unduly adv à tort
unearned: ~ dividend n (Stock) dividende fictif m; **~ income** n rentes f pl; **~ increment** n plus-value f; **~ interest** n (Bank) intérêt non gagné m, intérêt à courir m; **~ premium** n (Fin, Law) plus-value f, prime payée d'avance f; (Tax) plus-value de prime f
uneconomic adj (activity, work, methods) pas rentable, non rentable
unemployable adj inapte à travailler, inapte au travail
unemployed adj (capital) inutilisé; (person) au chômage, sans travail; **register as ~** s'inscrire au chômage; **the ~** n pl les chômeurs m pl, les sans-emploi m pl; **~ person** n chômeur/-euse m/f
unemployment n chômage m; **~ benefit** n BrE, **~ compensation** n AmE allocation chômage f, indemnité de chômage f; **~ figures** n pl chiffres du chômage m pl; **~ insurance** n assurance-chômage f; **~ pay** n indemnité de chômage f, indemnité-chômage

f; **~ rate** n taux de chômage m; **~ statistics** n statistiques du chômage f pl; **~ trap** n cercle vicieux du chômage m
unencumbered adj (Prop) non grevé d'hypothèque
unendorsed adj (cheque) non endossé
unenforceable adj inapplicable, non exécutoire; **~ contract** n contrat non exécutoire m
unequal adj inégal; **~ exchange** n change inégal m; **~ trade** n (international) marché inégal m
unequivocal adj sans équivoque
uneven adj (trend) irrégulier/-ière; (work, quality) inégal; **~ lot** n lot fractionnaire m
unexecuted adj (order) non satisfait
unexpended adj (money) non dépensé; **~ balance** n solde inemployé m
unexpired adj (contract) non expiré, toujours en vigueur
unexplained adj inexpliqué; **~ absence** n (habitual) absentéisme injustifié m; (once) absence injustifiée f
unfailing adj (remedy) infaillible; (optimism) à toute épreuve; (support) fidèle; (efforts) constant
unfair adj (advantage, decision, comparison, treatment) injuste; (strategy, tactics) irrégulier/-ière; **~ competition** n concurrence déloyale f; **~ contract** n contrat léonin m; **~ dismissal** n licenciement abusif m; **~ labor practice** AmE, **~ labour practice** BrE n pratique déloyale en matière de relations sociales f; **~ trade** n commerce illicite m; **~ trading practices** n pl pratiques commerciales déloyales f pl
unfavorable AmE, **unfavourable** BrE adj défavorable; (price, conditions, rate of exchange) défavorable; (moment) inopportun; **~ balance of trade** n balance commerciale défavorable f, balance commerciale déficitaire f, balance commerciale passive f; **~ trading conditions** n pl conditions défavorables pour le commerce f pl
unfeasible adj (plan) irréalisable
unfilled: ~ order n commande non satisfaite f, commande non exécutée f; **~ vacancy** n poste à pourvoir m, poste vacant m
unfinished adj (work) inachevé; (matter) en cours; **have ~ business** avoir des affaires à régler
unfit adj (sub-standard) inadéquat; (unsuitable) inapte; (Law) incapable; **~ for consumption** impropre à la consommation; **~ for work** inapte au travail; **~ to do** (person) inapte à faire
unfledged adj (person, company) sans expérience; **be ~** manquer d'expérience
unforeseeable adj imprévisible
unforeseen adj imprévu, inattendu
unformatted adj (disk, storage) non formaté
unfounded adj (rumour, suspicion, accusation, ⋯⟶

u

criticism) sans fondement

unfreeze *vt* (funds, capital) débloquer

unfriendly *adj* (bid, takeover) hostile; **environmentally-~** nuisible à l'environnement

unfulfilled *adj* (condition) non rempli; (promise) non tenu; (potential) non réalisé; (order) non satisfait, non exécuté

unfunded: **~ debt** *n* dette flottante *f*; **~ pension scheme** *n* régime de retraite sans capitalisation *m*

ungeared *adj* sans endettement; **~ balance sheet** *n* bilan bien équilibré *m*, bilan sans emprunts *m*

ungraded *adj* hors-série

unhedged *adj* non couvert

unification *n* unification *f*

unified credit *n* (Tax) crédit unifié *m*

uniform¹ *adj* uniforme

uniform² *n* uniforme *m*

uniform: **~ accounting** *n* comptabilité uniforme *f*; **~ practice code** *n* US code des usages *m*; **~ price** *n* prix unique *m*

Uniform Business Rate *n* UK impôt foncier local *m* (assis sur la valeur locative des bien fonciers bâtis et non batis utilisés à titre professionnel)

uniformed *adj* en uniforme

uniformity *n* uniformité *f*

uniformly *adv* uniformément

Uniform Resource Locator *n* adresse URL *f*, adresse réticulaire *f*

unify *vt* unifier

unifying *adj* (factor, feature) de cohésion; (theme) commun

unilateral *adj* unilatéral; **~ agreement** *n* accord unilatéral *m*; **~ measure** *n* mesure unilatérale *f*; **~ regulation** *n* réglementation unilatérale *f*

unilaterally *adv* unilatéralement

unimodal distribution *n* distribution normale *f*

unimpeachable *adj* (contract, evidence) inattaquable, incontestable

unimpeded *adj* (access, movement) libre; **be ~ by** ne pas être entravé par

unimpressive *adj* (performance) peu impressionnant, médiocre; (results, figures) médiocre

unincorporated business *n* entreprise non constituée en société *f*

uninfected *adj* (Comp) sain; (livestock) sain

uninstall *vt* désinstaller

uninsurable *adj* (Ins) non assurable

uninsured *adj* non assuré; **be ~** ne pas être assuré

uninvested *adj* (Bank) (money) non investi, non placé

union *n* union *f*; (trades union) syndicat *m*; **economic/monetary ~** union économique/

monétaire *f*; **join a ~** se syndiquer; **be a member of a ~** être syndiqué, être membre d'un syndicat; **~s and management** les syndicats et le patronat; **~ affiliation** *n* adhésion à un syndicat *f*; **~ agreement** *n* accord syndical *m*; **~-bashing** *n* (infrml) antisyndicalisme *m*; **~ dues** *n pl*, **~ fees** *n pl* cotisation syndicale *f*; **~ member** *n* membre d'un syndicat *m*, syndiqué/-e *m/f*; **~ movement** *n* mouvement syndical *m*; **~ officer** *n*, **~ official** *n* permanent *m*; **~ rate** *n* salaire proposé par les syndicats *m*; **~ representative** *n* délégué/-e syndical/-e *m/f*; **~ rights** *n pl* droits syndicaux *m pl*; **~ rules** *n pl* règlement syndical *m*; **~ shop** *n* monopole syndical de l'embauche *m*; **~ structure** *n* structure syndicale *f*

unionization *n* syndicalisation *f*

unionized *adj* syndicalisé

unique¹ *adj* unique

unique² *n* (website visitor) visiteur unique *m*; (selling point) argument clé de vente *m*

unique: **~ reference number** *n* numéro de référence unique *m*; **~ selling point** *n* argument clé de vente *m*; **~ selling proposition** *n* proposition unique de vente *f*

unissued *adj* (capital) non émis; **~ capital stock** *n* capital non émis *m*; **~ stock** *n* action non émise *f*, capital non émis *m*; **~ Treasury share** *n* action de capital non émise *f*

unit *n* (whole) unité *f*; (of measurement, currency) unité *f*; (Stock) combinaison de valeurs *f*, unité *f*; (department, building) service *m*; (Ind) unité *f*; (team) groupe *m*; (section of course, text) unité *f*; (coursework credit) unité de valeur *f*; (Prop) (flat) appartement *m*; (device) dispositif *m*; **industrial ~** local à usage industriel *m*; **~ of account** *n* moyenne d'un compte *f*, unité de compte *f*; **~ cost** *n* prix de revient unitaire *m*; **~ holder** *n* (Stock) détenteur d'unité *m*; **~ labor cost** AmE, **~ labour cost** BrE *n* (Acc) coût unitaire du personnel *m*; (Econ) coût unitaire de la main-d'œuvre *m*; **~ of measurement** *n* unité de mesure *f*; **~ price** *n* prix unitaire *m*; **~ pricing** *n* prix à l'unité *m*, tarification à l'unité *f*; **~ tax** *n* impôt unitaire *m*; **~ of trading** *n* quotité *f*, unité minimale de transaction *f*; **~ trust** *n* BrE société d'investissement à capital variable *f*, SICAV *f*, fonds commun de placement *m*; **~ value** *n* valeur unitaire *f*; **~ value index** *n* indice des valeurs unitaires *m*

unitary *adj* unitaire; **~ approach** *n* conception globale *f*; **~ elasticity** *n* élasticité unitaire *f*; **~ model** *n* modèle global *m*

unite **1** *vt* unir **2** *vi* s'unir

united *adj* (group, front, countries) uni; (attempt) conjoint; (effort) conjugé

United: **~ Kingdom Atomic Energy**

Authority n agence de l'énergie atomique du Royaume-Uni; ~ **Nations** n Nations Unies f pl, Organisation des Nations Unies f; ~ **Nations Association** n Association des Nations Unies f; ~ **Nations Organization** n Organisation des Nations Unies f; ~ **States Postal Service** n Poste des États-Unis f

unitization n multipropriété f

units-of-production method n méthode des unités de production f

universal adj (law, truth, message) universel/-elle; (education, health care) pour tous; (reaction, solution, acclaim, complaint) généralisé; **become** ~ se généraliser; ~ **agent** n (Law) agent général m, représentant général m; ~ **air waybill** n lettre de transport aérien universelle f; ~ **bank** banque universelle f; ~ **life insurance** n assurance-vie universelle f; ~**-life policy** n assurance vie-entière f; ~ **suffrage** n suffrage universel m

universe n (S&M) univers m

university[1] adj (course, town) universitaire; ~ **education** n formation universitaire f; ~ **lecturer** n enseignant/-e du supérieur m/f

university[2] n université f

unjust adj injuste

unjustified adj (Gen Comm, Law) injustifié; (Comp) non-justifié; ~ **absence** n (habitual) absentéisme injustifié m; (once) absence injustiée f

unknown[1] adj inconnu

unknown[2] n inconnue f

unladen adj à vide; ~ **weight** n poids à vide m, tare f

unlawful adj illégal, illicite; ~ **act** n acte illégal m, acte illicite m; ~ **contract** n contrat sans valeur légale m; ~ **picketing** n installation illégale de piquets de grève f; ~ **trespass** n intrusion illicite sur la propriété d'autrui f, violation de propriété f

unlawfully adv illégalement

unleaded gas AmE, **unleaded petrol** BrE n essence sans plomb f

unleveraged program AmE, **unleveraged programme** BrE n programme sans endettement m

unlicensed adj (activity) non autorisé; (dealer, trader) non agréé; ~ **broker** n courtier non agréé m

unlimited adj illimité; ~ **company** n entreprise illimitée f; ~ **liability** n responsabilité illimitée f; ~ **mileage** n (for car-hire) kilométrage illimité m; ~ **securities** n pl valeurs à cours non limité f pl

unliquidated adj (Fin) non acquitté

unlisted adj (Comms) AmE sur la liste rouge; (Stock) non admis (à la cote), non coté, non inscrit à la cote; ~ **company** n société non inscrite à la cote f; ~ **market** n second marché m; ~ **security** n valeur non cotée f; ~ **share** n action non cotée f

unload vt (vessel, vehicle, goods) décharger; (Fin, Stock) (shares) liquider

unloading n (Transp) déchargement m; (of shares) liquidation f

unlock vt (funds) débloquer; (Comp) (file) déverrouiller

unmanageable adj (business, staff, system) ingérable; (size, number) démesuré

unmanifested cargo n cargaison non déclarée f, marchandises non déclarées f pl

unmarketable adj (not commercially viable) non commercialisable; (unsaleable) invendable

unmarried adj célibataire

unmatched adj (dissimilar) dépareillé; (unequalled) inégalé

unmatured adj (coupon, debt) non échu

unmoderated (Comp) (newsgroup, chat) non modéré

unmortgaged adj libre d'hypothèque

unnamed adj sans nom; (buyer, company, source) dont le nom n'a pas été divulgué

unnegotiable adj non négociable

unnumbered adj (building) sans numéro; (page, seat, ticket) non numéroté

UNO abbr (▶United Nations Organization) ONU f (Organisation des Nations Unies)

unofficial adj (appointment) non officiel/-ielle; (report) non officiel/-ielle, officieux/-ieuse; (visit) privé; (market) hors cote; (strike) sauvage; (merchandise, biography) non autorisé; **in an** ~ **capacity** à titre non officiel

unpack vt (goods, belongings) déballer; (luggage) défaire

unpaid adj (debt) non acquitté; (work) non rémunéré; (leave) sans solde; ~ **bill** n impayé m; ~ **dividend** n dividende impayé m; ~ **tax** n impôt non payé m

unpalatable adj (decision, facts) désagréable; (advice) dur à avaler

unparalleled adj incomparable

unpatented adj non breveté

unplanned adj imprévu

unpopular adj impopulaire

unprecedented adj sans précédent

unpredictable adj imprévisible

unprejudiced adj (person) sans préjugés; (opinion, advice) impartial

unprepared adj (person) pas préparé; (speech, presentation) improvisé; **catch sb** ~ prendre qn au dépourvu

unpresented check AmE, **unpresented cheque** BrE n chèque non présenté m

unpriced adj (item, goods) dont le prix n'est pas marqué, sans indication de prix

unprocessed adj (data) non traité

unproductive adj (capital, labour, discussion) improductif/-ive; (land) stérile

unprofessional adj (attitude, approach) qui témoigne d'un manque de conscience ⋯▷

professionnelle; ∼ **conduct** n conduite
contraire au code professionnel f

unprofitable adj (firm, venture) peu rentable;
(discussion, debate) improductif/-ive

unpromising adj peu prometteur/-euse

unprotested adj (bill) non protesté

unpublished adj inédit

unpunctual adj (staff) tardif/-ive; **be** ∼ ne
pas être ponctuel/-elle

unqualified adj (staff) non qualifié; (support)
inconditionnel/-elle; **be** ∼ **for the job** ne pas
avoir les diplômes requis; **be an** ∼ **success**
être une grande réussite; ∼ **acceptance** n
acceptation inconditionnelle f; ∼ **opinion** n
opinion sans réserve f

unquestionable adj incontestable

unquoted adj (Stock) non admis à la cote,
non coté, non inscrit à la cote; ∼ **security** n
valeur non cotée f; ∼ **share** n action non
cotée f

unread adj (email, message) non lu

unrealistic adj (objective, target, expectation)
irréalisable; (person) qui manque de réalisme;
(depiction, portrayal) peu réaliste; **it is** ∼ **to
suggest that…** il n'est pas réaliste de
suggérer que…

unrealistically adv invraisemblablement

unrealized: ∼ **gains** n pl gains non
réalisés m pl; ∼ **loss** n perte non réalisée f;
∼ **profit** n bénéfice non réalisé m, profit non
réalisé m

unreasonable adj (request, price) excessif/
-ive; (views, expectations) irréaliste

unreceipted adj (bill, account) non acquitté,
sans la mention 'pour acquit'

unrecorded adj non enregistré

unrecoverable adj (Comp) (data, file)
irrémédiable; (Tax) non recouvrable

unredeemable adj non amortissable, non
remboursable

unredeemed adj (mortgage) non purgé;
(debt) non remboursé; (pledge) non retiré

unregistered adj (birth, person) non déclaré;
(worker) clandestin; (vehicle) non immatriculé;
(firm) non enregistré; ∼ **labor** AmE, ∼ **labour**
BrE n main-d'œuvre non déclarée f; ∼ **stock**
n action non enregistrée f, action non
nominative f; ∼ **trademark** n marque non
déposée f

unreliable adj (equipment) peu fiable;
(method, person) peu sûr; (evidence, figures)
douteux/-euse

unremunerative adj peu rémunérateur/
-trice

unreported adj (case, incident) non déclaré

unresolved adj (problem, question) irrésolu

unresponsive adj (market) insensible;
(person) peu réceptif/-ive

unrest n malaise m; (amongst workforce)
troubles m pl; (Pol) agitation f

unrestricted adj (power) illimité; (activity,

trade) non contrôlé; ∼ **access** n accès libre
m; ∼ **labor** AmE, ∼ **labour** BrE n main-
d'œuvre non réduite f; ∼ **letter of credit** n
lettre de crédit illimité f; ∼ **quota** n
contingent libre m

unrewarding adj (job) peu gratifiant

unrivalled adj sans rival

unsafe adj dangereux/-euse; (Law) (verdict)
douteux/-euse; ∼ **paper** n (Fin) effet douteux
m

unsalable AmE, **unsaleable** BrE adj
invendable

unscheduled adj (appearance) surprise;
(flight) supplémentaire; (event, break) qui n'a
pas été prévu

unscreened adj (not sorted) non trié

unscrupulous adj (person) sans scrupules;
(method, practice) peu scrupuleux/-euse

unseal vt (container) desceller; (envelope)
décacheter

unsealed adj (envelope) décacheté

unseat vt ∼ **the board** remplacer les
membres du conseil d'administration

unsecure adj (Comp) non sécurisé

unsecured adj (Bank) non-garanti,
chirographaire; ∼ **advance** n avance non
garantie f, avance à découvert f; ∼ **bond** n
obligation non garantie f; ∼ **creditor** n
créancier/-ière non garanti/-e m/f, créancier/
-ière ordinaire m/f; ∼ **debt** n dette non
garantie f; ∼ **loan** n emprunt non garanti m,
prêt non garanti m; ∼ **overdraft** n
découvert en blanc m

unsettle vt perturber

unsettled adj (Econ) instable; (bill, account)
impayé; (schedule) perturbé; ∼ **market** n
marché instable m

unsettling adj (influence) inquiétant;
(experience) troublant

unshipment n débarquement m,
déchargement m

unsigned adj non signé

unskilled adj (worker) non qualifié, non
spécialisé; ∼ **labor** AmE, ∼ **labour** BrE n
main-d'œuvre non qualifiée f, main-d'œuvre
non spécialisée f; ∼ **work** n travail non
spécialisé m

unsocial hours n pl heures indues f pl;
work ∼ travailler des heures indues

unsold adj invendu; ∼ **goods** n pl
invendus m pl

unsolicited adj non sollicité; ∼
application n candidature spontanée f; ∼
email n publicité rebut par courrier
électronique f, pourriel m Can

unsound adj (argument) peu valable; ∼ **risk**
n mauvais risque m

unspent adj (money) non dépensé; **remain** ∼
ne pas encore avoir été dépensé

unstable adj instable

unsteady adj (supply, output) irrégulier/-ière

unstructured *adj* non structuré; ∼ **interview** *n* entretien informel *m*

unstuck *adj* **come** ∼ (plan) tomber à l'eau; (person, organization) connaître un échec

unsubscribe *vi* se désabonner

unsubsidized *adj* non subventionné

unsubstantiated *adj* (accusation, rumour, claim) non corroboré

unsuccessful *adj* (attempt, bid) infructueux/-euse; (efforts, search) vain; (lawsuit) perdu; (person) malchanceux/-euse; **be ∼ in doing** ne pas réussir à faire; **his job application was ∼** sa candidature n'a pas été retenue

unsuitable *adj* (person) peu convenable; (place, time, equipment) inapproprié; **be ∼ ne pas convenir; be ∼ for a job** ne pas être fait pour un poste

unsuited *adj* inadapté; **be ∼ to the job** ne pas avoir le profil voulu pour le poste

unsupported *adj* (statement) non confirmé, sans preuves; (without IT backup) non pris en charge par le service informatique; (without maintenance) dont la maintenance n'est pas assurée

unsustainable *adj* (development) non durable; (pace) impossible à tenir; (level, rate) qui ne peut pas durer

untapped *adj* (resources) inexploité

untargeted *adj* (consumer base) insuffisamment ciblé

untaxed *adj* (goods) non imposé, libre

untenanted *adj* inoccupé, sans locataire

untested *adj* (invention, drug, product) non testé; (assertion, theory) non vérifié

until *prep* jusqu'à; ∼ **countermanded** jusqu'à nouvel avis, jusqu'à nouvel ordre; ∼ **further notice** jusqu'à nouvel avis, jusqu'à nouvel ordre; ∼ **such a time as** jusqu'à ce que

untimely *adj* inopportun

untrained *adj* (person) sans formation; **be ∼ in** n'avoir aucune formation en

untransferable *adj* (Law, Stock) incessible

untried *adj* (product) non testé; (method) non essayé; (case) qui n'a pas encore été jugé; (hypothesis) qui n'a pas été vérifié; (person) inexpérimenté

unused *adj* inutilisé, non utilisé

unusual *adj* (feature, case, event) peu commun, inhabituel/-elle; (original) original

unvalued policy *n* (Ins) police non évaluée *f*

unveil *vt* (proposals, plans, policy) dévoiler

unverified *adj* (product) non testé; (information) non vérifié

unwaged *adj* non salarié; **the ∼** *n pl* les chômeurs *m pl*, les sans-emploi *m pl*

unwanted *adj* (superfluous) superflu

unwarranted *adj* injustifié

unweighted *adj* (index, figures) non pondéré

unwired *adj* (Comp) sans fil

unworkable *adj* (plan, solution) impraticable; **prove ∼** s'avérer impraticable

unwrap *vt* défaire

unwritten (rule) tacite; ∼ **agreement** *n* accord verbal *m*

unzip *vt* (file) dézipper, décompresser

up¹ *adj* (Comp) (functioning) en marche; ∼ **14%** (Stock) en hausse de 14%; **sales are ∼ 10%** les ventes ont augmenté de 10 %; **XZ shares are ∼** les actions XZ sont en hausse; **prices are 2% ∼ on last year** les prix ont augmenté de 2% par rapport à l'an dernier; **when the 10 days are ∼** à la fin des 10 jours; **be ∼ and running** (equipment) être opérationnel/ -elle; (project, scheme) bien marcher

up² *adv* **be one ∼ on sb** faire mieux que qn; **from the age of 18 ∼** à partir de 18 ans; **from 40 euros ∼** à partir de 40 euros; **be ∼ with the leaders** faire partie des leaders; **be 2 points ∼ on** avoir 2 points d'avance sur

up³ *vt* (bid, offer, price) augmenter

up⁴ *prep* ∼ **to** jusqu'à; **be ∼ to scratch, be ∼ to standard** être au niveau; ∼ **the line** (Mgmnt) en remontant la hiérarchie; **we have ∼ to 300 calls a day** nous avons près de 300 appels par jour; **reductions of ∼ to 40%** réductions qui peuvent atteindre 40%; **it's ∼ to you** c'est à toi/vous de décider

up-and-coming *adj* (person) plein d'avenir, prometteur/-euse

upbeat *adj* (attitude, forecast) optimiste

updatable *adj* actualisable

update¹ *n* (Gen Comm, Comp) mise à jour *f*, actualisation *f*; **news ∼** dernières nouvelles *f pl*

update² *vt* (database, information) mettre à jour; (value, figure) actualiser; (person) mettre au courant; (image) remettre au goût du jour; (methods, system, equipment) moderniser; ∼ **sb on sth** mettre qn au courant de qch

updating *n* (Gen Comm, Comp) mise à jour *f*, actualisation *f*; (modernisation) modernisation *f*

upfront¹ *adj* payé d'avance; (conspicuous) en vue; (frank) franc/franche; ∼ **cost** *n* charge payable d'avance *f*

upfront² *adv* (pay) d'avance; **they want 6,000 euros ∼** ils demandent une avance de 6 000 euros

upgrade¹ *n* (Comp) mise à niveau *f*, amélioration *f*; (on flight) surclassement *m*

upgrade² *vt* (Comp) (memory) augmenter; (software) mettre à jour, passer à une version plus récente de; (hardware, system) améliorer, optimiser; (in quality) améliorer; (post, job) requalifier, revaloriser; (airline passengers) surclasser

upgradeability *n* évolutivité *f*

upgradeable *adj* (Comp) (memory) extensible; (system, software) évolutif/-ive

upgrading *n* (Comp) (of hardware) augmentation de puissance *f*, extension *f*, ····⟫

u

mise à niveau *f*; (of memory) augmentation *f*; (HRM) (promotion) reclassement *m*; ~ **of a loan** reclassement en amont d'un prêt *m*

upheaval *n* bouleversement *m*

uphold *vt* (law) faire respecter; (decision, sentence) confirmer; (right, principle, belief) soutenir

upkeep *n* (of property) entretien *m*; (costs) frais d'entretien *m pl*

upload *vt* (data) télécharger

upmarket *adv* **move** ~ se repositionner à la hausse

up-market *adj* (product, service) haut de gamme; (area, district) chic *inv*

upper *adj* **have the** ~ **hand** avoir le dessus; **get the** ~ **hand** prendre le dessus; ~ **case** *n* haut de casse *m*, majuscules *f pl*; ~**-case letter** *n* majuscule *f*; ~ **income bracket** *n* tranche des revenus élevés *f*; ~ **limit** *n* plafond *m*; (Stock) limite supérieure *f*, plafond *m*; ~ **quartile** *n* quartile supérieur *m*

ups and downs *n pl* hauts et bas *m pl*; (Econ, Stock) oscillations du marché *f pl*

upselling *n* vente incitative *f*, vente poussée *f*, vente d'un produit de gamme supérieure *f*

upset price *n* mise à prix *f*, prix de départ *m*, prix demandé *m*

upshift *n* augmentation *f*

upsize *vt* (company) restructurer avec embauche

upsizing *n* restructuration avec embauche *f*

upskilling *n* recyclage *m*

upstairs market *n* (Stock) négociation à un cours supérieur *f*, transaction hors parquet *f*

upstream *adj* (industry) en amont; ~ **direct marketing** *n* mercatique d'amont *f*; ~ **loans** *n pl* prêts en amont *m pl*

upsurge *n* (in activity) poussée *f*; (in debt, demand, incidence) augmentation *f*

upswing *n* (improvement) reprise *f*; (increase) augmentation *f*

uptick *n* (Stock) cours supérieur au cours précédent *m*

uptime *n* (Comp) temps de bon fonctionnement *m*, temps de disponibilité *m*

up-to-date *adj* (information, news) dernier/ -ière; (brochure, files, timetable, records) à jour; (person) au courant; **be** ~ (informed) être au courant; (contemporary) être dans le vent; **be** ~ **with** (developments) se tenir au courant de; **keep sb** ~ tenir qn au courant; **keep sth** ~ (records, files) tenir qch à jour; **bring sth** ~ mettre qch à jour, actualiser qch

up-to-sample *adj* conforme à l'échantillon

up-to-the-minute *adj* (information) dernier/ -ière; (equipment) moderne; (fashionable) à la mode

uptrend *n* orientation à la hausse *f*,

tendance à la hausse *f*

upturn *n* (Gen Comm) amélioration *f*; (Stock, Econ) reprise *f*

upvaluation *n* révision à la hausse *f*

upward[1] *adj* (Comp) ascendant, vers le haut; (trend) haussier/-ière, vers le haut, à la hausse

upward[2] *adv* vers le haut; (revise) à la hausse; **move** ~ monter

upward: ~ **compatibility** *n* (Comp) compatibilité ascendante *f*; ~ **mobility** *n* ascension sociale *f*; ~ **movement** *n* (Stock) mouvement à la hausse *m*, tendance haussière *f*, tendance à la hausse *f*; ~ **pressure** *n* (on budget) pression inflationniste *f*, pression à la hausse *f*; ~ **revision** *n* révision à la hausse *f*; ~ **spiral** *n* montée en spirale *f*, (in wages, prices) montée en spirale *f*, spirale ascendante *f*; ~ **trend** *n* (Stock) mouvement vers le haut *m*, mouvement à la hausse *m*, tendance haussière *f*, tendance à la hausse *f*

upwardly mobile *adj* en pleine ascension sociale

upwards[1] *adv* (Gen Comm) vers le haut; (revise) à la hausse; **move** ~ monter

upwards[2] *prep* ~ **of** plus de

urban *adj* urbain; ~ **area** *n* agglomération urbaine *f*; ~ **development zone** *n* zone à urbaniser en priorité *f*; ~ **planner** *n* urbaniste *mf*; ~ **planning** *n* urbanisme *m*; ~ **renewal** *n* rénovation urbaine *f*; ~ **sprawl** *n* mitage *m*

urbanization *n* urbanisation *f*

urbanize *vt* urbaniser

urgent *adj* (need, letter, demand) urgent; (measures, meeting) d'urgence; **be in** ~ **need of sth** avoir besoin de qch de toute urgence, avoir un besoin urgent de qch; ~ **matter** *n* affaire urgente *f*; ~ **order** *n* commande urgente *f*

urge: ~ **sb to do** *vt* inciter qn à faire

usability *n* facilité d'utilisation *f*

usable *adj* utilisable; (data) exploitable

usance *n* usance *f*; **at thirty days'** ~ à usance de trente jours; ~ **bill** *n* effet à usance *m*; ~ **credit** (Bank) crédit à usance *m*

US: ~ **dollar financial assets** *n pl* avoirs financiers libellés en dollars américains *m pl*; ~ **Treasury bond** *n* bon du Trésor américain à long terme *m*, obligation du Trésor américain *f*

use[1] *n* (act of using) emploi *m*, utilisation *f*, usage *m*; **conditions of** ~ conditions d'utilisation *f pl*; (Patents) (of mark) exploitation *f*; **be of** ~ être utile; **have the** ~ **of sth** pouvoir se servir de qch; **have no further** ~ **for sb/sth** ne plus avoir besoin de qn/qch; **for the** ~ **of sb** à l'usage de qn; **make** ~ **of** utiliser; **make full** ~ **of** tirer parti de; **put sth to good** ~ tirer bon parti de qch; ~**-by date** *n* (on food) date limite de consommation *f*; (on goods) date limite d'utilisation *f*; ~ **of funds** emploi de fonds *m*; ~ **value** *n* valeur d'usage *f*

use² *vt* se servir de, utiliser; (method, technique) employer; (opportunity) profiter de, saisir; (influence) faire jouer; (force) avoir recours à; (power, knowledge, information) utiliser; ~ **strong-arm tactics** employer la manière forte; ~ **up** (money, savings) dépenser; (stocks, supplies) épuiser

used *adj* (not new) d'occasion; ~ **assets** *n pl* (Tax) actif utilisé *m*; ~ **car** *n* voiture d'occasion *f*; ~ **vehicle** *n* véhicule d'occasion *m*

useful *adj* utile; (meeting, talks) profitable; ~ **to sb** utile à qn; ~ **life** *n* (of asset) durée de vie utile *f*; (of device, machine, tool) durée de vie *f*

usefully *adv* utilement

user *n* (of service, road, transport) usager *m*; (of product, equipment) utilisateur/-trice *m/f*; ~ **attitude** *n* attitude des utilisateurs *f*; ~ **cost** *n* coût utilisateur *m*; ~ **fee** *n* droits d'utilisation *m pl*, frais d'utilisation *m pl*; ~**-friendliness** *n* convivialité *f*; ~**-friendly** *adj* convivial, facile à utiliser; ~ **group** *n* groupe d'utilisateurs *m*; ~ **guide** *n* mode d'emploi *m*; ~**-hostile** *adj* non convivial; ~ **ID** *n* nom d'utilisateur *m*, code d'identification *m*; ~ **interface** *n* interface utilisateur *f*; ~ **interface ergonomist** *n* ergonome d'interfaces *mf*; ~ **manual** *n* guide de l'utilisateur *m*; ~ **name** *n* nom d'utilisateur *m*, code d'identification *m*; ~ **network** *n* réseau d'utilisateurs *m*; ~**-orientated** *adj* (Comp) personnalisé; (marketing) conçu en pensant à l'utilisateur; ~ **profile** *n* profil de l'utilisateur *m*; ~ **support** *n* assistance à l'utilisateur *f*; ~**-unfriendly** *adj* non convivial

USP *abbr* (▸**unique selling point**) argument clé de vente *m*; (▸**unique selling proposition**) proposition unique de vente *f*

USPS *abbr* (▸**United States Postal Service**) Poste des États-Unis *f*

usual *adj* habituel/-elle; **as** ~ comme d'habitude; **on the** ~ **terms** aux conditions habituelles; **with the** ~ **proviso** sous les réserves d'usage; **it is** ~ **to do** il est d'usage de faire; **it's business as** ~ les affaires continuent; **more/less than** ~ plus/moins que d'habitude

usufruct *n* usufruit *m*

usurer *n* usurier/-ière *m/f*

usurious *adj* usuraire

usurp *vt* usurper

usury *n* usure *f*

util *n* indice d'utilité *m*, util *m*

utilitarian *adj* utilitaire

utilitarianism *n* utilitarisme *m*

utilities sector *n* secteur public *m*, secteur exclu *m*

utility¹ *adj* (Gen Comm, Comp) utilitaire

utility² *n* (Comp) programme utilitaire *m*, utilitaire *m*; (usefulness) utilité *f*; (service) service public *m*

utility: ~ **average** *n* indice moyen des services publics *m*; ~ **company** *n* société chargée d'assurer un service public *f*; ~ **function** *n* fonction d'utilité *f*; ~ **program** *n* programme utilitaire *m*; ~ **revenue bond** *n* obligation à long terme émise par une collectivité *f*

utilization *n* utilisation *f*; ~ **percent** *n* taux de rendement *m*; ~ **rate** *n* taux d'utilisation *m*

utilize *vt* (object, idea, raw material) utiliser; (resource) exploiter

utilized capacity *n* potentiel de production utilisé *m*

utmost¹ *adj* (discretion, care) le plus grand/la plus grande; ~ **good faith** *n* (Ins) bonne foi absolue *f*; **be of the** ~ **importance** être extrêmement important

utmost² *n* maximum *m*; **do one's** ~ **to do** faire tout son possible pour faire

UVI *abbr* (▸**unit value index**) indice des valeurs unitaires *m*

u

v

Vv

VA *abbr* (▸**value analysis**) analyse de valeur *f*

vacancy *n* poste vacant *m*, poste à pourvoir *m*; **fill/create a** ~ pourvoir/libérer un poste; **advertise a** ~ faire paraître une offre d'emploi; **there is a** ~ **for an analyst** il y a un poste d'analyste à pourvoir; ~ **rate** *n* (in hotel) coefficient d'occupation *m*

vacant *adj* (unoccupied) libre, disponible; (job) vacant, à pourvoir; ~ **lot** *n* AmE terrain non bâti *m*; ~ **possession** *n* jouissance immédiate *f*

vacate *vt* (house, premises, job) quitter; (room) libérer

vacation *n* AmE congé *m*, vacances *f pl*; **on** ~ en congé, en vacances; **take a** ~ prendre ⋯⋡

des vacances; **do ~ work** travailler pendant les vacances; **~ pay** n congés payés m pl

vacationer n AmE vacancier/-ière m/f

vaccinate vt vacciner

vaccination n vaccination f

vacuum n vide m; **~ pack** n emballage sous vide m; **~ packaging** n conditionnement sous vide m; **~-packed** adj emballé sous vide

valid adj (passport, licence, invoice, contract) valide; (offer, ticket) valable; (argument, excuse) valable; (complaint) fondé; (comparison) légitime; (point) pertinent

validate vt (certificate, claim) valider; (Law, Tax) valider; (theory) prouver le bien-fondé de

validation n validation f

validity n (of document, argument, excuse, method) validité f; (of claim, objection) bien-fondé m; **~ period** n période de validité f

valorization n (Econ) valorisation f; (of commodity) maintien artificiel m

valorize vt (Econ) valoriser; (commodity) maintenir artificiellement le prix de

valuable adj (asset, item) de valeur; (advice, team member, information) précieux/-ieuse; **be ~** (asset, item) avoir de la valeur

valuables n pl objets de valeur m pl

valuation n (of property, asset, goods) évaluation f, estimation f; (of bid, submission) évaluation f; (of art, antique) expertise f; (of shares) évaluation f; **make a ~ of** (property, asset) évaluer; (artwork) expertiser; **have a ~ done on** (asset, property) faire évaluer; (artwork) faire expertiser; **~ allowance** n (Acc) provision pour moins-value f, provision pour évaluation d'actifs f; **~ clause** n (Ins) clause d'évaluation f; **~ criteria** n pl critères d'évaluation m pl; **~ price** n (Stock) cours estimatif m, prix estimatif m; **~ report** n rapport d'évaluation m

valuation basis n base d'évaluation f

value¹ n valeur f; **have a ~ of £2,000** valoir 2 000 livres sterling; **be good/bad ~ for money** avoir un bon/mauvais rapport qualité-prix; **be good ~** être avantageux; **get good ~ for money** en avoir pour son argent; **go up/down in ~** prendre/perdre de la valeur; **no ~ declared** sans valeur déclarée; **goods to the ~ of** des marchandises d'une valeur de; **a voucher/cheque to the ~ of** un bon/chèque d'un montant de; **put a ~ on sth** estimer la valeur de qch; **put the ~ of sth at 9,000 euros** évaluer qch à 9 000 euros; **be of ~** avoir de la valeur; **be of no ~** être sans valeur; **~ added** n valeur ajoutée f; **~-added network** n réseau à valeur ajoutée m; **~-added reseller** n (Comp) revendeur de systèmes à valeur ajoutée m; **~-added services** n pl services à valeur ajoutée m pl; **~-added tax** n UK taxe sur la valeur ajoutée f; **~ analysis** n (marketing) analyse de valeur f; **~ chain** n chaîne de valeur f; **~ at cost**

n valeur au prix coûtant f; **~ brand** n marque économique f; **~ date** n date de règlement f, jour de règlement m; **~ engineering** n analyse de valeur f, analyse des coûts f; **~ in exchange** n contre-valeur f, valeur d'échange f; **~ judgment** n jugement de valeur m; **~ pack** n lot économique m; **~ position** n (Stock) (short) position de compensation f; **~ share** n (Stock) action f; **~ test** n (Tax) critère de valeur m

value² vt (artwork, antique) expertiser; (asset, property) évaluer; (person, advice) apprécier; (reputation, freedom) tenir à; **~ sth for probate** évaluer qch pour l'homologation d'un testament

value at risk n valeur à risque f

valued adj (customer, employee, help, contribution) précieux/-ieuse; (Ins) (policy) évalué; **~ at** (Stock) coté à

valueless adj sans valeur

van n camionnette f, fourgonnette f

VAN abbr (▸value-added network) réseau à valeur ajoutée m

vanguard n be in the **~ of** être à l'avant-garde de; **in the ~ of progress** à la pointe du progrès

vanilla adj (infrml) (version) de base

vaporware n (Comp) fumiciel m, logiciel fictif m

VAR abbr (Comp) (▸value-added reseller) revendeur de systèmes à valeur ajoutée m

variability n variabilité f

variable¹ adj variable

variable² n variable f

variable: **~ capital** n capital variable m; **~ charge** n charge variable f, prix variable m; **~ cost** n coût variable m; **~ expenses** n pl frais variables m pl; **~ interest rate** n taux d'intérêt flottant m, taux d'intérêt variable m; **~ lending rate** n taux de crédit variable m; **~ rate** n taux flottant m, taux variable m; **~-rate bonds** n pl titres à taux variables m pl; **~-rate mortgage** n prêt sur hypothèque à taux variable m

variables sampling n échantillonnage de variables m

variance n (Acc) écart m; (statistics) variance f, écart m; **price ~s** écarts sur les prix m pl; **be at ~** (two statements) ne pas concorder; **be at ~ with sb about sth** avoir des divergences d'opinion avec qn au sujet de qch; **be at ~ with** (evidence, facts) être en désaccord avec; **~ analysis** n analyse de variance f; (statistics) (Acc) analyse des écarts f

variation n variation f; (Econ) (in revenue, expenditure) variation f; (Stock) variation f

variation margin n marge de variation f

varied adj varié

variety n (diversity) variété f; (type) type m; **they come in a ~ of colours** ils existent dans un grand choix de coloris

vary 1 *vt* (method, approach) modifier; (options, choices, products) varier
2 *vi* they ~ **in price** ils varient quant au prix; ~ **from sth** différer de qch

varying *adj* varié; **with ~ degrees of** avec plus ou moins de

vast *adj* (sum, amount, difference) considérable, énorme; (number, majority) très grand; (area, premises) vaste, immense

VAT *abbr* UK (▸value-added tax) TVA *f* (taxe sur la valeur ajoutée); **exclusive of ~** hors TVA; ~ **declaration** *n* déclaration de TVA *f*; ~ **inspector** *n* inspecteur/-trice de la TVA *m/f*; ~ **payments** *n pl* paiements de TVA *m pl*; ~ **registered trader** *n* commerçant inscrit à la TVA *m*; ~ **registration number** *n* numéro d'inscription à la TVA *m*; ~ **return** *n* déclaration de TVA *f*

vault *n* (Bank) salle forte *f*

VC *abbr* (▸variable charge) charge variable *f*; (▸venture capital) capital-risque *m*; (▸venture capitalist) capital-risqueur *m*

VCR *abbr* (▸video cassette recorder) magnétoscope *m*

VDU *abbr* (▸visual display unit) écran de visualisation *m*

vector *n* vecteur *m*

veep *n* AmE (infrml) (▸vice-president) V-P *m* (vice-président)

veer *vi* changer de direction, tourner

vega *n* véga *m*; ~ **coefficient** *n* AmE, ~ **factor** *n* BrE coefficient véga *m*, facteur véga *m*

vehicle *n* (Transp) véhicule *m*; (medium) véhicule *m*; ~ **exhaust emissions** *n pl* gaz d'échappement *m pl*; ~ **leasing** *n* location de véhicules *f*; ~ **turnaround time** AmE, ~ **turnround time** BrE *n* durée de rotation du véhicule *f*; ~ **unladen weight** *n* poids du véhicule à vide *m*, tare du véhicule *f*

velocity *n* vitesse *f*, vélocité *f*; ~ **of circulation** *n* (Fin) vitesse de circulation *f*

velvet *n* rentes *f pl*

vendee *n* acheteur/-euse *m/f*

vendible *adj* vendable

vending *n* distribution automatique *f*; ~ **machine** *n* distributeur automatique (de produits) *m*

vendor *n* (supplier) fournisseur *m*; (seller) vendeur/-euse *m/f*; ~ **company** *n* société apporteuse *f*; ~ **finance** *n* financement d'apport *m*; ~ **rating** *n* valuation de l'apporteur *f*, évaluation de l'apporteur *f*

vendue *n* US (auction) vente aux enchères *f*, vente à la criée *f*

Venn diagram *n* diagramme de Venn *m*

ventilate *vt* (concern) exprimer publiquement; (issue) livrer à la discussion

ventilation *n* ventilation *f*

venture¹ *n* (company) entreprise *f*;
(undertaking) aventure *f*, entreprise *f*; ~ **capital** *n* capital-risque *m*; ~ **capital company** *n*, ~ **capital corporation** *n* société de capital-risque *f*; ~ **capitalist** *n* capital-risqueur *m*; ~ **management** *n* gestion des risques *f*; ~ **team** *n* équipe chargée d'un nouveau produit *f*

venture² 1 *vt* (opinion) hasarder; (suggestion) se permettre; (money) risquer
2 *vi* ~ **into** (sector, activity) se lancer dans

venue *n* (for meeting, conference) lieu *m*; **the conference ~** le lieu du congrès *m*

VER *abbr* (▸voluntary export restraint) RVE *f* (restriction volontaire des exportations)

verbal *adj* verbal; ~ **agreement** *n* accord verbal *m*, convention verbale *f*; ~ **communication** *n* communication verbale *f*; ~ **offer** *n* offre verbale *f*; ~ **reasoning** *n* raisonnement verbal *m*; ~ **warning** *n* premier avertissement *m*

verbally *adv* verbalement

verbatim¹ *adj* (report, account) textuel/-elle

verbatim² *adv* (repeat) textuellement

verdict *n* verdict *m*

verge *n* be on the ~ **of bankruptcy** être au bord de la faillite; **be on the ~ of collapse** être sur le point de s'effondrer

verifiable *adj* vérifiable

verification *n* vérification *f*; ~ **of accounts** vérification comptable *f*

verify *vt* contrôler, vérifier

versatile *adj* (equipment, vehicle) polyvalent, à usages multiples; (person) plein de ressources, adaptable

versatility *n* (of hardware, system) polyvalence *f*; (of person) adaptabilité *f*

version *n* (Gen Comm, Comp) version *f*; (type, model) modèle *m*; (Media) version *f*; ~ **control** *n* gestion de versions *f*

verso *n* verso *m*

vertical *adj* vertical; ~ **amalgamation** *n* fusion verticale *f*; ~ **analysis** *n* analyse verticale *f*; ~ **business combination** *n* concentration verticale *f*; ~ **combination** *n* intégration verticale *f*; ~ **communication** *n* communication verticale *f*; ~ **discrimination** *n* discrimination verticale *f*; ~ **expansion** *n* croissance verticale *f*, développement vertical *m*; ~ **integration** *n* intégration verticale *f*; ~ **market** *n* marché vertical *m*; ~ **merger** *n* fusion verticale *f*, intégration verticale *f*; ~ **mobility** *n* mobilité verticale *f*; ~ **organization** *n* organisation verticale *f*; ~ **planning** *n* planification verticale *f*; ~ **portal** *n* portail vertical, vortail *m*, portail professionnel *m*; ~ **promotion** *n* avancement *m*; ~ **specialization** *n* spécialisation verticale *f*; ~ **spread** *n* (Stock) opération mixte sur options avec dates d'échéance différentes *f*, opération mixte verticale *f*; ~ **union** *n* ⋯⋗

syndicat professionnel *m*

vertically *adv* verticalement

vessel *n* bâtiment *m*, navire *m*, vaisseau *m*

vest *vt* (Stock) conférer; ～ **sb with sth** investir qn de qch; ～ **sth in sb** (Gen Comm) assigner qch à qn; (Stock) conférer qch à qn

vested *adj* (in trustee, beneficiary) dévolu; **have a ～ interest in** (Gen Comm) s'intéresser tout particulièrement à, être directement intéressé par; (Fin) être intéressé dans; ～ **benefits** *n pl* (Ins) avantages acquis *m pl*; ～ **interest** *n* (Law) droit acquis *m*

vestibule period *n* période d'attente *f*

vet *vt* (applicant, employee) mener une enquête approfondie sur; (document, publication) approuver

veto[1] *n* veto *m*; **exercise one's ～** exercer son droit de veto; **right of ～** droit de veto *m*

veto[2] *vt* mettre son veto à

vetting *n* contrôle de sécurité *m*, examen *m*

vexed question *n* question controversée *f*, question très débattue *f*

VGA *abbr* (**video graphics array**) (Comp) VGA *m*; ～ **card** *n* carte VGA *f*, carte vidéographique *f*

VHF *abbr* (**very high frequency**) VHF *f* (très haute fréquence)

via *prep* (Comms) par, via; (Transp) par, en passant par; (on ticket) via

viability *n* viabilité *f*

viable *adj* (company) viable; (project, plan) réalisable

vicarious liability *n* responsabilité civile *f*

vice: ～**-chairman** *n* vice-président *m*; ～**-president** *n* président/-e adjoint/-e *m/f*, vice-président/-e *m/f*

vice versa *adv* vice versa

vicious circle *n* cercle vicieux *m*

victimization *n* persécution *f*

victimize *vt* persécuter

video[1] *n* vidéo *f*; **promotional ～** vidéo publicitaire *f*; ～ **camera** *n* caméra vidéo *f*; ～ **card** *n* carte vidéo *f*; ～ **cassette** *n* cassette vidéo *f*, vidéocassette *f*; ～ **cassette recorder** *n* magnétoscope *m*; ～ **conference** *n* vidéoconférence *f*; ～ **conference over IP** *n* vidéoconférence sur IP *f*; ～ **conferencing** *n* vidéoconférence *f*; ～ **disk** *n* vidéodisque *m*; ～ **display** *n* écran vidéo *m*; ～ **display unit** *n* terminal à écran de visualisation *m*; ～ **game** *n* jeu-vidéo *m*; ～ **graphics** *n pl* vidéographie *f*; ～ **graphics array card** *n* carte VGA *f*; ～ **library** *n* vidéothèque *f*; ～**-on-demand** *n* vidéos à la demande *f pl*; ～ **piracy** *n* piratage de films vidéo *m*; ～ **RAM** *n* mémoire vidéo *f*; ～ **recorder** *n* magnétoscope *m*; ～ **show** *n* vidéoprésentation *f*; ～ **surveillance** *n* vidéosurveillance *f*; ～ **webcast** *n* webémission, émission diffusée sur le Web *f*

video[2] *vt* enregistrer sur bande vidéo

videophone *n* vidéophone *m*, visiophone *m*

videotape[1] *n* bande vidéo *f*; ～ **recorder** *n* magnétoscope *m*

videotape[2] *vt* enregistrer sur bande vidéo

videotex® *n* vidéographie interactive *f*, vidéotex® *m*

videotext® *n* vidéotexte® *m*

view[1] *n* (opinion) opinion *f*; (on website) impression *f*; ～ **of the world** vision du monde *f*; **in ～ of** (situation, facts) vu, étant donné; **take a different ～** voir autrement; **take a long ～** voir à long terme; **take a gloomy ～ of the situation** envisager la situation sous un jour pessimiste; **with a ～ to** en vue de; **with a ～ to doing** dans l'intention de faire; **with this in ～** à cette fin

view[2] *vt* (consider) considérer, envisager; (word processed document) visualiser; (documents) examiner; (property) visiter; (programme) regarder; ～**ed data** (on web) page vue *f*

viewdata® *n* vidéographie interactive *f*

viewer *n* téléspectateur/-trice *m/f*; (Comp) visionneur *m*; (Prop) visiteur/-euse *m/f*

viewing *n* (of house, exhibition) visite *f*; (of film) projection *f*; (of range, collection) présentation *f*; ～ **by appointment only** visites seulement sur rendez-vous; ～ **figures** *n pl* (Media) taux d'écoute *m*; ～ **room** *n* salle de projection *f*; ～ **time** *n* (airtime) temps d'antenne *m*

vie: ～ **with** *vt* (competitor) rivaliser avec

viewpoint *n* point de vue *m*

vigorous *adj* vigoureux/-euse

village shop *n*, **village store** *n* commerce de proximité rural *m*

vindicate *vt* (person, behaviour) justifier

vine *n* vigne *f*; ～ **grower** *n* viticulteur/-trice *m/f*; ～ **growing** *n* viticulture *f*; ～**-growing district** *n* région viticole *f*; ～ **harvest** *n* vendange *f*

vineyard *n* vignoble *m*

vintage *n* (year) millésime *m*

vintner *n* négociant/-e en vins *m/f*

violate *vt* (rule, regulation) enfreindre; (right, agreement, privacy) violer; ～ **the law** enfreindre la loi, violer la loi

violation *n* (of right, agreement, privacy) violation *f*; (minor crime) infraction *f*; **in ～ of** en violation de; **safety ～** non-respect des règles de sécurité *m*; ～ **of a law** violation d'un droit *f*

violence *n* violence *f*

VIP *abbr* (▸**very important person**) personnage de marque *m*

viral marketing *n* marketing viral *m*

vire *vt* effectuer un virement de, virer

virement *n* virement *m*

virtual *adj* (Comp) virtuel/-elle; (failure, collapse) quasi-total; ～ **bank** *n* banque en ligne *f*, banque sur Internet *f*; ～ **community** *n* communauté virtuelle *f*; ～ **coupon** *n*

coupon électronique m; ~ **environment** n
monde virtuel m; ~ **learning** n
apprentissage en ligne m, téléapprentissage
m; ~ **mall** n galerie marchande virtuelle f;
~ **marketplace** n place de marché
électronique f; ~ **mentoring** n mentorat en
ligne m; ~ **private network** n réseau privé
virtuel m, ~ **office** n bureau virtuel m; ~
reality n réalité virtuelle f; ~ **reality
modelling language** n VRML m; ~
shopping cart n panier (virtuel) m; caddie®
(virtuel) m; ~ **store** n boutique en ligne f,
cyberboutique f; ~ **storefront** n vitrine
virtuelle f; ~ **ticketing** n billetterie
électronique f

virtue n **by ~ of** en raison de, en vertu de;
by ~ of one's position de par ses fonctions

virus n (Comp) virus m; ~ **checker** n
logiciel antivirus; **~-free** adj non contaminé

visa n visa m; **entry/tourist ~** visa d'entrée/
de touriste m

viscous: ~ **demand** n viscosité de la
demande f; ~ **supply** n viscosité de l'offre f

visibility n (Gen Comm, S&M) visibilité f;
(Fin) transparence f

visible adj visible; ~ **export** n exportation
visible f; ~ **hand** n main visible f; ~ **import**
n importation visible f; ~ **trade balance** n
balance commerciale des visibles f

visibles n pl visibles m pl

vision n vision f; **project ~** vision du projet;
define a ~ définir une vision, élaborer une
vision

visioning n élaboration d'une vision f,
visioning m

visit[1] n visite f; (stay) séjour m; (to website)
visite f; ~ **counter** n (on website) compteur
de visiteurs m

visit[2] vt visiter; (inspect) inspecter

visitation n visite d'inspection f

visiting adj (person) de l'extérieur, en visite;
~ **card** n carte de visite f

visitor n (Gen Comm, Comp) visiteur m; ~**s'
book** n (Gen Comm, Comp) livre d'or m; ~**'s
tax** n taxe de séjour f

visual adj visuel/-elle; ~ **aid** n support
visuel m; ~ **appeal** n attrait visuel m,
intérêt visuel m; ~ **arts** n pl arts plastiques
m pl, arts visuels m pl; ~ **display unit** n
écran de visualisation m; ~ **impact** n
impact visuel m

visuals n pl (for presentation) supports visuels
m pl

vital adj essentiel/-elle (service, help)
indispensable; (factor) décisif/-ive; **it is ~ that**
il est indispensable que; **it is of ~
importance that** il est vital que; ~ **to sb/sth**
indispensable à qn/qch

vitiate vt (Law) vicier

VLCC abbr (**very large crude carrier**) très
gros transporteur de brut m

VLR abbr (▸**variable lending rate**) taux de

crédit variable m

VLS abbr (**very large-scale**) à très grande
échelle

v-mail abbr (**video mail**) courrier
électronique avec séquence vidéo m

vocation n métier m, vocation f

vocational adj professionnel/-elle; ~
course n stage de formation professionnelle
m; ~ **guidance** n orientation
professionnelle f; ~ **school** n école
professionnelle f; ~ **training** n formation
professionnelle f

VOD abbr (▸**video-on-demand**) vidéos à la
demande f pl

vogue n vogue f; **in ~** en vogue; **come into
~** entrer en vogue; **go out of ~** se démoder

voice: **~-activated** adj à commande
vocale; ~ **mail** n messagerie vocale f; ~
mail-box n boîte vocale f; ~ **messaging** n
messagerie vocale f; **~-over** n voix off f; ~
recognition n reconnaissance vocale f; ~
response unit n serveur vocal m

void[1] adj (contract, agreement) nul/nulle; ~ **of**
(resources) dépourvu de; **make ~, render ~**
annuler; ~ **policy** n police nulle f

void[2] vt annuler

voidable adj annulable, résiliable; ~
policy n police annulable f

voidance n (annulment) annulation f

VoIP abbr (**Voice over Internet Protocol**)
VoIP m, voix sur IP f

volatile adj (market, rate) instable

volatility n (of market, rate) instabilité f

volume n volume m; (capacity) capacité f; ~
of business n volume d'affaires m; ~
deleted n (Stock) volume des transactions
effacé m; ~ **discount** n ristourne sur
quantité f; ~ **of exports** n volume des
exportations m; ~ **mailing** n multipostage
m; ~ **of orders** volume des commandes m;
~ **of retail sales** n volume des ventes au
détail m; ~ **of trading** volume des
opérations m, volume des transactions m; ~
trading n (Stock) négociation de blocs
d'actions f

voluntarism n politique contractuelle f

voluntary adj (not imposed) volontaire;
(optional) facultatif/-ive; (unpaid) bénévole; ~
agency n agence bénévole f; ~ **arbitration**
n conciliation volontaire f; ~ **bankruptcy** n
dépôt de bilan m; ~ **body** n organisme
volontaire m; ~ **chain** n chaîne volontaire
de distribution f; ~ **compliance** n
observation volontaire f; ~ **contributions** n
pl UK (Tax) contributions volontaires f pl; ~
export restraint n restriction volontaire des
exportations f; ~ **insurance** n assurance
facultative f, assurance volontaire f; ~
liquidation n liquidation volontaire f; ~
redundancy n départ volontaire m; ~
retirement n départ volontaire à la retraite
m; ~ **winding-up** n (of business) liquidation ⋯⟩

v

volontaire *f*; **~ work** *n* travail volontaire *m*; **~ worker** *n* (travailleur/-euse) bénévole *m/f*

volunteer¹ *n* volontaire *mf*; (unpaid worker) bénévole *mf*

volunteer² *vt* (information) donner spontanément; (help, advice) offrir

vortal *n* vortail *m*, portail vertical *m*

vostro account *n* compte vostro *m*

vote¹ *n* vote *m*; (body of voters) voix *f pl*, vote *m*; **cast one's ~** voter; **take a ~** voter; **put sth to the ~** mettre qch aux voix; **~ against** voix contre *f*; **~ by proxy** vote par procuration *m*; **~ by show of hands** vote à mains levées *m*; **~ of confidence** vote de confiance *m*; **~ of thanks** discours de remerciement *m*

vote² ① *vt* (socialist, yes, no) voter; **~ sb in** élire qn; **~ sb into power** élire qn ② *vi* voter; **~ for/against sb** voter pour/contre qn; **~ for/against sth** voter en faveur de/contre qch; **~ on whether ...** voter pour décider si ...; **~ to strike** voter la grève; **~ by ballot** voter au scrutin

voter *n* électeur/-trice *m/f*; **~ turnout** *n* participation électorale *f*

voting *n* (at board meetings) vote *m*; (ballot, procedure) scrutin *m*; **~ booth** *n* isoloir *m*; **~ paper** *n* bulletin de vote *m*; **~ procedure** *n*

procédure électorale *f*; **~ right** *n* droit de vote *m*; **~ security** *n* (Stock) titre avec droit de vote *m*; **~ share** *n*, **~ stock** *n* action avec droit de vote *f*

vouch: ~ for *vt* se porter garant de

voucher *n* (proof, receipt) justificatif *m*, pièce justificative *f*; (for purchase, special offer) bon *m*; (Acc) justificatif comptable *m*; **~ system** *n* système de bons *m*

voyage *n* voyage *m*; **~ charter** *n* affrètement au voyage *m*; **~ charter party** *n* charte-partie au voyage *f*; **~ policy** *n* (Ins) (marine) police au voyage *f*

VP *abbr* (▸**vice-president**) V-P *m* (vice-président)

VPN *abbr* (▸**virtual private network**) réseau privé virtuel *m*

VRAM *abbr* (**video random access memory**) mémoire vidéo *f*

VRML *abbr* (▸**virtual reality modelling language**) VRML *m*

VRU *abbr* (▸**voice response unit**) serveur vocal *m*

vulgarize *vt* banaliser

vulnerable *adj* vulnérable

vulture fund *n* fonds prédateur *m*

Ww

W.A. *abbr* (▸**with average**) (Ins) avec avaries; **~ cover** *n* (marine) couverture avaries comprises *f*

wad *n* (of notes) liasse *f*

wage¹ *n* salaire *m*; **~ agreement** *n* accord salarial *m*, convention salariale *f*; **~-and-price guidelines** *n pl* directives en matière de salaires et de prix *f pl*; **~ arbitration** *n* arbitrage en matière de salaires *m*; **~ bargaining** *n* négociations salariales *f pl*; **~ bill** *n* masse salariale *f*; **~ bracket** *n* tranche de salaires *f*; **~ ceiling** *n* plafond *m*, plafonnement des salaires *m*; **~ claim** *n* revendication salariale *f*; **~ control** *n* contrôle des salaires *m*; **~ costs** *n pl* coûts salariaux *m pl*; **~ differential** *n* écart des salaires *m*, écart salarial *m*; **~ drift** *n* dérive des salaires *m*; **~ earner** *n* salarié/-e *m/f*; (breadwinner) soutien de famille *m*; **~ explosion** *n* explosion des salaires *f*; **~ floor** *n* plancher des salaires *m*; **~ freeze** *n* blocage des salaires *m*; **~ gap** *n* fossé entre les salaires *m*; **~ incentive** *n* stimulant salarial *m*; **~ increase** *n* augmentation de salaire *f*; **~ indexation** *n* indexation des

salaires *f*; **~ inflation** *n* inflation des salaires *f*; **~ lag** *n* décalage des salaires *m*; **~ negotiations** *n pl* négociations salariales *f pl*; **~ packet** *n* (envelope) enveloppe de paie *f*; (money) paie *f*; **~ policy** *n* politique salariale *f*; **~-price spiral** *n* spirale des salaires et des prix *f*; **~-push inflation** *n* inflation par les salaires *f*; **~ restraint** *n* limitation des salaires *f*; **~ round** *n* négociations salariales *f pl*; **~ scale** *n* échelle des salaires *f*; **~ settlement** *n* accord sur les salaires *m*; **~ slip** *n* feuille de paie *f*; **~ spread** *n* éventail des salaires *m*; **~ structure** *n* structure des salaires *f*; **~ subsidy** *n* subvention des salaires *f*; **~ talks** *n pl* négociations salariales *f pl*; **~-tax spiral** *n* montée de l'impôt sur les salaires *f*; **~ theory** *n* théorie des salaires *f*

wage² *vt* (campaign) mener; **~ a negative campaign** mener une campagne négative; **~ a war against** faire la guerre contre

waged *adj* salarié

wages *n pl* salaire *m*; **~ act** *n* loi sur les salaires *f*; **~ policy** *n* politique des revenus *f*, politique salariale *f*

wait¹ *n* attente *f*; **have a long ~** devoir attendre longtemps

wait² *vi* attendre; **~ for** attendre; **~ in line** faire la queue

wait-and-see policy *n* attentisme *m*

waiter *n* (Stock) commis *m*, coursier *m*

waiting *n* attente *f*; **~ game** attentisme *m*; **~ list** *n* liste d'attente *f*; **~ period** *n* délai d'attente *m*, période de latence *f*; **~ time** *n* période d'attente *f*

waive *vt* (claim, right, demand) renoncer à; (fee, duty, requirement) supprimer; (rule, regulation) déroger à

waiver *n* renonciation *f*; **~ clause** *n* (Ins) clause d'abandon *f*, clause d'exonération *f*

wake *n* **in the ~ of** à la suite de

wake-up call *n* (Comms) réveil téléphoné *m*

walkabout *n* bain de foule *m*; **go on a ~** prendre un bain de foule

walkaway *n* AmE victoire facile *f*

walkie-talkie *n* talkie-walkie *m*

walkout *n* grève *f*, grève surprise *f*; **stage a ~** (strikers) faire une grève surprise; (audience, delegates) partir en signe de protestation

walk: ~ out *vi* (strikers) cesser le travail; (audience, delegates) partir en signe de protestation

walkover *n* (infrml) victoire facile *f*

walk-up *n* US immeuble sans ascenseur *m*

wall¹ *n* **go to the ~** (company) couler, faire faillite; (person) perdre la partie; **have one's back to the ~** avoir le dos au mur

wall²: ~ out *vt* AmE (competition, foreign trade) dresser des barrières contre

wallflower *n* (Stock) action boudée *f*, titre déprécié *m*

wallpaper *n* (Comp) fond d'écran *m*

Wall Street *pr n* US Wall Street *n pr*; **~ Journal** *n* le journal de la Bourse de New-York; **~ crash** *n* krach de Wall Street *m*

WAN *abbr* (▶**wide area network**) grand réseau *m*, réseau longue distance *m*

wane *vi* (sector, industry) décliner; (enthusiasm, popularity) diminuer

wangle *vt* (infrml) réussir à obtenir; **~ sth out of sb** soutirer qch à qn; **~ it for sb to do** s'arranger pour que qn fasse

want ad *n* AmE petite annonce *f*

wanting *adj* **be ~** (not up to required standard) ne pas être à la hauteur; (lacking) manquer, faire défaut

WAP *abbr* (▶**wireless application protocol**) (protocole) WAP *m*; **~-enabled device** *n* terminal WAP portatif *m*; **~ phone** *n* téléphone WAP *m*; **~ portal** *n* portail mobile *m*; **~ server** *n* serveur d'applications WAP *m*, serveur de contenu WAP *m*; **~ technology** *n* technology WAP *f*; **~ user** *n* utilisateur/-trice WAP *m/f*

war *n* guerre *f*; (to eradicate sth) lutte *f*; (competition) guerre *f*; **go to ~** entrer en guerre, se mettre en guerre; **~ on crime** lutte contre le crime; **price ~** guerre des prix *f*; **~ babies** *n pl* valeurs des industries de défense *f pl*; **~ chest** *n* trésor de guerre *m*

ward: ~ off *vt* (bankruptcy, catastrophe) éviter; (threat) écarter

warehouse¹ *n* entrepôt *m*; **~ capacity** *n* capacité d'entreposage *f*; **~ charges** *n pl* frais d'entrepôt *m pl*, frais de magasinage *m pl*; **~ receipt** *n* récépissé d'entrepôt *m*, récépissé-warrant *m*; **~ supervisor** *n* chef magasinier *m*; **~ warrant** *n* récépissé-warrant *m*, warrant *m*

warehouse² *vt* entreposer

warehouseman *n* magasinier *m*, manutentionnaire *m*

warehousing *n* entreposage *m*, emmagasinage *m*; **~ charges** *n pl* frais d'entreposage *m pl*, frais d'emmagasinage *m pl*

wares *n pl* marchandises *f pl*

warez *n pl* (infrml) logiciels piratés *m pl*

warm¹ *adj* (welcome, reception) chaleureux/ -euse; **~ restart** *n* (Comp) redémarrage automatique *m*; **~-up session** *n* (Mgmnt) phase de mise en train *f*

warm²: ~ to, ~ towards *vt* (idea) s'enthousiasmer pour; (task, work) s'attaquer avec enthousiasme à

warn *vt* (alert) avertir, prévenir; (inform) avertir, aviser; **~ sb against sth** mettre qn en garde contre qch; **~ sb against doing sth** déconseiller à qn de faire qch; **~ sb that** prévenir qn que

warning *n* (alert) avertissement *m*; (formal notification) avis *m*; **a ~ against** une mise en garde contre; **official/written ~** avis officiel/ écrit; **without ~** à l'improviste; **without previous ~** sans préavis; **issue a ~** donner un avertissement; **~ device** *n* dispositif d'alarme *m*; **~ indicator** *n* signal d'alarme *m*; **~ list** *n* (Bank) liste d'oppositions *f*; **~ notice** *n* panneau avertisseur *m*; **~ shot** *n* coup de semonce *m*; **~ sign** *n* (notice) panneau avertisseur *m*; (early symptom) signe annonciateur *m*

warrant¹ *n* (receipt) récépissé *m*; (guarantee) garantie *f*; (for arrest, search) mandat *m*; (Stock) bon de souscription *m*; (Transp, Imp/Exp) warrant *m*; **~ of attorney** pouvoir *m*, procuration *f*; **~ discounting** *n* warrantage *m*; **~ for payment** ordonnance de paiement *f*; **~ holder** *n* (Stock) détenteur/-trice de bon de souscription *m/f*; **~ issue** *n* (Fin) émission de warrants *f*

warrant² *vt* (Bank) garantir; (justify) justifier

warranted *adj* garanti

warrantee *n* receveur d'une garantie *m/f*

warrantor *n* garant/-e *m/f*

warranty *n* garantie *f*; **be under ~** être ···>

sous garantie; **a two-year** ∼ une garantie de deux ans; ∼ **bond** *n* obligation garantie *f*; ∼ **card** *n* carte de garantie *f*; ∼ **of title** *n* attestation de titre *f*

Warsaw Convention *n* Convention de Varsovie *f*

washout *n* fiasco *m*

wash sale *n* (Stock) vente fictive (par achat et vente simultanés) *f*

WASP *abbr* (**wireless application service provider**) fournisseur de services WAP *m*

wastage *n* gaspillage *m*; (spillage) pertes *f pl*, fuites *f pl*; (of energy, heat) déperdition *f*; ∼ **rate** *n* (Econ) taux d'abandon *m*

waste¹ *n* (detritus) déchets *m pl*, ordures *f pl*; (squandering) gaspillage *m*; ∼ **of time** perte de temps *f*; **industrial/hazardous** ∼ déchets industriels/dangereux *m pl*; **let sth go to** ∼ gaspiller qch; ∼ **disposal** *n* traitement des déchets *m*; ∼ **dumping** *n* décharge de déchets *f*; ∼ **management** *n* gestion des déchets *f*; ∼ **processing** *n* transformation des déchets *f*; ∼ **product** *n* (made from waste) produit de récupération *m*; (of manufacturing process) déchet de fabrication *m*; ∼ **recycling** *n* recyclage des déchets *m*; ∼ **sorting** *n* tri des déchets *m*; ∼ **treatment** *n* traitement des déchets *m*; ∼ **treatment plant** *n* usine de traitement des déchets *f*

waste² *vt* (resources, money) gaspiller; (day, time, opportunity) perdre

wasted *adj* (effort, care) inutile; (commodity, energy) gaspillé; (energy, time) perdu; **a** ∼ **opportunity** une opportunité de perdue

wasteful *adj* (method, process) peu économique; (with money) dépensier/-ière; (with resources) gaspilleur/-euse; **be** ∼ **of** (commodity, resource) gaspiller; ∼ **expenditure** *n* dépenses inutiles *f pl*

wasteland *n* terrain vague *m*

wastepaper *n* vieux papiers *m pl*

wastewater *n* eaux usées *f pl*; ∼ **treatment** *n* traitement des eaux usées *m*; ∼ **treatment plant** *n* (Envir) station d'épuration des eaux usées *f*

wasting assets *n pl* actif défectif *m*, immobilisations défectives *f pl*

watch¹ *n* surveillance *f*; **keep a close** ∼ **on** surveiller de près; **be on the** ∼ **for sth** guetter qch; ∼ **list** *n* (Bank) liste de surveillance *f*; (Stock) liste de valeurs sous surveillance *f*

watch² *vt* (TV, video) regarder; (competitor, situation, share, value) surveiller; (progress, career, development) suivre; ∼ **one's back** surveiller ses arrières; ∼ **out for** (problem, person) guetter; (event) faire attention à; ∼ **over** (interests) veiller à

watchdog *n* (organization) organisme de surveillance *m*; (animal) chien de garde *m*; **consumer** ∼ organisme de défense des intérêts du consommateur *m*; **financial** ∼

observateur économique *m*; ∼ **committee** *n* comité de surveillance *m*

watcher *n* (at event) spectateur/-trice *m/f*; **fashion/industry** ∼ spécialiste de la mode/de l'industrie *mf*

watchman *n* gardien *m*

watchword *n* mot d'ordre *m*

water¹ *n* eau *f*; **keep one's head above** ∼ (Fin) faire face à ses engagements; **get into hot** ∼ avoir des ennuis; **that theory doesn't hold** ∼ cette théorie ne tient pas debout; ∼ **company** *n* compagnie hydraulique *f*; ∼ **damage** *n* dégâts des eaux *m pl*; ∼ **supplier** *n* distributeur d'eau *m*; ∼ **supply** *n* alimentation en eau *f*; ∼ **treatment** *n* traitement des eaux *m*

water²: ∼ **down** *vt* (idea, policy, statement) atténuer; (capital, stock) diluer

watered: ∼ **capital** *n* capital dilué *m*; ∼ **stock** *n* action diluée *f*, actions surveillées *f pl*

watermark *n* (Bank, Comp) filigrane *m*

watermarked *adj* (bank note) filigrané

waterproof *adj* imperméable

watershed *n* (turning point) tournant *m*; (Media) UK *l'heure à laquelle les émissions déconseillées aux enfants peuvent être diffusées*

watertight *adj* (argument) irréfutable; (regulations) incontestable; (container) étanche

wave *n* vague *f*; **make** ∼**s** créer des histoires; ∼ **power** *n* énergie des vagues *f*

way *n* façon *f*, manière *f*; ∼ **of doing** façon de faire; ∼ **of life** mode de vie *m*; **middle** ∼ juste milieu *m*; **be under** ∼ (in vehicle) être en route; (work, negotiations, project) être en cours; **get under** ∼ (in vehicle) se mettre en route; (event, work) commencer, démarrer; **pave the** ∼ **for** ouvrir la voie à; **make** ∼ **for** laisser la voie libre à, laisser la place à; **a** ∼ **out of our difficulties** un moyen de nous sortir de nos difficultés; **find a** ∼ **round a problem** contourner un problème; **find a** ∼ **forward** trouver une solution; **the** ∼ **ahead looks difficult** l'avenir s'annonce difficile

waybill *n* (air) lettre de transport aérien *f*; (road, rail) lettre de voiture *f*

ways and means *n pl* (Econ) voies et moyens *f pl*; ∼ **committee** *n* US (Fin) *commission des finances*

WBT *abbr* (▶**web-based training**) e-formation *f*, formation en ligne *f*

w.c. *abbr* (▶**without charge**) gratis, gratuitement, sans frais

weak *adj* (demand, economy, currency) faible; (government, performance) faible; (share) à prix bas; ∼ **market** *n* marché en baisse *m*; ∼ **point** *n* (point) faible *m*

weaken *vt* (authority, company, economy, currency value) affaiblir; (support, influence) diminuer

weakness *n* faiblesse *f*; ∼ **investigation** *n* (Acc) analyse des lacunes *f*

wealth *n* richesse *f*; **a** ∼ **of** (information) une

mine de; (talent, experience) énormément de;
(opportunities) beaucoup de; ~ **distribution** n
distribution de la richesse f; ~ **tax** n (Tax)
impôt sur la fortune m

Wealth of Nations n (Econ) Richesse des
nations f

wealthy adj riche; **the** ~ n pl les riches
m pl

wear[1] n usure f; ~ **and tear** n dégradation
f, usure f

wear[2] [1] vt (damage) user
[2] vi (get damaged) s'user; ~ **down**
(resistance) saper; ~ **off** (effect) se dissiper; **the
novelty will soon** ~ **off** ça n'aura bientôt
plus l'attrait de la nouveauté; ~ **out** [1] vt
user
[2] vi s'user

weather[1] n temps m; ~ **report** n bulletin
météorologique m

weather[2] vt (recession, crisis) surmonter

weaving trade n industrie du tissage f

web, Web n Web m, Toile f; **surf the** ~
surfer sur le Web, surfer sur la Toile; ~ **ad
broker** n courtier en publicité en ligne m; ~
address n adresse Web f; ~ **advertising** n
publicité en ligne f; ~ **agency** n agence de
communication sur la Toile f, Web agency f;
~ **application** n application Web f;
~**-assisted selling** n vente en ligne assistée
f; ~ **audience measurement** n audimètre
Web m, mesure d'audience sur Internet f; ~
authoring n création de pages Web f; ~
authoring program n outil de création de
pages Web m; ~**-based application** n
application Web f; ~**-based training** n
e-formation f, formation en ligne f; ~ **broker**
n courtier en publicité en ligne m; ~
browser n navigateur m, logiciel de
navigation m; ~ **callback** n option de
routage d'un appel sur un agent m; ~ **call
center** AmE, ~ **call centre** BrE n centre
d'appel sur Internet m; ~ **callthrough** n
liaison directe via la voix par téléphonie IP f;
~ **chat** n bavardage en ligne m; ~ **client** n
client/-e Web m/f; ~ **commerce** n
commerce en ligne m, cybercommerce m,
commerce sur Internet m; ~ **content** n
contenu (de sites Web) m; ~ **content
developer** n développeur/-euse de contenu
Web m/f; ~ **content management** n
gestion de contenu Web f; ~ **design** n
conception de sites Web f; ~ **designer** n
concepteur/-trice de sites Web m/f; ~
developer n développeur/-euse Web m/f; ~
document n page Web f; ~**-enabled
application** n application Web f;
~**-enabled device** n terminal portatif WAP
m; ~**-enabled phone** n téléphone portable
Internet m; ~ **ergonomist** n ergonome
d'interfaces m/f; ~ **front-end** n interface
utilisateur Web f; ~ **hosting** n hébergement
(de sites Web) m; ~ **hosting server** n
serveur d'hébergement m; ~ **media broker**

n courtier en publicité en ligne m; ~ **page** n
page Web f; ~ **presence** n présence sur
Internet f; ~ **request broker** n courtier de
recherches en ligne m; ~ **ring** n fédération
de sites f, anneau Web m; ~ **search** n
recherche sur Internet f; ~ **server** n serveur
Web m; ~ **session** n séance de navigation f;
~ **shop** n boutique en ligne f, cyberboutique
f; ~ **space** n espace Web m; ~ **space
provider** n hébergeur de sites Web m; ~
surf vi surfer (sur Internet); ~ **surfer** n
surfeur/-euse m/f; ~ **surfing** n surf (sur
Internet) m; ~ **telephony** n téléphonie sur
Internet f; ~ **tutor** n e-formateur/-trice m/f,
formateur/-trice en ligne m/f

webcam n webcam f

webcast[1] n émission diffusée sur Internet f

webcast[2] vt diffuser sur Internet

webcasting n diffusion sur Internet f

webification n transformation en format
HTML f

webify vt transformer en format HTML

webinar n séminaire en ligne m

webmaster n webmestre m,
administrateur/-trice de site Internet m/f

webmeeting n réunion en ligne f

webographics n + sing v étude du profil
comportemental des internautes f

website n site Web m; ~ **hosting** n
hébergement de sites Web m; ~ **plan** n plan
d'un site Web m; ~ **referencing** n
référencement (de sites) m

webzine n revue en ligne f

weed: ~ **out** vt (items, people) éliminer

week n semaine f; **at a** ~**'s notice** dans un
délai de sept jours; **a** ~ **in advance** une
semaine à l'avance; **a** ~ **today** aujourd'hui
en huit; **Friday** ~ vendredi en huit; **within a**
~ dans un délai de sept jours, dans une
semaine; **a** ~**'s wages** une semaine de
salaire

weekday n jour de (la) semaine m, jour
ouvrable m; **on** ~**s** en semaine

weekend n week-end m; **take a long** ~
prendre un week-end prolongé; **at the** ~
pendant le week-end; **at** ~**s** le week-end

weekly[1] adj hebdomadaire

weekly[2] n hebdomadaire m

weekly[3] adv (pay) à la semaine; (take place,
meet) une fois par semaine; (write, check)
chaque semaine

weekly: ~ **pay packet** n paie
hebdomadaire f, salaire hebdomadaire m; ~
rent n loyer hebdomadaire m; ~ **wage** n
paie hebdomadaire f, salaire hebdomadaire m

wef abbr (▶**with effect from**) avec effet à
compter du, à partir de

weigh vt (measure) peser; (arguments, evidence,
options) peser; (consequences) évaluer; ~ **up**
(benefits, risks) mettre en balance; (situation)
évaluer; ~ **up the pros and cons** peser le
pour et le contre; ~ **up whether to say yes** ⋯⋗

w

or no peser la situation pour savoir s'il faut dire oui ou non

weighbridge n pont-bascule m

weight¹ n (heaviness) poids m; (influence) poids m; (in statistics) coefficient m, pondérateur m; **~s and measures** poids et mesures m pl; **by ~** au poids; **lend ~ to sth** ajouter du poids à; **add one's ~ to sth** faire jouer son influence en faveur de qch; **throw one's ~ behind sth** soutenir qch à fond; **give equal ~ to** accorder une importance égale à; **pull one's ~** faire sa part de travail; **the ~ of responsibility** le poids des responsabilités; **carry ~** (argument, idea) avoir du poids; **~ allowed free** franchise de poids f; **~ limit** n limitation de poids f; **~ when empty** poids à vide m

weight² vt (index, average, variable) pondérer

weighted adj pondéré; **~ average** n moyenne pondérée f; **~ average cost** n coût moyen pondéré m; **~ index** n indice pondéré m

weighting n pondération f; (for cost of living) indemnité de vie chère f; **London ~** indemnité pour résidence à Londres f

welcome¹ adj (initiative, boost, news) opportun

welcome² n accueil m; **give sb a warm ~** faire un accueil chaleureux à qn

welcome³ vt (person) accueillir; (decision, news, change) se réjouir de; (move, initiative) accueillir favorablement; **I would ~ your opinion on this matter** j'aimerais savoir ce que vous pensez de cette affaire; **she would ~ a meeting** elle a dit qu'elle souhaiterait une rencontre

welcome: ~ message n (Comp) message d'accueil m; **~ page** n (Comp) page d'accueil m; **~ speech** n discours de bienvenue m

welcoming party n comité d'accueil m

welfare n AmE (state aid) assistance sociale f; (benefit) aide sociale f; (well-being) bien-être m; **be on ~** toucher des allocations; **go on ~** US demander de l'aide sociale; **person on ~** assisté/-e m/f; **~ benefits** n pl allocations de la Sécurité Sociale f pl, prestations sociales f pl; **~ department** n service social m, services d'assistance sociale m pl; **~ economics** n + sing v économie du bien-être f; **~ fund** n caisse de prévoyance f; **~ legislation** n législation sociale f; **~ office** n AmE bureau d'aide sociale m; **~ payment** n prestation sociale f; **~ payments** n pl allocations f pl; **~ recipient** n AmE allocataire mf, assisté/-e social/-e m/f; **~ services** n pl services d'assistance sociale m pl; **~ state** n État-providence m; **~ worker** n travailleur/-euse social/-e m/f

welfarist n partisan/-e de l'État-providence m/f

well adv bien; **be ~ advised to** faire bien de, être bien avisé de; **do ~** (succeed) réussir; (get rich) s'enrichir; **it might be as ~ to do** il

vaudrait mieux faire; **~-balanced** adj (person, mind) bien équilibré, équilibré; **~-educated** adj (person) instruit; **~-established** adj bien établi; **~-grounded** adj (belief) bien fondé; **~-informed** adj bien renseigné; **~-meaning** adj bien intentionné; **~-motivated** adj motivé; **~-off** adj aisé; **~-paid** adj (person, job) bien rémunéré; **~-placed, ~-positioned** adj bien placé; **~-stocked** adj bien approvisionné; **~-to-do** adj fortuné

wellhead: ~ cost n (for gas) coût brut d'extraction de gaz m; (for oil) coût brut d'extraction pétrolière m; **~ prices** n pl prix à la source m

well-known adj (famous) célèbre; **it's ~ that, it's a ~ fact that** il est bien connu que

Western: ~ Europe n Europe de l'Ouest f, Europe occidentale f; **~ World** n pays occidentaux m pl

wet adj mouillé; (Transp) liquide; **be ~ behind the ears** (infrml) manquer d'expérience, être un peu jeunot (infrml); **~ blanket** n (infrml) trouble-fête m; **~ bulk cargo** n vrac liquide m; **~ dock** n (port) bassin à flot m; **~ goods** n pl marchandises liquides f pl; **~ stock** n (spirits) spiritueux m pl

wetware n (infrml) (Gen Comm) capital humain m; (Comp) (developers) développeurs m pl; (users) utilisateurs m pl

WFSE abbr (▸World Federation of Stock Exchanges) FIBV f (Fédération internationale des bourses de valeurs)

WFTU abbr (▸World Federation of Trade Unions) FSM f (fédération syndicale mondiale)

wgt abbr (▸weight) poids m

wharf n quai m

wharfage n (tariff) frais de mise à quai m pl; **~ dues** n pl droits de quai m pl

wheel¹ n roue f; **the ~ has come full circle** la boucle est bouclée; **it's ~s within ~s** l'affaire est plus compliquée qu'elle n'en a l'air

wheel²: ~ and deal vi être toujours en train de chercher des combines

wheeler-dealer n (infrml) affairiste mf

wheeling and dealing n affairisme m

wheels n pl rouages m pl; **the ~ of government** les rouages du gouvernement m pl

when due adj (Stock) à l'échéance

whereas clauses n pl les attendus m pl, les considérants m pl

wherefore clauses n pl conclusions f pl

whichever pron **~ is the later** la date la moins rapprochée étant prise en considération; **~ is the sooner** la date la plus rapprochée étant prise en considération

whistle n sirène f; **blow the ~ on sb**

dénoncer qn; **blow the ~ on sth** révéler qch;
~-blower n dénonciateur/-trice m/f
whistlestop tour n (Pol) tournée
électorale f
whiteboard n tableau blanc m
white: ~ coal n houille blanche f;
~-collar crime n criminalité en col blanc f;
~-collar union n syndicat d'employés m;
~-collar worker n col blanc m, employé/-e
de bureau m/f; **~ good** n gros appareil
électro-ménager m, produit blanc m; **~
goods** n pl gros électro-ménager m, produits
blancs m pl; **~ information** n informations
financières f pl; **~ knight** n (Fin, Stock)
chevalier blanc m; **~ market** n marché blanc
m; **~ noise** n bruit blanc m, parasite m
White Paper n UK (Pol) livre blanc m
whitewash vt (action, truth) blanchir; (Fin)
(company) réhabiliter
whittle: ~ away at vt (advantage, lead)
réduire; **~ down** vt (amount, capital) rogner
sur; (reduce) réduire peu à peu
whizz kid n (infrml) jeune prodige m
WHO abbr (▸**World Health Organization**)
OMS f (Organisation mondiale de la santé)
whole¹ adj tout, entier/-ière; (emphatic) tout
entier/-ière; **in the ~ world** dans le monde
entier
whole² n tout m; **the ~ of** tout/-e; **sell sth
as a ~** vendre qch en bloc; **taken as a ~**
pris dans l'ensemble; **on the ~** dans
l'ensemble
whole: ~ cargo charter n affrètement
total m; **~-life insurance** n assurance vie-
entière f; **~-life insurance policy** n police
d'assurance-vie entière f; **~ years** n pl (Tax)
années accomplies f pl, années complètes f pl
wholesale¹ adj (huge) massif/-ive
wholesale² adv (buy, sell) en gros; (reject) en
bloc
wholesale³ n vente en gros f, gros m; **by
~** en gros
wholesale⁴ ① vt vendre en gros
② vi se vendre en gros
wholesale: ~ bank n banque
commerciale f; **~ banking** n banque de gros
f, services bancaires de gros m pl; **~
business** n, **~ company** n maison de gros
f; **~ coop** n coopérative de gros f; **~ dealer**
n grossiste m/f; **~ delivery** n livraison en
gros f; **~ distribution** n distribution en gros
f; **~ firm** n maison de gros f; **~ goods** n pl
marchandises de gros f pl, marchandises en
gros f pl; **~ manufacture** n fabrication en
série f; **~ market** n marché de gros m; **~
merchant** n grossiste m/f; **~ price** n prix de
gros m; **~ price inflation** n inflation des
prix de gros f; **~ trade** n commerce de gros
m; **~ trader** n grossiste m/f
wholesaler n grossiste m/f; **~ margin** n
marge du grossiste f
wholesaling n vente en gros f

wholly and exclusively adv
entièrement et exclusivement
wholly dependent adj (person)
entièrement à charge
wholly-owned subsidiary n filiale à
cent pour cent f
wicket n AmE guichet m, guichet de vente
des billets m
wide adj (broad) large; (extensive) grand; **a ~
choice** un grand choix; (survey, investigation) de
grande envergure; **be ~ of the mark** être
loin de la vérité; **wider share ownership** n
économie de partenariat f; **~ area network**
n grand réseau m, réseau longue distance m;
~-body aircraft n gros-porteur m, jumbo-jet
m; **~ monetary base** n (Fin) base monétaire
étendue f; **~ opening** n (Stock) écart
important à l'ouverture m; **~ range** n (of
goods) gamme étendue f; **~-ranging** adj
(enquiry, report) de grande envergure
widely adv (travel, vary) beaucoup; (used,
accepted) largement; **be ~ available** (product)
être en vente libre; **it is ~ accepted that** il
est largement admis que; **it is ~ believed
that** beaucoup de gens pensent que; **~-held
opinions** opinions très répandues f pl; **~
recognized** adj largement reconnu
widen ① vt (tax base) élargir; (powers)
étendre; (debate, scope, gap) élargir
② vi (gap) se creuser
widening n élargissement m
widespread adj (problem, occurrence)
généralisé; (belief, view) répandu; (damage)
étendu
widow n (in printing) veuve f; **~-and-orphan
stock** n action sans risque f
width n largeur f
wife n épouse f
wild card n (Comp) joker m; (unpredictable,
element) élément imprévisible m
wildcat: ~ drilling n forage d'exploration
m; **~ strike** n grève sauvage f; **~ venture** n
entreprise risquée f
wilful: ~ default n (Tax) omission
volontaire f; **~ misrepresentation of facts**
n fausse déclaration délibérée f
will n (Law) testament m; (mental strength)
volonté f; **at ~** à volonté
win¹ n victoire f
win² ① vt (customers, sb's confidence) gagner;
(contract, delay, amnesty, reprieve) obtenir;
(sympathy) s'attirer; (support) s'acquérir;
(election, votes) gagner; **~ the jackpot** gagner
le gros lot; **~ sb's favor** AmE, **~ sb's favour**
BrE s'attirer les bonnes grâces de qn; **~
some, lose some** on ne peut pas gagner à
tous les coups; **~ sb over to** (point of view)
convaincre qn de
② vi gagner; **~ or lose** quoi qu'il arrive; **~
back** (support) récupérer; (customers, market
share) reconquérir; **~ over** (persuade)
convaincre

w

winback n (S&M) (of clients) reconquête f

winch n treuil m

wind[1] n vent m; **get a second ~** trouver un second souffle; **take the ~ out of sb's sails** couper l'herbe sous le pied de qn; **the ~s of change** le vent du changement m; **get ~ of** avoir vent de, apprendre; **~ power** n énergie éolienne f

wind[2]: **~ down** vt (company, operations, campaign) démanteler; (activity) mettre fin à; **~ up** [1] vt (meeting) clôturer; (business) liquider; (project, campaign, career) mettre fin à; (estate) régler
[2] vi (meeting, speech) se terminer

windfall n aubaine f; **~ gain** n gain exceptionnel m; **~ loss** n perte exceptionnelle f; **~ profit** n bénéfice exceptionnel m; **~-profit tax** n impôt sur les bénéfices exceptionnels m; **~ tax** n impôt sur les gains exceptionnels m

winding-up n cessation de commerce f; (of corporation) liquidation f; (of meeting, account) clôture f; **~ arrangements** n pl concordat m; **~ order** n ordonnance de mise en liquidation f; **~ sale** n vente pour cessation de commerce f; **~ value** n valeur résiduelle de liquidation f

window n (Comp) fenêtre f; (of shop) vitrine f; **~ display** n étalage m; **~-dressing** n (in shop) composition de vitrines f; (Acc, Fin), habillage du bilan m, maquillage du bilan m; **~ envelope** n enveloppe à fenêtre f; **~ of opportunity** n créneau m, créneau favorable m, ouverture f, possibilité f

window-shopping n lèche-vitrines m; **go ~** faire du lèche-vitrines

wine n vin m; **~-bottling** n mise en bouteille du vin f; **~ grower** n viticulteur/ -trice m/f; **~ growing** n viticulture f; **~ harvest** n vendange f; **~ industry** n industrie viticole f; **~ merchant** n (shopkeeper) marchand/-e de vins m/f; (wholesaler) négociant en vins m; **~-producing area** n région viticole f

winner n gagnant/-e m/f; (bullish stock) valeur en hausse f; **be a ~** (product, film, design) avoir un gros succès; **~ takes all** le vainqueur ramasse tout; **be onto a ~** jouer gagnant

winning adj (number, team) gagnant; **be on a ~ streak** (infrml) avoir trouvé le bon filon (infrml)

winnings n pl gains m pl

win-win situation n situation où l'on gagne à tous les coups f

WIP abbr (▸**work in progress**) travail en cours m

wipe vt (tape) effacer; **~ the slate clean** passer l'éponge; **~ 20 points off ZDK shares** faire baisser les actions ZDK de 20 points; **~ out** (debt) liquider; (chances, losses, gains) annuler; (competitor, rival) anéantir

WIPO abbr (▸**World Intellectual Property Organization**) Organisation mondiale pour la propriété intellectuelle f

wire: **~ service** n service téléphonique m; AmE (news agency) agence de presse f; **~ transfer** n virement télégraphique m

wired adj (Comp) (population, homes) branché

wireless adj (communications) sans fil; **~ application protocol** n WAP m; **~ application server** n serveur WAP m; **~ commerce** n commerce mobile m, m-commerce m; **~ e-commerce** n commerce électronique mobile m; **~ Internet** n Internet mobile m; **~ portal** n portail mobile m; **~ web** n Internet mobile m, Internet nomade m

wiretapping n mise sur écoute téléphonique f

wishlist n desiderata m pl

with prep avec

withdraw [1] vt (money) retirer; (funds) prélever, retirer; (offer, suggestion, remark, application, permission, aid, product) retirer; (allegation, accusation) rétracter; (claim) renoncer à; **~ sth from sale** retirer qch de la vente
[2] vi (from business activity) se désengager; (back out of a meeting) se retirer; (applicant, candidate) se désister, se retirer

withdrawal n (of capital, money) retrait m; (Stock) (of shares) désengagement m; (of accusation) rétraction f; (of applicant, candidate) désistement m, retrait m; (of offer, aid, product, application) retrait m; **make a ~ from one's account** effectuer un retrait de son compte; **~ of an appeal** (Tax) désistement d'un appel m, désistement d'une plainte m; **~ of capital** retrait de fonds m; **~ from stocks** prélèvement sur stocks m; **~ of an objection** (Tax) retrait d'une opposition m; **~ plan** n (Stock) plan de désengagement m; **~ slip** n bordereau de retrait m; **~ warrant** n autorisation de remboursement f

withhold vt (information) ne pas divulguer; (consent) refuser; (payment) différer; (rent, tax) retenir

withholding n (of securities, taxes) détention f, retenue f; **~ tax** n retenue à la source f

within prep dans

without prep sans

with-profits endowment assurance n assurance mixte avec participation aux bénéfices f

witness[1] n témoin m; **give ~ on behalf of** témoigner en faveur de; **be a ~ to** (event) être témoin de; **~ for the defence** BrE, **~ for the defense** AmE témoin à décharge m; **~ for the prosecution** témoin à charge m

witness[2] vt (incident) être témoin de, assister à; (Law) (document) certifier; **~ a signature** contresigner

witnessing n (Law) certification f

wizard n génie m; (Comp) assistant m; **be a ~ at** (infrml) avoir le génie de

wk. *abbr* (▶week) semaine *f*
WML *abbr* (**Wireless Mark-up Language**)
WML *m*
wobbly *adj* (recovery) hésitant
wolf *n* (Stock) spéculateur expérimenté *m*
women's magazine *n* revue féminine *f*
won *n* won *m*
woods *n pl* **we're not out of the** ~ **yet** on
n'est pas encore sorti de l'auberge
word[1] *n* mot *m*; **have a** ~ **with sb about sth**
parler à qn au sujet de qch; **put in a good** ~
for sb glisser un mot en faveur de qn; **give
sb one's** ~ donner sa parole à qn; **keep/
break one's** ~ tenir/ne pas tenir sa parole;
take sb at his/her ~ prendre qn au mot;
take sb's ~ **for it** croire qn sur parole; **by** ~
of mouth de bouche à oreille; **by** ~ **of mouse**
d'internaute à internaute; ~**s per minute**
mots à la minute; **in other** ~**s** en d'autres
termes; **from the** ~ **go** dès le départ; ~ **has
it that** on dit que; ~ **of advice** *n* conseil *m*;
~ **count** *n* nombre de mots *m*; **do a** ~
compter les mots; ~ **length** *n* longueur de
mot *f*; ~**-of-mouth advertising** *n* publicité
de bouche à oreille *f*; ~**-of-mouth
marketing** *n* marketing de bouche à oreille
m; ~**-processing software** *n* traitement de texte *m*;
~**-processing software** *n* logiciel de
traitement de texte *m*; ~ **processor** *n*
machine à traitement de texte *f*; ~ **of
warning** *n* avertissement *m*; ~ **wrap** *n*
passage automatique à la ligne *m*
word[2] *vt* (letter, memo) formuler
wording *n* choix des termes *m*; (of contract)
libellé *m*, formulation *f*
work[1] *n* travail *m*; (building, construction)
travaux *m pl*; (published study) ouvrage *m*;
(essay, report) travail *m*; **at** ~ (machine) en
fonctionnement; **be at** ~ **on** travailler à; **get
down to** ~ se mettre au travail; **be off** ~ (on
holiday) être en congé; (ill) être en arrêt de
travail; **be out of** ~ être au chômage, être
sans emploi; **be in** ~ avoir un emploi; **put a
lot of of of** ~ **into** (essay, speech) travailler;
(plans, preparations, report) passer beaucoup de
temps sur; **day/night** ~ travail de jour/de
nuit *m*; ~ **by contract** *n* (HRM) travail à
forfait *m*; ~ **cycle** *n* cycle de travail *m*; ~
ethic *n* éthique du travail *f*; ~ **experience**
n expérience professionnelle *f*; (course) stage
(de formation) *m*; ~ **flow** *n* flux de travail *m*;
~ **history** *n* emplois précédents *m pl*; ~**-in**
n occupation du lieu de travail (sans arrêt de
production) *f*; ~ **in process** *n* AmE, ~ **in
progress** *n* travail en cours *m*; ~
measurement *n* analyse quantitative du
travail *f*; ~ **pack** *n* fiches de travail *f pl*; ~
permit *n* permis de travail *m*; ~ **phone
number** *n* numéro (de téléphone) au bureau
m; ~ **prospects** *n pl* perspectives de travail
f pl; ~ **sampling** *n* échantillonnage *m*; ~
schedule *n* calendrier des travaux *m*,
programme de travail *m*; ~ **sharing** *n*

partage du travail *m*; ~ **sheet** *n* (Ind) feuille
d'opérations *f*; (Acc) chiffrier *m*, tableau *m*;
(Comp) feuille de programmation *f*; ~
stoppage *n* arrêt de travail *m*; ~ **study** *n*
étude des méthodes de travail *f*, étude du
travail *f*; ~**-to-rule** *n* grève du zèle *f*
work[2] **1** *vt* (equipment, appliance) se servir
de; ~ **alternate weekends** devoir travailler
un week-end sur deux; ~ **full-time** travailler
à plein temps; ~ **one's way up in the
company** faire son chemin dans l'entreprise;
~ **overtime** faire des heures
supplémentaires; ~ **part-time** travailler à
mi-temps, travailler à temps partiel; ~
nights travailler de nuit; ~ **the system**
profiter du système
2 *vi* (person) travailler; (equipment)
fonctionner, marcher; (plan, idea) réussir;
(argument) tenir debout; ~ **alongside sb**
travailler côte à côte avec qn; ~ **against sb**
jouer en la défaveur de qn; ~ **as part of a
team** participer à un travail d'équipe; ~
closely with travailler en étroite
collaboration avec; ~ **flat out** travailler
d'arrache-pied; ~ **for a living** travailler pour
gagner sa vie; ~ **freelance** travailler en free-
lance, travailler en indépendant; ~ **in
insurance** travailler dans les assurances; ~
in partnership with travailler en association
avec; ~ **in shifts** travailler par équipes; ~ **in
tandem with** travailler en collaboration avec;
I've ~**ed things out so that...** j'ai arrangé les
choses de sorte que...; ~ **together** travailler
de concert, travailler ensemble; ~ **to sb's
advantage** tourner à l'avantage de qn; ~ **to
very tight deadlines** avoir des délais très
serrés; ~ **in** (mention) mentionner; ~ **off** (loan,
debt) travailler pour rembourser; ~ **on**
travailler sur; ~ **out** **1** *vt* (terms, details)
définir; (answer) trouver; (plan, scheme)
concevoir
2 *vi* (succeed) marcher; ~ **out at** BrE, ~
out to AmE (amount to) s'élever à; ~ **through**
(read) lire; ~ **towards** (solution) se diriger
vers; (compromise) s'acheminer vers; (settlement)
négocier
workable *adj* (compromise, arrangement)
possible; (plan, idea) réalisable; (system)
pratique
workaholic *n* (infrml) bourreau de travail *m*
workday *n* AmE jour de travail *m*; (of shop)
jour ouvrable *m*
worker *n* travailleur/-euse *m/f*; (manual)
ouvrier/-ière *m/f*; (white collar) employé/-e *m/f*;
~ **buyout** *n* rachat d'une entreprise par ses
employés *m*; ~ **compensation insurance** *n*
assurance contre les accidents du travail *f*,
assurance-accidents du travail *f*; ~ **control**
n autogestion *f*; ~ **director** *n* employé/-e
membre du conseil d'administration *m/f*; ~
participation *n* participation des
travailleurs à la gestion de l'entreprise *f*,
participation ouvrière *f*; ~ **representation**
n représentation du personnel *f*

W

workers': ~ **collective** n collectif de travailleurs m; ~ **compensation** n indemnisation des victimes d'accidents du travail f; ~ **control** n contrôle ouvrier m, autogestion f; ~ **cooperative** n coopérative ouvrière f; ~ **involvement** n implication des ouvriers f; ~ **participation** n participation des travailleurs à la gestion de l'entreprise f, participation ouvrière f

workfare n allocation conditionnelle f

workflow n (Comp) gestion électronique de processus f, workflow m

workforce n (manual) main-d'œuvre f; (white-collar) effectifs m pl

working n (functioning) fonctionnement m; (rough calculations) calculs m pl; (mine) chantier de mine m; (quarry) carrière f; (of an organization, administration) rouages m pl; ~ **account** n compte d'exploitation m; ~ **agreement** n modus vivendi m; ~ **capital** n fonds de roulement m; ~ **-capital ratio** n ratio du fonds de roulement m; ~ **conditions** n pl conditions de travail f pl; ~ **control** n contrôle effectif m; ~ **copy** n brouillon m, copie de travail f; ~ **day** n BrE jour de travail m; (of shop) jour ouvrable m; ~ **environment** n environnement professionnel m; ~ **group** n groupe de travail m; ~ **hours** n pl heures de travail f pl; ~ **hypothesis** n hypothèse de travail f; ~ **interest** n participation directe f; ~ **life** n vie active f; ~ **load** n charge de travail f; ~ **man** n homme actif m; ~ **paper** n document de travail m; ~ **party** n groupe de travail m; ~ **patterns** n pl modèles d'exploitation m pl; ~ **population** n population active f; ~ **practice** n pratique professionnelle f; ~ **ratio** n coefficient d'exploitation m; ~ **class** n classe ouvrière f, ~**-class** adj onvrier/-ière; (person) de la class ouvrière; ~ **masses** n pl masses laborieuses f pl; ~ **time** n heures de travail f pl; ~ **visa** n visa en cours de validité m; ~ **week** n BrE semaine de travail f; ~ **woman** n femme active f

work-life balance n équilibre entre la vie professionnelle et la vie privée m

workload n charge de travail f; **have a heavy/light** ~ avoir beaucoup/peu de travail; **reduce/increase sb's** ~ donner plus/moins de travail à qn

workman n ouvrier m

workmanship n **good** ~ du beau travail m; **the quality of** ~ la qualité du travail

workmate n camarade de travail m/f

workplace n lieu de travail m; ~ **bargaining** n négociation collective sur le lieu de travail f; ~ **shadowing** n stage d'observation-formation m (consistant à suivre une personne dans son travail)

works n pl usine f, établissement m; ~ **canteen** n restaurant d'usine m; ~ **committee** n UK comité d'entreprise m; ~

council n UK comité d'entreprise m; ~ **manager** n chef d'établissement m, directeur/-trice d'usine m/f

workshop n (on shop floor) atelier m; (training session) atelier m

workspace n espace de travail m

workstation n poste de travail m, station de travail f

workweek n AmE semaine de travail f

world¹ adj mondial; ~**-class** adj de classe mondiale

world² n monde m; (group, society) monde m; **the** ~ **of finance** le monde de la finance; **Western** ~ les pays occidentaux m pl; **the developing** ~ les pays en voie de développement m pl; **all over the** ~ dans le monde entier

world: ~**-beater** n (produit, company) leader mondial m; ~**-beating** adj qui surpasse tous les autres; ~ **consumption** n consommation mondiale f; ~ **economy** n économie mondiale f; ~**-famous** adj mondialement connu; ~ **export** n exportation mondiale f; ~ **inflation** n inflation mondiale f; ~ **leader** n (Pol) chef d'État m; (company) leader mondial m, numéro un mondial m; ~ **market** n marché mondial m; ~ **market price** n cours mondial m; ~ **price** n prix mondial m; ~ **record** n record du monde m; ~ **trade** n commerce mondial m; ~ **trade center** AmE, ~ **trade centre** BrE n (business hub) centre d'affaires international m

World: ~ **Bank** n Banque Mondiale f; ~ **Federation of Stock Exchanges** n Fédération internationale des bourses de valeurs f; ~ **Federation of Trade Unions** n Fédération syndicale mondiale f; ~ **Health Organization** n Organisation mondiale de la santé f; ~ **Intellectual Property Organization** n Organisation mondiale pour la propriété intellectuelle f; ~ **Trade Organization** n Organisation mondiale du commerce f

worldwide¹ adj dans le monde entier

worldwide² adv mondialement, partout dans le monde

World Wide Web n Toile (mondiale) f

worm¹ n (Comp) (virus) ver m

worm² abbr (Comp) (write once read many) disque optique inscriptible une seule fois à lectures multiples m

worsen vi (crisis, problem, shortage) s'aggraver; (condition, situation) se détériorer

worst: ~**-case projection** n (Econ) cas de figure le plus pessimiste m, projection catastrophe f; ~**-case scenario** n hypothèse pessimiste f, pire des cas m

worth¹ adj **be** ~ valoir

worth² n valeur f

worthless adj sans valeur

worthwhile adj (trip, enterprise) qui en vaut la peine; (job, project) intéressant; **be** ~ valoir la peine

WP *abbr* (▸**word processor**) machine à traitement de texte *f*; (▸**working party**) groupe de travail *m*; (**without prejudice**) sans préjudice; (**Ins**) sans constituer de précédent, sous toutes réserves

WPA *abbr* (**with particular average**) avec avaries particulières, avec avaries simples

wpm *abbr* (▸**words per minute**) mots à la minute

wraparound *n* (Comp) retour à la ligne automatique *m*; ~ **annuity** *n* annuité complémentaire *f*; ~ **mortgage** *n* hypothèque intégrante *f*

wrapped *adj* emballé

wrapper *n* papier d'emballage *m*

wrapping *n* emballage *m*; ~ **paper** *n* papier d'emballage *m*

wraps *n pl* keep under ~ garder secret; **take the** ~ **off** (plans, product, strategy) dévoiler

wrap-up *n* US résumé *m*, discours de clôture *m*

wrap: ~ **up** *vt* (goods) emballer; (deal, negotiations) conclure; (event, project) conclure

wreck[1] *n* épave *f*

wreck[2] *vt* (building) dévaster; (career, future) ruiner, détruire; (deal, talks, negotiations) faire échouer

wring *vt* ~ sth out of sb soutirer qch à qn

wrinkle *n* (infrml) tuyau *m*

writ *n* commandement *m*; **issue a** ~ **against sb** assigner qn en justice; **issue a** ~ **for libel against sb** assigner qn en justice pour diffamation; ~ **of attachment** commandement de saisie *m*, ordonnance de saisie-arrêt *f*; ~ **of sequestration** séquestre judiciaire *m*; ~ **of subpoena** assignation *f*, citation à comparaître *f*

writable *n* (Comp) inscriptible

write [1] *vt* écrire; ~ **a check** AmE, ~ **a cheque** BrE faire un chèque, libeller un chèque; ~ **a stock option** vendre une option [2] *vi* écrire; ~ **against** (Stock) vendre une option en face de; ~ **back** *vt* (Acc) contrepasser; *vi* (in correspondence) répondre; ~ **down** *vt* (price) réduire; (stocks) dévaluer; (debt) amortir; (record) noter; (Admin, Law) consigner par écrit; ~ **off** amortir; (Acc) (bad debt, loss) passer par pertes et profits; (vehicle) détruire; (condemn) enterrer; ~ **off over ten years** s'amortir sur dix ans; ~ **off an option against** vendre une option pour compenser

une position inverse; ~ **out** *vt* écrire; (copy) recopier; (cheque) faire, libeller; ~ **up** *vt* (Acc, Fin) augmenter la valeur de; (report) rédiger

write-down *n* dépréciation *f*, moins-value *f*, réduction *f*

write-off *n* (Acc) radiation *f*; (of debt) annulation *f*; (Fin) perte sèche *f*; **be a** ~-**off** (infrml) (vehicle) être une épave, être irréparable

write-protect (Comp) protéger en écriture

write-protected *adj* (Comp) protégé en écriture

writer *n* écrivain *m*; (Stock) vendeur *m*

write-up *n* rapport *m*

writing *n* écriture *f*, in ~ par écrit; **set down in** ~ mettre par écrit; ~ **back** *n* (Acc, Fin) contre-passation *f*; ~-**down allowance** *n* (Tax) abattement fiscal *m*; ~ **off** *n* (Acc) radiation *f*; (of debt) annulation *f*

written *adj* écrit; ~ **agreement** *n* contrat écrit *m*, convention *f*; ~ **declaration** *n* déclaration écrite *f*; ~-**down value** *n* valeur amortie *f*; ~ **evidence** *n* preuve écrite *f*; ~ **offer** *n* offre écrite *f*; ~ **option** *n* (Stock) option vendue *f*, option écrite *f*; ~ **warning** *n* avertissement écrit *m*

wrong[1] *adj* (ill-chosen) mauvais; (incorrect) erroné, faux/fausse; **be** ~ avoir tort, se tromper; **be** ~ **about** se tromper sur; **prove sb** ~ donner tort à qn; **be on the** ~ **track** faire fausse route; ~ **number** *n* (Comms) faux numéro *m*

wrong[2] *adv* get sth ~ (day, number, place, name) se tromper de; (calculations) se tromper dans; **go** ~ (person) se tromper; (machine) ne pas marcher

wrong[3] *n* (Law) délit *m*; **public/private** ~ délit civil/pénal *m*; **be in the** ~ être dans son tort

wrongdoing *n* faute professionnelle *f*

wrong-foot *vt* prendre au dépourvu

wrongful dismissal *n* licenciement arbitraire *m*

wrongly *adv* incorrectement

wt *abbr* (▸**weight**) p. (poids)

WTO *abbr* (▸**World Trade Organization**) OMC *f* (Organisation mondiale du commerce)

WWW *abbr* (▸**World Wide Web**) Toile (mondiale) *f*

WYSIWYG *abbr* (**what you see is what you get**) tel écran, tel écrit

w

Xx

XC *abbr* (▶**ex-coupon**) ex-c, ex-coup (ex-coupon)

XD *abbr* (▶**ex dividend**) ex-d, ex-div. (ex-dividende)

xenophobe *n* xénophobe *mf*

xenophobia *n* xénophobie *f*

Xerox¹® *n* (document) photocopie *f*

Xerox²® *vt* photocopier

XML *abbr* (**eXtensible Mark-up Language**) XML *m*

Yy

Yankee bond *n* US obligation Yankee *f*

yard *n* yard *m* (*0.9144m*); (for construction) chantier *m*; (for storage) dépôt *m*

yardstick *n* (of economy's progress) critère *m*; (to measure performance) étalon *m*, point de référence *m*

year *n* an *m*, année *f*; **company's** ∼ année sociale *f*; **each** ∼ chaque année; ∼ **ended** (Tax) exercice clos *m*; **every** ∼ chaque année; **in the** ∼ **to 1999** dans l'année précédent 1999; **from one** ∼ **to the next** d'une année à l'autre; **from** ∼ **to** ∼ d'année en année; **the current** ∼ l'année en cours; **earn £40,000 per** ∼ gagner 40 000 livres sterling par an; ∼ **of acquisition** *n* année d'acquisition *f*, ∼ **of assessment** *n* (Tax) année d'évaluation *f*; ∼ **of averaging** *n* (Tax) année d'étalement *f*; ∼ **end** *n* (Acc) clôture de l'exercice *f*, fin de l'exercice *f*; ∼**-end** *adj* de fin d'année; (Acc) de fin d'exercice; ∼**-end adjustment** *n* travaux de fin d'exercice *m pl*; ∼**-end audit** *n* audit de fin d'exercice *m*; ∼**-end dividend** *n* dividende de fin d'exercice *m*; ∼ **of issue** *n* (of bonds) année d'émission *f*; ∼ **to date** *n* (Acc, Tax) cumul annuel jusqu'à ce jour *m*, cumul sur l'exercice en cours *m*

yearbook *n* almanach *m*, annuaire *m*

yearling *n* BrE obligation à un an *f*

yearly¹ *adj* annuel/-elle

yearly² *adv* annuellement

yearly: ∼ **allowance** *n* (Tax) déduction annuelle *f*; ∼ **dividend** *n* dividende annuel *m*; ∼ **settlement** *n* (Acc) liquidation de fin d'année *f*

year-to-year *adj* d'une année à l'autre

Yellow: ∼ **Book** *n* UK *code de bonne conduite de la Bourse de Londres*; ∼ **Pages**® *n pl* UK Pages Jaunes® *f pl*

yellow metal *n* métal jaune *m*

yen *n* yen *m*

yes-man *n* (pej) lèche-bottes *m inv* (péj)

yield¹ *n* (product, quantity produced) production *f*, rendement *m*; (in agriculture) rendement *m*, récolte *f*; (of shares, investments) rendement *m*, rapport *m*; (output) productivité *f*; (Stock) taux de rendement *m*; ∼ **criterion** *n* critère de rentabilité *m*; ∼ **curve** *n* courbe de rendement *f*; ∼ **equivalence** *n* (Stock) équivalence de rendement *f*; ∼ **gap** *n* (Stock) courbe des taux *f*; ∼ **maintenance** *n* (Stock) ajustement du taux de rendement *m*; ∼ **per acre** *n* rendement à l'hectare *m*; ∼ **to call** *n* rendement minimum *m*; ∼ **to maturity** *n* rendement actualisé *m*, rendement à l'échéance *m*; ∼ **to worst** *n* rendement minimum *m*; ∼ **variance** *n* écart de rendement *m*

yield² **1** *vt* (bear, produce) rendre, produire; (interest, percentage, profit) rapporter; (result, information) donner, fournir

2 *vi* (surrender) céder; ∼ **to persuasion** se laisser persuader

young *adj* jeune; ∼ **people** *n pl* les jeunes *m pl*; ∼ **upwardly mobile professional** *n* jeune loup *m*, yuppie *m*

Yours: ∼ **faithfully,** ∼ **sincerely,** ∼ **truly** (letter ending) je vous prie d'agréer, Madame/Monsieur, l'expression de mes sentiments les meilleurs, veuillez agréer, Madame/Monsieur, mes salutations distinguées

youth: ∼ **market** *n* (S&M) marché de la jeunesse *m*; ∼ **training** *n* formation des jeunes *f*

yo-yo *vi* fluctuer

yo-yo stock *n* action fluctuante *f*, valeur yo-yo *f*

yr *abbr* (▶**your**) votre; (▶**year**) an *m*, année *f*; ∼ **ref.** (▶**your reference**) V/réf. (votre référence)

YTM *abbr* (▶**yield to maturity**) rendement

actualisé *m*, rendement à l'échéance *m*
yuan *n* yuan *m*

yuppie *n* (▸**young upwardly mobile professional**) jeune loup *m*, yuppie *m*

Zz

Z: ∼ **chart** *n* diagramme en Z *m*, graphique en dents de scie *m*; ∼ **score** *n* indice Z *m*
zap *vt* (Comp) effacer
ZBB *abbr* (▸**zero-base budgeting**) budget base zéro *m*, budgétisation base zéro *f*
zeal *n* zèle *m*
zero¹ *n* zéro *m*; ∼**-balance account** *n* compte à solde nul *m*; ∼**-base budget** *n* budget base zéro *m*; ∼**-base budgeting** *n* budget base zéro *m*, budgétisation base zéro *f*; ∼**-coupon bond** *n* obligation à coupon différé *f*, obligation à coupon zéro *f*, obligation à coupons détachés *f*; ∼**-coupon convertible security** *n* valeur convertible à coupon zéro *f*; ∼**-coupon security** *n* action coupon zéro *f*, valeur à coupon zéro *f*; ∼ **defect** *n* zéro défaut *m*; ∼ **growth** *n* croissance zéro *f*; ∼ **inflation** *n* inflation zéro *f*; ∼ **population growth** *n* croissance démographique nulle *f*, croissance démographique zéro *f*; ∼ **profit** *n* bénéfice nul *m*; ∼ **rate** *n* (Tax) taux zéro *m*; ∼ **rate of tax** *n* taux nul d'imposition *m*, taux nul de taxe *m*; ∼ **rate taxation** *n* fiscalité à taux zéro *f*; ∼**-rated good** *n* denrée au taux zéro *f*, denrée exempte de TVA *f*; ∼ **rating** *n* taux zéro *m*, exemption de la TVA *f*; ∼ **sum** *n* (Econ) somme nulle *f*; ∼**-sum game** *n* jeu à somme nulle *m*

zero² *vt* (counter) remettre à zéro; ∼ **in on** (issue, problem) cerner
zero-rated *adj* non assujetti à la TVA, taux zéro; **be** ∼ **for VAT** ne pas être assujetti à la TVA
zinc *n* zinc *m*; ∼ **ore** *n* minerai de zinc *m*
zip *vt* (Comp) (file) zipper, compresser
zip code, ZIP code *n* AmE code postal *m*
zip file *n* fichier zip *m*
Zip®: ∼ **disk** *n* disquette Zip® *f*; ∼ **drive** *n* lecteur Zip® *m*
zloty *n* zloty *m*
zone¹ *n* secteur *m*, zone *f*
zone² *vt* diviser en secteurs
Zone: ∼ **A credit institution** *n* établissement de crédit de la zone A *m*; ∼ **B credit institution** *n* établissement de crédit de la zone B *m*
zoned: ∼ **advertising** *n* publicité centrée sur une zone *f*; ∼ **campaign** *n* campagne centrée sur un secteur *f*
zoning *n* (Prop) zonage *m*
zoom¹ *n* (Comp) zoom *faire*
zoom²: ∼ **in on** *vt* faire un zoom sur